S0-FKK-411

University Casebook Series

April, 1976

ACCOUNTING AND THE LAW, Third Edition (1964), with Problem Pamphlet

The late James L. Dohr, Director, Institute of Accounting, Columbia University.
Ellis L. Phillips, Jr., Professor of Law, Columbia University.
George C. Thompson, Professor, Columbia University Graduate School of Business, and
William C. Warren, Professor of Law, Columbia University.

ACCOUNTING, MATERIALS ON, (1959), with 1968 Supplement

Robert Amory, Jr., Esq.,
W. Covington Hardee, Esq., Third Edition by
David R. Herwitz, Professor of Law, Harvard University, and
Donald T. Trautman, Professor of Law, Harvard University.

ADMINISTRATIVE LAW, Sixth Edition (1974), with 1974 Problems Supplement

Walter Gellhorn, University Professor, Columbia University, and
Clark Byse, Professor of Law, Harvard University.

ADMIRALTY (1969) with 1972 Supplement

Jo Desha Lucas, Professor of Law, University of Chicago.

ADMIRALTY (1954)

The late Stanley Morrison, Professor of Law, Stanford University, and
The late George W. Stumberg, Professor of Law, University of Texas.

ADVOCACY, INTRODUCTION TO, Second Edition (1976) with 1970 Supplementary Cases Pamphlet

Board of Student Advisers, Harvard Law School.

AGENCY–ASSOCIATIONS–EMPLOYMENT–PARTNERSHIPS (1972)

Reprinted from Conard, Knauss & Siegel's Enterprise Organization

AGENCY, see also Enterprise Organization

ARBITRATION (1968)

The late Shelden D. Elliott, Professor of Law, New York University.

BANKRUPTCY ACT (Annotated) 1967 Edition

The late James Angell MacLachlan, Professor of Law Emeritus, Harvard University.

BIOGRAPHY OF A LEGAL DISPUTE, THE: An Introduction to American Civil Procedure (1968)

Marc A. Franklin, Professor of Law, Stanford University.

BUSINESS ORGANIZATION, see also Enterprise Organization

BUSINESS PLANNING (1966) with 1976 Problem Supplement

David R. Herwitz, Professor of Law, Harvard University.

BUSINESS TORTS (1972)

Milton Handler, Professor of Law Emeritus, Columbia University.

CIVIL PROCEDURE, see Procedure

COMMERCIAL AND CONSUMER TRANSACTIONS (1972) with 1973 Supplement

William E. Hogan, Professor of Law, Cornell University.

William D. Warren, Dean of the School of Law, University of California, Los Angeles.

COMMERCIAL AND INVESTMENT PAPER, Third Edition (1964) with Statutory Materials

Roscoe T. Steffen, Professor of Law, University of California, Hastings College of the Law.

COMMERCIAL LAW, CASES & MATERIALS ON, Third Edition (1976)

E. Allan Farnsworth, Professor of Law, Columbia University.

John Honnold, Professor of Law, University of Pennsylvania.

COMMERCIAL PAPER, Second Edition (1976)

E. Allan Farnsworth, Professor of Law, Columbia University.

COMMERCIAL PAPER AND BANK DEPOSITS AND COLLECTIONS (1967) with Statutory Supplement

William D. Hawkland, Professor of Law, University of Illinois.

COMMERCIAL TRANSACTIONS—Text, Cases and Problems, Fourth Edition (1968)

Robert Braucher, Professor of Law, Harvard University, and

The late Arthur E. Sutherland, Jr., Professor of Law, Harvard University.

COMPARATIVE LAW, Third Edition (1970)

Rudolf B. Schlesinger, Professor of Law, Hastings College of the Law.

COMPETITIVE PROCESS, LEGAL REGULATION OF THE (1972) with Statutory Supplement and 1975 Supplement

Edmund W. Kitch, Professor of Law, University of Chicago.

Harvey S. Perlman, Professor of Law, University of Nebraska.

CONFLICT OF LAWS, Sixth Edition (1971), with 1975 Supplement

Willis L. M. Reese, Professor of Law, Columbia University, and

Maurice Rosenberg, Professor of Law, Columbia University.

CONSTITUTIONAL LAW, Fourth Edition (1973), with 1976 Supplement

Edward L. Barrett, Jr., Professor of Law, University of California, Davis.

Paul W. Bruton, Professor of Law, University of Pennsylvania.

CONSTITUTIONAL LAW, Ninth Edition (1975), with 1976 Supplement

Gerald Gunther, Professor of Law, Stanford University.

CONSTITUTIONAL LAW, INDIVIDUAL RIGHTS IN, Second Edition (1976), with 1976 Supplement

Gerald Gunther, Professor of Law, Stanford University.

CONTRACT LAW AND ITS APPLICATION (1971)

Addison Mueller, Professor of Law, University of California, Los Angeles.

Arthur I. Rosett, Professor of Law, University of California, Los Angeles.

CONTRACT LAW, STUDIES IN (1970)
Edward J. Murphy, Professor of Law, University of Notre Dame.
Richard E. Speidel, Professor of Law, University of Virginia.

CONTRACTS AND CONTRACT REMEDIES, Second Edition (1969)
John P. Dawson, Professor of Law, Harvard University, and
Wm. Burnett Harvey, Professor of Law, Indiana University.

CONTRACTS, Second Edition (1972) with Statutory Supplement
E. Allan Farnsworth, Professor of Law, Columbia University.
William F. Young, Jr., Professor of Law, Columbia University.
Harry W. Jones, Professor of Law, Columbia University.

CONTRACTS (1971) with Statutory and Administrative Law Supplement
Ian R. Macneil, Professor of Law, Cornell University.

COPYRIGHT, Unfair Competition, and Other Topics Bearing on the Protection of Literary, Musical, and Artistic Works, Second Edition (1974)
Benjamin Kaplan, Professor of Law Emeritus, Harvard University, and
Ralph S. Brown, Jr., Professor of Law, Yale University.

CORPORATE FINANCE (1972), with 1975 New Developments Supplement
Victor Brudney, Professor of Law, Harvard University.
Marvin A. Chirelstein, Professor of Law, Yale University.

CORPORATE READJUSTMENTS AND REORGANIZATIONS (1976)
Walter J. Blum, Professor of Law, University of Chicago.
Stanley A. Kaplan, Professor of Law, University of Chicago.

CORPORATION LAW, with Statutory Supplement (1973)
Detlev F. Vagts, Professor of Law, Harvard University.

CORPORATIONS, Fourth Edition—Unabridged (1969) with 1976 Supplement and 1976 Special Supplement
William L. Cary, Professor of Law, Columbia University.

CORPORATIONS, Fourth Edition—Abridged (1970) with 1976 Supplement and 1976 Special Supplement
William L. Cary, Professor of Law, Columbia University.

CORPORATIONS, THE LAW OF: WHAT CORPORATE LAWYERS DO (1976)
Jan G. Deutsch, Professor of Law, Yale University.
Joseph J. Bianco

CORPORATIONS COURSE GAME PLAN (1975)
David R. Herwitz, Professor of Law, Harvard University.

CORPORATIONS (1972)
Reprinted with Conard, Knauss & Siegels' Enterprise Organization.

CORPORATIONS, see also Enterprise Organization

CREDITORS' RIGHTS, Fifth Edition (1957)
The late John Hanna, Professor of Law Emeritus, Columbia University, and
The late James Angell MacLachlan, Professor of Law Emeritus, Harvard University.

CREDITORS' RIGHTS AND CORPORATE REORGANIZATION, Fifth Edition (1957)
The late John Hanna, Professor of Law Emeritus, Columbia University, and
The late James Angell MacLachlan, Professor of Law Emeritus, Harvard University.

CREDITORS' RIGHTS, see also Debtor-Creditor Law

CRIMINAL LAW (1973)

Fred E. Inbau, Professor of Law, Northwestern University.
James R. Thompson, U. S. Attorney for the Northern District of Illinois.
Andre A. Moenssens, Professor of Law, University of Richmond.

CRIMINAL PROCEDURE (1974) with 1975 Supplement

Fred E. Inbau, Professor of Law, Northwestern University.
James R. Thompson, U. S. Attorney for the Northern District of Illinois.
James B. Haddad, First Assistant State's Attorney, Cook County, Illinois.
James B. Zagel, Chief, Criminal Justice Division, Office of Attorney General of Illinois.
Gary L. Starkman, Assistant U. S. Attorney, Northern District of Illinois.

CRIMINAL JUSTICE, THE ADMINISTRATION OF, CASES AND MATERIALS ON, Second Edition (1969)

Francis C. Sullivan, Professor of Law, Louisiana State University.
Paul Hardin III, Professor of Law, Duke University.
John Huston, Professor of Law, University of Washington.
Frank R. Lacy, Professor of Law, University of Oregon.
Daniel E. Murray, Professor of Law, University of Miami.
George W. Pugh, Professor of Law, Louisiana State University.

CRIMINAL JUSTICE ADMINISTRATION AND RELATED PROCESSES, Successor Edition (1976)

Frank W. Miller, Professor of Law, Washington University.
Robert O. Dawson, Professor of Law, University of Texas.
George E. Dix, Professor of Law, University of Texas.
Raymond I. Parnas, Professor of Law, University of California, Davis.

CRIMINAL LAW, Second Edition (1975)

Lloyd L. Weinreb, Professor of Law, Harvard University.

CRIMINAL LAW AND ITS ADMINISTRATION (1940), with 1956 Supplement

The late Jerome Michael, Professor of Law, Columbia University, and
Herbert Wechsler, Professor of Law, Columbia University.

CRIMINAL LAW AND PROCEDURE, Fourth Edition (1972)

Rollin M. Perkins, Professor of Law, University of California, Hastings College of the Law.

CRIMINAL PROCESS, Second Edition (1974), with 1976 Supplement

Lloyd L. Weinreb, Professor of Law, Harvard University.

DAMAGES, Second Edition (1952)

The late Charles T. McCormick, Professor of Law, University of Texas, and
The late William F. Fritz, Professor of Law, University of Texas.

DEBTOR-CREDITOR LAW (1974) with 1975 Case-Statutory Supplement

William D. Warren, Dean of the School of Law, University of California, Los Angeles.
William E. Hogan, Professor of Law, Cornell University.

DECEDENTS' ESTATES (1971)

Max Rheinstein, Professor of Law Emeritus, University of Chicago.
Mary Ann Glendon, Professor of Law, Boston College Law School.

DECEDENTS' ESTATES AND TRUSTS, Fourth Edition (1971)

John Ritchie III, Professor of Law, University of Virginia,
Neill H. Alford, Jr., Dean of the School of Law, University of Georgia.
Richard W. Effland, Professor of Law, Arizona State University.

DECEDENTS' ESTATES AND TRUSTS (1968)

Howard R. Williams, Professor of Law, Stanford University.

DOMESTIC RELATIONS, Second Edition (1974)

Monrad G. Paulsen, Dean of the Law School, University of Virginia.
Walter Wadlington, Professor of Law, University of Virginia.
Julius Goebel, Jr., Professor of Law Emeritus, Columbia University.

DOMESTIC RELATIONS: STATUTORY MATERIALS, 1974 Edition

Monrad G. Paulsen, Dean of the Law School, University of Virginia.
Walter Wadlington, Professor of Law, University of Virginia.

DOMESTIC RELATIONS—Civil and Canon Law (1963)

Philip A. Ryan, Professor of Law, Georgetown University, and
Dom David Granfield, Associate Professor, Catholic University of America.

DYNAMICS OF AMERICAN LAW, THE: Courts, the Legal Process and Freedom of Expression (1968)

Marc A. Franklin, Professor of Law, Stanford University.

ENTERPRISE ORGANIZATION (1972)

Alfred F. Conard, Professor of Law, University of Michigan.
Robert L. Knauss, Dean of the School of Law, Vanderbilt University.
Stanley Siegel, Professor of Law, University of Michigan.

ENVIRONMENTAL PROTECTION, SELECTED LEGAL AND ECONOMIC ASPECTS OF (1971)

Charles J. Meyers, Professor of Law, Stanford University.
A. Dan Tarlock, Professor of Law, Indiana University.

EQUITY AND EQUITABLE REMEDIES (1975)

Edward D. Re, Adjunct Professor of Law, St. John's University.

EQUITY, RESTITUTION AND DAMAGES, Second Edition (1974)

Robert Childres, Professor of Law, Northwestern University.
William F. Johnson, Jr., Adjunct Professor of Law, New York University.

ESTATE PLANNING PROBLEMS (1973)

David Westfall, Professor of Law, Harvard University.

ETHICS, see Legal Profession

EVIDENCE, Third Edition (1976)

David W. Louisell, Professor of Law, University of California, Berkeley.
John Kaplan, Professor of Law, Stanford University.
Jon R. Waltz, Professor of Law, Northwestern University.

EVIDENCE, Sixth Edition (1973) with 1976 Supplement

John M. Maguire, Professor of Law Emeritus, Harvard University.
Jack B. Weinstein, Professor of Law, Columbia University.
James H. Chadbourn, Professor of Law, Harvard University.
John H. Mansfield, Professor of Law, Harvard University.

EVIDENCE (1968)

Francis C. Sullivan, Professor of Law, Louisiana State University.
Paul Hardin, III, Professor of Law, Duke University.

FEDERAL COURTS, Sixth Edition (1976)

The late Charles T. McCormick, Professor of Law, University of Texas.
James H. Chadbourn, Professor of Law, Harvard University, and
Charles Alan Wright, Professor of Law, University of Texas.

FEDERAL COURTS AND THE FEDERAL SYSTEM, Second Edition (1973)

The late Henry M. Hart, Jr., Professor of Law, Harvard University.
Herbert Wechsler, Professor of Law, Columbia University.
Paul M. Bator, Professor of Law, Harvard University.
Paul J. Mishkin, Professor of Law, University of California, Berkeley.
David L. Shapiro, Professor of Law, Harvard University.

FEDERAL RULES OF CIVIL PROCEDURE, 1973 Edition

FEDERAL TAXATION, see Taxation

FREE ENTERPRISE AND ECONOMIC ORGANIZATION, Fourth Edition (1972)

Louis B. Schwartz, Professor of Law, University of Pennsylvania.

FUTURE INTERESTS AND ESTATE PLANNING (1961) with 1962 Supplement

The late W. Barton Leach, Professor of Law, Harvard University, and
James K. Logan, Dean of the Law School, University of Kansas.

FUTURE INTERESTS (1958)

The late Philip Mechem, Professor of Law Emeritus, University of Pennsylvania.

FUTURE INTERESTS (1970)

Howard R. Williams, Professor of Law, Stanford University.

GOVERNMENT CONTRACTS, FEDERAL (1975)

John W. Whelan, Professor of Law, Hastings College of the Law.
Robert S. Pasley, Professor of Law, Cornell University.

HOUSING (THE ILL-HOUSED) (1971)

Peter W. Martin, Professor of Law, Cornell University.

INJUNCTIONS (1972)

Owen M. Fiss, Professor of Law, Yale University.

INSURANCE (1971)

William F. Young, Professor of Law, Columbia University.

INTERNATIONAL LAW, See also Transnational Legal Problems and United Nations Law

INTERNATIONAL LEGAL SYSTEM (1973) with Documentary Supplement

Noyes E. Leech, Professor of Law, University of Pennsylvania.
Covey T. Oliver, Professor of Law, University of Pennsylvania.
Joseph Modeste Sweeney, Dean of the School of Law, Tulane University.

INTERNATIONAL TRADE AND INVESTMENT, REGULATION OF (1970)

Carl H. Fulda, Professor of Law, University of Texas.
Warren F. Schwartz, Professor of Law, University of Virginia.

INTERNATIONAL TRANSACTIONS AND RELATIONS (1960)

Milton Katz, Professor of Law, Harvard University, and
Kingman Brewster, Jr., President, Yale University.

INTRODUCTION TO THE STUDY OF LAW (1970)
E. Wayne Thode, Professor of Law, University of Utah.
J. Leon Lebowitz, Professor of Law, University of Texas.
Lester J. Mazor, Professor of Law, University of Utah.

INTRODUCTION TO LAW, see also Legal Method, also On Law in Courts, also Dynamics of American Law

JUDICIAL CODE: Rules of Procedure in the Federal Courts with Excerpts from the Criminal Code, 1976 Edition
The late Henry M. Hart, Jr., Professor of Law, Harvard University, and Herbert Wechsler, Professor of Law, Columbia University.

JURISPRUDENCE (Temporary Edition Hard Bound) (1949)
Lon L. Fuller, Professor of Law, Harvard University.

JUVENILE COURTS (1967)
Hon. Orman W. Ketcham, Juvenile Court of the District of Columbia.
Monrad G. Paulsen, Dean of the Law School, University of Virginia.

JUVENILE JUSTICE PROCESS, Second Edition (1976)
Frank W. Miller, Professor of Law, Washington University.
Robert O. Dawson, Professor of Law, University of Texas.
George E. Dix, Professor of Law, University of Texas.
Raymond I. Parnas, Professor of Law, University of California, Davis.

LABOR LAW, Seventh Edition (1969) with Statutory Supplement and 1973 Case Supplement
Archibald Cox, Professor of Law, Harvard University, and
Derek C. Bok, President, Harvard University.

LABOR LAW (1968) with Statutory Supplement
Clyde W. Summers, Professor of Law, University of Pennsylvania.
Harry H. Wellington, Dean of the Law School, Yale University.

LAND FINANCING (1970)
Norman Penney, Professor of Law, Cornell University.
Richard F. Broude, Professor of Law, Georgetown University.

LAW, LANGUAGE AND ETHICS (1972)
William R. Bishin, Professor of Law, University of Southern California.
Christopher D. Stone, Professor of Law, University of Southern California.

LEGAL METHOD, Second Edition (1952)
Noel T. Dowling, late Professor of Law, Columbia University,
The late Edwin W. Patterson, Professor of Law, Columbia University, and
Richard R. B. Powell, Professor of Law, University of California, Hastings College of the Law.
Second Edition by Harry W. Jones, Professor of Law, Columbia University.

LEGAL METHODS (1969)
Robert N. Covington, Professor of Law, Vanderbilt University.
E. Blythe Stason, Professor of Law, Vanderbilt University.
John W. Wade, Professor of Law, Vanderbilt University.
The late Elliott E. Cheatham, Professor of Law, Vanderbilt University.
Theodore A. Smedley, Professor of Law, Vanderbilt University.

LEGAL PROFESSION (1970)
Samuel D. Thurman, Dean of the College of Law, University of Utah.
Ellis L. Phillips, Jr., Professor of Law, Columbia University.
The late Elliott E. Cheatham, Professor of Law, Vanderbilt University.

LEGISLATIVE AND ADMINISTRATIVE PROCESSES (1976)

Hans A. Linde, Professor of Law, University of Oregon.
George Bunn, Professor of Law, University of Wisconsin.

LEGISLATION, Third Edition (1973)

Horace E. Read, Vice President, Dalhousie University.
John W. MacDonald, Professor of Law, Cornell Law School.
Jefferson B. Fordham, Professor of Law, University of Utah, and
William J. Pierce, Professor of Law, University of Michigan.

LOCAL GOVERNMENT LAW, Revised Edition (1975)

Jefferson B. Fordham, Professor of Law, University of Utah.

MENTAL HEALTH PROCESS, Second Edition (1976)

Frank W. Miller, Professor of Law, Washington University.
Robert O. Dawson, Professor of Law, University of Texas.
George E. Dix, Professor of Law, University of Texas.
Raymond I. Parnas, Professor of Law, University of California, Davis.

MODERN REAL ESTATE TRANSACTIONS, Second Edition (1958)

Allison Dunham, Professor of Law, University of Chicago.

MUNICIPAL CORPORATIONS, see Local Government Law

NEGOTIABLE INSTRUMENTS, see Commercial Paper

NEW YORK PRACTICE, Third Edition (1973)

Herbert Peterfreund, Professor of Law, New York University.
Joseph M. McLaughlin, Dean of the Law School, Fordham University.

OIL AND GAS, Third Edition (1974)

Howard R. Williams, Professor of Law, Stanford University,
Richard C. Maxwell, Professor of Law, University of California, Los Angeles, and
Charles J. Meyers, Professor of Law, Stanford University.

ON LAW IN COURTS (1965)

Paul J. Mishkin, Professor of Law, University of California, Berkeley.
Clarence Morris, Professor of Law, University of Pennsylvania.

OWNERSHIP AND DEVELOPMENT OF LAND (1965)

Jan Krasnowiecki, Professor of Law, University of Pennsylvania.

PARTNERSHIP PLANNING (1970) (Pamphlet)

William L. Cary, Professor of Law, Columbia University.

PATENT, TRADEMARK AND COPYRIGHT LAW (1959)

E. Ernest Goldstein, Professor of Law, University of Texas.

PLEADING & PROCEDURE: STATE AND FEDERAL, Third Edition (1973)

David W. Louisell, Professor of Law, University of California, Berkeley, and
Geoffrey C. Hazard, Jr., Professor of Law, Yale University.

POLICE FUNCTION (1976) (Pamphlet)

Chapters 1–11 of Miller, Dawson, Dix & Parnas' Criminal Justice Administration, Second Edition.

PROCEDURE—Biography of a Legal Dispute (1968)

Marc A. Franklin, Professor of Law, Stanford University.

PROCEDURE—CIVIL PROCEDURE, Second Edition (1974)

James H. Chadbourn, Professor of Law, Harvard University, and
A. Leo Levin, Professor of Law, University of Pennsylvania.
Philip Shuchman, Professor of Law, University of Connecticut.

PROCEDURE—CIVIL PROCEDURE, Third Edition (1973)

Richard H. Field, Professor of Law, Harvard University, and
Benjamin Kaplan, Professor of Law, Harvard University.

PROCEDURE—CIVIL PROCEDURE, Third Edition (1976)

Maurice Rosenberg, Professor of Law, Columbia University.
Jack B. Weinstein, Professor, of Law, Columbia University.
Hans Smit, Professor of Law, Columbia University.
Harold L. Korn, Professor of Law, Columbia University.

PROCEDURE—FEDERAL RULES OF CIVIL PROCEDURE, 1975 Edition

PROCEDURE PORTFOLIO (1962)

James H. Chadbourn, Professor of Law, Harvard University, and
A. Leo Levin, Professor of Law, University of Pennsylvania.

PRODUCTS AND THE CONSUMER: DECEPTIVE PRACTICES (1972)

W. Page Keeton, Dean of the School of Law, University of Texas.
Marshall S. Shapo, Professor of Law, University of Virginia.

PRODUCTS AND THE CONSUMER: DEFECTIVE AND DANGEROUS PRODUCTS (1970)

W. Page Keeton, Dean of the School of Law, University of Texas.
Marshall S. Shapo, Professor of Law, University of Virginia.

PROFESSIONAL RESPONSIBILITY (1976)

Thomas D. Morgan, Professor of Law, University of Illinois.
Ronald D. Rotunda, Professor of Law, University of Illinois.

PROPERTY, Third Edition (1972)

John E. Cribbet, Dean of the Law School, University of Illinois,
The late William F. Fritz, Professor of Law, University of Texas, and
Corwin W. Johnson, Professor of Law, University of Texas.

PROPERTY—PERSONAL (1953)

The late S. Kenneth Skolfield, Professor of Law Emeritus, Boston University.

PROPERTY—PERSONAL, Third Edition (1954)

The late Everett Fraser, Dean of the Law School Emeritus, University of Minnesota—Third Edition by
Charles W. Taintor II, late Professor of Law, University of Pittsburgh.

PROPERTY—REAL—INTRODUCTION, Third Edition (1954)

The late Everett Fraser, Dean of the Law School Emeritus, University of Minnesota.

PROPERTY—REAL PROPERTY AND CONVEYANCING (1954)

Edward E. Bade, late Professor of Law, University of Minnesota.

PROPERTY, MODERN REAL, FUNDAMENTALS OF (1974)

Edward H. Rabin, Professor of Law, University of California, Davis.

PROPERTY, REAL, PROBLEMS IN (Pamphlet) (1969)

Edward H. Rabin, Professor of Law, University of California, Davis.

PROSECUTION AND ADJUDICATION (1976) (Pamphlet)

Chapters 12–16 of Miller, Dawson, Dix & Parnas' Criminal Justice Administration, Second Edition.

PUBLIC UTILITY LAW, see Free Enterprise, also Regulated Industries

REAL ESTATE PLANNING (1974) with Problems and Statutory Supplement and 1975 Supplement

Norton L. Steuben, Professor of Law, University of Colorado.

RECEIVERSHIP AND CORPORATE REORGANIZATION, see Creditors' Rights

REGULATED INDUSTRIES, Second Edition, 1976

William K. Jones, Professor of Law, Columbia University.

RESTITUTION, Second Edition (1966)

John W. Wade, Professor of Law, Vanderbilt University.

SALES AND SECURITY, Fourth Edition (1962), with Statutory Supplement

George G. Bogert, James Parker Hall Professor of Law Emeritus, University of Chicago.
The late William E. Britton, Professor of Law, University of California, Hastings College of the Law, and
William D. Hawkland, Professor of Law, University of Illinois.

SALES AND SALES FINANCING, Fourth Edition (1976)

John Honnold, Professor of Law, University of Pennsylvania.

SECURITY, Third Edition (1959)

The late John Hanna, Professor of Law Emeritus, Columbia University.

SECURITIES REGULATION, Third Edition (1972) with 1975 Statutory Supplement and 1975 Case Supplement

Richard W. Jennings, Professor of Law, University of California, Berkeley.
Harold Marsh, Jr., Professor of Law, University of California, Los Angeles.

SENTENCING AND THE CORRECTIONAL PROCESS, Second Edition (1976)

Frank W. Miller, Professor of Law, Washington University.
Robert O. Dawson, Professor of Law, University of Texas.
George E. Dix, Professor of Law, University of Texas.
Raymond I. Parnas, Professor of Law, University of California, Davis.

SOCIAL WELFARE AND THE INDIVIDUAL (1971)

Robert J. Levy, Professor of Law, University of Minnesota.
Thomas P. Lewis, Professor of Law, Boston University.
Peter W. Martin, Professor of Law, Cornell University.

TAX, FEDERAL INCOME, POLICY AND ANALYSIS (1976)

William A. Klein, Professor of Law, University of California, Los Angeles.

TAXATION, FEDERAL INCOME (1976)

Erwin N. Griswold, Dean Emeritus, Harvard Law School.
Michael J. Graetz, Professor of Law, University of Virginia.

TAXATION, FEDERAL ESTATE AND GIFT, 1961 Edition with 1973 Supplement

William C. Warren, Professor of Law, Columbia University, and
Stanley S. Surrey, Professor of Law, Harvard University.

TAXATION, FEDERAL INCOME (1972) with 1974 Supplement

James J. Freeland, Professor of Law, University of Florida.
Richard B. Stephens, Professor of Law, University of Florida.

TAXATION, FEDERAL INCOME, Volume I, Personal Tax (1972) with 1975 Supplement; Volume II, Corporate and Partnership Taxation (1973)

Stanley S. Surrey, Professor of Law, Harvard University.
William C. Warren, Professor of Law, Columbia University.
Paul R. McDaniel, Professor of Law, Boston College Law School.
Hugh J. Ault, Professor of Law, Boston College Law School.

TAXES AND FINANCE—STATE AND LOCAL (1974)
Oliver Oldman, Professor of Law, Harvard University.
Ferdinand P. Schoettle, Professor of Law, University of Minnesota.

TORT LAW AND ALTERNATIVES: INJURIES AND REMEDIES (1971), with 1976 Supplement
Marc A. Franklin, Professor of Law, Stanford University.

TORTS, Third Edition (1976)
The late Harry Shulman, Dean of the Law School, Yale University, and
Fleming James, Jr., Professor of Law, Yale University.
Oscar S. Gray, Professor of Law, University of Maryland.

TORTS, Sixth Edition (1976)
The late William L. Prosser, Professor of Law, University of California, Hastings College of the Law.
John W. Wade, Professor of Law, Vanderbilt University.
Victor E. Schwartz, Professor of Law, University of Cincinnati.

TRADE REGULATION (1975)
Milton Handler, Professor of Law Emeritus, Columbia University.
Harlan M. Blake, Professor of Law, Columbia University.
Robert Pitofsky, Professor of Law, Georgetown University.
Harvey J. Goldschmid, Professor of Law, Columbia University.

TRADE REGULATION, see Free Enterprise

TRANSNATIONAL LEGAL PROBLEMS, Second Edition (1976) with Documentary Supplement
Henry J. Steiner, Professor of Law, Harvard University.
Detlev F. Vagts, Professor of Law, Harvard University.

TRIAL ADVOCACY (1968)
A. Leo Levin, Professor of Law, University of Pennsylvania.
Harold Cramer, Esq., Member of the Philadelphia Bar, (Maurice Rosenberg, Professor of Law, Columbia University, as consultant).

TRUSTS, Fourth Edition (1967)
George G. Bogert, James Parker Hall Professor of Law Emeritus, University of Chicago.
Dallin H. Oaks, President, Brigham Young University.

TRUSTS AND SUCCESSION, Second Edition (1968)
George E. Palmer, Professor of Law, University of Michigan.

UNFAIR COMPETITION, see Competitive Process and Business Torts

UNITED NATIONS IN ACTION (1968)
Louis B. Sohn, Professor of Law, Harvard University.

UNITED NATIONS LAW, Second Edition (1967) with Documentary Supplement (1968)
Louis B. Sohn, Professor of Law, Harvard University.

WATER RESOURCE MANAGEMENT (1971) with 1973 Supplement
Charles J. Meyers, Professor of Law, Stanford University.
A. Dan Tarlock, Professor of Law, Indiana University.

WILLS AND ADMINISTRATION, 5th Edition (1961)
The late Philip Mechem, Professor of Law, University of Pennsylvania, and
The late Thomas E. Atkinson, Professor of Law, New York University.

WORLD LAW, see United Nations Law

University Casebook Series

CASES AND MATERIALS

ON THE

LAW OF TORTS

THIRD EDITION

By

HARRY SHULMAN
Late Dean of the Law School and Sterling Professor of Law, Yale University

FLEMING JAMES, Jr.
Sterling Professor of Law Emeritus, Yale University, and Visiting Professor of Law, University of Connecticut

and

OSCAR S. GRAY
Professor of Law, University of Maryland

Prepared with the assistance of

JOSEPH WARREN BISHOP, JR.
Richard Ely Professor of Law, Yale University

and

RALPH SHARP BROWN, JR.
Simeon E. Baldwin Professor of Law, Yale University

Mineola, N. Y.

THE FOUNDATION PRESS, INC.

1976

Library of Congress Catalog Card Number: 76–15440

PREFACE

This is the third edition of a casebook which was originally presented in 1942, and revised in 1952, by Harry Shulman and Fleming James, Jr. The first edition derived in part from materials previously used at Yale by Shulman and Walton Hamilton.

As stated in the preface to the first edition, while ". . . the focus of tort law is the adjustment of relationships between individuals, the quality of the adjustment here, as in all law, is referred to its effects upon the social good. Otherwise it would seem wasteful to spend social wealth and energy merely to shift money from the pocket of the defendant to that of the plaintiff. Accordingly in tort cases, as elsewhere, liability or immunity is sought to be justified by its larger effects: maintenance of peace and order by quieting the desire for vengeance or satisfying the wish for fairness between men, prevention of undesirable aggression or carelessness, encouragement of desirable activity, and so on. In this casebook, though we have doubtless failed to accomplish all we wished, we have tried to present the material in such a fashion as to emphasize social consequences and to invite inquiry and criticism as to underlying assumptions. The student should be constantly aware that the law is concerned not so much with rule or doctrine as with problems in human relations, that the problem must be understood before rule or doctrine can be properly fashioned or applied. . . . We have concentrated largely on the untoward physical harms incident to more or less legitimate activity because they constitute a large part of the law of torts and because it is in this area that there is the greatest change both in the nature of the problem and in the choice of adjustment. It is primarily here that we are beginning to see the potentialities of tort liability as a means of distributing losses in the socially desirable manner contemplated by the more direct methods of social insurance. We have tried also in all the material to retain whatever light is shed on the way in which the judicial process actually operates,—the role of the judge, the jury, the lawyer and the witnesses. This not merely because the readers will be training in law, but because the quality of the adjustments cannot be appraised without understanding as to the manner in which they are made."

Since the second edition much has changed in tort law: revolutions in products liability, the rights of those injured on the land of others, defamation and the compensation of automobile accident injuries, and significant evolution in the law of misrepresentation, and of medical malpractice. These changes have required substantial revisions in the casebook. Except for new developments, however, we have adhered in general to the principles set out in the preface to the second edition, "(1) that older leading cases should be retained, for the most part, since familiarity with them is a valuable part of the equipment of a student and a lawyer; (2) that cases which have proven good pedagogical tools should be retained even though they are not leading cases and even though more recent cases (but less satisfactory ones for this purpose) might easily have been substituted."

We have been greatly assisted in the preparation of this edition by Professors Joseph W. Bishop, Jr. and Ralph S. Brown, Jr. of Yale, who have contributed detailed suggestions as to content and have read and criticized most of the manuscript. Much of whatever credit this edition may merit is due to them, and appreciation is accordingly extended.

Harry Shulman died in 1955. In his lifetime he was known not only as a powerful teacher of torts, but also as a distinguished scholar in the field. This reputation was based largely on his work on the first Restatement of Torts. After his graduation from the Harvard Law School in 1926 he served first as Assistant to the Reporter, Professor Francis H. Bohlen, and later as an Adviser on Divisions 4–7 of the Restatement (Deceit, Defamation, Disparagement and Unjustifiable Litigation) and as Reporter in his own right for Division 9 (Interference with Business Relations). It is a satisfaction for a former colleague and for a former student of his to keep his name before a new generation of students with this edition.

FLEMING JAMES, JR.
OSCAR S. GRAY

June, 1976

ACKNOWLEDGEMENTS

Appreciation is expressed for permission to reprint excerpts identified herein from the Columbia, Harvard, Louisiana and Michigan Law Reviews, the Journal of Legal Studies, Law and Contemporary Problems, the Yale Law Journal and the International Encyclopedia of Comparative Law; from G. Calabresi, The Costs of Accidents: A Legal and Economic Analysis (Yale University Press); F. Harper and F. James, Jr., The Law of Torts (Little, Brown and Co.); Harvard Legal Essays and O. Holmes, The Common Law (Harvard University Press); E. Morgan, Introduction to the Study of Law (Callaghan and Co.); and from the Restatements of Torts (The American Law Institute).

*

TABLE OF CONTENTS

CHAPTER 7. DIGNITARY OR ECONOMIC INTERESTS: DEFAMATION AND THE "PRIVACY" TORTS; DISPARAGEMENT AND OTHER INVASIONS OF ECONOMIC INTERESTS

CHAPTER 8. ASSAULT AND BATTERY, FALSE IMPRISONMENT, MALICIOUS PROSECUTION, ETC. (p. 1010)

TABLE OF CASES

[Cases printed in italics are the cases reported as the text of this volume. Cases printed in roman are found in the footnotes and text. References are to pages.]

---

†

CASES AND MATERIALS
ON
THE LAW OF TORTS

Chapter 1

BASES OF LIABILITY FOR ACCIDENTAL [1] HARM

SECTION 1. INTRODUCTORY

IVES v. SOUTH BUFFALO R. CO.

Court of Appeals of New York, 1911, 201 N.Y. 271, 94 N.E. 431, 34 L.R.A.,N.S., 162, Ann.Cas.1912B, 156.

This is an action brought by an employee against his employer to recover compensation under article 14a of the Labor Law, being chapter 674 of the Laws of 1910, entitled compensation in certain dangerous employments.

The complaint alleges, in substance, that on the second day of September 1910, while the plaintiff was engaged in his work as a switchman on defendant's steam railroad, he was injured solely by reason of a necessary risk or danger of his employment; that at the time of the commencement of the action he had been totally incapacitated for labor for a period of three weeks, and that such incapacity would continue for four weeks longer, and demands judgment for compensation in accordance with the provisions of said act for a period of five weeks. The answer, after admitting all the allegations of the complaint, pleads as a defense the unconstitutionality of article 14–a of the Labor Law, upon the ground that it contravenes certain provisions of the Federal and State constitutions. The plaintiff demurred to this defense on the ground that it was insufficient in law upon the face thereof. The issue of law thus presented was tried at Special Term, where the demurrer was sustained. Final judgment was entered upon this decision, and the defendant appealed to the Appellate Division, where the judgment was affirmed by a divided court. * * *

WERNER, J. In 1909 the legislature passed a law (Chap. 518) providing for a commission of fourteen persons, six of whom were to

1. Chapters 1 through 5 deal primarily with accidental injuries of a physical nature to person and property. By accidental we mean that the injury is the more or less incidental (and usually undesired) by-product of carrying on legitimate activities of one sort or another.

be appointed by the governor, three by the president of the senate from the senate, and five by the speaker of the assembly from the assembly, "to make inquiry, examination and investigation into the working of the law in the State of New York relative to the liability of employers to employees for industrial accidents, and into the comparative efficiency, cost, justice, merits and defects of the laws of other industrial states and countries, relative to the same subject, and as to the causes of the accidents to employees." The act contained other provisions germane to the subject and provided for a full and final report to the legislature of 1910, if practicable, and if not practicable, then to the legislature of 1911, with such recommendations for legislation by bill or otherwise as the commission might deem wise or expedient. Such a commission was appointed and promptly organized by the election of officers and the appointment of sub-committees, the chairman being Senator Wainwright, from whom it has taken the name of the "Wainwright Commission," by which it is popularly known. No word of praise could overstate the industry and intelligence of this commission in dealing with a subject of such manifold ramifications and of such far-reaching importance to the state, to employers and to employees. We cannot dwell in detail upon the many excellent features of its comprehensive report, because the limitations of time and space must necessarily confine us to such of its aspects as have a necessary relation to the legal questions which we are called upon to decide. As a result of its labors the commission recommended for adoption the bill which, with slight changes, was enacted into law by the legislature of 1910, under the designation of article 14–a of the Labor Law. This act is modeled upon the English Workmen's Compensation Act of 1897, which has since been extended so as to cover every kind of occupational injury. Our commission has frankly stated in its report that the classification of the industries which will be immediately affected by the present statute is only tentative, and that other more extended classifications will probably be recommended to the legislature for its action.

The statute, judged by our common-law standards, is plainly revolutionary. Its central and controlling feature is that every employer who is engaged in any of the classified industries shall be liable for any injury to a workman arising out of and in the course of the employment by "a necessary risk or danger of the employment or one inherent in the nature thereof; * * * provided that the employer shall not be liable in respect of any injury to the workman which is caused in whole or in part by the serious and willful misconduct of the workman."[2] This rule of liability, stated in another form, is that the

2. The amount of compensation which might be recovered under the act was limited; it was computed on the basis of average weekly wages. § 219. Another section (§ 218) saved all existing rights of action at common law or under statute but provided that if any action was brought under the act, this should bar any other recovery. Section 219d provided that claims under the act might be settled, or arbitrated, or might be the basis for an action at law in any court of appropriate jurisdiction.

employer is responsible to the employee for every accident in the course of the employment, whether the employer is at fault or not, and whether the employee is at fault or not, except when the fault of the employee is so grave as to constitute serious and willful misconduct on his part. The radical character of this legislation is at once revealed by contrasting it with the rule of the common law, under which the employer is liable for injuries to his employee only when the employer is guilty of some act or acts of negligence which cause the occurrence out of which the injuries arise, and then only when the employee is shown to be free from any negligence which contributes to the occurrence. The several judicial and statutory modifications of this broad rule of the common law we shall further on have occasion to mention. Just now our purpose is to present in sharp juxtaposition the fundamentals of these two opposing rules, namely, that under the common law an employer is liable to his injured employee only when the employer is at fault and the employee is free from fault; while under the new statute the employer is liable, although not at fault, even when the employee is at fault, unless this latter fault amounts to serious and willful misconduct. The reasons for this departure from our long-established law and usage are summarized in the language of the commission as follows:

> "*First,* that the present system in New York rests on a basis that is economically unwise and unfair, and that in operation it is wasteful, uncertain and productive of antagonism between workmen and employers.
>
> "*Second,* that it is satisfactory to none and tolerable only to those employers and workmen who practically disregard their legal rights and obligations, and fairly share the burden of accidents in industries.
>
> "*Third,* that the evils of the system are most marked in hazardous employments, where the trade risk is high and serious accidents frequent.
>
> "*Fourth,* that, as matter of fact, workmen in the dangerous trades do not, and practically cannot, provide for themselves adequate accident insurance, and, therefore, the burden of serious accidents falls on the workmen least able to bear it, and brings many of them and their families to want."

This indictment of the old system is followed by a statement of the anticipated benefits under the new statute as follows: "These results can, we think, be best avoided by compelling the employer to share the accident burden in intrinsically dangerous trades, since by fixing the price of his product the shock of the accident may be borne by the community. In those employments which have not so great an element of danger, in which, speaking generally, there is no such imperative demand for the exercise of the police power of the state for the safeguarding of its workers from destitution and its consequences, we recommend, as the first step in this change of system, such amendment of the present law as will do away with some of its unfairness in theory and practice, and increase the workman's chance of recovery under the law. With such changes in the law we couple an elective plan of compensation which, if generally adopted, will do away with many of the evils of the present system. Its adoption will, we believe, be profitable to both employer and employee, and prove to be the simplest way for the State to change its system of liability without disturbance of industrial conditions. Not the least of the motives moving us is the hope that by these means a source of antagonism between employer and employed, pregnant with danger for the State, may be eliminated."

This quoted summary of the report of the commission to the legislature, which clearly and fairly epitomizes what is more fully set forth in the body of the report, is based upon a most voluminous array of statistical tables, extracts from the works of philosophical writers and the industrial laws of many countries, all of which are designed to show that our own system of dealing with industrial accidents is economically, morally and legally unsound. Under our form of government, however, courts must regard all economic, philosophical and moral theories, attractive and desirable though they may be, as subordinate to the primary question whether they can be molded into statutes without infringing upon the letter or spirit of our written constitutions. In that respect we are unlike any of the countries whose industrial laws are referred to as models for our guidance. Practically all of these countries are so called constitutional monarchies in which, as in England, there is no written constitution, and the Parliament or lawmaking body is supreme. In our country the Federal and State Constitutions are the charters which demark the extent and the limitations of legislative power; and while it is true that the rigidity of a written constitution may at times prove to be a hindrance to the march of progress, yet more often its stability protects the people against the frequent and violent fluctuations of that which, for want of a better name, we call public opinion. * * *

This legislation is challenged as void under the fourteenth amendment to the Federal Constitution and under section 6, article 1 of our State Constitution, which guarantee all persons against deprivation of life, liberty or property without due process of law. We shall not stop to dwell at length upon definitions of "life," "liberty," "property" and "due process of law." They are simple and comprehensive in themselves and have been so often judicially defined that there can be no misunderstanding as to their meaning. Process of law in its broad sense means law in its regular course of administration through courts of justice, and that is but another way of saying that every man's right to life, liberty and property is to be disposed of in accordance with those ancient and fundamental principles which were in existence when our Constitutions were adopted. "Due process of law implies the right of the person affected thereby to be present before the tribunal which pronounces judgment upon the question of life, liberty or property in its most comprehensive sense; to be heard by testimony or otherwise, and to have the right of controverting by proof every material fact which bears upon the question of right in the matter involved. If any question of fact or liability be conclusively presumed against him this is not due process of law." (Zeigler v. S. & N. Ala. R. Co., 58 Ala. 594.) Liberty has been authoritatively defined as "the right of one to use his faculties in all lawful ways, to live and work where he will, to earn his livelihood in any lawful calling, and to pursue any lawful trade or avocation." (Matter of Jacobs, 98 N.Y. 98, 106, 2 N.Y.Cr.R. 539, 50 Am.Rep. 636); and the right of property as "the right to acquire, possess and enjoy it in any way consistent with the equal rights of others and the just exactions and demands of the State." (Bertholf v. O'Reilly, 74 N.Y. 509, 515, 30 Am.Rep. 323.) The several industries and occupations enumerated in the statute before us are concededly lawful within any of the numerous definitions which might be referred to, and have always been so. They are, therefore, under the constitutional protection. One of the inalienable rights of every citizen is to hold and enjoy his property until it is taken from him by due process of law. When our Constitutions were adopted it was the law of the land that no man who was without fault or negligence could be held liable in damages for injuries sustained by another. That is still the law, except as to the employers enumerated in the new statute, and as to them it provides that they shall be liable to their employees for personal injury by accident to any workman arising out of and in the course of the employment which is caused in whole or in part, or is contributed to, by a necessary risk or danger of the employment or one inherent in the nature thereof, except that there shall be no liability in any case where the injury is caused in whole or in part by the serious and willful misconduct of the injured workman. It is conceded that this is a liability unknown to the common law and we think it plainly constitutes a deprivation of liberty and property under the Federal and State Constitutions, unless its imposition can be justified under the police power which will be discussed under a separate head. In arriving at this conclusion we do not overlook the cogent economic and sociological arguments which are urged in support of the statute. There can be no doubt as to the theory of this law. It is based upon the proposition that the inherent risks of an employment should in justice be placed upon the shoulders of the employer, who can protect himself against loss by insurance and by such an addition to the price of his wares as to cast the burden ultimately upon the consumer; that indemnity to an injured employee should be as much a charge upon the business as the cost of replacing or repairing disabled or defective machinery, appliances or tools; that, under our present system, the loss falls immediately upon the employee who is almost invariably unable to bear it, and ultimately upon the community which is taxed for the support of the indigent; and that our present system is uncertain, unscientific and wasteful, and fosters a spirit of antagonism between employer and employee which it is to the interests of the state to remove. We have already admitted the strength of this appeal to a recognized and widely prevalent sentiment, but we think it is an appeal which must be made to the people and not to the courts. The right of property rests not upon philosophical or scientific speculations nor upon the commendable impulses of benevolence or charity, nor yet upon the dictates of natural justice. The right has its foundation in the fundamental law. That can be changed by the people, but not by legislatures. In a government like ours theories of public goods or necessity are often so plausible or sound as to command popular approval, but courts are not permitted to forget that the law is the only chart by which the ship of state is to be guided. Law as used in this sense means the basic law and not the very act of legislation which deprives the citizen of his rights, privileges or property. Any other view would lead to the absurdity that the Constitutions protect only those rights which the legislatures do not take away. If such economic and sociologic arguments as are here advanced in support of this statute can be allowed to subvert the fundamental idea of property, then there is no private right entirely safe, because there is no limitation upon the absolute discretion of legislatures, and the guarantees of the Constitution are a mere waste of words. (Wynhamer v. People, 13 N.Y. 378; Taylor v. Porter & Ford, 4 Hill, 140, 145, 40 Am.Dec. 274; Norman v. Heist, 5 Watts. & Serg., Pa., 171, 40 Am.Dec. 493; Hoke v. Henderson, 14 N.C. 7, 15.) As stated by Judge Comstock in the case of Wynhamer v. People, "these constitutional safeguards, in all cases, require a judicial investigation, not to be governed by a law specially enacted to take away and destroy existing rights, but confined to the question whether, under the pre-existing rule of conduct, the right in controversy has been lawfully acquired and is lawfully possessed." (p. 395.) If the argument in support of this statute is sound we do not see why it cannot logically be carried much further. Poverty and misfortune from every cause are detrimental to the state. It would probably conduce to the welfare of all concerned if there could be a more equal distribution of wealth. Many persons have much more property than they can use to advantage and many more find it impossible to get the means for a comfortable existence. If the legislature can say to an employer, "you must compensate your employee for an injury not caused by you or by your fault," why can it not go further and say to the man of wealth, "you have more property than you need and your neighbor is so poor that he can barely subsist; in the interest of natural justice you must divide with your neighbor so that he and his dependents shall not become a charge upon the State?" The argument that the risk to an employee should be borne by the employer because it is inherent in the employment, may be economically sound, but it is at war with the legal principle that no employer can be compelled to assume a risk which is inseparable from the work of the employee, and which may exist in spite of a degree of care by the employer far greater than may be exacted by the most drastic law. If it is competent to impose upon an employer, who has omitted no legal duty and has committed no wrong, a liability based solely upon a legislative fiat that his business is inherently dangerous, it is equally competent to visit upon him a special tax for the support of hospitals and other charitable institutions, upon the theory that they are devoted largely to the alleviation of ills primarily due to his business. In its final and simple analysis that is taking the property of A and giving it to B, and that cannot be done under our Constitutions. Practical and simple illustrations of the extent to which this theory of liability might be carried could be multiplied *ad infinitum,* and many will readily occur to the thoughtful reader.[3] There is, of course in this country no direct legal authority upon the subject of the liability sought to be imposed by this statute, for the theory is not merely new in our system of jurisprudence, but plainly antagonistic to its basic idea. The English authorities are of no assistance to us, because in the king's courts the decrees of the Parliament are the supreme law of the land, although they are interesting in their discourses of the paternalism which logically results from a universal employers' liability based solely upon the relation of employer and employee, and not upon fault in the employer. There are a few American cases, however, which clearly state the legal principle which, we think, is applicable to the case at bar, and with a brief reference to them we shall close this branch of the discussion. In the nitroglycerine case (Parrot v. Wells, Fargo & Co., 15 Wall. 524, 21 L.Ed. 206) the plaintiff, who was the common landlord of the defendants and other tenants, sought to hold the defendants liable for damages occasioned to the premises occupied by the other tenants, by an explosion of nitroglycerine which had been delivered to the defendants as common carriers for shipment. It appeared that the defendants were innocently ignorant of the contents of the packages containing the dangerous explosives, and that they were guilty of no negligence in receiving or handling them. Upon these facts the Federal Supreme Court held that it was a case of unavoidable accident for which no one was legally responsible. In Ohio & Mississippi Ry. Co. v. Lackey (78 Ill. 55, 20 Am.Rep. 259) the question was whether the railroad company was liable under a statute which provided that

3. The similarities that run through the various schemes mentioned by the court are fairly obvious. Are there substantial differences among them? See, for example, Larson, The Welfare State & Workmen's Compensation, 5 N.A.C.C.A.L.J. 18 (1950); Larson, The Future of Workmen's Compensation, 6 id. 18 (1950). Cf. Lenhoff, Social Insurance Replacing Workmen's Compensation in England, 6 id. 49; note, 63 Harv.L.Rev. 330 (1949); Friedmann, Social Insurance & Tort Liability, 63 Harv.L.Rev. 241 (1949); Symposium on Workmen's Compensation, 16 Vand.L.Rev. 1021–1183 (1963); T. G. Ison, The Forensic Lottery 46–52 (1967); P. S. Atiyah, Accidents, Compensation and the Law, Chapters 14–17 (1970); G. Calabresi, The Costs of Accidents 39–47 (1970); Selmer, Interactions between Insurance and Tort Theories in the Norwegian Law of Personal Injuries, 18 A.J.Comp.L. 145 (1970); Harris, Accident Compensation in New Zealand: A Comprehensive Insurance System, 37 Modern L.Rev. 361 (1974). In Marxian socialist states tort law, with emphatic fault elements, "has not withered away in favor of socal insurance," but instead "has been strengthened" as "a major instrument of socialist morality." J. N. Hazard, Communists and Their Law 381 et seq. (1969). It appears that eastern European socialist states are in some respects more attached to the fault principle than the common law countries; see, e. g., Ionasco, The Fault Requirement in the Contract Liability of Socialist Organizations, 18 A.J.Comp.L. 31 (1970).

"every railroad company running cars within this State shall be liable for all the expense of the coroner and his inquest, and the burial of all persons who may die on the cars, or who may be killed by collision, or other accident occurring to such cars, or otherwise." In speaking of the effect of that section of the law Mr. Justice Breese observed: "An examination of the section will show that no default, or negligence of any kind, need be established against the railroad company, but they are mulcted in heavy charges if, notwithstanding all their care and caution, a death should occur on one of their cars, no matter how caused, even if by the party's own hand. Running of trains by these corporations is lawful and of great public benefit. It is not claimed that the liability attaches for the violation of any law, the omission of any duty or the want of proper care or skill in running their trains. The penalty is not aimed at anything of this kind. We say penalty, for it is in the nature of a penalty, and there is a constitutional inhibition against imposing penalties where no law has been violated or duty neglected. Neither is pretended in this case, nor are they in the contemplation of the statute. A passenger on a train dies from sickness. He is a man of wealth. Why should his burial expenses be charged to the railroad company? There is neither reason nor justice in it; and if he be poor, having not the means for a decent burial, the general law makes ample provision for such cases." To the same effect are the numerous cases arising under statutes passed by different states imposing upon railroad corporations absolute liability for killing or injuring upon their rights of way, horses, cattle, etc., by running over them, in which this liability was held to constitute a deprivation of property without due process of law. (Jensen v. Union Pacific Ry Co., 6 Utah 253, 21 P. 994, 4 L.R.A. 724; Zeigler v. South & North Alabama Ry Co., 58 Ala. 594; Birmingham Mineral Ry Co. v. Parsons, 100 Ala. 662, 13 So. 602, 27 L.R.A. 263, 46 Am.St.Rep. 92; Bielenberg v. Montana Union Ry Co., 8 Mont. 271, 20 P. 314, 2 L.R.A. 813; Schenck v. Union Pac. Ry. Co., 5 Wyo. 430, 40 P. 840.)

A different interpretation has been given to statutes imposing upon railroad corporations the duty to fence their rights of way, under which the liability is imposed for failure to obey the command of the statutes. (Quackenbush v. Wis. & M. R. Co., 62 Wis. 411, 22 N.W. 519; Missouri Pac. Ry. Co. v. Humes, 115 U.S. 512, 6 S.Ct. 110, 29 L.Ed. 463; Minneapolis & St. L. Ry. Co. v. Beckwith, 129 U.S. 26, 9 S.Ct. 207, 32 L.Ed. 585.) "But even such statutes," says Black in his work on Constitutional Law (2d ed. p. 351), "cannot go beyond the imposition of such a penalty in cases where the fault lies at the door of the company. If the law attempts to make such companies liable for accidents which were not caused by their negligence or disobedience of the law, but by the negligence of others or by uncontrollable causes, or does not give the company an opportunity to show these facts in its own defense, it is void." [4]

4. But compare the way the Federal Safety Appliance Act had already been interpreted. St. Louis, I. M. & S. R. Co. v. Taylor, 210 U.S. 281, 28 S.Ct. 616, 52 L.Ed. 1061 (1907). See James, Statutory Standards and Negligence in Accident Cases, 11 La.L.Rev. 95, 101 (1950).

We conclude, therefore, that in its basic and vital features the right given to the employee by this statute, does not preserve to the employer the "due process" of law guaranteed by the Constitutions, for it authorizes the taking of the employer's property without his consent and without his fault. * * *

If we are warranted in concluding that the new statute violates private right by taking the property of one and giving it to another without due process of law, that is really the end of this case. But the auspices under which this legislation was enacted, no less than its intrinsic importance, entitle its advocates to the fullest consideration of every argument in its support, and we, therefore, take up the discussion of the police power under which this law is sought to be justified. The police power is, of course, one of the necessary attributes of civilized government. In its most comprehensive sense it embraces the whole system by which the state seeks to preserve the public order, to prevent offenses against the law, to insure to citizens in their intercourse with each other the enjoyment of their own so far as is reasonably consistent with a like enjoyment of rights by others. Under it persons and property are subjected to all kinds of restraints and burdens in order to secure the general comfort, health and prosperity of the state. But it is a power which is always subject to the Constitution, for in a constitutional government limitation is the abiding principle, exhibited in its highest form in the Constitution as the deliberative judgment of the people, which moderates every claim of right and controls every use of power. In the language of Chief Justice Shaw, in Commonwealth v. Alger (7 Cush., Mass., 53): "It is much easier to perceive and realize the existence and sources of this power than to mark its boundaries or prescribe limits to its exercise." It covers a multitude of things that are designed to protect life, limb, health, comfort, peace and property according to the maxim sic utere tuo ut alienum non loedas, but its exercise is justified only when it appears that the interests of the public generally, as distinguished from those of a particular class, require it, and when the means used are reasonably necessary for the accomplishment of the desired end, and are not unduly oppressive. (Lawton v. Steele, 152 U.S. 133, 137, 14 S.Ct. 499, 38 L.Ed. 385; Colon v. Lisk, 153 N.Y. 188, 196, 47 N.E. 302, 60 Am. St.Rep. 609; Wright v. Hart, 182 N.Y. 330, 75 N.E. 404, 2 L.R.A.,N.S., 338.) In order to sustain legislation under the police power the courts must be able to see that its operation tends in some degree to prevent some offense or evil, or to preserve public health, morals, safety and welfare. If it discloses no such purpose, but is clearly calculated to invade the liberty and property of private citizens, it is plainly the duty of the courts to declare it invalid, for legislative assumption of the right to direct the channel into which the private energies of the citizen may flow, or legislative attempt to abridge or hamper the right of the citizen to pursue, unmolested and without unreasonable regulation, any lawful calling or avocation which he may choose, has always been condemned under our form of government. Concrete illustrations of what may and what may not be done uder the police power are to be found in this very Labor Law of which the new statute is a part. As this statute stood before article 14–a was added, it regulated electric work, the operation of elevators, work on scaffolds, work with explosives and compressed air, the construction of tunnels and railroad work. It regulated the hours of work in certain employments; it directed the payment of wages in cash at specified periods; it provided for the protection of employees engaged in the erection of buildings; it compelled the employer to guard dangerous and exposed machinery and to construct fire escapes and ventilating appliances; it required him to provide toilet facilities, pure drinking water and sanitary arrangements and prohibited the employment of women, and of children under certain ages, in specified occupations; it regulated the hours of labor of minors; it modified the fellow-servant rule, the law of contributory negligence and the assumption of risks; and, in short, it imposed upon the employer many restrictions and duties which were unknown to the common law. Broadly classified, all these and similar statutory provisions which are designed, in one way or another, to conserve the health, safety or morals of the employees and to increase the duties and responsibilities of the employer, are rules of conduct which properly fall within the sphere of the police power. (Holden v. Hardy, 169 U.S. 366, 18 S.Ct. 383, 42 L.Ed. 780; Missouri Pac. Ry. Co. v. Mackey, 127 U.S. 205, 8 S.Ct. 1161, 32 L.Ed. 107.) But the new addition to the Labor Law is of quite a different character. It does nothing to conserve the health, safety or morals of the employees, and it imposes upon the employer no new or affirmative duties or responsibilities in the conduct of his business. Its sole purpose is to make him liable for injuries which may be sustained wholly without his fault, and solely through the fault of the employee, except where the latter fault is such as to constitute serious and willful misconduct. Under this law, the most thoughtful and careful employer, who has neglected no duty, and whose workshop is equipped with every possible appliance that may make for the safety, health and morals of his employees, is liable in damages to any employee who happens to sustain injury through an accident which no human being can foresee or prevent, or which, if preventable at all, can only be prevented by the reasonable care of the employee himself. That this is the unmistakable theory and purpose of the act is made perfectly plain by the recital in section 215, which sets forth that from the nature, conditions or means of prosecution of the work in the employments which are classified as dangerous, "extraordinary risks to the life and limb of workmen engaged therein are inherent, necessary or substantially unavoidable, and as to each of which employments it is deemed necessary to establish a new system of compensation for accidents to workmen." And to make the matter still more plain, the learned counsel for the commission argues in his brief that "if it is competent for the legislature to say to the employer in a dangerous trade, 'use the utmost care in giving your workmen safe work, so that no act of yours, or implement of yours, or work that you set them to do shall hurt them, and if you fail you shall be liable in damages,' if it is competent to make such a law, then it is equally competent to say as in this new act directly, 'you shall be responsible for all damages caused by unsafe condition of work,' and that is just what the liability for trade risks under the new act means." In this argument the learned counsel ignores, or at least misses, as we think, the vital distinction between legislation which imposes upon an employer a legal duty, for the failure to perform which he may be penalized or rendered liable in damages, and legislation which makes him liable notwithstanding he has faithfully observed every duty imposed upon him by law. * * *

Conceding, as we do, that it is within the range of proper legislative action to give a workman two remedies for a wrong when he had but one before, we ask, by what stretch of the police power is the legislature authorized to give a remedy for no wrong? If, before the passage of this law, the employer had a right to a jury trial upon the question of liability, where and how did he lose it? Can it be taken from him by the mere assertion that this statute only reverses the common-law doctrine that the employee assumes the risk of his employment? It would be quite as logical and effective to argue that this legislation only reverses the laws of nature, for in everything within the sphere of human activity the risks which are inherent and unavoidable must fall upon those who are exposed to them. * * *

In support of this new statute we are also asked to consider the supposed analogies of the laws of deodands; the common-law liability of the husband for the torts of his wife; the liability of the master for the acts of his servant, and the liability of a ship for the care and maintenance of sick or disabled seamen. From the historical point of view, these subjects might be very entertainingly elaborated, but for the practical purposes of this discussion they may be very briefly disposed of. If the law of deodands was ever imported into this country it has never, to our knowledge, found expression in a single statute or judicial decision.[5] It was one of those primitive conceptions of justice under which a chattel which caused the death of a human being was forfeited to the king. We are unable to see what bearing it can have upon the question whether, under our Constitutions, it is due process of law to render a man liable for damages when he has been guilty of no fault. Quite as farfetched seems the argument based upon the common law

5. But see Act of March 31, 1868, sec. 5, 15 Stat. 58, 59, which provides for forfeiture of any distillery and distilling apparatus "used by" a distiller who shall "attempt to defraud the United States of the tax on * * * spirits", and Dobbins Distillery v. United States, 96 U.S. 395, 24 L.Ed. 637 (1877), where the distillery had been fraudulently operated by a lessee, but the statute was applied against the assertedly innocent lessor as well: "Nothing can be plainer * * * than * * * that the offense therein defined is attached primarily to the distillery * * *, without any regard whatsoever to the personal misconduct or responsibility of the owner * * *." The Supreme Court has indicated, without so ruling, that it might have constitutional qualms about "the broad scope of traditional forfeiture doctrine", United States v. U. S. Coin and Currency, 401 U.S. 715, 91 S.Ct. 1041, 28 L.Ed.2d 434 (1971), but such statutes continue to be applied against innocent parties, as in the forfeiture of automobiles used to transport contraband, where the principal financial interest in the vehicle is held by a moneylender-lienor, e. g., United States v. One 1969 Plymouth Fury Automobile, 476 F.2d 960 (5th Cir. 1973).

liability of the husband for the torts of his wife. Under the common-law unity of husband and wife, the latter was presumed to act under the compulsion of the former; and the wife could never be sued alone. As the marriage vested the husband with the personal property of the wife, it was simply logical that he should pay her obligations. So with the liability of the master for the acts of his servant, the whole theory is expressed in the maxim qui facit per alium facit per se. He who acts through another acts himself. How do these illustrations support the principle of liability without fault? Could a husband or master be held liable under the common law when the wife or servant had been guilty of no wrong? Would the common law have denied to the husband or master the right to prove that no tort had been committed by the wife or servant? The admiralty cases of The Osceola (189 U.S. 158, 23 S. Ct. 483, 47 L.Ed. 760), The City of Alexandria (17 F. 390, 399), and the case of Scarff v. Metcalf, (107 N.Y. 211, 13 N.E. 796, 1 Am.St.Rep. 807) seem to us equally inapplicable as authorities for the proposition that the law recognizes liability without fault. It is common knowledge that the contracts and services of seamen are exceptional in character. A seaman engages for the voyage. He is subject to physical discipline, and exposed to hardships and dangers peculiar to the sea. He is, in effect, a co-adventurer with the master, and shares in the risks of shipwreck and capture, often losing his wages by casualties which do not affect workmen on land. For these and many other obvious reasons the maritime law has wisely and benevolently built up peculiar rights and privileges for the protection of the seaman which are cognizable in the common law. When he is sick or injured he is entitled to be cared for at the expense of the ship, and for the failure of the master to perform his duty in this regard, the ship or the owner is liable. That is a right given to the seaman, and a duty enjoined upon the master, by the plainest dictates of justice, which arises out of the necessities of the case; and, because of the reason of the rule, the right and duty cease when the contract has terminated and the seaman has been returned to the port of shipment or discharge, or has been furnished with means to do so. But beyond this duty on the part of the master or owner, there seems to be no liability whatever for injuries sustained by the seaman in the course of his work. We think it may confidently be asserted that within the whole range of the maritime law there will be found no rule which renders master, owner or ship liable in damages for an injury sustained by the seaman without fault on the part of any one, or without any fault except his own. The case of Scarff v. Metcalf (107 N.Y. 211, 13 N.E. 796, 1 Am.St.Rep. 807) was not disposed of upon any such theory, but was based upon the neglect of the master to perform the duty of caring for the injured seaman imposed by the maritime law. The legal status of seamen is clearly illustrated in the case of Robertson v. Baldwin (165 U.S. 275, 17 S.Ct. 326, 41 L.Ed. 715), where it was held that compulsory personal service of a seaman in performance of his contract was not a violation of the thirteenth amendment to the Federal Constitution forbidding slavery or involuntary servitude. In that case the learned justice who wrote for the court suggested that enforced service under a seaman's contract was not involuntary within the Constitution, although the contract would not be enforced by the courts. But in the later case of Clyatt v. United States (197 U.S. 207, 25 S.Ct. 429, 49 L.Ed. 726) it was held that peonage or enforced service, whether under a voluntary contract of service or not, was involuntary servitude and forbidden by the Constitution in all cases save those arising out of the exceptional relations of the seaman to his ship, the child to its parents and the apprentice to his master. In the review in Robertson v. Baldwin (supra), of the various decisions in admiralty, it is made quite clear that the courts have always regarded seamen as irresponsible to a degree which makes them incapable of fully protecting their own rights. With the power given to the employer of seamen to compel specific performance of their contracts, there are imposed certain obligations unknown to any other relation. It is a relation which rests on affirmative law and not on natural right. We can find no analogy between a case arising out of such a relation and one in which an adult of sound mind and capable of freely contracting for himself voluntarily enters upon employment from which he is at liberty to withdraw whenever he will.

Great reliance is placed upon the case of St. Louis & San Francisco Ry. Co. v. Mathews (165 U.S. 1, 17 S.Ct. 243, 41 L.Ed. 611) in support of the contention that there may be liability where there is no delinquency. That was an action brought by an owner of land adjoining the defendant's railroad to recover damages for the destruction of his dwelling house and other buildings, caused by fire which spread from sparks emitted by the defendant's locomotives. The action was brought under a statute of the state of Missouri which provided that "each railroad corporation, owning or operating a railroad in this state, shall be responsible in damages to every person and corporation whose property may be injured or destroyed by fire communicated, directly or indirectly, by locomotive engines in use upon the railroad owned or operated by such railroad corporation; and each such railroad corporation shall have an insurable interest in the property upon the route of the railroad owned or operated by it, and may procure insurance thereon in its own behalf, for its protection against such damages." The statute was upheld as being within the legislative power of the state. That decision is amply supported by a number of reasons which have no application to the controversy at bar. To begin with, the Constitution of Missouri contained a clause, which was in force when the railroad company obtained its charter, providing that "the exercise of the police power of the state shall never be abridged, or so construed as to permit corporations to conduct their business in such manner as to infringe the equal rights of individuals, or the general well-being of the state." (Missouri Const. art 12, sec. 5.) Another ample reason is found in the fact that railroads alone "have the privilege of taking a narrow strip of land from each owner, without his consent, along the route selected for the track, and of traversing the same at all hours of the day and night, and at all seasons whether wet or dry, with locomotive engines that scatter fire along the margin of the land not taken, thereby subjecting all combustible property to extraordinary hazard of loss." (Grissell v. Housatonic R. R. Co., 54 Conn. 447, 9 A. 137, 1 Am. St.Rep. 138.) Then, again, "the right to use the agencies of fire and steam in the movement of railway trains is * * * derived from the legislation of the state, and it certainly cannot be denied that it is for the state to determine what safeguards must be used to prevent the escape of fire, and to define the extent of the liability for fires resulting from the operation of trains by means of steam locomotives. This is a matter within state control." (Hartford Fire Ins. Co. v. Chicago, M. & St. P. Ry. Co., 62 F. 904.) A legislature may, if it chooses, make it a condition of the right to run carriages propelled by the agency of fire, that the corporation employing them shall be responsible for all injuries which fire may cause. (Ingersoll v. Stockbridge & P. R. Co., 8 Allen, Mass., 438; Grand Trunk Ry. Co. v. Richardson, 9 U.S. 454, 23 L.Ed. 356.) And, finally, these statutes are designed to protect the rights of those who have no contractual relations to the corporations which inflict the injury. In such a case, when both parties are equally faultless, the legislature may properly consider it to be just that the duty of insuring private property against loss or injury caused by the use of the dangerous instruments should rest upon the railroad company, which employs the instruments and creates the peril for its own profit, rather than upon the owner of the property who has no control over or interest in these instruments. Quite aside from the considerations which support such a statutory liability against railroad corporations, it may be added that it is in no sense an extension of the rule of the common law to modern conditions, but in reality a return to the original common-law doctrine under which every person who permitted fire started by him to escape beyond his house or close was liable to every one who suffered loss or injury thereby. The severity of that early English rule was moderated by numerous statutes, among which are 6 Anne and 14 Geo. III. As to these two last-mentioned statutes it has been held that they became by adoption a part of the common law of this state (Thompson's Negligence, vol. 1, p. 148 et seq., notes under "Liability for Damages by Fire," and Webb v. Rome, W. & O. R. Co., 49 N.Y. 420, 426, 10 Am.Rep. 389), under which neither individuals nor corporations are liable for escaping fire unless there is negligence. The cited cases arising out of injuries inflicted by animals of known dangerous or vicious propensities, and the liability which has often been imposed for the maintenance of private nuisances, we shall not discuss, for we think they are governed by well-settled principles which clearly have no application to the questions now before us. * * *

The judgment of the Appellate Division should be reversed and judgment directed for the defendant, with costs in all courts.[6]

6. Contrast New York Cent. R. Co. v. White, 243 U.S. 188, 37 S.Ct. 247, 61 L.Ed. 667, L.R.A.1917D, 1, Ann.Cas. 1917D, 629 (1917), which recounts the subsequent constitutional history of workmen's compensation in New York and upholds such a scheme so far as the federal constitution is concerned. Cf. also Mountain Timber Co. v. Washington, 243 U.S. 219, 37 S.Ct. 260, 61

6. Note 6 Continued.

L.Ed. 685, Ann.Cas.1917D, 642 (1917); Opinion of the Justices, 209 Mass. 607, 96 N.E. 308 (1911); Kennerson v. Thames Towboat Co., 89 Conn. 367, 94 A. 372, L.R.A.1916A, 436 (1915).

While this case involves the issue of the constitutionality of a statute and might therefore be said to belong more appropriately in a course on constitutional law, it also states a proposition which to the extent that it may be true is fundamental to tort law. To be sure, the constitutionality of workmen's compensation legislation is no longer in doubt. But the extent to which liability may be imposed without "fault" is still subject to disagreement and the view has been tenaciously held that generally "fault" is requisite to tort liability and may be dispensed with only in "exceptional" cases. See, for example, the statement in Crowell v. Benson, 285 U.S. 22, 55–56, 52 S.Ct. 285, 76 L.Ed. 598 (1932): "Again, it cannot be maintained that the Congress has any general authority to amend the maritime law so as to establish liability without fault in maritime cases regardless of particular circumstances or relations. It is unnecessary to consider what circumstances or relations might permit the imposition of such a liability by amendment of the maritime law, but it is manifest that some suitable selection would be required." If there is such a fundamental limitation upon tort liability, it is worthy of notice at the outset. Compare, however, Bishop, The Validity Under the Constitution of the United States of Basic Protection Insurance and Similar Proposals for the Reform of the System of Compensating Victims of Automobile Accidents, in Department of Transportation Automobile Insurance and Compensation Study, Constitutional Problems in Automobile Accident Compensation Reform 35 (1970); Cowen, Due Process, Equal Protection and "No-Fault" Allocation of the Costs of Automobile Accidents, id at 1; Pinnick v. Cleary, 360 Mass. 1, 271 N.E.2d 592 (1971); Montgomery v. Daniels, 38 N.Y.2d 41, 367 N.Y.S.2d 419, 340 N.E.2d 444 (1975); similarly, Bridgeford v. U-Haul, —— Neb. ——, 238 N.W.2d 443 (1976); Godfrey v. State of Washington, 84 Wash.2d 959, 530 P.2d 630 (1975) (no vested right that contributory negligence defense not be changed).

But the case is here largely for a different purpose—to serve as an introduction to law and legal analysis. What is law and how does one find it? We read the legislation and know what to do if the legislation is law. But in some cases that is not enough because a higher law, for example, a constitution, may make what seems to be law not law at all. We read the constitution and find that the liability must not be such as to deprive the defendant of property "without due process of law." What is that and where do we find out? The court directs us to judicial decisions at the time of and prior to the adoption of the relevant constitution. How was the law found or made in those decisions? Is the law frozen as of that time or is change permissible? The court states that some change is surely permissible, but other change is not. How can we tell into which category a particular change falls?

The court makes its respectful bow to "the cogent economic and sociological arguments," "philosophical or scientific speculations," "the commendable impulses of benevolence or charity," and "the dictates of natural justice." But such an appeal, it feels, must not be made to the courts. Are the courts asses? Are they not at all concerned with economic or sociological consequences or the impulses of morality and philosophy? What is the relation between these factors and so-called "legal" factors? Upon what considerations does a court decide a new case?

This case was concededly one of first impression. There was no precedent precisely in point. In its search for light from prior judicial decisions, the court had, necessarily, to look to prior cases which were in many respects different from the one before it. Almost never are two cases precisely alike. At least the parties are different or may be of different height, age, color, or financial standing. Precedents therefore provide differences and similarities for the case in hand. Is it enough to find *a* similarity or *a* difference? If not, then we must look for *significant* differences or *significant* similarities. And we may have to determine whether the differences outweigh the similarities or vice versa. But how do we determine significance and the weight to which it is entitled?

Again, is it enough if we discover one prior decision with overpowering similarity or must we look for a "course" or "line" of decisions, for a consistent generalization of many cases? We study the decisions through the opinions of the courts which made them.

WESTERN & ATLANTIC RAILROAD v. HENDERSON et al.

Supreme Court of the United States, 1929.
279 U.S. 639, 49 S.Ct. 445, 73 L.Ed. 884.

APPEAL from a judgment of the Supreme Court of Georgia sustaining a recovery in an action for wrongful death. The case was twice before the Court of Appeals of Georgia, 35 Ga.App. 353, 133 S.E. 645; 36 Ga.App. 679, 137 S.E. 855. The appeal here was at first dismissed for want of a federal question, but a rehearing was granted, 278 U.S. 577, 49 S.Ct. 176, 73 L.Ed. 516. * * *

MR. JUSTICE BUTLER delivered the opinion of the Court.

Appellee, Mary E. Henderson, sued to recover damages for the death of her husband. He was killed near Tunnel Hill, Georgia, at a grade crossing of a public highway and appellant's railroad, in a collision between a motor truck that he was driving and one of appellant's railway trains. The jury returned a verdict for her and the judgment entered thereon was affirmed in the court of appeals and in the supreme court of the State.

The question presented is whether the due process clause of the Fourteenth Amendment is violated by section 2780 of the Georgia Civil Code. It follows: "A railroad company shall be liable for any damages done to persons, stock, or other property by the running of the locomotives, or cars, or other machinery of such company, or for damage done by any person in the employment and service of such company, unless the company shall make it appear that their agents have exercised all ordinary and reasonable care and diligence, the presumption in all cases being against the company."

Plaintiff's declaration charges that the collision and death were caused by negligence of defendant and its employees: in leaving the crossing in a dangerous condition; in failing to sound the whistle to give warning or to keep a lookout ahead as the train approached the

How much are we to be influenced by what is said in the opinions? Some opinions are well written and cogent. Others are ungrammatical, confused, illogical or otherwise unpersuasive. Can we disregard decisions resulting from reasoning of the latter type? How far can we accept or rely upon the statements in one opinion of what was decided in a prior case?

Reconsider the opinion in the Ives case. The court makes a number of statements of historical fact, for example, that when "our constitutions were adopted it was the law of the land that no man who was without fault or negligence could be held liable in damages for injuries sustained by another." Is the court's history accurate? What if it is wrong? The court also interprets quotations from other opinions. Do the interpretations seem indubitable? The court relies on prior decisions which are in many respects different from the case in hand. Are the similarities significant enough to justify the reliance or are the differences significant enough to distinguish the cases? The court also distinguishes away cases urged by the plaintiff. Are the differences stated enough to distinguish them away or are there significant enough similarities to justify reliance? Is significance a matter of ineluctable logic or choice? If the latter, what influences choice? Are "economic" or "sociological" differences or similarities relevant? Is the time factor—difference in general outlook and public opinion between two periods of time—relevant?

Questions of this character are raised by this case and they will recur throughout our study.

crossing; in that defendant's employees, after they saw the truck upon the crossing, failed to stop the train but accelerated its speed; in running at a dangerous speed; in not having the train under control when approaching the crossing; in operating the train by a "practically blind engineer." The answer denied that defendant or any of its employees was guilty of negligence and alleged that deceased came to his death as a result of his own fault.

Plaintiff proved that her husband was killed in the collision. She also offered some evidence of negligent maintenance and a dangerous condition of the crossing. And it necessarily appeared that the train failed to stop in time to avoid the collision. Plaintiff offered no evidence, and there was none in the case, to support her other allegations of negligence. Defendant offered much evidence tending to show that it and its employees exercised due care for the proper maintenance of the track and crossing and in the operation of the train and that neither it nor any employee was guilty of any negligence charged.

The court's charge included the following: "When it has been made to appear that injury or damage has occurred by reason of the operation of the locomotive and train of cars of a railroad company, the presumption arises that the railroad company and its employees were negligent in each of the particulars specified in the plaintiff's petition, and the burden thereupon shifts to the railroad company to show that its employees exercised ordinary care and diligence in the particulars wherein they are alleged to have been negligent, and, unless it does so, the fact of the injury or damage having been made to appear, the plaintiff, suing for recovery of damages by reason of such injury, would be entitled to recover. * * * The burden is upon the plaintiff in this case to establish her contentions by a preponderance of the evidence. That is subject to the qualification already given you, that, when the fact of the killing has been made to appear, the presumption arises that the defendant company was negligent in each of the particulars specified in the petition, and the burden thereupon shifts to the defendant company to show that its employees exercised ordinary care and diligence in such particulars."

Upon the mere fact of collision and resulting death, the statute is held to raise a presumption that defendant and its employees were negligent in each of the particulars alleged, and that every act or omission in plaintiff's specifications of negligence was the proximate cause of the death; and it makes defendant liable unless it showed due care in respect of every matter alleged against it. And, by authorizing the jury, in the absence of evidence, to find negligence in the operation of the engine and train, the court necessarily permitted the presumption to be considered and weighed as evidence against the testimony of defendant's witnesses tending affirmatively to prove such operation was not negligent in any respect.

Appellee insists that section 2780 is valid, and argues that the presumption, being one established by statute, has the effect of evidence and that it is for the jury to decide whether the company's evidence is sufficient to overcome the presumption; that "it should not as a matter of law be dissipated the instant any testimony is taken against it," and that the issue is to be determined on a consideration of all the evidence including the presumption.

Legislation declaring that proof of one fact or group of facts shall constitute prima facie evidence of an ultimate fact in issue is valid if there is a rational connection between what is proved and what is to be inferred. A prima facie presumption casts upon the person against whom it is applied the duty of going forward with his evidence on the particular point to which the presumption relates. A statute creating a presumption that is arbitrary or that operates to deny a fair opportunity to repel it violates the due process clause of the Fourteenth Amendment. Legislative fiat may not take the place of fact in the judicial determination of issues involving life, liberty or property. Manley v. Georgia, (279 U.S. 1, 49 S.Ct. 215, 73 L.Ed. 575) and cases cited.

The mere fact of collision between a railway train and a vehicle at a highway grade crossing furnishes no basis for any inference as to whether the accident was caused by negligence of the railway company or of the traveler on the highway or of both or without fault of anyone. Reasoning does not lead from the occurrence back to its cause. And the presumption was used to support conflicting allegations of negligence. Plaintiff claimed that the engineer failed to keep a lookout ahead, that he did not stop the train after he saw the truck on the crossing and that his eyesight was so bad that he could not see the truck in time to stop the train.

Appellee relies principally upon Mobile, J. & K. C. R. Co. v. Turnipseed, 219 U.S. 35, 31 S.Ct. 136, 55 L.Ed. 78, 32 L.R.A.,N.S., 226, Ann.Cas.1912A, 463. That was an action in a court of Mississippi to recover damages for the death of a section foreman accidentally killed in that State. While engaged about his work he stood by the track to let a train pass; a derailment occurred and a car fell upon him. A statute of the State provided: "* * * Proof of injury inflicted by the running of the locomotives or cars of such (railroad) company shall be prima facie evidence of the want of reasonable skill and care on the part of the servants of the company in reference to such injury." That provision was assailed as arbitrary and in violation of the due process clause of the Fourteenth Amendment. This court held it valid and said (p. 43) "The only legal effect of this inference is to cast upon the railroad company the duty of producing some evidence to the contrary. When that is done, the inference is at an end, and the question of negligence is one for the jury upon all of the evidence. * * * The statute does not * * * fail in due process of law, because it creates a presumption of liability, since its operation is only to supply an inference of liability in the absence of other evidence contradicting such inference." That case is essentially different from this one. Each of the state enactments raises a presumption from the fact of injury caused by the running of locomotives or cars. The Mississippi statute created merely a temporary inference of fact that vanished upon the introduction of opposing evidence. Gulf, M. &

N. R. Co. v. Brown, 138 Miss. 39, 66, 102 So. 855, et seq. Columbus & G. Ry. Co. v. Fondren, 145 Miss. 679, 110 So. 365. That of Georgia as construed in this case creates an inference that is given effect of evidence to be weighed against opposing testimony and is to prevail unless such testimony is found by the jury to preponderate.

The presumption raised by section 2780 is unreasonable and arbitrary and violates the due process clause of the Fourteenth Amendment. Manley v. Georgia, supra. McFarland v. American Sugar Refining Co., 241 U.S. 79, 36 S.Ct. 498, 60 L.Ed. 899. Bailey v. Alabama, 219 U.S. 219, 31 S.Ct. 145, 55 L.Ed. 191.

Judgment reversed.[7]

7. This case states another proposition, fundamental to tort law to the extent that the proposition is true. To state that a defendant is liable under certain circumstances, as for example, if he was negligent and his negligence proximately caused the harm, or that he is not liable under converse circumstances, is to state that the trier of the facts must be satisfied as to the existence or nonexistence of those circumstances. But in accident litigation the relevant circumstances are generally not facts which can be established beyond peradventure; and the trier of facts does not make a private independent investigation. The parties to the litigation must undertake to persuade the trier. Therefore, the determination of who bears the risk of nonpersuasion, that is, who loses if the trier is not satisfied as to what the circumstances were, is a matter of prime importance. The lawyer knows that it is not enough for him to be convinced as to what the facts are; he must worry also about whether and how he can prove the facts at the trial. So also in studying the following cases, the student must consider not merely the facts upon which liability or immunity are based, but also how those facts are established. He must develop an acute awareness of procedure and method at every point; for judgments are rendered not automatically or by omniscient powers, but by human beings informed only through certain processes.

This case holds that the plaintiff bears the risk of not persuading the trier that the harm was caused by negligence on the part of the defendant; that the plaintiff is to lose not only when the trier is persuaded that the harm was not so caused, but also when the trier is not persuaded either way, when the evidence is "in equipoise." As an original proposition, why is that so? Why must the plaintiff establish the conditions of liability rather than the defendant establish the conditions of non-liability?

The court in this case requires a "rational connection between what is proved and what is to be inferred." Does that mean "logical connection"? Is there any more logical connection between what is proved and what is inferred when the inference is temporary, as in the Mississippi case, than when it is not temporary, as in the Henderson case? May a presumption be rational though not logical? What of the "presumption" that a person accused of crime is innocent until proved guilty? Does the decision in this case in effect create a presumption that a railroad crossing accident is not caused by the negligence of the railroad company? Does the decision in this case hold that the Georgia legislature could not constitutionally make a railroad company liable for harm resulting from a crossing accident without reference to fault on the part of the company? It is now established that a state may render an employer liable to his employee for an accident in the course of employment whether or not the employer's negligence caused it. Would a statute be unconstitutional if it provided that in case of such a "work accident" the employer shall be presumed to have been negligent? Would the connection be rational? Logical? What is the difference in result between saying (a) the defendant is liable though he has not been at fault and (b) the defendant is presumed to have been at fault? Is the Georgia statute harsher or more lenient on the railroad than a statute imposing liability without fault?

Bear this decision in mind as you read the cases in this volume, particularly at pp. 249, 255 et seq. and consider the extent to which presumptions are ac-

SECTION 2. EARLIER DEVELOPMENTS

MORGAN, INTRODUCTION TO THE STUDY OF LAW
(Second Edition, 1948)

FORMS OF ACTION

[Pages 79–81.] After the Norman Conquest * * * the king's courts gradually absorbed all the judicial business of the kingdom. The method by which litigation was drawn into the royal tribunals was the issuance of a royal mandate, commonly called an original writ, that is, a writ originating an action or lawsuit. The development of the system of original writs may be briefly summarized as follows: At the beginning of the Norman period the jurisdiction actually exercised by the royal courts was very narrow. But the king had the power to draw to his courts, by the issuance of special writs, each manufactured for a particular case, such causes as he desired; and he exercised this power with increasing frequency. Under Henry II the royal judicial power was greatly extended. A royal writ was necessary to compel a

tually employed in assessing liability. Consider whether and how far presumptions and inferences are used as purposeful means for the accomplishment of desired results rather than as logical statements of probabilities. See also Bohlen, The Effect of Rebuttable Presumptions of Law upon the Burden of Proof, 68 U. of Pa.L. Rev. 307 (1920); Morgan, Some Observations Concerning Presumptions, 44 Harv.L.Rev. 906 (1931), and Instructing the Jury upon Presumptions and Burden of Proof, 47 id. 59 (1933); Carpenter, The Doctrine of Res Ipsa Loquitur, 1 U. of Chi.L.Rev. 519 (1934); Prosser, The Procedural Effect of Res Ipsa Loquitur, 20 Minn.L.Rev. 241 (1936); Malone, Res Ipsa Loquitur and Proof by Inference—A Discussion of the Louisiana Cases, 4 La.L.Rev. 70 (1941); James, Proof of the Breach in Negligence Cases (Including Res Ipsa Loquitur), 37 Va.L.Rev. 179 (1951).

The Supreme Court continues to invalidate legislation on the ground that it is based on presumptions which are impermissible as violative of due process. See, e. g., Vlandis v. Kline, 412 U.S. 441, 93 S.Ct. 2230, 37 L.Ed.2d 63 (1973) (conclusive presumption that students at state institutions with out-of-state addresses at the time of registration, or within a year earlier, are not bona fide residents for purposes of eligibility for reduced tuition charges); U. S. Department of Agriculture v. Murry, 413 U.S. 508, 93 S.Ct. 2832, 37 L.Ed.2d 767 (1973) (presumption that a household with a child over 18 who is a tax dependent of someone outside the household is not sufficiently needy for food stamps); Cleveland Board of Education v. La Fleur, 414 U.S. 632, 94 S.Ct. 791, 39 L.Ed.2d 52 (1974) (presumption of unfitness to teach elementary school after fourth or fifth month of pregnancy). See similarly Berger v. Board of Psychologist Examiners, 521 F.2d 1056 (D.C.Cir. 1975) presumption of professional incompetence absent a graduate psychology degree). But see Note, The Conclusive Presumption Doctrine: Equal Process or Due Protection? 72 Mich.L.Rev. 800 (1974); Note, The Irrebuttable Presumption Doctrine in the Supreme Court, 87 Harv.L.Rev. 1534 (1974).

Consider the jury instruction upheld in Felgner v. Anderson, 375 Mich. 23, 133 N.W.2d 136 (1965): "If you find that it was the defendant's gun that shot plaintiff, then it becomes the duty of the defendant to establish that he was completely without fault; that he was not negligent." See similarly Kavlich v. Kramer, 315 So.2d 282 (La. 1975) and Gonzales v. Winn-Dixie Louisiana, Inc., 326 So.2d 486 (La.1976) (in slip-and-fall on foreign substance on floor of self-service market, " * * * the duty of going forward with the evidence to exculpate the store * * * shifts to the store owner * * *. If the evidence * * * establishes that the owner is free from fault, there can be no liability.")

man to answer for his freehold. Actions for the recovery of possession of realty in the king's court were invented. In a steadily growing number of other classes of cases, the king through his chancery was issuing writs as of course. Indeed it began to look as if the royal courts, either through writs of course or special writs created for the purpose, might provide a remedy for every wrong. Under John a slight check occurred; but under Henry III the stream of writs issuing from chancery rapidly widened. As early as 1244 the barons and prelates protested. Gradually it was being perceived that the king by his invention of new writs was legislating and was frequently creating new rights. Finally in 1258 the barons extracted from the king, in the Provisions of Oxford, the pledge that his chancellor should be under oath to "seal no writs, excepting writs of course, without the commandment of the king and of his council, who shall be present." Thereafter no new writs could be granted by the chancery; and this meant that, so far as the royal courts were concerned, a litigant whose case could not be brought within the confines of a formed writ was remediless.

* * *

Importance of the Forms of Action. When the medieval litigant or his lawyer applied to chancery for a formed writ, he was in effect asking for a mandate to the royal judges to take jurisdiction of and to try a cause of action properly falling within the limits of that writ. The writ was no general order or authorization to try the validity of any claim which the plaintiff might choose to assert against the defendant. If plaintiff had selected and secured a writ in debt, he could not expect the judges to try a case in trespass. As Pollock and Maitland put it: [8]

"The metaphor which likens the chancery to a shop is trite; we will liken it to an armoury. It contains every weapon of medieval warfare from the two-handed sword to the poniard. The man who has a quarrel with his neighbor comes thither to choose his weapon. The choice is large; but he must remember that he will not be able to change weapons in the middle of the combat and also that every weapon has its proper use and may be put to none other. If he selects a sword, he must observe the rules of swordplay; he must not try to use his cross-bow as a mace. To drop metaphor, our plaintiff is not merely choosing a writ, he is choosing an action, and every action has its own rules."

And this remained true as long as the fomulary system endured. Professor Maitland, in pointing out the practical importance of distinguishing between the several forms of action, said:

"'A form of action' has implied a particular original process, a particular mesne process, a particular final process, a particular mode of pleading, of trial, of judgment. But further to a very considerable degree the substantive law administered in a given form of action has grown up independently of the law administered in other forms. Each

8. Pollock and Maitland, History of English Law (2d ed.), 561.

procedural pigeon-hole contains its own rules of substantive law, and it is with great caution that we may argue from what is found in one to what will probably be found in another; each has its own precedents. It is quite possible that a litigant will find that his case will fit some two or three of these pigeon-holes. If that be so he will have a choice, which will often be a choice between the old, cumbrous, costly, on the one hand, the modern, rapid, cheap, on the other. Or again he may make a bad choice, fail in his action, and take such comfort as he can from the hints of the judges that another form of action might have been more successful. The plaintiff's choice is irrevocable; he must play the rules of the game that he has chosen. Lastly he may find that, plausible as his case may seem, it just will not fit any one of the receptacles provided by the courts and he may take to himself the lesson that where there is no remedy there is no wrong." [9]

WEAVER v. WARD

King's Bench, 1617.
Hobart 134, 80 Eng.Rep. 284.

Weaver brought an action of trespass of assault and battery against Ward. The defendant pleaded, that he was amongst others by the commandment of the Lords of the Council a trained soldier in London, of the band of one Andrews captain; and so was the plaintiff, and that they were skirmishing with their musquets charged with powder for their exercise in re militari, against another captain and his band; and as they were so skirmishing, the defendant casualiter & per infortunium & contra voluntatem suam, in discharging of his piece did hurt and wound the plaintiff, which is the same, &c. absque hoc, that he was guilty aliter sive alio modo. And upon demurrer by the plaintiff, judgment was given for him; for though it were agreed that if men tilt or turney in the presence of the King, or if two masters of defence playing their prizes kill one another, that this shall be no felony; or if a lunatick kill a man, or the like, because felony must be done animo felonico: yet in trespass, which tends only to give damages according to hurt or loss, it is not so; and therefore if a lunatick hurt a man, he shall be answerable in trespass: and therefore no man shall be excused of a trespass (for this is the nature of an excuse, and not of a justification, prout ei bene licuit) except it may be judged utterly without his fault.

As if a man by force take my hand and strike you, or if here the defendant had said, that the plaintiff ran across his piece when it was discharging, or had set forth the case with the circumstances,

9. Maitland, Equity and the Forms of Action, 298. [Footnotes 8 and 9 from original, renumbered. For a brief history of writ procedure in the twelfth and thirteenth centuries see J. Baker, An Introduction to English Legal History 78 et seq. (1971), and R. Van Caenegem, The Birth of the English Common Law, Chapter 2 (1973).]

so as it had appeared to the Court that it had been inevitable, and that the defendant had committed no negligence to give occasion to the hurt.[10]

DICKENSON v. WATSON

King's Bench, 1682.
T. Jones 205, 84 Eng.Rep. 1218.

The plaintiff brought error on a judgment in the Court of the sheriffs of the City of York, in trespass for an assault, battery, and wounding of the plaintiff's eye, by discharging of a gun charged with powder and hail-shot, by which he lost the sight of his eye. The defendant pleaded *actio non,* because he is, and at the time of the trespass was an officer appointed for collecting the duty of hearth-money, and for the better discharge of his office, and more sure custody, and keeping of the money by him collected and to be collected, he provided himself with fire-arms, and having one of his pistols in his hands, and intending to discharge it *ne aliquod damnum eveniret,* he discharged it *(nemine in opposito vis. existente)* and while he discharged it, the plaintiff *casualiter viam illam proeterivit, & si aliquod malum ei inde accideret hoc fuit contra voluntat.* of the defendant. *Quoe est eadem transgressio.* Upon this the plaintiff demurred, and judgment was given for him; whereupon error was brought, and judgment was affirmed, nothing being urged besides the sufficiency of the plea. But the Court held it to be insufficient; for in trespass the defendant shall not be excused without unavoidable necessity, which is not shown here. Besides, the defendant did not traverse *absq;* [*absque*] *hoc quod aliter seu alio modo,* as was done in the case of Weaver and Ward, Hob. 134. And yet judgment there given for the plaintiff.

10. Cf. Brian, J., in The Case of Thorns, Y.B. 6 Edw. IV, 7, pl. 18 (1466). "And so if a man makes an assault upon me and I cannot avoid him, and he wants to beat me, and I in defence of myself raise my stick and strike him, and in raising it I hurt some man who is behind my back, this man will have an action against me. And yet it was lawful for me to raise my stick to defend myself, and it was against my will that I hurt him" (as set forth in 1 Street, Foundations of Legal Liability, 76) (dictum).

Note the discussion of Weaver v. Ward in Bohlen, Torts of Infants and Insane, 23 Mich.L.Rev. 9 (1924), Studies in the Law of Torts, 543, 547–552, in which the author views the case as the beginning by the court "to feel its way to a recognition of the excuse of inevitable accident." The case is also treated in most of the material cited at the end of this section.

GIBBONS v. PEPPER

King's Bench, 1695.
1 Ray. 38, 91 Eng.Rep. 922.

Trespass, assault and battery. The defendant pleads, that he rode upon a horse in the King's highway, and that his horse being affrighted ran away with him, persons standing in the way, among whom the plaintiff stood; so that he could not stop the horse; that there were several persons standing in the way, among whom the plaintiff stood; and that he called to them to take care, but that notwithstanding, the plaintiff did not go out of the way, but continued there; so that the defendant's horse ran over the plaintiff against the will of the defendant; quae est eadem transgressio, &c. The plaintiff demurred. And Serjeant Darnall for the defendant argued, that if the defendant in his justification shews that the accident was inevitable, and that the negligence of the defendant did not cause it, judgment shall be given for him. To prove which he cited Hob. 344, Weaver vers. Ward. Mo. 864, pl. 1192. 2 Roll.Abr. 548. 1 Brownl. Prec. 188.

Northey for the plaintiff said, that in all these cases the defendant confessed a battery, which he afterwards justified; but in this case he justified a battery, which is no battery. Of which opinion was the whole Court; for if I ride upon a horse, and J. S. whips the horse, so that he runs away with me and runs over any other person, he who whipped the horse is guilty of the battery, and not me. But if I by spurring was the cause of such accident, then I am guilty. In the same manner, if A. takes the hand of B. and with it strikes C., A. is the trespasser, and not B. And, Per Curiam, the defendant might have given this justification in evidence, upon the general issue pleaded. And therefore judgment was given for the plaintiff.[11]

11. See A.L.I. Restatement of Torts Second § 2 (1965), defining "act" as "an external manifestation of the actor's will", and § 8, defining "unavoidable accident * * * to denote the fact that the harm * * * is not caused by any tortious act * * *"; Bohlen, Cases on Torts (3d ed. 1930) 2–4; Steudle v. Rentchler, 64 Ill. 161 (1872) (boys frightened defendant's horse); Cunningham v. Pitzer, 2 W. Va. 264, 94 Am.Dec. 526 (1867) (trespass committed by confederate soldier under military compulsion).

Liability in trespass, as well as in case, had to be based on some *voluntary* conduct of defendant. Of course voluntary conduct can nearly always be shown if we look far enough back in the sequence of events. Pepper, we may assume, voluntarily went out to ride on the day that proved so eventful and by free choice rode to the place where his horse was affrighted. Would these acts support liability in trespass? in an action on the case?

What of the voluntary act of continuing to drive a car when sleepy, of getting drunk, and the like? See Lobert v. Pack, 337 Pa. 103, 9 A.2d 365 (1939), noted 38 Mich.L.Rev. 919 (1940); Diamond State Tel. Co. v. Hunter, 2 Terry 336, 21 A.2d 286 (Del.1941); Keller v. De Long, p. 153, infra; James, Qualities of the Reasonable Man in Negligence Cases, 16 Mo.L.Rev. 1, 19 (1951).

HALL v. FEARNLEY

Queen's Bench, 1842.
3 Q.B. 919, 114 Eng.Rep. 761.

Trespass for driving defendant's cart and horse with great violence against plaintiff, and thereby knocking him down, bruising and wounding him, &c.

Plea, not guilty.

On the trial, before WIGHTMAN, J., at the Middlesex sittings in Hilary term 1842, it was proved that the plaintiff was walking on a narrow part of the pavement in a public street, where there was a considerable curvature in it. The defendant was driving a cart in the road near the pavement at the edge of which the plaintiff was walking. The case for the plaintiff was that there was want of due care on the part of the defendant, who had driven so close to the pavement as to knock the plaintiff down, and run over and break his leg. The defendant endeavoured to shew that the plaintiff had slipped from the curb stone at the moment when the cart was passing, and had so got his leg under the wheel. The defendant called no witnesses.

WIGHTMAN, J. told the jury that the question for them was, whether the injury was occasioned by unavoidable accident or by the defendant's default; and that, if they thought the plaintiff had accidentally slipped off the pavement as the defendant's cart was passing, and had been run over in consequence of such accident, they ought to find for the defendant. Verdict for defendant.

In the same term Crowder obtained a rule nisi for a new trial on the ground that the Judge had misdirected the jury, by telling them that, on the issue, if the injury was accidental, the defendant was entitled to a verdict.

Knowles now shewed cause. The jury have in effect negatived all fault on the part of the defendant. This was an inevitable accident, as in Gibbon v. Pepper (2 Salk. 637), where the defendant's horse ran away with the rider, and struck the plaintiff, and the Court held it to be no trespass, and therefore properly evidence under not guilty. The new rules of pleading make no alteration in pleadings for trespass to the person; and the case therefore stands on the old forms of pleading. This was in fact no assault or battery at all; for to constitute one some degree of negligence is always necessary; 3 Starkie on Evidence, 1119, 3d ed. Gough v. Bryan (2 M. & W. 770), is to the same effect. There a special plea, alleging collision by the improper driving of the plaintiff himself, and concluding to the country, was held to be bad as amounting to the general issue. Griffin v. Parsons (1 Selw.N.P. 25, 26, note (1), 10th ed.), reported in Selwyn's Nisi Prius, tit. Assault and Battery, sect. 1, shews that a seizure of the person is not necessarily an assault, but that the animus with which the act was done is material; therefore, on a replication denying a prior assault, evidence was admitted to shew that the alleged assault was only to part the defendant and another who were fighting. It is at all events evidence in mitigation. (Lord Denman, C. J. If the plaintiff has suffered damage by a trespass not justified, the defendant should pay the whole amount without inquiry into the question of animus. The case would be different, if the defendant was not a voluntary agent. So it may be different where an action on the case for negligence is brought, and the negligence is denied; there negligence is the fact in issue.)

Crowder (with whom was H. S. Cooper) contra. The case of Gibbon v. Pepper, as reported in Lord Raymond's Reports (Gibbons v. Pepper, 1 Ld.Raym. 38), appears to have been one of mere involuntary accident occasioned by the act of a third person in frightening the defendant's horse. A flash of lightning may have the same effect, and would certainly exculpate the rider from all blame. But here there was nothing inevitable. Weaver v. Ward (Hob. 134, 5th ed.), is in point. There an accidental injury done by a soldier who was exercising was held to be actionable, for there was nothing to shew that it was unavoidable. Griffin v. Parsons (1 Selw.N.P. 25, 26, note (1), 10th ed.), is only a Nisi Prius case, and the doctrine contained is against the current of authorities. Milman v. Dolwell (2 Camp. 378), and Knapp v. Salsbury (2 Camp. 500), also shew that, if the trespass is in fact committed, the fact of its being excusable by some accident or by negligence of the plaintiff is matter for a special plea. (He was then stopped by the Court.)

LORD DENMAN, C. J. The authorities shew that if the accident had resulted entirely from a superior agency, that would have been a defence, and might have been proved under the general issue; but a defence admitting that the accident resulted from an act of the defendant would not have been so provable.

COLERIDGE, J. Any defence, which admits the trespass complained of to be the act of the defendant, must be pleaded specially.

WIGHTMAN, J. The act of the defendant was prima facie unjustifiable, and required an excuse to be shewn. When the motion in this case was first made, I had in my recollection the case of Wakeman v. Robinson (1 Bing. 213). It was there agreed that an involuntary act might be a defence on the general issue. The decision indeed turned on a different point; but the general proposition is laid down. I think the omission to plead the defence here deprived the defendant of the benefit of it, and entitled the plaintiff to recover.

Rule absolute for a new trial.[12]

12. Apparently in no reported common law action of trespass for assault and battery did the defendant actually prevail upon a showing that the injury, though caused directly by his voluntary act, did not result from any negligence on his part. Can it therefore be said that want of negligence was unavailable as a defense to an action of trespass? See, e. g., J. Baker, An Introduction to English Legal History 227–29 (1971). If freedom from fault was a defense at all to such an action, who had the burden of pleading and proving it? Compare this situation with the one which Georgia tried to bring about by statute. Cf. Western & Atlantic R. Co. v. Henderson, p. 16 supra.

SCOTT v. SHEPHERD

Common Pleas, 1773.
3 Wils. 403, 95 Eng.Rep. 1124.

This is an action of trespass and assault, wherein the plaintiff declares, that the defendant, on the 28th day of October, 1770, with force and arms, (to wit) with sticks, staves, clubs and fists, made an assault upon the plaintiff at Taunton, in the county of Somerset, and greatly bruised, wounded, and ill treated him, so that his life was greatly despaired of, and then and there threw, casted and tossed a lighted squib, consisting of gunpowder and other combustible materials, at and against the said plaintiff, and struck the said plaintiff on the face therewith, and so greatly burnt one of the eyes of the said plaintiff, that the plaintiff underwent and suffered great and excruciating pain and torment for a long time, (to wit) for the space of six months then next following, and afterwards wholly lost his said eye; * * *

The defendant by his guardian pleaded not guilty, whereupon issue being joined, this cause came on to be tried at the last Summer Assizes for the county of Somerset, before Mr. Justice Nares; when it appeared by the plaintiff's evidence that in the evening of the 28th day of October, 1770, at Milborne Port in the said county, it being the day the fair was held there, the defendant threw a lighted serpent, being a large squib, consisting of gunpowder and other combustible materials, from the street into the market-house, which is a covered building supported by arches, and inclosed at one end, but open at the other end and on both sides, when a large concourse of people were then assembled; and that the said lighted serpent or squib, so thrown by the defendant, fell upon the standing there of one William Yates, who was then exposing to sale gingerbread, cakes, pies, and other pastry wares upon his said standing; that one James Willis instantly, and to prevent injury to himself and to the said wares of the said William Yates, took the said lighted serpent or squib from off the said standing and then threw it across the said market-house, when it fell upon another standing there, of one James Ryall, on the said James Ryall instantly, and to save himself and his goods from being injured, took up the said lighted serpent or squib from off the said standing, and then threw it to another part of the said market-house, and in so throwing it struck the plaintiff then in said market-house in the face therewith, and the said lighted serpent or squib so striking against the plaintiff's face, and the combustible matter therein then bursting put out one of the plaintiff's eyes.

Upon this evidence the jury found a verdict for the plaintiff with £100. damages, subject to the opinion of this Court; whether upon these facts this action is maintainable against the defendant.

Serjeant Glynn [for the plaintiff].—It was objected at the trial that the plaintiff had mistaken his remedy, that trespass *vi et armis* will not lie because the damage the plaintiff received was not done immediately by the defendant, but was consequential. * * * In answer to this, I insist, that whoever does a *tortious* act is answerable in trespass * * * for the consequences. * * *

Serjeant Burland [for the defendant].—* * *

NARES, JUSTICE, for the Plaintiff.—The question is, whether, upon the facts proved at the trial, which have been reported, and before stated, this action of trespass of assault and battery vi et armis doth not well lie against the defendant? Or whether it should not have been an action upon the case against him, upon a supposal that the injury done to the plaintiff was consequential and not immediate?

I am of opinion that this action of trespass vi et armis doth well lie against the defendant.—The nature of the act, the time and place when and where it was done, make it highly probable that some personal damage would immediately happen thereby to somebody then present in a crowded market house on the fair-day; and I think the act in itself was illegal at common law; but the stat. 9 & 10 W. 3, ch. 7, which makes the throwing of squibs in any publick street, &c. a common nuisance, and gives a forfeiture for so doing, puts it out of doubt that the act was unlawful.

It is objected that the plaintiff's eye was not put out by the immediate act of the defendant but by the immediate act of James Ryall, and therefore this action will not lie against the defendant, but would well have laid against Ryall.

I answer, that the act of throwing the squib into the market-house was of a mischievous nature, and bespeaks a bad intention, and whether the plaintiff's eye was put out mediately or immediately thereby, the defendant, who first threw the squib, is answerable in this action: but supposing the defendant had no bad or mischievous intention when he threw the squib, yet as the injury done was not inevitable, this action well lies against him; for the malus animus of a defendant is not necessary to be alleged, proved or taken into consideration in this action; "but in felony it shall be considered, as where a man shoots (with a bow) arrows at butts and kills a man it is not felony, and it should be construed that he had no intent to kill him; and so of a tyler upon a house who with a tyle kills a man unknowingly, it is not felony: but where a man shoots at butts, and wounds a man, although that it be against his will, he shall be said to be a trespasser. 21 Hen. 7, 28a."—If the injury done be not inevitable, the person who doth it, or is the immediate cause thereof, even by accident, misfortune, and against his will, is answerable in this action of trespass vi et armis; so is 1 Stran. 596, Underwood versus Hewson. Hob. 134, Weaver versus Ward. Sir Thomas Jones, 205, Dickenson versus Watson. 6 Ed. 4, 7, 8. Sir Thomas Raym. 422. 4 Mod. 404, 5.—If the act in the first instance be unlawful, trespass will lie; but if the act is prima facie lawful, and the prejudice to another is not immediate, but consequential, it must be an action upon the case, and this is the distinction laid down by the Lord Chief Justice Raymond in Reynolds versus Clarke, 1 Stran. 635. 2 Lord Raym. 1399, S.C. In the case at Bar, the act in the first instance done by the defendant was unlawful, therefore trespass vi et armis well lies against him; every subsequent act in throwing the squib by Yates, and Ryall, did partake of the nature of the first act, and was quasi causa causata immediately and instanter. In the case of The Prior of Spalding in trespass against defendants for putting earth and mud into his sewer, whereby the water therein was stopped in its course and surrounded 40 acres of his land adjoining; it was objected that trespass vi et armis did not lie, and prayed judgment of the writ; but by Thirning Chief Justice, although the surrounding the land with water was not against the peace, yet the putting the earth and mud into the sewer may be against the peace; and the defendants have done what they ought not to have done, wherefore they must answer. 12 Hen. 4, 3 a. There are some cases where one may have either trespass vi et armis, or an action upon the case, as Hob. 180, Wheatley versus Stone. Cro.Jac. 122, 43, Dent versus Oliver.—"If a man be riding on the way, and another man striketh his horse by which the rider falleth and is hurt, he which is cast off his horse shall have trespass against the other" (whereby I suppose is meaned trespass vi et armis), F.N.B. 89 E. and 90 K., 91 A. 8vo. edit.—The stroke is given to the horse, and not to the rider, but he is instantly hurt by the fall, in consequence of the act of striking the horse.

It is objected that the squib, after it was thrown by the defendant, had a new direction given to it, whereby the plaintiff was injured, but was not hurt by the defendant's throwing it.—I answer, that the defendant was the first actor, and the cause of the cause of the putting out the eye of the plaintiff, the act was not compleat until the explosion; if a man turns out a mad bull, ox, or any other wild or mischievous beast towards A. who turns the brute towards B. who turns it again towards C. whom it hurts, he who was the first actor and turned out the beast is answerable in trespass vi et armis for the injury done to C.—But suppose the death of a man ensues from turning out such a wild beast by the owner, who knows it to be mischievous, the owner of the beast is guilty of murder, Rex versus Huggins, 2 Ld. Raym. 1583.—If a man doth an unlawful act, he shall be answerable for the consequences of it. 1 Ld.Raym. 480, per Holt Chief Justice. 5 Mod. 427, S.C. and S.P.

I shall conclude with what the Lord Chief Justice Wilmot, and the Court said in the case of Slater versus Baker and Stapleton, 1 Wilson 362, where it was objected that the defendants ought to have been charged as trespassers vi et armis, and not as trespassers upon the case; the Court said, "that the plaintiff in that case ought to receive a satisfaction, seemed to be admitted, so we will not look with eagle's eyes to see whether the evidence applies exactly or not to the case, when we can see the plaintiff has obtained a verdict for such damages as he deserves, but we will establish such verdict if possible:" so I am of opinion the plaintiff ought to have judgment.

BLACKSTONE, JUSTICE.—I am of a different opinion. I take it here is no verdict; the declaration and special case are stated for the opinion of the Court, whether the facts in the case amount to an assault and battery vi et armis by the defendant upon the plaintiff?

The declaration alleges that the defendant threw, cast and tost a lighted squib against the plaintiff, and struck him on the face therewith, whereby he lost his eye; this is laid as an immediate injury done by defendant to the plaintiff, which is the gist of this action of assault and battery; for if the injury received from the act of the defendant was not immediate, but a consequence, trespass vi et armis will not lie, but it must be an action on the case. * * *

The lawfulness or unlawfulness of an act is not the criterion between these two actions, for a man may become an immediate trespasser vi et armis, by doing a lawful act; as if a man doing an act lawful in itself, hurts another by accident, misfortune, and against the will of the actor, yet he shall be answerable in trespass vi et armis for immediate injury done; unless the injury was inevitable, 27 Hen. 7, 28a. 1 Stran. 596, and many other cases in the books to this purpose. Trespass on the case will lie for doing an unlawful act, if the damage sustained thereby be not immediate but consequential, 11 Mod. 108. The first act in the present case (I allow) was unlawful; but the squib by the first act did not strike the plaintiff, the first act was complete when it lay on Yates' stall, afterwards Willis a bystander threw it across the market-house, it fell on the stall of another man who threw it to another part of the market-house and struck the plaintiff therewith and put out his eye. Willis who took up the squib and threw it across the market-house is not answerable in trespass vi et armis, for he did that act to prevent injury to himself, and did no harm to anybody. Willis and Yates gave the squib two new directions, acting as free agents, not by the instigation, command, request, or as servants of the defendant, but in defence of their persons, so the injury which happened to the plaintiff was the consequence of, and not done immediately by the first act of the defendant. * * *

GOULD, J. I differ with my Brother BLACKSTONE, but with the utmost respect to his sentiments. I think that neither Willis nor Ryall are liable to an action in this case; if that be so, and this action will not lie against the defendant Shepherd who did the first act, which was unlawful, the plaintiff who has been greatly injured will be without remedy. The damage done did instantly arise by and from the act of the defendant: Willis and Ryall in defence of themselves and their goods, being in a state of fear, without power of recollection, instantly tossed and threw the squib away from themselves, what they did was inevitable, as it seemeth to me. Suppose a burning squib thrown into a coach passing along the street, and one of the persons therein throws it out, and the like misfortune as this happens; surely the person throwing the squib out of the coach might justify or excuse himself by pleading; though this is not so strong a case I think as the present. The defendant is the only wrong doer; his act put

Willis and Ryall under an inevitable necessity of acting as they did, so neither of them is liable to an action: upon the whole I am of opinion judgment must be for the plaintiff.

LORD CHIEF JUSTICE DE GREY. The distinction between actions of trespass on the case, and trespass vi et armis should be most carefully and precisely observed, otherwise we shall introduce much confusion and uncertainty; this is that kind of injury where the distinction is very nice. It strikes me thus; trespass vi et armis lies against the person from whom an injury is received by force. So the question is, whether this personal injury was received by the plaintiff by force from the defendant? Or whether the injury was received from, or resulting from a new force of another?

The real or true question (I think) is not whether the first act of throwing the squib by the defendant was lawful or not; for I see, that in doing a lawful act, trespass vi et armis will, in some cases, lie against the actor; and yet there are cases where trespass vi et armis will not lie against a person for doing an unlawful act. * * *

The throwing the squib by the defendant was an unlawful act at common law, the squib had a natural power and tendency to do mischief indiscriminately; but what mischief, or where it would fall, none could know; the fault egrediture e persona of him who threw the squib, it would naturally produce a defence to be made by every person in danger of being hurt thereby, and no line can be drawn as to the mischief likely to happen to any person in such danger; the two persons Willis and Ryall, did not act with or in combination with the defendant, and their removal of the squib for fear of danger to themselves seems to me to be a continuation of the first act of the defendant until the explosion of the squib; no man contracts guilt in defending himself; the second and third men were not guilty of any trespass, but all the injury was done by the first act of the defendant; here I lay the stress, and here I differ with my brother Blackstone; for I conceive all the facts of throwing the squib must be considered as one single act, namely the act of the defendant; the same as if it had been a cracker made with gunpowder which had bounded and rebounded again and again before it struck out the plaintiff's eye. I am of opinion that judgment must be for the plaintiff, and the postea was accordingly delivered to him, by the opinion of three judges against one.[13]

The relevance of the concepts of immediacy, force and negligence to trespass and case was further considered, inter alia, in Leame v. Bray, 3 East 593, 102 Eng.Rep. 724 (K.B.1803). Defendant had negligently driven his chaise into plaintiff's curricule, causing plaintiff's

13. Suppose a philanthropist grabs a bystander to shield himself from a terrorist dynamiter. See Laidlaw v. Sage, 2 App.Div. 374, 37 N.Y.S. 770 (1896), rev'd for insuffticent evidence of causation 158 N.Y. 73, 52 N.E. 679 (1899).

driver to be thrown to the ground, the horses to run away with the curricule, and plaintiff to jump for his life, fracturing his collarbone. No "blame" was "imputable" to the defendant except that on a dark night, when the parties could not see each other, he had driven on the wrong side of the road. Defendant contended that the injury here was "consequential and not immediately flowing from the forcible act of the defendant," and that therefore the only proper remedy was by an action on the case, not trespass vi et armis, no wilfulness having been shown. The court held that trespass did lie, notwithstanding defendant's negligence, and seemed to satisfy itself as to the requirement for immediacy in trespass on the basis of the continuity of activities resulting from defendant's application of force. For instance, Le Banc, J.:

> "* * * [W]here the injury is immediate on the act done, there trespass lies; but where it is not immediate on the act done, but consequential, there the remedy is in case. And the distinction is well instanced by the example put of a man's throwing a log into the highway: if at the time of its being thrown, it hit any person, it is trespass; but if after it be thrown, any person going along the road receive an injury by falling over it as it lies there, it is case. Neither does the degree of violence with which the act is done make any difference; for if the log were put down in the most quiet way upon a man's foot, it would be trespass; but if thrown into the road with whatever violence, and one afterwards fall over it, it is case and not trespass. So here, if the defendant had simply placed his chaise in the road, and the plaintiff had run against it in the dark, the injury would not have been direct, but in consequence only of the defendant's previous improper act. Here however the defendant was driving the carriage at the time with the force necessary to move it along, and the injury to the plaintiff happened from that immediate act: therefore the remedy must be trespass: and all the cases will support that principle. It is chiefly in actions for running down vessels at sea that difficulties may occur; because certainly the force which occasions the injury is not so immediate from the act of the person steering. The immediate agents of the force are the wind and waves, and the personal act of the party rather consists in putting the vessel in the way to be so acted upon: and whether that may make any difference in that case I will not now take upon me to determine. But here, where the personal force is immediately applied to the horse and carriage, the things acted upon and causing the damage, like a finger to the trigger of a gun, the injury is immediate from the act of driving, and trespass is the proper remedy for an immediate injury done by one to another: but where the injury is only consequential from the act done, there it is case."

The converse proposition, that case could lie where injury was immediate but occasioned by negligence was established in Williams v. Holland, Common Pleas (1833) 10 Bing. 112, despite earlier indications to the contrary, Day v. Edwards (1794) 5 Term Rep. 648.

EXCERPT FROM F. HARPER AND F. JAMES, JR., THE LAW OF TORTS (1956)

§ 12.2 * * * In trespass * * *, the gist of the action was certainly not fault. The notion was, rather, that he whose affirmative act directly caused the harm should ordinarily pay for it. Now it is perfectly true that this form of action was often used to redress the clearest type of wrongs, such as deliberate beatings and woundings, and the allegations in all cases savored of this kind of situation. But trespass was also the appropriate remedy for direct accidental harms. And a prima facie case in trespass was made out by showing that defendant's voluntary act directly produced the injury. This did not mean that liability for injuries so caused was absolute.[14] Defendant might justify even an intentional hurting of the plaintiff by showing that it was done in self-defense,[15] or to repel a trespass,[16] or to effect a lawful arrest,[17] for example. And there have been suggestions from early times that defendant could excuse himself by showing that the injury was caused through "inevitable accident." But it was never clear just what constituted an "inevitable accident." The phrase was sometimes used to describe a situation where there was really no voluntary act on the part of defendant at all "as if a man by force take my hand and strike you"; and such a state of facts was inconsistent with even a prima facie trespass and could be shown under the general issue. But the phrase seems also to have been used to refer to cases where defendant was utterly without fault, though the harm was caused by his voluntary act. This must be gathered from dicta; there is not a single recorded case before the nineteenth century in which a defendant successfully pleaded and proved such an excuse in an action of trespass. On the other hand, the pleas which were unsuccessful fell short of ruling out all possibilities of negligence as we know it today. Thus in Dickenson v. Watson, where defendant accidentally shot plaintiff, the defendant pleaded that he lawfully had the gun; that he discharged it intending no harm to happen, and when no one was in sight; that as he did so plaintiff came into the way. But it was not alleged that the presence of people in the vicinity was unlikely.

14. Winfield, The Myth of Absolute Liability, 42 L.Q.Rev. 37 (1926).

15. See Beale, Justification of Injury, 41 Harv.L.Rev. 553 (1927); Winfield, note 6 supra at 39; Pollock, Torts 113, 176 (13th ed. 1939).

16. See Winfield, The Myth of Absolute Liability; 42 L.Q.Rev. 37, at 44–45 (1926); Pollock, note 7 supra at 176.

17. Beale, Justification of Injury, 41 Harv.L.Rev. 553, 556 (1927); Pollock, Torts 113 (13th ed. 1939). [Footnotes 14–17 are from the original, renumbered; other footnotes in the original have been omitted.]

From the decisions, these conclusions seem warranted: (1) the gist of liability in trespass was that defendant's act directly produced the injury; (2) probably the complete absence of any negligence would defeat the action; (3) but if it would, this was matter of defense to be affirmatively pleaded and proved by defendant; it came in, so to speak, by the back door; (4) the concept of negligence was not dominant enough—at least in this form of action—and not well enough worked out in the mind of the profession so that its opposite was ever successfully formulated as a defense to an action of trespass before the nineteenth century.

BROWN v. KENDALL

Supreme Judicial Court of Massachusetts, 1850.
6 Cush. 292.

This was an action of trespass for assault and battery, originally commenced against George K. Kendall, the defendant, who died pending the suit, and his executrix was summoned in.

It appeared in evidence, on the trial, which was before Wells, C. J., in the court of common pleas, that two dogs, belonging to the plaintiff and the defendant, respectively, were fighting in the presence of their masters; that the defendant took a stick about four feet long, and commenced beating the dogs in order to separate them; that the plaintiff was looking on, at the distance of about a rod, and that he advanced a step or two towards the dogs. In their struggle, the dogs approached the place where the plaintiff was standing. The defendant retreated backwards from before the dogs, striking them as he retreated; and as he approached the plaintiff, with his back towards him, in raising his stick over his shoulder, in order to strike the dogs, he accidentally hit the plaintiff in the eye, inflicting upon him a severe injury.

Whether it was necessary or proper for the defendant to interfere in the fight between the dogs; whether the interference, if called for, was in proper manner, and what degree of care was exercised by each party on the occasion; were the subject of controversy between the parties, upon all the evidence in the case, of which the foregoing is an outline.

The defendant requested the judge to instruct the jury, that "if both the plaintiff and defendant at the time of the blow were using ordinary care, or if at that time the defendant was using ordinary care and the plaintiff was not, or if at that time both plaintiff and defendant were not using ordinary care, then the plaintiff could not recover."

* * *

The judge declined to give the instructions, as above requested, but left the case to the jury under the following instructions: "If the defendant, in beating the dogs, was doing a necessary act, or one which it was his duty under the circumstances of the case to do, and was doing it in a proper way; then he was not responsible in this action, provided he was using ordinary care at the time of the blow. If it was not a necessary act; if he was not in duty bound to attempt to part the dogs, but might with propriety interfere or not as he chose; the defendant was responsible for the consequences of the blow, unless it appeared that he was in the exercise of extraordinary care, so that the accident was inevitable, using the word inevitable not in a strict but a popular sense."

"If, however, the plaintiff, when he met with the injury, was not in the exercise of ordinary care, he cannot recover, and this rule applies, whether the interference of the defendant in the fight of the dogs was necessary or not. If the jury believe, that it was the duty of the defendant to interfere, then the burden of proving negligence on the part of the defendant, and ordinary care on the part of the plaintiff, is on the plaintiff. If the jury believe, that the act of interference in the fight was unnecessary, then the burden of proving extraordinary care on the part of the defendant, or want of ordinary care on the part of the plaintiff, is on defendant."

The jury under these instructions returned a verdict for the plaintiff; whereupon the defendant alleged exceptions. * * *

SHAW, C. J. This is an action of trespass, *vi et armis*, brought by George Brown against George K. Kendall, for an assault and battery; * * *

The facts set forth in the bill of exceptions preclude the supposition, that the blow, inflicted by the hand of the defendant upon the person of the plaintiff, was intentional. The whole case proceeds on the assumption, that the damage sustained by the plaintiff, from the stick held by the defendant, was inadvertent and unintentional; and the case involves the question how far, and under what qualifications, the party by whose unconscious act the damage was done is responsible for it. We use the term "unintentional" rather than involuntary, because in some of the cases, it is stated, that the act of holding and using a weapon or instrument, the movement of which is the immediate cause of hurt to another, is a voluntary act, although its particular effect in hitting and hurting another is not within the purpose or intention of the party doing the act.

It appears to us, that some of the confusion in the cases on this subject has grown out of the long-vexed question, under the rule of the common law, whether a party's remedy, where he has one, should be sought in an action of the case, or of trespass. This is very distinguishable from the question, whether in a given case, any action will lie. The result of these cases is, that if the damage complained of is the immediate effect of the act of the defendant, trespass *vi et armis* lies; if consequential only, and not immediate, case is the proper remedy. Leame v. Bray, 3 East, 593; Hugget v. Montgomery, 2 N.R. 446, Day's Ed. and notes.

In these discussions, it is frequently stated by judges, that when one receives injury from the direct act of another, trespass will lie.

But we think this is said in reference to the question, whether trespass and not case will lie, assuming that the facts are such, that some action will lie. These *dicta* are no authority, we think, for holding, that damage received by a direct act of force from another will be sufficient to maintain an action of trespass, whether the act was lawful or unlawful, and neither wilful, intentional, or careless. In the principal case cited, Leame v. Bray, the damage arose from the act of the defendant, in driving on the wrong side of the road, in a dark night, which was clearly negligent if not unlawful. In the course of the argument of that case, (p. 595,) Lawrence, J., said: "There certainly are cases in the books, where, the injury being direct and immediate, trespass has been holden to lie, though the injury was not intentional." The term "injury" implies something more than damage; but, independently of that consideration, the proposition may be true, because though the injury was unintentional, the act may have been unlawful or negligent, and the cases cited by him are perfectly consistent with that supposition. So the same learned judge in the same case says, (p. 597) "No doubt trespass lies against one who drives a carriage against another, whether done wilfully or not." But he immediately adds, "Suppose one who is driving a carriage is negligently and heedlessly looking about him, without attending to the road when persons are passing, and thereby runs over a child and kills him, is it not manslaughter? and if so, it must be trespass; for every manslaughter includes trespass;" showing what he understood by a case not wilful. * * *

In using this term, ordinary care, it may be proper to state, that what constitutes ordinary care will vary with the circumstances of cases. In general, it means that kind and degree of care, which prudent and cautious men would use, such as is required by the exigency of the case, and such as is necessary to guard against probable danger. A man, who should have occasion to discharge a gun, on an open and extensive marsh, or in a forest, would be required to use less circumspection and care, than if he were to do the same thing in an inhabited town, village or city. To make an accident, or casualty, or as the law sometimes states it, inevitable accident, it must be such an accident as the defendant could not have avoided by the use of the kind and degree of care necessary to the exigency, and in the circumstances in which he was placed.

We are not aware of any circumstances in this case, requiring a distinction between acts which it was lawful and proper to do, and acts of legal duty. There are cases, undoubtedly, in which officers are bound to act under process, for the legality of which they are not responsible, and perhaps some others in which this distinction would be important. We can have no doubt that the act of the defendant in attempting to part the fighting dogs, one of which was his own, and for the injurious acts of which he might be responsible, was a lawful and proper act, which he might do by proper and safe means. If, then, in doing this act, using due care and all proper precautions necessary to the exigency of the case, to avoid hurt to others, in raising his stick for that purpose, he accidentally hit the plaintiff in his eye and wounded him, this was the result of pure accident, or was involuntary and unavoidable, and therefore the action would not lie. Or if the defendant was chargeable with some negligence, and if the plaintiff was also chargeable with negligence, we think the plaintiff cannot recover without showing that the damage was caused wholly by the act of the defendant, and that the plaintiff's own negligence did not contribute as an efficient cause to produce it. * * *

The court are of opinion that [the instructions to the jury] were not conformable to law. If the act of hitting the plaintiff was unintentional, on the part of the defendant, and done in the doing of a lawful act, then the defendant was not liable, unless it was done in the want of exercise of due care, adapted to the exigency of the case, and therefore such want of due care became part of the plaintiff's case, and the burden of proof was on the plaintiff to establish it. * * *

Perhaps the learned judge, by the use of the term extraordinary care, in the above charge, explained as it is by the context, may have intended nothing more than that increased degree of care and diligence, which the exigency of particular circumstances might require, and which men of ordinary care and prudence would use under like circumstances, to guard against danger. If such was the meaning of this part of the charge, then it does not differ from our views, as above explained. But we are of opinion, that the other part of the charge, that the burden of proof was on the defendant, was incorrect. Those facts which are essential to enable the plaintiff to recover, he takes the burden of proving. The evidence may be offered by the plaintiff or by the defendant; the question of due care, or want of care, may be essentially connected with the main facts, and arise from the same proof; but the effect of the rule, as to the burden of proof, is this, that when the proof is all in, and before the jury, from whatever side it comes, and whether directly proved, or inferred from circumstances, if it appears that the defendant was doing a lawful act, and unintentionally hit and hurt the plaintiff, then unless it also appears to the satisfaction of the jury, that the defendant is chargeable with some fault, negligence, carelessness, or want of prudence, the plaintiff fails to sustain the burden of proof, and is not entitled to recover.

New trial ordered.[18]

---

18. Cf. Thorns case, fn. 10, p. 23 above. Cf. also United Electric Light Co. v. Deliso Constr. Co., 315 Mass. 313, 52 N.E.2d 553 (1943).

Brown v. Kendall effectively eliminated the difference between trespass and case in Massachusetts. This merger was less clear in English law for more than a century thereafter.

In Holmes v. Mather, (1875) L.R. 10 Ex. 261, defendant's horses, having been frightened by a dog, had run away with their carriage and knocked plaintiff down. Plaintiff sued in two counts, negligence and trespass, and defendant pleaded not guilty. The jury found "no negligence in any one." Bramwell B. ruled that the trespass action was accordingly not maintainable, stating, "For the convenience of mankind in carrying on the affairs of life, people as they go along roads must expect, or put up with, such mischief as reasonable care on the part of others cannot avoid. * * * [I]f the act that does an injury is an act of direct force vi et armis, trespass is the proper remedy (if there is any remedy) where the act is wrongful, either as being wilful or as being the result of negligence. Where the act is not wrongful for either of these reasons, no action is maintainable, though trespass would be the proper form of action if it were wrongful." He also concluded that the driver was not "immediately doing the act which did the mischief. * * *"

It has been argued that Baron Bramwell was assuming that wrongfulness was a necessary element in prima facie trespass, and that this reflected a general understanding of 19th century common lawyers, prevalent before 1875, that trespass would not lie except for a wrongful act. Diplock J., as he then was, so contended in Fowler v. Lanning [1959] 1 Q.B. 426. Most scholarly opinion had tended otherwise, assuming instead that, before Holmes v. Mather, negligence was relevant to trespass only as an affirmative defense, and not as a necessary element of the cause of action. It is clear in any event that a substantial body of English opinion considered Holmes v. Mather to have established a special exception for highway cases, perhaps based on the suggestion, reflected in Bramwell's opinion, that highway travellers voluntarily assume the risks of non-wrongful accidents. Until 1959 it was widely thought in England that, while plaintiffs must plead and prove negligence in actions of trespass arising from highway accidents, defendants must prove freedom from negligence in trespass arising otherwise. For instance, in Stanley v. Powell, L.R. [1891] 1 Q.B. 86, plaintiff, a beater (of bushes, for game), was wounded in a shooting accident which the jury found to be non-negligent; defendant's shot, aimed at a pheasant, had ricocheted. While plaintiff had alleged negligence and plaintiff had denied it, the question arose whether there might be liability, notwithstanding the lack of negligence, in trespass. Judge Denman ruled that there could be no such liability for unintentional gunshot injury without negligence; he seemed to assume, however, that the issue of negligence would arise in such a case only by way of defendant's pleading and proving an affirmative defense. That there was a distinction in this regard between highway and other cases was argued in National Coal Board v. Evans [1951] 2 K.B. 861, 865 (dicta by Lord Justice Cohen, disapproving the distinction but not ruling thereon because defendant was "utterly without fault" within Weaver v. Ward).

Not until 1959 did an English appellate court rule that an allegation "the defendant shot the plaintiff" (without alleging wilfulness, negligence or any other circumstances, "indeed with what weapon, from bow and arrow to atomic warhead") fails to state a cause of action, Fowler v. Lanning [1959] 1 Q.B. 426. Diplock J. said that trespass to the person "does not lie if the injury . . . was caused unintentionally and without negligence"; that trespass to the person on the highway does not differ in this respect from trespass to the person elsewhere; (referring to the argument reflected in Bramwell's opinion in Holmes v. Mather, which derived from the opinion of Blackburn J. in Fletcher v. Rylands, p. 53 below) that "* * * the plaintiff must today in this crowded world be considered as taking upon himself the risk of inevitable injury from any acts of his neighbor which, in the absence of damage to the plaintiff, would not in themselves be unlawful"; and that the "onus of proving negligence * * * lies upon the plaintiff, whether the action be framed in trespass or in negligence."

This did not quite merge trespass and case in the British Commonwealth. The High Court of Australia, for instance, rejected Fowler v. Lanning, McHale v. Watson, 111 Commw.L.R. 384 (Austl.1964). (The Supreme Court of New Zealand, on the other hand, followed Fowler v. Lanning, in Beals v. Hayward [1960] N.Z.L.R. 131, and British Columbia had anticipated it, Walmsley v. Humenick [1954] 2 D.L.R. 232.)

In England loose ends as to statutes of limitation remained until Letang v. Cooper [1965] 1 Q.B. 232 (C.A.). The defendant had driven his Jaguar car over a sunbather's legs. She sued nearly forty-three months later. The statute of limitations had been six years for actions founded "on tort", but had been reduced to three years for personal injuries from "negligence, nuisance or breach of duty." Plaintiff claimed that these words do not cover trespass to the person. The court disagreed. All three judges considered trespass to be at least "breach of duty". They furthermore thought, for slightly different reasons, that the action was also barred as "negligence." Diplock L. J., as he then was, defined a cause of action as "simply a factual situation the existence of which entitles one person to obtain from a court a remedy against another person." Since "trespass" and "negligence" were names for the forms of action, now abolished, which were formerly the means by which the remedy was sought, they are now merely convenient names for the factual situation which gives rise to liability, which may be called either trespass or negligence. "* * * [T]hat * * * does not mean that there are two causes of action. It does not cease to be the tort of negligence because it can also be called * * * an action for trespass to the person." Lord Denning M.R., on the other hand, with whom Dankwerts L.J. joined, stated that "* * * the distinction between trespass and case is obsolete. We have a different subdivision altogether

* * * according as the defendant did the injury intentionally or unintentionally. * * * If * * * [one] does not inflict injury intentionally but only unintentionally, the plaintiff has no cause of action today in trespass. His only cause of action is in negligence, and then only on proof of want of reasonable care."

Notwithstanding Lord Denning's position, there remains some Commonwealth opinion to the effect that a tort of "negligent trespass" survives as a different cause of action from "negligence". See, e. g., Trindade, Some Curiosities of Negligent Trespass to the Person—A Comparative Study, 20 Int'l Comp.L.Q. 706 (1971).

HOLMES, THE COMMON LAW (1881; Howe ed. 1963)

[Pages 76–78] To return to the example of the accidental blow with a stick lifted in self-defence, there is no difference between hitting a prson standing in one's rear and hitting one who was pushed by a horse within range of the stick just as it was lifted, provided that it was not possible, under the circumstances, in the one case to have known, in the other to have anticipated, the proximity. In either case there is wanting the only element which distinguishes voluntary acts from spasmodic muscular contractions as a ground of liability. In neither of them, that is to say, has there been an opportunity of choice with reference to the consequence complained of,—a chance to guard against the result which has come to pass. A choice which entails a concealed consequence is as to that consequence no choice.

The general principle of our law is that loss from accident must lie where it falls, and this principle is not affected by the fact that a human being is the instrument of misfortune. But relatively to a given human being anything is accident which he could not fairly have been expected to contemplate as possible, and therefore to avoid. In the language of the late Chief Justice Nelson of New York: "No case or principle can be found, or if found can be maintained, subjecting an individual to liability for an act done without fault on his part. * * * All the cases concede that an injury arising from inevitable accident, or, which in law or reason is the same thing, from an act that ordinary human care and foresight are unable to guard against, is but the misfortune of the sufferer, and lays no foundation for legal responsibility." If this were not so, any act would be sufficient, however remote, which set in motion or opened the door for a series of physical sequences ending in damage; such as riding the horse, in the case of the runaway, or even coming to a place where one is seized with a fit and strikes the plaintiff in an unconscious spasm. Nay, why need the defendant have acted at all, and why is it not enough that his existence has been at the expense of the plaintiff? The requirement of an act is the requirement that the defendant should have made a choice. But the only possible purpose of introducing this moral element is to make the power of avoiding the evil complained of a condition of liability. There is no such power where the evil cannot be foreseen. Here we reach the argument from policy, and I shall accordingly postpone for a moment the discussion of trespasses upon land, and of conversions, and will take up the liability for cattle separately at a later stage.

A man need not, it is true, do this or that act,—the term *act* implies a choice,—but he must act somehow. Furthermore, the public generally profits by individual activity. As action cannot be avoided, and tends to the public good, there is obviously no policy in throwing the hazard of what is at once desirable and inevitable upon the actor.

The state might conceivably make itself a mutual insurance company against accidents, and distribute the burden of its citizens' mishaps among all its members. There might be a pension for paralytics, and state aid for those who suffered in person or estate from tempest or wild beasts. As between individuals it might adopt the mutual insurance principle *pro tanto*, and divide damages when both were in fault, as in the *rusticum judicium* of the admiralty, or it might throw all loss upon the actor irrespective of fault. The state does none of these things, however, and the prevailing view is that its cumbrous and expensive machinery ought not to be set in motion unless some clear benefit is to be derived from disturbing the *status quo*.[19] State interference is an evil, where it cannot be shown to be a good.[20] Universal insurance, if desired, can be better and more cheaply accomplished by private enterprise. The undertaking to redistribute losses simply on the ground that they resulted from the defendant's act would not only be open to these objections, but, as it is hoped the preceding discussion has shown, to the still graver one of offending the sense of justice.[21] Unless my act is of a nature to threaten others, unless under the circumstances a prudent man would have foreseen the possibility of harm, it is no more justifiable to make me indemnify my neighbor against the consequences, than to make me do the same thing if I had fallen upon him in a fit, or to compel me to insure him against lightning.[22]

19. Compare G. Calabresi, The Costs of Accidents 261–63 (1970).

20. Compare Calabresi and Melamed, Property Rules, Liability Rules and Inalienability Rules: One View of the Cathedral, 85 Harv.L.Rev. 1089, 1090 (1972): "When a loss is left where it falls in an auto accident, it is not because God so ordained it. Rather it is because the state has granted the injurer an entitlement to be free of liability and will intervene to prevent the victim's friends if they are stronger, from taking compensation from the injurer. The loss is shifted in other cases because the state has granted an entitlement to compensation and will intervene to prevent the stronger injurer from rebuffing the victim's requests for compensation."

21. Compare Fletcher, Fairness and Utility in Tort Theory, 85 Harv.L.Rev. 537, 564 et seq. (1972).

22. See Smith, Sequel to Workmen's Compensation Acts, 27 Harv.L.Rev. 235 (1914), note 13, p. 239.

For various treatments of the material covered in this section, consult: Ames, Law and Morals, 22 Harv.L.Rev. 97 (1908); Selected Essays on the Law of Torts, 1; Holmes, The Common Law (1881) Chapters 1, 2, 3; Isaacs, Fault & Liability, 31 Harv.L.Rev. 954 (1918); Selected Essays on the Law of Torts,

SMITH, SEQUEL TO WORKMEN'S COMPENSATION ACTS

27 Harv.L.Rev. 235, 344 (1914).

(Pages 363–368). Of what has heretofore been said this is the sum: The result reached in many cases under the Workmen's Compensation Acts is absolutely incongruous with the results reached under the modern common law as to various persons whose cases are not affected by these statutes. For this difference there is no satisfactory reason.

It is believed that the incongruities heretofore pointed out, resulting from the difference between the statute and the modern common law, will not be permitted to continue permanently without protest. The public are not likely to be "content for long under these contradictory systems." In the end, one or the other of the two conflicting theories is likely to prevail. There is no probability, during the present generation, of a repeal of the Workmen's Compensation Acts. Indeed, the tendency is now in the direction of extension, rather than repeal, of this species of legislation. The only present available method to remove the inconsistency is by bringing about a change in the existing common law, either by legislation or by judicial decisions.

As to legislation (aided perhaps by constitutional amendments); there may be an attempt to bring about State Insurance, not confined to harm suffered by hired laborers. It may extend to an "outsider," who suffers harm from the non-culpable conduct of persons carrying on a business in which he is not a participant. It may not be con-

235; 1 Street, Foundations of Legal Liability Ch. 6 (1906); Wigmore, Responsibility for Tortious Acts, 7 Harv. L.Rev. 315, 383, 441 (1894); Selected Essays on the Law of Torts 18; Winfield, History of Negligence, 42 L.Q. Rev. 184 (1926); Winfield, Meaning of Absolute Liability, 42 L.Q.Rev. 37 (1926); Note, 67 L.Q.Rev. 434 (1951); Milsom, Trespass from Henry III to Edward III, 74 L.Q.Rev. 195, 407 and 561 (1958); Note, 75 L.Q.Rev. 161 (1959); Dworkin, The Case of the Misguided Missile, 22 Mod.L.Rev. 538 (1959); Davis, Trespass to the Person: Must Intention or Negligence be Proved?, 23 Mod.L.Rev. 674 (1960); Millner, The Retreat of Trespass, Current Legal Problems 1965 at 20; Dworkin, Trespass and Negligence—A Further Attempt to Bury the Forms of Action, 28 Mod.L.Rev. 92 (1965); James, Analysis of the Origin and Development of the Negligence Actions, in Department of Transportation Automobile Insurance and Compensation Study, The Origin and Development of the Negligence Action: Studies of the Role of Fault in Automobile Accident Compensation Law at 35 (1970); Malone, Ruminations on the Role of Fault in the History of Torts, id. at 1. 8 Holdsworth, A History of English Law, 446 et seq. (2d ed. 1937); as to the English court system see R. M. Jackson, The Machinery of Justice in England (1972).

Liability under Workmen's Compensation Acts has been called "a distinct revision to earlier conceptions that he who causes harm, however innocently, is, as its author, bound to make it good." Smith, op. cit., supra, p. 246. Is "absolute liability" imposed by Workmen's Compensation Acts for the same reasons that underlay liability in the early action of trespass? Are any factors present in workmen's compensation systems that did not exist in the ancient liability for trespass? See James, Accident Liability Reconsidered: The Impact of Liability Insurance, 57 Yale L.J. 549 (1948); Larson, The Welfare State & Workmen's Compensation, 5 N.A.C.C.A.L.J. 18, 25–31 (1950).

fined to the case where there is, in the chain of antecedents, the non-culpable conduct of some human being other than the damaged person himself. It may include the case of an independent workman, who is hurt by pure accident, without any human agency other than his own, while conducting his own business on his own account; e. g. a small farmer, or a blacksmith who runs his forge without an assistant.

A State Insurance Law may not merely insure against accident, but also against disease, either contracted in the service of another or while the claimant was working on his own account.

It may include damage wholly due to a natural cause, such as a stroke of lightning.

Whether legislation of the above descriptions *ought* to be enacted is a question upon which no opinion is here intimated. Our immediate point is, that the present Workmen's Compensation legislation will inevitably give rise to a plausible agitation for such further legislation.

As to a change in the common law, to be brought about by judicial decisions:

There may be an attempt to induce judges to repudiate the fundamental doctrine of the modern common law of torts that fault is generally requisite to liability, and to go back to the ancient common-law doctrine that an innocent actor must answer for harm caused by his non-culpable conduct.

Or the judges may be urged to adopt a middle or compromise view; that, as between two non-culpable actors, the loss shall be equally divided.

Several questions arise:

1. Can the judges change the law?

2. Ought they to change the law?

3. Will they change the law?

The objection may be raised that judges cannot make, or change, law; not merely that they cannot alter statute law, a result which is admittedly beyond their power; but that they cannot make or alter law on subjects not dealt with by the legislature.

There are at least three different theories as to judicial lawmaking:

1. That judges cannot "make" law; that they merely discover and apply law which has always existed.

2. (A middle view.) That judges can and do make new law on subjects not covered by previous decisions; but that judges cannot unmake old law, cannot even change an existing rule of "judge-made" law.

3. That judges can and do make new law; and also can and do unmake old law; i. e., law previously laid down by themselves or by their judicial predecessors.

We prefer the third view. But if the second view is adopted, the result here would not be to sustain and preserve unaltered (unless by legislation) the common law as declared by the courts in A.D. 1900; but, instead, to sustain the law as formerly declared in A.D. 1400 by the judges of that day. If judges have no power to change (i. e., if they cannot change) law "made" by their judicial predecessors, then, of course, they have not legally done that which they had no legal power to do (that which they could not do). Hence it would follow that the common law of 1400 is still in force; and that the decisions in more recent times, purporting to establish a contrary rule (i. e., the rule now known as the modern common-law doctrine), are simply instances of judicial usurpation.

But, as already intimated, we prefer the third view, that judges can and do make new law and unmake old law. Under this view the judges have heretofore changed the law of A.D. 1400 to the law of A.D. 1900, and still have now the power to change it back again. Assuming, then, that the judges can turn the hands of the legal clock back five centuries, the questions remain:

Ought they to make the change?

Will they make the change?

As to whether the change will be made: it is safe to say that, while it may take place, yet it is not likely to be done directly and avowedly. When courts change the substantive law, they generally do so very gradually, and often attempt to conceal (or perhaps unconsciously conceal) the fact of change by using various "fiction phrases."

Judges, however, are not insensible to public opinion; and legislation, evidencing public opinion, has a reflex action on courts.

Even if courts should shrink from directly and avowedly changing the law, the result could be, to a considerable extent, accomplished by indirect methods. By a very liberal construction of the *res ipsa loquitur* doctrine; by a broad view as to what constitutes *prima facie* evidence of negligence; and by inverting the burden of proof (putting on defendant the burden of proving that he was not negligent),—the court could go far towards practically reversing the common law of A.D. 1900 in a large proportion of cases.

Whether this change *ought* to be made (whether it is expedient for either courts or legislatures to make it) is a problem of immense importance, which we here make no attempt to solve. At the very beginning it was said: "The object of this paper is to give notice of an impending question of great importance; not to give an answer to the question, but to show how and why it arises at the present time."

SECTION 3. BASES OTHER THAN FAULT FOR IMPOSING OR WITHHOLDING LIABILITY

The cases in Section 1 suggested that tort liability must ordinarily rest on fault. The cases in Section 2 show that in the common law action of trespass fault was not the dominant theme, though it grew in importance along with the development of the action on the case until the attitude disclosed in the first section became pretty prevalent. The present section seeks to explore various bases of liability other than fault, which have actually found expression from time to time in our statutory and judge made law. We do not suggest that a common set of considerations or policies runs through all these cases and statutes; indeed quite the reverse. Our purpose is to point out the variety of objectives and aims which have been sought through the device of making one man pay for another's damage, or of refusing to do so. It is hoped that this will stimulate examination of the suitability and efficacy of the liability device in the pursuit of various aims in variant types of situations which present many different types of social and economic problems. The latter cannot be studied extensively in this course. Yet something will be gained if avenues for fruitful study are opened up.

13 Edw. 1 Statute 2 (1285)

c. 1. Forasmuch as from Day to Day, Robberies, Murthers, Burnings, & Theft, be more often used than they have been heretofore, and Felons cannot be attained by the Oath of Jurors, which had rather suffer Strangers to be robbed, and to pass without Pain, than to indite the Offenders, of whom great Part be People of the same Country, or at the least, if the Offenders be of another Country, the Receivers be of Places near; and they do the same, because an Oath is not given unto Jurors of the same Country where such Felonies were done, & the Restitution of Damages hitherto no Pain hath been limited for their Concealment and Laches: Our Lord the King, for to abate the Power of Felons, hath established a pain in this Case, so that from henceforth, for fear of the Pain more than for Fear of any Oath, they shall not spare any, nor conceal any Felonies; * * * [necessary inquests are to be held] And if the Country will not answer for the Bodies of such manner of Offenders, the Pain shall be such, that every Country, that is to wit, the People dwelling in the Country, shall be answerable for the Robberies done, and also the Damages; so that the whole Hundred where the Robbery shall be done * * * shall be answerable for the Robberies done. * * * And after that the Felony or Robbery is done, the Country shall have no longer Space than forty Days, within which * * * it shall behove them to agree for the Robbery or Offense, or else that they will answer for the Bodies of the Offenders."

This was amended 27 Eliz. c. 13 (1585) to provide "That the Inhabitants and Resiants of every or any such Hundred * * * wherein Negligence, Fault or Defect of Pursuit and fresh Suit, after Hue and Cry made, shall happen to be * * * shall answer & satisfy the one Moity or Half of * * * such Sum and Sums of Money & Damages, as shall [(by virtue of 13 Edw. 1 St. 2)] be recovered or had against * * * the said Hundred * * * in which any Robbery or Felony shall at any Time hereafter be committed or done: * * *." [23]

CLARK v. INHABITANTS OF THE HUNDRED OF BLYTHING, 3 Dowling & R. 489. (K.B.1823).

Action for civil damages under the Riot Acts (9 Geo. 1, c. 22). "The intention of the legislature in passing this & the other statutes of the same nature, was twofold; to render the inhabitants of hundreds vigilant for their own sake as well as that of the public, by making them interested in the prevention of offences; and where that is impossible, in the apprehension and conviction of offenders. This particular statute contains provisions which are applicable to both those objects, for section 7 renders the hundred liable to make satisfaction for the injury sustained, & section 9 provides, that they shall

23. A similar provision, requiring compensation of loss by the city and governor in whose jurisdiction a crime was committed, if the brigand was not captured, was contained in sections 22–24 of the Code of Hammurabi (circa 2250 B.C.).

State compensation for victims of violent crimes, whether or not the criminal is captured, has been provided under a number of modern statutes.

The California law provides for a special fine on conviction of violent crime, in addition to any other penalties, of up to $10,000, "commensurate with the offense * * * and the probable economic impact upon the victim", payable to the indemnity fund, if the criminal has the ability to pay and payment will not cause his dependents to require public welfare. The Maryland act imposes an "additional cost" of five dollars on any person convicted of any crime (with certain exceptions, such as motor vehicle offenses) after its effective date, to be deposited in the general funds of the State. In England a similar compensation scheme has been instituted administratively, see, e. g., Hirschel, The Criminal Injuries Compensation Board, 26 Current Legal Problems 40 (1973). "The first reported award by the Criminal Injuries Compensation Board to a footballer injured during a game arose from a match played in the second division of the Legal League, which consists of teams drawn from solicitors' firms in the London area. Compensation of £1,252 was awarded to Anthony Killingback, who, while playing for Messrs W. H. Thompson, was viciously and unfairly tackled by a player of the opposing team the equally august Messrs Wilkinson, Kimbers and Staddon—with the result that he now has a permanent slight deformity. The evidence given to the Board (which can make awards only if satisfied that the act leading to the injury was criminal) was to the effect that games in that league were particularly hard. The experienced referee told the board that the game in question was the worst of the 300 which he had refereed." The Times (London), March 25, 1976, p. 16, col. 7.

Such compensation is also available in New Zealand, Sweden, and a number of Canadian provinces. See, generally, H. Edelhertz and G. Geis, Public Compensation to Victims of Crime (1974). Northern Ireland, where sectarian violence has for years been the cause of serious injury to the persons and property of innocent people, has long had statutes providing compensation for the victims. Originally the cost was borne by the ratepayers (i. e., owners of taxable property) of the area in which the crime occurred, but the burden grew so great that it has been shifted to the taxpayers generally. See Miers, Compensation and Rights in Property, 24 N.Ir.Legal Q. 539 (1973).

not be so liable if the offender is apprehended & convicted within six months after the commission of the offense." [24]

VINCENT v. LAKE ERIE TRANSPORTATION CO.

Supreme Court of Minnesota, 1910.
109 Minn. 456, 124 N.W. 221, 27 L.R.A.,N.S., 312.

Action in the district court for St. Louis county to recover $1,200 for damage to plaintiffs' wharf, caused by defendant negligently keeping its vessel tied to it. * * * The case was tried before Ensign, J., who denied the defendant's motion to direct a verdict in its favor, and a jury which rendered a verdict in favor of plaintiffs for $500. From an order denying defendant's motion for judgment notwithstanding the verdict or for a new trial, it appealed. * * *

O'BRIEN, J. The steamship Reynolds, owned by the defendant, was for the purpose of discharging her cargo on November 27, 1905, moored to plaintiffs' dock in Duluth. While the unloading of the boat was taking place a storm from the northeast developed, which at about ten o'clock p. m., when the unloading was completed, had so grown in violence that the wind was then moving at fifty miles per hour and continued to increase during the night. There is some evidence that one, and perhaps two, boats were able to enter the harbor that night, but it is plain that navigation was practically suspended from the hour mentioned until the morning of the twenty-ninth, when the storm abated, and during that time no master would have been justified in attempting to navigate his vessel, if he could avoid doing so. After the discharge of the cargo the Reynolds signaled for a tug to tow her from the dock, but none could be obtained because of the severity of the storm. If the lines holding the ship to the dock had been cast off, she would doubtless have drifted away; but, instead, the lines were kept fast, and as soon as one parted or chafed it was replaced, sometimes with a larger one. The vessel lay upon the outside of the

24. The Riot Act of 1714, of which the one under consideration was an amendment, provided in sections 1 and 2 that where 12 or more are unlawfully assembled and have been ordered dispersed by the reading of a Proclamation (the form of which is set out) they shall be adjudged Felons without benefit of Clergy. (Hence the slang expression: "to read the riot act.") Section 6 provided that any property owner whose buildings should be demolished by unlawful riot could recover against the Hundred, the judgment to be raised and levied on inhabitants of the Hundred as in Stat. 27 Eliz. 1 Geo. 1, Statute 2, c. 5.

A number of states have similar statutes. See, e. g., Note, Riot Insurance, 77 Yale L.J. 541, 552 (1968); Comment, The Aftermath of the Riot: Balancing the Budget, 116 U.Pa.L.Rev. 649, 684 n. 166 (1968); Note, Municipal Liability for Riot Damage, 81 Harv.L. Rev. 653 (1968); Note, Compensation for Victims of Urban Riots, 68 Colum. L.Rev. 57, 67–76 (1968); Jackson v. Kansas City, Kansas, 448 F.2d 518 (10th Cir. 1971) (municipal liability for gang rape). For a different approach compare the Urban Property Protection and Reinsurance Act of 1968, 12 U.S.C. §§ 1749 bbb et seq.

Compare the liability imposed by the statutes dealt with in U. S. ex rel. Marcus v. Hess, 317 U.S. 537, 63 S. Ct. 379, 87 L.Ed. 443 (1943) (informer statute); Bowles v. Trowbridge, 60 F. Supp. 48 (N.D.Cal.1945) (O.P.A. treble damage provision).

dock, her bow to the east, the wind and waves striking her starboard quarter with such force that she was constantly being lifted and thrown against the dock, resulting in its damage, as found by the jury, to the amount of $500.

We are satisfied that the character of the storm was such that it would have been highly imprudent for the master of the Reynolds to have attempted to leave the dock or to have permitted his vessel to drift away from it. One witness testified upon the trial that the vessel could have been warped into a slip, and that, if the attempt to bring the ship into the slip had failed, the worst that could have happened would be that the vessel would have been blown ashore upon a soft and muddy bank. The witness was not present in Duluth at the time of the storm, and, while he may have been right in his conclusions, those in charge of the dock and the vessel at the time of the storm were not required to use the highest human intelligence, nor were they required to resort to every possible experiment which could be suggested for the preservation of their property. Nothing more was demanded of them than ordinary prudence and care, and the record in this case fully sustains the contention of the appellant that, in holding the vessel fast to the dock, those in charge of her exercised good judgment and prudent seamanship.

It is claimed by the respondent that it was negligence to moor the boat at an exposed part of the wharf, and to continue in that position after it became apparent that the storm was to be more than usually severe. We do not agree with this position. The part of the wharf where the vessel was moored appears to have been commonly used for that purpose. It was situated within the harbor at Duluth, and must, we think, be considered a proper and safe place, and would undoubtedly have been such during what would be considered a very severe storm. The storm which made it unsafe was one which surpassed in violence any which might have reasonably been anticipated.

The appellant contends by ample assignments of error that, because its conduct during the storm was rendered necessary by prudence and good seamanship under conditions over which it had no control, it cannot be held liable for any injury resulting to the property of others, and claims that the jury should have been so instructed. An analysis of the charge given by the trial court is not necessary, as in our opinion the only question for the jury was the amount of damages which the plaintiffs were entitled to recover, and no complaint is made upon that score.

The situation was one in which the ordinary rules regulating property rights were suspended by forces beyond human control, and if, without the direct intervention of some act by the one sought to be held liable, the property of another was injured, such injury must be attributed to the act of God, and not to the wrongful act of the person sought to be charged. If during the storm the Reynolds had entered the harbor, and while there had become disabled and been thrown against the plaintiffs' dock, the plaintiffs could not have recovered. Again, if while attempting to hold fast to the dock the lines had parted, without any negligence, and the vessel carried against some other boat or dock in the harbor, there would be no liability upon her owner. But here these in charge of the vessel deliberately and by their direct efforts held her in such a position that the damage to the dock resulted, and, having thus preserved the ship at the expense of the dock, it seems to us that her owners are responsible to the dock owners to the extent of the injury inflicted.

In Depue v. Flatau, 100 Minn. 299, 111 N.W. 1, 8 L.R.A.,N.S., 485, this court held that where the plaintiff, while lawfully in the defendants' house, became so ill that he was incapable of traveling with safety, the defendants were responsible to him in damages for compelling him to leave the premises. If, however, the owner of the premises had furnished the traveler with proper accommodations and medical attendance, would he have been able to defeat an action brought against him for their reasonable worth?

In Ploof v. Putnam, 81 Vt. 471, 71 A. 188, 20 L.R.A.,N.S., 152, 130 Am.St.Rep. 1072, 15 Ann.Cas. 1151, the supreme court of Vermont held that where, under stress of weather, a vessel was without permission moored to a private dock at an island in Lake Champlain owned by the defendant, the plaintiff was not guilty of trespass, and that the defendant was responsible in damages because his representative upon the island unmoored the vessel, permitting it to drift upon the shore, with resultant injuries to it. If, in that case, the vessel had been permitted to remain, and the dock had suffered an injury, we believe the shipowner would have been held liable for the injury done.

Theologians hold that a starving man may, without moral guilt, take what is necessary to sustain life; but it could hardly be said that the obligation would not be upon such person to pay the value of the property so taken when he became able to do so. And so public necessity, in times of war or peace, may require the taking of private property for public purposes; but under our system of jurisprudence compensation must be made.

Let us imagine in this case that for the better mooring of the vessel those in charge of her had appropriated a valuable cable lying upon the dock. No matter how justifiable such appropriation might have been, it would not be claimed that, because of the overwhelming necessity of the situation, the owner of the cable could not recover its value.

This is not a case where life or property was menaced by any object or thing belonging to the plaintiffs, the destruction of which became necessary to prevent the threatened disaster. Nor is it a case where, because of the act of God, or unavoidable accident, the infliction of the injury was beyond the control of the defendant, but is one where the defendant prudently and advisedly availed itself of the plaintiffs' property for the purpose of preserving its own more valuable property, and the plaintiffs are entitled to compensation for the injury done.

Order affirmed.

LEWIS, J. (dissenting). I dissent. It was assumed on the trial before the lower court that appellant's liability depended on whether the master of the ship might, in the exercise of reasonable care, have sought a place of safety before the storm made it impossible to leave the dock. The majority opinion assumes that the evidence is conclusive that appellant moored its boat at respondents' dock pursuant to contract, and that the vessel was lawfully in position at the time the additional cables were fastened to the dock, and the reasoning of the opinion is that, because appellant made use of the stronger cables to hold the boat in position, it became liable under the rule that it had voluntarily made use of the property of another for the purpose of saving its own.

In my judgment, if the boat was lawfully in position at the time the storm broke, and the master could not, in the exercise of due care, have left that position without subjecting his vessel to the hazards of the storm, then the damage to the dock, caused by the pounding of the boat, was the result of an inevitable accident. If the master was in the exercise of due care, he was not at fault. The reasoning of the opinion admits that if the ropes, or cables, first attached to the dock had not parted, or if, in the first instance, the master had used the stronger cables, there would be no liability. If the master could not, in the exercise of reasonable care, have anticipated the severity of the storm and sought a place of safety before it became impossible, why should he be required to anticipate the severity of the storm, and, in the first instance, use the stronger cables?

I am of the opinion that one who constructs a dock to the navigable line of waters, and enters into contractual relations with the owner of a vessel to moor the same, takes the risk of damage to his dock by a boat caught there by a storm, which event could not have been avoided in the exercise of due care, and further, that the legal status of the parties in such a case is not changed by renewal of cables to keep the boat from being cast adrift at the mercy of the tempest.

JAGGARD, J.

I concur with LEWIS, J.[25]

25. Cf. Holmes, The Common Law 148 (1881); Gardner, Insurance Against Tort Liability—An Approach to the Cosmology of the Law, 15 L. & Contemp.Prob. 455, 459 (1950); P. Atiyah, Accidents, Compensation and the Law 463–69 (1970); Restatement of Torts Second, §§ 197, 263 (1965); Keeton, Conditional Fault in the Law of Torts, 72 Harv.L.Rev. 401, 410–18 (1959). Contrast Morris v. Platt, 32 Conn. 75 (1864); Manor v. "Sir John Crosbie" (1965) 52 D.L.R.2d 48 (Can. Exch.); Ryan v. Thurston, 276 Md. 390, 347 A.2d 834 (1975) (pertinent issues apparently not argued).

THE MAYOR, &c. OF NEW-YORK v. LORD

New York Court for the Correction of Errors, 1837.
18 Wend. 126.

By the CHANCELLOR. The only real question in this case is, whether the lessee of the store, which was destroyed by direction of the public authorities of the city of New-York, during the great fire, is entitled, upon a fair construction of the statute on this subject, to compensation for the actual loss or damages which he sustained by the destruction of his goods, which, as such lessee, he had in the store at the time it was blown up; which loss, according to the finding of the jury, under the decision and charge of Judge Irving, must be considered as the direct and necessary consequence of the destruction of the store at the time and under the particular circumstances in which such destruction thereof took place or was effected. Upon this question I so fully concur with the able and conclusive reasoning of the first judge of the court of common pleas, and of the learned chief justice of the supreme court, who delivered the prevailing opinion of that court, that it appears to be almost a useless waste of time to attempt to go over any part of the same ground.

The principle appears to be well settled, that in a case of actual necessity, to prevent the spreading of a fire, the ravages of a pestilence, the advance of a hostile army, or any other great public calamity, the private property of an individual may be lawfully taken and used or destroyed, for the relief, protection or safety of the many, without subjecting those, whose duty it is to protect the public interests, by whom or under whose direction such private property was taken or destroyed, to personal liability for the damage which the owner has thereby sustained. Where the same extent of loss or injury would have been sustained by the individual, as the necessary consequence of the fire or other public calamity, if his property had not been thus taken and destroyed for the protection of others, it may be considered as at the least doubtful whether he has any equitable claim to compensation, either from the public in general or from that portion of the community for whose particular benefit or protection his private property was taken or sacrificed; for in such a case, although others have been benefitted, he has in fact sustained no damage thereby. It is very clear that the individual could not claim compensation for *such a loss,* under the statute we are now considering, which limits the amount of the assessment to *damages* actually sustained by the pulling down and destruction of the building. On the other hand, it is very evident that if the private property of an individual, the whole or a part of which might otherwise have been saved to the owner, is taken or destroyed for the benefit of the public, or of the inhabitants of a particular county, city, town, or other smaller section of the community, those for whose supposed benefit the sacrifice was made, ought in equity and justice to make good the loss which the individual has sustained for the common benefit of all. It is upon this great principle of natural equity that maritime contributions are founded; as in the case of a *jettison*, where the property of an individual is cast into the sea, or otherwise sacrificed, with a view to the safety of the vessel and the residue of the cargo, during an impending peril. In that case the vessel and freight and the residue of the cargo, which are thus saved by the sacrifice of a part, all contribute rateably to make good the loss to the individual whose property has been sacrificed for the common benefit. But where the jettison does not divert the impending evil, so that the same loss would have occurred to the individual by the same peril, if his property had not been thus sacrificed, he has no claim for contribution from the owners of the vessel and the residue of the cargo, who have all shared with him in a common calamity.[26]

REPORT BY PRIME MINISTER CHURCHILL TO PARLIAMENT ON THE PROGRESS OF THE WAR, OCTOBER 9, 1940

(As reported in the New York Times October 9, 1940.)

The diminution of damage done by blind bombing from what we had expected enables us to take an enormous step forward in spreading the risk over the property of all classes, rich and poor. The Chancellor of the Exchequer has virtually completed a bill for nation-wide compulsory insurance against damage to property. The immediate needs of food and shelter are already provided for. So is loss of life and limb so far as it is possible to compensate for such calamities.

But why should we have the whole value of the buildings of the country simultaneously discounted and discredited by the shadow of a sporadic sky vulture? An appropriate charge on the capital value of buildings of all kinds will provide a fund from which—supplemented if need be by a State subvention—every one can be sure that compensation will be made in one form or another at the end of the war, if not sooner, and where necessity arises means of carrying on will not be withheld. We also propose to provide insurance against war damage for all forms of movable property such as industrial plant machinery, household effects and other personal possessions not at the present time protected by insurance.

26. The Georgia court was apparently willing to accept this basis of compensation without the aid of a statute. Bishop & Parsons v. Macon, 7 Ga. 200, 50 Am.Dec. 400 (1849). Also see Burmah Oil Co. v. Lord Advocate [1965] A.C. 75, British War Damage Act 1965, and P. Atiyah, op. cit. supra note 25 at 466. But see Field v. City of Des Moines, 39 Iowa 575, 28 Am.Rep. 46 (1874); Hale v. Lawrence, 21 N.J.L. 714, 47 Am.Dec. 190 (1848); Russell v. Mayor, etc., of New York, 2 Denio. (N.Y.) 461 (1845) (denying compensation for property not covered by the statute).

See Bohlen, Incomplete Privilege to Inflict Intentional Invasions of Interests of Property and Personality, 39 Harv.L.Rev. 307 (1926); Restatement of Torts Second, §§ 196, 211, 262 (1965).

We must so arrange that when any district is smitten by bombs flung at random, strong mobile forces will descend on the scene to conquer the flames, rescue the sufferers, provide food and shelter, to whisk them away to places of rest and to reassure them that they have not lost all, because all will share their material loss.[27]

Here we see a method of administering losses which are the more or less inevitable consequence of socially desirable conduct (fire fighting, saving a ship, waging a war in the national interest). The outstanding characteristic of this method is the wide *distribution* of the loss. This distribution by itself confers some benefits on society and is one among a number of possible objectives which may be pursued in shaping the development of tort liability. Tort law has seldom until recently been expressly accepted by courts as a device for distributing losses. (Consider, for example, whether this was one of the purposes of the early statutes given at the beginning of this section.) Indeed there has until recently been scant machinery for doing so. Distribution in practice means either (a) holding each of many parties liable for a small fraction of the loss, or (b) shifting the loss to a party who has available the means for distributing it. The first alternative involves administrative difficulties of serious proportions. As to the second, until the eve of the present century there were few among the possible defendants who were equipped with the available means (Governmental units were virtually the only ones until the rise of large corporate enterprises). But modern developments, notably in the field of liability insurance, have vastly increased the practical effect of tort law as just such a device. More of this anon.[28]

FLETCHER v. RYLANDS

Court of Exchequer, 1865.
34 L.J.Rep.,N.S., 177.

This action came on to be tried at the Liverpool Summer Assizes, 1862, when a verdict was found for the plaintiff for 5,000£. and 40*s*. costs, subject to the award of an arbitrator, who afterwards was empowered by Judge's order to state a special case instead of making an award. [The material parts of the case are summarized as follows: Plaintiff was a tenant of certain beds of coal lying under certain lands belonging to the Earl of Wilton. By arrangement with Lord Wilton, plaintiff in 1850 sank a pit for the mining of coal under

27. Cf. the Act to Provide War Damage Insurance, 15 U.S.C.A. §§ 606b (5), 606b–1, 606b–2, 609q.

28. For an elaboration of this viewpoint see Ehrenzweig, Negligence Without Fault (1951), reprinted at 54 Calif. L.Rev. 1422 (1966); James, Accident Liability Reconsidered: The Impact of Liability Insurance, 57 Yale L.J. 549 (1948); Calabresi, Some Thoughts on Risk Distribution and the Law of Torts, 70 Yale L.J. 499 (1966); G. Calabresi, The Costs of Accidents 39 et seq. (1970).

other lands lying to the north of those first-mentioned. This was called the "Red House Pit," and the colliery worked thereby the "Red House Colliery."

In 1860 defendants, proprietors of a mill near the Red House Colliery, made a reservoir, to supply their mill with water, in certain other lands of Lord Wilton, lying north-west of the colliery.

The coal under the site of the reservoir and between it and the colliery had been partially worked at some time or other beyond living memory, but this was not known to defendants, or to anyone employed by them in selecting their site or constructing their reservoir. These old coal workings communicated with the plaintiff's coal workings.]

In the course of constructing and excavating for the bed of the reservoir, five old shafts running vertically downwards were met with in the portion of land selected for the site of the reservoir. At the time they were so met with, the sides or walls of at least three of them were constructed of timber, and were still in existence, but the shafts themselves were filled up with marl or soil of the same kind as the marl or soil which immediately surrounded them; and it was not known to or suspected by the defendants, or any of the persons employed by them in or about the planning or constructing of the reservoir that they were (as they afterwards proved to be) shafts which had been made for the purpose of getting the coal under the land in which the reservoir was made, or that they led down to coal workings under the site of the reservoir.

For the selection of the site of the reservoir, and for the planning and constructing thereof, it was necessary that the defendants should employ an engineer and contractors, and *they did employ for those purposes a competent engineer and competent contractors* by and under whom the site was selected, and the reservoir was planned and constructed; and, *on the part of the defendants themselves, there was no personal negligence or default whatever* in or about or in relation to the selection of the site, or in or about the planning or construction of the reservoir; *but, in point of fact, reasonable and proper care and skill were not exercised by or on the part of the persons so employed by them* with reference to the shafts so met with as aforesaid, to provide for the sufficiency of the reservoir, to bear the pressure of water which, when filled to the height proposed, it would have to bear.

The reservoir was completed about the beginning of December 1860, when the defendants caused the same to be partially filled with water; and on the morning of the 11th of December in the same year, whilst the reservoir was so partially filled, one of the shafts which had been so met with as aforesaid gave way and burst downwards; in consequence of which the water of the reservoir flowed into the old coal workings underneath, and by means of the underground communications, * * * large quantities of the water so flowing from the reservoir as aforesaid found their way into the coal workings in the Red House Colliery, and by reason thereof the said colliery became and was flooded, and the working thereof was obliged to be and was for a time necessarily suspended. * * * [Later the colliery was abandoned.]

The question for the opinion of the Court was, whether the plaintiff was entitled to recover damages from the defendants by reason of the matters stated in the case. * * *

BRAMWELL, B.—* * * I agree with Mr. Mellish, that the case is singularly wanting in authority, and, therefore, while it is always desirable to ascertain the principle on which a case depends, it is especially so here.

Now, what is the plaintiff's right? He had the right to work his mines to their extent, leaving no boundary between himself and the next owner. By so doing, he subjected himself to all consequences resulting from natural causes; among others, to the influx of all water naturally flowing in; but he had a right to be free from what has been called foreign water—that is, water artificially brought or sent to him directly, or indirectly by its being sent to where it would flow to him. * * *

I proceed to deal with the arguments the other way. It is said, there must be a trespass or nuisance with negligence. I do not agree with that, and I think Bonomi v. Blackhouse, 9 H.L.Cas. 903; s. c. 27 Law J.Rep., N.S., Q.B. 378, and ante, Q.B. 181, shews the contrary. But why is not this a trespass?—see Gregory v. Piper, 9 B. & C. 591. Wilfulness is not material—see Leame v. Bray, 3 East, 593. Why is it not a nuisance? The nuisance is not in the reservoir, but in the water escaping. As in Bonomi v. Blackhouse, 9 H.L.Cas. 903; s. c. 27 Law J.Rep., N.S., Q.B. 378, and ante, Q.B. 181, the act was lawful, the mischievous consequence was a wrong. Where two carriages come in collision, if there is no negligence in either, it is as much the act of the one driver as of the other that they meet. The cases of carriers and innkeepers are really cases of contract, and, though exceptional, furnish no evidence that the general law, in cases wholly independent of contract, is not what I have stated. The old common law liability for fire created a liability beyond what I contend for here.

I think, therefore, on the plain ground that the defendants have caused water to flow into the plaintiff's mines, which, but for the defendants' act, would not have gone there, this action is maintainable. I think that the defendants' innocence, whatever may be its moral bearing on the case, is immaterial in point of law. But I may as well add, that if the defendants did not know what would happen, their agents knew that there were old shafts on their land; knew, therefore, that they must lead to old workings; knew that those old workings might extend in any direction, and, consequently, knew damage might happen. The defendants surely are as liable as their agents would be.

Why should not both be held to act at their peril? But I own, this seems to me, rather to enforce the rule, that knowledge and wilfulness are not necessary to make the defendant liable, than to give the plaintiff a separate ground of action. My judgment is for the plaintiff. * * *

MARTIN, B.—* * * First, I think there was no trespass. In the judgment of my Brother Bramwell, to which I shall hereafter refer, he seems to think the act of the defendants was a trespass; but I cannot concur, as I own it seems to me that the cases cited by him, namely, Leame v. Bray, 3 East 593, and Gregory v. Piper, 9 B. & C. 591, prove the contrary. I think the true criterion of trespass is laid down in the judgment in the former case, namely, that to constitute trespass, the act doing the damage must be immediate, and that if the damage be not immediate but consequential, which I think the present was, it is not trespass. Secondly, I think there was no nuisance in the ordinary and generally understood meaning of that word,[29] that is to say, something hurtful or injurious to the senses. The making a pond for holding water is a nuisance to no one. The digging a reservoir on a man's own land is a lawful act. It does not appear that there was any embankment, or that the water in the reservoir was ever above the level of the natural surface of the land; but the water escaped from the bottom of the reservoir, and, in ordinary course, would descend by gravitation into the defendants' own land, and they did not know of the existence of the old workings. To hold the defendants liable, would therefore make them insurers against the consequence of a lawful act upon their own land, when they had no reason to believe or suspect that any damage was likely to ensue. No case was cited in which the question has arisen as to real property; but as to personal property the question arises every day, and there is no better established rule of law than that, when damage is done to personal property, or even to the person, by collision either upon land or at sea, there must be negligence in the party doing the damage to render him legally responsible; and, if there be no negligence, the party sustaining the damage must bear with it. The existence of this rule is proved by the exceptions to it, namely, the cases of the innkeeper and the common carrier of goods for hire, who are *quasi* insurers. These cases are said to be by the custom of the realm, treating them as exceptions from the ordinary rule of law. In the absence of authority to the contrary, I can see no reason why damage to real property should be governed by a different rule or principle than damage to personal property. There is an instance, also, of damage to real property, where the party causing it was at common law liable upon the custom of the realm as a *quasi* insurer; namely, in the case of the master of a house, if a fire had kindled

29. Cf. United Electric Light Co. v. Deliso Constr. Co., 315 Mass. 313, 52 N.E. 2d 553 (1943); Prosser, Nuisance Without Fault, 20 Tex.L.Rev. 399, 402, note 8 (1942); James, Accident Liability: Some Wartime Developments, 55 Yale L.J. 365, 369 (1946).

there, and consumed the house of another. In such case the master of the house was liable at common law without proof of negligence on his part. See Comyns's Digest, tit. "Action upon the Case for Negligence," (A. 6.) This seems to be an exception from the ordinary rule at law; and, in my opinion, affords an argument that in other cases such as the present there must be negligence to create a liability. * * *

There then arises the second question, namely, does it make any difference that reasonable and proper care and skill were not exercised by the engineer and contractors employed by the defendant (they being competent persons) with reference to the shafts, which were five old shafts running vertically downwards in that portion of the land selected for the reservoir, but which were not known or suspected by any one to be (as they afterwards proved to be) shafts which had been made for the purpose of getting coal under the land beneath the reservoir, or to lead to coal under it? Now, assuming that the want of reasonable and proper care and skill by the engineer and contractors constituted in point of law want of reasonable and proper skill by the defendants themselves (which is by no means a clear proposition), I nevertheless think that the defendants are not responsible.[30] The assumed facts are these: The defendants dig a reservoir in their own land; they do not know or suspect that their doing it in the manner they did would do any damage to their neighbour; is there any authority to shew that the law casts upon them a liability for damage, should it occur? In my opinion there is authority to the contrary. *Prima facie* a man may excavate a reservoir for water in his own land. Whether he does so carefully and skilfully would seem to be his own concern; and, if he be ignorant that any fact exists which makes it dangerous to his neighbour, it is difficult to see what duty is imposed upon him to take any peculiar care, or use any particular skill in the matter. When a man does an act upon his close, which of itself is lawful, but is alleged to be wrongful towards an adjoining neighbour by reason of the existence of some underground openings between their two closes, reason and good sense would seem to require that he should know or have the means of knowledge of the existence of the openings. How can a man be said to be negligent when he is ignorant of the existence of the circumstances which require the exercise of care? * * *

[The opinion of POLLOCK, C. B. is omitted.]

Judgment for the defendants.

30. This particular conclusion is against the current of later authority. Bohlen, The Rule in Rylands v. Fletcher, 59 U. of Pa.L.Rev. 298, 299, note 2 (1911); Smith, Tort & Absolute Liability, 30 Harv.L.Rev. 409, 410 (1917); Foster & Keeton, Liability Without Fault in Oklahoma, 3 Okla. L.Rev. 1, 31 (1950).

On error from this judgment, the decision of the court in the Exchequer Chamber is reported in (1866) L.R.Excheq. 265:

The judgment of the Court (WILLES, BLACKBURN, KEATING, MELLOR, MONTAGUE, SMITH, and LUSH, JJ.), was delivered by

BLACKBURN, J. * * * We have come to the conclusion that the opinion of BRAMWELL, B., was right, and that the answer to the question should be that the plaintiff was entitled to recover damages from the defendants, by reason of the matters stated in the case, and consequently, that the judgment below should be reversed. * * *

The plaintiff, though free from all blame on his part, must bear the loss, unless he can establish that it was the consequence of some default for which the defendants are responsible. The question of law therefore arises, what is the obligation which the law casts on a person who, like the defendant, lawfully brings on his land something which, though harmless whilst it remains there, will naturally do mischief if it escape out of his land. It is agreed on all hands that he must take care to keep in that which he has brought on the land and keeps there, in order that it may not escape and damage his neighbours, but the question arises whether the duty which the law casts upon him, under such circumstances, is an absolute duty to keep it in at his peril, or is, as the majority of the Court of Exchequer have thought, merely a duty to take all reasonable and prudent precautions, in order to keep it in, but no more. If the first be the law, the person who has brought on his land and kept there something dangerous, and failed to keep it in, is responsible for all the natural consequences of its escape. If the second be the limit of his duty, he would not be answerable except on proof of negligence, and consequently would not be answerable for escape arising from any latent defect which ordinary prudence and skill could not detect.

Supposing the second to be the correct view of the law, a further question arises subsidiary to the first, viz., whether the defendants are not so far identified with the contractors whom they employed, as to be responsible for the consequences of their want of care and skill in making the reservoir in fact insufficient with reference to the old shafts, of the existence of which they were aware, though they had not ascertained where the shafts went to.

We think that the true rule of law is, that the person who for his own purposes brings on his lands and collects and keeps there anything likely to do mischief if it escapes, must keep it in at his peril, and, if he does not do so, is prima facie answerable for all the damage which is the natural consequence of its escape. He can excuse himself by shewing that the escape was owing to the plaintiffs' default; or perhaps that the escape was the consequence of vis major, or the act of God; but as nothing of this sort exists here, it is unnecessary to inquire what excuse would be sufficient. The general rule, as above stated, seems on principle just. The person whose grass or corn is eaten down by the escaping cattle of his neighbour, or whose mine is flooded by the water from his neighbour's reservoir, or whose cellar is invaded by the filth of his neighbour's privy, or whose habitation is made unhealthy by the fumes and noisome vapours of his neighbour's alkali works, is damnified without any fault of his own; and it seems but reasonable and just that the neighbour, who has brought something on his own property which was not naturally there, harmless to others so long as it is confined to his own property, but which he knows to be mischievous if it gets on his neighbour's, should be obliged to make good the damage which ensues if he does not succeed in confining it to his own property. But for his act in bringing it there no mischief could have accrued, and it seems but just that he should at his peril keep it there so that no mischief may accrue, or answer for the natural and anticipated consequences. And upon authority, this we think is established to be the law whether the things so brought be beasts, or water, or filth, or stenches.

The case that has most commonly occurred, and which is most frequently to be found in the books, is as to the obligation of the owner of cattle which he has brought on his land, to prevent their escaping and doing mischief. The law as to them seems to be perfectly settled from early times; the owner must keep them in at his peril, or he will be answerable for the natural consequences of their escape; that is with regard to tame beasts, for the grass they eat and trample upon, though not for any injury to the person of others, for our ancestors have settled that it is not the general nature of horses to kick, or bulls to gore; but if the owner knows that the beast has a vicious propensity to attack man, he will be answerable for that too.

As early as the Year Book, 20 Ed. 4, 11. placitum 10, Brian, C. J., lays down the doctrine in terms very much resembling those used by Lord Holt in Tenant v. Goldwin, 2 Ld.Raym. 1089; 1 Salk. 360, which will be referred to afterwards. It was trespass with cattle. Plea, that the defendant's land adjoined a place where defendant had common, that the cattle strayed from the common, and defendant drove them back as soon as he could. It was held a bad plea. Brian, C. J., says: "It behoves him to use his common so that he shall do no hurt to another man, and if the land in which he has common be not enclosed, it behoves him to keep the beasts in the common and out of the land of any other." He adds, when it was proposed to amend by pleading that they were driven out of the common by dogs, that although that might give a right of action against the master of the dogs, it was no defence to the action of trespass by the person on whose land the cattle went. In the recent case of Cox v. Burbidge, 13 C.B., N.S., at p. 438; 32 L.J., C.P., 89, Williams, J., says: "I apprehend the general rule of law to be perfectly plain. If I am the owner of an animal in which by law the right of property can exist, I am bound to take care that it does not stray into the land of my neighbour, and I am liable for any trespass it may commit, and for the ordinary consequences of that trespass. Whether or not the escape of the animal is due to my negligence is altogether immaterial."

So in May v. Burdett, 9 Q.B. at p. 112, the Court, after an elaborate examination of the old precedents and authorities, came to the conclusion that, "a person keeping a mischievous animal, with knowledge of its propensities, is bound to keep it secure *at his peril.*" And in 1 Hale's Pleas of the Crown 430, Lord Hale states that where one keeps a beast, knowing its nature or habits are such that the natural consequence of his being loose is that he will harm men, the owner "must at his peril keep him up safe from doing hurt, for *though he use his diligence* to keep him up, if he escape and do harm, the owner is liable to answer damages;" though, as he proceeds to shew, he will not be liable criminally without proof of want of care. In these latter authorities the point under consideration was damage to the person, and what was decided was, that where it was known that hurt to the person was the natural consequence of the animal being loose, the owner should be responsible in damages for such hurt, though where it was not known to be so, the owner was not responsible for such damages; but where the damage is, like eating grass or other ordinary ingredients in damage feasant, the natural consequence of the escape, the rule as to keeping in the animal is the same. In Com. Dig. Droit (M.2.) it is said that, "if the owner of 200 acres in a common moor enfeoffs B. of 50 acres, B. ought to enclose *at his peril*, to prevent damage by his cattle to the other 150 acres. For if his cattle escape thither they may be distrained damage feasant. So the owner of the 150 acres ought to prevent his cattle from doing damage to the 50 acres *at his peril.*" The authority cited is Dyer, 372b., where the decision was that the cattle might be distrained; the inference from that decision, that the owner was bound to keep in his cattle *at his peril*, is, we think, legitimate, and we have the high authority of Comyns for saying that such is the law. In the note to Fitzherbert Nat. Brevium, 128, which is attributed to Lord Hale, it is said, "If A. and B. have lands adjoining, where there is no enclosure, the one shall have trespass against the other on an escape of their beasts respectively. Dyer 372, Rastal Ent. 621, 20 Ed. 4, 10, although wild dogs, &c., drive the cattle of the one into the lands of the other." No case is known to us on which in replevin it has ever been attempted to plead in bar to an avowry for distress damage feasant, that the cattle had escaped without any negligence on the part of the plaintiff, and surely if that could have been a good plea in bar, the facts must often have been such as would have supported it. These authorities, and the absence of any authority to the contrary, justify Williams, J., in saying, as he does in Cox v. Burbidge, 13 C.B., N.S., at p. 438; 32 L.J., C.P., 89, that the law is clear that in actions for damage occasioned by animals that have not been kept in by their owners, it is quite immaterial whether the escape is by negligence or not.

As has been already said, there does not appear to be any difference in principle, between the extent of the duty cast on him who brings cattle on his land to keep them in, and the extent of the duty imposed on him who brings on his land, water, filth, or stenches, or any other thing which will, if it escape, naturally do damage, to prevent their escaping and injuring his neighbour, and the case of Tenant v. Goldwin, 1 Salk. 21, 360; 2 Ld.Raym. 1089; 6 Mod. 311, is an express authority that the duty is the same, and is, to keep them in at his peril. * * *

No case has been found in which the question as to the liability for noxious vapours escaping from a man's works by inevitable accident has been discussed, but the following case will illustrate it. Some years ago several actions were brought against the occupiers of some alkali works at Liverpool for the damage alleged to be caused by the chlorine fumes of their works. The defendants proved that they at great expense erected contrivances by which the fumes of chlorine were condensed, and sold as muriatic acid, and they called a great body of scientific evidence to prove that this apparatus was so perfect that no fumes possibly could escape from the defendants' chimneys. On this evidence it was pressed upon the jury that the plaintiff's damage must have been due to some of the numerous other chimneys in the neighborhood; the jury, however, being satisfied that the mischief was occasioned by chlorine, drew the conclusion that it had escaped from the defendants' works somehow, and in each case found for the plaintiff. No attempt was made to disturb these verdicts on the ground that the defendants had taken every precaution which prudence or skill could suggest to keep those fumes in, and that they could not be responsible unless negligence were shewn; yet, if the law be as laid down by the majority of the Court of Exchequer, it would have been a very obvious defence. If it had been raised, the answer would probably have been that the uniform course of pleading in actions on such nuisances is to say that the defendant caused the noisome vapours to arise on his premises, and suffered them to come on the plaintiff's, without stating there was any want of care or skill in the defendant, and that the case of Tenant v. Goldwin, 1 Salk. 21, 360; 2 Ld.Raym. 1089; 6 Mod. 311, shewed that this was founded on the general rule of law, that he whose stuff it is must keep it that it may not trespass. There is no difference in this respect between chlorine and water; both will, if they escape, do damage, the one by scorching, and the other by drowning, and he who brings them there must at his peril see that they do not escape and do that mischief. What is said by Gibbs, C. J., in Sutton v. Clarke, 6 Taunt. at p. 44, though not necessary for the decision of the case, shews that that very learned judge took the same view of the law that was taken by Lord Holt. But it was further said by Martin, B., that when damage is done to personal property, or even to the person, by collision, either upon land or at sea, there must be negligence in the party doing the damage to render him legally responsible; and this is no doubt true, and as was pointed out by Mr. Mellish during his argument before us, this is not confined to cases of collision, for there are many cases in which proof of negligence is essential, as for instance, where an unruly horse gets on the footpath of a public street and kills a passenger; Hammack v. White, 11 C.B., N.S., 588; 31 L.J., C.P., 129;

or where a person in a dock is struck by the falling of a bale of cotton which the defendant's servants are lowering, Scott v. London Dock Company, 3 H. & C. 596; 34 L.J., Ex., 17, 220; and many other similar cases may be found. But we think these cases distinguishable from the present. Traffic on the highways, whether by land or sea, cannot be conducted without exposing those whose persons or property are near it to some inevitable risk; and that being so, those who go on the highway, or have their property adjacent to it, may well be held to do so subject to their taking upon themselves the risk of injury from that inevitable danger; and persons who by the license of the owner pass near to warehouses where goods are being raised or lowered, certainly do so subject to the inevitable risk of accident. In neither case, therefore, can they recover without proof of want of care or skill occasioning the accident; and it is believed that all the cases in which inevitable accident has been held an excuse for what prima facie was a trespass, can be explained on the same principle, viz., that the circumstances were such as to shew that the plaintiff had taken that risk upon himself. But there is no ground for saying that the plaintiff here took upon himself any risk arising from the uses to which the defendants should choose to apply their land. He neither knew what these might be, nor could he in any way control the defendants, or hinder their building what reservoirs they liked, and storing up in them what water they pleased, so long as the defendants succeeded in preventing the water which they there brought from interfering with the plaintiff's property.

The view which we take of the first point renders it unnecessary to consider whether the defendants would or would not be responsible for the want of care and skill in the persons employed by them, under the circumstances stated in the case. * * *

Judgment for the plaintiff.

The cause was then taken on error to the House of Lords. Its decision, reported in (1868) L.R. 3 H.L. 330, is as follows:

THE LORD CHANCELLOR (LORD CAIRNS) :—* * * My Lords, the principles on which this case must be determined appear to me to be extremely simple. The Defendants, treating them as the owners or occupiers of the close on which the reservoir was constructed, might lawfully have used that close for any purpose for which it might in the ordinary course of the enjoyment of land be used; and if, in what I may term the natural user of that land, there had been any accumulation of water, either on the surface or underground, and if, by the operation of the laws of nature, that accumulation of water had passed off into the close occupied by the Plaintiff, the Plaintiff could not have complained that that result had taken place. If he had desired to guard himself against it, it would have lain upon him to have done so, by leaving, or by interposing, some barrier between his close and the close of the Defendants in order to have prevented that operation of the laws of nature.

As an illustration of that principle, I may refer to a case which was cited in the argument before your Lordships, the case of Smith v. Kenrick in the Court of Common Pleas, 7 C.B. 515.

On the other hand if the Defendants, not stopping at the natural use of their close, had desired to use it for any purpose which I may term a nonnatural use, for the purpose of introducing into the close that which in its natural condition was not in or upon it, for the purpose of introducing water either above or below ground in quantities and in a manner not the result of any work or operation on or under the land,—and if in consequence of their doing so, or in consequence of any imperfection in the mode of their doing so, the water came to escape and to pass off into the close of the Plaintiff, then it appears to me that that which the Defendants were doing they were doing at their own peril; and, if in the course of their doing it, the evil arose to which I have referred, the evil, namely, of the escape of the water and its passing away to the close of the Plaintiff and injuring the Plaintiff, then for the consequence of that, in my opinion, the Defendants would be liable. As the case of Smith v. Kenrick is an illustration of the first principle to which I have referred, so also the second principle to which I have referred is well illustrated by another case in the same Court, the case of Baird v. Williamson, 15 C.B., N.S., 317, which was also cited in the argument at the Bar.

My Lords, these simple principles, if they are well founded, as it appears to me they are, really dispose of this case.

The same result is arrived at on the principles referred to by MR. JUSTICE BLACKBURN in his judgment, in the Court of Exchequer Chamber, * * *

My Lords, in that opinion, I must say I entirely concur. Therefore, I have to move your Lordships that the judgment of the Court of Exchequer Chamber be affirmed, and that the present appeal be dismissed with costs.

LORD CRANWORTH:—My Lords, I concur with my noble and learned friend in thinking that the rule of law was correctly stated by MR. JUSTICE BLACKBURN in delivering the opinion of the Exchequer Chamber. If a person brings, or accumulates, on his land anything which, if it should escape, may cause damage to his neighbour, he does so at his peril. If it does escape, and cause damage, he is responsible, however careful he may have been, and whatever precautions he may have taken to prevent the damage. * * *

Judgment of the Court of Exchequer Chamber affirmed.[31]

31. Rylands v. Fletcher was not received enthusiastically in this country and the principle it was taken to stand for was often expressly repudiated. See Bohlen, The Rule in Rylands v. Fletcher, 59 U. of Pa.L.Rev. 298, 373, 423 (1911); Thayer, Liability Without Fault, 29 Harv.L.Rev. 801 (1916). The course of later authority, however, suggests that the reluctance to impose strict liability in situations of the same general type has been greatly relaxed. See Green v. General Petroleum Corp., 205 Cal. 328, 270 P. 952,

YOMMER v. McKENZIE

Court of Appeals of Maryland, 1969.
255 Md. 220, 257 A.2d 138.

SINGLEY, JUDGE. Mr. and Mrs. McKenzie, the plaintiffs below, live at Little Crossing in Garrett County. Their immediate neighbors are the defendants, Mr. and Mrs. Yommer, who operate a grocery store and gasoline filling station. On 17 December 1967, Mr. McKenzie noticed a "smell" in his well water which, on analysis, proved to be caused by the presence of gasoline in the well. McKenzie complained

60 A.L.R. 475 (1928); Rozewski v. Simpson, 9 Cal.2d 515, 71 P.2d 72 (1937); Carpenter, 5 So.Cal.L.Rev. 263 (1932); Prosser, 20 Tex.L.Rev. 399 (1942); Burke, 22 Chi.-Kent L.Rev. 103 (1944); Note, 95 U. of Pa.L.Rev. 781 (1947); Note, 61 Harv.L.Rev. 515 (1948); Foster & Keeton, 3 Okl.L.Rev. 1, 29 et seq., 172 et seq. (1950); Prosser, The Principle of Rylands v. Fletcher, in W. Prosser, Selected Topics on the Law of Torts 135 et seq. (1954).

British developments may be traced in Stallybrass, 3 Camb.L.J. 376 (1920); Friedmann, 1 Mod.L.Rev. 39, 49–53 (1937); Friedmann, Social Insurance & Tort Liability, 63 Harv.L.Rev. 241, 246 (1949); Fridman, The Rise and Fall of Rylands v. Fletcher, 34 Can. B.Rev. 810 (1956); Ogus, Vagaries in Liability for the Escape of Fire, 27 Camb.L.J. 104 (1969).

It is sometimes emphasized that the harmful agent must have been brought on to the land by defendant, e. g., Pennsylvania Coal Co. v. Sanderson, 113 Pa. 126, 6 A. 453 (1886). Whether Lord Cairns intended to require more, i. e., that the use of the land be "unnatural", or only that the harmful agent be artificially on the land, rather than naturally so, is not clear from his opinion. Presumably agriculture would be considered a "natural" use, yet, as Blackburn points out, there has traditionally been strict liability for crop damage by escaping cattle. Nevertheless decisions often purport to turn on a characterization of the use, e. g., Rickards v. Lothian, Privy Council [1913] A.C. 263, [1911–1913] All E. R.Rep. 71 (supply of water to houses "ordinary and proper" use, so no liability for overflowing residential wash basin in absence of negligence); Duncans v. Regina [1966] Ex.C.R. 1080 (Can.Exch.) (strict liability for sewage seepage); Attorney-General v. Corke [1933] Ch. 89 (lease of land for gypsy encampment "abnormal use", so landowner strictly liable under injunction for damages to neighbors by off-site gypsies); Mihalchuk v. Ratke, (1966) 5 D.L.R. (2d) 269 (Sask.Q.B.) (spraying of crops from air unnatural use, as contrasted with customary boom spraying behind tractor); Mason v. Levy Auto Parts of England Ltd. [1967] 2 Q.B. 530 (bringing combustible materials onto land is nonnatural use, based on quantities of such materials, the method of storage, and the character of the neighborhood, so strict liability for escape of mysteriously caused fire).

As to whether a motor car should be treated as a wild beast, see masterful opinion by the Master of the Rolls in Haddock v. Thwale, reprinted in A. P. Herbert, Uncommon Law 124 (1935), approved by Mr. Justice Wool in Tripp v. The Milko Corp., Ltd., id. at 297.

In England the applicability of *Rylands* to personal injuries has been questioned, and the doctrine has been generally confined to escapes from defendant's land, Read v. J. Lyons & Co. [1947] A.C. 156, [1946] 2 All E.R. 471.

Strict liability, purportedly predicated on Rylands v. Fletcher has, however, been imposed by some courts for personal injury. See, e. g., Siegler v. Kuhlman, 81 Wash.2d 448, 502 P.2d 1181 (1972) (motorist killed by explosion from gasoline spilled on highway from defendant's trailer tank); Aldridge and O'Brien v. Van Patter [1952] 4 D.L.R. 93, [1952] O.R. 595 (Sup.Ct. Ont.) (escape of racing car); Hale v. Jennings Bros. [1938] 1 All E.R. 579 (rotating "chair-o-plane" at amusement park); also see Benning v. Wong, 122 Commw.L.R. 249, 43 A.L. J.R. 467 (High Ct. Austl. 1969) (dicta, in escaping gas case, where majority holds strict liability inapplicable, over strong dissent, because of statutory authority for defendant's activities, but a different majority considers personal injuries compensable under Rylands v. Fletcher.)

to Yommer, who arranged to have one of his storage tanks removed and replaced in January 1968. However, it was not until the McKenzies had a filter and water softener installed in April of 1968 that it was possible for them to use the water for cooking and bathing. At the time of the trial of the case in December of 1968 there was testimony that the McKenzies were still bringing drinking water from Grantsville, about a mile distant.

The McKenzies, alleging a nuisance, sued the Yommers for damages and recovered a verdict of $3,500. The Yommers had moved for a directed verdict at the end of the plaintiffs' case and renewed their motion at the end of the entire case. The Yommers have appealed from the judgment entered on the verdict, assigning as error the trial court's refusal to direct a verdict in their favor. We shall affirm.

The thrust of the Yommers' argument is threefold: (i) that the establishment of a gasoline filling station does not constitute a nuisance; (ii) that the McKenzies failed to show that the damage they sustained was occasioned by the Yommers' negligence in the operation of the filling station * * *.

The argument that the McKenzies must prove negligence in order to recover fails to take into account the doctrine of strict liability imposed by the rule of Rylands v. Fletcher which has been adopted by our prior decisions. * * * Dean Prosser states the rule of the English cases "[T]hat the defendant will be liable when he damages another by a thing or activity unduly dangerous and inappropriate to the place where it is maintained, in the light of the character of that place and its surroundings." Prosser, Torts (3d ed. 1964) § 77 at 522. * * * Or, as Mr. Justice Sutherland put it in describing a nuisance in Euclid, Ohio v. Ambler Co., 272 U.S. 365, 388, 47 S.Ct. 114, 118, 71 L.Ed. 303, 54 A.L.R. 1016 (1926), "[It is] merely a right thing in the wrong place, like a pig in the parlor instead of the barnyard."

Restatement, Torts (1938) § 519 at 41 relied on by the Yommers, limits the applicability of the rule of Rylands v. Fletcher to what it terms an "ultrahazardous activity" and incorporates a caveat, "The Institute expresses no opinion as to whether the construction and use of a large tank or artificial reservoir in which a large body of water or other fluid is collected is or is not an ultrahazardous activity." (at 44). Prosser, Torts, supra, § 77 at 527, is critical of the ultrahazardous activity concept which

> " * * * goes beyond the English rule in ignoring the relation of the activity to its surroundings, and falls short of it in the insistence on extreme danger and the impossibility of eliminating it with all possible care. The shift of emphasis is not at all reflected in the American cases, which have laid quite as much stress as the English ones upon the place where the thing is done."

Restatement, Torts 2d, for which Dean Prosser is the Reporter, §§ 519–520 at 52–68 (Tent.Draft No. 10, 1964) provides more guidance for us than its predecessor. For the "ultrahazardous activity" test an "abnormally dangerous activity" test has been substituted. The effect of this change is to enlarge the circumstances under which the rule of strict liability will apply. As the Reporter pointed out to the American Law Institute:

" 'Ultrahazardous,' as it is defined in the old Section, is misleading. There is probably no activity whatever, unless it be the use of atomic energy, which is not perfectly safe if the *utmost* care is used —which would of course include the choice of an absolutely safe place to carry it on." Restatement, Torts 2d, supra, Note to Institute at 57.

The black letter of new § 520 sets out the definition:

"520. *Abnormally Dangerous Activities*

In determining whether an activity is abnormally dangerous, the following factors are to be considered:

(a) Whether the activity involves a high degree of risk of some harm to the person, land or chattels of others;

(b) Whether the gravity of the harm which may result from it is likely to be great;

(c) Whether the risk cannot be eliminated by the exercise of reasonable care;

(d) Whether the activity is not a matter of common usage;

(e) Whether the activity is inappropriate to the place where it is carried on; and

(f) The value of the activity to the community."

* * *

The fifth and perhaps most crucial factor under the Institute's guidelines as applied to this case is the appropriateness of the activity in the particular place where it is being carried on. No one would deny that gasoline stations as a rule do not present any particular danger to the community. However, when the operation of such activity involves the placing of a large tank adjacent to a well from which a family must draw its water for drinking, bathing and laundry, at least that aspect of the activity is inappropriate to the locale, even when equated to the value of the activity.

In the Reporter's notes concerning the new rule of the Restatement, he is careful to make a distinction which is applicable to this case. While in the first Restatement no position was taken on the issue of the storage of water and other liquids, Restatement, Torts 2d takes a different view:

"The thing which stands out from the cases is that the important thing about the activity is not that it is extremely dangerous in itself, but that it is abnormally so in relation to its surroundings.

* * *

"The same is true of the storage of gasoline, or other inflammable liquids, in large quantities. In a populated area this is a matter of strict liability. [citing cases]. But in an isolated area it is not. [citing cases].

* * *

"The same distinction is found in the cases of water stored in quantity, as in a reservoir. Rylands v. Fletcher was a case of a reservoir in Lancashire, which was primarily coal mining country; and the basis of the decision in the House of Lords was clearly that this was a 'non-natural' use of the particular land. * * * Where water is stored in large quantity in [a] dangerous location in a city, there [h]as been strict liability. [citing cases]." Restatement, Torts 2d, supra Note to Institute at 57–58.

We accept the test of appropriateness as the proper one: that the unusual, the excessive, the extravagant, the bizarre are likely to be non-natural uses which lead to strict liability.

It is apparent to us that the storage of large quantities of gasoline immediately adjacent to a private residence comes within this rule and relieved the McKenzies of the necessity of proving negligence. * * * [32]

SPANO v. PERINI CORP.

Court of Appeals of New York, 1969.
25 N.Y.2d 11, 302 N.Y.S.2d 527, 250 N.E.2d 31.

FULD, CHIEF JUDGE. The principal question posed on this appeal is whether a person who has sustained property damage caused by blasting on nearby property can maintain an action for damages without a showing that the blaster was negligent. Since 1893, when this court decided the case of Booth v. Rome, W. & O. T. R. R. Co., 140 N.Y. 267, 35 N.E. 592, 24 L.R.A. 105, it has been the law of this State that proof of negligence was required unless the blast was accompanied by an actual physical invasion of the damaged property—

32. In 1934 the Restatement of Torts took the position that aerial navigation was an "ultrahazardous activity" giving rise to strict liability for personal injury or property damage caused thereby on the ground, § 520, Comment d. Thirty years later the Reporter for Restatement Second proposed a draft section which would have retained strict liability for ground damage only if caused by abnormally dangerous operations of aircraft, or by abnormally dangerous aircraft. Although approved by the Council of The American Law Institute, this proposal was rejected by the Institute itself in 1965. Instead Restatement Second § 520A retains strict liability for ground damage caused by the "ascent, descent or flight of any aircraft, or by the dropping or falling of any object therefrom." The comment suggests that abnormal danger exists for people on the ground in view of the gravity of the harm should a plane crash, unlikely as it may be for a crash to occur, and because people on the ground have no place to hide from falling aircraft. Alternatively the doctrine of res ipsa liquitur has been applied to unexplained air crashes, e. g., Cox v. Northwest Airlines, Inc., 379 F.2d 893 (7th Cir. 1967). As to claims by aircraft passengers see the Warsaw convention, page 100 below.

for example, by rocks or other material being cast upon the premises. We are now asked to reconsider that rule.

The plaintiff Spano is the owner of a garage in Brooklyn which was wrecked by a blast occurring on November 27, 1962. There was then in that garage, for repairs, an automobile owned by the plaintiff Davis which he also claims was damaged by the blasting. * * *

It is undisputed that, on the day in question * * * the defendants had set off a total of 194 sticks of dynamite at a construction site which was only 125 feet away from the damaged premises. Although both plaintiffs alleged negligence in their complaints, no attempt was made to show that the defendants had failed to exercise reasonable care or to take necessary precautions when they were blasting. Instead, they chose to rely, upon the trial, solely on the principle of absolute liability. * * * At the close of the plaintiff Spano's case, when defendants' attorney moved to dismiss the action on the ground, among others, that no negligence had been proved, the trial judge expressed the view that the defendants could be held liable even though they were not shown to have been careless. The case then proceeded, with evidence being introduced solely on the question of damages and proximate cause. Following the trial, the court awarded damages of some $4,400 to Spano and of $329 to Davis.

* * *

The Appellate Division affirmed; it called attention to a decision in the Third Department * * *, in which the court observed that "[i]f *Booth* is to be overruled, 'the announcement thereof should come from the authoritative source and not in the form of interpretation or prediction by an intermediate appellate court' ".

In our view, the time has come for this court to make that "announcement" and declare that one who engages in blasting must assume responsibility, and be liable without fault, for any injury he causes to neighboring property.

The concept of absolute liability in blasting cases is hardly a novel one. The overwhelming majority of American jurisdictions have adopted such a rule. (See Prosser, Torts [2d ed.], § 59, p. 336; 3 Restatement, Torts, §§ 519, 520, comment *c*; Ann., 20 A.L.R.2d 1372.)[33] Indeed, this court itself, several years ago, noted that a change in our law would "conform to the more widely (indeed almost universally) approved doctrine that a blaster is absolutely liable for any damages he causes, with or without trespass". (Schlansky v. Augustus V. Riegel, Inc., 9 N.Y.2d 493, 496, 215 N.Y.S.2d 52, 53, 174 N.E.2d 730, 731.)

33. See, e. g., Exner v. Sherman Power Constr. Co., 54 F.2d 510, 80 A.L.R. 686 (2d Cir.); Colton v. Onderdonk, 69 Cal. 155, 10 P. 395; Whitman Hotel Corp. v. Elliot & Watrous Eng. Co., 137 Conn. 562, 79 A.2d 591; FitzSimmons & Connell Co. v. Braun, 199 Ill. 390, 65 N.E. 249, 59 L.R.A. 421; Louden v. City of Cincinnati, 90 Ohio St. 144, 106 N.E. 970, L.R.A.1915E, 356; Hickey v. McCabe & Bihler, 30 R.I. 346, 75 A. 404, 27 L.R.A.,N.S., 425. [From original, renumbered.]

We need not rely solely however upon out-of-state decisions in order to attain our result. Not only has the rationale of the *Booth* case (140 N.Y. 267, 35 N.E. 592, supra) been overwhelmingly rejected elsewhere but it appears to be fundamentally inconsistent with earlier cases in our own court which had held, long before *Booth* was decided, that a party was absolutely liable for damages to neighboring property caused by explosions. (See, e. g., Hay v. Cohoes Co., 2 N.Y. 159; Heeg v. Licht, 80 N.Y. 579.) In the *Hay* case (2 N.Y. 159, supra), for example, the defendant was engaged in blasting an excavation for a canal and the force of the blasts caused large quantities of earth and stones to be thrown against the plaintiff's house, knocking down his stoop and part of his chimney. The court held the defendant *absolutely* liable for the damage caused, stating (2 N.Y., at pp. 160–161):

> "It is an elementary principle in reference to private rights, that every individual is entitled to the undisturbed possession and lawful enjoyment of his own property. The mode of enjoyment is necessarily limited by the rights of others—otherwise it might be made destructive of their rights altogether. Hence the maxim *sic utere tuo, &c.* The defendants had the right to dig the canal. The plaintiff the right to the undisturbed possession of his property. If these rights conflict, the former must yield to the latter, as the more important of the two, since upon grounds of public policy, it is better that one man should surrender a particular use of his land, than that another should be deprived of the beneficial use of his property altogether, which might be the consequence if the privilege of the former should be wholly unrestricted. The case before us illustrates this principle. For if the defendants in excavating their canal, in itself a lawful use of their land, could, in the manner mentioned by the witnesses, demolish the stoop of the plaintiff with impunity, they might, for the same purpose, on the exercise of reasonable care, demolish his house, and thus deprive him of all use of his property."

Although the court in *Booth* drew a distinction between a situation—such as was presented in the *Hay* case—where there was "a physical invasion" of, or trespass on, the plaintiff's property and one in which the damage was caused by "setting the air in motion, or in some other unexplained way" (140 N.Y., at p. 596, 35 N.E., at 279, 280), it is clear that the court, in the earlier cases, was not concerned with the particular manner by which the damage was caused but by the simple fact that any explosion in a built-up area was likely to cause damage. Thus, in Heeg v. Licht, 80 N.Y. 579, supra, the court held that there should be absolute liability where the damage was caused by the accidental explosion of stored gunpowder, even in the absence of a physical trespass (p. 581):

> "The defendant had erected a building and stored materials therein, which from their character were liable to and ac-

tually did explode, causing injury to the plaintiff. The fact that the explosion took place tends to establish that the magazine was dangerous and liable to cause damage to the property of persons residing in the vicinity. * * * The fact that the magazine was liable to such a contingency, which could not be guarded against or averted by the greatest degree of care and vigilance, evinces its dangerous character, * * * In such a case, the rule which exonerates a party engaged in a lawful business, when free from negligence, has no application."

Such reasoning should, we venture, have led to the conclusion that the *intentional* setting off of explosives—that is, blasting—in an area in which it was likely to cause harm to neighboring property similarly results in absolute liability. However, the court in the *Booth* case rejected such an extension of the rule for the reason that "[t]o exclude the defendant from blasting to adapt its lot to the contemplated uses, at the instance of the plaintiff, would not be a compromise between conflicting rights, but an extinguishment of the right of the one for the benefit of the other" (140 N.Y., at p. 281, 35 N.E., at p. 596). The court expanded on this by stating, "This sacrifice, we think, the law does not exact. Public policy is sustained by the building up of towns and cities and the improvement of property. Any unnecessary restraint on freedom of action of a property owner hinders this."

This rationale cannot withstand analysis. The plaintiff in *Booth* was not seeking, as the court implied, to "exclude the defendant from blasting" and thus prevent desirable improvements to the latter's property. Rather, he was merely seeking compensation for the damage which was inflicted upon his own property as a result of that blasting. The question, in other words, was not *whether* it was lawful or proper to engage in blasting but *who* should bear the cost of any resulting damage—the person who engaged in the dangerous activity or the innocent neighbor injured thereby. Viewed in such a light, it clearly appears that *Booth* was wrongly decided and should be forthrightly overruled.

In more recent cases, our court has already gone far toward mitigating the harsh effect of the rule laid down in the *Booth* case. Thus, we have held that negligence can properly be inferred from the mere fact that a blast has caused extensive damage, even where the plaintiff is unable to show "the method of blasting or the strength of the charges or the character of the soil or rock." (Schlansky v. Augustus V. Riegel, Inc., 9 N.Y.2d 493, 497, 215 N.Y.S.2d 52, 54, 174 N.E.2d 730, 732, supra; see, also, Brown v. Rockefeller Center, 289 N.Y. 729, 46 N.E.2d 348.) But, even under this liberal interpretation of *Booth*, it would still remain possible for a defendant who engages in blasting operations—which he realizes are likely to cause injury—to avoid liability by showing that he exercised reasonable care. Since blasting involves a substantial risk of harm no matter the degree of care exercised, we perceive no reason for ever permitting a person who engages in such an activity to impose this risk upon nearby persons or property without assuming responsibility therefor. * * * [34]

BOHAN v. THE PORT JERVIS GAS LIGHT COMPANY

Court of Appeals of New York, 1890.
122 N.Y. 18, 25 N.E. 246, 9 L.R.A. 711.

[Action to recover damages for the maintenance by the defendant of an alleged nuisance on its premises, and to restrain its continuance. At the trial of this case before a jury plaintiff gave no evidence of negligence on the part of defendant either in the construction or maintenance of its works or the conduct of its business. For failure to give such proof defendant moved to dismiss the complaint and excepted to the denial of this motion.]

BROWN, J. * * *

The court charged the jury that, to constitute a nuisance, it was essential that the smells and odors from the defendant's works should be sufficient "to contaminate and pollute the air and substantially interfere with the plaintiff's enjoyment of her property," and that the question for them to determine was: "Did the odor pollute the air so as to substantially render plaintiff's property unfit for comfortable enjoyment." An exception was taken by the defendant to this part of the charge.

The rule stated by the learned judge was in accordance with all the authorities. If one carry on a lawful trade or business in such a manner as to prove a nuisance to his neighbor, he must answer in damages, and it is not necessary to a right of action that the owner should be driven from his dwelling; it is enough that the enjoyment of life and property be rendered uncomfortable. * * *

It was claimed by the defendant, and the court refused a request to charge, "that unless the jury should find that the works of the defendant were defective, or that they were out of repair, or that the persons in charge of manufacturing gas at these works were un-

34. Occasionally Rylands v. Fletcher or nuisance is said to apply to activities like blasting, e. g., Himmelman v. Nova Construction Co. Ltd., 5 D.L.R. (3d) 56 (Sup.Ct. Nova Scotia 1969). As suggested in Judge Fuld's reference to Schlansky v. Riegel, a similar but not identical result is achieved under the doctrine of res ipsa loquitur; see, e. g., Vattilana v. George & Lynch, Inc., 154 A.2d 565 (Del.Super.1959), where the jury was permitted to infer negligence from the facts that defendant was blasting in connection with a highway construction job and defendant's property appeared to have been damaged by concussion, "since the damage alleged is unusual and would not normally occur if the user of the dangerous instrumentality had the required knowledge and if he had exercised the proper care"; such inference was, however, said to be subject to any explanation of defendant's, the burden of persuasion as to negligence remaining on the plaintiff. The general problem is ably dealt with in Smith, Liability for Damage to Land by Blasting, 22 Harv.L.Rev. 542 (1920) and Gregory, Trespass to Nuisance to Absolute Liability, 37 Va. L.Rev. 359 (1951).

skillful and incapable, their verdict should be for the defendant;" and "that if the odors which affect the plaintiff are those that are inseparable from the manufacture of gas with the most approved apparatus and with the utmost skill and care, and do not result from any defects in the works, or from want of care in their management, the defendant is not liable." An exception to this ruling raises the principal question discussed in the case.

While every person has exclusive dominion over his own property and may subject it to such uses as will subserve his wishes and private interests, he is bound to have respect and regard for his neighbor's rights.

The maxim "*Sic utere tuo ut alienum non laedas*" limits his power. He must make a reasonable use of his property, and a reasonable use can never be construed to include those uses which produce destructive vapors and noxious smells, and that result in material injury to the property and to the comfort of the existence of those who dwell in the neighborhood.

The reports are filled with cases where this doctrine has been applied, and it may be confidently asserted that no authority can be produced, holding that negligence is essential to establish a cause of action for injuries of such a character. * * *

The principle, that one cannot recover for injuries sustained from lawful acts done on one's own property without negligence and without malice, is well founded in the law. Everyone has the right to the reasonable enjoyment of his own property, and so long as the use to which he devotes it violates no rights of others, there is no legal cause of action against him.

The wants of mankind demand that property be put to many and various uses and employments, and one may have, upon his property, any kind of lawful business, and so long as it is not a nuisance, and is not managed so as to become such, he is not responsible for any damage that his neighbor accidently sustains as *damnum absque injuria.* And under this principle, if the steam boiler on the defendant's property, or the gas retort, or the naphtha tanks had exploded and injured the plaintiff's property, it would have been necessary for her to prove negligence, on the defendant's part, to entitle her to recover. (Losee v. Buchanan, 51 N.Y. 476, 10 Am.Rep. 623.)

But where the damage is the necessary consequence of just what the defendant is doing, or is incident to the business itself, or the manner in which it is conducted, the law of negligence has no application and the law of nuisance applies. * * *

The exception to the refusal to charge the first proposition above quoted was not, therefore, well taken.

It is contended, however, by the defendant, that the acts of the legislature relating to gas companies are a protection from liability or consequential injuries flowing from the manufacture of gas, or the prosecution of the business, when want of care forms no element of the cause of injury, and it is sought to apply to this case the broad principle that that which the law authorizes cannot be a nuisance, although it may occasion damages to individual rights and property.

The cases cited to sustain this proposition are ones where municipal corporations were engaged in grading and improving public streets and highways. (Radcliff's Ex'rs v. Brooklyn, 4 N.Y. 195, 53 Am.Dec. 357; Transportation Co. v. Chicago, 99 U.S. 635, 25 L.Ed. 336.) Or where the act causing the injury was done by corporations in the construction of works upon property acquired under the power of eminent domain. (Bellinger v. N. Y. C. R. Co., 23 N.Y. 42.)

In these cases, in doing the acts complained of, the defendants acted in the performance of a public duty imposed upon them by the legislature, or in the exercise of a right conferred by law, and it is well settled that persons appointed or authorized by law to perform a public duty, or to do acts of a public character are not answerable for consequential damages if they act within their jurisdiction and with care and skill. * * *

This principle cannot, however, be applied to cases like the one under consideration.

* * *

It may be conceded that the business of manufacturing and distributing gas through the public streets for public and private use is a business of a public character, and the individual possessing such right has a franchise granted by the state for a public object, and that it meets a public necessity for which the state may make provision.

But the state has not seen fit to confer upon the corporations formed under the act cited, the power of eminent domain, and they cannot, therefore, locate their works, where they will.

In their ability to acquire real estate upon which to establish their manufactory, they have no greater power than any citizen of the state, and having acquired property they rest under the same obligation as other citizens, to make a reasonable use of it and to respect and regard the rights of their neighbors.

The proposition contended for by the learned counsel for the defendant has, in recent years, received full consideration in the courts of England and of this country, and the rule is now established that the statutory authority which will justify an injury to private property and afford immunity for acts which would otherwise be a nuisance must be express, or must be a clear and unquestionable implication from powers expressly conferred, and it must appear that the legislature contemplated the doing of the very act which occasioned the injury. * * *

The legislature may authorize acts which would otherwise be a nuisance when they affect or relate to matters in which the public have an interest, or over which the public have control, such as highways or public streams.

In such cases the legislative authorization exempts from liability to suits civil or criminal at the instance of the state, but it does not affect the claims of a private citizen for damages for any special inconvenience and special discomfort not experienced by the public at large. * * *

These views lead to the conclusion that the defendant obtained no immunity from liability for consequential injuries sustained by property surrounding its works by reason of its incorporation, or the privilege conferred upon the business by the acts of the legislature, and that the facts of the case do not take it out of the operation of the rules of law applicable to ordinary common-law nuisances.

The legislature has given to the corporations created to manufacture gas the right to lay down their conductors in the public streets subject to the control and regulation of the municipal authorities, and for acts done in the execution of that privilege they are exempt from prosecution at the suit of the people.

The choice, however, of the place to locate their works, and the selection of materials from which to manufacture gas, has been left to the corporations, and those things must be performed with reference to the rights of others.

* * *

We think the proof permitted the conclusion that the defendant had created a nuisance, and that there was no error in the charge of the court, or the refusal to charge.

The judgment must be affirmed.

Fault is not always irrelevant in nuisance. See, e. g., McFarlane v. City of Niagara Falls, 247 N.Y. 340, 160 N.E. 391 (1928).

The Restatement has dealt with nuisance as an "invasion of another's interest in the private use and enjoyment of land", as distinguished from trespass, an invasion by "unprivileged entry or intrusion" of an interest in the exclusive possession of land. The Second Restatement suggests, as does the first, that the nuisance invasion is "non-trespassory", but adds that it is "not inconsistent with an accompanying trespass to the land", § 821D, Tent. Draft No. 16 (1970). See, e. g., Keeton, Trespass, Nuisance and Strict Liability, 59 Colum. L.Rev. 457 (1959); Renken v. Harvey Aluminum (Inc.), 226 F.Supp. 169 (D.Or.1963); and *Martin* case infra at page 87.

As to the relationship between fault and liability in nuisance, the first Restatement suggested a distinction between intentional and unintentional invasions (§ 822). For the latter there would be liability only if the invasion were "otherwise actionable under the rules governing liability for negligent, reckless or ultrahazardous conduct." If the invasion was "intentional" (either "for the purpose" of causing the harm, or known to be "resulting or * * * substantially certain to result" from the actor's conduct, § 825, e. g., typical industrial pollution, there would be liability only if it were also "unreasonable",

i. e., "unless the utility of the actor's conduct outweighs the gravity of the harm" (§ 826). When a similar formulation was proposed for Restatement Second, a dissenting memorandum was submitted by one of the Advisers:[35]

> "* * * The Restatement has built * * * an elaborate edifice for weighing in all cases the utility of defendant's enterprise * * * against the gravity of the harm inflicted on plaintiff's interest. * * *
>
> "This line of reasoning is, of course, quite in keeping with the late nineteenth and earlier twentieth century urge to reduce all tort liability to terms of fault. * * * But this reasoning unduly simplifies the matter by leaving out of account a basis of liability without fault the recognition of which gives greater flexibility to the law of nuisance and better explains some lines of cases than the Restatement's procrustean insistence on fault (except where conduct is abnormally dangerous).
>
> "* * * [W]here an actor's conduct will inevitably cause damage to another he may nevertheless be privileged to pursue it if its social utility is great enough. But where the actor is also the beneficiary of the conduct, the law may render his privilege incomplete; it may make him pay for the actual harm caused by its exercise. This, it is submitted, is the proper explanation of liability in some cases of nuisance * * * where the invasion of plaintiff's interest is so substantial that he should not be compelled to suffer it without compensation even though defendant's conduct entails no fault and is not abnormally dangerous. * * *
>
> "There is substantial authority for the position urged here. The Restatement position was at one time embraced by the English court of common pleas,[36] but in later cases repudiated by the Exchequer Chamber[37] and the House of Lords.[38] * * *
>
>> 'The reasoning has been accepted in a number of American decisions. A rather dramatic example is Madison v. Ducktown Sulphur, Copper & Iron Co.,[39] where the court specifically found that defendant's activity (open-air roasting of ores) was lawful and the only known method of conducting the operation; that defendants had used every method to eliminate the emis-

35. Fleming James, Jr., Memorandum, The element of fault in private nuisance, Restatement of Torts Second, Tent. Draft No. 16, at 131 (1970).

36. Hole v. Barlow, 4 C.B.N.S. 334, 140 Eng.Rep. 1113 (C.P.1858).

37. Bamford v. Turnley, 3 B&S 66, 122 Eng.Rep. 27 (Ex.Ch.1862); Tipping v. St. Helen's Smelting Co., 4 B&S 616, 122 Eng.Rep. 588, 591 (Ex.Ch.1864).

38. St. Helen's Smelting Co. v. Tipping, 11 H.L.Cas. 642, 11 Eng.Rep. 1483 (H.L.1865).

39. 113 Tenn. 331, 83 S.W. 658 (1904).

sions, spending large sums for the purpose; and that "There is no place more remote to which the operations referred to could be transferred." The lands of the farmer-plaintiffs were "all thin mountain lands, of little agricultural value," located from 2–8 miles from the plants in the mountains around Ducktown. Fumes and smoke from defendant's operations badly damaged the plaintiff's timber and crops. Defendants showed the utility of their operations and their economic value to the community. The court denied the injunction sought but ordered the award of damages, explaining: "* * * in the case of conflicting rights, where neither party can enjoy his own without in some measure restricting the liberty of the other in the use of property, the law must make the best arrangement it can between the contending parties, with a view to preserving to each one the largest measure of liberty possible under the circumstance * * *." This reasoning is surely inconsistent with a finding of fault on Ducktown's part; yet it was held in damages. In a number of other American cases defendants have been held liable in damages for substantial harm inflicted on plaintiff's property interest, although their operations have been lawful and carefully conducted in a suitable place.[40] Several of them use the reasoning of incomplete privilege or inverse condemnation.[41] And recently there have been similar rulings made on this basis awarding damages against airports for serious invasions of nearby land caused by low non-trespassory flights necessary for landing and taking off.[42] * * *

"The Restatement accepts abnormal danger as an appropriate basis for strict liability. The justification for it is the high degree of *risk* of injury caused by legitimate but dangerous activity. But if high risk of harm is a sufficient basis for strict liability, then the certainty (or substantial certainty) of harm in the cases under discussion is an even stronger basis for it.

40. See original for numerous citations.

41. See, e. g., Richards v. Washington Terminal Co., 233 U.S. 546, 34 S.Ct. 654, 58 L.Ed. 1088 (1914); Louisville and Nashville Terminal Co. v. Lellyett, 114 Tenn. 368, 85 S.W. 881 (1905). A classic statement is that of Baron Branwell in Banford v. Turnley, 3 B &S 66, 84–85, 122 Eng.Rep. 25, 33 (Ex. Ch.1862).

42. Thornburg v. Port of Portland, 233 Or. 178, 376 P.2d 100 (1963), on later appeal, 244 Or. 69, 415 P.2d 750 (1966); Martin v. Port of Seattle, 64 Wash.2d 309, 391 P.2d 540 (1961). (But see Batten v. United States, 306 F.2d 580 (10th Cir. 1962); Ferguson v. City of Keene, 108 N.H. 409, 238 A. 2d 1 (1968).) On the later appeal in *Thornburg,* supra, the court made it clear that if harm to plaintiff was substantial and peculiar, there would be no room for considering the airport's utility in determining whether compensation should be made.

"So far as policy goes, we have already noted how the progressive industrialization of our society increases both the danger of pollution and the means to meet it, and how the larger problems posed are essentially political, calling for political solutions. But this process may well be slow and incomplete. In the meantime, individuals will be in need of protection against serious abuse and they will have to rely largely on the private nuisance action to get it. * * *

"The foregoing reasoning would lead to the following rules:

'* * *

'Where the harm is inadvertently or unintentionally caused, liability will be imposed only if the invasion is negligent or reckless or actionable as an abnormally dangerous activity. This is the same as the Restatement rule.

'Where the invasion is intentional, liability will be imposed if the defendant's conduct has been unreasonable.

'Where the invasion is intentional, liability will be imposed even where the condition or conduct causing it is socially useful, is maintained and conducted with all due care and in a suitable and convenient location, if the harm caused is unreasonably great. This departs from Restatement rule but accords with what is believed to be the weight of judicial authority. This again involves weighing of utility against harm but within limits. * * * Persons who live in business or manufacturing districts must not, in Mellor's often quoted words "Stand upon extreme rights and bring actions in respect of every matter of annoyance." [43] But where material physical injury is inflicted upon persons or property or where annoyance is serious and long continued so as "visibly to diminish the value of the property and the enjoyment of it," [44] then "a thing of value has been taken from the plaintiff for the benefit of the defendant as the representative of the public, and for that thing compensation must be made." ' " [45]

In partial response to this memorandum, as well as to suggestions from Professor Robert Keeton, another adviser, the following pro-

43. Tipping v. St. Helen's Smelting Co., 4 B&S 608, 610–11, 122 Eng.Rep. 588, 589 (Q.B.1863).

44. Ibid.

45. Louisville & Nashville Terminal Co. v. Lellyett, 114 Tenn. 368, 397, 85 S.W. 881, 888 (1905), quoting from Cumberland Tel. & Tel. Co. v. United Electric Ry., 93 Tenn. 492, 520–521, 29 S.W. 104, 111, 27 L.R.A. 236 (1893). [Notes 36 to 39 and 41 to 45 have been adapted, renumbered, from the original; other notes in the original have been omitted. See also Brenner, Nuisance Law and the Industrial Revolution, 3 J.Leg.Studies 403 (1974).]

posed sections 826 and 829A were published in 1972 by the Reporter, Professor John W. Wade, to supplement the Restatement Second's probable revision of Section 822: [46]

§ 822. General Rule.

One is subject to liability for a private nuisance if, but only if, his conduct is a legal cause of an invasion of another's interest in the private use and enjoyment of land, and the invasion is either

(a) Intentional and unreasonable, or

(b) Unintentional and otherwise actionable under the principles controlling liability for negligent or reckless conduct, or for abnormally dangerous conditions or activities.

§ 826. Unreasonableness of Invasion.

An intentional invasion of another's interest in the use and enjoyment of land is unreasonable under the rule stated in § 822, if

(a) The gravity of the harm outweighs the utility of the actor's conduct, or

(b) The harm caused by the conduct is substantial and the financial burden of compensating for this and other harms does not render infeasible the continuation of the conduct.

§ 829A. Gravity vs. Utility—Serious Harm.

Under the rules stated in §§ 826–828, an intentional invasion of another's interest in the use and enjoyment of land is unreasonable and the actor is subject to liability if the harm resulting from the invasion is substantial and greater than the other should be required to bear without compensation.

BOOMER v. ATLANTIC CEMENT CO., INC.

Court of Appeals of New York, 1970.
26 N.Y.2d 219, 309 N.Y.S.2d 312, 257 N.E.2d 870.

BERGAN, JUDGE. Defendant operates a large cement plant near Albany. These are actions for injunction and damages by neighboring land owners alleging injury to property from dirt, smoke and vibration emanating from the plant. A nuisance has been found after trial, temporary damages have been allowed; but an injunction has been denied.

The public concern with air pollution arising from many sources in industry and in transportation is currently accorded ever wider

46. Restatement of Torts Second, Tent. Draft No. 18, at 1–6 (1972).

recognition accompanied by a growing sense of responsibility in State and Federal Governments to control it. Cement plants are obvious sources of air pollution in the neighborhoods where they operate.

But there is now before the court private litigation in which individual property owners have sought specific relief from a single plant operation. The threshold question raised by the division of view on this appeal is whether the court should resolve the litigation between the parties now before it as equitably as seems possible; or whether, seeking promotion of the general public welfare, it should channel private litigation into broad public objectives.

A court performs its essential function when it decides the rights of parties before it. Its decision of private controversies may sometimes greatly affect public issues. Large questions of law are often resolved by the manner in which private litigation is decided. But this is normally an incident to the court's main function to settle controversy. It is a rare exercise of judicial power to use a decision in private litigation as a purposeful mechanism to achieve direct public objectives greatly beyond the rights and interests before the court.

Effective control of air pollution is a problem presently far from solution even with the full public and financial powers of government. In large measure adequate technical procedures are yet to be developed and some that appear possible may be economically impracticable.

It seems apparent that the amelioration of air pollution will depend on technical research in great depth; on a carefully balanced consideration of the economic impact of close regulation; and of the actual effect on public health. It is likely to require massive public expenditure and to demand more than any local community can accomplish and to depend on regional and interstate controls.

A court should not try to do this on its own as a by-product of private litigation and it seems manifest that the judicial establishment is neither equipped in the limited nature of any judgment it can pronounce nor prepared to lay down and implement an effective policy for the elimination of air pollution. This is an area beyond the circumference of one private lawsuit. It is a direct responsibility for government and should not thus be undertaken as an incident to solving a dispute between property owners and a single cement plant—one of many—in the Hudson River valley.

* * * The total damage to plaintiffs' properties is, however, relatively small in comparison with the value of defendant's operation and with the consequences of the injunction which plaintiffs seek. [Permanent damages for all plaintiffs were found to total $185,000. Defendant had invested over $45,000,000 in plant and employed over 300 people.]

The ground for the denial of injunction, notwithstanding the finding both that there is a nuisance and that plaintiffs have been damaged substantially, is the large disparity in economic consequences of the nuisance and of the injunction. This theory cannot, however, be sustained without overruling a doctrine which has been consistently reaffirmed in several leading cases in this court and which has never been disavowed here, namely that where a nuisance has been found and where there has been any substantial damage shown by the party complaining an injunction will be granted. [See opinion of Judge Werner in Whalen v. Union Bag & Paper Co., 208 N.Y. 1, 101 N.E. 805.]

* * *

* * * [T]o follow the rule literally in these cases would be to close down the plant at once. This court is fully agreed to avoid that immediately drastic remedy; the difference in view is how best to avoid it.

One alternative is to grant the injunction but postpone its effect to a specified future date to give opportunity for technical advances to permit defendant to eliminate the nuisance; another is to grant the injunction conditioned on the payment of permanent damages to plaintiffs which would compensate them for the total economic loss to their property present and future caused by defendant's operations. For reasons which will be developed the court chooses the latter alternative.

If the injunction were to be granted unless within a short period—e. g., 18 months—the nuisance be abated by improved methods, there would be no assurance that any significant technical improvement would occur.

The parties could settle this private litigation at any time if defendant paid enough money and the imminent threat of closing the plant would build up the pressure on defendant. If there were no improved techniques found, there would inevitably be applications to the court at Special Term for extensions of time to perform on showing of good faith efforts to find such techniques.

Moreover, techniques to eliminate dust and other annoying byproducts of cement making are unlikely to be developed by any research the defendant can undertake within any short period, but will depend on the total resources of the cement industry nationwide and throughout the world. The problem is universal wherever cement is made.

For obvious reasons the rate of the research is beyond control of defendant. If at the end of 18 months the whole industry has not found a technical solution a court would be hard put to close down this one cement plant if due regard be given to equitable principles.

On the other hand, to grant the injunction unless defendant pays plaintiffs such permanent damages as may be fixed by the court seems to do justice between the contending parties. All of the attributions of economic loss to the properties on which plaintiffs' complaints are based will have been redressed.

The nuisance complained of by these plaintiffs may have other public or private consequences, but these particular parties are the only ones who have sought remedies and the judgment proposed will fully redress them. * * *

Thus it seems fair to both sides to grant permanent damages to plaintiffs which will terminate this private litigation. The theory of damage is the "servitude on land" of plaintiffs imposed by defendant's nuisance. (See United States v. Causby, 328 U.S. 256, 261, 262, 267, 66 S.Ct. 1062, 90 L.Ed. 1206, where the term "servitude" addressed to the land was used by Justice Douglas relating to the effect of airplane noise on property near an airport.)

The judgment, by allowance of permanent damages imposing a servitude on land, which is the basis of the actions, would preclude future recovery by plaintiffs or their grantees * * * [46a]

JASEN, JUDGE (dissenting).—* * *

I see grave dangers in overruling our long-established rule of granting an injunction where a nuisance results in substantial continuing damage. In permitting the injunction to become inoperative upon the payment of permanent damages, the majority is, in effect, licensing a continuing wrong. It is the same as saying to the cement company, you may continue to do harm to your neighbors so long as you pay a fee for it. Furthermore, once such permanent damages are assessed and paid, the incentive to alleviate the wrong would be eliminated, thereby continuing air pollution of an area without abatement.

* * *

This kind of inverse condemnation * * * may not be invoked by a private person or corporation for private gain or advantage. Inverse condemnation should only be permitted when the public is primarily served in the taking or impairment of property. * * * The promotion of the interests of the polluting cement company has, in my opinion, no public use or benefit.

* * *

SPUR INDUSTRIES, INC. v. DEL E. WEBB DEVELOPMENT CO.

Supreme Court of Arizona, 1972.
108 Ariz. 178, 494 P.2d 700.

[Spur's feedlot was established in 1956, about two miles south of a retirement community. In 1959 there were 25 cattle feeding operations within a seven-mile radius of Spur. About then Webb started acquiring land for urban development in the vicinity of the retirement community, and Spur also expanded.]

CAMERON, VICE CHIEF JUSTICE. * * *

Accompanied by an extensive advertising campaign, homes were first offered by Del Webb in January 1960 and the first unit to be

46a. For additional discussion of considerations applicable to choice of judicial remedy for nuisance see Harrison v. Indiana Auto Shredders Co., 528 F.2d 1107 (7th Cir. 1975). An ancient non-judicial remedy is also sometimes available: "abatement", i. e., self-help, when it can be accomplished without breach of peace, e. g., State ex rel. Herman v. Cardon, — Ariz. —, 544 P.2d 657 (1976).

completed was south of Grand Avenue and approximately 2½ miles north of Spur. By 2 May 1960, there were 450 to 500 houses completed or under construction. At this time, Del Webb did not consider odors from the Spur feed pens a problem and Del Webb continued to develop in a southerly direction, until sales resistance became so great that the parcels were difficult if not impossible to sell. * * *

By December 1967, Del Webb's property had extended south to Olive Avenue and Spur was within 500 feet of Olive Avenue to the north. * * * Del Webb filed its original complaint alleging that in excess of 1,300 lots in the southwest portion were unfit for development for sale as residential lots because of the operation of the Spur feedlot.

Del Webb's suit complained that the Spur feeding operation was a public nuisance because of the flies and the odor which were drifting or being blown by the prevailing south to north wind over the southern portion of Sun City. At the time of the suit, Spur was feeding between 20,000 and 30,000 head of cattle, and the facts amply support the finding of the trial court that the feed pens had become a nuisance to the people who resided in the southern part of Del Webb's development. The testimony indicated that cattle in a commercial feedlot will produce 35 to 40 pounds of wet manure per day, per head, or over a million pounds of wet manure per day for 30,000 head of cattle, and that despite the admittedly good feedlot management and good housekeeping practices by Spur, the resulting odor and flies produced an annoying if not unhealthy situation as far as the senior citizens of southern Sun City were concerned. There is no doubt that some of the citizens of Sun City were unable to enjoy the outdoor living which Del Webb had advertised and that Del Webb was faced with sales resistance from prospective purchasers as well as strong and persistent complaints from the people who had purchased homes in that area.

* * *

We have no difficulty, * * * in agreeing with the conclusion of the trial court that Spur's operation was an enjoinable public nuisance as far as the people in the southern portion of Del Webb's Sun City were concerned.

§ 36–601, subsec. A reads as follows:

> "§ 36–601. Public nuisances dangerous to public health
>
> "A. The following conditions are specifically declared public nuisances dangerous to the public health:
>
> "1. Any condition or place in populous areas which constitutes a breeding place for flies, rodents, mosquitoes and other insects which are capable of carrying and transmitting disease-causing organisms to any person or persons."

* * *

It is clear that as to the citizens of Sun City, the operation of Spur's feedlot was both a public and a private nuisance. They could have successfully maintained an action to abate the nuisance. Del Webb, having shown a special injury in the loss of sales, had a standing to bring suit to enjoin the nuisance. * * *

A suit to enjoin a nuisance sounds in equity and the courts have long recognized a special responsibility to the public when acting as a court of equity * * *.

In addition to protecting the public interest, * * * courts of equity are concerned with protecting the operator of a lawfully, albeit noxious, business from the result of a knowing and willful encroachment by others near his business.

In the so-called "coming to the nuisance" cases, the courts have held that the residential landowner may not have relief if he knowingly came into a neighborhood reserved for industrial or agricultural endeavors and has been damaged thereby * * *.

Were Webb the only party injured, we would feel justified in holding that the doctrine of "coming to the nuisance" would have been a bar to the relief asked by Webb, and, on the other hand, had Spur located the feedlot near the outskirts of a city and had the city grown toward the feedlot, Spur would have to suffer the cost of abating the nuisance as to those people locating within the growth pattern of the expanding city * * *.

We agree, however, with the Massachusetts court that:

> "The law of nuisance affords no rigid rule to be applied in all instances. It is elastic. It undertakes to require only that which is fair and reasonable under all the circumstances. In a commonwealth like this, which depends for its material prosperity so largely on the continued growth and enlargement of manufacturing of diverse varieties, 'extreme rights' cannot be enforced. * * *." Stevens v. Rockport Granite Co., 216 Mass. 486, 488, 104 N.E. 371, 373 (1914).

There was no indication in the instant case at the time Spur and its predecessors located in western Maricopa County that a new city would spring up, full-blown, alongside the feeding operation and that the developer of that city would ask the court to order Spur to move because of the new city. Spur is required to move not because of any wrongdoing on the part of Spur, but because of a proper and legitimate regard of the courts for the rights and interests of the public.

Del Webb, on the other hand, is entitled to the relief prayed for (a permanent injunction), not because Webb is blameless, but because of the damage to the people who have been encouraged to purchase homes in Sun City. It does not equitably or legally follow, however, that Webb, being entitled to the injunction, is then free of any liability to Spur if Webb has in fact been the cause of the damage Spur has sustained. It does not seem harsh to require a developer, who has taken advantage of the lesser land values in a rural area as well as the availability of large tracts of land on which to build and develop a new town or city in the area, to indemnify those who are forced to leave as a result.

Having brought people to the nuisance to the foreseeable detriment of Spur, Webb must indemnify Spur for a reasonable amount of the cost of moving or shutting down. It should be noted that this relief to Spur is limited to a case wherein a developer has, with foreseeability, brought into a previously agricultural or industrial area the population which makes necessary the granting of an injunction against a lawful business and for which the business has no adequate relief.

* * *

The "coming to the nuisance" doctrine has had a mixed acceptance. Sometimes it is asserted to protect a polluter whose activity began before the victim's, e. g., East St. John's Shingle Co. v. City of Portland, 195 Or. 505, 246 P.2d 554 (1952). In some circumstances there may be doubt as to the cleanliness of plaintiff's hands, e. g., Edwards v. Allouez Mining Co., 38 Mich. 46 (1878), where the land injured "was bought by the complainant with the preconceived purpose to force a sale of it upon the defendant"; even there, however, while an injunction was denied, the possibility of damages was left open. The reasonableness of plaintiff's use, e. g., the choice of an industrial area for a residence, may have a bearing on the substantiality of his damages, both as to their existence and their magnitude. Otherwise, however, the "coming to a nuisance" concept has been viewed with disfavor as a defense, on the ground that such a defense would enable a polluter to diminish the value of neighboring land without compensation. See, e. g., James, Assumption of Risk, 61 Yale L.J. 141, 144–45 (1952); F. Harper and F. James, The Law of Torts, § 21.1 at note 28 and § 22.8 at note 11 (1956 and Supp.1968); Prosser, Torts 611 (4th ed. 1971). Traditional precedents include Cooke v. Forbes, L.R. 5 Eq. 166 (1867–68) and Sturges v. Bridgman, 11 Ch.D. 852 (1879). In the Restatement of Torts Second, Tentative Draft No. 16 (1970), § 840D provides: "The fact that the plaintiff has acquired or improved his land after a nuisance interfering with it has come into existence is not in itself sufficient to bar his action, but is a factor to be considered in determining whether the nuisance is actionable."

"Public nuisance" is a great confusion. It has traditionally referred to certain low-level common law crimes offensive to the senses or sensibilities, for which damages may be available to victims who can show "special" or "particular" damages, usually of a "kind" not shared by the public. Some of these offenses may have nothing to do with the enjoyment of interests in land, the gravamen of private nuisance; others may coincidentally overlap. And sometimes "substantial" injury to person or property is said to qualify for redress for public nuisance although the public is affected by the same kind of injury, e. g. Hampton v. North Carolina Pulp Co., 223 N.C. 535, 27 S.E.2d 538 (1943) (river pollution damage to commercial fishery's interest in normal supply of migratory fish). "Substantial harm" is, however, necessary for liability for private nuisance as well, e. g., Phillips Ranch, Inc. v. Banta, — Or. —, 543 P.2d 1035 (1975). See, generally, Prosser, Private Action for Public Nuisance, 52 Va.L.Rev. 997 (1966).

A somewhat broadened concept has emerged in the drafting of the Restatement of Torts Second:

§ 821B Public Nuisance

(1) A public nuisance is an unreasonable interference with a right common to the general public.

(2) Factors conducing toward a determination that an interference with a public right is unreasonable, include the following:

(a) The circumstance that the conduct involves the kind of interference with the public health, the public safety, the public peace, the public comfort or the public convenience which sufficed to constitute the common law crime of public nuisance,

(b) The circumstance that the conduct is proscribed by a statute, ordinance or administrative regulation, or

(c) The circumstance that the conduct is of a continuing nature or has produced a permanent or long-lasting effect, that its detrimental effect upon the public right is substantial, and that the actor knows or has reason to know of that effect.

§ 821C Who Can Recover for Public Nuisance

(1) In order to recover damages in an individual action for a public nuisance, one must have suffered harm of a kind different from that suffered by other members of the public exercising the public right which was the subject of interference.

(2) In order to maintain a proceeding to enjoin or abate a public nuisance, one must

(a) Be qualified to sue for damages, as indicated in Subsection (1),

(b) Have authority as a public official or public agency to represent in such matters the State or a political subdivision, or

(c) Have standing to sue as a representative of the general public, or as a citizen in a citizen's action, or as a member of a class in a class action.

The editorial material accompanying these proposals, in Tentative Draft No. 17 (1971), recognizes that they may be "inadequate", particularly in continuing to require that compensable damages be "of a kind different" from the public's. The comments also state that some differences of degree may shade into differences of kind, and that pecuniary loss to a plaintiff, personal injury or physical damage to land would normally constitute damages different in kind.

MARTIN v. REYNOLDS METALS CO.

Supreme Court of Oregon, En Banc, 1959.
221 Or. 86, 342 P.2d 790.

O'CONNELL, JUSTICE. This is an action of trespass. The plaintiffs allege that during the period from August 22, 1951 to January 1, 1956 the defendant, in the operation of its aluminum reduction plant near Troutdale, Oregon, caused certain fluoride compounds in the form of gases and particulates to become airborne and settle upon the plaintiff's land rendering it unfit for raising livestock during that period. Plaintiffs allege that their cattle were poisoned by ingesting the fluorides which contaminate the forage and water on their land. They sought damages in the amount of $450,000 for the loss of use of their land for grazing purposes and for the deterioration of the land through the growth of brush, trees and weeds resulting from the lack of use of the premises for grazing purposes. * * *

The plaintiffs and the defendant each moved for a directed verdict, whereupon the trial court found that the plaintiffs had suffered damage in the amount of $71,500 in the loss of use of their land and $20,000 for the deterioration of their land and entered judgment accordingly. * * *

In the course of the pleadings the defendant raised the issue as to whether the complaint alleged a cause of action in trespass. The defendant contended that at most a cause of action in nuisance was stated. The trial court accepted the plaintiff's theory of the case. The principal assignments of error rest upon the defendant's contention that the trial court was mistaken in identifying the defendant's invasion of the plaintiffs' land as a trespass; that there was not sufficient evidence to establish a cause of action under any theory, but that if the court should find the evidence sufficient to give rise to liability the defendant's conduct constituted a nuisance and not a trespass.

Through appropriate pleadings the defendant set up the two-year statute of limitations applicable to nontrespassory injuries to land (ORS 12.110). If the defendant's conduct created a nuisance and not a trespass the defendant would be liable only for such damage as resulted from its conduct during a period of two years immediately preceding the date upon which plaintiffs' action was instituted. On the other hand, if the defendant's conduct resulted in a trespass upon plaintiff's land the six-year statute of limitations provided for in ORS 12.808 would be applicable and plaintiffs would be entitled to recover damages resulting from the trespasses by defendant during the period from August 22, 1959 to January 1, 1956.

The gist of the defendant's argument is as follows: a trespass arises only when there has been a "breaking and entering upon real property," constituting a direct, as distinguished from a consequential, invasion of the possessor's interest in land; and the settling upon the land of fluoride compounds consisting of gases, fumes and particulates is not sufficient to satisfy these requirements.

Before appraising the argument we shall first describe more particularly the physical and chemical nature of the substance which was deposited upon plaintiff's land. In reducing alumina (the oxide of aluminum) to aluminum the alumina is subjected to an electrolytic process which causes the emanation of fluoridic compounds consisting principally of hydrogen fluoride, calcium fluoride, iron fluoride and silicon tetrafluoride. The individual particulates which form these chemical compounds are not visible to the naked eye. A part of them were captured by a fume collection system which was installed in November, 1950; the remainder became airborne and a part of the uncaptured particles eventually were deposited upon plaintiff's land.

There is evidence to prove that during the period from August, 1951, to January, 1956 the emanation of fluorides from defendant's plant averaged approximately 800 pounds daily. Some of this discharge was deposited upon the plaintiff's land. There is sufficient evidence to support the trial court's finding that the quantity of fluorides deposited upon plaintiff's land was great enough to cause $91,500 damage to the plaintiffs in the use of their land for grazing purposes and in the deterioration of their land as alleged.

We must determine, however, whether all or only a part of this damage may be shown; all, if the invasion constitutes a trespass, a part only (i. e., the damage which resulted within the two-year period of the statute of limitations) if the invasion was a nuisance and not a trespass.

Trespass and private nuisance are separate fields of tort liability relating to actionable interference with the possession of land. They may be distinguished by comparing the interest invaded; an actionable invasion of a possessor's interest in the exclusive possession of land is a trespass; an actionable invasion of a possessor's interest in the use and enjoyment of his land is a nuisance. 4 Restatement, Torts 224, Intro. Note Chapter 40.

The same conduct on the part of a defendant may and often does result in the actionable invasion of both of these interests, in which case the choice between the two remedies is, in most cases, a matter of little consequence. Where the action is brought on the theory of nuisance alone the court ordinarily is not called upon to determine whether the conduct would also result in a trespassory invasion. In such cases the courts' treatment of the invasion solely in terms of the law of nuisance does not mean that the same conduct could not also be regarded as a trespass. Some of the cases relied upon by the defendant are of this type; cases in which the court holds that the interference with the plaintiff's possession through soot, dirt, smoke, cinders, ashes and similar substances constitute a nuisance, but where the court does not discuss the applicability of the law of trespass to the same set of facts. * * *

However, there are cases which have held that the defendant's interference with plaintiff's possession resulting from the settling upon his land of effluents emanating from defendant's operations is exclusively nontrespassory. Bartlett v. Grasselli Chemical Co., 1922, 92 W.Va. 445, 115 S.E. 451, 27 A.L.R. 54; O'Neill v. San Pedro, L.A. & S.L.R. Co., 1911, 38 Utah 475, 114 P. 127; Thackery v. Union Portland Cement Co., 1924, 64 Utah 437, 231 P. 813; see Ryan v. City of Emmetsburg, 1942, 232 Iowa 600, 4 N.W.2d 435. Although in such cases the separate particles which collectively cause the invasion are minute, the deposit of each of the particles constitutes a physical intrusion and, but for the size of the particle, would clearly give rise to an action of trespass. The defendant asks us to take account of the difference in size of the physical agency through which the intrusion occurs and relegate entirely to the field of nuisance law certain invasions which do not meet the dimensional test, whatever that is. In pressing this argument upon us the defendant must admit that there are cases which have held that a trespass results from the movement or deposit of rather small objects over or upon the surface of the possessor's land.

Thus it has been held that causing shot from a gun to fall upon the possessor's land is a trespass. * * *

The dropping of particles of molten lead upon the plaintiff's land has been held to be a trespass. Van Alstyne v. Rochester Telephone Corp., 163 Misc. 258, 296 N.Y.S. 726. And the defendant was held liable in trespass where spray from a cooling tower on the roof of its theater fell upon the plaintiff's land. B & R Luncheonette, Inc. v. Fairmont Theatre Corp., 278 App.Div. 133, 103 N.Y.S.2d 747.

The deposit of soot and carbon from defendant's mill upon plaintiff's land was held to be a trespass in Young v. Fort Frances Pulp and Paper Co., Canada 1919, 17 Ont.Wkly. Notes 6.

And liability on the theory of trespass has been recognized where the harm was produced by the vibration of the soil or by the concussion of the air which, of course, is nothing more than the movement of molecules one against the other. McNeill v. Redington, 1945, 67 Cal.App.2d 315, 154 P.2d 428. Liability on this basis was clearly recognized in Bedell v. Goulter, 1953, 199 Or. 344, 361, 261 P.2d 842, 850, where Justice Lusk, after discussing the rule of Rylands v. Fletcher, LR 3 HL 330, continued with the following observation:

> "* * * And there is slight difficulty in holding that one who engages in blasting operations which set in motion vibrations and concussions of the earth and air which reach to another's land—no matter how far distant—and shatter his dwelling, commits a trespass no less than one who accomplishes the same result by the propulsion of rocks or

> other material. Parcell v. United States, [D.C., 104 F.Supp. 110]; Bluhm v. Blanck & Gargaro, [62 Ohio App. 451, 24 N.E.2d 615], supra; 22 Am.Jur. 180, Explosions and Explosives, § 54. 'Is not a concussion of the air, and jarring, breaking, and cracking the ground with such force as to wreck the buildings thereon, as much an invasion of the rights of the owner as the hurling of a missile thereon?' Louden v. City of Cincinnati, supra [90 Ohio St. 144, 106 N.E. 970, 974, L.R.A.1915E, 356, Ann.Cas.1916C, 1171]."

The view recognizing a trespassory invasion where there is no "thing" which can be seen with the naked eye undoubtedly runs counter to the definition of trespass expressed in some quarters. 1 Restatement, Torts § 158, Comment h (1934); Prosser, Torts § 13 (2d Ed. 1955). It is quite possible that in an earlier day when science had not yet peered into the molecular and atomic world of small particles, the courts could not fit an invasion through unseen physical instrumentalities into the requirement that a trspass can result only from a *direct* invasion. But in this atomic age even the uneducated know the great and awful force contained in the atom and what it can do to a man's property if it is released. In fact, the now famous equation $E=mc^2$ has taught us that mass and energy are equivalents and that our concept of "things" must be reframed. If these observations on science in relation to the law of trespass should appear theoretical and unreal in the abstract, they become very practical and real to the possessor of land when the unseen force cracks the foundation of his house. The force is just as real if it is chemical in nature and must be awakened by the intervention of another agency before it does harm.

If, then, we must look to the character of the instrumentality which is used in making an intrusion upon another's land we prefer to emphasize the object's energy or force rather than its size. Viewed in this way we may define trespass as any intrusion which invades the possessor's protected interest in exclusive possession, whether that intrusion is by visible or invisible pieces of matter or by energy which can be measured only by the mathematical language of the physicist.

We are of the opinion, therefore, that the intrusion of the fluoride particulates in the present case constituted a trespass.

The defendant argues that our decision in Amphitheaters, Inc. v. Portland Meadows, 1948, 184 Or. 336, 198 P.2d 847, 851, 5 A.L.R.2d 690, requires a contrary conclusion. In discussing the distinction between trespass and nuisance the court referred to a difference between "a cannon ball and a ray of light" indicating that the former but not the latter could produce a trespassory invasion. The court also said "The mere suggestion that the casting of light upon the premises of a plaintiff would render a defendant liable without proof of any actual damage, carries its own refutation." 184 Or. 336, 343, 198 P.2d 847, 850. We do not regard this statement as a pronouncement that a trespass can *never* be caused by the intrusion of light rays or other intangible forces; more properly the case may be interpreted as stating that the conduct of the defendant in a particular case may not be actionable if it does not violate a legally protected interest of the plaintiff. The court states that the defendant is not liable *without proof of actual damage.* In that case the plaintiff contended that he had suffered damage in the form of a less efficient cinema screen due to the defendant's lights. In denying recovery the court found that there was no damage, apparently because whatever harm the plaintiff suffered was damnum absque injuria.

In every case in which trespass is alleged the court is presented with a problem of deciding whether the defendant's intrusion has violated a legally protected interest of the plaintiff. In most cases the defendant's conduct so clearly invades the well established possessory interest of the plaintiff that no discussion of the point is called for. But where neither the defendant's conduct nor the plaintiff's use fall within the familiar trespass pattern of the past the courts are faced with a preliminary inquiry as to whether the plaintiff has a protectible interest under the law of trespass. This in turn calls for the inquiry as to whether the defendant's conduct was such as to constitute an invasion of that interest.

In some cases the solution can be based upon the ground that the defendant's conduct is not substantial enough to be regarded as a trespassory intrusion. Thus, the casting of a candle beam upon the screen of a drive-in theater would not constitute an actionable invasion, simply because the intrusion is so trifling that the law will not consider it and the principle de minimis non curat lex is applicable. In some cases the solution may be arrived at by admitting that the intrusion is substantial but refusing to recognize that plaintiff has a legally protected interest in the particular possessory use as against the particular conduct of the defendant. And so the glare of flood lights upon an adjoining owner's cinema screen, as in the Amphitheaters case, may not be a trespass, not because the intrusion is trifling, but because the law does not wish to protect such a use from an invasion, whether the cause of the interference be viewed as a physical intrusion or as a nontrespassory act and covered by the law of nuisance.

The Amphitheaters case can be explained in terms of this latter point of view, i. e., that the glare of the defendant's lights could be regarded as an intrusion within the law of trespass, but that the plaintiff had no right to treat the intrusion as actionable in view of the nature of plaintiff's use and the manner in which the defendant interfered with it. Had the defendant purposely, and not as an incidence of his own legitimate use, directed the rays of light against the plaintiff's screen the court might well have taken the position that the plaintiff could have recovered in a trespass action. These illustrations demonstrate that the tort of trespass involves a weighing process, similar to that involved in the law of nuisance, although to a more limited extent than in nuisance and for a different purpose,

i. e., in the one case to define the possessor's interest in exclusive possession, and in the other to define the possessor's interest in use and enjoyment.

As stated earlier, normally no inquiry is made in the trespass cases as to whether the plaintiff's interest in making a particular use of his property is within the protection provided for under the law of trespass, because traditionally the interest has been regarded as one clearly entitled to protection in the trespass field. There are adjudicated cases which have refused to find a trespass where the intrusion is clearly established but where the court has felt that the possessor's interest should not be protected. Thus it has been held that the flight of aircraft over the surface of plaintiff's land does not constitute a trespass unless the intrusion interferes with the present enjoyment of property. Hinman v. Pacific Air Transport, 9 Cir., 1936, 84 F.2d 755. The same result would seem to follow if the intrusion interfered with the present use of the land but where such use was not entitled to legal protection as against the socially desirable conduct of the defendant. Here it is apparent that the law of trespass and the law of nuisance come very close to merging. This is so because when inquiry is made as to whether the plaintiff's interest falls within the ambit of trespass law the courts look at the interference with the plaintiff's *use and enjoyment* of his land to determine whether his interest in *exclusive possession* should be protected and thus the two torts coalesce.

The Amphitheaters case may also be viewed as a pronouncement that a possessor's interest is not invaded by an intrusion which is so trifling that it cannot be recognized by the law. Inasmuch as it is not necessary to prove actual damage in trespass the magnitude of the intrusion ordinarily would not be of any consequence. But there is a point where the entry is so lacking in substance that the law will refuse to recognize it, applying the maxim de minimis non curat lex. Thus it would seem clear that ordinarily the casting of a grain of sand upon another's land would not be a trespass. And so too the casting of diffused light rays upon another's land would not ordinarily constitute a trespass. Conceivably such rays could be so concentrated that their entry upon the possessor's land would result in a trespassory invasion. An appropriate illustration is found in Watson v. Mississippi River Power Co., 1916, 174 Iowa 23, 32, 156 N.W. 188, 191, L.R.A.1916D, 101, where the court said:

> "* * * If, for example, a person interests himself in solar phenomena, and, while experimenting with a powerful sunglass, he accidentally focuses the instrument upon some inflammable material on the lot of his nextdoor neighbor, starting a blaze which results in injury and loss to the latter, can it be said there was no trespass, no actual invasion of the neighbor's premises?"

But where the light is cast upon the plaintiff's premises in a manner which does no actual damage or causes no interference in any way with a legitimate use of the premises then there is no reason for recognizing an invasion of the plaintiff's possessory interest. Note 62 Harv.L.Rev. 704 (1949). Here again it is important to point out that the tort of trespass is composed of components which include the character (including the magnitude) of the defendant's conduct in causing an intrusion and the character (including the magnitude) of the harm visited on the plaintiff in interfering with his interest in the exclusive possession of the premises. Consequently the question as to whether a ray of light or any other intrusion is so unsubstantial that it is to be disregarded under the de minimis principle cannot be looked at solely from the standpoint of the defendant's conduct, but it must be evaluated with reference to the nature of the plaintiff's interest. The broader and more diverse the possessor's protectible interests the more sensitive they are to violation by the defendant and the easier it is to find that his conduct, although apparently inconsequential, gives rise to liability. The scope of the possessor's legitimate interest in the exclusive possession of land is broad and difficult to define specifically. Once recognizing that actual damage need not be shown in making out an actionable invasion, the plaintiff's right to insist upon freedom from interference with his possession seems almost limitless.

But there are limits and they can be found, if only vaguely, in the reasons for protecting the possessory interest of the landholder where no actual damage is suffered. * * * The modern law of trespass can be understood only as it is seen against its historical background. Originally all types of trespass, including trespass to land, was punishable under the criminal law because the trespasser's conduct was regarded as a breach of the peace. When the criminal and civil aspect of trespass were separated, the civil action for trespass was colored by its past, and the idea that the peace of the community was put in danger by the trespasser's conduct influenced the courts' ideas of the character of the tort. Therefore, relief was granted to the plaintiff where he was not actually damaged, partly at least as a means of discouraging disruptive influences in the community. Winfield on Torts (4th ed.) p. 305 expresses the idea as follows:

> "The law, on the face of it, looks harsh, but trespass was so likely in earlier times to lead to a breach of the peace that even unwitting and trivial deviations on to another person's land were reckoned unlawful. At the present day there is, of course, much greater respect for the law in general and appreciation of the security which it affords, and the theoretical severity of the rules as to land trespass is hardly ever exploited in practice."

The idea is similarly expressed in 1 Harper & James, Torts § 1.8 p. 25:

> "In the early law, emphasis was placed upon the criminal aspect of willful trespasses, as a breach of the peace or a wrong to the state. Compensation to the injured victim was regarded as of secondary importance. It came about,

therefore, that the rule developed that the plaintiff might recover nominal damages even though he sustained no actual pecuniary loss as a result of the trespass."

If then, we find that an act on the part of the defendant in interfering with the plaintiff's possession, does, or is likely to result in arousing conflict between them, that act will characterize the tort as a trespass, assuming of course that the other elements of the tort are made out. * * *

Probably the most important factor which describes the nature of the interest protected under the law of trespass is nothing more than a feeling which a possessor has with respect to land which he holds. It is a sense of ownership; a feeling that what one owns or possesses should not be interfered with, and that it is entitled to protection through law. This being the nature of the plaintiff's interest, it is understandable why actual damage is not an essential ingredient in the law of trespass. As pointed out in 1 Harper & James, Torts, § 1.8, p. 26, the rule permitting recovery in spite of the absence of actual damages "is probably justified as a vindicatory right to protect the possessor's proprietary or dignitary interest in his land."

We think that a possessor's interest in land as defined by the considerations recited above may, under the appropriate circumstances, be violated by a ray of light, by an atomic particle, or by a particulate of fluoride and contrariwise, if such interest circumscribed by these considerations is not violated or endangered, the defendant's conduct, even though it may result in a physical intrusion, will not render him liable in an action of trespass. Amphitheaters, Inc. v. Portland Meadows, supra.

We hold that the defendant's conduct in causing chemical substances to be deposited upon the plaintiff's land fulfilled all of the requirements under the law of trespass.

The defendant contends that trespass will not lie in this case because the injury was indirect and consequential and that the requirement that the injury must be direct and immediate to constitute a trespass was not met. We have held that the deposit of the particulates upon the plaintiff's land was an intrusion within the definition of trespass. That intrusion was direct. The damages which flowed from it are consequential, but it is well established that such consequential damage may be proven in an action of trespass. Van Alstyne v. Rochester Telephone Corp., supra; 1 Restatement, Torts § 163; Prosser, Torts (2d ed.) p. 57. The distinction between direct and indirect invasions where there has been a physical intrusion upon the plaintiff's land has been abandoned by some courts. See Prosser, Torts (2d ed.) p. 56; 1 Restatement, Torts, § 158, Comment h. Since the invasion in the instant case was direct it is not necessary for us to decide whether the distinction is recognized in this state.

* * *

It is also urged that the trial court erred in failing to enter a special finding requested by the defendant. The requested finding in effect stated that it was impossible in the operation of an aluminum reduction plant to capture all fluorides which are created in the manufacturing process; that the fume collection system was in operation during the period in question; and that it was the most efficient of the systems known in aluminum reduction plants in the United States.

* * * The complaint alleged that the defendant "carelessly, wantonly and willfully continuously caused to be emitted," from its plant the poisonous compounds. This allegation was denied in the defendant's answer. The issue thus raised, as to the character of defendant's conduct in making the intrusion upon plaintiff's land, would be material only with respect to the claim for punitive damages which * * * was rejected by the trial court. Since we hold that the intrusion in this case constituted a trespass it is immaterial whether the defendant's conduct was careless, wanton and willful or entirely free from fault. Therefore, the refusal to enter the requested finding is not error.

The judgment of the lower court is affirmed.

McAllister, Chief Justice (specially concurring).

I concur in the result of the above opinion but dissent from that portion thereof that attempts to reconcile the holding in this case with the holding in the case of Amphitheaters, Inc. v. Portland Meadows * * *.

Trespass to land is ordinarily said to require that the actor "intentionally" enters the land, e. g., Restatement of Torts Second § 158 (1965); "enters" is deemed to include "the presence upon the land of a third person or thing which the actor has caused to be or to remain there", id., Comment b. "Intent" is defined in § 8A "to denote that the actor desires to cause consequences of his act, or that he believes that the consequences are substantially certain to result from it." Also see Restatement §§ 164–166.

CONNECTICUT GENERAL STATUTES (1958)

Section 16–177. Fire communicated by railway engine. In an action to recover for any injury occasioned by fire communicated by any railroad locomotive engine in this state, the fact that such fire was so communicated shall be prima facie evidence of negligence on the part of the person or corporation who at the time of such injury by fire, is in the use and occupation of such railroad, either as owner, lessee or mortgagee, and of those who shall at such time have the care and management of such engine.

Section 16–175. Fire caused by engine; insurable interest. When property is injured by fire communicated by an engine of a railroad company, without contributory negligence on the part of the person entitled to the care and possession of such property, such company shall be held responsible in damages to the extent of such injury to the person so injured. Each such company shall have an insurable interest in the property for which it may be so held responsible in damages, and may procure insurance thereon in its own behalf.[47]

The preceding materials typically apply to conflicts between neighboring land users. The issues reflected in such conflicts have received intensive academic attention. Increasingly the modes of scholarly discourse diverge from the tone of the traditional literature. Considerable emphasis, for instance, has been placed on the analysis of such conflicts from the point of view of economic theory. See, e. g., Michelman, Pollution as a Tort: A Non-Accidental Perspective on Calabresi's *Costs,* 80 Yale L.J. 647 (1971); Calabresi and Hirschoff, Toward a Test for Strict Liability in Torts, 81 Yale L.J. 1055 (1972); and Calabresi and Melamed, Property Rules, Liability Rules, and Inalienability: One View of the Cathedral, 85 Harv.L.Rev. 1089 (1972). As described in the latter paper (at 1093 et seq.), these studies derive from an analytic framework established in G. Calabresi, The Costs of Accidents 135–97 (1970):

> "Economic efficiency asks that we choose the set of entitlements which would lead to that allocation of resources which could not be improved in the sense that a further change would not so improve the condition of those who gained by it that they could compensate those who lost from it and still be better off than before. This is often called Pareto optimality. * * *
>
> * * * [E]conomic efficiency standing alone would dictate that set of entitlements which favors knowledgeable choices between social benefits and the social costs of obtaining them, and between social costs and the social costs of avoiding them * * *. [T]his implies, in the absence of certainty as to whether a benefit is worth its costs to society, that the cost should be put on the party or activity best located to make such a cost-benefit analysis * * *. [I]n particular contexts like accidents or pollution this suggests putting costs on the party or activity which can most cheaply

47. The concept of "liability insurance" so familiar today was unknown at the time of this statute. That type of insurance was invented to protect employers from the increased litigation growing out of employers' liability acts —which date from the 1880's—and it did not become at all generally available until the present century. Crobaugh & Redding, Casualty Insurance, 395 (1928); McNeely, Illegality as a Factor in Insurance, 41 Col.L.Rev. 26, 28 (1941). This accounts for the awkward and indirect method devised by the legislature for allowing the railroads to pass on these losses through insurance—a device which is probably one of the early roots of liability insurance. McNeely op. cit., supra, 27. Cf. Eastern R. Co. v. Relief Fire Ins. Co., 98 Mass. 420 (1868).

What is now § 16–175 was upheld against constitutional challenge in Grissell v. Housatonic R. Co., 54 Conn. 447, 9 A. 137, 1 Am.St.Rep. 138 (1886). The exhaustive opinion in that case may profitably be compared with that in the Ives case.

avoid them * * *. [I]n the absence of certainty as to who that party or activity is, the costs should be put on the party or activity which can with the lowest transaction costs act in the market to correct an error in entitlements by inducing the party who can avoid social costs most cheaply to do so * * *. [S]ince we are in an area where by hypothesis markets do not work perfectly—there are transaction costs —a decision will often have to be made on whether market transactions or collective fiat is most likely to bring us closer to the Pareto optimal result the 'perfect' market would reach.

"* * * Economic efficiency is not, however, the sole reason which induces a society to select a set of entitlements. Wealth distribution preferences are another. * *"

For other perspectives inspired by economic analysis see Coase, The Problem of Social Cost, 3 J.Law & Econ. 1 (1960) and Posner, Strict Liability: A Comment, 2 J.Leg.Studies 205 (1973). Unlike the Calabresians, at least in emphasis, Posner concludes (at 221):

"1. Economic theory provides no basis, in general, for preferring strict liability to negligence, or negligence to strict liability, provided that some version of a contributory negligence defense is recognized. Empirical data might enable us to move beyond agnosticism but we do not have any.

"2. A strict liability standard without a contributory negligence defense is, in principle, less efficient than the negligence-contributory negligence standard. Empirical data could of course rebut the presumption derived from theory."

One difficulty in dealing with these materials has to do with the different senses in which the authors use the term "strict liability". Calabresi, for instance, as indicated above, uses it to refer to the allocation of accident costs, without regard to fault, to that party to the accident who is "best suited to make a cost-benefit analysis between accident costs and accident prevention costs", and not necessarily to the injurer. With regard to one of the goals of a tort system, that of minimizing the total costs of accidents and of accident prevention, which he calls "optimal deterrence", he views the fault system as effective only in those cases where the victim and others in his class can best decide whether accident avoidance is worthwhile and can in fact accomplish such avoidance most cheaply. In other cases (as well as in these), he argues, optimal deterrence could best be achieved by a combination of two techniques. Accident avoidance costs which can readily be determined by society to be worthwhile should be made mandatory, e. g., through the imposition of noninsurable fines. Where it is not certain that accident prevention—by either party or by both in coalition—is worthwhile, the system should attach incentives to decide that question correctly "to that class which is best suited to decide the question." For an elaboration see Calabresi, Optimal Deterrence and Accidents, 84 Yale L.J. 656 (1975).

Other studies of the same conflicts attempt to formulate non-economic terms of reference, e. g., Fletcher, Fairness and Utility in Tort Theory, 85 Harv.L.Rev. 537 (1972) and Epstein, A Theory of Strict Liability, 2 J.Leg.Studies 151 (1973).

BEHRENS v. BERTRAM MILLS CIRCUS LTD.

Queen's Bench Division, [1957] 2 Q.B. 13.

[Plaintiffs, married midgets, occupied a funfair concession between defendant's circus ring and the elephant house. Plaintiffs' manager and ticket seller brought his daughter to the funfair; she brought her small dog Simba. As the elephant procession passed the ticket booth, Simba got loose and ran out barking and snapping, frightening the elephants. One, Bullu, trumpeted in panic. Simba ran into plaintiff's booth. Bullu followed, knocking down the front of the booth, which caused physical injury and shock to plaintiffs.]

DEVLIN, J. read the following judgment:

* * * [P]laintiffs rely upon * * * breach of the absolute duty laid upon the keeper of a dangerous animal to confine and control it * * *.

A person who keeps an animal with knowledge (scienter retinuit) of its tendency to do harm is strictly liable for damage it does if it escapes; he is under an absolute duty to confine or control it so that it shall not do injury to others. All animals ferae naturae, that is, all animals which are not by nature harmless, such as a rabbit, or have not been tamed by man and domesticated, such as a horse, are conclusively presumed to have such a tendency, so that the scienter need not in their case be proved. All animals in the second class mansuetae naturae are conclusively presumed to be harmless until they have manifested a savage or vicious propensity; proof of such a manifestation is proof of scienter and serves to transfer the animal, so to speak, out of its natural class into the class of ferae naturae. * * * No doubt in its time * * * [this "primitive rule"] was a great improvement on the still more primitive notion that only the animal was "liable" for the harm it did. But now this sort of doctrine with all its rigidity—its conclusive presumptions and categorisations—is outmoded * * *.

The particular rigidity in the scienter action which is involved in this case —there are many others which are not—is the rule that requires the harmfulness of the offending animal to be judged not by reference to its particular training and habits, but by reference to the general habits of the species to which it belongs. The law ignores the world of difference between the wild elephant in the jungle and the trained elephant in the circus. The elephant Bullu is in fact no more dangerous than a cow; she reacted in the same way as a cow would do to the irritation of a small dog; if perhaps her bulk made her capable of doing more damage, her higher training enabled her to be more swiftly checked. But I am compelled to assess the defendants' liability in this case in just the same way as I would assess it if they had loosed a wild elephant into the funfair. This is a branch of the law, which * * * has been settled by authority rather than by reason. * * * [48]

TRESPASS BY DOMESTIC ANIMALS—FENCING STATUTES

Excerpt from F. Harper and F. James, The Law of Torts §§ 14.9 and 14.10 (1956).

By the common law of England, an owner of domestic animals was held strictly liable for their trespasses upon the land of others irrespective of the keeper's negligence. * * *

The common law rule of strict liability is the law in many states of this country in so far as it has not been altered or modified by statute. It is immaterial that the plaintiff's land is fenced and that the trespass is made possible by the lack of repair of the fences on the part of the plaintiff, unless the owner of the land is under a duty to the defendant or under a general duty imposed by law for the purpose of keeping such animals from intrusion upon his land. * * *

In some states, however, the common law rule has not been followed, due to differences of the conditions and pursuits of the people. * * * [S]ome Western states, early in their history, rejected the common law rule and allowed livestock to run at large. This was prompted in the main by economic reasons. The desire was to encourage the growth of the cattle industry and it was thought that a rule allowing for a wide open range would best implement that growth. Several of these states passed "fencing out" statutes. But times and conditions changed and the advent of large cities, heavily populated areas, thickly settled agricultural communities and the development of important heavy industries, led a number of these states either to abolish or modify the rule permitting cattle to run at large.

Some states enacted what are called "option" laws. Frequently these option laws allow local communities, generally at the county level of government, to determine for themselves whether the area will be under the common law rule or whether livestock will be permitted to run at large. This process of self-determination, so to speak,

48. See Restatement of Torts §§ 506 et seq. For contrary views as to dangerous animals cf. Vaughan v. Miller Bros. "101" Ranch Wild West Show, 109 W.Va. 170, 153 S.E. 289, 69 A.L.R. 497 (1930) and Ross v. Golden State Rodeo Co., —— Mont. ——, 530 P.2d 1166 (1975).

For a discussion of the proof necessary to establish that a domesticated animal has manifested a vicious propensity see Lee v. Weaver, —— Neb. ——, 237 N.W.2d 149 (1976).

English law on the entire subject has been revised by the Animals Act of 1971; see P. North, The Modern Law of Animals (1972).

sometimes extends to even smaller units of government than the county. Hence in the "option" law states it is possible to find a county which allows cattle to run at large and various townships within that county which have by local ordinance enacted the common law rule, or vice versa. In those counties which retain the rule allowing cattle to run at large, a "fence out" statute frequently is in force. * * *[49]

REVISED STATUTES ANNOTATED OF NEW HAMPSHIRE, 1955

466:19 *Liability of Owner or Keeper.* Any person to whom or to whose property damage may be occasioned by a dog not owned or kept by him shall be entitled to recover such damage of the person who owns or keeps the dog, or has it in possession, unless the damage was occasioned to him while he was engaged in the commission of a trespass or other tort.

* * *

466:21 *Liability of towns.* Any person whose sheep, lambs, fowls or other domestic creatures are killed, driven away, wounded or worried by dogs may recover of the town or city wherein such damage was done, in the manner herein provided, the amount of all damage thereby sustained by him, including the value of any creature so killed or lost, any depreciation in value of a creature so wounded or worried, and any other loss or expense to which he may be subjected by such killing, driving, wounding or worrying.

* * *

466:25 *Orders, How Payable.* All orders drawn and judgments rendered in favor of claimants under the three preceding sections shall be paid by the town or city treasurer out of the receipts from dog licenses if the same are sufficient, but in case of a deficiency thereof the balance shall be paid out of the general funds of the town or city.

LIABILITY FOR OIL POLLUTION

Excerpts from Sec. 311, Federal Water Pollution Control Act (1972).

(b)(1) The Congress hereby declares that it is the policy of the United States that there should be no discharges of oil or hazardous substances into or upon the navigable waters of the United States, adjoining shorelines, or into or upon the waters of the contiguous zone. * * *

49. Also see King v. Blue Mountain Forest Ass'n, 100 N.H. 212, 123 A.2d 151 (1956); Delaney v. Errickson, 10 Neb. 492, 6 N.W. 600 (1880); Webb, The Great Plains (1931); Restatement of Torts, Second § 504 (Tent. Draft No. 10, 1964); and cases collected in 1968 Supplement to Harper and James, §§ 14.9 and 14.10. As to liability for accidents caused by animals on public highways compare Jensen v. Nielson, — Nev. —, 537 P.2d 321 (1975) with Misterek v. Washington Mineral Products, Inc., 85 Wash.2d 166, 531 P.2d 805 (1975).

(f)(1) Except where an owner or operator can prove that a discharge was caused solely by (A) an act of God, (B) an act of war, (C) negligence on the part of the United States Government, or (D) an act or omission of a third party without regard to whether any such act or omission was or was not negligent, or any combination of the foregoing clauses, such owner or operator of any vessel from which oil or a hazardous substance is discharged in violation of * * * this section shall, notwithstanding any other provision of law, be liable to the United States Government for the actual costs incurred under subsection (c) for the removal of such oil or substancce by the United States Government in an amount not to exceed $100 per gross ton of such vessel or $14,000,000, whichever is lesser, except that where the United States can show that such discharge was the result of willful negligence or willful misconduct within the privity and knowledge of the owner, such owner or operator shall be liable to the United States Government for the full amount of such costs. Such costs shall constitute a maritime lien on such vessel which may be recovered in an action in rem in the district court of the United States for any district within which any vessel may be found. The United States may also bring an action against the owner or operator of such vessel in any court of competent jurisdiction to recover such costs.

LIABILITY TO INTERNATIONAL AIR PASSENGERS

A. Excerpts from Warsaw Convention (1929):[50]

Art. 17. The carrier shall be liable for damage sustained in the event of the death * * * of a passenger or any * * * bodily injury suffered by a passenger, if the accident which caused the damage so sustained took place on board the aircraft or in the course of any of the operations of embarking or disembarking.

Art. 20[1]. The carrier shall not be liable if he proves that he and his agents have taken all necessary measures to avoid the damage or that it was impossible for him or them to take such measures.

B. Excerpt from Montreal (IATA) Interim Agreement (1966):[51]

The undersigned carriers (hereinafter referred to as "the Carriers") hereby agree as follows:

> The Carrier shall not, with respect to any claim arising out of the death, wounding, or other bodily injury of a passenger, avail itself of any defense under Article 20(1) of said Convention * * *.

50. 49 Stat. 3000 et seq.

51. R. Mankiewicz (ed.), Yearbook of Air and Space Law 1966, at 119; see generally Lowenfeld and Mendelsohn, The United States and the Warsaw Convention, 80 Harv.L.Rev. 497 (1967).

THOMAS v. HUTCHINSON

Supreme Court of Pennsylvania, 1971.
442 Pa. 118, 275 A.2d 23.

JONES, JUSTICE. The facts underlying this appeal involve the claim of William E. Thomas, plaintiff-appellee, for personal injuries occasioned by the alleged negligence of Dr. Paul V. Hutchinson, appellant's decedent, in the performance of a surgical operation on plaintiff-appellee. Following receipt of all the evidence in the case, the court directed the jury to find a verdict in favor of plaintiff-appellee, leaving to the jury the assessment of damages. From a verdict in favor of the plaintiff-appellee in the sum of $120,000, appellant moved for judgment n. o. v. and for a new trial. These motions were denied by the court below and judgment was entered on the verdict. This appeal followed.

Plaintiff-appellee was a patient of Dr. Hutchinson, an orthopedic surgeon, on whose advice plaintiff-appellee underwent an operation to remove a ruptured vertebral disc. On August 22, 1963, Dr. Hutchinson, assisted by three orthopedic residents, i. e., medical doctors who were then receiving specialized training, performed the surgery in the operating room of St. Francis Hospital. These residents were selected from the hospital staff for this particular operation by the operating room supervisor, who was employed, as were the residents, by the hospital. After Dr. Hutchinson removed the disc and performed the related surgery, he left the operating room as he allowed the residents to close the surgical incision and remove the remaining sponges. As there was no general improvement in plaintiff-appellee's condition, a subsequent operation was performed by a Dr. Watson, who found a surgical sponge which was admitted by the appellant's decedent to be one of the sponges employed in the operation of August 22, 1963.
* * *

The major controversy between the parties, both in their briefs and in oral argument, concerns the question of vicarious liability on the part of the operating surgeon. The court's rationale for imposing vicarious liability rested on alternative grounds: an admission of agency and the "captain of the ship" theory. * * *

* * * Our reading of the record nowhere discloses any admission of agency. However, the same result would follow if the "captain of the ship" doctrine may properly be invoked.

This latter concept evolved from the language chosen by Mr. Justice (later Mr. Chief Justice) Horace Stern in his famous opinion in McConnell v. Williams, 361 Pa. 355, 362, 65 A.2d 243, 246 (1949): "in the course of an operation in the operating room of a hospital, and until the surgeon leaves that room at the conclusion of the operation, * * * he is in the same complete charge of those who are present and assisting him as is the captain of a ship over all on board [footnote omitted] * * *." *McConnell* reversed the entry of a nonsuit on behalf of an obstetrician as it held the doctor could be liable for the negligence of an assisting intern *if* the relationship between the obstetrician and the intern could be proven to be that of master-servant. * * *

* * * [T]he "captain of the ship" doctrine imposes liability on the surgeon in charge of an operation for the negligence of his assistants during the period when these assistants are under the surgeon's control, even though the assistants are also employees of the hospital. Stated differently, the "captain of the ship" concept is but the adaptation of the familiar "borrowed servant" principle in the law of agency to the operating room of a hospital.

As we noted earlier, the issue before us is whether the facts in this case warranted the court's directing the jury to find against the appellant on the issue of liability. Both *McConnell* and *Benedict* involved the propriety of a nonsuit entered on behalf of a doctor—effectively the exact opposite of the procedure employed by the court below. Particularly relevant is the closing paragraph of the *McConnell* opinion: "In the present case the court erred in entering a nonsuit. *It is for the jury to determine whether the relationship between defendant and the interne, at the time the child's eyes were injured, was that of master and servant.* If such was the relationship, defendant is legally liable for the injury caused by the interne's alleged negligence. In determining whether the interne was defendant's servant at that time, the mere fact that he was then in the general employ of the hospital would not prevent the jury from finding that he was also at that same time the servant of defendant if he was then subject to his orders in respect to the treatment of the child's eyes with the silver nitrate solution." * * * It appears to us that the question whether these residents were Dr. Hutchinson's deckhands is one of fact that ought properly be left to the jury.

In addition, we note that this doctrine was announced before the decision of this Court in Flagiello v. Pennsylvania Hosp., 417 Pa. 486, 208 A.2d 193 (1965), discarding the immunity from liability in tort previously enjoyed by public hospitals. In enunciating the "captain of the ship" theory in *McConnell*, it was no coincidence that this Court noted, "if operating surgeons were not to be held liable for the negligent performance of the duties of those then working under them, the law would fail in large measure to afford a means of redress for preventable injuries sustained during the course of such operations." 361 Pa. at 364, 65 A.2d at 247. Thus, any willingness to characterize a head surgeon as the "captain of the ship" in order to financially restore the patient should be clearly negated in light of the *Flagiello* opinion. If, in fact, the residents were negligent, either the hospital or the head surgeon could be vicariously liable, depending, of course, on whether the residents were "borrowed." Hence, this factual determination is well nigh dispositive of the case and should be decided by the jury.

The court below properly denied judgment n. o. v. but erred in dismissing the motion for a new trial. The question of Dr. Hutchinson's liability should have been submitted for determination by the jury rather than determined by the court.

SMITH, FROLIC AND DETOUR

(1923) 23 Colum.L.Rev. at 452.

No legal doctrine has been so generally criticized and yet so generally adhered to by courts as the doctrine of *respondeat superior*. Not only is it now irretrievably rooted in the law of the English speaking countries but it also exists to some extent in the law of Scotland, France, Italy, Germany, Spain, Portugal, Switzerland and other countries.[52] This phenomenon alone suggests that there is, perhaps, more justification for the doctrine than its critics have perceived. However, the criticisms cannot be ignored.

Mr. Justice Holmes in a series of lectures delivered at the Harvard Law School in the eighties, and afterwards published in the Harvard Law Review,[53] characterized the doctrine as an anomaly which "must be explained by some cause not manifest to common sense alone." The explanation offered was that the doctrine is a "survival from ancient times of doctrines which in their earlier form embodied certain rights and liabilities of heads of families based on substantive grounds which have disappeared long since, and that in modern days these doctrines have been generalized into a fiction, which, although nothing in the world but a form of words, has reacted upon the law and has tended to carry its anomalies still farther. That fiction is, of course, that, within the scope of the agency, principal and agent are one." [54]

52. See Baty, Vicarious Liability (1916) c. 9, for a summary of the extent to which *respondeat superior* exists in foreign countries. Japan appears to have rejected the doctrine.

53. Agency (1891) 4 Harvard Law Rev. 345 (1891) 5 Harvard Law Rev. 1.

54. [Ed. note] Of this explanation, Mr. Justice Holmes said:

"And this is equivalent to admitting, as I do, that the views here maintained are not favorites with the courts. How can they be? A judge would blush to say nakedly to a defendant: 'I can state no rational ground on which you should be held liable, but there is a fiction of law which I must respect and by which I am bound to say that you did the act complained of, although we both know perfectly well that it was done by somebody else whom the plaintiff could have sued if he had chosen, who was selected with the utmost care by you, who was in fact an eminently proper person for the employment in which he was engaged, and whom it was not only your right to employ, but much to the public advantage that you should employ.' That would not be a satisfactory form in which to render a decision against a master, and it is not pleasant even to admit to one's self that such are the true grounds upon which one is deciding. Naturally, therefore, judges have striven to find more intelligible reasons, and have done so in the utmost good faith; for whenever a rule of law is in fact a survival of ancient traditions, its ancient meaning is gradually forgotten, and it has to be reconciled to present notions of policy and justice, or to disappear." 5 Harv. L.Rev. at 22.

The writer does not profess sufficient knowledge of legal history to challenge the statements of Justice Holmes. However, Professor Wigmore in a subsequent series of articles published in the Harvard Law Review [55] makes out a strong case for the view that the ancient law to which Holmes relegates *respondent superior* had completely disappeared in England by the sixteenth century, and that the modern doctrine of the master's liability did not make its appearance until about two hundred years later.[56]

Furthermore, Pollock and Maitland state that the common law "when it took shape in Edward I.'s day did not, unless we are much misled, make masters pay for acts that they had neither commanded nor ratified." [57]

This view is also taken by Baty in his recent and excellent little book on vicarious liability.[58]

It would seem, therefore, that whatever relations there may be between the modern doctrine of *respondeat superior* and the ancient law to which Justice Holmes refers, must be traced through some process of legal reincarnation rather than attributed to undue old age.

According to Baty the modern law is attributable to unwarranted *dicta* by Lord Holt [59] beginning about 1698 and blindly repeated by judges and writers [60] until it was firmly established in 1796 by the decision of the King's Bench in Brucker v. Fromont.[61] This appears to be the prevailing view among legal historians.

It may be that Holt's side remarks were due to the fact that he was acquainted with Roman law doctrines and that he was influenced by the ancient law to which Justice Holmes refers. But if Wigmore, Pollock and Maitland, and Baty be right as to the actual state of English law prior to Holt's time, certainly Holt's observations were not the result of *stare decisis.*

However, whether Holmes on the one hand, or Wigmore, Pollock and Maitland, and Baty on the other, be right on the point of history, certainly the mere fact that in ancient times an absolute liability was imposed upon the head of a house for injuries done by members of his family, his servants and his slaves, is not a justification for courts in modern times imposing any such arbitrary liability upon employ-

55. Responsibility for Tortious Acts: Its History (1894) 7 Harvard Law Rev. 315, 383, 441.

56. Ibid., p. 383.

57. 2 Pollock and Maitland, History of English Law (2nd ed. 1899) 533. For a general discussion of the question see pp. 528 to 533, inclusive.

58. Baty, op. cit., c. 1.

59. "What one would like to know is the precise process by which Holt's dicta acquired the force of law between, say, 1698 ad 1725." Baty, op. cit., p. 28.

60. "And so we find Blackstone in 1765 observing that 'if a servant by his negligence does any damage to a stranger, the master shall answer for his neglect,' as if that had been the glory of English law *per saecula saeculorum.*" Baty, op. cit., p. 28.

61. "It was not until Brucker v. Fromont (1796) 6 T.R. 659, apparently, that the processual doctrine was authoritatively established. * * *" Baty, op. cit., p. 28.

ers for their employees' unauthorized torts. Neither does the fact, that Holt in his loose talk sponsored the idea justify the rule of law. At most these are mere explanations of its origin; not justifications of the doctrine. * * *

Is there any rational justification for the doctrine? * * *

In the last paragraph of Chapter VIII * * * [Baty] states: "In hard fact, the real reason for employers' liability is * * * : the damages are taken from a deep pocket."

The same idea finds expression in Pollock and Maitland: "Should we now-a-days hold masters answerable for the uncommanded torts of their servants if normally servants were able to pay for the damage that they do?" [62]

In view of the very able refutation by Baty and other writers of the * * * [other] reasons which have been assigned as justifications for the doctrine, the writer will not attempt to restate at length why none of * * * [them] are satisfactory.

Certainly the argument that the master should be liable because he has control neither explains nor justifies the distinction between frolic and detour [63] since obviously the master has as much control or, to be more accurate, as little control in the one case as in the other.

The argument that since the master has the selection of the servant, to make the master responsible would insure greater care in selecting the servant is not a very convincing reason, because even though the master exercises the greatest care, still he is responsible. Furthermore, this reason neither explains nor justifies the distinction between frolic and detour or the nonliability of one employing an independent contractor for the negligence of the contractor.

The same may be said of the arguments based upon revenge, identification, evidence, indulgence, danger, and satisfaction. None of these explanations would justify the distinction between frolic and detour once it is conceded the servant was entrusted by the master with the instrument with which the damage was done.

62. 2 Pollock and Maitland, op. cit., p. 532.

63. "The master is only liable where the servant is acting in the course of his employment. If he was going out of his way, against his master's implied commands, when driving on his master's business, he will make his master liable; but if he was going on a frolic of his own, without being at all on his master's business, the master will not be liable." Joel v. Morrison, 6 Car. & P. 501, 503, 172 Eng. Rep. 1338, 1339 (1834). The distinction is not always easy. See, e. g., Bejma v. Dental Development and Manufacturing Co., 356 F.2d 227 (6th Cir. 1966): travelling salesman who used his own automobile, subject to reimbursement for mileage, including authorized weekend trips home, got into accident while driving home, but in wrong direction and drunk, for Labor Day weekend; employer vicariously liable. Compare Keppel Bus Co. Ltd. v. Sa'ad bin Ahmad [1974] 2 All E.R. 700 (Privy Council): employer not liable for physical attack by Singapore bus conductor, while collecting fares, on seated passenger who had previously remonstrated concerning conductor's rudeness to elderly lady; conductor was not carrying out (wrongfully) his duty of maintaining order, since there was at time of his attack no disorder on bus. See Rose, The Carrier's Liability for Assaults, 91 L.Q.Rev. 17 (1975). Also see generally P. Atiyah, Vicarious Liability in the Law of Torts (1967).

The remaining reason mentioned by Baty is that the master is made responsible because he gets the profits from the undertaking. But one may derive profits from an undertaking and still not be responsible for injuries to others resulting from the operations. This is best illustrated by the cases holding that participation in the profits of a business does not necessarily render one responsible as a partner. True it is that frequently the master does receive part or all of the profits, but his liability for his servants' torts rests upon something other than the mere fact that he receives the profits from the undertaking.

Why, then, should the master be responsible?

A reason which occurs to the writer is that which has been offered in justification of workmen's compensation statutes. In substance it is the belief that it is socially more expedient to spread or distribute among a large group of the community the losses which experience has taught are inevitable in the carrying on of industry, than to cast the loss upon a few.[64]

CALABRESI, SOME THOUGHTS ON RISK DISTRIBUTION AND THE LAW OF TORTS

70 Yale L.J. 499 (1961).

* * * [W]hile many people have talked about "risk distribution," and some have even used it as a basis for proposed modifications in the law or torts, few have in recent years attempted to examine in any depth just what it is they are striving for when they say "distribute losses." They could mean one of three things. Do they wish as broad a spreading of all losses, both interpersonally and intertemporally, as is possible? Or do they want the burden of losses

64. "The justification of this policy is that the loss to wage-earners resulting from the accidents of industry should be regarded as an expense of production which the employer should bear as he bears the other expenses of production and which, since the burden falls on all employers alike, he will be able normally to recover in the somewhat high prices he will obtain for his goods." Seager, Principles of Economics (1918) 601.

"To the economist, the necessity of such legislation is abundantly evident. It is simply that the needs of the modern state require that the burden of loss of life, or personal injury in industry, shall be charged to the expenses of production, shall be borne, that is to say, by the employer. He knows well enough that eventually the cost will be paid by the community in the form of increased prices, but that is something it is not unwilling to pay." Laski, The Basis of Vicarious Liability (1916) 26 Yale Law Jour. 105, 126.

[Next is set forth the quotations in the Ives case, pp. 3, 4, supra, from the Report of the Wainwright Commission.]

[Footnotes numbered 52–64, except 54 and 63, by the author of the article, renumbered.]

In addition to the articles cited in the above footnotes, see Douglas, Vicarious Liability and Administration of Risk, 38 Yale L.J. 584 (1929); Seavey, Reflections on Respondeat Superior, Harv.Leg.Essays 433 (1934); Steffen, The Independent Contractor and The Good Life, 2 U. of Chi.L.R. 433 (1935); Ehrenzweig, Vicarious Liability in the Conflict of Laws, 69 Yale L.J. 978 (1960); Morris, Enterprise Liability and the Actuarial Process—The Insignificance of Foresight, 70 Yale L.J. 554 (1961).

to be borne by those classes of people "most able" to pay? Or do they seek something entirely different—that those "enterprises" which give rise to a loss "should" bear the burden, whether or not this accomplishes the prior two aims? The answer, I suppose, is that sometimes they mean each of these things, and at other times all of them. Unfortunately, these goals are not always consistent with each other. They are, moreover, supported by quite different ethical and economic postulates. * * *

The justification for allocation of losses on a nonfault basis which is found most often among legal writers is that if losses are broadly spread—among people and over time—they are least harmful. * * * The advantages of interpersonal loss spreading would probably be stated in terms of two propositions; (a) that taking a large sum of money from one person is more likely to result in economic dislocation, and therefore in secondary or avoidable losses, than taking a series of small sums from many people, and (b) that even if the total economic dislocation is the same, many small losses are preferable to one large one, simply because people feel they suffer less if 10,000 of them lost $1 than if one loses $10,000.

While the first of these propositions is an empirical generalization not too difficult to accept, the second is in its precise terms a variant of the economist's theory of the diminishing marginal utility of money. This theory has been in substantial disfavor among modern economists. The reason for this disfavor is illustrated by recent studies which have indicated, for example, that a loss of a relatively small amount of money, if it results in a change in social status, may be nearly as significant to an individual as a much larger loss which causes an approximately equal change in his social position. On the other hand, a relatively small loss, if it can be borne without giving up certain symbols of social status—be they the house on the right street or the television set—feels infinitely smaller to people than an only slightly larger loss which does involve a change in status. While this indicates the weaknesses of such a strict utilitarian pain-pleasure analysis as the marginal utility of money theory, with its implication that a loss of $5 divided among five people necessarily hurts less than $5 on one person, it does not detract much from the basic justification for loss spreading. We need merely take an additional step and recognize that social dislocations, like economic dislocations, will occur more frequently if one person bears a heavy loss than if many people bear light ones. One can, of course, conceive of situations where the extra $1 charged to one thousand people would be one thousand straws which would break one thousand backs and ruin one thousand homes or businesses, while $1,000 charged to one person would only ruin him, albeit thoroughly. But such situations seem mildly unlikely.

The economic bases of inter-*temporal* loss spreading are not dissimilar. There is less danger of economic dislocation, and hence of secondary losses, if losses are spread over time. Social dislocations are also less likely if individuals can buy their risk-of-loss burden on a long term credit plan.

Thus, there are substantial reasons for allocating losses in ways which spread the burden over as many people and over as long a time as is possible. If these were the only aims in allocating losses, however, the most desirable plan would be some sort of governmental accident relief program spread over the population through taxes * * *. But in view of the conflict between this system and the best system from the standpoint of resource allocations—enterprise liability—a government-responsibility plan should not be embraced without some consideration of what loss spreading is in fact accomplished by enterprise liability.

Insofar as enterprise liability places the burden of accidents on the most likely insurer, it accomplishes directly a fair amount of both interpersonal and intertemporal loss spreading. * * *

Respondeat superior—like workmen's compensation, to which it has often been analogized—was the forerunner of modern enterprise liability. * * * Respondeat superior applies it to injuries to third parties, while workmen's compensation applies it to the worker himself.

The effect * * * in terms of the justifications for enterprise liability is clear. The master is the best insurer, both in the sense of being able to obtain insurance at the lower rates and in the sense of being most aware of the risk.[65] Consequently, he is the best primary risk spreader. * * *

Equally strong allocation-of-resources arguments can be made. Unless wages reflect the risk of injuries the true cost of labor in an industry is not shown. Similarly, the failure to show injury costs means that the prices of the goods the industry sells understate their true costs, and that too much is produced in that industry compared to those which are less accident prone * * *.

The similarities between workmen's compensation and respondeat superior have led some writers to urge that the "scope of employment" rule of respondeat superior be read as broadly as the "arising out of and in the course of employment" test of workmen's compensation. On the basis of the theories analyzed here this is, of course, justified. These theories would suggest that *all* injuries caused by workmen which arise out of and in the course of their employment should result in the master's liability—whether or not the injury resulted from some activity which benefited the employer or was authorized by him, and whether it occurred through the servant's willfulness or through his negligence. Since insurance is probably available in each case, and since secondary risk spreading is certainly the same in each, there seems no reason for the distinctions on risk-spreading or "deep pocket" grounds. Similarly, allocation of resources would tend to support liability. For a cost of an activity is not any the less real because the

65. To some extent unions may have changed this. * * * Indeed, in some industries where management is small, poor, and disorganized, while the union is strong, wealthy, and large, the union may be more aware of the risks and in a better position to spread them and to make them a part of the appropriate prices.

employee was not authorized to undertake it, or because he acted willfully. If it arose out of an enterprise it should be just as chargeable to that enterprise as negligent torts; both should be reflected in prices. Of course, allocation of resources is not so exact or powerful a justification that it really matters too much where the line is drawn between activities arising, and those not arising, out of an enterprise; so long as it is in the general area. But since the other justifications are in accord with what formally seems the most "correct" line from the standpoint of resources it seems fair to say that allocation of resources also supports equating "scope of employment" and "arising out of or in the course of employment." To this extent courts like those in California, which have taken the lead in moving in this direction, have properly applied risk-distribution theories.[66]

This discussion, however, does not tell us why respondeat superior is in fact limited to injuries caused through the servant's *fault*. There is, of course, no answer to this question in terms of the theories analyzed in this Article, any more than there is an answer to why extra-hazardous activities are limited as they are, or to why tort liability generally retains a semi-fault basis. The answer must be found in the broad justifications for the fault requirement. * * *

SEAVEY, SPECULATIONS AS TO "RESPONDEAT SUPERIOR"

Harvard Legal Essays, at pp. 447–449 (1934).

Perhaps the strongest reason which can be given for the imposition of "absolute" liability applies even more strongly in the case of vicarious liability, that is, the fact that one who is responsible for all consequences is more apt to take precautions to prevent injurious consequences from arising. If the law requires a perfect score in result, the actor is more likely to strive for that than if the law requires only the ordinary precautions to be taken; the cases where, either *de jure* or *de facto*, an actor is made absolutely liable for consequences indicate that this reason plays a very large part. The extent to which the law of torts has a preventative function is of course debatable, and it is doubtful if reliable statistics can be obtained as to its effect upon the ordinary individual. To me, however, it seems fairly obvious that the likelihood of personal liability plays a very important part in our affairs. I have heard operators of trucks direct their employees to "get over the road," with a statement that their insurance will take care of accidents. My landowning neighbors in the country start brush fires with great care and no little trepidation, because of the liability to pay damages if the fire gets out of control. That defamation is usually spread through whispered confidence rather than upon

66. See, e. g., 2 Harper & James § 26.7 . . . n. 13 (collecting cases). [Notes 65 and 66 are from original, renumbered. Other notes in original have been omitted.]

the pages of responsible publishers is as well known as is the reason for it. Such situations and countless others, of which all of us are aware, indicate that the existence of tort liability is often the only substantial deterrent, and that frequently it is of more effect than that of a concurrent criminal liability.

But whether or not the law of torts has an appreciable deterrent effect upon individuals, it has important consequences where servants are employed. Without further investigation, our self-questioning inevitably leads us to believe that *respondent superior* results in greater care in the selection and instruction of servants than would be used otherwise. The master would, of course, be likely to be careful in any event in order to protect his own things; also, large corporations, at least, would necessarily use care to maintain friendly relations with the public, since an attitude towards public opinion such as that attributed to Commodore Vanderbilt has been found to reflect itself in loss of dividends. However, neither of these deterrents is as effective as an immediate pecuniary liability in cases where the employer is operating instrumentalities likely to harm others without injury to the operator. Because of this financial liability, it appears safe to assume that an employer can and does bring a pressure to bear upon his employees which has a greater effect upon them than would the chance of their being made defendants in suits, which, if action were permitted only against them, ordinarily would not be brought. The pressure upon the employee is thus two-fold.

It is sometimes stated that *respondent superior* does not tend to promote care by the employer because he is liable irrespective of his own care. Our everyday experience refutes this. The effect of being required to pay for an act of negligence by an employee has the same effect as has the certainty of paying compensation for death or fire upon insurance companies. These have learned that it pays to educate the persons they insure against, as witnessed by their advertisements in the public press, the precautions which fire insurance companies now require of those whose property they insure, and the reward they hold out by way of diminished premiums if safety devices are installed. In fact, the modern insurance broker has become an expert in inspection and safety devices in order to diminish both the premiums and the losses to the insurers. The history of the Employers' Liability Acts and of the Workmen's Compensation Acts, showing a decreasing mortality in an increasingly dangerous environment, indicates that the proper place to apply pressure is on the employer. * * *

POSNER, A THEORY OF NEGLIGENCE

1 J.Leg. Studies 29, 42–43 (1972).

* * * [T]he doctrine of respondeat superior * * * makes an employer liable to third parties for the torts of his employees committed in furtherance of their employment. The doctrine at first glance seems inconsistent with the economic theory of negligence. A careless workman is like a defective machine. A company should devote resources to screening out careless workmen just as it should devote resources to inspecting its machinery for defects but there comes a point where a further expenditure on supervision of employees or on inspection of machinery would exceed the accident costs that the expenditure would save. The law recognizes this quite clearly with respect to machinery. A firm was liable (in the * * * [late 19th century] at any rate) only for those defects that a reasonable inspection would have discovered. But the law seemingly takes an inconsistent position with respect to the careless workman. The employer is liable regardless of his care in attempting to prevent carelessness.

The inconsistency is more apparent than real. A machine is inanimate and undeterrable. A workman is not. But liability for negligence will not deter a workman who has no money to pay for the accidents he causes. This greatly complicates the formulation of an appropriate standard of care for the employer. Suppose that a railroad in hiring locomotive engineers makes a reasonable effort to screen out clumsy, irresponsible, accident-prone individuals. A serious problem would remain. An engineer—let him be as prudent and skillful as you want—is running behind schedule, so he opens the throttle. The resulting speed is dangerous to pedestrians at crossings but if the engineer is a coldly rational man the danger will not inhibit him. Being judgment-proof, he is not answerable for the consequences to pedestrians. Thus, a railroad not only must exercise care in hiring workers; it must impose sanctions on them for carelessness, because tort law cannot deter the judgment-proof. By making the railroad strictly liable for the torts of its employees in the scope of their employment, which is the effect of respondeat superior, the law creates a mechanism by which the railroad can decide for itself how much to invest in preventing its workers from being careless. It will invest until the last cent of its investment in worker safety saves one cent in accident costs. There will be cases where no reasonable expenditure would have averted the accident and where, therefore, the effect of respondeat superior is to shift losses without affecting the level of safety. But the only alternative would have been for the courts to regulate in great detail the company's methods of selecting, supervising, and disciplining employees.

Our interpretation of respondeat superior derives additional support from the distinction that the courts of the period made between employees and independent contractors. If you hired a contractor to do a job and left the manner of work entirely up to him, you were not liable for injuries caused by his negligence or the negligence of his employees. But if you supervised the details of his work you were liable. These distinctions are economically defensible. If there is no supervision of the work in which the accident occurs, there is no basis for anticipating that the work will be done more safely if the principal is liable. Nor is there a presumption that an independent contractor is insolvent and therefore undeterrable by the threat of tort liability from behaving, or permitting his employees to behave, carelessly. But the principal has a duty to select a competent contractor and if the work involves large risks to safety, such as bridge construction, this duty cannot be discharged, the courts held, by perfunctory inquiry.

The principle of respondeat superior was not applied to the family. Parents were liable for the torts of their children only if negligent in supervising them. Perhaps the reason for treating employers and parents differently is that employers in fact have greater control over the behavior of their employees on the job than do parents over their children. The employer can select his employees, discharge them, and prescribe rewards and punishments to which rational beings will respond. Children tend to be ungovernable; natural parents do not choose their children; children cannot be fired for having been careless. A rule of strict parental liability would have little regulatory effect * * *.

MALONEY v. RATH

Supreme Court of California, En Banc, 1968.
69 Cal.2d 442, 71 Cal.Rptr. 897, 445 P.2d 513.

TRAYNOR, CHIEF JUSTICE. Plaintiff brought this action to recover damages for injuries to her person and property incurred in an automobile accident. She appeals from an adverse judgment and from an order denying her motion for judgment notwithstanding the verdict on the issue of liability.

Plaintiff stopped her car in a left-turn lane to wait for a traffic signal to change. Defendant turned into the left-turn lane behind plaintiff and stepped on her brake pedal. Defendant's brakes failed, and a collision ensued.

Defendant neither knew nor had reason to know that her brakes were defective until they failed. The failure was caused by a rupture in a hydraulic hose that gave no warning to defendant of its impending occurrence. Defendant had the brakes completely overhauled by Peter Evanchik of Pete's Chevron Station about three months before the accident. Later, about two weeks before the accident, the car was involved in another collision, and defendant's husband had Evanchik inspect and repair it. Nothing was done to the brakes at that time. Defendant's expert witness testified that the brakes failed because of a hole in the hydraulic hose that was caused by rubbing of the hose against the right front wheel. The rubbing resulted from faulty installation of the hose at the time the brakes were overhauled. A qualified person inspecting the brakes before they failed would have detected the faulty installation and the evidence of the rubbing.

At the time of the accident section 26300 of the Vehicle Code provided that every motor vehicle "shall be equipped with brakes adequate to control the movement of the vehicle and to stop and hold the vehicle," and section 26453 provided that all "brakes and component parts thereof shall be maintained * * * in good working order." (See also Veh.Code, § 26454.) A defendant's failure to comply with these provisions gives rise to a presumption of negligence that he may rebut by proof "that he did what might reasonably be expected of a person of ordinary prudence, acting under similar circumstances, who desired to comply with the law." (Alarid v. Vanier (1958) 50 Cal.2d 617, 624, 327 P.2d 897, 900 * * *.)

Defendant offered sufficient evidence to rebut the presumption that she was negligent. The brakes had been overhauled three months before the accident; the car was inspected for damage and repaired after another accident in the interim; and the brakes gave no warning to defendant of their impending failure. Moreover, she was not negligent in failing to discover the faulty installation of or the growing damage to the hose, for those defects would be apparent only to a mechanic.

Plaintiff contends, however, that proof that defendant was not herself negligent should not absolve her from liability for the damage caused by the failure of her brakes. She contends that the court should reconsider the *Alarid* decision and hold that a motorist is strictly liable for damage caused by a brake failure or hold that the duty to exercise reasonable care to maintain adequate brakes is nondelegable.

We adhere to the holding of the *Alarid* case that a violation of a safety provision of the Vehicle Code does not make the violator strictly liable for damage caused by the violation. * * *

It does not follow, however, that the duty to exercise reasonable care to maintain brakes so that they comply with the provisions of the Vehicle Code can be delegated. This issue was not raised or considered in the *Alarid* case. * * * We believe * * * that the law governing nondelegable duties dictates imposing such a duty here.

Unlike strict liability, a nondelegable duty operates, not as a substitute for liability based on negligence, but to assure that when a negligently caused harm occurs, the injured party will be compensated by the person whose activity caused the harm and who may therefore properly be held liable for the negligence of his agent, whether his agent was an employee or an independent contractor. To the extent that recognition of nondelegable duties tends to insure that there will be financially responsible defendant available to compensate for the negligent harms caused by that defendant's activity, it ameliorates the need for strict liability to secure compensation. * * *

* * * [W]e have found nondelegable duties in a wide variety of situations and have recognized that the rules set forth in the Restatement of Torts with respect to such duties are generally in accord

with California law. Such duties include those imposed by a public authority as a condition of granting a franchise * * *; the duty of a condemning agent to protect a severed parcel from damage * * *; the duty of a general contractor to construct a building safely * * * the duty to exercise due care when an "* * * independent contractor is employed to do work which the employer should recognize as necessarily creating a condition involving an unreasonable risk of bodily harm to others unless special precautions are taken" * * *; the duty of landowners to maintain their property in a reasonably safe condition * * * and to comply with applicable safety ordinances * * * and the duty of employers and suppliers to comply with the safety provisions of the Labor Code * * *.

Section 423 of the Restatement Second of Torts provides that "One who carries on an activity which threatens a grave risk of serious bodily harm or death unless the instrumentalities used are carefully * * * maintained, and who employs an independent contractor to * * * maintain such instrumentalities, is subject to the same liability for physical harm caused by the negligence of the contractor in * * * maintaining such instrumentalities as though the employer had himself done the work of * * * maintenance." Section 424 provides that "One who by statute or by administrative regulation is under a duty to provide specified safeguards or precautions for the safety of others is subject to liability to the others for whose protection the duty is imposed for harm caused by the failure of a contractor employed by him to provide such safeguards or precautions." Both of these sections point to a nondelegable duty in this case. The statutory provisions regulating the maintenance and equipment of automobiles constitute express legislative recognition of the fact that improperly maintained motor vehicles threaten "a grave risk of serious bodily harm or death." The responsibility for minimizing that risk or compensating for the failure to do so properly rests with the person who owns and operates the vehicle. He is the party primarily to be benefited by its use; he selects the contractor and is free to insist upon one who is financially responsible and to demand indemnity from him; the cost of his liability insurance that distributes the risk is properly attributable to his activities; and the discharge of the duty to exercise reasonable care in the maintenance of his vehicle is of the utmost importance to the public. * * *

In the present case it is undisputed that the accident was caused by a failure of defendant's brakes that resulted from her independent contractor's negligence in overhauling or in thereafter inspecting the brakes. Since her duty to maintain her brakes in compliance with the provisions of the Vehicle Code is nondelegable, the fact that the brake failure was the result of her independent contractor's negligence is no defense.

The judgment and the order denying the motion for judgment notwithstanding the verdict on the issue of liability are reversed and the case is remanded to the trial court for a new trial on the issue of damages only.

HALL v. E. I. DU PONT DE NEMOURS CO.

United States District Court for the Eastern District of New York, 1972.
345 F.Supp. 353.

WEINSTEIN, DISTRICT JUDGE. These two cases arise out of eighteen separate accidents scattered across the nation in which children were injured by blasting caps. Damages are sought from manufacturers and their trade association, the Institute of Makers of Explosives (I.M.E.). The basic allegation is that the practice of the explosives industry during the 1950's—continuing until 1965—of not placing any warning upon individual blasting caps and of failing to take other safety measures created an unreasonable risk of harm resulting in plaintiffs' injuries.

In most instances the manufacturer of the cap is unknown. The question posed is whether a group of manufacturers and their trade association, comprising virtually the entire blasting cap industry of the United States, can be held jointly liable for injuries caused by their product. Our answer is that there are circumstances, illustrated by this litigation, in which an entire industry may be liable for harm caused by its operations. * * *

D. *Joint Liability*

The central question raised by defendants' motion is whether the defendants can be held responsible as a group under any theory of joint liability for injuries arising out of their individual manufacture of blasting caps. Joint tort liability is not limited to a narrow set of relationships and circumstances. It has been imposed in a wide range of situations, requiring varying standards of care, in which defendants cooperate in various degrees, enter into business and property relationships, and undertake to supply goods for public consumption. Developments in negligence and strict tort liability have imposed extensive duties on manufacturers to guard against a broad spectrum of risks with regard to the general population. The reasoning underlying current policy justifies the extension of established doctrines of joint tort liability to the area of industry-wide cooperation in product manufacture and design.

(1) *The Elements of Joint Liability*

Joint liability has historically been imposed in four distinguishable kinds of situations:

> (1) the actors knowingly join in the performance of the tortious act or acts; (2) the actors fail to perform a common duty owed to the plaintiff; (3) there is a special relationship between the parties (e. g., master and servant or joint entrepreneurs); (4) although there is no concerted action nevertheless the independent acts of several actors concur to produce indivisible harmful consequences. 1 Harper & James, The Law of Torts § 10.1 at 697–98 (1956).

See also Prosser, Joint Torts and Several Liability, 25 Calif.L.Rev. 413, 429 et seq. (1937).

These categories reflect three overlapping but distinguishable problems with which the law of joint liability has been concerned. The first is the problem of joint or group control of risk: the need to deter hazardous behavior by groups or multiple defendants as well as by individuals. The second is the problem of enterprise liability: the policy of assigning the foreseeable costs of an activity to those in the most strategic position to reduce them. The third is the problem of fairness with respect to burden of proof: the desire to avoid denying recovery to an innocent injured plaintiff because proof of causation may be within defendants' control or entirely unavailable. The complaint and defendants' motion to dismiss raise all three problems for consideration.

(2) *Joint Control of Risk*

The problem of joint control of risk was early posed in a case of group assault. In imposing joint liability, the court reasoned that "* * * [with] all coming to do an unlawful act, and of one party, the act of one is the act of all. * * *" See Sir John Heydon's Case, 11 Co.Rep. 5, 77 Eng.Rep. 1150 (1613), and other English cases cited in Prosser, Law of Torts § 46 at 291 (4th ed. 1971). Even in its earliest form the doctrine of joint liability for concerted action contained all the elements necessary for its future development: (1) causing harm (2) by cooperative or concerted activities (3) which violated a legal standard of care.

American courts have imposed joint liability for concerted action in cases involving a complex interaction of the three elements of the doctrine. "Cooperation" or "concert" has been found in various business and property relationships, group activities such as automobile racing, cooperative efforts in medical care or railroad work, and concurrent water pollution. "Express agreement is not necessary; all that is required is that there shall be a common design or understanding." Prosser, Joint Torts and Several Liability, 25 Cal.L.Rev. 413, 429–30 (1937). * * *

These diverse cases impose joint liability on groups whose actions create unreasonable hazards of risks of harm, even though only one member of the group may have been the "direct" or physical cause of the injury. Where courts perceive a clear joint control of risk—typically the racing and assault cases, as well as those involving common duties or joint enterprise—the issue of who "caused" the injury is distinctly secondary to the fact that the group engaged in joint hazardous conduct. * * *

Defendants argue that their participation in the I.M.E. safety program, and their cooperative or parallel activities regarding the safety features of blasting caps do not give them joint control over the risks of injury for purposes of tort liability. Joint control of risk and consequent joint responsibility arises, in their view, only when manufacturers enter into a conspiracy to commit intentional harm, or into a partnership or joint venture. The key to a joint venture, they assert, is an agreement to share profits and to pursue a limited number of business objectives over a short period of time. Since the defendants' membership in their trade association involves neither profit-sharing nor a limited time-span, they contend that no joint responsibility arises from the association and its members' activities.

The problem with this argument is that the elements of joint control of risk do not coincide with those in the formal doctrine of joint venture. * * *

[The court discusses Connor v. Great Western Savings & Loan Ass'n, 69 Cal.2d 850, 73 Cal.Rptr. 369, 447 P.2d 609 (1968). A savings bank which was financing a land developer was considered not to be in a joint venture with the developer, and therefore not vicariously liable for the developer's negligence. The bank was, however, held "liable for its own negligence in exercising what in practical effect was its joint control of the venture" by permitting, through its financing, the thinly capitalized builder to put up shoddy housing.]

* * * [J]oint control of risk can exist among actors who are not bound in a profit-sharing joint venture. This point is thoroughly confirmed by cases imposing joint liability on "joint enterprises," which are distinguished from "joint ventures" as being "non profit undertaking[s] for the mutual benefit or pleasure of the parties" * * * and on which joint liability is imposed because of the parties' effective joint control of the risk. * * *

Joint control may be shown in one of three ways. First, plaintiffs can prove the existence of an explicit agreement and joint action among the defendants with regard to warnings and other safety features—the classic "concert of action." Second, plaintiffs can submit evidence of defendants' parallel behavior sufficient to support an inference of tacit agreement or cooperation. Such cooperation has the same effects as overt joint action, and is subject to joint liability for the same reasons. Cf. Prosser, Joint Torts and Several Liability, 25 Calif.L.Rev. 413, 430 (1937); Posner, Oligopoly and the Antitrust Laws: A Suggested Approach, 21 Stan.L.Rev. 1562, 1576–78 (1969).

Third, plaintiffs can submit evidence that defendants, acting independently, adhered to an industry-wide standard or custom with regard to the safety features of blasting caps. Regardless of whether such evidence is sufficient to support an inference of tacit agreement, it is still relevant to the question of joint control of risk. The dynamics of market competition frequently result in explicit or implicit safety standards, codes, and practices which are widely adhered to in an entire industry. * * *

Where such standards or practices exist, the industry operates as a collective unit in the double sense of stabilizing the production costs of safety features and in establishing an industry-wide custom which influences, but does not conclusively determine, the applicable standard of care. * * * [T]he existence of industry-wide standards or practices alone will not support, in all circumstances, the imposition of joint liability. But where * * * individual defendant-manufacturers cannot be identified, the existence of industry-wide standards or practices could support a finding of joint control of risk and a shift of the burden of proving causation to the defendants. * * *

(3) *Enterprise Liability*

Joint liability has been traditionally imposed on multiple defendants who exercise actual collective control over a particular risk-creating product or activity. In a related but distinguishable fashion, joint or vicarious liability has been imposed on the most strategically placed participants in a risk-creating process, even though injuries are caused "directly" or partially by other participants under their general supervision. See 2 Harper & James, The Law of Torts, ch. 26, esp. at 1361–69, 1375–78 (1956) and Supplement (1968). As Judge Cardozo noted in a workmen's compensation case involving injury to one employee by another's carelessness:

> The risks of injury incurred in the crowded contacts of the factory through the acts of fellow workmen are not measured by the tendency of such acts to serve the master's business. Many things that have no such tendency are done by workmen every day. The test of liability under the statute is not the master's dereliction, whether his own or that of his representatives acting within the scope of their authority. The test of liability is the relation of the service to the injury, of the employment to the risk. Leonbruno v. Champlain Silk Mills, 229 N.Y. 470, 473, 128 N.E. 711, 712 (1920).

A similar principle of enterprise liability is embedded in the doctrine of respondeat superior—an employer's vicarious liability to third parties for employees' wrongs committed "in the scope of their employment." * * *

The rationale for an employer's vicarious liability to third parties has been analyzed as being very close to the enterprise liability basis of workmen's compensation. In both types of cases [w]e are not * * * looking for the master's fault but rather for risks that may fairly be regarded as typical of or broadly incidental to the enterprise he has undertaken. * * * [O]ne of the purposes for such a quest is to mark out in a broad way the extent of tort liability (as a cost item) that it is fair and expedient to require people to expect when they engage in such an enterprise, so there can be some reasonable basis for calculating this cost. * * * What is reasonably foreseeable in this context, however, is quite a different thing from the foreseeably unreasonable risk of harm that spells negligence. In the first place, we are no longer dealing with specific conduct but with the broad scope of a whole enterprise. Further, we are not looking for that which can and should reasonably be avoided, but with the more or less inevitable toll of a lawful enterprise. The foresight that should impel the prudent man to take precautions is not the same measure as that by which he should perceive the harm likely to flow from his long-run activity in spite of all reasonable precautions on his own part. * * * 2 Harper & James, The Law of Torts, § 26.7 at 1376–78 (1956) (citations omitted).

See also Calebresi, Some Thoughts on Risk Distribution and the Law of Torts, 70 Yale L.J. 449, 543 (1961).

Enterprise liability is also apparent in the long line of cases imposing joint and vicarious liability on owners, employers and manufacturers for breach of "non-delegable duties", or for miscarriage of "inherently dangerous activities" by their contractors, employees, and distributors. * * *

In many instances the most strategic point of foresight, precaution and risk distribution may be the individual manufacturer, supplier, or employer. In other situations—typically water or air pollution by multiple emitters—the only feasible method of ascertaining risks, imposing safeguards and spreading costs is through joint liability or other methods of joint risk control. * * * The point is not only that the damage is caused by multiple actors, but that the sole feasible way of anticipating costs or damages and devising practical remedies is to consider the activities of a group. We do not, of course, suggest that private actions are the best way to meet these problems but only that in the absence of preemptive legislation, tort principles will support a remedy. * * *

The allegations in this case suggest that the entire blasting cap industry and its trade association provide the logical locus at which precautions should be taken and liability imposed. It is unlikely that individual manufacturers would collect information about the nationwide incidence and circumstances of blasting-cap accidents involving children, and it is entirely reasonable that the manufacturers should delegate this function to a jointly-sponsored and jointly-financed association.

In the event that the evidence warrants it, the imposition of joint liability on the trade association and its members should in no way be interpreted as "punishment" for the establishment of industry-wide institutions. Such liability would represent rather the law's traditional function of reviewing the risk and cost decisions inherent in industry-wide safety practices, whether organized or unorganized. See, e. g., The T. J. Hooper, 60 F.2d 737 (2d Cir. 1932).

To establish that the explosives industry should be held jointly liable on enterprise liability grounds, plaintiffs, pursuant to their pleading, will have to demonstrate defendants' joint awareness of the risks at issue in this case and their joint capacity to reduce or affect those risks. By noting these requirements we wish to emphasize their special applicability to industries composed of a small number of units. What would be fair and feasible with regard to an industry of five or ten producers might be manifestly unreasonable if applied to a decentralized industry composed of thousands of small producers. * * *

LAIRD v. NELMS

United States Supreme Court, 1972.
406 U.S. 797, 92 S.Ct. 1899, 32 L.Ed.2d 499.

MR. JUSTICE REHNQUIST delivered the opinion of the Court.

Respondents brought this action in the United States District Court under the Federal Tort Claims Act, 28 U.S.C.A. §§ 1346(b), 2671–2680. They sought recovery for property damage allegedly resulting from a sonic boom caused by California-based United States military planes flying over North Carolina on a training mission. The District Court entered summary judgment for petitioners, but on respondents' appeal the United States Court of Appeals for the Fourth Circuit reversed. That court held that, although respondents had been unable to show negligence "either in the planning or operation of the flight," they were nonetheless entitled to proceed on a theory of strict or absolute liability for ultrahazardous activities conducted by petitioners in their official capacities. That court relied on its earlier opinion in United States v. Praylou, 4 Cir., 208 F.2d 291 (1953), which in turn had distinguished this Court's holding in Dalehite v. United States, 346 U.S. 15, 45, 73 S.Ct. 956, 972, 97 L.Ed. 1427 (1953). We granted certiorari. * * * *Dalehite* held that the Government was not liable for the extensive damage resulting from the explosion of two cargo vessels in the harbor of Texas City, Texas, in 1947. The Court's opinion rejected various specifications of negligence on the part of Government employees that had been found by the District Court in that case, and then went on to treat petitioners' claim that the Government was absolutely or strictly liable because of its having engaged in a dangerous activity. The Court said with respect to this aspect of the plaintiffs' claim:

> "[T]he Act does not extend to such situations, though of course well known in tort law generally. It is to be invoked only on a 'negligent or wrongful act or omission' of an employee. Absolute liability, of course, arises irrespective of how the tortfeasor conducts himself; it is imposed automatically when any damages are sustained as a result of the decision to engage in the dangerous activity." 346 U.S., at 44, 73 S.Ct., at 972.

This Court's resolution of the strict-liability issue in *Dalehite* did not turn on the question of whether the law of Texas or of some other State did or did not recognize strict liability for the conduct of ultrahazardous activities. It turned instead on the question of whether the language of the Federal Tort Claims Act permitted under any circumstances the imposition of liability upon the Government where there had been neither negligence nor wrongful act. The necessary consequence of the Court's holding in *Dalehite* is that the statutory language "negligent or wrongful act or omission of any employee of the Government," is a uniform federal limitation on the types of acts committed by its employees for which the United States has consented to be sued. Regardless of state law characterization, the Federal Tort Claims Act itself precludes the imposition of liability if there has been no negligence or other form of "misfeasance or nonfeasance," 346 U.S., at 45, 73 S.Ct. at 972, on the part of the Government.

It is at least theoretically possible to argue that since *Dalehite* in discussing the legislative history of the Act said that "wrongful" acts could include some kind of trespass, and since courts imposed liability in some of the early blasting cases on the theory that the plaintiff's action sounded in trespass, liability could be imposed on the Government in this case on a theory of trespass which would be within the Act's waiver of immunity. We believe, however, that there is more than one reason for rejecting such an alternate basis of governmental liability here.

The notion that a military plane on a high-altitude training flight itself intrudes upon any property interest of an owner of the land over which it flies was rejected in United States v. Causby, 328 U.S. 256, 66 S.Ct. 1062, 90 L.Ed. 1206 (1946). There this Court, construing the Air Commerce Act of 1926, 44 Stat. 568, as amended by the Civil Aeronautics Act of 1938, 52 Stat. 973, 49 U.S.C.A. § 401, said:

> "It is ancient doctrine that at common law ownership of the land extended to the periphery of the universe—*Cujus est solum ejus est usque ad coelum.* But that doctrine has no place in the modern world. The air is a public highway, as Congress has declared. Were that not true, every transcontinental flight would subject the operator to countless trespass suits. Common sense revolts at the idea. To recognize such private claims to the airspace would clog these highways, seriously interfere with their control and development in the public interest, and transfer into private ownership that to which only the public has a just claim." 328 U.S., at 260–261, 66 S.Ct., at 1065.

Thus, quite apart from what would very likely be insuperable problems of proof in connecting the passage of the plane over the owner's air space with any ensuing damage from a sonic boom, this version of the trespass theory is ruled out by established federal law. Perhaps the precise holding of United States v. Causby, supra, could be skirted by analogizing the pressure wave of air characterizing a sonic boom to the concussion that on occasion accompanies blasting, and treating the air waves striking the actual land of the property owner as a direct intrusion caused by the pilot of the plane in the mold of the classical common-law theory of trespass.

It is quite clear, however, that the presently prevailing view as to the theory of liability for blasting damage is frankly conceded to be strict liability for undertaking an ultrahazardous activity, rather than any attenuated notion of common law trespass. See Restatement of Torts §§ 519, 520(e); W. Prosser, Law of Torts § 75 (4th ed. 1971).
* * *

More importantly, however, Congress in considering the Federal Tort Claims Act cannot realistically be said to have dealt in terms of either the jurisprudential distinctions peculiar to the forms of action at common law or the metaphysical subtleties that crop up in even contemporary discussions of tort theory. See Prosser, supra, at 492–496. The legislative history discussed in *Dalehite* indicates that Congress intended to permit liability essentially based on the intentionally wrongful or careless conduct of Government employees, for which the Government was to be made liable according to state law under the doctrine of *respondeat superior,* but to exclude liability based solely on the ultrahazardous nature of an activity undertaken by the Government.

A House Judiciary Committee memorandum explaining the "discretionary function" exemption from the bill when that exemption first appeared in the draft legislation in 1942 made the comment that "the cases covered by that subsection would probably have been exempted * * * by judicial construction" in any event, but that the exemption was intended to preclude any possibility

> "that the act would be construed to authorize suit for damages against the Government growing out of a legally authorized activity, such as a flood-control or irrigation project, where no wrongful act or omission on the part of any Government agent is shown, and the only ground for suit is the contention that the same conduct by a private individual would be tortious * * *." Hearings on H.R. 5373 and H.R. 6463 before the House Committee on the Judiciary, 77th Cong., 2d Sess., ser. 13, pp. 65–66 (1942). * * *

* * * Liability * * * under the Act is not to be broadened beyond the intent of Congress by dressing up the substance of strict liability for ultrahazardous activities in the garments of common-law trespass. To permit respondent to proceed on a trespass theory here would be to judicially admit at the back door that which has been legislatively turned away at the front door. We do not believe the Act permits such a result.

Shortly after the decision of this Court in *Dalehite,* the facts of the Texas City catastrophe were presented to Congress in an effort to obtain legislative relief from that body. Congress, after conducting hearings and receiving reports, ultimately enacted a bill granting compensation to the victims in question. * * * At no time during these hearings was there any effort made to modify this Court's construction of the Tort Claims Act in *Dalehite.* Both by reason of *stare decisis* and by reason of Congress' failure to make any statutory change upon again reviewing the subject, we regard the principle enunciated in *Dalehite* as controlling here. * * *

Our reaffirmation of the construction put on the Federal Tort Claims Act in *Dalehite,* makes it unnecessary to treat the scope of the discretionary-function exemption contained in the Act, or the other matters dealt with by the Court of Appeals.

Reversed.

MR. JUSTICE DOUGLAS, having heard the argument, withdrew from participation in the consideration or decision of this case.

MR. JUSTICE STEWART, with whom MR. JUSTICE BRENNAN joins, dissenting.

Under the Federal Tort Claims Act, the United States is liable for injuries to persons or property

> "caused by the negligent or wrongful act or omission of any employee of the Government while acting within the scope of his office or employment, under circumstances where the United States, if a private person, would be liable to the claimant in accordance with the law of the place where the act or omission occurred." 28 U.S.C.A. § 1346(b).

The Court of Appeals in this case found that the law of North Carolina renders a person who creates a sonic boom absolutely liable for any injuries caused thereby, and that finding is not challenged here.[67] And while the petitioners argue that the conduct involved falls within one of the numerous express exceptions to the coverage of the Act contained in § 2680, the Court today does not reach that issue. Rather, the Court holds that the words "negligent or wrongful act or omission" preclude the application to the United States of any state law under which persons may be held absolutely liable for injuries caused by certain kinds of conduct. In my view, this conclusion is not justified by the language or the history of the Act, and is plainly contrary to the statutory purpose. * * *

In the vast majority of cases in the law of torts, liability is predicated on a breach of some legal duty owed by the defendant to the plaintiff, whether that duty involves exercising reasonable care in one's activities or refraining from certain activities altogether. The law of most jurisdictions, however, imposes liability for harm caused by certain narrowly limited kinds of activities even though those activities are not prohibited and even though the actor may have exercised the utmost care. Such conduct is "tortious," not because the actor is necessarily blameworthy, but because society has made a judgment that while the conduct is so socially valuable that it should not be prohibited, it nevertheless carries such a high risk of harm to others, even in the absence of negligence, that one who engages in

67. The question whether damage caused by sonic booms is recoverable on a theory of absolute liability has received considerable attention from commentators, most of whom have concluded that there should be such recovery, at least under certain conditions. See, e. g., Note, 32 J.Air Law & Commerce 596, 602–605 (1966); Note, 39 Tulane L.Rev. 145 (1964); Comment, 31 So.Cal.L.Rev. 259, 266–274 (1958); W. Prosser, Law of Torts 516 (4th ed. 1971).

it should make good any harm caused to others thereby. See generally, 2 F. Harper & F. James, Law of Torts 785–795, 815–816 (1956); W. Prosser, Law of Torts 442–496 (4th ed. 1971).

While the doctrine of absolute liability is not encountered in many situations even under modern tort law, it was nevertheless well established at the time the Tort Claims Act was enacted, and there is nothing in the language or the history of the Act to support the notion that this doctrine alone, among all the rules governing tort liability in the various States, was considered inapplicable in cases arising under the Act. The legislative history quoted by the Court relates solely to the "discretionary function" exception contained in § 2680, an exception upon which the Court specifically declines to rely.[68] As I read the Act and the legislative history, the phrase "negligent or wrongful act or omission" was intended to include the entire range of conduct classified as tortious under state law. The only intended exceptions to this sweeping waiver of governmental immunity were those expressly set forth and now collected in § 2680.[69] This

68. The Court's opinion refers to language in Dalehite v. United States, 346 U.S. 15, 73 S.Ct. 956, 97 L.Ed. 1427, which in turn relied on a fragment of legislative history, for the proposition that the words "wrongful act" as used in § 1346(b) refer only to trespasses. The legislative history cited by the Court in *Dalehite,* consisting of a statement by a Special Assistant to the Attorney General at a committee hearing, merely suggested trespass as one example of the kinds of conduct that would not be embraced by the word "negligence" but which the Act was intended to reach. As the Court today observes, many of the state cases applying what is essentially the doctrine of absolute liability for ultrahazardous activities speak in terms of "trespass." See, e. g., Guilford Realty & Ins. Co. v. Blythe Bros. Co., 260 N.C. 69, 131 S.E.2d 900 (1963); Enos Coal Mining Co. v. Schuchart, 243 Ind. 692, 188 N.E.2d 406 (1963); Whitney v. Ralph Myers Contracting Corp., 146 W.Va. 130, 118 S.E.2d 622 (1961). The similarity between the theories of trespass and absolute liability in the blasting cases leads the Court to conclude that the Act does not permit recovery on a "trespass" theory in this case because the Act does not permit recovery on an absolute liability theory. But if Congress intended, as the Court assumes, that "trespasses" be covered by the Act, * * * the similarity between the two theories would more logically lead to a conclusion that absolute-liability situations are likewise covered.

69. "The provisions of this chapter and section 1346(b) of this title shall not apply to—

"(a) Any claim based upon an act or omission of an employee of the Government, exercising due care, in the execution of a statute or regulation, whether or not such statute or regulation be valid, or based upon the exercise or performance or the failure to exercise or perform a discretionary function or duty on the part of a federal agency or an employee of the Government, whether or not the discretion involved be abused.

"(b) Any claim arising out of the loss, miscarriage, or negligent transmission of letters or postal matter.

"(c) Any claim arising in respect of the assessment or collection of any tax or customs duty, or the detention of any goods or merchandise by any officer of customs or excise or any other law-enforcement officer.

"(d) Any claim for which a remedy is provided by sections 741–752, 781–790 of Title 46, relating to claims or suits in admiralty against the United States.

"(e) Any claim arising out of an act or omission of any employee of the Government in administering the provisions of sections 1–31 of Title 50, Appendix.

"(f) Any claim for damages caused by the imposition or establishment of a quarantine by the United States.

"(g) Repealed.

"(h) Any claim arising out of assault, battery, false imprisonment, false arrest, malicious prosecution, abuse of process, libel, slander, misrepresenta-

interpretation was put upon the Act by the legislative committees that recommended its passage in 1946: "The present bill would establish a uniform system * * * permitting suit to be brought on *any tort claim* * * * with the exception of certain classes of torts *expressly exempted* from the operation of the act." (Emphasis supplied.) * * * See Peck, Absolute Liability and the Federal Tort Claims Act, 9 Stan.L.Rev. 433, 441–450 (1957).

The Court rests its conclusion on language from Dalehite v. United States, 346 U.S. 15, 73 S.Ct. 956, 97 L.Ed. 1427, where a four-man majority of the Court, in an opinion dealing primarily with the "discretionary function" exception, held the doctrine of absolute liability inapplicable in that extremely unusual case arising under the Federal Tort Claims Act. That language has been severely criticized,[70] it has not since been relied upon in any decision of this Court; and it was rejected as a general principle by at least one Court of Appeals less than a year after *Dalehite* was decided. United States v. Praylou, 4 Cir., 208 F.2d 291, 295. Moreover, *Dalehite* represented an approach to interpretation of the Act that was abruptly changed only two years later in Indian Towing Co. v. United States, 350 U.S. 61, 76 S.Ct. 122, 100 L.Ed. 48. That decision rejected the proposition that the United States was immune from liability where the activity involved was "governmental" rather than "proprietary"—a proposition that seemingly had been established in *Dalehite.*[71] And while the *Dalehite* opinion explicitly created a presumption in favor of sovereign immunity, to be overcome only where relinquishment by Congress was "clear," 346 U.S., at 30–31, 73 S.Ct. at 965, the Court in *Indian Towing* recognized that the Tort Claims Act "cuts the ground from under" the doctrine of sovereign immunity, and cautioned that a court should not "as a self-constituted guardian of the Treasury import immunity back into a statute designed to limit it." 350 U.S., at 65, 69, 76 S.Ct., at 126. See also Rayonier, Inc. v. United States, 352 U.S. 315, 319–320, 77 S.Ct. 374, 376–377, 1 L.Ed.2d 354. * * *

The rule announced by the Court today seems to me contrary to the whole policy of the Tort Claims Act. For the doctrine of absolute liability is applicable not only to sonic booms, but to other activities

tion, deceit, or interference with contract rights.

"(i) Any claim for damages caused by the fiscal operations of the Treasury or by the regulation of the monetary system.

"(j) Any claim arising out of the combatant activities of the military or naval forces, or the Coast Guard, during time of war.

"(k) Any claim arising in a foreign country.

"(*l*) Any claim arising from the activities of the Tennessee Valley Authority.

"(m) Any claim arising from the activities of the Panama Canal Company.

"(n) Any claim arising from the activities of a Federal land bank, a Federal intermediate credit bank, or a bank for cooperatives."

70. See, e. g., * * * Jacoby, Absolute Liability under the Federal Tort Claims Act, 24 Fed.Bar J. 139 (1964); 2 F. Harper & F. James, Law of Torts 860 (1956).

71. Four members of the Court dissented, saying that the failure of Congress to amend the Act after *Dalehite* should have been taken as indicating approval by Congress of the interpretation given to the Act in that case. 350 U.S., at 74, 76 S.Ct., at 129.

that the Government carries on in common with many private citizens. Absolute liability for injury caused by the concussion or debris from dynamite blasting, for example, is recognized by an overwhelming majority of state courts. A private person who detonates an explosion in the process of building a road is liable for injuries to others caused thereby under the law of most States even though he took all practicable precautions to prevent such injuries, on the sound principle that he who creates such a hazard should make good the harm that results. Yet if employees of the United States engage in exactly the same conduct with an identical result, the United States will not, under the principle announced by the Court today, be liable to the injured party. Nothing in the language or the legislative history of the Act compels such a result, and we should not lightly conclude that Congress intended to create a situation so much at odds with common sense and the basic rationale of the Act. We recognized that rationale in *Rayonier,* supra, a case involving negligence by employees of the United States in controlling a forest fire:

> "Congress was aware that when losses caused by such negligence are charged against the public treasury they are in effect spread among all those who contribute financially to the support of the Government and the resulting burden on each taxpayer is relatively slight. But when the entire burden falls on the injured party it may leave him destitute or grievously harmed. Congress could, and apparently did, decide that this would be unfair when the public as a whole benefits from the services performed by Government employees." 352 U.S., at 320, 77 S.Ct., at 377.

For the reasons stated, I would hold that the doctrine of absolute liability is applicable to conduct of employees of the United States under the same circumstances as those in which it is applied to the conduct of private persons under the law of the State where the conduct occurs. That holding would not by itself be dispositive of this case, however, for the petitioners argue that liability is precluded by the "discretionary function" exception in the Act. While the Court does not reach this issue, I shall state briefly the reasons for my conclusion that the exception is inapplicable in this case.

No right of action lies under the Tort Claims Act for any claim

> "based upon an act or omission of an employee of the Government, exercising due care, in the execution of a statute or regulation, whether or not such statute or regulation be valid, or based upon the exercise or performance or the failure to exercise or perform a discretionary function or duty on the part of a federal agency or an employee of the Government, whether or not the discretion involved be abused." 28 U.S.C.A. § 2680(a).

The Assistant Attorney General who testified on the bill before the House Committee indicated that this provision was intended to create no exceptions beyond those that courts would probably create without it:

> "[I]t is likely that the cases embraced within that subsection would have been exempted from [a bill that did not include the exception] by judicial construction. It is not probable that the courts would extend a Tort Claims Act into the realm of the validity of legislation or discretionary administrative action, but [the recommended bill] makes this specific." Hearings on H.R. 5373 and H.R. 6463 before the House Committee on the Judiciary, 77th Cong., 2d Sess., ser. 13, p. 29.

The *Dalehite* opinion seemed to say that no action of a Government employee could be made the basis for liability under the Act if the action involved "policy judgment and decision." 346 U.S., at 36, 73 S.Ct., at 968. Decisions in the courts of appeals following *Dalehite* have interpreted this language as drawing a distinction between "policy" and "operational" decisions, with the latter falling outside the exception. That distinction has bedeviled the courts that have attempted to apply it to torts outside routine categories such as automobile accidents, but there is no need in the present case to explore the limits of the discretionary function exception.

The legislative history indicates that the purpose of this statutory exception was to avoid any possibility that policy decisions of Congress, of the Executive, or of administrative agencies would be second-guessed by courts in the context of tort actions.[72] There is no such danger in this case, for liability does not depend upon a judgment as to whether Government officials acted irresponsibly or illegally. Rather, once the creation of sonic booms is determined to be an activity as to which the doctrine of absolute liability applies, the only questions for the court relate to causation and damages. Whether or not the decision to fly a military aircraft over the respondents' property, at a given altitude and at a speed three times the speed of sound, was a decision at the "policy" or the "operational" level, the

72. The policy behind the exception is explained by one leading commentator as follows: "[A]lmost no one contends that there should be compensation for all the ills that result from governmental operations. No one, for instance, suggests that there should be liability for the injurious consequence, of political blunders such as the unwise imposition of tariff duties or the premature lifting of OPA controls. * * * The separation of powers in our form of government and a decent regard by the judiciary for its co-ordinate branches should make courts reluctant to sit in judgment on the wisdom or reasonableness of legislative or executive political action. Moreover, courts are not particularly well suited to pursue the examinations that would be necessary to make this kind of judgment." James, The Federal Tort Claims Act and the "Discretionary Function" Exception: The Sluggish Retreat of an Ancient Immunity, 10 U.Fla.L.Rev. 184 (1957). [Notes 67–72 from the original, renumbered; other notes in original omitted.]

propriety of that decision is irrelevant to the question of liability in this case, and thus the discretionary function exception does not apply.[73]

HANSEN v. CITY OF SAINT PAUL

Supreme Court of Minnesota, 1974.
298 Minn. 205, 214 N.W.2d 346.

O. RUSSELL OLSON, JUSTICE. Two dogs attacked and bit plaintiff Ellen Hansen on a public sidewalk at 136 North Lexington Avenue in St. Paul on May 18, 1971, at 12:45 p. m. The attack resulted in extensive injuries and 2 months' hospitalization for Mrs. Hansen, a 59-year-old woman; seven reports of dog-biting, concerning the same dogs, had been made to the city officials during the prior 13-month period; the city officials knew the two dogs were vicious and prone to make unprovoked attacks upon public sidewalk pedestrians; the appropriate city health officer had notified the owner of the dogs that the dogs qualified as vicious under the city ordinance and the city knew the owner of the dogs ignored its requests that the dogs should be controlled or destroyed, pursuant to city ordinance requirements; the most recent of the other attacks had occurred 2 hours earlier against another sidewalk pedestrian who was also severely bitten; she had immediately reported the attack to the appropriate city officials; in response to that report, two city officers made a field investigation in the forenoon and discovered that the dogs were still running at large. It was while the officials interrupted this field investigation for their lunch break that the dogs attacked the plaintiff. * * *

With specified limitations and exceptions, Minn.St. c. 466 abolishes governmental (sovereign) immunity of municipalities as to tort claims. Section 466.02 reads as follows:

> "Subject to the limitations of Laws 1963, Chapter 798 [Minn.St. 466.01 to 466.15], every municipality is subject to liability for its torts and those of its officers, employees and agents acting within the scope of their employment or duties whether arising out of a governmental or proprietary function."

73. (a) Suppose a government surgeon operates on a portion of anatomy as to which patient had refused consent to operate, and patient is injured thereby. Is patient's claim against the government permitted under the FTCA as negligence, or barred as battery? See, e. g., Hulver v. United States, 393 F. Supp. 749 (W.D.Mo.1975).

(b) Consider the bidder for a government contract who is misled by negligent misrepresentations of the government; cf. Scanwell Laboratories, Inc. v. Thomas, 571 F.2d 941 (D.C.Cir. 1975).

(c) Note also that 28 U.S.C.A. § 2679(b) makes suit against the United States the exclusive remedy for damages caused by a government motor vehicle when operated within the scope of the driver's employment.

The exceptions or limitations are set forth in § 466.03, which provides in part:

> "Subdivision 1. Section 466.02 does not apply to any claim enumerated in this section. * * *
>
> * * * * * * * *
>
> "Subd. 6. Any claim based upon the performance or the failure to exercise or perform a discretionary function or duty, whether or not the discretion is abused. * * *

The cited exception, Minn.St. 466.03, subd. 6, is patterned after § 2680(a), the discretionary function exception, of the Federal Torts Claim Act, 62 Stat. 982, 28 U.S.C.A. § 2680(a). The leading United States Supreme Court decision first interpreting that exception is Dalehite v. United States, 346 U.S. 15, 73 S.Ct. 956, 97 L.Ed. 1427 (1953). Numerous Federal and other state court decisions have followed from Dalehite. In general, the judicial interpretations of the "discretionary acts" exception find greater applicability (and therefore immunity) for decisions made on the executive (planning) level of conduct than on the operational level. See, Dahlstrom v. United States, 228 F.2d 819 (8 Cir. 1956). Minnesota has followed this interpretation. Silver v. City of Minneapolis, 284 Minn. 266, 170 N.W.2d 206 (1969). In Silver, this court held that the deployment of police and fire-fighting resources in the face of threatened and actual riotous circumstances constituted the exercise of such a discretionary function and accordingly the city was immune from tort liability pursuant to the exception set forth in § 466.03, subd. 6. It appears reasonably clear that the facts in Silver v. City of Minneapolis, supra, represented an executive (planning) policy decision under circumstances clearly calling for the exercise of a discretionary function, i. e., how to deploy personnel. In the instant case, the failure of the city to act in the face of a known dangerous condition occurred in an entirely different circumstance, namely, at the operational level rather than the executive or administrative level.

We hold that the failure of the St. Paul City officials to control vicious dogs under circumstances wherein the city had knowledge that the identified and impoundable vicious dogs prowled uncontrolled on public sidewalks does not constitute a failure to exercise a discretionary function within the meaning of Minn.St. 466.03, subd. 6, and therefore the city of St. Paul is not immune from liability. * * * [74]

74. For further discussions of the "discretionary function" exception under the Federal Tort Claims Act see Driscoll v. United States, 525 F.2d 136 (9th Cir. 1975) (liability for negligent design of pedestrian crosswalks and warning devices on Air Force base) and Downs v. United States, 522 F.2d 990 (6th Cir. 1975) (exception inapplicable to shooting by FBI agent during aircraft hijacking).

JONES v. STATE OF NEW YORK

Court of Appeals of New York, 1973.
33 N.Y.2d 275, 352 N.Y.S.2d 169, 307 N.E.2d 236.

BURKE, JUDGE. Claimant seeks to recover damages from the State for the false imprisonment, pain and suffering and mental anguish which her decedent sustained prior to his death as well as for his wrongful death. The State moved in the Court of Claims to dismiss the claim on the grounds that workmen's compensation is claimant's sole remedy and that the claim failed to state a cause of action since the State is insulated against the alleged liability by the doctrine of sovereign immunity. * * * The Appellate Division, by a closely divided court, (3--2), * * * granted the State's motion and dismissed the claim.

The facts are simply stated. Claimant's decedent was employed by the Department of Correctional Services, a subdivision of the State of New York, in the capacity of accounts clerk at the Attica State Correctional Facility. His position was clerical and in no way was he involved in the guarding or disciplining of prisoners. On September 9, 1971, whle so employed, he was taken hostage during the occurrence of what is now recalled as the "Attica uprising". The claim alleges two causes of action. The first is based upon the negligence of the State in failing to warn the decedent of the impending riot of which the State had, or should have had, knowledge. The second cause of action is based upon intentional tort, alleging that during the forceful retaking of the prison on September 13, 1971 a State trooper "without just cause or provocation and with great force and violence, wilfully and intentionally assaulted and battered the Claimant's decedent by firing several shots of a gun at Claimant's decedent, one or more of which shot and struck him in the head, chest and back, thereby causing his death."

As to the first cause of action, the order appealed from should be affirmed. The cause of action is one in negligence. Since the claim alleges that the State was negligent while the decedent "was performing his clerical duties as an accounts clerk", the claim must be dismissed and the plaintiff is relegated to workmen's compensation as her exclusive remedy.

The second cause of action alleges that a State trooper "wilfully and intentionally assaulted" plaintiff's decedent causing his death. This claim states a cause of action and that part of the Appellate Division order which dismissed this claim is reversed. * * * The claim alleges a cause of action similar to the cause of action sustained by this court in the case of Kline v. State of New York, 278 N.Y. 615, 16 N.E.2d 124 [1938]. There, this court held that the State is liable for an assault committed upon the plaintiff by troopers which was "without cause or provocation and unjustifiable" (id., at p. 616, 16 N.E.2d 124), the precise words used in the instant claim.

The concept is not novel. A long line of cases has held the State or municipalities liable for the actions of their police officers in the line of duty. Hinton v. City of New York, 13 A.D.2d 475, 212 N.Y.S. 2d 97 [1st Dept., 1961]—plaintiff, while being lawfully arrested, was struck by several police officers; Franklin v. State of New York, 276 App.Div. 1038, 95 N.Y.S.2d 244 [3d Dept., 1950]—plaintiff was assaulted by State troopers during his detention; Huff v. State of New York, 271 App.Div. 1040, 68 N.Y.S.2d 365 [3d Dept., 1947]—plaintiff was assaulted by a State trooper in the course of a criminal investigation; Egan v. State of New York, 255 App.Div. 825, 7 N.Y. S.2d 64 [4th Dept., 1938]—plaintiff was assaulted by a State trooper during the course of his arrest. In each of these cases the troopers were engaged in activities which can only be described as "governmental" in nature. The theory upon which recovery from the State in these cases is premised is found in section 8 of the Court of Claims Act. Prior to the enactment of this section police officers were considered public officers whose actions in the area of governmental activities could not fasten liability upon the State * * * However, with the waiver of immunity effected by the enactment of section 12–a, the present section 8, of the Court of Claims Act, the State and its civil subdivisions became liable for the torts of their agents on the basis of *respondeat superior,* notwithstanding the fact that the agent was engaged in "governmental" activity. * * *

Nor should the fact that the decedent suffered his fatal injuries during the Attica riot bar his recovery. That fact is irrelevant in light of the settled law. The action of retaking the prison is no more "governmental" than making an arrest, maintaining someone in custody or investigating a traffic infraction. The use of excessive force by troopers during these activities was sufficient to fasten liability upon the State. A different rule should not apply here. Should the Judge in the Court of Claims find that the force used against the decedent was more than necessary under all the circumstances, then plaintiff is entitled to recover * * *.

JASEN, JUDGE (dissenting).

On this appeal from dismissal of a claim for damages for wrongful death, important questions are raised concerning the remedies for the torts of law enforcement officers. Affording the claimant the most liberal reading of the allegations of the claim, as is required on a motion to dismiss, I must nevertheless conclude that sovereign immunity is a bar to granting relief, and, accordingly, that claimant's exclusive remedy is in workmen's compensation. * * *

The immunity of the States and their civil subdivisions from liability for police torts may be traced to the pre-Civil War era. * * * In this State, the early cases dealt almost exclusively with the liability of municipal corporations for the torts of local law enforcement officers. Two theories were articulated for insulating the municipality from liability, each deriving from the maxim that "the King can do no wrong". The first was based on principles of agency—that policemen were not agents or servants of the municipality but "public servants of the state". * * * The second, a related rationale sometimes espoused alternatively with the agency theory, was that the functions of the police were "governmental" in nature, as opposed to "proprietary" or "corporate", and that in the performance of its "governmental" duties the municipality was not liable for the acts of its agents and officers. For half a century, in a variety of cases, "governmental" function stood as a bar to recovery. * * *

However, the need for an expanding concept of the law with respect to municipal tort liability soon became apparent. In Augustine v. Town of Brant, 249 N.Y. 198, 205, 163 N.E. 732, 734, this court noted that "[t]he modern tendency is against the rule of nonliability." And in Matter of Evans v. Berry, 262 N.Y. 61, 186 N.E. 203, we upheld an award by the New York City Board of Estimate for a bullet wound sustained by a bystander from a revolver fired by a policeman chasing robbers. Premised on a statutory provision empowering the city "to pay or compromise claims equitably payable * * * though not constituting obligations legally binding on it" * * * we held that the award was not an unconstitutional gift of public funds but "the legitimate recognition of an equitable claim" * * *. The decision was significant for its frank recognition of the injustice of the ancient rule that the innocent bystander, shot by stray bullets from the policemen pursing criminals or making arrests, must alone bear his loss.

Aided by two statutes, the destruction of immunity for police torts proceeded apace. One of these provided for municipal liability when a "municipally owned vehicle" caused injuries, if the operator were acting within the scope of his official duties. (Former Highway Law, § 282–g, L.1929, ch. 466; now General Municipal Law, Consol.Laws, c. 24, § 50–a.) The other was the notable section 8 of the Court of Claims Act (formerly § 12–a), which provided: "The state hereby waives its immunity from liability * * * and consents to have the same determined in accordance with the same rules of law as applied * * * against individuals or corporations". The gist of this waiver, although operative since 1929, was not fully apparent until this court decided the celebrated case of Bernardine v. City of New York, 294 N.Y. 361, 62 N.E.2d 604. *Bernardine* was an action in negligence to recover for injuries caused by a runaway police horse. We held the cause maintainable under either section 50–b of the General Municipal Law *or* section 8 of the Court of Claims Act, noting that the latter effected a waiver of immunity of the State *and* its civil divisions. (294 N.Y., at p. 365, 62 N.E.2d, at p. 605.)

There followed a host of cases recognizing municipal liability under the Court of Claims Act for the negligence of law enforcement officers in the line of duty. * * *

Similarly, under the Court of Claims Act, the courts found little difficulty in applying the principle of *respondeat superior* and imposing liability upon the State or its municipalities for the intentional torts of police officers committed in the performance of their official duties.[75] * * *

Thus, in the main it was the waiver of immunity in the Court of Claims Act that removed the bar that previously prevented actions based on police torts. * * * But as this court made clear in Weiss v. Fote (7 N.Y.2d 579, 200 N.Y.S.2d 409, 167 N.E.2d 63), although the State (and its civil divisions) has waived its immunity from liability arising from its sovereign character, the Court of Claims Act did not destroy all facets of governmental immunity (id., at pp. 586–587, 200 N.Y.S.2d at pp. 413–415, 167 N.E.2d at pp. 65–67). "It is proper and necessary to hold municipalities and the State liable for injuries arising out of the day-by-day operations of government * * * but to submit to a jury [or a court] the reasonableness of the lawfully authorized deliberations of executive bodies presents a different question." (Id., at p. 585, 200 N.Y.S.2d at p. 413, 167 N.E.2d at p. 65). That is akin to saying that discretionary determinations made by a co-ordinate branch of government must be immune from judicial scrutiny.

The question is, however, at what level a discretionary act becomes a political one, immune from judicial review. True, it may be difficult to define with precision what is a discretionary function for immunity purposes. But whatever the "line-drawing" difficulties in future cases, a workable definition will be one recognizing that "[m]uch of what is done by officers and employees of the government must remain beyond the range of judicial inquiry" (3 Davis, Administrative Law Treatise [1958], § 25.11, p. 484), and that obviously "it is not a tort for government to govern" (Dalehite v. United States, 346 U.S. 15, 57, 73 S.Ct. 956, 979, 97 L.Ed. 1427 [Jackson, J., dissenting]). But that it is not to say that all decisions by government officials involving the exercise of judgment should be immune from judicial review. Thus, semantical, purely literal, distinctions between ministerial and discretionary functions are not helpful. (Indeed, it is difficult to conceive of any official act that does not admit of some discretion in its performance.) Rather, the focus should be upon an assurance of judicial abstention in areas in which the responsibility for *basic policy decisions* has been committed to co-ordinate branches of government. Any wider review would place the courts in the unseemly position of passing upon the propriety of decisions expressly entrusted to a co-ordinate branch, a role and a function not consonant with the doctrine of separation of powers. Indeed, the very potentiality for such review might in the first instance affect the co-ordinate body's deliberative and decision making processes. (Jaffe, Judicial Control of Administrative Action, pp. 241–259; James, Tort Liability of Govern-

75. A municipality is not liable, however, for an act of positive and designed injury not done with a view to the municipality's service or for the purpose of executing its orders. (Burns v. City of New York, 6 A.D.2d 30, 32, 34–35, 36, 174 N.Y.S.2d 192, 195, 197–198, 199.) [Note from original renumbered.]

mental Units and Their Officers, 22 U.Chi.L.Rev. 610, 637–638, 640, 651; Note, The Discretionary Function Exception of the Federal Tort Claims Act, 66 Harv.L.Rev. 488, 498.)

So viewed, a rationale becomes apparent for the liability of the State and its civil divisions in the garden variety police tort case. * * * For example, with regard to the arrest situation where a policeman commits an intentional tort, doubtless it is true that in effecting the arrest the officer must exercise some discretion, perhaps a high degree. (Bivens v. Six Unknown Named Agents of Fed. Bur. of Narcotics, * * * [456 F.2d 1339, 1346 (2d Cir. 1972)]; Carter v. Carlson, 144 U.S.App.D.C. 388, 447 F.2d 358, 363, n. 9, revd. in part on other grounds sub nom. District of Columbia v. Carter, 409 U.S. 418, 93 S.Ct. 602, 34 L.Ed.2d 613.) But in reviewing the exercise of that discretion, basic policy decisions of a co-ordinate branch of government are not called into question, nor is the effective operation of a police department thereby impeded. Moreover, as to the latter, any threat posed thereto by the potentiality of damage suits would appear to be outweighed by the public interest in a tort remedy for police misconduct.

Were the case before us a simple police tort case, I would concur for reversal. But it is not. Looking to the substance of the claim for wrongful death, rather than the form of the pleading, however artfully drawn in terms of a conventional, intentional police tort * * *, the claimant is aggrieved by a basic discretionary policy decision—the manner and means of coping with the tragic uprising at Attica—made at the highest levels of the executive branch of government by officials entrusted with the responsibility for managing the correctional system. Involved is an area of quasi-legislative policy making in a co-ordinate branch of government sufficiently sensitive to warrant immunization from judicial review lest considerations of separation of powers be infringed and the executive's deliberative and decision making processes in crisis situations be invaded.

Neither McCrink v. City of New York, 296 N.Y. 99, 71 N.E.2d 419 nor Schuster v. City of New York, 5 N.Y.2d 75, 180 N.Y.S.2d 265, 154 N.E.2d 534, supra, undercuts this analysis. In *McCrink,* the city was held liable for the negligence of the police commissioner in failing to discharge an habitually drunken police officer who shot and killed a citizen. The power of dismissal called for an exercise of discretion which we held reviewable. But judicial review of that discretionary determination would not appear to pose a threat to the efficient administration of a police department, nor call into question the type of basic policy decisions warranting immunization. In the *Schuster* case, plaintiff's intestate supplied information to the Police Department of the City of New York leading to the arrest of a notorious criminal. Subsequent threats upon the informer's life were communicated to the police. Three weeks later, he was shot and killed. This court held that the public owes a *special* duty to use reasonable care to protect persons who have co-operated in the arrest or prosecution of criminals once it appears that they are in danger due to their collaboration. While it is true that a discretionary policy decision was involved—concerning the advisability and feasibility of providing security for the informer—and reviewed by this court, *Schuster* stands alone on its own facts and involves a special exception to traditional considerations of municipal tort liability. (See Riss v. City of New York, 22 N.Y.2d 579, 583, 293 N.Y.S.2d 897, 899, 240 N.E.2d 860, 861.)

For the reason stated, I would affirm the order of the Appellate Division.

FULD, C. J., and GABRIELLI and WACHTLER, JJ., concur with BURKE, J.

JASEN, J., dissents and votes to affirm in a separate opinion in which BREITEL and JONES, JJ., concur.

EVANS v. BOARD OF COUNTY COM'RS OF COUNTY OF EL PASO

Supreme Court of Colorado, 1971.
Colo., 482 P.2d 968.

GROVES, JUSTICE.

* * * The plaintiff alleged that while en route to jury duty she sustained a personal injury as a result of carelessness on the part of the county commissioners in permitting the concrete steps at the El Paso County Courthouse to deteriorate and to constitute a dangerous hazard. The court on motion dismissed the complaint under the doctrine of governmental immunity. We reverse and depart from that doctrine.

In opinions announced contemporaneously with this one, the majority of this court is rejecting the doctrines of governmental immunity of school districts (Flournoy v. School District No. 1 of Denver, Colo., 482 P.2d 966), and sovereign immunity of the State of Colorado (Proffitt v. State of Colorado, Colo., 482 P.2d 965). We use this opinion as the vehicle to express our views not only with respect to the instant matter but also as to the other two cases. * * *

One finds a certain sameness in many of the opinions of the appellate courts in the various states which, as here, overturn the doctrines of sovereign and governmental immunity, and in the dissents to those opinions which uphold the doctrines.[76] One finds frequently a

76. Stone v. Arizona Hwy. Comm., 93 Ariz. 384, 381 P.2d 107 (1963); Parish v. Pitts, 244 Ark. 1239, 429 S.W.2d 45 (1968); Muskopf v. Corning Hospital District, 55 Cal.2d 211, 11 Cal.Rptr. 89, 359 P.2d 457 (1961); Hargrove v. Town of Cocoa Beach, 96 So.2d 130 (Fla.1957); Smith v. Idaho, 93 Idaho 795, 473 P.2d 937 (1970); Molitor v. Kaneland Community Unit District, 18 Ill.2d 11, 163 N.E.2d 89 (1959); Haney v. City of Lexington, 386 S.W.2d 738 (Ky.1964); Spanel v. Mounds View School District, 264 Minn. 279, 118 N.W.2d 795 (1962); Holytz v. Milwaukee, 17 Wis.2d 26, 115 N.W.2d 618 (1962); and dissenting opinion of Roberts, J., in Smeltz v. Copeland, 440 Pa. 224, 269 A.2d 466 (1970). [From original, renumbered; other footnotes in original omitted.]

refutation of the proposition that the doctrines came from the common law. It is stated that the doctrine of sovereign immunity was not part of the common law, i. e., that there could be a petition of right under which the sovereign was in effect sued; or that the doctrine that the King (an individual) can do no wrong is not a proper basis for a declaration that a corporate state should have sovereign immunity; or that Russell v. The Men of Devon, 100 Eng.Rep. 359 (K.B.1788) (which so many times has been cited to show that the common law recognized the doctrine of governmental immunity) is no authority for application of the doctrine to political subdivisions, including municipal corporations, since *Men of Devon* was an action against the population of an unincorporated town.

It is possible that sovereign immunity as we know it stems in large part from the transformation in the English kingship, including augmented powers and divine and transcendental characteristics, which was occasioned by the Tudor monarchs, particularly Henry VIII, in pursuit of such ends as the split of the Church of England from the Church of Rome and the unity of temporal and spiritual life in England. The monarchical philosophies invented to solve the marital problems of Henry VIII are not sufficient justification for the denial of the right of recovery against the government in today's society. Assuming that there was sovereign immunity of the Kings of England, our forebears won the Revolutionary War to rid themselves of such sovereign prerogatives.

Frequently there has been mentioned the injustice and inequity—even absurdity—of having recovery for negligence against individuals and against firms for negligence of their employees, but no recovery against governmental units for the negligence of their employees. We see mentioned in the cases the incongruity of recovery against a municipality when it is engaging in a proprietary function for negligence of its employees, but no recovery if the employee—just as negligent—is engaged in a governmental function. It has been thought that the existence of legislatively authorized insurance for torts of governmental officers is inconsistent with continued insistence upon immunity. It has been repeatedly stated that the doctrines of sovereign and governmental immunity have been made by the courts and, when it appears that these rules were wrong when made and wrong currently, the courts should abolish the rule. Some courts and writers, while not wishing to state that the older decisions were wrong when decided, take the position that the intervening vicissitudes of society have necessitated a change in the law. We agree with these points of view. While there is a temptation to expound on them at length, they are so well—and ofttimes eloquently—discussed in many of the authorities to which attention has already been directed * * * that our comments will not be extended.

It can be stated frankly that this decision casting aside stare decisis results from a different philosophical outlook in the minds of the majority of the court today than was in the minds of the majority of the court as it pronounced and re-pronounced the doctrines through the past many years. Obviously, there is ample authority to continue application of the doctrine, and there is an abundance of authority to overturn it. A majority of us simply think that the doctrines are causing too great a degree of injustice.

In departing from these inequitable and untenable doctrines we are not in the vanguard. We have been preceded in varying degrees by the appellate courts of Arizona, Arkansas, California, Florida, Idaho, Illinois, Indiana, Kansas, Kentucky, Michigan, Minnesota, Nebraska, Nevada, New Jersey, Rhode Island and Wisconsin.[77]

The effect of this opinion and its two contemporaries is simply to undo what this court has done and leave the situation where it should have been at the beginning, or at least should be now: in the hands of the General Assembly of the State of Colorado. If the General Assembly wishes to restore sovereign immunity and governmental immunity in whole or in part, it has the authority to do so. * * * If the legislative arm of our government does not completely restore these immunities, then undoubtedly it will wish to place limitations upon the actions that may be brought against the state and its subdivisions. This, too, it has full authority to accomplish. * * *

We are not unmindful that to give the rule of this opinion immediate effect would constitute a disservice to governmental entities which will not be able to include in their budgets premiums for liability insurance coverage until a future time. Except as to the parties in this proceeding and in the two contemporaneous proceedings the ruling here shall be prospective only and shall be effective only as to causes of action arising after June 30, 1972. * * *

Another immunity, for charitable institutions, was formerly widespread. As liability insurance has become readily available the immunity has in recent years been increasingly repudiated, sometimes judicially, e. g., Abernathy v. Sisters of Saint Mary's, (Mo. banc.) 446 S.W.2d 599 (1969), and Colby v. Carney Hospital, 356 Mass. 527, 254 N.E.2d 407 (1969), and sometimes by statute, e. g., in Connecticut, C.G.S.A. § 52–557d: "The common law defense of charitable immunity is abolished and shall not constitute a valid defense to any cause of action. * * *" Also see Restatement of Torts, Second § 895 (Tentative Draft No. 18, 1972): "One engaged in a charitable, educational, religious or benevolent enterprise or activity is not for that reason immune from tort liability". Some states have modified the immunity partially; e. g., in Maryland the immunity has been abolished by statute for hospitals and "related" institutions, but liability is limited to the institution's insurance if it carries at least $100,000 coverage.

77. Citations omitted. For additional, later references see Campbell v. Indiana, 259 Ind. 55, 284 N.E.2d 733 (1972); Hicks v. State of New Mexico, 88 N.M. 588, 544 P.2d 1153 (1975); Merrill v. City of Manchester, 114 N.H. 722, 332 A.2d 378 (1975); Long v. City of Weirton, — W.Va. —, 214 S.E.2d 832 (1975); Nieting v. Blondell, — Minn. —, 235 N.W.2d 597 (1975); also cf. Brown v. Wichita State University, 217 Kan. 279, 540 P.2d 66 (1975).

Md.Ann.Code art. 43, § 556A; other charities remain immune, Howard v. Bishop Byrne Council Homes, Inc., 249 Md. 233, 238 A.2d 863 (1968).

Other immunities are sometimes recognized, based on relationships between the parties; these are discussed in Chapter 2, Section 4 infra.

FROM LEARNED HAND, HAVE THE BENCH AND BAR ANYTHING TO CONTRIBUTE TO THE TEACHING OF LAW?

24 Mich.L.Rev. 466 (1926).

(A paper read to an audience of law teachers):

"Since the advent of the Workmen's Compensation Acts, we have been getting used to the notion that in fixing liability for casual injuries, the old category of fault may not be universally applicable. It is of no concern to us why that idea became so firmly intrenched in our minds. It makes no difference whether it has a merely historical provenience from the criminal law, which canalized our instinctive demand for vengeance to prevent private warfare. We may agree that it still performs a high social service in securing a regard to the interests of others. But surely we have made a break away from it by reason of notions which are not yet finally worked out and whose limits are unknown. It is not very likely that so promising a start will be ignored by any class politically formidable enough to have its way, if a similar occasion arises for its application.

"Very well. You are going to be called upon to have opinions on the questions; no doubt you already have. What shall you say? The current theory is that when the conduct of an industry involves perils peculiar to itself and necessarily results in injuries which can be put down as inevitable incidents to its continuance, insurance of the individuals on whom fate chances to alight is a proper cost of production, and should be borne in the end by those who demand and enjoy the service. Does the same principle apply to persons crossing a railroad track? Does it apply to the rare cases where passengers are still not protected? Does it apply to motor-cars, those engines of death and mayhem? Does it apply to the carriage of goods at sea? When is it proper to insist that the individual shall bear his own insurance? When are perils peculiar to an industry? Is there any general principle about it at all, or is each case to be determined by weighing the relative position of the two opposed interests, the injured individual, and the persons enjoying the dangerous activity?

"Obviously we have to do with a matter which goes deep into the field of legal theory and social choice. You can hardly escape all reference to it if you propose an adequate treatment of modern torts. Yet in this I cannot think that your inquiries will be much helped by anything caught from bench or bar; if so, I should be much surprised.

We in practice have neither time nor capacity for that kind of thinking. We work along from step to step; we are apt to become irritated and we are sure to become confused when such questions are presented to us. When we speak at all, our solutions are usually as ineffectual as you would expect. Of course, I always except a few illustrious names, for now I am speaking only of general conditions. On this question you would, speaking largely, get no assistance at all. You must work it out for yourselves."

Chapter 2

THE ANATOMY OF FAULT

SECTION 1. STANDARDS OF CONDUCT

In this chapter attention is focused on "fault" as a basis of liability and particularly that type of fault known as "negligence." All the cases reprinted proceed on the assumption that negligence on the part of the defendant is a prerequisite of the liability sought to be imposed. Our concern is with what this thing, "negligence," is? The word is an ordinary one common in everyday language, but that is not to say that its connotations and meaning in various circumstances are clear or indisputable. Our search is not for dictionary definition but for function and operation. We wish to see who makes the determination, for example, judge or jury, how the decider is informed or limited for the performance of that function, what factors enter into the determination, and how the determination may be checked or reviewed. We may then inquire into the relation between liability so determined and "fault," and appraise the utility of this method of dealing with unintended physical harms as compared with alternative possibilities.

FREDERICK v. CITY OF DETROIT, DEP'T. OF STREET RAILWAYS

Supreme Court of Michigan, 1963.
370 Mich. 425, 121 N.W.2d 918.

SOURIS, JUSTICE (for affirmance). Plaintiff seeks reversal of an adverse jury verdict and denial of her subsequent motion for new trial on the ground that the trial judge instructed the jury improperly on the degree of care owed by a common carrier to its passengers. The case went to the jury on plaintiff's theory that defendant negligently permitted the rubber flooring of its bus to become worn and dirt to accumulate thereon and that it negligently omitted to provide a railing for the support of passengers alighting from its bus to the street. It was her claim that while leaving the bus she slipped on the worn, dirty flooring and, absent a railing which she could grasp for support, fell to the ground and suffered injuries.

The language of the instruction challenged by plaintiff is as follows:

> "Now, I will say this to you at this point; that the D.S.R. is not liable unless they were negligent. They are not an insurer. They are a common carrier. A common carrier has, in the vernacular, a higher degree,—owes a higher degree of care to its passengers than a person ordinarily owes to another person. Now, that definition is open to

question; because the actual definition reads that they have the duty,—anyone has the duty to exercise due care. That is the general test of negligence. Do you exercise due care? And, what do you mean by 'due care'? Due care means that amount of care that a reasonably prudent person would exercise under the circumstances then and there existing. But where the common carriers come into a different category, as it were, is the fact that it is more difficult for a common carrier to measure up to the standard of due care than it is for an ordinary person. The reason for that greater difficulty is precisely because he is a common carrier; he is carrying people for hire; and that makes him something less than an insurer, but someone who should exercise more care, in order to come up to the standard of due care, than an ordinary person. So, the Supreme Court in this state has sometimes referred,—and I personally believe erroneously,—to the fact that the common carrier owes a higher degree of care. I think that that is ultimately what it amounts to, but I think that is a very inaccurate way of stating it. They owe due care just like everybody else, but they have a harder time reaching that standard than the ordinary person does. * * * However, they do have that high standard to meet, that all public carriers have. They have to measure up to the test of due care owed by a bus company. * * *

"What is negligence? I will define it. Negligence is the failure to use that amount of care that a reasonably prudent person would use under the circumstances. * * * You must ask yourselves, did the D.S.R. use the usual amount of care in this case that a common carrier, a reasonable common carrier, would and should use. That is the standard you go by when you are determining liability * * *."

* * * [P]laintiff contends the trial judge erred in not clearly and concisely instructing the jury that she was owed a high degree of care, not just ordinary care, from the D.S.R. She claims that the instruction given, for all practical purposes, advised the jury that common carriers owe their passengers the same degree of care and diligence that others owe one another in the pursuit of their daily affairs. Without denying that the instruction can be read to impose upon carriers only a duty of due care as plaintiff contends, defendant maintains that it can, and should, be read as requiring no less than "a high degree of care," claimed by defendant to be a correct statement of its duty, by its reference to the greater difficulty a common carrier has in measuring up to a standard of due care than does an ordinary person and by its statement that a common carrier, because it carries people for hire, should exercise more care than an ordinary person. I agree with plaintiff that the instruction imposes upon defendant only the duty of due care, but that, in my view, is a correct statement of the law of this state, some of our prior opinions to the contrary notwithstanding and further notwithstanding the defend-

ant's apparent reluctance to urge upon us such interpretation of the law more favorable to it than that which it uncritically assumes to be the law.

We have recently expressed disapproval of contributory negligence instructions which expressly, or by fair inference, bar recovery by plaintiffs because of their own "slight negligence." * * * In those cases it was correctly conceded that the law imposed upon the plaintiffs no duty burden greater than ordinary or due care to avoid negligent injury to themselves and, hence, instructions which seemingly inferred the plaintiffs were barred from recovery for slight negligence or, put another way, for failure to exercise great care, were held erroneous. In this case of Frederick, however, while the parties assume that the law imposes upon the defendant a duty more stringent than due care,—a duty to exercise a high degree of care, or the highest degree of care for the safety of its fare paying passengers,—the law correctly stated requires no more than due care and, therefore, had the challenged instruction imposed a duty burden greater than due care, we would be obliged to strike it down.

* * * What an appellate court says in determining on review whether a trial record discloses factual compliance with the duty of reasonable care appropriately may be cast in terms of positive, comparative, or even superlative degrees, for then its task, as fact reviewer or determiner of fact sufficiency, is to apply the standard of reasonable care to the factual circumstances disclosed by the record,—circumstances which, because of the relation between the parties, because the instrument of harm is in the exclusive control of one party, or because the risk of physical harm is patently present, may reasonably require acts of great, greater or greatest diligence to meet the standard of care reasonable under such circumstances whereas other factual circumstances might reasonably require lesser acts of diligence. But its language thus used should not be, as it has been and is sought here to be, taken as a pronouncement of a different, more exacting, standard of care required of carriers nor should such appellate judicial language be considered appropriate for use in instructing juries. See 32 A.L.R. 1190. The common law standard of reasonable care is constant although it "may require an infinite variety of precautions, or acts of care, depending upon the circumstances, and * * * it is primarily for the jury to say just what precautions were appropriate to the danger apparent in the case at hand." 2 Harper and James, The Law of Torts, § 16.13.

That the standard of care imposed in this state upon common carriers of passengers is the common law standard of due care was authoritatively announced for a unanimous Court almost 90 years ago by Mr. Justice Campbell, speaking for himself and Chief Justice Graves and Justices Cooley and Christiancy, in Michigan Central Railroad Company v. Coleman, 28 Mich. 440.

* * * Justice Campbell * * * said that the care required in any business must be proportioned to its nature and risks, noting

that railroading involves great risks and, therefore, requires great caution. But the railroader's required caution which may be extraordinary when "compared with the care needed in a business involving no possible human risk," is no greater than that of a railroad company of ordinary care. As I read Justice Campbell's opinion it means to me that, absent statutory standards to the contrary, a carrier of passengers is obliged to use due care, but that the actions which conform with or violate that standard of due care will vary according to the circumstances in which care is required to be exercised and will depend *upon jury determination* of what the reasonably prudent person in similar circumstances would consider reasonably necessary for the safety of passengers. When trial judges describe the *standard of duty* in terms of "high care," "higher care," "highest care" or the like, they impinge upon the jury's function as finders of fact. * * *

* * * I would reaffirm the precepts of Michigan Central Railroad Company v. Coleman, supra, which endure in many of our sister states whose courts have carefully examined the carrier's liability at the common law and have resisted the now discredited theory that degrees of care or of negligence are recognized by the common law in such cases.[1] * * *

1. It is true that all other courts are not in agreement on the standard of liability of a common carrier to its passengers. Commentators and judges have written exhaustively on the subject, and on the more generalized, but directly related, topic of the common law's recognition or nonrecognition of degrees of care or of negligence. See Green, "High Care and Gross Negligence," 23 Ill.L.R. 4; Elliott, "Degrees of Negligence," 6 So.Cal.L.R. 91; 2 Harper and James, The Law of Torts, Chapter XVI, "The Nature of Negligence: Degrees of Care," § 16.13 et seq. For annotations of cases dealing with the liability of carriers to their passengers, see 96 A.L.R. 727, supplementing prior annotations; 117 A.L.R. 522; 126 A.L.R. 461; 9 A.L.R. 2d 938 and 74 A.L.R.2d 1336.

Also see Spence v. Three Rivers Builders & Masonry Supply, Inc., 353 Mich. 120, 128–131, 90 N.W.2d 873, 878 (1958): "Care does not increase or diminish by calling it names. We think the abstract concept of reasonable care is in itself quite difficult enough to grapple with and apply in our law without courts gratuitously conferring honorary degrees upon it. There is only one degree of care in the law, and that is the standard of care which may reasonably be required or expected under all the circumstances of a given situation. * * *"

A showing of "gross negligence" may also permit an employee to recover from his employer in tort in addition to workmen's compensation. See, e. g., Woolard v. Mobil Pipe Line Co., 479 F.2d 557 (5th Cir. 1973).

The principal case would require different degrees of vigilance under the single standard of due care, depending on the hazards in the circumstances. See, similarly, Goldstein v. Gontarz, — Mass. —, 309 N.E.2d 196 (1974) (single standard, but circumstances, i. e., backing truck, require special attention). It is sometimes unclear whether, under the common standard, different requirements of skill would apply to drivers who purport to possess special skill, such as professionals. See, e. g., Capital Raceway Promotions, Inc. v. Smith, 22 Md. App. 224, 237–240, 322 A.2d 238, 246 (1974): "Maryland has never established standards to be followed by classes of drivers on the basis of their experience with motor vehicles. Although the question has never been precisely asked or answered by our appellate courts, dicta strongly indicate that neither the inexperience of a novice nor the professional experience of a truck driver affects the standard of care required of a driver." Compare Restatement of Torts Second §§ 289(b), 298 and 299A; 2 F. Harper and F. James, The Law of Torts § 16.6 (1956: "* * * [I]f an actor has more than reasonable skill, he must probably exercise that which he has."

* * * [T]he common law duty of due care * * * may be defined simply as the duty to exercise such diligence as would be exercised in the circumstances by a reasonably prudent carrier. It then becomes the function of the jury to determine from the evidence what action, if any, should have been taken or omitted in order to measure up to the standard of a reasonably prudent carrier in the same circumstances. By instructing the jury that high care or the highest care is required of carriers, a court impinges upon the jury's obligation to determine the carrier's compliance with its duty of due care by consideration of the proofs of what a reasonably prudent carrier would have done in the circumstances disclosed by the evidence. It is for the jury to decide as a matter of fact, and not for the court to decide as a matter of law, whether a reasonably prudent carrier in similar circumstance would exercise greater or lesser diligence in performance of its duty of due care owed to passengers than would a reasonably prudent person engaged in other pursuits not involving the risks inherent in a common carrier's business.

Affirmed. Costs to defendant.

Orthodox doctrine today repudiates the notion of degrees of care, though in one fairly important field of automobile law (accidents to "guests") they have been resurrected by statute in many states, e. g., Clark v. Clark, — Va. —, 221 S.E.2d 123 (1976). See p. 459, infra. According to the great weight of American authority, however, a common carrier has been considered bound to exercise towards its passengers the "highest degree of care and forethought consistent with the practical operation of the carrier's business." Notes, 17 N.C.L.Rev. 453 (1937); 25 Va.L.Rev. 250 (1938). Prosser, Torts § 34 (4th ed. 1971).

Many questions arise as to when a person becomes or ceases to be a passenger so as to have the benefit of this rule. Cf. De Cicco v. Connecticut Co., 117 Conn. 677, 168 A. 879 (1933) (intending passenger); Zorotovich v. Washington Toll Bridge Authority, 80 Wash.

Suppose the driver is only a learner. Compare Lovelace v. Fossum et al. (No. 1), 24 D.L.R. (3d) 561, 564 (Brit. Col.Sup.Ct.1971): "The duty of the learner is to use the best skill he has and to obey the instructors to the limits of the understanding and ability he has acquired from his training", with Nettleship v. Weston [1971] 2 Q. B. 691, [1971] 3 W.L.R. 370 (C.A.) (per Lord Denning M.R.): "The learner driver may be doing his best, but his incompetent best is not enough. He must drive in as good a manner as a driver of skill, experience and care, who is sound in wind and limb, who makes no errors of judgment, has good eyesight and hearing, and is free from infirmity. * * * The reason is so that a person injured by a motor car should not be left to bear the loss on his own, but should be compensated out of the insurance fund. * * * [T]he injured person is only able to recover if the driver is liable in law. So the judges see to it that he is liable, unless he can prove care and skill of a high standard. * * * Thus we are, in this branch of the law, moving away from the concept: 'No liability without fault.' We are beginning to apply the test: 'On whom should the risk fall?' Morally the learner driver is not at fault; but legally she is liable to be because she is insured and the risk should fall on her."

2d 106, 491 P.2d 1295 (1971); Katamay v. Chicago Transit Authority, 53 Ill.2d 27, 32, 289 N.E.2d 623, 626 (1972); Suarez v. Trans World Airlines, Inc., 498 F.2d 612, 615–17 (7th Cir. 1974).

While it is not stated or explained in terms of degrees of care, a distinction is sometimes made in the extent of the duty owed to different classes of people. When such a distinction is applied as a matter of law by the court, it operates very much the way the ancient degrees of care did. Suppose, for example, the owner of a building has the elevator regularly inspected and repaired by the best firm of engineers in the locality, but that their inspector carelessly overlooks a defect which causes an accident although the elevator operator is using all possible care at the time. As to the owner's duty to use reasonable care with reference to the inspection, many courts would hold that (a) it was fulfilled towards employees by the owner's careful conduct in selecting the engineers and providing an adequate system for having inspection and repairs taken care of; (b) it was not fulfilled towards customers because as to them the owner could not "delegate" the duty but is bound to see that a careful inspection is actually made. See Sand Springs Park v. Shrader, 82 Okl. 244, 198 P. 983, 22 A.L.R. 593 (1921); Young v. Mason Stable Co., 193 N.Y. 188, 86 N.E. 15 (1908); Cohen v. Farmers' L. & T. Co., 70 Misc. 548, 551, 127 N.Y.S. 561, 564 (1911). Moreover, most courts agree that as to some classes of people (e. g., trespassers) no duty of inspection is owed at all. See ch. 3, infra.

Elevators can involve degrees of care in several ways. They may be considered common carriers, Springer v. Ford, 189 Ill. 430, 59 N.E. 953 (1910). In addition they are sometimes classified as "dangerous instrumentalities", in common with explosives and high-voltage electricity, for instance, as to which it is frequently said that a high degree of care is required, e. g., as to explosives, Kingsland v. Erie County Agricultural Society, 298 N.Y. 409, 84 N.E.2d 38 (1940); as to firearms, Reida v. Lund, 18 Cal.App.3d 698, 96 Cal.Rptr. 102, 165 (1971).

VAUGHAN v. MENLOVE

Common Pleas, 1837.
3 Bing.N.C. 468.

[Case. The declaration charged defendant with negligently maintaining a rick or stack of hay in such a way as to make spontaneous combustion unreasonably likely; that such combustion did take place and the fire consumed plaintiff's nearby cottages.]

At the trial it appeared that the rick in question had been made by the Defendant near the boundary of his own premises; that the hay was in such a state when put together, as to give rise to discussions on the probability of fire: that though there were conflicting opinions on the subject, yet during a period of five weeks, the Defendant was repeatedly warned of his peril; that his stock was insured; and that upon one occasion, being advised to take the rick down to avoid all danger, he said "he would chance it." He made an aperture or chimney through the rick; but in spite, or perhaps in consequence of this precaution, the rick at length burst into flames from the spontaneous heating of its materials; the flames communicated to the Defendant's barn and stables, and thence to the Plaintiff's cottages, which were entirely destroyed.

PATTESON, J. before whom the cause was tried, told the jury that the question for them to consider, was, whether the fire had been occasioned by gross negligence on the part of the Defendant; adding, that he was bound to proceed with such reasonable caution as a prudent man would have exercised under such circumstances.

A verdict having been found for the Plaintiff, a rule *nisi* for a new trial was obtained, on the ground that the jury should have been directed to consider, not, whether the Defendant had been guilty of gross negligence with reference to the standard of ordinary prudence, a standard too uncertain to afford any criterion; but whether he had acted *bona fide* to the best of his judgment; if he had, he ought not to be responsible for the misfortune of not possessing the highest order of intelligence. The action under such circumstances, was of the first impression. * * *

R. V. Richards, in support of the rule.

First, there was no duty imposed on the Defendant, as there is on carriers or other bailees, under an implied contract, to be responsible for the exercise of any given degree of prudence: the Defendant had a right to place his stack as near to the extremity of his own land as he pleased: * * * under that right, and subject to no contract, he can only be called on to act *bona fide* to the best of his judgment: if he has done that, it is a contradiction in terms, to inquire whether or not he has been guilty of gross negligence. At all events what would have been gross negligence ought to be estimated by the faculties of the individual, and not by those of other men. The measure of prudence varies so with the varying faculties of men, that it is impossible to say what is gross negligence with reference to the standard of what is called ordinary prudence. * * *

TINDAL, C. J. I agree that this is a case *primae impressionis*; but I feel no difficulty in applying to it the principles of law as laid down in other cases of a similar kind. Undoubtedly this is not a case of contract, such as a bailment or the like where the bailee is responsible in consequence of the remuneration he is to receive: but there is a rule of law which says you must so enjoy your own property as not to injure that of another; and according to that rule the Defendant is liable for the consequence of his own neglect: and though the Defendant did not himself light the fire, yet mediately, he is as much the cause of it as if he had himself put a candle to the rick; for it is well known that hay will ferment and take fire if it be not carefully stacked. It has been decided that if an occupier burns weeds so near the boundary of his own land that damage ensues to the property of his neighbour, he is liable to an action for the amount of injury done, unless the accident were occasioned by a sudden blast which he could not foresee: Turbervill v. Stamp (1 Salk. 13.). But put the case of a chemist making experiments with ingredients, singly innocent, but when combined, liable to ignite; if he leaves them together, and injury is thereby occasioned to the property of his neighbour, can any one doubt that an action on the case would lie?

It is contended, however, that the learned Judge was wrong in leaving this to the jury as a case of gross negligence, and that the question of negligence was so mixed up with reference to what would be the conduct of a man of ordinary prudence that the jury might have thought the latter the rule by which they were to decide; that such a rule would be too uncertain to act upon; and that the question ought to have been whether the Defendant had acted *honestly* and *bona fide* to the best of his own judgment. That, however, would leave so vague a line as to afford no rule at all, the degree of judgment belonging to each individual being infinitely various: and though it has been urged that the care which a prudent man would take, is not an intelligible proposition as a rule of law, yet such has always been the rule adopted in cases of bailment, as laid down in Coggs v. Bernard (2 Ld.Raym. 909.). Though in some cases a greater degree of care is exacted than in others, yet in "the second sort of bailment, viz. *commodatum* or lending *gratis*, the borrower is bound to the strictest care and diligence to keep the goods so as to restore them back again to the lender; because the bailee has a benefit by the use of them, so as if the bailee be guilty of the least neglect he will be answerable; as if a man should lend another a horse to go westward, or for a month; if the bailee put this horse in his stable, and he were stolen from thence, the bailee shall not be answerable for him: but if he or his servant leave the house or stable doors open, and the thieves take the opportunity of that, and steal the horse, he will be chargeable, because the neglect gave the thieves the occasion to steal the horse." The case taken by a prudent man has always been the rule laid down; and as to the supposed difficulty of applying it, a jury has always been able to say, whether, taking that rule as their guide, there has been negligence on the occasion in question.

Instead, therefore, of saying that the liability for the negligence should be co-extensive with the judgment of each individual, which would be as variable as the length of the foot of each individual, we ought rather to adhere to the rule which requires in all cases a regard to caution such as a man of ordinary prudence would observe. That was in substance the criterion presented to the jury in this case, and therefore the present rule must be discharged. * * * [2]

2. In Worthington v. Mencer, 96 Ala. 310, 11 So. 72, 17 L.R.A. 407 (1891), the court said that, if plaintiff was merely a person of dull mind who could nevertheless earn his living and needed no guardian, "he is chargeable with the same degree of care for his personal safety as one of higher intellect, as any attempt to frame and adapt varying rules of responsibility to varying degrees of intelligence would necessarily involve confusion and uncertainty

HOVER v. BARKHOOF

Court of Appeals of New York, 1870.
44 N.Y. 113.

* * * This action is for the recovery of damages sustained by the plaintiff, by the falling of a bridge over a stream in the town of Florida, in the county of Montgomery, which was alleged to be in an unsafe condition through the neglect of the defendants, who were commissioners of highways of that town, whereby the horses, wagon and harness of the plaintiff were injured. * * *

The jury found for the plaintiff $200 damages. On appeal to the General Term the judgment entered on this verdict was affirmed, and the defendants have appealed therefrom to the Court of Appeals.

LEONARD, C. * * * During the trial one of the defendants who had examined the bridge and contracted for repairs, being a witness for the defense, was asked, on their behalf, if he believed the defendants had made use of all of the means necessary to the safety of the bridge? The question was excluded, and the defendants excepted.

Their belief in the sufficiency of the means used, or of the structure, was of no consequence or materiality. The alleged neglect was a fact to be proven. The belief of the defendants as to the non-existence of the fact, did not tend to show how, in truth, the fact was or might be. The belief of the defendants, while it proved nothing as to the fact, might tend to mislead the mind of the jury. If the inquiry was for the purpose of proving that the defendants were not acting in bad faith or with malice, it was equally immaterial; the question was negligence or no negligence, as a fact. Mistaken belief in the soundness of the timbers, or the sufficiency of the repairs, did not tend to any conclusion as to the fact. The case of Seymour v. Wilson, 14 N.Y. 567, has no application. The rule there adopted should be confined to the class of cases in which it was introduced.

There appears to be no error, and the judgment should be affirmed with costs.[3]

in the law." Cf. Holmes, The Common Law, 108 (1881). In Georgia Cotton Oil Co. v. Jackson, 112 Ga. 620, 37 S. E. 873 (1901), an instruction charging contributory negligence to plaintiff if the defect was so obvious that "a person of his intelligence and understanding could perceive it," was held erroneous. Cf. Weirs v. Jones County, 86 Iowa 625, 53 N.W. 321, 17 L.R.A. 445 (1892) (plaintiff illiterate).

3. In Orr v. Bradley, 126 Mo.App. 146, 103 S.W. 1149 (1907), the collapse of a wall caused the damage in suit. Defendant showed that "competent persons, including city inspectors and his architect, considered the wall to be safe and that he, being a civil engineer himself, believed it to be safe." But plaintiff had a verdict and the trial court was upheld in refusing to require a defendant's verdict if the jury believed this evidence. "That was not a proper way to dispose of the question whether defendant was negligent. The question was one for the jury who were to judge of his conduct as measured by that of an ordinarily prudent man in the same circumstances."

In other tort situations, as the subsequent materials indicate, defendant's belief may be relevant and important.

MEMORIAL HOSPITAL OF SOUTH BEND, INC. v. SCOTT

Supreme Court of Indiana, 1973.
261 Ind. 27, 300 N.E.2d 50.

HUNTER, JUSTICE. The instant case involves a negligence action brought against a hospital for injuries sustained by a patient. Plaintiff Scott was severely burned by hot water (140° F.) while he was using a hospital toilet. Plaintiff activated a bed pan flusher hot water knob (shoulder level) which was located in proximity to the toilet flusher (small of back level) and was inundated by the scalding water. The facts set out below are those found by the trial court in support of his granting plaintiff's motion to correct error:

> "* * * [T]he patient was suffering from multiple sclerosis, that his known and recorded symptoms were lack of muscular co-ordination, difficiulty [sic] with vision, weakness in right arm and leg and in grip of right hand, occasional difficulty in walking and in distinguishing shapes. The plaintiff had hand trembles or intention tremors, vertical nystagumus or involuntary oscillatory eyeball movements, that sometimes his eyes would not focus and he would have some difficulty maintaining his balance. That on the morning of the accident he was subject to a spinal puncture and he was given an injection of thorazine. That the internist was of the opinion that he himself would not drive an automobile for four hours after being injected with thorazine. That a normal consequence of spinal puncture and thorazine injection was a headache. That the plaintiff, appellee, at sometime more than hour after the thorazine injection expressed the desire to use the bathroom. He was never instructed or warned about the bed pan flusher appliance mounted above and behind the toilet stool. That he remembers attempting to flush the toilet while he remained seated because he wasn't sure he was completed with his toilet function. He remembered touching a knob, and then he remembers the hot water. * * *"

In weighing the conflicting evidence, the trial court has concluded that the plaintiff, Scott, was not contributorily negligent. The reasons for this conclusion were based upon Scott's physical disabilities and the fact he had no knowledge of the bed pan flushing device and that he had no appreciation or awareness of a danger existing behind the toilet. The Court of Appeals decided as a matter of law that the reasons for granting a new trial were incorrect. The Court of Appeals held that the trial court did not apply the ordinary reasonable man test and, therefore, an inaccurate rule of law was applied in the court below. As enunciated by the Court of Appeals:

> "Therefore, assuming that Scott did not have actual knowledge of the danger, *if it were shown by Memorial Hospital that a reasonable and prudent person in like or similar*

> *circumstances would have known and appreciated the danger, then Scott still could have been guilty of contributory negligence.* * * *" 290 N.E.2d at 84–85. (Emphasis added.)

However, an examination of the record discloses that the trial court was cognizant of the proper test to be applied on the issue of contributory negligence. The trial court tendered the following instructions to the jury on this issue:

> "Contributory negligence is the failure of a plaintiff to use reasonable care to avoid injury to himself which failure is a proximate cause of the injuries for which he seeks to recover.
>
> "You are instructed that in determining ordinary care of Defendants as to Plaintiff in this case, you may consider the physical and mental ailments of Plaintiff which may have affected his ability to look after his own safety.
>
> "Similarly, you may consider such physical and mental ailments of Plaintiff in determining his ordinary care on the issue of contributory negligence." * * *

In our opinion the trial court did apply the correct standard when granting the new trial. Further, the Court of Appeals has made an incomplete statement of the law of contributory negligence.

The general rule on the issue of the plaintiff's contributory negligence is that the plaintiff must exercise that degree of care that an ordinary reasonable man would exercise in like or similar circumstances. * * * Contributory negligence is conduct on the part of the plaintiff, contributing as a legal cause to the harm he has suffered, *which falls below the standard to which he is required to conform for his own protection.* Restatement 2d of Torts § 463. Thus, the critical scope of inquiry here is an examination of the standard of care which Scott was required to exhibit. Lack of reasonable care is the factor upon which the presence or absence of negligence depends. * * * We hold that a departure from the general rule is required where the plaintiff is suffering from physical infirmities which impair his ability to function as an "ordinary reasonable man." The proper test to be applied in such cases is the test of a reasonable man *under the same disabilities and infirmities* in like circumstances. On the issue of contributory negligence, mental condition and/or physical incapacities are factors to be considered. * * * [4]

4. There is abundant case law authority supporting the proposition that physical infirmities are factors to be considered on the issue of contributory negligence: Millsaps v. Brogdon (1911), 97 Ark. 469, 134 S.W. 632 (cripple); Armstrong v. Day (1930), 103 Cal.App. 465, 284 P. 1083 (blind in one eye); Tomey v. Dyson (1946), 76 Cal.App.2d 212, 172 P.2d 739 (impaired hearing); Kerin v. Baccei (1939), 125 Conn. 335, 5 A.2d 876 (defective vision); Crawley v. Jermain (1920), 218 Ill.App. 51 (defective vision and hearing); Deshazer v. Cheatham (1930), 233 Ky. 59, 24 S.W.2d 936 (old age); Wilson v. Freeman (1930), 271 Mass. 438, 171 N.E. 469 (deaf); Heger v. Meissner (1954), 340

Dean Prosser has treated negligence with authoritative analysis and lends this discussion:

"As to his physical characteristics, the reasonable man may be said to be identical with the actor. The man who is blind or deaf, or lame, or is otherwise physically disabled, is entitled to live in the world and to have allowance made by others for his disability, and he cannot be required to do the impossible by conforming to physical standards which he cannot met [sic]. Similar allowance has been made for the weaknesses of age and sex. At the same time, the conduct of the handicapped individual must be reasonable in the light of his knowledge of his infirmity, which is treated merely as one of the circumstances under which he acts. A blind man may be negligent in going into a place of known danger, just as one who knows that he is subject to epileptic fits, or is about to fall asleep, may be negligent in driving a car. It is sometimes said that a blind man must use a greater degree of care than one who can see; but it is now generally agreed that as a fixed rule this is inaccurate, and that the correct statement is merely that he must take the precautions, be they more or less, which the ordinary reasonable man would take if he were blind. In theory the standard remains the same, but it is sufficiently flexible to take his physical defects into account." Prosser, Law of Torts, pp. 151–152 (4th ed., 1971).

As stated by the Florida Court of Appeals:

"* * *

"In determining whether a particular individual has been guilty of contributory negligence at a particular time, it is nessary to consider (1) the characteristics of that individual —age, intelligence, experience, knowledge, physical condition, etc.—which would affect his ability to detect dangerous conditions or appreciate the degree of hazards involved in conditions actually observed; (2) the physical facts—the extent to which the particular hazard is noticeable and the degree of alertness to avoid such a hazard reasonably called for by surrounding circumstances; and (3) the action taking place—the incidents of movement, sound and physical activities of the individual charged with contributory negligence and other persons and objects, animate and inanimate. * * *

"We think the rule is this: It is the duty of every person to exercise his individual faculties, physical and mental, to detect and avoid hazards to that degree that an ordinary and reasonable person having the same physical and mental abilities would exercise such faculties under the same circum-

Mich. 586, 66 N.W.2d 220 (cripple); Mackie v. McGraw (1948), 183 Or. 204, 191 P.2d 403 (defective hearing); Brunner v. John (1954), 45 Wash.2d 341, 274 P.2d 581 (cripple). [From original, renumbered.]

stances, taking into account the time, place, physical surroundings, and activities being pursued." Isenberg v. Ortona Park Recreational Center, Inc. (Fla.App.1964), 160 So.2d 132, 134–136.

And put another way by the Supreme Court of Errors of Connecticut:

> "'While the standard of care to be used [reasonable care] is an external standard taking no account of the personal equation of the man concerned, yet the amount of care required depends upon the circumstances of the particular case, and if a person suffers from a physical disability increasing the risk of harm to him that is among the circumstances to be considered.' Muse v. Page, 125 Conn. 219, 223, 4 A.2d 329, 331. Thus reasonable care in the case of one lacking normal co-ordination or obliged to use crutches is that amount of care which an ordinarily prudent person, similarly lacking in co-ordination or required to use crutches, would exercise under the same circumstances." Goodman v. Norwalk Jewish Center, Inc. (1958), 145 Conn. 146, 139 A.2d 812, 815.

In a California negligence case, the trial court had instructed the jury that one "whose faculties are impaired is required to use a greater amount of caution than one who does not suffer from any such disability." On appeal, the California Court of Appeals affirmed the granting of a new trial and said:

> "Instruction (d), supra, is not a correct statement of the law as to the quantum of care required of one whose faculties are impaired. Such person is bound to use that care which a person of ordinary prudence with faculties so impaired would use in the same circumstances. * * * This instruction, as requested by defendants and as given by the court, imposed upon the plaintiff a quantum of care which was not required of her. * * * Taken together, the trial court, upon the hearing of the motion for new trial, was justified in arriving at the conclusion that error in the instructions was prejudical to the plaintiff's case." Conjorsky v. Murray (1955), 135 Cal.App.2d 478, 287 P.2d 505, 508. * * *

As the rule is stated in C.J.S.:

> "A person laboring under any physical disability increasing his liability to injury must nevertheless exercise ordinary care to avoid injury, and if he fails to exercise that degree of care, and such failure contributes proximately to cause his injury, he is guilty of contributory negligence. Such a person is not required to exercise a higher degree of care to that end than is required of a person under no disability; ordinary care is all that is required.
>
> "However, in determining whether such a person exercised ordinary care for his own safety, his disability is a circum-

stance to be considered. Thus, while it has been said that ordinary care is such care as an ordinarily prudent person with the same disability would exercise under the same or similar circumstances, it has also been held that it may be incumbent on one with a physical disability to put forth a greater degree of effort than would otherwise be necessary in order to attain that standard of care which is required of everyone." C.J.S. Negligence § 142.

The Court of Appeals has extracted the general rule as to contributory negligence, but has not taken into account the facts and circumstances of the instant case. The correct test to be applied in determining Scott's standard of care is the test of a reasonably prudent man suffering from the same maladies and disabilities under like circumstances as those here. * * * [5]

KELLER v. DELONG

Supreme Court of New Hampshire, 1967.
108 N.H. 212, 231 A.2d 633.

DUNCAN, JUSTICE. The plaintiff's intestate, a registered nurse who was twenty-eight years of age, died in consequence of injuries suffered at Tyngsboro, Massachusetts at approximately 11:40 P.M. on April 14, 1963, when her automobile, operated by the defendant, collided with a utility pole at the side of the highway. She and the defendant had left Laconia late in the afternoon of the same day. Until shortly before the accident, the decedent had done the driving. A stop had been made at Bow, at which time both parties had some beer to drink. Thereafter they had sandwiches at a restaurant in Concord, and then proceeded toward Lowell, Massachusetts with the decedent at the wheel. At some place near the Massachusetts line, the defendant took the wheel at the decedent's request, and the decedent went to sleep. The accident occurred a few miles from where the defendant commenced to drive.

The Trial Court found "that the sole cause of the accident was the fact that the defendant dozed off to sleep and did not awaken in time to avoid collision with the pole." It further found: "While the defendant had been drinking, the evidence does not convince me that he was unable properly to control the vehicle while awake or that he had difficulty in doing so before dozing off. Neither is it found that after he took the wheel he had any warning that he was going to fall asleep." The Court granted the defendant's request as follows: "After taking over the wheel, Carl DeLong had no advance warning that he was about to doze, but suddenly and unexpectedly

5. Some of the authorities quoted refer to both physical and mental disabilities, while others refer only to physical disabilities. Is there a consistent basis for the difference, or do the former merely reject Vaughan v. Menlove? See, generally, F. Harper and F. James, The Law of Torts §§ 16.2, 16.7 and 16.8 (at notes 15 et seq.) (1956 and Supp.1968); compare Restatement of Torts Second §§ 283B and 464.

dozed at the time of the occurrence of the accident." After reasoning that dozing as a passenger "does not mean that a person cannot keep awake when charged with the responsibility of driving," the Trial Court was "not convinced * * * that in taking over the wheel * * * under all the circumstances was anything different than the ordinary man of average prudence would have done and I therefore do not find the defendant was negligent in doing so."

Under principles which receive general recognition an operator of a motor vehicle who permits himself to fall asleep while driving is guilty of ordinary negligence if he has continued to drive without taking reasonable precautions against sleeping after premonitory symptoms of drowsiness or fatigue. * * *

We are of the opinion that in the case before us, the Trial Court erred in the application of the law to the evidence. The error is best illustrated by the finding made at the defendant's request: "After taking over the wheel, Carl DeLong had no advance warning that he was about to doze, but suddenly and unexpectedly dozed at the time of occurrence of the accident." The effect of this finding, and of the like finding made by the Court of its own motion, was to isolate selected portions of the evidence in disregard of the evidence upon which the Court found that the defendant had dozed on a "couple of occasions" before he undertook to drive, and was "drowsy just before taking the wheel."

This evidence disclosed ample warning to the defendant that he might fall asleep. It was not disputed that when he took the wheel, the windows of the automobile were closed, and the heater turned on. There was no evidence that he took any precaution to arouse himself before proceeding, whether by walking around the vehicle, opening windows, or reducing the heat. * * * Under these circumstances, a finding that "after taking over the wheel" the defendant had "suddenly and unexpectedly dozed at the time of * * * the accident" cannot be sustained. Such an occurrence could not be unexpected in the absence of precaution to prevent it. * * * The plaintiff was entitled to have the defendant's care determined upon a basis of all of the evidence, rather than just what occurred after he took the wheel. * * * The verdict for the defendant must therefore be set aside. * * * [6]

6. Also see Lutzkovitz v. Murray, 339 A.2d 64 (Del.1975); consider Price v. Glosson Motor Lines, Inc., 509 F.2d 1033 (4th Cir. 1975).

DELLWO v. PEARSON

Supreme Court of Minnesota, 1961.
259 Minn. 452, 107 N.W.2d 859.

LOEVINGER, JUSTICE.

This case arises out of a personal injury to Jeanette E. Dellwo, one of the plaintiffs. She and her husband, the other plaintiff, were fishing on one of Minnesota's numerous and beautiful lakes by trolling at a low speed with about 40 to 50 feet of line trailing behind the boat. Defendant, a 12-year-old boy, operating a boat with an outboard motor, crossed behind plaintiffs' boat. Just at this time Mrs. Dellwo felt a jerk on her line which suddenly was pulled out very rapidly. The line was knotted to the spool of the reel so that when it had run out the fishing rod was pulled downward, the reel hit the side of the boat, the reel came apart, and part of it flew through the lens of Mrs. Dellwo's glasses and injured her eye. Both parties then proceeded to a dock where inspection of defendant's motor disclosed 2 to 3 feet of fishing line wound about the propeller.

The case was fully tried to the court and jury and submitted to the jury upon instructions which, in so far as relevant here, instructed the jury that: (1) In considering the matter of negligence the duty to which defendant is held is modified because he is a child, a child not being held to the same standard of conduct as an adult and being required to exercise only that degree of care which ordinarily is exercised by children of like age, mental capacity and experience under the same or similar circumstances * * *.

A more important point involves the instruction that defendant was to be judged by the standard of care of a child of similar age rather than of a reasonable man. There is no doubt that the instruction given substantially reflects the language of numerous decisions in this and other courts. However, the great majority of these cases involve the issue of contributory negligence and the standard of care that may properly be required of a child in protecting himself against some hazard. The standard of care stated is proper and appropriate for such situations.

However, this court has previously recognized that there may be a difference between the standard of care that is required of a child in protecting himself against hazards and the standard that may be applicable when his activities expose others to hazards. Certainly in the circumstances of modern life, where vehicles moved by powerful motors are readily available and frequently operated by immature individuals, we should be skeptical of a rule that would allow motor vehicles to be operated to the hazard of the public with less than the normal minimum degree of care and competence.

To give legal sanction to the operation of automobiles by teenagers with less than ordinary care for the safety of others is impractical today, to say the least. We may take judicial notice of the hazards of automobile traffic, the frequency of accidents, the often catastrophic results of accidents, and the fact that immature individuals are no less prone to accidents than adults. While minors are entitled to be judged by standards commensurate with age, experience, and wisdom when engaged in activities appropriate to their age, experience, and wisdom, it would be unfair to the public to permit a minor in the operation of a motor vehicle to observe any other standards of care and conduct than those expected of all others. A person observing children at play with toys, throwing balls, operating tricycles or velocipedes, or engaged in other childhood activities may anticipate conduct that does not reach an adult standard of care or prudence. However, one cannot know whether the operator of an approaching automobile, airplane, or powerboat is a minor or an adult, and usually cannot protect himself against youthful imprudence even if warned. Accordingly, we hold that in the operation of an automobile, airplane, or powerboat, a minor is to be held to the same standard of care as an adult.

Undoubtedly there are problems attendant upon such a view. However, there are problems in any rule that may be adopted applicable to this matter. They will have to be solved as they may present themselves in the setting of future cases. The latest tentative revision of the Restatement of Torts proposes an even broader rule that would hold a child to adult standards whenever he engages "in an activity which is normally undertaken only by adults, and for which adult qualifications are required." [7] However, it is unnecessary to this case to adopt a rule in such broad form, and, therefore, we expressly leave open the question whether or not that rule should be adopted in this state. For the present it is sufficient to say that no reasonable grounds for differentiating between automobiles, airplanes, and powerboats appears, and that a rule requiring a single standard of care in the operation of such vehicles, regardless of the age of the operator, appears to us to be required by the circumstances of contemporary life.

Reversed and remanded for a new trial.

7. Restatement, Torts, Tentative Draft No. 4, § 238A, comment c. This is quoted with apparent approval in Wittmeier v. Post, S.D., 105 N.W.2d 65. [From original, renumbered. Other notes in original omitted]. See, similarly, Daniels v. Evans, 107 N.H. 407, 224 A.2d 63 (1966). The concept of adult activities has been extended beyond the operation of motor vehicles; e. g., as to the game of golf as played by an 11-year-old, see Neumann v. Shlansky, 58 Misc.2d 128, 294 N.Y.S. 2d 628 (Westchester County Ct.1968); as to deerhunting (by a 17-year-old), on the other hand, compare Purtle v. Shelton, 251 Ark. 519, 474 S.W.2d 123, 47 A.L.R.3d 609 (1971).

It is commonly held that children of very tender years are incapable of negligence, e. g., DeLuca v. Bowden, 42 Ohio St.2d 392, 329 N.E.2d 109 (1975) (children under 7); Clark v. Circus-Circus, Inc., 525 F.2d 1328 (9th Cir. 1975); also see Alabama Power Co. v. Taylor, 293 Ala. 484, 306 So.2d 236 (1975) (evidentiary requirements as to capacity of children between ages of 7 and 14).

TERRANELLA v. UNION BLDG. & CONST. CO.

Supreme Court of New Jersey, 1949.
3 N.J. 443, 70 A.2d 753.

WACHENFELD, J. Appellant's eleven-year-old son was fatally injured while playing in a public playground in the City of Passaic. The City had entered into a contract with the respondent Union Building and Construction Co. for the installation of a storm sewer crossing the playground. About a week prior to the accident the construction company had placed on the playground fourteen concrete pipes each four feet long, five feet in diameter and weighing 5180 pounds. The pipes were not tied or secured and no watchman was placed over them.

During the week children in the playground had been playing with the pipes and rolling them around upon the ground. On the afternoon of the accident about eight boys between the ages of nine and twelve were rolling the pipes. The decedent fell between two pipes and sustained the fatal injuries. His father brought this action as administrator *ad prosequendum* against the two respondents and the Passaic Board of Education.

At the conclusion of the hearing, the trial court directed a verdict for all three defendants. [The court upheld the direction of the verdict for the city, and the appeal was discontinued against the Board of Education.]

The trial court predicated its direction of a verdict in favor of the construction company entirely upon the case of Friedman v. Snare & Triest Co., 71 N.J.L. 605, 61 A. 401, 403, 70 L.R.A. 147, 108 Am.St.Rep. 764, 2 Ann.Cas. 497 (E. & A.1905). There, however, the decision rested upon certain facts materially at variance with the facts in this case. The court found the girders which injured the plaintiff's child were stored on private property subject to a public easement for use as a sidewalk. The evidence showed the child was injured not while exercising the right of the easement for passage but in the course of playing about or resting upon the piled girders. This, the court found, exceeded the invitation implied in the easement and placed the child in the status of a licensee or trespasser. In this connection, the court said: "And further, an individual member of the public, if specially damnified by the nuisance while in the exercise of his rights in the street, may maintain a private action. But this refers only to parties injured while using the street as a street, and not to those whose injuries arise from their attempted use of the obstructing materials for their own purposes, whether of pleasure, convenience, or profit. For the building materials themselves do not in any sense become public property by being allowed to remain in the street. And neither a traveler, nor an idler, nor even a playful child, can gain rights against the landowner, or against his agent who stands in his rights, by using such building materials as a resting place or playground. In the absence of circumstances denoting invitation, one thus using the private property of another for his own purposes may be either a licensee or a mere trespasser, depending upon circumstances."

In the case presently before us we are concerned with the death of a child who, together with a group of other children, was using a restricted area specifically designated as a place for play. Their occupation and use of the premises was in the natural course of events and was or should have been anticipated and expected. The land was dedicated and posted as a playground, expressing an invitation to the children of the neighborhood to use it for that purpose.

Those making use of the grounds and equipment there provided were invitees acting within the precise scope and intent of the invitation. As such they were owed the duty of reasonable care. An owner of premises who by invitation, express or implied, induces a person to come upon the premises is under a duty to exercise ordinary care to render the premises safe for the purposes embraced in the invitation. Phillips v. Library Co., 55 N.J.L. 307, 27 A. 478 (E. & A.1893); Nolan v. Bridgeton & Millville Traction Co., 74 N.J.L. 559, 65 A. 992 (E. & A. 1907); Sefler v. Vanderbeek & Sons, 88 N.J.L. 636, 96 A. 1009 (E. & A.1916). This duty rests also upon an independent contractor employed by the owner of the lands. Connick v. John F. Craig, Inc., 107 N.J.L. 375, 153 A. 631 (E. & A.1931).

True, the pipes stored in the playground were not intended to be part of the facilities provided for play, but this does not, in the exercise of reasonable care, impose upon the immature children who are the ordinary users of the playground the duty of discriminating between the equipment which is intended for their use and enjoyment and that which, in an area devoted to their pleasure, is placed within their easy reach and access but is intended for other purposes. No sign, guard or warning was given or provided to assist them in differentiating between what was installed for their play and amusement and what was to be avoided under penalty of such dire consequences as here resulted.

To determine what constitutes reasonable care in any situation requires the consideration of all the surrounding facts and circumstances.

"* * * the rationale of the rule of due care is the reasonable exercise of 'the foresight for harm.'" Beck v. Hines, 95 N.J.L. 158, 112 A. 332, 333 (E. & A.1920).

In Niles v. Phillips Express Co., 118 N.J.L. 455, 193 A. 183, 186 (E. & A.1937), the court said: "There was laid upon him the common-law obligation to conform to the standard of conduct of a reasonable man so circumstanced. It is of the very nature of the term 'reasonable care' that it has a relative significance. It does not lend itself to a practical definition that will absolutely label the conduct under scrutiny in the individual case. Considered in the abstract, it is lacking in definitive quality. The common-law concept of negligence has relation to the facts and concomitant circumstances."

Where, as here, the obligation exists primarily in relation to groups of young children, that in itself is one of the concomitant circumstances to be weighed.

"No doubt, where a duty exists to take care with respect to the safety of children of tender years, their very age must be taken into account, so that what might be reasonable care with respect to the safety of adults, who are capable to some extent of looking out for themselves, might not be reasonable care with respect to children." Friedman v. Snare & Triest Co., supra.

A very similar situation occurred in Gottesman v. Cleveland, 142 Ohio St. 410, 52 N.E.2d 644, 645 (Sup.Ct.1944), where the court said: "This is not a case of attractive nuisance existing upon private property. The conduit pipes were in a park dedicated to the public and, so far as the duty of the defendant was concerned, the children playing there were in the position of all persons who visited the park for their advantage or pleasure. The unblocked pipes being attractive to the children and lacking anchorage became a dangerous plaything upon public property. Under these circumstances the issue of nuisance was property submitted to the jury."

Despite the size and weight of the pipes, they could be rolled about by children with relative ease and therefore became potentially dangerous instruments when left unguarded and unsecured in a public playground to be subjected to whatever treatment or use the minds and energies of curious and naturally mischievous youngsters could devise. Under these circumstances, whether the construction company exercised reasonable care was a question that should have been submitted to the jury for its determination.

The judgment is affirmed as to the respondent City of Passaic, but as to the respondent Union Building and Construction Co., it is reversed and a new trial ordered.[8]

GOULD v. SLATER WOOLEN COMPANY

Supreme Judicial Court of Massachusetts, 1888.
147 Mass. 315, 17 N.E. 531.

Tort to recover for personal injuries alleged to have been caused by the negligent use of poisonous dyes by the defendant in making woolen cloths purchased and used by the plaintiff, a manufacturer of caps. Writ dated September 22, 1884.

At the trial in the Superior Court, before Blodgett, J., the plaintiff's evidence tended to show that she was poisoned by using, in the ordinary course of her business, cloths manufactured by the defendant, and which she bought of its agent.

Dr. Charles Harrington, assistant chemist in the Harvard Medical School, called by the plaintiff as an expert, testified that he had made an analysis of the cloth in question, and had found in it quite a large amount of chrome compounds; that the chrome was in the cloth

8. Also cf. Neal v. Shiels, Inc., 166 Conn. 3, 347 A.2d 102 (1974); Brenna v. Melvie, —— Minn. ——, 231 N.W.2d 306 (1975) and Korbelik v. Johnson, 193 Neb. 356, 227 N.W.2d 21 (1975).

in an insoluble form, and that it would be hard to say what the compound was; that the cloth was mordanted by bichromate of potash in solution, and then passed through the dyeing process, so that a new compound was formed, the exact nature of which he could not tell; that bichromate of potash was the most common mordant used in dyeing woolen cloth to set the color; that all bichromate of potash was an irritant poison, and caused ulceration and more or less inflammation of the skin; that it was a well known fact that most workmen in factories where it was made had local ulcerations on the hands and nose; and that cloth dyed by bichromate of potash might be poisonous to susceptible persons. On cross-examination, he testified that bichromate of potash was very extensively used in dyeing cotton stockings black; that, so far as he knew, no cases of poisoning similar to that of the plaintiff had been published until he published four or five cases in 1886, but that since that time he had seen several more; that up to that time it had not been shown, so far as he could find out, that cases of poisoning had occurred from chrome mordanted cloth; that he did not know how poisoning could be effected from the presence of chrome compounds in cloth; and to the question, "Is there to-day anything further developed in relation to this kind of poisoning, other than that some people may be injured who have a disposition that way by the presence of this compound?" he replied, "Nothing more than occasionally persons may be injured by it, but the great majority of people not."

Upon this evidence, the judge ruled that the action could not be maintained, and ordered a verdict for the defendant; and the plaintiff alleged exceptions. * * *

C. ALLEN, J. The question in this case is whether there was any evidence, sufficient to go to the jury, to show that the defendant was negligent in the performance of any duty which it owed to the plaintiff, as one of the purchasers of the cloths manufactured by the defendant; and we are of the opinion that there was not. The plaintiff's action was brought on September 22, 1884. According to the testimony of the expert witness introduced by the plaintiff, it had never been shown, until 1886, that any cases of poisoning had occurred like the plaintiff's. For all that appears, the plaintiff's was the first instance of injury that ever was known to arise from the cause alleged in the declaration. All that the plaintiff showed against the defendant was, that it used an article for dyeing its cloths which was the most common mordant used in wool dyeing, which was also used very extensively in dyeing cotton stockings black, which so far as then known, had never caused injury to anybody who merely handled the cloths, and which the defendant did not know or suppose, and had no reason to know or suppose, to be injurious; and, under these circumstances, although there was evidence tending to show that, in point of fact, the plaintiff was injured by merely handling the cloths, this was not a result which the defendant was bound or ought to have contemplated as likely to happen. The facts of the present case do not call upon us to go any further than this. See Commonwealth v. Pierce, 138 Mass. 165, 179, 180, 52 Am.Rep. 264; Davidson v. Nichols, 11 Allen 514; Wellington v. Downer Kerosene Oil Co., 104 Mass. 64.

Exceptions overruled.[9]

9. Compare the reasonable accessibility of the facts (which might give foreknowledge of harm) to the defendants in Walstrom Optical Co. v. Miller, 59 S.W.2d 895 (Tex.Civ.App.1933); Pease v. Sinclair Ref. Co., 104 F.2d 183, 123 A.L.R. 933 (2d Cir. 1939); Palsgraf v. Long I. R. R., infra, p. 339.

For techniques of recovery in "allergy" cases, see Gober v. Revlon, Inc., 317 F.2d 47 (4th Cir. 1963); Bianchi v. Denholm & McKay Co., 302 Mass. 469, 19 N.E.2d 697, 121 A.L.R. 460 (1939); Hoar v. Rasmusen, 229 Wis. 509, 282 N.W. 652 (1938); Gerkin v. Brown & Sehler, 177 Mich. 45, 143 N.W. 48, 48 L.R.A.,N.S., 224 (1913). See, also, note 38 Mich.L.R. 233 (1939). A note, (1940) 121 A.L.R. 464, collects several cases and suggests their number will grow because of the increased use of cosmetics and the like. Other factors which may affect these cases are the increased knowledge of the field by the medical profession and the increased public awareness of allergies. How are these factors likely to make themselves felt?

Of what significance in the question of negligence would be (a) the knowledge by a vendor of strawberries that a certain number of people generally would suffer ill effects from eating strawberries; (b) the knowledge by the builders of a skyscraper that the enterprise will take an ascertainable toll in life and limb?

See F. Harper and F. James, The Law of Torts, § 16.5 at notes 21–61 (1956 and Supp.1968). The Restatement of Torts Second (1965) provides, in this connection:

"§ 290. What Actor is Required to Know

For the purpose of determining whether the actor should recognize that his conduct involves a risk, he is required to know

(a) the qualities and habits of human beings and animals and the qualities, characteristics, and capacities of things and forces in so far as they are matters of common knowledge at the time and in the community; and

(b) the common law, legislative enactments, and general customs in so far as they are likely to affect the conduct of the other or third persons.

"Comment"

* * *

"*e.* It is stated in § 283 that unless the actor is a child, the standard to which he must conform to avoid being negligent is that of a reasonable man under the circumstances. In determining whether the actor's conduct is negligent, his personal inability to conform to the standard is immaterial. He is treated as though he were a reasonable man and, therefore, he is treated as though he knew those things which the reasonable man at that time and place would know even though the actor is himself excusably ignorant of them. As a reasonable man, the actor is required to possess such scientific knowledge as is common among laymen at the time and in the community. Thus, he is required to know the ordinary operation of well-known natural laws. He is required, among other things, to know the poisonous qualities of many drugs, chemicals, and gases and the explosive or inflammable qualities of many chemical compounds and the intoxicating quality of certain liquids. So too, the actor as a reasonable man is required to know the ordinary operation of natural forces in the locality in which he lives which are likely to be affected by his conduct. Thus, a man living in the northern part of Minnesota is required to expect extremely cold temperature in early winter. A man living in the tropics is required to expect hot weather, even in winter. Every man should realize that heavy rainstorms are likely to produce floods in mountain streams. A Californian during the summer is not required to expect the fall of rain even though the morning is cloudy. On the other hand, a man living on the Atlantic coast may well be required to recognize that such conditions would make it imprudent to expose perishable goods to the risk of rain.

"In general, the actor is required to know everything with respect to the risk of harm which is a matter of common knowledge in the community in which his conduct occurs. There is a close relation between the minimum standard of knowledge required in negligence cases and those matters of

NATIONAL FOOD STORES, INC. v. UNION ELECTRIC CO.

Missouri Court of Appeals, St. Louis District, Division Two, 1973.
(Mo.App.) 494 S.W.2d 379.

MCMILLAN, JUDGE. * * *

National sued Union Electric for damages that resulted from the spoilage of certain perishable food items kept in its stores, because of an interruption by Union Electric of its electrical service to National. A jury verdict for $5800.00 was found for National. Upon Union Electric's motion * * * the court * * * set aside the verdict because there was no basis for legal liability. * * *

In June and July 1966 the City of St. Louis experienced a record breaking heat wave. The high temperatures put a great stress upon the capacity of Union Electric to meet the power needs of both its city and county consumers. During the morning of 11 July 1966, Union Electric was operating within 290 megawatts of its total capacity. In recognition of the gravity of the situation, Union Electric put into effect its five phase "Emergency Loan Reduction of Power Curtailment" plan.

At 7:55 A.M., 11 July 1966, Union Electric (Phase I) disconnected service to its "interruptable customers." For these contract customers neither reasons nor notices were necessary. Phase Two, which was a 5% voltage reduction, was not used. At 10:00 A.M., the same morning, the power drain continued; therefore, Union Electric (Phase Three) began to contact its 200 largest industrial consumers, and on a voluntary basis requested that each of them reduce their power consumption. By 12:30 P.M., all had been contacted.

At 1:47 P.M., the same afternoon, Union Electric (skipping phase four, which provided for a general notice to the general public by the media) put into operation phase five, which called for the involuntary curtailment of service periodically to certain specified geographical areas throughout the entire St. Louis Metropolitan area. It was the phase five interruption, without notice to National, which National claims resulted in spoilage to its food stuff in various stores throughout the area.

Union Electric contends * * * that it owed no duty to National to advise it of an interruption of electical service to each of its stores before an interruption occurred. * * *

* * * Generally speaking, an electric power company which undertakes to supply current, although not an insurer of service, has an obligation to provide a patron with adequate and continuous service, arising either from express contract, a regulatory enactment, or implied contract and the supplier is, ordinarily at least, subject to a

which a court will take judicial notice because they are generally known."

Also see James, The Qualities of the Reasonable Man in Negligence Cases, 16 Mo.L.Rev. 1 (1951); Tunc, Fault: A Common Name for Different Misdeeds, 49 Tul.L.Rev. 279 (1975).

duty to exercise reasonable care to fulfill such obligation. In Ellyson v. Missouri Power and Light Co., 59 S.W.2d 714 (Mo.App.1933), our court held that for an interruption of service by an electricity company a person may sue in tort as well as for breach of contract. In the Ellyson case the evidence disclosed that the defendant had contracted with plaintiff to maintain a continuous and sufficient supply of power at all times, and had additionally represented that it would furnish current from a secondary supply in the event of an emergency. The negligence charged was the failure to keep the secondary supply in good repair.

There are cases that hold when the action is based upon negligence, power suppliers are relieved from liability for unintended interruptions, either as a matter of general principle or because of an express contractual or regulatory provision, where the interruption resulted from an "Act of God" or from circumstances beyond the control of the supplier. * * *

While the instant case is not a breakdown by an "Act of God" or from circumstances beyond the control of the supplier as outlined in the above cases, this case does involve the cessation of power by the supplier due to an emergency situation over which the supplier had no control. We concede that under the conditions existing on the morning of 11 July 1966 Union Electric was justified in its decision to cut off service in various portions of the area throughout the afternoon and evening of that day and into July 12. However, the fact of an emergency does not relieve Union Electric of its general duty to exercise reasonable care to avoid undue harm to its consumers where the harm is reasonably foreseeable. Union Electric says there was no duty to advise National of the interruption of power.

In Heaven v. Pender, 11 Q.B.D. 503 (1883), Brett, M.R., afterwards Lord Esher, made the first attempt to state a formula of duty as follows:

> "* * * that whenever one person is by circumstances placed in such a position with regard to another, that every one of ordinary sense who did think would at once recognise that if he did not use ordinary care and skill in his own conduct with regard to those circumstances he would cause danger of injury to the person or property of the other, a duty arises to use ordinary care and skill to avoid such danger." [10]

10. Brett's formulation was not accepted in his time. It was, however, later adapted by Lord Atkin in a classic House of Lords speech which has become a landmark of twentieth century English negligence law. This statement, in Donoghue v. Stevenson, [1932] A.C. 562, [1932] All E.R.Rep. 1, was delivered in a product liability case (snail in bottle of ginger beer), and represents for the British the culmination of a process of doctrinal evolution from the preoccupation with remedies for particular offenses derived from the common law writs toward the expression of a general theory of liability for negligence:

"We are solely concerned with the question whether, as a matter of law in the circumstances alleged, the defender owed any duty to the pursuer to take care.

"It is remarkable how difficult it is to find in the English authorities statements of general application defining the relations between parties that give

So, in our opinion, Union Electric was by virtue of its own charter placed in a position to its customers so that if it did not use ordinary

rise to the duty. The Courts are concerned with the particular relations which come before them in actual litigation, and it is sufficient to say whether the duty exists in those circumstances. The result is that the Courts have been engaged upon an elaborate classification of duties as they exist in respect of property, whether real or personal, with further divisions as to ownership, occupation or control, and distinctions based on the particular relations of the one side or the other, whether manufacturer, salesman or landlord, customer, tenant, stranger, and so on. In this way it can be ascertained at any time whether the law recognizes a duty, but only where the case can be referred to some particular species which has been examined and classified. And yet the duty which is common to all the cases where liability is established must logically be based upon some element common to the cases where it is found to exist. To seek a complete logical definition of the general principle is probably to go beyond the function of the judge, for the more general the definition the more likely it is to omit essentials or to introduce non-essentials. The attempt was made by Brett M.R. in Heaven v. Pender ((1883) 11 Q.B.D. 503, 509), in a definition to which I will later refer. As framed, it was demonstrably too wide, though it appears to me, if properly limited, to be capable of affording a valuable practical guide.

"At present I content myself with pointing out that in English law there must be, and is, some general conception of relations giving rise to a duty of care, of which the particular cases found in the books are but instances. The liability for negligence, whether you style it such or treat it as in other systems as a species of 'culpa,' is no doubt based upon a general public sentiment of moral wrongdoing for which the offender must pay. But acts or omissions which any moral code would censure cannot in a practical world be treated so as to give a right to every person injured by them to demand relief. In this way rules of law arise which limit the range of complainants and the extent of their remedy. The rule that you are to love your neighbour becomes in law, you must not injure your neighbour; and the lawyer's question, Who is my neighbour? receives a restricted reply. You must take reasonable care to avoid acts or omissions which you can reasonably foresee would be likely to injure your neighbour. Who, then, in law is my neighbour? The answer seems to be—persons who are so closely and directly affected by my act that I ought reasonably to have them in contemplation as being so affected when I am directing my mind to the acts or omissions which are called in question. This appears to me to be the doctrine of Heaven v. Pender, as laid down by Lord Esher (then Brett M.R.) when it is limited by the notion of proximity introduced by Lord Esher himself and A. L. Smith, L.J. in Le Lievre v. Gould ([1893] 1 Q.B. 491, 497, 504). Lord Esher says: 'That case established that, under certain circumstances, one man may owe a duty to another, even though there is no contract between them. If one man is near to another, or is near to the property of another, a duty lies upon him not to do that which may cause a personal injury to that other, or may injure his property.' So A. L. Smith, L. J.: 'The decision of Heaven v. Pender was founded upon the principle, that a duty to take due care did arise when the person or property of one was in such proximity to the person or property of another that, if due care was not taken, damage might be done by the one to the other.' I think that this sufficiently states the truth if proximity be not confined to mere physical proximity; but be used, as I think it was intended, to extend to such close and direct relations that the act complained of directly affects a person whom the person alleged to be bound to take care would know would be directly affected by his careless act. * * * With this necessary qualification of proximate relationship as explained in Le Lievre v. Gould, I think the judgment of Lord Esher expresses the law of England * * * "

While Lord Atkin's speech is not often quoted in the United States, it reflects positions which are frequently at issue in American litigation. The notion, for instance, that there is a general requirement to take care, instead of a multiplicity of "duties" the breach of which constitutes negligence, is becoming increasingly familiar. As a consequence, the likelihood tends to diminish that exceptions to liability

care in the exercise of its franchise numerous injuries to both person and property could reasonably occur. Likewise, this general duty owed by a public utility to its customers is supplemented by the statutory obligation imposed on electrical corporations by § 393.130(1), RSMo 1969, which provides as follows:

> "Every * * * electrical corporation * * * shall furnish and provide such service instrumentalities and facilities as shall be safe and adequate and in all respects just and reasonable. * * *"

In Langley v. Pacific Gas & Electric Co., 41 Cal.2d 655, 262 P.2d 849 (Cal.Banc 1953), an owner of a trout hatchery sued to recover damages as a result of the death of 78,000 trout. Plaintiff claimed that the electric power necessary to pump water into the hatchery had gone off for about five hours due to a failure of defendant's voltage regulator. As a result of the power interruption the fish did not get sufficient water and died. The evidence showed that plaintiff had advised the defendant of the necessity of a continuous flow of power, and that defendant had agreed to notify them of the outage. Granted, the Langley case was founded upon contract, however, Justice Traynor clearly sets forth the general standard of conduct required of a public utility when he states:

> "* * * defendant agreed to furnish electricity in accordance with the applicable rules and regulations of the Public Utilities Commission * * * Defendant contends that under these provisions its duty is limited to exercising reasonable diligence to furnish a continuous and sufficient supply of electricity, and that it is under no duty to exercise reasonable care or diligence to prevent loss from power failure when it is not legally responsible for the power failure itself. These provisions deal with the duty to supply power, and they make clear that defendant is not an insurer or guarantor of service.

for damages resulting from negligence will be permitted; the more general the scope of the prototypical liability, the greater is the predisposition against recognition of such exceptions, some of which have been traditional, e. g., Sargent v. Ross, page 635 infra. The question of liability to whom remains a critical issue, and will be encountered repeatedly in the following materials, e. g., Palsgraf v. Long Island Ry. Co., page 339 infra; MacPherson v. Buick Motor Co., page 675 infra; Ultramares v. Touche, Niven & Co., page 811 infra; and Moch v. Rensselaer Water Co., page 682 infra (four important Cardozo opinions). Broad statements concerning the circumstances in which it is necessary to conform to the standard of reasonable care have been occasionally made by American courts, e. g., Wintersteen v. National Cooperage and Woodenware Co., 361 Ill. 95, 102, 103, 197 N.E. 578, 582 (1935):

> "It is axiomatic that every person owes a duty to all persons to exercise ordinary care to guard against any injury which may naturally flow as a reasonably probable and foreseeable consequence of his act, and the law is presumed to furnish a remedy for the redress of every wrong. This duty to exercise ordinary care to avoid injury to another does not depend upon contract, privity of interest, or the proximity of relationship between the parties. It extends to remote and unknown persons."

For limitations on the application of Donoghue v. Stevenson in English law see Winfield and Jolowicz on Tort 49–60 (10th ed. by W. Rogers 1975).

> *In no way, however do they*[11] *abrogate defendant's general duty to exercise reasonable care in operating its system to avoid unreasonable risks of harm to * * * property of its customers.* (Emphasis added.)
>
> "In the present case it is undisputed that defendant was not responsible for the power failure and that it exercised reasonable diligence to restore service. Accordingly, the question presented is whether * * * it could reasonably be concluded that its duty to exercise due care toward plaintiff in the operation of its system required it to give notice of the power failure when it knew that the failure to give notice would result in serious loss. In an analogous situation, a common carrier does not have a duty to transport goods immediately, but merely to use due diligence to deliver goods offered for shipment within a reasonable time * * *. Nevertheless, * * * if the carrier is aware that causes of unusual delay exist of which the shipper is unaware, and does not inform the shipper of the facts, the carrier is liable for injuries caused by delay. * * *
>
> * * *
>
> "* * * By undertaking to supply electricity to plaintiff, defendant obligated itself to exercise reasonable care toward him, and failure to exercise such care has the characteristics of both a *breach of contract and a tort* * * *" (Emphasis added.)

* * *

Public utilities occupy a unique position in our society. They furnish indispensable services while enjoying a privileged legal status. As consumers, our dependency upon their services is almost total. As such it is essential that such companies conduct themselves in a manner that does not take advantage of our dependency on them nor

11. "They" in this instance are the provisions of Rule 14 of the applicable rules and regulations of the California Public Utility Commission. Rule 14 requires, among other things, that the utility must exercise "reasonable diligence and care to supply energy to the customer but does not guarantee continuity of sufficiency of supply." [From original, renumbered; other notes in original omitted.]

For a suggestion, conversely, that an accident victim might in certain circumstances fare better against a public utility in contract than in tort, were a remedy in tort blocked, see Chipman v. Massachusetts Bay Transportation Authority, Mass., 316 N.E.2d 725, 729, note 9 (1974).

It is by no means always clear that a tort remedy is appropriate for disputes arising from the defective performance of a contract. Some typical problems are touched upon in Chapters 5 and 6 infra. For one thoughtful discussion see Gates Rubber Co. v. USM Corp., 508 F.2d 603 (7th Cir. 1975).

There are, however certain types of claims as to which courts commonly hold that tort or contract remedies are interchangeable, e. g., the liability of an insurer to pay a judgment against insured in excess of the policy limits, if the insurer wrongly failed to settle within policy limits, Rova Farms Resort, Inc. v. Investors Ins. Co. of America, 65 N.J. 474, 323 A.2d 495 (1974) and Johansen v. California State Automobile Association Inter-Ins. Bureau, 15 Cal.3d 9, 123 Cal.Rptr. 288, 538 P.2d 744 (1975).

of the privileged status granted to them by the state legislature. While we do not propose that public utilities, in this instance an electrical company, are insurers or guarantors of the safety of persons or of their property * * * we hold there is as a matter of law a duty on Union Electric to protect its customers from foreseeable damage from failure of electrical service. * * *

* * * [T]he right to interrupt service in the face of an emergency is a far different thing from relieving a utility of liability where it fails to give a reasonable notice to its consumers of its intentions to interrupt services when the utility knows or could reasonably anticipate a situation that would make it necessary to interrupt service and the utility knows or should know that by so failing to give notice the interruptions might result in loss or harm to its consumers.

Under the evidence in this case, a jury could have reasonably found that Union Electric could have reasonably anticipated that the steadily deteriorating environmental situation on July 11, 1966, would necessitate the interruption of service to its customers.

* * * [W]e find that Union Electric knew of the gravity of the situation and that it was well aware that it might have to have an area-wide cessation of power; therefore, we hold that it became a jury question as to whether Union Electric's failure to give a reasonable notice or warning of outages and interruptions of service was reasonably likely to cause harm or property loss to its consumers. It is a jury question as to whether or not the failure to give notice was a breach of that duty. * * *

A note on warning. Clearly many situations are dangerous only to those who do not know about them—to the knowing they carry no unreasonable dangers. The top of a flight of ordinary stairs is an example. Hunnewell v. Haskell, 174 Mass. 557, 55 N.E. 320 (1899). So may be the approach of a train to a grade crossing which a highway traveller is also approaching at moderate speed. One way to impart knowledge is by a suitable warning, and many negligence cases turn on questions of warning.

There may, for instance, be a question of whether reasonable care may be thought to require a warning. In this connection, consider the following: (a) The effect of defendant's knowledge or ignorance of the facts which threaten the danger. Contrast the Gould case with Gerkin v. Brown & Sehler, 177 Mich. 45, 143 N.W. 48, 48 L.R.A., N.S., 224 (1913). (b) The foreseeability of the human conduct which caused the dangers of the situation to be realized. Compare the Terranella case (p. 157, supra) with McDonald v. Fryberger, 233 Minn. 156, 46 N.W.2d 260 (1951). (c) The extent to which a defendant may reasonably rely on people's noticing the danger itself without further warning, and the kinds of circumstances which will affect this extent. (d) Whether warning is customary. (e) The extent to which the above factors are for the jury's consideration, rather than the court's.

There may also be a serious question as to whether warning is adequate. In this connection, consider the following: (a) Whether the warning given is likely to be perceived and understood. See, e. g., Rapp v. Public S.C.T., 15 N.J.Super. 305, 83 A.2d 355 (1951); Maize v. Atlantic Refining Co., 352 Pa. 51, 41 A.2d 850, 160 A.L.R. 449 (1945) (cleaner dangerous to inhale labelled conspicuously "Safety-Kleen," with warning in small letters); Spruill v. Boyle-Midway, Inc., 308 F.2d 79 (4th Cir. 1962); Hubbard-Hall Chemical Co. v. Silverman, 340 F.2d 402 (1st Cir. 1965). (b) The likelihood that people, if warned, will take effective self-protective measures. See, e. g., Reboni v. Case Bros., Inc., 137 Conn. 501, 78 A.2d 887 (1951); West Texas Utilities Co. v. Renner, 32 S.W.2d 264 (Tex.Civ.App.1930) (both dealing with high tension wires); but contrast LeVonas v. Acme Paper Board Co., 184 Md. 16, 40 A.2d 43 (1944). Also see Fleming v. Delta Airlines, 359 F.Supp. 339 (S.D.N.Y.1973). (c) The reciprocal rights and privileges of defendant and plaintiff to carry on their respective activities under the circumstances. See Bowen, L.J., in Thomas v. Quartermaine, 18 Q.B.D. 685, 696 (C.A.1887); Torts Restatement Second § 301 (1965), comments on subsections (1), (2). (d) The fact that the warning apparently is not being heeded. See, e. g., Locke v. Puget Sound International Ry. & Power Co., 100 Wash. 432, 171 P. 242, L.R.A.1918D, 1119 (1918); Huggans v. Southern Pac. Co., 92 Cal.App. 2d 599, 207 P.2d 864 (1949); Love v. Wolf, 226 Cal.App.2d 378, 38 Cal.Rptr. 183 (1964) (warning which complied with Food and Drug Administration's directive had been vitiated by other statements in drug supplier's promotional campaign among doctors). (e) Again, the extent to which the above factors are for the jury's consideration, rather than the court's.

Also see Dillard and Hart, Product Liability: Directions for Use and the Duty to Warn, 41 Va.L.Rev. 145 (1955) and Hiigel v. General Motors Corp., — Colo. —, 544 P.2d 983 (1975).

LUCCHESE v. SAN FRANCISCO-SACRAMENTO R. CO.

District Court of Appeal of California, First District, Division 2, 1930.
106 Cal.App. 242, 289 P. 188.

STURTEVANT, J. The plaintiff commenced an action against the defendants to recover a judgment for damages for injuries sustained in a collision. Both defendants answered, and the trial was had before the trial court sitting without a jury. The trial court made findings in favor of the plaintiff, and each defendant has appealed separately and each has brought up a typewritten record including the original exhibits.

Appeal of San Francisco-Sacramento Railroad Company.

On the afternoon of the 23d day of December, 1927, John Spingola was driving his truck on which he had a load of furniture. He was seated on the left-hand side, and the plaintiff, his helper, was seated at his right. The cab of the truck had a glass window in front and on the right-hand side it had a door. The door was closed, and on the right-hand side an ordinary automobile curtain was fastened down. The curtain had a small square lookout which resembled glass but was an imitation. After the truck left Bay Point in Contra Costa county, it proceeded toward Oakland. In a short distance the highway on which it was traveling crosses the railroad track of the defendant. When the truck was approximately fifteen hundred feet from the railroad track, one of the trains of the defendant was approaching from Sacramento and traveling toward Oakland and at that time was approximately two thousand feet from the crossing. The truck was traveling fifteen or sixteen miles an hour and the train was traveling thirty-five to forty miles an hour. Each was in clear view of the other. They were approaching each other on an angle of apparently sixty degrees. Immediately ahead of the truck were four distinct signs. One is a California state automobile sign which is a combination indicating a railroad crossing and a left-hand turn ahead. The next sign is an elevated cross-arm. The next one is apparently a county or state sign, "Slow—Turn." The last one is another elevated cross which is apparently on the further side of the railroad crossing. But all of said signs are clearly within the vision of one traveling on the highway. The approaching railroad train gave several signals with its whistle. However, the truck did not reduce its speed and a collision occurred at the crossing.

The defendant corporation attacks finding No. 12, which is the only finding which purports to charge it with negligence. That finding purports to find the defendant guilty under the doctrine of the last clear chance. In this attack the defendant is clearly right. The uncontradicted evidence is to the effect that the motorman had no reason to believe that danger of a collision existed until the motorman was within two hundred feet of the crossing and the truck in which the plaintiff was riding was about the same distance from the crossing. At that point the motorman threw loose the "dead-man" and stopped the train in the shortest distance possible by the use of that method. The plaintiff replies that there was another method for stopping the train which would have slowed it down, but more abruptly, and he argues that the latter method was not adopted because the use of the other method might have thrown some of the passengers to the floor and injured them. If the reason for selecting the method of stopping the train was as claimed, the reason was sound. The defendant owed to its passengers the first duty, and that was to exercise the utmost care for their safety. To the plaintiff it owed the duty of exercising ordinary care. It did so. The plaintiff may not complain. Moreover, if the second method had been adopted the evidence shows that under the same set of facts the accident might have been worse. The motorman was confronted with an emergency. The evidence does not show that he did not exercise the care an ordinary man would have exercised under similar circumstances.

As it is not claimed that this defendant was guilty of any other kind of negligence, the judgment as to the railroad company must be reversed.

It is so ordered.[12]

ADAMS v. BULLOCK

Court of Appeals of New York, 1919.
227 N.Y. 208, 125 N.E. 93.

CARDOZO, J. The defendant runs a trolley line in the city of Dunkirk, employing the overhead wire system. At one point, the road is crossed by a bridge or culvert which carries the tracks of the Nickle Plate and Pennsylvania Railroads. Pedestrians often use the bridge as a short cut between streets, and children play on it. On April 21, 1916, the plaintiff, a boy of 12 years, came across the bridge, swinging a wire about 8 feet long. In swinging it, he brought it in contact with the defendant's trolley wire, which ran beneath the structure. The side of the bridge was protected by a parapet 18 inches wide. Four feet 7¾ inches below the top of the parapet, the trolley wire was strung. The plaintiff was shocked and burned when the wires came together. He had a verdict at Trial Term, which has been affirmed at the Appellate Division by a divided court.

We think the verdict cannot stand. The defendant in using an overhead trolley was in the lawful exercise of its franchise. Negligence, therefore, cannot be imputed to it because it used that system and not another. Dumphy v. Montreal, etc., Co., 1907 A.C. 454. There was, of course, a duty to adopt all reasonable precautions to minimize the resulting perils. We think there is no evidence that this duty was ignored. The trolley wire was so placed that no one standing on the bridge or even bending over the parapet could reach it. Only some extraordinary casualty, not fairly within the area of ordinary prevision, could make it a thing of danger. Reasonable care in the use of a destructive agency imports a high degree of vigilance. * * * But no vigilance, however alert, unless fortified by the gift of prophecy, could have predicted the point upon the route where such an accident would occur. It might with equal reason have been expected anywhere else. At any point upon the route a mischievous or thoughtless boy might touch the wire with a metal pole, or fling another wire across it. Green v. W. P. Co., 246 Pa. 340, 92 Atl. 341, L.R.A.1915C, 151. If unable to reach it from the walk, he might stand upon a wagon or climb upon a tree. No special danger at this bridge warned the defendant that there was need of special measures of precaution. No like accident had occurred before. No custom had been disregarded. We think that ordinary caution did not involve forethought of this extraordinary peril. * * * There is, we may add, a distinction not to be ignored between electric light and trolley wires. The distinction

12. This case is noted in 44 Harv.L. Rev. 303 (1930).

is that the former may be insulated. Chance of harm, though remote, may betoken negligence, if needless. Facility of protection may impose a duty to protect. With trolley wires, the case is different. Insulation is impossible. Guards here and there are of little value. To avert the possibility of this accident and others like it at one point or another on the route, the defendant must have abandoned the overhead system, and put the wires underground. Neither its power nor its duty to make the change is shown. To hold it liable upon the facts exhibited in this record would be to charge it as an insurer.

The judgment should be reversed, and a new trial granted, with costs to abide the event.[13]

NOTE ON THE NEGLIGENCE CALCULUS:

In Conway v. O'Brien, 111 F.2d 611 (2d Cir. 1940) L. Hand, J. said:

> "The degree of care demanded of a person by an occasion is the resultant of three factors; the likelihood that his conduct will injure others, taken with the seriousness of the injury if it happens, and balanced against the interest which he must sacrifice to avoid the risk. All of these are practically not susceptible of any quantitative estimate, and the second two are generally not so, even theoretically. For this reason a solution always involves some preference, or choice between incommensurables, and it is consigned to a jury because their decision is thought most likely to accord with commonly accepted standards, real or fancied."

See also Judge Hand's opinion in United States v. Carroll Towing Co., 159 F.2d 169 (2d Cir. 1947) and discussion in Epstein, A Theory of Strict Liability, 2 J. Legal Studies 151, 154 et seq. (1973); compare Restatement of Torts Second § 291 (1965): ". . . the risk is unreasonable and the act is negligent if the risk is of such magnitude as to outweigh what the law regards as the utility of the act or of the particular manner in which it is done."

Despite Hand's disclaimer of quantifiability, his formulation has been explained in terms of the concepts of cost-benefit analysis; See Posner, A Theory of Negligence, 1 J. Leg. Studies 29, 32–34 (1972):

> "It is time to take a fresh look at the social function of liability for negligent acts. The essential clue, I believe, is

13. Compare Eckert v. Long Island R. Co., 43 N.Y. 502 (1871) discussed in Terry, 29 Harv.L.Rev. 40, 43 (1915) (whether conduct of rescuer of child from locomotive's path is reasonable); Cooley v. Public Service Co. of N. H., 90 N.H. 460, 10 A.2d 673 (1940) (discusses reasonableness of precautions which might protect telephone users from loud sudden noises but which would increase dangers of electrocution to travelers on highway); Nees v. Minneapolis St. Ry. Co., 218 Minn. 532, 16 N.W.2d 758 (1944) (hitting trolley rather than pedestrian); Green v. Guynes, 361 Mo. 606, 235 S.W.2d 298 (1951) (man not required to jeopardize his own life or limb to reduce danger to others).

provided by Judge Learned Hand's famous formulation of the negligence standard—one of the few attempts to give content to the deceptively simple concept of ordinary care. * * * In a negligence case, Hand said, the judge (or jury) should attempt to measure three things: the magnitude of the loss if an accident occurs; the probability of the accident's occurring; and the burden of taking precautions that would avert it. If the product of the first two terms exceeds the burden of precautions, the failure to take those precautions is negligence. Hand was adumbrating, perhaps unwittingly, an economic meaning of negligence. Discounting (multiplying) the cost of an accident if it occurs by the probability of occurrence yields a measure of the economic benefit to be anticipated from incurring the costs necessary to prevent the accident. The cost of prevention is what Hand meant by the burden of taking precautions against the accident. It may be the cost of installing safety equipment or otherwise making the activity safer, or the benefit forgone by curtailing or eliminating the activity. If the cost of safety measures or of curtailment—whichever cost is lower—exceeds the benefit in accident avoidance to be gained by incurring that cost, society would be better off, in economic terms, to forgo accident prevention. A rule making the enterprise liable for the accidents that occur in such cases cannot be justified on the ground that it will induce the enterprise to increase the safety of its operations. When the cost of accidents is less than the cost of prevention, a rational profit-maximizing enterprise will pay tort judgments to the accident victims rather than incur the larger cost of avoiding liability. Furthermore, overall economic value or welfare would be diminished rather than increased by incurring a higher accident-prevention cost in order to avoid a lower accident cost. If, on the other hand, the benefits in accident avoidance exceed the costs of prevention, society is better off if those costs are incurred and the accident averted, and so in this case the enterprise is made liable, in the expectation that self-interest will lead it to adopt the precautions in order to avoid a greater cost in tort judgments.

"One misses any reference to accident avoidance by the victim. If the accident could be prevented by the installation of safety equipment or the curtailment or discontinuance of the underlying activity by the victim at lower cost than any measure taken by the injurer would involve, it would be uneconomical to adopt a rule of liability that placed the burden of accident prevention on the injurer. Although not an explicit part of the Hand formula this qualification, as we shall see, is implicit in the administration of the negligence standard.

"Perhaps, then, the dominant function of the fault system is to generate rules of liability that if followed will bring about, at least approximately, the efficient—the cost-justified—level of accidents and safety. * * * Because we do not like to see resources squandered, a judgment of negligence has inescapable overtones of moral disapproval, for it implies that there was a cheaper alternative to the accident. Conversely, there is no moral indignation in the case in which the cost of prevention would have exceeded the cost of the accident. Where the measures necessary to avert the accident would have consumed excessive resources, there is no occasion to condemn the defendant for not having taken them.

"If indignation has its roots in inefficiency, we do not have to decide whether regulation, or compensation, or retribution, or some mixture of these best describes the dominant purpose of negligence law. In any case, the judgment of liability depends ultimately on a weighing of costs and benefits."

There are, however, other views as to whether traditional negligence rules are justified on grounds of economic efficiency. One approach would have it that, on certain assumptions, an optimal allocation of resources will come about whatever rules of liability a society may adopt, through market transactions among the potential parties to disputes.[14] The necessary assumption is the absence of "transaction costs"; these costs represent, inter alia, the lack of perfect information, the cost of obtaining information, and the administrative and similar costs of influencing the conduct of others, beyond the consideration which may be paid for changes of conduct (e. g., through theoretically legitimate market transactions sometimes called, nonpejoratively, "bribes"). A market without "transaction costs" is like a physical universe without friction; it does not exist, but thinking about it may advance understanding of that which does exist. Professor Guido Calabresi, on the other hand, has discussed in detail the effects of actual transaction costs as influencing whether any general rule for the allocation of accident costs, either predicated on negligence or not, will lead to optimality in resource allocation. The following example of such a discussion, from G. Calabresi, The Costs of Accidents: A Legal and Economic Analysis 133–38 (1970), is intended, as is the Posner excerpt above, to illustrate how economic analysis may assist in understanding the effect of legal rules, such as the negligence principle, but not to suggest that economic theory provides the sole benchmark for the evaluation of those rules:

" * * * Since in reality transactions are often terribly expensive, it is often not worthwhile spending both the cost of the transaction and the amount needed to bribe someone

14. This position is largely identified with a paper by Professor R. H. Coase, The Problem of Social Cost, 3 J.Law & Econ. 1 (1960), based on an analysis of nuisance problems.

else to diminish the accident-causing behavior. As a result, the accident cost is not avoided by society, while another allocation that could eliminate or lessen the transaction cost is available and would result in the avoidance of the accident cost. The aim of the pure market determination of which activity to hold liable is to find this other allocation.

"An overly simple example may be in order. Suppose car-pedestrian accidents currently cost $100. Suppose also that if cars had spongy bumpers the total accident costs would only be $10. Suppose finally that spongy bumpers cost $50 more than the present bumpers. Assuming no transaction costs, spongy bumpers would become established regardless of who was held responsible for car-pedestrian accidents. If car manufacturers were liable they would prefer to spend $50 for the new bumpers plus $10 in accident damages, instead of $100 for accident damages. If pedestrians were held responsible and could foresee the costs, they would prefer to bribe the car manufacturers $50 to put in spongy bumpers and bear $10 in damages, rather than bear $100 in damages. Exactly the same result would occur if an arbitrary third party, e. g. television manufacturers, were held liable initially; they too could lessen costs to themselves by bribing car manufacturers to put in spongy bumpers. The result is the same simply because the cost of avoiding the accident is in all instances smaller than the cost of compensating for it. Wherever this is so, and wherever it costs nothing to bribe (and people have the necessary knowledge), the market will seek the cheapest way and avoid the accident.

"Now let us alter the example to add transaction costs. Assume that any allocation other than leaving the cost where it falls (i. e. on the pedestrian) entails $5 in administrative costs. Assume also that for pedestrians to bribe anyone is very expensive, e. g. $65. (This is because it is costly to gather pedestrians together to bargain and to handle the problem of would-be free-loaders.[15]) Assume finally that it would cost television manufacturers $30 to bribe. What would happen in our example?

15. The free-loader is the person who refuses to be inoculated against smallpox because given the fact that almost everyone else is inoculated, the risk of smallpox to him is less than the risk of harm from the inoculation. If enough people are free-loaders it becomes necessary to compel inoculation to avoid smallpox epidemics. The free-loader is also the person who refuses to join a union because the fact that most other workers are union members assures him of the benefits of unionization without the cost. The use of compulsion in these areas suggests that the problem of free-loaders is crucial whenever many people must agree to bear a cost in order to bring about a change favorable to all of them. It would not be crucial if nonpayers could be excluded from the benefits of the change, but such exclusion is often extremely expensive. It is precisely that expense which justifies compulsion. [From original, renumbered; other notes in original omitted.]

"If car manufacturers were held liable, they would bear $100 in accident costs plus perhaps the $5 allocation cost. They could avoid this in the future by putting in spongy bumpers at $50, paying $10 in damages, and perhaps the same $5 in administrative costs (assuming for the sake of simplicity that these remained constant). Clearly they would install spongy bumpers.

"If pedestrians were held liable, they would bear $100 in accident costs. But to get spongy bumpers installed would cost them $50 (bribe) plus $65 (transaction costs), and they would still bear $10 in accident costs. Since $125 is more than $100, a change to spongy bumpers would not seem worth the expense. But the absence of spongy bumpers would in fact entail an unnecessary cost to society of the difference between $100 (accident costs when borne by pedestrians) and $65 (the cost to society when car manufacturers are held liable).

"If television manufacturers were held liable, the figures would be $100 plus $5 with no spongy bumpers, compared with $50 (bribe) plus $30 (transaction costs) plus $10 (remaining accident costs) plus perhaps $5 (administrative costs). Since $95 is less than $105, spongy bumpers would probably be installed. But this result would have been achieved in a more expensive, less efficient way than if car manufacturers had been liable, for $30 in unnecessary transaction costs would have been imposed on society.

"Clearly then, on the basis of our initial assumptions, it would be best to make automobile manufacturers liable."

LEHIGH & WILKES–BARRE COAL CO. v. HAYES

Supreme Court of Pennsylvania, 1889.
128 Pa. 294, 18 A. 387, 5 L.R.A. 441, 15 Am.St.Rep. 680.

Error to court of common pleas, Luzerne county; Woodward, Judge.

Trespass on the case by James Hayes and Ann Hayes, his wife, against the Lehigh & Wilkes-Barre Coal Company, a corporation, for the death of plaintiffs' son, a boy 14 years old, who worked in defendant's mine. It was alleged that the defendant's negligence caused the accident, which occurred by drawing a car of coal from the chute where deceased was at work, thus causing a large quantity of coal to be precipitated on him, causing his death. Plaintiffs contended that defendant's servants at the mouth of the shaft should have notified deceased that they intended to draw the car, but it appeared that the latter had sent word by another employe that the car should be drawn out. There was a verdict for plaintiffs, damages assessed at $1,500, judgment accordingly, and defendant brings error. * * *

GREEN, J. Upon the trial of this cause no evidence was given by the plaintiff to show that the defendant's breaker, and the machinery used in crushing and screening coal, was in any manner defectively built, or that it was not built in the same manner and with the same appliances as are used in all similar structures. The single act of negligence in this regard alleged against the defendant was that it had no appliance and used no means or method by which warning could be given to persons working in the pocket that a draw was about to be made. No evidence was given to show that it was customary among coal operators to give any such warning in the conduct of their collieries. It follows that there was no proof that the defendant neglected any of the precautions which were usually observed in carrying on the business of crushing, screening, and shipping coal. But the defendant did give testimony of importance upon this subject. G. M. Williamson, the mine inspector for the district in which this colliery was situated, testified that there were 62 collieries, or openings, altogether, in the district, and that this breaker, with its chutes and pockets, was constructed in the usual, ordinary way in which such breakers are constructed in that region. He also said he did not know that there was in use in any of the collieries of the district any signaling apparatus to indicate when coal is about to be drawn out of a chute to be lowered into a car. Joseph Tyrell, another witness, whose business was building breakers, and who built this one, testified that the breaker was built in the usual way in which breakers are built in that region, and that he knew of no breaker in the region in which, prior to this accident, any apparatus or device was used to signal before coal was drawn from the chutes into cars. There was affirmative testimony, therefore, that this breaker was built in the usual way in which all breakers were built in that district; and that there was no custom or use, known to the witnesses, of having appliances of any kind to signal the drawing of coal from the chutes. Against this there was no opposing testimony whatever. The rule in regard to the obligation of the employer, respecting the character of the tools and appliances furnished by him, has been repeatedly stated in the recent decisions of this court. Thus, in Pittsburgh & C. R. Co. v. Sentmeyer, 92 Pa.St. 276, 37 Am.Rep. 684, we said that, when the employer furnished his employees "with tools and appliances which, though not the best possible, may, by ordinary care, be used without danger, he has discharged his duty, and is not responsible for accidents." In Payne v. Reese, 100 Pa.St. 301, we said: "An employer is not bound to furnish for his workmen the 'safest' machinery, nor to provide the 'best methods' for its operation, in order to save himself from responsibility for accidents resulting from its use. If the machinery be of an ordinary character, and such as can, with reasonable care, be used without danger to the employe, it is all that can be required from the employer. This is the limit of his responsibility, and the sum total of his duty." In Allison Manufacturing Co. v. McCormick, 118 Pa.St. 519, 12 A. 273, 4 Am.St.Rep. 613, we said: "The general rule requires of the master that he provide materials and implements for the use of his servant such as are ordinarily used by persons in the same business; but he is not required to secure the best known materials, or to subject such as he does provide to a chemical analysis in order to settle, by experiment, what remote and possible hazard may be incurred by their use." In Delaware River Iron Ship-Building Works v. Nuttall, 119 Pa.St. 149, 13 A.Rep. 65, we held that the employer was under no obligation to give warning to his employes of the dangerous character of a circular saw, or to provide it with a spreader to prevent accidents. As to the spreader we said: "The testimony shows that such an attachment is not in general use, and that there is no general agreement among millowners or practical sawyers that it is a desirable or a useful attachment. It is not enough that some persons regard it as a valuable safeguard. The test is general use. Tried by this test the saw of the defendant is such a one as the company had a right to use, because it is such as is commonly used by millowners;. and it was error to leave to the jury any question of negligence based on the failure to provide a spreader." Applying these principles to the facts of the present case we fail to discover any evidence of negligence on the part of the defendant, so far as the character of the breaker and its appliances is concerned, and hence we can find nothing upon which to support a verdict for the plaintiff.

It was argued that the defendant should have given a warning to the deceased that the coal was about to be drawn; but, in view of the fact that the plaintiff gave evidence tending to show that the boy sent out word that they should draw the coal, he being at that time in the chute, the necessity for any such warning does not appear. It was a matter of no consequence, so far as he was concerned, whether his message was communicated to the parties outside or not. He, at least, was bound to avoid a danger which he must have had knowledge was likely to occur immediately. We think a verdict for the defendant should have been directed upon all the testimony. We sustain the first, second, third, seventh, and eighth assignments. Judgment reversed.[16]

16. With the principal case contrast Marsh Wood Prod. Co. v. Babcock & Wilcox Co., 207 Wis. 209, 240 N.W. 392 (1932).

Baltimore & O. R. Co. v. Groeger, 266 U.S. 521, 45 S.Ct. 169, 69 L.Ed. 419 (1925), involved the death of an engineman from a locomotive boiler explosion. Negligence was claimed in the construction of the crown sheet of the boiler without fusible plugs.

"If the question whether the standard of duty fixed by the act required defendant to have a fusible plug in the crown sheet of the boiler were one for the determination of a jury, we think there was evidence which could sustain a verdict in the affirmative or in the negative. But we think the question was not for the jury. * * * The act required a condition which would permit use of the locomotive without unnecessary danger. It left to the carrier the choice of means to be employed to effect that result. While the burden was on the plaintiff to prove a violation of the act by defendant, she was not bound to show that any particular contrivance or invention was suitable or necessary to have and keep the boiler in proper condition. There is a multitude of mechanical questions involved in determining the proper construction, maintenance and use of the boilers, other parts of locomotives, their tenders and appurtenances, all of which are covered by the Boiler Inspection Act, as amended, 45 U.S.C.A. section 23. Inventions are occurring frequently, and there are many devices to accomplish the same

LA SELL v. TRI-STATES THEATRE CORPORATION

Supreme Court of Iowa, 1943.
233 Iowa 929, 11 N.W.2d 36.

[Action for damages for personal injuries, suffered by the plaintiff from a fall, in an aisle of defendant's theater, allegedly caused by the negligence of the defendant. Judgment was rendered for defendant on a verdict by the jury. Plaintiff appealed.]

BLISS, JUSTICE. Appellant's assignments of error are based upon erroneous instructions, and the failure to properly instruct the jury. The appellee contends that if it be conceded the trial court so erred, it was error without prejudice, since its motion to direct a verdict because the appellant had failed to establish either negligence on the part of appellee, or her own freedom from contributory negligence should have been sustained. If there is merit in the appellee's contention it is decisive of this appeal, and makes it unnecessary to pass upon the merits of the errors assigned. Some review of the record is therefore first required.

The appellant, aged 64 years, weighing at the time about 223 pounds, accompanied by her daughter, and the latter's daughter, having paid the required admission, entered the Des Moines Theater, operated by the appellee, about 5 o'clock in the afternoon of June 8, 1941, to attend a moving picture show. Patrons, after passing through the entrance, traverse the lobby, foyer, and promenade, in succession, before taking their seats in the auditorium. * * * The entire

purpose. Comparative merits as to safety or utility are most difficult to determine. It is not for the courts to lay down rules which will operate to restrict the carriers in their choice of mechanical means by which their locomotives, boilers, engine tenders and appurtenances are to be kept in proper condition. Nor are such matters to be left to the varying and uncertain opinions and verdicts of juries. The interests of the carriers will best be served by having and keeping their locomotive boilers safe; and it may well be left to their officers and engineers to decide the engineering questions involved in determining whether to use fusible plugs or other means to that end."

Although decisions of this kind were found most frequently in master and servant cases, the rule was not confined to that relationship. See, e. g., Kilbride v. Carbon Dioxide & Magnesia Co., 201 Pa. 552, 51 A. 347, 88 Am. St.Rep. 829 (1902); James, Accident Liability: Some Wartime Developments, 55 Yale L.J. 365, 376 (1946). Under workmen's compensation laws the rule would have no relevance. And outside of that field, as the next case in the text points out, most modern courts hold that conformity to custom does not automatically preclude a finding of negligence. Maize v. Atlantic Refining Co., 352 Pa. 51, 41 A.2d 850, 160 A.L.R. 449 (1945) ("Other manufacturers * * * are not authorized to prescribe the standards of care by which the respective rights and liabilities of persons subject to the jurisdiction of Pennsylvania courts are determined."); James, op. cit. supra; Morris, Custom & Negligence, 42 Col. L.Rev. 1147, 1154 (1942). Under the circumstances of any given case, however, conformity to custom may tip the scale in favor of a finding that defendant's conduct was so obviously careful that a jury will not be allowed to call it negligent. Morris, op. cit. supra, 1155 et seq.

On the general subject, see James & Sigerson, Particularizing Standards of Conduct in Negligence Trials, 5 Van. L.Rev. 697 (1952).

floor of the auditorium extends from the stage toward the rear, south, on a gradually rising gradient or incline, until it reaches the third row of seats from the rear wall of the auditorium. From the elevation of this line, the level of the aisles gradually slopes downward toward the aisle entrances and coincides with the floor level of the promenade. But the level of the floor under the last three rows of seats in the auditorium, and between those parts of the aisles which slope southward and down, continues on a rising incline to the rear wall. As a result of this method of construction the passageway to the seats in the third row from the rear is on the same level as the aisle, and there is no step-up from the aisle into this passageway. But to enter the passageway to the seats in the second row from the back there is a step-up of approximately five inches, which continues as a ramp or upward-sloping way for a short distance into the passageway. Entrance from the aisle into the last row at the rear of the auditorium is in like manner except that the step-up is somewhat higher.

Appellant and her daughter and granddaughter entered the auditorium at aisle two, the second from the west wall. An usher, with a flashlight, seated them in the second row from the rear, in the section of seats on the left or west of this aisle. The granddaughter sat in the third seat from the aisle, the appellant in the second seat from the aisle, and the daughter in the seat on the aisle and just over the step-up. None of them had any difficulty in taking her seat, and the appellant testified that she did not notice the step-up. The usher did not call their attention to the step-up. Other patrons were passing along the aisle as they came in. Patrons were entering and leaving the auditorium throughout the entertainment. The picture was shown, as is customary, in partial darkness. After they had been in the theater for about three hours, the daughter went to the rest room. She almost fell in stepping to the aisle, but retained her balance. About five or ten minutes later, the appellant took hold of the granddaughter's hand with her left hand, and stepped toward the aisle. Not seeing the step-down because of darkness, and not knowing of its presence, and thinking there was no change in level of the floor on which she was walking, she lost her balance when her foot went to the aisle floor, and she fell forward, striking her head on the metal seat across the aisle. She had never been in this theater before. [The opinion then describes at length the testimony of plaintiff's witnesses.]

[Witnesses for defendant testified that the end of the step was painted with white enamel; that there was a hooded light with a 15 watt bulb immediately under the end seat of the second row which would illuminate the white portion of the step; that there were other lights which would more or less illuminate the place in question.]

No usher or any one else testified for the appellee, respecting the above matters, excepting a theater architect, who stated that "where it is necessary to have the level of the floor on which seats are placed above that which the aisle runs on, a step between the aisle and the floor on which the seats are placed is an approved method of construction." * * *

One ground of appellee's peremptory motion for a directed verdict is: "4. The theatre is constructed and lighted in an approved manner, and in accordance with the customary method of lighting and constructing theatres of similar character and nature."

[Appellee cited several cases.] Of these authorities, the appellee states: "Appellee respectfully submits that the above cases hold as a matter of law that it was not per se faulty construction for appellee to place the seats of the auditorium or theatre at a higher level than the aisle between them as such arrangement has advantages which are obvious; that there is nothing uncommon in this form of construction * * *."

[The court cited several other cases similar to those cited by appellee.] One witness testified that the lighting in appellee's theater was like that which he had seen in other moving picture theaters. There was also testimony that the use of a step to reach a row of seats was approved construction. All of this testimony was admitted without objection. We do not agree with the contention of appellee that because its lighting and construction was in accord with the customary or standard practice of theaters generally, in these respects, that these issues of alleged negligence were issues of law for the court, rather than issues of fact for the jury. The standard of custom cannot be substituted for the legal standard of reasonable or ordinary care under the circumstances. Following an approved method is merely evidentiary and is not conclusive on the question of ordinary care. The standard of care is ordinary care under the circumstances, and not what others have done under like circumstances. Habitual practice of any number, for any period of time, cannot make a negligent act an act of due care and caution. As said in Walgreen-Texas Co. v. Shivers, Tex.Civ.App., 131 S.W.2d 650, 657: "The fact that appellee and other companies had habitually and customarily used the same does not, of itself, show that they had exercised ordinary care. * * * Evidence of such use by other persons engaged in the same kind of business is admissible upon the issues of ordinary care, but the question * * * is whether, under the facts of the particular case, there has been an absence of ordinary care." The rule was tersely stated by Justice Holmes in Texas & P. R. Co. v. Behymer, 189 U.S. 468, 470, 23 S.Ct. 622, 623, 47 L.Ed. 905, 906, thus: "What usually is done may be evidence of what ought to be done, but what ought to be done is fixed by a standard of reasonable prudence, whether it usually is complied with or not." * * * The rule is aptly stated by the able court of the Second Circuit speaking through Learned Hand, J., in The T. J. Hooper, 60 F.2d 737, 739, 740. The owners of cargoes in towed barges sued the barge owners and tug owners for the loss of the cargoes through the negligence of the defendants, in not having radio receiving sets through which they would have been warned of the approaching storm. The defendants contended that it was not the general practice to carry such sets. In affirming judgments for plaintiffs, the court said: "Is it then a final answer that the business had not yet generally adopted receiving sets? There are, no doubt, cases where courts seem to make the general practice of the calling the standard of proper diligence; we have indeed given some currency to the notion ourselves. Ketterer v. Armour & Co., 2 Cir., 247 F. 921, 931, L.R.A.1918D, 798; Spang Chalfant & Co. v. Dimon, etc., Corp., 2 Cir., 57 F.2d 965, 967. Indeed in most cases reasonable prudence is in fact common prudence; but strictly it is never its measure; a whole calling may have unduly lagged in the adoption of new and available devices. It never may set its own tests, however persuasive may be its usages. Courts must in the end say what is required; there are precautions so imperative that even their universal disregard will not excuse their omission." (Citing Shandrew v. Chicago, St. P., M. & O. R. Co., 8 Cir., 142 F. 320, 324, 325, and other cases.) Speaking of evidence of customary conduct and standard methods, Wigmore, in 1 Evidence, Sect. 461, says: "The proper method is to receive it with an express caution that it is merely evidential and is not to serve as a legal standard." [17] In Smith v. Penn Federal Corp., 315 Pa. 20, 172 A. 147, 148, an action for damages against defendant as the operator of a moving picture show, based on inadequate lighting in view of the construction of the theater at the place of plaintiff's fall, there was a judgment for defendant on the jury's verdict, which was affirmed. The court said: "There is nothing in the complaint that defendant's witness was permitted to testify that the type of lighting in the theater was 'in accord with the best known practice in (his) profession in theater lighting'; the value of his evidence as to the use of the shaded light at the end of the second last row of seats, referred to above, was for the jury." In James v. Rhode Island Auditorium, 60 R.I. 405, 199 A. 293, 298, there was judgment on a verdict for plaintiff, and exceptions were overruled. The court said: "The defendant, relying upon the testimony of its expert, argues that it discharged its full duty to its invitees when it constructed its rink like other hockey rinks in various cities. We do not agree with this contention. The practice in other places and the opinion of the expert in this case are circumstances entitled to proper consideration as evidence, but they are not conclusive." Cited in Thurman v. Ice Palace, 36 Cal.App.2d 364, 97 P.2d 999. Respecting similar testimony in McCartan v. Park Butte Theater Co., 103 Mont. 342, 62 P.2d 338, the court held that the issue as to lighting was for the jury.

The decisions of this court are fully in accord with the sound and general rule announced by the various courts above noted.

There has been a tendency by a few courts to depart from the sound, general rule of reasonable or ordinary care and prudence owing

17. As the opinion in the text points out, courts today almost universally will admit evidence of custom as *tending to show* what conduct or what precautions are reasonable under the circumstances, provided the custom is shown to prevail under circumstances sufficiently like those in the case at bar to meet the test of relevancy. Good treatments of the basis for admitting this evidence are to be found in the section in Wigmore cited in the text, and in Morris, Custom & Negligence, 42 Colum.L.Rev. 1147 (1942). See, similarly, George v. Morgan Construction Co., 389 F.Supp. 253 (E.D.Pa. 1975) and Kaiser v. Cook, 67 Wis.2d 460, 227 N.W.2d 50 (1975).

to invitees and patrons, as it applies to moving picture exhibitors, with respect to lighting their theater auditoriums, by lessening and lightening that duty. The reason urged therefor is that since the pictures are best viewed in partial darkness the exhibitors may fulfill their legal obligation for the safety of their patrons, by keeping the lighting at the maximum least interfering with the presentation of the pictures. In other words, the interests of the exhibitors, and the better enjoyment of the patrons are given preference over the safety of the latter with respect to their lives and limbs. This doctrine was first announced, as we believe, in Rosston v. Sullivan, supra, 278 Mass. 31, 179 N.E. 173, 175. The Massachusetts court there said: "While pictures were being shown the defendant violated no duty to the plaintiff if the condition of light was that ordinarily used in exhibiting moving pictures to enable the audience to get a reasonably clear view of the image thrown on the screen. * * * The defendant undoubtedly had a duty to turn on the house lights for the convenience of its patrons within a reasonable time after the show was over."

The courts take judicial notice that it is the common practice of moving picture exhibitors to permit patrons to enter and leave the theater at all times during the show.

The rule of the Rosston case is adopted in Falk v. Stanley Fabian Corp., supra, 115 N.J.L. 141, 178 A. 740, 741. * * *

The Connecticut court subscribed to this same doctrine in Miller v. Poli's New England Theatres, Inc., supra, 125 Conn. 610, 7 A.2d 845, 847, saying: "Under the general rule of duty the issue is not to be decided solely upon the degree of visibility afforded an individual patron, as an isolated fact, without regard to the necessities arising from the nature of the entertainment, and as to these prevailing practice appears to afford a logical standard or test." That court in Falso v. Poli-New England Theatres, supra, 127 Conn. 367, 17 A.2d 5, 6, found this test was not applicable in doing justice to the injured patron, for whom a favorable judgment was affirmed. Evidently the plaintiff offered no express testimony that the lighting was not in accord with the usual standard, since the opinion states: "The defendant's principal contention as summarized in its brief is that there was 'no competent evidence upon which to predicate a finding of noncompliance with or deviation from standard practice.'" But instead of such evidence the plaintiff, by testimony of tests made by an electric cell photometer, showed that at the place of the fall the instrument registered "less than one-tenth of a foot candle," that is less than one-tenth of the light given by a one candle-power light located one foot therefrom—which was practically no light. The opinion also discloses that the stairway was covered by a wine-colored carpet which absorbed 80 per cent and reflected 20 per cent of the light falling upon it. The court therefore held: "That test (prevailing practice) is not exclusive. * * * Under such circumstances (the particular facts in the case) the test of that care which an ordinary reasonably prudent man would exercise under the circumstances is adequate without resort to that of the standard practice urged by the defendant." 17 A.2d at page 7.

The impracticability and the probative weakness of the standard practice test of negligence is made manifest when you consider the great variety of theater construction, the diversity of lighting in capacity and shading, the variety, presence, and absence of balconies, pillars, etc., which cast shadows, the reflecting powers of the carpeting, tapestries, wall coloring, and numerous other factors. There is ordinarily no absolute test, where human conduct is a controlling factor, of either negligence or due care, in a particular instance, unless it is by statute or statutory construction. * * *

It would have been no unreasonable burden for the appellee to have discontinued the use of the two rows of seats containing the dangerous steps. They constituted approximately one twentieth of the main floor seating capacity. Their discontinuance might have reduced the net income slightly, but it would have entirely eliminated the danger. As it was, after the appellant was injured, on the advice and under the direction of its expert witness, who would not say whether the danger was thereby lessened, the appellee replaced the steps with ramps. When one goes into a hazardous business—and it must be conceded that a darkened theater has its hazards—he must take that into consideration, and assume the burdens, and take the precautions which a reasonably and ordinarily prudent person would use under all of the circumstances. The fact that partial darkness is essential to the conduct of the business does not exempt him from this duty of reasonable care, nor does it lighten his burden thereunder. In fact it requires him to increase his care and watchfulness if necessary to make it commensurate with, and in proportion to, the patent, and to the reasonably expectable and foreseeable dangers which may injure his invitees and patrons. Such increased care, nevertheless, is nothing more than the legal standard of ordinary, or reasonable, care.

It appeared in the examination of appellee's theater architect that under his supervision the appellee's theater was remodeled somewhat, after the appellant's injury, by removing the step which caused the appellant's fall and other similar steps in the theater, and putting in their place ramps or gradually sloped inclines the lower ends of which were level and flush with the aisle floors. This expert witness had testified that the use of the steps was *necessary* and approved theater construction. The witness was cross-examined at length respecting this substitution and the reasons therefor, and the results effected. He admitted that both methods of construction were used. He testified that the ramp construction "is one practical way to do it. I don't think it is more dangerous to do it that way. Question. Now, as a matter of fact, isn't it less dangerous? Answer. I don't believe I can give you a yes or no on that, because there are some elements that enter into it. *We considered the danger of coming from this seat down to that change, lower level, stepping into that aisle, and whether there wasn't a possibility of that.* I am giving you the practical considerations that came into this argument. Anybody might form their opinion on it. * * * We debated over the safe method of construction. We don't know yet which way is the best. We did do it. * * * The only method we have is to hark back to experience and judgment and consultation with our client." This examination is an admission that the elevation of seats making it necessary to reach them by a "step construction" is dangerous. One of the factors entering into such construction of elevated seats, according to the witness, is "how many seats are required. Maybe how much money they can afford to spend." Approximately nineteen-twentieths of the seats in the ground floor of the auditorium were elevated so that all might see, but it was by a gradual incline of the floor from the stage to the rear of the auditorium and without any steps.

The matter of the discontinuance of the steps and the substitution of ramps had a very important relation to, and bearing upon, the claim of appellee, and the testimony of the expert that the step construction was necessary, and was approved construction. The jury was entitled to have the full benefit of the testimony relative to the remodeling, and all reasonable inferences deducible therefrom, with respect to this claim of the appellee and this testimony of the expert. Yet the court instructed the jury as follows: " * * * *and the fact that the building has been remodeled and changes made in the floor should not be considered by you in arriving at your verdict in this case.*" (Italics ours.) * * *

The italicized portion of Instruction 9 is clearly erroneous and prejudicial.[18] The testimony respecting the remodeling, both direct, and cross-examination, was all in the record and went to the jury. It was competent, relevant, and material. The weight and probative value of this testimony and of all reasonable inferences therefrom were for the jury to consider, and the court invaded the province of the jury in instructing them to give no consideration to the testimony. We are not questioning the rule that generally subsequent repairs or changes in the place causing the injury cannot be shown to prove the alleged negligence. * * *

Reversed and remanded. [Two judges dissented.]

18. In a note to this case it was said, "It is surprising that the majority, contrary to the overwhelming weight of authority says this is reversible error. * * *" 29 Iowa L.Rev. 511, 516 (1944). Compare the next case and note thereto.

STEVENS v. BOSTON ELEVATED R. CO.

Supreme Judicial Court of Massachusetts, 1903.
184 Mass. 476, 69 N.E. 338.

[Actions of tort for injuries and death of a hackman in a funeral whose carriage was struck by a car of defendant. Plaintiff had judgment and defendant alleges exceptions.]

The exception relied upon was as follows:

The plaintiff offered in evidence one of the rules in a certain book admitted by the defendant to be a book of rules issued by the defendant company to its motormen and conductors, and admitted to have been the book of rules that was in force on the day of the accident. The rule which the plaintiff offered was Rule 83, and was as follows:

"Gong Ringing. The gong must always be sounded before starting, when starting, and before reaching, and at all street crossings, when passing other cars or vehicles, and at all points where vehicles or foot passengers are crossing or are liable to cross the tracks. The gong must not be sounded wantonly or unnecessarily, and when passing places of worship during service hours, making as little noise as possible. Upon approaching streets or crossings the power must be shut off and the car kept under perfect control. This rule must be strictly observed during all hours of the day and night."

To the admission of this rule the defendant objected. The counsel for the plaintiff said: "I put it in as a rule of conduct for your motorman by which he is to be judged to some degree." The judge then said: "I suppose it is put upon the same ground that an ordinance is put upon as bearing upon the carelessness or negligence of the person by whom the rules are to be followed. I will admit the evidence and save Mr. Thompson his exception." The rule was then admitted in evidence. * * *

KNOWLTON, C. J. * * * The decisions in different jurisdictions are not entirely harmonious upon the question now raised, but we are of opinion that the weight of authority and of reason tends to support the ruling of the judge in the present case. * * *

It is contended by the defendant that there is no sound principle under which such evidence can be admitted. The evidence is somewhat analogous to proof of the violation of an ordinance or statute by the defendant or his servant, which is always received as evidence, although not conclusive, of the defendant's negligence. Wright v. Walden & Melrose Railroad Co., 4 Allen 283. Lane v. Atlantic Works, 111 Mass. 136. Hall v. Ripley, 119 Mass. 135. Hanlon v. South Boston Horse R. Co., 129 Mass. 310. Such an ordinance or statute, enacted by a body representing the interests of the public, imposes *prima facie* upon everybody a duty of obedience. Disobedience is, therefore, a breach of duty, unless some excuse for it can be shown which creates a different duty, that, as between man and man, overrides the duty imposed by the statute or ordinance. Such disobedience in a matter affecting the plaintiff is always competent upon the question whether the defendant was negligent. So a rule made by a corporation for the guidance of its servants in matters affecting the safety of others is made in the performance of a duty, by a party that is called upon to consider methods, and determine how its business shall be conducted. Such a rule, made known to its servants, creates a duty of obedience as between the master and the servant, and disobedience of it by the servant is negligence as between the two. If such disobedience injuriously affects a third person, it is not to be assumed in favor of the master that the negligence was immaterial to the injured person, and that his rights were not affected by it. Rather ought it to be held an implication that there was a breach of duty towards him, as well as towards the master who prescribed the conduct that he thought necessary or desirable for protection in such cases. Against the proprietor of a business, the methods which he adopts for the protection of others are some evidence of what he thinks necessary or proper to insure their safety.

A distinction may well be made between precautions taken voluntarily before an accident, and precautions which are suggested and adopted after an accident. This distinction is pointed out in Columbia & Puget Sound R. Co. v. Hawthorne, 144 U.S. 202, 207, 12 S.Ct. 591, 36 L.Ed. 405. Mr. Justice Gray, referring to changes made by a defendant after an accident, says in the opinion, "It is now settled, upon much consideration, by the decisions of the highest courts of most of the States in which the question has arisen, that the evidence is incompetent, because the taking of such precautions against the future is not to be construed as an admission of responsibility for the past, has no legitimate tendency to prove that the defendant had been negligent before the accident happened, and is calculated to distract the minds of the jury from the real issue, and to create a prejudice against the defendant." In Morse v. Minneapolis & St. Louis Ry., 30 Minn. 465, 16 N.W. 358, it is said, referring to the same subject, that "A person may have exercised all the care which the law required, and yet, in the light of his new experience, after an unexpected accident has occurred, and as a measure of extreme caution, he may adopt additional safeguards." See also Illinois Central R. v. Swisher, 61 Ill.App. 611. In Menard v. Boston & Maine R. Co., 150 Mass. 386, 23 N.E. 214, and in some of the earlier cases there is language which goes further than the decision, and which might imply that such evidence as was received in this case is incompetent, but the case is authority only for that which was decided.

Exceptions overruled.[19]

19. Accord (as to company rules) Atlanta Consol. St. Ry. Co. v. Bates, 103 Ga. 333, 30 S.E. 41 (1898); Montgomery v. Baltimore & O. R. Co., 22 F.2d 359 (6th Cir., 1927). Cf. Zinnel v. U. S. Shipping Board Emergency Fleet Corp., 10 F.2d 47 (2d Cir., 1925) (testimony that defendant had in fact furnished ropes for safety of seamen on deck in heavy seas held evidence of the proper standard of care for their safety. Here there was also evidence that the ropes had not been furnished and this warranted a finding of breach of duty). Some courts exclude evidence of company rules when offered to

BRUNE v. BELINKOFF

Supreme Judicial Court of Massachusetts, 1968.
354 Mass. 102, 235 N.E.2d 793.

SPALDING, JUSTICE. In this action of tort for malpractice Theresa Brune (plaintiff) seeks to recover from the defendant because of alleged negligence in administering a spinal anesthetic.
* * *

The plaintiff was delivered of a baby on October 4, 1958, at St. Luke's Hospital in New Bedford. During the delivery, the defendant, a specialist in anesthesiology practising in New Bedford, administered a spinal anesthetic to the plaintiff containing eight milligrams of pontocaine in one cubic centimeter of ten per cent solution of glucose. When the plaintiff attempted to get out of bed eleven hours later, she slipped and fell on the floor. The plaintiff subsequently complained of numbness and weakness in her left leg, an affliction which appears to have persisted to the time of trial.

Testimony was given by eight physicians. Much of it related to the plaintiff's condition. There was ample evidence that her condition resulted from an excessive dosage of pontocaine.

There was medical evidence that the dosage of eight milligrams of pontocaine was excessive and that good medical practice required a dosage of five milligrams or less. There was also medical evidence, including testimony of the defendant, to the effect that a dosage of eight milligrams in one cubic centimeter of ten per cent dextrose was

show what constitutes reasonable conduct. Louisville & N. R. Co. v. Vaughan's Adm'r, 183 Ky. 829, 210 S. W. 938 (1919) ("the care that employees of railroad companies must exercise towards the general public is to be determined by the principles of law, and not by the rules adopted by the company for the guidance of employees").

Perhaps the most thoughtful opinion of those excluding such rules is that in Fonda v. St. Paul City R. Co., 71 Minn. 438, 74 N.W. 166, 70 Am.St.Rep. 341 (1898) ("The effect of [admitting them] is that, the more cautious and careful a man is in the adoption of rules in the management of his business in order to protect others, the worse he is off, and the higher the degree of care he is bound to exercise. A person may, out of abundant caution, adopt rules requiring of his employees a much higher degree of care than the law imposes. This is a practice that ought to be encouraged, and not discouraged. But if the adoption of such a course is to be used against him as an admission, he would naturally find it to his interest not to adopt any rules at all.") Compare the reasoning behind the general exclusion of evidence of post-accident precautions, and consider whether the argument has greater force in one situation than it has in the other.

The violation of an industry-wide private safety code is sometimes admissible as evidence of negligence, e. g., Evans v. Howard R. Green Co., 231 N.W.2d 907 (Iowa 1975).

As to the admissibility of evidence showing repairs, etc., made after the accident, see Town of Waterbury v. Waterbury Traction Co., 74 Conn. 152, 50 A. 3 (1901); Shelton v. Southern R. Co., 193 N.C. 670, 139 S.E. 232 (1927); Chicago, B. & Q. R. Co. v. Kelley, 34 F.2d 80 (8th Cir., 1934); Arcement v. Southern Pacific Transportation Company, 517 F.2d 729 (5th Cir. 1975); Edwards v. Sears Roebuck & Co., 512 F.2d 276 5th Cir. 1975); doCanto v. Ametek, Inc., —— Mass. ——, 328 N.E.2d 873 (1975) (safety features adopted after sale but before injury); 2 Wigmore Evidence (3d ed. 1940) section 283; Federal Rules of Evidence, Rule 407 (1975).

proper. There was evidence that this dosage was customary in New Bedford in a case, as here, of a vaginal delivery.[20]

1. The plaintiffs' exception to the refusal to give their first request for instruction and their exception to a portion of the charge present substantially the same question and will be considered together. The request reads: "As a specialist, the defendant owed the plaintiff the duty to have and use the care and skill commonly possessed and used by similar specialist[s] in like circumstances." The relevant portion of the charge excepted to was as follows: "[The defendant] must measure up to the standard of professional care and skill ordinarily possessed by others in his profession in the community, which is New Bedford, and its environs, of course, where he practices, having regard to the current state of advance of the profession. If, in a given case, it were determined by a jury that the ability and skill of the physician in New Bedford were fifty percent inferior to that which existed in Boston, a defendant in New Bedford would be required to measure up to the standard of skill and competence and ability that is ordinarily found by physicians in New Bedford."

The basic issue raised by the exceptions to the charge and to the refused request is whether the defendant was to be judged by the standard of doctors practising in New Bedford.

The instruction given to the jury was based on the rule, often called the "community" or "locality" rule first enunciated in Small v. Howard, 128 Mass. 131, a case decided in 1880. There the defendant, a general practitioner in a country town with a population of 2,500 was consulted by the plaintiff to treat a severe wound which required a considerable degree of surgical skill. In an action against the defendant for malpractice this court defined his duty as follows: "It is a matter of common knowledge that a physician in a small country village does not usually make a specialty of surgery, and, however well informed he may be in the theory of all parts of his profession, he would, generally speaking, be but seldom called upon as a surgeon to perform difficult operations. He would have but few opportunities of observation and practice in that line such as public hospitals or large cities would afford. The defendant was applied to, being the practitioner in a small village, and we think it was correct to rule that 'he was bound to possess that skill only which physicians and surgeons of ordinary ability and skill, practising in similar localities, with opportunities for no larger experience, ordinarily possess; and he was not bound to possess that high degree of art and skill possessed by eminent surgeons practising in large cities, and making a specialty of the practice of surgery.'" The rule in Small v. Howard has been followed and applied in a long line of cases, some of which are quite recent. * * * Although in some of the later decisions the court

20. The defendant testified that such variations as there were in the dosages administered in Boston and New York, as distinct from New Bedford, were due to differences in obstetrical technique. The New Bedford obstetricians use suprafundi pressure (pressure applied to the uterus during delivery) which "requires a higher level of anesthesia."

has said that the doctor must exercise the care prevailing in "the locality where he practiced" it is doubtful if the court intended to narrow the rule in Small v. Howard where the expression "similar localities" was used.[21]

The rationale of the rule of Small v. Howard is that a physician in a small or rural community will lack opportunities to keep abreast with the advances in the profession and that he will not have the most modern facilities for treating his patients. Thus, it is unfair to hold the country doctor to the standard of doctors practising in large cities. The plaintiffs earnestly contend that distinctions based on geography are no longer valid in view of modern developments in transportation, communication and medical education, all of which tend to promote a certain degree of standardization within the profession. Hence, the plaintiffs urge that the rule laid down in Small v. Howard almost ninety years ago now be reëxamined in the light of contemporary conditions.

The "community" or "locality" rule has been modified in several jurisdictions and has been subject to critical comment in legal periodicals.[22]

One approach, in jurisdictions where the "same community rule" obtains, has been to extend the geographical area which constitutes the community. The question arises not only in situations involving the standard of care and skill to be exercised by the doctor who is being sued for malpractice, but also in the somewhat analogous situations concerning the qualifications of a medical expert to testify. See Sampson v. Veenboer, 252 Mich. 660, 666–667, 234 N.W. 170 (expert from another State permitted to testify as to standards in Grand Rapids, in view of evidence that he was familiar with standards in similar localities). In Connecticut which has the "same locality rule," it was said by the Supreme Court of Errors, "Our rule does not restrict the territorial limitation to the confines of the town or city in which the treatment was rendered, and under modern conditions there is perhaps less reason than formerly for such restriction. There is now no lack of opportunity for the physician or surgeon in smaller communities to keep abreast of the advances made in his profession, and to be familiar with the latest methods and practices adopted. It is not unreasonable to require that he have and exercise the skill of physicians and surgeons in similar localities in the same general neighborhood. It may not be sufficient if he exercise only that degree of skill possessed by other practitioners in the community in which he lives." Geraty v. Kaufman, 115 Conn. 563, 573–574, 162 A. 33, 36.

Other courts have emphasized such factors as accessibility to medical facilities and experience. See Tvedt v. Haugen, 70 N.D. 338,

21. For a general collection of cases dealing with the community or locality rule, see Annotation, 8 A.L.R.2d 772.

22. See note, 14 Stanford L.Rev. 884; note, 36 Iowa L.Rev. 681; note, 35 Minn.L.Rev. 186, 190; note, 60 Northwestern L.Rev. 834, 837; note, 36 Marquette L.Rev. 392; McCoid, The Care Required of Medical Practitioners, 12 Vanderbilt L.Rev. 549, 569 et seq. See also Prosser, Torts (3d ed.) § 32 (pp. 166–167).

294 N.W. 183, 132 A.L.R. 379, where the defendant doctor recognized that the plaintiff's injury required the care of a specialist but failed to call this to the attention of the plaintiff. The court said at p. 349, 294 N.W. at p. 188: "The duty of a doctor to his patient is measured by conditions as they exist, and not by what they have been in the past or may be in the future. Today, with the rapid methods of transportation and easy means of communication, the horizons have been widened, and the duty of a doctor is not fulfilled merely by utilizing the means at hand in the particular village where he is practicing. So far as medical treatment is concerned, the borders of the locality and community have, in effect, been extended so as to include those centers readily accessible where appropriate treatment may be had which the local physician, because of limited facilities or training, is unable to give." And in Cavallaro v. Sharp, 84 R.I. 67, 121 A.2d 669, a medical expert formerly of Philadelphia was allowed to testify as to required degree of care in Providence, the court saying at page 72, 121 A.2d at page 672, "The two localities cannot be deemed so dissimilar as to preclude an assumption that mastoidectomies are performed by otologists in Providence with the same average degree of careful and skillful technique as in Philadelphia. It is to be remembered in this connection that Providence is not a small city but is the metropolitan center of upwards of a million people, and moreover is in reasonable proximity to Boston, one of the principal medical centers of the country."

Other decisions have adopted a standard of reasonable care and allow the locality to be taken into account as one of the circumstances, but not as an absolute limit upon the skill required. See McGulpin v. Bessmer, 241 Iowa 1119, 43 N.W.2d 121; Viita v. Fleming, 132 Minn. 128, 135–137, 155 N.W. 1077, L.R.A.1916D, 644. In the case last cited the court said at page 137, 155 N.W. at page 1081, "Frequent meetings of medical societies, articles in the medical journals, books by acknowledged authorities, and extensive experience in hospital work put the country doctor on more equal terms with his city brother. * * * [W]e are unwilling to hold that he is to be judged only by the qualifications that others in the same village or similar villages possess."

Recently the Supreme Court of Washington (sitting en banc) virtually abandoned the "locality" rule in Pederson v. Dumouchel, Wash., 431 P.2d 973, 978. There the trial judge charged that the defendant doctor was required to exercise the care and skill of others in the same or similar localities. This instruction, on appeal, was held to be erroneous. In the course of its well reasoned opinion the court said, "the 'locality rule' has no present-day vitality except that it may be considered as *one* of the elements to determine the degree of care and skill which is to be expected of the average practitioner of the class to which he belongs. The degree of care which must be observed is, of course, that of an average, competent practitioner acting in the same or similar circumstances. In other words, local practice within geographic proximity is one, but not the only factor to be considered. No longer is it proper to limit the definition of the standard of care which a medical doctor or dentist must meet solely to the practice or custom of a particular locality, a similar locality, or a geographic area." In another recent case the Supreme Court of Appeals of West Virginia criticised the "locality" rule and appears to have abandoned it in the case of specialists. Hundley v. Martinez, W.Va., 158 S.E.2d 159.

In cases involving specialists the Supreme Court of New Jersey has abandoned the "locality" rule. See Carbone v. Warburton, 11 N.J. 418, where it was said at page 426, 94 A.2d 680, at page 683, " '[O]ne who holds himself out as a specialist must employ not merely the skill of a general practitioner, but also the special degree of skill normally possessed by the average physician who devotes special study and attention to the particular organ or disease or injury involved, having regard to the present state of scientific knowledge.' "

Because of the importance of the subject, and the fact that we have been asked to abandon the "locality" rule we have reviewed the relevant decisions at some length. We are of opinion that the "locality" rule of Small v. Howard which measures a physician's conduct by the standards of other doctors in similar communities is unsuited to present day conditions. The time has come when the medical profession should no longer be Balkanized by the application of varying geographic standards in malpractice cases. Accordingly, Small v. Howard is hereby overruled. The present case affords a good illustration of the inappropriateness of the "locality" rule to existing conditions. The defendant was a specialist practising in New Bedford, a city of 100,000, which is slightly more than fifty miles from Boston, one of the medical centers of the nation, if not the world. This is a far cry from the country doctor in Small v. Howard, who ninety years ago was called upon to perform difficult surgery. Yet the trial judge told the jury that if the skill and ability of New Bedford physicians were "fifty percent inferior" to those obtaining in Boston the defendant should be judged by New Bedford standards, "having regard to the current state of advance of the profession." This may well be carrying the rule of Small v. Howard to its logical conclusion, but it is, we submit, a reductio ad absurdum of the rule.

The proper standard is whether the physician, if a general practitioner, has exercised the degree of care and skill of the average qualified practitioner, taking into account the advances in the profession. In applying this standard it is permissible to consider the medical resources available to the physician as *one* circumstance in determining the skill and care required. Under this standard some allowance is thus made for the type of community in which the physician carries on his practice. See Prosser, Torts (3d ed.) § 32 (pp. 166–167); compare Restatement of Torts, Second § 299A, comment g.

One holding himself out as a specialist should be held to the standard of care and skill of the average member of the profession practising the specialty, taking into account the advances in the profession. And, as in the case of the general practitioner, it is permissible to consider the medical resources available to him.

Because the instructions permitted the jury to judge the defendant's conduct against a standard that has now been determined to be incorrect, the plaintiffs' exceptions to the charge and to the refusal of his request must be sustained.

2. The plaintiffs excepted to the refusal of the judge to give certain other requests for instructions. Of these we shall deal with only the eleventh, as the others are not likely to arise on a retrial of the case.[23] The ruling arose in this setting. There was evidence that in a brochure published by the manufacturers of pontocaine the use of two to five milligrams in dextrose was recommended for a vaginal (saddle block) delivery, and the defendant testified that he was familiar with the contents of this brochure. There was medical evidence that it was good medical practice to follow the recommendations of the manufacturer with respect to dosages for spinal anesthetics. There was, however, testimony by an anesthesiologist that the recommendations contained in the brochure were "intended as a guide to physicians, not to anesthesiologists." In support of their request the plaintiffs invoke the decisions holding that a violation of a rule previously adopted by a defendant in relation to the safety of third persons is admissible as tending to show negligence of the defendant's disobedient servant. Stevens v. Boston Elev. Ry., 184 Mass. 476, 69 N.E. 338. We think that this principle has no application here. The statement concerning dosages in the brochure was quite different from the rule adopted for the safety of third persons in the *Stevens* case. It was no more than a recommendation, and there was a difference of opinion among the anesthesiologists as to whether the failure to follow it was improper practice. The judge rightly refused to give the requested instruction.[24]

23. The eleventh request was: "The failure of the defendant to follow the instructions of the manufacturer in the use of Pontocaine is evidence of negligence." [Notes 20–23 from original, renumbered; other notes in original omitted.]

24. This case is noted at 82 Harv.L.Rev. 1781 (1969). Also see Anno., 37 A.L.R. 3d 420 (1971); Shier v. Freedman, 58 Wis.2d 269, 206 N.W.2d 166, rehearing denied 208 N.W.2d 328 (1973). As to admissibility of drug company warnings compare Ohligschlager v. Proctor Community Hospital, 55 Ill.2d 411, 303 N.E.2d 392 (1973).

Who is the "average" qualified practitioner? Are nearly half substandard? See Restatement of Torts Second § 299A, Comment e (1965); Blair v. Eblen, 461 S.W.2d 370 (Ky.1970) and Shilkret v. Annapolis Emergency Hospital Ass'n, 276 Md. 187, 349 A.2d 245 (1975) (substituting "reasonably competent practitioner in the same class to which he belongs"). The Kentucky and Maryland opinions introduce a different ambiguity, possibly insignificant: they refer to the degree of care and skill "expected of" (rather than customarily possessed or exercised by) such persons.

Proof that the medical care which was given accorded with any among the practices accepted as proper by any responsible physicians qualified in the particular field should ordinarily shield a doctor from liability for malpractice. See, e. g., Rytkonen v. Lojacono, 269 Mich. 270, 257 N.W. 703 (1934); Bolam v. Friern Hospital Management Committee [1957] 1 W.L.R. 582, 586–88, [1957] 2 All E.R. 118, 121–22 (Q.B.D.) ("* * * [T]here may be one or more perfectly proper stand-

HOMERE v. STATE OF NEW YORK

New York Supreme Court, Appellate Division, Third Department, 1975.
48 A.D.2d 422, 370 N.Y.S.2d 246.

MAIN, JUSTICE. This is an appeal from judgments in favor of claimants, entered December 5, 1974, upon a decision of the Court of Claims solely on the issue of liability for injuries which claimants sustained as the result of attacks by a former Pilgrim State Hospital patient.

On the morning of March 20, 1972, the two female claimants herein were assaulted at the Aqueduct Station of the Independent Subway Line, Queens County, New York. The identity of their assailant is conceded to be Melvin Samuels, a man who had been released from the Pilgrim State Hospital earlier that same morning and whose past record included repeated incidents of assaultive behavior and numerous confinements in State psychiatric hospitals. Finding that Samuels had been negligently discharged from the hospital, the trial court held that the State was thereby rendered liable for claimants' injuries resulting from the attacks. It is this decision which is challenged on this appeal.

We find that the judgments of the trial court must be affirmed. Although it is well settled that the State is not responsible for an

ards; and if a medical man conforms with one of those proper standards then he is not negligent. * * * A doctor is not guilty of negligence if he has acted in accordance with a practice accepted as proper by a responsible body of medical men skilled in that particular art. * * * [A] doctor is not negligent, if he is acting in accordance with such a practice, merely because there is a body of opinion that takes a contrary view. At the same time, that does not mean that a medical man can obstinately and pigheadedly carry on with some old technique if it has been proved to be contrary to what is really substantially the whole of informed medical opinion. Otherwise you might get men today saying: 'I don't believe in anaesthetics. I don't believe in antiseptics. I am going to continue to do my surgery in the way it was done in the eighteenth century.' That clearly would be wrong."); California Jury Instructions—Civil BAJI 6.03 (5th ed. 1969); Robinson v. Post Office and Another [1974] 1 W.L.R. 1176 (C.A.); Chumbler v. McClure, 505 F.2d 489 (5th Cir. 1974); see also Rickett v. Hayes, 256 Ark. 893, 511 S.W.2d 187 (1974). There are, however, occasional inconsistent decisions, e. g., Ault v. Hall, 119 Ohio 422, 164 N.E. 518, 60 A.L.R. 128 (1928) (refusing to direct verdict for defendant despite undisputed evidence of custom among surgeons in Cleveland to rely on sponge count of nurses); Helling v. Carey, 83 Wash.2d 514, 519 P.2d 981 (1974) (liability of ophthalmologists for failure to administer glaucoma pressure test, where test would have been cheap, easy and harmless, and would have saved 32-year-old patient loss of vision, despite undisputed expert testimony that the standards of the profession for that specialty do not require routine pressure tests for glaucoma on patients under 40 years of age; a concurring opinion on behalf of three justices suggests that this loss should have been imposed on the ophthalmologists in the circumstances as a matter of strict liability, so as not to stigmatise them with moral blame where they had followed all normal precautions of their profession; see similarly Justice Tobriner's concurring opinion in Clark v. Gibbons, page 273 infra). For an interesting general discussion applicable to issues raised not only in this chapter but also in Chapter 6 infra see Comment, Professional Negligence, 121 U.Pa.L.Rev. 627 (1973).

honest error of professional judgment made by qualified and competent doctors in its employ (Williams v. State of New York, 30 A.D. 2d 611, 290 N.Y.S.2d 263; St. George v. State of New York, 283 App. Div. 245, 127 N.Y.S.2d 147, affd., 308 N.Y. 681, 124 N.E.2d 320), this rule does not constitute an inflexible grant of total immunity to the State in all situations. Indeed, in St. George v. State of New York (supra, p. 248, 127 N.Y.S.2d p. 151), this court qualified its finding of no liability by saying that it would be unreasonable and unfair to hold the State responsible "unless there is something more present than is contained in this record".

Here, there is clearly "something more" which justifies the trial court's ruling in favor of claimants. In view of Samuels' past history, his treating psychiatrist, Dr. Chaudhary, termed his case "somewhat unusual" and found it necessary to convene a commission of three doctors to approve his discharge when, ordinarily, one doctor would make this decision. The commission thereupon made an evaluation of the patient and decided that he could be discharged on February 7, 1972, and, as conceded by claimants' expert witness, Dr. Orenstein, had Samuels been released at that time and the subsequent attacks had occurred, no liability would have attached to the State because of the rule enunciated in St. George v. State of New York (supra). However, in this case, the patient's ultimate release was delayed some (41) days until housing had been arranged for him outside of the hospital. In the intervening period, incidents occurred which effectively negated the commission's decision of February 7. On February 23, Samuels became violent and smashed windows and was throwing things. This conduct necessitated his being restrained in a straitjacket which he refused to come out of the next day. On the following two days, he suffered seizures and became uncontrollable and help was needed to restrain him, and yet, in spite of all these occurrences, there was no reevaluation of the patient's condition or suitability for release prior to his discharge on March 20.

In our opinion, these incidents plainly indicated a marked deterioration in the patient's condition which should have put the appropriate hospital authorities and the releasing doctor on notice that there had been a change for the worse in the patient's condition following the commission's recommendation for discharge. In such circumstances, while a reevaluation by "a commission" was not necessarily mandated, certainly another medical judgment was required to determine the patient's fitness for release, and we hold that the State's failure to make any further evaluation of Samuels prior to his discharge constitutes negligence, which was the proximate cause of claimants' injuries in a manner completely foreseeable.

In conclusion and at the risk of some repetition, we would reemphasize that we are in no way abrogating the rule enunciated in St. George v. State of New York (supra). We impose liability upon the State not for an erroneous medical judgment, but rather for its failure to make anything other than a purely administrative decision to release Samuels following the incidents of violence in February of 1972.

The judgments should be affirmed, with costs. * * * [25]

ZeBARTH v. SWEDISH HOSPITAL MEDICAL CENTER

Supreme Court of Washington, 1972.
81 Wash.2d 12, 499 P.2d 1.

HALE, ASSOCIATE JUSTICE. Defendant hospital administered to plaintiff a course of radiation therapy in treating him for Hodgkin's disease. About a year after the treatments had ended, plaintiff became paralyzed from injury to his spinal cord. He brought this action against the hospital alleging negligence in the treatment, and a jury returned a verdict in the sum of $450,280. Defendant hospital appeals a judgment entered upon that verdict * * *.

The doctors * * * told plaintiff that he had Hodgkin's disease, that it was a form of cancer, and that it would require extensive treatment. The record is not clear whether he was told it was a fatal disease although all experts agree that, if left unimpeded by therapy, it will with extremely rare exception prove fatal. It is a virtual certainty, however, that plaintiff knew he was very seriously ill. * * *

Dr. Frederick Warren Lovell, a specialist in pathology, called by the plaintiff, testified that * * * at the time plaintiff entered the defendant clinic, he was suffering from the "subgroup of malignant lymphoma" identified more particularly as "Hodgkin's sarcoma" or, as it is otherwise described, "reticulum cell sarcoma." * * * Corroborating other medical specialists on this point, Dr. Lovell said that the lymphoma afflicting plaintiff was one of a group that is very responsive to radiation, pointing out that lymphomas respond much better to radiation therapy than that other group of cancers known as carcinoma.

After reviewing the hospital records of myelograms that had been taken, and the records of bone marrow studies, and having examined the plaintiff's bone marrow, in response to the question as "to whether or not Mr. ZeBarth's present paraplegia is due to the radiation he received," Dr. Lovell testified that in his opinion, "[Mr. ZeBarth] has irradiation myelitis in the spinal cord at the level of approximately the 5th dorsal vertebra." Referring to external appearance and some apparent amendments or changes in the records of the amounts of radiation administered to the patient, the doctor testified that the defendant's skin showed a marked radiation scarring reaction on his back and that ZeBarth had probably received substantially more radiation to his back than the record indicated. * * *

Seven highly trained and certified medical specialists testified in the case, * * * There was no substantial conflict among them

25. Compare Hicks v. United States, 511 F.2d 407 (D.C.Cir. 1975).

* * * that a total dosage of 4,000 Roentgen (R.) of radiation administered over a 4-week period in fractionated doses did not depart from accepted medical standards, but there was a dispute as to whether a first dose in the amount of 1,000 R. was excessive and dangerous.

It was upon this initial 1,000 R. dose that the issue of negligence as a fact largely depended, but there were other claims of negligence, too. The evidence conflicted on whether the first treatment of 1,000 R. was properly administered, and whether the remaining total treatment did not in fact exceed the 3,000 R. as recorded. * * *

All of these varying considerations of fact were, we think, resolved at trial. There was a sharp conflict in the evidence given by highly trained and qualified medical specialists as to whether the plaintiff on his first visit to defendant institute was in such extreme emergency as to require a massive first dosage to preserve his life. There was an equally sharp conflict as to whether, assuming such an extreme emergency a lesser fractionated dosage at the outset would be expected to produce such a swelling of the trachea and adjacent tissue so as to deprive the patient of breath and thereby life. There was testimony to the contrary: that plaintiff, ambulatory and suffering little physical discomfort at the time of the first examination and treatment by defendant, was not in extremis and that, allowing for the normal and expected growth of the cancer, he still had many days over which the treatment could have been extended without further endangering his life and, moreover, with substantially less risk of myelopathy.

As earlier noted, defendant moved for a directed verdict and judgment non obstante veredicto, and assigns error to the denial of these motions. Our study of the record convinces us that there was sufficient evidence of negligence to take the case to the jury. * * *

The next assignment of error is directed to instruction No. 7 [26] concerning what has become known in medical malpractice cases as

26. The court's instruction No. 7 reads: "A doctor engaging in the practice of a medical specialty has the duty to comply with the standard of such practice with regard to informing his patient about the nature and probable results of any proposed radiation treatment and of any alternate methods of radiation treatment known or which should be known to the specialist, the nature and extent of any serious risks involved in any of the methods of treatment and in a refusal of treatment known or which should be known to the specialist but which the patient does not, but should know in order to enable the patient to weigh and balance the anticipated benefits from the respective methods of treatment as opposed to the risks and hazards involved in each and in a refusal of treatment, so the patient can determine whether to consent to the treatment.

"Failure to perform this duty is negligence even though the therapy might be administered and performed with that degree of skill otherwise required.

"This duty, however, is limited to those disclosures which, according to the recognized medical standards of that specialty, should be given by a reasonable doctor practicing the same specialty, in the same or similar circumstances. The standards must be proven by testimony of members of the medical profession practicing the same specialty.

"If therapy is administered without valid consent, it renders those responsible for such administration liable for any damages proximately resulting therefrom."

"informed consent." Informed consent, an obvious misnomer, identifies a principle covering situations where medical treatment involves a grave risk of collateral injury and puts the physician under a duty to advise the patient of such risks before initiating the treatment. Informed consent, therefore, is the name for a general principle of law that a physician has a duty to disclose what a reasonably prudent physician in the medical community in the exercise of reasonable care, would disclose to his patient as to whatever grave risks of injury may be incurred from a proposed course of treatment so that a patient, exercising ordinary care for his own welfare, and faced with a choice of undergoing the proposed treatment, or alternative treatment, or none at all, can, in reaching a decision, intelligently exercise his judgment by reasonably balancing the probable risks against the probable benefits. See Waltz & Scheuneman, Informed Consent to Therapy, 64 Nw.U.L.Rev. 628 (1969–70). Failure to impart such information to the patient is by the great weight of authority deemed negligence rendering the physician liable for injuries proximately caused thereby.

What proof is necessary to establish a duty to inform? From time to time cases may arise where the obligation upon the physician to inform his patient of the risks of treatment is so manifest that a layman, even without the benefit of medical testimony, could reasonably find that the benefits from the proposed therapy would be so slight in relation to the gravity of the risks of harm from it that no medical testimony would be required to prove the duty to inform. For example, high voltage, heavy dosage radiation therapy utilized to treat a wholly benign wart would undoubtedly call for a duty to inform without expert medical testimony to prove it. But in most instances, and as a general rule, the duty to inform the patient must be established by expert medical testimony or reasonable inferences to be drawn from it. Thus, as stated by Waltz & Scheuneman (64 Nw.U.L.Rev. 628, 636), "The great majority of courts follow some professional standard, variously worded. The largest group within this majority would measure the duty according to the custom and practice of physicians within the 'community.'" Some courts within the majority group require the disclosure that a reasonable practitioner would make under the circumstances; others require disclosure consistent with "good medical practice." Whatever may be the verbal formula, however, these courts generally require expert testimony to prove a duty to inform.

We deem it to be the prevailing view and one which should be followed by this court that generally the duty of the physician to inform and the extent of the information required should be established by expert medical testimony. This principle, we think, was suitably expressed in the court's instruction No. 7 * * *.

The duty of a medical doctor to inform his patient of the risks of harm reasonably to be expected from a proposed course of treatment does not place upon the physician a duty to elucidate upon all of the possible risks, but only those of a serious nature. Nor does it contemplate that the patient or those in whose charge he may be are completely ignorant of medical matters. A patient is obliged to exercise the intelligence and act on the knowledge which an ordinary person would bring to the doctors' office. The law does not contemplate that a doctor need conduct a short course in anatomy, medicine, surgery and therapeutics nor that he do anything which in reasonable standards for practice of medicine in the community might be inimical to the patient's best interests. The doctrine of informed consent does not require the doctor to risk frightening the patient out of a course of treatment which sound medical judgment dictates the patient should undertake, nor does the rule assume that the patient possesses less knowledge of medical matters than a person of ordinary understanding could reasonably be expected to have or by law should be charged with having. Nor should the rule declaring a duty to inform be so stated or applied that a physician, in the interest of protecting himself from an overburden of law suits and the attendant costs upon his time and purse, will always follow the most conservative therapy—which, while of doubtful benefit to the patient exposes the patient to no affirmative medical hazards and the doctor to no risks of litigation.[27] Thus, the information required of the doctor by the general rule is that information which a reasonably prudent physician or medical specialist of that medical community should or would know to be essential to enable a patient of ordinary understanding to intelligently decide whether to incur the risk by accepting the proposed treatment or avoid that risk by foregoing it. A doctor or specialist who fails to discharge this duty to inform would thus be liable as for negligence to the patient for the harm proximately resulting from the treatment to which the patient submitted. Whether the information should have been given at all and the nature, kind and extent of the disclosure thus must in most instances be established by expert medical testimony. Anderson v. Hooker, 420 S.W.2d 235 (Tex.Civ.App.1967); Simone v. Sabo, 37 Cal. 2d 253, 231 P.2d 19 (1951). And the standards are those of the medical community of which the physician is a part rather than the geographic location of his practice. Douglas v. Bussabarger, 73 Wash. 2d 476, 438 P.2d 829 (1968); Pederson v. Dumouchel, 72 Wash.2d 73, 431 P.2d 973 (1967).[28] We perceive the general rule to be—except in extraordinary circumstances where the duty to disclose is so clearly manifest that reasonable minds could not in reason differ on the question—that the standards of the medical profession are those to be applied by the jury in deciding that issue of fact. See Advise and Consent in Medicine: A Look at the Doctrine of Informed Consent, 16 N.Y.L.F. 863 (1970); Natanson v. Kline, 186 Kan. 393, 350 P.2d

27. See The Medical Malpractice Threat: A Study of Defensive Medicine, 1971 (No. 5) Duke L.J. 939.

28. In these cases Washington rejected the locality rule for medical malpractice. States which adhere to the locality rule generally in malpractice cases tend to apply it to informed consent cases as well. See, e. g., Karp v. Cooley, 493 F.2d 408, 420 (5th Cir. 1974) (Texas law).

1093, modified, 187 Kan. 186, 354 P.2d 670 (1960). Accord: Douglas v. Bussabarger, supra.

The rules imposing upon a doctor the duty to inform his patient of the possibilities of serious harm or injury from a proposed course of treatment, we are aware, may present dangers to patient and physician alike, and if extravagantly interpreted might in some degree impede the advancement of medical science or operate to deprive the patient of the most modern therapy and latest scientific developments, but these possibilities do not, we think, justify its abrogation. The duty to disclose remains; and the failure to discharge it is negligence.

The question is first a medical question going to the roots of medical judgment in determining what is best for the patient, and then a matter of law as to whether there is sufficient evidence to put the issue to the jury. When the issue is raised in the courts, it is a question of fact for the jury, after considering medical testimony, whether the physician met the standard of his profession under the circumstances. It is a question of fact, and only very rarely solely a question of law. * * *

Dr. Orliss Wildermuth, a highly trained specialist in radiation therapy, practicing on the staff of defendant tumor institute, said that from a medical standpoint a patient about to undergo radiation therapy should be advised in terms of ordinary understanding by his physician of the nature and effect of radiation therapy and the nature and effect of possible alternative treatments, and that the patient needed this medical information in order to reach an intelligent decision as to whether he would undergo the risks. Dr. Frederick Exner, a physician specialist in radiology, called by plaintiff, was more emphatic as to this duty and said in effect that the duty to inform the patient was specifically imposed by the very essence of good practice; and that this was done as a time-honored custom as well as a duty required of a physician in the practice of medicine.

None of the authorities nor the already extensive literature on the subject of informed consent * * * specifies the precise extent or degree of information which must be imparted to meet the medical standards of ordinary care in the practice of medicine. It is, however, generally recognized by the great weight of judicial and scholarly authority that the law does place this duty upon the physician and that the failure to meet it is characterized as a species of negligence.[29]

Because the rule declaring the duty cannot be stated with marked precision, the nature and extent of the disclosure required by it depends in each case upon the peculiar circumstances giving rise to the duty. Thus, our holding can be stated in general terms: a physi-

29. Prosser, Torts, § 32 at 165 (4th ed. 1971). A wholly unauthorized operation would constitute a battery as well as malpractice. Physicians' and Dentists' Business Bureau v. Dray, 8 Wash.2d 38, 111 P.2d 568 (1941). [Notes 26, 27 and 29 from original renumbered; other notes in original omitted.]

cian's duty to inform his patient is to inform his patient what a reasonably prudent medical specialist would tell a person of ordinary understanding of the serious risks and the possibility of serious harm which may occur from a proposed course of therapy so that the patient's choice will be an intelligent one, based upon sufficient knowledge to enable him to balance the possible risks against the probable benefits. * * * The extent of the disclosure is a matter of medical judgment. * * * For discussions and collections of case law on this point, see Fraser & Chadsey, Informed Consent in Malpractice Cases, 6 Willamette L.J. 183 (1970); Informed Consent in Medical Malpractice, 55 Cal.L.Rev. 1396 (1967); Sevier, The Hazards of Medical Treatment: The Duty to Inform and the Right to Know, A.B.A. Sec. of Ins., Neg. & Comp.Law 396 (1967); and Failure to Inform as Medical Malpractice, 23 Vand.L.Rev. 754 (1970). * * *

* * * [T]he court first had to determine whether the evidence warranted an instruction on the subject of informed consent * * * and then * * * whether it, nevertheless, should have been refused because the plaintiff did not testify directly that had he known the risks he would not have accepted the proposed treatment. * * *

Plaintiff professed little knowledge of the possible harmful effects of radiation therapy. He testified that he received no advice or information whatever from defendant institute or the treating physicians as to the hazards of radiation therapy or the harm that might result from it. Neither was the amount, duration and degree of fractionation mentioned to him. He realized that Hodgkin's is regarded as a fatal disease if unarrested; he was in no position to decline radiation therapy despite the hazards of treatment. He thus had no effective choice between some radiation treatment and the almost certain death without it.

But there was a vital choice open to him, had he been informed of the alternative: the initial large dose with the dangers of myelopathy, or a markedly lesser fractionated dose with its attendant danger of swelling. The totality of evidence permits an inference that, had plaintiff been informed that a massive initial dose carried with it a possible danger of a paralysis-inducing myelopathy, in contrast to the usual and lesser dosages so fractionated that the ultimate total amounted to the same, he would have chosen the latter course. * * *

The law does not encourage formulaic or catechistic responses, but looks instead to substance. For the plaintiff to say, after the fact of injury, that he would have refused the initial massive dose, adds little to the credible proof. Although admissible, a statement of that nature is little more than a transparently self-serving response, inviting the recital of a formulated catechism to put form above substance. * * *

We are of the opinion that the record warranted submitting the issue of informed consent to the jury * * *.

HOLLAND v. SISTERS OF SAINT JOSEPH OF PEACE

Supreme Court of Oregon, 1974.
— Or. —, 522 P.2d 208.

HOWELL, JUSTICE. * * *

The plaintiff suffered from cancer of the cervix and was treated by the defendant doctors, McMahan and Wilken. The diagnosis showed a large cancerous tumor affecting the vaginal area and the uterus. Dr. McMahan decided to treat plaintiff with radiation because he believed that alternative methods of treatment, such as surgery or chemotherapy, would be inappropriate in plaintiff's case. He did so treat her, using a cobalt treatment and placing radium capsules in her body for a period of time. Thereafter severe complications arose. Plaintiff went to the University of Oregon Medical Center where her condition was diagnosed and treated by a Dr. Benson, who discovered that she had an intestinal obstruction of both the large and small bowel and that the vault of the vagina, around the cervix, was scarred and very hard. Dr. Benson testified that plaintiff's condition was caused by excessive irradiation received by the plaintiff when she was being treated for the cancer.

Dr. Benson treated the plaintiff by performing a permanent colostomy.

The plaintiff contends that the doses of radiation were excessive and that the defendants should have used smaller doses of radiation over a longer period of time. Plaintiff argues that she was not informed of the dangers to healthy organs which could result from excessive radiation, and if she had been so informed she would have chosen the alternative treatment of lesser doses over a longer period of time.

The duty of a physician to inform his patient of the risks involved in a certain type of treatment and the availability of feasible alternatives was discussed by this court in Getchell v. Mansfield, 260 Or. 174, 489 P.2d 953 (1971). We stated the following regarding the physician's duty:

> " * * * A correct test would be to require the disclosure of all the 'material' risks, results that might well occur, not dangers that are extremely remote; risks that are of serious consequences, not unexpected results that are of little consequence." 260 Or. at 180, 489 P.2d at 956.

We also stated when medical testimony has been introduced showing that the risk is material, that alternatives are feasible, and that disclosure of the risk will not be detrimental to the patient, the duty to warn and advise of alternatives is not based upon the custom of physicians in the locality.

> " * * * The duty to warn and to advise of alternatives does not arise from and is not limited by the custom of physicians in the locality. Rather, it exists as a matter of law if

(1) the risk of injury inherent in the treatment is material; (2) there are feasible alternative courses available; and (3) the plaintiff can be advised of the risks and alternatives without detriment to his wellbeing. If there is evidence tending to prove all these elements, the plaintiff is entitled to have his case submitted to the jury under proper instructions. * * *" 260 Or. at 183, 489 P.2d at 957.

The plaintiff contends that the trial court erred in giving the following instruction:

"I instruct you it's a question for you to determine whether Doctor McMahan explained those risks and advised of those feasible alternative courses of treatment *which a reasonably prudent and skillful physician specializing in radiology would have explained* under the same or similar circumstances." (Emphasis supplied.)

Under our decision in *Getchell* the instruction was erroneous because the duty to inform follows as a matter of law and does not depend upon what a "reasonably prudent and skillful physician" would have explained under the circumstances. * * *

* * * [I]n *Getchell* we were referring to a situation where the doctor must disclose results that may well occur and which are of serious consequence; he need not inform the patient where the results are extremely remote and of little consequence. *Getchell* did not consider a case where the results are remote but of serious consequences, which could have been the situation under the facts in the instant case.

Unquestionably, the results of the radiation treatment were very serious to the plaintiff. There was medical testimony that a portion of the small bowel was stuck to the colon and a hole had formed in the intestine; part of the area was so stiff and fibriotic it would not hold a suture; the vaginal area was scarred and woody; and because of the condition of her intestines it was necessary to perform a colostomy. There was also evidence that plaintiff's condition was the result of excessive radiation treatment and that the proper treatment would have been a lesser dosage over a longer period of time.

The defendant Dr. McMahan, who gave plaintiff the radiation treatment, stated that he told plaintiff the tissues of the bladder and rectum could be damaged. He stated, "I told her these things were possible, but I felt it was not probable they would be serious." He admitted that there were other methods of treatment than the one he used and that protracting the treatment was a way of reducing the likelihood of radiation complications. However, it was his position that the treatment he administered was the proper treatment and "there was no true alternative * * * as I outlined it." He admitted that plaintiff's organs received more radiation "than they could tolerate," and that he did not advise her of the greater likelihood of complications from a high dosage.

We therefore have a situation where the results were serious but the treating doctor believed that the likelihood of the plaintiff being injured to the extent shown was only a possibility.

In *Getchell* we pointed out that the materiality of the risk is "the keystone of the physician's duty to disclose." 260 Or. 174 at 181, 489 P.2d at 956, citing 64 Nw.U.L.Rev. 638 (1969). The authors of that article, Waltz & Scheuneman, Informed Consent to Therapy, in discussing the materiality of the risk, endorse the following test, with which we agree:

> "A risk is thus material when a reasonable person, in what the physician knows or should know to be the patient's position, would be likely to attach significance to the risk or cluster of risks in deciding whether or not to undergo the proposed therapy." 64 Nw.U.L.Rev. at 640.

The factors which determine the significance of the risk or risks are the incidence of the injury from a certain treatment and the degree of harm which might be involved. A very small chance of serious harm may well be significant to the patient. Canterbury v. Spence, 150 U.S.App.D.C. 263, 464 F.2d 772 (1972). Thus, the jury should consider, when determining whether a risk is or is not material, the likelihood of any injury and its seriousness. If a serious injury might occur from a given method of treatment, the physician must inform the patient of all but extremely remote risks. However, if the potential injury is slight, then the patient need be informed of only those risks which might well occur. * * *

Reversed and remanded.

HOLMAN, JUSTICE (dissenting).

The majority opinion reverses the case for the failure to give a proper instruction upon the right of the plaintiff to have alternative methods of treatment explained to her by the defendants so that she could make a choice. This assumes that there was evidence of feasible alternative methods recognized by the medical profession as proper treatment for plaintiff's particular situation.

There is no substantial dispute as to what the evidence shows. The defendants' testimony was to the effect that the treatment which was given of two large doses of radium a week apart was the only proper treatment for plaintiff. The plaintiff's testimony, on the other hand, was to the effect that the only proper treatment for plaintiff was two smaller amounts of radium two weeks apart. There was no evidence by anyone that both methods of treatment were proper for plaintiff.

I diverge from the balance of the court on what I see as a question of logic. The majority sees the jury as being able to find that *both* methods were proper and, therefore, there was a basis upon which to give the jury an instruction on feasible alternative methods of treatment. I see the jury as being able to find that *one or the other* was proper and, therefore, there was no basis for finding that both were proper. The choice for the jury, as I see it, was whether the plaintiff's or the defendants' expert medical testimony was correct, and the jury made the choice in favor of defendants' testimony.

Before a physician should be required to explain alternative methods of treatment, there should be testimony that the medical profession objectively recognizes feasible alternative methods of treatment for the patient's particular condition. There was no such testimony in this case.

Because I believe plaintiff was not entitled to an instruction on alternative methods of treatment, I would affirm. Plaintiff could not have been prejudiced by the faulty instruction.[30]

"In order to sustain a verdict for the plaintiffs in an action for malpractice, the standard of medical practice * * * must be shown by affirmative evidence, and, unless there is evidence of such a standard, a jury may not be permitted to speculate as to what the required standard is, or whether the defendant has departed therefrom. * * * [N]egligence on the part of a physician or surgeon, by reason of his departure from the proper standard of practice, must be established by expert medical testimony, unless the negligence is so grossly apparent that a layman would have no difficulty in recognizing it." Boyce v. Brown, 51 Ariz. 416, 77 P.2d 455 (1938). See, similarly, Todd v. Eitel Hospital, —— Minn. ——, 237 N.W.2d 357 (1975).

The question occasionally arises whether there is a similar need for expert testimony in other areas of accident law.

In Zinnel v. U. S. Shipping Board Emergency Fleet Corp., 10 F. 2d 47 (2d Cir. 1925), the question was whether ropes could reasonably be required for the protection of seamen when passing across a deck load which raised the level of the well deck to the level of the forecastle head, leaving no protection by railings or the like. A majority of the court thought the jury could decide the issue without expert testimony. Judge Hough, dissenting, thought the case should not be dumped on a jury without proof "as to what skilled men habitually do under similar circumstances unless the occurrence at bar is so familiar to a jury of the vicinage as to need no such expositions [such as an ordinary traffic accident]. But the present decision invites, by easy possibility, a jury of tailors and haberdashers to pass judgment on how to make a wet and rolling deck in a seaway a 'safe place to work;' for there is no evidence at all as to what good seamanship, not the fears of tailors, require on such a ship at such a time."

30. Opinion withdrawn, 526 P.2d 577 (1974), for failure to except properly to instruction at trial.

Also see Scaria v. St. Paul Fire & Marine Ins. Co., 68 Wis.2d 1, 227 N.W. 2d 647 (1975); Capron, Informed Consent in Catastrophic Disease Research and Treatment, 123 U.Pa.L.Rev. 340 (1974). Additional materials on liability for medical injuries appear in Section 2 of this chapter and in Chapter 4 infra.

No doubt the matter to be dealt with is sometimes so esoteric that men of common judgment and experience cannot form a valid judgment as to whether the conduct of the party was reasonable without the aid of expert opinion. In such a case a plaintiff might be unable to make out a prima facie case of negligence without expert testimony. Likely examples of such situations occur in Air Reduction Co. v. Philadelphia Storage Battery Co., 14 F.2d 734 (3d Cir. 1926); Foley v. Pittsburgh-Des Moines Co., 363 Pa. 1, 68 A.2d 517 (1949) (in both these cases expert testimony was offered and the point here discussed was not raised). In any event, experts are usually called by both parties in cases involving complicated problems of engineering, and the like. An able and provocative treatment of the practical aspects of this problem may be found in Morris, The Role of Expert Testimony in the Trial of Negligence Issues, 26 Tex.L.Rev. 1 (1947). Outside of the malpractice field, however, there is no general rule requiring expert evidence on this issue in any particular type of case. Wigmore, Evidence § 2090 (3d ed. 1940). Occasionally, however, the same rules as in medical malpractice are said to apply to other professionals, such as design engineers, e. g., City of Eveleth v. Ruble, — Minn. —, 225 N.W.2d 521 (1974) (expert testimony as to departure from professional engineering standards normally required, but not where it is clear that failure of the professional to ascertain relevant facts was an omission inconsistent with the professional obligation assumed).

A problem that besets the use of expert testimony is the opinion rule, which will be studied in the course on evidence. This can scarcely be treated at length here. Suffice it to say that not so long ago there was some judicial hostility to receiving such evidence at all. See e. g., McNally v. Colwell, 91 Mich. 527, 52 N.W. 70, 30 Am.St.Rep. 494 (1892) and some pretty restrictive rules governing its admissibility. See, e. g., Ferguson v. Hubbell, 97 N.Y. 507, 513, 49 Am.R. 544 (1884); Hamilton v. Des Moines Valley R. Co., 36 Iowa 31 (1872). Today such evidence is received in a wide variety of cases to show the proper standard of care, skill, safety, and the like. The limits of its admissibility are still not agreed upon, but the most satisfactory test is that which excludes the opinion only where the situation is one "which the average trier can resolve as satisfactorily as an expert." Kelly v. City of Waterbury, 96 Conn. 494, 114 A. 530 (1921) (rejecting opinion as to whether certain conduct is careful automobile driving). See 7 Wigmore on Evidence, sections 1917–1929, 1949–1951 (3d ed. 1940).

LORENZO v. WIRTH

Supreme Judicial Court of Massachusetts, 1897.
170 Mass. 596, 49 N.E. 1010, 40 L.R.A. 347.

HOLMES, J. This is an action for personal injuries suffered by the plaintiff in consequence of her stepping into an open coal hole. The coal hole was situated about eighteen inches in front of a house held by the defendant under a lease, and upon land embraced in the lease. The house was set back from the street, and the coal hole was two feet or more outside the street line. But the paving over the space between the street line and the house was continuous with that of the street, and there was nothing in the usual conditions to give notice that it was not part of the street except the way in which it generally was used by tenants for the deposit of barrels, etc., and the fact that the steps of the house next to it on the side from which the plaintiff was coming came out to the line of the street.

At the time of the accident, a coal wagon was backed up to the side wall in front of the premises, and coal, which had been ordered by the defendant, was being delivered from it by the servants of a coal dealer. One of these had uncovered the coal hole, and was shoveling the last of the coal out of the wagon upon the sidewalk. The other stood by the hole, doing such work as was necessary to help the coal pour down the hole. The coal covered the whole sidewalk from the wagon to near the house. The plaintiff, a Spanish woman, who according to her own testimony never had seen coal put through a coal hole before, stepped upon the steps of the next building above mentioned, thence stepped upon the coal, and then with her other leg went into the coal hole, which was thirty inches from the corner of the steps. The judge was asked to direct a verdict for the defendant, which he refused to do, and the defendant excepted.

The question in its common form is whether these facts show any evidence of negligence proper to be left to the jury. But it will be seen that it is not a question of evidence in the ordinary sense. It is not whether there is anything tending to prove a disputed fact. The acts and omissions of the defendant as to the plaintiff are fully known and undisputed. The question is whether those acts and omissions made the defendant liable for the plaintiff's hurt,—in the common language of the law, whether they constituted a breach of duty to the plaintiff. It will be observed, further, that the facts on which the question arises are quite simple, and are likely to be repeated with slight variations as long as coal holes exist; that they are all matters of eyesight, capable of being photographed; and that theory must recognize that at some point the visible situation would be such as to warrant the defendant in assuming that the public were sufficiently warned, or, in other words, that the defendant would have done her whole duty. Chenery v. Fitchburg Railroad Co., 160 Mass. 211, 214, 35 N.E. 554, 22 L.R.A. 575. It is true that blind men and foreigners unused to our ways have a right to walk in the streets, and this fact must be taken into consideration in drawing the line of the defendant's duty; but the line when drawn is a physical line, so to speak,—it is a visible situation in which all the arrangements or precautions which the law requires of a defendant are there, upon the ground.

In simple cases of this sort courts have felt able to determine what in every case however complex, defendants are bound at their peril to know, and are presumed to know, namely, whether the given situation is on one or the other side of the line. The examples are numerous, and we take the first that come to our hand. Barron v. Eldredge,

100 Mass. 455, 460, 461, 1 Am.Rep. 126. Pinney v. Hall, 156 Mass. 225, 30 N.E. 1016. Crafter v. Metropolitan Railway, L.R. 1 C.P. 300. We think that the case at bar is not beyond our competence to decide. The greatest danger in attempting to do so is that of being misled by ready made generalizations, and of thinking only in phrases to which as lawyers the judges have become accustomed, instead of looking straight at things and regarding the facts in all their concreteness as a jury would do. Too broadly generalized conceptions are a constant source of fallacy. Thus it is easy to say that the continuity of the sidewalk was an invitation, and then to discuss in universals the duty of one who invites the public upon his land. But, invitation or no, the invitation is not the same, and the responsibility is not the same, when the place is seemingly in the middle of a clear highway, and looks safe and ready for travel to one who is walking straight along the open road, that it is where the place is in a snug corner and is capable of being reached only by going over steps which manifestly are not a part of the highway, and then by stepping into a pile of coal which surrounds the spot in question. Without considering whether under such circumstances the defendant would be freed from all duty in respect of the temporary dangers created by the coal dealer while he was doing his work, (Clapp v. Kemp, 122 Mass. 481), it is the opinion of a majority of the court that she was not called on to stand guard and to tell the public that they must not understand the continuity of the pavement under the coal, if they happened to know of it, as a present assurance that they might step blindly into the coal, and as a warranty that there was no hole in the place where the coal was pouring down. A heap of coal on a sidewalk in Boston is an indication according to common experience that there very possibly may be a coal hole to receive it. But without saying that it always is a sufficient warning to look out for one, we are of opinion that, as against a person coming from where the plaintiff came from, with a coal hole situated as this was, the coal in the condition shown, and the business of delivering then going on, in the absence of men with baskets or other indication of a different means of making the delivery, the defendant cannot be said to have been wanting in due care.[31]

Exceptions sustained.

KNOWLTON, J. I am unable to agree to the opinion of the majority in this case. The building occupied by the defendant, and the adjoining buildings for a considerable distance towards the west, stood back from the line of the street about three feet and eight inches. The buildings in the other direction, with their projections, came out to the line of the street. The space in front of the defendant's building and of the adjoining buildings towards the west was paved with

31. The opinion in this case reflects the consistently held view of its author. See, e. g., Holmes, The Common Law, 110 et seq., 124 (1881); Southern Pac. Co. v. Berkshire, 254 U.S. 415, 41 S.Ct. 162, 65 L.Ed. 335 (1920); Baltimore & O. R. Co. v. Goodman, p. 209, infra. Holmes did not however subscribe to the notion that the custom or practice of an industry was conclusive of the standard of care. Texas & P. R. Co. v. Behymer, 189 U.S. 468, 470, 23 S.Ct. 622, 47 L.Ed. 905 (1903).

the same kind of material, and on the same level all the way from the buildings to the curbstone, and was used as a sidewalk. The walk was not very wide, and there was nothing to mark the line of the street. In Holmes v. Drew, 151 Mass. 578, 580, 25 N.E. 22, is this language: "The jury might have inferred from the facts stated that the defendant laid out and paved the sidewalk on her own land in order that it should be used by the public as the sidewalk of the street, and allowed it to remain apparently the part of the street that was intended to be used by foot passengers. This would amount to an invitation to the public to enter upon and use as a public sidewalk the land so prepared, and the plaintiff so using it would have gone upon the defendant's land by her implied invitation, and she would owe to him the duty not to expose him to a dangerous condition of the walk which reasonable care on her part would have prevented." * * * I think that the jury might have found the circumstances under which the plaintiff was walking upon the sidewalk at the time of the accident to be such as entitled her to protection or warning against openings in it.

At the time of the accident the coal hole was being used for the defendant's benefit, by her authority. If this use would ordinarily be attended with danger to the public, the defendant was bound to see that proper precautions were taken for their safety, even if the work was being done by an independent contractor. Curtis v. Kiley, 153 Mass. 123, 26 N.E. 421. Woodman v. Metropolitan Railroad Co., 149 Mass. 335, 21 N.E. 482, 4 L.R.A. 213, 14 Am.St.Rep. 427. Pye v. Faxon, 156 Mass 471, 474, 31 N.E. 640. Pickard v. Smith, 10 C.B., N.S., 470. * * * There was testimony from several witnesses that the coal covered the sidewalk from the curbstone to the coal hole, and two others testified that it extended from the curbstone to the line of the defendant's house. The accident occurred at a little before six o'clock on the evening of November 15, and there was testimony that it was dark, and that there was no daylight. There was evidence from the plaintiff and from another witness who was present that they saw nobody about the coal hole before the accident. One of the two men who were delivering the coal was in the wagon, from which he had just shovelled the last of the coal, and was busy with his team, and he did not see the plaintiff until she was being lifted out of the hole. The other testified that he was about three feet from the coal hole, that he could not say what he was doing, that he thought his head was turned round looking up Eliot Street towards Tremont Street, which was in the direction opposite to that from which the plaintiff was coming. He also said in his testimony, "I was not shovelling coal at that time; I was trying to keep myself on my feet. There was a throng of people going up there each way."

Apparently the plaintiff was going as others were, except that they did not happen to step into the hole. According to her testimony she had just come from Spain, and had never seen coal put into a cellar through a coal hole. Eliot Street is travelled by many persons. Besides the plaintiff, others might have been expected there who had never seen coal put through holes in sidewalks. The wagon was backed up to the curbstone and there were electric cars and teams passing through the street. I think that the jury well might have found that a coal hole on a public sidewalk, where a throng of persons was passing in each direction, was left open on a dark evening with coal scattered about it from the curbstone to the side of the defendant's building, with a large two-horse wagon backed up against the curbstone, with nothing to indicate to pedestrians that there was an opening there, and with nobody to guard the hole or to warn them of danger. It seems to me that there was evidence of negligence on the part of those who left the hole open and unguarded.

What kind of conduct is required, under complex conditions, to reach the usual standard of due care, namely, the ordinary care of persons of common prudence, is a question of fact to be determined according to the observation and experience of common men. Even when there is no conflict of testimony, if there are acts and omissions of which some tend to show negligence and others do not, the question whether there was negligence or not is in my judgment a question for a jury. This proposition I deem to be established by such unanimity of decision as to need no citation of authorities in support of it. I think the case was rightly submitted to the jury.

MR. JUSTICE ALLEN concurs in this dissent.

BALTIMORE & OHIO R. R. CO. v. GOODMAN

Supreme Court of the United States, 1927.
275 U.S. 66, 48 S.Ct. 24, 72 L.Ed. 167, 56 A.L.R. 645.

CERTIORARI, 271 U.S. 658, 46 S.Ct. 632, 70 L.Ed. 1136, to a judgment of the Circuit Court of Appeals sustaining a recovery for death caused by alleged negligence of the Railroad, in an action by the widow and administratrix of the deceased. The action was removed from an Ohio state court on the ground of diversity of citizenship. * * *

MR. JUSTICE HOLMES delivered the opinion of the Court.

This is a suit brought by the widow and administratrix of Nathan Goodman against the petitioner for causing his death by running him down at a grade crossing. The defence is that Goodman's own negligence caused the death. At the trial, the defendant asked the Court to direct a verdict for it, but the request, and others looking to the same direction, were refused, and the plaintiff got a verdict and a judgment which was affirmed by the Circuit Court of Appeals. 10 F.2d 58.

Goodman was driving an automobile truck in an easterly direction and was killed by a train running southwesterly across the road at a rate of not less than sixty miles an hour. The line was straight, but it is said by the respondent that Goodman "had no practical view" beyond a section house two hundred and forty-three feet north of the crossing until he was about twenty feet from the first rail, or, as the respondent argues, twelve feet from danger, and that then the engine was still obscured by the section house. He had been driving at the rate of ten or twelve miles an hour, but had cut down his rate to five or six miles at about forty feet from the crossing. It is thought that there was an emergency in which, so far as appears, Goodman did all that he could.

We do not go into further details as to Goodman's precise situation, beyond mentioning that it was daylight and that he was familiar with the crossing, for it appears to us plain that nothing is suggested by the evidence to relieve Goodman from responsibility for his own death. When a man goes upon a railroad track he knows that he goes to a place where he will be killed if a train comes upon him before he is clear of the track. He knows that he must stop for the train, not the train stop for him. In such circumstances it seems to us that if a driver cannot be sure otherwise whether a train is dangerously near he must stop and get out of his vehicle, although obviously he will not often be required to do more than to stop and look. It seems to us that if he relies upon not hearing the train or any signal and takes no further precaution he does so at his own risk. If at the last moment Goodman found himself in an emergency it was his own fault that he did not reduce his speed earlier or come to a stop. It is true as said in Flannelly v. Delaware & Hudson Co., 32 S.Ct. 783, 225 U.S. 597, 603, 56 L.Ed. 1221, 44 L.R.A., N.S., 154, that the question of due care very generally is left to the jury. But we are dealing with a standard of conduct, and when the standard is clear it should be laid down once for all by the Courts. See Southern Pacific Co. v. Berkshire, 41 S.Ct. 162, 254 U.S. 415, 417, 419, 65 L.Ed. 335.

Judgment reversed.[32]

NIXON, CHANGING RULES OF LIABILITY IN AUTOMOBILE ACCIDENT LITIGATION 3 Law and Contemporary Problems, 476, 477, 478 (1936):

In the days of poor roads and low speeds, the facts of an accident could be reconstructed in the courtroom with some degree of accuracy, and the problem of determining fault did not present unusual difficulties. But with high-powered cars and concrete highways, the probability that an accident—often the consequence of a fractional mistake in management—can and will be described accurately in court has become increasingly remote, especially where court congestion has delayed the time of trial. The consequent uncertainties as to the facts have given to the jury in those cases where it determines the question of fault an almost unrestricted power to choose between the litigants

32. The subsequent fate of this decision may well be told from Note, 43 Harv. L.Rev. 926 (1930); Pokora v. Wabash R. Co., 292 U.S. 98, 54 S.Ct. 580, 78 L. Ed. 1149, 91 A.L.R. 1049 (1933); Erie R. Co. v. Tompkins, 304 U.S. 64, 58 S.Ct. 817, 82 L.Ed. 1188, 114 A.L.R. 1487 (1938). Where the view of the train is unobstructed for any considerable distance most courts hold that the driver of an automobile approaching a grade crossing is negligent "as a matter of law" if he fails to see it. Gianetta v. New York, N. H. & H. R. Co., 98 Conn. 743, 120 A. 560 (1923); cases collected in Notes, 1 A.L.R. 203; 41 A.L.R. 405.

at bar. And the notorious tendency of that body to prefer the plaintiff,[33] especially as against the defendant suspected of carrying insurance, has made "taking the case away from the jury" one of the primary objectives of the defense counsel.

To this end they have invoked the power of the trial judge to direct a verdict for the defendant if the evidence clearly demonstrates either the plaintiff's fault or the defendant's freedom from fault. But so long as the standard of care is that which a reasonable man would have exercised under the circumstances, the opportunity for such a demonstration is obviously limited. Where, however, the standard of care governing a specific situation has become crystallized in a rule of law, e. g., that a driver approaching a railroad crossing must "stop, look, and listen," the power of the trial judge is materially increased for the evidence may clearly show whether that standard was observed by the party to whom it is applicable.

It is not surprising then that it has been around the standard of care that some of the most important battles of automobile tort law have been waged. And the conflict has been most acute with respect to the standard of care applicable to the plaintiff. A specific standard of care is, as a rule, a more rigorous requirement than the general standard of the "reasonable man." For plaintiff's counsel, already enjoying the favor of the jury, the need to obtain a directed verdict based upon a proved deviation from a specific standard is less important than for a defendant's counsel who will strive to wrest the case from the jury by seeking a directed verdict based on the plaintiff's failure to observe such a standard. It is in the rise and decline of those specific standards of care most frequently invoked against plaintiff that the change in the rules of liability in automobile cases can best be marked.[34]

The specific standard of care in civil cases is usually either of judicial creation or adoption. When a judge has discovered through hearing a number of cases involving similar situations that certain conduct is generally blameworthy he may rule that a person guilty of such conduct is negligent as a matter of law.[35] If the appellate court

33. Thus in a survey covering courts of four cities it was found that verdicts for plaintiffs were rendered in approximately two-thirds of the cases. See Report by the Committee to Study Compensation for Automobile Accidents (1932) 34.

34. An example of a standard of care invoked against *defendants* is found in the development of the rules applicable to the horse-frightening cases. In the early cases, the common law standard of ordinary care was laid down. But as the number of cases of this type increased, the courts began to lay down exact rules for particular situations. Thus it was held to be negligent *per se* for the automobile driver not to stop if the driver of the horse signalled him or if the horse appeared frightened. The legislature passed statutes which were applied in civil cases. Finally a fairly exact set of rules governed the conduct of the automobile driver in this type of situation, and the driver of the horse had little difficulty in making out his case. See in general Berry, Rights and Duties of Automobile Drivers when Meeting and Passing Horse-Drawn Vehicles (1916) 82 Cent. L.J. 315.

35. See Holmes, The Common Law (1881) 122 et seq.

approves his ruling, or if that court itself so rules, the standard becomes a rule of law to be followed in all future cases involving similar facts. A similar power resides in the legislature, but it has acted principally through the creation of standards of care by which the *criminal* liability of an individual is to be measured. However, in a majority of the states, the courts in civil cases involving legislatively proscribed conduct have ruled that such conduct is negligence as a matter of law.[36] In other states, however, the courts have considered that the violation of the criminal statute is no more than evidence of negligence which the jury may weigh, along with the other facts of the case, in deciding the fault question.[37]

What is said here is by no means confined to *motor vehicle* accident cases. Note that specific standards of care may be applied as maximum standards or minimum standards. Of which type is Nixon writing? Would different considerations apply to the other application? How are the scales weighted by

(a) the requirement of expert testimony to show the standard of conduct?

(b) the refusal to allow expert testimony for such purpose?

(c) the admission or exclusion of company rules as bearing upon the proper standard of conduct?

(d) the exclusion of evidence showing precautions taken after the accident?

MARTIN v. HERZOG

Court of Appeals of New York, 1920.
228 N.Y. 164, 126 N.E. 814.

Action by Elizabeth Martin, as administratrix of William J. Martin, deceased, against Samuel A. Herzog and another. Judgment for the plaintiff against the named defendant was reversed by the Appellate Division (176 App.Div. 614, 163 N.Y.S. 189), and plaintiff appeals. Judgment of Appellate Division affirmed, and judgment absolute directed on stipulation in favor of defendant. * * *

CARDOZO, J. The action is one to recover damages for injuries resulting in death. Plaintiff and her husband, while driving toward Tarrytown in a buggy on the night of August 21, 1915, were struck by the defendant's automobile coming in the opposite direction. They were thrown to the ground, and the man was killed. At the point of the collision the highway makes a curve. The car was rounding the

36. Morris, The Relation of Criminal Statutes to Tort Liability (1933) 46 Harv.L.Rev. 453.

37. Ibid. [Footnotes 33–37 by the author of the article, renumbered.]

Cf. also Searl, Automobile Liability Law Development & Trend, 39 Best's Ins. News 583 (Fire & Cas. ed. 1938); James, Accident Liability: Some Wartime Developments, 55 Yale L.J. 365, 374 et seq. (1946); Chief Justice Maltbie & The Law of Negligence, 24 Conn. B.J. 61, 63 (1950).

curve, when suddenly it came upon the buggy, emerging, the defendant tells us from the gloom. Negligence is charged against the defendant, the driver of the car, in that he did not keep to the right of the center of the highway. Highway Law, section 286, subd. 3, and section 332 (Consol.Laws, c. 25). Negligence is charged against the plaintiff's intestate, the driver of the wagon, in that he was traveling without lights. Highway Law, section 329a, as amended by Laws 1915, c. 367. There is no evidence that the defendant was moving at an excessive speed. There is none of any defect in the equipment of his car. The beam of light from his lamps pointed to the right as the wheels of his car turned along the curve toward the left; and, looking in the direction of the plaintiff's approach, he was peering into the shadow. The case against him must stand, therefore, if at all, upon the divergence of his course from the center of the highway. The jury found him delinquent and his victim blameless. The Appellate Division reversed, and ordered a new trial.

We agree with the Appellate Division that the charge to the jury was erroneous and misleading. The case was tried on the assumption that the hour had arrived when lights were due. It was argued on the same assumption in this court. In such circumstances, it is not important whether the hour might have made a question for the jury. Todd v. Nelson, 109 N.Y. 316, 325, 16 N.E. 360. A controversy put out of the case by the parties is not to be put into it by us. We say this by way of preface to our review of the contested rulings. In the body of the charge the trial judge said that the jury could consider the absence of light "in determining whether the plaintiff's intestate was guilty of contributory negligence in failing to have a light upon the buggy as provided by law. I do not mean to say that the absence of light necessarily makes him negligent, but it is a fact for your consideration." The defendant requested a ruling that the absence of a light on the plaintiff's vehicle was "prima facie evidence of contributory negligence." This request was refused, and the jury were again instructed that they might consider the absence of lights as some evidence of negligence, but that it was not conclusive evidence. The plaintiff then requested a charge that "the fact that the plaintiff's intestate was driving without a light is not negligence in itself," and to this the court acceded. The defendant saved his rights by appropriate exceptions.

We think the unexcused omission of the statutory signals is more than some evidence of negligence. It *is* negligence in itself. Lights are intended for the guidance and protection of other travelers on the highway. Highway Law, section 329a. By the very terms of the hypothesis, to omit, willfully or heedlessly, the safeguards prescribed by law for the benefit of another that he may be preserved in life or limb, is to fall short of the standard of diligence to which those who live in organized society are under a duty to conform. That, we think, is now the established rule in this state. [Cases cited.]

Whether the omission of an absolute duty, not willfully or heedlessly, but through unavoidable accident, is also to be characterized as negligence, is a question of nomenclature into which we need not enter, for it does not touch the case before us. There may be times, when, if jural niceties are to be preserved, the two wrongs, negligence and breach of statutory duty, must be kept distinct in speech and thought. Pollock, Torts, 10th Ed., p. 458; Clark & Linsell, Torts, 6th Ed., p. 493; Salmond, Jurisprudence, 5th Ed., pp. 351, 363; Texas & Pac. Ry. Co. v. Rigsby, supra, 241 U.S. 43, 36 S.Ct. 482, 60 L.Ed. 874; Chicago, B. & Q. Ry. Co. v. U. S., 220 U.S. 559, 31 S.Ct. 612, 55 L.Ed. 582.

In the conditions here present they come together and coalesce. A rule less rigid has been applied where the one who complains of the omission is not a member of the class for whose protection the safeguard is designed. Amberg v. Kinley, supra [214 N.Y. 531, 108 N.E. 830]; Union Pac. Ry. Co. v. McDonald, 152 U.S. 262, 283, 14 S.Ct. 619, 38 L.Ed. 434; Kelley v. N. Y. State Rys., 207 N.Y. 342, 100 N.E. 1115; Ward v. Hobbs, 4 App.Cas. 13. Some relaxation there has also been where the safeguard is prescribed by local ordinance, and not by statute. Massoth v. Delaware & H. Canal Co., 64 N.Y. 524, 532; Knupfle v. Knickerbocker Ice Co., 84 N.Y. 488. Courts have been reluctant to hold that the police regulations of boards and councils and other subordinate officials create rights of action beyond the specific penalties imposed. This has led them to say that the violation of a statute is negligence, and the violation of a like ordinance is only evidence of negligence. An ordinance, however, like a statute, is a law within its sphere of operation, and so the distinction has not escaped criticism. [Cases cited.] Whether it has become too deeply rooted to be abandoned, even if it be thought illogical, is a question not now before us. What concerns us at this time is that, even in the ordinance cases, the omission of a safeguard prescribed by statute is put upon a different plane, and is held not merely some evidence of negligence, but negligence in itself. * * *

In the case at hand, we have an instance of the admitted violation of a statute intended for the protection of travelers on the highway, of whom the defendant at the time was one. Yet the jurors were instructed in effect that they were at liberty in their discretion to treat the omission of lights either as innocent or as culpable. They were allowed to "consider the default as lightly or gravely" as they would (Thomas, J., in the court below). They might as well have been told that they could use a like discretion in holding a master at fault for the omission of a safety appliance prescribed by positive law for the protection of a workman. Scott v. International Paper Co., 204 N.Y. 49, 97 N.E. 413; Fitzwater v. Warren, 206 N.Y. 355, 99 N.E. 1042, 42 L.R.A.,N.S., 1229; Texas & Pac. Ry. Co v. Rigsby, 241 U.S. 33, 36 S.Ct. 482, 60 L.Ed. 874. Jurors have no dispensing power, by which they may relax the duty that one traveler on the highway owes under the statute to another. It is error to tell them that they have. The omission of these lights was a wrong, and, being wholly unexcused, was also a negligent wrong. No license should have been conceded to the triers of the facts to find it anything else.

We must be on our guard, however, against confusing the question of negligence with that of the causal connection between the negligence and the injury. A defendant who travels without lights is not to pay damages for his fault, unless the absence of lights is the cause of the disaster. A plaintiff who travels without them is not to forfeit the right to damages, unless the absence of lights is at least a contributing cause of the disaster. To say that conduct is negligence is not to say that it is always contributory negligence. "Proof of negligence in the air, so to speak, will not do." Pollock, Torts (10th Ed.) p. 472.

We think, however, that evidence of a collision occurring more than an hour after sundown between a car and an unseen buggy, proceeding without lights, is evidence from which a causal connection may be inferred between the collision and the lack of signals. Lambert v. Staten Island R. R. Co., 70 N.Y. 104, 109, 110; Walsh v. Boston R. R. Co., 171 Mass. 52, 58, 50 N.E. 453. The Pennsylvania, 19 Wall. 125, 136, 137, 22 L.Ed. 148; Fisher v. Village of Cambridge, 133 N.Y. 527, 532, 30 N.E. 663. If nothing else is shown to break the connection, we have a case, prima facie sufficient, of negligence contributing to the result.

There may, indeed, be times when the lights on a highway are so many and so bright that lights on a wagon are superfluous. If that is so, it is for the offender to go forward with the evidence, and prove the illumination as a kind of substituted performance. The plaintiff asserts that she did so here. She says that the scene of the accident was illumined by moonlight, by an electric lamp, and by the lights of the approaching car. Her position is that, if the defendant did not see the buggy thus illumined, a jury might reasonably infer that he would not have seen it anyhow. We may doubt whether there is any evidence of illumination sufficient to sustain the jury in drawing such an inference; but the decision of the case does not make it necessary to resolve the doubt, and so we leave it open. It is certain that they were not required to find that lights on the wagon were superfluous. They might reasonably have found the contrary. They ought, therefore, to have been informed what effect they were free to give, in that event, to the violation of the statute. They should have been told, not only that the omission of the light was negligence, but that it was "prima facie evidence of contributory negligence"; i. e., that it was sufficient in itself unless its probative force was overcome (Thomas, J., in court below) to sustain a verdict that the decedent was at fault. Kelly v. Jackson, 6 Pet. 622, 632, 8 L.Ed. 523.

Here, on the undisputed facts, lack of vision, whether excusable or not, was the cause of the disaster. The defendant may have been negligent in swerving from the center of the road; but he did not run into the buggy purposely, nor was he driving while intoxicated, nor was he going at such a reckless speed that warning would of necessity have been futile. Nothing of the kind is shown. The collision was due to his failure to see at a time when sight should have been aroused and guided by the statutory warnings. Some explanation of the effect to be given to the absence of those warnings if the plaintiff failed to prove that other lights on the car or the highway took their place as equivalents, should have been put before the jury. The explanation was asked for and refused.

We are persuaded that the tendency of the charge, and of all the rulings following it, was to minimize unduly, in the minds of the triers of the facts, the gravity of the decedent's fault. Errors may not be ignored as unsubstantial, when they tend to such an outcome. A statute designed for the protection of human life is not to be brushed aside as a form of words, its commands reduced to the level of cautions, and the duty to obey attenuated into an option to conform.

The order of the Appellate Division should be affirmed, and judgment absolute directed on the stipulation in favor of the defendant, with costs in all courts.

HOGAN, J. (dissenting). * * * [38]

TEDLA v. ELLMAN

Court of Appeals of New York, 1939.
280 N.Y. 124, 19 N.E.2d 987.

LEHMAN, JUDGE. While walking along a highway, Anna Tedla and her brother, John Bachek, were struck by a passing automobile, operated by the defendant Ellman. She was injured and Bachek was killed. Bachek was a deaf-mute. His occupation was collecting and selling junk. His sister, Mrs. Tedla, was engaged in the same occupation. They often picked up junk at the incinerator of the village of Islip. At the time of the accident they were walking along "Sunrise Highway" and wheeling baby carriages containing junk and wood which they had picked up at the incinerator. It was about six o'clock, or a little earlier, on a Sunday evening in December. Darkness had

38. Though the distinction between the effect of a statute and ordinance in this respect is sometimes made, it is commonly repudiated outside of New York. See, e. g., Springer v. Joseph Schlitz Brewing Co., 510 F.2d 468 (4th Cir. 1974) (violation of municipal ordinance regulating sewage discharge subjects brewery to liability to downstream riparian owners for pollution damage); Lash v. J. J. Newberry Co., 510 F.2d 429 (2d Cir. 1975) (prima facie liability to injured pedestrian based on violation of municipal ordinance forbidding Vermont landowner from shoveling snow onto sidewalk). A regulation authorized by a non-criminal statute may also be deemed to "lay down a standard of care with which * * * [those regulated] must comply in the absence of circumstances * * * excusing such compliance", Petition of Kinsman Transit Company, 338 F.2d 708, 718 (2d Cir. 1964). On the other hand, as compliance with statutes is not necessarily conclusive as to care, e. g., Blasing v. P. R. L. Hardenbergh Co., —— Minn. ——, 226 N.W.2d 110 (1975), compliance with ordinances and regulations may also not necessarily be enough.

On the general subject of the relationship between criminal statutes and civil liability, see Thayer, Public Wrong and Private Action, 27 Harv.L. Rev. 317 (1913); Lowndes, Civil Liability by Criminal Legislation, 16 Minn. L.Rev. 361 (1932); Morris, Criminal Statutes & Tort Liability, 46 Harv.L. Rev. 453 (1932); Morris, The Role of Criminal Statutes in Negligence Actions, 49 Colum.L.Rev. 21 (1949); James, Statutory Standards and Negligence in Accident Cases, 11 La.L.Rev. 95 (1950).

already set in. Bachek was carrying a lighted lantern, or, at least, there is testimony to that effect. The jury found that the accident was due solely to the negligence of the operator of the automobile. The defendants do not, upon this appeal, challenge the finding of negligence on the part of the operator. They maintain, however, that Mrs. Tedla and her brother were guilty of contributory negligence as matter of law.

Sunrise Highway, at the place of the accident, consists of two roadways, separated by a grass plot. There are no footpaths along the highway and the center grass plot was soft. It is not unlawful for a pedestrian, wheeling a baby carriage, to use the roadway under such circumstances, but a pedestrian using the roadway is bound to exercise such care for his safety as a reasonably prudent person would use. The Vehicle and Traffic Law (Consol.Laws, c. 71) provides that "Pedestrians walking or remaining on the paved portion, or traveled part of a roadway shall be subject to, and comply with, the rules governing vehicles, with respect to meeting and turning out, except that such pedestrians shall keep to the left of the center line thereof, and turn to their left instead of right side thereof, so as to permit all vehicles passing them in either direction to pass on their right. Such pedestrians shall not be subject to the rules governing vehicles as to giving signals." Section 85, subd. 6. Mrs. Tedla and her brother did not observe the statutory rule, and at the time of the accident were proceeding in easterly direction on the east bound or right-hand roadway. The defendants moved to dismiss the complaint on the ground, among others, that violation of the statutory rule constitutes contributory negligence as matter of law. * * * The trial judge left to the jury the question whether failure to observe the statutory rule was a proximate cause of the accident; * * * Upon this appeal, the only question presented is whether, as matter of law, disregard of the statutory rule that pedestrians shall keep to the left of the center line of a highway constitutes contributory negligence which bars any recovery by the plaintiff.

Vehicular traffic can proceed safely and without recurrent traffic tangles only if vehicles observe accepted rules of the road. Such rules, and especially the rule that all vehicles proceeding in one direction must keep to a designated part or side of the road—in this country the right-hand side—have been dictated by necessity and formulated by custom. The general use of automobiles has increased in unprecedented degree the number and speed of vehicles. Control of traffic becomes an increasingly difficult problem. Rules of the road, regulating the rights and duties of those who use highways, have, in consequence, become increasingly important. The Legislature no longer leaves to custom the formulation of such rules. Statutes now codify, define, supplement, and, where changing conditions suggest change in rule, even change rules of the road which formerly rested on custom. * * *

* * * Until by chapter 114 of the Laws of 1933, it adopted subdivision 6 of section 85, quoted above, there was no special statutory

rule for pedestrians walking along a highway. Then for the first time it reversed, for pedestrians, the rule established for vehicles by immemorial custom, and provided that pedestrians shall keep to the left of the center line of a highway.

The plaintiffs showed by the testimony of a State policeman that "there were very few cars going east" at the time of the accident, but that going west there was "very heavy Sunday night traffic." Until the recent adoption of the new statutory rule for pedestrians, ordinary prudence would have dictated that pedestrians should not expose themselves to the danger of walking along a roadway upon which the "very heavy Sunday night traffic" was proceeding when they could walk in comparative safety along a roadway used by very few cars. It is said that now, by force of the statutory rule, pedestrians are guilty of contributory negligence as matter of law when they use the safer roadway, unless that roadway is left of the center of the road. Disregard of the statutory rule of the road and observance of a rule based on immemorial custom, it is said, is negligence which as matter of law is a proximate cause of the accident, though observance of the statutory rule might, under the circumstances of the particular case, expose a pedestrian to serious danger from which he would be free if he followed the rule that had been established by custom. If that be true, then the Legislature has decreed that pedestrians must observe the general rule of conduct which it has prescribed for their safety even under circumstances where observance would subject them to unusual risk; that pedestrians are to be charged with negligence as matter of law for acting as prudence dictates. It is unreasonable to ascribe to the Legislature an intention that the statute should have so extraordinary a result, and the courts may not give to a statute an effect not intended by the Legislature.

The Legislature, when it enacted the statute, presumably knew that this court and the courts of other jurisdictions had established the general principle that omission by a plaintiff of a safeguard, prescribed by statute, against a recognized danger, constitutes negligence as matter of law which bars recovery for damages caused by incidence of the danger for which the safeguard was prescribed. * * * Martin v. Herzog, 228 N.Y. 164, 168, 126 N.E. 814, 815 per Cardozo, J. The appellants lean heavily upon that and kindred cases and the principle established by them.

The analogy is, however, incomplete. The "established rule" should not be weakened either by subtle distinctions or by extension beyond its letter or spirit into a field where "by the very terms of the hypothesis" it can have no proper application. At times the indefinite and flexible standard of care of the traditional reasonably prudent man may be, in the opinion of the Legislature, an insufficient measure of the care which should be exercised to guard against a recognized danger; * * * Then the Legislature may by statute prescribe additional safeguards and may define duty and standard of care in rigid terms; and when the Legislature has spoken, the standard of the care required is no longer what the reasonably prudent man would do under the circumstances but what the Legislature has commanded. That is the rule established by the courts and "by the very terms of the hypothesis" the rule applies where the Legislature has prescribed safeguards "for the benefit of another that he may be preserved in life or limb." In that field debate as to whether the safeguards so prescribed are reasonably necessary is ended by the legislative fiat. Obedience to that fiat cannot add to the danger, even assuming that the prescribed safeguards are not reasonably necessary and where the legislative anticipation of dangers is realized and harm results through heedless or willful omission of the prescribed safeguard, injury flows from wrong and the wrongdoer is properly held responsible for the consequent damages.

The statute upon which the defendants rely is of different character. It does not prescribe additional safeguards which pedestrians must provide for the preservation of the life and limb or property of others, or even of themselves, nor does it impose upon pedestrians a higher standard of care. What the statute does provide is rules of the road to be observed by pedestrians and by vehicles, so that all those who use the road may know how they and others should proceed, at least under usual circumstances. A general rule of conduct—and, specifically, a rule of the road—may accomplish its intended purpose under usual conditions, but, when the unusual occurs, strict observance may defeat the purpose of the rule and produce catastrophic results.

Negligence is failure to exercise the care required by law. Where a statute defines the standard of care and the safeguards required to meet a recognized danger, then, as we have said, no other measure may be applied in determining whether a person has carried out the duty of care imposed by law. Failure to observe the standard imposed by statute is negligence, as matter of law. On the other hand, where a statutory general rule of conduct fixes no definite standard of care which would under all circumstances tend to protect life, limb or property but merely codifies or supplements a common-law rule, which has always been subject to limitations and exceptions; or where the statutory rule of conduct regulates conflicting rights and obligations in manner calculated to promote public convenience and safety, then the statute, in the absence of clear language to the contrary, should not be construed as intended to wipe out the limitations and exceptions which judicial decisions have attached to the common-law duty; nor should it be construed as an inflexible command that the general rule of conduct intended to prevent accidents must be followed even under conditions when observance might cause accidents. We may assume reasonably that the Legislature directed pedestrians to keep to the left of the center of the road because that would cause them to face traffic approaching in that lane and would enable them to care for their own safety better than if the traffic approached them from the rear. We cannot assume reasonably that the Legislature intended that a statute enacted for the preservation of the life and limb of pedestrians must be observed when observance would subject them to more imminent danger.

The distinction in the effect of statutes defining a standard of care or requiring specified safeguards against recognized dangers and the effects of statutes which merely codify, supplement or even change common-law rules or which prescribe a general rule of conduct calculated to prevent accidents but which under unusual conditions may cause accidents, has been pointed out often. Seldom have the courts held that failure to observe a rule of the road, even though embodied in a statute, constitutes negligence as matter of law where observance would subject a person to danger which might be avoided by disregard of the general rule. * * * [Cases cited].

The generally accepted rule and the reasons for it are set forth in the comment to section 286 of the Restatement of the Law of Torts. * * *

Even under that construction of the statute, a pedestrian is, of course, at fault if he fails without good reason to observe the statutory rule of conduct. The general duty is established by the statute, and deviation from it without good cause is a wrong and the wrongdoer is responsible for the damages resulting from his wrong. * * *

I have so far discussed the problem of the plaintiffs' right to compensation for the damages caused by defendants' negligence as if it depended solely upon the question of whether the pedestrians were at fault, and I have ignored the question whether their alleged fault was a proximate cause of the accident. In truth, the two questions cannot be separated completely. If the pedestrians had observed the statutory rule of the road they would have proceeded easterly along the roadway on the left of the center grass plot, and then, it must be conceded, they would not have been struck by the automobile in which the defendants were riding, proceeding in the same direction along the roadway on the right. Their presence on the roadway where they were struck was an essential condition of their injury. Was it also as matter of law a proximate cause of the accident? "The position of a vehicle which has been struck by another may or may not have been one of the causes of the striking. Of course, it could not have been struck if it had not been in the place where the blow came. But this is a statement of an essential condition, and not of a cause of the impact. The distinction is between that which directly or proximately produces or helps to produce, a result as an efficient cause and that which is a necessary condition or attendant cause of it. * * * That is, a contributing cause of an accident, is usually a question for a jury, to be determined by the facts of the particular case." Newcomb v. Boston Protective Department, 146 Mass. 596, 604, 16 N.E. 555, 559, 4 Am.St.Rep. 354. Here the jury might find that the pedestrians avoided a greater, indeed an almost suicidal, risk by proceeding along the east bound roadway; that the operator of the automobile was entirely heedless of the possibility of the presence of pedestrians on the highway; and that a pedestrian could not have avoided the accident even if he had faced oncoming traffic. Under those circumstances the question of negligence, was one of fact.

In each action, the judgment should be affirmed, with costs.

CRANE, C. J., and HUBBS, LOUGHRAN, and RIPPEY, JJ., concur.

O'BRIEN and FINCH, JJ., dissent on the authority of Martin v. Herzog, 228 N.Y. 164, 126 N.E. 814.

Judgments affirmed.[39]

JACKSON v. LEACH

Court of Appeals of Maryland, 1931.
160 Md. 139, 152 A. 813.

ADKINS, J. This is a suit for damages for injuries to the plaintiff resulting from a collision between the automobile of the plaintiff and that of Howard W. Jackson, one of the defendants, while being driven by Riall Jackson, the other defendant. The accident occurred at the intersection of Ellamont street and Clifton avenue in Baltimore city. The plaintiff was driving northerly on Ellamont street and Riall Jackson westwardly on Clifton avenue. * * * This appeal is from a judgment on a verdict in favor of the plaintiff. * * *

[The court found that there was enough evidence of excessive speed to take the issue of the defendant's negligence to the jury].

In addition to the testimony of Hall, plaintiff himself testified that, when he was within a distance of sixty feet from the intersection of the two streets traveling at a speed between fifteen and twenty miles an hour, he had a clear view of Clifton Avenue East of Ellamont street for a distance of one hundred and eighty feet, and there was no car in sight. If this be true, and it must be so accepted in considering [defendant's demurrer prayer] then the Jackson car must have been greatly exceeding the legal speed limit, and the prayer was properly refused.

Defendants' contributory negligence prayer was also properly refused. It is contended that, if plaintiff had looked to his right when he reached the intersection, he must have seen the Jackson car in time to have avoided the collision. But a like contention was unsuccessfully made in Taxicab Co. v. Ottenritter, [151 Md. 525, 135 A. 587]. In that case, in an opinion by Judge Urner, we said that plaintiff's duty in that respect was performed if he looked sufficiently far to his right to discover that there was no traffic approaching from that direction within a distance that would be traversed by a vehicle

39. Also see Sparkman v. Maxwell, Tex., 519 S.W.2d 852 (1975); Golden v. Springer, 238 N.W.2d 314 (Iowa 1975). In Tedla v. Ellman did the conduct of the pedestrians constitute an excusable violation of the statute, or no violation of it at all? See Morris, The Role of Criminal Statutes in Negligence Actions, 49 Colum.L.Rev. 21 (1949) and James, Statutory Standards and Negligence in Accident Cases, 11 La.L.Rev. 95 (1950).

driven at a speed permitted by law. He was not required to look always to his right while crossing the street, as he had to avoid endangering travel ahead of him, or approaching from his left. See, also Chiswell v. Nichols, 137 Md. 291, 112 A. 363. While it was incumbent upon the plaintiff to respect the rule giving the right of way at street intersections to vehicles approaching from the right, yet if at the time he looked on approaching, and within a short distance of the intersection, the way for a safe distance was clear of traffic coming from that direction, he should not judicially be declared negligent in not providing against the possibility of collision with a car which could not come into dangerous proximity to his own unless it were unlawfully operated.

Finding no error in the ruling presented for review the judgment must be affirmed. * * * [40]

40. Cf., however, Hensel v. Beckward, 20 Md. 544, 316 A.2d 309 (1974), page 377 infra (qualifying the rule of the principal case as to intersections with boulevards or through streets); Morris v. Bloomgren, 127 Ohio 147, 187 N.E. 2, 89 A.L.R. 831 (1933). See cases collected in notes 89 A.L.R. 838; 136 A.L.R. 1497.

Cf. Caines v. Wofsey, 117 Conn. 671, 167 A. 733 (1933); Baker v. Salvation Army, 91 N.H. 1, 12 A.2d 514 (1940). Even where plaintiff, coming from the disfavored direction, sees the other car he may nevertheless proceed if he reasonably thinks that such a course involves no danger of collision. Harman v. Bay Cities Transit Co., 36 Cal.App.2d 348, 98 P.2d 226 (1939); Boyd v. Close, 82 Colo. 150, 257 P. 1097 (1927); Korenkiewicz v. York Motor Express, 138 Pa.Super. 210, 10 A.2d 864 (1940). But cf. Ulman, A Judge Takes the Stand (1933), in which the author, a trial judge who had had wide experience in these matters, came to this conclusion: "In one collision case after another, I have found the factor that had conclusive weight with the jury was the bare rule of right of way, unaffected by any and all evidence of surrounding cicumstances, untouched by the qualifications and limitations that the judges have said should be imposed upon the application of the rule." (P. 30.)

The driver who approaches an intersection from the direction favored by the right of way statute is not entitled to rely blindly on his right of way but must exercise reasonable care under all the circumstances. Avery v. R. E. Guerin Trucking Co., 304 Mass. 500, 24 N.E.2d 330 (1939); Kerr v. Hayes, 250 Mich. 19, 229 N.W. 430 (1930) (driver having right of way may initially assume it will be yielded to him but this does not warrant a failure to look for cars approaching from disfavored direction).

See also Ferraro v. Garden City Fire Com'rs, 259 App.Div. 121, 18 N.Y.S.2d 194 (1940)—the driver who had the green light "in his favor was not absolutely entitled by that fact alone to go forward if he knew that by so doing an otherwise avoidable accident would happen, and * * * the fundamental obligation of using ordinary and reasonable care applied."

Cases dealing with these problems are collected in a note, 175 A.L.R. 1013.

Many statutes are so drawn as not to prescribe a particular course of conduct for all cases by rule of thumb, but instead to require the jury's aid in setting up the standard for each case. So where a statute commands one motorist in overtaking another to give a signal "whenever necessary to insure the safety of other users of the highway," a jury would determine the existence of the required necessity if there was room for reasonable doubt. Piper v. Adams Exp. Co., 270 Pa. 54, 113 A. 562 (1918). Cf. Tarry Warehouse & Storage Co. v. Duvall, 131 Tex. 466, 115 S.W.2d 401 (1938) (vehicles must park off pavement "when it is possible" to do so).

COMBS v. LOS ANGELES RY. CORPORATION

Supreme Court of California, in Bank, 1947.
29 Cal.2d 606, 177 P.2d 293.

EDMONDS, JUSTICE. Combs sued to recover damages for personal injuries, and the appeal of the Los Angeles Railway Corporation attacks the judgment in his favor upon the ground that he was contributorily negligent as a matter of law. As in Satterlee v. Orange Glenn School District, 29 Cal.2d 581, 177 P.2d 279, certain jury instructions are challenged upon the ground that they incorrectly state the law in regard to the effect of a plaintiff's violation of a statute upon his cause of action for negligence.

The accident occurred when a street car operated by the railway company collided with an automobile operated by Joseph Commodore. Combs was standing on the step of the car and the impact threw him to the street. He named both the corporation and Commodore as defendants. Each of them denied the charge of negligence and, as a separate defense, pleaded contributory negligence.

As Combs explained the circumstances of his case, late in the afternoon, he and several other persons were standing at a loading zone waiting for a street car. When it arrived, he made no observation as to the number of persons which it carried, nor did he notice that the rear platform was crowded. However, he saw several persons riding on the rear step.

He was the last person to board the car. He reached the second step and, after the car started, paid his fare to the conductor, received a transfer, and then endeavored to make his way to the platform. However, it was so crowded with passengers that he could not do so. As the street car approached the next stop, and while Combs was still on the second step, the car and the automobile of Commodore collided. The impact ripped the steps from the body of the car and Combs received injuries for which he now claims damages.

At the conclusion of the plaintiff's case, both defendants challenged the sufficiency of the evidence by motion for a nonsuit based upon the claim that the evidence conclusively established that, as a matter of law, Combs was guilty of contributory negligence. This motion was denied. Upon the same grounds, at the close of the trial, each defendant unsuccessfully moved for a directed verdict.

The jury returned its verdict in favor of Combs and Commodore and against the railway company. The appeal of the corporation is from the judgment and from the order denying its motion for judgment notwithstanding the verdict.

The appellant contends that the evidence conclusively established that Combs was guilty of contributory negligence as a matter of law because of his violation of a section of the Municipal Code of the City of Los Angeles which makes it unlawful for one to "ride upon the fenders, steps, or running board of any street car or vehicle." (§ 80.47.) And as there is no conflict in the testimony that Combs was "riding" upon the steps of the street car in violation of the statute and but one conclusion can be drawn from the facts, the question of proximate cause is one of law.

A further ground of attack upon the judgment is that prejudicial error resulted from the action of the trial court in refusing to instruct the jury that if it found Combs had violated the applicable ordinance, he was guilty of negligence as a matter of law. An instruction upon this point requested by appellant and given to the jury as modified is also challenged by the railway corporation as constituting prejudicial error. Violation of the ordinance was conclusive, not presumptive, evidence of negligence, since there were no circumstances presented which would justify or excuse violation. Furthermore, the modified instruction was conflicting, argumentative, and misleading. Also, says the appellant, the instruction given to the jury was erroneous because it failed to state in specific terms circumstances under which a violation of the ordinance is excused, but leaves this entire matter solely to conjecture without reference to legal principles.

On the other hand, Combs contends that the issue of contributory negligence was properly left to the jury. He urges that the evidence presented a question of fact as to whether he was "riding" upon the steps of the street car within the meaning of the ordinance and supports the jury's implied finding that he was not doing so.

The instruction given by the court on its own motion is defended by Combs as being a correct statement of law. Considering the circumstances, he says, the violation of the ordinance created merely a presumption of negligence, and it was a question of fact as to whether the evidence was such as to excuse such violation.

The railway company's proposed charge to the jury reads as follows: "If you find from the evidence * * * that at the time of the collision between the automobile and street car and immediately prior thereto, * * * Combs was riding upon one or more of the steps of said street car, then * * * Combs was * * * [violating] the Municipal Code * * * and as such was guilty of negligence as a matter of law. If you further find from the evidence that such negligence, if any, contributed proximately in any degree whatever, even the slightest, to the injuries sustained by * * * Combs, then [he] is not entitled to recover * * * against defendant * * corporation. * * *".

The instruction given by the court as a modification of one submitted by the appellant is No. 149 of California Jury Instructions, Third Revised Edition. It reads: "Conduct which is in violation of the [Municipal] code sections just read to you constitutes negligence per se. This means that if the evidence supports a finding, and you do find, that any party to this action did so conduct himself, it requires a presumption that he was negligent. However, such presumption is not conclusive. It may be overcome by other evidence showing that under all the circumstances surrounding the event, the conduct in question was excusable, justifiable and such as might reasonably have been expected from a person of ordinary prudence. In this connection you may assume that a person of ordinary prudence will reasonably endeavor to obey the law and will do so unless causes, not of his own intended making, induce him, without moral fault, to do otherwise."

The court also advised the jury that "a presumption is a deduction which the law expressly directs to be made from particular facts. It may be controverted by other evidence, direct or indirect; but unless so controverted, the jury is bound to find in accordance with the presumption."

These instructions present the same question which was decided in the Satterlee case, supra. The evidence concerning the injury to Combs required, first, a determination as to whether he had violated the ordinance and, if he had done so, the effect of such violation. The instruction refused by the court directed the jury to find that, if he did not comply with the mandate of the ordinance, he could not recover. Because of the omission of the important qualification that such conduct might be excused under certain circumstances, the court's ruling upon it was correct. See Satterlee v. Orange Glenn School District, supra, 29 Cal.2d 581, 177 P.2d 279.

The instruction given by the court was a complete and correct statement of the law. By it, the jury was first asked to determine whether Combs was "riding" upon the steps of the car. In view of the testimony of Combs that he was endeavoring to reach the rear platform and that the street car had traveled only a short distance before the collision, the fact of violation was correctly left to the jury. Connard v. Pacific Elec. R. Co., 14 Cal.2d 375, 94 P.2d 567.

If he was violating the ordinance in that particular at the time of the accident, the jury was told, the question then to be answered was whether the circumstances showed an excuse for his conduct. Bearing upon that issue was the testimony of Combs that when he boarded the street car he did not make any observation as to how many people it was carrying, that he did not notice the crowded condition of the rear platform until the car was proceeding on its way, that he endeavored to make his way into the car but found it was impossible to do so, and that the car had not stopped when the step upon which he was riding was struck by the automobile of Commodore. From this evidence, the jury could find that Combs reasonably thought that the people in front of him would soon move up into the car, but subsequent events beyond his control prevented him from doing so.

The appellant's contention that the instruction was conflicting, argumentative, and misleading and tended to confuse the jury is without merit. The statements in the instruction that violation of an ordinance requires a presumption of negligence and that the presumption may be overcome by "all the circumstances surrounding the event," are neither inconsistent nor confusing. In many other situations a jury is directed that, if it finds certain facts to be true, a certain conclusion follows; however, if additional facts are found then a different determination must be made. The challenged instruction does nothing more than this. In other words, to tell jurors that violation of an ordinance gives rise to a rebuttable presumption of negligence is to say that they are authorized by the law to look behind, beyond, around and outside the violation to see if there are circumstances that justify or excuse the conduct. The statements merely complement each other. This instruction, when combined with the instruction explaining the legal effect of a presumption, clearly states the applicable principles of law announced in Satterlee v. Orange Glenn School District, supra. It thus becomes unnecessary to decide whether a duty was owed to persons in the class of appellant so that it could take advantage of a violation of section 80.47 of the Los Angeles Municipal Code.

The verdict is an implied finding that, under the circumstances, the alleged violation of the ordinance was excusable and it is amply supported by the evidence.

The judgment is affirmed.

GIBSON, C. J., and SHENK, SCHAUER, and SPENCE, JJ., concurred.

CARTER, JUSTICE. I concur in the judgment of affirmance, but as the majority opinion is based upon the unsound reasoning in the Satterlee case, 29 Cal.2d 581, 177 P.2d 279, from which I dissented, I cannot agree with the legal theory upon which said opinion is based.

Once it is conceded, as it is in the majority opinion, that the violation of a penal statute or ordinance by one seeking to recover civil damages, does not necessarily bar a recovery, there is no common sense or logic in talking about presumptions or presumptive negligence arising from evidence of such violation. A person involved in an accident may be guilty of violating several statutes or ordinances but such violations may have no bearing upon his alleged negligent conduct. For example, he may be driving an automobile without a driver's license; his automobile may not have a current license number; and he may be operating his automobile at night without a taillight and have a head-on collision. Obviously, none of these violations can be said to have any bearing upon negligent conduct, and evidence relating to them would be immaterial and irrelevant. Even when we consider a statute or ordinance relating to conduct directly involved in the accident, it is first a question of fact as to whether there has been a violation, second, whether such violation was a proximate cause of the accident, and third, if both of the foregoing are answered in the affirmative, whether such violation was excused or justified. There must necessarily be involved in the latter the question of whether or not the person charged with such violation acted as a reasonably prudent person under the circumstances. If so, he could not be guilty of negligence. So the test must be in every case, what would a reasonably prudent person have done under the circumstances? * * *

From the foregoing discussion it is obvious that any error which existed in the instruction complained of was more favorable to defendant than to the plaintiff, and defendant could not have suffered prejudice thereby.

TRAYNOR, JUSTICE. I dissent. In my opinion plaintiff was guilty of contributory negligence as a matter of law. See my concurring opinion in Satterlee v. Orange Glenn School District, 29 Cal.2d 581, 177 P.2d 279. Under the instruction given by the trial court, riding on the street car steps in violation of the ordinance was merely evidence of negligence, and the jury was permitted to apply as a standard, the conduct of a man of ordinary prudence rather than the standard prescribed by the ordinance.

The principal issue in this case is whether the plaintiff was "riding" on the street car steps in violation of the ordinance. [The Justice concluded he was so riding.]

Before a verdict may be directed there must be not only a violation of the ordinance, but a causal relation between the conduct in violation of the ordinance and the injuries sustained by the plaintiff. The unconflicting evidence disclosed by the record shows that the automobile struck the side of the street car and ripped off the steps, including the step on which plaintiff was standing. If plaintiff had been standing on the platform or in the interior part of the car, he would not have been injured. No reasonable jury, therefore, could doubt that plaintiff's conduct in violation of the ordinance was in fact a contributing cause of his injuries.

It has been suggested that the ordinance does not provide a proper standard of conduct to determine the question of contributory negligence of persons riding on street car steps, since its purpose is to protect the passengers from harm rather than to protect street railways from liability. A statute or ordinance designed for the protection of the class of persons that includes the plaintiff provides the standard of conduct in determining contributory negligence, for "Unlike assumption of risk, the defense does not rest upon the idea that the defendant is relieved of any duty toward the plaintiff. Rather the plaintiff is denied recovery because his own conduct disentitles him to maintain the action. In the eyes of the law both parties are at fault." Prosser, Torts, § 393; see Rest., Torts, § 466, comment f. The purpose of the ordinance in question was to protect the users of street cars from injuries like that sustained by plaintiff. Violation of a duty to protect oneself, including a duty imposed by statute, constitutes contributory negligence. Meincke v. Oakland Garage, Inc., 11 Cal.2d 255, 256, 79 P.2d 91; Koeppel v. Daluiso, 118 Cal.App. 442, 446, 5 P.2d 457; see Connard v. Pacific Elec. R. Co., supra, 14 Cal.2d at page 376, 94 P.2d at page 568; Rest., Torts, §§ 469, 475.

Since the uncontradicted evidence showed that plaintiff was contributively negligent as a matter of law and that this negligence was a contributing cause of plaintiff's injuries, defendant's motion for a directed verdict should have been granted.

Rehearing denied; TRAYNOR, J., dissenting.

WHETZEL v. JESS FISHER MANAGEMENT CO.

United States Court of Appeals for the District of Columbia Circuit, 1960.
282 F.2d 943.

BAZELON, CIRCUIT JUDGE.

In Bowles v. Maloney, this court adhered to the common-law rule that "absent any statutory or contract duty, the lessor is not responsible for an injury resulting from a defect which developed during the term." Since that case was decided, the Commissioners of the District of Columbia have promulgated regulations concerning maintenance and repair of residential property. The primary question here presented is whether these regulations impose a "statutory * * * duty" on the lessor not presented in Bowles v. Mahoney. We conclude that they do.

The issue arises upon an appeal from a summary judgment entered against the plaintiffs below. Their amended complaint alleged that on March 1, 1956, Audrey Whetzel rented an apartment from the appellee for $75.00 per month upon a one-year lease which did not affirmatively place the burden of repairs, other than those caused by the tenant's negligence, on either party. On June 30, 1956, four months after she entered into possession, the entire bedroom ceiling fell, causing the injuries of which she complains. The principal theory of her action is that the appellee, with knowledge of the defect, negligently permitted the ceiling to remain in an unsafe condition.

I. The Applicable Law

Appellant contends that the Housing Regulations establish a standard of conduct for the landlord, which, if negligently breached, allows an injured tenant to recover. * * *

* * * Other jurisdictions have accepted the view that regulations which explicitly or implicitly require a landlord to repair may render him liable for injuries resulting from a failure to comply. Indeed, in our own case of Hill v. Raymond, 1935, 65 App.D.C. 144, 81 F.2d 278, we held that building regulations establishing certain standards for interior stairways were admissible as evidence of a landlord's negligence in failing to illuminate and to maintain a common stairway. * * *

The view expressed in these cases is fully consistent with "the almost universal American and English attitude * * * that where legislation prescribes a standard of conduct for the purpose of protecting life, limb, or property from a certain type of risk, and harm to the interest sought to be protected comes about through breach of the standard from the risk sought to be obviated, then the statutory prescription of the standard will at least be considered in determining civil rights and liabilities." 2 Harper & James, Torts 997 (1956). See also Restatement, Torts § 286 (1934); Prosser, Torts 152–64 (2d ed. 1955); Thayer, Public Wrong and Private Action, 27 Harv.L.Rev. 317 (1914).

This axiom of tort law tacitly recognizes that the continued vitality of the common law, including the law of torts, depends upon its ability to reflect contemporary community values and ethics. Holmes, The Common Law 1, 120–21, 149, 162–63 (1881); Cardozo, The Nature of the Judicial Process 24–25, 108 (1921); O'Meara, Natural Law and Everyday Law, 5 Natural Law Forum 85 (1960). An essential element of tort liability is the breach of a duty of care owed. Palsgraf v. Long Island R. R., 1928, 248 N.Y. 339, 162 N.E. 99, 59 A.L.R. 1253. Whether or not a duty of care exists is, basically, a question of law. Harper & James, Torts § 18.8 (1958). A penal statute which is imposed for the protection of particular individuals establishes a duty of care based on contemporary community values and ethics. The law of torts can only be out of joint with community standards if it ignores the existence of such duties. See Evers v. Davis, 1914, 86 N.J.L. 196, 90 A. 677; Morris, The Role of Criminal Statutes in Negligence Action, 49 Colum.L.Rev. 21 (1949).

The courts have not agreed, however, on the precise effect to be given a breach of a statute. A majority of American courts hold that the unexcused violation of a statute which is intended to protect a class of persons, of which the plaintiff is a member, against the type of harm which has in fact occurred is negligence *per se*. That is to say, such violation is negligence as a matter of law and the jury must be so instructed. Prosser, Torts 161 (1955). But a substantial and growing number of jurisdictions hold that violation of a penal statute is "only evidence of negligence which the jury may accept or reject as it sees fit." Ibid.

Commentators have pointed out that the *per se* rule may create serious rigidities and inequities. See, e. g., 2 Harper & James, Torts § 17.6 (1958); Morris, The Relation of Criminal Statutes to Tort Liability, 46 Harv.L.Rev. 453 (1933). Strictly applied, the *per se* rule can, for instance, render negligent as a matter of law a defendant who has taken all due precautions,[41] and bar recovery of a plaintiff who is likewise free from fault in all but a technical sense. Prosser, Torts 162–63 (1955); Morris, The Role of Criminal Statutes in Negligence Actions, 49 Colum.L.Rev. 21, 29 (1949); Prosser, Contributory Negligence as a Defense to a Violation of Statute, 32 Minn.L.Rev. 105 (1948). Courts adhering to the *per se* rule have generally recognized its inadequacies and developed such doctrines as "statutory purpose" and "justifiable violation" in an effort to return to the jury responsibility for determining whether reasonable care was exercised in the circumstances.

This jurisdiction has adopted these exceptions. In a leading case, we held that "violation of an ordinance intended to promote safety is negligence. If by creating the hazard which the ordinance was intended to avoid, it brings about the harm which the ordinance was

41. Harper & James give the example of a defendant whose automobile tail lights go out, despite all due precaution, shortly before an accident. Harper & James, Torts 999 (1958).

intended to prevent, it is a legal cause of the harm." Ross v. Hartman, 1943, 78 U.S.App.D.C. 217, 218, 139 F.2d 14, 15, 158 A.L.R. 1370.[42]

The doctrine of statutory purpose was subsequently refined in Peigh v. Baltimore & O. R. R., 1953, 92 U.S.App.D.C. 198, 200, 204 F.2d 391, 393, 44 A.L.R.2d 671, where we pointed out that "the doctrine of negligence *per se* is one which must be applied cautiously, with an eye to essential fairness. If its use in a particular case tends to produce liability based not on real fault, or on any real departure from standards of prudent conduct, but only on a technicality, the courts are justifiably reluctant to apply it." There each party contended that the other was negligent as a matter of law. We held the doctrine of negligence *per se* inapplicable to the defendant's illegal conduct (leaving a boxcar on the street for an unreasonable length of time) because the prime purpose of the regulation was, in our view, to expedite traffic and commerce and not to protect passing motorists. Such violation was, however, admissible as evidence of negligence. With respect to the plaintiff's possible violations of regulations requiring him to drive at a not "imprudent speed" and to stay "as closely as practicable" to the right-hand side of the road, we held that these were safety regulations, and that violation would be contributory negligence *per se.* But we further held that inasmuch as these regulations turned upon reasonableness and did not establish "precise and rigid standards," the question whether a violation had in fact occurred was for the jury to determine.

Thereafter, in Hecht Co. v. McLaughlin, 1954, 93 U.S.App.D.C. 382, 214 F.2d 212, we went one step further toward the doctrine of evidence of negligence. There the vestibule doors of defendant's department store were constructed in violation of District of Columbia Building Regulations. It was clear that the purpose of the regulation was to promote safety and that plaintiff was a member of the class to be protected. Although this would seem to meet the standards of the Peigh and Ross cases, supra, we held that violation of the regulations was not negligence *per se* because the defendant had secured the approval of architects and public authorities before installing its doors. We found this conduct was "indicative of care on the Company's part, quite inconsistent with the theory that violation of the regulation alone, all else aside, is negligence as a matter of law." Accordingly we held that:

> "The question of the Company's negligence is to be decided on all relevant evidence, including violation of any safety regulation found to be applicable, and consequently admissible in evidence, but including also facts tending to show due

42. There we found that a defendant, who had left his automobile unlocked in violation of traffic regulations, was negligent as a matter of law and liable for injuries sustained by third persons at the hands of one who stole the car. [Notes 41 and 42 from original, renumbered; other notes in original omitted.]

> care on the part of the Company in the selection and installation of the door." [93 U.S.App.D.C. at page 386, 214 F.2d at pages 215–216.]

Our holding was thus, in effect, although not in terms, that a jury might well find the defendant's violation "justifiable" or "excused." See 2 Harper & James, Torts 1007–11 (1958).

A review of these cases makes it clear that in this jurisdiction the rather rigid doctrine of negligence *per se* has been tempered by important limitations. Our law is clearly moving in the direction of leaving more and more of the question of negligence as derived from statutory standards for the jury to consider.

II. The Instant Case

* * *

Upon whom are the duties specified by the regulations imposed? Some are upon the landlord alone. Under § 2304, "No persons shall rent or offer to rent any habitation, or the furnishings thereof, unless such habitation and its furnishings are in a clean, safe and sanitary condition, in repair, and free from rodents or vermin." * * *

Appellee contends * * *, that * * * summary judgment was * * * appropriate because there are uncontradicted affidavits in the record showing that appellee had no notice of the defect in the ceiling. We think actual knowledge is not required for liability; it is enough if, in the exercise of reasonable care, appellee should have known that the condition of the ceiling violated the standards of the Housing Code. Prosser, Torts 6 (1955).

We cannot say that upon a trial a jury could not reasonably find that appellee should have known of the condition of the ceiling. The bathroom ceiling, located just off the bedroom in appellant's apartment, had fallen and been repaired not long before appellant took possession. On New Year's Eve of 1956, just two months before appellant moved in, the livingroom ceiling of the adjoining apartment also fell. On April 1, 1956, appellant noticed a leak in her bedroom ceiling, and reported it to the janitor who was able to stop the leak by adjusting the radiator in the apartment above. But there is no evidence that he then inspected appellant's ceiling to determine if it had been weakened. Just before appellant moved in, appellee hired a contractor to inspect and repair the plaster in appellant's apartment. The contractor's affidavit, executed three years after the event, stated that he "carefully inspected and examined the entire apartment" and found "the plaster in the ceiling of the bedroom * * * in good sound condition." Appellant filed no counter affidavits. But in the circumstances of this case, such failure does not "compel acceptance as true of fact alleged in the movant's affidavits" for the purpose of summary judgment.

In view of the fact that the ceiling fell only four months after the alleged inspection, the jury might reasonably find that the inspection was negligently performed. * * *

It follows from all that we have said that the District Court erred in granting summary judgment * * * We therefore reverse the judgment as to that count and remand with directions to proceed to trial. * * *

WILBUR K. MILLER, CIRCUIT JUDGE, dissents.

ROSS v. ROSS

Supreme Court of Minnesota, 1972.
294 Minn. 115, 200 N.W.2d 149.

OTIS, JUSTICE. The question for decision is whether persons who are not in the business of selling intoxicating liquor are liable under the Civil Damage Act, Minn.St. 340.95, for furnishing liquor to a minor, proximately causing his death. We hold that defendants are liable and affirm.

The facts are undisputed. On July 13, 1967, defendant-appellant Delmar Ross and defendant Joel Owen Johnson purchased liquor for Delmar's 19-year-old brother, Rodney Alan Ross, which, as the jury found, resulted in Rodney's becoming intoxicated. By special verdict, the jury also found that Rodney's intoxication proximately caused his death when the car he was driving left the road. These consolidated actions were brought on behalf of Rodney's infant son and by Rodney's parents.[43] The jury awarded damages in the sum of $4,680 for the son and $1,026.84 for the parents. * * *

Minn.St. 340.95, popularly known as the "Dramshop Act" or the "Civil Damage Act," has never been applied to permit recovery against a person not in the business of dispensing liquor.[44] Cases decided in appellate courts of Kansas, Michigan, and Illinois under similar statutes have denied recovery. Nevertheless, in searching for legislative intent, which is the only subject of our inquiry, we are persuaded that the purpose of the act was to impose liability on every violator, whether or not he was in the liquor business.

43. Although the negligence of a decedent is a defense in an ordinary wrongful death action, and one who voluntarily becomes intoxicated cannot recover for his own injury under the Dramshop Act, Heveron v. Village of Belgrade, 288 Minn. 395, 397, 181 N.W.2d 692, 693 (1970); Sworski v. Colman, 204 Minn. 474, 477, 283 N.W. 778, 780 (1939), a spouse, child, or parent may recover for loss of support notwithstanding the injured party or decedent became voluntarily intoxicated. Benes v. Campion, 186 Minn. 578, 244 N.W. 72 (1932); Fest v. Olson, 138 Minn. 31, 163 N.W. 798 (1917); Annotation, 4 A.L.R.3d 1332.

44. Minn.St. 340.95 provides:

"Every husband, wife, child, parent, guardian, employer, or other person who is injured in person or property, or means of support, by any intoxicated person, or by the intoxication of any person, has a right of action, in his own name, against any person who, by illegally selling, bartering or giving intoxicating liquors, caused the intoxication of such person, for all damages, sustained * * *.

Minn.St. 340.73 provides:

"Subdivision 1. It shall be unlawful for any person, except a licensed pharmacist to sell, give, barter, furnish, deliver, or dispose of, in any manner, either directly or indirectly, any spirituous, vinous, malt, or fermented liquors in any quantity, for any purpose, whatever, to any minor person, or to any intoxicated person, or to any public prostitute. * * *"

There is nothing in our other cases inconsistent with holding this defendant liable. * * * We have held that the Civil Damage Act is both penal and remedial, an inconsistency which we have recognized but resolved in favor of a liberal construction "to suppress the mischief and advance the remedy." (Italics omitted.) Hahn v. City of Ortonville, 238 Minn. 428, 436, 57 N.W.2d 254, 261. Our decisions have imposed on licensed liquor vendors strict liability because—

> " * * * such business or activity can best bear the loss occasioned by a violation of law regulating the business or activity, even though the violation was unintentional or did not involve any deviation from the standard of due care." Dahl v. Northwestern Nat. Bank, 268 Minn. 216, 220, 121 N.W.2d 321, 324.

It may well be that the legislature in light of our present holding will amend the Civil Damage Act to permit one who is not in the liquor business to assert the defense of due care. This, however, is not our prerogative.

Of the three jurisdictions called to our attention which have denied recovery, only one, Michigan, has a statute such as ours. Harris v. Hardesty, 111 Kan. 291, 207 P. 188 (1922), construed a statute which imposed liability for causing intoxication by selling liquor even if the sale was legal. The same kind of statute was applied in Miller v. Owens-Illinois Glass Co., 48 Ill.App.2d 412, 199 N.E.2d 300, 8 A.L.R. 3d 1402 (1964). The Illinois case arose out of damages inflicted by an employee of the defendant corporation who became intoxicated at a company picnic. The Illinois statute does not restrict liability to *illegal* sales. The Illinois Appellate Court found it was not the intention of the legislature to apply the act to social drinking provided by a friend or neighbor. To hold otherwise, the court said, would open the floodgates of litigation. If our statute also applied to every case for damage resulting from intoxication, whether the furnishing of liquor was legal or illegal, we might well find a different legislative intention also. The only cases of which we are aware construing a statute such as ours are LeGault v. Klebba, 7 Mich.App. 640, 152 N.W.2d 712 (1967); and Behnke v. Pierson, 21 Mich.App. 219, 175 N.W.2d 303 (1970). The LeGault case arose out of furnishing a guest liquor at a wedding reception, and the Behnke case stemmed from a company party where liquor was furnished an employee who was already intoxicated.

We have concluded that the circumstances surrounding the adoption of the Civil Damage Act in 1911 compel a finding that the legislature intended to create a new cause of action against every violator whether in the liquor business or not. It is significant that at that session the legislature seemed preoccupied with strengthening and tightening the liquor laws, using throughout * * * the words "any person" and making no mention anywhere of persons in the liquor business. Since the act applies only to illegal transactions, it is not unreasonable to assume that the legislature intended to include persons other than the licensed vendors. Where liquor is furnished in a purely social setting, ordinarily it may be expected that the donor will take some precautions to determine the age of the recipient or his state of intoxication. While the act applies to those invited to wedding receptions and company picnics as well as to other gatherings where supervision may be onerous, no reason occurs to us why those who furnish liquor to others, even on social occasions, should not be responsible for protecting innocent third persons from the potential dangers of indiscriminately furnishing such hospitality.[45] In any event it is not our duty to decide what the legislature would have intended had the act been adopted in 1971 rather than in 1911. Accordingly, we affirm.[46] * * *

ROGOSHESKE, JUSTICE (concurring specially).

While I am compelled to agree with the scope of application intended by the 1911 Legislature in enacting our Civil Damage Act, I cannot endorse the language of the opinion which might be read to imply that the strict liability we have held the statute imposes upon a commercial seller of liquor can, with equal justification, be imposed upon a social host even though he may or may not carry either the type of, or sufficient, liability insurance to protect against the risk of such liability.

Hopefully, everyone ought to share the view that we are our "brother's keeper," and that no social host worthy of another's visit to his home or to his party should be permitted to ignore his duty to exercise reasonable care for the sobriety of his guest because of the potential harm to innocent third parties which could result if he negligently permits his guest to become intoxicated. However, it must be understood that this is not the peculiar nature of the liability imposed upon a liquor dealer, and now a social host, by our Civil Damage Act. As briefly alluded to in the opinion, it is "strict liability" without regard to fault in the sense that the dealer, and now the host, engaged in any intentional or negligent misconduct. Dahl v. Northwestern

45. In a case where the majority refused to impose liability on those furnishing liquor on a social occasion absent a statute, Mr. Chief Justice Hallows, in a well considered dissent, in which he was joined by Justices Wilkie and Heffernan, said (Garcia v. Hargrove, 46 Wis.2d 724, 740, 176 N.W.2d 566, 573): "* * * We are still our brothers keepers, and it would be a rare host at a social gathering who would knowingly give more liquor to an intoxicated friend when he knows his invitee must take care of himself on the highway and will potentially endanger other persons. Social justice and common sense require the social host to see within reason that his guests do not partake too much of his generosity."

46. Subsequent to the release of this opinion, our attention was called to Williams v. Klemesrud, Iowa, 197 N.W.2d 614, decided May 11, 1972, in which the Iowa court reached exactly the same conclusion by remarkably similar reasoning. [Also see Brockett v. Kitchen Boyd Motor Co., 24 Cal.App.3d 87, 100 Cal.Rptr. 752 (1972) (office Christmas party); Brattain v. Herron, 309 N.E.2d 150 (Ind.App. 1974) (liability of hostess sister); Giardina v. Solomon, 360 F.Supp. 262 (M.D.Pa.1973) (liability of college fraternity); and, collecting cases contra, Anno., 8 A.L.R.3d 1412.]

Nat. Bank, 265 Minn. 216, 220, 121 N.W.2d 321, 324 (1963). As previously applied only to a commercial seller who makes a sale of liquor for consumption either on or off his premises, this means in plain language that if he sells or otherwise transfers liquor to a minor, causing his intoxication, or to one obviously intoxicated, and the intoxicated person injures a third party in his person, property, or means of support, the seller is strictly liable for all damages resulting. It is no defense to the seller that he exercised every reasonable precaution to avoid making such illegal sale. Hahn v. City of Ortonville, 238 Minn. 428, 57 N.W.2d 254 (1953). Nor is it a defense that the injured party was himself contributorily negligent. Kvanli v. Village of Watson, 272 Minn. 481, 139 N.W.2d 275 (1965).

The reason why this construction of our statute has evolved is our recognition that its ultimate purpose is a dual one involving both penal and remedial objectives; penal in that it intends to suppress the mischief of illegal sales by a liquor dealer to the end that there will be self-policing against illegal sales by dealers, and remedial in that the statute assures recovery of damages by an innocent person from a commercial activity which can best bear the burden of loss by insuring against it as a cost of engaging in a hazardous business for profit. * * *

However desirable it may appear to impose the same strict liability upon a social host as upon a commercial vendor, the consequences may mean jeopardy so far as at least the remedial purpose of our statute is concerned. The objective of advancing the remedy of recovery in future cases because the liquor industry can best bear the burden of loss is not present when recovery is sought from an uninsured private individual.

It thus seems to me that it is necessary to note that the result of our decision may be to effectively dull one edge of what has been a sharp two-edged tool fashioned by the legislature to protect the health, safety, and welfare of the public by carefully controlling the commercial sale or transfer of liquor to minors or intoxicated persons. Inevitably, attempts will now be made to amend the statute, or our construction of it, and to inject into it the element of fault or proof of negligence. I offer these observations in aid of those who will seek to improve the statute and its application. In this developing area of law, where we have not yet been directly confronted with whether or not nonstatutory common-law liability based on negligence should be imposed on private individuals, and indeed on commercial vendors,[47] it is important to keep clearly in mind the host of public policy considerations which must be weighed in resolving the threshold issue of whether such a remedy should be in addition to or a substitute for the liability imposed by our Civil Damage Act.

47. See, Note, 49 Minn.L.Rev. 1154; Hagglund & Arthur, Dram Shop Law in Minnesota, 28 Bench and Bar of Minn., Feb. 1972, p. 17. [Also see Rappaport v. Nichols, 31 N.J. 188, 156 A.2d 1 (1959) and Anno., 75 A.L.R.2d 833. Notes 43 and 45–47, except for bracketed material, from original, renumbered. Other notes in original omitted.]

JAMES, STATUTORY STANDARDS AND NEGLIGENCE IN ACCIDENT CASES, 11 La.L.Rev. 95, 104–105 (1950).

There is another point of view which has very occasionally found favor among American courts. The violator of penal statutes is after all a "criminal." He might therefore be treated as something of an outlaw who is liable for all the direct results of his misdeeds and disentitled to seek redress through the courts for any injury to which his criminal conduct contributed. Thus a defendant has been held liable without regard to negligence for injury to another person hit by a blow aimed at a horse he was maltreating contrary to statute.[48] A similar result has been reached by one court where defendant was violating a statute which forbade hunting on Sunday.[49] And Massachusetts treats an unregistered motor vehicle as a trespasser on the highway.[50] What little currency this notion enjoys today, however, is largely confined to cases where a law-breaking *plaintiff* is denied access to the courts, a fact which makes it run sharply counter to the objective of compensating accident victims.[51] The doctrine appears to be a barbarous relic of the worst there was in puritanism. Its application could be justified at all only as a stringent means of imposing additional sanctions to enforce a very important provision of the criminal law,[52] and it is questionable indeed whether it is wise for the courts

48. Osborne v. Van Dyke, 113 Iowa 557, 85 N.W. 784 (1901), a case which seemed to Thayer "hard to support." Thayer, * * * [Public Wrong and Private Action, 27 Harv.L.Rev. 317 (1913)] at 338, n. 62. Cf. La.R.S. (1950) 14:102.

49. White v. Levarn, 93 Vt. 218, 108 A. 564 (1918).

50. Koonovsky v. Quelette, 226 Mass. 474, 116 N.E. 243 (1917) (defendant driving unregistered car on the highway liable for all injury the direct result of that act even if not contemplatable as a probable result). * * * [Since changed by statute; cf. Mass. Gen.Laws Ann. c. 90, § 9 (1975); also see Falvey v. Hamelburg, 347 Mass. 430, 198 N.E.2d 400 (1964) (lack of registration not proximate cause of accident if accident "could just as well have happened had the car been legally registered.")]

51. Patrican v. Garvey, 287 Mass. 62, 90 N.E. 9 (1934) (eleven year old plaintiff denied recovery where he rode bicycle over middle line of road in violation of statute) (Cf. La.R.S. (1950) 32:-231); Johnson v. Boston & M. R. R., 83 N.H. 350, 143 A. 516 (1928) (plaintiff nonsuited where injuries in collision at railroad crossing with defendant's train because he had no driver's license). Contrast Rapee v. Beacon Hotel Corp., 293 N.Y. 196, 56 N.E.2d 548 (1944) (court refused to bar suit by plaintiff against hotel for damages merely because he had violated law by registering at hotel with woman not his wife). See Davis, The Plaintiff's Illegal Act as Defense in Actions of Tort, 18 Harv.L.Rev. 505 (1905).

A variation of this rule is that which deprives a plaintiff who is violating an ordinance or statute of the benefit of last clear chance. See Price v. Gabel, 162 Wash. 275, 298 P. 444 (1931) (photographer breaking city ordinance by taking pictures from the middle of street is a wrongdoer every moment he is so engaged; hence a defendant who injures him there can never be the last wrongdoer); Masters v. Man Lehmden, 36 Ohio App. 414, 173 N.E. 303 (1930) (where plaintiff is violating ordinance, he may recover only where defendant is wilfully and wantonly negligent). See contra Arnold v. Owens, 78 F.2d 495 (4th Cir. 1935).

52. Thayer half-heartedly suggested a curious pragmatic defense of the application of the doctrine in Massachusetts to plaintiffs only and not to defendants. Plaintiffs, he said, need only to have a statute regarded as evidence of negligence, for juries will generally find in their favor. "But when the plaintiff's conduct is in

to assume the responsibility of imposing such a sanction when the legislature has not seen fit to do so. It should be noted in passing that the limitations of the "statutory purpose" notion (described in the last section) have no logical relevance to the doctrine described in the present paragraph.

The following material does not deal with the ordinary assault and battery cases which involve fights, arrests, and efforts at self-help of one kind or another. Those are saved for later treatment (see Chapter 8). Here we are still inquiring into the problem of harms which are the more or less accidental by-product of legitimate activities not at all aimed at hurting people or property. Liability is for the most part imposed without regard to fault or for the fault of negligence. Yet even here notions of intentional or wilful injury play a part. It is that part that is sought to be explored in what follows. In making this exploration the following thought should be borne in mind. The general rule of liability for "negligence," which means unreasonably dangerous conduct, includes virtually all cases where defendant intended to bring about the harm that actually befell, for he will scarcely be heard to deny that his conduct involved an unreasonable risk of bringing about the very harm he purposed to consummate. For that and other reasons it is always *useful* to prove intent, or a wanton state of mind. But on the whole it is not *necessary* to do so in this field. There are, however, some rules of law which actually extend liability, enhance damages, or cut off defenses where some wrongdoing more serious than negligence is shown.

RESTATEMENT OF TORTS SECOND (1965)

Section 16. Character of Intent Necessary.

(1) If an act is done with the intention of inflicting upon another an offensive but not a harmful bodily contact, or of putting another in apprehension of either a harmful or offensive bodily contact, and such act causes a bodily contact to the other, the actor is liable to the other for a battery * * * although the act was not done with the intention of bringing about the resulting bodily harm.

question the *harshness* of contributory negligence as a defense and the relative situation of the parties often makes the jury grasp at any opportunity to exonerate the plaintiff of negligence even though he broke the law. *Justice* to the defendant thus requires that the lines be exactly drawn, protection which in the converse case the plaintiff does not need —forces the court to examine the principles more closely." A Draconian kind of "justice" that requires discrimination *against* accident victims to assure full force to the "harshness" of an outworn defense. In a slightly different connection the same author provides what should be a conclusive answer to the suggestion. "The reinforcement brought to this stringent defense by the suggested discrimination against the plaintiff would come oddly at a time when the defense itself is crumbling at many joints under attacks both legislative and judicial." Thayer, supra, * * * at 41–42. [Footnotes 48–52 (except for bracketed portion), by the author of the article, renumbered.]

(2) If an act is done with the intention of affecting a third person in the manner stated in Subsection (1), but causes a harmful bodily contact to another, the actor is liable to such other as fully as though he intended so to affect him.

Section 8A defines "Intent".

Comment b to Section 8A states, "As the probability that the consequences will follow decreases, and becomes less than substantial certainty, the actor's conduct loses the character of intent, and becomes mere recklessness, as defined in § 500. As the probability decreases further, and amounts only to a risk that the result will follow, it becomes ordinary negligence, as defined in § 282. All three have their important place in the law of torts, but the liability attached to them will differ."

VOSBURG v. PUTNEY

Supreme Court of Wisconsin, 1890 and 1891.
78 Wis. 84, 47 N.W. 99; 80 Wis. 523, 50 N.W. 403, 14 L.R.A. 226, 27 Am.St.Rep. 47.

ORTON, J. The facts of this case are briefly as follows: The plaintiff was about fourteen years of age, and the defendant about eleven years of age. On the 20th day of February, 1889, they were sitting opposite to each other across an aisle in the high school of the village of Waukesha. The defendant reached across the aisle with his foot, and hit with his toe the shin of the right leg of the plaintiff. The touch was slight. The plaintiff did not feel it, either on account of its being so slight or of loss of sensation produced by the shock. In a few moments he felt a violent pain in that place, which caused him to cry out loudly. The next day he was sick, and had to be helped to school. On the fourth day he was vomiting, and Dr. Bacon was sent for, but could not come, and he sent medicine to stop the vomiting, and came to see him the next day, on the 25th. There was a slight discoloration of the skin entirely over the inner surface of the tibia an inch below the bend of the knee. The doctor applied fomentations, and gave him anodynes to quiet the pain. This treatment was continued, and the swelling so increased by the 5th day of March that counsel was called, and on the 8th of March an operation was performed on the limb by making an incision, and a moderate amount of pus escaped. A drainage tube was inserted, and an iodoform dressing put on. On the sixth day after this, another incision was made to the bone, and it was found that destruction was going on in the bone, and so it has continued exfoliating pieces of bone. He will never recover the use of his limb. There were black and blue spots on the shin bone, indicating that there had been a blow. On the 1st day of January before, the plaintiff received an injury just above the knee of the same leg by coasting, which appeared to be healing up and drying down at the time of the last injury. The theory of at least one of the medical witnesses was that the limb was in a diseased condition when this touch or kick was given, caused by microbes entering in through the wound above the knee, and which were revivified by the touch, and that the touch was the exciting or remote cause of the destruction of the bone, or of the plaintiff's injury. It does not appear that there was any visible mark made or left by this touch or kick of the defendant's foot, or any appearance of injury until the black and blue spots were discovered by the physician several days afterwards, and then there were more spots than one. There was no proof of any other hurt, and the medical testimony seems to have been agreed that this touch or kick was the exciting cause of the injury to the plaintiff. The jury rendered a verdict for the plaintiff of $2,800.

The learned Circuit Judge said to the jury: "It is a peculiar case, an unfortunate case, a case, I think I am at liberty to say, that ought not to have come into court. The parents of these children ought, in some way, if possible, to have adjusted it between themselves." We have much of the same feeling about the case. It is a very strange and extraordinary case. The cause would seem to be very slight for so great and serious a consequence. And yet the plaintiff's limb might have been in just that condition when such a slight blow would excite and cause such a result, according to the medical testimony. That there is great uncertainty about the case cannot be denied. But perfect certainty is not required. It is sufficient that it is the opinion of the medical witnesses that such a cause even might produce such a result under the peculiar circumstances, and that the jury had the right to find, from the evidence and reasonable inferences therefrom, that it did. We will refrain from further comment on the case, as another trial will have to be had in it.

There were two errors committed on the trial and in the admission of testimony, too important and material to be overlooked.

On account of these two errors the judgment will have to be reversed.

BY THE COURT.—The judgment is reversed, and the cause remanded for a new trial.

[The two errors referred to were (1) the admission of a physician's answer to a question as to the "exciting cause of the condition of this leg" without laying the proper foundation for the answer and (2) the admission of answers by the plaintiff's father to questions relating "to his circumstances and concerning his employment and the number of his children."]

The case has been again tried in the circuit court, and the trial resulted in a verdict for plaintiff for $2,500. * * *

LYON, J. Several errors are assigned, only three of which will be considered.

1. The jury having found that the defendant, in touching the plaintiff with his foot, did not intend to do him any harm, counsel for defendant maintain that the plaintiff has no cause of action, and that defendant's motion for judgment on the special verdict should have been granted. In support of this proposition counsel quote from

2 Greenl. Ev. section 83, the rule that "the intention to do harm is of the essence of an assault." Such is the rule, no doubt, in actions or prosecutions for mere assaults. But this is an action to recover damages for an alleged assault and battery. In such case the rule is correctly stated, in many of the authorities cited by counsel, that plaintiff must show either that the intention was unlawful, or that the defendant is in fault. If the intended act is unlawful, the intention to commit it must necessarily be unlawful. Hence, as applied to this case, if the kicking of the plaintiff by the defendant was an unlawful act, the intention of defendant to kick him was also unlawful.

Had the parties been upon the play-grounds of the school, engaged in the usual boyish sports, the defendant being free from malice, wantonness, or negligence, and intending no harm to plaintiff in what he did, we should hesitate to hold the act of the defendant unlawful, or that he could be held liable in this action. Some consideration is due to the implied license of the play-grounds. But it appears that the injury was inflicted in the school, after it had been called to order by the teacher, and after the regular exercises of the school had commenced. Under these circumstances, no implied license to do the act complained of existed, and such act was a violation of the order and decorum of the school, and necessarily unlawful. Hence we are of the opinion that, under the evidence and verdict, the action may be sustained.

2. The plaintiff testified, as a witness in his own behalf, as to the circumstances of the alleged injury inflicted upon him by the defendant, and also in regard to the wound he received in January, near the same knee, mentioned in the special verdict. * * * Dr. Philler was called as a witness after the examination of the plaintiff and Dr. Bacon. On his direct examination he testified as follows: "I heard the testimony of Andrew Vosburg in regard to how he received the kick, February 20th from his playmate. I heard read the testimony of Miss More, and heard where he said he received this kick on that day." (Miss More had already testified that she was the teacher of the school, and saw defendant standing in the aisle by his seat, and kicking across the aisle, hitting the plaintiff.) The following question was then propounded to Dr. Philler: "After hearing that testimony, and what you know of the case of the boy, seeing it on the 8th day of March, what, in your opinion, was the exciting cause that produced the inflammation that you saw in that boy's leg on that day?" An objection to this question was overruled, and the witness answered: "The exciting cause was the injury received at that day by the kick on the shin-bone."

It will be observed that the above question to Dr. Philler calls for his opinion as a medical expert, based in part upon the testimony of the plaintiff, as to what was the proximate cause of the injury to plaintiff's leg. The plaintiff testified to two wounds upon his leg, either of which might have been such proximate cause. Without taking both of these wounds into consideration, the expert could give no intelligent or reliable opinion as to which of them caused the injury complained of; yet, in the hypothetical question propounded to him, one of these probable causes was excluded from the consideration of the witness, and he was required to give his opinion upon an imperfect and insufficient hypothesis,—one which excluded from his consideration a material fact essential to an intelligent opinion. A consideration by the witness of the wound received by the plaintiff in January being thus prevented, the witness had but one fact upon which to base his opinion, to wit, the fact that defendant kicked plaintiff on the shin-bone. Based, as it necessarily was, on that fact alone, the opinion of Dr. Philler that the kick caused the injury was inevitable, when, had the proper hypothesis been submitted to him, his opinion might have been different. The answer of Dr. Philler to the hypothetical question put to him may have had, probably did have, a controlling influence with the jury, for they found by their verdict that his opinion was correct.

Surely there can be no rule of evidence which will tolerate a hypothetical question to an expert, calling for his opinion in a matter vital to the case, which excludes from his consideration facts already proved by a witness upon whose testimony such hypothetical question is based, when a consideration of such facts by the expert is absolutely essential to enable him to form an intelligent opinion concerning such matter. The objection to the question put to Dr. Philler should have been sustained. The error in permitting the witness to answer the question is material, and necessarily fatal to the judgment.

3. Certain questions were proposed on behalf of defendant to be submitted to the jury, founded upon the theory that only such damages could be recovered as the defendant might reasonably be supposed to have contemplated as likely to result from his kicking the plaintiff. The court refused to submit such questions to the jury. The ruling was correct. The rule of damages in actions for torts was held in Brown v. Chicago, M. & St. P. R. Co., 54 Wis. 342, 11 N.W. 356, 911, 41 Am.Rep. 41, to be that the wrong-doer is liable for all injuries resulting directly from the wrongful act, whether they could or could not have been foreseen by him.

That case rules this on the question of damages. * * *

BY THE COURT.—The judgment of the circuit court is reversed, and the cause will be remanded for a new trial.

[In Vosburg v. Putney, 86 Wis. 278 (1893) Andrew's father recovered $1200 for medical expenses and loss of services resulting to him from Andrew's injury.] [53]

53. See Briese v. Maechtle, 146 Wis. 89, 130 N.W. 893, 35 L.R.A., N.S., 574, Ann.Cas.1912C, 176 (1911). This case is on the borderline between the problems presented in this section and those belonging to Chapter 8. It is put in here to show one of the possibilities a lawyer should always explore when dealing with personal injury caused by conduct that is not manifestly dangerous. Cf. Gould v. Slater Woolen Mills, supra, p. 159, and note.

The rule that defendant takes his victim as he finds him, the "thin-skull" doctrine, is general in personal injury cases, whether based on intentional wrongdoing or on negligence, e. g., Lebon v. B. L. & M. Bottling Co., Inc., — R.I. —, 339 A.2d 272 (1975).

COPE v. DAVISON

Supreme Court of California, in Bank, 1947.
30 Cal.2d 193, 180 P.2d 873, 171 A.L.R. 667.

[Action by an automobile guest against his host, driver of the automobile, for injuries sustained when the car skidded while going around a curve in wet weather. The testimony as to the speed of the car was in conflict. Defendant was familiar with the road and knew the danger of the curve. Defendant had a verdict and judgment. Plaintiff, on this appeal, claims error in instructions to the jury and in the admission, over objections, of testimony by defendant that he did not intend to injure anyone, including his wife, who was in the car. A third point raised on the appeal is immaterial for present purposes. In actions like the present the California Vehicle Code, § 403, restricted recovery to cases where the guest was injured by defendant's "willful misconduct."]

EDMONDS, JUSTICE. * * * The jury was instructed as follows: " 'Wilful misconduct' is defined as intentionally doing something in the operation of a motor vehicle which should not be done or intentionally failing to do something which should be done under circumstances disclosing knowledge on the part of the driver that injury to his passenger will be a probable result of his conduct or under circumstances disclosing a wanton and reckless disregard of the possible injurious results of his conduct.

"The terms 'wilful misconduct' have a meaning in the law, additional to that which they have in common usage. If we were to use the words in their ordinary sense, they would mean simply the indulging in wrongful conduct by conscious choice. Such conduct might consist of doing something which ought not to be done, or in failing to do something that ought to be done. But in order to be a basis for liability to a guest under our law the misconduct must be something more than intentional and wrongful; it must be done under circumstances which show either knowledge that serious injury to the guest probably will result, or a wanton and reckless disregard of the possible results."

"Wilful misconduct means intentional wrongful conduct, done either with knowledge that serious injury to the guest probably will result, [or] with a wanton and reckless disregard of the possible results.

"Although wilful misconduct is a form of negligence, it is something more than negligence; more even than what might be called gross negligence. A guest may not recover against his host driver for negligence; however, it might be classified, unless that negligence amounted to wilful misconduct, then that means intentional, wrongful conduct, done either with knowledge that serious injury to the guest probably will result, or with a wanton and reckless disregard of the possible results.

"When there is a question whether a vehicle driver conducted himself with knowledge that serious injury to a guest probably would result from the conduct, proof of such knowledge does not have to be by direct evidence. The jury has a right to infer that the driver had such knowledge, if such an inference may reasonably be drawn from facts in evidence, and if the judgment of the jury so directs."

These instructions, it is said, built up in the minds of the jurors the requirement of actual knowledge and a specific intent to order to constitute wilful misconduct. The deficiency in the definition of the standard of care required of Davison was not cured by the statement that the jurors might infer knowledge on the part of the driver as it presented merely a rule of evidence for their guidance. The second instruction was confusing, and the third one erroneous, says the appellant, because it leaves out the important word "or" and thus fails to distinguish between the two types of wilful misconduct. The appellant contends that his proposed instructions, refused by the trial court, would have cured these errors.

Wilful misconduct has been defined in various ways. In People v. Young, 20 Cal.2d 832, 836, 129 P.2d 353, 356 (quoting from Howard v. Howard, 132 Cal.App. 124, 129, 22 P.2d 279), it was said: " 'Willful misconduct implies at least the intentional doing of something either with a knowledge that serious injury is a *probable* (as distinguished from a possible) result, or the intentional doing of an act with a wanton and reckless disregard of its *possible* result.' " By two earlier decisions, Porter v. Hofman, 12 Cal.2d 445, 448, 85 P.2d 447, and Parsons v. Fuller, 8 Cal.2d 463, 468, 66 P.2d 430, 432, this court adopted the language of Helme v. Great Western Milling Co., 43 Cal.App. 416, 421, 185 P. 510, saying: "The term 'serious and willful misconduct' is described by the Supreme Judicial Court of Massachusetts as being something 'much more than mere negligence, or even gross or culpable negligence,' and as involving 'conduct of a quasi criminal nature, the intentional doing of something either with the knowledge that it is likely to result in serious injury or with a wanton and reckless disregard of its possible consequences.' * * * To constitute 'willful misconduct' there must be actual knowledge, or that which in the law is esteemed to be the equivalent of actual knowledge, of the peril to be apprehended from the failure to act, coupled with a conscious failure to act to the end of averting injury." [8 Cal.2d 463, 66 P.2d 432.] In the Porter case, supra [12 Cal.2d 445, 85 P.2d 448], the court stated: "To this must be added the element included in the definition approved in Meek v. Fowler, 3 Cal.2d 420, 425, 45 P.2d 194, and cases following it, of actual knowledge or its equivalent that an injury to a guest will be a probable result." The Meek case followed Turner v. Standard Oil, 134 Cal.App. 622, 626, 25 P.2d 988, and defined wilful misconduct " * * * as intentionally doing something in the operation of a motor vehicle which should not be done or intentionally failing to do something which should be done under circumstances disclosing knowledge, express or to be implied, that an injury to a guest will be a probable result." [3 Cal.2d 420, 45 P.2d 197.] * * *

Measured by these definitions, the instructions in the present case were not erroneous. The most recent opinion of this court (People v. Young, supra) defining wilful misconduct entirely omits the words "express or implied" when referring to knowledge of the defendant. Furthermore, the last quoted instruction, which was offered by Cope, bridged the gap left by the omission of these words. As stated in this instruction, the jury might infer knowledge by the driver that serious injury to a guest probably would result from his conduct, if such an inference could reasonably be drawn from the facts in evidence. The courts have treated "inferred" as synonymous with "implied" (see Davis v. Hearst, 160 Cal. 143, 162, 116 P. 530; State v. Millain, 3 Nev. 409), and it is presumed that the jury considered the instructions as a whole. Douglas v. Southern Pacific Co., 203 Cal. 390, 396, 264 P. 237; Stroud v. Hansen, 48 Cal.App.2d 556, 562, 120 P.2d 102.

In the Van Fleet case, supra, [51 Cal.App.2d 719, 125 P.2d 586] it was said that, for the purposes of determining whether the circumstances in a given situation are sufficient to disclose implied knowledge of the probability of injury from an act or omission, an external standard is applied. Such a probability, it was concluded, using the language of Stacey v. Hayes, 31 Cal.App.2d 422, 426, 88 P.2d 165, " 'must have been an apparent consequence to a man of ordinary prudence and intelligence.' " Considering the present record, the last-quoted instruction advised the jury, in substance, that they could draw their own inferences, and could charge the driver with knowledge "if the judgment of the jury so directs." This instruction presented for determination as an issue of fact the question as to whether Davison had implied knowledge of the probable consequences of his conduct. It allowed the jurors to draw from the evidence the inference that a man of ordinary prudence and intelligence would have realized the probable consequences of his conduct even though Davison himself did not do so.

Read as a whole, the instructions to the jury correctly and sufficiently disclosed the intention necessary to prove wilful misconduct, and they were neither misleading, nor confusing. The failure to include the word "or" between the two types of wilful misconduct in one of the instructions was probably a typographical error. In any event, it was cured by the other instructions which clearly distinguished between the kinds of conduct which fall within the statutory ban.

The objections to the questions asked of Davison concerning his intention to cause injury were made upon the grounds that they were immaterial, constituted an invasion of the province of the jury, and were leading and suggestive. Cope insists that "an intent to have an accident or an intent to injure" any one is not an element of wilful misconduct, and, therefore, the questions were immaterial. The prejudicial effect of this testimony was increased, the appellant argues, by the definition of wilful misconduct given to the jury.

The state of mind of a person, like the state or condition of the body, is a fact to be proved like any other fact when it is relevant to an issue in the case, and the person himself may testify directly thereto. See 20 Am.Jur. 312. Whenever the motive or intent with which an act was done is relevant, direct testimony is admissible, although not conclusive. * * * Also, when knowledge of a fact has important bearing upon the issues, evidence is admissible which relates to the question of the existence or nonexistence of such knowledge and a wide range of proof is allowed. * * *

It was said in Porter v. Hofman, supra, 12 Cal.2d page 447, 85 P.2d 448, and Parsons v. Fuller, supra, 8 Cal.2d page 468, 66 P.2d 432 (quoting from Norton v. Puter, 138 Cal.App. 253, 32 P.2d 172) that wilful misconduct "necessarily involves deliberate, intentional or *wanton* conduct in doing or omitting to perform acts, with knowledge or appreciation of the fact, on the part of the culpable person, *that danger is likely to result therefrom.* * * *" And in Meek v. Fowler, supra, 3 Cal.2d page 425, 45 P.2d page 197, the following language appears: " 'While the line between gross negligence and willful misconduct may not always be easy to draw, a distinction appears from the definition given in that gross negligence is merely such a lack of care as may be presumed to indicate a passive and indifferent attitude toward results, while willful misconduct involves a more positive intent actually to harm another or to do an act with a positive, active, and absolute disregard of its consequences. It seems clear that in excluding all forms of negligence as a basis for recovery in a guest case, the Legislature must have intended that to permit a recovery in such a case the thing done by a defendant must amount to misconduct as distinguished from negligence, and that this misconduct must be willful. While the word "willful" implies an intent, the intention referred to relates to the misconduct and not merely to the fact that some act was intentionally done. In ordinary negligence, and presumably more so in gross negligence, the element of intent to do the act is present and any negligence might be termed misconduct. But willful misconduct as used in this statute means neither the sort of misconduct involved in any negligence nor the mere intent to do the act which constitutes negligence. * * *' " * * *

Applying these principles to the present case, the evidence objected to was admissible. Although "an intent to injure anyone is not a necessary ingredient of wilful misconduct", "wilful misconduct involves a more positive intent actually to harm another" than gross negligence and could be established by proving such an intent. The questions were relevant to the issue of intent and knowledge, and were admissible to prove Davison's state of mind contemporaneously with the accident.

The judgment is affirmed.

SHENK and SPENCE, JJ., concur.

SCHAUER, J., concurs in the judgment.

CARTER, JUSTICE. I dissent.

The evidence would support the conclusion that defendant on a wet road, with the knowledge that it might be slippery and cause his car to skid, intentionally and deliberately drove his car toward the curve at 45 miles per hour, knowing that the curve was there and knowing that even on a dry pavement it was a dangerous curve unless approached very slowly.

Under the definition of wilful misconduct which has become standardized in this state this evidence was ample to support a finding of wilful misconduct.

Appellant proposed an instruction that:

"If you believe under the evidence in this case that the defendant Warren W. Davison intentionally did something or omitted to do something, in the operation of his automobile on the night in question, with knowledge express or implied, that injury to plaintiff was a probable consequence of his intentional act or failure to act, then I instruct you that defendant was guilty of wilful misconduct.

"I instruct you that in determining whether the said intentional act or omissions of said defendant, if such you find them to be, are sufficient to disclose implied knowledge of such probability of injury to plaintiff guest, an external standard is applied, and applying the 'external standard' the defendant Warren W. Davison is charged with knowledge of the probable consequences of his conduct, such consequence being apparent to any person of ordinary prudence of which you ladies and gentlemen of the jury are the exclusive judge." * * *

To instruct the jury that defendant must have actual knowledge is an instruction on a substantive fact which they are told must be proved to establish plaintiff's right to recover. To further instruct them that this actual knowledge may be proved by circumstantial evidence does not change the fact that under the instructions they must still find actual knowledge, and is not in any sense the same thing as telling them that they need not find that the defendant had actual knowledge if they do find that a person of ordinary prudence would have had such knowledge. * * *

This instruction contained no recognition of the fact that an intentional wrongful act coupled with implied knowledge of probable injury also constitutes wilful misconduct. It lays down an absolute requirement of actual knowledge in order to constitute wilful misconduct. It virtually requires an actual intent to injure. Under the "implied knowledge" part of the definition of wilful misconduct, as stated in Turner v. Standard Oil Company, Wright v. Sellers, supra, and distinctly pointed out in Van Fleet v. Heyler, and Hastings v. Serleto, supra, it is clear that a defendant may be held liable if he commits a wrongful act under circumstances indicating that he should have known that his conduct would probably result in the injuries to his guests. The above-quoted instruction entirely omits this possibility. Nor is the distinction pointed out in any of the other of the court's instructions.

This instruction is based upon the erroneous assumption that if a defendant believes he can drive his car with safety, such belief will exonerate him regardless of the highly dangerous quality of his acts and whether or not a reasonable person in his position should have known of the probability of resulting injury.

It is safe to say that the automobile driver involved in every "wilful misconduct" case to be found in the books believed that he could drive his car in the particular manner charged without injurying anyone. The reckless driver never intends, although he sometimes is apprehensive of, the disastrous results which occur. The defendant certainly should not be exonerated from the consequences of his misconduct as he was by this instruction because he might have thought that he could drive as he did with safety and did not as he stated intend the resulting injuries. If it were necessary to prove that a defendant driver believed that he could not drive as he did with safety and that he actually intended the accident, or was totally indifferent to possible results, or that he had actual knowledge that injury to his guest was probable, a plaintiff would have to prove in substance that the defendant driver was guilty of intent to commit murder or mayhem depending upon how lucky the guest was, and perhaps suicide as well, before a case of wilful misconduct could be made out. Under the cases already cited, this is not the law. * * *

There is not a single reported decision in which an actual intent to injure has been found to exist. The requirement of an actual intent to injure and actual knowledge of probability of injury was laid down as law in Walker v. Bacon, 132 Cal.App. 625, 23 P.2d 520, which was specifically overruled in Van Fleet v. Heyler, supra, which held that an intent to injure is not a necessary element of wilful misconduct.

Indeed it is the absence of an intent to injure which distinguishes wilful misconduct from one of several serious crimes. This distinction is very clearly brought out in the Restatement of the Law of Torts, as follows: "Reckless misconduct differs from intentional wrongdoing in a very important particular. While an act to be reckless must be intended by the actor, the actor does not intend to cause the harm which results from it. It is enough that he realizes or from facts which he knows should realize that there is a strong probability that harm may result, even though he hopes or even expects that his conduct will prove harmless. However, a strong probability is a different thing from the substantial certainty without which he cannot be said to intend the harm in which his acts results." Sec. 500f, p. 1296.

The Restatement of the Law of Torts, page 1293, sec. 500, specifically points out that an objective standard is to be applied in determining the question of implied knowledge of danger, as follows: "The actor's conduct is in reckless disregard of the safety of another if he intentionally does an act or fails to do an act which it is his duty to the other to do, knowing or having reason to know of facts which would lead a reasonable man to realize that the actor's conduct not only creates an unreasonable risk of bodily harm to the other but also involves a high degree of probability that substantial harm will result to him."

While the instruction points out the two different types of conducts constituting "wilful misconduct", they are so bound together in the instruction that it is difficult for the lawyer, let alone a layman juror to disintegrate and distinguish the two types through the maze of legal verbiage. Nowhere in the instructions given were they separately stated. Plaintiff, however, presented a detailed instruction setting forth in plain and concise language the two different types of conduct constituting wilful misconduct under the law. This was refused by the court. * * *

In addition to the rules involved in the above material, the notions of intentional or wanton misconduct may be useful to plaintiffs in personal injury litigation in the following ways:

(1) Damages may be enhanced, in either or both of two ways:

(a) the jury may be expressly told to award exemplary damages (in addition to those compensatory damages usually allowed in negligence cases). See McCormick, Damages (1935) ch. 10; 2 Sutherland, Law of Damages, ch. IX (4th ed. 1916); Restatement, Torts, section 908 (1939).

(b) the jury may be angered against a defendant and exercise unfavorably to him their discretion in awarding compensatory damages (and exemplary too if they are allowed). It must be remembered that in any personal injury case many items of damage (e. g. pain, suffering, etc.) are incapable of exact measurement and rest pretty much in the jury's discretion. The court, of course, sets limits to this power but there is some evidence that courts themselves are more lenient to plaintiff in setting these limits where defendant's misconduct has been wanton, or worse. Bauer, Fault as Affecting Damages 82 U. of Pa.L.Rev. 583 (1934).

(2) The effect of contributory negligence may be avoided. See p. 385 et seq., infra.

(3) More liberal rules of extent of duty and proximate cause may be applied. See, for example, Campbell, Duty, Fault, and Legal Cause [1938] Wis.L.Rev. 402, 409; Bauer, Degree of Moral Fault as Affecting Liability, 81 U. of Pa.L.Rev. 586 (1933). Cf. Scott v. Shepherd, p. 27, supra, in which the requirement of directness in the old action of trespass was similarly relaxed where defendant's wrong was grievous.

(4) Recovery may be had for an unseen trespasser or licensee who could not avail himself of ordinary negligence. See, for example, Bremer v. Lake Erie & W. R. Co., 318 Ill. 11, 148 N.E. 862, 41 A.L.R. 1345 (1925), and section 4, infra.

(5) Where plaintiff has given, in advance of the accident, a release of liability, this will not avail the defendant who has been wanton, or worse (though some courts uphold such a release as to acts of ordinary negligence). See, for example, note 38 Mich.L.Rev. 1310 (1940).

(6) Liability may be predicated on conduct not causing bodily impact but amounting to "assault." See chapter 8, infra.

(7) Procedural remedies such as body execution may be available for wanton or wilful misconduct, and not for negligence. See, e. g., Fanstiel v. Wright, 122 Colo. 451, 222 P.2d 1001 (1950).

(8) Immunity from suit such as that of a parent from suit by a minor child may more readily be avoided where the parent's misconduct transcends negligence. See e. g., Cowgill v. Boock, 189 Or. 282, 218 P.2d 445 (1950).

(9) Judgment claims may be not dischargeable in bankruptcy under Section 17, subdivision 2 of the Bankruptcy Act, 11 U.S.C.A. § 35, sub. 2. See, e. g., Greenfield v. Tuccillo, 129 F.2d 854 (2d Cir. 1942).

SECTION 2. PROOF OF THE BREACH

WINTEROWD v. CHRISTENSEN

Supreme Court of Utah, 1926.
68 Utah 546, 251 P. 360.

[Appeal by plaintiff from an order of nonsuit made at the close of plaintiff's evidence.]

CHERRY, J. * * *

The defendant as lessee conducted and operated a summer resort in Davis county, called the Lagoon Resort, devoted to pleasure and amusements, to which the public was invited and for admission to which a fee was charged. In connection with the resort the defendant maintained and conducted a baseball grounds, including an elevated grand stand with seats for the use of persons attending the ball games played there. The ball grounds adjoined the resort proper, and was inclosed with a fence. Gates permitted entrance to the ball park from the resort. On July 20, 1922, there was a meeting of the members of the Railway Mail Associations of Salt Lake City and Ogden, at the Lagoon Resort, and as a part of the entertainment a baseball game was played on the ball grounds above described. There was proof that permission to use the ball grounds for the purpose had been granted by the defendant.

The plaintiff attended the meeting with her husband, and paid for admission to the resort. In the afternoon a baseball game, between rival teams of the Railway Mail Associations of Salt Lake City and

Ogden, was being played. The gate between the resort proper and the ball grounds was open, and persons in considerable numbers were passing into the ball grounds and taking seats in the grand stand to witness the game. The plaintiff's husband was one of the baseball players. The plaintiff entered the grounds through the gate, and, while walking in the grand stand to obtain a seat, upon a floor or platform elevated two or three feet from the ground, a board in the floor broke and gave way under her, causing her to fall and her foot and leg to drop through the floor, in which manner she sustained the injuries complained of.

It was shown that the defendant had had control and possession of the premises for several years, during which time baseball games were frequently played at the ball grounds in connection with outings and excursions to the resort. The board in the floor which broke under the plaintiff's weight was described as a "2 × 10 plank," which was "decomposed and dark, soggy, pithy." "It broke without any splinters at all." It was further described as "rotten" and breaking easily. That it appeared like it might have been rotten and defective when first put in the floor. The board was wet from rain at the time of the accident. A witness said "when dry it would be rather porous" and observable to a man making an ordinary inspection of it.

The motion for nonsuit was based upon two grounds: (1) * * and (2) that there was no proof of negligence.

The trial court * * * sustained the motion [for nonsuit] on the second ground.

Whether or not the plaintiff by her evidence, and the fair and legitimate inferences therefrom, established a neglect of duty and failure to exercise the care required * * * is the test by which the case must be determined.

That the platform or floor was in an unsafe and dangerous condition was clearly made evident by the fact that the board which gave way was decomposed, and that it broke under the weight of one person. The particular fact of controlling importance is whether from the circumstances it can be fairly inferred that a reasonable inspection by defendant would have discovered the defect. As before seen, there was evidence that the board was decomposed and dark—porous when dry—and that the defective condition would be observable to a person making an ordinary inspection of it. The defect was not of recent origin. There was evidence tending to show it was old. This evidence, standing uncontradicted, and reviewed in the light most favorable to the plaintiff, is we think, sufficient, if believed and acted upon by the jury to warrant the conclusion that there was a neglect of duty on the part of the defendant in not discovering and repairing the defect, and that therefore the question of the defendant's negligence should have been submitted to the jury.

It follows that the court erred in granting the nonsuit, for which reason the judgment is reversed and a new trial granted; costs to appellant.

WELSH v. CORNELL

Court of Appeals of New York, 1901.
168 N.Y.Rep. 508, 61 N.E. 891.

PER CURIAM. This was an action to recover for personal injuries sustained by the plaintiff and alleged to have been caused by the negligence of the defendant. The plaintiff, his servant, was injured while in the defendant's employ by the breaking and falling of a portion of a clamp to which was attached the guy rope of a derrick owned by the defendant and in use upon his premises when the accident occurred. The plaintiff was at work under this guy rope and immediately in front of a post to which it was attached by the clamp which gave way. As negligence is not to be presumed, but must be proved to entitle the plaintiff to recover, it was necessary for him to show that the accident was the result of the defendant's negligence. It was the duty of the defendant to exercise reasonable and ordinary care to provide for the safety of his servants and to furnish appliances that were reasonably safe and suitable for the purpose for which they were employed. Unless there is proof in this case showing the absence of ordinary care upon the part of the master in furnishing or maintaining the appliance which was broken, the plaintiff cannot recover. Practically the only facts established by any tangible or substantial proof were the plaintiff's injury and that it was caused by the falling of a piece of the broken clamp. What occasioned the break was not shown, although there was some speculation or conjecture as to the cause. There was no proper proof, direct or inferential, that the clamp was made of defective iron, or that it was defectively made, or that it was not properly maintained, except such as might be inferred from the fact that it gave way. The only proof which even tended to show any defect in the clamp was that one witness testified that he glanced at the broken piece, that it looked like freshly broken iron, and that on the corner there was a little bit of rust, but he finally refused to swear it was rust and testified that it might have been paint instead. The main portion of the plaintiff's evidence was that of experts, by whom he at most proved that the clamp would not have broken unless in some way defective and that the defect which occasioned the break might have arisen from one of several causes, no one of which was proved to have existed. Nor was it proved that the defendant knew or with reasonable diligence might have ascertained the supposed defect. Upon that state of the evidence the court dismissed the plaintiff's complaint upon the ground that he had failed to show any negligence on the part of the defendant. The judgment entered upon such dismissal was reversed by the Appellate Division by a divided court. We think the trial judge was right and that the reversal by the Appellate Division was not justified. A persual of the evidence shows that the only proof relied upon by the plaintiff to establish the defendant's negligence was the mere speculations or conjecture of experts, with no sufficient proof upon which to base them. It is well established by the decisions of this court that parties may not enter the "realm of conjecture" and ask that a jury, in the absence of proof, may be allowed to guess that there was negligence on the part of a defendant. To entitle the plaintiff to recover in this case it was necessary for him to establish by a fair preponderance of competent evidence that the accident which caused his injury was occasioned by the omission of the defendant to discharge some duty which rested upon him. This we think he failed to do, and that the disposition of the case by the trial court was proper and should have been sustained.

We have patiently wandered through the maze of objections and exceptions contained in the record, but have found none which justified the learned Appellate Division in reversing the action of the trial court.

The order of the Appellate Division should be reversed and the judgment entered upon the decision of the Trial Term affirmed, with costs in all the courts.[54]

RISTAU v. E. FRANK COE COMPANY

Supreme Court of New York, Appellate Division, Second Department, 1907.
120 App.Div. 478, 104 N.Y.S. 1059.

APPEAL by the plaintiff, Edward Ristau, from a judgment of the Supreme Court in favor of the defendant, entered in the office of the clerk of the county of Kings on the 30th day of March, 1904, upon the dismissal of the complaint by direction of the court after a trial at the Kings County Trial Term.

The action was by servant against master for damages for negligence. The plaintiff was engaged in pushing by hand loaded trucks or

54. See also Brymer v. Southern Pac. Co., 90 Cal. 496, 27 P. 371 (1891) (unexplained breaking of chain); Removich v. Bambrick Bros. Const. Co., 264 Mo. 43, 173 S.W. 686, L.R.A.1917E, 233 (1915) (cable broke letting bucket of dirt fall on plaintiff); Grant v. Pennsylvania & N. Y. Canal & R. Co., 133 N.Y. 657, 31 N.E. 220 (1892) (breaking of drawbar); cases collected in note, L.R.A.1917E, 239. The distinction between proof of a defect's existence and proof that the defendant was careless in failing to discover it is neatly illustrated by Levine v. Union & N. H. Trust Co., 127 Conn. 435, 17 A.2d 500 (1941); Miller v. Hickey, 368 Pa. 317, 81 A.2d 910 (1951).

In South Baltimore Car Works v. Scheafer, 96 Md. 88, 105, 53 A. 665, 667 (1902), the court said: "It has been held in a number of cases that the sudden breaking of machinery is not sufficient, of itself, to warrant the court in sending the case to a jury. Thus the mere fact of the breaking of a chain, Brymer v. Southern Pacific Co., 90 Cal. 496, 27 P. 371 (1891); the unexplained bursting of an emery wheel, Simpson v. Pittsburgh Locomotive Works, 139 Pa. 245, 21 A. 386 (1891); the parting of a brake chain on a car, Sack v. Dolese, 137 Ill. 129, 27 N.E. 62 (1891); the bursting of a fly-wheel, Piehl v. Albany Ry., 30 App.Div. 166, 51 N.Y.S. 755 (3d Dep't 1898); the breaking of a car wheel from some cause unknown, Morrison v. Phillips-Colby Construction Co., 44 Wis. 410 (1878); the breaking of a derrick, Duffy v. Upton, 113 Mass. 544 (1873), were held not sufficient to justify an inference or presumption of negligence." Compare 37 Va.L.Rev. 179, 198 note 59 (1951).

Consider in light of the following two cases the distinction which can be drawn with respect to a "soap and grab" bathroom fixture which breaks loose from motel wall, as in Apper v. Eastgate Associates, 28 Md.App. 581, 347 A.2d 389 (1975).

cars along a track or tram on a trestle about 18 feet high. The product of the defendant's factory was thus taken from the factory to a storage place. The trestle collapsed and fell to the ground, and the plaintiff was thereby greatly injured. A nonsuit was granted on the plaintiff's case.

GAYNOR, J.: The plaintiff proved the collapse of the trestle and rested, relying on the maxim the thing speaks for itself. No particular defect to cause the collapse of the trestle was apparent, and the plaintiff did not try to prove any. There was nothing but the bare fact that the trestle collapsed while in the ordinary use for which it was constructed, and that it had been built only three years. The nonsuit was error. The maxim applied to the case. The learned counsel for respondent argues, following the broad language of some opinions, that the maxim is made applicable in a given case, if at all, only by facts and circumstances indicating negligence in the defendant proved in connection with the happening of the accident itself, and that as this case is bare of such facts and circumstances, there is not sufficient evidence for the application of the maxim. The fault of this is that if there were other facts showing negligence, the maxim would not be needed as evidence to carry the case to the jury at all; it is only where there is nothing but the bare happening of the accident that the plaintiff needs and the law gives him the help of the maxim to escape a nonsuit.

This case is not distinguishable from the fall of scaffolds, floors, or other places to work (Stewart v. Ferguson, 164 N.Y. 553, 58 N.E. 662; Lentino v. Port Henry Iron Ore Co., 71 App.Div. 466, 75 N.Y.S. 755; Muhlens v. Obermeyer & Liebmann, 83 App.Div. 88, 82 N.Y.S. 527). There are cases in which it is apparent that the accident may have happened by some omission or commission by some one other than the defendant. In such a case the mere happening of the accident does not prove the cause of it, but leaves it open to conjecture. In such cases the maxim cannot apply. It applies only where the accident apparently could not have happened unless through some negligence of the defendant (Fallon v. Mertz, 110 App.Div. 755, 97 N.Y.S. 417).

The judgment should be reversed.

It is pretty widely held that the doctrine does not apply to an unexplained fire. W. Prosser, Handbook of the Law of Torts 216 (4th ed. 1971). In Ruerat v. Stevens, 113 Conn. 333, 155 A. 219 (1931), Mrs. Ruerat showed that Stevens had called upon her and had been the only one to sit upon a davenport in the course of the evening, during which he had smoked many cigarettes. After defendant left a fire broke out in the davenport and destroyed some of the plaintiff's furniture. She had a judgment for the damage and defendant appealed, claiming there had been no proof of his negligence and asserting the unavailability of the *res ipsa loquitur* doctrine. In affirming the judgment, the court said, "The doctrine is ordinarily relied upon in cases of accidents resulting from defective machines, vehicles, or apparatus, where the evidence as to the true cause of the accident is accessible to the defendant but not to the plaintiff. It does not change the burden of proof, but its application satisfies the plaintiff's duty of producing evidence sufficient to go to the jury. The distinctive function of the rule is to permit an inference of negligence from proof of the injury and the physical agency inflicting it, without proof of facts pointing to the responsible human cause. If the proof includes facts tending to show negligence, the doctrine becomes simply a specific application of the general principle that negligence can be proved by circumstantial evidence. Here the injury was the destruction of the furnishings in the plaintiff's living room, and the physical agency which caused the destruction was the fire. But the plaintiff's evidence goes beyond the mere proof that her property was destroyed by fire. It includes evidence of the conduct of the defendant in placing the ash tray upon the inflammable arm of the davenport, and depositing his cigarette butts in it, and the evidence that when the plaintiff's daughter came into the room after defendant had left there were several butts in the tray, but not all that he had put down while he sat there. The defendant testified that he snuffed out all the cigarettes that he smoked on that occasion. The situation then was not one calling for the application of the *res ipsa loquitur* rule as a distinctive doctrine but for the determination of whether the circumstantial evidence was sufficient to justify an inference that the fire was caused by the defendant's negligence."

In a series of notes the position is put forth that "* * * in the situation to which res ipsa loquitur as a distinctive rule applies, there is no evidence, circumstantial or otherwise, at least none of sufficient probative value, to show negligence, apart from the postulate—which rests on common experience and not on the specific circumstances of the instant case—that physical causes of the kind which produced the accident in question do not ordinarily exist in the absence of negligence. * * *" 6 L.R.A.,N.S., 337; L.R.A.1917E, 4; 59 A.L.R. 468; 78 A.L.R. 731. Professor Prosser calls these attempts to distinguish the doctrine from the ordinary rules of circumstantial evidence "ill starred" and a source of confusion. 20 Minn.L.Rev. 241, 258 (1936). Certainly the statement of the inference of negligence is cast in a form just as logical when the doctrine is said to be invoked as when it is not. Certainly, also, there are some cases where the syllogism rests on a postulate like that described in the A.L.R. notes; and others where the syllogism falls for want of just such a postulate. Perhaps light may be shed on the dispute by asking when and on what basis the postulate has been adopted. Cf. introduction to section on proximate cause, infra. In Graham v. Badger, 164 Mass. 42, 41 N.E. 61 (1895), a rope broke where it had been spliced. A plaintiff's verdict was upheld with the comment: "Neither can we assume that the defect, if there was one, was hidden. If the jury were of opinion that defects in ropes, great enough to make them break under a strain slight in proportion to the normal power of rope generally, can be discovered by proper inspection, we know nothing to the contrary. It might be otherwise in the case of an iron chain." In another case an employee was killed when he was being transported from wharf to vessel in a travelling chute which fell when there was an unexplained break in the tackle. The court derived the postulate thus: "The appliances for loading vessels were such as were in ordinary use and, presumably, had been adopted by defendants as proper and suitable for the purpose designed. It is inconceivable that defendants would have adopted these means had they supposed that in the ordinary course of their operation, with proper care, such accidents as the one here were likely to occur." Koskela v. Albion Lumber Co., 25 Cal.App. 12, 142 P. 851 (1914). In Kleinman v. Banner Laundry Co., 150 Minn. 515, 186 N.W. 123, 23 A.L.R. 479 (1921), the court said: "Boilers sometimes explode. Comparing the number of explosions with the extent of the use of boilers, explosions are not frequent. If they are kept in proper condition and repair, and if they are operated properly, explosions are unusual. Whether the res ipsa loquitur doctrine, which permits an inference of negligence from the fact of an explosion, should apply, is largely a question of how justice in such cases is most practically and fairly administered. There is nothing legally illogical in permitting the inference to be drawn. Usually the party injured is without information upon which he may with certainty allege the exact cause, and is without direct proof. Perhaps the exact cause is incapable of ascertainment. The actual proof, if any, is with the party having the management of the instrumentality. These are practical considerations. We think the jury should have been permitted to draw an inference of negligence of the laundry company from the occurrence of the explosion. Though the holding may put us with the minority, we are content with it." For application to airplane accidents see Newing v. Cheatham, 15 Cal..3d 351, 124 Cal.Rptr. 193, 540 P.2d 33 (1975).

Try to formulate the major premise in the proof or attempted proof of negligence in the Winterowd case, in the Welsh and Ristau cases. Which, if any of them, is clearly demanded by common experience?

PFAFFENBACH v. WHITE PLAINS EXPRESS CORP.

Court of Appeals of New York, 1966.
17 N.Y.2d 132, 269 N.Y.S.2d 115, 216 N.E.2d 324.

BERGAN, JUDGE. Plaintiff was riding as a passenger in an automobile proceeding northerly on Route 117 near Mount Kisco. It was raining or snowing; there was slush on the road surface and it was slippery. A truck of defendant White Plains Express Corp., moving southerly on the road, came over into the northbound lane and struck the car in which plaintiff was riding. Plaintiff was injured.

Defendant at the trial gave no explanation for the accident, offered no proof on the issue of negligence, and the jury found a verdict for plaintiff. The Appellate Division by a divided court reversed the judgment on the law and dismissed the complaint.

The dismissal was for failure to make out a cause of action prima facie and was explicitly placed on the authority of two decisions * * [which] in the main stem back to Galbraith v. Busch, 267 N.Y. 230, 196 N.E. 36 and Lahr v. Tirrill, 274 N.Y. 112, 8 N.E.2d 298.

* * * Both *Galbraith* and *Lahr* were passenger actions against their own drivers.

* * * [D]ifferences of view within the Appellate Division, and its disagreement with the Trial Term on what is sufficient to show negligence prima facie, suggest the need for a restatement of the rule to be applied when a vehicle comes over onto the wrong side of the road and damage results.

In such a situation, showing this and nothing more, a case of negligence is made out prima facie sufficient to go to the jury to determine liability. The explanation of the defendant, if he gives one, will also usually be for the jury. The same rule, open to additional factual evaluation of his own responsibility for events, would apply to the passenger in a car which goes out of control.

The nice balance of knowledge and responsibility for some unknown "defect in the automobile" as a possible cause of an unexplained accident which the passenger guest, when he got in the car, was deemed to share equally with the owner and driver, and which it was held to be his burden to eliminate as part of his affirmative case has, in the 30 years since Galbraith v. Busch was handed down, been sapped of all practical application to the real world of motor vehicle operation (see 267 N.Y., p. 235, 196 N.E., p. 38).

Rigidity of legal rules which piece together conduct in the management and control of a moving vehicle in separate compartments under "negligent" and "non-negligent" labels has not only failed to succeed as an instrument of adjudication; it has succeeded in confusing the business of deciding motor vehicle accident cases consistently. Modern experience suggests we can be less certain of the precision of our categories in this field of adjudication than we had confidently assumed a generation or so ago.

Thus there should be more legal flexibility on what is negligence as applied to the control of moving vehicles and the question left open to factual judgments of the jury where the record shows a skid, or the explanation for a skid, or a car on the wrong side of the road, or the explanation of why it is there, or the need for the passenger in a car to act in relation to its operation.

It may, for one example, be quite as dangerous for a passenger to give unsolicited advice to the driver as to remain quiet. Either way the question is one of fact on the general obligation of the plaintiff to show himself free from negligence.

The order should be reversed, with costs, and, in view of the affirmance by the Appellate Division of the facts implicit in the verdict, the judgment for plaintiff reinstated.

BURKE, JUDGE (concurring). I would reverse solely on the ground that proof of "mere skidding" is prima facie evidence of negligence in this case where the plaintiff was *not* a passenger in defendant-respondent's car. There are obvious distinctions between a plaintiff who is a guest-passenger and one who is a stranger. The former not only assumes some risk in accepting the gratuitous transportation but also is in the advantageous position of having the opportunity to observe whether the defendant exercised reasonable care in the operation of the vehicle. * * * On the other hand, the stranger who is injured by defendant's vehicle's skidding into the opposite flowing lane of traffic or up onto a sidewalk, under conditions known to the defendant alone, is at a singular disadvantage. Therefore, the quantum of proof required to make a case in each situation ought to be measured according to the relationship of the parties. It is understandable why when a guest-passenger sues there ought to be additional proof to show that the defendant's negligent driving caused the skid and the consequent accident. The rule that a case is not made out without the additional evidence is reasonable because the accident may have occurred either through a defect in the car not known to the owner, the risk of which the passenger-guest assumes, or through the driver's negligent operation of the vehicle There the equal probability that the accident was caused by a defect in the car must be eliminated by other proof of negligence adduced by the plaintiff. However, in a suit by a person who is a stranger to the defendant and his vehicle, once the plaintiff adduced such evidence as is reasonably available to him (and it may be proof of defendant's skidding and nothing more), the burden of going forward with the proof ought to shift to the defendant. The defendant may then show that it was truly an unavoidable accident or elect to let the case go to the jury on the plaintiff's evidence. In such a case the plaintiff does not assume the same risk of unknown defects as would the owner of the vehicle or his guests. Such a rule is impartial. At all events, if the defendant refrains from giving any explanation, the plaintiff's evidence of the facts and circumstances leading up to the skid ought to be submitted to the jury to determine whether or not any inference of negligence may be drawn. This view does not cast as difficult a responsibility on the defendant as the ruling in the court below has imposed upon the plaintiff. On this theory, which I think is equitable, a nonsuit is here unjustifiable.

For these same reasons I believe that in the "skidding" cases we ought to draw a line between parties in disparate situations. The *Galbraith, Lahr, Gooch* rule that the assumption of risk by a passenger-guest for all defects in a car not known to the owner imposes on that plaintiff the obligation of introducing other evidence of the defendant's lack of due care in order to eliminate the inference of a defect in the car ought to be retained. If it is overruled the defendant owner will be unfairly penalized with a resulting unjustified windfall to the guest-passenger. But a limitation on that standard is justified in the situation of a stranger plaintiff in order to hold the scales even, and not place an undue burden on a party not in a position to know whether or not the defendant has acted in a negligent manner.

DESMOND, C. J., and FULD, VAN VOORHIS, SCILEPPI and KEATING, JJ., concur with BERGAN, J.

YBARRA v. SPANGARD

Supreme Court of California, 1944.
25 Cal.2d 486, 154 P.2d 687, 162 A.L.R. 1258.

GIBSON, CHIEF JUSTICE. This is an action for damages for personal injuries alleged to have been inflicted on plaintiff by defendants during the course of a surgical operation. The trial court entered judgments of nonsuit as to all defendants and plaintiff appealed.

On October 28, 1939, plaintiff consulted defendant Dr. Tilley, who diagnosed his ailment as appendicitis, and made arrangements for an appendectomy to be performed by defendant Dr. Spangard at a hospital owned and managed by defendant Dr. Swift. Plaintiff entered the hospital, was given a hypodermic injection, slept, and later was awakened by Drs. Tilley and Spangard and wheeled into the operating room by a nurse whom he believed to be defendant Gisler, an employee of Dr. Swift. Defendant Dr. Reser, the anesthetist, also an employee of Dr. Swift, adjusted plaintiff for the operation, pulling his body to the head of the operating table and, according to plaintiff's testimony, laying him back against two hard objects at the top of his shoulders, about an inch below his neck. Dr. Reser then administered the anesthetic and plaintiff lost consciousness. When he awoke early the following morning he was in his hospital room attended by defendant Thompson, the special nurse, and another nurse who was not made a defendant.

Plaintiff testified that prior to the operation he had never had any pain in, or injury to, his right arm or shoulder, but that when he awakened he felt a sharp pain about half way between the neck and the point of the right shoulder. He complained to the nurse, and then to Dr. Tilley, who gave him diathermy treatments while he remained in the hospital. The pain did not cease but spread down to the lower part of his arm, and after his release from the hospital the condition grew worse. He was unable to rotate or lift his arm, and developed paralysis and atrophy of the muscles around the shoulder. He received further treatments from Dr. Tilley until March, 1940, and then returned to work, wearing his arm in a splint on the advice of Dr. Spangard.

Plaintiff also consulted Dr. Wilfred Sterling Clark, who had X-ray pictures taken which showed an area of diminished sensation below the shoulder and atrophy and wasting away of the muscles around the shoulder. In the opinion of Dr. Clark, plaintiff's condition was due to trauma or injury by pressure or strain applied between his right shoulder and neck.

Plaintiff was also examined by Dr. Fernando Garduno, who expressed the opinion that plaintiff's injury was a paralysis of traumatic origin, not arising from pathological causes, and not systemic, and that the injury resulted in atrophy, loss of use and restriction of motion of the right arm and shoulder.

Plaintiff's theory is that the foregoing evidence presents a proper case for the application of the doctrine of res ipsa loquitur, and that the inference of negligence arising therefrom makes the granting of a nonsuit improper. Defendants take the position that, assuming that plaintiff's condition was in fact the result of an injury, there is no showing that the act of any particular defendant, nor any particular instrumentality, was the cause thereof. They attack plaintiff's action as an attempt to fix liability "en masse" on various defendants, some of whom were not responsible for the acts of others; and they further point to the failure to show which defendants had control of the instrumentalities that may have been involved. Their main defense may be briefly stated in two propositions: (1) that where there are several defendants, and there is a division of responsibility in the use of an instrumentality causing the injury, and the injury might have resulted from the separate act of either one of two or more persons, the rule of res ipsa loquitur cannot be invoked against any one of them; and (2) that where there are several instrumentalities, and no showing is made as to which caused the injury or as to the particular defendant in control of it, the doctrine cannot apply. We are satisfied, however, that these objections are not well taken in the circumstances of this case.

The doctrine of res ipsa loquitur has three conditions: "(1) the accident must be of a kind which ordinarily does not occur in the absence of someone's negligence; (2) it must be caused by an agency or instrumentality within the exclusive control of the defendant; (3) it must not have been due to any voluntary action or contribution on the part of the plaintiff." Prosser, Torts, p. 295. It is applied in a wide variety of situations, including cases of medical or dental treatment and hospital care. * * * [S]ee Shain, Res Ipsa Loquitur, 17 So. Cal.L.Rev. 187, 196.

There is, however, some uncertainty as to the extent to which res ipsa loquitur may be invoked in cases of injury from medical treatment. This is in part due to the tendency, in some decisions, to lay undue emphasis on the limitations of the doctrine, and to give too little attention to its basic underlying purpose. The result has been that a simple, understandable rule of circumstantial evidence, with a sound background of common sense and human experience, has occasionally been transformed into a rigid legal formula, which arbitrarily precludes its application in many cases where it is most important that it should be applied. If the doctrine is to continue to serve a useful purpose, we should not forget that "the particular force and justice of the rule, regarded as a presumption throwing upon the party charged the duty of producing evidence, consists in the circumstance that the chief evidence of the true cause, whether culpable or innocent, is practically accessible to him but inaccessible to the injured person." 9 Wigmore, Evidence, 3d Ed., § 2509, p. 382; see, also, Whetstine v. Moravec, 228 Iowa 352, 291 N.W. 425, 432; Ross v. Double Shoals Cotton Mills, 140 N.C. 115, 52 S.E. 121, 1 L.R.A.,N.S., 298; Maki v. Murray Hospital, 91 Mont. 251, 7 P.2d 228, 231. In the last-named case, where an unconscious patient in a hospital received injuries from a fall, the court declared that without the doctrine the maxim that for every wrong there is a remedy would be rendered nugatory, "by denying one, patently entitled to damages, satisfaction merely because he is ignorant of facts peculiarly within the knowledge of the party who should, in all justice, pay them."

The present case is of a type which comes within the reason and spirit of the doctrine more fully perhaps than any other. The passenger sitting awake in a railroad car at the time of a collision, the pedestrian walking along the street and struck by a falling object or the debris of an explosion, are surely not more entitled to an explanation than the unconscious patient on the operating table. Viewed from this aspect, it is diffficult to see how the doctrine can, with any justification, be so restricted in its statement as to become inapplicable to a patient who submits himself to the care and custody of doctors and nurses, is rendered unconscious, and receives some injury from instrumentalities used in his treatment. Without the aid of the doctrine a patient who received permanent injuries of a serious character, obviously the result of someone's negligence, would be entirely unable to recover unless the doctors and nurses in attendance voluntarily chose to disclose the identity of the negligent person and the facts establishing liability. See Maki v. Murray Hospital, 91 Mont. 251, 7 P.2d 228. If this were the state of the law of negligence, the courts, to avoid gross injustice, would be forced to invoke the principles of absolute liability, irrespective of negligence, in actions by persons suffering injuries during the course of treatment under anesthesia. But we think this juncture has not yet been reached, and that the doctrine of res ipsa loquitur is properly applicable to the case before us.

The condition that the injury must not have been due to the plaintiff's voluntary action is of course fully satisfied under the evidence produced herein; and the same is true of the condition that the accident must be one which ordinarily does not occur unless someone was negligent. We have here no problem of negligence in treatment, but of distinct injury to a healthy part of the body not the subject of treatment, nor within the area covered by the operation. The decisions in this state make it clear that such circumstances raise the inference of negligence and call upon the defendant to explain the unusual result. See Ales v. Ryan, 8 Cal.2d 82, 64 P.2d 409; Brown v. Shortlidge, 98 Cal.App. 352, 277 P. 134.

The argument of defendants is simply that plaintiff has not shown an injury caused by an instrumentality under a defendant's control, because he has not shown which of the several instrumentalities that he came in contact with while in the hospital caused the injury; and he has not shown that any one defendant or his servants had exclusive control over any particular instrumentality. Defendants assert that some of them were not the employees of other defendants, that some did not stand in any permanent relationship from which liability in tort would follow, and that in view of the nature of the injury, the number of defendants and the different functions performed by each, they could not all be liable for the wrong, if any.

We have no doubt that in a modern hospital a patient is quite likely to come under the care of a number of persons in different types of contractual and other relationships with each other. For example, in the present case it appears that Drs. Smith, Spangard and Tilley were physicians or surgeons commonly placed in the legal category of independent contractors; and Dr. Reser, the anesthetist, and defendant Thompson, the special nurse, were employees of Dr. Swift and not of the other doctors. But we do not believe that either the number or relationship of the defendants alone determines whether the doctrine of res ipsa loquitur applies. Every defendant in whose custody the plaintiff was placed for any period was bound to exercise ordinary care to see that no unnecessary harm came to him and each would be liable for failure in this regard. Any defendant who negligently injured him, and any defendant charged with his care who so neglected him as to allow injury to occur, would be liable. The defendant employers would be liable for the neglect of their employees; and the doctor in charge of the operation would be liable for the negligence of those who became his temporary servants for the purpose of assisting in the operation.

In this connection, it should be noted that while the assisting physicians and nurses may be employed by the hospital, or engaged by the patient, they normally become the temporary servants or agents of the surgeon in charge while the operation is in progress, and liability may be imposed upon him for their negligent acts under the doctrine of respondeat superior. Thus a surgeon has been held liable for the negligence of an assisting nurse who leaves a sponge or other object inside a patient, and the fact that the duty of seeing that such mistakes do not occur is delegated to others does not absolve the doctor from responsibility for their negligence. See Ales v. Ryan, 8 Cal.2d 82, 64 P.2d 409; Armstrong v. Wallace, 8 Cal.App.2d 429, 47 P.2d 740; Ault v. Hall, 119 Ohio St. 422, 164 N.E. 518, 60 A.L.R. 128; and see, also, Maki v. Murray Hospital, 91 Mont. 251, 7 P.2d 228, 233.

It may appear at the trial that, consistent with the principles outlined above, one or more defendants will be found liable and others absolved, but this should not preclude the application of the rule of res ipsa loquitur. The control at one time or another, of one or more of the various agencies or instrumentalities which might have harmed the plaintiff was in the hands of every defendant or of his employees or temporary servants. This, we think, places upon them the burden of initial explanation. Plaintiff was rendered unconscious for the purpose of undergoing surgical treatment by the defendants; it is manifestly unreasonable for them to insist that he identify any one of them as the person who did the alleged negligent act.

The other aspect of the case which defendants so strongly emphasize is that plaintiff has not identified the instrumentality any more than he has the particular guilty defendant. Here, again, there is a misconception which, if carried to the extreme for which defendants contend, would unreasonably limit the application of the res ipsa loquitur rule. It should be enough that the plaintiff can show an injury resulting from an external force applied while he lay unconscious in the hospital; this is as clear a case of identification of the instrumentality as the plaintiff may ever be able to make.

An examination of the recent cases, particularly in this state, discloses that the test of actual exclusive control of an instrumentality has not been strictly followed, but exceptions have been recognized where the purpose of the doctrine of res ipsa loquitur would otherwise be defeated. Thus, the test has become one of right of control rather than actual control. See Metz v. Southern Pac. Co., 51 Cal.App.2d 260, 268, 124 P.2d 670. In the bursting bottle cases where the bottler has delivered the instrumentality to a retailer and thus has given up actual control, he will nevertheless be subject to the doctrine where it is shown that no change in the condition of the bottle occurred after it left the bottler's possession, and it can accordingly be said that he was in constructive control. Escola v. Coca Cola Bottling Co., 24 Cal. 2d 453, 150 P.2d 436.[55] Moreover, this court departed from the single instrumentality theory in the colliding vehicle cases, where two defendants were involved, each in control of a separate vehicle. See Smith v. O'Donnell, 215 Cal. 714, 12 P.2d 933; Godfrey v. Brown, 220 Cal. 57, 29 P.2d 165, 93 A.L.R. 1092; Carpenter, 10 So.Cal.L.Rev. 170. Finally, it has been suggested that the hospital cases may properly be considered exceptional, and that the doctrine of res ipsa loquitur "should apply with equal force in cases wherein medical and nursing staffs take the place of machinery and may, through carelessness or lack of skill, inflict, or permit the infliction of injury upon a patient who is thereafter in no position to say how he received his injuries."

55. The question whether res ipsa loquitur may be applicable in bursting bottle cases (usually brought against the manufacturer or bottler) has vexed courts for some time. There is a split of authority. See, e. g., notes 31 Calif. L.Rev. 608 (1943); 42 Mich.L.Rev. 536 (1943); 17 So.Cal.L.Rev. 330 (1944); 16 Mo.L.Rev. 76 (1951); James, Accident Liability: Some Wartime Developments, 55 Yale L.J. 365, 388 et seq. (1946). Also see Smith v. Michigan Beverage Co., Inc., 495 F.2d 754 (7th Cir. 1974) (exploding soft drink bottle which may have been bumped); Green v. Safeway Stores, Inc., Okl., 541 P.2d 200 (1975); compare W. Prosser, Torts 217 (4th ed. 1971).

Even where a court is willing to apply the doctrine, plaintiff still must show that the probable negligence is that of the defendant, and not of another. See, e. g., Dunn v. Hoffman Beverage Co., 126 N.J.L. 556, 20 A.2d 352 (1941). For a doctrinaire application of the "exclusive control" test to preclude liability in such a situation, see Maybach v. Falstaff Brewing Corp., 359 Mo. 446, 222 S.W.2d 87 (1949) criticized in 16 Mo.L.Rev. 76 (1951).

Maki v. Murray Hospital, 91 Mont. 251, 7 P.2d 228, 231; see, also, Whetstine v. Moravec, 228 Iowa 352, 291 N.W. 425, 435, where the court refers to the "instrumentalities" as including "the unconscious body of the plaintiff."

In the face of these examples of liberalization of the tests for res ipsa loquitur, there can be no justification for the rejection of the doctrine in the instant case. As pointed out above, if we accept the contention of defendants herein, there will rarely be any compensation for patients injured while unconscious. A hospital today conducts a highly integrated system of activities, with many persons contributing their efforts. There may be, e. g., preparation for surgery by nurses and internes who are employees of the hospital; administering of an anesthetic by a doctor who may be an employee of the hospital, an employee of the operating surgeon, or an independent contractor; performance of an operation by a surgeon and assistants who may be his employees, employees of the hospital, or independent contractors; and post surgical care by the surgeon, a hospital physician, and nurses. The number of those in whose care the patient is placed is not a good reason for denying him all reasonable opportunity to recover for negligent harm. It is rather a good reason for re-examination of the statement of legal theories which supposedly compel such a shocking result.

We do not at this time undertake to state the extent to which the reasoning of this case may be applied to other situations in which the doctrine of res ipsa loquitur is invoked. We merely hold that where a plaintiff receives unusual injuries while unconscious and in the course of medical treatment, all those defendants who had any control over his body or the instrumentalities which might have caused the injuries may properly be called upon to meet the inference of negligence by giving an explanation of their conduct.[56]

The judgment is reversed.[57]

SHENK, CURTIS, EDMONDS, CARTER and SCHAUER, JJ., concurred.
Rehearing denied; TRAYNOR, J., dissenting.

56. Consider, Anderson v. Somberg, 67 N.J. 291, 338 A.2d 1 (1975); see Lavin, Somebody has to be Guilty, Medical Economics, January 12, 1976, at 151.

57. On a trial of the action all defendants testified that nothing untoward had happened during the operation. A verdict was had against them all. 93 Cal.App.2d 43, 208 P.2d 445 (1949).

This case had its share of law review comment. See, e. g., 33 Calif.L.Rev. 331 (1945); 40 Ill.L.Rev. 421 (1946).

Treatments of it, and its sequel, also occur in Seavey, Comment, *Res Ipsa Loquitur: Tabula in Naufragio*, 63 Harv.L.Rev. 643 (1950); James, Res Ipsa Loquitur in California, Proof of the Breach in Negligence Cases (Including Res Ipsa Loquitur), 37 Va.L. Rev. 179, 207 (1951).

The applicability of res ipsa loquitur to malpractice cases is also treated in notes, 9 Bklyn.L.Rev. 335 (1940); 40 Col.L.Rev. 161 (1940); 26 Ill.L.Rev. 350 (1931).

Contrast the justification of the doctrine given in the present case (unavailability of evidence to plaintiff) with Prosser's theory in the note to the Ristau case, p. —, supra. See also Prosser, Res Ipsa Loquitur in California, Proof of the Breach in Negligence Cases (Including Res Ipsa Loquitur), 37 Cal.L.Rev. 183, 203 (1949); James, 37 Va.L.Rev. 179, 213 (1951).

CLARK v. GIBBONS

Supreme Court of California, in Bank, 1967.
66 Cal. 399, 58 Cal.Rptr 125, 426 P.2d 525.

PETERS, JUSTICE. Plaintiff Eunice Clark brought this action against Dr. Selmants, an anesthesiologist, Dr. Gibbons and his partner Dr. Horn, orthopedic surgeons, and Sutter Community Hospital of Sacramento for damages for injuries resulting from an operation allegedly negligently performed in Sutter Community Hospital by Drs. Gibbons and Selmants. The jury returned verdicts of $27,500 against all of the doctors and exonerated the hospital. Motions for a new trial were denied, and the doctors have appealed from the judgment.

Defendants' contentions are that the verdicts are not supported by sufficient evidence of negligence, and that the trial court committed reversible error by giving conditional res ipsa loquitur instructions. Both contentions are unsound.

It must be kept in mind that in determining whether sufficient evidence of negligence was adduced against the doctors,[58] the power of an appellate court begins and ends with a finding that the record contains some substantial evidence, contradicted or uncontradicted, which supports the conclusion reached by the jury. The record must be read in the light most advantageous to the plaintiff. All conflicts must be resolved in her favor; and all legitimate and reasonable inferences must be indulged in to uphold the verdict, if that is possible. * * *

The record discloses that on October 30, 1960, at approximately 2 p. m., plaintiff Eunice Clark, who was 41 years old, obese and in good health, suffered a fractured right ankle when she slipped and fell on a waxed floor in her home. She was taken by ambulance to the Sutter Community Hospital and examined by her physician Dr. Smith. After viewing X-rays of the fracture, Dr. Smith told her that it was a case for an orthopedic surgeon. Mrs. Clark requested the services of Dr. Gibbons who had previously treated her husband and who happened to be in the hospital at that time. Dr. Gibbons determined from viewing the X-rays that plaintiff had a severe trimalleolar fracture of the right ankle and that an open reduction, i. e., reduction by surgery, should be performed as soon as possible. He informed plaintiff that he would prefer to operate that night since the ankle would be stiff by the next morning. Plaintiff agreed.

Dr. Selmants, one of the anesthesiologists on the hospital staff, undertook to administer the anesthesia. Plaintiff gave the doctor a preanesthesia history which revealed that she had eaten between 1 and 2 p. m. Dr. Selmants believed that a general anesthetic should not be given to one who had eaten in the 12 hours preceding surgery, and that a general anesthetic was dangerous for a patient who had eaten within six or seven hours of surgery. Dr. Selmants concluded that

58. Plaintiff did not produce any expert witnesses of her own. For expert testimony she relied upon the evidence of the defendants called under section 2055 of the Code of Civil Procedure.

plaintiff was not a safe subject for a general anesthetic. He told plaintiff that she should be given a spinal anesthetic, and she agreed to a spinal, although she said that she would prefer a general. Dr. Gibbons concurred in the decision to give a spinal.

Dr. Selmants selected the agent to be used for the spinal. He testified that it was the anesthesiologist's duty to know the time required for surgery and that he did not ask Dr. Gibbons how long the operation would take, because he knew from previously working with Dr. Gibbons that the surgeon averaged two hours for usual reductions of this kind. This case was not unusual, he believed, and would accordingly require two hours. The agent that Dr. Selmants chose was 10 milligrams of pontocaine. It was designed to maintain a level of T–10 for two hours plus or minus 15 minutes, and it was predictable in intensity and duration.

Dr. Gibbons testified that plaintiff's fracture was severe, and that he expected the operation to take from two to three hours. The anesthesiologist said that the anesthesia he selected could not be used unmodified for surgery of from two and a half to three hours, but that by adding epinephine to the pontocaine, he could have produced an agent with a predictable duration of over four and a half hours.

Prior to surgery plaintiff was nervous and anxious. She was not more upset however than any other person with an ankle injury and she was calmed by injections of vistaril and nembutal and taken into surgery at approximately 8 p. m.

Dr. Selmants then administered the spinal anesthetic and made pinprick tests to assure that the proper level of anesthesia had been achieved. After the anesthesia was injected and the numbness started up her legs, plaintiff felt that she could not breathe and her voice became squeaky. Dr. Selmants stated that a patient should not suffer from shortness of breath at a level of T–10, and that plaintiff's difficulty in breathing could have been "some undue effect [from] the way the anesthetic was given."

When the anesthesia reached the level necessary for surgery, Dr. Gibbons commenced the operation. The level of anesthesia remained adequate at first; but after about one hour the doctors noticed from plaintiff's unconscious movements that the anesthesia was beginning to wear off. At this point Dr. Gibbons had completed all of the reduction except for reduction of the posterior fragment of the tibia. Dr. Selmants believed than 20 minutes more were needed to complete the operation, but Dr. Gibbons testified that no less than another hour would have been required.

Dr. Selmants could have extended the surgical anesthesia without harm to the patient. He stated that intravenous demerol could have been used for that purpose and that there was no particular reason not to use it, although the extension obtained might still have been insufficient to complete the operation. Also, another spinal could have been given. Dr. Gibbons stated that he did not think that plaintiff "would have been up to" another spinal and that in turning her for the spinal all the prepping and draping would have to be undone and this might subject her to a risk of infection.

In any event, the operation was terminated, the incision was closed, and a cast was applied to plaintiff's ankle in an attempt to reduce the posterior fragment by external pressure. Dr. Gibbons' operative report mentioned that the operation was not completed because the anesthetic did not last for the required length of time. Dr. Selmants failed to note those facts, although he was supposed to make an accurate report of how the anesthesia proceeded with relation to the needs of the operation.

The decision to terminate surgery was made primarily by Dr. Gibbons. He was in control of the surgery and could have asked for an extension of the anesthesia. He had stated in his deposition that he became upset when the anesthesia began to wear off and that he did not consult with Dr. Selmants about extending the anesthesia but just said "I think we will quit for tonight and do this another time." At the trial, however, both he and Dr. Selmants testified that they discussed the question whether the anesthesia should be continued or the operation terminated and that Dr. Selmants agreed with the decision to terminate.

Dr. Gibbons testified that, when he made the decision to terminate, he expected to complete the operation later, but did not do so because blebs, infected blisters of the skin, developed; that it was very common for blebs to accompany an injury of this nature, that plaintiff's blebs healed at the normal rate, but that healing of blebs at the normal rate did not permit a second operation within the time when a second operation would have been of any value.

Three days after the operation Dr. Gibbons noticed that the posterior fragment had slipped back to some extent and that another open reduction was required. A second operation could not be performed, however, because pressure and resultant swelling, as pointed out, had caused blebs, which presented a serious risk of infection if the skin were cut.

Dr. Gibbons charged plaintiff less than the normal operating fee because his operation was unsuccessful. She now suffers from osteoarthritis in the ankle joint, which is painful. The arthritis might have resulted from the fracture even if a perfect union had been achieved. However, there is expert testimony that the chances of getting arthritis were increased by the failure to achieve a complete reduction; and the defendants do not claim that the evidence is insufficient to show that the arthritis was due, at least in part, to the failure to complete the operation.

Nothing but a fusion, which would impair the ankle's up and down movement could now give plaintiff a pain free ankle. Dr. Gibbons' partner, Dr. Horn, offered to fuse the ankle for a token fee of $100.

Plaintiff's position is that the jury received sufficient evidence to find that the imperfect reduction causing the present injury was the result of (1) the negligence of Dr. Selmants in selecting and administering an anesthetic which wore off before the operation was completed and (2) the negligence of Dr. Gibbons in (a) not informing Dr. Selmants that the operation might well take longer than the two hours which Selmants expected the operation to take and (b) terminating the operation prematurely rather than ordering an extension of the anesthesia.

The evidence upon which plaintiff primarily relies to show negligence in the selection or administration of the anesthetic is the following testimony of Dr. Selmants:

"Q. * * * if proper care is used, in the usual course of events, anesthetics like this don't run out or wear out, do they—surgical anesthetics? A. No, sir.

* * *

And I said 'no, sir.' What I mean is, they can. There is no control. There is—there is—there is a variable, as anything else we do in medicine. There is nothing exact that guarantees this will happen, this will not happen, how long this will last. You cannot ever predicate what you're doing on the basis that it's going to be 100 per cent; you have a certain area of predictability, and that's what you go on. Q. Now, my question was—you see, you misunderstood. I'll say it again. My question was, if proper care is used in a situation like this, anesthetics like this usually do not run out, do they? A. Yes, usually they do not run out." Dr. Gibbons stated in his deposition that if the anesthesiologist uses proper care and obtains proper information about the case, he can make a spinal anesthesia last long enough for an operation of this kind.

Later on direct examination Dr. Selmants and Dr. Horn testified that it is common knowledge in the field of anesthesia that there is always an inherent risk that, even when due care is used, a spinal anesthesia will not last as long as contemplated. Dr. Selmants explained that immediately upon the injection of any spinal anesthetizing agent a process of detoxification commences within the area of the nerve root blockage which ultimately causes the anesthesia to wear off. The speed of detoxification in any individual depends primarily upon the amount of circulation in the nerve area and the amount of myelin covering the nerve itself.

The evidence, independently of the doctrine of res ipsa loquitur, is sufficent to support the verdict against both doctors. So far as Dr. Selmants is concerned while the evidence shows that he and Dr. Gibbons were not negligent in making the initial decision to give a spinal rather than a general anesthetic,[59] there is evidence that Dr. Selmants

59. Even if the jury could find that a spinal was not absolutely necessary for the plaintiff's safety, there is no evidence that a general was necessarily preferable in this case. The mere giving of a spinal whenever the patient is experiencing the normal agitation due to an injury is certainly not sufficient to constitute negligence.

was negligent in selecting the agent to be used for the spinal. The orthopedic surgeon expected the operation would take from two to three hours to complete. Anesthetics were available that would have lasted at least that long without undue danger to the patient. Dr. Selmants did not use those anesthetics because he did not expect that the operation would take as long as three hours. Dr. Selmants admitted, however, that it was his responsibility to know the needs of the surgeon and that he did not inquire how long the surgeon would take in this case. Because he underestimated the probable length of the operation, he gave an anesthetic which was designed to last a maximum of two hours and 15 minutes and a minimum of one hour and 45 minutes. The jury could have found that this choice of anesthetic was negligent.

In addition, Dr. Selmants testified that anesthetics do not usually wear off prematurely if proper care is used. Premature termination can be caused by improper administration of the agent, and plaintiff's initial reaction to the injection, her squeaky voice and difficulty in breathing, is evidence that the anesthetic was improperly administered. Dr. Selmants failed to note the premature termination in his records relating to the progress of the anesthesia, as he should have done. The jury could infer from such omission that he possessed some guilty knowledge regarding the termination. From the symptoms of improper administration and the inference of guilty knowledge, the jury could properly imply that Dr. Selmants had administered the anesthetic improperly.

Although Dr. Selmants testified that inadequate anesthesia could have resulted from several unpredictable causes and that he used due care in the administration of the anesthetic, the credibility of this testimony was properly left to the jury.

There is also sufficient evidence of negligence to support the verdict against Dr. Gibbons. Dr. Gibbons could have been found responsible for the improper selection of an anesthetic. Although the anesthesiologist ordinarily has the duty to ask the surgeon about the projected length of the operation, Dr. Selmants testified that the surgeon should speak to the anesthesiologist if the operation is going to be unusually long. Dr. Selmants testified that Dr. Gibbons averaged two hours in operating on trimalleolar ankle fractures. Dr. Gibbons testified that Mrs. Clark's fracture was one of the most severe trimalleolars he had ever seen. Under those circumstances the jury could find that Dr. Gibbons expected an unusually long operation and was under a duty to warn Dr. Selmants of the need for an anesthetic that would last more than two hours.

Dr. Gibbons stated in his deposition that he became upset when the anesthesia began to wear off and, without consulting Dr. Selmants about the possibility of extending the anesthesia, said that the surgery would be terminated now and completed at a later time. He also admitted that healing of the skin at the normal rate did not permit a second operation to be performed within the necessary time.

Thus, from Dr. Gibbons' own statements, the jury could have found that in making the decision to terminate he acted rashly knowing the dangers, but without considering the possibility of extending the anesthesia and under the erroneous belief that the completion of the reduction could be accomplished by a second operation. Both the possibility of extending anesthesia and the possibility of further surgery are clearly major factors which should have been considered by a surgeon confronted with inadequate anesthesia. Under these circumstances, the jury could conclude without any other expert testimony that in making the decision to terminate surgery, Dr. Gibbons did not exercise that care and skill ordinarily practiced by other specialists in orthopedic surgery under similar circumstances.[60]

In addition, the facts of this case warrant the use of the conditional res ipsa loquitur instructions. As a general rule, res ipsa loquitur applies where the occurrence of the injury is of such a nature that it can be said, in the light of past experience, that it probably was the result of negligence by someone and that the defendant is probably the person who is responsible. In determining whether such probabilities exist with regard to a particular occurrence, the courts have relied both on common knowledge and on expert testimony. * * *

The doctrine of res ipsa loquitur is a doctrine fundamentally predicated upon inferences deducible from circumstantial evidence and the weight to be given to them. * * * As stated in Fowler v. Seaton, 61 Cal.2d 681, 686–687, 39 Cal.Rptr. 881, 884, 394 P.2d 697, 700:

> * * * "One of the frequently quoted statements of the applicable rules is to be found in the opinion of Chief Justice Erle in Scott v. London & St. Katherine Docks Co. (1865) 3 H. & C. 596, quoted in Prosser on Torts (2d ed. 1955) section 42, at page 201, as follows: 'There must be reasonable evidence of negligence; but where the thing is shown to be under the management of the defendant or his servants, and the accident is such as in the ordinary course of things does not happen if those who have the management use proper care, it affords reasonable evidence, in the absence of explanation by the defendants, that the accident arose from want of care.'

60. This court has held in one case that since a physician normally undertakes to exercise only that care and skill common to the profession and that since some mistakes are inherent in this exercise, proof of mistaken diagnosis or wrong method of treatment in itself is not sufficient to show lack of skill and care. (Patterson v. Marcus, 203 Cal. 550, 552–553, 265 P. 222.) However, as noted by Prosser, "Such decisions, together with the notorious unwillingness of members of the medical profession to testify against one another, may impose an insuperable handicap upon a plaintiff who cannot obtain the proof." (Prosser on Torts (3d ed. 1964) § 39, p. 231.) Each case must be determined on its own facts, and at least where, as here, there is evidence not only of improper treatment, but of the doctor's agitation and total failure to consider the alternative methods of treatment and their consequences, a jury is competent to find without the conclusion of an expert that the doctor did not exercise that degree of care and skill common to other specialists in the community. (Cf. Quintal v. Laurel Grove Hospital, 62 Cal.2d 154, 161, 41 Cal.Rptr. 577, 397 P.2d 161.)

"Of course negligence and connecting defendant with it, like other facts, can be proved by circumstantial evidence. There does not have to be an eyewitness, nor need there be direct evidence of defendant's conduct. There is no absolute requirement that the plaintiff explain how the accident happened. Res ipsa may apply where the cause of the injury is a mystery, if there is a reasonable and logical inference that defendant was negligent, and that such negligence caused the injury. (Prosser on Torts, supra, at p. 204.)" (See also Quintal v. Laurel Grove Hospital, supra, 62 Cal.2d 154, 164–165, 41 Cal.Rptr. 577, 397 P.2d 161.)

More than 20 years ago in Ybarra v. Spangard, 25 Cal.2d 486, 489 et seq., 154 P.2d 687, 162 A.L.R. 1258, this court had occasion to consider the application of the doctrine to cases where injury was received by a medical patient while unconscious under the influence of anesthesia. * * *

In *Ybarra,* it was pointed out that in a modern hospital a patient is quite likely to come under the care of a number of persons in different types of contractual relationships with each other, including physicians and surgeons, anesthetists, and nurses; that every defendant in whose custody the plaintiff was placed for any period was bound to exercise ordinary care to see that no unnecessary harm came to the plaintiff; that, although at the trial some of the defendants might be found liable and others absolved, this would not preclude application of the doctrine; and that, since each of the defendants in acting together to provide the medical treatment at one time or another was in control of the various agencies which might have harmed plaintiff, they should have the burden of initial explanation. (25 Cal.2d at pp. 491–492, 154 P.2d 687.)

Ybarra involved an injury which may not have been received during the operation, but Leonard v. Watsonville Community Hosp., 47 Cal.2d 509, 514 et seq., 305 P.2d 36, involved an injury during the operation and followed *Ybarra* in holding that where the conditions of the doctrine are satisfied all persons who had any control over the patient's body or the instrumentalities causing injury may properly be called upon to meet the inference of negligence by giving an explanation of their conduct. In *Leonard* it was further held that the inference of negligence arising under the doctrine is dispelled as a matter of law with regard to a particular doctor only where other evidence establishes as a matter of law that he is free from negligence. The evidence establishing the absence of negligence in such a case must be clear, positive, uncontradicted and of such a nature that it cannot be rationally disbelieved.

Ybarra and *Leonard* establish that, if the conditions giving rise to the doctrine are present when the medical personnel are treated as a group acting in concert and they collectively have access to the chief evidence as to the cause of the injury but the plaintiff does not, a single doctor may not escape the inference as a matter of law merely by showing that as to him alone it is more probable than not that he was free from fault. The basis of the application of the doctrine to all defendants in the cases is that the medical personnel acted as a group and that collectively, without regard to what any one may individually know, or did, they are in a position to explain the cause and produce the chief evidence bearing on the question whereas the plaintiff is not. To avoid the inference *as a matter of law* an individual doctor must go beyond showing that it was unlikely or not probable he was negligent and must establish that he is free from negligence by evidence which cannot be rationally disbelieved. Falling short of such a showing, it remains for the jury to determine whether the inference arising from the doctrine has been rebutted as to any particular doctor.

The fact that the patient may have received a local anesthetic rather than a general anesthetic does not eliminate the duty of explanation of those who had control over the procedure where the chief evidence as to the cause is accessible to them but not to the plaintiff. The plaintiff's lack of knowledge may exist not only where he is totally unconscious but also where he is partially unconscious and largely, if not entirely, unaware of what the medical personnel are doing.

The conditions giving rise to the doctrine here existed. This problem was recently discussed in Quintal v. Laurel Grove Hospital, supra, 62 Cal.2d 154, 41 Cal.Rptr. 577, 397 P.2d 161, a case involving injuries during an operation. There the plaintiff suffered a cardiac arrest during the administration of a general anesthetic, and it was held that an instruction on conditional res ipsa loquitur was proper even though the medical experts testified that a cardiac arrest, although a rare occurrence, is a known and calculated risk in the giving of a general anesthetic and though there was no expert testimony that when cardiac arrests do occur, they are more likely than not the result of negligence. There was evidence that a method of meeting the unusual risk existed. Experts testified that when due care is used, cardiac arrests do not ordinarily occcur, and, in addition, evidence was presented of fever and apprehension of the patient before administration of the anesthetic which tended to show that the cardiac arrest in that case was caused by negligence of the doctors.

Thus, we recognized in *Quintal* that proof that when due care is exercised an injury rarely occurs, accompanied by other evidence indicating negligence, may be sufficient to warrant an instruction on conditional res ipsa loquitur. * * * This is particularly true where, as in *Quintal* and in the present case, the injury occurred as the result of a normal procedure such as the administration of an anesthetic, rather than from a complex operation.

It is true that evidence that an accident rarely occurs when due care is used does not without more indicate that a particular occurrence is more likely than not the result of someone's negligence. (Siverson v. Weber, supra, 57 Cal.2d 834, 839, 22 Cal.Rptr. 337, 372 P.2d 97.) In *Siverson* it was stated:

"To permit an inference of negligence under the doctrine of res ipsa loquitur solely because an uncommon complication develops would place too great a burden upon the medical profession and might result in an undesirable limitation on the use of operations or new procedures involving an inherent risk of injury even when due care is used. Where risks are inherent in an operation and an injury of a type which is rare does occur, the doctrine should not be applicable unless it can be said that, in the light of past experience, such an occurrence is more likely the result of negligence than some cause for which the defendant is not responsible." (57 Cal.2d at p. 839, 22 Cal.Rptr. at p. 339, 372 P.2d at p. 99.) But in *Siverson* there was no evidence of a negligent act of a type that could have caused the accident, and none of the witnesses "testified that anything was done during the operation which was contrary to good medical practice." (57 Cal.2d at pp. 838–839, 22 Cal.Rptr. at p. 339, 372 P.2d at p. 99.) The court refused to permit an instruction on the doctrine where the only basis for it was evidence that the injury suffered by the patient rarely occurs as a result of the surgical procedure.

The likelihood of a negligent cause is increased if the low incidence of accidents when due care is used is combined with proof of specific acts of negligence of a type which could have caused the occurrence complained of. When those two facts are proved, the likelihood of a negligent cause may be sufficiently great that the jury may properly conclude that the accident was more probably than not the result of someone's negligence.

That a doctor has done a negligent act of a type that could have caused the accident, which does not ordinarily occur in the exercise of due care, greatly increases the probability that it was his negligence that caused the plaintiff's injury. Thus, the low incidence of accidents when due care is used plus negligent conduct of a type which could have caused the occurrence may make it probable that the occurrence was the result of someone's negligence and that the defendant is probably the person who was responsible. Those are the requirements for applying res ipsa loquitur.

The administration of an anesthetic is now a normal and tested procedure. Dr. Selmants stated that one of the reasons for selecting pontocaine in the instant case was its predictability as to duration. Medical experts testified that spinal anesthetics do not usually run out prematurely if proper care is used, and in explanation of this conclusion, Dr. Selmants stated only that the predictability of such anesthetics was not 100 percent. Dr. Gibbons stated in his deposition without qualification that if an anesthesiologist uses proper care and obtains proper information about the case, he can make a spinal anesthesia last long enough for an operation of this kind.

There is evidence that the injury here was caused by the anesthesia wearing off prematurely and that Dr. Selmants was responsible for selecting and administering an anesthetic which would be adequate for the length of surgery required. Dr. Selmants testified that he did not consult with the surgeon regarding the length of the operation and that he used an anesthetic which, according to the testimony of the surgeon, was inadequate for the estimated length of the operation. In addition, Dr. Selmants stated that plaintiff's unusual reaction to the anesthetic could have been caused by "some undue effect the way the anesthetic had been given."

There is also evidence, as we have seen, from which the jury could conclude that Dr. Gibbons in the exercise of due care should have advised Dr. Selmants of the anticipated extraordinary length of the surgery and that the former acted rashly in determining to terminate the surgery. It bears emphasis in this connection that the doctors were aware that the procedure should be performed and completed as soon as possible.

This evidence, taken as a whole, along with the evidence that there was a reasonable method of handling the risk when it occurred is certainly sufficient for the jury to find that the injury was probably the result of negligence of someone and that the defendants were probably the persons responsible.

Accordingly we conclude that it was proper to instruct the jury on the doctrine of res ipsa loquitur. It is not claimed that the form of the conditional instructions given was improper.

The judgment is affirmed.

MOSK, BURKE and PEEK, JJ., concur.

TOBRINER, JUSTICE (concurring).

I concur in the judgment, but I am unable to join either the majority opinion or the opinion of the Chief Justice. I propose here to explain my dissatisfaction with the present definition and application of the doctrine of res ipsa loquitur in that limited number of cases in which rare and inexplicable accidents occur in the operating room. In pursuing the laudable goal of shifting the losses occasioned by such accidents to the parties best able to protect against them through insurance, we have imposed the onus of negligence and malpractice upon capable and dedicated members of the medical profession, burdening the law of res ipsa loquitur with a sweep that is inaccurate, inefficient, and inequitable. I propose a redefinition of the doctrine governing these cases which seems to me more candid, more certain, and more consistent with our underlying objectives.

Initially, I set forth my reasons for joining the majority in affirming the judgments against both defendants. Given the evidence from which the jury could have found that the specific acts and omissions alleged by plaintiff were negligent and proximately caused her injury, I am unwilling to assume that the verdict against the defendants rested upon the trial court's instruction on res ipsa loquitur. * *

I cannot agree, however, with the route by which the majority reaches its result. As the Chief Justice demonstrates in his separate opinion herein, neither common knowledge nor expert testimony supported an inference in this case that accidents such as befell the plaintiff ordinarily bespeak a negligent cause.[61] To give a res ipsa instruction under such circumstances invites a purely speculative leap and entrusts the jury with unreviewable power to impose or withhold liability as it sees fit. If public policy demands that defendants be held responsible for unexplained accidents without a reasoned finding of fault, such responsibility should be fixed openly and uniformly, not under the guise of negligence and at the discretion of a jury. * *

I am likewise disturbed by the conclusion of the Chief Justice that the victims of accidents which do not truly "speak for themselves" should be required to present evidence that the kinds of accidents they suffered are ordinarily caused by negligence. Even if expert medical testimony were readily available to plaintiffs in malpractice cases,[62] such a rule would unfairly penalize the surgical patient who is injured by an accident of a type too rare or too little understood to permit meaningful statistical analysis of its probable cause.[63] Although I

61. Plaintiff adduced expert testimony to show that, when due care is used, premature termination of anesthetic is rare. The record contains no evidence, however, indicating that in those rare cases in which an anesthetic *does* terminate prematurely, a negligent cause is *more probable* than a non-negligent one. Although plaintiff presented evidence of specific negligent acts which *could* have caused premature termination, such evidence provided no rational basis for a conclusion that, of the various possible causes, a negligent one was *probably* responsible.

The majority asserts: "[I]f the low incidence of accidents when due care is used is combined with proof of specific acts of negligence of a type which could have caused the occurrence complained of. * * * the jury may properly conclude that the accident was more probably than not the result of someone's negligence." (Ante, p. 134, 426 P.2d 534.) I cannot agree.

Suppose, for example, that in 5 percent of all operations in which due care is used, a certain spinal anesthetic inevitably terminates prematurely because of an undetectable excess of myelin on the patient's nerves; suppose further that a specific technique for administering the anesthetic does not alter the likelihood of premature termination in patients with an excess of myelin but creates a 2 percent risk of premature termination in normal patients, whereas another available technique, equally desirable in all other relevant respects, creates only a 1 percent risk of premature termination in normal patients. Under these circumstances, the technique which creates twice as high a risk in normal patients and yields no compensating benefit would presumably be considered negligent.

If one were to examine 100 operations in which this negligent technique had been employed, one would expect to find 2 operations in which such negligence caused premature termination, compared with 5 in which an overabundance of myelin caused premature termination. Yet, in every one of these hypothetical operations, the majority would invite the jury to infer a negligent cause without further guidance from the evidence before it; I find it disturbing to note that in 5 out of every 7 cases of premature termination coupled with a specific negligent act, this inference would blame the doctor for an accident he did not cause.

62. The strong reluctance of doctors to testify against each other has frequently been noted (see, e. g., Huffman v. Lindquist (1951) 37 Cal.2d 465, 484, 234 P.2d 34, 29 A.L.R. 485 (Carter, J., dissenting); Belli, An Ancient Therapy Still Applied: The Silent Medical Treatment (1956) 1 Vill.L.Rev. 250, 259) and numerous corrective measures have been suggested (see, e. g., Note, Malpractice and Medical Testimony (1963) 77 Harv.L.Rev. 333, 338–350), but the problem apparently remains (see Note, Medical Malpractice-Expert Testimony (1966) 60 Nw.L.Rev. 834, 835–837).

63. Since the accidents with which we are here concerned by hypothesis occur rarely, there is little hope of obtaining broadly based statistics of the sort hypothesized for the computations in

agree with the Chief Justice that the above requirement for application of the res ipsa doctrine follows from its basic premises, I submit that use of the doctrine itself fails to serve the ends of justice in cases such as this. Indeed, even the expanded version of res ipsa loquitur espoused by the majority falls considerably short of truly protecting the victims of unfamiliar and unexplained surgical mishaps, since the majority would deny plaintiffs the benefit of a res ipsa instruction unless they could produce the kind of testimony which the Chief Justice would require, or could persuade a medical expert to characterize as substandard the conduct of those entrusted with their care.[64]

Upon reexamining what seem to me the grave shortcomings of these varying formulations of res ipsa loquitur in surgical accident cases, I have concluded that the basic error lies in primary reliance upon the concept of *negligence* and that the courts should undertake a fundamental reassessment of the largely fictitious and often futile search for fault which presently characterizes medical injury litigation of the kind here involved.

At the outset we must recognize that, in the present state of medical knowledge, risks which even the most cautious physician could not have prevented may lead to accidents which even the most expert cannot explain. Although the vast majority of medical practitioners are protected financially by liability insurance covering such accidents,[65] and although doctors and hospitals can readily transfer the cost of this insurance protection to their patients through higher medical fees, no technique yet devised can protect a doctor from the devastating impact which an adjudication of malpractice can have upon his professional standing.[66] Fearing, that his competence may thus be impugned whenever he adopts a procedure difficult to justify

footnote * * * [61], supra. The complexity of the concept of negligence as applied to medical techniques, coupled with the difficulties of determining the cause of the few accidents which might be included in any purported sample, render suspect the claim of any expert who asserts that in a representative group of cases he was able to determine the relative proportion of negligent and non-negligent causes.

64. The majority reaffirms the holding of Siverson v. Weber (1962) 57 Cal.2d 834, 839, 22 Cal.Rptr. 337, 372 P.2d 97, that rarity alone does not warrant a conditional res ipsa instruction, and limits the holding of Quintal v. Laurel Grove Hospital (1964) 62 Cal.2d 154, 164–166, 41 Cal.Rptr. 577, 397 P.2d 161, to cases in which rarity is coupled with "proof of specific acts of negligence of a type which could have caused the occurrence complained of." (Ante, p. 134, 426 P.2d 534.) Plaintiffs who cannot qualify under *Quintal* by obtaining such proof are thus relegated to the basic rule of *Siverson* that res ipsa is applicable only if common knowledge or expert witnesses establish that accidents of the sort which befells the plaintiff are "more likely the result of negligence than some cause for which the defendant is not responsible." (57 Cal.2d at 839, 22 Cal. Rptr. at 340, 372 P.2d at 100.)

65. A 1959 estimate showed that more than 92 percent of American doctors carried professional liability insurance with an average coverage ranging from $25,000 for general practitioners to $100,000 for specialists. (Silverman, Medicine's Legal Nightmare, Saturday Evening Post, April 25, 1959, pp. 36, 120.)

66. Indeed, many doctors genuinely fear that even if they win a malpractice case, they will be "all but destroyed professionally." (Shindell, Medicine versus Law: A Proposal for Settlement (1953) 151 A.M.A.J. 1078, 1079.)

to a lay jury, a surgeon may feel compelled to forego an unorthodox technique in order to protect his reputation from ruin.[67] Any system which thus diverts the doctor's attention from the operating room to the courtroom leaves much to be desired.[68]

In light of the expansion of res ipsa loquitur undertaken by such decisions as Quintal v. Laurel Grove Hospital, supra, 62 Cal.2d 154, 41 Cal.Rptr. 577, 397 P.2d 161, and by the majority opinion in the present case, there can be little doubt that the net effect of the doctrine is to shift from plaintiffs to defendants the cost of a certain number of unexplainable accidents in which no meaningful basis exists for finding the defendants at fault.[69] Thus the concept of negligence as a prerequisite to medical liability now provides only sporadic and illusory protection for the physician. At the same time, insistence under all circumstances upon a nominal finding of fault frustrates the risk-shifting purpose of the res ipsa doctrine as currently applied since it stands as an occasionally insuperable obstacle to the financial protection of inexplicably injured patients.

A system openly imposing liability without any pretense of negligence in this narrow range of cases can avoid unwarranted imputations of fault while permitting the rational development of badly needed doctrine. Simultaneously, such a system can insure that the burdens of unexplained accidents will not fall primarily upon the helpless but will be borne instead by those best able to spread their cost among all who benefit from the surgical operations in which these misfortunes occur.[70]

67. See Cohn, Medical Malpractice Litigation: A Plague on Both Houses (1966) 52 A.B.A.J. 32; McCoid, The Care Required of Medical Practioners (1959) 12 Vand.L.Rev. 549, 608; Silverman, op. cit. supra April 11, 1959, p. 48; The Urge To Sue, Time, Nov. 28, 1960, pp. 69, 70. A number of hospitals, for example, are said to have prohibited the use of spinal anesthetics, purportedly reacting to cases adjudicating that physicians employing their facilities were guilty of malpractice because of unfortunate results following the use of such anesthetics. (Silverman, ibid.)

68. When every patient is viewed largely as a potential plaintiff, the method of treatment chosen by the physician may well be that which appears easiest to justify in court rather than that which seems best from a purely medical standpoint. (See Siverson v. Weber, supra, 57 Cal.2d at 839, 22 Cal.Rptr. 337, 372 P.2d 97; Rubsamen, Res Ipsa Loquitur in California Medical Malpractice Law—Expansion of a Doctrine to the Bursting Point (1962) 14 Stan.L.Rev. 251, 282.) The probable victim of such litigation-oriented medical practice is of course the patient, who suffers first when he receives less than the best available care, and second when the doctor whom he decides to sue understandably appeals to the jury's inclination to protect a physician's professional standing. (See Fleming, Developments in the English Law of Medical Liability (1959) 12 Vand.L.Rev. 633, 634.)

69. See generally 2 Harper and James, Torts (1956) § 19.6, p. 1081; see also id., § 19.5, pp. 1080–1081 & fns. 16–18; § 19.7, p. 1089 & fn. 17; Ehrenzweig, Compulsory "Hospital-Accident" Insurance: A Needed First Step Toward the Displacement of Liability for "Medical Malpractice" (1964) 31 U.Chi.L.Rev. 279, 281–282 & fns. 8–9; Morris, Res Ipsa Loquitur—Liability Without Fault (1958) 25 Ins.Counsel J. 97.

70. See Ehrenzweig, op. cit. supra, passim; Calabresi, Some Thoughts on Risk Distribution and the Law of Torts (1961) 70 Yale L.J. 499, 548–549; James, Accident Liability Reconsidered: The Impact of Liability Insurance (1948) 57 Yale L.J. 549, 550 & fn. 1, 553 & fn. 8; cf. Greenman v. Yuba

The record in this case supports the conclusion that the plaintiff's arthritic condition resulted from the premature termination of anesthesia, bringing the operation to an untimely halt. We deal here neither with a complication flowing from an undetectable idiosyncrasy of the patient [71] nor with a risk which the patient voluntarily assumed in electing to undergo this type of surgery; we deal instead with a failure of the operation to accomplish the result that the patient, in light of her own physical condition, reasonably expected it to achieve.[72]

If this failure could have been traced to the anesthetic itself, or to some mechanical inadequacy in the hospital's surgical equipment, the plaintiff would not have been required to establish negligence as a prerequisite to recovery.[73] The wholly fortuitous circumstance that this plaintiff's injury resulted instead from some undetermined mishap in the operating room should make no difference: in neither case should the patient's right to recover turn on her ability to isolate a negligent cause for her surgical injury.

In such situations, the jury should be instructed that, if it finds that the plaintiff was injured in the course of an operation within the collective control of the defendants [74] and that this type of injury rarely occurs in such operations,[75] then it must return a verdict for the plaintiff unless the defendants establish that the injury resulted from

Power Products, Inc. (1963) 59 Cal.2d 57, 63–64, 27 Cal.Rptr. 697, 377 P.2d 897.

71. As the Chief Justice points out, expert testimony in this case supports the view that a certain number of patients are afflicted with a condition involving an overabundance of myelin surrounding their nerves. This rare condition, known as rachiresistance, apparently cannot be detected in advance and either prevents the deposit of an adequate quantity of the anesthetizing agent on the patient's nerves or accelerates the rate at which the agent disappears. One of the defendants testified that the patient "had good and profound anesthesia for the prescribed time before she did feel the pain" and that, for this reason, he concluded that the patient probably "detoxified faster than normal" because of rachiresistance. In light of the trial court's instructions and the jury's verdict, the jury evidently rejected this explanation, and I see no basis on which an appellate court could disturb the jury's conclusion in this regard.

72. I note in this connection that some courts have permitted injured patients to sue for breach of a warranty that surgery would not aggravate their malady. (See Recent Decisions (1962) 37 Notre Dame Law 725.) The transition from express to implied warranty, and thence to a legally imposed liability without fault, is too familiar to require detailed elucidation here. (See Greenman v. Yuba Power Products, Inc., supra, 59 Cal.2d 57, 61–63, 27 Cal. Rptr. 697, 377 P.2d 897.)

73. See, e. g., Greenman v. Yuba Power Products, Inc., supra, 59 Cal.2d 57, 27 Cal.Rptr. 697, 377 P.2d 897; see also Bowles v. Zimmer Manufacturing Co. (7th Cir. 1960) 277 F.2d 868, 874, 76 A.L.R.2d 120 (breach of warranty by manufacturer of surgical pin); cf. Note, The Medical Profession and Strict Liability for Defective Products—A Limited Extension (1965) 17 Hastings L.J. 359.

74. Compare Ybarra v. Spangard (1944) 25 Cal.2d 486, 154 P.2d 687, 162 A.L.R. 1258.

75. Compare Quintal v. Laurel Grove Hospital, supra, 62 Cal.2d 154, 41 Cal. Rptr. 577, 397 P.2d 161. Plaintiffs who suffer from injuries of a type which *commonly* accompany a given medical procedure could of course proceed against defendants on an ordinary negligence theory. (See fn. 78, infra.)

an idiosyncracy of the patient[76] or that the patient knowingly and voluntarily assumed the risk of incurring such an injury.[77]

Once the elusive and destructive search for an act or omission of "malpractice" has been restricted to those cases in which a negligent cause may actually be demonstrated,[78] a far higher percentage of all medical controversies will be settled out of court, without the "economic and emotional strain of protracted litigation requiring difficult or impossible proof." (Ehrenzweig, op. cit. supra, 31 U.Chi.L. Rev. at 288). In the relatively few cases which reach trial, the imposition of financial liability will not be aggravated by the ruinous consequences of a determination of malpractice unless the evidence points logically to such a finding.

We should not impose the stigma of negligence upon a doctor merely because an operation yields an uncommon and inexplicable result; in the present state of the medical art, the rarity of an event may well bear no relationship to negligence. Courts which ignore that fact in formulating the law of res ipsa loquitur unjustly penalize physicians and plunge the legal process into an abyss of uncertainty and obfuscation. Our proper concern for the financial protection of the patient gives us no warrant for faulting the doctor.

I must conclude that, in this limited category of cases, the attempt to fix liability exclusively in terms of traditional notions of fault has outlived its utility. Once it appears that an unexplained surgical accident has caused an unexpected injury, no useful end is advanced by rehearsing the ancient ritual of assessing blame.

76. Compare Prosser, The Fall of the Citadel (Strict Liability to the Consumer) (1966) 50 Minn.L.Rev. 791, 810–811 & fns. 104–106. A doctor who knew or should have learned of the patient's pecularity might theoretically be held liable if his negligence could be shown to have caused the injury.

77. Compare Farber v. Olkon (1953) 40 Cal.2d 503, 511, 254 P.2d 520, 525, in which we concluded that a malpractice plaintiff was not entitled to an instruction on res ipsa loquitur since undisputed testimony established that the bone fractures of which the plaintiff complained constituted "a calculated and even an expected risk of the [electroshock] treatment." In determining which risks a patient may voluntarily assume in submitting to a given medical procedure, the controlling consideration must of course be the reasonable expectations of the patient arising out of his relationship with the doctor, not the precise language of any prior agreement or understanding. * * *

78. Nothing in this opinion should be construed to suggest a change in the means by which a patient might prove actual negligence or in the defenses which a doctor might properly interpose to a negligence claim. Thus, for example, instructions on res ipsa loquitur would remain available when warranted by the evidence; there would no longer be any justification, however, for giving such instructions simply because rarity and specific acts of negligence might both be present in a given case. (See fn. [59], supra.) A verdict predicated upon inferred negligence under a res ipsa instruction would henceforth be sustained only under the conditions set forth in the separate opinion of the Chief Justice. [Notes 58–78 from original; other notes in original omitted; also cf. Brown v. Keaveny, 326 F.2d 660 (D.C. Cir. 1963). For other materials on the application of strict liability to medical accidents see page —— infra.]

TRAYNOR, CHIEF JUSTICE (concurring and dissenting).

I concur in the judgment under the compulsion of Quintal v. Laurel Grove Hospital, 62 Cal.2d 154, 41 Cal.Rptr. 577, 397 P.2d 161, but deem it appropriate to set forth why the evidence in this case, as in *Quintal,* does not justify a res ipsa loquitur instruction.

A physician's duty is to exercise that degree of care and skill ordinarily possessed and exercised by members of his profession under similar circumstances. (Sinz v. Owens (1949) 33 Cal.2d 749, 753, 205 P.2d 3, 8 A.L.R.2d 757.) He does not guarantee a cure. The doctrine of res ipsa loquitur cannot properly be invoked to make him an insurer of the recovery of persons he treats. The Latin words cannot obliterate the fact that much of the functioning of the human body remains a mystery to medical science and that risks inherent in a given treatment may occur unexplainably though the treatment is administered skillfully. The occurrence of an injury that is a calculated risk of an approved course of conduct, standing alone, does not permit an inference of negligence.

Such an inference must be based on more than speculation. If it is to be drawn from the happening of an accident, there must be common knowledge or expert testimony that when such an accident occurs, it is more probably than not the result of negligence. (Siverson v. Weber (1962) 57 Cal.2d 834, 836, 22 Cal.Rptr. 337, 372 P.2d 97; Davis v. Memorial Hospital (1962) 58 Cal.2d 815, 817, 26 Cal.Rptr. 633, 376 P.2d 561; Cavero v. Franklin Gen. Benef. Soc. (1950) 36 Cal.2d 301, 309, 223 P.2d 471.) A showing that such an accident rarely occurs does not justify an inference of negligence without a further showing that when the rare event happens, it is more likely than not caused by negligence. (Siverson v. Weber, supra; Seneris v. Haas (1956) 45 Cal.2d 811, 824–826, 291 P.2d 915, 53 A.L.R.2d 124.)

Nor does evidence of specific acts of negligence justify an inference of negligence based on res ipsa loquitur, for the inferences the jury may reasonably draw from the happening of the accident alone obviously cannot be determined by evidence of the defendant's conduct.

There is no support in the record for a res ipsa loquitur instruction. Two unfortunate events combined to cause the injury, namely, the premature termination of anesthesia and the premature termination of surgery. The former was in the area of Dr. Selmants' responsibility, the latter in Dr. Gibbons'.

Although there is evidence that premature termination of anesthesia is unusual, there is no evidence that when it occurs it is more probably than not caused by negligence. On the contrary, there is a satisfactory medical explanation consistent with due care. There is an inherent risk that a patient may have an excessive amount of myelin on his nerves. This condition cannot be detected in advance. It either prevents the deposit of an adequate quantity of the anesthetizing agent on the nerve or accelerates the rate at which it disappears. Physiological and pharmacological evidence indicated that it was such an overabundance of myelin that caused the premature termination of anesthesia in this case.

Accordingly, there is no basis for an inference that premature termination of anesthesia is probably the result of negligence. The hiatus in proof cannot logically be filled by invoking the rarity of the result and specific evidence of negligence. The facts that premature termination is rare, that plaintiff felt that she could not breathe and her voice became squeaky after anesthesia, and that defendants did not discuss the anticipated duration of surgery shed no light on the question whether premature termination of anesthesia is ordinarily caused by negligence.

The record is likewise devoid of any evidence that premature termination of surgery in cases of this kind is ordinarily the result of negligence. Indeed, there is not even evidence that such termination is rare. Although there is evidence that Dr. Gibbons was negligent in failing to consider the relevant factors before making his decision to terminate the operation, such evidence of specific negligence sheds no light on the inferences that may be drawn from the happening of the accident itself.

The absence of any basis for invoking res ipsa loquitur against either defendant individually also forecloses invoking it against them jointly under Ybarra v. Spangard (1945) 25 Cal.2d 486, 154 P.2d 687, 162 A.L.R. 1258. The *Ybarra* case involved an accident that was clearly the result of someone's negligence, and the court imposed a burden of explanation upon all the defendants who had assumed control of the unconscious plaintiff. That case cannot reasonably be invoked when the accident itself affords no evidence of negligence.

The expansion of res ipsa loquitur undertaken in *Quintal* places too great a burden on the medical profession and may result in an undesirable limitation on the use of procedures involving inherent risks of injury even when due care is used. (Siverson v. Weber, supra, 57 Cal.2d 834, 22 Cal.Rptr. 337, 372 P.2d 97.) An anesthesiologist and a surgeon, confronted with one of the inherent risks of an operation not susceptible to advance calculation, may be found liable for any unfortunate consequence. In planning a course of action they may therefore feel compelled to consider not simply the best interests of the patient but the procedure that will be most readily justified to a lay jury.

The essence of *Quintal* is restated in the majority opinion, which first discredits rarity alone as a basis for res ipsa, but then states: "The likelihood of a negligent cause is increased if the low incidence of accidents when due care is used is combined with proof of specific acts of negligence of a type which would have caused the occurrence complained of. When these two facts are proved, the likelihood of a negligent cause may be sufficiently great that the jury may properly conclude that the accident was more probably than not the result of someone's negligence." That statement might be appropriate for counsel to make in arguing to the jury that it could infer from evidence of defendants' negligent conduct that such conduct caused the injury. It has no relation, however, to res ipsa loquitur, which involves the inferences that may be drawn from the mere happening of the accident.

KANTER v. ST. LOUIS, SPRINGFIELD & PEORIA R. R.

Appellate Court of Illinois, 1921.
218 Ill.App. 565.

MR. JUSTICE HEARD delivered the opinion of the court.

This was an action of trespass on the case brought by Adele Kanter, as administratrix of the estate of Samuel C. Kanter, deceased, against the St. Louis, Springfield and Peoria Railroad, an electrically operated interurban railroad extending through Madison and other counties in Illinois. The suit was brought to recover damages for the death of Samuel C. Kanter, which occurred on October 26, 1916, following the derailment of a car of defendant a short distance north of Edwardsville about 10 o'clock in the evening.

The declaration consisted of four counts. The first count averred that Samuel C. Kanter was a passenger on October 26, 1916, on the electric motor car of the defendant railroad extending through Springfield and beyond Staunton; that while riding upon the car in the exercise of due care and caution, south of Staunton and near Edwardsville, by reason of the carelessness, negligence and recklessness of the defendant and without warning to the said Kanter, the car became derailed and wrecked and began to burn and by reason of said derailment the said Kanter became caught in said wreckage and was so injured and burned that he died.

The second count alleged that Kanter was a passenger on the car of the defendant and while riding, in the exercise of due care and caution, south of Staunton near Edwardsville, the defendant by its servants, so carelessly, negligently and recklessly drove, operated and managed said car that it became derailed and wrecked, etc.

The third count was withdrawn by the plaintiff before trial.

[The fourth count charged specific acts of negligence in failing properly to maintain its equipment. Defendant pleaded the general issue and a special plea. The sustaining of a demurrer to this plea was upheld.]

The only other assignment of error argued by appellant in its brief and argument is "that the verdict and judgment are contrary to the overwhelming preponderance of the evidence."

We do not think there was any evidence tending to prove the fourth count of the declaration and the judgment must have been based upon the first and second counts, which are the counts where the charges of negligence were general, and the only question here is whether or not the evidence in the case is sufficient to sustain a judgment on these counts.

The evidence shows that deceased became a passenger on defendant's car at Springfield, Illinois, having purchased a ticket for St. Louis, Missouri. The train consisted of a single car in charge of a motorman and conductor.

The car left the track between Staunton and Edwardsville at a point where one of the rails was a half foot out of line; ran a distance of about 300 feet, part of the time on the side of the roadbed, tearing up and splintering ties, breaking two telegraph poles, one on the east and one on the west side of the track, striking and breaking off the 3-foot concrete abutment of a bridge and finally landing on its side in a ravine several feet below the level of the track, where it was burned by fire from an overturned stove.

Deceased at the time of the accident was riding in the front part of the car in the smoking compartment, which was separated by a partition from the main passenger compartment. He was in the exercise of ordinary care for his own safety. There were some trunks in the smoking compartment.

When the car was overturned deceased was pinned down by the trunks and before he could be extricated was burned to death.

Upon proof of these circumstances the question arises whether the doctrine of *res ipsa loquitur* applies. * * *

In this case the charges of negligence in the first and second counts of the declaration were general. The cars, tracks and equipment were under the control and management of appellant and the accident was such as in the ordinary course of things would not happen if those who had such control and management used proper care, and hence under the evidence heretofore mentioned the doctrine of *res ipsa loquitur* applies.

Applying this doctrine to such evidence, a *prima facie* case of negligence sufficient to justify a verdict was made against appellant and the burden rested upon it to overcome this presumption by evidence. Appellant attempted to overcome this presumption and prove that the derailment and death of deceased was the result of acts of vandalism committed by persons unknown.

The evidence clearly shows that at a point immediately north of the place of derailment, a curve, described by plaintiff's witness Shaffer as a 35-minute curve and by defendant's witness Martin as a 1-degree curve, began, which extended about 300 feet down a slight grade to a bridge, over a small creek or bottom. Plaintiff's witness Shaffer, who surveyed the premises, described the grade as a 7/10 of 1 per cent grade. Beginning at this curve, which at the northerly end was about 300 feet from the bridge, spikes were found, immediately after the accident, removed from the ties and rails for a distance of approximately 80 feet. In the first 40 feet the spikes were pulled by persons unknown from each side of the rail and in the 40 feet nearest to the bridge, the outside spike was pulled from the north rail from all of the ties. In all 45 spikes were found, which had been drawn, leaving straight, clean, vertical holes. The point where the car went off from the rails was about 40 feet from the beginning of the curve. North of the place where the marks of the car were first discerned on the track, at one place one spike had been driven under the rail from the inside, and a few ties further on from that place, two other spikes had been placed under the rail, one on top of the other, crosswise, in position, and these had also been driven from the inside, that is, their heads were inside of the rail and the points forced under the rail. This caused that rail to be 6 inches out of alignment with the other rails, and a few feet from there was the place where the car left the track and went onto the right of way.

Proof of these facts was sufficient to overcome the *prima facie* case and require a verdict for appellant unless there was other evidence in the case showing negligence on the part of appellant in the control, management or operation of the car in question which, combined with the acts of vandalism of the persons unknown, constituted the proximate cause of the accident. * * *

Edward L. Gass, who was the motorman in charge of the car, testified that as he approached the place of derailment he observed that a rail on the right-hand side 25 feet in front of him was half a foot out of line; that the car was equipped with an electric headlight which when set high enough cast a reflection for 900 or 1,000 feet, but that he could not see the rail further than 30 feet in front of him; that the light could be regulated by setting it higher or lower to reflect a greater or shorter distance ahead; that he as motorman had control of the regulation of the carbon; that he had it carrying high so that he could see a great distance ahead; that turning it up gives you a chance to see further ahead and turning it down gives you a chance to see the track closer to you; that when he saw the rail out of alignment he applied the automatic air brakes to the full extent, but was unable to stop the car before it landed down at the bottom of the grade at the bridge; that at Graney Siding, a little over half a mile before reaching the place of derailment, he put off the power and did not put it on again. Witness was not interrogated and did not testify as to what he was doing, if anything, from the time he shut off the power at Graney Siding until he saw the rail out of alignment. He was not interrogated and did not testify as to whether or not he was watching the track ahead.

A. G. Wilcoxon, who at the time of the accident was chief dispatcher for appellant, in answer to the question, "How far ahead could you see rails with that headlight?" testified, "A headlight will throw a distance—that headlight will throw possibly a distance of 900 or 1,000 feet on the rails; the rails will shine; it would have a glaring effect." Of course if the motorman had sooner seen the defect in the track he would have sooner applied the brakes and so checked the speed of the car somewhat if not entirely before the derailment. * * *

Appellant owed to deceased the duty of exercising the highest degree of care consistent with the practical operation of the road and the mode of conveyance adopted. Whether or not the evidence showed such an explanation of the accident as to relieve appellant from the charge of negligence contributing to bring about the accident was a question of fact for the jury. It was also a question of fact for the jury whether or not a car equipped as this car was and so operated that a rail 6 inches out of alignment was not seen by the motorman until within 25 feet of it was operated with the highest degree of care consistent with the practical operation of the road and the mode of conveyance adopted. The jury have evidently found against appellant on these questions.

Under the evidence the jury were justified in finding that appellant was negligent in the management, control and operation of the car in question and that such negligence, combined with the intervening acts of parties unknown, constituted the proximate cause of the accident and resultant death of deceased.

The judgment is affirmed.

Affirmed.

NIEHAUS, J., took no part.[79]

79. For a more successful defense which also included a showing of sabotage but was thought to negative the possibility of careless operation, see Gray v. Baltimore & O. R. Co., 24 F.2d 671, 59 A.L.R. 461 (7th Cir., 1928) (saboteur had opened switch and turned the signal so that it showed a clear track to the engineer).

Less spectacular, but more often available, is a demonstration that the accident was caused solely by a defect which could not be prevented nor detected by reasonable care in the present stage of the arts. Chesapeake & O. R. Co. v. Baker, 149 Va. 549, 140 S.E. 648; 149 Va. 549, 141 S.E. 753; 150 Va. 647, 143 S.E. 299 (1927–1928) (derailment due to transverse fissure in a steel rail. Today such fissures may be detected by the Sperry car. See N. Y. Times, Dec. 17, 1941, p. 7, col. 6.) Ash v. Child's Dining Hall Co., 231 Mass. 86, 120 N.E. 396, 4 A.L.R. 1556 (1918) (injury caused by infinitesimal tack in blueberry pie). Is there a logical basis for distinguishing such cases from the Kanter case?

Even where such evidence is not strong enough to entitle defendant to judgment as matter of law, the court or jury may find as a matter of fact that reasonable men would not have found the defect. Rayl v. Syndicate Bldg. Co., 118 Cal.App. 396, 5 P.2d 476 (1931); Levine v. Union & N. H. Trust Co., 127 Conn. 435, 17 A.2d 500 (1941).

Probably the most common line of defense in these cases is a showing of the precautions that defendant did take together with evidence or argument that these precautions were reasonable under the circumstances. A typical case of this kind is Fallo v. New York, N. H. & H. R. Co., 123 Conn. 81, 192 A. 712 (1937), in which plaintiff, a highway traveler, was struck by a flying bolt at the time when a passenger train of defendant was passing nearby. The evidence showed the bolt to be of the type used in defendant's braking mechanism. The defendant offered evidence that three trains, one of which was that which was passing the automobile at the time of the accident, had been inspected before it occurred and that no bolts such as that which caused the injury were missing or defective.

The record in this case further characterizes the evidence on inspection thus: "The Defendant makes a regular ex-

SECTION 3. CAUSATION AND ITS COUSINS

This section deals with the *extent* of a defendant's liability for the injuries that follow after an admittedly wrongful act. For the most part the problem concerns the limits within which the trier of fact *may* impose liability, through some attention has been given in the cases to the language in which instructions to the jury should be cast.

Probably no subject in the law of torts has been more written about than proximate cause. It is the kind of thing that involves interesting cases and invites speculation.[80] Yet the sort of problem which is most challenging to the theorist is presented only by the rare, freak case (the Polemis and Palsgraf cases furnish examples). The practitioner, to be sure, will often be vexed with questions of cause. Plaintiff has the burden of proof on the issue of proximate cause. This means that before he can get to the jury he must put in direct or circumstantial evidence which tends to show that *more probably than not* his injury resulted in fact from some act or neglect of the defendant. In most cases this will be easy, but in a significant number it is not. A man is found dead alongside a railroad track near a crossing. The marks on his body may point to his being killed by a train. Perhaps the time he was killed may be narrowed down by medical testimony and testimony as to when he was seen walking in the general direction of the tracks, and all this may afford an inference as to the identity of the train that struck him. It will then be possible—it always is—to get testimony that the bell and whistle were not sounded for the crossing. In a state where the burden of proving contributory negligence is on defendant, has the plaintiff made a case for the jury? He has shown that a negligently

amination of all its trains leaving New York, and again at New Haven. These inspections are designed to discover any defects in the equipment and would include any bolts of this kind. The four car inspectors who made the inspection in New Haven of these trains on that day found no bolts of this kind missing in any of the three trains in question. The men who have charge of the inspections at both the Grand Central and Pennsylvania stations produced the records of the inspections made of these trains on that day, and these inspections showed no bolts missing or defective." Other typical cases where defendant relied—at least, in part—on direct evidence of inspection are Jianou v. Pickwick Stages System, 111 Cal.App. 754, 296 P. 108 (1931); Sand Springs Park v. Shrader, 82 Okl. 244, 198 P. 983, 22 A.L.R. 593 (1921).

80. Even courts are easily led into long and scholarly—often quite unnecessary—dissertations on proximate cause. Three Wisconsin cases may serve as examples, Berrafato v. Exner, 194 Wis. 149, 216 N.W. 165 (1927); Hamus v. Weber, 199 Wis. 320, 226 N.W. 392 (1929); Osborne v. Montgomery, 203 Wis. 233, 234 N.W. 372 (1931). In the first case a very simple question as to cause was presented. The trial court's charge could have been understood by the jury to mean that there could in law be only *one* proximate cause of an accident. Under the facts presented there was considerable likelihood that the jury—if properly instructed—would have found two such causes. The charge was quite properly held to be misleading under the circumstances. In the last two cases there was no possible problem of proximate cause (even of cause in fact if negligence was established) yet the opinions all contain an elaborate treatment of the whole problem.

operated train struck his decedent. But has he shown any basis for a conclusion by the jury that the decedent was struck *because* the train was negligently run? The want of a signal may have had no part in the tragedy. Deceased may have fainted on the track, he may have seen the train and used poor judgment in trying to beat it, he may have been so preoccupied that he would have failed to hear the whistle just as he failed to hear the roar of the train or see its headlight, and so on. A good many judges would say the issue was left in the realm of speculation, surmise, and conjecture, and take it from the jury.

Other serious problems arise where each of several wrongdoers causes *some* of the total damage and the plaintiff is confronted with the demand that he show the separate damage attributable to each or forego damages altogether; conversely there may be several wrongdoers, with harm caused by less than all.

The tort practitioner is probably troubled more by such questions of cause-in-fact and the burden of proving a causal relation than he is by all the rest of the subject put together. Yet this branch of the matter has received relatively scant attention from scholars. It is after the relation of cause-in-fact has been established that the more obvious applications of social policy, philosophy, and jurisprudence are brought into play to limit the *extent* of defendant's liability for the results of his wrong. And most of the cases in the following section treat judicial reaction to this problem. Yet, because it is so seldom noted, it is worth while to point out here how much room there really is for the interplay of political and other non-logical considerations in applying the canons of proof. The rules themselves are supposed to be (1) mere incidents of procedure, and (2) mere applications of rules of general, scientific reasoning. Consider, however, the case of the pedestrian and train, mentioned above. On the facts given many courts would say that the plaintiff had not sustained his burden of proof upon the issue of proximate cause. This ruling means (1) the plaintiff loses his case as effectively as though he had been barred by some substantive rule of law, like contributory negligence, and (2) the court happened to choose a scientific premise, but on a basis which from this point of view is little short of capricious. The premise is something like this: Of the total number of pedestrians struck at railway crossings by engines which have not whistled it cannot be said that a majority would have been avoided being struck if the whistle had been blown. Now the premise itself is unassailable enough. So complete is our present lack of accurate quantitative data about human behavior, that an agnostic premise is generally not only safe but demanded by any scientific standard. Of course some generalizations would command wide popular acceptance (though they may someday be shown not to have deserved it). But the area is vast wherein thoughtful men would either disagree or refuse to guess on which side of the line the greater probability lies. To adopt an agnostic premise throughout this field would paralyze too much of the law, and courts do not do so. They are constantly asserting or assuming generalizations about human behavior which either rest on the court's own very fallible notions about it, or spring from considerations of policy and expediency. This is more apparent in *res ipsa loquitur* cases than elsewhere, but it marks the whole field of circumstantial proof.

Throughout these materials both interplay and confusion will be evident between notions expressed under the rubric of "causation" and a range of other concepts, often tagged as relating to "duty", which are concerned instead with the basis for tort liability, the interests to be protected and the relations to be recognized between parties, standards of care and, generally, the extent of liability, when liability is imposed.[81]

WOLF v. KAUFMANN

Supreme Court of New York, Appellate Division, First Department, 1929.
227 App.Div. 281, 237 N.Y.S. 550.

FINCH, J. The defendants appeal from an order setting aside the verdict of a jury in their favor and granting a new trial. The order should be reversed in so far as it grants a new trial, and the complaint dismissed, upon the ground that, assuming the existence of all the facts claimed by the plaintiff upon the trial, no cause of action exists against the defendants.

The action is in negligence to recover damages for the death of plaintiff's intestate. The plaintiff's cause of action is based upon the fact that the deceased was found injured and unconscious at the foot of a flight of stairs in premises owned by the defendants, coupled with the fact that the hallway was unlighted, in violation of section 76 of the Tenement House Law (as amended by Laws 1923, c. 796) which provides:

"Every light required by this section * * * shall be kept burning by the owner every night from sunset to sunrise throughout the year."

There was a sharp issue of fact as to whether the accident happened before or after sunset, and a controversy over the admission in evidence of a hospital record containing the report of a police officer based upon hearsay information obtained by him after the accident. The receipt of this report was error, under section 374–a of the Civil Practice Act, as added by chapter 532 of the Laws of 1928, for the reasons set forth in our decision of even date in the case of Needle v. New York Railways Corporation, 227 App.Div. 276, 237 N.Y.S. 547, and in itself justified the setting aside of the verdict.

81. The problems treated in this section are discussed in H. Hart and A. Honoré, Causation in the Law (1959); R. Keeton, Legal Cause in the Law of Torts (1963); James and Perry, Legal Cause, 60 Yale L.J. 761 (1951); Malone, Ruminations on Cause-In-Fact, 9 Stan.L.Rev. 60 (1956); and Calabresi, Concerning Cause and the Law of Torts: An Essay for Harry Kalven, 43 U.Chi.L.Rev. 69 (1975).

A fatal defect exists, however, in the case of the plaintiff, in that, assuming the accident to have occurred after sunset and the hallway to have been unlighted, there is a total absence of proof of any causal connection between the accident and the absence of flight. The deceased was shown to have entered the premises and was heard by tenants upon the stairs and in the hallway. Following a thud, also heard by tenants, he was found at the foot of the stairs. No one saw him fall. Without further proof, it would be solely a conjecture for a jury to draw the conclusion that the deceased fell down the stairs because of the absence of light. A case closely analogous to the one at bar upon the facts, but containing an element not present in the case before us, serves to differentiate the case at bar from one where a failure to furnish light might be found to be a proximate cause of the accident. In Bornstein v. Faden, 149 App.Div. 37, 133 N.Y.S. 608, affirmed 208 N.Y. 605, 102 N.E. 1099, the action was brought against the owner of a tenement house to recover for the death of a tenant due to the alleged negligence of the defendant in failing to light the public hallways as required by section 76 of the Tenement House Law.

In that case there was an eyewitness to the accident, who came out of an apartment with the decedent, and was within a few feet of her when she fell. This witness testified that the deceased was walking slowly with her hand on the railing, and that, as she turned to go down the stairs, she slipped and fell. The court held that the Legislature, in enacting section 76 of the Tenement House Law, contemplated that the light to be maintained should be sufficient to light the lower stairway and to enable people lawfully using the stairs, by exercising proper care, to see the steps and avoid slipping or missing their foothold. The court further held that the evidence tended to show that the decedent slipped, and that there was sufficient evidence of negligence on the part of the defendants to take the case to the jury, since the evidence there placed the decedent in the act of descending the stairs in the usual way, and that the absence of light sufficient to light the entire lower stairway created the inference that she slipped because of the darkness.

In the case at bar there is nothing to show that the accident occurred in the use of the stairs in the ordinary manner. In the absence of such proof, there are many possible conjectures for the accident. It follows that the order appealed from should be reversed in so far as it grants a new trial, with costs, and the complaint dismissed, with costs.

Order in so far as it grants a new trial reversed, with costs and disbursements, and the complaint dismissed, with costs. Order filed. All concur.[82]

82. Compare Ingersoll v. Liberty Bank of Buffalo, 278 N.Y. 1, 14 N.E.2d 828 (1938); Mutterperl v. Lake Spofford Hotel, Inc., 106 N.H. 538, 216 A.2d 35 (1965).

REYNOLDS v. TEXAS & PAC. R. CO.

Supreme Court of Louisiana, 1885.
37 La.Ann. 694.

The opinion of the Court was delivered by FENNER, J. The plaintiff and his wife claim damages of the defendant company for injuries suffered by the wife and caused by the alleged negligence of the company.

Mr. Reynolds, with his wife, sister-in-law, three small children and two colored attendants, had purchased tickets as passengers on the defendant road, and were at the depot at Morrogh Station for the purpose of boarding the east-bound train, which was due at that station at about midnight, but, being behind time, did not reach there till about two o'clock in the morning.

[The court decided that the evidence justified a finding of negligence in failing sufficiently to light the stairway down which plaintiff fell, in view of the lack of railing and the narrowness of the platform at the bottom of it.]

The train was behind time. Several witnesses testify that passengers were warned to "hurry up." Mrs. Reynolds, a corpulent woman, weighing two hundred and fifty pounds, emerging from the bright light of the sitting-room which naturally exaggerated the outside darkness, and hastening down these unlighted steps, made a misstep in some way and was precipitated beyond the narrow platform in front and down the slope beyond, incurring the serious injuries complained of.

Upon what grounds do the company claim exemption from liability? * * *

2nd. It contends that, even conceding the negligence of the company in the above respect, it does not follow that the accident to plaintiff was necessarily caused thereby, but that she might well have made the misstep and fallen even had it been broad daylight. We concede that this is possible, and recognize the distinction between post hoc and propter hoc. But where the negligence of the defendant greatly multiplies the chances of accident to the plaintiff, and is of a character naturally leading to its occurrence, the mere possibility that it might have happened without the negligence is not sufficient to break the chain of cause and effect between the negligence and the injury. Courts, in such matters, consider the natural and ordinary course of events, and do not indulge in fanciful suppositions. The whole tendency of the evidence connects the accident with the negligence.

[The judgment for plaintiff was affirmed.]

DILLON v. TWIN STATE GAS & ELECTRIC CO.

Supreme Court of New Hampshire, 1932.
85 N.H. 449, 163 A. 111.

[Plaintiff's decedent, a trespassing boy, fell off bridge, grabbed power company's charged high voltage line.]

ALLEN, J.

* * *

The evidence tended to show that changes in the construction and arrangement of the lamp and its wires were practical. * * *

The defendant, however, makes the contention that it owed no duty of care to those not using the bridge in a rightful manner to make their wrongful use safe. If a duty might arise towards such a person as a workman painting the girders, yet it says there was none towards a boy in the decedent's position of climbing and mounting the girders without right.

The present state of the law here in force does not support the claim. * * *

A rule that no care is due one engaged in wrongful conduct is unreasonable without substantial qualifications. * * *

* * * [C]onceding no right to mount the framework of a bridge in play, the defendant here may not be relieved from duty towards those of whose probable presence it had notice, however their conduct is to be regarded. * * *

If A's conduct towards B is wrongful, it should also be wrongful towards C if the only difference between B and C is that B is not, while C is, engaged in a wrong unrelated to A. C's wrong is not legally causal of his injury merely if it places him in the same position as B is in, and he should recover as well as B. Reasonable care is due both. The only qualification is that C's wrong might be a circumstance affecting A's care in his case. It may be that in reasonable conduct one will use less care towards wrongdoers than others. But the duty to use such care as the circumstances demand is not modified, and the difference is an issue of fact and not of law. * * *

If on a private road two stolen cars meet, one driven by its thief and with a passenger ignorant of the theft, and the other driven by an innocent purchaser from its thief and with a passenger aware of its theft, the varying wrongs of the drivers and passengers towards the owners of the cars would not be enough in any instance to affect their respective rights and duties to receive and use care. If the differences are circumstances affecting care, the standard of duty to use the care reasonably required is not lowered. Their wrongs towards the owners are not the causes of injury from negligence among themselves or from others, and recovery for the injury gives no profit from their own wrongdoing. * * *

The circumstances of the decedent's death give rise to an unusual issue of its cause. In leaning over from the girder and losing his balance he was entitled to no protection from the defendant to keep from falling. Its only liability was in exposing him to the danger of charged wires. If but for the current in the wires he would have fallen down on the floor of the bridge or into the river, he would without doubt have been either killed or seriously injured. Although he died from electrocution, yet, if by reason of his preceding loss of balance he was bound to fall except for the intervention of the current, he either did not have long to live or was to be maimed. In such an outcome of his loss of balance, the defendant deprived him, not of a life of normal expectancy, but of one too short to be given pecuniary allowance, in one alternative, and not of normal, but of limited, earning capacity, in the other.

If it were found that he would have thus fallen with death probably resulting, the defendant would not be liable, unless for conscious suffering found to have been sustained from the shock. In that situation his life or earning capacity had no value. To constitute actionable negligence there must be damage, and damage is limited to those elements the statute prescribes.

If it should be found that but for the current he would have fallen with serious injury, then the loss of life or earning capacity resulting from the electrocution would be measured by its value in such injured condition. Evidence that he would be crippled would be taken into account in the same manner as though he had already been crippled.

His probable future but for the current thus bears on liability as well as damages. Whether the shock from the current threw him back on the girder or whether he would have recovered his balance, with or without the aid of the wire he took hold of, if it had not been charged, are issues of fact, as to which the evidence as it stands may lead to different conclusions.

Exception overruled.[83]

83. See Peaslee, Multiple Causation and Damage, 47 Harv.L.Rev. 1127 (1934). If plaintiff's life expectancy was shortened by silicosis caused by wrongful exposure to industrial dust, liability for which is barred by a statute of limitations, and his remaining life expectancy is further reduced by additional exposures as to which action is not barred, defendant is liable only for the further shortening caused by the exposure within the limitation period, Pieczonka v. Pullman Co., 89 F.2d 353 (2d Cir. 1937); cf. Golden v. Lerch Bros., 203 Minn. 211, 281 N.W. 249, 253 (1937). Similarly if a physician's malpractice aggravates a preexisting illness he is theoretically liable only to the extent of the aggravation; as a practical matter, however, the burden may be placed on the doctor to bear all the damages of plaintiff's illness following the negligent treatment unless he can establish a reasonable apportionment, Fosgate v. Corona, 66 N.J. 268, 330 A.2d 355 (1974).

Where it seems clear that a patient would have died even if the doctor had not been negligent, the doctor's malpractice may be considered not to be a cause of the patient's death, Barnett v. Chelsea and Kensington Hospital Management Committee [1969] 1 Q.B. 428 (arsenic poisoning; victim came to hospital too late, the court thought, to have been saved by proper treatment); compare Rewis v. United States, 503 F.2d 1202 (5th Cir. 1974), where doctor

SUMMERS v. TICE

Supreme Court of California, in Bank, 1948.
33 Cal.2d 80, 199 P.2d 1, 5 A.L.R.2d 91.

CARTER, JUSTICE. Each of the two defendants appeals from a judgment against them in an action for personal injuries. Pursuant to stipulation the appeals have been consolidated.

Plaintiff's action was against both defendants for an injury to his right eye and face as the result of being struck by bird shot discharged from a shotgun. The case was tried by the court without a jury and the court found that on November 20, 1945, plaintiff and the two defendants were hunting quail on the open range. Each of the defendants was armed with a 12 gauge shotgun loaded with shells containing 7½ size shot. Prior to going hunting plaintiff discussed the hunting procedure with defendants, indicating that they were to exercise care when shooting and to "keep in line." In the course of hunting plaintiff proceeded up a hill, thus placing the hunters at the points of a triangle. The view of defendants with reference to plaintiff was unobstructed and they knew his location. Defendant Tice flushed a quail which rose in flight to a ten foot elevation and flew between plaintiff and defendants. Both defendants shot at the quail, shooting in plaintiff's direction. At that time defendants were 75 yards from plaintiff. One shot struck plaintiff in his eye and another in his upper lip. Finally it was found by the court that as the direct

had misdiagnosed aspirin poisoning as virus and had prescribed aspirin, for example of determined judicial resistance to expert suggestions that the victim would have died anyway. And, where fish would have died anyway, because of drop in temperature of river water, had a nuclear power plant not been warming the stream, it has been held that the plant is not liable for fish kills during shutdown, State, Dep't of Environmental Protection v. Jersey Central Power & Light Co., 69 N.J. 102, 351 A.2d 337 (1976).

Consider Kuhn v. Banker, 133 Ohio St. 304, 13 N.E.2d 242, 115 A.L.R. 292 (1938), where plaintiff was able to prove that defendant, a surgeon who had set her fractured leg, was negligent in failing to detect loss of bony union by absorption after removal of the cast. Nevertheless plaintiff was unable to recover anything because the testimony showed that even if the condition had been detected the chances were somewhat against the successful production of a new bony union (though the chance was great enough to warrant making the attempt). While this testimony should clearly have affected the measure of recovery, why could not the court have evaluated the chance of which defendant's negligence had deprived his patient? See valuable discussion in McCormick, Damages, section 31 (1935).

Suppose plaintiff suffers permanent leg injury, with ascertainable prospective damages, as a result of the defendant's negligent driving, but before the trial he is shot in that leg by a robber and it is amputated. See Baker v. Willoughby [1970] A.C. 467; McGregor, Successive Causes of Personal Injury, 33 Modern L.Rev. 378 (1970); Strachan, The Scope and Application of the "But For" Causal Test, 33 Modern L. Rev. 386 (1970). Is this problem the same as that in Mayor, etc., of New York v. Lord, page 51 above? See Cohn, Note, 86 L.Q.Rev. 449 (1970). Also see Buchalski v. Universal Marine Corporation, 393 F.Supp. 246 (D.W.D.Wash.1975) (disabling heart attack after and unrelated to injury caused by fault of defendant); compare Jurney v. Lubeznik, 72 Ill.App.2d 117, 218 N.E.2d 799 (1966) (injured leg amputated because of subsequent unrelated injury); Victorson v. Milwaukee & Sub. Transport Co., 70 Wis.2d 336, 234 N.W.2d 332 (1975) (disabling stroke after and unrelated to injuries for which defendant was liable).

result of the shooting by defendants the shots struck plaintiff as above mentioned and that defendants were negligent in so shooting and plaintiff was not contributorily negligent.

[The court felt that a finding in plaintiff's favor on the issues of negligence, contributory negligence, and assumption of risk was warranted.]

The problem presented in this case is whether the judgment against both defendants may stand. It is argued by defendants that they are not joint tort feasors, and thus jointly and severally liable, as they were not acting in concert, and that there is not sufficient evidence to show which defendant was guilty of the negligence which caused the injuries—the shooting by Tice or that by Simonson. * *

[The trial court] determined that the negligence of both defendants was the legal cause of the injury—or that both were responsible. Implicit in such finding is the assumption that the court was unable to ascertain whether the shots were from the gun of one defendant or the other or one shot from each of them. The one shot that entered plaintiff's eye was the major factor in assessing damages and that shot could not have come from the gun of both defendants. It was from one or the other only.

It has been held that where a group of persons are on a hunting party, or otherwise engaged in the use of firearms, and two of them are negligent in firing in the direction of a third person who is injured thereby, both of those so firing are liable for the injury suffered by the third person, although the negligence of only one of them could have caused the injury. * * * The same rule has been applied in criminal cases (State v. Newberg, 129 Or. 564, 278 P. 568, 63 A.L.R. 1225), and both drivers have been held liable for the negligence of one where they engaged in a racing contest causing an injury to a third person. Saisa v. Lilja, 1 Cir., 76 F.2d 380. These cases speak of the action of defendants as being in concert as the ground of decision, yet it would seem they are straining that concept and the more reasonable basis appears in Oliver v. Miles, supra. There two persons were hunting together. Both shot at some partridges and in so doing shot across the highway injuring plaintiff who was travelling on it. The court stated they were acting in concert and thus both were liable. The court then stated [110 So. 668]: "We think that * * * each is liable for the resulting injury to the boy, although no one can say definitely who actually shot him. *To hold otherwise would be to exonerate both from liability, although each was negligent, and the injury resulted from such negligence.*" [Emphasis added.] 110 So. p. 668. It is said in the Restatement: "For harm resulting to a third person from the tortious conduct of another, a person is liable if he * * * (b) knows that the other's conduct constitutes a breach of duty and gives substantial assistance or encouragement to the other so to conduct himself, or (c) gives substantial assistance to the other in accomplishing a tortious result and his own conduct, separately considered, constitutes a breach of duty to the third person." (Rest., Torts, sec. 876(b)(c).) Under subsection (b) the example is given: "A and B are members of a hunting party. Each of them in the presence of the other shoots across a public road at an animal, this being negligent as to persons on the road. A hits the animal. B's bullet strikes C, a traveler on the road. A is liable to C." (Rest., Torts, sec. 876(b), Com., Illus. 3.) An illustration given under subsection (c) is the same as above except the factor of both defendants shooting is missing and joint liability is not imposed. It is further said that: "If two forces are actively operating, one because of the actor's negligence, the other not because of any misconduct on his part, and each of itself is sufficient to bring about harm to another, the actor's negligence may be held by the jury to be a substantial factor in bringing it about." (Rest., Torts, sec. 432.) Dean Wigmore has this to say: "When two or more persons by their acts are possibly the sole cause of a harm, or when two or more acts of the same person are possibly the sole cause, and the plaintiff has introduced evidence that the one of the two persons, or the one of the same person's two acts, is culpable, then the defendant has the burden of proving that the other person, or his other act, was the sole cause of the harm. (b) * * * The real reason for the rule that each joint tortfeasor is responsible for the whole damage is the practical unfairness of denying the injured person redress simply because he cannot prove how much damage each did, when it is certain that between them they did all; let them be the ones to apportion it among themselves. Since, then, the difficulty of proof is the reason, the rule should apply whenever the harm has plural causes, and not merely when they acted in conscious concert. * * *" (Wigmore, Select Cases on the Law of Torts, sec. 153.) Similarly Professor Carpenter has said: "[Suppose] the case where A and B independently shoot at C and but one bullet touches C's body. In such case, such proof as is ordinarily required that either A or B shot C, of course fails. It is suggested that there should be a relaxation of the proof required of the plaintiff * * * where the injury occurs as the result of one where more than one independent force is operating, and it is impossible to determine that the force set in operation by defendant did not in fact constitute a cause of the damage, and where it may have caused the damage, but the plaintiff is unable to establish that it was a cause." (20 Cal.L.Rev. 406.)

When we consider the relative position of the parties and the results that would flow if plaintiff was required to pin the injury on one of the defendants only, a requirement that the burden of proof on that subject be shifted to defendants becomes manifest. They are both wrongdoers—both negligent toward plaintiff. They brought about a situation where the negligence of one of them injured the plaintiff, hence it should rest with them each to absolve himself if he can. The injured party has been placed by defendants in the unfair position of pointing to which defendant caused the harm. If one can escape the other may also and plaintiff is remediless. Ordinarily defendants are in a far better position to offer evidence to determine which one caused the injury. This reasoning has recently found favor in this Court. In a quite analogous situation this Court held that a patient injured while unconscious on an operating table in a hospital could hold all or any of the persons who had any connection with the operation even though he could not select the particular acts by the particular person which led to his disability. Ybarra v. Spangard, 25 Cal.2d 486, 154 P.2d 687, 162 A.L.R. 1258. There the Court was considering whether the patient could avail himself of res ipsa loquitur, rather than where the burden of proof lay, yet the effect of the decision is that plaintiff has made out a case when he has produced evidence which gives rise to an inference of negligence which was the proximate cause of the injury. It is up to defendants to explain the cause of the injury. It was there said: "If the doctrine is to continue to serve a useful purpose, we should not forget that 'the particular force and justice of the rule, regarded as a presumption throwing upon the party charged the duty of producing evidence, consists in the circumstance that the chief evidence of the true cause, whether culpable or innocent, is practically accessible to him but inaccessible to the injured person.'" 25 Cal.2d at page 490, 154 P.2d at page 689, 162 A.L.R. 1258. Similarly in the instant case plaintiff is not able to establish which of defendants caused his injury.

The foregoing discussion disposes of the authorities cited by defendants such as Kraft v. Smith, 24 Cal.2d 124, 148 P.2d 23, and Hernandez v. Southern California Gas Co., 213 Cal. 384, 2 P.2d 360, stating the general rule that one defendant is not liable for the independent tort of the other defendant, or that ordinarily the plaintiff must show a causal connection between the negligence and the injury. There was an entire lack of such connection in the Hernandez case and there were not several negligent defendants, one of whom must have caused the injury.

Defendants rely upon Christensen v. Los Angeles Electrical Supply Co., 112 Cal.App. 629, 297 P. 614, holding that a defendant is not liable where he negligently knocked down with his car a pedestrian and a third person then ran over the prostrate person. That involves the question of intervening cause which we do not have here. Moreover it is out of harmony with the current rule on that subject and was properly questioned in Hill v. Peres, 136 Cal.App. 132, 28 P.2d 946 (hearing in this Court denied), and must be deemed disapproved. See, Mosley v. Arden Farms Co., 26 Cal.2d 213, 157 P.2d 372, 158 A.L.R. 872; Sawyer v. Southern California Gas Co., 206 Cal. 366, 274 P. 544; 6 Cal.Jur. Ten Yr.Supp., Automobiles, sec. 349; 19 Cal. Jur. 570–572.

Cases are cited for the proposition that where two or more tort feasors acting independently of each other cause an injury to plaintiff, they are not joint tort feasors and plaintiff must establish the portion of the damage caused by each, even though it is impossible to prove the portion of the injury caused by each. * * * In view of the foregoing discussion it is apparent that defendants in cases like the present one may be treated as liable on the same basis as joint tort feasors, and hence the last cited cases are distinguishable inasmuch as they involve independent tort feasors.

In addition to that, however, it should be pointed out that the same reasons of policy and justice shift the burden to each of defendants to absolve himself if he can—relieving the wronged person of the duty of apportioning the injury to a particular defendant, apply here where we are concerned with whether plaintiff is required to supply evidence for the apportionment of damages. If defendants are independent tort feasors and thus each liable for the damage caused by him alone, and, at least, where the matter of apportionment is incapable of proof, the innocent wronged party should not be deprived of his right to redress. The wrongdoers should be left to work out between themselves any apportionment. See, Colonial Ins. Co. v. Industrial Acc. Com., 29 Cal.2d 79, 172 P.2d 884. Some of the cited cases refer to the difficulty of apportioning the burden of damages between the independent tort feasors, and say that where factually a correct division cannot be made, the trier of fact may make it the best it can, which would be more or less a guess, stressing the factor that the wrongdoers are not in a position to complain of uncertainty. California Orange Co. v. Riverside P. C. Co., supra.

It is urged that plaintiff now has changed the theory of his case in claiming a concert of action; that he did not plead or prove such concert. From what has been said it is clear that there has been no change in theory. The joint liability, as well as the lack of knowledge as to which defendant was liable, was pleaded and the proof developed the case under either theory. We have seen that for the reasons of policy discussed herein, the case is based upon the legal proposition that, under the circumstances here presented, each defendant is liable for the whole damage whether they are deemed to be acting in concert or independently.

The judgment is affirmed.

GIBSON, C. J., and SHENK, EDMONDS, TRAYNOR, SCHAUER, and SPENCE, JJ., concur.[84]

84. See, similarly, Haddigan v. Harkins, 441 F.2d 844 (3d Cir. 1970), where decedent was whacked substantially simultaneously by two negligently driven cars, and no one knows which whack killed her.

HALL v. E. I. DU PONT DE NEMOURS & CO., INC.

United States District Court for the Eastern District of New York, 1972.
345 F.Supp. 353.

[The facts and discussion of the bases of liability are set out at page 115 et seq. above.

WEINSTEIN, DISTRICT JUDGE.

* * *

Plaintiffs contend that they should be relieved of the usual burden of proving a causal connection between each of their injuries and a particular manufacturer. Their problem is that a blasting cap found and exploded by a child often destroys what will be the only reliable evidence of its manufacturer—markings on the casing. As a solution they invoke Section 433B of the Second Restatement of Torts, which provides in pertinent part:

> (2) Where the tortious conduct of two or more actors has combined to bring about harm to the plaintiff, and one or more of the actors seeks to limit his liability on the ground that the harm is capable of apportionment among them, the burden of proof as to the apportionment is upon each such actor.
>
> (3) Where the conduct of two or more actors is tortious, and it is proved that harm has been caused to the plaintiff by only one of them, but there is uncertainty as to which one has caused it, the burden is upon each such actor to prove that he has not caused the harm.

Subsection (2) is based primarily on cases in which water pollution has been caused by independent actors. Its applicability depends on an initial showing by the plaintiff that each defendant has done something—not necessarily simultaneously—to cause the damage although it cannot be demonstrated "that any one defendant was responsible for the entire injury or any specified part of it." 1 Harper & James, The Law of Torts § 10.1 at 708 (1956). Courts have held that where the injury "cannot be apportioned with reasonable certainty among the individual wrongdoers, all of the wrongdoers will be held jointly and severally liable for the entire damages. * * *" Landers v. East Texas Salt Water Disposal Co., 151 Tex. 251, 256, 248 S.W.2d 731, 734 (1952); see also cases cited in 1 Harper & James, supra, § 10.1 at 706–09.

In the instant case plaintiffs have alleged that defendants' conduct combined to cause injury at the point of the labeling and designing of the caps. The rule embodied in Section 433B(2) of the Second Restatement of Torts, shifting the burden of apportionment to the defendants, is applicable only as a corollary principle of proof to plaintiffs' main theories that defendants engaged in concerted action, or operated as a joint enterprise, with respect to the labeling and design of the caps.

Subsection (3) of Section 433B shifts the burden of proving causation to independently-acting defendants. It arises not from the problem of combined causation but rather from alternative causation of injury. The best known example is Summers v. Tice, 33 Cal. 2d 80, 199 P.2d 1 (1948), in which a hunter's injury could have been caused by only one of his two independently negligent companions. The reason for shifting the burden of proving causation, as with the burden of proving apportionment, is

> the injustice of permitting proved wrongdoers, who among them have inflicted an injury upon the entirely innocent plaintiff, to escape liability merely because the nature of their conduct and the resulting harm has made it difficult or impossible to prove which of them has caused the harm. Restatement of Torts, Second § 433B, comment f (1965).

* * * See also Wigmore, Joint Tortfeasors and Severance of Damages: Making the Innocent Party Suffer Without Redress, 17 Ill.L.Rev. 458 (1923).

* * *

* * * Defendants argue that * * * the caps may have been made by other, unnamed manufacturers. In their supporting papers defendants raise the possibility that the caps involved in the accidents may have come from Canadian or other foreign manufacturers or from domestic firms no longer in business and not named in the complaint. * * *

The possibility—admitted by plaintiffs—that the caps may have come from other, unnamed sources, does not affect plaintiffs' burden of proof. Plaintiffs must show by a preponderance of the evidence—i. e., that it is more probable than not—that the caps involved in the accidents were the products of the named defendant-manufacturers. Plaintiffs do not have to identify which one of the defendant-manufacturers made each injury-causing cap. * * * It must be more probable than not that an injury was caused by a cap made by some one of the named defendant manufacturers, though which one is unknown. See, e. g., Ball, The Moment of Truth: Probability Theory and Standards of Proof, 14 Vand.L.Rev. 807 (1961); Tribe, Trial by Mathematics: Precision and Ritual in the Legal Process, 84 Harv. L.Rev. 1329, 1341 n. 37 (1971); J. M. Maguire et al., Cases and Materials on Evidence, 547, 550 (5th ed. 1965); citations in Rosado v. Wyman, 322 F.Supp. 1173 (E.D.N.Y.1970).

Defendants argue further that the requisite causal connection between the unknown member or members of the group and the injuries cannot be established because the defendants' conduct was not in "close physical and chronological connection to the injurious results." * * * The key requirement thus far imposed in the cases has been that the risk-creating conduct be "simultaneous in time, or substantially so, and [be] * * * of substantially the same character, creating substantially the same risk of harm, on the part of each actor." Restatement of Torts, Second § 433B, comment h (1965). The required chronological nexus, in other words, is not between defendants' conduct and injury, but among the conduct of the several defendants. Plaintiffs' allegations satisfy these criteria.

If plaintiffs can establish by a preponderance of the evidence that the injury-causing caps were the product of some unknown one of the named defendants, that each named defendant breached a duty of care owed to plaintiffs and that these breaches were substantially concurrent in time and of a similar nature, they will be entitled to a shift of the burden of proof on the issue of causation. * * * [85]

COREY v. HAVENER

Supreme Judicial Court of Massachusetts, 1902.
182 Mass. 250, 65 N.E. 69.

TWO ACTIONS OF TORT by the same plaintiff against different defendants for injuries to the plaintiff and to his wagon caused by the alleged negligence of both defendants each operating a separate gasoline motor tricycle at an illegal and dangerous rate of speed and frightening the plaintiff's horse. * * *

In the Superior Court the two cases were tried together before Pierce, J. It appeared, that the plaintiff, who was very deaf and could only hear by the use of an ear trumpet, was driving slowly in a wagon along Shrewsbury Street, a public street and main thoroughfare in Worcester; that the defendants came up from behind and passed the plaintiff at a high rate of speed one on each side; that each defendant was mounted on a motor tricycle with a gasoline engine making a loud noise and emitting steam, some of the plaintiff's witnesses saying that the machines emitted steam and smoke making a cloud about the defendants as they rode.

The plaintiff testified that his horse took fright when the defendants first passed but was under control and guidance until he overtook the defendants, and that running between them the horse shied and he then lost control. His wagon wheel struck another wagon going in the same direction, and the injuries to himself and his wagon occurred.

The plaintiff and each of his witnesses was asked on cross-examination if he could tell which defendant or which vehicle caused the horse to take fright, and each witness was unable to tell.

The defendants requested the judge to instruct the jury that the evidence showing that they were on two separate vehicles entirely independent of each other, and there being two different suits for the same injury, the burden was on the plaintiff to show which one of

85. Suppose it is clear that one, but only one, of a group was negligent and caused the injury. See, e. g., Jackson v. Magnavox Corp., 115 N.J.Super. 1, 280 A.2d 692 (1971); Nopco Chemical Division v. Blaw-Knox Co., 59 N.J. 274, 281 A.2d 793 (1971).

the defendants, if either, was to blame; and that, if it was not clearly shown which one of the defendants caused the accident, the plaintiff could not recover.

The defendants also requested the judge to instruct the jury, that there being two defendants and two separate suits, and the cause of action against each being for the same injury, if the jury found for the plaintiff they must assess the full damages and determine against which defendant, and that they could not assess full damages against both, as that would be giving double damages.

The judge refused to give either of these instructions. The jury found for the plaintiff in each case and in each case assessed the damages in the sum of $700. The defendants alleged exceptions. * * *

LATHROP, J. The only question which arises in these cases is whether the judge erred in refusing to give the instructions requested. The bill of exceptions does not set forth what instructions were given, and we must assume that they were appropriate to the case as presented by the evidence, and were correct.

The verdict of the jury has established the fact that both of the defendants were wrongdoers. It makes no difference that there was no concert between them, or that it is impossible to determine what portion of the injury was caused by each. If each contributed to the injury, that is enough to bind both. Whether each contributed was a question for the jury. Boston & Albany R. v. Shanly, 107 Mass. 568, 578, and cases cited.

It makes no difference that the defendants were sued severally and not jointly. If two or more wrongdoers contribute to the injury, they may be sued either jointly or severally. McAvoy v. Wright, 137 Mass. 207. The first request for instructions was therefore rightly refused.

Nor was there any error in refusing to give the second request. If both defendants contributed to the accident, the jury could not single out one as the person to blame. There being two actions, the plaintiff was entitled to judgment against each for the full amount. There is no injustice in this, for a satisfaction of one judgment is all that the plaintiff is entitled to. Elliott v. Hayden, 104 Mass. 180. * *

Compare or contrast with the foregoing cases and with each other the problems presented by the following:

(a) an attempt to join as parties defendant two wrongdoers who have successively injured the plaintiff. See McGannon v. Chicago & N. W. R. Co., 160 Minn. 143, 199 N.W. 894 (1924); Sherlock v. Manwaren, 208 App.Div. 538, 203 N.Y.S. 709 (1924); Clark, Cases on Pl. & Proc., 736 et seq. (2d ed. 1940); Federal Rules of Civil Procedure, rules 18(a), 20(a), 28 U.S.C.A. following section 723c.

(b) the substantive liability of and the measure of recovery from each of such wrongdoers (whether sued in the same action or not).

(c) the way in which the first wrongdoer's liability may be affected if his act foreseeably exposes plaintiff to the second wrongdoer's negligence. See Sawdey v. R. W. Rasmussen Co., 107 Cal.App. 467, 290 P. 684 (1930); O'Quinn v. Alston, 213 Ala. 346, 104 So. 653, 39 A.L.R. 1263 (1925).

(d) the measure of recovery from one whose wrongful act aggravates a diseased condition for which he is in no way responsible.

(e) the measure of recovery from one whose wrongful act causes greater injury than could be foreseen, because of some unsuspected weakness or condition of the victim.

MICHIE v. GREAT LAKES STEEL DIVISION

United States Court of Appeals for the Sixth Circuit, 1974.
495 F.2d 213.

Before EDWARDS and CELEBREZZE, CIRCUIT JUDGES, and KRUPANSKY, DISTRICT JUDGE.

EDWARDS, CIRCUIT JUDGE. This is an interlocutory appeal from a District Judge's denial of a motion to dismiss filed by three corporations which are defendants-appellants herein. The District Court certified that the appeal presented a controlling issue of law and this court granted leave to appeal under 28 U.S.C.A. § 1292(b) (1970).

Appellants' motion to dismiss was based upon the contention that each plaintiff individually had failed to meet the requirement of a $10,000 amount in controversy for diversity jurisdiction set forth in 28 U.S.C.A. § 1332 (1970).[86]

The facts in this matter, as alleged in the pleadings, are somewhat unique. Thirty-seven persons, members of thirteen families residing near LaSalle, Ontario, Canada, have filed a complaint against three corporations which operate seven plants in the United States immediately across the Detroit River from Canada. Plaintiffs claim that pollutants emitted by plants of defendants are noxious in character and that their discharge in the ambient air violates various municipal and state ordinances and laws. They assert that the discharges represent a nuisance and that the pollutants are carried by air currents onto their premises in Canada, thereby damaging their persons and property. Each plaintiff individually claims damages ranging

86. 28 U.S.C.A. § 1332 provides:
"(a) The district courts shall have original jurisdiction of all civil actions where the matter in controversy exceeds the sum or value of $10,000, exclusive of interest and costs, and is between—

* * * * *

(2) citizens of a State, and foreign states or citizens or subjects thereof; and . . . ."

from $11,000 to $35,000 from all three corporate defendants jointly and severally. There is, however, no assertion of joint action or conspiracy on the part of defendants.

Additionally, plaintiffs jointly seek $1,000,000 from each defendant, presumably as exemplary or punitive damages, because the nuisance complained of was "wilful and wanton."

This action was originally brought as a class action under Rule 23(b)(3) of the Federal Rules of Civil Procedure but when defendants filed a motion to dismiss the class action aspect of the case, plaintiffs conceded the motion and were allowed to substitute allegations of permissive joinder under Rule 20(a) of the Federal Rules of Civil Procedure. See Zahn v. International Paper Co., 414 U.S. 291, 94 S.Ct. 505, 38 L.Ed.2d 511 (1973).

We believe the principal question presented by this appeal may be phrased thus: Under the law of the State of Michigan, may multiple defendants, whose independent actions of allegedly discharging pollutants into the ambient air thereby allegedly create a nuisance, be jointly and severally liable to multiple plaintiffs for numerous individual injuries which plaintiffs claim to have sustained as a result of said actions, where said pollutants mix in the air so that their separate effects in creating the individual injuries are impossible to analyze.

Appellants argue that the law applicable is that of the State of Michigan and that Michigan law does not allow for joint and several liability on the part of persons charged with maintaining a nuisance. They cite and rely on an old Michigan case. Robinson v. Baugh, 31 Mich. 290 (1875). They also quote and rely upon Restatement of Torts § 881:

> "Where two or more persons, each acting independently, create or maintain a situation which is a tortious invasion of a landowner's interest in the use and enjoyment of land by interfering with his quiet, light, air or flowing water, each is liable only for such proportion of the harm caused to the land or of the loss of enjoyment of it by the owner as his contribution to the harm bears to the total harm."

They also rely upon the comment under § 881:

> "The rule stated in this Section is applicable whether or not there has been a physical or chemical union of materials and whether or not fumes or polluted matter sent out by the defendant have united with those sent out by others before entry upon the plaintiff's land, since the unity of the means by which the harm is caused does not prevent recovery."

See also 1 T. Cooley, Torts § 86 (4th ed. 1932).

Appellees rely strongly upon the opinion of the District Judge in denying the motion to dismiss:

> This court is of the view that this is not the state of the law in Michigan with respect to air pollution. In the absence

of any Michigan cases on point, analogous Michigan cases in the automobile negligence area involving questions of joint liability after the simultaneous impact of vehicles and resultant injuries, are instructive.

In Watts v. Smith, 375 Mich. 120, 134 N.W.2d 194, quoting Meier v. Holt, 347 Mich. 430, 80 N.W.2d 207, the Michigan Supreme Court said:

> "Although it is not always definitely so stated the rule seems to have become generally established that, although there is no concert of action between tort feasors, if the cumulative effects of their acts is a single indivisible injury which it cannot certainly be said would have resulted but for the concurrence of such acts, the actors are to be held liable as joint tort feasors."

In Maddux v. Donaldson, 362 Mich. 425, [108 N.W.2d 33] the Michigan Supreme Court cites Landers v. East Texas Salt Water Disposal Company, 151 Tex. 251, 248 S.W.2d 731, a pollution case, in support of the above stated proposition. The court indicated that

> "* * * [i]t is clear that there is a manifest unfairness in 'putting on the injured party the impossible burden of proving the specific shares of harm done by each. * * * Such results are simply the law's callous dullness to innocent sufferers. One would think that the obvious meanness [sic] of letting wrongdoers go scot free in such cases would cause the courts to think twice and to suspect some falacy in their rule of law'."

Plaintiffs contend that the *Maddux,* id, and *Watts,* supra, language applies here since there is no possibility of dividing the injuries herein alleged to have occurred and that it is impossible to judge which of the alleged tortfeasors caused what harm.

It is the opinion of this court that the rule of *Maddux,* supra, and *Landers,* supra, cited therein is the better, and applicable rule in this air pollution case.

On this point we affirm the decision of the District Judge. This complaint appears to have been filed under the diversity jurisdiction of the federal courts. All parties have agreed that Michigan law alone controls.[87]

Like most jurisdictions, Michigan has had great difficulty with the problems posed in tort cases by multiple causes for single or in-

87. Arguably there may be a federal common law of nuisance applicable to injuries by pollution of water or air across state boundaries. See Illinois v. Milwaukee, 406 U.S. 91, 92 S.Ct. 1385, 31 L.Ed.2d 712 (1972); Texas v. Pankey, 441 F.2d 236 (10th Cir. 1971). Thus far, however, no case has been decided under federal nuisance doctrine except where the action has been brought by a state.

Clearly, a suit for injunctive relief could have been (but was not) brought under federal environment law. See 42 U.S.C.A. § 1857h–2 (Supp.1973).

divisible injuries. Meier v. Holt, 347 Mich. 430, 80 N.W.2d 207 (1957); De Witt v. Gerard, 281 Mich. 676, 275 N.W. 729 (1937); De Witt v. Gerard, 274 Mich. 299, 264 N.W. 379 (1936); Frye v. City of Detroit, 256 Mich. 466, 239 N.W. 886 (1932). *Compare* Watts v. Smith, 375 Mich. 120, 134 N.W.2d 194 (1965); Maddux v. Donaldson, 362 Mich. 425, 108 N.W.2d 33 (1961).

The first four of these cases clearly support the rule of law argued for by appellants. But the last two represent the more recent rule adopted by the Michigan Supreme Court and relied upon by the District Judge.

We believe that the issue was decided in the lengthy consideration given by the Michigan court in the *Maddux* case. There Justice Talbot Smith (now Senior Judge, United States District Court for the Eastern District of Michigan, Southern Division) in an opinion for the court majority (joined by the writer of this opinion) held:

It is our conclusion that if there is competent testimony, adduced either by plaintiff or defendant, that the injuries are factually and medically separable, and that the liability for all such injuries and damages, or parts thereof, may be allocated with reasonable certainty to the impacts in turn, the jury will be instructed accordingly and mere difficulty in so doing will not relieve the triers of the facts of this responsibility. This merely follows the general rule that "where the independent concurring acts have caused distinct and separate injuries to the plaintiff, or where some reasonable means of apportioning the damages is evident, the courts generally will not hold the tort-feasors jointly and severally liable."

But if, on the other hand, the triers of the facts conclude that they cannot reasonably make the division of liability between the tort-feasors, this is the point where the road of authority divides. Much ancient authority, not in truth precedent, would say that the case is now over, and that plaintiff shall take nothing. Some modern courts, as well, hold that his is merely the case of the marauding dogs and the helpless sheep relitigated in the setting of a modern highway. The conclusion is erroneous. Such precedents are not apt. When the triers of the facts decide that they cannot make a division of injuries we have, by their own finding, nothing more or less than an indivisible injury, and the precedents as to indivisible injuries will control. They were well summarized in Cooley on Torts in these words: "Where the negligence of two or more persons concur in producing a single, indivisible injury, then such persons are jointly and severally liable, although there was no common duty, common design, or concert action." Maddux v. Donaldson, 362 Mich. 425, 432–433, 108 N.W.2d 33, 36 (1961). (Footnotes omitted.)

The *Maddux* case has been the subject of an extensive annotation wherein the A.L.R. concludes:

> American decisions, statutes, and rules of court have modified and liberalized the common-law rule as to joinder of defendants, and although there is apparently no satisfactory

> general rule as to when various persons acting independently may be joined in a tort action, many jurisdictions evidently would now permit joinder of two or more drivers who were involved in successive collisions or accidents with a plaintiff or his vehicle. See Am Jur Parties (1st ed §§ 40–43); Am Jur, Negligence (1st ed § 257); Prosser, Torts 2d ed § 46; 1 Harper and James, Torts § 10.1. 100 A.L.R.2d 16, 29 n. 13 (1965).

We recognize, of course, that the *Maddux* and *Watts* cases both involve multiple collisions causing allegedly indivisible injuries. Hence, appellants are free to argue that the rule stated does not necessarily apply to the nuisance category of torts with which we deal here. Indeed, appellants call our attention to what appears to be a contrary rule applicable to nuisance cases referred to in the *Maddux* opinion. Restatement of Torts § 881.

In the latest Restatement, however, both the old and the newer rule are recognized and as the Michigan court held in *Maddux,* the question of whether liability of alleged polluters is joint or several is left to the trier of the facts. Where the injury itself is indivisible, the judge or jury must determine whether or not it is practicable to apportion the harm among the tortfeasors. If not, the entire liability may be imposed upon one (or several) tortfeasors subject, of course, to subsequent right of contribution among the joint offenders.

Perhaps the best summary of the rationale for such a rule is found in Harper and James:

> In the earlier discussion of the substantive liability of joint tort-feasors and independent concurring wrongdoers who have produced indivisible harm it was indicated that there were four categories into which these parties may be placed: situations in which (1) the actors knowingly join in the performance of the tortious act or acts; (2) the actors fail to perform a common duty owed to the plaintiff; (3) there is a special relationship between the parties (e. g., master and servant or joint entrepreneurs); (4) although there is no concerted action nevertheless the independent acts of several actors concur to produce indivisible harmful consequences.
>
> * * * * * * * * * *
>
> While the Restatement of Torts contains a short and apparently simple statement of the rule in category four, this type of situation has caused a great deal of disagreement in the courts. Here joint and several liability is sometimes imposed for the harm caused by the independent concurring acts of a number of persons. In all the situations in which such recovery is permitted the court must find first that the harm for which the plaintiff seeks damages is "indivisible." This can mean that the harm is not even theoretically divisi-

ble (as death or total destruction of a building) or that the harm, while theoretically divisible, is single in a practical sense so far as the plaintiff's ability to apportion it among the wrongdoers is concerned (as where a stream is polluted as a result of refuse from several factories). In the first type of case almost uniformly courts will permit entire recovery from any or all defendants. There is conflict, however, in the second situation, with some well-reasoned recent cases recognizing that the plaintiff's right to recover for his harm should not depend on his ability to apportion the damage but that this is a problem which is properly left with the defendants themselves. 1 F. Harper & F. James, The Law of Torts § 10.1 at 697–98, 701–02 (1956) (Footnotes omitted.)

* * *

In the diversity case Michigan law is not finally and conclusively declared. The District Judge, under Erie R. Co. v. Tompkins, 304 U.S. 64, 58 S.Ct. 817, 82 L.Ed. 1188 (1938), had to seek to establish what the Supreme Court of Michigan would do with this case on the basis of what it has already decided. Like the District Judge, we believe that the Michigan courts would apply the *Maddux* principles to the case at bar. Under *Maddux,* each plaintiff's complaint should be read as alleging $11,000 or more in damages against each defendant.[88] Therefore, the principle of Zahn v. International Paper Co., 414 U.S. 291, 94 S.Ct. 505, 38 L.Ed.2d 511 (1973), which would disallow aggregation of plaintiffs' claims for the purpose of establishing diversity jurisdiction, does not apply to this case.

88. Michigan law, of course, does not allow collection of the judgment more than once. Maddux v. Donaldson, 362 Mich. 425, 451, 108 N.W.2d 33 (1961) (Black, J., concurring). It also allows for the joint defendant who pays the judgment to seek contribution from his joint tortfeasors. Mich.Comp.Laws Ann. § 600.2925 (1967) [notes 86, 87 and the preceding portion of 88 from original.] Contribution statutes vary widely. Compare Uniform Contribution Among Tort-Feasors Act (e. g., Md.Ann.Code art. 50, §§ 16–24): "The right to contribution exists among joint tort-feasors", defined as "two or more persons jointly or severally liable in tort for the same injury to person or property, whether or not judgment has been recovered against all or some of them." A settlement with one tortfeasor can raise complex issues under these statutes, both for the tort-feasor (to assure that he does not remain liable for contribution), and for the claimant (to assure that the balance of his claim against the other tortfeasors is not reduced by more than the amount he collects under the settlement); see, e. g., Pulvari v. Greyhound Corp., 287 F.Supp. 104 (D.D.C.1968); Butters v. Kane, Me., 347 A.2d 602 (1975). Some states, such as Illinois and Ohio, have no contribution statute but allow common-law indemnity. For another variation see Dole v. Dow Chemical Co., 30 N.Y.2d 143, 331 N.Y. S.2d 382, 282 N.E.2d 288 (1972). See, generally, James, Contribution Among Joint Tortfeasors: A Pragmatic Criticism, 54 Harv.L.Rev. 1156 (1941); Gregory, Contribution Among Joint Tortfeasors: A Defense, 54 Harv.L. Rev. 1170 (1941); James, Contribution Among Joint Tortfeasors: Replication, 54 Harv.L.Rev. 1178 (1941); and James, Indemnity, Subrogation and Contribution and the Efficient Distribution of Accident Costs, 21 NACCA L.J. 360 (1958).

VICARS v. WILCOCKS

Court of King's Bench, 1806.
8 East's Reports 1.

In an action on the case for slander, * * *

It appeared at the trial before Lawrence, J. at Stafford, that the plaintiff had been retained by J. O. as a journeyman for a year at certain wages, and that before the expiration of the year his master had discharged him in consequence of the [allegedly slanderous] words spoken by the defendant [to J. O.]. That the plaintiff afterwards applied to R. P. for employment, who refused to employ him, in consequence of the words, *and because his former master had discharged him for the offence imputed to him.* The plaintiff was thereupon nonsuited; it being admitted that the words in themselves were not actionable without special damages; and the learned judge being of opinion that the plaintiff having been retained by his master under a contract for a certain time then unexpired, it was not competent for the master to discharge him on account of the words spoken; but it was a mere wrongful act of the master, for supposed special damage was the loss of those advantages which the plaintiff was entitled to under his contract with his master; which he could not in law be considered as having lost, as he still had a right to claim them of his master, who without a sufficient cause had refused to continue the plaintiff in his service. 2dly, With respect to the subsequent refusal of R. P. to employ the plaintiff, that it did not appear to be merely on account of the words spoken; but rather on account of his former master having discharged him in consequence of the accusation; without which he might not have regarded the words.

Jervis now moved to set aside the nonsuit, and urged that it was always deemed sufficient proof of special damage in these cases to shew that the injury arose in fact from the slander of the defendant, and it was not less a consequence of it because the act so induced was wrongful on the part of the master. He said, that he could find no case where such a distinction was laid down, and that the practice of *Nisi Prius* was understood to be otherwise. 2dly, That the refusal of R. P. to employ the plaintiff was clear of that objection; and that such refusal had proceeded upon the alleged cause of discharge by the first master, and not upon the bare act itself of discharge.

LORD ELLENBOROUGH, C. J. said, that the special damage must be the legal and natural consequence of the words spoken, otherwise it did not sustain the declaration: and here it was an illegal consequence; a mere wrongful act of the master; for which the defendant was no more answerable, than if, in consequence of the words, other persons had afterwards assembled and seised the plaintiff, and thrown him into a horsepond by way of punishment for his supposed transgression. And his Lordship asked whether any case could be mentioned of an action of this sort sustained by proof only of an injury sustained by the tortious act of a third person. Upon the second ground, *non liquet* that the refusal by R. P. to employ the plaintiff was in consequence of the words spoken, as it is alleged to be: there was at least a concurrent cause, the act of his former master in refusing to continue him in his employ; which was more likely to weigh with R. P. than the mere words themselves of the defendant.

The other Judges concurring.

Rule refused.[89]

89. The last wrongdoer rule has received its share of comment. See for example, Bohlen, Contributory Negligence, 21 Harv.L.Rev. 233 (1908); Eldredge, Culpable Intervention as Superseding Cause, 86 U. of P.L.R. 121 (1937). It has also received occasional commendation and application. Wharton, Negligence, section 134 (1st ed. 1874); Stone v. City of Philadelphia, 302 Pa. 340, 153 A. 550 (1931). As a test for limiting defendant's liability in ordinary negligence cases, however, it has never commanded wide support. Perhaps it is significant that the case where the rule first found expression was not a personal injury action at all but one of the disfavored type of slander. And most of the applications in Pennsylvania, noted in Mr. Eldredge's valuable article, deal with highway defects and exonerate the governmental unit (town, county, etc.) charged with the duty of highway repair. There defendants had no liability for such defects apart from statute and they have not infrequently been the object of especial tenderness by the courts. An example, quite suggestive of the Pennsylvania cases, is the early New England rule (by no means dead) that no action could be maintained against the town unless the injury arose *solely* from the defect. This resulted from no application of the last-wrongdoer rule but was placed upon what seems a distorted interpretation of statute. See elaborate discussion in Bartram v. Town of Sharon, 71 Conn. 686, 43 A. 143, 46 L.R.A. 144, 71 Am.St.Rep. 225 (1889). Cf. Hayes v. Hyde Park, 153 Mass. 514, 27 N.E. 522, 12 L.R.A. 249 (1891); Holmes-Pollock Letters, 34–38 (Howe ed. 1941); James and Perry, Legal Cause, 60 Yale L.J. 761, 807 (1951).

Examples of liability for failure to exercise reasonable care to protect victims from the wrongdoing of others include Schuster v. City of New York, 5 N.Y.2d 75, 180 N.Y.S.2d 265, 154 N.E. 2d 534 (1958) (failure by police to protect informer from underworld murder); Danile v. Oak Park Arms Hotel, Inc., 55 Ill.App.2d 2, 203 N.E.2d 706 (1964) and Tobin v. Slutsky, 596 F.2d 1097 (2d Cir. 1974) (liability of hotels for sexual assaults on guests by employees); Elliott v. James, 165 U.S. App.D.C. 356, 507 F.2d 1179 (1974) (liability for murder by third party based on defendant's negligence in locking decedent in building at night); Samson v. Saginaw Professional Building, Inc., 393 Mich. 393, 224 N.W.2d 843 (1975) (liability of office building landlord to tenant's employee robbed and stabbed in building elevator by patient of mental health clinic, another tenant); and Homere v. State of New York, page 193 supra. Also consider Tarasoff v. Regents of the University of Caifornia, 13 Cal.3d 177, 118 Cal. Rptr. 129, 529 P.2d 553 (1974); cf. Fleming and Maximov, The Patient or His Victim: The Therapist's Dilemma, 62 Calif.L.Rev. 1025 (1974) and Curran, Confidentiality and the Prediction of Dangerousness in Psychiatry, 293 N. Engl.J.Med. 285 (1975).

ILLIDGE v. GOODWIN

Court of Common Pleas, 1831.
5 Carrington & Payne's Reports 100.

The declaration stated, that the plaintiff was possessed of certain goods and porcelain, in a certain shop window; and that the defendant was possessed of a cart and horse, which, through the negligence of his servant, was backed against the window, and broke the china; whereby the plaintiff was put to expense, &c.

It appeared, from the evidence of the plaintiff's shopman, that the plaintiff was a china-man in St. Paul's Church Yard, and that, between eight and nine in the morning of a day in June, a scavenger's cart, with the name of Joseph Goodwin upon it, backed against the window of the plaintiff's shop, and broke a quantity of china; and that the carman was not there at the time, but came up very soon after.

* * *

To make out the defence opened by Spankie, Serjt., two witnesses were called, who swore to the striking of the horse by a person passing by; and one added, that the horse backed against the window in consequence of the bad management of the plaintiff's shopman, who came out and laid hold of his head. During the cross-examination of the second of these witnesses, the Jury interposed, and said they did not believe the evidence of either of them.

TINDAL, C. J.—After all, supposing them to be speaking the truth, it does not amount to a defence. If a man chooses to leave a cart standing in the street, he must take the risk of any mischief that may be done. * * *

The Jury then, under his Lordship's direction, found a Verdict for the plaintiff—18*l*, 14*s*.

VESELY v. SAGER

Supreme Court of California, In Bank, 1971.
5 Cal.3d 153, 95 Cal.Rptr. 623, 486 P.2d 151.

WRIGHT, CHIEF JUSTICE. In this case we are called upon to decide whether civil liability may be imposed upon a vendor of alcoholic beverages for providing alcoholic drinks to a customer who, as a result of intoxication, injures a third person. * * *

Defendant Sager owned and operated the Buckhorn Lodge, a roadhouse located near the top of Mount Baldy in San Bernardino County, and was engaged in the business of selling alcoholic beverages to the general public. Beginning about 10 p. m. on April 8, 1968, Sager served or permitted defendant O'Connell to be served large quantities of alcoholic beverages. At the time the beverags were served, Sager knew that O'Connell was becoming excessively intoxicated and that O'Connell was "incapable of exercising the same degree of volitional control over his consumption of intoxicants as the average reasonable person." Sager also knew that the only route leaving the Buckhorn Lodge was a very steep, winding, and narrow mountain road and that O'Connell was going to drive down that road. Nevertheless, Sager continued to serve O'Connell alcoholic drinks past the normal closing time of 2 a. m. until 5:15 a. m. on April 9. After leaving the lodge, O'Connell drove down the road, veered into the opposite lane, and struck plaintiff's vehicle. * * *

Defendant Sager demurred to the complaint on the ground that a "seller of intoxicating liquors is not liable for injuries resulting from intoxication" of a buyer thereof * * *.

The trial court sustained the demurrer * * *. Plaintiff appeals. * * *

Until fairly recently, it was uniformly held that an action could not be maintained at common law against the vendor of alcoholic beverages for furnishing such beverages to a customer who, as a result of being intoxicated, injured himself or a third person * * *. The rationale for the common law rule was that the consumption and not the sale of liquor was the proximate cause [90] of injuries sustained as a result of intoxication. * * * "The rule was based on the obvious fact that one cannot be intoxicated by reason of liquor furnished him if he does not drink it." (Nolan v. Morelli (1967), 154 Conn. 432, 226 A.2d 383 * * *) The common law rule has been substantially abrogated in many states by statutes which specifically impose civil liability upon a furnisher of intoxicating liquor under specified circumstances. (See Comment, 57 Cal.L.Rev. 995, 996, fn. 6, listing the 20 states that have such statutes.) California, however, has not enacted similar legislation.

* * * [V]arious courts in other jurisdictions have reevaluated the common law rule that the vendor of intoxicating liquor cannot be held liable for injuries resulting from intoxication, and in particular the rule that the seller cannot be held liable for furnishing alcoholic beverages to a customer who injures a third person. A substantial number, if not a majority, have decided that the sale of alcoholic beverages may be the proximate cause of such injuries and that liability may be imposed upon the vendor in favor of the injured third person. * * *

The two leading cases abrogating or modifying the common law rule are Waynick v. Chicago's Last Department Store * * * 269

90. "The term proximate cause comes from one of Bacon's maxims. 'In jure non remota causa sed proxima spectatur.' (In law not the remote but only the proximate cause is looked to.) In many discussions, however, the term 'legal' cause is used in the hope that it will be less misleading than 'proximate cause'." Epstein, A Theory of Strict Liability, 2 J.Leg.Studies 151, 161, n. 26 (1973), discussing causation at length. Compare Lord Denning's version of the maxim: "[C]*ausa proxima non remota spectatur.* (Look at the significant cause and not the insignificant one)." Hoveringham Gravels Ltd. v. Secretary of State for the Environment, Law Report (Court of Appeal), The Times (London) March 15, 1975, page 5, col. 5, holding, *inter alia*, that the determination of "cause" in this sense was "a matter for the trained lawyer . . . too difficult for a layman", and therefore a question of law, not fact. In the United States, similarly, while "cause in fact" is generally considered a jury question under American procedures for fact-finding in civil cases, it has been said that "the question whether the defendant should be legally responsible for what he has caused * * * whether the conduct has been so significant and important a cause that the defendant should be legally responsible * * * whether the policy of the law will extend the responsibility for the conduct to the consequences which have in fact occurred" is "not a question of causation, or even of fact, but quite removed from both", and is instead "essentially a problem of law." W. Prosser, The Law of Torts 240, 244 (4th ed. 1971). Compare Restatement of Torts Second § 434 and Comment C (1965).

F.2d 322 [(7th Cir. 1959)], and Rappaport v. Nichols * * * 31 N. J. 188, 156 A.2d 1 [(1959)]. In *Waynick* the plaintiffs, residents of Michigan, brought an action for personal injuries against three Illinois tavern keepers for selling liquor to two Illinois residents who drove an automobile into Michigan and there collided with a vehicle in which the plaintiffs were riding. The sale by each defendant was alleged to have been made in violation of an Illinois criminal statute prohibiting the sale of liquor to an intoxicated person. Although both Michigan and Illinois had dram shop acts expressly providing for civil liability, the court concluded that neither applied to the case before it because the state courts had decided that the statutes did not apply extraterritorially. Nevertheless, the court held that the complaint stated a cause of action under the common law of Michigan. The court determined that the Illinois statute prohibiting the sale of liquor to an intoxicated person was enacted "for the protection of any member of the public who might be injured or damaged as a result of the drunkenness to which the particular sale of alcoholic liquor contributes" and that the statute imposed a duty upon the sellers of alcoholic beverages in favor of those who might be injured as a result of a violation of the statute. Without analyzing at length the question of proximate cause, the court held that "under the facts appearing in the complaint, the tavern keepers are liable in tort for the damages and injuries sustained by plaintiffs, as a proximate result of the unlawful acts of the former." (269 F.2d at p. 326.)

Rappaport involved a wrongful death action by a widow against the operators of four taverns for selling liquor to an intoxicated minor who negligently killed her husband in an automobile accident. Although New Jersey had repealed its dram shop act, the New Jersey Supreme Court held that the action was permissible under common law negligence principles. The court stated that "Where a tavern keeper sells alcoholic beverages to a person who is visibly intoxicated or to a person he knows or should know from the circumstances to be a minor, he ought to recognize and foresee the unreasonable risk of harm to others through action of the intoxicated person or the minor." (31 N.J. at p. 201, 156 A.2d at p. 8.) The court determined that a criminal statute and administrative regulations forbidding the sale of alcoholic beverages to a minor or an intoxicated person were intended to protect members of the general public and concluded that "If the patron is a minor or is intoxicated when served, * * * and if the circumstances are such that the tavern keeper knows or should know that the patron is a minor or is intoxicated, his service to him may * * * constitute common law negligence." (Id. at p. 202, 156 A.2d at p. 9.) Finally, the court rejected the defendants' contention that their conduct, if negligent, was not the proximate cause of the injuries suffered. It stated: "But a tortfeasor is generally held answerable for the injuries which result in the ordinary course of events from his negligence and it is generally sufficient if his negligent conduct was a substantial factor in bringing about the injuries. [Citations.] The fact that there were also intervening causes which were foreseeable or were normal incidents of the risk created would not relieve the tortfeasor of liability. [Citations.] Ordinarily these questions of proximate and intervening cause are left to the jury for its factual determination." (Id. at p. 203, 156 A.2d at p. 9.) * * *

To the extent that the common law rule of nonliability is based on concepts of proximate cause, we are persuaded by the reasoning of the cases that have abandoned that rule. The decisions in those jurisdictions which have abandoned the common law rule invoke principles of proximate cause similar to those established in this state by cases dealing with matters other than the furnishing of alcoholic beverages. * * * Under these principles an actor may be liable if his negligence is a substantial factor in causing an injury, and he is not relieved of liability because of the intervening act of a third person if such act was reasonably foreseeable at the time of his negligent conduct. (* * * Restatement of Torts, Second, §§ 302, 302A, 431, 447.) Moreover, "If the likelihood that a third person may act in a particular manner is the hazard or one of the hazards which makes the actor negligent, such an act whether innocent, negligent, intentionally tortious or criminal does not prevent the actor from being liable for harm caused thereby." (Restatement of Torts, Second § 449 * * *.)

Insofar as proximate cause is concerned, we find no basis for a distinction founded solely on the fact that the consumption of an alcoholic beverage is a voluntary act of the consumer and is a link in the chain of causation from the furnishing of the beverage to the injury resulting from intoxication. Under the above principles of proximate cause, it is clear that the furnishing of an alcoholic beverage to an intoxicated person may be a proximate cause of injuries inflicted by that individual upon a third person. If such furnishing is a proximate cause, it is so because the consumption, resulting intoxication, and injury-producing conduct are foreseeable intervening causes, or at least the injury-producing conduct is one of the hazards which makes such furnishing negligent.

The central question in this case, therefore, is not one of proximate cause, but rather one of duty: Did defendant Sager owe a duty of care to plaintiff or to a class of persons of which he is a member?

In the instant case a duty of care is imposed upon defendant Sager by Business and Professions Code section 25602, which provides: "Every person who sells, furnishes, gives, or causes to be sold, furnished, or given away, any alcoholic beverage to any habitual or common drunkard or to any obviously intoxicated person is guilty of a misdemeanor." * * *

This provision * * * was adopted for the purpose of protecting members of the general public from injuries to person and damage to property resulting from the excessive use of intoxicating liquor. * * *

The judgment of dismissal is reversed.

LINEY v. CHESTNUT MOTORS, INC.

Supreme Court of Pennsylvania, 1966.
421 Pa. 26, 218 A.2d 336.

EAGEN, JUSTICE. In this action in trespass, the lower court sustained preliminary objections to the complaint in the nature of a demurrer and dismissed the action. This appeal challenges the correctness of that order.

* * *

The defendant operates an automobile sales agency and garage. About ten o'clock a. m. on the day involved, a customer's automobile was delivered to the garage for repairs. The defendant's employees allowed the automobile to remain outside the building, double-parked in the street and with the key in the ignition. About three hours later, it was stolen by an adult stranger who then drove it around the block in such a careless manner that it mounted a sidewalk, struck the plaintiff, a pedestrian thereon, causing her serious injury. Defendant's garage was located in a Philadelphia area experiencing a high and increasing number of automobile thefts in the immediate preceding months.

The lower court's order was correct and we affirm. The complaint failed to state a cause of action against the defendant.

Assuming that defendant's employees were negligent in permitting the automobile to remain outside in the street under the circumstances described, it is clear that the defendant could not have anticipated and foreseen that this carelessness of its employees would result in the harm the plaintiff suffered. See, Rapczynski v. W. T. Cowan, Inc., 138 Pa.Super. 392, 10 A.2d 810 (1940), and Roscovich v. Parkway Baking Co., 107 Pa.Super. 493, 163 A. 915 (1933). In other words, the defendant violated no duty owed to the plaintiff. This being so, the plaintiff was not harmed by the defendant's negligence. See, Dahlstrom v. Shrum, 368 Pa. 423, 84 A.2d 307 (1951), and Zilka v. Sanctis Construction, Inc., 409 Pa. 396, 186 A.2d 897 (1962). Assuming also that the defendant should have foreseen the likelihood of the theft of the automobile, nothing existed in the present case to put it on notice that the thief would be an incompetent or careless driver. Under the circumstances, the thief's careless operation of the automobile was a superseding cause of the injury suffered, and defendant's negligence, if such existed, only a remote cause thereof upon which no action would lie. See, Restatement, Torts, Second, §§ 448, 449, and § 302B, Illustration 2 (1965); Prosser, Law of Torts (2d ed. 1941), at 140–41–42 * * *.

It is true that the question of proximate cause is generally for the jury. However, if the relevant facts are not in dispute and the remoteness of the causal connection between the defendant's negligence and the plaintiff's injury clearly appears, the question becomes one of law: Klimczak v. 7–Up Bottling Co. of Phila., 385 Pa. 287, 122 A.2d 707 (1956), and Green v. Independent Oil Co., supra.

Finally, it is strenuously argued that Anderson v. Bushong Pontiac Co., 404 Pa. 382, 171 A.2d 771 (1961), is controlling. We do not agree. In *Anderson,* several salient facts were present which are absent here. Those facts clearly put the defendant in that case on notice, not only that the automobile was likely to be stolen, but also that it was likely to be stolen and operated by an incompetent driver. In *Anderson,* we cited Murray v. Wright, 166 Cal.App.2d 589, 333 P.2d 111 (1958), as persuasive authority for sustaining liability under the facts therein presented. We note that the same court has denied liability in a situation similar to the one now before us. See, Richards v. Stanley, 43 Cal.2d 60, 271 P.2d 23 (1954). Other jurisdictions have reached the same result. * * *

Order affirmed.[91]

MODAVE v. LONG ISLAND JEWISH MEDICAL CENTER

United States Court of Appeals for the Second Circuit, 1974.
501 F.2d 1065.

[Plaintiff, injured in an automobile accident, was taken to a private hospital, Long Island Jewish Medical Center ("LIJ"), where, she alleged, she was subjected to malpractice through failure to diagnose a spinal injury, and failure to safeguard her against aggravation of the injury as she was moved about during reception and examination. LIJ had no room to keep her, so she was transferred to a Nassau County hospital, Meadowbrook, where, she claimed, her injury was further aggravated negligently. She sued both LIJ and the county. The jury awarded $50,000 against LIJ and $650,000 against the county. The trial judge having set aside the verdict against the county on procedural grounds, plaintiff unsuccessfully moved to amend the judgment against LIJ to include the $650,000 awarded against the county.]

Before MOORE, FRIENDLY and MANSFIELD, CIRCUIT JUDGES.

FRIENDLY, CIRCUIT JUDGE.

* * *

Plaintiff's motion to amend the judgment against LIJ to include the $650,000 awarded against Nassau County takes off from the unassailable proposition of New York law "that a wrongdoer is liable for the ultimate result, though the mistake or even negligence of the physician who treated the injury may have increased the damage which would otherwise have followed from the original wrong," Milks v. McIver, 264 N.Y. 267, 270, 190 N.E. 487, 488 (1934). See ALI Restatement (Second) of Torts § 457 (1965); Prosser, Torts § 44, at 278–79 (4th ed. 1971). In Ferrara v. Galluchio, 5 N.Y.2d 16, 176 N.Y.S.2d 996, 152 N.E.2d 249 (1958), the Court of Appeals applied

91. Compare Ross v. Hartman, page 331 below, and Peck, An Exercise Based Upon Empirical Data: Liability for Harm Caused by Stolen Automobiles, 1969 Wis.L.Rev. 909 (indicating, inter alia, that the accident rate for stolen cars appears to be about 200 times the normal accident rate).

this principle in a case where malpractice by the defendant x-ray specialists led to plaintiff's consulting a dermatologist who advised her that her radiodermatitis might develop into cancer, with consequent emotional disturbance. The Court stated that the employment of the dermatologist was "a natural consequence of the original wrongdoers' tort because the necessity for such employment was imposed upon the plaintiff by the original wrongdoers' fault." The risk of emotional injury from an alarming remark of the dermatologist, the court concluded, "must be borne by the wrongdoers who started the chain of circumstances without which the cancerophobia would not have developed," 5 N.Y.2d at 20–21, 176 N.Y.S.2d at 999, 152 N.E.2d at 252. It cannot be questioned that if the driver who caused Miss Modave's injury was negligent, he would be liable for the malpractice of both hospitals. Counsel argues that on a parity of reasoning a first malpractitioner is liable as a matter of law for the malpractice of a second * * *.

Plaintiff reads the malpractice aggravation rule too broadly. It is true that a negligent driver normally is responsible for all the harm occasioned by subsequent malpractice in the course of treatment, whether the malpractice is by one hospital or by two; the driver's negligence is plainly a cause-in-fact of all the subsequent harm, and the intervening malpractice is regarded as being within the scope of the risk created by the negligent conduct. But where a third party has inflicted the original injury, the first hospital to treat the victim, even if negligent, is not necessarily responsible for any subsequent malpractice. At least where apportionment is practicable, the first hospital will be liable for subsequent damage only if its malpractice was a legal cause of the injury suffered at the hands of the second. The distinction that counsel's argument overlooks is the need to show a sufficient causal connection between LIJ's negligence and the harm inflicted by Meadowbrook.[92]

If proper handling at LIJ would have enabled Miss Modave to have been discharged on the night of the accident without need of further hospitalization and it was her maltreatment at LIJ that necessitated her hospitalization at Meadowbrook, her case against LIJ would indeed fall within the decisions of the Court of Appeals in *Milks* and

92. A hypothetical will make this clear. A plaintiff who has suffered a stroke is brought to a hospital where he is given an overdose of medicine, which results in permanent damage to his eyesight. He is then transferred to a second hospital, which has better facilities for stroke victims. The staff of the second hospital negligently fails to recognize the seriousness of his condition, and, as a result, he suffers brain damage. Plainly the first hospital is liable only for the injury to the plaintiff's eyesight, and the second is liable only for the brain damage. If the malpractice of each had contributed substantially to the same brain injury, both would probably be liable for all the damages attributable to that injury. This, however, would be because it would be impossible for the jury rationally to apportion each tortfeasor's contribution to the single indivisible injury, not because, as counsel insists, the first hospital's malpractice automatically becomes "an original injury" as to the second hospital in any case involving successive acts of malpractice. [From original, renumbered; other notes in original omitted.]

Ferrara. But plaintiff sensibly has not pressed any such contention. Her condition was concededly serious enough to require further hospitalization, regardless of the quality of the emergency care she received at LIJ. Going a step further, when malpractice of a first hospital creates a condition not inherent in the original injury and this causes a second hospital to carry out measures which would not otherwise have been needed and which result in further harm, the first hospital might likewise be held liable. There was some evidence in this case to support a theory that the acts of malpractice at Meadowbrook would not have occurred but for the faulty handling at LIJ, but absent a request to charge in accordance with such a theory, the judge quite properly refrained from submitting it to the jury on his own. * * *

Plaintiff's second attack on the court's charge, presented in tandem with the first, is that the judge should not have permitted the jury to apportion damages in a case in which there was no logical basis for apportioning the harm caused by each defendant. However, there was evidence to support the jury's conclusion that plaintiff's injuries were separable, and in view of her failure to raise the point below it is not necessary for us to consider whether, upon request, the judge should have instructed the jury more extensively as to the limitations on their prerogative to apportion damages. * * *

We may indeed wonder at the jury's ability to calculate that the damage inflicted by LIJ amounted to $50,000 and the damage at Meadowbrook to $650,000. Had we been the jurors, we might well have availed ourselves of the option, accorded by the trial judge, to find apportionment impracticable and award a judgment against both parties. Compare ALI, Restatement (Second) of Torts, supra, § 433B, Illustration 8; Prosser, Torts, supra, § 52, at 313–16. But if the jurors found themselves capable of this feat, it is not for us to say them nay. * * * [93]

93. "The risk theory generalizes the notion that liability should extend but also be restricted to those types of harm the chance or risk of which formed *the* reason or *a* reason for the imposition of liability. * * * The risk theory * * * applies not merely to negligence but also to strict liability; harm is, in this context, said to be within the risk if it is of the sort the chance of which led to the imposition of strict liability." H. Hart and A. Honoré, Causation in the Law 256–57 (1959); for a critique of the risk theory, in which these authors question its applicability to "ulterior harm", such as malpractice following negligently caused injury, cf. id. at 256–60. Compare Seavey, Principles of Torts, 56 Harv.L.Rev. 72, 90–93 (1942); James and Perry, Legal Cause, 60 Yale L.J. 761, 787 et seq. (1951); and Note, The Risk Theory and Proximate Cause—A Comparative Study, 32 Neb.L.Rev. 72 (1952). For an alternative proposition see Restatement of Torts, Second §§ 431, 433 and 435 (1965), relating "legal cause" to whether the "actor's negligent conduct * * * is a substantial factor in bringing about the harm." Also compare civil law concept of "adequate cause", e. g., "A given contingency will be an *adequate cause* of harm if and only if it satisfies two conditions: (i) it must be a *sine qua non* of the harm, (ii) it must have 'increased the probability' of the harm by a significant amount." H. Hart and A. Honoré, supra, at 415.

WHEELER v. GLENS FALLS INSURANCE CO.

Supreme Court of Tennessee, 1974.
Tenn., 513 S.W.2d 179.

McCANLESS, JUSTICE. This is a workman's compensation case in which the employee, Joseph G. Wheeler, sustained an injury from a fall in the course of his employment, but in which death resulted from complications arising out of chronic alcoholism. * * *

The record in the trial shows that Wheeler, an Oak Ridge policeman, was injured on January 13, 1970, when he slipped on an icy street and fell on his back. The fall aggravated degenerative arthritis in his back and neck, resulting in extreme pain in these areas. Wheeler continued to work until January 24, when the pain forced him to stay home until February 20, 1970. His return to work lasted only two days, when the pain forced him to quit again. He returned on April 6, 1970, but on this day was able to work for only two hours. * * *

At the time of his injury, the decedent had a history of alcoholism and its related diseases. The family physician, Dr. Charles Gurney, first saw him in 1965 and found evidence of alcoholism. Wheeler was hospitalized in the Oak Ridge Hospital in 1966 and was found to have pancreatitis and cirrhosis of the liver. He was hospitalized again in 1967 and the same diseases were diagnosed. The record shows that the decedent was drinking heavily at this time as a result of marital difficulties.

There is no medical record of any treatment of these diseases between his discharge from Oak Ridge Hospital in 1967 and the injury in January, 1970. Following Wheeler's absences from work because of pain resulting from his accident, he was admitted to Oak Ridge Hospital again on April 27, 1970. He had been drinking heavily, according to the testimony of his wife, to relieve the pain in his back and neck. Shortly after admittance, he was treated for acute delirium tremens. His doctors again found pancreatitis and cirrhosis to be present. After his discharge, Wheeler was found to have a marked enlargement of the liver on July 1, 1970. On July 23, 1970, he was admitted to the hospital in a comatose state. He died early the next morning. Dr. Alex Carabia, who performed the autopsy, stated that the immediate cause of death was "acute necrotizing pancreatitis, and he has as a contributing factor bilateral lobular pneumonia, and also cirrhosis of the liver." * * *

The first two assignments of error arise out of the basic disagreement between the parties as to the cause of death and its relation to the injury. The plainiff contends that her husband drank heavily, and unintentionally precipitated his own death in order to alleviate the pain and despair which resulted from his injury. The defendants contend that Wheeler's death resulted from longstanding alcoholism which originated before the decedent's compensable injury, and which was unrelated to the injury. * * *

* * * While we agree that the decedent had a background of alcoholism before the injury, we are persuaded by testimony in the record that his consumption of alcohol increased greatly after, and as a direct result of, the injury. * * *

We think the * * * testimony from the decedent's wife, doctors, and fellow employees is material evidence to support the trial court's conclusion that, while the decedent was an alcoholic before the accident, the injury precipitated a flurry of heavy drinking which drastically deteriorated his condition and resulted in death. * * *

The first issue challenges the proposition that the work-related injury was the proximate cause of the death, which it must be in order for the plaintiff to recover. The general rule is expressed in 1 Larson, Workmen's Compensation Law, Section 13.00 at 3–279:

> "When the primary injury is shown to have arisen out of and in the course of employment, every natural consequence that flows from the injury likewise arises out of the employment, unless it is the result of an independent intervening cause attributable to claimant's own intentional conduct."

There is no question in this case but that the death of the employee was causally related to the injury, assuming momentarily no intentional conduct on his part. In fact, we have already determined this causal connection in a case with similar facts, Fennell v. Maryland Casualty Co., 208 Tenn. 116, 344 S.W.2d 352 [1961]. There the employee suffered an on-the-job injury and began drinking to relieve the subsequent pain. As a result of his drinking combined with a state of malnutrition, the employee died. The court awarded his widow compensation because of the unbroken chain of causation emanating from the injury: he was injured on the job, the injury caused great pain, medicine did not relieve the pain, decedent drank to relieve the pain, and he died from the intake of alcohol. In short, the court reasoned that, but for the injury, the employee would not have died when he did. * * *

Defendants * * * cite the *Fennell* case in support of their contention that the employee's drinking constituted "willful misconduct" or "self-inflicted injury" within the meaning of Section 50–910, T.C.A., which provides in pertinent part:

> "No compensation shall be allowed for an injury or death due to the employee's willful misconduct or intentional self-inflicted injury * * *." * * *

In our opinion, the evidence in this case reveals the conduct of the employee Wheeler to be below that which would comprise an intervening, willful intent. The contention of the defendants necessarily assumes that the decedent was a person who was warned not to drink, who understood that warning and its consequences, and who had the ability to make a rational and deliberate choice to violate the prohibition. We cannot, in the face of all the evidence, make the assumption that a chronic alcoholic could meet all these conditions. The evidence paints the picture of a man who drank, not out of a perverse intent to ignore his doctors' advice, but because the pain, despair, and idleness resulting from his injury forced him to do so. The record reveals that the medication prescribed to alleviate his pain was ineffective * * * Also, we note that Wheeler chose to drink in the face of warnings that it could lead to his own death. We find it difficult to assume from that fact that the decedent willfully and deliberately chose to make that decision. Rather, it seems more to be the choice of a person who, as a chronic alcoholic, was yielding to a natural inability to resist the lure of alcohol. In short, we feel that the evidence indicates that Wheeler had no reasonable control over his decision to continue drinking.

We take judicial notice of the fact that chronic alcoholism can carry with it an irresistable and uncontrollable desire to drink alcohol, and that a substantial school of thought supports the proposition that alcoholism is a disease. * * *

This case is analogous to those in which an injury aggravates a pre-existent disease or condition, and that disease or condition eventually causes death. We have previously held, for example, that the death of an employee who had cancer, when the injury accelerates the growth of the disease until it results in premature death, is compensable. Boyd v. Young, 193 Tenn. 272, 246 S.W.2d 10 [1951]. This decedent had a history of excessive drinking in times of stress, as he had done in 1966–67 when he and his wife were temporarily separated, and had proved on that occasion that he was unable to heed the advice of his physician to quit drinking. Of course, an employer must take his employees as he hires them, assuming the risk that he may have a condition such as alcoholism or cancer which could be aggravated by an injury that would have consequences greater than those that would be suffered by an otherwise healthy employee. * * *

GREEN–WHEELER SHOE CO. v. CHICAGO, R. I. & P. RY. CO.

Supreme Court of Iowa, 1906.
130 Iowa 123, 106 N.W. 498.

McClain, C. J. In the agreed statement on which the case was tried without other evidence being introduced it is stipulated that the defendant was guilty of negligent delay in the forwarding of the goods of plaintiff from Ft. Dodge to Kansas City, where they were lost or injured on May 30, 1903, by a flood which was so unusual and extraordinary as to constitute an act of God, and that if there had been no such negligent delay the goods would not have been caught in the flood referred to or damaged thereby.

We have presented for our consideration, therefore, the simple question whether a carrier who by a negligent delay in transporting goods has subjected them, in the course of transportation, to a peril which has caused their damage or destruction and for the consequence of which the carrier would not have been liable had there been no negligent delay intervening, is liable for the loss. On this question there is a well-recognized conflict in the authorities. In several well-considered cases decided by courts of high authority it was decided, while the question was still new, that the negligent delay of the carrier in transportation could not be regarded as the proximate cause of an ultimate loss by a casualty which in itself constituted an act of God, as that term is used in defining the carrier's exemption from liability, although had the goods been transported with reasonable diligence they would not have been subjected to such casualty, and these cases are very similar to the one before us inasmuch as the loss in each instance was due to the goods being overtaken by an unprecedented flood for the consequence of which the carrier would not be responsible. Morrison v. Davis, 20 Pa. 171, 57 Am.Dec. 695; Denny v. New York Cent. R. Co., 13 Gray, Mass., 481, 74 Am.Dec. 645; * * * These cases are predicated upon the view that if the carrier could not reasonably have foreseen or anticipated that the goods would be overtaken by such a casualty as a natural and probable result of the delay, then the negligent delay was not the proximate cause of the loss, and should be disregarded in determining the liability for such loss. A similar course of reasoning has been applied in other cases, where the loss has been due immediately to some cause such as accidental fire involving no negligence on the part of the carrier and within a valid exception in the bill of lading, but the goods have been brought within the peril stipulated against by negligent delay in transportaton. * * * For similar reasons it has been held that loss of or injury to the goods by reason of their inherent nature, as by freezing or the like, will not render the carrier liable, even after negligent delay in transportation, if such casualty could not have been foreseen or anticipated as the natural and probable consequence of such delay. * * *

On the other hand it was held by the Court of Appeals of New York in a case arising out of the same flood which caused the destruction of the goods involved in Denny v. New York Cent. R. Co., 13 Gray, Mass., 481, 74 Am.Dec. 645, supra, that the preceding negligent delay on the part of the carrier, in consequence of which the goods were overtaken by the flood, was sufficient ground for holding the carrier to be liable for the loss. Michaels v. New York Cent. R. Co., 30 N.Y. 564, 86 Am.Dec. 415; Read v. Spaulding, 30 N.Y. 630, 86 Am.Dec. 426. And the same court has adhered to this view in case of a loss by fire covered by valid exception in the bill of lading. Condict v. Grand Trunk R. Co., 54 N.Y. 500. * * * [Citations from other jurisdictions omitted.]

The irreconcilable conflict in the authorities is recognized by text-writers, and while the weight of general authority has in many cases been said to support the rule announced in Massachusetts and Pennsylvania cases (1 Thompson, Negligence, section 74; Schouler, Bailments [Ed. 1905] section 348; Hale, Bailments and Carriers, 361; 6 Cyc. 382; notes in 36 Am.St.Rep. 838), other authorities prefer the

New York rule (Hutchinson, Carriers [2d Ed.] section 200; Ray, Negligence of Imposed Duties, 177). In the absence of any express declaration of this court on the very point, and in view of the fact that in most recent cases the conflict of authority is still recognized (see 5 Cur.Law, 517) it seems necessary that the reasons on which the two lines of cases are supported shall be considered in order that we may now reach a conclusion which shall be satisfactory to us. Mere negligence will not render one person liable to another for a loss which the latter would not have sustained had there been no such negligence, unless the negligence consists in some violation of a duty which the one person owes to the other. * * * And, on the other hand, it is well settled that if the negligence of one person with reference to the duty owed to another concurs with an accidental cause resulting in injury to another to whom such duty is owed the negligent person must answer for the consequences as though his negligence were the sole cause of the loss. * * *

The real difficulty seems to be in determining to what extent if at all, it is necessary that the negligent party must have been able to foresee and anticipate the result of his negligent act in order to render him liable for the consequences thereof resulting from a concurrence of his negligence and another cause for which he is not responsible. In an action on contract the party who is at fault is only liable for such consequences as arise according to the usual course of things from his breach, or such as may reasonably be supposed to have been in the contemplation of both parties at the time the contract was made as the probable result of the breach. Hadley v. Baxendale, 9 Exch. 341; Sedgwick, Elements of Damage, 17. But in an action for tort, and the present action is of that character, recovery is not limited to the consequences within the contemplation of the parties or either of them, but includes all the consequences "resulting by ordinary natural sequence, whether foreseen by the wrongdoer or not, provided that the operation of the cause of action is not interrupted by the intervention of an independent agent or overpowering force, and that but for the operation of the cause of action the consequence would not have ensued." Sedgwick, Elements of Damage, section 54. It is true that for the purpose of determining whether the injury suffered by the party complaining was the natural and probable result of the wrong complained of a convenient test is to consider whether in general such a result might have been foreseen as the consequence of the wrong, but it is not necessary "that the injury in the precise form in which it in fact resulted should have been foreseen. It is enough that it now appears to have been the natural and probable consequence." * * * [A number of cases are here cited.] [94]

Now, while it is true that defendant could not have anticipated this particular flood and could not have foreseen that its negligent de-

94. It was not until 1967 that the House of Lords stated explicitly, albeit by dicta, that it would recognize liability in contract only for more predictable damages than the limit permissible in tort, applying, however, the rhetoric of "natural" consequences to the test for contracts, Koufos v. C. Czarnikow, Ltd. [1969] 1 A.C. 350, 411, 422.

lay in transportation would subject the goods to such a danger, yet it is now apparent that such delay did subject the goods to the danger, and that but for the delay they would not have been destroyed; and defendant should have foreseen, as any reasonable person could foresee, that the negligent delay would extend the time during which the goods would be liable in the hands of the carrier to be overtaken by some such casualty, and would therefore increase the peril that the goods should be thus lost to the shipper. This consideration that the peril of accidental destruction is enhanced by the negligent extension of time during which the goods must remain in the carrier's control and out of the control of the owner, and during which some casualty may overtake them, has not, we think, been given sufficient consideration in the cases in which the carrier has been held not responsible for a loss for which he is not primarily liable, but which has overtaken the goods as a consequence of the preceding delay in their transportation.

It is not sufficient for the carrier to say by way of excuse that while a proper and diligent transportation of the goods would have kept them free from the peril by which they were in fact lost it might have subjected them to some other peril just as great. He cannot speculate on mere possibilities. A pertinent illustration is furnished by the well-settled rule with reference to deviation which is that if the carrier transports the goods over some other route than that specified in the contract or reasonably within the contemplation of the parties, he must answer for any loss or damage occurring during such deviation, although it is from a cause which would not in itself render him liable. In such a case it is said "that no wrongdoer can be allowed to apportion or qualify his own wrong, and that as a loss has actually happened whilst his wrongful act was in operation and force, and which is attributable to his wrongful act, he cannot set up as an answer to the action the bare possibility of a loss if his wrongful act had never been done. It might admit of a different construction if he could show, not only that the same loss might have happened, but that it must have happened if the act complained of had not been done." Davis v. Garrett, 6 Bing. 716. * * * It is true that the analogy to the case of a deviation is denied in the case which announce the rule of the Pennsylvania and Massachusetts cases but the distinction attempted to be made that a deviation amounts to a conversion rendering the carrier absolutely liable is too technical to be considered as persuasive. The analogy between the two classes of cases has been recognized in Constable v. National Steamship Co., 154 U.S. 51, 14 S.Ct. 1062, 38 L.Ed. 903, and in Hutchinson, Carriers (2d Ed.) section 200. This court has expressed itself in favor of the liability of the carrier in classes of cases very analogous to that of deviation. Where goods were shipped with the agreement that they should be carried to their destination without change of cars, and in violation of this contract the goods were unloaded at Chicago which was not their destination, for the purpose of transporting them in other cars, and they were destroyed by the Chicago fire, it was held that the carriers were liable although the loss by fire was within a valid exemption from liability contained in the bill of lading. Robinson v. Merchants' Dispatch Transp. Co., 45 Iowa 470; Stewart v. Merchants' Dispatch Transp. Co., 47 Iowa 229, 29 Am.Rep. 476.

Certainly the act of the carrier in unloading the goods at Chicago, instead of carrying them through to their destination in the cars in which they were originally loaded, would not amount even to a technical conversion, nor could it have been anticipated that the result of such an act would be the destruction of the goods; nevertheless this court reached the conclusion that such a departure from the terms of the contract rendered the carrier liable for a loss for which it would not have been liable had it resulted without such departure. * * * As supporting the same view we may also refer to Hewett v. Chicago, B. & Q. R. Co., 63 Iowa 611, 19 N.W. 790, in which it was held that negligent delay in forwarding goods which were liable to damage by freezing rendered the carrier accountable for the loss thus resulting. * * *

We are satisfied that the sounder reasons, supported by good authority, require us to hold that in this case the carrier is liable for the loss of and damage to plaintiff's goods, and the judgment of the trial court is therefore reversed.

BERRY v. SUGAR NOTCH

Supreme Court of Pennsylvania, 1899.
191 Pa. 345, 43 A. 240.

Opinion by MR. JUSTICE FELL: The plaintiff was a motorman in the employ of the Wilkes-Barre and Wyoming Valley Traction Company on its line running from Wilkes-Barre to the borough of Sugar Notch. The ordinance by virtue of which the company was permitted to lay its track and operate its cars in the borough of Sugar Notch contained a provision that the speed of the cars while on the streets of the borough should not exceed eight miles an hour. On the line of the road, and within the borough limits, there was a large chestnut tree, as to the condition of which there was some dispute at the trial. The question of the negligence of the borough in permitting it to remain must, however, be considered as set at rest by the verdict. On the day of the accident the plaintiff was running his car on the borough street in a violent wind-storm, and as he passed under the tree it was blown down, crushing the roof of the car and causing the plaintiff's injury. There is some conflict of testimony as to the speed at which the car was running, but it seems to be fairly well established that it was considerably in excess of the rate permitted by the borough ordinance.

We do not think that the fact that the plaintiff was running his car at a higher rate of speed than eight miles an hour affects his right to recover. It may be that in doing so he violated the ordinance by virtue of which the company was permitted to operate its cars in the streets of the borough, but he certainly was not for that reason without rights upon the streets. Nor can it be said that the speed was the cause of the accident, or contributed to it. It might have been otherwise if the tree had fallen before the car reached it; for in that case a high rate of speed might have rendered it impossible for the plaintiff to avoid a collision which he either foresaw or should have foreseen. Even in that case the ground for denying him the right to recover would be that he had been guilty of contributory negligence, and not that he had violated a borough ordinance. The testimony however shows that the tree fell upon the car as it passed beneath. With this phase of the case in view, it was urged on behalf of the appellant that the speed was the immediate cause of the plaintiff's injury, inasmuch as it was the particular speed at which he was running which brought the car to the place of the accident at the moment when the tree blew down. This argument, while we cannot deny its ingenuity, strikes us, to say the least, as being somewhat sophistical. That his speed brought him to the place of the accident at the moment of the accident was the merest chance, and a thing which no foresight could have predicted. The same thing might as readily have happened to a car running slowly, or it might have been that a high speed alone would have carried him beyond the tree to a place of safety. It was also argued by the appellant's counsel that, even if the speed was not the sole efficient cause of the accident, it at least contributed to its severity, and materially increased the damage. It may be that it did. But what basis could a jury have for finding such to be the case; and, should they so find, what guide could be given them for differentiating between the injury done this man and the injury which would have been done a man in a similar accident on a car running at a speed of eight miles an hour or less?

The judgment is affirmed.[95]

GORRIS v. SCOTT

Court of Exchequer, 1874.
L.R. 9 Exch. 125.

On demurrer to declaration.

KELLY, C. B. This is an action to recover damages for the loss of a number of sheep which the defendant, a shipowner, had contracted to carry, and which were washed overboard and lost by reason (as we must take it to be truly alleged) of the neglect to comply with a certain order made by the Privy Council, in pursuance of the Contagious Diseases (Animals) Act, 1869. The Act was passed merely for sanitary purposes, in order to prevent animals in a state of infectious disease from communicating it to other animals with which they might come in contact. Under the authority of that Act, certain

95. Defendant negligently causes highway accident. Members of medical rescue team are killed in helicopter crash as a result of either pilot error or mechanical malfunction. See Maltman v. Sauer, 84 Wash.2d 975, 530 P.2d 254 (1975).

orders were made; amongst others, an order by which any ship bringing sheep or cattle from any foreign port to ports in Great Britain is to have the place occupied by such animals divided into pens of certain dimensions, and the floor of such pens furnished with battens or foot-holds. The object of this order is to prevent animals from being overcrowded, and so brought into a condition in which the disease guarded against would be likely to be developed. This regulation has been neglected, and the question is, whether the loss, which we must assume to have been caused by that neglect, entitles the plaintiffs to maintain an action.

The argument of the defendant is, that the Act has imposed penalties to secure the observance of its provisions, and that, according to the general rule, the remedy prescribed by the statute must be pursued; that although, when penalties are imposed for the violation of a statutory duty, a person aggrieved by its violation may sometimes maintain an action for the damage so caused, that must be in cases where the object of the statute is to confer a benefit on individuals, and to protect them against the evil consequences which the statute was designed to prevent, and which have in fact ensued; but that if the object is not to protect individuals against the consequences which have in fact ensued, it is otherwise; that if, therefore, by reason of the precautions in question not having been taken, the plaintiffs had sustained that damage against which it was intended to secure them, an action would lie, but that when the damage is of such a nature as was not contemplated at all by the statute, and as to which it was not intended to confer any benefit on the plaintiffs, they cannot maintain an action founded on the neglect. The principle may be well illustrated by the case put in argument of a breach by a railway company of its duty to erect a gate on a level crossing, and to keep the gate closed except when the crossing is being actually and properly used. The object of the precaution is to prevent injury from being sustained through animals or vehicles being upon the line at unseasonable times; and if by reason of such a breach of duty, either in not erecting the gate, or in not keeping it closed, a person attempts to cross with a carriage at an improper time, and injury ensues to a passenger, no doubt an action would lie against the railway company, because the intention of the legislature was that, by the erection of the gates and by their being kept closed individuals should be protected against accidents of this description. And if we could see that it was the object, or among the objects of this Act, that the owners of sheep and cattle coming from a foreign port should be protected by the means described against the danger of their property being washed overboard, or lost by the perils of the sea, the present action would be within the principle.

But, looking at the Act, it is perfectly clear that its provisions were all enacted with a totally different view; there was no purpose, direct or indirect, to protect against such damage; but, as is recited in the preamble, the Act is directed against the possibility of sheep or cattle being exposed to disease on their way to this country. The preamble recites that "it is expedient to confer on Her Majesty's most honourable Privy Council power to take such measures as may appear from time to time necessary to prevent the introduction into Great Britain of contagious or infectious diseases among cattle, sheep, or other animals, by prohibiting or regulating the importation of foreign animals," and also to provide against the "spreading" of such diseases in Great Britain. Then follow numerous sections directed entirely to this object. Then comes section 75, which enacts that "the Privy Council may from time to time make such orders as they think expedient for all or any of the following purposes." What, then, are these purposes? They are "for securing for animals brought by sea to ports in Great Britain a proper supply of food and water during the passage and on landing," "for protecting such animals from unnecessary suffering during the passage and on landing," and so forth; all the purposes enumerated being calculated and directed to the prevention of disease, and none of them having any relation whatever to the danger of loss by the perils of the sea. That being so, if by reason of the default in question the plaintiffs' sheep had been overcrowded, or had been caused unnecessary suffering, and so had arrived in this country in a state of disease, I do not say that they might not have maintained this action. But the damage complained of here is something totally apart from the object of the Act of Parliament, and it is in accordance with all the authorities to say that the action is not maintainable.

PIGOTT, B. * * * The legislature never contemplated altering the relations between the owners and carriers of cattle, except for the purposes pointed out in the Act; and if the Privy Council had gone out of their way and made provisions to prevent cattle from being washed overboard, their act would have been *ultra vires*. If, indeed, by reason of the neglect complained of, the cattle had contracted a contagious disease, the case would have been different. * * *

POLLOCK, B. I also think this demurrer must be allowed. * * *

AMPHLETT, B. I am of the same opinion.

Judgment for the defendant.

KERNAN v. AMERICAN DREDGING CO.

United States Supreme Court, 1958.
355 U.S. 426, 78 S.Ct. 394, 2 L.Ed.2d 382.

[Plaintiff's decedent was a seaman who was killed in an explosion; an open-flame kerosene lamp on the deck of a scow, three feet above water, had ignited inflammable petroleum vapors over the river surface. A Coast Guard navigation rule had required the lamp to be at least eight feet high, in which case the vapor would not have been ignited.]

MR. JUSTICE BRENNAN delivered the opinion of the Court.

* * *

The District Court held that the violation of the rule "whether * * * [it] be called negligence or be said to make the flotilla unseaworthy," did not impose liability because "the Coast Guard regulation had to do solely with navigation and was intended for the prevention of collisions, and for no other purpose. In the present case there was no collision and no fault of navigation. True, the origin of the fire can be traced to the violation of the regulation, but the question is not causation but whether the violation of the regulation, of itself, imposes liability." * * *

The petitioner urges first that the statutory violation made the flotilla unseaworthy, creating liability without regard to fault. But the remedy for unseaworthiness derives from the general maritime law, and that law recognizes no cause of action for wrongful death whether occasioned by unseaworthiness or by negligence. * * * Before the Jones Act,[96] federal courts of admiralty resorted to the various state death acts to give a remedy for wrongful death. * * * The Jones Act created a federal right of action for the wrongful death of a seaman based on the statutory action under the Federal Employers' Liability Act. In Lindgren v. United States, 281 U.S. 38, 50 S.Ct. 207, 74 L.Ed. 686, the Court held that the Jones Act remedy for wrongful death was exclusive and precluded any remedy for wrongful death within territorial waters,[97] based on unseaworthiness, whether derived from federal or state law. * * *

The petitioner also urges that, since the violation of the rule requiring the lights to be eight feet above the water resulted in a defect

96. "Any seaman who shall suffer personal injury in the course of his employment may, at his election, maintain an action for damages at law, with the right of trial by jury, and in such action all statutes of the United States modifying or extending the common-law right or remedy in cases of personal injury to railway employees shall apply; and in case of the death of any seaman as a result of any such personal injury the personal representative of such seaman may maintain an action for damages at law with the right of trial by jury, and in such action all statutes of the United States conferring or regulating the right of action for death in the case of railway employees shall be applicable. [I. e., Federal Employers' Liability Act, 35 Stat. 65, as amended, 45 U.S.C. §§ 51–60, 45 U.S.C.A. §§ 51–60.] Jurisdiction in such actions shall be under the court of the district in which the defendant employer resides or in which his principal office is located." 41 Stat. 1007, 46 U.S.C. § 688, 46 U.S.C.A. § 688.

97. Where death occurs beyond a marine league from state shores, the Death on the High Seas Act, 41 Stat. 537, 46 U.S.C. §§ 761–768, 46 U.S.C.A. §§ 761–768, provides a remedy for wrongful death. Presumably any claims, based on unseaworthiness, for damages accrued prior to the decedent's death would survive, at least if a pertinent state statute is effective to bring about a survival of the seaman's right. See Holland v. Steag, Inc., D.C., 143 F.Supp. 203; cf. Cox v. Roth, 348 U.S. 207, 75 S.Ct. 242, 99 L.Ed. 260; Just v. Chambers, 312 U.S. 383, 668, 61 S.Ct. 687, 85 L.Ed. 903. Claims for maintenance and cure survive the death of the seaman. Sperbeck v. A. L. Burbank & Co., 2 Cir., 190 F.2d 449. For a discussion of the applicability of a state wrongful-death statute to an action for death of a nonseaman based upon a breach of the warranty of seaworthiness, see Skovgaard v. The Tungus, 3 Cir., 252 F.2d 14.

or insufficiency in the flotilla's lighting equipment which in fact caused the seaman's death, liability was created without regard to negligence under the line of decisions of this Court in actions under the FELA based upon violations of either the Safety Appliance Acts [98] or the Boiler Inspection Act.[99] That line of decisions interpreted the clause of § 1 of the FELA, 45 U.S.C. § 51, 45 U.S.C.A. § 51, which imposes liability on the employer "by reason of any defect or insufficiency, due to its negligence, in its cars, engines, appliances, machinery, track, roadbed, works, boats, wharves, or other equipment." The cases hold that under this clause, a defect resulting from a violation of either statute which causes the injury or death of an employee creates liability without regard to negligence. * * *

The FELA and the Jones Act impose upon the employer the duty of paying damages when injury to the worker is caused, in whole or in part, by the employer's fault. This fault may consist of a breach of the duty of care, analogous but by no means identical to the general common-law duty, or of a breach of some statutory duty. The tort doctrine which the lower courts applied imposes liability for violation of a statutory duty only where the injury is one which the statute was designed to prevent. However, this Court has repeatedly refused to apply such a limiting doctrine in FELA cases. In FELA cases based upon violations of the Safety Appliance Acts or the Boiler Inspection Act, the Court has held that a violation of either statute creates liability under FELA if the resulting defect or insufficiency in equipment contributes in fact to the death or injury in suit, without regard to whether the injury flowing from the breach was the injury the statute sought to prevent. * * *

The decisive question in this case, then, is whether the principles developed in this line of FELA cases permit recovery for violation of this navigation statute or are limited as the dissenting opinion would have it, to cases involving the Safety Appliance and Boiler Inspection Acts. * * *

* * * [I]t is argued that the Safety Appliance and Boiler Inspection Acts are special safety statutes and thus may easily be assimilated to the FELA under general common-law principles. But there is no magic in the word "safety." In the cases * * * it was regarded as irrelevant that the defects in the appliances did not disable them from performing their intended safety function. * * * We think that the irrelevance of the safety aspect in these cases demonstrates that the basis of liability is a violation of statutory duty without regard to whether the injury flowing from the violation was the injury the statute sought to guard against. It must therefore be concluded that the nature of the Acts violated is not a controlling consideration; the basis of liability is the FELA.

* * *

98. 27 Stat. 531, as amended, 45 U.S.C. §§ 1–16, 45 U.S.C.A. §§ 1–16.

99. 36 Stat. 913, as amended, 45 U.S.C. §§ 24–34, 45 U.S.C.A. §§ 22–34. [Notes 96–99 from original, renumbered; other notes in original omitted.]

We find no difficulty in applying these principles, developed under the FELA, to the present action under the Jones Act, for the latter Act expressly provides for seamen the cause of action—and consequently the entire judicially developed doctrine of liability—granted to railroad workers by the FELA. The deceased seaman here was in a position perfectly analogous to that of the railroad workers allowed recovery in the line of cases we have discussed, and the principles governing those cases clearly should apply here.

* * *

Reversed.

MR. JUSTICE HARLAN, whom MR. JUSTICE FRANKFURTER, MR. JUSTICE BURTON, and MR. JUSTICE WHITTAKER join, dissenting.

* * *

The Court neither casts doubt on the District Court's finding that respondent was not negligent in carrying the tug's lantern at three feet above the water surface nor disputes that the sole purpose of the Coast Guard regulation was to guard against the risk of collision, but it nevertheless decides that violation of the regulation in and of itself rendered the respondent liable for *all* injuries flowing from it. This holding is said to follow from the decisions of this Court in a series of FELA cases based on violations of the Safety Appliance Act, 27 Stat. 531, as amended, 45 U.S.C. §§ 1–16, 45 U.S.C.A. §§ 1–16, and the Boiler Inspection Act, 36 Stat. 913, as amended, 45 U.S.C. §§ 22–34, 45 U.S.C.A. §§ 22–34. These decisions as the Court here properly states, have created under the FELA an absolute liability—that is, a liability "without regard to negligence"—for injuries resulting from violations of the other Acts. From this, the Court concludes that there is no reason not to extend this absolute liability to cases based on the violation of a statutory duty which are brought under the Jones Act.

This conclusion I cannot share. * * *

In the course of its development of an absolute liability under the FELA for injuries traceable to violations of the Safety Appliance Act or the Boiler Inspection Act, the Court has faced two distinct problems. First, was it necessary for the plaintiff to show that the violation of either of these safety statutes was due to negligence? The answer has uniformly been "no." * * * Second, was the defendant's liability for the injuries suffered limited to those within the character of the risks which these statutes were designed to eliminate? * * * the answer here has also been "no." * * *

The rationale for * * * earlier cases is not entirely clear, but after a good deal of uncertainty it finally became established in 1948 and 1949 that railway employees suffering injuries in consequence of a violation of safety regulations found in or promulgated under either the Safety Appliance Act or the Boiler Inspection Act could maintain an action under the FELA *without reference* to the law of negligence. * * * As a result of these cases, the scope of § 1 of the FELA, 35 Stat. 65, as amended, 45 U.S.C. § 51, 45 U.S.C.A. § 51, has been enlarged by making compensable not only injuries "resulting in whole or in part from the negligence" of the carrier, but also those resulting from violation of the two regulatory Acts, so that in effect these Acts give rise, through the medium of the FELA, to a "non-negligence" * * * cause of action. * * *

These cases then certainly do not establish any broad rule under the FELA that the term "*negligence*" as used in that Act is not subject to the limiting doctrine of Gorris v. Scott, supra, which the District Court applied. Rather, they are based on a theory of liability wholly divorced from negligence. And in fact, the Court today invokes these decisions to support its conclusion that a "*non-negligence*" action based on violation of this Coast Guard regulation lies under the Jones Act. Its reasons for this conclusion are that the Jones Act "incorporates the provisions of the FELA" and "expressly provides for seamen the cause of action—and consequently the entire judicially developed doctrine of liability—granted to railroad workers by the FELA." The Court thus reads these decisions to establish a doctrine under the FELA that injuries following *any* violation of *any* statute, not simply the Safety Appliance and Boiler Inspection Acts, are actionable without any showing of negligence, and it is this doctrine which, the Court argues, the Jones Act absorbs.

So unjustifiably broad a view of the doctrine this Court is said to have established disregards the basis upon which these earlier decisions proceed. In brief, they concentrate and explicitly rest upon the peculiar relationship between the Safety Appliance and the Boiler Inspection Acts, on the one hand, and the FELA, on the other. * *

These express indications of congressional intent to impose strict liability for injuries traceable to violations of these statutes underlay the holdings on which the Court relies. * * *

* * * I think it is evident that this Court's past interpretation of the FELA to provide a cause of action based on absolute liability for injuries traceable to violations of these two *particular* safety statutes has rested entirely on its view of congressional intent, and that no general rule of absolute liability without regard to negligence for injuries resulting from violation of *any* statute can fairly be said to emerge from these decisions.

* * *

Whatever may be one's views of the adequacy of "negligence" liability as the means of dealing with occupational hazards in these fields, Congress has not legislated in terms of absolute liability. "The basis of liability under the Act is and remains negligence." Wilkerson v. McCarthy, 336 U.S. 53, 69, 69 S.Ct. 413, 421, 93 L.Ed. 497 (concurring opinion of Douglas, J.). And, except as expressly modified by Congress, the term "negligence" as it appears in § 1 of the FELA has always been taken to embody common-law concepts. * *

I cannot agree that Congress intended the federal courts to roam at large in devising new bases of liability to replace the liability for negligence which these Acts imposed on employers.

I would affirm.

* * *

ROSS v. HARTMAN

United States Court of Appeals, District of Columbia, 1943.
78 U.S.App.D.C. 217, 139 F.2d 14, 158 A.L.R. 1370.

EDGERTON, ASSOCIATE JUSTICE. This is an appeal by the plaintiff from a judgment for the defendant in a personal injury action.

The facts were stipulated. Appellee's agent violated a traffic ordinance of the District of Columbia [100] by leaving appellee's truck unattended in a public alley, with the ignition unlocked and the key in the switch. He left the truck outside a garage "so that it might be taken inside the garage by the garage attendant for night storage," but he does not appear to have notified anyone that he had left it. Within two hours an unknown person drove the truck away and negligently ran over the appellant.

The trial court duly directed a verdict for the appellee on the authority of Squires v. Brooks.[101] That case was decided in 1916. On facts essentially similar to these, and despite the presence of a similar ordinance, this court held that the defendant's act in leaving the car unlocked was not a "proximate" or legal cause of the plaintiff's injury because the wrongful act of a third person intervened.[102] We cannot reconcile that decision with facts which have become clearer and principles which have become better established than they were in 1916, and we think it should be overruled.

Everyone knows now that children and thieves frequently cause harm by tampering with unlocked cars. The danger that they will do so on a particular occasion may be slight or great. In the absence of an ordinance, therefore, leaving a car unlocked might not be negligent in some circumstances, although in other circumstances it might be both negligent and a legal or "proximate" cause of a resulting accident.[103]

100. "Locks on Motor Vehicles. Every motor vehicle shall be equipped with a lock suitable, to lock the starting lever, throttle, or switch, or gear-shift lever, by which the vehicle is set in motion, and no person shall allow any motor vehicle operated by him to stand or remain unattended on any street or in any public place without first having locked the lever, throttle, or switch by which said motor vehicle may be set in motion." Traffic and Motor Vehicle Regulations for the District of Columbia, Section 58.

101. 44 App.D.C. 320.

102. Slater v. T. C. Baker Co., 1927, 261 Mass. 424, 158 N.E. 778, and Castay v. Katz & Besthoff, Ltd., La.App.1933, 148 So. 76, are to similar effect; but cf. Malloy v. Newman, 1941, 310 Mass. 269, 37 N.E.2d 1001.

103. Lee v. Van Beuren & New York Bill Posting Co., 190 App.Div. 742, 180 N.Y.S. 295; Gumbrell v. Clausen-Flanagan Brewery, 199 App.Div. 778,

But the existence of an ordinance changes the situation. If a driver causes an accident by exceeding the speed limit, for example, we do not inquire whether his prohibited conduct was unreasonably dangerous. It is enough that it was prohibited. Violation of an ordinance intended to promote safety is negligence. If by creating the hazard [104] which the ordinance was intended to avoid it brings about the harm which the ordinance was intended to prevent, it is a legal cause of the harm.[105] This comes only to saying that in such circumstances the law has no reason to ignore and does not ignore the causal relation which obviously exists in fact. The law has excellent reason to recognize it, since it is the very relation which the makers of the ordinance anticipated. This court has applied these principles to speed limits and other regulations of the manner of driving.[106]

The same principles govern this case. The particular ordinance involved here is one of a series which require, among other things, that motor vehicles be equipped with horns and lamps. Ordinary bicycles are required to have bells and lamps,[107] but they are not required to be locked. The evident purpose of requiring motor vehicles to be locked is not to prevent theft for the sake of owners or the police, but to promote the safety of the public in the streets. An unlocked motor vehicle creates little more risk of theft than an unlocked bicycle, or for that matter an unlocked house, but it creates much more risk that meddling by children, thieves or others will result in injuries to the public. The ordinance is intended to prevent such consequences. Since it is a safety measure, its violation was negligence.[108] This negligence created the hazard and thereby brought about the harm which the ordinance was intended to prevent. It was therefore a legal or "proximate" cause of the harm.[109] Both negli-

192 N.Y.S. 451; Connell v. Berland, 223 App.Div. 234, 228 N.Y.S. 20.

Contra, Rhad v. Duquesne Light Co., 255 Pa. 409, 100 A. 262, L.R.A.1917D, 864.

The New York Court of Appeals has said broadly that "If one is negligent in leaving a motor vehicle improperly secured, if as a result thereof and in immediate sequence therewith some other event occurs, which would not have occurred except for such negligence, and if injury follows, such a one is responsible, even though the negligent act comes first in order of time." Maloney v. Kaplan, 233 N.Y. 426, 135 N.E. 838, 839, 26 A.L.R. 909.

104. Cf. Boronkay v. Robinson & Carpenter, 247 N.Y. 365, 160 N.E. 400.

105. Clements v. Potomac Electric Power Co., 26 App.D.C. 482; Janof v. Newsom, 60 App.D.C. 291, 53 F.2d 149; Martin v. Herzog, 228 N.Y. 164, 126 N.E. 814; DeHaen v. Rockwood Sprinkler Co., 258 N.Y. 350, 179 N.E. 764; Osborne v. McMasters, 40 Minn. 103, 41 N.W. 543, 12 Am.St.Rep. 698; Restatement, Torts, §§ 286, 449.

106. Capital Traction Co. v. Apple, 34 App.D.C. 559; Danzansky v. Zimbolist, 70 App.D.C. 234, 105 F.2d 457.

107. §§ 53(c), 47(e).

108. In Rosenberg v. Murray, 73 App.D.C. 67, 116 F.2d 552, on which appellee relies, it did not appear that either the owner of the car or any agent whom he had employed to drive it had acted negligently.

109. This does not mean that one who violates a safety ordinance is responsible for all harm that accompanies or follows his negligence. He is responsible for the consequences of his negligence but not for coincidences. If in the present case, for example, the intermeddler had simply released the brake of appellee's truck, without making use of the ignition key or the un-

gence and causation are too clear in this case, we think, for submission to a jury.

The fact that the intermeddler's conduct was itself a proximate cause of the harm, and was probably criminal, is immaterial. Janof v. Newsom [110] involved a statute which forbade employment agencies to recommend servants without investigating their references. An agency recommended a servant to the plaintiff without investigation, the plaintiff employed the servant, and the servant robbed the plaintiff. This court held the agency responsible for the plaintiff's loss. In that case as in this, the conduct of the defendant or his agent was negligent precisely because it created a risk that a third person would act improperly. In such circumstances the fact that a third person does act improperly is not an intelligible reason for excusing the defendant.[111]

There are practical as well as theoretical reasons for not excusing him. The rule we are adopting tends to make the streets safer by discouraging the hazardous conduct which the ordinance forbids. It puts the burden of the risk, as far as may be, upon those who create it. Appellee's agent created a risk which was both obvious and prohibited. Since appellee was responsible for the risk, it is fairer to hold him responsible for the harm than to deny a remedy to the innocent victim.

Reversed.[112]

locked switch, and the truck had thereupon rolled downhill and injured appellant, appellee would not have been responsible for the injuries because of the negligence of his agent in leaving the switch unlocked, since it would have had no part in causing them. In other words the fact that the ignition was unlocked, which alone gave the agent's conduct its negligent character, would have had nothing to do with bringing about the harm.

Neither do we suggest that the ordinance should be interpreted as intended to apply in all possible circumstances. In some emergencies, no doubt, the act of leaving a car unlocked and unattended in a public place would not be a violation of the ordinance, fairly interpreted, and would therefore entail no responsibility for consequences. A classic illustration of the same general principle is the Bologna ordinance against blood-letting in the streets, which did not make criminals of surgeons.

110. 60 App.D.C. 291, 53 F.2d 149.

111. Restatement, Torts, § 449. Cf. Butts v. Ward, 227 Wis. 387, 279 N.W. 6, 116 A.L.R. 1441. [Footnotes 100–111 by the court, renumbered.]

112. For opposing attitudes towards the principal case, see notes, 32 Geo.L.J. 202 (1944); 92 U.P.L.Rev. 467 (1944). See also Peck, op. cit. note 91 supra; as to proposition covered by footnote 109 supra, see also Archibeque v. Homrich, 88 N.M. 527, 543 P.2d 820 (1975).

BROWN v. SHYNE

Court of Appeals of New York, 1926.
242 N.Y. 176, 151 N.E. 197, 44 A.L.R. 1407.

APPEAL, by permission, from a judgment of the Appellate Division of the Supreme Court in the fourth judicial department, entered May 25, 1925, unanimously affirming a judgment in favor of plaintiff entered upon a verdict. * * *

LEHMAN, J. The plaintiff employed the defendant to give chiropractic treatment to her for a disease or physical condition. The defendant had no license to practice medicine, yet he held himself out as being able to diagnose and treat disease, and under the provisions of the Public Health Law (Cons.Laws, ch. 45) he was guilty of a misdemeanor. The plaintiff became paralyzed after she had received nine treatments by the defendant. She claims, and upon this appeal we must assume, that the paralysis was caused by the treatment she received. She has recovered judgment in the sum of $10,000 for the damages caused by said injury.

The plaintiff in her complaint alleges that the injuries were caused by the defendant's negligence. If negligence on the part of the defendant caused the injury, the plaintiff may recover the consequent damages. Though the defendant held himself out, and the plaintiff consulted him, as a chiropractor and not as a regular physician, he claimed to possess the skill requisite for diagnosis and treatment of disease, and in the performance of what he undertook to do he may be held to the degree of skill and care which he claimed to possess. At the trial the plaintiff gave testimony in regard to the manner in which she was treated. She supplemented this testimony by evidence that the treatment was not in accordance with recognized theory or practice, that it produced the injury which followed and that a person qualified to treat disease should have foreseen that the treatment might have such result. Though her testimony was contradicted, the jury might well have resolved the conflict in her favor, and if the only question submitted to the jury had been whether or not this evidence showed that plaintiff's injury was caused by the defendant's negligence, the defendant could not complain of any substantial error at the trial. Indeed, it would seem that in some respects the rulings of the trial judge may have been too favorable to the defendant.

At the close of the plaintiff's case the plaintiff was permitted to amend the complaint to allege "that in so treating the plaintiff the defendant was engaged in the practice of medicine contrary to and in violation of the provisions of the Public Health Law of the State of New York in such case made and provided, he at the time of so treating plaintiff not being a duly licensed physician or surgeon of the State of New York." Thereafter the trial judge charged the jury that they might bring in a verdict in favor of the plaintiff if they found that the evidence established that the treatment given to the plaintiff was not in accordance with the standards of skill and care which prevail among those treating disease. He then continued: "This is a little different from the ordinary malpractice case, and I am going to allow you, if you think proper under the evidence in the case, to predicate negligence upon another theory. The public health laws of this State prescribe that no person shall practice medicine unless he is licensed so to do by the Board of Regents of this State and registered pursuant to statute * * *. This statute to which I have referred is a general police regulation. Its violation, and it has been violated by the defendant, is some evidence, more or less cogent, of negligence which you may consider for what it is worth, along with all the other evidence in the case. If the defendant attempted to treat the plaintiff and to adjust the vertebrae in her spine when he did not possess the requisite knowledge and skill as prescribed by the statute to know what was proper and necessary to do under the circumstances, or how to do it, even if he did know what to do, you can find him negligent." In so charging the jury that from the violation of the statute the jury might infer negligence which produced injury to the plaintiff, the trial justice in my opinion erred.

The provisions of the Public Health Law prohibiting the practice of medicine without a license granted upon proof of preliminary training and after examination intended to show adequate knowledge, are of course intended for the protection of the general public against injury which unskilled and unlearned practitioners might cause. If violation of the statute by the defendant was the proximate cause of the plaintiff's injury, then the plaintiff may recover upon proof of violation; if violation of the statute has no direct bearing on the injury, proof of the violation becomes irrelevant. For injury caused by neglect of duty imposed by the penal law there is civil remedy; but of course the injury must follow from the neglect.

Proper formulation of general standards of preliminary education and proper examination of the particular applicant should serve to raise the standards of skill and care generally possessed by members of the profession in this State; but the license to practice medicine confers no additional skill upon the practitioner; nor does it confer immunity from physical injury upon a patient if the practitioner fails to exercise care. Here, injury may have been caused by lack of skill or care; it would not have been obviated if the defendant had possessed a license yet failed to exercise the skill and care required of one practicing medicine. True, if the defendant had not practiced medicine in this State, he could not have injured the plaintiff, but the protection which the statute was intended to provide was against risk of injury by the unskilled or careless practitioner, and unless the plaintiff's injury was caused by carelessness or lack of skill, the defendant's failure to obtain a license was not connected with the injury. The plaintiff's cause of action is for negligence or malpractice. The defendant undertook to treat the plaintiff for a physical condition which seemed to require remedy. Under our law such treatment may be given only by a duly qualified practitioner who has obtained a license.

The defendant in offering to treat the plaintiff held himself out as qualified to give treatment. He must meet the professional standards of skill and care prevailing among those who do offer treatment lawfully. If injury follows through failure to meet those standards, the plaintiff may recover. The provisions of the Public Health Law may result in the exclusion from practice of some who are unqualified. Even a skilled and learned practitioner who is not licensed commits an offense against the State; but against such practitioners the statute was not intended to protect, for no protection was needed, and neglect to obtain a license results in no injury to the patient and, therefore, no private wrong. The purpose of the statute is to protect the public against unfounded assumption of skill by one who undertakes to prescribe or treat for disease. In order to show that the plaintiff has been injured by defendant's breach of the statutory duty, proof must be given that defendant in such treatment did not exercise the care and skill which would have been exercised by qualified practitioners within the State, and that such lack of skill and care caused the injury. Failure to obtain a license as required by law gives rise to no remedy if it has caused no injury. No case has been cited where neglect of a statutory duty has given rise to private cause of action where it has not appeared that private injury has been caused by danger against which the statute was intended to afford protection, and which obedience to the statute would have obviated. It is said that in the case of Karpeles v. Heine, 227 N.Y. 74, 124 N.E. 101, this court held that liability *per se* arises from breach of the statute which prohibits employment of a child under sixteen years of age, but in that case this court merely decided that the statute was intended to protect the child against danger arising from its own lack of foresight in the course of such employment, and that, therefore, an action against the employer by a child unlawfully employed "for injuries arising in the course of such employment and as the proximate result thereof cannot be defeated by his contributory negligence." In that case the court was considering the legal effect of the proven negligence of the child who was unlawfully employed; only upon proof in the present case of negligence on the part of the chiropractor would any analogy be apparent.

It is said that the trial justice did not charge that plaintiff might recover for defendant's failure to obtain a license but only that failure to obtain a license might be considered "some evidence" of defendant's negligence. Argument is made that even if neglect of the statutory duty does not itself create liability, it tends to prove that injury was caused by lack of skill or care. That can be true only if logical inference may be drawn from defendant's failure to obtain or perhaps seek a license that he not only lacks the skill and learning necessary for the physical manipulation he gave to this plaintiff. Evidence of defendant's training, learning and skill and the method he used in giving the treatment was produced at the trial and upon such evidence the jury could base finding either of care or negligence, but the absense of a license does not seem to strengthen inference that might be drawn from such evidence, and *a fortiori* would not alone be a basis for such inference. Breach or neglect of duty imposed by statute or ordinance may be evidence of negligence only if there is logical connection between the proven neglect of statutory duty and the alleged negligence.

Our decision in the case of People v. Meyer, 239 N.Y. 608, 147 N.E. 216, is not in conflict with these views. The defendant there was charged with causing death by "culpable negligence." Negligence was shown by independent evidence, but the charge of manslaughter could be sustained only if the defendant's negligence reached beyond the bounds of lack of skill and foresight where civil liability begins to a point where criminal is imposed because the negligence is not merely venal but is "culpable," involving fault for which the State may demand punishment. We held that the circumstance that the defendant practiced medicine without those qualifications which the law demands as a prerequisite to practice was relevant and material upon the question whether the defendant's proven negligence was venal or culpable. We did not hold that the absence of license tended to prove negligence itself.

For these reasons the judgments should be reversed and a new trial granted, with costs to abide the event.

CRANE, J. (dissenting).

* * *

The prohibition against practicing medicine without a license was for the very purpose of protecting the public from just what happened in this case. The violation of this statute has been the direct and proximate cause of the injury. The courts will not determine in face of this statute whether a faith healer, a patent medicine man, a chiropractor, or any other class of practitioner acted according to the standards of his own school, or according to the standards of a duly licensed physician. The law, to insure against ignorance and carelessness, has laid down a rule to be followed, namely, examinations to test qualifications, and a license to practice. If a man, in violation of this statute, takes his chances in trying to cure disease, and his acts result directly in injury, he should not complain if the law, in a suit for damages, says that his violation of the statute is some evidence of his incapacity.[113]

* * *

* * * The Public Health Law was intended to guard individual members of the public from the injuries which might result from resorting to unexamined practitioners. The violation of the law in this case has brought about the very thing which the Legislature has tried to prevent. * * *

113. Attitudes have varied as to whether chiropractors should be licensed to practice without meeting physicians' standards; for a review see England v. Louisiana State Board of Medical Examiners, 259 F.2d 626 (5th Cir. 1958).

* * * The defendant held himself out as a doctor, able to cure laryngitis. He had an office where his name appeared, as though he were a duly licensed physician. The plaintiff could not tell whether or not the doctor was licensed according to the Health Law; she was not obliged to look up the records before going to him; nor was she expected to understand all the requirements of the Regents. She was one of that public which the law sought to protect by declaring that the so-called doctor was forbidden to do the very thing he did do, and which resulted in injury. * * *

In recent times the difficulty with these statutes in the courts has been to determine whether the violation was negligence *per se,* or only some evidence of negligence. I have not been able to find any case where the violation of a statute or an ordinance was not at least some evidence of negligence, where the violation was the direct and proximate cause of the injury, that is, that the act done resulting in injury, was prohibited, and the aim and purpose of the statute or ordinance was to prevent such injuries by such prohibition. * * *

* * * I am convinced that the plaintiff in this case was a part of that public for whose benefit the Public Health Law in this particular was passed. It was to prevent injury to such as she that the Legislature forbade the unlicensed practice of medicine. The plaintiff was injured through the defendant's disobedience of the law. He was treating her for laryngitis by pushing her vertebra. In pushing her vertebra and twisting her head, that is, by doing the very thing the law said he must not do, he caused paralysis. Thus by these authorities, the plaintiff could prove in connection with his acts that he was practicing medicine without a license, and such violation was, to say the least, some evidence of negligence. This is as far as the trial judge went in charging the jury. Personally, I am of the opinion that where an injury is the direct and proximate result of practicing medicine without a license, a recovery can be had, as for an act negligent *per se;* but we do not need to go so far in this case. * * *

* * * In this case we * * * have the question of negligence, and as bearing upon it the judge permitted the jury to consider together with all the other facts the practice of medicine without a license.

The ruling was correct, and the judgments below should be affirmed, with costs.

HISCOCK, CH. J., POUND and ANDREWS, JJ., concur with LEHMAN J.; CRANE, J., writes dissenting opinion, in which MCLAUGHLIN, J., concurs; CARDOZO, J., absent.

Judgments reversed, etc.[114]

114. Contrast the approach of the New Hampshire court in Johnson v. Boston & M. R. R., 83 N.H. 350, 143 A. 516, 61 A.L.R. 1173 (1928), with which should be compared Mandell v. Dodge-Freedman Poultry Co., 94 N.H. 1, 45 A.2d 577, 163 A.L.R. 1370 (1946). Also see Gerltch v. Gerber, 193 Neb. 181, 226 N.W.2d 132 (1975) (fifteen year old unlicensed driver, but car skidded on ice, no evidence that driver was negligent); and Koninklijke Rotterdamsche Lloyd (N.V.) v. Western Steamship Co. Ltd. (The Empire Jamaica) [1957] A.C.

PALSGRAF v. LONG ISLAND R. CO.

Court of Appeals of New York, 1928.
248 N.Y. 339, 162 N.E. 99, 59 A.L.R. 1253.

APPEAL from a judgment of the Appellate Division of the Supreme Court in the second judicial department, entered December 16, 1927, affirming a judgment in favor of plaintiff entered upon a verdict. * * *

CARDOZO, CH. J. Plaintiff was standing on a platform of defendant's railroad after buying a ticket to go to Rockaway Beach. A train stopped at the station, bound for another place. Two men ran forward to catch it. One of the men reached the platform of the car without mishap, though the train was already moving. The other man, carrying a package, jumped aboard the car, but seemed unsteady as if about to fall. A guard on the car, who had held the door open, reached forward to help him in, and another guard on the platform pushed him from behind. In this act, the package was dislodged, and fell upon the rails. It was a package of small size, about fifteen inches long, and was covered by a newspaper. In fact it contained fireworks, but there was nothing in its appearance to give notice of its contents. The fireworks when they fell exploded. The shock of the explosion threw down some scales at the other end of the platform, many feet away. The scales struck the plaintiff, causing injuries for which she sues.

The conduct of the defendant's guard, if a wrong in its relation to the holder of the package, was not a wrong in its relation to the plaintiff, standing far away. Relatively to her it was not negligence at all. Nothing in the situation gave notice that the falling package had in it the potency of peril to persons thus removed. Negligence is not actionable unless it involves the invasion of a legally protected interest, the violation of a right. "Proof of negligence in the air, so to speak, will not do" (Pollock, Torts (11th ed.), p. 455; Martin v. Herzog, 228 N.Y. 164, 170, 126 N.E. 814; cf. Salmond, Torts (6th ed.), p. 24). "Negligence is the absence of care, according to the circumstances" (Willes, J., in Vaughan v. Taff Vale Ry. Co., 5 H. & N. 679, 688; 1 Beven, Negligence (4th ed.), 7; Paul v. Consol. Fireworks Co., 212 N.Y. 117, 105 N.E. 795; Adams v. Bullock, 227 N.Y. 208, 211, 125 N.E. 93; Parrott v. Wells-Fargo Co., 15 Wall. 524, 21 L.Ed. 206). The plaintiff as she stood upon the platform of the station might claim to be protected against intentional invasion of her bodily security. Such invasion is not charged. She might claim to be protected against unintentional invasion by conduct involving in the thought of reasonable men an un-

386 (statutory liability of shipowner only for actual negligence or "privity"; "neglilgent mate" was not certificated, as required by statute, but had appeared "fully competent", could have obtained waiver of certification requirement had application been made.)

For divergent points of view among commentators, see Gregory, Breach of Criminal Licensing Statutes in Civil Litigation, 36 Corn.L.Q. 622 (1951); James, Wartime Tort Liability, 55 Yale L.J. 365, 393 (1946); Legal Cause, 60 Yale L.J. 761, 772 (1951).

reasonable hazard that such invasion would ensue. These, from the point of view of the law, were the bounds of her immunity, with perhaps some rare exceptions, survivals for the most part of ancient forms of liability, where conduct is held to be at the peril of the actor (Sullivan v. Dunham, 161 N.Y. 290, 55 N.E. 923, 47 L.R.A. 715, 76 Am.St.Rep. 274). If no hazard was apparent to the eye of ordinary vigilance, an act innocent and harmless, at least to outward seeming, with reference to her, did not take to itself the quality of a tort because it happened to be a wrong, though apparently not one involving the risk of bodily insecurity, with reference to some one else. "In every instance, before negligence can be predicated of a given act, back of the act must be sought and found a duty to the individual complaining, the observance of which would have averted or avoided the injury." McSherry, C. J., in West Va. Central & P. R. Co. v. State, 96 Md. 652, 666, 54 A. 669, 61 L.R.A. 574. The plaintiff sues in her own right for a wrong personal to her, and not as the vicarious beneficiary of a breach of duty to another.

A different conclusion will involve us, and swiftly too, in a maze of contradictions. A guard stumbles over a package which has been left upon a platform. It seems to be a bundle of newspapers. It turns out to be a can of dynamite. To the eye of ordinary vigilance, the bundle is abandoned waste, which may be kicked or trod on with impunity. Is a passenger at the other end of the platform protected by the law against the unsuspected hazard concealed beneath the waste? If not, is the result to be any different, so far as the distant passenger is concerned, when the guard stumbles over a valise which a truckman or a porter has left upon the walk? The passenger far away, if the victim of a wrong at all, has a cause of action, not derivative, but original and primary. His claim to be protected against invasion of his bodily security is neither greater nor less because the act resulting in the invasion is a wrong to another far removed. In this case, the rights that are said to have been violated, the interests said to have been invaded, are not even of the same order. The man was not injured in his person nor even put in danger. The purpose of the act, as well as its effect, was to make his person safe. If there was a wrong to him at all, which may very well be doubted, it was a wrong to a property interest only, the safety of his package. Out of this wrong to property, which threatened injury to nothing else, there has passed, we are told, to the plaintiff by derivation or succession a right of action for the invasion of an interest of another order, the right to bodily security. The diversity of interests emphasizes the futility of the effort to build the plaintiff's right upon the basis of a wrong to some one else. The gain is one of emphasis, for a like result would follow if the interests were the same. Even then, the orbit of the danger as disclosed to the eye of reasonable vigilance would be the orbit of the duty. One who jostles one's neighbor in a crowd does not invade the rights of others standing at the outer fringe when the unintended contact casts a bomb upon the ground. The wrongdoer as to them is the man who carries the bomb, not the one who explodes it without suspicion of the danger. Life will have to be made over, and human nature transformed, before prevision so extravagant can be accepted as the norm of conduct, the customary standard to which behavior must conform.

The argument for the plaintiff is built upon the shifting meanings of such words as "wrong" and "wrongful," and shares their instability. What the plaintiff must show is "a wrong" to herself, i. e., a violation of her own right, and not merely a wrong to some one else, nor conduct "wrongful" because unsocial, but not "a wrong" to any one. We are told that one who drives at reckless speed through a crowded city street is guilty of a negligent act and, therefore, of a wrongful one irrespective of the consequences. Negligent the act, is and wrongful in the sense that it is unsocial, but wrongful and unsocial in relation to other travelers, only because the eye of vigilance perceives the risk of damage. If the same act were to be committed on a speedway or a race course, it would lose its wrongful quality. The risk reasonably to be perceived defines the duty to be obeyed, and risk imports relation; it is risk to another or to others within the range of apprehension (Seavey, Negligence, Subjective or Objective, 41 H.L.Rv. 6; Boronkay v. Robinson & Carpenter, 247 N.Y. 365, 160 N.E. 400). This does not mean, of course, that one who launches a destructive force is always relieved of liability if the force, though known to be destructive, pursues an unexpected path. "It was not necessary that the defendant should have had notice of the particular method in which an accident would occur, if the possibility of an accident was clear to the ordinarily prudent eye" (Munsey v. Webb, 231 U.S. 150, 156, 34 S.Ct. 44, 58 L.Ed. 162; Condran v. Park & Tilford, 213 N.Y. 341, 345, 107 N.E. 565; Robert v. United States Emergency Fleet Corp., 240 N.Y. 474, 477, 148 N.E. 650). Some acts, such as shooting, are so imminently dangerous to any one who may come within reach of the missile, however unexpectedly, as to impose a duty of prevision not far from that of an insurer. Even today, and much oftener in earlier stages of the law, one acts sometimes at one's peril (Jeremiah Smith, Tort and Absolute Liability, 30 H.L.Rv. 328; Street, Foundations of Legal Liability, vol. 1, pp. 77, 78). Under this head, it may be, fall certain cases of what is known as transferred intent, an act willfully dangerous to A resulting by misadventure in injury to B (Talmage v. Smith, 101 Mich. 370, 374, 59 N.W. 656, 45 Am.St.Rep. 414). These cases aside, wrong is defined in terms of the natural or probable, at least when unintentional (Parrot v. Wells-Fargo Co. (The Nitro-Glycerine Case), 15 Wall. 524, 21 L.Ed. 206). The range of reasonable apprehension is at times a question for the court, and at times, if varying inferences are possible, a question for the jury. Here, by concession, there was nothing in the situation to suggest to the most cautious mind that the parcel wrapped in newspaper would spread wreckage through the station. If the guard had thrown it down knowingly and willfully, he would not have threatened the plaintiff's safety, so far as appearances could warn him. His conduct would not have involved, even then, an unreasonable probability of invasion of her bodily security. Liability can be no greater where the act is inadvertent.

Negligence, like risk, is thus a term of relation. Negligence in the abstract, apart from things related, is surely not a tort, if indeed it is understandable at all (Bowen, L. J., in Thomas v. Quartermaine, 18 Q.B.D. 685, 694). Negligence is not a tort unless it results in the commission of a wrong, and the commission of a wrong imports the violation of a right, in this case, we are told, the right to be protected against interference with one's bodily security. But bodily security is protected, not against all forms of interference or aggression, but only against some. One who seeks redress at law does not make out a cause of action by showing without more that there has been damage to his person. If the harm was not willful, he must show that the act as to him had possibilities of danger so many and apparent as to entitle him to be protected against the doing of it though the harm was unintended. Affront to personality is still the keynote of the wrong. Confirmation of this view will be found in the history and development of the action on the case. Negligence as a basis of civil liability was unknown to mediaeval law (8 Holdsworth, History of English Law, p. 449; Street, Foundations of Legal Liability, vol. 1, pp. 189, 190). For damage to the person, the sole remedy was trespass, and trespass did not lie in the absence of aggression, and that direct and personal (Holdsworth, op. cit. p. 453; Street, op. cit. vol. 3, pp. 258, 260, vol. 1, pp. 71, 74). Liability for other damage, as where a servant without orders from the master does or omits something to the damage of another, is a plant of later growth (Holdsworth, op. cit. 450, 457; Wigmore, Responsibility for Tortious Acts, vol. 3, Essays in Anglo-American Legal History, 520, 523, 526, 533). When it emerged out of the legal soil, it was thought of as a variant of trespass, an offshoot of the parent stock. This appears in the form of action, which was known as trespass on the case (Holdsworth, op. cit. p. 449; cf. Scott v. Shepard, 2 Wm. Black 892; Green, Rationale of Proximate Cause, p. 19). The victim does not sue derivatively, or by right of subrogation, or vindicate an interest invaded in the person of another. Thus to view his cause of action is to ignore the fundamental difference between tort and crime (Holland, Jurisprudence (12th ed.), p. 328). He sues for breach of a duty owing to himself.

The law of causation, remote or proximate, is thus foreign to the case before us. The question of liability is always anterior to the question of the measure of the consequences that go with liability. If there is no tort to be redressed, there is no occasion to consider what damage might be recovered if there were a finding of a tort. We may assume, without deciding, that negligence, not at large or in the abstract, but in relation to the plaintiff, would entail liability for any and all consequences, however novel or extraordinary (Bird v. St. Paul F. & M. Ins. Co., 224 N.Y. 47, 54, 120 N.E. 86, 13 A.L.R. 875; Ehrgott v. Mayor, etc., of N. Y., 96 N.Y. 264, 48 Am.Rep. 622; Smith v. London & S. W. R. Co., L.R. 6 C.P. 14; 1 Beven, Negligence, 106;

Street, op. cit. vol. 1, p. 90; Green, Rationale of Proximate Cause, pp. 88, 118; cf. Matter of Polemis, L.R. [1921] 3 K.B. 560; 44 Law Quarterly Review, 142). There is room for argument that a distinction is to be drawn according to the diversity of interests invaded by the act, as where conduct negligent in that it threatens an insignificant invasion of an interest in property results in an unforeseeable invasion of an interest of another order, as, e. g., one of bodily security. Perhaps other distinctions may be necessary. We do not go into the question now. The consequences to be followed must first be rooted in a wrong.

The judgment of the Appellate Division and that of the Trial Term should be reversed, and the complaint dismissed, with costs in all courts.

ANDREWS, J. (dissenting). * * * The result we shall reach depends upon our theory as to the nature of negligence. Is it a relative concept—the breach of some duty owing to a particular person or to particular persons? Or where there is an act which unreasonably threatens the safety of others, is the doer liable for all its proximate consequences, even where they result in injury to one who would generally be thought to be outside the radius of danger? This is not a mere dispute as to words. We might not believe that to the average mind the dropping of the bundle would seem to involve the probability of harm to the plaintiff standing many feet away whatever might be the case as to the owner or to one so near as to be likely to be struck by its fall. If, however, we adopt the second hypothesis we have to inquire only as to the relation between cause and effect. We deal in terms of proximate cause, not of negligence.

Negligence may be defined roughly as an act or omission which unreasonably does or may affect the rights of others, or which unreasonably fails to protect oneself from the dangers resulting from such acts. Here I confine myself to the first branch of the definition. Nor do I comment on the word "unreasonable." For present purposes it sufficiently describes that average of conduct that society requires of its members.

There must be both the act or the omission, and the right. It is the act itself, not the intent of the actor, that is important. (Hover v. Barkhoof, 44 N.Y. 113; Mertz v. Connecticut Co., 217 N.Y 475, 112 N.E. 166.) In criminal law both the intent and the result are to be considered. Intent again is material in tort actions, where punitive damages are sought, dependent on actual malice—not on merely reckless conduct. But here neither insanity nor infancy lessens responsibility. (Williams v. Hays, 143 N.Y. 442, 38 N.E. 449, 26 L.R.A. 153, 42 Am.St.Rep. 743.)

As has been said, except in cases of contributory negligence, there must be rights which are or may be affected. Often though injury has occurred, no rights of him who suffers have been touched. A licensee or trespasser upon my land has no claim to affirmative care on my part that the land be made safe. (Meiers v. Fred Koch Brewery, 229 N.Y. 10, 127 N.E. 491, 13 A.L.R. 633.) Where a railroad is required to fence its tracks against cattle, no man's rights are injured should he wander upon the road because such fence is absent. (Di Caprio v. New York Central R. Co., 231 N.Y. 94, 131 N.E. 746, 16 A.L. R. 940.) An unborn child may not demand immunity from personal harm. (Drobner v. Peters, 232 N.Y. 220, 133 N.E. 567, 20 A.L.R. 1503.)

But we are told that "there is no negligence unless there is in the particular case a legal duty to take care, and this duty must be one which is owed to the plaintiff himself and not merely to others." (Salmond, Torts (6th ed.), 24.) This, I think too narrow a conception. Where there is the unreasonable act, and some right that may be affected there is negligence whether damage does or does not result. That is immaterial. Should we drive down Broadway at a reckless speed, we are negligent whether we strike an approaching car or miss it by an inch. The act itself is wrongful. It is a wrong not only to those who happen to be within the radius of danger but to all who might have been there—a wrong to the public at large. Such is the language of the street. Such the language of the courts when speaking of contributory negligence. Such again and again their language in speaking of the duty of some defendant and discussing proximate cause in cases where such a discussion is wholly irrelevant on any other theory. (Perry v. Rochester Line Co., 219 N.Y. 60, 113 N.E. 529, L.R.A.1917B, 1058.) As was said by Mr. Justice Holmes many years ago, "The measure of the defendant's duty in determining whether a wrong has been committed is one thing, the measure of liability when a wrong has been committed is another." (Spade v. Lynn & Boston R. Co., 172 Mass. 488, 52 N.E. 747, 43 L.R.A. 832, 70 Am.St.Rep. 298.) Due care is a duty imposed on each one of us to protect society from unnecessary danger, not to protect A, B or C alone.

It may well be that there is no such thing as negligence in the abstract. "Proof of negligence in the air, so to speak, will not do." In an empty world negligence would not exist. It does involve a relationship between man and his fellows. But not merely a relationship between man and those whom he might reasonably expect his act would injure. Rather, a relationship between him and those whom he does in fact injure. If his act has a tendency to harm some one, it harms him a mile away as surely as it does those on the scene. We now permit children to recover for the negligent killing of the father. It was never prevented on the theory that no duty was owing to them. A husband may be compensated for the loss of his wife's services. To say that the wrongdoer was negligent as to the husband as well as to the wife is merely an attempt to fit facts to theory. An insurance company paying a fire loss recovers its payment of the negligent incendiary. We speak of subrogation—of suing in the right of the insured. Behind the cloud of words is the fact they hide, that the act, wrongful as to the insured, has also injured the company. Even if it be true that the fault of father, wife or insured will prevent recovery, it is because we consider the original negligence not the proximate cause of the injury. (Pollock, Torts (12th ed.), 463.) * * *

The proposition is this. Every one owes to the world at large the duty of refraining from those acts that may unreasonably threaten the safety of others. Such an act occurs. Not only is he wronged to whom harm might reasonably be expected to result, but he also who is in fact injured, even if he be outside what would generally be thought the danger zone. There needs be duty due the one complaining but this is not a duty to a particular individual because as to him harm might be expected. Harm to some one being the natural result of the act, not only that one alone, but all those in fact injured may complain. We have never, I think, held otherwise. Indeed in the Di Caprio case we said that a breach of a general ordinance defining the degree of care to be exercised in one's calling is evidence of negligence as to every one. We did not limit this statement to those who might be expected to be exposed to danger. Unreasonable risk being taken, its consequneces are not confined to those who might probably be hurt. * * *

The right to recover damages rests on additional considerations. The plaintiff's rights must be injured, and this injury must be caused by the negligence. We build a dam, but are negligent as to its foundations. Breaking it injures property down stream. We are not liable if all this happened because of some reason other than the insecure foundation. But when injuries do result from our unlawful act we are liable for the consequences. It does not matter that they are unusual, unexpected, unforeseen and unforeseeable. But there is one limitation. The damages must be so connected with the negligence that the latter may be said to be the proximate cause of the former.

These two words have never been given an inclusive definition. What is a cause in a legal sense, still more what is a proximate cause, depend in each case upon many considerations, as does the existence of negligence itself. Any philosophical doctrine of causation does not help us. A boy throws a stone into a pond. The ripples spread. The water level rises. The history of that pond is altered to all eternity. It will be altered by other causes also. Yet it will be forever the resultant of all causes combined. Each one will have an influence. How great only omniscience can say. You may speak of a chain, or if you please, a net. An analogy is of little aid. Each cause brings about future events. Without each the future would not be the same. Each is proximate in the sense it is essential. But that is not what we mean by the word. Nor on the other hand do we mean sole cause. There is no such thing.

Should analogy be thought helpful, however, I prefer that of a stream. The spring, starting on its journey, is joined by tributary after tributary. The river, reaching the ocean, comes from a hundred sources. No man may say whence any drop of water is derived. Yet for a time distinction may be possible. Into the clear creek, brown swamp water flows from the left. Later, from the right comes water stained by its clay bed. The three may remain for a space, sharply divided. But at last, inevitably no trace of separation remains. They are so commingled that all distinction is lost.

As we have said, we cannot trace the effect of an act to the end, if end there is. Again, however, we may trace it part of the way. A murder at Serajevo may be the necessary antecedent to an assassination in London twenty years hence. An overturned lantern may burn all Chicago. We may follow the fire from the shed to the last building. We rightly say the fire started by the lantern caused its destruction.

A cause, but not the proximate cause. What we do mean by the word "proximate" is, that because of convenience, of public policy, of a rough sense of justice, the law arbitrarily declines to trace a series of events beyond a certain point. This is not logic. It is practical politics. Take our rule as to fires. Sparks from my burning haystack set on fire my house and my neighbor's. I may recover from a negligent railroad. He may not. Yet the wrongful act as directly harmed the one as the other. We may regret that the line was drawn just where it was, but drawn somewhere it had to be. We said the act of the railroad was not the proximate cause of our neighbor's fire. Cause it surely was. The words we used were simply indicative of our notions of public policy. Other courts think differently. But somewhere they reach the point where they cannot say the stream comes from any one source.

Take the illustration given in an unpublished manuscript by a distinguished and helpful writer on the law of torts. A chauffeur negligently collides with another car which is filled with dynamite, although he could not know it. An explosion follows. A, walking on the sidewalk nearby, is killed. B, sitting in a window of a building opposite, is cut by flying glass. C, likewise sitting in a window a block away, is similarly injured. And a further illustration. A nursemaid, ten blocks away, startled by the noise, involuntarily drops a baby from her arms to the walk. We are told that C may not recover while A may. As to B it is a question for court or jury. We will all agree that the baby might not. Because, we are again told, the chauffeur had no reason to believe his conduct involved any risk of injuring either C or the baby. As to them he was not negligent.

But the chauffeur, being negligent in risking the collision, his belief that the scope of the harm he might do would be limited is immaterial. His act unreasonably jeopardized the safety of any one who might be affected by it. C's injury and that of the baby were directly traceable to the collision. Without that, the injury would not have happened. C had the right to sit in his office, secure from such dangers. The baby was entitled to use the sidewalk with reasonable safety.

The true theory is, it seems to me, that the injury to C, if in truth he is to be denied recovery, and the injury to the baby is that their several injuries were not the proximate result of the negligence. And here not what the chauffeur had reason to believe would be the result of his conduct, but what the prudent would foresee, may have a bearing. May have some bearing for the problem of proximate cause is not to be solved by any one consideration.

It is all a question of expediency. There are no fixed rules to govern our judgment. There are simply matters of which we may take account. We have in a somewhat different connection spoken of "the stream of events." We have asked whether that stream was deflected—whether it was forced into new and unexpected channels. (Donnelly v. Piercy Contracting Co., 222 N.Y. 210). This is rather rhetoric than law. There is in truth little to guide us other than common sense.

There are some hints that may help us. The proximate cause, involved as it may be with many other causes, must be, at the least, something without which the event would not happen. The court must ask itself whether there was a natural and continuous sequence between cause and effect. Was the one a substantial factor in producing the other? Was there a direct connection between them, without too many intervening causes? Is the effect of cause on result not too attenuated? Is the cause likely, in the usual judgment of mankind, to produce the result? Or by the exercise of prudent foresight could the result be foreseen? Is the result too remote from the cause, and here we consider remoteness in time and space. (Bird v. St. Paul F. & M. Ins. Co., 224 N.Y. 47, 120 N.E. 86, 13 A.L.R. 875, where we passed upon the construction of a contract—but something was also said on this subject.) Clearly we must so consider, for the greater the distance either in time or space, the more surely do other causes intervene to affect the result. When a lantern is overturned the firing of a shed is a fairly direct consequence. Many things contribute to the spread of the conflagration—the force of the wind, the direction and width of streets, the character of intervening structures, other factors. We draw an uncertain and wavering line, but draw it we must as best we can.

Once again, it is all a question of fair judgment, always keeping in mind the fact that we endeavor to make a rule in each case that will be practical and in keeping with the general understanding of mankind.

Here another question must be answered. In the case supposed it is said, and said correctly, that the chauffeur is liable for the direct effect of the explosion although he had no reason to suppose it would follow a collision. "The fact that the injury occurred in a different manner than that which might have been expected does not prevent the chauffeur's negligence from being in law the cause of the injury." But the natural results of a negligent act—the results which a prudent man would or should foresee—do have a bearing upon the decision as to proximate cause. We have said so repeatedly. What should be foreseen? No human foresight would suggest that a collision itself might injure one a block away. On the contrary, given an explosion, such a possibility might be reasonably expected. I think the direct connection, the foresight of which the courts speak, assumes prevision of the explosion, for the immediate results of which, at least, the chauffeur is responsible.

It may be said this is unjust. Why? In fairness he should make good every injury flowing from his negligence. Not because of tenderness toward him we say he need not answer for all that follows his wrong. We look back to the catastrophe, the fire kindled by the spark, or the explosion. We trace the consequences—not indefinitely, but to a certain point. And to aid us in fixing that point we ask what might ordinarily be expected to follow the fire or the explosion.

This last suggestion is the factor which must determine the case before us. The act upon which defendant's liability rests is knocking an apparently harmless package onto the platform. The act was negligent. For its proximate consequences the defendant is liable. If its contents were broken, to the owner; if it fell upon and crushed a passenger's foot, then to him. If it exploded and injured one in the immediate vicinity, to him also as to A in the illustration. Mrs. Palsgraf was standing some distance away. How far cannot be told from the record—apparently twenty-five or thirty feet. Perhaps less. Except for the explosion, she would not have been injured. We are told by the appellant in his brief "it cannot be denied that the explosion was the direct cause of the plaintiff's injuries." So it was a substantial factor in producing the result—there was here a natural and continuous sequence—direct connection. The only intervening cause was that instead of blowing her to the ground the concussion smashed the weighing machine which in turn fell upon her. There was no remoteness in time, little in space. And surely, given such an explosion as here it needed no great foresight to predict that the natural result would be to injure one on the platform at no greater distance from its scene than was the plaintiff. Just how no one might be able to predict. Whether by flying fragments, by broken glass, by wreckage of machines or structures no one could say. But injury in some form was most probable.

Under these circumstances I cannot say as a matter of law that the plaintiff's injuries were not the proximate result of the negligence. That is all we have before us. The court refused to so charge. No request was made to submit the matter to the jury as a question of fact, even would that have been proper upon the record before us.

The judgment appealed from should be affirmed, with costs.

POUND, LEHMAN and KELLOGG, JJ., concur with CARDOZO, CH. J.; ANDREWS, J., dissents in opinion in which CRANE and O'BRIEN, JJ., concur.[115]

115. Compare Prosser, Palsgraf Revisited, 52 Mich.L.Rev. 1 (1953) with Seavey, Mr. Justice Cardozo and The Law of Torts, 39 Colum.L.Rev. 20, 29–39, 52 Harv.L.Rev. 372, 381–91, and 48 Yale L.J. 390, 399–409 (1939) and with F. Harper and F. James, The Law of Torts §§ 18.2 and 20.1, at notes 2 and 4 (1956 and Supp.1968). Additional references are collected in W. Prosser, The Law of Torts 254, note 50 (4th ed. 1971). Also compare Smith v. London & South Western Ry., 1870, L.R. 5 C.P. 98, Common Pleas, and L.R. 6 C.P. 14, Exchequer Chamber (sparks from locomotive foreseeably ignited hedge trimmings along tracks; fire unforeseeably crossed adjoining stubble field, a road, and burned plaintiff's cottage 200 yards from railroad; held that there was issue of "negligence" for jury, that if defendants were aware that the

YANIA v. BIGAN

Supreme Court of Pennsylvania, 1959.
397 Pa. 316, 155 A.2d 343.

BENJAMIN R. JONES, JUSTICE. A bizarre and most unusual circumstance provides the background of this appeal.

On September 25, 1957, John E. Bigan was engaged in a coal strip-mining operation in Shade Township, Somerset County. On the property being stripped were large cuts or trenches created by Bigan when he removed the earthen overburden for the purpose of removing the coal underneath. One cut contained water 8 to 10 feet in depth with side walls or embankments 16 to 18 feet in height; at this cut Bigan had installed a pump to remove the water.

At approximately 4 p. m. on that date, Joseph F. Yania, the operator of another coal strip-mining operation, and one Boyd M. Ross went upon Bigan's property for the purpose of discussing a business matter with Bigan, and, while there, were asked by Bigan to aid him in starting the pump. Ross and Bigan entered the cut and stood at the point where the pump was located. Yania stood at the top of one of the cut's side walls and then jumped from the side wall—a height of 16 to 18 feet—into the water and was drowned.

Yania's widow, in her own right and on behalf of her three children, instituted wrongful death and survival actions against Bigan contending Bigan was responsible for Yania's death. * * *

Since Bigan has chosen to file preliminary objections, in the nature of demurers, every material and relevant fact well pleaded in the complaint and every inference fairly deducible therefrom are to be taken as true. * * *

The complaint avers negligence in the following manner: (1) "The death by drowning of * * * [Yania] was caused entirely by the acts of [Bigan] * * * in *urging, enticing, taunting and inveigling* [Yania] to jump into the water, which [Bigan] knew or ought to have known was of a depth of 8 to 10 feet and dangerous to the life of anyone who would jump therein" (emphasis supplied); * * *.

(3) "After [Yania] was in the water, a highly dangerous position, having been induced and inveigled therein by [Bigan], [Bigan]

heaps were likely to catch fire, even if defendants were not bound to anticipate that plaintiff's cottage would be burned, they "were responsible for all the natural consequences" of the fire; that "once * * * there is evidence of negligence, the person guilty of it is equally liable for its consequences, whether he should have foreseen them or not"; a concurring opinion expressed doubts as to the existence of "negligence", on the ground that "[i]t can hardly be negligent not to provide against that which no one would anticipate"). Contrast Ryan v. New York Central R. Co., 35 N.Y. 210, 91 Am.Dec. 9 (1866), establishing peculiar New York rule that liability for negligently started fire is limited to the first building affected. (This rule was later slightly modified to cover the first other property affected, Webb v. Rome, W. and O.R.Co., 49 N.Y. 420 (1872) and Homac Corp. v. Sun Oil Co., 258 N.Y. 462, 180 N.E. 172 (1932); also, see Rose v. Pennsylvania R. Co., 236 N.Y. 568, 142 N.E. 287 (1923) for special rule on forest fires.)

failed and neglected to take reasonable steps and action to protect or assist [Yania], or extradite [Yania] from the dangerous position * * * [Bigan] had placed him".

Appellant initially contends that Yania's descent from the high embankment into the water and the resulting death were caused "entirely" by the spoken words and blandishments of Bigan delivered at a distance from Yania. The complaint does not allege that Yania slipped or that he was pushed or that Bigan made any *physical* impact upon Yania. On the contrary, the only inference deducible from the facts alleged in the complaint is that Bigan, by the employment of cajolery and inveiglement, caused such a *mental* impact on Yania that the latter was deprived of his volition and freedom of choice and placed under a compulsion to jump into the water. Had Yania been a child of tender years or a person mentally deficient then it is conceivable that taunting and enticement could constitute actionable negligence if it resulted in harm. However, to contend that such conduct directed to an adult in full possession of all his mental faculties constitutes actionable negligence is not only without precedent but competely without merit.

Lastly, it is urged that Bigan failed to take the necessary steps to rescue Yania from the water. The mere fact that Bigan saw Yania in a position of peril in the water imposed upon him no legal, although a moral, obligation or duty to go to his rescue unless Bigan was legally responsible, in whole or in part, for placing Yania in the perilous position. Restatement, Torts, § 314. Cf. Restatement, Torts, § 322. * * * The complaint does not aver any facts which impose upon Bigan legal responsibility for placing Yania in the dangerous position in the water and, absent such legal responsibility, the law imposes on Bigan no duty of rescue.

Recognizing that the deceased Yania is entitled to the benefit of the presumption that he was exercising due care and extending to appellant the benefit of every well pleaded fact in this complaint and the fair inferences arising therefrom, yet we can reach but one conclusion: that Yania, a reasonable and prudent adult in full possession of all his mental faculties, undertook to perform an act which he knew or should have known was attended with more or less peril and it was the performance of that act and not any conduct upon Bigan's part which caused his unfortunate death. * * * [116]

116. This case, and others like it, have been severely criticized, e. g., W. Prosser, The Law of Torts 340 (4th ed. 1971) ("* * * unappetizing * * *"), but they derive from a point of view sufficiently well established to be reflected in Restatement of Torts Second § 314 (1965) (knowledge "that action * * * is necessary for another's aid * * * does not of itself impose * * * a duty to take such action.") The second Restatement identifies certain special relationships in which a "duty * * * to take reasonable action" to protect or give first aid is recognized, e. g., carrier-passengers, innkeeper-guests, master-servant, §§ 314A and 314B; it also contains an amended § 322, which proposes a duty to exercise reasonable care to prevent further bodily harm to another who has been harmed and is helpless as a result of the actor's conduct, "whether tortious or innocent"; the first Restatement spoke only of "tortious conduct", with a comment

CARNEY v. BUYEA

Supreme Court of New York, Appellate Division, Fourth Department, 1946.
271 App.Div. 338, 65 N.Y.S.2d 902.

DOWLING, JUSTICE. The defendant, at all times herein mentioned, was the owner and in possession of a farm and farm buildings located on Route 5, the main road leading from Oneida to Syracuse. The defendant did not reside on the farm. The farm house was occupied by Isaac A. Barriger and his wife. Mr. Barriger was employed on the farm by the defendant. The farm and the farm buildings are located on the southerly side of the highway. The farm buildings stand on an elevation above the highway and about one hundred fifty feet distant therefrom. To reach the buildings from the highway one has to ascend a considerable grade as indicated in the photograph Ex. 1.

On the afternoon of October 30, 1945, the defendant drove to her farm on business. She parked her car in the lane leading to the cow barn, entered the barn and engaged in conversation with Mr. and Mrs. Barriger. While the defendant was in the barn with the Barrigers, the plaintiff, his wife and three of the plaintiff's brother's children arrived at the farm. The plaintiff had brought the children to the farm to visit their grandparents, Mr. and Mrs. Barriger. The plaintiff parked his car in the driveway leading to the house. Leaving two children in the car and taking the baby with them, the plaintiff and his wife went to the barn to notify the Barrigers of their arrival and while in the barn they met the defendant. Shortly thereafter the defendant left the barn, entered her car, backed it around so that it faced down the incline to the main highway. The plaintiff left the barn with the defendant to move his car out of the way if necessary. The defendant drove her car part way down the incline, stopped it, left the car, walked down the incline ahead of the car for a distance of twenty feet, about faced, bent over to pick up some soft drink bottles which were lying in the path her car would take. While she was so engaged, her car, without the assistance of anyone or the application of any external force began to move down the incline towards the defendant. The defendant was oblivious of the approaching car. Noticing that the car was gaining speed, the plaintiff holloed to the defendant "Look out," rushed down, pushed her out of the path of the approaching car and to safety. In order to rescue the defendant, the plaintiff was obliged to get into the pathway of the defendant's car.

which expressed no opinion as to the existence of such a duty "to aid or protect one whom the actor's non-tortious conduct has rendered helpless." Note that one who undertakes a rescue although under no duty to do so must not negligently increase the danger to the victim, e. g., United States v. DeVane, 306 F.2d 182 (5th Cir. 1962).

For an example of judicial progress away from restrictions on the application of normal negligence principles to situations where someone needs to be rescued, see Pridgen v. Boston Housing Authority, 364 Mass. 696, 308 N.E.2d 467 (1974).

Should doctors have to stop for every apparently serious highway accident to render aid if it should prove necessary? Should you, as a passing motorist? Why, or why not? See Franklin, Vermont Requires Rescue: A Comment, 25 Stan.L.Rev. 51 (1972).

Before he could extricate himself, he was struck by the moving car sustaining severe personal injuries. The plaintiff brought action against the defendant, recovered a judgment in the amount of $2,000 damages and $86.30 costs. The defendant has appealed to this court.

The plaintiff alleged in his complaint "she parked her automobile on a downgrade or hill without applying the emergency brake or placing the said automobile in gear or without taking some precaution to prevent the automobile from moving when she left same" and by reason of such parking the car started down the grade and struck him inflicting the injuries complained of.

The plaintiff succeeded on the theory that the defendant, without fault on his part, negligently injured him while he was engaged in rescuing her from the perilous position in which the defendant had placed herself.

It is the claim of the defendant that the plaintiff was a mere licensee when he sustained his injuries. That she owed the plaintiff no duty except to refrain from wantonly or intentionally injuring him; that she was guilty of no actionable negligence which contributed to the plaintiff's injuries and that she could be guilty of no actionable negligence against herself.

The Court, in substance, charged the jury (1) that it was the duty of the defendant to exercise reasonable care to avoid injury to the plaintiff. (2) That if the jury found that the defendant parked her car on the incline without taking proper precaution to prevent it from starting down the grade, they could find her negligent in that regard, if her negligence was a direct cause of the accident. The Court left it to the jury to say whether the defendant was in imminent danger of being injured when the plaintiff undertook to rescue her and whether the plaintiff was injured in rescuing the defendant or in an attempt to stop the defendant's car.

If the plaintiff was a mere licensee at the time of the accident, the defendant owed him the duty of not inflicting on him intentional or wanton injury. She also owed him the duty of not injuring him by her own affirmative negligence. Vaughan v. Transit Development Company, 222 N.Y. 79, 82, 118 N.E. 219. We think the parking of the car on the incline as disclosed by the evidence constituted an act of affirmative negligence. But the plaintiff was on the premises at the implied invitation of the defendant's tenants, at least the jury could have so found. * * * Obviously the plaintiff was not a trespasser while he was engaged in the act of rescuing the defendant. * * *

It was the duty of the defendant under the existing circumstances when she parked her car to leave it in such condition that it could not be put in motion except by the application of external force. * * *

In Eckert v. Long Island Railroad Co., 43 N.Y. 502, 3 Am.Rep. 721, decided in January 1871, the plaintiff's intestate was standing in the afternoon of the day named, in conversation with another person about fifty feet from the defendant's track, in East New York, as a train of cars was coming in from Jamaica. A child three or four years old was sitting or standing upon the track of the defendant's road and was in danger of being run over, if not removed. The plaintiff's intestate, seeing the danger of the child, ran to it, seized it, threw it clear of the track, but before he could cross the track he was struck by the engine, was thrown down receiving injuries which caused his death shortly thereafter. In affirming a judgment for the plaintiff, Judge Grover, speaking for the majority of the court, said at page 505 of 43 N.Y. that the intestate seeing the child in such a critical position and that she must inevitably be crushed by the moving train owed her "a duty of important obligation" to rescue her from her extreme peril if he could do so without incurring great danger to himself; that it was not wrongful in him to make every effort in his power to rescue the child compatible with a reasonable regard for his own safety; that it was his duty to exercise his judgment as to whether he could probably save the child without serious injury to himself and if, from appearances, he believed that he could, it was not negligence to make an attempt so to do, although believing possibly that he might fail and receive an injury himself; that he had no time for deliberation; that he must act instantly, if at all, as a moment's delay would have been fatal to the child; that the law has so high a regard for human life that it will not impute negligence to an effort to preserve it, unless made under such circumstances as to constitute rashness in the judgment of prudent persons. * * * The learned trial court followed the Eckert case in submitting the case to the jury. While the Eckert case defines the duty of the plaintiff in this case it does not directly touch upon the obligation which the defendant owed to the plaintiff under the circumstances. So far as we know, after extended research, the question of the defendant's duty to the plaintiff under the facts of this case has never been determined by the courts of this state. The rigid rules of an action at law for negligence bend before a situation where the life of a person is imperilled and without penalty to his rights permit a casual bystander to take risks in the attempt to save life which would be prohibited under any other circumstances. * * * Whether negligence should be imputed to the plaintiff in making the rescue was, upon the facts, a question for the jury. Danger invites rescue. Wagner v. International Railway Company, 232 N.Y. 176, 180, 133 N.E. 437, 19 A.L.R. 1 * * *.

Negligence on the part of the defendant towards the plaintiff which induced him to undertake her rescue must be established before the plaintiff can sustain a recovery. The defendant claims that she could not be guilty of negligence as against herself; that she owed no legal duty of care toward herself * * *.

The incline on which the car was parked led onto the main highway. In parking her car as she did, the defendant endangered the safety not only of the bystanders on her farm but also the safety of herself and the probable safety of the users of the highway who might be passing her farm in case her car should run onto the highway. May not a lack of self protective care be negligent towards any person in whose vicinity one exposes oneself to an undue risk of injury? We think so. The act, however, must be wrongful to the person injured as at least tending to create an undue risk of injury to him. The rescuer need have no interest in the person rescued such as a husband has in the services of his wife or a master in the services of his servant. We think Professor Bohlen, in his Studies in the Law of Torts, lays down the proper rule in footnote 33, page 569, when he says: "The rescuer's right of action, therefore, must rest upon the view that one who imperils another, at a place where there may be bystanders, must take into account the chance that some bystander will yield to the meritorious impulse to save life or even property from destruction, and attempt a rescue. If this is so, the right of action depends not upon the wrongfulness of the defendant's conduct in its tendency to imperil the person whose rescue is attempted, but upon its tendency to cause the rescuer to take the risk involved in the attempted rescue. And it would seem that a person who carelessly exposes himself to danger or who attempts to take his life in a place where others may be expected to be, does commit a wrongful act towards them in that it exposes them to a recognizable risk of injury." The Law Quarterly Review (London) Vol. 58, page 300, agrees with the rule stated by Professor Bohlen.

We think the defendant, by parking her car as she did, exposed herself to undue risk of injury. Her act in that respect was wrongful to the plaintiff since it brought about an undue risk of injury to him causing him to undertake her rescue to his injury and damage. Brugh v. Bigelow, 310 Mich. 74, 16 N.W.2d 668, 671, 158 A.L.R. 184; Vol. 43 Michigan Law Review, pages 980–982. We think there was a legal duty owing by the defendant to the plaintiff not to create an undue risk of injury to him and not merely a moral duty as was held in Saylor v. Parsons, 122 Iowa 679, 98 N.W. 500, 64 L.R.A. 542, 101 Am. St.Rep. 283, supra.

We do not regard the verdict as excessive under the facts. The judgment should be affirmed with costs.

Judgment affirmed with costs. All concur.[117]

117. Also see Talbert v. Talbert, 199 N.Y.S.2d 212 (1960) (liability of suicide to rescuer).

"It is straining the idea of foreseeability past the breaking point to say that when a defendant fails to inspect the brakes of his car he should foresee that the brakes may fail to hold while a child is crossing the street, and that the plaintiff may be standing on the sidewalk at the precise instance of time when as a reasonable man he would regard it possible to rescue the child with reasonable safety to himself. Yet to hold that the defendant in such case is liable because he should have foreseen that the plaintiff would imperil himself to save the child requires the defendant to have had all this in mind. Such a use of the word 'foreseeable' is altogether different from that 'ordinary prevision to be looked for in a busy world' which Judge Cardozo has said is all that the law exacts in order that the actor may be free from negligence. [Greene v. Sibley, Lindsay & Curr Co., 257 N.Y. 190, 192, 177 N.E. 416, 417 (1931).]" Bohlen, Book Review (of F. Harper, A Treatise on The Law of Torts), 47 Harv.L.Rev. 556, 557 (1934).

IN RE POLEMIS AND FURNESS, WITHY & CO.

Court of Appeal [1921] L.R. 3 K.B. 560.

APPEAL from the judgment of SANKEY, J., on an award in the form of a special case.

The owners of the Greek Steamship Thrasyvoulos claimed to recover damages for the total loss of the steamship by fire.

By a charter party, dated February 21, 1917, Messrs. Polemis and Boyazides, the owners of the Greek steamship Thrasyvoulos (hereinafter called the owners), chartered the steamship to Furness, Withy & Co., Ld. (hereinafter called the charterers), * * * By clause 3, the owners were to provide and pay for all the provisions and wages of the captain, officers, engineers, firemen, and crew, * * * By clause 4, the charterers were to provide and pay for * * * all other charges whatsoever, except those before stated. By clause 5, the charterers were to pay for the use and hire of the vessel at the rate of 9572£. 16*s.* per calendar month commencing on the day of delivery as above with a clean and clear hold, "hire to continue from the time specified for commencing the charter until the hour of her redelivery to owners (unless lost) at a port in the United Kingdom or continent in same good order and condition as when delivered to them fair wear and tear excepted." By clause 21: "The act of God, the King's enemies, loss or damage from fire on board in hulk or craft, or on shore, arrest and/or restraint of princes, rulers, and people, collision, any act, neglect, or default whatsoever of pilot, master, or crew in the management or navigation of the ship, and all and every of the dangers and accidents of the seas, canals, and rivers, and of navigation of whatever nature or kind always mutually excepted." * * *

The vessel by the directions of the charterers * * * loaded at Nantes * * * for Casablanca, Morocco. She then proceeded to Lisbon and was loaded with further cargo, consisting of cases of benzine and/or petrol and iron for Casablanca and other ports on the Morocco coast. She arrived at Casablanca on July 17, and there discharged a portion of her cargo. The cargo was discharged by Arab workmen and winchmen from the shore supplied and sent on board by the charterers' agents. The cargo in No. 1 hold included a considerable quantity of cases of benzine or petrol which had suffered somewhat by handling and/or by rough weather on the voyage, so that there had been some leakage from the tins in the cases into the hold. On July 21 it had become necessary to shift from No. 1 lower hold a number of the cases of benzine which were required to be taken on by the ship to Safi, and for this purpose the native stevedores had placed heavy planks across the forward end of the hatchway in the 'tween decks using it as a platform in the process of transferring the cases from the lower hold to the 'tween decks. There were four or five of the Arab shore labourers in the lower hold filling the slings which, when filled, were hove up by means of the winch situated on the upper deck to the 'tween decks level of the platform on which some of the Arabs in the 'tween decks were working. In consequence of the breakage of the cases there was a considerable amount of petrol vapour in the hold. In the course of heaving a sling of the cases from the hold the rope by which the sling was being raised or the sling itself came into contact with the boards placed across the forward end of the hatch, causing one of the boards to fall into the lower hold, and the fall was instantaneously followed by a rush of flames from the lower hold, and this resulted eventually in the total destruction of the ship.

The owners contended (so far as material) that the charterers were liable for the loss of the ship; that fire caused by negligence was not an excepted peril; and that the ship was in fact lost by the negligence of the stevedores, who were the charterers' servants, in letting the sling strike the board, knocking it into the hold, and thereby causing a spark which set fire to the petrol vapour and destroyed the ship.

The charterers contended that fire however caused was an excepted peril; that there was no negligence for which the charterers were responsible, inasmuch as to let a board fall into the hold of the ship could do no harm to the ship and therefore was not negligence towards the owners; and that the danger and/or damage were too remote—i. e., no reasonable man would have foreseen danger and/or damage of this kind resulting from the fall of the board.

The three arbitrators made the following findings of fact:—

"(a) That the ship was lost by fire.

"(b) That the fire arose from a spark igniting petrol vapour in the hold.

"(c) That the spark was caused by the falling board coming into contact with some substance in the hold.

"(d) That the fall of the board was caused by the negligence of the Arabs (other than the winchmen) engaged in the work of discharging.

"(e) That the said Arabs were employed by the charterers or their agents the Cie. Transatlantique on behalf of the charterers, and that the said Arabs were the servants of the charterers.

"(f) That the causing of the spark could not reasonably have been anticipated from the falling of the board, though some damage to the ship might reasonably have been anticipated.

"(g) There was no evidence before us that the Arabs chosen were known or likely to be negligent.

"(h) That the damages sustained by the owners through the said accident amount to the sum of 196,165£. 1*s*. 11*d*. as shown in the second column of the schedule hereto."

Subject to the opinion of the Court on any questions of law arising the arbitrators awarded that the owners were entitled to recover from the charterers the before-mentioned sum.

If the Court should be of opinion that the above award was wrong, then the arbitrators awarded that the owners should recover nothing from the charterers.

SANKEY, J. affirmed the award. The charterers appealed. * * *

BANKES, L. J. * * * These findings are no doubt intended to raise the question whether the view taken, or said to have been taken, by Pollock C.B. in Rigby v. Hewitt, 5 Ex. 243, and Greenland v. Chaplin, 5 Ex. 248, or the view taken by Channell B., and Blackburn J. in Smith v. London and South Western Ry. Co., L.R. 6 C.P. 21, is the correct one. * * * Assuming the Chief Baron to have been correctly reported in the Exchequer Reports, the difference between the two views is this: According to the one view, the consequences which may reasonably be expected to result from a particular act are material only in reference to the question whether the act is or is not a negligent act; according to the other view, those consequences are the test whether the damages resulting from the act, assuming it to be negligent, are or are not too remote to be recoverable. Sir F. Pollock in his Law of Torts, 11th ed., pp. 39, 40, refers to this difference of view, and calls attention to the fact that the late Mr. Beven, in his book on Negligence, supports the view founded on Smith v. London and South Western Ry. Co., L.R. 6 C.P. 21. In two recent judgments dealing with the question, the view taken by the Court in Smith v. London and South Western Ry. Co., L.R. 6 C.P. 21, has been adopted—namely, by the late President (Sir Samuel Evans) in H.M.S. London [1914] P. 72, 76, and by Lord Sumner in Weld-Blundell v. Stephens, [1920] A.C. 983, 984. * * * In the latter case Lord Sumner said, [1920] A.C. 983, 984: "What are 'natural, probable and necessary' consequences? Everything that happens, happens in the order of nature and is therefore 'natural.' Nothing that happens by the free choice of a thinking man is 'necessary,' except in the sense of predestination. To speak of 'probable' consequence is to throw everything upon the jury. It is tautologous to speak of 'effective' cause or to say that damages too remote from the cause are irrecoverable, for an effective cause is simply that which causes, and in law what is ineffective or too remote is not a cause at all. I still venture to think that direct cause is the best expression. Proximate cause has acquired a special connotation through its use in reference to contracts of insurance. Direct cause excludes what is indirect, conveys the essential distinction, which *causa causans* and *causa sine qua non* rather cumbrously indicate and is consistent with the possibility of the concurrence of more direct causes than one, operating at the same time and leading to a common result as in Burrows v. March Gas & Coke

Co., (1872) L.R. 7 Ex. 96, and Hill v. New River Co., (1868) 9 B. & S. 303. As, however, these different epithets and formulae are used almost indiscriminately, something more must be done than to choose an epithet which has been used in a decided case. It is necessary to consider whether the facts of the case cited raise a question of causation belonging to the same category as that under discussion." * * *

In the present case the arbitrators have found as a fact that the falling of the plank was due to the negligence of the defendants' servants. The fire appears to me to have been directly caused by the falling of the plank. Under these circumstances I consider that it is immaterial that the causing of the spark by the falling of the plank could not have been reasonably anticipated. The appellants' junior counsel sought to draw a distinction between the anticipation of the extent of damage resulting from a negligent act, and the anticipation of the type of damage resulting from such an act. He admitted that it could not lie in the mouth of a person whose negligent act had caused damage to say that he could not reasonably have foreseen the extent of the damage, but he contended that the negligent person was entitled to rely upon the fact that he could not reasonably have anticipated the type of damage which resulted from his negligent act. I do not think that the distinction can be admitted. Given the breach of duty which constitutes the negligence, and given the damage as a direct result of that negligence, the anticipations of the person whose negligent act has produced the damage appear to me to be irrelevant. I consider that the damages claimed are not too remote.

The other point relied upon by the appellants was that the damage having been caused by fire they were protected by clause 21 of the charter party. To this it was replied that the clause had no application in the case of a fire caused by the negligence of the charterers' servants. * * *

For these reasons I think that the appeal fails, and must be dismissed with costs.

WARRINGTON, L. J. * * *

The presence or absence of reasonable anticipation of damage determines the legal quality of the act as negligent or innocent. If it be thus determined to be negligent, then the question whether particular damages are recoverable depends only on the answer to the question whether they are the direct consequence of the act. Sufficient authority for the proposition is afforded by Smith v. London and South Western Ry. Co., L.R. 6 C.P. 14, in the Exchequer Chamber, and particularly by the judgments of Channell, B. and Blackburn, J. * * * In the present case it is clear that the act causing the plank to fall was in law a negligent act, because some damage to the ship might reasonably be anticipated. If this is so then the appellants are liable for the actual loss, that being on the findings of the arbitrators the direct result of the falling board: see per Lord Sumner in Weld-Blundell v. Stephens, [1920] A.C. 983, 984.

On the whole in my opinion the appeal fails and must be dismissed with costs.

SCRUTTON, L. J. * * *

The second defence is that the damage is too remote from the negligence, as it could not be reasonably foreseen as a consequence. On this head we were referred to a number of well known cases in which vague language, which I cannot think to be really helpful, has been used in an attempt to define the point at which damage becomes too remote from, or not sufficiently directly caused by, the breach of duty, which is the original cause of action, to be recoverable. For instance, I cannot think it useful to say the damage must be the natural and probable result. This suggests that there are results which are natural but not probable, and other results which are probable but not natural. I am not sure what either adjective means in this connection; if they mean the same thing, two need not be used; if they mean different things, the difference between them should be defined. And as to many cases of fact in which the distinction has been drawn, it is difficult to see why one case should be decided one way and one another. Perhaps the House of Lords will some day explain why, if a cheque is negligently filled up, it is a direct effect of the negligence that some one finding the cheque should commit forgery: London Joint Stock Bank v. Macmillan, [1918] A.C. 777; while if some one negligently leaves a libellous letter about, it is not a direct effect of the negligence that the finder should show the letter to the person libelled: Weld-Blundell v. Stephens, [1920] A.C. 956. In this case, however, the problem is simpler. To determine whether an act is negligent, it is relevant to determine whether any reasonable person would foresee that the act would cause damage; if he would not, the act is not negligent. But if the act would or might probably cause damage, the fact that the damage it in fact causes is not the exact kind of damage one would expect is immaterial, so long as the damage is in fact directly traceable to the negligent act, and not due to the operation of independent causes having no connection with the negligent act, except that they could not avoid its results. Once the act is negligent, the fact that its exact operation was not foreseen is immaterial. * * * In the present case it was negligent in discharging cargo to knock down the planks of the temporary staging, for they might easily cause some damage either to workmen, or cargo, or the ship. The fact that they did directly produce an unexpected result, a spark in an atmosphere of petrol vapour which caused a fire, does not relieve the person who was negligent from the damage which his negligent act directly caused.

For these reasons the experienced arbitrators and the judge appealed from came, in my opinion, to a correct decision, and the appeal must be dismissed with costs.

Appeal dismissed.

During the 1960's the questions reflected in *Polemis* were intensely considered on both sides of the Atlantic.

In 1961, for instance, the Privy Council purported to repudiate *Polemis*, in Overseas Tankship (U.K.) Ltd. v. Morts Dock and Engineering Co. Ltd. [1961] A.C. 388. Defendant had chartered the tankship *Wagon Mound;* its servants had carelessly allowed bunkering oil to spill over the harbor in Sydney, Australia. That the oil might have fouled plaintiff's drydock was foreseeable. The Privy Council accepted, however, the finding of the trial court that "defendant did not know and could not reasonably be expected to have known that * * * [the oil] was capable of being set afire when spread on water." A fire nevertheless ensued, apparently when cotton waste in the water was ignited by molten metal falling from the wharf where defendant's servants were welding, and plaintiff's property was burned. The Privy Council held for defendant, on the ground that liability should be limited to "the probable consequences" of an act. "To demand more is too harsh * * *." Even "if B's * * * act has been shown to be negligent and has caused some foreseeable damage to A * * * to hold B liable for conseqences however unforeseeable of a careless act, if, but only if, he is at the same time liable for some other damage however trivial, appears to be neither logical nor just. * * * It is irrelevant to the question whether B is liable for unforeseeable damage that he is liable for foreseeable damage, as irrelevant as would the fact that he had trespassed on Whiteacre be to the question that he has trespassed on Blackacre." Rejecting the proposition that "unforeseeability is irrelevant if damage is 'direct' ", their Lordships insisted that "the essential factor in determining liability is whether the damage is of such a kind as the reasonable man should have foreseen * * *. [L]iability * * * [should not be] made to depend solely on the damage being the 'direct' or 'natural' consequence of the precedent act. Who knows or can be assumed to know all the processes of nature? But if it would be wrong that a man should be held liable for damage unpredictable by a reasonable man because it was 'direct' or 'natural', equally it would be wrong that he should escape liability, however 'indirect' the damage, if he foresaw or could reasonably foresee the intervening events which led to its being done."

Somewhat similarly in the same year in the United States defendants prevailed in litigation arising from the Texas City disaster, Republic of France v. United States, 290 F.2d 395 (5th Cir. 1961). A cargo of Fertilizer Grade Ammonium Nitrate (FGAN) had exploded, causing over 500 deaths, 3000 personal injuries, and "tremendous destruction" of property. The ship's master was found negligent in permitting the fire to start, and in failing to extinguish it early. It was further found by the district court that he "should have foreseen and anticipated the danger of a disastrous fire, with the *possibility* of explosion", but that, "[f]rom the literature and information generally available * * * in the exercise of ordinary care, the Master could [not] have foreseen the probability of an explosion *of this sort,* even in the presence of fire." (Emphasis by appellate court.) On appeal defendants were held "not liable for any claim arising out of or consequent upon the explosion of the steamship." The court emphasized, in a split decision, that there had been no previous known instance of explosion of FGAN in storage or transit; that "it is only the operation of natural forces theretofore recognized as normal which one is charged with foreseeing"; and that "the explosion as distinguished from the fire could not reasonably have been foreseen." The court also quoted a Supreme Court reference, in an earlier case involving somewhat different issues, to a Cardozo statement, in a products liability case not involving causation, that " 'There must be knowledge of a danger, not merely possible, but probable', MacPherson v. Buick Motor Co., 217 N.Y. 382, 389, 145 N.Y.S. 462, 111 N.E. 1050, 1053, * * * " (page —— below).

Then the wind shifted.

HUGHES v. LORD ADVOCATE

House of Lords [1963] A.C. 837; [1963] 2 W.L.R. 779; 107 S.J. 232; [1963] 1 All E.R. 705; 1963 S.C. (H.L.) 31; 1963 S.L.T. 150.

[Workers had left unguarded an open manhole covered by a tent, with paraffin-fueled burning warning lights. Two children entered, took and dropped a lamp. Paraffin (kerosene) spilled, vaporized, was ignited and exploded. The explosion knocked a child into the hole and spread hot paraffin, which burned him as he tried to get out. The court below, ruling for defendants, found that there was a low probability that this sequence of events should occur, and that it was so unforeseeable that a reasonable man would be excused if he disregarded it.]

LORD REID. * * *

It was argued that the appellant cannot recover because the damage which he suffered was of a kind which was not foreseeable. * * * [T]he facts proved do not, in my judgment, support that argument. The appellant's injuries were mainly caused by burns, and it cannot be said that injuries from burns were unforeseeable. As a warning to traffic the workmen had set lighted red lamps round the tent which covered the manhole, and if boys did enter the dark tent it was very likely that they would take one of these lamps with them. If the lamp fell and broke it was not at all unlikely that the boy would be burned and the burns might well be serious. No doubt it was not to be expected that the injuries would be as serious as those which the appellant in fact sustained. But a defender is liable, although the damage may be a good deal greater in extent than was foreseeable. He can only escape liability if the damage can be regarded as differing in kind from what was foreseeable. * * *

* * * The cause of this accident was a known source of danger, the lamp, but it behaved in an unpredictable way.

* * * [I]n my judgment, that affords no defence. I would therefore allow the appeal.

LORD JENKINS. * * *

It is true that the duty of care expected in cases of this sort is confined to reasonably foreseeable dangers, but it does not necessarily follow that liability is escaped because the danger actually materialising is not identical with the danger reasonably foreseen and guarded against. * * *

To my mind, the distinction drawn between burning and explosion is too fine to warrant acceptance. Supposing the pursuer had on the day in question gone to the site and taken one of the lamps, and upset it over himself, thus setting his clothes alight, the person to be considered responsible for protecting children from the dangers to be found there would presumably have been liable * * *.

* * * If there is a risk of such a fire as that, I do not think the duty of care * * * is prevented from coming into operation by the presence of the remote possibility of the more serious event of an explosion. * * *

LORD GUEST.

* * *

* * * In order to establish a coherent chain of causation it is not necessary that the precise details leading up to the accident should have been reasonably foreseeable: it is sufficient if the accident which occurred is of a type which should have been foreseeable by a reasonably careful person * * *. An explosion is only one way in which burning can be caused. * * * [T]he explosion was an immaterial event in the chain of causation. It was simply one way in which burning might be caused by the potentially dangerous paraffin lamp. * * *

LORD PEARCE. * * *

* * * The obvious risks were burning and conflagration and a fall. All these in fact occurred, but unexpectedly the mishandled lamp instead of causing an ordinary conflagration produced a violent explosion. Did the explosion create an accident and damage of a different type from the misadventure and damage that could be foreseen? In my judgment it did not. The accident was but a variant of the foreseeable. It was, to quote the words of Denning L. J. in Ros v. Minister of Health,[118] "within the risk created by the negligence."

No unforeseeable, extraneous initial occurrence fired the train. * * * [I]t would be, I think, too narrow a view to hold that those who cre-

118. [1954] 2 Q.B. 66, 85; [1954] 2 W.L. R. 915; [1954] 2 All E.R. 131, C.A.

ated the risk of fire are excused from the liability for the damage by fire because it came by way of explosive combustion. The resulting damage, though severe, was not greater than or different in kind from that which might have been produced had the lamp spilled and produced a more normal conflagration in the hole. * * *

OVERSEAS TANKSHIP (U.K.) LTD. v. THE MILLER STEAMSHIP CO. PTY. (THE WAGON MOUND NO. 2)

Privy Council [1967] 1 A.C. 617.

[Action arising from the same accident as Wagon Mound No. 1, discussed at page 360 above. In this case plaintiffs are the owners of ships which were damaged by the fire. Unlike Morts Dry Dock and Engineering Co., which was constrained by considerations of contributory negligence, these plaintiffs contended that the inflammability of the oil was foreseeable.]

LORD REID. * * *

The findings of the learned trial judge are as follows:

"(1) Reasonable people in the position of the officers of the *Wagon Mound* would regard the furnace oil as very difficult to ignite upon water. (2) Their personal experience would probably have been that this had very rarely happened. (3) If they had given attention to the risk of fire from the spillage, they would have regarded it as a possibility, but one which could become an actuality only in very exceptional circumstances. (4) They would have considered the chances of the required exceptional circumstances happening whilst the oil remained spread on the harbour waters as being remote. (5) I find that the occurrence of damage to the plaintiff's property as a result of the spillage was not reasonably foreseeable by those for whose acts the defendant would be responsible. (6) I find that the spillage of oil was brought about by the careless conduct of persons for whose acts the defendant would be responsible. (7) I find that the spillage of oil was a cause of damage to the property of each of the plaintiffs. (8) Having regard to those findings, and because of finding (5), I hold that the claim of each of the plaintiffs, framed in negligence, fails."

* * *

The crucial finding of Walsh J. in this case is in finding (5): that the damage was "not reasonably foreseeable by those for whose acts the defendant would be responsible." That is not a primary finding of fact but an inference from the other findings, and it is clear from the learned judge's judgment that in drawing this inference he was to a large extent influenced by his view of the law. The vital parts of the findings of fact which have already been set out in full are (1) that the officers of the *Wagon Mound* "would regard furnace oil as very difficult to ignite upon water"—not that they would regard this as impossible; (2) that their experience would probably have been "that this had very rarely happened"—not that they would never have heard of a case where it had happened, and (3) that they would have regarded it as a "possibility, but one which could become an actuality only in very exceptional circumstances"—not, as in *The Wagon Mound (No. 1)*, that they could not reasonably be expected to have known that this oil was capable of being set afire when spread on water. The question which must now be determined is whether these differences between the findings in the two cases do or do not lead to different results in law.

In *The Wagon Mound (No. 1)* the Board were not concerned with degrees of foreseeability because the finding was that the fire was not foreseeable at all. So Lord Simonds had no cause to amplify the statement that the "essential factor in determining liability is whether the damage is of such a kind as the reasonable man should have foreseen." But here the findings show that some risk of fire would have been present to the mind of a reasonable man in the shoes of the ship's chief engineer. So the first question must be what is the precise meaning to be attached in this context to the words "foreseeable" and "reasonably foreseeable."

Before Bolton v. Stone [119] the cases had fallen into two classes: (1) those where, before the event, the risk of its happening would have been regarded as unreal either because the event would have been thought to be physically impossible or because the possibility of its happening would have been regarded as so fantastic or far-fetched that no reasonable man would have paid any attention to it —"a mere possibility which would never occur to the mind of a reasonable man" (per Lord Dunedin in Fardon v. Harcourt-Rivington [120] —or (2) those where there was a real and substantial risk or chance that something like the event which happens might occur, and then the reasonable man would have taken the steps necessary to eliminate the risk.

Bolton v. Stone posed a new problem. There a member of a visiting team drove a cricket ball out of the ground onto an unfrequented adjacent public road and it struck and severely injured a lady who happened to be standing in the road. That it might happen that a ball would be driven onto this road could not have been said to be

119. [1951] A.C. 850; [1951] 1 T.L.R. 977; [1951] 1 All E.R. 1078, H.L. [See Goodhart, Note, 57 L.Q.Rev. 480 (1951); Tunc, Tort Law and The Moral Law, 30 Cam.L.J. 247, 253 et seq. (1972).]

120. (1932) 146 L.T. 391. [Unbracketed portions of footnotes 119 and 120 from original, renumbered; other notes in original omitted.]

a fantastic or far-fetched possibility: according to the evidence it had happened about six times in 28 years. And it could not have been said to be a far-fetched or fantastic possibility that such a ball would strike someone in the road: people did pass along the road from time to time. So it could not have been said that, on any ordinary meaning of the words, the fact that a ball might strike a person in the road was not foreseeable or reasonably foreseeable—it was plainly foreseeable. But the chance of its happening in the foreseeable future was infinitesimal. A mathematician given the data could have worked out that it was only likely to happen once in so many thousand years. The House of Lords held that the risk was so small that in the circumstances a reasonable man would have been justified in disregarding it and taking no steps to eliminate it.

But it does not follow that, no matter what the circumstances may be, it is justifiable to neglect a risk of such a small magnitude. A reasonable man would only neglect such a risk if he had some valid reason for doing so, e. g., that it would involve considerable expense to eliminate the risk. He would weigh the risk against the difficulty of eliminating it. If the activity which caused the injury to Miss Stone had been an unlawful activity, there can be little doubt but that Bolton v. Stone would have been decided differently. In their Lordships' judgment Bolton v. Stone did not alter the general principle that a person must be regarded as negligent if he does not take steps to eliminate a risk which he knows or ought to know is a real risk and not a mere possibility which would never influence the mind of a reasonable man. What that decision did was to recognise and give effect to the qualification that it is justifiable not to take steps to eliminate a real risk if it is small and if the circumstances are such that a reasonable man, careful of the safety of his neighbour, would think it right to neglect it.

In the present case there was no justification whatever for discharging the oil into Sydney Harbour. Not only was it an offence to do so, but it involved considerable loss financially. If the ship's engineer had thought about the matter, there could have been no question of balancing the advantages and disadvantages. From every point of view it was both his duty and his interest to stop the discharge immediately.

It follows that in their Lordships' view the only question is whether a reasonable man having the knowledge and experience to be expected of the chief engineer of the *Wagon Mound* would have known that there was a real risk of the oil on the water catching fire in some way: if it did, serious damage to ships or other property was not only foreseeable but very likely. * * *

In their Lordships' view a properly qualified and alert chief engineer would have realised there was a real risk here and they do not understand Walsh J. to deny that. But he appears to have held that if a real risk can properly be described as remote it must then be held to be not reasonably foreseeable. * * * [O]n principle their Lordships cannot accept this view. If a real risk is one which would occur to the mind of a reasonable man in the position of the defendant's servant and which he would not brush aside as far-fetched,[121] and if the criterion is to be what that reasonable man would have done in the circumstances, then surely he would not neglect such a risk if action to eliminate it presented no difficulty, involved no disadvantage, and required no expense.

In the present case the evidence shows that the discharge of so much oil onto the water must have taken a considerable time and a vigilant ship's engineer would have noticed the discharge at an early stage. The findings show that he ought to have known that it is possible to ignite this kind of oil on water, and that the ship's engineer probably ought to have known that this had in fact happened before. The most that can be said to justify inaction is that he would have known that this could only happen in very exceptional circumstances. But that does not mean that a reasonable man would dismiss such a risk from his mind and do nothing when it was so easy to prevent it. If it is clear that the reasonable man would have realised or foreseen and prevented the risk, then it must follow that the appellant is liable in damages. * * *

121. See speech of Lord Upjohn in C. Czarnikow Ltd. v. Koufos [1969] 1 A.C. 350, 422: "The test in tort * * * is that the tortfeasor is liable for any damage which he can reasonably foresee may happen as a result of the breach however unlikely it may be, unless it can be brushed aside as far fetched. See the *Wagon Mound* cases."

Compare § 435, Restatement of Torts Second (1965):

"(1) If the actor's conduct is a substantial factor in bringing about harm to another, the fact that the actor neither foresaw nor should have foreseen the extent of the harm or the manner in which it occurred does not prevent him from being liable.

"(2) The actor's conduct may be held not to be a legal cause of harm to another where after the event and looking back from the harm to the actor's negligent conduct, it appears to the court highly extraordinary that it should have brought about the harm."

"It is enough to say that negligence is tested by foresight but proximate cause is determined by hindsight." Loevinger, J., in Dellwo v. Pearson, 259 Minn. 452, 107 N.W.2d 859 (1962). Compare Atlantic Tubing & Rubber Co. v. International Engraving Co., 528 F.2d 1272, 1277 (1st Cir. 1976) (" * * * reasonable foreseeability is an important factor in placing practical limits on a defendant's liability for negligence").

PETITION OF KINSMAN TRANSIT COMPANY

United States Court of Appeals for the Second Circuit, 1964.
338 F.2d 708.

[A ship (the "Shiras") owned by Kinsman Transit Co., loaded with grain owned by Continental Grain Co., was moored for the winter in the Buffalo River, at Continental's dock, three miles upstream from a lift bridge maintained by the City of Buffalo. Because of the negligence of both Kinsman and Continental the ship broke loose under the pressure of floating ice during a thaw. The ship collided with another ship (the "Tewksbury"), which had been properly moored, and both ships drifted downstream toward the bridge. The bridge crew was notified in time to have lifted the bridge, had the operator not been off at a tavern. Since the bridge was not lifted in time, the ships crashed into it so as to dam the entire flow of the river. The ice and water backed up, flooding the shores for about three miles, and the bridge tower later collapsed, damaging the adjacent property. The flooded and otherwise injured property owners sued Kinsman, Continental, and the City of Buffalo, *inter alia.*]

BEFORE WATERMAN, MOORE and FRIENDLY, CIRCUIT JUDGES.

FRIENDLY, CIRCUIT JUDGE:

* * *

III. *The allegedly unexpectable character of the events leading to much of the damage.*

The very statement of the case suggests the need for considering Palsgraf v. Long Island RR., 248 N.Y. 339, 162 N.E. 99, 59 A.L.R. 1253 (1928), and the closely related problem of liability for unforeseeable consequences.

In Sinram v. Pennsylvania R.R., 61 F.2d 767, 770 (2 Cir. 1932), which received Palsgraf into the admiralty, Judge Learned Hand characterized the issue in that case as "whether, if A. omitted to perform a positive duty to B., C., who had been damaged in consequence, might invoke the breach, though otherwise A. owed him no duty; in short, whether A. was chargeable for the results to others of his breach of duty to B." Thus stated, the query rather answers itself; Hohfeld's analysis tells us that once it is concluded that A. had no duty to C., it is simply a correlative that C. has no right against A. The important question is what was the basis for Chief Judge Cardozo's conclusion that the Long Island Railroad owed no "duty" to Mrs. Palsgraf under the circumstances.

Certainly there is no general principle that a railroad owes no duty to persons on station platforms not in immediate proximity to the tracks, as would have been quickly demonstrated if Mrs. Palsgraf had been injured by the fall of improperly loaded objects from a passing train. Cf. the decision with respect to the husband in Carey v. Pure Distributing Corp., 133 Tex. 31, 124 S.W.2d 847 (1939). Neither is there any principle that railroad guards who jostle a package-carrying passenger owe a duty only to him; if the package had contained bottles, the Long Island would surely have been liable for injury caused to close bystanders by flying glass or spurting liquid. The reason why the Long Island was thought to owe no duty to Mrs. Palsgraf was the lack of any notice that the package contained a substance demanding the exercise of any care toward anyone so far away; Mrs. Palsgraf was not considered to be within the area of apparent hazard created by whatever lack of care the guard had displayed to the anonymous carrier of the unknown fireworks.[122] The key sentences in Chief Judge Cardozo's opinion are these:

> "Here, by concession, there was nothing in the situation to suggest to the most cautious mind that the parcel wrapped in newspaper would spread wreckage through the station. If the guard had thrown it down knowingly and willfully, he would not have threatened the plaintiff's safety, so far as appearances could warn him. Liability can be no greater where the act is inadvertent." 248 N.Y. at 345, 162 N.E. at 101.

We see little similarity between the Palsgraf case and the situation before us. The point of Palsgraf was that the appearance of the newspaper-wrapped package gave no notice that its dislodgement could do any harm save to itself and those nearby, and this by impact, perhaps with consequent breakage, and not by explosion. In contrast, a ship insecurely moored in a fast flowing river is a known danger not only to herself but to the owners of all other ships and structures downriver, and to persons upon them. No one would dream of saying that a shipowner who "knowingly and wilfully" failed to secure his ship at a pier on such a river "would not have threatened" persons and owners of property downstream in some manner.[123] The shipowner

122. There was exceedingly little evidence of negligence of any sort. The only lack of care suggested by the majority in the Appellate Division was that instead of endeavoring to assist the passenger, the guards "might better have discouraged and warned him not to board the moving train." 222 App.Div. 166, 167, 225 N.Y.S. 412, 413 (2d Dept. 1927). Chief Judge Cardozo said: "The man was not injured in his person nor even put in danger. The purpose of the act, as well as its effect, was to make his person safe.

If there was a wrong to him at all, which may very well be doubted, it was a wrong to a property interest only, the safety of his package." 248 N.Y. at 343, 162 N.E. at 100. Judge Andrews' dissent said the Long Island had been negligent, 248 N.Y. at 347, 162 N.E. 99, but did not state in what respect.

How much ink would have been saved over the years if the Court of Appeals had reversed Mrs. Palsgraf's judgment on the basis that there was no evidence of negligence at all!

123. The facts here do not oblige us to decide whether the Shiras and Continental could successfully invoke Palsgraf against claims of owners of shoreside property upstream from the Concrete Elevator or of non-riparian property other than the real and personal property which was sufficiently close to the bridge to have been damaged by the fall of the towers.

and the wharfinger in this case having thus owed a duty of care to all within the reach of the ship's known destructive power, the impossibility of advance identification of the particular person who would be hurt is without legal consequence. Jackson v. B. Lowenstein & Bros., 175 Tenn. 535, 136 S.W.2d 495 (1940); Pfeifer v. Standard Gateway Theater, 262 Wis. 229, 55 N.W.2d 29 (1952). Similarly the foreseeable consequences of the City's failure to raise the bridge were not limited to the Shiras and the Tewksbury. Collision plainly created a danger that the bridge towers might fall onto adjoining property, and the crash of two uncontrolled lake vessels, one 425 feet and the other 525 feet long, into a bridge over a swift ice-ridden stream, with a channel only 177 feet wide, could well result in a partial damming that would flood property upstream. As to the City also, it is useful to consider, by way of contrast, Chief Judge Cardozo's statement that the Long Island would not have been liable to Mrs. Palsgraf had the guard wilfully thrown the package down. If the City had deliberately kept the bridge closed in the face of the onrushing vessels, taking the risk that they might not come so far, no one would give house-room to a claim that it "owed no duty" to those who later suffered from the flooding. Unlike Mrs. Palsgraf, they were within the area of hazard.

The case is quite different from this Court's ruling in Sinram, where a tug which had negligently rammed a barge was held free of liability for the loss of coal that the bargee subsequently allowed to be loaded into his barge without first having inspected her for damage. That case illustrates the principle, noted in Judge Hand's opinion, 61 F.2d at 771, "that there must be a terminus somewhere, short of eternity, at which the second party becomes responsible in lieu of the first," Prosser, Torts, 280—a principle now explicitly recognized in the Restatement of Torts, Second § 452(2) (Tent. Draft No. 9, April, 1963): "Where, by contract or otherwise, all responsibility for the protection of the other against the threatened harm is shifted to the third person, his intentional or negligent failure to act to prevent such harm is a superseding cause." * * *[124]

Since all the claimants here met the Palsgraf requirement of being persons to whom the actors owed a "duty of care," we are not obliged to reconsider whether that case furnishes as useful a standard for determining the boundaries of liability in admiralty for negligent conduct as was thought in Sinram, when Palsgraf was still in its infancy. But this does not dispose of the alternative argument that the manner in which several of the claimants were harmed, particularly by flood damage, was unforeseeable and that recovery for this may

124. Compare Professor Beale's "come to rest" rule, The Proximate Consequences of an Act, 33 Harv.L.Rev. 633, 651 ff. (1920), and Professor Seavey's "termination of risk" principle. Principles of Torts, 56 Harv.L.Rev. 72, 93 (1942).

not be had—whether the argument is put in the forthright form that unforeseeable damages are not recoverable or is concealed under a formula of lack of "proximate cause." [125]

* * *

* * * Foreseeability of danger is necessary to render conduct negligent; where as here the damage was caused by just those forces whose existence required the exercise of greater care than was taken—the current, the ice, and the physical mass of the Shiras, the incurring of consequences other and greater than foreseen does not make the conduct less culpable or provide a reasoned basis for insulation.[126] See Hart and Honoré, Causation in the Law, 234–48 (1959). The oft encountered argument that failure to limit liability to foreseeable consequences may subject the defendant to a loss wholly out of proportion to his fault seems scarcely consistent with the universally accepted rule that the defendant takes the plaintiff as he finds him and will be responsible for the full extent of the injury even though a latent susceptibility of the plaintiff renders this far more serious than could reasonably have been anticipated. See Prosser, Torts, 260.

The weight of authority in this country rejects the limitation of damages to consequences foreseeable at the time of the negligent conduct when the consequences are "direct," and the damage, although other and greater than expectable, is of the same general sort that

125. It is worth underscoring that the *ratio decidendi* in Palsgraf was that the Long Island was not required to use *any* care with respect to the package vis-a-vis Mrs. Palsgraf; Chief Judge Cardozo did not reach the issue of "proximate cause" for which the case is often cited. 248 N.Y. at 346–347, 162 N.E. 99.

126. The contrasting situation is illustrated by the familiar instances of the running down of a pedestrian by a safely driven but carelessly loaded car, or of the explosion of unlabeled rat poison, inflammable but not known to be, placed near a coffee burner. Larrimore v. American Nat. Ins. Co., 184 Okl. 614, 89 P.2d 340 (1939). Exoneration of the defendant in such cases rests on the basis that a negligent actor is responsible only for harm the risk of which was increased by the *negligent aspect* of his conduct. See Keeton, Legal Cause in the Law of Torts, 1–10 (1963); Hart & Honoré, Causation in the Law, 157–58 (1959). Compare Berry v. Borough of Sugar Notch, 191 Pa. 345, 43 A. 240 (1899).

This principle supports the judgment for the defendant in the recent case of Doughty v. Turner Mfg. Co., [1964] 2 W.L.R. 240 (C.A.). The company maintained a bath of molten cyanide protected by an asbestos cover, reasonably believed to be incapable of causing an explosion if immersed. An employee inadvertently knocked the cover into the bath, but there was no damage from splashing. A minute or two later an explosion occurred as a result of chemical changes in the cover and the plaintiff, who was standing near the bath, was injured by the molten drops. The risk against which defendant *was* required to use care—splashing of the molten liquid from dropping the supposedly explosion proof cover—did not materialize, and the defendant was found not to have lacked proper care against the risk that did. As said by Lord Justice Diplock, [1964] 2 W.L.R. at 247, "The former risk was well known (that was foreseeable) at the time of the accident; but it did not happen. It was the second risk which happened and caused the plaintiff damage by burning." Moreover, if, as indicated in Lord Pearce's judgment, [1964] 2 W.L.R. at 244, the plaintiff was not within the area of potential splashing, the case parallels Palsgraf; Lord Justice Diplock's statement, [1964] 2 W.L.R. at 248, that defendants "would have been under no liability to the plaintiff if they had intentionally immersed the cover in the liquid" is reminiscent of Chief Judge Cardozo's quoted above.

was risked. See the many cases cited in Prosser, Torts, 260–62, fns. 75–78, and 263–64, and the recent reaffirmation, Dellwo v. Pearson, 259 Minn. 452, 107 N.W.2d 859, 97 A.L.R.2d 866 (1961), of Mr. Justice Mitchell's statement in Christianson v. Chicago, St. P., M. & O. Ry., 67 Minn. 94, 96, 69 N.W. 640, 641 (1896), that the rule of Hadley v. Baxendale, 9 Exch. 341 (1854), has no place in negligence law. Other American courts, purporting to apply a test of foreseeability to damages, extend that concept to such unforeseen lengths as to raise serious doubt whether the concept is meaningful * * *.[127]

We see no reason why an actor engaging in conduct which entails a large risk of small damage and a small risk of other and greater damage, of the same general sort, from the same forces, and to the same class of persons, should be relieved of responsibility for the latter simply because the chance of its occurrence, if viewed alone, may not have been large enough to require the exercise of care. By hypothesis, the risk of the lesser harm was sufficient to render his disregard of it actionable; the existence of a less likely additional risk that the very forces against whose action he was required to guard would produce other and greater damage than could have been reasonably anticipated should inculpate him further rather than limit his liability. This does not mean that the careless actor will always be held for all damages for which the forces that he risked were a cause in fact. Somewhere a point will be reached when courts will agree that the link has become too tenuous—that what is claimed to be consequence is only fortuity. Thus, if the destruction of the Michigan Avenue Bridge had delayed the arrival of a doctor, with consequent loss of a patient's life, few judges would impose liability on any of the parties here, although the agreement in result might not be paralleled by similar unanimity in reasoning; perhaps in the long run one returns to Judge Andrews' statement in Palsgraf, 248 N.Y. at 354–355, 162 N.E. at 104 (dissenting opinion). "It is all a question of expediency, * * * of fair judgment, always keeping in mind the fact that we endeavor to make a rule in each case that will be practical and in keeping with the general understanding of mankind." It would be pleasant if greater certainty were possible, see Prosser, Torts, 262, but the many efforts that have been made at defining the *locus* of the "uncertain and wav-

127. An instance is In re Guardian Casualty Co., 253 App.Div. 360, 2 N.Y.S.2d 232 (1st Dept.), aff'd, 278 N.Y. 674, 16 N.E.2d 397 (1938), where the majority gravely asserted that a foreseeable consequence of driving a taxicab too fast was that a collision with another car would project the cab against a building with such force as to cause a portion of the building to collapse twenty minutes later, when the cab was being removed, and injure a spectator twenty feet away. Surely this is "straining the idea of foreseeability past the breaking point," Bohlen, Book Review, 47 Harv.L.Rev. 556, 557 (1934), at least if the matter be viewed as of the time of the negligent act, as the supposedly symmetrical test of The Wagon Mound demands, [1961] 1 All Eng.R. at 415. On the other hand, if the issue of foreseeability is viewed as of the moment of impact, see Seavey, Mr. Justice Cardozo and the Law of Torts, 52 Harv.L.Rev. 372, 385 (1939), the test loses functional significance since at that time the defendant is no longer able to amend his conduct so as to avert the consequences. [Notes 122–127 from original, renumbered.]

ering line," 248 N.Y. at 354, 162 N.E. 99, are not very promising; what courts do in such cases makes better sense than what they, or others, say. Where the line will be drawn will vary from age to age; as society has come to rely increasingly on insurance and other methods of loss-sharing, the point may lie further off than a century ago. Here it is surely more equitable that the losses from the operators' negligent failure to raise the Michigan Avenue Bridge should be ratably borne by Buffalo's taxpayers than left with the innocent victims of the flooding; yet the mind is also repelled by a solution that would impose liability solely on the City and exonerate the persons whose negligent acts of commission and omission were the precipitating force of the collision with the bridge and its sequelae. We go only so far as to hold that where, as here, the damages resulted from the same physical forces whose existence required the exercise of greater care than was displayed and were of the same general sort that was expectable, unforeseeability of the exact developments and of the extent of the loss will not limit liability. Other fact situations can be dealt with when they arise. * * *

MOORE, CIRCUIT JUDGE (concurring and dissenting):

* * *

I cannot agree * * * merely because "society has come to rely increasingly on insurance and other methods of loss-sharing" that the courts should, or have the power to, create a vast judicial insurance company which will adequately compensate all who have suffered damages. Equally disturbing is the suggestion that "[H]ere it is surely more equitable that the losses from the operators' negligent failure to raise the Michigan Avenue Bridge should be ratably borne by Buffalo's taxpayers than left with the innocent victims of the flooding." Under any such principle, negligence suits would become further simplified by requiring a claimant to establish only his own innocence and then offer, in addition to his financial statement, proof of the financial condition of the respective defendants. Judgment would be entered against the defendant which court or jury decided was best able to pay. Nor am I convinced that it should be the responsibility of the Buffalo taxpayers to reimburse the "innocent victims" in their community for damages sustained. In my opinion, before financial liability is imposed, there should be some showing of legal liability.

Unfortunate though it was for Buffalo to have had its fine vehicular bridge demolished in a most unexpected manner, I accept the finding of liability for normal consequences because the City had plenty of time to raise the bridge after notice was given. Bridges, however, serve two purposes. They permit vehicles to cross the river when they are down; they permit vessels to travel on the river when they are up. But no bridge builder or bridge operator would envision a bridge as a dam or as a dam potential. * * *

My dissent is limited to that portion of the opinion which approves the awarding of damages suffered as a result of the flooding of various properties upstream. I am not satisfied with reliance on hindsight or on the assumption that since flooding occurred, therefore, it must have been foreseeable. In fact, the majority hold that the danger "of flooding would not have been unforeseeable under the circumstances to anyone who gave them thought." But believing that "anyone" might be too broad, they resort to that most famous of all legal mythological characters, the reasonably "prudent man." Even he, however, "carefully pondering the problem," is not to be relied upon because they permit him to become prudent "[W]ith the aid of hindsight."

The majority, in effect, would remove from the law of negligence the concept of foreseeability because, as they say, "[T]he weight of authority in this country rejects the limitation of damages to consequences foreseeable at the time of the negligent conduct when the consequences are 'direct.'" Yet lingering thoughts of recognized legal principles create for them lingering doubts because they say: "This does not mean that the careless actor will always be held for all damages for which the forces that he risked were a cause in fact. Somewhere a point will be reached when courts will agree that the link has become too tenuous—that what is claimed to be consequence is only fortuity." The very example given, namely, the patient who dies because the doctor is delayed by the destruction of the bridge, certainly presents a direct consequence as a factual matter yet the majority opinion states that "few judges would impose liability on any of the parties here," under these circumstances.

In final analysis the answers to the questions when the link is "too tenuous" and when "consequence is only fortuity" are dependent solely on the particular point of view of the particular judge under the particular circumstances. In differing with my colleagues, I must be giving "unconscious recognition of the harshness of holding a man for what he could not conceivably have guarded against because human foresight could not go so far." (L. Hand, C. J., in Sinram v. Pennsylvania R. Co., 61 F.2d 767, 770, 2 Cir. 1932.) If "foreseeability" be the test, I can foresee the likelihood that a vessel negligently allowed to break its moorings and to drift uncontrolled in a rapidly flowing river may well strike other ships, piers and bridges. Liability would also result on the "direct consequence" theory. However, to me the fortuitous circumstance of the vessels so arranging themselves as to create a dam is much "too tenuous."

* * * The line of demarcation will always be "uncertain and wavering," Palsgraf v. Long Island R.R., 248 N.Y. 339, 354, 162 N.E. 99, 59 A.L.R. 1253 (1928), but if, concededly, a line exists, there must be areas on each side. The flood claimants are much too far on the non-liability side of the line. As to them, I would not award any recovery even if the taxpayers of Buffalo are better able to bear the loss.[128]

128. Since the river was blocked by this accident, shipping was disrupted. As to economic losses from such disruption, see Petition of Kinsman Transit Co., 338 F.2d 821 (2d Cir. 1968).

For another thoughtful causation discussion see Marshall v. Nugent, 222

SECTION 4. IMPEDIMENTS TO RECOVERY BECAUSE OF PLAINTIFF'S OWN CONDUCT OR RELATIONSHIPS

BUTTERFIELD v. FORRESTER

Court of King's Bench, 1809.
11 East's Reports 59, 103 Eng.Rep. 926.

This was an action on the case * * *. At the trial before Bayley, J. at Derby, it appeared that the defendant, for the purpose of making some repairs to his house, which was close by the road side at one end of the town, had put up a pole across this part of the road, a free passage being left by another branch or street in the same direction. That the plaintiff left a public house not far distant from the place in question at 8 o'clock in the evening in August, when they were just beginning to light candles, but while there was light enough left to discern the obstruction at 100 yards distance: and the witness, who proved this, said that if the plaintiff had not been riding very hard he might have observed and avoided it: the plaintiff, however, who was riding violently, did not observe it, but rode against it, and fell with his horse, and was much hurt in consequence of the accident; and there was no evidence of his being intoxicated at the time. On this evidence Bayley, J. directed the jury, that if a person riding with reasonable and ordinary care could have seen and avoided the obstruction; and if they were satisfied that the plaintiff was riding along the street extremely hard, and without ordinary care, they should find a verdict for the defendant: which they accordingly did.

Vaughan, Serjt. now objected to this direction, on moving for a new trial; and referred to Buller's No. Pri.* 26. (The book cites Carth. 194 and 451 in the margin, which references do not bear on the point in question.), where the rule is laid down, that "if a man lay logs of wood across a highway; *though a person may with care ride safely by,* yet if by means thereof my horse stumble and fling me, I may bring an action."

F.2d 604 (1st Cir. 1955) (defendant trucker negligently forces auto off icy road; while trucker tries to tow car from snow drift, plaintiff passenger goes down the road to flag down approaching motorists, one of whom skids into plaintiff; trucker liable: "Though this particular act of negligence was over and done with when the truck pulled up alongside of the stalled Chevrolet without having actually collided with it, still the consequences of such past negligence were in the bosom of time, as yet unrevealed.") Compare Riggle v. Wadell, — Va. —, 221 S.E.2d 142 (1976) (first defendant may have negligently obstructed highway; second defendant, negligently speeding, collided; held, first defendant's negligence a "remote", rather than a "proximate" cause of collision, second defendant's negligence "the sole proximate cause of the accident." Also see Weirum v. RKO General, Inc., 15 Cal.3d 40, 123 Cal.Rptr. 468, 539 P.2d 36 (1975) (liability of radio station for wrongful death of motorist forced off road by driver participating in defendant's contest to locate peripatetic disk jockey).

BAYLEY, J. The plaintiff was proved to be riding as fast as his horse could go, and this was through the streets of Derby. If he had used ordinary care he must have seen the obstruction; so that the accident appeared to happen entirely from his own fault.

LORD ELLENBOROUGH, C. J. A party is not to cast himself upon an obstruction which has been made by the fault of another, and avail himself of it, if he do not himself use common and ordinary caution to be in the right. In cases of persons riding upon what is considered to be the wrong side of the road, that would not authorize another purposely to ride up against them. One person being in fault will not dispense with another's using ordinary care for himself. Two things must concur to support this action, an obstruction in the road by the fault of the defendant, and no want of ordinary care to avoid it on the part of the plaintiff.

PER CURIAM. Rule refused.[1]

RAISIN v. MITCHELL

Court of Common Pleas, 1839.
9 C. & P. 613.

The declaration stated that on the 20th November, 1837, the plaintiff was possessed of a sloop which was at anchor in that part of the river Thames which is called the Lower Hope, and that the defendants were possessed of a brig which they by their servants so unskilfully and negligently navigated, that it ran against the plaintiff's sloop, and caused it to sink. Plea, not guilty.

Atcherley, Serjt., stated the plaintiff's case.—The sloop was of thirty-nine tons burthen, and on the day in question, being on a voyage from Cherburg, laden with eggs for the London market, came to an anchor about six in the evening in the Lower Hope; and the brig, which was called the Arethusa, and was of more than 300 tons burthen, came towards the sloop, and having its anchor a-cockbill, ran it into the side of the sloop and sunk the sloop. The brig had not a proper pilot, but only a waterman on board. The question will be whether or no the brig was in fault. I contend that she was, for three reasons: —1st, the sloop was at anchor; 2nd, the ground was ordinary anchoring ground; and, 3rdly, it is contrary to all seamanship for a vessel to sail with the anchor a-cockbill. * * *

1. See, in general, Bohlen, Contributory Negligence 21 Harv.L.Rev. 233 (1908); Green, Contributory Negligence & Proximate Cause, 6 N.C.L. Rev. 3 (1927); Lowndes, Contributory Negligence, 22 Geo.L.J. 674 (1934); Cooley, Problems in Contributory Negligence, 89 U.Pa.L.Rev. 335 (1941); Leflar, The Declining Defense of Contributory Negligence, 1 Ark.L.Rev. 1 (1946); Malone, The Formative Era of Contributory Negligence, 41 Ill.L. Rev. 151 (1946); Lord Wright, Contributory Negligence, 13 Mod.L.Rev. 2 (1950); Philbreck,. Loss Apportionment in Negligence Cases, 99 U.Pa. L.Rev. 572 (1951); Williams, Joint Torts & Contributory Negligence (1951); James, Contributory Negligence, 62 Yale L.J. 691 (1953); Prosser, Comparative Negligence, 51 Mich. L.Rev. 465 (1953).

Thesiger, for the defendants.—1st, The captain of the French vessel, not himself understanding English, and having a crew who did not understand English, was bound to have a pilot who did understand it, to navigate his vessel; 2nd, the French vessel, according to my case, was not at anchor, but on the larboard tack, and that being so, and the brig being on the starboard tack, the French vessel ought to have given way and allowed the brig to keep her course; 3rd, as to the question of whether the sloop was in fact at anchor, the witnesses say the wind was stronger than the tide, and if that be so, the head of the vessel would have been in a different position from that in which they say it was. * * *

Atcherley, Serjeant, replied.

TINDAL, C. J., in summing up, said, the question is, whether the plaintiff has made out a case to entitle him to damages. You must be satisfied that the injury was occasioned by the want of care or the improper conduct of the defendants, and was not imputable in any degree to any want of care or any improper conduct on the part of the plaintiff.

The jury found for the plaintiff, damages £250, the amount claimed by him being upwards of £500.

Atcherley, Serjeant, for the plaintiff.—There must be some mistake.

R. V. Richards, for the defendants.—There is not any mistake at all.

TINDAL, C. J., asked the jury how they made up their verdict.

The Foreman answered that there were faults on both sides.

TINDAL, C. J.—Then you have considered the whole matter.

The Foreman replied in the affirmative.

R. V. Richards submitted to his Lordship that the fact which the foreman of the jury had stated entitled the defendant to the verdict.

TINDAL, C. J.—No. There may be faults to a certain extent.

R. V. Richards requested his Lordship to take a note of his having made the objection.

TINDAL, C. J. assented, and the verdict was entered by the associate for £250.[2]

2. [The following note by the original reporter reveals the confusion of concepts current at the time.] "The verdict in this case, as well as the opinion of the learned Chief Justice, seem to be quite correct, and sustainable in point of law, according to the most modern authorities.—In the case of Bridge v. The Grand Junction Railway Company, 3 Mee. & Wels. 244, which was an action on the case for the negligent management of a train of railway carriages, Mr. Baron Parke said—"There may have been negligence in both parties, and yet the plaintiff may be entitled to recover. The rule of law is laid down with perfect correctness in the case of Butterfield v. Forrester, [11 East. 60], and that rule is, that although there may have been negligence on the part of the plaintiff, yet, unless he might, by the exercise of ordinary care, have avoided the consequences of the defendant's negligence, he is entitled to recover: if by ordinary care he might have avoided them, he is the author of his own wrong. That is the only way

HENSEL v. BECKWARD

Court of Appeals of Maryland, 1974.
273 Md. 426, 330 A.2d 196.

DIGGES, JUDGE. In Creaser v. Owens, 267 Md. 238, 240–241, 297 A.2d 235 (1972), the most recent case of this Court which discusses Maryland's motor vehicle "boulevard rule," Maryland Code (1957, 1970 Repl. Vol.) Art. 66½, § 11–403,[3] we indicated our hope that, with the views expressed there, no longer would this statute give rise to either "lingering doubts about the absoluteness of its application," or, other than through legislative enactment, further "attempts to create new exceptions to it." The present litigation, however, has dashed this hope, as once again we are faced with a case in which the application of the "boulevard rule" is sought to be avoided. Like the Rock of Gibraltar we remain firm and will not allow the legislative

in which the rule, as to the exercise of ordinary care, is applicable to questions of this kind." In the case of Marriott v. Stanley, 1 Scott New Cases, p. 392, it was held, that in an action to recover compensation in damages, for an injury occasioned by an obstruction in a highway, it was not a misdirection on the part of the Judge to leave it to the jury, to say —'whether or not the plaintiff was himself in any degree *the cause of the injury*—whether he had acted with *such a want* of reasonable and ordinary *care as to disentitle him* to recover?' See also the cases there cited and referred to of Smith v. Pelah, 2 Stra. 1264, and Bird v. Holbrook, 1 Moo. & Payne, 607, and 4 Bing. 628.

"The result of the cases seems to be, that the fault of the plaintiff, in order to prevent his recovering, must be one directly *tending to produce the* injury; as, for instance, if a person be on the wrong side of the road, or in a state of drunkenness, though in such case they would neither of them be altogether free from blame, yet they might recover in an action for damages, unless the being on the wrong side of the road in the one case, or the being in a state of drunkenness in the other, directly contributed to the occurrence of the injury. On this point see particularly the concluding observations of Mr. Justice Coleridge, in the case of Sills v. Brown, ante, p. 601."

This was not an admiralty case, presumably because admiralty jurisdiction over collisions was then limited in England to acts "committed on the high seas outside the body of any county", 1 Halsbury's Laws of England 47–8 (3d ed. by Simonds 1952). Since 1824 it had been the rule in admiralty in England that damages would be divided equally among parties at fault, regardless of the relative degree of their faults. This was followed in United States admiralty law in 1854. It was replaced in England in 1911 by a rule for apportionment of damages in proportion to fault. The apportionment rule became virtually universal in admiralty except for the United States, which retained the equal division rule until it was replaced by the apportionment rule in United States v. Reliable Transfer Co., Inc., 421 U.S. 397, 95 S.Ct. 1708, 44 L.Ed.2d 251 (1975).

3. Maryland Code (1957, 1970 Repl. Vol.) Art. 66½, § 11–403 in relevant part states:

"(a) [Provides for the erection of stop or yield signs.]

(b) *Stopping at entrance to through highway.*—The driver of a vehicle shall come to a full stop as required by this subtitle at the entrance to a through highway and shall yield the right-of-way to other vehicles approaching on the through highway.

(c) *Stopping in obedience to stop signs.*—The driver of a vehicle likewise shall come to a full stop in obedience to a stop sign and yield the right-of-way to a vehicle approaching on the intersecting highway as required herein at an intersection where a stop sign is erected at one or more entrances thereto although not a part of a through highway.

(d) [Obligation of motorist when approaching intersection marked by yield sign.]" [Note from original, renumbered.]

mandates contained in this right-of-way statute to be judicially either bypassed or otherwise eroded through new waves of attack.

* * * [T]he accident, which gave rise to this case, occurred on a clear but moonless night in February 1970, when an automobile driven by the respondent, Garfield Beckward, collided with a vehicle driven by the petitioner, Russell William Hensel. That collision occurred in Allegany County at the unilluminated intersection of Vocke Road, a four-lane divided highway running east and west, and Maryland Route 49, a two-lane highway running north and south with a stop sign which controlled the entry of traffic on Route 49 into its intersection with Vocke Road. The evidence also shows that when Beckward approached that intersection he came to a complete stop on Route 49, whereupon he, together with his wife who was beside him on the front seat, each looked twice, both to the east and to the west, for traffic proceeding on Vocke Road. Seeing no vehicular movement and therefore satisfied as to the apparent safety of moving out into the intersection, Beckward began to drive very slowly across the two eastbound lanes of Vocke Road toward the median, while both he and his wife continued to watch for traffic which might approach from their left. When the Beckwards were about half way across that side of the highway, the petitioner's car suddenly appeared in the illumination of their headlights. This second vehicle was about 20 to 25 feet away when first spotted by the Beckwards, and was proceeding, they say at a fast rate of speed in an easterly direction with unlit headlights. The collision which followed caused Beckward to be catapulted from his automobile onto the road curb, and tragically resulted in his being hospitalized for six months, after which he returned to his home permanently paralyzed from the neck down.

After all the evidence was presented, Judge Getty, relying principally on our decision in Creaser v. Owens, supra, directed a verdict, and we think quite correctly, in favor of Hensel on the ground that, under the "boulevard rule," Beckward as the unfavored driver, though he halted at the stop sign, was contributorily negligent as a matter of law in failing to yield the right-of-way to the Hensel vehicle traveling on the favored highway.

In *Creaser*, a school bus driver, traveling on an unfavored highway, properly stopped at the stop sign and looked for traffic proceeding on the favored highway before venturing into the intersection. Though her visability beyond 200 feet to her left was obstructed by a hill and a curve in the "boulevard," the bus driver slowly "creeped out" into the intersection, only to be surprised by a speeding car which "jumped" over the hill and collided with the bus. While recognizing the possible harshness of the result, this Court held that because the bus driver failed to yield the right-of-way to the favored driver as required by the "boulevard" statute, the unfavored operator was guilty of contributory negligence as a matter of law. In so ruling we stated:

> "In order to make crystal clear our holding here, we emphasize that if an unfavored driver is involved in an accident

> with a favored vehicle under circumstances where the boulevard law is applicable then in a suit based on that collision the unfavored driver is deemed to be negligent as a matter of law. And, if the unfavored driver is a plaintiff, his suit is defeated unless the doctrine of last clear chance rescues his claim. Whereas, if the unfavored driver is a defendant he is liable except in the rare case when the issue of contributory negligence on the part of the favored driver is properly submitted to a jury, i. e., whether he was guilty of negligence that was a proximate cause of the accident." (all citations omitted) * * *

* * * [T]he "boulevard rule," developed over the years, and whose meaning is explained in *Creaser* and similar cases, applies to the facts present here so as to prohibit recovery by the respondent as a matter of law * * *.

SMITH, JUDGE (dissenting). * * *

NORTH BEND LUMBER CO. v. CITY OF SEATTLE

Supreme Court of Washington, 1921.
116 Wash. 500, 199 P. 988, 19 A.L.R. 415.

Action by the North Bend Lumber Company against the City of Seattle to recover damages for the flooding of plaintiffs' property. From a judgment granting new trial after verdict for defendant, it appeals. * * *

BRIDGES, J. Boxley creek is a small mountain stream in King county, having its source near Rattlesnake Lake, and running thence in a southerly direction for some three miles, empties into the south fork of the Snoqualmie river. The plaintiff, North Bend Lumber Company, had its sawmill located on both sides of this creek, at a point about one mile above its mouth. The Druid Lumber Company's sawmill was located on the same creek, but very near its mouth. These mills were built during the years 1905 and 1906, and from time to time since have been enlarged. The plaintiff built a dam across the creek a short distance above its mill for the purpose of creating a pond of water in which to store its sawlogs. A platform crossed the creek from one part to another of the sawmill. This platform rests upon piling driven in the banks and bed of the stream.

Cedar river flows through Cedar Lake, which is located near the foot of Mt. Washington. The river, after flowing out of the lake, takes, for a number of miles, a general westerly course. In 1914 the city of Seattle constructed a large dam in this river, at a point about two miles west of the lake. The purpose of the dam was to impound waters in the canyon of the river between the lake and the dam, to be used by the city in generating electric power. The northerly bank of this reservoir is for the most part a glacial moraine. Whether this moraine formation would permit much of the water of the reservoir to leak out has been a question from the beginning, and has, to a considerable extent, disturbed the minds of the city authorities. This glacial moraine covers several hundred acres, and a part of it is within the watershed of Boxley creek, and a part within the Cedar river watershed. The divide between the two watersheds is less than one mile in width.

Immediately prior to December 23, 1918, there had been heavy rains, which caused the waters of Boxley creek to become very considerably swollen. On that date the sawmills of the North Bend Lumber Company and of the Druid Lumber Company were either wholly or partially destroyed by high water. The plaintiff sued the city of Seattle for its damage, and also for damage to the property of the Druid Lumber Company, the latter having assigned to the former its claim of damages. The plaintiff contends that its damage was caused by the waters from defendant's reservoir. Seeping through the coarse ground forming the moraine and tending in a westerly direction, they suddenly broke out in great quantities near the westerly edge of the moraine, thence being conveyed into the watershed of Boxley creek, and ultimately into that creek above plaintiff's works.

The plaintiff charged the city with negligence in the construction and maintenance of its reservoir, and particularly the north bank thereof, and in permitting the waters of Cedar river to be diverted in part into the channels of Boxley creek. The city denied negligence upon its part, and denied that any of the waters had found their way into Boxley creek, to the damage of the plaintiff, and alleged that the damage done to its property was caused by the waters coming from the natural watershed of Boxley creek. It further alleged contributory negligence on the part of the plaintiff in building and maintaining its log pond in the creek, and in partially closing up the creek by means of piling, logs, and debris.

Upon these issues the case went to trial before a jury, which returned its verdict in favor of the defendant. The plaintiff's motion for a new trial was granted by the trial court, and the defendant has appealed therefrom.

The trial court gave three instructions on contributory negligence, wherein, among other things, it told the jury that it was to determine whether the plaintiff used such degree of care and prudence as an ordinarily prudent person, under the same or similar circumstances, would have used, and that in determining whether it did use such degree of care and caution the jury had the right to, and should, take into consideration any knowledge which the plaintiff had of the danger, and should consider all the circumstances and conditions surrounding the situation.

At the hearing of the motion for a new trial, the court concluded that it had erred in giving these instructions on contributory negligence, and for that reason granted a new trial. The respondent argues that there is not, and cannot be, in this case any question of contributory negligence; that the only question involved is whether, because of the negligence of the appellant, any of the waters belonging to the Cedar river watershed were suddenly diverted into the watershed of Boxley creek to the respondent's damage, and that if this question be answered in the negative, then, under no circumstances, could the appellant be held liable, and that if it be answered in the affirmative, then, even if respondent's works in the bed of the creek did block the stream more or less, and did cause or aggravate the injury to its property, still, there would be no question of contributory negligence, because respondent would not be required, under any circumstances, to so use its property as to protect itself against the wrongful act of the appellant in diverting large quantities of the waters of Cedar river into their unnatural watershed and into Boxley creek.

If the destruction of respondent's property was caused by the waters naturally coming from the watershed of Boxley creek, or if appellant was not guilty of the negligence charged against it, then that would be an end of the case, for it is plain that under those circumstances contributory negligence could not be involved, because contributory negligence of the plaintiff grows out of, and is necessarily associated with, the negligence of the defendant. But appellant argues that the question of its negligence was for the jury, and that if the finding was against it in that regard, then it would be proper for the jury to consider whether respondent contributed to its damage by putting its dam across the creek and by driving piling in the bed of the stream, thus restricting its natural capacity. In this connection it asserts that there was testimony to show that some of respondent's officers had lived many years in the immediate vicinity of Cedar Lake; knew that the appellant was creating the great reservoir; knew that its north bank was a moraine, and knew as much as the city officers concerning whether it was pervious to water, and because of this information had reason to anticipate that the very thing which happened might happen; that notwithstanding all this knowledge it afterwards caused the channel of the creek to be blocked in such a way as to impede the flow of the waters therein. To these facts (and it may be conceded that there was testimony tending to show such to be the facts), it applies the doctrine that one must protect himself and his property against such acts of negligence of others as a reasonably prudent person would have reason to anticipate.

Appellant's reasoning is plausible, but not sound. We need not here decide whether one may use and improve his property in total disregard of a danger, resulting from the negligence of some one else, which he knows exists, and which he is morally certain will damage him. There is no evidence showing or tending to show this condition. We hold, however, that one is not bound to use his property in anticipation of a situation arising, which, because of the negligence of some one else, known to or suspected by him may or may not cause him damage. The use one may make of his property is not to be measured or limited by any such unstable rule as that contended for by appellant. At least, up to the point where one has become morally certain that the negligence of another will injure him he may make any proper and customary use of his property in total disregard of any negligence of that other, whether such negligence be known to him or not. One owns real estate for the use he may make of it. Being the owner, he may make such use of it as he sees fit, so long as he does not injure his neighbor or violate some principle of the doctrine of police regulation. His neighbor may not say to him:

"You must not improve your land nor plant it to crop, because I have been guilty of such negligence as may cause your improvements or your crop to be damaged or destroyed."

Any other rule would permit one guilty of wrongdoing to deprive another of the right of making any lawful use of his property. If appellant's theory of the law is to prevail, then every man who owns real estate below a reservoir of water must use it at his peril, if he have reason to suspect the dam, through the negligence of the owner, has become weakened; and a farmer takes his chances in planting his land to crop, simply because he knows a culvert has been so negligently built by another that it will not carry away flood waters, but may cause them to wash over his land to his damage. The rule which requires one to make a reasonable effort to protect his person from the known negligence of another is a rule of personal conduct, and in the nature of things, cannot be extended to the use of property. Respondent knew something about the moraine, and it knew that it formed the northerly bank of appellant's reservoir. It did not know that it was or was not impervious to water. From its standpoint there was no certainty that what it claims happened, would happen. Must it then at its peril make use of the land because of the knowledge it had? If it was guilty of contributory negligence in putting a dam in Boxley creek, it was guilty of contributory negligence in constructing its mills on the bank of the stream.

An extensive examination of the authorities on this question convinces us that they are not in entire accord, and that the subject has not always been treated with the thoroughness its difficulties and importance deserve. * * *

[The court then discusses a number of cases.]

We, therefore, conclude that the question of contributory negligence is in no wise involved in this case, and that the court was right in granting a new trial because he had erred in instructing the jury on that question. But appellant contends that, aside from the question of contributory negligence, the court erred in granting a new trial because there was not sufficient evidence of its negligence to carry the case to the jury. We cannot sustain this position. At the trial the appellant's contention was that the waters which damaged respondent's property were those belonging to the natural watershed of Boxley creek, and that none of them came from appellant's reservoir. On the other hand, respondent contended that the waters which injured it seeped from the reservoir through the moraine, and were there stored in great quantities, till they suddenly broke out and found their way into Boxley creek, and that appellant knew, or should have known, of the pervious character of the moraine. There was testimony to support each of these theories or contentions. It was therefore the duty of the court to submit to the jury the question of appellant's negligence.

The judgment is affirmed. * * * [4]

KOENIG v. PATRICK CONST. CORPORATION

Court of Appeals of New York, 1948.
298 N.Y. 313, 3 N.E.2d 133, 10 A.L.R.2d 848.

FULD, JUDGE. We are called upon to determine whether, in an action for damages brought by an injured worker on the strength of section 240 of the Labor Law, Consol.Laws, c. 3, a defendant may assert the worker's contributory negligence as a defense.

Plaintiff, a window cleaner, had been hired as an independent contractor by defendant to do the work necessary on the windows of a school which defendant was engaged in constructing. On the day of the accident, February 7, 1941, plaintiff was atop a ladder, some 16 or 17 feet above the floor, scraping and removing paint from one of the large windows in the auditorium. While plaintiff was thus engaged, the ladder which had been placed by him against the wall, with its base some 4 feet from the wall slipped out and hurled him to the floor. It was plaintiff's claim that, in spite of his protests, he had been directed by defendant's employees to use the ladder in order to reach the windows; that the ladder, a straight, wooden, rung-type affair about 20 feet long, was without the usual devices at the bottom —called "safety shoes"—to prevent slipping when the ladder was in use; and that it likewise lacked notches to which such safety shoes could be fitted.

Plaintiff, seriously injured, commenced this suit for damages predicated primarily upon defendant's asserted failure to comply with the requirements of section 240 of the Labor Law. That statute provides, in part, that a person "employing or directing another to per-

4. Distinguish the situation underlying this case from those in which the plaintiff is said to assume the risk. What difference in this regard would it make if defendant controlled all the lower riparian rights in Boxley creek and plaintiff put his mill and dam there as a licensee of the defendant? Contrast also the legal effect of plaintiff's using, with all possible care, a stairway he knows is defective (1) upon premises leased from defendant to plaintiff, (2) upon defendant's own premises (P being a business visitor), (3) in a common approach to a group of apartments owned by defendant, one of which is leased to plaintiff. See ch. 3, infra; James, Assumption of Risk, 61 Yale L.J. 141 (1952).

A leading case on the question presented by the principal case is Leroy Fibre Co. v. Chicago, M. & St. P. R. Co., 232 U.S. 340 (1914).

Does the notion involved in the principal case apply to all situations where plaintiff encounters a known danger which he has a right to be free from and which is imposed upon him by defendant's wrongful conduct? How far, for instance, may a driver insist on maintaining his right of way without being negligent?

form labor of any kind in the erection * * * repairing * * * painting, cleaning or pointing of a building or structure shall furnish * * * or cause to be furnished * * * scaffolding * * * ladders," or any other safe equipment required for the worker's protection.

Upon the trial, the court charged, that under section 240, plaintiff could recover only if he proved (1) that defendant "assumed to furnish this ladder to the plaintiff to be used under the circumstances under which it was used, and that those circumstances were such that the danger of an accident was foreseeable by the defendant"; (2) that defendant "failed in its duty", and (3) that plaintiff had not "contributed any negligence to the accident himself."

The jury returned a verdict in favor of defendant, and because of the last item of instruction, the possibility is present that that verdict in defendant's favor was predicated upon a finding that plaintiff had been guilty of contributory negligence. In the view which we take of the law, that would be an erroneous basis for the verdict. That error in the charge requires reversal, despite the fact that it is quite likely considering the entire record that the jury found that defendant did not violate section 240, and, accordingly, did not even reach the question of plaintiff's contributory negligence.

Though defendant was also charged with common-law negligence, the gravamen of the complaint, as indicated, was that defendant was liable for having violated its statutory duty to furnish plaintiff safe equipment. Of course, if defendant did actually direct the work, it is of no moment—we simply note in passing—that plaintiff happened to be an independent contractor rather than an ordinary employee. See, e. g., Sdoia v. Cawley, 290 N.Y. 847, 50 N.E.2d 240; Weber v. State, Ct.Cl., 53 N.Y.S.2d 598. Plaintiff, being thus included within the class protected, is entitled to the full benefit of the statute.

Firmly established is the principle of law that a plaintiff's carelessness is no bar to his recovery under a statute which imposes liability "regardless of negligence". See Schmidt v. Merchants Despatch Transp. Co., 270 N.Y. 287, 305, 306, 200 N.E. 824, 830, 104 A.L.R. 450. Obviously, not every statute which commands or prohibits particular conduct is within this principle. Only when the statute is designed to protect a definite class of persons from a hazard of definable orbit, which they themselves are incapable of avoiding, is it deemed to create a statutory cause of action and to impose a liability unrelated to questions of negligence. This rule is based upon the view that, not being dependent upon proof of specific acts of negligence on defendant's part, the cause of action may not be defeated by proof of plaintiff's want of care. Thus, it has been said, "If the defendant's negligence consists in the violation of a statute enacted to protect a class of persons from their inability to exercise self-protective care, a member of such class is not barred by his contributory negligence from recovery for bodily harm caused by the violation of such statute". Restatement, Torts, § 483.

Irrespective of how the courts may once have viewed the question * * * it is our judgment that both sound reason and persuasive decisions, involving statutes whose content and purpose are similar to those of section 240, require the conclusion that that statute does not permit the worker's contributory negligence to be asserted as a defense. * * * For example, in construing a statute of nearly identical import—section 202 of the Labor Law which requires that safe devices be supplied to window washers who work on public buildings from the outside—this court observed not long ago that "Since * * * liability of defendant depends upon violation of the statute, contributory negligence would be no defense. Stern v. Great Island Corp., 250 App.Div. 115, 293 N.Y.S. 608; Osborne v. Salvation Army, 2 Cir., 107 F.2d 929." See Pollard v. Trivia Bldg. Corp., supra, 291 N.Y. at page 24, 50 N.E.2d at page 290. And in the Stern case, supra, the court had written, 250 App.Div. at page 116, 293 N.Y.S. at page 611: "Since the plaintiff's cause of action does not rest on negligence, contributory negligence does not constitute a defense. Indeed, the very purpose of the statute was to protect plaintiff's intestate and others in like position from the consequences of their own negligence. It would be strange, therefore, if the same negligence could defeat the operation of the statute. Karpeles v. Heine, 227 N.Y. 74, 124 N.E. 101; Corwin v. New York & Erie, R. Co., 13 N.Y. 42."

The safe-ladder provision of section 240 comes squarely within this doctrine. By its force, certain safeguards have been legislatively commanded for the safety of those engaging in the work described. Instead of simply defining the general standard of care required and then providing that violation of that standard evidences negligence, the legislature imposed upon employers or those directing the particular work to be done, a flat and unvarying duty. This the language of the section makes crystal clear: the employer or one directing the work "*shall furnish*" or cause to be furnished equipment or devices "which shall be so constructed, placed and operated as *to give proper protection*" to the one doing the work. (Emphasis supplied.) For breach of that duty, thus absolutely imposed, the wrongdoer is rendered liable without regard to his care or lack of it.

And, what the statute declares, its reason confirms. Workmen such as the present plaintiff, who ply their livelihoods on ladders and scaffolds, are scarcely in a position to protect themselves from accident. They usually have no choice but to work with the equipment at hand, though danger looms large. The legislature recognized this and to guard against the known hazards of the occupation required the employer to safeguard the workers from injury caused by faulty or inadequate equipment. If the employer could avoid this duty by pointing to the concurrent negligence of the injured worker in using the equipment, the beneficial purpose of the statute might well be frustrated and nullified. That possibility we long ago perceived and provided for, declaring that "this statute is one for the protection of workmen from injury, and undoubtedly is to be construed as liberally as may be for the accomplishment of the purpose for which it was thus framed". See Quigley v. Thatcher, 207 N.Y. 66, 68, 100 N.E. 596. Such an interpretation manifestly rules out contributory negligence as a defense to an action predicated upon violation of the statute to the injury of one in the protected class. See, e. g., Laurin v. Patrick Constr. Corp., 263 App.Div. 1013, 33 N.Y.S.2d 928; Weber v. State of New York, Ct.Cl., 53 N.Y.S.2d 598, supra.

A different case would be before us if the injured person were a passerby or a workman struck by a falling ladder; as to them—persons outside the class for whose special benefit the statute was designed—a violation might do no more than evidence negligence. That, however, is not this case. Here, to recapitulate, we have an action based upon a statute whose cardinal purpose was to protect plaintiff and others in his calling, without reference to questions of negligence, from the occurrence of just such an accident as befell him. In spite of this, the trial court left the jury free to bring in a verdict against plaintiff if it found him guilty of contributory negligence. Such instructions were in open conflict with the purpose and aim of the statute, and, since they may have improperly influenced the result, there must be a new trial.

The judgments should be reversed and a new trial granted, with costs to abide the event.

LOUGHRAN, C. J., and LEWIS, CONWAY, DESMOND and DYE, JJ., concur.

Judgments reversed, etc.[5]

ELLIOTT v. PHILADELPHIA TRANSP. CO.

Supreme Court of Pennsylvania, 1947.
356 Pa. 643, 53 A.2d 81.

LINN, JUSTICE. The plaintiff was run down by a street car on Haverford Avenue at the intersection of Preston Street in Philadelphia. He sued the Transportation Company and recovered a verdict of $1,500. The trial court entered judgment for the defendant notwithstanding the verdict. Plaintiff appealed to the Superior Court, which reversed the judgment. We allowed this appeal.

Haverford Avenue, between 40th and 41st Streets, has a cartway 44 feet between curbs and sidewalks 18 feet wide. The block from 41st Street on the west, to 40th Street on the east, is intersected at right angles by three streets mentioned in the evidence, Budd Street, Ludwick Street and Preston Street. At the northeast corner of Preston Street and Haverford Avenue is a fire station housing a city fire engine. Defendant's single street car track is somewhat south of the center of the Avenue. Plaintiff called a surveyor from the city's Survey Bureau who testified that the distance from 41st Street to

5. See Prosser, Contributory Negligence as Defense to Violation of Statute, 32 Minn.L.Rev. 105 (1948).

Preston Street was 421 feet 9 inches; from Budd Street to Preston Street 232 feet 4 inches; and from Ludwick Street to Preston Street 74 feet 10 inches, distances to be kept in mind in considering plaintiff's conduct. Preston Street is 50 feet wide with a cartway of 26 feet.

Plaintiff described an extraordinary occurrence. Defendant, on the other hand, called three eye witnesses, whose evidence, if the jury had accepted it, would have justified a finding that it was a case of simple contributory negligence with nothing extraordinary about it. We of course take the oral evidence supporting the verdict and reject the rest. So considered, plaintiff's contention is that the effect of his contributory negligence drops out of the case and, notwithstanding such negligence, he may recover because defendant was guilty of wanton misconduct resulting in his injury: Kasanovich v. George, 348 Pa. 199, 34 A.2d 523. Defendant contends that plaintiff's own testimony shows that he exposed himself unnecessarily and recklessly to an obvious danger and to consequences that were obvious to him and for that reason the law does not permit recovery. The trial court adopted defendant's view; the Superior Court rejected it; the courts differed as to the effect to be given to plaintiff's conduct.

At about 10:30 a. m., May 27, 1943, a clear day, plaintiff, a paper hanger by trade, was at the northwest corner of Haverford Avenue and Preston Street when he heard and saw a fire engine about a block away on Preston Street approaching southward toward Haverford Avenue; it was returning to the fire house on the northeast corner of Preston Street and Haverford Avenue. He also saw a street car approaching from the west on Haverford Avenue. He testified that on seeing the fire engine, he "went out in the middle of the street [Haverford Avenue] and I stood there right in the middle of the car track" and "waved to the trolley car" which was then "at 41st and Haverford Avenue." The distance between him and 41st Street was 421 feet. He was familiar with the neighborhood. He gave the speed of the trolley car as "about 25 or 30 miles an hour." At first he was "facing the trolley car" but after a while he turned, facing northward, and "waved for the fire engine to come on, and the trolley car kept moving toward me." The car "was coming about the same speed, around 30 miles an hour." When the car struck him he was "looking toward the fire engine." The car stopped within its own length. The plaintiff had an unobstructed view as there was no other traffic on Haverford Avenue between 41st Street and the plaintiff. He testified that he had been facing the approaching car until it was between Budd Street and Ludwick Street, when he "turned around and had my hands up and waved for the fire engine to come on * * *." Budd Street was 232 feet from Preston Street where plaintiff stood and Ludwick Street was 75 feet from there. At the time he turned from facing the street car it must then have been at some point within the 232 feet distance between Budd and Preston Streets and must reach him within five or six seconds at the rate at which he said it was moving.

There was no reason why he remained standing in the car track to give the signals he described; he was not asked to give them. He appears to have volunteered to "flag" the fire engine into Haverford Avenue. There is nothing to show that such "flagging" was needed nor that the motorman on the street car should have known what plaintiff intended by "waving" his arms. He might have given his signals just as well and in perfect safety while standing in the Avenue outside the range of the rapidly approaching car. He continued to stand in the tracks although a step or two would have taken him out of danger. By remaining on the track he also endangered the street car passengers.

The court may not hold and the jury cannot be permitted to find, that plaintiff did not realize the gravity of the risk involved in remaining on the track in the circumstances he described.

By his evidence he brought himself clearly within section 482(2) of the Restatement of Torts: "(2) A plaintiff is barred from recovery for harm caused by the defendant's reckless disregard for the plaintiff's safety, if knowing of the defendant's reckless misconduct and the danger involved to him therein, the plaintiff recklessly exposes himself thereto." See also Section 503(2) and Section 893. Comment (a) to Section 482, reads: "In order that the plaintiff's conduct may bar him from recovering it is necessary that he not only know of the defendant's reckless conduct but also realize the gravity of the risk involved therein so that he is not only unreasonable but reckless in exposing himself to it."

Defendant had the right to operate its cars. The motorman may properly have assumed that the plaintiff would step off the track when it became apparent to him, as it must have become apparent, that the car was not coming to a stop at Preston Street. As it approached without reducing speed, the plaintiff saw that it would not stop and that he must leave the track or risk injury. The movement of the car from 41st Street to Preston Street, a distance of 421 feet, at the rate at which the plaintiff said the car was moving, would take about 10 seconds; it was only 5 seconds from him when he turned and looked away from it. By staying on the track when he might have left it in safety, he must be held to have assumed the consequences of his rashness. This element of assumption of risk by the plaintiff was not present in Kasanovich v. George, 348 Pa. 199, 34 A.2d 523, referred to above, a fact which distinguishes this case from that, because there was no evidence that Kasanovich, who was struck by the street car, knew that it was approaching behind him.

Plaintiff's reckless conduct bars recovery for the result of defendant's wanton misconduct for the same reason that contributory negligence constitutes a defense to an action based on mere negligence. Contributory negligence is a defense because it introduces into a case a new cause of plaintiff's injury making defendant's negligence no longer the legal cause. So in this case, defendant's wanton misconduct, as a legal cause of injury, was superseded by plaintiff's wanton or reckless misconduct which became the legal cause of his injury. * *

Plaintiff concedes the principle; in his brief it is said: "Plaintiff is barred from recovery if, being cognizant of the peril threatening him, his disregard for his own safety represents conduct of the same character as that of the defendant. In short, if defendant is guilty of negligence, plaintiff will be barred by contributory negligence. If defendant is guilty of reckless misconduct, plaintiff will be barred by his own recklessness. It is submitted that this is the purport of the decisions."

The judgment of the Superior Court is reversed and the judgment for the defendant entered by Court of Common Pleas No. 1 is reinstated.[6]

ALLEN M. STEARNE, JUSTICE (dissenting).

* * *

While I concur in the principles of law set forth in the majority opinion, I do not agree that these principles are properly applied to the facts as narrated by the plaintiff and which must be accepted in the light most favorable to the plaintiff's contention. It should not be held, on the present facts, as matter of law, that despite defendant's wanton negligence, plaintiff is barred from recovery because of his own wanton misconduct. In my view, plaintiff did *not* recklessly or unnecessarily expose himself to a known danger created by defendant's negligence. Plaintiff, of course, had no authority to assume the function of a traffic officer. According to plaintiff's testimony he became apprehensive that there might be a right angle collision between an approaching trolley car and fire truck. When he first stood between the rails of the single line trolley tracks and waved for the trolley car to stop before it reached the intersection, *the trolley car was approximately 400 feet away,* approaching at an estimated speed of 25 to 30 miles per hour. Defendant's testimony was that the trolley car was in full view of the plaintiff and, conversely, the plaintiff was in full view of the motorman. At a point less than 230 feet away, plaintiff turned around, still holding his hands up, and waved for the fire truck to come on. The trolley car, however, continued toward the plaintiff with unslackened speed. After the accident, the driver of the fire truck asked the motorman: "What is the idea of hitting

6. Does the explanation in terms of proximate cause make sense if we use here the same test which would be used in determining defendant's liability to a third person hurt by the accident (e. g. a passenger injured by the jolt of the collision)? Is there anything here that makes plaintiff's conduct "proximate" to the exclusion of defendant's, except the gravity of his wrong? Why is not the wantonness of *each* party a proximate cause of the damage? Although the possibility of plural legal causes has become generally accepted, when the question arises between a negligent plaintiff and a negligent defendant, the quest for a *single* "proximate" or "decisive" cause sometimes enables a court to disregard completely the negligence of one of the parties. As between two wrongs which are equally causes in fact, how is this choice to be made? Compare note, p. 300, supra; Lord Wright, Contributory Negligence, 13 Modern L.Rev. 2 (1950); Gordon, Wrong Turns in the Volens Cases, 61 L.Q.Rev. 140 (1945). Contrast Green, Contributory Negligence, 6 N.C.L.Rev. 3 (1927); James, Last Clear Chance: A Transitional Doctrine, 47 Yale L.J. 704 (1938); Williams, Joint Torts & Contributory Negligence, § 62 (1951).

that man? Didn't you see that man?" The motorman replied: "Sure, I saw the man, but what the hell is he doing on the track?" I agree with the Superior Court that if the motorman saw plaintiff on the track (which it is admitted that he did) *and that the plaintiff obviously was not going to move,* and there was sufficient time for the motorman to have stopped the car (which is conceded), then it was the duty of the motorman to stop to prevent injury or death rather than run the man down. The motorman could have stopped his car and either caused plaintiff's arrest for obstructing traffic or have forcibly removed him from the tracks.

For these reasons I dissent.

SMITHWICK v. HALL & UPSON CO.

Supreme Court of Errors of Connecticut, 1890.
59 Conn. 261, 21 A. 924.

TORRANCE, J. The general question reserved for our advice in this case is whether the plaintiff, upon the facts found, is entitled to the substantial damages or only to the nominal damages found by the court below. Inasmuch as that court has expressly found that the negligence of the defendant caused or contributed to the injury for which the plaintiff seeks to recover, the decision of the above general question depends upon this single point, namely, whether the acts and conduct of the plaintiff, as set forth upon the record, constitute or amount to such contributory negligence on his part as will bar his right to substantial damages. The facts found, so far as they bear upon the question for decision, are in substance the following: The plaintiff was a workman in the service of the defendant, and at the time of the injury complained of was engaged in helping to store ice for the defendant in a certain brick building. In doing this work the plaintiff stood upon a platform about 5 feet wide and 17 feet long, raised 15 feet above the ground, and extending from the west side of the building easterly to a point about 2 feet east of the door or aperture through which the ice was taken into the building. A stout plank of suitable height and strength extended along the outer side of the platform as far as the west side of the door, and served as a protective railing or guard to that portion of the platform. In front of the door, and east of it, the platform was without guard or railing of any kind. A short time prior to the injury the foreman of the defendant stationed the plaintiff on the platform just west of the door, and inside the railing, and showed him what his duties were there, and told him 'not to go upon the east end of the platform east of the slide and door, as it was not safe to stand there.' He did not tell the plaintiff why it was not safe, but the danger which he had in mind was the narrowness and unrailed condition of the platform, and the liability by inadvertence to misstep or fall or slip off, the latter being aggravated by the liability of the platform to become slippery from broken ice. These dangers were all manifest. The peril resulting from the accident which happened to the building was not in contemplation. After the foreman went away the plaintiff, in spite of the orders so given to him, and for reasons of his own apparently, went over to the east end of the platform, and worked there. It is found that there was no sufficient reason or excuse for the change of position. One of his fellow-workmen, seeing the plaintiff in that place, told him that 'it was not safe, and to stand on the other side,' but the plaintiff, notwithstanding such warning, remained at work there. While so at work the brick wall of the building above the platform, in consequence of the negligence of the defendant, gave way, the brick falling upon the platform, and thence to the ground. The plaintiff was struck by portions of the descending mass, and fell to the earth. He was either knocked off, or his fall, in the condition in which he stood, was inevitable; indeed, had he not fallen when he did, his injuries, which were very serious, would have been worse. Most of the injuries which he actually sustained were occasioned by the fall. The plaintiff had no knowledge that the wall would be likely to fall, or was in any way unsafe, and it is found that "no fault or negligence can be imputed to him in this regard." In contemplation of the peril from the falling wall, it is found that "the spot where the plaintiff stood could not have been considered more dangerous than the place where he was directed to stand, though in fact most of the brick fell upon the side where he stood, and the result demonstrated, therefore, that the other side would have been safer in the event which occurred."

Upon these facts the defendant contends that the plaintiff, in going to and remaining on the east end of the platform, contrary to he orders and in spite of the warning given him, and in view of the obvious and manifest danger in so doing, was guilty of such contributory negligence as bars him of his right to recover more than nominal damages. If the plaintiff's injuries had resulted from any of the perils and dangers attendant upon the mere fact of his standing and working on the east end of the platform, which were obvious and manifest to any one in his place, which were in the mind of the foreman when he told the plaintiff not to go there, and in view of which his fellow-workman warned him, then this claim of the defendant would be a valid one. But upon the facts found it is without foundation. The injury to the plaintiff was not the result of any such dangers, but was caused through the negligence of the defendant by the falling walls. This was a source of danger of which he had no knowledge whatever. He was justified in supposing that the wall was safe, and would not be likely to fall upon him, no matter where he stood on the platform. He had no reason to anticipate even the slightest danger from that source before or after he changed his position. This being so, he could be guilty of no negligence with respect to this source of danger by changing his position contrary to orders; for negligence presupposes a duty of taking care, and this, in turn, presupposes knowledge or its legal equivalent. With respect to that danger, the plaintiff, upon the facts found, must be held to have acted as any reasonably careful man would have acted under the same circumstances. In changing his position contrary to orders, he voluntarily took the risk of all perils and dangers which a man of ordinary care in his place ought to have known or could reasonably have anticipated; but as to dangers arising through the defendant's negligence from other sources,—dangers which he was not bound to anticipate and of whose existence he had no knowledge,—he took no risk and assumed no duty of taking care. It was the duty of the defendant, on the facts found, to warn the plaintiff against the danger from the falling wall. Now, the act or omission of a party injured, which amounts to what is called "contributory negligence," must be a negligent act or omission, and in the production of the injury it must operate as a proximate cause or one of the proximate causes, and not merely as a condition. In the case at bar the conduct of the plaintiff, as we have seen, was, with respect to the danger from the falling wall, not negligent, for the want of knowledge or its equivalent on the part of the plaintiff. Nor was his conduct, legally considered, a cause of the injury. It was a condition, rather. If he had not changed his position, he might not have been hurt. And so, too, if he had never been born, or had remained at home on the day of the injury, it would not have happened; yet no one would claim that his birth, or his not remaining at home that day, can in any just or legal sense be deemed a cause of the injury. The court below has found that the plaintiff's fall, in the position in which he stood was due to the giving way of the wall, and that most of his injuries were occasioned by the fall. His position there, upon the facts found, can no more be considered as a cause of the injury, than it could be in a case where the defendant, in doing some act near the platform without the plaintiff's knowledge, had negligently knocked him to the ground, or had negligently hit him with a stone. Had the injury been occasioned by a misstep or slip from the platform by the carelessness of the plaintiff, or for the want of a railing, the casual connection between the change of position and the injury would, legally speaking, be quite obvious; but, from a legal point of view, no such connection exists between the change of position and the giving way of the wall.

* * * Under these circumstances, the failure or neglect to heed the warning does not constitute contributory negligence. Gray v. Scott, 66 Pa.St. 345. * * * The defendant seems to claim, however, that, although some of the plaintiff's injuries were caused by falling bricks, yet most of them were caused by his fall; and that, as he probably would not have fallen had he remained behind the railing, he contributed to his injury by placing himself where, in case of such accident, there was nothing to prevent his fall. Whether the claim that he would probably not have fallen had he remained where he was stationed be true or not, must forever remain matter of conjecture. But if its truth could be demonstrated it would not, as we have seen, change the relation of the plaintiff's act to the legal cause of his injury, or make that act, from a legal stand-point, a contributing cause when it was but a condition. And if the claim means that the plaintiff by his act increased the injury, merely, then, if this were true, it would

not be such contributory negligence as would defeat the action. To have that effect it must be an act or omission which contributes to the happening of the act or event which caused the injury. An act or omission that merely increases or adds to the extent of the loss or injury will not have that effect, though, of course, it may affect the amount of damages recovered in a given case. Gould v. McKenna, 86 Pa.St. 297; Stebbins v. Railroad Co., 54 Vt. 464. This claim, however, on the facts found, is wholly without foundation. The plaintiff is entitled to judgment in his favor for $1,000, and the superior court is so advised. The other judges concurred.[7]

DERHEIM v. N. FIORITO CO.

Supreme Court of Washington, En Banc, 1972.
80 Wash.2d 161, 492 P.2d 1030.

HUNTER, ASSOCIATE JUSTICE. The plaintiff, Lawrence Derheim (respondent), recovered a jury verdict for personal injuries incurred in a collision with a dump truck owned by defendant, N. Fiorito Company, Inc. (appellant), and operated by defendant's employee. Defendant's appeal to * * * the Court of Appeals was certified to this court. Specifically, the so-called "seat belt defense" is a principal issue in the case, and as this court has not addressed itself to the appropriateness of this defense in automobile litigation, the Court of Appeals concluded that a fundamental issue of broad public interest is presented. * * *

The impact occurred when plaintiff, overtaking the defendant's truck, struck the left front of defendant's truck which was engaged in a left-turn maneuver preparatory to crossing the two lanes of old Highway 99 to reach the on ramp. There seems to be no dispute but that defendant's truck commenced its left turn from the right lane, swinging over to the right-hand shoulder of the road and back across both lanes to the left, or inside lane, at which point the impact occurred. The testimony conflicts as to whether or not the truck's left turn signal was on. Plaintiff received a fracture of his right kneecap and injury to his mouth. * * *

* * * Shortly before the trial commenced, defendant filed an amended answer raising the issue of contributory negligence on the part of the plaintiff for failure to wear an available seat belt and

7. Consider Mahoney v. Beatman, 110 Conn. 184, 147 A. 762 (1929) (plaintiff's Nash automobile on wrong side of road collided with defendant's speeding Rolls-Royce; defendant's speed did not contribute to the collision, but may have contributed to loss of control after the collision, with aggravation of damage; judgment directed to be entered, over dissent by Maltbie, J., for full repair costs); Kinderavich v. Palmer, 127 Conn. 85, 15 A.2d 83 (1940) (plaintiff contributorily negligent with respect to first railroad injury, knocked unconscious onto another track, where he was struck again).

Suppose plaintiff failed to wear automobile seat belt. For one interpretation of the effect of *Southwick* and *Mahoney* see Brown v. Case, 31 Conn. Sup. 207, 327 A.2d 267 (1974) and Melesko v. Riley, 32 Conn.Sup. 82, 339 A. 2d 479 (1975).

to sound the horn. The trial court allowed the amendment insofar as the horn was concerned, but denied the portion relating to the seat belt issue. In addition the trial court ruled, on plaintiff's motion in limine, that during the trial the defendant was prohibited from making any reference to plaintiff's failure to wear a seat belt. These pretrial rulings are assigned as errors. Specifically, defendant asserts that the plaintiff's failure amounted to contributory negligence, or in the alternative, that evidence should have been admitted in mitigation of damages or in proof of an avoidable consequence.

By way of offer of proof, defendant offered plaintiff's admission that his 1959 Chevrolet was equipped with seat belts and that he was not wearing one at the time of the accident. The defendant offered testimony of Dr. William Snell, a physician and surgeon in charge of the Department of Orthopedics at the University of Oregon Medical School, to the effect that plaintiff's knee injury would not have been sustained if his seat belt had been properly fastened. * * * We are thus called upon to determine the rule in this state with respect to the so-called "seat belt defense". No subject in the field of automobile accident litigation, with the possible exception of no-fault insurance, has received more attention in recent years than has the seat or lap belt defense. The question being one of first impression in this state, we have reviewed the published material extensively, concluding that while the research and statistical studies indicate a far greater likelihood of serious injuries in the event of nonuse, nevertheless the courts have been inconsistent in their handling of the defense.[8] This inconsistency seems to result from the fact that the defense does not fit conveniently into the familiar time-honored doctrines traditionally used by the courts in deciding tort cases. Thus, the conduct in question (failure to buckle up) occurs *before* the defendant's negligence, as opposed to contributory negligence which cutomarily is thought of in terms of conduct contributing to the accident itself. While more precisely, contributory negligence is conduct contributing, with the negligence of the defendant in bringing about the plaintiff's harm, it is a rare case indeed where the distinction need be made. Furthermore, while states with comparative negligence do not have the problem to the same extent, contributory negligence in many

8. A complete list of cases dealing with the seat belt defense is found in a symposium on the seat belt defense reported in 53 Marq.L.Rev. 172, 226 (1970). To this list we would add the most recent cases, following in alphabetical order: Britton v. Doehring, 286 Ala. 498, 242 So.2d 666 (1970); Clark v. State, 28 Conn.Supp. 398, 264 A.2d 366 (1970); D. W. Boutwell Butane Co. v. Smith, 244 So.2d 11 (Miss. 1971); Dziedzic v. St. John's Cleaners & Shirt Laund., Inc., 53 N.J. 157, 249 A.2d 382 (1969); Estate of Abrams v. Woods, 64 Misc.2d 1093, 316 N.Y.S.2d 750 (1970); Genger v. Campbell, Or., 469 P.2d 776 (1970); Henderson v. United States, 429 F.2d 588 (10th Cir. 1970); MacDonnell v. Kaiser, 68 D.L.R.2d 104 (1968); Miller v. Haynes, 454 S.W.2d 293 (Mo.App.1970); Petersen v. Klos, 426 F.2d 199 (5th Cir. 1970).

An even longer list of annotations and recent articles on the seat belt defense is contained in an appendix bibliography commencing on page 227 in the above referenced law review article. [From original, renumbered; other notes in original omitted.]

states (such as Washington) is a complete bar to any recovery by a plaintiff—an obvious unjust result to apply in seat belt cases. The same result would be reached if the defense were presented in terms of assumption of risk, that is, that one who ventures upon the highway without buckling up is voluntarily assuming the risk of more serious injuries resulting from a possible accident proximately caused by the negligence of another.

The doctrine of avoidable consequences has been suggested as a possible solution to this conceptual dilemma, but here again, the problem is one of appearing to stretch the doctrine to fit an unusual fact pattern. As a legal theory, avoidable consequences is closely akin to mitigation of damages, and customarily is applied when plaintiff's conduct *after* the occurrence fails to meet the standards of due care. Moreover, courts have traditionally said that a defendant whose negligence proximately causes an injury to plaintiff, "takes the plaintiff as he finds him."

The practical implications of allowing seat belt evidence, has also given the courts pause. For example, most automobiles are now manufactured with shoulder straps in addition to seat belts, and medical evidence could be anticipated in certain cases that particular injuries would not have resulted if both shoulder belts and seat belts had been used. Additionally, many automobiles are now equipped with headrests which are designed to protect on from the so-called whiplash type of injury. But to be effective, its height must be adjusted by the occupant. Should the injured victim of a defendant's negligence be penalized in ascertainment of damages for failure to adjust his headrest? Furthermore the courts are aware that other protective devices and measures are undergoing testing in governmental and private laboratories, or are on the drawing boards. The concern is, of course, that if the seat belt defense is allowed, would not the same analysis require the use of all safety devices with which one's automobile is equipped. A further problem bothers the courts, and that is the effect of injecting the seat belt issue into the trial of automobile personal injury cases. The courts are concerned about unduly lengthening trials and if each automobile accident trial is to provide an arena for a battle of safety experts, as well as medical experts, time and expense of litigation might well be increased.

These problems, legal and practical, are found in reviewing the most recent cases decided by other jurisdictions confronting the issue. In 1966, the Supreme Court of South Carolina held in Sams v. Sams, 247 S.C. 467, 148 S.E.2d 154 (1966), that a defendant should be allowed to prove, if he can, that the failure of the plaintiff to use a seat belt under the facts and circumstances of the case amounted to a contributing cause of plaintiff's injuries, as opposed to the trial court's striking of the defense simply on the pleadings. The following year, the Supreme Court of Wisconsin in Bentzler v. Braun, 34 Wis.2d 362, 149 N.W.2d 626 (1967), concluded that there is a common law duty to use available seat belts, and that where credible evidence is presented by one qualified to express the opinion of how the use or nonuse of seat belts would have affected the particular injuries, the jury should be instructed in this regard.

In 1968, the Supreme Court of North Carolina decided a leading case in this area, Miller v. Miller, 273 N.C. 228, 160 S.E.2d 65 (1968). There, the plaintiff, a passenger, sued the driver for personal injuries incurred when the car negligently left the road. The defendant, asserting that plaintiff failed to buckle an available seat belt which, if buckled would have prevented the injuries, alleged no unusual circumstances prior to the accident which created any hazard over and above the ordinary risks incident to highway travel. The court held that, since there is no statutory or common law duty to wear seat belts in routine travel, the defendant had alleged no facts which would constitute contributory negligence or breach of the duty to minimize damages. Also in 1968, the Supreme Court of Oregon reached the same result, deferring to its legislature to resolve the question of whether or not available seat belts should be worn. Robinson v. Lewis, 254 Or. 52, 457 P.2d 483 (1968). * * *

In 1970, the Alabama Supreme Court, after a detailed analysis of the case law to date, held that evidence of failure to wear available seat belts is inadmissible to mitigate damages or in proof of avoidable consequences, and that the admission of the evidence was tantamount to the adoption of comparative negligence. The court was careful to point out, however, that it was not faced with, and actually was reserving its decision on, the question of whether nonuse of seat belts may constitute contributory negligence, since the case was tried solely on a wanton negligence theory. Britton v. Doehring, 286 Ala. 498, 242 So.2d 666 (1970).

The Supreme Court of Mississippi held in 1971, in a case where the defense was raised but no evidence introduced as to whether or not the use of a seat belt would have affected the injuries received, that the plaintiff was not guilty of comparative negligence as a matter of law for failure to avail herself of an available seat belt, and the question was properly kept from the jury by the trial court. D. W. Boutwell Butane Co. v. Smith, 244 So.2d 11 (Miss.1971).

The same divergence of approach is noted in law review articles and texts. See 47 Or.L.Rev. 204, 213 (1968); 10 Ariz.L.Rev. 523, 535 (1968), and 38 Fordham L.Rev. 94, 103 (1969). Also see W. Prosser, Handbook of the Law of Torts, 423 (4th ed. 1971); 2 Restatement (Second) of Torts § 465 (1965).

We believe the cases in those jurisdictions rejecting the "seat belt defense" are the better reasoned cases. It seems extremely unfair to mitigate the damages of one who sustains those damages in an accident for which he was in no way responsible, particularly when, as in this jurisdiction, there is no statutory duty to wear seat belts.

Moreover, in the state of Washington the installation of seat belts is required only in cars sold in this state manufactured after 1964. RCW 46.37.510. The problem of unequal treatment of owners and occupants of motor vehicles immediately arises. To charge a person with negligence for failure to wear an available seat belt and thereby require a mitigation of his damages resulting therefrom, would constitute preferential treatment to owners of vehicles who failed to have their cars equipped with seat belts, and passengers who knowingly entered cars not equipped with seat belts who sustained injuries. Under the proposed rule, no mitigation of their damages resulting from their failure to wear seat belts would be required. The resolution of this problem encompasses the legislative judgment of whether all vehicles on the roads or highways should be equipped with seat belts.

In addition, the state of Washington has not adopted the doctrine of comparative negligence. As viewed by the court of Alabama, Britton v. Doehring, supra, the admission of evidence on the "seat belt defense" issue is tantamount to adopting the rule of comparative negligence. Also see D. W. Boutwell Butane Co. v. Smith, supra. This poses a question of a change in public policy as to the doctrine of comparative negligence, which issue is not properly before us in this case.

For the reasons heretofore stated, we believe the trial court was correct in refusing admission of evidence on the "seat belt defense."

The judgment of the trial court is affirmed.

SPIER v. BARKER

Court of Appeals of New York, 1974.
35 N.Y.2d 444, 363 N.Y.S.2d 916, 323 N.E.2d 164.

GABRIELLI, JUDGE. Presented for our consideration, for the first time, is the question of what effect, if any, the failure of a plaintiff to wear a seat belt has upon his right to recovery in an action for personal injuries incurred in a motor vehicle accident. * * *

* * * Plaintiff testified that when she neared the intersection, she reduced the speed of her automobile from 40 to 20 miles per hour and simultaneously turned on her left directional indicator; and as she was doing this, plaintiff looked in her rear view mirror and saw a set of headlights "way back"; she then neared the center line of Route 31, and, while she was turning left to enter Camp Road, was struck in the westbound lane of Route 31 by the defendants' tractor-trailer which was in the process of attempting to pass her automobile. The right front fender of the tractor-trailer came into contact with the left front portion of the plaintiff's automobile, and, as a result of the initial impact, the plaintiff was ejected from her vehicle, which then rolled over her in such a way that her legs were pinned under the left rear wheel. Although the plaintiff's automobile was equipped with seat belts, she was not using the device at the time of the accident.

The tractor-trailer driver's account of the accident differed in several significant respects from plaintiff's version. * * * Although the plaintiff was not sure whether she made a gradual or an abrupt turn, the defendant driver stated that she "cut right across in front" of him, taking a "sharp lefthand turn". * * *

Upon the trial defendants called, as an expert witness, a professor of mechanical and aerospace engineering, who had also been previously employed as a consulting engineer in the field of accident analysis and reconstruction. He testified to an extensive background in the use of seat belts in both the aircraft and automotive industries. Over plaintiff's objection, the expert was permitted to give his opinion that "The seat belt is an extremely effective device in either preventing or alleviating injury." More specifically, he stated that the seat belt is the most effective improvement that has been made in the automobile in the last 20 years. After viewing photographs of the vehicles and the accident scene, the expert opined that had the plaintiff been wearing a seat belt, she would not have been ejected from her automobile; and that had she not been ejected, she probably would not have been seriously injured. When asked on cross-examination if the fact that plaintiff was ejected from her automobile might have saved her life, the engineer stated that "the worst thing that could have happened to her [was] being ejected from the vehicle."

Having permitted the defense expert to testify as to what would have probably happened to the plaintiff had she used the seat belt available to her, the trial court charged the jury as follows: "If you find that a reasonably prudent driver would have used a seat belt, and that she would not have received some or all of her injuries had she used the seat belt, then you may not award any damages for those injuries you find she would not have received had she used the seat belt. The burden of proving that some or all of her injuries would not have been received had she used the seat belt rests upon the [defendants]". Although the plaintiff's counsel took no exception to the trial court's charge, he requested the court to charge the jury "that there isn't any law in the State of New York that requires a person to wear a seat belt or to anticipate the happening of an accident." The trial court so charged.

When called upon to resolve the conflicting testimony and to decide the validity of the plaintiff's personal injury action, her husband's derivative claim and the defendant trucking company's property damage counterclaim, the jury returned verdicts of no cause of action against both plaintiffs and the trucking company's counterclaim as well. Only the plaintiff operator has appealed.

In unanimously affirming the judgment of the trial court, the Appellate Division found that the Trial Judge had correctly charged the law of negligence and contributory negligence, and then concluded as follows: "The jury, having determined that none of the parties had a cause of action, it is clear that at the very least the jury found negligence on the part of plaintiff and defendants. On this verdict, the jury never reached the issue of damages and thus never considered the seat belt defense which was raised and submitted to it in mitigation of damages." However, the Appellate Division then proceeded to state that the charge relating to the doctrine of avoidable consequences would have been error if the issue of liability had been resolved in favor of the plaintiff. In reaching this determination, it noted that allowing the triers of fact to apportion damages for nonuse of an available seat belt "would permit the jury to engage in sheer speculation and apply an apportionment similar to computing damages under comparative negligence" (42 A.D.2d 428, 430–431, 348 N.Y.S.2d 581, 583, supra). Although we are in accord with the Appellate Division's conclusion that the verdicts indicate that the jury found negligence on the part of the plaintiff driver and the defendants as well and, therefore, never considered the issue of damages, we are unable to agree with its determination that the trial court's charge would have been error had the issue of liability been resolved in favor of the plaintiff.

Despite the fact that the "seat belt defense", as it is commonly known, has received extensive examination in other jurisdictions as well as several legal periodicals, it is raised as a matter of first impression in this court. We today hold that nonuse of an available [9] seat belt, and expert testimony in regard thereto, is a factor which the jury may consider, in light of all the other facts received in evidence, in arriving at its determination as to whether the plaintiff has exercised due care, not only to avoid injury to himself, but to mitigate any injury he would likely sustain (Mount v. McClellan, 91 Ill.App.2d 1, 234 N.E.2d 329). However, as the trial court observed in its charge, the plaintiff's nonuse of an available seat belt should be strictly limited to the jury's determination of the plaintiff's damages and should not be considered by the triers of fact in resolving the issue of liability. Moreover, the burden of pleading and proving that nonuse thereof by the plaintiff resulted in increasing the extent of his injuries and damages, rests upon the defendant. That is to say, the issue should not be submitted to the jury unless the defendant can demonstrate, by competent evidence, a causal connection between the plaintiff's nonuse of an available seat belt and the injuries and damages sustained (Kircher, Seat Belt Defense—State of the Law, 53 Marq.L.Rev. 172, 186).

The cases from other jurisdictions suggest that three approaches have been advanced by defendants in support of the seat belt de-

9. It has been intimated that reducing recovery solely in cases of nonuse of an available seat belt creates an invidious distinction (Robinson v. Bone, D.C., 285 F.Supp. 423, 424). However, as one author has asserted, the distinction is not only justified but rational since the effort entailed in using an available seat belt is far less than the expense of arranging to have seat belts installed (see Comment, Self-Protection Safety Devices: An Economic Analysis, 40 U.Chi.L.Rev. 421, 439). Furthermore, the distinction will eventually become academic in as much as section 383 of the Vehicle and Traffic Law, Consol.Laws, c. 71, requires seat belts to be installed for each passenger seat position in all new passenger cars sold or registered in New York after January 1, 1968. (See, also, 23 C.F.R., § 255.21 [1968] [Standard 208].)

fense: first, it is urged that a plaintiff's nonuse of an available seat belt constitutes negligence per se which would, of course, entirely preclude the plaintiff from recovery; secondly, it is argued that, in failing to make use of an available seat belt, the plaintiff has not complied with the standard of conduct which would have been pursued by a reasonable man under similar circumstances, and, therefore, the plaintiff may be found to have been contributorily negligent; and, thirdly, it is asserted that by not fastening his seat belt the plaintiff may, under the circumstances of the particular case, be found to have acted unreasonably and in disregard of his own best interests, and, thus, should not be permitted to recover damages for those injuries which a seat belt would have obviated (see, Kircher, Seat Belt Defense—State of the Law, 53 Marq.L.Rev. 172, 173). We reject both the first and the second of these approaches; and, with the modifications made herein, we accept the third.

Since section 383 of the Vehicle and Traffic Law does not require occupants of a passenger car to make use of available seat belts, we hold that a plaintiff's failure to do so does not constitute negligence per se. Even in jurisdictions in which some form of the seat belt defense has been adopted, the negligence per se approach has been rejected because legislation, which does not require use of the device, "cannot be considered a safety statute in a sense that it is negligence *per se* for an occupant of an automobile to fail to use available seat belts." (Bentzler v. Braun, 34 Wis.2d 362, 385, 149 N.W.2d 626, 639.) Likewise, we do not subscribe to the holdings of those cases in which the plaintiff's failure to fasten his seat belt may be determined by the jury to constitute contributory negligence as a matter of common law (Bentzler v. Braun, supra; Sams v. Sams, 247 S.C. 467, 148 S.E.2d 154; Mays v. Dealers, Tr., 7 Cir., 441 F.2d 1344). In our view, the doctrine of contributory negligence is applicable only if the plaintiff's failure to exercise due care causes, in whole or in part, *the accident*, rather than when it merely exacerbates or enhances the severity of his injuries (Dillon v. Humphreys, 56 Misc.2d 211, 214, 288 N.Y.S.2d 14, 18; Abrams v. Woods, 64 Misc.2d 1093, 1094, 316 N.Y.S.2d 750, 751; Noth v. Scheurer, D.C., 285 F.Supp. 81, 85). That being the case, holding a nonuser contributorily negligent would be improper since it would impose liability upon the plaintiff for all his injuries though use of a seat belt might have prevented none or only a portion of them. Having disapproved of these two variations of the seat belt defense, we address ourselves to the defendants' contention that nonuse of an available seat belt may be considered by the jury in assessing the plaintiff's damages where it is shown that the seat belt would have prevented at least a portion of the injuries.

As Prosser has indicated, the plaintiff's duty to mitigate his damages is equivalent to the doctrine of avoidable consequences, which precludes recovery for any damages which could have been eliminated by reasonable conduct on the part of the plaintiff (Prosser, Torts [4th ed.], § 65, pp. 422–424). Traditionally both of these concepts have been applied only to postaccident conduct, such as a plaintiff's failure to obtain medical treatment after he has sustained an injury. To do otherwise, it has been argued, would impose a preaccident obligation upon the plaintiff and would deny him the right to assume the due care of others (Kleist, Seat Belt Defense—An Exercise in Sophistry, 18 Hastings L.J. 613, 616). We concede that the opportunity to mitigate damages prior to the occurrence of an accident does not ordinarily arise, and that the chronological distinction, on which the concept of mitigation damages rests, is justified in most cases. However, in our opinion, the seat belt affords the automobile occupant an unusual and ordinarily unavailable means by which he or she may minimize his or her damages *prior* to the accident. Highway safety has become a national concern; we are told to drive defensively and to "watch out for the other driver". When an automobile occupant may readily protect himself, at least partially, from the consequences of a collision, we think that the burden of buckling an available seat belt may, under the facts of the particular case, be found by the jury to be less than the likelihood of injury when multiplied by its accompanying severity.

At this juncture, there can be no doubt whatsoever as to the efficiency of the automobile seat belt in preventing injuries.[10] Simply stated, "[t]he seat belt, properly installed *and properly worn,* still offers the single best protection available to the automotive occupant exposed to an impact." (Synder, Seat Belt as a Cause of Injury, 53 Marq.L.Rev. 211). Furthermore, though it has been repeatedly suggested that the seat belt itself causes injury, to date the device has never been shown to worsen an injury, but, on the contrary, has prevented more serious ones (p. 213). The studies on the subject overwhelmingly indicate that the seat belt fulfills its primary purpose of restraining the automobile occupant during and immediately after the initial impact; in so doing, it significantly reduces the likelihood of ejection and frequently prevents "the second collision" of the occupant with the interior portion of the vehicle.

Another objection frequently raised is that the jury will be unable to segregate the injuries caused by the initial impact from the injuries caused by the plaintiff's failure to fasten his seat belt. In addition to underestimating the abilities of those trained in the field of accident reconstruction, this argument fails to consider other instances in which the jury is permitted to apportion damages (i. e., as between an original tort-feasor and a physician who negligently treats the original injury). Furthermore, if the defendant is unable to show that the seat belt would have prevented some of the plaintiff's injuries, then the trial court ought not submit the issue to the jury.

10. See Huelke, Practical Defense Problems—The Expert's View, 53 Marq.L.Rev. 203; Miller, Crashworthiness of Automobiles, Scientific Am., Feb. 1973, at p. 81; Synder, Seat Belt as a Cause of Injury, 53 Marq. L.Rev. 211 and studies referred to in footnotes 1–5 thereof. [Notes 9 and 10 from original, renumbered; other notes in original omitted.]

In the instant case, the plaintiff was ejected from her car, which subsequently rolled over her body causing a broken leg. The defense expert stated that she would have remained in the car had she used her seat belt, and that she would have sustained only minor injuries had she not been ejected. On cross-examination, plaintiff's counsel was unsuccessful in his attempts to undermine either of these opinions of the expert. In view of what has previously been stated, we hold that the trial court properly submitted this issue to the jury.

For the reasons stated, the order of the Appellate Division should be affirmed.[11]

BRINKMOELLER v. WILSON

Supreme Court of Ohio, 1975.
41 Ohio St.2d 223, 325 N.E.2d 233.

[Action against taxicab company for negligence in stopping at unnecessarily hazardous location to permit visibly intoxicated plaintiff to alight for visit to an inn; plaintiff staggered into the path of another automobile, whose driver is not involved in this litigation. The trial court granted defendant's motion for directed verdict.]

CORRIGAN, JUSTICE.

* * *

In passing on the motion in question the trial court ruled * * * that Mrs. Brinkmoeller was negligent as a matter of law, which negligence contributed proximately to the accident. * * *

11. Compare the rule adopted in England by the Court of Appeal, Froom and Others v. Butcher, The Times (London) July 22, 1975, at 7, [1975] 2 Lloyd's L.R. 478:

"The question is not what was the cause of the accident. It is rather what was the cause of the damage. In seat belt cases the cause of the accident is one thing. The cause of the damage another. The accident was caused by bad driving; the damage was caused partly by the defendant's bad driving and partly by the plaintiff's failure to wear a seat belt. If the plaintiff was to blame for not wearing a seat belt his damages fell to be reduced to such extent as the court thought just and equitable. * * *

"There might be exceptions to the ordinary run of cases. A man who was unduly fat or a pregnant woman might rightly be excused because a strap across the abdomen might do more harm than good. But apart from such cases a person failing to wear a seat belt should accept some share of responsibility for the damage if it could have been prevented or lessened by wearing one. * * *

"* * * The question should not be prolonged by an expensive inquiry into the degree of blameworthiness which would be hotly disputed. Suffice it to assess a share of responsibility which would be just and equitable in the majority of cases.

"Sometimes the evidence would show that the failure made no difference and in such cases the damages should not be reduced at all. At other times the evidence would show that the failure made all the difference and the injuries would have been prevented altogether if a belt had been worn. In such cases damages should be reduced by 25 per cent. Often the evidence would only show that the failure made a considerable difference; the injuries would have been a good deal less severe if a seat belt had been worn. There the damages should be reduced by 15 per cent."

The trial judge did not so state, but, if he concluded that Mrs. Brinkmoeller was contributorily negligent as a matter of law because of her intoxicated condition which served as a proximate cause of her injuries, and used that as a reason to grant the motion for a directed verdict, then he was in error in arriving at that conclusion. See Fagan v. Atlantic Coast Line R. R. Co. (1917), 220 N.Y. 301, 115 N.E. 704, with Judge Cardozo concurring in the opinion and judgment, which, at page 312, 115 N.E. at page 709 held: "The intoxication of the intestate at the time he was assisted from the train was not contributory negligence. He was negligent in becoming intoxicated, but the defendant was bound to reasonably care for him as he was. * * * His intoxication previous to and at the time the defendant unlawfully placed him, as its passenger, in the hazardous situation is not a direct and proximate cause of the injury, and therefore, not contributory negligence. * * *"

DAVIES v. MANN

Court of Exchequer, 1842.
10 M. & W. 545.

CASE for negligence. * * *

The defendant pleaded not guilty.

At the trial, before Erskine, J., at the last Summer Assizes for the county of Worcester, it appeared that the plaintiff, having fettered the fore feet of an ass belonging to him, turned it into a public highway, and at the time in question the ass was grazing on the off side of a road about eight yards wide when the defendant's wagon, with a team of three horses, coming down a slight descent, at what the witness termed a smartish pace, ran against the ass, knocked it down, and the wheels passing over it, it died soon after. The ass was fettered at the time, and it was proved that the driver of the wagon was some little distance behind the horses. The learned Judge told the jury, that though the act of the plaintiff, in leaving the donkey on the highway so fettered as to prevent his getting out of the way of carriages traveling along it, might be illegal, still, if the proximate cause of the injury was attributable to the want of proper conduct on the part of the driver of the wagon, the action was maintainable against the defendant; and his Lordship directed them, if they thought that the accident might have been avoided by the exercise of ordinary care on the part of the driver, to find for the plaintiff. The jury found their verdict for the plaintiff, damages 40*s*.

Godson now moved for a new trial, on the ground of misdirection.—The act of the plaintiff in turning the donkey into the public highway was an illegal one, and, as the injury arose principally from that act, the plaintiff was not entitled to compensation for that injury which, but for his own unlawful act, would never have occurred. (PARKE, B.—The declaration states that the ass was lawfully on the highway, and the defendant has not traversed that allegation; therefore it must be taken to be admitted.) The principle of law, as deducible from the cases, is, that where an accident is the result of faults on both sides, neither party can maintain an action. Thus, in Butterfield v. Forrester, 11 East, 60, it was held that one who is injured by an obstruction on a highway, against which he fell, cannot maintain an action, if it appear that he was riding with great violence and want of ordinary care, without which he might have seen and avoided the obstruction. So, in Vennall v. Garner, 1 C. & M. 21, in case for running down a ship, it was held, that neither party can recover when both are in the wrong; and Bayley, B., there says, "I quite agree that if the mischief be the result of the combined negligence of the two, they must both remain in *statu quo* and neither party can recover against the other." Here the plaintiff, by fettering the donkey, had prevented him from removing himself out of the way of accident; had his fore feet been free, no accident would probably have happened. Pluckwell v. Wilson, 5 Carr. & P. 375; Luxford v. Large, Ibid, 421, and Lynch v. Nurdin, 1 Ad. & E., N.S., 29; 4 P. & D. 672, are to the same effect.

LORD ABINGER, C. B.—I am of opinion that there ought to be no rule in this case. The defendant has not denied that the ass was lawfully on the highway, and therefore we must assume it to have been lawfully there; but even were it otherwise, it would have made no difference, for as the defendant might, by proper care, have avoided injuring the animal, and did not, he is liable for the consequences of his negligence though the animal may have been improperly there.

PARKE, B.—This subject was fully considered by this Court in the case of Bridge v. The Grand Junction Railway Company, 3 M. & W. 246, where, as appears to me, the correct rule is laid down concerning negligence, namely, that the negligence which is to preclude a plaintiff from recovering in an action of this nature, must be such as that he could, by ordinary care, have avoided the consequences of the defendant's negligence. I am reported to have said in that case, and I believe quite correctly, that "the rule of law is laid down with perfect correctness in the case of Butterfield v. Forrester, that, although there may have been negligence on the part of the plaintiff, yet unless he might, by the exercise of ordinary care, have avoided the consequences of the defendant's negligence, he is entitled to recover; if by ordinary care he might have avoided them, he is the author of his own wrong." In that case of Bridge v. Grand Junction Railway Company, there was a plea imputing negligence on both sides; here it is otherwise; and the Judge simply told the jury, that the mere fact of negligence on the part of the plaintiff in leaving his donkey on the public highway, was no answer to the action, unless the donkey's being there was the immediate cause of the injury; and that, if they were of opinion that it was caused by the fault of the defendant's servant in driving too fast, or, which is the same thing, at a smartish pace, the mere fact of putting the ass upon the road would not bar the plaintiff of his action. All that is perfectly correct; for, although the ass may have been wrongfully there, still the defendant was bound to go along the road at such a pace as would be likely to prevent mischief. Were this not so, a man might justify the driving over goods left on a public highway, or even over a man lying asleep there, or the purposely running against a carriage going on the wrong side of the road.

GURNEY, B., and ROLFE, B., concurred.

Rule refused.

MOSSO v. E. H. STANTON CO.

Supreme Court of Washington, 1913.
75 Wash. 220, 134 P. 941, L.R.A.1916A, 943.

ELLIS, J.—The plaintiff was struck and injured by defendant's motor truck, at a point in Howard Street, in the city of Spokane, a few feet south of the concrete bridge crossing the Spokane river. The Centennial mill is situated just north of the Spokane river on the west side of Howard Street, which extends from in front of the mill in a straight line southerly for a distance of about 400 feet, the bridge being the same width as the street. There is no cross-walk throughout this distance, nor for over three blocks to the south. A double-tracked street car line occupies the middle of the street. On October 27, 1911, at about 15 minutes past noon, the plaintiff, having purchased a two-bushel sack of chicken feed at the Centennial mill, carrying it on his left shoulder, walked down the west side of Howard street for a distance of something over 300 feet, to a point estimated by different witnesses at from 15 to 35 feet south of the south end of the bridge, at which point he stepped into the street and proceeded diagonally across the street with the intention of reaching the sidewalk on the east side. He testified that, before stepping into the street, he turned and looked north along the street and bridge, there being an unobstructed view to the Centennial mill, and saw no vehicle of any kind; that, when he had proceeded to about the middle of the street and was between the two car tracks, something struck him in the back and left side rendering him unconscious. The testimony of three other witnesses introduced in behalf of the plaintiff, was to the effect that he had reached a point between the two car tracks about the middle of the street, when he was struck in the back, "doubled up" in a crouching position under the front end of the motor truck, and shoved a distance of three or four feet; that the motor was running "pretty fast" or "12 to 15 miles an hour," did not swerve or change its direction as it approached the plaintiff, and stood about the middle of the street between the two car tracks and straight with the street when it came to a stop.

The testimony of the chauffeur and three other witnesses who testified in defendant's behalf was to the effect that the plaintiff was struck either a little east of, or a short distance west of, the west rail of the west car track and shoved over onto the track; that the truck swerved toward the car track just as it struck him, and came to a standstill pointing slightly to the southeast. The chauffeur testified that the man stepped into the street immediately in front of the motor truck, and that the brakes were at once applied and the machine stopped as quickly as possible. The machine was muffled, and all the witnesses agree that it made very little noise. All the witnesses testified that they failed to hear any horn or gong sounded from the motor truck. Neither of the men in the motor truck testified to the giving of any alarm, save that one of them said he called to the man just as he was struck. The plaintiff suffered a fracture of the second lumbar vertebra, causing a deformity of the back and a permanent injury. The jury returned a verdict for $5,500. At appropriate times the defendant moved for a directed verdict, for judgment notwithstanding the verdict and for a new trial, all of which were denied. Judgment was entered on the verdict. The defendant has appealed.

I. It is contended that the undisputed physical facts show that respondent did not look north before starting across the street, and hence was guilty of contributory negligence, as a matter of law, under the rule announced in Fluhart v. Seattle Elec. Co., 65 Wash. 291, 118 P. 51; Hellieson v. Seattle Elec. Co., 56 Wash. 278, 105 P. 458, and Skinner v. Tacoma Ry. & Power Co., 46 Wash. 122, 89 P. 488. The so-called physical facts relied upon are respondent's estimate that he was walking at the rate of about three miles an hour, and that he had walked about 40 feet from the curb before he was struck; that the highest estimate of any witness as to the speed of the motor truck was 15 miles an hour, and that the distance, with an unobstructed view from the Centennial mill to the point of accident, was 327 feet. It is argued that, since the motor truck was not running over five times as fast as the man walked, it could not go over 200 feet while he walked 40 feet; that, therefore, he did not look north just as he stepped into the street or he would have seen the motor truck, hence the physical facts show him guilty of contributory negligence in not so looking.

The vice of this argument is in the assumption that the speed of both man and machine as testified to were indisputably established physical facts, whereas they were mere estimates. Either one or both of these estimates may have been incorrect. Mere estimates, given as such, can hardly discredit positive testimony to the point of incredibility, as a matter of law. It would be equally as sound to take respondent's testimony that he looked north and saw no vehicle, as a physical fact. The irresistible inference would then be either that the speed of the man was overestimated or that of the machine was underestimated. Soundly, neither the speed of the machine, nor its position at the time when the respondent stepped into the street, nor the speed of the man, nor the fact that he looked north just after he stepped into the street, were admitted or indisputably established facts, physical or otherwise. They were all questions for the jury upon the evidence.

On the other hand, all of the evidence strongly tends to show that the appellant was guilty of negligence in failing to keep a reasonably vigilant lookout, in failing to sound a horn or gong, and in running in or near the middle of the street. Even if the respondent was also guilty of negligence in failing to look north when he first started to cross the street, he was not necessarily negligent at the time he was struck. Every witness who testified as to the collision, save the driver of the truck, placed the respondent at the time practically outside of the zone of danger reasonably to be anticipated from automobiles coming from the north, and where it would be his duty to begin looking south for vehicles which might be approaching from that direction. A city ordinance in evidence made it the duty of drivers of automobiles "to keep to the right and as near the right hand curb as possible." Every witness, save the chauffeur and one other, testified that the respondent, when he was struck, had reached a point inside of the west rail of the west car track, and the respondent and three eyewitnesses testified that, when he was struck, he had reached the middle of the street between the east rail of the west car track and the west rail of the east car track. Obviously, he could not have been struck in either place had the driver of the motor truck observed the ordinance, a course of action upon which the respondent had the right to rely.

II. It is next contended that the court erred in submitting to the jury the question whether the appellant, by an observance of the rule of "last clear chance," could have avoided the accident. It is first argued that this rule cannot be invoked because the complaint did not admit contributory negligence on the respondent's part. The answer, however, denied any negligence of the appellant and alleged affirmatively that the respondent's injury was due to his own negligence. This was equivalent to an allegation that contributory negligence of the respondent was the proximate cause of the injury. It was put in issue by the denial in the reply.

The rule of last clear chance is grounded in the doctrine of proximate cause. Like any other phase of proximate cause, evidence to sustain it may be submitted to the jury under the general issue. We cannot subscribe to the doctrine that the rule of last clear chance can only be invoked by a plea in confession and avoidance. It would be more logical to say that the defense of contributory negligence could not be made or submitted to the jury without confession of the primary negligence of the appellant. We have never so held, notwithstanding the fact that contributory negligence is in this state an affirmative defense which must be specially pleaded.

The denial of contributory negligence is not necessarily a denial of any negligence on the part of the injured person. It is only a denial of negligence contributing directly to the injury. The doctrine of last clear chance, while presupposing some negligence on a plaintiff's part, relieves that negligence of its contributory character where the injury results proximately from the failure of a defendant to embrace the last clear chance to avoid the injury. Moreover, the allegation of the complaint (in addition to specific allegations of negligence) that the appellant was operating the motor truck "recklessly and without regard to the safety of pedestrians on the highway," was sufficient to admit evidence of a violation of the last clear chance rule, in the absence of a motion to make more specific.

III. It is also claimed that the evidence shows that both parties were concurrently negligent up to the time of the accident, and that, therefore, the last clear chance rule cannot apply. Whether the respondent negligently failed to look for approaching vehicles before entering upon the street was clearly a question for the jury. But assuming that he did fail to look, he was not negligent, as a matter of law, in failing to be continuously thereafter looking to ascertain if auto-cars were approaching from behind him, especially impeded as he was by the sack of grain upon his left shoulder. * * * Even assuming, therefore, that he was negligent in the first instance, it was for the jury to say whether his negligence continued up to the time of the accident, or whether it terminated after he got into the street so as to be in plain view of drivers of auto-cars. This is especially true in view of the almost conclusive evidence that no horn or gong was sounded.

The appellant cites certain authorities, most of them railroad or street car cases, and some of them cases arising on injuries to trespassers on railroad tracks, to sustain the contention that in no case can a plaintiff recover where his negligence continues up to the time of the injury. The authorities cited hardly bear that construction. * * * At any rate, this court has held, in accordance with many courts and with what we conceive to be the more logical as well as the more humane rule, that where the peril of a traveler on the highway is actually discovered and should be appreciated by the operator of a street car, or other agency of danger, there arises a new duty to exercise all reasonable care to avoid injury, and the failure to exercise such care, if it results in injury, will render a defendant liable notwithstanding the continuance of the plaintiff's negligence up to the instant of the injury. * * *

IV. Finally, it is contended that, even conceding that the last chance doctrine applies, the instructions given as embodying that doctrine were erroneous. They were as follows:

"(24) If you should find from the evidence that the plaintiff was guilty of contributory negligence in not seeing the defendant's automobile approaching, yet this negligence will not defeat the plaintiff's right to recover, if the driver of the defendant's automobile actually saw, *or if by keeping a reasonably vigilant lookout could have seen,* the exposed condition of danger of the plaintiff, if you so find, in time to have avoided the injury by the exercise of reasonable care, and negligently failed to exercise such reasonable care."

"(25) If you believe from the evidence that at the time of the alleged injury the plaintiff was walking across Howard Street in the city of Spokane, diagonally from the west side of said street to the east side thereof, and at the same time the driver of defendant's automobile was driving an automobile belonging to the defendant along said street in the direction of said plaintiff, and that said driver saw, *or by the exercise of reasonable care and caution could have seen the plaintiff in season to have stopped the automobile, altered its course, or in some way avoided the accident,* and if the jury further believes, from the evidence that the said driver did not do so, but carelessly and negligently permitted the said automobile to run against plaintiff and knock him down, and thereby injure him, as charged in the complaint, this would be negligence on the part of said driver, and the defendant is liable for such negligence."

The objection is directed to the parts which we have italicized. The courts are wide of an agreement as to the extent of the last chance docrine as applied to the operation of trains, street cars, automobiles and the like. But what we conceive to be the sounder view is this: assuming that a traveler has negligently placed himself in a dangerous situation upon the highway, then as we have seen, whenever the person in control of such agency actually sees the traveler's situation and should appreciate his danger, the last chance rule applies, without regard to the continuing negligence of the traveler concurring with that of the operator up to the very instant of the injury. A second situation to which the rule applies is this: where the person in control of such agency, by keeping a reasonably careful lookout commensurate with the dangerous character of the agency and the nature of the locality, could have discovered and appreciated the traveler's perilous situation in time, by the exercise of reasonable care, to avoid injuring him, and injury results from the failure to keep such lookout and to exercise such care, then the last chance rule applies, regardless of the traveler's prior negligence, whenever that negligence has terminated or culminated in a situation of peril from which the exercise of ordinary care on his part would not thereafter extricate him. This last phase of the rule applies whenever injury results from new negligence or from a continuance of the operator's negligence after that of the traveler has so ceased or culminated.

The application of the rule to the first situation, as above indicated, needs no support outside of simple considerations of humanity. Any other view would condone wilful or wanton injury. The application of the rule to the second situation indicated has been sustained by this court, and we think soundly, in a case of injury to an automobile stalled through its owner's negligence on a railway crossing. Nicol v. Oregon-Washington R. & Nav. Co., 71 Wash. 409, 128 P. 628, 43 L.R.A.,N.S., 174. Another court has upheld it in case of injury to a portable steam engine similarly situated. Bullock v. Wilmington

& W. R. Co., 105 N.C. 180, 10 S.E. 988. The law will hardly hold more cheap, or view with less solicitude, the safety or life of a human being. We have recognized the same principle in cases of personal injury. * * *

An examination of a vast number of authorities induces our conviction that the application of the rule as above outlined is much broader than that countenanced by many courts, and is as broad as can be applied without in effect overruling all of our own decisions sustaining the defense of contributory negligence and adopting in its stead the doctrine of comparative negligence, a doctrine against which this court has set its face from the beginning. * * * There is much in the evidence in the case in hand from which the jury might reasonably have found that respondent was free from negligence at the time he was injured, or that his negligence, if any, was only slight. To hold slight negligence as contributory would be to impose the rule of extraordinary care. Lamoon v. Smith Cement Brick Co., 74 Wash. 164, 132 P. 880.

From what we have said as to the proper limits of the rule of last clear chance as a ground of liability, it is clear that the instructions complained of are erroneous. In the first place, the reference in instruction No. 24 to the plaintiff's negligence as "contributory" is inaccurate and confusing, as connected with the rule of last clear chance. If the rule applies, then it relieves the respondent's negligence of its contributory quality. In the second place, the italicized words in both instructions should have been qualified so as to embody the thought that if the jury found that the plaintiff's negligence had, prior to the instant of injury, terminated or culminated by placing him in a situation of danger such that the exercise of ordinary care on his part alone would not thereafter have avoided injury without the cooperation of care on the appellant's part, and that the driver of the appellant's motor truck by keeping a reasonably vigilant lookout could have seen and appreciated the exposed condition of the plaintiff in time to avoid the injury by the exercise of reasonable care, and negligently failed to keep such lookout or to exercise such care, then the plaintiff's prior negligence would not defeat his right to recover. Better words, of course, could easily be found, but the instruction should have embodied in some manner the thought which we have endeavored to express. Both instructions, so far as they state the rule as to actual discovery of peril, are practically faultless.

The court also instructed the jury to the effect that if it found the plaintiff's failure to look after stepping into the street was contributory negligence, and that such negligence continued up to the last moment before the accident and contributed to it as a proximate cause, he cannot recover. This instruction was in direct conflict with the two instructions above quoted. It is impossible to know what effect the giving of the two erroneous instructions and their manifest conflict with this instruction had upon the verdict of the jury. In such a case a new trial is imperative.

In order that this decision may not be construed as narrowing the questions properly submitted to the jury in such cases, we deem it proper to state that, although the rule of the last clear chance is a phase of the question of proximate cause, it does not cover the whole ground of proximate cause. It applies only to a status of danger usually originating in the plaintiff's negligence, and relieves that negligence of its contributory character under certain conditions. It must not be forgotten that the failure of the operator of a locomotive, train, street car, automobile or other agency of danger to travelers on the highway to keep a vigilant lookout is negligence in any event, entailing a liability for injury proximately resulting therefrom. Where there are counter charges of contributory negligence, the jury may find the negligence of either party proximate and that of the other remote, according to all of the circumstances. The usual instruction as to proximate cause is, therefore, always proper even when an instruction as to the last clear chance would not be. * * *

The judgment is reversed, and the cause is remanded for a new trial. The payment of the costs may await the final disposition of the cause.

MORRIS and MAIN, JJ., concur.[12]

FULLERTON, J., (concurring). I am of the opinion that the second instruction above quoted (No. 25) is not erroneous. I therefore concur in the result.

12. While there has been some diversity in last clear chance doctrine, distinctions have usually been drawn depending upon whether, immediately before the accident, plaintiff could have avoided it by the exercise of reasonable care. See, e. g., Restatement of Torts, Second §§ 479 and 480 (1965) (if plaintiff was then helpless, defendant is liable if he knew or should have known of plaintiff's situation and realized or should have realized plaintiff's peril; if plaintiff was then merely inattentive, defendant is liable only if he actually knew the situation and realized or had reason to realize the peril). In Missouri, however, the "humanitarian doctrine" obtains that defendant is liable in either case if plaintiff's peril should have been apparent to defendant had he exercised reasonable vigilance. For a similar result see Dendy v. Watkins, 288 N.C. 447, 219 S.E.2d 214 (1975), couched in terms that "duty" arises for defendant motorist only when he sees or should have seen that pedestrian is unaware of approaching danger; quaere effect of this formulation in a state which has adopted comparative negligence. See, generally, James, Last Clear Chance: A Transitional Doctrine, 47 Yale L.J. 704, 713 (1938).

Also see, in general, Schofield, Davies v. Mann: Theory of Contributory Negligence, 3 Harv.L.Rev. 263 (1890); MacIntyre, Rationale of Last Clear Chance, 53 Harv.L.Rev. 1225 (1940); Goodhart, The Last Opportunity Rule, 65 L.Q.Rev. 237 (1949); Williams, Joint Torts & Contributory Negligence (1951).

BROWN v. SAN FRANCISCO BALL CLUB, INC.

District Court of Appeal of California, First District, Division 1, 1950.
99 Cal.App.2d 484, 222 P.2d 19.

FRED B. WOOD, JUSTICE. This is an appeal by plaintiff from a judgment entered upon a directed verdict for the defendant in an action against San Francisco Ball Club, Inc., for damages for personal injuries sustained while attending a professional baseball game at Seals' Stadium, San Francisco.

The appeal is also from an order denying plaintiff's motion for new trial. That phase of the appeal should be dismissed, for such an order is not appealable.

Appellant, a woman of 46 years, attended the game as the guest of friends, one of whom furnished and purchased the tickets which were for seats in an unscreened portion of the stadium near the first-base line. The game was in progress when they arrived and about an hour later the accident occurred while the players were changing sides. Appellant was struck by some object and sustained serious injury. Evidence is lacking whether or not it was a baseball, or from what direction it came. However, the motion for directed verdict appears to have been made, and the issues discussed by the parties upon this appeal, upon the assumption that appellant was hit by a baseball, possibly thrown from second to first base, touching the first baseman's glove and passing thence into the stand.

Respondent owned and operated the stadium which had a seating capacity of 18,601, divided into screened and unscreened areas. Approximately 5,000 seats were behind a screen back of the home plate. The remainder were unscreened and in two sections behind the first-base and third-base lines respectively. Tickets for seats were sold at separate windows, one window for each of these three sections, each window marked for a particular section. Patrons decided where they would sit, and went to the appropriate window for their seats. It is generally true of all the games held in this stadium that a great majority of the patrons are situated in the unscreened sections, because they prefer an unobstructed view.

The attendance at this particular game was approximately 5,000. There were many vacant seats in each seating area. Most of the spectators were seated in the first-base and third-base unscreened sections, very few in the home-plate screened area.

For this game, held October 14, 1945, after the close of the Pacific Coast League season, respondent rented the stadium to others and had no control over the conduct of the game or the players; nor did it publicize the game or fix the admission price. Ticket sales at the stadium were handled by respondent's employees and the ushers who escorted patrons to their seats were its employees. The rental charged was a percentage of the gross receipts, not of the profits.

Accordingly, the duty of care, if any, which respondent owed to appellant was that of proprietor, toward a patron, of the stadium at which this game was played.

The applicable general principle is that the owner of property, insofar as an invitee is concerned, is not an insurer of safety but must use reasonable care to keep his premises in a reasonably safe condition and give warning of latent or concealed perils. He is not liable for injury to an invitee resulting from a danger which was obvious or should have been observed in the exercise of reasonable care. * * * To the extent that the duty of self-protection rests upon the invitee, the duty of the invitor to protect is reduced. The extent of these relative duties depends upon many factors involving the capacity and opportunity of the invitor to protect the invitee and the capacity and opportunity of the invitee to protect himself.

In baseball, one of these factors is that the patron participates in the sport as a spectator and in so doing subjects himself to certain risks necessarily and usually incident to and inherent in the game; risks that are obvious and should be observed in the exercise of reasonable care. This does not mean that he assumes the risk of being injured by the proprietor's negligence but that by voluntarily entering into the sport as a spectator he knowingly accepts the reasonable risks and hazards inherent in and incident to the game.

The duty of the proprietor or operator of a baseball stadium toward his patrons is specifically defined, as follows: " 'With respect to the law governing cases of this kind, it has been generally held that one of the natural risks assumed by spectators attending professional games is that of being struck by batted or thrown balls; that the management is not required, nor does it undertake to insure patrons against injury from such source. All that is required is the exercise of ordinary care to protect patrons against such injuries (Edling v. Kansas City Baseball, etc., Co., 181 Mo.App. 327, 168 S.W. 908), and, in doing so, the management is not obliged to screen all seats, because, as pointed out by the decisions, many patrons prefer to sit where their view is not obscured by a screen. Moreover, the management is not required to provide screened seats for all who may apply for them. The duty imposed by law is performed when screened seats are provided for as many as may be reasonably expected to call for them on any ordinary occasion (Wells v. Minneapolis Baseball, etc., Ass'n, 122 Minn. 327, 142 N.W. 706, 46 L.R.A.,N.S., 606, Ann.Cas.1914D, 922; Brisson v. Minneapolis Baseball, etc., Ass'n, 185 Minn. 507, 240 N.W. 903); and if as in the cases of Wells v. Minneapolis Baseball, etc., Ass'n, supra, and Kavafian v. Seattle Baseball Club Ass'n, 105 Wash. 215, 177 P. 776, 181 P. 679, a spectator chooses to occupy an unscreened seat, or, as in the Brisson Case, supra, is unable to secure a screened seat and consequently occupies one that is not protected, he assumes the risk of being struck by thrown or batted balls; and, if injured thereby, is precluded from recovering damages therefor. As aptly said in Cincinnati Baseball Club Co. v. Eno, 112 Ohio St. 175, 147 N.E.

86, it is common knowledge that in baseball games hard balls are thrown and batted with such great swiftness they are liable to be thrown or batted outside the lines of the diamond, and spectators occupying positions which may be reached by such balls assume the risk of injury therefrom.' " Quinn v. Recreation Park Ass'n, 3 Cal.2d 725, 729–730, 46 P.2d 144, 146.

It would seem necessarily to follow that respondent fully discharged its duty toward appellant, as concerns the risk to her of being hit by thrown or batted baseballs, when it provided screened seats for all who might reasonably be expected to request them, in fact many more screened seats than were requested. Hence, the injury suffered by her when struck by a thrown ball, while voluntarily occupying an unscreened seat, did not flow from, was not caused by, any failure of performance by respondent of any duty owed her, and did not give rise to a cause of action in her favor against respondent for damages for such injury.

Appellant seeks to take this case out of the application of the rule upon the theory that she was ignorant of the game of baseball and the attendant risks, hence cannot be said to have knowingly assumed the risk. The point is not well taken. Although she had a limited experience with baseball, she was a mature person in possession of her faculties with nothing about her to set her apart from other spectators and require of her a lower standard of self-protection from obvious inherent risks than that required of other spectators. She was, at the time of the accident, 46 years of age; had lived in the San Francisco area since 1926; was about to go to a school for training and to have a job as saleswoman in a real estate office; had seen one baseball game prior to this, in 1928, played in a big field, not a ball park, when she observed the game from an automobile and did not see balls thrown or knocked into the crowd; and had seen kids in the street pitching balls. At the game at which this accident happened she knew there was no screen in front of her seat but failed to notice if any of the seats were behind a screen. She was in attendance for about an hour before the accident, which should have apprised her of the risk of being struck by a ball. Instead of observing, she paid no particular attention to the game and spent her time visiting with a friend. We find nothing here to take appellant outside the usual rule, whether it be said that this "common knowledge" of these obvious and inherent risks are imputed to her or that they are obvious risks which should have been observed by her in the exercise of ordinary care. * * *

Of the cases relied upon by appellant herein, only one, Ratcliff v. San Diego Baseball Club, etc., 27 Cal.App.2d 733, 81 P.2d 625, relates to the peculiar liability to their patrons of operators of baseball stadiums. That case involved a plaintiff who had elected to occupy a seat within a screened section and was injured while approaching her seat through an unscreened passageway. That case called for the application of a rule of liability materially different from that available to a person injured while occupying a seat in an unscreened section.

We conclude that the evidence herein, viewing it most favorably to the appellant, does not take her outside the application of the rule announced in the Quinn case; that she assumed the risk of injury in respect to which she complains; that the injury was not caused by any negligence upon the part of the respondent; and that determination thereof was a proper function of the trial court upon motion for directed verdict.

In the absence of negligence upon the part of the respondent, it is unnecessary to consider the question of contributory negligence upon the part of the appellant.

The judgment is affirmed and the appeal from the order denying a new trial is dismissed.

PETERS, P. J., and BRAY, J., concur.[13]

WOOLDRIDGE v. SUMNER

Court of Appeal [1963] 2 Q.B. 43; [1962] 3 W.L.R. 616; 106 S.J. 489; [1962] 2 All E.R. 978.

[Action by spectator against participant in National Horse Show. Plaintiff claimed that defendant had ridden too fast and had erred in guiding the horse, which injured plaintiff, away from shrubs near which plaintiff had been standing.]

DIPLOCK, L. J. * * *

To treat Lord Atkin's statement: "You must take reasonable care to avoid acts or omissions which you can reasonably foresee would be likely to injure your neighbour," as a complete exposition of the law of negligence is to mistake aphorism for exegesis. It does not purport to define what is reasonable care and was directed to identifying the persons to whom the duty to take reasonable care is owed. What

13. This seems to be the general rule in the baseball cases as the cases cited by the court show. The experienced hockey spectator takes similar risks as to flying pucks. How about the inexperienced hockey spectator? Compare Modec v. City of Eveleth, 224 Minn. 556, 29 N.W.2d 453 (1947) with Tite v. Omaha Coliseum Corp., 144 Neb. 22, 12 N.W.2d 90, 149 A.L.R. 1164 (1943).

See, in general, Warren, Volenti Non Fit Injuria, 8 Harv.L.Rev. 457 (1895); Bohlen, Voluntary Assumption of Risk, 20 Harv.L.Rev. 14, 91 (1910); Gow, The Defense of Volenti Non Fit Injuria, 61 Jurid.Rev. 37 (1949); James, Assumption of Risk, 61 Yale L.J. 141 (1952); Keeton, Personal Injuries Resulting From Open & Obvious Conditions, 100 U.P.L.Rev. 629 (1952); Green, Assumed Risk as a Defense, 22 La.L.Rev. 77 (1961); P. Keeton, Assumption of Risk and the Landowner, id. 108; R. Keeton, Assumption of Risk in Products Liability Cases, id. 122; Mansfield, Informed Choice in the Law of Torts, id. 17; Pedrick, Taken for a Ride: The Automobile Guest and Assumption of Risk, id. 90. Wade, The Place of Assumption of Risk in the Law of Negligence, id. 5 (1961); R. Keeton, Assumption of Risk of Products Risks, 19 Sw.L.J. 61 (1965); James, Assumption of Risk: Unhappy Reincarnation, 78 Yale L.J. 185 (1968). Restatement, Second, Torts §§ 496A–496G (1965). Formerly the doctrine found its commonest acceptance in master and servant cases. But there are not many situations today wherein it has not been eliminated from this field by workmen's compensation laws or other statutory modifications of the common law. The last great stronghold of the de-is reasonable care in a particular circumstance is a jury question [14] and where, as in a case like this, there is no direct guidance or hindrance from authority it may be answered by inquiring whether the ordinary reasonable man would say that in all the circumstances the defendant's conduct was blameworthy.

The matter has to be looked at from the point of view of the reasonable spectator as well as the reasonable participant; not because of the maxim volenti non fit injuria, but because what a reasonable spectator would expect a participant to do without regarding it as blameworthy is as relevant to what is reasonable care as what a reasonable participant would think was blameworthy conduct in himself. The same idea was expressed by Scrutton L. J. in Hall v. Brooklands: "What is reasonable care would depend upon the perils which might be reasonably expected to occur, *and the extent to which the ordinary spectator might be expected to appreciate and take the risk of such perils.*"

A reasonable spectator attending voluntarily to witness any game or competition knows and presumably desires that a reasonable participant will concentrate his attention upon winning, and if the game or competition is a fast-moving one, will have to exercise his judgment and attempt to exert his skill in what, in the analogous context of contributory negligence, is sometimes called "the agony of the moment." If the participant does so concentrate his attention and consequently does exercise his judgment and attempt to exert his skill in circumstances of this kind which are inherent in the game or competition in which he is taking part, the question whether any mistake he makes amounts to a breach of duty to take reasonable care must take account of those circumstances. * * *

Furthermore, the duty which he owes is a duty of care, not a duty of skill. Save where a consensual relationship exists between a plaintiff and a defendant by which the defendant impliedly warrants his skill a man owes no duty to his neighbour to exercise any special skill beyond that which an ordinary reasonable man would acquire before indulging in the activity in which he is engaged at the relevant time. It may well be that a participant in a game or competition would be guilty of negligence to a spectator if he took part in it when he knew or ought to have known that his lack of skill was such that even if he exerted it to the utmost he was likely to cause injury to a spectator watching him. No question of this arises in the present case. It was common ground that Mr. Holladay was an exceptionally skilful and experienced horseman.

fense was in actions under the Federal Employers' Liability Act, but it was abolished here by amendment of 1939. See Tiller v. Atlantic Coast Line R. Co., 318 U.S. 54, 63 S.Ct. 444, 87 L.Ed. 610, 143 A.L.R. 967 (1943); James 1952 op. cit., supra, 61 Yale L.J. at 154 et seq.

14. By "jury question" Lord Diplock means a question of fact, to be determined by the court. Juries have not been used in negligence cases in England essentially since the first World War, Conrad, The Jury (1968).

The practical result of this analysis of the application of the common law of negligence to participant and spectator would, I think, be expressed by the common man in some such terms as these: "A person attending a game or competition takes the risk of any damage caused to him by any act of a participant done in the course of and for the purposes of the game or competition notwithstanding that such act may involve an error of judgment or a lapse of skill, unless the participant's conduct is such as to evince a reckless disregard of the spectator's safety."

The spectator takes the risk because such an act involves no breach of the duty of care owed by the participant to him. He does not take the risk by virtue of the doctrine expressed or obscured by the maxim *volenti non fit injuria.* That maxim states a principle of estoppel applicable originally to a Roman citizen who consented to being sold as a slave. * * * In my view, the maxim in the absence of expressed contract has no application to negligence *simpliciter* where the duty of care is based solely upon proximity or "neighbourship" in the Atkinian sense. The maxim in English law presupposes a tortious act by the defendant. The consent that is relevant is not consent to the risk of injury but consent to the lack of reasonable care that may produce that risk (see Kelly v. Farrans Ltd. ([1954] N.I. 41, 45) *per* Lord MacDermott) and requires on the part of the plaintiff at the time at which he gives consent full knowledge of the nature and extent of the risk that he ran (Osborne v. London and North Western Railway ((1888) 21 Q.B.D. 220, 224), per Wills J., approved in Letang v. Ottawa Electric Railway ([1926] A.C. 725)).
* * *

Since the maxim has in my view no application to this or any other case of negligence *simpliciter*, the fact that the plaintiff owing to his ignorance of horses did not fully appreciate the nature and extent of the risk he ran did not impose upon Mr. Holladay any higher duty of care towards him than that which he owed to any ordinary reasonable spectator with such knowledge of horses and vigilance for his own safety as might be reasonably expected to be possessed by a person who chooses to watch a heavyweight hunter class in the actual arena where the class is being judged. He cannot rely upon his personal ignorance of the risk any more than the plaintiff in Murray v. Harringay Arena ([1951] 2 K.B. 529) could rely upon his ignorance of the risk involved in ice-hockey, excusable though such ignorance may have been in a six-year-old child. * * *

MEISTRICH v. CASINO ARENA ATTRACTIONS, INC.

Supreme Court of New Jersey, 1959.
31 N.J. 44, 155 A.2d 90.

WEINTRAUB, C. J.

Plaintiff was injured by a fall while iceskating on a rink operated by defendant. The jury found for defendant. The Appellate Division reversed * * *.

The Appellate Division found error in the charge of assumption of the risk. It also concluded there was no evidence of contributory negligence and hence that issue should not have been submitted to the jury.

Defendant urges there was no negligence and therefore the alleged errors were harmless. * * * We think there was sufficient proof to take the issue to the jury. There was evidence that defendant departed from the usual procedure in preparing the ice, with the result that it became too hard and hence too slippery for the patron of average ability using skates sharpened for the usual surface. From plaintiff's account of his fall, a jury could infer the stated condition of the ice was the proximate cause.

We however agree with defendant that the issue of contributory negligence was properly left to the trier of the facts. Plaintiff had noted that his skates slipped on turns. A jury could permissibly find he carelessly contributed to his injury when, with that knowledge, he remained on the ice and skated cross-hand with another.

The remaining question is whether the trial court's charge with respect to assumption of risk was erroneous. * * *

The Appellate Division also found the trial court failed to differentiate between assumption of risk and contributory negligence. The Appellate Division added * * *:

> "We note that contributory negligence involves some breach of duty on the part of a plaintiff. His actions are such as to constitute a failure to use such care for his safety as the ordinarily prudent man in similar circumstances would use. On the other hand, assumption of risk may involve no fault or negligence, but rather entails the undertaking of a risk of a known danger. Hendrikson v. Koppers Co., Inc., 11 N.J. 600, 607, 95 A.2d 710 (1953)."

As we read the charge, the trial court expressed essentially the same thought, i. e., that assumption of risk may be found if plaintiff knew or reasonably should have known of the risk, notwithstanding that a reasonably prudent man would have continued in the face of the risk. We think an instruction to that effect is erroneous in the respect hereinafter delineated. The error is traceable to confusion in the opinions in our State.

Assumption of risk is a term of several meanings. For present purposes, we may place to one side certain situations which sometimes are brought within the sweeping term but which are readily differentiated from the troublesome area. Specifically we place beyond present discussion the problem raised by an express contract not to sue for injury or loss which may thereafter be occasioned by the covenantee's negligence, and also situations in which actual consent exists, as, for example, participation in a contact sport.

We here speak solely of the area in which injury or damage was neither intended nor expressly contracted to be nonactionable. In this area, assumption of risk has two distinct meanings. In one sense (sometimes called its "primary" sense), it is an alternate expression for the proposition that defendant was not negligent, i. e., either owed no duty or did not breach the duty owed. In its other sense (sometimes called "secondary"), assumption of risk is an affirmative defense to an established breach of duty. In its primary sense, it is accurate to say plaintiff assumed the risk whether or not he was "at fault", for the truth thereby expressed in alternate terminology is that defendant was not negligent. But in its secondary sense, i. e., as an affirmative defense to an established breach of defendant's duty, it is incorrect to say plaintiff assumed the risk whether or not he was at fault.

A discussion of the subject must start with the common-law action of a servant against his master, for it was there that assumption of risk emerged or at least was distinctly developed. The master owed a duty to provide a reasonably safe place to work. If he discharged that duty, he was not liable for damages due to the inherent risks that remained. The master, upon that postulate, was not negligent. He might be liable if he failed to warn the uninitiate of those inherent risks, 3 Labatt, Master and Servant (2d ed. 1913), § 1151, p. 3059, but the experienced workman was said to have assumed them. Quite obviously, the expression simply stated in other terms the basic thought that the master had not breached his duty. 3 Labatt, Master and Servant (2d ed. 1913), § 1186a, p. 3188. Assumption of risk, in that sense, was not a separate defense. It was not required to be pleaded and the burden of proof was not upon the master. Taylor v. Chicago, R. I. & P. Ry. Co., 186 Iowa 506, 170 N.W. 388, 390 (Sup. Ct.1919). On the contrary, the servant had to prove the injury was caused by a risk other than one inherent in a well-run establishment, that is to say, that the master was negligent. That assumption of risk as thus used was not a separate defense but rather another way of saying the defendant was not negligent, is further evident from the frequent statement that a servant did *not* assume the risk of his master's *negligence.* * * *

Hence if the servant established that his injury was caused by a risk created by the master's breach of duty to furnish a reasonably safe place to work, assumption of the risk in the primary sense necessarily was negated. But the master could press an affirmative defense, as to which the burden of pleading and proof was his, that plaintiff should nonetheless fail because he voluntarily exposed himself to a risk negligently created by the master. Unhappily, that defense was also called assumption of risk. Thus two utterly distinct thoughts bore the same label with inevitable confusion. Martin v. Des Moines Edison Light Co., 131 Iowa 724, 106 N.W. 359, 363 (Sup. Ct.1906).

The confusion was aided by the practice of pleading assumption of risk as a separate defense without indicating whether the purpose was merely to deny negligence or to assert an affirmative defense on the hypothesis that defendant was negligent. So also a single form of charge to the jury came into usage attended by the same obscurity. Thus where the facts were such that assumption of risk was pertinent only as a denial of negligence, the jury was instructed to deal first with the issue of negligence, and if negligence should be found, then to consider the "defense." Thus instructed, a jury might find negligence (a finding which in legal effect negates assumption of risk in its primary sense) and yet find for defendant under a misapprehension that assumption of risk in its primary sense somehow constituted a bar. Still further, although it would be technically accurate with respect to assumption of risk in its primary sense to say that plaintiff assumed the risk of non-negligent injury even though he was free of fault, that same instruction, if given where assumption of risk in its secondary sense is in issue, would lead to the exculpation of a negligent defendant upon the erroneous notion that a plaintiff assumed the risk of that negligence even though he was free of blame. And, we believe, the confusion has been further compounded by treating assumption of risk in its secondary sense as an affirmative defense different in its essential ingredients from the defense of contributory negligence, thus creating the potential of a verdict for defendant notwithstanding a jury's finding under the issue of contributory negligence that plaintiff exercised the care of the reasonably prudent man under all the circumstances.

The proposition we have just advanced, that assumption of risk in its secondary sense is indistinguishable in its nature from contributory negligence, requires further discussion. We may note at once that our cases describe these two "defenses" as "barely distinguishable," Castino v. Di Menzo, 124 N.J.L. 398, 401, 11 A.2d 738 (Sup.Ct.1940); "virtually identical," White v. Ellison Realty Corp., 5 N.J. 228, 235, 74 A.2d 401, 19 A.L.R.2d 264 (1950); "convertible" or "interchangeable," Benton v. Y.M.C.A. of Westfield, 27 N.J. 67, 69, 141 A.2d 298 (1958); * * * and "twins," Scheirek v. Izsa, 26 N.J.Super. 68, 72, 97 A.2d 167 (App.Div.1953). Indeed in Hartman v. City of Brigantine, 23 N.J. 530, 537, 129 A.2d 876, 880 (1957), it was suggested that in the interest of clarity assumption of risk in the secondary sense "might well be subsumed" under the defense of contributory negligence.

To determine if assumption of risk in its secondary sense differs from contributory negligence, the critical test is whether a plaintiff's conduct under the former is measured by the standard of the reasonably prudent man, for if it is, nothing remains to distinguish it from contributory negligence.

Reverting again to the soil of origin, we find the servant was held to have assumed the risk of a negligently created hazard if he continued to work with knowledge of it. Indeed, actual knowledge was not required, for the doctrine was applied to a risk which a reasonable man would have detected. Seaboard Air Line Railway v. Horton, 233 U.S. 492, 34 S.Ct. 635, 58 L.Ed. 1062 (1914). If the employee knew or ought to have known of the hazard, he was barred even though he was guilty of no "fault" beyond continuing to work. Cetola v. Lehigh Valley R. Co., 89 N.J.L. 691, 692, 99 A. 310 (E. & A.1916). The rigor of that rule was later tempered by permitting an employee to rely for a reasonable period upon the master's promise to rectify the negligent condition. Seaboard Air Line Railway v. Horton, supra; 3 Labatt, Master and Servant (2d ed. 1913), § 1197, p. 3242.

Although the rationalization of the foregoing common-law view was threaded with the fiction that the servant "contracted" for his master's immunity as a *quid pro quo* for the wages paid, it seems likely that it was but a harsh and improvident application of the familiar standard of the behavior of the reasonable man. In short the courts thought it indisputable that a reasonably prudent man would not continue to work with such knowledge, and thus finding no room for difference of opinion, took the matter from the jury. But if this be an incorrect view of the underlying thought process and if assumption of risk was then something other than a misguided application of the broad principle of contributory negligence, it would not matter today, for the common-law concept, however viewed, was discredited long ago at the very scene of its flowering. Thus in our State, the Legislature, the final arbiter of public policy, abolished that defense in the Workmen's Compensation Act, ordaining that where the parties choose to retain the common-law remedy, relief shall not be denied on the ground that the employee "assumed the risks * * * arising from the failure of the employer to provide and maintain safe premises and suitable appliances." R.S. 34:15–2, N.J.S.A.; Brost v. Whitall-Tatum Co., 89 N.J.L. 531, 99 A. 315, L.R.A.1917D, 71 (E. & A.1916)

In the light of the history of the subject and legislative action just described, it would be improvident to transplant the doctrine of assumption of risk into other areas with the discredited notion that one who knew (or should have known) of a negligently created risk is barred even though free of fault, i. e., even though a reasonably prudent man would have incurred the risk despite that knowledge. Rather the just approach, as with respect to other applications of contributory negligence, is to leave the issue to the jury if reasonable men may disagree or to decide it as a matter of law if there is no room for difference in evaluation. So it may be one thing to raise the bar as a matter of law if a man entered a blazing structure to retrieve a fedora, but something else thus to bar him if his purpose was to rescue a child. See Eckert v. Long Island R. Co., 43 N.Y. 502 (Ct.App. 1871); Wagner v. International Ry. Co., 232 N.Y. 176, 133 N.E. 437, 19 A.L.R. 1 (Ct.App.1921). This approach has been embraced in our State. In applying assumption of risk in its secondary sense in areas other than that of master and servant, our cases have consistently recognized the ultimate question to be whether a reasonably prudent man would have moved in the face of a known risk, dealing with the issue as one of law or leaving it to the jury upon the same standard which controls the handling of the issue of contributory negligence. * * *

Hence we think it clear that assumption of risk in its secondary sense is a mere phase of contributory negligence, the total issue being whether a reasonably prudent man in the exercise of due care (a) would have incurred the known risk and (b) if he would, whether such a person in the light of all of the circumstances including the appreciated risk would have conducted himself in the manner in which plaintiff acted.

Thus in the area under discussion there are but two basic issues: (1) defendant's negligence, and (2) plaintiff's contributory negligence. In view of the considerations discussed above, it has been urged that assumption of risk in both its primary and secondary senses serves merely to confuse and should be eliminated. Editorial, Assumption of the Risk—A False Issue, 73 N.J.L.J. 346 (1950); James, Assumption of Risk, 61 Yale L.J. 141, 169 (1952); 2 Harper and James, Law of Torts (1956), § 21.8, p. 1191. Dean Prosser agrees that in the area with which we are here concerned "assumption of risk serves no useful purpose, since it introduces nothing that is not fully covered either by the idea of an absence of duty on the part of the defendant, or by that of contributory negligence of the plaintiff." Prosser, Torts (2d ed. 1955), § 55, p. 305. He however suggests the terminology does focus attention upon the nature of the ultimate issues and hence may well be retained.

Perhaps a well-guarded charge of assumption of risk in its primary sense will aid comprehension. But we cannot see how a charge of the concept in its secondary sense will contribute a net gain. And it seems too much to expect a jury to grasp the issues when assumption of risk is advanced in both of its senses. The present case is of that character, for here defendant may urge in the primary sense that plaintiff assumed the risk inherent in a carefully operated rink and also in the secondary sense that plaintiff assumed the risk of a negligently created hazard because he imprudently skated with awareness of the added danger. We think it likely in such circumstances that a jury will think there are three or four issues rather than the two of negligence and contributory negligence.

We are satisfied there is no reason to charge assumption of the risk in its secondary sense as something distinct from contributory negligence, and hence that where the thought is projected in that aspect, the terminology of assumption of risk should not be used. Rather, as suggested in Hartman v. City of Brigantine, supra (23 N.J. at page 537, 129 A.2d at page 880), the subject should be subsumed under the charge of contributory negligence. With respect to its primary sense, it will not matter whether a trial court makes or omits a reference to assumption of the risk, provided that if the terminology is used the jury is plainly charged it is merely another way of expressing the thought that a defendant is not liable in the absence of negligence; that a plaintiff does not assume a risk defendant negligently created, cf. Ford v. Reichert, 23 N.J. 429, 434, 129 A.2d 439 (1957); and that if defendant is found to have been negligent, plaintiff is barred only if defendant carries the burden of proving contributory negligence, i. e., plaintiff's failure to use the care of a reasonably prudent man under all of the circumstances either in incurring the known risk or in the manner in which he proceeded in the face of that risk.

Still another reason has been advanced for the retention of assumption of the risk in its primary sense. The thesis is that "in that situation, though the assumption of risk gives rise to a lack of duty on the defendant's part, nevertheless (notwithstanding that the plaintiff usually has the burden of proving that the defendant owes him a duty) the defendant here has the burden of proving the assumption of risk—that is, the burden of proving the lack of duty." Klinsky v. Hanson Van Winkle Munning Co., 38 N.J.Super. 439, 444, 119 A.2d 166, 168 (App.Div.1955), certification denied 20 N.J. 534, 120 A.2d 661 (1956). With this, we disagree. See, 2 Harper and James, Law of Torts (1956), § 21.7, p. 1190. * * *

A plaintiff has the burden of proving negligence. If a defendant challenges the existence or extent of the duty asserted or disputes a breach of that duty, the burden of proof remains with plaintiff, even though defendant may be defeated in that inquiry if he fails to adduce facts to negate the duty or the breach suggested by plaintiff's proof. The burden of proof as to negligence of defendant does not shift to him merely because he chooses to express his denial of negligence in terms that plaintiff assumed (may not complain of) risks which inhered notwithstanding that defendant properly discharged the duty he owed in the circumstances. For example, if a passenger upon a common carrier is thrown by the movement of the vehicle, the burden is his to prove an unusual (negligently created) jerk or jar even though defendant asserts the fall resulted from an incidental, non-negligent movement. Perhaps the confusion flows from those situations in which a defendant may have a duty to warn of the existence of a risk which itself is not the product of negligence, just as for example at common law the master was bound to warn the inexperienced employee. The fact that there plaintiff's knowledge of the risk is crucially involved in the issue of defendant's breach of duty should not obscure the obligation of the plaintiff to prove that breach, i. e., a failure to warn. Different, of course, is a case in which the risk itself was negligently created and defendant as part of his affirmative defense of contributory negligence seeks to prove that plaintiff was warned or knew of it.

In short, each case must be analyzed to determine whether the pivotal question goes to defendant's negligence or to plaintiff's contributory negligence. If the former, then what has been called assumption of risk is only a denial of breach of duty and the burden of proof is plaintiff's. If on the other hand assumption of risk is advanced to defeat a recovery despite a demonstrated breach of defendant's duty, then it constitutes the affirmative defense of contributory negligence and the burden of proof is upon defendant.

With the modifications expressed above, the judgment of the Appellate Division is affirmed.[15]

JAMES, ASSUMPTION OF RISK: UNHAPPY REINCARNATION, 78 Yale L.J. 185 (1968).

The second Restatement of Torts states that implied assumption of risk should be recognized as a separate defense.[16] In a leading article over sixty years ago, Bohlen [17] took the contrary position. A plaintiff's *reasonable* assumption of risk would not bar him unless the risk was one which defendant had a legal right to put up to plaintiff; and in such a case defendant breached no relevant duty. A plaintiff's *unreasonable* assumption of risk would constitute contributory negligence on his part; and this would be a defense without the need to invoke any separate doctrine.[18] Bohlen was the reporter for the original

15. "Experience * * * indicates the term 'assumption of risk' is so apt to create mist that it is better banished from the scene. We hope we have heard the last of it. Henceforth let us stay with 'negligence' and 'contributory negligence.'" McGrath v. v. American Cyanamid Co., 41 N.J. 272, 276, 196 A.2d 238, 240-41 (1963).

Also cf. Lyons v. Redding Construction Co., 83 Wash.2d 86, 515 P.2d 821 (1973); compare dicta in Nelson v. Brunswick Corp., 503 F.2d 376, 383 (9th Cir. 1974). And see, for clear repudiation of assumption of risk, Farley v. M M Cattle Co., Tex., 529 S.W.2d 751 (1975).

16. Restatement of Torts, Second §§ 496A–496G (1965).

17. Bohlen, Voluntary Assumption of Risk, 20 Harv.L.Rev. 14, 91 (1906), reprinted in F. Bohlen, Studies in the Law of Torts 441 (1926).

18. This statement, which was mine, not Bohlen's, is an oversimplification. Where defendant's conduct is wilful or wanton, or entails strict liability, ordinary contributory negligence is not a defense, but the deliberate and voluntary assumption of an unreasonable risk may be. See, e. g., Restatement of Torts, Second § 402A, comment n, § 496A, comment d (1965); W. Prosser, Handbook of the Law of Torts 454, 455 (3d ed. 1964) [hereinafter cited as Prosser, Torts—the edition will be noted]. In such a situation there will be need to distinguish what may be called the unreasonable assumption of risk from ordinary contributory negligence.

Under a rule of proportional or comparative negligence, the question will arise whether the unreasonable assumption of a risk constitutes a complete defense or whether damages are to be apportioned. Different answers have been given to this question. See, e. g., Tiller v. Atlantic Coast Line R. R., 318 U.S. 54, 62 et seq. (1943) (describing the situation under the Federal Employers' Liability Act both before and after the 1939 amendment which abolishes the defense of assumption of risk); Baird v. Cornelius, 12 Wis. 2d 284, 107 N.W.2d 278 (1961); McConville v. State Farm Mut. Auto. Ins. Co., 15 Wis.2d 374, 113 N.W.2d 14 (1962). The better view is clearly that such assumption of risk is a form of contributory negligence to be compared with defendant's breach of duty. Prosser, Torts 455 (3d ed. 1964); Re-part of the first Restatement of Torts, which reflected his view by giving no separate treatment to the doctrine of assumed risk. * * *

Harper and I have always been inclined to accept, in the main, Bohlen's analysis, as our textbook on torts shows. In the decade which followed that book's publication in 1956 there came to be substantial judicial and scholarly support for the point of view it espoused, namely, that the doctrine deserves no separate existence (except for *express* assumption of risk) and is simply a confusing way of stating certain no-duty rules or, where there has been a breach of duty toward plaintiff, simply one kind of contributory negligence.

In the course of the discussion of the second Restatement, the Reporter proposed to the advisors the adoption of new sections which would refine Section 893 of the first Restatement. What happened is well told by Justice Greenhill in Halepeska v. Callihan Interests, Inc.:

> In preparing Restatement of the Law of Torts, Second, the advisers sharply divided. A group mainly of distinguished deans and professors, favored striking the entire chapter of Assumption of Risk. They would use contributory negligence. The group includes Deans Page Keeton and Wade, and Professors James, Malone, Morris, Seavey and Thurman. Mr. Eldredge prepared a "dissent" for this group. The group is referred to in the notes to the draft as "The Confederacy." Others including Prosser, Professor Robert Keeton, and Judges Fee, Flood, Traynor and Goodrich supported the existence of the defense of assumed risk. The distinguished scholars refer to the debate, among themselves, as "The Battle of the Wilderness." The Reporter, Prosser, states in the draft that the American Law Institute Council voted unanimously to follow the recommendations of the sections on assumption of the risk.[19]

The upshot was adoption by the American Law Institute of Sections 496A–496G of the second Restatement.[20]

statement of Torts, Second § 496A, comment d, illustration 3, at 564.

This article will not be concerned with the unreasonable assumption of a risk.

19. 371 S.W.2d 368, 378 n. 3 (Tex.1963). See also City of Tucson v. Holliday, 3 Ariz.App. 10, 411 P.2d 183, 188 (1966).

20. Section 496A states the general principle that plaintiff's voluntary assumption of a risk arising from defendant's negligent or reckless conduct bars his recovery for harm resulting from that risk.

Section 496B deals with express assumption of risk.

Section 496C states that a plaintiff who fully understands a risk caused by defendant's conduct, or the condition of defendant's land or chattels, "and who nevertheless voluntarily chooses to enter or remain * * * within the area of that risk, under circumstances that manifest his willingness to accept it," is barred from recovery "for harm within that risk." The section also covers plaintiff's things, but it excepts situations where express assumption of risk "would be invalid as contrary to public policy."

Section 496D makes plaintiff's knowledge and appreciation of the risk conditions to the doctrine's application.

Section 496E requires that the assumption be voluntary. * * *

Section 496F deals with the assumption of a risk created by defendant's breach of statute.

By far the most serious difference between these sections and my position concerns the question whether a defendant who has breached his duty of care toward plaintiff may nevertheless defend an action for injury resulting to plaintiff from that breach on the ground that plaintiff *reasonably but voluntarily* encountered that risk. * * * [In] cases in which defendant's wrong may be said to restrict unduly plaintiff's freedom of choice or to put him under a kind of duress * * * a plaintiff will not be barred simply because he knowingly incurs the risk (unless his conduct is *unreasonable* under the circumstances). On the other hand, where injury comes from use of defendant's land or chattels, there are (as all concede) large though diminishing areas wherein defendant's only duty to plaintiff is one of care to acquaint him with risks inherent in the land or chattel. Here no duty is owed to such a plaintiff who encounters the condition with full knowledge of its risks, however carefully he does so. And here again both sides are in agreement.

The difference between the Restatement view and that taken here is significant only in that narrow area in which defendant's wrong "does not cause the plaintiff's choice to be made under duress," but in which defendant does not have the right to withhold or condition the plaintiff's use of land or chattels or the other terms of a mutually voluntary association. A hypothetical case posed by Keeton illustrates the difference. Black and Blue "are persons to whom the purchaser of a defectively designed motorcycle lends it, after discovering the defect and with full warning to Black but not to Blue, the plaintiffs having need of a vehicle and reasonably choosing to take this, the only vehicle available." Both Keeton and I would no doubt agree that Black would not recover against the *lender* for injury caused by the defect. Under prevailing law the lender has fully discharged his duty to Black; [21] alternatively the result might be described in terms of Black's assumption of risk. But Keeton, and presumably the Restatement,[22] would also bar Black's recovery *against the maker* even where Black's knowing acceptance of the risk was reasonable and even where the maker's duty to a foreseeable user of the motorcycle was not satisfied by warning.[23]

The latter result, it is submitted, is unfortunate. The maker has, by hypothesis, put out a product which is unreasonably dangerous even to one who knows of the defect. Whether he is held strictly or only for negligence, why should he be freed of liability merely because the plaintiff knew of the defect but used the thing carefully? If the individualism embodied in assumption of risk is to be justified by the

Section 496G states that if defendant "would otherwise be subject to liability to the plaintiff," defendant has the burden of proving plaintiff's assumption of risk. * * *

21. See 2 F. Harper & F. James, Law of Torts 1163–64, 1181 (1956). But cf. Pfaffenbach v. White Plains Express Corp., 17 N.Y.2d 132, 135–36, 269 N.Y.S.2d 115, 116–17, 216 N.E.2d 324, 325 (1966).

22. Restatement of Torts, Second § 496C, comments e, f & g (1965).

23. R. Keeton, [Assumption of Risks in Products Liability Cases], 22 La.L.Rev. 122, 157–59 [(1961)].

unwillingness to inhibit the maker's activities in such a way as to diminish or defeat the flow of advantages to plaintiff's class (customers and users), then surely it is unrealistic to think that in the case put the withholding of liability will materially promote that objective.[24] The maker, negligent by hypothesis, will be subject to liability to plaintiffs ignorant of the risk, and if the fear of this liability does not keep him from producing the product, it is unlikely indeed that he will go out of production to avoid the prospect of additional liability to the occasional informed victim. Except where products are extremely dangerous, liability in both instances is more likely to induce care in manufacture than cessation of production.

Although the difference between the second Restatement position and mine is a narrow one, its scope is widening and will probably continue to grow in importance. The two views will produce the same result wherever the defendant's duty to plaintiff will be fulfilled by adequate warning. Then if the plaintiff has full knowledge and appreciation of the risks inherent in the condition or the conduct which injures him, he is not hurt by the hazard (ignorance) which underlay the duty to warn him of these risks. The two views will produce different results only in those situations where defendant's duty to plaintiff goes beyond mere warning or full disclosure and includes the taking of some additional precaution for plaintiff's safety. But the tendency of courts today is to require (or to let a jury require) additional precautions in many situations where a warning of the danger, or its obviousness, was held to satisfy defendant's duty of care a generation ago.

Examples come readily to mind. The traditional view was that an occupier of land would in most cases satisfy his duty of care to an invitee by full disclosure of the dangers of his premises. Similarly, the maker of goods had only to acquaint the user of the dangers of the goods (and he had this duty only when the dangers were not obvious). Today courts are increasingly reluctant to abide by such rules of thumb; there is a substantial tendency to recognize that circumstances may call for precautions in addition to warning. The second Restatement itself adopts the newer view in these cases, though guardedly.[25]

The adoption of this view represents a judgment that the dangers of the premises or the product are unreasonable ones *even to those who are fully aware of them.* Thus, if the maker of an appliance with obvious and exposed moving parts is held to the duty to equip it with some safety appliance, then the law no longer accepts the user's ability to take care of himself as an adequate safeguard of interests which society seeks to protect; the law has put some of the burden

24. See Mansfield, Informed Choice in the Law of Torts, 22 La.L.Rev. 17, 67–68 (1961).

25. Restatement of Torts, Second § 343 A, & comments & illustrations (1966); id. Appendix 233–35 (1966) (Reporter's Notes) (dealing with occupier's liability for obvious dangers); id. § 389 & comments d, e & f.

of looking out for the plaintiff on the defendant. If now the law should relieve the defendant from liability for breach of that duty because plaintiff encountered the unreasonable danger voluntarily but carefully, then indeed the law would defeat itself. It would be applying a doctrine born of the notion that an actor owes no duty of affirmative care for the protection of others to a situation in which the law has imposed just such a duty. The increasing judicial rejection of the assumption of risk doctrine reflects a recognition that this defense is inconsistent with newer policies which underlie the imposition of a duty to take care of others that extends beyond merely warning them. * * * [T]his repudiation has attained substantial proportions during recent years. * * *

* * * I quite agree with Professor Keeton that the difference in the no-duty cases is essentially a semantic one, that courts often prefer the language of assumption of risk, and that all of us should learn to be bilingual. What I fear from his usage is that it may lead others, as it has led him,[26] to adopt a substantive result that would bar the knowing but careful plaintiff from recovering for harm caused by defendant's negligence, thus neutralizing the judgment (made on the negligence issue) that the situation produced by the negligence is unreasonably dangerous even to one who has full knowledge of its risks. * * *

LI v. YELLOW CAB COMPANY OF CALIFORNIA

Supreme Court of California, in Bank, 1975.
13 Cal.3d 804, 119 Cal.Rptr. 858, 532 P.2d 1226.

SULLIVAN, JUSTICE. In this case we address the grave and recurrent question whether we should judicially declare no longer applicable in California courts the doctrine of contributory negligence, which bars all recovery when the plaintiff's negligent conduct has contributed as a legal cause in any degree to the harm suffered by him, and hold that it must give way to a system of comparative negligence, which assesses liability in direct proportion to fault. As we explain in detail infra, we conclude that we should. In the course of reaching our ultimate decision we conclude that: (1) The doctrine of comparative negligence is preferable to the "all-or-nothing" doctrine of contributory negligence from the point of view of logic, practical experience, and fundamental justice; (2) judicial action in this area is not precluded by the presence of section 1714 of the Civil Code, which has been said to "codify" the "all-or-nothing" rule and to render it immune from attack in the courts except on constitutional grounds; (3) given the possibility of judicial action, certain practical difficulties attendant upon the adoption of comparative negligence should not dissuade us from charting a new course—leaving the resolu-

26. R. Keeton, Assumption of Products Risks, 19 Sw.L.J. 61, 68 (1965); cf. R. Keeton, Assumption of Risk in Products Liability Cases, 22 La.L.Rev. 122, 160–61 (1961). [Notes 16–26 from original, renumbered; other notes in original omitted.]

tion of some of these problems to future judicial or legislative action; (4) the doctrine of comparative negligence should be applied in this state in its so-called "pure" form under which the assessment of liability in proportion to fault proceeds in spite of the fact that the plaintiff is equally at fault as or more at fault than the defendant; and finally (5) this new rule should be given a limited retrospective application.

The accident here in question occurred near the intersection of Alvarado Street and Third Street in Los Angeles. At this intersection Third Street runs in a generally east-west direction along the crest of a hill, and Alvarado Street, running generally north and south, rises gently to the crest from either direction. At approximately 9 p. m. on November 21, 1968, plaintiff Nga Li was proceeding northbound on Alvarado in her 1967 Oldsmobile. She was in the inside lane, and about 70 feet before she reached the Third Street intersection she stopped and then began a left turn across the three southbound lanes of Alvarado, intending to enter the driveway of a service station. At this time defendant Robert Phillips, an employee of defendant Yellow Cab Company, was driving a company-owned taxicab southbound in the middle lane on Alvarado. He came over the crest of the hill, passed through the intersection and collided with the right rear portion of plaintiff's automobile, resulting in personal injuries to plaintiff as well as considerable damage to the automobile.

The court, sitting without a jury, found as facts that defendant Phillips was traveling at approximately 30 miles per hour when he entered the intersection, that such speed was unsafe at that time and place, and that the traffic light controlling southbound traffic at the intersection was yellow when defendant Phillips drove into the intersection. It also found, however, that plaintiff's left turn across the southbound lanes of Alvarado "was made at a time when a vehicle was approaching from the opposite direction so close as to constitute an immediate hazard." The dispositive conclusion of law was as follows: "That the driving of NGA LI was negligent, that such negligence was a proximate cause of the collision, and that she is barred from recovery by reason of such contributory negligence." Judgment for defendants was entered accordingly.

I

"Contributory negligence is conduct on the part of the plaintiff which falls below the standard to which he should conform for his own protection, and which is a legally contributing cause cooperating with the negligence of the defendant in bringing about the plaintiff's harm." (Restatement of Torts, Second § 463.) Thus the American Law Institute, in its second restatement of the law, describes the kind of conduct on the part of one seeking recovery for damage caused by negligence which renders him subject to the doctrine of contributory negligence. What the effect of such conduct will be is left to a further section, which states the doctrine in its clearest essence: "Except where the defendant has the last clear chance, the plaintiff's contributory negligence *bars recovery* against a defendant whose negligent conduct would otherwise make him liable to the plaintiff for the harm sustained by him." (Restatement of Torts, Second § 467.) (Italics added.)

This rule, rooted in the long-standing principle that one should not recover from another for damages brought upon oneself (see Baltimore & P. R. Co. v. Jones (1877) 95 U.S. 439, 442, 24 L.Ed. 506; * * * has been the law of this state from its beginning. * * * Although criticized almost from the outset for the harshness of its operation, it has weathered numerous attacks, in both the legislative and the judicial arenas, seeking its amelioraton or repudiation. We have undertaken a thorough reexamination of the matter, giving particular attention to the common law and statutory sources of the subject doctrine in this state. As we have indicated, this reexamination leads us to the conclusion that the "all-or-nothing" rule of contributory negligence can be and ought to be superseded by a rule which assesses liability in proportion to fault.

It is unnecessary for us to catalogue the enormous amount of critical comment that has been directed over the years against the "all-or-nothing" approach of the doctrine of contributory negligence. The essence of that criticism has been constant and clear: the doctrine is inequitable in its operation because it fails to distribute responsibility in proportion to fault.[27] Against this have been raised several arguments in justification but none have proved even remotely adequate to the task.[28] The basic objection to the doctrine—grounded in

27. Dean Prosser states the kernel of critical comment in these terms: "It [the rule] places upon one party the entire burden of a loss for which two are, by hypothesis, responsible." (Prosser, Torts (4th ed. 1971) § 67, p. 433.) Harper and James express the same basic idea: "[T]here is no justification—in either policy or doctrine—for the rule of contributory negligence, except for the feeling that if one man is to be held liable because of his fault, then the fault of him who seeks to enforce that liability should also be considered. But this notion does not require the all-or-nothing rule, which would exonerate a very negligent defendant for even the slight fault of his victim. The logical corollary of the fault principle would be a rule of comparative or proportional negligence, not the present rule." (2 Harper & James, The Law of Torts (1956) § 22.3, p. 1207.)

28. Dean Prosser, in a 1953 law review article on the subject which still enjoys considerable influence, addressed himself to the commonly advanced justificatory arguments in the following terms: "There has been much speculation as to why the rule thus declared found such ready acceptance in later decisions, both in England and in the United States. The explanations given by the courts themselves never have carried much conviction. Most of the decisions have talked about 'proximate cause,' saying that the plaintiff's negligence is an intervening, insulating cause between the defendant's negligence and the injury. But this cannot be supported unless a meaning is assigned to proximate cause which is found nowhere else. If two automobiles collide and injure a bystander, the negligence of one driver is not held to be a superseding cause which relieves the other of liability; and there is no visible reason for any different conclusion when the action is by one driver against the other. It has been said that the defense has a penal basis, and is intended to punish the plaintiff for his own misconduct; or that the court will not aid one who is himself at fault, and he must come into court with clean hands. But this is no explanation of the many cases, particularly those of the last clear chance, in which a plaintiff clearly at fault is permitted to re-

the primal concept that in a system in which liability is based on fault, the extent of fault should govern the extent of liability—remains irresistible to reason and all intelligent notions of fairness.

Furthermore, practical experience with the application by juries of the doctrine of contributory negligence has added its weight to analyses of its inherent shortcomings: "Every trial lawyer is well aware that juries often do in fact allow recovery in cases of contributory negligence, and that the compromise in the jury room does result in some diminution of the damages because of the plaintiff's fault. But the process is at best a haphazard and most unsatisfactory one." (Prosser, Comparative Negligence, supra, p. 4; fn. omitted.) (See also Prosser, Torts, supra, § 67, pp. 436–437; Comments of Malone and Wade in Comments on Maki v. Frelk—Comparative v. Contributory Negligence: Should the Court or Legislature Decide? (1968) 21 Vand.L.Rev. 889, at pp. 934, 943; Ulman, A Judge Takes the Stand (1933) pp. 30–34; cf. Comment of Kalven, 21 Vand.L.Rev. 889, 901–904.) It is manifest that this state of affairs, viewed from the standpoint of the health and vitality of the legal process, can only detract from public confidence in the ability of law and legal institutions to assign liability on a just and consistent basis. (See Keeton, Creative Continuity in the Law of Torts (1962) 75 Harv.L.Rev. 463, 505; Comment of Keeton in Comments on Maki v. Frelk, supra, 21 Vand.L. Rev. 889, at p. 916 [29]; Note (1974) 21 U.C.L.A.L.Rev. 1566, 1596–1597.)

cover. It has been said that the rule is intended to discourage accidents, by denying recovery to those who fail to use proper care for their own safety; but the assumption that the speeding motorist is, or should be, meditating on the possible failure of a lawsuit for his possible injuries lacks all reality, and it is quite as reasonable to say that the rule promotes accidents by encouraging the negligent defendant. Probably the true explanation lies merely in the highly individualistic attitude of the common law of the early nineteenth century. The period of development of contributory negligence was that of the industrial revolution, and there is reason to think that the courts found in this defense, along with the concepts of duty and proximate cause, a convenient instrument of control over the jury, by which the liabilities of rapidly growing industry were curbed and kept within bounds." (Prosser, Comparative Negligence (1953) 41 Cal.L.Rev. 1, 3–4; fns. omitted. For a more extensive consideration of the same subject, see 2 Harper & James, supra, § 22.2, pp. 1199–1207.)

To be distinguished from arguments raised in justification of the "all or nothing" rule are practical considerations which have been said to counsel against the adoption of a fairer and more logical alternative. The latter considerations will be discussed in a subsequent portion of this opinion.

29. Professor Keeton states the matter as follows in his Vanderbilt Law Review comment:

"In relation to contributory negligence, as elsewhere in the law, uncertainty and lack of evenhandedness are produced by casuistic distinctions. This has happened, for example, in doctrines of last clear chance and in distinctions between what is enough to sustain a finding of primary negligence and what more is required to sustain a finding of contributory negligence. Perhaps even more significant, however, is the casuistry of tolerating blatant jury departure from evenhanded application of the legal rules of negligence and contributory negligence with the consequence that a kind of rough apportionment of damages occurs, but in unpoliced, irregular, and unreasonably discriminatory fashion. Moreover, the existence of this practice sharply reduces the true scope of the substantive change

It is in view of these theoretical and practical considerations that to this date 25 states,[30] have abrogated the "all or nothing" rule of contributory negligence and have enacted in its place general apportionment *statutes* calculated in one manner or another to assess liability in proportion to fault. In 1973 these states were joined by Florida, which effected the same result by *judicial* decision. (Hoffman v. Jones (Fla.1973) 280 So.2d 431.) We are likewise persuaded that logic, practical experience, and fundamental justice counsel against the retention of the doctrine rendering contributory negligence a complete bar to recovery—and that it should be replaced in this state by a system under which liability for damage will be borne by those whose negligence caused it in direct proportion to their respective fault.

The foregoing conclusion, however, clearly takes us only part of the way. It is strenuously and ably urged * * * that whatever our views on the relative merits of contributory and comparative negligence, we are precluded from making those views the law of the state by judicial decision. Moreover, it is contended, even if we are not so precluded, there exist considerations of a practical nature which should dissuade us from embarking upon the course which we have indicated. We proceed to take up these two objections in order.

II

It is urged that any change in the law of contributory negligence must be made by the Legislature, not by this court. Although the doctrine of contributory negligence is of judicial origin—its genesis being traditionally attributed to the opinion of Lord Ellenborough in Butterfield v. Forrester (K.B.1809) 103 Eng.Rep. 926—the enactment of section 1714 of the Civil Code [31] in 1872 codified the doctrine as it

effected by openly adopting comparative negligence. [¶] Thus, stability, predictability, and evenhandedness are better served by the change to comparative negligence than by adhering in theory to a law that contributory fault bars when this rule has ceased to be the law in practice." (21 Vand. L.Rev. at p. 916).

A contrary conclusion is drawn in an article by Lewis F. Powell, Jr., now an Associate Justice of the United States Supreme Court. Because a loose form of comparative negligence is already applied in practice by independent American juries, Justice Powell argues, the "all-or-nothing" rule of contributory negligence ought to be retained as a check on the jury's tendency to favor the plaintiff. (Powell, Contributory Negligence: A Necessary Check on the American Jury (1957) 43 A.B.A.J. 1005.)

30. Arkansas, Colorado, Connecticut, Georgia, Hawaii, Idaho, Maine, Massachusetts, Minnesota, Mississippi, Nebraska, Nevada, New Hampshire, New Jersey, North Dakota, Oklahoma, Oregon, Rhode Island, South Dakota, Texas, Utah, Vermont, Washington, Wisconsin, Wyoming. (Schwartz, Comparative Negligence (1974), Appendix A, pp. 367–369.) [Also, later in 1975, New York, by statute, and Alaska, judicially, Kaatz v. State, Alaska, 540 P.2d 1037. Comparative negligence obtains, furthermore, throughout Great Britain, Australia, Canada and New Zealand. (Eds.)]

In the federal sphere, comparative negligence of the "pure" type (see infra) has been the rule since 1908 in cases arising under the Federal Employers' Liability Act (see 45 U.S.C.A. § 53) and since 1920 in cases arising under the Jones Act (see 46 U.S.C.A. § 688) and the Death on the High Seas Act (see 46 U.S.C.A. § 766.)

31. Section 1714 of the Civil Code has never been amended. It provides as follows: "Everyone is responsible, not only for the result of his willful acts,

stood at that date and, the argument continues, rendered it invulnerable to attack in the courts except on constitutional grounds. Subsequent cases of this court, it is pointed out, have unanimously affirmed that—barring the appearance of some constitutional infirmity—the "all-or-nothing" rule is the law of this state and shall remain so until the Legislature directs otherwise. The fundamental constitutional doctrine of separation of powers, the argument concludes, requires judicial abstention.

We are further urged to observe that a basic distinction exists between the situation obtaining in Florida prior to the decision of that state's Supreme Court abrogating the doctrine (Hoffman v. Jones, supra, 280 So.2d 431), and the situation now confronting this court. There, to be sure, the Florida court was also faced with a statute, and the dissenting justice considered that fact sufficient to bar judicial change of the rule. The statute there in question, however, merely declared that the general English common and statute law in effect on July 4, 1776, was to be in force in Florida except to the extent it was inconsistent with federal constitutional and statutory law and acts of the state Legislature. (Fla.Stat., § 2.01, F.S.A.) The majority simply concluded that there was no clear-cut common law rule of contributory negligence prior to the 1809 *Butterfield* decision (Butterfield v. Forrester, supra, 103 Eng.Rep. 926), and that therefore that rule was not made a part of Florida law by the statute.[32] (280 So.2d at pp. 434–435.) In the instant case, defendants and the amici curiae who support them point out, the situation is quite different: here the Legislature has specifically enacted the rule of contributory negligence as the law of this state. In these circumstances, it is urged, the doctrine of separation of powers requires that any change must come from the Legislature.

We have concluded that the foregoing argument, in spite of its superficial appeal, is fundamentally misguided. * * * [I]t was not the intention of the Legislature in enacting section 1714 of the Civil Code, as well as other sections of that code declarative of the common law, to insulate the matters therein expressed from further judicial development; rather it was the intention of the Legislature to announce and formulate existing common law principles and definitions for purposes of orderly and concise presentation and with a distinct view toward continuing judicial evolution.

* * *

but also for an injury occasioned to another by his want of ordinary care or skill in the management of his property or person, *except so far as the latter has, willfully or by want of ordinary care, brought the injury upon himself.* The extent of liability in such cases is defined by the Title on Compensatory Relief." (Italics added.)

32. It should be observed that the Florida court held alternatively that even if contributory negligence *was* recognized by the common law prior to the day of American independence, and therefore was made a part of Florida law by the statute, it remained subject to judicial overruling because of its common law origin. (280 So.2d at pp. 435–436.)

III

We are thus brought to the second group of arguments which have been advanced by defendants and the amici curiae supporting their position. Generally speaking, such arguments expose considerations of a practical nature which, it is urged, counsel against the adoption of a rule of comparative negligence in this state even if such adoption is possible by judicial means.

The most serious of these considerations are those attendant upon the administration of a rule of comparative negligence in cases involving multiple parties. One such problem may arise when all responsible parties are not brought before the court: it may be difficult for the jury to evaluate relative negligence in such circumstances, and to compound this difficulty such an evaluation would not be res judicata in a subsequent suit against the absent wrongdoer. Problems of contribution and indemnity among joint tortfeasors lurk in the background. (See generally Prosser, Comparative Negligence, supra, 41 Cal.L.Rev. 1, 33–37; Schwartz, Comparative Negligence, supra, §§ 16.1–16.9, pp. 247–274.)

A second and related major area of concern involves the administration of the actual process of fact-finding in a comparative negligence system. The assigning of a specific percentage factor to the amount of negligence attributable to a particular party, while in theory a matter of little difficulty, can become a matter of perplexity in the face of hard facts. The temptation for the jury to resort to a quotient verdict in such circumstances can be great. (See Schwartz, supra, § 17.1, pp. 275–279.) These inherent difficulties are not, however, insurmountable. Guidelines might be provided the jury which will assist it in keeping focussed upon the true inquiry (see, e. g., Schwartz, supra, § 17.1, pp. 278–279), and the utilization of special verdicts or jury interrogatories can be of invaluable assistance in assuring that the jury has approached its sensitive and often complex task with proper standards and appropriate reverence. (See Schwartz, supra, § 17.4, pp. 282–291; Prosser, Comparative Negligence, supra, 41 Cal. L.Rev., pp. 28–33.)

The third area of concern, the status of the doctrines of last clear chance and assumption of risk, involves less the practical problems of administering a particular form of comparative negligence than it does a definition of the theoretical outline of the specific form to be adopted. Although several states which apply comparative negligence concepts retain the last clear chance doctrine (see Schwartz, supra, § 7.2, p. 134), the better reasoned position seems to be that when true comparative negligence is adopted, the need for last clear chance as a palliative of the hardships of the "all-or-nothing" rule disappears and its retention results only in a windfall to the plaintiff in direct contravention of the principle of liability in proportion to fault. (See Schwartz, supra, § 7.2, pp. 137–139; Prosser, Comparative Negligence, supra, 41 Cal.L.Rev., p. 27.) As for assumption of risk, we have recognized in this state that this defense overlaps that of contributory negligence to some extent and in fact is made up of at least two distinct defenses. "To simplify greatly, it has been observed * * * that in one kind of situation, to wit, where a plaintiff *unreasonably* undertakes to encounter a specific known risk imposed by a defendant's negligence, plaintiff's conduct, although he may encounter that risk in a prudent manner, is in reality a form of contributory negligence * * *. Other kinds of situations within the doctrine of assumption of risk are those, for example, where plaintiff is held to agree to relieve defendant of an obligation of reasonable conduct toward him. Such a situation would not involve contributory negligence, but rather a reduction of defendant's duty of care." (Grey v. Fibreboard Paper Products Co. (1966) 65 Cal.2d 240, 245–246, 53 Cal.Rptr. 545, 548, 418 P.2d 153, 156; see also * * *; 2 Harper & James, The Law of Torts, supra, § 21.1, pp. 1162–1168; cf. Prosser, Torts, supra, § 68, pp. 439–441.) We think it clear that the adoption of a system of comparative negligence should entail the merger of the defense of assumption of risk into the general scheme of assessment of liability in proportion to fault in those particular cases in which the form of assumption of risk involved is no more than a variant of contributory negligence. (See generally, Schwartz, supra, ch. 9, pp. 153–175.)

Finally there is the problem of the treatment of willful misconduct under a system of comparative negligence. In jurisdictions following the "all-or-nothing" rule, contributory negligence is no defense to an action based upon a claim of willful misconduct (see Restatement of Torts, Second, § 503; Prosser, Torts, supra, § 65, p. 426), and this is the present rule in California. (Williams v. Carr (1968) 68 Cal.2d 579, 583, 68 Cal.Rptr. 305, 440 P.2d 505.) As Dean Prosser has observed, "[this] is in reality a rule of comparative fault which is being applied, and the court is refusing to set up the lesser fault against the greater." (Prosser, Torts, supra, § 65, p. 426.) The thought is that the difference between willful and wanton misconduct and ordinary negligence is one of kind rather than degree in that the former involves conduct of an entirely different order,[33] and under this conception it might well be urged that comparative negligence concepts should have no application when one of the parties has been guilty of willful and wanton misconduct. It has been persuasively argued, however, that the loss of deterrent effect that would occur upon application of comparative fault concepts to willful and wanton misconduct as well as ordinary negligence would be slight, and that a comprehensive system of comparative negligence should allow for the apportionment of damages in all cases involving misconduct which falls short of being intentional. (Schwartz, supra, § 5.3, p. 108.)

33. "Disallowing the contributory negligence defense in this context is different from last clear chance; the defense is denied not because defendant had the last opportunity to avoid the accident but rather because defendant's conduct was so culpable it was different in 'kind' from the plaintiff's. The basis is culpability rather than causation." (Schwartz, supra, § 5.1, p. 100; fn. omitted.)

The law of punitive damages remains a separate consideration. (See Schwartz, supra, § 5.4, pp. 109–111.)

The existence of the foregoing areas of difficulty and uncertainty (as well as others which we have not here mentioned—see generally Schwartz, supra, § 21.1, pp. 335–339) has not diminished our conviction that the time for a revision of the means for dealing with contributory fault in this state is long past due and that it lies within the province of this court to initiate the needed change by our decision in this case. Two of the indicated areas (i. e., multiple parties and willful misconduct) are not involved in the case before us, and we consider it neither necessary nor wise to address ourselves to specific problems of this nature which might be expected to arise. As the Florida court stated with respect to the same subject, "it is not the proper function of this Court to decide unripe issues, without the benefit of adequate briefing, not involving an actual controversy, and unrelated to a specific factual situation." (Hoffman v. Jones, supra, 280 So.2d 431, 439.)

Our previous comments relating to the remaining two areas of concern (i. e., the status of the doctrines of last clear chance and assumption of risk, and the matter of judicial supervision of the finder of fact) have provided sufficient guidance to enable the trial courts of this state to meet and resolve particular problems in this area as they arise. As we have indicated, last clear chance and assumption of risk (insofar as the latter doctrine is but a variant of contributory negligence) are to be subsumed under the general process of assessing liability in proportion to fault, and the matter of jury supervision we leave for the moment within the broad discretion of the trial courts.

Our decision in this case is to be viewed as a first step in what we deem to be a proper and just direction, not as a compendium containing the answers to all questions that may be expected to arise. Pending future judicial or legislative developments, we are content for the present to assume the position taken by the Florida court in this matter: "We feel the trial judges of this State are capable of applying [a] comparative negligence rule without our setting guidelines in anticipation of expected problems. The problems are more appropriately resolved at the trial level in a practical manner instead of theoretical solution at the appellate level. The trial judges are granted broad discretion in adopting such procedures as may accomplish the objectives and purposes expressed in this opinion." (280 So.2d at pp. 439–440.)

It remains to identify the precise form of comparative negligence which we now adopt for application in this state. Although there are many variants, only the two basic forms need be considered here. The first of these, the so-called "pure" form of comparative negligence, apportions liability in direct proportion to fault in all cases. This was the form adopted by the Supreme Court of Florida in Hoffman v. Jones, supra, and it applies by statute in Mississippi, Rhode Island, and Washington. Moreover, it is the form favored by most scholars and commentators. (See, e. g., Prosser, Comparative Negligence, supra, 41 Cal.L.Rev. 1, 21–25; Prosser, Torts, supra, § 67, pp. 437–438; Schwartz, supra, § 21.3, pp. 341–348; Comments on Maki v. Frelk—Comparative v. Contributory Negligence: Should the Court or Legislature Decide?, supra, 21 Vand.L.Rev. 889 (Comment by Keeton at p. 906, Comment by Leflar at p. 918).) The second basic form of comparative negligence, of which there are several variants, applies apportionment based on fault *up to the point* at which the plaintiff's negligence is equal to or greater than that of the defendant—when that point is reached, plaintiff is barred from recovery. Nineteen states have adopted this form or one of its variants by statute. The principal argument advanced in its favor is moral in nature: that it is not morally right to permit one more at fault in an accident to recover from one less at fault. Other arguments assert the probability of increased insurance, administrative, and judicial costs if a "pure" rather than a "50 percent" system is adopted, but this has been seriously questioned. (See authorities cited in Schwartz, supra, § 21.3, pp. 344–346; see also Vincent v. Pabst Brewing Co. (1970) 47 Wis.2d 120, 138, 177 N.W.2d 513 (dissenting opinion).)

We have concluded that the "pure" form of comparative negligence is that which should be adopted in this state. In our view the "50 percent" system simply shifts the lottery aspect of the contributory negligence rule [34] to a different ground. As Dean Prosser has noted, under such a system "[i]t is obvious that a slight difference in the proportionate fault may permit a recovery; and there has been much justified criticism of a rule under which a plaintiff who is charged with 49 percent of a total negligence recovers 51 percent of his damages, while one who is charged with 50 percent recovers nothing at all." [35] Prosser, Comparative Negligence, supra, 41 Cal.L.Rev. 1, 25; fns. omitted.) In effect "such a rule distorts the very principle it recognizes, i. e., that persons are responsible for their acts to the extent their fault contributes to an injurious result. The partial rule simply lowers, but does not eliminate, the bar of contributory negligence." (Juenger, Brief for Negligence Law Section of the State Bar of Michigan in Support of Comparative Negligence as Amicus Curiae, Parsonson v. Construction Equipment Company, supra, 18 Wayne L. Rev. 3, 50; see also Schwartz, supra, § 21.3, p. 347.)

34. "The rule that contributory fault bars completely is a curious departure from the central principle of nineteenth century Anglo-American tort law—that wrongdoers should bear the losses they cause. Comparative negligence more faithfully serves that central principle by causing the wrongdoers to share the burden of resulting losses in reasonable relation to their wrongdoing, rather than allocating the heavier burden to the one who, as luck would have it, happened to be more seriously injured." (Comments on Maki v. Frelk, supra, 21 Vand.L.Rev. 889, Comment by Keeton, pp. 912–913.)

35. This problem is compounded when the injurious result is produced by the combined negligence of several parties. For example in a three-car collision a plaintiff whose negligence amounts to one-third or more recovers nothing; in a four-car collision the plaintiff is barred if his negligence is only one-quarter of the total. (See Juenger, Brief for Negligence Law Section of the State Bar of Michigan in Support of Comparative Negligence as Amicus Curiae, Parsonson v. Construction Equipment Company (1972) 18 Wayne L.Rev. 3, 50–51.)

We also consider significant the experience of the State of Wisconsin, which until recently was considered the leading exponent of the "50 percent" system. There that system led to numerous appeals on the narrow but crucial issue whether plaintiff's negligence was equal to defendant's. (See Prosser, Comparative Negligence, supra, 41 Cal.L.Rev. 1, 23–25.) Numerous reversals have resulted on this point, leading to the development of arcane classifications of negligence according to quality and category. (See cases cited in Vincent v. Pabst Brewing Co., supra, 47 Wis.2d 120, at p. 137, 177 N.W.2d 513 (dissenting opinion).) This finally led to a frontal attack on the system in the *Vincent* case, cited above, wherein the state supreme court was urged to replace the statutory "50 percent" rule by a judicially declared "pure" comparative negligence rule. The majority of the court rejected this invitation, concluding that the Legislature had occupied the field, but three concurring justices and one dissenter indicated their willingness to accept it if the Legislature failed to act with reasonable dispatch. The dissenting opinion of Chief Justice Hallows, which has been cited above, stands as a persuasive testimonial in favor of the "pure" system. We wholeheartedly embrace its reasoning. (See also, Hoffman v. Jones, supra, 280 So.2d 431, 438–439.)

For all of the foregoing reasons we conclude that the "all-or-nothing" rule of contributory negligence as it presently exists in this state should be and is herewith superseded by a system of "pure" comparative negligence, the fundamental purpose of which shall be to assign responsibility and liability for damage in direct proportion to the amount of negligence of each of the parties. Therefore, in all actions for negligence resulting in injury to person or property, the contributory negligence of the person injured in person or property shall not bar recovery, but the damages awarded shall be diminished in proportion to the amount of negligence attributable to the person recovering. The doctrine of last clear chance is abolished, and the defense of assumption of risk is also abolished to the extent that it is merely a variant of the former doctrine of contributory negligence; both of these are to be subsumed under the general process of assessing liability in proportion to negligence. Pending future judicial or legislative developments, the trial courts of this state are to use broad discretion in seeking to assure that the principle stated is applied in the interest of justice and in furtherance of the purposes and objectives set forth in this opinion.

It remains for us to determine the extent to which the rule here announced shall have application to cases other than those which are commenced in the future. * * * Upon mature reflection, in view of the very substantial number of cases involving the matter here at issue which are now pending in the trial and appellate courts of this state, and with particular attention to considerations of reliance applicable to individual cases according to the stage of litigation which they have reached, we have concluded that a rule of limited retroactivity should obtain here. Accordingly we hold that the present opinion shall be applicable to all cases in which trial has not begun before the date this decision becomes final in this court, but that it shall not be applicable to any case in which trial began before that date (other than the instant case)—except that if any judgment be reversed on appeal for other reasons, this opinion shall be applicable to any retrial.

* * *

WRIGHT, C. J., and TOBRINER and BURKE, JJ., concur.

MOSK, JUSTICE (concurring and dissenting).

Although I concur in the judgment and agree with the substance of the majority opinion, I dissent from its cavalier treatment of the recurring problem of the manner of applying a new court-made rule.

* * *

CLARK, JUSTICE (dissenting).

I dissent.

For over a century this court has consistently and unanimously held that Civil Code section 1714 codifies the defense of contributory negligence. Suddenly—after 103 years—the court declares section 1714 shall provide for comparative negligence instead. In my view, this action constitutes a gross departure from established judicial rules and role.

* * *

The majority decision also departs significantly from the recognized limitation upon judicial action—encroaching on the powers constitutionally entrusted to the Legislature. * * *

Further, the Legislature is the branch best able to effect transition from contributory to comparative or some other doctrine of negligence. Numerous and differing negligence systems have been urged over the years, yet there remains widespread disagreement among both the commentators and the states as to which one is best. (See Schwartz, Comparative Negligence (1974) Appendix A, pp. 367–369 and § 21.3, fn. 40, pp. 341–342, and authorities cited therein.) This court is not an investigatory body, and we lack the means of fairly appraising the merits of these competing systems. Constrained by settled rules of judicial review, we must consider only matters within the record or susceptible to judicial notice. That this court is inadequate to the task of carefully selecting the best replacement system is reflected in the majority's summary manner of eliminating from consideration *all but two* of the many competing proposals—including models adopted by some of our sister states.[36]

Contrary to the majority's assertions of judicial adequacy, the courts of other states—with near unanimity—have conceded their in-

36. "It remains to identify the precise form of comparative negligence which we now adopt for application in this state. Although there are many variants, only the two basic forms need be considered here." (Ante, p. 874 of 119 Cal.Rptr., p. 1242 of 532 P.2d.)

ability to determine the best system for replacing contributory negligence, concluding instead that the legislative branch is best able to resolve the issue.[37]

By abolishing this century old doctrine today, the majority seriously erodes our constitutional function. We are again guilty of judicial chauvinism.

McCOMB, J., concurs.

IMPERIAL CHEMICAL INDUSTRIES v. SHATWELL

House of Lords [1965] A.C. 656; [1964] 3 W.L.R. 329; 108 S.J. 578; [1964] 2 All E.R. 999.

LORD REID: My Lords, this case arises out of the accidental explosion of a charge at a quarry belonging to the appellants which caused injuries to the respondent George Shatwell and his brother James, who were both qualified shot firers. On June 28, 1960, these two men and another shot firer, Beswick, had bored and filled fifty shot holes and had inserted electric detonators and connected them up in series. Before firing it was necessary to test the circuit for continuity. This should have been done by connecting long wires so that the men could go to a shelter some eighty yards away and test from there. They had not sufficient wire with them, and Beswick went off to get more. The testing ought not to have been done until signals had been given so that other men could take shelter and these signals were not due to be given for at least another hour.

Soon after Beswick had left George said to his brother: "Must we test them?" meaning shall we test them, and James said "Yes." The testing is done by passing a weak current through the circuit in which a small galvanometer is included and if the needle of the instrument moves when a connection is made the circuit is in order. So George got a galvanometer and James handed two short wires to him. Then George applied the wires to the galvanometer and the needle did not move. This showed that the circuit was defective so the two men went round inspecting the connections. They saw nothing wrong and George said that that meant there was a dud detonator somewhere, and decided to apply the galvanometer to each individual detonator. James handed two other wires to him and George used them to apply the galvanometer to the first detonator. The result was an explosion which injured both men.

37. See, e. g., Codling v. Paglia (1973) 32 N.Y.2d 330, 344–345, 345 N.Y.S.2d 461, 298 N.E.2d 622; McGraw v. Corrin (Del.Supr.1973) 303 A.2d 641, 644; Bridges v. Union Railroad Company (1971) 26 Utah 2d 281, 488 P.2d 738; Parsonson v. Constr. Equipment Co. (1970) 386 Mich. 61, 191 N.W.2d 465 (concurring opinion); Krise v. Gillund (N.D.1971) 184 N.W.2d 405; Peterson v. Culp (1970) 255 Or. 269, 465 P.2d 876; Vincent v. Pabst Brewing Co. (1970) 47 Wis.2d 120, 177 N.W.2d 513; Maki v. Frelk (1968) 40 Ill.2d 193, 239 N.E.2d 445; compare Hoffman v. Jones (Fla.1973) 280 So.2d 431. [Notes 27–37 from original, renumbered; other notes in original omitted.]

This method had been regularly used without mishap until the previous year. Then some research done by the appellants showed that it might be unsafe and in October 1959, the appellants gave orders that testing must in future be done from a shelter and a lecture was given to all the shot firers, including the Shatwells, explaining the position. Then in December 1959, new statutory regulations were made (1959, No. 2259) probably because the Ministry had been informed of the results of the appellants' research. These regulations came into operation in February 1960, and the Shatwells were aware of them. But some of the shot firers appear to have gone on in the old way. An instance of this came to the notice of the management in May 1960, and the management took immediate action and revoked the shot firing certificate of the disobedient man, and told the other shot firers about this. George admitted in evidence that he knew all this. He admitted that they would only have had to wait ten minutes until Beswick returned with the long wires. When asked why he did not wait, his only excuse was that he could not be bothered to wait.

George now sues the appellants on the ground that he and his brother were equally to blame for this accident, and that the appellants are vicariously liable for his brother's conduct. He has been awarded £1,500, being half the agreed amount of his loss. There is no question of the appellants having been in breach of the regulation because the duty under the regulation is laid on the shot firer personally. So counsel for George frankly and rightly admitted that if George had sued James personally instead of suing his employer the issue would have been the same. If this decision is right it means that if two men collaborate in doing what they know is dangerous and is forbidden and as a result both are injured, each has a cause of action against the other.

The appellants have two grounds of defence, first that James' conduct had no causal connection with the accident, the sole cause being George's own fault, and secondly, *volenti non fit injuria.* I am of opinion that they are entitled to succeed on the latter ground but I must deal shortly with the former ground * * *.

* * * I think that James' conduct did have a causal connection with this accident. It is far from clear that George would have gone on with the test if James had not agreed with him. But perhaps more important James did collaborate with him in making the test in a forbidden and unlawful way. His collaboration may not have amounted to much but it was not negligible. * * *

* * * [R]ecently it appears to have been thought in some quarters that, at least as between master and servant, *volenti non fit injuria* is a dead or dying defence. That I think is because in most cases where the defence would now be available it has become usual to base the decision on contributory negligence. Where the plantiff's own disobedient act is the sole cause of his injury it does not matter in the result whether one says 100 per cent. contributory negligence or *volenti non fit injuria.* But it does matter in a case like the pres-

ent. If we adopt the inaccurate habit of using the word "negligence" to denote a deliberate act done with full knowledge of the risk it is not surprising that we sometimes get into difficulties. I think that most people would say, without stopping to think of the reason, that there is a world of difference between two fellow-servants collaborating carelessly so that the acts of both contribute to cause injury to one of them, and two fellow-servants combining to disobey an order deliberately though they know the risk involved. It seems reasonable that the injured man should recover some compensation in the former case but not in the latter. If the law treats both as merely cases of negligence it cannot draw a distinction. But in my view the law does and should draw a distinction. In the first case only the partial defence of contributory negligence is available. In the second *volenti non fit injuria* is a complete defence if the employer is not himself at fault and is only liable vicariously for the acts of the fellow-servant. If the plaintiff invited or freely aided and abetted his fellow-servant's disobedience, then he was *volens* in the fullest sense. He cannot complain of the resulting injury either against the fellow-servant or against the master on the ground of his vicarious responsibility for his fellow-servant's conduct. I need not here consider the common case where the servant's disobedience puts the master in breach of a statutory obligation and it would be wrong to decide in advance whether that would make any difference. * * *

I entirely agree that an employer who is himself at fault in persistently refusing to comply with a statutory rule could not possibly be allowed to escape liability because the injured workman had agreed to waive the breach. * * * [38]

KALECHMAN v. DREW AUTO RENTAL, INC.

Court of Appeals of New York, 1973.
33 N.Y.2d 397, 353 N.Y.S.2d 414, 308 N.E.2d 886.

WACHTLER, JUDGE.

On April 2, 1968, Hersz Kalechman, a 26-year-old sales technician employed by Speizman Knitting Machine Company (Speizman) was killed in a collision between a truck and an automobile owned by the defendant Drew Auto Rental, Inc. At the time of the accident, Kalechman was a passenger in the defendant's automobile en route to Mexico to develop new territory for his employer. The car which was on an extended lease to Speizman was being driven by David Trigub, Kalechman's father-in-law, who although not an employee of Speizman, had gone along to share expenses and help Kalechman with the driving.

38. This case is discussed in Atiyah, Causation, Contributory Negligence and Volenti Non Fit Injuria, 43 Can. B.Rev. 609 (1965); Brodetsky, Employees' Joint Breach of Statutory Duty: *Volenti* Not Barred, 27 Mod. L.Rev. 733 (1964); Dias, Consent of Parties and *Voluntas Legis*, [1966] Cam.L.J. 75; and Lewis, Master and Servant—Breach of Statutory Duty—*Volenti non fit injuria*, [1964] Cam.L. J. 194.

The accident occurred when Trigub, proceeding westbound on a two-lane highway, crossed the dividing line and entered the eastbound lane, accelerating to approximately 60 hours an hour in order to pass two trucks. After passing one truck he drew abreast of the other which suddenly turned left in front of him.

Kalechman was survived by two infant children (one born posthumously) and his wife, the plaintiff, who as administratrix of his estate commenced this action for wrongful death and conscious pain and suffering. Drew Auto Rental, the owner of the vehicle, is the only defendant named in the action and its liability rests entirely on section 388 of the Vehicle and Traffic Law, McK.Consol.Laws, c. 71, which states: "Every owner of a vehicle used or operated in this state shall be liable and responsible for death or injuries to person or property resulting from negligence in the use or operation of such vehicle, in the business of such owner or otherwise, by any person using or operating the same with the permission, express or implied, of such owner."

The sole issue on this appeal is whether the driver's negligence should be imputed to the passenger so as to bar any recovery against the owner under section 388 of the Vehicle and Traffic Law.

* * * The Appellate Division, Second Department * * * [held] that the deceased, as custodian of the vehicle "had dominion and control over Trigub and the latter's negligence must therefore be imputed to him in an action against the owner". * * *

The leading case is Gochee v. Wagner, 257 N.Y. 344, 178 N.E. 553. In *Gochee* the plaintiff passenger was the owner of the automobile which was being driven by his wife when it collided with the defendant's vehicle. In a suit by the plaintiff for personal injuries and property damage to his vehicle the jury found that both drivers were negligent.

This court held that the contributory negligence of the driver should be imputed to the owner because "he was present and had the legal right to control [the] operation" of the vehicle (*Gochee*, supra, at p. 348, 178 N.E. at p. 554).

Subsequently in a brief series of cases the doctrine was alternately extended and limited. It has been extended to impute the driver's negligence to a passenger who is either a lessee (Ullery v. National Car Rental System, 23 N.Y.2d 677, 295 N.Y.S.2d 929, 243 N.E.2d 148) or a sublessee (Kleinman v. Frank, 34 A.D.2d 121, 309 N.Y.S.2d 651, affd., 28 N.Y.2d 603, 319 N.Y.S.2d 852, 268 N.E.2d 648) in an action against the owner or a third party. It has been limited so that the driver's negligence will not be imputed to the passenger where the driver has an equal right (Jenks v. Veeder Contr. Co., 264 App.Div. 979, 37 N.Y.S.2d 230, affd., 290 N.Y. 810, 50 N.E.2d 231) or a superior right to control the operation of the vehicle (Ullery v. National Car Rental System, supra) or where the action is against the driver himself. (Kleinman v. Frank, supra.)

The rule that has emerged can be stated as follows:

> The driver's negligence will be imputed to the passenger to defeat his action whenever the passenger has the exclusive authority to control the operation of the vehicle, except in a case where the driver himself is the defendant.

Turning to the case at bar, it is obvious that the passenger Kalechman, as the employee of the lessee, had custody and control of the vehicle. Unless the plaintiff was able to show that Trigub had been granted equal or superior authority over the operation of the vehicle the driver's negligence must be imputed to the passenger. On this point the plaintiff notes that certain officers of the Speizman Co. had been informed that Kalechman intended to take his father-in-law on the trip; but since there is no allegation or indication that Trigub was given any right to control the operation of the vehicle, the plaintiff has failed to demonstrate a triable issue (compare Ullery v. National Car Rental System, supra).

Thus the application of *Gochee* and its progeny is clear * * *.

One of the most frequently made and obvious criticisms of the doctrine of imputed contributory negligence is that it rests on a legal fiction which has no basis in reality. (See, e. g., * * *. Lessler, Proposed Discard of the Doctrine of Imputed Contributory Negligence, 20 Fordham L.Rev. 156; Imputed Negligence in Automobile Accident Cases, 16 St.John's L.Rev. 222.)

However in fairness to the rule it should be noted that at the time of its inception it apparently represented a realistic appraisal of the relationship between passenger and driver. One commentator has offered the following explanation of the genesis of the rule: "If the owner of a wagon and team handed the reins over to a passenger and let him drive, control of the horses was within easy reach. If he didn't think the driver reined up fast enough at a railroad crossing, he could reach out and resume control. * * * Actual control was a possibility, not a fiction." (Op. cit., 16 St.John's L.Rev. 222.) But with the advent of the modern automobile there is no longer any basis for assuming that the passenger, no matter what his relationship to the driver may be, has the capacity to assert control over or direct the operation of a moving automobile. The design of the vehicle, the high speeds at which it travels, the split second timing which is often necessary to avoid collision have all combined to erode the assumption that anyone other than the driver can effectively control the operation of the vehicle in traffic.

In fact, under modern driving conditions anyone who "allows another to drive would only increase the risk of accidents by interfering with the driver's control of the car or by diverting his attention" (op. cit., 16 St.John's L.Rev. 222). Although it might have been practical in the past, the modern highway is clearly the wrong place to assert the right to control. "Certainly assertion of such rights in the course of operation is not timely, nor in the interest of public safety." * * *

Thus the concept now rests on a pure legal fiction, which insofar as it assumes or encourages interference with the driver's function, conflicts with public policy. All this serves to illustrate the wisdom of CARDOZO'S celebrated observation that "Precedents drawn from the days of travel by stage coach do not fit the conditions of travel to-day." (MacPherson v. Buick Motor Co., 217 N.Y. 382, 391, 111 N.E. 1050, 1053.)

A more telling criticism of the doctrine of imputed or vicarious contributory negligence is that it is an illegitimate offspring of the vicarious liability concept, which only serves to frustrate the broad policy goals of the parent rule.

Obviously if the doctrine has any conceptual validity it must work both ways. If the passenger's responsibility for the driver's conduct is sufficient to destroy his claim against a third party, it should also be sufficient to impose liability on the passenger in an action by a third party. (See, e. g., Little v. Hackett, 116 U.S. 366, 6 S.Ct. 391, 29 L.Ed. 652; Gregory, Vicarious Responsibility and Contributory Negligence, 41 Yale L.Rev. 831; Prosser, Torts, [4th ed.] p. 488; 2 Harper and James, Torts, 1264; Restatement of Torts, Second § 485.) This so-called "both-ways test" which has the appeal of formal symmetry and fairness was originally envisioned as a "vehicle for humane law reform" (2 Harper and James, op. cit., p. 1273).

This limitation is undoubtedly correct as far as it goes, for it would clearly be absurd to hold the plaintiff passenger guilty of contributory negligence when he would bear no responsibility for the driver's acts had he (the passenger) been made a defendant in the action. However even with this limitation the doctrine of imputed contributory negligence remains indefensible. To treat it as a natural compliment to vicarious liability leads to a paradox for "a rule which departed from the common law in response to an urge towards wider liability is being used to curtail liability by expanding the scope of a defense to it." (2 Harper and James, op. cit., p. 1274; see, also, Continental Auto Lease Corp. v. Campbell, 19 N.Y.2d 350, 280 N.Y.S. 2d 123, 227 N.E.2d 28.)

But the most unfortunate consequence of the doctrine of imputed contributory negligence as it presently functions in this State is that it primarily serves to bar claims for personal injury and death. It is only in suits for property damage that we have been able—to some extent—to limit its application. Thus in Continental v. Campbell (supra) we reaffirmed the rule of Mills v. Gabriel, 284 N.Y. 755, 31 N.E.2d 512, holding that section 388 of the Vehicle and Traffic Law which imputes to an absentee owner the negligence of his driver, for the purpose of imposing liability for injury to a third party, may not be used to impute contributory negligence to the absentee owner in an action to recover for property damages to his vehicle.

In sum the *Gochee* rule is based on an unrealistic fiction, conceptually flawed, serves no useful social purpose and frustrates the express public policy "that one injured by the negligent operation of a motor vehicle should have recourse to a financially responsible defendant. The owner of the automobile [being] the obvious candidate". *Continental*, supra, 19 N.Y.2d at p. 352, 280 N.Y.S.2d at p. 124, 227 N.E.2d at p. 29.) It survives only as a remnant of the past reflecting a period in the history of the common law when the relationship between the passenger and the driver was generally considered to be a relevant circumstance in determining the passenger's right to recover for injuries. (See Prosser, op. cit., p. 488.)

But it no longer has any place in the present scheme of tort liability where the paramount consideration is to give full effect to the "vital interest of society in protecting people from losses resulting from [vehicular] accidents" (Gelbman v. Gelbman, 23 N.Y.2d 434, 439, 297 N.Y.S.2d 529, 532, 245 N.E.2d 192, 194). In accord with this policy the modern tendency, both in this court and the Legislature, has been to abolish or refuse to adopt defenses based on the relationship between the passenger and the negligent driver and to substitute the more desirable rule that the passenger's right to recover should depend solely upon his own conduct in actually controlling the vehicle or in failing to exercise control or to take such action as is reasonably required by the circumstances. Thus in this State we have abandoned the defense of intra-family immunity (Gelbman v. Gelbman, supra), rejected the guest statute concept (see Babcock v. Jackson, 12 N.Y.2d 473, 482, 240 N.Y.S.2d 743, 749, 191 N.E.2d 279, 283) and abolished the common-law doctrines imputing the negligence of a parent to a child (Domestic Relations Law, McK.Consol.Laws, c. 14, former § 73), the child to the parent (4 N.Y.Jurisprudence, Automobiles, § 416) or one spouse to another spouse (Michelson v. Stuhlman, 272 N.Y. 163, 5 N.E.2d 185).

Clearly we have reached the point where the general rule now is that the passenger's right to recover should not be barred merely because he bears some special relationship to the driver—a rule to which *Gochee* represents a somewhat incongruous exception. * * *

We have therefore concluded that Gochee v. Wagner should be overruled, and that the general rule should be applied without exception by allowing the plaintiff passenger to recover for negligent operation of the vehicle—no matter what his relationship to the driver may be—unless it is shown that his own personal negligence contributed to the injury. * * *

DASHIELL v. KEAUHOU-KONA COMPANY

United States Court of Appeals for the Ninth Circuit, 1973.
487 F.2d 957.

Before KOELSCH, WRIGHT and TRASK, CIRCUIT JUDGES.

TRASK, CIRCUIT JUDGE:

This is an appeal from a judgment of the district court, pursuant to a special verdict by a six-member jury, that the contributory negligence of Mrs. Dashiell barred both herself and her husband from recovering for injuries received when the golf cart which Mrs. Dashiell was driving and in which Mr. Dashiell was riding, collided with a truck following a ride down an incline during which Mrs. Dashiell lost control of the cart. * * *

The theories of liability pleaded against the golf course defendants centered around negligent construction of and directions on the cart paths; negligence in supplying a cart that was dangerous to use on steep inclines and in failing to warn of that danger; and negligence in failing to warn of the defects alleged in the braking system and steering mechanism of the cart. * * *

The jury found in the form of a special verdict that (1) the golf course defendants were negligent, and their negligence was a proximate cause of the acccident; * * * (3) Mr. Dashiell was not contributorily negligent; (4) Mrs. Dashiell was contributorily negligent, and her negligence was a proximate cause of the accident * * *. * * *

The trial court found as a matter of law that because the Dashiells were engaged in a joint enterprise, the negligence of Mrs. Dashiell that contributed to the accident so as to bar her recovery must be imputed to her husband so as to bar his recovery. * * *

The appellants argue that the facts of this case do not support a finding of a joint enterprise or venture, and that even if they did, this theory of tort law is so discredited that the Hawaiian courts would not today apply the rule of imputed contributory negligence. * * *

Appellees contend that Mrs. Dashiell was acting as agent for her husband while driving the golf cart, and that the Supreme Court of Hawaii in Wong v. McCandless, 31 Haw. 750, 761–762 (1931), has at least by way of dictum adopted the imputed contributory negligence theory.

We find that on the facts of this case, at no time did the relationship of joint enterprise or joint venture exist between Mr. and Mrs. Dashiell within the meaning of imputed negligence. This is not a typical case of a business venture of a character similar to a partnership where two or more parties undertake, for some pecuniary purpose, a contractual obligation resulting in the liability of each for the negligence of the other. Because the evidence was insufficient to allow the issue of joint enterprise to go to the jury where a husband

and wife were merely enjoying a round of golf, the trial court should have ruled as a matter of law that any contributory negligence of Mrs. Dashiell could not be imputed to her husband. * * *

The concept of imputed contributory negligence developed on the basis of a fictitious agency applied to defeat the recovery of an injured plaintiff by imputing the negligence of another to him, even though the plaintiff would not have been liable for that negligence had he been sued as a defendant. It had its beginnings in England where it was followed for a relatively short period of time before being overruled.[39] It has been severely criticized by both courts and commentators in this country.[40] Prosser notes that

> "[e]xcept for vestigial remnants which are at most moribund historical survivals, 'imputed contributory negligence' in its own right has now disappeared." W. Prosser, Law of Torts § 74 at 488 (4th ed. 1971). * * *

Several reasons persuade us to reject the imputation of Mrs. Dashiell's negligence to Mr. Dashiell. The Restatement of Torts, Second § 491 at 548, comment c, states the law to be:

> "The elements which are essential to a joint enterprise are commonly stated to be four: (1) an agreement, express or implied, among the members of the group; (2) a common purpose to be carried out by the group; (3) a community of pecuniary interest in that purpose, among the members; and (4) an equal right to a voice in the direction of the enterprise, which gives an equal right to control. * * *"

In Dias v. Kamalani, * * * 39 Haw. [474] at 477–479 [(1952)], the Supreme Court of Hawaii stated that among other considerations, a joint enterprise is "voluntarily assumed and arising wholly *ex contractu*," and that the factor of joint control "is more readily inferable where the trip is for a business venture than where it is for a pleasure venture." There is no suggestion in the present case that appellants' activities were anything more than social, nor can there by any reasonable inference by reason of the marital relationship alone that appellants undertook any contractual obligation which should cause each to be chargeable for the negligence of the other. "* * * [T]he great weight of modern authority finds no basis for imputing the negligence of one spouse to another merely because of the marital

39. Thorogood v. Bryan, 8 C.B. 115, 137 Eng.Rep. 452 (1849), overruled, The Bernina, 13 App.Cas. 1 (1888). See Clerk & Lindsell, Torts, 995 (13th ed. 1969); Salmond, Torts, 1704–05 (15th ed.), where it is discussed under the name of "the doctrine of identification". See also, Harper & James, The Law of Torts, ¶ 23.2, at 1267 (1956).

40. Miller v. Union Pacific R. R. Co., 290 U.S. 227, 231–232, 54 S.Ct. 172, 78 L.Ed. 285 (1933); 3 Cooley, Torts, ¶ 492, at 440–45 (4th ed. 1932); Harper & James, The Law of Torts, supra, ¶ 23.2, at 1267–70; W. Prosser, The Law of Torts, § 74 (4th ed. 1971); Restatement of Torts, Second ¶ 485 at 542 (1965). [Notes 39 and 40 from original, renumbered; other notes in original omitted.]

relationship itself." Harper & James, The Law of Torts ¶ 23.4 at 1271 (1956). See also W. Prosser, The Law of Torts, 490 (4th ed. 1971) * * *.

The only exception is found in the law of some community property states to prevent the negligent spouse from profiting from his own wrongdoing, as a result of his community ownership of a part of the recovery by the non-negligent spouse. * * *

Additionally, applying the concept of imputed contributory negligence to the facts of this case would needlessly frustrate some basic policies of tort law. Mr. Dashiell was found by the jury to be blameless, and since negligence law is based on personal fault, it would be both illogical and inequitable to deny him recovery unless he were under a duty to control the actions of Mrs. Dashiell as she drove the golf cart. The record reflects no basis on which to find any duty of control. The original purpose of defining the joint enterprise relationship was vicarious liability, in order to increase the number of those liable to provide a financially responsible person to injured third parties. See Pierson v. Edstrom, 286 Minn. 164, 174 N.W.2d 712, 715 (1970). That purpose is absent when related to the Dashiells; in fact, application of the imputed contributory negligence rule would have the opposite effect of freeing from liability another party who is at fault even though the person denied recovery is blameless. * *

We reject the bar against Mr. Dashiell's recovery based upon imputation of Mrs. Dashiell's negligence merely by reason of their common recreational interest or any supposed shared right of control of the golf cart. * * *

KOELSCH, CIRCUIT JUDGE (dissenting).

* * *

This court, until now, has consistently taken the position that, in diversity cases such as this, "The district court's considered view as to the law of the state in which it sits is entitled to great weight, and will be accepted on review unless shown to be clearly wrong." * * *

HANDELAND v. BROWN

Supreme Court of Iowa, 1974.
Iowa, 216 N.W.2d 574.

MCCORMICK, JUSTICE. In this case of first impression we are required to decide whether a parental claim for medical expense and loss of services, companionship and society under rule 8, Rules of Civil Procedure, is subject to a defense based on the injured child's contributory negligence. Trial court held it is. We disagree and reverse and remand.

Vincent Handeland is the minor son of plaintiff Ronald D. Handeland. On September 10, 1971, Vincent was operating a borrowed motorcycle in Des Moines. He was injured when he collided at an intersection with an automobile driven by defendant Jane Eileen Brown and owned by defendant Dennis Brown.

Litigation ensued. Vincent, through plaintiff as next friend, brought a negligence action against defendants seeking to recover for his injuries. Plaintiff joined the action individually to assert his rule 8 claim based on Vincent's injuries. Rule 8, R.C.P., provides, "A parent, or the parents, may sue for the expense and actual loss of services, companionship and society resulting from injury to or death of a minor child." Defendants pleaded a defense based on Vincent's alleged contributory negligence in bar of plaintiff's claim as well as Vincent's claim. * * *

The jury returned its verdict for defendants on both claims. Plaintiff alone appealed. The sole issue, squarely presented, is whether trial court erred in instructing the jury a defense of contributory negligence good against Vincent would also be good against plaintiff.

The position taken by trial court is supported by cases decided in other jurisdictions but not by logic. Our choice is whether we will be persuaded to follow a rule because it is generally followed elsewhere or reject it because we believe it is unsound.

The general rule is stated in § 494, Restatement of Torts, Second:

> "The plaintiff is barred from recovery for an invasion of his legally protected interest in the health or life of a third person which results from the harm or death of such third person, if the negligence of such third person would have barred his own recovery."

In the Appendix to that section the authors say the rule is supported by the great majority of cases which have considered it. Cases from several jurisdictions are cited for the principle. The authors recognize the rule has been much criticized on the ground the action is independent and not derivative. A number of law review citations are listed. A Canadian case, Wasney v. Jurazsky, 41 Man. 46, 1 D.L.R. 616 (Can.1933), is cited in opposition to the rule. See Restatement of Torts, Second, § 494 (App.1966). Other authorities are collected in an annotation at 21 A.L.R.3d 469 et seq.

Analysis of the cases shows four independent bases relied on by the courts applying the restatement rule: (1) the plaintiff's action is "derivative"; (2) the negligence of the injured party is "imputed" to the plaintiff; (3) the plaintiff receives his cause of action by "assignment" from the injured person; and (4) the rule should be followed because it is well-settled. Although defendants cite cases from other jurisdictions in support of each basis, they choose to defend only the fourth basis. Since its strength depends upon the persuasiveness of the cases by which the general rule arose, we will discuss each basis.

I. *The derivative action theory.* Illustrative of cases in the first category is Dudley v. Phillips, 218 Tenn. 648, 405 S.W.2d 468 (1966). There, without saying why, the court held, "[A] cause of action arising in favor of the parent resulting from a tort committed against the child is derivative in nature and such action is subject to the same defenses that are available in the action arising in favor of the child." 405 S.W.2d at 471.

We rejected the derivative action rationale as applied to a rule 8 claim in Irlbeck v. Pomeroy, 210 N.W.2d 831, 833 (Iowa 1973) ("Under rule 8 the parent has a cause of action for a legal wrong to himself independent of that of the child."); see also Wardlow v. City of Keokuk, 190 N.W.2d 439, 443 (Iowa 1971). In Irlbeck we distinguished rule 8 claims from truly derivative actions, such as wrongful death actions, which are brought by one person to redress a wrong done to another rather than himself. A rule 8 claim is brought by a parent to redress a wrong done to himself rather than another.

We cannot use the derivative action shibboleth as a basis for adopting the restatement rule.

II. *The imputed negligence theory.* The imputed negligence rationale had its genesis in a federal case purporting to apply Iowa law, Chicago, B. & Q. R. Co. v. Honey, 63 F. 39 (8 Cir. 1894). It was an action by a husband for medical expense and lost consortium by reason of injuries to his wife. The court held the plaintiff was barred from recovery by his wife's contributory fault because he vouched for her ability to avoid injury by permitting her to go out unattended, and it is thus reasonable to hold him responsible for the manner in which her faculties of self-preservation were exercised. This rule was equated to a rule then extant in Iowa which would impute the wife's contributory negligence to the husband in an action against a third party for damages to a horse and carriage owned by the husband but operated with his consent by the wife.

The latter rule was repudiated when the family purpose doctrine was rejected in McMartin v. Saemisch, 254 Iowa 45, 116 N.W.2d 491 (1962), where the Honey case was referred to as "an interesting discussion of the old law" and distinguished. The court held the family use doctrine was based on obsolete concepts. Since they were no longer viable, the doctrine itself was repudiated. Cf. Stuart v. Pilgrim, 247 Iowa 709, 74 N.W.2d 212 (1956).

Another strand of reasoning in the Honey case treated the family relationship itself as a reason for imputing contributory negligence. Permitting recovery where someone in the household was contributorily negligent was considered unjust enrichment of the family treasury. That thinking was rejected by this court long ago. See Wymore v. Mahaska County, 78 Iowa 396, 43 N.W. 264 (1889) (parent's negligence not imputed to his child); Watson v. Wabash, 66 Iowa 164, 23 N.W. 380 (1885) (child's negligence not imputed to his parent).
* * *

The reasoning of the Honey case cannot withstand critical analysis. We have implicitly disapproved it; now we explicitly do so. It rests on an archaic and discredited view of familial responsibility. We refuse to accept imputed negligence as a basis for adopting the restatement rule.

III. *The assignment theory.* The third category of cases is rooted in an assignment theory posited in Callies v. Reliance Laundry Co., 188 Wis. 376, 206 N.W. 198 (1925). This theory essentially rests on the same foundation as the derivative action theory with which it is often equated. Basically, the assignment rationale is an effort to explain why the parental action can be called derivative. The Wisconsin court held the parental cause of action for lost services is assigned to the parent by operation of law in return for the parental support obligation. The court said, "The parent takes by operation of law a part of the child's cause of action, and he must take it as the child leaves it." Id., 188 Wis. at 381, 206 N.W. at 200.

This theory has been subjected to devastating and persuasive criticism. See, e. g., James, Imputed Contributory Negligence, 14 La. L.Rev. 340, 354–360 (1954); Gregory, The Contributory Negligence of Plaintiff's Wife or Child in an Action for Loss of Services, 2 U. Chi.L.Rev. 173, 180–193 (1935); Prosser, Law of Torts, § 125 (Fourth Ed.1971); 1 Harper and James, The Law of Torts, § 8.8 (1956). The assignment basis is a convenient legal fiction without historical validity.

Wisconsin recently limited and perhaps undermined the rationale of the Callies case in Schwartz v. City of Milwaukee, 54 Wis.2d 286, 195 N.W.2d 480 (1972).

Our holdings in Irlbeck v. Pomeroy and Wardlow v. City of Keokuk, supra, in which we identify the independent nature of a parental claim under rule 8 make it clear we do not accept the assignment rationale as a basis for adopting the restatement rule.

IV. *The well-settled rule theory.* The fourth category of cases is illustrated by Ross v. Cuthbert, 239 Or. 429, 397 P.2d 529 (1964), where the court, in the context of a wife's consortium action, by a four to three margin held the fact the rule is so well-settled in the courts overrides the logic of modern textwriters and commentators. * * * The dissent in Ross noted, "This does not answer the criticism levied against the rule, and it does not discharge our responsibility as an appellate court to recognize only those principles of law that can be supported by sound reason." 397 P.2d at 533. We agree. * * *

* * * [W]e decline to perpetuate an erroneous doctrine simply to avoid a departure from the past. * * *

Similarly, we have no obligation to adopt a rule just because it has generally been adopted elsewhere. Although cases from other states may be persuasive authority, they have no greater cogency than the reasoning by which they were decided.

The development of the common law did not end with the Declaration of Independence. Its genius is its flexibility and capacity for growth and adaptation. See Miller v. Monsen, 228 Minn. 400, 406, 37 N.W.2d 543, 547 (1949). When common-law principles are no longer supportable in reason they are no longer supportable in fact.

The majority opinion in Ross v. Cuthbert, supra, suggests the courts which follow the principle incorporated in the restatement rule may believe it results in justice even if it is not logical. The Oregon court speculates about two possible reasons. One is the idea that courts may oppose permitting a plaintiff to recover all his damages from a third party when a family member was responsible for them in part. The second is the possibility that courts wish to prevent a family from "teaming up" to pursue a claim against the third party. 397 P.2d at 531–532.

Such reasoning is not articulated in the cases prior to Ross, and what is more important, is contrary to reasoning long articulated in our own cases and the restatement itself. * * * [W]e have rejected the doctrine that the proximate concurring negligence of a parent will bar either a child's recovery from a third party for his injuries or the other parent's recovery under rule 8 for parental damages caused by injury to the child. * * * We have also rejected the view that one spouse is barred from recovering from a third party for his loss by the proximate concurring negligence of the other spouse. * * * Nor have we accepted the contention that an injured parent should be barred from recovery from a third party by his child's concurring proximate negligence. * * * The restatement is in accord. [§§ 488(1) and (2) and 494A.]

If justice is served when family members are permitted to recover damages despite the concurring proximate negligence of another member of the immediate family in all these situations, it is surely as well served by application of the same standard in this rule 8 action.

Negligence law in Iowa includes the principle that the merely concurrent proximate negligence of another is not a bar to recovery from one whose negligence proximately caused the plaintiff's damages. Henneman v. McCalla, 260 Iowa 60, 67, 148 N.W.2d 447, 452 (1967) ("proximate negligence need not be the sole cause of an injury"). This permits a plaintiff to recover his total damages from one whose negligence merely concurs in proximately causing his loss. We do not believe any proper basis exists for excluding from the operation of that principle only situations where concurrent proximate negligence of the injured person is pleaded as a defense to the claim of one who holds a legally protected interest in the health or life of such injured person. Specifically we are aware of no rational justification in precedent or policy to say a parent may not recover his loss under rule 8 simply because his child is barred from recovery of his separate loss by the child's contributory negligence.

The gist of the parental action under rule 8 is a wrong done to the parent in consequence of injury to his child by the actionable negligence of another. We are not in this case deciding whether such cause of action exists. It exists under rule 8. See Wardlow v. City of Keokuk, supra. We are deciding whether it will be extinguished by a contributory negligence defense good against the child. In Irlbeck v. Pomeroy, supra, we held, contrary to the rule generally followed elsewhere, that a defense good against the child is not automatically good against the parent. Cf. C.J.S. Parent and Child § 45; 59 Am. Jur.2d Parent and Child § 121. The fact the defense in Irlbeck was based on statute instead of common law is not a controlling distinction.

The eccentricity of the rule in Restatement of Torts, Second § 494, is most graphically demonstrated by its effect in this case if Vincent had been operating a motorcycle owned by plaintiff. In that event plaintiff's negligence action against defendants for damages to the motorcycle would not have been subject to a defense based on Vincent's contributory negligence. * * * Similarly, if plaintiff had been injured as a passenger on the vehicle his action based on his injuries would not have been subject to that defense. Nor, if Vincent wore clothing owned by his father, would plaintiff's action for its loss have been subject to a defense based on Vincent's contributory negligence. In each of these situations the general principle would be applicable. The merely concurrent negligence of the child would not bar parental redress. By the same logic the father's rule 8 claim should not be subject to a defense predicated on the merely concurrent negligence of the child.

Faced with the choice of following a rule simply because it has generally been followed elsewhere or rejecting it because we believe it is unsound, we choose to reject it. We hold a child's contributory negligence, not the sole proximate cause of his injury, is not a defense to a parental claim under rule 8 for the expense and actual loss of services, companionship and society resulting from injury to or death of the child. * * *

MASON, RAWLINGS, REYNOLDSON and HARRIS, JJ., concur.

MOORE, C. J., and UHLENHOPP, LEGRAND, and REES, JJ., dissent. * * *

A number of special contributory negligence problems are presented in connection with claims arising from death. Ordinarily the right to recover damages for wrongful death is statutory.[41] Some statutes provide for the inheritance of decedent's claims. Others provide for compensation to specified survivors of decedent for their loss resulting from the death. The Restatement of Torts Second (1965) provides, in part:

§ 493. Beneficiary Under a Death Statute

(1) Unless otherwise provided by statute the contributory negligence of one beneficiary under a death statute does not bar recovery for the benefit of any other beneficiary.

(2) Whether the contributory negligence of a beneficiary under a death statute bars or reduces recovery to the extent of his own benefit depends upon the statute.

For an example of the application of these concepts see Baca v. Baca, 71 N.M. 468, 379 P.2d 765 (1963).

41. This is conventional doctrine, but see Gaudette v. Webb, 362 Mass. 60, 284 N.E.2d 222 (1972); compare Meagher v. Electrolux Corp., 388 F. Supp. 1009 (D.Mass.1975).

SMITH v. KAUFFMAN

Supreme Court of Virginia, 1971.
212 Va. 181, 183 S.E.2d 190.

GORDON, JUSTICE. A seven year old child brought this action against the administrator of her stepfather's estate to recover for injuries suffered in an automobile accident, allegedly as a result of the stepfather's negligence. The trial court held that the plaintiff-child could not maintain the action because her stepfather, who stood *in loco parentis* to the child, was immune from liability. The court held alternatively that if the plaintiff could maintain the action, her stepfather owed only slight care because she was a gratuitous guest-passenger. Va.Code Ann. § 8–646.1 (1957). The court dismissed the action, and this appeal ensued.

We are called on to reexamine the rule of intra family tort immunity. If the plaintiff passes that barrier, we will decide whether the operator of an automobile owes the duty of ordinary care or only slight care to a seven year old passenger who is gratuitously transported.

I

In 1934 we adopted the rule that an unemancipated minor child cannot maintain an action against his parent to recover for personal injuries caused by the parent's negligence. Norfolk Southern R. R. v. Gretakis, 162 Va. 597, 174 S.E. 841 (1934).[42]

Other courts have reasoned that intra family tort actions should be proscribed because of the possibility of fraud or collusion. W. Prosser, Law of Torts, § 122 at 865–66 (4th ed., 1971). But we rejected that theory in Midkiff v. Midkiff, 201 Va. 829, 113 S.E.2d 875 (1960), involving an action between brothers. We pointed out that "[i]f actions were barred because of the possibility of fraud many wrongs would be permitted to go without redress". Id. at 833, 113 S.E.2d at 878. In the same vein, the Supreme Court of New Jersey recently said: "We do not believe that the judiciary should continue to refuse to hear an entire class of actions simply because some of these claims may be the product of venality". France v. A. P. A. Transport Corp., 56 N.J. 500, 505, 267 A.2d 490, 493 (1970).

Courts have also reasoned that parental immunity could be supported on an analogy to the common law rule proscribing interspousal personal injury actions. W. Prosser, Law of Torts, supra. We rejected that theory in Worrell v. Worrell, 174 Va. 11, 4 S.E.2d 343 (1939).

The rule in this State is therefore grounded solely on the theory that a suit by a child against his parent "tends to disturb the peace

42. This rule was first adopted in this country in Hewellette v. George, 68 Miss. 703, 9 So. 885 (1891). It was followed by many other courts in this country, perhaps under the mistaken belief that the rule was part of the English common law. See Worrell v. Worrell, 174 Va. 11, 18, 4 S.E.2d 343, 346 (1939).

and tranquillity of the home, or disrupt the voluntary and natural course of disposal of the parents' exchequer". Worrell v. Worrell, supra at 19, 4 S.E.2d at 346.

The intra family immunity rule applies only to personal injury actions, not to property damage actions. See Midkiff v. Midkiff, 201 Va. 829, 113 S.E.2d 875 (1960). Within the family, the rule encompasses only actions between husband and wife and between parent and child, not actions between two children. Id. And exceptions have been carved out of the rule of immunity in actions by child against parent. An emancipated child can maintain a personal injury action against his parent, see Brumfield v. Brumfield, 194 Va. 577, 74 S.E. 2d 170 (1953), and, even though unemancipated, a child can bring a personal injury action against his parent if they stand in the relation of servant and master, see Norfolk Southern R. R. v. Gretakis, supra.

In Worrell v. Worrell, supra, we added another exception to the rule of parental immunity. That case involved an action by an unemancipated child against her father for personal injuries suffered when a bus collided with another motor vehicle. The plaintiff-child was a ticketed passenger in the bus; the defendant-father was the owner of the bus, which was operated as a common carrier.

Speaking of the rule of parental immunity adopted five years earlier, we said in *Worrell:*

> "In later years, economic, social and legislative changes have caused a judicial reaction to the earlier views. Modern methods of business, new or enlarged occupational capacities and the advent of the automobile and liability indemnity insurance have placed the parties in a different position. Therefore, the effect of the earlier decisions must be considered in relation to the occasion, facts and laws upon which they were based. A correct determination of each case must necessarily depend upon its facts and circumstances and the law applicable thereto. Rules of thumb must give way to rules of reason."

Id., 174 Va. at 20, 4 S.E.2d at 346–347.

In view of the changed circumstances in 1939, we held in *Worrell* that an unemancipated child could maintain an action against her parent for personal injuries incurred while riding as a passenger on a common carrier:

> "[W]e think that the statutes of this State providing for compulsory insurance indemnity to passengers of a common carrier for damages resulting from the negligent operation of its vehicles, evidence a purpose and policy to afford protection to all such persons from damages arising in tort from the relationship of passenger and carrier."

Id. at 28, 4 S.E.2d at 350.

The enactment of Virginia uninsured motorist laws in 1958 has effected a further and major change of circumstances. One of these laws requires an uninsured motor vehicle endorsement to each policy of automobile liability insurance issued or delivered by an insurer licensed in this State covering a motor vehicle principally garaged or used in this State. Va.Code Ann. § 38.1–381 (1970). Under the endorsement, the insurer must agree to pay to the insured all sums that he may be legally entitled to recover as damages from the owner or operator of an uninsured motor vehicle or unknown operator of a motor vehicle, within the limits prescribed by statute: $20,000 for bodily injury to or death of any one person and $30,000 for bodily injury to or death of two or more persons in any one accident, and $5,000 for damage to property in any one accident. Va.Code Ann. §§ 38.1–381(b) (1970) and 46.1–1(8) (Supp.1971).

A complementary law, first enacted in 1958, encourages the obtaining of insurance coverage by requiring that every person who seeks registration of an "uninsured motor vehicle" pay a $50 fee to the State Uninsured Motorists Fund. This fee must be paid as a prerequisite to registration of a motor vehicle unless the vehicle has liability insurance coverage up to the limits described in the preceding paragraph or unless the owner (i) qualifies the vehicle as an "insured motor vehicle" by giving a bond or depositing cash or securities in lieu of insurance or (ii) qualifies as a self-insurer. Va.Code Ann. §§ 46.1–167.2(b) (1967), –395 (1967), –504 (Supp.1971). According to the records of the State Division of Motor Vehicles, only 1.57% of the motor vehicles registered in Virginia are "uninsured motor vehicles".

The very high incidence of liability insurance covering Virginia-based motor vehicle, together with the mandatory uninsured motorist endorsements to insurance policies, has made our rule of parental immunity anachronistic when applied to automobile accident litigation. In such litigation, the rule can be no longer supported as generally calculated to promote the peace and tranquillity of the home and the advantageous disposal of the parents' exchequer. A rule adopted for the common good now prejudices the great majority.

What the New Jersey Supreme Court said while abrogating interspousal immunity in automobile accident litigation is equally pertinent to this case:

> "[R]ealistically, it must be remembered when dealing with the question of conjugal harmony that today virtually every owner of a motor vehicle with a sense of responsibility carries liability insurance coverage.[43] The presence of insurance militates against the possibility that the interspousal relatonship will be disrupted since a recovery will in most cases be paid by the insurance carrier rather than by the de-

43. "The Department of Motor Vehicles indicates that between June 1, 1969 and May 31, 1970, 98.24% of New Jersey motor vehicle owners registered their vehicles as insured." [Notes 42 and 43 from the original, renumbered; other notes in original omitted.]

> fendant spouse. In fact, it is ironic that the presence of insurance has spawned the second rationale, i. e., that of protecting the insurance carriers against fraud and collusion. That rationale belies the possibility that domestic harmony will be disturbed since its very premise is that the interspousal relationship is so harmonious that fraud and collusion will result. Domestic harmony may be more threatened by denying a cause of action than by permitting one where there is insurance coverage. The cost of making the injured spouse whole would necessarily come out of the family coffers, yet a tortfeasor spouse surely anticipates that he will be covered in the event that his negligence causes his spouse injuries. This unexpected drain on the family's financial resources could likely lead to an interference with the normal family life. And it is doubtful that this void in insurance coverage would comport with the reasonable expectations of the insured that this Court has so often sought to protect. * * * In short, the immunity doctrine cannot be fairly sustained on the basis that negligence suits between husbands and wives will disrupt the harmony of the family.

Immer v. Risko, 56 N.J. 482, 489–490, 267 A.2d 481, 484–485 (1970); see France v. A. P. A. Transport Corp., 56 N.J. 500, 267 A.2d 490 (1970) (abrogating parental immunity in automobile accident litigation).

Recognizing that today's changed circumstances vitiate the underlying reason for a rule of parental immunity in automobile accident litigation, we follow the precedent of Worrell v. Worrell, supra, and abrogate that rule. The plaintiff can therefore maintain this action. Our decision of course relates only to the kind of action before us, an action by child against parent to recover for injuries sustained in a motor vehicle accident.[44]

II

Under a Virginia statute, which codifies the rule of Boggs v. Plybon, 157 Va. 30, 160 S.E. 77 (1931), a person transported in a motor vehicle "as a guest without payment for such transportation" cannot recover for death or injuries resulting from the operation of the motor vehicle except upon proof of the owner's or operator's gross negligence or willful and wanton conduct. Va.Code Ann. § 8–646.1 (1957). Plaintiff's counsel contends that Code § 8–646.1 is not appli-

44. On the same day that it decided the *Smith* case the Virginia Supreme Court also abolished interspousal immunity in actions for personal injury sustained in automobile accidents, Surratt v. Thompson, 212 Va. 191, 183 S.E.2d 200 (1971).

See, similarly, Maestas v. Overton, 87 N.M. 213, 531 P.2d 947 (1975). Where interspousal immunity is retained the defense may be denied to a spouse's employer charged with vicarious liability, e. g., Fields v. Synthetic Ropes, Inc., 215 A.2d 427 (Del.1965). As to parental immunity see also Small v. Rockfeld, 66 N.J. 231, 330 A.2d 335 (1974); Sorensen v. Sorensen, Mass., 339 N.E.2d 907 (1975).

cable to the case now before us because a seven year old child is not capable of being a "guest without payment". Counsel therefore contends that recovery can be predicated upon proof of ordinary negligence. * * *

Some courts have held that guest statutes encompass young children who are transported gratuitously only if they are transported with parental consent. Other courts disregard parental consent. They hold either that a young child cannot assume the status of guest-passenger or, conversely, that a young child automatically assumes that status if he is gratuitously transported. See Rosenbaum v. Raskin, 45 Ill.2d 25, 29, 257 N.E.2d 100, 102 (1970).

We agree with the courts that hold a child can become a guest in a motor vehicle and subject himself to the gross negligence rule only if he can knowingly and voluntarily accept an invitation to become a guest. Rosenbaum v. Raskin, supra; Green v. Jones, 136 Colo. 512, 319 P.2d 1083 (1957); see W. Prosser, Law of Torts § 60 at 385 (4th ed. 1971). We adopt that rule and will fix the dividing line between those children who can and those who cannot knowingly and voluntarily accept an invitation to become a guest.

Virginia has adopted the rule that "a child under 7 years of age cannot be guilty of negligence, and that as to children between 7 and 14 years of age the presumption is they are incapable of exercising care and prudence and this presumption prevails unless rebutted by sufficient proof to the contrary". Morris v. Peyton, 148 Va. 812, 821, 139 S.E. 500, 502–503 (1927). We are now dealing with capacity to assume a risk, rather than capacity to be negligent. See Boggs v. Plybon, supra. So we will borrow from, rather than adopt entirely, the rule respecting the capacity of young children to exercise care and prudence.

We hold that a child under the age of fourteen years is incapable of knowingly and voluntarily accepting an invitation to become a guest in an automobile so as to subject himself to the gross negligence rule. Accordingly, the plaintiff in this case was owed the duty of ordinary care, rather than slight care.

Reversed and remanded.[45]

I'ANSON, COCHRAN and HARMAN, JJ., concurring in part and dissenting in part. * * *

45. Guest statutes in some states have been held to violate the equal protection clause of the applicable state or the federal constitution, or both, e. g., Brown v. Merlo, 8 Cal.3d 855, 106 Cal. Rptr. 388, 506 P.2d 212 (1973); Primes v. Tylor, 43 Ohio St.2d 195, 331 N.E. 2d 723 (1975); Manistee Bank & Trust Co. v. McGowan, 394 Mich. 655, 232 N.W.2d 636 (1975); McGeehan v. Bunch, 88 N.M. 308, 540 P.2d 238 (1975); contra, e. g., Botsch v. Reisdorff, 193 Neb. 165, 226 N.W.2d 121 (1975) and White v. Hughes, 257 Ark. 627, 519 S.W.2d 70 (1975). Another treatment is to construe such statutes strictly, e. g., Naber v. Thompson, 274 Or. 309, 546 P.2d 467 (1976) (husband of guest not barred concerning his separate action for loss of consortium).

SECTION 5. DAMAGES

(A) GENERAL CONSIDERATIONS [1]

FETTER v. BEAL

King's Bench, 1699.
1 Raymond's Rep. 339.

SPECIAL action of trespass and battery for a battery committed by the defendant upon the plaintiff, and breaking his skull. The plaintiff declares of the battery &c. and that he brought an action for it against the defendant and recovered 11£. and no more; and that after that recovery part of his skull by reason of the said battery came out of his head, *per quod, &c.* The defendant pleaded the said recovery in bar. Upon which the plaintiff demurred. And Shower for the plaintiff argued, that this action differed from the nature of the former, and therefore would well lie, notwithstanding the recovery in the other; because the recovery in the former action was only for the bruise and battery, but here there is a maihem by the loss of the

1. The term "special damage" is used in so many different senses by courts and lawyers that a very brief indication of the more common uses may be helpful:

a. The substantive law may give a plaintiff no civil remedy unless he has suffered some private or individual injury, rather than a harm in common with the general public. Such an injury is sometimes called "special damage" as, for example, in the reference to a public nuisance causing "special" harm to the plaintiff.

b. A rule of the substantive law of contracts denies recovery for those consequences of a breach which accrue to a plaintiff because of his special circumstances unless these circumstances were brought home to the defendant when he made the bargain. Hadley v. Baxendale, 9 Ex. 341 (1854). Damages for the loss of an especially favorable opportunity to resell the subject of the principal contract furnish an example. These are often called "special damages." While such a limitation is not applicable to ordinary accidents, it may vex cases where defendant's negligent wrong is also a breach of contract. See Buskey v. New England Telephone & Telegraph Co., 91 N.H. 522, 23 A.2d 367 (1941).

c. While the substantive law (of proximate cause or duty, as in the Palsgraf case) in accident cases lets a plaintiff recover for all proximate consequences of the defendant's wrong, there is a rule of *pleading* which requires any consequence which is unusual and not standardized to be specifically alleged. See C. Clark, Code Pleading 350 (2d ed. 1947); F. James, Civil Procedure 124–25 (1965).

This rule has nothing to do with foreseeability of the consequence from the time of the accident. It is designed simply to give the defendant a reasonable basis to tell from the pleadings what the plaintiff will claim at trial. These unusual consequences are frequently called "special damages." See, e. g., Restatement, Torts (1939) section 904.

d. In some localities, at least, claim men and lawyers often refer to expenses (for doctors, medicine, hospitalization, nursing, etc.) and pecuniary losses (property damage, loss of wages or salary, etc.) as "special damages" or "the specials," as distinguished from, e. g., general damages for pain and suffering or loss of limb, Rosenstein v. Chicago Transit Authority, 12 Ill.App.3d 1089, 299 N.E.2d 396 (1973); Beranek v. Mulcare, page 489 infra. This loose sense usually, but not always, coincides with that given in paragraph c.

e. In the law of libel and slander the term "special damage" is used in still another special sense. See chapter 7, infra.

skull. As if a man brings an action against another for taking and detaining of goods for two months, and afterwards he brings another action for taking and detaining for two years, the recovery in the former action is not pleadable in bar of the second. If death ensues upon the battery of a servant, this will take away the action *per quod servitium amisit.* And then if a consequence will take away an action, for the same reason it will give an action. If a man brings an action for uncovering his house, by which his goods were spoiled, and afterwards by reason of the said uncovering new goods are spoiled, he shall have a new action. *Quod Holt negavit.* And *per totam curiam,* the jury in the former action considered the nature of the wound, and gave damages for all the damages that it had done to the plaintiff; and therefore a recovery in the said action is good here. And it is the plaintiff's fault, for if he had not been so hasty, he might have been satisfied for this loss of the skull also. Judgment for the defendant, nisi &c.

SAME CASE, SUB NOM

FERRER v. BEALE

King's Bench, 1702.
1 Raymond's Rep. 692.

Sir Bartholomew Shower moved in this case for judgment for the plaintiff, because this special subsequent damage is a sufficient foundation for an action, and that for great reason, because the jury could not have consideration of it in giving damages. And he compared it to the case of a nuisance, that a man might have an action for every new dropping of the water from the eaves of the house. 2. There is a maim laid here, and therefore the prior recovery in the action of assault cannot be a bar. Mr. Montague, of the same side said, that if *A.* breaks a sea wall, and the owner of the land recovers damages for it in an action, and erects a new wall, and before it is dry and settled the sea throws it down again, and overflows the land, &c. for this special subsequent damage the owner may have a new action. Holt chief justice. This is a new case to which there is no parallel in the books. Every one shall recover damages in proportion to his prejudice which he hath sustained; and if this matter had been given in evidence, as that which in probability might have been the consequence of the battery, and the greatness or consequence of that is only in aggravation of damages. In some cases the damage is the foundation of the action as in the action by the master for battery of his servant, *per quod servitium amisit,* but here the battery only is the foundation of the action, and this damage, which might probably ensue, might and ought to have been given in evidence, in the former action, and that the jury gave damages for all the hurt that he suffered; for if the nature of the battery was such, as probably to produce this effect, the jury might give damages for it before it happened. As to the case of the sea wall, the plaintiff would recover damages enough in the first action, to rebuild it; and if he rebuilds it ill, the fault is his own. And as to the nuisance every new dropping is a new nuisance. As to the maihem, that is nothing; for a recovery in battery, &c. is a bar in appeal of maihem, 4 Co. 43 a. because in battery the plaintiff may give a maihem in evidence, and recover damages for it. And Holt chief justice said, that the original cause was tried before him eight years ago, and the plaintiff and defendant appeared to be both in drink, and the jury did not well know which of them was in fault, and therefore they gave the less damages. The plaintiff could not obtain judgment, the court inclining strongly against him.

As this case suggests there are situations where successive recoveries may be had but in torts they are confined to cases of continuing trespass or continuing nuisance. The question of when a trespass or nuisance is continuing is often difficult. See on the whole problem Clark, Cases on Pl. and Procedure (2d ed. 1941) ch. 16. These cases aside, the decision reprinted gives the rule for dealing with personal injury and property damage cases (whether the wrong is negligent, or something worse).

An alternative way of handling prospective loss is widely employed in administering workmen's compensation laws. Here the notion of the single recovery, with all its limitations, is rejected in favor of an award calling for periodic payments (cf. technique sometimes used in handling claims for alimony). This award may be modified from time to time on a showing that disability has increased, decreased, or ceased; or that some other change in the material circumstances has taken place. See, e. g., Conn.C.G.S.A. § 31–315 (1972); N. Y. Workmen's Comp.L., sections 22, 123; Pa. 77 P.S., section 772.

Another alternative is to provide a paid-up insurance policy covering the contingency, a device particularly attractive to insurance companies. See, e. g., Bishop, Book Review, 69 Yale L.J. 925, 928 (1960).

A variation appears in a settlement made in 1974 by a university medical center in California, whose admitted negligence during surgery left a 50-year-old woman in an apparently permanent coma, likely to spend the rest of her life as an otherwise normal sleeping person. The hospital agreed to provide for the patient's needs for the rest of her life, estimated at 23.5 years. The cost of care was said to range from $334 to $380 per day at present prices, and was estimated to reach a total of between $3.5 million and $4.5 million, considering inflation. The settlement also included the establishment of a contingency fund to pay the patient $100,000 if she should recover, and the payment of $100,000 existing medical bills and attorneys' fees of $445,000. Cf. 31 The Citation 49 (1975). Consider the relative advantages and disadvantages of these alternative methods with respect to flexibility, difficulties of proof, the probable results of mistaken prognosis, possible effect on the plaintiff's recovery. On the last point, see, e. g., Norcross, Vocational Rehabilitation & Workmen's Compensation (1936); Karnosh, Traumatic Neuroses and Psychoses (1941) 49 Western J. of Surgery O. & G. 606, 612 (treatment of post-concussion syndrome: "If compensation is involved there should be a quick settlement with a lump sum"; a commissioner is usually empowered to make such an award); Kessler, Accidental Injuries (1941) 618 (distinguishing in this regard "traumatic hysteria" from "traumatic neurosis").

In trespass, at common law, if plaintiff made out the trespass he was entitled to at least nominal damages, though he had to plead substantial damages in order to recover them. In case, damages were usually an essential element of liability. Shipman, Common Law Pl. (3d ed. 1923) 211, 223. The effect of the plaintiff's election, where he had one at later common law, and of the codes, is well analyzed in McCormick, Damages (1935) section 22. "In cases of negligence, there is no such invasion of rights as to entitle a plaintiff to recover at least nominal damages * * * Although there has been negligence in the performance of a legal duty, yet it is only those who have suffered damage therefrom that may maintain an action therefor." Sullivan v. Old Colony Street Ry., 200 Mass. 303, 86 N.E. 511 (1908).

FELDMAN v. ALLEGHENY AIRLINES, INC.

United States Court of Appeals for the Second Circuit, 1975.
524 F.2d 384.

Before FRIENDLY and OAKES, CIRCUIT JUDGES, and LASKER, DISTRICT JUDGE.*

LASKER, DISTRICT JUDGE.

On June 7, 1971, an Allegheny Airlines flight crashed in fog while approaching New Haven Airport. Nancy Feldman, a passenger, died, in the crash. Allegheny conceded liability, and the parties submitted the issue of damages to Judge Blumenfeld of the United States District Court for the District of Connecticut. The airline appeals from Judge Blumenfeld's judgment awarding $444,056. to Reid Laurence Feldman, as administrator of the estate of his late wife.

Determination of damages in this diversity wrongful death action is governed by Connecticut law, specifically Conn.Gen.Stats. § 52–555, which measures recovery by the loss to the decedent of the value of her life rather than by the value of the estate she would have left had she lived a full life. * * * In accordance with Connecticut law, the judgment represented the sum of (1) the value of Mrs. Feldman's lost earning capacity and (2) the destruction of her capacity to enjoy life's non-remunerative activities, less (3)

* Of the United States District Court for the Southern District of New York, sitting by designation.

deductions for her necessary personal living expenses. No award was made for conscious pain and suffering before Mrs. Feldman's death because the evidence on this point was too speculative, nor did the award include pre-judgment interest.

Damages in a wrongful death action must of necessity represent a crude monetary forecast of how the decedent's life would have evolved. Prior to stating his specific findings, the district judge noted, and we agree, that "[t]he whole problem of assessing damages for wrongful death * * * defies any precise mathematical computation," citing Floyd v. Fruit Industries, Inc., supra, 144 Conn. at 675, 136 A.2d at 927 (382 F.Supp. at 1282).

It is clear from Judge Blumenfeld's remarkably detailed and precise analysis that he nevertheless made a prodigious effort to reduce the intangible elements of an award to measurable quantities. It is with reluctance, therefore, that we conclude that his determination of loss of earnings and personal living expenses must be remanded.

I.

Damages for Destruction of Earning Capacity.

Nancy Feldman was 25 years old at the time of her death. From 1968 until shortly before the plane crash, she lived and worked in New Haven while her husband studied at Yale Law School. On Mr. Feldman's graduation from law school in the spring of 1971 the Feldmans moved to Washington, D. C., where they intended to settle. At the time of her death, Mrs. Feldman had neither accepted nor formally applied for employment in Washington, although she had been accepted by George Washington Law School for admission in the Fall of 1971 and had made inquiries about the availability of employment.

A key objection of appellant Allegheny runs to Judge Blumenfeld's calculation of the discount rate at 1½% in determining the present value of Mrs. Feldman's lost earning capacity on the grounds that the court has no right to take inflation into account in any way in its assessment of damages. The district court decided that the appropriate rate of discount would be the "price of capital," such to be "obtained by adjusting interest rates on 'risk-free' investments so as to exclude the additional interest demanded by the investment market as compensation for investors' assumption of the risk of inflation." * * *

In calculating the discount rate, the appellee's expert, relied on by the district court, used an average earnings of 4.14% (from mutual savings bank investments) as representative of a prudent, non-sophisticated investment and subtracted 2.87% as the average yearly inflation rate revealed in the Department of Labor's Consumer Price Index over an 18-year period, yielding a 1.27% difference which was rounded up to 1.5%. Judge Blumenfeld corroborated this "inflation-adjusted discount rate" of 1.5% by calculating the real yields of investments since 1940 in federal government securities (with inflation factored out) from the 1974 Economic Report of the President, a source referred to by appellant Allegheny's expert. The district court made this calculation according to its view of Connecticut's law and policies on the subject of inflation accounting in wrongful death damages.

We agree with the district court's interpretation of Connecticut law as leaving open the question how inflation may be accounted for in such damages.[2] We believe that Judge Blumenfeld, a long-time Connecticut lawyer and district court judge for 14 years, appropriately hypothesized the Connecticut Supreme Court's favorable reaction to a discount rate adjustment, since Connecticut, unlike most jurisdictions, reduces what would otherwise be inflated judgments for wrongful death injuries by requiring deduction of income taxes payable on future earnings. Floyd v. Fruit Industries, Inc., supra, 144 Conn. at 673, 136 A.2d at 926.

The district court was fully aware that in a way it was being speculative in what it was doing, as every trier of fact is required to some extent to be whenever it engages in calculating future earnings and a lump sum discount rate. * * * As a matter of federal law we do not necessarily vouchsafe either the principle of making an "inflation adjustment" in setting a discount rate or the means by which it was done in this instance. Yet we note that consideration of inflation has historically been approved in a number of state courts. See, e. g., Halloran v. New England Telephone & Telegraph Co., 95 Vt. 273, 276, 115 A. 143, 144 (1921) and cases cited in Judge Blumenfeld's opinion, 382 F.Supp. at 1290. As a matter of federal law, at least one circuit has approved jury consideration of the impact of inflation and even reversed for charging that it should not consider "future increases or decreases in the purchasing power of money." Bach v. Penn Central Transportation Co., 502 F.2d 1117, 1122 (6th Cir. 1974); see also Sleeman v. Chesapeake & Ohio Railway Co., 414 F.2d 305 (6th Cir. 1969). Our own Perry v. Allegheny Airlines, Inc., supra, 489 F.2d 1349, affirmed a $369,400. judgment on a jury verdict for the estate of another victim of the very same crash here involved; while the point was not discussed specifically in the opinion it is interesting that Judge Blumenfeld's charge to the jury referred to the plaintiff's expert's testimony on a 1.5% discount rate and the underlying rationale therefor, a reference duly attacked on appeal by Allegheny. Commentators have supported an accounting for inflation in damage awards, see Eco-

2. Connecticut law requires discounting the lump sum representing loss of earning capacity (Chase v. Fitzgerald, 132 Conn. 461, 45 A.2d 789 (1946)), less income taxes that would be paid (Floyd v. Fruit Industries, Inc., 144 Conn. 659, 136 A.2d 918 (1957)). In Quednau v. Langrish, 144 Conn. 706, 714, 137 A.2d 544, 549 (1957), the court reserved judgment whether a case "could arise in which it would be proper to charge the jury that they should take into consideration the depreciated value of the dollar in assessing damages." The Connecticut courts' position thus does not pose the bar to explicit consideration of an inflation factor by the fact-finder which the Nebraska court's position did in Riha v. Jasper Blackburn Corp., 516 F.2d 840, 843 (8th Cir. 1975).

nometrics and Damages, 44 Wash.L.Rev. 351, 360–61 (1969); Comment, 6 U.S.F.L.Rev. 311 (1972). It has even been suggested that a trial court may be in error in failing to account fully for inflation in wrongful death damages in a non-diversity case. See Mills v. Tucker, 499 F.2d 866, 868 (9th Cir. 1974).[3] As Judge Friendly himself said in McWeeney v. New York, New Haven and Hartford Railroad Co., 282 F.2d 34, 38 (2d Cir. 1960):

> "There are few who do not regard some degree of continuing inflation as here to stay and would be willing to translate their own earning power into a fixed annuity, and it is scarcely to be expected that the average personal injury plaintiff will have the acumen to find investments that are proof against both inflation and depression—a task formidable for the most expert investor." (Footnote omitted.)

Within the latitude afforded by the Connecticut decisions, note 2 supra, and with the support in the historical and other economic evidence before him that Judge Blumenfeld had, we cannot fault him for computing the discount rate by offsetting the anticipated rate of earnings from investment of the lump sum to be awarded, by an inflation factor.

In computing the value of Mrs. Feldman's lost earning capacity, the trial judge found that Mrs. Feldman's professional earnings in her first year of employment would have been $15,040, and that with the exception of eight years during which she intended to raise a family and to work only part time, she would have continued in full employment for forty years until she retired at age 65. The judge further found that during the period in which she would be principally occupied in raising her family, Mrs. Feldman would have remained sufficiently in contact with her profession to maintain, but not increase, her earning ability. Pointing out that under Connecticut law damages are to be based on "the loss of earning *capacity*, not future earnings per se * * *" (382 F.Supp. at 1282) (emphasis in original), the judge concluded that when a person such as Mrs. Feldman, who possesses significant earning capacity, chooses to forego remunerative employment in order to raise a family, she manifestly values child rearing as highly as work in her chosen profession and her loss of the opportunity to engage in child rearing "may thus fairly be measured by reference to the earning capacity possessed by the decedent" * * *. Applying this rationale, the trial judge made an award for the eight year period of $17,044. per year, the salary which he computed Mrs. Feldman would have reached in the year preceding the first child-bearing year, but did not increase the amount during the period.

3. But see Johnson v. Penrod Drilling Co., 510 F.2d 234 (5th Cir. 1975) (en banc, 12–3 on issue of inflation), petition for cert. filed, 43 U.S.L.W. 3684 (June 24, 1975). [Notes 2 and 3 from original, renumbered; other notes in original omitted.]

We believe the trial judge erred in automatically valuing Mrs. Feldman's loss for the child-bearing period at the level of her salary. As Judge Blumenfeld's opinion points out, the Connecticut cases distinguish clearly between loss of earning capacity and loss of capacity to carry on life's non-remunerative activities. As we read Connecticut law, where a decedent suffers both kinds of loss for the same period each must be valued independently in relation to the elements particular to it.

The court in Floyd v. Fruit Industries, Inc., supra, equated "earning capacity" with "the capacity to carry on the particular activity of earning money." 144 Conn. at 671, 136 A.2d at 925. Here the evidence established, and the trial court found, that Mrs. Feldman would have worked only part-time while raising a family. In the circumstances, we believe that under the Connecticut rule the plaintiff is entitled to recover "loss of earnings" for the child raising years only to the extent that the court finds that Mrs. Feldman would actually have worked during those years. For example, if the court finds that she would have worked 25% of the time during that period, the plaintiff would properly be credited only with 25% of her salary for each of the eight years.

This conclusion is consistent with the other leading authority in Connecticut. In Chase v. Fitzgerald, 132 Conn. 461, 45 A.2d 789 (1946), an award for "loss of future earnings" was denied in respect of a decedent who had been employed as a housekeeper, but who at the time of her death was a housewife with no intention of seeking outside employment. The court held that any award for wrongful death in such a case should be based not on the decedent's loss of earning capacity, but rather on her "loss of the enjoyment of life's activities." 132 Conn. at 470, 45 A.2d at 793. Consistently with the holding in *Chase*, we conclude that any award in relation to the portion of the child-raising period during which Mrs. Feldman would not have been working must be predicated on her "loss of the enjoyment of life's activities" rather than on loss of earnings, and on remand the district judge should re-evaluate the elements accordingly.

We recognize that thus computed the total award for Mrs. Feldman's child-raising years may be similar to that already made, but conclude that the conceptual framework we have described is required by Connecticut's distinctive law of damages.

II.

Deductions for Decedent's Necessary Personal Living Expenses.

Where the decedent had been subject to the expense of self-maintenance, Connecticut case law provides for the deduction of "personal living expenses" from damages otherwise recoverable for the loss of earning capacity. Floyd v. Fruit Industries, Inc., supra, 144 Conn. at 674, 136 A.2d at 926. Judge Blumenfeld properly held that although a husband under Connecticut law has a duty to support his spouse, (see, e. g., Conn.Gen.Stats. §§ 46–10; 53–304), that duty does not exempt an income-earning wife from an obligation to apportion a part of her income for her own support. The *Floyd* court defined the term "personal living expenses" as:

> "* * * those personal expenses which, under the standard of living followed by a given decedent, it would have been reasonably necessary for him to incur in order to keep himself in such a condition of health and well-being that he could maintain his capacity to enjoy life's activities, including the capacity to earn money." 144 Conn. at 675, 136 A. 2d at 926–927.

The trial judge concluded that, under Connecticut law, deductions for Mrs. Feldman's personal living expenses should include the cost, at a level commensurate with her standard of living, of food, shelter, clothing and health care. The judge fixed such costs in Washington, D. C. for the year following her death at $2,750., increasing that figure by 3% per year to the age of retirement. After retirement, living expenses were deducted at the rate of $5,000. annually. These figures were discounted annually by 1.5% to reduce the deduction to present value. Although the process by which the trial judge determined the level of Mrs. Feldman's living expenses was proper, we believe that he substantially underestimated the actual costs of food, shelter, clothing and health care.

On direct examination, Mr. Feldman testified that his wife's personal living expenses in New Haven had been approximately $2,120. per year. On cross-examination, this figure was shown to have been unduly conservative with regard to clothing and food, and the trial judge rounded the amount to $2,200. He found that the Feldmans' cost of living would have increased after they moved to Washington, where living expenses were higher and their social and economic status would have changed from that of students to that of young professionals. Accordingly, the judge adjusted the $2,200. figure upward by 25% for the first year Mrs. Feldman would have resided in Washington, and by 3% annually until she would have reached the age of sixty-five and retired. Personal living expenses for that year were calculated to be $6,675., but during the years of retirement deductions were lowered to $5,000., a level which the trial judge felt was consistent with a high standard of living but also reflected the fact that the cessation of work often produces a reduction in personal expenditures.

We recognize the perils involved in an appellate court dealing de novo with factual matters. We would not venture to do so in this case if we did not feel we have the right to take judicial notice of the facts of life, including the cost of living for those in the position of the Feldmans in such metropolitan areas as Washington, D. C. We reluctantly conclude that the trial judge was in error in computing living expenses at $2,750. for the year after Mrs. Feldman's death, and building on that base for later years.

Without attempting to specify what the results of such a computation should be, we believe that it would fall more nearly in the area of $4,000., including approximately $25. per week for food, $125 per month for rent, $1,000. annually for clothing and $400. annually for health care. For one year the difference between the trial judge's figure of $2,750. and the suggested figure of $4,000. may be considered de minimis in relation to the total award. However, projected over the 52 years of Mrs. Feldman's life expectancy, and at an annual increase of 3%, the difference is sufficiently large to require us to remand the matter for further determination by the trial judge.

We have considered the other points raised by Allegheny and find them to be without merit.

The judgment is affirmed in part, reversed in part and remanded.

FRIENDLY, CIRCUIT JUDGE (concurring dubitante):

This case is another example of a federal court's being compelled by the Congressional grant of diversity jurisdiction to determine a novel and important question of state law on which state decisions do not shed even a glimmer of light. The question here, how far awards of damages for disabling personal injury or for death shall attempt to make allowance for future inflation, is of great concern to the states since awards like that made here will further escalate the heavily mounting burden of liability insurance costs. The state decisions and the federal cases endeavoring to ascertain state law are in a stage of uncertainty and flux. So too are the decisions with respect to federal law. Compare Sleeman v. Chesapeake & Ohio Railway Co., 414 F.2d 305 (6 Cir. 1969), with Bach v. Penn Central Transportation Co., 502 F.2d 1117, 1122 (6 Cir. 1974). In a case of federal law, the Fifth Circuit recently granted *en banc* consideration and by a vote of twelve to three expressly disapproved a district court's effort, in computing lost future earnings, to take account of possible inflationary trends over a period of several decades on the ground that "the influence on future damages of possible inflation or deflation is too speculative a matter for judicial determination." Johnson v. Penrod Drilling Co., 510 F.2d 234, 236, 241 (5 Cir. 1975) (en banc), petition for certiorari filed, 43 U.S. L.W. 3684.

Both plaintiff's expert and the court allowed for inflation not by building cost-of-living increases into future earnings but by applying a rate of only 1.5% in discounting to present value estimated lost future earnings and other recoverable values calculated in 1971 dollars. The district court derived this 1.5% figure by comparing rates of return on a number of "risk-free" securities issued by the federal government (plaintiff's expert examined other types of "risk-free" fixed income investments and reached similar conclusions) since 1940 with rates of inflation during the same period as reflected by annual changes in the Consumer Price Index. The court subtracted the latter from the former on the theory that the latter amounted to that portion of the return representing what investors have historically demanded as protection against inflation. The difference varied from year to year, but the court determined that 1.5% was a representative figure for the period. This was deemed to be "that part of the annual yield which constitutes payment for the use of capital" or "real yield"—presumably the rate of return which investors would be willing to accept in an inflation-free economy; while the rate of inflation might rise and fall, investors could be expected to demand about 1.5% return on safe investments in addition to protection against expected inflation. The court recognized that other courts have been reluctant to take explicit account of the effects of future inflation (see 510 F.2d at 236 n. 1) but stated that its approach in fact was "a means to avoid undue speculation" with respect to future inflation and even suggested that when, as in this case, the effects of future inflation have been expressly excluded in the calculation of the amount to be discounted, the "appropriate rate of discount" must necessarily be adjusted so that "the additional interest demanded by the investment market as compensation for investors' assumption of the risk of inflation" is excluded. The distinction drawn between this method and the one more commonly used—adjusting the amount to be discounted so as to include a sum reflecting assumptions about future inflation—apparently given some weight by the majority—is more apparent than real. Plaintiff's expert acknowledged that "another approach" or "alternative calculation" for this problem would be to increase estimated lost future compensation and living expenses to take account of the effects of future inflation and not reduce the rate of return used for discounting by any amount reflecting inflation. The outcome of the calculation under either approach would be very nearly identical. Indeed, at one point counsel for plaintiff asked his expert to calculate the present value in 1971 dollars of the deceased's lost earnings based upon the "speculative" assumption of an inflation rate of 4.5% and a rate of return of 6%. This approach would have reduced the recovery by less than $2,000 out of approximately a quarter of a million dollars.

In any event, plaintiff's expert came up with a $253,424 present value of Mrs. Feldman's projected earnings. Using higher starting and ending salary figures and a different percentage deduction for income taxes, the judge arrived at an initial sum of $499,953 to which he added $100,000, admittedly drawn from the atmosphere, "for the destruction of the decedent's capacity to enjoy life's activities", an element recognized as appropriate for consideration by Connecticut law, and from which he subtracted $155,897 as the discounted sum of personal living expenses, yielding a total recovery of $444,056. On the judge's computations, Mrs. Feldman, who had been earning $10,000 a year at the time of her death in 1971, would be earning $33,757 in 1971 dollars in 2011 as a "legislative analyst" for the National League of Cities and United States Conference of Mayors (NLC/USCM), when she would have attained the age of 65. However, as counsel for Allegheny points out, without dispute from counsel for Mr. Feldman and apparently based upon the testimony of plaintiff's expert about an alternative method of calculation discussed above, a calculation deducting 4.5% for inflation from a 6% interest rate assumed to be attainable on an investment free from risks other than inflation implicitly carries the prediction that Mrs. Feldman, and also all federal employees in the GS 16–7 category (which Mrs. Feldman hypothetically would reach after 40 years under the scheme for predicting merit pay increases adopted by the court), would in fact be earning $122,823 in the year 2011. Similar calculations based upon maintaining the 1.5% differential could yield even more striking results, which are largely veiled by the court's approach. One point that immediately occurs is why, if Mrs. Feldman's salary would rise to such a figure, income tax, deductible from damages under Connecticut law, should be computed at only 25%, a rate which the court found would achieve "substantial justice." It is common knowledge that one effect of inflation is that the same progressive rates of income tax take an ever larger bite out of real income, and it is unlikely in the last degree that, in an era of increasing budgets, due in considerable part to inflation, Congress would make the accommodation needed to prevent this.

Save for this important point not urged by Allegheny and the two corrections made by the majority, I have no reason to question the meticulous calculations of the able district judge. Indeed one could argue that, at a time when the national goal is simply to bring back the golden age of single rather than double digit inflation, without too much question what the single digit should be, the entire interest return on otherwise risk-free investments, today probably in excess of 6%, represents compensation against the risk of inflation; in other words, investors in fixed income securities are willing, for the time being, to forego any return if they can keep the real amount of their investment intact. Indeed, insofar as the return is subject to income tax, they are not even achieving that. Yet common sense suggests that investors will not tolerate such a situation indefinitely.

I doubt whether judges, or anyone else, can peer so far into the future; the district court's computations suffer from what Mr. Justice Holmes, in another context, called "[t]he dangers of a delusive exactness," Truax v. Corrigan, 257 U.S. 312, 342, 42 S.Ct. 124, 133, 66 L.Ed. 254 (1921) (dissenting opinion). Instead of recognizing the plethora of uncertainties as the Fifth Circuit has done, see Johnson v. Penrod Drilling Co., supra, 510 F.2d at 236, compare Frankel v. United States, 321 F.Supp. 1331, 1346 (E.D.Pa.1970), aff'd, 466 F.2d 1226 (3 Cir. 1972), the court below endeavored to construct an iron-clad guaranty against the unknown and unknowable future effects of inflation. The estate of a young woman without dependents is hardly an outstanding candidate for a forty-year protection against inflation not enjoyed at all by millions of Americans who depend on pensions or investment income and not fully enjoyed by millions more whose salaries have in no wise kept pace with inflation.

The court necessarily assumed not only continued inflation, which unhappily seems likely in some degree, but continued responsiveness to it by equivalent wage increases. Yet we have seen in recent months that employers, particularly municipalities, simply cannot maintain these. Thousands of New York City's employees have been dismissed and the rest are being subjected to a wage freeze. Other important cities may not be far behind in having to resort to similar measures. Under such conditions can we be sure that NLC/USCM would continue to grant automatic cost-of-living pay increases for 40 years, as the court assumed? Perhaps so, since the main business of NLC/USCM is seeking to obtain federal funds for cities, which surely is a boom industrv if any there be; but perhaps not.

I would also question the likelihood—indeed, the certainty as found by the court—that, despite her ability, determination and apparent good health, Mrs. Feldman would have worked full time for forty years until attaining age 65, except for the eight years she was expected to devote to the bearing and early rearing of two children. Apart from the danger of disabling illness, temporary or permanent, there would be many attractions to which the wife of a successful lawyer might yield: devoting herself to various types of community service, badly needed but unpaid, or to political activity; accompanying her husband on business trips—often these days to far-off foreign countries; making pleasure trips for periods and at times of the year inconsistent with the demands of her job; perhaps, as the years went on, simply taking time off for reflection and enjoyment. Granted that in an increasing number of professional households both spouses work full time until retirement age, in more they do not. Surely some discount can and should be applied to the recovery for these reasons.

My guess is also that, even if inflation should be taken into account, neither a Connecticut nor a federal jury would have made an award as large as was made here: I say this despite the $369,400 jury verdict for another death arising out of the same crash which we sustained in Perry v. Allegheny Airlines, Inc., supra, 489 F.2d 1349, where we did not expressly discuss the inflation question. Even though the existence of dependents is legally irrelevant under the Connecticut survival statute, a jury would hardly have ignored that, whereas Perry was survived by a dependent wife and five children ranging from 6 to 14 years in age, Mrs. Feldman had no dependents. More significant to me is that in Perry's case the jury awarded only $369,400 as against the $535,000 estimate of Mrs. Perry's expert for economic loss alone; here the judge was more generous in important respects than plaintiff's expert.

However, I am loathe to require a busy federal judge to spend still more time on this diversity case, especially when I do not know what instructions to give him about Connecticut law. Some of the questions I have raised are not open for exploitation by the defendant since its own expert made his calculations on the basis that Mrs. Feldman would work until age 65. Although intuition tells me that the

Supreme Court of Connecticut would not sustain the award made here, I cannot prove it. I therefore go along with the majority, although with the gravest doubts. I do this on the basis that, as far as I am concerned, the decision will not constitute a precedent on the inflation problem in a case arising under federal law. Judgments like Mr. Feldman's and Mrs. Perry's also inevitably raise serious policy questions with respect to damages in airline accident cases beyond those here considered, but these are for Congress and not for the courts.[4]

4. For another method of considering inflation see Pierce v. New York Central Railroad Co., 304 F.Supp. 44 (W.D.Mich.1969); other discussions include Beaulieu v. Elliott, Alaska, 434 P.2d 665 (1967); Hinzman v. Palmanteer, 81 Wash.2d 327, 501 P.2d 1228 (1972), Restatement of Torts, Second § 913A and Comment (Tent. Draft No. 19, 1973); Johnson v. Serra, 521 F.2d 1289 (8th Cir. 1975); United States v. English, 521 F.2d 63 (9th Cir. 1975); Tenore v. Nu Car Carriers, Inc., 67 N.J. 466, 341 A.2d 613 (1975); Huddell v. Levin, 395 F.Supp. 64, 83 (D.N.J.1975).

As to allowance for future income taxes compare McWeeney v. New York, N. H. & H. R. R. Co., 282 F.2d 34 (2d Cir. 1960); Petition of Marina Mercante Nicaraquense, S.A., 364 F.2d 118 (2d Cir. 1966); and Cox v. Northwest Airlines, Inc., 379 F.2d 893 (7th Cir. 1967).

See, generally, F. Harper and F. James, The Law of Torts § 25.12 (1956 and Supp.1968) ("The argument for computing damages on estimated income after taxes is a clear one: this will measure the actual loss. * * * [F]uture taxes are no more speculative than many other items that go into prophesies about future losses * * * witness the future earnings of a young child or the future trends of the dollar's value."); Nordstrom, Income Taxes and Personal Injury Awards, 19 Ohio St.L.J. 212 (1958); Morris and Nordstrom, Personal Injury Recoveries and the Federal Income Tax Law, 56 A.B.A.J. 274 (1960); Annotation, 63 A.L.R.2d 1394; Restatement of Torts, Second § 914A and comments (Tent. Draft No. 19, 1973). American decisions under state law typically require that the effect of future income taxes be ignored, e. g., Culley v. Pennsylvania R.R., 244 F.Supp. 710 (D.Del. 1965) (Md. law; low-income wage-earner, but doctrine not explicitly so limited), but there is some authority otherwise, e. g., Floyd v. Fruit Industries, Inc., 144 Conn. 659, 136 A.2d 918, 63 A.L.R.2d 1378 (1957) (high-income earner); Tenore v. Nu Car Carriers, Inc., 67 N.J. 466, 341 A.2d 613 (1975). The House of Lords requires that income taxes be deducted from estimated future earnings, British Transport Commission v. Gourley [1965] A.C. 185, and that the lump-sum damages so computed, which a "prudent person * * * is expected to invest * * * and to use * * * up gradually", be then increased to take account of future income taxes on the investment income, Taylor v. O'Connor [1971] A.C. 115. The Supreme Court of Canada has rejected *Gourley* for personal injury damages, The Queen (in Right of the Province of Ontario) v. Jennings, 57 D.L.R. (2d) 644 (1966), but the Ontario High Court distinguishes death claims by survivors, which it requires to be based on estimates of the decedent's lost future earnings net of estimated taxes, May et al. v. Municipality of Metropolitan Toronto, 2 D.L.R. (3d) 659 (1969).

As to a related question, whether the trial court may, or should, instruct the jury that compensatory damage awards are not taxable, see Domeracki v. Humble Oil & Refining Co., 443 F.2d 1245 (3d Cir. 1971); compare Kawamoto v. Yasutake, 49 Haw. 42, 410 P.2d 976 (1966); Coleman v. New York City Transit Authority, 37 N.Y. 2d 137, 332 N.E.2d 850 (1975).

LANGE v. HOYT

Supreme Court of Errors of Connecticut, 1932.
114 Conn. 590, 159 A. 575, 82 A.L.R. 486.

[Consolidated actions brought by Minelda Lange, a minor, through her next friend, for personal injuries and by Minette B. Lange, her mother, for expenses, etc. Plaintiffs had a verdict and defendant appeals.]

AVERY, J. * * * The plaintiff Minelda sustained a fracture of her left arm, and a fracture and dislocation of the pelvis. Upon the trial, evidence was offered and the plaintiff claimed that there was a deformity of the pelvis whereby the right side of the pelvis was displaced upward about one half inch, so as to diminish the size of the pelvic outlet; and that this deformity was permanent and would interfere with normal childbirth when the plaintiff reached maturity.

It was the claim of the defendant that the condition of the arm and pelvis was aggravated by lack of proper medical treatment after the accident. The plaintiff Minette B. Lange was a believer in Christian Science and had brought her daughter, Minelda, up in the same belief. On the day of the accident, the mother called a medical practitioner who gave first-aid treatment, and advised the removal of the child to the Danbury Hospital. She was removed to the hospital on the same day, where efforts were made by the physicians to reduce the fracture, and a temporary splint was applied, and X-rays taken. The defendant claims that the mother then took the child home against the advice of the physicians; and that, thereafter, medical advice was not had for the child's injuries until May 15th, when a physician visited the plaintiffs on behalf of the defendant and recommended that medical and surgical treatment be secured immediately, but that such medical and surgical treatment was not obtained until May 27th, when Minelda was taken to New York for X-ray examination; and, thereafter, was treated by a surgeon. In substance, the claim of the defendant is that because of lack of surgical treatment from the day of the accident until May 27th, the plaintiff's injuries were aggravated; and that proper treatment by regular physicians and surgeons from the beginning would have effected a substantial cure of her injuries so that no permanent disability would have resulted therefrom.

On the other hand, the plaintiff Minelda Lange claims that she reasonably relied upon her mother to provide such curative agencies as the latter thought necessary; and the mother claimed that on the day of the accident, in addition to first-aid treatment by a regular surgeon, she secured the services of a surgical nurse and had Minelda's arm set by a qualified surgeon at the Danbury Hospital; that from the time of the accident to the time of the trial Minelda was cared for by a competent nurse, had frequent X-rays and treatments by a competent surgeon, and between May 2d and May 25th was kept quiet and in bed at home; that no other treatment was suggested by the surgeons nor was she ever informed that further surgical treatments would be useful until the defendant's physician so recommended about May 21st; after which, and as soon as possible, the services of a competent orthopedist and a competent X-ray specialist were engaged on behalf of her daughter.

In view of these claims, the defendant in six of her requests for instructions asked the court to inform the jury as to the duty of one injured to exercise ordinary care to cure and restore herself, and assigns error in the charge as delivered upon this subject. The defendant was undoubtedly entitled to have the jury instructed upon this phase of the case. We think, however, the charge as delivered covered the substance of defendant's requests so far as they were proper. * * * It is a rule of general application that one who has been injured by the negligence of another must use reasonable care to promote recovery and prevent any aggravation or increase of the injuries. Flint v. Connecticut Hassam Paving Co., 92 Conn. 576, 578, 103 A. 840. In Morro v. Brockett, 109 Conn. 87, 92, 145 A. 659, we stated that the requirement of this rule is met "when the plaintiff does what a reasonably prudent person would be expected to do under the same circumstances." * * *

The charge of the court is to be tested by the situation disclosed by the claims of proof. Minelda was a child eight years of age, and even if there had been neglect of proper surgical treatment by her mother, the negligence of the parent would not be imputable to the child. * * * The jury were, in substance, told that if they found the negligence of the defendant was a substantial factor in producing Minelda's injuries, she would be entitled to recover, even though negligence on behalf of the parent in failing to obtain proper surgical treatment might have concurred with the negligence of the defendant. As regards the plaintiff Minette B. Lange, the jury were in effect told that she was entitled to recover for expenses incurred by her for nursing, surgery, etc., in connection with her daughter's injuries in so far as the wrongful conduct of the defendant was a substantial factor in producing the injuries. If the injuries were in any way aggravated by the failure of the parent to exercise reasonable care to obtain proper medical and surgical treatment, the parent could not recover for any aggravation of the injuries so caused.

The jury were told that the conduct of both plaintiffs with reference to the presence or absence of reasonable care was to be judged in the light of all the surrounding circumstances including whatever belief as to the methods of treatment the jury might have found they conscientiously held. The reference in the last clause of this charge was to the fact that the plaintiff Minette B. Lange was a Christian Scientist and her conduct in the effort to promote the recovery of her daughter was in part at least actuated by the tenets of that belief. While the test of conduct on the part of a plaintiff in promoting a recovery from injuries suffered is one of reasonable care and cannot be made to depend upon the idiosyncrasies of personal belief no matter how honestly held, courts cannot disregard theories as to proper curative methods, held by a large number of reasonable and intelligent people. Reading the charge in the light of the facts claimed to have been proved, it went no farther than saying that in determining whether the plaintiff Minette B. Lange exercised a reasonable degree of care, the jury were entitled to consider, with all the other evidence, her conduct in the light of her belief in the doctrines of the Christian Science Church and the extent to which she acted in accordance with them. This was as favorable a charge to the defendant as she was entitled to have upon this feature of the case.

The defendant further complains that the charge was inadequate in that it did not sufficiently explain to the jury the effect which negligence on the part of the mother in failing to afford proper surgical treatment to her daughter might have as an intervening cause which would relieve the defendant from liability for such part of her injuries as would otherwise have been avoided. * * * Where an injured plaintiff uses reasonable care in the selection of a physician or surgeon, the right of recovery is not affected by the negligence or improper action of the latter. Wright v. Blakeslee, 102 Conn. 162, 166, 128 A. 113. Primarily the defendant is liable for all the pain, suffering and injury resulting from his wrongdoing, and to relieve him of any of it there must be some act or neglect intervening sufficient to break the causal connection between the injuries actually suffered, and that wrongdoing; and where the plaintiff has performed his full duty in using reasonable care in employing a physician or surgeon, the latter's neglect or default is not deemed in law sufficient to produce that result. Stover v. Inhabitants of Blue Hill, 51 Me. 439; Sauter v. New York Central & H. R. Co., 66 N.Y. 50, 53, 23 Am.Rep. 18; Pullman Palace Car Co. v. Bluhm, 109 Ill. 20, 24, 50 Am.Rep. 601. A child of the age of eight years is necessarily dependent upon her parents as regards the steps to be taken to bring about a recovery from an injury, and if she is not herself guilty of any negligence or improper conduct, the failure of the parents to take proper steps to that end, by a parity of reasoning, cannot be such a cause of any portion of the injuries as will defeat a recovery for all the results of the defendant's wrongdoing. The charge of the trial court was too favorable to the defendant in suggesting that the mother's negligence in failing to secure surgical attention to her daughter might be such an intervening cause as would defeat a recovery for damages for such part of the latter's injury as might have been avoided thereby.

There is no error.[5]

5. Suppose an operation would probably alleviate a disability, but would involve serious risks, or suffering; see, e. g., Stark v. Shell Oil Company, 450 F.2d 994 (5th Cir. 1971).

COYNE v. CAMPBELL

Court of Appeals of New York, 1962.
11 N.Y.2d 372, 230 N.Y.S.2d 1, 183 N.E.2d 891.

FROESSEL, JUDGE. On July 5, 1957 plaintiff sustained a whiplash injury when his automobile was struck in the rear by a motor vehicle driven by defendant. Inasmuch as plaintiff is a practicing physician and surgeon, he received medical treatment, physiotherapy and care from his professional colleagues and his nurse, and incurred no out-of-pocket expenses therefor. Nevertheless, in his bill of particulars, he stated that his special damages for medical and nursing care and treatment amounted to $2,235. The trial court ruled that the value of these services was not a proper item of special damages, and that no recovery could be had therefor since they had been rendered gratuitously. He thus excluded evidence as to their value. The sole question here presented is the correctness of this ruling.

In the leading case of Drinkwater v. Dinsmore, 80 N.Y. 390, we unanimously reversed a plaintiff's judgment entered upon a jury verdict, because defendant was precluded from showing that plaintiff had been paid his wages by his employer during the period of his incapacitation. We held such evidence admissible on the theory that plaintiff was entitled to recover only his pecuniary losses, of which wages gratuitously paid were not an item. With respect to medical expenses, we stated (p. 393) that "the plaintiff must show what he paid the doctor, and can recover only so much as he paid or was bound to pay". Although decided more than 80 years ago, the Drinkwater case has continuously been and still is recognized as the prevailing law of this State * * *.

As recently as 1957, the Legislature declined to enact a proposed amendment to the Civil Practice Act, the avowed purpose of which (1957 Report of N.Y.Law Rev.Comm., p. 223) was "to abrogate the rule of Drinkwater v. Dinsmore, 80 N.Y. 390 (1880) and to conform New York law to the rule followed in most states that payments from collateral sources do not reduce the amount recoverable in a personal injury action." The proposed legislation (Sen.Int. No. 264, Assem. Int. No. 361) was supported by a comprehensive study of the Law Revision Commission (1957 Report, pp. 225–255), which criticized the New York rule as "unfair, illogical and unduly complex" (id., p. 227). The Legislature and not the judiciary is the proper body to decide such a policy question involving the accommodation of various interests. We should not now seek to assume their powers and overrule their decision not to change the well-settled law of this State. No matter what may be the rule in other jurisdictions, Drinkwater is still the law in this State.

We find no merit in plaintiff's contention that the medical and nursing services for which damages are sought were supported by consideration. Plaintiff testified that he did not have to pay for the physiotherapy, and his counsel confirmed the fact that "these various items were not payable by the doctor nor were they actual obligations of his, and that he will not have to pay them".

Plaintiff's colleagues rendered the necessary medical services gratuitously as a professional courtesy. It may well be that as a result of having accepted their generosity plaintiff is under a moral obligation to act for them in a similar manner should his services ever be required; such need may never arise, however, and in any event such a moral obligation is not an injury for which tort damages, which "must be compensatory only" (Steitz v. Gifford, 280 N.Y. 15, 20, 19 N.E.2d 661, 664, 122 A.L.R. 292), may be awarded. A moral obligation, without more, will not support a claim for legal damages. * * *

We are also told that the physiotherapy treatments which plaintiff received from his nurse consumed approximately two hours per week, and that they were given during the usual office hours for which she received her regular salary. Plaintiff does not claim that he was required to or in fact did pay any additional compensation to his nurse for her performance of these duties, and, therefore, this has not resulted in compensable damage to plaintiff.

Finally, we reject as unwarranted plaintiff's suggestion that our decision in Healy v. Rennert, 9 N.Y.2d 202, 206, 213 N.Y.S.2d 44, 46, 173 N.E.2d 777, 778 casts doubt on the continued validity of the Drinkwater rule in a case such as the instant one. In Healy, we held that it was error to permit defendants to establish on cross-examination that plaintiff was a member of a health insurance plan and that he was receiving increased disability pension benefits. In that case, however, the plaintiff had given value for the benefits he received; he paid a premium for the health insurance, and had worked for 18 years, in order to be eligible for the disability retirement benefits. We were not confronted with—and did not attempt to pass upon—a situation where the injured plaintiff received wholly gratuitous services for which he had given no consideration in return and which he was under no legal obligation to repay. In short, insurance, pension, vacation and other benefits which were contracted and paid for are not relevant here. Gratuitous services rendered by relatives, neighbors and friends are not compensable.

* * * It would hardly be fair in a negligence action, where damages are compensatory and not punitive, to change the Drinkwater rule of long standing in the face of the Legislature's refusal to do so, and to punish a defendant by requiring him to pay plaintiff for a friend's generosity. If we were to allow a plaintiff the reasonable value of the services of the physician who treated him gratuitously, logic would dictate that the plaintiff would then be entitled to the reasonable value of such services, despite the fact that the physician charged him but a fraction of such value. Such a rule would involve odd consequences, and in the end simply require a defendant to pay a plaintiff the value of a gift.

The judgment appealed from should be affirmed.

DESMOND, CHIEF JUDGE (concurring).

The reason why this plaintiff cannot include in his damages anything for physicians' bills or nursing expense is that he has paid nothing for those services. It has always been the rule in tort cases that "damages must be compensatory only" (Steitz v. Gifford, 280 N.Y. 15, 20, 19 N.E.2d 661, 664, 122 A.L.R. 292). If this were—and it is not—a case of "payment from collateral source", Healy v. Rennert, 9 N.Y. 2d 202, 213 N.Y.S.2d 44, 173 N.E.2d 777 would be authority for recovery.

* * * Diminution of damages because medical services were furnished gratuitously results in a windfall of sorts to a defendant but allowance of such items although not paid for would unjustly enrich a plaintiff.

* * *

FULD, JUDGE (dissenting).

It is elementary that damages in personal injury actions are awarded in order to compensate the plaintiff, but, under an established exception, the collateral source doctrine—which we recognized in Healy v. Rennert, 9 N.Y. 2d 202, 213 N.Y.S.2d 44, 173 N.E.2d 777—a wrongdoer will not be allowed to deduct benefits which the plaintiff may have received from another source. To put the matter broadly, the defendant should not be given credit for an amount of money, or its equivalent in services, received by the plaintiff from other sources. "The rationale of the collateral source doctrine in tort actions", it has been said, "is that a tort-feasor should not be allowed to escape the pecuniary consequences of his wrongful act merely because his victim has received benefit from a third party" (Note, 26 Fordham L.Rev. 372, 381).

In the Healy case (9 N.Y.2d 202, 213 N.Y.S.2d 44, 173 N.E.2d 777 supra), this court held that, if one is negligently injured by another, the damages recoverable from the latter are diminished neither (1) by the fact that the injured party has been indemnified for his loss by insurance effected by him nor (2) by the fact that his medical expenses were paid by HIP or some other health insurance plan (p. 206, 213 N.Y.S.2d p. 46, 173 N.E.2d p. 778). In the case before us, the plaintiff suffered injuries and required medical and nursing care. He had no health insurance, but he received the necessary medical care and services from fellow doctors without being required to pay them in cash. In addition, he received physiotherapy treatments from the nurse employed by him in his office and to whom he, of course, paid a salary.

I fail to see any real difference between the situation in Healy v. Rennert and the case now before us. In neither case was the injured person burdened with any charges for the medical services rendered and, accordingly, when the defendant is required to pay as "damages" for those services or their value, such damages are no less "compensatory" in the one case than in the other. Nor do I understand why a distinction should be made depending upon whether the medical services were rendered gratuitously or for a consideration.[6] What difference should it make, either to the plaintiff or to the defendant whether an injured plaintiff has his medical bills taken care of by an insurer or by a wealthy uncle or by a fellow doctor? Certainly, neither the uncle, who acted out of affection, nor the doctor, impelled by so-called professional courtesy, intended to benefit the tort-feasor.

The crucial question in cases such as this is whether the tort-feasor should, in fairness and justice, be given credit for the amounts, or their equivalent in services, which the plaintiff has received from some collateral source. The collateral source doctrine is not, and should not be, limited to cases where the plaintiff had previously paid consideration (in the form of insurance premiums, for instance) for the benefits or services which he receives or where there has been a payment of cash or out-of-pocket expenses. The rationale underlying the rule is that a wrongdoer, responsible for injuring the plaintiff, should not receive a windfall. Were it not for the fortuitous circumstance that the plaintiff was a doctor, he would have been billed for the medical services and the defendant would have had to pay for them. The medical services were supplied to help the plaintiff, not to relieve the defendant from any part of his liability or to benefit him. * * * It should not matter, in reason, logic or justice, whether the benefit received was in return for a consideration or given gratuitously, or whether it represented money paid out or its equivalent in services.[7]

* * *

6. I shall assume that in this case the doctors' services were given gratuitously, though a strong argument could be made to the contrary, that is, that they were supported by consideration in that the plaintiff came under a duty to reciprocate and render medical services to his colleagues. Be that as it may, though, I see no basis for labeling the physiotherapy treatments given by the plaintiff's salaried nurse gratuitous. They were given during the nurse's normal working day for which she received wages from the plaintiff. Had she not been required to give such treatments, she would undoubtedly have been free to perform other work for the plaintiff.

7. It is not amiss to note that the courts of a number of other jurisdictions permit the plaintiff to recover from the defendant the reasonable value of nursing care and services furnished him by his wife or other members of his family. (See, e. g., Strand v. Grinnell Auto. Garage Co., 136 Iowa, 68, 70, 113 N.W. 488; Wells v. Minneapolis Baseball & Athletic Ass'n, 122 Minn. 327, 332–334, 142 N.W. 706, 46 L.R.A.,N.S., 606, supra; Houston & Tex. Cent. Ry. Co. v. Gerald, 60 Tex.Civ.App. 151, 157–158, 128 S.W. 166; see, also, Ann., 128 A.L.R. 686.) If the injured person is a man of means, he can hire nurses and he will be reimbursed for the amounts which he pays them in wages. Why should the rule be different if, unable to afford nurses, he has to rely upon his wife or others close to him for the necessary nursing services? There is certainly no reason why the defendant should be subject to less damages when sued by a poor man rather than by one who is rich. [Notes 6 and 7 from original, renumbered. For a subsequent discussion of the right of a wife to be reimbursed for nursing services, beyond the performance of "ordinary household tasks" under a workmen's compensation statute which requires the employer to pay for "medical * * * and hospital services * * * or other attendance", see Kushay v. Sexton Dairy Company, 394 Mich. 69, 228 N.W.2d 205 (1975). On the collateral source

(B) PROPERTY DAMAGE

BIRMINGHAM RAILWAY LIGHT & POWER CO. v. HINTON

Supreme Court of Alabama, 1908.
157 Ala. 630, 47 So. 576.

Action by Walter L. Hinton against the Birmingham Ry. L. & P. Co., to recover as damages the value of certain household goods alleged to have been destroyed by fire set out by one of defendant's engines. [Request to] Charge 1, was as follows: If the jury find for the plaintiff they can assess no more than nominal damages in this case. Judgment for plaintiff and defendant appeals. * * *

ANDERSON, J.—The witness was the owner of the goods and was familiar with them, and this was the only predicate essential to an opinion from him as to their value.—Southern R. R. Co. v. Morris, 143 Ala. 631, 42 So. 17, and authorities there cited. The plaintiff testified as to the worth of the goods, and this evidence was to be considered by the jury in determining the value of same. It may be that the cost of same could not have been shown as evidence of their value, or, if the witness had not knowledge of their value and based his estimate solely on what they cost, that an opinion advanced by him should be excluded. But it was not shown that Hinton based his valuation solely on the cost of the articles, or that he could not give an opinion of their value regardless of the cost. On the other hand, he stated upon cross-examination that the basis of his estimate was the amount they cost "and what they are really worth." There was no effort to exclude from his consideration the cost of the goods or to show that his opinion was based entirely upon the cost, and, as there was proof of value not based entirely upon the cost of the goods, the jury was authorized to fix the value beyond a nominal sum.

While we treat this case upon the idea that the market value of the goods at the time of destruction was the criterion of their value, and affirm it upon the idea that the jury had some evidence of said market value, yet we do not mean to hold that the marketable value should be the test as to articles of the character in question, or that the owner could not have shown the cost of same as a factor in arriving at their value. Household goods, such as furniture, bedding, and wearing apparel, kept for use and not for sale, and which have in fact been used, may have a real intrinsic value to the owner, and yet little or no market value. In some instances it would be difficult, as well as expensive, to replace them, and yet, if put upon the market there would be little or no demand for them, and in such cases the value should be fixed or ascertained in some rational way, other than by showing what they would bring in a particular market or if hawked

rule in general, see Fleming, The Collateral Source Rule and Loss Allocation in Tort Law, 54 Calif.L.Rev. 1478 (1966), and Fleming, Collateral Benefits, ch. 11 of vol. XI (Torts), International Encyclopedia of Comparative Law (1971).]

off by a secondhand dealer.—Denver, South Park & Pac. R. R. v. Frame, 6 Colo. 382; Southern Express Co. v. Owens, 146 Ala. 412, 41 So. 752, 8 L.R.A.,N.S. 369, 119 Am.St.Rep. 41; Howard College v. Turner, 71 Ala. 430, 46 Am.Rep. 326.

The trial court did not err in refusing charge 1, requested by the defendant The judgment of the city court is affirmed.

Affirmed.

AUTOMOBILE DAMAGE. In some states the measure of damages is simply the difference in value immediately before and after the accident, McCormick, Handbook on the Law of Damages 472 (1935); sometimes it is said to be merely the cost of repairs, e. g., Bauer v. Armour & Co., 84 Pa.Super. 174 (1924); Compare Restatement of Torts (1939) § 928, which would allow either difference in value or, at plaintiff's election, reasonable cost of repair with due allowance for any difference between the original value and the value after repairs; cf. Travelers Indemnity Co. v. Skyway Marine, Inc., 251 So.2d 327 (Fla.App.1971); O'Connor v. Schwartz, —— Minn. ——, 229 N.W.2d 511 (1975).

A customary formula is cost of repairs necessary to restore the car to substantially similar condition as before the accident, but not more than the diminution in market value due to the injury, e. g., Kruvant v. Dickerman, 18 Md.App. 1, 305 A.2d 227 (1973).

LOSS OF USE. Damages for loss of use of the property injured are widely but not universally allowed, if proper evidence of the value of such loss is introduced. See annotation 18 A.L.R.3d 497; Bos v. Dolajak, —— Mont. ——, 534 P.2d 1258 (1975) (silo, "programmed as an integral part of a total dairy farming operation"); Jones v. Herrin, 252 Ark. 837, 481 S.W.2d 362 (1972) (denying recovery for such loss). Where the property is repaired, the time reasonably necessary for repairs measures the loss of use. What can be allowed for this item if an automobile is traded in for a new one, or is a total wreck? See Barnes v. United R. & E. Co., 140 Md. 14, 116 A. 855 (1922).

OTHER EXPENSES. Loss caused by decreasing plaintiff's earnings or profits, or increasing the expenses of his business has been allowed, Myers Const. Co. v. Wood R. D. & L. Dist., 221 Ill.App. 473 (1921) (expenses incident to tie-up in plaintiff's construction work caused by backing up water); Marland Ref. Co. v. Duffy, 94 Okl. 16, 220 P. 846, 35 A.L.R. 52 (1923) (loss of 10 days from brokerage business because of damage to auto); Caso v. Keboni, 55 Cal.App. 601, 203 P. 1025 (1921) (earnings of taxi in suit for personal injury to driver and damage to taxi); but nothing on this score, above the loss of use, may be recovered unless for some reason other similar property was unavailable. Conley v. Kansas City Rys. Co., 259 S.W. 153 (Mo.App. 1921); Francischini v. McMullen, 142 A. 651, 6 N.J.Misc. 736 (1928); Cincinnati Traction Co. v. Feldkamp, 19 Ohio App. 421 (1924).

How does the doctrine of avoidable consequences affect recovery for expenses of repairing, salvaging, etc., the property? Cf. Northern Tex. Traction Co. v. Stone, 230 S.W. 754 (Tex.Civ.App.1921); Lamon v. Perry, 33 Ga.App. 248, 125 S.E. 907 (1924); and Doolittle v. Otis Elevator Co., 98 Conn. 248, 118 A. 818 (1922).

CHICAGO, MILWAUKEE, ST. PAUL AND PACIFIC RAILROAD COMPANY v. TINDAL

United States District Court for the Southern District of Iowa, 1966.
249 F.Supp. 988.

STEPHENSON, CHIEF JUDGE.

* * *

On April 10, 1964, a fire destroyed plaintiff's freight depot. Although the walls remained standing after the fire, the frame building had no practical value after the fire and it was later destroyed and the building site restored to ground level. At the time of the fire defendant was in possession of the premises by virtue of a lease with plaintiff. Defendant utilized the building for the storage of fertilizer and at the time in question its employees had been engaged in loading out fertilizer from the building. The fertilizer was in fifty (50) pound bags which were emptied into the buyer's spreader at the site. The empty paper bags were then placed in a pile on the ground approximately twenty-five to thirty feet southeast from the southeast part of the freight depot where an employee then set them afire. * *

* * * The Court * * * finds that defendant's employees were negligent in failing to take ordinary care in ascertaining that the fire was out before leaving the premises. Said negligence was the proximate cause of the damage to plaintiff's building. * * *

This leaves the issue of damages. Plaintiff contended the building destroyed had no market value and therefore offered evidence as to its replacement cost less depreciation. Plaintiff also asks the Court to consider that the property was income producing property not only as to the rent received, but because of the increased freight revenue accruing to plaintiff because of its use in the fertilizer business. Defendant contends the proper measure of damages is the difference in the fair market value of the property before and after the fire. In this connection defendant offered the testimony of two experts that this value was nominal, if any. Defendant further asks the Court to consider that the evidence indicates a very limited use for a building of this type and thus the value is slight.

The Court finds the property in question had little market value, if any. Under these circumstances the actual value of the premises is the measure of recovery. McMahon v. City of Dubuque, 107 Iowa 62, 77 N.W. 517 (1898). Actual value can best be determined by considering the replacement cost less depreciation, taking into consideration the age, condition, utility and use to which the building is being put or can be reasonably used. Its value as income producing property should also be considered.

The freight depot is of heavy frame construction. It was originally built in 1903. It has been kept in a reasonable state of repair through annual, periodic inspections and repairs. About six to seven years before the fire a new roof and major foundation repairs were made to the building. It was in fair condition as a storage facility. It had not been painted for several years and windows were boarded up. There were no utilities provided to the building. The floors had developed cracks. The dimensions of the frame building were thirty feet by eighty feet. In addition there was a loading dock eight feet by eighty feet. In summary, the building was old but durable for storage purposes. It was not suitable for other than rough storage. It was not rodent tight. The building was being used for storing fertilizer in bags. It was suitable for that purpose. Defendant paid plaintiff an annual rental of $284.00 for use of the building. In addition, use of the building for storage purposes increased the freight revenue coming to plaintiff railroad.

On the basis of replacement at a cost of approximately twenty thousand dollars ($20,000) less depreciation of at least sixty percent, the building had a value of about eight thousand dollars ($8,000). However, the limited use to which the building was or could be put reduced its value materially.

The Court finds that the actual value of the building at the time it was destroyed was three thousand dollars ($3,000). The reasonable cost of restoring the site and clearing the rubble was one hundred dollars ($100).

The foregoing shall constitute the Court's findings of fact and conclusions of law. Judgment will enter in favor of the plaintiff and against the defendant in the sum of $3,100.

(C) PERSONAL INJURIES

Loss of Time; Wages, Salary, and Profits.

When the accident victim has a job and loses time from it because of the injury, he is entitled to recover damages based on this loss. The principal questions which arise about damages of this nature are these:

1. Is the measure of recovery the reasonable value of the plaintiff's time, or the wage he was actually getting? In most cases it would not matter which rule is chosen for all courts agree that the actual wage or salary is presumptive evidence of what the man's time is worth. But the two rules might bring about different results in some situations. For example may the defendant put in evidence to show that plaintiff was overpaid in the job he had when injured?

2. Where the plaintiff is not employed at a regular salary by another but works on commission or for profit may he prove his average earnings or profits before the injury as tending to show what his lost time is worth? This should be divided into separate questions for

(a) the salesman working on commission,

(b) the "fee" man (lawyer, doctor, dentist, etc.),

(c) the entrepreneur who has little or no capital invested in his enterprise,

(d) the entrepreneur whose profits flow from the investment of capital as well as his own activities. The rule of "certainty" is often invoked to exclude a showing of profits in this case, such items being regarded as too "speculative," "remote," or "contingent."

It is hard to tell from the opinions whether the courts are simply deciding that the proof before them did not support recovery based on profits, or whether they are laying down a rule which would preclude evidence of profits in all cases, no matter how carefully the effectiveness of the plaintiff's management could be isolated and its share in producing profits could be traced.

3. If the plaintiff is not gainfully employed but is, for example, a child in grade school, an unemployed man, a housewife, how can the value of lost time be measured?

4. How can plaintiff show the probable future loss of earnings? The principle of the single recovery clearly permits a recovery based on future earnings if a proper showing can be made. The problems which surround such a showing include

(a) the requirement of certainty of proof. The probable duration and extent of the incapacity must be shown by proof which meets the test of "certainty." Then there must be evidence on the basis of which prospective earnings may be found. Past earnings will usually afford such a basis (except in the case of profits where, as we have seen, another branch of the rule of "certainty" may impede the proving of loss of profits even as to a period which is past at the time of trial).

(b) As bearing on the duration of a permanent injury the probable length of plaintiff's life is obviously an important factor. The usual way of showing this is to introduce mortality tables in evidence. Problems which arise are

(i) whether a finding of probable life expectancy may be made in the absence of such tables.

(ii) what tables to use. The American Experience Table is the most widely used by insurance companies and by courts in this country. For a history of this and other tables, see Sources and Characteristics of the Principal Mortality Tables (rev. ed. 1932) pub. by Actuarial Society of America. Some states have adopted statutes governing the matter. See McCormick, Cases on Damages (1935)

228–230. For a compilation of alternative tables see Institute of Life Insurance, Life Insurance Fact Book 1974, at 108–09.

(iii) how to get the table in evidence. In the absence of statute, this is often done by agreement of counsel. Otherwise it may be necessary to call an actuary.

(iv) what factors should be considered in applying the tables to the case in hand (e. g. health, occupation, effect of the injury sued for on probable life span, etc.), e. g., Chester v. United States, 403 F.Supp. 458 (W.D.Pa.1975). In this connection it should be noted that courts have almost universally used the figure in the "expectation of life" column as the base for computation. For an economist's analysis of the significance of this column, see Maclean, Life Insurance (3d ed. 1932) 72, 73.

(v) May the possibility of advancement be considered?

(c) the effect of recovery in the present upon the amount allowable for loss which will occur in the future. This is offset by allowing plaintiff only the present worth of his prospective loss. Annuity tables may generally be used by the jury as an aid in computing this. For a treatment of the problems of evidence and instructions on this point, see McCormick, Cases on Damages (1935) 228 et seq. If the rate that can be earned on money is reduced in the future, how will this affect the use of mortality tables? of annuity tables?

5. Need loss of earnings be specially pleaded to be recoverable?

As to the above questions, consult Restatement of Torts, Second (Tent. Draft No. 19, 1973) section 912, comments d and e; section 924, comments d, e, and f; McCormick, Damages (1935) sections 86, 87; anno., 50 A.L.R.2d 419. See also Dublin and Lotka, The Money Value of a Man (1930); Fleming, The Lost Years: A Problem in the Computation and Distribution of Damages, 50 Calif.L.Rev. 598 (1962); P. Atiyah, Accidents, Compensation and the Law (1970) 194 et seq., and Komesar, Toward a General Theory of Personal Injury Loss, 3 J. Legal Studies 457 (1974).

REID'S BRANSON INSTRUCTIONS TO JURIES (3d ed. 1936)

Charge from Wisconsin Court, Section 1398.

(1) The court instructs the jury that you will name such sum as you find from a preponderance of all the credible evidence in the case, to a reasonable certainty, will be required fairly and reasonably to compensate the plaintiff in money for such loss of earnings and such pain and suffering, both mental and physical, as you are satisfied is chargeable to the injury, and, also for such loss of earnings, if any, and the impairment, if any, of capacity to earn a livelihood in the future, as it is reasonably certain will result from the injury, and such pain and suffering, both mental and physical, if any, as it is reasonably certain he will suffer in the future.

(2) The fifth question is this [the jury having been instructed to return a special verdict answering specific questions]: What sum of money would fairly compensate plaintiff for the damages he suffered by falling over a barrel-skid at the time and place in question? * * *

In arriving at your answer to this question you should, in measuring the results of plaintiff's personal injury, take into consideration the following elements of damage, so far as they are proved by the evidence to a reasonable certainty to have been produced by the personal injury in question: First, all pain and suffering, both bodily and mental, which the plaintiff has undergone; second, all reasonable expenses which the plaintiff has in good faith incurred, or will be required to incur in endeavoring to cure or relieve himself of the said personal injuries; third, all earnings, if any which the plaintiff has lost by reason of disability resulting from said injuries; and fourth, in case the jury become satisfied by the evidence to a reasonable certainty that the plaintiff will in the future continue to suffer further similar loss or losses or pain as the result of this injury, then you should take that into consideration and make a just provision therefor.

The amount that would fairly compensate the plaintiff for pain and suffering is not capable of any mathematical computation, but the jury should consider the facts as disclosed by the evidence in respect to pain and suffering caused to the plaintiff, all mental worry, both as to the immediate or future effects of the injury, and deprivation of usual pleasurable activities and enjoyments, and you should fix upon such sum as in the sound judgment of the jury would be a fair compensation to the plaintiff therefor.

In respect to the plaintiff's medical and surgical expenses and expenses incurred for care and nursing, and in respect to earnings lost by the plaintiff, these elements are more nearly capable of exact computation and you should give careful attention to what the evidence shows these to be.

The total sum found by you should be such, and only such, as the evidence shows to a reasonable certainty would be required to fairly and justly compensate the plaintiff for actual damages sustained as the result of the injury in question. Nothing should be added by way of punishment or by reason of any feeling of sympathy or resentment, nor should anything be deducted by reason of doubt of the defendant's liability, or because of the weight of the burden that may be put upon the defendant.

Some courts are less liberal than this in several particulars. Compare, for example, Northern Indiana Public Service Co. v. Robinson, 106 Ind.App. 210, 18 N.E.2d 933 (1939), noted in 38 Mich.L.Rev. 97 (1939) (injury may not consider plaintiff's inability to enjoy life in the manner to which she had become accustomed); Hogan v. Santa Fe

Trail Transp. Co., 148 Kan. 720, 85 P.2d 28, 120 A.L.R. 521 (1938), noted in 13 So.Cal.L.Rev. 152 (1939) (inability to play violin on account of her injuries); contrast Hayes v. Nanaimo Shipyards, Ltd. (1972) W.W.R. 337 (Brit.Col.) (inability to sail ocean-going ketch off-shore, instead of merely along coast); also see McNulty v. Southern Pacific Co., 96 Cal.App.2d 841, 216 P.2d 534 (1950). As to anguish, humiliation, etc., because of disfiguring injuries, see Merrill v. Los Angeles Gas & Electric Co., 158 Cal. 499, 111 P. 534, 31 L.R.A.,N.S. 559, 139 Am.St.Rep. 134 (1910). And as to the loss of a woman's childbearing years, see Feldman v. Allegheny Airlines Inc., page 463 supra.

There has been considerable Commonwealth attention to the questions whether, if plaintiff is unconscious for life, or has only partial awareness of a helpless existence, there is pain and suffering, or any other compensable loss in respect of the lost opportunity for hapiness; see e. g., Wise v. Kaye [1962] 1 Q.B. 638; H. West & Son Ltd. v. Shephard [1964] A.C. 326; Skelton v. Collins, 115 Commw.L.R. 94 (Austl.1966).

Plaintiffs' counsel often attempt a form of argument known as the unit of time or per diem argument, involving a request that the jury multiply the number of time units during which pain has been suffered (e. g., hours, days, months, etc.) by the amount of compensation contended to be proper for the suffering endured during each such unit of time. The reaction of the courts has varied, from disapproval, e. g., Botta v. Brunner, 26 N.J. 82, 138 A.2d 713 (1958), through intermediate positions, e. g., Boutang v. Twin City Motor Bus Co., 248 Minn. 240, 80 N.W.2d 30 (1960) (permitting the argument as a form of illustration by counsel, but not to be used by the jury in actual calculations), to outright approval in a number of jurisdictions, e. g., Grossnickle v. Village of Germantown, 3 Ohio St.2d 96, 209 N.E.2d 442 (1965). Also see Ratner v. Arrington, 111 So.2d 82 (Fla.1959) and Rush v. Cargo Ships & Tankers, Inc., 360 F.2d 766 (2d Cir. 1966).

On the general subject of damages for pain see Plant, Damages for Pain and Suffering, 19 Ohio St.L.J. 200 (1958); Morris, Liability for Pain and Suffering, 59 Colum.L.Rev. 476 (1959); Olender, Proof and Evaluation of Pain and Suffering in Personal Injury Litigation, 3 Duke L.J. 344 (1962); O'Connell and Simon, Payment for Pain & Suffering: Who Wants What, When & Why? 1972 U.Ill.L.Forum 1; Peck, Compensation for Pain: A Reappraisal in the Light of New Medical Evidence, 72 Mich.L.Rev. 1355 (1974).

BERANEK v. MULCARE

Supreme Court of Oregon, In Banc, 1974.
269 Or. 324, 524 P.2d 1214.

HOWELL, JUSTICE. Plaintiff was riding his motorcycle when it was hit from the rear by an auto owned and operated by defendant. Plaintiff filed this action seeking general and special damages for personal injuries and, in a second count, for damages to his motorcycle.

A jury returned a verdict for plaintiff for his damages to the motorcycle and awarded plaintiff $5,429.23 as special damages for medical expenses and lost wages. The jury awarded no general damages. Counsel for plaintiff then moved for a mistrial. However, the trial court send the jury back for further deliberations after instructing them that they must find general damages before they could award special damages. The court then granted plaintiff's motion for a mistrial. Later, the court accepted and filed the original verdict and entered a judgment thereon. Plaintiff appeals.

As a general rule, a verdict for special damages without an allowance for general damages is improper. Flansberg v. Paulson, 239 Or. 610, 399 P.2d 356 (1965). However, in Saum v. Bonar, 258 Or. 532, 484 P.2d 294 (1971), we held that where the issue of general damages is controverted in the pleadings and the evidence, and the jury could have concluded that plaintiff had not suffered any substantial injuries, a verdict for special damages only is a valid verdict.

In Brannan v. Slemp, 260 Or. 336, 490 P.2d 979 (1971), we found a verdict for special damages and no general damages to be improper where there was uncontroverted medical testimony that plaintiff sustained some pain and suffering and that he had some permanent injury, although not extensive.

In the instant case, plaintiff alleged that he suffered lacerations and injury to the muscles and tissues of his right leg and ankle. The defendant's answer admitted "some" injury to plaintiff but denied the extent of the injury.

The evidence as to the permanency of plaintiff's injuries and the extent of his injuries was seriously controverted.

However, there was uncontroverted evidence that plaintiff was hospitalized for five days with his leg elevated and that he was in some pain at that time. There was also evidence that he was at home in bed with his leg elevated for three weeks and that he would have some permanent scars on his leg. This is evidence of general damages.

Under the circumstances we believe that the facts fall within the rule of Flansberg v. Paulson, supra, and that the verdict for special damages only was improper. The trial court should not have entered the verdict. * * *

O'CONNELL, CHIEF JUSTICE (dissenting).

* * * Regardless of what refinements this court makes in distinguishing general and special damages, the present case, as well as our previous cases, demonstrates that juries view plaintiff's damages as an indivisible unit rather than a composite of the separate legal elements of general and special damages.

There is no reason why a jury should not be permitted to measure defendant's fault solely in terms of plaintiff's medical costs or other items which are denominated special damages, even though the plaintiff received injuries which caused him pain and suffering. * * *

DeMAURO v. CENTRAL GULF SS CORP.

United States Court of Appeals for the Second Circuit, 1975.
514 F.2d 403.

VAN GRAAFEILAND, CIRCUIT JUDGE. Patrick DeMauro, a longshoreman, was injured by the collapse of a tier of wooden boxes while he was unloading cargo from the hatch of a ship docked at Bayonne, N. J. This appeal is from a judgment in his favor against the shipowner. * * *

It is on the issue of damages that we feel appellants have cause to complain. DeMauro sustained a fractured femur, which was fixed by open reduction and pinning, and a non-displaced fracture of the fibula. Both fractures healed properly and with good union. The medical experts disagreed concerning DeMauro's ability to perform the heavy manual labor and climbing required by his former job, but all were in accord that he was able to work. According to DeMauro, his attending physician discharged him from treatment in April of 1972, one year following the accident, and advised him at that time that he could return to work. DeMauro's medical specials were $5,049.37.

We conclude that the jury's verdict of $200,000 must have been based in large measure upon a finding of permanent disability from employment which was not justified by the testimony and is therefore grossly excessive. We reverse and remand the case to the trial court for a new trial solely on the issue of plaintiff's damages unless plaintiff is willing to remit all damages in excess of $100,000. In the event that such remittitur is made within ten (10) days, the judgment will be affirmed with costs to plaintiff-appellee.[8]

8. Awards are sometimes reversed for being too low, e. g., Mills v. Telenczak, Del.Supr., 345 A.2d 424 (1975) ($4,000 for hideous permanent injuries "so grossly out of proportion to the injuries suffered as to shock the Court's conscience and sense of justice * * "); Drummond v. Mid-West Growers Cooperative Corp., — Nev. —, 542 P.2d 198 (1975).

SPADE v. LYNN & BOSTON R. R.

Supreme Judicial Court of Massachusetts, 1897.
168 Mass. 285, 47 N.E. 88, 38 L.R.A. 512, 60 Am.St.Rep. 393.

TORT, for personal injuries occasioned to the plaintiff by the alleged negligence of the defendant. * * *

At the trial in the Superior Court, before MASON, C. J., there was evidence tending to show that the accident complained of occurred while the plaintiff was being conveyed to her home in Chelsea upon a crowded car of the defendant company, after 10:30 P.M., on February 16, 1895.

The plaintiff testified in substance that two men somewhat intoxicated were allowed, during a part of the trip from Boston to Chelsea, to stand near her in the car, one of them in a position where he was leaning or lurching toward her in such a way that she was obliged to move to avoid him; that a controversy occurred between one of the intoxicated persons and the conductor about the payment of a fare, and that the conductor said to the intoxicated person, after some other conversation, that if he did not keep quiet he would throw him off the car, even if he broke his head; that as she neared the place where she was to leave the car, "the first thing I saw was the conductor * * * grab this man by the collar; the next thing I saw was * * * another man from the other end of the car, whom I did not know, come down; but the other man, as he pulled him lurched over on me; then it seemed as though I turned to solid ice. My breath was cut right off. I could not have spoken; I tried to speak, but I chilled so I kept growing stiffer and stiffer, until I did not know, I do not know when they got me off the car." She further stated that nothing had occurred of any sort or description that gave any suggestion of a warning that the conductor was going to rush at the drunken man at this time; that he did it "just as quick as a man could jump"; and that the intoxicated person standing directly in front of her "lurched over so it kind of pushed me back against the car."

The plaintiff further testified:

"Q. Your body was not injured in any way by contact with this man? A. Oh, no, I was not injured. There were not any marks on me, anything like that.

"Q. You suffered no pain from this man touching you? A. No, not any injury from that.

"Q. What was the cause of this man's touching you, the one that lurched forward? A. When the conductor jumped and grabbed this man that I told about, on the opposite side of the car, that made a commotion, and as he twitched him it pushed this other man over on to me."

The jury returned a verdict for the plaintiff; and the defendant alleged exceptions. * * *

ALLEN, J. This case presents a question which has not heretofore been determined in this Commonwealth, and in respect to which the decisions elsewhere have not been uniform. It is this: whether in an action to recover damages for an injury sustained through the negligence of another, there can be a recovery for a bodily injury caused by mere fright and mental disturbance. The jury were instructed that a person cannot recover for mere fright, fear, or mental distress occasioned by the negligence of another, which does not result in bodily injury; but that when the fright or fear or nervous shock produces a bodily injury, there may be a recovery for that bodily injury, and for all the pain, mental or otherwise, which may arise out of that bodily injury. * * *

The case calls for a consideration of the real ground upon which the liability or non-liability of a defendant guilty of negligence in a case like the present depends. The exemption from liability for mere fright, terror, alarm, or anxiety does not rest on the assumption that these do not constitute an actual injury. They do in fact deprive one of enjoyment and of comfort, cause real suffering, and to a greater or less extent disqualify one for the time being from doing the duties of life. If these results flow from a wrongful or negligent act, a recovery therefor cannot be denied on the ground that the injury is fanciful and not real. Nor can it be maintained that these results may not be the direct and immediate consequence of the negligence. Danger excites alarm. Few people are wholly insensible to the emotions caused by imminent danger, though some are less affected than others.

It must also be admitted that a timid or sensitive person may suffer not only in mind, but also in body, from such a cause. Great emotion may and sometimes does produce physical effects. The action of the heart, the circulation of the blood, the temperature of the body, as well as the nerves and the appetite, may well be affected. A physical injury may be directly traceable to fright, and so may be caused by it. We cannot say, therefore, that such consequences may not flow proximately from unintentional negligence, and if compensation in damages may be recovered for a physical injury so caused, it is hard on principle to say why there should not also be a recovery for the mere mental suffering when not accompanied by any perceptible physical effects.

It would seem therefore that the real reason for refusing damages sustained from mere fright must be something different; and it probably rests on the ground that in practice it is impossible satisfactorily to administer any other rule. The law must be administered in the courts according to general rules. Courts will aim to make these rules as just as possible, bearing in mind that they are to be of general application. But as the law is a practical science, having to do with the affairs of life, any rule is unwise if in its general application it will not as a usual result serve the purposes of justice. A new rule cannot be made for each case, and there must therefore be a certain generality in rules of law, which in particular cases may fail to meet what would be desirable if the single case were alone to be considered.

Rules of law respecting the recovery of damages are framed with reference to the just rights of both parties; not merely what it might be right for an injured person to receive, to afford just compensation for his injury, but also what it is just to compel the other party to pay. One cannot always look to others to make compensation for injuries received. Many accidents occur, the consequences of which the sufferer must bear alone. And in determining the rules of law by which the right to recover compensation for unintended injury from others is to be governed, regard must chiefly be paid to such conditions as are usually found to exist. Not only the transportation of passengers and the running of trains, but the general conduct of business and of the ordinary affairs of life, must be done on the assumption that persons who are liable to be affected thereby are not peculiarly sensitive, and are of ordinary physical and mental strength. If, for example, a traveller is sick or infirm, delicate in health, specially nervous or emotional, liable to be upset by slight causes, and therefore requiring precautions which are not usual or practicable for travellers in general, notice should be given, so that, if reasonably practicable, arrangements may be made accordingly, and extra care be observed. But, as a general rule, a carrier of passengers is not bound to anticipate or to guard against an injurious result which would only happen to a person of peculiar sensitiveness. This limitation of liability for injury of another description is intimated in Allsop v. Allsop, 5 H. & N. 534, 538, 539. One may be held bound to anticipate and guard against the probable consequences to ordinary people, but to carry the rule of damages further imposes an undue measure of responsibility upon those who are guilty only of unintentional negligence. The general rule limiting damages in such a case to the natural and probable consequences of the acts done is of wide application, and has often been expressed and applied. * * *

The law of negligence in its special application to cases of accidents has received great development in recent years. The number of actions brought is very great. This should lead courts well to consider the grounds on which claims for compensation properly rest, and the necessary limitations of the right to recover. We remain satisfied with the rule that there can be no recovery for fright, terror, alarm, anxiety, or distress of mind, if these are unaccompanied by some physical injury; and if this rule is to stand, we think it should also be held that there can be no recovery for such physical injuries as may be caused solely by such mental disturbance, where there is no injury to the person from without. The logical vindication of this rule, is, that it is unreasonable to hold persons who are merely negligent bound to anticipate and guard against fright and the consequences of fright; and this would open a wide door for unjust claims, which could not successfully be met. * * *

It is hardly necessary to add that this decision does not reach those classes of actions where an intention to cause mental distress or to hurt the feelings is shown, or is reasonably to be inferred, as, for example, in cases of seduction, slander, malicious prosecution, or arrest, and some others. Nor do we include cases of acts done with gross carelessness or recklessness, showing utter indifference to such consequences, when they must have been in the actor's mind. * * *

In the present case, no such considerations entered into the rulings or were presented by the facts. The entry therefore must be, Exceptions sustained.

Cf. Homans v. Boston El. Ry. Co., 180 Mass. 456, 62 N.E. 737, 57 L.R.A. 291, 91 Am.St.Rep. 324 (1902); Freedman v. Eastern Mass. St. Ry. Co., 299 Mass. 246, 12 N.E.2d 739 (1938); Sullivan v. H. P. Hood & Sons, 341 Mass. 216, 168 N.E.2d 80 (1960).

This rule obtained quite a following though the modern trend is distinctly away from it. See, in general, Goodrich, Emotional Disturbance as Legal Damage, 20 Mich.L.Rev. 497 (1922); Magruder, Mental and Emotional Disturbance in the Law of Torts, 49 Harv.L. Rev. 1033 (1936); Smith, Relation of Emotions to Injury and Disease: Legal Liability for Psychic Stimuli, 30 Va.L.Rev. 193 (1944); F. Harper and F. James, The Law of Torts § 18.4 (1956 and Supp.1968); W. Prosser, Law of Torts § 54 (4th ed. 1971); Restatement, Second, Torts §§ 306, 413, 436, 436A, and comments (1965); D'Ambra v. United States, 354 F.Supp. 810 (D.R.I.1973); Id. — R.I. —, 338 A.2d 524 (1975); Id. 518 F.2d 275 (1st Cir. 1975). Two things about the rule deserve special mention. It does not preclude recovery for the nervous or mental consequences of a physical injury. Homans v. Boston El. Ry. Co., 180 Mass. 456, 63 N.E. 737, 57 L.R.A. 291, 91 Am.St.Rep. 324 (1902) (in which Holmes, J., characterized the rule in the Spade cases as "an arbitrary exception, based upon a notion of what is practicable.") And it has never been held to require physical contact between defendant (or his vehicle) and plaintiff (or his vehicle), though many laymen—and even a few claim adjusters—have the notion that there is some such requirement for liability. Impact from "an external force" is sometimes still required, e. g., Gilliam v. Stewart, 291 So.2d 593 (Fla.1974) (but see strong dissent at 596 et seq.). A somewhat more liberal variation denies compensation for emotional damage unless it is "manifested" or "accompanied" by physical injury; e. g., Piorkowski v. Liberty Mutual Insurance Co., 68 Wis.2d 455, 228 N.W.2d 695 (1975). See, similarly, Rosman v. Transworld Airlines, Inc., 34 N.Y.2d 385, 358 N.Y.S.2d 97, 314 N.E. 2d 848 (1974) (liability for "bodily injuries" under Warsaw Convention includes damages for mental distress resulting from skin rash resulting from fear of hijacked airplane passenger, "but not for the trauma as such or for the nonbodily or behavioral manifestations of the trauma"); compare Husserl v. Swiss Air Transport Company, Ltd., 388 F.Supp. 1238, 1251 (S.D.N.Y.1975), which would allow damages for "mental injury alone" under Warsaw Convention language "en cas de mort, de blessure ou de toute autre lésion corporelle * * *").

In this and the next few cases the problems could easily be treated under some other head than "damages," since the question in each of them is whether defendant shall be held liable at all. Some prefer to deal with this line of cases as raising primarily the question of the scope and kinds of interests (on plaintiff's side) which will receive the law's protection against various kinds of possible invasion by defendants. This alternative arrangement tends to emphasize the increasing protection which some of those interests are receiving. Surely here we are at one of the frontiers of tort law. There are others; liability is being expanded, and occasionally contracted too, by manipulation of various doctrines of torts and procedure. So long as that is kept in mind, any peculiar advantage inhering in the arrangements of materials according to interests to be protected is thought to be retained. The problem is here included under "damages" because it is widely felt that one of its most important aspects is the difficulty of telling the real from the feigned cases, and this subsidiary problem in turn runs through the whole field of compensatory damages, including those awarded by workmen's compensation tribunals.

Where plaintiff has suffered mental or physical injury without trauma, the lawyer should always explore the possibilities of recovery which may be opened up by showing that defendant was guilty of an intent to frighten or injure, or of some other aggravated wrong. See material, chapter 8, infra. Sometimes special statutory provisions apply, e. g., Westview Cemetery, Inc. v. Blanchard, 234 Ga. 540, 216 S.E.2d 776 (1975) (damages to widow for wrongful disinterment of husband's body, under statute concerning torts where "the entire injury is to the peace, happiness, or feelings of the plaintiff").

PRICE v. YELLOW PINE PAPER MILL CO.

Court of Civil Appeals of Texas, 1922.
240 S.W. 588.

O'QUINN, J. Mary Price, joined by her husband, R. A. Price, sued the Yellow Pine Paper Mill Company for damages to Mrs. Price, * * *.

The case went to trial before a jury; but, when the testimony was closed, the court instructed a verdict for defendant, upon which judgment was rendered, and from which plaintiffs appealed. * * *

[The facts stated in the petition are substantially those found by the court in its opinion on motion for rehearing, infra.]

Generally, it is held that damages for mental suffering, accompanied by physical injuries, negligently inflicted, may be recovered; but many courts hold that for injuries resulting merely from fright or other mental emotions caused by the wrongful act or omission of another, but which do not accompany such mental emotions, no recovery can be had. The question in Texas seems to be well settled that no recovery can be had for mere fright which is neither attended nor followed by any other injury. Railway v. Trott, 86 Tex. 412, 25 S.W. 419, 40 Am.St.Rep. 866. But where physical injury, such as sickness, insanity, miscarriage, etc., results from fright or other mental shock caused by the willful act or omission of another, and such wrongful act or omission is the proximate cause of the injury, and the injury ought, in the light of all the circumstances, to have been foreseen as a natural and probable consequence thereof, the injured party is entitled to recover, and as a rule these questions are for the jury to determine. Railway Co. v. Hayter, 93 Tex. 239, 54 S.W. 944, 47 L.R.A. 325, 77 Am.St.Rep. 856; Hill v. Kimball, 76 Tex. 210, 13 S.W. 59, 7 L.R.A. 618. * * *

We think plaintiffs' petition stated a cause of action, and that the evidence was sufficient to raise a question of fact for the jury. We do not express any opinion as to the sufficiency of the evidence to support a verdict for appellants, but only hold that the petition stated a cause of action, and the evidence was sufficient to raise an issue of fact to go to the jury; and hence that the court erred in directing the verdict for defendant, for which error the judgment is reversed, and the cause remanded.

On motion for rehearing.

* * * At the suggestion and on motion of appellee, we make the following findings of fact, to wit:

"R. A. Price was an employé of the Yellow Pine Paper Mill Company, defendant in error and while in the discharge of his duty in the course of his employment received injuries * * *.

That when the accident occurred by which R. A. Price, husband of Mary Price, was injured, George S. Holmes, who was the general manager of appellee, assumed control in rendering first aid to the injured employés, and said Holmes took said Price in an automobile from the place of the accident to the home of said Price, and that while on the way Price told said Holmes not to take him (Price) home in the condition he (Price) was in; that his wife, Mrs. Price, was in the family way and not in condition to see him (Price) in his then condition, and to let him out of the car, but that Holmes did not let Price out of the car; but carried him on to his (Price's) home; that at the time Price arrived at his home he was bruised and bloody and exhibited external appearances of his injured condition, and Mrs. Price was so mentally shocked and excited at his appearance that she became sick and continued to suffer until she miscarried, and has continued to suffer ever since; that at the time of the accident Mrs. Price was some six months advanced in pregnancy, and that her general health and condition was good up to that time, but has been bad ever since. * * *

JOHNSON v. STATE OF NEW YORK

Court of Appeals of New York, 1975.
37 N.Y.2d 378, 372 N.Y.S.2d 638, 334 N.E.2d 590.

BREITEL, CHIEF JUDGE. On claimant Fleeter Thorpe's appeal, the issue is whether the daughter of a patient in a State hospital, falsely advised that the patient, her mother, had died, may recover from the State for emotional harm. She sustained the harm as a direct result of the negligent misinformation provided by the hospital in the course of it advising relatives of the death of a patient. The mother was in fact alive and well.

Claimant and her aunt, Nellie Johnson, since deceased, had filed a claim against the State for funeral expenses incurred, emotional harm and punitive damages. The Court of Claims awarded claimant $7,500 for funeral expenses undertaken on the false information, and for emotional harm. It denied her punitive damages, and dismissed the aunt's claim for insufficiency. The State appealed to the Appellate Division and claimants cross-appealed. The Appellate Division modified, limiting the daughter's award to her pecuniary losses of $1,658.47, and otherwise affirmed as to both claimants. * * *

There should be a reversal. The daughter of a hospital patient may recover for emotional harm sustained by her as a result of negligent misinformation given by the hospital that her mother had died. Key to liability, of course, is the hospital's duty, borne or assumed, to advise the proper next of kin of the death of a patient.

Claimant's mother, Emma Johnson, had been a patient in the Hudson River State Hospital since 1960. On August 6, 1970, another patient, also named Emma Johnson, died. Later that day, the hospital sent a telegram addressed to Nellie Johnson of Albany, claimant's aunt and the sister of the living Emma Johnson. The telegram read:

"REGRET TO INFORM YOU OF DEATH OF EMMA JOHNSON PLEASE NOTIFY RELATIVES MAKE BURIAL ARRANGEMENTS HAVE UNDERTAKER CONTACT HOSPITAL BEFORE COMING FOR BODY HOSPITAL WISHES TO STUDY ALL DEATHS FOR SCIENTIFIC REASONS PLEASE WIRE POST MORTEM CONSENT.

HUDSON RIVER STATE HOSPITAL

In accordance with the instructions in the telegram, claimant was notified of her mother's death by her aunt. An undertaker was engaged; the body of the deceased Emma Johnson was released by the hospital and taken to Albany that night. A wake was set for August 11, with burial the next day. In the interim claimant incurred expenses in preparing the body for the funeral, and in notifying other relatives of her mother's death.

On the afternoon of the wake, claimant and her aunt went to the funeral home to view the body. After examining the body, both claimant and her aunt remarked that the mother's appearance had changed. Nellie Johnson also expressed doubt that the corpse was that of her sister Emma. Thereafter the doubts built up, and upon returning that evening for the wake, claimant, in a state of extreme distress, examined the corpse more closely and verified that it was not that of her mother. At this point, claimant became "very, very hysterical", and had to be helped from the funeral chapel.

The hospital was called, and the mistake confirmed. Claimant's mother was alive and well in another wing of the hospital. Later that evening at the hospital, the deputy director, with the authorization of the director, admitted the mistake to claimant and her aunt. Upon the trial it appeared that the hospital had violated its own procedures and with gross carelessness had "pulled" the wrong patient record.

After this incident, claimant did not work in her employment for more than 11 days. She complained of "[r]ecurrent nightmares, terrifying dreams of death, seeing the coffin * * * difficulty in concentrating, irritability, inability to function at work properly, general tenseness and anxiety." Her psychiatrist testified that "She appeared to be somewhat depressed, tremulous. She seemed to be under a considerable amount of pressure. She cried easily when relating events that occurred. I thought that she spoke rather rapidly and obviously perspiring." Both her psychiatrist and that of the State agreed that, as a result of the incident, claimant suffered "excessive anxiety", that is, anxiety neurosis. Her expert, as indicated, testified that she showed objective manifestations of that condition.

One to whom a duty of care is owed, it has been held, may recover for harm sustained solely as a result of an initial, negligently-caused psychological trauma, but with ensuing psychic harm with residual physical manifestations (Battalla v. State of New York, 10 N.Y.2d 237, 238–239, 219 N.Y.S.2d 34, 35, 176 N.E.2d 729; Ferrara v. Galluchio, 5 N.Y.2d 16, 21–22, 176 N.Y.S.2d 996, 999–1000, 152 N.E.2d 249, 252; cf. Restatement, Torts 2d, § 313, subd. [1]; see, generally, Tobin v. Grossman, 24 N.Y.2d 609, 613, 301 N.Y.S.2d 554, 556, 249 N.E.2d 419, 420; Prosser, Torts [4th ed.] § 54, pp. 330–333; 2 Harper and James, Law of Torts, § 18.4, pp. 1032–1034; Torts —Emotional Disturbances, Ann., 64 A.L.R.2d 100, 143, § 11 et seq.). In the absence of contemporaneous or consequential physical injury, courts have been reluctant to permit recovery for negligently caused psychological trauma, with ensuing emotional harm alone (see Restatement, Torts 2d, § 436A; Prosser, Torts [4th ed.] op. cit., pp. 328–330, and cases collected; 2 Harper and James, Law of Torts, op. cit., pp. 1031–1032, and cases collected; Torts—Emotional Disturbances, Ann., 64 A.L.R.2d 100, 115, § 7; cf. Weicker v. Weicker, 22 N.Y.2d 8, 11, 290 N.Y.S.2d 732, 733, 237 N.E.2d 876). The reasons for the more restrictive rule were best summarized by Prosser (op. cit., p. 329): "The temporary emotion of fright, so far from serious that it does no physical harm, is so evanescent a thing, so easily counterfeited, and usually so trivial, that the courts have been quite unwilling to protect the plaintiff against mere negligence, where the elements of extreme outrage and moral blame which have had such weight in the case of the intentional tort are lacking". Contemporaneous or consequential physical harm, coupled with the initial psychological trauma, was, however, thought to provide an index of reliability otherwise absent in a claim for psychological trauma with only psychological consequences.

There have developed, however, two exceptions. The first is the minority rule permitting recovery for emotional harm resulting from negligent transmission by a telegraph company of a message announcing death (see cases collected in Restatement, Torts 2d, App., § 436A; Prosser, op. cit., p. 329; but see Western Union Tel. Co. v. Speight, 254 U.S. 17, 18, 41 S.Ct. 11, 65 L.Ed. 104; Curtin v. Western Union Tel. Co., 13 App.Div. 253, 255–256, 42 N.Y.S. 1109, 1110–1111 [majority rule denying recovery]. The Federal rule does, however, permit recovery where the psychological trauma results in physical illness * * *.

The second exception permits recovery for emotional harm to a close relative resulting from negligent mishandling of a corpse (see Prosser, op. cit., pp. 329–330, and cases collected). Recovery in these cases has ostensibly been grounded on a violation of the relative's quasi-property right in the body (see Darcy v. Presbyterian Hosp., 202 N.Y. 259, 262, 95 N.E. 695, 696; but cf. Owens v. Liverpool Corp. [1939] 1 KB 394, 400 [CA] [applying negligence principles], disapproved in Hay or Bourhill v. Young [1943] AC 92, 110 [HL] [per Lord WRIGHT], but applied in Behrens v. Bertram Mills Circus [1957] 2 QB 1, 28 [DEVLIN, J.]) It has been noted, however, that in this context such a "property right" is little more than a fiction; in reality the personal feelings of the survivors are being protected (Prosser, op. cit., p. 59).

In both the telegraph cases and the corpse mishandling cases, there exists "an especial likelihood of genuine and serious mental distress, arising from the special circumstances, which serves as a guarantee that the claim is not spurious" (p. 330). Prosser notes that "[t]here may perhaps be other such cases" (p. 330; see Nieman v. Upper Queens Med. Group, City Ct., 220 N.Y.S.2d 129, 130, in which plaintiff alleged emotional harm due to negligent misinformation by a laboratory that his sperm count indicated sterility; and defendant's motion for judgment on the pleadings was denied). The instant claim provides an example of such a case.

As the Appellate Division correctly found and the State in truth concedes, the hospital was negligent in failing to ascertain the proper next of kin when it mistakenly transmitted the death notice to claimant's aunt and through her, at its behest, to claimant. * * * The false message and the events flowing from its receipt were the proximate cause of claimant's emotional harm. Hence, claimant is entitled to recover for that harm, especially if supported by objective manifestations of that harm.

Tobin v. Grossman (24 N.Y.2d 609, 301 N.Y.S.2d 554, 249 N.E.2d 419, supra) is not relevant. In the *Tobin* case, the court held that no cause of action lies for unintended harm sustained by one, solely as a result of injuries inflicted directly upon another, regardless of the relationship and whether the one was an eyewitness to the incident which resulted in the direct injuries (p. 611, 301 N.Y.S.2d pp. 554–555, 249 N.E.2d pp. 419–420). In this case, however, the injury was inflicted by the hospital directly on claimant by its negligent sending of a false message announcing her mother's death. Claimant was not indirectly harmed by injury caused to another; she was not a mere eyewitness of or bystander to injury caused to another. Instead, she was the one to whom a duty was directly owed by the hospital, and the one who was directly injured by the hospital's breach of that duty. Thus, the rationale underlying the *Tobin* case, namely, the real dangers of extending recovery for harm to others than those directly involved, is inapplicable to the instant case. * * *

Moreover, not only justice but logic compels the further conclusion that if claimant was entitled to recover her pecuniary losses she was also entitled to recover for the emotional harm caused by the same tortious act. The recovery of the funeral expenses stands only because a duty to claimant was breached. Such a duty existing and such a breach of that duty occurring, she is entitled to recover the proven harmful consequences proximately caused by the breach. In the light of the *Battalla* and *Ferrara* cases (supra), and the reasoning upon which they were based, recovery for emotional harm to one subjected directly to the tortious act may not be disallowed so long as the evidence is sufficient to show causation and substantiality of the harm suffered, together with a "guarantee of genuineness" to which the court referred in the *Ferrara* case. * * *

Accordingly, the order of the Appellate Division should be reversed, with costs, and the matter remitted to that court for a determination of the facts in accordance with CPLR 5613.

* * *

STEINHAUSER v. HERTZ CORPORATION

United States Court of Appeals, Second Circuit, 1970.
421 F.2d 1169.

FRIENDLY, CIRCUIT JUDGE. On September 4, 1964, plaintiff Cynthia Steinhauser, a New Jersey citizen then 14 years old, her mother and father were driving south through Essex County, N. Y. A northbound car, owned by defendant Hertz Corporation, a Delaware corporation authorized to do business in New York, and operated by defendant Ponzini, a citizen of New York, crossed over a double yellow line in the highway into the southbound lane and struck the Steinhauser car heavily on the left side. The occupants did not suffer any bodily injuries.

The plaintiffs' evidence was that within a few minutes after the accident Cynthia began to behave in an unusual way. Her parents observed her to be "glassy-eyed," "upset," "highly agitated," "nervous" and "disturbed." When Ponzini came toward the Steinhauser car, she jumped up and down and made menacing gestures until restrained by her father. On the way home she complained of a headache and became uncommunicative. In the following days things went steadily worse. Cynthia thought that she was being attacked and that knives, guns and bullets were coming through the windows. She was hostile toward her parents and assaulted them; becoming depressed, she attempted suicide.

The family physician recommended hospitalization. After observation and treatment in three hospitals, with a final diagnosis of "schizophrenic reaction—acute—undifferentiated," she was released in December 1964 under the care of a psychiatrist, Dr. Royce, which continued until September 1966. His diagnosis, both at the beginning and at the end, was of a chronic schizophrenic reaction; he explained that by "chronic" he meant that Cynthia was not brought to him because of a sudden onset of symptoms. She then entered the Hospital of the University of Pennsylvania and, one month later, transferred to the Institute of Pennsylvania Hospital for long-term therapy. Discharged in January 1968, she has required the care of a psychiatrist. The evidence was that the need for this will continue, that reinstitutionalization is likely, and that her prognosis is bad.

As the recital makes evident, the important issue was the existence of a causal relationship between the rather slight accident and Cynthia's undoubtedly serious ailment.[9] The testimony was uncontradicted that prior to the acccident she had never displayed such exaggerated symptoms as thereafter. However, she had fallen from a horse about two years earlier and suffered what was diagnosed as a minor concussion; she was not hospitalized but missed a month of school. The other evidence relied on by the defendants to show prior psychiatric abnormality was derived largely from the history furnished, apparently in large part by Cynthia, at her admission to the first of the three hospitals on September 20, 1964, which we set out in the margin.[10]

9. The fact that no physical harm was suffered as a result of the accident does not affect plaintiff's right to recover. New York has abandoned the rule disallowing recovery for mental disturbance in the absence of a physical impact, see Battalla v. State, 10 N.Y.2d 237, 219 N.Y.S.2d 34, 176 N.E. 2d 729 (1961), and although some courts deny recovery for mental disturbance unaccompanied by physical injuries, see Prosser, Torts 348–49 (3d ed. 1964); A.L.I. Restatement 2d Torts § 436A, New York allows such recovery if the "mental injury [is] marked by definite physical symptoms which are capable of clear medical proof," Ferrara v. Galluchio, 5 N.Y.2d 16, 176 N.Y.S.2d 996, 152 N.E.2d 249 (1958), quoting Prosser, Torts 212 (1st ed. 1941); see also Battalla v. State, supra, and "A. A." v. State, 43 Misc.2d 1004, 252 N.Y.S.2d 800 (Ct. Cl.1964) (awarding damages where slight physical impact "aggravated and exacerbated that pre-existing condition" to produce schizophrenia).

10. She was a normal child except one incident when at the age of nine one of the friends of her uncle molested her three times. Two years before

Dr. Royce testified that a person may have a predisposition to schizophrenia which, however, requires a "precipitating factor" to produce an outbreak. As a result of long observation he believed this to have been Cynthia's case—that "she was a rather sensitive child and frequently exaggerated things and distorted things that happened within the family" but that the accident was "the precipitating cause" of her serious mental illness. Under cross-examination he stated that prior to the accident Cynthia had a "prepsychotic" personality but might have been able to lead a normal life. Dr. Stevens, attending psychiatrist at the Institute of Pennsylvania Hospital, who had treated Cynthia, in answer to a hypothetical question which included the incidents relied on by the defendants to show prior abnormality, was of the opinion that the accident "was the precipitating cause of the overt psychotic reaction," "the last straw that breaks the camel's back." In contrast defendants' expert, Dr. Brock, while agreeing that "with a background of fertile soil" schizophrenia can be induced by emotional strain, was of the opinion, based largely on the matters recited in footnote * * * [18], that Cynthia was already schizophrenic at the time of the accident.

* * * [T]he judge said he would put the case to the jury on the basis of proximate cause. * * * Efforts by counsel to explain that his theory was one of "precipitating cause of a quiescent disease" proved unavailing; the judge insisted that he choose between saying "that this plaintiff was perfectly normal and that she got this schizophrenia as a result of the accident" or admitting "that she had schizophrenia before this accident, and that this accident only aggravated a pre-existing condition. There is no inbetween position." Counsel remarked that there were "a host of other positions" between Cynthia's being "the most perfect child" or being schizophrenic before the accident, but the judge was not persuaded. * * *

It is plain enough that plaintiffs were deprived of a fair opportunity to have the jury consider the case on the basis of the medical evidence they had adduced. The testimony was that before the accident Cynthia was *neither* a "perfectly normal child" *nor* a schizophrenic, but a child with some degree of pathology which was activated into schizophrenia by an emotional trauma although it otherwise might not have blossomed. Whatever the medical soundness of this theory may or may not be, and there does not seem in fact to have

while in camp she fell down from a horse. There she liked one horse called Silverfox, which she wanted to buy and felt much attached to him. Against her wishes, she saw that horse sold to another party. She felt depressed. Food seemed the only answer. She ate and felt better. As a result of it she became fat and felt further depressed. Later on she felt attached to a Riviera automobile but the family bought a Cadillac, which she hated very much. "Horses go away, car goes away but food never does." One year before she got involved with "hoods." They were fast and did everything—also in quotes. Quote, I felt much better among them. I wished to be liked and did everything to please them, unquote.

There was evidence that in fact the first incident was exposure by the brother of an uncle rather than molestation.

been any dispute about it, see Guttmacher and Weihofen, Psychiatry and the Law 43–55 (1952), plaintiffs were entitled to have it fairly weighed by the jury. They could not properly be pinioned on the dilemma of having either to admit that Cynthia was already suffering from active schizophrenia or to assert that she was wholly without psychotic tendencies. The jury's question showed how well they had perceived the true issue. When they were told in effect that plaintiffs could recover only if, contrary to ordinary experience, the accident alone produced the schizophrenia, the result was predestined.

It is unnecessary to engage in exhaustive citation of authority sustaining the legal validity of plaintiffs' theory of the case. Since New York law governs, the oft-cited decision in McCahill v. New York Transportation Co., 201 N.Y. 221, 94 N.E. 616, 48 L.R.A.,N.S. 131 (1911), which plaintiffs' appellate counsel has discovered, would alone suffice. There the defendant's taxicab negligently hit McCahill, broke his thigh and injured his knee. After being hospitalized, he died two days later of delirium tremens. A physician testified that "the injury precipitated his attack of delirium tremens, and understand I mean precipitated not induced"; he explained that by "precipitated," he meant "hurried up,"—just what plaintiffs' experts testified to be the role of the accident here. The Court of Appeals allowed recovery for wrongful death. In Champlin Refining Co. v. Thomas, 93 F.2d 133, 136 (10 Cir. 1937), the court held that "where one who has tubercular germs in his system suffers injuries due to the negligence of another, and the injuries so weaken the resistance of the tissues that as a direct consequence tubercular infection sets up therein, the negligence is the proximate cause of the tubercular infection and renders the negligent person liable in damages therefor." There was no suggestion that plaintiff was required either to admit that he already "had" tuberculosis or to assert that the accident "caused" the development of the germs. Accord, Hazelwood v. Hodge, 357 S.W.2d 711 (Ky.1961). In Pigney v. Pointer's Transport Services, Ltd., [1957] 1 W.L.R. 1121, recovery for wrongful death was allowed where head injuries induced an anxiety neurosis leading to suicide. Our own decision in Evans v. S. J. Groves & Sons Co., 315 F.2d 335, 346–349 (1963) [thrombosis of sinus possibly due in part to ear disease but "triggered" by blow to head] is also quite relevant. If more were needed, the New York Court of Claims decision in "A. A." v. State, supra, note * * * [119], seems directly on point. For further discussion of this familiar tort doctrine,[11] see A.L.I. Restatement of Torts 2d § 461; Prosser, Torts 300–301 (3d ed. 1964); 2 Harper & James, The Law of Torts 1127–28 (1956); Hart and Honoré, Causation in the Law 160–62 (1959); Keeton, Legal Cause in the Law of Torts 67–69 (1963). * * *

We add a further word that may be of importance on a new trial. Although the fact that Cynthia had latent psychotic tendencies would

11. The seeming severity of this doctrine is mitigated by the prevalence of liability insurance which spreads the risks. [Notes 9–11 from original, renumbered; other notes in original omitted.]

not defeat recovery if the accident was a precipitating cause of schizophrenia, this may have a significant bearing on the amount of damages. The defendants are entitled to explore the probability that the child might have developed schizophrenia in any event. While the evidence does not demonstrate that Cynthia already had the disease, it does suggest that she was a good prospect. Judge Hiscock said in *McCahill*, "it is easily seen that the probability of later death from existing causes for which a defendant was not responsible would probably be an important element in fixing damages, but it is not a defense." 201 N.Y. at 224, 94 N.E. at 617. In Evans v. S. J. Groves & Sons Company, supra, we noted that if a defendant "succeeds in establishing that the plaintiff's pre-existing condition was bound to worsen * * * an appropriate discount should be made for the damages that would have been suffered even in the absence of the defendant's negligence." 315 F.2d at 347–348. See also the famous case of Dillon v. Twin State Gas & Electric Co., 85 N.H. 449, 163 A. 111 (1932), and 2 Harper & James, supra, at 1128–1131. It is no answer that exact prediction of Cynthia's future apart from the accident is difficult or even impossible. However taxing such a problem may be for men who have devoted their lives to psychiatry, it is one for which a jury is ideally suited.

Reversed for a new trial.

DILLON v. LEGG

Supreme Court of California, in Bank, 1968.
68 Cal.2d 728, 69 Cal.Rptr. 72, 441 P.2d 912.

TOBRINER, JUSTICE. That the courts should allow recovery to a mother who suffers emotional trauma and physical injury from witnessing the infliction of death or injury to her child for which the tortfeasor is liable in negligence would appear to be a compelling proposition. As Prosser points out, "All ordinary human feelings are in favor of her [the mother's] action against the negligent defendant. If a duty to her requires that she herself be in some recognizable danger, then it has properly been said that when a child is endangered, it is not beyond contemplation that its mother will be somewhere in the vicinity, and will suffer serious shock." (Prosser, Law of Torts (3d ed. 1964) p. 353.)

Nevertheless, past American decisions have barred the mother's recovery. Refusing the mother the right to take her case to the jury, these courts ground their position on an alleged absence of a required "duty" of due care of the tortfeasor to the mother. Duty, in turn, they state, must express public policy; the imposition of duty here would work disaster because it would invite fraudulent claims and it would involve the courts in the hopeless task of defining the extent of the tortfeasor's liability. In substance, they say, definition of liability being impossible, denial of liability is the only realistic alternative.

We have concluded that neither of the feared dangers excuses the frustration of the natural justice upon which the mother's claim rests. We shall point out that in the past we have rejected the argument that we should deny recovery upon a legitimate claim because other fraudulent ones may be urged. We shall further explain that the alleged inability to fix definitions for recovery on the different facts of future cases does not justify the denial of recovery on the specific facts of the instant case; in any event, proper guidelines can indicate the extent of liability for such future cases.

In the instant case plaintiff's first cause of action alleged that on or about September 27, 1964, defendant drove his automobile in a southerly direction on Bluegrass Road near its intersection with Clover Lane in the County of Sacramento, and at that time plaintiff's infant daughter, Erin Lee Dillon, lawfully crossed Bluegrass Road. The complaint further alleged that defendant's negligent operation of his vehicle caused it to "collide with the deceased Erin Lee Dillon resulting in injuries to decedent which proximately resulted in her death." (Complaint, p. 3.) Plaintiff, as the mother of the decedent, brought an action for compensation for the loss.

Plaintiff's second cause of action alleged that she, Margery M. Dillon, "was in close proximity to the * * * collision and personally witnessed said collision." She further alleged that "because of the negligence of defendants * * * and as a proximate cause [*sic*] thereof plaintiff * * * sustained great emotional disturbance and shock and injury to her nervous system" which caused her great physical and mental pain and suffering.

Plaintiff's third cause of action alleged that Cheryl Dillon, another infant daughter, was "in close proximity to the * * * collision and personally witnessed said collision." Because of the negligence, Cheryl Dillon "sustained great emotional disturbance and shock and injury to her nervous system," which caused her great physical and mental pain and suffering.

On December 22, 1965, defendant, after he had filed his answer, moved for judgment on the pleadings, contending that "No cause of action is stated in that allegation that plaintiff sustained emotional distress, fright or shock induced by apprehension of negligently caused danger or injury or the witnessing of negligently caused injury to a third person. Amaya v. Home Ice, Fuel & Supply Co., 59 Cal.2d 295, 29 Cal.Rptr. 33, 379 P.2d 513 (1963). Even where a child, sister or spouse is the object of the plaintiff's apprehension no cause of action is stated, Supra, p. 303, 29 Cal.Rptr. 33, 379 P.2d 513, *unless the complaint alleges that the plaintiff suffered emotional distress, fright or shock as a result of fear for his own safety.* Reed v. Moore, 156 Cal. App.2d 43 (1957) at page 45 [319 P.2d 80]." (Italics added.) The court granted a judgment on the pleadings against the mother's count, the second cause of action, and denied it as to the sister's count, the third cause of action. The court, further, dismissed the second cause of action. Margery M. Dillon, the mother appealed from that judgment.

Thereafter, on January 26, further proceedings took place as to the third cause of action, Cheryl Dillon's claim for emotional trauma from witnessing her sister's death while "watching her sister lawfully cross Bluegrass Road."

Defendant moved for summary judgment on this count. In opposition plaintiff contended that the declaration of one McKinley disclosed that Mrs. Dillon testified at her deposition that when she saw the car rolling over Erin she noted that Cheryl was on the curb, but that the deposition of Cheryl Dillon contradicts such statements. Plaintiff therefore submitted that "Since the declarations filed by defendant are contradictory and the testimony contained in the testimony of Mrs. Dillon does not establish as a matter of law that Cheryl Dillon was not in the zone of danger or had fear for her own safety, plaintiff respectfully submits that the motion must be denied."

The court denied the motion for summary judgment on the third cause as to Cheryl on the ground that the pretrial order precluded it. The trial court apparently sustained the motion for judgment on the pleadings on the second cause as to the mother because she was not within the zone of danger and denied that motion as to the third cause involving Cheryl because of the possibility that she was within such zone of danger or feared for her own safety. Thus we have before us a case that dramatically illustrates the difference in result flowing from the alleged requirement that a plaintiff cannot recover for emotional trauma in witnessing the death of a child or sister unless she also feared for her own safety because she was actually within the zone of physical impact.

The posture of this case differs from that of Amaya v. Home Ice, Fuel & Supply Co. (1963) 59 Cal.2d 295, 298, 29 Cal.Rptr. 33, 35, 379 P.2d 513, 515, which involved "fright or nervous shock (with consequent bodily illness) induced solely by * * * apprehension of negligently caused danger or injury to a third person" because the complaint here presents the claim of the emotionally traumatized mother, who admittedly was *not* within the zone of danger, as contrasted with that of the sister, who *may have been* within it. The case thus illustrates the fallacy of the rule that would deny recovery in the one situation and grant it in the other. In the first place, we can hardly justify relief to the sister for trauma which she suffered upon apprehension of the child's death and yet deny it to the mother merely because of a happenstance that the sister was some few yards closer to the accident. The instant case exposes the hopeless artificiality of the zone-of-danger rule. In the second place, to rest upon the zone-of-danger rule when we have rejected the impact rule becomes even less defensible. We have, indeed, held that impact is not necessary for recovery (Cook v. Maier (1939) 33 Cal.App.2d 581, 584, 92 P.2d 434.) The zone-of-danger concept must, then, inevitably collapse because the only reason for the requirement of presence in that zone lies in the fact that one within it will fear the danger of *impact.* At the threshold, then, we point to the incongruity of the rules upon which any rejection of plaintiff's recovery must rest.

* * *

We turn then to an analysis of the concept of duty, which, as we have stated, has furnished the ground for the rejection of such claims as the instant one. Normally the simple facts of plaintiff's complaint would establish a cause of action: the complaint alleges that defendant drove his car (1) negligently, as a (2) proximate result of which plaintiff suffered (3) physical injury. Proof of these facts to a jury leads to recovery in damages; indeed, such a showing represents a classic example of the type of accident with which the law of negligence has been designed to deal.

The assertion that liability must nevertheless be denied because defendant bears no "duty" to plaintiff "begs the essential question—whether the plaintiff's interests are entitled to legal protection against the defendant's conduct. * * * It [duty] is a shorthand statement of a conclusion, rather than an aid to analysis in itself. * * * But it should be recognized that 'duty' is not sacrosanct in itself, but only an expression of the sum total of those considerations of policy which lead the law to say that the particular plaintiff is entitled to protection." (Prosser, Law of Torts, supra, at pp. 332–333.)

The history of the concept of duty in itself discloses that it is not an old and deep-rooted doctrine but a legal device of the latter half of the nineteenth century designed to curtail the feared propensities of juries toward liberal awards. "It must not be forgotten that 'duty' got into our law for the very purpose of combatting what was then feared to be a dangerous delusion (perhaps especially prevalent among juries imbued with popular notions of fairness untempered by paramount judicial policy), viz. that the law might countenance legal redress for all foreseeable harm." (Fleming, An Introduction to the Law of Torts (1967) p. 47.)

Indeed, the idea of court-imposed restrictions on recovery by means of the concept of "duty" contrasted dramatically with the preceding legal system of fuedal society.[12] In the enclosed fuedal society, the actor bore responsibility for any damage he inflicted without regard to whether he was at fault or owed a "duty" to the injured per-

12. "The gradual development of the law in the matter of civil liability is discussed and traced by the late Sir William Holdsworth with ample learning and lucidity in his History of English Law, vol. 8, pp. 446 et seq., and need not here be rehearsed. Suffice it to say that the process of evolution has been from the principle that every man acts at his peril and is liable for all the consequences of his acts to the principle that a man's freedom of action is subject only to the obligation not to infringe any duty of care which he owes to others. The emphasis formerly was on the injury sustained and the question was whether the case fell within one of the accepted classes of common law actions; the emphasis now is on the conduct of the person whose act has occasioned the injury and the question is whether it can be characterized as negligent." (Read v. J. Lyons & Co., Ltd. (1947) A.C. 156, 171.)

son. Thus, at that time, the defendant owed a duty to all the world to conduct himself without causing injury to his fellows. It may well be that the physical contraction of the fuedal society imposed an imperative for maximum procurable safety and a corresponding absolute responsibility upon its members.

The Industrial Revolution, which cracked the solidity of the fuedal society and opened up wide and new areas of expansion, changed the legal concepts. Just as the new competitiveness in the economic sphere figuratively broke out of the walls of the fuedal community, so it broke through the rule of strict liability. In the place of strict liability it introduced the theory that an action for negligence would lie only if the defendant breached a duty which he owed to plaintiff. As Lord Esher said in Le Lievre v. Gould (1893) 1 Q.B. 491, 497: "A man is entitled to be as negligent as he pleases towards the whole world if he owes no duty to them."

We have pointed out that this late 19th century concept of duty, as applied to the instant situation, has led the courts to deny liability. We have noted that this negation of duty emanates from the twin fears that courts will be flooded with an onslaught of (1) fraudulent and (2) indefinable claims. We shall point out why we think neither fear justified.

1. *This court in the past has rejected the argument that we must deny recovery upon a legitimate claim because other fraudulent ones may be urged.*

The denial of "duty" in the instant situation rests upon the prime hypothesis that allowance of such an action would lead to successful assertion of fraudulent claims. (See, e. g, Waube v. Warrington (1935) 216 Wis. 603, 613, 258 N.W. 497.) The rationale apparently assumes that juries, confronted by irreconcilable expert medical testimony, will be unable to distinguish the deceitful from the bona fide. The argument concludes that only a per se rule denying the entire class of claims that potentially raises this administrative problem [13] can avoid this danger.

In the first instance, the argument proceeds from a doubtful factual assumption. Whatever the possibilities of fraudulent claims of physical injury by disinterested spectators of an accident, a question not in issue in this case, we certainly cannot doubt that a mother who sees her child killed will suffer physical injury from shock. "It seems sufficiently obvious that the shock of a mother at danger or harm to her child may be both a real and a serious injury." (Prosser, Law of Torts, supra, at p. 353.)

Over a half-century ago this court recognized the likelihood that such fright and fear would cause physical injury. In Sloane v. South-

13. To the extent that this argument shades into the contention that such claims should be denied because otherwise courts would experience a "flood of litigation," we point out that courts are responsible for dealing with cases on their merits, whether there be few suits or many; the existence of a multitude of claims merely shows society's pressing need for legal redress.

ern California Ry. Co. (1896) 111 Cal. 668, 680, 44 P. 320, 322, we affirmed a judgment for damages for a plaintiff who alleged physical injury resulting from mental suffering, saying: "It is a matter of general knowledge that an attack of sudden fright or an exposure to imminent peril has produced in individuals a complete change in their nervous system, and rendered one who was physically strong and vigorous weak and timid." Since no one can seriously question that, fear or grief for one's child is as likely to cause physical injury as concern over one's own well-being, rejection of the fraudulent claims contention in *Sloane* clearly applies here.

In the second instance, and more fundamentally, the possibility that fraudulent assertions may prompt recovery in isolated cases does not justify a wholesale rejection of the entire class of claims in which that potentiality arises. The "contention that the rule permitting the maintenance of the action would be impractical to administer * * * is but an argument that the courts are incapable of performing their appointed tasks, a premise which has frequently been rejected." (Emden v. Vitz (1948) 88 Cal.App.2d 313, 319, 198 P.2d 696, 700.) "[F]ear that unfounded claims may be put forward, and may result in erroneous conclusions of fact, ought not to influence us to impose legal limitations as to the nature of the facts that it is permissible to prove." (Owens v. Liverpool Corp. (1939) 1 K.B. 394, 400.) "Certainly it is a very questionable position for a court to take, that because of the possibility of encouraging fictitious claims compensation should be denied those who have actually suffered serious injury through the negligence of another." (Orlo v. Connecticut Co. (1941) 128 Conn. 231, 239, 21 A.2d 402, 405. See also Goodhart, The Shock Cases and Area of Risk (1953) 16 Modern L.Rev. 14, 23; Throckmorton, Damages for Fright, supra, 34 Harv.L.Rev. 260, 276.)

On the analogous issue of whether the possibility of collusive fraud in intrafamily tort actions justified a per se rule denying recovery in all such cases, this court held that the interests of meritorious plaintiffs should prevail over alleged administrative difficulties. Upholding the claim of a minor child in that situation we said: "The interest of the child in freedom from personal injury caused by the tortious conduct of others is sufficient to outweigh any danger of fraud or collusion. * * * [T]he fact that there may be greater opportunity for fraud or collusion in one class of cases than another does not warrant courts of law in closing the door to all cases of that class. Courts must depend upon the efficacy of the judicial processes to ferret out the meritorious from the fraudulent in particular cases." (Emery v. Emery (1955) 45 Cal.2d 421, 431, 289 P.2d 218, 224; see also Klein v. Klein (1962) 58 Cal.2d 692, 695–696, 26 Cal.Rptr. 102, 376 P.2d 70.)

The possibility that some fraud will escape detection does not justify an abdication of the judicial responsibility to award damages for sound claims: if it is "to be conceded that our procedural system for the ascertainment of truth is inadequate to defeat fraudulent claims * * *, the result is a virtual acknowledgment that the courts are unable to render justice in respect to them." (Chiuchiolo v. New England Wholesale Tailors (1930) 84 N.H. 329, 335, 150 A. 540, 543.)

Indubitably juries and trial courts, constantly called upon to distinguish the frivolous from the substantial and the fraudulent from the meritorious, reach some erroneous results. But such fallibility, inherent in the judicial process, offers no reason for substituting for the case-by-case resolution of causes an artificial and indefensible barrier. Courts not only compromise their basic responsibility to decide the merits of each case individually but destroy the public's confidence in them by using the broad broom of "administrative convenience" to sweep away a class of claims a number of which are admittedly meritorious. The mere assertion that fraud is possible, "a possibility [that] exists to some degree in all cases" (Klein v. Klein, supra, 58 Cal.2d 692, 695, 26 Cal.Rptr. 102, 104, 376 P.2d 70, 72), does not prove a present necessity to abandon the neutral principles of foreseeability, proximate cause and consequential injury that generally govern tort law.

Indeed, we doubt that the problem of the fraudulent claim is substantially more pronounced in the case of a mother claiming physical injury resulting from seeing her child killed than in other areas of tort law in which the right to recover damages is well established in California. For example, a plaintiff claiming that fear for his own safety resulted in physical injury makes out a well recognized case for recovery.[14] (Lindley v. Knowlton (1918) 179 Cal. 298, 176 P. 440; Webb v. Francis J. Lewald Coal Co. (1931) 214 Cal. 182, 4 P.2d 532; Vanoni v. Western Airlines (1967) 247 Cal.App.2d 793, 56 Cal.Rptr. 115.) Moreover, damages are allowed for "mental suffering," a type of injury, on the whole, less amenable to objective proof than the physical injury involved here; the mental injury can be in aggravation of, or "parisitic to," an established tort. * * * In fact, fear for another, even in the absence of resulting physical injury, can be part of these parisitic damages. (Acadia, California, Ltd. v. Herbert, * * * 54 Cal.2d 328, 337, 5 Cal.Rptr. 686, 353 P.2d 294; Easton v. United Trade School Contracting Co., * * * 173 Cal. 199, 202, 159 P. 597.) And emotional distress, if inflicted intentionally, constitutes

14. California's rule that plaintiff's fear for his own safety is compensable also presents a strong argument for the same rule as to fear for others; otherwise, some plaintiffs will falsely claim to have feared for themselves, and the honest parties unwilling to do so will be penalized. (Cf. 2 Harper & James, The Law of Torts (1956) § 16.15, p. 961.) Moreover, it is incongruous and somewhat revolting to sanction recovery for the mother if she suffers shock from fear for her own safety and to deny it for shock from the witnessed death of her own daughter. To the layman such a ruling must appear incomprehensible; for the courts to rely upon self-contradictory legalistic abstractions to justify it is indefensible. We concur with Judge Magruder's observation in 49 Harvard Law Review 1033, at page 1039: "Once accepting the view that a plaintiff threatened with an injurious impact may recover for bodily harm resulting from shock without impact, it is easy to agree with Atkin, L.J. ([Hambrook v. Stokes Bros., [1925] 1 K.B. 141, 158–159]), that to hinge recovery on the speculative issue whether the parent was shocked through fear for herself or for her children 'would be discreditable to any system of jurisprudence.'"

an independent tort. (State Rubbish Collectors Ass'n v. Siliznoff (1952) 38 Cal.2d 330, 338, 240 P.2d 282.) The danger of plaintiffs' fraudulent collection of damages for nonexistent injury is at least as great in these examples as in the instant case.

In sum, the application of tort law can never be a matter of mathematical precision. In terms of characterizing conduct as tortious and matching a money award to the injury suffered as well as in fixing the extent of injury, the process cannot be perfect. * * * Yet we cannot let the difficulties of adjudication frustrate the principle that there be a remedy for every substantial wrong.

2. *The alleged inability to fix definitions for recovery on the different facts of future cases does not justify the denial of recovery on the specific facts of the instant case; in any event, proper guidelines can indicate the extent of liability for such future cases.*

In order to limit the otherwise potential infinite liability which would follow every negligent act, the law of torts holds defendant amenable only for injuries to others which to defendant at the time were reasonably foreseeable.

In the absence of "overriding policy considerations * * * foreseeability of risk [is] of * * * primary importance in establishing the element of duty." (Grafton v. Mollica (1965) 231 Cal.App. 2d 860, 865, 42 Cal.Rptr. 306, 310. * * * As a classic opinion states: "The risk reasonably to be perceived defines the duty to be obeyed." (Palsgraf v. Long Island R. R. Co. (1928) 248 N.Y. 339, 344, 162 N.E. 99, 100.) Defendant owes a duty, in the sense of a potential liability for damages, only with respect to those risks or hazards whose likelihood made the conduct unreasonably dangerous, and hence negligent, in the first instance. (See Keeton, Legal Cause in the Law of Torts (1963) 18–20; Seavey, Mr. Justice Cardozo and the Law of Torts (1939) 52 Harv.L.Rev. 372; Seavey, Principles of Torts (1942) 56 Harv.L.Rev. 72.)

Harper and James state the prevailing view. The obligation turns on whether "the offending conduct foreseeably involved unreasonably great risk of harm to the interests of someone other than the actor. * * * [T]he obligation to refrain from * * * particular conduct is owed only to those who are foreseeably endangered by the conduct and only with respect to those risks or hazards whose likelihood made the conduct unreasonably dangerous. Duty, in other words, is measured by the scope of the risk which negligent conduct foreseeably entails." (2 Harper & James, The Law of Torts, supra, at p. 1018; fns. omitted.)

This foreseeable risk may be of two types. The first class involves actual physical impact. A second type of risk applies to the instant situation. "In other cases, however, plaintiff is outside the zone of physical risk (or there is no risk of physical impact at all), but bodily injury or sickness is brought on by emotional disturbance which in turn is caused by defendant's conduct. Under general principles recovery should be had in such a case if defendant should foresee fright or shock severe enough to cause substantial injury in a person normally constituted. Plaintiff would then be within the zone of risk in very much the same way as are plaintiffs to whom danger is extended by acts of third persons, or forces of nature, or their own responses (where these things are foreseeable)." (2 Harper & James, The Law of Torts, supra, at pp. 1035–1036; fns. omitted.) [15]

Since the chief element in determining whether defendant owes a duty or an obligation to plaintiff is the foreseeability of the risk, that factor will be of prime concern in every case. Because it is inherently intertwined with foreseeability such duty or obligation must necessarily be adjudicated only upon a case-by-case basis. We cannot now predetermine defendant's obligation in every situation by a fixed category; no immutable rule can establish the extent of that obligation for every circumstance of the future. We can, however, define guidelines which will aid in the resolution of such an issue as the instant one.

We note, first, that we deal here with a case in which plaintiff suffered a shock which resulted in physical injury and we confine our ruling to that case. In determining, in such a case, whether defendant should reasonably foresee the injury to plaintiff, or, in other terminology, whether defendant owes plaintiff a duty of due care, the courts will take into account such factors as the following: (1) Whether plaintiff was located near the scene of the accident as contrasted with one who was a distance away from it. (2) Whether the shock resulted from a direct emotional impact upon plaintiff from the sensory and contemporaneous observance of the accident, as contrasted with learning of the accident from others after its occurrence. (3) Whether plaintiff and the victim were closely related, as contrasted with an absence of any relationship or the presence of only a distant relationship.

The evaluation of these factors will indicate the *degree* of the defendant's foreseeability: obviously defendant is more likely to foresee that a mother who observes an accident affecting her child will suffer harm than to foretell that a stranger witness will do so. Similarly, the degree of foreseeability of the third person's injury is far greater in the case of his contemporaneous observance of the accident than that in which he subsequently learns of it. The defendant is more likely to foresee that shock to the nearby, witnessing mother will cause physical harm than to anticipate that someone distant from the accident will suffer more than a temporary emotional reaction. All these

15. The concept of the zone of danger cannot properly be restricted to the area of those exposed to *physical* injury; it must encompass the area of those exposed to *emotional* injury. The courts, today, hold that no distinction can be drawn between physical injury and emotional injury flowing from the physical injury; indeed, in the light of modern medical knowledge, any such distinction would be indefensible. As a result, in awarding recovery for emotional shock upon witnessing another's injury or death, we cannot draw a line between the plaintiff who is in the zone of danger of physical impact and the plaintiff who is in the zone of danger of emotional impact. The recovery of the one, within the guidelines set forth *infra*, is as much compelled as that of the other.

elements, of course, shade into each other; the fixing of obligation, intimately tied into the facts, depends upon each case.

In light of these factors the court will determine whether the accident and harm was *reasonably* foreseeable. Such reasonable foreseeability does not turn on whether the particular defendant as an individual would have in actuality foreseen the exact accident and loss; it contemplates that courts, on a case-to-case basis, analyzing all the circumstances, will decide what the ordinary man under such circumstances should reasonably have foreseen. The courts thus mark out the areas of liability, excluding the remote and unexpected.

In the instant case, the presence of all the above factors indicates that plaintiff has alleged a sufficient prima facie case. Surely the negligent driver who causes the death of a young child may reasonably expect that the mother will not be far distant and will upon witnessing the accident suffer emotional trauma. As Dean Prosser has stated: "when a child is endangered, it is not beyond contemplation that its mother will be somewhere in the vicinity, and will suffer serious shock." (Prosser, The Law of Torts, supra, at p. 353. See also 2 Harper & James, The Law of Torts, supra, at p. 1039.)

We are not now called upon to decide whether, in the absence or reduced weight of some of the above factors, we would conclude that the accident and injury were not reasonably foreseeable and that therefore defendant owed no duty of due care to plaintiff. In future cases the courts will draw lines of demarcation upon facts more subtle than the compelling ones alleged in the complaint before us.

* * *

The fear of an inability to fix boundaries has not impelled the courts of England to deny recovery for emotional trauma caused by witnessing the death or injury of another due to defendant's negligence. We set forth the holdings of some English cases merely to demonstrate that courts can formulate and apply such limitations of liability.

The first and classic case, Hambrook v. Stokes Bros., supra 1 K.B. 141, rejected the argument that recovery should be denied because of possible administrative difficulty. In *Hambrook* the defendant's servant left a truck parked at the top of a steep and narrow street with the engine running. The deceased, a pregnant woman, had walked with her children on their way to school to the point where they turned onto the street where the truck was parked. Because the driver did not take proper precautions, the truck started itself down the hill and struck one of the children. Although she herself was never in danger, the mother saw the runaway truck and feared greatly for the safety of her children. Upon inquiry she found that one of the children had been seriously injured; several months later both the mother and the foetus were dead. The trial court directed the jury that the father's suit for loss of services could succeed only if the death were caused by the mother's fear for her own safety, but the appellate court held that the plaintiff could recover even if the fear for the children brought about her demise.

Faced with the contention that their holding would increase the number of suits and foment possible fraudulent claims, Lord Justice Atkin quoted this passage: " 'I should be sorry to adopt a rule which would bar all such claims on grounds of policy alone, and in order to prevent the possible success of unrighteous or groundless actions. Such a course involves the denial of redress in meritorious cases, and it necessarily implies a certain degree of distrust, which I do not share, in the capacity of legal tribunals to get at the truth in this class of claim.' " (Hambrook v. Stokes Bros., supra, quoting from Dulieu v. White and Sons [1901] 2 K.B. 669, 681, opinion by Kennedy, J.)

In a recent application of the *Hambrook* rule, an English court permitted recovery by a widow of a man who developed severe psychoneurotic symptoms as a result of harrowing experiences, not involving his personal safety, while serving as a rescuer at a gruesome train wreck. The court stated that the " 'test of liability for shock is foreseeability of injury by shock.' " (Chadwick v. British Railways Board [1967] 1 W.L.R. 912, 920, quoting from King v. Phillips [1953] 1 Q.B. 429, 441, opinion by Denning, L.J.)

Professor John Fleming of the School of Law, Boalt Hall, University of California, in a careful analysis of the development of English law on this subject, first explains, "It is evident, of course, that to the extent of denying redress for certain kinds of negligently inflicted harm, the law is in effect withholding its protective mantle from corresponding human interests that may accordingly be infringed with impunity. To refuse a remedy for nervous shock is the equivalent of refusing to accede to an individual's claim for safeguarding his emotional security. It is also the same as saying that there is no 'duty' owed to exercise reasonable care to avoid inflicting this type of loss or injury. Although no longer quite as fashionable in this particular context, the same idea can also, finally, be expressed by asserting that such damage is 'too remote' or, what amounts to the same thing, that the defendant's negligence was not its 'proximate cause'." (Fleming, An Introduction to the Law of Torts (1967) p. 46.)

After explaining that certain English cases manipulated doctrinal approaches "to subserve ulterior purposes" in granting recovery in some situations and denying it in others, Fleming states that "a long-delayed change in attitude may perhaps be discerned in the latest decision by the Court of Appeal [Boardman v. Sanderson (1964) 1 W.L.R. 1317 (C.A.)], which sustained a father's claim for a mental shock he suffered upon hearing the screams of his boy when the latter's foot was negligently caught under the wheel of the defendant's car from which father and son had just alighted inside a service garage. Neither did the father fear for his own safety nor did he so much as even see the accident. Indeed, the claimant was not even a female—the prototype plaintiff in these cases being almost exclusively concerned with pregnancy injuries. Yet the court considered it sufficient to say that a duty was owed not only to the boy but also to his *near relatives*, who, to the defendant's *knowledge*, were on the premises within earshot and likely to come upon the scene if any injury befell him. It remains to be seen whether this relaxation, slight as it may be, might not eventually be extended to relatives whose presence, though not actually known, was yet *foreseeable* in accordance with the prevailing test customarily applied to claims for physical injuries." (Italics in original; fn. omitted.) (Fleming, An Introduction to the Law of Torts, supra, at p. 54.)

The English courts have likewise marked out areas of liability, excluding those injuries that are remote and unexpected. Thus a distinguished English court has held that the physical injury of a casual bystander resulting from shock or fright upon witnessing an accident would present so unusual and hence unforeseeable an event as to warrant a directed verdict for defendant. "The driver of a car or vehicle, even though careless, is entitled to assume that the *ordinary frequenter* of the streets has sufficient fortitude to endure such incidents as may from time to time be expected to occur in them, including the noise of a collision and the sight of injuries to others, and is not to be considered negligent towards one who does not possess the customary phlegm." (Italics added.) (Bourhill v. Young (1943) A.C. 92, 117 (Porter, L.J.); see, id. at pp. 98 (Thankerton, L.J.), 101 (Russell, L.J.), 104 (MacMillan, L.J.), and 107 (Wright, L.J.); King v. Phillips, supra, 1 Q.B. 429, 442.)

Thus we see no good reason why the general rules of tort law, including the concepts of negligence, proximate cause, and foreseeability, long applied to all other types of injury, should not govern the case now before us. Any questions that the cause raises "will be solved most justly by applying general principles of duty and negligence, and * * * mechanical rules of thumb which are at variance with these principles do more harm than good." (2 Harper & James, The Law of Torts, supra, p. 1039; fn. omitted.) "The refusal to apply these general rules to actions for this particular kind of physical injury is nothing short of a denial of justice." (Throckmorton, Damages for Fright (1921) 34 Harv.L.Rev. 260, 277; fn. omitted.)

In short, the history of the cases does not show the development of a logical rule but rather a series of changes and abandonments. Upon the argument in each situation that the courts draw a Maginot Line to withstand an onslaught of false claims, the cases have assumed a variety of postures. At first they insisted that there be no recovery for emotional trauma at all. (Amaya v. Home Ice, Fuel & Supply Co., supra, 59 Cal.2d 295, dissenting opinion by Peters, J., p. 328 fn. 9, 29 Cal.Rptr. 33, 379 P.2d 513.) Retreating from this position, they gave relief for such trauma only if physical impact occurred. (Id. at p. 325 fn. 4, 29 Cal.Rptr. 33, 379 P.2d 513.) They then abandoned the requirement for physical impact but insisted that the victim fear for her own safety (Amaya v. Home Ice, Fuel & Supply

Co., supra, 59 Cal.2d 295, 29 Cal.Rptr. 33, 379 P.2d 513), holding that a mother could recover for fear for her children's safety if she simultaneously entertained a personal fear for herself. (Lindley v. Knowlton, supra, 179 Cal. 298, 176 P. 440.) [16] They stated that the mother need only be in the "zone of danger" (Reed v. Moore (1957) 156 Cal. App.2d 43, 47, 319 P.2d 80). The final anomaly would be the instant case in which the sister, who observed the accident, would be granted recovery because she was in the "zone of danger," but the *mother*, not far distant, would be barred from recovery.

The successive abandonment of these positions exposes the weakness of artificial abstractions which bar recovery contrary to the general rules. As the commentators have suggested, the problem should be solved by the application of the principles of tort, not by the creation of exceptions to them. Legal history shows that artificial islands of exceptions, created from the fear that the legal process will not work, usually do not withstand the waves of reality and, in time, descend into oblivion.

* * *

To deny recovery would be to chain this state to an outmoded rule of the 19th century which can claim no current credence. No good reason compels our captivity to an indefensible orthodoxy.

The judgment is reversed.

PETERS, MOSK, and SULLIVAN, JJ., concur.

DISSENTING OPINION

TRAYNOR, CHIEF JUSTICE.

I dissent for the reasons set forth in Amaya v. Home Ice, Fuel & Supply Co. (1963) 59 Cal.2d 295, 297–315, 29 Cal.Rptr. 33, 379 P.2d 513. In my opinion that case was correctly decided and should not be overruled.

16. In *Lindley* a 165-pound chimpanzee had entered plaintiff's house and attacked her children, whom she rescued from it. The court recognized that the concern of the mother for the safety of the children as well as concern for her own safety could have contributed to her fright. It states: "While, of course, Mrs. Lindley was greatly and perhaps chiefly concerned for her children * * * there is nothing in the testimony to indicate that she was not concerned for her own safety." (179 Cal. 302, 176 P. p. 441.) As a basis for reversal of plaintiff's verdict defendant urged that the court should have instructed the jury that "no recovery may be had on account of fright produced by apprehended danger or peril to a third person." The court affirmed, saying that the circumstances made "it impossible that she should have been devoid of fear for herself" and that the instruction was therefore properly refused. Hence the court in substance sustained recovery for fright based upon a combination of fears, those arising from fear of the mother for the children as well as for herself.

DISSENTING OPINION

BURKE, JUSTICE.

* * *

Every one of the arguments advanced in today's opinion was considered by this court and rejected, expressly or by fair implication, in *Amaya.*[17] * * * As we asked in *Amaya*: What if the plaintiff was honestly *mistaken* in believing the third person to be in danger or to be seriously injured? What if the third person had assumed the risk involved? How "close" must the relationship be between the plaintiff and the third person? I. e., what if the third person was the plaintiff's beloved niece or nephew, grandparent, fiancé, or lifelong friend, more dear to the plaintiff than her immediate family? Next, how "near" must the plaintiff have been to the scene of the accident, and how "soon" must shock have been felt? Indeed, what is the magic in the plaintiff's being actually present? Is the shock any less real if the mother does not know of the accident until her injured child is brought into her home? On the other hand, is it any less real if the mother is physically present at the scene but is nevertheless unaware of the danger or injury to her child until after the accident has occurred? No answers to these questions are to be found in today's majority opinion. Our trial courts, however, will not so easily escape the burden of distinguishing between litigants on the basis of such artificial and unpredictable distinctions.

* * *

The assertion of the majority * * * that "The denial of 'duty' in the instant situation [i. e., physical impairment resulting from emotional distress occasioned by apprehension of the peril of others] rests upon the *prime hypothesis* that allowance of such an action would lead to successful assertion of fraudulent claims," (italics added) is controverted by the very case cited in support. (Waube v. Warrington, * * * 216 Wis. 603, 613, 258 N.W. 497, 501.) Instead of reliance on any such "prime hypothesis," the Wisconsin court had this to say in *Waube*: "* * * Such consequences are so unusual and extraordinary, viewed after the event, that a user of the highway may be said not to subject others to an unreasonable risk of them by the careless management of his vehicle. Furthermore, the liability imposed by such a doctrine is wholly out of proportion to the culpability of the negligent tort-feasor, would put an unreasonable burden upon users of the highway, open the way to fraudulent claims, and enter a field that has no sensible or just stopping point."

17. In *Amaya* the trial court sustained a general demurrer to the complaint and dismissed the action. The Court of Appeal reversed, and in its opinion pronounced the doctrine that is revived in the majority opinion here. (See Cal.App., 23 Cal.Rptr. 131.) Upon petition this court granted a hearing, thereby nullifying the Court of Appeal opinion. Our opinion affirmed the trial court. [Footnotes 12–17 from original, renumbered; other notes in original omitted.]

As this court declared in *Amaya* (p. 315 of 59 Cal.2d, p. 45 of 29 Cal.Rptr., p. 529 of 379 P.2d), there is good sense in the conclusion of the court in *Waube* that "the liability imposed by such a doctrine is wholly out of proportion to the culpability of the negligent tortfeasor"; further, to permit recovery by every person who might adversely feel some lingering effect of the defendant's conduct would throw us into "the fantastic realm of infinite liability." Yet the majority opinion in the present case simply omits to either mention or discuss the injustice to California defendants flowing from such a disproportionate extension of their liability—an injustice which plainly constituted a "prime hypothesis" for rejection of the liability sought to be imposed by the plaintiffs in *Waube* and in *Amaya*. * * *

I would affirm the judgment.

McCOMB, J., concurs.[18]

18. (a) Tobriner, J. had been the author of the California Court of Appeals opinion in *Amaya*, which was overruled 4–3 by the state Supreme Court. He was thereafter appointed to that Supreme Court.

(b) In *Bourhill* (liability rejected) the presence of plaintiff, who was not related to the person whose injury shocked her, was unknown to defendant. In *Boardman* (liability allowed) the plaintiff's presence, within earshot of his injured son, was known to defendant. In *King* (liability rejected) plaintiff-mother was at window 70–80 yards from child whose scream attracted her attention as he was crushed by cab backing into his bicycle on the street. In *Chadwick* (liability allowed) the plaintiff-rescuer came to the scene after the train wreck, and was not related to the accident victims. Consider applicability of general negligence principles.

(c) Also see Toms v. McConnell, 45 Mich.App. 647, 207 N.W.2d 140 (1973). Compare Leong v. Takasaki, 55 Haw. 398, 520 P.2d 758 (1974) (liability for shock to child who witnessed traffic death of step-grandmother with whom he lived, where child was not physically injured, and court explicitly rejected a zone-of-danger test) with Kelley v. Kokua Sales and Supply, Ltd., —— Haw. ——, 532 P.2d 673 (1975) (liability denied for shock, resulting in fatal heart attack, to father in California, who had been informed by telephone of death, earlier the same day, of his daughter and granddaughter, as a result of a traffic accident in Hawaii negligently caused by defendant; *held* over strong dissent by Chief Justice Richardson, defendant "owed no duty of care" to the father.) Earlier Hawaii had recognized liability for negligent infliction of emotional distress resulting from flood damage to plaintiffs' home, Rodrigues v. State, 52 Haw. 156, 472 P.2d 509 (1970). Compare H. & R. Block, Inc. v. Testerman, 275 Md. 36, 338 A.2d 48 (1975). There is little American case law allowing liability for psychic injury arising after the accident the sight of the result of which shocked plaintiff. For one example see Archibald v. Braverman, 275 Cal. App.2d 253, 79 Cal.Rptr. 723 (1969) (mother viewed injured child minutes after accident). A Canadian court has held that liability for emotional shock to a wife, who sees the badly injured body of her husband shortly after the accident, depends on the foreseeability of such injury to her, Marshall v. Lionel Enterprises Inc., 25 D.L.R. (3d) 141 (Ont.1971); similarly, in Australia, Benson v. Lee, [1972] Vict. 879. See also Fleming, Comment: Distant Shock in Germany (and Elsewhere), 20 Am.J.Comp.L. 485 (1972).

HINZ v. BERRY

Court of Appeal, [1970] 1 Q.B. 40.

LORD DENNING M. R. It happened on April 19, 1964. It was bluebell time in Kent. Mr. and Mrs. Hinz had been married some 10 years, and they had four children, all aged nine and under. The youngest was one. Mrs. Hinz was a remarkable woman. In addition to her own four, she was foster-mother to four other children. To add to it, she was two months pregnant with her fifth child.

On this day they drove out in a Bedford Dormobile van from Tonbridge to Canvey Island. They took all eight children with them. As they were coming back they turned into a lay-by at Thurnham to have a picnic tea. The husband, Mr. Hinz, was at the back of the Dormobile making the tea. Mrs. Hinz had taken Stephanie, her third child, aged three, across the road to pick bluebells on the opposite side. There came along a Jaguar car driven by Mr. Berry, out of control. A tyre had burst. The Jaguar rushed into this lay-by and crashed into Mr. Hinz and the children. Mr. Hinz was frightfully injured and died a little later. Nearly all the children were hurt. Blood was streaming from their heads. Mrs. Hinz, hearing the crash, turned round and saw this disaster. She ran across the road and did all she could. Her husband was beyond recall. But the children recovered.

An action has been brought on her behalf and on behalf of the children for damages against Mr. Berry, the defendant. The injuries to the children have been settled by various sums being paid. The pecuniary loss to Mrs. Hinz by reason of the loss of her husband has been found by the judge to be some £15,000; but there remains the question of the damages payable to her for her nervous shock—the shock which she suffered by seeing her husband lying in the road dying, and the children strewn about.

The law at one time said that there could not be damages for nervous shock; but for these last 25 years, it has been settled that damages can be given for nervous shock caused by the sight of an accident, at any rate to a close relative. Very few of these cases have come before the courts to assess the amount of damages. O'Connor J. fixed the damages at the sum of £4,000 for nervous shock. The defendant appeals, saying that the sum is too high.

* * * In English law no damages are awarded for grief or sorrow caused by a person's death. No damages are to be given for the worry about the children, or for the financial strain or stress, or the difficulties of adjusting to a new life. Damages are, however, recoverable for nervous shock, or, to put it in medical terms, for any recognisable psychiatric illness caused by the breach of duty by the defendant.

* * * Somehow or other the court has to draw a line between sorrow and grief for which damages are not recoverable, and

nervous shock and psychiatric illness for which damages are recoverable. The way to do this is to estimate how much Mrs. Hinz would have suffered if, for instance, her husband had been killed in an accident when she was 50 miles away: and compare it with what she is now, having suffered all the shock due to being present at the accident. The evidence shows that she suffered much more by being present. I will consider first the grief and sorrow if she had *not* been present at the accident. The consultant psychiatrist from the hospital in Maidstone said:

> "It is common knowledge and there is a 'mourning period' for all of us, and that normally time dispels this. In the average person it might be a year, but in a predisposed person it can be greatly prolonged. * * * "

Mrs. Hinz was not predisposed at all. She was a woman of great capacity, level-headed, hard working, happily married. She would have got over the loss of her husband in, say, a year.

Consider next her condition, as it is, due to being present at the accident. Two years after the accident, the consultant psychiatrist said:

> "There is no medical doubt at all that she is suffering from a morbid depression; she is now officially ill." He went on to give some of the symptoms. She said to him: "It does not seem worth going on. I feel I cannot cope at all. I get so dreadfully irritable with the children too. It is wrong but I feel like killing him," that is, the posthumous child. The consultant went on: "She feels exhausted, has frequent suicidal ruminations and at the same time is covered with guilt at being like this." The posthumous baby "now saddens her even more because it cries 'Dad, Dad,' " and one of the elder children persists in saying "You have not got a Dad"; and then the other fatherless children join in the chorus. The consultant concluded: "In other circumstances I would probably have brought her into hospital, at least for a rest, but possibly for electrical treatment and it may come to that yet."

At the trial, five years after the accident, she frequently broke down when giving her evidence. She brought the children to court. They were very well turned out. The judge summed up the matter in this way:

> "I am satisfied that she was of so robust a character that she would have stood up to that situation, that she would have been hurt, sorrowful, in mourning, Yes; but in a state of morbid depression, No."

He awarded her £4,000 on this head. There is no suggestion that he misdirected himself. We can only interfere if it is a wholly erroneous estimate. I do not think it is erroneous. I would dismiss the appeal.

(D) WRONGFUL DEATH—AND LIFE

FIRST NATIONAL BANK OF MEADVILLE, PENNSYLVANIA v. NIAGARA THERAPY MANUFACTURING CORPORATION

United States District Court for the Western District of Pennsylvania, 1964.
229 F.Supp. 460.

WILLSON, DISTRICT JUDGE. The plaintiff in this case is the First National Bank of Meadville, Pennsylvania, Executor under the will of Kenneth W. Rice, deceased. Mr. Rice was killed in an airplane accident at the Port Erie Airport on January 22, 1962. * * *

Kenneth W. Rice of Meadville, Pennsylvania, was general counsel for the defendant, Niagara Therapy Manufacturing Corporation. Edward R. Donegan was the Vice President of the corporation. Roger G. Counselman was the regularly employed pilot of the Aero-Commander 680 B aircraft owned by the defendant. On January 21, 1962, Mr. Counselman piloted the aircraft with Mr. Rice and Mr. Donegan as passengers from Meadville to Buffalo for the purpose of taking a deposition in that city the next morning. * * *

Plaintiff contends and strongly urges that the evidence discloses that the pilot Counselman was negligent in taking off from Buffalo under the weather conditions existing and in the face of unfavorable weather forecasts. This was especially so urges plaintiff because the aircraft was not equipped with any deicing boots or any other method of removing ice from the surface of the aircraft. Further says plaintiff, the negligence of the pilot in taking off was compounded by his failure to return to the Buffalo Airport which he had an opportunity to do very soon after encountering ice. * * *

Applying the ruling of ordinary negligence, this Court does not hesitate to find that the pilot Counselman failed in his duty to exercise reasonable care in making his plans for his flight, and thereafter during the course of his flight in failing to return to Buffalo when he had the opportunity to do so. * * *

DAMAGES

Plaintiff brought suit under both the "Wrongful Death Statutes" (12 P.S. §§ 1602–1604) and the "Survival Statute" (20 P.S. § 320.603) of Pennsylvania for the benefit of the surviving widow and the two daughters of the decedent.

* * *

It is clear from the evidence that Mr. Rice had a lucrative practice in Crawford County and northwestern Pennsylvania. He was well and favorably known to this Court as a practicing member of the Bar. The President Judge of Crawford County testified as to the type of practice engaged in by Mr. Rice and the number of cases on the dockets in Crawford County Courts in which Mr. Rice was counsel. His tax returns for several years were introduced as evidence. It is conservative to say that his average net income during five years prior to his death was $25,000.00 a year. He provided generously for his family. On the day he was killed he was just four days short of his forty-ninth birthday, and thus was in the prime of his life so far as a lawyer is concerned. He had been married to his surviving wife for twelve years. He and his wife had recently completed and paid for a dwelling and furnishings therein which cost $65,000.00. He owned a half interest in each of two small office buildings. His interest in one building was appraised at $9,200.00 and in the other building was appraised at $17,500.00. He had accumulated securities valued at $63,000.00 at the time of his death. He himself drove a Cadillac automobile and provided his wife with an Oldsmobile 88. Both his daughters were in college at the time Mr. Rice died. The foregoing is mentioned not as showing the measure of the damages to be awarded in this case, but as indicating the earning capacity of the decedent, as the record indicates that his accumulations and earnings came from his law practice and not from inheritance or gifts.

This Court will apply the principle announced in Ferne v. Chadderton, 363 Pa. at 197, 69 A.2d at 107, with respect to the amounts which the plaintiff is to recover for the benefit of the wife and daughters. That opinion says the rule is:

> "Under the Death Statutes the administratrix was entitled to recover for the benefit of the daughter and herself as widow the amount of the pecuniary loss they suffered by reason of decedent's death, that is to say, the present worth of the amount they probably would have received from his earnings for their support during the period of his life expectancy and while the family relationship continued between them, but without any allowance for mental suffering, grief, or loss of companionship; in other words, the measure of damages is the value of the decedent's life to the parties specified in the statute: Minkin v. Minkin, 336 Pa. 49, 55, 7 A.2d 461, 464. Recovery is also allowed for the expense incurred for medical and surgical care, for nursing of the deceased, and for the reasonable funeral expenses. Act of May 13, 1927, P.L. 992, 12 P.S. § 1604. Under the Survival Statute, 20 P.S. §§ 771, 772, the administratrix was entitled to recover for the loss of decedent's earnings from the time of the accident until the date of his death, and compensation for his pain and suffering during that period. Recovery may also be had for the present worth of his likely earnings during the period of his life expectancy, but diminished by the amount of the provision he would have made for his wife and children as above stated (thus avoiding duplication: Pezzulli, Administrator v. D'Ambrosia, 344 Pa. 643, 650, 26 A.2d 659, 662) and diminished also by the probable cost of his own maintenance during the time he would likely have lived but for the accident: Murray, Administrator, v. Philadelphia Transportation Co., 359 Pa. 69, 73, 74, 58 A.2d 323, 325."

As indicated Mr. Rice was survived by his widow, Mary T. Rice, and two daughters, Cynthia and Barbara. The older daughter, Cynthia, was born August 22, 1940, and lived with her father and Mrs. Rice in the new dwelling house. She had a room and bath for her own use. Barbara, the younger daughter, was born November 29, 1942. She lived with her mother; Mr. Rice's first wife. However, she was supported by her father. He provided her with a money allowance each month and paid for her clothing, medical and dental bills, and additional miscellaneous expenses, and paid the child's mother $50.00 a month in addition for maintenance. When Barbara entered Oberlin College, Mr. Rice paid for tuition, books, room, clothing, and medical and incidental expenses. She enrolled there in 1960, at which time the tuition was $1,031.00 per semester. In 1961 her college expenses were $2,047.25; in 1962 the expenses were $2,047.00. In addition, Mr. Rice gave her approximately $700.00 per year as spending money. By virtue of her father's death, Barbara was deprived of the cost of two and one half years of her college education and other living expenses, which she had been receiving from her father.

The older daughter, Cynthia, was 21 years of age at the time of her father's death, but she had one semester to complete at Wooster College. Her father paid for all of her college expenses which amounted to over $2,000.00 per year, provided her with a substantial allowance, and paid for all of her clothing, medical, and dental bills. His checking account showed that from 1958 to January 12, 1962, he had deposited $1,930.00 as spending money for Cynthia.

Under the evidence it is believed fair and just to award the plaintiff the sum of $7,500.00 for the loss of the contributions which the two children would have received had it not been for their father's death.

The widow, Mary T. Rice, had the benefit of the generosity of a husband who provided her with the good things in life commensurate with his $25,000.00 a year income. It seems conservative of this Court to say that she had the benefit of at least $10,000.00 a year of that income. She enjoyed the use of a new automobile every two years. She had an unlimited checking account. She bought clothes of up to $2,500.00 in price annually. They lived among friends commensurate with a house and furnishings of the value of $65,000.00. Again but only as indicating the manner in which Mr. Rice spent his money, the records showed that he would borrow $20,000.00 from the bank, invest it in stock, and pay off the debt over a period of about three years. It is apparent that the rest of his money was spent in good living, as he had no cash savings at the time he died. He had been some twenty-five years in the practice of law, and it is believed his income had leveled off. But under the testimony he had a life expectancy of approximately twenty-four years on January 22, 1962. Counsel for plaintiff argues that decedent's earnings would increase during his remaining working life. This is so, says counsel, because a lawyer's earnings will increase as he advances in wisdom and maturity. On the other hand, counsel for the defendant contended that it is more likely that decedent's earnings would fall off during the remainder of his life. Balancing the two theories together, it seems to the Court that $25,000.00 a year averaged out for his life expectancy is reasonable. In this Court's opinion, Mrs. Rice had the benefit of $10,000.00 per year contributions from her husband. She received the benefit of this sum by way of her general maintenance in the home on a rather luxurious standard of living, her expenses for her clothing, medical and incidental bills, and in the expenditure of funds for her own and her husband's pleasure. There was a two year interval between the date of death, which occurred January 22, 1962, and the trial. Mrs. Rice's pecuniary loss during that period is not reduced, so for her benefit the Executor in this instance recovers $20,000. Under the various life expectancy tables, it appears that twenty-two years is the proper number of years to be used in computing the present worth of likely earnings and contributions. Thus in Mrs. Rice's case $10,000.00 a year for twenty-two years amounts to a gross of $220,000.00. Under the tables, Am.Jur.2d Desk Book, Doc. No. 133, the present value of $1.00 per year, computed at 6 per cent as required by state law, for twenty-two years is 12.042 dollars. $10,000.00 is $120,420.00. Thus, under the Wrongful Death Acts, the Executor is entitled to recover for the benefit of Mrs. Rice, $120,420.00. Also, the Executor is claiming the sum of $2,000.00, covering reasonable funeral and administration expenses, and this sum is awarded the Executor. Under the Wrongful Death Act then the damages are computed as follows:

Loss of contributions by the two daughters	$ 7,500.00
Loss of contributions by widow to date of trial	20,000.00
Loss of future contributions to widow (reduced to present worth by 6 per cent method)	120,420.00
Funeral and administration expenses	2,000.00
TOTAL DAMAGES UNDER WRONGFUL DEATH ACT:	$149,920.00

The damages awarded in the foregoing amount under the Wrongful Death Acts are amply supported by the evidence. In the computation of damages under the Survival Act, however, the problem is not as clearly defined.

It is this Court's experience that under the Survival Act damages to be awarded a decedent's estate are generally based on evidence which must be estimated with some degree of elasticity. There has lately been considerable discussion as to what the rule is with respect to this type of award. See a discussion in the Pennsylvania Bar Journal, Vol. 32, p. 47 (Oct. 1960), "Has The Measure Of Damages Under The Survival Act In Pennsylvania Been Modified?" In the instant case, the problem is made somewhat difficult because the record is bare of any specific testimony as to the money spent by Mr. Rice for his own maintenance during his lifetime. The last decision of the Supreme Court of Pennsylvania, Skoda v. West Penn Power Co., 411 Pa. 323, 191 A.2d 822, 829 (1963), states the rule as follows:

> " 'Recovery may also be had for the present worth of his likely earnings during the period of his life expectancy, but diminished by the amount of the provision he would have made for his wife and children as above stated, thus avoiding duplication. Pezzulli, Administrator, v. D'Ambrosia, 344 Pa. 643, 650, 26 A.2d 659, 662, and diminished also by the probable cost of his own maintenance during the time he would likely have lived but for the accident. Murray, Administrator v. Philadelphia Transportation Co., 359 Pa. 69, 73, 74, 58 A.2d 323, 325.' (Emphasis supplied)".

Counsel for plaintiff strongly urge that under the rule in the various decisions, including Skoda, the award to the Executor in this case should run over $127,000.00. Although the award to be made under the Survival Statute is not to be based on savings and not to be based on accumulations, nevertheless, the history of Mr. Rice's financial status indicates that he shows not only the ability to save but also to accumulate. Following the rule, however, in Ferne v. Chadderton, and other cases, the present worth of decedent's likely earnings during the remaining period of the decedent's life expectancy is to be computed. This sum is to be diminished by the amount of the awards to the family under the Wrongful Death Acts and also diminished by the probable cost of his own maintenance during the time he would likely have lived but for the accident.

Therefore, in accordance with the rule and the tables, the present worth of $25,000.00 a year for twenty-two years is $301,050.00. From this sum the amount awarded to the family under the Wrongful Death Acts is to be deducted. This sum is $147,920.00. Deducting this figure from the $301,050.00 leaves $153,130.00 as the present worth of the pecuniary earnings lost to the state. To arrive at an award from this sum, it is necessary to deduct decedent's own maintenance expenses which he would have incurred had he lived. Under the cases and decisions these items, of course, include his cost of living, medical expenses, reasonable amounts for recreation, and general expenses of living. This is the area in the evidence in which there is very little proof, but it seems to this Court safe to conclude that his maintenance expenses are certainly equal to the amount he provided for his wife, that is, $10,000.00 a year. They both lived on the same scale. On this basis then, $120,420.00 is to be deducted from $153,130.00, leaving $32,710.00. This sum represents the loss of future earnings to the estate reduced to present worth. This sum also represents the diference between the likely gross earnings during decedent's lifetime diminished by the family contributions and less also the amount of his own maintenance during his life expectancy. To this sum is added the two years' gross earnings which are not to be reduced to present worth.

> "In applying the doctrine of 'present worth,' it should be borne in mind that compensation, both for loss of earning power under the Survival Act and for loss of contributions under the Death Act, accruing from the date of the accident until the date of trial, is not reduced to present worth." See Pennsylvania Bar Association Quarterly, Vol. XXIII, No. 1, October 1951, p. 19.

The two years' gross earnings between the decedent's death and the trial amount to $50,000.00. But, however, during the two years preceding the trial decedent would have expended $20,000.00 on his own maintenance. Therefore, from his gross earnings that amount is to be deducted leaving the sum of $30,000.00 to be added to the $32,710.00, leaving a net recovery under the Survival Act of $62,710.00.

In summary then, the damages to be awarded the Executor are as follows:

Under the Wrongful Death Acts,	$149,920.00
Under the Survival Act	62,710.00
TOTAL DAMAGES:	$212,630.00

Under the Federal Employers' Liability Act, 45 U.S.C.A. section 51 et seq., which contains a provision for survival of deceased's right of action (section 9), as well as one creating rights in named beneficiaries for the wrongful death (section 1), the formula for awarding damages under the two sections has been summarized as follows: "Although originating in the same wrongful act or neglect, the two claims are quite distinct, no part of either being embraced in the other. One is for the wrong to the injured person and is confined to his personal loss and suffering before he died, while the other is for the wrong to the beneficiaries and is confined to their pecuniary loss through his death. One begins where the other ends, and a recovery upon both in the same action is not a double recovery for a single wrong but a single recovery for a double wrong." St. Louis, Iron Mountain & S. Ry. Co. v. Craft, 237 U.S. 648, 658, 35 S.Ct. 704, 706, 59 L.Ed. 1160 (1915). Cf. Hindmarsh v. Sulpho-Saline Bath Co., 108 Neb. 168, 187 N.W. 806 (1922); Farrington v. Stoddard, 115 F.2d 96, 131 A.L.R. 1344 (1st Cir., 1940).

See, for further problems, the cases collected in Green et al., Cases on Injuries to Relations (1968) 176–223.

Whether the survivors' benefits are to be confined to pecuniary loss depends on the applicable statute. See, e. g., Md.Ann.Code (1974) CJ § 3–904, which provides for an action for the benefit of the "wife, husband, parent, and child of the deceased person", damages to be divided among the beneficiaries in shares directed by the verdict;

it further provides that, for the death of a "spouse or minor child" (but apparently not for the death of a parent) the damages "are not limited or restricted by the 'pecuniary loss' or 'pecuniary benefit' rule but may include damages for mental anguish, emotional pain and suffering, loss of society, companionship, comfort, protection, marital care, parental care [sic], filial care, attention, advice, counsel, training, guidance, or education where applicable."

WATSON v. FISCHBACH

Supreme Court of Illinois, 1973.
54 Ill.2d 498, 301 N.E.2d 303.

UNDERWOOD, CHIEF JUSTICE. Plaintiff Beverly A. Watson, as personal representative of her deceased husband and for the benefit of her minor daughter and herself, brought this dramshop action against defendant tavern keepers for injury to plaintiff's means of support and for property damage. It was alleged that decedent's death, which occurred as a result of his car leaving the paved road and striking a telephone pole while he was the driver and sole occupant, resulted from his intoxication caused in whole or in part by alcoholic liquor purchased and consumed in the several places of business owned and operated by defendants. A jury trial resulted in a verdict for all defendants upon which judgment was entered. * * *

Plaintiff urges here that the trial court rulings permitting the jurors to be informed of her remarriage and interrogated regarding their acquaintanceship with her second husband, when coupled with cross-examination which established that the family was living in the same home occupied during the first marriage and that a son had been born to the second marriage, constituted reversible error necessitating a retrial. * * *

The propriety of reference, in the trial of an action for the wrongful death of a deceased spouse, to the remarriage of the surviving spouse must be examined both as to its relevancy in determining damages and its relevancy in the selection of a fair and impartial jury. A very substantial majority of the jurisdictions which have considered the first question have held that remarriage of the surviving spouse, or the possibility thereof, does not affect the damages recoverable for the wrongful death of the deceased spouse. (Annot. (1963), 87 A.L.R.2d 252 (Michigan now appears to have reversed its minority position cited in the annotation; see Bunda v. Hardwick (1965), 376 Mich. 640, 138 N.W.2d 305); Stuart v. Consolidated Foods Corp. (1972), 6 Wash. App. 841, 496 P.2d 527; Dubil v. Labate (1968), 52 N.J. 255, 245 A.2d 177; Wiesel v. Cicerone (1970), 106 R.I. 595, 261 A.2d 889.) This view prevails in Illinois * * *.

Stating that rule, however, is not dispositive of the more troublesome question of the relevancy of plaintiff's remarriage to the selection of a fair and impartial jury. Defendants, generally, urge that their right to jurors uninfluenced by possible relationships or acquaintanceships with plaintiff's new spouse or members of that family necessitates revealing to the jury the fact of plaintiff's remarriage and the identity of the new mate. Some, of course, would go further and adopt the Wisconsin rule (Jensen v. Heritage Mutual Insurance Co. (1964), 23 Wis.2d 344, 127 N.W.2d 228) which holds remarriage or the possibility of it are proper factors for the jury's consideration in assessing damages in a wrongful death action. (See, also, Campbell v. Schmidt (Miss.1967), 195 So.2d 87.) Conversely, plaintiffs, generally, urge that such revelation inevitably results in a greater likelihood of a not guilty verdict, or, at the very least, a diminution of the damages which would otherwise have been awarded, and that this occurs despite cautionary instructions by the judge that the plaintiff's remarriage is totally irrelevant to the issues of liability and damages.

We are not persuaded that jurors will so far abdicate their responsibilities as to consider a remarriage in determining liability, assuming a properly restrictive and cautionary instruction has been requested and given. * * * And the possibility that the amount of damages awarded may be affected by knowledge of the fact that plaintiff has remarried, if it exists, must be weighed against what seems to us an element essential to the integrity of the jury trial process: that the parties to the litigation have a reasonable opportunity to ascertain that the fact-finding body is free from influence-producing relationships unfavorable to them.

There is no unanimity among the courts which have considered the relevance of a plaintiff's remarriage in the context of *voir dire* examination. The opposing views are perhaps best illustrated by Wiesel v. Cicerone (1970), 106 R.I. 595, 261 A.2d 889, and Dubil v. Labate (1968), 52 N.J. 255, 245 A.2d 177. In *Dubil* the Supreme Court of New Jersey concluded that "It would be offensive to the integrity of the judicial process if the plaintiff, after taking an oath to be truthful, were permitted to misrepresent her marital status to the jury. Of course, the defendants may not inquire into the details of the remarriage nor may they offer evidence concerning it. However, the desirable exclusion of evidence relating to the remarriage may not be carried to the point of affirmatively misrepresenting the truth to the jury. It seems to us that in the course of the trial of a wrongful death case, it would be virtually impossible to avoid mention of a remarriage without resorting to untruths. [Citations omitted.] Thus, we believe that—while evidence of the details of a remarriage, such as the earnings of the new spouse or the birth of a child, is to be excluded—the mere fact of a plaintiff's remarriage should not be kept from the jury." (52 N.J. at 261–262, 245 A.2d at 180.) In *Wiesel* the Supreme Court of Rhode Island characterized the disclosure of the remarriage as "putting a premium on form and overlooking substance." (106 R.I. at 607, 261 A.2d at 895.) That court concluded that an instruction telling the jurors that evidence of the remarriage was not to be considered by them would not "outweigh the likelihood of misuse of such evidence by the jury." (106 R.I. at 607, 261 A.2d at 895.) Accordingly, it determined to follow the practice approved by the trial and intermediate courts of California, Ohio and New York * * * pursuant to which no disclosure of the fact of remarriage is permitted. Adequate protection from partial jurors is thought to be secured by permitting *voir dire* examination of prospective jurors regarding their acquaintanceship with a person by the name of the new spouse, not disclosing the relationship of that person to plaintiff. While the factual situations vary in that the new spouse may or may not have been physically present so that the jurors might view him or her in determining their acquaintance, the Rhode Island court apparently held that either method was permissible. Additionally, it held that other witnesses related to the new spouse could be presented in similar fashion, or questions might be asked about them or their businesses in order to determine whether the prospective jurors were in any manner acquainted with them; it is clear, however, that no disclosure of the fact of the remarriage would be permitted.

We are inclined to agree with the position taken by the New Jersey Supreme Court. There is, to us, a patent offensiveness in a rule which countenances false statements made under oath in a judicial proceeding on the theory that, unless false testimony is permitted, jurors will disregard the instructions of the court to the prejudice of the plaintiff.

We believe the judicial process in its search for truth need not resort to the condonation of perjury to accomplish its objective, and we accordingly hold that prospective jurors may be told by the judge that a plaintiff has remarried. Beyond this point, however, we believe defendants have no legitimate interest in exploring. They are, in our judgment, sufficiently protected in their right to an impartial jury by disclosure of the fact of remarriage and identification of the new spouse, coupled with the opportunity to determine the extent of acquaintanceship between the prospective jurors and new spouse. And, we believe, the plaintiff's right to a trial free from factors irrelevant to the issues of liability and damages is adequately assured by the fact that the judge will in his initial identification of the parties state the fact of remarrriage, identify the new spouse and advise the prospective jurors that the plaintiff's remarriage is not to be considered by them on the issues of liability or damages. A similar instruction, if requested by plaintiff, will be given at the close of the case as a part of the written instructions. Beyond the *voir dire,* questions, comments or argument relating to the remarriage will, ordinarily, be improper.

We come now to an assessment of the effect of the cross-examination of plaintiff regarding her remarriage which she contends constituted reversible error. That cross-examination, as noted by the appellate court, clearly exceeded the scope of the direct examination. Its purpose was to and it did emphasize plaintiff's remarriage and disclose to the jury that plaintiff had a child by the new husband and that she and the new family were living in the home formerly occupied by plaintiff and her deceased husband. The questions resulting in these disclosures were vigorously objected to and a mistrial was sought.

The objections were overruled and a mistrial denied. The questions and resulting answers were clearly irrelevant * * * and, in our judgment, constitute reversible error. * * * [19]

SOUTHERN PACIFIC TRANSPORTATION COMPANY v. LUECK

Supreme Court of Arizona, in Banc, 1975.
111 Ariz. 560, 535 P.2d 599.

STRUCKMEYER, VICE CHIEF JUSTICE. This is an appeal from a verdict of a jury and a judgment in an action for wrongful death at a railroad crossing. The jury in a unanimous verdict awarded $2,000,000, compensatory, and $1,080,000, punitive damages to Melanie Lueck, the surviving widow of William T. Lueck, deceased, and their two children, ages six years and 18 months. * * *

The railroad crossing where the accident occurred was protected by all the usual railroad crossing signs. In addition to the standard crossbucks, highway and pavement markings, there were four flashing red lights, eight inches in diameter with warning bells located at the sides of the crossing and two flashing red lights on an overhead cantilever extending over the center of the inside traffic lane with warning bells and a square sign warning "stop on red signal." * * * It is plaintiff's position that * * * all the facts and circumstances then existing at the crossing tended to confuse and mislead the deceased. She points to 25 inferences which she derives from the evidence to support her claim of wanton negligence.

From the * * * [evidence] the jury could conclude that the Southern Pacific Transportation Company was either willfully or wantonly negligent in failing to inform its agents and employees in its Arizona Division or other interested persons in Arizona of facts which, at the time of increasing the speed limit in 1965 from 30 to 60 miles per hour through the City of Willcox, would have required the installation of automatic crossing gates at Maley Street to ensure the safety of the public.

DAMAGES

This brings us to the questions raised by appellant as to the claimed excessiveness of the damages awarded by the jury. In our most recent case on punitive damages, where damages of $3,600 actual damages and $15,000 exemplary or punitive damages was awarded, we said:

> "Punitive damages are allowed on grounds of public policy * * * and are based on aggravated, wanton, reckless or maliciously intentional wrongdoing. * * * Such damages are not to be awarded to compensate a plaintiff for the

19. Compare State v. Cress, 22 Ariz. App. 490, 528 P.2d 876 (1974) (following California-New York procedure.) Also see for Texas rule Conway v. Chemical Leaman Tank Lines, Inc., 525 F.2d 927 (5th Cir. 1976).

> loss sustained, but, rather, are awarded for the avowed purpose of punishing the wrongdoer for his intentional misconduct and they also act as a deterrent to further wrongdoing. * * * Restatement of the Law, Torts, § 908 Comment a." Acheson v. Shafter, 107 Ariz. 576, 578, 490 P.2d 832, 834 (1971)

and we also said:

> "In Arizona, the law is well settled that the amount of an award for damages is a question peculiarly within the province of the jury and such award will not be disturbed on appeal except for the most cogent of reasons, i. e., the verdict is so exorbitant as to indicate passion, prejudice, mistake or a complete disregard of the evidence and instructions of the court. * * * We have, in the past, held that punitive damages will be upheld unless the verdict is 'so manifestly unfair, unreasonable and outrageous as to shock the conscience of the Court.' * * * 107 Ariz. at 579, 490 P.2d at 835.

The purpose of punitive damages is to punish a wrongdoer for his wrongdoing. The wealth or financial status of the wrongdoer is therefore relevant and may be known to the jury so that it may impose an appropriate punishment. * * * As to this, the plaintiff's evidence established that the net assets of defendant were $1,712,-727,000 for the year 1972 and that its annual income after expenses but before income taxes was $165,555,000.

Applying the foregoing to the evidence in this case, it is apparent that if the jury concluded that the Southern Pacific Transportation Company had either deliberately or through wanton or gross negligence withheld from its employees facts which would have required and resulted in the upgrading of the Maley Street crossing by the installation of crossing gates, the punitive damages awarded were not so manifestly unfair, unreasonable and outrageous as to shock the conscience.

In examining defendant's argument that the award of actual damages by the jury is excessive, we consider that the decision of the United States Supreme Court in Grunenthal v. Long Island Railroad Company, 393 U.S. 156, 89 S.Ct. 331, 21 L.Ed.2d 309 (1968), has particular significance. There, a jury in the Southern District of New York awarded actual damages in the sum of $305,000. On appeal, the Second Circuit ordered a remittitur of $105,000. The Supreme Court observed that the discussion by the Court of Appeals concerning the amount of damages was limited to the bald statement that it could not in any rational manner consistent with the evidence arrive at a sum greater than $200,000. The Supreme Court in reinstating the jury's verdict held that if damages are ordered reduced by an appellate court an appraisal of the evidence must be made which discloses the excessive nature thereof.

The defendant does not attempt to evaluate the evidence other than pointing to the deceased's income tax returns, which showed that in the five years preceding his death he had taxable income in his best year of $5,834.37, and an assumed economic loss to plaintiff of $691,769 reduced to present value of $281,863. Defendant argues that $281,863 would not provide a basis for a two million dollars compensatory award. The figure of $281,863 is taken from the testimony of Edward Heller, by profession an economist with a specialty in the field of manpower economy, resource economics. He testified that there were studies available as to future earning capacity of an individual as it relates to inflation and the purchasing power of the dollar, and that by means of these he was able to project what a person of a given education and training could reasonably earn in the future.

Heller made a study or evaluation of the earning capacity of deceased. In arriving at his conclusions, among the factors considered were that the deceased was a high school graduate with vocational training in welding and had operated a welding shop from his high school days until 1961 when he started the business known as Lueck's Construction Materials. He testified:

> "A. * * * In terms of surveying the job market, Mr. Lueck, as a—what we would call a heavy-duty welder, heavy-duty concrete—I can't now remember the exact title now, but it's a—concrete journeyman; a person who could pour, finish, do the molding work necessary with heavy concrete construction—could have expected to earn around the same $800 per month at the—in 1966.
>
> * * * * * * * * * *
>
> "Q. Would I be correct, then, the fringe benefits, plus the 800 a month, are the figures you used to make your ultimate conclusion?
>
> "A. Yes. Plus the cost of replacing his services, less his personal consumption.
>
> "Q. * * * What I was driving at, if Mr. Lueck had been in the job market, rather than in a self-employed situation, would the additional fringe benefits he would expect to have mean that he would have had a greater earning capacity in a job market, as opposed to being self-employed?
>
> "A. Very definitely.
>
> "Q. And yet you used the lesser end of those two figures?
>
> "A. Yes."

It is therefore apparent that the deceased's earning capacity over his life expectancy of 41 years was predicated on the assumption that Lueck could be employed as an expert welder or journeyman concrete worker.

The jury was not, however, compelled to accept as conclusive the statistical approach used by Heller. Other evidence disclosed that deceased was a well-liked, industrious, hard-working male of the age of 30 years, that the business of Lueck's Construction Materials involved manufacturing and selling ready-mixed concrete for buildings and irrigation ditches; that in addition deceased operated a gravel pit and sold gravel; that in the course of the five years since he started the business, he had acquired by the time of his death three mixers, three dump trucks, three loaders, a rock crusher, a steam shovel and blade, and a batching plant.

The Iowa Court in Nicoll v. Sweet, 163 Iowa 683, 144 N.W. 615 (1913) has probably best summarized the difficulties in the assessment of damages for wrongful death:

> " It is correct to say, as does the appellant, that the only true measure of recovery for the death of an individual is the value of his life to his estate, had he not come to such untimely end. It is hardly too much to say that this rule is vague, uncertain, and speculative, if not conjectural, but it is the best which judicial wisdom and experience has yet been able to formulate. No evidence is possible of the time which deceased would have lived but for the injury complained of. Had he avoided this injury, death may have met him the next day, week, or year in some other form. In business he might have become a phenomenal success and accumulated millions, or he might have lived to old age and died a pauper. From a man of good habits and prudence and industry, he might have become a spendthrift or a tramp, or if a man of dissolute habits he might have reformed into an efficient and prosperous citizen. But the demands of justice will not tolerate the idea that human life may be extinguished by the tort of another without the wrongdoer being held to answer therefor in damages, and the rule we have stated is the one which has been devised for this purpose. The principle which underlies it is of unquestionable soundness, but the difficulty which besets its practical application is in the fact that it calls for an estimate or conclusion which must be arrived at by a balancing of mere probabilities and possibilities which we deduce by way of inference from the age, character, habits, condition, education, employment, surroundings, and apparent capacity of the deceased. Fairness to the beneficiaries of the estate on the one hand and of the defendant on the other require that the jury be put in possession of all the facts having the slightest legitimate bearing upon this intricate problem." 163 Iowa at 687–688, 144 N.W. 615 at 617.

Plaintiff points to the recent Florida case of Compania Dominicana de Aviacion v. Knapp, 251 So.2d 18 (Fla.App.1971), in which a verdict for $1,800,000 was upheld in favor of a father and mother for the wrongful death of their 15-year-old son. The son was a graduate of a junior high school about to enter high school, a good student, friendly, polite, warm, active, religious, and at the time of his death was working in his father's paint and body shop. There was also testimony as to the grief and anguish of the parents. The Florida court noted that the amount of the verdict was determined by a carefully chosen jury after a lengthy trial before an experienced and knowledgeable judge with the assistance of expert counsel. It said in concluding that the verdict and judgment were supported in law and fact: "No one doubts that the verdict is large. No one doubts the enduring pain which the parents have suffered."

While it is true the deceased's net earnings for taxes were relatively small, we think it can be said that the jury could make its own evaluation of the earning capacity of the deceased over his lifetime from the establishment of a successful, going business at the age of thirty, which evaluation would be much greater than the purely statistical approach used by Heller.

The jury could consider other matters for which the members of deceased's family should be compensated: For the wife her loss, of love, affection, companionship, consortium, and her personal anguish, sorrow, suffering and pain and shock which resulted from her husband's death. For the six-year-old son, it was shown that following the accident he commenced to draw pictures of train wrecks, that he refused to go to school and developed head and stomach aches and that these problems were determined to have been caused by the emotional loss of his father, and that it was three years before he overcame them. For the 18-month-old child, it was shown that after the accident he would not leave the presence of his moher even to be held by his grandparents and if his mother left he would scream until she returned, and he refused to sleep in his own bed until some six months after the death of his father. The jury could also consider what the sons were to be compensated for the loss of love, affection, comfort, guidance and companionship which they would have received from their father.

* * * [N]o interrogatories or separate forms of verdicts were requested from the jury segregating the damages suffered by each survivor. There is accordingly now no way of determining what the jury believed the plaintiffs individually suffered. We are not convinced the verdict is so outrageously excessive that it compels the conclusion that it must have been based on passion and prejudice. * * *[20]

20. Serious questions can arise as to whether punitive damages are covered by liability insurance. See, e. g., Southern Farm Bureau Casualty Insurance Co. v. Daniel, 246 Ark. 849, 440 S.W.2d 582 (1969); R. Keeton, Basic Text on Insurance Law § 5.3(f) (1971).

TROPPI v. SCARF

Court of Appeals of Michigan, Div. 1, 1971.
31 Mich.App. 240, 187 N.W.2d 511.

LEVIN, PRESIDING JUDGE. In this case we consider the civil liability of a pharmacist who negligently supplied the wrong drug to a married woman who had ordered ar oral contraceptive and, as a consequence, became pregnant and delivered a normal healthy child.

I.

A summary judgment was entered dismissing the complaint of the plaintiffs, John and Dorothy Troppi, on the ground that it does not state a claim upon which relief can be granted. In our appraisal of the correctness of the trial judge's ruling we accept as true plaintiffs' factual allegations.

In August 1964, plaintiffs were the parents of seven children, ranging in age from six to sixteen years of age. John Troppi was 43 years old, his wife 37.

While pregnant with an eighth child, Mrs. Troppi suffered a miscarriage. She and her husband consulted with their physician and decided to limit the size of their family. The physician prescribed an oral contraceptive, Norinyl, as the most desirable means of insuring that Mrs. Troppi would bear no more children. He telephoned the prescription to defendant, Frank H. Scarf, a licensed pharmacist. Instead of filling the prescription, Scarf negligently supplied Mrs. Troppi with a drug called Nardil, a mild tranquilizer.

Believing that the pills she had purchased were contraceptives, Mrs. Troppi took them on a daily basis. In December 1964, Mrs. Troppi became pregnant. She delivered a well-born son on August 12, 1965.

Plaintiffs' complaint alleges four separate items of damage: (1) Mrs. Troppi's lost wages; (2) medical and hospital expenses; (3) the pain and anxiety of pregnancy and childbirth; and (4) the economic costs of rearing the eighth child.

In dismissing the complaint the judge declared that whatever damage plaintiff suffered was more than offset by the benefit to them of having a healthy child.

II.

Contraception, conjugal relations, and childbirth are highly charged subjects. It is all the more important, then, to emphasize that resolution of the case before us requires no intrusion into the domain of moral philosophy. At issue here is simply the extent to which defendant is civilly liable for the consequences of his negligence. In reversing and remanding for trial, we go no further than to apply settled common-law principles.

We begin by noting that the fundamental conditions of tort liability are present here. The defendant's conduct constituted a clear breach of duty. A pharmacist is held to a very high standard of care in filling prescriptions. When he negligently supplies a drug other than the drug requested, he is liable for resulting harm to the purchaser. * * *

We assume, for the purpose of appraising the correctness of the ruling dismissing the complaint, that the defendant's negligence was a cause in fact of Mrs. Troppi's pregnancy. The possibility that she might become pregnant was certainly a foreseeable consequence of the defendant's failure to fill a prescription for birth control pills; we therefore, could not say that it was not a proximate cause of the birth of the child.

Setting aside, for the moment, the subtleties of the damage question, it is at least clear that the plaintiffs have expended significant sums of money as a direct and proximate result of the defendant's negligence. The medical and hospital expenses of Mrs. Troppi's confinement and her loss of wages arose from the defendant's failure to fill the prescription properly. Pain and suffering, like that accompanying childbirth, have long been recognized as compensable injuries.

This review of the elements of tort liability points up the extraordinary nature of the trial court's holding that the plaintiffs were entitled to no recovery as a matter of law. We have here a negligent, wrongful act by the defendant, which act directly and proximately caused injury to the plaintiffs.

What we must decide is whether there is justification here for a departure from generally applicable, well-established principles of law * * *.

III.

The trial judge based his decision upon what he perceived to be the law "announced by a majority of the courts in this country." But, as yet, no appellate court has passed upon the liability of a pharmacist for negligently dispensing oral contraceptives. Several cases have, indeed, dealt with the liability of physicians for failure to exercise due care in the therapeutic or elective sterilization of patients. Because the elements of damage in these cases correspond to some of the damages prayed for here, the decisions deserve scrutiny.

In Christensen v. Thornby (1934), 192 Minn. 123, 255 N.W. 620, 93 A.L.R. 570, a physician had warned that the plaintiff's wife might not survive the birth of another child. Plaintiff consented to a sterilization operation which the defendant surgeon performed. Although the surgeon represented that the operation was successful, the plaintiff's wife subsequently became pregnant and delivered a healthy child. The plaintiff sued for the medical expenses and his anxiety occasioned by fears for his wife's health.

The Minnesota Supreme Court affirmed an order of the trial court sustaining defendant's demurrer upon two grounds. The first was that since the plaintiff had sued for deceit, not negligence, proof of fraudulent intent was required. Second, the plaintiff had suffered no damage (p. 126, 255 N.W. at 622):

> "The purpose of the operation was to save the wife from the hazards to her life which were incident to childbirth. It was not the alleged purpose to save the expense incident to pregnancy and delivery. The wife has survived. Instead of losing his wife, the plaintiff has been blessed with the fatherhood of another child."

That case, is, of course, distinguishable from the one before us. The plaintiff husband in *Christensen* made no claim that the child itself or the economic consequences of its birth were unwanted. The operation was directed at the threat to his wife's health. Since her health remained unimpaired, no damage was suffered. That the husband could not have foreseen that his wife would emerge unscathed and his anxiety was therefore quite justified was a factor the court did not discuss.

In Shaheen v. Knight (Pa.1957), 11 Pa.Dist. & Co.R.2d 41, 45, 46, a Pennsylvania *nisi prius* court ruled that a physician who violated his promise to perform an effective, elective sterilization operation was not liable for the consequences of his breach of contract. Plaintiff, the father of four children, wanted no more. As a result of an ineffective sterilization, plaintiff was able to impregnate his wife, who delivered a healthy baby. After finding defendant in breach of contract, the court said:

> "Defendant argues, however, and pleads, that plaintiff has suffered no damage. We agree with defendant. The only damages asked are the expenses of rearing and educating the unwanted child. We are of the opinion that to allow damages for the normal birth of a normal child is foreign to the universal public sentiment of the people.
>
> "Many consider the sole purpose of marriage a union for having children. * * *
>
> "To allow damages in a suit such as this would mean that the physician would have to pay for the fun, joy and affection which plaintiff Shaheen will have in the rearing and educating of this, [plaintiff's] fifth child. Many people would be willing to support this child were they given the right of custody and adoption, but according to plaintiff's statement, plaintiff does not want such. He wants to have the child and wants the doctor to support it. In our opinion to allow damages would be against public policy."

Underlying the *Shaheen* opinion are two principal ideas. The first is that the birth of a healthy child confers such an undoubted benefit upon the plaintiff as to outweigh, as a matter of law, the expenses of delivering and rearing the child. The second is that if the child is really unwanted, plaintiff has a duty to place him for adoption, in effect to mitigate damages. We defer for the moment our evaluation of these concepts, while noting their relevance to the issues at hand.

Different questions were presented to the New Jersey Supreme Court in Gleitman v. Cosgrove (1967), 49 N.J. 22, 29, 227 A.2d 689, 693, 22 A.L.R.3d 1411. Mrs. Gleitman contracted rubella (German measles) during her pregnancy and subsequently gave birth to a deformed child. The infant and his parents sued the defendant physician for malpractice, alleging that he had negligently failed to warn Mrs. Gleitman of the likelihood that her child would be born defective. As a result of his negligence, Mrs. Gleitman did not seek a therapeutic abortion.

The majority of the court assumed that Mrs. Gleitman could have obtained a lawful abortion, but nonetheless affirmed the decision of the trial court dismissing the complaint as to all three plaintiffs.

The majority distinguished between the rights of the infant plaintiff and those of his parents. As to the infant, the court held in essence that it could not countenance an action for "wrongful life."

A more difficult question was presented by the parents' claim for compensatory damages. The court disposed of this claim in extraordinary fashion. Of principal relevance to the case before us is the holding that compensatory damages were too uncertain to be awarded:

> "In order to determine their compensatory damages a court would have to evaluate the denial to them of the intangible, unmeasurable, and complex human benefits of motherhood and fatherhood and weigh these against the alleged emotional and money injuries."

Three of the seven justices were of the view that money damages were ascertainable with reasonable precision and would have allowed the parents' claim to be presented to the trier of fact.

In Milde v. Leigh (1947), 75 N.D. 418, 28 N.W.2d 530, 173 A.L.R. 738, the defendant negligently performed a therapeutic sterilization operation upon the plaintiff's wife and she subsequently delivered a healthy child. The appeal was taken by the defendant from an order of the trial court rejecting his defense of the statute of limitations. In affirming this order, the North Dakota Supreme Court declared that the plaintiff could recover for loss of his wife's services, society and companionship during her pregnancy, as well as for medical expenses occasioned by her confinement.

A comprehensive review of the cases dealing with negligent sterilization was conducted by a California intermediate appellate court in Custodio v. Bauer (1967), 251 Cal.App.2d 303, 325, 59 Cal.Rptr. 463, 477, 476, 27 A.L.R.3d 884. Plaintiffs, husband and wife, had eight children. The defendant physician recommended that Mrs. Custodio be sterilized, citing her large family and uncertain health. After the operation, she became pregnant and delivered a healthy baby. The plaintiffs sued for medical expenses, Mrs. Custodio's physical damage, her pain and suffering, and the cost of supporting the child until he reached maturity. The trial court dismissed the suit before trial.

Expressly rejecting Christensen v. Thornby, supra, and Shaheen v. Knight, supra, the California appeals court reversed, noting "some trend of change in social ethics with respect to the family establishment" and declared:

> "It is clear that if successful on the issue of liability, [plaintiffs] have established a right to more than nominal damages."

How the excess over nominal damages was to be determined was not specified, beyond this suggestion:

> "Where the mother survives without casualty there is still some loss. She must spread her society, comfort, care, protection and support over a larger group. If this change in the family status can be measured economically it should be as compensable as the former losses." (Custodio, supra, 323, 324, 59 Cal.Rptr. at 476.)

Additional decisions recognizing that there is a cause of action for negligent sterilization are Jackson v. Anderson (Fla.App., 1970), 230 So.2d 503; Bishop v. Byrne (S.D.W.Va., 1967), 265 F.Supp. 460; cf. Doerr v. Villate (1966), 74 Ill.App.2d 332, 334, 335, 220 N.E.2d 767, 768.[21]

IV.

Our review has been conducted to determine whether the defendant in this case should be exempted from the consequences of his negligence. We conclude that there is no valid reason why the trier of fact should not be free to assess damages as it would in any other negligence case.

21. Cf. Ball v. Mudge (1964), 64 Wash. 2d 247, 250, 391 P.2d 201, 204. A physician had performed a vasectomy upon the plaintiff. This operation had been prompted by fears for the health of Mrs. Ball if she became pregnant again, as well as by a desire on the part of Mr. and Mrs. Ball to avoid the expense of rearing a fourth child. Despite the vasectomy, Mrs. Ball again became pregnant and delivered a healthy baby. The plaintiffs appealed a *jury verdict* in favor of the physician and argued that they should have been granted a directed verdict on the issue of negligence. This was rejected on the ground that subsequent fertility is not conclusive proof that a vasectomy was negligently performed. As to damages, the Court observed:

"As reasonable persons, the *jury* may well have concluded that appellants suffered no damage in the birth of a normal, healthy child, whom they dearly love, would not consider placing for adoption, and 'would not sell for $50,000,' and that the cost incidental to such birth was far outweighed by the blessing of a cherished child, albeit an unwanted child at the time of conception and birth." (Emphasis supplied.) * * *

Public Policy. The trial court found that "to allow damages such as claimed here would be in contravention of public policy." A judicial declaration of preemptive public policy should express the manifest will of the people. Not only does contraception not violate the public policy of the State of Michigan, the legislature has recently enacted two separate statutes designed to foster the use of contraceptives. Family planning services may be supplied to medically indigent women by the State, upon request * * *.

Where the State's advocacy of family planning is so vigorous as to include payments for contraceptives as part of the welfare program, public policy cannot be said to disfavor contraception. The notion that public policy may favor contraception for the poor, yet disapprove of it for the more affluent, is unworthy of serious discussion.

Contraceptives are used to prevent the birth of healthy children. To say that for reasons of public policy contraceptive failure can result in no damage as a matter of law ignores the fact that tens of millions of persons use contraceptives daily to avoid the very result which the defendant would have us say is always a benefit, never a detriment. Those tens of millions of persons, by their conduct, express the sense of the community.

Contraception has been held to be within a constitutionally protected "zone of privacy" that surrounds the marital relationship.[22] The State may not infringe upon the rights of husband and wife to use contraceptives to limit the size of their family. Since the State may not infringe upon this right, it may not constitutionally denigrate the right by completely denying protection provided as a matter of course to like rights.[23]

In theory at least, the imposition of civil liability encourages potential tortfeasors to exercise more care in the performance of their duties, and, hence, to avoid liability-producing negligent acts.[24] Applying this theory to the case before us, public policy favors a tort scheme which encourages pharmacists to exercise great care in filling prescriptions. To absolve defendant of all liability here would be to remove one deterrent against the negligent dispensing of drugs. Given the great numbers of women who currently use oral contraceptives, such absolution cannot be defended on public policy grounds.

Overriding Benefit. It is arguable that the birth of a healthy child confers so substantial a benefit as to outweigh the expenses of his birth and support. In the great majority of cases, this is no doubt true, else, presumably, people would not choose to multiply so freely. But can we say, as a matter of law, that a healthy child always confers such an overriding benefit?

22. Griswold v. Connecticut (1965), 381 U.S. 479, 485, 85 S.Ct. 1678, 14 L.Ed. 2d 510. See Brodie, Marital Procreation, 49 Or.L.Rev. 245 (1970).

23. Compare 1 Antieau, Modern Constitutional Law, § 7:13, p. 542; § 8:10, p. 574.

24. Prosser, Torts (3d ed.), § 4, p. 23; 2 Harper and James, Torts, § 11.5, p. 742.

The so-called "benefit rule" is pertinent. The Restatement declares:

> "Where the defendant's tortious conduct has caused harm to the plaintiff or to his property and in so doing has conferred upon the plaintiff a special benefit to the interest which was harmed, the value of the benefit conferred is considered in mitigation of damages, where this is equitable." Restatement, Torts, § 920, p. 616.

Thus, if the defendant's tortious conduct conferred a benefit to the same interest which was harmed by his conduct the dollar value of the benefit is to be subtracted from the dollar value of the injury in arriving at the amount of damages properly awardable.

Since pregnancy and its attendant anxiety, incapacity, pain and suffering are inextricably related to child bearing, we do not think it would be sound to attempt to separate those segments of damage from the economic costs of an unplanned child in applying the "same interest" rule. Accordingly, the benefits of the unplanned child may be weighed against all the elements of claimed damage.

The trial court evidently believed, as did the court in Shaheen v. Knight, supra, that application of the benefits rule prevents any recovery for the expenses of rearing an unwanted child. This is unsound. Such a rule would be equivalent to declaring that in every case, as a matter of law, the services and companionship of a child have a dollar equivalent greater than the economic costs of his support, to say nothing of the inhibitions, the restrictions, and the pain and suffering caused by pregnancy and the obligation to rear the child.

There is a growing recognition that the financial "services" which parents can expect from their offspring are largely illusory. As to companionship, cases decided when "loss of companionship" was a compensable item of damage for the wrongful death of a child reveal no tendency on the part of juries to value companionship so highly as to outweigh expenses in every foreseeable case.

Our discussion should not be construed as an expression of doubt as to the efficacy of the benefits rule in cases like the one before us. On the contrary, we believe that rule to be essential to the rational disposition of this case and the others that are sure to follow. The benefits rule allows flexibility in the case-by-case adjudication of the enormously varied claims which the widespread use of oral contraceptives portends.

What must be appreciated is the diversity of purposes and circumstances of the women who use oral contraceptives. Unmarried women who seek the pleasures of sexual intercourse without the perils of unwed motherhood, married women who wish to delay slightly the start of a family in order to retain the career flexibility which many young couples treasure, married women for whom the birth of another child would pose a threat to their own health or the financial security of their families, all are likely users of oral contraceptives. Yet it is clear that in each case the consequences arising from negligent interference with their use will vary widely. A rational legal system must award damages that correspond with these differing injuries. The benefits rule will serve to accomplish this objective.

Consider, for example, the case of the unwed college student who becomes pregnant due to a pharmacist's failure to fill properly her prescription for oral contraceptives. Is it not likely that she has suffered far greater damage than the young newlywed who, although her pregnancy arose from the same sort of negligence, had planned the use of contraceptives only temporarily, say while she and her husband took an extended honeymoon trip? Without the benefits rule, both plaintiffs would be entitled to recover substantially the same damages.

Application of the benefits rule permits a trier of fact to find that the birth of a child has materially benefitted the newly wed couple, notwithstanding the inconvenience of an interrupted honeymoon, and to reduce the net damage award accordingly. Presumably a trier of fact would find that the "family interests" of the unmarried coed has been enhanced very little.

The essential point, of course, is that the trier must have the power to evaluate the benefit according to all the circumstances of the case presented. Family size, family income, age of the parents, and marital status are some, but not all, the factors which the trier must consider in determining the extent to which the birth of a particular child represents a benefit to his parents. That the benefits so conferred and calculated will vary widely from case to case is inevitable.

Mitigating Damages. It has been suggested that parents who seek to recover for the birth of an unwanted child are under a duty to mitigate damages by placing the child for adoption. If the child is "unwanted", why should they object to placing him for adoption, thereby reducing the financial burden on defendant for his maintenance?

However, to impose such a duty upon the injured plaintiff is to ignore the very real difference which our law recognizes between the avoidance of conception and the disposition of the human organism after conception. This most obvious distinction is illustrated by the constitutional protection afforded the right to use contraceptives, while abortion is still a felony in most jurisdictions. At the moment of conception, an entirely different set of legal obligations is imposed upon the parents. A living child almost universally gives rise to emotional and spiritual bonds which few parents can bring themselves to break.

Once a child is born he obviously should be treated with love regardless of whether he was wanted when he was conceived. Many, perhaps most, persons living today are conceptional accidents in the sense that their parents did not desire that a child result from the particular intercourse in which the person was conceived. Nevertheless, when the child is born, most parents accept him with love. That the plaintiffs accepted their eighth child does not change the fact that the birth of another child, seven years younger than the youngest of their previously born children, unbalanced their life style and was not desired by them.

The doctrine which requires a plaintiff to take measures to minimize the financial consequences of a defendant's negligence requires only that reasonable measures be taken.

> "If the effort, risk, sacrifice, or expense which the person wronged must incur in order to avoid or minimize a loss or injury is such that under all the circumstances a reasonable man might well decline to incur it, a failure to do so imposes no disability against recovering full damages." McCormick, Damages, § 35, p. 133.

It should be noted that the standards by which reasonable conduct is determined are less stringent when used to evaluate the subsequent acts of the injured party than when used to evaluate the tortious act itself.[25]

In determining reasonableness the best interests of the child must be considered. The law has long recognized the desirability of permitting a child to be reared by his natural parents. The plaintiff may have believed that the hazards of adoption would damage the child.

A child will not be taken from his mother without her consent, without regard to whether the child was conceived or born in wedlock, unless the child is neglected or the mother is unfit. The mother's right to keep the child is not dependent on whether she desired the conception of the child.

As a matter of personal conscience and choice parents may wish to keep an unwanted child. Indeed, parents have been known to keep children that many think should be institutionalized, e. g., mentally retarded children, not because of any anticipated joy or happiness that the child will bring to them but out of a sense of obligation. So, too, the parents of an unplanned, healthy child may feel, and properly so, that whether they wanted the child or not is beside the point once the child is born and that they have an obligation to rear the child as best they can rather than subject him to rearing by unknown persons.

Further, even though the parents may not want to rear the child they may conclude that the psychological impact on them of rejecting the child and placing him for adoption, never seeing him again, would be such that, making the best of a bad situation, it is better to rear the child than to place him for adoption.

25. Courts have been reluctant, for example, to require that plaintiffs submit to surgical procedures that are more than routine. Where ethical or religious scruples prevent a plaintiff from submitting to relatively minor surgery, the trier of fact may consider these scruples as part of the circumstances which bear upon the reasonableness of his conduct. McCormick, Damages, § 36, p. 136; 22 Am.Jur.2d, Damages, § 39, p. 63. Cf. Romankewiz v. Black (1969), 16 Mich. App. 119, 167 N.W.2d 606. [Notes 21–25 from original, renumbered; other notes in original omitted.]

Many women confronted with an unwanted pregnancy will abort the fetus, legally or illegally. Some will bear the child and place him for adoption. Many will bear the child, keep and rear him. The defendant does not have the right to insist that the victim of his negligence have the emotional and mental makeup of a woman who is willing to abort or place a child for adoption. If the negligence of a tortfeasor results in conception of a child by a woman whose emotional and mental makeup is inconsistent with aborting or placing the child for adoption, then, under the principle that the tortfeasor takes the injured party as he finds him, the tortfeasor cannot complain that the damages that will be assessed against him are greater than those that would be determined if he had negligently caused the conception of a child by a woman who was willing to abort or place the child for adoption.

While the reasonableness of a plaintiff's efforts to mitigate is ordinarily to be decided by the trier of fact, we are persuaded to rule, as a matter of law, that no mother, wed or unwed, can reasonably be required to abort (even if legal) or place her child for adoption. The plaintiffs are entitled to have the jurors instructed that if they find that negligence of the defendant was a cause in fact of the plaintiffs' injury, they may not, in computing the amount, if any, of the plaintiffs' damages, take into consideration the fact that the plaintiffs might have aborted the child or placed the child for adoption.

Uncertainty of Damages. Of the four items of damage claimed by plaintiffs, each is capable of reasonable ascertainment. The medical and hospital expenses and Mrs. Troppi's lost wages may be computed with some exactitude. Plaintiffs' claimed pain and anxiety, if not capable of precise determination, is a component of damage which triers of fact traditionally have been entrusted to ascertain. As to the costs of rearing the child until his majority, this is a computation which is routinely performed in countless cases.

It should be clear that ascertainment of *gross* damages is a routine task. Whatever uncertainty attends the final award arises from application of the benefits rule, which requires that the trier of fact compute the dollar value of the companionship and services of an unwanted child. Placing a dollar value on these segments may well be more difficult than assessing damages for, say, Mrs. Troppi's lost wages. But difficulty in determining the amount to be subtracted from the gross damages does not justify throwing up our hands and denying recovery altogether.

Michigan law is clear that there need only be a basis for reasonable ascertainment of the amount of the damages. Where the fact of liability is proven, difficulty in determining damages will not bar recovery. As the Michigan Supreme Court noted in Allison v. Chandler (1863), 11 Mich. 542, 554:

> "The law does not require impossibilities; and can not, therefore, require a higher degree of certainty than the nature of the case admits."

More recently, the Court said in Purcell v. Keegan (1960), 359 Mich. 571, 576, 103 N.W.2d 494, 496:

> "But where injury to some degree is found, we do not preclude recovery for lack of precise proof. We do the best we can with what we have. We do not, 'in the assessment of damages, require a mathematical precision in situations of injury where, from the very nature of the circumstances, precision is unattainable.' Particularly is this true where it is defendant's own act or neglect that has caused the imprecision."

Moreover, the Michigan Supreme Court has repeatedly recognized that the dollar value of a child's services and companionship is not too uncertain to be left to the judgment of the trier of fact. Beginning in 1960 with Wycko v. Gnodtke (1960), 361 Mich. 331, 105 N.W.2d 118, recovery for the wrongful death of a child was measured by considering, among other elements of damage, the value of his services and companionship. Although there was spirited dissent as to the statutory basis of this rule, subsequent cases reflected no feeling on the part of the Court that these damages were too uncertain to be entrusted to determination by the trier of fact. The recent disavowal of Wycko in Breckon v. Franklin Fuel Company (1970), 383 Mich. 251, 174 N.W. 2d 836, involved a question of statutory interpretation, and not the specificity of the measure of damages.

The assessment of damages in this case is properly within the competence of the trier of fact. The element of uncertainty in the net recovery does not render the damages unduly speculative.

Reversed and remanded for trial.[26]

26. Compare Terrell v. Garcia, 496 S.W. 2d 124 (Tex.Civ.App.1973) and Coleman v. Garrison, 327 A.2d 757 (Del. Super.1974). What about damages to other siblings, whose share of love, affection and worldly interest is diluted by a birth caused by a druggist's or doctor's negligence? See Aronoff v. Snider, 292 So.2d 410 (Fla. App.1974). Unwillingness persists to recognize a cause of action for wrongful birth for the benefit of a deformed child, e. g., Stewart v. Long Island College Hospital, 35 A.D.2d 531, 313 N.Y.S.2d 502 (1970), aff'd 30 N.Y.2d 695, 283 N.E.2d 616, 332 N.Y.S.2d 640 (1972); Dumer v. St. Michael's Hosptial, 69 Wis.2d 766, 233 N.W.2d 372 (1975). See, however, Friedman, Legal Implications of Amniocentesis, 123 U.Pa.L.Rev. 92, 143 et seq. (1974).

(E) LOSS OF "RELATIVE RIGHTS"

HITAFFER v. ARGONNE CO.

United States Court of Appeals, D. C., 1950.
183 F.2d 811.

CLARK, CIRCUIT JUDGE.[27] The appeal in the instant case presents * * * the question of whether or not a wife has a cause of action for loss of *consortium* resulting from a negligent injury to her husband * * *.

Appellant's husband was injured while in appellee's employ. As a result thereof he suffered and sustained severe and permanent injuries to his body and in particular in and about his abdomen, and as a consequence appellant has been deprived of his aid, assistance, and enjoyment, specifically sexual relations. * * *

Although this is the first time this question has been presented to this court, we are not unaware of the unanimity of authority elsewhere denying the wife recovery under these circumstances. As a matter of fact we have found only one case in which the action was allowed, and that authority has since been effectively overruled. But after a careful examination of these cases we remain unconvinced that the rule which they have laid down should be followed in the District of Columbia. On the contrary, after piercing the thin veils of reasoning employed to sustain the rule, we have been unable to disclose any substantial rationale on which we would be willing to predicate a denial of a wife's action for loss of *consortium* due to a negligent injury to her husband.

Analysis of the cases in opposition to the position which we are taking in this opinion will reveal that the synthesizations which follow are fairly representative of the sundry reasons assigned for denying the wife a right of recovery.

One group of cases base their results on the theory that although in the abstract the term "*consortium*" contains, in addition to material services, elements of companionship, love, felicity, and sexual relations, in cases of injury to the *consortium* resulting from negligence the material services are the predominant factor for which compensation is given. From this point they variously argue: (1) That since the wife has no right as such to her husband's services, she has no cause of action, although, of course, the husband, having always been entitled to his wife's services, still has a right of action; (2) That the Emancipation Acts, having given a wife a right to the fruits of her own services, have placed the husband in the same position as the wife in number (1) so that neither may bring an action, except that a husband may recover for monies actually expended. The difficulty with adhering to these authorities is that they sound in the false premise that in these actions the loss of services is the predom-

27. The extensive footnotes to the opinion are omitted.

inant factor. This distinction lacks precedent. It is nothing more than an arbitrary separation of the various elements of *consortium* devised to circumvent the logic of allowing the wife such an action. The development of this fiction has been attributed to the use of words. * * *

Consortium, although it embraces within its ambit of meaning the wife's material services, also includes love, affection, companionship, sexual relations, etc., all welded into a conceptualistic unity. And, although loss of one or the other of these elements may be greater in the case of any one of the several types of invasions from which *consortium* may be injured, there can be no rational basis for holding that in negligent invasions suability depends on whether there is a loss of services. It is not the fact that one or the other of the elements of *consortium* is injured in a particular invasion that controls the type of action which may be brought but rather that the *consortium* as such has been injured at all. Hence we are constrained to reject the cases which refuse to allow the wife to sue in these actions for the reason that we are unable to accept the premise. We likewise reject those cases which go one step further in disallowing the husband such an action for the further reason that he has always been allowed to sue for loss of his *consortium* due to negligence in this jurisdiction.

Another group of cases which similarly appear to place principal emphasis on the element of services in these actions hold that in negligent invasions of the *consortium* the wife has no cause of action because the husband, who is under a legal duty to support his wife according to his station in life, recovers in his action for the tort, as an element of his damages, for any impairment of his ability to perform his obligation, and thus the wife indirectly recovers for the value of any loss of her *consortium.* Any other conclusion, they reason, would result in a double recovery. The husband, on the other hand, is allowed the action when the wife is injured, because she is under no corresponding duty to him. Of course, as we have already pointed out, there is no foundation for the statement that the predominant factor involved in negligence cases of this type is the element of material services. For that reason we cannot accept their argument. There is more to *consortium* than the mere services of the spouse. Beyond that there are the so-called sentimental elements to which the wife has a right for which there should be a remedy. We do agree, however, that if the wife is allowed to sue, there could be a double recovery in regard to the service element of *consortium,* if the husband's recovery is not taken into account in measuring the wife's damages and we shall deal with the problem hereinafter in more detail.

Other cases following the reasoning of the foregoing authorities have realized, however, that the sentimental elements of the *consortium* are injured in negligent invasions. Thus, in order to deny the wife a right to recover for love, affection, conjugal relations, etc., they have variously concluded: (1) That in negligence cases the purpose of the damages is to compensate the injured person for the direct consequences of the wrong. The injury to the wife is indirect and so not compensable; (2) That her injuries are too remote and consequential to be capable of measure; (3) That the common law recognized no cause of action for the loss of the so-called sentimental elements of *consortium* and the acts have given the wife no new cause of action; and (4) That no action for loss of *consortium* was ever allowed in which there was no showing of the loss of some services, and since the wife cannot show such a loss she has no action. None of these cases commend themselves to us on the basis of their logic.

As to those authorities which hold that the injury to the wife is not compensable because it is indirect, we simply state that if that be so then it would likewise be true in the husband's suit. But such is not the rule here. Invasion of the *consortium* is an independent wrong directly to the spouse so injured. The mere fact that the loss of one or the other of the elements thereof may have been indirectly redressed in another's suit, does not make the injury to the remaining elements any less direct.

The argument that the injuries of which a wife complains are too remote and consequential fails for two reasons. In the first place, we are committed to the rule in negligence cases that where in the natural and continual sequence, unbroken by any intervening cause, an injury is produced which, but for the negligent act would not have occurred, the wrongdoer will be liable. And it makes no difference whether or not that particular result was foreseeable. Secondly, if such a rule were valid there could be no basis for distinguishing between an action by a husband and one by the wife. In both cases the damages for the sentimental elements would be too remote and consequential; and yet we do not apply such a rule in the husband's action. And, furthermore, there could be no reason for the allowance of an action for criminal conversation or alienation of affections in cases where the husband condoned the wife's conduct, for obviously there would be no disruption of services; yet under such circumstances, it has been held that the husband may sue the seducer. The same would also be true in cases where it has been held that a husband has a cause of action for criminal conversation though living apart from his wife. Here too there could be no showing of a loss of services. In both cases the only injury to the spouse's *consortium* lies in the sentimental area.

Within the rationale of the cases just cited, allowing a husband recovery in cases where he can show no loss of services, lies the destruction of the authorities which hold that the common law recognized no cause of action for the loss of the so-called sentimental elements of the *consortium* alone, and the cases which further refine the rule by holding that an action for the loss of the sentimental elements cannot be allowed unless there is a showing of a loss of some material services. There is no judicial precedent for these rules, and the allowance of the action where no loss of material service is shown effectively destroys them.

Finally, there are a few cases which hold that the wife's interest in the marital relation is not a right of property or derived from a contract of bargain and sale and it lies in an area into which the law will not enter except of necessity. But be that as it may for those jurisdictions, we are nonetheless here committed to a different rule. * * *

The incongruity of the position taken by the authorities is further demonstrated in those cases where they have attempted to explain the reason for allowing the wife to sue for the so-called intentional or malicious invasions to her *consortium,* while denying her the right to sue when the very same interest is injured due to the defendant's negligence. Where this denial is predicated on the rationale that a wife's interest in the marital relation lies in an area into which the law will not enter, they hold that in cases of alienation of affections, etc., necessity compels the law to step in in order to inflict the seducer or enticer with heavy damages by way of punishment and atonement rather than compensation. The civil side of the court cannot permit an award of punitive damages except as incidental to an actionable civil wrong.

There can be no doubt, therefore, that if a cause of action in the wife for the loss of *consortium* from alienation of affections or criminal conversation is to be recognized it must be predicated on a legally protected interest. Now then, may we say that she has a legally protected and hence actionable interest in her *consortium* when it is injured from one of these so-called intentional invasions, and yet, when the very same interest is injured by a negligent defendant, deny her a right of action? It does not seem so to us. Such a result would be neither legal nor logical. On the contrary, it has already been held in this jurisdiction that her interest in the marriage relation is coextensive with that of her husband, and that any interference therewith is a violation of her legal rights. When a legally protected interest of a person has been injured by the wrongful act of another, it is no less actionable because the invasion was negligent rather than intentional or malicious. Some authorities seek to avoid the impact of such logic by holding that in the cases involving intentional invasions to the *consortium* the injury to the wife is direct, because the husband, having participated with the defendant, cannot join with her and benefit from his own wrong. The wife therefore has a cause of action. But we are unable to see how the injury to the *consortium* is any less direct when the invasion is by a negligent act. Certainly the directness or remoteness of the injury cannot be affected by the fact that in such cases the measure of the wife's damages may be less because of the husband's recovery of the diminished value of his obligation to support his wife. All that it could possibly do is remove from the arena of compensable injuries those already redressed.

In only a few cases has the theory been advanced that in these intentional invasions the wife has lost her husband's services and so has a suable base for her action. The rule is predicated on the proposition that a wife cannot sue in cases of negligent invasions because in order to sustain an action for loss of *consortium* she must be able to show a loss of material services. The untenability of this position has been sufficiently dealt with, *ubi supra,* where we pointed to those cases where a husband recovers though he shows no loss of services. * * *

Furthermore, we can conceive of no reasons for denying the wife this right for the reason that in this enlightened day and age they simply do not exist. On the contrary it appears to us that logic, reason and right are in favor of the position we are now taking. The medieval concepts of the marriage relation to which other jurisdictions have reverted in order to reach the results which have been handed to us as evidence of the law have long since ceased to have any meaning. It can hardly be said that a wife has less of an interest in the marriage relation than does the husband or in these modern times that a husband renders services of such a different character to the family and household that they must be measured by a standard of such uncertainty that the law cannot estimate any loss thereof. The husband owes the same degree of love, affection, felicity, etc., to the wife as she to him. He also owes the material service of support, but above and beyond that he renders other services as his mate's helper in her duties, as advisor and counselor, etc. Under such circumstances it would be a judicial fiat for us to say that a wife may not have an action for loss of *consortium* due to negligence.

It is therefore the opinion of this court that in light of the existing law of this jurisdiction, in light of the specious and fallacious reasoning of those cases from other jurisdictions which have decided the question, and in light of the demonstratable desirability of the rule under the circumstances, a wife has a cause of action for loss of *consortium* due to a negligent injury to her husband.

This result poses no problems in ascertaining the wife's damages. Simple mathematics will suffice to set the proper *quantum.* For inasmuch as it is our opinion that the husband in most cases does recover for any impairment of his duty to support his wife, and, since a compensable element of damages must be subject to measure, it is a simple matter to determine the damages to the wife's *consortium* in exactly the same way as those of the husband are measured in a similar action and subtract therefrom the value of any impairment of his duty of support. Of course, in cases where it can be shown that the husband realized no such recovery in his action, as for example under our Workman's Compensation statute where the schedule of compensations makes no effort to distinguish between married and unmarried male claimants entitled to compensation, the wife should also be able to include in her claim for damages the worth of any loss of this recognized element of her *consortium.* * * * [28]

28. Accord: Rodriguez v. Bethlehem Steel Corporation, 12 Cal.3d 382, 115 Cal.Rptr. 765, 525 P.2d 669 (1974) and numerous references in notes 4–6 thereto. Also see Sea-Land Services, Inc. v. Gaudet, 414 U.S. 573, 94 S.Ct. 806, 39 L.Ed.2d 9 (1974). Compare Best v. Samuel Fox & Co. [1952] A.C. 716, [1952] 2 All E.R. 394.

JACKIEWICZ v. UNITED ILLUMINATING CO.

Supreme Court of Errors of Connecticut, 1927.
106 Conn. 310, 138 A. 151.

[This and its companion case, Edward Jackiewicz, p. p. a., v. United Illuminating Co., were tried together before a jury. Edward, aged three and a half, had been badly burned by a charged electric wire which, it was claimed, had broken and fallen because of defendant's negligence. In the child's own case the jury awarded $7,500 damages. Error was found in this judgment in instructions bearing on the issue of liability, and a new trial ordered. 106 Conn. 302, 138 A. 147. The following case was argued and decided on the same days as the child's.]

WHEELER, C. J. The trial court ordered the verdict set aside conditionally on three grounds: (1) That there had been no evidence of pecuniary loss to the plaintiff's parent from loss of earnings of his minor son; (2) that the instruction of the court upon this subject was inadequate; and (3) that the verdict in favor of the minor son had probably included the amount awarded the parent in this case for loss of the son's earnings during his minority, and hence was excessive.

Nothing appears in the record which enables us to know, or which enabled the trial court to know, that the jury included, in the action brought in behalf of the son, the amount due his father for loss of the son's earnings during his minority. If the jury followed the instruction of the court, they did not include such amount. Moreover the verdict in the action brought in behalf of the son was not set aside by the trial court as excessive because of the inclusion of such earnings. The setting aside of a verdict by the trial judge for error in his instruction to the jury should be exercised by him with great caution and never done unless he is entirely satisfied, upon the authorities or the statutes, that his error is unmistakable and must have been unquestionably harmful. The conclusion as to the inadequacy of the charge is predicated by the court upon his failure to charge that special damages cannot be recovered without proof of them by evidence. Tomlinson v. Derby, 43 Conn. 562, 567; Smith v. Whittlesey, 79 Conn. 189, 191, 63 A. 1085, 7 Ann.Cas. 114.

This rule is not applicable to the action brought by a parent for loss of earnings of a minor child of tender years resulting from injuries suffered by the minor through the negligence of another. Evidence of loss of earnings of an adult, and perhaps of a boy between 14 and 21, may be available, but evidence of the loss of earnings of a minor child, 3½ years of age, from the time he suffered injuries from the negligence of another to the time when he shall become 21, is problematical and speculative. It is uncertain what part of this period he will live, or what his condition of health will be during such period. It cannot be told what character, competency, and capacity or personality he may develop, or what field of usefulness he may be fitted for, or what his earnings will be. To procure evidence of the future earning capacity of a child of tender years, would, in most cases, be impossible, and result in the denial of a recovery by a parent for such loss. At best the ascertainment of the loss for a personal injury to an adult is difficult and incapable of exact measurement, but in the case of the minor child it depends upon so many contingencies as to be incapable of definite ascertainment, and must be largely an estimate based upon conjecture and speculation, weighed in the light of experience, and left upon the facts proven, to the sound judgment, experience, and conscience of the trier, court, or jury, whose judgment or verdict will not be disturbed unless it be so unreasonable as to be excessive, when the court will cause the excess to be remitted, or order a new trial. * * * [Citing many cases.]

The trial court instructed the jury that, if they found in favor of the plaintiff's father, the recovery should include whatever loss of earnings they might find would result from the impairment of his son's earning capacity from the time he went to work until he became of age, and that the jury were bound to consider the fact that the son is subject to all of the ordinary vicissitudes of life; that he is no more free from accident, sickness, and death than anybody else, and that any award made for his impaired earning capacity in the future represents a present cash payment to him.

As far as it went, the instruction was correct. The father was entitled to recover reasonable payments made by him for the cure and care of his son and for any loss suffered by him from the impairment of his son's earning capacity during his minority. The instruction should have pointed out that the extent of the damage for the loss of the minor's services was his total earning capacity, since the father was bound to support his son during his minority, after as before his injuries. Galligan v. Woonsocket Ry. Co., 27 R.I. 363, 365, 62 A. 376; Sedgwick on Damages, section 7.

It should also have pointed out with greater emphasis the contingencies which made an award for the prospective earnings of the minor necessarily a matter of conjecture and speculation and imposed upon the jury the most careful weighing of all the factors involved in determining what the prospective earnings of the minor were. The instruction should have made it clearer to the jury that their estimate of prospective earnings of the plaintiff's son should be confined to finding the present worth of the total estimated amount by which the son's earning capacity was diminished during the period of his minority from 14 to 21 years, when he might under our law be free from the obligation of attending school. The court should also have instructed the jury as to the method of ascertaining the present worth; that is, that the jury should first find the total diminution of the minor's earning capacity during all of this period, reaching their estimate after a consideration of all of the facts in evidence, weighed in the scales of their own experience, and making all reasonable deductions for the contingencies to which we have referred, and then ascertaining the sum which would represent the present worth of the ascertained loss from the diminution of earning capacity. Kost v. Ashland Borough, 236 Pa. 164, 169, 84 A. 691. The instruction upon such a subject should also ordinarily contain a caution to the jury that the sum so awarded for the loss by a parent of the minor's earnings should be such as would fairly and reasonably compensate him for such loss, and that in making their estimate the jury should be careful to separate sentiment from the ascertainment of the pecuniary loss. * * * [29]

SHOCKLEY v. PRIER

Supreme Court of Wisconsin, 1975.
66 Wis.2d 394, 225 N.W.2d 495.

DAY, JUSTICE. The question raised on this appeal is, should a parent be permitted to recover damages for loss of the aid, comfort, society and companionship of a minor child who has been injured by the negligent acts of another?

* * *

The complaint of Paul Shockley and his parents alleges that on July 23, 1971, Mrs. Shockley gave birth prematurely to twins at Milwaukee St. Joseph Hospital of Franciscan Sisters. Only Paul survived and was placed in a premature infant-care unit. The complaint alleges that due to the negligence of the defendants Paul was given excessive amounts of oxygen which caused retrolental fibroplasia, resulting in total and permanent blindness and disfigurement. The complaint sets forth a cause of action for damages sustained by the infant Paul. That portion of the complaint is not involved in this appeal. The complaint also sets forth as a cause of action by Paul's father that "he was deprived of his minor son's aid, comfort, society and companionship, and will in the future continue to be deprived of the same, to which he is entitled * * *." A similar cause of action is set forth for Paul's mother.

It is that part of the complaint alleging damages for loss of aid, comfort, society and companionship to which Drs. Prier and Tacke and their insurer The Medical Protective Company demur on the ground the facts alleged do not state a cause of action.

* * *

Counsel for the plaintiffs stated at the time of oral argument that the complaint prayed for damages only for loss of Paul's aid, comfort, society and companionship during his minority. * * * We therefore confine this opinion to the question of whether such damages are allowable to a parent during the minority of an injured child.

29. For the right of action for prenatal injuries see Jasinsky v. Potts, 153 Ohio St. 529, 92 N.E.2d 809 (1950); Jorgensen v. Meade Johnson Laboratories, Inc., 483 F.2d 237 (10th Cir. 1973) (right of action by Mongoloid children for pre-conception injury to mother's chromosomes). For the right of action for the death of an unborn but viable child see Chrisafogeorgis v. Brandenberg, 55 Ill.2d 368, 304 N.E. 2d 88 (1973); Libbee v. Permanente Clinic, 268 Or. 258, 518 P.2d 636 (1974); Mone v. Greyhound Lines, Inc., — Mass. —, 331 N.E.2d 916 (1975); compare Endresz v. Friedberg, 24 N.Y.2d 478, 301 N.Y.S.2d 65, 248 N.E.2d 901 (1969).

At the present time, by statute, a parent can recover for loss of society and companionship of a child in the case of wrongful death but only if there is no surviving spouse or unemancipated or dependent children of the deceased.[30]

There is no statute defining what damages may be recovered by a parent for injuries to a child. The law in that area is common law and was enunciated 50 years ago in the case of Callies v. Reliance Laundry Co. (1925), 188 Wis. 376, 380, 206 N.W. 198, 200. In that case, this court said:

> "But when a minor child is injured by the negligence of another * * * the parent can recover (1) for loss of the minor's earning capacity during minority and (2) for reasonable medical and nursing expenses during minority."

The plaintiffs argue that the common law is a developing body of law which changes with the changing times and that the rule limiting recovery to the monetary loss sustained by a parent for an injured child harks back to the days when children were regarded as economic assets and no longer applies.

The defendants-respondents argue that if such a change is to be made, it should be made by the legislature and not by the court. This is an area where either this court or the legislature may act.

The rule against such recovery was created by the courts and not by the legislature and it is as much our responsibility, as the legislature's, to make changes in the law, if the common-law rule no longer fits the social realities of the present day. This court in recent years has made changes in the common law affecting personal injury actions as a result of changing concepts as to the relationship of members of the family to each other. * * * [The court referred to Wisconsin decisions allowing damages to a wife for loss of consortium and abrogating parental immunity.]

In the majority of family situations, children are no longer an economic asset but on the contrary are usually sources of great expenditure on the part of parents. Wisconsin's lowering of the age of majority from 21 to 18 years has made the possibility of a parent acquiring the earnings of a minor child even more remote.

In an article in the Washington Law Review, Vol. 43, p. 654 (1967), entitled "Wrongful Death of a Minor Child: The Changing Parental Injury," the author points out, pp. 655, 656, 668:

> "Honest application of a pecuiary standard does not, in today's world, allow adequate recovery for child-death. The cost-accounting technique for measuring damages—value of

30. "895.04 *Plaintiff in wrongful death action* (4) Judgment for damages for pecuniary injury from wrongful death, and additional damages not to exceed $5,000 for loss of society and companionship, may be awarded to the spouse, unemancipated or dependent children or parents of the deceased. * * *"

services less cost of support—is archaic in a society which is not structured on child labor and the family chore framework of an agricultural community. * * *

Tort law seeks to compensate injuries as those injuries are understood in light of changing social and economic conditions. * * *

* * * [B]oth court and legislature have recognized that today the injury sustained by a parent on the death of his child is not primarily economic. The law recognizes an interest in emotional and mental well-being. If this is the primary interest invaded when a parent loses his minor child, tort law should look to that injury, and fashion an appropriate remedy."

What is said with respect to parental loss in the event of death of a child is equally true in the case of injury. Our wrongful death statute already recognizes the loss of society and companionship as an element of damages in the case of death. It seems reasonable to recognize this same type loss where there has been injury to a minor child.

In Family Law Quarterly, Vol. 7 (1973) 211, published by the American Bar Association, Professor Sanford N. Katz and Messrs. William A. Schroeder and Lawrence R. Sidman, in an article entitled "Emancipating Our Children—Coming of Legal Age in America," point out, pp. 212, 214, 215, 224, 225:

"In colonial America children occupied the lowest rungs of the social ladder. Various enactments of the Massachusetts Bay Colony suggest that children and servants were treated similarly before the law and were subject to the harshest punishments for relatively trivial offenses. Apprenticeship 'was often merely a specialized form of servitude.' Children owed the strictest obedience toward parents and were expected to assume completely subservient positions within the family unit. Since child labor was crucial to the economic system, the parental right to a minor child's services and wages was also a practical necessity."

* * * [U]nder a heritage of the past, the parent is also entitled to the child's services and, by derivation, to his or her earnings.

* * * Due to a changed economic climate and altered perceptions of the parent-child relationship, the predominant cultural expectation is increasingly that the child be allowed to keep his or her earnings and decide how to expend them. Indeed, actions for recovery of a child's wages have become something of a rarity. Nevertheless, collateral actions for loss of a child's time and impairment to his or her earning capacity are still brought by parents."

The "remedy" of loss of minor's earning capacity during minority is of diminishing significance. Since our court last laid down the rule in 1925, the family relationship has changed. Society and companionship between parents and their children are closer to our present day family ideal than the right of the parents to the "earning capacity during minority," which once seemed so important when the common law was originally established.

In the case at bar one needs little imagination to see the shattering effect that Paul's blindness will have on the relationship between him and his parents. The loss of the enjoyment of those experiences normally shared by parents and children need no enumeration here.

We conclude that the law should recognize the right of parents to recover for loss of aid, comfort, society and companionship of a child during minority when such loss is caused by the negligence of another.

Defendants point out that several states have declined to create a cause of action for loss of a child's society and companionship. These states include Alabama, New York, North Dakota, Pennsylvania, Mississippi, Rhode Island, and New Jersey. [Footnote citations omitted.]

One of the cases called to our attention by the defendants is McGarr v. National & Providence Worsted Mills (1902), 24 R.I. 447, 53 A. 320, 325, 326. The supreme court of Rhode Island in denying a mother the right to recover for loss of the society and comfort of her injured daughter said:

> "In short, the measure of damages in such a case is the same as that which obtains in a case brought by a master for the loss of services of his servant or apprentice. It is therefore practically a business and commercial question only, and the elements of affection and sentiment have no place therein."

We submit that today's relationship between parents and children is, or should be, more than that between master and servant.

* * *

There are presently two standard jury instructions which could serve as models for a proper instruction as to damages for the loss of aid, comfort, society and companionship of an injured minor child.[31]

31. Wis J I—Civil:

"1895 Death of Child: Parent's Loss of Society and Companionship

Subdivision ______ of Question ______ makes inquiry as to what sum will reasonably compensate the plaintiff (father) (mother) for loss of society and companionship of the child.

You will carefully consider all of the credible evidence and reasonable inferences therefrom, bearing on this inquiry, and in answer, name such sum as will fairly and reasonably compensate (him) (her) for the loss of the society and companionship of (his) (her) deceased (son) (daughter).

You should take into consideration the ages of both the deceased child and the parent. You should also consider the relationship of the parent and the child; the love and affection and conduct of each towards the other; the society and companionship that was afforded to the parent by the child; the personality, disposition, and character of the child; the disposition and susceptibility of the parent to suffer from such loss; and name an amount which will in your judgment reasonably compensate the parent for such loss as (he) (she) sustained by being deprived of such society and companionship as the child afforded (him) (her) during (his) (her) lifetime and which you are reasonably certain would have continued during the na-

The right recognized in this decision may be enlarged by the legislature, * * * or it may abolish the cause of action or may limit the amount recoverable, as it has in the wrongful death statute.

In summary, this court concludes that a parent may maintain an action for loss of aid, comfort, society and companionship of an injured minor child against a negligent tortfeasor provided, and on condition, that the parent's cause of action is combined with that of the child for the child's personal injuries. * * *

The change in the rule announced in this opinion is to be limited to causes of action arising on or after February 4, 1975, the date of the filing of this opinion, except that it is to be applicable to the instant case. * * *

Order reversed, with costs to the appellants.

(F) ECONOMIC LOSSES

UNION OIL COMPANY v. OPPEN

United States Court of Appeals for the Ninth Circuit, 1974.
501 F.2d 558.

SNEED, CIRCUIT JUDGE. This is another case growing out of the Santa Barbara oil spill of 1969. The plaintiffs are commercial fishermen. Each of their complaints alleges * * * that the defendants joined in an enterprise, the day-to-day operation of which was within the control and under the management of defendant Union Oil Company, to drill for oil in the waters of the Santa Barbara Channel; that during the period commencing on or about January 28, 1969, vast quantities of raw crude oil were released and subsequently carried by wind, wave and tidal currents over vast stretches of the

tural life of the parent except for the death of the child."

Wis J I—Civil:

"1816 INJURY TO HUSBAND: SERVICES, SOCIETY, AND COMPANIONSHIP: PAST AND FUTURE

In answer to Question ____ with respect to loss of services, society, and companionship of her husband, you should name such sum as you feel will fairly and reasonably compensate (name) for such loss as she has sustained by being deprived of his aid, assistance, comfort, society and companionship during such period as he was unable to render such services because of his injuries. In considering the amount to be awarded, you will bear in mind the evidence as to the relationship which existed between the husband and wife before his injury.

If you are satisfied to a reasonable certainty that for any appreciable time in the future he will be unable to render such services and/or provide such society and companionship, you should make a proper allowance therefor for the period such disability will exist.

You will not include in your finding any sum, which you are required to determine in any other question, representing loss of earning capacity sustained by (name), the husband, by reason of his injuries. To do so would be to allow double damages for such loss of earning capacity, which you must not do." [Notes 30 and 31 from original, renumbered; other notes in original omitted.]

coastal waters of Southern California; and that as a consequence the plaintiffs have suffered various injuries for which damages are sought. * * *

On May 1, 1970, counsel for all parties to this suit entered into a Stipulation which was approved by the district court. * * * Paragraph 3 of the Stipulation, which sets out the defendants' undertaking to pay damages, provides as follows:

> In order to provide a basis for the disposition of the above referenced claims it is agreed by the undersigned defendants that they will pay to the above referenced persons and/or plaintiffs who are, or who by reason of subsequent joinder herein become, parties hereto, *all legally compensable damages arising from a legally cognizable injury* caused by the aforementioned occurrence as such damages are determined pursuant to the following provisions; *provided however, that the payment assumed hereby will not exceed such amount and such claim as said defendants or their contractors would be responsible for in the case of negligence.* Payment of said damages pursuant hereto shall operate as an assignment of said claims to said defendants. No claim for punitive or exemplary damages shall be asserted and no such damages shall be awarded. (emphasis added).

In May of 1972, the defendants moved for partial summary judgment before the special masters to strike from plaintiffs' prayers "that item of damage usually denominated as 'ecological damage'." More specifically, the defendants sought to eliminate from the prayers any element of damages consisting of profits lost as a result of the reduction in the commercial fishing potential of the Santa Barbara Channel which may have been caused by the occurrence. According to the defendants, such long-term ecological damage is not compensable under the law and thus is not within their undertaking as set forth in the Stipulation.

The motion was denied by the special masters in a brief order which recognized that injuries resulting from "an interference by defendants with [plaintiffs'] economic right to fish in public waters" were legally compensable. The defendants then went into district court to object to this order, and again moved for a partial summary judgment.

Once more the motion was denied. In his order the district judge first observed that paragraph 3 of the Stipulation, although carefully phrased, had the practical effect of a confession of liability for tort negligence. Continuing, the judge accepted the defendants' statement of the issue, viz:

> Does the alleged diminution of the aquatic life of the Santa Barbara Channel claimed to have resulted from the occurrence constitute a legally compensable injury to the Commercial Fishermen claimants?

The district judge then went on to hold that such a question must be answered in the affirmative. This result, he pointed out, is in no way dependent on whether the plaintiffs have a proprietary interest in, or ownership of, the sea life in the Santa Barbara Channel. As the district judge saw it, "the loss of a prospective economic advantage occasioned by the alleged diminishment of the quantities of available sea life formed a sufficient basis for the recovery under the law of negligence."

* * * [T]he issue now before us is whether the district court properly denied the defendants' motion. We hold that the district court properly interpreted paragraph 3 of the Stipulation, and that its action in denying the defendants' motion was proper.

I.

The Applicable Law.

* * *

We are, * * * not driven to the choice between maritime law and the law of California. So far as our research reveals, neither forum has made a definitive ruling on the precise issue before us. * * *

* * * [W]e shall proceed in a manner that we believe is faithful to the spirit of California tort law in disposing of the issue before us. For this reason we are content to say that for purposes of this case we regard it as irrelevant whether our efforts are designated as an exposition of admiralty law or the law of California.

II.

Recovery for Pure Economic Loss in Negligence: The General Rule.

Defendants support their motion for partial summary judgment by pointing to the widely recognized principle that no cause of action lies against a defendant whose negligence prevents the plaintiff from obtaining a prospective pecuniary advantage. See, e. g., Prosser, Law of Torts 952 (4th ed. 1971) (hereinafter Prosser); Harvey, Economic Losses and Negligence, 50 Can.Bar Rev. 580 (1972); Note, 49 Can. Bar Rev. 619 (1971); Note, Negligence and Economic Loss, 117 The Solicitors' Jour. 255 (1971); Note, Negligent Interference with Economic Expectancy: The Case for Recovery, 16 Stan.L.Rev. 664 (1964). See also Restatement (Second) of Torts, Tent. Draft No. 14, § 766B. As the defendants see it, any diminution of the sea life in the Santa Barbara Channel caused by the occurence, which, it must be remembered, is attributable to the defendants' negligence by reason of the parties' Stipulation, consists of no more than the loss of an economic advantage which is not a "legally cognizable injury" and thus not "legally compensable."

Their argument has strength. It rests upon the proposition that a contrary rule, which would allow compensation for all losses of economic advantages caused by defendant's negligence, would subject the defendant to claims based upon remote and speculative injuries which he could not foresee in any practical sense of the term. Accordingly, in some cases it has been stated as the general rule that the negligent defendant owes no duty to plaintiffs seeking compensation for such injuries.[32] In other of the cases, the courts have invoked the doctrine of proximate cause to reach the same result;[33] and in yet a third class of cases the "remoteness" of the economic loss is relied upon directly to deny recovery.[34] The consequence of these cases is that a defendant is normally relieved of the burden to defend against such claims, and the courts of a class of cases the resolution of which is particularly difficult.

The general rule has been applied in a wide variety of situations. Thus, the negligent destruction of a bridge connecting the mainland with an island, which caused a loss of business to the plaintiff who was a merchant on the island, has been held not to be actionable. Rickards v. Sun Oil Company, 41 A.2d 267, 23 N.J.Misc. 89 (1945). A plaintiff engaged in commercial printing has been held unable to recover against a negligent contractor who, while engaged in excavation pursuant to a contract with a third party, cut the power line upon which the plaintiff's presses depended. Byrd v. English, 117 Ga. 191, 43 S.E. 419 (1903); contra, J. W. Moore (North Shields) Ltd. v. Sharp, 108 Sol.J. 453 (1964). But see S. C. M. (U. K.) v. W. J. Whittall & Sons, Ld., [1970] 3 All E.R. 245; Seaway Hotels Ltd. v. Gragg, [1959] Ont. 177, 17 D.L.R.2d 292 (High Ct.), aff'd [1959] Ont. 581, 21 D.L.R.2d 264 (Ct.App.1960). A defendant who negligently injures a third person entitled to life-care medical services by the plaintiff is liable to the third person but not to the plaintiff. Fifield Manor v. Finston, 54 Cal.2d 632, 7 Cal.Rptr. 377, 354 P.2d 1073 (1960) (subrogation also denied because third party's claim not assignable). The operators of a dry dock are not liable in admiralty to charterers of a ship, placed by its owners in the dry dock, for negligent injury to the ship's propeller where the injury deprived the charterer of the use of the ship. Robins Dry Dock & Repair Company v. Flint, 275 U.S. 303, 48 S.Ct. 134, 72 L.Ed. 290 (1927). Mr. Justice Holmes, in writing this opinion, observed that " * * * a tort to the person or property of one man does not make the tort-feasor liable to another merely be-

32. See, e. g., The Federal No. 2, 21 F. 2d 313 (2d Cir., 1927); Chelsea Moving & Trucking Co. v. Ross Towboat Co., 280 Mass. 282, 182 N.E. 477 (1932); Byrd v. English, 117 Ga. 191, 43 S.E. 419 (1903); Brink v. Wabash R. R., 160 Mo. 87, 60 S.W. 1058 (1901); Attorney General for New South Wales v. Perpetual Trustee Co., 85 Commw.L.R. 237, 286 (K.B.1951) (Austr.).

33. See, e. g., The Federal 2, supra note 4; Chelsea Moving & Trucking Co. v. Ross Towboat Co., supra note 4; Byrd v. English, supra note 4; La Societe Anonyme de Remorguage a Helice v. Bennetts [1911] 1 K.B. 243 (1910); Cattle v. Stockton Waterworks Co., L.R. 10 Q.B. 453 (1875).

34. See, e. g., Northern States Contracting Co. v. Oakes, 191 Minn. 88, 253 N.W. 371 (1934). For a discussion of this area, see particularly Note, Negligent Interference with Economic Expectancy: The Case for Recovery, supra at 674–75.

cause the injured person was under a contract with that other, unknown to the doer of the wrong." 275 U.S. at 309, 48 S.Ct. at 135.

The citation of cases applying the general rule could be extended, but this abridged collection is sufficient to emphasize the point that it operates in a wide variety of settings. For purposes of our analysis, however, one further setting in which the rule has been applied requires mention—that being the area of the law dealing with products liability. In this area, the issue is usually couched in terms of whether a purchaser can recover in tort from a negligent manufacturer, with whom the purchaser is not in privity, for economic losses caused by the failure of the purchased article to perform in accordance with the purchaser's reasonable expectations. Defendants in the present action rely heavily on California cases which indicate that no such recovery is possible.

In Seely v. White Motor Company, 63 Cal.2d 9, 45 Cal.Rptr. 17, 403 P.2d 145 (1965), for example, the plaintiff, who had purchased a truck for use in his business, sought to recover from the manufacturer damages representing both the cost of repairs and lost profits attributable to defects in the performance of the truck as well as that portion of the purchase price which he had previously paid. The manufacturer had expressly warranted the truck "to be free from defects in material and workmanship under normal use and service" and had limited its liability thereunder "to making good at its factory any part or parts thereof. * * *" The trial court permitted a recovery of the lost profits and the previously paid portion of the purchase price, but denied recovery for the cost of repairs. On appeal, the manufacturer contended that the damage award allowed by the trial court had exceeded that permissible under the theory of strict liability in tort, which theory had superseded the law of warranty in California by reason of Greenman v. Yuba Power Products, Inc., 59 Cal. 2d 57, 27 Cal.Rptr. 697, 377 P.2d 897 (1962).[35]

The Supreme Court of California held that the abandonment of warranty did not extend to the commercial aspects of a transaction. As to those aspects, it was held that recovery must be based on the principles of warranty law and not on strict liability in tort. Inasmuch as the defendant in *Seely* had warranted that the truck was "free from defects in material and workmanship under normal use and service," the damages allowed by the trial court were held to have been proper. This was true, observed the court, even though they

35. In *Greenman*, the California Supreme Court held that a consumer, not in privity with the manufacturer of a defective product, could not recover under a theory based on breach of warranty for personal injuries which he had sustained as a result of the product's malfunction. In its opinion, the court indicated that such damages were cognizable under strict liability in tort, and in doing so stated that:

> * * * rules defining and governing warranties that were developed to meet the needs of commercial transactions cannot properly be invoked to govern the manufacturer's liability to those injured by their defective products unless those rules also serve the purposes for which such liability is imposed.

59 Cal.2d at 63, 27 Cal.Rptr. at 701, 377 P.2d at 901.

would not have been had the doctrine of strict liability in tort been applicable. The court's observation was bolstered by dictum, upon which the defendants in this case place great reliance, which stated that under California law pure economic losses are not recoverable in an action based on negligence. The dictum consists of the following statement:

> A consumer should not be charged at the will of the manufacturer with bearing the risk of physical injury when he buys a product on the market. * * * *Even in actions for negligence, a manufacturer's liability is limited to damages for physical injuries and there is no recovery for economic loss alone.*

63 Cal.2d at 18, 45 Cal.Rptr. at 23, 403 P.2d at 151. (emphasis added).

Two things should be said concerning the court's reference to the scope of liability in negligence. The first is that it must be understood as having been made in the context of an unavoidable undertaking to fix the spheres in the field of products liability within which warranties and strict liability were to operate. Too much should not be made of a restraint imposed on the scope of liability for negligence when it has been developed for the purpose of preserving an area within which warranties can function.[36] The second is that this restraint has been cogently criticized as being unnecessary to an appropriate accommodation of warranty and tort liability. See Franklin, When Worlds Collide: Liability Theories and Disclaimers in Defective Product Cases, 18 Stan.L.Rev. 974, 1002–03 (1966). The recovery of economic losses sustained by an ultimate consumer, even absent privity with a negligent manufacturer, may or may not be desirable; but its allowance, in any event, would not make warranty principles redundant.

III.

Some Exceptions to the General Rule.

Doubt concerning the scope of *Seely* dictum is strengthened when the numerous exceptions or qualifications to the general rule are considered.

Prosser recognizes that a recovery for pure economic losses in negligence has been permitted in instances in which there exists "some special relation between the parties." Prosser at 952. The failure of the plaintiff to obtain a contract because of a telegraph company's negligent transmission of a message has been held to be legally cognizable, and is cited as an example of the "special relationship" quali-

36. The dictum of the California Supreme Court in *Seely*, quoted above, has been applied by this Court to deny recovery in the products liability setting where the plaintiff has brought an action in negligence rather than under a theory of strict liability. See Bright v. Goodyear Tire & Rubber Co., 463 F.2d 240 (9 Cir. 1972). While our opinion does contain language sufficiently broad to suggest that the *Seely* distinction between warranty and tort recovery may be applicable beyond this setting, we are of the view that such a reading unduly expands our decision in that case. For the reasons outlined in the text, we therefore decline to so apply it.

fication. Id., at 952, n. 79. See also McQuilkin v. Postal Telegraph Cable Company, 27 Cal.App. 698, 151 P. 21 (1915) (injury from lost advantageous contract must not be remote and uncertain). Other examples which have been cited are the negligent failure to perform a gratuitous promise to obtain insurance, and the negligent delay in acting upon an application for insurance. See Prosser, at 952, n. 80, 81.

A more recent development in California law involves the right to recover, absent privity, from a defendant whose negligent failure to obtain a proper attestation of the will of a third party has deprived the plaintiff of a bequest which had been granted in the improperly attested will. Biakanja v. Irving, 49 Cal.2d 647, 320 P.2d 16 (1958). On appeal to the Supreme Court of California, the plaintiff's pure economic loss was held to be a legally cognizable injury, a position which has been subsequently reaffirmed in Lucas v. Hamm, 56 Cal.2d 583, 15 Cal.Rptr. 821, 364 P.2d 685 (1961) (recovery denied because of the absence of negligence).

The approach adopted by the California Supreme Court in *Biakanja* is particularly instructive. After stating that the question before it was "whether defendant was under a duty to exercise due care to protect plaintiff from injury and was liable for damages caused plaintiff by his negligence even though they were not in privity of contract," the court stated:

> The determination whether in a specific case the defendant will be held liable to a third person not in privity is a matter of policy and involves the balancing of various factors, among which are the extent to which the transaction was intended to affect the plaintiff, the foreseeability of harm to him, the degree of certainty that the plaintiff suffered injury, the closeness of the connection between the defendant's conduct and the injury suffered, the moral blame attached to the defendant's conduct, and the policy of preventing future harm.

49 Cal.2d at 650, 320 P.2d at 19 (1958). It is thus obvious that California does not blindly follow the general rule upon which the defendants here rely.

It is but a short step from these two California cases to a body of law existing both in this country and in the British Commonwealth in which defendants engaged in certain professions, businesses, or trades have been held liable for economic losses resulting from the negligent performance of tasks within the course of their callings. One Commonwealth scholar has stated that "in a proper case a person may recover economic loss caused by the negligence of persons such as bankers, commission agents, real estate agents, accountants, surveyors, valuers, analysts, insurance brokers, stock brokers, government employees, doctors, architects, car salesmen who undertake to have cars insured, car testers, and drawers of cheques." Harvey, Economic

Losses and Negligence, 50 Can.Bar Rev. 580, 603–04 (1972). See also, Hedley Byrne & Co. Ltd. v. Heller & Partners Ltd. [1964] A.C. 465.

The American cases reflect a similar development. There are numerous cases indicating that economic losses may be recovered for the negligence of pension consultants, accountants, architects, attorneys, notaries public, test hole drillers, title abstractors, termite inspectors, soil engineers, surveyors, real estate brokers, drawers of checks, directors of corporations, trustees, bailees and public weighers.[37]

Recovery for pure economic loss legally attributable to the defendant's negligence has also been recognized in traditional maritime settings. Thus, fishermen in Scotland who worked under a profit-sharing arrangement with the owner of a trawler damaged by the defendant's negligence have been permitted to recover their portion of the anticipated profits of the fishing venture even though they suffered no physical injury. Main v. Leask [1910] S.C. 771 (Ct. of Session). More important, however, is the fact that this Circuit has reached precisely the same conclusion in an admiralty proceeding. Carbone v. Ursich, The Del Rio, 209 F.2d 178 (9th Cir., 1953). In so doing, we refused to apply the teaching of Robins Dry Dock and Repair Company v. Flint, supra, to the situation with which the fishermen were confronted, and observed:

> This long recognized rule [the right of fishermen to recover their share of the prospective catch] is no doubt a manifestation of the familiar principle that seamen are the favorites of admiralty and their economic interests entitled to the full-

37. Gediman v. Anheuser Busch, Inc., 299 F.2d 537 (2nd Cir., 1962) (pension consultant); Rusch Factors, Inc. v. Levin, 284 F.Supp. 85 (D.C.R.I.1968) (accountant); United States v. Rogers & Rogers, 161 F.Supp. 132 (S.D. Cal.1958) (architect); Lucas v. Hamm, 56 Cal.2d 583, 15 Cal.Rptr. 821, 364 P.2d 685, cert. denied, 368 U.S. 987, 82 S.Ct. 603, 7 L.Ed.2d 525 (1962) (attorney); Biakanja v. Irving, 49 Cal. 2d 647, 320 P.2d 16 (1958) (notary public); Gagne v. Bertran, 43 Cal.2d 481, 275 P.2d 15 (1954) (test hole driller); Northwestern Title Ins. Co. v. Flack, 6 Cal.App.3d 134, 85 Cal.Rptr. 693 (1970) (title abstractor); Viotti v. Giomi, 230 Cal.App.2d 730, 41 Cal. Rptr. 345 (1964) (title abstractor); Hardy v. Carmichael, 207 Cal.App. 2d 218, 24 Cal.Rptr. 475 (1962) (termite inspector); M. Miller Co. v. Central Contra Costa Sanitary Dist., 198 Cal.App.2d 305, 18 Cal.Rptr. 13 (1961) (soil engineer); Roberts v. Karr, 178 Cal.App.2d 535, 3 Cal.Rptr. 98 (1960) (surveyor); Granberg v. Turnham, 166 Cal.App.2d 390, 333 P. 2d 423 (1958) (real estate broker); Hawkins v. Oakland Title Ins. & Guar. Co., 165 Cal.App.2d 116, 331 P.2d 742 (1958) (title abstractor); Park State Bank v. Arena Auto Auction, Inc., 59 Ill.App.2d 235, 207 N.E.2d 158 (1965) (drawer of check); Ryan v. Kanne, 170 N.W.2d 395 (Iowa 1969) (accountant); Shatterproof Glass Corp. v. James, 466 S.W.2d 873, 46 A.L.R.3d 968 (Tex.Civ.App.1971) (accountant); Durham v. Wichita Mill & Elevator Co., 202 S.W. 138 (Tex.Civ.App.1918) (director of corporation); Doyle v. Chatham & Phenix Nat'l Bank, 253 N.Y. 369, 171 N.E. 574 (1930) (trustee); New York Int'l Products Co. v. Erie R. R., 244 N.Y. 331, 155 N.E. 662 (1927) (bailee); Glanzer v. Shepard, 233 N.Y. 236, 135 N.E. 275 (1922) (public weigher). See, generally Freeman, Opinion Letters and Professionalism, 1973 Duke L.J. 371 (1973). [Notes 32–37 from original, renumbered; other notes in original omitted.]

est possible legal protection. These considerations have given rise to a special right comparable to that of a master to sue for the loss of services of his servant, or the right of a husband or father to sue for the loss of services of wife or child.

209 F.2d at 182.

Another instance in which a claim for economic loss, unaccompanied by any physical injury to the person or property of the claimant, has been recognized under admiralty law is illustrated by Aktieselskabet Cuzco v. The Sucarseco, 294 U.S. 394, 55 S.Ct. 467, 79 L.Ed. 942 (1935). The issue before the Court in that case was whether the owners of cargo, shipped on a vessel which ultimately collided with defendant's vessel, could recover for their general average contribution when both vessels were at fault and both were damaged. The Supreme Court held in the affirmative. Although the cargo was physically damaged by the collision, this fact appears to have had no bearing on the Court's resolution of the issue. Rather, the Court recognized that the right of the cargo owners to have their general average contribution restored sprang directly from the tort and was in no sense derivative or parasitically dependent upon the presence of a physical injury.

The right to recover for economic losses which are parasitic to an injury occurring to person or property is not questioned. See e. g., Reynolds v. Bank of America National Trust and Savings Association, 53 Cal.2d 49, 345 P.2d 926 (1959) (loss of use of airplane destroyed by defendant's negligence held to be recoverable). Furthermore, this is the case even though frequently the magnitude of the economic loss so far overshadows that of the physical injury as to warrant the assertion that the general rule, barring recovery absent a physical injury, is but a formalism. *See* Harvey, supra at 585, 594–95.

This much abridged catalogue of exceptions and qualifications to the general rule can be brought to a close for purposes of our analysis by calling attention to several cases in which pollution of a stream has enabled one whose business is injured thereby to recover his lost profits. For example, in Fort Worth & Rio Grande Railway Company v. Hancock, 286 S.W. 335 (Tex.Civ.App.1926) the plaintiff, who operated a swimming pool in the channel of a river was permitted to recover lost profits which had resulted from the defendant's negligent pollution of the river. Similarly, downstream riparian owners, engaged in operating a business dependent upon fishing, have been permitted to recover for the injury to their business caused by the pollution of the stream. See Masonite Corporation v. Steede, 198 Miss. 530, 547, 23 So.2d 756 (1945); Hampton v. North Carolina Pulp Company, 223 N.C. 535, 27 S.E.2d 538 (1943). It should be noted that in each of these cases the plaintiff was a riparian owner, and in the latter two there was no indication that the defendant's conduct was merely negligent and not intentional. However, in neither *Masonite* nor *Hampton* does there appear any recognition that mere negligence would have absolved the defendants. Both assumed the existence of a nuisance which could well have rested upon the defendants' negligent conduct. See Prosser at 575.

Moreover, the plaintiffs' status as riparians does not make improper the classification of these cases as exceptions to, or qualifications of, the general rule which is relied upon by the defendants in the present action. The injury for which damages were sought in each case was the loss of anticipated profits—a pure economic loss as that term is normally understood. To permit riparianship to transmute this loss into an ordinary property loss for the purpose of allowing recovery does no harm. However, harm would be done if the fact that the plaintiffs in this case are not riparian owners was held to deprive them of the comfort these authorities provide.

IV.

The Instant Action.

It is thus apparent that we are not forclosed by precedent from examining on its merits the issue presented by the defendants' motion for partial summary judgment. As we see it, the issue is whether the defendants owed a duty to the plaintiffs, commercial fishermen, to refrain from negligent conduct in their drilling operations, which conduct reasonably and foreseeably could have been anticipated to cause a diminution of the aquatic life in the Santa Barbara Channel area and thus cause injury to the plaintiffs' business.

In finding that such a duty exists, we are influenced by the manner in which the Supreme Court of California has approached the duty issue in tort law. In holding that the mother of a child, killed by the defendant's negligent operation of an automobile, could recover for emotional disturbance and shock even though she was not within the zone of physical impact, the court in Dillon v. Legg, 68 Cal.2d 728, 69 Cal.Rptr. 72, 441 P.2d 912 (1968) stated that:

> Defendant owes a duty, in the sense of a potential liability for damages, only with respect to those risks or hazards whose likelihood made the conduct unreasonably dangerous, and hence negligent, in the first instance. (See Keeton, Legal Cause in the Law of Torts (1963) 18–20; Seavey, Mr. Justice Cardozo and the Law of Torts (1939) 52 Harv.L. Rev. 372; Seavey, Principles of Torts (1942) 56 Harv.L.Rev. 72.)
>
> Harper and James state the prevailing view. The obligation turns on whether 'the offending conduct foreseeably involved unreasonably great risk of harm to the interests of someone other than the actor. * * * [T]he obligation to refrain from * * * particular conduct is owed only to those who are foreseeably endangered by the conduct and only with respect to those risks or hazards whose likelihood made the conduct unreasonably dangerous. Duty, in other

> words, is measured by the scope of the risk which negligent conduct foreseeably entails.' (2 Harper & James, The Law of Torts, supra, at p. 1018; fns. omitted.)
>
> * * *
>
> Since the chief element in determining whether defendant owes a duty or an obligation to plaintiff is the foreseeability of the risk, that factor will be of prime concern in every case. Because it is inherently intertwined with foreseeability such duty or obligation must necessarily be adjudicated only upon a case-by-case basis.

68 Cal.2d at 739–740, 69 Cal.Rptr. at 79, 441 P.2d at 919–920.

While it is true that the earlier decision of the California Supreme Court in *Biakanja* does not accord "foreseeability of the risk" the commanding position which it was afforded in Dillon v. Legg, we can not escape the conclusion that under California law the presence of a duty on the part of the defendants in this case would turn substantially on foreseeability. That being the crucial determinant, the question must be asked whether the defendants could reasonably have foreseen that negligently conducted drilling operations might diminish aquatic life and thus injure the business of commercial fishermen. We believe the answer is yes. The dangers of pollution were and are known even by school children. The defendants understood the risks of their business and should reasonably have foreseen the scope of its responsibilities. To assert that the defendants were unable to foresee that negligent conduct resulting in a substantial oil spill could diminish aquatic life and thus injure the plaintiffs is to suppose a degree of general ignorance of the effects of oil pollution not in accord with good sense.

An examination of the other factors mentioned in *Biakanja* only strengthens our conclusion that the defendants in this case owed a duty to the plaintiffs. Thus, the fact that the injury flows directly from the action of escaping oil on the life in the sea, Askew v. American Waterways Operators, Inc., 411 U.S. at 333 n. 5, 93 S.Ct. 1590, the public's deep disapproval of injuries to the environment and the strong policy of preventing such injuries, all point to existence of a required duty.

The same conclusion is reached when the issue before us is approached from the standpoint of economics. Recently a number of scholars have suggested that liability for losses occasioned by torts should be apportioned in a manner that will best contribute to the achievement of an optimum allocation of resources. See e. g., Calabresi, The Cost of Accidents, 69–73 (1970) (hereinafter Calabresi); Coase, The Problem of Social Cost, 3 J.Law & Econ. 1 (1960). This optimum, in theory, would be that which would be achieved by a perfect market system. In determining whether the cost of an accident should be borne by the injured party or be shifted, in whole or in part, this approach requires the court to fix the identity of the party who can avoid the costs most cheaply. Once fixed, this determination then controls liability.

It turns out, however, that fixing the identity of the best or cheapest cost-avoider is more difficult than might be imagined. In order to facilitate this determination, Calabresi suggests several helpful guidelines. The first of these would require a rough calculation designed to exclude as potential cost-avoiders those groups/activities which could avoid accident costs only at an extremely high expense. Calabresi at 140–43. While not easy to apply in any concrete sense, this guideline does suggest that the imposition of oil spill costs directly upon such groups as the consumers of staple groceries is not a sensible solution. Under this guideline, potential liability becomes resolved into a choice between, on an ultimate level, the consumers of fish and those of products derived from the defendants' total operations.

To refine this choice, Calabresi goes on to provide additional guidelines which, in this instance, have proven none too helpful. For example, he suggests an evaluation of the administrative costs which each party would be forced to bear in order to avoid the accident costs. Calabresi at 143–44. He also states that an attempt should be made to avoid an allocation which will impose some costs on those groups or activities which neither consume fish nor utilize those products of the defendants derived from their operations in the Santa Barbara Channel. Calabresi at 144–50. On the record before us, we have no way of evaluating the relative administrative costs involved. However, we do recognize that it is probable that by imposing liability on the defendants some portion of the accident costs in this case may be borne by those who neither eat fish nor use the petroleum products derived from the defendants' operations in Santa Barbara.

Calabresi's final guideline, however, unmistakably points to the defendants as the best cost-avoider. Under this guideline, the loss should be allocated to that party who can best correct any error in allocation, if such there be, by acquiring the activity to which the party has been made liable. Calabresi at 150–52. The capacity "to buy out" the plaintiffs if the burden is too great is, in essence, the real focus of Calabresi's approach. On this basis there is no contest—the defendants' capacity is superior.

Our holding that the defendants are under a duty to commercial fisherman to conduct their drilling and production in a reasonably prudent manner so as to avoid the negligent diminution of aquatic life is not foreclosed by the fact that the defendants' negligence could constitute a public nuisance under California law. Contrary to the situation that existed in Oppen v. Aetna Insurance Company, [485 F.2d 252 (9th Cir. 1973)] in which we held that an interference with the public's right of navigation in the navigable waters of California did not vest a private cause of action in those who lost the use of their private pleasure craft, in the case now before us the plaintiffs assert an injury to their commercial enterprises, not to their "occasional Sunday piscatorial pleasure." Id. at 260. The right of commercial fishermen to recover for injuries to their businesses caused by pollution of public waters has been recognized on numerous occasions. See Masonite Corporation v. Steede, supra; Hampton v. North Carolina Pulp Company, supra; Prosser, Private Action for Public Nuisance, 52 Va.L.Rev. 997, 1013–16 (1966). The injury here asserted by the plaintiff is a pecuniary loss of a particular and special nature, limited to the class of commercial fishermen which they represent.

This injury must, of course, be established in the proceedings that will follow this appeal. To do this it must be shown that the oil spill did in fact diminish aquatic life, and that this diminution reduced the profits the plaintiffs would have realized from their commercial fishing in the absence of the spill. This reduction of profits must be established with certainty and must not be remote, speculative or conjectural. *See* McCormick, Damages, 97–101 (1935). These are not small burdens, nor can they be eased by our abhorrence of massive oil spills. All that we do here is to permit the plaintiffs to attempt to prove their case, and to reject the idea urged upon us by the defendants that a barrier to such an effort exists in the form of the rule that negligent interference with an economic advantage is not actionable.

Finally, it must be understood that our holding in this case does not open the door to claims that may be asserted by those, other than commercial fishermen, whose economic or personal affairs were discommoded by the oil spill of January 28, 1969. The general rule urged upon us by defendants has a legitimate sphere within which to operate. Nothing said in this opinion is intended to suggest, for example, that every decline in the general commercial activity of every business in the Santa Barbara area following the occurrences of 1969 constitutes a legally cognizable injury for which the defendants may be responsible. The plaintiffs in the present action lawfully and directly make use of a resource of the sea, *viz.* its fish, in the ordinary course of their business. This type of use is entitled to protection from negligent conduct by the defendants in their drilling operations. Both the plaintiffs and defendants conduct their business operations away from land and in, on and under the sea. Both must carry on their commercial enterprises in a reasonably prudent manner. Neither should be permitted negligently to inflict commercial injury on the other. We decide no more than this.

Affirmed.[38]

38. Also see James, Limitations on Liability for Economic Loss Caused by Negligence: A Pragmatic Appraisal, 25 Vand.L.Rev. 43 (1972); Spartan Steel & Alloys, Ltd. v. Martin & Co. (Contractors), Ltd., [1973] Q.B. 27.

Chapter 3

OCCUPIERS AND OWNERS OF LAND

In this chapter attention will be focused on cases in which the harm to the plaintiff is caused on premises occupied or owned by the defendant. In these cases, as in the preceding ones, the plaintiff suffered physical harm to interests which are ordinarily legally protected against intentional or negligent invasions. No new issues revolving about the nature of the plaintiff's interest are here involved. But the fact that the defendant is owner or occupier of the premises on which the harm was suffered seems to affect the nature of the defendant's duty. In the preceding cases the nature of the defendant's duty was usually determined by the potentialities of harm involved in his conduct and the position of the plaintiff in the zone of danger. In the cases in this chapter, a new element is added, namely, the occasion for the plaintiff's presence in the zone of danger. Here we have been traditionally told to ask first, what is the plaintiff's relation to the land, how did he happen to be there when he was hurt. For the extent of defendant's duty has been said to depend on the answer to these questions; so that of two people hurt on the same premises as a result of the same danger one may properly claim that the defendant owed him a duty of reasonable care and the other may not.

When the technical detail of the following cases is mastered, a number of general questions remain: To what extent are the added concepts effective in altering the course of decisions that would have been made without them on the basis of the guides in the preceding pages? Or conversely, to what extent, in some of the situations at least, are the added concepts useless symbols receiving lip service but deprived of vitality by suffocation in logomachy designed only for this lethal purpose? What do we seek to accomplish by these added ideas, and by the determination of liability or immunity in the cases in which they are employed? To what social purpose are the added ideas relevant? Prevention of harm by encouragement of precaution? Distribution of loss? Retribution? Better utilization of economic resources?

When dealing with harm incident to industrial activity, is there point in concern with the privileges of occupiers of land? Consider the appropriateness of differentiation between various kinds of land occupancy: the farm, the home and its surrounding yard, the apartment house, the factory, the railroad right of way, vacant land in the country, vacant lots in the city, etc. Or between the various kinds of activity on land: cultivation, hunting, operation of trains, etc. In assessing liability for harm is there unifying significance in the fact that both the railroad and the home owner occupy or use land? It is said that the liability of the occupier for harm caused by his "*active* conduct on the land must be sharply distinguished from the liability arising out of *conditions* existing upon the land." See Eldredge, Modern Tort Problems (1941) 163, 195. To what extent is the differentiation made? Why should it be made?

The cases in this chapter, as in the preceding ones, involve also, of course, the usual questions of negligence, contributory negligence, causation and proof. The recent cases further exemplify a trend which we find throughout torts law, of development from a jurisprudence of particularized categories, toward a system of liability based upon more generalized principles.

SECTION 1. GENERAL

OSTERMAN v. PETERS

Court of Appeals of Maryland, 1971.
260 Md. 313, 272 A.2d 21.

SINGLEY, JUDGE. This case is the aftermath of the tragic death of Lawrence Bruce Osterman, a four and a half year old boy, who was drowned when he fell into the swimming pool at a neighbor's vacant house while attempting, with a friend, to retrieve a ball. The boy's father, as administrator of his son's estate, and in his own right as parent, brought suit for damages in the Circuit Court for Montgomery County against Mr. and Mrs. Barry J. Peters, the owners of the property upon which the pool was located. At the end of the entire case, the Peters' motion for a directed verdict was granted and judgment was entered in their favor for costs, from which Dr. Osterman has appealed.

In [citations omitted] we had occasion to reiterate the Maryland rule that the owner of land owes no duty to a trespasser or licensee, even one of tender years, except to abstain from willful or wanton misconduct or entrapment, since trespassers or bare licensees, including trespassing children, take the premises as they find them. * * *

Dr. Osterman, doubtless aware that Maryland is one of only seven states which reject the doctrine of attractive nuisance without qualification, Prosser, Law of Torts § 59, at 373, n. 44 (3d ed. 1964), argues that there are four reasons why this case should be taken from under the rule of our prior decisions and should have gone to the jury on the issue of negligence.

First, he relies on the age of the child, who was four and a half. However, in both Herring v. Christensen, * * * 252 Md. 240, 249 A.2d 718 and Barnes v. Housing Authority of Baltimore City, 231 Md. 147, 189 A.2d 100 (1963), we declined to make an exception for a three year old child, and our predecessors were unwilling to except a mentally subnormal boy of 11 years of age [citation omitted].

Next, the appellant argues that the child came on the Peters' property for the sole purpose of retrieving a ball, and not to play or swim in the pool. We view this argument as inapposite, since it is reminiscent of the concept of allurement, once thought to be essential to recovery in attractive nuisance cases, but now largely discredited in states which accept the attractive nuisance doctrine, McGettigan v. National Bank of Washington, 115 U.S.App.D.C. 384, 320 F.2d 703 (1963) * * *.

There was testimony that the Peters had vacated their house on 9 May, three days before the accident, leaving the pool filled with water for the convenience of the new occupants, who planned to move in on 2 June. This, the appellant argues, was "almost criminal indifference" to the rights of the Peters' neighbors. Assuming for purposes of argument that it was an act of indifference, this is not the sort of willful or wanton misconduct or entrapment identified in our prior decisions. In Hensley v. Henkels & McCoy, Inc., 258 Md. 397, 412, 265 A.2d 897, 905, we held that a contracting firm which left unguarded a rope dangling between transmission towers, within reach of a 10 year old boy who was injured when swinging on the rope, created "no covert change or entrapment" and "no hidden danger or secret pitfall." It seems to us that the filled swimming pool may well have been less of a hazard than the dangling rope.

Finally, the appellant points out that Montgomery County Code (1965) § 105–2 requires that private pools be fenced or surrounded with impenetrable planting, and that gates be equipped with self-closing and self-latching devices. The Peters' pool was fenced, but there was testimony that there were apertures about twelve inches high in the fence and that the gate was kept closed by placing a stone in front of it. The boys had pushed the stone aside to gain access to the pool itself. The Peters' violation of this statute, the appellant says, is evidence of negligence. And so it may be, assuming that there was a violation, * * *. The difficulty with the appellant's contention is that this precise point was made in State to Use of Potter v. Longeley, supra, 161 Md. 563, 158 A. 6 where it was alleged that a 12 year old boy had drowned in an abandoned quarry which the owners had failed to inclose with a six foot fence, as required by a Baltimore City ordinance. In rejecting this contention, our predecessors said:

> "The ordinance in this case was passed for the benefit of the public. Any violation of it subjects the owner of a quarry to a fine. But, before an individual can hold such owner liable for an injury alleged to have resulted from such violation, there must be shown a right on the part of the plaintiff, a duty on the part of the defendant with respect to that right, and a breach of that duty by the defendant whereby the plaintiff has suffered injury. Maenner v. Carroll, supra [46 Md. 193 (1877)]. A trespasser can acquire no such right except in case of willful injury. The mere violation of a statute would not give it. The effect of such violation is only to raise a presumption of negligence in favor of one entitled to assert it. See an interesting discussion on 27 Harvard Law Review, p. 333." 161 Md. at 569–570, 158 A. 8.

For these reasons, we conclude that Dr. Osterman could no more take his case from under the Maryland rule than could the plaintiff in Hensley v. Henkels & McCoy, Inc., supra, 258 Md. 397, 265 A.2d 897, who attempted to do so by alleging that the contractor knew that the area where the accident occurred was customarily traversed by children.

What Chief Judge McSherry, speaking for the Court, said in Demuth v. Old Town Bank of Baltimore, 85 Md. 315, 37 A. 266 (1897), * * * is equally appropriate to the distressing situation which this case presents:

> "This is a case of exceedingly great hardship, and we have diligently, but in vain, sought for some tenable ground upon which the appellants could be relieved from the loss that an affirmance of the decree appealed from will necessarily subject them to. But hard cases, it has often been said, almost always make bad law; and hence it is, in the end, far better that the established rules of law should be strictly applied, even though in particular instances serious loss may be thereby inflicted on some individuals, than that by subtle distinctions, invented and resorted to solely to escape such consequences, long-settled and firmly-fixed doctrines should be shaken, questioned, confused, or doubted. Lovejoy v. Irelan, 17 Md. [525] 527. It is often difficult to resist the influence which a palpable hardship is calculated to exert; but a rigid adherence to fundamental principles at all times, and a stern insensibility to the results which an unvarying enforcement of those principles may occasionally entail, are the surest, if not the only, means by which stability and certainty in the administration of the law may be secured. It is for the legislature, by appropriate enactments, and not for the courts, by metaphysical refinements, to provide a remedy against the happening of hardships which may result from the consistent application of established legal principles." 85 Md. at 319–320, 37 A. at 266.

Judgment affirmed * * *.[1]

---

1. Is defendant's immunity here due to "fault" on the part of the plaintiff, like contributory negligence, or the reasonableness or merit of defendant's conduct? It has been held that a child of six is liable in trespass for damage to a stranger's shrubbery and flowers. Huchting v. Engel, 17 Wis. 230, 84 Am.Dec. 741 (1863). And compare Vosburg v. Putney, p. 238, supra. On the other hand some courts have held that a child of six is *prima facie* incapable of negligence. See, for example, Chicago City R. Co. v. Tuohy, 196 Ill. 410, 63 N.E. 997, 58 L.R.A. 270 (1902) and p. 156, supra.

The student will find assistance in handling the material of this section in James, Tort Liability of Occupiers of Land: Duties Owed to Trespassers, 63 Yale L.J. 144 (1953); James, Tort Liability of Occupiers of Land: Duties Owed to Licensees and Invitees, 63 Yale L.J. 605 (1954); Hughes, Duties to Trespassers: A Comparative Survey and Revaluation, 68 Yale L.J. 633 (1959); Prosser, Trespassing Children, 47 Calif.L.Rev. 427 (1959); Comment, Land Occupant's Liability to Invitees, Licensees and Trespassers, 31 Tenn.L.Rev. 485 (1965); Annotation, "Modern status of rules condi-

The Maryland position in *Osterman* is unusual today, as will be seen below in this chapter, but it reflects traditional doctrine. See, e. g., Santora v. New York, N. H. & H. R. Co., 211 Mass. 464, 98 N.E. 90 (1912) and Robert Addie & Sons (Collieries) Ltd. v. Dumbreck [1929] A.C. 358. Compare British Railways Board v. Herrington [1972] A.C. 877, in which the House of Lords unanimously overruled *Addie,* particularly Lord Diplock's speech at 931:

> "*Addie's* case was one of trespass by a child aged four and a half years. It was decided in the year that I started to read for the Bar. Even at that time it offended against what Lord Atkin, only three years later, was to call "a general public sentiment of moral wrongdoing for which the offender must pay" (Donoghue v. Stevenson [1932] A.C. 562, 580). I well recall the disappointment with which it was received by those who thought that previous cases in this House had shown the common law as moving towards a less draconian treatment of those who trespassed innocently upon other people's land.
>
> "If the facts in the instant appeal are compared with those in *Addie's* case * * *, I do not think it possible to say that * * * the conduct of those engaged in operating the appellants' railway in the instant case was any more blameworthy than the conduct of those engaged in running the colliery of the successful appellant in *Addie's* case. Yet all nine judges who have been concerned with the instant case in its various stages are convinced that the plaintiff's claim ought to succeed; and, if I may be permitted to be candid, are determined that it shall. The problem of judicial technique is how best to surmount or to circumvent the obstacle presented by the speeches of the Lord Chancellor and Viscount Dunedin in *Addie's* case * * *."

GAUTRET v. EGERTON

Court of Common Pleas, 1867.
L.R. 2 C.P. 371.

The declaration in the first of these actions stated that the defendants were possessed of a close of land, and of a certain canal and cutting intersecting the same, and of certain bridges across the said canal and cuttings, communicating with and leading to certain docks of the defendants, which said land and bridges had been and were from time to time used with the consent and permission of the defendants by persons proceeding towards and coming from the said docks; that the defendants, well knowing the premises, wrongfully, negligent-

tioning landowner's liability upon status of injured party as invitee, licensee, or trespasser", 32 A.L.R.3d 508; Note, Smith v. Arbaugh's Restaurant Inc., and the Invitee-Licensee-Trespasser Distinction, 121 U. Pa.L.Rev. 378 (1972). See also Green, Judge and Jury, pp. 126–135 (1930); Restatement of Torts, Second Chapter 13 (1965).

ly, and improperly kept and maintained the said land, canal, cuttings, and bridges, and suffered them to continue and be in so improper a state and condition as to render them dangerous and unsafe for persons lawfully passing along and over the said land and bridges towards the said docks, and using the same as aforesaid; and that Leon Gautret, whilst he was lawfully in and passing and walking along the said close and over the said bridge, and using the same in the manner and for the purpose aforesaid, by and through the said wrongful, negligent, and improper conduct of the defendants as aforesaid, fell into one of the said cuttings of the defendants, intersecting the said close as aforesaid, and thereby lost his life. * * *

[On demurrer to the declarations:]

WILLES, J. I am of opinion that our judgment must be for the defendants in each of these cases. * * * The consequences of these accidents are sought to be visited upon these defendants, because they have allowed persons to go over their land, not alleging it to have been upon the business or for the benefit of the defendants, or as the servants or agents of the defendants; nor alleging that the defendants have been guilty of any wrongful act, such as digging a trench on the land, or misrepresenting its condition, or anything equivalent to laying a trap for the unwary passengers; but simply because they permitted these persons to use a way with the condition of which, for anything that appears, those who suffered the injury were perfectly well acquainted. That is the whole sum and substance of these declarations. If the docks to which the way in question led were public docks, the way would be a public way, and the township or parish would be bound to repair it, and no such liability as this could be cast upon the defendants merely by reason of the soil of the way being theirs. * * * Assuming that these were private docks, the private property of the defendants, and that they permitted persons going to or coming from the docks, whether for their own benefit or that of the defendants, to use the way, the dedication of a permission to use the way must be taken to be in the character of a gift. The principle of law as to gifts is, that the giver is not responsible for damage resulting from the insecurity of the thing, unless he knew its evil character at the time, and omitted to caution the donee. There must be something like fraud on the part of the giver before he can be made answerable. It is quite consistent with the declarations in these cases that this land was in the same state at the time of the accident that it was in at the time the permission to use it was originally given.[2] To create a cause of action, something like fraud must be

2. Plaintiff, an employee of defendant dairy, was injured when he fell into an unguarded excavation which had been dug the previous day in a driveway at defendant's plant. On the day of the accident plaintiff quit work at 5:30 P.M., but returned on a personal errand between 8 and 9 o'clock that evening. Plaintiff testified that he was not aware of the excavation. The driveway was commonly used by the public with defendant's knowledge and acquiescence. Judgment for plaintiff affirmed. John v. Reick-McJunkin Dairy Co., 281 Pa. 543, 127 A. 143 (1924). See Restatement of Torts, Second §§ 342 and 343A (1965).

shewn. No action will lie against a spiteful man who, seeing another running into a position of danger, merely omits to warn him.[3] To bring the case within the category of actionable negligence, some wrongful act must be shewn, or a breach of some positive duty: otherwise, a man who allows strangers to roam over his property would be held to be answerable for not protecting them against any danger which they might encounter whilst using the license. * * *

Judgment accordingly.

INDERMAUR v. DAMES

English Common Pleas, 1866.
L.R. 1 C.P. 274.

WILLES, J. This was an action to recover damages for hurt sustained by the plaintiff's falling down a shaft at the defendant's place of business, through the actionable negligence, as it was alleged, of the defendant and his servants.

At the trial before the Lord Chief Justice at the sittings here after Michaelmas Term, the plaintiff had a verdict for 400£ damages, subject to leave reserved. * * *

It appears that the defendant was a sugar-refiner, at whose place of business there was a shaft four feet three inches square, and twenty-nine feet three inches deep, used for moving sugar. The shaft was necessary, usual, and proper in the way of the defendant's business. Whilst it was in use, it was necessary and proper that it should be open and unfenced. When it was not in use, it was sometimes necessary, with reference to ventilation, that it should be open. It was not necessary that it should,when not in use, be unfenced; and it might then without injury to the business have been fenced by a rail. Whether it was usual to fence similar shafts when not in use did not distinctly appear; nor is it very material, because such protection was unquestionably proper, in the sense of reasonable, with reference to the safety of persons having a right to move about upon the floor where the shaft in fact was, because in its nature it formed a pit-fall there. At the time of the accident it was not in use, and it was open and unfenced.

The plaintiff was a journeyman gas-fitter in the employ of a patentee who had supplied the defendant with his patent gas-regulator, to be paid for upon the terms that it effected a certain saving: and, for the purpose of ascertaining whether such saving had been effected, the plaintiff's employer required to test the action of the regulator. He accordingly sent the plaintiff to the defendant's place of business

3. Compare Pridgen v. Boston Housing Authority, 364 Mass. 696, 308 N.E.2d 467, 475–77. Also see Restatement of Torts, Second § 337 (1965); Ames, Law and Morals, 22 Harv.L.Rev. 97 (1908), Selected Essays on the Law of Torts 1; Bohlen, the Moral Duty to Aid Others as a Basis of Tort Liability, 56 U. of Pa.L.Rev. 217, 316, (1908); Bohlen, Studies in the Law of Torts, 291.

for that purpose; and, whilst the plaintiff was engaged upon the floor where the shaft was, he (under circumstances as to which the evidence was conflicting, but) accidentally, and, as the jury found without any fault or negligence on his part, fell down the shaft and was seriously hurt. * * *

It was also argued that the plaintiff was at best in the condition of a bare licensee or guest who, it was urged, is only entitled to use the place as he finds it, and whose complaint may be said to wear the colour of ingratitude, so long as there is no design to injure him: see Hounsell v. Smith, 7 C.B., N.S., 731; 29 L.J.C.P., 203.

We think this argument fails, because the capacity in which the plaintiff was there was that of a person on lawful business in the course of fulfilling a contract in which both the plaintiff and the defendant had an interest, and not upon bare permission. * * *

The authorities respecting guests and other bare licensees, and those respecting servants and others who consent to incur a risk, being therefore inapplicable, we are to consider what is the law as to the duty of the occupier of a building with reference to persons resorting thereto in the course of business, upon his invitation, express or implied. The common case is that of a customer in a shop: but it is obvious that this is only one of a class; for, whether the customer is actually chaffering at the time, or actually buys or not, he is, according to an undoubted course of authority and practice, entitled to the exercise of reasonable care by the occupier to prevent damage from unusual danger, of which the occupier knows or ought to know such as a trap-door left open, unfenced, and unlighted.

* * * This protection does not depend upon the fact of a contract being entered into in the way of the shopkeeper's business during the stay of the customer, but upon the fact that the customer has come ino the shop in pursuance of a tacit invitation given by the shopkeeper, with a view to business which concerns himself. And, if a customer were, after buying goods, to go back to the shop in order to complain of the quality, or that the change was not right, he would be just as much there upon business which concerned the shopkeeper, and as much entitled to protection during this accessory visit, though it might not be for the shopkeeper's benefit, as during the principal visit, which was. And if, instead of going himself, the customer were to send his servant, the servant would be entitled to the same consideration as the master.

The class to which the customer belongs includes persons who go not as mere volunteers, or licensees, or guests, or servants, or persons whose employment is such that danger may be considered as bargained for, but who go upon business which concerns the occupier, and upon his invitation, express or implied.

BROSNAN v. KOUFMAN

Supreme Judicial Court of Massachusetts, 1936.
294 Mass. 495, 2 N.E.2d 441, 104 A.L.R. 1177.

PIERCE, JUSTICE. This is an action of tort for personal injuries sustained by the plaintiff while upon a certain stairway in the Carney building in Boston, which collapsed while the plaintiff was passing over it. * * *

At the trial there was ample evidence to warrant a finding that the plaintiff was in the exercise of due care, as well as a finding that the defendant was negligent in the maintenance of the stairway upon which the plaintiff was injured, if the defendant owed a duty to the plaintiff to exercise reasonable care to maintain the stairway in a reasonably safe condition for travel over it. * * *

Upon the evidence most favorable to the plaintiff it appeared that the Carney building was located upon a parcel of land which had a frontage on Tremont street and a rear frontage on Pemberton Square, both public highways. The entrance to the building from Tremont street led into a marble corridor which was about eight feet wide. This corridor extended to a flight of stairs which led to Pemberton Square. The building had been under the control of the defendant since 1921, and this corridor had been used for a long time by a large number of people in walking between Tremont street and Pemberton Square. The defendant had seen many persons making such use of the corridor. * * *

The evidence showed that as one goes along the corridor from the Tremont street entrance he passes a bulletin board containing the names of the tenants of the building; that further on, at about fifteen feet from the entrance to the building, he passes three elevators; that beyond the elevators is a stand at which cigars, cigarettes and fruit are sold; that there is also a telephone booth and nearly opposite the elevators is a United States mail box; that beyond the cigar stand there is a right angle turn to the right in the corridor, then more steps, and then another sharp turn, to the left, leading to the iron stairway of seven steps which leads to Pemberton Square. The evidence warranted a finding that the plaintiff had frequently passed over the corridor in question, and at the time of his injury he had entered the building by the Tremont street entrance for the purpose of mailing letters; that he had done so by using the mail box in the corridor, and that when injured he was about to leave the premises by the Pemberton Square exit. * * *

The only fundamental question is as to whether the plaintiff, in going upon the defendant's premises, was an invitee or business visitor to whom was owed a duty of care with reference to the maintenance of the stairway which collapsed to his physical injury, or whether he was a licensee to whom no such duty was owed. * * *

Persons using a way over private land for their own convenience, with the acquiescence of the owner thereof, are held in many cases to be licensees only, unless the way is so constructed or maintained as to induce people to believe it to be a public street or way. Holmes v. Drew, 151 Mass. 578, 580, 25 N.E. 22. It is the contention of the plaintiff in the case at bar that invitation was implied from the whole condition of things, including the relation of the corridor to Tremont street and Pemberton Square, the fact that there was no sign at the entrance to the corridor at Pemberton Square, the presence of the sales stand in the corridor, and particularly the presence of a United States mail receptacle in the corridor, assuming the jury might properly find that the mail box was put there with the purpose and design that it should be used by the public at large, of whom the plaintiff was one.

When a building is adapted for business uses, it is generally held that one who comes upon the premises for a purpose connected with the business carried on or in the interest of the occupant, does so under an implied invitation as one to whom is owed a duty of due care. * * * If, however, one comes upon such premises for his own convenience, to gratify curiosity, or with the expectation of gratuitous favors, he is at the best a licensee. * * * The facts in the case at bar * * * establish, on the plaintiff's own testimony, that he was within the corridor for the purpose of mailing his own letters. Leaving out any consideration of the federal statute governing the establishing of mail boxes, the plaintiff has not made out his case. He has not shown that the mail box was intended for the use of the public generally, rather than for the use of the tenants of the building. It may be noted in this connection that there is no testimony in the record that there was any sign on the outside of the building indicating to the public that there was a mail box within the building, from which an invitation to make use of the box could be implied. Compare Sullivan v. New York Telephone Co., 157 App. Div. 642, 643–645, 142 N.Y.S. 735, affirmed 215 N.Y. 678, 109 N.E. 1093. It is not shown that the use of the mail box was for the common or mutual advantage of the defendant and the plaintiff, or that the defendant derived any revenue from its presence or had any direct pecuniary interest in its maintenance, from which it might be implied that he authorized the public having letters to mail to come on the premises to do so. Even though it appears that those using the corridor were not forbidden to use the mail box, such silence would import no more than a tolerance or license to make use of the mail box for personal convenience.

* * *

* * * It is immaterial that a cigar stand and public telephone were maintained in the corridor, or that on some other occasion he had come on the premises for purposes connected with the sale of tobacco or with the use of the telephone. Had he done so on the day of the accident he might have been there under an implied invitation of the defendant. Compare Fleckenstein v. Great Atlantic & Pacific

Tea Co., 91 N.J.L. 145, 146, 102 A. 700, L.R.A. 1918C, 179; Kelley v. City of Columbus, 41 Ohio St. 263, * * *.[4]

---

4. Is this in effect an invitation to perjury? For example:

"*Client*: I broke my leg on a bad stair in the Carney Bldg. Do you think I can get damages?

"*Lawyer*: Well that depends. Tell me the whole story. What were you doing in the Carney Bldg. and so forth. You know there was a similar accident there in 1936. Terrible. The whole stairway collapsed while a fellow named Brosnan was on it. Hurt him pretty bad. The jury gave him $9,900. But our Supreme Court threw him out. They said he couldn't get anything at all because he went into the building just to mail a letter. If a fellow goes into a building just for his own convenience, he can't expect much from the owner. But the Court said that if the fellow went in there on business with some tenant or to buy tobacco at the stand in the lobby he could have kept the $9,900 verdict. Pretty well settled law here.

"*Client*: Really? That's funny as hell. Why, there are dozens of people in and out of that building all the time. It's just a fluke that it was my leg and not that of one of the dozens of people who go to the dentists, lawyers, finance companies and other tenants in the building. Well, in my case * * * I was walking along Tremont Street to go to the Court House at Pemberton Square and thought I would cut through the building. I mean I found I needed cigarettes and thought I'd get them in the lobby and then go out the Pemberton Square side.

"*Lawyer*: You're sure you went in to buy cigarettes? Because if you were just using the building for a short cut, you'd be out of luck.

"*Client*: Why, I'm positive. You know I was laid up for a couple of months and still haven't paid my medical bills.

"*Lawyer*: Well, I just wanted to make sure. So far you're in the clear. Go on."

Of course, perjury is conceivable in any case. But in situations like that in Brosnan v. Kaufman, is the temptation too great? Is it checked by objective facts or the availability of testimony other than that of the plaintiff? May a plaintiff's testimony be influenced by the existence of a statute such as the one quoted in the case which seems to give him not merely permission but a right to enter the building to mail a letter? Does the rule of the Brosnan case as applied do more than trap the honest or ignorant? What more?

Is the defendant's non-liability based on a desire to relieve him from the necessity of expending money for repairs, as in the case of a gift of an old car or as perhaps in Gautret v. Egerton where the premises are adequate for defendant's own use and he has no interest in their use by any other people? Or is it based on a desire to relieve him from liability for consequences of a state of disrepair which he, and perhaps he alone, can, must and should rectify in any event? Or is it based on lack of sympathy for the interest of the plaintiff?

See Baird v. Goldberg, 283 Ky. 558, 562, 142 S.W.2d 120, 122 (1940): Plaintiff was injured when he tripped over a scale in the open vestibule at the entrance of defendant's corner store. The vestibule, triangular in shape and level with the sidewalk, was commonly used by pedestrians to "cut the corner" with defendant's knowledge and acquiescence. The scale had been installed four days before the accident against the post at the apex of the triangle directly opposite the door. The platform of the scale was about two feet long. When injured plaintiff was cutting through the vestibule in order to avoid the midday crowd. Judgment on directed verdict for defendant affirmed. "It is not necessary for us to determine whether or not the plaintiff was guilty of contributory negligence as a matter of law, since we have reached the conclusion that he was a mere licensee, therefore the only duty owed him by defendant, Goldberg, was not to injure him wilfully or wantonly, or to express it another way, not to injure him through active negligence."

This Massachusetts opinion typifies conventional doctrine. Massachusetts law itself, however, has moved forward. Mounsey v. Ellard, Mass. (1973), 297 N.E.2d 43, noted on page 618 below.

In off-hand generalization, judicial opinions and textwriters differentiate between "invitees"—to whom the occupier is said to owe an affirmative duty of care to discover unreasonably dangerous conditions and to protect the visitor from them—and "licensees." As a result of developments since Gautret v. Egerton, there is conventionally a duty to warn "licensees" of concealed dangers actually known to the occupier or of which "he has reason to know," and which are likely not to be discovered by the licensee. Restatement of Torts, Second §§ 342 and 343. (For the difference between "should know" and "reason to know" see Restatement § 12). There can also be liability to both "invitees" and "licensees" for unreasonably dangerous active conduct, but under somewhat different conditions, id., sections 341 and 341A. These terms imply that the differentiating criterion is the fact of invitation from the occupier. See, for example, 36 A.L.R. 37–38: "In considering the duty of the owner or occupier of premises to persons who come thereon, the law divides them into three categories—trespassers, licensees, and invitees. Invitees are persons who are invited to come upon the premises. * * * Licensees are persons whose presence is not invited, but tolerated." And in some cases much effort is expended on determining whether the occupier requested the visitor to come or rather granted the visitor's request for permission. See, e. g., Myers v. Gulf Public Service Corp., 15 La.App. 589, 132 So. 416 (1931). Frequently too, the difference is said to be between a visit for the visitor's benefit only and one for the mutual benefit of visitor and occupier. But more careful analysis of the cases indicates that the differentiating factor is not merely the fact of invitation or the mutuality of interest. Yet much of the conventional doctrine cannot easily be explained without reference to these factors.

Two important differences have contributed to confusion in the literature. One has to do with nomenclature—whether to use the categories of "licensees" and "invitees", or to reclassify "invitees" as a specially protected subcategory of "licensees." An ill-fated attempt at such a reclassification, in the first Restatement of Torts, is described below. The second has to do with the differentiating criterion between "mere" (or "bare") "licensees" and the other, more protected class of visitor, whether designated "invitees" or something else.

The first Restatement of Torts was prepared for the American Law Institute between 1923 and 1939 by a committee led until 1937 by Professor Francis H. Bohlen of the University of Pennsylvania (the "Reporter"). That Restatement avoided the term "invitee." Instead it dealt solely with "trespassers" and licensees", and defined a licensee as a person who is privileged to be on the land by virtue of the possessor's consent "whether given by invitation or permission." It stated: "The important fact is that the entry is by consent of the possessor and it is immaterial that the suggestion of the visit originates with him or with his licensee", section 330, Comment a. The Restatement, sections 331 and 332, then divided "licensees" into two subclasses: (1) "gratuitous licensee," elsewhere frequently belittled by the adjectives "mere" or "bare", and (2) "business visitor." The latter was defined as being on the land with the possessor's consent "for a purpose directly or indirectly connected with business dealings between them"; the former was any licensee other than the latter. And in some situations, a special class of "business visitors," i. e., patrons, was to be differentiated. Section 332, Comment a.

Professor Bohlen had for years been identified with the notion that the basis for the increased liability to the more protected class of visitor lay in the economic benefit expected by the occupier of the land from the visit; cf. Bohlen, The Basis of Affirmative Obligations in the Law of Torts, 53 U. of Pa.L.Rev. 209 (1905). Under his influence the first Restatement adopted this view. Despite some significant scholarly and judicial support, this explanation came under massive attack. See, e. g., Prosser, Business Visitors and Invitees, 26 Minn.L.Rev. 573 (1942); Harper and James, The Law of Torts, § 27.12 (1956 and Supp.1968). "The alternative theory * * * is that the basis of liability is not any economic benefit to the occupier, but a representation to be implied when he encourages others to enter to further a purpose of his own, that reasonable care has been exercised to make the place safe for those who come for that purpose." Prosser, Torts 388–89 (4th ed. 1971).

In 1965 the Restatement of Torts, Second, Professor Prosser now serving as Reporter, reverted to traditional terminology. It reinstated the "invitee", defining him as either a "public invitee" ("a person who is invited to enter or remain on land as a member of the public for a purpose for which the land is held open to the public") or a "business visitor" ("a person who is invited to enter or remain on land for a purpose directly or indirectly connected with business dealings with the possessor of the lands"), section 332. "Licensee" was redefined as "a person who is privileged to enter or remain on land only by virtue of the possessor's consent," section 330. The comments to section 330 use "consent" and "permission" interchangeably. Comment b to section 330 refers to comment b of section 332 for "the distinction between 'consent' or 'permission' and 'invitation' ". The latter comment defines "invitation" as "conduct which justifies others in believing that the possessor desires them to enter the land", and "permission" as "conduct justifying others in believing that the possessor is willing that they shall enter if they desire to do so."

Suppose you are hurt in a department store. Does it matter that you are there, without a dime or a charge account, merely to waste a little time, or to procure a date for some evening with one of the employees, or to solicit a contribution to the Red Cross from the manager or one of the employees, or to persuade an employee to join your labor union, or to sell an insurance policy, etc.? How would a court know with confidence what the purpose of your visit was? Cf. Fraters v. Keeling, 20 Cal.App.2d 490, 67 P.2d 118 (1937).

Or suppose you are "working your way through college" by selling magazine subscriptions, hosiery, aluminum or what not from house to house. Does it matter that the lady of the house is a known "sucker" always willing so to help a boy work his way through college, or is a battle axe who hates college boys or reading? Does it matter that you don't know this when you go to the house? And see Lord Justice Denning's opinion in Dunster v. Abbott, [1954] 1 W.L.R. 58, 61–62: "A canvasser who comes without your consent is a trespasser. Once he has your consent, he is a licensee. Not until you do business with him is he an invitee. Even when you have done business with him it seems rather strange that your duty to him should be different when he comes up to the door than when he goes away. Does he really change his colour in the middle of the conversation? And what is the position when you discuss business with him and it comes to nothing? No confident answer can be given to these questions. Such is the morass into which the law has floundered in trying to distinguish between licensees and invitees."

MORRIS v. GRANATO

Supreme Court of Errors of Connecticut, 1946.
133 Conn. 295, 50 A.2d 416.

DICKENSON, JUDGE. This is an action to recover damages for personal injuries claimed to have been caused the plaintiff as an invitee of the defendants by their negligence in the care of their restaurant. It was tried to the jury and a verdict was rendered for the plaintiff. The sole ground of appeal is the denial of a motion to set aside the verdict.

Viewing the evidence in the light most favorable to the plaintiff, the jury might reasonably have found the facts as follows: The defendants conduct a restaurant on Main Street, Hartford, with a license to sell beer. Upon entering the restaurant, there is a bar to the right and a double line of booths to the left extending nearly the depth of the room. Passage to the rear of the room may be had through an aisle between the booths or in the space between the bar and the booths. In the wall which extends along back of the bar are three doors. The first of these is behind the bar and leads to the cellar. The second is the door to the men's toilet and is about four feet from the cellar door and opposite the rear end of the bar. The third door is to the women's toilet and is about four feet from the door to the men's toilet. There is a screen between the door to the men's room and that to the women's room extending out a few feet from the wall and at right angles to it. The partition is nearer the women's room and between it and the men's room is a pinball machine extending into the restaurant to a point about opposite the rear end of the bar. Access to the men's room and to the cellar door is had by passing between the end of the bar and the pinball machine. Access to the women's room is had by passing to the left of the pinball machine and the screen. At the time of the plaintiff's fall, there was no sign on the door to the men's room or on the cellar door. Both of these doors opened in. The door to the women's room opened out, and a sign, which projected at right angles from the left casing at the height of the top of the door, bore the word "Ladies." A partition part way to the ceiling separates the main room of the restaurant from the kitchen.

The plaintiff and a man companion entered the restaurant about 11 p. m. on October 21, 1944, and seated themselves in one of the booths facing in the direction of the entrance door. They ordered sandwiches, and beer for the man. While the plaintiff was eating, her companion went to the men's toilet. When he returned, the plaintiff in turn started to go to a toilet. She proceeded down the aisle to the rear of the line of booths, passed between these and the kitchen partition, crossed to the passage between the end of the bar and the pinball machine and entered the men's toilet. In her course, the women's toilet was to her left. The sign "Ladies" was hidden at first from her view by the partition wall separating the kitchen from the main room, and as she got beyond this the "Ladies" sign was at an angle to her line of vision. She did not see this sign or the door to the women's room and entered the men's room. She had been in the restaurant but once before and had not gone to a toilet on that occasion. Her companion's attention was called to the fact that she had entered the men's toilet. He went to the door, called to her that she was in the wrong room, and returned to his seat. She came out quite embarrassed and turned to her left. She opened the door leading to the cellar and stepped in, falling down the stairs to the cellar floor. There was no light in the cellar. Had the plaintiff looked to her left just before entering the passageway between the pinball machine and the end of the bar, she could have seen the sign over the women's room.

* * * The contention of the defendants on these facts is that the plaintiff was not an invitee with relation to that part of the restaurant where the cellar door was * * *.

In Knapp v. Connecticut Theatrical Corporation, 122 Conn. 413, at page 417, 190 A. 291, at page 293, we said: "In most of the cases of this character the question of the status of the visitor has been determined as one of fact, and this would ordinarily be so, since it depends upon whether the owner should have known that the visitor would be led to believe that the door was one which he was expected to use." Whether an invitee exceeded the limits of the invitation depends upon whether his use of the premises went beyond that which the owner might reasonably have contemplated. Guilford v. Yale University, 128 Conn. 449, 454, 23 A.2d 917; Smith v. L. & S. Corporation, 133 Conn. 105, 107, 48 A.2d 239. The defendants recognized the need for toilets for both sexes in their establishment and provided them. The three doors in question were in line and an equal distance apart. While the women's room was separated from the men's room by a screen, the jury might have found that it was in a corner where it might readily have been overlooked, whereas the other two doors were in plain view of one entering the passageway between the pinball machine and the end of the bar, and on neither was a visible sign indicating its purpose. The fact that the door to the men's room was about opposite the rear end of the bar and that the cellar door was behind the bar does not vitally affect a conclusion of invitation by the jury. The defendants can hardly contend that the men's room was not in a proper location for a toilet. The jury reasonably could have concluded that the cellar door, four feet away, might be mistaken for a toilet, and could have found that the plaintiff was an invitee as to that part of the restaurant. * * * [5]

A prime anomaly under the nomenclature of either Restatement is the situation of the social guest. Social guests are fairly uniformly said to be "mere", "bare" or "gratuitous licensees" to whom is owed a lesser duty than that owed to business visitors, Southcote v. Stanley, 1 H. & N. 247 (1856); Page v. Murphy, 194 Minn. 607, 261 N.W. 443 (1935), even when the host and the guest are really fond of each other and derive mutual pleasure from the visit. The criterion, then, is neither invitation nor mutuality of benefit broadly, but business purpose. But query. Suppose a salesman comes to defendant's store to sell defendant a line of goods. Having made the sale, he says to defendant "let me take you to dinner and the theatre to-night"; the saleman returns to the store at six and is hurt by a condition of the floor which would subject defendant to liability to a "business visitor." Or suppose that the parties could not agree by dinner time and defendant says: "Come home with me for dinner; perhaps a couple of cocktails will open your eyes to my proposition and we'll close the deal." Plaintiff accepts the invitation and is hurt by a condition of the floor in defendant's home.

Some states reject the Restatement's categories. One variation is to divide licensees into two groups, the "bare licensee" who, "like a trespasser * * * is owed no duty * * * except that he may not

5. Plaintiffs who have entered premises in one capacity, such as business visitor, are frequently held to have changed status to that of licensee or trespasser if they visit and are injured upon a different portion of the premises. See, e. g., West v. Shizuko Tan, 322 F.2d 924 (9th Cir. 1963) (restaurant patron "invitee" in dining room, but "mere licensee" on bandstand, where she fell); Carey v. Gray, 98 N.J.L. 217, 119 A. 176 (1922) (plaintiff employed to disinfect defendant's house and working therein at night received a call of nature, went to the outdoor toilet in the dark and fell in because the toilet had no floor); McMullen v. M. & M. Hotel Co., 227 Iowa 1061, 290 N.W. 3 (1940) (plaintiff went behind counter in drug store to use private telephone); Wall v. F. W. Woolworth Co., 209 Ky. 258, 272 S.W. 730 (1925) (customer stepped behind counter to help clerk); Ellington v. Ricks, 179 N.C. 686, 102 S.E. 510 (1920); Trask v. Shotwell, 41 Minn. 66, 42 N.W. 699 (1889); Annotation, "Landlords' liability for one injured while using for a purpose for which it was not intended property remaining in former's control," 30 A.L.R. 1390. Harper and James, Law of Torts § 27.12 at notes 40–48 (1956 and Supp.1968); Prosser, Torts 391–92 (4th ed. 1971); Restatement of Torts, Second § 332 Comment 1. Also see, similarly, Paris v. Howard D. Johnson Co., 340 Mass. 739, 166 N.E.2d 735 (1960) (restaurant patron inadvertently enters through wrong door, an emergency exit, falls over unlit step, held not business visitor where accident occurred, because defendant had not extended an invitation to use that entrance.) Sometimes status is said to change as the visitor's purpose changes. Compare Braun v. Vallade, 33 Cal.App. 279, 164 P. 904 (1917) with Kneiser v. Belasco-Blackwood Co., 22 Cal.App. 205, 133 P. 989 (1913) (injuries to barroom patrons who entered premises in order to use toilet but also had drinks).

be wilfully or wantonly injured of entrapped * * * once his pressence is known," and a "licensee by invitation", defined as the "social guest", who is owed the Restatement Second's section 342 duty of care concerning known dangerous conditions. Bramble v. Thompson, 264 Md. 518, 287 A.2d 265 (1972). Florida distinguishes between licensees by express or reasonably implied invitation, including social guests, who are accorded the same duty of reasonable care as invitees, and uninvited licensees, who get less. Wood v. Camp, 284 So.2d 691 (Fla. 1973). Illinois, on the other hand, is said to exclude liability to social guests except for "willful and wanton misconduct," Madrazo v. Michaels, 1 Ill.App.3d 583, 274 N.E.2d 635 (1971).

Customs, tax and sanitary inspectors, postmen, garbage collectors and water meter readers are generally classified as business visitors.[6] Firemen and policemen, however, have generally been called licensees in the United States, Aravenis v. Eisenberg, 237 Md. 242, 206 A.2d 148 (1965); Kinney v. Sun Oil Co., 437 Pa. 80, 262 A.2d 128 (1970);[7] but see Shypulski v. Waldorf Paper Products Co., 232 Minn. 394, 45 N.W.2d 549 (1951), Dini v. Naiditch, 20 Ill.2d 406, 170 N.E.2d 881 (1960) and Cameron v. Abatiell, 127 Vt. 111, 241 A.2d 310 (1968); compare Cook v. Demetrakas, 108 R.I. 397, 275 A.2d 919 (1971), which suggests a distinction depending upon whether the policeman enters the premises on a routine security check, in which case he might be an invitee, or to chase a thief, in which case he is only a licensee. Also see Restatement of Torts, Second § 345(2) (1965) (liability to public officer or employee who enters land in performance of duty and suffers harm because of condition of part of land held open to the public same as liability to an invitee); in England public officers and employees were apparently considered invitees at common law, Hartley v. Mayoh & Co. [1954] 1 Q.B. 383. As to civilian rescuers, see 73 U.Pa.L.Rev. 409 (1925).

As to students or other sightseers permitted to take an observation tour through a plant, see Public Service Co. v. Elliott, 123 F.2d 2 (1st Cir. 1941); Gilliland v. Boudurant, 332 Mo. 881, 59 S.W.2d 679 (1933); 3 U.Chi.L.Rev. 514 (1936). As to workmen seeking employment, see 13 Notre D.L.Rev. 330 (1938); relative bringing lunch to an employee in plant, Gotch v. K. & B. Packing & Provision Co., 93 Colo. 276, 25 P.2d 719, 89 A.L.R. 753 (1933).[8]

6. See Prosser, Torts 396 (4th ed. 1971); Annotations, "Liability of owner or occupant of premises for injuries sustained by mail carrier", 21 A.L.R.3d 1099; "Liability of owner or occupant of premises to building or construction inspector coming upon premises in discharge of duty," 28 A.L.R.3d 891; "Liability of owner or operator of premises for injury to meter reader or similar employee of public service corporation coming to premises in course of duties," 28 A.L.R.3d 1344; and "Premises liability: liability of owner or occupant to garbage or trash man coming on premises in course of duty," 36 A.L.R.3d 610.

7. Also see 26 Colum.L.Rev. 116 (1926); 35 Mich.L.Rev. 1157 (1937); Annotations, "Duty and liability of owner or occupant of premises to fireman or policeman coming thereon in discharge of his duty", 13 A.L.R. 637, 86 A.L.R.2d 1205.

8. In an influential article, "Business Visitors and Invitees," 26 Minn.L.Rev. 573 (1942), Prof. William L. Prosser provided a useful collection of cases

HERRICK v. WIXOM

Supreme Court of Michigan, 1899.
121 Mich. 384, 80 N.W. 117, 81 N.W. 333.

MONTGOMERY, J. This is an action of trespass on the case, * * *. Defendant was possessed of and managed a tent show or circus. * * * Plaintiff went to the circus grounds on the afternoon of this day in company with his cousin. There is testimony to show that while there he and his cousin were invited by a son of the defendant, who had been selling tickets in the ticket wagon, to enter the tent with him, the entertainment being in progress. This plaintiff did, taking a seat on the lower tier of seats. The testimony on the part of defense tended to show that plaintiff was not invited into the show, and that the son of defendant had no authority to invite him in. * * * A part or feature of the entertainment consisted in the ignition and explosion of a giant firecracker attached to a pipe set in an upright position in one of the show rings. This was done by one of the clowns. There is testimony to show that plaintiff sat 30 or 40 feet from the place where the cracker was exploded, but when the same was exploded a part of the firecracker flew and struck plaintiff in the eye, putting it out, whereby he lost the sight and use of the eye.

on the status of various entrants on land in a variety of circumstances. The article answered a number of the questions raised in this chapter in light of the first Restatement and suggested rationalizations for the decisions in various situations dealt with in this chapter. Prof. Prosser's conclusions as to his principal question were:

"* * * By and large the courts have not talked of business interest or expected financial gain; they have talked of invitation. Invitation is an unfortunate word, since it applies equally to the customer who is entitled to protection and the social guest who is not. It is unfortunate also in that it connotes some initiative on the part of the occupier; and one who is permitted to come in response to his own proposal to do work on the premises may still expect to be protected. But the idea which it conveys, of encouragement to enter under circumstances which carry an implied assurance of care taken to make the place safe for the purpose, is essentially sound.

"The conclusions which it is hoped may be drawn from the foregoing discussion are these:

"1. In the early cases dealing with the liability of the occupier, business interest and pecuniary gain had only incidental mention, and did not affect the decision.

"2. The decisions which have turned on the presence or absence of business interest are few in comparison with the large number which cannot be accounted for on that basis.

"3. When premises are thrown open to the public, the occupier assumes responsibility for their safe condition toward any member of the public who may enter for the purpose for which they are open, regardless of whether he brings with him the hope of profit or 'benefit.'

"4. When premises are not open to the public, the individual may still be entitled to protection if he enters under circumstances which give him reasonable assurance that care has been taken to make the place safe for his reception. Visits for the performance of contracts, and for other economic advantage to the occupier, usually are made upon such implied assurance.

"5. When premises are not open to the public, the individual is not entitled to protection where he does not enter under circumstances giving him reasonable assurance that the place has been made safe for him; and this is true whether or not he confers benefit upon the occupier.

"6. The Restatement of the Law of Torts is wrong.*"

* So also, in several particulars, is Prosser, Torts, 626–630, 635–642 (1941). To that learned author, a thoroughgoing reprimand. [Note by Prof. Prosser.]

* * * Upon the trial of the cause a verdict of no cause for action was rendered, and judgment for the defendant entered accordingly. Plaintiff brings error.

* * *

The circuit judge charged the jury as follows: "The negligence charged in this case is, gentlemen, that Mr. Wixom exploded a firecracker, of the dimensions that the plaintiff claims this firecracker was, in the inside of this tent, and in the presence of his audience. They claim that was negligence. And that is the question for you to determine, under the evidence, and under the rules of law that I have given you and that I shall give you hereafter. Now, you must further find, in order that the plaintiff recover, that the plaintiff was in the tent, where he was injured, by the invitation of some person having authority to allow him to go in there. If he was a mere trespasser, who forced his way in, then the defendant owed him no duty that would enable him to recover under the declaration and proofs in this case. * * * We think this instruction faulty, in so far as it was intended to preclude recovery in any event if the plaintiff was found to be a trespasser. It is true that a trespasser who suffers an injury because of a dangerous condition of premises is without remedy. But, where a trespasser is discovered upon the premises by the owner or occupant, he is not beyond the pale of the law, and any negligence resulting in injury will render the person guilty of negligence liable to respond in damages. * * * In this case the negligent act of the defendant's servant was committed after the audience was made up. The presence of plaintiff was known, and the danger to him from a negligent act was also known. The question of whether a dangerous experiment should be attempted in his presence, or whether an experiment should be conducted with due care and regard to his safety, cannot be made to depend upon whether he had forced himself into the tent. Every instinct of humanity revolts at such a suggestion. For this error the judgment will be reversed, and a new trial ordered.[9]

The extent to which the occupier has a duty to warn seen trespassers of a dangerous condition of the premises is an unsettled question. The Restatement finds such a duty when the condition is an "artificial" one and involves danger of "death or serious bodily harm," Section 337. The Restatement also suggests that "it may reasonably be expected" that the duty exists when the condition is either natural or one that threatens lesser harm. Ibid. Comment b.

The Restatement also proposes further variations, concerning duties in respect of "activities" (section 334) and "artificial conditions" (section 335) highly dangerous to trespassers who "constantly intrude upon a limited area of the land." See, e. g., Franc v. Pennsylvania Railroad, 424 Pa. 99, 225 A.2d 528 (1967).

9. The Restatement of Torts, Second follows Herrick v. Wixom; see section 336 concerning the liability of a possessor of land "who knows or has reason to know of the presence of another." Also see Peaslee, Duty to Seen Trespassers, 27 Harv.L.Rev. 403 (1914).

LYNCH v. NURDIN

Court of Queen's Bench, 1841.
1 A. & E.,N.S., 29.

On a rule *nisi* for a new trial, "on the grounds of misdirection and that the verdict was against evidence" :

LORD DENMAN, C. J. delivered the judgment of the Court.

This case was an action of tort for negligence by the defendant's servant, in leaving his cart and horse half an hour in the open street at the door of a house in which the servant remained during that period. The evidence for the plaintiff proved that, at the end of the first half hour, he, a child of very tender age, being between six and seven years old, was heard crying, and, on the approach of the witnesses, was found on the ground, and a wheel of the defendant's cart going over his leg, which was thereby fractured. * * * Witnesses * * * proved that, after the servant had been about a quarter of an hour in the house, the plaintiff and several other children came up, and began to play with the horse, and climb into the cart and out of it. While the plaintiff was getting down from it, another boy made the horse move, in consequence of which the plaintiff fell, and his leg was broken as before mentioned. On this undisputed evidence (for there was no cross-examination of the witnesses), the defendant's counsel claimed the Judge's direction in his favour, contending that, as the plaintiff had obviously contributed to the calamity, it could not be said in point of law to have been caused by the negligence of the defendant's servant. My learned brother, however, thought himself bound to lay all the facts before the jury, and take their opinion on that general point. They found a verdict for the plaintiff. It is now complained that such direction was not given; and at all events the jury are said to have given a verdict contrary to the evidence. * * *

It is urged that the mischief was not produced by the mere negligence of the servant as asserted in the declaration, but at most by that negligence in combination with two other active causes, the advance of the horse in consequence of his being excited by the other boy, and the plaintiff's improper conduct in mounting the cart and so committing a trespass on the defendant's chattel. On the former of these two causes no great stress was laid, and I do not apprehend that it can be necessary to dwell at any length. For if I am guilty of negligence in leaving any thing dangerous in a place where I know it to be extremely probable that some other person will unjustifiably set it in motion to the injury of a third, and if that injury should be so brought about, I presume that the sufferer might have redress by action against both or either of the two, but unquestionably against the first. * * * But in the present case an additional fact appears. The plaintiff himself has done wrong: he had no right to enter the cart, and, abstaining from doing so, would have escaped the mischief. Certainly he was a cooperating cause of his own misfortune by doing an unlawful act: and the question arises, whether that fact alone must deprive the child of his remedy. * * * We have here express authorities for our guidance. In Ilott v. Wilkes (3 B. & Ald. 304), a decision which excited great attention both in Westminster Hall and beyond it, this Court indeed held that a trespasser in a wood, where he well knew spring guns to be placed, could not sue for the injury received by him from the explosion of one of them. But Lord Tenterden and his three brethren cautiously and repeatedly declared that their opinion was founded on the plaintiff's knowing of the danger, and voluntarily incurring it. Best J., who was supposed to carry to the greatest extent the right of protecting property against invaders by placing dangerous instruments, took infinite pains, when Chief Justice of the Common Pleas, to explain that his opinion in Ilott v. Wilkes rested exclusively on the notice. In Bird v. Holbrook (4 Bing. 628) his expressions are most remarkable. * * * Bird v. Holbrook is a decisive authority against the general proposition that misconduct, even wilful and culpable misconduct, must necessarily exclude the plaintiff who is guilty of it from the right to sue. I remember being present at a trial at Warwick before Lord Chief Baron Richards, where the same law prevailed. * * *

A distinction may here by taken between the wilful act done by the defendant in those cases, in deliberately planting a dangerous weapon in his ground with the design of deterring trespassers, and the mere negligence of the defendant's servant in leaving his cart in the open street. But between wilful mischief and gross negligence the boundary line is hard to trace: I should rather say impossible. The law runs them into each other, considering such a degree of negligence as some proof of malice. It is then a matter strictly within the province of a jury deciding on the circumstances of each case. They would naturally enquire whether the horse was vicious or steady; whether the occasion required the servant to be so long absent from his charge, and whether in that case no assistance could have been procured to watch the horse: whether the street was at that hour likely to be clear or thronged with a noisy multitude (It appeared in the present case that Compton Street was more thronged than usual, in consequence of a neighboring street being stopped.): especially whether large parties of young children might be reasonably expected to resort to the spot. If this last mentioned fact were probable, it would be hard to say that a case of gross negligence was not fully established.

But the question remains, can the plaintiff then, consistently with the authorities, maintain his action, having been at least equally in fault. The answer is that, supposing that fact ascertained by the jury, but to this extent, that he merely indulged the natural instinct of a child in amusing himself with the empty cart and deserted horse, then we think that the defendant cannot be permitted to avail himself of that fact. The most blameable carelessness of his servant having tempted the child, he ought not to reproach the child with yielding to that temptation. He has been the real and only cause of the mischief. He has been deficient in ordinary care: the child, acting without prudence or thought, has, however, shown these qualities in as great a degree as he could be expected to possess them. His misconduct bears no proportion to that of the defendant which produced it.

For these reasons, we think that nothing appears in the case which can prevent the action from being maintained. It was properly left to the jury, with whose opinion we fully concur.

Rule discharged.

SIOUX CITY & P. R. CO. v. STOUT

Supreme Court of the United States, 1873.
17 Wall. 657, 21 L.Ed. 745.

Error to the Circuit Court for the District of Nebraska.

Henry Stout, a child six years of age * * * sued * * * the Sioux City and Pacific Railroad Company * * * to recover damages for an injury sustained upon a turntable belonging to the said company. The turntable was in an open space, about eighty rods from the company's depot, in a hamlet or settlement of one hundred to one hundred and fifty persons. Near the turntable was a travelled road passing through the depot grounds, and another travelled road near by. * * * There were but few houses in the neighborhood of the turntable, and the child's parents lived in another part of the town, and about three-fourths of a mile distant. The child, without the knowledge of his parents, set off with two other boys, the one nine and the other ten years of age, to go to the depot, with no definite purpose in view. When the boys arrived there, it was proposed by some of them to go to the turntable to play. The turntable was not attended or guarded by any servant of the company, was not fastened or locked, and revolved easily on its axis. Two of the boys began to turn it, and in attempting to get upon it, the foot of the child (he being at the time upon the railroad track) was caught between the end of the rail and the turntable as it was revolving and the end of the iron rail on the main track of the road, and was crushed.

One witness, then a servant of the company, testified that he had previously seen boys playing at the turntable, and had forbidden them from playing there. But the witness had no charge of the table, and did not communicate the fact of having seen boys playing there to any of the officers or servants of the company having the table in charge.

One of the boys, who was with the child when injured, had previously played upon the turntable when the railroad men were working on the track, in sight, and not far distant.

It appeared from the testimony that the child had not, before the day on which he was now injured, played at the turntable, or had, indeed, ever been there.

The table was constructed on the railroad company's own land, and, the testimony tended to show, in the ordinary way. * * * There was an iron latch fastened to it which turned on a hinge, and, when in order, dropped into an iron socket on the track, and held the table in position while using. The catch of this latch was broken at the time of the accident. The latch, which weighed eight or ten pounds, could easily be lifted out of the catch and thrown back on the table, and the table was allowed to be moved about. This latch was not locked, or in any way fastened down before it was broken, and all the testimony on that subject tended to show that it was not usual for railroad companies to lock or guard turntables, but that it was usual to have a latch with a catch, or a draw-bolt, to keep them in position when used. * * *

On the question whether there was negligence on the part of the railway Company in the management or condition of its turntable, the judge charged the jury—

"That to maintain the action it must appear by the evidence that the turntable, in the condition, situation, and place where it then was, was a dangerous machine, one which, if unguarded or unlocked, would be likely to cause injury to children; that if in its construction and the manner in which it was left it was not dangerous in its nature, the defendants were not liable for negligence; that they were further to consider whether, situated as it was as the defendants' property in a small town, somewhat remote from habitations, there was negligence in not anticipating that injury might occur if it was left unlocked or unguarded; that if they did not have reason to anticipate that children would be likely to resort to it, or that they would be likely to be injured if they did resort to it, then there was no negligence."

The jury found a verdict of $7500 for the plaintiff, from the judgment upon which this writ of error was brought. * * *

MR. JUSTICE HUNT delivered the opinion of the court. * * *

The record expressly states that "the counsel for the defendant disclaim resting their defence on the ground that the plaintiff's parents were negligent, or that the plaintiff (considering his tender age) was negligent, but rest their defence on the ground that the company was not negligent, and claim that the injury to the plaintiff was accidental or brought upon himself."

This disclaimer ought to dispose of the question of the plaintiff's negligence, whether made in a direct form, or indirectly under the allegation that the plaintiff was a trespasser upon the railroad premises, and therefore cannot recover.

A reference to some of the authorities on the last suggestion may, however, be useful.

In the well-known case of Lynch v. Nurdin, the child was clearly a trespasser in climbing upon the cart, but was allowed to recover. * * *

In Bird v. Holbrook, the plaintiff was injured by the spring guns set in the defendant's grounds, and although the plaintiff was a trespasser the defendant was held liable.

There are no doubt cases in which the contrary rule is laid down. But we conceive the rule to be this: that while a railway company is not bound to the same degree of care in regard to mere strangers who are unlawfully upon its premises that it owed to passengers conveyed by it, it is not exempt from responsibility to such strangers for injuries arising from its negligence or from its tortious acts.

2d. Was there negligence on the part of the railway company in the management or condition of its turntable?

The charge on this point was an impartial and intelligent one. * * *

That the turntable was a dangerous machine, which would be likely to cause injury to children who resorted to it, might fairly be inferred from the injury which actually occurred to the plaintiff. There was the same liability to injury to him, and no greater, that existed with reference to all children. When the jury learned from the evidence that he had suffered a serious injury, by his foot being caught between the fixed rail of the roadbed and the turning rail of the table they were justified in believing that there was a probability of the occurrence of such accidents.

So, in looking at the remoteness of the machine from inhabited dwellings, when it was proved to the jury that several boys from the hamlet were at play upon the turntable on other occasions, and within the observation and to the knowledge of the employes of the defendant, the jury were justified in believing that children would probably resort to it, and that the defendant should have anticipated that such would be the case.

As it was in fact, on this occasion, so it was to be expected that the amusement of the boys would have been found in turning this table while they were on it or about it. This could certainly have been prevented by locking the turntable when not in use by the company. It was not shown that this would cause any considerable expense or inconvenience to the defendant. It could probably have been prevented by the repair of the broken latch. * * * The evidence is not strong and the negligence is slight, but we are not able to say that there is not evidence sufficient to justify the verdict. We are not called upon to weigh, to measure, to balance the evidence, or to ascertain how we should have decided if acting as jurors. The charge was in all respects sound and judicious, and there being sufficient evidence to justify the finding, we are not authorized to disturb it. * * *

Affirmed.[10]

10. See McKiddy v. Des Moines Electric Co., 202 Iowa 225, 206 N.W. 815 (1926); Goodrich, Landowner's Duty to Strangers on His Premises (1922) 7 Iowa L.Bull. 67.

In Edgington v. Burlington, C. R. & N. Ry. Co., 116 Iowa 410, 90 N.W. 95, 57 L.R.A. 561 (1902), a turntable case, the Iowa court followed the Stout case. The opinion by Weaver, J., contains a very lengthy discussion of the earlier authorities. The following are portions of the opinion:

These cases are all strongly alike in their circumstances, and, generally speaking, the story of one is the story of all,—an open lot; a turntable insecurely fastened, or wholly unfasten-

10. Note 10 cont'd

ed; children gathering upon it, some riding while others work the levers; a misstep, a fall, and a little body is maimed, or young life is extinguished. It is useless to moralize upon the instinct for play which controls the action of a child, or argue for its control by parental authority and guidance. It exists, ingrained in the child's being, and we must deal with it as we find it. Nothing seems to appeal to it more strongly than some device in the form of a merry-go-round; and the temptation to ride it, if the opportunity offers, is practically irresistible, until approaching maturity brings some reasonable measure of judgment and discretion. Accepting these facts before us: Is a landowner who exposes dangerous but attractive machinery upon an open lot in close proximity to a public way or other place where he may reasonably expect young children will pass or resort for play under any duty to fasten or guard such machinery, or to exercise care to provide against children interfering with it to their injury? * * * Ordinarily the owner of property, real or personal, may use or deal with it as he likes; but this right can never be divorced from the responsibility suggested by the maxim, "*Sic utere tuo alien um non laedas.*" In other words, no man is at liberty, under the law, to so use his own as to endanger the person or property of his neighbor. This is a necessary result of social organization, and an indispensable requisite of social order. So long as one lives in comparative isolation, this rule rests lightly upon him, and he need scarcely feel its restraint; but, as population multiplies, and he is brought into proximity with his kind, he finds the range in which he may exercise absolute control over his own is constantly being narrowed. * * * But we are told that, conceding all this, the law makes no provision for the protection of a trespasser, and that he who enters unbidden upon the land of another assumes all risk of pitfalls, traps, and other sources of danger which may be there encountered, and that he who officiously or needlessly intermeddles with property of any kind to which he has no legal right has no cause of complaint if thereby injured. This is a general rule of unquestioned authority and justice, but, as we have said, like other rules, is not without limitation. * * * Ryan v. Towar, 128 Mich. 463, 87 N.W. 644, 55 L.R.A. 310, 92 Am.St.Rep. 481, vividly depicts the woes which children inflict upon society in general. We quote: "There are no more lawless class than children, and none more annoyingly resent an attempt to prevent their trespasses. The average citizen has learned that the surest way to be overrun by children is to give them to understand that their presence is distasteful. The consequences is that they roam at will over private premises, and, as a rule, this is tolerated so long as no damage is done. The remedy which the law affords for trifling trespasses of children is inadequate. No one ever thinks of suing them, and an attempt to remove a crowd of boys from private premises by gently laying on of hands, and using no more force than is necessary to put them off, would be a roaring farce, with all honor to the juveniles." If this sweeping indictment of boyhood and these gloomy prophesies are intended as a sober argument, they demonstrate a failure upon the part of the authors to fairly interpret the doctrine against which they array themselves; and, if intended as sarcasm, it is proper to observe that there is not a rule known to the law, no matter how sacred or universally recognized, which cannot, by an extreme and exaggerated application of its principle, be made to appear ridiculous. * * * [I]t is sufficient to say that the hoodlums there described find no immunity or protection on the law as we interpret it. Their mental acuteness is open to no discount or disparagement. They know the difference between right and wrong, and understand the meaning of trespass as well as the property owner. Ordinarily, they are at no loss to care for themselves. They disregard property right from mere love of mischief, and take risks out of mere bravado, or in conscious defiance of moral and legal restraint. When a boy is thus injured, we may pity his folly, but justly say, as the law says, that having intelligently assumed the risk, he ought not to recover damages. This has no application whatever to infants who are yet without judgment or discretion, and the argument built upon such circumstances is wholly irrelevant to the question in controversy. * * *

UNITED ZINC & CHEMICAL CO. v. BRITT

Supreme Court of the United States, 1922.
258 U.S. 268, 42 S.Ct. 299, 66 L.Ed. 615, 36 A.L.R. 28.

MR. JUSTICE HOLMES delivered the opinion of the Court.

This is a suit brought by the respondents against the petitioner to recover for the death of two children, sons of the respondents. The facts that for the purposes of decision we shall assume to have been proved are these. The petitioner owned a tract of about twenty acres in the outskirts of the town of Iola, Kansas. Formerly it had there a plant for the making of sulphuric acid and zinc spelter. In 1910 it tore the buildings down but left a basement and cellar, in which in July, 1916, water was accumulated, clear in appearance but in fact dangerously poisoned by sulphuric acid and zinc sulphate that had come in one way or another from the petitioner's works, as the petitioner knew. The respondents had been travelling and encamped at some distance from this place. A travelled way passed within 120 or 100 feet of it. On July 27, 1916, the children, who were eight and eleven years old, came upon the petitioner's land, went into the water, were poisoned and died. The petitioner saved the question whether it could be held liable. At the trial the Judge instructed the jury that if the water looked clear but in fact was poisonous and thus the children were allured to it the petitioner was liable. The respondents got a verdict and judgment, which was affirmed by the Circuit Court of Appeals. 264 Fed. 785.

Union Pacific Ry. Co. v. McDonald, 152 U.S. 262, 14 Sup.Ct. 619, 38 L.Ed. 434, and kindred cases were relied upon as leading to the result, and perhaps there is language in that and in Sioux City & Pacific Ry. Co. v. Stout, 17 Wall. 657, 21 L.Ed. 745, that might seem to justify it; but the doctrine needs very careful statement not to make an unjust and impracticable requirement. If the children had been adults they would have had no case. They would have been trespassers and the owner of the land would have owed no duty to remove even hidden danger; it would have been entitled to assume that they would obey the law and not trespass. The liability for spring guns and mantraps arises from the fact that the defendant has not rested on that assumption, but on the contrary has expected the trespasser and prepared an injury that is no more justified than if he had held the gun and fired it. Chenery v. Fitchburg R. R. Co., 160 Mass., 211, 213, 35 N.E. 554, 22 L.R.A. 575. Infants have no greater right to go upon other people's land than adults, and the mere fact that they are infants imposes no duty upon landowners to expect them and to prepare for their safety. On the other hand the duty of one who invites another upon his land not to lead him into a trap is well settled, and while it is very plain that temptation is not invitation, it may be held that knowingly to establish and expose, unfenced, to children of an age when they follow a bait as mechanically as a fish, something that is certain to attract them, has the legal effect of an invitation to them although not to an adult. But the principle if accepted must be very cautiously applied.

In Sioux City & P. Railroad Co. v. Stout, 17 Wall. 657, 21 L.Ed. 745, the well-known case of a boy injured on a turntable, it appeared that children had played there before to the knowledge of employees of the railroad, and in view of that fact and the situation of the turntable near a road without visible separation, it seems to have been assumed without much discussion that the railroad owed a duty to the boy. Perhaps this was as strong a case as would be likely to occur of maintaining a known temptation, where temptation takes the place of invitation. A license was implied and liability for a danger not manifest to a child was declared in the very similar case of Cooke v. Midland Great Western Ry. of Ireland [1909], A.C. 229.

In the case at bar it is at least doubtful whether the water could be seen from any place where the children lawfully were and there is no evidence that it was what led them to enter the land. But that is necessary to start the supposed duty. There can be no general duty on the part of a landowner to keep his land safe for children, or even free from hidden dangers, if he has not directly or by implication invited or licensed them to come there. The difficulties in the way of implying a license are adverted to in Chenery v. Fitchburg R. R. Co., 160 Mass. 211, 212, 35 N.E. 554, 22 L.R.A. 575, but need not be considered here. It does not appear that children were in the habit of going to the place; so that foundation also fails.

Union Pacific Ry. Co. v. McDonald, 152 U.S. 262, 14 Sup.Ct. 619, 38 L.Ed. 434, is less in point. There a boy was burned by falling into burning coal slack close by the side of a path on which he was running homeward from other boys who had frightened him. It hardly appears that he was a trespasser and the path suggests an invitation; at all events boys habitually resorted to the place where he was. Also the defendant was under a statutory duty to fence the place sufficiently to keep out cattle. The decision is very far from establishing that the petitioner is liable for poisoned water not bordering a road, not shown to have been the inducement that led the children to trespass, if in any event the law would deem it sufficient to excuse their going there, and not shown to have been the indirect inducement because known to the children to be frequented by others. It is suggested that the roads across the place were invitations. A road is not an invitation to leave it elsewhere than at its end.

Judgment reversed.

MR. JUSTICE CLARKE, with whom concurred THE CHIEF JUSTICE and MR. JUSTICE DAY, dissenting. * * * [11]

11. "The Britt case with its requirement of 'allurement' has been condemned by every American writer whose views I have read. It has been repeatedly rejected by courts all over the United States, though a few cases are to the contrary. It has been rejected in the Restatement. It has no place in modern law." Eldredge, Modern Tort Problems, 203–04 (1911).

GOULD v. DeBEVE

United States Court of Appeals, District of Columbia Circuit, 1964.
330 F.2d 826.

McGOWAN, CIRCUIT JUDGE. In a complaint filed in the District Court, two causes of action were asserted in respect of the fall by a small boy, 2½ years old at the time of the accident, from the third-floor window of an apartment house. * * * The principal issue on this appeal is whether the trial court, after having found the boy to be a trespasser upon defendants' premises as a matter of law, erred in permitting the jury to pass upon the question of defendants' liability to him. We hold this not to have been error * * *.

I

Defendants are the owners and operators of rental housing accommodations. In March of 1960, they leased an apartment to one Mrs. Dodd for use by her and her two children. In June of 1960, Mrs. DeBeve and her son Jacques (the boy subsequently injured) came to stay with Mrs. Dodd temporarily. Shortly thereafter Mrs. DeBeve decided to remain indefinitely, under an arrangement with Mrs. Dodd whereby the latter was reimbursed for one-half of the rent paid by her to defendants. This arrangement was not made known to defendants nor consented to by them in any way. It was, in fact, contrary to a provision in Mrs. Dodd's lease which restricted permanent occupancy to Mrs. Dodd and her family; and it was because of this lease provision that the trial court ruled the two and one-half year-old boy to be a trespasser in legal contemplation.

The accident occurred July 6, 1960. The DeBeve boy and the Dodd children (aged approximately three and five) were getting dressed for bed in one of the bedrooms, and Mrs. Dodd and Mrs. DeBeve were seated in an adjoining room. A bed was next to the window, which was open but with a screen in place. Suddenly one of the Dodd children screamed and said "Jackie fell." On entering the bedroom, the mothers found the screen gone from the window and the DeBeve boy fallen through the window to the ground three floors below.

There was uncontradicted testimony to the effect that the screen was warped and cracked, and that it did not fit securely into the grooves in the window frame because of the rotting away of the latter. The screen had fallen or been knocked by a child from the window on earlier occasions; and there was testimony by Mrs. Dodd, corroborated by Mrs. DeBeve, that the former had on several occasions notified defendants of the hazard represented by the screen and urgently requested that suitable repair or replacement be made. The absence of any response to these appeals had caused the window to be kept closed as a safety measure, but it was open on July 6—the day of the injury—because of the extreme heat. The lease obligated the landlord to make all repairs required on the premises, except those necessitated by damage caused by the tenants.

II

These, then, are the circumstances in which the trial court accorded the status of trespasser to the $2\frac{1}{2}$ year-old boy and proceeded to define the legal obligations owed to him in that capacity by defendants. There is no attack here upon the finding of trespass and, for purposes of this appeal, we must accept it as technically accurate. But, on these facts, we are vividly reminded that the concept of trespass, like other legal abstractions, casts its net very widely indeed, and that meaningful classification for particular purposes can only begin after the catch and not before. There are, obviously, trespassers and trespassers. The poacher upon the manorial estate of 18th Century England—that figure about whom revolved so much of the developing law of landowners' liabilities to unauthorized visitors—defies identification with the child in this case, albeit a common legal label has been affixed to them. The manifest differences between them suggest strongly that projecting the label from the one to the other can not rationally be an automatic determinant of the result in each case in which injuries attributable to the landlord have been sustained.

But, as the appellee here does not resist the designation given him by the trial court, so the appellants do not quarrel with the court's instructions to the jury as to the measure of the duty owed by a landlord to a trespasser. These were lengthy and detailed and may best be described in the court's own culminating words:

> "[The plaintiffs] must prove by a fair preponderance of the evidence that the defendant was guilty of wilful or wanton misconduct which proximately caused the injuries to the child. * * * [W]ilful or wanton misconduct is defined as wilfully performing or wilfully failing to perform any act with knowledge that the performance or non-performance of that act was likely to result in injury, or performing or not performing that act with ruthless and wanton disregard of its probable consequence."

Appellants complain, we repeat, not of what was said to the jury by way of definition of their duty, but of the opportunity given the jury to weigh that definition against the proof produced. The contention, in short, is that, on the evidence received, no jury could rationally find a level of fault rising to that established in the instructions. We are no more persuaded of this than was the trial judge.

Defendants were in the business of owning and operating rental housing. By their own contractual undertaking, as well as by reason of legislative command, they were obligated to provide and maintain decent and safe quarters where ordinary life might go on. That obligation certainly comprehends, in the Washington summer when windows must be raised, screens which keep flies out and young children in. There was substantial evidence that the screen was defective in respect of its safety function; and there was also corroborated testimony (which appellants in their brief say "for purposes of this appeal must be conceded as true") that defendants had repeatedly been notified of the dangerous condition of the screen and requested to discharge their obligations with respect to it. These requests were ignored, and what was feared would happen did happen. We think a jury might well have concluded from these facts that defendants were guilty, in the language of the instruction, of "wilfully failing to perform [an] act with knowledge that * * * non-performance of that act was likely to result in injury." We think, in any event, that the trial court committed no error in leaving the matter to the jury to decide.

Had the DeBeve boy been one of Mrs. Dodd's children, there would seem to us to be little question as to the crystallization on the evidence of a jury issue. We do not think calling him a trespasser dictates a different result. He was well within the range of foreseeability in terms of those persons to whom injury might result from an unsafe screen, and, at least as to him, we do not think that the terms of the lease are the outer limits of defendants' vision. His mother might have been required to remove him and herself from continuing residence in the apartment, but he appears to us to be one of the many children, of differing legal relationships to the premises, who were likely to be physically present in it, and for whom the defective screen presented a hazard. To hold otherwise would be to ignore reality in favor of technicality in administering justice.

One who puts his land to profitable use by building apartments and inviting significant numbers of people to lead their lives therein inevitably takes on an aspect different from the country squire who wants mainly to be left alone on his rural acres. Those who come without express permission on the premises of each also have differing guises and purposes. Defining the liability of the one to the other cannot be divorced from the factual context, nor can the law be sensibly applied in this area without taking account of diverging circumstances. There obviously continue to be many situations where an intruder upon the property of another will not be covered by the law of negligence. All we hold here is that this 2½ year-old boy was not such an intruder upon defendants' premises as to be beyond the reach of defendants' duty to accommodate those premises safely to the incidents of normal living.

* * *

WILBUR K. MILLER, CIRCUIT JUDGE, dissenting.

The language and length of the foregoing opinion demonstrate the difficulty the majority met with in affirming a judgment which was based on sympathy instead of legal liability. In the circumstances, the appellant owed Mrs. DeBeve and her child no duty whatever with respect to screens; they were plainly trespassers, as the District Court said and as the majority opinion says.

Even as to an actual tenant, the appellants' only duty under § 2806 of the Housing Code was to provide screens which would effectively keep insects out. I think the majority err in adding another requirement: that owners of residential buildings must provide "screens which keep flies out and children in." This addition is unjustified under applicable regulations or otherwise. The notion that screens are to "keep children in" has no foundation whatever, as far as I know. The Housing Code does not require screens to be of such strength as to form protective barriers which will withstand the violent impact of a child's body. * * * The regulation here involved was promulgated, as its terms clearly show, to require screens for the protection of tenants against flies and mosquitoes during the season when such insects appear. It was not designed to prevent the sort of harm which occurred in this case: the safety of children was not its goal.

Leaving small children, unattended, to play on a bed placed beside an open third-story window, protected only by a screen which they knew to be defective, was an inexcusably reckless act on the part of the two mothers, but for which the unfortunate accident would not have occurred. It does not appear that the child would not have fallen if the screen had not been defective; this alone is enough to prevent recovery. Moreover, the screen involved in this case, though defective, was in place, serving its purpose of keeping out flies and mosquitoes; so § 2806 of the Housing Code was not violated.

I cannot agree to this opinion which imposes liability upon a landlord for injury sustained by a person to whom he owed no duty because a screen could not withstand violence it was not designed to meet. My view is that the judgment should be reversed * * *.

JONES v. BILLINGS

Supreme Court of Maine, 1972.
289 A.2d 39.

WEBBER, JUSTICE. Plaintiff brought action as personal representative of Michael L. Jones, deceased, seeking damages for the alleged wrongful death and conscious suffering of the decedent. The complaint alleges the deceased child, aged three years, climbed or fell into a cesspool on the premises of the defendant, negligently left open and unprotected by the defendant. The complaint does not recite the claimed status of the decedent on defendant's premises nor does it allege the nature of the duty claimed to be owed by the defendant to the decedent. The defendant elected to attack the complaint by a motion to dismiss for failure to state a claim on which relief can be granted, * * *. Without elaborating reasons for his action the Justice below granted the motion and dismissed the complaint. Plaintiff appeals.

* * *

The plaintiff * * * contends that, assuming arguendo that decedent is shown to have been a trespassing child, she should nevertheless be able to proceed on the theory of "attractive nuisance." This doctrine originated with the so-called "turntable cases" and was based upon the judicial fiction that the turntable or other similar hazardous condition attracts the young child and this enticement substitutes for an invitation and imposes upon the landowner the duties and obligations owed to an invitee. In a series of cases culminating in Lewis v. Mains (1954) 150 Me. 75, 104 A.2d 432 we have steadfastly declined to incorporate this fiction into our law. Our reluctance stemmed not from a stubborn adherence to a feudal concept that property rights are more sacred than the safety of children but rather from a serious doubt as to whether such a patently contrived fiction should be employed to lift from the shoulders of the parents their primary responsibility for the supervision and protection of their children and place that burden upon strangers. In an effort to avoid the fictional approach, the authors of the Restatement of the Law of Torts devised a rule which would forthrightly recognize the status of the child as a trespasser but would impose a duty upon the landowner *under carefully limited circumstances.* The suggested rule was further refined and is stated in the Restatement of the Law of Torts, 2d Ed., Vol. 2, Page 197, Sec. 339 as follows:

> "Sec. 339 Artificial Conditions Highly Dangerous to Trespassing Children
>
> "A possessor of land is subject to liability for physical harm to children trespassing thereon caused by an artificial condition upon the land if
>
> (a) the place where the condition exists is one upon which the possessor *knows or has reason to know* that children are likely to trespass, and
>
> (b) the condition is one of which the possessor knows or has reason to know and which he realizes or should realize will involve *an unreasonable risk of death or serious bodily harm* to such children, and
>
> (c) the children because of their youth do not discover the condition or realize the risk involved in intermeddling with it or in coming within the area made dangerous by it, and
>
> (d) the utility to the possessor of maintaining the condition and the burden of eliminating the danger are slight as compared with the risk to children involved, and
>
> (e) the possessor fails to exercise reasonable care to eliminate the danger or otherwise to protect the children." (Emphasis ours)

It is apparent that the Restatement Rule was very carefully stated so as to limit the duty owed by the possessors of property to trespassing children to specific and well defined situations. It was not to be equated with the obligation "to exercise ordinary care to keep the premises reasonably safe" since it applies only to conditions "which involve an unreasonable risk of death or serious bodily harm." For some time we have observed with interest the development of the law in the ever increasing number of states which have adopted the principles of the Restatement Rule. Our reluctance heretofore to change our position has stemmed in part from our recognition that courts which have adopted the Rule have been subjected to constant pressure to depart from or overlook the limitations on recovery which were so carefully built into the Rule by its authors. The application of the Rule by some courts to some fact situations has the practical effect of making the defendant an absolute insurer of the safety of trespassing children and of imposing a duty to "childproof" his premises, a result not within the contemplation of the Rule itself. On the other hand, we have become satisfied from a reading of the cases that when courts have vigilantly respected the limits of liability contemplated by the Rule and clearly stated therein, the burden imposed upon the possessor of property has not been intolerable or unjust. When the Rule is properly understood and applied, liability will attach only with respect to conditions involving an "unreasonable risk of death or serious bodily harm" and not to those innocuous conditions which are normally considered perfectly safe but which the ingenuity of the childish mind can sometimes convert to an instrument of harm.

We recognize that the adoption of the Restatement Rule is a radical departure from our prior case law. We think it important, therefore, to emphasize at the outset that we contemplate a careful adherence to the limitations imposed by the Rule itself. The element of foreseeability is important. It must be shown by preponderating proof that the possessor of land knows or has reason to know that children are likely to trespass in the area where the dangerous condition exists. As we have already noted, the duty is not the same as is owed to an invitee, that is, to exercise reasonable care to keep the premises reasonably safe. It is rather to exercise reasonable care to protect against dangerous conditions which *"involve an unreasonable risk of death or serious bodily harm."* The distinction is well illustrated by an application of the two rules to the facts presented in the recent case of Orr v. First National Stores, Inc. (1971–Me.) 280 A.2d 785. There the child was an invitee who was injured while playing on a guard rail in defendant's store. A divided Court held that it was a jury question as to whether under the existing circumstances the defendant had exercised reasonable care to keep the premises reasonably safe for its youthful invitee. If the child were a trespasser seeking recovery in an identical factual situation we would not view the rail, installed for the protection of customers and not structurally defective, as presenting an "unreasonable risk of death or serious bodily harm" to children within the meaning of the Restatement Rule as we interpret it. The authors of the Restatement Rule recognized that the element of invitation might properly add to the protective duty imposed upon the one issuing the invitation. The distinction found expression in the Restatement, Vol. 2, Page 223 wherein it was stated in Comment c, "Because of his status as * * * an invitee, the child may be entitled to greater protection than that afforded to a trespasser. This Section (Sec. 343B) is intended to say only that he is entitled to at least as much."

On balance we have finally concluded that the legitimate interests of children too immature to appreciate and guard against dangerous conditions which present an unreasonable risk of death or serious bodily harm require that we provide them with the protection afforded by a *strict interpretation* of the above quoted Restatement Rule. It follows that this plaintiff is entitled to proceed, if she so desires, to offer proof of facts which satisfy the several requirements of the Rule and warrant recovery thereunder. We are satisfied, however, that such an abrupt and drastic departure from our prior case law on the subject should be given only limited application in order to reduce transitional impact. This fatal accident is alleged to have occurred on November 29, 1969. The rule of liability herein announced with respect to trespassing children will be applied in other cases only if the injury causing event occurred on or after that date.

The entry will be

Appeal sustained. * * *

The court also noted:

> "We are aware that until recently Maine was one of only seven states which had not adopted either the "attractive nuisance" theory or the Restatement Rule. This number was reduced to six when the Rhode Island Court in Haddad v. First National Stores, Inc. (1971–R.I.) 280 A.2d 93 overruled its prior case law and adopted the Restatement Rule." (Id., footnote 4.)

The first Restatement required in section 339 that the dangerous artificial condition be one "of which the possessor knows or should know"; this was changed in the Restatement Second to "* * * knows or has reason to know."

As to the requirement of artificiality Restatement, Second contains a Caveat that the American Law Institute "expresses no opinion as to whether the rule stated in this Section [339] may not apply to natural conditions on the land." Some earlier cases excluded from section 339 coverage man-made conditions which "duplicate the work of nature and are not uncommon," including pools of water and sand piles, e. g., Knight v. Kaiser Co., 48 Cal.2d 778, 312 P.2d 1089 (1957); also see Haden v. Hockenberger & Chambers Co., 193 Neb. 713, 228 N.W.2d 883 (1975); compare, however, King v. Lennen, 53 Cal.2d 340, 1 Cal.Rptr. 665, 348 P.2d 98 (1959) (swimming pool deceptive as to depth, and presence of very small children, unlikely to appreciate the danger, foreseeable.)

The Supreme Court of Oregon has refused to extend section 339 liability to natural dangerous conditions, stating that it has found no case where any court has done so. The court relied in part on "public policy" based on state statutes which encourage landowners to make their land available to the public for recreation. One of those statutes, for instance, ORS 105.665, provides in part that

> "(1) An owner of land owes no duty of care to keep the land safe for entry or use by others for any recreational purpose or to give any warning of a dangerous condition, use, structure or activity on the land to persons entering thereon for any such purpose.
>
> "(2) An owner of land who either directly or indirectly invites or permits any person to use his land for any recreational purpose without charge does not thereby:
>
> > '(a) Extend any assurance that the land is safe for any purpose;
> >
> > '(b) Confer upon such person the legal status of an invitee or licensee to whom a duty of care is owed; or
> >
> > '(c) Assume responsibility for or incur liability for any injury, death or loss to any person or property caused by an act or omission of that person.' "

In Loney v. McPhillips, 268 Or. 378, 521 P.2d 340 (1974), the court ruled that a duty of care to trespassing children with respect to natural dangerous conditions "would tend toward the closure of private open-space land" and would accordingly "work adversely to the public policy of Oregon as declared by the Oregon legislature." Chief Justice O'Connell dissented on the ground that, while "the legislature has declared that it is in the interest of the public to provide outdoor recreation areas, * * * the legislature did not say that this public interest is to be served by insulating from liability landowners who expose children to unreasonable risks which could be avoided without undue or disproportionate expense to the landowner * * *. The extension of the attractive nuisance doctrine to natural conditions which are dangerous to children will not impose upon a defendant any greater burden to protect them than he has where the condition is created by him. In either case, the landowner has the burden only of taking reasonable precautions against exposing the child to danger, and in either case '* * * [i]f nothing effective can be done to protect him without undue and disproportionate trouble and expense to the defendant, there is no liability even for a clearly recognizable risk, demonstrated by past experience, that children may get into trouble, so long as the risk is not too extreme' [citing Prosser, Trespassing Children, 47 Calif.L.Rev. 427, 465 (1959)]."

Dangers from water, or from falling, are sometimes said to be outside the coverage of Restatement section 339 because they should be so obvious to a child that the risk is not "unreasonable" for purposes of paragraph (b) of the section. On the other hand it has been held that obviousness is not a defense where the occupier should anticipate that the danger would not be fully appreciated by a child, as when the child's attention is foreseeably distracted from the danger. Cargill, Incorporated v. Zimmer, 374 F.2d 924 (8th Cir. 1967).

EXCERPTS FROM OCCUPIERS' LIABILITY ACT 1957

(5 & 6 Eliz. 2 c. 31).

1.—(1) The rules enacted by the two next following sections shall have effect, in place of the rules of the common law, to regulate the duty which an occupier of premises owes to his visitors in respect of dangers due to the state of the premises or to things done or omitted to be done on them. * * *

2.—(1) An occupier of premises owes the same duty, the "common duty of care," to all his visitors, except in so far as he is free to and does extend, restrict, modify or exclude his duty to any visitor or visitors by agreement or otherwise.

(2) The common duty of care is a duty to take such care as in all the circumstances of the case is reasonable to see that the visitor will be reasonably safe in using the premises for the purposes for which he is invited or permitted by the occupier to be there.

(3) The circumstances relevant for the present purpose include the degree of care, and of want of care, which would ordinarily be looked for in such a visitor, so that (for example) in proper cases—

(a) an occupier must be prepared for children to be less careful than adults; and

(b) an occupier may expect that a person, in the exercise of his calling, will appreciate and guard against any special risks ordinarily incident to it, so far as the occupier leaves him free to do so.

(4) In determining whether the occupier of premises has discharged the common duty of care to a visitor, regard is to be had to all the circumstances, so that (for example)—

(a) where damage is caused to a visitor by a danger of which he had been warned by the occupier, the warning is not to be treated without more as absolving the occupier from liability, unless in all the circumstances it was enough to enable the visitor to be reasonably safe * * *

* * *

(6) For the purposes of this section, persons who enter premises for any purpose in the exercise of a right conferred by law are to be treated as permitted by the occupier to be there for that purpose, whether they in fact have his permission or not.

This Act provides for a common duty of care in England and Wales to visitors formerly classified as invitees or licensees, but not to common law trespassers.

Such a distinction in principle does not apply in Scotland, where Section 2(1) of the Occupiers Liability (Scotland) Act, 1960, requires an occupier "to show towards a person entering thereon * * * such care as in all the circumstances of the case is reasonable * * *." This section "* * * applies both to trespassers and to persons entering properly by invitation or license expressed or implied. But that does not mean that the occupier must always show equal care for the safety of all such persons. The care required is such care as is reasonable and it may be reasonable to require a greater degree of care in one such case than in another * * *. [I]t may often be reasonable to hold that an occupier must do more to protect a person whom he permits to be on his property than he need do to protect a person who enters his property without permission." McGlone v. British Railways Board, 1966 S.L.T. 2, 9 (H.L.Sc.) (speech of Lord Reid).

SMITH v. ARBAUGH'S RESTAURANT

United States Court of Appeals for the District of Columbia Circuit, 1972.
469 F.2d 97.

Before BAZELON, CHIEF JUDGE, and WRIGHT and LEVENTHAL, CIRCUIT JUDGES.

BAZELON, CHIEF JUDGE. This is an appeal from a jury verdict for the appellee after trial on appellant Smith's claim that Arbaugh's negligently maintained a set of greasy metal stairs on which he fell and was injured. The relevant facts are not in dispute.

On March 4, 1966, the appellant Ralph Smith, a Health Inspector in the employment of the District of Columbia, was directed by his supervisor to inspect the barbecue kitchen in appellee's restaurant. A grease fire had occurred in one of the barbecue pits several weeks previously, and the purpose of the inspection was to determine whether kitchen repairs had been completed.

The barbecue kitchen was located in the basement of a building adjacent to the premises of the actual restaurant. Large quantities of spareribs were barbecued in two pits in the basement, transported up approximately twenty metal steps and carried into the kitchen of the restaurant building to be stored before serving to patrons.

On his tour of inspection, appellant Smith descended these metal stairs to examine the barbecue pits. Just before reaching the bottom, his left foot skidded out from under him and he fell backwards, losing his grip on the handrail. Smith landed on his back and bounced to the bottom of the stairs. * * *

Smith and his wife commenced this action in the District Court seeking $65,000.00 in damages for personal injury and loss of consortium resulting from the negligence of the defendant corporation in creating, and failing to correct or warn the plaintiff of, a hazardous condition on its premises—namely, worn, wet and slippery metal steps with accumulated grease thereon. * * * Both Smith and his supervisor testified that they had observed grease on the steps, which were also smooth and rounded from continuous wear. James Lane, the barbecue cook, testified for the defendant and substantiated the story of Smith's fall. He also stated that cartons of uncooked spareribs were delivered to the barbecue kitchen twice a day. At the close of the trial, the jury returned a verdict in favor of the defendant.

Smith moved for a new trial on the grounds that the trial court erred in instructing the jury to determine for itself whether Smith was a "business invitee" or merely a "licensee" on Arbaugh's premises, and thus whether Arbaugh's owed him the duty of care to keep the premises reasonably safe or merely the duty of warning him of any known but concealed dangers. This motion was denied.

Smith maintained on appeal that the undisputed facts reveal the business purpose of his visit to Arbaugh's, and that therefore the trial court should have ruled as a matter of law that he was a "business invitee" toward whom Arbaugh's owed a duty of reasonable care. He contends that the verdict in favor of the defendant could have been based on the jury's erroneous decision that Smith was instead a "licensee" toward whom a lesser duty is owed, and that he is therefore entitled to a new trial with proper jury instructions.

I.

In examining this contention, we are once again struck by the awkwardness of fitting the circumstances of modern life into the rigid common law classifications of trespassers, licensees, and invitees. More importantly, we do not believe the rules of liability imposed by courts in the eighteenth century are today the proper tools with which to allocate the costs and risk of loss for human injury.

Ordinarily, liability for negligence is based on the failure to exercise reasonable care in the conduct of one's personal activities. However, the landowner/occupier's duty of care—the actions he should take by reason of dangerous conditions on his property—depends solely on the circumstances of the injured party's entry onto his property. To the trespasser, the landowner owes a duty only to refrain from intentional, wanton or willful conduct and from maintaining a "hidden engine of destruction." Toward a licensee, the landowner must refrain from active negligence, which includes failure to warn of known but hidden perils. Only for the invitee must the landowner exercise ordinary care and prudence to render his premises reasonably safe for the visit. These distinctions are crucial for a plaintiff's case, since whether Arbaugh's will be held liable for maintaining its greasy stairs will depend not on the jury's evaluation of this conduct, but largely on whether the injured party happened to be an employee, a Health Inspector, a fireman, a patron invited to the kitchen or simply a curious child.

Rather than continue to predicate liability on the status of the entrant, we have decided to join the modern trend [citing, inter alia, Rowland v. Christian, 69 Cal.2d 108, 70 Cal.Rptr. 97, 443 P.2d 561 (1968); Pickard v. City and County of Honolulu, 51 Haw. 134, 452

P.2d 445 (1969); Mile High Fence Co. v. Radovich, 489 P.2d 308 (Colo.S.Ct.1971)] and to apply ordinary principles of negligence to govern a landowner's conduct: A landowner must act as a reasonable man in maintaining his property in a reasonably safe condition in view of all the circumstances, including the likelihood of injury to others, the seriousness of the injury, and the burden of avoiding the risk.

II.

Almost fifteen years ago, the United States Supreme Court commented on the decreasing viability of the common law approach to landowner liability in a case dealing with a shipowner's duty to those aboard his vessel. In deciding whether to import into admiralty law the distinction between the duty owed an invitee and a licensee, Mr. Justice Stewart wrote for the Court:

> The distinctions which the common law draws between licensee and invitee were inherited from a culture deeply rooted to the land, a culture which traced many of its standards to a heritage of feudalism.
>
> * * *
>
> For the admiralty law at this late date to import such conceptual distinctions would be foreign to its traditions of simplicity and practicality. * * * [Such] appears particularly unwarranted when it is remembered that they originated under a legal system *in which status depended almost entirely upon the nature of the individual's estate with respect to real property*, a legal system in that respect entirely alien to the law of the sea. [Kermarec v. Compagnie Generale Transatlantique, 358 U.S. 625, at 630–632, 79 S.Ct. 406, at 410 (1959) (emphasis added).]

We believe that the common law classifications are now equally alien to modern tort law, primarily because they establish immunities from liability which no longer comport with accepted values and common experience. Perhaps the protection afforded to landowners by these rules was once perceived as necessary in view of the sparseness of land settlements, and the inability of owners to inspect or maintain distant holdings. The prestige and dominance of the landowning class in the nineteenth century contributed to the common law's emphasis on the economic and social importance of free use and exploitation of land over and above the personal safety of those who qualified as trespassers or licensees. [Citing, inter alia, 2 Harper and James, The Law of Torts, § 27.2 at 1432, n. 13].

Today, the preeminence of land over life is no longer accepted. Human safety may be more important than a landowner's unrestricted freedom. "A man's life or limb does not become less worthy of protection by the law nor a loss less worthy of compensation under the law because he has come upon the land of another without permission or with permission but without a business purpose." [Rowland v. Christian, 69 Cal.2d 108, 70 Cal.Rptr. 97, 443 P.2d 561, 568 (1968).]

This realignment of values is being recognized in all of tort law. There is a general trend away from immunities conferred on certain classes by reason of their technical status. The law of products' liability has become a field of strict liability, [citing Restatement Torts, Second § 402A and 2 Harper & James, The Law of Torts, §§ 28.15–.28] and there is continual movement away from *fault* as the governing principle for allocation of losses, in favor of enterprise liability or the distribution of losses over a larger segment of society through insurance. [citing Prosser, Torts, § 3 (3d ed. 1964) and 2 Harper & James §§ 13.1–.7] There is no sound reason to immunize landowners from the community's perception of values.

We do not believe, as the concurrence suggests, that the problem of allocating the costs and risks of human injury is a simple one. Nor do we believe that one value—human safety—should be advanced above all others. We recognize that the allocation of costs requires the resolution of a complex equation, one for which society has not as yet provided a computer. Rather, for centuries the costs of personal negligence have been allocated by a jury according to the standard of reasonable care under all the circumstances.

This court has frequently recognized that questions which involve moral and empirical judgments are best handled by representatives of the community as a whole, specifically in cases involving landowner responsibilities to children of tender years [citing McGettigan v. National Bank of Washington, 320 F.2d 703 (D.C.Cir. 1963)]. Therefore, in the absence of legislative action to the contrary, we believe that the most effective way to achieve an allocation of the costs of human injury which is acceptable to the community is to allow the jury to function under the standard of "reasonable care under all the circumstances."

If immunities from liability are to exist they should be based on consideration of factors which are relevant in modern society and unrelated to classifications of trespassers, licensees and invitees. In the words of the California Supreme Court, the jury should consider "the closeness of the connection between the injury and the defendant's conduct, the moral blame attached to the defendant's conduct, the policy of preventing future harm, and the prevalence and availability of insurance" [citing Rowland v. Christian, 69 Cal.2d 108, 70 Cal.Rptr. 97, 443 P.2d 561, 567 (1968)].

Beyond establishing immunities, the common law labels and the varying duties of care attached to them may have once provided relevant standards of foreseeability of presence to guide the jury in determining what was reasonable conduct for the landowner.

The realities of modern life teach us that these labels are today irrelevant to the jury's task. Personal status no longer depends on one's relation to real property. [citing Reich, The New Property, 73

Yale L.J. 731, 739 (1964).] With urbanized society comes closer living conditions and a more gregarious population. The trespasser who steps from a public sidewalk onto a private parking lot today is not the "outlaw" or "poacher" whose entry was both unanticipated and resented in the nineteenth century. It is contrary to reason to accept as a settled principle of law that a parking lot owner actually varies his conduct according to the status of those who walk across his boundaries.

III.

A further indication that the classifications have become increasingly difficult to apply is that the current trend in modern tort law is a process of erosion of the once sharply defined categories into "increasingly subtle verbal refinements, * * * subclassifications among traditional common-law categories, * * * [and] fine graduations in the standards of care which the landowner owes to each." [Kermarec v. Compagnie Generale Transatlantique, 358 U.S. 625, 630, 79 S.Ct. 406, 3 L.Ed.2d 550 (1959)] There are two reasons for this: first, the harsh results produced by rigid classification cause courts to broaden certain classifications and expand the duties owed; and second, this expansion has produced even further confusion and conflict and a toleration of exceptions which apply only to individual cases.

* * *

An examination of the law in the District reveals the difficulties which confront the courts. Harshness results because the essential task of judging a landowner's conduct under prevailing community standards is removed from the province of the jury. Through motions for dismissal, for directed verdicts, and for judgment notwithstanding the verdict, courts resolve the issue of liability solely on the facts which establish the status of the person injured. Mechanical legal decisions made by judges eliminate jury scrutiny of the actual conduct of the visitor and the landowner.

An unwillingness to tolerate harsh results has led courts to expand certain categories of visitors and to create overlap between them. We have drawn a distinction between "bare licensee" and "licensee by invitation" in order to extend the duty of reasonable care to injured parties who could not qualify as "invitees" under District of Columbia law. * * *

This court has also placed trespassers who diverge from public highways into the category of licensees because of the obvious absurdity of treating them as unforeseeable "wrongdoers" in the context of modern urban life. [Daisey v. Colonial Parking, Inc., 331 F. 2d 777 (D.C.Cir. 1963).]

In Gould v. DeBeve, [page 597 above] in order to uphold the obviously equitable verdict which the jury had returned in favor of a two-year old "trespasser" who fell out of a loosely screened window, this court recognized that "types" of trespassers exist and must be differentiated. The opinion indicated that the foreseeability of the child's presence might justify the imposition of a higher standard of care on the landowner than is usually owed to trespassers, but left the test of liability essentially unchanged. To our way of thinking, this approach will only generate further confusion over the duty owed to various "types" of trespassers. Some doubt already exists over the duty owed social guests and other licensees.

IV.

It is the genius of the common law that it recognizes changes in our social, economic, and moral life. Legal classifications such as trespasser and licensee are judicial creations which should be cast aside when they are no longer useful as controlling tools for the jury. The principle of stare decisis was not meant to keep a stranglehold on developments which are responsive to new values, experiences, and circumstances. In our opinion, the time has come to put an end to our total reliance on these common law labels and to allow the finder of fact to focus on whether the landowner has exercised "reasonable care under all the circumstances." That standard contains the flexibility necessary to allow the jury to take account of the infinite variety of fact situations which affect the foreseeability of presence and injury, and the balance of values which determines the allocation of the costs and risks of human injury.

Eliminating reliance on the common law classifications does not leave the jury awash, without standards to guide its determination of reasonable conduct. The principles which are now to be applied are those which have always governed personal negligence under our jurisprudence. The factors to be weighed in the determination of the degree of care demanded in a specific situation are "the likelihood that [the landowner's] conduct will injure others, taken with the seriousness of the injury if it happens, and balanced against the interest which [the landowner] must sacrifice to avoid the risk," [citing Conway v. O'Brien, 111 F.2d 611, 612 (2d Cir. 1940) (L. Hand, J.)].

Thus, we do not hold that landowners are now insurers of their property, or that they must endure unreasonable burdens to maintain it. We do hold that the status of an entrant onto the property is not solely determinative of the duty of care owed him.

Of course, the circumstances of the visitor's entry have some relation to the question of landowner liability. Foreseeability of the visitor's presence determines in part the likelihood of injury to him, and the extent of the interest which must be sacrificed to avoid the risk of injury.

Nor do we think that the status of the landowner should exclusively define the duty of care he owes to those who enter his property. The concurring opinion suggests that we apply the standard of "reasonable care under all the circumstances" to owners of business establishments but retain the common law classifications and duties for owners of residential property. Beyond creating new problems of drawing lines between these "types" of property-owners, such a distinction would also prolong the squabbles over the duty owed by homeowners to firemen vs. building inspectors, to door-to-door salesmen vs. habitual trespassers, to social guests who help with the housekeeping vs. those who don't—all of which seem exceedingly awkward attempts to fit the circumstances of modern life into common law categories.

Furthermore, the harsh results which the concurrence predicts upon application of the standard of reasonable care to homeowners of limited means and apartment dwellers need never occur. There is sufficient flexibility retained in the determination of what is reasonable "under all the circumstances" for the jury to avoid undue harshness. In certain cases there may well be, as Judge Leventhal would hold, "rough common sense" to the notion that a host should take no greater care of his social guests than of his own family. If so, the jury can find the host's conduct "reasonable." On the other hand, the jury might consider that a host must be more careful towards those who have no notice of any dangers or defects. Also, what might be a "reasonable" maintenance burden for one homeowner may require unreasonable sacrifices for another. We cannot set these standards in the abstract. All these considerations are crucial to the jury's evaluation of the degree of care demanded "under all the circumstances" of a specific situation.

All three factors to be balanced by the jury—the likelihood and seriousness of injury, and the sacrifice required to avoid the risk—"are practically not susceptible of any quantitative estimate, and the second two are generally not so, even theoretically. For this reason a solution always involves some preference, or choice between incommensurables, and it is consigned to a jury because their decision is thought most likely to accord with commonly accepted standards, real or fancied." [Citing Conway v. O'Brien, 111 F.2d 611, at 612 (2d Cir. 1940).]

Since we see our task in this field as being the promotion of the resolution of negligence disputes according to community standards of acceptable behavior, it is no more proper for us to dictate to the jury what standards govern owners of residential property than what governs owners of business property. The reasoning of our decision today admits of no distinctions between landowners, since what is "reasonable" for any landowner, of necessity, varies with the circumstances of each and every case.

Accordingly, appellant Smith is entitled to a new trial at which the jury is instructed that Arbaugh's owed him the duty of maintaining its property in a condition reasonably safe under all the circumstances. Whether or not Arbaugh's breached this duty is for the jury to resolve.

Reversed and remanded.

LEVENTHAL, CIRCUIT JUDGE, concurring.

The majority understands this case to pose a clear conflict in values: the value of human safety on the one hand, and the value of a landowner's unrestricted exploitation of his property on the other. With all respect, I believe this overly simplifies the issues. What is ultimately at issue here is not "people" versus "property," but rather how to allocate the costs and risk of loss for human injury.

Those who advocate change in the rules governing the liability of persons controlling real property frequently refer to the commercial and industrial necessities of modern life, and the strong differences from the pastoral life of yesteryear. I am completely convinced as to the reasons of policy which would lead the court to announce an end to the differential duties of a possessor of land with respect to trespassers, invitees or licensees, where the land is used as a business establishment. I am not so clear as to the broader sweep of the majority's rule. I therefore limit myself to concurring in the result, and to a separate statement of my reasons.

The use of the common law distinctions with respect to business establishments is mischievous because, in the context of a business establishment, it is generally almost impossible to tell the trespassers from the licensees, or either from the invitees. If a man scales the fence and uses my back yard as a shortcut, I have little difficulty in saying he is a trespasser, on my premises without my consent. But if he takes a shortcut through my parking lot or store, classification is beclouded. While a businessman may not prefer his premises to be used as a thoroughfare, he does value goodwill of individuals, often prospective customers. In the totality, such goodwill is a business asset. Given the probable ambiguity of the status of anyone on business property, I am satisfied that the proper rule in such circumstances is one which gives the jury broad latitude to affix liability under a general standard of reasonable care in all of the circumstances of the case. I assume it is understood that the "circumstances" of the case include the factual and legal relationships of the parties. Presumably the jury will not be awarding verdicts to burglars.

A second factor which underscores a change of rule as to business establishments is the matter of loss-distribution. The costs of foreseeable harms can, in a business context, be distributed among all customers by means of insurance or self-insurance.

However, this loss-distribution capability does not necessarily apply in nonbusiness situations. The occupier of residential property is not in a position to distribute either the costs of foreseeable losses or the cost of insurance against those losses. He must bear such costs himself.

Today's decision exposes many less-affluent homeowners—whose modest home represents their major capital asset—and apartment dwellers, to lawsuits not previously permitted, where there is no concealed defect—e. g., a sliding rug. It may increase the costs of insuring against such risks, and it may increase the risks of not insuring at all. This may not be sound public policy. Furthermore, the rule may be unwise insofar as it permits recoveries, where insurance is available, with the too-ready acquiescence of the owner or resident of the home or apartment. In the broad, I am concerned that this rule of law may furnish incentives for redressing loss through litigation, and a corresponding disincentive for persons to insure *themselves* against losses due to personal injury.

As to residential premises, while I see a good case for a rule that places business and social visitors on the same footing, I also discern some rough common-sense in the notion that a social guest, broadly, takes a host as he is, expecting that the host will take as much care of his guest as he takes of himself, and that he will point out latent defects. I certainly see some rough common sense in the broad notion that a householder has no legal duty, as to trespassers entering without his consent, to fill up holes and otherwise tidy up his property so that it is in reasonably safe condition—though this is a broad conception subject to limited exceptions. I do not find these principles "awkward * * * in the circumstances of modern life" or contrary to "accepted values and modern experience." Perhaps my difficulty is that I have not studied these problems deeply enough. But then, they are not involved in the case at bar, and were not argued.

COOPER v. GOODWIN

United States Court of Appeals, District of Columbia Circuit, 1973.
478 F.2d 653.

Before BAZELON, CHIEF JUDGE, SIMON E. SOBELOFF, SENIOR CIRCUIT JUDGE for the Fourth Circuit, and LEVENTHAL, CIRCUIT JUDGE.

BAZELON, CHIEF JUDGE. This is an appeal from a directed verdict for the appellees on appellant Cooper's claim that he was injured by reason of Mr. and Mrs. William Goodwin's negligent maintenance of their basement stairs. We reverse and remand this case for trial under the standard established by this court's opinion in Smith v. Arbaugh's Restaurant, Inc.

I.

The relevant facts are not in dispute. On November 26, 1967, the appellant Cooper was invited for a social visit at the home of his friends the Goodwins. At the conclusion of his call, the Goodwins indicated to Cooper that he should leave through the basement area of the house. As Cooper started to descend the final three stairs down into the basement, he slipped. He reached for a handrail, but there was none. He fell and injured his back. * * *

* * * [A]t the close of Cooper's case, the Goodwins moved for a directed verdict on the ground that since Cooper was a social

guest toward whom the homeowners owed only the duty of refraining from *active* negligence, no actionable negligence had been shown. The trial court agreed, * * *.

From this ruling, Cooper now appeals.

II.

This case illustrates the problems which, as we pointed out in our recent ruling in Smith v. Arbaugh's, result from rigid applications of the common law classifications of trespasser, licensee and invitee to determine the duty of care owed by a landowner/occupier to persons entering upon his property. Harshness inheres because the trial judge removed from the province of the jury the determination of crucial factual issues and resolved them himself. Confusion over the exact duty owed to Mr. Cooper, a social guest responding to an explicit invitation to use the basement stairs, is apparent in the cases cited by counsel for their respective contentions. The trial court undoubtedly relied on the legal rule that a social guest may recover for active negligence only. This ruling, while it may have once comported with existing case law, we now hold to be in error.

The standard adopted in *Smith*—that "a landowner must act as a reasonable man in maintaining his property in a reasonably safe condition in view of all the circumstances," seeks to eliminate the harshness of and confusion over the common law classifications. Furthermore, as discussed in *Smith,* we believe that this standard places the crucial determination—whether Cooper suffered from an unfortunate accident, from his own carelessness, or from the Goodwins' negligence—where it should be, with the jury and not the court. It is for the jury to consider and weigh *all the circumstances* of Cooper's fall, including those which affect the foreseeability of the injury, the burden of avoiding the injury, and the care which appellant as a reasonable man could be expected to take for his own safety. [Note by the Court: "It would appear, although we need not decide, that the question of what degree of care should be exercised toward those traditionally labelled "trespassers" will, under the logic of this standard, depend to a large extent on the foreseeability of their presence and hence the foreseeability of the injury."]

There may be some concern that less-affluent home owners and apartment dwellers will be severely penalized for the hazards of their dwelling places which they cannot afford to repair or remove. However, the financial capacity of the occupant to undertake safety precautions should be taken into account in determining what was, for him, reasonable maintenance conduct. Financial hardship should be no excuse for failing to take those measures which are within a defendant's capacity—for example, an adequate warning. Despite the fears expressed in the concurrence, both this and the *Smith* opinion hold that the duty to maintain one's property might be fully discharged by a warning of a dangerous condition. We are therefore not persuaded that owners of residential property should be excluded from the standard of reasonable care under all the circumstances.

Under this standard, the jury will have wide latitude to exercise its own rough common sense as to the degree of care which was reasonable for particular home owners or dwellers to take toward their guests. As we said in *Smith* this standard cannot be set in the abstract but will vary according to the circumstances of each and every case. Rather than rely on rigid labels and rules of law to provide the illusion of certainty and fairness, we choose the jury as the mature institution to take account of the infinite variety of fact situations which affect the reasonableness of human conduct.

Accordingly, appellant Cooper is entitled to a new trial at which the jury is instructed that the Goodwins owed him the duty of maintaining their property in a condition reasonably safe under all the circumstances. Whether or not the Goodwins breached this duty is a question for the jury.

* * *

LEVENTHAL, CIRCUIT JUDGE, concurring:

* * *

* * * I agree with the majority that the sound evolution that is the hallmark of the common law has brought it at the present time to the point where the traditional distinction between licensees and invitees is properly considered the relic of a bygone age. * * * [This] concept * * * has been applied in the United States by the Supreme Court in an admiralty decision, [citing Kermaric v. Compagnie Generale Transatlantique, supra.] and then by the courts of California, Hawaii, Colorado, and recently, after our *Smith* opinion, by the Minnesota Supreme Court. [Citing Peterson v. Balach, 294 Minn. 161, 199 N.W.2d 639 (1972).]

This does not, however, mean that the requirements of judicial administration in a modern, largely urban, industrialized society necessarily extend so far as to require a change in the liability of an occupant of land to a trespasser. I would follow the example of the Minnesota court, and defer, as a separate question, the issue of liability to trespassers, which was left unchanged in England. This was the problem that particularly prompted my separate opinion in *Smith.* The restraint counseled by the Minnesota court, on the ground that the issue of a plaintiff-trespasser was not before the court, is enhanced as to this court by the circumstances that it is no longer the authoritative expositor of the common law of the District of Columbia. So long as our modification of doctrine is not automatically extended for the benefit of trespassers, I agree that the general statement of doctrine need not distinguish between business and residential properties. In the case of trespassers, a higher duty may rightly be put on the occupier of a business property by virtue of both accessibility of insurance and the business reasons that tolerate what is technically a trespass. As for the majority's comment that owners of residences may soundly be put under an obligation to trespassers because the owners' financial position can be taken into account, if this means what it says, and owners of side-by-side residences may have different legal obligations depending on their financial means, it is an extraordinary statement for a judicial opinion, and in my view it is, as stated, an unsound proposition.

I don't think it is proper to instruct the jury that the Goodwins owed plaintiff Cooper "the duty of maintaining their property in a condition reasonably safe under all the circumstances." To begin with, language should be selected so as to provide in the direct statement of the rule for awareness that the liability may be discharged by giving a warning. More important, I would limit myself, at this time, to a statement of duty that is focused both on a person invited or permitted on the premises and on his reasonably expected use. I would follow the Minnesota opinion: * * *, and instruct the jury that a person who occupies land (or is otherwise responsible for its condition) has the duty to take such care, as in all the circumstances of the case is reasonable, to see that any person invited or permitted on the premises will be reasonably safe in using the premises for a purpose that was reasonably to be expected.

SOBELOFF, SENIOR CIRCUIT JUDGE, concurring:

My brethren, Judges Bazelon and Leventhal, are in agreement that the traditional distinctions between licensees and invitees are an archaic remnant of the common law and tend to confuse rather than assist in reaching a just resolution of disputed questions of liability. They agree further that with regard to all but trespassers no distinction should be made in the standard used to adjudicate the liability of occupiers of business and the occupiers of residential properties. In these sentiments, I fully concur.

Judge Bazelon would have the trial judge instruct the jury that the Goodwins owed Cooper "the duty of maintaining their property in a condition reasonably safe under all the circumstances." Judge Leventhal, on the other hand, would phrase this instruction as "the duty to take such care, as in all circumstances is reasonable, to see that any person invited or permitted on the premises will be reasonably safe in using the premises for a purpose that was reasonably to be expected." In respect to all but the question of the duty owed a trespasser, I see no meaningful distinction between the two formulations, although Judge Bazelon's seems preferable as it is a simpler, more lucid explanation of the law and will be more easily understood by a jury. Under either proposed instruction, the jury is to consider in its deliberations all the circumstances surrounding the injury.

Only on the question of liability to a trespasser do Judges Bazelon and Leventhal lock horns. Judge Bazelon would extend the "all the circumstances" test to include the duty of care owed a trespasser. * * * Judge Leventhal seemingly would have the circumstances test govern only the liability to trespassers upon business property, but would maintain the rule that "a householder has no legal duty, as to trespassers entering without his consent, * * * subject to limited exceptions." Actually, the question of the degree of care owed by property owners to trespassers is not presented in this case; it was neither briefed nor argued. The discussion about the duty to trespassers is entirely gratuitous and without foundation in the record. I would refrain, under these circumstances from fully endorsing the position of either of my two distinguished colleagues in respect to the property owner's liability to trespassers and would defer deciding this question until it is properly before the court and has been maturely developed in briefs and arguments upon a record that squarely raises the issue.

In MOUNSEY v. ELLARD, Mass., 297 N.E.2d 43 (1973), plaintiff was a police officer, on duty, who was injured on defendant's premises. The court reversed a directed verdict for the allegedly negligent defendant. Citing Smith v. Arbaugh's Restaurant, Inc., inter alia, it stated: "[W]e no longer follow the common law distinction between licensees and invitees and, instead, create a common duty of reasonable care which the occupier owes to all lawful visitors." In footnote No. 7, the court went on to say:

> "We feel that there is significant difference in the legal status of one who trespasses on another's land as opposed to one who is on the land under some color of right—such as a licensee or invitee. For this reason, among others, we do not believe they should be placed in the same legal category. For example, one who jumps over a six foot fence to make use of his neighbor's swimming pool in his absence does not logically belong in the same legal classification as a licensee or invitee. Frankly, we are not persuaded as to the logic and reasoning in Rowland v. Christian, 69 Cal.2d 108, 70 Cal.Rptr. 97, 443 P.2d 561, in placing trespassers in the same legal status as licensees and invitees. The possible difference in classes of trespassers is miniscule compared to the others. These differences can be considered when they arise in future cases."

JUSTICE KAPLAN concurred in a separate opinion:

> "I go along with the court but I am taken somewhat aback by footnote 7 which seems unfaithful to the rest of the opinion. The court holds that the measure of responsibility of an occupier should no longer depend on whether the injured person is characterized as a 'licensee' rather than an 'invitee,' or vice versa; the question is to turn on other, more vital factors. But footnote 7 seems to say that 'trespassers' stand apart, that that characterization is to remain decisive or highly influential. This tends to perpetuate, although on a smaller scale, the kind of tradition-bound and mistaken analysis that I had supposed the court was aiming to correct.

For it is sometimes just as hard to distinguish trespassers from licensees or invitees, as to distinguish licensees from invitees; and the class of trespassers is probably just as various as either of the other classes. The very effort at dry classification and differentiation puts the emphasis at the wrong places. Thus it is awkward to leave the suggestion that the basic reasoning of the court's opinion may stop short of so called trespassers. See Rowland v. Christian, 69 Cal.2d 108, 70 Cal.Rptr. 97, 443 P.2d 561, and note the unsatisfactory condition of English law as to trespassers after they were excluded from the Occupiers' Liability Act, 1957 * * *. Millner, Negligence in Modern Law, c. 1, p. 11, c. 2, pp. 47–54 (1967). North, Occupiers' Liability, c. 11 (1971). Herrington v. British Rys. Bd. [1971] 2 Q.B. 107, affd. sub nom. British Rys. Bd. v. Herrington [1972] A.C. 877."

BRITISH RAILWAYS BOARD v. HERRINGTON

House of Lords.
[1972] A.C. 877.

LORD REID, My Lords, on June 7, 1965, the respondent, then a child of six years old, was playing with other children on National Trust property at Mitcham which is open to the public. Immediately adjoining this property the appellants have an electrified railway line a few yards from the boundary. Their boundary is marked by a fence which, if it had been in good repair, would have sufficed to prevent the respondent from reaching the railway line. But it was in very bad repair so that when the respondent strayed away from his playmates he was able to get through or over it. He then went a few yards farther and came in contact with the live electrified rail. * * *

The appellants' main contention is that they owed no duty to this child. They found on the leading case Robert Addie & Sons (Collieries) Ltd. v. Dumbreck [1929] A.C. 358. * * *

The speeches in this House in *Addie's* case appear to me to be intended to lay down a general rule that no occupier is under any duty to potential trespassers, whether adults or children, to do anything to protect them from danger on his land, however likely it may be that they will come and run into danger and however lethal the danger may be. * * *

The first matter to be determined is the nature of the duty owed by occupiers to trespassers. * * *

* * * Normally the common law applies an objective test. If a person chooses to assume a relationship with members of the public, say by setting out to drive a car or to erect a building fronting a highway, the law requires him to conduct himself as a reasonable man with adequate skill, knowledge and resources would do. He will not be heard to say that in fact he could not attain that standard.

If he cannot attain that standard he ought not to assume the responsibility which that relationship involves. But an occupier does not voluntarily assume a relationship with trespassers. By trespassing they force a "neighbour" relationship on him. When they do so he must act in a humane manner—that is not asking too much of him—but I do not see why he should be required to do more.

So it appears to me than an occupier's duty to trespassers must vary according to his knowledge, ability and resources. It has often been said that trespassers must take the land as they find it. I would rather say that they must take the occupier as they find him.

So the question whether an occupier is liable in respect of an accident to a trespasser on his land would depend on whether a conscientious humane man with his knowledge, skill and resources could reasonably have been expected to have done or refrained from doing before the accident something which would have avoided it. * * *

LORD WILBERFORCE. * * * We have not, in England, any general law as to public enterprise liability. * * * So if the plaintiff is to recover, he must rely on our outdated law of fault liability. * * *

* * * Just as in the 19th century the introduction of turntables, attractive to children, accessible and dangerous, gave rise to a jurisprudence known by their name, so we must take account of the placing of electrical conductors above or on the ground all over our overcrowded island and see where this leads as regards foresight and care. The ingredients of such duty as may arise must stem from the inevitable proximity to places of access, including highways, from the continuous nature of the danger, from the lethal danger of contact and from the fact that to children the danger may not be apparent. There is no duty to make the place safe, but a duty does arise because of the existence, near to the public, of a dangerous situation. The greater the proximity, the greater the risk, and correspondingly the need of foresight and a duty of care.

* * * What is reasonable depends on the nature and degree of the danger. It also depends on the difficulty and expense of guarding against it. The law, in this context, takes account of the means and resources of the occupier or other person in control—what is reasonable for a railway company may be very unreasonable for a farmer, or (if this is relevant) a small contractor. * * *

* * * I am left with the feeling that cases such as these would be more satisfactorily dealt with by a modern system of public enterprise liability devised by Parliament. * * *

LORD PEARSON. * * * In my opinion, the occupier of premises * * * does *not* owe to the trespasser a duty to take such care as in all the circumstances of the case is reasonable to see that the trespasser will be reasonably safe in using the premises for the purposes for which he is trespassing. * * *

It does not follow that the occupier never owes any duty to the trespasser. If the presence of the trespasser is known to or reasonably to be anticipated by the occupier, then the occupier has a duty to the trespasser, but it is a lower and less onerous duty than the one which the occupier owes to a lawful visitor. Very broadly stated, it is a duty to treat the trespasser with ordinary humanity. * * * [I]t is normally sufficient for the occupier to make reasonable endeavours to keep out or chase off the potential or actual intruder who is likely to be or is in a dangerous situation. The erection and maintenance of suitable notice boards or fencing or both, or the giving of suitable oral warning, or a practice of chasing away trespassing children, will usually constitute reasonable endeavours for this purpose. * * * If the trespasser, in spite of the occupier's reasonable endeavours to deter him, insists on trespassing or continuing his trespass, he must take the condition of the land and the operations on the land as he finds them. * * * But that statement is subject to this proviso: if the occupier knows or as good as knows that some emergency has arisen whereby the trespasser has been placed in a position of imminent peril, ordinary humanity requires further steps to be taken. * * *

There are several reasons why an occupier should not have imposed upon him onerous obligations to a trespasser—

(1) There is the unpredictability of the possible trespasser both as to whether he will come on the land at all and also as to where he will go and what he will do if he does come on the land. * * * Occupiers are entitled to farm lands, operate quarries and factories, run express trains at full speed through stations, fell trees and fire shots without regard to the mere general possibility that there might happen to be in the vicinity a trespasser who might be injured. * * *

(3) It would in many, if not most, cases be impracticable to take effective steps to prevent (instead of merely endeavouring to deter) trespassers from going into or remaining in situations of danger. The cost of erecting and maintaining an impenetrable and unclimbable or, as it has been put, "boy-proof" fence would be prohibitive, if it could be done at all. * * *

(4) There is also a moral aspect. Apart from trespasses which are inadvertent or more or less excusable, trespassing is a form of misbehaviour, showing lack of consideration for the rights of others. It would be unfair if trespassers could by their misbehaviour impose onerous obligations on others. One can take the case of a farmer. He may know well from past experience that persons are likely to trespass on his land for the purpose of tearing up his primroses and bluebells, or picking his mushrooms or stealing his turkeys, or for the purpose of taking country walks in the course of which they will tread down his grass and leave gates open and watch their dogs chasing the farmer's cattle and sheep. It would be intolerable if a farmer had to take expensive precautions for the protection of such persons in such activities. * * *

In my opinion the Addie v. Dumbreck formulation of the duty of occupier to trespasser is plainly inadequate for modern conditions, and its rigid and restrictive character has impeded the proper development of the common law in this field. It has become an anomaly and should be discarded. But in my opinion the duty of occupier to trespasser should remain limited. * * *

[Generally concurring opinions of LORD MORRIS of Borth-y-Gest and LORD DIPLOCK omitted.]

Lord Denning M.R. summarized his understanding of *Herrington's* case in Pannett v. McGuinness & Co. [1972] 3 W.L.R. 386, 389–91, C.A. (construction contractor held liable to 5-year old trespasser who had previously been chased off site several times, where contractor set rubbish fire and stationed men to chase off children, but they neglected to do so):

> "The long and short of it is that you have to take into account all the circumstances of the case and see then whether the occupier ought to have done more than he did. (1) You must apply your common sense. You must take into account the gravity and likelihood of the probable injury. Ultra-hazardous activities require a man to be ultra-cautious in carrying them out. The more dangerous the activity, the more he should take steps to see that no one is injured by it. (2) You must take into account also the character of the intrusion by the trespasser. A wandering child or a straying adult stands in a different position from a poacher or a burglar. You may expect a child when you may not expect a burglar. (3) You must also have regard to the nature of the place where the trespass occurs. An electrified railway line or a warehouse being demolished may require more precautions to be taken than a private house. (4) You must also take into account the knowledge which the defendant has, or ought to have of the likelihood of trespassers being present. The more likely they are, the more precautions may have to be taken."

The Privy Council has also attempted to formulate a special "humanitarian" duty toward trespassers, broader than *Addie* but different from the duty toward lawful visitors, Southern Portland Cement Ltd. v. Cooper [1974] 2 W.L.R. 152 (again through Lord Reid):

> "Their Lordships are breaking no new ground in holding that the nature and extent of an occupier's duty to a trespasser must be based on considerations of humanity. As long ago as 1820 in Holt v. Wilkes (1820) 3 B. & Ald. 304, a case dealing with injury to a trespasser by a spring gun. Best J. said, at p. 319: "the law of England will not

sanction what is inconsistent with humanity." In Grand Trunk Railways Co. of Canada v. Barnett [1911] A.C. 361, the judgment of the Board refers, at p. 370, to "wilful or reckless disregard of ordinary humanity rather than mere absence of reasonable care."

"Next comes the question to whom does the occupier owe a duty. Their Lordships have * * * rejected the view that no duty is owed unless the advent of a trespasser is extremely probable. It was argued that the duty could be limited to cases where the coming of trespassers is more probable than not. Their Lordships can find neither principle nor authority nor any practical reason to justify such a limitation. The only rational or practical answer would seem to be that the occupier is entitled to neglect a bare possibility that trespassers may come to a particular place on his land but is bound at least to give consideration to the matter when he knows facts which show a substantial chance that they may come there. * * *

"The problem then is to determine what would have been the decision of a humane man with the financial and other limitations of the occupier."

The preceding cases deal with the special privileges or defenses available to a defendant on the ground that he was in possession of the premises on which the plaintiff was hurt. It is the possessor or occupant who has the legally protected interest of exclusive possession which entitles him to exclude or admit others on the land. See Restatement, Torts, Chapter 7. Frequently there is no occasion to differentiate between owner and possessor, as when the owner is also the occupant or when the land is unoccupied. But frequently, too, the owner and possessor are different persons, as for example, in the cases below in this chapter which deal with the liability of the lessor of premises occupied by a lessee.

In Humphrey v. Twinstate Gas & Electric Co., 100 Vt. 414, 139 A. 440, 56 A.L.R. 1011 (1927), plaintiff was hurt by coming in contact with a wire fence which became charged with electricity through the fall of electric wires strung over the land by the defendant with the permission of Thomas, the owner or occupant of the land. Defendant resisted the suit on the ground that plaintiff was a trespasser on the land. Said the court: "We do not stop to consider this question. He was not an invitee, and for the purposes of this discussion we will assume that he was a trespasser. Being such, he could recover nothing from Thomas for injuries resulting from the condition of the premises, though these existed through the latter's carelessness. This result follows from the fact that Thomas owned him no duty to keep the premises safe for his unlawful use. The defendant takes the position that, so far as the plaintiff's rights go, it stands in Thomas' position and can make the same defense that he could; that it owed the plaintiff no duty, and consequently any negligence proved against it is not actionable so far as the plaintiff can assert. * * * The object of the law being to safeguard and protect the various rights in land, it is obviously going quite far enough to limit the immunity to the one whose rights have been invaded. Nor does logic or justice require more. A trespass is an injury to the possession; and as it is only he whose possession is disturbed who can sue therefor, so it should be that he, alone, could assert the unlawful invasion when suit is brought by an injured trespasser. One should not be allowed 'to defend an indefensible act' by showing that the party injured was engaged in doing something which, as to a third person, was unlawful. Authorities sustaining this view of the law are not wanting." But see McPheters v. Loomis, 125 Conn. 526, 7 A.2d 437 (1939).

According to the Restatement of Torts, Second §§ 382–385, the rules relating to the liability or immunity of the possessor of land apply also to "members of the household" of the possessor, and to others "acting on his behalf." Trespassers are subject to liability (1) to the possessor and members of his household, regardless of negligence, for physical harm caused by "any act done, activity carried on or condition created" by the trespasser while upon the land (Section 162) and (2) to anyone whom the trespasser "should recognize as likely to be on the land," for physical harm caused by such act, activity or condition, "which he should recognize as involving an unreasonable risk of causing such harm" (Section 381).

The notions of trespass, license and invitation have been employed also with reference to property other than land. See, for example, Falardeau v. Malden & Melrose Cas. Co., 275 Mass. 196, 175 N.E. 474 (1931) and cf. Lynch v. Nurdin, supra, p. 589.

We are concerned in this chapter with cases in which the plaintiff is hurt on the defendant's premises. If the plaintiff is outside the defendant's premises when he is hurt by some act or force from the defendant's land, liability is said to be governed by the general principles disclosed in the preceding chapters and the defendant enjoys no special immunity as land occupier. His use of the land may of course be a factor in appraising the social utility of his conduct in the light of the risks involved. For the liability for harm to persons outside the land, see Restatement of Torts, Second §§ 363–379A, 382–387. But in some cases, though the harm occurs on defendant's land, defendant is deprived of the immunities incident to his possession and is held to the standard of reasonable care because the land appears to be a public highway or the dangerous condition is so close to a public highway or the land of another that there is an unreasonable risk that persons thereon will accidentally deviate and be hurt by the condition. See Holmes v. Drew, 151 Mass. 578, 25 N.E. 22 (1890); White v. Suncook Mills, 91 N.H. 92, 13 A.2d 729 (1940); Restatement of Torts, Second §§ 367–369.

In some cases, a defendant is held liable for his failure to protect the plaintiff from the harmful conduct of third persons. This duty to protect is in some cases, thought to be incident to the defendant's possession of land. For example, in the chapter of the Torts Restatement dealing with the "liability for condition and use of land" is section 344, which states that "a possessor of land who holds it open to the public for entry for his business purposes is subject to liability" under stated circumstances for bodily harm caused to members of the public while on the land for such a purpose by "the accidental, negligent or intentionally harmful acts of third persons or animals." And see Mastad v. Swedish Brethren, 83 Minn. 40, 85 N.W. 913, 53 L.R.A. 803, 85 Am.St.Rep. 446 (1901); Sinn v. Farmers' Deposit Savings Bank, 300 Pa. 85, 150 A. 163 (1930); Barnes v. J. C. Penney Co., 190 Wash. 633, 70 P.2d 311 (1937); Corcoran v. McNeal, 400 Pa. 14, 161 A.2d 367 (1960). The courts have been generous to patrons of enterprises, like carriers, which traditionally are subjected to a "high duty of care", e. g., Neering v. Illinois Central R. R. Co., 383 Ill. 366, 50 N.E.2d 497 (1943) (passenger assaulted while waiting for train) and like innkeepers (see Annotation, "Liability of innkeeper, restauranteur, or tavern keeper for injury occurring on or about premises to guest or patron by person other than proprietor or his servant, 70 A.L.R.2d 628). They have been less generous to customers injured in bank hold-ups, Boyd v. Racine Currency Exchange, 56 Ill.2d 95, 306 N.E.2d 39 (1973) (teller under no duty to accede to robber's demands, when robber held gun to head of customer, plaintiff's decedent), and Nigido v. First National Bank of Baltimore, 264 Md. 702, 288 A.2d 127 (1972). Also see Lee v. National League Baseball Club of Milwaukee, 4 Wis.2d 168, 89 N.W.2d 811 (1958) (proprietor of sports arena responsible for reasonable care to protect patrons from disturbances); Goldberg v. Housing Authority of Newark, 38 N.J.2d 578, 186 A.2d 291 (1962) (owner of multi-family structure not responsible for failure to protect milk delivery man); Compare Braitman v. Overlook Terrace Corp., 68 N.J. 368, 346 A.2d 76 (1975); Kline v. 1500 Massachusetts Ave. Apt. Corp., 439 F.2d 477 (D.C.Cir.1970) noted at page 643 below. Compare "duty to control conduct of third persons" Restatement of Torts, Second §§ 315–320. Of course the defendant's possession of the premises is a necessary condition in the situation. But it seems more intelligible to think of the liability as incident to defendant's business and his business relation to the plaintiff rather than to his status as land occupant. The third person in such a case is of course also subject to liability.

The defendant's duty as owner or occupier of premises to exercise proper care to put or keep the premises in a properly safe condition is said to be in some circumstances non-delegable. This does not mean, of course, that defendant may not employ another to do the required work. It means rather that defendant remains subject to liability for harm caused even though the culpable misconduct is that of the person employed to do the work and even though that person is an independent contractor rather than an employee of defendant. See

Misiulis v. Mibrand Maintenance Corp., 52 Mich.App. 494, 218 N.W.2d 68 (Mich.App.1974); Besner v. Central Trust Co. of New York, 230 N.Y. 357, 130 N.E. 577, 23 A.L.R. 1081 (1921); 31 Yale L.J. 99; Restatement of Torts, Second § 422. Compare the vicarious liability for the misconduct of an independent contractor in the course of so-called abnormally dangerous activity, Restatement of Torts, Second § 427A.

"The duty of maintaining a highway [including sidewalks] in a condition safe for travel is, in America, in some States by statute and in others by common law, placed upon the municipal subdivision which holds the highway open to the public for travel." Restatement, Torts, section 349, Comment b. That appears to be true whether title to the land is in the municipality or in the private person who owns also the abutting land. Accordingly section 349 states that the possessor of land is not subject to liability for failure to maintain the highway in safe condition or to warn of dangerous conditions thereon, unless (section 350) the dangerous condition is "created in the highway by him for his sole benefit subsequent to dedication." See Gabrielsen v. City of Seattle, 150 Wash. 157, 272 P. 723, 63 A.L.R. 200 (1928); Washington Gaslight Co. v. District of Columbia, 161 U.S. 316, 16 S.Ct. 564, 40 L.Ed. 712 (1895); Callaway v. Newman Mercantile Co., 321 Mo. 766, 12 S.W.2d 491, 62 A.L.R. 1056 (1928); Korricks Dry Goods Co. v. Kendall, 33 Ariz. 325, 264 P. 692, 58 A.L.R. 145 (1928).

In the case of a state highway maintained by the state, the state's sovereign immunity to suit may make questions of liability academic. (In some cases it has been urged that a private person contracting with a state to construct or repair a highway for it partakes of the state's immunity from liability for harm caused by his negligent work. See Taylor v. Westerfield, 233 Ky. 619, 26 S.W.2d 557, 69 A.L.R. 482 (1930).) But some states have waived the immunity and have consented to be sued for physical harm caused by defective conditions of their highways under prescribed conditions. See, e. g., Mass.Gen.L. (Ter. ed. 1932) c. 81, section 18. Conn.Gen.Stat. (1930) section 1481. Statutes also regulate the liability of muncipalities for defective conditions of streets and sidewalks. Requirements of notice within a specified period after the accident and of bringing of suit within another given period are common in statutes or municipal ordinances.

The municipality's obligation and the possessor's immunity extend to accumulations of snow and ice which render travel on the highway (including sidewalks) dangerous. Hanley v. Fireproof Bldg. Co., 107 Neb. 544, 186 N.W. 534, 24 A.L.R. 382 (1922). But the possessor is also subject to liability if the snow or ice is artifically thrown upon the highway from the possessor's building because of the way in which it is constructed. Klepper v. Seymour House Corp., of Ogdensburg, 246 N.Y. 85, 158 N.E. 29, 62 A.L.R. 955 (1927); cf. Farolato v. Springfield Five Cents Sav. Bank, 310 Mass. 806, 39 N.E. 2d 948 (1942). Legislation may, however, impose upon the abutting landowner the duty to clear sidewalks of snow and ice or to maintain them otherwise in safe condition. Such legislation may be interpreted as subjecting the owner to liability to the traveller for physical harm caused by the breach of duty or as subjecting him merely to a fine or to liability to the municipality for the cost of repair. See Hanley v. Fireproof Bldg. Co., supra. These are matters peculiarly requiring investigation of local legislation and decisions.

SECTION 2. LESSORS

O'MALLEY v. TWENTY-FIVE ASSOCIATES

Supreme Judicial Court of Massachusetts, 1901.
178 Mass. 555, 60 N.E. 387.

HOLMES, C. J. This is an action for personal injuries caused by the fall of the basket of coal upon the plaintiff's head. The plaintiff was hoisting the coal to a tenement in a building owned by the defendant, by means of a pulley and tackle attached to a crane by a hook, and the hook broke. * * *

The jury were instructed that if the tenant did not know and could not have known by the exercise of ordinary care and inspection what the condition of the tackle was, but the defendant did know or ought to have known by the exercise of ordinary care and inspection what the condition of the tackle was, but the defendant did know or ought to have known that it was unsuitable, they might find for the plaintiff on the ground of the original construction. The ruling, it will be seen, made the defendant answerable not only for what it knew, but for what the jury might say that it ought to have known.

The knowledge of the tenant of course would be immaterial except on the hypothesis that the plaintiff was to recover, if at all, as standing on the tenant's right. * * * [I]f the recovery was to be on this ground we are of opinion that the instruction went too far * * *.

There was no evidence that the defendant knew of any secret defect in the hook which would make it a trap to a tenant not equally informed. If, then, the hoisting apparatus had been let with the upper tenement to which it was attached, the principle of *caveat emptor* would have been applied. * * *

If merely the use of the hoisting apparatus was let in connection with this and other tenements, the rule as to the original condition of the apparatus would be the same. It would be anomalous to apply one rule to the principal object demised and another and severer one to something incidentally annexed. No doubt when the lessor retains controls he owes a duty, and, in some cases where the point which we now are considering was not before the mind of the court, the duty has been spoken of in a general way as a duty to keep the article or place reasonable safe. But when attention has been directed in any way to the condition of things at the beginning of the lease, it has been recognized as the general rule that the tenant must take things as he finds them, and if they then are unsafe, cannot complain. There is no implied undertaking or duty on the landlord's part to make things better than they are. * * *

The only extension of liability beyond this limit is in the case of hidden defects actually known to exist. As the landlord makes no contract concerning the condition of the premises at the time, the only ground on which he can be held is that he unconscionably is leading the other party into a trap. * * * The duty when it exists is only a duty to inform the tenant of the danger, and "there can be no such duty without knowledge of the defect." * * * The duty to use reasonable care to keep a staircase safe, up to the standard of the date of the lease, might not be met by a proof of ignorance that the staircase had decayed. * * * [12]

Our decision seems to us in accord with the more authoritative cases. Doyle v. Union Pacific Railway, 147 U.S. 413, 424, 13 S.Ct. 333, 37 L.Ed. 223 et seq.; Edwards v. New York & Harlem Railroad, 98 N.Y. 245, 50 Am.Rep. 659. The views expressed in Willcox v. Hines, 100 Tenn. 538, 46 S.W. 297, 66 Am.St.Rep. 770, 41 L.R.A. 278; Hines v. Willcox, 96 Tenn. 148, 33 S.W. 914 and 34 L.R.A. 824, 54 Am.St.Rep. 823, do not command our assent. No doubt a duty to take reasonable care to secure reasonable safety might be imposed upon the landlords on grounds of policy, irrespective of the condition at the date of the lease. But we see no sufficient reason for departing from the general rule when we consider the relation of landlord and tenant from the point of view of contract, and if there is no im-

12. The doctrine of caveat lessee may also be important in the determination of a lessee's liability to pay rent for an uninhabitable dwelling house. See Young v. Povich, 121 Me. 141, 116 A. 26, 29 A.L.R. 48 (1922); Ingalls v. Hobbs, 156 Mass. 348, 31 N.E. 286, 16 L.R.A. 51, 32 Am.St.Rep. 400 (1892). But see Annotation, Modern statute of rules as to existence of implied warranty of habitability or fitness for use of leased premises, 40 A.L.R.3d 646.

Steel v. Latimer, 214 Kan. 329, 521 P.2d 304 (1974); Green v. The Superior Court of the City and County of San Francisco, 10 Cal.3d 616, 111 Cal. Rptr. 704, 517 P.2d 1168 (1974); Boston Housing Authority v. Hemingway, 293 N.E.2d 831 (Mass.1973); Mease v. Fox, 200 N.W.2d 791 (Iowa 1972); Jack Spring, Inc. v. Little, 50 Ill.2d 351, 280 N.E.2d 208 (1972); and other cases cited in the Green opinion; also Sargent v. Ross, 113 N.H. 388, 308 A. 2d 528 (1973), page 635 below.

For background information relevant to this section generally see the materials cited in Note, "Developments in Contemporary Landlord-Tenant Law: An Annotated Bibliography," 26 Vand.L. Rev. 689 (1973).

The extent of a landlord's liability is treated in Jacobs, Tort Liability of a Connecticut Landlord, 15 Conn.Bar J. 315 (Oct.1941); Calandriello, Landlord's Liability for Defective Premises, 29 Geo.L.J. 1046 (1941); Bohlen, Fifty Years of Torts, 50 Harv.L.Rev. 725, 740–748 (1937); Eldredge, Landlord's Tort Liability for Disrepair, 84 U.Pa. L.Rev. 467 (1936); Eldredge, Modern Tort Problems, p. 113 (1941); Harkrider, Tort Liability of a Landlord, 26 Mich.L.Rev. 260, 383, 531 (1928); Bohlen, Landlord and Tenant, 35 Harv.L.Rev. 633 (1922); Bohlen, Studies in the Law of Torts, p. 202 (1926); Selected Essays on the Law of Torts, p. 429 (1924); Note, Landlord and Tenant: Defects Existing at the Time of the Lease, 35 Ind.L.J. 361 (1960); Tiffany, Landlord and Tenant (1912) c. 10; Restatement of Torts, Second §§ 355–362 (1965). Annotations, in addition to those cited later, are found in 13 A.L.R. 837; 25 A.L.R. 1273; 26 A.L.R. 1253, 1265; 52 A.L.R. 864; 58 A.L.R. 1411, 1428, 1432; 40 A.L.R.3d 795.

plied undertaking to give the tenant more than he hires, we can see no ground for holding a landlord liable in tort for not making the same improvement or for not mentioning what he did not know. In the opinion of the majority of the court the exceptions should be sustained.

Compare Restatement of Torts, Second § 358(1)(b) (1965) (liability for non-disclosure to tenant of dangerous condition if lessor "knows or has reason to know of the condition, and realizes or should realize the risk involved, and has reason to expect that the lessee will not discover the condition or realize the risk"); Wagner v. Kepler, 411 Ill. 368, 104 N.E.2d 231 (1951) (liability where landlord "knew or in the exercise of reasonable care might have known" of dangerous latent condition); Cummings v. Prater, 95 Ariz. 20, 386 P.2d 27 (1963) (duty of landlord to use ordinary care to inspect for latent defects when he has "reason to suspect" their existence at the time tenancy begins); Noel, Landlord's Tort Liability in Tennessee, 30 Tenn.L.Rev. 368 (1963) (duty of landlord to use reasonable care to discover latent defects existing at the commencement of tenancy).

ROMAN v. KING

Supreme Court of Missouri, 1921.
289 Mo. 641, 233 S.W. 161, 25 A.L.R. 1263.

BROWN, C. Suit for damages sustained by falling on the steps of a two-story flat building, known as Nos. 3209 and 3209–A North Newstead avenue, in the city of St. Louis, owned and leased as residences by defendant. The plaintiff was tenant of the upper flat. A porch extended across the entire front on Newstead avenue, which was reached from the street by a granitoid walk to the steps about the middle of the porch. These consisted of a lower step of granitoid, with four wooden steps leading from it to the porch floor. Each flat was reached by a front door leading into the house from this porch, which was not divided by rail or otherwise, but was common to both flats. There was also a back door, reached by stairs. The plaintiff occupied the upper flat as tenant from month to month of the defendant; the lower flat being occupied by a tenant holding by like tenure.

* * *

The four wooden steps leading up to the front porch were supported upon carriers of wood, and for a long time one of them had been loose at one end so that it could be moved out several inches in front of the riser beneath it. The tenants of the respective flats washed the steps alternatively. The loose step had first been observed in that condition in December previous to the accident, which occurred May 18, 1914, and the plaintiff had, on several occasions, driven nails into the loose end, but the wooden carrier was so rotten that these would not take hold of it. Plaintiff, about two weeks before the accident, directed defendant's attention to its condition and told him she would move out unless he fixed it, which he promised, but failed to do until after the accident occurred. Mr. King, the defendant, denied this, and says, in substance, that if a tenant should so address him he would tell him to move out.

On the day of the accident the plaintiff was descending the steps with a pan full of chicken feed held in front of her; the loose steps slipped out and she fell down the steps, striking on her head and back, suffering thereby the injuries complained of. * * * Whenever the owner of a house demises a portion of it to which access is had by way of halls, stairways, or other approaches to be used in common with the owner or tenants of other portions of the same premises, the owner, by such transaction, retains as to the tenant the possession and control of the undemised facilities, and it is his duty to keep them, or to use reasonable care to keep them, in safe condition for the use of the tenant in the enjoyment of his own possession. Without the application of this rule in his favor the tenancy is a farce, and the tenant from month to month, as in this case, may be evicted without notice by the simple refusal of his landlord to maintain the only means of access. The principle is well illustrated by the evidence in this case, in which the owner testified that, if his tenant had threatened to leave unless such repairs should be made as to enable her to enter her apartment with safety, he would simply have told her to go. It is impossible that the application of the rules of the common law should create such a condition.

It is a principle too well established to be now thoughtlessly abandoned that one who invites another to come upon his premises is bound in law to see that those premises are in such condition that the invitation may be safely accepted. In this case the lease was an invitation to the plaintiff to enter the flat by the way already apparently provided. In return the owner exacted a monthly rental. She could only enter by crossing his own premises by the use of the steps that gave way under her feet, and she was entitled to have them maintained so that she could do so in safety. Her rights under the lease constituted the measure of his duty in that respect.

The property was constructed for the purpose of a residence, and was so used. This use implies free entrance and exit for business and social purposes, and the most of the cases to which we have already referred hold that all persons so entering and leaving do so upon the implied invitation of the owner, and are equally entitled to the same protection as the tenant himself.

* * * [A]nother rule which has become thoroughly established in our jurisprudence, and is expressed by the Kentucky Court of Appeals in Home Realty Co. v. Carius, supra, as follows:

> "It is urged that plaintiff's equal knowledge with defendant of the condition of the steps bars her right to re-

> cover herein. We cannot agree with this contention. These steps constituted practically the only means of access to the two apartments, and were used by both tenants, facts necessarily known to the landlord. Because of their inaccessibility and condition the other entrances were seldom used. * * * Mere continued use of a common passageway, after knowledge of its dangerous condition, is not of itself conclusive evidence of a lack of due care on the part of the tenant, since such knowledge does not require the tenant to desist from using same in a careful manner, nor render the careful use of same contributory negligence. Looney v. McLean, 129 Mass. 33, 37 Am.Rep. 295."

We think the proposition expressed in these and other cases is a sound one. We do not think the law should encourage the wrongdoer in interposing his own wrong as a defense against one who has suffered from its effects. It is true that in this case the plaintiff had access through a rear door to her back yard, and we will presume that this way wound somewhere safely to a street. It may also be that under some circumstances it might have been plaintiff's duty to protect her landlord from loss by subjecting herself to the same roundabout process, but she also had the right to consider, to some extent at least, her own convenience secured to her by her lease, even to the extent of encountering a danger which might possibly react upon the landlord who violates it. The law will not compel her, without good reason, to abandon her front door, the full and free use of which was included in her monthly rental.

* * * The plaintiff was, at the time of her injuries, as tenant of the premises from month to month, entitled to use all these steps, not only for personal access to her own premises, but for the access of others having business or social relations with her, which might make it necessary or desirable to her. All such persons passing in such capacity to and from her flat were, by the fact of her tenancy, entitled to reasonable care on the part of the owner of the premises with respect to such conditions of safety. She had paid her rent in advance and her title to these facilities was complete. The free and constant use of these steps was necessary to the enjoyment of her own residence, and the law does not require her to cease that enjoyment the moment the owner chooses to permit it to become dangerous. While the approach is in the possession of the owner, the easement is a part of her own premises, and the tenant may still continue to use it in the exercise of reasonable care to be determined in view of the extent and nature of the danger created by the owner's neglect or refusal to perform his duty, and her own right of enjoyment. * *

If upon due notice or with knowledge of such dangerous condition he still fails to make the necessary repairs, she is not bound to vacate the premises and resort to her suit in damages for relief, but may, in the exercise of such care as is indicated by the danger, continue to use, the premises, if practicable to do so with reasonable safety. The landlord may not set a deadfall before the front door of his tenant, and claim exemption from damages for the consequent injury on the sole ground that he had succeeded in making it dangerous to enter or leave by that route. In such a case the jury may weigh the need of the tenant in the same balance into which the cupidity of the owner has already been cast. * * *

WEBEL v. YALE UNIVERSITY

Supreme Court of Errors of Connecticut, 1939.
125 Conn. 515, 7 A.2d 215, 123 A.L.R. 863.

MALTBIE, CHIEF JUSTICE. This case is an appeal from a judgment entered upon the sustaining of a demurrer to the complaint filed by the defendant Yale University. The complaint contained the following allegations: The plaintiff was in a beauty shop conducted by the defendants Segal, for the purpose of having her hair waved. She went into the ladies' room connected with the shop and on leaving it fell at the entrance. The floor of the ladies' room was some seven inches higher than the floor of the shop, the door extending down to the level of the shop floor. The building is owned by Yale University, to which we shall hereafter refer as the defendant, and the Segals were occupying it at the time of and had occupied it for a long time before, the accident as lessees of the defendant. The structural condition at the entrance to the ladies' room existed when the shop was leased to the Segals and "it was intended by the defendant Yale University that said condition be continued in the manner and for the purpose set out and used by said defendants, which use for such purposes and in such a manner was a nuisance." * * *

In Reardon v. Shimelman, 102 Conn. 383, 128 A. 705, 39 A.L.R. 287, we directly repudiated the doctrine that one who comes upon premises at the invitation of a tenant can have no greater right to recover for an injury suffered thereon than would the tenant. * * * It is true that in that case we were dealing with a defective condition of a common approach to a tenement house, but under the principle there stated one who comes upon leased premises at the invitation of the tenant may have, as regards defects therein, other rights than a tenant would have. Colorado Mortgage & Investment Co. v. Giacomini, 55 Colo. 540, 559, 136 P. 1039, L.R.A.1915B, 364. Indeed, from the standpoint of practical justice, there are strong reasons for applying the doctrine in such a case. The freedom from liability of the landlord to the tenant for defects in the premises is based upon the notice of the conditions of the premises which the tenant has or with which he is chargeable; but it certainly is not just to charge one who visits the premises at the invitation of the tenant with the knowledge which the tenant has or with which he is chargeable when the invitee may have neither actual notice nor, upon the facts known or reasonably observable by him, be chargeable with notice. Gibson v. Hoppman, 108 Conn. 401, 410, 143 A. 635, 75 A.L.R. 148.

Even where the rule that one who visits the premises at the invitation of a tenant has no greater rights to recover against the landlord than would the tenant applies, an exception has not infrequently been made and the landlord has been held liable to persons who visit them at the express or implied invitation of the tenant for injuries due to defects in the leased premises existing at the time the lease was made. In a number of the cases the premises in question were let for a use which involved a general invitation to the public to visit them; thus in Edwards v. New York & H. R. Co., 98 N.Y. 245, 50 Am.Rep. 659, the premises were leased for an exhibition open to the general public; in Camp v. Wood, 76 N.Y. 92, 32 Am.Rep. 282, the premises were let for a dance open to the public; in Barrett v. Lake Ontario Beach Imp. Co., 174 N.Y. 310, 66 N.E. 968, 61 L.R.A. 829; in Joyce v. Martin, 15 R.I. 558, 10 A. 620, in Albert v. State, 66 Md. 325, 7 A. 697, 59 Am.Rep. 159, the premises were used as a beach resort, and in Folkman v. Lauer, 244 Pa. 605, 91 A. 218, the injury occurred as the result of the collapse of a grandstand at a baseball park. On the other hand, in Swords v. Edgar, 59 N.Y. 28, 17 Am.Rep. 295, a longshoreman recovered for injuries on a leased pier, and while that case was criticized and limited in the majority opinion in Edgar v. New York & H. R. Co., supra, it was cited as authority in Barrett v. Lake Ontario Beach Imp. Co., supra, and has been quite generally referred to in other states as sustaining a recovery in like actions. * * * [W]e have no need, in the situation before us, to consider whether liability of a landlord would extend to an employee of the tenant. We confine our attention to a situation where one enters upon leased premises as a business patron of the lessee.

* * * in the Restatement of the Law of Torts, section 359, it is stated: "A lessor who leases land for a purpose which involves the admission of a large number of persons as patrons of his lessee, is subject to liability for bodily harm caused to them by an artificial condition existing when the lessee took possession, if the lessor (a) knew or should have known of the condition and realized or should have realized the unreasonable risk to them involved therein, and (b) had reason to expect that the lessee would admit his patrons before the land was put in a reasonably safe condition for their reception." If the liability of a landlord for defects existing when the lease was made to those who enter upon leased premises as patrons of the lessee is to be sanctioned, as we think it should, we are not able to see any distinction in law depending merely upon the number of persons who enter upon the premises. The legal relationship between the proprietor of a beach open upon payment of a fee for general use and those who resort to it is no different than that which exists between the proprietor of a store and people generally invited to it in hope that they will buy goods there for sale; and an attempt to distinguish situations based solely upon the number of persons who visit premises as patrons of the tenant would make liability depend upon a test unsatisfactory and im-

practical to apply.[13] The basis of liability in such a case, as is repeatedly stated in the decisions we have cited, is that the landowner leases premises on which he knows or should know that there are conditions likely to cause injury to persons entering upon them, that the purpose for which the premises are leased involves the fact that people will be invited upon the premises as patrons of the tenant, and that the landowner knows or should know that the tenant cannot reasonably be expected to remedy or guard against injury from the defect. * * *

An important limitation upon the landlord's liability is that such liability does not arise unless he has reason to expect that the tenant will not take steps to remedy or guard against injury from the defect. * * * The question whether the landlord had reason to expect that the tenant would not remedy the defect or otherwise safeguard patrons entering the premises would ordinarily present a question of fact.

The quotation we have made from the Restatement does not purport to determine in what field of law the right of the plaintiff to recover lies, and an examination of the cases we have cited shows that in some of them the liability is treated as one in nuisance, while in others it is treated as in negligence. One who enters premises at the express or implied invitation of a tenant does not come upon them in the exercise of any public right, but is there by reason of a right extended to him by the tenant; and, if injured, the visitor to the premises cannot base his right to recover upon the existence of a public nuisance. A private nuisance exists only where one is injured in relation to a right which he enjoys by reason of his ownership of an interest in land. * * *

The liability in this case, if one exists, belongs in the field of negligence. * * *

The complaint squarely placed the claimed right of the plaintiff to recover against the defendant upon the ground of nuisance. Had the demurrer been upon the ground that the only possible liability of the defendant was in negligence and not in nuisance, it might have been sound. It took, however, the broader ground that the plaintiff could not recover because the exclusive control of the premises was in the tenants, the Segals, and the plaintiff was in the shop at their invi-

13. The New Jersey Court considered this criticism and found it wanting. "Certainly, the use of a private dwelling as an 'office' for the practice of medicine by the physician-lessee cannot be fairly termed a 'public' use in the sense contemplated by our adjudications and the rule enunciated in the restatement." La Freda v. Woodward, 125 N.J.L. 489, 15 A.2d 798, 130 A.L.R. 1269 (1940).

But see Prosser, Business Visitors and Invitees (1942) 26 Minn.L.Rev. 573 (1942); Spain v. Kelland, 93 Ariz. 172, 379 P.2d 149 (1963). In the Restatement of Torts, Second § 359 has been amended to replace "a large number of persons as patrons of the lessee" with "the public"; according to Comment (d), it "is not necessary that the public should enter in large numbers at one time;" the new section would apply equally "where the purpose of the lease involves the admission of the public two or three at a time, as in the case of a small beauty shop, or a doctor's office." Quaere, why not one at a time?

tation; and this was the basis upon which the trial court decided the case. These facts were not sufficient to defeat the plaintiff's right of recovery and the demurrer should have been overruled.[14]

SARGENT v. ROSS

Supreme Court of New Hampshire, 1973.
113 N.H. 388, 308 A.2d 528.

KENISON, CHIEF JUSTICE. The question in this case is whether the defendant landlord is liable to the plaintiff in tort for the death of plaintiff's four-year-old daughter who fell to her death from an outdoor stairway at a residential building owned by the defendant in Nashua. The defendant resided in a ground-floor apartment in the building, and her son and daughter-in-law occupied a second story apartment serviced by the stairway from which the child fell. At the time of the accident the child was under the care of the defendant's daughter-in-law who was plaintiff's regular baby-sitter.

Plaintiff brought suit against * * * the defendant for negligent construction and maintenance of the stairway which was added to the building by the defendant about eight years before the accident. There was no apparent cause for the fall except for evidence that the stairs were dangerously steep, and that the railing was insufficient to prevent the child from falling over the side. The jury returned a verdict * * * in favor of the plaintiff * * *. The defendant seasonably excepted to the denial of her motions for a nonsuit, directed verdict, judgment n. o. v. and to have the verdict set aside * * *

Claiming that there was no evidence that the defendant retained control over the stairway, that it was used in common with other tenants, or that it contained a concealed defect, defendant urges that there was accordingly no duty owing to the deceased child for the defendant to breach. This contention rests upon the general rule which has long obtained in this and most other jurisdictions that a landlord is not liable, except in certain limited situations, for injuries caused by defective or dangerous conditions in the leased premises. E. g. * * * 2 Powell, Real Property ¶ 234 (rev. ed. 1971); Prosser, Torts § 63 (4th ed. 1971); 1 Tiffany, Real Property §§ 104, 107 (3d ed. 1939). The plaintiff does not directly attack this rule of nonliability but in-

14. See Notes 38 Mich.L.Rev. 429 (1940), 24 Minn.L.Rev. 283 (1940); Eldredge, Modern Tort Problems, 152 (1941); Jacobs, Tort Liability of a Connecticut Landlord, 15 Conn.Bar J. 315 (Oct. 1941).

Compare with the court's discussion of whether the action should be nuisance or negligence, its decision and opinion in Bergman v. Jacob, 125 Conn. 486, 7 A.2d 219 (1939), decided on the same day as the Webel case.

Also see Austin v. Buettner, 211 Md. 61, 76, 124 A.2d 793, 801 (1955), which follows *Webel*, and Bluemer v. Saginaw Oil Service, 356 Mich. 399, 97 N.W.2d 90 (1959), which uses nuisance doctrine. In Restatement of Torts, Second § 359 (1965), the phrase "knew or should have known of the condition and realized or should have realized the unreasonable risk" has been changed to "knows or by the exercise of reasonable care could discover that the condition involves an unreasonable risk", and the requirement that the dangerous condition be "artificial" has been dropped.

stead attempts to show, rather futilely under the facts, defendant's control of the stairway. She also relies upon an exception to the general rule of nonliability, to wit, that a landlord is liable for injuries resulting from his negligent repair of the premises. * * * Prosser, supra at 410–12; 1 Tiffany, supra at § 105; Restatement of Torts, Second § 362 (1965). The issue, as framed by the parties, is whether the rule of nonliability should prevail or whether the facts of this case can be squeezed into the negligent repair or some other exception to the general rule of landlord immunity.

General principles of tort law ordinarily impose liability upon persons for injuries caused by their failure to exercise reasonable care under all the circumstances. * * * Restatement of Torts, Second § 283 (1964). A person is generally negligent for exposing another to an unreasonable risk of harm which foreseeably results in an injury. Quint v. Porietis, 107 N.H. 463, 225 A.2d 179 (1966); State v. Dodge, 103 N.H. 131, 166 A.2d 467 (1960); Restatement of Torts, Second § 282 (1965). But, except in certain instances, landlords are immune from these simple rules of reasonable conduct which govern other persons in their daily activities. This "quasi-sovereignty of the landowner" (2 Harper and James, Law of Torts 1495 (1956)) finds its source in an agrarian England of the dark ages. * * * Due to the untoward favoritism of the law for landlords, it has been justly stated that "the law in this area is a scandal." Quinn and Phillips, The Law of Landlord-Tenant: A Critical Evaluation of the Past with Guidelines for the Future, 38 Ford.L.Rev. 225 (1969). "For decades the court persistently refused to pierce the hardened wax that preserved the landlord-tenant relationship in its agrarian state." Note, 59 Geo.L.J. 1153, 1163 (1971). But courts and legislatures alike are beginning to reevaluate the rigid rules of landlord-tenant law in light of current needs and principles of law from related areas. See * * * Lemle v. Breeden, 51 Haw. 426, 462 P.2d 470 (1969); Kline v. 1500 Massachusetts Ave. Apt. Corp., 141 U.S.App.D.C. 370, 439 F.2d 477 (1970); 2 Powell, Real Property ¶ 220, at 174–75 (rev. ed. 1971); 1970/71 Am. Survey of American Law 365; Note, 121 U.Pa. L.Rev. 378 (1972). "Justifiable dissatisfaction with the rule" of landlord tort immunity (2 Harper and James, supra at 1510) compels its reevaluation in a case such as this where we are asked either to apply the rule, and hold the landlord harmless for a foreseeable death resulting from an act of negligence, or to broaden one of the existing exceptions and hence perpetuate an artificial and illogical rule. See Note, Lessor's Duty to Repair: Tort Liability to Persons Injured on the Premises, 62 Harv.L.Rev. 669 (1949).

One court recognized at an early date that ordinary principles of tort liability ought to apply to landlords as other persons. "The ground of liability upon the part of a landlord when he demises dangerous property has nothing special to do with the relation of landlord and tenant. It is the ordinary case of liability for personal misfeasance, which runs through all the relations of individuals to each other." Wilcox v. Hines, 100 Tenn. 538, 548–549, 46 S.W. 297, 299 (1898).

Most courts, however, while recognizing from an early date that "the law is unusually strict in exempting the landlord from liability" (Bowe v. Hunking, 135 Mass. 380, 386 (1883)), sought refuge from the rigors of the rule by straining other legal principles such as deceit * * * and by carving out exceptions to the general rule of nonliability. 2 Harper and James, supra at 1510. Thus, a landlord is now generally conceded to be liable in tort for injuries resulting from defective and dangerous conditions in the premises if the injury is attributable to (1) a hidden danger in the premises of which the landlord but not the tenant is aware, (2) premises leased for public use, (3) premises retained under the landlord's control, such as common stairways, or (4) premises negligently repaired by the landlord. See generally 2 Powell, Real Property ¶ 234 (rev. ed. 1971); Prosser, Torts § 63 (4th ed. 1971); Restatement of Torts, Second §§ 358–62 (1965).[15]

As is to be expected where exceptions to a rule of law form the only basis of liability, the parties in this action concentrated at trial and on appeal on whether any of the exceptions applied, particularly whether the landlord or the tenant had control of the stairway. 1 Tiffany, Real Property § 109 (3d ed. 1939). The determination of the question of which party had control of the defective part of the premises causing the injury has generally been considered dispositive * * * This was a logical modification to the rule of nonliability since ordinarily a landlord can reasonably be expected to maintain the property and guard against injuries only in common areas and other areas under his control. A landlord, for example, cannot fairly be held responsible in most instances for an injury arising out of the tenant's negligent maintenance of the leased premises. * * * But the control test is insufficient since it substitutes a facile and conclusive test for a reasoned consideration of whether due care was exercised under all the circumstances. * * *

15. There has been a protracted controversy over the question whether a landlord might also be liable in tort for damages caused by the breach of a covenant to repair. Most states formerly denied any such tort liability to the lessee or his invitees or guests, on the theory that tort liability is an incident to occupation or control. See, e. g., Cullings v. Goetz, 256 N.Y. 287, 176 N.E. 397 (1931); the requisite "control" was sometimes found in the reservation by lessor of the right to enter the premises for the purpose of making repairs, Noble v. Marx, 298 N.Y. 106, 81 N.E.2d 40 (1948). The Restatement, on the other hand, proposed liability if "the lessor fails to exercise reasonable care to perform his contract" (section 357), and the Restatement view is said to have become the majority rule, Prosser, Torts 408–409 (4th ed. 1971). Also see Harper and James, The Law of Torts § 27.16 at notes 44 et seq. (1956 and Supp. 1968). Further distinctions have been drawn between promises for a consideration and gratuitous promises to repair, e. g., that in the former case lessor has tort liability for negligence in performance to both the tenant and other persons who within the contemplation of the parties were to use the premises, but in the latter case there is liability only to the promisee, and only for gross negligence. Bergeron v. Forest, 233 Mass. 392, 124 N.E. 74 (1919); the Massachusetts court has, however, indicated more recently that it "might well be inclined toward a reconsideration of the rules of tort liability of lessors," DiMarzo v. S. & P. Realty Corp., Mass. (1974), 306 N.E. 2d 432. As for the liability of lessor where a statute imposes a duty to repair, see Altz v. Leiberson, 233 N.Y. 16, 134 N.E. 703 (1922).

There was evidence from which the jury could find that the landlord negligently designed or constructed a stairway which was dangerously steep or that she negligently failed to remedy or adequately warn the deceased of the danger. A proper rule of law would not preclude recovery in such a case by a person foreseeably injured by a dangerous hazard solely because the stairs serviced one apartment instead of two. But that would be the result if the control test were applied to this case, since this was not a "common stairway" or otherwise under the landlord's control. See generally Annot., 26 A.L.R.2d 468 (1952). While we could strain this test to the limits and find control in the landlord (Gibson v. Hoppman, 108 Conn. 401, 143 A. 635 (1928)), as plaintiff suggests, we are not inclined to so expand the fiction since we agree that "it is no part of the general law of negligence to exonerate a defendant simply because the condition attributable to his negligence has passed beyond his control before it causes injury * * *." 2 Harper and James, Law of Torts § 27.16, at 1509 (1956); see id. at 207 (Supp. to vol. 2 1968).

The anomaly of the general rule of landlord tort immunity and the inflexibility of the standard exceptions, such as the control exception, is pointedly demonstrated by this case. A child is killed by a dangerous condition of the premises. Both husband and wife tenants testify that they could do nothing to remedy the defect because they did not own the house nor have authority to alter the defect. But the landlord claims that she should not be liable because the stairs were not under her control. Both of these contentions are premised on the theory that the other party should be responsible. So the orthodox analysis would leave us with neither landlord nor tenant responsible for dangerous conditions on the premises. This would be both illogical and intolerable, particularly since neither party then would have any legal reason to remedy or take precautionary measures with respect to dangerous conditions. In fact, the traditional "control" rule actually discourages a landlord from remedying a dangerous condition since his repairs may be evidence of his control. * * * Nor can there be serious doubt that ordinarily the landlord is best able to remedy dangerous conditions, particularly where a substantial alteration is required. * * *

* * * [T]he issue of control is relevant to the determination of liability only insofar as it bears on the question of what the landlord and tenant reasonably should have believed in regard to the division of responsibility for *maintaining* the premises in a safe condition. The basic claim in this case involves only the design or construction of the steps; the maintenance of the stairs was not seriously in issue, except perhaps concerning the lack of precautions, since the evidence was clear that the stairway was dry and free of debris. The inquiry should have centered upon the unreasonableness of the pitch of the steps and the unreasonableness of failing to take precautionary measures to reduce the danger of falls.

Similarly, the truly pertinent questions involved in determining who should bear responsibility for the loss in this case were clouded by the question of whether the accident was caused by a hidden defect or secret danger. * * * The mere fact that a condition is open and obvious, as was the steepness of the steps in this case, does not preclude it from being unreasonably dangerous, and defendants are not infrequently "held liable for creating or maintaining a perfectly obvious danger of which plaintiffs are fully aware." 2 Harper and James, supra at 1493 * * *. Additionally, while the dangerous quality of the steps might have been obvious to an adult, the danger and risk would very likely be imperceptible to a young child such as the deceased. * * *

Finally, plaintiff's reliance on the negligent repairs exception to the rule of nonliability * * * would require us to broaden the exception to include the negligent construction of improvements to the premises. We recognize that this would be no great leap in logic (see Bohlen, Landlord and Tenant 35 Harv.L.Rev. 633, 648 (1922)), but we think it more realistic instead to consider reversing the general rule of nonliability (Note, 62 Harv.L.Rev. 669 (1949)) since "[t]he exceptions have * * * produced a twisting of legal concepts which seems undesirable." Id. at 676. And "it appears to us that to search for gaps and exceptions in a legal doctrine * * * which exists only because of the somnolence of the common law and the courts is to perpetuate further judicial fictions when preferable alternatives exist. * * * The law of landlord-tenant relations cannot be so frail as to shatter when confronted with modern urban realities and a frank appraisal of the underlying issues." Lemle v. Breeden, 51 Haw. 426, 435, 462 P.2d 470, 475 (1969) (establishing an implied warranty of habitability in dwelling leases). The emphasis on control and other exceptions to the rule of nonliability, both at trial and on appeal, unduly complicated the jury's task and diverted effort and attention from the central issue of the unreasonableness of the risk. * * *

This conclusion springs naturally and inexorably from our recent decision in Kline v. Burns, 111 N.H. 87, 276 A.2d 248 (1971). *Kline* was an apartment rental claim suit in which the tenant claimed that the premises were uninhabitable. Following a small vanguard of other jurisdictions, we modernized the landlord-tenant contractual relationship by holding that there is an implied warranty of habitability in an apartment lease transaction. As a necessary predicate to our decision, we discarded from landlord-tenant law "that obnoxious legal cliché, *caveat emptor*." Pines v. Perssion, 14 Wis.2d 590, 596, 111 N.W.2d 409, 413 (1961). In so doing, we discarded the very legal foundation and justification for the landlord's immunity in tort for injuries to the tenant or third persons. * * * To the extent that Kline v. Burns did not do so, we today discard the rule of "caveat lessee" and the doctrine of landlord nonliability in tort to which it gave birth. We thus bring up to date the other half of landlord-tenant law. Henceforth, landlords as other persons must exercise reasonable care not to subject others to an unreasonable risk of harm. * * * A landlord must act as a reasonable person under all of the circumstances including the likelihood of injury to others, the probable seriousness of such injuries, and the burden of reducing or avoiding the risk.

* * * We think this basic principle of responsibility for landlords as for others "best expresses the principles of justice and reasonableness upon which our law of torts is founded." Dowd v. Portsmouth Hosp., 105 N.H. 53, 59, 193 A.2d 788, 792 (1963) (on rehearing).

* * * The questions of control, hidden defects and common or public use, which formerly had to be established as a prerequisite to even considering the negligence of a landlord, will now be relevant only inasmuch as they bear on the basic tort issues such as the foreseeability and unreasonableness of the particular risk of harm. * * *

Can a landlord absolve himself from liability by a suitably drawn lease? In Clarke v. Ames, 267 Mass. 44, 165 N.E. 696 (1929), a tenant of an office building injured by negligent operation of an elevator provided by the landlord was held barred from recovery by a covenant to "save the Lessor harmless and indemnified from all loss, damage, liability, or expense, incurred, suffered, or claimed by reason of * * * any injury, loss, or damage from any cause to any person or property upon or about the demised premises or while in transit thereto or thereupon upon the hallways, stairways, elevators, or other approaches to the demised premises." In Kirshenbaum v. General Outdoor Advertising Co., 258 N.Y. 489, 180 N.E. 245, 84 A.L.R. 645 (1932), a tenant storekeeper whose merchandise was damaged by a leaky roof was denied recovery against the landlord's indemnitor because of a covenant exempting the landlord from all liability for injury to person or property caused by water or rain which might leak into any part of the building, whether or not the damage should be caused by the landlord's negligence. Accord, where the exculpatory clause was couched in more general language, Inglis v. Garland, 19 Cal.App. 2d 767, 2 Cal.Supp. 213, 64 P.2d 501 (1936). But see Excellent Holding Co. v. Richman, 155 Misc. 257, 279 N.Y.S. 587 (1935), where despite an exculpatory clause similar to that approved in Kirshenbaum v. General Outdoor Advertising Co., supra, a lower New York court allowed recovery to a tenant of a tenement injured because of a leaky roof, on the theory that the clause was void as opposed to the policy of the Multiple Dwelling Law.

In Illinois legislative efforts to void exculpatory clauses have been frustrated by both the judicial and executive branches of the state government. See Strauch v. Charles Apartments Co., 1 Ill.App. 3d 57, 273 N.E.2d 19 (Ill.App.1971), in which tenant was permitted to submit evidence as to disparity of bargaining power. Nearly all courts construe exculpatory clauses strictly against the landlord. For example, in Baldwin v. McEldowney, 324 Pa. 399, 188 A. 154 (1936), the court construed the following covenant not to apply to a fire-escape used as a common passageway by the tenants of an apartment building and known by the landlord to be defective at the time the lease was signed: "The Lessor shall not be liable for any injury or damage to any person or to any property at any time on said premises or building from any cause whatever which may arise from the use or condition of said premises or building—or from any other cause, during said term or any renewal thereof."

See generally as to exculpatory clauses Notes 15 Temple L.Q. 427 (1941), 7 Fordham L.Rev. 126 (1938), 11 So.Cal.L.Rev. 296 (1937), 37 Col.L.Rev. 248 (1937), 84 A.L.R. 654 (1933), Kessler, Contracts of Adhesion—Some Thoughts About Freedom of Contract, 43 Colum.L. Rev. 629 (1943), and, in English law, Lowe, The Exclusion of Liability for Negligence, 37 Mod.L.Rev. 218 (1974).

See also Restatement, Contracts, sections 574, 575.

THE DEFECTIVE PREMISES ACT 1972

In force in England and Wales as of 1st January 1974.

* * *

4.—(1) Where premises are let under a tenancy which puts on the landlord an obligation to the tenant for the maintenance or repair of the premises, the landlord owes to all persons who might reasonably be expected to be affected by defects in the state of the premises a duty to take such care as is reasonable in all the circumstances to see that they are reasonably safe from personal injury or from damage to their property caused by a relevant defect.

(2) The said duty is owed if the landlord knows (whether as the result of being notified by the tenant or otherwise) or if he ought in all the circumstances to have known of the relevant defect.

(3) In this section "relevant defect" means a defect in the state of the premises existing at or after the material time and arising from, or continuing because of an act or omission by the landlord which constitutes or would if he had had notice of the defect, have constituted a failure by him to carry out his obligation to the tenant for the maintenance or repair of the premises; and for the purposes of the foregoing provision "the material time" means—

(a) where the tenancy commenced before this Act, the commencement of this Act; and

(b) in all other cases, the earliest of the following times, that is to say—

(i) the time when the tenancy commences;

(ii) the time when the tenancy agreement is entered into;

(iii) the time when possession is taken of the premises in contemplation of the letting.

(4) Where premises are let under a tenancy which expressly or impliedly gives the landlord the right to enter the premises to carry out any description of maintenance or repair of the premises, then, as from the time when he first is, or by notice or otherwise can put himself, in a position to exercise the right and so long as he is or can put himself in that position, he shall be treated for the purposes of subsections (1) to (3) above (but for no other purpose) as if he were under an obligation to the tenant for that description of maintenance or repair of the premises; but the landlord shall not owe the tenant any duty by virtue of this subsection in respect of any defect in the state of the premises arising from, or continuing because of, a failure to carry out an obligation expressly imposed on the tenant by the tenancy. * * *

JOHNSTON v. HARRIS

Supreme Court of Michigan, 1972.
387 Mich. 569, 198 N.W.2d 409.

T. M. KAVANAGH, CHIEF JUSTICE. Plaintiff was an elderly tenant in decedent's 4-unit apartment building located in the Detroit inner city. Returning home at about 7:30 p. m. on October 7, 1965, plaintiff approached the front door. As he reached for the doorknob, the door was jerked open and he was assaulted, struck and robbed by an unknown youth who was lurking in the poorly lighted, unlocked vestibule.

Plaintiff commenced action in Wayne circuit court against defendants' decedent, asserting that the assault, robbery and consequent injuries were proximately caused by the failure of decedent to provide adequate lighting and door locks. * * *

The Court of Appeals apparently treated the action as solely based on a theory that decedent's failure to provide proper locks and lighting had resulted in plaintiff's injuries. Viewed as such, a fatal logical void existed as to the element of proximate cause. However, to so narrowly view plaintiff's pleadings and proofs is to wholly ignore the interwoven assertion that decedent was negligent in creating a condition conducive to criminal assaults.

The crux of plaintiff's case was that in a high crime district it is reasonably foreseeable that inadequate lighting and unlocked doors would create conditions to which criminals would be attracted to carry out their nefarious deeds. Thus, on a theory not unlike that contemplated by sections 302B, 448 and 449 of 2 Restatement Torts, 2d, pp. 88, 480 and 482, plaintiff asserted that decedent's negligence consisted of enhancing the likelihood of exposure to criminal assaults by failing to provide adequate lighting and locks. Plaintiff argued, in effect, that decedent set a trap. * * *

Section 302B provides:

"An act or an omission may be negligent if the actor realizes or should realize that it involves an unreasonable risk of harm to another through the conduct of the other or a third person which is intended to cause harm, even though such conduct is criminal."

Section 448 provides:

"The act of a third person in committing an intentional tort or crime is a superseding cause of harm to another resulting therefrom, although the actor's negligent conduct created a situation which afforded an opportunity to the third person to commit such a tort or crime, *unless the actor at the time of his negligent conduct realized or should have realized the likelihood that such a situation might be created, and that a third person might avail himself of the opportunity to commit such a tort or crime.*" (Emphasis supplied.)

Section 449 provides:

"If the likelihood that a third person may act in a particular manner is the hazard or one of the hazards which makes the actor negligent, such an act whether innocent, negligent, intentionally tortious, or criminal does not prevent the actor from being liable for harm caused thereby." * * *

Contrary to the statement of the trial court, we hold that actionable negligence may lie in these circumstances. * * *

BRENNAN, JUSTICE (dissenting).

I disagree. I believe the majority extends the rule of tort law too far.

Public safety is the business of government.

Today's decision concedes the failure of government to make the streets and homes of certain areas reasonably safe and in effect transfers the governmental function of public protection to the unfortunate owners of real property in such places.

Already overburdened by taxes largely laid to pay for public safety, these owners will now be required to maintain additional lighting, guards, enclosures, alarms, locks and take every other precaution to avoid reasonably foreseeable conditions which attract criminals to carry out their nefarious deeds.

At a time when concerned citizens and public officials are seeking ways to involve the broader community in resolving the plight of so-called "high crime areas", our Court would place an additional burden upon the land and the resources of such areas.

The intrusion of private industry into the business of public safety has been one of the most unfortunate phenomena of the 1960's and the 1970's. Already, there are subdivisions which operate their own patrol cars; private police and private guards are multiplying; vigilante forces of private citizens roam the streets with walkie-talkies; store owners and apartment managers arm themselves and set traps for burglars; and now this Court would give further impetus to such developments by imposing civil liability on the unfortunate victims of crime in "high crime areas."

No member of this Court lives in such an area. None are voting to increase his own insurance premium, or that of his neighbors. What we do in the name of liberality is regressive. It is a mistake.[16]

16. In Kline v. 1500 Massachusetts Avenue Corp., 439 F.2d 477 (D.C.Cir. 1970), the court found "a duty * * * on a landlord to take steps to protect tenants from foreseeable criminal acts committed by third parties", where it was within the power of the lessor of an apartment building, but of no individual apartment lessee, to "take measures to guard the garage entranceways, to provide scrutiny at the main entrance of the building, to patrol the common hallways and elevators, to set up any kind of a security alarm system in the building, to provide additional locking devices on the main doors, to provide a system of announcement for authorized visitors only, to close the garage doors at appropriate hours, and to see that the entrance was manned at all times."

See other similar and contrasting cases cited on page 625.

Chapter 4

APPLICATIONS OF ACCIDENT LAW RECONSIDERED

A. TUNC, TORTS: INTRODUCTION, International Encyclopedia of Comparative Law 3–6 (1974):

1. *The paradoxical situation of the law of tort in industrialized countries.*—In most industrialized countries, the law of tort is at the moment in a paradoxical situation. On the one hand, there has been a great increase in the number of civil liability suits, in their variety, in the amounts they involve, and an abrupt change of the rules which govern them. This is attributable in part to the enormous increase in the number of accidental personal injuries, as a result of the industrial revolution; the safety measures introduced in factories and, to a certain extent, on the roads and in cars only act as a gentle brake on this increase. Every year in the United States alone 115,000 persons die as the result of accidents, more than 11 million suffer temporary disablement, and more than 50 million others (making a total of one person out of four) suffer some kind of injury. The cost of accidents is permanently increasing and must be in the neighbourhood of US $30 billion *per annum.*

The present importance of civil liability is also due to a greater intolerance of misfortunes. In a welfare state anybody who has suffered damage by reason of another's act feels more or less justified in suing him for compensation. The imagination and skill of the lawyers in finding new grounds for actions in tort or new heads of recoverable damages has enabled compensation to be recovered which, by its nature or amount, would never have been conceived of a few decades ago. Malpractice suits against physicians and surgeons have become so common in the United States that many insurance companies now hesitate to cover medical liability. Disappointed shareholders bring suits against stockbrokers. Manufacturers are threatened, not only by an enormous increase of individual claims based on product liability, but also by collective claims derived from a greater awareness of the evils of pollution, which have now taken on an international dimension. The complexities of business law explain in part why the big industrial firms are permanently involved, either as plaintiffs or defendants, in law suits each involving hundreds of millions, if not billions, of dollars. The increased role of tort litigation has created a real problem for the administration of justice in many industrialized countries, as well as a permanent problem for the insurance companies covering tort liability.

On the other hand, the principles and functions of tort liability are at present unsettled, and indeed the very applicability of the law of tort itself, at least in certain fields, is often disputed. In a welfare state personal injuries are compensated, at least in part, by some social security scheme. Furthermore, in an affluent society, the personal injuries of many citizens will be covered by a personal insurance policy which they will have taken out. The need for tort liability is, therefore, smaller than it used to be. In fact, in the industrialized countries, tort liability is no longer the main source of indemnification for personal injuries; and it even plays a very secondary role in the compensation of industrial accidents, i. e., injuries suffered by workers in connection with their employment * * *. Furthermore, the spreading of liability insurance has completely changed the meaning of what is called tort liability. When the driver of a car is "liable" for the damage he has caused, perhaps by serious recklessness, his "liability" is purely nominal provided he is insured. Criminal courts may, of course, impose a punishment on him; but civil courts are powerless towards him. Whatever may be the amount of the damages awarded to the victim, he will have no part whatsoever in its payment if he is fully insured. In fact, he is no longer liable. He is no longer responsible for the consequences of his behaviour, except to the extent to which he may incur an increase of the insurance premiums. Similarly, the liability of directors and officers in large companies has more or less disappeared: it is currently covered by insurance—at the cost of the company itself.

The law of tort, therefore, is in a state of crisis. It may have reached its zenith: at the very moment where it occupies a position without precedent, it is impregnated and surrounded by institutions which deeply modify its traditional working and put into question its functions and its domain. Inherited from a time when there was neither social security nor insurance, it is now threatened by the rise of these institutions of loss distribution. Furthermore, it has been designed to govern individuals and it now mainly applies to private and public enterprises. The notions according to which western societies have lived for centuries are no longer true: it is no longer true that we are liable for the harm we have done by a tort, since it is likely that we will be either employed or insured; by reason of social security it is no longer true that no-one can recover for the damage he suffers as a consequence of his own fault. In certain respects man is more responsible than ever: his power to cause harm (as is his power to help his fellow men) is multiplied by increased industrialization and by the general development of technology. In other respects, as a result of the emergence of social security and insurance, his responsibility disappears. * * *

2. *Developing countries.*—In the developing countries the problems encountered by the law of tort are equally deep, if of a different nature. The law has been adjusted to suit rapidly changing activities and situations.

The consequences of personal injuries used to be covered, not by a scheme of social security, but by familial solidarity. This solidarity is, however, threatened by personal mobility, by the impact of more individualistic philosophies, and even by statutes which, in order to give an incentive to work, restrict the scope and strength of the family unit. It is doubtful whether social security will, in the foreseeable future, be able to replace it. Because of this the law of tort is likely to take on an increasing importance.

On the other hand, since collective liability is rapidly declining, most tortfeasors are insolvent and the ones who are solvent usually enjoy such a social status that the ordinary citizen will not dare to sue them before a court or has no means of doing so * * *.

In the developing countries, therefore, the importance of tort liability will probably increase in the years to come, but no more rapidly than the institutions which contribute to its decline in the industrialized countries: insurance and workman's compensation laws. * *[1]

STAFF REPORT, DRIVER BEHAVIOR AND ACCIDENT INVOLVEMENT: IMPLICATIONS FOR TORT LIABILITY (Department of Transportation Automobile Insurance and Compensation Study 1970), Excerpts from Part II, Chapter III, "The Limits of Driver Capability", pp. 151–169, and Chapter IV, "Normal and Deviant Driver Behavior, at 171:

* * * [T]raffic law has not been framed in the context of the perceptual, conceptual and motor skills needed by the driver to meet different driving demands in different driving environments at all times. The law, in simply stating the objective behavior desired, seemed to reflect the assumption that most if not all drivers had it within their capacity to meet the legal standard. That assumption, that the driver would be uniformly capable of safe driving behavior, and its complement, that it would be the driver's avoidable error that produces unsafe driving behavior, will be examined below. * * *

A. PERCEPTION AND FORECASTING

* * * [E]ven the normal driver's visual limitations may be sufficiently severe so that he cannot always perceive his driving environment well enough to permit the safe operation of his vehicle.

The normal driver's visual capacity would seem to limit to some degree his ability to sense his vehicle's motion. The normal driver's field of vision is a rather broad cone that widens from the driver's eyes to the front and sides of the car. While the average driver's peripheral vision is rather wide, its normal limits make him incapable of responding to certain stimuli. An example of this kind of limitation is the driver's ability to perceive motion.

* * *

More important than motion perception, however, is visual acuity. The limits on the width of the driver's vision require the driver periodically to divert his attention from the road to read signs and pick

1. Notes in original omitted; punctuation as in original except for minor changes.

up other driving-relevant stimuli. In addition, the average driver will respond to roadside distractions, further reducing the time he is visually fixing on the road ahead. * * *

B. CAR FOLLOWING

According to the National Safety Council, 3,850,000 out of the 14,600,000 vehicular accidents in 1969 were rear end collisions. The importance of "rear-enders" in automobile insurance is much greater, since tort liability's scope is largely limited to two-car accidents. According to a survey of personal injury accident claims sponsored by the Automobile Insurance and Compensation Study of the U.S. Department of Transportation, 40 percent of the claims involved rear-end collisions. The rear-end collision is the most common form of vehicular mishap, and has become what can be viewed as a rather commonplace occurrence.

The rear-end collision is frequently used to justify the assertion that "fault" is easy to determine in car accidents. However, a closer examination of this particular phenomenon and its circumstances may help put the role of the driver in rear-end collisions in a somewhat different perspective.

1. The Shock Wave

First to be considered is what can be called "shock waves" that are generated by cars moving in congested traffic patterns. The effect of these "waves" has been described by means of a mathematical theory of traffic flow by Robert Herman of the General Motors Research Laboratories * * *.

The principal stimulus to a "following" driver is found to be the relative speed between his car and the car ahead. A time lag occurs between the creation of this stimulus and the response of the driver, and this time lag varies *inversely* with the distance between the two cars. Herman's equation, based on these factors and applied to the situation of a chain of following cars responding to a change in the lead car's velocity, found that the resultant collisions in the chain became inevitable under certain circumstances * * *.

The severely congested nature of modern, urban "stop and start" traffic should make the foregoing painfully realistic to most drivers today. Another point should be noted, however. A driver attempting to maintain an adequate distance between cars to ensure his safety during traffic acceleration and deceleration would likely find this impossible. Gaps left open between cars, deliberately or inadvertently, on multiple lane roads are quickly filled in by drivers from the other lane. And in streets with only a single lane in each direction, cars entering from side streets or pulling away from the curb tend to fill gaps left in the traffic flow.

At least one implication of Herman's research regarding the assessment of "fault" is that while the driver factor may be asserted as being responsible in rear-end collisions, the individual can hardly be shown to be "at fault" in the sense of being morally culpable for running into the rear of someone else's car under truly congested traffic conditions.

2. The Freeway Ramp

A common scene of rear-end collisions is the freeway entrance ramp. A series of studies in Texas indicated that the design of the freeway ramp could make some rear-end collisions virtually inevitable. * * * The reasons for the concentration of rear-end collisions at these points in the highway system were addressed by the author, who referred to a specific accident which was viewed by the researchers.

> * * * as in the case of most entrance ramp accidents, the accident resulted from a false start by the leading vehicle and a collision by the trailing vehicle. The driver of a trailing vehicle on an entrance ramp is put in an unfortunate position of needing to look in two directions at the same time. He must accept a gap in the freeway traffic stream and also keep an eye on the vehicle ahead. The trailing driver often assumes that the lead vehicle is going into the freeway and looks back while his vehicle is moving forward. If the lead vehicle stops, a rear-end collision often results. * * *

Again, as in the case of the traffic "shock wave" patterns, it seems to be difficult to assert with much confidence that crashes in these circumstances derived from driver "error" in a fault sense.

C. PASSING

Among the most severe automobile crashes are head-on collisions between two cars. According to National Safety Council figures, 17 percent of all fatal accidents occur in crashes by two cars moving in opposite directions. Most of these accidents occur on rural two-lane roads at high speeds. As one researcher pointed out about drivers on such roads, "Every time one passes he must get on the wrong side of the road; he must face oncoming vehicles; and he must take chances in getting out and back into his lane of traffic."

"Passing" behavior and capabilities of drivers and the closely related matter of "car following" have been the subjects of several empirical studies in recent years. The concensus [sic] of their findings is that drivers, even when operating their vehicles under "laboratory" conditions giving maximum attention to the performance of their task, are unable to make decisions to ensure safe passing on two-lane roadways. As one review of the material put it,

> It had been indicated that drivers are relatively good judges (a 20% error or less, 95% of the time) of distances to oncoming cars in passing situations, but very poor judges of either closing rate or oncoming car speed. Farber's research emphasized that at normal passing distances drivers cannot accurately estimate oncoming car speeds. * * *

Inherent human limitations on drivers' abilities to operate their vehicles safely *do* exist; they have been acknowledged by some members of the automobile industry and the federal government. As Ralph Nader has noted,

> The limitations of human beings in coping with the increasingly complex driving task even under the most rigid law enforcement or the most ambitious education programs, make it unrealistic to expect all drivers to control their vehicles perfectly all the time.

A driver's normal abilities can be reduced further by certain debilitating agents, some of which, like carbon monoxide, are almost universally present. Environmental factors, such as darkness or weather conditions, also constrict the range of driver effectiveness. The literature reviewed does indicate that driver "error" is not always avoidable. * * *

The studies reviewed seem to indicate that most drivers commit errors regularly. These drivers are deviant only in that they depart from ideal or optimum behavior. Deviant drivers, in the sense of deviating from the average, do exist, but they are few in number in comparison with the average drivers who commit most of the errors and become involved in most of the crashes. A certain magnitude of driver error for any driver must be considered normal.[2]

D. KLEIN AND J. A. WALLER, CAUSATION, CULPABILITY AND DETERRENCE IN HIGHWAY CRASHES (Department of Transportation Automobile Insurance and Compensation Study 1970), 62–74 and 209–18:

The basic concept that has guided safety programs during the past half century—and that remains a major influence today—is that crashes are caused by avoidable inappropriate actions on the part of the driver or the pedestrian. One kind of inappropriate action popularly believed to cause crashes is the deliberate violation of traffic laws. Indeed, one manual of crash investigation widely used by police departments states, "When the investigation is completed, the officer should know that he has accomplished something worthwhile, such as showing the person who caused the accident that he violated the law, thus helping him avoid future accidents" * * *.

In order clearly to implicate traffic violations as a cause of accidents, one would have to demonstrate that violations occur with greater frequency among drivers who have crashes than among drivers who do not. Although such a relationship has been demonstrated for some kinds of violation and for some types of drivers * * *, the over-all relationship is not sufficiently strong to implicate violations in general. Indeed, a study * * * made of overt driving behavior immediately preceding a crash concluded that drivers traveling at substantially greater *or lower* speeds than the general flow of traffic were more likely to crash than those traveling at the same

2. Notes omitted; for extensive references see original.

speed as the general flow. Since in many cases—notably on limited-access highways—the general flow exceeds the posted limits by a few miles per hour, the driver who complies with the law by driving at or below the limit conceivably runs a greater risk of a crash than the driver who breaks the speed limit by a slight margin.

When the driver's or the pedestrian's inappropriate response does not involve deliberate violation of the law, it is frequently interpreted as involving "error," carelessness, risk-taking, or some other form of avoidable "improper behavior." This view assumes that every individual is omniscient, omnipotent, and totally rational, and that he become culpably involved in crashes through intentional lapses from this state of omniscience, omnipotence, and rationality. As one police manual expresses it, "Most * * * accidents are due to CARELESSNESS, NEGLIGENCE, or other AVOIDABLE CIRCUMSTANCES. THE LARGE MAJORITY CAN BE AVOIDED" * * *. So widespread is this view, among police authorities as well as the general public, that state and city traffic authorities, according to the 1968 edition of the National Safety Council's *Accident Facts,* specify, on the basis of reports embodying this assumption and reflecting conventional police training, that "improper driving" was involved in 83% of fatal crashes, 88% of injury-producing crashes, and 91% of all crashes.

As in the case of violations, "improper" driving can be implicated as a causal factor only if it can be demonstrated that it occurs more frequently among drivers involved in crashes than among those not involved. Good evidence on this relationship is lacking, and as least two studies appear to document a lack of any relationship. In one of these * * * drivers were covertly observed during one to two miles of city driving and were scored on the basis of safe or unsafe driving behavior. Of the sample, 48% "were judged entirely safe," 41% committed more safe driving acts than unsafe ones, 9% committed an equal number of safe and unsafe acts, and 1% drove unsafely more often than safely. However, when the behavior of these drivers was checked against their official driving records, "comparison of average scores with accident involvement revealed no significant tendency among persons demonstrating different degrees of safeness or unsafeness to have accidents." A similar conclusion appears warranted from the results of the second study as well * * *.

The fundamental difficulty with the concept of "driver error," however, is twofold: first, the term is too broad and too vague for either administrative or research purposes; second, its pejorative connotation implies that the driver who commits an error is morally delinquent, since presumably he could have avoided the crash if he had only been "more careful," and it implies that the remedy lies in punishing or rehabilitating the individual instead of attempting to change other factors.

Both of these difficulties may be somewhat alleviated if we borrow two concepts from the vocabulary of systems analysis. First, we shall talk of "faults" not as moral lapses but as inevitable malfunctions in a system—malfunctions which may or may not result from intentional negligence or other avoidable deficiencies. Second, we shall refine the broad concept of driver error into "faults of input," "faults of processing," and "faults of output." In the process we may be able to point out that certain kinds of error may occur even when the driver or the pedestrian is being as "careful" as he can and that other kinds require for their correction basic changes in the entire system rather than rehabilitation of the "defective" individual driver or pedestrian.

Faults of input. A fault of input involves the failure of a driver or a pedestrian to perceive a cue which can lead him to avoid a crash. The failure to perceive a stop sign, for example, may be due to inattention or distraction, but it may also be due to (1) inappropriate or unusual location or design of the sign, (2) snow covering the sign, (3) inability to see the sign because of a sudden rain squall or direct or reflected sun glare.

Similarly, the failure to note a vehicle approaching at right angles at an intersection may be due to distraction, but it may also be due to "tunnel vision," a visual deficiency which is not checked for in most licensing vision tests and of which the individual himself is likely to be totally unaware. * * *

Failure to monitor the rear-view mirror may be due not to carelessness but to a sudden sleet storm or to fogging of the car's windows—a technical problem which the industry seems unable to solve except by means of expensive optional equipment. Similarly, a driver may be unable to see a cyclist to his right rear because the design of the vehicle precludes the possibility of such observation.

Various kinesthetic cues of vehicle behavior—the effects of a slowly deflating tire, for example, or the effects of a seriously misaligned wheel, or the "feel" of the first one or two seconds of a skid—may not be perceived simply because the driver was never trained to perceive them. Very few driver-education courses offer training in coping with such critical phenomena as skids, blow-outs, or drifting off the road onto the shoulder, and consequently the conscientious driver's first experience with such events may occur only moments before a crash. Moreover, the industry's emphasis that modern cars need virtually no owner-maintenance may lead to neglect of tire, steering-gear, and other maintenance not because the owner is negligent but because he is excessively credulous of advertising claims. Perhaps more important, the industry's efforts to provide a "soft" ride with low levels of noise and vibration has resulted in minimal feedback on changes in conditions of road or vehicle; consequently the driver may need an unusual degree of skill to identify and interpret very subtle cues that in fact are signals of serious danger.

Faults of processing. Even when the input of a cue is adequate, fault or failure may occur in its processing—that is, in the driver's interpretation of its meaning. A driver may, for example, perceive an on-coming car but decide to make a pass anyhow, not because he wants to take risks but because he makes an inappropriate judgment due to inexperience or to a perceptually misleading visual environment. At night a driver may see an on-coming car, judge its distance by the distance between its headlights, and make an error because it turns out to be a European compact, whose headlights are closer together and thus create an impression of greater distance. Or he may see a single headlight and assume it to be a motorcycle instead of a passenger vehicle with a defective left headlight. A substantial number of motorcycle crashes at intersections are apparently caused by the inexperience of automobile drivers in correctly judging both the speed and the distance of an on-coming motorcycle. * * *

Especially when coming from a high-speed expressway onto a rural road or local street, a driver may exceed the speed limit quite unintentionally because like the majority of drivers, he cannot gauge his speed within 10 to 20% without constantly monitoring his speedometer. Many drivers use road noise, engine noise, and the speed of accompanying traffic as gauges of their own speed, and the transition from one kind of road to another or one vehicle to another renders these cues unreliable.

A child pedestrian may hear a warning automobile horn and nevertheless run into the path of the automobile because young children have not yet developed the ability to determine the direction of the source of a sound.

Faults of output. Even if he perceives and interprets cues correctly, an individual may not be able to respond promptly and properly. * * *

There is also the likelihood that the appropriate response will be inhibited because the driver is overwhelmed with cues which he cannot sort out. * * *

The Learning Curve and Driving Skill. The process of learning any skill—whether it be driving an automobile, speaking French, or delivering a lecture—can be depicted graphically as a curve in which, as experience is gained, "inappropriate responses," or errors, decrease and are replaced by "appropriate responses," or correct behavior * * *. This concept of a curve implies that the commission and correction of errors is inherent in the learning process and that correct performance cannot be achieved unless errors are made and are understood to be errors. Hence, the insufficiently experienced driver—and this includes the graduate of driver education courses—is virtually certain to commit errors, some of them likely to result in violations or crashes.

* * *

Specific research on the relationship between an individual's driving skill and his likelihood of involvement in violations or crashes is difficult to undertake. * * *

* * * [Nevertheless], several studies have attempted to determine whether drivers who pass the skill test with high scores differ in subsequent crash experience from those who pass with low scores. These studies have shown that drivers with higher scores do have somewhat fewer crashes than those with lower scores. The differences, however, though statistically significant, are not substantial * * *. To the extent that basic skill can be evaluated by currently available techniques, therefore, such skill would appear to be a distinquishing factor in crash experience but not an overriding one.

Random Error. Although it may be possible to characterize an individual as a generally "safe" or generally "unsafe" driver, it is important to note that no individual performs even a thoroughly familiar task at precisely the same level of skill at all times. Everyone—from the professional athlete to the housewife—has "off days" or "bad moments" during which a normally high level of skill deteriorates sharply, for any of a multiplicity of reasons. Hence a substantial but largely unmeasureable number of violations and crashes occur which involve generally competent drivers who are suffering temporary lapses from their normally adequate levels.

Common sense would lead to the conclusion that such lapses, if they are indeed temporary and infrequent, might lead to a record of only one or two violations or crashes over a considerable period of time—certainly not a "bad" record. This is undoubtedly true for many drivers, and it probably accounts for a very high proportion of violations and of less severe crashes. Increasingly sophisticated statistical techniques demonstrate, however, that infrequent events, such as violations and crashes, do not distribute themselves in random fashion but may, instead, cluster in a quite "improbable" way. Thus it is possible for a generally "safe" driver to accumulate a "bad" record over a short period of time despite the fact that his lapses from "good" driving behavior are few. As Daniel P. Moynihan * * * has noted in connection with the "point" system employed by many states, the high-point driver may be a habitually unsafe driver, but he may also be a generally safe driver "who is the innocent victim of a statistically illiterate bureaucracy."

The foregoing analysis has several implications. It indicates that although intentional risk-taking and gross negligence undoubtedly play a part in some crashes—especially the more severe ones—many, if not most, cases of driver error are not intentional or negligent but are beyond conscious control. Some are the result of inherent biological limitations, transitory or permanent, of which the individual is unaware * * *. Others may be triggered by an environment (of highway, vehicle, etc.) that, at best, fails to inhibit, prevent, or forgive error and, at worst, actually promotes the likelihood or the inevitability of error * * *. In such cases error may be the proximate cause of a crash—the cause most easily noted in superficial investigation—but the remote causes, which lie elsewhere, may in fact be not only more significant but also more amenable to change. Still others may result from a combination of these factors.

A parallel situation existed for several centuries in the field of medicine. Before the discovery that many illnesses were caused by bacteria and viruses, it was common practice to assign the cause of death to miasma, air currents, or other climatic conditions that prevailed at the seasons of the year when certain microorganisms were more prevalent. In other cases death was attributed to such immediate causes as fever, wasting, or other end results of the action of microorganisms. As medicine developed into a true science, the stage was set for a more rational approach to prevention and treatment based on underlying, and more remote, rather than proximate and immediately visible causes.

Once the underlying causes were understood, the most dramatic accomplishments in medicine were achieved not by changing the behavior of the individual so much as by modifying the environment. Inoculations and improvements in personal sanitation, which required education of and cooperation from countless individuals, were far less effective in the reduction of contagious diseases than were such environmental changes as purification of water supply, regulation of food processing, and other measures which reduced the likelihood of the individual's coming into contact with the harmful microorganisms, no matter how "careful" or "careless" he might be.

The very sharp reduction in industrial injuries, too, was accomplished not by educational efforts to make the worker "more careful" but by changes in his environment through the adoption of machinery guards, air brakes and other fail-safe devices, factory fire laws, limitations on the concentration of coal dusts and other hazards in the air, etc. The few industries which still suffer a relatively high rate of industrial injuries are those in which technological devices for environmental safety have not yet been sufficiently developed (e. g., construction) or which for economic or ideological reasons generate extensive lobbying against their mandatory adoption (e. g., coal mining).

As we review the further data on causation, therefore, we must bear in mind that the human behavior involved in causation is itself the outcome of more remote causes, that attempting to change the proximate human behavior may be futile unless these more remote causes are modified, that there may be alternatives to the changing of human behavior, and that in connection with the highway problem these alternatives may be more effective than the traditional efforts to "improve" the driver. * * *

A Shift in Focus and Priorities

By far the most important inference to be drawn from this report is that efforts need to be shifted from the pre-crash phase of the crash sequence to the crash and post-crash phases—from the prevention or reduction of the number of crashes to the prevention or reduction of the human and economic losses that result from crashes.

A very substantial proportion of current countermeasures focuses on changing the behavior of the driver, apparently on the assumption that, since the driver is recognized, both in law and in public opinion, as being primarily responsible, countermeasures ought to be concentrated on him. Both the assumption and the policies based upon it, however, are open to serious question. First, as we have noted in many parts of this report, driver responsibility for crashes is rarely unilateral and is often impossible to isolate from the multiplicity of causes involved in almost every crash. Second, considerations of cost-benefit would dictate an emphasis on the *most effective* means of loss-reduction rather than a choice based on the faulty syllogism that since the driver is responsible for crashes, changing his behavior will reduce the number of crashes.

Given the present level of technology and the present economic and political system, it would appear that primary emphasis should be devoted to vehicle design improvements to increase crashworthiness—essentially an acceleration of some of the efforts that have been going on for the past several years and have already shown positive results. Second priority should be given to improving emergency health services because, relatively speaking, the costs are low and the return in terms of lives saved is high. Third priority should be given to improving the highway system—since highway changes require more time for legislative approval and both more time and more money for implementation. Lastly, efforts should be devoted to changing driver behavior, but such efforts must be based in sound research and must be implemented not on a happenstance basis, as they currently are, but systematically, tentatively, and under careful professional scrutiny—in the manner of other public health countermeasures. * * *

Although the narrow concept of individual culpability (or responsibility) is still very common among policy-makers and laymen alike with respect to traffic safety and is reinforced both by the legal profession and by the vast amounts of negligence litigation currently on court calendars, it has been largely abandoned (or substantially broadened) in other areas of pathology or deviance. The broadening of this concept has been accompanied almost invariably by a clearer understanding of the total process, and this understanding has led in some cases to more effective countermeasures, and—equally important—in others to the abandonment of traditional countermeasures which, though ineffective, absorbed substantial social resources and provided a false sense of accomplishment.

Recommendation

Since personal culpability is rarely the sole cause of a crash, since it is virtually impossible to isolate in the complexity of contributing factors, and since, even when isolated, it is more difficult to modify than many of the other contributing factors, it is recommended that a very substantial proportion of the resources now devoted to the determination of individual culpability be diverted to the development of environmental modifications which would make human "error" (both driver and pedestrian) less likely to occur and less severe in its consequences.

Deterrent Countermeasures

The conventional deterrent countermeasures, which are based essentially on punishing the driver for his "errors"—e. g., the issuance of citations, the punishment of traffic offenses through fines and imprisonment, the suspension or revocation of licenses, increases in insurance premiums, etc.—have proved to be substantially less effective than are measures based on protecting the driver in an inherently dangerous environment. Punitive measures have been largely ineffective for several reasons.

To begin with, most such countermeasures are based on the assumption that the behavior to be deterred is causally related to the initiation of a crash; but for a wide range of driving behavior this has not been satisfactorily demonstrated. Hence, even if the behavior is deterred effectively, a reduction in crash rates may not necessarily follow.

More important, the advocates of deterrence assume that those who do not conform to "safe" driving behavior (however it is defined) can be motivated to conform by current methods of deterrence —perhaps with more severe penalties attached to them. They overlook the fact that the population of those who *do not* conform consists, in substantial but unmeasurable part, of two subpopulations: those who *will not* conform and those who *cannot* conform. Those who *will not* conform to "safe" driving behavior do, in fact, conform to a set of deviant norms which are antithetical not only to safe driving but to a wide variety of socially acceptable behavior and they have demonstrated (by criminal recidivism, by driving with revoked licenses, by repeated citations, and by other nonvehicular forms of social deviance) that they are largely immune to conventional deterrent measures.

Those who *cannot* conform, no matter how well motivated, may be prevented by personal impairment either permanent or transitory —for example, physical, chemical, psychological, the effects of intense social pressure—or by defects in their immediate or remote environment—in the vehicle, the highway, etc. This "cannot conform" population is neither small nor stable. Every driver who has ever received a citation for a violation that was not intentional has been a member of it. And, like the "will not conform" population, such individuals are not deterrable, though for different reasons.

Recommendation

As long as deterrent measures concentrate on a punitive approach to the correction of "driver error," they are likely to remain relatively ineffective. The only route for "improvement" of their effectiveness is an increase in the severity of punishment—but any substantial increase in severity will cause intolerable economic and social dislocations and will have little effect on the "do not conform" group and no effect on the "cannot conform" group.

For example, the reduction of exposure—through improvements in urban planning and mass transit—seems promising, and this step is already being taken at the federal level. Modification of education and the mass media to change the symbolic meaning that driving and the automobile have for certain subcultural groups may be effective. Broad social and cultural changes which would offer the young person a meaningful social role and a means of establishing his identity would not only modify the traffic behavior of adolescents but would also reduce the incidence of a wide variety of social pathologies. * * *

Conclusion

As the review of the literature embodied in the preceding sections indicates, most efforts to modify driver behavior in the direction of "safer" driving are either demonstrably ineffective or of indeterminable effectiveness or exceedingly expensive from a cost-benefit point of view—especially in view of the availability of demonstrably more effective and less costly alternatives. It is our firm opinion that if much of the resources—money, manpower, and legislative and public support—now devoted to the identification and correction of human "error" were redirected to a clearer understanding and modification of the driver's and pedestrian's environment (this term being used in its very broadest sense), progress in the reduction of losses due to crashes would be substantially accelerated.[3]

ECONOMIC CONSEQUENCES OF AUTOMOBILE ACCIDENT INJURIES (Department of Transportation Automobile Insurance and Compensation Study 1970), Summary, pp. 1–4:

This report presents the results of a probability sample survey of police-reported injuries and fatalities due to automobile accidents in the 48 contiguous states and the District of Columbia.

Injured persons were identified as seriously injured if they responded to a screening questionnaire that they had been hospitalized for two weeks or more, *or* that they had $500 or more of medical

3. Notes omitted; for extensive references see original.

costs, other than hospital costs, *or* that, if working, they had missed three weeks of work, *or,* if not working, they had missed six weeks or more of normal activities.

Projected to universe totals, the study represents 500,000 fatalities and seriously injured persons according to the above definition.

Average economic losses to the date of interview (18 to 30 months after the accident) for seriously injured persons were $4,200. About 45% of this was wage loss, 38% was medical cost and 12% was property damage.

Nearly all had medical costs.

About two-thirds suffered wage losses.

About one-tenth of seriously injured persons suffered losses in future earnings. Half of such persons had losses whose present value (discounted) was over $25,000.

Average economic losses to fatality cases was $2,300, exclusive of lost earnings. Funeral and related costs contributed over half of this amount. Less than half incurred medical expense.

Economic losses to families who had one or more seriously injured members or fatalities averaged $4,200 to date of interview plus $6,100 in future lost earnings. Future lost earnings include wages of heads of households, and their spouses and an imputed earnings equivalent of $4,000 per year for homemakers. They exclude all earnings of other adults living with the family and potential earnings of children who died as a result of the accident. A maintenance cost of $2,000 per year was subtracted from future earnings of wage earners (or homemakers) killed in the accident. All future earnings were discounted to present values as 6%, adjusted for a 3% inflation rate.

Total societal losses in future earnings amounted to $13,600 per person seriously injured or killed. Adjusted for savings in maintenance and losses of persons without known dependents, the average personal and family loss was $5,900 per person seriously injured or killed.

On the average, about half of total personal and family economic loss was recovered.

> Over twice the amount of economic loss was recovered when such loss was under $500.
>
> Only 30% was recovered when total losses exceeded $25,000.
>
> About 9 out of 10 recovered some losses.

About one-third of recovery for personal and family losses due to serious injury or fatality was from tort (claims against another party or his insurance company), 15% from medical and auto medical insurance, 14% from life insurance, 6% from collision insurance, and 24%

from wage replacement sources (sick leave, workmen's compensation, Social Security, and other sources of replacement for actual or future wage losses).

Almost half received some medical insurance benefits.

35% recovered from auto medical insurance.

45% recovered from tort claims.

30% received benefits from collision insurance.

About 65% of seriously injured and fatalities were covered by some form of medical and hospital insurance. About 54% were covered by auto medical policies.

Legal costs amounted to about one-fourth of total recovery under tort for serious injury or fatality cases.

Claims against another party were made in 65% of serious injury or fatality cases. About 65% of those who made such claims retained counsel, and 74% of those retaining counsel actually filed lawsuits. About 8% of lawsuits filed actually reached verdict.

On the average, 16 months elapsed between date of accident and final settlement of tort claim. Larger economic losses were settled after longer delays and small losses after shorter delays.

30% of families with incomes under $5,000 retained counsel, compared to 42% of families with incomes over $10,000. The ratio of reparations to loss was 0.38 for low income families and 0.61 for high income families.

Persons with higher educational achievement had a greater tendency to retain counsel and also had a higher ratio of recovery to loss.

Males in the age group 15 to 44 constituted 20% of the population but suffered 39% of the serious injuries and fatalities.

Both actual and future wage losses of serious injuries or fatalities were poorly compensated for—about 15% from sick leave, workmen's compensation, Social Security and similar sources and an unknown amount from tort. Total net tort recovery, however, was only about one-fifth of total wage loss, so it is clear that total recovery of wage loss was relatively small.

A. TUNC, TORTS: TRAFFIC ACCIDENT COMPENSATION: LAW AND PROPOSALS, International Encyclopedia of Comparative Law 34 (1971):

* * *

69. *A general view.*—The need for law reform in the field of traffic accident compensation is today widely felt, even in countries which already have legislation imposing strict liability in this field. The most obvious arguments are practical in nature. They are based on court congestion, current injustices, costs, delays in the payment of compensation, etc.

However, it may be felt that most of the shortcomings of present systems are merely the consequences of a more fundamental defect: i. e., the inappropriate foundation of traffic accident compensation within the law of tort, especially when this involves the proof of negligence or fault.

The various arguments in support of the reform of the law will be summarized, starting with the more practical considerations, and continuing with the more theoretical ones. * * *

71. *Court congestion.*—In many countries, the most obvious impact of traffic accidents on the law and its administration is the congestion they produce in the courts. * * *

In the United States * * * the number of traffic accidents involving lawsuits is considered the main reason lying behind an unquestionable congestion in the courts. "According to a study published in 1966, the flood of automobile accident trials has produced an *average* delay of 31.1 months for personal injury trials in metropolitan areas. The longest average delay was 69.5 months in Chicago * * *. In their overwhelming number and time-consuming nature, these automobile cases are choking the court calendars and delaying the administration of justice in other types of case as well. Typically, automobile accident cases are two-thirds or more of a court's civil jury docket." One can say that "the present system of automobile insurance is preventing the American legal system from functioning properly."

72. *Delays in settlement.*—A similar observation can be made as regards cases which are settled out of court. There again, settlement is usually very slow. And what is worse, often the greater the loss, the slower the settlement. The reasons for this are (a) the sheer number of cases, (b) the reluctance on the part of many insurance companies to offer reasonable indemnity in the hope that the victim will become discouraged, and (c) delay in the courts, since settlement is often only reached when the imminence of trial induces the maximum effort to find an acceptable compromise. But these factors could all be reduced if the law could be made clearer and more certain. In itself, the sheer delay involved in reaching settlement would seem to justify Professor *Street*'s remark: "It is no exaggeration to state that the present tort system is endurable at all only because of the social security system. Although the tort system purports to be independent of the social security system it would be an utter failure if social security did not prop it up at every stage." [4]

73. *Tangible and intangible costs of indemnification.*—One of the most striking findings of Professor *Conard*'s research * * * relates to the costs of the process of indemnification. Taking into account all items of expense (insurance companies' administrative expenses, lawyers' and experts' fees), the study concludes that "in the

4. Elliott and Street, Road Accidents 247 (1968).

aggregate, the total burden is more than twice the net reparation delivered * * *. At the other end of the scale is social security, where the operating expense rate appears to be about 3 per cent of the reparation delivered".[5]

In another study, Professor *Conard* commented on the findings of the Michigan research as follows: "This summation indicated that the operating costs of the damage system are about 120 per cent of the net benefits that go to the injury victims themselves; the net amounts that the victims get are less than the total retained by insurance companies, law offices and courts. Presumably, the cost ratio would be even higher in such States as New York and Illinois, where it appears that the legal expenses are substantially higher than in Michigan." [6]

Such findings have obviously been disputed. However, a thorough study of the contradictory calculations recently made by various insurance associations and experts led Professor *Keeton* to the conclusion that "the practical performance of automobile liability insurance had been even worse than previously estimated". This conclusion is supported by the following results of his research: "Combined data from various studies reveal the stunning fact that, of the premium dollar collected for automobile bodily injury liability insurance, the part that is paid net to victims in compensation for out-of-pocket losses not already compensated from other sources amount to only 14½ cents. Even the additional net payments to victims for other items—8 cents for losses also compensated from other sources and 21½ cents for payments above loss, made in theory for pain and suffering—bring the net sum that victims receive to only 44 cents of the premium dollar." [7]

Three factors seem to account for the cost of the present system: "the refined objectives of tort reparation, which is 'custom made' for each injury victim;" the fact that "tort damages have many other objectives beyond mere reparation, including the deterrence of negligence"; the multiplicity of insurance companies, which results in high costs in the consequential competition for new clients, and in mutual settlements.

Besides the financial costs of the present system, there is also "a disturbing stream of evidence that many beneficiaries of the services of accident reparation carry away reactions of disappointment and even bitterness". "Other observations * * * painted an emphatic

5. Conard, et al., Automobile Accident Costs and Repayments 8 (1964).

6. Conard, The Economic Treatment of Automobile Injuries, 63 Mich.L.Rev. 279, 290 (1964).

7. R. Keeton, Compensation Systems: The Search for a Viable Alternative to Negligence Law 32–38 (1969). On the cost of litigation, see also *Department of Transportation,* Automobile Accident Litigation (1970) 7, 33–40 (especially 40: "at the output side of the legal process victims received about $.7 billion in net returns in 1968, and lawyers received about $.6 billion in fees and $.1 billion in expenses reimbursement"), 40–44 (especially 44: "the court administrative costs seem to be $4,200 per trial before a state court and $7,800 per trial before a federal court) * * *.

picture of anxiety, frustration, disappointment, and resentment felt by injury victims in the course of the adjustment and litigation processes. It is clear that there is room for tremendous improvement in the relations between injury victims and the people who deal with them": such is the conclusion reached by Professor *Conard* and his colleagues.

74. *Uncertainty as to the judgment of the respective liabilities of the parties.*—The uncertainty which parties usually feel as to their rights after a collision—or sometimes even after an accident not involving a collision—falls into two types: uncertainty as to the quantum of damage suffered; and uncertainty as to the respective liabilities of the parties.

The second type of uncertainty springs from a number of factors. First, there is in many cases the difficulty of reconstructing the circumstances of the accident (which may have occurred in a split second) with sufficient accuracy to pass judgment on the parties' respective behaviour. Even though the extent of this difficulty has been queried, it is certainly predominant in many cases, and would be fundamental in most cases if they were actually decided according to the criterion of the conduct of "the reasonable man".

Secondly, this difficulty is aggravated by the fact that the law does not recognize "accidents" as such. An "accident" is not regarded as a merely fortuitous event save in exceptional cases: in the eyes of the law it must result from the fault of one or other of the parties, or of both * * *. If, therefore, to borrow an example from daily life, a pedestrian walks on to a pedestrian crossing (not protected by lights) but, on seeing a car approaching, turns back and is hurt whilst doing so, the question in many countries * * * is in substance whether the car was being driven in a direction and at a speed which would allow it either to pass the pedestrian with a reasonable margin of safety, or to stop within a reasonable distance of him, and in a manner which made a reasonable allowance for any unfortunate reaction of fear on the part of the pedestrian, who is assumed to be a reasonable man. Perhaps an objective answer could be given if an expert had been warned that an accident was to occur and had watched both car and pedestrian (so far as that was possible). In many cases, however, the question cannot be answered, even by a witness who saw the accident until the very last moment, and, in most cases, it certainly cannot be answered by the judge or jury months (or even years) after the accident. It must be stressed that the case just discussed is in no way exceptional in the problem it involves. It is, in fact, typical of hundreds of accidents which occur every day in industrialized countries, often as a result of similar types of misunderstanding * * *.

75. *Uncertainty as to the assessment of damages.*—Whilst damages should, subject to some qualification, compensate so far as is possible the damage suffered by the injured party, there is strong evidence that in fact the practice greatly differs from the theory.

In the United States, the Columbia Study had found that relatively slight injuries were being promptly and vastly overcompensated; and that, in contrast, the more seriously hurt (or the dependent survivors of a decedent) were being grossly undercompensated, and then only after a long delay.[8] This pattern has remained the same, as is shown by two recent surveys. The University of Pennsylvania Survey, which embraced minor as well as serious injuries, revealed that in cases with less than US $100 of "tangible loss" reparation was frequently five times this loss, whilst, in cases where the loss exceeded US $3,000, it was frequently less than half.[9] Similarly, the results of the Michigan Survey have been summarized as follows: "At one end of the scale were one fifth of the injury victims, recovering less than a quarter of their economic loss; and at the other end were another fifth, who recovered more than one and a half times their economic loss. The smaller the loss, the greater the chance of generous compensation. * * * These observations relate to reparation from all sources; when tort reparation alone is considered, the disparity between the level of reparation becomes even more striking." [10]

These findings must be read with caution. For one thing, "tangible" or "economic" losses are not the only ones which deserve to be taken into consideration * * *. For another thing, the reparation taken into account is the total of what is received by the injured party under tort law, insurance, and in respect of social security. Thus, the fact that the reparation exceeds the loss, does not mean that too much has been paid. * * *

76. *Influence of insurers and lawyers in the settlement of accident claims.*—Uncertainty in the determination of liability and in the assessment of damages is in itself a serious evil. * * * Furthermore, this dual uncertainty opens the door to two evils, which, in turn, serve to increase the uncertainty: the scope for insurers to deny compensation, and for lawyers to press for unreasonably large fees. * * *

77. *Futility of litigation among insurers.*—The futility of litigation between insurers is another reason for establishing special rules dealing with traffic accidents. To the extent to which a case is a conflict between an insurer and a private person, it creates a risk of oppression by the former over the latter. To the extent to which it is a conflict between two insurers, it is a waste of time and money. If the argument is of a legal nature, one may be certain that, given the sheer number of traffic accidents occurring daily, the two opponents are probably arguing from opposite positions in some other case. If the argument is of a practical nature and relates, for example, to the question of whether such and such a party has been negligent, the dis-

8. R. Keeton and J. O'Connell, Basic Protection for the Traffic Victim 36–37 (1965).

9. Morris and Paul, The Financial Impact of Automobile Accidents, 110 U. Pa.L.Rev. 913, 917 (1962).

10. Conard, op. cit. note 6 supra, at 6–7.

cussion is as meaningless as in the former case, since there is no reason why the clients of insurer A should be either more or less careful than those of insurer B; and it would seem logical, therefore, that a set-off arrangement should take the place now occupied by the argument of individual cases. * * *

78. *Distortion of the law by juries and judges.*—It is a well-known fact that in countries where the decision on fact is entrusted to juries—especially in the United States—most lawyers do their best to manipulate the juries, and with the help of books and professional journals, they have attained in this art a high degree of expertise and skill. Obviously, they take advantage of the uncertainties of the circumstances of the accident * * *, and as to the extent of the damage * * *. But what should be emphasized is that in most cases juries incline towards the plaintiff: "there is a widespread popular revulsion against failure to care for the economic loss of injured persons regardless of negligence and contributory negligence. This is not particularly identified with the idea that the causers of loss should pay; on the contrary, the feeling seems to be that it should be taken care of by insurance without regard to what kind."

What is even more remarkable is that this bias in favour of the injured person regardless of negligence or contributory negligence is even to be found amongst judges—who are professional men. * * * In practice, this means that those with control over the operation of the law do not in fact believe in it. * * *

80. *Defects in the protection of the driver.*—All the foregoing trends point to a very serious deficiency in the protection of road users against traffic hazards. Granted that compensation of all (or nearly all) victims is desirable on human grounds and justified on legal ones * * *, it seems hardly tolerable that in some countries a majority of victims receive no compensation whatsoever under the law of tort.[11]

11. Only 37% of the victims considered by the Michigan Study received compensation under the law of tort. Another 40% received compensation from other sources, mainly their own insurance. See Conard, op. cit. note 6 supra, at 138–139 (and also 145–155); Keeton and O'Connell, op. cit. note 8 supra, at 43–46, 49–53. [Notes 4–11 adapted from original; other notes in original omitted.]

EXCERPT FROM REPORT OF PROFESSOR ROGER C. HENDERSON TO SPECIAL COMMITTEE ON UNIFORM MOTOR VEHICLE ACCIDENT REPARATIONS ACT, NATIONAL CONFERENCE OF COMMISSIONERS ON UNIFORM STATE LAWS (April 1976):

* * *

II. STATUS OF NO-FAULT COMPENSATION SYSTEMS FOR TRAFFIC ACCIDENTS IN THE UNITED STATES

* * * Massachusetts was the first state to enact a scheme denominated as no-fault automobile insurance. Since this landmark legislation, effective January 1, 1971, there have been twenty-three more so called no-fault automobile insurance statutes passed in the United States. This legislation has varied markedly in detail as well as basic structure, leading some of those in favor of reform to charge that a good number of these statutes are not genuine no-fault laws. In addition to the variety of plans passed by the state legislatures, other plans are being considered, including some by the federal congress and by those states which have already passed no-fault legislation, that are still different.

Although the enacted and proposed plans vary considerably, certain patterns have emerged. At least in regard to compensation schemes for bodily injury, the no-fault plans which have been enacted and which are being proposed can be grouped into three basic categories without doing too much violence to them. The first category has been denominated as "add-on" plans, the second "modified" plans, and the third "pure" no-fault plans.

A. Add-On Plans

This first category includes those plans that merely prescribe that additional coverages be added to the present standard automobile liability insurance policy. These plans are generally referred to as "add-on" plans because they merely add to the present tort-liability insurance system and do not abolish tort liability. This type of plan, in addition to the present standard coverages protecting against the possibility of tort liability, as well as collision and comprehensive coverages, medical payments, and uninsured motorist coverage, afford coverages which would include increased benefits for medical and related expenses and new benefits for lost wages and for loss of essential nonincome producing services. A few of the add-on plans would include a life insurance benefit in the event of death. These additional coverages are no-fault coverages like the present collision, comprehensive, and medical payments coverages, but are limited to damages arising from bodily injury. Of the 24 states enacting so called no-fault automobile insurance plans, eight are add-on type schemes.

These add-on plans can be further subcategorized into three types. The first sub-type includes those that require that any insurance company that writes automobile liability insurance in the enacting state must offer these additional coverages to anyone purchasing a standard automobile liability insurance policy. The automobile owner has the option either to buy or reject the additional coverages, just as he * * * may do today with collision, comprehensive, medical payments, and, in some states, uninsured motorist coverage. These plans are referred to as providing optional add-on no-fault coverage. The states of South Dakota [12], Texas [13], and Virginia [14] presently have such a plan. Minnesota previously enacted such a scheme only to supersede it in 1974 with a much more extensive type of plan to be discussed below. Apparently, there is a similar move * * * in South Dakota * * *.

The second sub-type of add-on plan includes those plans that require the additional coverages to be included in any automobile liability insurance policy sold or issued for delivery in the enacting state so that when one buys that type of policy there is no choice as the additional no-fault coverages are included as part of the package. Arkansas [15] and Oregon [16] have adopted this type of plan which is referred to as providing mandatory add-on no-fault insurance. One is not required to buy the automobile liability insurance policy under the financial responsibility law of these states, but if the policy is purchased one has no choice and receives the additional no-fault coverages as a part of the package.

The third sub-type includes those plans that require not only that the additional coverages must be included in every automobile liability insurance policy sold or issued for delivery in the enacting state, but that one must purchase the policy before he * * * can legally operate an automobile on the highways of that state. This type of law is referred to as compulsory add-on no-fault insurance and has been adopted in Delaware,[17] Maryland,[18] and South Carolina.[19]

The no-fault coverages in the add-on plans range from $1,000 to about $15,000. The add-on coverages also are sometimes conditioned on the loss being incurred within a certain time from the date of the accident, for example one year. Under this type of plan there is no change in the legal system that now exists which determines when one may or may not successfully sue or be sued in tort for personal injury or property damage resulting from the operation or use of a motor vehicle. Before or after collecting the additional no-fault benefits, a person is free to pursue his * * * claim under the fault-based tort system, usually subject to certain rights of off-set, or reimbursement or subrogation on behalf of the no-fault insurer.

12. S.D.Comp.Laws §§ 58–23–6 –8 (Supp. 1974).

13. Tex.Ins.Code Ann. art. 5.06–3 (Supp. 1975).

14. Va.Code Ann. § 381.1–380.2 (Supp. 1975).

15. Ark.Stat.Ann. §§ 66–4014 –4021 (Supp.1975).

16. Ore.Rev.Stat. §§ 743.800–.835 (1973).

17. Del.Code Ann. tit. 21, § 2118 (1974).

18. Md.Ann.Code art. 48A, §§ 538–546 (Supp.1975).

19. S.C.Code §§ 46–750.101 –154 (Supp. 1974).

B. Modified Plans

The second basic category of plans is referred to as modified no-fault and differs from the add-on plans in that the former eliminates some part of the present tort liability system for bodily injury. When injured in an automobile accident the victim receives benefits from the additional no-fault coverages under the modified plans, which would be similar in type but in some instances much larger in dollar amounts than those described in the add-on plans. The victim, however, would be limited to some extent in his * * * right to sue the tortfeasor under the rules of law pertaining to negligence. He * * * would also be free, usually to the same extent, from being sued. The modified no-fault plans can be broken down into two sub-types depending upon the extent to which different types of damages under the tort liability system are abolished. The plans in the first sub-type would limit one's right to sue under the tort system for general damages only. One would still be able to sue in tort for any economic loss suffered as a result of an automobile accident, but the right to sue for pain and suffering and similar damages would be limited. Typically the limitation placed on the recovery for these noneconomic losses applies only in the less-than-serious injury cases. This is accomplished through the use of techniques called "thresholds". The first technique employed is related to the amount of medical expense that one incurs as a result of the accident. The second technique is to describe certain injuries for which a cause of action for pain and suffering is retained. Thus, the right to recover for general damages is eliminated in cases in which the medical expenses do not exceed a certain figure, for example $500, or do not meet narrative thresholds which attempt to delineate certain serious injuries, for example, death, permanent serious disfigurement, fracture, or loss of body function. Conversely, where the medical expense threshold or a narrative threshold is met there is no limitation and one can still claim the full amount of general damages suffered. As mentioned, these plans do not involve any limitation or restriction on the tort cause of action for economic loss such as medical bills or loss of earnings. A right of subrogation or reimbursement is usually provided for the no-fault insurer so as to adhere to the principle of indemnity by preventing the insured from collecting twice for the same economic loss. Of the fourteen states adopting modified no-fault insurance plans, seven fall into the sub-type described above: Colorado [20], Georgia [21], Kansas [22], Kentucky [23], Minnesota [24], New Jersey [25], and Utah [26].

20. Colo.Rev.Stat.Ann. §§ 13–25–1 –23 (Supp.1974).

21. Ga.Code Ann. §§ 56–3501b –3413b, § 56–9915.2 (Supp.1975).

22. Kan.Stat.Ann. §§ 40–3101 –3121 (Supp.1975).

23. Ky.Rev.Stat.Ann., §§ 304.39–010–340, § 304.99–050 (Supp.1974).

24. Minn.Stat.Ann. §§ 65B.14, 65B.41–71 (Supp.1976).

25. N.J.Stat.Ann. §§ 39:6A–1 –20 (1973).

26. Utah Code Ann. §§ 31–41–1 –13.4 (1974).

The second sub-type of modified no-fault insurance plan includes those plans that not only limit one's right to recover general damages in the minor or less-than-serious personal injury cases, but * * * also eliminate the right to sue or be sued in tort for economic loss to the extent that one is entitled to collect the no-fault benefits. Each insured injured party would collect for economic loss from his * * * own insurance carrier up to the limits provided, and to that extent the cause of action for negligence against the other motorist would be abolished. A cause of action would be retained for any economic loss above that compensated by the no-fault benefits. It is this second type of modified plan that Massachusetts adopted.[27] The states of Connecticut [28], Florida [29], Hawaii [30], Nevada [31], North Dakota [32], and Pennsylvania [33] have also followed the same track. All of the plans falling in both sub-types make the additional no-fault insurance coverages compulsory, save Kentucky.

C. Plans Approaching Pure No-Fault

The third basic category includes those plans which more nearly approach what has been denominated as pure no-fault insurance proposals. A pure no-fault insurance plan would eliminate the negligence system as the basis for compensating traffic victims for bodily injury entirely and substitute in lieu thereof a comprehensive no-fault insurance scheme. None of the plans which have been included in the third category go this far, but they do provide for much more extensive compulsory no-fault benefits and concomitant abolition of tort liability than those in the modified no-fault plans described above. For these reasons they deserve to be distinguished because they constitute a more definite decision to favor compensating traffic accident victims solely on a no-fault basis. Like most of the modified no-fault plans, the additional no-fault coverages are always compulsory. New York [34] and Michigan [35] have taken the largest steps in abolishing the negligence system and substituting therefore a no-fault insurance scheme. Neither, however, has gone as far as the Uniform Motor Vehicle Accident Reparations Act (UMVARA) although much of the language and basic structure of the New York and Michigan acts are taken from the Uniform Act.

The New York act provides up to $50,000 of no-fault benefits for most personal injury losses suffered as a result of a motor vehicle ac-

27. Mass.Gen.Laws Ann. ch. 90, §§ 34A, 34D, 34H, 34K, 34M, 34N, 34O (1975), ch. 231, § 6D (Supp.1974).

28. Conn.Gen.Stat.Rev. §§ 38–319 –351a (Supp.1975).

29. Fla.Stat.Ann. §§ 627.730–.741 (1974).

30. Hawaii Rev.Laws §§ 294–1 –41 (Supp.1974).

31. Nev.Rev.Stat. §§ 698.010 –.510 (1973).

32. N.D.Cent.Code §§ 26–41–01–19 (Supp.1975).

33. Pa.Stat. tit. 40, §§ 1009.101–, 603 (Supp.1975).

34. N.Y.Ins.Law §§ 670–677 (McKinney Supp.1975).

35. Mich.Comp.Laws §§ 500.3101 –.3179 (Supp.1975).

cident, and to the same extent abolishes causes of action for pecuniary losses arising out of negligent motor vehicle operation. Death cases are not covered by the New York plan. The Michigan act provides for unlimited medical loss reimbursement and up to $1,000 per month for three years for certain other economic loss. It likewise abolishes negligence actions for economic loss to the extent no-fault benefits are payable. In regard to causes of action for general damages, the Michigan act is designed to eliminate all causes of action for general damages save those involving very serious injury. Thus, the act abolishes the great majority of causes of action arising out of the ownership, maintenance, or use of motor vehicles which heretofore have been based on negligence concepts. It more clearly involves a shift to a different system of compensating traffic accident victims. * * *

The literature on no-fault compensation plans for accidents is enormous. Among many other contributions, reference can fruitfully be made to R. Keeton and J. O'Connell, Basic Protection for The Traffic Victim (1965); Blum and Kalven, Ceilings, Costs, and Compulsion in Auto Compensation Legislation, 1973 Utah L.Rev. 341; Keeton, Compensation Systems and Utah's No-Fault Statute, 1973 Utah L.Rev. 383; and J. O'Connell and R. Henderson, Tort Law, No-Fault and Beyond (1975). Also of interest are a celebrated exchange: Blum and Kalven, Public Law Perspectives on a Private Law Problem —Auto Compensation Plans, 31 U.Chi.L.Rev. 641 (1964); Calabresi, Fault, Accidents and the Wonderful World of Blum and Kalven, 75 Yale L.J. 216 (1965); and Blum and Kalven, The Empty Cabinet of Dr. Calabresi: Auto Accidents and General Deterrence, 34 U.Chi.L. Rev. 239 (1967); and symposia at 71 Colum.L.Rev. 189–273 (1971) and 44 Miss.L.J. 1–181 (1973).

Similar suggestions have been made concerning other kinds of accidents. For no-fault approaches to medical injuries, for instance, see Havighurst and Tancredi, "Medical Adversity Insurance"—A No-Fault Approach to Medical Malpractice and Quality Assurance, 1974 (February) Ins.L.J. 69; O'Connell, Elective No-Fault Liability by Contract—With or Without An Enabling Statute, 1975 Ill.L.Forum 59; Havighurst, "Medical Adversity Insurance": Has Its Time Come? 1975 Duke L.J. 1233; but see Keeton, Compensation for Medical Accidents, 121 U.Pa.L.Rev. 590 (1973). For a review of less drastic alternatives see Comment, An Analysis of State Legislative Responses to the Medical Malpractice Crisis, 1975 Duke L.J. 1417.

For more general discussions see also T. Ison, The Forensic Lottery (1967); P. Atiyah, Accidents, Compensation and the Law (2d ed. 1975); and G. Calabresi, The Costs of Accidents (1970).

Chapter 5

SUPPLIERS OF GOODS AND REMOTE CONTRACTORS

INTRODUCTORY NOTE

In this Chapter we shall be concerned with the liability to the person physically harmed of the persons who, as manufacturers or as wholesale or retail distributors through sale or bailment, put out the defective commodities which caused the harm. The matter of quality and fitness of goods is important for sellers and buyers quite apart from the relatively very small percentage of cases in which the goods contain defects that ultimately cause physical harm. A large body of law exists, therefore, with respect to the obligations of sellers and buyers which comprises at least one course in law school curricula and is unrelated to torts. But when the sold goods, because defective, cause physical harm (as distinguished from the mercantile harm resulting when the buyer gets a $.50 piece of glass though he thought he was buying a $500 diamond) torts and sales overlap.

Accordingly, the materials included in this chapter cut across the lines of jurisdiction in curriculum. We do not usurp the domain of sales law. But we do enter so much of it as is relevant. Our view of it here may leave room for emendation in the course on Sales, but we shall have a fair picture of the way in which physical harms caused by defective commodities are dealt with in the *law*—not merely in the part of it called torts.[1]

WINTERBOTTOM v. WRIGHT

Court of Exchequer, 1842.
10 M. & W. 109, 11 L.J.Ex. 415, 152 Eng.Rep. 402.

The declaration stated, that the defendant was a contractor for the supply of mail-coaches, and had in that character contracted for hire and reward with the Postmaster-General, to provide the mail-coach for the purpose of conveying the mail-bags from Hartford, in

1. The material covered by this chapter is discussed generally in L. Frumer and M. Friedman, Products Liability (1966) and D. Noel and J. Phillips, Products Liability in a Nutshell (1974).

For penetrating policy discussions see Symposium, Products Liability: Economic Analysis and the Law, 38 U. Chi.L.Rev. 1 et seq. (1970), particularly two articles which tend to resist the extension of producer liability: McKean, Products Liability: Trends and Implications, id. at 3, and Buchanan, In Defense of *Caveat Emptor*, id. at 64, and two rebuttals, Calabresi and Bass, Right Approach, Wrong Implications: A Critique of McKean on Products Liability, id. at 74 (from a point of view involving economic analysis) and Gilmore, Products Liability: A Commentary, id. at 103 (from a historical perspective, staunchly aloof from economic theory).

For other useful symposia on products liability see 2 Hofstra L.Rev. 445 et seq. (1974) and 12 Duquesne L.Rev. 425 et seq. (1974).

the county of Chester, to Holyhead: That the defendant, under and by virtue of the said contract, had agreed with the said Postmaster-General that the said mail-coach should, during the said contract, be kept in a fit, proper, safe, and secure state and condition for the said purpose, and took upon himself, to wit, under and by virtue of the said contract, the sole and exclusive duty, charge, care, and burden of the repairs, state, and condition of the said mail-coach; and it had become and was the sole and exclusive duty of the defendant, to wit, under and by virtue of his said contract, to keep and maintain the said mail-coach in a fit, proper, safe, and secure state and condition for the purpose aforesaid: That Nathaniel Atkinson and other persons, having notice of the said contract, were under contract with the Postmaster-General to convey the said mail-coach from Hartford to Holyhead, and to supply horses and coachmen for that purpose, and also, not, on any pretence whatever, to use or employ any other coach or carriage whatever than such as should be so provided, directed, and appointed by the Postmaster-General: That the plaintiff, being a mail-coachman, and thereby obtaining his livelihood, and whilst the said several contracts were in force, having notice thereof, and trusting to and confiding in the contract made between the defendant and the Postmaster-General, and believing that the said coach was in a fit, safe, secure and proper state and condition for the purpose aforesaid, and not knowing and having no means of knowing to the contrary thereof, hired himself to the said Nathaniel Atkinson and his co-contractors as mail-coachman, to drive and take the conduct of the said mail-coach, which but for the said contract of the defendant he would not have done. The declaration then averred, that the defendant so improperly and negligently conducted himself, and so utterly disregarded his aforesaid contract, and so wholly neglected and failed to perform his duty in this behalf, that heretofore, to wit, on the 8th of August, 1840, whilst the plaintiff, as such mail-coachman so hired, was driving the said mail-coach from Hartford to Holyhead, the same coach, being a mail-coach found and provided by the defendant under his said contract, and the defendant then acting under his said contract, and having the means of knowing and then well knowing all the aforesaid premises, the said mail-coach being then in a frail, weak, infirm, and dangerous state and condition, to wit, by and through certain latent defects in the state and condition thereof, and unsafe and unfit for the use and purpose aforesaid, and from no other cause, circumstance, matter, or thing whatsoever, gave way and broke down, whereby the plaintiff was thrown from his seat, and, in consequence of injuries then received, had become lamed for life.

To this declaration the defendant pleaded several pleas, to two of which there were demurrers; but as the Court gave no opinion as to their validity, it is not necessary to state them.

LORD ABINGER, C. B. I am clearly of opinion that the defendant is entitled to our judgment. We ought not to permit a doubt to rest upon this subject, for our doing so might be the means of letting in upon us an infinity of actions. This is an action of the first impression, and it has been brought in spite of the precautions which were taken, in the judgment of this Court in the case of Levy v. Langridge, [2 M. & W. 519, 4 M. & W. 337] to obviate any notion that such an action could be maintained. We ought not to attempt to extend the principle of that decision, which, although it has been cited in support of this action, wholly fails as an authority in its favour; for there the gun was bought for the use of the son, the plaintiff in that action, who could not make the bargain himself, but was really and substantially the party contracting. Here the action is brought simply because the defendant was a contractor with a third person; and it is contended that thereupon he became liable to everybody who might use the carriage. If there had been any ground for such an action, there certainly would have been some precedent of it; but with the exception of actions against innkeepers, and some few other persons, no case of a similar nature has occurred in practice. That is a strong circumstance, and is of itself a great authority against its maintenance. It is however contended, that this contract being made on the behalf of the public by the Postmaster-General, no action could be maintained against him, and therefore the plaintiff must have a remedy against the defendant. But that is by no means a necessary consequence—he may be remediless altogether. There is no privity of contract between these parties; and if the plaintiff can sue, every passenger, or even any person passing along the road who was injured by the upsetting of the coach, might bring a similar action. Unless we confine the operation of such contracts as this to the parties who entered into them, the most absurd and outrageous consequences, to which I can see no limit, would ensue. Where a party becomes responsible to the public, by undertaking a public duty, he is liable, though the injury may have arisen from the negligence of his servant or agent. So in cases of public nuisances, whether the act was done by the party as a servant, or in any other capacity, you are liable to an action at the suit of any person who suffers. Those, however, are cases where the real ground of the liability is the public duty, or the commission of the public nuisance. There is also a class of cases in which the law permits a contract to be turned into a tort; but unless there has been some public duty undertaken, or public nuisance committed, they are all cases in which an action might have been maintained upon the contract. Thus, a carrier may be sued either in *assumpsit* or case; but there is no instance in which a party, who was not privy to the contract entered into with him, can maintain any such action. The plaintiff in this case could not have brought an action on the contract; if he could have done so, what would have been his situation, supposing the Postmaster-General had released the defendant? that would, at all events, have defeated his claim altogether. By permitting this action, we should be working this injustice, that after the defendant had done every thing to the satisfaction of his employer, and after all matters between them had been adjusted, and all accounts settled on the footing of their contract, we should subject them to be ripped open by this action of tort being brought against him.

ALDERSON, B. I am of the same opinion. The contract in this case was made with the Postmaster-General alone: and the case is just the same as if he had come to the defendant and ordered a carriage, and handed it at once over to Atkinson. If we were to hold that the plaintiff could sue in such a case, there is no point at which such actions would stop. The only safe rule is to confine the right to recover to those who enter into the contract: if we go one step beyond that, there is no reason why we should not go fifty. The only real argument in favour of the action is, that this is a case of hardship; but that might have been obviated, if the plaintiff had made himself a party to the contract. Then it is urged that it falls within the principle of the case of Levy v. Langridge. But the principle of that case was simply this, that the father having bought the gun for the very purpose of being used by the plaintiff, the defendant made representations by which he was induced to use it. There, a distinct fraud was committed on the plaintiff; the falsehood of the representation was also alleged to have been within the knowledge of the defendant who made it, and he was properly held liable for the consequences. How are the facts of that case applicable to those of the present? Where is the allegation of misrepresentation or fraud in this declaration? It shows nothing of the kind. Our judgment must therefore be for the defendant.

GURNEY, B., concurred.

ROLFE, B. * * * The duty [with breach of which defendant is charged], therefore, is shown to have arisen solely from the contract; and the fallacy consists in the use of that word "duty." If a duty to the Postmaster-General be meant, that is true; but if a duty to the plaintiff be intended (and in that sense the word is evidently used), there was none. This is one of those unfortunate cases in which there certainly has been *damnum,* but is it *damnum absque injuria*; it is, no doubt, a hardship upon the plaintiff to be without a remedy, but, by that consideration we ought not to be influenced. Hard cases, it has been frequently observed, are apt to introduce bad law.

Judgment for the defendant.[2]

2. This case comes down to us, and has been consistently treated, as the leading case for the proposition that a manufacturer or seller is not liable to a remote purchaser with whom he is not in "privity of contract" for harm caused even by the lack of care on his part in putting out the product; because, it is said, the manufacturer or seller is not under a duty to the remote purchaser, not in privity of contract, to exercise care. It is enlightening toward an understanding of the development of law to see how far the case supports this proposition for which alone the case is remembered. What features of the case would indicate a much narrower principle? But, of course, the opinions may express a common-sense judgment of much wider applicability. "The wide acceptance of this rule is remarkable in as much as it was based on dictum by Lord Abinger in a case which involved a contractor rather than a manufacturer, and the matter was before the court on a demurrer." Anderson v. Linton, 178 F.2d 304, 307 (7th Cir. 1949). The judges treat the case as one of first impression. No precedent for the plaintiff's claim, but also no precedent denying his claim. How

MacPHERSON v. BUICK MOTOR CO.

Court of Appeals of New York, 1916.
217 N.Y. 382, 111 N.E. 1050, L.R.A.1916F, 696, Ann.Cas.1916C, 440.

CARDOZO, J. The defendant is a manufacturer of automobiles. It sold an automobile to a retail dealer. The retail dealer resold to the plaintiff. While the plaintiff was in the car, it suddenly collapsed. He was thrown out and injured. One of the wheels was made of defective wood, and its spokes crumbled into fragments. The wheel was not made by the defendant; it was bought from another manufacturer. There is evidence, however, that its defects could have been discovered by reasonable inspection, and that inspection was omitted. There is no claim that the defendant knew of the defect and willfully concealed it. The case, in other words, is not brought within the rule of Kuelling v. Roderick Lean Mfg. Co., 183 N.Y. 78, 75 N.E. 1098, 2 L.R.A., N.S., 303, 111 Am.St.Rep. 691, 5 Ann.Cas. 124. The charge is one, not of fraud, but of negligence. The question to be determined is whether the defendant owed a duty of care and vigilance to any one but the immediate purchaser.

The foundations of this branch of the law, at least in this state, were laid in Thomas v. Winchester, 6 N.Y. 397, 57 Am.Dec. 455. A poison was falsely labeled. The sale was made to a druggist, who in turn sold to a customer. The customer recovered damages from the seller who affixed the label. "The defendant's negligence," it was said, "put human life in imminent danger." A poison falsely labeled is likely to injure any one who gets it. Because the danger is to be foreseen, there is a duty to avoid the injury. Cases were cited by way of illustration in which manufacturers were not subject to any duty irrespective of contract. The distinction was said to be that their conduct, though negligent, was not likely to result in injury to any one except the purchaser. We are not required to say whether the chance of injury was always as remote as the distinction assumes. Some of the illustrations might be rejected today. The *principle* of the distinction is for present purposes the important thing.

Thomas v. Winchester became quickly a landmark of the law. In the application of its principle there may at times have been uncertainty or even error. There has never in this state been doubt or disavowal of the principle itself. The chief cases are well known, yet to

then is the law determined for such a new case? The court does not mean that *no* new liability can be created—or does it? If not, then what considerations are to guide choice? How well suited was the decision to the life of 1842? How well suited to the present? What kind of life does the decision subsume?

Note that even in 1842 there was troublesome precedent. Is the court's treatment of Levy v. Langridge satisfying? What would be plaintiff's argument to show similarity rather than difference? The following cases sketch the life of the doctrine of Winterbottom v. Wright. What doomed it?

See Bohlen, Liability of Manufacturers to Persons Other Than Their Immediate Vendees, 45 L.Q.Rev. 343 (1929).

recall some of them will be helpful. Loop v. Litchfield, 42 N.Y. 351, 1 Am.Rep. 543, is the earliest. It was the case of a defect in a small balance wheel used on a circular saw. The manufacturer pointed out the defect to the buyer, who wished a cheap article and was ready to assume the risk. The risk can hardly have been an imminent one, for the wheel lasted five years before it broke. In the meanwhile the buyer had made a lease of the machinery. It was held that the manufacturer was not answerable to the lessee. Loop v. Litchfield was followed in Losee v. Clute, 51 N.Y. 494, 10 Am.Rep. 638, the case of the explosion of a steam boiler. That decision has been criticised (Thompson on Negligence, 233; Shearman & Redfield on Negligence [6th ed.], section 117); but it must be confined to its special facts. It was put upon the ground that the risk of injury was too remote. The buyer in that case had not only accepted the boiler, but had tested it. The manufacturer knew that his own test was not the final one. The finality of the test has a bearing on the measure of diligence owing to persons other than the purchaser (Beven, Negligence [3d ed.], pp. 50, 51, 54; Wharton, Negligence [2d ed.] section 134).

These early cases suggest a narrow construction of the rule. Later cases, however, evince a more liberal spirit. * * *

It may be that Devlin v. Smith and Statler v. Ray Mfg. Co.[3] have extended the rule of Thomas v. Winchester. If so, this court is committed to the extension. The defendant argues that things imminently dangerous to life are poisons, explosives, deadly weapons—things whose normal function it is to injure or destroy. But whatever the rule in Thomas v. Winchester may once have been, it has no longer that restricted meaning. A scaffold (Devlin v. Smith, supra) is not inherently a destructive instrument. It becomes destructive only if imperfectly constructed. A large coffee urn (Statler v. Ray Mfg. Co., supra) may have within itself, if negligently made, the potency of danger, yet no one thinks of it as an implement whose normal function is destruction. What is true of the coffee urn is equally true of bottles of aerated water (Torgeson v. Schultz, 192 N.Y. 156, 84 N.E. 956) * * *

Devlin v. Smith was decided in 1882. A year later a very similar case came before the Court of Appeal in England (Heaven v. Pender, L.R. 11 Q.B.D. 503). We find in the opinion of BRETT, M.R., after-

3. In Statler v. George A. Ray Mfg. Co., 195 N.Y. 478, 88 N.E. 1063 (1909), defendant was a manufacturer of coffee urns for restaurant use. It sold to a jobber who sold one to a hotel company of which plaintiff was an officer. After the urn was put into use in the hotel it exploded, killed one person and scalded the plaintiff and one other. Said the court (Hiscock, J.):

"We think further that there was evidence which permitted a jury to say that the defendant, knowing the uses for which the urn was intended when it marketed the same, was guilty of, and of course chargeable with knowledge of, defective and unsafe construction. This leaves on this branch of the case simply the question whether a manufacturer and vendor of such an inherently dangerous appliance as this was may be made liable to a third party on the theory invoked by plaintiff, and we think that this question must be regarded as settled in the latter's favor. * * *"

wards Lord Esher (p. 510), the same conception of a duty, irrespective of contract, imposed upon the manufacturer by the law itself: "Whenever one person supplies goods, or machinery, or the like, for the purpose of their being used by another person under such circumstances that every one of ordinary sense would, if he thought, recognize at once that unless he used ordinary care and skill with regard to the condition of the thing supplied or the mode of supplying it, there will be danger of injury to the person or property of him for whose use the thing is supplied, and who is to use it, a duty arises to use ordinary care and skill as to the condition or manner of supplying such thing." He then points out that for a neglect of such ordinary care or skill whereby injury happens, the appropriate remedy is an action for negligence. The right to enforce this liability is not to be confined to the immediate buyer. The right, he says, extends to the persons or class of persons for whose use the thing is supplied. It is enough that the goods "would in all probability be used at once * * * before a reasonable opportunity for discovering any defect which might exist," and that the thing supplied is of such a nature "that a neglect of ordinary care or skill as to its condition or the manner of supplying it would probably cause danger to the person or property of the person for whose use it was supplied, and who was about to use it." On the other hand, he would exclude a case "in which the goods are supplied under circumstances in which it would be a chance by whom they would be used or whether they would be used or not, or whether they would be used before there would probably be means of observing any defect," or where the goods are of such a nature that "a want of care or skill as to their condition or the manner of supplying them would not probably produce danger of injury to person or property." What was said by Lord ESHER in that case did not command the full assent of his associates. His opinion has been criticised "as requiring every man to take affirmative precautions to protect his neighbors as well as to refrain from injuring them" (Bohlen, Affirmative Obligations in the Law of Torts, 44 Am.Law Reg., N.S., 341). It may not be an accurate exposition of the law of England. Perhaps it may need some qualification even in our own state. Like most attempts at comprehensive definition, it may involve errors of inclusion and of exclusion. But its tests and standards, at least in their underlying principles, with whatever qualification may be called for as they are applied to varying conditions, are the tests and standards of our law.

We hold, then, that the principle of Thomas v. Winchester is not limited to poisons, explosives, and things of like nature, to things which in their normal operation are implements of destruction. If the nature of a thing is such that it is reasonably certain to place life and limb in peril when negligently made, it is then a thing of danger. Its nature gives warning of the consequences to be expected. If to the element of danger there is added knowledge that the thing will be used by persons other than the purchaser, and used without new tests, then, irrespective of contract, the manufacturer of this thing of danger is under a duty to make it carefully. That is as far as we are required to go for the decision of this case. There must be knowledge of a danger, not merely possible, but probable. It is *possible* to use almost anything in a way that will make it dangerous if defective. That is not enough to charge the manufacturer with a duty independent of his contract. Whether a given thing is dangerous may be sometimes a question for the court and sometimes a question for the jury. There must also be knowledge that in the usual course of events the danger will be shared by others than the buyer. Such knowledge may often be inferred from the nature of the transaction. But it is possible that even knowledge of the danger and of the use will not always be enough. The proximity or remoteness of the relation is a factor to be considered. We are dealing now with the liability of the manufacturer of the finished product, who puts it on the market to be used without inspection by his customers. If he is negligent, where danger is to be foreseen, a liability will follow. We are not required at this time to say that it is legitimate to go back of the manufacturer of the finished product and hold the manufacturers of the component parts.[4] To make their negligence a cause of imminent danger, an independent cause must often intervene; the manufacturer of the finished product must also fail in *his* duty of inspection. It may be that in those circumstances the negligence of the earlier members of the series is too remote to constitute, as to the ultimate user, an actionable wrong (Beven on Negligence [3d ed.], 50, 51, 54; Wharton on Negligence [2d ed.] section 134; Leeds v. New York Tel. Co., 178 N.Y. 118, 70 N.E. 219; Sweet v. Perkins, 196 N.Y. 482, 90 N.E. 50; Hayes v. Hyde Park, 153 Mass. 514, 516, 27 N.E. 522, 12 L.R.A. 249). We leave that question open. We shall have to deal with it when it arises. The difficulty which it suggests is not present in this case. There is here no break in the chain of cause and effect. In such circumstances, the presence of a known danger, attendant upon a known use, makes vigilance a duty. We have put aside the notion that the duty to safeguard life and limb, when the consequences of negligence may be foreseen, grows out of contract and nothing else. We have put the source of the obligation where it ought to be. We have put its source in the law.

From this survey of the decisions, there thus emerges a definition of the duty of a manufacturer which enables us to measure this defendant's liability. Beyond all question, the nature of an automobile gives warning of probable danger if its construction is defective. This automobile was designed to go fifty miles an hour. Unless its wheels were sound and strong, injury was almost certain. It was as much a thing of danger as a defective engine for a rail-

4. See Smith v. Peerless Glass Co., 259 N.Y. 292, 181 N.E. 576 (1932) where the manufacturer of a bottle was held liable for harm caused to a waitress by explosion of the bottle after it had been filled with soda water by a soda company and sold as a bottle of pop. Compare Ford Motor Co. v. Mathis, 322 F.2d 267 (5th Cir. 1973) (assembler vicariously liable for negligence of component manufacturer although unable reasonably to have discovered defect by inspection).

road. The defendant knew the danger. It knew also that the car would be used by persons other than the buyer. This was apparent from its size; there were seats for three persons. It was apparent also from the fact that the buyer was a dealer in cars, who bought to resell. The maker of this car supplied it for the use of purchasers from the dealer just as plainly as the contractor in Devlin v. Smith supplied the scaffold for use by the servants of the owner. The dealer was indeed the one person of whom it might be said with some approach to certainty that by him the car would not be used. Yet the defendant would have us say that he was the one person whom it was under a legal duty to protect. The law does not lead us to so inconsequent a conclusion. Precedents drawn from the days of travel by stage coach do not fit the conditions of travel today. The principle that the danger must be imminent does not change, but the things subject to the principle do change. They are whatever the needs of life in a developing civilization require them to be.

In reaching this conclusion, we do not ignore the decisions to the contrary in other jurisdictions. * * *

There is nothing anomalous in a rule which imposes upon A, who has contracted with B, a duty to C and D and others according as he knows or does not know that the subject-matter of the contract is intended for their use. We may find an analogy in the law which measures the liability of landlords. If A leases to B a tumble-down house he is not liable, in the absence of fraud, to B's guests who enter it and are injured. This is because B is then under the duty to repair it, the lessor has the right to suppose that he will fulfill that duty, and, if he omits to do so, his guests must look to him (Bohlen, supra, at p. 276). But if A leases a building to be used by the lessee at once as a place of public entertainment, the rule is different. There injury to persons other than the lessee is to be foreseen, and foresight of the consequences involves the creation of a duty (Junkermann v. Tilyou Realty Co., 213 N.Y. 404, 108 N.E. 190, L.R.A.1915F, 700, and cases there cited). * * *

We think the defendant was not absolved from a duty of inspection because it bought the wheels from a reputable manufacturer. It was not merely a dealer in automobiles. It was a manufacturer of automobiles. It was responsible for the finished product. It was not at liberty to put the finished product on the market without subjecting the component parts to ordinary and simple tests (Richmond & Danville R. Co. v. Elliott, 149 U.S. 266, 272, 13 S.Ct. 837, 37 L.Ed. 728). Under the charge of the trial judge nothing more was required of it. The obligation to inspect must vary with the nature of the thing to be inspected. The more probable the danger, the greater the need of caution. There is little analogy between this case and Carlson v. Phoenix Bridge Co., 132 N.Y. 273, 30 N.E. 750, 43 N.Y.St.Rep. 942, where the defendant bought a tool for a servant's use. The making of tools was not the business in which the master was engaged. Reliance on the skill of the manufacturer was proper and almost inevitable. But that is not the defendant's situation. Both by its relation to the work and by the nature of its business, it is charged with a stricter duty.

Other rulings complained of have been considered, but no error has been found in them.

The judgment should be affirmed with costs.

WILLARD BARTLETT, Ch. J. (dissenting). * * *

BAXTER v. FORD MOTOR CO.

Supreme Court of Washington, 1932.
168 Wash. 456, 12 P.2d 409, 88 A.L.R. 521.

HERMAN, J. During the month of May, 1930, plaintiff purchased a model A Ford town sedan from defendant St. John Motors, a Ford dealer, who had acquired the automobile in question by purchase from defendant Ford Motor Company. Plaintiff claims that representations were made to him by both defendants that the windshield of the automobile was made of nonshatterable glass which would not break, fly, or shatter. October 12, 1930, while plaintiff was driving the automobile through Snoqualmie pass, a pebble from a passing car struck the windshield of the car in question, causing small pieces of glass to fly into plaintiff's left eye, resulting in the loss thereof. Plaintiff brought this action for damages for the loss of his left eye and for injuries to the sight of his right eye. The case came on for trial, and, at the conclusion of plaintiff's testimony, the court took the case from the jury and entered judgment for both defendants. From that judgment, plaintiff appeals. * * *

The principal question in this case is whether the trial court erred in refusing to admit in evidence, as against respondent Ford Motor Company, the catalogues and printed matter furnished by that respondent to respondent St. John Motors to be distributed for sales assistance. Contained in such printed matter were statements which appellant maintains constituted representations or warranties with reference to the nature of the glass used in the windshield of the car purchased by appellant. A typical statement, as it appears in appellant's exhibit for identification No. 1, is here set forth:

"Triplex Shatter-Proof Glass Windshield. All of the new Ford cars have a Triplex shatter-proof glass windshield—so made that it will not fly or shatter under the hardest impact. This is an important safety factor because it eliminates the dangers of flying glass—the cause of most of the injuries in automobile accidents. In these days of crowded, heavy traffic, the use of this Triplex glass is an absolute necessity. Its extra margin of safety is something that every motorist should look for in the purchase of a car—especially where there are women and children."

Respondent Ford Motor Company contends that there can be no implied or express warranty without privity of contract, and warranties as to personal property do not attach themselves to, and run with, the article sold. * * *

An ordinary person would be unable to discover by the usual and customary examination of the automobile whether glass which would not fly or shatter was used in the windshield. In that respect the purchaser was in a position similar to that of the consumer of a wrongly labeled drug, who has bought the same from a retailer, and who has relied upon the manufacturer's representation that the label correctly set forth the contents of the container. For many years it has been held that, under such circumstances, the manufacturer is liable to the consumer, even though the consumer purchased from a third person the commodity causing the damage. Thomas v. Winchester, 6 N.Y. 397, 57 Am.Dec. 455. The rule in such cases does not rest upon contractual obligations, but rather on the principle that the original act of delivering an article is wrong, when, because of the lack of those qualities which the manufacturer represented it as having, the absence of which could not be readily detected by the consumer, the article is not safe for the purposes for which the consumer would ordinarily use it. * * *

Since the rule of *caveat emptor* was first formulated, vast changes have taken place in the economic structures of the English speaking peoples. Methods of doing business have undergone a great transition. Radio, billboards, and the products of the printing press have become the means of creating a large part of the demand that causes goods to depart from factories to the ultimate consumer. It would be unjust to recognize a rule that would permit manufacturers of goods to create a demand for their products by representing that they possess qualities which they, in fact, do not possess, and then, because there is no privity of contract existing between the consumer and the manufacturer, deny the consumer the right to recover if damages result from the absence of those qualities, when such absence is not readily noticeable. * * *

We hold that the catalogues and printed matter furnished by respondent Ford Motor Company for distribution and assistance in sales (appellant's exhibits for identification Nos. 1, 2, 3, 4 and 5) were improperly excluded from evidence, because they set forth representations by the manufacturer that the windshield of the car which appellant bought contained Triplex nonshatterable glass which would not fly or shatter. The nature of nonshatterable glass is such that the falsity of the representations with reference to the glass would not be readily detected by a person of ordinary experience and reasonable prudence. Appellant, under the circumstances shown in this case, had the right to rely upon the representations made by respondent Ford Motor Company relative to qualities possessed by its products, even though there was no privity of contract between appellant and respondent Ford Motor Company. * * *

Reversed with directions to grant a new trial with reference to respondent Ford Motor Company; affirmed as to respondent St. John Motors.

On the new trial, the jury returned a verdict for the plaintiff and Ford appealed. The Supreme Court affirmed, saying, per Holcomb, J. (Baxter v. Ford Motor Co., 179 Wash. 123, 35 P.2d 1090 (1934):

"In the former decision * * * we held that, in an action for breach of warranty of nonshatterable glass in a windshield, catalogues and printed statements furnished the dealer for sales assistance are admissible against the manufacturer, although there was no privity of contract, since the falsity of the representations could not be readily detected, and that, in an action for a breach of warranty of nonshatterable glass in a windshield, plaintiff is entitled to show his absence of familiarity with nonshatterable glass, and that he had had no experience enabling him to recognize the difference between it and ordinary glass. * * *

"A new point, arising out of the last trial, claimed as error, was in excluding testimony of an expert witness on behalf of appellant to the effect that there was no better windshield made than that used in respondent's car and in sustaining the objection to appellant's offer of proof on that point.

"No authorities are cited by appellant to sustain this claim, and we know of none. Indeed, it would seem that whether there was any better make of shatter-proof glass manufactured by any one at that time would be wholly immaterial, under the law as decided by us on the former appeal, since it was the duty of appellant to know that the representations made to purchasers were true. Otherwise it should not have made them. If a person states as true material facts susceptible of knowledge to one who relies and acts thereon to his injury, if the representations are false, it is immaterial that he did not know they were false, or that he believed them to be true. * * *"[5]

MOCH CO. v. RENSSELAER WATER CO.

Court of Appeals of New York, 1928.
247 N.Y. 160, 159 N.E. 896, 62 A.L.R. 1199.

CARDOZO, CH. J. The defendant, a water works company under the laws of this State, made a contract with the city of Rensselaer for the supply of water during a term of years. Water was to be furnished to the city for sewer flushing and streetsprinkling; for service to schools and public buildings; and for service at fire hydrants, the latter service at the rate of $42.50 a year for each hydrant. Water

5. Is this contract liability, or tort? Or both?

Like the law of contract in general, which itself grew out of tort, the law of warranty began with an action on the case, known as the action of deceit upon a false warranty. The tort was viewed, not as the breach of a promise, but as the wrong of selling goods which did not conform to a warranty. See Ames, The History of Assumpsit, 2 Harv.L.Rev. 2, 8 (1888).

For the proposition that contract law is being reabsorbed into tort see G. Gilmore, The Death of Contract (1974) 87 et seq.

was to be furnished to private takers within the city at their homes and factories and other industries at reasonable rates, not exceeding a stated schedule. While this contract was in force, a building caught fire. The flames, spreading to the plaintiff's warehouse near by, destroyed it and its contents. The defendant according to the complaint was promptly notified of the fire, "but omitted and neglected after such notice, to supply or furnish sufficient or adequate quantity of water, with adequate pressure to stay, suppress or extinguish the fire before it reached the warehouse of the plaintiff, although the pressure and supply which the defendant was equipped to supply and furnish, and had agreed by said contract to supply and furnish, was adequate and sufficient to prevent the spread of the fire to and the destruction of the plaintiff's warehouse and its contents." By reason of the failure of the defendant to "fulfill the provisions of the contract between it and the city of Rensselaer," the plaintiff is said to have suffered damage, for which judgment is demanded. A motion, in the nature of a demurrer, to dismiss the complaint, was denied at Special Term. The Appellate Division reversed by a divided court.

Liability in the plaintiff's argument is placed on one or other of three grounds. The complaint, we are told, is to be viewed as stating: (1) A cause of action for breach of contract within Lawrence v. Fox, 20 N.Y. 268; (2) a cause of action for a common-law tort, within MacPherson v. Buick Motor Company, 217 N.Y. 382, 111 N.E. 1050, L.R.A.1916F, 696, Ann.Cas.1916C, 440; or (3) a cause of action for the breach of a statutory duty. These several grounds of liability will be considered in succession.

(1) We think the action is not maintainable as one for breach of contract.

No legal duty rests upon a city to supply its inhabitants with protection against fire (Springfield Fire & Marine Ins. Co. v. Village of Keeseville, 148 N.Y. 46, 42 N.E. 405, 30 L.R.A. 660, 51 Am.St.Rep. 667). That being so, a member of the public may not maintain an action under Lawrence v. Fox against one contracting with the city to furnish water at the hydrants, unless an intention appears that the promisor is to be answerable to individual members of the public as well as to the city for any loss ensuing from the failure to fulfill the promise. No such intention is discernible here. On the contrary, the contract is significantly divided into two branches: one a promise to the city for the benefit of the city in its corporate capacity, in which branch is included the service at the hydrants; and the other a promise to the city for the benefit of private takers, in which branch is included the service at their homes and factories. In a broad sense it is true that every city contract, not improvident or wasteful, is for the benefit of the public. More than this, however, must be shown to give a right of action to a member of the public not formally a party. The benefit, as it is sometimes said, must be one that is not merely incidental and secondary (cf. Fosmire v. National Surety Co., 229 N.Y. 44, 127 N.E. 472). It must be primary and immediate in such a sense and to such a degree as to bespeak the assumption of a duty to make reparation directly to the individual members of the public if the benefit is lost. The field of obligation would be expanded beyond reasonable limits if less than this were to be demanded as a condition of liability. A promisor undertakes to supply fuel for heating a public building. He is not liable for breach of contract to a visitor who finds the building without fuel, and thus contracts a cold. The list of illustrations can be indefinitely extended. The carrier of the mails under contract with the government is not answerable to the merchant who has lost the benefit of a bargain through negligent delay. The householder is without a remedy against manufacturers of hose and engines, though prompt performance of their contracts would have stayed the ravages of fire. "The law does not spread its protection so far" (Robins Dry Dock & Repair Co. v. Flint, 275 U.S. 303, 48 S.Ct. 134, 72 L.Ed. 290).

So with the case at hand. By the vast preponderance of authority, a contract between a city and a water company to furnish water at the city hydrants has in view a benefit to the public that is incidental rather than immediate, an assumption of duty to the city and not to its inhabitants. * * * Only a few States have held otherwise (Page, Contracts, Sec. 2401). An intention to assume an obligation of indefinite extension to every member of the public is seen to be the more improbable when we recall the crushing burden that the obligation would impose (cf. Hone v. Presque Isle Water Co., 104 Me. 217, at 232, 71 A. 769, 21 L.R.A.,N.S., 1021). The consequences invited would bear no reasonable proportion to those attached by law to defaults not greatly different. A wrongdoer who by negligence sets fire to a building is liable in damages to the owner where the fire has its origin, but not to other owners who are injured when it spreads. The rule in our State is settled to that effect, whether wisely or unwisely. * * * If the plaintiff is to prevail, one who negligently omits to supply sufficient pressure to extinguish a fire started by another, assumes an obligation to pay the ensuing damage, though the whole city is laid low. A promisor will not be deemed to have had in mind the assumption of a risk so overwhelming for any trivial reward. * * *

(2) We think the action is not maintainable as one for a common-law tort.

"It is ancient learning that one who assumes to act, even though gratuitously, may thereby become subject to the duty of acting carefully, if he acts at all" (Glanzer v. Shepard, 233 N.Y. 236, 239, 135 N.E. 275, 23 A.L.R. 1425; Marks v. Nambil Realty Co., Inc., 245 N.Y. 256, 258, 159 N.E. 129). The plaintiff would bring its case within the orbit of that principle. The hand once set to a task may not always be withdrawn with impunity though liability would fail if it had never been applied at all. A time-honored formula often phrases the distinction as one between misfeasance and nonfeasance. Incomplete the formula is, and so at times misleading. Given a relation involving in its existence a duty of care irrespective of a contract, a tort may result as well from acts of omission as of commission in the fulfillment of the duty thus recognized by law (Pollock, Torts (12th ed), p. 555; Kelley v. Metropolitan Ry. Co. [1895] 1 Q. B. 944). What we need to know is not so much the conduct to be avoided when the relation and its attendant duty are established as existing. What we need to now is the conduct that engenders the relation. It is here that the formula, however incomplete, has its value and significance. If conduct has gone forward to such a stage that inaction would commonly result, not negatively merely in withholding a benefit, but positively or actively in working an injury, there exists a relation out of which arises a duty to go forward (Bohlen, Studies in the Law of Torts, p. 87). So the surgeon who operates without pay, is liable though his negligence is in the omission to sterilize his instruments (cf. Glanzer v. Shepard, supra); the engineer, though his fault is in the failure to shut off steam (Kelley v. Metropolitan Ry. Co., supra; cf. Pittsfield Cottonwear Mfg. Co. v. Pittsfield Shoe Co., 71 N.H. 522, 529, 533, 53 A. 807, 60 L.R.A. 116); the maker of automobiles, at the suit of some one other than the buyer, though his negligence is merely in inadequate inspection (MacPherson v. Buick Motor Co., 217 N.Y. 382, 111 N.E. 1050, L.R.A.1916F, 696, Ann.Cas.1916C, 440). The query always is whether the putative wrongdoer has advanced to such a point as to have launched a force or instrument of harm, or has stopped where inaction is at most a refusal to become an instrument for good (cf. Fowler v. Athens City Waterworks Co., 83 Ga. 219, 222, 9 S.E. 673, 20 Am.St.Rep. 313).

The plaintiff would have us hold that the defendant, when once it entered upon the performance of its contract with the city, was brought into such a relation with every one who might potentially be benefited through the supply of water at the hydrants as to give to negligent performance, without reasonable notice of a refusal to continue, the quality of a tort. There is a suggestion of this thought in Guardian Trust & Deposit Co. v. Fisher, 200 U.S. 57, 26 S.Ct. 186, 50 L.Ed. 367, but the dictum was rejected in a later case decided by the same court (German Alliance Ins. Co. v. Homewater Supply Co., 226 U.S. 220, 23 S.Ct. 32, 57 L.Ed. 195, 42 L.R.A.,N.S., 1000) when an opportunity was at hand to turn it into law. We are satisfied that liability would be unduly and indeed indefinitely extended by this enlargement of the zone of duty. The dealer in coal who is to supply fuel for a shop must then answer to the customers if fuel is lacking. The manufacturer of goods, who enters upon the performance of his contract, must answer, in that view, not only to the buyer, but to those who to his knowledge are looking to the buyer for their own sources of supply. Every one making a promise having the quality of a contract will be under a duty to the promisee by virtue of the promise, but under another duty, apart from contract, to an indefinite number of potential beneficiaries when performance has begun. The assumption of one relation will mean the involuntary assumption of a series of new relations, inescapably hooked together. Again we may say in the words of the Supreme Court of the United

States, "The law does not spread its protection so far" (Robins Dry Dock & Repair Co. v. Flint, supra * * *). We do not need to determine now what remedy, if any, there might be if the defendant had withheld the water or reduced the pressure with a malicious intent to do injury to the plaintiff or another. We put aside also the problem that would arise if there had been reckless and wanton indifference to consequences measured and foreseen. Difficulties would be present even then, but they need not now perplex us. What we are dealing with at this time is a mere negligent omission, unaccompanied by malice or other aggravating elements. The failure in such circumstances to furnish an adequate supply of water is at most the denial of a benefit. It is not the commission of a wrong.

(3) We think the action is not maintainable as one for the breach of a statutory duty.

The defendant, a public service corporation, is subject to the provisions of the Transportation Corporations Act. The duty imposed upon it by that act is in substance to furnish water, upon demand by the inhabitants, at reasonable rates, through suitable connections at office, factory or dwelling, and to furnish water at like rates through hydrants or in public buildings upon demand by the city, all according to its capacity * * *. We find nothing in these requirements to enlarge the zone of liability where an inhabitant of the city suffers indirect or incidental damage through deficient pressure at the hydrants. The breach of duty in any case is to the one to whom service is denied at the time and at the place where service to such one is due. The denial, though wrongful, is unavailing without more to give a cause of action to another. We may find a helpful analogy in the law of common carriers. A railroad company is under a duty to supply reasonable facilities for carriage at reasonable rates. It is liable, generally speaking, for breach of a duty imposed by law if it refuses to accept merchandise tendered by a shipper. The fact that its duty is of this character does not make it liable to some one else who may be counting upon the prompt delivery of the merchandise to save him from loss in going forward in his work. If the defendant may not be held for a tort at common law, we find no adequate reason for a holding that it may be held under the statute.

The judgment should be affirmed with costs.[5A]

5A. See Sunderland, Liability of Water Companies for Fire Losses, 3 Mich.L. Rev. 442 (1905); Kales, Liability of Water Companies for Fire Losses, 3 Mich.L.Rev. 501 (1905); Corbin, Liability of Water Companies for Losses by Fire, 19 Yale L.J. 425 (1910); Seavey, Mr. Justice Cardozo and the Law of Torts, 39 Colum.L.Rev. 20, 52 Harv.L.Rev. 372, 48 Yale L.J. 390 (1939); Seavey, The Water Works Cases and Stare Decisis, 66 Harv.L. Rev. 84 (1952); James, Scope of Duty in Negligence Cases, 47 Nw.U.L.Rev. 778, 806–09 (1953).

Compare Doyle v. South Pittsburgh Water Co., 414 Pa. 199, 199 A.2d 875 (1964); Harris v. Board of Water and Sewer Commissioners of City of Mobile, 294 Ala. 606, 320 So.2d 624 (1975).

Consider also in connection with the problems of these cases Ultramares Corp. v. Touche, Niven & Co., infra, p. 811.

RYAN v. PROGRESSIVE GROCERY STORES

Court of Appeals of New York, 1931.
255 N.Y. 388, 175 N.E. 105, 74 A.L.R. 339.

CARDOZO, CH. J. The action is for breach of warranty.

Plaintiff through his wife, who acted as his agent, bought a loaf of bread at the defendant's grocery. The loaf had concealed in it a pin, which hurt the plaintiff's mouth. There has been a judgment for the damage.

(1) "Where the buyer, expressly or by implication, makes known to the seller the particular purpose for which the goods are required, and it appears that the buyer relies on the seller's skill or judgment (whether he be the grower or manufacturer or not), there is an implied warranty that the goods shall be reasonably fit for such purpose" (Pers.Prop.Law; Cons.Laws, ch. 41, section 96, subd. 1).

The plaintiff did not rely on the seller's skill or judgment. His wife stated to the salesman that she wished to have a loaf of "Ward's bread." The salesman gave her what she asked for, wrapped in a sealed package as it had come from the Ward Baking Company, the baker. She made her own choice, and used her own judgment.

The leading case in this State as to the meaning of the statute quoted is Rinaldi v. Mohican Co., 255 N.Y. 70, 121 N.E. 471. The sale was one of pork, which turned out to be diseased. We held that reliance on the seller's skill and judgment might be gathered from the purchase as a reasonable inference. We left the question open whether a like inference would be drawn upon a sale in the original package as bought by the vendor from others.

Since Rinaldi v. Mohican Co., the scope of the implied warranty upon a sale of food in sealed containers has been discussed in other courts. There are decisions to the effect that even in such circumstances an implied warranty ensues if the seller's judgment has been trusted for the selection of the bread or make * * * We assume for present purposes that so the rule should be declared. Invariably, however, the limitation has been added that there can be no inference of reliance where the buyer selects the brand and gets what he selects. * * * There is no room for a holding that choice shall be imputed to the seller when the transaction shows upon its face that the judgment of the seller was superseded, and choice determined by the buyer.

The award of damages, if it is to be upheld, must rest upon some other basis than the imputation of reliance.

(2) "Where the goods are bought by description from a seller who deals in goods of that description (whether he be the grower or manufacturer or not), there is an implied warranty that the goods shall be of merchantable quality" (Pers.Prop.Law, section 96, subd. 2).

The facts excluding a warranty under subdivision 1, we are to inquire whether there is a warranty under subdivision 2.

Under the common-law rule long in force in this State, the warranty of merchantable quality was limited to sales by a manufacturer or grower. * * * All this has been changed since the coming of the Sales Law. * * * Dealer as well as manufacturer or grower affirms as to anything he sells, if purchased by description, that it is of merchantable quality. The burden may be heavy. It is one of the hazards of the business.

Most of the sales of defective food stuffs have been dealt with by the courts as if subdivision 1 of the section defining warranties gave the exclusive rule to be applied. In some instances the goods were not purchased by description. In others, the courts may have been unmindful of the fact that the warranty of merchantable quality is no longer confined to manufacturers or growers. Innovations of this order are slow to make their way. Gradually, however, as the statute has become better known, the bearing of subdivision 2 upon sales of food in sealed containers has been perceived by court and counsel. The nature of the transaction must determine in each instance the rule to be applied. There are times when a warranty of fitness has no relation to a warranty of merchantable quality. This is so, for example, when machinery competently wrought is still inadequate for the use to which the buyer has given notice that it is likely to be applied. There are times on the other hand when the warranties coexist, in which event a recovery may be founded upon either. "Fitness for a particular purpose may be merely the equivalent of merchantability" (Williston, Sales, vol. 1, section 235, and cases there cited).

A dual warranty is thus possible for food stuffs as for anything else. Both in this court and in others the possibility is recognized. * * *

Loaves baked with pins in them are not of merchantable quality. The dealer is thus charged with liability though the buyer selects the brand, just as he would be liable for concealed defects upon a sale of wool or silk. Assume that the sale had been made by a manufacturer or a grower, and that there had been a request for a special brand. There would then be no warranty of fitness for any "particular" purpose. Would any one dispute, however, that a defect of this order, destroying value altogether, would be covered by the warranty of merchantable quality? The question carries its own answer. The rule is different, to be sure, upon a sale of specific goods, not purchased by description (Hight v. Bacon, 126 Mass. 10, 30 Am.Rep. 639). It may even be different, though the purchase is by description, if the goods are subject to inspection and the defects are of such a nature that inspection will reveal them (Williston, Sales, section 234; Pers.Prop. Law, section 96, subd. 3). Here the sale was by description, the defect was wholly latent, and inspection was impossible. In such circumstances, the law casts the burden on the seller, who may vouch in the manufacturer, if the latter was to blame. The loss in its final incidence will be borne where it is placed by the initial wrong.

The argument is made that the only damage to be recovered for the breach of the warranty of mechantable quality is the price of the bread, the difference between the value of a good loaf and a bad one. The rule is not so stubborn. Undoubtedly, the difference in value supplies the ordinary measure (Pers.Prop.Law, section 150, subds. 6 and 7; section 151). The measure is more liberal where special circumstances are present with proof of special damage (section 150, subd. 7; section 151). Here the dealer had notice from the nature of the transaction that the bread was to be eaten. Knowledge that it was to be eaten was knowledge that the damage would be greater than the price * * *. For damages thus foreseen, the buyer has his remedy, whether the warranty is one of fitness or of merchantable quality.

The judgment should be affirmed with costs. * * * [6]

The interplay between warranty and negligence was further manifested in certain lines of cases dealing with foodstuffs and related products. Some courts held that an implied warranty of quality ran to a consumer, notwithstanding lack of privity, from a producer of foods, e. g., Klein v. Dutchess Sandwich Co., Ltd., 14 Cal.2d 272, 93 P.2d 799 (1939), or from a brand-name distributor, e. g., Armour Co. v. Leasure, 177 Md. 393, 9 A.2d 572 (1939); courts which would not accept this doctrine required proof of negligence, e. g., Crigger v. Coca-Cola Bottling Co., 132 Tenn. 545, 179 S.W. 155 (1915) (decomposed mouse in bottle of Coca-Cola); East Kentucky Beverage Co. v. Stumbo, 313 Ky. 66, 230 S.W.2d 106 (1950) (rubber prophylactic in bottle of Pepsi Cola).

Other courts recognized a *MacPherson*-like exception, in the case of foodstuffs, to their ordinary privity requirement as a condition for negligence liability for defective products; in these courts it became necessary to determine whether contaminated marginal products, like chewing tobacco, qualified as food.

6. Cf. Tonsman v. Greenglass, 248 Mass. 275, 142 N.E. 756 (1924). There, too, plaintiff was hurt by a piece of metal imbedded in a loaf of bread. But plaintiff sued, not the immediate vendor, but the remote baker. The action was for negligence and plaintiff recovered. In this suit would plaintiff's burden of proof be lighter, or chances of recovery greater, if the liability were based on breach of warranty? How is the case different from that against the immediate vendor? Is he subject to a greater liability than the manufacturer? Are his opportunities for prevention of the harm greater?

When one says "retailer" what does he denote? Sears Roebuck, Montgomery Ward, Atlantic & Pacific Tea Stores, May Department Stores, Macy's are all retailers. So is also the corner druggist or small grocer who works long hours and makes little money. There is a difference not merely in economic power and capacity to bear losses. There are differences also in buying methods, inspection, representation to the public, and influence on the manufacturers.

While the Sales Act warranty provisions have been replaced by §§ 2–313 through 2–318 of the Uniform Commercial Code (1962, as amended 1966), text at page 719 infra, Cardozo's discussion in *Ryan* is still generally applicable.

See, e. g., Liggett & Myers Tobacco Co. v. Cannon, 132 Tenn. 419, 178 S.W. 1009, L.R.A.1916A, 940, Ann.Cas.1917A, 179 (1915): Plaintiff was injured by chewing "plug" tobacco in which was embedded a bug. The tobacco was manufactured by defendant and purchased by plaintiff from a retailer who had purchased it through intermediate wholesale dealers. The plaintiff was denied recovery for lack of privity of contract, the court being of opinion that tobacco was not a food and, therefore, not within the "exception" applied in the preceding cases; that recovery could be had only by showing "knowledge, or a reasonable means of knowledge from anything brought to the notice of the manufacturer, that use by the consumer would be dangerous. In that event knowledge or notice disregarded gives to the transaction the color of fraud." Although the court below erred in thinking that negligence was a sufficient ground for recovery, yet, since it arrived at a correct result by directing a verdict for defendant, on the ground that negligence was not shown but negatived, the judgment was affirmed. The court said: "We think it manifest that tobacco is not a foodstuff. It does not tend to build bodily tissue, and as to the average adult its tendency is widely thought to retard the building up of fatty tissue. In respect of its use by the young, it cannot be doubted that it tends to stunt normal development and even growth in stature. The desire or appetite for food is natural and common to all of the human race, while the desire for tobacco must be created. * * *

"The admission of foodstuffs among those classes of commodities excepted from the general rule of non-liability to the ultimate consumer on the part of the manufacturer is comparatively recent, and this was done because of the close analogy of such commodity to drugs. * * *

"Such inclusion of foods among the excepted articles of commerce was based upon public policy and compelling necessity. * *

"Foods are used as a matter of necessity in the support of life by all mankind, from the infant to the aged. * * *

"It is, we think, apparent that the same consideration of public welfare cannot support the enlargement of the class of foodstuffs proper, so as to include tobacco, even in the form of chewing tobacco, and that public policy as thus far declared is, as it should continue to be, not favorable to a classification that would protect its ultimate consumer under the rule above outlined.

"The liability of a manufacturer of tobacco should not be carried to the extent asked by plaintiff, when there is thus a failure to justify its imposition. The door to fraud would be opened wide for false claims on the part of consumers against distant manufacturers, who would be under serious handicaps in making defense. The rule would invite a flood of litigation, in which the parties would lack much of having an equal opportunity to adduce proof that a claimed defect did or did not exist, or that there was or was not negligence imputable to the manufacturer as to the particular article purchased in open market. * * * "

Compare Pillars v. R. J. Reynolds Tobacco Co., 117 Miss. 490, 78 So. 365 (1918): The plaintiff was made sick by chewing a plug of tobacco in which was embedded "a human toe in a state of putrefaction." This suit was brought against the manufacturer and the wholesaler who sold to the retailer from whom the plaintiff bought. No evidence of negligence seems to have been introduced. The trial judge directed a verdict for both defendants. The Supreme Court affirmed, as to the wholesaler, because it "could not have suspected that human toes were concealed in the plug, and was not negligent in not discovering the noxious contents"; but it reversed as to the manufacturer because it could "imagine no reason why, with ordinary care, human toes could not be left out of chewing tobacco, and if toes are found in chewing tobacco, it seems to us that somebody has been very careless." The court agreed with the Tennessee Court that "tobacco is not food," but argued that the food exception was based on the probability of impairment of health when poisons are concealed in foods and that this probability exists as well in the case of tobacco, since we know that it "is taken into the mouth, that a certain proportion will be absorbed by the mucous membrane of the mouth, and that some, at least, of the juice or pulp will and does find its way into the alimentary canal, there to be digested and ultimately to become a part of the blood." [7]

Consider the cigarette. Do implied warranties of merchantability and fitness include a warranty that the product can be used without causing physical injury? Or merely that it is made of commercially satisfactory tobacco? Do the same considerations apply to whisky? To pure butter, or salted peanuts, sold to a consumer who should be on a nonfat or salt-free diet? See, e. g., Pritchard v. Liggett & Meyers Tobacco Co., 295 F.2d 292 (3d Cir. 1961); Ross v. Phillip Morris & Co., 328 F.2d 3 (8th Cir. 1964); Green v. American Tobacco Co., 154 So.2d 169 (Fla.1963), 391 F.2d 97 (5th Cir. 1968), 409 F.2d 1166 (5th Cir. 1969).

7. Almost all the states now have statutes prohibiting the sale of adulterated or misbranded goods in language similar to that of the federal Food and Drugs Act of 1906, now superseded by the Federal Food, Drug, and Cosmetic Act of 1938, 52 Stat. 1040, 21 U.S.C.A. section 301 et seq. The possible uses of these statutes in connection with civil liability are indicated in some of the cases in this chapter.

Food cases have received special attention and are sometimes spoken of as exceptional. See the criticism by Llewellyn of writers who see "food (plus drink: stomach stuff) as a special and separate problem" rather than "as what it is in truth: merely a peculiarly poignant point from which the whole line of civil protection of the uninformed consumer branches out." Llewellyn, On Warranty of Quality, and Society, 36 Col.L.Rev. 699, 704, n. 14 (1936).

Finally, in 1972, Congress passed similar legislation covering consumer products other than food, drugs, cosmetics, tobacco and certain other exceptions. See Consumer Product Safety Act, page 740 infra.

doCANTO v. AMETEK, INC.

Supreme Judicial Court of Massachusetts, 1975.
— Mass. —, 328 N.E.2d 873.

WILKINS, JUSTICE. The defendant, a manufacturer of ironing machinery used in commercial laundries, argues various exceptions arising out of a trial which resulted in verdicts for the plaintiffs aggregating $467,000.

On July 16, 1968, Ezila C. doCanto (Ezila) was one of two operators of a "Troy Speedline 8 Roll Flat Work Ironer" at the Boston premises of Hospital Laundry Association, Inc. (Laundry). The defendant, Ametek, Inc. (Ametek), had sold the ironer to Laundry and installed it in the latter part of 1961. Ezila's job was to put sheets into the ironer from one side, while another operator did so on the other side. As she was feeding a sheet into the ironer that day, her right hand, caught in a sheet, was pulled into the ironer under a safety bar. Although the electricity which powered the ironer shut off when her hand activated the safety mechanism, the momentum of the rollers in the ironer caused her hand to be pulled farther into the machine. The coasting of the machine after the electricity has been shut off is described as overtravel, can be measured in inches and varies with the circumstances, particularly the speed at which the rollers were operating. At the time of Ezila's injury the ironer was operating at its maximum speed, 115 feet a minute. Ezila sustained serious injuries from the heat and pressure of the ironer. Subsequently she lost all of her fingers, except her thumb, and underwent four operations during about eight weeks of hospitalization. * * *

* * * Facts relating to each area of contention will be set forth in the relevant discussion below.

1. Evidence of safety features developed by Ametek after the sale of the ironer to Laundry and before Ezila's injury properly was admitted for limited purposes. These design improvements principally involved (a) the addition of a device which reduced the overtravel of the ironer after activation of the safety mechanism, and (b) the relocation of the safety bar farther from the point at which an operator's fingers would be pinched by the pressure rolls of the ironer. The judge allowed evidence of post-sale safety improvements for three purposes: (1) to demonstrate the feasibility of redesign of the machine's safety features; (2) to show Ametek's knowledge, if any, of inadequacies in the "existing safety features" of the ironer; and (3) to establish Ametek's duty, if any, to warn purchasers of the ironer of any deficiency in the ironer's safety features. The judge instructed the jury that the evidence of safety improvements "is not in and of itself any evidence of negligence."

Ametek argues that evidence of pre-injury improvements "should be considered in the same light as evidence of subsequent improvements or repairs." The theory behind the general rule which excludes evidence of post-accident improvements as evidence of negligence rests in considerable degree on the belief that a contrary rule would discourage owners from making repairs to dangerous property. Wigmore, Evidence, § 283 (3d ed. 1940).

Without accepting Ametek's premise that evidence of pre-accident safety improvements should be treated the same as evidence of post-accident improvements, we note that evidence of a post-accident improvement may be admissible, in the judge's discretion and subject to limiting instructions, on a variety of other issues in a case. * *

* * * For example, evidence of such a change is admissible to prove the practical possibility of making a safety improvement. * * * Likewise, evidence of such a safety improvement may be admissible on the issue whether the defendant knew or should have known of the danger at the time of the plaintiff's injury. * * * It is clear, therefore, that on the issues of feasibility and knowledge of the risk, two of the three grounds on which the judge admitted evidence of pre-accident safety improvements, post-accident evidence would have been admissible in his discretion. We see no reason why evidence of pre-accident remedial measures should be any less admissible for the same purposes.

The evidence of pre-accident improvements was admissible also on the third ground specified by the judge: the question of Ametek's duty to warn of any deficiency in the ironer's safety. Ametek contends that by admitting the evidence on this ground, the judge in effect ruled erroneously that there was a continuing duty to warn purchasers of safety improvements made to a machine which was reasonably safe at sale. However, the evidence was not admitted for such a narrow purpose, if indeed it was admitted at all for that purpose. The duty to warn for which the evidence was admitted could have been a duty to warn at the time of sale because the overtravel of the machine when operating at full speed exceeded the distance between the safety bar and the danger point on the rollers. Moreover, a duty to warn of post-sale safety measures may have existed because of the negligent design of the machine as originally sold. Consequently, the admission of the evidence as bearing on a duty to warn of safety deficiencies did not involve necessarily the question of a manufacturer's continuing duty, if any, to notify customers of post-manufacture improvements to a properly designed machine. * * *

2. Ametek argues in support of its motion for directed verdicts that expert testimony concerning the design safety of the ironer was an indispensable and unsatisfied element of the plaintiffs' case. It contends that, because of the complex technology involved, expert opinion evidence was necessary to prove that Ametek failed to use reasonable care in designing the ironer.

* * * There was ample evidence to support the submission of the case to the jury. The jury could have found, on the basis of their own lay knowledge, that the ironer's overtravel was not consistent with Ametek's duty to design the machine with reasonable care. * * * Moreover, there was evidence that Ametek never advised

Laundry of this particular danger. Indeed, Ametek stated in a catalogue that "a magnetic brake stops the rolls with no coasting from residual momentum." There was evidence that an Ametek employee who had designed the machine knew that this statement was incorrect. He also believed that a machine which failed adequately to prevent a hand from being pulled into the mechanism was improperly designed and that the ironer did permit a hand to be pulled under the safety bar. Clearly this evidence was sufficient to send the case to the jury on both the question of negligent design and the question of negligent failure to warn. * * *

There was evidence that Ezila's hand was unusually small, smaller than ninety-nine percent of the female hands measured in a survey conducted for the Air Force. There was evidence, however, that Ezila's hand was not abnormal in size. Ametek requested instructions concerning its lack of liability to a person whose characteristics depart from its reasonable expectations. The judge was under no duty to focus in his charge on this disputed factual circumstance. * * * He did instruct the jury that Ametek was required to design a product which was reasonably safe and that Ametek had no obligation to develop safety devices to protect against every remotely possible danger. He also told the jury to determine whether the danger was a likely one or an unlikely one and whether that danger "involved a reasonably foreseeable risk to a person such as Mrs. doCanto, *as you find her to be*" (emphasis supplied). These instructions adequately covered the law pertaining to any abnormality in the size of Ezila's hand. * * *

Finally, Ametek argues that the judge should have instructed the jury that Ametek "was under no duty to inform purchasers of its machines of any facts regarding changes or improvements it later decided to incorporate in the manufacture of similar machines." This request did not embody a correct statement of the law in light of the evidence.

There was evidence from which the jury could have found that the machine was negligently designed and its braking capacity misrepresented. When the manufacturer of such a machine learns or should have learned of the risk created by its fault, it has a duty to take reasonable steps to warn at least the purchaser of the risk. * * * One such reasonable step may be to warn at least the purchaser of changes which eliminate or tend to eliminate the risk created by the manufacturer's initial fault.

The judge charged the jury that in determining Ametek's negligence, if any, they would probably want to determine what warnings after sale, if any, Ametek should have given. Ametek did not object to this portion of the judge's charge. It made no attempt to focus the judge's attention on the distinction between a duty to warn of post-sale safety improvements in a properly designed machine and such improvements in a machine which was designed improperly. There was no error in the denial of Ametek's request concerning a duty to warn, or in the judge's treatment in his charge of the general subject of a duty to warn.[8]

Exceptions overruled.

ESCOLA v. COCA COLA BOTTLING CO.

Supreme Court of California, 1944.
24 Cal.2d 453, 150 P.2d 436.

GIBSON, CHIEF JUSTICE. Plaintiff, a waitress in a restaurant, was injured when a bottle of Coca Cola broke in her hand. * * * This appeal is from a judgment upon a jury verdict in favor of plaintiff.

Defendant's driver delivered several cases of Coca Cola to the restaurant, placing them on the floor, one on top of the other, under and behind the counter, where they remained at least thirty-six hours. Immediately before the accident, plaintiff picked up the top case and set it upon a near-by ice cream cabinet in front of and about three feet from the refrigerator. She then proceeded to take the bottles from the case with her right hand, one at a time, and put them into the refrigerator. Plaintiff testified that after she had placed three bottles in the refrigerator and had moved the fourth bottle about 18 inches from the case "it exploded in my hand." The bottle broke into two jagged pieces and inflicted a deep five-inch cut, severing blood vessels, nerves and muscles of the thumb and palm of the hand. * * * The broken bottle was not produced at the trial, the pieces having been thrown away by an employee of the restaurant shortly after the accident. Plaintiff, however, described the broken pieces, and a diagram of the bottle was made showing the location of the "fracture line" where the bottle broke in two.

One of defendant's drivers, called as a witness by plaintiff, testified that he had seen other bottles of Coca Cola in the past explode and had found broken bottles in the warehouse when he took the cases out, but that he did not know what made them blow up.

Plaintiff then rested her case, having announced to the court that being unable to show any specific acts of negligence she relied completely on the doctrine of res ipsa loquitur. * * *

8. No inference should be drawn from what we have said that the manufacturer of a properly designed product does not have a duty to warn of dangers in his product of which he knew or should have known at the time of sale. * * * Moreover, there may be a duty to give reasonable warning of a product's dangers which are discovered after sale. See Comstock v. General Motors Corp., 358 Mich. 163, 176–178, 99 N.W.2d 627 (1959) (latent defect discovered shortly after product put on the market); Rekab, Inc. v. Frank Hrubetz & Co., Inc., 261 Md. 141, 146–147, 274 A.2d 107 (1971) (expensive machine improperly designed); Braniff Airways, Inc. v. Curtiss-Wright Corp., 411 F.2d 451, 453 (2d Cir. 1969), cert. den. 396 U.S. 959, 90 S.Ct. 431, 24 L.Ed.2d 423 (1969), cert. den. sub nom. Addabbo v. Curtiss-Wright Corp., 400 U.S. 829, 91 S.Ct. 59, 27 L.Ed.2d 59 (1970) (deficiencies in airplane engine, discovered after sale and before accident). [From original, renumbered; other notes in original omitted.]

Many jurisdictions have applied the doctrine in cases involving exploding bottles of carbonated beverages. * * *

Upon an examination of the record, the evidence appears sufficient to support a reasonable inference that the bottle here involved was not damaged by any extraneous force after delivery to the restaurant by defendant. It follows, therefore, that the bottle was in some manner defective at the time defendant relinquished control, because sound and properly prepared bottles of carbonated liquids do not ordinarily explode when carefully handled.

The next question, then, is whether plaintiff may rely upon the doctrine of res ipsa loquitur to supply an inference that defendant's negligence was responsible for the defective condition of the bottle at the time it was delivered to the restaurant. Under the general rules pertaining to the doctrine, as set forth above, it must appear that bottles of carbonated liquid are not ordinarily defective without negligence by the bottling company. * * *

An explosion such as took place here might have been caused by an excessive internal pressure in a sound bottle, by a defect in the glass of a bottle containing a safe pressure, or by a combination of these two possible causes. The question is whether under the evidence there was a probability that defendant was negligent in any of these respects. If so, the doctrine of res ipsa loquitur applies.

The bottle was admittedly charged with gas under pressure, and the charging of the bottle was within the exclusive control of defendant. As it is a matter of common knowledge that an overcharge would not ordinarily result without negligence, it follows under the doctrine of res ipsa loquitur that if the bottle was in fact excessively charged an inference of defendant's negligence would arise. If the explosion resulted from a defective bottle containing a safe pressure, the defendant would be liable if it negligently failed to discover such flaw. If the defect were visible, an inference of negligence would arise from the failure of defendant to discover it. Where defects are discoverable, it may be assumed that they will not ordinarily escape detection if a reasonable inspection is made, and if such a defect is overlooked an inference arises that a proper inspection was not made. A difficult problem is presented where the defect is unknown and consequently might have been one not discoverable by a reasonable, practicable inspection. * * * In the present case, however, we are supplied with evidence of the standard methods used for testing bottles.

A chemical engineer for the Owens-Illinois Glass Company and its Pacific Coast subsidiary, maker of Coca Cola bottles, explained how glass is manufactured and the methods used in testing and inspecting bottles. * * *

It thus appears that there is available to the industry a commonly-used method of testing bottles for defects not apparent to the eye, which is almost infallible. Since Coca Cola bottles are subjected to these tests by the manufacturer, it is not likely that they contain defects when delivered to the bottler which are not discoverable by visual inspection. Both new and used bottles are filled and distributed by defendant. The used bottles are not again subjected to the tests referred to above, and it may be inferred that defects not discoverable by visual inspection do not develop in bottles after they are manufactured. Obviously, if such defects do occur in used bottles there is a duty upon the bottler to make appropriate tests before they are refilled and if such tests are not commercially practicable the bottles should not be re-used. This would seem to be particularly true where a charged liquid is placed in the bottle. It follows that a defect which would make the bottle unsound could be discovered by reasonable and practicable tests.

Although it is not clear in this case whether the explosion was caused by an excessive charge or a defect in the glass there is a sufficient showing that neither cause would ordinarily have been present if due care had been used. Further, defendant had exclusive control over both the charging and inspection of the bottles. Accordingly, all the requirements necessary to entitle plaintiff to rely on the doctrine of res ipsa loquitur to supply an inference of negligence are present.

It is true that defendant presented evidence tending to show that it exercised considerable precaution by carefully regulating and checking the pressure in the bottles and by making visual inspections for defects in the glass at several stages during the bottling process. It is well settled, however, that when a defendant produces evidence to rebut the inference of negligence which arises upon application of the doctrine of res ipsa loquitur, it is ordinarily a question of fact for the jury to determine whether the inference has been dispelled.

The judgment is affirmed.[9]

TRAYNOR, JUSTICE. I concur in the judgment, but I believe the manufacturer's negligence should no longer be singled out as the basis of a plaintiff's right to recover in cases like the present one. In my opinion it should now be recognized that a manufacturer incurs an absolute liability when an article that he has placed on the market, knowing that it is to be used without inspection, proves to have a defect that causes injury to human beings. MacPherson v. Buick Motor Co., 217 N.Y. 382, 111 N.E. 1050, L.R.A.1916F, 696, Ann.Cas. 1916C, 440 established the principle, recognized by this court, that irrespective of privity of contract, the manufacturer is responsible for an injury caused by such an article to any person who comes in lawful contact with it. Sheward v. Virtue, 20 Cal.2d 410, 126 P.2d 345; Kalash v. Los Angeles Ladder Co., 1 Cal.2d 229, 34 P.2d 481. In these cases the source of the manufacturer's liability was his negligence in the manufacturing process or in the inspection of component parts

9. For application of both res ipsa loquitur and implied warranty of merchantability, in exploding Coca Cola bottle case, against supermarket retailer but not against bottler, see Giant Food, Inc. v. Washington Coca-Cola Bottling Co., Inc., 273 Md. 592, 332 A.2d 1 (1975).

supplied by others. Even if there is no negligence, however, public policy demands that responsibility be fixed wherever it will most effectively reduce the hazards to life and health inherent in defective products that reach the market. It is evident that the manufacturer can anticipate some hazards and guard against the recurrence of others, as the public cannot. Those who suffer injury from defective products are unprepared to meet its consequences. The cost of an injury and the loss of time or health may be an overwhelming misfortune to the person injured, and a needless one, for the risk of injury can be insured by the manufacturer and distributed among the public as a cost of doing business. It is to the public interest to discourage the marketing of products having defects that are a menace to the public. If such products nevertheless find their way into the market it is to the public interest to place the responsibility for whatever injury they may cause upon the manufacturer, who, even if he is not negligent in the manufacture of the product, is responsible for its reaching the market. However intermittently such injuries may occur and however haphazardly they may strike, the risk of their occurrence is a constant risk and a general one. Against such a risk there should be general and constant protection and the manufacturer is best situated to afford such protection.

The injury from a defective product does not become a matter of indifference because the defect arises from causes other than the negligence of the manufacturer, such as negligence of a submanufacturer of a component part whose defects could not be revealed by inspection (see Sheward v. Virtue, 20 Cal.2d 410, 126 P.2d 345; O'Rourke v. Day & Night Water Heater Co., Ltd., 31 Cal.App.2d 364, 88 P.2d 191; Smith v. Peerless Glass Co., 259 N.Y. 292, 181 N.E. 576), or unknown causes that even by the device of res ipsa loquitur cannot be classified as negligence of the manufacturer. The inference of negligence may be dispelled by an affirmative showing of proper care. If the evidence against the fact inferred is "clear, positive, uncontradicted, and of such a nature that it can not rationally be disbelieved, the court must instruct the jury that the nonexistence of the fact has been established as a matter of law." Blank v. Coffin, 20 Cal.2d 457, 461, 126 P.2d 868, 870. An injured person, however, is not ordinarily in a position to refute such evidence or identify the cause of the defect, for he can hardly be familiar with the manufacturing process as the manufacturer himself is. In leaving it to the jury to decide whether the inference has been dispelled, regardless of the evidence against it, the negligence rule approaches the rule of strict liability. It is needlessly circuitous to make negligence the basis of recovery and impose what is in reality liability without negligence. If public policy demands that a manufacturer of goods be responsible for their quality regardless of negligence there is no reason not to fix that responsibility openly.

In the case of foodstuffs, the public policy of the state is formulated in a criminal statute. Section 26510 of the Health and Safety Code, St.1939, p. 989, prohibits the manufacturing, preparing, compounding, packing, selling, offering for sale, or keeping for sale, or advertising within the state, of any adulterated food. Section 26470, St.1941, p. 2857, declares that food is adulterated when "it has been produced, prepared, packed or held under insanitary conditions whereby it may have become contaminated with filth, or whereby it may have been rendered diseased, unwholesome or injurious to health." The statute imposes criminal liability not only if the food is adulterated, but if its container, which may be a bottle (§ 26451, St.1939, p. 983), has any deleterious substance (§ 26470(6), or renders the product injurious to health (§ 26470(4). The criminal liability under the statute attaches without proof of fault, so that the manufacturer is under the duty of ascertaining whether an article manufactured by him is safe. People v. Schwartz, 28 Cal.App.2d Supp. 775, 70 P.2d 1017. Statutes of this kind result in a strict liability of the manufacturer in tort to the member of the public injured. * * *

The statute may well be applicable to a bottle whose defects cause it to explode. In any event it is significant that the statute imposes criminal liability without fault, reflecting the public policy of protecting the public from dangerous products placed on the market, irrespective of negligence in their manufacture. * * *

The retailer, even though not equipped to test a product, is under an absolute liability to his customer, for the implied warranties of fitness for proposed use and merchantable quality include a warranty of safety of the product. * * * This warranty is not necessarily a contractual one (Chamberlain Co. v. Allis-Chalmers, etc., Co., 51 Cal.App.2d 520, 524, 125 P.2d 113; see 1 Williston on Sales, 2d ed., §§ 197–201), for public policy requires that the buyer be insured at the seller's expense against injury. * * * The courts recognize, however, that the retailer cannot bear the burden of this warranty, and allow him to recoup any losses by means of the warranty of safety attending the wholesaler's or manufacturer's sale to him. See Waite, Retail Responsibility and Judicial Law Making, 34 Mich.L. Rev. 494, 509. Such a procedure, however, is needlessly circuitous and engenders wasteful litigation. Much would be gained if the injured person could base his action directly on the manufacturer's warranty. * * *

This court and many others have extended protection according to such a standard to consumers of food products, taking the view that the right of a consumer injured by unwholesome food does not depend "upon the intricacies of the law of sales" and that the warranty of the manufacturer to the consumer in absence of privity of contract rests on public policy. * * * Dangers to life and health inhere in other consumers' goods that are defective and there is no reason to differentiate them from the dangers of defective food products. * * *

In the food products cases the courts have resorted to various fictions to rationalize the extension of the manufacturer's warranty to the consumer: that a warranty runs with the chattel; that the cause of action of the dealer is assigned to the consumer; that the consumer is a third party beneficiary of the manufacturer's contract with the dealer. They have also held the manufacturer liable on a mere fiction of negligence. * * * Such fictions are not necessary to fix the manufacturer's liability under a warranty if the warranty is severed from the contract of sale between the dealer and the consumer and based on the law of torts as a strict liability. * * * Warranties are not necessarily rights arising under a contract. An action on a warranty "was, in its origin, a pure action of tort," and only late in the historical development of warranties was an action in assumpsit allowed. Ames, The History of Assumpsit, 2 Harv.L.Rev. 1, 8; 4 Williston on Contracts (1936) § 970. * * * On the basis of the tort character of an action on a warranty, recovery has been allowed for wrongful death [10] as it could not be in an action for breach of contract. Greco v. S. S. Kresge Co., 277 N.Y. 26, 12 N.E.2d 557, 115 A.L.R. 1020 * * *

As handicrafts have been replaced by mass production with its great markets and transportation facilities, the close relationship between the producer and consumer of a product has been altered. Manufacturing processes, frequently valuable secrets, are ordinarily either inaccessible to or beyond the ken of the general public. The consumer no longer has means or skill enough to investigate for himself the soundness of a product, even when it is not contained in a sealed package, and his erstwhile vigilance has been lulled by the steady efforts of manufacturers to build up confidence by advertising and marketing devices such as trade-marks. * * * The manufacturer's obligation to the consumer must keep pace with the changing relationship between them; it cannot be escaped because the marketing of a product has become so complicated as to require one or more intermediaries. Certainly there is greater reason to impose liability on the manufacturer than on the retailer who is but a conduit of a product that he is not himself able to test. * * *

British products liability law is exemplified by the Privy Council's Grant v. Australian Knitting Mills [1936] A.C. 85. Plaintiff sued the selling retailer and the manufacturer for severe dermatitis allegedly contracted from chemical contaminants in underpants. Proof was based on inferences, from a great deal of circumstantial evidence, including residues in washed garments, that the dermatitis may have been caused by sulphites which could have remained in the garments if one of the manufacturing processes was not properly carried out. The manufacturer testified that in the six previous years 4,737,600 of these items had been sold without any complaints.

10. But see contra, Goodwin v. Misticos, 207 Miss. 361, 42 So.2d 397 (1949); Burkhardt v. Armour & Co., 115 Conn. 249, 161 A. 385, 90 A.L.R. 1260 (1932). [From original, renumbered.]

An employee testified that an excess of sulphite "would be bound to be somebody's fault", that the workers had to be "very careful", and that "something might go wrong, someone might be negligent". It was held that, as against the manufacturer, the liability "must be in tort, and the gist of the cause of action is negligence", but that the total evidence was sufficient and that, on the strength of Donoghue v. Stevenson [1932] A.C. 562, the manufacturer would be liable to the consumer notwithstanding lack of privity. (The Donoghue case, in which MacPherson v. Buick Motor Co. was liberally cited, became a landmark in British negligence jurisprudence, not only for its applicability to products liability, but more generally for the proposition in dicta, page 163 supra, that there is a "duty" of reasonable care to one's "neighbour", essentially those who would foreseeably be affected by one's conduct, i. e., that there is a general tort of negligence.) The retailer, who was not negligent, was held to be liable "in contract" for breach of warranties under the South Australia Sale of Goods Act, both the implied warranty of fitness for the purpose for which the goods were purchased, and the implied warranty of merchantability, which were held to overlap.

For a discussion of the British cases see generally J. Fleming, The Law of Torts (4th ed. 1971) 439 et seq.; Winfield and Jolowicz on Tort (10th ed. by W. Rogers 1975) 202 et seq. Also see J. Weir, A Casebook on Tort (3d ed. 1974) 22:

> "So the law now is that the vendor is liable to the purchaser whenever the goods are defective, but the manufacturer is liable to the consumer only if the goods are dangerous by reason of a defect attributable to his carelessness. Many members of our consumptive society think it shocking that if I am burnt by the contents of a defective hot water bottle I have just bought, I get damages automatically from the shop, whereas my scalded girl-friend has to sue the rubber plant and show that someone there was careless. But it is just as odd that the vendor is strictly liable as that the manufacturer is liable only for carelessness."

Compare, among many extant American variations, Serksnas v. Engine Support, Inc., 392 F.Supp. 392 (S.D.Fla.1975), discussing the Florida action of breach of implied warranty, which is described as a "tort which closely resembles the doctrine of strict liability", and, which is said not to apply to retailers.

Whether breach of warranty is considered to be a ("sound in * * * ") tort or breach of contract may matter for a number of reasons which vary from one jurisdiction to another. There can, for instance, be differences in statutes of limitations, e. g., Barfield v. United States Rubber Co., 234 So.2d 374 (Fla.App.1970); Romano v. Westinghouse Electric Co., —— R.I. ——, 336 A.2d 555 (1975); in measure of damages, e. g., the availability of punitive damages in tort, or the psychological preference for the use of "warranty" as non-"tort", e. g., presumably contract, to cover commercial losses, as reflected in Seely v. White Motor Co., 63 Cal.2d 9, 45 Cal.Rptr. 17, 403 P.2d 145 (1965), page 561 supra; compare Santor v. A. M. Karagheusian, Inc., 44 N.J. 52, 207 A.2d 305, 16 A.L.R.3d 670 (1965); in choice of law rules, e. g., compare Uppgren v. Executive Aviation Services, Inc., 326 F.Supp. 709 (D.Md.1971) with Volkswagen of America, Inc. v. Young, 272 Md. 201, 321 A.2d 737 (1974) as to whether breach of warranty is governed by the law of the state where the injury occurred or where the sale occurred; and in the requirement for and application of doctrines concerning privity, e. g., Allen v. Ortho Pharmaceutical Corp., 387 F.Supp. 364 (S.D.Tex.1974), the statute of frauds, the parol evidence rule and consideration. There are further implications arising from the notion that a tort happens when and where the tortious conduct results in injury to the victim. First, it is conceptually easy for tort liability to attach to injuries long after the date of manufacture of a product, assuming the accident can be attributed to a defect in design or construction, e. g., Mickle v. Blackmon, 252 S.C. 202, 166 S.E.2d 173 (1969) (liability by automobile manufacturer for injuries in 1962, when passenger was impaled on gearshift lever of 1949 Ford, because gearshift knob was made of white plastic, which became more embrittled by exposure to ultraviolet rays of sunlight than would black plastic, and therefore shattered on impact). In addition, if viewed as a tort, breach of warranty may subject an out-of-state manufacturer to the jurisdiction of courts of the state where the accident occurred, under a "long arm" statute of the latter state, e. g., Keckler v. Brookwood Country Club, 248 F.Supp. 645 (N.D.Ill.1965); Dawkins v. White Products Corporation of Middleville, Michigan, 443 F.2d 589 (5th Cir. 1971); Alliance Clothing Ltd. v. District Court, — Colo. —, 532 P.2d 351 (1975), anno., 19 A.L.R.3d 13. There may also be questions as to whether a state's wrongful death statute applies to a non-tort cause of action, e. g., Denny v. Seaboard Lacquer, Inc., 487 F.2d 485 (4th Cir. 1973).

HENNINGSEN v. BLOOMFIELD MOTORS, INC.

Supreme Court of New Jersey, 1960.
32 N.J. 358, 161 A.2d 69.

FRANCIS, J. Plaintiff Claus H. Henningsen purchased a Plymouth automobile, manufactured by defendant Chrysler Corporation, from defendant Bloomfield Motors, Inc. His wife, plaintiff Helen Henningsen, was injured while driving it and instituted suit against both defendants to recover damages on account of her injuries. Her husband joined in the action seeking compensation for his consequential losses. The complaint was predicated upon breach of express and implied warranties and upon negligence. At the trial the negligence counts were dismissed by the court and the cause was submitted to the jury for determination solely on the issues of implied warranty of merchantability. Verdicts were returned against both defendants and in favor of the plaintiffs. Defendants appealed * * *.

The facts are not complicated, but a general outline of them is necessary to an understanding of the case.

On May 7, 1955 Mr. and Mrs. Henningsen visited the place of business of Bloomfield Motors, Inc., an authorized De Soto and Plymouth dealer, to look at a Plymouth. * * * The record indicates that Mr. Henningsen intended the car as a Mother's Day gift to his wife. He said the intention was communicated to the dealer. When the purchase order or contract was prepared and presented, the husband executed it alone. His wife did not join as a party.

The purchase order was a printed form of one page. On the front it contained blanks to be filled in with a description of the automobile to be sold, the various accessories to be included, and the details of the financing. The particular car selected was described as a 1955 Plymouth, Plaza "6", Club Sedan. The type used in the printed parts of the form became smaller in size, different in style, and less readable toward the bottom where the line for the purchaser's signature was placed. The smallest type on the page appears in the two paragraphs, one of two and one-quarter lines and the second of one and one-half lines, on which great stress is laid by the defense in the case. These two paragraphs are the least legible and the most difficult to read in the instrument, but they are most important in the evaluation of the rights of the contesting parties. They do not attract attention and there is nothing about the format which would draw the reader's eye to them. In fact, a studied and concentrated effort would have to be made to read them. De-emphasis seems the motive rather than emphasis. More particularly, most of the printing in the body of the order appears to be 12 point block type, and easy to read. In the short paragraphs under discussion, however, the type appears to be six point script and the print is solid, that is, the lines are very close together.

The two paragraphs are:

> "The front and back of this Order comprise the entire agreement affecting this purchase and no other agreement or understanding of any nature concerning same has been made or entered into, or will be recognized. I hereby certify that no credit has been extended to me for the purchase of this motor vehicle except as appears in writing on the face of this agreement.
>
> "I have read the matter printed on the back hereof and agree to it as a part of this order the same as if it were printed above my signature. I certify that I am 21 years of age, or older, and hereby acknowledge receipt of a copy of this order."

On the right side of the form, immediately below these clauses and immediately above the signature line, and in 12 point block type, the following appears:

> "CASH OR CERTIFIED CHECK ONLY ON DELIVERY."

On the left side, just opposite and in the same style type as the two quoted clauses, but in eight point size, this statement is set out:

> "This agreement shall not become binding upon the Dealer until approved by an officer of the company."

The two latter statements are in the interest of the dealer and obviously an effort is made to draw attention to them.

The testimony of Claus Henningsen justifies the conclusion that he did not read the two fine print paragraphs referring to the back of the purchase contract. And it is uncontradicted that no one made any reference to them, or called them to his attention. With respect to the matter appearing on the back, it is likewise uncontradicted that he did not read it and that no one called it to his attention.

The reverse side of the contract contains 8½ inches of fine print. It is not as small, however, as the two critical paragraphs described above. The page is headed "Conditions" and contains ten separate paragraphs consisting of 65 lines in all. The paragraphs do not have headnotes or margin notes denoting their particular subject, as in the case of the "Owner Service Certificate" to be referred to later. In the seventh paragraph, about two-thirds of the way down the page, the warranty, which is the focal point of the case, is set forth. It is as follows:

> "7. It is expressly agreed that there are no warranties, express or implied, *made* by either the dealer or the manufacturer on the motor vehicle, chassis, of parts furnished hereunder except as follows.
>
> " 'The manufacturer warrants each new motor vehicle (including original equipment placed thereon by the manufacturer except tires), chassis or parts manufactured by it to be free from defects in material or workmanship under normal use and service. Its obligation under this warranty being limited to making good at its factory any part or parts thereof which shall, within ninety (90) days after delivery of such vehicle *to the original purchaser* or before such vehicle has been driven 4,000 miles, whichever event shall first occur, be returned to it with transportation charges prepaid and which its examination shall disclose to its satisfaction to have been thus defective; *this warranty being expressly in lieu of all other warranties expressed or implied, and all other obligations or liabilities on its part,* and it neither assumes nor authorizes any other person to assume for it any other liability in connection with the sale of its vehicles. * * *.' " (Emphasis ours.)

After the contract had been executed, plaintiffs were told the car had to be serviced and that it would be ready in two days. According to the dealer's president, a number of cars were on hand at the time; they had come in from the factory about three or four weeks earlier and at least some of them, including the one selected by the Henningsens, were kept in the back of the shop for display purposes. When sold, plaintiffs' vehicle was not "a serviced car, ready to go." The testimony shows that Chrysler Corporation sends from the factory to the dealer a "New Car Preparation Service Guide" with each new automobile. The guide contains detailed instructions as to what has to be done to prepare the car for delivery. The dealer is told to "Use this form as a guide to inspect and prepare this new Plymouth for delivery." It specifies 66 separate items to be checked, tested, tightened or adjusted in the course of the servicing, but dismantling the vehicle or checking all of its internal parts is not prescribed. The guide also calls for delivery of the Owner Service Certificate with the car.

This Certificate, which at least by inference is authorized by Chrysler, was in the car when released to Claus Henningsen on May 9, 1955. It was not made part of the purchase contract, nor was it shown to him prior to the consummation of that agreement. The only reference to it therein is that the dealer "agrees to promptly perform and fulfill all terms and conditions of the owner service policy." The Certificate contains a warranty entitled "Automobile Manufacturers Association Uniform Warranty." The provisions thereof are the same as those set forth on the reverse side of the purchase order, except that an additional paragraph is added by which the dealer extends that warranty to the purchaser in the same manner as if the word "Dealer" appeared instead of the word "Manufacturer."

The new Plymouth was turned over to the Henningsens on May 9, 1955. * * * It had no servicing and no mishaps of any kind before the event of May 19. That day, Mrs. Henningsen drove to Asbury Park. On the way down and in returning the car performed in normal fashion until the accident occurred. She was proceeding north on Route 36 in Highlands, New Jersey, at 20–22 miles per hour. The highway was paved and smooth, and contained two lanes for northbound travel. She was riding in the right-hand lane. Suddenly she heard a loud noise "from the bottom, by the hood." It "felt as if something cracked." The steering wheel spun in her hands; the car veered sharply to the right and crashed into a highway sign and a brick wall. No other vehicle was in any way involved. A bus operator driving in the left-hand lane testified that he observed plaintiffs' car approaching in normal fashion in the opposite direction; "all of a sudden [it] veered at 90 degrees * * * and right into this wall." As a result of the impact, the front of the car was so badly damaged that it was impossible to determine if any of the parts of the steering wheel mechanism or workmanship or assembly were defective or improper prior to the accident. The condition was such that the collision insurance carrier, after inspection, declared the vehicle a total loss. It had 468 miles on the speedometer at the time.

The insurance carrier's inspector and appraiser of damaged cars, with 11 years of experience, advanced the opinion, based on the history and his examination, that something definitely went "wrong from the steering wheel down to the front wheels" and that the untoward happening must have been due to mechanical defect or failure; "something down there had to drop off or break loose to cause the car" to act in the manner described.

As has been indicated, the trial court felt that the proof was not sufficient to make out a *prima facie* case as to the negligence of either the manufacturer or the dealer. The case was given to the jury, therefore, solely on the warranty theory, with results favorable to the plaintiffs against both defendants.

I.

The Claim of Implied Warranty against the Manufacturer.

In the ordinary case of sale of goods by description an implied warranty of merchantability is an integral part of the transaction. R.S. 46:30–20, N.J.S.A. If the buyer, expressly or by implication, makes known to the seller the particular purpose for which the article is required and it appears that he has relied on the seller's skill or judgment, an implied warranty arises of reasonable fitness for that purpose. R.S. 46:30–21(1), N.J.S.A. The former type of warranty simply means that the thing sold is reasonably fit for the general purpose for which it is manufactured and sold. * * * As Judge (later Justice) Cardozo remarked in Ryan, supra, the distinction between a warranty of fitness for a particular purpose and of merchantability in many instances is practically meaningless. In the particular case he was concerned with food for human consumption in a sealed container. Perhaps no more apt illustration of the notion can be thought of than the instance of the ordinary purchaser who informs the automobile dealer that he desires a car for the purpose of business and pleasure driving on the public highway.

* * *

Of course such sales, whether oral or written, may be accompanied by an express warranty. Under the broad terms of the Uniform Sale of Goods Law any affirmation of fact relating to the goods is an express warranty if the natural tendency of the statement is to induce the buyer to make the purchase. R.S. 46:30–18, N.J.S.A. And over the years since the almost universal adoption of the act, a growing awareness of the tremendous development of modern business methods has prompted the courts to administer that provision with a liberal hand. * * * Solicitude toward the buyer plainly harmonizes with the intention of the Legislature. That fact is manifested further by the later section of the act which preserves and continues any permissible implied warranty, despite an express warranty, unless the two are inconsistent. R.S. 46:30–21(6), N.J. S.A.

The uniform act codified, extended and liberalized the common law of sales. The motivation in part was to ameliorate the harsh doctrine of *caveat emptor,* and in some measure to impose a reciprocal obligation on the seller to beware. The transcendent value of the legislation, particularly with respect to implied warranties, rests in the fact that obligations on the part of the seller were imposed by operation of law, and did not depend for their existence upon express agreement of the parties. And of tremendous significance in a rapidly expanding commercial society was the recognition of the right to recover damages on account of personal injuries arising from a breach of warranty. * * * Prosser, Law of Torts, p. 493 (1955). The particular importance of this advance resides in the fact that under such circumstances strict liability is imposed upon the maker or seller of the product. Recovery of damages does not depend upon proof of negligence or knowledge of the defect. * * *

As the Sales Act and its liberal interpretation by the courts threw this protective cloak about the buyer, the decisions in various jurisdictions revealed beyond doubt that many manufacturers took steps to avoid these ever increasing warranty obligations. Realizing that the act governed the relationship of buyer and seller, they undertook to withdraw from actual and direct contractual contact with the buyer. They ceased selling products to the consuming public through their own employees and making contracts of sale in their own names. Instead, a system of independent dealers was established; their products were sold to dealers who in turn dealt with the buying public, ostensibly solely in their own personal capacity as sellers. In the past in many instances, manufacturers were able to transfer to the dealers burdens imposed by the act and thus achieved a large measure of immunity for themselves. But, * * * such marketing practices, coupled with the advent of large scale advertising by manufacturers to promote the purchase of these goods from dealers by members of the public, provided a basis upon which the existence of express or implied warranties was predicated, even though the manufacturer was not a party to the contract of sale.

* * * It must be noted, however, that the sections of the Sales Act, to which reference has been made, do not impose warranties in terms of unalterable absolutes. R.S. 46:30–3, N.J.S.A., provides in general terms that an applicable warranty may be negatived or varied by express agreement. As to disclaimers or limitations of the obligations that normally attend a sale, it seems sufficient at this juncture to say they are not favored, and that they are strictly construed against the seller. 2 Harper & James, supra § 28.25; Vold, supra p. 459; "Warranties of Kind & Quality," 57 Yale L.J. 1388, 1400–1401 (1948).

With these considerations in mind, we come to a study of the express warranty on the reverse side of the purchase order signed by Claus Henningsen. At the outset we take notice that it was made only by the manufacturer and that by its terms it runs directly to Claus Henningsen. On the facts detailed above, it was to be extended to him by the dealer as the agent of Chrysler Corporation. The consideration for this warranty is the purchase of the manufacturer's product from the dealer by the ultimate buyer. * * *

Although the franchise agreement between the defendants recites that the relationship of principal and agent is not created, in particular transactions involving third persons the law will look at their conduct and not to their intent or their words as between themselves but to their factual relation. Restatement of Agency, Second § 27 (1958). The normal pattern that the manufacturer-dealer relationship follows relegates the position of the dealer to the status of a way station along the car's route from maker to consumer. This is indicated by the language of the warranty. Obviously the parties knew and so intended that the dealer would not use the automobile for 90 days or drive it 4,000 miles. And the words "original purchaser," taken in their context, signify the purchasing member of the public. * * * Moreover, the language of this warranty is that of the uniform warranty of the Automobile Manufacturers Association, of which Chrysler is a member. See Automotive Facts & Figures, 1958 Edition, published by Automotive Manufacturers Association, p. 69 * * *. And it is the form appearing in the Plymouth Owner Service Certificate mentioned in the servicing instruction guide sent with the new car from the factory. The evidence is overwhelming that the dealer acted for Chrysler in including the warranty in the purchase contract. * * *

The terms of the warranty are a sad commentary upon the automobile manufacturers' marketing practices. Warranties developed in the law in the interest of and to protect the ordinary consumer who cannot be expected to have the knowledge or capacity or even the opportunity to make adequate inspection of mechanical instrumentalities, like automobiles, and to decide for himself whether they are reasonably fit for the designed purpose. * * * 1 Williston, supra, pp. 625, 626. But the ingenuity of the Automobile Manufacturers Association, by means of its standardized form, has metamorphosed the warranty into a device to limit the maker's liability. * * *

The manufacturer agrees to replace defective parts for 90 days after the sale or until the car has been driven 4,000 miles, whichever is first to occur, *if the part is sent to the factory, transportation charges prepaid, and if examination discloses to its satisfaction that the part is defective.* It is difficult to imagine a greater burden on the consumer, or less satisfactory remedy. Aside from imposing on the buyer the trouble of removing and shipping the part, the maker has sought to retain the uncontrolled discretion to decide the issue of defectiveness. Some courts have removed much of the force of that reservation by declaring that the purchaser is not bound by the manufacturer's decision. Mills v. Maxwell Motor Sales Corporation, 105 Neb. 465, 181 N.W. 152, 22 A.L.R. 130 (Sup.Ct.1920); Cannon v. Pulliam Motor Company, 230 S.C. 131, 94 S.E.2d 397 (Sup.Ct. 1956). In the Mills case, the court said:

> "It would nevertheless be repugnant to every conception of justice to hold that, if the parts thus returned for examination were, in point of fact, so defective as to constitute a breach of warranty, the appellee's right of action could be defeated by the appellant's arbitrary refusal to recognize that fact. Such an interpretation would substitute the appellant for the courts in passing upon the question of fact, and would be unreasonable." Supra, 181 N.W. at page 154.

Also suppose, as in this case, a defective part or parts caused an accident and that the car was so damaged as to render it impossible to discover the precise part or parts responsible, although the circumstances clearly pointed to such fact as the cause of the mishap. Can it be said that the impossibility of performance deprived the buyer of the benefit of the warranty?

Moreover, the guaranty is against defective workmanship. That condition may arise from good parts improperly assembled. There being no defective parts to return to the maker, is all remedy to be denied? One court met that type of problem by holding that where the purchaser does not know the precise cause of inoperability, calling a car a "vibrator" would be sufficient to state a claim for relief. It said that such a car is not an uncommon one in the industry. The general cause of the vibration is not known. Some part or parts have been either defectively manufactured or improperly assembled * *. The difficulty lies in locating the precise spot and cause. * * * But the warranty does not specify what the purchaser must do to obtain relief in such case, if a remedy is intended to be provided. Must the purchaser return the car, transportation charges prepaid, over a great distance to the factory? It may be said that in the usual case the dealer also gives the same warranty and that as a matter of expediency the purchaser should turn to him. But under the law the buyer is entitled to proceed against the manufacturer. Further, dealers' franchises are precarious (see, Automobile Franchise Agreements, Hewitt (1956)). For example, Bloomfield Motors' franchise may be cancelled by Chrysler on 90 days' notice. And obviously dealers' facilities and capacity, financial and otherwise, are not as sufficient as those of the primarily responsible manufacturer in his distant factory.

The matters referred to represent only a small part of the illusory character of the security presented by the warranty. Thus far the analysis has dealt only with the remedy provided in the case of a defective part. What relief is provided when the breach of the warranty results in personal injury to the buyer? (Injury to third persons using the car in the purchaser's right will be treated hereafter.) As we have said above, the law is clear that such damages are recoverable under an ordinary warranty. The right exists whether the warranty sued on is express or implied. See, e. g., Ryan v. Progressive Grocery Stores, supra. And, of course, it has long since been settled that where the buyer or a member of his family driving with his permission suffers injuries because of negligent manufacture or construction of the vehicle, the manufacturer's liability exists. Prosser, supra, §§ 83, 84. But in this instance, after reciting that defective parts will be replaced at the factory, the alleged agreement relied upon by Chrysler provides that the manufacturer's "obligation under this warranty" is limited to that undertaking; further, that such remedy is "in lieu of all other warranties, express or implied, and all other obligations or liabilities on its part." The contention has been raised that such language bars any claim for personal injuries which may emanate from a breach of the warranty. * * *

Putting aside for the time being the problem of the efficacy of the disclaimer provisions contained in the express warranty, a question of first importance to be decided is whether an implied warranty of merchantability by Chrysler Corporation accompanied the sale of the automobile to Claus Henningsen.

Preliminarily, it may be said that the express warranty against defective parts and workmanship is not inconsistent with an implied warranty of merchantability. Such warranty cannot be excluded for that reason. * * *

Chrysler points out that an implied warranty of merchantability is an incident of a contract of sale. * * * Then Chrysler urges that since it was not a party to the sale by the dealer to Henningsen, there is no privity of contract between it and the plaintiffs, and the absence of this privity eliminates any such implied warranty.

There is no doubt that under early common-law concepts of contractual liability, only those persons who were parties to the bargain could sue for a breach of it. In more recent times a noticeable disposition has appeared in a number of jurisdictions to break through the narrow barrier of privity when dealing with sales of goods in order to give realistic recognition to a universally accepted fact. The fact is that the dealer and the ordinary buyer do not, and are not expected to, buy goods, whether they be foodstuffs or automobiles, exclusively for their own consumption or use. Makers and manufacturers know this and advertise and market their products on that assumption; witness the "family" car, the baby foods, etc. The limitations of privity in contracts for the sale of goods developed their place in the law when marketing conditions were simple, when maker and buyer frequently met face to face on an equal bargaining plane and when many of the products were relatively uncomplicated and conducive to inspection by a buyer competent to evaluate their quality. * * * With the advent of mass marketing, the manufacturer became remote from the purchaser, sales were accomplished through intermediaries, and the demand for the product was created by advertising media. In such an economy it became obvious that the consumer was the person being cultivated. Manifestly, the connotation of "consumer" was broader than that of "buyer." He signified such a person who, in the reasonable contemplation of the parties to the sale, might be expected to use the product. Thus, where the commodities sold are such that if defectively manufactured they will be dangerous to life or limb, then society's interests can only be protected by eliminating the requirement of privity between the maker and his dealers and the reasonably expected ultimate consumer. In that way the burden of losses consequent upon use of defective articles is borne by those who are in a position to either control the danger or make an equitable distribution of the losses when they do occur. As Harper & James put it, "The interest in consumer protection calls for warranties by the maker that *do* run with the goods, to reach all who are likely to be hurt by the use of the unfit commodity for a purpose ordinarily to be expected." 2 Harper & James, supra 1571, 1572; also see, 1535; Prosser, supra, 506–511.

* * *

Although only a minority of jurisdictions have thus far departed from the requirement of privity, the movement in that direction is most certainly gathering momentum. Liability to the ultimate consumer in the absence of direct contractual connection has been predicated upon a variety of theories. Some courts hold that the warranty runs with the article like a covenant running with land; others recognize a third-party beneficiary thesis; still others rest their decision on the ground that public policy requires recognition of a warranty made directly to the consumer. * * *

Most of the cases where lack of privity has not been permitted to interfere with recovery have involved food and drugs. * * * In fact, the rule as to such products has been characterized as an exception to the general doctrine. But more recently courts, sensing the inequity of such limitation, have moved into broader fields * * * [citations to cases concerning a home permanent wave set, soap detergent, inflammable cowboy suit, exploding bottle, and defective emery wheel, wire rope and cinder blocks].

We see no rational doctrinal basis for differentiating between a fly in a bottle of beverage and a defective automobile. The unwholesome beverage may bring illness to one person, the defective car, with its great potentiality for harm to the driver, occupants, and others, demands even less adherence to the narrow barrier of privity. 2 Harper & James, supra, 1572; 1 Williston, supra, § 244a, p. 648; Note, 46 Harv.L.Rev. 161 (1932). * * *

Under modern conditions the ordinary layman, on responding to the importuning of colorful advertising, has neither the opportunity nor the capacity to inspect or to determine the fitness of an automobile for use; he must rely on the manufacturer who has control of its construction, and to some degree on the dealer who, to the limited extent called for by the manufacturer's instructions, inspects and services it before delivery. In such a marketing milieu his remedies and those of persons who properly claim through him should not depend "upon the intricacies of the law of sales. The obligation of the manufacturer should not be based alone on privity of contract. It should rest, as was once said, upon 'the demands of social justice.'" Mazetti v. Armour & Co., 75 Wash. 622, 135 P. 633, 635, 48 L.R.A.,N.S., 213 (Sup.Ct.1913). * * *

Accordingly, we hold that under modern marketing conditions, when a manufacturer puts a new automobile in the stream of trade and promotes its purchase by the public, an implied warranty that it is reasonably suitable for use as such accompanies it into the hands of the ultimate purchaser. Absence of agency between the manufacturer and the dealer who makes the ultimate sale is immaterial.

II.

The Effect of the Disclaimer and Limitation of Liability Clauses on the Implied Warranty of Merchantability.

Judicial notice may be taken of the fact that automobile manufacturers, including Chrysler Corporation, undertake large scale advertising programs over television, radio, in newspapers, magazines and all media of communication in order to persuade the public to buy their products. As has been observed above, a number of jurisdictions, conscious of modern marketing practices, have declared that when a manufacturer engages in advertising in order to bring his goods and their quality to the attention of the public and thus to create consumer demand, the representations made constitute an express warranty running directly to a buyer who purchases in reliance thereon. The fact that the sale is consummated with an independent dealer does not obviate that warranty. * * *

In view of the cases in various jurisdictions suggesting the conclusion which we have now reached with respect to the implied warranty of merchantability, it becomes apparent that manufacturers who enter into promotional activities to stimulate consumer buying may incur warranty obligations of either or both the express or implied character. These developments in the law inevitably suggest the inference that the form of express warranty made part of the Henningsen purchase contract was devised for general use in the automobile industry as a possible means of avoiding the consequences of the growing judicial acceptance of the thesis that the described express or implied warranties run directly to the consumer.

In the light of these matters, what effect should be given to the express warranty in question which seeks to limit the manufacturer's liability to replacement of defective parts, and which disclaims all other warranties, express or implied? In assessing its significance we must keep in mind the general principle that, in the absence of fraud, one who does not choose to read a contract before signing it, cannot later relieve himself of its burdens. Fivey v. Pennsylvania R. R. Co., 67 N.J.L. 627, 52 A. 472, (E. & A.1902). And in applying that principle, the basic tenet of freedom of competent parties to contract is a factor of importance. But in the framework of modern commercial life and business practices, such rules cannot be applied on a strict, doctrinal basis. The conflicting interests of the buyer and seller must be evaluated realistically and justly, giving due weight to the social policy evinced by the Uniform Sales Act, the progressive decisions of the courts engaged in administering it, the mass production methods of manufacture and distribution to the public, and the bargaining position occupied by the ordinary consumer in such an economy. This history of the law shows that legal doctrines, as first expounded, often prove to be inadequate under the impact of later experience. In such case, the need for justice has stimulated the necessary qualifications or adjustments. * * *

In these times, an automobile is almost as much a servant of convenience for the ordinary person as a household utensil. For a multitude of other persons it is a necessity. Crowded highways and filled parking lots are a commonplace of our existence. There is no need to look any farther than the daily newspaper to be convinced that when an automobile is defective, it has great potentiality for harm.

No one spoke more graphically on this subject than Justice Cardozo in the landmark case of MacPherson v. Buick Motor Co. * * * In the 44 years that have intervened since that * * * [opinion], the average car has been constructed for almost double the speed mentioned; 60 miles per hour is permitted on our parkways. The number of automobiles in use has multiplied many times and the hazard to the user and the public has increased proportionately. The Legislature has intervened in the public interest, not only to regulate the manner of operation on the highway but also to require periodic inspection of motor vehicles and to impose a duty on manufacturers to adopt certain safety devices and methods in their construction. * * * It is apparent that the public has an interest not only in the safe manufacture of automobiles, but also, as shown by the Sales Act, in protecting the rights and remedies of purchasers, so far as it can be accomplished consistently with our system of free enterprise. * * * Consequently, the courts must examine purchase agreements closely to see if consumer and public interests are treated fairly.

* * * It seems obvious in this instance that the motive was to avoid the warranty obligations which are normally incidental to such sales. The language gave little and withdrew much. In return for the delusive remedy of replacement of defective parts at the factory, the buyer is said to have accepted the exclusion of the maker's liability for personal injuries arising from the breach of the warranty, and to have agreed to the elimination of any other express or implied warranty. An instinctively felt sense of justice cries out against such a sharp bargain. But does the doctrine that a person is bound by his signed agreement, in the absence of fraud, stand in the way of any relief?

In the modern consideration of problems such as this, Corbin suggests that practically all judges are "chancellors" and cannot fail to be influenced by any equitable doctrines that are available. And he opines that "there is sufficient flexibility in the concepts of fraud, duress, misrepresentation and undue influence, not to mention differences in economic bargaining power" to enable the courts to avoid enforcement of unconscionable provisions in long printed standardized contracts. 1 Corbin on Contracts (1950) § 128, p. 188. Freedom of contract is not such an immutable doctrine as to admit of no qualification in the area in which we are concerned. As Chief Justice Hughes said in his dissent in Morehead v. People of State of New York ex rel. Tipaldo, 298 U.S. 587, 627, 56 S.Ct. 918, 930, 80 L.Ed. 1347, 1364 (1936):

> "We have had frequent occasion to consider the limitations on liberty of contract. While it is highly important to preserve that liberty from arbitrary and capricious interference, it is also necessary to prevent its abuse, as otherwise it could be used to override all public interests and thus in the end destroy the very freedom of opportunity which it is designed to safeguard."

That sentiment was echoed by Justice Frankfurter in his dissent in United States v. Bethlehem Steel Corp., 315 U.S. 289, 326, 62 S.Ct. 581, 599, 86 L.Ed. 855, 876 (1942):

> "It is said that familiar principles would be outraged if Bethlehem were denied recovery on these contracts. But is there any principle which is more familiar or more firmly embedded in the history of Anglo-American law than the basic doctrine that the courts will not permit themselves to be used as instruments of inequity and injustice? Does any principle in our law have more universal application than the doctrine that courts will not enforce transactions in which the relative positions of the parties are such that one has unconscionably taken advantage of the necessities of the other? * * *"

The traditional contract is the result of free bargaining of parties who are brought together by the play of the market, and who meet each other on a footing of approximate economic equality. In such a society there is no danger that freedom of contract will be a threat to the social order as a whole. But in present-day commercial life the standardized mass contract has appeared. It is used primarily by enterprises with strong bargaining power and position. "The weaker party, in need of the goods or services, is frequently not in a position to shop around for better terms, either because the author of the standard contract has a monopoly (natural or artificial) or because all competitors use the same clauses. His contractual intention is but a subjection more or less voluntary to terms dictated by the stronger party, terms whose consequences are often understood in a vague way, if at all." Kessler, "Contracts of Adhesion—Some Thoughts About Freedom of Contract," 43 Colum.L.Rev. 629,

632 (1943); Ehrenzweig, "Adhesion Contracts in the Conflict of Laws," 53 Colum.L.Rev. 1072, 1075, 1089 (1953). * * *

The warranty before us is a standardized form designed for mass use. It is imposed upon the automobile consumer. He takes it or leaves it, and he must take it to buy an automobile. No bargaining is engaged in with respect to it. In fact, the dealer through whom it comes to the buyer is without authority to alter it; his function is ministerial—simply to deliver it. The form warranty is not only standard with Chrysler but, as mentioned above, it is the uniform warranty of the Automobile Manufacturers Association. * * *

The gross inequality of bargaining position occupied by the consumer in the automobile industry is thus apparent. There is no competition among the car makers in the area of the express warranty. Where can the buyer go to negotiate for better protection? Such control and limitation of his remedies are inimical to the public welfare and, at the very least, call for great care by the courts to avoid injustice through application of strict common-law principles of freedom of contract. * * *

Although the courts, with few exceptions, have been most sensitive to problems presented by contracts resulting from gross disparity in buyer-seller bargaining positions, they have not articulated a general principle condemning, as opposed to public policy, the imposition on the buyer of a skeleton warranty as a means of limiting the responsibility of the manufacturer. They have endeavored thus far to avoid a drastic departure from age-old tenets of freedom of contract by adopting doctrines of strict construction, and notice and knowledgeable assent by the buyer to the attempted exculpation of the seller. * * * Accordingly to be found in the cases are statements that disclaimers and the consequent limitation of liability will not be given effect if "unfairly procured," * * * if not brought to the buyer's attention and he was not made understandingly aware of it * * * or if not clear and explicit * * *.

The rigid scrutiny which the courts give to attempted limitations of warranties and of the liability that would normally flow from a transaction is not limited to the field of sales of goods. Clauses on baggage checks restricting the liability of common carriers for loss or damage in transit are not enforceable unless the limitation is fairly and honestly negotiated and understandingly entered into. If not called specifically to the patron's attention, it is not binding. It is not enough merely to show the form of a contract; it must appear also that the agreement was understandingly made. * * * The same holds true in cases of such limitations on parcel check room tickets, * * *; on automobile parking lot or garage tickets or claim checks * * *; as to exculpatory clauses in leases releasing a landlord of apartments in a multiple dwelling house from all liability for negligence where inequality of bargaining exists, see Annotation, 175 A.L.R. 8 (1948). And the validity of release clauses in orders signed by a depositor directing a bank to stop payment of his check, exonerating the bank from liability for negligent payment, has been seriously questioned on public policy grounds in this State * * *. Elsewhere they have been declared void as opposed to public policy.

* * *

It is undisputed that the president of the dealer with whom Henningsen dealt did not specifically call attention to the warranty on the back of the purchase order. The form and the arrangement of its face, as described above, certainly would cause the minds of reasonable men to differ as to whether notice of a yielding of basic rights stemming from the relationship with the manufacturer was adequately given. The words "warranty" or "limited warranty" did not even appear in the fine print above the place for signature, and a jury might well find that the type of print itself was such as to promote lack of attention rather than sharp scrutiny. * * *

But there is more than this. Assuming that a jury might find that the fine print referred to reasonably served the objective of directing a buyer's attention to the warranty on the reverse side, and, therefore, that he should be charged with awareness of its language, can it be said that an ordinary layman would realize what he was relinquishing in return for what he was being granted? Under the law, breach of warranty against defective parts or workmanship which caused personal injuries would entitle a buyer to damages even if due care were used in the manufacturing process. Because of the great potential for harm if the vehicle was defective, that right is the most important and fundamental one arising from the relationship. Difficulties so frequently encountered in establishing negligence in manufacture in the ordinary case make this manifest. 2 Harper & James, supra, §§ 28.14, 28.15; Prosser, supra, 506. Any ordinary layman of reasonable intelligence, looking at the phraseology, might well conclude that Chrysler was agreeing to replace defective parts and perhaps replace anything that went wrong because of defective workmanship during the first 90 days or 4,000 miles of operation, but that he would not be entitled to a new car. It is not unreasonable to believe that the entire scheme being conveyed was a proposed remedy for physical deficiencies in the car. *In the context* of this warranty, only the abandonment of all sense of justice would permit us to hold that, as a matter of law, the phrase "its obligation under this warranty being limited to making good at its factory any part or parts thereof" signifies to an ordinary reasonable person that he is reliquishing any personal injury claim that might flow from the use of a defective automobile. * * *

The task of the judiciary is to administer the spirit as well as the letter of the law. On issues such as the present one, part of that burden is to protect the ordinary man against the loss of important rights through what, in effect, is the unilateral act of the manufacturer. The status of the automobile industry is unique. Manufacturers are few in number and strong in bargaining position. In the matter of warranties on the sale of their products, the Automotive Manufacturers Association has enabled them to present a united front. From the standpoint of the purchaser, there can be no arms length negotiating on the subject. Because his capacity for bargaining is so grossly unequal, the inexorable conclusion which follows is that he is not permitted to bargain at all. He must take or leave the automobile on the warranty terms dictated by the maker. He cannot turn to a competitor for better security.

* * *

* * * In the area of sale of goods, the legislative will has imposed an implied warranty of merchantability as a general incident of sale of an automobile by description. * * * The judicial process has recognized a right to recover damages for personal injuries arising from a breach of that warranty. The disclaimer of the implied warranty and exclusion of all obligations except those specifically assumed by the express warranty signify a studied effort to frustrate that protection. True, the Sales Act authorizes agreements between buyer and seller qualifying the warranty obligations. But quite obviously the Legislature contemplated lawful stipulations (which are determined by the circumstances of a particular case) arrived at freely by parties of relatively equal bargaining strength. The lawmakers did not authorize the automobile manufacturer to use its grossly disproportionate bargaining power to relieve itself from liability and to impose on the ordinary buyer, who in effect has no real freedom of choice, the grave danger of injury to himself and others that attends the sale of such a dangerous instrumentality as a defectively made automobile. In the framework of this case, illuminated as it is by the facts and the many decisions noted, we are of the opinion that Chrysler's attempted disclaimer of an implied warranty of merchantability and of the obligations arising therefrom is so inimical to the public good as to compel an adjudication of its invalidity. * * *

III.

The Dealer's Implied Warranty.

The principles that have been expounded as to the obligation of the manufacturer apply with equal force to the separate express warranty of the dealer * * *. [T]he purchaser must take or leave the automobile, accompanied and encumbered as it is by the uniform warranty.

Moreover, it must be remembered that the actual contract was between Bloomfield Motors, Inc., and Claus Henningsen, and that the description of the car sold was included in the purchase order. Therefore, R.S. 46:30–21(2), N.J.S.A., annexed an implied warranty of merchantability to the agreement. * * * It has been said that this doctrine is harsh on retailers who generally have only a limited opportunity for inspection of the car. But, as Chief Judge Cardozo said in Ryan, supra:

> "The burden may be heavy. It is one of the hazards of the business.

* * * * * *

"* * * In such circumstances, the law casts the burden on the seller, who may vouch in the manufacturer, if the latter was to blame. The loss in its final incidence will be borne where it is placed by the initial wrong." 175 N.E. at pages 106 and 107.

Re-examination of the purchase contract discloses an ambiguous situation with respect to the warranty position of the dealer. Section 7, on the reverse side thereof, says no warranties, express or implied, are made by the dealer or manufacturer except the express warranty of the manufacturer discussed above. However, the last paragraph of the section says that: "The dealer also agrees to promptly perform and fulfill all terms and conditions of the owner service policy." That policy, as noted above, sets forth the same manufacturer's warranty and then adds a stipulation substituting "dealer" in the context wherever "manufacturer" appears. Presumably the intention was to incorporate the policy into the sales contract by reference. Accepting that to be the dealer's intention, the binding character of the limitation on its liability to the buyer under the warranty is even less apparent than in the case of Chrysler. The uncontradicted proof shows that the policy was not shown or given to Henningsen prior to or at the time of execution of the sales agreement; it was delivered with the car. No one suggests that the clause limiting the dealer's liability to replacement of defective parts and excluding implied warranties as well as responsibility for personal injury claims was specifically brought to Henningsen's attention, or that any attempt was made to make him understand that he was yielding his right, and that of any third person claiming in his right, to recover for such injuries.

For the reasons set forth in Part I hereof, we conclude that the disclaimer of an implied warranty of merchantability by the dealer, as well as the attempted elimination of all obligations other than replacement of defective parts, are violative of public policy and void. * * *

V.

The Defense of Lack of Privity Against Mrs. Henningsen.

* * * In the present matter, the basic contractual relationship is between Claus Henningsen, Chrysler, and Bloomfield Motors, Inc. The precise issue presented is whether Mrs. Henningsen, who is not a party to their respective warranties, may claim under them. * * * We are convinced that the cause of justice in this area of the law can be served only by recognizing that she is such a person who, in the reasonable contemplation of the parties to the warranty, might be expected to become a user of the automobile. Accordingly, her lack of privity does not stand in the way of prosecution of the injury suit against the defendant Chrysler.

The context in which the problem of privity with respect to the dealer must be considered, is much the same. Defendant Bloomfield Motors is chargeable with an implied warranty of merchantability to Claus Henningsen. * * * His understanding of the expected use of the car by persons other than the buyer is the same as that of the manufacturer. And so, his claim to the doctrine of privity should rise no higher than that of the manufacturer.

* * *

* * * [I]t is our opinion that an implied warranty of merchantability chargeable to either an automobile manufacturer or a dealer extends to the purchaser of the car, members of his family, and to other persons occupying or using it with his consent. It would be wholly opposed to reality to say that use by such persons is not within the anticipation of parties to such a warranty of reasonable suitability of an automobile for ordinary highway operation. Those persons must be considered within the distributive chain.

Harper and James suggest that this remedy ought to run to members of the public, bystanders, for example, who are in the path of harm from a defective automobile. 2 Harper & James, supra, note 6, p. 1572. Section 2–318 of the Uniform Commercial Code proposes that the warranty be extended to "any natural person who is in the family or household of his buyer or who is a guest in his home if it is reasonable to expect that such person may use, consume or be affected by the goods and who is injured in person by breach of the warranty." And the section provides also that "A seller may not exclude or limit the operation" of the extension. * * *

It is not necessary in this case to establish the outside limits of the warranty protection. For present purposes, with respect to automobiles, it suffices to promulgate the principle set forth above.

* * *

Under all of the circumstances outlined above, the judgments in favor of the plaintiffs and against the defendants are affirmed.

EXCERPTS FROM UNIFORM COMMERCIAL CODE 1962 OFFICIAL TEXT WITH 1966 AMENDMENTS

§ 2–313. Express Warranties by Affirmation, Promise, Description, Sample

(1) Express warranties by the seller are created as follows:

(a) Any affirmation of fact or promise made by the seller to the buyer which relates to the goods [11] and becomes part of the basis of the bargain creates an express warranty that the goods shall conform to the affirmation or promise.

11. "Seller" and "Buyer" are defined in § 2–103 to include a person who contracts to sell or buy as well as one who sells or buys goods. Compare note 9 infra. "Goods" is defined in § 2–105 to mean "all things (including specially manufactured goods) which are movable at the time of identification to the contract for sale other than the money in which the price is to be paid, investment securities (Article 8) and things in action. "Goods" also includes the unborn young of animals and growing crops and [certain] other identified things attached to realty * * *."

(b) Any description of the goods which is made part of the basis of the bargain creates an express warranty that the goods shall conform to the description.

(c) Any sample or model which is made part of the basis of the bargain creates an express warranty that the whole of the goods shall conform to the sample or model.

(2) It is not necessary to the creation of an express warranty that the seller use formal words such as "warrant" or "guarantee" or that he have a specific intention to make a warranty, but an affirmation merely of the value of the goods or a statement purporting to be merely the seller's opinion or commendation of the goods does not create a warranty.

§ 2–314. Implied Warranty: Merchantability; Usage of Trade

(1) Unless excluded or modified (Section 2–316), a warranty that the goods shall be merchantable is implied in a contract for their sale if the seller[12] is a merchant[13] with respect to goods of that kind. Under this section the serving for value of food or drink to be consumed either on the premises or elsewhere is a sale.

(2) Goods to be merchantable must be at least such as

(a) pass without objection in the trade under the contract description; and

(b) in the case of fungible goods, are of fair average quality within the description; and

(c) are fit for the ordinary purposes for which such goods are used; and

(d) run, within the variations permitted by the agreement, of even kind, quality and quantity within each unit and among all units involved; and

(e) are adequately contained, packaged, and labeled as the agreement may require; and

(f) conform to the promises or affirmations of fact made on the container or label if any.

(3) Unless excluded or modified (Section 2–316) other implied warranties may arise from course of dealing or usage of trade.

12. Cf. Md.Ann.Code Art. 95B, § 2–314: "* * * Notwithstanding any other provisions of this subtitle, in §§ 2–314 through 2–318 of this subtitle, 'seller' shall include the manufacturer, distributor, dealer, wholesaler or other middleman, and/or the retailer; and any previous requirement of privity is abolished as between the buyer and any of the aforementioned parties in any action brought by the buyer. * * *"

13. "Merchant" is defined in § 2–104 to mean "a person who deals in goods of the kind or otherwise by his occupation holds himself out as having knowledge or skill peculiar to the practices or goods involved in the transaction or to whom such knowledge or skill may be attributed by his employment of an agent or broker or other intermediary who by his occupation holds himself out as having such knowledge or skill."

§ 2-315. Implied Warranty: Fitness for Particular Purpose

Where the seller at the time of contracting has reason to know any particular purpose for which the goods are required and that the buyer is relying on the seller's skill or judgment to select or furnish suitable goods, there is unless excluded or modified under the next section an implied warranty that the goods shall be fit for such purpose.

§ 2-318. Third Party Beneficiaries of Warranties Express or Implied

Note: *If this Act is introduced in the Congress of the United States this section should be omitted. (States to select one alternative.)*

Alternative A

A seller's warranty whether express or implied extends to any natural person who is in the family or household of his buyer or who is a guest in his home if it is reasonable to expect that such person may use, consume or be affected by the goods and who is injured in person by breach of the warranty. A seller may not exclude or limit the operation of this section.

Alternative B

A seller's warranty whether express or implied extends to any natural person who may reasonably be expected to use, consume or be affected by the goods and who is injured in person by breach of the warranty. A seller may not exclude or limit the operation of this section.

Alternative C

A seller's warranty whether express or implied extends to any person who may reasonably be expected to use, consume or be affected by the goods and who is injured by breach of the warranty. A seller may not exclude or limit the operation of this section with respect to injury to the person of an individual to whom the warranty extends.[14]

14. Compare Md.Ann.Code § 2-318: "A seller's warranty whether express or implied extends to any natural person who is in the family or household of his buyer or who is a guest in his home or any other ultimate consumer or user of the goods or person affected thereby if it is reasonable to expect that such person may use, consume or be affected by the goods and who is injured in person by breach of the warranty. A seller may not exclude or limit the operation of this section."

GREENMAN v. YUBA POWER PRODUCTS, INC.

Supreme Court of California, In Bank, 1963.
59 Cal.2d 57, 27 Cal.Rptr. 697, 377 P.2d 897.

TRAYNOR, JUSTICE. Plaintiff brought this action for damages against the retailer and the manufacturer of a Shopsmith, a combination power tool that could be used as a saw, drill, and wood lathe. He saw a Shopsmith demonstrated by the retailer and studied a brochure prepared by the manufacturer. He decided he wanted a Shopsmith for his home workshop, and his wife bought and gave him one for Christmas in 1955. In 1957 he bought the necessary attachments to use the Shopsmith as a lathe for turning a large piece of wood he wished to make into a chalice. After he had worked on the piece of wood several times without difficulty, it suddenly flew out of the machine and struck him on the forehead, inflicting serious injuries. About ten and a half months later, he gave the retailer and the manufacturer written notice of claimed breaches of warranties and filed a complaint against them alleging such breaches and negligence.

After a trial before a jury, the court ruled that there was no evidence that the retailer was negligent or had breached any express warranty and that the manufacturer was not liable for the breach of any implied warranty. Accordingly, it submitted to the jury only the cause of action alleging breach of implied warranties against the retailer and the causes of action alleging negligence and breach of express warranties against the manufacturer. The jury returned a verdict for the retailer against plaintiff and for plaintiff against the manufacturer in the amount of $65,000. The trial court denied the manufacturer's motion for a new trial and entered judgment on the verdict. The manufacturer and plaintiff appeal. Plaintiff seeks a reversal of the part of the judgment in favor of the retailer, however, only in the event that the part of the judgment against the manufacturer is reversed.

Plaintiff introduced substantial evidence that his injuries were caused by defective design and construction of the Shopsmith. His expert witnesses testified that inadequate set screws were used to hold parts of the machine together so that normal vibration caused the tailstock of the lathe to move away from the piece of wood being turned permitting it to fly out of the lathe. They also testified that there were other more positive ways of fastening the parts of the machine together, the use of which would have prevented the accident. The jury could therefore reasonably have concluded that the manufacturer negligently constructed the Shopsmith. The jury could also reasonably have concluded that statements in the manufacturer's brochure were untrue, that they constituted express warranties,[14A] and that plaintiff's injuries were caused by their breach.

14A. In this respect the trial court limited the jury to a consideration of two statements in the manufacturer's brochure. (1) "WHEN SHOPSMITH IS IN HORIZONTAL POSITION—Rugged construction of frame provides rigid support from end to end. Heavy centerless-ground steel tubing insures

The manufacturer contends, however, that plaintiff did not give it notice of breach of warranty within a reasonable time and that therefore his cause of action for breach of warranty is barred by section 1769 of the Civil Code. Since it cannot be determined whether the verdict against it was based on the negligence or warranty cause of action or both, the manufacturer concludes that the error in presenting the warranty cause of action to the jury was prejudicial.

Section 1769 of the Civil Code provides: "In the absence of express or implied agreement of the parties, acceptance of the goods by the buyer shall not discharge the seller from liability in damages or other legal remedy for breach of any promise or warranty in the contract to sell or the sale. But, if, after acceptance of the goods, the buyer fails to give notice to the seller of the breach of any promise or warranty within a reasonable time after the buyer knows, or ought to know of such breach, the seller shall not be liable therefor."

Like other provisions of the uniform sales act (Civ.Code, §§ 1721–1800), section 1769 deals with the rights of the parties to a contract of sale or a sale. It does not provide that notice must be given of the breach of a warranty that arises independently of a contract of sale between the parties. Such warranties are not imposed by the sales act, but are the product of common-law decisions that have recognized them in a variety of situations. * * * It is true that in many of these situations the court has invoked the sales act definitions of warranties (Civ.Code, §§ 1732, 1735) in defining the defendant's liability, but it has done so, not because the statutes so required, but because they provided appropriate standards for the court to adopt under the circumstances presented. * * *

The notice requirement of section 1769, however, is not an appropriate one for the court to adopt in actions by injured consumers against manufacturers with whom they have not dealt. * * *

"As between the immediate parties to the sale [the notice requirement] is a sound commercial rule, designed to protect the seller against unduly delayed claims for damages. As applied to personal injuries, and notice to a remote seller, it becomes a booby-trap for the unwary. The injured consumer is seldom 'steeped in the business practice which justifies the rule,' [James, Product Liability, 34 Texas L.Rev. 44, 192, 197] and at least until he has had legal advice it will not occur to him to give notice to one with whom he has had no dealings." (Prosser, Strict Liability to the Consumer, 69 Yale L.J. 1099, 1130, footnotes omitted.) * * * We conclude, therefore, that even if plaintiff did not give timely notice of breach of warranty to the manufacturer, his cause of action based on the representations contained in the brochure was not barred.

perfect alignment of components." (2) "SHOPSMITH maintains its accuracy because every component has positive locks that hold adjustments through rough or precision work."

Moreover, to impose strict liability on the manufacturer under the circumstances of this case, it was not necessary for plaintiff to establish an express warranty * * * A manufacturer is strictly liable in tort when an article he places on the market, knowing that it is to be used without inspection for defects, proves to have a defect that causes injury to a human being. Recognized first in the case of unwholesome food products, such liability has now been extended to a variety of other products that create as great or greater hazards if defective. * * *

Although in these cases strict liability has usually been based on the theory of an express or implied warranty running from the manufacturer to the plaintiff, the abandonment of the requirement of a contract between them, the recognition that the liability is not assumed by agreement but imposed by law * * *, and the refusal to permit the manufacturer to define the scope of its own responsibility for defective products * * * make clear that the liability is not one governed by the law of contract warranties but by the law of strict liability in tort. Accordingly, rules defining and governing warranties that were developed to meet the needs of commercial transactions cannot properly be invoked to govern the manufacturer's liability to those injured by their defective products unless those rules also serve the purposes for which such liability is imposed.

We need not recanvass the reasons for imposing strict liability on the manufacturer. (See 2 Harper and James, Torts, §§ 28.15–28.16, pp. 1569–1574; Prosser, Strict Liability to the Consumer, 69 Yale L.J. 1099; Escola v. Coca Cola Bottling Co., 24 Cal.2d 453, 461, 150 P.2d 436, concurring opinion.) The purpose of such liability is to insure that the costs of injuries resulting from defective products are borne by the manufacturers that put such products on the market rather than by the injured persons who are powerless to protect themselves. Sales warranties serve this purpose fitfully at best. (See Prosser, Strict Liability to the Consumer, 69 Yale L.J. 1099, 1124–1134.) In the present case, for example, plaintiff was able to plead and prove an express warranty only because he read and relied on the representations of the Shopsmith's ruggedness contained in the manufacturer's brochure. Implicit in the machine's presence on the market, however, was a representation that it would safely do the jobs for which it was built. Under these circumstances, it should not be controlling whether plaintiff selected the machine because of the statements in the brochure, or because of the machine's own appearance of excellence that belied the defect lurking beneath the surface, or because he merely assumed that it would safely do the jobs it was built to do. It should not be controlling whether the details of the sales from manufacturer to retailer and from retailer to plaintiff's wife were such that one or more of the implied warranties of the sales act arose. * * * "The remedies of injured consumers ought not to be made to depend upon the intricacies of the law of sales." (Ketterer v. Armour & Co., D.C., 200 F. 322, 323; Klein v. Duchess Sandwich Co., 14 Cal.2d 272, 282, 93 P.2d 799.) To establish the manufacturer's liability it was sufficient that plaintiff proved that he was injured while using the Shopsmith in a way it was intended to be used as a result of a defect in design and manufacture of which plaintiff was not aware [15] that made the Shopsmith unsafe for its intended use.

EXCERPT FROM RESTATEMENT OF TORTS, SECOND (1965)

§ 402A. Special Liability of Seller of Product for Physical Harm to User or Consumer

(1) One who sells any product [16] in a defective condition unreasonably dangerous to the user or consumer or to his property is subject to liability for physical harm thereby caused to the ultimate user or consumer, or to his property, if

(a) the seller is engaged in the business of selling such a product, and

(b) it is expected to and does reach the user or consumer without substantial change in the condition in which it is sold.

15. It was later made clear that plaintiff need not prove lack of awareness, Luque v. McLean, 8 Cal.3d 136, 104 Cal.Rptr. 443, 501 P.2d 1163 (1972). Also see Butaud v. Suburban Marine & Sporting Goods, Inc., 543 P.2d 209 (Alaska 1975).

16. Under both warranty law and § 402A there have been attempts to avoid supplier liability by distinguishing "services" from "sales", and non-"products" from "products". A particularly serious problem concerns blood transfusions, because it has in the past been very difficult, if not impossible, to screen out blood containing hepatitis virus. Some cases have denied strict liability on the ground that the transfusion is a service, not a sale, e. g., Perlmutter v. Beth David Hospital, 308 N.Y. 100, 123 N.E.2d 792 (1954) (under warranty law); St. Luke's Hospital v. Schmaltz, — Colo. —, 534 P.2d 781 (1975) (under either warranty or strict tort liability); or simply on policy grounds, e. g., Brody v. Overlook Hospital, 66 N.J. 448, 332 A.2d 596 (1975). Strict liability has, on the other hand, been imposed on the ground that there is a sale of blood, e. g., Cunningham v. MacNeal Memorial Hospital, 47 Ill.2d 443, 266 N.E. 2d 897 (1970) (under § 402A), or on the ground that implied warranties apply whether the transaction is a sale or a service, Hoffman v. Misercordia Hospital of Philadelphia, 439 Pa. 501, 267 A.2d 867 (1970). A number of states, including Illinois after *Cunningham*, have passed statutes exempting blood from warranty; cf. e. g., McDaniel v. Baptist Memorial Hospital, 469 F.2d 230, 234 (6th Cir. 1972); Heirs of Fruge v. Blood Services, 506 F.2d 841 (5th Cir. 1975). For an extensive policy discussion advocating strict liability for blood see Franklin, Tort Liability for Hepatitis: An Analysis and a Proposal, 24 Stan.L. Rev. 439 (1972).

Other applications of strict liability in the case of services, or hybrid product-service combinations, or non-conventional "products", in which New Jersey has led the way, include Cintrone v. Hertz Truck Leasing, 45 N.J. 434, 212 A.2d 769 (1965) (vehicle hire bailment); Newmark v. Gimbel's Incorporated, 54 N.J. 585, 258 A.2d 697 (1969) (permanent wave, using lotion; the court distinguished beauty parlor operators—"commercial"—from doctors and dentists—"professional"); and Schipper v. Levitt & Sons, Inc., 44 N.J. 70, 207 A.2d 314 (1965) (builder-vendor of development houses). Also see Schwartz, Statutory Strict Liability for an Insurer's Failure to Settle: A Balanced Plan for an Unresolved Problem, 1975 Duke L.J. 901.

(2) The rule stated in Subsection (1) applies although

(a) the seller has exercised all possible care in the preparation and sale of his product, and

(b) the user or consumer has not bought the product from or entered into any contractual relation with the seller.

PIKE v. FRANK G. HOUGH COMPANY

Supreme Court of California, In Bank, 1970.
2 Cal.3d 465, 85 Cal.Rptr. 629, 467 P.2d 229.

MOSK, ACTING CHIEF JUSTICE.

On July 15, 1964, at 3:10 a. m., Robert Pike was killed when he was struck by a Hough Model D–500 Paydozer, which was being used in the construction of the Oroville Dam. Pike was working the night shift as a "spotter" for Oro-Dam Constructors, and his assignment was to direct dump trucks in the area in which dumped fill was to be spread and tamped down by the paydozer. On the morning of the accident, the men were filling in a corner of the dam surface, and in doing so it was necessary for the paydozer to go forward and then backward within a short distance to accomplish the spreading and tamping of the earth. Decedent was some 30 to 40 feet behind the paydozer, standing on an angle with his back to the paydozer when it backed up and struck him.

Decedent's widow and minor children brought this action for wrongful death against the manufacturer of the paydozer. The case was tried to a jury. Plaintiffs sought to establish the liability of the defendant on either a negligence or a strict liability theory, based on the design of the paydozer. At the conclusion of plaintiffs' case, defendant moved for a nonsuit which was granted. Plaintiffs appeal. * * *

The record establishes the following evidence most strongly in favor of plaintiffs: The area in which the accident occurred was well illuminated with mercury lights and visibility was good despite the hour of the morning. When decedent was struck, the paydozer was in the process of reversing to position itself to then move forward to spread and tamp down fill; behind the paydozer decedent was directing dump trucks in depositing fill which was to be spread and tamped by the paydozer at a later time. Prior to backing up, the operator of the paydozer, who had not observed Pike for about five minutes, looked to the rear to ascertain if it was clear, but he did not see Pike, who was standing 30 to 40 feet behind the vehicle and wearing a luminous jacket. The operator testified that there was a substantial blind spot to the rear of the paydozer because of its design. He also testified that the lighting was clear enough so that workers on the other side of the dam were visible.

The Hough paydozer was a large, noisy earth-moving machine. It was designed to move backward as well as forward and, as here, to perform in confined areas. It was equipped with two white headlights, and, on the rear, two red taillights and two white lights. At the time of the accident, only the red taillights were illuminated; the headlights were turned off because the dump truck operators complained of the glare, and the rear white lights were off because they blinded other equipment operators working in the vicinity. The paydozer had no rearview mirrors and no audible or visible backup warning signal.

Robert Snyder, a registered mechanical engineer, appeared as an expert for plaintiffs. According to his testimony, the design of the paydozer with its large engine box to the rear created a blind area behind the paydozer of such dimension that, if the operator looked behind him while sitting in the cab, he could not see a man six feet tall standing anywhere between one and 48 feet to the rear of the machine. The blind area extended laterally at least 10 feet to each side of the midline of the paydozer. Snyder testified that the blind area could be reduced from a rectangle 48 feet by 20 feet to a cone-shaped area with a maximum length behind the machine of 12 feet by installation of two rearview mirrors located four feet out from each side of the cab. The four-foot distance, he pointed out, would not project the mirrors beyond the vertical line of the huge tires on the tractor. The mirrors he described were similar to those he had seen on ditchdigging equipment. He also recommended a blinking amber light or a tooting horn to alert persons within the remaining blind area.

In nonsuiting plaintiffs on their negligence cause of action, the trial court held as a matter of law that a vehicle intended to move backward is not negligently designed although the operator cannot see a man 30 to 40 feet behind him in the direct path of the vehicle and although simple mirrors and lights could alleviate the danger. The court was in error; this was essentially a question of fact for determination by the jury.

The duty of a manufacturer with respect to the design of products placed on the market is defined in the Restatement Second of Torts, section 398: "A manufacturer of a chattel made under a plan or design which makes it dangerous for the uses for which it is manufactured his subject to liability to others whom he should expect to use the chattel or to be endangered by its probable use for physical harm caused by his failure to exercise reasonable care in the adoption of a safe plan or design." Thus, the manufacturer must use reasonable care " 'to so design his product as to make it not accident-proof, but safe for the use for which it was [*sic*] intended.' " (Varas v. Barco Mfg. Co. (1962) 205 Cal.App.2d 246, 258, 22 Cal.Rptr. 737, 744, quoting from 76 A.L.R.2d 91, 94.) What is "reasonable care," of course, varies with the facts of each case, but it involves a balancing of the likelihood of harm to be expected from a machine with a given design and the gravity of harm if it happens against the burden of the precaution which would be effective to avoid the harm. (2 Harper and James, The Law of Torts (1956) § 28.4, p. 1542.)

Applying the foregoing standards to the case at bar, it would seem a jury could conclude that a manufacturer of a vehicle intended to go backward should have been aware that the machine's structural design made it impossible for the operator to see a man standing anywhere between one and 48 feet behind the machine and in its direct path. And, having so found, a jury could decide that a manufacturer who failed to correct this deficiency with two rearview mirrors, or any comparable device, violated his duty to produce a product reasonably safe for its intended use. Although that result may not have been compelled, the evidence was sufficient to justify such findings, and plaintiffs need do no more than produce such evidence to avoid a nonsuit. * * *

The * * * case at bar * * * [is] distinguishable from Hatch v. Ford Motor Co. (1958) 163 Cal.App.2d 393, 329 P.2d 605. In *Hatch*, plaintiff, a young child, lost his eye when he walked into a nine and three-fourths inch hood ornament on a parked Ford automobile. The court affirmed a judgment for defendant entered upon a general demurrer, but carefully delineated the reasons for its holding: "There is not involved in this case any question of a defect which created a risk of injury to its driver or passengers therein or to persons upon the highway through its use in the normal manner for which it was manufactured to be used * * *. If we were to hold that there was a duty to render a vehicle safe to collide with rather than simply a duty to so manufacture it as to make it safe for the use for which it is intended, i. e., to move upon the highways or to be safely parked, that duty would apply not only to ornaments * * * but to functional parts of the vehicle. * * * In other words, each case in which a person collided with a standing vehicle and received some injury from a part of the vehicle which injury he might not have sustained had the vehicle been constructed in some other manner would raise a question of fact as to whether the manufacturer was liable to that person." (Id. at pp. 396–397, 329 P.2d at p. 607.) By contrast, in the instant case, a jury could find the decedent was killed as a result of defects in the design of the paydozer which created a substantial and unreasonable risk of injury to persons working in the vicinity of the paydozer while it was engaged in its normal backing-up operations necessary to the moving and compacting of earth.

Defendant contends that the danger of being struck by the paydozer was a patent peril and, therefore, that it had no duty to install safety devices to protect against an obvious danger. We do not agree. First, although all vehicles contain the potential of impact, it is not necessarily apparent to *bystanders* that the machine operator is incapable of observing them though they are 30 to 40 feet behind the vehicle and in its direct path. The danger to bystanders is not diminished because the purchaser of the vehicle is aware of its deficiencies of design. The manufacturer's duty of care extends to all persons within the range of potential danger. Second, the obviousness of peril is relevant to the manufacturer's defenses, not to the issue of duty. If a bystander does not exercise due care to protect himself from an evident peril, he may be contributorily negligent. * * * But the issue of contributory negligence is one normally for the jury; clearly the evidence here did not justify nonsuiting plaintiffs on the ground of decedent's contributory negligence as a matter of law. * * * Indeed, " '[w]here a person must work in a place of possible danger the amount of care he is bound to exercise for his own safety may well be less by reason of the necessity of his giving attention to his work than would otherwise be the case.' " * * *

Finally, even if the obviousness of the peril is conceded, the modern approach does not preclude liability solely because a danger is obvious. "Today, however, the negligence principle has been widely accepted in products liability cases; and the bottom does not logically drop out of a negligence case against the maker when it is shown that the purchaser knew of the dangerous condition. Thus if the product is a carrot-topping machine with exposed moving parts, or an electric clothes wringer dangerous to the limbs of the operator, and if it would be feasible for the maker of the product to install a guard or a safety release, it should be a question for the jury whether reasonable care demanded such a precaution, though its absence is obvious. Surely reasonable men might find here a great danger, even to one who knew the condition; and since it was so readily avoidable they might find the maker negligent. Under this analysis the obviousness of a condition will still preclude liability if the obviousness justifies the conclusion that the condition is not unreasonably dangerous; otherwise it would simply be a factor to consider on the issue of negligence. * * * The greatest conceptual obstacle to recovery * * * comes in the case where the buyer himself is hurt by the article. * * * Surely it is well within the framework and spirit of [recent] common law modifications to require reasonable care to protect even the buyer himself from what may be foreseen as an unreasonable danger to him. But even if courts are unwilling to go so far, without legislation, in the case of the adult buyer or user, the existing law of negligence demands this duty of care where *others* are threatened by want of a feasible safety device wherever the foreseeable danger to them is unreasonable." (Harper and James, The Law of Torts, supra, § 28.5, pp. 1543, 1545.)

To the same effect see 71 Yale Law Journal 816, in which Professor Noel wrote (at p. 838): "Any definite requirement that the defect or the danger must be latent seems to revert to the concept that a chattel must be 'inherently' dangerous, and this concept has been replaced under the modern decisions, by the rule that the creation of any unreasonable danger is enough to establish negligence. Under the modern rule, even though the absence of a particular safety precaution is obvious, there ordinarily would be a question for the jury as to whether or not a failure to install the device creates an unreasonable risk." [17]

17. The contrary proposition, that "the duty owed by a manufacturer to remote users does not require him to guard against hazards apparent to the

We conclude, therefore, that it was error to nonsuit plaintiffs in their cause of action based on the negligent design of the paydozer. The issue should have gone to the jury. We now discuss their cause of action based on a strict liability concept.

California has pioneered in the development and extension of the theory that manufacturers are strictly liable in tort for injuries to persons caused by defects in their products. * * * In our landmark opinion in Greenman v. Yuba Power Products, Inc. * * * we held that "[a] manufacturer is strictly liable in tort when an article he places on the market, knowing that it is to be used without inspection for defects, proves to have a defect that causes injury to a human being." In Vandermark v. Ford Motor Co. (1964) 61 Cal.2d 256, 37 Cal.Rptr. 896, 391 P.2d 168, we applied such strict liability to retailers, and in Elmore v. American Motors Corp. (1969) * * * 70 Cal.2d 578, 585–587, 75 Cal.Rptr. 652, 451 P.2d 84, we extended protection beyond users and consumers of defective products to bystanders within "the risk of the maker's enterprise."

Here the trial court held as a matter of law that the paydozer was not defectively designed and that the doctrine of strict liability was inapplicable. We cannot agree. * * *

Most reported cases in California and other jurisdictions have applied strict liability to products containing defects in their manufacture; few have involved defects in design. However, there is no rational distinction between design and manufacture in this context, since a product may be equally defective and dangerous if its design subjects protected persons to unreasonable risk as if its manufacture does so. Indeed, in Greenman v. Yuba Power Products, Inc. * * * we held that plaintiff could recover on a strict liability theory if he proved "that he was injured while using the Shopsmith in a way it was intended to be used as a result of a defect in *design and manufacture* * * *." (Italics added.) * * *

Persuasive authorities in other jurisdictions have * * * reached the conclusion that products lacking safety devices may be defective. In Wright v. Massey-Harris, Incorporated (1966) 68 Ill. App.2d 70, 215 N.E.2d 465, defendant's motion to dismiss was reversed on the ground that plaintiff had stated a good cause of action in both negligence and strict liability, based on the design of the defendant's cornpicker. "The present case involves a claimed defect in design rather than a defect in manufacture and we interpret Suvada [18] to mean that the strict liability imposed upon a manufac-

casual observer", is particularly identified with Judge Fuld's opinion in Campo v. Scofield, 301 N.Y. 468, 95 N.E.2d 802 (1950); see, however, Messina v. Clark Equipment Co., 263 F. 2d 291, 293 (Clark, C.J., dissenting) (2d Cir. 1959).

18. Suvada v. White Motor Company (1965) 32 Ill.2d 612, 210 N.E.2d 182. *Suvada*, like its *Greenman* counterpart in California, established the liability of sellers of defective and unreasonably dangerous products without privity of contract. [From original, renumbered; other notes in original omitted.]

turer includes injuries which arise from defects in design as well as defects in manufacture. Whether the design defect in the present case is of a nature upon which liability can be imposed involves the factual question of whether it creates an unreasonably dangerous condition, or, in other words, whether the product in question has lived up to the required standard of safety." (Id. at p. 470.) The defects alleged in the cornpicker were that it lacked a shield over the area in which ears of corn could jam in the chain mechanism and a guard over the shucking rollers from which ears of corn were manually extracted. Thus, on the basis of a case no broader in scope than *Greenman,* the Illinois court applied strict liability to a machine defective in design because it lacked safety devices which would have reduced the risk of harm. * * * We adapt a similar rule to this case. Whether the paydozer was unreasonably dangerous due to faulty design when it left the hands of the manufacturer is clearly a question of fact to be determined by the jury. * * *

Of course, we do not decide whether the paydozer is in fact unreasonably dangerous for its intended use, but only that plaintiffs' evidence was sufficient to support a jury verdict in their favor. A jury could decide that an earth-moving machine with a 48-foot by 20-foot rectangular blind spot was dangerous "to an extent beyond that which would be contemplated by the ordinary consumer who purchases it [or by a bystander], with the ordinary knowledge common to the community as to its characteristics." (Restatement of Torts, Second § 402A, com. i, at p. 352.) * * * [19]

NANDA v. FORD MOTOR COMPANY

United States Court of Appeals for the Seventh Circuit, 1974.
509 F.2d 213.

TONE, CIRCUIT JUDGE. The principal issue before us in this diversity case is whether under Illinois law an automobile manufacturer has a duty so to design and to manufacture its product that its occupants will not be subjected to an unreasonable risk of injury if a collision occurs which is not itself caused by any defects in the condition of the automobile. We hold that such a duty exists in the circumstances of this case and affirm the District Court's judgment on a jury verdict in favor of the plaintiff. * * *

19. Compare Volkswagen of America, Inc. v. Young, 272 Md. 201, 220–21, 321 A.2d 737, 747 (1974): "Regardless of whether the theory of § 402A * * * should be accepted in other contexts, we are convinced that it has no proper application to liability for *design* defects in motor vehicles. * * * Since the existence of a defective design depends upon the reasonableness of the manufacturer's action, and depends upon the degree of care which he has exercised, it is wholly illogical to speak of a defective *design* even though the manufacturer has exercised all possible care in the preparation of his product." What about the liability of the retailer? Contrast Seattle-First Nat. Bank v. Tabert, 86 Wash.2d 145, 542 P.2d 774 (1975), which also analyzes the relationship between "defective" and "unreasonably dangerous", largely in terms of the consumer's reasonable expectations as to safety.

At about 8:30 P.M. on October 29, 1967 plaintiff Chitta R. Nanda, driving alone in his 1967 Ford Cortina, stopped in the inner northbound lane of Route 45 in Urbana, Illinois, to wait for an opening in southbound traffic so he could turn left into an access road. While stopped, the Cortina was struck in the rear by a 1962 Oldsmobile traveling at a speed the jury could have found was as low as 10 miles per hour. This collision injured no one and caused only relatively minor damage to the front of the Oldsmobile. The Cortina, however, was spun around and pushed into the southbound lanes, where it was struck in the rear by a southbound Rambler. * * *

The jury could have found that the collision with the Oldsmobile caused a small fire on the rear of the Cortina, which was the size and shape of a grapefruit with a stream coming up from it and which, when the Rambler struck the Cortina, grew into a huge ball, enveloping the Cortina and the front of the Rambler. Almost instantaneously after the second collision the inside of the Cortina was engulfed in flames. Plaintiff suffered permanently disfiguring and disabling burns.

Plaintiff contends that design defects in the Cortina caused his injury. The fuel tank in the 1967 Cortina, like that in at least some other models manufactured by defendant, was "dropped into" a hole in the floor of the trunk, the top of the fuel tank serving as a portion of the floor of the trunk. The only shield separating the fuel tank from the passenger compartment was a piece of cardboard. Other automobile manufacturers in the United States provided a trunk floor consisting of some kind of continuous metal panel which shielded the fuel tank from the passenger compartment, and after 1971 defendant itself abandoned the "drop-in" fuel tank installation. * * *

I.

The Duty of the Manufacturer Under Illinois Law

Courts have differed on the issue of the liability of an automobile manufacturer for injuries to occupants of the automobile resulting from a collision not itself caused by any defects in the condition of the automobile, sometimes called the "second collision" issue.[20] The two leading cases are one in this court applying Indiana law, Evans v. General Motors Corp., 359 F.2d 822 (7th Cir. 1966), cert. denied, 385 U.S. 836, 87 S.Ct. 83, 17 L.Ed.2d 70 (1966), and one in the Eighth Circuit applying Minnesota law, Larsen v. General Motors Corp., 391 F.2d 495 (8th Cir. 1968). *Evans,* in which the court reasons that the intended use of an automobile does not include participa-

20. In the jargon of automobile tort law, the "first collision" is the accident in which the vehicle strikes another vehicle or object, and the "second collision" occurs when the occupants of the vehicle are exposed to an unreasonably dangerous condition because of the design of the vehicle. The "first collision" is not caused by the allegedly defective design, but the "second collision" is. A second collision with still another vehicle, which occurred in the case at bar, is not necessarily a part of a "second collision" case and is not the "second collision" to which that term refers.

tion in collisions despite their foreseeability, holds that the manufacturer is not liable. *Larsen,* on the other hand, holds that since injury-producing impacts are foreseeable, the manufacturer has a duty so to design its vehicle that the user will not be subjected to an unreasonable risk of injury in the event of collision. We are, of course, not bound by *Evans,* because in this case the law of Illinois rather than Indiana is controlling.

The Illinois Supreme Court recently considered the *Evans* and *Larsen* cases and the divergent lines of cases following them in Mieher v. Brown, 54 Ill.2d 539, 301 N.E.2d 307 (1973). In the *Mieher* case the court held that the manufacturer of a truck was not liable for the death of the driver of an automobile that had run under the rear of the trunk bed, the truck having no rear bumper or shield to prevent such an occurrence. The controlling issue, in the words of the court, was "whether the defendant and the decedent stood in such a relationship to one another that the law imposed upon the defendant an obligation of reasonable conduct for the benefit of the decedent." (54 Ill.2d at 541, 301 N.E.2d at 308.) After analyzing the *Evans* and *Larsen* lines of cases, the court did not expressly adopt either view. Rather it distinguished those cases:

> "The question in *Larsen* and *Evans* concerned the duty of the manufacturer to design a vehicle in which it was safe to ride. The question in our case involves the duty of the manufacturer to design a vehicle with which it is safe to collide." (54 Ill.2d at 543, 301 N.E.2d at 309.)

In deciding that question, the court said, the controlling considerations are whether "it appears to the court highly extraordinary that it [the defendant's conduct] should have brought about the harm,"[21] and whether the defendant has created "an unreasonable risk of injury" or "an unreasonable danger."[22]

The Illinois Supreme Court followed and applied Mieher v. Brown in Cunis v. Brennan, 56 Ill.2d 372, 308 N.E.2d 617 (1974) * * * in which the plaintiff, when the automobile in which he was riding and another automobile collided, had been thrown approximately 30 feet to a parkway, where one of his legs was impaled on an object protruding from the ground. In holding that the municipality was not liable for permitting a dangerous condition to remain on the parkway, the court applied the "unreasonable danger" test of *Mieher* and concluded that the municipality's duty did not extend to maintaining the parkway to guard against "the remote possibility" of the "tragically bizarre" and perhaps "unique" occurrence for which the plaintiff sued. Again Justice Goldenhersh dissented.

Application of the principles stated in the *Mieher* and *Cunis* opinions requires affirmance here. Viewing the evidence in the light most

21. Restatement of Torts, Second § 435 (2) (1965) is quoted and relied upon by the court, as is Prosser, Palsgraf Revisited, 52 Mich.L.Rev. 1, 27 (1953).

22. The phrase "an unreasonable risk of injury" appears in Larsen v. General Motors, supra, 391 F.2d at 502.

favorable to the plaintiff, it does not appear to us to be "highly extraordinary" that the absence of a firewall or shield between the fuel tank and the passenger compartment and the condition of the filler-pipe assembly would bring about the harm for which plaintiff sues. The jury could have found that those conditions, in the words of the *Mieher* opinion, constituted an "unreasonable danger" and subjected the user of the product to "an unreasonable risk of injury." A rear-end collision is the most common of highway mishaps, and it is not "extraordinary," "bizarre," "unique," or "freakish and fantastic" [23] for such a collision to impel the victim vehicle into a collision with a third vehicle. We believe the law of Illinois to be that when an automobile is so constructed that its occupants are subjected to an unreasonable risk of being severely injured if it becomes involved in an accident that is not of a highly extraordinary kind, the manufacturer is liable fo resulting injuries to occupants of the automobile. * * * [24]

BERKEBILE v. BRANTLY HELICOPTER CORPORATION

Supreme Court of Pennsylvania, 1975.
— Pa. —, 337 A.2d 893.

JONES, CHIEF JUSTICE.

* * *

* * * [E]vidence which would be admissible in a negligence case to prove "abnormal use" is admissible in a strict liability case only for the purpose of rebutting the plaintiff's contentions of defect and proximate cause. It is not properly submitted to the jury as a separate defense.[25]

The trial court's charge on "abnormal use" permitted the jury to conclude that an alleged failure on decedent's part to determine the amount of gas available for flight precluded plaintiff's recovery on any theory. A plaintiff cannot be precluded from recovery in a

23. The last phrase is from a passage in Prosser, Palsgraf Revisited, 52 Mich.L.Rev. 1, 27 (1953), quoted in Mieher v. Brown, 54 Ill.2d at 545, 301 N.E.2d at 310. [Notes 20–24 from original, renumbered.]

24. Also see Dreisenstok v. Volkswagenwerk, A. G., 489 F.2d 1066 (4th Cir. 1974); Wooten v. White Trucks, 514 F.2d 634 (1975).

25. As to "normality" of use, it is familiar doctrine in negligence cases that defectiveness is measured by foreseeable misuses and abuses as well as by intended uses, e. g., Spruill v. Boyle-Midway, Inc., 308 F.2d 79 (4th Cir. 1962) (as to duty to warn of dangers incident to use of Old English Red Oil Furniture Polish, which appeared harmless but if ingested was lethal in small amounts to children, the manufacturer should have anticipated the environment which was normal for use of the product and the reasonably foreseeable risks of the use of the product in that environment); Haberly v. Reardon Co., 319 S.W.2d 859 (Mo. 1958) (manufacturer should have anticipated that paint might get into the eye of a user or bystander); Boyl v. California Chemical Co., 221 F.Supp. 669, 674 (D.Or.1963) (foreseeable that weed killer on grass could injure sunbather). Misuse can, however, be a defense against even strict liability, if the abuse is unreasonable, e. g., Maiorino v. Weco Products Co., 45 N.J. 570, 214 A.2d 18 (1965).

strict liability case because of his own negligence. He is precluded from recovery only if he knows of the specific defect eventually causing his injury [26] and voluntarily proceeds to use the product with knowledge of the danger caused by the defect. Ferraro v. Ford Motor Co., 423 Pa. 324, 327, 223 A.2d 746, 748 (1966); Restatement of Torts, Second § 402A, comment *n*.[27] Furthermore, a finding of assumption of risk must be based on the individual's own subjective knowledge, not upon the objective knowledge of a "reasonable man." See Dorsey v. Yoder, 331 F.Supp. 753, 765 (E.D.Pa., 1971); Restatement of Torts, Second § 496D, comment *c*. Such a defense can be charged upon by the court only if there is evidence introduced by defendant that the decedent knew of the specific defect causing his death and appreciated the danger it involved before using the aircraft. See Restatement of Torts, Second §§ 496C and 496D.[28]

26. Also see McCown v. International Harvester Co., —— Pa. ——, 342 A.2d 381 (1975). Compare Codling v. Paglia, 32 N.Y.2d 330, 345 N.Y.S.2d 461, 469, 298 N.E.2d 622, 628 (1973), which applied "a doctrine of strict products liability" on the part of the manufacturer, without specifying whether the liability was based on warranty, tort or both, to any person injured or damaged by "a defective product", provided (before the enactment in 1975 of New York's comparative negligence statute) "that if the person injured or damaged is himself the user of the product he would not by the exercise of reasonable care have both discovered the defect and perceived its danger."

27. Comment *n* would bar from recovery the user or consumer who "discovers the defect and is aware of the danger, and nevertheless proceeds *unreasonably* to make use of the product and is injured by it * * *" (emphasis added). See, e. g., Brooks v. Dietz, 218 Kan. 698, 545 P.2d 1104 (1976). Compare Weakley v. Fischback & More, Inc., 515 F.2d 1260 (5th Cir. 1975).

28. Should an employee be barred by assumption of risk for using machinery provided by the employer? Is it unreasonable for him to do so? See, e. g., Rhoads v. Service Machine Co., Inc., 329 F.Supp. 367, 381 (E.D. Ark.1971): "The 'voluntariness' with which a worker assigned to a dangerous machine in a factory 'assumes the risk of injury from the machine' is illusory." Compare Wooten v. White Trucks, 514 F.2d 634 (5th Cir. 1975), which assumes that under Kentucky law an encounter with a known or obvious danger would be reasonable only "under conditions of urgent necessity, 'such as to save a life * * *'", but that "matters more exigent than job security are required to ground an excuse from knowing encounter," and Ralston v. Illinois Power Co., 13 Ill.App.3d 95, 299 N.E.2d 497 (1973) (order from supervisor does not make employee's conduct involuntary).

Since the assumption of risk defense requires a "voluntary" and "knowing" encounter, it is often arguable that knowledge of a potentially hazardous condition may not be equivalent to full appreciation of the danger presented by the condition, a distinction which is also used to rebut contributory negligence, e. g., Krugh v. Miehle Co., 503 F.2d 121, 127 (6th Cir. 1974); Devors v. Mobil Chemical Corp., 488 F.2d 258 (5th Cir. 1974).

Also see, generally, Noel, Defective Products: Abnormal Use, Contributory Negligence, and Assumption of Risk, 25 Vand.L.Rev. 93 (1972).

CUNNINGHAM v. CHARLES PFIZER & CO., INC.

Supreme Court of Oklahoma, 1975.
Okl., 532 P.2d 1377.

BERRY, JUSTICE:

Plaintiff brought this action to recover damages for injuries allegedly sustained from ingesting oral polio vaccine manufactured by Charles Pfizer & Company, Inc. [defendant].

The jury returned a verdict for plaintiff for $340,000 and the trial court entered judgment accordingly. Defendant appeals. * *

The Sabin oral vaccine contains live attenuated polio virus. Producers of the vaccine, including defendant, are licensed by the United States Government.

There are three types of polio virus, Type I, Type II and Type III. There are three corresponding types of monovalent Sabin vaccine, Type I, Type II and Type III. One must take each vaccine in order to be immunized against all three polio viruses.

There is also a trivalent vaccine which contains all three types of attenuated viruses.

Prior to 1963 the Surgeon General appointed a committee to investigate cases of polio which might have been caused by the vaccine.

In 1963 the Tulsa County Medical Society and the Tulsa City-County Health Department sponsored a mass polio immunization clinic using Sabin oral polio vaccine manufactured by defendant.

A licensed doctor was available at each distribution point to answer questions.

It was stipulated that the vaccine furnished by defendant was produced and manufactured in accordance with U. S. Government specifications.

The evidence indicated members of the medical society sponsoring the program were aware of all existing information concerning any relationship between ingestion of the vaccine and the onset of polio. However, defendant made no effort to furnish this information to participants in the mass immunization program.

On January 20, 1963, plaintiff, who was 15 years old at the time, took Type I vaccine as a part of this program. Defendant gave no direct warning to plaintiff or his parents concerning possible untoward effects of the vaccine.

Within five weeks after he took the vaccine plaintiff contracted a paralytic disease.

Plaintiff's theory in the trial court was to the effect defendant failed to warn him, or his parents, of the risk of contracting polio from the polio vaccine, and this failure to warn rendered defendant liable for all damages plaintiff incurred as a result of taking the vaccine. * * *

Defendant * * * contends the trial court erred in submitting the case to the jury because there was no proof of a defect in the vaccine.

Subsection k of the comments under § 402A, supra, states:

> "k. *Unavoidably unsafe products.*
>
> "There are some products which, in the present state of human knowledge, are quite incapable of being made safe for their intended and ordinary use. These are especially common in the field of drugs. * * * Such a product, properly prepared, and accompanied by proper directions and warning, is not defective nor is it *unreasonably* dangerous. The same is true of many other drugs, vaccines, and the like, many of which for this very reason cannot legally be sold except to physicians, or under the prescription of a physician. * * * The seller of such products, again with the qualification that they are properly prepared and marketed, and proper warning is given, where the situation calls for it, is not to be held to strict liability for unfortunate consequences at tending their use merely because he has undertaken to supply the public with an apparently useful and desirable product, attended with a known but apparently reasonable risk."

In applying § 402A, supra, courts have construed this comment to mean that in certain circumstances a drug manufacturer has a duty to ensure consumers are warned of known risks involved in taking a drug and a failure to fulfill this duty renders the drug defective within the meaning of § 402A, supra. Davis v. Wyeth Laboratories, Inc., 9 Cir., 399 F.2d 121; Alman Bros. Farms and Feed Mill, Inc. v. Diamond Lab., Inc., 5 Cir., 437 F.2d 1295.

Therefore, if a duty to warn existed in the present case, we conclude plaintiff was not required to establish the vaccine was otherwise defective.

Our research has led us to only three cases which have considered the duty of a manufacturer of polio vaccine to warn consumers of the risk of contracting polio from the vaccine. Davis v. Wyeth Laboratories, Inc., supra; Stahlheber v. American Cyanamid Company, Mo., 451 S.W.2d 48; Reyes v. Wyeth Laboratories, 5 Cir., 498 F.2d 1264. All three of these cases held the manufacturer had a duty to warn of the risk of contracting polio from the vaccine.

At the time plaintiff herein took the vaccine defendant was aware of a report of the special advisory committee on oral poliomyelitis vaccine dated December 18, 1962. This report indicated the committee had considered 23 cases of polio associated with administration of Type I vaccine causation, six were inconclusive and ten were not compatible with vaccine causation. The report also indicates 31 million doses of Type I vaccine were given in non-epidemic areas during 1962.

Evidence in the record indicates the 1962 paralytic polio rate from all three types of polio was between 4.0–7.0 per million. There is no evidence indicating the incidence of Type I polio during this period.

There was testimony there were 12 cases of polio in Tulsa during October and November, 1962, and Oklahoma was an epidemic state prior to 1963.

A duty to warn of known potential risks of drugs had been found to exist even though the chances of the adverse reaction occurring are statistically small. Parke-Davis and Company v. Stromsodt, 8 Cir., 411 F.2d 1390; Sterling Drug, Inc. v. Cornish, 8 Cir., 370 F.2d 82. Therefore, we conclude defendant had a duty to warn plaintiff or his parents of the risk of contracting polio from the vaccine and the failure to warn of this risk rendered the vaccine defective within the meaning of § 402A, supra.

Defendant next contends the trial court erred in instructing the jury that defendant had a duty to warn plaintiff of risks involved in taking the vaccine rather than instructing that defendant's duty was limited to warning the members of the medical society under whose supervision the vaccination was given.

As a general rule it has been held that in cases involving prescription drugs the drug manufacturer has only a duty to warn the prescribing physician.

In Davis v. Wyeth Laboratories, Inc., supra, the court noted the reason for this rule to be as follows:

> "* * * In such cases the choice involved is essentially a medical one involving an assessment of medical risks in the light of the physician's knowledge of his patient's needs and susceptibilities. Further it is difficult under such circumstances for the manufacturer, by label or direct communication, to reach the consumer with a warning. A warning to the medical profession is in such cases the only effective means by which a warning could help the patient."

However, with reference to a mass immunization program the court stated:

> "Here * * * although the drug was denominated a prescription drug it was not dispensed as such. It was dispensed to all comers at mass clinics without an individualized balancing by a physician of the risks involved. In such cases (as in the case of over-the-counter sales of nonprescription drugs) warning by the manufacturer to its immediate purchaser will not suffice. The decision (that on balance and in the public interest the personal risk to the individual was worth taking) may well have been that of the medical society and not that of appellee. * * *
>
> "We conclude that appellee did not meet its duty to warn.

> "This duty does not impose an unreasonable burden on the manufacturer. * * * means of communication such as advertisements, posters, releases to be read and signed by recipients of the vaccine, or oral warnings were clearly available and could easily have been undertaken or prescribed by appellee."

See also Reyes v. Wyeth Laboratories, supra.

In the present case the vaccine was administered as part of a mass immunization program and the evidence does not indicate the doctor present at each center assessed medical risks in light of his knowledge of each patient's needs and susceptibilities. We conclude instruction 7 was not erroneous insofar as it stated defendant had a duty to warn plaintiff, rather than the medical society sponsoring the program, of the risks involved in taking the vaccine.

Defendant next contends the trial court erred in submitting the case to the jury because there was no evidence plaintiff would have refused to take the vaccine if he or his parents had been informed of risks involved in taking the vaccine.

In Reyes v. Wyeth Laboratories, supra, the court considered a similar contention. There the defendant requested the trial court to submit a special interrogatory to the jury concerning whether failure to warn was the proximate cause of a child's contracting polio in view of the fact that "even with warning they may have proceeded with immunization."

The trial court refused to give such an instruction.

The Court of Appeals held there are two causation issues in most products liability cases (1) was defendant's product the cause in fact of plaintiff's injuries and (2) did the plaintiff's injuries result from the alleged defect in the defendant's product [i. e., the failure to warn].

However, that court held failure to submit the latter question to the jury did not constitute reversible error in that case. In so doing the court stated:

> "* * * Where a consumer, whose injury the manufacturer should have reasonably foreseen, is injured by a product sold without a required warning, a rebuttable presumption will arise that the consumer would have read any warning provided by the manufacturer, and acted so as to minimize the risks. In the absence of evidence rebutting the presumption, a jury finding that the defendant's product was the producing cause of the plaintiff's injury would be sufficient to hold him liable.
>
> "* * * According to the test we have distilled above, we must assume in the absence of evidence to the contrary that Anita's parents would have acted on the warning, had it been given. * * *"

We agree with defendant's contention that as part of plaintiff's cause of action plaintiff must establish he would have refused to take the vaccine if adequate warning had been given.

However, we conclude plaintiff was not required to present any direct evidence upon this point because he was entitled to a rebuttable presumption he would have heeded any warning which might have been given. Reyes v. Wyeth Laboratories, supra.

In the present case there was evidence which tended to overcome the presumption. This evidence indicates when plaintiff took the vaccine there was considerable risk of contracting polio from natural sources, there had been 12 cases of polio in Tulsa during October and November 1962, and Oklahoma was an epidemic state prior to 1963.

In these circumstances we conclude the issue of whether the plaintiff as a reasonably prudent person would have refused to take the vaccine if adequate warning had been given should have been submitted to the jury.

We further conclude the test applied should be an objective test, i. e., in light of all circumstances existing on the date plaintiff took the vaccine, would a reasonably prudent person in plaintiff's position have refused the vaccine if adequate warning of risks had been given. See Cobbs v. Grant, 8 Cal.3d 229, 104 Cal.Rptr. 505, 502 P.2d 1, Canterbury v. Spence, 150 U.S.App.D.C. 263, 464 F.2d 772. * * *

We conclude the trial court's failure to instruct the jury that defendant would be liable only if its failure to warn was the cause of plaintiff's injury constituted a failure to instruct upon a material issue and was fundamental error. Furthermore, we conclude instruction 7 was erroneous because it allowed the jury to find for plaintiff if no warning was given and the vaccine caused plaintiff's injuries, and did not require the jury to find the failure to warn caused the injury.

The judgment of the trial court is reversed and remanded with instructions to grant defendant a new trial.[29]

EXCERPTS FROM CONSUMER PRODUCT SAFETY ACT OF 1972

15 U.S.C.A. §§ 2051 et seq.

§ 2051. (a) The Congress finds that—

(1) an unacceptable number of consumer products which present unreasonable risks of injury are distributed in commerce;

(2) complexities of consumer products and the diverse nature and abilities of consumers using them frequently result in an inability of users to anticipate risks and to safeguard themselves adequately;

29. See Merrill, Compensation for Prescription Drug Injuries, 59 Va.L.Rev. 1 (1973).

(3) the public should be protected against unreasonable risks of injury associated with consumer products;

(4) control by State and local governments of unreasonable risks of injury associated with consumer products is inadequate and may be burdensome to manufacturers;

(5) existing Federal authority to protect consumers from exposure to consumer products presenting unreasonable risks of injury is inadequate; and

(6) regulation of consumer products the distribution or use of which affects interstate or foreign commerce is necessary to carry out this chapter. * * *

§ 2056. (a) The [Consumer Product Safety] Commission may * * * promulgate consumer product safety standards. A consumer product safety standard shall consist of one or more of any of the following types of requirements:

(1) Requirements as to performance, composition, contents, design, construction, finish, or packaging of a consumer product.

(2) Requirements that a consumer product be marked with or accompanied by clear and adequate warnings or instructions, or requirements respecting the form of warnings or instructions.

Any requirement of such a standard shall be reasonably necessary to prevent or reduce an unreasonable risk of injury associated with such product. The requirements of such a standard (other than requirements relating to labeling, warnings, or instructions) shall, whenever feasible, be expressed in terms of performance requirements. * * *

§ 2072. (a) Any person who shall sustain injury by reason of any knowing (including willful) violation of a consumer products safety rule, or any other or order issued by the Commission may sue any person who knowingly (including willfully) violated any such rule or order in any district court of the United States in the district in which the defendant resides or is found or has an agent, subject to the provisions of section 1331 of Title 28 as to the amount in controversy, and shall recover damages sustained, and the cost of suit, including a reasonable attorney's fee, if considered appropriate in the discretion of the court.

(b) The remedies provided for in this section shall be in addition to and not in lieu of any other remedies provided by common law or under Federal or State Law.

(a) Compliance with consumer product safety rules or other rules or orders under this chapter shall not relieve any person from liability at common law or under State statutory law to any other person.

(b) The failure of the Commission to take any action or commence a proceeding with respect to the safety of a consumer product shall not be admissible in evidence in litigation at common law or under State statutory law relating to such consumer product.

(c) Subject to sections 2055(a)(2) and 2055(b) of this title but notwithstanding section 2055(a)(1) of this title, (1) any accident or investigation report made, under this chapter by an officer or employee of the Commission shall be made available to the public in a manner which will not identify any injured person or any person treating him, without the consent of the person so identified, and (2) all reports on research projects, demonstration projects, and other related activities shall be public information.

§ 2075. (a) Whenever a consumer product safety standard under this chapter is in effect and applies to a risk of injury associated with a consumer product, no State or political subdivision of a State shall have any authority either to establish or to continue in effect any provision of a safety standard or regulation which prescribes any requirements as to the performance, composition, contents, design, finish, construction, packaging, or labeling of such product which are designed to deal with the same risk of injury associated with such consumer product, unless such requirements are identical to the requirements of the Federal standard.

(b) Nothing in this section shall be construed to prevent the Federal Government or the government of any State or political subdivision thereof from establishing a safety requirement applicable to a consumer product for its own use if such requirement imposes a higher standard of performance than that required to comply with the otherwise applicable Federal standard.

(c) Upon application of a State or political subdivision thereof, the Commission may by rule, after notice and opportunity for oral presentation of views, exempt from the provisions of subsection (a) of this section (under such conditions as it may impose) a proposed safety standard or regulation described in such application, where the proposed standard or regulation (1) imposes a higher level of performance than the Federal standard, (2) is required by compelling local conditions, and (3) does not unduly burden interstate commerce.
* * *

EXCERPTS FROM MAGNUSON–MOSS WARRANTY–FEDERAL TRADE COMMISSION IMPROVEMENT ACT

Public Law 93–237, 88 Stat. 2183, approved January 4, 1975.

* * *

WARRANTY PROVISIONS

Sec. 102. (a) In order to improve the adequacy of information available to consumers, prevent deception, and improve competition in the marketing of consumer products, any warrantor warranting a consumer product to a consumer by means of a written warranty shall, to the extent required by rules of the [Federal Trade] Commission, fully and conspicuously disclose in simple and readily understood language the terms and conditions of such warranty. Such rules may require inclusion in the written warranty of any of the following items among others:

(1) The clear identification of the names and addresses of the warrantors.

(2) The identity of the party or parties to whom the warranty is extended.

(3) The products or parts covered.

(4) A statement of what the warrantor will do in the event of a defect, malfunction, or failure to conform with such written warranty—at whose expense—and for what period of time.

(5) A statement of what the consumer must do and expenses he must bear.

(6) Exceptions and exclusions from the terms of the warranty.

(7) The step-by-step procedure which the consumer should take in order to obtain performance of any obligation under the warranty, including the identification of any person or class of persons authorized to perform the obligations set forth in the warranty.

(8) Information respecting the availability of any informal dispute settlement procedure offered by the warrantor and a recital, where the warranty so provides, that the purchaser may be required to resort to such procedure before pursuing any legal remedies in the courts.

(9) A brief, general description of the legal remedies available to the consumer.

(10) The time at which the warrantor will perform any obligations under the warranty.

(11) The period of time within which, after notice of a defect, malfunction, or failure to conform with the warranty, the warrantor will perform any obligations under the warranty.

(12) The characteristics or properties of the products, or parts thereof, that are not covered by the warranty.

(13) The elements of the warranty in words or phrases which would not mislead a reasonable, average consumer as to the nature or scope of the warranty.

(b)(1)(A) The Commission shall prescribe rules requiring that the terms of any written warranty on a consumer product be made available to the consumer (or prospective consumer) prior to the sale of the product to him.

(B) The Commission may prescribe rules for determining the manner and form in which information with respect to any written warranty of a consumer product shall be clearly and conspicuously presented or displayed so as not to mislead the reasonable, average consumer, when such information is contained in advertising, labeling, point-of-sale material, or other representations in writing. * *

(c) No warrantor of a consumer product may condition his written or implied warranty of such product on the consumer's using, in connection with such product, any article or service (other than article or service provided without charge under the terms of the warranty) which is identified by brand, trade, or corporate name; except that the prohibition of this subsection may be waived by the Commission if—

(1) the warrantor satisfies the Commission that the warranted product will function properly only if the article or service so identified is used in connection with the warranted product, and

(2) the Commission finds that such a waiver is in the public interest.

* * *

(e) The provisions of this section apply only to warranties which pertain to consumer products actually costing the consumer more than $5. * * *

Remedies

Sec. 110. (a)(1) Congress hereby declares it to be its policy to encourage warrantors to establish procedures whereby consumer disputes are fairly and expeditiously settled through informal dispute settlement mechanisms.

(2) The Commission shall prescribe rules setting forth minimum requirements for any informal dispute settlement procedure which is incorporated into the terms of a written warranty to which any provision of this title applies. Such rules shall provide for participation in such procedure by independent or governmental entities.

(3) One or more warrantors may establish an informal dispute settlement procedure which meets the requirements of the Commission's rules under paragraph (2). If—

(A) a warrantor establishes such a procedure,

(B) such procedure, and its implementation, meets the requirements of such rules, and

(C) he incorporates in a written warranty a requirement that the consumer resort to such procedure before pursuing any legal remedy under this section respecting such warranty, then (i) the consumer may not commence a civil action * * * under subsection (d) of this section unless he initially resorts to such procedure * * *

(d)(1) Subject to subsections (a)(3) and (e), a consumer who is damaged by the failure of a supplier, warrantor, or service contractor to comply with any obligation under this title, or under a written warranty, implied warranty, or service contract, may bring suit for damages and other legal and equitable relief—

(A) in any court of competent jurisdiction in any State or the District of Columbia; or

(B) in an appropriate district court of the United States, subject to paragraph (3) of this subsection.

(2) If a consumer finally prevails in any action brought under paragraph (1) of this subsection, he may be allowed by the court to recover as part of the judgment a sum equal to the aggregate amount of cost and expenses (including attorneys' fees based on actual time expended) determined by the court to have been reasonably incurred by the plaintiff for or in connection with the commencement and prosecution of such action, unless the court in its discretion shall determine that such an award of attorneys' fees would be inappropriate.

(3) No claim shall be cognizable in a suit brought under paragraph (1)(B) of this subsection—

(A) if the amount in controversy of any individual claim is less than the sum or value of $25;

(B) if the amount in controversy is less than the sum or value of $50,000 (exclusive of interests and costs) computed on the basis of all claims to be determined in this suit; or

(C) if the action is brought as a class action, and the number of named plaintiffs is less than one hundred.

(e) No action (other than a class action or an action respecting a warranty to which subsection (a)(3) applies) may be brought under subsection (d) for failure to comply with any obligation under any written or implied warranty or service contract * * * unless the person obligated under the warranty or service contract is afforded a reasonable opportunity to cure such failure to comply. * *

Effect on Other Laws

Sec. 111 * * *

(b)(1) Nothing in this title shall invalidate or restrict any right or remedy of any consumer under State law or any other Federal law.

(2) Nothing in this title (other than sections 108 and 104(a)(2) and (4)) shall (A) affect the liability of, or impose liability on, any

person for personal injury, or (B) supersede any provision of State law regarding consequential damages for injury to the person or other injury.

(c)(1) Except as provided in subsection (b) and in paragraph (2) of this subsection, a State requirement—

> (A) which relates to labeling or disclosure with respect to written warranties or performance thereunder;
>
> (B) which is within the scope of an applicable requirement of sections 102, 103, and 104 (and rules implementing such sections), and
>
> (C) which is not identical to a requirement of section 102, 103, or 104 (or a rule thereunder),

shall not be applicable to written warranties complying with such sections (or rules thereunder).

(2) If, upon application of an appropriate State agency, the Commission determines (pursuant to rules issued in accordance with section 109) that any requirement of such State covering any transaction to which this title applies (A) affords protection to consumers greater than the requirements of this title and (B) does not unduly burden interstate commerce, then such State requirement shall be applicable (notwithstanding the provisions of paragraph (1) of this subsection) to the extent specified in such determination for so long as the State administers and enforces effectively any such greater requirement. * * *

Chapter 6

MISREPRESENTATION [1]

SECTION 1. INTRODUCTORY

F. HARPER AND F. JAMES, THE LAW OF TORTS 527–28 (1956):

The modern law of misrepresentation evolved from the action on the case of deceit. * * *

The type of interest protected by the law of deceit is the interest in formulating business judgments without being misled by others—in short, in not being cheated. Misrepresentation may induce action exposing one to danger of bodily injury or property damage; misrepresentation may injure one's reputation which in turn may or may not cause financial loss; misrepresentation may affect adversely the marketability of one's land or personal property or may cause third persons to break their contracts thus causing pecuniary damage. Such misrepresentations and their legal consequences are not dealt with in this chapter but are to be found in the chapters on negligence, defamation, disparagement and interference with contractual relations. What is usually included in the law of deceit is limited to misrepresentations which mislead another into an unwise judgment in some business enterprise which results in financial loss.

It is for this reason that this phase of the law is, as it has always been, closely associated with the mores of the commercial world. * *

The effect of misrepresentation is considered in a number of courses in the law school curriculum: procedure, equity, contracts, property, finance, credit or security transactions, bills and notes, etc. Accordingly, the treatment here is in a sense introductory. While the main emphasis here is on the action for damages, the cases have been selected and arranged to stress the choice of remedies available, to invite comparison between them and to bring out the considerations relevant in making the choice. A useful description and comparison of these remedies may be found in Keeton, Actionable Misrepresentation: Legal Fault as a Requirement, 1 Okla.L.Rev. 21 (1948), 2 id. 56 (1949).

The characteristics and incidents of the various remedies have retained much of their importance under the Codes of Procedure. This is true even under liberal procedures which have genuinely abolished the old distinctions among the forms of action and between law and equity. It is even more true, of course, where the distinctions

1. See generally James and Gray, Misrepresentation, 36 Md.L.Rev. 1 (1976).

linger under one guise or another. It may be well to review the extent to which pleading reform does or can affect the situation.

1. Under the older system it was fatal to bring an action in the wrong *form* and as a general thing only one form of action could be pursued at a time. If plaintiff brought an action on the case for fraud and deceit, for example,

(a) he could not join with it a count in assumpsit for breach of the contract;

(b) he could not recover for a breach of contract even though,

i. all the elements needed for an action of assumpsit were set forth in the pleadings,

ii. all these elements were admitted or proved, and

iii. all the parties to the contract were before the court.

(c) Similarly the action could not include a prayer for rescission of the contract because of the misrepresentations alleged, no matter how appropriate such a remedy would be if suit had been brought in equity.

(d) Nor could plaintiff recover by showing that he had already rescinded the contract at law.

Modernized procedure should make impossible results like these. Many courts no longer tolerate them, e. g., Edward Greenband Enterprises of Arizona v. Pepper, 112 Ariz. 115, 538 P.2d 389 (1975). But the old rigid formalism recurs sporadically as the "theory of the pleadings doctrine," or the "doctrine of election of remedies," even under the Codes. See in general Clark, Code Pleading §§ 43, 77 (2d ed. 1947); James, Civil Procedure 90 et seq. (1965). One may not, of course, both rescind a contract and have damages for fraud in inducing its execution, for the latter are based on the assumption that the contract continues in force. See, e. g. 2 Williston on Sales section 648 et seq. (Rev. ed. 1948); note, 2 U.Fla.L.Rev. 142 (1949). But the question remains at how early a step should a defrauded plaintiff be regarded as having made this election irrevocably. And note that rescission may be accompanied by recovery of consequential damages, Banco Frances E Brasileiro S. A. v. Doe, 36 N.Y.2d 592, 370 N.Y.S. 2d 534, 331 N.E.2d 502 (1975), or punitive damages, Z. D. Howard Co. v. Cartright, Okl., 537 P.2d 345 (1975).

2. The substantive rules of liability were not meant to be changed by the procedural reforms (although the substantive doctrines themselves have undergone some change during the same period of time). Thus in general only the promisor was liable on a contract, the seller on a warranty, and the like; while since Pasley v. Freeman, infra, third parties have been liable for fraud and deceit. There is nothing about procedural reforms which would justify imposing liability on such a third party on a showing of facts which would not have supported recovery against him in *any* of the old forms of action

available at law or in equity. This does not mean that his liability should not be extended; it means only that its extension must be put on some other ground.

In like manner the Codes were never intended to change the kind of a showing which must be made to entitle a plaintiff to any given relief, or any particular measure of damages (though they should keep him from being turned out of court simply because he asks for one remedy and shows himself entitled to another).

3. Perhaps the most vexing problem injected into this matter by procedural reforms is that of jury trial. Where the ancient remedy was by common law action in any form this mode of trial obtained as a matter of course, and the right to it (unless waived) is preserved by the federal and most state constitutions. The problem becomes particularly acute (a) where the plaintiff had a choice of legal or equitable remedy before the code, and (b) where he seeks an equitable remedy (e. g. rescission or reformation) but by his proof shows himself entitled to damages (as for breach of contract) only. This problem is dealt with elsewhere but should be kept in mind here.

4. The parol evidence rule will be invoked (if otherwise applicable) where plaintiff relies on contract or warranty theories of recovery. This rule excludes consideration of promises and probably of representations which are not contained in the written contract (if there is one which may be considered as an "integration" of the previous negotiations between the parties). If the action is grounded on a theory of fraud or misrepresentation, however, the rule does not apply. Wigmore, Evidence sections 2423, 2439 (3d ed. 1940).

PASLEY v. FREEMAN

Court of King's Bench, 1789.
3 D. & E. [3 Term Rep.] 51, 100 Eng.Rep. 450.

This was an action in the nature of a writ of deceit; to which the defendant pleaded the general issue. And after a verdict for the plaintiffs on the third count, a motion was made in arrest of judgment.

The third count was as follows: "And whereas also the said Joseph Freeman, * * * intending to deceive and defraud the said John Pasley and Edward, did wrongfully and deceitfully encourage and persuade the said John Pasley and Edward, to sell and deliver to the said John Christopher Falch divers other goods, wares, and merchandizes, * * * of the value of 2634£. 16s. 1d. upon trust and credit; and did for that purpose then and there falsely, deceitfully, and fraudulently, assert and affirm to the said John Pasley and Edward, that the said John Christopher then and there was a person safely to be trusted and given credit to in that respect; and did thereby falsely, fraudulently, and deceitfully, cause and procure the said John Pasley and Edward to sell and deliver the said last-mentioned goods, wares, and merchandizes, upon trust and credit, to the said John Christopher; and in fact they the said John Pasley and Edward, confiding in and giving credit to the said last-mentioned assertion and affirmation of the said Joseph, and believing the same to be true, and not knowing the contrary thereof, did afterwards * * * sell and deliver the said last-mentioned goods, wares, and merchandizes, upon trust and credit, to the said John Christopher; whereas in truth and in fact, at the time of the said Joseph's making his said last-mentioned assertion and affirmation, the said John Christopher was not then and there a person safely to be trusted and given credit to in that respect, and the said Joseph well knew the same. * * * And the said John Pasley and Edward further say, that the said John Christopher hath not, nor hath any other person on his behalf, paid to the said John Pasley and Edward, or either of them, the said sum of 2634£. 16s. 1d. last mentioned, or any part thereof, for the said last-mentioned goods, wares, and merchandizes; but on the contrary the said John Christopher then was, and still is, wholly unable to pay the said sum of money last mentioned, or any part thereof. * * *

Application was first made for a new trial, which, after argument, was refused: and then this motion in arrest of judgment. * *

GROSE, J.—Upon the face of this count in the declaration, no privity of contract is stated between the parties. No consideration arises to the defendant; and he is in no situation in which the law considers him in any trust, or in which it demands from him any account of the credit of Falch. He appears not to be interested in any transaction between the plaintiffs and Falch, nor to have colluded with them. * * * Then this is an action against the defendant for making a false affirmation, or telling a lie, respecting the credit of a third person, with intent to deceive, by which the third person was damnified; and for the damages suffered, the plaintiffs contend that the defendant is answerable in an action upon the case. It is admitted, that the action is new in point of precedent; but it is insisted that the law recognizes principles on which it may be supported. The principle on which it is contended to lie is, that wherever deceit or falsehood is practised to the detriment of another, the law will give redress. This proposition I controvert. * * * If the action can be supported, it must be upon the ground that there exists in this case what the law deems *damnum cum injuria.* If it does, I admit that the action lies; and I admit that upon the verdict found, the plaintiffs appear to have been damnified. But whether there has been *injuria,* a wrong, a tort, for which an action lies, is matter of law. The tort complained of is the false affirmation made with intent to deceive; and it is said to be an action upon the case analogous to the old writ of deceit. When this was first argued at the Bar, on the motion for a new trial, I confess I thought it reasonable that the action should lie; but, on looking into the old books for cases in which the old action of deceit has been maintained upon the false affirmation of the defendant, I have changed my opinion. The cases on this head are brought together in Bro. tit. Deceit, pl. 29, & in Fitz. Abr. I have likewise looked into Danvers, Kitchins, and Comyns, and I have not met with any case of an action upon a false affirmation, except against a party to a contract, and where there is a promise, either express or implied, that the fact is true, which is misrepresented: and no other case has been cited at the Bar. Then if no such case has ever existed, it furnishes a strong objection against the action, which is brought for the first time for a supposed injury, which has been daily committed for centuries past; for I believe there has been no time when men have not been constantly damnified by the fraudulent misrepresentations of others: and if such an action would have lain, there certainly has been, and will be, a plentiful source of litigation, of which the public are not hitherto aware. * * * In this very case, if the action lies, the plaintiffs will stand in a peculiarly fortunate predicament, for then they will have the responsibility both of Falch and the defendant. And they will be in a better situation than they would have been if, in the conversation that passed between them and the defendant, instead of asserting that Falch might safely be trusted, the defendant had said, "if he do not pay for the goods, I will": for then undoubtedly an action would not have lain against the defendant. * * * So far from a person being bound in a case like the present to tell the truth, the books supply me with a variety of cases in which even the contracting party is not liable for a misrepresentation. There are cases of two sorts, in which, though a man is deceived, he can maintain no action. The first class of cases (though not analogous to the present) is, where the affirmation is that the thing sold has not a defect which is a visible one: there the imposition, the fraudulent intent, is admitted, but it is no tort. The second head of cases is, where the affirmation is (what is called in some of the books) a nude assertion; such as the party deceived may exercise his own judgment upon; as where it is matter of opinion, where he may make inquiries into the truth of the assertion, and it becomes his own fault from laches that he is deceived. 1 Ro.Abr. 101. Yelv. 20, 1 Sid. 146. Cro. Jac. 386, Bayly v. Merrel. In Harvey v. Young, Yelv. 20 J.S., who had a term for years, affirmed to J.D. that the term was worth 150£. to be sold, upon which J.D. gave 150£. and afterwards could not get more than 100£. for it, and then brought his action: and it was alleged that this matter did not prove any fraud, for it was only a naked assertion that the term was worth so much, and it was the plaintiff's folly to give credit to such assertion. But if the defendant had warranted the term to be of such a value to be sold, and upon that the plaintiff had bought it, it would have been otherwise; for the warranty given by the defendant is a matter to induce confidence and trust in the plaintiff. * * * The misrepresentation stated in the declaration is respecting the credit of Falch; * * * but credit to which a man is entitled is matter of judgment and opinion, on which different men might form different opinions, and upon which the plaintiffs might form their own; to mislead which no fact to prove the good credit of Falch is falsely asserted. It seems to me therefore that any assertion relative to credit, especially where the party making it has no interest, nor is in any collusion with the person respecting whose credit the assertion is made, is like the case in Yelverton respecting the value of the term. But at any rate it is not an assertion of a fact peculiarly in the knowledge of the defendant. Whether Falch deserved credit depended on the opinion of many; for credit exists on the good opinion of many. Respecting this, the plaintiffs might have inquired of others, who knew as much as the defendant; it was their fault that they did not, and they have suffered damage by their own laches. It was owing to their own gross negligence that they gave credence to the assertion of the defendant, without taking pains to satisfy themselves that that assertion was founded in fact, as in the case of Bayly v. Merrel. I am therefore of opinion, that this action is as novel in principle as it is in precedent, that it is against the principles to be collected from analogous cases, and consequently that it cannot be maintained.

BULLER, J.— * * * Fraud without damage, or damage without fraud, gives no cause of action; but where these two concur, an action lies. Per Croke, J. 3 Bulst. 95. * * * I agree that an action cannot be supported for telling a bare naked lie; but that I define to be, saying a thing which is false, knowing or not knowing it to be so, and without any design to injure, cheat, or deceive, another person. Every deceit comprehends a lie; but a deceit is more than a lie on account of the view with which it is practised, it's being coupled with some dealing, and the injury which it is calculated to occasion, and does occasion, to another person. Deceit is a very extensive head in the law; and it will be proper to take a short view of some of the cases which have existed on the subject, to see how far the Courts have gone, and what are the principles upon which they have decided. I lay out of the question the case in 2 Cro. 196, and all other cases which relate to freehold interests in lands: for they go on the special reason that the seller cannot have them without title, and the buyer is at his peril to see it. But the cases cited on the part of the defendant, deserving notice, are Yelv. 20. Carth. 90. Salk. 210. The first of these has been fully stated by my brother Grose: but it is to be observed that the book does not affect to give the reasons on which the Court delivered their judgment: but it is a case quoted by counsel at the Bar, who mentions what was alleged by counsel in the other case. If the Court went on a distinction between the words warranty and affirmation, the case is not law: for it was rightly held by Holt, C. J. in the subsequent cases, and has been uniformly adopted ever since, that an affirmation at the time of a sale is a warranty, provided it appear on evidence to have been so intended. But the true ground of that determination was, that the assertion was of mere matter of judgment and opinion; of a matter of which the defendant had no particular knowledge, but of which many men will be of many minds, and which is often governed by whim and caprice. Judgment or opinion, in such case, implies no knowledge. And here this case differs materially from that in Yelverton: my brother Grose considers this assertion as mere matter of opinion only; but I differ from him in that respect. For it is stated on this record, that the defendant knew that the fact was false. The case in

Yelv. admits, that if there had been fraud, it would have been otherwise. The case of Crosse v. Gardner, Carth. 90, was upon an affirmation that oxen, which the defendant had in his possession, and sold to the plaintiff were his, when in truth they belonged to another person. The objection against the action was that the declaration neither stated that the defendant deceitfully sold them, or that he knew them to be the property of another person; and a man may be mistaken in his property and right to a thing without any fraud or ill intent. *Ex concessis* therefore, if there were fraud or deceit the action would lie; and knowledge of the falsehood of the thing asserted is fraud and deceit. But notwithstanding these objections, the Court held that the action lay, because the plaintiff had no means of knowing to whom the property belonged but only by the possession. And in Cro.Jac. 474, it was held, that affirming them to be his, knowing them to be a stranger's is the offence, and cause of action. The case of Medina v. Stoughton (Salk. 210), in the point of decision, is the same as Crosse v. Gardner; but there is an *obiter dictum* of Holt, Ch. J., that where the seller of a personal thing is out of possession, it is otherwise, for there may be room to question the seller's title, and *caveat emptor* in such case to have an express warranty, or a good title. This distinction by Holt is not mentioned by Lord Raym. 598, who reports the same case: and if an affirmation at the time of sale be a warranty, I cannot feel a distinction between the vendor's being in or out of possession. The thing is bought of him, and in consequence of his assertion: and if there be any difference, it seems to me that the case is strongest against the vendor when he is out of possession, because then the vendee has nothing but the warranty to rely on. These cases then are so far from being authorities against the present action, that they shew that, if there be fraud or deceit, the action will lie; and that knowledge of the falsehood of the thing asserted is fraud and deceit. * * *

Some general arguments were urged at the Bar, to shew that mischiefs and inconveniences would arise if this action were sustained; for if a man, who is asked a question respecting another's responsibility, hesitate, or is silent, he blasts the character of the tradesman: and if he say that he is insolvent, he may not be able to prove it. But let us see what is contended for: it is nothing less than that a man may assert that which he knows to be false, and thereby do an everlasting injury to his neighbour, and yet not be answerable for it. This is as repugnant to law as it is to morality. Then it is said, that the plaintiffs had no right to ask the question of the defendant. But I do not agree in that; for the plaintiffs had an interest in knowing what the credit of Falch was. It was not the inquiry of idle curiosity, but it was to govern a very extensive concern. The defendant undoubtedly had his option to give an answer to the question, or not: but if he gave none, or said he did not know, it is impossible for any Court of Justice to adopt the possible inferences of a suspicious mind as a ground for grave judgment. All that is required of a person in the defendant's situation is, that he shall give no answer, or that if he do, he shall answer according to the truth as far as he knows. The reasoning in the case of Coggs v. Barnard which was cited by the plaintiff's counsel, is I think very applicable to this part of the case. If the answer import insolvency, it is not necessary that the defendant should be able to prove that insolvency to a jury; for the law protects a man in giving that answer, if he does it in confidence and without malice. No action can be maintained against him for giving such an answer unless express malice can be proved. From the circumstance of the law giving that protection, it seems to follow, as a necessary consequence, that the law not only gives sanction to the question, but requires that, if it be answered at all, it shall be answered honestly. * * * And if a man will wickedly assert that which he knows to be false, and thereby draws his neighbour into a heavy loss, even though it be under the specious pretence of serving his friend, I say *ausis talibus istis non jura subserviunt.*

ASHHURST, J.— * * * It is admitted that a fraudulent affirmation, when the party making it has an interest, is a ground of action; as in Risney v. Selby (Salk. 211), which was a false affirmation made to a purchaser as to the rent of a farm which the defendant was in treaty to sell to him. But it was argued that the action lies not unless where the party making it has an interest, or colludes with one who has. I do not recollect that any case was cited which proves such a position; but if there were any such to be found, I should not hesitate to say that it could not be law; for I have so great a veneration for the law as to suppose that nothing can be law which is not founded in common sense or common honesty. For the gist of the action is the injury done to the plaintiff, and not whether the defendant meant to be a gainer by it: what is it to the plaintiff whether the defendant was or was not to gain by it; the injury to him is the same. And it should seem that it ought more emphatically to lie against him, as the malice is more diabolical, if he had not the temptation of gain. * * *

LORD KENYON, CH. J. * * * There are many situations in life, and particularly in the commercial world, where a man cannot by any diligence inform himself of the degree of credit which ought to be given to the persons with whom he deals; in which cases he must apply to those whose sources of intelligence enable them to give that information. The law of prudence leads him to apply to them, and the law of morality ought to induce them to give the information required. In the case of Bulstrode the carrier might have weighed the goods himself: but in this case the plaintiffs had no means of knowing the state of Falch's credit but by an application to his neighbours. The same observation may be made to the cases cited by the defendant's counsel respecting titles to real property. For a person does not have recourse to common conversations to know the title of an estate which he is about to purchase: but he may inspect the title deeds; and he does not use common prudence if he rely on any other security. * * * It is admitted that the defendant's conduct was highly immoral, and detrimental to society. And I am of opinion that the action is maintainable on the grounds of deceit in the defendant, and injury and loss to the plaintiffs.

Rule for arresting the judgment discharged.[2]

SECTION 2. WHERE THE PARTY INJURED WAS BROUGHT INTO LEGAL RELATIONS WITH THE PERSON MAKING THE MISREPRESENTATION

In Pasley v. Freeman plaintiff was in the last analysis trying to recover the unpaid purchase price for goods he had sold Falch. It was useless for him to pursue his rights against Falch because of the latter's insolvency. Further exploration of his rights against third parties is postponed to the next section. Ordinarily where the seller seeks redress from the buyer because the goods are not paid for, a suit on the contract for the purchase price is adequate, available, and easy to prove. Often, too, there is collateral security which may be proceeded against as in the case of conditional sales of chattels. Notions of fraud, with all their attendant difficulties need not usually be resorted to. Yet they are occasionally useful even in such a quest (witness the following case and note).

DEZERO v. TURNER

Supreme Court of Vermont, 1941.
112 Vt. 194, 122 A.2d 173.

JEFFORDS, JUSTICE. This is an action in tort for deceit. The plaintiff in his complaint alleges that he sold to the defendant and installed in the home of the latter a certain oil burning heating system upon the following express representations of the defendant: "I (defendant) have an interest in an estate being probated in the Fair Haven Probate Court and I have just received $1500.00 from this estate, and I have this money now in my possession and I will keep $825.75 of this money and pay it to you immediately after you have installed the heating system in my home on the Gleason Road." Then follow allegations of falsity of the above representations, scienter by the defendant, reliance by the plaintiff on the representations, installation of the heating system, failure to pay for the same on demand, total loss of the goods and labor of installation resulting from the facts previously alleged, to the damage of the plaintiff.

2. "This decision * * * marks a new point of departure in the law of fraud. Prior to [it] the use of the action of deceit upon a false representation, if not strictly limited to situations where the false representation was made by a seller to his vendee as an inducement to the sale, was at least restricted to situations where the party injured was brought into legal relations with the persons making the false representation." 1 Street, Foundations of Legal Liability 392 (1906).

The defendant in his demurrer to the complaint specified as reasons for its claimed insufficiency that there was no false representation alleged of any existing fact to secure credit but merely an allegation of a promise to pay for services at some future time. The demurrer was sustained and the cause passed to this Court under P.L. 2072.

Certain false representations alleged to have been made by the defendant were that he had an interest in an estate and had received a stated amount of money from the estate which he then possessed. There can be no question but that these alleged false statements, admitted by the demurrer to have been made, were of existing facts which the jury could reasonably find were spoken for the purpose of securing credit for the transaction in question alleged to have been given in reliance upon said representations. Consequently grounds for an action of fraud or deceit are set forth and the pleading is not defective because these false representations were followed by others looking to the future, reliance upon which is also alleged. The false statements of existing facts alleged in the complaint could be found by the jury to have constituted a material inducement to the dealings between the parties and the right of the plaintiff to recover would not be changed because the jury could also find that he was induced to some extent in the matter by the alleged future representations. It is not essential that a misrepresentation of a material fact be the sole cause or inducement of the contract or transaction in question. It is enough that it constitute a material inducement. * * *

Judgment reversed and cause remanded.[3]

3. See, similarly, Casale v. Dooner Laboratories, Inc., 503 F.2d 303 (4th Cir. 1973) (employee persuaded to change jobs on basis of oral (i) promises, which were broken, of higher salary and other employee benefits, and (ii) false representations as to the nature, extent and degree of establishment of defendant's business). Note the requirement that the misrepresentation be one of fact. Could the promise to pay be turned into such a misrepresentation by showing that when it was made the defendant (a) had the formed intention not to pay? (b) had no reasonable prospect of resources from which to pay? See e. g. Ahmed v. Collins, 23 Ariz.App. 54, 530 P.2d 900 (1975); Grefe v. Ross, Iowa, 231 N.W.2d 863 (1975); 2 Williston on Sales, section 630, 637 (Rev. ed. 1948); Llewellyn, Cases & Materials on Sales 57 (1930); Sternberg v. American Snuff Co., 69 F.2d 307 (8th Cir. 1934); In re Penn Table Co., 26 F.Supp. 887 (D.C.W.Va.1939). Cf. Note 11, U.Pitts.L.Rev. 666 (1951). It is familiar history that the notion of a broken promise as a sort of deceit played an important part in the development of assumpsit from case. 3 Street, Foundations of Legal Liability, c. XIV (1900) But this kind of *ex post facto* deceit will not serve where fraud is to be proved today.

Why did plaintiff in the above case take on himself the burden of proving fraud? Several possibilities suggest themselves, viz. to get (a) punitive damages (McCormick, Damages, ch. 10 (1935)); (b) a judgment not dischargeable in bankruptcy; see section 17 of the Bankruptcy Act, 11 U.S.C.A. § 35; Abbott v. Regents of University of California, 516 F.2d 830 (9th Cir. 1975) (fraudulent application for student loan); (c) attachment or execution of the body of the defendant. The Vermont statutes have provided for body execution, 12 V.S.A. § 2741 (1973) except in certain cases among which are actions founded on contract, § 3521. And in tort actions the imprisoned defendant shall not be admitted to the liberties of the jail, if the court adjudges that the cause of action arose from a wilful and malicious act of the defendant, § 3624; nor in such a case may he be dis-

CABOT v. CHRISTIE

Supreme Court of Vermont, 1869.
42 Vt. 121, 1 Am.Rep. 313.

Case for false warranty in the sale of a farm. Plea, not guilty. Trial by jury, May term, 1868, BARRETT, J., presiding. The plaintiff gave evidence tending to show that he bought the farm at the time and for the price stated in the declaration, and that the defendant made representations in respect to the number of acres, as of his own knowledge, designedly intending to induce the plaintiff to suppose and believe, and thereby the plaintiff was induced to and did suppose and believe, that the farm contained at least one hundred and thirty acres of land, and relying thereupon, the plaintiff made the purchase; that the defendant knew that there was not one hundred and thirty acres, or he didn't know that there was that quantity; that in fact there was only one hundred and seventeen acres and a few rods in the farm; that the plaintiff had no knowledge of the quantity except from the defendant's representation. The defendant gave evidence tending to show that he supposed there was one hundred and thirty acres and a little more in the farm, derived from what he had heard said, and from various deeds in his possession of various grantors and of various parcels, but that he did not know, and did not profess or represent to the plaintiff that he knew, how many acres there were in fact; that he gave the plaintiff all the information and sources of information he had on the subject, neither making any false representation, nor fraudulent concealment, nor any undertaking as to the number of acres in the farm. There was no evidence or claim that the farm was sold by the acre; but it appeared that it was sold in lump, or as a farm entire. The plaintiff requested the court to charge the jury: *First,* That under the declaration, the plaintiff is entitled to recover if he proves a warranty of the number of acres in the farm, or if he proves a fraudulent representation of the number of acres. *Second,* That the fraudulent representation may be proved either by evidence of false representations, known to the defendant to be false, and relied upon by the plaintiff, or by proof of an absolute representation of the number of acres, which representation was made with intent that the plaintiff should rely upon it, and was made upon professed

charged on taking the poor debtor's oath, § 3673. A situation may well be imagined where defendant himself has no property that can be reached by legal process, but where other members of the family who do have property (sometimes held in secret and unprovable trust for defendant himself) would be willing to pay the judgment rather than let defendant be imprisoned.

Aside from the present action, and the contract suit, plaintiff might also have had rescission "at law," on the showing made here. This would have involved his tendering any money already paid him on the oil burner, and recovering the burner itself by appropriate action if necessary. See Pritchett v. Fife, 8 Ala.App. 462, 62 So. 1001 (1913) (detinue); Comment, 37 Yale L.J. 1141 (1928); Williston op. cit., supra section 647. No doubt this would have been a less satisfactory remedy in the instant case but there are situations where it is the best one available, e. g. typical bankruptcy situation. See citations in first paragraph of this note.

knowledge, but without actual knowledge, and which was in fact false, but was relied upon by the plaintiff as true. The court complied with said requests only so far as is shown by the charge, and charged as follows: In order to entitle the plaintiff to recover, he must satisfy the jury that the defendant knew the farm did not contain one hundred and thirty acres, or that he did not believe it contained one hundred and thirty acres; and that in order to induce the plaintiff to buy the farm, he falsely represented it to contain one hundred and thirty acres; and that the plaintiff was by such false representation induced to make the purchase, believing it to contain that quantity. If he honestly believed it contained one hundred and thirty acres, the plaintiff can not recover, though the defendant was in error about it. Honest mistake is not fraud. Incorrect is not the same as false. You must find that he represented the quantity different from what he knew or believed to be true, with the fraudulent intent. Also, that the plaintiff was thus induced to make the purchase. That is, that the plaintiff would not have made the purchase if the defendant had not represented it to be one hundred and thirty acres. Inquire as to these several points. Fraud is not presumed, but must be proved. The jury returned a verdict for the defendant. The plaintiff excepted to the charge in the respects in which it failed to comply with or was against said requests. In other respects the charge was satisfactory. The declaration counted both upon a false warranty of the defendant in regard to the number of acres contained in the farm, and a warranty in regard to said quantity. * * *

STEELE, J. I. The plaintiff can not recover upon the ground of a parol warranty of the quantity of the land. If the quantity was warranted it should be provable by the deed. It is true that a deed of conveyance need not contain all the stipulations of the parties. For example, the agreements as to consideration and mode of payment need not be embraced in the deed, for the instrument purports to be the deed of but one of the parties. But it does purport to contain the covenants of the grantor with respect to the property conveyed. To add a new covenant by parol proof would be a palpable violation of the familiar rule that written contracts are not to be varied by oral testimony. Such a parol stipulation, it has been held, could not be proved in respect to an ordinary bill of sale of personal property.

Nor is the plaintiff entitled to recover in this action upon the ground of mistake. A mutual and material mistake, by which the purchaser was misled as to the quantity of land, would be a more appropriate ground for relief in a court of chancery than in a court of law.

If, then, the plaintiff was entitled to recover at all in this case, it was by reason of some fraud on the part of the defendant by which the bargain was induced.

II. The plaintiff complains of the ruling of the county court upon the subject of fraud. It is conceded that the quantity of land was represented incorrectly. The court properly told the jury that this, in itself, would not amount to fraud. To entitle the plaintiff to a recovery upon that ground, the defendant must have made some representation upon the subject that he did not believe to be true. The plaintiff claims, and his evidence tended to prove, that the defendant did make such a representation by stating the quantity of land as a matter within his own knowledge, when, in fact, as the defendant concedes, it was a matter upon which he had only a belief. We think it very clear that a party may be guilty of fraud by stating his belief as knowledge. Upon a statement of the defendant's mere belief, judgment, or information, the plaintiff might have regarded it prudent to procure a measurement of the land before completing his purchase. A statement as of knowledge, if believed, would make a survey or measurement seem unnecessary. A representation of a fact, as of the party's own knowledge, if it proved false, is, unless explained, inferred to be willfully false and made with an intent to deceive, at least in respect to the knowledge which is professed. A sufficient explanation however sometimes arises from the nature of the subject itself, or from the situation of the parties being such that the statement of knowledge could only be understood as an expression of strong belief or opinion. But the quantity of land in a farm is a matter upon which accurate or approximately accurate knowledge is not at all impossible or unusual. If the defendant had only a belief or opinion as to the quantity of land, it was an imposition upon the plaintiff to pass off such belief as knowledge. So, too, if he made an absolute representation as to quantity, which was understood and intended to be understood as a statement upon knowledge, it is precisely the same as if he had distinctly and in terms professed to have knowledge as to the fact. It is often said that a representation is not fraudulent if the party who makes it believes it to be true. But a party who is aware that he has only an opinion how a fact is, and represents that opinion as knowledge, does not believe his representation to be true. As is well said in a note to the report of the case of Taylor v. Ashton, 11 Mees. & Wels. 418, Phila.Ed., the belief of a party to be an excuse for a false representation must be "a belief in the representation as made. The *scienter* will, therefore, be sufficiently established by showing that the assertion was made as of the defendant's own knowledge, and not as mere matter of opinion with regard to facts of which he was aware that he had no such knowledge." The same principle of law has been repeatedly recognized. Hammatt v. Emerson, 27 Me. 308, 326; Bennett v. Judson, 21 N.Y. 238; Stone v. Denny, 4 Metc., Mass., 151; Hazard v. Irwin, 18 Pick., Mass., 95.

In the case before us, the plaintiff, under the charge of the court, was denied the benefit of this rule of law, although there was evidence tending to show every necessary element of a fraud of the nature we have been considering. The plaintiff's request was refused, and the jury were instructed that the plaintiff could only recover in case they found "that the defendant represented the quantity of land different from what he knew or believed to be true." Under these instructions it would be immaterial whether he made the representation as a matter of knowledge or as a matter of opinion so long as he kept within his belief as to the quantity of land. In this we think there was error. The court properly instructed the jury that the representation, to warrant a recovery must have been relied on and have been an inducement to the purchase. The subsequent remark, that the jury, to hold the defendant, must find that the plaintiff would not have made the purchase but for the representation, we regard as probably inadvertent.

What the plaintiff would have done but for the false representation, is often a mere speculative enquiry, and is not the test of the plaintiff's right. If the false representations were material and relied upon, and were intended to operate and did operate as one of the inducements to the trade, it is not necessary to enquire whether the plaintiff would or would not have made the purchase without this inducement.

The judgment of the county court is reversed and the cause is remanded.

In most states one of the elements of the action for damages for fraud is *scienter*. But cf. Clements Auto Company v. Service Bureau Corporation, page 770 infra; Rosenberg v. Cyrowski, p. 796, infra and note. Where the defendant actually knew the falsity of his statements this requirement is satisfied. Such knowledge may, of course, be proven circumstantially and is often to be found in these cases. No jurisdiction, however, *requires* the jury to find actual conscious knowledge of falsity. Stein v. Treger, 86 U.S.App.D.C. 400, 182 F.2d 696 (1950), 49 Mich.L.Rev. 450 (1951); Atkinson v. Charlotte Builders, Inc., 232 N.C. 67, 59 S.E.2d 1 (1950), 29 N.C.L.Rev. 328 (1951). It is, however, frequently stated that proof of knowledge that the representation is false, or of reckless disregard of whether it is true or not, must be "clear, strong, and convincing", e. g., Knudson v. Weeks, 394 F.Supp. 963, 973 (W.D.Okla.1975); Lubbe v. Barba, — Nev. —, 540 P.2d 115 (1975); Bausch v. Myers, — Or. —, 541 P.2d 817 (1975). See Green, Deceit, 16 Va.L.Rev. 749 (1930). In an action on a warranty *scienter* need not be shown. Hill v. Snider, 217 N.C. 437, 8 S.E. 2d 202 (1940); 1 Street, Foundations of Legal Liability, 390 (1906).

Note here that in pursuing a remedy on the warranty plaintiff avoided the issue of *scienter* but ran afoul of the parol evidence rule; in counting on fraud he exchanged one of these hurdles for another. Could he have succeeded in any way if the representation was oral and there was no *scienter*? Should the codes be given the effect of allowing an action for damages in such a case?

See § 2–313 of the Uniform Commercial Code, page 719 above. Official Comment 8 thereto states: " * * * The provisions of subsection (2) [relating to affirmation of value and seller's opinion or commendation of goods] are included * * * since common experience discloses that some statements or predictions cannot fairly be viewed as entering into the bargain. Even as to false statements of value, however, the possibility is left open that a remedy may be provided by the law relating to fraud or misrepresentation." The Comment contains a cross-reference to U.C.C. § 1–103, which provides that " * * * the principles of law and equity * * * including the law relative to * * * fraud, misrepresentation * * * shall supplement * * * [the Code's] provisions."

CONTROL DATA CORP. v. GARRISON

Supreme Court of Minnesota, 1975.
— Minn. —, 223 N.W.2d 740.

SHERAN, CHIEF JUSTICE.

* * *

The appeal follows an action instituted by Control Data Corporation (CDC) against Allan Garrison, individually and doing business as Garrison Construction Company, for damages which resulted when a commercial building constructed by Garrison and thereafter acquired by CDC proved defective.

Garrison owned and was in possession of the building site during construction. CDC took possession of the building originally as a tenant and acquired title approximately 8 months later, on October 1, 1969. Within a year, the northwest corner of the building had settled so much that this part of the structure was unsafe for occupancy and was evacuated to permit necessary reconstruction.

At the conclusion of the trial, the jury returned a special verdict, reading in part as follows:

> "QUESTION 1: Did defendant Garrison represent to plaintiff Control Data, at the time of the events leading up to the sale here involved, that the office portion of the building in question was structurally sound?
>
> "ANSWER: Yes
> Yes or No
>
> "QUESTION 2: If you answer Question 1 'Yes', then answer this question: Was that representation false?
>
> "ANSWER: Yes
> Yes or No
>
> * * * * * * * * * *
>
> "QUESTION 3: Did that representation have to do with a past or present fact?
>
> "ANSWER: Yes
> Yes or No
>
> "QUESTION 4: Was the fact material?
>
> "ANSWER: Yes
> Yes or No

"QUESTION 5: Was that fact susceptible of knowledge?

"ANSWER: No
Yes or No

"QUESTION 6: Did defendant Garrison know that representation to be false, or in the alternative, assert it as of his or its own knowledge without knowing whether it was true or false?

"ANSWER: Yes
Yes or No

"QUESTION 7: Did defendant Garrison intend to have the plaintiff induced to act, or justified in acting upon it?

"ANSWER: Yes
Yes or No

"QUESTION 8: Was plaintiff Control Data induced to act or justified in so acting?

"ANSWER: Yes
Yes or No

"QUESTION 9: Did plaintiff Control Data act in reliance upon that representation?

"ANSWER: Yes
Yes or No

"QUESTION 10: Did plaintiff Control Data suffer damage?

"ANSWER: Yes
Yes or No

"QUESTION 11: Was damage attributable to the misrepresentation so as to be the proximate cause of the damage?

"ANSWER: Yes
Yes or No"

Damages in the amount of $106,000 were awarded to plaintiff.

The trial court directed that judgment be entered for plaintiff in the amount of $106,000. Defendant then moved for an order vacating and setting aside the special verdict and for an order granting judgment notwithstanding the verdict in favor of defendant or, in the alternative, for a new trial. These motions were denied. Judgment was entered, and this appeal followed.

An essential element in an action for fraud is that the fact misrepresented must be "susceptible of knowledge." * * * The parties have not cited any authority dealing with the precise meaning of the quoted words. Webster's New International Dictionary (2 ed. 1947) p. 2541, gives as the preferred meaning of the word "susceptible" this definition:

> " * * * Of such a nature, character, or constitution as to admit or permit; capable of submitting successfully to the

> action, process, or operation;—with *of*, followed usually by an action noun (or, less often, a verbal noun); as, a theory *susceptible* of proof; a gem *susceptible* of a brilliant polish; a theme *susceptible* of being developed (or of development)."

The essential question on this appeal is whether the answer to special interrogatory No. 5 (asserting in effect that the unsound character of the construction was not susceptible of knowledge) can be reconciled with the answers to the other interrogatories and with the entry of judgment in favor of plaintiff. We affirm because, in our view, the evidence in this case establishes as a matter of law that the representation found to have been made by the defendant, i. e. that the portion of the building in question was structurally sound, was susceptible of knowledge. * * *

Plaintiff advanced two factual theories in support of its claim that the building was not structurally sound, as Garrison represented it to be: (1) That the soil composition was such as to provide inadequate support for the structure; and (2) that pilings driven into the ground to give additional support for the structure may have been broken during the pile-driving process, making the pilings unsuitable for the purpose intended.

It is clear to us that the load-bearing capacity of the ground on which a structure is built is subject to scientific analysis by appropriate borings and tests. Where, as here, a building is constructed by the person who owns and is in possession of the land, in the absence of evidence of extraordinary circumstances, not present here, we hold that the capacity of the building site to bear the load placed on it is susceptible of knowledge. Further, the evidence is clear that defendant had preconstruction knowledge of the peculiarities of the soil at the construction site which could have caused "negative load," a phenomenon which could explain the unusual deterioration of the foundation in the northwest section of the building.

The problem is complicated, however, by the fact that in this case the jury could have determined that the building settled, not because of the failure of the site-owning builder to ascertain the load-bearing potential of the site, but, instead, because pilings driven into the ground to give added support for the structure were sheared during the process in such a way as to make the support capacity of these pilings inadequate for the intended purpose.

Defendant calls our attention to testimony given by an expert called by plaintiff:

> "Q. * * * [Do you] have an opinion as to the cause of the looseness of the piling you observed on the premises * * *?
>
> "A. Yes, sir.
>
> "Q. Will you please state that opinion?

* * * * * * * * * *

"THE WITNESS: I believe the pile was broken during driving.

* * * * * * * * * *

"Q. Could this phenomena * * * have been obtained without the knowledge of a Structural Engineer?

"A. Yes, sir.

"Q. Without the benefit of a Structural Engineer?

"A. Yes, sir.

"Q. So he, too, could have been fooled under the circumstances * * *?

"A. Yes, sir."

From this testimony defendant argues:

> " * * * Taking the evidence in the light most favorable to support the jury's decision on a question of fact, the jury could find that the pilings were broken at the time they were driven in and that the plaintiff had failed to prove, as it had the burden of doing, that Garrison could reasonably have known of that fact at or prior to the time that the building was sold to CDC."

It must be conceded that the determination of whether a piling driven into the ground has remained intact would be difficult. It is entirely possible that in the ordinary situation the cost of making such an inspection would be excessive, in view of the likelihood of breakage to be discovered. But, however difficult ascertainment of the fact might have been, defendant, who owned and was in possession of the building site, who was responsible for the construction, and who, through his agent, drove the pilings into the ground, must, we believe, be held able, as a matter of law, to measure the in-place characteristics of his work product, at least in the absence of extraordinary circumstances not disclosed by this record. A fact is "susceptible" of knowledge within the definition set out above, even though physical circumstances in a given situation make determination of that fact burdensome and difficult. The question is not whether defendant acted reasonably in assuming the pilings were intact. The question is whether a defective piling can be distinguished from one which is not defective. Except for the difficulty of making the required inspection, the fact was clearly ascertainable. It was therefore susceptible of knowledge within the meaning of the interrogatory submitted to the jury. We hold as a matter of law that the answer to interrogatory No. 5 should have been in the affirmative. This being so, the answers to the interrogatories are consistent, and the trial court's conclusion that judgment should be entered in favor of plaintiff was correct.

Affirmed.

Compare Harris v. Delco Products, 305 Mass. 362, 25 N.E.2d 740 (1940) (representations by well-digger that "we would get good sweet water" and that he knew what the conditions were on the basis of drillings held non-actionable because customer "must have known that no one could tell whether fresh or salt water would be encountered" and that the misrepresentation "must be held to have been, at most, expressions of an opinion * * *."). The court's assumption may seem inconceivable to a generation which knows not about wells, but it was essentially universal knowledge at the time.

What should be the result if the matter is not actually susceptible of knowledge but plaintiff reasonably believed it is? See *Clements*, page 770 infra.

Prophesies are apt to be regarded as opinion. See Forsberg v. Baker, 300 N.W. 371 (1941); Nielson v. Leamington Mines & Exploration Co., 87 Utah 69, 48 P.2d 439 (1935). And there was at one time a distinct disposition to treat statements of the capacity a machine, etc. would have or of the performance it would render, as statements of opinion merely. Cummings v. Cass, 52 N.J.L. 77, 18 A. 972 (1889) (that horse would go eight miles in an hour or an hour and a half); Davis Calyx Drill Co. v. Mallory, 137 F. 332, 69 L.R.A. 973 (8th Cir. 1905) (capacity of drill). But the tendency is away from such strict holdings, in cases where the statement is made by one in a position to know the facts. Connelly Co. v. Schlueter Bros., 69 Mont. 65, 220 P. 103 (1923) (capacity of road machinery); Maxwell Ice Co. v. Brackett Shaw & Lunt, 80 N.H. 236, 116 A. 34 (1921) (same of saw mill engine); Clements Auto Co. v. Service Bureau Corp., infra page 770; Williston on Sales (Rev. ed. 1948) section 202; for a reactionary case, see American Laundry Machinery Co. v. Skinner, 225 N.C. 285, 34 S.E.2d 190 (1945), 24 N.C.L.Rev. 49 (1945).

Judgments as to the capacity of people may be regarded as more speculative, e. g., Parker v. Arthur Murray, Inc., 10 Ill.App.3d 1000, 295 N.E.2d 487 (1973) (representations to plaintiff that he had "exceptional potential to be a fine and accomplished dancer" and that he was a "natural born dancer" and a "terrific dancer", in connection with sale of a course of dancing lessons, considered "mere expression of opinion", pertaining to "future or contingent events, expectations or probabilities", "speculation or opinion", rather than "averment of fact").

Statements of *value* are often just dealers' talk or opinion. But often too the circumstances make them pregnant with implications of fact, and so actionable. Hecht v. Metzler, 14 Utah 408, 48 P. 37, 60 Am.St.Rep. 906 (1897) (rental from real estate); Beaver Drug Co. v. Hatch, 61 Utah 597, 217 P. 695 (1923) (inventory value of stock of goods sold); Whitney v. Richards, 17 Utah 226, 53 P. 1122 (1898) (where representer is in position to know the value of note and victim has no experience, information, opportunity to investigate, etc.). But cf. Babb v. Bolyard, 194 Md. 603, 72 A.2d 13 (1950), 29 Tex.L.Rev. 646 (1951) (misrepresentation by second hand car dealer of list price of new Buicks, during post-war automobile shortage).

SENECA WIRE & MFG. CO. v. A. B. LEACH & CO.

Court of Appeals of New York, 1928.
247 N.Y. 1, 159 N.E. 700.

CRANE, J. At the end of the plaintiff's case the complaint was dismissed. The judgment of dismissal has been affirmed by the Appellate Division, two of the justices dissenting. We are of the opinion that the facts proved made out a cause of action, and that the rulings below must be reversed.

A. B. Leach & Co., Inc., is a New York corporation engaged in the business of selling and marketing corporate securities. Mr. V. M. Bates was its duly authorized salesman and representative. The plaintiff is an Ohio corporation, of which Lucian E. Kinn is president and general manager. The corporation, and the president individually, bought securities of the defendant through Bates, but in this opinion I shall speak of but one plaintiff, as the evidence is the same for both. Kinn told Bates, when approached about buying securities, that the company was considering the purchase only of listed securities, because the funds available were surplus funds from inventory, and might be needed on quick notice to put back in the business, and also as an additional safety. Bates recommended 8 per cent. notes of the Island Oil & Transport Corporation, calling attention to the fact that application would be made to list the securities. This occurred in September, 1921. On the 23d of that month the defendant, through its Cleveland office, wrote the plaintiff full particulars about these 8 per cent. participating secured gold notes, and stated:

"The common stock of the company is listed on the New York Stock Exchange, and application will be made to list these securities."

In closing, the letter stated:

"Mr. Bates will be glad to call on you and go into further detail on either of these issues, if you desire it."

A circular accompanying the letter also contained the statement:

"Application will be made to list these notes on the New York Stock Exchange."

When Mr. Bates again called shortly after the receipt of this letter and circular, he stated to Mr. Kinn that application "had already been made, and that the notes would be listed."

Kinn testified that, relying upon these representations, he and his company bought the notes, and paid their purchase price to the defendant.

A few months later the company went into the hands of a receiver, and the plaintiff then learned that no application had been made to list the securities, and, what is more, he was informed that the defendant never intended to make such application; that the statements made by Bates were false and untrue. The plaintiff had been deceived in making the purchase. It is not claimed that Bates made willful and fraudulent misrepresentations, but it was insisted in the immediate correspondence between the parties that Bates' statements were false in fact, and that he had knowingly stated that about which he had no positive knowledge.

The plaintiff, immediately upon ascertaining the facts, rescinded the sale, offered to return the securities, and demanded back the purchase price. * * *

We therefore have a case where the plaintiff bought securities, relying upon false representations, and immediately rescinded the transaction. Two questions remain. Were the representations material? In the first place, the parties themselves made the representations material, because Kinn told Bates that they only desired to purchase listed securities or those which were to be listed. And in the next place, Michael J. Murphy, vice president of the Federation Bank of New York, testified that it would be a favorable factor from the standpoint of a purchaser to know that securities were listed, or would be listed, on the New York Stock Exchange; that there is value in the statement that application is to be made for listing, as it is a factor in purchasing. William D. Williams, assistant secretary of the New York Stock Exchange, described the care with which securities and corporations were investigated when application was made to list them. And Kinn swore:

"I banked on that the company would not make application to list unless they were of a quality that would pass the requirements, and I took it for granted that they knew what the requirements were. I accepted the statements that an application to list meant listing."

There was, therefore, sufficient evidence regarding these representations to make their materiality a question for the jury.

Another question arises regarding the remedy. The plaintiff brought this action at law on the rescission to get its money back. It has not proved, or attempted to prove, that the misrepresentations were willfully false or fraudulently made. It seeks relief on the same ground that rescission might be maintained in equity by proving that the representations were false in fact, and misled the plaintiff into making the purchase. Bloomquist v. Farson, 222 N.Y. 375, 118 N.E. 855; Hammond v. Pennock, 61 N.Y. 145. As no equitable relief was required, it was inappropriate, if not impossible, for the plaintiff to maintain an action for rescission in equity. All it wanted was the return of its money. Action at law was therefore proper. The proof required was no different from that which would be required in equity. No reason exists for a distinction. Schank v. Schuchman, 212 N.Y. 352, 106 N.E. 127. It is not necessary, in order that a contract may be rescinded for fraud or misrepresentation, that the party making the misrepresentation should have known that it was false. Innocent misrepresentation is sufficient, and this rule applies to actions at law based upon rescission as well as to actions for rescission in equity. Continental Ins. Co. v. Equitable Trust Co. of New York, 127 Misc. Rep. 45, 215 N.Y.S. 281; 2 Williston on Sales (2d Ed.) section 632; 2 Parsons on Contracts (9th Ed.) p. 775; Montgomery Door & Sash

Co. v. Atlantic Lumber Co., 206 Mass. 144, 92 N.E. 71; McKinnon v. Vollmar, 75 Wis. 82, 43 N.W. 800, 6 L.R.A. 121, 17 Am.St.Rep. 178; American Educational Co. v. Taggert, 124 Ill.App. 567; Helvetia Copper Co. v. Hart-Parr Co., 137 Minn. 321, 163 N.W. 665.

That a purchaser who has relied upon a material misrepresentation may rescind the transaction, if he acts without delay, is established by such authorities as Weigel v. Cook, 237 N.Y. 136, 142 N.E. 444; Schank v. Schuchman, 212 N.Y. 352, 106 N.E. 127; Vail v. Reynolds, 118 N.Y. 297, 23 N.E. 301; Smith v. Countryman, 30 N.Y. 655.

A distinction in the nature of the proof, therefore, does not exist between the action at law and the action in equity, but does exist between the action in rescission and the action for damages based upon fraud and deceit. Here there must be proof of willful and fraudulent misrepresentation, knowingly made, resulting in damage. Reno v. Bull, 226 N.Y. 546, 124 N.E. 144. * * *

Judgments reversed.[4]

For the availability of rescission as a remedy for breach of warranty, see 2 Williston, op. cit., supra, sections 608, 608a.

The present court's attitude towards *scienter* in a case of rescission is common but not universal. See e. g. Chattanooga Beauty Supply Co. v. Fanin, 61 Ga.App. 736, 7 S.E.2d 302 (1940); note 29 N.C. L.Rev. 328, 330 (1951). The issues that are properly made in such a case are triable to the jury.

The notion underlying rescission "at law" is that the bargain, being tainted with fraud, is voidable at the election of the victim. The election is exercised by his returning what he has received in the transaction, or by making tender of it if return is not accepted. He is then entitled to get back what he has parted with, in an appropriate legal action, or to treat any obligations assumed by him as at an end. Procedurally, the effects of rescission may be called into play in one of three ways:

1. Suit for the consideration parted with and retained by defendant as in the instant case. Where the seller of goods seeks such a remedy, a possessory action or a petition for reclamation (in bankruptcy) may be the appropriate form of remedy.

2. As a defense to an action, e. g. on the purchase price. See e. g., Societe Titanor v. Sherman Machine & Iron Works, 172 Okl. 213, 45 P.2d 144 (1935).

3. As an avoidance of a defense to an action. Typical is a suit on a tort or contract obligation to which defendant interposes the defense of accord and satisfaction (compromise and release). To avoid the accord, plaintiff claims it was procured by misrepresentation and has been rescinded (thus leaving the original claim intact).

4. In a comment, 29 Tex.L.Rev. 644 (1951), there is a good treatment of materiality, pointing out that the right to rely is generally gauged on an objective basis, but that if special factors show that defendant knew plaintiff would in fact rely on the representation, then it would be material. See also Keeton, Actionable Misrepresentation, 2 Okla.L.Rev. 56, 59–60 (1949).

See e. g. Whitney v. Richards, 17 Utah 226, 53 P. 1122 (1898); Gould v. Cayuga County Nat. Bank, 86 N.Y. 75 (1881); with which compare N.Y.C.P.A. § 112g; note, 15 Minn.L.Rev. 805 (1931).

Where the action, defense, or avoidance is regarded as resting on the theory of a rescission "at law," return or tender of what he has received by the rescinding party *before* suit is regarded as a condition precedent to the successful use of the theory. Chattanooga Beauty Supply Co. v. Fann, supra; Gould v. Cayuga County Nat. Bank, supra. See 2 Williston, op. cit., supra, section 649a, for exceptions to rule. If there has been no tender, should the court avoid this difficulty by regarding the claim as an equitable proceeding for a rescission? See Gould v. Cayuga County Nat. Bank, supra; note 11 Minn.L.Rev. 277 (1927). Of course, in some cases the question of restoring the benefits of the bargain is more fundamental than the formalities of tender before suit. Consider the availability of the rescission technique in Harris v. Delco Prod. Co., supra, p. 764; Glanzer v. Shepard, infra, p. 809.

The right to rescind either by returning the consideration or by action for a rescission may be lost by conduct affirming the bargain or by an unreasonable delay, if either comes after discovery of the facts. Prosser, Law of Torts 689 (4th ed. 1971). Cf. Neff v. Engler, 205 Cal. 484, 271 P. 744 (1928) (contrasting rescission with damage action in this respect).

Compare the remedy of rescission with other alternatives with respect to the measure, and the difficulties of proof of damages in various situations.

The federal Securities Act of 1933 and Securities and Exchange Act of 1934 have provided statutory grounds for civil liability for misrepresentations affecting securities in transactions which are subject to federal jurisdiction. The principal provisions include Sections 11, 12(2) and 17(a) of the 1933 Act, 15 U.S.C.A. §§ 77k, 77*l*(2) and 77q(a); and, under the 1934 Act, sections 10(b) and 14(a), 15 U.S.C.A. §§ 78j(b) and 78n, and Rules 10b–5, 17 C.F.R. § 240.10b–5, and 14a–9(a), 17 C.F.R. § 240.14a–9(a). Under these provisions the common law requirements of reliance, scienter, causation and materiality are often substantially modified or eliminated. See, generally, 3 L. Loss, Securities Regulation 1431 et seq. (2d ed. 1961) and 6 id. 3534 et seq. (1969). For representative opinions see Gerstle v. Gamble Skogmo, Inc., 478 F.2d 1281 (2d Cir. 1973); Madigan, Incorporated v. Goodman, 498 F.2d 233 (7th Cir. 1974); Chris-Craft Industries, Inc. v. Piper Aircraft Corporation, 516 F.2d 172 (2d Cir. 1975); Hilton v. Mumaw, 522 F.2d 588 (9th Cir. 1975); Odette v. Shearson-Hammill & Co., Inc., 394 F.Supp. 946 (S.D.N.Y.1975); Goodman v. Poland, 395 F.Supp. 660 (D.Md.1975); and Fox v. Kane-Miller Corp., 398 F.Supp. 609 (D.Md.1975); but check against Ernst & Ernst v. Hochfelder, —— U.S. ——, 96 S.Ct. 1375, —— L.Ed.2d —— (1976).

CLEMENTS AUTO COMPANY v. SERVICE BUREAU CORPORATION

United States Court of Appeals for the Eighth Circuit, 1971.
444 F.2d 169.

HEANEY, CIRCUIT JUDGE. The Service Bureau Corporation, a wholly-owned subsidiary of International Business Machines Corporation, appeals from a judgment awarding SM Supply Company [5] $480,811 in damages, the basis of the award being actionable misrepresentations made by SBC to SM in connection with the sale of data processing services. * * *

SBC is engaged in the business of electronic data processing, offering to the public its services in eighty-four branch offices throughout the United States. It sells data processing services in the following areas: payroll, personnel records, accounts receivable, billing, sales accounting, marketing studies, cost accounting, inventory record, budgets and general accounting.

SM operates wholesale supply houses at Mankato and Rochester, Minnesota, and at Eau Claire, Wisconsin. It operated a similar supply house in LaCrosse, Wisconsin, through 1965. It deals in automotive parts and supplies, electrical construction materials, and electronic parts, supplies and equipment. * * *

* * * In February, 1963, SM signed two contracts dated December 20, 1962, under which SBC agreed to provide certain basic data processing services to SM. * * * Twelve additional contracts providing for additional services were signed by the parties during the succeeding four years. * * *

The nature of the data processing services provided during the four-year relationship between SBC and SM may be conveniently categorized into three basic stages. Initially, SBC automated SM's accounting and billing. At the same time, SBC used this input material to prepare certain monthly sales analysis reports and a weekly report of inventory movement. The inventory reports contained a six-week history of sales for all of SM's inventory. * * *

Second generation inventory reports began in January, 1965, and continued through December 4, 1965. These were bi-weekly reports which provided a twelve-week movement history, a record of inventory purchases, receipts and inter-branch transfers, and, for the first time, an on-hand balance of items for certain vendors selected by SM.

Finally, in December, 1965, SM signed a contract to obtain a third generation of inventory reports. These reports were to contain a detailed history for each item for the previous year, a movement history during specified months, an on-hand figure, and a computation of the number of weeks' supply of each item on hand. * * *

5. Business name of Clements Auto Company.

The services proved to be unsatisfactory to SM. It charges that the input method was slow and expensive, and that the reports were too error-prone and voluminous to be of use in purchasing inventory. SM finally terminated all contracts with SBC in January, 1967.

SM then brought the present lawsuit against SBC in September of 1967. It proceeded on the theories of rescission, breach of implied warranty, breach of contract, reformation and fraudulent misrepresentation. SBC counterclaimed for payments due.

The action was tried to the court without a jury. * * * The court denied recovery on all grounds other than misrepresentation, but found that SBC had made one central actionable misrepresentation to SM, *i. e.*, that the proposed data processing system would, when fully implemented, be capable of providing SM sufficient information in a form such that when properly utilized, it would constitute an effective and efficient tool to be used in inventory control.

It further found that SBC had made several other specific actionable misrepresentations to SM:

> (1) that the only way SM would ever get an inventory control system such as that in use at the Chevrolet dealership would be by automating the firm's accounting;
>
> (2) that there were controls built into the system which were adequate to prevent any but a minimal number of errors;
>
> (3) that Friden Flexowriters were a suitable input device to be used in the data processing system * * *; and
>
> (4) that weekly sales management reports provided by the contract would allow management by exception.

* * * [T]he trial court properly relied on Hanson v. Ford Motor Company, 278 F.2d 586 (8th Cir. 1960), in enumerating the essential elements of a fraud action in Minnesota:

> "1. There must be a representation;
>
> "2. That representation must be false;
>
> "3. It must have to do with a past or present fact;
>
> "4. That fact must be material;
>
> "5. It must be susceptible of knowledge;
>
> "6. The representer must know it to be false, or in the alternative, must assert it as of his known knowledge without knowing whether it is true or false;
>
> "7. The representer must intend to have the other person induced to act, or justified in acting upon it;
>
> "8. That person must be so induced to act or so justified in acting;
>
> "9. That person's action must be in reliance upon the representation;

"10. That person must suffer damage;

"11. That damage must be attributable to the misrepresentation, that is, the statement must be the proximate cause of the injury."

Id. at 591.

It is important to emphasize that in Minnesota, the element of scienter, or intent to deceive, or even recklessness, is not necessary to actionable fraud. As the Minnesota Supreme Court stated in Swanson v. Domning, 251 Minn. 110, 86 N.W.2d 716, 720–721 (1957):

> "It is immaterial whether a statement made as of one's own knowledge is made innocently or knowingly. An intent to deceive no longer is necessary. Nor is it necessary to prove that defendants knew the representations were false.
>
> " * * * It is not necessary that the statement be recklessly or carelessly made. It makes no difference how it is made if it is made as an affirmation of which defendant has knowledge and it is in fact untrue. The right of recovery in a case of this kind is based on the fact that such statement, being untrue in fact, relied upon by the other party in entering into the transaction, has resulted in the loss to him which he should not be required to bear." (Footnotes omitted.) * *

While accepting the above as a correct statement of Minnesota law, SBC raises two arguments in opposition to the trial court's finding of liability for fraud. It first argues that the trial court erred in applying the Minnesota law of fraud to the present situation. The argument is rooted in what SBC considers to be a legal inconsistency in the trial court's findings. It is developed by SBC as follows:

> (1) The trial court found certain aforementioned representations made to SM to be actionable under the Minnesota law of fraud.
>
> (2) The trial court found that these same representations did not give rise to an express warranty because there was no valid agreement by the parties incorporating these representations into the contract, and that a disclaimer in the various contracts effectively negated all implied warranties.
>
> (3) Under the relevant law, innocent misrepresentations and warranties, either express or implied, are substantially similar in nature.
>
> (4) The passage of the Uniform Commercial Code by the legislature evinced an intent to have that body of law control all commercial transactions. * * *
>
> We cannot agree that this argument dictates a result other than that reached by the trial court. * * *

The first argument raised by SBC necessarily rests on two assumptions, both of which must be valid to sustain SBC's position:

(1) That the trial court's ruling as to the warranties was a correct assessment of Minnesota law.

(2) That the Minnesota Supreme Court would not permit the same representations to result in liability for fraud, but not for breach of warranty.

Assuming, arguendo, that the trial court correctly found the warranty disclaimer valid, we nevertheless believe that the Minnesota Supreme Court would find liability for fraud. SBC's conclusion that liability for innocent misrepresentation cannot exist without liability for breach of warranty compels two further conclusions:

(1) A contract provision which validly negates warranties is sufficient to negate liability for innocent misrepresentations.

(2) The Minnesota Supreme Court would be willing to distinguish between innocent and intentional misrepresentations. Both of these conclusions appear to be contrary to the main thrust of Minnesota law. * * *

* * * In the case of National Equipment Corporation v. Volden, 190 Minn. 596, 252 N.W. 444 (1934), the Minnesota Court dealt with a fraud action based on misrepresentations in the sale of a "dumptor," a piece of construction equipment used in earth moving operations. The court first * * * [ruled] that parole evidence was properly introduced to prove that the contract had been procured by fraudulent representations. It then went on to find that fraud had been committed and, in so doing, relied on its earlier opinion in Helvetia Copper Co. v. Hart-Parr Co., 137 Minn. 321, 163 N.W. 665 (1917), for its definition of fraud. In *Helvetia Copper*, the court had specifically held that an action in fraud required no showing of scienter:

> "The damage to plaintiff, arising from the fact that * * * [the representations were false] * * * is the same whether the representations * * * were known to be false by defendant, and made with intent to deceive, or whether they were made innocently and in perfect good faith. The good faith of defendant is no defense.
>
> * * *
>
> "Defendant was the manufacturer of the engine, and presumptively possessed of knowledge of its condition and whether the improvements suggested would overcome the defects theretofore complained of. The representations were unqualified and must be treated as assertions of a fact within the knowledge of defendant, *the falsity of which constitutes fraud as a matter of law.*" (Emphasis added.)

Id. at 163 N.W. 667.

The court in *National Equipment* then faced the issue pertinent here. The sales contract contained a provision that:

> "* * * no representations made by an agent not included herein shall be binding * * *."

The court * * * [found] the contract provision ineffective to negative the fraud action:

> "A party who makes fraudulent representations to induce another to make a contract cannot escape liability for his fraud by incorporating a disclaimer of fraud in the contract."

Id. at 252 N.W. 445.

* * * Considering the court's definition of fraud and the fact that we can find no indication in the opinion that deceitful intent was in fact demonstrated, we believe this decision must be read as holding that a general disclaimer clause is ineffective to negate reliance on even innocent misrepresentations. This view is further supported by Goldfine v. Johnson, 208 Minn. 449, 294 N.W. 459 (1940) * * *.

There is no indication that the disclaimer of warranty negates reliance on false representations made with or without intent to deceive.

The only situation in which the Minnesota courts have held that a contract provision negatives a claim of fraud is where the provision explicitly states a fact completely antithetical to the claimed misrepresentations. * * *

SBC's argument that the passage of the Uniform Commercial Code would lead the Minnesota Court to a contrary result is unpersuasive.

* * * [T]he Uniform Commercial Code was, in part, a replacement for the Uniform Sales Act which had been the basis of existing commercial law in Minnesota since 1917. * * * A governing policy of national uniformity in commercial transactions was a motivating influence in the passage of both of these uniform acts. Moreover, the passage of the U.C.C. did not substantially alter Minnesota law as to disclaimer of warranties. These factors tend to undercut SBC's contention that the passage of the U.C.C. would alter the relationship in Minnesota between the law of fraud and the law of warranty. Similarly, the fact that the U.C.C. has not brought a radical change to Minnesota contract law would give added authority to the earlier decisions of the Minnesota Court.

In viewing these earlier decisions, we believe it is relevant that the Minnesota Court has stated that:

> "The fact that one who has been defrauded has a remedy on the contract or on a guaranty or warranty is not any impediment or defense to an action for the fraud or deceit. * * *"
>
> Osborn v. Will, 183 Minn. 205, 236 N.W. 197, 200 (1931). * * *

SBC argues alternatively that even if the trial court was correct in applying the Minnesota law of fraud to this situation, it erred in finding that the representations proven by SM met the requirements for actionable fraud. Specifically, SBC contends that the representations found actionable by the trial court cannot be considered "past or present facts susceptible of knowledge" or that they were such that SM "was induced or justified in acting upon" them. * * *

We believe that the trial court was correct in finding that the representations as a whole were more than mere predictions and that SM relied upon them in entering into the contract.

We have previously stated the central representation to be "that the proposed data processing system would, when fully implemented, be capable of providing SM sufficient information in a form such that when properly utilized, it would constitute an effective and efficient tool to be used in inventory control." While this statement is in a sense a prediction of what the system will do, it is also, under existing Minnesota law, a statement of the inherent capabilities of a particular product. * * *

SBC relies to a great extent on our decision in First Acceptance Corp. v. Kennedy, 8 Cir., 194 F.2d 819 (1952), wherein we held that, under Iowa law, statements to the effect that an air conditioning system "would do the job" were statements of opinion rather than fact.

In our view, *First Acceptance* is factually distinguishable. In *First Acceptance,* the party bringing the fraud action had designed a completely novel method of storing onions. He realized that his new system was somewhat of a "revolutionary experiment" and that his present air conditioning would be inadequate to preserve onions if he implemented the new storage system. He thereafter came into contact with an employee of an air conditioning company. Together they studied the problem carefully, and ultimately an air conditioning system was designed and installed by the air conditioning company. The system was unsuccessful. A large number of onions deteriorated and a large financial loss was incurred.

In finding that representations that the air conditioning system "would do the job" were predictions only, the Court relied heavily upon the fact that both parties knew that the storage system and the air conditioning system were completely new and experimental concepts. The onion grocer recognized the problems he faced and had enlisted the aid of the air conditioning expert. However, in the circumstances of the case, it was unreasonable to expect either party to be completely assured of the success of the venture. * * *

In a less extraordinary situation, the Minnesota Supreme Court has indicated that the statement that "an ice machine, * * * when installed, could and would keep the buyer's ice box at a temperature low enough to prevent meat from spoiling" was a statement of an existing fact—the inherent capacity or power of the machine. Schmitt v. Ornes Esswein & Co., * * * [149 Minn. 370, 183 N.W. 840 (1921)].

While the representation in question here would appear to fall somewhere between these two cases, we think that there was sufficient evidence from which the trial court could determine that the statement was one of fact rather than opinion and could reasonably have been relied upon as such. SBC was clearly an expert in the data processing area and was known to have extensive experience in the area of inventory control. There is nothing in the record to indicate that SM presented or thought it presented any special problems in regard to designing data processing services for inventory control. SM sought inventory control and was told by the expert in the field that the system designed would provide it.

* * *

SBC next argues that there was no actual or justifiable reliance by SM on any representations made by SBC. We think this contention is without merit when applied to the initial relationship between SM and SBC. * * *

* * * [W]e take notice of the inequality of knowledge as between the two parties. SBC was clearly the expert in the computer field and must be held responsible for superior knowledge in that field. The Minnesota Court has frequently looked to the relative knowledge of the parties in determining whether reliance on the representations was justified. * * *

* * * SBC urges * * * that because of contract provisions, the total award cannot exceed the total charges for services, and that no special or consequential damages can be awarded * * *.

The contracts between SBC and SM contained the following provision:

> "* * * SBC's liability with respect to this agreement is limited to the total charge for the services provided herein and no special or consequential damages may be recovered."

SBC argues that this provision validly limits the damages which can be awarded here. * * *

In many ways, this question is substantially similar to SBC's earlier contention that a merger and warranty provision is effective to negate fraud. As it did there, SBC concedes that the contract provision is ineffective against intentional deceit, but argues it must be given effect where the fraud is based on "innocent misrepresentations." SBC again emphasizes the anomaly of obtaining different results in contract actions as opposed to fraud actions which do not include an element of bad faith.

However, we remain unconvinced that this difference in result would lead the Minnesota Court to give effect to the contract provision. In reaching this decision, we have relied to a large extent on our earlier analysis of the Minnesota law of fraud vis-a-vis Minnesota contract law. Minnesota's strong policy of providing an effective remedy in fraud would be substantially undermined were we to give effect to this severe restriction on the amount of liability. Having previously held that Minnesota would not give effect to a contract provision which would negate the fact of liability, we believe it inconsistent to hold that the court would then give effect to a provision limiting the amount of liability.[6] * * *

The appellant's final contention is that evidence as to damages is so speculative and the evidence as to benefits received so negligible that the trial court erred in granting any award. We cannot agree. The Supreme Court and this Court have stated on a number of occasions that, once the fact of damages has been established, the courts are allowed considerable leeway in arriving at the amount of damages. Eastman Kodak Co. of New York v. Southern Photo Materials Corp., 273 U.S. 359, 47 S.Ct. 400, 71 L.Ed. 684 (1927) * * *.[7]

EXCERPT FROM RESTATEMENT OF TORTS, SECOND (TENT. DRAFT NO. 3, 1958)

524A. Misrepresentation in Sale, Rental or Exchange Transaction

(1) One who, in a sale, rental or exchange transaction with another, makes a misrepresentation of a material fact for the purpose of inducing the other to act or to refrain from action in reliance upon it, is subject to liability to the other for the harm caused by his justifiable reliance upon the misrepresentation, even though it is made without knowledge of its falsity or negligence.

(2) If such a misrepresentation is made without knowledge of its falsity or negligence, the damages recoverable for it are limited to the difference between the value of what the other has parted with and the value of what he has received in the transaction.[8]

6. A recent case comment has reached the opposite conclusion. 54 Minn.L. Rev. 846 (1970). The article, however, is primarily a theoretical discussion of what the law ought to be, rather than an attempt to predict what the Minnesota Supreme Court would decide. Further, its analysis of the policy considerations in this area appears to deviate from the orthodox analyses of the Minnesota Court. Its reliance on our decision in Lack Industries, Incorporated v. Ralston Purina Company, 327 F.2d 266 (8th Cir. 1964), for the general proposition that "the degree of fault warrants a narrower liability for nonintentional than for intentional misrepresentation" is misplaced. *Lack Industries* stands only for the proposition that statements concerning future action will not, in the absence of intentional deceit, support an action in fraud. [From original, renumbered; other notes in original omitted.]

7. Compare Hill, Damages for Innocent Misrepresentation, 73 Colum.L. Rev. 679 (1973): "If the defendant's innocent, non-negligent representation is promissory, it should be governed by the law relating to broken promises—contract law. * * * If such a representation is not promissory, it should not be the basis of liability in damages (apart from what may be recoverable in an action in rescission). A representation is deemed promissory within the meaning of the foregoing if a promise to 'make good' the representation is express or can fairly be implied * * *.", id. at 684. Also see Restatement of Torts, Second § 552B (Tent. Draft No. 10, 1964).

8. See Hill, Breach of Contract as a Tort, 74 Colum.L.Rev. 40 (1974).

SELMAN v. SHIRLEY

Supreme Court of Oregon, 1938.
161 Or. 582, 85 P.2d 384.

ROSSMAN, JUSTICE.

* * *

The property with which this suit is concerned is 160 acres of land * * * [which] the plaintiffs agreed to purchase this property for a consideration of $2,000 * * *.

The findings state: "The defendant, H. E. Shirley, knowingly and falsely represented to plaintiff that there was at least 4000 cords of wood on said premises; that said representations was false and was made by defendant H. E. Shirley with the intention of inducing plaintiffs to purchase said premises; that the plaintiffs in purchasing said premises relied upon said representations."

We have read carefully the transcript of evidence and are well satisfied that it fully supports the above findings. The uncontradicted testimony also indicates that Shirley represented that timber of that kind was worth fifty cents a cord as stumpage. These were material representations, and it is clear that the plaintiffs would not have signed the contract of purchase had they not been deceived into the belief that 4,000 cords of firewood were upon the place. * * *

* * * As a matter of fact there were only 200 cords of wood upon the property. * * *

The plaintiffs also claim that they were deceived by a representation that a stream which they saw upon their visit to the land in May, 1933, flowed throughout the year and supplied enough water to irrigate ten acres. Besides inquiring about the timber, the plaintiffs had also inquired of Blakely [defendant's real estate agent] about the stream. In a letter to them Blakely stated: "This stream does run the year round and the owner told me the next day after you were here that it is a dandy trout stream and that he has caught lots of trout in it. There is plenty of water in this stream, as I told you, to irrigate ten acres of the farm. You need have no fear that you wouldn't always have good water in this creek." Blakely knew nothing concerning the stream from his own observations and swore that the letter was a true narrative of Shirley's statement. A witness who had overheard the conversation between the two men corroborated Blakely, stating that Shirley had said, "It was a year round stream and that he (Shirley) had irrigated ten acres." * * * However, the witnesses swore that the stream dries up in the summer months and, under the best of circumstances, does not flow sufficient water to irrigate even a small garden patch. The circuit court found that Shirley had made the statement contained in Blakely's letter, but made no finding concerning its truthfulness. We are satisfied that the evidence warrants a conclusion that the representation was false.

The findings state that the property was "of the fair market value of $2,000 at the time said contract was entered into, to-wit: July 1, 1933; that plaintiffs have suffered no damages, having agreed to pay $2,000 for said premises." The sole issue upon which we deem it necessary to express an opinion is whether the plaintiffs are entitled to (1) the benefits of their bargain; or (2) no damages because the market value of the land equals the sum which they agreed to pay.

* * * [T]he plaintiffs retained possession of the property after they discovered the fraud which had been practiced upon them. It has been many times stated by this court that a defrauded party is not required to rescind the contract in order to sue for deceit, and that if he affirms the contract he does not thereby waive his right to recover damages for the fraud which had been practiced upon him.

The plaintiffs argue that they are entitled to the benefit of their bargain which contemplated that they should have, not only 160 acres of land, but also a growth of timber upon the land aggregating 4000 cords and a good irrigating stream; and that the rule which measures their damages should be based upon that premise. The defendants contend that this court has rejected the benefit-of-the-bargain rule in favor of the rule which grants damages equal only to the out-of-pocket loss. The rule championed by the plaintiffs would certainly be available if this action were based upon a warranty and were, therefore, contractual in nature. * * *

The rule which gives to the defrauded party the benefit of his bargain is favored by the textbook writers. The following is quoted from Williston on Contracts (Rev.Ed.) § 1392: "Not all courts allow the same damages to a buyer who has been induced to buy by fraudulent representations and sues for the deceit as to a buyer who sues for breach of warranty. The contrary view, confining the damages in deceit to the value of what the plaintiff parted with, less the value of what he received, has the support of the Supreme Court of the United States, and of some state courts. This also seems to be the law of England. At first sight it may seem that the latter rule is clearly and universally correct, confining as it does the plaintiff's recovery to a restitution of what he lost by entering into the transaction. The real explanation of the broader rule, at least in cases of sales of goods, seems to be that the defendant in deceit is not simply a fraudulent person; he is a warrantor of the truth of his statements. The injured person may, because of fraud, elect to rescind the transaction and claim restitution of what he has parted with, or he may demand that the representations be made good. Ordinary warranties where no fraud exists may be enforced by action of tort. The addition of the element of deceit cannot deprive the injured person of the rights which would be his if this element were lacking, and if the representation on which he relied were a warranty and nothing more. Nor is a strictness of pleading to be defended that denies to a plaintiff the relief that would be his if he omitted an allegation that the representation of the quality of goods, of which he complains, was fraudulent. A practical reason for the enforcement of the broader rule may be found in the fact that under the other rule a fraudulent person can in no event lose anything by his fraud. He runs the chance of making a profit if he successfully carries out his plan and is not afterward brought to account for it; and if he is brought to account, he at least will lose nothing by his misconduct. * * * Any universal statement, therefore, that the damages for fraudulent misrepresentation are the difference between the law governing sales of goods and that governing other transactions may explain some apparently inconsistent decisions."

Sedgwick on Damages (9th Ed.), § 1027, in stating the measure of damages where fraud is employed in the course of a sale of land, declares: "In such actions, as in actions for fraud in the sale of chattels, it has usually been held that the measure of damages is the difference in value between the land as it would have been if as represented and as it actually was."

The rule is thus stated in 27 C.J., Fraud, § 243, p. 92: "The measure of the damages sustained by the purchaser where a purchase has been induced by fraud, is according to the weight of authority, the difference between the real value of the property purchased and the value which it would have had had the representations been true. This rule is based upon the theory that a defrauded party is entitled to the benefit of his bargain and should be placed in the same position that he would have occupied had the false representations upon which he acted been true."

Sutherland on Damages (4th Ed.), § 1172, in criticizing the out-of-pocket-loss rule, states: "As said by Mr. Justice Gray, 'to allow the plaintiff only the difference between the real value of the property and the price which he was induced to pay for it would be to make any advantage lawfully secured to the innocent purchaser in the original bargain inure to the wrongdoer; and, in proportion as the original price was low, would afford a protection to the party who had broken, at the expense of the party who was ready to abide by, the terms of the contract.' The amount paid is evidence of the value, but on principle and according to the general course of decision is not conclusive of the value as it was represented to be."

However, the Restatement of the Law of Torts, § 549, embraces the out-of-pocket-loss rule. We quote from it the following:

"The measure of damages which the recipient of a fraudulent misrepresentation is entitled to recover from its maker as damages under the rule stated in § 525 is the pecuniary loss which results from the falsity of the matter misrepresented, including

"(a) the difference between the value of the thing bought, sold or exchanged and its purchase price or the value of the thing exchanged for it,

"(b) * * *"

Williston on Contracts (Rev.Ed.), § 1392, referring to the section of the Restatement just quoted, declares that it "adopts the minority rule." Professor Williston continues that under the maxim adopted by the Restatement, "if fraudulent representations constitute a warranty also, recovery may be had on that basis"; that is, the defrauded party obtains the benefit of his bargain. * * *

Professor Charles T. McCormick, in a treatise appearing in 28 Ill.Law Rev. 1050, states: "In few of the states have the courts seized upon one of these formulas and applied it with entire consistency in all classes of cases. * * * In land sales also many courts seem to treat differently cases where the quality or character of the land has been misrepresented from those in which the false statement relates to its title, identity or quantity." As a footnote to this statement he quotes from that part of Mr. Justice Harris' opinion in Lichtenthaler v. Clow, supra, which indicates that the rule governing the measurement of damages in fraud actions has been applied in a flexible manner. In a preceding paragraph of this opinion we set forth the same excerpt. * * * McCormick approves the nonuniform manner in which these rules for the measurement of damages have been applied by the courts, and urges that "a technique should be developed by which both of these formulas shall be made available, so that one or the other may be used as the circumstances of the case may demand." * * *

We come now to an effort to reconcile our decisions and to deduce a rule therefrom. First of all, it is evident that the party guilty of fraud is liable for such damages as naturally and proximately resulted from the fraud. This is the universal rule. Next, our decisions warrant the conclusions: (1) If the defrauded party is content with the recovery of only the amount that he actually lost, his damages will be measured under that rule; (2) if the fraudulent representation also amounted to a warrany, recovery may be had for loss of the bargain because a fraud accompanied by a broken promise should cost the wrongdoer as much as the latter alone; (3) where the circumstances disclosed by the proof are so vague as to cast virtually no light upon the value of the property had it conformed to the representations, the court will award damages equal only to the loss sustained; and (4) where, * * * the damages under the benefit-of-the-bargain rule are proved with sufficient certainty, that rule will be employed.

In the present instance, the plaintiffs are clearly the victims of a fraud. The representations which deceived them concerned the quality or condition of the property; they were willful, were phrased in positive terms and were made in writing. They were made with knowledge upon the part of Shirley that the plaintiffs were ignorant of the facts and desired information. A determination of the value of the property, had it been as represented, does not carry one into the field of conjecture, but resort may be had to values for which Shirley and other witnesses vouched; that is, 4,000 cords of stumpage were worth $2,000. Had Shirley's representations been true, the plaintiffs would now have, not only the land, but also the timber. They should not be compelled, because Shirley was dishonest, to be content with the land only. Through false representations Shirley should not be permitted to obtain for the logged-off land a sum which would have been refused him had he been honest and truthful. In this case we are satisfied that Shirley must have known that through his deceit the plaintiffs would lose the benefit of the bargain which he was inducing them to enter into. Thus, we get back to the one rule which is of universal application: the party guilty of the fraud is liable for such damages as naturally and proximately result from the fraud. We conclude that the plaintiffs are entitled to damages awarded upon the basis of 50 cents per cord for the difference between the represented 4,000 cords and the actual 200 cords. The balancing of these accounts will indicate that there is now $650 owing to the plaintiffs. * * * It may appear that under these circumstances the plaintiffs will obtain the land for virtually nothing. There is, however, substantial evidence in the record indicating that without the timber and water for irrigation the land possesses virtually no value. While it is true that Shirley, Blakely and two other real estate agents expressed the opinion that this logged-off tract was worth $2,000, the effect of this evidence is greatly discredited by the representation, which induced the plaintiffs to make the purchase, that the land plus the 4,000 cords and served by a good irrigating stream was worth $2,000. But, be this as it may, courts ought not to be overnice in trying to save one who has willfully deceived another from the vicissitudes resulting from his wrong.

* * *

RAND and KELLY, JJ., concur.

BELT, JUSTICE (dissenting).

* * *

The measure of damages set forth in the majority opinion enables plaintiffs to acquire the 160-acre ranch for $100. If the representation had been 8,000 cords of wood, plaintiffs would get the ranch for nothing and the sum of $1,900 in addition. As stated in Curtis v. Buzard, 254 Pa. 61, 98 A. 777, and quoted in note 27 C.J. § 244, p. 96: "One defrauded 'can deduct from the purchase-money the difference between what he agreed and what it was then actually worth, and in our opinion no more, for if he could exceed that measure of damages a vendee of land might get a man's land for nothing, by showing that had the land been as represented it would have been worth enough more than its actual value to wipe out all the purchase-money, and thus give the vendee the land for nothing.' "

* * *

Neither am I able to agree that the land without the timber as represented is "virtually of no value." The conclusion as expressed in the majority opinion is contrary to the findings of the trial court and is not supported by the record. * * *

The combination rule of the Oregon court has been followed by Idaho, Massachusetts, New Jersey and Washington, and is adopted in § 549 of the Restatement Second. According to the Restatement Reporter, nine states plus the District of Columbia have followed the out-of-pocket rule (Arkansas, California, Iowa, Maryland, Minnesota, Montana, New York, Pennsylvania and Texas). As to New York, however, the leading case, Reno v. Bull, 226 N.Y. 546, 124 N.E. 144 (1919), is somewhat qualified by statement in Hotaling v. A. B. Leach Co., 247 N.Y. 84, 159 N.E. 870 (1928); in Texas the rule has been changed by statute for real estate and corporate stock transactions; and Maryland has since endorsed the *Selman* rule, Hinkle v. Rockville Motor Co., 262 Md. 502, 278 A.2d 42 (1971). Thirty-one states are said to provide only for the benefit of the bargain. For detailed citations see Restatement of Torts Second, Tent. Draft No. 10, 161–62 (1964); compare Restatement Second § 552B.

Expenses incurred because of fraud are recoverable and so, usually, is "consequential" damage which proximately results from it. See Maxwell Ice Co. v. Brackett Shaw & Lunt Co., 80 N.H. 236, 116 A. 34 (1921) (temporary shut-down of mill); Applied Data Processing, Inc. v. Burroughs Corp., 394 F.Supp. 505 (D.Conn.1975); Banco Frances E. Brasileiro S. A. v. Doe, 36 N.Y.2d 592, 331 N.E.2d 502 (1975) (special damages allowed for penalty imposed on illegal foreign exchange transaction, in action for rescission of the transaction). But some courts have applied the rule of Hadley v. Baxendale, 9 Exch. 341 (1854) in this connection. McCormick, Damages, 459, 460 (1935).

Under the loss of bargain rule it may be hard to prove what value the thing would have had if the representations had been true. See McCormick, op. cit., supra, section 122. But it seems that the price actually paid for it will afford some evidence of this. Morrell v. Wiley, 119 Conn. 578, 178 A. 121 (1935). (Note that where this evidence is accepted there is no difference in effect between the two rules.)

A more serious question (which besets both rules alike) is one dealt with in Hotaling v. A. B. Leach & Co., 247 N.Y. 84, 159 N.E. 870 (1928), where something fraudulently sold, e. g., securities, has a market value at the time of sale equivalent to the amount paid, value is subject to fluctuations based on market conditions as well as intrinsic worth, and item is purchased for investment. Difficulties which courts have sometimes been unable to surmount spring from (1) want of proof of value at the time of sale, see Kinnear v. Prows, 81 Utah 135, 16 P.2d 1094 (1932); Guaranty Mortg. Co. v. Flint, 66 Utah 128, 240 P. 175 (1925); (2) want of proof that the fact misrepresented actually contributed to a later decline in value (even if that would otherwise be considered as a basis for computing the loss) Morrell v. Wiley, supra. These requirements cannot always be met. Where they cannot be, will plaintiff ever be able to avoid them by resorting to rescission? The methods for measuring damages in such a proceeding are neatly contrasted with those in deceit in Mullin v. Gano, 299 Pa. 251, 149 A. 488 (1930) (land sale case). See also Pomeroy, Equity Jurisprudence, section 898a (5th ed. 1941); and Restatement of Torts § 549, comment (c) (in case of widespread belief in misrepresentation, value to be determined after discovery of the fraud).

SEEGER v. ODELL

Supreme Court of California, 1941.
18 Cal.2d 409, 115 P.2d 977, 136 A.L.R. 1291.

TRAYNOR, JUSTICE. Plaintiffs have appealed from a judgment on the pleadings in favor of defendants A. J. Odell, Mary Gibbs, William G. McAdoo and R. T. Colter. The allegations of the complaint must therefore be considered true as though the complaint were before the court upon a general demurrer. * * *

The complaint alleges: The plaintiffs, an elderly couple, were the owners of a lot located in Huntington Beach, California. In 1926 they executed a note and mortgage on this lot to William G. McAdoo and R. T. Colter as security for the payment of a loan of $2,255. McAdoo and Colter assigned the note and mortgage to Mary Gibbs, who in 1933 secured a final judgment of foreclosure. Shortly thereafter, A. J. Odell and Mary Gibbs requested the plaintiffs to confer with them on the disposition of the property. At the conference, McAdoo, Colter, Gibbs and Odell were represented by their attorney, Ben H. Neblett. Neblett told plaintiffs that as an attorney he had superior knowledge of many facts concerning the land and that they could rely upon all he had to say. McAdoo and Colter had previously secured a money judgment against plaintiffs in another action, and Neblett stated that, acting on behalf of Colter and McAdoo, he had secured an execution on plaintiffs' land to satisfy the judgment, that the sheriff had levied on the land and sold it to McAdoo and Colter for the amount of the judgment debt, and that McAdoo and Colter were the owner of any interest which plaintiffs previously had in the land. McAdoo and Colter, he represented, were going to submit to the foreclosure sale, which had been set for August, 1933, and would not exercise their equity of redemption. Neblett went on to assure the plaintiffs, however, that he and his clients were plaintiffs' friends and would make an unselfish proposal solely to enable the plaintiffs to receive some return from the land out of which they would otherwise get nothing. The proposal was that plaintiffs join with Mary Gibbs in a lease of the land to Odell for the purpose of drilling for oil, with the understanding that they would receive a specific royalty from the oil produced.

The complaint further alleges: The plaintiffs believed Neblett's representation that their land had been sold at an execution sale to Colter and McAdoo. They therefore joined in executing a lease to Odell and made no attempt to pay the mortgage debt or to exercise the equity of redemption after the foreclosure sale, although during this period many persons offered to lease the land from them with advances sufficient to cover the mortgage indebtedness. After Mary Gibbs bought in the property at the foreclosure sale in August, 1933, Odell took possession under his lease and drilled a well, from which he has received profits of more than $100,000.

The complaint alleges further: No execution actually had been levied on the land. The representation that the land had been sold to McAdoo and Colter was known to be false by Neblett and his clients. It was made to induce the plaintiffs to refrain from paying the mortgage indebtedness or from exercising their equity of redemption and to induce them to join in leasing the property to Odell. Plaintiffs did not discover the falsity of the representations until May, 1936. The records covering the facts involved were situated in a city at some distance from the city where plaintiffs reside. They are both elderly; neither drives an automobile; and they had no reason to suspect that the representations were false. Following the discovery of the misrepresentation, plaintiffs notified Odell of their rescission of the lease. They then brought this action against Odell, McAdoo, Colter and Gibbs, asking that the foreclosure sale to Mary Gibbs be set aside, that the title to the property be quieted in them except as to existent sub-leases in the hands of innocent sublessees, and that a judgment be awarded them for all moneys received as royalties by Mary Gibbs or her assigns from the oil well and for all moneys received by Odell from the oil well. Plaintiffs offer to do all things required of them by the court, including the paying of the mortgage indebtedness on the property. The oil companies were made nominal defendants solely to have their rights, if any, adjudicated.

It is well established in California and other jurisdictions that a person who has been induced by fraudulent misrepresentations to enter into a contract or to make a conveyance may have the contract or conveyance set aside and secure a restitution of those benefits lost to him by the transaction. * * * It must appear, however, not only that the plaintiff acted in reliance on the misrepresentation but that he was justified in his reliance. * * * He may not justifiably rely upon mere statements of opinion, including legal conclusions drawn from a true state of facts (Rest.Torts, sec. 545; see cases cited in 12 Cal.Jur. 730–33), unless the person expressing the opinion purports to have expert knowledge concerning the matter or occupies a position of confidence and trust. Rest.Torts, sec. 542; see cases cited in 12 Cal.Jur. 725 et seq. If, however, the opinion or legal conclusion misrepresents the facts upon which it is based or implies the existence of facts which are nonexistent, it constitutes an actionable misrepresentation. Rest.Torts, sec. 539; see cases cited in 12 Cal.Jur. 727, 728. Negligence on the part of the plaintiff in failing to discover the falsity of a statement is no defense when the misrepresentation was intentional rather than negligent.[9]

9. Cf. treatment of contributory negligence in Bohlen, Misrepresentation as Deceit, Negligence, or Warranty (1929) 42 Harv.L.Rev. 733; National Surety

See cases cited in 12 Cal.Jur. 758, 759; Prosser, Torts, 748. As a general rule negligence of the plaintiff is no defense to an intentional tort. See Prosser, Torts, 402. The fact that an investigation would have revealed the falsity of the misrepresentation will not alone bar his recovery (Rest.Torts, sec. 540; see cases cited in 12 Cal.Jur. 758, 759), and it is well established that he is not held to constructive notice of a public record which would reveal the true facts. Rest. Torts, sec. 540[b]; see cases cited in 12 Cal.Jur. 764, 759; Prosser, Torts, 750, 751. The purpose of the recording acts is to afford protection not to those who make fraudulent misrepresentations, but to bona fide purchasers for value. Nor is a plaintiff held to the standard of precaution or of minimum knowledge of a hypothetical, reasonable man. Exceptionally gullible or ignorant people have been permitted to recover from defendants who took advantage of them in circumstances where persons of normal intelligence would not have been misled. See cases cited in 6 Cal.Jur.Supp. 45 (note 13); Prosser, Torts, 749. "No rogue should enjoy his ill-gotten plunder for the simple reason that his victim is by chance a fool." Chamberlin v. Fuller, 59 Vt. 247, 9 A. 832, 835, 836. If the conduct of the plaintiff in the light of his own intelligence and information was manifestly unreasonable, however, he will be denied a recovery. Rest. Torts, sec. 541; see cases cited in 12 Cal.Jur. 757; Prosser, Torts, 747, 748. "He may not put faith in representations which are preposterous, or which are shown by facts within his observation to be so patently and obviously false that he must have closed his eyes to avoid discovery of the truth * * *" Prosser, Torts, 749.

In the present case the allegations of the plaintiffs' complaint, if true, are sufficient to establish the right to relief on the basis of a fraudulent misrepresentation. * * * The fact that an examination of the record would have revealed to plaintiffs the falsity of the representation or that they may have been negligent in failing to make further investigations does not bar their right to relief. The

Corp. v. Lybrand, 256 App.Div. 226, 9 N.Y.S.2d 554 (1939); Gould v. Flato, 170 Misc. 378, 10 N.Y.S.2d 361 (1938); Restatement of Torts, Second §§ 545A (no bar to recovery for fraudulent misrepresentation) and 552A (bar to recovery for negligent misrepresentation) (Tent. Draft No. 10, 1964).

There are at least occasional *dicta* today that plaintiff must show that he exercised reasonable diligence to discover the truth, even where actual fraud is relied on. See, e. g. Crossman v. Bacon & Robinson Co., 119 Me. 588, 109 A. 487 (1920); Murphy v. Cady, 30 F.Supp. 466 (D.C.Me.1939) (recovery for deceit denied on this ground, but recovery under the Securities Act allowed).

Under the Federal Securities Act of 1933 a plaintiff is barred from civil recovery if he knew the falsity of the representation. Section 11(a), 15 U.S.C.A. § 77k(a). And it seems he may lose his rights under the act by failing for the period of limitation to use reasonable diligence towards discovering the fraud after the transaction is completed. Rosenberg v. Hano, 121 F.2d 818 (3d Cir. 1941). Shonts v. Hirliman, 28 F.Supp. 478 (S.D.Cal.1939) suggests plaintiff would be required on his own initiative to discover the fraud, and that this would be no hardship because of his access to corporate books, etc. This would in many cases bring in a rule very like contributory negligence, but with a vengeance! See Comment, 50 Yale L.J. 90, 100 (1940); Loss, Securities Regulation 1031 (1951) (contrasting the high standard of diligence required of an investor with the low standard required of an accountant).

misrepresentation is not such that its falsity must have been so obvious to the plaintiffs as to preclude any justifiable reliance thereon by them. The defendants cannot urge as a defense that plaintiffs were more credulous than the average person. The representation that a levy of execution and sale of the property had occurred was a false statement of fact and is not rendered less actionable because it also contained legal conclusions.

Defendants contend that under the case of Robins v. Hope, 57 Cal. 493, an owner of property in California is "conclusively presumed" to know the state of his own title and therefore may not justifiably rely upon misrepresentations as to ownership. Since a "conclusive presumption" is simply a statement of the rule of law applicable in a given situation, defendants are contending for the establishment of a rule that no action will lie for a fraudulent misrepresentation when it concerns the title to property owned by the party misled. Such a rule would give legal sanction to the perpetration of fraud and permit the cunning to take unfair advantage of the ignorant. The average property owner knows nothing more about the state of his own title than that it is presumably in himself. He usually purchases his property in reliance upon a policy of title insurance and does not search the record for possible adverse claims. While situations might arise where the owner of property would not be justified in relying upon a misrepresentation as to its title, the circumstances of each case should determine whether or not justification exists as in any other action based upon fraud. The defense should not be conclusively presumed against the owner without giving him a chance to show justifiable reliance. Numerous cases in other jurisdictions have permitted a vendor of realty to rescind a contract of sale because the vendee had fraudulently misrepresented to the vendor the value, quantity, or state of the title of the land being conveyed. No attempt is made to presume, conclusively or otherwise, knowledge by the ignorant vendor of the facts concerning his own land. * * * See 9 A.L.R. 1062. In the California case of Conlan v. Sullivan, 110 Cal. 624, 42 P. 1081, a vendee purchased land from a vendor for far less than its value by concealing from the vendor the fact that a mortgage with which the vendor believed the land to be encumbered actually applied to another piece of land. This court held that the fraudulent conduct of the vendee justified the trial court in rescinding the contract of sale on behalf of the vendor. There was no conclusive presumption against the vendor that he knew the state of the title to his land. In the recent case of Glickman v. New York Life Insurance Co., 16 Cal.2d 626, 107 P.2d 252, 131 A.L.R. 1292, this court held that the holder of an insurance policy was not so chargeable with notice of the terms of his policy as to be precluded from rescinding a surrender of the policy when he was misled by fraudulent statements as to his rights made by the insurer's agent. The same considerations which prompted the court to refuse to hold the policyholder to a knowledge of the terms of his policy apply against conclusively presuming knowledge of the state of his title on the part of the owner of realty. The case of Robins v. Hope, supra, is therefore overruled to the extent that it holds that an owner of realty is conclusively presumed to know the state of the title to his land.

Because of the alleged fraudulent misrepresentation plaintiffs ask for a setting aside of the foreclosure sale to Mary Gibbs and a rescission of the lease to Odell, with an accounting of the profits received by these defendants from the property. Since the action is one for equitable relief rather than for damages at law, it is sufficient for the plaintiffs to allege that they have been wrongfully deprived of certain property by the misrepresentation and they need not set forth in detail the extent to which they have been damaged. See cases cited in 12 Cal.Jur. 813, 814. As a condition of restitution, however, the plaintiffs must restore to the defendants any benefits which they have received as a result of the transaction. Rest.Restitution, sec. 65; Cal.Civ.Code, sec. 1691(2); see cases cited in Cal.Annotations to Rest.Restitution, sec. 65; 12 Cal.Jur. 781. Plaintiffs must therefore pay to Mary Gibbs the amount of the mortgage debt before they can recover the property. A restoration of the royalties received by plaintiffs is not necessary since they need not restore property which is rightfully theirs. See Rest.Restitution, sec. 65 and Cal. Annotations. Defendants contend that plaintiffs have not properly offered to make the necessary restitution. It is well established, however, that a court granting equitable relief has the power to make its decrees contingent upon compliance by the plaintiff with certain conditions. See cases cited in 10 Cal.Jur. 508–11, 512. The interests of the defendants can thus be well protected by a decree making any relief granted to plaintiffs conditional upon their paying the mortgage debt. Plaintiffs' offer in their complaint to "do and perform all things of them in equity required by the court to be done by them in the premises" and to subtract the amount of the mortgage debt from any sum awarded them from Mary Gibbs is a sufficient offer of restitution.

Defendants finally contend that plaintiffs are barred from a recovery by the statute of limitations and laches. In California the statute of limitations in an action based upon fraud begins to run from the time when the fraud was discovered or should reasonably have been discovered. Cal.Code Civ.Proc. sec. 338(4). It is necessary for a plaintiff to allege facts showing that suit was brought within a reasonable time after discovery of the fraud without unnecessary delay and that failure to make the discovery sooner was not due to negligence. See cases cited in 12 Cal.Jur. 795–799. The present action was brought more than three years after the date when the misrepresentation was allegedly made but only sixty days after it was discovered. Plaintiffs allege that the discovery did not occur sooner because of their advanced age, the considerable distance of the available records from their home, and the absence of any occasion on their part to examine the records or otherwise inquire into the truth of the representation. The alleged facts, if believed, would justify a trial court in finding that the plaintiffs were sufficiently diligent in discovering the fraud, and that the action was brought within a reasonable time thereafter.

The judgment is reversed.[10]

The theory of equitable relief is not that the bargain has already been rescinded, but that in an appropriate case the court will by its decree rescind it, cancel any instrument that represents it, put the parties back in *statu quo,* and do whatever else is necessary for complete justice. Note the difference between the necessity of tender here and under the "legal" theory, and the flexibility of the relief.

A limitation commonly found in dealing with equitable remedies is that they are unavailable where the legal remedy is adequate. In this country—though probably not in England—that limitation has vexed the field of misrepresentation. 3 Pomeroy, Equity Jurisprudence, sections 912–914a (5th ed. 1940). When law and equity were administered separately the consequence of the limitation was significant and fairly clear. If a suit for cancellation was brought in equity, it would be dismissed where the remedy at law (by action or defense) was thought adequate. Under a procedure where equity and law are united this should not be the result if it appears that plaintiff is entitled to any remedy. But there is still a significant consequence of the old rule. In cases where equity would have granted relief the parties have no right to jury trial; where equity would have dismissed, jury trial is assured by the federal and most state constitutions (though it can be waived). See Clark, Cases on Pleading and Procedure, ch. 13 (1940); James, Trial by Jury and the New Federal Rules of Procedure, 45 Yale L.J. 1022 (1936). Thus one who fears suit on an obligation, cannot by suing for cancellation defeat his adversary's right to jury trial on the issue of fraud, if that is available as a defense to an action on the obligation and if a favorable outcome of such action will fully protect the defrauded party. Enelow v. New York Life Ins. Co., 293 U.S. 379, 55 S.Ct. 310, 79 L.Ed. 440 (1934). See Abbott, Fraud as a Defense at Law in the Federal Courts, 15 Col.L.Rev. 489 (1915). In this connection, two things should be noted:

(a) This problem differs from the one posed by declaratory judgment procedure as to whether a party who fears suit on an asserted obligation may himself start proceedings and thus have relief from peril and insecurity. The granting of such a remedy is not inconsistent with having a jury trial on all issues where that is appropriate by conventional tests. See Borchard, Declaratory Judgments 399–404 (2d ed. 1941).

(b) Ordinarily the affirmative form of relief by "cancellation" means nothing, and the net substantive result of the "equity suit"

10. This case is noted 30 Calif.L.Rev. 197 (1942).

is precisely the same as though there had been rescission "at law," and successful action or defense thereafter, based on the rescission. Would that be true in this case and the last one? See also 3 Pomeroy, op. cit., supra, section 914a.

Cancellation or rescission is by no means the only remedy equity has to give in cases of fraud. Reformation, specific performance of the bargain as represented, the constructive trust device, receivership, and any other appropriate relief may be granted in a proper case. See Pomeroy, Equity Jurisprudence, section 910 (5th ed. 1941). And these remedies are all available to enforce the liabilities created by the Securities Act. Independence Shares Corp. v. Deckert, 311 U.S. 282, 61 S.Ct. 229, 85 L.Ed. 189 (1940), note 27 Va.L.Rev. 554 (1941).

SMITH v. POPE

Supreme Court of New Hampshire, 1961.
103 N.H. 555, 176 A.2d 321.

Action at law alleging deceit and breach of warranty in the sale of certain premises in Harrisville. The plaintiffs alleged false and fraudulent representations that an artesian well on the premises furnished water "fit for human consumption" when in fact it did not because of the presence of kerosene in the well. * * *

At the time the defendant was residing with a nephew in Dublin, and the plaintiffs resided in Keene in property which was ultimately exchanged for the Harrisville store. Later in the year the defendant resumed her residence above the store, and the defendants visited the premises on several occasions to inspect the property and to have an accountant examine the business records of the store.

In the course of the negotiations, the plaintiff husband observed stains on a sink in the store, and inquired "what was in the water which made it so red and [the defendant] said it was mineral in the water."

Shortly before the sale the plaintiff husband learned that the water was reputed to be questionable. A selectman with whom he had discussed the matter, testified that he advised the plaintiff that it "would behoove him to inquire into the water" and that the plaintiff had replied "Do you mean about the oil?" The plaintiff himself testified that he was told by the selectman that there might be kerosene in the water. As a result the plaintiff again inquired about the water, and as the Trial Court found, was told by the defendant that it had a mineral taste but that it was "drinkable and usable."

The evidence indicated that the artesian well in question was drilled in 1949, and that in 1951 a leak developed in an underground tank used for the storage of kerosene. The Court found that the defendant and her husband believed "that this leak had permeated the soil and in some fashion had come into the artesian well."

The defendant's evidence was that the well was nevertheless used for drinking and all other household purposes up to the time of the sale, although spring water was used for drinking purposes by some members of the family in the summertime.

The defendant conceded that the water tasted and smelled of kerosene, although she maintained that she herself was unable to smell the kerosene, and that "to me it was more an iron taste than it was a kerosene taste." She denied that she was ever asked by the plaintiffs if the water contained kerosene, or that she told them anything that was untrue.

The plaintiff testified that when he told the defendant that he had heard rumors that there was kerosene in the water, and asked her about it, "she evaded me again. * * * All she said was there was mineral in the water." He testified that he did not look at the water at any time, and neither tasted nor smelled it. By way of explanation he stated that "Most generally an artesian well is sealed off properly" and "I felt if I bought the place I could put a filter on to get the iron out of it."

The Trial Court found and ruled in part as follows:

> "The Court finds that the defendant did not disclose to either of the plaintiffs that the oil tank had leaked into the ground and that the cause of this mineral taste was thought to be from kerosene.
>
> "There is no evidence that the water had a bacteria count of note, or that it had ever produced any untoward results upon those persons who had used it over the years. It is found, however, that it was somewhat discolored, that it contained a sediment, and that it had a definite odor and taste of kerosene, and that the average person would have found it to be unpleasant for drinking.
>
> "It is also found that at no time did Mrs. Pope do anything actively to conceal the source of the kerosene taste and odor, nor did she prevent the plaintiffs from sampling the water, although the Court feels that under all the circumstances of the case she was somewhat less than candid in the matter, and that her failure to mention the probable cause of the contamination was for the purpose of facilitating and bringing about the ultimate sale to the plaintiffs and that she was successful in that purpose. The plaintiffs, although quite able at any time to have sampled the water or tested it, apparently did not (which would have been quite simple to have done) but rather chose to accept the defendant's statement that it was usable and drinkable, and that it tasted of minerals."

In response to requests filed by the defendant, the Court found and ruled that the plaintiffs did not use reasonable care to investigate after they were told that the water had minerals in it, and that there was kerosene in it, and they had seen the red stains made by the water; and that they did not use "ordinary care to investigate the water prior to the purchase although they had every opportunity to do so and the defendant in no way attempted to dissuade them from so doing."

The Court further found and ruled: "However, on what the Court believes to be the New Hampshire doctrine of contributory negligence as a defense in actions sounding in deceit, the Court finds in favor of the plaintiffs" in the amount of the verdict.

DUNCAN, JUSTICE.

The defendant maintains that the plaintiffs are not entitled to recover because there is no finding that the defendant made any intentional misrepresentations, because she was under no duty to disclose that kerosene had leaked into the well some years previously, and because it was found that the plaintiffs themselves were contributorily negligent.

While there was no finding of intentional misrepresentation in so many words, there were findings that the defendant believed that kerosene "had come into the artesian well," that she "did not disclose * * * that the cause of [the] mineral taste was thought to be from kerosene," and that this "was for the purpose of facilitating and bringing about the ultimate sale * * *." The plain implication is that the defendant's failure to disclose the facts was an intentional concealment, for a fraudulent purpose.

In asserting that she was under no duty to disclose the past presence of kerosene, the defendant relies upon Benoit v. Perkins, 79 N.H. 11, 15, 104 A. 254, 256, where it was said: "The duty to speak must arise from the circumstances, or there must be some relation of trust and confidence between the parties upon which to build the duty to disclose before the failure to disclose can be deemed a fraud whatever motive led to the concealment." Also cited by the defendant is Charlton v. Brunelle, 81 N.H. 13, 15, 120 A. 726, 727, where it appeared however that the "element of the dishonest mental state upon [the defendant's] part [was] wholly lacking."

Had the defendant made no representations concerning the water her position would be well taken. I Harper & James: The Law of Torts, § 7.14. But in this case, the defendant undertook to describe the quality of the water, and did so in an accurate, but findably incomplete manner. The Trial Court found that her failure to state the probable cause of the contamination was "somewhat less than candid," or in effect a half-truth, tantamount to falsehood. Restatement, Torts, § 529; I Harper & James, supra, § 7.14 at 587. See Swinton v. Whitinsville Savings Bank, 311 Mass. 677, 678, 42 N.E.2d 808, 141 A.L.R. 905. Since she undertook to speak, the circumstances imposed upon her a duty not to mislead. Benoit v. Perkins, supra.[11]

11. The extent to which half-truths and partial non-disclosure of facts may be a basis for actionable misrepresentation is treated in Equitable Life Insurance Co. of Iowa v. Halsey, Stuart & Co., 312 U.S. 410, 424–26 (1941)

The case resolves itself into a question of whether the plaintiffs were justified in accepting the defendant's statements at face value, and if so, whether they could be found to have relied upon them and been misled thereby. * * * I Harper & James, supra, § 7.13.

Despite the possibility that the plaintiffs were not misled into believing that the water was free from kerosene but preferred to run the risk of poor water for the sake of acquiring the property in exchange for their own, the record did not compel a finding that this was so. The finding by the Trial Court that the defendant was "successful in [her] purpose" (to bring about the sale) and that the plaintiffs "chose to accept the defendant's statement" was a finding that they relied upon her statement and were misled.

The plaintiffs correctly assert that contributory negligence is no defense to an action for intentional wrong. Wright v. Noyes, 80 N.H. 172, 115 A. 273. The older cases upon which the defendant relies state an earlier rule, since disavowed by later cases. See Seavey: Fraud and Misrepresentation in New Hampshire, 1 N.H.B.J. No. 1, pp. 23–24; Prosser on Torts (2d ed.) § 89 at 552–553. In a case of intentional wrong, the standard applied to the plaintiffs' conduct is not that of ordinary care, but an individual standard, based upon his own capacity and knowledge. Prosser on Torts, supra, § 89 at 552.

In Restatement, Torts, § 541, one rule with respect to reliance is stated thus:

"The recipient in a business transaction of a fraudulent misrepresentation is not justified in relying upon its truth if its falsity is obvious." The comment is then made that while the recipient is not barred because he could have discovered the falsity by investigation, "he is nonetheless required to use his senses and cannot recover if he blindly relies upon a misrepresentation the falsity of which would be patent to him if he had utilized his opportunity to make a cursory inspection of the article." Id., comment a. See also, I Harper & James, supra § 7.12; Annot. 174 A.L.R. 1010, 1027–1030.

The other side of the coin is portrayed in Restatement, Torts, § 540, where it is said that the recipient of a fraudulent misrepresentation of fact is justified in relying upon its truth although investigation might have disclosed its falsity; and the comment is made that the rule applies not only when investigation would be difficult, "but also when it could be made without any considerable trouble or expense." Id., comment a.

("a statement of a half truth is as much a misrepresentation as if the facts stated were untrue"); Simmons v. Evans, 185 Tenn. 282, 206 S.W.2d 295 (1948), noted 20 Tenn.L.Rev. 392 (1948); Metropolitan Life Ins. Co. v. Hedgepeth, 182 Tenn. 296, 185 S.W.2d 906 (1945) (intent to commit suicide undisclosed by applicant for life insurance); Neuman v. Corn Exch. Nat. Bank & Trust Co., 356 Pa. 442, 51 A.2d 759 (1947), noted 21 Temple L.Q. 368 (1948); Rex v. Kylsant [1932] 1 K.B. 442, noted 45 Harv.L.Rev. 1078 (1932), 48 L.Q.Rev. 43 (1932); L. Loss, Securities Regulation 1433–34, 1439 (2d ed. 1961). Also see Restatement of Torts § 527. As to liability for total non-disclosure see Griffith v. Byers Construction Co. of Kansas, Inc., infra p. 798.

Although the Trial Court's findings indicate that an investigation in this case would have involved no particular trouble, the conclusion that the plaintiffs' reliance was justified is implicit in the verdict. If a different view might have been taken upon the evidence, we cannot say that the trier of the facts who heard and saw the parties was compelled as a matter of law to adopt it.

Any defects in the water disclosed by the defendant's disarming statements were such as the plaintiffs might reasonably expect to be able to remedy without abandonment of the water supply. While the vendors of property should not be expected to volunteer information as to every adverse feature however patent, the "law of the present day does not assume in all cases that [they] are endeavoring to defraud the vendees by false and fraudulent representations, and consequently require vendees to distrust such representations and seek the information elsewhere, or suffer the consequences." Sipola v. Winship, 74 N.H. 240, 248, 66 A. 962, 967. * * *

Judgment on the verdict.

Affirmative acts of concealment of defects, or of other unattractive qualities of the object of a transaction, have long been considered the equivalent of fraudulent misrepresentation, e. g., Campbell v. Booth, 526 S.W.2d 167 (Tex.Civ.App.1975) (alleged use of deodorant, during inspection by home buyers, to conceal temporarily dog urine damage to carpets). A classic example of common law concealment has been the tampering with an automobile's odometer, now also subject to statutory treble damages (or $1500, whichever is greater) under the Motor Vehicle Information and Cost Savings Act, 15 U.S.C.A. § 1981 et seq.; see, e. g., Klein v. Pincus, 397 F.Supp. 847 (E.D.N.Y.1975); the common law remedy may be worth more than the statutory remedy, if punitive damages are available, e. g., Edgar v. Fred Jones Lincoln Mercury of Oklahoma City, Inc., 524 F.2d 162 (10th Cir. 1975).

SECTION 3. WHERE THE PARTY INJURED WAS NOT BROUGHT INTO LEGAL RELATIONS WITH THE PERSON MAKING THE MISREPRESENTATION

SMITH v. BADLAM

Supreme Court of Vermont, 1941.
112 Vt. 143, 22 A.2d 161.

SHERBURNE, JUSTICE. This is an action of fraud and deceit, in which it is alleged that the plaintiff was induced to buy an apple orchard by the false and fraudulent representation of the defendant that the orchard contained 3,500 trees, whereas it only contained 2,500 trees, as the defendant knew or ought to have known. * * *

This case turns upon whether the defendant made an absolute representation as to the number of trees, which was understood and intended to be understood as a statement upon knowledge, for, if he did, it is precisely the same as if he had distinctly and in terms professed to have knowledge as to the fact. * * * However, the fact that the representations took a declaratory form does not of itself necessarily imply that the defendant made the representations "as of his own knowledge." Adams v. Ladeau, 84 Vt. 460, 464, 79 A. 996, 997.

Viewing the evidence most favorably for the plaintiff, it appears that the defendant, a real estate agent, in endeavoring to induce the plaintiff to buy the orchard of one Anderson, called the plaintiff on the telephone and told him that he had a proposition in which he might be interested. As a result the plaintiff went to ride with the defendant on the following day, and on the way the defendant said he wanted to sell him an apple orchard of 3,500 trees owned by Anderson. They proceeded to the Anderson orchard and saw in general what it looked like, and the defendant then told him that there were 3,500 trees of different varieties. The plaintiff asked for an inventory, and in a few days the defendant gave him a paper in his handwriting on which were listed the numbers of the different varieties with the total of 3,500, also the acreage, buildings, and some articles of personal property. At the time this inventory was given the defendant had not told the plaintiff that he been over the orchard, or that he knew about or was familiar with it, and the plaintiff did not understand that he had ever had anything to do with it. The plaintiff did not understand that the defendant had counted the trees, but he did understand that he had seen Anderson. Later, before the plaintiff closed the trade with Anderson for the purchase of the orchard, Anderson also stated to him that there were 3,500 trees.

In fact, the defendant knew nothing about the number of trees except as Anderson had told him. Anderson had given him the number of 3,500 trees divided up into varieties, as shown on the inventory furnished by the defendant to the plaintiff. The defendant testified in cross-examination that when he gave the inventory to the plaintiff he did not know whether it was true or false, and was not permitted to testify in re-examination that he believed it was true.

In view of the fact that the defendant represented a known principal, it cannot reasonably be inferred from the foregoing that the plaintiff understood that the defendant made the statements and inventory as of his own knowledge, or that the defendant intended him to so understand.

In this connection Sec. 348, Comment b, of the Restatement of Agency is pertinent: "An agent is not liable because of misrepresentations of the principal or of another agent unless he should know of them. He is not affected by the knowledge of facts which the principal or another agent has and which, if known to him, would cause his representations to be fraudulent. An agent who makes untrue statements based upon the information given to him by the principal is not liable because of the fact that the principal knew the information to be untrue. He may rely upon statements of the principal to the same extent as upon statements from any other similarly reputable source." See also Pollock on Torts, 14th Ed., 240, where, in the case that the principal knows the representation to be false and authorizes the making of it, it states: "Here the principal is clearly liable; the agent is or is not liable according as he does not or does himself believe the representation to be true." Some illustrative cases are Kuehl v. Parmenter, 195 Iowa 497, 192 N.W. 429; State v. Katcef, 159 Md. 271, 150 A. 801; Harriss v. Tams, 258 N.Y. 229, 179 N.E. 476; Lasman v. Calhoun, Denny & Ewing, 111 Wash. 467, 191 P. 409.

Defendant's motion for a verdict should have been granted.[12]

ROSENBERG v. CYROWSKI

Supreme Court of Michigan, 1924.
227 Mich. 508, 198 N.W. 905.

SHARPE, J. The plaintiffs are real estate agents in the city of Detroit. In June, 1919, they arranged with Paul Cyrowski to sell certain property owned by him to one Steinberg. It is their claim that a 3 per cent commission was agreed upon. They went to the office of Cyrowski's brother, the defendant, who was a practicing attorney, to have the papers prepared. Rosenberg testified that while there he said to defendant:

"'Mr. Cyrowski, make out an agreement for our commission.' He said, 'What commission?' 'Three per cent.' August said to Paul, 'Is that right?' 'Yes.' 'Do you know how much it is?' He takes a pencil and figures $1,050, and he says, 'That is right.' Paul said, 'That is right.' I said, 'Make out an agreement.' He said, 'You don't need any agreement.' I said, 'August, I want an agreement; I want a writing.' He said, 'It aint necessary; I am a lawyer, and that is my brother, and you will get every cent; take my word of honor.' And that was all there was about it." * * *

The sale was consummated, but the commission has not been paid.

Plaintiffs' declaration is grounded on a claimed false and fraudulent representation made by defendant that a written agreement was not necessary to enable them to recover a commission on the sale, on which they relied to their damage, the loss of the commission agreed upon. It does not count on any breach of duty arising from the relationship of attorney and client. Recovery is not sought based on any negligence of the defendant in giving advice in conflict with the statute, and we therefore do not consider it.

12. Would rescission be available here? See Connelly v. Glenny, 233 App.Div. 198, 251 N.Y.S. 288 (1931); But cf. Federal Securities Act of 1933, as amended, section 12 (15 U.S.C.A. § 77*l*); Cady v. Murphy, 113 F.2d 988 (1st Cir. 1940), noted in 54 Harv.L. Rev. 150 (1940); Comment, 50 Yale L.J. 90, 97 (1940).

The trial court charged that, if defendant stated that a written agreement was not necessary, and that he so stated either "knowing it to be false or with reckless disregard of its truth or falsity," and plaintiffs relied and acted on it to their damage, they might recover. [Judgment for plaintiff and defendant appealed.]

There was no privity of contract between the plaintiffs and the defendant. Neither does it appear that defendant in any way personally profited by the plaintiffs' having been misled to their damage by his utterance. When action is brought to recover for false and fraudulent representations made by one party to another in a transaction between them, any representations which are false in fact and actually deceive the other and are relied on by him to his damage are actionable, irrespective of whether the person making them knew them to be false or acted in good faith in making them, when the loss of the party deceived inured to the benefit of the other. [Citing a number of Michigan cases.]

But when the person making the representations is not a party to the transaction, and in no way profits by the act of the party defrauded in reliance on the representations made by him, he is liable for damage only in case he knows the representations made by him to be false, and makes them for the purpose of deception, and with the intent that they shall be relied on and acted on by the person to whom they are made and loss or damage results therefrom. * * *

Applying these rules to the facts here presented, it is clear that this instruction given was erroneous. To hold the defendant liable the jury must find that he made the representation as testified to by plaintiffs; that he knew he was not stating the truth; that he intended to deceive the plaintiffs and induce them to act on his advice; that they acted in reliance upon it, and sustained damages as a result thereof.

The more serious question is whether, under the proof submitted by plaintiffs, any liability attaches to the defendant. He was under no obligation to give legal advice to the plaintiffs. He might have declined to do so. He was acting for his brother, the vendor, in preparing the contract of sale with the vendee whom plaintiffs had produced, a person ready, willing, and able to purchase the property. The plaintiffs had at that time earned the commission agreed upon between themselves and the vendor. In order that they might be in a position to enforce payment, they believed (and were right about it) that they must have the commission agreement reduced to writing. By the advice given, defendant relieved his client from a liability which would have been incurred by him, had such advice not been given. If he knowingly, and with the intent to deceive them and relieve his client from such payment, falsely represented to them that it was not necessary to have a written agreement in order to enforce collection of their commission, and they relied and acted upon it, we are of the opinion that plaintiffs may recover. In 1 Thornton on Attorneys at Law, section 295, it is said:

"An attorney's liability does not end with being answerable to his client. He is also liable to third persons who have suffered injury or loss in consequence of fraudulent or tortious conduct on his part."

The cases cited in support of the text are mostly those in which the attorney actively participated in the enforcement of process illegally issued. In some of them the purpose knowingly to aid the client to do an illegal act was presented.

It is the general rule that "fraud cannot be predicated upon misrepresentations as to matters of law." 12 R.C.L. 295. The writer, however, adds that the rule "may be rendered inapplicable by the existence of peculiar facts and circumstances." Page 296. The cases cited afford little help in determining the question here presented. The rule is founded on the maxim that "all men are presumed to know the law." Experience teaches us that this maxim finds but little support in fact. It may be doubted if it was ever intended to excuse fraud. * * *

The judgment is reversed, and a new trial granted, with costs to appellant.[13]

GRIFFITH v. BYERS CONSTRUCTION CO. OF KANSAS, INC.

Supreme Court of Kansas, 1973.
212 Kan. 65, 510 P.2d 198.

FROMME, JUSTICE. The purchasers of new homes in Woodlawn East Addition, City of Wichita, Kansas, brought separate actions for damages because of the saline condition of the soil of their homesites. These actions were filed on alternative theories, (1) breach of an implied warranty of fitness and (2) fraud in the concealment of a material matter. The actions were brought against the developer. This appeal is from an order granting summary judgments in favor of the developer, Byers Construction Co. of Kansas, Inc. (Byers).

The petitions allege that Byers developed and advertised the addition as a choice residential area. Prior to the time of development the addition was part of an abandoned oil field which contained salt water disposal areas which Byers knew or should have known would

13. Has the doctrine of *scienter* been repudiated in some jurisdictions? See Green, Deceit, 16 Va.L.Rev. 745, 750 (1930); Forsberg et al. v. Baker, 211 Minn. 59, 300 N.W. 371 (1941); Ford v. Buffalo Eagle Colliery Co., 122 F. 2d 555 (4th Cir. 1941); Osborne v. Holt, 92 W.Va. 410, 114 S.E. 801 (1922); Horton v. Tyree, 104 W.Va. 238, 139 S.E. 737 (1937); National Bank of Pawnee v. Hamilton, 202 Ill. App. 516 (1916). Compare the objective test of knowledge as stated in Chatham Furnace Co. v. Moffatt, 147 Mass. 403, 18 N.E. 168, 9 Am.St.Rep. 727 (1888), with the subjective test of Nash v. Minnesota Title Insurance & Trust Co., 163 Mass. 574, 40 N.E. 1039, 28 L.R.A. 753, 47 Am.St.Rep. 489 (1895). Assuming defendant's client had been plaintiff and had suffered injury, what would his rights have been against the defendant? See McGregor v. Wright et al., 117 Cal. App. 186, 3 P.2d 624 (1931); Holland v. Brown, 66 S.W.2d 1095 (Tex.Civ. App.1933); Goodrich-Lockhart Co. v. Sears, 270 F. 971 (D.C.Ky.1919).

not sustain vegetation because of the saline content of the soil. It was alleged that Byers graded and developed the whole addition for homesites in such a manner that it became impossible for a purchaser to discover the presence of these salt areas. It further appears from allegations in the petitions and testimony in depositions that each of the plaintiffs selected a homesite which was located within a salt water disposal area. After houses were constructed attempts to landscape the homesites failed. Grass, shrubs and trees were planted and died because of the saline content of the soil. * * *

* * * [T]he district court entered summary judgments in favor of the defendant Byers * * *. This appeal followed.

These additional allegations or facts, gleaned from the pleadings and depositions, should be noted. The purchase of the homesites and the construction of the homes was handled in this manner. Each prospective homeowner contracted with a separate building contractor to construct a home on a homesite to be chosen by the owner. The homesites in Woodlawn East Addition were advertised by the developer and considered to be in a restricted residential area developed for choice homes. Each prospective homeowner picked out a homesite without personally consulting the developer Byers but each was influenced by billboard advertising and by the general reputation of the area. When a homesite was chosen the respective building contractor then purchased the lot. The contractors obtained warranty deeds from Byers. When the houses were completed in accordance with specifications titles were transferred and the homeowners then received deeds to the improved homesites. No inquiry was made and no assurance was given by Byers on soil fertility.

The facts of this case appear to be unique for, although many cases can be found on a vendor-builder's liability for the sale of a defective home (see 25 A.L.R.3d, p. 383), no cases are cited and we find none which discuss a developer's liability for defects arising from sterility of soil. The saline content of the soil of these homesites does not affect the structural qualities of the homes. The allegations of the petitions and deposition testimony indicate that landscaping is either impossible or highly expensive.

The appellants contend there is or should be an implied warranty on the part of a developer of homesites that the soil will sustain grass, shrubs and trees. They argue there is no reasonable distinction between implied warranties in product liability cases and in cases involving the sales of developed homesites. In either case an implied warranty of fitness for use should attach, they argue, to the product sold. We cannot agree.

In product liability cases the manufacturers and the vendors are dealing in products which may be dangerous to the personal health of the public. There is imposed a special liability for the protection of the health of consumers. In such cases the implied warranty does not arise from any particular transaction or agreement, but is imposed by operation of law on the basis of public policy for the protection of the health, safety and welfare of the public. * * * Any injury in the present case arises from sterility of the soil and is to the pocketbook, not to the person.

Appellee-Byers points out that cases cited by the appellants involve construction of houses in an unworkmanlike manner by a builder who sells to a purchaser. The defects complained of are generally in the nature of sewer trouble, water in the basement or structural defects which affect the quality of the structure sold. The implied covenants recognized in such cases arise from the terms, conditions and nature of the construction contract entered into between the contractor and the homeowner. Byers points out he is only a developer selling vacant homesites. There appears to be some distinction. * * *

A contract between a purchaser and vendor-builder contemplates more than the mere transfer of title to real estate; it contemplates the construction of a structurally sound building. The rationale for the implication of a warranty in the vendor-builder cases is that when a vendee buys a development house from plans and specifications he clearly relies on the skill and integrity of his builder. He relies on the builder to erect the house in a workmanlike manner and to furnish a completed house reasonably suited for habitation. In the present case the soil defect does not affect the structural quality of the dwelling. Therefore the defect relates only to the real estate, the fertility of the soil.

The sales of the homesites in the present cases were accomplished by delivery of ordinary warranty deeds. There is a presumption that when a deed is prepared, executed and delivered by a grantor and accepted by a grantee any contract is merged in the deed. * * * Implied covenants or warranties as to land are not favored and the tendency of modern decisions is not to imply covenants which might and ought to have been expressed by the parties if intended. * * *

A real estate developer by subdividing and offering lots for sale as choice residential homesites does not by implication warrant the fertility of the soil of said lots. * * * The trial court properly held there was no implied warranty of soil fertility on which plaintiffs might maintain their actions.

Our next inquiry is directed to the claims based on fraud. The trial court held as a matter of law no claims for fraud could be maintained because of lack of privity between the developer and these appellants. The residential lots were sold to the builders who in turn constructed the houses and then deeded the improved lots to the appellants.

In support of the trial court's holding the appellee, Byers, contends not only was there a lack of privity but that the appellants wholly failed to produce any evidence to support their claim of fraud. * * *

* * * As to the second question we do not believe the record conclusively establishes the inability of the appellants to support their charges of fraud nor did the trial court dispose of the motion on that

ground. It is true the appellants and the builders stated in their depositions they had talked to no one who said the appellee Byers knew the soil of the lots was incapable of growing vegetation. However, this does not mean they had no evidence to support their claim of fraud. It was alleged in the petitions that appellee Byers developed the area and at that time the salt water disposal areas were apparent, that Byers knew or should have known of their nature and presence, that it graded the whole addition and the areas thereafter became latent, and that appellee was guilty of fraud in failing to disclose the presence of the salt areas to appellants. Byers' knowledge of the defect did not depend on testimony of appellants and the contractors. Fifteen other witnesses were listed by appellants in the pretrial order.

A summary judgment proceeding is not a trial by affidavits or depositions and the parties are entitled to trial when there is a good faith dispute of facts. * * * Any doubt as to the existence of an issue of fact must be resolved against the movant and the opponent's evidence is entitled to the benefit of all reasonable inferences. * * *

The allegations of fraud appear to be viable issues for trial if nondisclosure of a known material defect in the lots constitutes actionable fraud as to the appellants.

This court has held that the purchaser may recover on the theory of fraud from a vendor-builder for nondisclosure of defects. In Jenkins v. McCormick, 184 Kan. 842, 339 P.2d 8, it is stated:

> "Where a vendor has knowledge of a defect in property which is not within the fair and reasonable reach of the vendee and which he could not discover by the exercise of reasonable diligence, the silence and failure of the vendor to disclose the defect in the property constitutes actionable fraudulent concealment."

* * *

This *Jenkins* rule approximates that stated in Restatement, Second, Torts, § 551 (Ten.Draft No. 12, 1966):

> "(1) One who fails to disclose to another a thing which he knows may justifiably induce the other to act or refrain from acting in a business transaction is subject to the same liability to the other as though he had represented the nonexistence of the matter which he has failed to disclose, if, but only if, he is under a duty to the other to exercise reasonable care to disclose the matter in question.
>
> "(2) One party to a business transaction is under a duty to disclose to the other before the transaction is consummated.
>
> * * *
>
> "(e) Facts basic to the transaction, if he knows that the other is about to enter into the transaction under a mistake as to such facts, and that the other, because of the relationship

> between them, the customs in the trade, or other objective circumstances, would reasonably expect a disclosure of such facts." [14]

A similar rule has been recognized in other states. See Bethlahmy v. Bechtel, 91 Idaho 55, 415 P.2d 698, where a drainage ditch underlay a garage and was not disclosed to the purchaser. See also Buist v. C. Dudley DeVelbiss Corp., 182 Cal.App.2d 325, 6 Cal.Rptr. 259; Cohen v. Vivian, 141 Colo. 443, 349 P.2d 366, where there was a failure by vendors to disclose that the homes sold were built on filled land and subsidence of the land damaged plaintiffs' homes. Many such cases are collected in 80 A.L.R.2d 1453. We see no reason why the rule in *Jenkins* should not be extended in the present case to a developer of residential lots.

The appellee Byers next contends, without agency, there can be no privity and without privity there can be no duty to disclose. Here, of course, appellants never dealt with the appellee, Byers. The duty to disclose the saline nature of the soil must extend to appellants if their fraud claims are to be upheld. However, the doctrine of privity provides no defense to appellee Byers if appellants were within a class of persons appellee intended to reach. Liability for misrepresentation is not necessarily limited to the person with whom the misrepresenter deals. The rule is embodied in Restatement, Second, Torts, § 531 (Ten.Draft No. 10, 1964):

> "One who makes a fraudulent misrepresentation is subject to liability for pecuniary loss
>
> "(a) To the persons or class of persons whom he intends or has reason to expect to act or to refrain from action in reliance upon the misrepresentation; and
>
> "(b) For pecuniary loss suffered by them through their reliance in the type of transaction in which he intends or has reason to expect their conduct to be influenced."

Liability may exist in a situation similar to that of the present case without a specific finding of agency. In Massei v. Lettunich, 248 Cal.App.2d 68, 56 Cal.Rptr. 232, Lettunich owned hillside property and in the course of laying out lot plans for a residential subdivision had the land filled. An engineering firm advised him regarding the depth to which the foundation should be laid to insure safety. Without informing a builder of the engineering report or that the land had been

14. The clauses of § 551(a)(2) skipped by the court are:

"(a) Such matters known to him as the other is entitled to know because of a fiduciary or other similar relation of trust and confidence between them; and

"(b) Such additional matters known to him as he knows to be necessary to prevent his partial statement of the facts from being misleading; and

"(c) Subsequently acquired information which he knows will make untrue or misleading a previous representation which when made was true or believed to be so; and

"(d) The falsity of a representation not made with the expectation that it would be acted upon. If he subsequently learns that the other is about to act in reliance upon it in a transaction with him * * *"

filled, Lettunich sold the land to the builder. Massei and others purchased homes from the builder and were damaged when the filled dirt subsided. The court found that the ultimate purchasers could recover from Lettunich because of the nondisclosure. In the opinion it was stated:

> "The contention of Lettunich that he had no contact with appellants and that therefore it was impossible for him to be guilty of deceit toward them is without merit. 'The law is well settled that "representations made to one person with intention that they will be repeated to another and acted upon by him and which are repeated and acted upon to his injury gives the person so acting the same right to relief as if the representations had been made to him directly."' [Citations omitted.] No reason appears why this same rule should not be applicable to nondisclosures as well as misrepresentations. The jury could easily have found that Lettunich, in failing to disclose to the Trents that the lots had been filled, did so because he was fearful that the prospective purchasers would in turn learn that fact and be dissuaded. * * *" (p. 73, 56 Cal.Rptr. p. 235)

In Anderson v. Rexroad, 175 Kan. 676, 266 P.2d 320, this court refused to accept the defense of lack of privity in an action brought by owners of property damaged by a contractor. The improvement contract was entered into between the officers of a city and a street improvement contractor. The contractor agreed to stand liable for damages to buildings, trees and shrubbery arising from the work necessitated by the street improvement. In disapproving a previous case decided on privity the court said:

> "* * * Be that as it may there are other sound reasons for holding the rule in the Mott case, to the effect there was no such privity of contract between the parties as would authorize the plaintiff to maintain the action, is no longer to be regarded as sound and should be disapproved. In the years since its decision there has been steady progress on the part of the courts in the extension of the right of a third party to sue on a contract made for his benefit and it has been stated frequently that in the light of modern developments privity in the sense it was used prior to recognition of the present third party beneficiary doctrine is no longer necessary in order for the beneficiary to maintain an action or recover on a contract intended for his benefit." (p. 681, 266 P. 2d p. 325)

Under the alleged facts of our present case, accepting the same in the light most favorable to the appellants, we must assume the appellee, Byers, had knowledge of the saline content of the soil of the lots it placed on the market. After the grading and development of the area this material defect in the lots was not within the fair and reasonable reach of the vendees, as they could not discover this latent defect by the exercise of reasonable care. The silence of the appellee, Byers, and its failure to disclose this defect in the soil condition to the purchasers could constitute actionable fraudulent concealment under the rule in Jenkins v. McCormick, supra. One who makes a fraudulent misrepresentation or concealment is subject to liability for pecuniary loss to the persons or class of persons whom he intends or has reason to expect to act or to refrain from action in reliance upon the misrepresentation or concealment.

Of course, the fraudulent concealment to be actionable has to be material to the transaction. A matter is material if it is one to which a reasonable man would attach importance in determining his choice of action in the transaction in question. (Restatement, Second, Torts, § 538 [Ten.Draft No. 10, 1964].) There is little doubt in this case a prospective purchaser of a residential building site would consider the soil condition a material factor in choosing a lot on which to build his home. It materially affected the value and acceptability of the homesite.

As to privity we do not believe it is important to categorize its existence under a particular legal theory. Suffice it to say the appellants were in that class of persons desiring building lots in a choice residential area whom appellee intended and had reason to expect would purchase and build their homes. The fact that title was first taken in the names of the builders did not change the identity of those who would be ultimately affected by any fraudulent misrepresentations or nondisclosure of material defects in the lots. The building contractors were acting on behalf of their respective purchasers as a conduit or temporary way station for the legal title which, it was understood, would pass on completion of the homes to the appellants. There is no lack of privity in this case which would prevent causes of action based on fraud, and, in this, the district court erred in entering summary judgments for the appellee, Byers. * * * [15]

RENO v. BULL

Court of Appeals of New York, 1919.
226 N.Y. 546, 124 N.E. 144.

McLaughlin, J. Action to recover damages for fraud and deceit, by reason of which it is claimed plaintiff was induced to purchase fifty shares, each of the par value of $100, of the capital stock of the American Oriental Company, a Maine corporation. Plaintiff had a verdict for $6,000, and from the judgment entered thereon defendants appealed to the Appellate Division, where the same was unanimously affirmed, and by permission they now appeal to this court.

15. For liability of state banking official to defrauded depositors, for fraudulent non-disclosure of truth concerning misrepresentation by bank's officers, see Tcherepnin v. Franz, 393 F. Supp. 1197 (N.D.Ill.1975).

The unanimous affirmance of the judgment conclusively establishes that the findings of the jury are sustained by evidence. The judgment, therefore, must be affirmed, unless errors, presented by proper exceptions, were committed by the trial court which affect the substantial rights of the defendants.

After a careful consideration of the record, the briefs and argument of respective counsel, I have reached the conclusion that there are at least two errors of this character which are so fundamental that they necessitate the reversal of the judgment. They are instructions given to the jury as to the duty and obligations of the defendants and as to the measure of damages.

As to the duty and obligations of the defendants: At the time the stock was purchased, they were, with others, directors of the corporation. It had a plant, which cost several hundred thousand dollars, for refining crude oil located on San Francisco bay, in the state of California. The corporation was organized with a capital stock of four million dollars, two million common and two million preferred, and one million of the latter it was desirous of inducing the public to buy. To that end, it made an arrangement with Charles D. Barney & Company, prominent bankers in New York and Philadelphia, to offer the same for sale. Prior to the offering, Barney & Company prepared a circular, or prospectus, signed by them, which consisted of a letter from one Ertz, the president of the corporation, addressed to Barney & Company, which contained statements as to the capacity of the plant, probable earnings of the corporation, crude oil supplied in the state of California, advantages in securing trade in the Orient and large dividends that would be received by holders of the preferred stock. The circular also contained the names of the directors, the advisory committee and other matters unnecessary to state. This circular was adopted and approved by the directors of the corporation. The statements contained in the circular, which the plaintiff claimed were and which the jury have found to be false, were: (a) that the plant was well built, fully completed and had a capacity of refining 2,000 barrels of crude oil in the state of California; and (c) that there was a profitable Oriental market for the sale of the refined products. In connection with these alleged false statements, it was also claimed that the defendants were liable, by reason of a statement made by Ertz, the president of the corporation, to the plaintiff, at or immediately prior to the time he purchased the stock, to the effect that the corporation would begin business with $1,000,000 cash capital.

No evidence was offered at the trial, nor was the claim there made, or upon the argument before us, that the defendants or any of them had actual knowledge of the alleged false statements set forth in the circular or the statement made by the president, or that they had any connection with such statements other than as directors of the corporation, and all except one of them testified at the trial that they, at the time the circular was issued, believed the statements therein made to be true.

The action, as indicated, was to recover for fraud and deceit and to maintain it the plaintiff had to prove that the defendants, as directors, by adopting and authorizing Barney & Company to issue the circular, made the representations alleged; that such representations were false; that they knew they were false; that they were made for the purpose of deceiving the public, and that he, believing the same to be true, made the purchase and was thereby damaged; in other words, the plaintiff had to prove, as this court has recently said, "Representation, falsity, *scienter,* deception and injury." (Ochs v. Woods, 221 N.Y. 335, 117 N.E. 305.) This rule is so well settled in this state that the citation of authorities seems almost unnecessary. * * * The jury should have been so instructed. The trial court, however, in utter disregard of this rule, said to the jury that it was the duty of the defendants, when they, as directors of the corporation, approved of the circular, to know the truth of the facts stated therein and if they did not know whether such facts were true, they were bound to know if they had a reasonable opportunity to ascertain the same. He said, "It is their duty before they allow these representations to be made to the public * * * to know the facts * * * even though they believe the representations to be true * * *; if they had ample time to know * * * they are bound * * *. In other words, if although they did not know these facts and did not know them to be false, if they authorized the issuance of the prospectus, and authorized the statements to be made, then they are liable, * * * if in the exercise of ordinary care in the conduct of the business they would have been given means of knowing that they were false * * * If they authorized a false statement to be made, when by common prudence and the exercise of ordinary care, they could have discovered that these representations were false, then they are just as liable as if they had actual personal knowledge that they were false."

When the instructions thus given are subjected to the rule above stated, it at once becomes apparent that the same were erroneous. Erroneous, because there was substituted as the test of defendants' liability, negligence, instead of a purpose to deceive. Negligence and fraud are not synonymous terms; nor in legal effect are they equivalent terms. Fraud presupposes a willful purpose resorted to with intent to deprive another of his legal rights. It is positive in that the purpose concurs with the act, designedly and knowingly committed. Negligence, whatever be its grade, does not include a purpose to do a wrongful act. It may be some evidence of, but is not fraud. (Gardner v. Heartt, 3 Den. 232.) Fraud always has its origin in a purpose, but negligence is an omission of duty minus the purpose. * * * This distinction was clearly pointed out in Kountze v. Kennedy, supra, 147 N.Y. 129, 41 N.E. 414, 29 L.R.A. 360, 49 Am.St.Rep. 651, the court saying: "Misjudgment, however gross, or want of caution, however marked, is not fraud. Intentional fraud, as distinguished from a mere breach of duty or the omission to use due care, is an essential factor in an action for deceit."

But it is suggested by counsel for respondent that this distinction and the "ancient rule of *scienter*" in actions for deceit has been changed by this court. (Downey v. Finucane, 205 N.Y. 251, 98 N.E. 391, 40 L.R.A.,N.S., 307.) In this, he is mistaken. It was not the intention of this court in the Downey case to overrule prior decisions of the court as to what was necessary to be established in order to recover for fraud and deceit. No such question was presented, considered or passed upon. There, the defendants were hald liable for the acts of one Fenn, not upon the ground that he was a co-director, but because defendants had made him their agent as the manager of a syndicate. This was pointed out in Rives v. Bartlett, 215 N.Y. 33, 109 N.E. 83.

In the instant case, the defendants, in approving the circular and authorizing Barney & Company to offer the stock for sale, acted solely for the corporation. They were not members of a syndicate to promote the sale, nor were they nor any of them, underwriters of the stock offered to the public. So far as they were concerned, the corporation alone was interested in the sale. Barney & Company was its agent and not the agent of the defendants. (Arthur v. Griswold, supra [55 N.Y. 400]; Rives v. Bartlett, supra.)

The rule as to the measure of damages was not the one to be applied. The court said to the jury that if the plaintiff were entitled to recover, then he should be awarded "the difference between the value of the stock at the time it was sold to him * * * and the value of the stock as it would have been at that time if the representations were true." The purpose of an action for deceit is to indemnify the party injured. All elements of profit are excluded. The true measure of damage is indemnity for the actual pecuniary loss sustained as the direct result of the wrong. * * * The plaintiff paid $5,000 for the stock purchased by him. If he were entitled to recover at all, it was the difference between that amount and the value of the stock which he received with interest from that time. He was not entitled to anything else. * * *

Judgments reversed, etc.

Derry v. Peek (1889) 14 A.C. 337, a classic case, was a shareholder's action in deceit against the directors of a corporation, alleging misrepresentation in the prospectus, reliance, and consequent injury and loss. Compare the following excerpts from the opinion by Lord Herschell: "This action is one which is commonly called an action of deceit, a mere common law action. * * * I think it important that it should be borne in mind that such an action differs essentially from one brought to obtain rescission of a contract on the ground of a misrepresentation of a material fact. * * * Where rescission is claimed it is only necessary to prove that there was misrepresentation: then, however honestly it may have been made, however free from blame the person who made it, the contract, having been obtained by misrepresentation, cannot stand. In an action of deceit, on the contrary, it is not enough to establish misrepresentation alone. * * *

"There is another class of actions which I must refer to also for the purpose of putting it aside. I mean those cases where a person within whose special province it lay to know a particular fact, has given an erroneous answer to an enquiry made with regard to it by a person desirous of ascertaining the fact for the purpose of determining his course accordingly, and has been held bound to make good the assurance he has given. * * * In cases like this it has been said that the circumstance that the answer was honestly made in the belief that it was true affords no defense to the action. * * *

"I may now pass to Foster v. Charles (7 Bing. 105). It was there contended that the defendant was not liable, even though the representation he had made was false to his knowledge, because he had no intention of defrauding. * * * This contention was not upheld by the court. * * * Wilfully to tell a falsehood, intending that another shall be led to act upon it as if it were the truth, may well be termed fraudulent, whatever the motive which induces it, though it be neither gain to the person making the assertion nor injury to the person to whom it was made.

"The next case * * * is one * * * of great importance. * * * The jury found the defendants not guilty of fraud, but expressed the opinion that they had been guilty of gross negligence. * * * it was contended that their verdict was sufficient to render the defendants liable; Park, B., however, said: 'It is insisted that even that (viz., the gross negligence * * *), accompanied with a damage to the plaintiff in consequence of that gross negligence, would be sufficient to give him a right of action. From this proposition we entirely dissent * * * no one can be made responsible for a representation unless it be *fraudulently* made. * * * It is not necessary to shew that the defendants knew the facts to be untrue: if they stated a fact which was untrue for a fraudulent purpose, they at the same time *not believing* that fact to be true, in that case it would be both a legal and moral fraud.'

"* * * A man's mere assertion that he believed the statement he made to be true is not accepted as conclusive proof that he did so. There may be such an absence of reasonable ground for his belief as, in spite of his assertion, to carry conviction to the mind that he had not really the belief he alleges. If the Learned Lord intended to go further * * * and to say that though the belief was really entertained, yet if there was no reasonable grounds for it, the person making the statement was guilty of fraud * * * I say * * * that the previous authorities afford no warrant for the view that an action of deceit would lie under such circumstances.

"* * * I proceed to state briefly the conclusions to which I have been led. * * * First, in order to sustain an action of deceit, there must be proof of fraud, and nothing short of that will suffice.

Secondly, fraud is proved when it is shewn that a false representation has been made * * * knowingly, or * * * without belief in its truth, or * * * recklessly, careless whether it be true or false. Although I have treated the second and third as distinct cases. I think the third is but an instance of the second, for one who makes a statement under such circumstances can have no real belief in the truth of what he states. To prevent a false statement being fraudulent, there must, I think, always be an honest belief in its truth. * * * Thirdly, if fraud be proved, the motive of the person guilty of it is immaterial.

"In my opinion, making a false statement through want of care falls far short of, and is a very different thing from fraud, and the same may be said of a false representation honestly believed though on insufficient grounds."

See note to Rosenberg v. Cyrowski, p. 798, supra, in reference to objective and subjective tests of knowledge. Note the broad group of persons who may be held liable under the provisions of the Securities Act, 48 Stat. 74, 1933, amended, 48 Stat. 905, 1934, 15 U.S.C.A. § 77a et seq. See, in this regard, Comment, 44 Yale L.J. 456, 470 et seq. (1935). For liability generally under the act, see Comment, 50 Yale L.J. 90 (1940); Shulman, Civil Liability and the Securities Act, 43 Yale L.J. 227 (1933); 27 Va.L.Rev. 554 (1941).

Note that while scienter is said to be required for claims arising under § 17(a) of the Securities Act of 1933, partly because of the defense provided by § 12(2) of that act, 15 U.S.C.A. § 77*l*(2), that defendant did not know and in the exercise of reasonable care could not have known of the misrepresentation—but "[s]cienter may be inferred where the lack of knowledge consists of ignorance of facts which any ordinary person under similar circumstances should have known," Stone v. United States, 113 F.2d 70, 75 (6th Cir. 1970)—it was sometimes said that scienter need not be proved in an action under § 10(b) of the Securities Exchange Act of 1934, 15 U.S.C.A. § 78j(b), e. g., Tomera v. Galt, 511 F.2d 504 (7th Cir. 1975); compare, however, 6 L. Loss, Securities Regulation 3883 et seq. (1969) and Ernst & Ernst v. Hochfelder, — U.S. —, 96 S.Ct. 1375, — L.Ed.2d — (1976).

GLANZER v. SHEPARD

Court of Appeals of New York, 1922.
233 N.Y. 236, 135 N.E. 275, 23 A.L.R. 1425.

CARDOZO, J. Plaintiffs bought of Bech, Van Siclen & Co., a corporation, 905 bags of beans. The beans were to be paid for in accordance with weight sheets certified by public weighers. Bech, Van Siclen & Co., the seller, requested the defendants, who are engaged in business as public weighers, to make return of the weight and furnish the buyers with a copy. A letter to the weighers, dated July 20, 1918, informed them that the bags were on the dock, that the beans had been sold to Glanzer Bros., the plaintiffs, who would accept delivery Tuesday, July 23, and that the defendants were to communicate with the plaintiffs, and ascertain whether it would "be in order" to be on the pier Tuesday morning to weigh the beans before delivery. The defendants did as bidden. They certified the weight of the 905 bags to be 228,380 pounds, and were paid for the service by the seller. Their return recites that it has been made "by order of" Bech, Van Siclen & Co., "for G. Bros." One copy of the return they sent to the seller, and a duplicate to the buyers. Later, 17 bags, containing 4,136 pounds, were withdrawn from the shipment. The others were accepted and paid for on the faith of the certificates. The plaintiffs, upon attempting a resale, found that the actual weight was less by 11,854 pounds than the weight as certified in the return. Upon learning this, they brought suit against the defendants in the City Court of New York for $1,261.26, the amount overpaid. The trial judge, upon motions made by each side for the direction of a verdict, ordered judgment for the plaintiffs. The Appellate Term reversed upon the ground that the plaintiffs had no contract with the defendants, and must seek their remedy against the seller. The Appellate Division reversed the Appellate Term, and reinstated the verdict. The defendants are the appellants here.

We think the law imposes a duty toward buyer as well as seller in the situation here disclosed. The plaintiffs' use of the certificates was not an indirect or collateral consequence of the action of the weighers. It was a consequence which, to the weighers' knowledge, was the end and aim of the transaction. Bech, Van Siclen & Co. ordered, but Glanzer Brothers were to use. The defendants held themselves out to the public as skilled and careful in their calling. They knew that the beans had been sold, and that on the faith of their certificate payment would be made. They sent a copy to the plaintiffs for the very purpose of inducing action. All this they admit. In such circumstances, assumption of the task of weighing was the assumption of a duty to weigh carefully for the benefit of all whose conduct was to be governed. We do not need to state the duty in terms of contract or of privity. Growing out of a contract, it has none the less an origin not exclusively contractual. Given the contract and the relation, the duty is imposed by law (cf. MacPherson v. Buick Motor Co. * * *).

There is nothing new here in principle. If there is novelty, it is in the instance only. * * * It is ancient learning that one who assumes to act, even gratuitously, may thereby become subject to the duty of acting carefully, if he acts at all. * * * The most common examples of such a duty are cases where action is directed toward the person of another or his property (Street, supra). A like principle applies, however, where action is directed toward the governance of conduct. The controlling circumstance is not the character of the consequence, but its proximity or remoteness in the thought and purpose of the actor. * * * Here the defendants are held, not merely for careless words (Le Lievre v. Gould, 1893, 1

Q.B.D. 491; Pollock, Torts (10th ed.), pp. 301, 302; Jeremiah Smith, Liability for Negligent Language, 14 Harv.L.Rev. 184, 195), but for the careless performance of a service—the act of weighing—which happens to have found in the words of a certificate its culmination and its summary (cf. Corey v. Eastman, 166 Mass. 279, 287, 44 N.E. 217, 55 Am.St.Rep. 401). The line of separation between these diverse liabilities is difficult to draw. It does not lose for that reason its correspondence with realities. Life has relations not capable always of division into inflexible compartments. The moulds expand and shrink.

We state the defendants' obligation, therefore, in terms, not of contract merely, but of duty. Other forms of statement are possible. They involve, at most a change of emphasis. We may see here, if we please, a phase or an extension of the rule in Lawrence v. Fox, 20 N.Y. 268, as amplified recently in Seaver v. Ransom, 224 N.Y. 233, 120 N.E. 639, 2 A.L.R. 1187. If we fix our gaze upon that aspect, we shall stress the element of contract, and treat the defendants' promise as embracing the rendition of a service, which though ordered and paid for by one, was either wholly or in part for the benefit of another (De Cicco v. Schweizer, 221 N.Y. 431, 117 N.E. 807, L.R.A. 1918E, 1004, Ann.Cas.1918C, 816; Rector, etc., St. Mark's Church v. Teed, 120 N.Y. 583, 24 N.E. 1014). We may find analogies again in the decisions which treat the sender of a telegram as the agent of the recipient (Wolfskehl v. Western Union Tel. Co., 46 Hun 542; Milliken v. Western Union Tel. Co., 110 N.Y. 403, 18 N.E. 251, 1 L.R.A. 281). These other methods of approach arrive at the same goal, though the paths may seem at times to be artificial or circuitous. We have preferred to reach the goal more simply. The defendants, acting, not casually nor as mere servants, but in the pursuit of an independent calling, weighed and certified at the order of one with the very end and aim of shaping the conduct of another. Diligence was owing, not only to him who ordered, but to him also who relied. * * *

The judgment should be affirmed with costs. * * * [16]

ULTRAMARES CORP. v. TOUCHE, NIVEN & CO.

Court of Appeals of New York, 1931.
255 N.Y. 170, 174 N.E. 441, 74 A.L.R. 1139.

CARDOZO, CH. J. The action is in tort for damages suffered through the misrepresentations of accountants, the first cause of action being for misrepresentations that were merely negligent and the second for misrepresentations charged to have been fraudulent.

In January, 1924, the defendants, a firm of public accountants, were employed by Fred Stern & Co., Inc., to prepare and certify

16. See Green, Deceit, 16 Va.L.Rev. 749, 759 et seq. (1930); Carpenter, Responsibility for Intentional, Negligent and Innocent Misrepresentation, 24 Ill.Rev. 749, 754 et seq. (1930).

a balance sheet exhibiting the condition of its business as of December 31, 1923. They had been employed at the end of each of the three years preceding to render a like service. Fred Stern & Co., Inc., which was in substance Stern himself, was engaged in the importation and sale of rubber. To finance its operations, it required extensive credit and borrowed large sums of money from banks and other lenders. All this was known to the defendants. The defendants knew also that in the usual course of business the balance sheet when certified would be exhibited by the Stern company to banks, creditors, stockholders, purchasers or sellers, according to the needs of the occasion, as the basis of financial dealings. Accordingly when the balance sheet was made up, the defendants supplied the Stern company with thirty-two copies certified with serial numbers as counterpart originals. Nothing was said as to the persons to whom these counterparts would be shown or the extent or number of the transactions in which they would be used. In particular there was no mention of the plaintiff, a corporation doing business chiefly as a factor, which till then had never made advances to the Stern company, though it had sold merchandise in small amounts. The range of the transactions in which a certificate of audit might be expected to play a part was as indefinite and wide as the possibilities of the business that was mirrored in the summary.

By February 26, 1924, the audit was finished and the balance sheet made up. It stated assets in the sum of $2,550,671.88 and liabilities other than capital and surplus in the sum of $1,479,956.62, thus showing a net worth of $1,070,715.26. Attached to the balance sheet was a certificate as follows:

"We have examined the accounts of Fred Stern & Co., Inc., for the year ending December 31, 1923, and hereby certify that the annexed balance sheet is in accordance therewith and with the information and explanations given us. We further certify that, subject to provision for federal taxes on income, the said statement, in our opinion, presents a true and correct view of the financial condition of Fred Stern & Co., Inc., as at December 31, 1923.

"TOUCHE, NIVEN & CO.
"Public Accountants."

Capital and surplus were intact if the balance sheet was accurate. In reality both had been wiped out, and the corporation was insolvent. The books had been falsified by those in charge of the business so as to set forth accounts receivable and other assets which turned out to be fictitious. The plaintiff maintains that the certificate of audit was erroneous in both its branches. The first branch, the asserted correspondence between the accounts and the balance sheet, is one purporting to be made as of the knowledge of the auditors. The second branch, which certifies to a belief that the condition reflected in the balance sheet presents a true and correct picture of the resources of the business, is stated as a matter of opinion. In the view of the plaintiff, both branches of the certificate are either fraudulent or negligent. As to one class of assets, the item of accounts receivable, if not also as to others, there was no real correspondence, we are told, between balance sheet and books, or so the triers of the facts might find. If correspondence, however, be assumed, a closer examination of supporting invoices and records, or a fuller inquiry directed to the persons appearing on the books as creditors or debtors, would have exhibited the truth.

The plaintiff, a corporation engaged in business as a factor, was approached by Stern in March, 1924, with a request for loans of money to finance the sales of rubber. Up to that time the dealings between the two houses were on a cash basis and trifling in amount. As a condition of any loans the plaintiff insisted that it receive a balance sheet certified by public accountants, and in response to that demand it was given one of the certificates signed by the defendants and then in Stern's possession. On the faith of that certificate the plaintiff made a loan which was followed by many others. The course of business was for Stern to deliver to the plaintiff documents described as trust receipts which in effect were executory assignments of the moneys payable by purchasers for goods thereafter to be sold. When the purchase price was due, the plaintiff received the payments reimbursing itself therefrom for its advances and commissions. Some of these transactions were effected without loss. Nearly a year later, in December, 1924, the house of cards collapsed. In that month, plaintiff made three loans to the Stern company, one of $100,000, a second of $25,000, and a third of $40,000. For some of these loans no security was received. For some of the earlier loans the security was inadequate. On January 2, 1925, the Stern company was declared a bankrupt.

This action, brought against the accountants in November, 1926, to recover the loss suffered by the plaintiff in reliance upon the audit, was in its inception one for negligence. On the trial there was added a second cause of action asserting fraud also. The trial judge dismissed the second cause of action without submitting it to the jury. As to the first cause of action, he reserved his decision on the defendants' motion to dismiss, and took the jury's verdict. They were told that the defendants might be held liable if with knowledge that the results of the audit would be communicated to creditors they did the work negligently, and that negligence was the omission to use reasonable and ordinary care. The verdict was in favor of the plaintiff for $187,576.32. On the coming in of the verdict, the judge granted the reserved motion. The Appellate Division affirmed the dismissal of the cause of action for fraud, but reversed the dismissal of the cause of action for negligence, and reinstated the verdict. The case is here on cross-appeals.

The two causes of action will be considered in succession, first the one for negligence and second that for fraud.

(1) We think the evidence supports a finding that the audit was negligently made, though in so saying we put aside for the moment the question whether negligence, even if it existed, was a wrong to

the plaintiff. To explain fully or adequately how the defendants were at fault would carry this opinion beyond reasonable bounds. A sketch, however, there must be, at least in respect of some features of the audit, for the nature of the fault, when understood, is helpful in defining the ambit of the duty.

We begin with the item of accounts receivable. (Defendant's employees did not investigate a suspicious looking entry in the ledger of $706,843.07 made by a Stern employee after the ledger had been posted by defendant's employee. The entry was false and the falsity could easily have been discovered.)

The December entry of accounts receivable was not the only item that a careful and skillful auditor would have desired to investigate. There was ground for suspicion as to an item of $113,199.60, included in the accounts payable as due from the Baltic Corporation. As to this the defendants received an explanation, not very convincing, from Stern and Romberg. A cautious auditor might have been dissatisfied and have uncovered what was wrong. There was ground for suspicion also because of the inflation of the inventory. The inventory as it was given to the auditors, was totaled at $347,219.08. The defendants discovered errors in the sum of $303,863.20, and adjusted the balance sheet accordingly. Both the extent of the discrepancy and its causes might have been found to cast discredit upon the business and the books. There was ground for suspicion again in the record of assigned accounts. Inquiry of the creditors gave notice to the defendants that the same accounts had been pledged to two, three and four banks at the same time. The pledges did not diminish the value of the assets, but made in such circumstances they might well evoke a doubt as to the solvency of a business where such conduct was permitted. There was an explanation by Romberg which the defendants accepted as sufficient. Caution and diligence might have pressed investigation farther.

If the defendants owed a duty to the plaintiff to act with the same care that would have been due under a contract of employment, a jury was at liberty to find a verdict of negligence upon a showing of a scrutiny so imperfect and perfunctory. No doubt the extent to which inquiry must be pressed beyond appearances is a question of judgment, as to which opinions will often differ. No doubt the wisdom that is born after the event will engender suspicion and distrust when old acquaintances and good repute may have silenced doubt at the beginning. All this is to be weighed by a jury in applying its standard of behavior, the state of mind and conduct of the reasonable man. Even so, the adverse verdict, when rendered, imports as alignment of the weights in their proper places in the balance and a reckoning thereafter. The reckoning was not wrong upon the evidence before us, if duty be assumed.

We are brought to the question of duty, its origin and measure.

The defendants owed to their employer a duty imposed by law to make their certificate without fraud, and a duty growing out of contract to make it with the care and caution proper to their calling. Fraud includes the pretense of knowledge when knowledge there is none. To creditors and investors to whom the employer exhibited the certificate, the defendants owed a like duty to make it without fraud, since there was notice in the circumstances of its making that the employer did not intend to keep it to himself * * *. A different question develops when we ask whether they owed a duty to these to make it without negligence. If liability for negligence exists, a thoughtless slip or blunder, the failure to detect a theft or forgery beneath the cover of deceptive entries, may expose accountants to a liability in an indeterminate amount for an indeterminate time to an indeterminate class. The hazards of a business conducted on these terms are so extreme as to enkindle doubt whether a flaw may not exist in the implication of a duty that exposes to these consequences. We put aside for the moment any statement in the certificate which involves the representation of a fact as true to the knowledge of the auditors. If such a statement was made, whether believed to be true or not, the defendants are liable for deceit in the event that it was false. The plaintiff does not need the invention of novel doctrine to help it out in such conditions. The case was submitted to the jury and the verdict was returned upon the theory that even in the absence of a misstatement of a fact there is a liability also for erroneous opinion. The expression of an opinion is to be subject to a warranty implied by law. What, then, is the warranty, as yet unformulated, to be? Is it merely that the opinion is honestly conceived and that the preliminary inquiry has been honestly pursued, that a halt has not been made without a genuine belief that the search has been reasonably adequate to bring disclosure of the truth? Or does it go farther and involve the assumption of a liability for any blunder or inattention that could fairly be spoken of as negligence if the controversy were one between accountant and employer for breach of a contract to render services for pay?

The assault upon the citadel of privity is proceeding in these days apace. * * * In the field of the law of contract there has been a gradual widening of the doctrine of Lawrence v. Fox, 20 N.Y. 268, until today the beneficiary of a promise, clearly designated as such, is seldom left without a remedy (Seaver v. Ransom, 224 N.Y. 233, 238, 120 N.E. 639, 2 A.L.R. 1187). Even in that field, however, the remedy is narrower where the beneficiaries of the promise are indeterminate or general. Something more must then appear than an intention that the promise shall redound to the benefit of the public or to that of a class of indefinite extension. The promise must be such as to "bespeak the assumption of a duty to make reparation directly to the individual members of the public if the benefit is lost" (Moch Co. v. Rensselaer Water Co., 247 N.Y. 160, 164, 159 N.E. 896, 897, 62 A.L.R. 1199; American Law Institute, Restatement of the Law of Contracts, section 145). In the field of the law of torts a manufacturer who is negligent in the manufacture of a chattel in circumstances pointing to an unreasonable risk of serious bodily harm to those using it thereafter may be liable for negligence though privity is lacking between manufacturer and user. * * * A force or instrument of harm having been launched with potentialities of danger manifest to the eye of prudence, the one who launches it is under a duty to keep it within bounds. * * * We are now asked to say that a like liability attaches to the circulation of a thought or a release of the explosive power resident in words.

Three cases in this court are said by the plaintiff to have committed us to the doctrine that words, written or oral, if negligently published with the expectation that the reader or listener will transmit them to another, will lay a basis for liability though privity be lacking. These are Glanzer v. Shepard, 233 N.Y. 236, 238, 135 N.E. 275, 23 A.L.R. 1425; International Products Co. v. Erie R. R. Co., 244 N.Y. 331, 155 N.E. 662, 56 A.L.R. 1377, and Doyle v. Chatham & Phenix Nat. Bank, 253 N.Y. 369, 171 N.E. 574.

In Glanzer v. Shepard * * * was a case where the transmission of the certificate to another was not merely one possibility among many, but the "end and aim of the transaction," as certain and immediate and deliberately willed as if a husband were to order a gown to be delivered to his wife, or a telegraph company, contracting with the sender of a message, were to telegraph it wrongly to the damage of the person expected to receive it. * * * The intimacy of the resulting *nexus* is attested by the fact that after stating the case in terms of legal duty, we went on to point out that viewing it as a phase or extension of Lawrence v. Fox (supra), or Seaver v. Ransom (supra), we could reach the same result by stating it in terms of contract. * * * The bond was so close as to approach that of privity, if not completely one with it. Not so in the case at hand. No one would be likely to urge that there was a contractual relation, or even one approaching it, at the root of any duty that was owing from the defendants now before us to the indeterminate class of persons who, presently or in the future, might deal with the Stern company in reliance on the audit. In a word, the service rendered by the defendant in Glanzer v. Shepard was primarily for the information of a third person, in effect, if not in name, a party to the contract, and only incidentally for that of the formal promisee. In the case at hand, the service was primarily for the benefit of the Stern company, a convenient instrumentality for use in the development of the business, and only incidentally or collaterally for the use of those to whom Stern and his associates might exhibit it thereafter. Foresight of these possibilities may charge with liability for fraud. The conclusion does not follow that it will charge with liability for negligence.

In the next of the three cases (International Products Co. v. Erie R. R. Co., supra) the plaintiff, an importer, had an agreement with the defendant, a railroad company, that the latter would act as bailee of goods arriving from abroad. The importer, to protect the goods by suitable insurance, made inquiry of the bailee as to the location of the storage. The warehouse was incorrectly named, and the policy did not attach. Here was a determinate relation, that of bailor and bailee, either present or prospective, with peculiar opportunity for knowledge on the part of the bailee as to the subject-matter of the statement and with a continuing duty to correct it if erroneous. Even the narrowest holdings as to liability for unintentional misstatement concede that a representation in such circumstances may be equivalent to a warranty. There is a class of cases "where a person within whose special province it lay to know a particular fact, has given an erroneous answer to an inquiry made with regard to it by a person desirous of ascertaining the fact for the purpose of determining his course accordingly, and has been held bound to make good the assurance he has given." (Herschell, L.C., in Derry v. Peek, L.R. 14 A.C. 337, 360). So in Burrowes v. Lock, 10 Ves. 470, a trustee was asked by one who expected to make a loan upon the security of a trust fund whether notice of any prior incumbrance upon the fund had been given to him. An action for damages was upheld though the false answer was made honestly in the belief that it was true (cf. Brownlie v. Campbell, L.R. 5 A.C. 925, 935; Doyle v. Chatham & Phenix Nat. Bank, supra, at p. 379).

In one respect the decision in International Products Co. v. Erie R. R. Co. is in advance of anything decided in Glanzer v. Shepard. The latter case suggests that the liability there enforced was not one for the mere utterance of words without due consideration, but for a negligent service, the act of weighing, which happened to find in the words of the certificate its culmination and its summary. This was said in the endeavor to emphasize the character of the certificate as a business transaction, an act in the law, and not a mere casual response to a request for information. The ruling in the case of the Erie Railroad shows that the rendition of a service is at most a mere circumstance and not an indispensable condition. The Erie was not held for negligence in the rendition of a service. It was held for words and nothing more. So in the case at hand. If liability for the consequences of a negligent certificate may be enforced by any member of an indeterminate class of creditors, present and prospective, known and unknown, the existence or non-existence of a preliminary act of service will not affect the cause of action. The service may have been rendered as carefully as you please, and its quality will count for nothing if there was negligence thereafter in distributing the summary.

Doyle v. Chatham & Phenix Nat. Bank (supra), the third of the cases cited, is even more plainly indecisive. A trust company was a trustee under a deed to secure an issue of bonds. It was held liable to a subscriber for the bonds when it certified them falsely. A representation by a trustee intended to sway action had been addressed to a person who by the act of subscription was to become a party to the deed and a *cestui que* trust.

The antidote to these decisions and to the over-use of the doctrine of liability for negligent misstatement may be found in Jaillet v. Cashman, 235 N.Y. 511, 139 N.E. 714, and Courteen Seed Co. v. Hong Kong & Shanghai Banking Corp., 245 N.Y. 377, 381, 157 N.E. 272, 273, 56

A.L.R. 1186. In the first of these cases the defendant supplying ticker service to brokers was held not liable in damages to one of the broker's customers for the consequences of reliance upon a report negligently published on the ticker. If liability had been upheld, the step would have been a short one to the declaration of a like liability on the part of proprietors of newspapers. In the second the principle was clearly stated by Pound, J., that "negligent words are not actionable unless they are uttered directly with knowledge or notice that they will be acted on, to one to whom the speaker is bound by some relation of duty, arising out of public calling, contract or otherwise, to act with care if he acts at all."

From the foregoing analysis the conclusion is, we think, inevitable that nothing in our previous decisions commits us to a holding of liability for negligence in the circumstances of the case at hand, and that such liability, if recognized, will be an extension of the principle of those decisions to different conditions, even if more or less analogous. The question then is whether such an extension shall be made.

The extension, if made, will so expand the field of liability for negligent speech as to make it nearly, if not quite, coterminous with that of liability for fraud. Again and again, in decisions of this court, the bounds of this latter liability have been set up, with futility the fate of every endeavor to dislodge them. *Scienter* has been declared to be an indispensable element except where the representation has been put forward as true of one's own knowledge. (Hadcock v. Osmer, 153 N.Y. 604, 47 N.E. 923), or in circumstances where the expression of opinion was a dishonorable pretense * * *. Even an opinion, especially an opinion by an expert, may be found to be fraudulent if the grounds supporting it are so flimsy as to lead to the conclusion that there was no genuine belief back of it. Further than that this court has never gone. Directors of corporations have been acquitted of liability for deceit though they have been lax in investigation and negligent in speech (Reno v. Bull, 226 N.Y. 546, 124 N.E. 144, and cases there cited; Kountze v. Kennedy, 147 N.Y. 124, 129, 41 N.E. 414, 29 L.R.A. 360, 49 Am.St.Rep. 651). This has not meant, to be sure, that negligence may not be evidence from which a trier of the facts may draw an inference of fraud (Derry v. Peek, L.R. 14 A.C. 337, 369, 375, 376), but merely that if that inference is rejected, or, in the light of all the circumstances, is found to be unreasonable, negligence alone is not a substitute for fraud. Many also are the cases that have distinguished between the willful or reckless representation essential to the maintenance at law of an action for deceit, and the misrepresentation, negligent or innocent, that will lay a sufficient basis for rescission in equity (Bloomquist v. Farson, 222 N.Y. 375, 118 N.E. 855; Seneca Wire & Mfg. Co. v. A. B. Leach & Co., 247 N.Y. 1, 159 N.E. 700). If this action is well conceived, all these principles and distinctions, so nicely wrought and formulated, have been a waste of time and effort. They have even been a snare, entrapping litigants and lawyers into an abandonment of the true remedy lying ready to the call. The suitors thrown out of court because they proved negligence, and nothing else, in an action for deceit, might have ridden to triumphant victory if they had proved the self-same facts, but had given the wrong another label, and all this in a State where forms of action have been abolished. So to hold is near to saying that we have been paltering with justice. A word of caution or suggestion would have set the erring suitor right. Many pages of opinion were written by judges the most eminent, yet the word was never spoken. We may not speak it now. A change so revolutionary, if expedient, must be wrought by legislation (Landell v. Lybrand, 264 Pa. 406, 107 A. 783, 8 A.L.R. 461).

We have said that the duty to refrain from negligent representation would become coincident or nearly so with the duty to refrain from fraud if this action could be maintained. A representation even though knowingly false does not constitute ground for an action of deceit unless made with the intent to be communicated to the persons or class of persons who act upon it to their prejudice (Eaton, Cole & Burnham Co. v. Avery, supra).[17] Affirmance of this judgment would require us to hold that all or nearly all the persons so situated would suffer an impairment of an interest legally protected if the representation had been negligent. We speak of all "or nearly all," for cases can be imagined where a casual response, made in circumstances insufficient to indicate that care should be expected, would permit recovery for fraud if willfully deceitful. Cases of fraud between persons so circumstanced are, however, too infrequent and exceptional to make the radii greatly different if the fields of liability for negligence and deceit be figured as concentric circles. The like may be said of the possibility that the negligence of the injured party, contributing to the result, may avail to overcome the one remedy, though unavailing to defeat the other.

Neither of these possibilities is noted by the plaintiff in its answer to the suggestion that the two fields would be coincident. Its answer has been merely this, *first,* that the duty to speak with care does not arise unless the words are the culmination of a service, and *second,* that it does not arise unless the service is rendered in the pursuit of an independent calling, characterized as public. As to the first of these suggestions, we have already had occasion to observe that given a relation making diligence a duty, speech as well as conduct must conform to that exacting standard (International Products Co. v. Erie R. R. Co., supra). As to the second of the two suggestions, public accountants are public only in the sense that their services are offered to any one who chooses to employ them. This is far from saying that those who do not employ them are in the same position as those who do.

Liability for negligence if adjudged in this case will extend to many callings other than an auditor's. Lawyers who certify their opinion as to the validity of municipal or corporate bonds with knowledge

17. But cf. Rosenbluth v. Sackadorf, 190 Misc. 665, 76 N.Y.S.2d 447 (1947), rev'd 274 App.Div. 794, 79 N.Y.S.2d 524 (1948), noted 33 Minn.L.Rev. 194 (1949); Benton v. Pratt, 2 Wend. 385 (N.Y.1829); Merchant's Nat. Bank v. Robison, 8 Utah 256, 30 P. 985 (1892). And see Advance Music Corp. v. American Tobacco Co., 183 Misc. 645, 649, 50 N.Y.S.2d 287, 291 (1944).

In general, see Keeton, The Ambit of the Fraudulent Representor's Liability, 17 Tex.L.Rev. 1 (1938).

that the opinion will be brought to the notice of the public, will become liable to the investors, if they have overlooked a statute or a decision, to the same extent as if the controversy were one between client and adviser. Title companies insuring titles to a tract of land, with knowledge that at an approaching auction the fact that they have insured will be stated to the bidders, will become liable to purchasers who may wish the benefit of a policy without payment of a premium. These illustrations may seem to be extreme, but they go little, if any, farther than we are invited to go now. Negligence, moreover, will have one standard when viewed in relation to the employer, and another and at times a stricter standard when viewed in relation to the public. Explanations that might seem plausible, omissions that might be reasonable, if the duty is confined to the employer, conducting a business that presumably at least is not a fraud upon his creditors, might wear another aspect if an independent duty to be suspicious even of one's principal is owing to investors. * * *

Our holding does not emancipate accountants from the consequences of fraud. It does not relieve them if their audit has been so negligent as to justify a finding that they had no genuine belief in its adequacy, for this again is fraud. It does no more than say that if less than this is proved, if there has been neither reckless misstatement nor insincere profession of an opinion, but only honest blunder, the ensuing liability for negligence is one that is bounded by the contract, and is to be enforced between the parties by whom the contract has been made. We doubt whether the average business man receiving a certificate without paying for it and receiving it merely as one among a multitude of possible investors, would look for anything more.

(2) The second cause of action is yet to be considered.

The defendants certified as a fact, true to their own knowledge, that the balance sheet was in accordance with the books of account. If their statement was false, they are not to be exonerated because they believed it to be true * * *.[18] We think the triers of the facts might hold it to be false.

Correspondence between the balance sheet and the books imports something more, or so the triers of the facts might say, than correspondence between the balance sheet and the general ledger, unsupported or even contradicted by every other record. The correspondence to be of any moment may not unreasonably be held to signify a correspondence between the statement and the books of original entry, the books taken as a whole. If that is what the certificate means, a

18. But cf. Brodsky, The Twilight Zone Between Negligence and Fraud in the Accountants' Cases, 3 Intramural L. Rev. 11, 13 (1947) ("This portion of the opinion does not recognize an important distinction between negligence and fraud. If a person pretends that he knows his statement is true when he merely believes that it is probably true, he has not the sort of belief which would remove his case from the realm of consciousness of false representation. But if he believes it is definitely true, and says it is, but it isn't, then the element of scienter is lacking and he shouldn't be held liable for fraud.").

jury could find that the correspondence did not exist and that the defendants signed the certificates without knowing it to exist and even without reasonable grounds for belief in its existence. The item of $706,000, representing fictitious accounts receivable, was entered in the ledger after defendant's employee Seiss had posted the December sales. He knew of the interpolation, and knew that there was need to verify the entry by reference to books other than the ledger before the books could be found to be in agreement with the balance sheet. The evidence would sustain a finding that this was never done. By concession the interpolated item had no support in the journal, or in any journal voucher, or in the debit memo book, which was a summary of the invoices, or in anything except the invoices themselves. The defendants do not say that they ever looked at the invoices, seventeen in number, representing these accounts. They profess to be unable to recall whether they did so or not. They admit, however, that if they had looked, they would have found omissions and irregularities so many and unusual as to have called for further investigation. When we couple the refusal to say that they did look with the admission that if they had looked, they would or could have seen, the situation is revealed as one in which a jury might reasonably find that in truth they did not look, but certified the correspondence without testing its existence.

In this connection we are to bear in mind the principle already stated in the course of this opinion that negligence or blindness, even when not equivalent to fraud, is none the less evidence to sustain an inference of fraud. At least this is so if the negligence is gross. Not a little confusion has at times resulted from an undiscriminating quotation of statements in Kountze v. Kennedy (supra), statements proper enough in their setting, but capable of misleading when extracted and considered by themselves. "Misjudgment, however gross," it was there observed, "or want of caution, however marked, is not fraud." This was said in a case where the trier of the facts had held the defendants guiltless. The judgment in this court amounted merely to a holding that a finding of fraud did not follow as an inference of law. There was no holding that the evidence would have required a reversal of the judgment if the finding as to guilt had been the other way. Even Derry v. Peek, as we have seen, asserts the probative effect of negligence as an evidentiary fact. We had no thought in Kountze v. Kennedy of upholding a doctrine more favorable to wrongdoers, though there was a reservation suggesting the approval of a rule more rigorous. * * *

The defendants attempt to excuse the omission of an inspection of the invoices proved to be fictitious by invoking a practice known as that of testing and sampling. A random choice of accounts is made from the total number on the books, and these, if found to be regular when inspected and investigated, are taken as a fair indication of the quality of the mass. The defendants say that about 200 invoices were examined in accordance with this practice, but they do not assert that any of the seventeen invoices supporting the fictitious sales were among the number so selected. Verification by test and sample was very likely a sufficient audit as to accounts regularly entered upon the books in the usual course of business. It was plainly insufficient, however, as to accounts not entered upon the books where inspection of the invoices was necessary, not as a check upon accounts fair upon their face, but in order to ascertain whether there were any accounts at all. If the only invoices inspected were invoices unrelated to the interpolated entry, the result was to certify a correspondence between the books and the balance sheet without any effort by the auditors, as to $706,000 of accounts, to ascertain whether the certified agreement was in accordance with the truth. How far books of account fair upon their face are to be probed by accountants in an effort to ascertain whether the transactions back of them are in accordance with the entries, involves to some extent the exercise of judgment and discretion. Not so, however, the inquiry whether the entries certified as there, are there in very truth, there in the form and in the places where men of business training would expect them to be. The defendants were put on their guard by the circumstances touching the December accounts receivable to scrutinize with special care. A jury might find that with suspicions thus awakened, they closed their eyes to the obvious, and blindly gave assent.

We conclude, to sum up the situation, that in certifying to the correspondence between balance sheet and accounts the defendants made a statement as true to their own knowledge, when they had, as a jury might find, no knowledge on the subject. If that is so, they may also be found to have acted without information leading to a sincere or genuine belief when they certified to an opinion that the balance sheet faithfully reflected the condition of the business.

Whatever wrong was committed by the defendants was not their personal act or omission, but that of their subordinates. This does not relieve them, however, of liability to answer in damages for the consequences of the wrong, if wrong there shall be found to be. It is not a question of constructive notice, as where facts are brought home to the knowledge of subordinates whose interests are adverse to those of the employer (Henry v. Allen, 151 N.Y. 1, 45 N.E. 355, 36 L.R.A. 658; see, however, American Law Institute, Restatement of the Law of Agency, section 506, subd. 2–a). These subordinates, so far as the record shows, had no interests adverse to the defendants', nor any thought in what they did to be unfaithful to their trust. The question is merely this, whether the defendants, having delegated the performance of this work to agents of their own selection, are responsible for the manner in which the business of the agency was done. As to that the answer is not doubtful (Fifth Ave. Bank of New York v. 42d St. & G. St. Ferry R. R. Co., 137 N.Y. 231, 33 N.E. 378, 19 L.R.A. 331, 33 Am.St.Rep. 712; Gleason v. Seaboard Air Line Ry. Co., 278 U.S. 349, 356; American Law Institute, Restatement of the Law of Agency, section 481).

Upon the defendants' appeal as to the first cause of action, the judgment of the Appellate Division should be reversed, and that of the Trial Term affirmed, with costs in the Appellate Division and in this court.

Upon the plaintiff's appeal as to the second cause of action, the judgment of the Appellate Division and that of the Trial Term should be reversed, and a new trial granted, with costs to abide the event. * * * [19]

HEDLEY BYRNE & CO. v. HELLER & PARTNERS LTD.

House of Lords.
[1964] A.C. 465, [1963] 2 All E.R. 575.

[Plaintiff advertising agency, committing itself for television time and advertising space on behalf of a client ("Easipower"), tried to check on the client's credit through inquiries by the agency's bank to defendant, the client's bank, whether Easipower would be good for an advertising contract, on first inquiry in the amount of £8000–9000, and on a later inquiry in the amount of £100,000. Defendant replied to plaintiff's bank "without responsibility on the part of the Bank or its officials" that Easipower was "respectably constituted and considered good for its normal business engagements", and, on the second inquiry, "Your figures are larger than we are accustomed to see." Plaintiff lost £17,000 when Easipower went into liquidation. There was no suggestion of dishonesty on the part of defendant; indeed, the evidence as to negligence is not clear, although there is some discussion in the report about defendant's knowledge of its own large loans to Easipower, and of the financial difficulties of Easipower's parent company.]

LORD REID. * * *

* * * Apart altogether from authority, I would think that the law must treat negligent words differently from negligent acts. * * * [20] The most obvious difference between negligent words

19. Compare Chandler v. Crane, Christmas & Co., [1951] 1 A.E. 426 [1951] 2 K.B. 164, noted 65 Harv.L.Rev. 355; Seavey, Chandler v. Crane, Christmas & Co., Negligent Misrepresentations by Accountants, 67 L.Q.Rev. 466 (1951). The Securities Act adopts a negligence theory of liability, placing the burden of proof upon the defendant. Section 11(b)(3)(B), 15 U.S.C.A. § 77k(b)(3)(B). But see Shonts v. Hirliman, 28 F.Supp. 478, 483 (D.C.Cal.1939), where accountant is held to a "surprisingly low" standard of care which might not advance the accountant's statutory liability far beyond that imposed by the principal case. See L. Loss, Securities Regulation 1021 (1951). Cf. State St. Trust Co. v. Ernst, 278 N.Y. 104, 15 N.E.2d 416, 120 A.L.R. 1250 (1938). Mr. Loss' excellent book discusses the whole problem of civil liabilities under SEC statutes. The principal case is excellently noted by Green, (1931) 26 Ill.L.Rev. 49. See National Surety Corp. v. Lybrand, 256 App.Div. 226, 9 N.Y.S.2d 554 (1939), where the question of contributory negligence is treated. Gould v. Flato, 170 Misc. 378, 10 N.Y.S.2d 361 (1938), is not a third-party plaintiff case, but a valuable discussion of liability for deceit and negligent language is found in the opinion.

20. Donoghue v. Stevenson [1932] A.C. 562; 48 T.L.R. 494, H.L. [See note 10, page 163 supra.]

and negligent acts is this. Quite careful people often express definite opinions on social or informal occasions even when they see that others are likely to be influenced by them; and they often do that without taking that care which they would take if asked for their opinion professionally or in a business connection. * * * But it is at least unusual casually to put into circulation negligently made articles which are dangerous. A man might give a friend a negligently-prepared bottle of home-made wine and his friend's guests might drink it with dire results. But it is by no means clear that those guests would have no action against the negligent manufacturer.

Another obvious difference is that a negligently made article will only cause one accident, and so it is not very difficult to find the necessary degree of proximity or neighbourhood between the negligent manufacturer and the person injured. But words can be broadcast with or without the consent or the foresight of the speaker or writer. It would be one thing to say that the speaker owes a duty to a limited class, but it would be going very far to say that he owes a duty to every ultimate "consumer" who acts on those words to his detriment. It would be no use to say that a speaker or writer owes a duty but can disclaim responsibility if he wants to. He, like the manufacturer, could make it part of a contract that he is not to be liable for his negligence: but that contract would not protect him in a question with a third party, at least if the third party was unaware of it.

So it seems to me that there is good sense behind our present law that in general an innocent but negligent misrepresentation gives no cause of action. There must be something more than the mere misstatement. * * * The most natural requirement would be that expressly or by implication from the circumstances the speaker or writer has undertaken some responsibility * * *. Where there is a contract there is no difficulty as regards the contracting parties: the question is whether there is a warranty. Then there are cases where a person does not merely make a statement but performs a gratuitous service. * * * [I]n some cases that person owes a duty of care apart from any contract, and to that extent * * * there can be a duty of care in making a statement of fact or opinion which is independent of contract.

Much of the difficulty in this field has been caused by Derry v. Peek.[21] The action was brought against the directors of a company in respect of false statements in a prospectus. It was an action of deceit based on fraud and nothing else. But it was held that the directors had believed that their statements were true although they had no reasonable grounds for their belief. The Court of Appeal held that this amounted to fraud in law, but naturally enough this House held that there can be no fraud without dishonesty and that credulity is not dishonesty. The question was never really considered whether the facts had imposed on the directors a duty to exercise care. It

21. (1889) 14 App.Cas. 337; 5 T.L.R. 625, H.L. [From original, renumbered. See page 807 supra.]

must be implied that on the facts of that case there was no such duty. But that was immediately remedied by the Directors' Liability Act, 1890, which provided that a director is liable for untrue statements in a prospectus unless he proves that he had reasonable ground to believe and did believe that they were true.

It must now be taken that Derry v. Peek did not establish any universal rule that in the absence of contract an innocent but negligent misrepresentation cannot give rise to an action. * * * We cannot * * * now accept as accurate the numerous statements to that effect in cases between 1889 and 1914, and we must now determine the extent of the exceptions to that rule.

* * *

A reasonable man, knowing that he was being trusted or that his skill and judgment were being relied on, would, I think, have three courses open to him. He could keep silent or decline to give the information or advice sought: or he could give an answer with a clear qualification that he accepted no responsibility for it or that it was given without that reflection or inquiry which a careful answer would require: or he could simply answer without any such qualification. If he chooses to adopt the last course he must, I think, be held to have accepted some responsibility for his answer being given carefully, or to have accepted a relationship with the inquirer which requires him to exercise such care as the circumstances require. * *

* * * [H]ere [the agency's] bank, who were their agents in making the inquiry, began by saying [according to defendant's records] that "they wanted "to know in confidence and without responsibility on our part," that is, on the part of the respondents. So I cannot see how the appellants can now be entitled to disregard that and maintain that the respondents did incur a responsibility to them. * * *

I am therefore of opinion that it is clear that the respondents never undertook any duty to exercise care in giving their replies. The appellants cannot succeed unless there was such a duty and therefore in my judgment this appeal must be dismissed.

LORD MORRIS OF BORTH-Y-GEST.

* * * It is, I think, a reasonable and proper inference that the bank must have known that the National Provincial were making their inquiry because some customer of theirs was or might be entering into some advertising contract in respect of which Easipower Ltd. might become under a liability to such customer to the extent of the figures mentioned. * * * The bank must have known that the inquiry was being made by someone who was contemplating doing business with Easipower Ltd. and that their answer or the substance of it would in fact be passed on to such person. The conditions subject to which the bank gave their answers are important but the fact that the person to whom the answers would in all probability be passed on was unnamed and unknown to the bank is not important * * *.

My Lords, it seems to me that if A assumes a responsibility to B to tender him deliberate advice, there could be a liability if the advice is negligently given. * * *

* * * There was in the present case no contemplation of receiving anything like a formal and detailed report such as might be given by some concern charged with the duty (probably for reward) of making all proper and relevant inquiries concerning the nature, scope and extent of a company's activities and of obtaining and marshalling all available evidence as to its credit, efficiency, standing and business reputation. There is much to be said, therefore, for the view that if a banker gives a reference in the form of a brief expression of opinion in regard to credit-worthiness he does not accept, and there is not expected from him, any higher duty than that of giving an honest answer. I need not, however, seek to deal further with this aspect of the matter, which perhaps cannot be covered by any statement of general application, because, in my judgment, the bank in the present case, by the words which they employed, effectively disclaimed any assumption of a duty of care. They stated that they only responded to the inquiry on the basis that their reply was without responsibility. If the inquirers chose to receive and act upon the reply they cannot disregard the definite terms upon which it was given. They cannot accept a reply given with a stipulation and then reject the stipulation. * * *

[LORD HODSON agreed generally with LORD MORRIS of BORTH-Y-GEST.]

LORD DEVLIN.

* * *

Originally it was thought that the tort of negligence must be confined entirely to deeds and could not extend to words. That was supposed to have been decided by Derry v. Peek. I cannot imagine that anyone would now dispute that if this were the law, the law would be gravely defective. The practical proof of this is that the supposed deficiency was in relation to the facts in Derry v. Peek immediately made good by Act of Parliament. Today it is unthinkable that the law could permit directors to be as careless as they liked in the statements they made in a prospectus.

A simple distinction between negligence in word and negligence in deed might leave the law defective but at least it would be intelligible. [H]owever, the distinction * * * is one which would be unworkable. A defendant who is given a car to overhaul and repair if necessary is liable to the injured driver (a) if he overhauls it and repairs it negligently and tells the driver it is safe when it is not; (b) if he overhauls it and negligently finds it not to be in need of repair and tells the driver it is safe when it is not; and (c) if he negligently omits to overhaul it at all and tells the driver that it is safe when it is not. It would be absurd in any of these cases to argue that the proximate cause of the driver's injury was not what the defendant did or failed to do but his negligent statement on the faith of which the driver drove the car and for which he could not recover. In this type of case, where if there were a contract there would undoubtedly be a duty of service, it is not practicable to distinguish between the inspection or examination, the acts done or omitted to be done, and the advice or information given. * * *

This is why the distinction is now said to depend on whether financial loss is caused through physical injury or whether it is caused directly. The interposition of the physical injury is said to make a difference of principle. I can find neither logic nor common sense in this. If irrespective of contract, a doctor negligently advises a patient that he can safely pursue his occupation and he cannot and the patient's health suffers and he loses his livelihood, the patient has a remedy. But if the doctor negligently advises him that he cannot safely pursue his occupation when in fact he can and he loses his livelihood, there is said to be no remedy. Unless, of course, the patient was a private patient and the doctor accepted half a guinea for his trouble: then the patient can recover all. I am bound to say, my Lords, that I think this to be nonsense. It is not the sort of nonsense that can arise even in the best system of law out of the need to draw nice distinctions between borderline cases. It arises, if it is the law, simply out of a refusal to make sense. The line is not drawn on any intelligible principle. It just happens to be the line which those who have been driven from the extreme assertion that negligent statements in the absence of contractual or fiduciary duty give no cause of action have in the course of their retreat so far reached. * * *

I have had the advantage of reading all the opinions prepared by your Lordships and of studying the terms which your Lordships have framed by way of definition of the sort of relationship which gives rise to a responsibility towards those who act upon information or advice and so creates a duty of care towards them. I do not understand any of your Lordships to hold that it is a responsibility imposed by law upon certain types of persons or in certain sorts of situations. It is a responsibility that is voluntarily accepted or undertaken, either generally where a general relationship, such as that of solicitor and client or banker and customer, is created, or specifically in relation to a particular transaction. * * * Responsibility can attach only to the single act, that is, the giving of the reference, and only if the doing of that act implied a voluntary undertaking to assume responsibility. This is a point of great importance because it is, as I understand it, the foundation for the ground on which in the end the House dismisses the appeal. * * *

I shall therefore content myself with the proposition that wherever there is a relationship equivalent to contract, there is a duty of care. Such a relationship may be either general or particular. Examples of a general relationship are those of solicitor and client and of banker and customer. * * * Where there is a general relationship of this sort, it is unnecessary to do more than prove its existence and the duty follows. Where, as in the present case, what is relied on is a particular relationship created ad hoc, it will be necessary to examine the particular facts to see whether there is an express or implied undertaking of responsibility. * * *

* * * I should consider it necessary to examine [plaintiff's] contentions were it not for the general disclaimer of responsibility which appears to me in any event to be conclusive. I agree entirely with the reasoning and conclusion on this point of my noble and learned friend, Lord Reid. A man cannot be said voluntarily to be undertaking a responsibility if at the very moment when he is said to be accepting it he declares that in fact he is not. The problem of reconciling words of exemption with the existence of a duty arises only when a party is claiming exemption from a responsibility which he has already undertaken or which he is contracting to undertake. For this reason alone, I would dismiss the appeal.

LORD PEARCE.

* * *

How wide the sphere of the duty of care in negligence is to be laid depends ultimately upon the courts' assessment of the demands of society for protection from the carelessness of others. Economic protection has lagged behind protection in physical matters where there is injury to person and property. It may be that the size and the width of the range of possible claims has acted as a deterrent to extension of economic protection. * * *

* * * The true rule is that innocent misrepresentation per se gives no right to damages. If the misrepresentation was intended by the parties to form a warranty between two contracting parties, it gives on that ground a right to damages * * *. If an innocent misrepresentation is made between parties in a fiduciary relationship it may, on that ground, give a right to claim damages for negligence. There is also, in my opinion, a duty of care created by special relationships which, though not fiduciary, give rise to an assumption that care as well as honesty is demanded.

* * * If * * * [the circumstances of the transaction] disclosed a casual social approach to the inquiry, no such special relationship or duty of care would be assumed * * * To import such a duty the representation must normally, I think, concern a business or professional transaction whose nature makes clear the gravity of the inquiry and the importance and influence attached to the answer. * * * A most important circumstance is the form of the inquiry and of the answer. Both were here plainly stated to be without liability. * * * [Those words] clearly prevent a special relationship from arising. They are part of the material from which one deduces whether a duty of care and a liability for negligence was assumed. If both parties say expressly (in a case where neither is

deliberately taking advantage of the other) that there shall be no liability, I do not find it possible to say that a liability was assumed. * * * [22]

RHODE ISLAND HOSPITAL TRUST NATIONAL BANK v. SWARTZ, YAVNER & JACOBS

United States Court of Appeals for the Fourth Circuit, 1972.
455 F.2d 847.

WINTER, CIRCUIT JUDGE. Rhode Island Hospital Trust National Bank ("Bank") sued Swartz, Bresenoff, Yavner & Jacobs, a firm of certified public accountants ("Accountants"), each of the partners of the firm and the estate of a deceased partner, alleging, *inter alia,* that Accountants had negligently audited the financial statements of International Trading Corporation and related companies ("Borrower") in consequence of which Bank had made loans to Borrower which was unable to repay them and Bank sustained a loss in excess of $100,000.00. The district court, sitting nonjury, * * * dismissed the complaint. We disagree with the district court's conclusions with regard to negligence. We, therefore, reverse and remand for further proceedings.

I

Borrower, an importer of cement, became a customer of Bank in 1962 * * * Borrower obtained a line of credit from Bank, to be secured by a pledge of inventories and accounts receivable, in the amount of 75% of collateral but not to exceed $200,000.00. At approximately the same time, Borrower undertook to change its method of loading and unloading cement imports from handling in bags to handling in bulk.

This change in method necessitated a modification of facilities and the expenditure of considerable sums for leasehold improvements. * * *

In 1963 Borrower sought long-term financing of leasehold improvements from Bank, but Bank was unwilling to lend on this basis. Bank, however, did accede to Borrower's request that the maximum amount of its line of credit be exceeded upon Borrower's assurance

22. After *Hedley Byrne* what was the liability of English accountants to third parties for negligent misrepresentation? The Council of the Institute of Chartered Accountants in England and Wales issued the following statement:

"In counsel's view, third parties entitled to recover damages under the *Hedley Byrne* principle will be limited to those who by reason of accountants' negligence in preparing reports, accounts or financial statements on which the third parties place reliance suffer financial loss in circumstances where the accountants knew or ought to have known that the reports, accounts or financial statements in question were being prepared for the specific purpose or transaction which gave rise to the loss and that they would be shown to and relied on by third parties in that particular connection." J. Accountancy, July 1965, at 66.

that economies from savings on labor costs expected to result from bulk handling would enable Borrower to operate more profitably and to meet greater loan obligations.

In June 1964 Borrower represented to Bank that during 1963 it had expended $212,000.00 for leasehold improvements to its facilities at Palm Beach, Florida, Brunswick, Georgia, and Providence, Rhode Island. The work was purportedly done by Borrower, using its own labor and materials. *In fact, the claimed 1963 leasehold improvements were totally fictitious.* The labor expenses claimed to have been incurred were incurred as operating expenses of handling and storing cement. No materials were purchased. An inspection in 1964 of all three of the facilities disclosed that they were in the same condition as they were at the end of 1962.

In accordance with the loan agreement establishing the line of credit, Borrower was obligated to furnish Bank with financial statements for each year, ending December 31; and, beginning March 27, 1964, Bank pressed to obtain the statements for the year 1963. They were not forthcoming until June 24, 1964. The income statement showed that total operating expenses, amounting to $609,956.42, were reduced by $212,000.00, designated "Estimated Expenses Contained in Operating Expenses Representing Cost of Leasehold Improvements," with the net effect that Borrower had a net profit after taxes of $9,257.60. The balance sheet similarly capitalized this sum on the asset side, together with other leasehold improvements, and showed a net worth of $339,427.48. If the $212,000.00 had not been capitalized, the income statement would have shown a substantial loss from operations and the balance sheet would have shown a substantial depletion of net worth (both of approximately $200,000.00).

When Accountants transmitted the financial statements to their client they wrote a covering letter expressing certain reservations about the "fairness of the accompanying statements." They stated that they had reviewed the balance sheet and profit and loss statement of Borrower and "[o]ur examination included a general review of accounting procedures and such tests of accounting records as we were permitted to make." Next, they stated that cash in banks had been verified by direct confirmations and reconciled, but that only 80.98% of the total trade accounts receivable had been confirmed. Physical inventories had been taken in Georgia, Florida and Rhode Island by correspondent accountants and various items of inventory valuation examined, with the result that the inventory as priced by management and the total of inventories as shown on the statements appeared to be correct.

The letter then discussed the crucial item concerned in this litigation—the leasehold improvements—and set forth the following:

> *Additions* to fixed assets in 1963 *were found* to include principally warehouse improvements and installation of machinery and equipment in Providence, Rhode Island, Brunswick, Georgia, and Palm Beach, Florida. Practically

> *all of this work was done by company employees and materials and overhead was borne by the International Trading Corporation and its affiliates.* Unfortunately, fully complete detailed cost records were not kept of these capital improvements and no exact determination could be made as to the actual cost of said improvements. (emphasis added) * *
>
> Management has obtained appraisals from * * * [certain named] companies, *which support* the amounts set up for leasehold improvements in the warehouses * * *. Copies of their appraisals are attached hereto and are part of this report.[23] (emphasis added)
>
> With reference to the appraisal from A. H. Leeming and Sons of Rhode Island, Inc., this report did not include engineering services, electrical service, crane service and concrete installation forms and drilling. Management was able to identify these items from invoices recorded on its books and are submitted herewith in conjunction with said appraisal. This work *was done* in Providence, Rhode Island. (emphasis added)

Next, the letter discussed amounts invested in machinery and equipment, trade accounts payable, certain drafts payable, disputed as to amount and unconfirmed, and concluded:

> Because of the limitations upon our examination expressed in the preceding paragraphs and the material nature of the items not confirmed directly by us, we are unable to express an opinion as to the fairness of the accompanying statements.

Because of the death of the partner of Accountants who made the examination of Borrower's accounts the proof was not complete as to what examination and what inquiries had been made. The deceased partner's work papers were produced and they showed that the deceased had attempted to segregate the cost of labor, which Borrower had recorded as operating expenses, attributable to the purported leasehold improvements, but the work papers showed that no item of building material cost had been recorded.

* * * [W]hat the Bank did after copies, together with the Accountants' letter, were delivered to it appears from a memorandum,

23. While termed "appraisals" the documents attached to the letter are more correctly described as estimates of cost of construction. Specifically, there was an estimate from a general contractor to perform work at Palm Beach, Florida, and at Brunswick, Georgia, and another estimate of another general contractor to perform work at Providence, Rhode Island. * * * The estimate for Providence was to do certain described items of work, and specified that it did not include silos or their foundations or any foundations under the walls which contain the cement, or any responsibility for the steel building column strength.

Also appended was a memorandum, authorship undisclosed, that various installation work for improvements at Providence, not included in the contractor's estimate, cost $8,904.69, exclusive of any labor expense of Borrower.

made on the day the financial statements were received by the Bank's loan officer servicing the account, that the statements "show continued effect of the cost-cutting automation expenses initiated * * * in 1962 and completed shortly before the end of 1963." It called attention to the fact that $400,000.00 had been invested in new equipment and leasehold improvements and this investment had enabled Borrower drastically to "reduce the cost of handling cement both in unloading it from the ships and loading it into the tank trucks." The statements were referred to the analysis department of the Bank for closer study.

The analysis department reported critically on the statements on September 24, 1964.

As of the date of receipt of its copies of the financial statements, Bank had lent Borrower $220,000.00. There was testimony, not disputed, that if it had known on the date that $212,000.00 of leasehold improvements were fictitious, it would have refused further loans and immediately begun efforts to effect collection of the amount outstanding. Since Bank claimed that it did not know this crucial fact, the loan balance was allowed to increase during the summer of 1964 until it reached the level of $336,685.61 on September 24, 1964, the date of the adverse report of Bank's analysis department. Thought was given to taking additional collateral, but this was not done because additional property which could be pledged was in other jurisdictions and would be impractical to service. After the analysis department reported critically on Borrower's financial statements, no further loans or commitments were made. After that date, collections were effected from collateral pledges, and they were routinely applied to the oldest loan standing on Bank's books. Total collections reduced the unpaid balance to $116,685.61, and this sum has become uncollectible.

II

* * * The Accountants' financial statements were prepared in Virginia, but they were delivered to Bank in Rhode Island where, allegedly, reliance on them and subsequent injury took place. Under such circumstances * * * the law of Rhode Island governs.

As stated by the district court, the liability, if any, of Accountants for negligence is to be determined by the rule that "[a]ccountants owe a duty to their employer, and others whom they know or expect to rely on the report, to make the report in good faith without fraud or collusion and with care and caution of experts." While the Rhode Island Supreme Court has not spoken on the problem, a district court, analyzing Rhode Island decisions, concluded, in full accord with the trial court here, that "an accountant should be liable in negligence for careless financial misrepresentations relied upon by actually foreseen and limited classes of persons." Rusch Factors, Inc. v. Levin, 284 F. Supp. 85, 93 (D.R.I.1968). Since the evidence here is uncontroverted that Accountants not only knew but acknowledged that Bank sought Borrower's financial statements in connection with loans, that is the rule which will be applied.[24] In accord are Ryan v. Kanne, 170 N.W. 2d 395 (Iowa, 1969); Gammel v. Ernst & Ernst, 245 Minn. 249, 72 N.W.2d 364 (1955); Restatement of Torts § 552 (1938); Restatement of Torts, Second § 552(h) (Tent. Draft No. 12, 1966); United States v. Neustadt, 281 F.2d 596 (4 Cir. 1960); and also the English cases, Hedley Byrne & Co. v. Heller [1963] 2 All E.R. 575 (although defendant found not to have assumed responsibility for statements); and Candler v. Crane, Christman & Co. [1951] 1 All E.R. 426 (Lord Denning's dissent).

III

By application of the rule stated, we think that Accountants are liable for negligence on either of alternate theories.

From the Accountants' work papers and the other evidence in the case, either of two inferences may be drawn. First, Accountants, having identified some of the purported labor costs of the purported leasehold improvements, failed, from pressure of work or other reason, to search for material costs. Second, Accountants, having identified some of the purported labor costs of the purported leasehold improvements, searched for material costs and, not finding any, failed to conduct any independent investigation of the existence of the leasehold improvements and their value [25] and failed to disclose that there was no verification that the leasehold improvements were in being. In either event, Accountants certified the financial statements, saying overall only that they could not express an opinion with regard to their fairness. This disclaimer, however, followed other reference to the purported leasehold improvements which expressed no reservation about their existence but only about their precise value. We think that a fair reading of Accountants' covering letter and disclaimer indicates that while the leasehold improvements may have had a value of more or less than $212,000.00, there was no question but that they existed and that they had substantial value. Whether Accountants failed to look or, having looked, failed to find, they were guilty of actionable negligence if Bank, in reliance on the statements, made further loans.

Our conclusions with respect to the report and disclosure are reinforced by reference to industry standards of what should have been done in these circumstances. While industry standards may not always be the maximum test of liability, certainly they should be deemed the minimum standard by which liability should be determined. Brief

24. In arriving at this conclusion, we recognize that other jurisdictions have adopted rules establishing a more stringent test to find liability for negligence. See, e. g., Ultramares v. Touche, * * *; Stephens Industries, Inc. v. Haskins, 438 F.2d 357 (10 Cir. 1971) (liability to those not in privity only upon a showing of deceit or gross negligence).

25. It should be noted that Accountants did not hesitate to employ correspondents to verify the existence of inventories. Of course, the duty to investigate may arise only where the employment contract permits. Ryan v. Kanne, supra. But if the employment contract would not permit an independent investigation, at least the lack of verification should be disclosed. [Notes 23–25 from original, renumbered.]

references to American Institute of Certified Public Accountants, Statements on Auditing Procedure No. 33 (1963) are sufficient to prove the point.

Chapter 10 ¶ 1 of the Statements reads, "[t]he report shall either contain an expression of opinion regarding the financial statements, taken as a whole, or an assertion to the effect that an opinion cannot be expressed. *When an overall opinion cannot be expressed, the reasons therefor should be stated.* * * *" (emphasis added) When Accountants said only that "fully complete detailed cost records were not kept of these capital improvements and no exact determination could be made as to the actual cost of said improvements," we do not think that the reasons assigned were sufficiently stated. The documentary evidence shows that *no* cost records for material were kept, so that Accountants' statement, viewed even in the most charitable light, was a major understatement, whatever Accountants failed to do. * * * Accountants failed to comply * * * too, when they failed to disclose that the absence of any records for material purchases led them to resort to "appraisals." Had the absence of any records for material purchases been assigned as a reason for resort to "appraisals," Bank would have been charged with knowledge that the existence of the leasehold improvements might have been in question. The disclaimer, read in conjunction with the preceding paragraphs, conveyed the impression that the leasehold improvements unquestionably existed. * * * The district court failed to make a finding as to whether or not Bank relied upon the financial statements in making loans up to September 24, 1964, when the analysis department completed a report critical of the financial statements, and in forebearing from the collection of outstanding indebtedness. * * * Manifestly, it is the district court * * * which should make the requisite finding. Of course, if reliance is found the district court should proceed to assess damages.[26]

Reversed and remanded.

WILLIAMS v. POLGAR

Supreme Court of Michigan, 1974.
391 Mich. 6, 215 N.W.2d 149.

WILLIAMS, JUSTICE (To Affirm).

While important, the issue in this case is a relatively narrow one.

Michigan already permits a buyer of property who has relied on a faulty abstract to his detriment to recover from the abstracter, even though there is no clear contractual privity between them, if the abstracter in fact knew the buyer would rely on the abstract.[27]

26. Should a bank have relied in any way on an audit report which was late, which disclaimed an opinion as to the fairness of the statements submitted, and which called a cost estimate an "appraisal"?

27. See * * * Beckovsky v. Burton Abstract & Title Co., 208 Mich. 224, 175 N.W. 235, 178 N.W. 238 (1919) * * *.

This case presents the issue whether a faulty abstracter should likewise be liable to a buyer *he should have foreseen would rely* on the abstract as well as to the buyer *he knew would rely* on it. The question boils down to whether there should be liability for *foreseeable* as well as *known* reliance.

This Court has answered that question affirmatively in a related fact situation, and in categorical terms relieved Michigan jurisprudence of the restrictions of "privity." [28] In this opinion, we reaffirm our general decision eliminating privity and specifically apply it to abstracters. * * *

Plaintiffs Williams purchased certain property situated in the City of Warren, Macomb County, from defendants Polgar on a land contract dated August 1, 1959. At the time of purchase, as provided in the land contract, defendants furnished to plaintiffs an abstract of title certified to July 15, 1959 by Abstract and Title Guaranty Company. This abstract was originally issued on February 4, 1926 by the Macomb County Abstract Company and was extended by said company in 1936, 1937, 1943, 1944, 1945, 1946, 1948, 1951, and 1952. Defendant American Title Insurance Company is the successor in interest to Macomb County Abstract Company.

The abstract of title failed to include a deed dated May 1, 1926 which was recorded on May 24, 1926 in Liber 242 of Deeds at page 174 of Macomb County records. This deed conveyed the southerly 60 feet of the property in question to the Macomb County Board of Road Commissioners.

After execution of the land contract on August 1, 1959, plaintiffs learned, allegedly for the first time, of the existence of this omitted deed. As the result thereof, plaintiffs claim they were required to completely remove a building and that certain other damages were incurred.

* * *

III—DEFENSE OF PRIVITY

A. *Cessante Ratione Legis, Cessat et Ipsa Lex* [29]

The early common law rule restricting liability to those in contractual privity with an abstracter was based on a system where abstracts would only be used by real estate owners. 1 Fitch, Abstracts

28. Spence v. Three Rivers Builders & Masonry Supply, Inc., 353 Mich. 120, 90 N.W.2d 873 (1958) [a products liability case].

29. Justice Cardozo in extending a weigher's liability to a known third party beneficiary against the defense of privity, among other reasons stated:

"Constantly the bounds of duty are enlarged by knowledge of a prospective use."

In making this statement he relied upon, as we shall, a products liability case, his famous case of MacPherson v. Buick Motor Co., 217 N.Y. 382, 111 N.E. 1050, L.R.A.1916F, 696. Glanzer v. Shepard, 233 N.Y. 236, 240, 135 N.E. 275, 23 A.L.R. 1425 (1922). In dicta, Judge Cardozo found this same lack of immunity specifically applicable to abstracters:

"No such immunity, it has been held, protects the searcher of a title, who, preparing an abstract at the order of a client, delivers it to another to induce action on the faith of it." (Citations omitted.) 233 N.Y. 240, 135 N.E. 276.

and Titles to Real Property, § 9, p. 9; and see § 3. As time went on the actual usage of abstracts and the class of people relying on them expanded. This historical change in circumstance and the corresponding change in law is noted in numerous cases of which the following two quotations will serve as examples. The first, Brown v. Sims, 22 Ind.App. 317, 325, 53 N.E. 779, 781, 72 Am.St.Rep. 308 (1899) illustrates a judicial expansion of liability to a known third party beneficiary:

> "It is very well known that the owner of real estate seldom incurs the expense of procuring an abstract of the title from an abstracter, except for the purpose of thereby furnishing information to some third person or persons who are to be influenced by the information thus provided. If the abstracter in all cases be responsible only to the person under whose employment he performs the service, it is manifest that the loss occasioned thereby must in many cases, if not in most cases, be remediless."

The second, Gate City Abstract Co. v. Post, 55 Neb. 742, 746, 76 N.W. 471, 472 (1898), represents judicial support of legislation that purports to create liability "for the payment by such abstracters of any or all damages that may accrue to any party or parties, by reason of any error, deficiency or mistake in any abstract":

> "By the common law, as we interpret it, the owner of real estate could only utilize an abstract as an argument to reinforce his own assertions concerning the state of his title. It might be persuasive, but was without legal efficacy. He may now use it as evidence in an action to enforce the specific performance of a contract of sale, and in every other form of action in which the validity of his title or the existence or non-existence of liens or incumbrances are questions directly or collaterally involved. The right to use an abstract as evidence is not even limited to the person to whom it is issued. Any one may use it, and any one against whom it is employed may be injured in consequence of the certificate being false. Having thus widened the abstract's sphere of action, it was quite natural that the legislature should also widen the abstracter's liability."

Responding to the actual change in use of abstracts and the additional classes of persons relying on them, * * * exceptions have been grafted onto the supposed common law requirement of strict contractual privity. * * *

Whereas the common law rule limiting abstracter liability provided immunity from all who were injured by a faulty abstract except those in actual contractual privity, of the 35 jurisdictions (outside of Michigan) addressing themselves to this matter only seven retain a rule of strict contractual privity: Arizona, California, Florida, Illinois, Ohio, Texas and Wisconsin. On the other hand, 11 extend liability to known third-parties relying thereon: Alabama, District of Columbia, Hawaii, Idaho, Indiana, Maryland, Missouri, New Jersey, New York, Pennsylvania and Tennessee. Two jurisdictions have allowed recovery by undiscovered principals: Iowa and Washington. Fourteen purport to extend liability by statute to "any person" relying on the abstract: Arkansas, Colorado, Kansas, Minnesota, Montana, Nebraska, Nevada, New Mexico, North Dakota, Oklahoma, Oregon, South Dakota, Utah and Wyoming. And one jurisdiction extends liability to foreseeable relying third-parties by court decision: Louisiana.[30] * * *

Michigan's own jurisprudence records the categorical elimination of privity. This Court had previously extended abstracter liability consonant with the historical growth in reliance and use of abstracts and the corresponding changes in the law to known relying third-parties. Confronted now as of first impression with the question of abstracter liability to foreseeable relying third-parties, we have but to apply our own persuasive precedent of categorical elimination of privity to an analogous situation, and we do so.

IV—ABSTRACTER LIABILITY IN TORT FOR NEGLIGENT MISREPRESENTATION

On the basis of *Three Rivers* and a plethora of jurisdictions in the United States a good case is made for abolishing contractual privity and permitting suit in "negligence or implied warranty" by any foreseeable third-party who would and does rely on the abstract. We consider now the matter of suit in "negligence."

In Clark v. Dalman, 379 Mich. 251, 150 N.W.2d 755 (1967), for example, it was held that breach of a contract to repair, clean, and paint a water storage tank, also gave rise to an action in tort in favor of a non-contracting third-party. Chief Justice (then Justice) T. M. Kavanagh explained this relationship of a tort action to the underlying contract:

> "Actionable negligence presupposes the existence of a legal relationship between parties by which the injured party is owed a duty by the other, and such duty must be imposed by law * * *. Such duty of care may be a specific duty owing to the plaintiff by the defendant, or it may be a general one owed by the defendant to the public, of which the plaintiff is a part. *Moreover, while this duty of care, as an essential element of actionable negligence, arises by operation of law, it may and frequently does arise out of a contractual relationship, the theory being that accompanying every contract is a common-law duty to perform with ordinary care the thing agreed to be done, and that a negligent performance constitutes a tort as well as a breach of contract.* But it must be kept in mind that the contract cre-

30. See Appendices A and B. [Omitted; see 215 N.W.2d at 159–65.]

ates only the relation out of which arises the common-law duty to exercise ordinary care. Thus in legal contemplation the contract merely creates the state of things which furnishes the occasion of the tort. This being so, the existence of a contract is ordinarily a relevant factor, competent to be alleged and proved in a negligence action to the extent of showing the relationship of the parties and the nature and extent of the common-law duty on which the tort is based." (Emphasis added.) 379 Mich. 251, 260–261, 150 N.W.2d 755, 759, 760. * * *

With respect to the particular type of tort action arising from breach of an abstracter's contractual duty, we hold it to be an action in negligent misrepresentation. Numerous cases and law review articles have debated the precise tort cause of action most appropriate in this context.[31] The theories of fraud, deceit, warranty, and strict liability have all been the subject of extensive discussion with respect to professional misrepresentations of this sort. None of these theories has been found to adequately deal with this particular problem; negligent misrepresentation, on the other hand, precisely fits this situation.

The obvious difficulty with a fraud or deceit action is the requisite element of scienter. The issue we are dealing with in the instant case does not, on the pleadings, involve *intentional* misrepresentation. To supply the element of intent constructively is to do great violence to existing law on the subject of fraud. Note the discussion of this point by Prof. Francis Bohlen in "Should Negligent Misrepresentations Be Treated As Negligence or Fraud," 18 Va.L.R. 703, 706–707 (1932):

> "In all other fields of tort law the line is sharply drawn between intentional and unintentional injury. The persistence of this distinction can only be explained by recognizing the fact that it is in accord with the normal reactions of the mass of mankind. If negligent misrepresentation is called fraud, and, therefore, comes to be regarded by courts as tantamount thereto, there is danger that the unintentional character of the one and the intentional character of the other will be overlooked. There is danger that that liability, which is regarded both by lawyers and laymen as just where there is conscious dishonesty, will be imposed although there is no purpose to deceive. Call any two essentially different things by the same name and the two are likely to be treated as identical for all purposes."

31. See especially [Hill] "Damages for Innocent Misrepresentation," 73 Col. L.R. 679 (1973); [Bohlen,] "Misrepresentation As Deceit, Negligence or Warranty," 42 Harv.L.R. 733 (1929); Prosser, "Misrepresentation and Third Persons," 19 Vand.L.R. 231 (1966); Green, "The Duty To Give Accurate Information," 12 U.C.L.A.L.R. 464 (1965); [Bohlen,] "Should Negligent Misrepresentations Be Treated as Negligence or Fraud," 18 Va.L.R. 703 (1932). [Notes 27–31 from original, renumbered; other notes in original omitted.]

Further, to treat this cause of action as sounding in warranty or strict liability might serve to extend an abstracter's duty beyond the duty anticipated by the original contract. It is important to repeat that the tort cause of action created by an abstracter's nonfeasance or misfeasance stems from the contractual duty originally imposed and does not render an abstracter liable for action beyond such contractually-imposed duty, i. e., to perform in a diligent and reasonably skillful workmanlike manner.

Thus, we adopt the tort action of negligent misrepresentation in this context. See 1 Harper & James, The Law of Torts, § 7.6; C.J.S. Contracts § 154c. It should be noted that this action is premised on negligence in title search; an abstracter is not converted into a title insurer by virtue of our decision today. * * *

As to the measure of the duty required to be exercised by the abstracter, Chief Justice Kavanagh noted in Nash v. Sears Roebuck & Co., * * * 383 Mich. [136 (1970)] at page 142, 174 N.W.2d [818,] at page 821:

> "Every contract of employment includes an obligation, whether express or implied to perform in a diligent and reasonably skillful workmanlike manner."

This is clearly a form of the traditional negligence standard. Since the legal duty which, when breached, gives rise to a tort cause of action, springs from the contractual duty imposed, this *Nash* standard governs an abstracter's legal obligation to non-contracting parties. Because an abstracter is hired to determine what is in the public record, misstatements of, or failure to include, relevant items contained in that record are obviously examples of acts constituting failure to perform abstracting services in a diligent and reasonably skillful workmanlike manner.

This cause of action arising from breach of the abstracter's contractual duty runs to those persons an abstracter could reasonably foresee as relying on the accuracy of the abstract put into motion. * * * There is a clearly foreseeable class of potential injured persons which would obviously include grantees where his or her grantor or any predecessor in title of the grantor has initiated the contract for abstracting services with the abstracter. * * * [32]

32. Compare Anderson v. Boone County Abstract Co., 418 S.W.2d 123 (Mo. 1967) (liability for abstracter's negligence limited to persons dealing with the employer of the supplier of the information); with which contrast Rozny v. Marnul, 43 Ill.2d 54, 250 N.E.2d 656, 35 A.L.R.3d 487 (1969) (negligent surveyor liable to purchasers from purchaser of land from surveyor's customer, the court observing, inter alia, that "potential liability in this case is restricted to a comparatively small group, and that, ordinarily, only one member of that group will suffer loss." Also consider Dutton v. Bognor Regis United Building Co. Ltd. [1972] 1 All E.R. 462, [1972] 1 Q.B. 373 (liability of local housing authority to remote purchaser from builder whose foundations authority's inspector negligently passed, for repair costs and diminution of value caused by subsidence), and Note, The Aftermath of Hedley Byrne v. Hellers, 1973 Scots L.Times 109.

Chapter 7

DIGNITARY OR ECONOMIC INTERESTS: DEFAMATION AND THE "PRIVACY" TORTS; DISPARAGEMENT AND OTHER INVASIONS OF ECONOMIC INTERESTS

SECTION 1. INTRODUCTORY

The actions of libel and slander afford redress for harm to reputation resulting from disparaging or defamatory statements. Such harm often arises out of petty personal quarrels and idle village gossip. Today, however, it often results from the activities of the great business enterprises which have become important in the dissemination of information and opinion. The law's attempt to cover both types of situations with the same set of rules has its parallel in other branches of torts. Another parallel is found in the availability of the same possible bases of liability, viz., intent, negligence, and strict liability.

In the past strict liability prevailed in defamation law, together with other benefits for plaintiffs: the burden was on defendant to establish truth as a defense, not on plaintiff to establish falsity, and in many situations plaintiff did not have to prove damages. (Indeed the entire distinction between libel and slander, and much of the law of slander itself, and of libel in some states, turned on the need, or not, for plaintiff to prove damages.)

All these features of traditional defamation law have now been substantially if not entirely changed as a result of a series of decisions of the United States Supreme Court, which are summarized in Stone v. Essex County Newspapers, Inc., infra page 896. These decisions assert First (and Fourteenth) Amendment constitutional limitations on the right of states to impose liability for defamation without fault, in one degree or another, at least as to publishers and broadcasters (but not necessarily limited to such defamers); they also limit the availability of general damages.

Given the ensuing state of flux in defamation law, the subject is difficult to approach except from the perspective of what it has been, in order to appreciate how it is being changed. The initial cases on defamation law as it was should accordingly be read with the anticipation that much of what will be learned first is merely prologue.

The same tension, between plaintiff's interest in not being defamed, and the defamer's interest in freedom of speech, is evident where the protection of other dignitary interests, e. g., "privacy", would require curtailment of the freedom of the invaders of such interests to look, listen, speak, compete or otherwise act.

SECTION 2. THE LEGAL DOCTRINES

(A) THE TRADITONAL "ELEMENTS" OF AN ACTION FOR LIBEL OR SLANDER

1 STREET, THE FOUNDATIONS OF LEGAL LIABILITY, (1906) 300:

Where the language alleged to be defamatory does not appear to be such on its face, the plaintiff is required to state fully in his declaration the circumstances which make the words actionable. This is done by setting forth, in addition of course to the words actually used, what is called the inducement, the colloquium, and the innuendo. The first term is applied to the narrative of the extrinsic circumstances under which the words were used and which are necessary to be known before the defamatory meaning can attach. The office of the colloquium is to connect the spoken or written words with the circumstances disclosed in the inducement, while the innuendo interprets the meaning of the language used in the light of the surrounding circumstances and discloses its sting to the court. The purpose of all this elaborate apparatus is merely to enable the court to ascertain with certainty the meaning which the language was really intended and understood to have. Consequently, it is settled that there can be no enlargement of the meaning of words by innuendo beyond that which they may properly bear under the facts disclosed in the inducement and colloquium.

BALL v. ROANE

Court of King's Bench, 1593.
1 Croke's Rep. 308.

ACTION for these words: "There was never a robbery committed within forty miles of Wellingborough, but thou hadst thy part in it." After verdict it was moved in arrest of judgment, that the action did not lie, because it was not averred there was any robbery committed within forty miles, &c. for otherwise it is no slander—*Et sic opinio Cur'*; and judgment for the defendant. Mich. 36. & 37. Eliz. 6. R. Placito 11.

BALL v. ROANE

Court of King's Bench, 1594.
1 Croke's Rep. 342.

ACTION FOR WORDS. "There was never a purse cut within twenty miles of Wellingborough, but thou hadst thy part in it." And avers, that such a purse was cut, &c. and he had no part in it.—And it was moved, that an action lieth not; for it is not said he had a part of it as a partaker in the felony; for he may have a part in it in the loss, and so it is no slander.—But it was adjudged for the plaintiff; for the words shall be taken to be spoken in the worst sense, in disgrace and reproach of the plaintiff.—Nota, Serjeant Yelverton cited a case, Pasch. 32. Eliz. Sir Edward Hastings brought an action for these words: "You have procured a perjured man to seek my blood;" and ruled, that an action did not lie. But Fenner said the case was not adjudged, but ended by his arbitrament.

ANTHONY THEOBALD v. BROOK

Court of King's Bench, 1598.
1 Croke's Rep. 618.

ACTION for these words, which the defendant spake to one Gurney: "Bring me to the constable's house, for I am robbed this night: and bring me to Bonaventure Theobalds' house to arrest him; for old Theobalds (*innuendo* the plaintiff) setteth his sons to rob me (*innuendo dictum Bonaventure, et quendam Johannem, filium ipsus Anthonii*) from time to time." The defendant pleaded not guilty and found against him. After verdict it was moved in arrest of judgment, that the words were not actionable, because it is not alleged that any of Anthony's sons robbed him; and it is but an intent of setting to rob, and no act done: the words also are insensible.—But notwithstanding it was held by The Court, that the words were very slanderous, and that the action was maintainable. And so it had been adjudged in this court, that "one such lay in wait to murder me;" or, that "he sent his servant to murder me." Wherefore it was adjudged for the plaintiff.—NOTE. Error was hereof brought, because it is not precisely affirmed *of* the plaintiff, but it is said Old Theobalds, and he doth not name the plaintiff, and an *innuendo* will not serve. Whereupon it was reversed.[1]

1. As the foregoing cases indicate, words which charge the plaintiff with the commission of some crimes have been considered slanderous in traditional defamation law (even though no special damage is alleged). The accusation need not recount all the elements of the crimes; the word by which it is commonly called (e. g., murder, theft, arson, and the like) clearly may suffice. So may synonyms and slang words if the court feels their meaning is clear enough, and would be taken to refer to the crime. Lander v. Wald, 218 App.Div. 514, 219 N.Y.S. 57 (1926), affirmed 245 N.Y. 590, 157 N.E. 870 (1927) ("pimp"); Kammerer v. Sachs, 131 Misc. 640, 227 N.Y.S. 641 (1928) ("bootlegger"); Weiner v. Leviton, 230 App.Div. 312, 244 N.Y.S. 176 (2d Dept. 1930) ("crook"). *Contra,* as to "crook" Villemin v. Brown, 193 App.Div. 777, 184 N.Y.S. 570 (1st Dept. 1920).

Words which are capable of describing a crime may, however, be spoken under circumstances which make it clear that they are not used in such a sense. Morrisette v. Beatte, 66 R.I. 73, 17 A.2d 464 (1941) ("buggar" used as an insult).

More serious questions arise where the defamer does not use a word that covers the whole crime, but accuses plaintiff of specific facts. Of the rule in such cases Pollock has said, "The practical inference seems to be that minute and copious vituperation is safer than terms of general reproach, such as 'thief,' inasmuch as a layman who enters on details will probably make some impossible combination." Pollock, Torts (14th ed. 1939) 193. But even here all the elements of the crime need not be specified if the implication is clear. Keller v. Safeway Stores, 111 Mont. 28, 108 P.2d

GOODSTEIN v. CHALFONTE HOTEL CORP.

Supreme Court of New York, Trial Term, New York County, Part 17, 1950.
198 Misc. 1068, 101 N.Y.S.2d 851.

DI FALCO, JUSTICE. Plaintiff, a tenant of the defendant, Chalfonte Hotel, sues the hotel and its bookkeeper, the defendant, Kathleen Nolan, alleging * * * slander against both defendants * *. The testimony before me reveals that, on the morning of March 25, 1949, plaintiff personally presented himself and requested his mail at the desk in the lobby of defendant hotel where he resided. Plaintiff and the defendant Nolan, who was waiting at the desk at the time, became embroiled in a heated argument. While the testimony as to the cause of the argument is partially in conflict, plaintiff has established that Nolan did say of plaintiff, in the presence of others, "You dirty Jew", "You're a no good bum", "the ladies say he is drunk". It is for the public utterance of these words that plaintiff seeks damages from both defendants. Plaintiff conceded at the trial that, if the words complained of were not slanderous per se, he has not established his cause of action therefor, inasmuch as he has not pleaded or proven special damages.

It is settled law that where utterances or words charged as being slanderous are not such per se, special damages must be pleaded. * * *

After studied consideration of the cases cited by counsel and my own independent research and examination of the authorities, I am constrained to hold that the epithets, including the words "You dirty Jew" uttered by Nolan, of plaintiff, while malodorous, offensive, distasteful and outrageous, are not slanderous per se. However offending the words bespoken may be, wounded pride and outraged sensibilities are not actionable in the absence of an allegation of special damages. The words cannot be said to be slanderous per se in light of the holdings. * * *

Coming now to the words "You're a no good bum", I find the authorities decided that the use of the spoken word "bum" is not slanderous per se. * * *

In respect of the words "the ladies say he is drunk", again, I find the authorities decided that the use of the word "drunk" is not slanderous per se. * * * Plaintiff's claim, that Sec. 1221, Penal Law, makes the word "drunk" slanderous per se as being a charge of committing a crime under this section, is untenable and without merit. Sec. 1221 of the Penal Law, which makes intoxication in a public place a misdemeanor, by its very express provision does not

605 (1940) (charge of passing bad check actionable without statement that plaintiff knew the check was bad and intended to defraud).

Not all crimes will do to make a charge slanderous. After all, parking too long may be a crime. The tests most commonly used are that the offence must be indictable, or entail "infamous punishment," or involve "moral turpitude."

apply to the City of New York, as the very last sentence of the last subdivision "h" of that section reads: "The provisions of section twelve hundred and twenty-one shall not apply to the city of New York. As amended L.1911, c. 700, § 2, eff. July 19, 1911". * * *

Upon these considerations, I have no alternative but to dismiss the first cause of action for slander against both defendants.[2]

2. Whether being called a crook is actionable at all may depend on the circumstances, e. g., Prince v. Peterson, — Utah 2d —, 538 P.2d 1325 (1975): " 'clever crook,' etc. 'who is stealing from his own children * * *' referring to his operation of a business, and his efforts to sell it * * *". Some of the Southern States have actionable words statutes like the following one from Mississippi: "All words which, from their usual construction and common acceptation, are considered as insults, and calculated to lead to a breach of the peace, shall be actionable." Virginia recognizes a similar action for insulting words at common law, Tweddy v. J. C. Penney Co., Inc., 216 Va. 596, 221 S.E.2d 152 (1976). The story and purpose of these statutes are engagingly told in Malone, Insult in Retaliation, 11 Miss.L.Rev. 333 (1939). See also note, 15 A.L.R.2d 108. Contrast this purpose (suppression of duelling) with that of (1) the conventional civil defamation action, (2) criminal libel. One consequence of the notion that the action of defamation lay to redress injury to reputation is the requirement of *publication*, viz. that the words to be actionable must be spoken so that some third person heard and understood them.

DAVIES AND WIFE v. SOLOMON

Court of Queen's Bench, 1871.
L.R. 7 Q.B. 112.

(Action of slander for the following words) "I can prove that John Davies' wife had connection with a man named Labrach two years ago, but I would rather have the tongue cut out of my mouth than separate man and wife," whereby the plaintiff Isabella was injured in her character and reputation, and became alienated from and deprived of the companionship and ceased to receive the hospitality of divers friends, and especially of her husband, John Davies, "and one M. D. and one G. H. T. and one A. J. M.," who have by reason of the premises withdrawn from the companionship and ceased to be hospitable to or friendly with the plaintiff Isabella.

Demurrer and joinder in demurrer. * * *

BLACKBURN, J. The sole difficulty in deciding the case is caused by the opinion of Lord Wensleydale in Lynch v. Knight. (9 H.L.C. 577) He held that no action would lie for slander of a wife when the only special damage alleged was the loss to the plaintiff of the consortium of her husband. In the present case, however, it is unnecessary to decide this question, for the declaration, after alleging the loss of cohabitation by the wife, proceeds to aver that "she lost, and was deprived of the companionship, and ceased to receive the hospitality of divers friends." Now, first, was that consequence such as might reasonably and naturally be expected to follow from the speaking of slanderous words? Judging from the habits and manners of society, of all the consequences that might be expected to result from a statement that a woman had committed adultery, or had been guilty of unchastity, the most natural would be that those who had invited her and given her hospitality would thenceforth cease to do so. Then Moore v. Meagher (1 Taunt. 39) decides that the loss of the hospitality of friends is sufficient special damage to sustain an action like the present; and the hospitality, as the word is there used, means simply that persons receive another into their houses, and give him meat and drink gratis. Perhaps such a definition may rather extend the signification of the word, but it is true in effect—for if they do not receive him, or if they make him pay for his entertainment, that is not hospitality. In Roberts v. Roberts [5 B. & S. 384; 33 L.J. (Q.B.) 249], it is to be observed, that the loss suffered by the plaintiff in being excluded from a religious society, was not temporal, and was therefore held not to be enough. But in the present case there is a matter of temporal change—small though it be—laid in the declaration. It is also argued, that inasmuch as this action is brought by the wife, the husband being merely joined for conformity, the damage necessary to give the right to recover must be damage to her alone, and that the loss of hospitality which she has hitherto enjoyed, is only pecuniary loss to her husband and not to her. * * * I am, however, unwilling to agree with such artificial reasoning, and I think the real damage in this case is to the wife herself. Notwithstanding that it is the husband's duty to support his wife, he is only bound to provide her with necessaries suitable to his station in life; and she might, by visiting friends in a higher position than himself, enjoy luxuries which he either could not or might not choose to afford her * * *. I am therefore of opinion that the declaration is good; and the demurrer must be overruled.[3]

3. Adultery and fornication were not crimes in the temporal courts of England or many of our states. See Buys v. Gillespie, 2 Johns., N.Y., 115, 3 Am. Dec. 404 (1807). By contrast, adultery was a capital offense in early New Hampshire, though fornication was a crime only in the man—which meant that an unmarried woman could be called a "whore" with impunity. Woodbury v. Thompson, 3 N.H. 194 (1823) (Webster for the plaintiff). Many states by statute or judicial decision have made it slander *per se* to charge a woman with unchastity. Cf. Justice for Men, Aley v. Fish, in A. P. Herbert, Uncommon Law, 320 (1935).

Also see Restatement of Torts, Second § 574, which refers instead to the imputation "of serious sexual misconduct to another", and comment c thereto (Tent. Draft No. 20, 1974).

Mental suffering and impairment of health were generally not regarded as special damage so as to support an action for words not otherwise slanderous. Allsop v. Allsop, 5 Hurl. & N. 534 (Ex.1860); Terwilliger v. Wands, 17 N.Y. 54, 72 Am.Dec. 420 (1858); Clark v. Morrison, 80 Or. 240, 156 P. 429 (1916); Restatement of Torts, Second § 575, Comments c and d (Tent. Draft No. 20, 1974).

The rule protecting a defendant from liability for damages caused by the *unauthorized repetition* of the slander [Pettibone v. Simpson, 66 N.Y. 492 (1873)], still has vitality, though some courts reject it. Morrill v. Crawford, 278 Mass. 250, 179 N.E. 609 (1932); Seelman, Law of Libel and Slander in New York, 683 (1933); Dell v. K. E. McKay's Market of Coos Bay, Inc., — Or. —, 543 P.2d 678 (1975).

Compare Vicars v. Wilcocks, 8 East 1 (1806), page 307 supra, which New York has rejected. Moody v. Baker, 5 Cow. 351 (N.Y.1826).

THORLEY v. LORD KERRY

Court of Exchequer Chamber, 1812.
4 Taunt. 355, 128 Eng.Rep. 367.

[Defendant sent by messenger an unsealed letter to the plaintiff, which the messenger read, stating that the plaintiff "under the cloak of religious and spiritual reform, hypocritically, and with the grossest impurity, deals out his malice, uncharitableness, and falsehoods." The plaintiff sued for libel and gained a verdict and judgment. On writ of error:]

MANSFIELD, C. J. * * * There is no doubt that this was a libel, for which the plaintiff in error might have been indicted and punished; because, though the words impute no punishable crimes, they contain that sort of imputation which is calculated to vilify a man, and bring him, as the books say, into hatred, contempt, and ridicule; for all words of that description an indictment lies; and I should have thought that the peace and good name of individuals was sufficiently guarded by the terror of this criminal proceeding in such cases. The words, if merely spoken, would not be of themselves sufficient to support an action. But the question now is, whether an action will lie for these words so written, notwithstanding that such an action would not lie for them if spoken; and I am very sorry it was not discussed in the Court of King's Bench, that we might have had the opinion of all the twelve judges on the point, whether there be any distinction as to the right of action, between written and parol scandal; for myself, after having heard it extremely well argued, and especially, in this case, by Mr. Barnewall, I cannot, upon principle, make any difference between words written and words spoken, as to the right which arises on them of bringing an action. For the plaintiff in error it has been truly urged, that in the old books and abridgments no distinction is taken between words written and spoken. But the distinction has been made between written and spoken slander as far back as Charles the Second's time, and the difference has been recognized by the Courts for at least a century back. It does not appear to me that the rights of parties to a good character are insufficiently defended by the criminal remedies which the law gives, and the law gives a very ample field for retribution by action for words spoken in the cases of special damage, of words spoken of a man in his trade or profession, of a man in office, of a magistrate or officer; for all these on action lies. But for mere general abuse spoken, no action lies. In the arguments both of the judges and counsel, in almost all the cases in which the question has been, whether what is contained in a writing is the subject of an action or not, it has been considered, whether the words, if spoken, would maintain an action. It is curious that they have also adverted to the question, whether it tends to produce a breach of the peace: but that is wholly irrelevant, and is no ground for recovering damages. So it has been argued that writing shews more deliberate malignity; but the same answer suffices, that the action is not maintainable upon the ground of the malignity, but for the damage sustained. So, it is argued that written scandal is more generally diffused than words spoken, and is therefore actionable; but an assertion made in a public place, as upon the Royal Exchange, concerning a merchant in London, may be much more extensively diffused than a few printed papers dispersed, or a private letter: it is true that a newspaper may be very generally read, but that is all casual. These are the arguments which prevail on my mind to repudiate the distinction between written and spoken scandal; but that distinction has been established by some of the greatest names known to the law, Lord Hardwicke, Hale, I believe, Holt, C. J., and others. Lord Hardwicke, C. J. especially has laid it down that an action for a libel may be brought on words written, when the words, if spoken, would not sustain it. Co.Dig. tit. Libel, referring to the case in Fitzg. 122, 253, says, there is a distinction between written and spoken scandal. By his putting it down there as he does, as being the law, without making any query or doubt upon it, we are led to suppose that he was of the same opinion. I do not now recapitulate the cases, but we cannot, in opposition to them, venture to lay down at this day, that no action can be maintained for any words written, for which an action could not be maintained if they were spoken: upon these grounds we think the judgment of the Court of King's Bench must be affirmed. The purpose of this action is to recover a compensation for some damage supposed to be sustained by the plaintiff by reason of the libel. The tendency of the libel to provoke a breach of the peace, or the degree of malignity which actuates the writer, has nothing to do with the question. If the matter were for the first time to be decided at this day, I should have no hesitation in saying, that no action could be maintained for written scandal which could not be maintained for the words if they had been spoken.

Judgment affirmed.[4]

4. Where defendant procures the publication of defamatory matter in a newspaper it is libel; where he tells his story in the presence of an undisclosed reporter it is not. Conflict appears where the reporter elicits the story, but his profession and purpose are known. Compare Valentine v. Gonzalez, 190 App.Div. 490, 179 N.Y.S. 711 (1920) with Johnson v. Gerasimos, 247 Mich. 248, 225 N.W. 636 (1929). There are divergent views, too, as to whether the dictation of a letter to a stenographer is slander or libel. See Osborn v. Boulter [1930] 2 K.B. 226; Allen v. American Indemnity Co., 63 Ga.App. 894, 12 S.E.2d 127 (1940); Paton, Reform and English Law of Defamation, 33 Ill.L.Rev. 669, 673 (1939); Restatement of Torts, Second § 577, Comment (h) (Tent. Draft No. 20, 1974).

For a discussion of the question whether reading a written communication aloud to a third person constitutes the publication of a *libel* (rather than slander), see Hartmann v. Winchell, 296 N.Y. 296, 73 N.E.2d 30, 171 A.L.R. 759 (1947); Meldrum v. Australian Broadcasting Co. (1932) Victoria L.R. 425.

The question may also arise whether the dictation of a letter amounts to *publication*. It has been suggested that when the corporation which employs both the composer and the stenographer is sued, the act of dictation, being done solely within the corporate personnel, is not publication. Green, Relational Interests, 31 Ill.L.Rev. 35 (1936); Bryanston Finance Ltd. v. de Vries [1975] 2 All E.R. 609; United States Steel Corp. v. Darby, 516 F.2d 961 (5th Cir. 1975). But as a general rule communication to one's own agent or to the agent of the person defamed is publication. Restatement of Torts,

ATKINSON v. EQUITABLE LIFE ASSURANCE SOC. OF UNITED STATES

United States Court of Appeals for the Fifth Circuit, 1975.
519 F.2d 1112.

GEE, CIRCUIT JUDGE.

* * * Appellee Kenneth W. "Tex" Atkinson (Atkinson) brought suit * * * against his former employer, The Equitable Life Assurance Society of the United States (Equitable). * * *

The evidence supporting Atkinson's slander action, together with authorities epitomizing Florida law on the question presented, are well stated in Atkinson's brief:

> [A successor agent], acting as the representative of Equitable, visited Herbert Enfinger, a client of Atkinson's. [The agent] confused Enfinger about the details of a policy of insurance which had been sold to Enfinger by Atkinson. When Enfinger indicated that he wanted to talk to Atkinson because of the confusion generated by [the agent, he] made the following statements about Atkinson:
>
> > It is the man that sold it to you * * * he was selling for his own gain and not yours * * * he ain't looking out for you.
>
> Enfinger continued:
>
> > Well, he [the agent] informed me that his (Atkinson's) commissions was all that he was interested in, he (Atkinson) wasn't interested in my part of the policy. (A 363–365)
>
> Equitable argues that these and other statements made about an insurance agent to his client do not constitute slander per se as a matter of law. The authorities relied upon by Equitable, however, do not support its position. There is no dispute about the law applicable to the defamatory statements made by [the successor agent].

Second § 577, Comment (e) (Tent. Draft No. 20, 1974); Note, 116 A.L.R. 114. Contrast this with still another question, *viz.* whether, if the statement is qualifiedly privileged, the communication of it through or to an agent is a reasonable means of doing so. See Osborn v. Boulter, supra; Beck v. Oden, 64 Ga.App. 407, 13 S.E. 2d 468 (1941).

The sending of a sealed letter to the plaintiff himself is not a publication, even though he may thereafter show it to a third person. Restatement of Torts, Second § 577, Comment b, Ill. (2) (Tent. Draft No. 20, 1974). But the law with cynical realism regards the sending of defamatory matter on a postcard as publication. And, obviously, the sending of a telegram, Brandon v. Arkansas Fuel Oil Co., 64 Ga. App. 139, 12 S.E.2d 414 (1940).

Is a statement made by a husband to his wife thereby published? See Dyer v. MacDougall, 93 F.Supp. 484 (E.D.N.Y. 1950); Evans, 24 Minn.L.Rev. 607, 613 (1940).

In Campbell v. Jacksonville Kennel Club, 66 So.2d 495 (Fla.1953), the Supreme Court of Florida, adopting the Restatement view and the majority view of other jurisdictions held:

> It is established in most jurisdictions that an oral communication is actionable per se—that is, without a showing of special damages—if it imputes to another (a) a criminal offense amounting to a felony, or (b) a presently existing venereal or other loathsome and communicable disease, or (c) conduct, characteristics, or a condition incompatible with the proper exercise of his lawful business, trade, profession, or office, or (d) the other being a woman, acts of unchastity. 66 So.2d 495, at 497.

This principle of law expanding the categories of words considered as slanderous per se is the controlling law in this case. The history of the development of slander per se in Florida was recently summarized in Wolfson v. Kirk, 273 So.2d 774 (Fla.App. 4th 1973). The Defendant Kirk stated that when he was running a brokerage office he invited the plaintiff out of the office. That was *all* he said. The Court held that a complaint alleging those facts stated a cause of action for slander per se:

> We conclude, however, that from the language of the comment, it does not seem unreasonable to infer that persons hearing the same and possessed of a common mind might have taken it to mean that the plaintiff was a person with whom commercial relations were undesirable. Given this meaning, the comment attributes to the plaintiff a characteristic which is incompatible with the conduct of any lawful business. Hence the comment could come within one of the categories of slander per se recognized in Campbell v. Jacksonville Kennel Club and Teare v. Local Union No. 295 [98 So.2d 79], supra. Of course the communication might also have been intended to convey and perhaps did convey only innocuous meanings. *Where, however, a communication is ambiguous and is reasonably susceptible of a meaning which is defamatory, it is for the trier of fact to decide whether or not the communication was understood in the defamatory sense.* Diplomat Electric, Inc. v. Westinghouse Electric Supply Co., 5 Cir. 1967, 378 F.2d 377. Wolfson v. Kirk, 273 So.2d at 778–779. (Emphasis original.)

For a full picture, there need only be added to the above that Enfinger, the sole source of testimony for Atkinson's slander case, gave no evidence that he repeated these assertions to anyone, and admitted that they had no effect to denigrate Atkinson in his estimation. Indeed, after taking the matter up with Atkinson and being reassured, he cashed in his Equitable policies despite Atkinson's advice to the contrary because he was unwilling to maintain any relationship with a concern related, however tenuously, to such assertions. For them the jury mulcted Equitable, in general damages, $15,000 (a figure not far from Atkinson's average annual earned commission income), and $125,000 punitive damages.

The disproportion of such damages as compensation, or as punishment, for the nasty gossip of a commission employee—remarks not shown by any faintest evidence to have been authorized, tolerated, or even known of by Equitable—requires no comment. It is intolerable that Tex Atkinson should be so blackguarded behind his back. It is equally so that he should receive $140,000 in compensation and salve for the single smear, made to one client and neither credited nor passed on. Attempting a remittitur from such a slash would amount to restoring a reasonable portion of the severed head. We decline to do so. Without relish, and recognizing fully that we are, in this function, not finders but "unfinders," we conclude that another attempt must be made, by another finder of fact, at a rational award. It sometimes happens that when one continues to receive unmeaning answers, the wrong question is being asked. It may be that the slander cause should be retried in whole, rather than merely as to damages * * *. But this is for the trial court.

Reversed and remanded.

REMINGTON v. BENTLEY

United States District Court, S.D. New York, 1949.
88 F.Supp. 166.

CONGER, DISTRICT JUDGE. The defendants' motion to dismiss the complaint under Rule 12(b)(6) of the Federal Rules of Civil Procedure, 28 U.S.C.A., presents problems in connection with the application of the laws of slander and libel to the medium of television.

The complaint alleges that the plaintiff, an economist by profession has been, since May, 1940, an employee of the United States Government in various capacities; that in assuming his positions he was required to, and did take an oath that he did not belong to any organization which advocated the overthrow of the Government by force and violence; that the Attorney General of the United States has consistently ruled that the Communist Party was such an organization.

The complaint further alleges that the plaintiff is not and never has been a Communist nor a member of the Party, nor a Communist sympathizer, of which facts the defendants knew or should have known at the time of the remarks in controversy.

The complaint further alleges that on July 30, 1948, the defendant Bentley testified before a Senate Sub-Committee, among other things, that she had joined the Communist Party in 1935 and had remained a member for approximately ten years; that she had acted as a spy for the Party, realizing that information obtained was going to the Soviet Government; that using a fictitious name and hiding her true identity, she obtained confidential information from the plaintiff in his capacity as an employee of the United States Government; and that plaintiff was a member of the Communist Party.

The complaint alleges that the plaintiff denied under oath the charges made by the defendant Bentley before the same Sub-Committee * * *.

On the evening of September 12, 1948, it is alleged, the defendant Bentley appeared on a certain television broadcast known as "Meet the Press" * * * and the program was seen and heard by hundreds of thousands of persons; that in the course of the program, the defendant Bentley repeated the charge that she had made before the Senate Sub-Committee * * *.

The complaint further alleges that such program was permanently recorded in writing, on phonograph records and otherwise by the corporate defendants and others; that her statements were intended to and did convey the meaning that plaintiff was and is a member of the Communist Party, and was such while an employee of the Government, contrary to his oaths, his testimony before the Sub-Committee and the laws of the United States; * * * that the statements are untrue, false and defamatory of plaintiff as an economist and employee of the Government, and have greatly injured him and damaged him in his employment and in his profession.

The complaint demands judgment in the sum of $100,000.

Specifically, the defendants' objections are * * *: [1] that the broadcast of extemporaneous defamatory matter constitutes slander; and the statements attributed to the defendant Bentley, not being slanderous per se, are not actionable without proof of special damage * * *

* * * [S]lander is tortious if the oral defamation falls within certain classes of cases which are actionable per se or if it causes special damage, while libel is actionable by itself.

It is this distinction upon which the defendants base the initial ground of their motion.

In Hartman v. Winchell, 296 N.Y. 296, 73 N.E.2d 30, 171 A.L.R. 759, the Court of Appeals held that the broadcast of defamatory matter read from a script constitutes libel, but the Court expressly stated that it was not required to pass upon the question "whether broadcasting defamatory matter which has not been reduced to writing should be held to be libellous." 296 N.Y. at page 300, 73 N.E.2d at page 32.

Prior to this decision, however, the point was considered in Locke v. Gibbons, Supreme Court, N.Y. County, Special Term, 164 Misc. 877, 299 N.Y.S. 188, affirmed 253 App.Div. 887, 2 N.Y.S.2d 1015, and there Mr. Justice Pecora held that extemporaneous defamatory matter not contained in a script was slander. Compare Locke v. Benton & Bowles, Inc., 253 App.Div. 369, 2 N.Y.S.2d 150, where the Appellate

Division found it unnecessary to determine whether the same matter involved in the Gibbons case was slander or libel, the Court remarking that it would be actionable in any event if it injured the plaintiff in his work. Actually, the case was decided on a question of pleading, the alleged defamatory remarks not having been set forth in the complaint.

The defendants assert that the analogy between broadcasting and the method of publication in suit is valid, and therefore that precedent requires that the statements be deemed slanderous. I accept the analogy to the extent that it applies to extemporaneous oral expression, and I feel that the additional factor of pictorial representation along with the statements adds no more to the form of defamation than would the circumstance of a great audience in a stadium or the like listening to the spoken word. I adopt this view keeping in mind and in spite of the fact that defamation in motion pictures has been treated as libel. See Brown v. Paramount Publix Corp., 240 App.Div. 520, 270 N.Y.S. 544; Youssopoff v. Metro-Goldwyn-Mayer, 50 Times L.R. 581, 99 A.L.R. 864 [English Court of Appeal].

If the age-old difference between libel and slander is to be maintained, as an adherence to precedent compels, then it seems to me that the rule as set forth by Mr. Justice Cardozo in Ostrowe v. Lee, 256 N.Y. 36, at page 39, 175 N.E. 505, 506, is most pertinent to the question at issue.

"The schism in the law of defamation between the older wrong of slander and the newer one of libel is not the product of mere accident * * * It has its genesis in evils which the years have not erased. Many things that are defamatory may be said with impunity through the medium of speech. Not so, however, when speech is caught upon the wing and transmuted into print. What gives the sting to the writing is its permanence of form. The spoken word dissolves, but the written one abides and 'perpetuates the scandal.' * * *

Generally, slander is actionable without a showing of special damage if the publication imputes a crime, a loathsome disease, or some conduct, condition or trait tending to injure another in his trade or profession. See Seelman, The Law of Libel and Slander, p. 599 et seq.; Restatement, supra, p. 170.

The complaint charges that the defendant Bentley's statements imputed various crimes to the plaintiff; and in his brief the plaintiff points out that the accusation, if true, would subject him to prosecution for violation of § 1001 of Title 18 of the New United States Code Annotated which makes it a crime with dire punishment to state falsely in any matter within the jurisdiction of any department or agency of the United States Government; for violation of § 1621 of Title 18 of the New Code relating to perjury in connection with his testimony before the Sub-Committee; for violation of the Hatch Act, 5 U.S.C.A. § 118(j), with respect to membership of Federal employees in any political party or organization advocating the overthrow of our constitutional form of Government; and for violation of the Smith

Act, 18 U.S.C.A. § 2385, which interdicts advocacy of the overthrow of the Government by force and violence.

The defendants assert that none of the facts showing the commission of a crime were contained in the remarks of the defendant Bentley; and they argue that the case is, therefore, one of defamation by extrinsic fact supplied by the pleading, under which circumstances special damages must be pleaded, citing for the proposition O'Connell v. Press Publishing Co., 214 N.Y. 352, 108 N.E. 556.[5]

Plaintiff urges that the facts indicating the commission of a crime are not extrinsic within the meaning of the O'Connell case. In this I must disagree. If there were on the statute books a law which stated that it was a crime to be a Communist, then of course the defendant's remarks would accuse plaintiff of the commission of a crime. However, there being no such statute, it is necessary to prove by extrinsic facts that plaintiff took an oath that he was not a Communist, or that he swore before a certain legislative body that he was not a Communist. The crime is in the false oath.

However, the complaint as heretofore indicated, charges that the defendant Bentley's statements have greatly injured and damaged the

5. A confusing ambiguity has been introduced into some of the modern cases by use of the expression "libel *per se.*"

1. There is a rule of practice and pleading that, if words need extrinsic facts to make them appear libellous or slanderous (as the case may be), the plaintiff will fail unless he pleads and proves those facts. In such cases written words are sometimes described as "not libellous *per se*" (more rarely spoken words in like cases are said not to amount to "slander *per se*").

2. There was a rule of substantive law that, if spoken words together with all the extrinsic facts pleaded and proven come short of charging a crime, loathsome disease, unchastity (in women), or incompetence to pursue one's calling, they are not actionable unless they cause special damage. When it is said that words are not "slander *per se*" this rule is generally referred to; the expression meaning that special damage must be shown. There was no closely analogous rule for libel though conceivably words might fail to hold the plaintiff up to scorn, ridicule, etc. (even in all their setting of surrounding circumstances) yet be actionable for the special damage they cause.

3. The O'Connell case was taken to lay down the rule that whenever written words needed extrinsic facts to make them appear defamatory, (a) not only must the facts be pleaded and proven, (b) but also special damages must be shown. See also note 26 Iowa L.R. 893 (1941) (attributing similar rule to Kansas and Kentucky); Sauerhoff v. Hearst Corporation, 388 F. Supp. 117 (D.Md.1974) (discussing Maryland's "irrational animals known as libel 'per quod' and libel 'per se', and the Merlinesque touchstones which attach to them"). So far as doctrinal orthodoxy goes, *O'Connell* was clearly the illegitimate offspring of the two rules noted above, and the result has been unequivocally repudiated by a later decision of the same court, which did not however expressly overrule the O'Connell case. Sydney v. MacFadden Newspaper Pub. Corp., 242 N.Y. 208, 151 N.E. 209, 44 A.L.R. 1419 (1926). The lower New York courts were just as likely to follow one as the other of these inconsistent precedents, until the rule which had been attributed to the O'Connell case was in effect repudiated in Hinsdale v. Orange County Publications, Inc., 17 N.Y.2d 284, 270 N.Y.S.2d 592, 217 N.E.2d 650 (1966). For excellent analyses see Seelman, The Law of Libel & Slander in New York State, Ch. II and Supp. (1933). See also, Sharratt v. Housing Innovation, Inc., 365 Mass. 141, 310 N.E.2d 343 (1974); and Restatement of Torts Second §§ 569, 580A and 580B (Tent. Draft No. 21, 1975) and Questions Suggested for Discussion (Tent. Draft No. 20, 1974 at xiv).

plaintiff in his employment and profession. A slanderous statement affecting one in this respect has always been actionable *per se.* * * *

The defendants argue that the words must be spoken in relation to plaintiff's occupation and must be peculiarly injurious to the plaintiff because of his particular calling. And they assert that the words complained of, if defamatory, are not so because plaintiff is an economist and a Government employee, but would be equally injurious to any reputable citizen whether a lawyer, a teacher, etc.

I know of no accusation more discreditive of a United States Government official with respect to the proper conduct of his office than that he is a Communist. * * * Generally, Communists are looked upon as representatives of a foreign Government. * * *

Certainly, in accord with present day thinking officers of our Government and the public at large would distrust the honesty, the impartiality and the judgment of an economist in the employ of our Government who was known as a Communist. His usefulness as a public servant would be ended.

In addition, the statement injures plaintiff in his profession as an economist. It is natural to presume that an economist who is a Communist adheres to the economic theories of Communism, which are repugnant to the theories historically accepted in this Country.

I do not agree with defendants that a defamation injurious to one in his business or profession must refer to him in his practice of that business or profession. It is not necessary to say that the plaintiff is an unfit Government official or economist because he is a Communist. It is sufficient to charge what he stands for and the relationship is obvious. * * *

I conclude that the defendant Bentley's remarks are injurious to plaintiff as a Government official and economist and are, therefore, slanderous *per se,* and that special damage need not be alleged. * * *

Motion denied.[6]

6. In the present climate of opinion there seems to be little doubt that it would be a libel to charge in writing that a man is a communist, though this may not always have been so. See, e. g., Cahill v. Hawaiian Paradise Park Corp., — Haw. —, 543 P.2d 1356 (1975); note, 58 Yale L.J. 1387, note 4 (1949); 24 Temple L.Q. 247 (1950). But cf. Dilling v. Illinois Pub. & Printing Co., 340 Ill.App. 303, 91 N.E.2d 635 (1950), noted 45 Ill.L. Rev. 525 (1950) ("subversive"); and McAndrew v. Scranton Republican Publishing Co., 364 Pa. 504, 514, 72 A.2d 780, 784 (1950). As to the charge that a journalist is a "fellow traveller" of "fascists", see Buckley v. Littell, 394 F.Supp. 918 (S.D.N.Y.1975).

The principal case was much commented upon in the law reviews. See, e. g., 50 Col.L.Rev. 526 (1950); 25 N.Y.U.L. Q.Rev. 416 (1950); 23 So.Cal.L.Rev. 618 (1950).

The question whether defamation by radio (and now television) is to be regarded as libel, or slander, or as a new tort has naturally received a great deal of attention. See, for example, Bohlen, Fifty Years of Torts, 50 Harv. L.Rev. 725, 729–731 (1937); Donnelly, Defamation by Radio: A Reconsideration, 34 Iowa L.Rev. 12 (1948); Finley, Defamation by Radio, 19 Can.Bar Rev. 353 (1941); Vold, Defamatory Interpolations in Radio Broadcasts, 88 U.P. L.Rev. 256 (1940); note [1950] Wash. U.L.Q. 95.

For definitive discussion of underlying principles (in the "notorious Gramophone-Libel case") see Chicken v. Ham,

PECK v. CHICAGO TRIBUNE

Supreme Court of the United States, 1909.
214 U.S. 185, 53 L.Ed. 960, 16 Ann.Cas. 1075.

MR. JUSTICE HOLMES delivered the opinion of the court.

This is an action on the case for a libel. The libel alleged is found in an advertisement printed in the defendant's newspaper, the Chicago Sunday Tribune, and so far as is material is as follows: "Nurse and Patients Praise Duffy's—Mrs. A. Schuman, One of Chicago's Most Capable and Experienced Nurses, Pays an Eloquent Tribute to the Great Invigorating, Life-Giving and Curative Properties of Duffy's Pure Malt Whiskey. * * * " Then followed a portrait of the plaintiff, with the words "Mrs. A. Schuman" under it. Then, in quotation marks, "After years of constant use of your Pure Malt Whiskey, both by myself and as given to patients in my capacity as nurse, I have no hesitation in recommending it as the very best tonic and stimulant for all weak and run-down conditions," &c., &c., with the words "Mrs. A. Schuman, 1576 Mozart st., Chicago, Ill.," at the end, not in quotation marks, but conveying the notion of a signature, or at least that the words were hers. The declaration alleged that the plaintiff was not Mrs. Schuman, was not a nurse, and was a total abstainer from whiskey and all spirituous liquors. There was also a count for publishing the plaintiff's likeness without leave. The defendant pleaded not guilty. At the trial, subject to exceptions, the judge excluded the plaintiff's testimony in support of her allegations just stated, and directed a verdict for the defendant. His action was sustained by the Circuit Court of Appeals. 154 F. 330; s. c., 83 C.C.A. 202.

Of course the insertion of the plaintiff's picture in the place and with the concomitants that we have described imported that she was the nurse and made the statements set forth, as rightly was decided in Wandt v. Hearst's Chicago American, 129 Wis. 419, 421, 109 N.W. 70, 6 L.R.A.,N.S., 919, 116 Am.St.Rep. 959, 9 Ann.Cas. 864. Morrison v. Smith, 177 N.Y. 366, 69 N.E. 725. Therefore the publication was of and concerning the plaintiff, notwithstanding the presence of another fact, the name of the real signer of the certificate, if that was Mrs. Schuman, that was inconsistent, when all the facts were known, with the plaintiff's having signed or adopted it. Many might recognize the plaintiff's face without knowing her name, and those who did know it might be led to infer that she had sanctioned the publication under an alias. There was some suggestion that the defendant published the portrait by mistake, and without knowledge that it was the plaintiff's portrait or was not what it purported to be. But the fact, if it was one, was no excuse. If the publication was libellous the defendant took the risk. As was said of such matters by Lord Mansfield,

in A. P. Herbert, Uncommon Law 71 (1935). The relevance of the distinction is fading in light of constitutional developments, page 880 et seq. infra. To the extent that relevance remains the weight of opinion appears to favor libel; see, e. g., Restatement of Torts, Second § 568A (Tent. Draft No. 20, 1974).

"Whatever a man publishes he publishes at his peril." The King v. Woodfall, Lofft, 776, 781. See further Hearne v. Stowell, 12 A. & E. 719, 726; Shepheard v. Whitaker, L.R. 10 C.P. 502; Clark v. North American Co., 203 Pa. 346, 351, 352, 53 A. 237. The reason is plain. A libel is harmful on its face. If a man sees fit to publish manifestly hurtful statements concerning an individual, without other justification than exists for an advertisement or a piece of news, the usual principles of tort will make him liable, if the statements are false or are true only of some one else. See Morasse v. Brochu, 151 Mass. 567, 575, 25 N.E. 74, 8 L.R.A. 524, 21 Am.St.Rep. 474.

The question, then, is whether the publication was a libel. It was held by the Circuit Court of Appeals not to be, or at most to entitle the plaintiff only to nominal damages, no special damage being alleged. It was pointed out that there was no general consensus of opinion that to drink whiskey is wrong or that to be a nurse is discreditable. It might have been added that very possibly giving a certificate and the use of one's portrait in aid of an advertisement would be regarded with irony, or a stronger feeling, only by a few. But it appears to us that such inquiries are beside the point. It may be that the action for libel is of little use, but while it is maintained it should be governed by the general principles of tort. If the advertisement obviously would hurt the plaintiff in the estimation of an important and respectable part of the community liability is not a question of a majority vote.

We know of no decision in which this matter is discussed upon principle. But obviously an unprivileged falsehood need not entail universal hatred to constitute a cause of action. No falsehood is thought about or even known by all the world. No conduct is hated by all. That it will be known by a large number and will lead an appreciable fraction of that number to regard the plaintiff with contempt is enough to do her practical harm. Thus if a doctor were represented as advertising, the fact that it would affect his standing with others of his profession might make the representation actionable, although advertising is not reputed dishonest and even seems to be regarded by many with pride.[7] See Martin v. The Picayune, 115 La. 979, 40 So.

7. Suppose a naval officer is portrayed in a movie as a warm-hearted, courageous, impetuous hero in such a way as to endear him to the movie-going public but to make him seem undisciplined and irresponsible to his fellow professional officers. Plaintiff was one of the heroes of the PT Boat exploits depicted in They Were Expendable. Kelly v. Loew's, Inc., 76 F. Supp. 473 (D.Mass.1948).

Do those who would be likely to think less of the plaintiff because of a defamatory charge have to be "right-thinking" people? Consider the case of the filling station operator who was falsely charged with habitually carrying out his manifest civic duty of informing on truck drivers who violated regulations of the I.C.C. Connelley v. McKay, 176 Misc. 685, 28 N.Y.S.2d 327 (Sup.Ct.1941); The Community Segment in Defamation Actions: A Dissenting Essay, 58 Yale L.J. 1387 (1949). And see discussion by L. Hand, J., in Grant v. Reader's Digest Ass'n, 151 F.2d 733, 735 (2d Cir. 1945). ("We do not believe, therefore, that we need say whether 'right-thinking' people would harbor similar feelings towards a lawyer, because he had been an agent for the Communist Party, or was a sympathizer with its aims and means. It is enough if

376, 4 L.R.A., N.S., 861. It seems to us impossible to say that the obvious tendency of what is imputed to the plaintiff by this advertisement is not seriously to hurt her standing with a considerable and respectable class in the community. Therefore it was the plaintiff's right to prove her case and go to the jury, and the defendant would have got all that it could ask if it had been permitted to persuade them, if it could, to take a contrary view. Culmer v. Canby, 101 F. 195, 197, 41 C.C.A. 302; Twombly v. Monroe, 136 Mass. 464, 469. See Gates v. New York Recorder Co., 155 N.Y. 228, 49 N.E. 769.

It is unnecessary to consider the question whether the publication of the plaintiff's likeness was a tort *per se*. It is enough for the present case that the law should at least be prompt to recognize the injuries that may arise from an unauthorized use in connection with other facts, even if more subtlety is needed to state the wrong than is needed here. In this instance we feel no doubt.

Judgment reversed.[8]

CARDILLO v. DOUBLEDAY & CO., INC.

United States Court of Appeals for the Second Circuit, 1975.
518 F.2d 638.

OAKES, CIRCUIT JUDGE. Robert Cardillo, presently incarcerated at the United States Federal Penitentiary at Lewisburg, Pennsylvania, appeals from an order of the United States District Court for the Southern District of New York * * * dismissing petitioner's civil libel suit and granting summary judgment for the appellees * * *. We affirm. * * *

* * * [W]e consider as a matter of law that appellant is, for purposes of this case, libel-proof, i. e., so unlikely by virtue of his life

there be some, as there certainly are, who do feel so, even if they would be 'wrong-thinking' people if they did.")

Would it be a libel to call an ardent and life-long Democrat a Republican, or vice versa?

8. The requirement that the words be published "of and concerning" the plaintiff has for the most part, like other aspects of interpreting the challenged statement, been worked out along the lines of the objective test so consistently espoused by Holmes. Hulton v. Jones, [1910] A.C. 20, 79 L.J.K.B. 198 (1909); Newstead v. London Express Newspaper, Ltd., [1940] 1 K.B. 377, noted (1941) 7 Camb.L.J. 275, 89 U. of Pa.L.Rev. 676 (1941); Restatement of Torts, sections 563, 564 (test whether recipient "correctly, or mistakenly but reasonably, understands" the statement to mean what is claimed). In Massachusetts it was held otherwise as to the reference to plaintiff, Hanson v. Globe Newspaper Co., 159 Mass. 293, 34 N.E. 462, 20 L.R.A. 856 (1893). Knowlton wrote the opinion; Holmes dissented. The same fundamental divergence between these two judges may be seen in another field. Nash v. Minnesota Title Insurance & Trust Co., 163 Mass. 574, 40 N.E. 1039, 28 L.R.A. 753, 47 Am.St. Rep. 489 (1895) (misrepresentation).

Under either test it is clear that plaintiff need not be named or identified by pictures, etc., if the meaning (subjective or objective) is reasonably apparent. See Corrigan v. Bobbs-Merrill Co., 228 N.Y. 58, 126 N.E. 260, 10 A.L.R. 662 (1920) (fictitious name); Kelly v. Loew's Inc., 76 F.Supp. 473 (D.Mass. 1948) (the court here also deals with the exceedingly familiar "any resemblance * * *" statement).

as a habitual criminal to be able to recover anything other than nominal damages as to warrant dismissal of the case, involving as it does First Amendment considerations. * * * We by no means intend to suggest that prison inmates can be deprived of access to federal diversity jurisdiction to obtain redress of wrongs, including libels, committed against them whether they are in or out of prison. But here appellant is serving 21 years, sentenced for assorted federal felonies, including separate convictions for stolen securities and bail-jumping in the United States District Court for the Southern District of Florida, bail-jumping in the District of Maryland, and conspiracy and interstate transportation of stolen securities in the District of New Hampshire. He has been previously convicted of receiving stolen property and numerous minor infractions of the law in Massachusetts where he lived. His answers to interrogatories indicate that he was in Teresa's company "frequently" from 1963–69, knew Teresa to be a petty thief and confidence man, and was "directly involved" with Teresa "in several minor crimes, none of which were noteworthy or profitable." While he denies participation in a robbery mentioned by Teresa (*My Life in the Mafia* at 176) at, or above, Lindenbaum's Laundromat and claims that much of Teresa's story is fantasy, from 1967 to early 1969 he admits that Teresa, who was then in possession of a considerable quantity of money, and a "Joe Black" each told him they were in a "shylocking and bookmaking operation" (although he says Teresa was swindled by Black). He denies participation in numerous other specific crimes referred to in the appellees' book, including fixing a specific race, the Constitution Handicap at Suffolk Downs, but he was indicted in Massachusetts for fixing races at that track and apparently not tried only because of his present incarceration. The records of the House Select Committee on Crime, 92d Cong., 2d Sess., on Organized Crime in Sports (Racing) contain testimony at page 738 (May 24, 1972) of Joseph "The Baron" Barboza, a former organized crime "enforcer," substantiating Teresa's claim that Cardillo frequented the "Ebb Tide" which was where "the mob generally hung out" and that Cardillo fixed races at Suffolk by slowing down the favorites with drug injections. With Cardillo himself having a record and relationships or associations like these, we cannot envisage any jury awarding, or court sustaining, an award under any circumstances for more than a few cents' damages, even if Cardillo were to prevail on the difficult legal issues with which he would be faced.

Accordingly, we affirm the judgment below.

Judgment affirmed.

BURTON v. CROWELL PUB. CO.

Circuit Court of Appeals of the United States, Second Circuit, 1936.
82 F.2d 154.

L. HAND, CIRCUIT JUDGE. This appeal arises upon a judgment dismissing a complaint for libel upon the pleadings. The complaint alleged that the defendant had published an advertisement—annexed and incorporated by reference—made up of text and photographs; that one of the photographs was "susceptible of being regarded as representing plaintiff as guilty of indecent exposure and as being a person physically deformed and mentally perverted"; that some of the text, read with the offending photograph, was "susceptible of being regarded as falsely representing plaintiff as an utterer of salacious and obscene language"; and finally that "by reason of the premises plaintiff has been subjected to frequent and conspicuous ridicule, scandal, reproach, scorn, and indignity." The advertisement was of "Camel" cigarettes; the plaintiff was a widely known gentleman steeple-chaser, and the text quoted him as declaring that "Camel" cigarettes "restored" him after "a crowded business day." Two photographs were inserted; the larger, a picture of the plaintiff in riding shirt and breeches, seated apparently outside a paddock with a cigarette in one hand and a cap and whip in the other. This contained the legend, "Get a lift with a Camel"; neither it, nor the photograph, is charged as part of the libel, except as the legend may be read upon the other and offending photograph. That represented him coming from a race to be weighed in; he is carrying his saddle in front of him with his right hand under the pommel and his left under the cantle; the line of the seat is about twelve inches below his waist. Over the pommel hangs a stirrup; over the seat at his middle a white girth falls loosely in such a way that it seems to be attached to the plaintiff and not to the saddle. So regarded, the photograph becomes grotesque, monstrous, and obscene; and the legends, which without undue violence can be made to match, reinforce the ribald interpretation. That is the libel. The answer alleged that the plaintiff had posed for the photographs and been paid for their use as an advertisement; a reply, that they had never been shown to the plaintiff after they were taken. On this showing the judge held that the advertisement did not hold the plaintiff up to the hatred, ridicule, or contempt of fair-minded people, and that in any event he consented to its use and might not complain.

We dismiss at once so much of the complaint as alleged that the advertisement might be read to say that the plaintiff was deformed, or that he had indecently exposed himself, or was making obscene jokes by means of the legends. Nobody could be fatuous enough to believe any of these things; everybody would at once see that it was the camera, and the camera alone, that had made the unfortunate mistake. If the advertisement is a libel, it is such in spite of the fact that it asserts nothing whatever about the plaintiff, even by the remotest implications. It does not profess to depict him as he is;

it does not exaggerate any part of his person so as to suggest that he is deformed; it is patently an optical illusion, and carries its correction on its face as much as though it were a verbal utterance which expressly declared that it was false. It would be hard for words so guarded to carry any sting, but the same is not true of caricatures, and this is an example; for, notwithstanding all we have just said, it exposed the plaintiff to overwhelming ridicule. The contrast between the drawn and serious face and the accompanying fantastic and lewd deformity was so extravagant that, though utterly unfair, it in fact made of the plaintiff a preposterously ridiculous spectacle; and the obvious mistake only added to the amusement. Had such a picture been deliberately produced, surely every right-minded person would agree that he would have had a genuine grievance; and the effect is the same whether it is deliberate or not. Such a caricature affects a man's reputation, if by that is meant his position in the minds of others; the association so established may be beyond repair; he may become known indefinitely as the absurd victim of this unhappy mischance. Literally, therefore, the injury falls within the accepted rubric; it exposes the sufferer to "ridicule" and "contempt." Nevertheless, we have not been able to find very much in the books that is in point, for although it has long been recognized that pictures may be libels, and in some cases they have been caricatures, in nearly all they have impugned the plaintiff at least by implication, directly or indirectly uttering some falsehood about him. * * *

The defendant answers that every libel must affect the plaintiff's character; but if by "character" is meant those moral qualities which the word ordinarily includes, the statement is certainly untrue, for there are many libels which do not affect the reputation of the victim in any such way. Thus, it is a libel to say that a man is insane (Totten v. Sun Printing & Pub. Co. [C.C.] 109 F. 289; Southwick v. Stevens, 10 Johns. [N.Y.] 443; Belknap v. Ball, 83 Mich. 583, 47 N.W. 674, 11 L.R.A. 72, 21 Am.St.Rep. 622); or that he has negro blood if he professes to be white (Stultz v. Cousins [C.C.A.6] 242 F. 794); or is too educated to earn his living (Martin v. Press Pub. Co., 93 App.Div. 531, 87 N.Y.S. 859); or is desperately poor (Moffatt v. Cauldwell, 3 Hun [N.Y.] 26); or that he is a eunuch (Eckert v. Van Pelt, 69 Kan. 357, 76 P. 909, 66 L.R.A. 266); or that he has an infectious disease, even though not venereal (Villers v. Monsley, 2 Wils. 403; Simpson v. Press Pub. Co., 33 Misc. 228, 67 N.Y.S. 401); or that he is illegitimate (Shelby v. Sun P. & P. Ass'n, 38 Hun [N.Y.] 474, affirmed on opinion below, 109 N.Y. 611, 15 N.E. 895); or that his near relatives have committed a crime (Van Wiginton v. Pulitzer Pub. Co., 218 F. 795 [C.C.A.8]; Merrill v. Post Pub. Co., 197 Mass. 185, 83 N.E. 419); or that he was mistaken for Jack Ketch (Cook v. Ward, 6 Bing. 409); or that a woman was served with process in her bathtub (Snyder v. New York Press Co., 137 App.Div. 291, 121 N.Y.S. 944). It is indeed not true that all ridicule (Lamberti v. Sun P. & P. Ass'n, 111 App.Div. 437, 97 N.Y.S. 694), or all disagreeable comment (Kimmerle v. New York Evening Journal, Inc., 262 N.Y. 99, 186 N.E. 217;

Cohen v. New York Times Co., 153 App.Div. 242, 138 N.Y.S. 206), is actionable; a man must not be too thin-skinned or a self-important prig; but this advertisement was more than what only a morbid person would not laugh off; the mortification, however ill-deserved, was a very substantial grievance.

A more plausible challenge is that a libel must be something that can be true or false, since truth is always a defense. It would follow that if, as we agree, the picture was a mistake on its face and declared nothing about the plaintiff, it was not a libel. We have been able to find very little on the point. In Dunlop v. Dunlop Rubber Co. (1920) 1 Irish Ch. & Ld.Com. 280, 290–292, the picture represented the plaintiff in foppish clothes, and the opinion seems to rely merely upon the contempt which that alone might have aroused, but those who saw it might have taken it to imply that the plaintiff was in fact a fop. In Zbyszko v. New York American, 228 App.Div. 277, 239 N.Y.S. 411, however, though the decision certainly went far, nobody could possibly have read the picture as asserting anything which was in fact untrue; it was the mere association of the plaintiff with a gorilla that was thought to lower him in others' esteem. Nevertheless, although the question is almost tabula rasa, it seems to us that in principle there should be no doubt. The gravamen of the wrong in defamation is not so much the injury to reputation, measured by the opinions of others, as the feelings, that is, the repulsion or the light esteem, which those opinions engender. We are sensitive to the charge of murder only because our fellows deprecate it in most forms; but a head-hunter, or an aboriginal American Indian, or a gangster, would regard such an accusation as a distinction, and during the Great War an "ace," a man who had killed five others, was held in high regard. Usually it is difficult to arouse feelings without expressing an opinion, or asserting a fact; and the common law has so much regard for truth that it excuses the utterance of anything that is true. But it is a non sequitur to argue that whenever truth is not a defense, there can be no libel; that would invert the proper approach to the whole subject. In all wrongs we must first ascertain whether the interest invaded is one which the law will protect at all; that is indeed especially important in defamation, for the common law did not recognize all injuries to reputation, especially when the utterance was oral. But the interest here is by hypothesis one which the law does protect; the plaintiff has been substantially enough ridiculed to be in a position to complain. The defendant must therefore find some excuse, and truth would be an excuse if it could be pleaded. The only reason why the law makes truth a defense is not because a libel must be false but because the utterance of truth is in all circumstances an interest paramount to reputation; it is like a privileged communication, which is privileged only because the law prefers it conditionally to reputation. When there is no such countervailing interest, there is no excuse; and that is the situation here. In conclusion therefore we hold that because the picture taken with the legends was calculated to expose the plaintiff to more than trivial ridicule, it was prima facie actionable; that the fact that it did not assume to state a fact or an opinion is irrelevant; and that in consequence the publication is actionable.

Finally, the plaintiff's consent to the use of the photographs for which he posed as an advertisement was not a consent to the use of the offending photograph; he had no reason to anticipate that the lens would so distort his appearance. If the defendant wished to fix him with responsibility for whatever the camera might turn out, the result should have been shown him before publication. Possibly any one who chooses to stir such a controversy in a court cannot have been very sensitive originally, but that is a consideration for the jury, which, if ever justified, is justified in actions for defamation.

Judgment reversed; cause remanded for trial.[9]

FARRELL v. TRIANGLE PUBLICATIONS, INC.

Supreme Court of Pennsylvania, 1960.
399 Pa. 102, 159 A.2d 734.

CHARLES ALVIN JONES, CHIEF JUSTICE.

On January 29, 1958, The Inquirer, Philadelphia's morning newspaper of wide circulation, published the following under the headline "$900,000, Trash Deal 'Split' for Commissioners Probed":

> "The Delaware county District Attorney's office yesterday began investigating a report that a $900,000 slice of the canceled $1,600,000 Upper Darby incinerator deal was earmarked for division among a number of township commissioners and others.
>
> "This startling development arose on the eve of the opening today of the Delaware county grand jury investigation into the abortive deal that was quickly dropped after an expose by the Inquirer. Investigators studying the report of the $900,000 jackpot declined to elaborate, but it was learned they would question the 13 commissioners, former office holders. * * * "

John H. Farrell, the plaintiff, was at the time one of the Commissioners of Upper Darby Township, of whom there were thirteen. Farrell brought this action against Triangle Publications, Inc., the publisher of the Philadelphia Inquirer, for damages on the ground that the article libeled him. The defendant filed preliminary objections to the complaint, asserting that it failed to state a cause of action. The court sustained the preliminary objections and entered judgment for the defendant. This appeal followed.

The sole question involved is whether the article referred to Farrell as an object of its charges and insinuations with sufficient

9. Compare Restatement of Torts, Second § 566 (Tent. Draft No. 21, 1975, as amended).

particularity to invest him with a cause of action for libel. That the article was defamatory cannot be seriously disputed.

Where a defamatory publication or utterance is directed toward a class or group whose membership is so numerous that no one individual member can reasonably be deemed an intended object of the defamatory matter, no cause of action for libel or slander arises therefrom. For example, if someone should speak or write defamatorily of all the members of one of the professions, such as the law, medicine or ministry, no particular lawyer, doctor or minister could maintain a personal action for the defamation for the reason that no one would be sufficiently identified as an object thereof to justifiably warrant a conclusion that his individual reputation had been substantially injured. Where, however, a defamatory publication or utterance is directed toward a comparatively small class or group all of whose constituent members may be readily identified and the recipients of the defamatory matter are likely to identify some, if not all, of them as intended objects of the defamation, an individual member of the group may sue for the damages done his reputation thereby.

If a newspaper should publish defamatory statements about a person by referring to him by name, it would, of course, lay itself open to liability for damages to the injured person in a suit for libel. That being so, it would indeed be irrational, as well as unconscionable, to permit a publication to escape responsibility under the libel law simply by confining the objects of its defamation to "a number of", "some of", or even to "one of" a relatively small group of persons all of whom are readily identifiable by recipients of the defamatory matter. To hold otherwise would be to make liability for libel depend upon the form of the defamation rather than its content.

On the other hand, if it is clear that, because of the large number in the group referred to in the printed matter, or for any other reason, a recipient of a defamatory publication could not reasonably conclude that it referred to the particular person claiming to have been libeled thereby, the complaint should be dismissed for failure to state a cause of action. But, if the defamatory publication can reasonably be interpreted as referring to a particular complainant, whether recipients did so conclude is for a jury to determine.

The Restatement of Torts, § 564, states the principle as follows:

> "*Applicability of Defamatory Communication to Plaintiff:* A defamatory communication is made concerning the person to whom its recipient correctly, or mistakenly but reasonably, understands it as intended to refer."

Illustrations:

> "2. A newspaper publishes the statement that some member of B's household has committed murder. In the absence of any circumstances indicating that some particular member of B's household was referred to, the newspaper has defamed each member of B's household."

One of the most noted cases of group libel in recent years is Gross v. Cantor, 1936, 270 N.Y. 93, 200 N.E. 592. In that case, Eddie Cantor, the singer-comedian, had written an article which was published in the magazine "Radio Guide" in which he inveighed against "those New York radio editors who are experts at logrolling, who use their columns for delving into personalities that have nothing to do with radio and whose various rackets are a disgrace to the newspaper profession." The author further asserted that "There is but one person writing on radio in New York City who has the necessary background, dignity and honesty of purpose." He did not, however, name the person so exonerated of the charges. A New York radio editor sued Cantor for damages in an action for libel and obtained a judgment which the New York Court of Appeals affirmed. In its opinion, the court quoted with approval from Ryckman v. Delavan, 1840, 25 Wend., N.Y., 186, 202, as follows: "But if the words may by any reasonable application, import a charge against several individuals, under some general description or general name, the plaintiff has the right to go on to trial, and it is for the jury to decide, whether the charge has the personal application averred by the plaintiff."

A case in this State, in no way distinguishable from the present case so far as the sufficiency of the plaintiff's complaint, in stating the cause of action, is concerned, is Egan v. Dubois Printing & Publishing Company, 1916, 64 Pa.Super. 115. In the Egan case, a newspaper printed a defamatory story about "a number of [former] national organizers" for the United Mine Workers of America who were in DuBois. The plaintiffs in the action were two such organizers, but were not specifically referred to or identified in the article. The Superior Court held (at page 122) that, "Whether the descriptions of the persons referred to in the article applied to the plaintiff[s] was a question of fact properly submitted to the jury."

* * *

Here, the ordinary reader of the Philadelphia Inquirer could naturally and reasonably infer that the defamatory publication referred to the plaintiff, among others. Certain it is that a substantial number of readers, particularly those resident in Upper Darby Township, knew that the plaintiff was one of the thirteen commissioners of the township. Moreover, it is not unreasonable to conclude that many other Upper Darby readers of the Inquirer who, prior to the defamatory article, had not known the identity of all of the township's commissioners, were impelled by the scandalous nature of the charges to make inquiry and find out who the commissioners were—a process which would almost inevitably lead to connecting the plaintiff's name with the alleged corruption in office.

The fact that the article did not state that all of the commissioners of the township were parties to the reported corrupt deal could not operate to exclude the plaintiff from being one of the relatively small and officially designated group to which the article indisputably made reference. The publication also declared that the district attorney's office would question all thirteen of the commissioners, one of whom was the plaintiff. That statement at least implied that, in the mind of the district attorney, none of the commissioners was above suspicion of knowledge, guilty or otherwise, of the alleged "split". The effect of the article could be to impugn the integrity and honesty of the plaintiff in the estimation of the public. Even persons favorably disposed toward him might, upon reading the article, reasonably conclude that the plaintiff was one of the commissioners referred to as being corrupt. This would be a sufficient maligning of his reputation to give him a cause of action for libel.

On preliminary objections to a complaint for libel on the ground that it fails to state a cause of action, it was the duty of the court to determine whether the words employed were defamatory or capable of a defamatory meaning, and if so, whether a recipient of the communication could reasonably conclude that it referred to the plaintiff. We hold that, under the facts pleaded, the trial court should have concluded as a matter of law that the publication was defamatory and that the plaintiff was sufficiently referred to so that a recipient might reasonably conclude that the plaintiff was an object of the defamation. Whether recipients did so conclude is a question for a jury to determine. The court was therefore in error in dismissing the complaint and in entering judgment for the defendant. * * * [10]

10. Also see Restatement of Torts, Second § 564A (Tent. Draft No. 21, 1975) on defamation of a group or a class. Compare Fowler v. Curtis Publishing Co., 78 F.Supp. 303 (D.D.C.1948), aff'd 182 F.2d 377 (D.C.Cir. 1950) (article unfavorable to Washington taxi drivers, with illustration showing a Columbia Taxicab: no liability either to a cab owner, or to one of sixty Columbia drivers); DeWitt v. Kearney & Treaker Corp., 265 Wis. 132, 60 N.W.2d 748 (1953) (liability to the four officers of a local union for a statement attributing misconduct to "the small group of officers" of a union); Neiman-Marcus Co. v. Lait, 13 F.R.D. 311 (S.D.N.Y.1952) (as to sufficiency of complaint, potential liability undisputed to the entire group of models, nine, for statement that "some Neiman-Marcus models are call girls—the top babes in town"; no liability to thirty suing saleswomen, out of total of 382, for statement, "The salesgirls are good, too—pretty and often much cheaper * * * more fun, too, not as snooty as the models"; potential liability to fifteen suing salesmen, of total of twenty-five for statement that "most of the [men's store] sales staff are fairies").

Even where individual members of the group are not well-enough identified to warrant action by any of them, what of the right of the group itself to sue? There has been some development in this field. It is now clear, for instance, that a corporation may recover for defamation of itself (as distinguished from its product) whether it is a business or a non-profit corporation. New York Soc. for Suppression of Vice v. MacFadden Publications, Inc., 260 N.Y. 167, 183 N.E. 284, 86 A.L.R. 440 (1932). And recovery has been allowed to a labor union (an unincorporated association) of 17,000 members. Kirkman v. Westchester Newspapers, Inc., 287 N.Y. 373, 39 N.E.2d 919 (1942), 41 Col.L.Rev. 937 (1941). A lower court case in Pennsylvania has allowed recovery by the ADA, an unincorporated political organization. This decision is the subject of an able and provocative note in 98 U.Pa.L.Rev. 865 (1950). See also 24 Temple L.Q. 247 (1950).

Excellent treatment of the problem of group libel and some of its ramifications (e. g. defamation of racial and other minority groups) may be found in Chafee, Government and Mass Communications, ch. 5 (1947); Riesman, Democracy and Defamation: Control of Group Libel, 42 Colum.L.Rev. 727 (1942); Donnelly, Law of Defamation: Proposals for Reform, 33 Minn.L.Rev.

(B) DEFENSES AND CONSTITUTIONAL LIMITATIONS

GABAUER v. WOODCOCK

United States Court of Appeals for the Fifth Circuit, 1975.
520 F.2d 1084.

VAN OOSTERHOUT, SENIOR CIRCUIT JUDGE.

* * * Count II of plaintiff's complaint alleges common law libel against individual defendants Leonard Woodcock, President of the United Automobile, Aerospace and Agricultural Implement Workers of America (UAW), and Emil Mazey, Secretary-Treasurer of the UAW. * * * At the close of all of the evidence the trial court granted defendants' motion for a directed verdict * * *. We affirm * * *.

At all times relevant Gabauer and Claude Huskey were members of the UAW and Local 25 of the UAW in St. Louis, Mo. They were both employees of General Motors' Chevrolet Unit in St. Louis. Both had been employed there since 1957 or 1958.

In 1968 Gabauer was Chairman of the Shop Committee in the Chevrolet Unit of Local 25. Huskey was a district committeeman in the same Unit. In 1969 a strike occurred at the General Motors plant which began April 10th and ended June 6th of that year. Gabauer, Huskey and other local committeemen of the Chevrolet Unit opposed this strike by voting against it and by advising defendant Woodcock, then vice-president of the UAW, of their opposition by letter dated April 1, 1969. Woodcock, through local UAW officers, attempted unsuccessfully to persuade Huskey and other Chevrolet Unit Committeemen to support the strike. The "Green and White" slate, as Gabauer, Huskey and their political faction were known, made their opposition to the 1969 strike the basis for Huskey's and Gabauer's successful campaign for election in March of 1970 as delegates to the national UAW convention.

In June 1969 shortly after the strike ended Gabauer was reelected Chairman of the Shop Committee and Huskey was elected a zone committeeman. * * * [The court recites a history of further friction between plaintiff and the international union, culminating in the imposition by the international of a trusteeship over the local unit.]

In July of 1970, following imposition of the Trusteeship, the UAW undertook to audit the finances of Local 25 with respect to union funds paid to committee members for time lost from work on account of authorized union employment. When a trusteeship is imposed a general audit is routine practice. Defendant Mazey, as

609, 623 (1949); Tanenhaus, Group Libel, 35 Corn.L.Q. 261 (1950); Beth, Group Libel and Free Speech, 39 Minn. L.Rev. 167 (1955); Belton, The Control of Group Defamation: A Comparative Study of Law and its Limitations, 34 Tul.L.Rev. 299 (1960); note, Statutory Prohibition of Group Defamation, 47 Col.L.Rev. 595 (1947); note, Group Libel Laws: Abortive Efforts to Combat Hate Propaganda, 61 Yale L.J. 252 (1952).

Secretary-Treasurer of the UAW and supervisor of union auditors, ordered a lost time audit as well as a general audit after learning from Mattix of complaints of alleged "double-dipping." [11] The audit revealed that Huskey, Gabauer and others may have wrongfully received amounts ranging from $159 (Huskey) and $74.69 (Gabauer) down to $5.80 (for a total of $319) for alleged "double-dipping." Five of the six found to have wrongfully received union funds were those commiteemen who had opposed the 1969 strike and had passed out handbills in violation of Mattix's censorship order. On August 19, 1970, union auditor Berry made his final report to Mazey. On August 22, 1970, Mazey wrote Huskey and Gabauer a letter, the text of which reads:

> A recent audit of the financial records of UAW Local 25 revealed possible overcharges of lost time that you received from the Local Union.
>
> Attached is a summary of the lost time in question.
>
> You will be given an opportunity to appear before representatives of the International Union on Thursday, August 27, 1970, to explain what appears to be an overcharge of lost time. You are requested to appear at the UAW Region 5 office, located at 130 South Bemiston Avenue, St. Louis, Missouri, at 2:00 P.M., in the office conference room.

Copies of the August 22nd letter were sent to Worley, Administrator and Regional Director of UAW; Irv Bluestone, Co-Director of the UAW's General Motors Department; Roy Hartzell, Financial Secretary of Local 25; Mattix, Deputy Administrator; and the auditor who conducted the audit. Similar letters were sent to other committeemen who were accused of "double-dipping." All such accused persons appeared and presented evidence at a hearing August 27, 1970, conducted by UAW's chief auditor Bateman. On September 1, 1970, Bateman wrote a report to Mazey detailing the results of the auditor's hearing. Mazey then forwarded written findings and recommendations to Woodcock. After a consideration of the record Woodcock wrote the following letter to Gabauer on September 15, 1970:

> As a result of an audit by the International Union, it appears by convincing evidence that you are responsible for misappropriation of funds in the amount of $74.69.
>
> You were given an opportunity at a hearing held on August 27, 1970 * * * to explain alleged misappropriation of funds from Local 25. I have been advised by the office of the Secretary-Treasurer that your explanations were unsatisfactory and did not in any way change the finding of the Auditor that you had misappropriated funds from Local 25.

11. "Double-dipping" is charging the local union for the same hours for which pay is received from the employer.

Therefore, be advised that you are summarily suspended; upon receipt of this letter, from any office or position you may now hold within the Local Union and you are further prohibited from seeking election to any office or position within the Local Union (elected or appointed), until you have made full restitution of the misappropriated funds claimed against you or such prohibition has been lifted by a two-thirds (⅔) vote of the International Executive Board.

* * * You have the right, under this provision, to appeal your suspension within thirty (30) days.

You are hereby requested to make full restitution to Local 25 in the amount of $74.69 which you improperly received from the Local Union.

The above action is effective and binding upon you and the Local Union upon receipt of this letter.

A similar letter accusing Huskey of misappropriation of $159.04 was mailed to Huskey September 15th. Copies were mailed to the same persons who received copies of Mazey's August 22nd letter. On September 18, 1970, Woodcock wrote another letter to Huskey and Gabauer making a correction in the September 15th letter, the effect of which was to require both repayment *and* a two-thirds vote of the Executive Board before either could be restored to candidacy or elective office.

Gabauer and Huskey repaid the money as requested and appealed Woodcock's action to the Appeals Committee of the UAW Executive Board. The Appeals Committee absolved Gabauer completely from any wrongdoing in February of 1971 * * *.

The trial court directed a verdict at the close of all the evidence in favor of all defendants on Count II of plaintiff's complaint. As a basis for directing a verdict on Count II, Judge Regan found (1) that communications in question were at least qualifiedly privileged and that there was insufficient evidence to support a finding of actual malice needed to overcome privilege, and (2) the legal element of publication was absent.

On appeal plaintiff argues that there was actual publication of the letters in question and that there was sufficient evidence of actual malice to overcome the qualified privilege, if it exists.

* * * We agree with the trial court that the controlling Missouri law on libel actions of this type is found in Pulliam v. Bond, 406 S.W.2d 635 (Mo.1966). Pulliam was a union official who had differences with other officials of the union. A statement charging Pulliam with financial misconduct (including "double-dipping") was prepared, signed and filed by a majority of the Executive Committee of the union of which Pulliam was a member. Copies of these charges were sent to the Secretary-Treasurer of the union Board and to Pulliam. * * * A jury returned a verdict in favor of plaintiff Pulliam after the trial court overruled defendant's motions for

a directed verdict. On appeal the Missouri Supreme Court reversed the trial court, holding that a verdict should have been directed in defendant's favor. The court stated:

> It seems to be generally recognized that a qualified privilege attaches to statements and communications made in connection with the various activities of such organizations as * * * labor unions * * *. Thus, it is well settled that members of such bodies may * * * prefer charges against fellow members * * * and make proper publication of any disciplinary action that may be taken, without liability for any resultant defamation so long as they act without malice. [Citations omitted]. The * * manner in which the charges were preferred were within the framework of the organization. The trial court correctly held that the communication in question was entitled to the protection of a qualified or conditional privilege. [Citations omitted].
>
> By accepting membership in the [union], the plaintiff must be held to have consented to be subjected to having written charges filed against him and to have such charges processed in the manner provided by the constitution and bylaws of the organization and by applicable statutes. [406 S.W.2d at 641].

In the instant case copies of the allegedly libelous letters were mailed only to officials of either the local or national union.

Assuming without deciding that the letters in question were both false and defamatory, the publications are not necessarily actionable. A communication in Missouri is qualifiedly made in good faith upon any subject matter in which the person making the communication has an interest or in reference to which he has a duty, and to a person having a corresponding interest or duty. Estes v. Lawton-Byrne-Bruner Ins. Agency Co., 437 S.W.2d 685, 690 (St. Louis Ct.App.1969). The recipients of the three letters, as officers of the union involved, certainly had the requisite interest in and, in the case of Worley, Mattix and Auditor Bateman, a duty to implement the directives maintained in the letters. Just as in Pulliam v. Bond, supra, the plaintiff consented to be subjected to having such charges processed according to local by-laws and those of the national union by accepting membership in the union. There is no evidence that the charges against plaintiff were processed other than by guidelines found in the UAW Constitution.

There is evidence that persons other than those who received the allegedly libelous letters eventually learned of their contents. There is no evidence, however, that any of the defendants were responsible for such publication. There is evidence that plaintiff himself is responsible for the excessive publication. Defendants are not legally responsible for such unauthorized publication. Pulliam v. Bond, supra, at 643.

We think that the persons who received the allegedly libelous publications were qualifiedly privileged to receive those communications. In the absence of evidence of malice, there was thus no actionable publication of the letters.

Once a qualified privilege is found [12] a plaintiff may still recover if he presents substantial evidence that the defendant has acted outside the privilege. This may be done by showing that a publication was done with actual or express malice. Pulliam v. Bond, supra at 641. Although the question of the existence of actual malice is for the jury, if there is no substantial evidence to support a finding of malice, the court should direct a verdict. Estes v. Lawton-Byrne-Bruner Ins. Agency Co., 437 S.W.2d 685, 691 (St. Louis App.Ct. 1969). The finding that a qualified privilege exists "precludes an inference of malice from the communication of false and defamatory matter and the plaintiff has the burden of proving express malice." Pulliam v. Bond, supra at 641. In Missouri "actual malice" means "with knowledge that it was false or with reckless disregard of whether it was false or not." Woolbright v. Sun Communications, Inc., 480 S.W.2d 864, 867 (Mo.1972). See New York Times v. Sullivan, 376 U.S. 254, 280, 84 S.Ct. 710, 11 L.Ed.2d 686 (1964).[13] We think plaintiff's evidence clearly fails to meet this burden. Although Gabauer was later exonerated of any wrongdoing, the evidence shows that a prima facie case of "double-dipping" was revealed by the audit. Mazey's letter of August 22nd merely informed Gabauer of the nature of the charges and where and when he would have an opportunity to be heard. Woodcock's letters of September 15th and 18th were sent in accordance with and the requirements of Article 48 § 5 of the UAW Constitution. There is no substantial evidence that the letters were sent "with knowledge of their falsity or with reckless disregard of whether they were true or false." Woolbright v. Sun Communications, supra, at 868.

Finding (1) that a qualified privilege exists and (2) that there is no substantial evidence of actual malice, we conclude that there was no error in directing a verdict in favor of defendants on Count II of plaintiff's complaint. * * *

---

12. The determination of whether a qualified privilege exists is a question for the court and not a jury. Hellesen v. Knaus Truck Lines, Inc., 370 S.W. 2d 341, 345 (Mo.1963). [Notes 11 and 12 from original, renumbered; other notes in original omitted.]

13. Other courts reject "actual malice" as the requirement for defeat of this kind of conditional privilege, on the ground that it is a constitutional term of art under New York Times v. Sullivan, relating solely to a specific constitutional privilege under the First Amendment, e. g., Calero v. Del Chemical Corp., 68 Wis.2d 487, 228 N.W.2d 737 (1975) (preferring "common law malice" or "express malice", equated with "ill will, envy, spite, revenge"). In England the test is "express malice", defined by the House of Lords as a "desire to injure the person who is defamed", which desire must be "the dominant motive for the defamatory publication", Horrocks v. Lowe [1974] 1 All E.R. 662, 669.

TRUTH

In several states truth has been a defense only if there are no improper motives for publishing it, if it is published for justifiable ends, or the like. See Torts Restatement, Caveat to section 582; Ray, Truth: A Defense to Libel, 16 Minn.L.Rev. 43 (1931). Elsewhere malice will not avoid the defense. See, e. g. Alabama Ride Co. v. Vance, 235 Ala. 263, 178 So. 438 (1938). On the whole subject see Harnett & Thornton, The Truth Hurts: A Critique of a Defense to Defamation, 35 Va.L.Rev. 425 (1949); Donnelly, Law of Defamation: Proposals for Reform, 33 Minn.L.Rev. 609 (1949). At least one court has held such a statute unconstitutional, Farnsworth v. Tribune Co., 43 Ill.2d 286, 253 N.E.2d 408 (1969).

In most states truth has been an affirmative defense, e. g., Cowman v. LaVine, Iowa, 234 N.W.2d 114 (1975). In view of recent constitutional developments, however, pages 880 et seq. infra, to the extent that a showing of fault becomes necessary for recovery in defamation, plaintiffs may have to prove falsity in the typical case. See, e. g., Restatement of Torts Second, §§ 558, 580A, 580B and Comment i, and 582 (Tent. Draft No. 21, 1975).

In any event the traditional defense of truth would fail unless the charge was shown to be substantially true in all material particulars.

Moreover, a showing of literal truth would not always avail a defendant if his statement carried implications which the facts shown did not warrant. English & Scottish C. P. M. & I. Co., Ltd. v. Odhams Press, Ltd., [1940] 1 K.B. 440, (noted in 56 L.Q.Rev. 293 (1940); cf. Duncan v. Record Pub. Co., 145 S.C. 196, 143 S.E. 31; Wettach, Developments in Newspaper Libel, 13 Minn.L.Rev. 21, 27–31 (1928).

A restriction on the defense of truth, where the defamation charges a crime, is to be found in the rule (applied in South Carolina and England) that it must be proven beyond a reasonable doubt. See Wettach, op. cit., supra.

In Leevy v. North Carolina Mut. Life Ins. Co., 184 S.C. 111, 191 S.E. 811 (1937), the following instruction was held proper: "If the defendants undertook to justify the slander and prove the truth of the statements, and failed because justification is unsupported by the evidence, it may be considered a circumstance of aggravation, and a continued and express malice, and may properly be considered by the jury in estimating damages." This suggests a danger to defendants in seeking to prove truth. On the other hand, the defendant may reap certain advantages even from an unsuccessful attempt to do this, if

(a) he shows partial truth, or any other discrediting facts, which tend to indicate that the injured reputation was none too good before the defamation. See for example Fleckenstein v. Friedman, 266 N.Y. 19, 193 N.E. 537 (1934) (attack on professional football player's tactics and methods of play. Repetition of similar charges in defendant's answer held available for either truth or to reduce damages as case may be—depending on whether enough is proven to show attack substantially true),

(b) he succeeds in showing grounds for an honest, if mistaken, belief. This is not a defense, but it may be considered by the jury on the question of damages.

The plaintiff's bad character in general, or for the particular trait involved in the defamation, may be shown to mitigate damages. Paddock v. Salisbury, 2 Cow. 811 (N.Y.1824); Bowen v. Hall, 20 Vt. 232 (1848). But there is a dispute as to whether defendant may put in evidence common report of specific acts of wrongdoing. The opposing points of view are well set forth in the following passages:

"Compensatory damages were only such as were occasioned by the false defamatory matter contained in the publication, less whatever damage, if any, had already been occasioned to plaintiff by common current report of the same false, defamatory matter circulated without the agency of the defendant before the publication thereof by the defendant." Republican Pub. Co. v. Mosman, 15 Colo. 399, 24 P. 1051 (1890).

"These very stories may have originated in slander, and character could not be protected, if the third or fourth circulator should be able to defend himself or reduce the damages, because he only gave more publicity, and added the weight of his character, to calumny which had been originated by others." Bodwell v. Swan, 3 Pick. 376 (Mass. 1826).

A thoughtful opinion on this question is that in Abell v. Cornwall Industrial Corp., 241 N.Y. 327, 150 N.E. 132, 43 A.L.R. 880 (1925). See note 43 A.L.R. 887.

The dangers to a plaintiff from having the truth proven are serious, and for the most part obvious. A dramatic illustration is afforded by the case of Oscar Wilde. For a graphic brief account of this see Ernst & Lindey, Hold Your Tongue, pp. 270–276 (1933) (not reprinted in 2d ed.). See Donnelly, The Right of Reply: An Alternative to an Action for Libel, 34 Va.L.Rev. 867, 871 et seq. (1948).

BARR v. MATTEO

United States Supreme Court, 1959.
360 U.S. 564, 79 S.Ct. 1335, 3 L.Ed.2d 1434.

MR. JUSTICE HARLAN announced the judgment of the Court, and delivered an opinion, in which MR. JUSTICE FRANKFURTER, MR. JUSTICE CLARK, and MR. JUSTICE WHITTAKER join.

We are called upon in this case to weigh in a particular context two considerations of high importance which now and again come into sharp conflict—on the one hand, the protection of the individual citizen against pecuniary damage caused by oppressive or malicious action on the part of officials of the Federal Government; and on the other, the protection of the public interest by shielding responsible governmental officers against the harassment and inevitable hazards of vindictive or ill-founded damage suits brought on account of action taken in the exercise of their official responsibilities.

This is a libel suit, brought in the District Court of the District of Columbia by respondents, former employees of the Office of Rent Stabilization. The alleged libel was contained in a press release issued by the office on February 5, 1953, at the direction of petitioner, then its Acting Director. The circumstances which gave rise to the issuance of the release follow.

In 1950 the statutory existence of the Office of Housing Expediter, the predecessor agency of the Office of Rent Stabilization, was about to expire. Respondent Madigan, then Deputy Director in charge of personnel and fiscal matters, and respondent Matteo, chief of the personnel branch, suggested to the Housing Expediter a plan designed to utilize some $2,600,000 of agency funds earmarked in the agency's appropriation for the fiscal year 1950 exclusively for terminal-leave payments. The effect of the plan would have been to obviate the possibility that the agency might have to make large terminal-leave payments during the next fiscal year out of general agency funds, should the life of the agency be extended by Congress. In essence, the mechanics of the plan were that agency employees would be discharged, paid accrued annual leave out of the $2,600,000 earmarked for terminal-leave payments, rehired immediately as temporary employees, and restored to permanent status should the agency's life in fact be extended.

Petitioner, at the time General Manager of the agency, opposed respondents' plan on the ground that it violated the spirit of the Thomas Amendment, 64 Stat. 768,[14] and expressed his opposition to the Housing Expediter. The Expediter decided against general adoption of the plan, but at respondent Matteo's request gave permission for its use in connection with approximately fifty employees, including both respondents, on a voluntary basis. Thereafter the life of the agency was in fact extended.

Some two-and-a-half years later, on January 28, 1953, the Office of Rent Stabilization received a letter from Senator John J. Williams of Delaware, inquiring about the terminal-leave payments made under the plan in 1950. Respondent Madigan drafted a reply to the letter, which he did not attempt to bring to the attention of petitioner, and then prepared a reply which he sent to petitioner's office for his signature as Acting Director of the agency. Petitioner was out of the

14. This statute, part of the General Appropriation Act of 1951, provided that:

"No part of the funds of, or available for expenditure by any corporation or agency included in this Act, including the government of the District of Columbia, shall be available to pay for annual leave accumulated by any civilian officer or employee during the calendar year 1950 and unused at the close of business on June 30, 1951 * * *."

office, and a secretary signed the submitted letter, which was then delivered by Madigan to Senator Williams on the morning of February 3, 1953.

On February 4, 1953, Senator Williams delivered a speech on the floor of the Senate strongly criticizing the plan, stating that "to say the least it is an unjustifiable raid on the Federal Treasury, and heads of every agency in the Government who have condoned this practice should be called to task." The letter above referred to was ordered printed in the Congressional Record. Other Senators joined in the attack on the plan. Their comments were widely reported in the press on February 5, 1953, and petitioner, in his capacity as Acting Director of the agency, received a large number of inquiries from newspapers and other news media as to the agency's position on the matter.

On that day petitioner served upon respondents letters expressing his intention to suspend them from duty, and at the same time ordered issuance by the office of the press release which is the subject of this litigation, and the text of which appears in the margin.[15]

Respondents sued, charging that the press release, in itself and as coupled with the contemporaneous news reports of senatorial reaction to the plan, defamed them to their injury, and alleging that its publication and terms had been actuated by malice on the part of petitioner. Petitioner defended, inter alia, on the ground that the issuance of the press release was protected by either a qualified or an absolute privilege. The trial court overruled these contentions, and instructed the jury to return a verdict for respondents if it found the release defamatory. The jury found for respondents.

Petitioner appealed, raising only the issue of absolute privilege. The judgment of the trial court was affirmed by the Court of Appeals,

15. "William G. Barr, Acting Director of Rent Stabilization today served notice of suspension on the two officials of the agency who in June 1950 were responsible for the plan which allowed 53 of the agency's 2,681 employees to take their accumulated annual leave in cash.

"Mr. Barr's appointment as Acting Director becomes effective Monday, February 9, 1953, and the suspension of these employees will be his first act of duty. The employees are John J. Madigan, Deputy Director for Administration, and Linda Matteo, Director of Personnel.

"'In June 1950,' Mr. Barr stated, 'my position in the agency was not one of authority which would have permitted me to stop the action. Furthermore, I did not know about it until it was almost completed.

"'When I did learn that certain employees were receiving cash annual leave settlements and being returned to agency employment on a temporary basis, I specifically notified the employees under my supervision that if they applied for such cash settlements I would demand their resignations and the record will show that my immediate employees complied with my request.

"'While I was advised that the action was legal, I took the position that it violated the spirit of the Thomas Amendment and I violently opposed it. Monday, February 9th, when my appointment as Acting Director becomes effective, will be the first time my position in the agency has permitted me to take any action on this matter, and the suspension of these employees will be the first official act I shall take.'

"Mr. Barr also revealed that he has written to Senator Joseph McCarthy, Chairman of the Committee on Government Operations, and to Representative John Phillips, Chairman of the House Subcommittee on Independent Offices Appropriations, requesting an opportunity to be heard on the entire matter."

which held that "in explaining his decision [to suspend respondents] to the general public [petitioner] * * * went entirely outside his line of duty" and that thus the absolute privilege, assumed otherwise to be available, did not attach. * * * We granted certiorari, vacated the Court of Appeals' judgment, and remanded the case "with directions to pass upon petitioner's claim of a qualified privilege." * * * On remand the Court of Appeals held that the press release was protected by a qualified privilege, but that there was evidence from which a jury could reasonably conclude that petitioner had acted maliciously, or had spoken with lack of reasonable grounds for believing that his statement was true, and that either conclusion would defeat the qualified privilege. * * *

The law of privilege as a defense by officers of government to civil damage suits for defamation and kindred torts has in large part been of judicial making, although the Constitution itself gives an absolute privilege to members of both Houses of Congress in respect to any speech, debate, vote, report, or action done in session.[16] This Court early held that judges of courts of superior or general authority are absolutely privileged as respects civil suits to recover for actions taken by them in the exercise of their judicial functions, irrespective of the motives with which those acts are alleged to have been performed, Bradley v. Fisher (US) 13 Wall. 335, 20 L.Ed. 646, and that a like immunity extends to other officers of government whose duties are related to the judicial process. Yaselli v. Goff (NY) 12 F.2d 396, 56 A.L.R. 1239 (2d Cir. 1926) affd. per curiam 275 U.S. 503, 48 S.Ct. 155, 72 L.Ed. 395, involving a Special Assistant to the Attorney General.[17] Nor has the privilege been confined to officers of the legislative and judicial branches of the Government and executive officers of the kind involved in Yaselli. In Spalding v. Vilas, 161 U.S. 483, 16 S.Ct. 631, 40 L.Ed. 780, petitioner brought suit against the Postmaster General, alleging that the latter had maliciously circulated widely among postmasters, past and present, information which he knew to be false and which was intended to deceive the postmasters to the detriment of the plaintiff. This Court sustained a plea by the Postmaster General of absolute privilege, stating that (498, 499):

> "In exercising the functions of his office, the head of an Executive Department, keeping within the limits of his authority, should not be under an apprehension that the motives that control his official conduct may, at any time, become the subject of inquiry in a civil suit for damages. It would seriously cripple the proper and effective administration of public affairs as entrusted to the executive branch of the government, if he were subjected to any such restraint. He may have legal authority to act, but he may have such large

16. U.S.Const, Art. 1 § 6. See Kilbourn v. Thompson, 103 U.S. 168, 26 L.Ed. 377.

17. See also Cooper v. O'Connor, 69 App.D.C. 100, 99 F.2d 135, 118 A.L.R. 1440; compare Brown v. Shimabukuro, 73 App.D.C. 194, 118 F.2d 17. [Notes 14–17 from original, renumbered; other notes in original omitted.]

discretion in the premises that it will not always be his absolute duty to exercise the authority with which he is invested. But if he acts, having authority, his conduct cannot be made the foundation of a suit against him personally for damages, even if the circumstances show that he is not disagreeably impressed by the fact that his action injuriously affects the claims of particular individuals."

The reasons for the recognition of the privilege have been often stated. It has been thought important that officials of government should be free to exercise their duties unembarrassed by the fear of damage suits in respect of acts done in the course of those duties—suits which would consume time and energies which would otherwise be devoted to governmental service and the threat of which might appreciably inhibit the fearless, vigorous, and effective administration of policies of government. The matter has been admirably expressed by Judge Learned Hand:

"It does indeed go without saying that an official, who is in fact guilty of using his powers to vent his spleen upon others, or for any other personal motive not connected with the public good, should not escape liability for the injuries he may so cause; and, if it were possible in practice to confine such complaints to the guilty, it would be monstrous to deny recovery. The justification for doing so is that it is impossible to know whether the claim is well founded until the case has been tried, and that to submit all officials, the innocent as well as the guilty, to the burden of a trial and to the inevitable danger of its outcome, would dampen the ardor of all but the most resolute, or the most irresponsible, in the unflinching discharge of their duties. Again and again the public interest calls for action which may turn out to be founded on a mistake, in the face of which an official may later find himself hard put to it to satisfy a jury of his good faith. There must indeed be means of punishing public officers who have been truant to their duties; but that is quite another matter from exposing such as have been honestly mistaken to suit by anyone who has suffered from their errors. As is so often the case, the answer must be found in a balance between the evils inevitable in either alternative. In this instance it has been thought in the end better to leave unredressed the wrongs done by dishonest officers than to subject those who try to do their duty to the constant dread of retaliation. * * *

"The decisions have, indeed, always imposed as a limitation upon the immunity that the official's act must have been within the scope of his powers; and it can be argued that official powers, since they exist only for the public good, never cover occasions where the public good is not their aim, and hence that to exercise a power dishonestly is necessarily to overstep its bounds. A moment's reflection shows, however, that that cannot be the meaning of the limitation without defeating the whole doctrine. What is meant by saying that the officer must be acting within his power cannot be more than that the occasion must be such as would have justified the act, if he had been using his power for any of the purposes on whose account it was vested in him. * * *" Gregoire v. Biddle (2d Cir. 1949) 177 F.2d 579, 581.

We do not think that the principle announced in Vilas can properly be restricted to executive officers of cabinet rank, and in fact it never has been so restricted by the lower federal courts. The privilege is not a badge or emolument of exalted office, but an expression of a policy designed to aid in the effective functioning of government. The complexities and magnitude of governmental activity have become so great that there must of necessity be a delegation and redelegation of authority as to many functions, and we cannot say that these functions become less important simply because they are exercised by officers of lower rank in the executive hierarchy.

To be sure, the occasions upon which the acts of the head of an executive department will be protected by the privilege are doubtless far broader than in the case of an officer with less sweeping functions. But that is because the higher the post, the broader the range of responsibilities and duties, and the wider the scope of discretion, it entails. It is not the title of his office but the duties with which the particular officer sought to be made to respond in damages is entrusted—the relation of the act complained of to "matters committed by law to his control or supervision," Spalding v. Vilas, supra (161 U.S. at 498)—which must provide the guide in delineating the scope of the rule which clothes the official acts of the executive officer with immunity from civil defamation suits.

Judged by these standards, we hold that petitioner's plea of absolute privilege in defense of the alleged libel published at his direction must be sustained. The question is a close one, but we cannot say that it was not an appropriate exercise of the discretion with which an executive officer of petitioner's rank is necessarily clothed to publish the press release here at issue in the circumstances disclosed by this record. Petitioner was the Acting Director of an important agency of government, * * * The integrity of the internal operations of the agency which he headed, and thus his own integrity in his public capacity, had been directly and severely challenged in charges made on the floor of the Senate and given wide publicity; and without his knowledge correspondence which could reasonably be read as impliedly defending a position very different from that which he had from the beginning taken in the matter had been sent to a Senator over his signature and incorporated in the Congressional Record. The issuance of press releases was standard agency practice, as it has become with many governmental agencies in these times. We think that under these circumstances a publicly expressed statement of the position of the agency head, announcing personnel action which he planned to take in reference to the charges so widely disseminated to the public, was an appropriate exercise of the discretion which an officer of that rank must possess if the public service is to function effectively. It would be an unduly restrictive view of the scope of the duties of a policy-making executive official to hold that a public statement of agency policy in respect to matters of wide public interest and concern is not action in the line of duty. That petitioner was not *required* by law or by direction of his superiors to speak out cannot be controlling in the case of an official of policy-making rank, for the same considerations which underlie the recognition of the privilege as to acts done in connection with a mandatory duty apply with equal force to discretionary acts at those levels of government where the concept of duty encompasses the sound exercise of discretionary authority.

The fact that the action here taken was within the outer perimeter of petitioner's line of duty is enough to render the privilege applicable, despite the allegations of malice in the complaint, for as this Court has said of legislative privilege:

> "The claim of an unworthy purpose does not destroy the privilege. Legislators are immune from deterrents to the uninhibited discharge of their legislative duty, not for their private indulgence but for the public good. One must not expect uncommon courage even in legislators. The privilege would be of little value if they could be subjected to the cost and inconvenience and distractions of a trial upon a conclusion of the pleader, or to the hazard of a judgment against them based upon a jury's speculation as to motives." Tenney v. Brandhove, 341 U.S. 367, 377, 71 S.Ct. 783, 95 L.Ed. 1019, 1027.

We are told that we should forbear from sanctioning any such rule of absolute privilege lest it open the door to wholesale oppression and abuses on the part of unscrupulous government officials. It is perhaps enough to say that fears of this sort have not been realized within the wide area of government where a judicially formulated absolute privilege of broad scope has long existed. It seems to us wholly chimerical to suggest that what hangs in the balance here is the maintenance of high standards of conduct among those in the public service. To be sure, as with any rule of law which attempts to reconcile fundamentally antagonistic social policies, there may be occasional instances of actual injustice which will go unredressed, but we think that price a necessary one to pay for the greater good. And there are of course other sanctions than civil tort suits available to deter the executive official who may be prone to exercise his functions in an unworthy and irresponsible manner. We think that we should not be deterred from establishing the rule which we announce today by any such remote forebodings.

Reversed.

[JUSTICE BLACK concurred. CHIEF JUSTICE WARREN and JUSTICES DOUGLAS, BRENNAN and STEWART dissent.]

BROWN v. SHIMABUKURO

United States Court of Appeals for the District of Columbia, 1940.
73 App.D.C. 194, 118 F.2d 17.

EDGERTON, ASSOCIATE JUSTICE. This appeal is from an order dismissing on the ground of privilege, a complaint charging libel. The alleged libel is in an affidavit which defendant Shimabukuro executed, and defendant Wattawa filed, in a previous suit.

In that suit Shimabukuro's wife was seeking a divorce, and Wattawa was his attorney. In the course of that suit Shimabukuro moved for a rehearing on his wife's motion for counsel fees, suit money, and alimony *pendente lite.* The offending affidavit was filed in support of that motion. In the affidavit Shimabukuro made various charges of misconduct against his wife, and various statements tending to show his own poverty and lack of earning capacity. He stated, among other things, that his wife "and her father preferred charges against him before the U.S. Attorney's Office; that such charges were wholly false and in affiant's opinion were made for the sole purpose of intimidating and blackmailing him; that as a result of the persistent litigation against him by plaintiff and her father and the preferment of these false charges, and of the notoriety and publicity, and certain race feeling, which their litigation and actions have caused and by reason of the severe financial reverses which he has sustained, affiant has suffered great mental anguish, and is unable intelligently and consistently to carry on any business or occupation, even if he should be able to find the same." "Her father," referred to in the affidavit, is the present plaintiff. He alleges that the charge of blackmail was false and was intended to injure him.

In this jurisdiction, among others, statements in pleadings and affidavits are absolutely privileged if they have enough appearance of connection with the case in which they are filed so that a reasonable man might think them relevant. They need not be relevant in any strict sense.[18] A reasonable man might think that the statements of the defendants regarding the plaintiff were relevant, for they had some appearance of connection with the questions what the wife deserved, what her motives were in bringing the divorce suit, and what the husband could pay, questions which might influence a court's discretion in fixing alimony. They were therefore privileged, and the complaint was rightly dismissed.

Affirmed.[19]

18. Young v. Young, 57 App.D.C. 157, 18 F.2d 807. Cf. Sacks v. Stecker, 2 Cir., 60 F.2d 73.

A narrower view is sometimes taken. Union Mut. Life Ins. Co. v. Thomas, 9 Cir., 83 F. 803. [Footnote by the court, renumbered.]

19. In Johnston v. Schlarb, 7 Wash.2d 528, 134 A.L.R. 474, 110 P.2d 190 (1941), the disparaging statements had been made in the defendant's answer in another suit, and were stricken on motion as irrelevant to the issues made in that suit. Nevertheless, in the present case they were thought to

NEW YORK TIMES CO. v. SULLIVAN

Supreme Court of the United States, 1964.
376 U.S. 254, 84 S.Ct. 710, 11 L.Ed.2d 686.

MR. JUSTICE BRENNAN delivered the opinion of the Court.

We are required in this case to determine for the first time the extent to which the constitutional protections for speech and press limit a State's power to award damages in a libel action brought by a public official against critics of his official conduct.

Respondent L. B. Sullivan is one of the three elected Commissioners of the City of Montgomery, Alabama. He testified that he was "Commissioner of Public Affairs and the duties are supervision of the Police Department, Fire Department, Department of Cemetery and Department of Scales." He brought this civil libel action against the four individual petitioners, who are Negroes and Alabama clergymen, and against petitioner the New York Times Company, a New York corporation which publishes the New York Times, a daily newspaper. A jury in the Circuit Court of Montgomery County awarded him damages of $500,000, the full amount claimed, against all the petitioners, and the Supreme Court of Alabama affirmed. 273 Ala. 656, 144 So.2d 25.

Respondent's complaint alleged that he had been libeled by statements in a full-page advertisement that was carried in the New York Times on March 29, 1960. Entitled "Heed Their Rising Voices," the advertisement began by stating that "As the whole world knows by now, thousands of Southern Negro students are engaged in widespread non-violent demonstrations in positive affirmation of the right to live in human dignity as guaranteed by the U. S. Constitution and the Bill of Rights." It went on to charge that "in their efforts to uphold these guarantees, they are being met by an unprecedented wave of terror by those who would deny and negate that document which the whole world looks upon as setting the pattern for modern freedom. * * *" Succeeding paragraphs purported to illustrate the "wave of terror" by describing certain alleged events. The text concluded with an appeal for funds for three purposes: support of the student movement, "the struggle for the right-to-vote," and the legal defense of Dr. Martin Luther King, Jr., leader of the movement, against a perjury indictment then pending in Montgomery.

The text appeared over the names of 64 persons, many widely known for their activities in public affairs, religion, trade unions, and the performing arts. Below these names, and under a line reading "We in the south who are struggling daily for dignity and freedom warmly endorse this appeal," appeared the names of the four individual petitioners and of 16 other persons, all but two of whom were iden-

have had enough connection with the former litigation to be privileged. For proposition that tavern license application proceedings are "quasi-judicial" and accordingly provide absolute privilege see Hartman v. Buerger, 71 Wis. 2d 393, 238 N.W.2d 505 (1976).

tified as clergymen in various Southern cities. The advertisement was signed at the bottom of the page by the "Committee to Defend Martin Luther King and the Struggle for Freedom in the South," and the officers of the Committee were listed.

Of the 10 paragraphs of text in the advertisement, the third and a portion of the sixth were the basis of respondent's claim of libel. They read as follows:

Third paragraph:

> "In Montgomery, Alabama, after students sang 'My Country, 'Tis of Thee' on the State Capitol steps, their leaders were expelled from school, and truckloads of police armed with shotguns and tear-gas ringed the Alabama State College Campus. When the entire student body protested to state authorities by refusing to re-register, their dining hall was padlocked in an attempt to starve them into submission."

Sixth paragraph:

> "Again and again the Southern violators have answered Dr. King's peaceful protests with intimidation and violence. They have bombed his home almost killing his wife and child. They have assaulted his person. They have arrested him seven times—for 'speeding,' 'loitering' and similar 'offenses.' And now they have charged him with 'perjury'—a *felony* under which they could imprison him for *ten years*. * * *"

Although neither of these statements mentions respondent by name, he contended that the word "police" in the third paragraph referred to him as the Montgomery Commissioner who supervised the Police Department, so that he was being accused of "ringing" the campus with police. He further claimed that the paragraph would be read as imputing to the police, and hence to him, the padlocking of the dining hall in order to starve the students into submission. As to the sixth paragraph, he contended that since arrests are ordinarily made by the police, the statement "They have arrested [Dr. King] seven times" would be read as referring to him; he further contended that the "They" who did the arresting would be equated with the "They" who committed the other described acts and with the "Southern violators." Thus, he argued, the paragraph would be read as accusing the Montgomery police, and hence him, of answering Dr. King's protests with "intimidation and violence," bombing his home, assaulting his person, and charging him with perjury. Respondent and six other Montgomery residents testified that they read some or all of the statements as referring to him in his capacity as Commissioner.

It is uncontroverted that some of the statements contained in the two paragraphs were not accurate descriptions of events which occurred in Montgomery. Although Negro students staged a demonstration on the State Capitol steps, they sang the National Anthem and not "My Country, 'Tis of Thee." Although nine students were expelled by the State Board of Education, this was not for leading the demonstration at the Capitol, but for demanding service at a lunch counter in the Montgomery County Courthouse on another day. Not the entire student body, but most of it, had protested the expulsion, not by refusing to register, but by boycotting classes on a single day; virtually all the students did register for the ensuing semester. The campus dining hall was not padlocked on any occasion, and the only students who may have been barred from eating there were the few who had neither signed a preregistration application nor requested temporary meal tickets. Although the police were deployed near the campus in large numbers on three occasions, they did not at any time "ring" the campus, and they were not called to the campus in connection with the demonstration on the State Capitol steps, as the third paragraph implied. Dr. King had not been arrested seven times, but only four; and although he claimed to have been assaulted some years earlier in connection with his arrest for loitering outside a courtroom, one of the officers who made the arrest denied that there was such an assault.

On the premise that the charges in the sixth paragraph could be read as referring to him, respondent was allowed to prove that he had not participated in the events described. Although Dr. King's home had in fact been bombed twice when his wife and child were there, both of these occasions antedated respondent's tenure as Commissioner, and the police were not only not implicated in the bombings, but had made every effort to apprehend those who were. Three of Dr. King's four arrests took place before respondent became Commissioner. Although Dr. King had in fact been indicted (he was subsequently acquitted) on two counts of perjury, each of which carried a possible five-year sentence, respondent had nothing to do with procuring the indictment.

Respondent made no effort to prove that he suffered actual pecuniary loss as a result of the alleged libel.[20] One of his witnesses, a former employer, testified that if he had believed the statements, he doubted whether he "would want to be associated with anybody who would be a party to such things that are stated in that ad," and that he would not re-employ respondent if he believed "that he allowed the Police Department to do the things that the paper say he did." But neither this witness nor any of the others testified that he had actually believed the statements in their supposed reference to respondent.

The cost of the advertisement was approximately $4800, and it was published by the Times upon an order from a New York advertising agency acting for the signatory Committee. The agency submitted the advertisement with a letter from A. Philip Randolph, Chairman of the Committee, certifying that the persons whose names appeared on the advertisement had given their permission. Mr. Randolph was known to the Times' Advertising Acceptability Department as a re-

20. Approximately 394 copies of the edition of the Times containing the advertisement were circulated in Alabama. Of these, about 35 copies were distributed in Montgomery County. The total circulation of the Times for that day was approximately 650,000 copies.

sponsible person, and in accepting the letter as sufficient proof of authorization it followed its established practice. There was testimony that the copy of the advertisement which accompanied the letter listed only the 64 names appearing under the text, and that the statement, "We in the south * * * warmly endorse this appeal," and the list of names thereunder, which included those of the individual petitioners, were subsequently added when the first proof of the advertisement was received. Each of the individual petitioners testified that he had not authorized the use of his name, and that he had been unaware of its use until receipt of respondent's demand for a retraction. The manager of the Advertising Acceptability Department testified that he had approved the advertisement for publication because he knew nothing to cause him to believe that anything in it was false, and because it bore the endorsement of "a number of people who are well known and whose reputation" he "had no reason to question." Neither he nor anyone else at the Times made an effort to confirm the accuracy of the advertisement, either by checking it against recent Times news stories relating to some of the described events or by any other means.

Alabama law denies a public officer recovery of punitive damages in a libel action brought on account of a publication concerning his official conduct unless he first makes a written demand for a public retraction and the defendant fails or refuses to comply. Alabama Code, Tit. 7, § 914. Respondent served such a demand upon each of the petitioners. None of the individual petitioners responded to the demand, primarily because each took the position that he had not authorized the use of his name on the advertisement and therefore had not published the statements that respondent alleged had libeled him. The Times did not publish a retraction in response to the demand, but wrote respondent a letter stating, among other things, that "we * * * are somewhat puzzled as to how you think the statements in any way reflect on you," and "you might, if you desire, let us know in what respect you claim that the statements in the advertisement reflect on you." Respondent filed this suit a few days later without answering the letter. The Times did, however, subsequently publish a retraction of the advertisement upon the demand of Governor John Patterson of Alabama, who asserted that the publication charged him with "grave misconduct and * * * improper actions and omissions as Governor of Alabama and Ex-Officio Chairman of the State Board of Education of Alabama." When asked to explain why there had been a retraction for the Governor but not for respondent, the Secretary of the Times testified: "We did that because we didn't want anything that was published by The Times to be a reflection on the State of Alabama and the Governor was, as far as we could see, the embodiment of the State of Alabama and the proper representative of the State and, furthermore, we had by that time learned more of the actual facts which the ad purported to recite and, finally, the ad did refer to the action of the State authorities and the Board of Education presumably of which the Governor is the ex-officio chairman

* * *." On the other hand, he testified that he did not think that "any of the language in there referred to Mr. Sullivan."

The trial judge submitted the case to the jury under instructions that the statements in the advertisement were "libelous per se" and were not privileged, so that petitioners might be held liable if the jury found that they had published the advertisement and that the statements were made "of and concerning" respondent. The jury was instructed that, because the statements were libelous *per se*, "the law * * * implies legal injury from the bare fact of publication itself," "falsity and malice are presumed," "general damages need not be alleged or proved but are presumed," and "punitive damages may be awarded by the jury even though the amount of actual damages is neither found nor shown." An award of punitive damages—as distinguished from "general" damages, which are compensatory in nature—apparently requires proof of actual malice under Alabama law, and the judge charged that "mere negligence or carelessness is not evidence of actual malice or malice in fact, and does not justify an award of exemplary or punitive damages." He refused to charge, however, that the jury must be "convinced" of malice, in the sense of "actual intent" to harm or "gross negligence and recklessness," to make such an award, and he also refused to require that a verdict for respondent differentiate between compensatory and punitive damages. The judge rejected petitioners' contention that his rulings abridged the freedoms of speech and of the press that are guaranteed by the First and Fourteenth Amendments.

In affirming the judgment, the Supreme Court of Alabama sustained the trial judge's rulings and instructions in all respects. * * * It held that "[w]here the words published tend to injure a person libeled by them in his reputation, profession, trade or business, or charge him with an indictable offense, or tends to bring the individual into public contempt," they are "libelous per se"; that "the matter complained of is, under the above doctrine, libelous per se, if it was published of and concerning the plaintiff"; and that it was actionable without "proof of pecuniary injury * * *, such injury being implied." * * * It approved the trial court's ruling that the jury could find the statements to have been made "of and concerning" respondent, stating: "We think it common knowledge that the average person knows that municipal agents, such as police and firemen, and others, are under the control and direction of the city governing body, and more particularly under the direction and control of a single commissioner. In measuring the performance or deficiencies of such groups, praise or criticism is usually attached to the official in complete control of the body." * * * In sustaining the trial court's determination that the verdict was not excessive, the court said that malice could be inferred from the Times' "irresponsibility" in printing the advertisement while "the Times in its own files had articles already published which would have demonstrated the falsity of the allegations in the advertisement"; from the Times' failure to retract for respondent while retracting for the Governor, whereas the falsity of some of the allegations was then known to the Times and "the matter contained in the advertisement was equally false as to both parties"; and from the testimony of the Times' Secretary that apart from the statement that the dining hall was padlocked, he thought the two paragraphs were "substantially correct." * * * The court reaffirmed a statement in an earlier opinion that "There is no legal measure of damages in cases of this character." * * * It rejected petitioners' constitutional contentions with the brief statements that "The First Amendment of the U. S. Constitution does not protect libelous publications" * * *.

Because of the importance of the constitutional issues involved, we granted the separate petitions for certiorari of the individual petitioners and of the Times. * * * We reverse the judgment. We hold that the rule of law applied by the Alabama courts is constitutionally deficient for failure to provide the safeguards for freedom of speech and of the press that are required by the First and Fourteenth Amendments in a libel action brought by a public official against critics of his official conduct. We further hold that under the proper safeguards the evidence presented in this case is constitutionally insufficient to support the judgment for respondent.

* * *

II.

Under Alabama law as applied in this case, a publication is "libelous per se" if the words "tend to injure a person * * * in his reputation" or to "bring [him] into public contempt"; the trial court stated that the standard was met if the words are such as to "injure him in his public office, or impute misconduct to him in his office, or want of official integrity, or want of fidelity to a public trust * * *." The jury must find that the words were published "of and concerning" the plaintiff, but where the plaintiff is a public official his place in the governmental hierarchy is sufficient evidence to support a finding that his reputation has been affected by statements that reflect upon the agency of which he is in charge. Once "libel per se" has been established, the defendant has no defense as to stated facts unless he can persuade the jury that they were true in all their particulars. * * * His privilege of "fair comment" for expressions of opinion depends on the truth of the facts upon which the comment is based. * * * Unless he can discharge the burden of proving truth, general damages are presumed, and may be awarded without proof of pecuniary injury. A showing of actual malice is apparently a prerequisite to recovery of punitive damages, and the defendant may in any event forestall a punitive award by a retraction meeting the statutory requirements. Good motives and belief in truth do not negate an inference of malice, but are relevant only in mitigation of punitive damages if the jury chooses to accord them weight. * * *

The question before us is whether this rule of liability, as applied to an action brought by a public official against critics of his official conduct, abridges the freedom of speech and of the press that is guaranteed by the First and Fourteenth Amendments.

Respondent relies heavily, as did the Alabama courts, on statements of this Court to the effect that the Constitution does not protect libelous publications. Those statements do not foreclose our inquiry here. None of the cases sustained the use of libel laws to impose sanctions upon expression critical of the official conduct of public officials. * * *

In deciding the question now, we are compelled by neither precedent nor policy to give any more weight to the epithet "libel" than we have to other "mere labels" of state law. * * * Like insurrection, contempt, advocacy of unlawful acts, breach of the peace, obscenity, solicitation of legal business, and the various other formulae for the repression of expression that have been challenged in this Court, libel can claim no talismanic immunity from constitutional limitations. It must be measured by standards that satisfy the First Amendment.

The general proposition that freedom of expression upon public questions is secured by the First Amendment has long been settled by our decisions. The constitutional safeguard, we have said, "was fashioned to assure unfettered interchange of ideas for the bringing about of political and social changes desired by the people." Roth v. United States, 354 U.S. 476, 484, 77 S.Ct. 1304, 1308, 1 L.Ed.2d 1498. "The maintenance of the opportunity for free political discussion to the end that government may be responsive to the will of the people and that changes may be obtained by lawful means, an opportunity essential to the security of the Republic, is a fundamental principle of our constitutional system." Stromberg v. California, 283 U.S. 359, 369, 51 S.Ct. 532, 536, 75 L.Ed. 1117. "[I]t is a prized American privilege to speak one's mind, although not always with perfect good taste, on all public institutions," Bridges v. California, 314 U.S. 252, 270, 62 S.Ct. 190, 197, 86 L.Ed. 192, and this opportunity is to be afforded for "vigorous advocacy" no less than "abstract discussion." N. A. A. C. P. v. Button, 371 U.S. 415, 429, 83 S.Ct. 328, 9 L.Ed.2d 405. The First Amendment, said Judge Learned Hand, "presupposes that right conclusions are more likely to be gathered out of a multitude of tongues, than through any kind of authoritative selection. To many this is, and always will be, folly; but we have staked upon it our all." United States v. Associated Press, 52 F.Supp. 362, 372 (D.C.S.D. N.Y.1943). Mr. Justice Brandeis, in his concurring opinion in Whitney v. California, 274 U.S. 357, 375–376, 47 S.Ct. 641, 648, 71 L.Ed. 1095, gave the principle its classic formulation:

> "Those who won our independence believed * * * that public discussion is a political duty; and that this should be a fundamental principle of the American government. They recognized the risks to which all human institutions are subject. But they knew that order cannot be secured merely through fear of punishment for its infraction; that it is hazardous to discourage thought, hope and imagination; that

> fear breeds repression; that repression breeds hate; that hate menaces stable government; that the path of safety lies in the opportunity to discuss freely supposed grievances and proposed remedies; and that the fitting remedy for evil counsels is good ones. Believing in the power of reason as applied through public discussion, they eschewed silence coerced by law—the argument of force in its worst form. Recognizing the occasional tyrannies of governing majorities, they amended the Constitution so that free speech and assembly should be guaranteed."

Thus we consider this case against the background of a profound national commitment to the principle that debate on public issues should be uninhibited, robust, and wide-open, and that it may well include vehement, caustic, and sometimes unpleasantly sharp attacks on government and public officials. * * * The present advertisement, as an expression of grievance and protest on one of the major public issues of our time, would seem clearly to qualify for the constitutional protection. The question is whether it forfeits that protection by the falsity of some of its factual statements and by its alleged defamation of respondent.

Authoritative interpretations of the First Amendment guarantees have consistently refused to recognize an exception for any test of truth—whether administered by judges, juries, or administrative officials—and especially one that puts the burden of proving truth on the speaker. * * * The constitutional protection does not turn upon "the truth, popularity, or social utility of the ideas and beliefs which are offered." N. A. A. C. P. v. Button, 371 U.S. 415, 445, 83 S.Ct. 328, 344, 9 L.Ed.2d 405. As Madison said, "Some degree of abuse is inseparable from the proper use of every thing; and in no instance is this more true than in that of the press." 4 Elliot's Debates on the Federal Constitution (1876), p. 571. In Cantwell v. Connecticut, 310 U.S. 296, 310, 60 S.Ct. 900, 906, 84 L.Ed. 1213, the Court declared:

> "In the realm of religious faith and in that of political belief, sharp differences arise. In both fields the tenets of one man may seem the rankest error to his neighbor. To persuade others to his own point of view, the pleader, as we know, at times, resorts to exaggeration, to vilification of men who have been, or are, prominent in church or state, and even to false statement. But the people of this nation have ordained in the light of history, that, in spite of the probability of excesses and abuses, these liberties are, in the long view, essential to enlightened opinion and right conduct on the part of the citizens of a democracy."

That erroneous statement is inevitable in free debate, and that it must be protected if the freedoms of expression are to have the "breathing space" that they "need * * * to survive," N. A. A. C. P. v. Button, 371 U.S. 415, 433, 83 S.Ct. 328, 338, 9 L.Ed.2d 405, was also recognized by the Court of Appeals for the District of Columbia Circuit in Sweeney v. Patterson, 76 U.S.App.D.C. 23, 24, 128 F.2d 457, 458 (1942), cert. denied, 317 U.S. 678, 63 S.Ct. 160, 87 L.Ed. 544. Judge Edgerton spoke for a unanimous court which affirmed the dismissal of a Congressman's libel suit based upon a newspaper article charging him with anti-Semitism in opposing a judicial appointment. He said:

> "Cases which impose liability for erroneous reports of the political conduct of officials reflect the obsolete doctrine that the governed must not criticize their governors. * * * The interest of the public here outweighs the interest of appellant or any other individual. The protection of the public requires not merely discussion, but information. Political conduct and views which some respectable people approve, and other condemn, are constantly imputed to Congressmen. Errors of fact, particularly in regard to a man's mental states and processes, are inevitable. * * * Whatever is added to the field of libel is taken from the field of free debate." [21]

Injury to official reputation error affords no more warrant for repressing speech that would otherwise be free than does factual error. Where judicial officers are involved, this Court has held that concern for the dignity and reputation of the courts does not justify the punishment as criminal contempt of criticism of the judge or his decision. Bridges v. California, 314 U.S. 252, 62 S.Ct. 190, 86 L.Ed. 192. This is true even though the utterance contains "half-truths" and "misinformation." Pennekamp v. Florida, 328 U.S. 331, 342, 343, n. 5, 345, 66 S.Ct. 1029, 90 L.Ed. 1295. Such repression can be justified, if at all only by a clear and present danger of the obstruction of justice. See also Craig v. Harney, 331 U.S. 367, 67 S.Ct. 1249, 91 L.Ed. 1546; Wood v. Georgia, 370 U.S. 375, 82 S.Ct. 1364, 8 L.Ed.2d 569. If judges are to be treated as "men of fortitude, able to thrive in a hardy climate," Craig v. Harney, supra, 331 U.S., at 376, 67 S.Ct., at 1255, 91 L.Ed. 1546, surely the same must be true of other government officials, such as elected city commissioners. Criticism of their official conduct does not lose its constitutional protection merely because it is effective criticism and hence diminishes their official reputations.

If neither factual error nor defamatory content suffices to remove the constitutional shield from criticism of official conduct, the combination of the two elements is no less inadequate. This is the lesson to be drawn from the great controversy over the Sedition Act of

21. See also Mill, On Liberty (Oxford: Blackwell, 1947), at 47:

"* * * [T]o argue sophistically, to suppress facts or arguments, to misstate the elements of the case, or misrepresent the opposite opinion * * * all this, even to the most aggravated degree, is so continually done in perfect good faith, by persons who are not considered, and in many other respects may not deserve to be considered, ignorant or incompetent, that it is rarely possible, on adequate grounds, conscientiously to stamp the misrepresentation as morally culpable; and still less could law presume to interfere with this kind of controversial misconduct."

1798, 1 Stat. 596, which first crystallized a national awareness of the central meaning of the First Amendment. See Levy, Legacy of Suppression (1960), at 258 et seq.; Smith, Freedom's Fetters (1956), at 426, 431 and *passim.* That statute made it a crime, punishable by a $5,000 fine and five years in prison, "if any person shall write, print, utter or publish * * * any false, scandalous and malicious writing or writings against the government of the United States, or either house of the Congress * * *, or the President * * *, with intent to defame * * * or to bring them, or either of them, into contempt or disrepute; or to excite against them, or either or any of them, the hatred of the good people of the United States." The Act allowed the defendant the defense of truth, and provided that the jury were to be judges both of the law and the facts. Despite these qualifications, the Act was vigorously condemned as unconstitutional in an attack joined in by Jefferson and Madison. * * *

Although the Sedition Act was never tested in this Court, the attack upon its validity has carried the day in the court of history. Fines levied in its prosecution were repaid by Act of Congress on the ground that it was unconstitutional. * * * Calhoun, reporting to the Senate on February 4, 1836, assumed that its invalidity was a matter "which no one now doubts." * * * Jefferson, as President, pardoned those who had been convicted and sentenced under the Act and remitted their fines, stating: "I discharged every person under punishment or prosecution under the sedition law, because I considered, and now consider, that law to be a nullity, as absolute and as palpable as if Congress had ordered us to fall down and worship a golden image." * * * The invalidity of the Act has also been assumed by Justices of this Court. * * * These views reflect a broad consensus that the Act, because of the restraint it imposed upon criticism of government and public officials, was inconsistent with the First Amendment.

There is no force in respondent's argument that the constitutional limitations implicit in the history of the Sedition Act apply only to Congress and not to the States. It is true that the First Amendment was originally addressed only to action by the Federal Government, and that Jefferson, for one, while denying the power of Congress "to controul the freedom of the press," recognized such a power in the States. * * * But this distinction was eliminated with the adoption of the Fourteenth Amendment and the application to the States of the First Amendment's restrictions. * * *

What a State may not constitutionally bring about by means of a criminal statute is likewise beyond the reach of its civil law of libel. The fear of damage awards under a rule such as that invoked by the Alabama courts here may be markedly more inhibiting than the fear of prosecution under a criminal statute. * * * Alabama, for example, has a criminal libel law which subjects to prosecution "any person who speaks, writes, or prints of and concerning another any accusation falsely and maliciously importing the commission by such person of a felony, or any other indictable offense involving moral turpitude," and which allows as punishment upon conviction a fine not exceeding $500 and a prison sentence of six months. Alabama Code, Tit. 14, § 350. Presumably a person charged with violation of this statute enjoys ordinary criminal-law safeguards such as the requirements of an indictment and of proof beyond a reasonable doubt. These safeguards are not available to the defendant in a civil action. The judgment awarded in this case—without the need for any proof of actual pecuniary loss—was one thousand times greater than the maximum fine provided by the Alabama criminal statute, and one hundred times greater than that provided by the Sedition Act. And since there is no double-jeopardy limitation applicable to civil lawsuits, this is not the only judgment that may be awarded against petitioners for the same publication.[22] Whether or not a newspaper can survive a succession of such judgments, the pall of fear and timidity imposed upon those who would give voice to public criticism is an atmosphere in which the First Amendment freedoms cannot survive. Plainly the Alabama law of civil libel is "a form of regulation that creates hazards to protected freedoms markedly greater than those that attend reliance upon the criminal law." Bantam Books, Inc. v. Sullivan, 372 U.S. 58, 70, 83 S.Ct. 631, 639, 9 L.Ed.2d 584.

The state rule of law is not saved by its allowance of the defense of truth. A defense for erroneous statements honestly made is no less essential here than was the requirement of proof of guilty knowledge which, in Smith v. California, 361 U.S. 147, 80 S.Ct. 215, 4 L.Ed.2d 205, we held indispensable to a valid conviction of a bookseller for possessing obscene writings for sale. We said:

> "For if the bookseller is criminally liable without knowledge of the contents, * * * he will tend to restrict the books he sells to those he has inspected; and thus the State will have imposed a restriction upon the distribution of constitutionally protected as well as obscene literature. * * * And the bookseller's burden would become the public's burden, for by restricting him the public's access to reading matter would be restricted. * * * [H]is timidity in the face of his absolute criminal liability, thus would tend to restrict the public's access to forms of the printed word which the State could not constitutionally suppress directly. The bookseller's self-censorship, compelled by the State, would be a censorship affecting the whole public, hardly less virulent for being privately administered. Through it, the distribution of all books, both obscene and not obscene, would be impeded." * * *

A rule compelling the critic of official conduct to guarantee the truth of all his factual assertions—and to do so on pain of libel judgments

22. The Times states that four other libel suits based on the advertisement have been filed against it by others who have served as Montgomery City Commissioners and by the Governor of Alabama; that another $500,000 verdict has been awarded in the only one of these cases that has yet gone to trial; and that the damages sought in the other three total $2,000,000.

virtually unlimited in amount—leads to a comparable "self-censorship." Allowance of the defense of truth, with the burden of proving it on the defendant, does not mean that only false speech will be deterred.[23] * * * Under such a rule, would-be critics of official conduct may be deterred from voicing their criticism, even though it is believed to be true and even though it is in fact true, because of doubt whether it can be proved in court or fear of the expense of having to do so. They tend to make only statements which "steer far wider of the unlawful zone." * * * The rule thus dampens the vigor and limits the variety of public debate. It is inconsistent with the First and Fourteenth Amendments.

The constitutional guarantees require, we think, a federal rule that prohibits a public official from recovering damages for a defamatory falsehood relating to his official conduct unless he proves that the statement was made with "actual malice"—that is, with knowledge that it was false or with reckless disregard of whether it was false or not.[24] * * *

Such a privilege for criticism of official conduct [25] is appropriately analogous to the protection accorded a public official when *he* is sued for libel by a private citizen. In Barr v. Matteo, 360 U.S. 564, 575, 79 S.Ct. 1335, 1341, 3 L.Ed.2d 1434, this Court held the utterance of a federal official to be absolutely privileged if made "within the outer

23. Even a false statement may be deemed to make a valuable contribution to public debate, since it brings about "the clearer perception and livelier impression of truth, produced by its collision with error." Mill, On Liberty (Oxford: Blackwell, 1947), at 15; see also Milton, Areopagitica, In Prose Works (Yale, 1959), Vol. II, at 561.

24. E. g., Ponder v. Cobb, 257 N.C. 281, 299, 126 S.E.2d 67, 80 (1962); Lawrence v. Fox, 357 Mich. 134, 146, 97 N.W.2d 719, 725 (1959); Stice v. Beacon Newspaper Corp., 185 Kan. 61, 65–67, 340 P.2d 396, 400–401, 76 A.L.R.2d 687 (1959); Bailey v. Charleston Mail Assn., 126 W.Va. 292, 307, 27 S.E.2d 837, 844, 150 A.L.R. 348 (1943); Salinger v. Cowles, 195 Iowa 873, 889, 191 N.W. 167, 174 (1922); Snively v. Record Publishing Co., 185 Cal. 565, 571–576, 198 P. 1 (1921); McLean v. Merriman, 42 S.D. 394, 175 N.W. 878 (1920). Applying the same rule to candidates for public office, see, e. g., Phoenix Newspapers v. Choisser, 82 Ariz. 271, 276–277, 312 P.2d 150, 154 (1957); Friedell v. Blakely Printing Co., 163 Minn. 226, 230, 203 N.W. 974, 975 (1925). And see Chagnon v. Union-Leader Corp., 103 N.H. 426, 438, 174 A.2d 825, 833 (1961), cert. denied, 369 U.S. 830, 82 S.Ct. 846, 7 L.Ed.2d 795. The consensus of scholarly opinion apparently favors the rule that is here adopted. E. g., 1 Harper and James, Torts, § 5.26, at 449–450 (1956); Noel, Defamation of Public Officers and Candidates, 49 Col.L.Rev. 875, 891–895, 897, 903 (1949); Hallen, Fair Comment, 8 Tex.L.Rev. 41, 61 (1929); Smith, Charges Against Candidates, 18 Mich.L.Rev. 1, 115 (1919); Chase, Criticism of Public Officers and Candidates for Office, 23 Am.L.Rev. 346, 367–371 (1889); Cooley, Constitutional Limitations (7th ed., Lane, 1903), at 604, 616–628. But see, e. g., American Law Institute, Restatement of Torts, § 598, Comment a (1938) (reversing the position taken in Tentative Draft 13, § 1041(2) (1936)); Veeder, Freedom of Public Discussion, 23 Harv.L.Rev. 413, 419 (1910).

25. The privilege immunizing honest misstatements of fact is often referred to as a "conditional" privilege to distinguish it from the "absolute" privilege recognized in judicial, legislative, administrative and executive proceedings. See, e. g., Prosser, Torts (2d ed 1955), § 95. [Notes 24–29 from original, renumbered; other notes in original omitted.]

perimeter" of his duties. The States accord the same immunity to statements of their highest officers, although some differentiate their lesser officials and qualify the privilege they enjoy. But all hold that all officials are protected unless actual malice can be proved. The reason for the official privilege is said to be that the threat of damage suits would otherwise "inhibit the fearless, vigorous, and effective administration of policies of government" and "dampen the ardor of all but the most resolute, or the most irresponsible, in the unflinching discharge of their duties." Barr v. Matteo, supra, 360 U.S., at 571, 79 S. Ct., at 1339, 3 L.Ed.2d 1434. Analogous considerations support the privilege for the citizen-critic of government. It is as much his duty to criticize as it is the official's duty to administer. See Whitney v. California, 274 U.S. 357, 375, 47 S.Ct. 641, 648, 71 L.Ed. 1095 (concurring opinion of Mr. Justice Brandeis), quoted supra, pp. 720, 721. As Madison said, see supra, p. 723, "the censorial power is in the people over the Government, and not in the Government over the people." It would give public servants an unjustified preference over the public they serve, if critics of official conduct did not have a fair equivalent of the immunity granted to the officials themselves.

We conclude that such a privilege is required by the First and Fourteenth Amendments.

III.

We hold today that the Constitution delimits a State's power to award damages for libel in actions brought by public officials against critics of their official conduct. Since this is such an action, the rule requiring proof of actual malice is applicable. While Alabama law apparently requires proof of actual malice for an award of punitive damages, where general damages are concerned malice is "presumed." Such a presumption is inconsistent with the federal rule. "The power to create presumptions is not a means of escape from constitutional restrictions," Bailey v. Alabama, 219 U.S. 219, 239, 31 S.Ct. 145, 151, 55 L.Ed. 191; "[t]he showing of malice required for the forfeiture of the privilege is not presumed but is a matter for proof by the plaintiff * * *." Lawrence v. Fox, 357 Mich. 134, 146, 97 N.W.2d 719, 725 (1959). Since the trial judge did not instruct the jury to differentiate between general and punitive damages, it may be that the verdict was wholly an award of one or the other. But it is impossible to know, in view of the general verdict returned. Because of this uncertainty, the judgment must be reversed and the case remanded. * * *

Since respondent may seek a new trial, we deem that considerations of effective judicial administration require us to review the evidence in the present record to determine whether it could constitutionally support a judgment for respondent. * * *

* * * [W]e consider that the proof presented to show actual malice lacks the convincing clarity which the constitutional standard demands, and hence that it would not constitutionally sustain the

judgment for respondent under the proper rule of law. The case of the individual petitioners requires little discussion. Even assuming that they could constitutionally be found to have authorized the use of their names on the advertisement, there was no evidence whatever that they were aware of any erroneous statements or were in any way reckless in that regard. The judgment against them is thus without constitutional support.

As to the Times, we similarly conclude that the facts do not support a finding of actual malice. The statement by the Times' Secretary that, apart from the padlocking allegation, he thought the advertisement was "substantially correct," affords no constitutional warrant for the Alabama Supreme Court's conclusion that it was a "cavalier ignoring of the falsity of the advertisement [from which], the jury could not have but been impressed with the bad faith of The Times, and its maliciousness inferable therefrom." The statement does not indicate malice at the time of the publication; even if the advertisement was not "substantially correct"—although respondent's own proofs tend to show that it was—that opinion was at least a reasonable one, and there was no evidence to impeach the witness' good faith in holding it. The Times' failure to retract upon respondent's demand, although it later retracted upon the demand of Governor Patterson, is likewise not adequate evidence of malice for constitutional purposes. Whether or not a failure to retract may ever constitute such evidence, there are two reasons why it does not here. *First,* the letter written by the Times reflected a reasonable doubt on its part as to whether the advertisement could reasonably be taken to refer to respondent at all. *Second,* it was not a final refusal, since it asked for an explanation on this point—a request that respondent chose to ignore. Nor does the retraction upon the demand of the Governor supply the necessary proof. It may be doubted that a failure to retract which is not itself evidence of malice can retroactively become such by virtue of a retraction subsequently made to another party. But in any event that did not happen here, since the explanation given by the Times' Secretary for the distinction drawn between respondent and the Governor was a reasonable one, the good faith of which was not impeached.

Finally, there is evidence that the Times published the advertisement without checking its accuracy against the news stories in the Times' own files. The mere presence of the stories in the files does not, of course, establish that the Times "knew" the advertisement was false, since the state of mind required for actual malice would have to be brought home to the persons in the Times' organization having responsibility for the publication of the advertisement. With respect to the failure of those persons to make the check, the record shows that they relied upon their knowledge of the good reputation of many of those whose names were listed as sponsors of the advertisement, and upon the letter from A. Philip Randolph, known to them as a responsible individual, certifying that the use of the names was authorized. There was testimony that the persons handling the advertisement saw nothing in it that would render it unacceptable under the Times' policy of rejecting advertisements containing "attacks of a personal character"; their failure to reject it on this ground was not unreasonable. We think the evidence against the Times supports at most a finding of negligence in failing to discover the misstatements, and is constitutionally insufficient to show the recklessness that is required for a finding of actual malice. * * *

We also think the evidence was constitutionally defective in another respect: it was incapable of supporting the jury's finding that the allegedly libelous statements were made "of and concerning" respondent. Respondent relies on the words of the advertisement and the testimony of six witnesses to establish a connection between it and himself. Thus, in his brief to this Court, he states:

> "The reference to respondent as police commissioner is clear from the ad. In addition, the jury heard the testimony of a newspaper editor * * *; a real estate and insurance man * * *; the sales manager of a men's clothing store * * *; a food equipment man * * *; a service station operator * * *; and the operator of a truck line for whom respondent had formerly worked * * *. Each of these witnesses stated that he associated the statements with respondent * * *." (Citations to record omitted.)

There was no reference to respondent in the advertisement, either by name or official position. A number of the allegedly libelous statements—the charges that the dining hall was padlocked and that Dr. King's home was bombed, his person assaulted, and a perjury prosecution instituted against him—did not even concern the police; despite the ingenuity of the arguments which would attach this significance to the word "They," it is plain that these statements could not reasonably be read as accusing respondent of personal involvement in the acts in question. The statements upon which respondent principally relies as referring to him are the two allegations that did concern the police or police functions: that "truckloads of police * * * ringed the Alabama State College Campus" after the demonstration on the State Capitol steps, and that Dr. King had been "arrested * * * seven times." These statements were false only in that the police had been "deployed near" the campus but had not actually "ringed" it and had not gone there in connection with the State Capitol demonstration, and in that Dr. King had been arrested only four times. The ruling that these discrepancies between what was true and what was asserted were sufficient to injure respondent's reputation may itself raise constitutional problems, but we need not consider them here. Although the statements may be taken as referring to the police, they did not on their face make even an oblique reference to respondent as an individual. Support for the asserted reference must, therefore, be sought in the testimony of respondent's witnesses. But none of them suggested any basis for the belief that respondent himself was attacked in the advertisement beyond the bare fact that he was in overall charge of the Police Department and thus bore official responsibility for police conduct; to the extent that some of the witnesses thought respondent to have been charged with ordering or approving the conduct or otherwise being personally involved in it, they based this notion not on any statements in the advertisement, and not on any evidence that he had in fact been so involved, but solely on the unsupported assumption that, because of his official position, he must have been. This reliance on the bare fact of respondent's official position was made explicit by the Supreme Court of Alabama. That court, in holding that the trial court "did not err in overruling the demurrer [of the Times] in the aspect that the libelous matter was not of and concerning the [plaintiff,]" based its ruling on the proposition that:

> "We think it common knowledge that the average person knows that municipal agents, such as police and firemen, and others, are under the control and direction of the city governing body, and more particularly under the direction and control of a single commissioner. In measuring the performance or deficiencies of such groups, praise or criticism is usually attached to the official in complete control of the body." * * *

This proposition has disquieting implications for criticism of govermental conduct. For good reason, "no court of last resort in this country has ever held, or even suggested, that prosecutions for libel on government have any place in the American system of jurisprudence." City of Chicago v. Tribune Co., 307 Ill. 595, 601, 139 N.E. 86, 88, 28 A.L.R. 1368 (1923). The present proposition would sidestep this obstacle by transmuting criticism of government, however impersonal it may seem on its face, into personal criticism, and hence potential libel, of the officials of whom the government is composed. There is no legal alchemy by which a State may thus create the cause of action that would otherwise be denied for a publication which, as respondent himself said of the advertisement, "reflects not only on me but on the other Commissioners and the community." Raising as it does the possibility that a good-faith critic of government will be penalized for his criticism, the proposition relied on by the Alabama courts strikes at the very center of the constitutionally protected area of free expression. We hold that such a proposition may not constitutionally be utilized to establish that an otherwise impersonal attack on governmental operations was a libel of an official responsible for those operations. Since * * * there was no other evidence to connect the statements with respondent, the evidence was constitutionally insufficient to support a finding that the statements referred to respondent.

* * *

Reversed and remanded.

[JUSTICE BLACK concurred on the ground that the press should have "absolute immunity for criticism of the way public officials do their public duty." JUSTICE GOLDBERG concurred similarly. JUSTICE DOUGLAS joined both BLACK and GOLDBERG.]

STONE v. ESSEX COUNTY NEWSPAPERS, INC.

Supreme Judicial Court of Massachusetts, 1975.
— Mass. —, 330 N.E.2d 161.

HENNESSEY, JUSTICE.

The plaintiff had a jury verdict in the Superior Court in a tort action for libel. The case came before us on the defendant's outline bill of exceptions and was decided on May 6, 1974. Stone v. Essex County Newspapers, Inc., 365 Mass. 246, 311 N.E.2d 52 (1974). Thereafter, on June 25, 1974, the Supreme Court of the United States decided Gertz v. Robert Welch, Inc., 418 U.S. 323, 94 S.Ct. 2997, 41 L.Ed.2d 789 (1974). The plaintiff thereupon filed a petition, based on the holdings of the Supreme Court in the *Gertz* case, for a rehearing of the instant case. We granted the petition for rehearing, and have reconsidered the matter on new briefs filed by the parties.

The defendant claimed exceptions to the judge's denial of the defendant's motion for a directed verdict, and to certain of the judge's instructions to the jury. We conclude that there was no error in the refusal to direct a verdict, but by reason of errors now apparent in the judge's charge to the jury as considered in light of the holdings of the *Gertz* case, this case must be remanded to the Superior Court for a new trial.

In particular, as will be seen, we hold that a plaintiff who is not a public officer or a public figure may recover damages in an action for libel by proof of negligence in the publishing of the libel by the defendant, its agents or servants, even though the libel occurred in the reporting of an event of public or general concern. We further hold that a plaintiff who is a public officer or a public figure may in such an action recover only on proof of "actual malice" (wilful or reckless disregard of the truth in the publishing of the libel). Also, while it now appears that punitive damages may be constitutionally permissible in certain cases, we, placing primary emphasis on the necessity for protection of freedom of speech and the press, decline to adopt a rule allowing punitive damages. Rather, we affirm the principle that damages for defamation in this Commonwealth may be assessed only for actual injury and only on a compensatory basis, subject to searching judicial scrutiny at the trial and appellate levels. Finally, in any case where the plaintiff must show knowledge of falsity or reckless disregard of the truth, he must establish his proof, not merely by the fair preponderance of the evidence, but by "clear and convincing proof."

We restate the facts as presented in the original hearing before this court. On November 4, 1969, Jeffrey C. Stone, the then twenty year old son of the plaintiff, appeared in District Court charged with being present where narcotic drugs were illegally kept and with illegal possession of narcotics. A tablet alleged to be a "harmful drug" was introduced in evidence. The city marshal, Robert F. Jones, testified that the other defendants in the District Court case had indicated to him that the defendant Stone was the owner of the harmful drug.

The plaintiff from 1963 to 1972 served on the Newburyport Redevelopment Authority, owned a catering business, and was food service director for the Newburyport schools.

Anthony Pearson, a reporter for the defendant's newspaper, the Newburyport Daily News, was in court covering the proceedings. Pearson had been at work just four months as a reporter and had received only several hours of instruction in the work. Unaware that there was a reporter's table near the witness stand, Pearson sat in the back of the court room. So positioned, he had trouble hearing some of the witnesses, including Jones.

Pearson interpreted Jones's testimony to be that "Mr. Stone" was the owner of the "harmful drug," and inferred that the title "Mister" was used to distinguish the father, who was in the court room, from the son.

That evening, Pearson wrote his story on the trial, translating the "Mr. Stone" of his notes to "John J. Stone," which he had discovered the father's name to be. He submitted it to William Coltin, the editor who ordinarily checked over and edited his copy. Coltin testified that he read it about midnight and was "surprised" at the information about the plaintiff (whom he had known for twenty years and whom he considered an "excellent citizen"), but accepted it as the testimony of a reliable public official under oath. He "may have" been surprised enough to question Pearson but did not see the reporter's notes on the story; he very rarely went back to check a reporter's notes. The article, which had been written for inclusion on November 5, 1969, the day following the trial, was crowded out and its publication postponed for twenty-four hours. During that time Coltin did not communicate any concern about the story to his superiors.

There also was evidence from which the jury could infer that police testimony was produced in the District Court proceeding to show that the substance in question was not a harmful drug or narcotic, and that Pearson's notes and the news story did not include an account of that testimony.

The article was published on November 6, 1969. Shortly after it reached the public, the plaintiff called Coltin to complain of its inaccuracy. Coltin discussed the matter with John J. O'Neil, the managing editor, and then checked with Jones and discovered the plaintiff had had nothing to do with the case. O'Neil next consulted the editor and general manager of the paper, and then called the plaintiff and discussed on which page a retraction would be printed. O'Neil offered to get the plaintiff's approval of the retraction before printing it and they met the next morning for that purpose. The plaintiff "said it was fine but the damage had already been done."

1. We turn first to a consideration of the instructions to the jury. The defendant's preliminary argument, which is apposite to the directed verdict issue as well as to the instructions, is that the article did not charge the plaintiff with a crime as it only referred to his ownership of the drug, and the crime, if any, would have been in its sale or giving away. Even if we accept the defendant's understanding of the criminal law as correct, this argument avails it nothing. While an imputation of crime is defamatory per se, Lynch v. Lyons, 303 Mass. 116, 118–119, 20 N.E.2d 953 (1939), the general test for libel is much broader; written words which would tend to hold the plaintiff up to scorn, hatred, ridicule or contempt, in the minds of any considerable and respectable segment in the community. Ingalls v. Hastings & Sons Publishing Co., 304 Mass. 31, 22 N.E.2d 657 (1939). The judge's charge clearly and properly left these issues to the jury, who were instructed to consider damages only if they found the publication libellous, either by imputing commission of a crime or otherwise harming the plaintiff's reputation.

2. The defendant excepted to the judge's failure, in instructing on the issue of the common law privilege for reports of a judicial proceeding, to charge that the accuracy required to claim the privilege is substantial accuracy and does not require correctness in all particulars. Thompson v. Boston Publishing Co., 285 Mass. 344, 348–349, 189 N.E. 210 (1934). We find no error. The standard supplied by the trial judge, "fair and accurate report," was at least as favorable to the defendant as it had any right to expect. We have previously held that accuracy is required "at least in regard to all material matters." Sweet v. Post Publishing Co., 215 Mass. 450, 102 N.E. 660 (1913). Our statement in another mistaken identity case is almost directly applicable here: "A publication which identifies a person who had nothing to do with the proceedings as the one against whom the proceedings were directed can be neither fair nor accurate." Whitcomb v. Hearst Corp., 329 Mass. 193, 199, 107 N.E.2d 295, 299 (1952). The jury were wholly warranted in concluding that this privilege did not apply.

3. There was error in the judge's instructions on the constitutional aspects of the case. The judge ruled that the standards enunciated in New York Times Co. v. Sullivan, 376 U.S. 254, 84 S.Ct. 710, 11 L.Ed.2d 686 (1964), were inapplicable. He charged the jury, in substance, that a verdict for the plaintiff was warranted on proof, without more, of publication by the defendant of a falsehood which was defamatory of the plaintiff. Essentially, the judge thus instructed that the defendant newspaper could be found liable without fault. This, whether the plaintiff is a private person, or a public figure or public official, was error. Accordingly, there must be a new trial and the jury must be charged in accordance with the holdings of this opinion.

We turn now to the constitutional issues raised by the decision in Gertz v. Robert Welch, Inc., 418 U.S. 323, 94 S.Ct. 2997, 41 L.Ed.

2d 789 (1974), a decision that in large measure prompted our grant of this rehearing. We appreciate that we are dealing here with conflicting interests. On the one hand, the tort law of this Commonwealth has long recognized a right of redress to one who suffers injury to his reputation by the publishing of a defamatory falsehood. On the other hand, freedom of expression is guaranteed by the First Amendment to the United States Constitution as applicable to the States through the Fourteenth Amendment. In this case, involving as it does the right of the press to publish and disseminate news and the right of an individual to be free from a defamatory mark on his reputation, a balancing of interests is necessary.

"[T]o insure the ascertainment and publication of the truth about public affairs, it is essential that the First Amendment protect some erroneous publications as well as true ones." St. Amant v. Thompson, 390 U.S. 727, 732, 88 S.Ct. 1323, 1326, 20 L.Ed.2d 262 (1968). The suggestion has been made that the First Amendment provides absolute protection for the press, protection extending even to knowing publication of falsehoods, but this suggestion has been rejected and is not the law.[26] As a result, the issue is under what circumstances the publication of certain statements is expression not protected by the First Amendment's proscription of any law "abridging the freedom of speech, or of the press." Thus in this case we must define as matter of State Law the standards by which a publisher or broadcaster is to be adjudged liable for the publication of falsehoods, to wit, we must decide whether such publication need simply be proved negligent or whether a heavier burden such as publication with reckless or intentional disregard of the truth is required.

Limitations on the power of State courts to award damages in libel actions were established by certain decisions of the United States Supreme Court. New York Times Co. v. Sullivan, 376 U.S. 254, 283, 84 S.Ct. 710, 11 L.Ed.2d 686 (1964), held that public officials cannot recover damages against critics of their official conduct without proof of actual malice (i. e., reckless or wilful disregard of the truth) in the publishing. The rule in turn was extended to include public figures who are not public officials. Curtis Publishing Co. v. Butts, 388 U.S. 130, 155, 87 S.Ct. 1975, 18 L.Ed.2d 1094 (1967) (Harlan, J.).

Further extending the doctrine of the *New York Times Co.* and *Butts* cases, the Supreme Court, in a plurality opinion, decided that the actual malice standard applied not only to criticism of a public figure or of the official conduct of a public officer but also to the reporting of an event of public or general concern. Rosenbloom v. Metromedia, Inc., 403 U.S. 29, 44, 91 S.Ct. 1811, 29 L.Ed.2d 296 (1971) (Brennan, J.). Thereafter, we set the standard in this Common-

26. New York Times Co. v. Sullivan, 376 U.S. 254, 293, 84 S.Ct. 710, 11 L.Ed.2d 686 (1964) (Black, J., concurring). Garrison v. Louisiana, 379 U.S. 64, 80, 85 S.Ct. 209, 13 L.Ed.2d 125 (1964) (Douglas, J., concurring). Curtis Publishing Co. v. Butts, 388 U.S. 130, 170, 87 S.Ct. 1975, 18 L.Ed.2d 1094 (1967) (Black, J., concurring and dissenting). The majority of the court, however, declined to go that far.

wealth for invoking the First Amendment protection for libellous material published without actual malice by holding, in accordance with the apparent requirements of the *Metromedia* case, that the relevant issue was not the status of the particular plaintiff involved, but rather the events which were the subject of the publication. Priestley v. Hastings & Sons Publishing Co. of Lynn, 360 Mass. 118, 123, 271 N.E.2d 628 (1971). See Twohig v. Boston Herald-Traveler Corp., 362 Mass. 807, 291 N.E.2d 398 (1973).

Accordingly we held, on first deciding the instant case on May 6, 1974, that because the event which was reported was a matter of public interest, the *New York Times Co.* standard applied and the plaintiff was required to show that the libel was a wilful or reckless publication of a defamatory falsehood. We held, also, that in these circumstances involving a public prosecution, it was immaterial whether the plaintiff was a public person or a private person, since the matter was one of public interest under the *Metromedia* case. Cf. Cox Bdcst. Corp. v. Cohn, 420 U.S. 734, 95 S.Ct. 1029, 43 L.Ed. 2d 328 (1975) [27] However, we remanded the case for a new trial because the judge had essentially charged that liability could be imposed without fault.

Thereafter, the case of Gertz v. Robert Welch, Inc., 418 U.S. 323, 94 S.Ct. 2997, 41 L.Ed.2d 789 (1974), the case which impelled us to allow the plaintiff's petition for reconsideration of the instant case, was handed down. In an opinion written by Mr. Justice Powell for five members [28] of the court, the *Gertz* case held, inter alia, that (1)

27. As stated in Cox Bdcst. Corp. v. Cohn, 420 U.S. 734, 95 S.Ct. 1029, 1045, 43 L.Ed.2d 328 (1975) [1975], "The commission of crime, prosecutions resulting from it, and judicial proceedings arising from the prosecutions, however, are without question events of legitimate concern to the public."

28. In actuality, seven of the Justices of the Supreme Court indicated a willingness to digress from the plurality view expressed in the *Metromedia* case. Chief Justice Burger and Mr. Justice White dissented in the Gertz case on the ground that they would depart even more emphatically from the *Metromedia* rule, by permitting recovery by a private person without proof of fault, even where a matter of public interest was concerned. The reasoning of Chief Justice Burger, in his dissent, that the court is now embarking "on a new doctrinal theory which has no jurisprudential ancestry" (418 U.S. at 355, 94 S.Ct. at 3014 [1974]), presumably refers to the fact that, prior to the advent of New York Times Co. v. Sullivan, supra, civil liability could be imposed on a defendant for a defamatory publication without a showing of fault and general damages for loss of reputation were presumed without proof of actual injury, such presumed damages being based on a judgment that the publication was per se likely to cause injury. See Gertz v. Robert Welch, Inc., 418 U.S. at 371–380, 94 S.Ct. 2997 (1974) (White, J., dissenting). Moreover, in this Commonwealth evidence of express malice, that is malice in the common law sense of ill will, was material only where the defense pleaded was truth. In such cases, malice could be found sufficient to overcome both the affirmative defense of truth and the conditional privilege which accrued to the press in instances of substantially accurate reporting of a judicial proceeding. Thompson v. Boston Publishing Co., 285 Mass. 344, 352–353, 189 N.E. 210 (1934). Cf. Sharratt v. Housing Innovations, Inc., 365 Mass. 141, 310 N.E.2d 343 (1974) (Mass.Adv.Sh. [1974] 575). See Beckley Newspapers Corp. v. Hanks, 389 U.S. 81, 88 S.Ct. 197, 19 L.Ed.2d 248 (1967). See generally, Prosser, Torts, § 116, pp. 796–797 (4th ed. 1971); Harper & James, Torts, § 5.27 (1956).

the First Amendment protection afforded to defendants against defamation suits by public persons is not to be extended to defamation suits by private individuals even though the defamatory statements concern an issue of public or general interest, id. at 346, 94 S.Ct. 2997, (2) so long as they do not impose liability without fault, the States may define for themselves the appropriate standard of liability for a publisher or broadcaster of defamatory falsehood injurious to a private individual, id. at 347, 94 S.Ct. 2997, and (3) the States may not permit recovery of presumed or punitive damages, at least when liability is not based on a showing of knowledge of falsity or reckless disregard for the truth, id. at 349, 94 S.Ct. 2997.

Accordingly, we hold that private persons, as distinguished from public officials and public figures, may recover compensation on proof of *negligent* publication of a defamatory falsehood. But see Walker v. Colorado Springs Sun, Inc., Colo., 538 P.2d 450 (1975). See also AAFCO Heating & Air Conditioning Co. v. Northwest Publications, Inc., Ind.App., 321 N.E.2d 580 (1974). Publishers and broadcasters of defamatory falsehoods concerning public officers or figures must be protected by the *New York Times Co.* standard, but "injury to the reputation of private individuals requires that a different rule should obtain with respect to them." Gertz v. Robert Welch, Inc., supra, 418 U.S. at 343, 94 S.Ct. at 3009.[29] The State's interest here resides in the private individual's right to the protection of his own good name, for this "reflects no more than our basic concept of the essential dignity and worth of every human being—a concept at the root of any decent system of ordered liberty." Rosenblatt v. Baer, 383 U.S. 75, 92, 86 S.Ct. 669, 679, 15 L.Ed.2d 597 (1966) (Stewart, J., concurring).

In considering whether private individuals should be governed by a different rule from that governing public persons, we find the *Gertz* case convincing in its reasoning that public officials and public figures usually enjoy greater access to the channels of effective communication and hence have a more realistic opportunity to counteract false statements than private individuals normally enjoy, and

29. Clearly the *Gertz* case in one sense narrows the scope of a defendant's protection under the First Amendment as it was assumed to be by reason of the *Metromedia* opinion. In another sense, however, the *Gertz* case can be said to have broadened the protection afforded to a defendant by the First Amendment, since no plaintiff, whether a public or private person, can now recover in a defamation action without proving at least negligence in the publication of the falsehood. This rule of negligence is one part of an apparently unprecedented modification by the Supreme Court of the civil common law of the States. Other parts of the modification, referred to elsewhere in this opinion, are: the requirements that plaintiffs who are public persons must prove actual malice, and that actual malice must be proved by clear and convincing proof, and the restriction on punitive damages. [Compare Chapadeau v. Utica Observer-Dispatch, Inc., 38 N.Y. 2d 196, 379 N.Y.S.2d 61, 341 N.E.2d 569 (1975) (where private person is defamed by a publisher in an article "arguably within the sphere of legitimate public concern, * * * reasonably related to matters warranting public exposition", plaintiff must establish, by a preponderance of the evidence, that "publisher acted in a grossly irresponsible manner without due consideration for the standards of information gathering and dissemination ordinarily followed by responsible parties.")]

that public persons have thrust themselves forward, have invited attention and comment, and thus (unlike private persons) have voluntarily exposed themselves to increased risk of injury from defamatory falsehoods. Thus, private individuals are not only more vulnerable to injury than public officials and public figures—they are also more deserving of recovery. Gertz v. Robert Welch, Inc., supra, 418 U.S. at 344, 94 S.Ct. 2997.[30]

4. We turn now to a consideration of the principles which we hold shall control the assessment of damages in defamation actions in this Commonwealth. The rule defining the limits of damages, like the rules defining liability, must take cognizance of the need to reconcile the State interest in permitting defamation actions against the competing values of the First Amendment. The *Gertz* case so requires: "[T]he States have no substantial interest in securing for plaintiffs such as this petitioner gratuitous awards of money damages far in excess of any actual injury." Gertz v. Robert Welch, Inc., supra, at 349, 94 S.Ct. at 3012. However, the *Gertz* opinion also apparently provides that a State may constitutionally permit the award of punitive damages to a plaintiff who proves under the *New York Times Co.* standard, wilful or reckless defamation by a publisher or broadcaster. Id. at 349, 94 S.Ct. 2997. Presumably in such aggravated cases, the damages may be permitted as private fines levied by civil juries to punish reprehensible conduct and to deter its future occurrence.

We reject the allowance of punitive damages in this Commonwealth in any defamation action, on any state of proof, whether based in negligence, or reckless or wilful conduct. We so hold in recognition that the possibility of excessive and unbridled jury verdicts, grounded on punitive assessments, may impermissibly chill the exercise of First Amendment rights by promoting apprehensive self-censorship.

We reaffirm the following as the controlling principles in this Commonwealth. In a case of defamation the plaintiff's recovery is limited to actual damages, which are compensatory for the wrong done by the defendant. Ellis v. Brockton Publishing Co., 198 Mass. 538, 84 N.E. 1018 (1908). Where specific harm is alleged to have resulted from the defendant's tortious conduct, such harm may be pleaded and damages recovered. Muchnick v. Post Publishing Co., 332 Mass. 304, 125 N.E.2d 137 (1955). Cf. Lewis v. Vallis, 356 Mass. 662, 255 N.E.2d 337 (1970). Otherwise the plaintiff is limited

30. We observe that there may be a recognition in Restatement of Torts Second of a right of recovery even by a public official or public figure, on proof of negligent publication, where the defamation relates to a private matter. Restatement of Torts, Second (Tent. draft No. 21, 1975), § 580B, which was formulated after the *Gertz* case came down, reads as follows: "One who publishes a false and defamatory communication concerning a private person, or *concerning a public official or a public figure in relation to a private matter,* is subject to liability, if, but only if, he (a) knows that the statement is false and that it defames the other, (b) acts in reckless disregard of these matters, or (c) acts negligently in failing to ascertain them" (emphasis supplied).

to compensatory damages for actual injury, which include mental suffering, Chesley v. Tompson, 137 Mass. 136, 137 (1884); Pion v. Caron, 237 Mass. 107, 111, 129 N.E. 369 (1921), and harm to reputation. Ellis v. Brockton Publishing Co., supra. Punitive damages are prohibited, Ellis v. Brockton Publishing Co., supra, even on proof of actual malice. G.L. c. 231, § 93, as appearing in St.1943, c. 360. In addition, the defendant may introduce evidence of a retraction in mitigation of damages, G.L. c. 231, § 94, as appearing in St.1943, c. 361, but the degree of mitigation, if any, is for the jury. Whitcomb v. Hearst Corp., 329 Mass. 193, 107 N.E.2d 295 (1952).

The United States Supreme Court has recognized, at least by implication the difficulties in instructing a jury on compensatory damages for such abstract elements as impairment of reputation and mental suffering. In the Gertz case, 418 U.S. at 349–350, 94 S.Ct. at 3012 (1974), it is stated: "We need not define 'actual injury,' as trial courts have wide experience in framing appropriate jury instructions in tort actions. Suffice it to say that actual injury is not limited to out-of-pocket loss. Indeed, the more customary types of actual harm inflicted by defamatory falsehood include impairment of reputation and standing in the community, personal humiliation, and mental anguish and suffering. Of course, juries must be limited by appropriate instructions, and all awards must be supported by competent evidence concerning the injury, although there need be no evidence which assigns an actual dollar value to the injury."

Because of constitutional considerations, and the potential difficulties in assessing fair compensation in such cases, in our view both trial and appellate judges have a special duty of vigilance in charging juries and reviewing verdicts to see that damages are no more than compensatory. Thus, Chief Justice Shaw's solution to the difficulty of measuring libel damages, that "the court will be slow to pronounce a verdict excessive," Treanor v. Donahoe, 9 Cush. 228, 231 (1852), has limited applicability since First Amendment values are at stake. Cf. Curtis Publishing Co. v. Butts, 388 U.S. 130, 138, 87 S.Ct. 1975, 18 L.Ed.2d 1094 (1967) (Harlan, J.); Rosenbloom v. Metromedia, Inc., 403 U.S. 29, 40, 91 S.Ct. 1811, 29 L.Ed.2d 296 (1971) (Brennan, J.).

5. Finally, we discuss several concepts that will be crucial in the retrial of this case, or in similar cases: concepts involving the nature of "public official," "public figure," and "actual malice." "Negligence," a more familiar concept, needs no such discussion. Of necessity, our discussion is broader than is required by the evidence at the prior trial of the instant case, because we have no way of knowing what the evidence will be on retrial, or what jury instructions will be required based on that evidence.

We turn first to the meaning of "public official." When we first heard and decided this case, this term was unimportant in our consideration, because under the law then controlling the case clearly turned on the fact that the judicial proceeding which was reported was an event of public or general concern. Under the present law, the determination whether the plaintiff is a public official becomes a paramount issue in this case.

The determination of the plaintiff's status, whether public official or public figure or private person, "as is the case with questions of privilege generally, . . . is for the trial judge in the first instance." Rosenblatt v. Baer, 383 U.S. 75, 88, 86 S.Ct. 669, 677, 15 L.Ed.2d 597 (1966). In Lewis v. Vallis, 356 Mass. 662, 668, 255 N.E. 2d 337 (1970), where the point did not affect the decision, we interpreted this to mean that the question whether the plaintiff was a public figure "was a question of law for the court." [31] A full statement of the rule would seem to be that the question whether the plaintiff is a public official or a public figure is one for the court to answer whenever (a) all of the facts bearing thereon are uncontested or agreed by the parties (b) the case is tried before a judge without a jury, or (c) all of the facts bearing thereon are specially found and reported by the jury by way of answers to special questions submitted to them; and that otherwise, in a case tried to a jury, it is a question for the jury to answer after instructions by the judge on the applicable law and on what facts must be found to constitute the plaintiff a public official or a public figure.

It is not crucial that the newspaper article did not refer to the plaintiff's public capacity. It is clear that the defendant did not criticize the plaintiff's official conduct per se as in New York Times Co. v. Sullivan, 376 U.S. 254, 283, 84 S.Ct. 710, 11 L.Ed.2d 686 (1964), and Rosenblatt v. Baer, 383 U.S. 75, 87, 86 S.Ct. 669, 15 L.Ed.2d 597 (1966). Similarly unlike the plaintiffs in Monitor Patriot Co. v. Roy, 401 U.S. 265, 271, 91 S.Ct. 621, 28 L.Ed.2d 35 (1971), and Ocala Star-Banner Co. v. Damron, 401 U.S. 295, 299, 91 S.Ct. 628, 28 L.Ed.2d 57 (1971), the plaintiff was not at the time of the publication a candidate for public office. To a large extent his public position seems irrelevant to the defendant's article. Yet that is not controlling, for "a charge of criminal conduct against an official or a candidate, no matter how remote in time or place, is always 'relevant to his fitness for office' for purposes of applying the *New York Times* rule of knowing falsehood or reckless disregard of the truth." Ocala Star-Banner Co. v. Damron, 401 U.S. 295, 300, 91 S.Ct. 628, 632, 28 L.Ed.2d 57 (1971). Monitor Patriot Co. v. Roy, 401 U.S. 265, 91 S.Ct. 621, 28 L.Ed.2d 35 (1971).

The mere fact that a plaintiff was a government employee is also not determinative, for such employees in the lower ranks are clearly not public officials for purposes of the rule, but the designation of public official applies at least to government employees who have, or publicly appear to have, substantial responsibility for control of public affairs. Rosenblatt v. Baer, 383 U.S. at 85, 86 S.Ct. 669 (1966). New York Times Co. v. Sullivan, 376 U.S. at 283, 84 S.Ct. 710 (1964).

31. Cf. Rosenblatt v. Baer, 383 U.S. at 96, 86 S.Ct. [669] at 681 (1966) (Black, J., concurring and dissenting): "Statements like this have a way of growing and I fear that the words 'in the first instance' will soon be forgotten."

In Rosenblatt v. Baer, supra, 383 U.S. at 86, 86 S.Ct. at 676, the court stated: "Where a position in government has such apparent importance that the public has an independent interest in the qualifications and performance of the person who holds it, beyond the general public interest in the qualifications and performance of all government employees, both elements we identified in *New York Times* are present and the *New York Times* malice standards apply." With respect to this statement the court continued: "It is suggested that this test might apply to a night watchman accused of stealing state secrets. But a conclusion that the *New York Times* malice standards apply could not be reached merely because a statement defamatory of some person in government employ catches the public's interest; that conclusion would virtually disregard society's interest in protecting reputation. The employee's position must be one which would invite public scrutiny and discussion of the person holding it, entirely apart from the scrutiny and discussion occasioned by the particular charges in controversy." Id., at 86–87 (fn. 13), 82 S.Ct. at 676.

The *New York Times Co.* standard has been held to apply in cases involving an elected city commissioner of Montgomery, Alabama (New York Times Co. v. Sullivan); the mayor of a small city who was a candidate for county tax assessor (Ocala Star-Banner Co. v. Damron); a candidate for the United States Senate (Monitor Patriot Co. v. Roy); and a deputy chief of detectives for a large city police department (Time, Inc. v. Pape, 401 U.S. 279, 91 S.Ct. 633, 28 L.Ed.2d 45 [1971]). However a lawyer was not held to be a public official, merely because he was an officer of the court. Gertz v. Robert Welch, Inc.

The plaintiff in this case was employed by the school department of the city of Newburyport; he was also a member of the Newburyport Redevelopment Authority. His position with the city's school department was entitled "food service director." His duties involved the purchasing of food and equipment for two school cafeterias, preparation of menus and hiring and firing of employees with the approval of the school committee. His salary, which was set by agreement with the school committee rather than by statute or ordinance, was in the amount of $150 or $160 a week in 1969, with $40 a week added during the football season for the handling of athletic funds.

In addition, the plaintiff was a member of the Newburyport Redevelopment Authority from 1963 to 1972. At the time of the publication of the alleged libel he was treasurer of the authority, bonded in the sum of $25,000 and in this position he was authorized to co-sign checks, thus exercising a degree of management over $1,000,000 in authority funds during his term of office. It does not appear whether he was remunerated for these services, what his exact duties were and whether and to what extent he made policy decisions on public issues.

All of these facts must be considered at a new trial in light of the consideration that the purpose of the *New York Times Co.* privilege is to further "first, a strong interest in debate on public issues, and, second, a strong interest in debate about those persons who are in a position significantly to influence the resolution of those issues." Rosenblatt v. Baer, 383 U.S. 75, 85, 86 S.Ct. 669, 675, 15 L.Ed.2d 597 (1966).

Since the inquiry into relevant facts such as remuneration, duties, and participation in decisions on public issues was limited at the prior trial, we express no opinion or prediction whether the plaintiff here was a public official at the time of the publication. We leave that ruling for development at a new trial.

Although we have before us for review the defendant's exception to the denial of its motion for a directed verdict, this does not necessitate any further consideration of the public official issue. Since we have held, as shown later in this opinion, that the evidence warranted an inference of actual malice on the defendant's part, the case was one for the jury's consideration even if the plaintiff was ruled to be a public official.

6. If a ruling is required that the plaintiff was a public official, there would be no necessity for consideration whether he is also a public figure. Assuming that the "public figure" concept may be material, however, we turn to a discussion of its meaning. Whether a plaintiff is to be considered a "public figure" is also a matter not easily resolved by any sort of precise classification. In the *Gertz* case, the plaintiff was held not to be a public figure. This result was reached despite the facts that the plaintiff was a lawyer well known in legal circles, had published several books and articles on legal subjects, served as an officer of local civil groups and professional organizations and had long been active in community and professional affairs.

In the *Gertz* case, the court said: "That designation [public figure] may rest on either of two alternative bases. In some instances an individual may achieve such pervasive fame or notoriety that he becomes a public figure for all purposes and in all contexts. More commonly, an individual voluntarily injects himself or is drawn into a particular public controversy and thereby becomes a public figure for a limited range of issues. In either case such persons assume special prominence in the resolution of public questions. * * * We would not lightly assume that a citizen's participation in community and professional affairs rendered him a public figure for all purposes. Absent clear evidence of general fame or notoriety in the community, and pervasive involvement in the affairs of society, an individual should not be deemed a public personality for all aspects of his life. It is preferable to reduce the public figure question to a more meaningful context by looking to the nature and extent of an individual's participation in the particular controversy giving rise to the defamation." 418 U.S. at 351–352, 94 S.Ct. at 3013 (1974).

On the evidence presented at the trial of the instant case, it is our view that the plaintiff clearly was not shown to be a public figure. Although he was, aside from his official duties, an active participant in community affairs and a member of certain fraternal organizations, he had not "thrust himself into the vortex of * * * public issue[s], nor did he engage the public's attention in an attempt to influence * * * [the] outcome [thereof]." Gertz v. Robert Welch, Inc., supra, 418 U.S. at 352, 94 S.Ct. at 3013 (1974).

7. We turn next to a consideration of the meaning of "actual malice." This concept becomes relevant, of course, if the plaintiff is shown to be a public official or a public figure.

Mr. Justice Harlan's plurality opinion in the earlier case of Curtis Publishing Co. v. Butts, 388 U.S. 130, 155, 87 S.Ct. 1975, 1991, 18 L.Ed.2d 1094 (1967) (Harlan, J.), had allowed recovery, at least for a "public figure" who was not a public official, on a showing of "highly unreasonable conduct constituting an extreme departure from the standards of investigation and reporting ordinarily adhered to by responsible publishers." This language implies an objective test and a requirement of something less than recklessness. This requirement fell short of actual malice and was never adopted by a majority of the court, however. Cf. Gertz v. Robert Welch, Inc., 471 F.2d 801, 806, fn. 11 (7th Cir. 1972).

Actual malice is not necessarily proved in terms of ill will or hatred, but is proved rather by a showing that the defamatory falsehood was published with knowledge that it was false or reckless disregard of whether it was false. See New York Times Co. v. Sullivan, 376 U.S. 254, 279–280, 84 S.Ct. 710, 11 L.Ed.2d 686 (1964). "[D]efeasance of the privilege is conditioned, not on mere negligence, but on reckless disregard for the truth." Garrison v. Louisiana, 379 U.S. 64, 79, 85 S.Ct. 209, 218, 13 L.Ed.2d 125 (1964).

" 'Reckless disregard,' it is true, cannot be fully encompassed in one infallible definition. * * * [H]owever * * * [t]here must be sufficient evidence to permit the conclusion that the defendant in fact entertained serious doubts as to the truth of his publication. Publishing with such doubts shows reckless disregard for truth or falsity and demonstrates actual malice." St. Amant v. Thompson, 390 U.S. 727, 730–731, 88 S.Ct. 1323, 1325, 20 L.Ed.2d 262 (1968). Thus, the test is entirely a subjective one. That information was available which would cause a reasonably prudent man to entertain serious doubts is not sufficient. In order to negate the privilege, the jury must find that such doubts were in fact entertained by the defendant, or by the defendant's servant or agent acting within the scope of his employment. The jury may, of course, reach this conclusion on the basis of an inference drawn from objective evidence, since it would perhaps be rare for a defendant in such a circumstance to admit to having had serious, unresolved doubts, but the jury must draw this conclusion in order to hold the defendant liable.

The constitutionally mandated standard of recklessness in this civil context thus requires actual malice.[32] In this regard it is conceptually narrower than the Massachusetts common law concept of

32. "It may be that jury instructions that are couched only in terms of knowing or reckless falsity, and omit reference to 'actual malice,' would

recklessness sufficient to impose criminal liability, e. g., in a homicide case. In the criminal law we have held that an objective standard of recklessness and thus proof of implied malice will suffice, and said of a defendant that although " 'in fact he did not realize the grave danger, he cannot escape the imputation of wanton or reckless conduct in his dangerous act or omission, if an ordinary normal man under the same circumstances would have realized the gravity of the danger.' " Commonwealth v. Welansky, 316 Mass. 383, 398–399, 55 N.E.2d 902, 910 (1944). Commonwealth v. Pierce, 138 Mass. 165 (1884). Cf. Am.Law Inst., Model Penal Code, § 2.02(2)(c) (Proposed Official Draft May 4, 1962).

Subsequent decisions, both in this court and in the United States Supreme Court, adopt and apply the subjective formulation in the *St. Amant* case rather than the objective standard of the criminal law. Twohig v. Boston Herald-Traveler Corp., 362 Mass. 807, 291 N.E.2d 398 (1973). Time Inc. v. Pape, 401 U.S. 279, 91 S.Ct. 633, 28 L.Ed.2d 45 (1971).

8. In reviewing the denial of the defendant's motion for a directed verdict we consider the evidence in light of the concept of actual malice. Thus we are faced with the issue whether the evidence adduced at trial constituted sufficient proof of the requisite state of mind for recklessness so as to warrant the jury in returning a verdict for the plaintiff. New York Times Co. v. Sullivan, supra. Despite evidence of what the jury could find to be gross carelessness on the part of Pearson, it does not appear that the evidence would have been sufficient to warrant a conclusion of recklessness on his part. Of course, we have no way of knowing what the evidence at a new trial may show as to his state of mind.

However, the evidence concerning the defendant's news editor Coltin was sufficient to warrant submission of the case to the jury. Coltin allowed the story to be printed despite serious doubts as to its accuracy with respect to the plaintiff. Coltin admitted he was "surprised" by the report of the plaintiff's involvement. He denied that this term was an understatement and stated that he accepted the reported testimony of the city marshal. Nevertheless, combining this admission with his testimony that he considered the plaintiff, whom he knew well, to be an "excellent citizen," and the fact that the article was written by an inexperienced reporter, of whose minimal training Coltin was fully aware, a jury might draw the inference that the news editor had in fact entertained doubts as to the story's accuracy. The detailed evidence of Coltin's knowledge of the plaintiff's reputation and character, all of which evidence could be found to be inconsistent with the nature of the crime charged, might well support such a finding.

Assuming a jury so found, the amount of time necessary and available for checking the accuracy of the story might be considered

further a proper application of the New York Times standard to the evidence." Rosenbloom v. Metromedia, Inc., 403 U.S. 29, 52, fn. 18, 91 S.Ct. 1811, 1824, 29 L.Ed.2d 296 (1971) (Brennan, J.).

relevant to determine whether pushing aside or disregarding those doubts rose to the level of recklessness. In this regard, there was evidence of a delay of a full day in the publication of the story. Cf. Priestley v. Hastings & Sons Publishing Co. of Lynn, 360 Mass. 118, 123–125, 271 N.E.2d 628 (1971), and Curtis Publishing Co. v. Butts, 388 U.S. 130, 159, 87 S.Ct. 1975, 18 L.Ed.2d 1094 (1967). All told, there was sufficient evidence to warrant consideration by the jury. Therefore, it is appropriate for us to order a new trial of the case, rather than order that judgment should enter for the defendant.

9. In any case where the plaintiff is required to prove actual malice he must do so, not merely by the fair preponderance of the evidence, but by "clear and convincing proof." See Gertz v. Robert Welch, Inc., 418 U.S. 323, 342, 94 S.Ct. 2997, 41 L.Ed.2d 789 (1974); New York Times Co. v. Sullivan, 376 U.S. 254, 285–286, 84 S.Ct. 710, 11 L.Ed.2d 686 (1964); Restatement 2d: Torts (Tent. draft No. 21, 1975), § 580A, comment (f). It is an unusual development, indeed, that requires as matter of constitutional law that the jury must find facts according to such a standard, and must be charged accordingly; yet that is the apparent holding of the Supreme Court.[33] In ruling on a defendant's motion for a directed verdict in a defamation case, the judge certainly must apply the "clear and convincing proof" standard. That is to say, the judge must determine whether the jury would be warranted in concluding that malice was proved by clear and convincing evidence.[34] Further, at least until the Supreme Court makes additional comment on the issue, if it does, the jury should be charged according to that standard.[35]

33. Traditionally, in those few instances where "clear and convincing proof" has been required in civil cases, it has related ordinarily to findings and rulings of the judge. See, e. g., Stockbridge Iron Co. v. Hudson Iron Co., 107 Mass. 290 (1871) (mutual mistake sufficient to justify reformation of an instrument); Foley v. Coan, 272 Mass. 207, 172 N.E. 74 (1930) (gift causa mortis); Coghlin v. White, 273 Mass. 53, 172 N.E. 786 (1930) (contents of a lost will); Kidder v. Greenman, 283 Mass. 601, 187 N.E. 42 (1933) (cancellation of lease).

34. There is no suggestion here that the trial judge must *himself* be convinced. See the warning against such a practice in the concurring and dissenting opinion of Quirico, J., * * *

35. The language of the Supreme Court, by Mr. Justice Powell, writing for the court in the *Gertz* case, is clearly directive (rather than merely rhetorical, as the opinion of Quirico, J., contends) as shown by the following statement: "The *New York Times* standard defines the level of constitutional protection appropriate to the context of defamation of a public person. Those who, by reason of the notoriety of their achievements or the vigor and success with which they seek the public's attention, are properly classed as public figures and those who hold governmental office may recover for injury to reputation *only on clear and convincing proof* that the defamatory falsehood was made with knowledge of its falsity or with reckless disregard for the truth. This standard administers an extremely powerful antidote to the inducement to media self-censorship of the common-law rule of strict liability for libel and slander. And it exacts a correspondingly high price from the victims of defamatory falsehood" (emphasis supplied). 418 U.S. at 342, 94 S.Ct. at 3008 (1974).

Decisions of the Federal Courts bearing on the issue of clear and convincing proof of actual malice support the conclusion that this burden of proof is required as matter of constitutional law. [Citations omitted.]

The *New York Times* and the *Gertz* cases offer no definition of the meaning of "clear and convincing proof," to assist in formulating jury instructions. However, from other sources we find the phrase defined. Clear and convincing proof involves a degree of belief greater than the usually imposed burden of proof by a fair preponderance of the evidence, but less than the burden of proof beyond a reasonable doubt imposed in criminal cases. See Foley v. Coan, supra; Coghlin v. White, supra. It has been said that the proof must be "strong, positive and free from doubt" (Coghlin v. White, supra, 273 Mass. at 55, 172 N.E. at 786 (quoting from Newell v. Homer, 120 Mass. 277, 280 [1876]), and "full, clear and decisive" (Kidder v. Greenman, supra, 283 Mass. at 613, 187 N.E. 42, and cases cited). See generally, Wigmore Evidence, § 2498(3) (3d ed. 1940).

10. The defendant's exceptions are sustained and the case is remanded to the Superior Court for a new trial on all issues.

So ordered.

QUIRICO, JUSTICE (concurring in part and dissenting in part).

I concur with all of the opinion in this case except part 9 thereof. Specifically, I disagree that as a matter of constitutional law (1) "[i]n any case where the plaintiff is required to prove actual malice he must do so, not merely by the fair preponderance of the evidence, but by 'clear and convincing proof' " which "involves a degree of belief greater than the usually imposed burden of proof by a fair preponderance of the evidence, but less than the burden of proof beyond a reasonable doubt imposed in criminal cases," (2) "the jury must find facts according to such a standard, and must be charged accordingly," and (3) "[i]n ruling on a defendant's motion for a directed verdict in a defamation case, the judge certainly must apply the 'clear and convincing proof' standard."

I recognize that in New York Times Co. v. Sullivan, 376 U.S. 254, 285–286, 84 S.Ct. 710, 11 L.Ed.2d 686 (1964), the Supreme Court, through Mr. Justice Brennan, indicated that the proof of actual malice presented in that case would not constitutionally sustain the judgment because it lacked "convincing clarity." I also recognize that in Rosenbloom v. Metromedia, Inc., 403 U.S. 29, 52, 91 S.Ct. 1811, 29 L.Ed.2d 296 (1971), Mr. Justice Brennan, for three members of the court, transposed his *New York Times Co.* "convincing clarity" language into a requirement that actual malice be proved by "clear and convincing proof." I further recognize that in Gertz v. Robert Welch, Inc., 418 U.S. 323, 342, 94 S.Ct. 2997, 3008, 41 L.Ed.2d 789 (1974), a majority of the court interpreted the *New York Times Co.* standard as permitting a public official or public figure to "recover for injury to reputation only on clear and convincing proof that the defamatory falsehood was made with knowledge of its falsity or with reckless disregard for the truth." It is doubtless possible to read these excerpts, as the court today has done, to require that juries be instructed to find for the defendant on the issue of malice unless they view the evidence on that issue as "clear and convincing" in the plaintiff's favor. It is also possible to infer that this standard involves a degree of belief lying somewhere between that required to support a verdict in an ordinary civil case and that required to support a verdict of conviction in a criminal case. It may even be possible to interpret this language as requiring the trial judge in a jury case to direct a verdict[36] for the defendant unless *he* is *personally* satisfied that the evidence establishing malice is clear and convincing. And perhaps the language can also be construed as demanding that members of appellate courts review trial transcripts and exhibits and thereafter reverse a denial of a motion for a directed verdict unless *they* are *personally* satisfied that the evidence establishing malice is clear and convincing. I, however, view this language as little more than confusing rhetoric—words which have been given no content by the United States Supreme Court. For reasons hopefully explained below, I would not give these words the content given them by the court today.

1. The Supreme Court has not defined "convincing clarity" or "clear and convincing." Neither has it stated whether these undefined terms raise questions of law or of fact. The court today creates a definition for these phrases and seemingly rules that they raise questions of both law and fact. In considering these holdings, it is helpful to bear in mind that they are not explicitly mandated by the Supreme Court.

2. My feeling that the phrases "convincing clarity" and "clear and convincing" are essentially rhetorical is reinforced by the fact that in the *Gertz* case the court said: "Absent *clear evidence* of general fame or notoriety in the community, and pervasive involvement in the affairs of society, an individual should not be deemed a public personality for all aspects of his life" (emphasis supplied). 418 U.S. at 352, 94 S.Ct. at 3013 (1974). It seems to me that if, as the court today holds, the plaintiff in a defamation action has a special burden of proof in regard to the issue of malice, then the defendant has a similar (although perhaps not identical) burden of proof on the issue whether the plaintiff is a public personality.

The question thus arises whether the burden of adducing "clear" evidence on an issue is less than the burden of adducing "clear and convincing" evidence on an issue. If these phrases are not mere rhetoric, then each must set a precise, independent standard. If we hold, as the court apparently does, that one implication of the existence of such precise, independent standards is that juries must be instructed to find facts according to those standards, we raise the spectre of requiring trial judges in defamation cases to instruct juries as to four separate and distinct burdens of proof, falling various-

36. Although the court focuses on the trial judge's duty in considering a motion for a directed verdict, it would seem that the same duty would inhere, if at all, in considering a motion for judgment notwithstanding the verdict or a motion, perhaps accompanied by affidavits, for summary judgment. See Mass.R.Civ.P. 50(a), 50(b), and 56 (b), — Mass. — (1974). [Unbracketed portions of notes 26–36 from original, renumbered; other notes in original omitted.]

ly on the plaintiff and defendant. That is to say that since the court today defines "clear and convincing" evidence as that which would satisfy a burden somewhere between those imposed by the ordinary preponderance of the evidence and reasonable doubt standards utilized in civil and criminal cases, and since "clear" evidence is presumably stronger than a preponderance of the evidence but not so strong as "clear and convincing" evidence, then a trial judge must instruct the jury as to the meaning of: (1) "a preponderance" of the evidence, by which most of the facts in issue must be found, (2) "beyond a reasonable doubt," so that the standard can help define other terms, (3) "clear and convincing" evidence, by which malice must be proved, and (4) "clear" evidence, by which the public character of the plaintiff's personality must be proved. A juror listening to a judge instructing him to draw such fine distinctions in his levels of belief would likely agree with Mr. Bumble: "If the law supposes that, * * * the law is a ass, a idiot." Dickens, Oliver Twist, ch. 51.

Moreover, it is by no means entirely clear that the problem of special burdens of proof is limited to the issues of malice and whether the plaintiff is a public personality. Circuit Judge Bell, specially concurring in Firestone v. Time, Inc., 460 F.2d 712, 722–723 (5th Cir. 1972) cert. den. 409 U.S. 875, 93 S.Ct. 120, 34 L.Ed.2d 127 (1972), said: "The Supreme Court has not expressly added the requirement of clear and convincing proof of falsity to the plaintiff's burden of proof. * * * Such a standard of proof seems implicit however, in the stated requirement in *New York Times* that plaintiff has the burden of showing by clear and convincing proof that publication was with knowledge of falsity or with reckless disregard as to falsity *vel non.* I conclude for the same constitutional reasons giving rise to this stringent proof requirement that the clear and convincing proof standard would also apply to proving that the statement was false in the first instance." If I were to agree that a special burden of proof were properly applicable to any of the issues in a defamation case, I, like Circuit Judge Bell, would find it difficult to isolate one among many issues to which to apply such a special burden.

3. Even assuming that the "convincing clarity" and "clear and convincing" language in the *New York Times Co., Rosenbloom,* and *Gertz* cases does require some special instructions to the jury, I do not believe that this language requires that juries in this Commonwealth be instructed that they find certain facts with "a degree of belief greater than the usually imposed burden of proof by a fair preponderance of the evidence, but less than the burden of proof beyond a reasonable doubt imposed in criminal cases." * * * In Kidder v. Greenman, 283 Mass. 601, 613–614, 187 N.E. 42, 48 (1933), we said: "It is settled that where reformation of an instrument is sought on the ground of a mutual mistake the proof must be 'full, clear, and decisive.' * * * Whether this rule requires proof 'beyond a reasonable doubt' as those words are used in the criminal law * * * or merely recognizes that, *in determining the preponderance of evidence,* a completed instrument is evidence of great weight of the in-

tention of the parties thereto and such evidence is not readily overcome by parol evidence of such intention, need not be considered, for the rule, however stated, is not applicable to the present case" (emphasis supplied). In Matter of Mayberry, 295 Mass. 155, 167, 3 N.E. 2d 248, 253 (1936), this court held "that cause for disbarment may be established by a fair preponderance of the evidence as in other civil causes and that proof beyond reasonable doubt as in criminal cases is not required." We added: "Nor do we think that there is in this commonwealth any rule of law establishing for such cases an intermediate standard of proof, such as that the evidence must be 'clear and convincing' or 'not of doubtful character.' Such midway expressions may have some place in emphasizing the care with which the trier of fact should approach the decision of an issue so important to the respondent as the loss of his profession. * * * But such terms are too vague to serve generally as a practical guide in the trial of cases." Cf. Commonwealth v. Bell, 356 Mass. 724, 725, 252 N.E.2d 414 (1969).

In my view, we could accommodate our trial practice to the evidentiary requirements of *New York Times Co.*, *Rosenbloom*, and *Gertz* simply by having judges instruct juries to find for the defendant in a defamation action unless the plaintiff proves every necessary element of his claim for relief by a preponderance of the evidence, but that on the issue of malice they should scrutinize the evidence with special care, not lightly inferring the presence of malice, and that they should find that the defendant acted with malice only if they find the evidence on that issue clear enough to convince them by a preponderance of the evidence. A similar instruction, running in favor of the plaintiff, could be given on whether the plaintiff is a public personality. Such instructions should be adequate to satisfy any constitutional requirements imposed by the Supreme Court without formally incorporating into our jurisprudence an unworkable standard of proof, a standard of proof which will be unintelligible to juries, and which we have heretofore generally eschewed.

4. The court's opinion states that, "[i]n ruling on a defendant's motion for a directed verdict in a defamation case, the judge certainly must apply the 'clear and convincing proof' standard. That is to say, the judge must determine whether the jury would be warranted in concluding that malice was proved by clear and convincing evidence." This statement, touching, as it does, on our historic allocation of functions between judge and jury, seems to me to raise a serious problem. Despite the court's disclaimer of an intention to do so, it appears inevitable that, by reason of the statement that the trial judge must make a preliminary determination whether the jury could find the evidence on the malice issue clear and convincing, the judge must to some degree evaluate the weight and credibility of possibly conflicting and ambiguous evidence and draw his own inferences therefrom. I would prefer a statement to the effect that, in so far as malice is concerned, a case must go to the jury if there is *any* evidence from which malice could be inferred, and that it is for the jury

alone to determine whether that evidence is clear and convincing. It is true that some Federal Courts have adopted or advocated a practice in defamation cases being tried to juries of having judges grant directed verdicts in the face of conflicting or ambiguous evidence on the malice issue if personally unconvinced that the defendant in fact acted maliciously. I regard such a practice as improvident and would proscribe it in our courts unless the United States Supreme Court were unequivocally to require it as matter of Federal constitutional law. I do not believe that the Supreme Court has imposed such a requirement. * * *

ALIOTO v. COWLES COMMUNICATIONS, INC.

United States Court of Appeals for the Ninth Circuit, 1975.
519 F.2d 777.

CHOY, CIRCUIT JUDGE.

The September 23, 1969, issue of LOOK magazine contained an article entitled "The Web That Links San Francisco's Mayor Alioto and the Mafia: A LOOK report on the private Joseph Alioto and his relationships with organized crime." The article, written by two young employees of a San Francisco television station, accused Alioto of using his position as chairman of the board of a San Francisco bank to obtain loans for a trucking company run by James Fratianno, a convicted felon alleged to be a West Coast Mafia operative. The source of the information upon which this accusation was based was Fratianno's son-in-law, Tommy Thomas. Thomas claimed that Fratianno had told him of a number of meetings between Alioto and several underworld figures at the Nut Tree, a Bay Area restaurant. Thomas also claimed knowledge of connections between the Mafia and other prominent politicians. FBI and California law enforcement authorities were unable to corroborate the alleged meeting or other relationships between Alioto and the Mafia.

After agreeing to buy the article, LOOK editors had the authors interview Alioto. The authors asked Alioto about his connections with Fratianno, but did not tell him of their forthcoming Nut Tree accusations. When Alioto later learned that an article was to be published, he demanded, in a series of telegrams, a meeting with LOOK editors. LOOK officials replied that such a meeting would serve no useful purpose, since the story had already been sent to the printers.

Alioto responded by filing a libel suit in federal district court against LOOK's publisher, Cowles Communications, Inc. The first trial ended in a hung jury. On retrial, the jury returned a special verdict, finding that the article was false and that it was defamatory. The jury was unable to agree whether the article had been published with the requisite actual malice, however.

Despite this inconclusive verdict, the district judge awarded judgment to Cowles. He held that a finding of actual malice by both judge and jury was required in order for Alioto to recover, and that he found that actual malice "was not shown with convincing clarity." Therefore, he granted Cowles' motion for judgment n. o. v. Furthermore, he found that Alioto was entitled only to special damages because he had not complied with the requirements of Cal.Civ.Code § 48a by demanding a retraction within 20 days of publication; Alioto had demanded only general and punitive damages, so the judge granted Cowles' motion for summary judgment.

Alioto appeals. We reverse and remand for a new trial on the issue of actual malice.

RETRACTION

California permits a publisher or broadcaster to escape liability for general damages in a libel suit if he publishes or broadcasts a retraction upon proper demand:

> 1. In any action for damages for the publication of a libel in a newspaper, or of a slander by radio broadcast, plaintiff shall recover no more than special damages unless a correction be demanded and be not published or broadcast, as hereinafter provided. Plaintiff shall serve upon the publisher, at the place of publication or broadcaster at the place of broadcast, a written notice specifying the statements claimed to be libelous and demanding that the same be corrected. Said notice and demand must be served within 20 days after knowledge of the publication or broadcast of the statements claimed to be libelous.

Cal.Civ.Code § 48a(1).

On its face, section 48a does not apply to magazines. One division of the California Court of Appeal has held explicitly that magazines are not covered by either the letter or the rationale of section 48a. Morris v. National Federation of the Blind, 192 Cal.App.2d 162, 13 Cal.Rptr. 336 (1961). Other divisions have applied section 48a to magazines without apparent notice that the statute specifies libels in newspapers, not all printed media. * * *

The California Supreme Court has added to the confusion in an opinion applying section 48a to the Reader's Digest. Briscoe v. Reader's Digest Association, 4 Cal.3d 529, 93 Cal.Rptr. 866, 483 P.2d 34 (1971). In two sentences near the end of a long opinion, the *Briscoe* court stated only that the plaintiff had not complied with the requirements of section 48a, and thus was limited to recovery of special damages. The court did not discuss the contrary decision in *Morris,* nor the fact that it was construing "newspaper" to include magazines.

In a case decided this year, a division of the Court of Appeal has refused to acknowledge *Briscoe* as requiring extension of 48a to publishers of magazines. Montandon v. Triangle Publications, Inc., 45 Cal.App.3d 938, 120 Cal.Rptr 186 (1975). The *Montandon* court carefully analyzed the judicial history of the issue, observing that *Morris* had been the only reasoned decision to date. The court observed that section 48a(3) requires that a retraction be published within three weeks of the demand. While publication within this time would have been possible for the weekly magazine involved in the *Montandon* litigation, the *Montandon* court was unwilling to adopt a construction of the statute which would require a distinction between weekly and biweekly magazines on the one hand and monthly magazines on the other. The court also emphasized the validity of the distinction made in *Morris* between newspapers and broadcast media, which are under pressure to disseminate "news while it is new," and magazines, which have the advantage of greater leisure in which to ascertain the truth of accusations before publishing them. Finally, in examining the legislative history of section 48a, the *Montandon* court observed that the statute originally applied only to newspapers, but had been amended in 1945 and again in 1949 to extend coverage to radio and then to television. The legislature had not seen fit, however, to amend the statute again in 1961 following the *Morris* decision in order to extend coverage explicitly to magazines.

We find the reasoning presented by the *Montandon* opinion persuasive. The California Supreme Court has declined to review *Montandon*. Although this action does not of itself indicate approval of the *Montandon* decision, we conclude that if it were confronted with the issue it would decide that, notwithstanding its decision in *Briscoe*, section 48a's requirement of a demand for retraction does not extend to libels appearing in magazines. * * *

Actual Malice

In order to recover damages for publication of libelous statements relating to official conduct, a public official must establish that the defendant published the falsehood with actual malice—"that is, with knowledge that it was false or with reckless disregard of whether it was false or not." New York Times Co. v. Sullivan, 376 U.S. 254, 280, 84 S.Ct. 710, 726, 11 L.Ed.2d 686 (1964). "Reckless disregard" does not refer to an objective "reasonable man" standard. The defendant must be proved to have subjectively "entertained serious doubts as to the truth of his publication." St. Amant v. Thompson, 390 U.S. 727, 731, 88 S.Ct. 1323, 1325, 20 L.Ed.2d 262 (1968). To protect first amendment values, the Court requires a higher standard of proof than the usual "preponderance of the evidence"; the recklessness must be demonstrated by "clear and convincing proof." See, e. g., Rosenbloom v. Metromedia, Inc., 403 U.S. 29, 30, 91 S.Ct. 1811, 29 L.Ed.2d 296 (1971). Because of the importance of the interests in freedom of speech and press which are at stake, a court must review the facts to determine whether the jury applied the proper standard; simply ascertaining that the jury was properly instructed does not suffice. New York Times, 376 U.S. at 285, 84 S.Ct. 710; Rosenbloom, 403 U.S. at 55, 91 S.Ct. 1811.

In his opinion granting Cowles' motion for judgment n. o. v., the district judge stated that a jury could justifiably find that the evidence proved with convincing clarity that the libel was published either with or without actual malice. He then weighed for himself the persuasiveness of the evidence and the credibility of witnesses, took into account that Alioto had twice failed to convince a jury of Cowles' actual malice, and decided that Alioto had failed to establish actual malice.

The court thus implied that a plaintiff in a libel action must persuade two triers of fact: both judge and jury. Judge Skelly Wright has stated the proposition:

> "[T]he trial court at the close of the plaintiff's case must decide whether actual malice has been shown with 'convincing clarity.' In making this judgment the court will judge the credibility of the witnesses and draw its own inferences from the evidence. If the trial is permitted to proceed, the court will be called upon again to make a judgment on the actual malice issue at the close of all of the evidence. If the motion for a directed verdict at this stage of the trial is denied, the actual malice issue, along with the other issues, is then submitted to the jury under the *Times* instruction without any indication from the court or counsel that the court has decided that the evidence shows actual malice with 'convincing clarity.'
>
> This two-step procedure in which both the trial judge and the jury must find actual malice before there can be judgment for the plaintiff provides the protection of the First Amendment freedom that *Times* sought to make secure in areas of public concern".

Wasserman v. Time, Inc., 138 U.S.App.D.C. 7, 424 F.2d 920, 922–923, cert. denied, 398 U.S. 940, 90 S.Ct. 1844, 26 L.Ed.2d 273 (1970) (Wright, J., concurring); see Bon Air Hotel, Inc. v. Time, Inc., 426 F.2d 858 (5th Cir. 1970).

Following the district court's decision, however, we repudiated Judge Wright's two-step approach in Guam Federation of Teachers, Local 1581 v. Ysrael, 492 F.2d 438 (9th Cir.), cert. denied, 419 U.S. 872, 95 S.Ct. 132, 42 L.Ed.2d 111 (1974). A district judge on motion for judgment n. o. v., or an appellate judge on review, must examine the evidence to see whether, if all permissible inferences were drawn in the plaintiff's favor and all questions of credibility were resolved in his behalf, the evidence then would demonstrate by clear and convincing proof that the libelous material was published with actual malice. Once this question has been resolved in the plaintiff's favor, the jury's findings as to those inferences and as to witness credibility are determinative.

The district court, while granting Cowles' motion for judgment n. o. v., found that:

> Judging the whole matter objectively on the whole record I think that a jury justifiably could find that the evidence showed with convincing clarity that the authors (and as of the date of publication their states of mind could be imputed

> to defendant) were ambitious young men, anxious to sell a sensational story to a national magazine; that the Tommy Thomas statements as to the Nut Tree meetings added greatly to the sensational nature and salability of the article; that the authors must have had doubts about the veracity of Tommy Thomas (the sole source of the Nut Tree statements); that they deliberately failed to cross-check on the validity of his statements because they did not want to find them to be untrue, and so published the statements with a reckless disregard for truth.

Our review of the record convinces us that the district judge fairly summarized the permissible inferences which a jury might draw from the evidence. Having found the evidence that LOOK's editors entertained doubts as to the truth of the Nut Tree allegations to be sufficiently clear and convincing in nature were the jury to decide questions of credibility and draw permissible inferences in Alioto's favor, the court was without power to award Cowles judgment notwithstanding the jury's failure to arrive at a verdict. The judgment must be reversed and the case remanded for a new trial on the sole issue of actual malice.

Reversed and remanded.

Gertz is not clear as to whether its First Amendment rules apply to the defamation of non-public figures by private persons other than publishers or broadcasters. The Restatement of Torts Second generally assumes that the First Amendment fault requirement will not be limited to defamation by publishers and broadcasters, and that, if it is limited in terms of the type of subject matter, the limitation may possibly be narrower than that which would be permitted by a test related broadly to matters of public or general interest, e. g., there may be exclusion from the constitutional privilege of particular kinds of activities which may give rise to defamation, such as private gossip or "commercial speech" (which could include both advertising and reports of credit rating bureaus); see § 580B, Comments d and e (Tent. Draft 21, 1975); Retail Credit Co. v. Russell, 234 Ga. 765, 218 S.E.2d 54 (1975); Phillips, Defamation, Invasion of Privacy and the Constitutional Standard of Care, 16 Santa Clara L.Rev. 77, 93–95 (1975).

JACRON SALES CO., INC. v. SINDORF

Court of Appeals of Maryland, 1976.
276 Md. 580, 350 A.2d 688.

LEVINE, J. We are asked here to determine the extent to which the First and Fourteenth Amendments to the Federal Constitution are applicable to actions for defamation by private individuals against defendants who are not publishers or broadcasters; alternatively, we shall decide as a matter of state law whether the law of defamation should be changed in view of recent decisions of the Supreme Court. See Gertz v. Robert Welch, 418 U.S. 323, 94 S.Ct. 2997, 41 L.Ed.2d 789 (1974). These questions arise from an action for slander brought by appellee, Jack Sindorf (Sindorf), against his former employer, Jacron Sales Co., Inc. (Jacron). When the case came on for trial * * * the court directed a verdict for Jacron at the close of all the evidence. On appeal, the Court of Special Appeals reversed the judgment and remanded the case to the circuit court for a new trial. * * * We then granted certiorari.

Early in 1972, Sindorf entered the employ of Jacron, a Philadelphia-based company, as a construction tools salesman. Sindorf submitted a letter of resignation terminating that relationship some 18 months later, and within a few days thereafter began working in a similar capacity for a Maryland company known as the Tool Box Corporation. In his letter of resignation to Jacron, Sindorf had acknowledged that he was in possession of inventory belonging to Jacron worth $2,451.77, and further stated that although he regarded the material in his possession as part payment of commissions due him, he would return the property "at such time as" he received the sum of $2,561.50, representing unpaid commissions of $2,100 and other miscellaneous amounts owed to him by Jacron. In addition to enclosing invoices for the inventory in his possession, he expressed his regret at the need for proceeding in such a manner, which was pursuant to the advice of counsel, but noted that his efforts to "collect the money" due him "through normal business channels" had been unsuccessful.

Within two days after he commenced his employment with Tool Box, Sindorf was asked to come from his Pennsylvania home to Maryland for a conference with William R. Brose (Brose), the president of the company. At that meeting, Brose related a recorded telephone conversation between him and one Robert Fridkis (Fridkis), vice president of Jacron Sales of Virginia, a subsidiary of Jacron, who had never been Sindorf's employer. The tape recording was played for the jury, and a transcript of the dialogue was received in evidence. As related by Brose, the substance of Fridkis' statement was that there were "quite a few cash sales and quite a bit of merchandise that were uncounted [sic] for." This suggested to Brose, according to his testimony, that possibly Sindorf "had taken items, either for possibly for his own use * * * or for a cash sale," i. e., implying that they had been stolen by Sindorf. When confronted by Brose with Fridkis' statements, Sindorf branded them as untrue; furthermore, despite an "extremely careful" check of the Tool Box inventory entrusted to Sindorf during his nine months of employment, nothing was ever found to be missing. We note that neither in the Court of Special Appeals nor in this Court has appellant contended that Fridkis' statement did not constitute slander per se.

Testimony revealed that Fridkis had placed the call to Brose on instructions from the president of the parent corporation in Philadelphia. Those instructions, however, had not implicated Sindorf in any theft or other criminal conduct. In the president's own words he told Fridkis:

> ". . . to call the Tool Box and see if Mr. Sindorf was working for them. We explained to Bob how the man had left us, keeping the merchandise in his possession, our merchandise, and we wanted to verify his employment, whether he was working there while he was still on our payroll or had he just started with Tool Box."

Apparently, when Fridkis reported to the president the outcome of his discussion with Brose, he merely "verified [Sindorf's] employment * * *."

In directing a verdict for the defendant, the trial court ruled that although Sindorf had established a case of slander per se warranting its submission to the jury, Jacron was protected by a common law conditional privilege which had not been lost because Sindorf had failed "to show actual malice." Shortly after an appeal had been lodged, the Court of Special Appeals ordered the parties to address their briefs, in part, to the decision in Gertz v. Robert Welch, Inc., supra, which the Supreme Court had handed down in June 25, 1974, more than two months after the trial of this case. The Court of Special Appeals held that Sindorf had presented sufficient evidence of malice to warrant submission of the question of abuse of the common law conditional privilege to the jury, thus compelling a reversal of the circuit court decision. Further, the Court of Special Appeals said that since the defamatory statements here were of a "purely private" nature, this case was beyond the reach of *Gertz.*

I

Although we too regard this case as one of defamation of a private individual as to a purely private matter, we think the Court of Special Appeals has misread *Gertz* in concluding that the holding there applies "only when a private individual is defamed as to a matter of general or public interest." * * * No consideration of *Gertz,* however, would be productive without first referring, at the very least, to three prior decisions of the Supreme Court: New York Times Co. v. Sullivan, 376 U.S. 254, 84 S.Ct. 710, 11 L.Ed.2d 686 (1964); Curtis Publishing Co. v. Butts, 388 U.S. 130, 87 S.Ct. 1975, 18 L.Ed.2d 1094 (1967); and Rosenbloom v. Metromedia, 403 U.S. 29, 91 S.Ct. 1811, 29 L.Ed.2d 296 (1971).

At common law, the only defenses available to a publisher of defamatory material were truth and the common law privileges. Then, in its landmark decision in *New York Times,* the Supreme Court held that in a state libel trial, a public official must establish "malice," defined as a knowing falsity or a reckless disregard for the truth, on the part of the publisher to recover damages for defamatory statements concerning the plaintiff's official conduct. The traditional defense of truth, the Court held, did not provide adequate protection to the First Amendment rights of the press.

Three years later, in Curtis Publishing Co. v. Butts, supra, another unanimous Court expanded the class of plaintiffs subject to the *New York Times* test to include "public figures." Although Mr. Justice Harlan wrote the opinion for the Court, a majority agreed with Mr. Chief Justice Warren's definition of a public figure, which included not only public officials but also those individuals who are "nevertheless intimately involved in the resolution of important public questions or, by reason of their fame, shape events in areas of concern to society at large." 388 U.S. at 164. The Chief Justice assumed that involvement in public issues or events itself guaranteed access to the means by which defamatory criticism might be controverted.

In Rosenbloom v. Metromedia, supra, in an opinion joined by only two other members of the Court, Mr. Justice Brennan appeared to extend the constitutional privilege enunciated in *New York Times* yet another step further by applying it to defamatory falsehoods if the statements concern matters of public or general interest, regardless of the status of the person defamed. The essence of the opinion is this:

> "If a matter is a subject of public or general interest, it cannot suddenly become less so merely because a private individual is involved, or because in some sense the individual did not 'voluntarily' choose to become involved. The public's primary interest is in the event; the public focus is on the conduct of the participant and the content, effect, and significance of the conduct, not the participant's prior anonymity or notoriety. * * *" 403 U.S. at 43.

Subsequent history has proved the separate dissenting opinions of Mr. Justice Harlan and Mr. Justice Marshall more durable than the purality opinion of Mr. Justice Brennan. Justice Harlan urged in his dissent in *Rosenbloom* that the *New York Times* privilege should not apply to private persons because of the diminished likelihood of "securing access to channels of communication sufficient to rebut falsehoods." 403 U.S. at 70. To this extent, Mr. Justice Marshall, joined by Mr. Justice Stewart, was in general agreement. The disagreement between the two dissenting opinions was over the matter of punitive damages. Justice Harlan was of the view that the states might allow such damages in amounts bearing "a reasonable and purposeful relationship to the actual harm done," 403 U.S. at 75, while

Justice Marshall expressed the view that both punitive and presumed damages should not be allowed because they resulted in self-censorship.

Thus was the stage set for *Gertz.* There, the plaintiff was a Chicago attorney prosecuting a civil action for the family of a youth who had been shot and killed by a police officer. The officer had previously been convicted of second degree murder in the incident, but the plaintiff had neither participated in the criminal proceeding nor discussed the officer with media representatives. Nevertheless, the defendant published an article characterizing the plaintiff as the "architect of the criminal prosecution" which it portrayed as part of a nationwide Communist conspiracy to discredit local law enforcement agencies. The article falsely accused the plaintiff of membership in Communist-front organizations and of having a criminal record. After a jury had awarded the plaintiff $50,000 in damages, the trial court, anticipating *Rosenbloom* and granting the defendant's motion for a judgment n. o. v., ruled that the *New York Times* standard should govern even though the plaintiff was neither a public official nor a public figure. On appeal, the United States Court of Appeals upheld the trial court on the ground that, regardless of whether the plaintiff was a public figure, the defamatory statements concerned an issue of significant public interest. Gertz v. Robert Welch, Inc., 471 F.2d 801 (7th Cir. 1972).

The Supreme Court, with a majority of five, held that the constitutional privilege articulated in *New York Times* does not extend to defamatory falsehoods concerning an individual who is neither a public official nor a public figure. Rather than expand the *New York Times* standard to falsehoods relating to private persons when made in connection with events of public interest, as the *Rosenbloom* plurality had done, the Court applied a number of restrictions to the law of libel designed to accommodate freedom of the press with the state's interest in protecting a private person's reputation. The Court held that in cases of defamation of private persons (1) the state may not impose liability without fault, but with that limitation may adopt any other standard of media liability, and (2) in cases where the *New York Times* test of knowing or reckless falsity is not met, the state may permit recovery for "actual injury" but not presumed or punitive damages. Such "actual injury" was not confined to out-of-pocket loss, but may include "impairment of reputation and standing in the community, personal humiliation, and mental anguish and suffering." 418 U.S. at 350. After then determining that Gertz was neither a public official nor a public figure, the Court reversed and remanded the case for a new trial.

The Court's shift in emphasis from First Amendment protection of free expression to the state interest in protecting the reputation of the plaintiff who is a private individual represented a rejection of the rationale underlying the plurality opinion in *Rosenbloom.* In sum, the Court held that a private individual deserves a greater degree of protection than does a public figure because the latter usually has a greater access to the media to rebut defamatory charges and, unlike the private individual, usually has chosen to run "the risk of closer public scrutiny." 418 U.S. at 344. Thus, the *Rosenbloom* test, whether the matter is of "public or general" concern, did not afford sufficient recognition of the legitimate state interest in enforcing a remedy for injury to a private person's reputation. Additionally, the *Gertz* Court found the *Rosenbloom* plurality approach unacceptable because it imposed on courts the task of deciding on an "ad hoc" basis what issues were of "general or public interest," a task which the Court doubted the wisdom of committing "to the conscience of judges." 418 U.S. at 346. * * *

The Court of Special Appeals' conclusion that the *Gertz* holding applies only where a private person is defamed in regard to a matter of public or general interest finds no support in the *Gertz* decision itself. To the contrary, the opinion for the Court by Mr. Justice Powell is punctuated with manifestations that the "public or general interest" test was being jettisoned. 418 U.S. at 343–44. The Court stated that the "extension of the *New York Times* test proposed by the *Rosenbloom* plurality would abridge [the] legitimate state interest to a degree that [it found] unacceptable," and declared that the " 'public or general interest' test for determining the applicability of the *New York Times* standard to private defamation actions inadequately serves both of the competing values at stake." Id. at 346. That *Gertz* was regarded as having rejected the *Rosenbloom* plurality opinion and as a withdrawal "to the factual limits of the pre-*Rosenbloom* cases" is confirmed by the concurring opinion of Mr. Justice Blackmun, 418 U.S. at 353, which gave Justice Powell's opinion the approval of a majority, and even more forcefully by Mr. Justice White's dissent where he stated that "[t]he Court now repudiates the plurality opinion in *Rosenbloom* * * *." Id. at 378–79.

The very essence of the *Gertz* decision, as we noted early on, was the shift in focus from the protection of free expression, which undergirded *New York Times* and its progeny, including *Rosenbloom,* to the state interest in protecting private persons who have been defamed. It was because the *Rosenbloom* approach did not afford sufficient recognition of this state interest that the *Gertz* Court found it unacceptable and sounded the death knell for the "public or general interest" test as a constitutional requirement. See Anderson, Libel and Press Self-Censorship, 53 Texas L.Rev. 422, 445 (1975) ; Brosnahan, From Times v. Sullivan to Gertz v. Welch: Ten Years of Balancing Libel Law and the First Amendment, 26 Hastings L.J. 777, 791–92 (1975) ; Comment, The Law of Libel—Constitutional Privilege and The Private Individual: Round Two—Gertz v. Robert Welch, Inc., 12 San Diego L.Rev. 455, 466 (1975) ; Note, Gertz v. Welch: Reviving the Libel Action, 48 Temp.L.Q. 450, 459 (1975). * * *

Undeniably, the *Gertz* holding effects sweeping changes in the law of defamation. The Court seeks to eliminate in cases of private plaintiffs the threat of self-censorship, the very objective of the *New York Times* rule, but instead of shielding the media from private plaintiffs with the *New York Times* privilege, it does so by protecting them against strict liability as well as presumed and punitive damages. Beyond this, the states are free to fashion their own rules. We read *Gertz* to apply to actions brought by private persons regardless of whether the subject matter of the defamation is one of public or general interest. * * *

II

This case also presents the question whether a non-media defendant, such as Jacron, is within the class of defendants to be afforded the protection of the *Gertz* holding. It is plain that the holding in *Gertz* was limited to media expression. See Brosnahan, supra, 26 Hastings L.J. at 792–93; Frakt, The Evolving Law of Defamation: New York Times Co. v. Sullivan to Gertz v. Robert Welch, Inc. and Beyond, 6 Rutgers-Camden L.J. 471, 507–509 (1975); Nimmer, Introduction—Is Freedom of the Press a Redundancy: What Does it Add to Freedom of Speech? 26 Hastings L.J. 639, 649–50 (1975); see also Restatement of Torts, Second § 580B, Comment e (Tent. Draft No. 21, 1975). Apart from the fact that the defendant in *Gertz* was a member of the media, whose defamatory act consisted of the publication of a libelous statement, the majority opinion is riddled with references to "publishers and broadcasters," "the press and broadcast media," and "the news media." Similar terms appear in the concurring opinion of Justice Blackmun and the dissenting opinions of the Chief Justice and Justice Brennan. Justice White stands alone in his view that *Gertz* applies to all defamation actions. We must nevertheless make an informed prediction as to whether at some future date the Supreme Court will extend the *Gertz* holding to defamatory expression of any kind by non-media defendants. Even if we were to decide here that the Court will not so extend *Gertz,* we would consider whether, in any event, we should do so as a matter of state law.

The history of *New York Times* provides an instructive analogy. Although that case arose in a media context, the holding contained no caveat restricting its application to media publications; nor has the Supreme Court hesitated to apply it in non-media cases. In Garrison v. Louisiana, 379 U.S. 64, 85 S.Ct. 209, 13 L.Ed.2d 125 (1964), the defamatory comments were made during a press conference, and in St. Amant v. Thompson, 390 U.S. 727, 88 S.Ct. 1323, 20 L.Ed.2d 262 (1968), they were made during a televised speech. In both instances, the media merely served as a vehicle for the defamatory statements by the defendants and the Court focused on free speech and public debate rather than on the protection of the media. In Henry v. Collins, 380 U.S. 356, 85 S.Ct. 992, 13 L.Ed.2d 892 (1965), the Court in a short per curiam opinion applied *New York Times* where an individual who had been arrested by a police chief charged in a letter to a deputy sheriff and in a statement read to several wire services that the arrest was a "diabolical plot." Similarly, in non-media cases arising from labor disputes the Court has found the constitutional privilege applicable. Letter Carriers v. Austin, 418 U.S. 264, 94 S.Ct. 2770, 41 L.Ed.2d 745 (1974); Linn v. Plant Guard Workers, 383 U.S. 53, 86 S.Ct. 657, 15 L.Ed.2d 582 (1966). A number of lower courts have also applied the *New York Times* standard in non-media cases, and one court has applied *New York Times* in an action by an officer of a private club for defamations arising out of communications between club members concerning his activities. Evans v. Lawson, 351 F. Supp. 279 (W.D.Va.1972).

Nor do we discern any persuasive basis for distinguishing media and non-media cases. The rationale for the application of a constitutional privilege in *New York Times, Curtis* and *Gertz* is that the defense of truth is not alone sufficient to assure free and open discussion of important issues. Issues of public interest may equally be discussed in media and non-media contexts, and the need for a constitutional privilege, therefore, obtains in either case. See Restatement of Torts, Second § 580A, Comment h (Tent. Draft No. 21, 1975); but cf. Nimmer, supra. The proposition that the press enjoys greater rights than members of the public generally was rejected by the Supreme Court in Pell v. Procunier, 417 U.S. 817, 834–35, 94 S.Ct. 2800, 41 L.Ed.2d 495 (1974), where a newspaper argued that it had a constitutional right to interview inmates of a state correctional system despite a regulation prohibiting such contacts.

Wholly apart from any possible Supreme Court holding in the future based on constitutional grounds, we conclude as a matter of state law that the *Gertz* holding should apply to media and non-media defendants alike, and to both libel and slander. As one commentator stated:

> "* * * Regardless of constitutional strictures, it would be a bizarre result as a matter of tort law to hold individual defendants liable without fault while the media were liable only for negligence. The standard tort rationale for strict liability is that it serves to spread the cost of injury over all the users of a given product; in short, it is a theory of enterprise liability. Further, an individual's defamatory statement is, on the whole, likely to create a smaller risk of harm than a media publication. Finally, the media are more likely to be aware of the risk of liability, and thus more likely to insure against it. * * *" The Supreme Court, 1973 Term, 88 Harv.L.Rev. 41; 148 n. 52 (1974).

Any rule according less favorable treatment to certain types of non-media defendants might well present "difficult questions concerning the roles of the press and other speakers in our society." Anderson, supra, 53 Texas L.Rev. at 442–43 n. 95. Furthermore, most non-media private defamations arise in the context of one of the common law privileges; "[t]he completely gratuitous private defamation is rare." Thus, experience suggests that liability without fault is unusual in non-media private defamation cases. Frakt, supra, 6 Rutgers-Camden L.J. at 511.

Yet another reason for applying the *Gertz* holding to non-media defendants and to slander as well as libel is the compelling need for consistency and simplicity in the law of defamation. To limit the *Gertz* principles to media defendants and to cases of libel would mean one test, that of *New York Times,* for defamation of public officials and figures; another, which imposes a greater degree of proof than strict liability, and bans presumed and punitive damages, for cases brought by private plaintiffs against media defendants; and at least one more based on existing common law principles for all other defamation, an area of tort law which wholly apart from the advent of constitutional considerations, has traditionally been noted for its complexity. The rationale for applying the *Gertz* holding to non-media defendants and to slander as well as libel is aptly stated in the Restatement of Torts, Second § 580B, Comment e (Tent. Draft No. 21, 1975):

> "* * * As the Supreme Court declares, the protection of the First Amendment extends to freedom of speech as well as to freedom of the press, and the interests which must be balanced to obtain a proper accommodation are similar. It would seem strange to hold that the press, composed of professionals and causing much greater damage because of the wider distribution of the communication, can constitutionally be held liable only for negligence, but that a private person, engaged in a casual private conversation with a single person, can be held liable at his peril if the statement turns out to be false, without any regard to his lack of fault.
>
> "* * * There is little reason to conclude that the states would now be disposed to take the traditional strict liability approach for libel actions against the communications media, which has now been declared unconstitutional, and apply it to slander actions against private individuals, where it has not previously been significant."

III

We hold, therefore, that the rules announced in *Gertz* apply to cases of libel and slander alike brought against non-media defendants. Consequently, the principles of *Gertz* are applicable to the instant case. We must here decide, however, the standard of liability which should govern this case, recognizing that there cannot be recovery on strict liability. While holding that "so long as they do not impose liability without fault, the States may define for themselves the appropriate standard of liability," 418 U.S. at 347, the *Gertz* Court left little doubt of its assumption that most states would adopt a negligence standard. At one point, the Court stated: "Our inquiry would involve considerations somewhat different from those discussed above if a State purported to condition civil liability on a factual misstatement whose content did not warn a *reasonably prudent* editor or broadcaster of its defamatory potential." Id. at 348 (emphasis added).

In prohibiting punitive damages, the Court stated that such "damages are wholly irrelevant to the state interest that justifies a negligence standard for private defamation actions." Id. at 350. Justice Blackmun, concurring, flatly states that "the Court now conditions a libel action by a private person upon a showing of negligence * * *," id. at 353, and Chief Justice Burger characterizes the majority opinion as introducing to defamation law the concept of "negligence," id. at 355. Justice Brennan refers to "a reasonable-care standard," id. at 366, and Justice White's dissent contains similar language.

Nevertheless, we are free to adopt a stricter standard than negligence. In the wake of the *Gertz* decision, courts in Colorado, Walker v. Colorado Springs Sun, Inc., —— Colo. ——, 538 P.2d 450 (1975), cert. denied 44 U.S.L.W. 3342 (U.S. Dec. 9, 1975), and in Indiana, AAFCO Heating & Air Con. Co. v. Northwest Pub., Inc., 321 N.E.2d 580 (Ind.App.1974), both media-defendant and private-plaintiff cases, have opted, as a matter of state law, for the adoption of the *New York Times* standard of knowing falsity or reckless disregard, but only where the defamatory matter is of public or general interest. The Supreme Court of Illinois, however, in Troman v. Kingsley Wood, No. 47429 (Sup.Ct.Ill., filed November 25, 1975), a case involving a media-defendant and a private plaintiff, chose a standard of negligence. And in another case decided after *Gertz,* in which a private plaintiff alleged a defamation by a media-defendant, a negligence standard was adopted "even though the libel occurred in the reporting of an event of public or general concern." Stone v. Essex County Newspapers, Inc., —— Mass. ——, 330 N.E.2d 161, 164 (1975). Cf. Gobin v. Globe Publishing Co., 216 Kan. 223, 531 P.2d 76 (1975) (negligence standard adopted in case of private plaintiff and media defendant for defamation in reporting judicial proceedings).

In the only other post-*Gertz* case, of which we are aware, that has considered the question, the Wisconsin Supreme Court, in Calero v. Del Chemical Corp., 68 Wisc.2d 487, 228 N.W.2d 737 (1975), a case which also involved a defamation suit by a private individual against his former employer and thus not involving the media, retained its common law test. It concluded that *Gertz,* by its own terms, did not literally apply because of the non-media defendant context presented in the Wisconsin case. We decline to follow that authority, since the court there simply limited its examination to the question of whether it was bound by *Gertz.*

The adoption of a negligence standard in cases of purely private defamation hardly introduces a radical concept to tort law. The application of the negligence standard in tort cases is so well established that juries can safely be expected to comprehend the term when applied in defamation cases. Nor is the negligence standard unknown to common law defamation. In some jurisdictions, the lack of a reasonable ground to believe in the truth of a published statement is deemed sufficient to defeat a common law conditional privilege. See 1 F. Harper & F. James, Law of Torts § 5.27 n. 16 (1956), and the cases therein cited; Restatement of Torts § 601 (1938). And in connection with the issue of publication, the usual rule of strict liability has been relaxed in favor of a negligence standard. W. Prosser, Law of Torts § 113 (4th ed. 1971).

We hold, therefore, that a standard of negligence, as set forth in Restatement of Torts, Second § 580B (Tent. Draft No. 21, 1975), which we here adopt, must be applied in cases of purely private defamation. Section 580B states:

"§ 580B. Defamation of Private Person.

"One who publishes a false and defamatory communication concerning a private person, or concerning a public official or public figure in relation to a purely private matter not affecting his conduct, fitness or role in his public capacity, is subject to liability, if, but only if, he

"(a) Knows that the statement is false and that it defames the other,

"(b) acts in reckless disregard of these matters, or

"(c) acts negligently in failing to ascertain them."

It is to be noted that under the negligence standard which we adopt here, truth is no longer an affirmative defense to be established by the defendant, but instead the burden of proving falsity rests upon the plaintiff, since, under this standard, he is already required to establish negligence with respect to such falsity.

We turn, then, to the quantum of proof by which the plaintiff must establish the fault of the defendant. We address the question merely to dispel any possible notion that the plaintiff must prove negligence by "clear and convincing" evidence. The "clear and convincing" test, applied in the public-official and public-figure sphere, apparently derives from the *New York Times* requirement of "convincing clarity," 376 U.S. at 285–86, with respect to the "actual malice" standard articulated there. See Rosenbloom v. Metromedia, supra, 403 U.S. at 30. The *Gertz* opinion, however, does not suggest that the standard of clear and convincing proof must be applied in the negligence context, saying only that the states may adopt any standard except strict liability.

* * *

IV

* * *

[The court discusses the showing necessary to overcome common law conditional privileges, expressed in Maryland as "actual malice" or "express malice", requiring more than negligence, at least "reckless disregard" of truth, and draws attention to the difference between § 601 of the first Restatement of Torts (" * * * no reasonable grounds for so believing * * * ") and § 600 of Restatement of Torts, Second (Tent. Draft No. 21, 1975) (" * * * knows * * * or acts in reckless disregard * * *).]

* * * We agree with the Court of Special Appeals that the trial court erred in ruling that there was insufficient evidence of malice, as defined in our cases, to defeat the conditional privilege. Reasonable minds could have concluded that the suggestion of Sindorf's discharge for stealing was not only false, but far exceeded the facts that had been related to Fridkis by the corporation president who had done little more than instruct him to verify Sindorf's employment. This was evidence on which a finding by the trier of fact of malice in the form of reckless disregard of truth overcoming the conditional privilege could have been based. Hence, the Court of Special Appeals was correct in reversing the judgment of the circuit court and in remanding the case for a new trial.

Unless a conditional privilege is found to have existed, the plaintiff shall be required at the new trial of this case to establish the liability of the defendant through proof of negligence by the preponderance of the evidence, and may recover compensation for actual injury, as defined in *Gertz* and outlined earlier, but neither presumed nor punitive damages, unless he establishes liability under the more demanding *New York Times* standard of knowing falsity or reckless disregard for the truth. Should the court determine that a common law conditional privilege existed, the question of its forfeiture vel non shall be governed by the views expressed herein.[37]

TIME, INC. v. FIRESTONE

United States Supreme Court, 1976.
— U.S. —, 96 S.Ct. 958, 47 L.Ed.2d 154.

MR. JUSTICE REHNQUIST delivered the opinion of the Court.

Petitioner is the publisher of Time, a weekly news magazine. The Supreme Court of Florida affirmed a $100,000 libel judgment against petitioner which was based on an item appearing in Time that purported to describe the result of domestic relations litigation between respondent and her husband. We granted certiorari * * to review petitioner's claim that the judgment violates its rights under the First and Fourteenth Amendments to the United States Constitution.

I

Respondent, Mary Alice Firestone, married Russell Firestone, the scion of one of America's wealthier industrial families, in 1961. In 1964, they separated, and respondent filed a complaint for separate maintenance in the Circuit Court of Palm Beach County, Fla.

37. For an extensive survey see Eaton, The American Law of Defamation Through Gertz v. Robert Welch, Inc. and Beyond: An Analytic Primer, 61 Va.L.Rev. 1349 (1975). Other post-*Gertz* decisions adopting a negligence standard for liability to private plaintiffs include Troman v. Wood, 62 Ill.2d 184, 340 N.E.2d 292 (1975) and Martin v. Griffin Television, Inc., — P.2d — (Okl.1976), both involving media defendants.

Her husband counterclaimed for divorce on grounds of extreme cruelty and adultery. After a lengthy trial the Circuit Court issued a judgment granting the divorce requested by respondent's husband. In relevant part the court's final judgment read:

> "This cause came on for final hearing before the court upon the plaintiff wife's second amended complaint for separate maintenance (alimony unconnected with the causes of divorce), the defendant husband's answer and counterclaim for divorce on grounds of extreme cruelty and adultery, and the wife's answer thereto setting up certain affirmative defenses. * * *
>
> * * *
>
> "According to certain testimony in behalf of the defendant, extramarital escapades of the plaintiff were bizarre and of an amatory nature which would have made Dr. Freud's hair curl. Other testimony, in plaintiff's behalf, would indicate that defendant was guilty of bounding from one bedpartner to another with the erotic zest of a satyr. The court is inclined to discount much of this testimony as unreliable. Nevertheless, it is the conclusion and finding of the court that neither party is domesticated, within the meaning of that term as used by the Supreme Court of Florida. * * *
>
> * * *
>
> "In the present case, it is abundantly clear from the evidence of marital discord that neither of the parties has shown the least susceptibility to domestication, and that the marriage should be dissolved.
>
> * * *
>
> "The premises considered, it is thereupon
>
> "ORDERED AND ADJUDGED as follows:
>
> "1. That the equities in this cause are with the defendant; that defendant's counterclaim for divorce be and the same is hereby granted, and the bonds of matrimony which have heretofore existed between the parties are hereby forever dissolved.
>
> * * *
>
> "4. That the defendant shall pay unto the plaintiff the sum of $3,000 per month as alimony beginning January 1, 1968, and a like sum on the first day of each and every month thereafter until the death or remarriage of the plaintiff. * * *"

Time's editorial staff, headquartered in New York, was alerted to the fact that a judgment had been rendered in the Firestone divorce proceeding by a wire service report and an account in a

New York newspaper. The staff subsequently received further information regarding the Florida decision from Time's Miami bureau chief and from a "stringer" working on a special assignment basis in the Palm Beach area. On the basis of these four sources, Time's staff composed the following item which appeared in the magazine's "Milestones" section the following week:

> "DIVORCED. By Russell A. Firestone Jr., 41, heir to the tire fortune: Mary Alice Sullivan Firestone, 32, his third wife; a onetime Palm Beach schoolteacher; on grounds of extreme cruelty and adultery; after six years of marriage, one son; in West Palm Beach, Fla. The 17-month intermittent trial produced enough testimony of extramarital adventures on both sides, said the judge, 'to make Dr. Freud's hair curl.' "

Within a few weeks of the publication of this article respondent demanded in writing a retraction from petitioner, alleging that a portion of the article was "false, malicious and defamatory." Petitioner declined to issue the requested retraction.[38]

Respondent then filed this libel action against petitioner in the Florida Circuit Court. Based on a jury verdict for respondent, that court entered judgment against petitioner for $100,000, and after review in both the Florida District Court of Appeal and the Supreme Court of Florida the judgment was ultimately affirmed. Petitioner advances several contentions as to why the judgment is contrary to decisions of this Court holding that the First and Fourteenth Amendments of the United States Constitution limit the authority of state courts to impose liability for damages based on defamation.

II

Petitioner initially contends that it cannot be liable for publishing any falsehood defaming respondent unless it is established that the publication was made "with actual malice," as that term is defined in New York Times Co. v. Sullivan, 376 U.S. 254, 84 S.Ct. 710, 11 L.Ed.2d 686 (1964). Petitioner advances two arguments in support of this contention: that respondent is a "public figure" within this Court's decisions extending *New York Times* to defamation suits brought by such individuals. See, e. g., Curtis Publishing Co. v. Butts, 388 U.S. 130, 87 S.Ct. 1975, 18 L.Ed.2d 1094 (1967); and that the Time item constituted a report of a judicial proceeding, a class of subject matter which petitioner claims deserves the protection of the "actual malice" standard even if the story is proven to be defamatorily false or inaccurate. We reject both arguments.

38. Under Florida law the demand for retraction was a prerequisite for filing a libel action, and permits defendants to limit their potential liability to actual damages by complying with the demand. Fla.Stat.Ann. §§ 770.01–770.02 (1963).

In Gertz v. Robert Welch, Inc., 418 U.S. 323, 94 S.Ct. 2997, 41 L.Ed.2d 323 (1974), we have recently further defined the meaning of "public figure" for the purposes of the First and Fourteenth Amendments:

> "For the most part those who attain this status have assumed roles of especial prominence in the affairs of society. Some occupy positions of such persuasive power and influence that they are deemed public figures for all purposes. More commonly, those classed as public figures have thrust themselves to the forefront of particular public controversies in order to influence the resolution of the issues involved."

Respondent did not assume any role of especial prominence in the affairs of society, other than perhaps Palm Beach society, and she did not thrust herself to the forefront of any particular public controversy in order to influence the resolution of the issues involved in it.

Petitioner contends that because the Firestone divorce was characterized by the Florida Supreme Court as a "cause célèbre," it must have been a public controversy and respondent must be considered a public figure. But in so doing petitioner seeks to equate "public controversy" with all controversies of interest to the public. Were we to accept this reasoning, we would reinstate the doctrine advanced in the plurality opinion in Rosenbloom v. Metromedia, Inc., 403 U.S. 29, 91 S.Ct. 1811, 29 L.Ed.2d 296 (1971), which concluded that the *New York Times* privilege should be extended to falsehoods defamatory of private persons whenever the statements concern matters of general or public interest. In *Gertz,* however, the Court repudiated this position, stating that "extension of the *New York Times* test proposed by the *Rosenbloom* plurality would abridge [a] legitimate state interest to a degree that we find unacceptable." 418 U.S., at 346.

Dissolution of a marriage through judicial proceedings is not the sort of "public controversy" referred to in *Gertz,* even though the marital difficulties of extremely wealthy individuals may be of interest to some portion of the reading public. Nor did respondent freely choose to publicize issues as to the propriety of her married life. She was compelled to go to court by the State in order to obtain legal release from the bonds of matrimony. We have said that in such an instance "[r]esort to the judicial process * * * is no more voluntary in a realistic sense than that of the defendant called upon to defend his interests in court." Boddie v. Connecticut, 401 U.S. 311, 376, 91 S.Ct. 780, 28 L.Ed.2d 113 (1971). Her actions, both in instituting the litigation and in its conduct, were quite different from those of General Walker in Curtis Publishing Co., supra.[39] She assumed no "special prominence in the resolution of public questions." *Gertz,* 418 U.S., at 351. We hold respondent was not a "public figure" for the purpose of determining the constitutional protection afforded petitioner's report of the factual and legal basis for her divorce.

For similar reasons we likewise reject petitioner's claim for automatic extension of the *New York Times* privilege to all reports of judicial proceedings. It is argued that information concerning proceedings in our Nation's courts may have such importance to all citizens as to justify extending special First Amendment protection to the press when reporting on such events. We have recently accepted a significantly more confined version of this argument by holding that the Constitution precludes States from imposing civil liability based upon the publication of truthful information contained in official court records open to public inspection. Cox Broadcasting Corp. v. Cohn, 420 U.S. 469, 95 S.Ct. 1029, 43 L.Ed.2d 328 (1975).

Petitioner would have us extend the reasoning of *Cox Broadcasting* to safeguard even inaccurate and false statements, at least where "actual malice" has not been established. But its argument proves too much. It may be that all reports of judicial proceedings contain some informational value implicating the First Amendment, but recognizing this is little different from labeling all judicial proceedings matters of "public or general interest," as that phrase was used by the plurality in *Rosenbloom.* Whatever their general validity, use of such subject matter classifications to determine the extent of constitutional protection afforded defamatory falsehoods may too often result in an improper balance between the competing interests in this area. It was our recognition and rejection of this weakness in the *Rosenbloom* test which led us in *Gertz* to eschew a subject matter test for one focusing upon the character of the defamation plaintiff. * * * By confining inquiry to whether a plaintiff is a public officer or a public figure who might be assumed to "have voluntarily exposed themselves to increased risk of injury from defamatory falsehood," we sought a more appropriate accommodation between the public's interest in an uninhibited press and its equally compelling need for judicial redress of libelous utterances. Cf. Chaplinsky v. New Hampshire, 315 U.S. 568, 62 S.Ct. 766, 86 L.Ed. 1031 (1942).

Presumptively erecting the *New York Times* barrier against all plaintiffs seeking to recover for injuries from defamatory falsehoods

39. Nor do we think the fact that respondent may have held a few press conferences during the divorce proceedings in an attempt to satisfy inquiring reporters converts her into a "public figure." Such interviews should have had no effect upon the merits of the legal dispute between respondent and her husband or the outcome of that trial, and we do not think it can be assumed that any such purpose was intended. Moreover, there is no indication that she sought to use the press conferences as a vehicle by which to thrust herself to the forefront of some unrelated controversy in order to influence its resolution. See Gertz v. Robert Welch, Inc., 418 U.S. 323, 345, 94 S.Ct. 2997, 41 L.Ed.2d 789 (1974).

published in what are alleged to be reports of judicial proceedings would effect substantial depreciation of the individual's interest in protection from such harm, without any convincing assurance that such a sacrifice is required under the First Amendment. And in some instances such an undiscriminating approach might achieve results directly at odds with the constitutional balance intended. Indeed, the article upon which the *Gertz* libel action was based purported to be a report on the murder trial of a Chicago police officer. * * * Our decision in that case should make it clear that no such blanket privilege for reports of judicial proceedings is to be found in the Constitution.

It may be argued that there is still room for application of the *New York Times* protections to more narrowly focused reports of what actually transpires in the courtroom. But even so narrowed, the suggested privilege is simply too broad. Imposing upon the law of private defamation the rather drastic limitations worked by *New York Times* cannot be justified by generalized references to the public interest in reports of judicial proceedings. The details of many, if not most, courtroom battles would add almost nothing towards advancing the uninhibited debate on public issues thought to provide principal support for the decision in *New York Times.* * * * And while participants in some litigation may be legitimate "public figures," either generally or for the limited purpose of that litigation, the majority will more likely resemble respondent, drawn into a public forum largely against their will in order to attempt to obtain the only redress available to them or to defend themselves against actions brought by the State or by others. There appears little reason why these individuals should substantially forfeit that degree of protection which the law of defamation would otherwise afford them simply by virtue of their being drawn into a courtroom. The public interest in accurate reports of judicial proceedings is substantially protected by *Cox Broadcasting Co.,* supra. As to inaccurate and defamatory reports of facts, matters deserving no First Amendment protection, see 418 U.S., at 340, we think *Gertz* provides an adequate safeguard for the constitutionally protected interests of the press and affords it a tolerable margin for error by requiring some type of fault.

III

Petitioner has urged throughout this litigation that it could not be held liable for publication of the "Milestones" item because its report of respondent's divorce was factually correct. In its view the Time article faithfully reproduced the precise meaning of the divorce judgment. But this issue was submitted to the jury under an instruction intended to implement Florida's limited privilege for accurate reports of judicial proceedings * * * By returning a verdict for respondent the jury necessarily found that the identity of meaning which petitioner claims does not exist even for laymen. The Supreme Court of Florida upheld this finding on appeal, rejecting petitioner's contention that its report was accurate as a matter of law. Because demonstration that an article was true would seem to preclude finding the publisher at fault, see *Cox Broadcasting Co.*, 420 U.S., at 498–500 (POWELL, J., concurring), we have examined the predicate for petitioner's contention. We believe the Florida courts properly could have found the "Milestones" item to be false.

For petitioner's report to have been accurate, the divorce granted Russell Firestone must have been based on a finding by the divorce court that his wife had committed extreme cruelty towards him *and* that she had been guilty of adultery. This is indisputably what petitioner reported in its "Milestones" item, but it is equally indisputable that these were not the facts. Russell Firestone alleged in his counterclaim that respondent had been guilty of adultery, but the divorce court never made any such finding. Its judgment provided that Russell Firestone's "counterclaim for divorce be and the same is hereby granted," but did not specify that the basis for the judgment was either of the two grounds alleged in the counterclaim. The Supreme Court of Florida on appeal concluded that the ground actually relied upon by the divorce court was "lack of domestication of the parties," a ground not theretofore recognized by Florida law. The Supreme Court nonetheless affirmed the judgment dissolving the bonds of matrimony because the record contained sufficient evidence to establish the ground of extreme cruelty. * * *

Petitioner may well argue that the meaning of the trial court's decree was unclear, but this does not license it to choose from among several conceivable interpretations the one most damaging to respondent. Having chosen to follow this tack, petitioner must be able to establish not merely that the item reported was a conceivable or plausible interpretation of the decree, but that the item was factually correct. We believe there is ample support for the jury's conclusion, affirmed by the Supreme Court of Florida, that this was not the case. There was, therefore, sufficient basis for imposing liability upon petitioner if the constitutional limitations we announced in *Gertz* have been satisfied. These are a prohibition against imposing liability without fault * * * and the requirement that compensatory awards "be supported by competent evidence concerning the injury." * * *

As to the latter requirement little difficulty appears. Petitioner has argued that because respondent withdrew her claim for damages to reputation on the eve of trial, there could be no recovery consistent with *Gertz*. Petitioner's theory seems to be that the only compensable injury in a defamation action is that which may be done to one's reputation, and that claims not predicated upon such injury are by definition not actions for defamation. But Florida has obviously decided to permit recovery for other injuries without regard to measuring the effect the falsehood may have had upon a plaintiff's reputation. This does not transform the action into something other than an action for defamation as that term is meant in *Gertz*. In that opinion we made it clear that States could base awards on elements other than injury to reputation, specifically listing "personal humiliation, and mental anguish and suffering" as examples of injuries which might be compensated consistently with the Constitution upon a showing of fault. Because respondent has decided to forgo recovery for injury to her reputation, she is not prevented from obtaining compensation for such other damages that a defamatory falsehood may have caused her.

The trial court charged, consistently with *Gertz,* that the jury should award respondent compensatory damages in "an amount of money that will fairly and adequately compensate her for such damages," and further cautioned that "It is only damages which are a direct and natural result of the alleged libel which may be recovered." * * * There was competent evidence introduced to permit the jury to assess the amount of injury. Several witnesses[40] testified to the extent of respondent's anxiety and concern over Time inaccurately reporting that she had been found guilty of adultery, and she herself took the stand to elaborate on her fears that her young son would be adversely affected by this falsehood when he grew older. The jury decided these injuries should be compensated by an award of $100,000. We have no warrant for re-examining this determination. * * *

IV

Gertz established, however, that not only must there be evidence to support an award of compensatory damages, there must also be evidence of some fault on the part of a defendant charged with publishing defamatory material. No question of fault was submitted to the jury in this case, because under Florida law the only findings required for determination of liability were whether the article was defamatory, whether it was true, and whether the defamation, if any, caused respondent harm.

The failure to submit the question of fault to the jury does not, of itself establish noncompliance with the constitutional requirements established in *Gertz,* however. Nothing in the Constitution requires that assessment of fault in a civil case tried in a state court be made by a jury, nor is there any prohibition against such a finding being made in the first instance by an appellate, rather than a trial, court. The First and Fourteenth Amendments do not impose upon the States any limitations as to how, within their own judicial systems, factfinding tasks shall be allocated. If we were satisfied that one of the Florida courts which considered this case had supportably ascertained petitioner was at fault, we would be required to affirm the judgment below.

40. These included respondent's minister, her attorney in the divorce proceedings, plus several friends and neighbors, one of whom was a physician and testified to having to administer a sedative to respondent in an attempt to reduce discomfort wrought by her worrying about the article.

But the only alternative source of such a finding, given that the issue was not submitted to the jury, is the opinion of the Supreme Court of Florida. That opinion appears to proceed generally on the assumption that a showing of fault was not required,[41] but then in the penultimate paragraph it recites:

> "Furthermore, this erroneous reporting is clear and convincing evidence of the negligence in certain segments of the news media in gathering the news, Gertz v. Welch, Inc., supra. Pursuant to Florida law in effect at the time of the divorce judgment (Section 61.08, Florida Statutes), a wife found guilty of adultery could not be awarded alimony. Since petitioner had been awarded alimony, she had not been found guilty of adultery nor had the divorce been granted on the ground of adultery. A careful examination of the final decree prior to publication would have clearly demonstrated that the divorce had been granted on the grounds of extreme cruelty, and thus the wife would have been saved the humiliation of being accused of adultery in a nationwide magazine. This is a flagrant example of 'journalistic negligence.'" 304 So.2d, at 178.

It may be argued this is sufficient indication the court found petitioner at fault within the meaning of *Gertz.* Nothing in that decision or in the First or Fourteenth Amendments requires that in a libel action an appellate court treat in detail by written opinion all contentions of the parties, and if the jury or trial judge had found fault in fact, we would be quite wiling to read the quoted passage as affirming that conclusion. But without some finding of fault by the judge or jury in the Circuit Court, we would have to attribute to the Supreme Court of Florida from the quoted language not merely an intention to affirm the finding of the lower court, but an intention to find such a fact in the first instance.

Even where a question of fact may have constitutional significance, we normally accord findings of state courts deference in reviewing constitutional claims here. * * * But that deference

41. After reiterating its conclusion that the article was false, the Florida court noted that falsely accusing a woman of adultery is libelous *per se* and normally actionable without proof of damages. The court then recognized that our opinion in *Gertz* necessarily displaced this presumption of damages but ruled that the trial court's instruction was consistent with *Gertz* and that there was evidence to support the jury's verdict—conclusions with which we have agreed. The court went on to reject a claim of privilege under state law, pointing out that the privilege shielded only "fair and accurate" reports and the jury had resolved these issues against petitioner. The court appears to have concluded its analysis of petitioner's legal claims with this statement, which immediately precedes the paragraph set out in the text:
"Careful examination and consideration of the record discloses that the judgment of the trial court is correct and should have been affirmed on appeal to the District Court." 305 So.2d, at 177–178.

There is nothing in the court's opinion which appears to make any reference to the relevance of some concept of fault in determining petitioner's liability.

is predicated on our belief that at some point in the state proceedings some factfinder has made a conscious determination of the existence or nonexistence of the critical fact. Here the record before us affords no basis for such a conclusion.

It may well be that petitioner's account in its "Milestones" section was the product of some fault on its part, and that the libel judgment against it was, therefore, entirely consistent with *Gertz*. But in the absence of a finding in some element of the state court system that there was fault, we are not inclined to canvass the record to make such a determination in the first instance. Cf. Rosenblatt v. Baer, 383 U.S. 75, 87–88, 86 S.Ct. 669, 15 L.Ed.2d 597 (1966). Accordingly, the judgment of the Supreme Court of Florida is vacated and the case remanded for further proceedings not inconsistent with this opinion.

So ordered.

MR. JUSTICE STEVENS took no part in the consideration or decision of this case.

* * *

MR. JUSTICE POWELL, with whom MR. JUSTICE STEWART joins, concurring.

A clear majority of the Court adheres to the principles of Gertz v. Robert Welch, Inc., 418 U.S. 323, 94 S.Ct. 2997, 41 L.Ed.2d 789 (1974). But it is evident from the variety of views expressed that perceptions differ as to the proper application of such principles to this bizarre case. In order to avoid the appearance of fragmentation of the Court on the basic principles involved, I join the opinion of the Court. I add this concurrence to state my reaction to the record presented for our review.

In *Gertz* we held that "so long as they do not impose liability without fault, the States may define for themselves the appropriate standard of liability for a publisher or broadcaster of defamatory falsehood injurious to a private individual." Id., at 347. Thus, while a State may elect to hold a publisher to a lesser duty of care,[42] there is no First Amendment constraint against allowing recovery upon proof of negligence. The applicability of such a fault standard was expressly limited to circumstances where, as here, "the substance of the defamatory falsehood makes 'substantial danger to reputation apparent.'" * * *[43] By requiring a showing of fault the Court in *Gertz* sought to shield the press and broadcast media from a rule of strict liability that could lead to intolerable

42. A State, if it elected to do so, could require proof of gross negligence before holding a publisher or broadcaster liable for defamation. In *Gertz*, we concluded "that the States should retain substantial latitude in their efforts to enforce a legal remedy for defamatory falsehood injurious to the reputation of a private individual." 418 U.S. at 345–346.

43. In amplification of this limitation, we referred to the type of "factual misstatement whose content [does] not warn a reasonably prudent editor or broadcaster of its defamatory potential." 418 U.S. at 348.

self-censorship and at the same time recognize the legitimate state interest in compensating private individuals for wrongful injury from defamatory falsehoods.

In one paragraph near the end of its opinion, the Supreme Court of Florida cited *Gertz* in concluding that Time was guilty of "journalistic negligence." But, as the opinion of the Court recognizes * * *, it is not evident from this single paragraph that any type of fault standard was in fact applied. Assuming that Florida now will apply a negligence standard in cases of this kind, the ultimate question here is whether Time exercised due care under the circumstances: did Time exercise the reasonably prudent care that a State may constitutionally demand of a publisher or broadcaster prior to a publication whose content reveals its defamatory potential?

The answer to this question depends upon a careful consideration of all the relevant evidence concerning Time's actions prior to the publication of the Milestones article. But in its conclusory paragraph finding negligence, the Supreme Court of Florida mentioned only the provision of Florida law that proscribed an award of alimony to a wife found guilty of adultery, arguing that the award of alimony to respondent clearly demonstrated that the divorce was granted on other grounds. There is no recognition in the opinion of the ambiguity of the divorce decree and no discussion of any of the efforts made by Time to verify the accuracy of its news report. Nor was there any weighing of the evidence to determine whether there was actionable negligence by Time under the *Gertz* standard.

There was substantial evidence, much of it uncontradicted, that the editors of Time exercised considerable care in checking the accuracy of the story prior to its publication. The Milestones item appeared in the December 22, 1967, issue of Time. This issue went to press on Saturday, December 16, the day after the Circuit Court rendered its decision at about 4:30 in the afternoon. The evening of the 15th the Time editorial staff in New York received an Associated Press dispatch stating that Russell A. Firestone, Jr., had been granted a divorce from his third wife, whom "he had accused of adultery and extreme cruelty." Later that same evening, Time received the New York Daily News edition for December 16, which carried a special bulletin substantially to the same effect as the AP dispatch.

On the morning of December 16, in response to an inquiry sent to its Miami Bureau, Time's New York office received a dispatch from the head of that Bureau quoting excerpts from the Circuit Court's opinion that strongly suggested adultery on the part of both parties. Later that day the editorial staff received a message from Time's Palm Beach stringer that read, in part: "The technical grounds for divorce according to Joseph Farrish, Jr., attorney for Mary Alice Firestone, were given as extreme cruelty and adultry [*sic*]." App.

532. The stringer's dispatch also included several quotations from the Circuit Court opinion.[44] At trial the senior editor testified that although no member of the New York editorial staff had read the Circuit Court's opinion, he had believed that both the stringer and the chief of Time's Miami Bureau had read it.

The opaqueness of the Circuit Court's decree is also a factor to be considered in assessing whether Time was guilty of actionable fault under the *Gertz* standard. Although it appears that neither the head of the Miami Bureau nor the stringer personally read the opinion or order, the stringer testified at trial that respondent's attorney Farrish and others read him portions of the decree over the telephone before he filed his dispatch with Time.[45] The record does not reveal whether the limited portions of the decree that shed light on the grounds for the granting of the divorce were read to the stringer.[46] But the ambiguity of the divorce decree may well have contributed to the stringer's view, and hence the Time editorial staff's conclusion, that a ground for the divorce was adultery by respondent.

However one may characterize it, the Circuit Court decision was hardly a model of clarity. Its opening sentence was as follows

> "This cause came on for final hearing before the court upon the plaintiff wife's second amended complaint for separate maintenance (alimony unconnected with the causes of divorce), the defendant husband's answer and counterclaim for divorce on grounds of extreme cruelty and adultery, and the wife's answer thereto setting up certain affirmative defenses." * * *

After commenting on the conflicting testimony as to respondent's "extramarital escapades" and her husband's "bounding from one

44. Based on these news items and dispatches, the Time editorial team, consisting of a researcher, writer, and senior editor in charge of the Milestones section of the magazine, wrote, edited, and checked the article for accuracy. At trial they testified as to their complete belief in the truth of the news item at the time of publication.

45. Several hours after filing his dispatch, the stringer spoke with the divorce judge by telephone. According to testimony of the stringer at trial the divorce judge read him portions of the decree, and none of this information was inconsistent with that contained in his dispatch to Time; otherwise, he would have alerted Time's New York office immediately.

46. Time did not consider the stringer to be an employee. He worked for Time part-time and was compensated at an hourly rate, although he was guaranteed a minimum amount of work each year. In this case, he was contacted by the chief of the Miami Bureau and requested to investigate the Firestone divorce decree. There is thus a question whether the fault, if any, of the stringer in not personally reading the entire opinion and order, is even a factor that may be considered in assessing whether there was actionable fault by Time under *Gertz*. Cf. Cantrell v. Forest City Publishing Co., 419 U.S. 245, 253–254 (1974).

bedpartner to another," the opinion states that "it is the conclusion and finding of the court that neither party is domesticated. * * *" Finally, the Circuit Court "ORDERED AND ADJUDGED":

> "That the equities in this cause are with the defendant; that defendant's counterclaim for divorce be and the same is hereby granted, and the bonds of matrimony which have heretofore existed between the parties are hereby forever dissolved." * * *

The remaining paragraphs in the order portion of the decision relate to child custody and support, disposition of certain property, attorney's fees, and the award of $3,000 per month to the wife (respondent) as alimony. There is no reference whatever in the "order" portion of the decision either to "extreme cruelty" or "adultery," the only grounds relied upon by the husband. But the divorce was granted to him following an express finding "that the equities * * * are with the defendant [the husband]."

Thus, on the face of the opinion itself, the husband had counterclaimed for divorce on the grounds of extreme cruelty and adultery, the court had found the equities to be with him and had granted his counterclaim for divorce. Apart from the awarding of alimony to the wife there is no indication, either in the opinion or accompanying order, that the husband's counterclaim was not granted on both of the grounds asserted. This may be a redundant reading, as either ground would have sufficed. But the opinion that preceded the order was full of talk of adultery and made no explicit reference to any other type of cruelty. In these circumstances, the decision of the Circuit Court may have been sufficiently ambiguous to have caused reasonably prudent newsmen to read it as granting divorce on the ground of adultery.

As I join the opinion of the Court remanding this case, it is unnecessary to decide whether the foregoing establishes as a matter of law that Time exercised the requisite care under the circumstances. Nor have I undertaken to identify all of the evidence that may be relevant or to point out conflicts that arguably have been resolved against Time by the jury. My point in writing is to emphasize that, against the background of a notorious divorce case * * * and a decree that invited misunderstanding, there *was* substantial evidence supportive of Time's defense that it was not guilty of actionable negligence. At the very least the jury or court assessing liability in this case should have weighed these factors and this evidence before reaching a judgment.[47] There is no indication in the record before us that this was done in accordance with *Gertz.*

MR. JUSTICE BRENNAN, dissenting. * * *

47. Indeed, I agree with the view expressed by MR. JUSTICE MARSHALL in his dissenting opinion: unless there exists some basis for a finding of fault other than that given by the Supreme Court of Florida there can be no liability.

I

In a series of cases beginning with New York Times Co. v. Sullivan, 376 U.S. 254, 84 S.Ct. 710, 11 L.Ed.2d 686 (1964), this Court has held that the laws of libel and defamation, no less than other legal modes of restraint on the freedoms of speech and press, are subject to constitutional scrutiny under the First Amendment. The Court has emphasized the central meaning of the free expression guarantee is that the body politic of this Nation shall be entitled to the communications necessary for self-governance, and that to place restraints on the exercise of expression is to deny the instrumental means required in order that the citizenry exercise that ultimate sovereignty reposed in its collective judgment by the Constitution.[48] Accordingly, we have held that laws governing harm incurred by individuals through defamation or invasion of privacy, although directed to the worthy objective of ensuring the "essential dignity and worth of every human being" necessary to a civilized society, Rosenblatt v. Baer, 383 U.S. 75, 92, 86 S.Ct. 669, 15 L.Ed.2d 597 (1966) (STEWART, J., concurring), must be measured and limited by constitutional constraints assuring the maintenance and well-being of the system of free expression. Although "calculated falsehood" is no part of the expression protected by the central meaning of the First Amendment, Garrison v. Louisiana, 379 U.S. 64, 75, 85 S.Ct. 209, 13 L.Ed.2d 125 (1964), error and misstatement is recognized as inevitable in any scheme of truly free expression and debate. New York Times, 376 U.S., at 271–272. Therefore, in order to avoid the self-censorship that would necessarily accompany strict or simple fault liability for erroneous statements, rules governing liability for injury to reputation are required to allow an adequate margin for error—protecting some misstatements so that the "freedoms of expression * * * have the 'breathing space' that they 'need * * * to survive.'" Ibid. "[T]o insure the ascertainment and publication of the truth about public affairs, it is essential that the First Amendment protect some erroneous publications as well as true ones." St. Amant v. Thompson, 390 U.S. 727, 732, 88 S.Ct. 1323, 20 L.Ed.2d 262 (1968). For this reason, *New York Times* held that liability for defamation of a public official may not be imposed in the absence of proof of actual malice on the part of the person making the erroneous statement. Id., at 279–280.[49]

48. See Kalven, The New York Times Case: A Note on "The Central Meaning of the First Amendment," 1964 Sup.Ct.Rev. 191; Meiklejohn, The First Amendment Is An Absolute, 1961 Sup.Ct.Rev. 245. See also Bloustein, The First Amendment and Privacy: The Supreme Court Justice and the Philosopher, 28 Rut.L.Rev. 41 (1974); Meiklejohn, Public Speech in the Supreme Court Since New York Times v. Sullivan, 26 Syr.L.Rev. 819 (1975).

49. The protection of the actual malice test extends to erroneous statements that in any way "might touch on * * * [the] fitness for office" of a public official, Garrison v. Louisiana, 379 U.S., at 77, or a candidate for public office, Monitor Patriot Co. v. Roy, 401 U.S. 265, 274, 91 S.Ct. 621, 28 L.Ed.2d 35 (1971). The actual malice standard has been applied "at the very least to those among the hierarchy of government employees

Identical considerations led the Court last Term in Cox Broadcasting Corp. v. Cohn, 420 U.S. 469, 95 S.Ct. 1029, 43 L.Ed.2d 328 (1975), to hold that the First Amendment commands an absolute privilege to truthfully report the contents of public records reflecting the subject matter of judicial proceedings. Recognizing the possibility of injury to legitimate privacy interests of persons affected by such proceedings, the Court was nevertheless constrained in light of the strong First Amendment values involved to conclude that no liability whatever could be imposed by the State for reports damaging to those concerns. Following the reasoning of *New York Times* and its progeny, the Court in *Cox Broadcasting* noted that

> "* * * in a society in which each individual has but limited time and resources with which to observe at first hand the operations of his government, he relies necessarily upon the press to bring to him in convenient form the facts of those operations. Great responsibility is accordingly placed upon the news media to report fully and accurately the proceedings of government, and official records and documents open to the public are the basic data of governmental operations. Without the information provided by the press most of us and many of our representatives would be unable to vote intelligently or to register opinions on the administration of government generally. With respect to judicial proceedings in particular, the function of the press serves to guarantee the fairness of trials and to bring to bear the beneficial effects of public scrutiny upon the administration of justice.
>
> * * *
>
> "Public records by their very nature are of interest to those concerned with the administration of government, and a public benefit is performed by the reporting of the true contents of the records by the media. The freedom of the press to publish that information appears to us to be of

who have, or appear to the public to have, substantial responsibility for or control over the conduct of governmental affairs," Rosenblatt v. Baer, 383 U.S., at 85, and further to "public figures" who are "intimately involved in the resolution of important public questions or, by reason of their fame, shape events in areas of concern to society at large." Curtis Publishing Co. v. Butts, 388 U.S. 130, 164, 87 S.Ct. 1975, 18 L.Ed.2d 1094 (1967) (Warren, C. J., concurring in the result).

As an erroneous judgment of liability is, in view of the First Amendment values at stake, of more serious concern than an erroneous judgment in the opposite direction, Rosenbloom v. Metromedia, Inc., 403 U.S. 29, 50, 91 S.Ct. 1811, 29 L.Ed.2d 296 (1971), the Court has held that actual malice must be demonstrated with "convincing clarity." *New York Times*, 376 U.S., at 285–286. The actual malice standard requires a showing that the erroneous statements were made in knowing or reckless disregard of their falsity, id., at 280, and has been otherwise defined as requiring a showing that the statements were made by a person who in fact was entertaining "serious doubts" as to their truth. St. Amant v. Thompson, 390 U.S., at 731.

critical importance to our type of government in which the citizenry is the final judge of the proper conduct of public business." Id., at 491–492, 495.

Crucial to the holding in *Cox Broadcasting* was the determination that a "reasonable man" standard for imposing liability for invasion of privacy interests is simply inadequate to the task of safeguarding against "timidity and self-censorship" in reporting judicial proceedings. Id., at 496. Clearly, the inadequacy of any such standard is no less in the related area of liability for defamation resulting from inadvertent error in reporting such proceedings.

II

It is true, of course, that the Court in Gertz v. Robert Welch, Inc., 418 U.S. 323, 94 S.Ct. 2997, 41 L.Ed.2d 789 (1974), cut back on the scope of application of the *New York Times* privilege as it had evolved through the plurality opinion in Rosenbloom v. Metromedia, Inc., 403 U.S. 29, 91 S.Ct. 1811, 29 L.Ed.2d 296 (1971). *Rosenbloom* had held the *New York Times* privilege applicable to "all discussion and communication involving matters of public or general concern, without regard to whether the persons involved are famous or anonymous." * * * But in light of the Court's perception of an altered balance between the conflicting values at stake where the person defamed is in some sense a "private individual," *Gertz,* supra, at 347, 349–350, held First Amendment interests adequately protected in such circumstances so long as defamation liability is restricted to a requirement of "fault" and proof of "actual injury" resulting from the claimed defamation.[50] However, the exten-

50. In this case, the $100,000 damage award was premised entirely on the injury of mental pain and anguish. All claims as to injury to reputation were withdrawn prior to trial, and no evidence concerning damage to reputation was presented at trial. (Indeed, it appears that petitioner was affirmatively precluded from offering evidence to refute any possible jury assumption in this regard by a pretrial order granting "Plaintiff's Motion to Limit Testimony," App. 77). It seems clear that by allowing this type of recovery the State has subverted whatever protective influence the "actual injury" stricture may possess. *Gertz* would, of course, allow for an award of damages for such injury after proof of injury to reputation * * *. But to allow such damages without proof "by competent evidence" of any other "actual injury" is to do nothing less than return to the old rule of presumed damages supposedly outlawed by *Gertz* in instances where the *New York Times* standard is not met. * * * See Anderson, Libel and Press Self-Censorship, 53 Tex.L.Rev. 422, 472–473 (1975). Eaton, The American Law of Defamation through Gertz v. Robert Welch, Inc., and Beyond: An Analytical Primer, 61 Va.L.Rev. 1349, 1436–1437 (1975). The result is clearly to invite "gratuitous awards of money damages far in excess of any actual injury" and jury punishment of "unpopular opinions rather than [compensation to] individuals for injury sustained by the publication of a false fact." *Gertz,* supra, at 349.

Furthermore, the allowance of damages for mental suffering alone will completely abrogate the use of summary judgment procedures in defamation litigation. Cf. Anderson, supra, at 469 n. 218. The use of such summary procedures may be a critical factor enabling publishers to avoid large litigation expenses in marginal and frivolous defamation suits. The spectre of such expenses may be as potent a force for self-censorship as any threat of an ultimate damage award. See generally ibid.

sion of the relaxed standard of *Gertz* to news reporting of events transpiring in and decisions arising out of public judicial proceedings is unwarranted by the terms of *Gertz* itself, contrary to other well-established precedents of this Court and, most importantly, savaging of the cherished values encased in the First Amendment.

There is no indication in *Gertz* of any intention to overrule the *Rosenbloom* decision on its facts. Confined to those facts, *Rosenbloom* holds that in instances of erroneous reporting of the public actions of public officials, the *New York Times* actual malice standard must be met before liability for defamation may be imposed in favor of persons affected by those actions. Although *Gertz* clearly altered the broader rationale of *Rosenbloom,* until the Court's decision today it could not have been supposed that *Rosenbloom* did not remain the law roughly to the extent of my Brother WHITE's concurring statement therein:

> "[I]n defamation actions, absent actual malice as defined in New York Times Co. v. Sullivan, the First Amendment gives the press and the broadcast media a privilege to report and comment upon the official actions of public servants in full detail, with no requirement that the reputation or the privacy of an individual involved in or affected by the official action be spared from public view." Id., at 62.

At stake in the present case is the ability of the press to report to the citizenry the events transpiring in the Nation's judicial systems. There is simply no meaningful or constitutionally adequate way to report such events without reference to those persons and transactions that form the subject matter in controversy. * * *

Also no less true than in other areas of government, error in reporting and debate concerning the judicial process is inevitable. Indeed, in view of the complexities of that process and its unfamiliarity to the laymen who report it, the probability of inadvertent error may be substantially greater.

"There is perhaps no area of news more inaccurately reported factually, on the whole, though with some notable exceptions, than legal news.

"Some part of this is due to carelessness * * *. But a great deal of it must be attributed, in candor, to ignorance which frequently is not at all blameworthy. For newspapers are conducted by men who are laymen to the law. With too rare exceptions their capacity for misunderstanding the significance of legal events and procedures, not to speak of opinions, is great. But this is neither remarkable nor peculiar to newsmen. For the law, as lawyers best know, is full of perplexities.

"In view of these facts any standard which would require strict accuracy in reporting legal events factually or in commenting upon them in the press would be an impossible one. Unless the courts and judges are to be put above criticism, no such rule can obtain. There must be some room for misstatement of fact, as well as for misjudgment, if the press and others are to function as critical agencies in our democracy concerning courts as for all other instruments of government." Pennekamp v. Florida, 328 U.S. 331, 371–372, 66 S.Ct. 1029, 90 L.Ed. 1295 (1946) (Rutledge, J., concurring).[51]

* * *

MR. JUSTICE WHITE, dissenting.

I would affirm the judgment of the Florida Supreme Court because First Amendment values will not be furthered in any way by application to this case of the fault standards newly drafted and imposed by Gertz v. Robert Welch, Inc., 418 U.S. 323, 94 S.Ct. 2997, 41 L.Ed.2d 789 upon which my Brother REHNQUIST relies, or the fault standards required by Rosenbloom v. Metromedia, Inc., 403 U.S. 29, 91 S.Ct. 1811, 29 L.Ed.2d 296, upon which my Brother BRENNAN relies; and because, in any event, any requisite fault was properly found below.

The jury found on ample evidence that the article published by petitioner Time, Inc., about respondent Firestone was false and defamatory. This Court has held, and no one seriously disputes, that, regardless of fault, "there is no constitutional value in false statements of fact." "They belong to that category of utterances which '* * * are of such slight social value as' " to be worthy of no First Amendment protection. Gertz v. Robert Welch, Inc., 418 U.S., at 340, quoting Chaplinsky v. New Hampshire, 315 U.S. 568, 572, 62 S.Ct. 766, 86 L.Ed. 1031. This Court's decisions from New York Times Co. v. Sullivan, 376 U.S. 254, 84 S.Ct. 710, 11 L.Ed.2d 686, through Gertz v. Robert Welch, Inc., supra, holding that the Constitution requires a finding of some degree of fault as a precondition to a defamation award, have done so for one reason and one reason alone: unless innocent falsehood is allowed as a defense, some true speech will also be deterred. * * *

At the time of the defamatory publication in this case—December 1967—the law clearly authorized liability without fault in defamation cases of the sort involved here. Whatever the chilling effect of that rule of law on publication of "speech that matters" in 1967 might have been, it has already occurred and is now irremediable. The goal of protecting "speech that matters" by announcing rules, as this Court did in Gertz v. Welch, supra, and Rosenbloom v. Metromedia, Inc., 403 U.S. 29, 91 S.Ct. 1811, 29 L.Ed.2d 296 (1971), requiring fault as a precondition to a defamation recovery under circumstances such as are involved here, is *fully* achieved so long as fault is required for cases in which the publication occurred *after* the dates of those decisions. This is not such a case.

51. Judge Frank's opinion of the phenomenon and its cause appears to have been roughly comparable. J. Frank, Courts On Trial 1–3 (Antheneum ed. 1963). [Notes 38–51 from original, renumbered; other notes in original omitted.]

Therefore, to require proof of fault in this case—or in any other case predating *Gertz* and *Rosenbloom* in which a private figure is defamed—is to interfere with the State's otherwise legitimate policy of compensating defamation victims without furthering First Amendment goals *in any way at all.* In other areas in which the Court has developed a rule designed not to achieve justice in the case before it but designed to induce socially desirable conduct by some group in the future, the Court has declined to apply the rule to fact situations predating its announcement, e. g., Williams v. United States, 401 U.S. 646, 653, 91 S.Ct. 1148, 28 L.Ed.2d 388. The Court should follow a similar path here. * * *

MR. JUSTICE MARSHALL, dissenting.

The Court agrees with the Supreme Court of Florida that the "actual malice" standard of New York Times Co. v. Sullivan, 376 U.S. 254, 84 S.Ct. 710, 11 L.Ed.2d 686 (1964), does not apply to this case. Because I consider the respondent, Mary Alice Firestone, to be a "public figure" within the meaning of our prior decisions, Gertz v. Robert Welch, Inc., 418 U.S. 323, 94 S.Ct. 2997, 41 L.Ed.2d 789 (1974); Curtis Publishing Co. v. Butts, 388 U.S. 130, 87 S.Ct. 1975, 18 L.Ed.2d 1094 (1967), I respectfully dissent. * * *

I

Mary Alice Firestone was not a person "first brought to public attention by the defamation that is the subject of the lawsuit." Rosenbloom v. Metromedia, Inc., 403 U.S. 29, 78, 86, 91 S.Ct. 1811, 29 L.Ed. 2d 296 (1971) (MARSHALL, J., dissenting). On the contrary, she was "prominent among the '400' of Palm Beach Society," and an "active [member] of the sporting set," Firestone v. Time, Inc., 271 So. 2d 745, 751 (1972), whose activities predictably attracted the attention of a sizeable portion of the public. Indeed, Mrs. Firestone's appearances in the printed press were evidently frequent enough to warrant her subscribing to a press clipping service.

* * *

If *Gertz* is to have any meaning at all, the focus of analysis must be on the actions of the individual, and the degree of public attention that had already developed, or that could have been anticipated, before the report in question. Under this approach, the class of public figures must include an individual like Mrs. Firestone, who acquired a social prominence that could be expected to attract public attention, initiated a lawsuit that predictably attracted more public attention, and held press conferences in the course of and in regard to the lawsuit. I would hold that, for purposes of this case, Mrs. Firestone is a public figure, who must demonstrate that the report in question was published with "actual malice"—that is, with knowledge that it was false or with reckless disregard of whether it was false or not.

II

While the foregoing discussion is sufficient to dispose of the case under my reading of the law, two other aspects of the Court's opinion warrant comment. First, the Court appears to reject the contention that a rational interpretation of an ambiguous document is always entitled to some constitutional protection. * * *

* * * The choice of one of several rational interpretations of an ambiguous document, without more, is insufficient to support a finding of fault under *Gertz.*

Finally, assuming that the Court is correct in its assessment of the law in this case, I find the Court's disposition baffling. The Court quotes that portion of the Supreme Court of Florida's opinion which, citing *Gertz,* states in no uncertain terms that Time's report was a "flagrant example of 'journalistic negligence.'" Firestone v. Time, Inc., 305 So.2d 172, 178 (1974). But the Court is unwilling to read that statement as a "conscious determination" of fault, and accordingly the Court remands the case for an assessment of fault.

Surely the Court cannot be suggesting that the quoted portion of the Supreme Court of Florida's opinion, which contained a citation to *Gertz,* had no meaning at all. And if it did have meaning, it must have reflected either an intention to find fault or an intention to affirm a finding of fault. It is quite clear that the opinion was not intended to affirm any finding of fault, for as the Court observes there was no finding of fault to affirm. * * * The absence of any prior finding of fault only reinforces what the Supreme Court of Florida's language itself makes clear—that the Court was not simply affirming a finding of fault, but making such a finding in the first instance.

[H]owever, * * * it is a determination that is wholly unsupportable. The sole basis for that Court's determination of fault was that under Florida law a wife found guilty of adultery cannot be, as Mrs. Firestone was, awarded alimony. Time, the Court reasoned, should have realized that a divorce decree containing an award of alimony could not, consistent with Florida law, have been based on adultery. But that reasoning assumes that judicial decisions can always be squared with the prior state of the law. If we need be reminded that courts occasionally err in their assessment of the law, we need only refer to the subsequent history of the divorce decree involved in this case: when the divorce case reached the Supreme Court of Florida, that court found that the divorce had been granted for lack of "domestication" and pointed out that that was not one of the statutory grounds for divorce. Firestone v. Firestone, 263 So.2d 223 (1972). Time's responsibility was to report accurately what the trial court did, not what it could or should have done. If the trial court awarded alimony while basing the divorce on a finding of adultery by the wife, Time cannot be faulted for reporting that fact. Unless there is some basis for a finding of fault other than that given by the Supreme Court of Florida, I think it clear that there can be no liability.

EXCERPT FROM RESTATEMENT OF TORTS SECOND, TENTATIVE DRAFT NO. 21, 1975, pp. 81–85

(NOTE BY REPORTER JOHN W. WADE):

SPECIAL NOTE ON REMEDIES FOR DEFAMATION OTHER THAN DAMAGES

The tort law of libel and slander has been conceived of as serving three separate functions: (1) to compensate the plaintiff for the injury to his reputation, for his pecuniary losses and for his emotional distress, (2) to vindicate him and aid in restoring his reputation, and (3) to punish the defendant and dissuade him and others from publishing defamatory statements. The traditional remedy has been an award of damages, whether compensatory, nominal or punitive. The award of damages has served all three purposes, to a greater or lesser degree.

But the damage remedy has proved to have many inadequacies, and it has become much less useful as a remedy for the injured party as a result of recent developments in the law of defamation. In the first place, there has always been a serious anomaly in trying to convert damage to reputation in the absence of proof of specific pecuniary loss and injury to feelings into exact monetary figures.

Second, and more important, the damage remedy is frequently not available even though the communication is both false and defamatory and causes actual provable harm. The defendant is often found to be privileged. If he is absolutely privileged, there is certainly no point in bringing suit for damages. The common law of conditional privilege has been built up over the years as a careful balancing of the conflicting interests of the plaintiff and of the defendant, together with those of other people. But no matter how desirable it is to protect significant interests of other parties the fact remains that it is the plaintiff who has innocently suffered the damage. Now that strict liability for defamation is no longer constitutional, the plaintiff may lose because he was unable to prove that the defendant published the statement with knowledge of its falsity or in reckless disregard of its truth or falsity, or even negligently in this regard. If the plaintiff fails to win on any one of these bases, he not only fails to obtain damages, but the impression created among those who were aware of the suit is that the defamatory charge must have been true. As a result, the plaintiff's reputation is damaged all the more, and he would have been better off never to have brought the suit.

Third, the damage remedy has sometimes proved to be unfair to the defendant. Defamation actions have not infrequently been brought—or jury verdicts have been rendered, irrespective of the plaintiff's motivation in bringing the action—not to compensate for actual pecuniary loss or to vindicate the plaintiff, but instead to cudgel the defendant and to mulct him for substantial damages which may be like a windfall to the plaintiff. It is cases of this sort which have helped to persuade the Supreme Court to intervene and set restrictions and standards which will protect the country's commitment to free speech and free press.

These inadequacies make it very doubtful whether the damage remedy fully serves the purposes for which the law of defamation was established, especially the vindication of plaintiff's reputation. Consideration should therefore be given to alternative legal remedies which may more adequately serve one or more of the purposes enumerated. Several of these alternatives may be considered.

(1) *Declaratory relief.* In a jurisdiction where declaratory relief is available as a general remedy and statutory provisions do not preclude it, resort may be had to a suit for a declaratory judgment that the defamatory statement is untrue. This action would provide no compensation for injury but it could vindicate the plaintiff and aid in restoring his reputation. Libel or slander suits similar to this are those in which the plaintiff seeks only nominal damages or announces that he will donate to charity any award which he receives.

There is presently no established practice for bringing suit to obtain a declaratory judgment that a defamatory statement about the plaintiff is false, and a number of questions will arise if the practice develops. Thus, since there is no request for award of damages, can an action for slander be maintained for a communication which was not slanderous per se, even in the absence of any proof of special damages? Again, now that the common law strict liability for defamation is no longer constitutional (see §§ 580A, 580B), would it still be necessary to prove fault on the part of the defendant in order to maintain an action solely for declaratory relief? Could the declaratory action be sustained even though the defendant was able to claim a privilege, on the basis that the purpose of the privilege is to protect the defendant from the burden of a monetary obligation? Should the affirmative defense of truth in a regular defamation action be converted into a specific element of the plaintiff's cause of action in a suit for declaratory relief, so that the burden of proof as to falsity is on the plaintiff? How should costs of suit be allocated? Would it be desirable to develop a technique for eliminating suits based on trivial defamation? Substantial policy issues abound in each of these problems.

If the remedy of a formal action for a declaratory judgment is not available in a particular jurisdiction there remain two possible methods of using the ordinary action for defamation to obtain declaratory relief. The first is to bring the action expressly requesting only nominal damages, and stating that the suit is for the purpose of vindicating the plaintiff's reputation and not for the purpose of recovering compensatory damages. It has been tacitly assumed that a suit of this nature would be subject to all of the defenses and restrictions of a suit for regular damages. But the issues involved are different, and the competing interests may produce a different balance. Decisions consciously treating these issues have not been rendered. A suit brought solely for nominal damages may well come to be treated as one for declaratory relief, with different restrictions and defenses.

The second possible method of obtaining declaratory relief in a regular defamation suit involves the utilization of a special verdict. Thus, if a fact issue is presented as to whether the defendant published a defamatory communication negligently (or recklessly or with knowledge of the falsity), and the case goes to the jury, the trial judge may call for a special verdict indicating (1) whether the communication was true or false and (2) whether the defendant acted negligently. In this way, even if the jury finds that the defendant was not negligent, so that he wins the suit, the plaintiff will have had an opportunity to obtain a formal declaration that the defamatory statement about him was false.

(2) *Retraction.* There are numerous retraction statutes in the United States. They usually provide that if a newspaper receives a notification as to the falsity of a defamatory news item and complies with a request for retraction, its liability for damages will be reduced. At an earlier time the English manorial courts sometimes required an apology and the ecclesiastical courts required the defendant to acknowledge his false witness and beg the pardon of the injured party. The core of the idea might be utilized today as a supplement to the action for declaratory relief. A news medium for example, might be directed to publish a news item covering the judgment against it and thus aid in vindicating the plaintiff's repuation. As to the constitutionality of a statute to this effect, see Miami Herald Pub. Co. v. Tornillo, 418 U.S. 241, 258, 94 S.Ct. 2831, 41 L.Ed.2d 730 (1974) (Brennan, J., concurring).

(3) *Injunctive relief.* Equity courts have never been inclined to grant freely injunctive remedies against personal defamation, and ever since Near v. Minnesota ex rel Olson, 283 U.S. 697, 51 S.Ct. 625, 75 L.Ed.2d 1357 (1931) it has been recognized that prior restraint of a publication runs afoul of the First Amendment. Nevertheless, it remains possible that injunctive relief might become, on some occasions, a suitable supplement to declaratory relief. When it has been formally determined by a court that a statement is both defamatory and untrue and the defendant persists in continuing to publish it, a carefully worded injunction might meet the need and be available against further publication of the statement which has already been determined by the court to be false and defamatory.

(4) *Self-help.* The Supreme Court has said: "The first remedy of any victim of defamation is self-help—using available opportunities to contradict the lie or correct the error and thereby to minimize its adverse impact on reputation." This remedy, of course, does not require suit or court action. The law can nevertheless help. It gives a conditional privilege to a person who is seeking to protect his reputation by answering a defamatory charge. (See § 594). But a statute requiring a news medium to publish a reply offered to a statement made by it would apparently be unconstitutional. The party seeking to vindicate his reputation by self-help must find his own means of publication. If he finds the means, he may, at least in some situations, succeed in fully vindicating himself.

But self-help may be resorted to, not only to reveal the falsity of the defamatory statement and to vindicate the reputation, but also to punish the defamer and retaliate against him. In earlier times, the principal method of this type of self-help was the clan or blood feud. They were supplanted for a time by the challenge to a duel and the horsewhip. One of the primary reasons for developing the tort law of defamation was to induce the defamed person to resort to the courts for relief instead of wreaking his own vengeance. With the increasing unavailability of the damage remedy for defamation and the consequent heightened temptation to resort to extralegal methods like these which are presently regarded as uncivilized, the need grows for making available legal and civilized methods of protecting the defamed person's reputation. Development of a declaratory remedy seems best calculated to do this.

Further Reform of the Damage Remedy. The Supreme Court has on numerous occasions expressed concern regarding the rendering of verdicts for large sums of damages, and the effect of this in unconstitutionally impairing freedom of speech and freedom of the press by producing a form of self-censorship to avoid the possibility of these verdicts. The Court has now held in Gertz v. Robert Welch, Inc., 418 U.S. 323, 94 S.Ct. 2997, 41 L.Ed.2d 789 (1974), that the constitution limits recoverable damages to "compensation for actual injury * * * at least when liability is not based on a showing of knowledge of falsity or reckless disregard for the truth." But actual injury is "not limited to out-of-pocket loss" and may include "impairment of reputation and standing in the community, personal humiliation, and mental anguish and suffering." While this places much more restraint on discretion to determine the size of the damage award and gives more control over jury conduct to the courts, it still leaves a considerable amount of uncertainty regarding the ultimate figure. At the same time it leaves out one important element of pecuniary or out-of-pocket damages, for which the amount can be determined on an objective basis. This is for the cost of reasonable attorney's fees.

The normal common law rule in America is not to award damages for attorney's fees in a tort action. At the same time it has been the traditional, though unexpressed, practice to treat the award for emotional distress as providing the funds for paying the plaintiff's counsel fees. The common law rule can be changed by a statute providing for recovery of the counsel fees. Since this might, however, create constitutional problems because of the potential overall size of verdicts, a provision in the statute would be advisable, indicating that if counsel fees are sought, other damages will be limited to pecuniary loss. Perhaps the statute should leave the election as to whether to seek attorney's fees and forego recovery for mental suffering to the plaintiff; perhaps it should make the choice for him.[51a]

SECTION 3. THE "PRIVACY" TORTS

HAMBURGER v. EASTMAN

Supreme Court of New Hampshire, 1965.
106 N.H. 107, 206 A.2d 239.

The plaintiffs, husband and wife, brought companion suits for invasion of their privacy against the defendant who owned and rented a dwelling house to the plaintiffs. The plaintiffs allege that the defendant installed and concealed "a listening and recording device" in their bedroom, which was in the dwelling house rented to them by the defendant and that this device was connected to the defendant's adjacent residence by wires "capable of transmitting and recording any sounds and voices originating in said bedroom." * * *

KENISON, CHIEF JUSTICE.

The question presented is whether the right of privacy is recognized in this state. There is no controlling statute and no previous decision in this jurisdiction which decides the question. Inasmuch as invasion of the right of privacy is not a single tort but consists of four distinct torts, it is probably more concrete and accurate to state the issue in the present case to be whether this state recognizes that intrusion upon one's physical and mental solitude or seclusion is a tort. The most recent, as well as the most comprehensive, analysis of the problem is found in Prosser, Torts, s. 112 (3d ed. 1964).

In capsule summary the invasion of the right of privacy developed as an independent and distinct tort from the classic and famous article by Warren and Brandeis, The Right to Privacy, 4 Harv.L.Rev. 193 (1890), although Judge Cooley had discussed "the right to be let alone" some years previously. Cooley, Torts 29 (1st ed. 1879). In 1902 the New York Court of Appeals decided that the right of privacy did not have "an abiding place in our jurisprudence." Roberson v. Rochester Folding Box Co., 171 N.Y. 538, 556, 64 N.E. 442. The following year the New York Legislature acted promptly to remedy this deficiency. Laws of N.Y. 1903 ch. 132; N.Y. Civil Rights Law, McKinney's Consol.Laws, c. 6, §§ 50 and 51. Shortly thereafter in 1905 Pavesich v. New England Life Ins. Co., 122 Ga. 190, 50 S.E. 68 upheld the right of privacy and became the leading case on the subject. Since that time the right of privacy has been given protection in a majority of the jurisdictions in this country, generally without benefit of statute, and only a small minority have rejected the concept and some of these minority decisions are not recent. See Henry v. Cherry & Webb, 30 R.I. 13, 73 A. 97 (1909). See also 1 Harper and James, Torts ss. 9.5–9.7 (1956); Annots. 138 A.L.R. 22, 168 A.L.R. 446, 14 A.L.R.2d 750. "Today, with something over three hundred cases in the books, some rather definite conclusions are possible.

What has emerged is no very simple matter. It is not one tort, but a complex of four. The law of privacy comprises four distinct kinds of invasion of four different interests of the plaintiff which are tied together by the common name, but otherwise have almost nothing in common except that each presents an interference with the right of the plaintiff 'to be let alone.' " Prosser, Torts, s. 112, p. 832 (3d ed. 1964).

The four kinds of invasion comprising the law of privacy include: (1) intrusion upon the plaintiff's physical and mental solitude or seclusion; (2) public disclosure of private facts; (3) publicity which places the plaintiff in a false light in the public eye; (4) appropriation, for the defendant's benefit or advantage, of the plaintiff's name or likeness. In the present case, we are concerned only with the tort of intrusion upon the plaintiffs' solitude or seclusion. See Ezer, Intrusion on Solitude: Herein of Civil Rights and Civil Wrongs, 21 Law in Transition 63 (1961).

"It is evident that these four forms of invasion of privacy are distinct, and based on different elements. It is the failure to recognize this which has been responsible for much of the apparent confusion in the decisions. Taking them in order—intrusion, disclosure, false light, and appropriation—the first and second require the invasion of something secret, secluded or private pertaining to the plaintiff; the third and fourth do not. The second and third depend upon publicity, while the first does not, nor does the fourth, although it usually involves it. The third requires falsity or fiction; the other three do not. The fourth involves a use for the defendant's advantage which is not true of the rest." Prosser, Torts, s. 112 pp. 842–843 (3d ed. 1964).

The tort of intrusion upon the plaintiff's solitude or seclusion is not limited to a physical invasion of his home or his room or his quarters. As Prosser points out, the principle has been carried beyond such physical intrusion "and extended to eavesdropping upon private conversations by means of wire tapping and microphones." Prosser, supra, p. 833. Examples of wire tapping in which the right of privacy has been protected as an invasion of the plaintiff's solitude or seclusion are Rhodes v. Graham, 238 Ky. 225, 37 S.W.2d 46; LaCrone v. Ohio Bell Telephone Co., 114 Ohio App. 299, 182 N.E.2d 15 and LeCrone v. Ohio Bell Telephone Co., 120 Ohio App. 129, 201 N.E.2d 533, decided September 10, 1963 but not reported until 1964. The right of privacy has been upheld in situations where microphones have been planted to overhear private conversations. Roach v. Harper, 143 W.Va. 869, 105 S.E.2d 564; McDaniel v. Atlanta Coca-Cola Bottling Co., 60 Ga.App. 92, 2 S.E.2d 810.

We have not searched for cases where the bedroom of husband and wife has been "bugged" but it should not be necessary—by way of understatement—to observe that this is the type of intrusion that would be offensive to any person of ordinary sensibilities. What married "people do in the privacy of their bedroom is their own business so long as they are not hurting anyone else." Ernst and Loth,

For Better or Worse, 79 (1952). The Restatement, Torts s. 867 provides that "a person who unreasonably and seriously interferes with another's interest in not having his affairs known to others * * * is liable to the other." As is pointed out in *comment d* "liability exists only if the defendant's conduct was such that he should have realized that it would be offensive to persons of ordinary sensibilities. It is only where the intrusion has gone beyond the limits of decency that liability accrues. These limits are exceeded where intimate details of the life of one who has never manifested a desire to have publicity are exposed to the public * * *."

The defendant contends that the right of privacy should not be recognized on the facts of the present case as they appear in the pleadings because there are no allegations that anyone listened or overheard any sounds or voices originating from the plaintiffs' bedroom. The tort of intrusion on the plaintiffs' solitude or seclusion does not require publicity and communication to third persons although this would affect the amount of damages, as Prosser makes clear. Prosser, supra, 843. The defendant also contends that the right of privacy is not violated unless something has been published, written or printed and that oral publicity is not sufficient. Recent cases make it clear that this is not a requirement. Carr v. Watkins, 227 Md. 578, 177 A.2d 841; Bennett v. Norba, 396 Pa. 94, 151 A.2d 476, 71 A.L.R.2d 803; Norris v. Moskin Stores, Inc., 272 Ala. 174, 132 So.2d 321.

If the peeping Tom, the big ear and the electronic eavesdropper (whether ingenious or ingenuous) have a place in the hierarchy of social values, it ought not to be at the expense of a married couple minding their own business in the seclusion of their bedroom who have never asked for or by their conduct deserved a potential projection of their private conversations and actions to their landlord or to others. Whether actual or potential such "publicity with respect to private matters of purely personal concern is an injury to personality. It impairs the mental peace and comfort of the individual and may produce suffering more acute than that produced by a mere bodily injury." III Pound, Jurisprudence 58 (1959). The use of parabolic microphones and sonic wave devices designed to pick up conversations in a room without entering it and at a considerable distance away makes the problem far from fanciful. Dash, Schwartz & Knowlton, The Eavesdroppers pp. 346–358 (1959).

It is unnecessary to determine the extent to which the right of privacy is protected as a constitutional matter without the benefit of statute. See Beaney, The Constitutional Right to Privacy in the Supreme Court in 1962 The Supreme Court Review 212 (Kurland ed. 1962); Olmstead v. United States, 277 U.S. 438, 478, 48 S.Ct. 564, 72 L.Ed. 944 (1928) (dissenting opinion of Brandeis, J.); Dykstra, The Right Most Valued by Civilized Man, 6 Utah L.Rev. 305 (1959); Pound, The Fourteenth Amendment and the Right of Privacy, 13 W.Res.L.Rev. 34 (1961). For the purposes of the present case it is sufficient to hold that the invasion of the plaintiffs' solitude or seclusion, as alleged in the pleadings, was a violation of their right of privacy and constituted a tort for which the plaintiffs may recover damage; to the extent that they can prove them. "Certainly, no right deserves greater protection, for, as Emerson has well said, 'solitude, the safeguard of mediocrity, is to genius the stern friend.'" Ezer, Intrusion on Solitude: Herein of Civil Rights and Civil Wrongs, 21 Law in Transition 63, 75 (1961).

The motion to dismiss should be denied. * * *

The late Dean William Prosser's four-fold classification of "privacy" torts was incorporated in the Restatement of Torts Second, at his suggestion as Reporter, § 652A (Tent. Draft No. 13, 1967). This formulation was reaffirmed by the American Law Institute at its 1975 Annual Meeting, after a spirited debate. Some of the objections, shared by Dean John W. Wade, Prosser's successor as Reporter, concerned the drafting problem of how to limit the concept of privacy to a right only against invasions which are unreasonable. Another objection concerned the use of the word "privacy" to describe interests which have nothing to do with privacy. There is, furthermore, a serious body of opinion, referred to in the *Briscoe* case, page 968 infra, which questions the existence of a common law "false light" tort apart from defamation. The question becomes of particular interest if the distinction should be used to justify a difference in terms of constitutional protection for the defendant.

GALELLA v. ONASSIS

United States Court of Appeals for the Second Circuit, 1973.
487 F.2d 986.

J. JOSEPH SMITH, CIRCUIT JUDGE. Donald Galella, a free-lance photographer, appeals from a summary judgment dismissing his complaint against three Secret Service agents for false arrest, malicious prosecution and interference with trade * * * and the grant of injunctive relief to defendant Onassis on her counterclaim and to the intervenor, the United States, on its intervening complaint * * *. In addition to numerous alleged procedural errors, Galella raises the First Amendment as an absolute shield against liability to any sanctions. The judgments dismissing the complaints are affirmed; the grant of injunctive relief is affirmed as herein modified. * * *

Galella is a free-lance photographer specializing in the making and sale of photographs of well-known persons. Defendant Onassis is the widow of the late President John F. Kennedy, mother of the two Kennedy children, John and Caroline, and is the wife of Aristotle Onassis, widely known shipping figure and reputed multimillionaire. John Walsh, James Kalafatis and John Connelly are U. S. Secret Service agents assigned to the duty of protecting the Kennedy children under 18 U.S.C.A. § 3056, which provides for protection of the children of deceased presidents up to the age of 16.

Galella fancies himself as a "paparazzo" (literally a kind of annoying insect, perhaps roughly equivalent to the English "gadfly.") Paparazzi make themselves as visible to the public and obnoxious to their photographic subjects as possible to aid in the advertisement and wide sale of their works.[52]

Some examples of Galella's conduct brought out at trial are illustrative. Galella took pictures of John Kennedy riding his bicycle in Central Park across the way from his home. He jumped out into the boy's path, causing the agents concern for John's safety. The agents' reaction and interrogation of Galella led to Galella's arrest and his action against the agents; Galella on other occasions interrupted Caroline at tennis, and invaded the children's private schools. At one time he came uncomfortably close in a power boat to Mrs. Onassis swimming. He often jumped and postured around while taking pictures of her party notably at a theater opening but also on numerous other occasions. He followed a practice of bribing apartment house, restaurant and nightclub doormen as well as romancing a family servant to keep him advised of the movements of the family.

After detention and arrest following complaint by the Secret Service agents protecting Mrs. Onassis' son and his acquittal in the state court, Galella filed suit in state court against the agents and Mrs. Onassis. Galella claimed that under orders from Mrs. Onassis, the three agents had falsely arrested and maliciously prosecuted him, and that this incident in addition to several others described in the complaint constituted an unlawful interference with his trade.

Mrs. Onassis answered denying any role in the arrest or any part in the claimed interference with his attempts to photograph her, and counterclaimed for * * * injunctive relief, charging that Galella had invaded her privacy, assaulted and battered her, intentionally inflicted emotional distress and engaged in a campaign of harassment. * * *

* * * [T]he government intervened requesting injunctive relief from the activities of Galella which obstructed the Secret Service's ability to protect Mrs. Onassis' children.[53]

Certain incidents of photographic coverage by Galella, subsequent to an agreement among the parties for Galella not to so engage, resulted in the issuance of a temporary restraining order to prevent further harassment of Mrs. Onassis and the children. Galella was enjoined from "harassing, alarming, startling, tormenting, touching the person of the defendant * * * or her children * * * and from blocking their movements in the public places and

52. The newspapers report a recent incident in which one Marlon Brando, annoyed by Galella, punched Galella, breaking Galella's jaw and infecting Brando's hand.

53. The Secret Service is responsible for protecting the children of former presidents until the age of 16. 18 U.S.C.A. § 3056.

thoroughfares, invading their immediate zone of privacy by means of physical movements, gestures or with photographic equipment and from performing any act reasonably calculated to place the lives and safety of the defendant * * * and her children in jeopardy." Within two months, Galella was charged with violation of the temporary restraining order; a new order was signed which required that the photographer keep 100 yards from the Onassis apartment and 50 yards from the person of the defendant and her children. Surveillance was also prohibited.

Upon notice of consolidation of the preliminary injunction hearing and trial for permanent injunction, plaintiff moved for a jury trial * * *. Just prior to trial Galella deposed Mrs. Onassis. Under protective order of this court, the defendant was allowed to testify at the office of the U. S. Attorney and outside the presence of Galella.

After a six-week trial the court dismissed Galella's claim and granted relief to both the defendant and the intervenor. Galella was enjoined from (1) keeping the defendant and her children under surveillance or following any of them; (2) approaching within 100 yards of the home of defendant or her children, or within 100 yards of either child's school or within 75 yards of either child or 50 yards of defendant; (3) using the name, portrait or picture of defendant or her children for advertising; (4) attempting to communicate with defendant or her children except through her attorney.

We conclude that grant of summary judgment and dismissal of Galella's claim against the Secret Service agents was proper. Federal agents when charged with duties which require the exercise of discretion are immune from liability for actions within the scope of their authority. Ordinarily enforcement agents charged with the duty of arrest are not so immune. Bivens v. Six Unknown Named Agents of Fed. Bur. of Narc., 456 F.2d 1339 (2d Cir. 1972). The protective duties assigned the agents under this statute, however, require the instant exercise of judgment which should be protected. The agents saw Galella jump into the path of John Kennedy who was forced to swerve his bike dangerously as he left Central Park and was about to enter Fifth Avenue, whereupon the agents gave chase to the photographer. Galella indicated that he was a press photographer listed with the New York City Police; he and the agents went to the police station to check on the story, where one of the agents made the complaint on which the state court charges were based. Certainly it was reasonable that the agents "check out" an individual who has endangered their charge,[54] and seek prosecution for apparent violation of state law which interferes with them in the discharge of their duties. * * *

54. Even where an absolute privilege has been denied police officers charged with false arrest, good faith and reasonable belief in the validity of the arrest is an affirmative defense. See Pierson v. Ray, 386 U.S. 547, 555–557, 87 S.Ct. 1213, 18 L.Ed.2d 288 (1967) (§ 1983 action); *Bivens*, supra, 456 F.2d at 1341, 1348; Boyd v. Huffman, 342 F.Supp. 787, 789 (N.D.Ohio, W.D.1972).

Discrediting all of Galella's testimony the court found the photographer guilty of harassment, intentional infliction of emotional distress, assault and battery, commercial exploitation of defendant's personality, and invasion of privacy. Fully crediting defendant's testimony, the court found no liability on Galella's claim. Evidence offered by the defense showed that Galella had on occasion intentionally physically touched Mrs. Onassis and her daughter, caused fear of physical contact in his frenzied attempts to get their pictures, followed defendant and her children too closely in an automobile, endangered the safety of the children while they were swimming, water skiing and horseback riding. Galella cannot successfully challenge the court's finding of tortious conduct.[55]

Finding that Galella had "insinuated himself into the very fabric of Mrs. Onassis' life * * *" the court framed its relief in part on the need to prevent further invasion of the defendant's privacy. Whether or not this accords with present New York law, there is no doubt that it is sustainable under New York's proscription of harassment.[56]

55. Harassment is a criminal violation under New York Penal Law § 240.25 (McKinney's Consol.Laws, c. 40, 1967) when with intent to harass a person follows another in a public place, inflicts physical contact or engages in any annoying conduct without legitimate cause. Galella was found to have engaged in this proscribed conduct. Conduct sufficient to invoke criminal liability for harassment may be the basis for private action. Cf. Long v. Beneficial Finance Co. of New York, 39 A.D.2d 11, 330 N.Y.S.2d 664 (1972).

56. Although the New York courts have not yet recognized a common law right of privacy, if we were required to reach the question, we would be inclined to agree with the court below that when again faced with the issue the Court of Appeals may well modify or distinguish its 1902 holding in Roberson v. Rochester Folding Box Co., 171 N.Y. 538, 64 N.E. 442 (1902), that "The so-called right of privacy has not as yet found an abiding place in our jurisprudence." There is substantive support today for the proposition that privacy is a "basic right" entitled to legal protection, Time v. Hill, 385 U.S. 374, 415, 87 S.Ct. 534, 17 L.Ed.2d 456 (1967) (Fortas, J., dissenting), nor can the "power of a State to control and remedy such intrusion [even] for news gathering purposes * * * be denied." Id. at 404, 87 S.Ct. at 550 (Harlan, J., concurring and dissenting). Privacy essential to individual dignity and personal liberty underlies the fundamental rights guaranteed in the Bill of Rights. See Katz v. United States, 389 U.S. 347, 350 n. 5, 88 S.Ct. 507, 19 L.Ed.2d 576 (1967); Tehan v. U. S. ex rel. Shott, 382 U.S. 406, 416, 86 S.Ct. 459, 15 L.Ed.2d 453 (1966) (Fifth Amendment); Stanley v. Georgia, 394 U.S. 557, 564–566, 89 S.Ct. 1243, 22 L.Ed.2d 542 (1969) (First and Fourteenth Amendments). See also Time v. Hill, supra, 385 U.S. at 412–415, 87 S.Ct. 534; Bloustein, Privacy As An Aspect of Human Dignity: An Answer to Dean Prosser, 39 N.Y.U.L. Rev. 962, 971 (1964); Fried, Privacy, 77 Yale L.J. 475, 482ff (1968). There is an emerging recognition of privacy as a distinct, constitutionally protected right. Roe v. Ingraham, 480 F.2d 102 (2d Cir., 1973), (Friendly, J.)

While the Constitution provides protection for specific manifestations of privacy "* * * the protection of a person's general right to privacy—his right to be let alone by other people is like the protection of his property and his very life left largely to the law of the individual states. * * *" *Katz*, supra 389 U.S. at 350–351, 88 S. Ct. at 511, citing Warren & Brandeis, Right to Privacy, 4 Harv.L.Rev. 193 (1890).

The vast majority of states have now recognized and protect a right to privacy. Restatement of Torts, Second § 652(a), comment a (Tent. Draft No. 13, 1967). Statutory protection has been afforded the right in New York through imposition of criminal sanctions for invasion of privacy through

Of course legitimate countervailing social needs may warrant some intrusion despite an individual's reasonable expectation of privacy and freedom from harassment. However the interference allowed may be no greater than that necessary to protect the overriding public interest. Mrs. Onassis was properly found to be a public figure and thus subject to news coverage. See Sidis v. F. R. Publishing Corp., 113 F.2d 806 (2d Cir.), cert. denied 311 U.S. 711, 61 S.Ct. 393, 85 L.Ed. 462 (1940). Nonetheless, Galella's action went far beyond the reasonable bounds of news gathering. When weighed against the *de minimis* public importance of the daily activities of the defendant, Galella's constant surveillance, his obtrusive and intruding presence, was unwarranted and unreasonable. If there were any doubt in our minds, Galella's inexcusable conduct toward defendant's minor children would resolve it.

Galella does not seriously dispute the court's finding of tortious conduct. Rather, he sets up the First Amendment as a wall of immunity protecting newsmen from any liability for their conduct while gathering news. There is no such scope to the First Amendment right. Crimes and torts committed in news gathering are not protected. See Branzburg v. Hayes, 408 U.S. 665, 92 S.Ct. 2646, 33 L.Ed.2d 626 (1972); Rosenbloom v. Metromedia, 403 U.S. 29, 91 S. Ct. 1811, 29 L.Ed.2d 296 (1971); Dietemann v. Time, Inc., 449 F.2d 245, 249–250 (9th Cir. 1971). See Restatement of Torts, Second § 652(f), comment k (Tent. Draft No. 13, 1967). There is no threat to a free press in requiring its agents to act within the law. * * *

Injunctive relief is appropriate. Galella has stated his intention to continue his coverage of defendant so long as she is newsworthy, and his continued harassment even while the temporary restraining orders were in effect indicate that no voluntary change in his technique can be expected. New York courts have found similar conduct sufficient to support a claim for injunctive relief. * * *

The injunction, however, is broader than is required to protect the defendant. Relief must be tailored to protect Mrs. Onassis from the "paparazzo" attack which distinguishes Galella's behavior from that of other photographers; it should not unnecessarily infringe on reasonable efforts to "cover" defendant. Therefore, we modify the court's order to prohibit only (1) any approach within twenty-five (25) feet of defendant or any touching of the person of the defendant Jacqueline Onassis; (2) any blocking of her movement in public places and thoroughfares; (3) any act foreseeably or reasonably

the use of mechanical devices for wiretap and eavesdropping and for tampering with certain private communications. New York Penal Code §§ 250.00–250.35 (McKinney, 1967).

Although not recognizing a right to privacy as such except as defined by statute, the New York courts have softened this rule in many cases by recognizing and liberally applying freedom from emotional distress as a protectable interest. * * * [Citations omitted. Notes 52–56 from original, reunmbered; other notes in original omitted.]

calculated to place the life and safety of defendant in jeopardy; and (4) any conduct which would reasonably be foreseen to harass, alarm or frighten the defendant.

Any further restriction on Galella's taking and selling pictures of defendant for news coverage is, however, improper and unwarranted by the evidence. * * * Likewise, we affirm the grant of injunctive relief to the government modified to prohibit any action interfering with Secret Service agents' protective duties. Galella thus may be enjoined from (a) entering the children's schools or play areas; (b) engaging in action calculated or reasonably foreseen to place the children's safety or well being in jeopardy, or which would threaten or create physical injury; (c) taking any action which could reasonably be foreseen to harass, alarm, or frighten the children; and (d) from approaching within thirty (30) feet of the children. * * *

TIMBERS, CIRCUIT JUDGE (concurring in part and dissenting in part):

With one exception, I concur in the judgment of the Court and in the able majority opinion of Judge Smith.

With the utmost deference to and respect for my colleagues, however, I am constrained to dissent from the judgment of the Court and the majority opinion to the extent that they modify the injunctive relief found necessary by the district court to protect Jacqueline Onassis and her children, Caroline B. and John F. Kennedy, Jr., from the continued predatory conduct of the self-proclaimed paparazzo Galella. * * *

* * * I feel very strongly that such findings should not be set aside or drastically modified by our Court unless they are clearly erroneous; and I do not understand the majority to suggest that they are.

But here is what the majority's modification of the critical distance provisions of the injunction has done:

DISTANCES GALELLA IS REQUIRED TO MAINTAIN	AS PROVIDED IN DISTRICT COURT INJUNCTION	AS MODIFIED BY COURT OF APPEALS MAJORITY
From home of Mrs. Onassis and her children	100 yards	No restriction
From children's schools	100 yards	Restricted only from entering schools or play areas
From Mrs. Onassis personally	50 *yards*	25 *feet* and not to touch her
From children personally	75 *yards*	30 *feet*

With deference, I believe the majority's modification of the injunction in the respects indicate above to be unwarranted and unworkable. Briefly summarized, the following are the reasons for my dissent from the modification of the injunction:

* * *

(3) It results in no restriction whatsoever against Galella's hovering at the entrance to the home of Mrs. Onassis and her children (where he has caused such agonizing humiliation in the past), or at the schools attended by the children—just so he does not physically enter their schools or play areas. This strikes me as an invitation for trouble.

* * *

(7) Finally, I am utterly unable to find any basis in the record or any justification as a matter of law for the majority's modification of the injunction so as to limit the protection provided for the children to the "grant of injunctive relief to the *government* modified to prohibit any action interfering with Secret Service agents' protective duties." (emphasis added). * * * The judgment entered July 20, 1972 provided, in paragraph 4, for injunctive relief for the protection of Mrs. Onassis and both of her children * * * As I read the majority's modification of the injunction, to the extent that it distinguishes between protection for Mrs. Onassis and that for the children, limiting the latter to the grant of injunctive relief to the government, the net effect is to strip the children of any protection under the injunction after they reach age 16 when their protection by the Secret Service ceases. 18 U.S.C.A. § 3056 (1970). For Caroline, who was born November 27, 1957, this means that one of her birthday presents—less than two months away—will be exposure to the resumed predatory conduct of the paparazzo Galella who will be totally unrestrained with respect to her by the injunction as modified by the majority. For John, who was born November 25, 1960, he has only three years to wait for similar exposure. To strip these children, before they reach their majority, of the protection of the injunction of the United States District Court below, is to deny to them and to their mother the very least to which they are entitled under the law.

I most respectfully dissent.

EXCERPT FROM WARREN AND BRANDEIS, THE RIGHT TO PRIVACY

4 Harv.L.Rev. 193, 196 (1890).

* * * The press is overstepping in every direction the obvious bounds of propriety and of decency. Gossip is no longer the resource of the idle and of the vicious, but has become a trade, which is pursued with industry as well as effrontery. To satisfy a prurient taste the details of sexual relations are spread broadcast in the columns of the daily papers. To occupy the indolent, column upon column is filled with idle gossip, which can only be procured by intrusion upon the domestic circle. The intensity and complexity of life, attendant upon advancing civilization, have rendered necessary some retreat from the world, and man, under the refining influence of culture, has become more sensitive to publicity, so that solitude and privacy have become more essential to the individual; but modern enterprise and invention have, through invasions upon his privacy, subjected him to mental pain and distress, far greater than could be inflicted by mere bodily injury. Nor is the harm wrought by such invasions confined to the suffering of those who may be made the subjects of journalistic or other enterprise. * * * Each crop of unseemly gossip * * * becomes the seed of more, and, in direct proportion to its circulation, results in a lowering of social standards and of morality. Even gossip apparently harmless, when widely and persistently circulated, is potent for evil. It both belittles and perverts. It belittles by inverting the relative importance of things, thus dwarfing the thoughts and aspirations of a people. * * * Triviality destroys at once robustness of thought and delicacy of feeling. No enthusiasm can flourish, no generous impulse can survive under its blighting influence.

SIDIS v. F–R PUB. CORPORATION

Circuit Court of Appeals of the United States, Second Circuit, 1940.
113 F.2d 806, 138 A.L.R. 15.

CLARK, CIRCUIT JUDGE. William James Sidis was the unwilling subject of a brief biographical sketch and cartoon printed in The New Yorker weekly magazine for August 14, 1937. Further references were made to him in the issue of December 25, 1937, and in a newspaper advertisement announcing the August 14 issue. He brought an action in the district court against the publisher, F-R Publishing Corporation. His complaint stated three "causes of action": The first alleged violation of his right of privacy as that right is recognized in California, Georgia, Kansas, Kentucky, and Missouri; the second charged infringement of the rights afforded him under sections 50 and 51 of the N. Y. Civil Rights Law (Consol.Laws, c. 6); the third claimed malicious libel under the laws of Delaware, Florida, Illinois, Maine, Massachusetts, Nebraska, New Hampshire, Pennsylvania, and Rhode Island. Defendant's motion to dismiss the first two "causes of action" was granted, and plaintiff has filed an appeal from the order of dismissal. Since a majority of this court believe that order appealable, for reasons referred to below, we may consider the merits of the case.

William James Sidis was a famous child prodigy in 1910. His name and prowess were well known to newspaper readers of the period. At the age of eleven, he lectured to distinguished mathematicians on the subject of Four-Dimensional Bodies. When he was sixteen, he was graduated from Harvard College, amid considerable public attention. Since then, his name has appeared in the press only sporadically, and he has sought to live as unobtrusively as possible. Until the articles objected to appeared in The New Yorker, he had apparently succeeded in his endeavor to avoid the public gaze.

Among The New Yorker's features are brief biographical sketches of current and past personalities. In the latter department, which appears haphazardly under the title of "Where Are They Now?" the article on Sidis was printed with a subtitle "April Fool." The author describes his subject's early accomplishments in mathematics and the wide-spread attention he received, then recounts his general break down and the revulsion which Sidis thereafter felt for his former life of fame and study. The unfortunate prodigy is traced over the years that followed, through his attempts to conceal his identity, through his chosen career as an insignificant clerk who would not need to employ unusual mathematical talents, and through the bizarre ways in which his genius flowered, as in his enthusiasm for collecting streetcar transfers and in his proficiency with an adding machine. The article closes with an account of an interview with Sidis at his present lodgings, "a hall bedroom of Boston's shabby south end." The untidiness of his room, his curious laugh, his manner of speech, and other personal habits are commented upon at length, as is his present interest in the lore of the Okamakammessett Indians. The subtitle is explained by the closing sentence, quoting Sidis as saying "with a grin" that it was strange, "but, you know, I was born on April Fool's Day." Accompanying the biography is a small cartoon showing the genius of eleven years lecturing to a group of astounded professors.

It is not contended that any of the matter printed is untrue. Nor is the manner of the author unfriendly. Sidis today is described as having "a certain childlike charm." But the article is merciless in its dissection of intimate details of its subject's personal life, and this in company with elaborate accounts of Sidis' passion for privacy and the pitiable lengths to which he has gone in order to avoid public scrutiny. The work possesses great reader interest, for it is both amusing and instructive; but it may be fairly described as a ruthless exposure of a once public character, who has since sought and has now been deprived of the seclusion of private life.

The article of December 25, 1937, was a biographical sketch of another former child prodigy, in the course of which William James

Sidis and the recent account of him were mentioned. The advertisement published in the New York World-Telegram of August 13, 1937, read: "Out Today. Harvard Prodigy. Biography of the man who astonished Harvard at age 11. Where are they now? by J. L. Manley. Page 22. The New Yorker."

The complaint contains a general allegation, repeated for all the claims, of publication by the defendant of The New Yorker, "a weekly magazine of wide circulation throughout the United States." Then each separate "cause" contains an allegation that the defendant publicly circulated the articles or caused them to be circulated in the particular states upon whose law that cause is assumed to be founded. Circulation of the New York World-Telegram advertisement is, however, alleged only with respect to the second "cause," for asserted violation of New York law.

1. Under the first "cause of action" we are asked to declare that this exposure transgresses upon plaintiff's right of privacy, as recognized in California, Georgia, Kansas, Kentucky, and Missouri.[57] Each of these states except California grants to the individual a common law right, and California a constitutional right,[58] to be let alone to a certain extent. The decisions have been carefully analyzed by the court below,[59] and we need not examine them further. None of the cited rulings goes so far as to prevent a newspaper or magazine from publishing the truth about a person, however intimate, revealing or harmful the truth may be. Nor are there any decided cases that confer such a privilege upon the press. Under the mandate of Erie R. Co. v. Tompkins, 304 U.S. 64, 58 S.Ct. 817, 82 L.Ed. 1188, 114 A.L.R. 1487, we face the unenviable duty of determining the law of five states on a broad and vital public issue which the courts of those states have not even discussed.[60]

57. Green, The Right of Privacy, 27 Ill. L.Rev. 237, 248; Ragland, The Right of Privacy, 17 Ky.L.J. 85, 110–113; Moreland, The Right of Privacy Today, 19 Ky.L.J. 101; Lisle, The Right of Privacy (A *Contra* View), 19 Ky.L.J. 137; Larremore, The Law of Privacy, 12 Col.L.Rev. 693; Harper and McNeely, Wis.L.Rev. 426, 458 [1938]; 5 Mo.L.Rev. 343.

58. Melvin v. Reid, 112 Cal.App. 285, 297 P. 91. But cf. Metter v. Los Angeles Examiner, 35 Cal.App.2d 304, 95 P. 2d 491.

59. Judge Goddard's decision is reported in 34 F.Supp. 19. The cases he reviewed are Melvin v. Reid, supra note 58; Pavesich v. New England L. I. Co., 122 Ga. 190, 50 S.E. 68, 69 L.R.A. 101, 106 Am.St.Rep. 104, 2 Ann.Cas. 561; Bazemore v. Savannah Hospital, 171 Ga. 257, 155 S.E. 194; Goodyear Tire & Rubber Co. v. Vandergriff, 52 Ga. App. 662, 184 S.E. 452; Kunz v. Allen, 102 Kan. 883, 172 P. 532, L.R.A.1918D, 1151; Brents v. Morgan, 221 Ky. 765, 299 S.W. 967, 55 A.L.R. 964; Douglas v. Stokes, 149 Ky. 506, 149 S.W. 849, 42 L.R.A.,N.S., 386, Ann.Cas.1914B, 374; Foster-Milburn Co. v. Chinn, 134 Ky. 424, 120 S.W. 364, 34 L.R.A.,N.S., 1137, 135 Am.St.Rep. 417; Jones v. Herald Post Co., 230 Ky. 227, 18 S.W.2d 972; Rhodes v. Graham, 238 Ky. 225, 37 S. W.2d 46; Munden v. Harris, 153 Mo. App. 652, 134 S.W. 1076. See also Metter v. Los Angeles Examiner, supra note 58.

60. The cases most nearly in point are Jones v. Herald Post Co., supra note [59] and Metter v. Los Angeles Examiner, supra note [58]. But both these decisions involved news events of great current interest to the community.

All comment upon the right of privacy must stem from the famous article by Warren and Brandeis on The Right of Privacy in 4 Harv.L.Rev. 193. The learned authors of that paper were convinced that some limits ought to be imposed upon the privilege of newspapers to publish truthful items of a personal nature. * * *

Warren and Brandeis realized that the interest of the individual in privacy must inevitably conflict with the interest of the public in news. Certain public figures, they conceded, such as holders of public office, must sacrifice their privacy and expose at least part of their lives to public scrutiny as the price of the powers they attain. But even public figures were not to be stripped bare. "In general, then, the matters of which the publication should be repressed may be described as those which concern the private life, habits, acts, and relations of an individual, and have no legitimate connection with his fitness for a public office. * * * Some things all men alike are entitled to keep from popular curiosity, whether in public life or not, while others are only private because the persons concerned have not assumed a position which makes their doings legitimate matters of public investigation." Warren and Brandeis, supra at page 216.

It must be conceded that under the strict standards suggested by these authors plaintiff's right of privacy has been invaded. Sidis today is neither politician, public administrator, nor statesman. Even if he were, some of the personal details revealed were of the sort that Warren and Brandeis believed "all men alike are entitled to keep from popular curiosity."

But despite eminent opinion to the contrary, we are not yet disposed to afford to all of the intimate details of private life an absolute immunity from the prying of the press. Everyone will agree that at some point the public interest in obtaining information becomes dominant over the individual's desire for privacy. Warren and Brandeis were willing to lift the veil somewhat in the case of public officers. We would go further, though we are not yet prepared to say how far. At least we would permit limited scrutiny of the "private" life of any person who has achieved, or has had thrust upon him, the questionable and indefinable status of a "public figure." See Restatement, Torts, section 867, comments c and d * * *; cf. Hillman v. Star Pub. Co., 64 Wash. 691, 117 P. 594, 35 L.R.A.,N.S., 595, criticized in 10 Mich.L.Rev. 335.

William James Sidis was once a public figure. As a child prodigy, he excited both admiration and curiosity. Of him great deeds were expected. In 1910, he was a person about whom the newspapers might display a legitimate intellectual interest, in the sense meant by Warren and Brandeis, as distinguished from a trivial and unseemly curiosity. But the precise motives of the press we regard as unimportant. And even if Sidis had loathed public attention at that time, we think his uncommon achievements and personality would have made the attention permissible. Since then Sidis has cloaked himself in obscurity, but his subsequent history, containing as it did the answer to the question of whether or not he had fulfilled his early promise, was still a matter of public concern. The article in The New Yorker sketched the life of an unusual personality, and it possessed considerable popular news interest.

We express no comment on whether or not the news worthiness of the matter printed will always constitute a complete defense. Revelations may be so intimate and so unwarranted in view of the victim's position as to outrage the community's notions of decency. But when focused upon public characters, truthful comments upon dress, speech, habits, and the ordinary aspects of personality will usually not transgress this line. Regrettably or not, the misfortunes and frailties of neighbors and "public figures" are subjects of considerable interest and discussion to the rest of the population. And when such are the mores of the community, it would be unwise for a court to bar their expression in the newspapers, books, and magazines of the day.

Plaintiff in his first "cause of action" charged actual malice in the publication, and now claims that an order of dismissal was improper in the face of such an allegation. We cannot agree. If plaintiff's right of privacy was not invaded by the article, the existence of actual malice in its publication would not change that result. Unless made so by statute, a truthful and therefore nonlibelous statement will not become libelous when uttered maliciously. Restatement, Torts, section 582, comment a * * *.[61] A similar rule should prevail on invasions of the right of privacy. "Personal ill-will is not an ingredient of the offence, any more than in an ordinary case of trespass to person or to property." Warren and Brandeis, supra at page 218. Nor does the malice give rise to an independent wrong based on an intentional invasion of the plaintiff's interest in mental and emotional tranquility. This interest, however real, is one not yet protected by the law. Restatement, Torts, section 46, comment c.

If the article appearing in the issue of August 14, 1937, does not furnish grounds for action, then it is clear that the brief and incidental reference to it contained in the article of December 25, 1937, is not actionable.

2. The second "cause of action" charged invasion of the rights conferred on plaintiff by sections 50 and 51 of the N. Y. Civil Rights Law. Section 50 states that "A person, firm or corporation that uses for advertising purposes, or for the purposes of trade, the name, portrait or picture of any living person without having first obtained the written consent of such person, or if a minor of his or her parent or guardian, is guilty of a misdemeanor." Section 51 gives the injured person the right to an injunction and to damages.

61. In several states the rule is to the contrary, and the basis of plaintiff's third cause of action is the doctrine of "malicious libel" recognized in those jurisdictions. But that doctrine does not appear to be recognized by the law of the five states concerned in the first cause of action.

Before passage of this statute, it had been held that no common law right of privacy existed in New York. Roberson v. Rochester Folding Box Co., 171 N.Y. 538, 64 N.E. 442, 59 L.R.A. 478, 89 Am. St.Rep. 828. Any liability imposed upon defendant must therefore be derived solely from the statute, and not from general considerations as to the right of the individual to prevent publication of the intimate details of his private life. The statute forbids the use of a name or picture only when employed "for advertising purposes, or for the purposes of trade." In this context, it is clear that "for the purposes of trade" does not contemplate the publication of a newspaper, magazine, or book which imparts truthful news or other factual information to the public. Though a publisher sells a commodity, and expects to profit from the sale of his product, he is immune from the interdict of sections 50 and 51 so long as he confines himself to the unembroidered dissemination of facts. Publishers and motion picture producers have occasionally been held to transgress the statute in New York, but in each case the factual presentation was embellished by some degree of fictionalization. See, for example, Blumenthal v. Picture Classics, Inc., 235 App.Div. 570, 257 N.Y.S. 800, affirmed without opinion 261 N.Y. 504, 185 N.E. 713. The cases are collected and the distinction between fact and fiction explained as vital in Sarat Lahiri v. Daily Mirror, 162 Misc. 776, 295 N.Y.S. 382. See also Neyland v. Home Pattern Co., 2 Cir., 65 F.2d 363; Sweenek v. Pathé News, Inc., D.C.E.D.N.Y., 16 F.Supp. 746. The New Yorker articles limit themselves to the unvarnished, unfictionalized truth.[62]

The case as to the newspaper advertisement announcing the August 14 article is somewhat different, for it was undoubtedly inserted in the World-Telegram "for advertising purposes." But since it was to advertise the article on Sidis, and the article itself was unobjectionable, the advertisement shares the privilege enjoyed by the article. Humiston v. Universal Film Mfg. Co., 189 App.Div. 467, 476, 178 N.Y.S. 752. Besides, the advertisement, quoted above, did not use the "name, portrait or picture" of the plaintiff.

Affirmed.

BRISCOE v. READER'S DIGEST ASSOCIATION

Supreme Court of California, In Bank, 1971.
4 Cal.3d 529, 93 Cal.Rptr. 866, 483 P.2d 34.

PETERS, JUSTICE. Plaintiff Marvin Briscoe filed suit against defendant Reader's Digest Association, alleging that defendant had willfully and maliciously invaded his privacy by publishing an article which disclosed truthful but embarrassing private facts about plaintiff's past life. A demurrer was sustained without leave to amend, and

62. In this respect they differ also from the libelous publications considered in cases such as Triggs v. Sun Printing & Pub. Ass'n, 179 N.Y. 144, 71 N.E. 739, 66 L.R.A. 612, 103 Am.St.Rep. 841, 1 Ann.Cas. 326; and Burton v. Crowell Pub. Co., 2 Cir., 82 F.2d 154, which are cited by plaintiff as showing a refusal by the courts to sanction "journalistic license." [Footnotes 57–62 by court, renumbered.]

plaintiff has appealed from the ensuing judgment. Thus, we are presented simply with a pleading problem—does the complaint state a cause of action?

The allegations of the complaint may be summarized as follows: On December 15, 1956, plaintiff and another man hijacked a truck in Danville, Kentucky. "[I]mmediately subsequent to said incident, plaintiff abandoned his life of shame and became entirely rehabilitated and has thereafter at all times lived an exemplary, virtuous and honorable life * * * he has assumed a place in respectable society and made many friends who were not aware of the incident in his earlier life."

"The Big Business of Hijacking," published by defendant 11 years after the hijacking incident, commences with a picture whose caption reads, "Today's highwaymen are looting trucks at a rate of more than $100 million a year. But the truckers have now declared all-out war." The article describes various truck thefts and the efforts being made to stop such thefts. Dates ranging from 1965 to the time of publication are mentioned throughout the article, but none of the described thefts is itself dated.

One sentence in the article refers to plaintiff: "Typical of many beginners, Marvin Briscoe and [another man] stole a 'valuable-looking' truck in Danville, Ky., and then fought a gun battle with the local police, only to learn that they had hijacked four bowling-pin spotters." There is nothing in the article to indicate that the hijacking occurred in 1956.

As a result of defendant's publication, plaintiff's 11-year-old daughter, as well as his friends, for the first time learned of this incident. They thereafter scorned and abandoned him.

Conceding the truth of the facts published in defendant's article, plaintiff claims that the public disclosure of these private facts has humiliated him and exposed him to contempt and ridicule. Conceding that the *subject* of the article may have been "newsworthy," he contends that the use of his *name* was not, and that the defendant has thus invaded his right to privacy.

The concept of a legal right to privacy was first developed by Warren and Brandeis in their landmark law review article, The Right to Privacy (1890) 4 Harv.L.Rev. 193. Warren and Brandeis characterized the right to privacy as the individual's "right of determining, ordinarily, to what extent his thoughts, sentiments, and emotions shall be communicated to others." (Id., at p. 198; see also A. Westin, Privacy and Freedom (1967) p. 7; Gross, The Concept of Privacy (1967) 42 N.Y.U.L.Rev. 34, 35–36.) [63] Try as they might, Warren

63. Although other ways in which the word "privacy" is used—to indicate an interest in mental repose, physical solitude, or autonomy—are weaker senses of the word (Gross, supra, at pp. 36–39), the "right of privacy" has also served as a general rallying point for those concerned about "deep intrusions on human dignity by those in possession of economic or governmental power." (Havighurst, Foreward (1966) 31 Law & Contemp.Prob. 251, 252.)

and Brandeis had a difficult time tracing a right of privacy to the common law. In many respects a person had less privacy in the small community of the 18th century than he did in the urbanizing late 19th century or he does today in the modern metropolis. Extended family networks, primary group relationships, and rigid communal mores served to expose an individual's every deviation from the norm and to straitjacket him in a vise of backyard gossip. Yet Warren and Brandeis perceived that it was mass exposure to public gaze, as opposed to backyard gossip, which threatened to deprive men of the right of "scratching wherever one itches." (Westin, Science, Privacy, and Freedom: Issues and Proposals for the 1970's (1966) 66 Colum. L.Rev. 1003, 1025.)

Acceptance of the right to privacy has grown with the increasing capability of the mass media and electronic devices with their capacity to destroy an individual's anonymity, intrude upon his most intimate activities, and expose his most personal characteristics to public gaze.

In a society in which multiple, often conflicting role performances are demanded of each individual, the original etymological meaning of the word "person"—mask—[64] has taken on new meaning. Men fear exposure not only to those closest to them; much of the outrage underlying the asserted right to privacy is a reaction to exposure to persons known only through business or other secondary relationships. The claim is not so much one of total secrecy as it is of the right to *define* one's circle of intimacy—to choose who shall see beneath the quotidian mask. Loss of control over which "face" one puts on may result in literal loss of self-identity (Westin, supra, at p. 1023; cf. Fried, Privacy (1968) 77 Yale L.J. 475), and is humiliating beneath the gaze of those whose curiosity treats a human being as an object.*

A common law right to privacy, based on Warren and Brandeis' article, is now recognized in at least 36 states. * * *

The right to keep information private was bound to clash with the right to disseminate information to the public. We early noted the potential conflict between freedom of the press and the right of privacy (Gill v. Curtis Publishing Co., 38 Cal.2d 273, 277–278, 239 P.2d 630; Gill v. Hearst Publishing Co., 40 Cal.2d 224, 228, 253 P.2d 441), as did Warren and Brandeis themselves, who suggested that the right should not apply to matters of "public or general interest." (Warren and Brandeis, supra, 4 Harv.L.Rev. 193, 214.) [65]

64. Webster's New International Dictionary (2d ed. 1958) at p. 1827.

65. One writer suggests that the First Amendment's scope is so great as to "swallow the tort." (See Kalven, Privacy in Tort Law—Were Warren and Brandeis Wrong? (1966) 31 Law & Contemp.Prob. 326.) Most commentators place greater emphasis on the right to privacy. (See Bloustein, Privacy, Tort Law, and the Constitution: Is Warren and Brandeis' Tort Petty and Unconstitutional as Well? (1968) 46 Tex.L.Rev. 611; see also Nimmer, The Right to Speak from TIMES to TIME: First Amendment Theory Applied to Libel and Misapplied to Privacy (1968) 56 Cal.L.Rev. 935.)

The instant case, pitting a rehabilitated felon's right to anonymity against a magazine's right to identify him, compels us to consider the character of these competing interests.

The central purpose of the First Amendment "is to give to every voting member of the body politic the fullest possible participation in the understanding of those problems with which the citizens of a self-governing society must deal. * * * "[66] (A. Meiklejohn, Political Freedom: The Constitutional Powers of the People (1960) p. 75.) Nor is freedom of the press confined to comment upon public affairs and those persons who have voluntarily sought the public spotlight. "Freedom of discussion * * * must embrace all issues about which information is needed or appropriate to enable the members of society to cope with the exigencies of their period. * * * " (Thornhill v. Alabama (1940) 310 U.S. 88, 102, 60 S.Ct. 736, 744, 84 L.Ed. 1093; see Time, Inc. v. Hill (1967) 385 U.S. 374, 388, 87 S.Ct. 534, 17 L.Ed. 2d 456.) The scope of the privilege thus extends to almost all reporting of recent events, even though it involves the publication of a purely private individual's name or likeness. (See, e. g., Metter v. Los Angeles Examiner, 35 Cal.App.2d 304, 95 P.2d 491; Coverstone v. Davies, 38 Cal.2d 315, 239 P.2d 876.)[67]

Particularly deserving of First Amendment protection are reports of "hot news," items of possible immediate public concern or interest. The need for constitutional protection is much greater under these circumstances, where deadlines must be met and quick decisions made, than in cases where more considered editorial judgments are possible. (Rosenbloom v. Metromedia, Inc. (3d Cir. 1969) 415 F.2d 892, 895–896).[68] Most factual reporting concerns current

66. Almost any truthful commentary on public officials or public affairs, no matter how serious the invasion of privacy, will be privileged. By volunteering his services for public office the official (as opposed to the ordinary employee) waives much of his right to privacy.

Other individuals who voluntarily seek the public eye are also subject to fair comment and criticism. * * * Because discussion of such figures is not so vital to the maintenance of our self-governing democracy as is discussion of public officials and public affairs, such figures may have greater protection from media exposure or untruths. (See Curtis Publishing Co. v. Butts (1967) 388 U.S. 130, 155, 87 S.Ct. 1975, 18 L.Ed.2d 1094.)

67. The publisher need not intend to educate the public. "The line between * * * informing and * * * entertaining is too elusive * * *. Everyone is familiar with instances of propaganda through fiction. What is one man's amusement, teaches another's doctrine. * * * " (Winters v. New York (1948) 333 U.S. 507, 510, 68 S.Ct. 665, 667, 92 L.Ed. 840.)

68. This is not to say, however, that *all* factual reports of current events have been held absolutely privileged. (See, e. g., Commonwealth v. Wiseman, supra, 356 Mass. 251, 249 N.E.2d 610 [film showing conditions in mental hospital, including naked inmates, forced feedings, masturbation, sadism; individuals identifiable]; Lambert v. Dow Chemical Company (La.App.1968) 215 So.2d 673 [identified picture of plaintiff's unsightly wounds]; Daily Times Democrat v. Graham (1964) 276 Ala. 380, 162 So.2d 474 [identifiable picture of plaintiff with dress blown above her waist]; Harms v. Miami Daily News, Inc. (Fla.App.1961) 127 So.2d 715 [phone number of woman identified as having sexy voice]; Tribune Review Publishing Company v. Thomas (3d Cir. 1958) 254 F.2d 883 [picture of criminal defendant in courthouse]; In re Mack (1956) 386 Pa. 251, 126 A.2d 679, cert. denied 352

events. For example, in Time, Inc. v. Hill, supra, 385 U.S. 374, 383–384, fn. 7, 87 S.Ct. 534, 17 L.Ed.2d 456, the court cited 22 cases in which the right of privacy gave way to the right of the press to publish matters of public interest. Seventeen of these 22 cases (77.3 percent) involved events which had occurred quite recently.[69]

There can be no doubt that reports of current criminal activities are the legitimate province of a free press. The circumstances under which crimes occur, the techniques used by those outside the law, the tragedy that may befall the victims—these are vital bits of information for people coping with the exigencies of modern life. Reports of these events may also promote the values served by the constitutional guarantee of a public trial. Although a case is not to be "tried in the papers," reports regarding a crime or criminal proceedings may encourage unknown witnesses to come forward with useful testimony and friends or relatives to come to the aid of the victim.

It is also generally in the social interest to identify adults currently charged with the commission of a crime. While such an identification may not presume guilt, it may legitimately put others on notice that the named individual is suspected of having committed a crime. Naming the suspect may also persuade eye witnesses and character witnesses to testify. For these reasons, while the suspect or offender obviously does not consent to public exposure, his right to privacy must give way to the overriding social interest.

In general, therefore, truthful reports of *recent* crimes and the names of suspects or offenders will be deemed protected by the First Amendment.[70]

U.S. 1002, 77 S.Ct. 559, 1 L.Ed.2d 547 [picture of convicted murderer in courthouse just prior to sentencing]; Barber v. Time, Inc. (1942) 348 Mo. 1199, 159 S.W.2d 291 [name and picture of woman with humiliating disease]; cf. Tollefson v. Price (1967) 247 Or. 398, 430 P.2d 990 [advertising that plaintiff owed business debts]; Trammell v. Citizens News Co., Inc. (1941) 285 Ky. 529, 148 S.W.2d 708 [advertising that plaintiff owed business debts]; York v. Story (9th Cir. 1963) 324 F.2d 450, cert. denied 376 U.S. 939, 84 S.Ct. 794, 1 L.Ed.2d 659 [indecent photos of plaintiff in poses induced by police officer].)

69. Another of these cases (Thompson v. Curtis Publishing Co. (3d Cir. 1952) 193 F.2d 953) clearly involved voluntary waiver. In Samuel v. Curtis Pub. Co. (N.D.Cal.1954) 122 F.Supp. 327, a photograph of plaintiff restraining a would-be suicide was republished two years after the event. The court found that there was nothing offensive or discreditable to a reasonable man in the photograph. In Miller v. National Broadcasting Company (D.Del. 1957) 157 F.Supp. 240, plaintiff was presently incarcerated, and would not be heard to complain of a dramatic reenactment of his crime four years later. Of the 22 cases cited, only Barbieri v. News-Journal Company (Del. 1963) 189 A.2d 773, which explicitly rejects our landmark decision of Melvin v. Reid, supra, 112 Cal.App. 285, 297 P. 91, and Smith v. Doss (1948) 251 Ala. 250, 37 So.2d 118, is the recall of past events involving nonpublic figures at issue. In the latter case the spectacular disappearance of plaintiff's father, who was thought murdered, the accusation of an innocent man, and the discovery 25 years later of the facts (the father had deserted his family) was said to be so imprinted on the community's collective history that publication was privileged.

70. We do not mean to imply that the First Amendment gives the media the unmitigated right to publish the identity of suspected offenders or victims. In some jurisdictions, for example, the Legislature has decided that the re-

The instant case, however, compels us to consider whether reports of the facts of *past* crimes and the identification of *past* offenders serve these same public-interest functions.

We have no doubt that reports of the facts of past crimes are newsworthy. Media publication of the circumstances under which crimes were committed in the past may prove educational in the same way that reports of current crimes do. The public has a strong interest in enforcing the law, and this interest is served by accumulating and disseminating data cataloguing the reasons men commit crimes, the methods they use, and the ways in which they are apprehended. Thus in an article on truck hijackings, Reader's Digest certainly had the right to report the *facts* of plaintiff's criminal act.

However, identification of the *actor* in reports of long past crimes usually serves little independent public purpose. Once legal proceedings have terminated, and a suspect or offender has been released, identification of the individual will not usually aid the administration of justice. Identification will no longer serve to bring forth witnesses or obtain succor for victims. Unless the individual has reattracted the public eye to himself in some independent fashion, the only public "interest" that would usually be served is that of curiosity.

There may be times, of course, when an event involving private citizens may be so unique as to capture the imagination of all. In such cases—e. g., the behavior of the passengers on the sinking *Titanic,* the heroism of Nathan Hale, the horror of the Saint Valentine's Day Massacre—purely private individuals may by an accident of history lose their privacy regarding that incident for all time. There need be no "reattraction" of the public eye because the public interest never wavered. An individual whose name is fixed in the public's memory, such as that of the political assassin, never becomes an anonymous member of the community again. But in each case it is for the trier of fact to determine whether the individual's infamy is such that he has never left the public arena; we cannot do so as a matter of law.

The Restatement of Torts some time ago balanced the considerations relevant here, concluding that criminals "are the objects of legitimate public interest during a period of time after their conduct * * * has brought them to the public attention; until they have reverted to the lawful and unexciting life led by the great bulk of the community, they are subject to the privileges which publishers have to satisfy the curiosity of the public as to their leaders, heroes, villains and victims." (§ 867, com. c.) Where a man has reverted to that "lawful and unexciting life" led by others, the Restatement implies that he no longer need "satisfy the curiosity of the public."

habilitative goals of the juvenile law are so important as to override the right of the press to identify juvenile defendants. * * * Similarly, some states have prohibited the naming of rape victims in news reports. [But see Cox Broadcasting Corporation v. Cohn, 420 U.S. 469, 95 S.Ct. 1029, 43 L.Ed.2d 328 (1975).]

Another factor militating in favor of protecting the individual's privacy here is the state's interest in the integrity of the rehabilitative process. Our courts recognized this issue four decades ago in Melvin v. Reid, supra, 112 Cal.App. 285, 297 P. 91. There, plaintiff had been a prostitute. She was charged with murder and acquitted after a long and very public trial. She thereafter abandoned her life of shame, married, and assumed a place in respectable society, making many friends who were not aware of the incidents of her earlier life.

Seven years after the trial defendants made a movie based entirely on Mrs. Melvin's early life. They used only facts found in the public record, and did not falsify or create false innuendoes regarding that period of her life. Defendants used Mrs. Melvin's true maiden name in the film.

The Court of Appeal, in a decision cited ceaselessly since, held that the *subject* of the film was protected. No cause of action accrues from the use of "incidents of a life * * * so public as to be spread upon a public record," the court reasoned, since these matters "cease to be private." (112 Cal.App. at pp. 290–291, 297 P. at p. 93.) The court took a different view of defendants' use of Mrs. Melvin's *name*. Although that, too, had been spread upon a public record, the court held that defendants' use of plaintiff's name was improper. The lapse of time between the incidents in issue and the making of the film was a relevant, but not conclusive, factor to the court.[71] Rather, the Court of Appeal emphasized that "[o]ne of the major objectives of society * * * and of the administration of our penal system, is the rehabilitation of the fallen and the reformation of the criminal. * * * Where a person has * * * rehabilitated himself, we, as right-thinking members of society, should permit him to continue in the path of rectitude rather than throw him back into a life of shame or crime. Even the thief on the cross was permitted to repent during the hours of his final agony." (112 Cal.App. at p. 292, 297 P. at p. 93.) The plaintiff was held to have stated a cause of action for invasion of privacy.

One of the premises of the rehabilitative process is that the rehabilitated offender can rejoin that great bulk of the community from which he has been ostracized for his anti-social acts. In return for becoming a "new man," he is allowed to melt into the shadows of obscurity.

We are realistic enough to recognize that men are curious about the inner sanctums of their neighbors—that the public will create its heroes and villains. We must also be realistic enough to realize that full disclosure of one's inner thoughts, intimate personal characteristics, and past life is neither the rule nor the norm in these United States. We have developed a variegated panoply of professional listeners to whom we confidentially "reveal all"; otherwise we

71. See Note, The Right of Privacy: Normative-Descriptive Confusion in the Defense of Newsworthiness (1963) 30 U.Chi.L.Rev. 722, 733–734.

keep our own counsel. The masks we wear may be stripped away upon the occurrence of some event of public interest. But just as the risk of exposure is a concomitant of urban life, so too is the expectation of anonymity regained. It would be a crass legal fiction to assert that a matter once public never becomes private again.[72] Human forgetfulness over time puts today's "hot" news in tomorrow's dusty archives. In a nation of 200 million people there is ample opportunity for all but the most infamous to begin a new life.

Plaintiff is a man whose last offense took place 11 years before, who has paid his debt to society, who has friends and an 11-year-old daughter who were unaware of his early life—a man who has assumed a position in "respectable" society. Ideally, his neighbors should recognize his present worth and forget his past life of shame. But men are not so divine as to forgive the past trespasses of others, and plaintiff therefore endeavored to reveal as little as possible of his past life. Yet, as if in some bizarre canyon of echoes, petitioner's past life pursues him through the pages of Reader's Digest, now published in 13 languages and distributed in 100 nations, with a circulation in California alone of almost 2,000,000 copies.

In a nation built upon the free dissemination of ideas, it is always difficult to declare that something may not be published. But the great general interest in an unfettered press may at times be outweighed by other great societal interests. As a people we have come to recognize that one of these societal interests is that of protecting an individual's right to privacy. The right to know and the right to have others *not* know are, simplistically considered, irreconcilable. But the rights guaranteed by the First Amendment do not require total abrogation of the right to privacy. The goals sought by each may be achieved with a minimum of intrusion upon the other.

In Time, Inc. v. Hill, supra, 385 U.S. 374, 383, 87 S.Ct. 534, 17 L.Ed.2d 456, the United States Supreme Court considered some of these same balancing problems with regard to a different form of invasion of privacy, that of placing the individual in a false light in the public eye. The New York statute construed in *Time* did not

72. "A public figure * * * can be so far removed from his former position in the public eye, that the publisher will no longer enjoy the prophylactic treatment accorded him when he deals with those persons who truly are public officials or public figures. * * *" (Johnston v. Time, Inc. (M.D.N.C.1970) 321 F.Supp. 837 [former professional basketball player no longer a public figure, had regained right to privacy].) "[I]t is erroneous * * * to assume that privacy, though lost for a certain time or in a certain context, goes forever unprotected * * *." (Spahn v. Julian Messner, Inc. (1966) 18 N.Y.2d 324, 328, 274 N.Y.S.2d 877, 879, 221 N.E.2d 543, 545; accord, Leverton v. Curtis Pub. Co. (3d Cir. 1951) 192 F.2d 974; Mau v. Rio Grande Oil, Inc. (N.D.Cal. 1939) 28 F.Supp. 845; see Note, supra, 30 U.Chi.L.Rev. 722, 726–727.)

In Time, Inc. v. Hill, supra, 385 U.S. 374, 87 S.Ct. 534, 17 L.Ed.2d 456, plaintiffs had been held hostage in their own home by escaped criminals three years prior to publication of the article in Life magazine. Their plight had been fully reported at the time. The court did not even question whether that previously publicly reported event remained public; the Hills were assumed to have a right to privacy concerning the event.

create a right of action for the truthful report of newsworthy people or events.[73] The Supreme Court stated, however, that "[t]his limitation to newsworthy persons and events does not of course foreclose an interpretation * * * to allow damages where 'Revelations may be so intimate and so unwarranted in view of the victim's position as to outrage the community's notions of decency.' * * * ". (385 U.S. at p. 383, fn. 7, 87 S.Ct. at p. 539.) Thus a truthful publication is constitutionally protected if (1) it is newsworthy and (2) it does not reveal facts so offensive as to shock the community's notions of decency.

We have previously set forth criteria for determining whether an incident is newsworthy. We consider "[1] the social value of the facts published, [2] the depth of the article's intrusion into ostensibly private affairs, and [3] the extent to which the party voluntarily acceded to a position of public notoriety. [Citations.]" (Kapellas v. Kofman, 1 Cal.3d 20, 36, 81 Cal.Rptr. 360, 370, 459 P.2d 912, 922.)

On the assumed set of facts before us we are convinced that a jury could reasonably find that plaintiff's identity as a former hijacker was not newsworthy. First, as discussed above, a jury could find that publication of plaintiff's identity in connection with incidents of his past life was in this case of minimal social value. There was no independent reason whatsoever for focusing public attention on Mr. Briscoe as an individual at this time. A jury could certainly find that Mr. Briscoe had once again become an anonymous member of the comunity. Once legal proeedings have concluded, and particularly once the individual has reverted to the lawful and unexciting life led by the rest of the community, the public's interest in knowing is less compelling.

Second, a jury might find that revealing one's criminal past for all to see is grossly offensive to most people in America. Certainly a criminal background is kept even more hidden from others than a humiliating disease (Barber v. Time, Inc., supra, 348 Mo. 1199, 159 S.W.2d 291) or the existence of business debts (Trammell v. Citizens News Co., Inc., supra, 285 Ky. 529, 148 S.W.2d 708; Tollefson v. Price, supra, 247 Or. 398, 430 P.2d 990).[74] The consequences of

73. New York does not recognize a common law right to privacy. Its statutory right to privacy provides no relief for the publication of truthful but embarrassing private facts so long as the reports concern newsworthy persons or events. (Spahn v. Julian Messner, Inc., supra, 18 N.Y.2d 324, 328, 274 N.Y.S.2d 877, 221 N.E.2d 543, vacated on other grounds, 387 U.S. 239, 87 S.Ct. 1706, 18 L.Ed.2d 744, judgment affirmed 21 N.Y.2d 124, 286 N.Y.S.2d 832, 233 N.E.2d 840, appeal dismissed (1968) 393 U.S. 1046, 89 S.Ct. 676, 21 L.Ed.2d 600.)

74. The instant case must be contrasted with the situation in Time, Inc. v. Hill, supra, 385 U.S. 374, 87 S.Ct. 534, 17 L.Ed.2d 456; most people would not consider their former momentary status as a hostage of escaped criminals to be so offensive or discreditable as to render the disclosure of this fact outrageous. * * * Compare Commonwealth v. Wiseman, supra, 356 Mass. 251, 249 N.E.2d 610, limiting public access to defendant's film on Bridgewater Hospital (Titicut Follies) because the film invaded the inmates' right to privacy by showing scenes of forced feeding, masturbation, etc.

revelation in this case—ostracism, isolation, and the alienation of one's family—make all too clear just how deeply offensive to most persons a prior crime is and thus how hidden the former offender must keep the knowledge of his prior indiscretion.

Third, in no way can plaintiff be said to have voluntarily consented to the publicity accorded him here. He committed a crime. He was punished. He was rehabilitated. And he became, for 11 years, an obscure and law-abiding citizen. His every effort was to forget and have others forget that he had once hijacked a truck.

Finally, the interests at stake here are not merely those of publication and privacy alone, for the state has a compelling interest in the efficacy of penal systems in rehabilitating criminals and returning them as productive and law-abiding citizens to the society whence they came. A jury might well find that a continuing threat that the rehabilitated offender's old identity will be resurrected by the media is counter-productive to the goals of this correctional process.

Mindful that "the balance is always weighted in favor of free expression" (Liberty Lobby, Inc. v. Pearson (1968) 129 U.S.App. D.C. 74, 390 F.2d 489, 491), and that we must not chill First Amendment freedoms through uncertainty,[75] we find it reasonable to require a plaintiff to prove, in each case, that the publisher invaded his privacy with reckless disregard for the fact that reasonable men would find the invasion highly offensive.[76]

We do not hold today that plaintiff must prevail in his action. It is for the trier of fact to determine (1) whether plaintiff had become a rehabilitated member of society, (2) whether identifying him as a former criminal would be highly offensive and injurious to the reasonable man, (3) whether defendant published this information with a reckless disregard for its offensiveness, and (4) whether any independent justification for printing plaintiff's identity existed. We hold today only that, as pleaded, plaintiff has stated a valid cause of action, sustaining the demurrer to plaintiff's complaint was improper, and that the ensuing judgment must therefore be reversed.

75. * * * Because the categories with which we deal—private and public, newsworthy and nonnewsworthy—have no clear profile, there is a temptation to balance interests in ad hoc fashion in each case. Yet history teaches us that such a process leads too often to discounting society's stake in First Amendment rights. (See Nimmer, supra, 56 Cal.L.Rev. 935, 939–941.) We therefore strive for as much predictability as possible within our system of case-by-case adjudication, lest we unwittingly chill First Amendment freedoms. "One steers clear of a barbed wire fence * * * he stays even farther away if he is not sure exactly where the fence is. * * *" (Wright, supra, 46 Tex.L.Rev. 630, 634.)

However, there is little uncertainty here. A publisher does have every reason to know, *before* publication, that identification of a man as a former criminal will be highly offensive to the individual involved. It does not require close reading of "Les Miserables" or "The Scarlet Letter" to know that men are haunted by the fear of disclosure of their past and destroyed by the exposure itself.

76. In alleging malice and willfulness in his complaint, plaintiff has complied with this initial requirement.

Plaintiff also claims that defendant's article placed him in a false light in the public eye by implying that his criminal activity was of recent vintage. He refers to the words "today" and "now" in the opening caption to the article, and the numerous recent dates mentioned, and contends that these imply to the reasonable man that the incident described took place recently.

We have previously stated that a "false light" cause of action "is in substance equivalent to * * * [a] libel claim, and should meet the same requirements of the libel claim * * * including proof of malice (cf. Time, Inc. v. Hill (1967) 385 U.S. 374, 87 S.Ct. 534, 17 L.Ed.2d 456) and fulfillment of the requirements of section 48a [of the Civil Code]. * * * [77]

VIRGIL v. TIME, INC.

United States Court of Appeal for the Ninth Circuit, 1975.
527 F.2d 1122.

MERRILL, CIRCUIT JUDGE. This suit was brought in California state courts by appellee, Virgil, complaining of a violation of his right of privacy. It was removed to federal court by appellant, Time, Incorporated, on grounds of diversity. This interlocutory appeal, taken pursuant to 28 U.S.C.A. § 1292(b), is from an order of the district court denying the motion of appellant for a summary judgment.

The facts are stated by the district court in its memorandum decision as follows:

> "The complaint is based upon an article that appeared in the February 22, 1971, issue of *Sports Illustrated* magazine [owned by appellant], entitled 'The Closest Thing to Being Born.' The article concerned the sport of body surfing as practiced at the 'Wedge,' a public beach near Newport Beach, California, reputed to be the world's most dangerous site for body surfing. The article attempted to describe and explore the character of the unique breed of man who enjoys meeting the extreme hazards of body surfing at the Wedge. Plaintiff is well known as a constant frequenter of the Wedge and is acknowledged by body surfers there to be the more daredevil of them all. He was extensively interviewed by Thomas Curry Kirkpatrick, the author of the article, and much of the information obtained from these interviews was used in the *Sports Illustrated*

77. Section 48a requires a libelled individual, within 20 days of learning of the publication, to advise the publisher specifically what statements he claims to be libelous and to request that the statements be corrected. Recovery of general damages is possible only if the section is complied with and if the publisher fails to correct the libelous statement. [Notes 63–77 from original, renumbered; other notes in original omitted.]

story. Photographs showing plaintiff surfing and lying on the public beach were taken and used to illustrate the article.

"Plaintiff admits that he willingly gave interviews to Kirkpatrick and that he knew that his name and activities as a body surfer might be used in connection with a forthcoming article in *Sports Illustrated.* But plaintiff now alleges that he 'revoked all consent' upon learning that the article was not confined solely to testimonials to his undoubted physical prowess.

"The article complained of was written by Kirkpatrick, a *Sports Illustrated* staff writer. In the summer of 1969 he received authorization from the senior editor of the magazine to do a story about the Wedge and the men who surf there. He was supplied with names and information about prominent body surfers, including the plaintiff, by the Beverly Hills bureau of Time, Inc. He began researching the article that summer, and contacted many surfers at the Wedge. Through these sources Kirkpatrick heard about the plaintiff and his daredevil attitude toward body surfing and life in general. He returned to the Newport Beach area the following summer to complete his research. It was during this period that Kirkpatrick first met the plaintiff and conducted several interviews with him.

"The photographs complained of were taken by a local freelance photographer who was commissioned by the defendants to photograph the Wedge and the body surfers. The photographer arranged, through one of the surfers, to have a group of surfers, including the plaintiff, come to the Wedge to have their pictures taken in connection with the article.

"Before publication the Kirkpatrick article was checked and researched by another *Sports Illustrated* staff member. For that purpose the checker telephoned the plaintiff's home and verified some of the information with the plaintiff's wife. The checker also talked to the plaintiff concerning the article, at which point, for the first time, the plaintiff indicated his desire not to be mentioned in the article at all, and that he wanted to stop the story. While not disputing the truth of the article or the accuracy of the statements about him which it contained, and while admitting that he had known that his picture was being taken, the plaintiff indicated that he thought the article was going to be limited to his prominence as a surfer at the Wedge, and that he did not know that it would contain references to some rather bizarre incidents in his life that were not directly related to surfing.

"In spite of the plaintiff's expressed opposition to the article, the article was published following its approval by the editorial staff and legal counsel for Sports Illustrated. In its published form, the article is eleven pages long and contains approximately 7,000 words. The article refers by name to many people who surf at the Wedge, and concludes in the last two pages with an account of the plaintiff's daredevil feats at the Wedge and a series of anecdotes about him that emphasize the psychological characteristics which presumably explain the reckless disregard for his own safety which his surfing demonstrates.

"Along with the photographs of the plaintiff, he complains of these references to incidents in his private, or nonsurfing, life." [78]

Respecting the applicable state law, the district court stated:

"California has adopted Dean Prosser's analysis of the tort of invasion of privacy. Kapellas v. Kofman, 1 C.3d 20, 35, n. 16, 459 P.2d 912, 81 Cal.Rptr. 360 (1969). According to that analysis, four separate torts are included within the broader designation of invasion of privacy.

1. *Intrusion* upon the plaintiff's seclusion or solitude, or into his private affairs;

78. E.g.: "He is somewhat of a mystery to most of the regular personnel, partly because he is quiet and withdrawn, usually absent from their get-togethers, and partly because he is considered to be somewhat abnormal."

"Virgil's carefree style at the Wedge appears to have emanated from some escapades in his younger days, such as the time at a party when a young lady approached him and asked where she might find an ashtray. 'Why, my dear, right here,' said Virgil, taking her lighted cigarette and extinguishing it in his mouth. He also won a small bet one time by burning a hole in a dollar bill that was resting on the back of his hand. In the process he also burned two holes in his wrist."

The article quoted a statement Virgil made to the author about a trip to Mammoth Mountain: " 'I quit my job, left home and moved to Mammoth Mountain. At the ski lodge there one night I dove headfirst down a flight of stairs—just because. Because why? Well, there were these chicks all around. I thought it would be groovy. Was I drunk? I think I might have been.' "

The article quotes Virgil as saying: " 'Every summer I'd work construction and dive off billboards to hurt myself or drop loads of lumber on myself to collect unemployment compensation so I could surf at the Wedge. Would I fake injuries? No, I wouldn't fake them. I'd be damn injured. But I would recover. I guess I used to live a pretty reckless life. I think I might have been drunk most of the time.' "

Again quoting Virgil, the author relates: " 'I love tuna fish. Eat it all the time. I do what feels good. That's the way I live my life. If it makes me feel good, whether it's against the law or not, I do it. I'm not sure a lot of the things I've done weren't pure lunacy.' Cherilee [plaintiff's wife] says, 'Mike also eats spiders and other insects and things.' "

Virgil was further quoted as saying, " 'I've always been determined to find a sport I could be the best in. I was always aggressive as a kid. You know, competitive, mean. Real mean. I bit off the cheek of a Negro in a six-against-30 gang fight. They had tire irons with them. But that was a long time ago. At the Wedge, there are a lot of individualists.' "

The articles notes: "Perhaps because most of his time was spent engaged in such activity, Virgil never learned how to read."

A photo caption reads: "Mike Virgil, the wild man of the Wedge, thinks it possible his brain is being slowly destroyed."

2. Public *disclosure of embarrassing private facts* about the plaintiff;

3. Publicity which places the plaintiff in a *false light* in the public eye;

4. *Appropriation,* for the defendant's advantage, of plaintiff's name or likeness.

Prosser, Law of Torts (4th ed. 1971) 804–14. See also Prosser, *Privacy,* 48 Cal.L.Rev. 383, 389 (1960)."

The district court concluded that of these four separate torts the one alleged by plaintiff was that of public disclosure of embarrassing private facts. We agree.[79]

The most recent definition of this tort and discussion of its elements is that to be found in The American Law Institute Restatement (Second) of Torts (Tentative Draft No. 21, 1975). Section 652D gives a new name to the tort, "Publicity Given to Private Life." The black letter reads:

"One who gives publicity to a matter concerning the private life of another is subject to liability to the other for unreasonable invasion of his privacy, if the matter publicized is of a kind which

(a) would be highly offensive to a reasonable person, and

(b) is not of legitimate concern to the public."

With respect to "publicity" comment *b* reads in part:

" 'Publicity,' as it is used in this Section, differs from 'publication,' as that term is used in § 577 in connection with liability for defamation. 'Publication,' in that sense, is a word of art, which includes any communication by the defendant to a third person. 'Publicity,' on the other hand, means that the matter is made public, by communicating it to the public at large, or to so many persons that the matter must be regarded as substantially certain to become one of public knowledge. The difference is not one of the means of com-

79. While the district court also determined that the "false light" theory applied, Virgil has expressly abandoned this theory on appeal. In the complaint appellee included other claims that can be regarded as dismissed from the case:

(A.) Intentional infliction of emotional distress. Under California law this is found only in cases of extreme or outrageous conduct, State Rubbish Collectors Association v. Siliznoff, 38 Cal. 2d 330, 240 P.2d 282 (1952). Such conduct, apart from the invasion of privacy by the publication of private facts, is not present here, and the case is thus best treated on the basis of the publication tort only.

(B.) Intrusion into private areas. It is clear that Kirkpatrick did not intrude on appellee's solitude and that all interviews were freely given.

(C.) Libel. Virgil expressly denies that this is a libel action.

(D.) Publication of the photograph. Under California law one who voluntarily adopts a pose in public view waives any right of privacy in so far as that particular pose is concerned, Gill v. Hearst Publishing Co., 40 Cal.2d 224, 253 P.2d 441 (1953).

munication, which may be oral, written, or by any other means. It is one of communication which reaches, or is sure to reach the public.

"Thus it is not an invasion of the right of privacy, within the rule stated in this Section, to communicate a fact concerning the plaintiff's private life to a single person, or even to a small group of persons. On the other hand, any publication in a newspaper or a magazine, even of small circulation, or in a handbill distributed to a large number of persons, or any broadcast over the radio, or statement made in an address to a large audience, is sufficient to give publicity within the meaning of the term as it is used in this Section. The distinction, in other words, is one between private and public communication."

With respect to "private life," comment *c* reads in part:

"The rule stated in this Section applies only to publicity given to matters concerning the private, as distinguished from the public, life of the individual. There is no liability when the defendant merely gives further publicity to information about the plaintiff which is already public. * * *

"Likewise there is no liability for giving further publicity to what the plaintiff himself leaves open to the public eye."

It is argued that by voluntary disclosure of the facts to Kirkpatrick, knowing that he proposed to write an article including information about appellant, appellant had himself rendered public the facts disclosed. We cannot agree.

It is not the manner in which information has been obtained that determines whether it is public or private. Here it is undisputed that the information was obtained without commission of a tort and in a manner wholly unobjectionable. However, that is not determinative as to this particular tort. The offense with which we are here involved is not the intrusion by means of which information is obtained * * *; it is the publicizing of that which is private in character. The question, then, is whether the information disclosed was public rather than private—whether it was generally known and if not, whether the disclosure by appellant can be said to have been to the public at large.

Talking freely to someone is not in itself, under comment *c*, making public the substance of the talk. There is an obvious and substantial difference between the disclosure of private facts to an individual—a disclosure that is selective and based on a judgment as to whether knowledge by that person would be felt to be objectionable—and the disclosure of the same facts to the public at large. The former, as the Restatement recognizes, does not constitute publicizing or public communication (see comment *b* as quoted supra) and accordingly does not destroy the private character of the facts disclosed. * * *

Talking freely to a member of the press, knowing the listener to be a member of the press, is not then in itself making public. Such communication can be said to anticipate that what is said will be made public since making public is the function of the press, and accordingly such communication can be construed as a consent to publicize. Thus if publicity results it can be said to have been consented to. However, if consent is withdrawn prior to the act of publicizing, the consequent publicity is without consent.

We conclude that the voluntary disclosure to Kirkpatrick did not in itself constitute a making public of the facts disclosed.

Appellant contends that since Virgil has not denied the truth of the statements made in the article, the publication was privileged under the First Amendment. The law has not yet gone so far.

The most recent Supreme Court expression on the subject, Cox Broadcasting Corp. v. Cohn, 420 U.S. 469, 95 S.Ct. 1029, 43 L.Ed.2d 328 (1975), dealt with the same tort as is involved here, characterized by the Court as "the right [of one] to be free from unwanted publicity about his private affairs, which, although wholly true, would be offensive to a person of ordinary sensibilities." Id. at 489, 95 S.Ct. at 1043. The Court noted:

> "* * * the appellants urge upon us the broad holding that the press may not be made criminally or civilly liable for publishing information that is neither false nor misleading but absolutely accurate, however damaging it may be to the reputation or individual sensibilities."

Id. The Court refused to reach this broad question "whether truthful publications may ever be subjected to civil or criminal liability consistently with the First and Fourteenth Amendments * * *." Id. at 491, 95 S.Ct. at 1044. It chose instead to deal with a "narrower interface between press and privacy," id., focusing on the protectable area of privacy and excluding from it material to be found in judicial records open to inspection by the public.

The Supreme Court, then, has not held in accordance with the contentions of appellant. Instead it has expressly declined to reach the issue presented. That issue seems to us to be whether, despite California's recognition and the recognition elsewhere given, this tortious violation of privacy is, as a tort, to be written out of the law. It seems to us to contemplate the further question whether the private individual is hereafter to be able to enjoy a private life save with leave of the press; whether (at least so far as the press is concerned) the concept of "private facts" continues to have meaning.[80]

80. In this respect we note that privacy is not only a personal interest, but is also one of concern to society as a whole, Rosenblatt v. Baer, 383 U.S. 75, 92–94, 86 S.Ct. 669, 679, 680, 15 L.Ed.2d 597 (1966) (Stewart, J., concurring).

To hold that privilege extends to all true statements would seem to deny the existence of "private" facts, for if facts be facts—that is, if they be true—they would not (at least to the press) be private, and the press would be free to publicize them to the extent it sees fit. The extent to which areas of privacy continue to exist, then, would appear to be based not on rights bestowed by law but on the taste and discretion of the press. We cannot accept this result.

To test the validity of such a rule we might start with the public's right to know under the First Amendment. Does the spirit of the Bill of Rights require that individuals be free to pry into the unnewsworthy private affairs of their fellowmen? In our view it does not. In our view fairly defined areas of privacy must have the protection of law if the quality of life is to continue to be reasonably acceptable. The public's right to know is, then, subject to reasonable limitations so far as concerns the private facts of its individual members.

If the public has no right to know, can it yet be said that the press has a constitutional right to inquire and to inform? In our view it cannot. It is because the public has a right to know that the press has a function to inquire and to inform.[81] The press, then, cannot be said to have any right to give information greater than the extent to which the public is entitled to have information.

We conclude that unless it be privileged as newsworthy (a subject we discuss next), the publicizing of private facts is not protected by the First Amendment.

The privilege to publicize newsworthy matters is included in the definition of the tort set out in Restatement of Torts, Second § 652D (Tentative Draft No. 21, 1975). Liability may be imposed for an invasion of privacy only if "the matter publicized is of a kind which * * * is not of legitimate concern to the public." While the Restatement does not so emphasize, we are satisfied that this provision is one of constitutional dimension delimiting the scope of the tort and that the extent of the privilege thus is controlled by federal rather than state law.

Restatement comment casts light on the nature of matter that "is not of legitimate concern to the public." The privilege extends to "voluntary public figures," comment *c*,[82] and to some "involuntary

81. *See* Columbia Broadcasting System, Inc. v. Democratic National Committee, 412 U.S. 94, 122, 93 S.Ct. 2080, 2096, 36 L.Ed.2d 772 (1973), indicating that the foremost First Amendment concern is the interest of the public; see also Red Lion Broadcasting Co. v. FCC, 395 U.S. 367, 390, 89 S.Ct. 1794, 1806, 23 L.Ed.2d 371 (1969).

82. Comment *c*, as well as the other comments cited or referred to in the text, is taken from the comments to Restatement of Torts, Second § 652F (Tentative Draft No. 13, 1967). That section, which spoke of the privilege to publicize matters of public interest, has now been eliminated; the provision of § 652F pertinent to the tort involved here has now been directly incorporated within § 652D by Restatement of Torts, Second (Tentative Draft No. 21, 1975). The preliminary note to Tentative Draft No. 21, p. 86, indicates that the purpose of this change was to treat the element of "legitimate concern to the public" as a restriction on the cause of action rath-

public figures" (those "who have not sought publicity or consented to it, but through their own conduct or otherwise have * * * become 'news,' ") comment *d.* It extends to "all matters of the kind customarily regarded as 'news,' " comment *e*; and also "giving information to the public for purposes of education, amusement or enlightenment, where the public may reasonably be expected to have a legitimate interest in what is published," comment *h.*

That this privilege extends to private facts is made clear by comment *f.* It is emphasized, however, that the privilege is not unlimited. The comment states:

> "In determining what is a matter of legitimate public interest, account must be taken of the customs and conventions of the community; and in the last analysis what is proper becomes a matter of the community mores. The line is to be drawn when the publicity ceases to be the giving of information to which the public is entitled, and becomes a morbid and sensational prying into private lives for its own sake, with which a reasonable member of the public, with decent standards, would say that he had no concern. * * * "

In our judgment such a standard for newsworthiness does not offend the First Amendment; by the extreme limits it imposes in defining the tort [83] it avoids unduly limiting the breathing space needed by the press for the exercise of effective editorial judgment. See Miami Herald Publishing Co v. Tornillo, 418 U.S. 241, 94 S.Ct. 2831, 41 L.Ed.2d 730 (1974). The definition of the "line to be drawn" is not as clear as one would wish, but it expresses the distinction between that which is of legitimate public interest and that which is not as well as we could do.[84] Where competing values are involved, unless one competitor is to be sacrificed outright, those involved with the competition must accept that risks are inherent and the problem lies in attempting to minimize them to the extent that the conflict permits. In our view this the Restatement has done. Accordingly we accept the Restatement's standard for newsworthiness.

We move, then, to the question whether, with such a standard to be applied, the district court correctly ruled that factual issues re-

er than as a privilege; nothing is said to indicate that a substantive change with respect to any matter in the comments is intended. Accordingly, we shall treat the comments to the now eliminated § 652F as applicable to § 652D as it presently exists.

83. We do not intend that "morbid and sensational" be taken too literally. This language is not, in our view, to be regarded as a statement of a prerequisite but rather as illustrative of the degree of offensiveness which should be present.

84. The fact that the standard is made to depend on community mores does not, to us, make it constitutionally infirm. Community standards play a role of constitutional dimension in other areas of free speech—e. g., as to the obscene nature of a publication, Miller v. California, 413 U.S. 15, 24, 93 S.Ct. 2607, 2615, 37 L.Ed.2d 419 (1973). While determinations regarding community standards are subject to close judicial scrutiny, Jenkins v. Georgia, 418 U.S. 153, 160–61, 94 S.Ct. 2750 (1974), they nonetheless are essential in the resolution of free speech questions which are predicated on community values.

mained to be resolved on trial. Here appellant makes a vigorous attack upon the order appealed from. Appellant contends: "A press which must depend upon a governmental determination as to what facts are of 'public interest' in order to avoid liability for their truthful publication is not free at all. * * * [However,] protection of the editor's discretion need not result in a rule which abdicates all responsibility to the press. A constitutional rule can be fashioned which protects all the interests involved. This goal is achieved by providing a privilege for truthful publications which is defeasible only when the court concludes as a matter of law that the truthful publication complained of constitutes a clear abuse of the editor's constitutional discretion to publish and discuss subjects and facts which in his judgment are matters of public interest."

We cannot agree that the First Amendment requires that the question must be confined to one of law to be decided by the judge. Courts have not yet gone so far in other areas of the law involving First Amendment problems, such as libel and obscenity. The testing of facts against a standard founded on community mores does entail judgment of the court itself. But if there is room for differing views as to the state of community mores or the manner in which it would operate upon the facts in question, there is room for the jury function. The function of the court is to ascertain whether a jury question is presented.[85]

This court, in Guam Federation of Teachers, Local 1581, A.F.T. v. Ysrael, 492 F.2d 438, 441 (9th Cir. 1974), cert. denied 419 U.S. 872, 95 S.Ct. 132, 42 L.Ed.2d 111 (1974), stated:

> "We agree * * * that it is important that judges focus attention on the summary judgment, directed verdict and judgment notwithstanding the verdict procedures in libel actions. When civil cases may have a chilling effect on First Amendment rights, special care is appropriate. Thus, a judicial examination at these stages of the proceeding, closely scrutinizing the evidence to determine whether the case should be terminated in a defendant's favor, provides a buffer against possible First Amendment interferences. The Supreme Court has instructed trial courts to 'examine for [themselves] the statements in issue and the circumstances

85. The determination whether a matter is of public interest thus differs from the determination whether an individual is a public official or figure, which at least in the first instance is a matter for the trial judge, Rosenblatt v. Baer, 383 U.S. 75, 88, 86 S.Ct. 669, 677, 15 L.Ed.2d 597 (1966). The rationale advanced for this latter approach is to lessen the possibility that jury will use the general verdict as a cloak to punish unpopular ideas or speakers, id. at 88 n. 15, Monitor Patriot Co. v. Roy, 401 U.S. 265, 267–77, 91 S.Ct. 621, 28 L.Ed.2d 35 (1971). While this danger is also present in the area of privacy, we believe that a determination founded on community mores must be largely resolved by a jury subject to close judicial scrutiny to ensure that the jury resolutions comport with First Amendment principles, New York Times Co. v. Sullivan, 376 U.S. 254, 285, 84 S.Ct. 710, 11 L.Ed.2d 686 (1964). [Notes 78 to 85 from original, renumbered; other notes in original omitted.]

> under which they were made to see * * * whether they are of a character which the principles of the First Amendment * * * protect.' * * *
>
> * * *
>
> The *standard* against which the evidence must be examined is that of *New York Times* and its progeny. But the *manner* in which the evidence is to be examined in the light of that standard is the same as in all other cases in which it is claimed that a case should not go to the jury. If the evidence, so considered, measures up to the *New York Times* standard, the case is one for the jury, and it is error to grant a directed verdict, as the trial judge did in this case." * * *

The final question, then, is whether in application of the standard for newsworthiness taken from the Restatement, jury questions are presented.

We may concede, arguendo, that the privilege to publicize newsworthy matter would, as matter of law, extend to the general subject of the article here in question: body surfing at the Wedge. While not hot news of the day, this subject quite properly can be regarded as of general public interest.

However, accepting that it is, as matter of law, in the public interest to know about some area of activity, it does not necessarily follow that it is in the public interest to know private facts about the persons who engage in that activity. The fact that they engage in an activity in which the public can be said to have a general interest does not render every aspect of their lives subject to public disclosure. Most persons are connected with some activity, vocational or avocational, as to which the public can be said as matter of law to have a legitimate interest or curiosity. To hold as matter of law that private facts as to such persons are also within the area of legitimate public interest could indirectly expose everyone's private life to public view. Limitations, then, remain to be imposed and at this point factual questions are presented respecting the state of community mores.

Among the questions so presented here are: Whether (and, if so, to what extent), private facts respecting Virgil, as a prominent member of the group engaging in body surfing at the Wedge, are matters in which the public has a legitimate interest; whether the identity of Virgil as the one to whom such facts apply is matter in which the public has a legitimate interest. (Additional questions, related not to privilege but to other elements of the tort are: whether, for reasons other than the voluntary and knowing communication to Kirkpatrick, the facts had become matter of public knowledge; if not, whether the publicizing of these facts would prove highly offensive to a reasonable person—one of ordinary sensibilities.)

On these questions the function of the court on motion for summary judgment is to decide whether, on the record, reasonable minds could differ. If in the judgment of the court reasonable minds could not differ, and the answer on which reasonable minds agree favors invocation of the privilege, then summary judgment for the appellant would be proper.

We have no way of knowing whether, in denying summary judgment, the court had in mind matters we have here discussed. *Guam Federation of Teachers,* supra, had not then been decided and the court did not have before it the language of that case stressing the importance of close judicial scrutiny of the evidence as a buffer against possible First Amendment interferences. We think, on balance, the desirable remand would be one that invites reconsideration of the motion in the light of our views here expressed.

* * *

CANTRELL v. FOREST CITY PUBLISHING CO.

Supreme Court of the United States, 1974.
419 U.S. 245, 95 S.Ct. 465, 42 L.Ed.2d 419.

MR. JUSTICE STEWART delivered the opinion of the Court.

* * *

In Time, Inc. v. Hill, 385 U.S. 374, 87 S.Ct. 534, 17 L.Ed.2d 456, the Court considered a similar false light, invasion of privacy action. The New York Court of Appeals had interpreted New York Civil Rights Law, McKinney's Consol.Laws, c. 6, §§ 50–51 to give a "newsworthy person" a right of action when his or her name, picture or portrait was the subject of a "fictitious" report or article. Material and substantial falsification was the test for recovery. Id., at 384–386, 87 S.Ct. at 540–541. Under this doctrine the New York courts awarded the plaintiff James Hill compensatory damages based on his complaint that Life Magazine had falsely reported that a new Broadway play portrayed the Hill family's experience in being held hostage by three escaped convicts. This Court, guided by its decision in New York Times Co v. Sullivan, 376 U.S. 254, 84 S.Ct. 710, 11 L.Ed.2d 686, which recognized constitutional limits on a State's power to award damages for libel in actions brought by public officials, held that the constitutional protections for speech and press precluded the application of the New York statute to allow recovery for "false reports of matters of public interest in the absence of proof that the defendant published the report with knowledge of its falsity or in reckless disregard of the truth." Id., 385 U.S. at 388, 87 S.Ct. at 542. Although the jury could have reasonably concluded from the evidence in the *Hill* case that Life had engaged in knowing falsehood or had recklessly disregarded the truth in stating in the article that "the story reenacted" the Hill family's experience, the Court concluded that the trial judge's instructions had not confined the jury to such a finding as a predicate for liability as required by the Constitution. Id., at 394, 87 S.Ct. at 545.

The District Judge in the case before us, in contrast with the trial judge in Time, Inc. v. Hill, did instruct the jury that liability could be imposed only if it concluded that the false statements in the Sunday Magazine feature article on the Cantrells had been made with knowledge of their falsity or in reckless disregard of the truth. No objection was made by any of the parties to this knowing-or-reckless-falsehood instruction. Consequently, this case presents no occasion to consider whether a State may constitutionally apply a more relaxed standard of liability for a publisher or broadcaster of false statements injurious to a private individual under a false-light theory of invasion of privacy, or whether the constitutional standard announced in Time, Inc. v. Hill applies to all false-light cases. Cf. Gertz v. Welch, Inc, * * *.

Does the false light category add anything significant to the substantive law of privacy? A false statement may, of course, constitute defamation or an injurious falsehood. If it does neither of these things it might nevertheless invade a person's privacy if it recites a fact which *if true* would constitute an unjustified disclosure of private matters. Is not that the only thing that would render the statement actionable *as an invasion of privacy?* And if so, does the false light concept deserve separate recognition as a branch of the law of privacy?

When we come to constitutional privilege, however, falsity may assume importance. If the fact disclosed falls within the field protected by the First Amendment the States may not hold it actionable unless the statement of purported fact was knowingly false or made with reckless disregard of its truth or falsity, or perhaps meets lower *Gertz* standards, all of which would include a requirement that the statement must be false.

SECTION 4. THE FIELD OF BUSINESS, COMPETITION, AND MARKETING

HANSCHKE v. MERCHANTS' CREDIT BUREAU

Supreme Court of Michigan, 1931.
256 Mich. 272, 239 N.W. 318.

McDONALD, J. This is an action to recover damages for libel. In December, 1926, the plaintiff was employed in the city of Detroit as auditor and salesman for the Chelsea Rubber Company. The defendant Merchants' Credit Bureau is a corporation organized for the benefit and protection of merchants in the city of Detroit. Its secretary testified: "Our corporation is engaged in the business of procuring and preserving information regarding persons and corporations, partnerships and companies, for the purpose of protecting our subscribers and our membership, and furnishing them with such information upon request."

The defendant Boyer is a member of the Merchants' Credit Bureau. On information furnished by him, the bureau published the following matter of and concerning the plaintiff: "Hanschke: It has been reported that the above party, representing the Chelsea Rubber Co., Chelsea, Michigan, presented a check for merchandise in the amount of $47.65 to a local member, and while they were seeking information on the telephone, he disappeared. The check was drawn on the Grand Rapids National bank. If this party comes to your attention, notify this office."[86]

It is conceded that the publication was false. On demand, defendant published a retraction. This suit was brought. The plaintiff was given a judgment for $3,500 in a trial by the court without a jury. The defendant appealed.

The defendants' plea of qualified privilege presents the principal question in the case. The Merchants' Credit Bureau is a corporation organized for profit. Its articles of association announce the purpose of the corporation to be as follows: "Collecting, compiling, preserving of reports and information concerning the financial standing, reputation and responsibility of individuals, firms and corporations, and for the purpose of furnishing and selling such reports to members of and subscribers to this corporation, and to other persons, firms and corporations; and for the further purpose of collecting accounts, claims and demands of any individual, firm or corporation desiring said service."

In carrying out the purpose of its organization, it contracts with subscribers and members to furnish such information on request, and provides that all information furnished shall be for the sole use and benefit of the subscribers, and shall be held by them in strict confidence. One feature of the service not required by the contract is the publication and circulation of a weekly bulletin which: "gives a summary of all the cautionary notices received during the week, such as fraudulent checks passed, illegal buying, forgery, stolen checks, and post office money orders, names upon whom the bureau has received important information, lost and found addresses, and any other items of general interest to the membership."

86. It has been held that if a bank wrongfully dishonors a customer's check, the latter may recover "general compensatory damages" if the customer is a merchant or trader. Svendsen v. State Bank of Duluth, 64 Minn. 40, 65 N.W. 1086, 31 L.R.A. 552, 58 Am.St.Rep. 522 (1896).

Cf. J. M. James Co. v. Bank, 105 Tenn. 1, 58 S.W. 261, 51 L.R.A. 255 (1900) (on allegation that he was a trader, plaintiff entitled to "temperate but substantial damages."); Weaver v. Grenada Bank, 180 Miss. 876, 178 So. 105, 179 So. 564 (1938) (charge suggesting nominal damage verdict would be acceptable held error where jury brought in $5 verdict). See note 9 N.C.L.Rev. 94 (1930).

As to disparagement of a bank by false rumors, see Ridgeway State Bank v. Bird, 185 Wis. 418, 202 N.W. 170, 37 A.L.R. 1343 (1925); Ernst and Lindey, Hold Your Tongue 67 (1932) (omitted from 2d ed.).

In Meyerson v. Hurlbut, 68 App.D.C. 360, 98 F.2d 232, 118 A.L.R. 313 (1938), charges that various Washington jobbers had cut plaintiff off an open account, and had refused to sell merchandise to him, were held capable of a meaning defamatory to a merchant's credit.

In one of such bulletins, the libel declared upon in this suit was published. It was sent to the 700 paid members in Detroit, and gratuitously to others outside of the city, including the Border Cities' Credit Bureau of Windsor, Ont., the credit bureau of Flint, Mich., the credit bureau of Pontiac and of Saginaw and Port Huron.

If it may be said that a privilege relation existed between the defendant bureau and its subscribers, it certainly cannot be extended to outsiders.

"A communication from a mercantile agency is privileged only when made to one having an interest in the particular matter and not when it is published in a report for general circulation among subscribers." 36 C.J., page 1267, section 253, citing Pollasky v. Minchener, 81 Mich. 280, 46 N.W. 5, 9 L.R.A. 102, 21 Am.St.Rep. 516.

The information contained in the publication in question was not requested by any of the subscribers. Their contract did not call for it. The added feature of the bureau service in conveying information by bulletin was voluntary. It was given a wide circulation not only in the city of Detroit, but elsewhere. It carried the defamatory matter not only to subscribers, but to others. It was not privileged. Pollasky v. Minchener is controlling. * * *

The judgment is affirmed, with costs to the plaintiff.[87]

EVANS v. HARLOW

Court of Queen's Bench, 1844.
5 Adolph & E.N.S. 624, 13 L.J.Q.B. 120.

[Case for a libel. The declaration stated that plaintiff was the inventor and manufacturer of a registered article called the self acting tallow syphon or lubricator; that he had built up a profitable trade in these articles; and that defendant published in a newspaper, "of and concerning the plaintiff, and of and concerning him in the way of his said trade and business, and of and concerning the said design and the plaintiff as the inventor and proprietor thereof, * * * etc.," the following statement.]

"This is to caution parties employing steam power from a person (meaning the plaintiff) 'offering what he' (meaning the plaintiff) 'calls *Self acting tallow syphons or lubricators*' (meaning the said

87. An early case where the majority and dissenting opinions work out elaborately the divergent points of view is King v. Patterson, 49 N.J.L. 417, 9 A. 705, 60 Am.Rep. 622 (1887).

The weight of American authority inclines towards recognizing a qualified privilege where the agency furnishes information "based upon careful investigation" in response to a specific request by a subscriber. Restatement, Torts, section 595, comment g; Smith, Conditional Privilege for Mercantile Agencies, 14 Col.L.R. 187, 296 (1914). See Hooper—Holmes Bureau v. Bunn, 161 F.2d 102 (5th Cir. 1947). Some states, however, recognize no such privilege, e. g., Hood v. Dun & Bradstreet, 486 F.2d 25 (5th Cir. 1973) (Georgia law).

Compare the problem of such services as Consumers' Research and Consumers' Union. See Ernst & Lindey, Hold Your Tongue 64, 66 (1932) (omitted from 2d ed.).

design, and meaning the said goods and articles which the plaintiff had so sold and had on sale as aforesaid), 'stating that he' (meaning the plaintiff) 'is the sole inventor, manufacturer and patentee, thereby monopolizing high prices at the expense of the public. *Robert Harlow*' (meaning himself the defendant), 'brass-founder, *Stockport*, takes this opportunity of saying that such a patent does not exist, and that he' (meaning the defendant) 'has to offer an improved lubricator, which dispenses with the necessity of using more than one to a steam engine, thereby constituting a saving of 50 per cent. over every other kind yet offered to the public. Those who have already adopted the lubricators' (meaning the said design of the plaintiff, and meaning his goods and articles which the plaintiff has so sold and had on sale as aforesaid), 'against which R. H.' (meaning himself the defendant) 'would caution, will find that the tallow is wasted instead of being effectually employed as professed.' "

By means of which premises the plaintiff was greatly injured in his credit, reputation and circumstances, and was prevented from selling divers articles made according to the said design, and also divers of the said other articles and goods, which he might and otherwise would have sold, and was thereby prevented from acquiring divers great gains which he might and otherwise would have acquired, and was and is greatly injured in the way of his said trade and business and otherwise. To the plaintiff's damage, of &c.

General demurrer, and joinder. The ground stated in the margin of the demurrer was, "that there is nothing in the alleged libel which is actionable." * * *

LORD DENMAN, C. J. I am of opinion that the statement complained of does not amount to a libel. It contains no real imputation upon the plaintiff of fraud or misrepresentation. There are indeed words intimating that the plaintiff stated himself to be the sole inventor and patentee of the lubricators, whereas no such patent existed; but it does not appear by the record that the plaintiff had or claimed to have any patent in respect to these. The gist of the complaint is, the defendant's telling the world that the lubricators sold by the plaintiff were not good for their purpose, but wasted the tallow. A tradesman offering goods for sale exposes himself to observations of this kind; and it is not by averring them to be "false, scandalous, malicious and defamatory" that the plaintiff can found a charge of libel upon them. To decide so would open a very wide door to litigation, and might expose every man who said his goods were better than another's to the risk of an action. There is, in this case, a caution given by the defendant against the plaintiff; but it is not against fraud in him; it is simply on account of his selling defective goods. Any one selling the same articles would have as much right to complain as he has. The imputation is only on the goods, and is not ground for an action. * * *

Judgment for defendant.

TEX SMITH, THE HARMONICA MAN, INC. v. GODFREY

Supreme Court of New York, Special Term, Part III, New York County, 1951.
198 Misc. 1006, 102 N.Y.S.2d 251.

STEUER, JUSTICE. The corporate plaintiff sells a ukulele for two dollars and ninety-nine cents, which activity it advertises widely. The individual plaintiff is its chief stockholder. The individual defendant is a radio and television performer and the corporate defendant operates radio and television stations over which the matter to be referred to was broadcast. On April 11, 1950, the individual defendant, on a television broadcast produced one of plaintiff's ukuleles and made some remarks concerning it. While the plaintiffs' name was not mentioned, the price was, and as the complaint alleges that plaintiff was the only producer at that price and was well known on account of it, no point is made on this motion that plaintiff was not referred to and that the listening audience so understood.

The complaint sets out the exact words of the individual defendant but as they are extensive, repetition would be inconvenient as well as needless. The fair purport of the remarks follows. Three different makes of ukuleles were exhibited. The first was stated to retail at about eleven dollars and was described as a good instrument. The second, retailing at about half that price, was stated to be suitable for learning to play and for beginners in the art. Third, plaintiff's was inferred to be unsuitable for either study or performance. It was pointed out that there were no frets but merely a painted line to indicate the fret. The tone was illustrated to indicate its poverty. The opinion was expressed that to sell the instrument as a ukulele might not be contrary to law but that people who did it should be jailed. The conclusion is that no one should be deceived into buying it.

The first cause of action is against the individual defendant, the third against the corporation. The fourth is against both for a radio rebroadcast of the same remarks. The second is in favor of the individual plaintiff against both defendants. The motion is to dismiss the complaint or in the alternative each cause of action for failure to make out a cause of action.

The gist of the motion is the claim that the words used are not actionable, or in other words, not slanderous per se. While the progressive development of the law of defamation discloses a field in which general statements can rarely be made without challenge, there are a few principles concerning which there is general accord. Words, slanderous per se, are limited to those which impute unchastity to a woman, charge the commission of a crime or tend to injure the person spoken of in his business or profession. The first two grounds are not applicable here. The fair import of the statement deplores the state of the criminal code but charges no violation of it as constituted. As regards the third category distinction has always been made between the product and the manufacturer or seller. Slander of the product is not slander per se of the maker or seller. Words tending to injure in a business are those which impugn solvency or would directly have an adverse effect on credit, or charge unethical or unfair practices in the conduct of the business.

It is sometimes difficult to say whether words impeach the product or the sale of it. This is particularly true where, as here, they assert the marketing of inferior merchandise. It is, however, clear that in this statement the method as well as the goods are within the field of the remarks. Their intendment is that a purchaser is duped into buying a worthless article by grossly unfair advertising. It is not only that plaintiff is inept, unskillful or ignorant in manufacture, but that it is unethical. This is actionable.

If the words are regarded purely as a reflection on the instruments, the same result would be reached. Here the words only become actionable if it is shown that damage followed upon their utterance. There was a time when such damage had to be specifically shown—the loss of a contract, a position, or the like. It is practically impossible for one selling to the general public at retail or by mail order to show loss of particular sales. Under such circumstances those people were without remedy from the most groundless calumny. It is, however, now recognized that allegations and proof of a general loss of sales is sufficient, leaving it to the trier of the facts to determine whether the loss is properly to be attributed to the slander or not. The allegations of the complaint on this subject are sufficient by this standard.

No point has been raised in regard to differentiating between the plaintiffs. Although it may not be immediately apparent how the individual plaintiff could have suffered through words spoken of the corporation, that question has not been raised.

Motion denied.

DIRECT IMPORT BUYERS ASSOCIATION v. KSL, INC.

Supreme Court of Utah, 1975.
— Utah —, 538 P.2d 1040.

ELLETT, JUSTICE. This is an appeal by plaintiff from a summary judgment in favor of the defendant for no cause of action.

The plaintiff was selling a product called Econo-Jets, which when used in the carburetor of an automobile was claimed to increase gas mileage and reduce pollution. It advertised its products through KSL and claims that its sales were numerous until November 14 and December 31, 1973, at which time Lynn Packer, an announcer for KSL, Inc., made false statements over the air deprecating plaintiff's products, and as a result thereof plaintiff sustained a great loss of sales.

The defendant claims that due to gasoline shortage at the time, the product was a news item and that the information broadcast was of a public interest and was true. It makes a further claim that the statements made over the air were conditionally privileged.

The substance of the statement as made was to the effect that the Econo-Jets sold in stores for $5.95 a pair; that the inventor said they cost twenty cents per pair to manufacture but the price was driven up by royalties, packaging, marketing and profits; and that Econo-Jets advertising says the product can add up to six miles per gallon when installed on a car.

The announcer also stated:

(a) That KSL News had sent a set to Motor Vehicle Research Laboratories in New Hampshire and that Director A. J. White said that the device can slightly increase mileage by leaning the fuel mixture, but the leaner mixture created by the units he's seen could cause burned valves and the hole could admit dust into the engine and that in his opinion the jets do not improve mileage. White said further that the rules of the U. S. Clean Air Act prohibit disturbing a car's existing idle screws.

(b) A spokesman for Econo-Jets said his product was being tested by the New Orleans Police Department and the test was going "very well," but in New Orleans Captain Herman Saacks today said he's noticed no gas mileage improvement with the jets installed in his personal police car.

(c) A local auto executive said he personally thinks such devices are a waste of money.

(d) Doctor Grant Winn of the Utah Air Conservation Committee said the Econo-Jets would be unlawful, if they alter—for the worse—a car's air pollution control equipment.

(e) In 1971, a California government agency tested Econo-Jets and found the units decreased carbon monoxide emission but increased hydrocarbon and nitrogen oxides emissions.

The announcer concluded on one occasion by saying, "Inventor Rock says thirty thousand units in successful operation prove the skeptics wrong. He says he is now developing a new engine that will yield 60–70 miles per gallon. And to top that, the Utahn says he's close to a cure for cancer and the common cold."

The basis upon which plaintiff claims a right to recover is libel and slander, but it is actually for injurious falsehood. The principle of slander of title, while similar, is not quite the same, for in this case there is no disparagement of plaintiff's title. It is merely a depreciation of the quality of plaintiff's product.

In order for plaintiff here to recover, it must prove falsity of the statements made, malice, and special damages.[88]

Mr. Packer, the announcer, filed an affidavit in which he averred that he, in good faith, attempted to introduce into the broadcast the relevant and reliable facts about the product and that he utilized his best efforts to state the same fairly and evenhandedly.

88. Drug Research Corp. v. Curtis Publishing Co. et al., 7 N.Y.2d 435, 199 N.Y.S.2d 33, 166 N.E.2d 319 (1960). [From original, renumbered.]

The plaintiff filed affidavits wherein it was stated that Lynn Packer did not make a reasonable effort to verify the information which he published and that he did not publish all of the material and pertinent information on hand but published only those portions of the information which tended to cast doubt on the product.

The malice which plaintiff must show in order to overcome a conditional privilege is simply an improper motive such as a desire to do harm or that the defendant did not honestly believe his statements to be true or that the publication was excessive. * * *

In view of the fact that the announcer stated, "And to top that, the Utahn says he's close to a cure for cancer and the common cold," it would seem to present a jury question as to whether malice existed. This statement has absolutely no relevance to the efficiency of Econo-Jets and might be considered by the triers of the facts along with other matters in determining whether malice existed. The question of the truth of the statement and the matter of special damages are, of course, for the jury.

We think there are disputed issues of fact in this case which prevent the granting of a summary judgment. Therefore, the judgment is reversed and the case remanded for such further proceedings as may be proper not in conflict with this opinion. Costs are awarded to the appellant.

HENRIOD, CHIEF JUSTICE (dissenting).

I dissent and believe the lower court should be affirmed.

I have read the two broadcasts upon which this case is bottomed and I see nothing in them that would approach in infamy the critical analysis of a Consumers Guide. * * * As to evidence of malice with the intention seriously and wilfully to damage the distributor of this article, there is no evidence thereof, as I can see, save the possibility of zealous inquiry on the part of the newscaster * * *. It is difficult to see how the news media would hate a carburetor * * *.

ADVANCE MUSIC CORPORATION v. AMERICAN TOBACCO CO.

Court of Appeals of New York, 1946.
296 N.Y. 79, 70 N.E.2d 401.

LOUGHRAN, CHIEF JUDGE. The amended complaint in this action is attacked by motion under rule 106 of the Rules of Civil Practice for insufficiency on its face. Three separately stated causes of action are pleaded therein.

By way of inducement, the first cause makes these allegations: The plaintiff is a corporation engaged in the business of publishing musical compositions. Its revenue is chiefly derived from sales of sheet music made to the public and from licenses for use of its compositions in the entertainment field. It expends large sums of money for advertising in an effort to create a general impression that its compositions are or will be among the most popular song successes of the day. Methods employed by the plaintiff to that end include performances of its compositions by bandleaders and entertainers through the media of radio, phonograph recordings and motion pictures. Jobbers, dealers and the general public normally purchase musical compositions which are currently made popular by means of advertising of that kind. Sheet music is handled by jobbers and dealers on consignment. Premature return or other failure to promote sales thereof brings about serious loss to the publisher.

In respect of the wrong asserted by the plaintiff, the first cause of action goes on to say: The defendants—a tobacco company and an advertising concern—are the creators of a commercial coast-to-coast radio program which is broadcast each Saturday night. "A wide listening audience estimated to be in excess of fifteen million people per week is attracted to this program by reason of the constant representations * * * made by the defendants that said program consists of the rendition of the nine or ten most popular songs of the week in the relative order of their popularity based upon an extensive and accurate survey conducted throughout the nation." Weekly lists of the songs thus classified by the defendants upon their radio program are widely circulated by them, "so that the public, dealers, jobbers, motion picture companies, phonograph companies, electrical transcription companies, radio station performers and entertainers, and others, may be induced to rely upon such lists and purchase and use the music stated to be the most popular." In pursuing this course, the defendants act wantonly and without good faith. Their selections and ratings of the nine or ten most popular songs of the week "are in fact the choice or result of caprice or of other considerations foreign to a selection based on an accurate and extensive survey of the nation-wide popularity of such songs and the relative order of their popularity for the current week of such broadcast." Songs published by the plaintiff which are among the first nine or ten most popular musical compositions of the nation are either passed over by the defendants or placed on their radio program and weekly lists in an improper order of popularity.

In respect of the damages complained of by the plaintiff, the first cause of action sets forth the following particulars: Music jobbers and dealers, bandleaders, entertainers, supervisors of radio programs, phonograph recording companies and motion picture producers in choosing songs are largely influenced by the selections and ratings which the defendants disseminate by way of their radio program and weekly lists. On that account, jobbers and dealers prematurely return songs of the plaintiff and thereby prevent distribution thereof to retail outlets for sale to the public. For the same reason, most users of music are induced to accept the songs heralded by the defendants and to neglect songs published by the plaintiff. In consequence of all this, the measures taken by the plaintiff for exploitation of its songs are frustrated; the value of its musical compositions is depreciated; its revenue is diminished; and its property rights and business prestige are impaired.

The foregoing parts of the first cause of action are incorporated by reference into the second cause of action and are there followed by the further allegation that "the aforesaid acts and representations on the part of the defendants are made with intent to injure the plaintiff." Thus in sum and substance the second cause of action constitutes a statement to this effect: The defendants are wantonly causing damage to the plaintiff by a system of conduct on their part which warrants an inference that they intend harm of that type. So read, the second cause of action is, we think, adequate in its office as a plaintiff's pleading.

In Skinner & Co. v. Shew & Co. [1893], 1 Ch. 413, 422, Lord Justice Bowen said: "At Common Law there was a cause of action whenever one person did damage to another wilfully and intentionally, and without just cause or excuse". So, in Aikens v. State of Wisconsin, 195 U.S. 194, 25 S.Ct. 3, 49 L.Ed. 154, the court said: "It has been considered that, prima facie, the intentional infliction of temporal damages is a cause of action, which, as a matter of substantive law, whatever may be the form of pleading requires a justification if the defendant is to escape." 195 U.S. at page 204, 25 S.Ct. at page 5, 49 L.Ed. 154, per Holmes, J. These broad propositions were approved by Sir Frederick Pollock as authority for his doctrine that all willful harm is actionable unless the defendant justify or excuse his conduct. Pollock, The Law of Torts, 14th Ed., 17, 18.

"On the other hand the view that all intentional wrongdoing is prima facie tortious has been rejected by other high authorities who contrariwise maintain that every plaintiff must bring his case under some accepted head of tort liability. "The only adequate answer to many claims for damages [said Sir John Salmond] is the mere ipse dixit of the law that no such cause of action is recognized." Salmond on Torts, 10th Ed., 15–16, note m. So, Mr. P. A. Landon, as editor of the fourteenth edition of Pollock's Law of Torts, says (p. 46): "The law is to-day, is it has always been, that only that harm which falls within one of the specified categories of wrong-doing entitles the person aggrieved to a legal remedy. The categories of tort (not, of course, the categories of particular torts) are closed."

This difference over the general principles of liability in tort was composed for us in Opera on Tour, Inc., v. Weber, 285 N.Y. 348, 34 N.E.2d 349, 136 A.L.R. 267. We there adopted from Aikens v. State of Wisconsin, supra, the declaration that "prima facie, the intentional infliction of temporal damages is a cause of action, which * * * requires a justification if the defendant is to escape." The above second cause of action alleges such a prima facie tort and, therefore, is sufficient in law on its face. American Guild of Musical Artists v. Petrillo, 286 N.Y. 226, 231, 36 N.E.2d 123, 125. * * *

The justification that is required in a case like this must, of course, be one which the law will recognize. Beardsley v. Kilmer, 236 N.Y. 80, 140 N.E. 203, 27 A.L.R. 1411; Langan v. First Trust & Deposit Co., 293 N.Y. 604, 608, 59 N.E.2d 424. See Winfield, The Law of Tort, 2d Ed. pp. 15–21; Ames, Miscellaneous Legal Essays, 399 et seq., and the cases in this court there cited.

The judgment of the Appellate Division should be reversed and the order of Special Term affirmed, with costs in this court and in the Appellate Division.

LEWIS, CONWAY, DESMOND, THACHER and DYE, JJ., concur.

Judgment accordingly.[89]

KEENE LUMBER CO. v. LEVENTHAL

Circuit Court of Appeals, First Circuit, 1948.
165 F.2d 815.

MAGRUDER, CIRCUIT JUDGE. This is an appeal from a judgment dismissing a complaint brought by Keene Lumber Company, a New Hampshire corporation, against four individual defendants and three Massachusetts corporations owned and controlled by various of the individual defendants.

* * *

[The court proceeded to deal with the question of federal jurisdiction.]

We state in summary form the allegations of the complaint, not inaptly described by appellant's brief as "perhaps inartistically" drawn: For some time prior to December 1, 1943, plaintiff had been doing business with Davenport-Brown, Inc., a Massachusetts corporation, by selling to it lumber on terms of credit. Becoming apprehensive of the financial standing of Davenport-Brown, Inc., the plaintiff refused it further credit. Defendants conceived a general scheme to defraud Davenport-Brown, Inc., and its creditors, including the plaintiff. As part of the scheme, defendant, Koritz, in November, 1943, "spoke" to plaintiff's treasurer, "stating that he had come into Davenport-Brown, Inc., as a partner; that he had invested in the business $50,000 and that he had unlimited funds to invest in the business of Davenport-Brown, Inc., if and when needed." He asked plaintiff's treasurer to make further sales of lumber to Davenport-Brown, Inc., on terms of credit, stating that the bills would be paid as and when due. Such representations were false, were known by Koritz to be

89. An excellent note to this case appears in 41 Ill.L.Rev. 661 (1947).

This case—for for the most part this section—merely marks a boundary of the present treatment. The significant problems here opened up have little in common, save as to name and form, with those we have been studying. They can be far more profitably dealt with in courses which include other aspects of business and competition and the controls placed upon them. Courses in equity also often deal with the remedial aspects of trade libel or disparagement.

false, and "were made with the intention to deceive the plaintiff and to cause the plaintiff to extend credit terms to Davenport-Brown, Inc., and thus enhance the value of the assets and property of said Davenport-Brown, Inc." before certain foreclosure sales about to be mentioned. In reliance on the said representations, plaintiff, during the period November 17, 1943, to January 20, 1944, sold and delivered to Davenport-Brown, Inc., on credit, lumber to the value of $7,809.76. Meanwhile a series of chattel mortgages had been acquired on the stock in trade, machinery, fixtures and other business property of Davenport-Brown, Inc., in the name of the defendant Federal Studios, Inc., and in the name of the defendant Prime Business Company. At least one of these chattel mortgages is alleged to have been executed by Davenport-Brown, Inc., without consideration. "In each of the said mortgages was a clause covering property therein named, together with any and all after-acquired property and in each of them provision was made in event of default, for sale by public auction." The mortgagor "had many creditors, including the plaintiff, and was indebted to them for much money, all of which was known to all of the defendants." In further pursuit of the conspiracy by defendants to take over the business and property of Davenport-Brown, Inc., and the property of the plaintiffs "without paying adequate consideration therefor," defendants went through an elaborate pretense of foreclosure sales at public auction on January 20 and 21, 1944, at which the purported auctioneer sold the properties to various of the defendants at rigged and prearranged prices amounting in the aggregate to "less than one-fourth of the fair value." Prior to these "sales," defendant Leventhal had lulled Mr. Paeff, president of the mortgagor, Davenport-Brown, Inc., into acquiescence by assuring him that the procedure "was a mere matter of form necessary as protection against creditors and that Paeff was not to be concerned with them, and advised Mr. Paeff not to proceed to raise money to pay off these mortgages, or any of them, or to attempt to raise capital for the purpose of buying in the property at the proposed foreclosure sales." In fact there "were no sales by public auction as provided for in all of the aforementioned mortgages." Immediately after the purported sales, and again as had been agreed upon in defendants' scheme to defraud, further conveyances of the property were made to defendant Finley Wood Products, Inc., a corporation wholly owned and controlled by defendant Finley. Davenport-Brown, Inc., was adjudicated bankrupt in March, 1944, "having no assets except a chose in action against some or all of the named defendants for alleged wrongful foreclosure of the mortgages as hereinabove stated." Plaintiff has not been paid any part of said sum of $7,809.76, and has suffered damage to that extent by reason of the various acts of the defendants in pursuance of the fraudulent scheme aforesaid.

To the complaint, above summarized, the several defendants filed motions to dismiss upon the ground that the complaint failed to state a claim upon which relief could be granted. In support of the motion, defendants urged a defense under Mass.Gen.Laws (Ter.Ed.) c. 259,

§ 4, the section of the Massachusetts Statute of Frauds patterned after Lord Tenterden's Act, 9 Geo. IV, C. XIV, par. VI (1828). Since it appeared from the face of the complaint that the alleged fraudulent representations of defendant Koritz were oral, this defense was properly raised by motion to dismiss. * * *

At the hearing on the motions to dismiss, the District Judge questioned counsel for the plaintiff as to his understanding of the nature of the cause of action sought to be presented in the complaint. In response, plaintiff's counsel "disclaimed any intention of seeking relief under the Uniform Fraudulent Conveyance Act, Mass.Gen.Laws, Chap. 109A." Counsel also accepted as correct the court's analysis of the complaint as presenting a cause of action in deceit and a conspiracy to commit deceit. The District Judge took the matter under advisement, and a few days later handed down his memorandum granting the motions to dismiss. He ruled that the alleged oral misrepresentations of Koritz made to induce plaintiff to sell goods on credit to Davenport-Brown, Inc., were representations concerning the "credit" of another person within the meaning of Mass.Gen.Laws, c. 259, § 4, and therefore that no action for deceit could be brought thereon; and further, that the cases against the other defendants for their alleged participation in the scheme thus to practice deceit upon the plaintiff necessarily fell with the case against Koritz. We agree with the District Judge's conclusion of law on this point, and have nothing to add to the full discussion in his memorandum. 71 F.Supp. 598.

With the cause of action for deceit based upon the misrepresentations by Koritz eliminated from the complaint, the question is, whether the remaining allegations are sufficient to set forth a claim upon which relief could be granted.

The complaint contained no reference to the uniform fraudulent conveyance law of Massachusetts, and, as previously stated, counsel for plaintiff specifically disclaimed before the District Court any intention to assert a claim thereunder. The District Judge accordingly left that possibility out of account in ruling on the motions to dismiss, and we do not pass upon the point at this time.

Certain other allegations in the complaint appear to be predicated on the theory, not that Davenport-Brown, Inc., had made conveyances with intent to hinder, delay, or defraud its creditors, but that the defendants, with knowledge of the indebtedness of Davenport-Brown, Inc., to the plaintiff and other creditors, and pursuant to a concerted plan to hinder and defraud Davenport-Brown, Inc., and its creditors, including the plaintiff, had tortiously appropriated the property of that company under the guise of pretended foreclosure sales at which, by the stratagems aforesaid, they acquired the property at a fraction of its real value. These allegations make out a tort to Davenport-Brown, Inc., the right of action for which became vested in the trustee in bankruptcy. But under the law of Massachusetts, which is controlling here, we think that these allegations also make out a direct and independent tort liability to the creditors of Davenport-Brown, Inc., for such pecuniary loss as may be proved to have resulted from the conduct of the defendants in substantially stripping Davenport-Brown, Inc., of its assets and thus disabling it from performing its contract obligations to its creditors.

There is ample precedent in the law of torts for the imposition of liability upon a conscious wrongdoer whose tortious act, directly injuring the person or the property interests of X, intentionally causes a pecuniary loss to the plaintiff from the resulting interference with a relationship between X and the plaintiff known to the wrongdoer at the time he acted. The proposition is illustrated by the old landmark case of Tarleton v. M'Gawley, Peake 204 (1793). There the defendant, claiming that a tribe of African natives owed him a debt, determined that he would not suffer them to trade with any ship until they paid the debt. Natives put out in a canoe to trade with plaintiffs' ship which was lying off the coast. The defendant, with the purpose aforesaid, and intending to prevent the natives from trading with the plaintiffs, shot at the canoe and killed one of the natives therein, whereby the natives were deterred from trading with the plaintiffs, and the plaintiffs suffered damages from the loss of their trade. Lord Kenyon held that the plaintiffs had made out a case, saying: "Had this been an accidental thing, no action could have been maintained, but it is proved that the Defendant had expressed an intention not to permit any to trade, until a debt due from the natives to himself was satisfied."

Tarleton v. M'Gawley was cited with approval by the Supreme Judicial Court in Walker v. Cronin, 1871, 107 Mass. 555, 563.

It is to be observed that, in Tarleton v. M'Gawley, the defendant's act was not done with the motive or purpose of causing pecuniary loss to the plaintiffs—his malevolence was not directed against the plaintiffs—but it was enough that defendant intended by the battery upon the natives to interrupt and prevent their trade with the plaintiffs until the natives should satisfy defendant's claim against them. The relationship which defendant interfered with as the indirect effect of his assault and battery upon the natives was merely an advantageous trade expectancy, not a contractual relationship. The liability which Lord Kenyon recognized was but an application of a fundamental tort principle that "prima facie, the intentional infliction of temporal damage is a cause of action, which, as a matter of substantive law, whatever may be the form of pleading, requires a justification if the defendant is to escape." Holmes, J., in Aikens v. Wisconsin, 1904, 195 U.S. 194, 204, 25 S.Ct. 3, 49 L.Ed. 154. Within this principle, the case for the plaintiff is even stronger when the interference is with an existing contractual relationship. In Massachusetts, as elsewhere, it is settled that inducing a promisor to commit a breach of contract is prima facie a tort to the promisee, with the burden on the defendant to establish some justification or privilege. Beekman v. Marsters, 1907, 195 Mass. 205, 80 N.E. 817, 11 L.R.A.,N.S., 201, 122 Am.St.Rep. 232, 11 Ann.Cas. 332; Lumley v. Gye, 2 E. & B. 216 (1853). But a tortious interference with a contract relationship may also be perpetrated in other ways. See Carpenter, Interference with Contract Relations, 41 Harv.L.Rev. 728 (1928). Thus, if inducing the promisor to commit a breach of contract may be a tort to the promisee, it would seem to be a fortiori case where the defendant, by an unprivileged act, and with knowledge of its inevitable consequence, actually prevented the promisor from performing his contract. Carroll v. Chesapeake & Ohio Coal Agency Co., 4 Cir., 1903, 124 F. 305; St. Johnsbury & L. C. R. R. Co. v. Hunt, 1882, 55 Vt. 570, 45 Am.Rep. 639. See Walden v. Conn, 1886, 84 Ky. 312, 315, 1 S.W. 537, 4 Am.St.Rep. 204. And see Prosser on Torts, § 104. As was pointed out by Learned Hand, J., in Sidney Blumenthal & Co., Inc. v. United States, 2 Cir., 1929, 30 F. 2d 247, 248: "The case is stronger than Lumley v. Gye, 2 E. & B. 216, and the many cases which have followed it, in respect of the nature of the interference, which in those cases was usually persuasion, while here it was physical prevention." And where the promisee sues for a pecuniary loss intentionally caused by the defendant by acts which not only disabled the promisor from performing but also were independently tortious as against the promisor, it is of course impossible for the defendant to establish a justification or privilege for inflicting such loss upon the promisee. The means used is itself unlawful, and hence unprivileged, quite apart from the resulting harm to the promisee.

For these reasons we conclude that, upon a not-too-indulgent reading of the complaint, it makes out a tort claim upon which relief could be granted, leaving out of account altogether the cause of action for deceit founded upon the oral representations by Koritz. It is true that, in the court below, counsel for the plaintiff concentrated on what he thought was the strong point in the case, the liability based upon Koritz's alleged misrepresentations. But it is not an inflexible rule that the plaintiff must in all cases be held to his theory of the complaint as urged in the trial court, where the allegations of the complaint, even though inartistically drawn, are sufficient to set forth a tort claim well-founded in principle and in precedent. It may serve the interest of justice to give the plaintiff a chance to establish its case by proof, even though counsel for the plaintiff did not urge an acceptable theory of liability upon the District Judge and thus, in a sense, may be said to have induced the adverse judgment now complained of. We think such is the case here.

* * *

The judgment of the District Court is vacated and the case is remanded for further proceedings not inconsistent with this opinion.

SLOAN v. CLARK

New York Court of Appeals, 1966.
18 N.Y.2d 570, 277 N.Y.S.2d 411, 223 N.E.2d 893.

BURKE, JUDGE. Plaintiffs in each of these actions are limited partners of Ira Haupt & Co. The Haupt partnership went into bankruptcy because of its inability to meet its obligations on large loans made to Allied Crude Vegetable Oil Refining Co. upon the strength of warehouse receipts allegedly issued by defendant American Express Company (Amexco) through a wholly owned subsidiary. Plaintiffs sued Amexco contending that defendant's tortious acts resulted in Haupt's insolvency and the loss of plaintiffs' investment in the partnership. The complaints were dismissed by the trial court on the grounds that plaintiffs lacked capacity to sue and that the complaint and amended complaints failed to state facts sufficient to constitute a cause of action. This dismissal was properly affirmed by the Appellate Division.

We are not confronted on these appeals with the issue whether limited partners can bring a representative action on a claim which the general partners have refused to prosecute because of an alleged conflict of interest (see Lichtyger v. Franchard Corp., 18 N.Y.2d 528, 277 N.Y.S.2d 377, 223 N.E.2d 869, decided herewith). No similar charges are leveled by plaintiffs against the general partners of Haupt. The question here presented is whether the limited partners can prosecute an action as individuals when at the same time their partnership's trustee in bankruptcy is suing the same defendant on behalf of the partnership and all its creditors for some $52,000,000 which amount includes the damages sought by the limited partners herein. We answer this question in the negative.

[The court held that the limited partners had no individual causes of action against Amexco for injury done to the partnership, this right of action being vested in the trustee.]

* * *

Plaintiffs also allege, however, that their complaints state facts upon which relief can be granted based on a theory of prima facie tort. With this we cannot agree. The limited partners refer us to the case of Ultramares Corp. v. Touche, 255 N.Y. 170, 174 N.E. 441, 74 A.L.R. 1139 [1931] as precedent for such a recovery, but their reliance is ill-founded. Prevalent throughout Chief Judge Cardozo's opinion therein is the awareness that there existed a *reliance* upon the allegedly fraudulent financial statement and that such reliance was the *sine qua non* for recovery. Plaintiffs here did not rely upon the integrity of the warehouse receipts and consequently that element is missing to prosecute a cause of action in fraud. For that reason, fraud as such was dropped as a gravamen of these suits. Without such reliance, and without fraud as the basis of the complaint, plaintiffs can find no support in *Ultramares* for their prima facie tort theory. " 'The assumption of one relation will mean [if recovery were allowed] the involuntary assumption of a series of new relations, inescapably hooked together' * * * 'The law does not spread its protection so far' ". (Ultramares Corp. v. Touche, supra, p. 189, 174 N.E. p. 448, 74 A.L.R. 1139.)

Keene Lbr. Co. v. Leventhal, 165 F.2d 815 (1st Cir., 1948), upon which plaintiffs also place their reliance, does not persuade us otherwise. The facts in that case are quite different from those presented here: defendant, after directly and apparently with malice inducing plaintiff to continue its dealings with Davenport-Brown, Inc., on the promise that defendant had invested large sums of money in said company and would see to it that any and all bills thereof would be satisfied, tortiously stripped Davenport of all its assets, with the result that it became bankrupt to the damage of plaintiff. While it is true that Keene, a creditor of the bankrupt lumber company, was permitted to sue the alleged tort-feasor, the wrong had been perpetrated directly upon Keene by the defendant. It was only through defendant's direct dealings with and promises to Keene that the latter was induced to continue its financial transactions with the bankrupt firm. No such situation exists here. Defendant Amexco had no business dealings with and made no promises to the limited partners of Haupt, and it must be remembered that plaintiffs here are *not* suing on behalf of the partnership. Plaintiffs contend that "The *Keene* case thus demonstrates that suit will lie in favor of anyone whose contractual expectations have been indirectly injured by socially undesirable conduct, at least where it is claimed that the injury was foreseeable by defendant." Under this theory it might well be argued that, anytime a debtor refused to pay a creditor, the creditors of that creditor would have a cause of action against the debtor for interfering with the contract between the debtor's creditor and this creditor's creditor. As was stated earlier, "The law does not spread its protection so far."

* * *

The orders of the Appellate Division, affirming the dismissal of the plaintiffs' complaints, should be affirmed, with costs.

REINFORCE, INC. v. BIRNEY

Court of Appeals of New York, 1954.
308 N.Y. 164, 124 N.E.2d 104.

DESMOND, JUDGE. Plaintiffs (Reinforce, Inc. a corporation organized to carry on a lathing business, and Foley, its principal officer and owner) were awarded money damages by a jury, on their complaint that defendant union and its members had maliciously conspired to prevent plaintiffs from carrying on their business and had put an end to such business operations by causing some of the union members to quit their employment with plaintiffs, and by causing all the union's members to refuse to work for plaintiffs. The Appellate Division reversed plaintiffs' judgment on the law, and dismissed the complaint for failure of proof. The members of that court were not, however, in full agreement as to the applicable law. The Trial Justice had charged the jury that its task was to determine whether defendants' acts had been motivated by malice, or by a desire to improve employment conditions, and had instructed the jurors that, if the motivation was malicious, plaintiffs would be entitled to their damages. The majority Justices in the Appellate Division took the view that since the union members "had the absolute right to refuse to work for the plaintiffs for any reason or for no reason at all" [282 App.Div. 736, 122 N.Y.S.2d 369], malice was immaterial. The Presiding Justice, however, coming to the same result (reversal and dismissal) by a different route, did not agree that the element of malice was immaterial. Defendants' acts, he pointed out, were concerted and so, if prompted by malice alone, would cast defendants in damages. But the evidence here, as he saw it, was insufficient to show that malice was the only spur to the union's activity, or that damage to plaintiffs was the union's sole purpose. We agree with the Presiding Justice's analysis of the proof and with his statement of the law.

Plaintiff Foley was for many years a construction worker and member of the operating engineers' union. After attending law school and being admitted to the Bar, he again took up construction work and in 1937 became president of one of the locals of his union. While so acting as a union representative, he, in 1940, 1945, and 1946, had three serious disagreements with the representatives of defendant union. The first of those controversies had to do with a complaint by defendants' officers that plaintiff Foley was siding with a contractor who, according to defendants, was violating a certain building contract, to defendants' disadvantage, by installing fewer steel rods than were called for in the specifications. In the second, or 1945 dispute, Foley lined up on the side of certain contractors and against defendant union, which was resisting efforts of the contractors to eliminate double pay for Saturday work. The third difference of opinion came in 1946, when, after a Federal board had authorized a seven-hour day in the construction industry, defendant union tried to obtain an agreement whereby its members would get eight hours pay for seven hours work, but the contractors (and Foley) insisted that the regular workday remain at eight hours.

Later in 1946, Foley resigned as his union's president and became a labor relations consultant. Again, trouble broke out between Foley and defendants' officers, who blamed him for grievances which defendant union had suffered at the hands of a contractors' organization with which Foley was associated.

In 1948, Foley organized the plaintiff corporation to go into the lathing business as a so-called "lumper", that is, one whose contracts require it to supply labor only on construction work, the general contractor furnishing the materials. Foley had never done lathing work, or operated as a "lumper" previously. On behalf of plaintiff Reinforce, he consulted one of defendants' principal officers, Matthews, who recommended one of the union members for the job of Reinforce's superintendent. Foley, for Reinforce, then signed a lathing contract on an apartment house job, and got some workers for it (between ten and thirty men, at various times) from defendant union. No contract, however, was ever made by the union, with either plaintiff. Late in 1948, Reinforce obtained several more lathing jobs. However, after a union hearing at which Foley appeared and at which there was some discussion of the old grievances, defendant union notified plaintiffs that Reinforce had been denied approval as a contractor to which defendant union would supply men, and that, after the next pay roll date, no members of the union would work for plaintiff Reinforce. None of the members ever did work for Reinforce thereafter, and so, since defendants' members included all the metal lathers in the vicinity, Reinforce was out of business. The union sent to Reinforce's general contractors some letters informing them of the union action, and we will mention those letters again, at another place in this opinion. All the above facts, including the recurring difficulties between Foley and the union, were undisputed at the trial.

The Trial Justice submitted to the jury questions of fact as to whether Foley was "anti-union" or "guilty of anti-union acts". In another part of his instructions he told the jurors that it was for them to decide whether defendants' purpose was to further the proper aims of union labor or whether their motive was vengeful and spiteful. Finally, he told them that if they should conclude that defendants had acted maliciously and without cause or justification, damages might be awarded to plaintiff. The charge does not say in so many words (although perhaps it is sufficiently suggested) that if the motives were found to be mixed—good and bad—defendants must win the case, provided their acts had some reasonable relation to wages, hours of employment, collective bargaining or some other valid union objective. But, whether or not the charge was adequate, the complaint was, in our opinion, properly dismissed by the Appellate Division, because plaintiffs did not carry their burden of showing that defendants' acts were solely "malicious", that is, that they were done "without legal or social justification". Campbell v. Gates, 236 N.Y. 457, 460, 141 N.E. 914, 915.

Just as (when there is no binding contract) an employer may hire, or refuse to hire, at will, so may a worker or a group of workers refuse, or quit employment for any reason or no reason, Opera on Tour, Inc., v. Weber, 285 N.Y. 348, 353, 34 N.E.2d 349, 351, 136 A.L.R. 267; Hunt v. Crumboch, 325 U.S. 821, 825, 65 S.Ct. 1545, 89 L.Ed. 1954. But when men quit work in concert, they offend against the law if their sole and unmixed motive or purpose is to injure an employer, Exchange Bakery & Restaurant, Inc., v. Rifkin, 245 N.Y. 260, 262, 157 N.E. 130, 132; see Gray, J., in National Protective Ass'n, of Steam Fitters & Helpers v. Cumming, 170 N.Y. 315, 334, 63 N.E. 369, 374, 58 L.R.A. 135; Bossert v. Dhuy, 221 N.Y. 342, 359, 117 N.E. 582, 585; Williams v. Quill, 277 N.Y. 1, 12 N.E.2d 547; see Dorchy v. State of Kansas, 272 U.S. 306, 311, 47 S.Ct. 86, 71 L.Ed. 248. But, if the acts of unions "have any reasonable connection with wages, hours of employment, health, safety, the right of collective bargaining, or any other condition of employment or for the protection from labor abuses, then the acts are justified." Opera on Tour, Inc. v. Weber, supra, 285 N.Y. at page 355, 34 N.E.2d at page 352. The result is not changed by the fact that the work stoppage or refusal injures an employer. Such harm, athough intentionally done, is actionable only if not justified, Lough v. Outerbridge, 143 N.Y. 271, 283, 38 N.E. 292, 296, 25 L.R.A. 674; Grombach Productions, Inc., v. Waring, 293 N.Y. 609, 59 N.E.2d 425, and cases cited; Aikens v. State of Wisconsin, 195 U.S. 194, 204, 25 S.Ct. 3, 49 L.Ed. 154. If the doers, by means not in themselves unlawful, of acts not in themselves unlawful, have any proper purpose to serve, they are not liable for the damage they cause, Stephen Peabody, Jr., & Co. v. Travelers Ins. Co., 240 N.Y. 511, 519, 148 N.E. 661, 664, 42 A.L.R. 1090; Al Raschid v. News Syndicate Co., 265 N.Y. 1, 191 N.E. 713. Unions, as well as everyone else, may claim the benefit of the settled rule that "the genesis which will make a lawful act unlawful must be a malicious one unmixed with any other and exclusively directly to injury and damage of another", Beardsley v. Kilmer, 236 N.Y. 80, 90, 140 N.E. 203, 206, 27 A.L.R. 1411, citing American Bank & Trust Co. v. Federal Reserve Bank, of Atlanta, 256 U.S. 350, 358, 41 S.Ct. 499, 65 L.Ed. 983, for the epigrammatic phrase: "disinterested malevolence"; and see John D. Park & Sons Co. v. National Wholesale Druggists' Ass'n, 175 N.Y. 1, 67 N.E. 136, 62 L.R.A. 632; Roseneau v. Empire Circuit Co., 131 App.Div. 429, 436, 115 N.Y.S. 511, 517. The Beardsley decision rejects the idea that the motive is immaterial if the act be lawful, since a concurring opinion to that effect, in Beardsley, represented the view of one Judge only.

The modern application, to controversies between unions and employers, of these rules, is illustrated by Rochette & Parzini Corp. v. Campo, 301 N.Y. 228, 93 N.E.2d 652. There, the defendant union whose members were the only ones available in the metropolitan New York area for certain kinds of stone work, decided not to supply labor to any subcontractors, and so put plaintiff, a subcontractor for such work, out of business. Just as in the present case, the question in Rochette was not as to the fairness, propriety or necessity of such a determination by the union. In the absence of proof that the motivation was entirely malicious, plaintiff had no remedy at law. In the Rochette situation, the union withdrew its members from an employment because the union thought it to its interest so to do. In each case it was impossible, on the record, to find that the sole motivation was "malicious", hence, there was no basis for a judgment against the union.

In Rochette & Parzini Corp. v. Campo, supra, there was another question, too, and some support was found there for a finding of illegal union activity by the union in sending, to other unions, letters coercing those unions not to work for plaintiff, and in sending letters to contractors describing plaintiff as "non-union", etc. However, the letters sent by the defendant union in the present case were in no way unlawful since they merely gave simple notification that "Reinforce, Inc. has not been approved by Local Union 46 as one of the lathing contractors to whom it will furnish union members", and that, "Effective as of the next pay roll date no members of Local Union 46 will accept employment with, or continue in the employ of, Reinforce, Inc."

The judgment should be affirmed, with costs.

[Van Voorhis, J., dissented in an opinion in which Lewis, Ch. J., and Conway, J., concurred.]

Chapter 8

ASSAULT AND BATTERY, FALSE IMPRISONMENT, MALICIOUS PROSECUTION, ETC.

RESTATEMENT OF THE LAW OF TORTS, SECOND—American Law Institute—Chapter 2:

§ 18. BATTERY: OFFENSIVE CONTACT

(1) An actor is subject to liability to another for battery if

(a) he acts intending to cause a harmful or offensive contact with the person of the other or a third person, or an imminent apprehension of such a contact, and

(b) an offensive contact with the person of the other directly or indirectly results.

(2) An act which is not done with the intention stated in Subsection (1, a) does not make the actor liable to the other for a mere offensive contact with the other's person although the act involves an unreasonable risk of inflicting it and, therefore, would be negligent or reckless if the risk threatened bodily harm.[1]

§ 21. ASSAULT

(1) An actor is subject to liability to another for assault if

(a) he acts intending to cause a harmful or offensive contact with the person of the other or a third person, or an imminent apprehension of such a contact, and

(b) the other is thereby put in such imminent apprehension.

(2) An action which is not done with the intention stated in Subsection (1, a) does not make the actor liable to the other for an apprehension caused thereby although the act involves an unreasonable risk of causing it and, therefore, would be negligent or reckless if the risk threatened bodily harm.

1. When one man intentionally beats another up, there is little question about legal liability in the absence of consent or privilege, although, of course, there may be and usually is very serious dispute as to the facts. See Vold, Legal Allocation of Risk in Assault, Battery and Imprisonment, 17 Neb.L.Rev. 149, 151, 152 (1938).

WHITE v. SANDER

Supreme Judicial Court of Massachusetts, 1897.
168 Mass. 296, 47 N.E. 90.

These were two actions of tort, one by Benjamin White, and the other by Emma White, his wife, against F. H. Sander, to recover damages for personal injuries caused by a fright caused by defendant throwing a stone into a room where the wife was. The jury returned a verdict for the husband for $179.30, and for the wife for $847.47, and the defendant excepted. Exceptions sustained.

ALLEN, J. There was no evidence that the defendant had any intention to injure the female plaintiff, or that he was aware of her condition of health. The house did not belong to her, but to her father, with whom the defendant had an altercation. The defendant's declared purpose was to injure the house, and he threw a large stone against it, in her presence. She then ran into the front room, with her little child, whereupon a large stone was willfully thrown by the defendant, which passed through one of the blinds, all of the blinds upon the front windows being closed. This greatly frightened her, though she was not struck or touched. We do not understand by the bill of exceptions that the defendant knew that she was in that room, or that he had any purpose either to hit or to frighten her, or that it was designed to present to us a case of an intentional injury to her or to her property. These elements being absent, the defendant was not responsible in damages for her fright or the consequent injury to her health. Spade v. Lynn & B. Railroad Co., 168 Mass. 285, 47 N.E. 88, 38 L.R.A. 512, 60 Am.St.Rep. 393. Under the order taking off the default, the defendant was responsible for nominal damages. Exceptions sustained.

BARTOW v. SMITH

Supreme Court of Ohio, 1948.
149 Ohio St. 301, 78 N.E.2d 735, 15 A.L.R.2d 94.

Without the caption, prayer and verification, the amended petition reads as follows:

"Plaintiff Kathryn V. Bartow, for her cause of action against the defendant, R. D. Smith, represents:

"That on Saturday afternoon, September 8, 1945, in the city of Norwalk, Huron county, Ohio, in front of No. 31 East Main street, in the presence and hearing of many people, the defendant in a loud voice and malicious manner, falsely slandered plaintiff in that he called her a 'God damned son of a bitch' and 'a dirty crook,' repeating the slanderous and defamatory statements many times.

"That defendant knew plaintiff was advanced in pregnancy, highly nervous and very sensitive, and chose the time and place to wreak the maximum of opprobrium upon her.

"That by reason of defendant's language as aforesaid plaintiff was greatly shocked and humiliated, her nerves were deranged, her health impaired and her rest disturbed, and she believes and so alleges that her nerves will continue to be deranged, her health impaired and her rest disturbed, for a considerable time in the future, the exact termination whereof she is not now able to ascertain, all to her great damage in the sum of $5,000."

To such petition defendant filed a general denial. The cause came on for trial, and, after the jury was sworn, counsel for plaintiff in the opening statement to the jury read the amended petition and, in addition, [elaborated the facts somewhat more in detail].

Before any testimony was taken at the trial, counsel for defendant moved the court to render judgment in favor of the defendant and to dismiss the plaintiff's amended petition, on the opening statement of counsel for the plaintiff and the allegations of the amended petition combined, which motion the court sustained.

The Court of Appeals reversed the judgment of the Court of Common Pleas and held that plaintiff, on the amended petition and opening statement, was entitled to submit her evidence to the jury.

The case is before this court on appeal from the judgment of the Court of Appeals, a motion to certify the record having been allowed.

STEWART, JUDGE. Obviously the theory upon which the trial court dismissed the plaintiff's amended petition is that spoken words are not slander per se, unless they impute a crime, subject a person to disgrace, ridicule, odium or contempt in the estimation of friends or acquaintances or the public, impute to a person an infectious disease likely to exclude him from society, impute the unfitness of one to perform the duties of an office or employment, or tend to prejudice him in his profession or trade; and that an action for slander per quod does not lie unless special damages are pleaded.

The Court of Appeals was of the opinion that if the instant action were treated as one for slander the trial court's disposition of it was correct, and the Court of Appeals stated: "While it is alleged that from the verbal assault defendant is said to have committed upon plaintiff, great emotional disturbance and bodily harm resulted to her, it is not claimed that she sustained any loss or damage in the estimation of those who heard it, or even those who may have heard of it."

However, the Court of Appeals, in its opinion, said that under the liberal construction to be given our procedural law, the plaintiff has the right to go to the jury on any basis which the facts alleged permit; and that the physical condition of the plaintiff, known to the defendant, gave rise to the hazard of an emotional disturbance and bodily injury to her nerves, which disturbance and injury the petition alleges she experienced and which, it is alleged, defendant must well have anticipated from his conduct.

It is axiomatic that opprobrious epithets, even if malicious, profane and in public, are ordinarily not actionable. There is no right to recover for bad manners. But it is contended here that plaintiff has the right to recover because defendant was aware of her physical condition and designed to use the language he did for the purpose of hurting her and causing her physical injury, and his remarks did cause her physical injury. There can be no doubt that personal injury may be produced through emotional or mental disturbance caused by fright, terror, shock and other similar experiences, and there likewise can be no doubt that in proper cases pecuniary damages may be recovered for nervous shock and emotional disturbance and injuries directly resulting therefrom.

Where one is in a situation in which he is entitled to protection from another, such as would be due to a guest from an innkeeper, to a patron from a theater, or to a passenger from a common carrier, he may recover for any injuries, including fright and terror, which result from a wilful breach of duty, insult or unlawful treatment. Cincinnati Northern Traction Co. v. Rosnagle, an Infant, 84 Ohio St. 310, 95 N.E. 884, 35 L.R.A.,N.S., 1030, Ann.Cas.1912C, 639.

The weight of authority seems to be, and certainly it is the rule in Ohio, that there is no liability for merely negligent acts which cause fright or shock unaccompanied by contemporaneous physical injury, even though subsequent illness results, where the negligent acts complained of are neither wilful nor malicious. Miller v. Baltimore & Ohio Southwestern Rd. Co., 78 Ohio St. 309, 85 N.E. 499, 18 L.R.A., N.S., 949, 125 Am.St.Rep. 699.

However, in the present case, construing, as we must, the allegations of the plaintiff's petition and the opening statement of her counsel most strongly in her favor, the action of the defendant in using the vile epithets, which it is alleged he did, was wilful and malicious, and the question we must solve is, was his conduct actionable.

There are many authorities to the effect that, where a defendant, knowing of a plaintiff's unusual physical condition and that insults and vile epithets might reasonably be anticipated to cause her mental and emotional disturbance and illness, such defendant would be liable for any deleterious effects of insults or epithets which he purposely and maliciously uttered. An examination of the authorities will demonstrate, however, that, where such liability was recognized, almost without exception the defamatory, insulting and profane words were accompanied by either threats, menacing actions which amounted to an assault, or a violation of the privacy and serenity of a home. * * *

There is no allegation or statement in the present case, either in the amended petition or the opening statement of counsel, of anything which could be construed as a threat or an assault. The inexcusable words alleged to have been used by the defendant were uttered on the sidewalk of a public street. Plaintiff made no claim that she was frightened or terrified. There is no allegation that defendant was guilty of any menacing actions or attitudes. All the allegations state merely the use of profane and vulgar words with the malicious intention of wreaking the maximum of opprobrium upon the plaintiff.

It is true that in the opening statement it was said that the defendant stepped right up to the plaintiff and started the resumption of a former wrangling, and, in the presence of people on the sidewalk, he used profane words in a loud voice and with a flushed face. It is also true it was stated that plaintiff's mother took her quickly by the arm and rushed her into a store. Neither of those statements, however, was of an assault or a causing of fright and terror. Consequently, the question before us is: does profane and atrocious language not slanderous and unaccompanied by menacing actions or attitudes, threats, trespass, or invasions of the serenity of private premises or a home give rise to a cause of action? We do not think so. * * *

The reason for not extending the right of action, in the instant case, for insulting and profane words uttered on a public highway, and unaccompanied by threats or conduct amounting to an assault, is well stated by the Court of Appeals of Kentucky in Reed v. Ford, 129 Ky. 471, 112 S.W. 600, 601, 19 L.R.A.,N.S., 225, and quoted with approval by the same court in Smith v. Gowdy, 196 Ky. 281, 285, 244 S.W. 678, 29 A.L.R. 1353: "The damages sought to be recovered are too remote and speculative. The injury is more sentimental than substantial. Being easily simulated and hard to disprove, there is no standard by which it can be justly, or even approximately, compensated."

If the allegations in the amended petition and the opening statement in the present case are true, and for the purposes of our decision they must be assumed to be true, the conduct of the defendant was atrocious, inexcusable and certainly unworthy of any one claiming to be a gentleman. However, plaintiff did not allege that she was put in fear or terror or that defendant was guilty of any conduct which amounted to even a slight assault, and it is apparent, since the episode occurred on a public sidewalk, that there was no violation of the serenity, peace and quiet of the home. The actions of the defendant, therefore, however reprehensible, amount to damnum absque injuria.

The judgment of the Court of Appeals is reversed and that of the Court of Common Pleas affirmed.

Judgment reversed.

WEYGANDT, C. J., and MATTHIAS and SOHNGEN, JJ., concur.

TURNER, HART and ZIMMERMAN, JJ., dissent.

HART, JUDGE (dissenting). The question presented in the instant case is whether, under the circumstances described in the amended petition and the opening statement of counsel to the jury, which admittedly must be taken as the truth, the boisterous, atrocious and inexcusable verbal assault of the defendant upon the plaintiff in a public place and in the hearing of many people with knowledge that she was in an advanced state of pregnancy, causing her nervous shock, mental distress, impairment of health and a period of illness requiring medical treatment, gives the plaintiff a cause of action against the defendant, in the absence of physical contact with, or menacing threats of physical harm toward, the plaintiff.

Liability for nervous shock or its harmful consequences, in the absence of some physical impact, is a comparatively recent doctrine in the law. Until about a half century ago, no reported cases had appeared in which claims were made for a recovery for the consequences of fright, mental distress or shock. And, until a quarter of a century ago, it was almost universally held that to support an action for physical harm, there must have been some physical impact so applied as to actually work a direct and immediate physical injury. The three leading cases in this country supporting this doctrine are Mitchell v. Rochester Ry. Co., 151 N.Y. 107, 45 N.E. 354, 34 L.R.A. 781, 56 Am.St.Rep. 604; Spade v. Lynn & Boston R. Co., 168 Mass. 285, 47 N.E. 88, 38 L.R.A. 512, 60 Am.St.Rep. 393; and Ewing v. Pittsburgh, C. & St. L. Ry. Co., 147 Pa. 40, 23 A. 340, 14 L.R.A. 666, 30 Am.St.Rep. 709.

The reasons assigned by the courts for denial of recovery for the physical consequences of fright, shock or mental distress, unaccompanied by contemporaneous physical impact or injury, are that such claims cannot be placed in the mold of any category of tort actions known to the law; that there is a lack of judicial precedent for the legal recognition of such claims; that mental suffering and its consequences are so evanescent and intangible that they cannot be foreseen or anticipated and for that reason have no reasonable proximate causal connection with the act of the defendant; that the recognition of such claims would open the door not only to fictitious and fraudulent claims but to litigation in the field of trivialities and mere bad manners; and that such claims present administrative difficulties for the courts which make judicial consideration inadvisable.

In recent years, the courts have, in most instances, abandoned the idea that no action is maintainable for a tort unless it comes within a specified type or category of tort actions. They have discarded the lack of precedent as a reason for denying recovery, as such a theory would deny all progress and vitality in the law, and they have determined that it is the responsibility of the law to grant a remedy for a substantial wrong even though a new term must be invented to describe it.

Sir Frederick Pollock, perhaps the greatest authority in his day on the law of torts, said (Pollock on Torts [14 Ed.], 16):

"Down to our own time it was difficult to find any definite authority for stating as a general proposition of English law that it is a wrong to do wilful harm to one's neighbour without lawful justification or excuse. * * * Law begins not with authentic general principles, but with enumeration of particular remedies. * * * [There is no] law of delicts, but only a list of certain kinds of injury which have certain penalties assigned to them. Thus in the Anglo-Saxon and other early Germanic laws we find minute assessments of the compensation due for hurts to every member of the human body, but there is no general prohibition of personal violence * * *. Whatever agreements are outside the specified forms of obligation and modes of proof are incapable of enforcement; whatever injuries are not in the table of compensation must go without legal redress. The phrase damnum sine injuria, which for the modern law is at best insignificant, has meaning and substance enough in such a system. Only that harm which falls within one of the specified categories of wrong-doing entitles the person aggrieved to a legal remedy.

* * *

"Such is not the modern way of regarding legal duties or remedies. * * * So we can be no longer satisfied in the region of tort with a mere enumeration of actionable injuries. The whole modern law of negligence, with its many developments, enforces the duty of fellow-citizens to observe in varying circumstances an appropriate measure of prudence to avoid causing harm to one another. * * * If there exists, then, a positive duty to avoid harm, much more must there exist the negative duty of not doing wilful harm, subject, as all general duties must be subject, to the necessary exceptions. The three main heads of duty with which the law of torts is concerned—namely, to abstain from wilful injury, to respect the property of others, and to use due diligence to avoid causing harm to others—are all alike of a comprehensive nature.

"In fact, there are dicta of the late Lord Bowen's which appear fully to recognize the doctrine here contended for. He said, as Lord Justice, in 1892: 'At common law there was a cause of action whenever one person did damage to another, wilfully and intentionally, and without just cause or excuse.' Skinner & Co. v. Shew & Co., 1 Ch. 413, 422, 62 L.J.Ch. 196. * * * [after further quotation from Pollock, the opinion quotes at length from Harper and Prosser.]

The courts for many years have allowed recoveries for insult, mental shock, and the violation of other personal rights against defendants who, because of a special relationship, are charged with a special duty of care toward persons within such relationship. For such violations of protective care, recoveries have been allowed to passengers of public carriers and to patrons of places of public entertainment such as hotels and theaters.

In other situations where a defendant commits a traditional tort, even though a wrongful touching or an essential element, such as menacing threats, slander and libel per se, alienation of affections or false imprisonment, is not present, the courts, with great unanimity, have allowed recoveries for distress and humiliation. Incidentally, it should be observed that in allowing recoveries in the classes of cases above mentioned, the courts have disregarded or have overcome the same objections and difficulties of administration as are present in cases such as the one at bar. Consequently, little validity should now attach to the reasons originally given for refusal to consider injuries due to shock and mental distress when they demand consideration at the hands of the courts.

At the present time, the courts in most American jurisdictions permit recovery for physical harm or injury caused by mental distress for which the defendant is wrongfully responsible, even though there is an absence of contemporaneous impact. There is in this country, however, a sharp conflict of authority as to whether there may be a recovery where a physical injury or illness results from fright or mental shock caused by the *negligent* act of another, in the absence of physical impact or the commission of an independent tort. * * *

In the instant case, the verbal attack of the defendant upon the plaintiff was made wilfully, intentionally and even maliciously, resulting in mental distress and subsequent illness. The courts almost universally hold, even those which recognize the rule denying liability for injuries resulting from fright or shock caused by negligence where there is no physical impact, that such rule cannot be invoked where it is shown that the fright or shock was due to a wilful or intentional and unreasonable wrongful act resulting in illness or physical injury. This is because the law is more willing to charge the defendant with the consequence of a wilful than a negligent wrong. See "Intentional Infliction of Mental Suffering: A New Tort," by Prosser, 37 Michigan Law Review, 874. And, besides, in cases of wilful and intentional conduct, the court is not burdened with the problem of foreseeability, except possibly as to the unreasonableness of the defendant's act.

The majority opinion in this case takes the position that notwithstanding the insulting and brutal language of the defendant toward the plaintiff, causing her mental distress and nervous shock resulting in physical illness, she is not entitled to recover for such physical illness because the defendant did not commit any technical physical assault upon her by striking her or making menacing threats of physical harm toward her, or commit any other independent or traditional tort against her.

As I see it, the majority opinion undertakes to test liability in this case by postulating the tort of assault, and then assuming the position that, since the words spoken did not constitute a technical assault, no recovery can be had. In case of assault, the wrong which gives a right of action is the act of assault itself, and damages for mental distress are allowed as parasitic damages, as incidental to the principal damages for the physical harm caused by the assault. But, if violent words directed against a plaintiff, even though they do not rise to the magnitude of an assault, are so vicious as to cause mental distress and consequent physical injury and damages, there arises a cause of action.

I maintain that the doctrine, which requires the commission of an independent concomitant and traditional tort in connection with the verbal onslaught, which in this case was sufficient in itself to cause emotional distress so acute as to result in physical illness, before there can be a recovery for such physical harm, has no application in this action. When any person wilfully, intentionally and without excuse sets in motion forces which cause physical injury to another by whatever means he may choose, he becomes liable under the law for such physical injury or harm. * * *

Under the law as I interpret it, upon the allegations of plaintiff's amended petition together with the statement of counsel as to the evidence to be offered thereunder, plaintiff was entitled to go to the court and jury with her evidence.[2]

KATKO v. BRINEY

Supreme Court of Iowa, 1971.
Iowa, 183 N.W.2d 657.

MOORE, CHIEF JUSTICE. The primary issue presented here is whether an owner may protect personal property in an unoccupied boarded-up farm house against trespassers and thieves by a spring gun capable of inflicting death or serious injury.

We are not here concerned with a man's right to protect his home and members of his family. Defendants' home was several miles from the scene of the incident to which we refer infra.

Plaintiff's action is for damages resulting from serious injury caused by a shot from a 20–gauge spring shotgun set by defendants in a bedroom of an old farm house which had been uninhabited for several years. Plaintiff and his companion, Marvin McDonough, had broken and entered the house to find and steal old bottles and dated fruit jars which they considered antiques.

At defendants' request plaintiff's action was tried to a jury consisting of residents of the community where defendants' property was located. The jury returned a verdict for plaintiff and against defendants * * *.

For about 10 years, 1957 to 1967, there occurred a series of trespassing and housebreaking events with loss of some household items, the breaking of windows and "messing up of the property in general". The latest occurred June 8, 1967, prior to the event on July 16, 1967 herein involved.

Defendants through the years boarded up the windows and doors in an attempt to stop the intrusions. They had posted "no trespass"

2. See Hallen, Hill v. Kimball—A Milepost in the Law, 12 Tex.L.Rev. 1 (1933); Magruder, Mental and Emotional Disturbance in the Law of Torts, 49 Harv.L.Rev. 1033 (1936); Prosser, Intentional Infliction of Mental Suffering: A New Tort, 37 Mich. L.Rev. 874 (1939); Smith, Relation of Emotions to Injury & Disease: Legal Liability for Psychic Stimuli, 30 Va.L. Rev. 193 (1944); A.L.I. Restatement of Torts Second § 40 ("Outrageous Conduct Causing Severe Emotional Distress") and comments.

Compare this with the kindred problem of liability for harm resulting from mental suffering or shock caused by negligence. See p. 491ff, supra.

An excellent opinion dealing with this problem in the context of high-pressure bill collection methods is to be found in Clark v. Associated Retail Credit Men of Washington, 70 App. D.C. 183, 105 F.2d 62 (1939); as to conduct in bad faith by insurer see, e. g., World Insurance Co. v. Wright, 308 So.2d 612 (Fla.App.1975).

signs on the land several years before 1967. The nearest one was 35 feet from the house. On June 11, 1967 defendants set "a shotgun trap" in the north bedroom. After Mr. Briney cleaned and oiled his 20–gauge shotgun, the power of which he was well aware, defendants took it to the old house where they secured it to an iron bed with the barrel pointed at the bedroom door. It was rigged with wire from the doorknob to the gun's trigger so it would fire when the door was opened. Briney first pointed the gun so an intruder would be hit in the stomach but at Mrs. Briney's suggestion it was lowered to hit the legs. He admitted he did so "because I was mad and tired of being tormented" but "he did not intend to injure anyone". He gave no explanation of why he used a loaded shell and set it to hit a person already in the house. Tin was nailed over the bedroom window. The spring gun could not be seen from the outside. No warning of its presence was posted.

Plaintiff lived with his wife and worked regularly as a gasoline station attendant in Eddyville, seven miles from the old house. He had observed it for several years while hunting in the area and considered it as being abandoned. He knew it had long been uninhabited. In 1967 the area around the house was covered with high weeds. Prior to July 16, 1967 plaintiff and McDonough had been to the premises and found several old bottles and fruit jars which they took and added to their collection of antiques. On the latter date about 9:30 p. m. they made a second trip to the Briney property. They entered the old house by removing a board from a porch window which was without glass. While McDonough was looking around the kitchen area plaintiff went to another part of the house. As he started to open the north bedroom door the shotgun went off striking him in the right leg above the ankle bone. Much of his leg, including part of the tibia, was blown away. Only by McDonough's assistance was plaintiff able to get out of the house and after crawling some distance was put in his vehicle and rushed to a doctor and then to a hospital. He remained in the hospital 40 days.

Plaintiff's doctor testified he seriously considered amputation but eventually the healing process was successful. Some weeks after his release from the hospital plaintiff returned to work on crutches. He was required to keep the injured leg in a cast for approximately a year and wear a special brace for another year. He continued to suffer pain during this period.

There was undenied medical testimony plaintiff had a permanent deformity, a loss of tissue, and a shortening of the leg.

The record discloses plaintiff to trial time had incurred $710 medical expense, $2056.85 for hospital service, $61.80 for orthopedic service and $750 as loss of earnings. In addition thereto the trial court submitted to the jury the question of damages for pain and suffering and for future disability.

Plaintiff testified he knew he had no right to break and enter the house with intent to steal bottles and fruit jars therefrom. He further testified he had entered a plea of guilty to larceny in the nighttime of property of less than $20 value from a private building. He stated he had been fined $50 and costs and paroled during good behavior from a 60-day jail sentence. Other than minor traffic charges this was plaintiff's first brush with the law. On this civil case appeal it is not our prerogative to review the disposition made of the criminal charge against hm.

The main thrust of defendants' defense in the trial court and on this appeal is that "the law permits use of a spring gun in a dwelling or warehouse for the purpose of preventing the unlawful entry of a burglar or thief". They repeated this contention in their exceptions to the trial court's instructions 2, 5 and 6. * * *

In the statement of issues the trial court stated plaintiff and his companion committed a felony when they broke and entered defendants' house. In instruction 2 the court referred to the early case history of the use of spring guns and stated under the law their use was prohibited except to prevent the commission of felonies of violence and where human life is in danger. The instruction included a statement breaking and entering is not a felony of violence.

Instruction 5 stated: "You are hereby instructed that one may use reasonable force in the protection of his property, but such right is subject to the qualification that one may not use such means of force as will take human life or inflict great bodily injury. Such is the rule even though the injured party is a trespasser and is in violation of the law himself."

Instruction 6 stated: "An owner of premises is prohibited from willfully or intentionally injuring a trespasser by means of force that either takes life or inflicts great bodily injury; and therefore a person owning a premise is prohibited from setting out 'spring guns' and like dangerous devices which will likely take life or inflict great bodily injury, for the purpose of harming trespassers. The fact that the trespasser may be acting in violation of the law does not change the rule. The only time when such conduct of setting a 'spring gun' or a like dangerous device is justified would be when the trespasser was committing a felony of violence or a felony punishable by death, or where the trespasser was endangering human life by his act." * * *

Prosser on Torts, Third Edition, pages 116–118, states:

> "* * * the law has always placed a higher value upon human safety than upon mere rights in property, it is the accepted rule that there is no privilege to use any force calculated to cause death or serious bodily injury to repel the threat to land or chattels, unless there is also such a threat to the defendant's personal safety as to justify a self-defense. * * * spring guns and other man-killing devices are not justifiable against a mere trespasser, or even a petty thief.

They are privileged only against those upon whom the landowner, if he were present in person would be free to inflict injury of the same kind."

Restatement of Torts, section 85, page 180, states: "The value of human life and limb, not only to the individual concerned but also to society, so outweighs the interest of a possessor of land in excluding from it those whom he is not willing to admit thereto that a possessor of land has, as is stated in § 79, no privilege to use force intended or likely to cause death or serious harm against another whom the possessor sees about to enter his premises or meddle with his chattel, unless the intrusion threatens death or serious bodily harm to the occupiers or users of the premises. * * * A posessor of land cannot do indirectly and by a mechanical device that which, were he present, he could not do immediately and in person. Therefore, he cannot gain a privilege to install, for the purpose of protecting his land from intrusions harmless to the lives and limbs of the occupiers or users of it, a mechanical device whose only purpose is to inflict death or serious harm upon such as may intrude, by giving notice of his intention to inflict, by mechanical means and indirectly, harm which he could not, even after request, inflict directly were he present."

In Volume 2, Harper and James, The Law of Torts, section 27.3, pages 1440, 1441, this is found: "The possessor of land may not arrange his premises intentionally so as to cause death or serious bodily harm to a trespasser. The possessor may of course take some steps to repel a trespass. If he is present he may use force to do so, but only that amount which is reasonably necessary to effect the repulse. Moreover if the trespass threatens harm to property only—even a theft of property—the possessor would not be privileged to use deadly force, he may not arrange his premises so that such force will be inflicted by mechanical means. If he does, he will be liable even to a thief who is injured by such device." * * *

In United Zinc & Chemical Co. v. Britt, 258 U.S. 268, 275, 42 S.Ct. 299, 66 L.Ed. 615, 617, the court states: "The liability for spring guns and mantraps arises from the fact that the defendant has * * expected the trespasser and prepared an injury that is no more justified than if he had held the gun and fired it."

In addition to civil liability many jurisdictions hold a land owner criminally liable for serious injuries or homicide caused by spring guns or other set devices. * * *

The legal principles stated by the trial court in instructions 2, 5 and 6 are well established and supported by the authorities cited and quoted supra. There is no merit in defendants' objections and exceptions thereto.

Affirmed.[3]

All Justices concur except LARSON, J., who dissents.

LARSON, JUSTICE. I respectfully dissent, first, because the majority wrongfully assumes that by installing a spring gun in the bedroom of their unoccupied house the defendants intended to shoot any intruder who attempted to enter the room. * * * Unless it is held that these property owners are liable for any injury to an intruder from such a device regardless of the intent with which it is installed, liability under these pleadings must rest upon two definite issues of fact, i. e., did the defendants intend to shoot the invader, and if so, did they employ unnecessary and unreasonable force against him? * * *

* * * [The court] utterly failed to tell the jury it could find the installation was not made with the intent or purpose of striking or injuring the plaintiff. There was considerable evidence to that effect. * * * Both defendants stated the installation was made for the purpose of scaring or frightening away any intruder, not to seriously injure him. It may be that the evidence would support a finding of an intent to injure the intruder, but obviously that important issue was never adequately or clearly submitted to the jury.

Unless, then, we hold for the first time that liability for death or injury in such cases is absolute, the matter should be remanded for a jury determination of defendant's intent in installing the device under instructions usually given to a jury on the issue of intent. * *

STRAWN v. INGRAM

Supreme Court of Appeals of West Virginia, 1937.
118 W.Va. 603, 191 S.E. 401.

HATCHER, JUDGE. In a fight between plaintiff, Ray Strawn, and defendant, Arley Ingram, the former received personal injuries, for which he recovered a judgment. Defendant alleges error.

The physician who treated plaintiff after the fight testified without contradiction that his skull was fractured, his brain severely concussed and permanently contused, his face and head lacerated, and his vision permanently impaired. The plaintiff, aged 36 years, testified without contradiction that, since the assault, his head has pained him intermittently at the place where his skull was fractured, that his eyes have ached almost continuously, that he can "scarcely see" with his left eye and can see "not more than half" with his right eye, that he has been dizzy at times and "night after night" has not "known what sleep is." The verdict specified that actual damages were assessed at $800 and punitive damages at $25. * * *

1. The plea [of justification] was stricken because not filed within the time required by a court rule, as construed by the court. This action, however, need not be considered seriously. Defendant testified unequivocally that he and plaintiff mutually agreed to fight.

3. See, similarly, McKinsey v. Wade, 136 Ga.App. 109, 220 S.E.2d 30 (1975) (booby-trapped cigarette vending machine; owner liable for death of burglar).

Defendant admitted striking plaintiff on the head with an iron bar "not exactly to protect" himself. He admitted intentionally gouging plaintiff's eye with his thumb and hitting plaintiff with his fist after having him on the ground. Under such circumstances, the law recognizes no justification for the injuries inflicted, and striking defendant's plea did not prejudice him. "If men fight the state will punish them. If one is injured, the law will not listen to an excuse based on a breach of the law. * * * The rule of law is therefore clear and unquestionable, that consent to an assault is no justification. Where a combat involves a breach of the peace, the mutual consent of the parties thereto is generally regarded as unlawful, and as not depriving the injured party, or for that matter, each injured party, from recovering damages for injuries received from the unlawful acts of the other." Cooley on Torts (4th Ed.) section 97. * * *

2 and 4. Because the combat was by mutual consent and no counterclaim was interposed, verdict for plaintiff was properly directed. The fact that plaintiff was also at fault is no defense. Brown v. Patterson, 214 Ala. 351, 108 So. 16, 47 A.L.R. 1093. That fact may be taken by the jury to preclude or mitigate punitive damages but not to reduce actual damages. Grotton v. Glidden, 84 Me. 589, 24 A. 1008, 30 Am.St.Rep. 413. And because there was no material conflict in the evidence as to the infliction or the extent of plaintiff's injuries, instruction on the burden of proof and preponderance of evidence was uncalled for. * * *

5. * * * It was error, however, to direct the jury, either orally or in writing, to assess punitive damages. Though the existence of elements may be established which warrant the assessment of exemplary damages, "it is with a jury to say whether or not they shall be given." Fink v. Thomas, 66 W.Va. 487, 66 S.E. 650, 19 Ann.Cas. 571. The assessment thereof, however, is only $25. * * *

The judgment will be modified [by deducting $25] and affirmed.

Modified and affirmed.[3a]

3a. This case is noted in 22 Min.L.Rev. 546 (1938).

Compare Restatement of Torts, Second § 60 (1965).

An interesting variant to the problem posed in the Strawn case is presented in Hudson v. Craft, 33 Cal.2d 654, 204 P.2d 1, 7 A.L.R.2d 696 (1949) (minor plaintiff who engaged in boxing match conducted by proprietor of carnival without license required by law, held entitled to recover for injuries sustained in such match). Also see Restatement of Torts Second § 61 (1965).

MILLER v. BENNETT

Supreme Court of Appeals of Virginia, 1940.
190 Va. 162, 56 S.E.2d 217.

HUDGINS, CHIEF JUSTICE. Raymond J. Bennett, Adm'r of Kerneda C. Bennett, instituted this action against Iva Rodeffer Davis Coffman to recover $15,000 damages for the wrongful death of decedent. It was alleged that the death of decedent was the result of an abortion, or an attempted abortion, performed by defendant upon Mrs. Bennett. The trial court overruled defendant's contention that proof that decedent consented to the commission of the illegal or immoral act barred recovery. The jury returned a verdict for plaintiff in the sum of $8,000, on which judgment was entered.

This action was commenced before Mrs. Coffman was convicted under Code Michie's 1942, sec. 4401, of an attempted abortion. After her conviction, and while she was confined in the State penitentiary, Francis S. Miller was appointed committee of her estate, and in his name the action was contested.

There is no substantial difference in the evidence introduced in this case, and that introduced in the criminal case, which need not be repeated, as a full statement of it is found in Coffman v. Commonwealth, 188 Va. 553, 50 S.E.2d 431, to which reference is made.

The decisive question presented is, whether consent of a mature married woman to an attempt to produce an illegal abortion, resulting in death, bars recovery, under Lord Campbell's Act, in an action by her administrator against the party attempting to procure the abortion. This question has not been decided in this jurisdiction.

It is conceded that if the consent of decedent to the commission of the immoral or illegal act would have been a bar to decedent's right to recover had she survived, such consent bars recovery in an action by her administrator for her wrongful death under the provisions of Code Michie's 1942, secs. 5786, 5787. See Street v. Consumers Min. Corp., 185 Va. 561, 39 S.E.2d 271, 167 A.L.R. 886, and cases there cited.

The general rule, that a party who consents to and participates in an immoral or illegal act cannot recover damages from other participants for the consequence of that act, is well settled. The rule itself, and the reasons therefor, are clearly stated in the often quoted excerpt from the opinion of Lord Mansfield, in Holman v. Johnson, 98 Eng.Rep. 1120, which is as follows:

"No Court will lend its aid to a man who founds his cause of action upon an immoral or an illegal act. If, from the plaintiff's own stating or otherwise, the cause of action appears to arise ex turpi causa, or the transgression of a positive law of this country, there the Court says he has no right to be assisted. It is upon that ground the Court goes; not for the sake of the defendant, but because they will not lend their aid to such a plaintiff. So if the plaintiff and defendant were to change sides, and the defendant was to bring his action against the plaintiff, the latter would then have the advantage of it; for where both are equally in fault, potior est conditio defendentis."

This general rule has been applied in Virginia in at least four cases, and in most, if not all, of the American courts. * * *

The principle applies to civil actions, whether based on tort or contract. When applied to actions in tort, it is said that consent or participation in an immoral or unlawful act by plaintiff precludes recovery for injuries sustained as a result of that act, on the maxim volenti non fit injuria. It is conceded that Mrs. Bennett consented to and participated in the immoral and illegal act when she solicited the services of Mrs. Coffman and submitted herself to treatment to produce abortion. If the general rule is applicable, then this action is barred.

Appellee contends that there is an exception to the general rule, and cites numerous authorities to support his contention. Each is based on the reasons stated in 1 Cooley on Torts, 4th Ed., sec. 97, p. 326, thus:

"The life of an individual is guarded in the interest of the state, and not in the interest of the individual alone; and not his life only is protected but his person as well. Consent cannot justify an assault. * * * Consent is generally a full and perfect shield when that is complained of as a civil injury which was consented to. * * * But in the case of a breach of the peace it is different. The state is wronged by this, and forbids it on public grounds. If men fight, the state will punish them. If one is injured, the law will not listen to an excuse based on a breach of the law. There are three parties here, one being the state, which for its own good, does not suffer the others to deal on a basis of contract with the public peace. The rule of law is therefore clear and unquestionable, that consent to an assault is no justification."

Mr. Francis H. Bohlen, in an article entitled "Consent as Affecting Civil Liability for Breaches of the Peace," XXIV Columbia Law Review, 819, states that the origin of this exception to the general rule is based on dictum in Matthew v. Ollerton (Comberbach 218), an old English case, decided in 1693. At the time this case was decided, both the Crown and the individual were interested in the outcome of the writ of trespass, the Crown in the fine to be imposed, and the individual for damages sustained. Subsequently, misdemeanors were punished by prosecutions in the name of the Crown and the writ of trespass was used exclusively by the individual to recover compensation for the wrong. Hence, Mr. Bohlen said: "So long as the writ of trespass was the only machinery by which breaches of the King's peace, falling short of felony, could be punished, it is obvious that the consent of the private individual could no more defeat an action of trespass than his consent today can bar a criminal prosecution by the Crown."

Mr. Bohlen, in pointing out the fallacious reasoning upon which the exception is founded, said: "The statement that the State is a party in interest was, as has been seen, true, at least in theory until 1694. It has not been true since then. If, however, Chief Justice Cooley is not alluding to the State's interest as litigant, but to the State's interest in deterring persons contemplating breaches of the peace from their commission, his language would apply equally to make consent to any invasion of any legally protected interest which involved any element of criminality inoperative to prevent liability. Thus he would make the civil remedy of a person aggrieved by tortious conduct a prop to the inefficient administration of the criminal law, for unless the criminal law is inefficiently administered or unless the penalties imposed are insufficient deterrents, there is no need to pervert what is today a purely private remedy into a device to punish and so prevent crime, and to force this ill-mated couple, the civil and criminal functions of trespass, happily divorced in 1694, to masquerade occasionally as husband and wife. If the State really feels that its good order has been seriously disturbed by the assault or battery, it can and does prosecute the participants. Usually the State regards the offense done it as so trivial as not to warrant the trouble and expense of prosecution. It is curious to find courts so tender of the interests of the State as to preserve the civil liability of the participants in an offense which the State itself does not think is sufficiently serious to justify the trouble of prosecuting them."

Notwithstanding the fact that the State as such is no longer interested in an action of trespass instituted by an individual to obtain redress for private injuries, the exception to the general rule is extended in a few jurisdictions to permit recovery where the woman consented to an illegal abortion resulting in personal injuries to her. * * *

The better reasoned cases support the view that no recovery can be had in such cases. * * *

In some states the anti-abortion statutes make the woman who consents to the procurement of an abortion upon herself an accomplice, and in others such a woman is not made an accomplice. But whether such a woman is or is not declared to be an accomplice is not regarded as material in a civil action brought by her to recover damages for injuries resulting from the abortion, or the illegal attempt to procure abortion. * * *

Appellee further contends that while there is no Virginia case deciding whether a person consenting to an abortion can recover for injuries resulting therefrom, yet Virginia is committed to the doctrine that recovery can be had for personal injuries sustained in affray notwithstanding both parties voluntarily participated therein. Hence, by analogy, consent to an illegal abortion would not bar recovery.

This contention is based upon the opinion in Matthews v. Warner, 29 Grat. 570, 26 Am.Rep. 396. The facts, as stated in the report of the case, were that Warner used "very abusive language" to Matthews, who, in retaliation, shot and killed him. The court held that the killing was done under circumstances which indicated that if Matthews was not guilty of murder, he was at least guilty of voluntary manslaughter. The pertinent and precise point decided was that the trial court correctly refused an instruction which read "that if the jury believed, from the evidence, that the death of the deceased, Montesco Warner, was the result of his own misconduct or neglect, then the jury must find for the defendant."

The court said: "This is not a case in which contributory negligence can be pleaded. The death in this case was not caused by negligence; it was caused by violence—by a wrongful act."

There is nothing in the statement of the case from which it can be inferred that Warner consented to engage in an affray, but even if he did, there was no justification for Matthews' use of a deadly weapon. The abusive language could, and doubtless would, have been considered in mitigation of punishment in a criminal prosecution, and in mitigation of damages in the civil action, but such language was not a defense to the criminal prosecution or a bar to recovery in the civil action.

A number of cases are cited in the briefs in which a distinction is made between the purpose of an anti-abortion statute and assault and battery and dueling statutes. These cases hold that the former class of statutes are not designed for the protection of the woman, but only of the unborn child and through it society, while the assault and battery, dueling etc. statutes are designed for the protection of the individuals concerned. Hence recovery is allowed in one class of cases and denied in the other. See Herman v. Julian, 117 Kan. 733, 232 P. 864; Bowlan v. Lunsford, 176 Okl. 115, 54 P.2d 666.

However, we do not deny recovery in this case on the distinction between the two classes of statutes, but upon the ground that the plaintiff's decedent, a mature married woman, was guilty of moral turpitude and participated in the violation of a general anti-abortion statute, enacted to effectuate a public policy.

The judgment of the trial court is reversed, the verdict of the jury set aside, and final judgment entered for defendant.

Reversed and final judgment.[4]

4. Contrast these cases with McAdams v. Windham, 208 Ala. 492, 94 So. 742, 30 A.L.R. 194 (1922); Bennan v. Parsonnet, 83 N.J.L. 20, 83 A. 948 (1912).

McMURREY CORPORATION v. YAWN

Court of Civil Appeals of Texas, 1940.
143 S.W.2d 664.

HALL, JUSTICE. Addie Yawn, surviving wife, and the minor children of Girardus H. Yawn, appellees, instituted this suit against the McMurrey Corporation, the McMurrey Petroleum Corporation, the McMurrey Interests, the McMurrey Pipe Line Company, the McMurrey Refining Company, Marvin H. McMurrey, Jim McMurrey, and Lucille McMurrey, for damages occasioned by the alleged wrongful death of Girardus H. Yawn, hereinafter referred to as deceased. It was alleged that the McMurreys were partners, joint adventurers, or joint associates in the ownership and operation of certain oil properties located in Rusk County, among which was the oil lease known as the Pinkston lease, and that one Rudolph Loesewitz was employed by them to guard, supervise and manage said lease; that said Loesewitz as their agent and while acting within the scope or apparent scope of his authority as watchman, manager and operator of said lease, and not in his own self-defense, negligently and carelessly shot and killed deceased. In the alternative it was alleged that the killing of deceased was intentionally brought about by the conspiracy of the McMurreys acting by and through their agent, Loesewitz. All the McMurreys including the several companies answered denying partnership, and all except Jim McMurrey denied that Loesewitz was their employee or agent in any capacity. Jim McMurrey answered that after he purchased the Pinkston lease he employed Loesewitz to look after said lease "generally" and to flow the oil wells located thereon; that at the time Loesewitz killed deceased, he Loesewitz, "was outside of his employment or the scope of his employment by this defendant; that said Rudolph Loesewitz, at the time of such killing, and immediately prior thereto, was acting in his own self-defense, for all of which this defendant is in no way liable for damages or any part of the damages sued for herein."

The record reflects that deceased operated and managed the Pinkston lease before it was purchased by Jim McMurrey. Shortly after its purchase he was discharged, and Loesewitz was employed in his stead. While deceased was working on the Pinkston lease he lived in a house located thereon. This house was purchased either by Jim McMurrey or some one for him, and was being moved on the day deceased was killed. Deceased had removed from the lease before his death. Loesewitz also lived in a house located on the lease about 200 or 300 feet from the house formerly occupied by deceased. After deceased had been discharged by appellant and before his death, some of the oil wells located on this lease had on two occasions been turned on at night, causing the tanks to overflow. Loesewitz thought that deceased was the party who turned on the wells and he so informed Jim McMurrey. On the day of the killing Loesewitz was informed that deceased was on the lease near the house where he had formerly lived. On receiving this information, Loesewitz took his shotgun, went to where deceased was, and after speaking a few words to him shot and killed him. Loesewitz testified that threats by deceased to take his life had been, on two occasions, communicated to him; one on the night before, and the other a few minutes before the killing. Loesewitz also testified that, at the time of the killing, deceased by acts committed evidenced an intention to carry said threats into execution and that he shot him in self-defense. It later developed, however, that deceased was unarmed. The jury verdict upon special issues and the judgment rendered thereon were for appellees and against defendants Jim McMurrey, M. H. McMurrey, and the McMurrey Corporation, jointly and severally, who prosecute this appeal. The other defendants were dismissed from the case. * * *

Self-defense was relied on as a justification for said killing. The court below charged the jury as follows:

"You are charged that by the term 'wrongful' as used in Special Issue No. 1, means the use of a greater degree of force than was reasonable and necessary under the circumstances then existing.

"Now bearing in mind the foregoing definitions and instructions, you will answer the following special issues, to-wit: Special Issue No. 1:

"Do you find from a preponderance of the evidence that the action of Rudolph Loesewitz in shooting and killing the deceased, Girardus H. Yawn, was wrongful? Answer Yes or No."

Jury answer: "Yes."

By proposition No. 9 appellants challenge the correctness of this definition when applied to the facts and circumstances surrounding the defense of self-defense as shown by the testimony in the record. Appellants' proposition is: "In a civil suit to recover damages for the alleged wrongful death of the deceased, where the defendant's pleadings and evidence raised the issue that the deceased had made threats against the life of the defendant, which were communicated to the defendant, and that, by the demonstration made by the deceased, the defendant believed the deceasd intended to carry out such threat, and, in defense of himself, he killed the deceased, it is error for the court to submit to the jury the bald question whether the action of the defendant in killing the deceased was wrongful, without instructing the jury upon the law of threats and self-defense and justifiable homicide. An instruction that the term 'wrongful,' as used in the question, means the use of a greater degree of force than is reasonable and necessary under the circumstances then existing, is entirely inadequate, misleading, and gives to the jury the impression that the killing of the deceased was the exercise of a greater degree of force than was necessary, and was, therefore, wrongful."

If Loesewitz was acting in his own self-defense at the time he shot and killed deceased, the killing in law would not be wrongful but justifiable. This is true in a civil action as well as in a criminal action. It was said in the early case of March v. Walker, 48 Tex. 372: "The law of self-defense is the same as in a criminal prosecution, with the exception of the rule of evidence which, in a criminal cause, gives the defendant the benefit of a reasonable doubt. That doubt, however, is as to the facts,—not as to the extent of the right. The stage of the difficulty at which self-defense ceases is just the same, whether the question be investigated civilly or criminally." * * *

This defense was not only available to Loesewitz had he been sued, but also to his principals, appellants herein. Cameron Compress Co. v. Kubecka, Tex.Civ.App., 283 S.W. 285, writ refused. Loesewitz testified that he thought deceased on two occasions at night had turned on the oil wells located on said lease, causing the oil tanks to overflow; that he had deceased make tracks for comparison with "boot tracks" found near the oil wells; that he reported to the sheriff's office of Rusk County and to the officers of the Railroad Commission that said oil wells had been turned on. Loesewitz testified further that he went to see the district attorney of Rusk County for the purpose of having deceased placed under a peace bond to avoid having trouble with him. On the night before deceased was killed Loesewitz testified that his (Loesewitz's) wife told him that deceased "was coming on the lease and get me"; that about fifteen minutes before the killing "T. M. Hill came up and told me that Buck Yawn (deceased) was down on the lease and had a gun and was going to—he said, 'going to kill you the first time he saw you.'" Loesewitz testified further:

"Q. When Hill told you that, what did you do? A. I got me a gun and went down there to get him to carry him to town.

"Q. Well, how near did you get to him before you saw him? A. I judge between 20 and 30 steps.

"Q. Did you say steps? A. I said steps but I mean feet, between 20 and 30 feet.

"Q. What did you say to him, if anything? A. I said, 'All right, Buck come and go with me, you are going to town.'

"Q. What did he do if anything? A. He made about two steps and went left hand to his waist—

"Q. What did you say or do, if anything? A. I did not say anything or do anything, I just raised my gun and shot.

"Q. Then what did you do? A. I turned around and went to the Lispen Gasoline plant and called the sheriff's department and told them to call Jim McMurrey, told them about what had happened.

"Q. Who was the first person you saw after you had shot Buck Yawn? A. My wife—I believe it was my wife.

"Q. Do you know Mr. Larner? A. Yes, I know him.

"Q. Did you see him first or your wife? A. I can not say for sure whether it was him or my wife.

"Q. What statement, if any, did you make to Mr. Larner about Buck? A. The same statement I made to every one, the only statement I made was to go and watch him and don't let them take that gun off of him.

"Q. How long was that after you had fired the shot that had killed Buck Yawn? A. About as long as it would take you to walk around—say 100 feet.

"Q. What was Buck Yawn doing, just prior to the time that you fired the shot that killed him? A. He was walking toward me.

"Q. Was he doing anything else? A. Well, when I first seen him he had his back towards me and was walking off.

"Q. When he started towards you what movement did he make with his hands? A. He went left-handed for his shirt, like he was going in his shirt after something.

"Q. What did you think he was going to do? A. I thought my time had come; I thought he would probably kill me.

"Q. What did you think he was going to kill you with? A. I thought he had a gun in his belt.

"Q. Did you know the reputation that Buck Yawn bore in that neighborhood, and in that vicinity, for being a law-abiding man? A. I had heard about him toting a pistol and shooting out lights out of those honkey-tonks up and down the highway.

* * *

"Q. When you put the Ford pick-up in the Rushing garage and walked home, who was it that you were afraid of that night, who was it you were afraid would come, or might? A. Well my wife told me it was Buck Yawn.

"Q. From what your wife had told you about what was going on up at the store, they were going to get you that night, you left it there because you were afraid that Buck Yawn and whoever might be with him would come? A. Yes.

"Q. That was Friday night before the killing on Saturday? A. Yes, sir."

This testimony, in our opinion, clearly raises the issue of communicated threats and self-defense, and the court's definition of the term "wrongful" as applied to the facts in this case is incorrect. If at the time of the killing the deceased by his acts and conduct reasonably induced Loesewitz to believe that deceased was about to attack him with a deadly weapon which would probably cause Loesewitz' death or some serious bodily injury; or if by the acts of the deceased it reasonably appeared to Loesewitz at the time, viewed from his standpoint alone, that deceased was then about to attack him with a deadly weapon which would probably cause Loesewitz' death or some serious bodily injury, and if same was reasonably calculated to create in the mind of Loesewitz, and did create in his mind, a reasonable expectation of fear of death or some serious bodily injury, and that Loesewitz then and there moved and actuated by such reasonable expectation of fear of death or serious bodily injury, shot and killed deceased, then under such circumstances the killing would be in his lawful self-defense and would not be "wrongful." Where a person accused of murder seeks to justify himself on the ground of threats against his own life, he may be permitted to introduce evidence of the threats made, but the same shall not be regarded as affording a justification for the offense, unless it be shown that at the time of the homicide the person killed by some act then done manifested an intention to execute the threats so made. If deceased did make threats against the life of Loesewitz and at the time of the killing deceased made such an act or demonstration as reasonably to produce in the mind of Loesewitz, viewed from his standpoint at the time, a belief that deceased then and there intended to execute such threats and to take the life of Loesewitz, or to do him some serious bodily harm, then the killing would not be "wrongful." It is not essential to the right of self-defense that real danger should exist. If from Loesewitz' standpoint, taking into consideration all the facts and circumstances surrounding the parties, it reasonably appeared to him that he was in danger of death or serious bodily injury, under the law he had the right to defend against such apparent danger to the same extent as if the danger were real, and if he shot and killed the deceased under such circumstances the killing would not be "wrongful." Kelly v. State, 68 Tex.Cr.R. 317, 151 S.W. 304. This omission from the definition of the term "wrongful" in the court's charge preceding Special Issue No. 1 is vital, and calls for a reversal of this case, Barrow v. Barclay, Tex.Civ.App., 269 S.W. 235, writ refused; Whitaker v. Haynes, Tex. Civ.App., 128 S.W.2d 532. The converse of the above is also true; that is to say, if Loesewitz used a greater degree of force than was reasonable and necessary under the circumstances existing at the time of the killing and was not acting in his own necessary self-defense as explained above, the killing would be "wrongful." * * *

The judgment is reversed, and the cause remanded.[5]

5. Other cases dealing with the master's liability for assault and battery committed by the servant and its limitations are Crawford v. Exposition Cotton Mills, 63 Ga.App. 458, 11 S.E.2d 234 (1940) (majority and dissenting opinion); Healey v. Playland Amusements Co., 199 So. 682 (La.App.1941) (test of vicarious responsibility not the servant's motive but whether he was doing something contemplated by his employment which, if he should do it lawfully, he might do in the employer's name); Fields v. Sanders, 29 Cal.2d 834, 180 P.2d 684, 172 A.L.R. 525 (1947) (defendant's driver who struck plaintiff with wrench during altercation arising after collision on highway between the parties' automobiles, held within scope of employment).

A privilege to defend others from threatened attack is also recognized. This was once limited to those who stood in some relationship to the one assailed which involved a moral or legal duty to protect him, but the limitation probably has little modern vitality. Harper, Torts section 48 (1933).

C. I. T. CORPORATION v. BREWER

Supreme Court of Florida, 1941.
146 Fla. 247, 200 So. 910.

PER CURIAM. On writ of error we review judgment in favor of the plaintiff in a suit for damages alleged to have been inflicted by an assault and battery. The facts to sustain a verdict as gleaned from the record are, in effect:

One Amos had bought an automobile under conditional sales contract. The conditional sales contract had been assigned to C. I. T. Corporation, a corporation. J. B. Brewer was president and manager of J. B. Brewer, Inc., a Florida corporation, engaged in the business commonly known as an automobile garage in Fort Pierce, Florida. Amos had delivered the automobile to J. B. Brewer, Inc., to be repaired. The automobile had been repaired. Amos had not paid the repair bill. The automobile was in possession of J. B. Brewer, Inc., just outside of the garage building on the premises of J. B. Brewer, Inc. The ignition key had been removed from the automobile by the garage owner or its agent.

One Denmark was agent for C. I. T. Corporation with authority to collect instalments due under conditional sales contract and to repossess automobiles in event of default in payment. Amos and Denmark went into the garage of J. B. Brewer, Inc., and requested J. B. Brewer to make payment for Amos of the amounts in default under the conditional sales contract. Brewer declined to do so, whereupon Denmark said that he would repossess the automobile. J. B. Brewer told Denmark that he was holding the car for the amount due his corporation for repairs and also told Denmark that he could not remove the car from his possession without paying the repair bill. While they were discussing the matter Brewer's attention was called somewhere else and as he turned away Denmark got into the automobile, found the ignition key was not in it and hereupon attempted to remove the automobile from the premises by using the starter as motive power. The noise of the operation of the starter attracted Brewer; he returned and attempted to get Denmark out of the automobile. Denmark resisted and put up a fight. Brewer called on some of his employees to assist him and together they separated Denmark from the automobile. But, in the fight or altercation over possession of the automobile Denmark injured Brewer by either striking him or kicking him in or about the abdomen, thereby causing a serious hernia resulting in great pain and suffering and in permanent injury.

Other questions which may be raised by this privilege are the effect of reasonable mistake or to whether intervention or force is necessary the degree of force that may be used to protect oneself (or another) from a merely offensive bodily touching, from a battery which does not menace life or limb, and the like; and the circumstances under which the one assailed may stand his ground rather than retreat.

Plaintiff in error has posed seven questions for our consideration, stated as follows:

"1. Has the holder of a conditional sales contract upon an automobile the right to take possession of the automobile when it is parked on the premises of an automobile sales agency and garage serving the public when the holder or his agent is rightfully on the premises and did not commit a breach of the peace or trespass in entering into and taking possession of the automobile?

"2. Has the holder of a conditional sales contract on an automobile the right to defend his possession of the automobile after he has rightfully repossessed it and is in complete charge and control of it?

"3. Has the holder of a mechanic's and materialmen's lien on an automobile the right to physically and forcibly take possession of the automobile from one holding the conditional sales contract of prior date and effect, who is actually in custody and possession thereof? * * *

The first and second questions indulge the unwarranted assumption that the agent of the holder of the conditional sales contract repossessed the automobile in question without committing a breach of the peace or a trespass in taking possession of the automobile.

In C.I.T. Corporation et al. v. Reeves, 112 Fla. 424, 150 So. 638, 639, in discussing the rights of the holder of retain title contract to retake property, we said: "Without doubt, trespasses or assaults perpetrated in exercising the right to peaceably retake possession, as conferred by the contract, are not contemplated by any of the contractual provisions, and if any such trespasses or assaults are committed by the title holder or his agent, in the course of exercising the contract right given, an action on the case for damages will clearly lie. See Silverstin v. Kohler & Chase, 181 Cal. 51, 183 P. 451, 9 A.L.R. 1177."

Authorities are legion to support that enunciation. See Percifield v. State, 93 Fla. 247, 111 So. 519; Annotation and authorities cited 9 A.L.R. 1180 et seq., also annotations and authorities cited 105 A.L.R. 926 et seq.

The third question unwarrantedly assumes that the agent of the holder of the conditional sales contract had accomplished taking possession of the automobile, that is of divesting J. B. Brewer, Inc., of the possession of the automobile when Brewer undertook to remove Denmark from the automobile. The jury was warranted in finding a contrary condition. There is ample evidence to establish it as a fact that Denmark was attempting to forcibly and against the will of the person in possession of the property remove that property from the possession of the garage owner.

In Crews et al. v. Parker, 192 Ala. 383, 68 So. 287, 288, that court said: "Any act or action manifesting force or violence, or naturally calculated to provoke a breach of the peace, in the recaption of property renders the actor a trespasser, and precludes him from availing of his right to retake the property. To enter one's premises, and notwithstanding the possessor's protest, and in a rude and rough manner to take chattels against his will, is, we think, clearly not an assertion of a right in a peaceful manner."

In Singer Sewing Machine Co. v. Phipps, 49 Ind.App. 116, 94 N.E. 793, it was held: "A corporation is liable in damages as an individual for a tort committed by its agent in the line of his employment and within the scope of his authority, though it be malicious and against its express order." * * *

So it may be said that the attempt to seize manual control of a chattel and to remove it from the premises of one who is in lawful possession thereof by one claiming the right to repossess it under conditional sales contract after he had been expressly denied the right by the person in lawful possession constitutes a trespass for which damages may be awarded; and where such trespass is committed by the agent of the owner of a conditional sales contract when the agent is shown to have general authority to repossess property covered by such contracts the employer is liable for the trespass or assault and battery committed and may be required to answer in damages for the same. * * *

A consideration of the entire record discloses no reversible error. The judgment is affirmed.

So ordered.[6]

6. If the C.I.T. Corporation did have the right to immediate possession as against Brewer, it would not become a converter of the automobile by taking it with unprivileged force. Silverstin v. Kohler & Chase, 181 Cal. 51, 183 P. 451, 9 A.L.R. 1177 (1919).

For the extent of the privilege to use force to recapture chattels in fresh pursuit, see Restatement of Torts, Second §§ 100–111 (1965). In the absence of fresh pursuit the one entitled to immediate possession of personal property may generally retake it if he can do so without using any force. See notes 19 Minn.L.Rev. 602 (1935) (collecting many cases; some where seller by contract sought to reserve privilege to retake with force); 31 Mich.L.Rev. 987 (1938).

The rules concerning reentry upon land are not quite the same. In England, though forcible entry is a criminal offense under a statute of 1381, no civil action lies for the regaining of possession by the use of reasonably necessary force. Hemmings v. Stoke Poges Golf Club [1920] 1 K.B. 720. This case overruled earlier decisions giving redress "in respect of independent wrongful acts which are done in the course of or after the forcible entry [i. e. acts of force against the person]." See Pollock, Torts 305–308 (14th ed. 1939). The governing statutes in this country vary. There is a distinct tendency, however, to follow the earlier (overruled) English cases. Cf. the analogy of recaption of chattels. A different question is presented when some force is used—but not against a person—to gain entry. That is not treated here. See Harper, Law of Torts, section 50 (1933); Tiffany, Real Property, sections 180, 181 (3d ed. 1939).

CUMMINS v. ST. LOUIS AMUSEMENT CO.

St. Louis Court of Appeals, Missouri, 1941.
147 S.W.2d 190.

BENNICK, COMMISSIONER. This is an action for damages for an assault and battery allegedly committed upon plaintiff by one of defendant's ushers while in the act of ejecting plaintiff from the Gravois motion picture theater, in the City of St. Louis, on September 9, 1936. Tried to a jury, a verdict was returned in favor of defendant; and from the judgment which was entered in conformity with the verdict, plaintiff's appeal to this court has followed in the usual course.

The evidence disclosed that plaintiff, a boy then about thirteen years of age, was admitted into the theater after paying the required admission price of 10 cents, and took a seat next to the aisle in the fourth or fifth row from the front.

During the showing of the picture, projection trouble of some sort developed, causing the picture to go off the screen temporarily while the necessary steps were being taken by the operator to remedy the difficulty.

The usher's testimony was to the effect that when the picture went off the screen, plaintif began shouting, "I want to see the picture," so as to disturb every one else in the theater; that no one else was creating a disturbance at that particular time; that he gave plaintiff three different warnings to be quiet, but all to no avail; that when plaintiff persisted in the disturbance, he requested him to leave, and took hold of his right arm to escort him back up the aisle and out of the theater; that he did not at any time twist plaintiff's arm or bring it up behind his back; that whatever force was employed was occasioned by plaintiff's own conduct in twisting and jerking in an attempt to get away from the usher instead of leaving the theater peaceably when he was told that "he had to go out"; and that when the usher reached the head of the aisle with plaintiff, he called the manager, who then took plaintiff in charge, and put him out of the theater.

Plaintiff's testimony, on the other hand, was that while "most of the people" started clapping their hands, stamping their feet, and whistling when the picture went off the screen, all he did was merely to clap his hands; that he had done no shouting or stamping at any time; that notwithstanding his innocence of any disturbance, the usher came down to where he was sitting and pulled him out of his seat, telling him to "come into the back of the show"; and that when the usher took hold of him, he twisted his arm up behind his back and forced him up the aisle to the rear door, where the manager took him over and completed his ejection from the premises.

In plaintiff's petition, to which defendant answered by a general denial, it was averred that while plaintiff was present in the theater as a patron, "defendant did wrongfully threaten plaintiff and use abusive language to him and assault and strike and beat plaintiff and twist and distort his limbs and force part of one of plaintiff's arms behind and over his back," whereby he was injured in the manner and to the extent thereafter alleged.

Tried upon the controverted issues of fact in the case, the jury found in favor of defendant, as we have already indicated; and now the judgment is assailed by plaintiff upon the ground of error in the giving of two instructions for defendant, one of which was the latter's instruction No. 5, which read as follows:

"You are instructed that under the law the theater ticket purchased by plaintiff on the occasion mentioned in evidence was only a license to him to enter said theater, which license might at the pleasure of the defendant, with or without any good reason therefor, be revoked or canceled by requesting plaintiff to leave the theater or by returning his admission fee. Upon such cancellation or revocation of such license, if any, it then became the duty of plaintiff to leave the theater quietly and peaceably; and it made no difference whether or not defendant had any reason for requesting plaintiff to leave.

"Therefore, if you find and believe from the evidence herein that the defendant, through its agents, servants, and employees, canceled or revoked plaintiff's ticket of admission by requesting him to leave the theater upon the occasion mentioned in the evidence and by returning his admission fee, that plaintiff refused so to do, and that said agents, servants, and employees used no more force in ejecting plaintiff than was reasonably necessary, then your verdict herein should be in favor of defendant.

"You are further instructed that whether or not plaintiff was making any noise or creating any disturbance in the treater is of no consequence with respect to the right of defendant to eject him from the theater, for the reason that plaintiff had no irrevocable right but only a license to be in the theater, which license could be canceled or revoked by defendant at any time, and for any reason, or for no reason at all."

Plaintiff challenges the correctness of the instruction in charging the jury that defendant had the right to eject him from its theater either with or without any reason for his expulsion.

The instruction was obviously prepared by defendant in the light of the rule which is said to prevail in this country, * * * 62 C.J. 861–863; 26 R.C.L. 704; Ayres v. Middleton Theater Co., Mo.App., 210 S.W. 911, 913; Pearce v. Spalding, 12 Mo.App. 141, 144.

While the instruction, in its abstract terms, was not incorrect in so far as it contemplated the general doctrine with respect to defendant's power of revocation of the license granted by the ticket sold to plaintiff and its right to remove him with reasonable and necessary force when such power of revocation was exercised, we nevertheless cannot escape the conclusion that it went entirely too far, not only in its unqualified statement that defendant had the right to demand plaintiff's removal "with or without any good reason therefor" or "for any reason," but especially so, under the facts and issues in the case, in its concluding assertion that "whether or not plaintiff was making any noise or creating any disturbance" was of no consequence upon the question of defendant's right to eject him from the theater.

A case which we cannot read except as supporting our conclusion about the error inherent in the instruction is Hoagland v. Forest Park Highlands Amusement Co., 170 Mo. 335, 70 S.W. 878, 880, 94 Am.St.Rep. 740, in which our Supreme Court had occasion to consider the question of good cause as the same affects the right of the proprietor of an amusement enterprise to eject one of his patrons from the premises. * * *

[In that case the court held defendant not privileged to eject a patron for the latter's reasonable refusal to turn over to defendant's manager a pocketbook which the patron had found, until the patron was assured of the manager's identity.]

It follows, therefore, that regardless of the revocable nature of the license granted by the sale of a ticket to a theater or other place of amusement, the proprietor nevertheless has no right to eject one of his patrons "without any good reason therefor," or "for any reason," if that reason happens to be wrongful and unfounded; and in directing the jury to the contrary so far as the instance under consideration was concerned, defendant's instruction No. 5 erroneously claimed for defendant an unlimited power of revocation which it did not in fact possess.

If defendant's evidence was to be believed that plaintiff was guilty of creating a disturbance in the theater, then it had perfectly good cause to ask him to depart, and, upon his refusal, to employ all reasonable and necessary force to accomplish his removal. But on the other hand, if plaintiff's evidence was to be believed that he had created no disturbance, then, to adopt defendant's own language, it had no right to eject him based upon a "wrongful demand" or a "supposed right," which did not in fact exist. So far as its evidence was concerned, defendant had no misapprehension about the necessity for showing good cause for plaintiff's expulsion; and with the evidence in direct conflict upon the sole issue of fact by which defendant had sought to justify its course of action, it was especially harmful and prejudicial to tell the jury that "whether or not plaintiff was making any noise or creating any disturbance" was of no consequence as regards defendant's right to have ejected him from the theater. On the contrary, that question was of consequence in the case for the reason that defendant itself had made it so by putting its demand for plaintiff's removal upon that ground; and if, in resisting plaintiff's cause of action for damages for an alleged assault and battery committed upon him, defendant thought it important to have the jury instructed about its power of revocation of the license granted by the ticket sold to plaintiff, it should not have assumed a proper and justifiable exercise of the power except upon a finding by the jury of the truth of the facts upon which its action had been predicated.

The question of error in the giving of the other instruction complained of by plaintiff may not appear upon a retrial of the case.

For the error noted in the giving of defendant's instruction No. 5, it follows that the judgment rendered by the circuit court should be reversed and the cause remanded, and the Commissioner so recommends.

PER CURIAM.

The foregoing opinion of BENNICK, C., is adopted as the opinion of the court.

The judgment of the circuit court is, accordingly, reversed and the cause remanded.[7]

S. H. KRESS & CO. v. BRADSHAW

Supreme Court of Oklahoma, 1940.
186 Okl. 588, 99 P.2d 508.

BAYLESS, CHIEF JUSTICE. Frances Bradshaw sued S. H. Kress & Co., a corporation, in the district court of Garfield County, Oklahoma, to recover compensatory damages. In her petition, in a first cause of action based upon alleged false imprisonment, she claimed damages in amount of $1500, and in a second cause of action based upon alleged personal injuries, she claimed damages in amount of $1400. The jury returned a verdict finding generally in her favor, and in relation to the first cause of action fixing the amount of her recovery at $1500, and in relation to the second cause of action fixing the amount of recovery at $300. Judgment was rendered on the verdict, and the defendant has appealed.

From the evidence, as same relates to the first cause of action, the following is made to appear: On May 21, 1937, at about 12:30, noon, Mrs. Frances Bradshaw, a resident on Enid, Oklahoma, made a purchase of postage stamps at the post office in that city, and in the transaction received as part of the change due her a certain half dollar. From the post office, and accompanied by her five year old daughter, she proceeded to the defendant's store in Enid, intent upon there purchasing some work sox for her husband. In making the purchase, which came to the amount of forty-one cents, she tendered to Miss Reinwald, the defendant's clerk there waiting upon her, the half dollar which she had received over at the post office. Miss Reinwald,

7. For limits on the amount of force which may be used to eject a trespasser (or to prevent a threatened trespass) see Gargotto v. Isenberg, 244 Ky. 493, 51 S.W.2d 443 (1932); Restatement of Torts, section 77–79; Mitsu Nakashima v. Takase, 8 Cal.App.2d 35, 46 P.2d 1020 (1935) (felonious trespass). Compare the similar problem posed by (1) self defense against an insulting but not dangerous battery; (2) apprehension of a misdemeanant. See Laney v. Rush, 152 S.W.2d 491 (Tex.Civ.App.1941); (3) recapture of chattels in fresh pursuit. Prosser, Torts section 24 (1941). Cf. also Bogrett v. Hromada, 91 N.H. 351, 19 A.2d 432 (1941) (defendant may use reasonable force to gain exit he has right to use. No deadly force involved.)

from sounding the half dollar on a marble slab attached to the cash register, became of the belief that said coin might be counterfeit. She did not, however, inform Mrs. Bradshaw of this belief; but under pretext of having to procure change in order to complete the sale transaction absented herself from the presence of Mrs. Bradshaw and carried the half dollar to the store's office which was located on a balcony in the rear of the store room, leaving Mrs. Bradshaw in waiting at the counter where the merchandise had been selected. Upon reaching the office Miss Reinwald turned the half dollar over to another of the defendant's employees, a Miss Glenn, who then held the position of assistant cashier in the store. There Miss Glenn made certain tests of the half dollar, from which she became convinced said coin was counterfeit. Miss Glenn thereupon proceeded to call the city police station by telephone, and advised the desk sergeant then on duty at the station, that the Kress store "had a bad half dollar," and that "if they care to, to send a man over." Upon receiving this call from Miss Glenn, the desk sergeant directed a uniformed city policeman, Officer Bennell, to forthwith proceed to the store; and the distance from the police station to the store being only fifty or sixty feet, Bennell arrived at the store very shortly after Miss Glenn's call came into the station. He had proceeded from the police station to the store along an alley, and he entered the store through one of the doorways in the rear of the building. Miss Reinwald, it appears, after turning the half dollar over to Miss Glenn in the office, was informed by Miss Glenn that the half dollar was counterfeit. Whereupon Miss Reinwald immediately returned to the counter where Mrs. Bradshaw had remained in waiting and there proceeded to engage Mrs. Bradshaw in casual conversation. Bennell, upon entering the store, was approached by Miss Glenn who there handed to him the half dollar in question and pointed in the direction where Mrs. Bradshaw and Miss Reinwald were standing at the hosiery counter. Miss Glenn was in the act of leaving the store, to go out for lunch, at the time she met the policeman, and after handing him the coin she immediately departed from the store.

With respect to occurrences subsequent to Bennell's arrival at the store, Mrs. Bradshaw testified that she "noticed a policeman coming in at the back door"; that he first approached some one in the store, and then walked up to where she was standing, and said to her: "Lady, where did you get that fifty cent piece?" and that she said: "At the post office"; that the policeman then said to her: "Are you sure you got it at the post office?" that she replied, "I certainly am"; that he then said to her, "You come and tell that to the desk sergeant"; that she was afraid to resist him; that she suggested, "let's ride in the car," and explained to the officer that her car was parked "out in front"; that the officer said: "No, let's go out this way," meaning, "out the back door." Bennell testified that, upon entering the store at the rear, he "stood there and one of the girls brought the money to me"; that he did not remember which of the girls it was; that he "had some instructions that there was some counterfeit money over there and she handed it to me and I looked at it and there was some chips in it and it looked very similar to some we had gotten before and I looked at it and the lady that had passed it walked up there." That he said to Mrs. Bradshaw, "It looks like counterfeit to me all right"; and further, "we will go over to the police station and see what the sergeant says, and if you remember where you got it we will get your money back for you," and, "I started out the back door and she followed me out." Bennell also testified that, while in the store on this occasion, none of the store employees or clerks asked him to take Mrs. Bradshaw out of the store, or said anything other or further to him than that to which he testified.

Mrs. Bradshaw, her small daughter, and Bennell left the store together, departing therefrom through a doorway in the rear, and Bennell proceeded with Mrs. Bradshaw and the little girl along the alley to the police station. At the police station she was interrogated by the desk sergeant concerning the source from which she had come into possession of the half dollar in question. In this connection, Bennell testified: "I throwed the half dollar on the desk and he looked at it and he had several others in the drawer and he pulled them out and compared them and dropped them on the desk and they sounded exactly alike, and he asked her if she remembered where she got it, and she said she got it in change at the post office. And he asked her if she wanted to go over with me to get her money and she said 'yes,' and I went over to the post office and got her money for the half dollar." Mrs. Bradshaw testified, however, that it was at the suggestion of a police matron who was present that she was taken over to the post office. Bennell further testified that after they had left the store, and either on the way to the police station or at the station, the following occurred: "She made the statement that she was excited and nervous and trying to do right, and never had been arrested, and I told her we were not arresting her, that it was our duty to help people the same as anything else, and we would try to help her."

At the post office, the postal clerk from whom Mrs. Bradshaw had made the purchase of stamps was interviewed by Bennell in the presence of Mrs. Bradshaw, and the clerk readily remembered that Mrs. Bradshaw had that day made a purchase of stamps from him. Bennell testified that upon arriving at the post office with Mrs. Bradshaw, the following occurred: "I throwed the half dollar in the window and asked (the clerk) if he remembered giving the lady the half dollar in change and he say, 'yes, I did': that, He (the clerk) took the half and looked at it and dropped it down on the metal plate in the window and said, 'That half dollar is all right,' and throwed it in the drawer and picked out another half and throwed it out." At the conclusion of the interview Mrs. Bradshaw and Bennell left the post office together, and upon reaching the street Mrs. Bradshaw was released from further custody.

It was further disclosed by the evidence that the defendant had previously issued written instructions to its employees, on the subject of counterfeit money as follows: "Check the money received from customers to determine counterfeit money, coin and bills. If in doubt whether a coin or bill is good refer it to the manager, or authorized person on the floor. This may be done on the excuse of securing change, as the customer might otherwise be offended."

And, Mr. W. L. Casselman, local manager of the defendant's store in Enid at the time Mrs. Bradshaw made the purchase aforementioned and also holding that position at the time of the trial in the court below, testified that he was not in or about the store at or during the time Mrs. Bradshaw was there, but he had previously instructed clerks and employees of the store "that whenever counterfeit coins were handed them or detected on their registers to call the police."

False imprisonment, it is said in 25 C.J. 443, sec. 1, "consists in the unlawful restraint against his will of an individual's personal liberty or freedom of locomotion." And in 22 Am.Jur. 353, sec. 2, the following appears: "False imprisonment has been said to be the unlawful restraint by one person of the physical liberty of another. In this phrase the word 'false' seems to be exactly synonymous with 'unlawful,' * * *. The following comprehensive definition is given by the American Law Institute: 'An act which directly or indirectly, is a legal cause of confinement of another within boundaries fixed by the actor for any time, no matter how short in duration, makes the actor liable to the other irrespective of whether harm is caused to any legally protected interest of the other, if the act is intended to confine the other or a third person, and the other is conscious of the confinement, and the confinement is not otherwise privileged.' "

With respect to the detention of Mrs. Bradshaw in the defendant's store up to the time Miss Glenn, the defendant's employee, became convinced the half dollar was counterfeit it properly may be said that the proof adduced at the trial warrants no conclusion other than that Mrs. Bradshaw was not at the time conscious of the fact that she was being intentionally detained. The fact that she had tendered in payment for merchandise selected by her from the defendant's stock a half dollar which Miss Reinwald, the defendant's clerk, then believed to be counterfeit, undoubtedly warranted and justified her detention in the store for a reasonable time thereafter in order that the defendant's clerks and employees who had interested themselves in the matter might become satisfied as to the genuineness of the coin in question. Otherwise they might have been placed in the position of permitting their employer's merchandise to be exchanged for a coin proving to be counterfeit. In 11 R.C.L. 805, sec. 18, we find the statement that: "* * * the right of defense of one's person and property may sometimes require and justify the restraint of any person who seeks to interfere with and injure them."

And in Collyer v. S. H. Kress & Co., et al., 5 Cal.2d 175, 54 P.2d 20, it was held that: "Ordinarily, owner of property in exercise of his inherent right to protect it may restrain another who seeks to interfere with or injure it." * * *

In Jacques v. Childs Dining Hall Co., [244 Mass. 438, 138 N.E. 843, 26 A.L.R. 1329] it was held: "The proprietor of a restaurant may detain a patron who apparently has not paid for food purchased, a reasonable time to investigate the circumstances."

It does not appear that Mrs. Bradshaw has complained to the effect that her detention was for an unreasonable length of time. And since she was not at the time conscious of an intentional detention, and the right to protect the defendant's property having intervened, we are of the opinion the detention of Mrs. Bradshaw in the defendant's store was not unlawful up to the time Miss Glenn became convinced through tests made by her that the half dollar in question was counterfeit.

With respect to further detention Mrs. Bradshaw alleged in her petition that:

"* * * she had been retained and restrained at said store by agents of said defendant * * * and on the arrival of the policemen, * * * said agents and employees caused this plaintiff to be arrested without cause.

"* * * At the instance of defendant's agents, * * * plaintiff was taken by the policemen to the police station * * * and subjected to detention there * * *. The policeman * * * took plaintiff to the post office * * *.

"* * * plaintiff was taken into the custody of the policeman, who was the agent of defendant, without warrant and without authority at the instance and request of defendant through its employees, * * * that said arrest greatly frightened plaintiff and humiliated her * * * and her reputation and standing in the community greatly damaged * * *. That said arrest and shock caused plaintiff nervous illness, injured her reputation and standing," etc.

In 22 Am.Jur. 354, sec. 3, it is said that, "false arrest and false imprisonment as causes of action are indistinguishable. The only distinction lies in the manner in which they arise." In Hepworth v. Covey Bros., etc., Co., Utah, 91 P.2d 507, 509, the following may be noted: "False arrest may be committed only by one who has legal authority to arrest or who has pretended legal authority to arrest. False imprisonment may be committed by anyone who imprisons without legal right. One who commits a false arrest of another may be liable in damages for false imprisonment, but from this we must not reason that if there is a failure of proof of false arrest, of necessity there is a failure of proof or false imprisonment. False arrest is merely one means of committing a false imprisonment. False imprisonment may be committed without any thought of attempting an arrest."

See, also, Fox v. McCurnin, 205 Iowa 752, 218 N.W. 499, wherein it was held: "Where plaintiff in action for false imprisonment was driven from apartment house in which he had rooms by owner, and under direction of owner was placed under arrest, whereupon he brought action against owner alleging false arrest and false imprisonment, held that they were not distinguishable, and therefore charge amounted only to charge of false imprisonment, and did not state distinct causes of action, in view of Code 1924, section 13465, defining arrest, and section 13468, providing occasions upon which police officer may make an arrest."

In 22 Am.Jur. 356, sec. 4, the following statement appears: "The primary right involved in an action for false imprisonment is the liberty of the citizen, or, in other words, the right of freedom of locomotion, the right to come and go or stay when or where one may choose, * * *. The constituent elements of a cause of action for false imprisonment, as seen from the definition and essential elements of the tort, as distinguished from other similar wrongs, are (1) the detention or restraint of one against his will, and (2) the unlawfulness of such detention or restraint. It is not necessary that the wrongful act which results in detention or restraint be under color of any legal or judicial proceeding, nor do lack of malice, the presence of good faith, or the presence of probable cause for the imprisonment affect the existence of the wrong when the detention is unlawful. There need be no actual force, threats, or injury done to the individual person, character, or reputation.[8]

False imprisonment may be accomplished without actual arrest, assault, or imprisonment, and may be committed by words alone or by acts alone, or by both. Harris & Co. v. Caldwell, Tex.Civ.App., 276 S.W. 298; Riley v. Stone, 174 N.C. 588, 94 S.E. 434; Newton v. Rhoads Bros., Tex.Com.App., 24 S.W.2d 378.

In the instant case there was proof on the part of Mrs. Bradshaw going to establish that she was taken into custody by Bennell, a policeman, without warrant, and required against her will to proceed under that custody to places other than where she wished to go.

The following statement appears in the brief (p. 26) of the plaintiff in error: "As shown by the evidence the plaintiff was not arrested as there was no intention on the part of the clerks or the police officer to arrest the plaintiff but merely an intention to investigate

8. Suppose that defendant's conduct does not bring about plaintiff's confinement, but that defendant simply fails to take affirmative steps to release plaintiff from confinement. Would this amount to false imprisonment? See Davis & Alcott Co. v. Boozer, 215 Ala. 116, 110 So. 28, 49 A.L.R. 1307 (1926); Timmons v. Fulton Bag & Cotton Mills, 45 Ga.App. 670, 166 S.E. 40 (1932), noted in 7 So.Cal.L.Rev. 102 (1933). The note discusses the existence and extent of a duty to take affirmative steps to release a plaintiff from confinement. Cf. Whittaker v. Sandford, 110 Me. 77, 85 A. 399, Ann. Cas.1914B, 1202 (1912); Talcott v. National Exhibition Co., 144 App.Div. 337, 128 N.Y. 1059 (1911).

A good conventional treatment of what constitutes confinement appears in Vold, Legal Allocation of Risk in Assault, Battery, and Imprisonment, 17 Neb.L.Bull. 149, 180 et seq. (1938). If confinement is not complete, so that the traditional requirements of false imprisonment are not satisfied, does this mean that plaintiff must go without remedy? See Cullen v. Dickenson, 33 S.D. 27, 144 N.W. 656, 50 L.R.A., N.S., 987, Ann.Cas.1916B, 115 (1913). Also see Restatement of Torts, Second § 120A, Temporary Detention for Investigation (1965) and the Reporter's Notes to that section.

for the purpose of tracing the counterfeit coin, but had she been arrested the defendant and the police officer would have been justified."

It will be remembered that Mrs. Bradshaw testified, that, while standing in the defendant's store, she "noticed a policeman coming in at the back door," and that in the course of her conversation which he there had with her, he said to her: "You come and go tell that to the desk sergeant." Hence, in effect, as much as to say: "I am a police officer, as you know, and what I am now doing and commanding you to do is by legal authority." From Mrs. Bradshaw's testimony it may fairly and reasonably be inferred that the policeman's appearance and his acts and words tended to create in Mrs. Bradshaw's mind the belief of a necessity of conforming to the demands thus made upon her or suffer the consequences, and that she conformed rather than chance the consequences, and thereby was restrained of her liberty. So, whether she was arrested or not, the restraint was just as effective. Hepworth v. Covey Bros., etc., supra.

In the brief of plaintiff in error no authority is cited as sustaining or supporting the right or authority of Bennell as an officer or otherwise to take Mrs. Bradshaw into custody and further detain her while such investigation as is referred to in the statement quoted above was being carried on. In section 2780, Okl.St.1931, 22 Okl.St. Ann. section 196, it is provided that a peace officer may without a warrant arrest a person:

"1. For a public offense, committed or attempted in his presence.

"2. When the person arrested has committed a felony, although not in his presence.

"3. When a felony has in fact been committed, and he has reasonable cause for believing the person arrested to have committed it.

"4. On a charge, made upon reasonable cause, of the commission of a felony by the party arrested."

Section 2783, Id., 22 Okl.St.Ann. section 199, provides: "When arresting a person without a warrant, the officer must inform him of his authority and the cause of the arrest, except when he is in actual commission of a public offense, or is pursued immediately after an escape."

And section 2765, Id., 22 Okl.St.Ann. section 181, provides: "The defendant must, in all cases, be taken before the magistrate without unnecessary delay."

Section 2138, Id., 21 Okl.St.Ann. section 1591, provides: "Every person who has in his possession any counterfeit of any gold or silver coin, whether of the United States or any foreign country or government, knowing the same to be counterfeit, with intent to sell or to use, circulate or export the same, as true or as false, or by causing the same to be uttered or passed, is guilty of forgery in the second degree."

Considering that, according to Mrs. Bradshaw's testimony, Bennell said to her: "You come and go tell that to the desk sergeant"; and also, that, according to Bennell's testimony, he told her while in the store: "We will go over to the police station and see what the sergeant says, and if you remember where you got it we will get your money back for you"; and, further, that he told her, after they had departed from the store, he was not "arresting" her, we think it may be said that no conclusion may fairly and reasonably be drawn other than that Bennell was not in the matter of taking Mrs. Bradshaw into custody proceeding by virtue of any provision of, or authority contained in, section 2780, supra.

In connection with the detention of Mrs. Bradshaw which ensued from the time Miss Glenn became convinced that the half dollar in question was counterfeit, it is to be remembered the evidence disclosed that Mr. Casselman had previously instructed the clerks and employees "to call the police" in instances wherein counterfeit coins were tendered to said clerks or employees; that the evidence also disclosed that Miss Glenn, after completing tests which she made on the questioned half dollar while Miss Reinwald was with her in the office, there advised Miss Reinwald that said half dollar was counterfeit; that thereupon Miss Reinwald left the office and returned to the hosiery counter where she had left Mrs. Bradshaw in waiting for her change; that Miss Reinwald, upon returning to the hosiery counter, made no tender of change nor explanation for not so doing, but proceeded to engage Mrs. Bradshaw in casual conversation. From this evidence it may fairly and reasonably be inferred that Mrs. Bradshaw was then and there being intentionally and purposely detained pending arrival of an officer. It is also to be kept in mind that the evidence disclosed the telephone call to the police station as being made by Miss Glenn, after she had become convinced that the half dollar was counterfeit; that upon arrival of Bennell, the officer, Miss Glenn approached him while he yet was in the rear of the store, handed the half dollar to him and pointed in the direction where Mrs. Bradshaw was standing; that Bennell, as heretofore stated, then accosted Mrs. Bradshaw, and after conversing with her took her into custody and proceeded with her to the police station.

A well established principle of law is that all who by direct act or indirect procurement, personally participate in, or proximately cause, the false imprisonment or unlawful detention of another are liable therefor. 22 Am.Jur. 371, sec. 31; 25 C.J. 497, sec. 69; Halliburton-Abbott Co. v. Hodge, 172 Okl. 175, 44 P.2d 122. And as to each participant, the law is unconcerned with the extent or degree of his activity when it comes to consider the question of liability, and places all on the same footing, each equally liable, jointly and severally. And this is true, regardless of whether a conspiracy to do the act theretofore had been entered into. 22 Am.Jur. 371, sec. 30; 25 C.J. 497, sec. 69; Meints v. Huntington et al., 8 Cir., 276 F. 245, 19 A.L.R. 664.

In the court below, and with respect to each cause of action, the defendant demurred to the plaintiff's evidence, subsequently renewed same and also moved for a directed verdict. The trial judge overruled the demurrer and also refused to direct a verdict, and in this appeal these adverse rulings are assigned as error.

As we view and consider the evidence adduced on the part of Mrs. Bradshaw same tends to show that, on the occasion of her appearance at the defendant's store, referred to in her petition and in the testimony, she was restrained of her liberty under circumstances from which the presumption would follow in law that the restraint effected was not lawful; and further, said evidence and the inferences fairly and reasonably arising therefrom tended to show employees of the defendant as having contributed to said restraint. The evidence, in our opinion, sufficiently made out as against the defendant a *prima facie* case of unlawful restraint or detention. See 22 Am.Jur. 422, sec. 107; 25 C.J. 538, sec. 146; Fox v. McCurnin, 205 Iowa 752, 218 N.W. 499; Smith v. Clark, 37 Utah 116, 106 P. 653, 658, 26 L.R.A.,N.S., 953, Ann.Cas.1912B, 1366. In Smith v. Clark, supra, it was said that: "* * * When by proof of facts or circumstances tending to show that the plaintiff was restrained or detained or imprisoned by the defendant, without a warrant, or other process, or by threats or force, or other facts or circumstances which naturally give rise to the inference or presumption that the restraint or imprisonment was wrongful or unlawful, he undoubtedly has made a *prima facie* case. The duty of proceeding to show a legal justification for such restraint, detention, or imprisonment then rests upon the defendant. * * *"

With respect to the demurrer to the evidence, so far as same was directed against the evidence adduced on Mrs. Bradshaw's part in making out a *prima facie* case of unlawful restraint and detention, we hold said demurrer to be without merit.

In her petition, in stating her second cause of action, Mrs. Bradshaw alleged in part the following: "* * * agents of defendant named herein detained and restrained * * * plaintiff until the officer arrived and then * * * W. L. Casselman, the manager of the store or Mable Reinwald or other agents of defendant to plaintiff unknown opened a door in the rear of the store not intended for entrance or departure from said store and directed or caused the policeman, Bennell, who was the agent of defendant, to take this plaintiff out said door, * * *. That plaintiff, over her protest was arrested by the policeman and taken out of this rear door. This door was elevated nearly three feet above the alley and was not intended for egress or entrance to the store but the agents and manager of defendant caused the policeman to compel the plaintiff to jump from the floor to the alley, * * *. This jump seriously and permanently injured this plaintiff and caused a miscarriage. Said jump caused shock and injury to her nervous system and injured her back so that she has suffered pain and nervousness since said jump and has been permanently injured thereby. * * *"

From the foregoing allegations it would appear that the claim of damages asserted under the second cause of action is based, not upon the fact of Mrs. Bradshaw having been unlawfully detained and restrained of her liberty, but upon the alleged fact that she was compelled to "jump from the floor to the alley," and that the "jump" resulted in alleged injuries to her, in that it "caused a miscarriage," caused "shock and injury to her nervous system," and, "injured her back so that she has suffered pain and nervousness since said jump and has been permanently injured thereby."

There was not, however, as we read the record, any evidence adduced on the part of Mrs. Bradshaw which either directly or inferentially tended to support the allegation, that clerks or employees of the defendant "directed and caused" the policeman to use a rear doorway in taking her out of the store; and the same also applies with respect to the further allegation that "the agents and manager of defendant caused the policeman to compel the plaintiff to jump from the floor to the alley." Evidence tending to support these allegations being essential in order to establish in the second cause of action a right of recovery as against the defendant, and there being no such evidence, we are of the opinion the trial court should have sustained the demurrer to the evidence, so far as said demurrer related to the second cause of action. * * *

The judgment on the first cause of action is hereby affirmed. But said judgment, on the second cause of action, is hereby reversed, and the cause is remanded to the trial court with directions to dismiss said second cause of action.

Affirmed in part; reversed in part, and remanded with directions.[9]

9. Treatments of the law of arrest, with and without a warrant, appear in Perkins, Law of Arrest, 25 Iowa L.B. 201 (1940), and LaFave, Arrest: The Decision to Take a Suspect into Custody (1965).

Compare Walton v. Will, 66 Cal.App.2d 509, 152 P.2d 639 (1944) (arrest of wrong man on a warrant).

A note, 37 Mich.L.Rev. 311 (1938) discusses a possible police privilege to stop and question suspects.

In Central Motor Co. v. Roberson, 154 S.W.2d 180 (Tex.Civ.App.1941), defendant told the Waco police that Roberson had left town with a car sold on time on which there was an unpaid balance. The police were asked to pick up the car and according to one version, to pick up Roberson. Acting under instructions from the Waco police, the Ft. Worth police arrested Roberson without a warrant, which under the circumstances was not privileged. It was held that defendant did not authorize an *improper* arrest of Roberson, under any of the evidence, so it was not liable for false imprisonment. Cf. Winegar v. Chicago, B. & Q. R. Co., 163 S.W.2d 357 (Mo.App.1942). Contrast Oldham v. Smith, 201 Ark. 903, 147 S.W.2d 361 (1941) (where conditional vendor swore out warrant for plaintiff's arrest and was held for malicious prosecution, other elements being present). Other cases where defendant was held to have instigated the arrest by an officer are Carter v. Casey, 153 S.W.2d 744 (Mo.App.1941); McGill v. Walnut Realty Co., 235 Mo. App. 874, 148 S.W.2d 131 (1941); Jillson v. Caprio, 86 U.S.App.D.C. 169, 181 F.2d 523 (D.C.Cir.1950). Compare Hammond v. Eckerd's of Asheville, 220 N.C. 596, 18 S.E.2d 151 (1942) (clerk held to lack authority to get policeman to search plaintiff for cigars thought to have been stolen from employer) with Zentko v. G. M. McKelvey, Inc., 88 N.E.2d 265 (Oh.App.1948) (Store owner held for arrest made by detective agency hired by it as inde-

HUBBARD v. BANKER ET AL.

Livingston County Court of New York, 1940.
24 N.Y.S.2d 289.

Action by Gervase N. Hubbard against Dan Banker, Warren S. Morey, and Eugene J. Stiegler for damages growing out of the issuance and execution of a warrant of attachment. On motion by the defendants for an order dismissing the complaint, and on motion by Dan Banker for judgment against the plaintiff.

Motions denied.

Order affirmed in 260 App.Div. 901, 23 N.Y.S.2d 198.

WHEELER, JUDGE. The defendants each move for an order dismissing the plaintiff's complaint; and the defendant Dan Banker asks that judgment be entered against the plaintiff in his favor in accordance with the provisions of Rule 113 of Civil Practice Act on "the ground that the action has no merit."

The plaintiff's complaint is for damages against the defendants, growing out of the issuance and execution of a warrant of attachment in an action entitled, "Justice's Court, Town of North Dansville. Dan Banker, Plaintiff, against Gervase N. Hubbard, Defendant."

Upon the return day of the summons the defendant appeared specially by his attorney and moved to vacate the warrant of attachment and to set aside the service of the summons. The Justice denied the motions and continued the case rendering judgment against the defendant for $115 damages and $10.35 costs.

The defendant appealed to this Court from the decision of the Justice denying his motion to vacate the warrant of attachment, and the decision of the Justice was reversed on appeal, and the attachment vacated and service of the summons set aside, pursuant to the provisions of Section 87, Justice Court Act. Misc., 24 N.Y.S.2d 286.

In the Justice Court action, Dan Banker was the plaintiff, who applied for the warrant of attachment; Warren S. Morey, a defendant, was the Justice who granted the application for the warrant; and Eugene J. Stiegler was the constable who received the warrant and executed it, and each of the above named for his connection with the case in Justice's Court is made a defendant in this action, by the plaintiff Gervase N. Hubbard, to recover damages which he claims he suffered and sustained by reason of the unlawful issuance and execution of the warrant of attachment.

The defendants' answer was by way of a general denial, and demand judgment dismissing plaintiff's complaint with costs.

pendent contractor). See note 18 A.L.R.2d 402; Sindle v. New York City Transit Authority, 33 N.Y.2d 293, 352 N.Y.S.2d 183, 307 N.E.2d 245 (1973); Montgomery Ward & Co., Inc. v. Keulemans, 275 Md. 441, 340 A.2d 705 (1975); Orso v. City and County of Honolulu, — Haw. —, 534 P.2d 489 (1975); Clark v. I. H. Rubenstein, Inc., 326 So.2d 497 (La.1976); and Vandermeer v. Pacific Northwest Development Corp., 274 Or. 221, 545 P.2d 868 (1976).

The plaintiff makes application by way of cross motion asking that the answer be stricken out and for summary judgment against the defendants in accordance with the provisions of Rule 113 of the Rules of Civil Practice.

The plaintiff takes the position on this motion that the amended complaint is to recover damages for a malicious abuse of process and upon this theory alone.

The process issued upon which it is sought to predicate malicious abuse of process was the warrant of attachment issued by the Justice.

The legal purpose of a warrant of attachment is for the levying upon so much of the personal or real property of the defendant, within his county, not exempt from levy and sale by virtue of an execution, as will satisfy the plaintiff's demand, with the costs and expenses. He must safely keep the property attached, to be disposed of as prescribed in "Article 5," section 74 et seq., of Justice's Court Act and immediately make an inventory thereof stating therein the estimated value of each item or article. Section 78, Justice Court Act.

"The gist of the action for abuse of process lies in the improper use of process after it is issued." Hauser v. Bartow, 273 N.Y. 370, 375, 7 N.E.2d 268, 269. (citing Dean v. Kochendorfer, 237 N.Y. 384–390, 143 N.E. 229).

The question is, in what manner was this process abused; How was it diverted from its lawful purpose?

Section 78 of the Justice Court Act provides: "The constable to whom the warrant of attachment is delivered must execute it at least six days before the return day of the summons by levying upon and taking into his custody so much of the goods and chattels of the defendant, not exempt from levy and sale by virtue of an execution * * * which he finds within his county, as will satisfy the plaintiff's demand, with the costs and expenses. He must safely keep the property attached, to be disposed of as prescribed in this article, and immediately must make an inventory thereof, stating therein the estimated value of each item or article."

The complaint alleges a substantial compliance with the provisions of Section 78 of the Justice Court Act. Paragraph numbered "Third" reads: "That pursuant to said warrant of attachment, the defendant Eugene J. Stiegler on the day aforesaid and in the village of Dansville, Livingston County, N. Y., seized, attached and took into his custody and then detained certain chattels and goods of the plaintiff, consisting of one 1938 Chevrolet truck bearing engine no. 1663069 and serial no. 2204— and 90 bales of hay, and on said day served Stanley Hubbard, the father of this plaintiff, with a copy of the summons, warrant of attachment and the inventory of the property so taken, and that since said day to the commencement of this action has detained said chattels and goods of the plaintiff."

The Court said in the course of his opinion in the Hauser v. Bartow case: " 'The action is not for the wrongful bringing of an action or prosecution, but for the improper use * * * of process in connection therewith * * *. The process of law must be used improperly. * * * If he is content to use the particular machinery of the law for the immediate purpose for which it was intended, he is not ordinarily liable, notwithstanding a vicious * * * motive. But the moment he attempts to attain some collateral objective, outside the scope of the operation of the process employed, a tort has been consummated,' " and he becomes liable for resultant damages. " 'The tortious character of the defendant's conduct consists of his attempts to employ a legitimate process for a legitimate purpose in an improper manner, and this point must be clearly shown by the plaintiff to entitle him to maintain his action.' " Harper on the Law of Torts, Sec. 272, pp. 593–595.

This must be discovered in the complaint if the complaint is sufficient to maintain an action for malicious abuse of process, a perversion of the process, from its statutory function or purpose.

In the pleading we have the defendants admittedly using the process of the Court for the purposes for which it was intended. Nowhere can it be found, by any allegation in the complaint, that the defendant did any act under color of his warrant of attachment, except what the statute contemplated in its execution.

The conclusion of the Court is that the complaint fails to state a cause of action for abuse of process.

The question then presents itself: Does the complaint state a cause of action for malicious prosecution, as has been intimated?

It is immaterial whether the action be labeled an action for abuse of process or malicious prosecution, or how it may be classified or named, if the complaint is sufficiently broad and pointed to maintain an action to right a wrong, however tabulated. Keller v. Butler, 246 N.Y. 249, 254, 158 N.E. 510, 55 A.L.R. 349.[10]

A "malicious prosecution" is one that begins in malice, without probable cause to believe it can succeed and which finally ends in failure.

10. This, of course, has not always been fully true; nor is it where the forms of action, or a "theory of the pleadings" doctrine, obtains. See Gibson v. Chaters, 2 Bos. & P. 129 (1800); Cowen v. Kuich, 39 D. & C. 530 (Pa.1940). Cf. Clissold v. Cratchley, [1910] 2 K.B. 244 (C.A.1910). False imprisonment or wrongful attachment of property was remediable in an action of trespass. The direct and *prima facie* unwarranted interference with person or property was the gist of the action, and called for justification. Malicious prosecution was the subject of an action on the case. Here the legal forms were observed and the legal steps taken. An action would lie, if at all, only where the elements set forth in the court's opinion were present. Under the Codes of Procedure it should make no difference that the complaint may have been framed with a view to one of these ancient forms rather than another. If the facts of *either* are alleged and proved, the court should permit recovery, as it does here. See Clark, Code Pleading, section 43 (2d ed. 1948).

Cf. White v. Miami Home Milk Producers Ass'n, 143 Fla. 518, 197 So. 125 (1940), where a similar approach was used under modified common law pleading which allowed joinder of counts for the different forms of action (a device not available at common law), though plaintiff was not successful under any of them.

The complaint must allege malice; that the action was commenced without probable cause and that the action ended in failure.

The essential allegations in the complaint set forth that the defendant Dan Banker applied to the defendant Warren S. Morey for a warrant of attachment in a Justice Court action; that the warrant was delivered to the defendant Eugene J. Stiegler for service and that he took into his custody, and detained, certain property; that he stored it with the full knowledge and consent of the other two defendants, without proper care, causing damage to the plaintiff.

That the seizure was unlawful, because the warrant of attachment was void, in that the papers upon which it was granted, was insufficient to confer jurisdiction.

That the defendant Dan Banker wilfully and maliciously and without probable cause, procured the issuance of the warrant of attachment, against the property of the plaintiff, with the intent and purpose to vex and harass the plaintiff, and that defendant Eugene J. Stiegler knowingly and wilfully did aid, assist and abet the defendants, and each of them, in such purpose.

That by virtue of the wrongful and malicious acts of each of the defendants, the plaintiff incurred legal expense in his defense, in the employing of counsel to appear in the Justice Court action to move to vacate the warrant and stating the reasons therefor; that the plaintiff appeared by counsel and opposed the motion, which was denied; that a motion was made to increase security given at the time of the application for the warrant, which was similarly opposed and denied; that the opposition to the motions and the defendant Warren S. Morey's refusal to grant same were calculated to further embarrass and vex the plaintiff and deprive him of his property.

That by reason of the wrongful and malicious acts of the defendants, plaintiff has been damaged in the sum of $2,500, and closes with a prayer for judgment.

An action for malicious prosecution is usually based upon an arrest in criminal proceedings, although it may be founded upon a civil action when commenced simply to harass and oppress the defendant. Burt v. Smith, 181 N.Y. 1–5, 73 N.E. 495, 2 Ann.Cas. 576.[11]

Damages are rarely recovered, however, for the malicious prosecution of a civil action, unless person or property is interfered with by some remedy such as arrest, attachment or injunction.

11. See also Melvin v. Pence, 76 U.S. App.D.C. 154, 130 F.2d 423 (1942), noted 41 Mich.L.Rev. 549, 29 Va.L.Rev. 118 (1942) (malicious prosecution of proceedings before an administrative board leading to loss of license); Christopher v. Henry, 284 Ky. 127, 143 S.W.2d 1069 (1940) (proceedings for commitment to insane asylum); note 22 Minn.L.Rev. 1060 (1938) (juvenile delinquency proceedings). It is an interesting problem whether a counterclaim for malicious prosecution may be filed in the very action which is alleged to constitute such tort. See Herendeen v. Ley Realty Co., 75 N.Y.S.2d 836 (Sup.Ct.1947); Mayflower Industries v. Thor Corp., 15 N.J.Super. 139, 83 A.2d 246 (1951).

Malice is the root of the action. Malice alone is not sufficient; want of probable cause must also be shown. Burt v. Smith, supra.

Probable cause is the knowledge of facts, actual or apparent, showing enough to justify a reasonable man in the belief that he has lawful grounds for prosecuting the defendant in the manner complained of.

Thus an innocent person may be prosecuted unjustly and subjected to expense and disgrace, with no right to call the prosecutor to account, provided he act upon an honest and reasonable belief in commencing the proceedings complained of.

Peace and good order exact this hardship from the individual for the benefit of the people at large, so the citizens may not be prevented by fear of the consequence, from attempting to assert their own rights or to vindicate the cause of public justice by an appeal to the courts. Hazzard v. Flury, 120 N.Y. 223, 24 N.E. 194; Heyne v. Blair, 62 N.Y. 19; Farnam v. Feeley, 56 N.Y. 451; Carl v. Ayers, 53 N.Y. 14; Long Island Bottlers' Union v. Seitz, 180 N.Y. 243, 73 N.E. 20.

It has been held that a judgment rendered by a justice of the peace, and subsequently reversed on appeal, is not conclusive but only *prima facie* evidence of probable cause. Burt v. Place, 4 Wend. 591; Nicholson v. Sternberg, 61 App.Div. 51, 70 N.Y.S. 212.[12]

If probable cause exists, it is an absolute protection against an action for malicious prosecution. Even when express malice has been proved, this is the rule supported by ample judicial authority.

Probable cause existed for the commencement of this action. The answer discloses that the action in Justice Court was commenced by the plaintiff Dan Banker now defendant in this action, to recover on a check given by Gervaise N. Hubbard to pay him for hay sold and

12. Cf. Addington v. Bates, 101 Colo. 293, 73 P.2d 529 (1937), noted in, 22 Minn.L.Rev. 740 (1938). What effect on the issue of probable cause in the civil case do the following events in the criminal proceeding have: waiver of preliminary examination; binding over or committal for trial in higher court, by magistrate; an unreversed conviction obtained by fraud and perjury?

A different question is presented by the requirement in malicious prosecution that the former proceedings must have ended in failure. See Hyde v. Southern Grocery Stores, 197 S.C. 263, 15 S.E.2d 353 (1941) (civil action with attachment brought against H and N for N's sole debt. On N's payment of debt the justice marked the bill paid and put papers in drawer for finished cases. This satisfied the requirement here treated); Gardner v. Bank of Pinehurst, 35 F.Supp. 727 (D.C.N.C. 1940) (prosecuting attorney, convinced there was no breach of the statute, nolled the charge. This satisfies present requirement but does not preclude showing in the later action that statute was breached); but cf. Fogg v. First National Bank, 268 Mass. 25, 167 N.E. 251 (1929) (*nolle prosequi* for lack of evidence not a successful termination). A note, 135 A.L.R. 784, deals with dismissal of the charge by a magistrate, for lack of evidence. Of course, where the proceedings are dismissed as result of compromise (as where the criminal charge is dropped upon restitution; where there is a plea bargain, etc.) there is no foundation for a later civil action. See cases collected in note 67 A.L.R. 509. Cf. Hughes v. Georgia Power Co., 65 Ga. App. 163, 15 S.E.2d 466 (1941) (plaintiff after being fined $5 for smoking on trolley allowed to go free "on his own recognizance.")

delivered to him at the agreed price and fair value of $113, an ordinary business transaction, a sale of goods at the agreed price for which check was given in payment.

The complaint fails to state a cause of action for malicious prosecution.

The question remaining is: Does the complaint state a cause of action containing allegations sufficient to support any cause of action, a triable issue against these defendants or any of them?

The complaint alleges that the defendant Dan Banker applied to Justice of the Peace defendant Warren J. Morey for a warrant of attachment against the plaintiff; that the warrant was issued to the defendant Eugene J. Stiegler by the Justice, for execution; that defendant Stiegler seized property; that he failed, by reason of negligence, to safely keep the property seized by him, while in his possession, to the damage of the plaintiff; that the warrant was unlawful and void in that the papers presented were insufficient as a matter of law to confer jurisdiction upon the Justice; that the defendant Banker without probable cause procured the issuance of the warrant; that by reason of the wrongful and unlawful acts of the defendants, he was compelled to incur legal expenses in his defense and was deprived of the use of his property and the same was, while being held under the warrant, damaged.

The complaint alleges a cause of action for damages growing out of the issuance and execution of an alleged void warrant of attachment, in other words, a trespass action for damages growing out of an unlawful seizure of property, without resultant damages, under an unlawful or void process.

The answer is in the nature of a general denial.

This Court, as it appears heretofore in this decision, has already vacated the warrant of attachment.

The defendants' answer by way of a general denial seeks to put in issue the validity of the warrant, which validity has, however, been adjudicated.

It therefore appears that there is no triable issue of fact raised by the answer, other than the question of damages for which judgment might be granted.

Having reached this conclusion,

The answer of the defendants, and each of them, should be stricken out as insufficient as a matter of law, and that an assessment to determine the amount of damages which plaintiff has suffered, if any, should be granted for a hearing to be held by a referee to be appointed by the Court pursuant to the provisions of Rule 113 of the Rules of Civil Practice.

The motion, therefore, of the defendants Warren S. Morey and Eugene J. Stiegler, for a dismissal of the complaint should be denied, and the motion of the defendant Dan Banker for a summary judgment after assessment of damages, should be denied.

Costs, however, to either party as against the other, are disallowed in all motions presented.

Submit order accordingly.[13]

SOFFOS v. EATON

United States Court of Appeals, District of Columbia, 1945.
80 U.S.App.D.C. 306, 152 F.2d 682.

EDGERTON, ASSOCIATE JUSTICE. This appeal is from a judgment of the Municipal Court of Appeals for the District of Columbia, one judge dissenting, which sustained the action of the Municipal Court in dismissing a complaint for malicious prosecution. 39 A.2d 865.

Appellant's complaint includes substantially the following allegations. Appellee B. M. Eaton leased a house to appellant for use as a dwelling. The rent was afterwards reduced from $63 a month to $55 in order to comply with the Emergency Rent Act. The appellees thereupon brought or instigated four successive suits against appellant to recover possession of the house. In July, 1942, appellee B. M. Eaton sued for possession on the alleged ground that he wished to remodel the premises into two apartments. Trial resulted in favor of appellant. In August appellee Eaton sued for possession on an alleged breach of covenant in that appellant and his wife were disorderly and committing a nuisance. This suit also resulted in favor of appellant. Appellee Eaton and his wife then "sold" the house to their daughter, appellee Jenkins. In October Jenkins sued appellant for possession on the alleged ground that she wanted the house for her own use as a dwelling. This suit was dismissed. In December, 1942, appellee Jenkins again sued appellant on the same ground, and the court rendered judgment for appellant on a finding that appellee did not seek in good faith to recover the house for her own use as a dwelling.

13. If Morey had been acting within his "jurisdiction" he would not have been liable even though actuated by malice. Linder v. Foster, 209 Minn. 43, 295 N.W. 299 (1940) (citing authorities); note 173 A.L.R. 836. Cf. also Springfield v. Carter, 175 F.2d 914 (8th Cir. 1949) (city authorities alleged to have acted falsely and maliciously in initiating prosecution); Gregoire v. Biddle, 177 F.2d 579 (2d Cir. 1949) (attorney general alleged to have procured plaintiff's detention maliciously).

Contrast Dyer v. Dyer, 178 Tenn. 234, 156 S.W.2d 445 (1941) (affidavits of doctors filed in lunacy proceedings held absolutely privileged) with Jillson v. Caprio, 86 U.S.App.D.C. 169, 181 F.2d 523 (1950) (where doctor failed to follow statutory procedure).

For extensive recent discussion of abuse of process see Hyde Construction Co. v. Koehring Co., 387 F.Supp. 702 (S.D.Miss.1974). Also, for a more recent New York case imposing liability for abuse of process, as well as discussing "prima facie tort" for unprivileged intentional infliction of economic harm through such abuse, see Board of Education v. Farmingdale Classroom Teachers Ass'n, Inc., 38 N.Y.2d 397, 380 N.Y.S.2d 635, 343 N.E.2d 278 (1975).

The complaint alleges that the two suits of appellee B. M. Eaton were brought for himself and his wife and that the two suits of appellee Jenkins were brought for herself and her parents. It alleges that all four suits were instigated by the Eatons and were brought "maliciously without just cause and in bad faith." It claims damages for the expense of defending the suits, injury to appellant's reputation by the charges of disorderliness and nuisance, and mental anguish caused by threatened loss of a home. If the suit is maintainable, all these are proper elements of damage.[14] The question is whether the complaint states a claim upon which relief can be granted.

The law tries to avoid both too much discouragement and too much encouragement of litigation. Some sort of balance has to be struck between the social interests in preventing unconscionable suits and in permitting honest assertion of supposed rights. These interests conflict because a suit which its author thinks honest may look unconscionable to a jury. Probably some suits which ought to be brought would not brought if the inevitable risk of losing a suit always carried with it the further risk of having to defend a charge that it was brought maliciously and without probable cause. By something like half the courts which have dealt with the question, this consideration has been thought to justify a rule which confers immunity, within limits, for malicious prosecution of civil suits. This court said in 1931 that " * * * no action will lie for the recovery of damages sustained by the prosecution of a civil action with malice, and without probable cause, when there has been no arrest of the person or seizure of the property of the defendant, and no special injury sustained, which would not necessarily result in all suits prosecuted to recover for like causes of action." [15]

But we have also said that "the right to litigate is not the right to become a nuisance." [16] The burden of being compelled to defend successive unconscionable suits is not one which would "necessarily result in all suits prosecuted to recover for like causes of action." The burden increases in more than arithmetical proportion. As the dissenting opinion in the Municipal Court of Appeals points out, successive suits may even wear a defendant down to the point of capitulation. We see no good reason why the law should tolerate repeated abuse of its processes. To allow redress for such abuse will not seriously hamper the honest assertion of supposed rights. No one is likely to be deterred from litigating an honest claim by fear that some future jury may erroneously decide that he has brought *two* suits maliciously and without probable cause.[17] We hold accordingly that

14. Melvin v. Pence, 76 U.S.App.D.C. 154, 159, 130 F.2d 423, 143 A.L.R. 149.

15. Peckham v. Union Finance Co., 60 App.D.C. 104, 105, 48 F.2d 1016, 1017. If this was "in accordance with generally accepted law" at that time, Melvin v. Pence, 76 U.S.App.D.C. 154, 157, 130 F.2d 423, 143 A.L.R. 149, it is not clearly so today. 150 A.L.R. 897, 899.

16. Melvin v. Pence, 76 U.S.App.D.C. 154, 157, 130 F.2d 423, 426, 143 A.L.R. 149.

17. Since two errors are less likely than one, erroneous findings that both of two civil suits were brought maliciously and without probable cause are

one who twice sues another maliciously and without probable cause is responsible to him in damages.[18] Appellant's complaint therefore states a claim upon which relief may be granted.

Reversed.

SMITH ET AL. v. HENSLEY

Supreme Court of Colorado, 1941.
107 Colo. 180, 109 P.2d 909.

Action by C. E. Hensley against Violet A. Smith and another, for alleged malicious prosecution wherein defendants filed a counterclaim. To review an adverse judgment, defendant Violet A. Smith brings error.

PER CURIAM. Judgment affirmed without written opinion.

On Rehearing.

BURKE, JUSTICE. Plaintiff and her husband (an attorney at law, deceased since this suit was started) are hereinafter referred to as Mr. and Mrs. Smith, respectively, and defendant in error as Hensley.

Because the record herein left plaintiff in error without the shadow of right to relief, we were obliged to affirm this judgment; and because the law applicable thereto was so simple that an intelligent layman should not have been misled, we could write nothing in explanation in this particular case without apparent reflection upon counsel. Overanxious, possibly, to avoid such reflection, we affirmed without written opinion. Within the time limited, following, a petition for rehearing was filed. Since that petition is signed only by Mr. O. A. Johnson the followng comment must be taken as applying to him alone.

This petition recites that plaintiff in error does "respectfully petition," and closes with the statement that, "We therefore respectfully submit." Nothing else about it is respectful. It opens with a charge that affirmance without written opinion was prompted by the court's desire to avoid the work of writing, and its inability, if it attempted to give reasons, to affirm without overruling a long and unbroken line of decisions to the contrary. The fact that a decision against counsel by the very able trial judge was approved by a department consisting of a majority of the judges of this court, seems never to have raised a suspicion in his mind that he might have blundered, and the nonchalance with which he has led his client into this costly review of a judgment of $55 is perhaps consistent with the slip-

less likely than an erroneous finding that one criminal prosecution was so brought.

18. Shedd v. Patterson, 302 Ill. 355, 134 N.E. 705, 26 A.L.R. 1004. Cf. Pope v. Pollock, 46 Ohio St. 367, 21 N.E. 356, 4 L.R.A. 255, 15 Am.St.Rep. 608; Cincinnati Daily Tribune Co. v. Bruck, 61 Ohio St. 489, 56 N.E. 198, 76 Am.St. Rep. 433. Contra, Pye v. Cardwell, 110 Tex. 572, 222 S.W. 153; Myhre v. Hessey, 242 Wis. 638, 9 N.W.2d 106, 150 A.L.R. 889. [Footnotes 15–19 by the court, renumbered.]

shod work appearing on the face of the petition before us. We commend to counsel a rereading of the second paragraph of the oath administered to newly admitted members of the bar, (Rule 83, R.C.P. Colo. 223) and our Rule 83a (Rule 224, R.C.P.Colo.) immediately following that oath.

Mr. and Mrs. Smith claimed a shack located in the little town of Nederland. This claim rested upon a bill of sale by the alleged agent of the alleged owner. Hensley claimed the same shack by virtue of a tax deed to the land on which it stood. In the course of the dispute Hensley got possession and moved the shack. Plaintiff and her husband induced the deputy district attorney to prosecute Hensley for larceny. Hensley was acquitted and thereupon brought this action against Mr. and Mrs. Smith for malicious prosecution. They counterclaimed for the value of the property. The cause was tried to a jury which found that the Smiths owned the property and that its value was $25, but that the Smiths were guilty of malicious prosecution and that Hensley's actual damages amounted to $40, and awarded him exemplary damages of $40, or a balance of $55. Such, briefly, is the story of the judgment before us, to reverse which we have here, on behalf of Mrs. Smith, a transcript of 190 pages, typewritten abstract (wholly superfluous) of 60 pages, 10 assignments of error, petition for supersedeas and final judgment thereon, 30 pages of briefs, and five pages of this petition for rehearing.

Since no question presented by the assignments found the slightest support in the record we mention here only the one reargued (in plain defiance of our Rule 48) in the petition before us—i. e.—that Mrs. Smith made a full, fair, and accurate disclosure of all material facts to her husband and to the deputy district attorney and thereby became impregnable to this attack.

Admittedly the interest and conduct of Mr. and Mrs. Smith were identical. The claims and acts of one were those of the other and both were made defendants. If two lawyers were sued for damages for malicious prosecution they could scarcely defend on the ground that each had made a full and fair disclosure to the other and acted on his advice. For the same reason Mrs. Smith can not defend on the advice of her husband. No legal knowledge is essential to a comprehension of that conclusion, hence we dismiss all reference to what Mrs. Smith may have told Mr. Smith or what advice he may have given her.

It is next asserted that a full and fair disclosure was made to the deputy district attorney who instituted the prosecution with complete knowledge of all material facts, hence Mrs. Smith was not liable. In support of that proposition the following, inter alia, are cited. Climax Dairy Co. v. Mulder, 78 Colo. 407, 242 P. 666; Van Meter v. Bass, 40 Colo. 78, 90 P. 637, 18 L.R.A.,N.S., 49; 18 R.C.L. sec. 21, p. 36.

Before examining these we should here interpolate that counsel's argument in his 26-page opening brief is divided into eight propositions and that now under consideration is not one of them. Also that the record discloses that the Smiths were putting much pressure on the deputy district attorney to bring this prosecution, and that their most potent argument, and the one apparently finally effective, was that the Smiths were residents and taxpayers whereas Hensley was an outsider.

In the Climax Dairy case, supra, the statute in question made certain acts misdemeanors, irrespective of intent, and the question was did "other beverages," as used therein, include milk? The district attorney thought it did and so advised Snow who made affidavit for a search warrant and filed the complaint following. We held the contrary and that Mulder had been prosecuted under an inapplicable statute for acts not amounting to a misdemeanor, basing our decision upon the Van Meter case. The latter depended upon the applicability of a statute concerning the practice of medicine to one limiting his practice to osteopathy. It will be readily seen that this, like the preceding, involved the interpretation of a questionable statute and presented a problem for a lawyer, not a layman, and one who in good faith and with a full disclosure took such advice and acted upon it should not be held liable for his error.

R.C.L., supra, states the majority rule that "probable cause" has reference to the state of mind of the instigator of the prosecution, i. e., honest belief in guilt supported by facts sufficiently strong to warrant that belief in a cautious man. Apparently counsel too soon grew weary in his reading. Had he followed it to section 30, page 48, id., he would have learned, what reason without authority should teach, that advice of counsel, to be a defense, must be acted upon in good faith. For example, a shrewd lawyer who induced an ignorant, careless, or dishonest prosecutor to persecute his enemy, well knowing no crime had been committed, could not, in a suit for malicious prosecution, hide behind "advice of counsel" and "official conduct." For the same reason a layman, irrespective of full disclosure, would not be protected if he charged B with the murder of C by striking him with a knife in the city of Denver on the tenth day of January, 1938, at the same time well knowing that throughout that entire month B was in the city of Chicago. Advice of counsel is no defense for one who, by statements known to him to be false, instigates a criminal prosecution, and there is no law to the contrary. 38 C.J. section 82, p. 435; Burke v. Watts, 188 Cal. 118, 204 P. 578.

Applying the foregoing to the facts before us what do we find? Mrs. Smith, well knowing that Hensley never intended to steal anything, but was making a *bona fide* claim to the shack in question, and grounding that claim upon a tax deed to the lot on which it stood, and simply attempting to exercise acts of ownership over property he believed to be his, instigated a criminal prosecution explicitly charging that Hensley "did willfully, unlawfully and feloniously take, steal, and carry away a certain frame building, the property of one Violet A. Smith of the value of $50.00." On the question of which owned the property she may well have taken legal advice, and that advice followed in good faith after a full disclosure, would have been a complete defense. But on the question of Hensley's intent, and the charge that he willfully stole, no legal advice was necessary and such advice is no defense because she knew better than the deputy district attorney that Hensley claimed to be the owner, and she knew upon what he based that claim. The judge knew and carefully and correctly instructed the jury that if she "acted in good faith upon the advice of such attorney in instituting and carrying on the prosecution against the plaintiff for the protection of the public" this would be "a full and complete defense." Of course the jury found that she had not "acted in good faith" and to emphasize that finding returned a small verdict for exemplary damages. Such findings and verdict are not only supported by the record, but the jury could not well have found the contrary since all the evidence was that Hensley believed himself to be the owner and had no intention to steal.

We pass over the apparent incongruity that a counterclaim for the value of this shack was allowed and set off in a suit for malicious prosecution, and the further fact that since Hensley had a tax deed for the lot and the shack was attached to it he probably owned the shack. Since both these questions were decided in favor of Mrs. Smith we give them no further consideration.

We regret the necessity for the use herein of some of the foregoing language, but counsel asked for it. Whatever note of harshness it may contain is in fact excessive tenderness when read in the light of this record and the state of the law.

Rehearing denied.[19]

19. What evidence of "malice" is presented in the above case? Compare the malice here required with (a) that said to be a requisite in defamation; (b) that which will defeat a qualified privilege to utter a defamatory statement.

Light may perhaps be shed on malice and want of probable cause and their interrelationship by comparing Gardner v. Bank of Pinehurst, 35 F.Supp. 727 (D.C.N.C.1940) with Cooper v. Shirrmeister, 176 Misc. 474, 26 N.Y. S.2d 668 (1941). In each of these cases the prosecution arose out of attempts to collect a debt. See note 10 A.L.R. 2d 1200.

The issue of probable cause has much in common with the issue of reasonable care in a negligence case. Both may involve (1) a determination of the facts, in the sense of what actually happened, from conflicting evidence; (2) an evaluation of a party's conduct as to its reasonableness under the circumstances. In both types of cases the first question is left to the jury where the evidence permits a dispute; but the second question receives divergent treatments. In the negligence field the evaluation of conduct is also generally left to the jury (within the bounds always imposed on them). But cf. Holmes, J., in Lorenzo v. Wirth, p. 205, supra, Martin v. Herzog, p. 212, supra. In malicious prosecution it is for the court to say whether given facts amount to probable cause. This potentially gives the judge greater control of the latter issue than he has of negligence. Whether this control is made effective may depend on his choice of procedural techniques. See Thayer, Preliminary Treatise on Evidence, 222–228 (1898); Green, Judge and Jury, 341–347 (1930); Arnold & James, Cases on Trials, Judgments and Appeals, 664, 689, 702–712 (1936); James, Functions of Judge & Jury in Negligence Cases, 58 Yale L. J. 667 (1949).

POSTSCRIPT

There are other torts as well. Some have no names; see e. g., Seidel v. Greenberg, 108 N.J.Super. 248, 260 A.2d 863 (1969) (liability of arsonist to innocent employee who fell under suspicion and, not being cleared by defendant, suffered anguish and defense expenses). Some have familiar names; see, e. g., Breiner v. Olson, — Neb. —, 237 N.W.2d 118 (1975) (alienation of affections and criminal conversation). Most can be readily dealt with on the basis of some research in standard treatises, although a few, e. g., trover and conversion [20], are highly technical. In certain fields, furthermore, e. g., privacy [21] and civil rights[22], statutory remedies are becoming important. In all these cases, however, which are not explictly discussed in this coursebook, the basic principles which have been developed are relevant in large part, and should assist in the study and practice of such tort law as has been necessarily omitted from consideration here because of limitations of space.

20. See, e. g., Restatement of Torts Second §§ 222A–244 and Comments thereto; also, in addition to standard American texts, Clerk & Lindsell on Torts paras. 1071–1185 (14th ed. by A. Armitage, R. Dias and others 1975) (including discussion of detinue and replevin).

21. E. g., Freedom of Information Act, 5 U.S.C. § 552, and Privacy Act of 1974, 5 U.S.C. § 552a.

22. E. g., Civil Rights Acts of 1866 and 1964, 42 U.S.C. §§ 1981 et seq. and 2000a. As to civil rights suits against executive branch governmental officials on basis of qualified immunity instead of the absolute immunity suggested in Barr v. Matteo, page 872 supra, see Economou v. Dep't of Agriculture, — F.2d —, 44 U.S.L.W. 2516 (2d Cir. 1976).

*

INDEX

References are to Pages

END OF VOLUME

Luxemburger Juristische Studien –
Luxembourg Legal Studies

edited by

Faculty of Law, Economics and Finance
University of Luxembourg

Volume 8

Dr. Sandra V. I. Schmitz

The Struggle in Online Copyright Enforcement

Problems and Prospects

The research of Sandra Schmitz has been supported by the Fonds National de la Recherche, Luxembourg.

The Deutsche Nationalbibliothek lists this publication in the Deutsche Nationalbibliografie; detailed bibliographic data are available on the Internet at http://dnb.d-nb.de

a.t.: Luxemburg, Univ., Diss., 2014

ISBN: HB (Nomos) 978-3-8487-2428-4
ePDF (Nomos) 978-3-8452-6587-2

British Library Cataloguing-in-Publication Data
A catalogue record for this book is available from the British Library.

ISBN: HB (Hart) 978-1-5099-0566-9

Library of Congress Cataloging-in-Publication Data
Schmitz, Sandra V. I.
The Struggle in Online Copyright Enforcement
Problems and Prospects
Sandra V. I. Schmitz
800 p.
Includes bibliographic references.

ISBN 978-1-5099-0566-9 (hardcover Hart)

1. Edition 2015

Table of Contents

Introduction

Copyright enforcement on the Internet constitutes a controversial subject. One side in the debate, mostly the rights-holders, argue that copyright infringement takes place on a new scale and that there is not enough protection with the insufficient ability to enforce existing laws in "cyberspace".[1] The opposing side in the debate takes the position that traditional copyright concepts are outdated in a digital world, and current enforcement goes beyond what was initially intended by copyright law.[2] Some argue that cyberspace has created its own norms that do not correspond to the law of nation states.[3] Against this background, States are finding it increasingly difficult to apply to cyberspace domestic laws that are traditionally delimited by the borders of a State's territory, so that they protect copyright efficiently. Thus, new legislation, specifically adapted to the Internet, has been on the agenda of many, including the European Union and its Member States.[4] This research will analyse the problems of copyright enforcement on the Internet with a special focus on newly enacted legislation in some Member States and the struggle of applying existing

---

1 See for instance Spiegel online, *Sven Regener zum Urheberrecht: "Man pinkelt uns ins Gesicht!"*, Der Spiegel Online (22.03.2012); Spiegel Online, *Urheberrechtskampagne: 1500 Künstler gegen Gier und Geiz*, Der Spiegel Online (10.05.2012). In the UK, Simon Cowell, Roger Daltrey, Professor Green, Elton John, Andrew Lloyd-Webber, Brian May, Robert Plant, Roger Taylor, Tinie Tempah and Pete Townshend have signed an open letter to British Prime Minister David Cameron urging the British government to implement the antipiracy-focused Digital Economy Act 2010, see *Musicians need strong copyright laws to excel globally*, The Telegraph (24.07.2012).

2 Cf. for instance the call by Pirate Party MEP Christian Engström with support from the Greens/EFA-group in the European Parliament to reform copyright legislation, Christian Engström/Rick Falkvinge, *The case for copyright reform* (2012). See also Hector MacQueen/Charlotte Waelde/Graeme Laurie/Abbe Brown, *Contemporary Intellectual Property, Law and Policy* (2nd ed. 2011), pp. 244–246.

3 See Chris Reed, *Making laws for cyberspace* (2012), pp. 5 et seq. with further references.

4 For instance on a multilateral level: The draft for an *Anti-Counterfeiting Trade Agreement (ACTA)*; on a European Union level: revision of the *Intellectual Property Rights Enforcement Directive*; on national level: *Loi HADOPI* in France, *Digital Economy Act* in the UK.

laws in an online environment. In addition, the prospects of current approaches will be discussed, in particular since some of them fail to strike a fair balance between fundamental rights.

A. Defining Copyright

It has been difficult for consumers to regard copyright as property, due to its inherent immaterial nature. However, as long as the printing press has existed, there has been copyright, which grants the author of original work exclusive rights to the use of the work and its distribution,[5] and sanctions for infringing it.

Copyright does not only protect the author but also the exploiters of the work. Due to the many actors being involved in the creation and exploitation of works in music and audio-visual media, these actors are often referred to as the content industry or creative industry. The protection of the author is a prerequisite for the protection of the exploiters. The concept of copyright is based on the idea that creators of intellectual wealth receive compensation for their work and are able to financially support themselves, which would give them a motive to continue publishing. Without copyright, authors of creative works would have to find other ways for financial support.

The idea of copyright protection can also be based on utilitarian thoughts for copyright protection, which emphasises the promotion of cultural and economic progress as reason and justification for copyright.[6] The author of a work should be honoured and an incentive to create should be given. At the same time, the creative industry, meaning those who exploit

5 Generally, it is "the right to copy", but also gives the copyright owner the right to be credited for the work, to determine who may adapt the work to other forms, who may perform the work, who may financially benefit from it, and other related rights. See generally on this Wilhelm Nordemann/Anke Nordemann-Schiffel in: Ulrich Löwenheim (ed.), *Handbuch des Urheberrechts* (2nd ed. 2010), § 4 Urheberrechtliche Grundbegriffe in vergleichender Sicht, paras. 10–16; Hector MacQueen/ Charlotte Waelde/Graeme Laurie/Abbe Brown, *Contemporary Intellectual Property, Law and Policy* (2nd ed. 2011), pp. 104–118, and 124–128.

6 See Ulrich Löwenheim in: Ulrich Löwenheim (ed.), *Handbuch des Urheberrechts* (2nd ed. 2010), § 1 Gegenstand Zweck und Bedeutung des Urheberrechts, para. 4.

copyright, should be encouraged to invest in the production of cultural goods.[7]

Copyright is also said to be beneficial to society: by protecting authors and exploiters of creative works, copyright is promoting the creation and dissemination of cultural goods and thereby serving cultural life and cultural diversity within a society.[8]

Accordingly, copyright is important: from a cultural point of view, it is essential for the personality of creative persons, and for the process of creation and exploitation of the work; from an economic point of view, important industries depend on copyright protection. These industries include enterprises that contribute to employment and innovation on a large scale, such as publishers, film and television, print media, and software industries.

B. Defining Copyright Enforcement

Copyright primarily refers to "the right to copy", but it also includes the right to be credited for the work, to determine who may adapt the work to other forms, who may perform the work, who may financially benefit from it, and other related rights.

Copyright was initially conceived as a way for governments to restrict printing. By giving authors the control of copyright and the legal framework to profit economically from it, the contemporary intent of copyright is to promote the creation of works.

Copyrights are territorial, which means that they do not extend beyond the territory of a specific state unless that state is a party to an international agreement. Today, however, this is less relevant since most countries are parties to at least one such agreement including most prominently the *Berne Convention*[9] and the UN's *World Intellectual Property Organisation (WIPO) Copyright Treaty*[10].

7 *Ibid.*

8 *Ibid.*

9 *Berne Convention for Protection of Literary and Artistic Works,* adopted in Berne on 09.09.1886. The Berne Convention was the first multi-lateral copyright treaty, and established rights but no enforcement mechanisms.

10 *WIPO Copyright Treaty*, adopted in Geneva on 20.12.1996.

While many aspects of national copyright laws have been standardised through these international copyright agreements, this is not the case with enforcement – although the *Agreement on Trade Related Aspects of Intellectual Property Rights (TRIPS)*[11] provides minimum standards of intellectual property rights enforcement. Generally, copyright is enforced as a civil matter, though some jurisdictions also apply criminal sanctions, in particular when copyright infringements are committed on a commercial scale. In contrast to TRIPS, the Council of Europe *Cybercrime Convention*[12] addresses enforcement on the Internet in specific. Article 10 of said Convention requires its signatory states to "adopt such legislative and other measures as may be necessary to establish as criminal offences under its domestic law the infringement of copyright,…where such acts are committed wilfully, on a commercial scale and by means of a computer system". In the European Union, copyright enforcement on the Internet is part of the European Commission's policy "Digital Agenda for Europe"[13] and partly covered by legislative acts, for instance the *Information Society Directive*[14] and the *Intellectual Property Rights Enforcement Directive*[15]. The aim of the European Commission is to ensure that copyright and licensing stay fit for purpose in a digital context.

C. The Problem: When Copyright and Technology Clash

Before copyright existed, authors generally requested a one-off payment from the printer of their book before publication. With copyright in place,

---

11 *Agreement on Trade-Related Aspects of Intellectual Property Rights,* Annex 1C to *the Agreement establishing the World Trade Organisation* (*TRIPS*, Marrakesh 1994). *TRIPS* was negotiated at the end of the Uruguay Round of the *General Agreement on Tariffs and Trade* (*GATT*).

12 *Convention on Cybercrime*, CETS No. 185.

13 See European Commission, *Digital agenda for Europe, A Europe 2020 initiative*, Pillar I: Digital Single Market, Action 6: Protecting intellectual property rights online, http://ec.europa.eu/digital-agenda/en/pillar-i-digital-single-market/action-6-protecting-intellectual-property-rights-online.

14 *Directive 2001/29/EC of the European Parliament and of the Council of 22.05.2001 on the harmonisation of certain aspects of copyright and related rights in the information society (InfoSoc Directive), OJ L 167 (22.6.2001*), 10-19

15 *Directive 2004/48/EC of the European Parliament and of the Council of 29 April 2004 on the enforcement of Intellectual Property Rights*, OJ L 157 (30.04.2004), 16-25. The directive is also known as "(IPR) Enforcement Directive" or "IPRED".

and assuming efficient enforcement, authors of creative works can publish their creations immediately, and license subsequent use or re-publication of their works by third parties. A means for instant publication is for instance the Internet, which for many people has created the opportunity to become publishers themselves. It has never been as easy to publish while at the same time reaching – at least potentially – a worldwide audience as it is nowadays. Similarly, it has never been easier to copy, or disseminate copyrighted content without the authorisation of the rights-holder. In addition, it has never been easier to access information and share it with others. The assumption that "Internet changes everything" is thus even truer in the area of copyright.

I. Ordinary Users Easily Become Infringers

In the early days of the Internet, the Internet used to be all about communication. Like the telephone network or mail, people used email and other services to communicate with each other. This has changed within the last decade.

While it is now common to communicate via Internet using additionally video and voice over IP, the growth of the Web meant, that the Internet is becoming more about content than about communication.[16] The Web is used to find and access information including intellectual property creations. In an information society, access to information is becoming more important than ever. The Internet has in principle become the repository of thoughts, the memory of mankind. It thereby also stimulates creation. However, access to information does not mean that one is allowed to use this information freely, reproduce it, or adapt it.

In the context of the above, it has been argued that until twenty years ago, copyright hardly concerned "ordinary" people.[17] This is partly true, because at least copyright enforcement did not concern them. If someone wanted to copy a poem and send it to his loved one, or record his favourite songs from the radio, or copy an audio cassette and give it to a friend, he would not need to worry about becoming the target of legal action. Although he committed a breach of copyright in most jurisdictions when

---

16 Andrew S. Tanenbaum/David J. Wetherall, *Computer Networks* (5th ed. 2011), p. 734.

17 Christian Engström/Rick Falkvinge, *The case for copyright reform* (2012), p. 4.

he copied the works with the intent to pass them on to a third party, he hardly risked punishment or claims for damages. Today however, the technological means to which anyone has access have changed not only the way media is consumed, but it has also changed the way we deal with creative works. The hand-written letter is more often replaced by email; friendships sometimes only exist in digital format (the Facebook "friends" with whom one is not personally acquainted), thus communication and passing on of messages take place online in a digital format; instead of phoning a friend, people chat or post messages on social media platforms. If someone wants to copy a poem, he can do so by just pressing the copy and paste keys on the keyboard; if someone wants to share music with friends, he may do so by publishing a link leading to a digital copy stored in the "cloud"; copying the content of a CD is only a few clicks, sharing it as well. Technological progress means that what ordinary people can do with creative works has changed. However, just because one can do it, does not mean that one is allowed to do it. While the way we enjoy and deal with creative content, copying and sharing it, has changed, the law has not. As a consequence, copyright is infringed all the time.

One may argue that the extent to which enforcement is practically possible has an effect on the individual's perception of the applicability of a law.[18] This means that a law which is never enforced or is clearly unenforceable may send the message that it is not really intended to be complied with.[19] Accordingly, copying in the analogue world that has not been subject to civil or criminal enforcement may have sent the message that it is alright "because no one cares". In that regard, many Internet users may underestimate the range of availability of online content. A link which was published in a forum and directs to content stored on a file-hosting service is regularly not just made available to the participants in that online discussion group, but to every Internet user. The poem published on a Facebook page may not be visible only to the person to whom the personal profile belongs, or his friends, but to every Internet user. A file uploaded to a peer-to-peer network is not just made available to another peer, but usually to everyone else that joins the "swarm" of sharers of a particular file. The disseminating factor plays an important role why rights-holders

18 Chris Reed, *Making laws for cyberspace* (2012), p. 15.

19 *Ibid.* At least does the likelihood of detection and enforcement have a substantial effect on the behaviour of those that are subject to the law. See *ibid*, p. 55 with further references.

disapprove of content sharing. At the same time, rights-holders face problems in enforcing their rights, such as difficulties of identifying infringers who hide behind pseudonyms, which are completely anonymous or of whom they can only get hold via the IP address tied to the infringement. While in the physical world, infringements are usually detected by geographical presence, on the internet, the infringement may be visible for the rights-holder, but the infringer may be located in a jurisdiction where it is difficult to get hold of him, if not impossible, in order to enforce his rights.

That omnipresence of content makes it also difficult for users to comply with copyright. Even if a user had some level of understanding of national copyright law, he is likely to be ignorant of the multiplicity of foreign laws that may equally apply to his online activities.[20]

Thus, it is not surprising that even scholars suggest that "beneath some threshold of activity – and that would have to be determined carefully – copyright infringement should not be an actionable offence...leave[ing] everyone free to devote resources to the infringers above that threshold, and it would remove ordinary people, going about ordinary use of innovative products and services, from the long arm of copyright law".[21]

II. Changed Concept of Ownership

Besides the emergence of new forms of adaption of content such as mashups, voice-overs, remixes that also infringe copyright, one may also wonder whether the concept of how one owns music has changed.

Digital music sales are growing[22] as is the use of streaming portals such as Spotify[23]. With more content "owned" and being consumed in a digital format, it may well be that ownership becomes a different "feeling". Questions arise such as whether it makes a difference for digital natives,

---

20 Cf. *ibid*, p. 13.

21 Jeff Lynn, *Copyright for growth*, in: Ian Hargreaves/Paul Hofheinz (eds.), *Intellectual property and innovation. A framework for 21st century growth and jobs*, p. 15.

22 See for instance Bart Cammaerts/Robin Mansell/Bingchun Meng, *Copyright & Creation, A case for promoting inclusive online sharing* (September 2013), London School of Economics and Political Science, Media Policy Brief 9, p. 7.

23 According to the ranking by web traffic ranking service Alexa, as of June 2014, Spotify is within the 1000 most popular websites globally, see http://www.alexa.com/siteinfo/spotify.com (last accessed on 06.06.2014).

whether they download a music track from the online music store iTunes or whether they listen to music on the music streaming service Spotify. Do they lose the relationship of owning an album because they cannot touch and feel it, because it is not tangible? Do they value immaterial "stuff" differently than other generations used to value tangible products? Will they feel the same if they lose their "record collection" because the service where it was stored went bankrupt, because their hardware broke, because licenses are withdrawn? Especially the latter may lead to confusion, because essentially what users acquire when they purchase an mp3 album is merely a licence to use the digital files. With digital content, one does not have the same rights as for instance with vinyl, CDs or print books. This is an issue that many people are not yet aware of. They may only become aware, if something goes wrong like for instance when Amazon deleted a Disney Christmas movie from their servers of which they had previously "sold" digital copies to consumers.[24] Amazon had to delete the movie, because Disney had withdrawn the licence from Amazon in order to exclusively stream the movie via its own streaming channel. Consumers are also rarely aware that while vinyl or CD collections can be passed on to third parties and can be inherited, this is not the case with music that is purchased online only in a digital format (as long as it is not moved to an external hard disk). Against this background, one may argue that the idea of ownership seems in a process of gradually disappearing.[25] This assumption triggers a new question, namely what is the benefit of purchasing digital content? If one only acquires a licence, and has thus limited options regarding the use of the data, for instance not being able to sell a used copy or inheriting it, what is the benefit of purchasing digital music or E-books online – especially if it is sold at (almost) the same price as a hard copy?

Again, this system makes it difficult for users to relate to the idea of copyright and may lead to frustration. One may also argue that it may be difficult for users to develop guilt for producing illegal copies, if they cannot relate to the idea of copyright and see no benefit in legal copies.

24 Felix Knoke, *Streaming: Disney löscht Weihnachtsfilm für Amazon-Kunden,* Der Spiegel Online (16.12.2013).

25 Cf. Dan Gillmor, *The Bruce Willis dilemma? In the digital era, we own nothing,* The Guardian (03.09.2012).

III. Do Consumers Understand the System and Vice Versa?

The aspects mentioned above are only a few examples of what makes the copyright system difficult for consumers to understand. History has shown that the system, and also to some extent the rights-holders, do not understand the consumer. One may argue that copyright infringement, in particular file-sharing, is the result of ignorance and missed opportunities by rights-holders: File-sharing probably became the norm because the music industry refused to make its music available in a downloadable form.[26] Instead they sued the innovators of file-sharing technology and introduced copyright protection measures that also prohibited consumers from making private copies, which is legitimate in most civil law copyright systems. They ignored that consumers want easy access to music that can be played on all of their devices. Technical protection measures that hinder copying, or allow data only to be played on certain devices, interfered with this desire.

Similarly, consumers want easy, convenient and reliable access to music and films. Most piracy websites are far from reliable. Most of them are also not convenient to use because advertisements windows pop up, and they may even be infected with viruses. These piracy websites nevertheless attract many users, with probably a substantial number of users paying for premium accounts insofar as file-hosting services are concerned. The reasons for their popularity may be manifold, with the primary reason being presumably the variety of content available, including content that is otherwise not or hardly available.[27] While window releases (i.e. content being published region after region and for type of service

---

26 As regards the latter see Chris Reed, *Making laws for cyberspace* (2012), p. 12.

27 This may include the desire of many users for example in Germany to watch US or UK movies and TV serial dramas in their original language as they do not want to wait for the release date in German or just prefer the original. Streaming services in Germany will however only have acquire a license for the German language version. Copyright infringement may thus be driven by the lack of legal alternative sources and the current system of windowing releases (See Lilian Edwards, *Next steps in the UK*, in: Ian Hargreaves/Paul Hofheinz (eds.), *Intellectual property and innovation. A framework for 21st century growth and jobs*, pp. 39 et seq. with reference to Christopher Williams, *E-books drive older women to piracy*, The Telegraph (17.05.2011). Further many TV programmes are not available elsewhere after they have been broadcast. While some German TV stations still offer their so-called "Mitschnittservice" (see e.g. http://www.ndr-mitschnittservice.de/ [last accessed on 06.06.2014]) where copies of TV programmes are sold

after type of service) were not such a problem in pre-Internet days, today users are more aware of the content's availability.[28] In a networked world it may be difficult to understand why content is circulating in the US and discussed in online fora or online newspapers for example, while users in another state must wait to access the materials after a later official regional release date. Worldwide attention and awareness trigger worldwide demand. It is questionable whether users develop guilt when they have no legal or comparably easy to use legal alternatives to consume the desired content.

Users may also not develop guilt if enforcement is perceived as "rip-off"[29] and if they consider infringement claims as "bogus".[30] In this regard, businesses with great economic dependence upon copyright, such as those in the music business, have been advocating the extension and expansion of their intellectual property rights, and seek additional legal and technological enforcement.

D. The Research Topic: Copyright Enforcement on the Internet

As aforementioned, new technologies have altered the dimensions and the scale of copyright issues. The development of digital media and computer network technologies has prompted reinterpretation of for instance private copying and fair use exceptions[31], introduced new difficulties in enforcing copyright, and inspired additional challenges to copyright law's philosophic basis.

When the recording of a lecture by Harvard Law School professor and co-founder of the non-profit Creative Commons Lawrence Lessig was blocked on the online video portal YouTube based on copyright infringe-

---

on DVD-R or Blu-Ray, the acquisition of such a copy may involve too much hassle and take too long for some consumers.

28 Markus Brauck/Isabell Hülsen/Alexander Kühn/Ann-Kathrin Nezik, *Was glotzen Sie so?*, Der Spiegel online (13.01.2014).

29 Spiegel Online, *Gesetz gegen Abzocke: Bundestag setzt Massenabmahnungen Grenzen*, Der Spiegel online (27.06.2013).

30 See for instance Electronic Frontier Foundation, *Lawrence Lessig strikes back against bogus copyright takedown,* EFF press release of 22.08.2013.

31 Most jurisdictions recognize copyright limitations, allowing "fair" exceptions to the creator's exclusivity of copyright, and giving users certain rights.

ment allegations,[32] one may ask whether this was intended by the idea to give copyright to the creators.[33] Did the rights-holders lose any revenues due to Lessig's lecture being disseminated via YouTube? Did the band members lose their incentive to create further songs and/or perform them? Although this may be considered an extreme case, the list of similar cases is long.[34] Questions may be raised of whether the protection of intellectual property rights goes beyond what was initially intended, namely to guarantee that creators can live on revenues generated by their creations and have an incentive to create. While the issue of whether the scope of infringements raises questions of legitimacy of the law is a more philosophical question, this research will focus on copyright as it stands today. It is accepted that copyright has always been a controversial issue with regard to its subject-matter, scope and methods of enforcement.[35] Based on the fact that ignorance of the law is no defence, this research examines current and proposed enforcement schemes in terms of their respect to technology and fundamental rights.

---

32 Lessig had included in his presentation several short clips of amateur dance videos set to a song by a French band in order to highlight emerging styles of cultural communication on the Internet.

33 While US copyright law allows for the fair use of works for purposes such as criticism, comment, and teaching, the license-holder of the song filed a takedown notice with YouTube. Following threats that they will sue Lessig, Lessig withdrew his counter-notice and sought clarification before a US court. See Electronic Frontier Foundation, *Lawrence Lessig strikes back against bogus copyright takedown*, EFF press release of 22.08.2013. In February 2014, Lawrence Lessig and the rights-holders agreed on a settlement, see Electronic Frontier Foundation, *Lawrence Lessig settles fair use lawsuit over Phoenix music snippets*, EFF press release of 27.02.2014.

34 The first prominent case was presumably the case of Stephanie Lenz, who recorded her toddler dancing to a song by the artist Prince. Because she wanted to show the cuteness of her little boy to friends and family, she uploaded the video clip on YouTube. Although the audio was of poor quality, and the song was audible for only approximately twenty seconds, Universal Music group asked YouTube to take the video clip down. Lenz is currently asking for a declaratory judgment that her home video does not infringe any copyright nor trigger damages, and is seeking injunctive relief restraining Universal from bringing further claims in connection with the video. For a case history and the briefs that have been filed see Electronic Frontier Foundation, *Lenz v Universal*, https://www.eff.org/cases/lenz-v-universal (last accessed on 06.06.2014).

35 Cf. Irini A. Stamatoudi, *Preface*, in: Irini A. Stamatoudi (ed.), *Copyright enforcement and the Internet* (2010), p. xv.

If one looks at common enforcement schemes, it becomes clear that legislators follow the approach that "rights without sanctions are no rights"[36]. Thus, one will encounter enforcement via criminal law, meaning that the government becomes the arbitrator for private rights. Copyright is nevertheless primarily enforced via private law. If rights-holders want to pursue civil claims, they need an identifiable and locatable addressee of their infringement claim who is ideally located within the same jurisdiction or at least situated in a jurisdiction in which the rights-holder is able to enforce a judgment. If the infringer does not fulfil these conditions, rights-holders may search for other actors that fulfil these criteria. Thus, lately one can witness an increase in lawsuits being filed against online intermediaries: when action against host providers did not promise any results, access providers became targets. On which basis such action could be pursued and what can be required from online intermediaries that not necessarily themselves participated in the act of infringing copyright will be discussed throughout this work.

E. Macrolevel Approaches to Fight Online Copyright Infringements

As this contribution focusses on copyright enforcement, it is necessary to also address the level of enforcement. With copyright being territorial, enforcement naturally has been territorial as well. The Internet however neither knows nor respects national borders. Applying laws in an online environment means that an appropriate link to the territory of the legislator must be established. Private international law has developed techniques and rules for such localisation. These, however, are of limited use, if not all States share the same approach. Operators of websites dedicated to copyright infringement know well enough how to hide their identities and settle down their business in "safe havens". Thus, States have been seeking agreements whereby enforcement of copyright would be strengthened and cooperation encouraged. Already in 2005, the EU published a Strategy for the enforcement of intellectual property rights in third countries[37] as

36 Michael Keplinger, *Enforcement of IP rights in the digital environment: The role of the World Intellectual Property Organisation,* Gewerblicher Rechtsschutz und Urheberrecht – Internationaler Teil 2007, 648.

37 European Commission, *Strategy for the enforcement of intellectual property rights in third countries,* OJ C 129 (26.05.2005), 3–16.

a logical consequence of EU internal enforcement instruments. Although the Strategy focusses on counterfeit tangible goods, the strategy's main statement also applies to digital piracy: Instead of unilateral solutions, approaches are needed which recognise that any proposed solution can only be effective if it is received positively by the recipient country.[38]

I. Unilateral or Multilateral Enforcement: Strengthening Enforcement within and outside of National Borders

Enforcement on EU level, the focus of this research, must be divided into trade-related external enforcement measures and internal enforcement measures that are part of safeguarding the functioning of the Internal Market.[39] For instance, the *EU Intellectual Property Rights Enforcement Directive*[40]only concerns the internal market. In order to ensure external enforcement, copyright enforcement must be tackled in the framework of multilateral and bilateral negotiations with third countries. While the WIPO Copyright Treaty and its predecessors provided for some protections for copyright deemed necessary due to advances in information technology, it did not contain any enforcement mechanisms. TRIPS closed this gap on a multinational level by specifying enforcement procedures, remedies, and dispute resolution procedures.

However, these instruments only provided a general umbrella for copyright protection and enforcement. In particular Europe and the US have identified the use of foreign-based and foreign-controlled websites and web services as a growing problem for domestic intellectual property rights. In the very recent past, an attempt to agree on a multilateral anti-piracy mechanism, the *Anti-Counterfeiting Trade Agreement (ACTA)*,[41]

---

38 *Ibid,* p. 4.

39 See Jörg Reinbothe, *The EU Enforcement Directive 2004/48/EC as a tool for copyright enforcement,* in: Stamatoudi, Irini (ed.), *Copyright enforcement and the Internet* (2010), p. 5. The legal framework for enforcement measures inside the EU is the *acquis communautaire,* which includes horizontal measures like the *Intellectual Property Rights Enforcement Directive,* and provisions on sanctions and remedies in the various harmonising instruments.

40 The Directive was based on Article 95 *EC Treaty* (now Article 114 *TFEU*).

41 For the full text of the *ACTA* draft cf. http://register.consilium.europa.eu/pdf/en/11/st12/st12196.en11.pdf (last accessed on 06.06.2014).

has prominently failed.[42] Similarly unilateral attempts as for instance the US *Stop Online Piracy Act (SOPA)*[43] and *Protect-IP Act (PIPA)*[44] did not become law. One reason for their failure was the strong public opposition which caused policymakers and legislators to reconsider their approach. With the public perception that these instruments are over-regulating and giving preferential treatment to rights-holders whereas end-users' rights are not respected, the EU legislators find it difficult to revise the current enforcement regime. It is obvious that legislators find it difficult to pass legislation within a tough climate for "anti-piracy" legislation.

II. Multilateral: Proposal for New Trade Agreement ACTA

ACTA was supposed to be a multilateral treaty for the purpose of establishing international standards for intellectual property rights enforcement targeting inter alia copyright infringement on the Internet.[45] This approach to combat the proliferation of counterfeiting and online piracy within the global economy was met by extensive protests all over the world and membership to *ACTA* was subsequently rejected by the European Parliament on 4 July 2012,[46] meaning that neither the EU nor its individual Member States can join the Agreement. The rejection obviously was a result of strong opposition to the Agreement with a single petition from

---

42 Cf. Duncan Matthews/Petra Zikovska, *The rise and fall of the Anti-counterfeiting Trade Agreement (ACTA): lessons for the European Union*, International Review of Intellectual Property and Competition Law 2013, Vol. 44 Issue 6, 626–655.

43 *H.R. 3261*, 112th Congress (2011), available online at http://www.gpo.gov/fdsys/pkg/BILLS-112hr3261ih/pdf/BILLS-112hr3261ih.pdf (last accessed on 06.06.2014). *SOPA* was initially entitled *Enforcing and Protecting American Rights Against Sites Intent on Theft and Exploitation Act (E-PARASITE Act).*

44 *S. 968*, 112th Congress (2011), available online at http://www.gpo.gov/fdsys/pkg/BILLS-112s968rs/pdf/BILLS-112s968rs.pdf (last accessed on 06.06.2014). The *Protect-IP Act*, also known as *PIPA*, is the abbreviation for *Preventing Real Online Threats to Economic Creativity and Theft of Intellectual Property Act of 2011.*

45 For an analysis of the regulation foreseen by *ACTA* see Luc Pierre Devigne/Pedro Velasco-Martins/Alexandra Iliopoulou, *Where is ACTA taking us? Policies and politics*, in: Irini Stamatoudi (ed.), *Copyright enforcement and the Internet* (2010), pp. 29–42.

46 By 478 votes to 39, with 165 abstentions. See European Parliament, *ACTA before the European Parliament,* press release Ref. no. 20120217BKG38488 of 04.06.2012.

citizens calling on MEPs to reject *ACTA* having been signed by over 2.8 million people from all over the world.[47] David Martin himself, the MEP responsible for steering the *ACTA* dossier through Parliament, gave the recommendation to reject *ACTA* following identification of some unintended consequences such as individual criminalisation, the definition of "commercial scale" infringements, and the role of Internet service providers.[48]

It is striking that the most controversial enforcement measures, proposed in the initial stages of the negotiations of *ACTA,* had been narrowed down or abandoned in its final version, which did not require the parties to introduce "Three Strikes Laws" as discussed during negotiations. This, however, neither silenced the protests, nor did it prevent the negative vote in the European Parliament. One of the major points of criticism was and still is that *ACTA* contains a number of broad and vague provisions.[49] Article 27(1) of *ACTA*, for example, provides that the parties to *ACTA* shall ensure the availability of civil and criminal enforcement proceedings under their domestic law, including expeditious remedies to prevent infringements and remedies that constitute a deterrent to further infringements. As concerns enforcement proceedings, *ACTA* encourages "cooperative efforts with the business community". There is no explanation what is actually meant by this and thus it leaves plenty of room for speculation.

Accordingly, this obligation has been interpreted as legitimising and promoting the policing and even sanctioning of alleged infringers outside the regular judicial frameworks.[50]A lack of judicial oversight is, however, one of the core concerns when private actors are involved in the enforcement of intellectual property rights.[51]

---

47 *Ibid.*

48 *Ibid.*

49 Cf. Roberto D'Erme/Christophe Geiger/Henning Große Ruse-Khan/Christian Heinze/Thomas Jaeger and Others, *Opinion of European academics on anti-counterfeiting trade agreement*, Journal of Intellectual Property, Information Technology and E-Commerce Law 2011, Vol. 2 Issue 1, 65–72.

50 European Digital Rights, *ACTA fact sheet*, EDRi (02.02.2012).

51 Obviously, businesses have to be profitable and hence, may not be interested – from an economic point of view – in investigating alleged infringements any further once they are notified of an infringement. In the light of the costs and efforts involved inter alia for further investigations, it is likely that even legal materials will be taken down.

Finally, the most problematic premise for *ACTA*'s success was the secrecy of its negotiations.[52] Negotiators ignored that such an important agreement, which has the potential to have a broad impact on consumers and businesses alike, cannot be negotiated behind closed doors with minimal non-industry input.[53] Controversial parts of the confidential draft version were subsequently leaked to the public,[54] and largely influenced the general public's perception of the Agreement as "jeopard[ising] free speech by prioritising private sector repressive measures aimed at copyright protection over the fundamental rights to privacy and freedom of communication...without guarantees of due process and equality of arms".[55] The lawmakers learnt from the protest against the bill that in order to gain the support of the public, drawing up laws relating to intellectual property rights enforcement in a digital context requires transparency and participation of the public rather than one-sided lobbying of the entertainment industry.[56]

It must be noted that with the EU and its Member States' rejection of *ACTA* the Agreement is not "dead" on an international level as the EU is considered to be a single negotiating party and ratification by six parties to the negotiations is sufficient for the agreement to come into force.

This does not mean that an international agreement on the enforcement of intellectual property rights has disappeared from the agenda of the EU. Currently, negotiations are ongoing with the US regarding a *Transatlantic Trade and Investment Partnership (TTIP),* which will also include a chapter on intellectual property rights. Unsurprisingly, this has caused a lot of *ACTA*-related bells to ring[57] and needs to be watched.

---

52 Only following the eighth round of negotiations, a draft version of ACTA has been released. For further information on the negotiations see Peter Yu, *Six secret (and now open) fears of ACTA,* Southern Methodist University Law Review 2011, Vol. 64 Issue 3, 975, 978 et seq. and 1011 et seq.

53 *Ibid*, 1018.

54 Paul Meller, *Leaked ACTA draft reveals plans for Internet clampdown*, Computerworld (20.02.2010).

55 European Digital Rights, *ACTA fact sheet*, EDRi (02.02.2012).

56 Cf. Duncan Matthews/Petra Zikovska, *The rise and fall of the Anti-counterfeiting Trade Agreement (ACTA): lessons for the European Union,* International Review of Intellectual Property and Competition Law 2013, Vol. 44 Issue 6, 626, 653.

57 Ana Ramalho, *The EU mandate to negotiate the TTIP: should copyright be an outcast?*, Kluwer Copyright Blog (21.05.2013).

III. United States: SOPA and PIPA – Initiatives to Strengthen Enforcement Globally

Parallel to the negotiations on *ACTA*, States also looked into combatting the global reach problem on a domestic basis. In order to have an effect outside national borders, these approaches were deemed to interfere with legitimate interests of third parties. Thus, opposition to the US initiatives has not been limited to the US and escalated on 18 January 2012 when a number of Internet sites including the English language version of Wikipedia turned black as a demonstration of their opposition to the *Stop Online Piracy Act (SOPA)*.[58] Besides *SOPA*, which is a US House of Representatives initiative, the US Senate had been discussing an almost identical bill, known as *Protect-IP Act (PIPA)*.

Like many recent initiatives, both bills were the result of lobbying of the "content industry", primarily the Hollywood movie industry and record labels, whose representatives argue to suffer economic loss from the fact that pirated content is readily available on the worldwide web.[59] They reflect the US Government's policy of strengthening enforcement of Intellectual property rights internationally – outlined in the 2010 Joint Strategic Plan on Intellectual Property.[60]

The bills aimed to "crack down" on international infringement of intellectual property rights held by US companies/authors by restricting access to sites that host or facilitate the trading of pirated content. Their main tar-

---

58 Jimmy Wales, founder of Wikipedia, defended the blackout as "a broad global message that the internet as a whole will not tolerate censorship in response to mere allegations of copyright infringement", see Emma Barnett, *Wikipedia founder Jimmy Wales defends SOPA protest blackout,* The Telegraph (17.01.2012). For a list of opponents of the bills as of December 2011, see http://www.net-coalition.com/wp-content/uploads/2011/12/Opposition_Dec16.pdf (last accessed on 17.05.2014). Fierce opposition against SOPA was seen all around the globe. While previously so called net activists fought their battle against Internet content blocking initiatives more or less on their own, this was the first time that they got massive public backup by Internet giants like Google, Wikipedia and co.

59 The bills are supported by predominately media companies and associations such as the Motion Picture Association of America and the Recording Industry Association as well as such that have an interest in banning counterfeit goods entering the US market like the NBA, NFL or MLB.

60 Executive Office of the President of the United States, *US Intellectual Property Enforcement Coordinator, Joint Strategic Plan on Intellectual Property Enforcement* (June 2010).

gets are so called "rogue" overseas sites such as the torrent hub "The Pirate Bay" that are a trove for illegal downloads and against which the US content industry finds it particularly difficult to take action, or enforce US judgements.[61]

As the servers of the (in)famous torrent hub "The Pirate Bay" are physically located in Sweden, the newly proposed acts aimed at "cutting off the oxygen"[62] by requiring US search engines, advertising networks and other providers to withhold their services in relation to such websites. As a result, the piracy websites would be cut off from US-based funding and visibility in the US.

As regards search engines, this would have meant that websites flagged as "rogue" would not appear among the search results. Payment services like Paypal would have been obliged to stop processing payments to these websites, and advertising services would have been required to cease providing their services to offending websites.[63] Although the proposed legislation was US legislation, it would have had a deep impact on websites around the world as many of the major search engines, payment services and social networking sites are based in the US.

Generally, besides the risk of over-censoring, two severe side-effects were identified, namely a chilling effect on websites containing user-generated content and an impact on the critically fundamental internet architecture and security.[64] As regards the latter, the major concern was that requiring service providers to bar access to foreign websites may break the Internet's core technical infrastructure by interfering with the Internet's fundamental interconnection principle.[65]

---

61 SOPA utilised a very broad definition of infringing websites, extending its applicability to any site that facilitates copyright infringement, meaning that potentially all user-generated content sites were to be included.

62 Julianne Pepitone, *SOPA explained: What is is and why it matters*, CNN (20.01.2012).

63 For an in-depth outline and analysis of the proposed provisions see Sandra Schmitz, *The US SOPA and PIPA – A European Perspective*, International Review of Law, Computers & Technology 2013, Vol. 27 Issue 1–2, 213–229.

64 For an analysis of the threat, see *ibid*, 218 et seq.

65 Peter Eckersley/Parker Higgins, *An Open Letter From Internet Engineers to the U.S. Congress*, EFF (15.12.2011). Both bills proposed DNS (Domain name Server) blocking. This blocking system will be outlined in the third Chapter of this work. The interconnection principle would be at risk, if countries decide unilaterally who can find what on the Internet. The principle of domain name universality requires that all domain name servers, irrespective of their location, will return the

Although the bills targeted "rogue" websites directed at US residents, they were clearly designed to have an extra-territorial effect. If they had become law, this would have had a severe impact on European website operators. This means that the risks addressed above also apply to European Internet sites. They are not shielded from the collateral damage that may arise and may be affected by the broad scope of these bills.

However, it was unsustainable that both bills meant in practice that the US claimed jurisdiction over the property of non-US sites: The bills allowed for court orders requiring service providers to block sites and Internet search engines to stop linking to them. Irrespective of the severe sanction of content blocking, in an ever-growing Web, linking is essential for an Internet site to be found. Considering that most search engines are US-based, they would have been required to comply with an order. Accordingly, a search engine like Google would have been obliged to stop linking to content that infringes US laws. Even Chinese content blocking (the often colloquially referred to as "Great Firewall of China")[66] does not require content to be blocked for users outside of China.[67] But this is exactly what *SOPA* and *PIPA* proposed to do: irrespective of the user's location, search engines would not link to the allegedly infringing content. Thus, US law would have applied directly to third State citizens outside of US jurisdiction.

Should a website operator have wished to challenge a court order, he would necessarily have had to consent to the jurisdiction of US courts.

Consequently, one might go as far as to conclude that the US government would force compliance with US IP laws on third countries. From a third country point of view, this is not acceptable. Non-US citizens would have to comply with domestic laws and may have been bound by international treaties and agreements, but not by unilateral US initiatives. However, the US IP enforcement strategy seemed to export its rules to other countries, including European countries.

---

same answer when queried with respect to an Internet address. This core principle would be undermined if domain servers ceased resolving specific domain names to the respective IP address.

66 The Chinese web content blocking scheme is officially named the "Golden Shield Project".

67 See Ronald Deibert/John Palfrey/Rafal Rohozinski/Jonathan Zittrain, *Access denied, the practice and policy of global Internet filtering* (2008), Country summary China, pp. 263–268.

The protests against *SOPA* and *PIPA* were remarkably effective and none of the bills might ever be turned into law.[68] Thus, on the day of the Wikipedia blackout, a bipartisan group of US lawmakers introduced the *Online Protection and Enforcement of Digital Trade Act (OPEN)* and asked for public contribution so that the Act "becomes a digital citizen's bill of rights".[69] Whether this project, on which everyone can comment, criticise and collaborate will be successful and will lead to a feasible result remains to be seen. It shows, however, a change in the attitude towards law-making where laws affect basically each citizen.

IV. EU: IPRED2

In the European Union, remedies and sanctions for intellectual property rights infringements are foreseen in several EU Directives, with the most detailed being the *Intellectual Property Rights Enforcement Directive (IPR Enforcement Directive* or *IPRED)*.[70] The *IPR Enforcement Directive* harmonises inter alia the rules on standing, evidence, provisional measures, seizure and injunctions in civil matters. The primary aim of the Directive is to provide for civil remedies necessary to enforce intellectual property rights. Initially, it was foreseen that the Directive is supplemented by a further Directive, known as *IPRED2*, which was to provide for criminal measures aiming at ensuring the enforcement of intellectual property rights.[71] However, the second Directive was never passed and the European Com-

---

68 PIPA has already been voted out of the Senate Judiciary Committee in September. A vote on SOPA had been scheduled for 23 January 2012, but due to the public protest and a White House statement that it will not support SOPA, see Victoria Espinel/Aneesh Chopra/Howard Schmidt, *Combating online piracy while protecting an open and innovative Internet*, Official White House response to the petitions "Stop the E-Parasite Act" and "VETO the SOPA bill and any other future bills that threaten to diminish the free flow of information" (14.01.2012), and US Senate, Committee on the Judiciary, *Statement from Chairman Smith on Senate Delay of Vote on PROTECT IP Act*, Senate press release of 20.01.2012.

69 See http://keepthewebopen.com/ (last accessed on 06.06.2014).

70 *Directive 2004/48/EC of the European Parliament and of the Council of 29 April 2004 on the enforcement of Intellectual Property Rights,* OJ L 157 (30.04.2004), 16–25.

71 See European Commission, *Proposal for a European Parliament and Council Directive on criminal measures aimed at ensuring the enforcement of intellectual property rights,* COM(2005) 276 final (12.07.2005).

mission decided to withdraw the proposal for the Directive in 2010.[72] Criminal sanctions for enforcement of intellectual property rights are therefore currently not harmonised.

The effective fight against counterfeiting and piracy is still on the European Commission's agenda. In order to encourage greater collaboration in the area of intellectual property rights enforcement, in April 2009 the Commission launched the "European Observatory on Counterfeiting and Piracy", which shall provide evidence-based contributions and data to enable EU policymakers to shape effective intellectual property enforcement policies and to support innovation and creativity.[73]

However, as the need for a stronger, horizontal and harmonised instrument at EU level to combat piracy, in particular online piracy, is still perceived, the *IPR Enforcement Directive* is currently under review. The EU Commission intended to publish a revised draft version of the *IPR Enforcement Directive* which is intended to be fit for the digital age, in autumn 2012.[74] However, in the current harsh climate for anti-piracy legislation, it seems that the Commission is not in a hurry to publish the draft bill. Being faced with protests all around and with the rejection of *ACTA* in the European Parliament, the Commission decided to extend its review of *IPRED1* and postpone the publication of a draft version for a revised Directive. In this regard a public consultation on the efficiency of proceedings and accessibility of measures was conducted in 2013.[75]

Against the background of *ACTA*, *SOPA* and *PIPA*, the public carefully watches anti-piracy initiatives and the follow-ups of the Commission consultation remain to be seen.

---

72 See *Withdrawal of obsolete Commission proposals*, OJ C 252 (18.09.2010), 7.

73 In June 2012, the European Observatory on Counterfeiting and Piracy has been transferred to the Office for Harmonization in the Internal Market (OHIM) in Alicante on the basis of *Regulation (EU) 386/2012* (OJ L 129 (16.05.2012), 1–6), and has been renamed as "the European Observatory on Infringements of Intellectual Property Rights".

74 See European Commission, *Proposal for a revision of the Directive on the enforcement of intellectual property rights (Directive 2004/48/EC).*

75 European Commission, *Civil enforcement of intellectual property rights: public consultation on the efficiency of proceedings and accessibility of measures, consultation period 30.11.2012 to 30.03.2013* (July 2013). For a summary of the responses see http://ec.europa.eu/internal_market/consultations/2012/intellectual-property-rights_en.htm (last accessed on 06.06.2014).

V. Copyright Enforcement in the EU: No Uniform Approach in Member States

Due to little progress on EU level intellectual property rights enforcement, Member States are increasingly adapting specific online legislation in order to respond to copyright infringements on the Internet. These regimes include the *Lois HADOPI*[76] in France, the *Ley Sinde*[77] in Spain and the *Digital Economy Act 2010*[78] in the UK. These schemes are targeted at different actors, but primarily seek to enforce copyright against end-users by way of graduated response schemes. Graduated response schemes foresee the sanctioning of an infringer following a certain number of notifications of infringements that also inform him about possible sanctions. The Member States thereby respond to the problem that enforcement schemes that functioned in the offline world, reach their limits when applied in the online world.

The major issue in this regard is that in the online world, it is difficult and often impossible to identify the actual infringer. The only digital trace infringers leave in Cyberspace are usually their IP addresses. An IP address, however, only allows the identification of the subscriber of a specific Internet access service. Thus, new legislation constructs responsibility of subscribers, which would make the identification of the actual infringer more or less obsolete. Where criminal sanctions are concerned in this respect, issues arise with regard to the proportionality of criminal sanctions against non-infringers. Some proposed and implemented sanctions even go so far to ban subscribers from the Internet. In this regard, this research will also examine the legal implications for other users affected by a disconnection order. As opposed to the offline world, sanctions that interfere with the subscriber's Internet access service will likely affect users other than the subscriber. The suspension or limitation of Internet access is a novel instrument, nothing comparable ever existed before; it is unknown whether the disconnection of telephone lines in con-

---

76 *Loi no. 2009-669 du 12.06.2009 favorisant la diffusion et la protection de la création sur Internet* and *Loi no. 2009-1311 du 28.10.2009 relative à la protection pénale de la propriété littéraire et artistique sur Internet.*

77 *Ley 2/2012, de 4 de marzo, de Economía Sostenible,* available at http://www.boe.es/boe/dias/2011/03/05/pdfs/BOE-A-2011-4117.pdf.

78 *Digital Economy Act 2010,* available at http://www.legislation.gov.uk/ukpga/2010/24/pdfs/ukpga_20100024_en.pdf.

nection with criminal offences has been on anyone's agenda in the past. The Internet is, however, not only a means of one-to-one communication, but also a means to seek, receive and impart information. Consequently, any interference with Internet access must be balanced against the fundamental rights of the users concerned.

Where no Internet-specific legislation is passed, Member States seek to apply their traditional regime to Internet scenarios. An example for such an approach would be Germany, where courts construed responsibility of Internet access service subscribers by applying a liability concept that derives from liability for dangerous property. The same regime is also applied by German courts to host providers when requiring them to stop the continuation of an infringement. While the approach to establishing online intermediary liability differs in the EU, the European legal framework provides for common liability exemptions for online intermediaries. In that respect, all Member States are faced with indefinite legal concepts that call for clarification by the Court of Justice of the European Union (CJEU).

F. Limits of the Research

Against all the issues that have already been touched, it is necessary to identify the limits of the scope of this research. Obviously a multitude of issues arise in respect of copyright enforcement on the Internet, which include inter alia: questions of digital evidence, in particular the collecting of evidence and its reliability; identification of infringers; liability of potential non-infringers, in particular liability of online intermediaries and subscribers of Internet access services; colliding rights and interests, such as the conflict between copyright protection on the one hand and freedom of speech and information, data protection and privacy on the other; private international law issues, such as the applicable law when infringements are committed online; enforcement of rights where the targets of legal action are located elsewhere.

Addressing all these issues would go beyond the scope of this book as the main focus of this research, the issue of online copyright enforcement, would perish in discussions of national copyright law. The territoriality of copyright and a lack of complete harmonisation of copyright laws, makes it impossible to compare enforcement one-to-one. Thus, only selected questions with regard to the establishment of an infringement will be discussed, for instance whether sharing of bits and pieces of a work amounts to a copyright infringement, or whether back-up copies on file-hosters are legitimate under the private copying exception. The issues addressed are carefully selected and solely intend to highlight that already the establishment of an infringing activity is not so easy as it may seem at first glance. In that respect also technology issues, such as the reliability of digital evidence, will be briefly addressed without clarifying them exhaustively.

Further, although this research refers to online copyright enforcement with a focus on enforcement within the EU, it was necessary to restrict the national instruments that are examined to three EU Member States, namely France, Germany and the United Kingdom. Again, these Member States have been carefully selected because they do not only stand for different and innovative approaches but also provide more case law than other States with regard to copyright enforcement on the Internet. The assessment of these measures will focus on their compliance with secondary EU Law and fundamental rights. As regards the assessment of fundamental rights, in particular a fair balance between copyright enforcement and the rights of others, it will be discussed to what extent or to what human rights' cost copyright on the Internet can and should be enforced. In this respect, social policy and behaviour questions such as whether we should enforce copyright on the Internet at all will not be addressed. The assessment of the legitimacy and proportionality of responses to copyright infringement constitutes the centre of consideration of this work.

The research will finally show that as of now governments are not moving from constraining human behaviour with laws to indirectly constraining behaviour by regulating software, a scenario that Lawrence Lessig was worried about in his influential work "Code: Version 2.0".[79]

G. Terminology

It is important to clarify some of the terminology that is used throughout this work. Infringement in this work refers to the unauthorised copying, distribution or use of a copyrighted work. As stated above, it is not the intention of this work to define what constitutes an infringement under dif-

79 As regards Lessig's worries in relation to a shift from "East Coast Code" to "West Coast Code" see Lawrence Lessig, *Code: Version 2.0* (2006), pp. 4 et seq. and pp. 74 et seq.

ferent national laws, but to analyse how infringements are sanctioned, eliminated and ultimately also prevented, hence how copyright is enforced.

Different terms are used to describe the increasing phenomenon of online copyright infringements and they are used interchangeably. The most common terms are: Internet or online piracy, illegal downloading or illegal file-sharing. The basic statement of all of these notions is that the activity referred to is in violation of the law. In order to use a uniform notion throughout this work, the terminology used in the following when addressing the fight against these activities will be copyright enforcement. Copyright enforcement does not only include the imposition of sanctions for copyright infringements but also the prevention of such infringements. It further encompasses infringements of copyright and related rights.

H. Sources

This research encompasses principally legislation and jurisprudence from the EU Member States France, Germany and the UK. Further, the analysis of EU secondary legislation, in particular the relevant Directives, builds an essential part of this research. In order to identify the fundamental rights concerned and potential justifications for interferences with these rights, the jurisprudence of the European Court of Human Rights (ECtHR) and the Court of Justice of the European Union (CJEU) are important sources. The latter plays a significant role when it comes to the interpretation of the applicable Directives.

Further legal doctrine, opinions, legal commentaries, legal papers as well as scientific papers discussing technology are important sources for this work.

I. Outline of the Research

This work is divided into three main chapters. In order to provide some general background to the subsequent research, the first Chapter begins by outlining the history of online copyright infringements and enforcement (A.). When examining the status quo of copyright enforcement, it is instructive to also look at the predecessor technology and be familiar with new technologies that facilitated copyright infringements. The second part of the first Chapter provides some background on the functioning of information and communications technology (ICT) (B. I.), identifies the fundamental rights that may be interfered with and defines the scope of protection guaranteed by these rights (B. II.).

The second and third Chapter are both in a similar way structured, with the second Chapter discussing enforcement measures that are targeted at end-users, and the third Chapter discussing enforcement measures that are targeted at the infringing content itself and are addressed to online intermediaries. To facilitate the legal assessment, both Chapters at first outline the activities addressed and the reasons for addressing either users or online intermediaries (A. I.–II.). In the following, both Chapters outline the respective technological challenges that enforcement is faced with (A. III.). On this basis, both Chapters will then set out the applicable European legal framework before enforcement in the Member States is assessed (B. I.).

In the second Chapter, the assessment of national enforcement is divided into two major parts. First, enforcement by criminal sanctions by way of graduated response schemes is discussed (B. II.). In this regard the French approach (B. II. 1.) is compared to the approach in the UK (B. II. 2.), before the concerns relating to technology, secondary EU legislation and fundamental rights are focussed on (B. II. 3.). The same structure is employed with regard to enforcement against end-users through private litigation (B. III.). In this respect, the German approach will be focussed on (B. III. 1.), and the UK approach only addressed briefly, highlighting the concerns of the UK courts when the German model of cease and desist letters was imported to the UK (B. III. 2.). On the basis of the prior assessment of criminal enforcement, the final section will discuss the concerns relating to technology, secondary EU legislation and fundamental rights (B. III. 3.).

In the third Chapter, the assessment of national enforcement measures is divided into three major parts. The first part discusses the failed attempts to enforce copyright upon the initiative of administrative authorities (B. II.). Due to diverging approaches to this subject matter, all three Member States (France, Germany and the UK) will be addressed in this context. In the following, enforcement upon initiative of the rights-holders via access providers is analysed (B. III.). In this regard, the focus is on the approach conducted in the UK (B. III. 1.), which is then contrasted against the German refusal of granting injunctions against access providers (B. III. 2.). Similar to the second Chapter, the outline of the enforcement scheme is followed by an assessment of the concerns in relation to technology and fundamental rights (B. III. 3.). The final section of the third Chapter addresses enforcement upon the initiative of the rights-holders that is directed against host providers (B. IV.). In this respect, the German (B. IV. 1.) and French (B. IV. 2.) approach will be compared and subsequently analysed in terms of how technological issues are dealt with and in terms of compliance with secondary EU law and fundamental rights (B. IV. 3.).

The three main Chapters will be followed by a general conclusion which addresses the problems and prospects of online copyright enforcement in brief.

First Chapter: Legal and Technological Background

A. The Status Quo – or How Did We Get to Where We Are Today?

I. Copyright in a Digitalised World

In simple terms, copyright is a legal concept that grants the author of an original work exclusive rights to its use and distribution, usually for a limited time, with the intention of enabling the author to receive compensation for his work and be able to financially support himself. In a digital world these rights are challenged more than ever due to the dissemination factor of the Internet and the ease by which works can be reproduced by everyone without a loss in quality. The following sections seek to explore the fundamentals of copyright and its enforcement in order to understand, where the core ideas of copyright derive from and to explore the challenges for copyright in an online environment. In this respect, it will also be necessary to look at the scope of copyright infringement. This being said, the challenges for copyright that derive from technological progress and the scope of technology are put forward as justifications for new legislation in this field of law.

1. A Short History of Copyright and Copyright Enforcement in the Offline World

In civil law tradition, the scope of copyright extends beyond being a mere economic right for the distribution of creative content and it includes also moral rights of the author. It first developed in the early modern period as a response to the printing technology that facilitated the vast and fast multiplication of copies of written works.[80]

At the "heart" of copyright law lies the assumption that respect needs to be paid to intellectual property. It grants the author of an original work

80 Thomas Dreier in: Thomas Dreier/Gernot Schulze, *Urheberrechtsgesetz* (4th ed. 2013), Einleitung para. 10.

exclusive rights to it for a limited time. These exclusive rights give the copyright-holder the right to charge third parties for accessing the work. This basic principle does not only serve as an incentive for authors to create, but also establishes a system whereby intellectual property can be marketed. A work in the sense of copyright law as defined in Article 2 (1) of the *Berne Convention for Protection of Literary and Artistic Works* includes productions in the literary and artistic domain, whatever may be the mode or form of their expression, such as books and other writings, musical compositions, cinematographic works, drawings, paintings and photographic works.

Today, copyright promotes the creation of new works by giving authors control of and profit from them. Copyright is confined to specific territories, which means that it does not extend beyond the territory of a specific state, unless that state is a party to an international agreement.[81] Most countries are parties to at least one such international copyright agreement with the result, that many aspects of national copyright laws have been standardised. Nevertheless, national copyright laws may have some unique features such as the fair use exception in US copyright law.[82] Most jurisdictions recognise certain copyright limitations, allowing for example exceptions to the creator's exclusivity of copyright, and giving users certain rights such as the aforementioned fair use of protected works.

The birth of copyright was the attempt of governments to regulate and control the output of printers in the 15th century. Before the 18th century, the term of copyright was not used, instead the concept was referred to simply as the "copy", which was substituted for the word "licence".[83] The modern concept of copyright is believed to stem from the early 16th century.[84] At that time, it was tied to the ownership of printing presses and was a right to print and distribute printed materials; it was not linked to the author as it is in the contemporary context. Unlike today, it was a mere economic right, associated with the book trade, and it was not seen as a property right or as having any regard to culture.[85] Hence, up to the 18th century, copyright was characterised by state licenced printers holding a

81 *Ibid*, Einleitung, para. 42.

82 17 *US Code* § 107: Limitations on exclusive rights: Fair use.

83 Monica Horten, *The Copyright Enforcement Enigma* (2011), p. 14.

84 *Ibid.*

85 *Ibid.*

monopoly over the printing and distribution of books.[86] In return for control of the market, printing licensees had to comply with state censorship demands.[87] The first known copyright statute is the English *Statute of Anne* of 1709,[88] which marked a change in the approach to licensing by giving the "copyright" to authors who could then authorise the printing of their own work for a limited time. Since the *Statute of Anne*, copyright is associated with the author of a work rather than the printer or publisher.[89] The Statute also contained copyright enforcement mechanisms when giving copyright-holders the right to sue for damages, as well as setting forth that unauthorised book copies could be seized by the rights-holders.[90] The Statute also introduced a concept of indirect liability, whereby booksellers, who knew of an unauthorised copy might also be sanctioned.[91] The move from the monopoly of printers to a limited monopoly right, where authors were given the copyright in their works marked the recognition of copyright as an economic incentive to create.[92] While under common law the focus was on the economic interests of the author, a number of civil law jurisdiction such as Germany, France, and Belgium also recognised the importance of moral rights of an author.[93]

Once copyright had become a statutory right guaranteed by law,[94] the rights-holders turned to the judicature to enforce their rights. Subsequently, many disputes dealt with territoriality or technical formats.[95] Territori-

---

86 For the situation in France see *ibid*, pp. 19 et seq.

87 *Ibid*, pp. 15–17; Thomas Dreier in: Thomas Dreier/Gernot Schulze, *Urheberrechtsgesetz* (4th ed. 2013), Einleitung para. 10.

88 Ian J. Lloyd, *Information Technology Law* (6th ed. 2011), p. 285.

89 Monica Horten, *The Copyright Enforcement Enigma* (2011), p. 18.

90 *Statute of Anne 1709*, p. 262.

91 *Ibid.*

92 Cf. Monica Horten, *The Copyright Enforcement Enigma* (2011), pp. 18 et seq.

93 Thomas Dreier in: Thomas Dreier/Gernot Schulze, *Urheberrechtsgesetz* (4 th ed. 2013), Einleitung para. 10.

94 In France, it only became a statutory right after the French Revolution with the Loi du 13 janvier 1791, relative aux théâtres et au droit de représentation et d'exécution des œuvres dramatiques et musicales which was amended by the *Loi du juillet 1793, relative à la propriété littéraire et artistique.* In Germany, a first statutory regulation of the relationship author – publisher can be found in the *Allgemeines Preußisches Landrecht 1794;* the basis for the modern German copyright code was the *Badisches Landrecht 1809.*

95 For the so-called Battle of the Booksellers, see Monica Horten, *The Copyright Enforcement Enigma* (2011), pp. 22 et seq.

ality became such an important issue as copyright is national and early statutes did not necessarily grant protection to foreign works. This resulted in the ability of publishers to take works from one country and publish them in another without paying the original authors. Territorial disputes, even between the small German states[96], led to the signing of the *Berne Convention* in 1886, the first multi-lateral copyright treaty, which established rights but no enforcement mechanisms.[97] Not until 1994, were the latter introduced by the *Agreement on Trade-Related Aspects of Intellectual Property Rights* (*TRIPS*).[98] In the 20th century, new technologies allowed for improved publishing and reproduction formats, providing a catalyst for copyright reforms.[99] Cross-border business and interaction had made it necessary to agree upon a basic international copyright framework. The *Berne Convention* sets up minimum standards for copyright protection and requires the parties to the Agreement to recognise the copyright of works of authors from other signatory states in the same way as it recognises the copyright of its own nationals.

While new technologies like piano role, records, radio, television, copy machines, video recorder, digital storage media, and data networks are content-neutral, they have required adaptions of copyright, once the economic changes brought by these technologies as well as the societal changes in the wake of new communication formats became known. Protection had to be extended and adapted to cover new forms of works (i.e. photography, film, sound recording, or software), of multiplication (i.e. printing press, tape recorders, or photocopiers) and of transmission (inter alia broadcasting, cable transmissions, Internet).

Already at the end of the 19th century, sheet music publishers started fighting new technologies, i.e. the piano roll and gramophone records, by accusing the emerging record industry of breaching copyright.[100] The dispute was settled in 1909 when the US Congress introduced a mechanical

---

96 Thomas Dreier in: Thomas Dreier/Gernot Schulze, *Urheberrechtsgesetz* (4th ed. 2013), Einleitung para. 42.

97 The US did not sign the *Berne Convention* until 1989.

98 *Agreement on Trade-Related Aspects of Intellectual Property Rights, Annex 1C to the Agreement establishing the World Trade Organisation (TRIPS, Marrakesh 1994)*. *TRIPS* was negotiated at the end of the Uruguay Round of the *General Agreement on Tariffs and Trade (GATT)*.

99 Thomas Dreier in: Thomas Dreier/Gernot Schulze, *Urheberrechtsgesetz* (4 th ed. 2013), Einleitung para. 11.

100 See Monica Horten, *The Copyright Enforcement Enigma* (2011), pp. 23 et seq.

licence, requiring a fee to be paid to the composer for the right to make a recording.[101] The next copyright battle was fought in the 1970s when the video recorder enabled copyright infringement by consumers. The Walt Disney Company and Universal Studios wanted to make Sony as the producer of the Betamax recorders responsible for contributory infringement. The US Supreme Court held that it was legal to manufacture and sell standardised copying equipment, and that it "does not constitute contributory infringement if the product is widely used for legitimate, unobjectionable purposes".[102] While the Hollywood industry feared the wide availability of video recorders, in particular blank tapes, videotapes and their successor the digital video disc (DVD)[103] became a lucrative product line for the film industry.[104] The movie industry is nowadays seeking to protect exactly this product line. The same development can be seen in the music industry: with rising popularity of cassette recorders, the music industry feared that people recording music from the radio onto cassettes would cause a decline in record sales. Thus, music industry trade groups like the British Phonographic Industry (BPI) started to campaign against private copying with the slogan "Home Taping is Killing Music".[105] Similar campaigns were run when new reproduction products entered the market, such as the "Don't Copy That Floppy" anti-copyright infringement campaign run by the US Software Publishers Association (SPA) in 1992.[106] Rightsholders associated with new technologies feared a loss of control over their rights as protected by law, and beside their campaigning, demanded a strengthening of their position. In the context of industry campaigning and lobbying, it needs to be mentioned, that the current developments are characterised by a material Zeitgeist and a strong economic-oriented perspective, which protects investment rather than the creativity of an author.[107]

---

101 *Ibid*, p. 25.

102 *US Supreme Court, Sony Corp. of America v Universal City Studios Inc.*, 464 U.S. 417 (1984), 442.

103 Nowadays the abbreviation DVD stands for digital versatile disc.

104 Monica Horten, *The Copyright Enforcement Enigma* (2011), p. 26.

105 The logo consisted of a Jolly Roger formed from the silhouette of a compact cassette.

106 Cf. Software & Information Industry Association (SIAA), *SIIA Releases Sequel to Classic Anti-Piracy Music Video "Don't Copy That Floppy"*, Reuters (09.09.2009).

107 Thomas Dreier in: Thomas Dreier/Gernot Schulze, *Urheberrechtsgesetz* (4th ed. 2013), Einleitung, para. 17a.

This economic component reflects the concentration of individual rights in the hands of global players, namely collecting societies and associations.[108]

The integration of the World Intellectual Property Organization (WIPO) into the United Nations marked a transition for WIPO from the mandate it inherited from the Bureaux Internationaux Réunis pour la Protection de la Propriété Intellectuelle (BIRPI)[109] in 1967, promoting protection of intellectual property, to one that involved the more complex task of promoting technology transfer and economic development.[110] Enforcement mechanisms, however, were not implemented at an international level until *TRIPS* in 1994.[111] *TRIPS* as such is the result of intense lobbying by the US supported by the EU and other developed nations. Ratification of *TRIPS* is a compulsory requirement of World Trade Organisation membership and for this reason, it has become the most important multilateral instrument for the globalisation of IP laws. The Agreement has a detailed chapter dedicated to the setting of minimum standards of intellectual property rights enforcement and technical cooperation and provides for a structure responsible for monitoring the implementation of the provisions of the Agreement and for consultation between Member States. Under Part 3 of *TRIPS* (Articles 41–61), governments must ensure that intellectual property rights can be enforced under their domestic laws, and that the remedies constitute deterrents to further infringements. The provisions oblige WTO Member States to provide enforcement procedures, including civil or administrative remedies, as well as criminal penalties, that permit effective action against any act of copyright infringement. The *TRIPS* enforcement provisions describe in some detail how enforcement should be handled,

---

108 *Ibid.*

109 The WIPO is the successor of Bureaux Internationaux Réunis pour la Protection de la Propriété Intellectuelle (BIRPI), which was established in 1893, and administered the *Berne Convention.*

110 Preamble to the *Convention Establishing the World Intellectual Property Organization,* signed in Stockholm on 14.07.1967.

111 The so-called Berne-plus minima for substantive protection. "Berne-plus" means that the minimum standard for international copyright protection has risen beyond the Berne standard in the ways enumerated in the substantive section of the *TRIPS Agreement* on copyright (Section II, Articles 9-14). A detailed discussion of the substantive standards of *TRIPS* and to what degree these go further than the standards of the *Berne Convention* would be beyond the scope of this research.

including rules for obtaining provisional measures, injunctions, damages and other penalties, as well as rules for obtaining evidence. Key to the *TRIPS* enforcement standard is, that remedies must constitute a "deterrent to further infringements". Article 61 *TRIPS* also requires Member States to provide that wilful copyright piracy is a criminal offence, and that criminal enforcement must be used by governments against copyright piracy "on a commercial scale".

However, *TRIPS* did not yet contain provisions concerning digital enforcement. This began to change with the adoption of the 1996 *WIPO Copyright Treaty*, which addressed questions raised by new economic, social, cultural and technological developments.[112] The *WIPO Copyright Treaty* was the basis for the US *Digital Millennium Copyright Act* and was implemented into EU law by *Directive 91/250/EC creating copyright protection for software*[113], *Directive 96/9/EC on copyright protection for databases*[114] and the *InfoSoc Directive 2001/29/EC*[115]. The Treaty does not directly introduce new enforcement mechanisms, but obliges the contracting parties to provide legal remedies against the circumvention of technological measures (the so-called "anti-circumvention" clause), e.g. encryption, used by authors in connection with the exercise of their rights and against the removal or altering of information, such as certain data that identify works or their authors, necessary for the management (e.g. licensing, collecting and distribution of royalties) of their rights.[116] The digital rights management is a first response to copyright challenges that arose with the digitalisation of content and that will be addressed in the following section. The *WIPO Copyright Treaty* as well as the *WIPO Performances and Phonograms Treaty* also introduced the "making available" right, a concept that considers the necessity to control the use of material in addition to control the existence of physical copies. With an increasing

---

112 See Preamble to the *WIPO Copyright Treaty*, adopted in Geneva on 20.12.1996.

113 *Council Directive 91/250/EEC of 14.05.1991 on the legal protection of computer programs, OJ L 122 (17.05.1991),* pp. 42–46.

114 *Directive 96/9/EC of the European Parliament and of the Council of 11.03.1996 on the legal protection of databases,* OJ L 077 (27.03.1996), pp. 20–28.

115 *Directive 2001/29/EC of the European Parliament and of the Council of 22.05.2001 on the harmonisation of certain aspects of copyright and related rights in the information society (InfoSoc Directive),* OJ L 167 (22.6.2001), pp. 10–19.

116 See Article 11 *WIPO Copyright Treaty.*

dematerialisation of content, control over the use of material becomes essential.

2. Copyright Challenges in an Online Environment

History shows that copyright is a response to evolving technology, from the past until today. The resistance with regard to offline copying equipment gives an idea of what to expect in the digital age where copying is becoming increasingly easier. Major copyright challenges in a digitalised world are the growing use of the Internet and communication technologies that allow the instantaneous copying of materials as well as the emergence of user-generated content. In addition, many users find it more and more difficult to distinguish between legal and illegal use of intellectual property.

a) Technological Progress

The development of digital media and computer network technologies introduced new challenges for rights-holders to enforce copyright. These days, it requires not much effort to produce and distribute a work that itself required a certain degree of effort and investment to be created. It does not require a high degree of computer skills to copy a CD; neither does it require elaborated skills to download content from the Internet or upload content to the Internet. The dissemination of content in general has never been as easy; neither has been the copying. Copying now also plays a significant role in the creation of new content: users use existing works to remix them, create mash-ups or alter them in another way.

Technological progress means that some goods and services can nowadays be traded independently from any physical medium. In this context, one may speak of the aforementioned digital "dematerialisation". Music, films and books can be consumed remotely without the need to acquire a physical copy.

Historically, music was the first digital content that was available on the Internet. With increased broadband capacity, the distribution of larger files, for example cinematographic works, became faster and easier. With increased popularity of e-book readers, e-books are the newest form of media affected by piracy. Nowadays, access to content is quick and easy.

E-books for instance can be downloaded directly from the e-book reader onto the reader via an Internet connection. At the same time the publication of own works on open electronic networks is easier than ever before.

While digitalisation facilitates or improves many aspects of our daily life, it also opens the door to new types of criminal offences. Intellectual property rights infringements are not a new phenomenon, but they are tremendously facilitated by digitalisation. The basis for digital copyright infringements is fast and accurate reproduction. During the pre-digital age, people recorded songs played on the radio onto tape. This kind of recording as well as the copying of a record or a video-tape necessarily resulted in a degree of loss of quality. Today the popular self-produced "mix-tapes" have been replaced by digital recordings from Internet radio channels. The self-produced copy commonly does not lack quality when compared with the original. Similar to the way of copying, the distribution of unauthorised copies has changed. In the past, an actual physical copy had to be handed over physically one-to-one. Accordingly, the self-produced mix-tape was actually given to friends in face-to-face. Similarly, professional counterfeit products such as illegal pressings of records were sold by street vendors or at car boot sales. This was due to the fact that copies were intrinsically linked to a tangible good. Today, a copy is distributed one-to-many or many-to-many. It is possible to duplicate digital sources without loss of quality anytime and anywhere, and also to make copies from any copy. Content can be rapidly multiplied and distributed worldwide at no cost. As previously mentioned, it is essential, that copying does not lead to reduced quality and does neither involve huge effort nor disproportional costs.

Since the launch of the original Napster website in 1999, copyright violation has become a mass phenomenon. Simultaneously, enforcement of copyright has become significantly more difficult. While some argue that the anonymity of the Internet lowers the threshold for illegal behaviour,[117] it is obvious that anonymity, by nature, at least makes copyright enforcement more difficult.

---

117 Boris Paal/Moritz Hennemann, *Schutz von Urheberrechten im Internet, ACTA, Warnhinweismodell und Europarecht,* MultiMedia und Recht 2012, 288.

Rights-holders are most commonly faced with the exchange of copyright-protected works in peer-to-peer[118] file-sharing networks and the dissemination of copyright-protected works via file-hosting services[119] or streaming websites[120]. File-sharing systems are being used to exchange any kind of computer data, including music files, videos or software. Especially during the first decade of the 21st century, peer-to-peer technology was extremely popular for exchanging music files and later on, with increasing bandwidth, also for (HD) movies. Techniques of exchanging computer data have become highly sophisticated and now also enable the exchange of large files within short time.

As technology progresses, file-sharing systems have moved on from such using a central server to decentralized networks. While centralised file-sharing models enabled rights-holders to take action against unauthorised file-sharing, the decentralised structure of modern file-sharing networks makes it more difficult for rights-holders to trace infringers.

Technological progress also meant that the scale of copyright infringement grew. More and more people gain access to the Internet, which also allows for copyright infringement to become a large-scale, global phenomenon that causes worldwide concern.

b) Failure of Technological Protection Measures

Early responses to copyright infringements saw rights-holders protecting their works with Technical Protection Measures (TPMs) against unauthorised access and copying. The digital format also allowed for the so-called Digital Rights Management (DRM), which was used to prevent actual access to copyright works, to prevent unauthorised copying, or to control the use of a copyrighted work, which the user was authorised to access.[121] The use of TPMs and DRM was paralleled by legal provisions in the *WIPO Copyright Treaty* and the *WIPO Performances and Phonograms*

---

118 Peer-to-peer (P2P) describes direct connectivity between participants in networks instead of communicating over centralised server-based structures. As regards the functioning of peer-to-peer file-sharing see A. II. 1. Peer-to-Peer File-Sharing.

119 Such as Rapidshare or Megaload.

120 Most prominently kino.to, whose providers were convicted for copyright infringements in Germany.

121 Diane Rowland/Uta Kohl/ Andrew Charlesworth, *Information Technology Law* (4th ed. 2012), p. 348.

Treaty supporting their use. In the EU, Article 6 *InfoSoc Directive* implemented the international obligations of Article 11 *WIPO Copyright Treaty* and Article 18 *WIPO Performances and Phonograms Treaty*. The Directive required Member States to provide for protection against acts of circumventing protective technological measures (Article 6 (1)) and against dealings in such circumvention devices (Article 6(2) *InfoSoc Directive*). According to the Directive, the protection of TPM complements the protection of copyright.[122]

However, TPMs, in particular DRM, was of limited success in the beginning: CDs with DRM schemes could not be played on various CD players because they are rather CD-ROM media[123] than standard audio CDs.[124] Computers running Microsoft Windows have been reported to have crashed when attempting to play these types of CDs.[125] DRM policies also did not allow for legal uses, such as making backup copies of CDs, or DVDs or fair use. Accordingly, DRM was not appreciated by consumers. Notably, Article 11 of the *WIPO Copyright Treaty 1996*, implicitly allows circumvention of anti-copying measures for acts that would be permitted by law, but it does not give any practical guidance as to how this should or could be accomplished. The circumvention of anti-copying mechanisms, however, raises questions relating to the ability and the legality of de-compilation or disassembly of a computer program, which will not be discussed here.[126]

In January 2007, music recording and publishing company, EMI, stopped publishing audio CDs with DRM, arguing that "the costs of DRM do not measure up to the results".[127] This example was followed by other

---

122 Commission of the European Communities, Commission Staff Working Document, *Report to the Council, the European Parliament and the Economic and Social Committee on the application of Directive 2001/29/EC on the harmonisation of certain aspects of copyright and related rights in the information society* (30.11.2007), SEC(2007) 1556, p. 7.

123 CD-ROMs are identical in appearance to audio CDs, but differ from audio CDs in the standards used to store the data.

124 Rita Lewis, *What is DRM and why should I care?,* Firefox News (08.01.2008).

125 *Ibid.*

126 For more information on these issues see Diane Rowland/Uta Kohl/Andrew Charlesworth, *Information Technology Law* (4th ed. 2012), p. 348.

127 The Economist, *Criminalising the consumer – Where digital rights went wrong,* The Economist (27.04.2007).

record labels and a number of online music stores including Apple's iTunes.[128]

The failure of CDs with embedded DRM schemes showed that the approach to see a criminal in every consumer is not a good starting point to protect and enforce copyright. One may even argue that the interoperability, which was also linked with some schemes such as Apple iTunes and the fact that legitimately acquired CDs could not be played on every CD player, backfired. It may as well have raised awareness of users in terms of circumvention tools or made them turn to file-sharing networks, where they could get a "ripped copy",[129] which they could play on all their devices without restrictions.

c) Lack of Understanding Intellectual Property Rights

It is important to understand that file-sharing as such is not illegal. There is also legitimate use of file-sharing networks, for example the exchange of authorised copies or works from the public domain. A variety of business models exists online, such as free downloads supported by advertising or free browser games with premium charges for advanced use. For consumers, it is not always obvious whether a music service is providing copyrighted material without authorisation unless the service – as Hargreaves puts it his *Digital Opportunity Report*[130] – puts the "skull and

---

128 *Ibid.* Apple has its own DRM system called FairPlay which is used by the iPhone, iPod, iPad, Apple TV, iTunes, and iTunes Store and the App Store. FairPlay has however been abolished in relation to music files in 2009, but is still used in relation to videos.

129 Ripping is the process of copying audio or video content to a hard disk, typically from removable media such as CD or DVD, although the word refers to all forms of media. "Ripping" is often used to shift formats, and to edit, duplicate or back up media content, thus must not be confused with simple file copying. Ripping always involves reformatting the content. Accordingly, a "ripped copy" is a copy in a format that is distinct from the original format.

130 Ian Hargreaves, *Digital Opportunity, A Review of Intellectual Property and Growth* (2011). The Hargreaves Review of Intellectual Property and Growth, or Digital Opportunity – A review of Intellectual Property and Growth, was an independent review of the United Kingdom's IP system, focusing on domestic copyright law. Professor Ian Hargreaves was commissioned to chair a review of how the IP framework supports economic growth and innovation in November 2010 by Prime Minister David Cameron. The review was published in May 2011.

crossbones" on its mainsail (like the Swedish download service, the Pirate Bay, did).[131]

So it came to no surprise that face to face interviews with British adults conducted in September 2009 showed that 73 % of consumers are unaware of what they are allowed to replicate or record.[132]

This indicates that consumers are confused by the concept of ownership in the digital age. In the analogue world, the situation was different: Intellectual creations were intrinsically tied to movable things, i.e. books, cassettes, vinyl or film reels. An infringing copy commonly came with a lack of quality unless made by using professional equipment. In a digital world of intangible goods, copied works come in the same quality and format as the originals. Users may get an electronic version of a book or record, either through a retailer like Amazon or via a file-hosting platform like Rapidshare, without being able to tell, if there is a difference between the original and a pirated version. Against this background, users may be confused why downloading from some sources is legal and from other sources it is illegal. They may be unaware, that the act of downloading copyright-protected digital content can be qualified as a copyright-relevant reproduction and that essentially, every form of downloading involves copying. [133] If a user wants to be on the safe side, he will need the copyright owner's prior permission in order not to contravene copyright laws. Such prior permission can be acquired by a licence, including an implicit licence.[134] A licence, however, does not necessarily imply that the user needs to pay for the content. Several business models exist, that are funded by advertisements, making it difficult for users to distinguish between legal and illegal content. These platforms as well as websites with user-generated content are also used by newcomers to become known to a large public, or by established musicians for promotion purposes. Similarly, peer-to-peer networks are increasingly used by artists as a new form of promotion.[135] The band Georgia Wonder for instance seeded its songs in peer-to-peer net-

---

131 *Ibid*, para. 8.6.

132 Consumer Focus, *Outdated copyright law confuses consumers,* press release (24.02.2010).

133 European Parliament, DG for Internal Policies, Policy Department C: Citizens' Rights and Constitutional Affairs, *File Sharing* (2011), p. 8.

134 The latter will for example be granted where the copyright owner himself offers a work for downloading on his website.

135 European Parliament, DG for Internal Policies, Policy Department C: Citizens' Rights and Constitutional Affairs, *File Sharing* (2011), p. 8.

works and became the 14th most downloaded band in the world, and only thus known to the wider audience.[136] So called viral marketing can also mean that content is initially offered free of charge before it goes on sale.[137]

Some users may also be confused by the "private copying exception" which exists in most Member States[138] and allows them to make a copy without the copyright owner's permission for private use.[139] Where such an exception does not exist, the reproduction of a legitimate copy that the user purchased for his personal use – for example, making a private back-up of the copy, would constitute a copyright infringement.[140] This is difficult for users to understand. Particularly in regard to copies for back-up in a cloud service or elsewhere, the exclusion of a private copying exception

---

136 Techradar, *Cheap promotion, Twitter and peer-to-peer, How one band used YouTube, Twitter and file-sharing to create a community of fans,* Techradar (16.01.2010).

137 *Ibid.*

138 Notably, the UK has no such exception. However, the UK government intends to introduce a narrow private copying exception which will allow individuals to copy content under the condition that they own the content, and have acquired the content lawfully. Under this circumstances, they will be allowed to copy the content to another medium or device for their own personal use. See HM Government, *Modernising Copyright: A modern, robust and flexible framework, Government Response to Consultation on Copyright Exceptions and Clarifying Copyright Law* (December 2012), p. 25. The House of Lords proposed to insert the following new clause into section 28 of the *Copyright Designs and Patents Act 1988*: "(5) Any provisions of this Chapter relating to an exception for private copying shall not apply where further copies of copyright works are commercially available, under the terms of the acquisition of the copy of the copyright work concerned, by or with the authority of the copyright owner." See *Intellectual Property Bill [HL],* Session 2012–14, 17.07.2013.

139 Exception or limitation for private copying is enshrined in Article 5(2)(b) of the *InfoSoc Directive*, which foresees that "Member States may provide for exceptions or limitation to the reproduction right provided for in Article 2 in the following cases: ...(b) in respect of reproductions on any medium made by a natural person for private use and for ends that are neither directly nor indirectly commercial, on condition that the rights-holders receive fair compensation which takes account of the application or non-application of technological measures referred to in Article 6 to the work or subject-matter concerned".

140 As regards the lack of a private copying exception in the UK, see HM Government, *Modernising Copyright: A modern, robust and flexible framework, Government Response to Consultation on Copyright Exceptions and Clarifying Copyright Law (December 2012)*, p. 22.

or defence, is considered unfair.[141] Adding to the confusion of legitimacy, is the fact that where a private copying exception exists, the exception may even encompass downloading materials from the Internet.[142] The conditions for the private copying exception however vary, but regularly have their limits where the making of multiple copies for friends or other third parties is concerned.[143] Downloading from peer-to-peer networks, in particular BitTorrent networks, is also generally not considered as copying for private use, especially since the content is both, uploaded and downloaded simultaneously.[144] Although downloading is commonly conducted for private use, the fact that the content is made publicly available to a third party, excludes the application of the private copying exceptions. Therefore, the user's option to block the upload function is irrelevant.

One condition for applying the private copying exception is also the absence of any direct or indirect commercial aim.[145] If one argued, that every download constituted a lost sale, the download without payment would imply a commercial benefit for the downloader. As noted above, an unauthorised download cannot be equalled with a lost sale.[146] A private copy exemption implies that a fair compensation system must be put in place.[147]

In relation to private copies, it is also discussed whether it is relevant or not that the copy is made from an evidently illegal source.[148] Germany, for

---

141 Cf. *Ibid.*

142 European Parliament, DG for Internal Policies, Policy Department C: Citizens' Rights and Constitutional Affairs, *File Sharing* (2011), p. 8.

143 Limitations can be found in the national Copyright Acts or the national interpretations of private use. As regards the interpretation of "private use" in Germany, see Thomas Dreier in: Thomas Dreier/Gernot Schulze, *Urheberrechtsgesetz* (4th ed. 2013), para. 7 with further references.

144 See below Second Chapter, II. Peer-to-Peer File-Sharing: Scope,Specific Functioning and Consequences.

145 European Parliament, DG for Internal Policies, Policy Department C: Citizens' Rights and Constitutional Affairs, *File Sharing* (2011), p. 9.

146 See also *ibid.*

147 Such a system is required by Article 5(2)(b) of the *InfoSoc Directive*.

148 The question whether a law which allows copying from illegal sources for private use is compliant with EU copyright law has recently been subject before the CJEU in the case C-435/12 *ACI Adam v Stichting de Thuiskopie*. In concreto, the Dutch Supreme Court sought guidance from the CJEU, asking: "Should Article 5(2)(b) – whether or not in conjunction with Article 5(5) of the [InfoSoc] Directive be interpreted as meaning that the limitation on copyright referred to therein applies to reproductions which satisfy the requirements set out in that provision,

instance, prohibits downloading from an evidently illegal source,[149] whereby the Dutch copying regime considers the legality/illegality of the origin of the downloaded material as irrelevant.[150] While there is less discussion about what constitutes an illegal source (either the content copied is distributed without the rights-holder's permission or the file from which the content is downloaded has been created without the rights-holder's consent), the question is to determine when the illegality is evident. For the average user it is regularly difficult to determine if the source is illegal. Especially with regard to streaming this question has recently been in focus in Germany, when thousands of users were addressed by rights-holders for watching copyrighted streams of porn clips.[151] In this regard, it is even questionable whether the consumer of stream is actually infringing copyright or not. At least the illegality of the source may not be obvious to him.

Finally, there are also users that argue that the Internet is about sharing, meaning that once content has been published on the Internet, this shall imply that the author wants it to be shared. Of course this is a radical view, only shared by a few, but it highlights that there is also opposition to accept the application of the traditional concept of copyright being applied to the World Wide Web. For instance, the operators of Heftig.co, [152] a platform that "copies" content from other websites, announced in May 2014,

---

regardless of whether the copies of the works from which the reproductions were taken became available to the natural person concerned lawfully – that is to say: without infringing the copyright of the rights-holders – or does that limitation apply only to reproductions taken from works which have become available to the person concerned without infringement of copyright?". The Opinion by AG Cruz Villalón in this subject-matter has been released in January 2014. The AG concludes that the private copying exception is to be restricted to copies from legitimate sources (See Opinion of the Advocate General in C-435/12 *ACI Adam v Stichting de Thuiskopie* of 09.01.2014). The Court essentially followed the AG's opinion in its judgment of 10 April 2014, see CJEU, C-435/12 *ACI Adam v Stichting de Thuiskopie,* Judgment of 10.04.2014.

149 See § 53 (1) *Urheberrechtsgesetz – UrhG.*

150 See Article 16c (1) *Auteurswet.*

151 The RedTube case in Germany has been outlined in Sandra Schmitz, *The RedTube copyright infringement affair in Germany: Shame on who?,* International Review of Law, Computers & Technology 2015, Vol. 29 Issue 1, 33–49.

152 As of June 2014, heftig.co was ranked as the 84th most popular website in Germany. See the page ranking by Alexa at http://www.alexa.com/siteinfo/heftig.co (last accessed on 06.06.2014). As of June 2015, the website also had more than 1,700,000 Facebook fans.

that they do not consider their service to be illegal. Although they, for more or less obvious reasons, first operated anonymously out of Belize[153], they suddenly revealed their identities in order to rebut the allegations that they were infringing copyright by declaring that every user, that creates "viral" content and disseminates this content "intends uncontrollable effects" in order to maximise attention for his creation.[154] It is certainly true, that authors are happy to reach a vast audience and receive many clicks on their uploaded files, for instance on YouTube or their own website, but it certainly is questionable whether that also applies to clicks on content that has been copied by heftig.co and been republished on the heftig.co website. Such generalising statements show that the Internet also changes how we perceive traditional legal instruments. The operators of platforms like heftig.co do not lack an understanding of copyright in a strict sense. They rather interpret the act of original online publication as a copyright waiver.

d) User-Generated Content and a Participatory Internet

In the light of the fast growing market of social media sites and social networks that rely on the creation and upload of online content by end-users (user-generated content)[155], specific attention must be given to the fact, that consumers become recipients, users and authors at the same time.[156] Web 2.0 applications (inter alia blogs, podcasts, wikis, social media) enable users easily to create and share content, and to play a more active and collaborative role in content creation and knowledge dissemination.[157] In this context, it is necessary to distinguish between purely user-created

153 Their domain was also registered anonymously via a service from Panama, see Lars Wienand, *Das ist heftig: Die Viralseiten-Macher und ihr Verhältnis zu Urheberrechten*, Rhein-Zeitung (27.05.2014).

154 *Ibid.*

155 User-generated content appears in various formats, including blogs, podcasts, comments, Wikis, mash-ups of music files and videos, voice-overs, etc.

156 Commission of the European Communities, *Green Paper, Copyright in the Knowledge Economy* (16.07.2008), COM(2008) 466 final, p. 19.

157 For the evolution from web 1.0 to web 2.0 see Andrew Murray, *Information Technology Law, The law and society* (2nd ed. 2013), pp. 109 et seq.

content[158] and existing (copyright protected) content, which is simply uploaded by users or which has been adapted in some way by the user. As regards the latter, Internet users make "use" of copyrighted content, but not in a sense where they themselves exploit the work commercially, they rather use it as a means to express themselves.[159] In this context, one may speak of "prosumers" as a merger of producer and consumer.[160] On YouTube, for example, movie excerpts with user-made voice-overs are popular as well as video-clips where users mime to pop songs. While this might not be a new phenomenon of persiflage, the dissemination of the material via an online portal adds another quality to this. In the offline world, such a voice-over generally would have been shown only to friends and family in a private setting. An upload onto YouTube, however, means a worldwide dissemination and, especially in relation to YouTube, also adds a commercial context. YouTube as a business entity generates profits from advertisements; each click on their website increases its revenues. This is something that many copyrights-holders will no longer tolerate. Though the issue of user-generated adaptions of works is not the key issue of the current copyright debate, the example highlights two of the main problems of today's challenges for copyrights-holders: the ease by which content can be copied and disseminated and the fact that third parties generate revenues from infringing content.

Copyright laws as they exist are not designed for these scenarios. Although there have been calls for the acceptance of an exception for transformative, user-created content,[161] the *InfoSoc Directive*[162] does not currently contain an exception, which would allow the use of existing

---

158 In a study on user-created content conducted by the OECD, user-created content is defined as "i) content made publicly available over the Internet, ii) which reflects a "certain amount of creative effort", and iii) which is "created outside of professional routines and practices". See OECD, Directorate for Science, Technology and Industry, Committee for Information, Computer and Communications Policy, Working Party on the Information Economy, *Participative Web: User-Created Content* (12.04.2007), DSTI/ICCP/IE(2006)7/FINAL, p. 4.

159 *Ibid.*

160 See Deutscher Bundestag, *Bundestagsdrucksache 17/7899* (23.11.2011), p. 8.

161 Cf. Commission of the European Communities, *Green Paper, Copyright in the Knowledge Economy* (16.07.2008), COM(2008) 466 final, p. 19. See also Deutscher Bundestag, *Bundestagsdrucksache 17/7899* (23.11.2011), p. 8.

162 Directive 2001/29/EC of the European Parliament and of the Council of 22.05.2001 on the harmonisation of certain aspects of copyright and related rights in the information society, OJ L 167 (22.06.2001), pp. 10–19.

copyright protected content for creating new or derivative works. In particular the UK *Gowers Review* recommended the introduction of an exception for "creative, transformative or derivative works within the parameters of the Berne Three Step Test to clearly legitimise the reworking of existing material for a new purpose or to give it a new meaning, and to align the law in the EU with that of the US.[163] However, under the existing regimes, the user in the YouTube example would need to acquire a licence, if he wanted to adapt a cinematographic or musical work. Ignorance of the law is no defence, and thus, users may find themselves exposed to a claim for damages or at least the request to delete the content. While legal action is only taken in a limited number of cases, the situation is somehow different when it comes to the dissemination of rather substantial parts of copyrighted films and musical works and not just excerpts thereof.[164]

Although there is a growing realisation that solutions are needed to make it easier and affordable for amateur users to integrate third-party copyright protected content for non-commercial purposes in their own creations, this issue is being explored further and as of now, users must face infringement proceedings.[165]

---

163 Andrew Gowers, *Gowers Review of Intellectual Property* (December 2006), p. 6, Recommendation 11. For the *Berne Convention* three-step test see Hector MacQueen/Charlotte Waelde/Graeme Laurie/Abbe Brown, *Contemporary Intellectual Property, Law and Policy* (2nd ed. 2011), pp. 258 et seq. The *Gowers Review* however acknowledges that the introduction of such an exception would be contrary to the *InfoSoc Directive* and hence calls for its amendment.

164 Some uses of short takings may fall under the exceptions of Article 5(23)(d) *InfoSoc Directive* which allows quotations "for purposes such as criticism or review". Because the Directive uses the term "such as", criticism and review are only examples for possible justifications for using small takings. A further justification for quotations can be found in Article 5(3)(k) of the *InfoSoc Directive* which exempts uses "for the purposes of caricature, parody or pastiche".

165 European Commission, Communication from the Commission to the European Parliament, the Council, the European Economic and Social Committee and the Committee of the Regions, *A Single Market for intellectual property rights – Boosting creativity and innovation to provide economic growth, high quality jobs and first class products and services in Europe*, Com(2011) 287 final, p. 12.

e) Necessity to Reform Copyright Law?

As mentioned above, the aim of this work is not to make a proposal for a new copyright law.[166] The elaboration of a revised copyright law for the digital age goes beyond the scope of this study. It intends to examine and to analyse current legislative measures in relation to illegal content on the web with a focus on copyright infringements. Irrespective of the scope of this study, a brief introduction into the current debate on copyright in a networked world is necessary in order to outline the problem at its root. This work intends to show, that courts struggle to apply liability regimes, developed in the 20th century, to new Internet phenomena. This results in great uncertainty when it comes to monitoring obligations that may arise, for example, once an infringement has taken place. Notice and take down regimes that apply to host providers fail when users share content in peer-to-peer networks; there is no host provider that may be notified. They equally seem to fail when it comes to new forms of content storage like file-hosting and cloud computing; although notification may be feasible, the upload as such, is under most copyright regimes not illegal, whereas the act of making the link to the stored copyrighted work publicly available constitutes an infringement. Monitoring obligations that were more or less feasible with traditional user-generated content sites, such as YouTube or eBay, reach their limits when the upload as such does not constitute an illegal act. This work also shows the deficiencies of recently developed schemes that aim at holding users of file-sharing networks criminally liable.

3. Scope of Online Copyright Infringement

In 2013, the European Commission carried out an interactive online consultation on the civil enforcement of intellectual property rights,[167] in

---

166 Legal scholars, politicians and the net community currently discuss a revision of copyright law and new business models for collecting societies, see Deutscher Bundestag, *Dritter Zwischenbericht der Enquete-Kommission 'Internet und digitale Gesellschaft'*, Bundestagsdrucksache 17/7899 (23.11.2011); Thomas Darnstädt, *Wem gehören die Gedanken?*, Der Spiegel online (21.05.2012).

167 European Commission, *Civil enforcement of intellectual property rights: public consultation on the efficiency of proceedings and accessibility of measures, consultation period 30.11.2012 to 30.03.2013.*

which is considered that unpaid license fees cost the audiovisual industry 500 million Euros per year.[168] The following sections outline that such estimates must be seen critically, in particular when research on the scale and scope of infringements is conducted on behalf of creative industries.

a) Difficulties in Determining the Scope of Online Copyright Infringements

Infringements of intellectual property rights at large are a global phenomenon and are causing worldwide concern. A 2009 Organisation for Economic Cooperation and Development (OECD) study estimates that international trade in counterfeit goods has increased from 100 billion USD to 250 billion USD in 2007.[169] The statistics published by the European Commission on national customs activities show a continuous upward trend in the number of cases of goods suspected to violate intellectual property rights. The number of cases increased by more than 240% from 2005 (26,704 cases) to 2011 (more than 91,000 cases).[170] The figures relating to customs detentions of articles suspected of infringing intellectual property rights are only those of registered cases, meaning, that the overall figure of counterfeited goods imported to or traded within the European Union and its scope can only be estimated. However, in the case of physical goods, figures of physical goods seizures and detected cases by national/European authorities, may serve as a basis to determine the scope of infringements of intellectual property. When it comes to infringements of intellectual property rights on the Internet, in particular copyright infringements, there are no official figures.

The reasons for this are twofold. First, most online copyright infringements are enforced in civil law and no state authority screens the Net for infringements in a way customs examines goods at the border. A consumer, who buys counterfeited or even unlicensed physical goods from a

168 European Commission, *Synthesis of the responses "Civil enforcement of intellectual property rights: public consultation on the efficiency of proceedings and accessibility of measures"* (July 2013), p. 5.

169 OECD, *Magnitude of counterfeiting and piracy of tangible products* – November 2009 update.

170 For the numbers of registered cases see http://ec.europa.eu/taxation_customs/customs/customs_controls/counterfeit _piracy/statistics/index_en.htm (last accessed on 30.04.2014).

foreign country on the Internet, will often be confronted with the seizure of these good. This will not happen to him, if he downloads an unauthorised digital copy from a foreign website, due to a missing screening process. Regarding the civil enforcement of copyrights, many cases are settled outside of court and thus, statistics are non-existent on the actual number of copyright infringements that occur online. Second, as with all illegal activities committed with cyberspace the extent of such activities is uncertain. This uncertainty is inherent to all cybercrime.[171] It is unclear how the statistics represent the scope and economic impact of cybercrime.[172] This further applies to online copyright infringement: its extent and economic impact, specifically the reliability of information on the degree of losses, are difficult to quantify. Studies in relation to online copyright infringement must rely on estimates, whereby the range of estimates differs significantly. Sales figures show a more coherent picture, measuring a continued decrease in physical music sales (i.e. CD, vinyl) in parallel with rising popularity of Internet. For instance, statistics of 2009 show a decrease in the turnover of record labels within most European countries.[173] While it is difficult to obtain data on unpaid media consumption, it is equally difficult to link unpaid media consumption to data on paid music consumption. Even if data on unpaid media consumption was available, the causal effect of unauthorised copying on legal purchases is challenging to prove. While the music industry may be quick in assuming that every second to fifth download equals a non-purchase,[174] this ignores

---

171 International Telecommunication Union, *Understanding Cybercrime: A guide for developing countries* (April 2009), p. 62.

172 Regarding the related difficulties see: United Nations Conference on Trade and Development, *Information Economy Report 2005*, UNCTAD/SDTE/ECB/2005/1, p. 229.

173 Bundesverband Musikindustrie, *Musikindustrie in Zahlen 2009*, p.57. While there has been a decrease in most European countries, Poland, Belgium and the Czech Republic saw an increase in sales from 2007 to 2008.

174 The substitution rate of IP rights infringements against licit sales that is reported by copyright owners varies from sector to sector. In the European Commission's public consultation on the civil enforcement of intellectual property rights, respondents from the cinema sector reported 20 %, while respondents from the digital music sector have reported substitution rates up to 50 %. Notably book publishers have reported almost a 1:1 ratio. See European Commission, *Synthesis of the responses "Civil enforcement of intellectual property rights: public consultation on the efficiency of proceedings and accessibility of measures"* (July 2013), p. 5.

aspects of "try before you buy" and downloading or streaming as a mere substitution for radio consumption.[175] Such figures also seem to ignore that many factors other than peer-to-peer file-sharing can influence creative industry revenues[176], for example change in demand levels per GDP/capita of a country,[177] growth of alternative consumer goods on which to spend income,[178] or a loss of innovation within music and film markets[179]. Furthermore, some downloads may be of material that was otherwise legally unavailable and thus, they do not replace sales. Recent studies on illegal music downloads further conclude, that illegal music downloads have little or no effect on legal digital sales.[180] Moreover, a European Commission research project analysing the clicks on legal purchase websites and illegal downloading websites suggests, that the vast majority of

175 See Lilian Edwards, *Role and responsibility of Internet intermediaries in the field of copyright and related rights* (2011), p. 16.

176 The term "creative industries" is commonly used in the EU policy debates and primarily refers to the audio-visual industries (film, broadcasting and music), but arguably also includes print publishing. See Monica Horten, *The Copyright Enforcement Enigma* (2012), p. 28.

177 Cf. European Commission, Synthesis of the responses "Civil enforcement of intellectual property rights: public consultation on the efficiency of proceedings and accessibility of measures" (July 2013), p. 5.

178 Charles Arthur, *Are downloads really killing the music industry? Or is it something else?,* The Guardian (09.06.2009).

179 Lilian Edwards, *Role and responsibility of Internet intermediaries in the field of copyright and related rights* (2011), p. 16.

180 Irène Bastard/Marc Bourreau/François Moreau, *L'impact du piratage sur l'achat et le telechargement legal: une comparaison de quatre filieres culturelles* (2012): The authors of this study use survey data on a sample of 2000 French individuals. They conclude that while piracy has a negative effect on the probability to purchase music in CD format, it has a positive effect on the probability of downloading music legally. Hence legal and illegal music downloading are complements rather than substitutes. Robert G. Hammond, *Profit Leak? Pre-release File-sharing and the music industry* (2013): the author of this study focuses on pre-release file-sharing, in which file-sharers download music files that are not yet publicly available for sale. Hammond suggests that the causal effect of file-sharing of music titles on their sales is essentially zero. Godefroy Dang Nguyen/Sylvain Dejean/François Moreau, *Are streaming and other music consumption modes substitutes or complements?* (2012): the authors found that consuming music as streams has no significant effect on CD purchases but is complement to buying music online.

the music that is consumed illegally would not have been legally purchased, if illegal downloading websites were unavailable.[181]

The information above speaks of a direct link between the usage of illegal copies and a decrease in sales figures, although the extent is not manifestly proven.[182] However, from an empirical perspective, one cannot equate an illegal copy with a lost sale.

A 2010 Swedish study by Aldermon and Liang[183] suggests such a link: it measured Internet traffic before and after the transposition of *the Intellectual Property Rights Enforcement Directive 2004/48/EC*[184] into national law. Within the six months following implementation of the new legal provisions, Internet traffic in Sweden decreased by 18%, whereas there was no such decrease in Norway or Finland within that same time period.[185] Due to the fact that physical copies of music increased by 27% and sales of digital music by 48%, Adermon and Liang concluded, that the Swedish decrease in traffic resulted from users refraining from illegal activities.[186]

Furthermore, a 2010 German study on the usage of digital content in Germany, conducted on behalf of the music industry, suggests a link between unauthorised file-sharing and a decrease in sales. The study concluded that 185 million single music files, 46 million music albums, 6 million audio books, 14 million e-books, 54 million films and 23 million TV

181 Luis Aguiar/Bertin Martens, *Digital music consumption on the Internet: Evidence from clickstream data* (2013), European Commission JRC Technical Reports, Institute for Prospective Technological Studies.

182 Rolf Schwartmann, *Vergleichende Studie über Modelle zur Versendung von Warnhinweisen durch Internet-Zugangsanbieter an Nutzer bei Urheberrechtsverletzungen, Studie im Auftrag des Bundesministerium für Wirtschaft und Technologie* (Januar 2012), p. 63.

183 Adrian Adermon/Che-Yuan Liang, *Piracy, music, and movies: A natural experiment*, Uppsala Universitet Working Paper 2010: 18.

184 *Directive 2004/48/EC of the European Parliament and of the Council of 29 April 2004 on the enforcement of Intellectual Property Rights,* OJ L 157 (30.04.2004), pp. 16–25. The directive is also known as "(IPR) Enforcement Directive" or "IPRED".

185 Adrian Adermon/Che-Yuan Liang, *Piracy, music, and movies: A natural experiment*, Uppsala Universitet Working Paper 2010: 18, p. 15.

186 *Ibid.*

series had been illegally downloaded.[187] In the same year the total sales volume decreased by 4.6%.[188]

The *Hargreaves Report on Intellectual Property and Growth*[189] of May 2011 noted that "…in the Review's four months of evidence gathering, we have failed to find a single UK survey that is demonstrably statistically robust. For many surveys, methodology is not available for peer review".[190] The Review team has neither been able to examine the methodology of the surveys nor discover problems with the identified methodology.[191]

The *Hargreaves Report* identified additional reasons to the above mentioned, why digital copyright infringement is difficult to measure: for example respondents to survey questions may have an insufficient understanding of the law.[192] In addition, free downloads are not necessarily illegal and paid downloads must not necessarily be legitimate.[193] Considering that online copyright infringement often takes place across international borders, users may be unaware that what is legal in one country may not be in another country. What is more, peer-to-peer file-sharing or the use of file-hosting services is per se not illegal.[194]

---

187 GfK Consumer Panel, *Studie zur digitalen Content-Nutzung* (DCN-Studie) 2011 (2011). The conductors of the study defined illegal downloads as such downloads that have been undertaken from file-sharing networks, sharehosters, private websites, blogs, fora, ftp servers, or newsgroups.

188 *Ibid.*

189 Ian Hargreaves, *Digital Opportunity, A Review of Intellectual Property and Growth* (2011).

190 *Ibid*, para. 8.9.

191 *Ibid*, para. 8.16. A 2010 report by the US Government Accountability Office also questions the estimates, see United States Government Accountability Office, *Observations on Efforts to Quantify the Economic Effects of Counterfeit and Pirated Goods, Report to Congressional Committees* (12.04.2010).

192 Ian Hargreaves, *Digital Opportunity, A Review of Intellectual Property and Growth* (2011), para. 8.10.

193 *Ibid.*

194 See also *ibid.*

b) The Impact of Illegal Downloads on Sales Figures

There are numerous studies[195] examining the impact of illegal downloads on the sale of music and/or films. However, as aforementioned the robustness of the collected statistics is questionable.[196] Identifying the effects of file-sharing on the economy "is not a straight forward matter".[197] In this regard, it is not the place of this research to adjudicate on the empirical evidence for and against the extent of unauthorised file-sharing and its economic effects. Since the extent of file-sharing is regularly used to justify new legislation, it is important to have a basic understanding of illegal downloads statistics.

If one compares the figures on illegal downloads of the *BPI Digital Music Nation 2010 report*[198] with that of *MidemNet's 2010 Global Music Study*[199], there is significant discrepancy in regard to the percentage of downloads that are illegal: BPI claims that 76% are illegal,[200] whereas MidemNet claims that 13% of UK downloads are illegal.[201] Taking into

---

195 For example: Envisional, *Technical Report: An estimate of infringing use of the Internet* (2011); Norbert Michel, *The impact of digital file sharing on the music industry: An empirical analysis,* B.E. Journal of Economic Analysis & Policy 2006, Vol. 6 Issue 1; Alejandro Zentner, *Measuring the effect of file sharing on music purchases,* Journal of Law and Economics 2006, Vol. 49 Issue 1, 63–90; Felix Oberholzer-Gee/Koleman Strumpf, *The effect of file sharing on record sales: An empirical analysis,* Journal of Political Economy 2007, Vol. 115 Issue 1, 1–42; Martin Peitz/Patrick Waelbroeck, *The effect of Internet piracy on music sales: Cross-section evidence,* Review of Economic Research on Copyright Issues 2004, Vol. 1 Issue 2, 71–79.

196 See also with regard to the US: United States Government Accountability Office (GAO), *Intellectual Property, Observations on Efforts to Quantify the Economic Effects of Counterfeit and Pirated Goods* (April 2010).

197 European Parliament, DG for Internal Policies, Policy Department C: Citizens' Rights and Constitutional Affairs, *File Sharing* (2011), p. 17.

198 The British Record Music Industry (BPI), *Digital Music Nation 2010, the UK's legal and illegal digital music landscape* (2010).

199 See the reference in Ian Hargreaves, *Digital Opportunity, A Review of Intellectual Property and Growth* (2011), para. 8.11 to the Music Matters/Synovate/MidemNet, *Global Music Study* (2010), which consisted of a survey of 8,500 adult users (aged 18+) in 13 countries

200 The British Record Music Industry (BPI), *Digital Music Nation 2010, the UK's legal and illegal digital music landscape* (2010), p. 27.

201 As regards the percentage claimed in the Midem Global Music Survey Ian Hargreaves, *Digital Opportunity, A Review of Intellectual Property and Growth* (2011), para. 8.11.

account a number of studies from the UK and elsewhere, the *Hargreaves Report* concluded that it is difficult to assess the impact of copyright piracy on growth.[202]

Using industry estimates, he further attempted to quantify the scale of copyright infringement expressed as a percentage of the economy as a whole. [203]

The *Hargreaves Report* concluded that "copyright infringement appears to account for just under 0.1 per cent of economic activity". [204]

A study by Business Action to Stop Counterfeiting and Piracy estimated the losses from piracy as equivalent to 1.24% of the contribution made by the core copyright industries to the UK economy. [205] According to Hargreaves 1.24% is "at the upper end of probability".[206]

Undeniably, the economic value of the creative industry is high and the creative industry constitutes an important business segment of the European economy.[207] Furthermore, illegal file-sharing is concurrently causative to a decline of sales of physical copies.[208] However, the conclusion that "a CD copied is a CD less sold" appears to be untenable.[209] An illegal download does not equal a lost sale and money that is not spent on a legal copy is not lost to the economy.[210]

Although some businesses suffered dramatically following the rise of digital downloads, the overall music industry has been growing in recent years.[211] In Germany, individual businesses that have been affected are

202 *Ibid*, para. 8.15.

203 *Ibid*, para. 8.17.

204 *Ibid*, para. 8.17.

205 *Ibid*, para. 8.19.

206 *Ibid.*

207 In Germany for example, the cultural and creative industries' share of the 2006 German gross national product was 2.6 %. See Bundesministerium für Wirtschaft und Technologie, *Gesamtwirtschaftliche Perspektiven der Kultur- und Kreativwirtschaft in Deutschland*, Forschungsbericht Nr. 577 (2009).

208 Cf. European Parliament, DG for Internal Policies, Policy Department C: Citizens' Rights and Constitutional Affairs, *File Sharing* (2011), p. 17.

209 *Ibid.*

210 Ian Hargreaves, *Digital Opportunity, A Review of Intellectual Property and Growth* (2011), para. 8.15; see also Markus Beckedahl/Falk Lüke, *Wie die Musikbranche zum Internetgegner wurde*, Der Spiegel Online (23.05.2012).

211 Ian Hargreaves, *Digital Opportunity, A Review of Intellectual Property and Growth* (2011), para. 8.20 with further references}. In Germany for example, the sales of the creative industries increased from 117 to 131 billion Euros in the

primarily small independent labels.[212] One also has to take into account that following the introduction of the medium CD sales increased as many consumers purchased records they already owned on vinyl. A decrease in sales at the beginning of the century was also related to the fact that the market launch of CDs led to a peak in sales, which slowly declined.[213] Accordingly, figures cited such as those by the German content industry, which claims to have suffered a decrease in sales of 740 million Euros in 2008 alone, must be viewed critically.[214]

Although illegal downloading has some, truly difficult to measure, effects on the economy, it can also be said, that it has some form of positive influence. One possible positive advantage of file-sharing on the purchase is, that consumers may be introduced to content, artists or genres that they might have otherwise not encountered, and this may create demand; this is known as the sampling effect. [215] A report by the European Parliament lists inter alia the following as positive effects: a complementary demand by increasing demand for concerts and related products, and a network effect, meaning that file-sharing enhances the popularity of products, and thereby boosts demand driven by a lack of purchasing power.[216] File-sharing also meets a demand for products that are not available on the market, for example, foreign TV programmes that are not available, neither for free nor for purchase, outside the original broadcasting area. Some research concludes that (illegal) downloaders are clearly buyers, and that they buy more than non-downloaders.[217] This is apparently due to the fact that they are more active users and a consequence of the aforementioned sampling effect.[218]

---

years 2003 to 2009, see Bundesministerium für Wirtschaft und Technologie, *Gesamtwirtschaftliche Perspektiven der Kultur- und Kreativwirtschaft in Deutschland,* Forschungsbericht Nr. 577 (2009), p. 23.

212 Markus Beckedahl/Falk Lüke, *Wie die Musikbranche zum Internetgegner wurde*, Der Spiegel Online (23.05.2012).

213 *Ibid.*

214 Rolf Schwartmann, *Filesharing, Sharehosting & Co, Funktionsweise und rechtliche Bewertung aktueller Erscheinungsformen von Urheberrechtsverletzungen im Internet,* Kommunikation &Recht 2011, Beihefter 2, 3.

215 Cf. European Parliament, DG for Internal Policies, Policy Department C: Citizens' Rights and Constitutional Affairs, *File Sharing* (2011), p. 17.

216 *Ibid.*

217 *Ibid*, p.18.

218 *Ibid.*

The Hargreaves Report concludes that "…many creative businesses are experiencing turbulence, which translates into fears about the further, future impact of copyright infringement on sales, profitability and sources of investment. However, at the level of the whole economy or even at the level of whole creative business sectors, the measured impacts to date are not as stark as is sometimes suggested by the language used to describe them. That said, copyright infringement is a stubborn fact of the digital landscape which might well get worse and which justifies serious government effort in identifying the right mix of measures to address it".[219] The impact of illegal file-sharing on music sales is not questioned, but clearly controversy exists over the extent and economic impact of unauthorised file-sharing, to include other forms of copyright infringement on the Internet.[220] This shall be born in mind, when assessing legal solutions and their proportionality.

II. The History of File-Sharing: From Peer-to-Peer Technology to Sharehosting and Streaming

Digital files can be shared in many ways. Outside of the Internet, digital files can be shared physically for instance by burning music and films to CDs, DVDs or BluRays, or by copying onto a USB stick. Also via the Internet, files can be shared in many ways. Users may share files within a limited circle of recipients by attaching the file to an e-mail. They may also post copyrighted content to a website. The dominant techniques for file-sharing are however peer-to-peer file-sharing, the distribution of files via file-hosting services, USENET-related forms of sharing and streaming.

1. Peer-to-Peer File-sharing

Peer-to-peer applications as the basic and literally first mass-scale technology to share data online will at this point explained in more detail. As such

219 Ian Hargreaves, *Digital Opportunity, A Review of Intellectual Property and Growth* (2011), para. 8.23.

220 See also European Parliament, DG for Internal Policies, Policy Department C: Citizens' Rights and Constitutional Affairs, *File Sharing* (2011), p. 17.

this technology accounts for a large amount of all Internet traffic.[221] Though it is in general associated with unauthorised sharing of copyrighted works, the technology as such is perfectly legal. A variety of applications is covered by the broad term of peer-to-peer technology.

Peer-to-peer file-sharing, also known as P2P file-sharing, is a means by which data can be shared between computers using a specific peer-to-peer software client.[222] Traditionally, a home computer needed to connect to a central web server to download files that the users wanted to access. Because storing large amounts of data on a server is costly for the provider, new means of file-sharing were developed that do not rely on a centralised server and would also not require the provision of large amounts of bandwidth. Peer-to-peer technology that does not require a "major" server emerged in the 1990s and became highly popular with the launch of the file-sharing service Napster in 1999. Napster managed to link users who had specific files with those who requested those files via a central server.[223] Basically, instead of accessing a central server, home computers connected to each other to download files from each other. By this, the resources of the computers were pooled and performance could be enhanced.[224]

Napster was one of the first peer-to-peer networks to become widely known and available, having about 50 million users.[225] It marked a profound change in the balance of power between rights-holders and consumers by basically changing the dynamics of distribution and cost.[226] While pre-Napster, the record industry had enjoyed an effective monopoly and control over the release and distribution of content, peer-to-peer technology changed this by turning users into distributors.With Napster, users could share music via the Internet on a large scale, so that comprehensive

221 Envisional, *Technical Report: An estimate of infringing use of the Internet* (2011), p. 47; Andrew Tanenbaum/David Wetherall, *Computer networks* (5th ed. 2011), p. 748.
Such as for example Gnutella or Kazaa.

222 "Peers" are computer systems connected to each other through the Internet. The concrete functioning of peer-to-peer file-sharing will be outlined in Chapter 2.

223 See Andrew Tanenbaum/ David Wetherall, *Computer networks* (5th ed. 2011), p. 748.

224 *Ibid*, p. 749.

225 *Ibid.*

226 Nick Scharf, *Napster's long shadow: copyright and peer-to-peer technology*, Journal of Intellectual Property Law & Practice 2011, Vol. 6 No.11, 806, 806.

digital music collections became available for them. At the same time, the capabilities of home PCs got increasingly better as well as the bandwidth available for home pc users.

In a peer-to-peer file-sharing network, numerous computer systems are connected to each other via the Internet. Files can be shared directly between systems on the network without the need for a central server. A distinctive feature of peer-to-peer networks is, that each computer on the network can be a file server as well as a client.

The term peers in this context refers to all the computers being used which can alternately act as a client to another peer, fetching its content, and as a server, providing content to other peers.[227] Unlike a traditional content delivery network, peer-to-peer systems have no dedicated infrastructure.[228] Everyone participates in the distribution of content.

In order to join a peer-to-peer file-sharing network, users need an Internet connection and need to install a specific peer-to-peer application software on their computer like for example BitTorrent, µTorrent or eDonkey. Once connected to the Internet, the peer-to-peer software allows a user to search for files on the computers of fellow users. At the same time, other online users may search for files on the given user's computer.[229]

While the first generation of file-sharing networks like the original version of Napster, where the operators of the network run a central server which allowed users to search for the desired file and linked them to a distributor,[230] in current networks there is no such central server. The reason

227 Andrew S. Tanenbaum/David J. Wetherall, *Computer networks* (5th ed. 2011), p. 748.

228 *Ibid.*

229 Mark Taylor/John Haggerty/David Gresty/Tom Berry, *Digital evidence from peer-to-peer networks*, Computer Law & Security Review 2011, Vol. 27 Issue 6, 647.

230 As regards Napster, central servers would index all of the current users and search their computers for shareable files. When a user searched for a file, the server would find all of the available copies of the requested file and present them to the user. The file would then be transferred between the two private computers. Napster allowed only for music files to be shared. As the downloading occurred via a central server, Napster was held liable of contributory and vicarious copyright infringement and ordered to monitor the activities of its network and to block access to infringing material when notified of that material's location (17 U.S.C. *A&M Records. Inc. v Napster. Inc.* 114 F. Supp. 2d 896 (N. D. Cal. 2000), confirmed by *A&M Records Inc. v Napster Inc.*, 239 F.3d 1004 (9th Cir. 2001). As Napster was unable to comply with the judgement it eventually

for this is that US courts found Napster liable for contributory infringement, because its services were designed to enable users to locate and download music files.[231] In addition, the 9th Circuit Court also held Napster vicariously liable for its users' infringing activities, because the central index allowed Napster to monitor its users.[232] The original[233] Napster eventually shut down in July 2001 as it was not able to prevent copyright infringements taking place.[234] This was due to the fact that the central catalogue, which was hosted by Napster, was constantly being modified as users connected and disconnected to the Internet.

The second generation of networks[235], which was developed to be more robust and avoid legal liability after the US *Napster* case,[236] learnt its lessons from the findings of the US courts. The succeeding generation connected users remotely to each other. With a lot of second generation networks, the amount of the downloaded material and the downloading speed depends on the extent to which the user makes files available himself.[237] Thus, users are encouraged to share data. Because of the structure of peer-to-peer sharing, where users generally act both as a client and a server (i.e. uploader as well as downloader), each participant provides resources to the network such as bandwidth, storage space and computing power, thereby increasing capacity as the network grows. The speed by which files can be shared, is one of the why peer-to-peer file-sharing remains popular.

The newest (third) generation provides for files being searched and retrieved almost without any form of database being involved. The third generation protocols work decentralised; the so called BitTorrent protocol

---

shut down its service in July 2001. It later re-emerged as an online music store. For the history of Napster see also Nick Scharf, *Napster's long shadow: copyright and peer-to-peer technology*, Journal of Intellectual Property Law & Practice 2011, Vol. 6 Issue 11, 806–812.

231 *A&M Records, Inc. v Napster, Inc.*, 239 F.3d 1004 (9th Cir. 2001) at 1024.

232 *Ibid.*

233 Napster later re-emerged as a commercial online music store.

234 Vickie L. Feeman/William S. Coats/Heather D. Rafter/John G. Given, *Revenge of the Record Industry Association of America: The rise and fall of Napster*, Villanova Sports & Entertainment Law Journal 2002, Vol. 35 Issue 9, 53.

235 Such as for example Grokster or KaZaa.

236 See Lilian Edwards, *Role and responsibility of Internet intermediaries in the field of copyright and related rights,* p. 16.

237 European Parliament, DG for Internal Policies, Policy Department C: Citizens' Rights and Constitutional Affairs, *File Sharing* (2011), p. 6.

does not download a whole file from one single user but small blocks of data (bits) from different users that together form the desired content. By dividing the files into bits, sharing gains in efficiency and enables the simultaneous sharing of even very large files such as HD movies and video files. How this works in detail will be outlined in the Second Chapter. At this point, it is sufficient to be aware that in contrast to the second generation peer-to-peer file-sharing technologies, there is no single file-sharing network where all the files are being shared. Instead a different network (a so called swarm) is created for each and every file to be shared. Users within a swarm share blocks of data with each other that assembled together form the desired content.[238] Information on how these blocks need to be assembled, and more importantly information on the blocks of data that are distributed, is contained in the so called torrent file, which – at the start of each sharing process – is created by the torrent client and distributed by the user on certain notorious platforms. As will be outlined in the second Chapter, the utilisation of the BitTorrent protocol means that it has become more difficult for rights-holders to track and identify infringements, especially, when swarms are formed within closed groups.

A 2010 study conducted by Envisional for the content industry estimates that BitTorrent usage makes up 14.6% of all Internet bandwidth worldwide.[239] It is an extremely efficient way of transferring files, which provides for substantial non-infringing uses. Thus, it is not surprising that collected data strongly suggests that BitTorrent is the most used file-sharing protocol worldwide.[240] However, the Envisional analysis of BitTorrent traffic, conducted in 2010, found that more than 99% of all material (excluding pornography) in the top 10,000 swarms was copyright infring-

---

238 Gaetano Dimita, *Six characters in search of infringement: potential liability for creating, downloading, and disseminating .torrent files,* Journal of Intellectual Property Law & Practice 2012, Vol. 7 Issue 6, 466, 466.

239 In its study from January 2011, Envisional measured over eight million users simultaneously connected to the bittorent network Envisional, *Technical Report: An estimate of infringing use of the Internet* (2011), p. 7. In addition the distributor of two of the most-used BitTorrent clients µTorrent and BitTorrent Mainline, claims that the clients have over 100 million unique users worldwide and 20 million daily users, see Business Wire, BitTorrent, Inc. grows to over 100 million active monthly users, Business Wire (03.01.2011).

240 Envisional, *Technical Report: An estimate of infringing use of the Internet* (2011), p. 7.

ing,[241] which gives some impression of what BitTorrent is predominantly used for.

In summary, what is important to know is that users that download a file onto their computer, at the same time become a supplier for the given file in the network; they generally act both as a client and a server.[242] It seems that most users are not aware of this fact,[243] and thus, also do not make use of potentially available deactivation or blocking of the uploading function.[244]

2. File Hosting Services

File-hosting services, also known as one-click hosts or sharehosters, basically offer remote storage space. Users can upload data to the servers of the file-hosting service and then allow third parties to access the data by providing them with the respective link to the stored data. As such, this facilitates the sharing of files that would be too large to be sent as eMail attachments. It also may be used for data back-up, or as a storage place which users – other than data stored on a desktop PC – may access from anywhere. Cloud storage services operate similar, and recently, these kind of services have become an almost essential part of mobile technology.

The crux is however, that file-hosters may be used to share copyrighted content without the consent of the rights-holders. As mentioned above, third parties may access the data if they are provided with a specific link that tells the location of the file. These links are usually distributed on link directories or so called indexing websites. A popular German example for such directories is the website serienjunkies.org, where users may search for links leading them to their favourite TV series.

As we will see in the third Chapter, most file-hosting services operate a freemium model, by which user are granted basic access for free but will

---

241 *Ibid,* p. 10.

242 Rolf Schwartmann, *Filesharing, Sharehosting & Co, Funktionsweise und rechtliche Bewertung aktueller Erscheinungsformen von Urheberrechtsverletzungen im Internet,* Kommunikation &Recht 2011, Beihefter 2, 9.

243 European Parliament, DG for Internal Policies, Policy Department C: Citizens' Rights and Constitutional Affairs, *File Sharing* (2011), p. 6.

244 *Ibid.*

have to pay for more convenient usage including increased download capacities and advertisement-free services.

3. USENET

Outside of the above described environments, there are further ways that music is unlawfully distributed and acquired. One of this is USENET, which actually is also a form of peer-to-peer. In USENET, files are placed into news groups on decentralised servers. These news groups are analogous to a virtual bulletin board where users post messages similar to emails with attachments for reading or download by other news group participants. The term USENET refers to the set of people who exchange articles tagged with one or more universally-recognised labels (called "newsgroups").[245] A newsgroup as such is a discussion forum, in which Internet users can read and post messages and reply to postings from other users. They can be private, or of limited distribution. Newsgroups are organised around common themes and follow a hierarchical structure.[246] What makes USENET global in scope is that multiple hosts each carry selected newsgroups, add postings they have received to their own copies of the newsgroup database, and periodically swap updates with other USENET hosts.[247] Thus, a posting can be quickly distributed to other news servers which carry the newsgroup in which the posting was made.[248] Accordingly, USENET can also be described as a world-wide distributed discussion system without a higher authority than the people who own the servers on which USENET traffic is carried.[249]

---

245 There is often some confusion about the precise set of newsgroups that constitute Usenet; one commonly accepted definition is that it consists of newsgroups listed in the periodic "List of Active Newsgroups" postings which appear regularly in news.lists.misc and other newsgroups. A broader definition of Usenet would include the newsgroups listed in the article "Alternative Newsgroups Hierarchies". An even broader definition includes also newsgroups that are restricted to specific geopgraphic regions or organisations. See Chris Reed, *Internet Law, Text and Materials* (2nd ed. 2004), p. 29.

246 Chip Salzenberg/Gene Spafford/Mark Moraes, *What is Usenet?* (1998).

247 Chris Reed, *Internet Law, Text and Materials* (2nd ed. 2004), p. 28.

248 *Ibid*, p. 29.

249 Chip Salzenberg/Gene Spafford/Mark Moraes, *What is Usenet?* (1998).

Fact is, that it is one of the oldest Internet communications technologies around.

Although it may be considered a legacy technology, newsgroups are used for the unlawful sharing of copyright content.[250]

An important difference with the forms of peer-to-peer described earlier is the fact that the user does not need to be active in supplying files. Sticking to downloading exclusively is not only possible, it is the chief form of use.[251]

An example for a successful surviving USENET service is Newzbin, which will be thoroughly dealt with in the third Chapter.

4. Streaming

Unlike downloading, streaming does not require the prior storing of material on the computer's harddrive before it can be used. Instead, the material is delivered in "real time" (as on radio and television), where a "stream" of data is received and converted into sound (and picture). Although conversion usually occurs simultaneously with the reception of data, the data received in a given time span may exceed the volume required. When this happens, such excess data must be temporarily stored in a "buffer" (usually in the random access memory (RAM) of the computer) until it is needed in the streaming process. Therefore, bits of, e.g. a music or film file may be temporarily copied, but no permanent copy of the material is kept unless the receiver chooses (and has the technology) to download the stream.

As we will learn in the third Chapter, streaming is increasingly being used by public and private broadcasters to allow consumers to catch up with TV programme that they have missed. Smart TVs and other portable devices thereby allow access to TV programmes from anywhere at any time.

---

250 See for example *Ellison v Robertson*, 357 F.3d 1072 (9th Cir. 2004).

251 Cf. European Parliament, DG for Internal Policies, Policy Department C: Citizens' Rights and Constitutional Affairs, *File Sharing* (2011), p. 6.

5. File-Sharing as of Today

Although the notion of file-sharing is commonly associated with unauthorised downloading and making available of copyrighted works without the consent of the copyright owners, new technologies mean that works are also "shared" by the rights-holders themselves. Streaming, for instance, is nothing else than sharing a file.

First of all, none of the file-sharing technologies described above, has disappeared. Peer-to-peer technologies are becoming more and more sophisticated, while file-hosting sees many legitimate users, who use remote storing to synchronise their devices or have access to their data from anywhere, turning to cloud storage providers. USENET has become more of a special interest forum that is not widely being used by average users. At the same time, streaming is seen as the technology of the future considering its role in the net neutrality debate[252], where Internet service providers make deals with services like Netflix or Amazon allowing those companies to pay to stream their products to online viewers through a faster "express lane" on the web.[253] Obviously the streaming operators fear that they will lose customers if they subscription-based services do not offer better service than piracy streaming platforms. Similar direct download delivery sites like Apple's iTunes not only have to compete with free streaming portals, but also with persisting "free services" such as BitTorrent, which makes it hard for them to develop their market.

To the short history of file-sharing in this section, it needs to be added that commercial platforms, where users can download works, have been very complicated to use in the beginning, while file-sharing platforms turned out to be rather user-friendly.[254] Not surprisingly the latter attracted more users. Some users even felt that it is their right to share or download

---

252 For the background of the net neutrality debate, see Andrew Murray, *Information Technology Law, the law and society* (2nd ed. 2013), pp. 25 et seq.; Christopher Marsden, *Net Neutrality: Towards a co-regulatory solution* (2010).

253 As regards the Internet service provider Verizon in the US, see Edward Wyatt, *Rebuffing F.C.C. in 'Net Neutrality' Case, court allows streaming deals*, The New York Times (14.01.2014); Joseph Schumpeter, *Net Neutraliy, More equal than others*, The Economist (25.04.2014).

254 Deutscher Bundestag, *Dritter Zwischenbericht der Enquete-Kommission 'Internet und digitale Gesellschaft'*, Bundestagsdrucksache 17/7899 (23.11.2011), p. 11.

copyrighted files as the creative industries did not offer legal alternatives.[255]

Today, the basic situation has changed, there are now numerous legal online music stores.[256] As of June 2015, there are about 60 legal alternatives in Germany.[257] An increase in online music sales is intrinsically tied to the launch of Apple's iPod.[258] While Apple started to sell music files in a specific Apple format employing a digital rights management which also only allowed the files to be played whilst using the Apple iTunes software, this changed in 2007: the Digital rights management tool was abandoned and users free to play the music on devices that do not depend on iTunes software.[259]

This basically constituted a shift away from digital copyright protection. Users were now free to play their music on any device – and at the same time easily make copies of their music collection. Hence, it has also become easy to distribute one's music collection, because no copyright protection had to be circumvented. On the other hand, this also meant, that iTunes became more accepted by users and has become the major player when it comes to sales of digital media.

Convenience and easy-to-use services go in line with acceptance. This can lately be witnessed with the aforementioned online players of broadcaster to allow users to catch up with TV programmes that they have missed or watch live TV streams. Usage increased with modern Internet-enabled TVs, and the popularity of tablet PCs which are primarily being used for entertainment, which includes the consumption of streams. The reason why the first wave of connected TVs, called "Web TVs," failed, was because it had been assumed that people would use their TVs as computers, i.e. for browsing the Internet and reading eMail.[260] The new gener-

---

255 Boris Paal/Moritz Hennemann, *Schutz von Urheberrechten im Internet, ACTA, Warnhinweismodell und Europarecht,* MultiMedia und Recht 2012, 288.

256 For a list of legal online music stores in Europe, Africa and Russia see http://www.pro-music.org/Content/GetMusicOnline/stores-europe.php (last accessed 17.05.2014).

257 See country list Germany at http://www.pro-music.org/legal-music-services-europe.php (last accessed 07.07.2015).

258 Markus Beckedahl/Falk Lüke, *Wie die Musikbranche zum Internetgegner wurde*, Der Spiegel Online (23.05.2012).

259 *Ibid.*

260 See Mark Holzel, *The connected TV landscape: Why smart TVs and streaming gadgets are conquering the living room*, Business Insider (03.03.2014).

ation of Internet-enabled TVs has been considered a success story because they enhance the everyday experience of watching TV by offering a better viewing experience, as well as an alternative to TV recorders.[261] It needs to be noted, that – having an in-built browser – smart TVs also allow access to streaming websites that offer pirated content, which explains the fight of on-demand streaming services to provide their customers a better service than anyone else by having their digital traffic be treated favourably by Internet access providers. As long as this is not the case, rights-holders which seek revenues for the communication of their works to the public, are now seeking to have piracy websites blocked. Hence, already at this point, there is an indication that peer-to-peer file-sharers are becoming to some degree less interesting targets for rights-holders.

III. Existing Model Regimes for Online Intermediary Liability

1. Early Responses to File-Sharing: Legal Action against the Innovators

As aforementioned devices that make it possible for end-users to make copies of protected works are not novel. Accordingly, comparable conflict situations between the legitimate interests of authors on the one hand and the users of technical innovations on the other hand have already been addressed by case law in the past. The starting point has always been the same: a medium is made available that in addition to a lawful use can also be used to infringe copyright. The history of attempts to ban unauthorised copying by attempting to ban the device proves that going for the innovators is no solution to stop unauthorised copying. The earliest response to peer-to-peer file-sharing has been one that has been often employed to innovative copying devices in the past: the music industry sued the innovators like they had previously done with e.g. the Sony Betamax

261 *Ibid.*

recorder[262] or twin-deck tape recorders[263].[264] The US Supreme Court's decision in the *Betamax* case (*Sony Corp. v Universal City Studios*), at its time, created a legal safe haven for non-commercial home use recording of complete television programmes for purposes of time-shifting. While the entertainment industry argued that Sony was manufacturing a device that could be used for copyright infringement, and thus, Sony should be liable for any infringement committed by its purchasers, the Supreme Court held, that time-shifting, i.e. the process of recording television programmes so that they could be consumed at another time, constituted a commercially significant non-infringing use and was fair use. Accordingly, Sony could not be described as "contributing" to copyright infringement. Many of the same points of law that were litigated in the Betamax case were argued in the peer-to-peer lawsuits in the 1990s. Unsurprisingly, also the arguments used by the entertainment industry back in 1984 in the Betamax case are the same that were made against peer-to-peer technology in 1999 (Napster)[265] and 2005 (Grokster)[266].[267] With Napster gaining popularity during the late 1990s, a number of record companies and music publishers brought various claims, including contributory and vicarious liability for copyright infringement under US law. Napster, for its part, argued that its users could avail themselves of the fair use defence under US law, first on the basis of sampling the music before buying, and second, on the basis of space-shifting – that is, using the Napster system to

262 *Sony Corp. of America v Universal City Studios*, 464 U.S. 417 (1984).

263 In *CBS Songs v Amstrad* [1988] AC 1013, the House of Lords held that by marketing twin-deck tape recorders Armstrad did not "sanction, approve or countenance an infringing use of [its] model", it just "conferred on the purchaser the power to copy but did not grant or purport to grant the right to copy" and Amstrad had no "control over the use of [its] models once they [were] sold".Accordingly, Amstrad did not authorise copyright infringements and was not liable.

264 Lawsuits were filed against Scour, Aimster, AudioGalaxy, Morpheus, Grokster, Kazaa, iMesh, and LimeWire. See Electronic Frontier Foundation, *RIAA v the People: Five years later* (2008), p. 1.

265 17 U.S.C. *A&M Records. Inc. v Napster*. Inc. 114 F. Supp. 2d 896 (N. D. Cal. 2000), confirmed by *A&M Records, Inc. v Napster, Inc.*, 239 F.3d 1004 (9th Cir. 2001).

266 *Metro-Goldwyn-Mayer Studios, Inc. v Grokster, Ltd.* 125 S. Ct. 2764 (U.S.S.C. 2005), 380 F.3d 1154 (9th Cir. 2004), 259 F.Supp.2d 1029 (C.D. Calif. 2003).

267 A comparison of the arguments brought forward against the new technologies can be accessed at http://w2.eff.org/ legal/cases/betamax/.

make a copy of an audio CD of which they were already the legitimate owner.[268] Examining inter alia, the effect of the alleged fair use on the market, the US court in Napster considered a number of reports on the use of Napster and its effect of the sale of recorded music, and concluded that "having digital downloads for free on the Napster system necessarily harms the copyright-holders' attempts to charge for the same downloads".[269] The court concluded that file-sharing was not protected by the fair use provisions. The US Ninth Circuit Court of Appeals rejected the time-shifting argument that prevailed in the Betamax case. Napster was distinguished on the basis that the defendants operated a system that allowed them to monitor and control the potentially infringing activities of its users. In contrast to the time-shifting function of the Betamax recorder, which was held to be fair use, the crux with Napster was also the fact that while downloading the users made the copyright materials available to other members of the public.[270] Having established that there was no fair use and that Napster's users were directly infringing copyright, the court considered whether Napster could be liable for contributory infringement. Contributory liability required Napster to know, or having reason to know, of the direct infringement. While in the Betamax case, there had neither been evidence of actual knowledge of specific cases of infringement, nor did the Supreme Court assign constructive knowledge to Sony for infringing uses of its Betamax recorders (on the grounds that the equipment could be used for both infringing and "substantial non-infringing" uses), the Court of Appeals in Napster found that Napster had "actual knowledge that specific infringing material is available using its system, that it could block access to the system by suppliers of the infringing material, and that it failed to remove the material".[271] Napster's demise was primarily its centralised architecture, and its consequently alleged ability to both control content and prevent infringement. For subsequent peer network developers, it was hence important to create decentralised networks without a

---

268 The second argument was also used by Sony in the Betamax case, see *Sony Corp. of America v Universal City Studios*, 464 U.S. 417 (1984 *Sony Corp. of America v Universal City Studios*, 464 U.S. 417 (1984).

269 *A&M Records, Inc. v Napster, Inc.*, 239 F.3d 1004 (9th Cir. 2001), 1017.

270 "It is obvious that once a suers lists a copy of music he already owns on the Napster system in order to access the music from another location, the song becomes available to millions of other individuals, not just the original CD owner". *A&M Records, Inc. v Napster, Inc.*, 239 F.3d 1004 (9th Cir. 2001), 1019.

271 *Ibid*, 1022.

central entity that may control the content of the files being shared. This assumption was also being relied on by the defendants in Re: Aimster Copyright Litigation who argued that unlike Napster, they designed their technology in such a way that they had no way of monitoring the content of the files that were shared.[272] However, they could not escape liability. The US Seventh Circuit Appeals Court concluded that although Aimster could be used for entirely innocuous purposes, the defendants were turning a blind eye to the extent to which its system was being used to infringe copyright.[273] As "wilful blindness is knowledge in copyright law"[274], the defendants were liable for contributory infringement. In similar terms, the US Supreme Court held in 2005 that Grokster, which also worked decentralised, was liable as "one who distributes a device with the object of promoting its use to infringe copyright, as shown by clear expression or other affirmative steps taken to foster infringement, is liable for the resulting acts of third parties".[275] In the circumstances of Grokster, there was ample evidence that there had been both intent to promote, and actual promotion of infringing use sufficient to find Grokster liable for contributory infringement. This conduct went beyond the "equivocal conduct of selling an item with lawful and unlawful uses" in the Sony Betamax case.[276] The inducement arguments used in Grokster, enabled in the following more music industry victories in the US.[277]

Although the most prominent cases derive from the US, the US was not the only jurisdiction in which such cases were being heard. The supernode architecture which was employed by Grokster, was originally developed

---

272 *In Re: Aimster Copyright Litigation* 334 F 3d 643 (7th Cir. 2003) the Seventh Circuit addressed copyright infringement claims brought against Aimster, concluding that a preliminary injunction against the file-sharing service was appropriate, because the copyright owners were likely to prevail on their claims of contributory infringement.

273 In fact the only examples given in the explanatory tutorial about Aimster involved the sharing of copyrighted material, see *ibid*, 650.

274 *Ibid*, 650.

275 *MGM v Grokster*, 125 S. Ct. 2764 (2005), 2780.

276 *Ibid*, 2768.

277 This also in context of non-peer-to-peer technology in the case of *Arista Records LLC v Usenet.com Inc* (633 F.Supp.2d 124 (S.D.N.Y. 2009), where inducement was one of several grounds on which liability of an actual host provider was found. In a number of cases, the mere threat of court action has also been enough to close down sites. See Lilian Edwards, *Role and responsibility of Internet intermediaries in the field of copyright and related rights*, p. 22.

by the Dutch company KaZaa which was subsequently sued for distributing file-sharing software by the Dutch licensing organisation BUMA/STEMRA in the Netherlands. The Amsterdam Appeal Court found that although individual users might infringe copyright when file-sharing, the distributor of the software, KaZaa, was not liable on the basis that, because there was no central server, there could be no control over the files that were shared once the software had been installed on a user's computer. As in Grokster, it was also the case that the software could be, and was being, used for legal purposes, including the exchange of both copyright material with the permission of the copyright owner and also non-copyright-material. This reasoning was subsequently upheld by the Dutch Supreme Court in December 2003.[278] When the licence to distribute KaZaa was transferred to an Australian company, it was the Australian's courts time to give its opinion on the subject matter.[279]

Also in Germany, one of the countries which is in the focus of this research, developers and distributors of peer-to-peer software became subject to lawsuits for secondary liability. In Cybersky[280] for example, a German pay-TV provider sued the developers and intended distributor of a new free-of-charge peer-to-peer software called Cybersky TV and demanded that they refrain from offering, disseminating and/or operating the Cybersky TV software as long as this software could be used by end-users to send and/or receive encoded content (i.e. pay-per view and subscription only TV channels) on the Internet from the claimant's pay-TV programme as part of a peer-to-peer system.[281] Although the Court refused to give an opinion on the lawfulness of peer-to-peer software in light of

278 Gerechtshof Amsterdam, Decision of 28.03.2002 – 1370/01SKG *(KAZAA B.V.v. BUMA/STEMRA),* unauthorised English translation available at http://www.eff.org/IP/P2P/BUMA_v_KaZaA/20020328_KaZaA_ appeal_judgment.html (last accessed 17.05.2014).

279 *Universal Music Australia Pty Ltd v Sharman License Holdings Ltd* [2005] FCA 1242 [30]. The Australian Court found that the company was well aware that Kazaa was widely used to infringe copyright and concluded that Sharman was liable for copyright infringement because it had "authorised" Kazaa's users to infringe the record companies' copyrights.

280 OLG Hamburg, Decision of 08.02.2006 – 5 U 78/05 (*Cybersky*), International Review of Intellectual Property and Competition Law 2006, 989 with comment by Hannes Rösler.

281 The Cybersky designers described Cybersky TV as "free pay-TV". It was claimed that Cybersky TV could be as revolutionary for TV as the original Napster was for the music industry. See Hannes Rösler, *Comment to OLG Hamburg,*

intellectual property and competition law in general, it concluded that the supplier of a peer-to-peer software has a responsibility to take appropriate protective measures to the benefit of intellectual property rights-holder, in particular if the software developer has, in the product announcement, sales advertising or description of use, offered potential users the opportunity to infringe rights of others.[282] This responsibility exists irrespective of any primary or secondary liability for copyright infringements of the defendants. The Court stressed that if an – although possibly only small – percentage of the purchasers use the software for purposes that do not interfere in third-party copyright, a general prohibition on the marketing of the medium may constitute an abuse of the law.[283] Nevertheless, the Court issued the requested interlocutory injunction which practically constituted a complete prohibition on sales.[284] To avoid a further injunction against distribution, the defendants would have to employ reasonable and suitable mechanisms necessary to prevent future infringements as effectively as possible. Although the court explicitly rejected a reference to the US *Grokster* case, it accepts the "Janus-faced nature" of peer-to-peer networks with similar standards.[285]

In France or the UK, on which this study focusses, there have been no major cases taken against the developers and distributors of file-sharing software. However, especially in the UK, there has been some speculation as to whether the courts would follow the approach by the Australian court in the KaZaa case or whether they would use a similar approach as in the twin-deck tape recorders case, in which the House of Lords held that Amstrad's production of twin-deck tape recorders did not, of itself, indicate that Amstrad authorised copyright infringement, because the devices

---

decision of 08.02.2006 – 5 U 78/05 (Cybersky), International Review of Intellectual Property and Competition Law 2006, 994.

282 OLG Hamburg, Decision of 08.02 – 5 U 78/05 (*Cybersky*), International Review of Intellectual Property and Competition Law 2006, 989, 991. It has to be noted that by the time the German pay-TV provider took the defendants to court, Cybersky TV had not yet been launched. Thus, the claimant sought to obtain an injunction preventing the launch of Cybersky TV in its planned format.

283 *Ibid*, 992 et seq.

284 For the reasons see *ibid*, 993 et seq.

285 Hannes Rösler, *Comment to OLG Hamburg, decision of 08.02.2006 – 5 U 78/05 (Cybersky)*, International Review of Intellectual Property and Competition Law 2006, 994, 996.

could be used for both infringing and non-infringing purposes.[286] In this respect, it has to be noted that the US case law with regard to Napster and Grokster is of limited guidance when discussing the issue of primary infringement by authorisation under UK law. The concept of secondary liability discussed in the US cases does not exist in the majority of civil law countries in Europe.[287] This also applies to the Dutch and German cases even if the German court applied similar standards. At all, an analysis of this subject matter would go beyond the scope of this research, but the discussion highlights that courts will struggle to find a developer and provider of file-sharing software liable if he has no control over the individual usage of the software, and if there are substantial non-infringing purposes. Where liability had been established, this always was due to the developer or operator having some kind of control over a central server or inciting the use of the software for infringing purposes.

The worldwide case law with regard to early file-sharing technology highlight that although Napster and subsequent file-sharing systems were content-neutral, meaning that they could and in fact were also being used for non-infringing purposes, including sharing of authorised songs, public domain works, the record industry has won most of these lawsuits.[288] From an economical point of view, the victories ultimately did not bring the sought after results. Already the lawsuit against Napster showed that this track is not very effective: the attention that Napster got due to the media publicity let to an increase in users, and following its eventual shutdown, new networks with new technologies quickly emerged. The latter responded to the legal developments. While the early peer-to-peer technology was likely to trigger liability (provided that there has been some sort of encouragement or incitement to indulge in illegal file-sharing and the

---

286 As regards the discussion of whether the providers of file-sharing software authorise copyright infringement see Haflidi Kristjan Larusson, *Uncertainty in the scope of copyright: the case of illegal file-sharing in the UK*, European Intellectual Property Review 2009, Vol. 31 Issue 3, 124, 128; Simon Stokes, *Digital Copyright* (2nd ed. Hart Publishing 2005), pp.134–135.

287 Diane Rowland/Uta Kohl/ Andrew Charlesworth, *Information Technology Law* (4th ed. 2012), p. 340.

288 As regards Napster: 17 U.S.C. *A&M Records. Inc. v Napster. Inc.* 114 F. Supp. 2d 896 (N. D. Cal. 2000), confirmed by *A&M Records, Inc. v Napster, Inc.*, 239 F.3d 1004 (9th Cir. 2001); as regards Aimster: *Re Aimster Copyright Litigation* 334 F 3d 643 (7th Cir. 2003); as regards Grokster: *Metro-Goldwyn-Mayer Studios, Inc. v Grokster, Ltd.* 125 S. Ct. 2764 (U.S.S.C. 2005).

operators failed to prevent or reduce the extent of infringements), the third generation of file-sharing technology makes it difficult to establish liability on part of the developers or providers. BitTorrent software now enables users to download large files in small blocks of data from multiple sources, while the software itself does not provide users with the tools to actually locate files. BitTorrent users act completely autonomous and there is no central chokepoint. This makes it more difficult to actually prove intent on behalf of the providers of BitTorrent software with regard to induce users to breach copyright.[289] In fact, many providers are now being more careful and ask users not to use the software for infringing purposes. New variations of peer-to-peer technology may also provide for encryption of the content being shared, so that the legal detection of copyright infringement becomes more difficult.[290] Encryption is perfectly legal, and the users sharing files may also have legitimate reasons to hide the content.

The road to sue the innovators thus may have reached a dead end, and this seems to be the reason why lately the rights-holders refrained from suing the innovators of peer-to-peer file-sharing software for copyright infringements. However, recently, the popularity of file-hosting services meant that rights-holders turned their attention towards these providers. The case law in this regard will be assessed in the third Chapter, but at this point it shall already be stressed, that file-hosters are unlikely to be held liable for copyright infringements by their users, but may be liable to prevent repeat infringements from taking place via their servers.[291] With regard to file-hosters, more or less the same technology is used as regards cloud computing, which is an accepted lawful service. Accordingly, the file-hosting service as such has been declared lawful within several jurisdictions,[292] as long as they do not employ a scheme that rewards uploaders based on the number of downloads that they generate and by this make it attractive for users to upload copyrighted works in order to trigger as

---

289 See Diane Rowland/Uta Kohl/ Andrew Charlesworth, *Information Technology Law* (4th ed. 2012), p. 339.

290 These systems may not be used by the majority file-sharers for lack of advanced IT literacy.

291 See Chapter 3.

292 For a summary of the German case law, see Rolf Danckwerts, *Neues vom Störer: Was ist ein „von der Rechtsordnung gebilligtes Geschäftsmodell"?,* GRUR-Prax 2011, 260. The sharehosting models that have been declared legitimate do not use reward systems for uploading content.

many downloads as possible.[293] For example, Megaupload used to reward one million downloads with $ 1,500.[294] Such reward schemes may obviously encourage users to upload copyrighted materials and publish the link granting access to the material to the general public. This again can be regarded as an incitement to infringe copyright and trigger liability (civil as well as criminal) for an otherwise content-neutral service. In fact, in the case of Megaupload, this lead to the seizure of Megaupload's assets, the detention of its operators, and the shutdown of the site on 19 January 2012 by the US Department of Justice.[295] Similarly, kino.to[296], a streaming portal targeting German consumers was shut down, its assets seized,[297] and its operators held criminally liable by a German criminal court for making publicly available copyrighted works.[298] In this case, it was again not the technology as such that led to the convictions of the operators, but the fact that they had actual knowledge of every single infringing file that was disseminated via their service as they operated a scheme where every file had to be approved manually.[299] Because the operators of kino.to resided within the European Union, they could be arrested and brought before a German court. In contrast, the operators of Megaupload have not been convicted yet, and as they reside in New Zealand enforcement depends on extradition to the US.[300]

---

293 Such as for example Megaupload.

294 Tobias Lauinger/Engin Kirda/Pietro Michiardi, *Paying for Piracy? An Analysis of One-Click Hosters' Controversial Reward Schemes,* in: Davide Balzarotti/ Salvatore J. Stolfo/Marco Cova (eds.), *Research in attacks, intrusions, and defenses 2012,* Lecture Notes in Computer Science Vol. 7462 (2012), p. 169.

295 See Ben Sisario, *7 Charged as F.B.I. Closes a Top File-Sharing Site*, The New York Times (20.01.2012).

296 According to the Internet ranking website Alexa, kiNo.to was accessed up to 4 million times per day, and could be ranked within the 50 most visited websites in Germany until June 2011. See LG Leipzig, Decision of 14.06.2012 – 11 KLs 390 Js 191/11 (*kiNo.to*), Zeitschrift für Urheber- und Medienrecht 2013, 338, 340.

297 Thorsten Ricke/Fabian Wild, *Konten in Sachen „kiNo.to" beschlagnahmt*, MultiMedia und Recht-Aktuell 2011, 319492.

298 LG Leipzig, decision of 14.06.2012 – 11 KLs 390 Js 191/11 (*kino.to*), Zeitschrift für Urheber- und Medienrecht 2013, 338.

299 *Ibid*, 340 and 345.

300 David Fisher, *Dotcom trial may not occur*, The New Zealand Herald (21.04.2012). An extradition hearing was set for June 2015, but has been delayed to September 2015, see Morgan Tait, *Dotcom extradition hearing delayed,* The New Zealand Herald (01.05.2015).

Although these cases do not directly concern the innovators of new technologies, but moreover those of new business schemes, they highlight additional hurdles that rights-holders may have to face, namely that the innovators/operators reside outside a jurisdiction where they could be held accountable. Additionally, they once more prove that the operators need to play an active role that goes beyond the mere provision of a content-neutral technology so that liability may established.[301]

Hence, as aforementioned, taking the innovators of new technologies to court, can only be successful under very limited circumstances and is a route that most rights-holders have left. In a bid to constrain unlawful file-sharing, the rights-holders have also initiated actions against Internet service providers. Internet service providers are an obvious target for those wishing to gain some recompense for violation of their rights, especially in situations where the actual infringer cannot be identified or is located in another jurisdiction. There are some different approaches to the question of the extent of the liability of service providers depending on whether they are acting merely as a conduit, provide the means of transmission, or are capable of having some control over at least some of the material to which they provide access. Access providers as the natural gatekeepers to the Internet were seen as the most effective actors to control the distribution of illegal and harmful content as they are not only identifiable actors, but also locatable, and in most cases situated in the same jurisdiction.[302] However, turning to these gatekeepers also turned out impractical. They effectively lacked practical control: the volume of material and the dynamic nature of it was impossible for them to control.[303] They also

---

301 In this respect, it can also be assumed that the severity of the custodial sentences of the defendants in the Swedish The Pirate Bay case results from the attitude of the defendants to file-sharing and copyright infringement evidenced by their comments on the website – they "had made it clear that they were not going to take any action to put an end to such dissemination, even in cases where there could be no doubt that it was in violation of individual identified rights" (Jerker Edstrom/Henrik Nillson, *The Pirate Bay verdict – predictable, and yet...*, European Intellectual Property Review 2009, Vol. 31 Issue 9, 483, 487).

302 Diane Rowland/Uta Kohl/ Andrew Charlesworth, *Information Technology Law* (4th ed. 2012), p. 341.

303 BT Internet estimated in 1999 that just to effectively monitor news-group traffic alone, they would need 1500 employees working 24 hours a day. See Lilian Edwards, *Role and responsibility of Internet intermediaries in the field of copyright and related rights*, p. 5, citing material from a WIPO Workshop on Service Provider Liability.

lacked the legal control to monitor all communication of their customers and feared liability for interferences that later would turn out unjustified. While in the advent of the Internet, the distinction between different types of intermediaries was relatively clear cut, this changed in the 1990s in the advent of web 2.0. The distinction between a traditional Internet access provider, who merely provided "fundamental communication services such as success, information storage etc."[304] and an Internet service provider, who provided "some additional service which facilitates a transaction between end users, e.g. identifying one of the parties, providing search facilities etc."[305] became less important with service providers giving access to large amounts of in-house as well as third party produced content.[306] The arrival of interactive user-generated content or user-mediated content further meant that host provider liability has become increasingly controversial. Holding host providers as well as access providers and other intermediaries responsible equals "shooting the messenger". The new millennium started with a number of immunity regimes for copyright infringements such as § 512 of the US *Digital Millennium Copyright Act 1998* (*DMCA*) and the *E-Commerce Directive* of 2000. These legal instruments introduced liability exemptions for Internet service providers in relation to copyright infringements, of which in particular the provisions for hosting content are of interest, because more than the access provider which is a mere communications carrier, does the host provider have certain control over the content hosted. Both instruments purport to provide Internet service providers with immunity from suit provided that they are not acting as a content provider and have no involvement with the actual information transmitted via their networks. This was necessary in order to not disturb the proper functioning and development of the worldwide net. While it is obvious from the wording of the provisions on access providers that they cannot be held accountable for copyright infringements committed via their service, host providers – as already mentioned – are in a position to have or acquire knowledge of the contents hosted and hence, remove or block access to illegal content. Due to the vast case law on this subject matter, the following sections will address the development of limited liability in the US and Europe in more detail.

---

304 Chris Reed, *Internet Law: Texts and Materials* (2nd ed. 2004), p. 89.

305 *Ibid.*

306 See Lilian Edwards, *Role and responsibility of Internet intermediaries in the field of copyright and related rights,* p. 4.

2. The Development of Limited Liability

Early cases, mainly from the US, that had to deal with liability for hosting, transmitting or publishing material that was illegal, saw traditional concepts applied to news publishers applied to Internet service providers.[307] For example, the New York Supreme Court held that the Internet service provider *Prodigy* was liable as a publisher of the content generated by its users because it exercised editorial control over the messages on its bulletin boards by posting guidelines for users and enforcing these with the help of so called board leaders as well as utilising screening software designed to remove offensive language.[308]

The decision was widely seen as encouraging Internet service providers not to monitor the content of bulletin boards since they might become subject to the strict liability standard applied to publishers rather than the knowledge standard applicable to distributors. Internet service providers were also not keen to check the legality of content due to sheer amount of material passing through their servers. However, while it may not be possible for them to manually check all content, Yahoo proved to be unsuccessful with its defense that it was also technically impossible for Yahoo US to block access to "all persons from France" to pages on its site selling Nazi Memorablia in a case before a French court in 2000.[309] A technical sub-committee reported to the court that Yahoo! had the capacity to identify and thus block access to 90% of French Citizens. While this decision concerned location-based blocking and not content-based blocking, it latter turned out ineffective as the judgement condemning Yahoo to take steps to prevent French Internet users from accessing the sections of the Yahoo auction site containing Nazi memorabilia, could not be enforced in the US, domicile of Yahoo Inc. An US court granted a summary judgement in favour of Yahoo Inc. declaring that the "First Amendment pre-

307 Cf. for example *Cubby v CompuServe* 766 F Supp 135 (SDNY 1991), *Stratton Oakmont, Inc. v Prodigy Services Co.*, 1995 WL 323710 (NY Sup. Ct. 1995).

308 *Stratton Oakmont, Inc. v Prodigy Services Co.*, 1995 WL 323710 (NY Sup. Ct. 1995).

309 TGI Paris, Decision of 20.11.2000 – RG No. 00/05308 (*La Ligue contre le racisme et l'antisémitisme et al. v Yahoo Inc)*, available at http://www.juriscom.net/txt/jurisfr/cti/tgiparis20001120.pdf (last accessed 10.05.2011).

cludes enforcement within the United States of a French order intended to regulate the content of its speech over the Internet".[310]

Irrespective of monitoring capacities, Internet service providers also argued that they were mere messengers and not content providers, and thus it would be inequitable to hold them responsible.[311] Liability for content generated by third parties would also mean uneconomic burdens and pose a threat to a necessary evolving information infrastructure and emerging businesses.[312]

Thus, legal frameworks for Internet service provider developed from the mid-1990s onwards. The legal regimes took different approaches: either "horizontal", dealing with the liability of Internet service providers across all types of content such as for example the German *Gesetz über die Nutzung von Telediensten* (*TDG*) of 1997 or the *E-Commerce Directive* of 2000, or "vertical", regulating specific domains such as for example § 230 (c) of Title V of the *Telecommunications Act of 1996*[313] or the UK *Defamation Act of 1996*. The first vertical regulatory models did not address copyright, which came into the focus from 1998 onwards.

a) The Leading Model Regimes Relating to Intellectual Property

aa) The US Digital Millennium Copyright Act

The *Digital Millenium Copyright Act* constitutes the US implementation of the 1996 *WIPO Copyright Treaty*.[314] The *DMCA* was "designed to facilitate the robust development and world-wide expansion of electronic commerce, communications, research, development, and education in the

---

310 *Yahoo Inc. v La Ligue contre le racisme et l'antisémitisme and others,* 169 F.Supp. 2d 1181 (N.D. Cal. 2001), p. 22.

311 Cf. Lilian Edwards, *Role and responsibility of Internet intermediaries in the field of copyright and related rights,* p. 6.

312 *Ibid.*

313 § 230 (c) is commonly known the *Communications Decency Act of 1996* and bars immunity from all kinds of liability for third party content except IP.

314 *World Intellectual Property Organization Copyright Treaty*. The text of the Treaty is available at: http://www.wipo.int/ treaties/en/ip/wct/trtdocs_wo033.htm l; an up-to-date list of the Contracting Parties can be found at: http://www.wipo.i nt/treaties/en/ShowResults.jsp?lang=en&treaty_id=16.

digital age."[315] The relevant provision with regard to immunity of Internet service providers within the *Copyright Act* is 17 U.S.C. § 512, or the *Online Infringement Liability Limitation Act* (*OCILLA*). In order to strike a balance between the respective interests of service providers and copyright owners, the OCILLA seeks to "preserve ... strong incentives for service providers and copyright owners to cooperate to detect and deal with copyright infringements that take place in the digital networked environment".[316] § 512 distinguishes between different functions carried out by intermediaries: "mere conduit",[317] system caching,[318] hosting[319] and information location tools[320]. Accordingly, it sets up four conditional liability exemptions with regard to copyright infringement liability, that are commonly referred to as "safe harbours".

A service provider in the sense of § 512 (b) to (d) is defined as "a provider of online services or network access, or the operator of facilities therefor" [321]. The latter definition is broader than definitions of service providers in earlier drafted statutes such as § 230 of the *Communications Decency Act 1996* (*CDA*), which is due to the fact that it was drafted in the advent of web 2.0.[322] The legislator paid regard to the variety of functionalities of web 2.0 services available at that time and courts thus could apply the provision on typical web 2.0 online merchants such as Amazon.com's shops[323] or eBay[324] without any problems.

---

315 See Senate, *Digital Millennium Copyright Act*, Report, S. Rep. No. 105–190 (1998), 1 et seq.

316 *Ibid*, 20; House of Representatives, *Digital Millennium Copyright Act of 1998*, Report, H.R. Rep. No. 105–551 (1998), Part II, 49.

317 § 512 (a) "Transitory digital network communications"; A service provider in the sense of § 512 (a) is defined as "an entity offering transmission, routing, or providing connections for digital online communications, between or among points specified by a user, of material of the user's choosing, without modification to the content of the material as sent or received" (§ 512 (k)(1)(A)).

318 § 512 (b) "system caching".

319 § 512 (c) Information Residing on Systems or Networks at Direction of Users

320 § 512 (d).

321 § 512 (k) (1) (B).

322 Lilian Edwards/Waelde, Charlotte, *Online intermediaries and liability for copyright infringement* (2005), p.11.

323 *Corbis Corp. v Amazon.com. Inc.*, 351 F. Supp. 2d 1090, 1100 (W.D. Wash. 2004) ("There is no doubt that Amazon fits within the definition.").

324 *Hendrickson v eBay, Inc.*, 165 F. Supp. 2d 1082, 1088 (C.D. Cal.) ("eBay clearly meets the *DMCA*'s broad definition of online 'service provider.'").

Each limitation bars monetary damages for direct, vicarious and contributory infringement, and restricts the availability of injunctive relief in various respects.

In order to qualify for any of the limitations on liability the service provider must adopt and reasonably implement "a policy that provides for the termination in appropriate circumstances of subscribers and account holders of the service provider's system or network who are repeat infringers".[325] Additionally, the service provider must accommodate and not interfere with "standard technical measures"[326], meaning such measures that copyright owners use to identify or protect copyrighted works.[327] Systems that interfere with certain anti-piracy devices will not be able to benefit from the liability limitations established by the *DMCA*.

In addition to the two general requirements listed above, all four safe harbour provisions impose additional requirements to benefit from immunity.

§ 512 (a), which limits the liability of mere passive conduits for the transmission of copyright infringing material, applies if infringing material is being transmitted at the request of a third party to a designated recipient, is handled by an automated process without human intervention, is not modified in any way, and is only temporarily stored on the system.[328]

The key difference in scope between this section, and § 512 (b) to (d) relates to the location of the material in question. § 512 (b) to (d) refer to infringing material that resides on a system controlled by the service provider.

The liability exemption for system caching applies when a service provider engages in caching of online content for purposes of improving

---

325 Section 512 (i) (1) (A). This policy must also be communicated to the users. Courts have been very liberal with regard to valid communication, holding that it requires nothing more than a warning to users in their terms of use statements of their repeat-infringer policy, see *Corbis Corp v Amazon.com, Inc*, 351 F. Supp. 2d 1090, 1101 (W.D. Wash. 2004); In *re Aimster Copyright litigation*, 252 F.Supp.2d 634, 658 (N.D. Ill. 2002).

326 Section 512 (i) (1) (B).

327 The measures must have been developed pursuant to a broad consensus of copyright owners and service providers in an open, fair and voluntary multi-industry process, and must be available to anyone on reasonable nondiscriminatory terms. Further, they must not impose substantial costs or burdens on service providers. See § 512 (i).

328 § 512 (a) (1)–(5).

network performance. The exemption applies under the condition that the cached material is not modified, the service provider complies with industry standard rules regarding the refreshing, reloading, or other updating of the cached material, and the service provider does not interfere with the ability of technology that returns hit count information that would otherwise have been collected had the website not been cached.[329] In addition, the service provider must impose the same conditions that the original poster of the material required for access, and he must remove or block access to any material that is posted without the copyright owner's authorisation, upon being notified that such material has been previously removed from the originating site, or that the copyright owner has obtained a court order for the material to be removed from the originating site or access to the material be disabled.[330]

§ 512 (d) creates a safe harbour for service providers that links users, through a tool such as a web search engine, to an online location that contains infringing material, under the condition that the service provider does not know the material is infrining. Once the service provider becomes aware of facts or circumstances from which infringing activity is apparent, he must expeditiously remove or disable access to the content.[331] If the service provider controls the infringing activity, he must not derive any financial benefit through the provision of the link.[332]

Of specific interest in the context of file-sharing is § 512(c), which limits the liability of service providers for infringing material on websites hosted on their systems. A service provider is only protected from liability if copyrights have been infringed by reason of the storage of material at the direction of a user. Information will not be stored at the direction of a user when "it resides on the system or network operated by or for the service provider through its own acts or decisions".[333] Courts interpreted the notion broadly and in at least one case a service provider was not precluded from the § 512 (c) safe harbour even when his employees engaged in

329 § 512 (b) (2) (A)–(C).

330 § 512 (b) (2) (D)–(E).

331 § 512 (d) (1), (3).

332 § 512 (d) (2).

333 House of Representatives, *Digital Millenium Copyright Act of 1998*, Report, H.R. Rep. No. 105–551 (1998), Part II, 53.

some brief review of submitted materials before posting them on the website.[334]

In order to be eligible for the limitation the service provider must not know of the infringement or act expeditiously to remove or disable access to the material when it has actual knowledge, is aware of facts or circumstances from which infringing activity is apparent or has received *DMCA*-compliant notice; and additionally does not have the right and ability to control the infringing activity, or – if he does – does not receive a financial benefit directly attributable to the infringing activity. A right and ability to control infrining activities requires some kind of direct supervision by the service provider of the direct infringers.[335] If an ability to control content is established then there must be no fincancial benefit deriving from the infringing activity.[336]

Three types of knowledge of infringement can be identified which can take a service provider out of the safe harbour: (1) the service provider can have actual knowledge of infringement; (2) it can be aware of facts which

---

334 *CoStar Group Inc. v LoopNet, Inc*, 164 F.Supp. 2d 688, 701 et seq. (D. Md. 2001), affirmed by 373 F.3d 544 (4th Cir. 2004). In *Costar Group, Inc. v LoopNet, Inc.,* the defendant offered a service that enabled subscribers to upload real estate photos to a folder on the defendant's system. Defendant's employees briefly reviewed the submitted photos and posted to the website only those that met defendant's criteria-that is, any photos that did not depict real estate or which obviously were copyrighted by a third-party would not be posted. The court held that defendant nonetheless satisfied the requirement that material be stored at the direction of a user.

335 See *Corbis Corp. v Amazon.com. Inc*., 351 F. Supp. 2d 1090, 1109 (W.D. Wash. 2004). Courts have also held that the mere ability to disable access to or remove infringing content (*IO Group, Inc. v Veoh Networks*, Inc., 586 F. Supp. 2d 1132, 1151 (N.D. Cal. 2008); Perfect 10, Inc. V CCBill LLC, 488 F.3d 1102, 1117 (9th Cir. 200/); *Corbis Corp. v Amazon.com. Inc*., 351 F. Supp. 2d 1090, 1109 (W.D. Wash. 2004); *Hendrickson v eBay, Inc*., 165 F. Supp. 2d 1082 (C.D. Cal. 2001)), or enforcing policies that prohibit users from engaging in illegal or unauthorised conduct (*IO Group, Inc. v Veoh Networks*, Inc., 586 F. Supp. 2d 1132, 1153 et seq. (N.D. Cal. 2008)), do not constitute sufficient prove for the right and ability to control. On the other hand, screening and filtering of content may establish exercising an ability to control content (*Corbis Corp. v Amazon.com. Inc*., 351 F. Supp. 2d 1090, 1110 (W.D. Wash. 2004)).

336 The House Report instructs that there will be no financial benefit "where the infringer makes the same kind of payment as non-infringing users of the provider's service", see House of Representatives, *Digital Millenium Copyright Act of 1998*, Report, H.R. Rep. No. 105–551 (1998), Part II, 54.

raise a "red flag" that its users are infringing; or (3) the copyright owner can notify the service provider in a manner "substantially" conforming with § 512 (c) (3) that its works are being infringed. A court will first examine whether the service provider had actual knowledge of infringing activity. The dominant means by which knowledge will be established is a notification satisfying the statutory requirements of § 512 (c) (2) (A), (c) (3) (A).[337] In addition to the formal requirements described above, the *DMCA* also provides that a take-down notice must be notified to the alleged infringer, who then has the opportunity to file a counter-notice with the service provider's designated agent and protest that the material should not be removed.[338]

---

337 To be effective the notification of a claimed infringement has to be in writing and fulfil the following requirements: it must include sufficient information to contact the complaining party and a signature (either physical or electronic) of the complaining party, sufficient information to identify the copyrighted work or works claimed to have been infringed, the infringing matter and its Internet location, a statement by the complaining party that it has a good faith belief that there is no legal basis for the use of the materials complained of, and a statement of the accuracy of the notice and, under penalty of perjury, that the complaining party is authorised to act on behalf of the owner of an exclusive right that is allegedly infringed. If a notification fails to comply substantially with the requirements it will not be considered in determining knowledge or awareness of illegal content (§ 512 (c) (3) (B) (i)). However, if the notifier identifies the allegedly infringed work, and the material that is allegedly being infringed and contact information for the comlaining party is provided, then the service provider must contact the copyright owner and request the rest of the notice requirements (§ 512 (c) (3) (B) (ii)). If the service provider fails to contact the copyright owner and does not insist upon receiving a correct notice, then the service provider will be deemed to have received correct notice (Debra Weinstein, *Defining expeditious: Uncharted territory of the DMCA safe harbor provision – A survey of what we know and do not know about the expeditiousness of service provider responses to take down notifications*, 26 Cardozo Arts & Entertainment Law Journal 2009, Vol. 26, 589, 601).

338 § 512 (g) (3) "counternotification"; A valid counter-notification requires inter alia a "statement under penalty of perjury that the subscriber has a good faith belief that the material was removed or disabled as a result of mistake or misidentification of the material to be removed or disabled". In case that the alleged infringer protests against the removal, the content in question must be "put back" by the Internet service provider. If the original notifier continues to dispute the legality of the content in question, the argument must be taken to court. Within that period of time – while the dispute is in progress – the Internet service provider is free from liability, even if in the end a court finds the content was illicit. This procedure serves as a safeguard to discourage unfounded take down requests and pre-

If the notification is insufficient, the notifier may seek to prove under § 512 (c) (1) (A) (ii) that the service provider is aware of "facts or circumstances from which infringing activity is apparent". The test to establish awareness consists of two elements: the first determining whether the service provider is aware of circumstances of infringement (objective component) and the second determines whether infringing activity would have been apparent to a reasonable person operating under the same or similar circumstances (subjective component).[339]

Infringing material needs to be removed or disabled access to it expeditiously. The meaning of "expeditious" is to be determined by the US courts. During the legislative process the US Senate argued that because "factual circumstances and technical parameters may vary from case to case, it is not possible to identify a uniform time limit for expeditious action".[340]

bb) The E-Commerce Directive 2000/31/EC

The *E-Commerce Directive* 2000/31/EC, via its national transpositions, constitutes the main regulatory framework on liability for Internet services throughout the European Union. The *E-Commerce Directive* was drafted at a time when only few Member States already had specific E-Commerce provisions in place. The consensus reached in the negotiations on the Directive was that so far the limitations on liability for online content should only deal with the most general and problematic barriers to Internet service providers.[341] It is drafted very broadly, and thus its liability regimes does not only apply to the traditional Internet service providers,

---

vents any overhasty take down of contents. It is not for the Internet service provider to examine whether the content provider has a defence, e.g. fair use, as the Internet service provider also regularly lacks the legal expertise.

339 House of Representatives, *Digital Millenium Copyright Act of 1998*, Report, H.R. Rep. No. 105 – 551 (1998), Part II, 53; see also Liliana Chang, *The red flag test for apparent knowledge under the DMCA § 512 (c) Safe Harbor*, Cardozo Arts & Entertainment Law Journal, Vol. 28, 195, 201 et seq.

340 See Senate, *Digital Millenium Copyright Act*, Report, S. Rep. No. 105-190 (1998), 44.

341 Department of Trade and Industry, *Consultation Document on Electronic Commerce Directive: the liability of Hyperlinkers, Location Tool Services and Content Aggregators* (June 2005), http://www.berr.gov.uk/files/file13986.pdf, p.10.

but a much wider range of actors including e-commerce merchants, social network sits and even cloud computing services.[342]

As is the case with EC Directives generally, the provisions of the *E-Commerce Directive* are not directly applicable in the Member States; it requires implementing measures by the Member States and is only binding as to a specific result to be achieved without dictating the means of achieving that result. It thereby leaves a margin of discretion to the Member States. In many Member States the Directive was implemented into national law almost verbatim from the specific language version.[343]

In order to assess the impact the Directive had on the liability regime in Europe it is necessary to examine the individual national implementation and its application. The underlying question is whether the attempt to harmonise the law regarding the liability of Internet service providers has been successful.

The *E-Commerce Directive* applies to "information society services" which are defined in Article 2 (a) as "any service normally provided for remuneration, at a distance, by means of electronic equipment for the processing (including digital compression) and storage of data, and at the individual request of a recipient of a service".[344] Recital 18 of the Directive states explicitly that services which are free of charge to the recipient do not fall outside the scope of an "information society service" if they broadly form part of an economic activity. Thus, not only the traditional Internet service provider sector but also providers offering online information or search tools are covered under certain conditions.[345] Although the CJEU held that the Google's "Adwords" referencing service falls, under certain conditions, within the scope of a host provider, this does not conclusively settle the matter of whether Google's cost-free search engine ser-

342 Cf. Lilian Edwards, *Role and responsibility of Internet intermediaries in the field of copyright and related rights*, p. 8.

343 Cf. *Electronic commerce (EC Directive) Regulation 2002* (UK); *Loi du 14 août 2000 relative au commerce électronique* (Luxembourg).

344 Article 2 (a) *E-Commerce Directive* refers back to the definition in Article1 (2) of *Directive 98/34/EC* as amended by *Directive 98/48/EC.*

345 This has recently been confirmed by the CJEU in Joined cases C-236/08 to C-238/08, *Google France, Google Inc. v Louis Vuitton Malletier, Google France v Viaticum Luteciel, Google France v CNRRH Pierre-Alexis Thonet, Bruno Raboin, Tiger, a franchisee of Unicis,* Judgment of 23.03.2010, ECR [2010] I-02417 *(Google Adwords).*

vice falls within the application of the Directive, as the Directive itself does not contain a provision on linking liability immunity.

Articles 12–14 of the *E-Commerce Directive* sets up liability limitations of Internet service providers for third party content when they act in one of the intermediary roles identified by the Directive, i.e. mere conduit (Article 12), caching (Article 13), and hosting (Article 14). These various activities are addressed separately.

Unlike the US, the European Community chose to take a horizontal approach in determining intermediary service provider liability. So rather than focusing on a single area of law, the liability regime deals with all content issues. The rationale behind this seems to be that all intermediaries are carrying out the same technical activities regardless of the content involved.[346] Thus, the liability limitations apply to all kinds of illegal material provided by third parties, including inter alia copyright, trademark, defamatory statements, hate speech and pornography. However, certain activities are excluded including the activities of notaries and gambling. The limitations apply to civil as well as criminal liability, but do not prevent the imposition of injunctions upon Internet service providers.

The liability limitations set forth by the Directive have been classified as defences[347] and as a kind of pre-filter in proceedings where a claim is directed against an intermediary with regard to third-party content.[348]

An intermediary who falls within the definition of a mere conduit is essentially no more than a telephonic network. Pursuant to Article 12 *E-Commerce Directive*, a mere conduit that does not 'initiate the transmission', 'select the receiver of the transmission' or 'select or modify the information', is absolved from all liability. This service provider is thus not liable for damages or for any criminal sanction as a result of any transmission of information.

Caching describes the process by which intermediary service provider store information temporarily in order to allow users the access to web pages more quickly. The service provider retains the material so that sub-

---

346 Miquel Peguera, *The DMCA Safe Harbors and Their European Counterparts: A Comparative Analysis of Some Common Problems,* Columbia Journal of Law & the Arts 2009, Vol. 32, 481, 482.

347 Andrew Murray, *Information Technology Law* (2nd ed. 2013), p. 185.

348 Deutscher Bundestag, Bundestagsdrucksache 13/7385 (09.04.1997), p. 51; BGH, Decision of 23.09. 2003 – VI ZR 335/02, GRUR 2004, 74; Köhler/Arndt/Fezer, *Recht des Internet* (6th ed. 2008), para. 746.

sequent requests for the same material can be fulfilled by transmitting the retained copy, rather than retrieving the material from the original source on the network. Pursuant to Article 13 *E-Commerce Directive*, this kind of automatic, temporary storage of information for the sole purpose of making more efficient onward transmission of information does not render a service provider liable for the content of the cached pages. The immunity is lost if the service provider does not act quickly to remove a copy of a page where it has actual knowledge that the initial source has been removed or that a court has ordered its removal.

The most relevant and at the same time the most controversial liability regime is the regime governing the act of hosting. Pursuant to Article 14 of the *E-Commerce Directive* hosting services are services that "consist of the storage of information provided by a recipient of the service". Furthermore hosting services are "of a mere technical, automatic and passive nature, which implies that the information society service provider has neither knowledge of nor control over the information which is transmitted or stored".[349]

Under Article 14 of the *E-Commerce Directive* a host provider shall not be liable for the information stored at the request of a recipient on the condition that :

> "(a) the provider does not have actual knowledge of illegal activity or information and, as regards claims for damages, is not aware of facts or circumstances from which the illegal activity or information is apparent; or
> (b) the provider, upon obtaining such knowledge or awareness, acts expeditiously to remove or to disable access to the information."

The last condition imposes a duty of care on the provider. He has to take expeditious action if he obtains knowledge or awareness of the illegality of information. Recital 48 provides that the Directive does not affect the possibility for Member States to require host providers to apply duties of care, which can reasonably be expected from them and which are specified by national law, in order to detect and prevent certain types of illegal activities.[350] However,

349 Recital 42 of the *E-Commerce Directive*.

350 It has been understood that such duties of care mean those imposed by criminal or public law e.g. aid in investigation of crime or security matters, not as extending to duties under private law, such as to help prevent copyright infringement – since that would negate the point of Article 15 as well as that of Article 14 gener-

Article 15 of the *E-Commerce Directive* prohibits Member States from imposing a general obligation on information society services to monitor the information which they transmit or store, or to request that providers actively seek out facts or circumstances indicating illegal activity. This does not mean that monitoring is in general prohibited. Moreover, Article 14 (3) clarifies that the prohibition of general monitoring does not affect the possibility for a court or national authority of requiring the service provider to terminate or prevent an infringement, or of establishing procedures governing the removal or disabling of access to information. In practice, Article 14 (3) is increasingly invoked as a way by which prior monitoring or filtering may be imposed on host providers by court order. In that regard the prevention of future infringements is a sensible issue as unlawful content can hardly be avoided without the monitoring of all uploaded information.

Even if a host provider receives notice of unlawful content, it can avoid liability under the condition that it takes down or blocks access to that content expeditiously. This imports the US "notice and take down" approach. At the time when the *E-Commerce Directive* was adopted, the European legislator decided that notice and take down procedures should not be regulated in the Directive itself.[351] Member States are merely encouraged to implement "rapid and reliable procedures for removing and disabling access to illegal information".[352] Like the US *DMCA*, the Directive gives no guidance as to the interpretation of the vague expression of "expeditous". Also national implementations of the *E-Commerce Directive* refrained from specifying what "expeditious" means, with some defining it with the equally uncertain notion of "undue delay".[353]

---

ally. See Cf. Lilian Edwards, *Role and responsibility of Internet intermediaries in the field of copyright and related rights*, p. 10.

351 European Commission, *Report from the Commission to the European Parliament, the Council and the European Economic and Social Committee – First Report on the Application of Directive 2000/31/EC of the European Parliament and of the Council of 8.06.2000 on Certain Legal Aspects of Information Society Services, in particular Electronic Commerce, in the Internal Market (Directive on Electronic Commerce)* COM/2003/0702, para.4.7.

352 Recital 40 of the *E-Commerce Directive*.

353 In Germany, the term "expeditious" is defined in § 121 I 1 of the *Bürgerliches Gesetzbuch* (*BGB*) as meaning "without undue delay". Undue delay" is also used in Austria in order to define the notion of "expeditious". Annotation to § 16 of the Regierungsvorlage 817, available at: www.parlament.gv.at/PG/DE/XXI/I/I_0

cc) The US and EU Regimes: Similarities and Deficits

The liability regime by the *E-Commerce Directive* is very similar to that of the earlier drafted *DMCA*. Unlike the US, the European Union took a horizontal approach in determining intermediary service provider liability. Under both regimes, mere conduits are not liable for damages or for criminal sanctions as a result of any transmission of information. Also the liability for caching is constructed similar. However, the regimes differ in some aspects when it comes to liability for hosting and information location tools. While the *DMCA* explicitly introduces a safe harbour provision for information location tools, the *E-Conmerce Directive* only foresees an examination "for the need for proposals concerning the liability of providers of hyperlinks and location tool services".[354] Although the European legislator was aware that problems may arise with regard to the liability of link providers, he explicitly refrained from regulation without having assessed its necessity in practice. In relation to host provider liability, the *E-Commerce Directive* does not foresee a statutory "notice and take down" (NTD) procedure as introduced by the *DMCA*, but simply requires intermediaries to take down or bar access to illegal content or activity upon acquiring knowledge of the content in question. Member States are free to adopt NTD procedures, but there is no uniform proce-

0817/fnameorig_000000.html (last accessed 4.12.2009). The Austrian Supreme Court held that one week did not fulfil the criterion of undue delay (see OGH, Decision of 21.12.2006 – 6 Ob 178/04a. In the UK, legislation dealing with terroristic offences indicates that two working days might fulfil the requirement expeditious. The specialised *Electronic Commerce Directive (Terrorism Act 2006) Regulations 2007* – which provides immunities for Internet service providers from offences under the *Terrorism Act 2006* – also requires expeditious removal of Internet postings constituting terrorism-related offences. For such postings the *Terrorism Act 2006* contains a notice and take down regime applying to website operators which requires them to modify or remove offending material within two working days after having received a notice by a police constable. The period of two working days is fixed in Section 3 subsection 2 (b) of the *Terrorism Act 2006*. "Working days" is further defined as "any day other than a Saturday or a Sunday, Christmas Day or good Friday or a day which is a bank holiday under the *Banking and Financial Dealings Act 1971* (c. 80) in any part of the United Kingdom" (Section 3 subsection 9 of the *Terrorism Act 2006*).

354 Article 21(2) *E-Commerce Directive*.

dure throughout the EU.[355] Thus, the indefinite concepts of "actual knowledge" and "awareness of facts and circumstances from which the illegal activity or information is apparent" are crucial for determining provider liability. In this regard, it is necessary to define the preconditions of knowledge or awareness (e.g. positive knowledge or negligent ignorance) and the notion of manifestly illegal content. Specifically in the area of IP law, the infringing nature of content may often not be apparent. An image uploaded on Facebook does regularly not contain any information with regard to the author. Knowledge or awareness will thus usually be acquired by notification. It will then be the provider itself who has to determine whether or not a complaint is legitimate.[356] There is a risk that, in the interest of avoiding litigation, service provider would be best served by removing or blocking access to any content hosted by them which was brought to their notice regardless how unfounded or trivial the objection might seem to be. Not having the legal knowledge of a court or legally-trained person, there is a presumption that Internet service providers are likely to delete or block access.[357]

Although statutory NTD procedures have received criticism for having a potential chilling effect on freedom of speech, and – being a self-regulatory measure – constituting privatized censorship, this criticism is not restricted to statutory NTD procedures.[358] Any legal obligation to remove illegal material upon notification, may induce intermediaries to over-comply with take down notices in order to limit their liability and as a result suppress legitimate content.

355 Some Member States introduced statutory NTD procedures, e.g. France (Article 6-I-5° *Loi n° 2004-575 de 21 Juin 2004 pour la confiance dans l'économie numérique* (*LCEN*)) and Finland, which has set out copyright-specific NTD procedure (Section 22 *Laki tietoyhteiskunnan palvelujen tarjoamisesta* (458/2002) of 05.06.2002).

356 Christian Ahlert/Chris Marsden/Chester Yung, How "liberty" disappeared from Cyberspace: The mystery shopper tests Internet content self-regulation, p.7.

357 *Ibid.*

358 Wendy Seltzer, *Free Speech Unmoored in Copyright's Safe Harbor: Chilling Effects of the DMCA on the First Amendment,* Harvard Journal of Law & Technology 2010, Vol. 24 No. 1, 171 et seq.; See also Lilian Edwards, *Role and responsibility of Internet intermediaries in the field of copyright and related rights,* p. 11.

Research has shown that the incentive to take down or bar access to material is higher than facing a potential lawsuit and its costs.[359] Associated with a high compliance-rated with take down requests, is a risk of censorship when perfectly legal material is taken down. A non-representative survey conducted in the field of notice and take down procedures showed that an European Internet service provider took down content although the complaint related to it was unfounded and very little information related to the infringement was given, whereas an Internet service provider in the US requested further information in accordance with the *DMCA*.[360] A Dutch study[361] confirmed that Internet service providers prefer to take down content over which they received a complaint rather than investigating the matter. It proved that it only takes a free email-account to take content down. There is some concern over potential abuse of complaints where standardised notice and take down procedure are lacking, when Internet service providers consider default take down on demand as their safest and easiest option.[362] The *DMCA* tries to address these concerns by

---

359 The thesis that Internet service providers are more likely to remove alleged illegal material than to question complaints has been proven by an empirical research conducted by Oxford researchers in 2004 on Notice and Take down procedures. The researchers investigated how Internet service providers make use of notice and take down by making a complaint by email to several Internet service providers about alleged copyright infringement on a website which they had previously uploaded and which contained perfectly legal material. See: Christian Ahlert/Chris Marsden/Chester Yung, *How "liberty" disappeared from Cyberspace: The mystery shopper tests Internet content self-regulation*, p.12. See also a similar study from India, which came to the same conclusion: Rishabh Dara, *Intermediary Liability in India: Chilling Effects on Free Expression on the Internet* (2011), pp. 29 et seq.

360 The outcome of the research project is not representative as only two Internet service providers were tested, one US IPS and one UK Internet service provider; Christian Ahlert/Chris Marsden/Chester Yung, *How "liberty" disappeared from Cyberspace: The mystery shopper tests Internet content self-regulation.*

361 The research was carried out by Sjoera Nas at Bits of Freedom, a Dutch digital human rights group. Ten Internet service providers were chosen and a text uploaded which clearly stated that the text belongs to the public domain. A fake society was created to act as a copyright-holder, which then sent complaints to the providers from a Hotmail email account. 7 out of the 10 providers removed the text without any further investigation. See Sjoera Nas, *The Multatuli Project ISP Notice & take down* (27.10.2004).

362 Christian Ahlert/Chris Marsden/Chester Yung, *How "liberty" disappeared from Cyberspace: The mystery shopper tests Internet content self-regulation*, p. 26.

introducing safeguards to discourage an abuse of the system. Any take down notice must be notified to the content provider, who then has the opportunity to protest. Where then a dispute arises between the notifier and the content provider, the case will be taken to court. False allegations of infringement are penalised (§ 512 (f)).

So, while in the EU no guidelines exist with regard to an appropriate notice and take down procedure, the complex procedure in the US does not leave room for uncertainties and tries to ensure that overblocking is avoided.

b) The Necessity to Go Beyond Notice and Take down

NTD was and is an effective solution when sites physically host infringing content, but when content is shared via decentraslised peer-to-peer networks, there is no longer a host provider that can be held accountable or that may delete or block access to infringing materials.

With centralised peer-to-peer networks like Napster, the service provider could be held liable to direct and contributory infringement if it received reasonable knowledge of specific infringing material, knew or should have known these were available, and failed to prevent its distribution.[363] Napster's downfall was its centralised server system, which technically allowed Napster to monitor the activities of its network and to restrict access to infringing material when informed of that material's location.

While the first generation of peer-to-peer networks operated a centralised database, already the second generation of decentralised sharing made it impossible to hold the providers of the file-sharing software accountable. Providers of second generation peer-to-peer file-sharing software lacked a central server or index function, meaning that they actually could not acquire knowledge of specific files being exchanged, at least at

363 *A&M Records, Inc. v Napster, Inc.*, 239 F.3d 1004 (9th Cir. 2001), at 1027. The case highlights that liability for contributory infringement exists if one engages in personal conduct that encourages or assists copyright infringement. For an analysis of the case see Nick Scharf, *Napster's long shadow: copyright and peer-to-peer technology*, Journal of Intellectual Property Law & Practice 2011, Vol. 6 Issue 11), 806 et seq.

the moment of exchange itself.[364] Conceptually, peer-to-peer clients and torrent sites are also rather "pointing to" infringing material than transmitting it.[365]

An ongoing issue with respect to online file-sharing is that some users resist attempts to limit their perceived rights of free exchange of information, ideas and content, and have demonstrated such resistance by developing and implementing new methods to mask their activities.[366] The third generation of file-sharing networks reflect this: they are decentralised, fast and sometimes anonymised or encrypted.

Technological progress posses a challenge for notice and take down. This does not mean that notice and take down became useless as such, it still is a good solution with regard to traditional host providers including providers of user-generated content. But, as mentioned previously, with increased use of information technologies by consumers from the millenium onwards, we could also see an increase in infringing materials being available and a lot of these infringing materials are not shared on YouTube or DailyMotion. While host providers such as YouTube or Dailymotion are originally based around the idea of users sharing their self-generated content with others, new types of host providers such as sharehosters or cloud computing providers have entered the scene; their primary service is hosting and not distributing user-generated content. However, these platforms are also being used to share copyrighted content with some of them being founded with the purpose of facilitating copyright infringements; the operators of the latter are usually at least difficult to identify, may be difficult to locate, and frequently located outside domestic jurisdiction. The German operator's of kino.to for instance had their servers located in Russia: Because they blocked access to Russian consumers, Russian authorities were reluctant to ban the copyright infringing activities and the rightsholders had no chance to have the service shut-down until the operators

364 *Metro-Goldwyn-Mayer Studios Inc. v Grokster, Ltd.,* 380 F.3d 1154 (2004) (9 th Circuit) 1162; See also Colin Nasir, *Taming the beast of file-sharing – Legal and technological solutions to the problem of copyright infringement over the Internet: Part 2,* Entertainment Law Review 2005, Vol. 16 Issue 4, 82–88, at 83.

365 See Lilian Edwards, *Role and responsibility of Internet intermediaries in the field of copyright and related rights,* p. 16.

366 Robert C. Piasentin, Unlawful? Innovative? Unstoppable? A comparative analysis of the potential legal liability facing P2P end-users in the United States, United Kingdom and Canada, International Journal of Law and Information Technology 2006, No. 14, 195, 211.

who were still located in the European Union could be arested. In such scenarios, questions arise as to whether special duties should and could be imposed on online intermediaries (in the case of kino.to, on access providers) to block access to these materials. Where the host providers are identifiable, and situated in the same jurisdiction or in a jurisdiction where judicial decisions from another state are recognised and enforceable, such obligations could also include filtering obligations by the hosts providers themselves (sharehosters or providers that provide links to unauthorised copies). In this regard, rights-holders and collecting societies call for European rules on notice and take down, that go beyond the existing limited liability scheme enshrined in the *E-Commerce Directive*.[367] The case law from Germany, France and the UK relating to potential blocking and filtering obligations, which will be outlined in Chapter 3, shows that courts are struggling to apply duties upon online intermediaries that go beyond mere take down of infringing content.

B. The Technological and Legal Challenges of Online Copyright Enforcement

Copyright enforcement on the Internet compared to the analogue world faces additional challenges. While with hard-copies some form of contact was necessary between infringer and beneficiary, or seller and buyer, this is not the case with digital copies. File-sharing often takes place anonymously, or at least the actors hide behind pseudonyms. Sometimes it can be almost impossible to identify an uploader, or the person who made a work available to the public. Similarly, downloaders are difficult to track. The reasons for this may be manifold, but an important role is definitely played by technology as such.

367 European Commission, *Synthesis of Comments on the Commission Report on the Application of Directive 2004/48/EC of the European Parliament and the Council of 29.04.2004 on the Enforcement of Intellectual Property Rights* (July 2011), COM(2010) 779 final, p. 11.

I. The Technological Challenges

In how far technology allows for the identification of the different actors involved, or for the gathering of evidence, will be briefly discussed at this stage. The particular challenges involved when trying to enforce copyright against end-user or intermediaries will be outlined at the beginning of the respective chapters.

1. Technological Context

For the purpose of legal analysis, it may be misleading to speak of "the Internet" without having a clear idea what this collective noun refers to in specific. First of all, there is no "recognisable controller of the Internet, who might ultimately be responsible for it"; secondly, the Internet has no "fixed, definable infrastructure; and thirdly, "the information and services obtainable via the Internet" are not provided by a single entity called "the Internet".[368]

Due to this reasons, it is impossible to discuss the law without referring to the functioning of the technology behind the Internet, a brief overview shall help to understand the following discussions.

a) The Evolution of the Internet in a Nutshell

A basic understanding of how the Internet operates is important for any consideration of copyright enforcement mechanisms and user sanctions. Therefore, this section provides a brief overview of the functioning of the Internet with an emphasis on relevant implications for the identification of users and for how access to materials may be blocked.

The basic function performed by the Internet is extremely simple: it transports digital information from one computer to another.[369] It is a simple communications infrastructure.

The birth of the Internet can be seen with the development of ARPANET, a US defence project funded by the Advanced Research

---

368 Chris Reed, *Internet Law, Text and Materials* (2nd ed. 2004), p. 7.

369 See Chris Reed, *Internet Law, Text and Materials* (2nd ed. 2004), p. 8.

Projects Agency (ARPA), in the late 1960s.[370] The system would link a number of computers or 'nodes', so that messages could be forwarded from one computer to another. Every message would be divided up into a number of segments (packets) that would each be labelled with its intended destination and with information as to its position in the message as a whole.[371] Passing from node to node, the packets would be reassembled when they arrived at the intended destination. The next major development was, when during the 1970s, US universities, the US government and high-tech companies, and finally commercial communication providers took leading roles in what began as a military project.[372] The evolution of the communication standard Transmission Control Protocol (TCP) and Internet Protocol (IP) paved the way to the global network of today.[373] A protocol is, in essence, an algorithm for recognising and dealing with a piece of information.[374] The TCP component is responsible for converting messages into streams of packets for transmission and recombines them at the receiving end, whilst the IP is responsible for addressing and routing the packets to their intended destination. All digital devices linked to the Internet are allocated an IP address as a unique identifier. The TCP/IP protocols enable any user to connect to the vast network of communications network – that is the Internet.[375] IP addresses in that regard enable the transmission of communications between for instance the user's web browser and the server hosting the website that he wants to browse.

While the early Internet was predominately a tool for academia and the technology literates, more user-friendly navigational tools were introduced

---

370 For the history and development of ARPANET see Andrew S. Tanenbaum/David J. Wetherall, *Computer Networks* (5th ed. 2011), pp. 55 et seq.; Andrew Murray, *Information Technology Law, The law and society* (2nd ed. 2013), pp. 16 et seq.

371 Ian J. Lloyd, *Information Technology Law* (4th ed. 2004), p. 12.

372 Andrew S. Tanenbaum/David J. Wetherall, *Computer Networks* (5th ed. 2011), p. 456.

373 For a brief outline of how the modern Internet functions, see Andrew Murray, *Information Technology Law, the law and society* (2nd ed. 2013), pp. 21 et seq.

374 Chris Reed, *Internet Law, Text and Materials* (2nd ed. 2004), p. 11. To communicate using the Internet system, a host computer must implement the layered set of protocols comprising the Internet protocol site; for more information on the different protocol layers, cf. *ibid*, pp. 12 et seq.

375 Ian J. Lloyd, *Information Technology Law* (4th ed. 2004), p. 31. For the functioning of the TCP/IP protocols see Andrew S. Tanenbaum/David J. Wetherall, *Computer Networks* (5th ed. 2011), pp. 45 et seq.

in the early 1990s.[376] The most significant technical innovation at that time was the introduction of the World Wide Web (WWW).[377] The WWW is not synonymous with the Internet, but is a higher-level network which uses the Internet as a network or computer networks as its carrier medium.[378] It uses the so called hypertext to create links between documents, allowing users to click on a marked link to move to a document. Initially all Internet connections were referred to solely by an IP number. However, as the Internet grew, more memorable means of identification were needed. In 1987 the system of domain names which transcribe into IP addresses came into effect and meant that webpage could be accessed by typing a readable domain name into a web browser such as Internet Explorer or Mozilla Firefox. Today uniform resource locater (URL), also known as web address, serve as references to a resource. The format combines the system of domain names with file path syntax, where slashes are used to separate directory and file names.

When a user requests a webpage, he will enter the URL of that page into his browser software. This client software generates a request for the page, which is sent via the Internet to the computer on which the page is stored. Web server software running on this computer responds to the request by sending the streams of data packets that make up the web page to the browser software. The browser then reassembles the information once the packets have arrived and displays the page.[379] A user's client software and the web server software are able to exchange data packets across the Internet because all the computers involved use common protocols (the aforementioned TCP and IP) to define how a packet should dealt with.

---

376 Ian J. Lloyd, *Information Technology Law* (4th ed. 2004), p. 13.

377 *Ibid.* Its invention is usually credited to Sir Tim Berners-Lee, cf. Andrew Murray, *Information Technology Law, The law and society* (2nd ed. 2013), p. 33. See also Tim Berners-Lee, *Weaving the Web: The original design and ultimate destiny of the World Wide Web by its inventor* (2000).

378 See Andrew Murray, Information Technology Law, The law and society (2nd ed. 2013), p. 33.

379 See Chris Reed, *Internet Law, Text and Materials* (2nd ed. 2004), p. 10.

b) IP Address Allocation

The issuance of IP addresses can be compared with the issuance of a phone number. As mentioned above, every computer linked to the Internet is allocated a unique IP address. This IP address consists of 32 binary digits in length (IPv 4 standard).[380] Because the number of computers and other devices connecting to the Internet is outgrowing the IP addresses that are available, a new standard is being introduced.[381] The IPv 6 standard brings an increase in number length to 128-bit numbers to provide capacity for some 2^{128} addresses, more than 7.9×10^{28} times as many as IPv 4.[382] While still the majority of Internet traffic is carried by IPv 4, computers are allocated dynamic IP addresses. This means that each time a computer connects to the Internet, it will be assigned a new IP address by its Internet access provider, who has a limited block of addresses available. When the computer becomes inactive, the IP address will be taken away again and be assigned to another computer that becomes active. Accordingly, while websites will usually have a fixed IP address, users that are not online 24/7 will be allocated a new IP address every time they connect to the Internet.

c) Domain Name System

Because IP address are hard for people to remember and may change[383], readable names were introduced in order to decouple machine names from machine addresses. Typing in the readable address in a web browser initiates a process of trying to match the name with the appropriate IP number. The process of looking up a name and finding an address is called domain

---

380 Andrew S. Tanenbaum/David J. Wetherall, *Computer Networks* (5th ed. 2011), p. 439.

381 *Ibid*, p. 455.

382 See Andrew Murray, Information Technology Law, The law and society (2nd ed. 2013), p. 23.

383 For example if a company's website that could be accessed under a certain IP number was moved to a different server with a different IP address, everyone needed to be told the new IP address. See Andrew S. Tanenbaum/David J. Wetherall, *Computer Networks* (5th ed. 2011), p. 611.

name resolution.[384] A query about a domain name passes first to a local name server, if it fails to make a match, the query will be passed on to a remote server.[385] The definite tables of names and numbers are maintained on so called root servers. There are 13 root DNS servers, of which most are present in multiple geographical locations.[386]

Domain names can be categorised into two categories – generic (e.g. .com, .info, .org) and country code (e.g. .fr, .de, .uk, .lu). The Internet Corporation for Assigned Numbers and Names (ICANN) delegates the administration of generic top level domains to third party organisations to oversee the domain registry activity. Country code top level domains are administered by national independent registries operating on a country by country basis. When an individual or company purchases a domain name from a registrar they are asked to complete domain contact details including their email and postal addresses. These details are entered into DNS WHOIS, a service provided by the DNS Registry that allows queries to the Domain Name database, such that the ownership of a particular domain can be established. However, this simply gives the information provided by the registrant, which may not necessarily be correct or informative.[387]

2. The Difficulties to Identify an Infringer That Result from Technology as such

Technological progress means that it is becoming more and more difficult to identify infringers. A starting point is usually the collecting of an IP address from which an infringement took place. This information however may only help to identify the subscriber of that IP address of a specific given time. Notorious infringers or users who value privacy may also browse the web anonymously.

---

384 For a detailed explanation on how domain name resolution works, see *ibid*, pp. 620 et seq.

385 *Ibid*, p. 620.

386 *Ibid*, p. 621.

387 Cf. Richard Clayton et al., *A study of Whois privacy and proxy services abuse*, National Physical Laboratory (20.09.2013).

a) "On the Internet, Nobody Knows You're a Dog"

"On the Internet, nobody knows you're a dog" is an adage which began as the caption of a cartoon by the American cartoonist Peter Steiner that was published by The New Yorker on 5 July 1993 and became the most reproduced cartoon of The New Yorker.[388] The cartoon features two dogs sitting in front of a computer, with one telling the caption to the other. It symbolises an understanding of Internet privacy that stresses the ability of users to send and receive messages in general anonymity. Internet communication lacks clear identification of the communication parties. This does not only apply to two users communicating with each other, but also to users requesting web pages, where the request is made via a communication that identifies only the host through which the user accessed the Internet and does not identify the user that made the request.[389]

General anonymity in this context means, that Internet protocols do not force users to identify themselves. An identification may only be required at local access points such as universities or libraries, when users log onto the Internet via the university's or library's access, but the log on information will then be privately held by the local access point and will not become part of the Internet transaction itself.[390] Though it is often possible to identify the device with which the Internet was accessed, the user is not identified. The identification of an IP address thus, in general, only leads to the identification of a specific Internet access point and, without further information, not to the person that used the IP address at a given time.

In those cases where only an IP address can be identified, this does not automatically lead to the identification of the actual infringer.

b) Dynamic IP Addresses

Although it is possible to log an IP address, the fact that most IP addresses that are allocated to end-users are dynamic addresses, make it difficult for rights-holders to identify a subscriber. A prerequisite for identification is that IP data is retained by the Internet service provider. However, under

---

388 Glenn Fleishman, *Cartoon Captures Spirit of the Internet,* The New York Times (14.12.2000).

389 Chris Reed, *Internet Law, Text and Materials* (2nd ed. 2004), p. 141.

390 Cf. Lawrence Lessig, *Code: Version 2.0* (2006), p. 35.

the general data protection principles of data reduction and data economy, Internet service providers are obliged to retain as little data as possible. They may thus only retain data as long as necessary. Telecommunication service providers or operators store customers' personal data for the purposes of transmitting communications, invoices as well as marketing and certain other value-added services. Only in the context of the transmission of communication and invoicing it is necessary to retain communications data, i.e. the "envelope" or "metadata" consisting of information on the identity of the subscriber (e.g. IP address), traffic data (communication-associated information e.g. logs of connections), and data on the location of the user at the time of the communication.[391]

However, with flat rate plans becoming the common choice for customers,[392] it is no longer necessary to retain data for several weeks as it used to be when Internet access was paid for by the minute or by traffic. Although the latter becomes in some way relevant again in mobile telecommunications, where transfer speed may be reduced after a certain amount of traffic, the providers do not need to store all connection processes for billing their customers. Hence many rights-holders complain that data often are not retained long enough by Internet access providers to allow them to obtain the information they need to enforce their rights.[393] At least under European law, there is no obligation to store data (on a temporary basis) for the purpose of disclosing information related to intellectual property rights infringements. In contrast to the perception of many

---

391 These types of data are also reflected in the *Data Retention Directive,* see Article 5(1) of the *Data Retention Directive* i.e. from whom (sub-article a)) and to whom (b) the communication was sent, when it was sent and how long it lasted (c), what sort of communication (d), how the communication was sent i.e. what equipment was used (e) and where the communication was sent (f). For definitions see European Telecommunications Standards Institute, ETSI TS 101 331(2001-08), pp. 6 et seq.

392 In Germany, the proportion of private Internet users with such flat rate plans rose from 18 % in 2005 to 87 % in 2009. See European Commission, *Evidence Dossier – Evidence for Necessity of Data Retention in the EU (2013),* p.5 Fn. 13, http://ec.europa.eu/dgs/home-affairs/pdf/policies/police_cooperation/evidence_en .pdf

393 European Commission, Synthesis of Comments on the Commission Report on the Application of Directive 2004/48/EC of the European Parliament and the Council of 29.04.2004 on the Enforcement of Intellectual Property Rights (July 2011), COM/2010/779 final, p. 12.

lay people, the *Data Retention Directive* [394] did not contain a legal basis by which Internet service providers are obliged to retain telecommunications data for private law enforcement.

The *Data Retention Directive*, which has recently been declared invalid by the CJEU,[395] required telecommunication operators to retain certain categories of data for identifying users and details of phone calls made and emails sent (excluding the content of those communications) for a period between six months and two years and to make them available, on request, to law enforcement authorities for the purposes of investigating, detecting and prosecuting serious crime and terrorism.[396] The Directive as well as the *Data Protection Directive* was quite specific in its balancing of principles and exceptions related to data retention for specific purposes and the use of this data. None of the provisions required data retention for the purposes of enforcing intellectual property rights. Thus, often data can only be obtained by way of a quick request to preserve certain communications data ("quick freeze") under which operators served with a court order are obliged to retain data relating only to specific circumstances.[397]

---

394 Directive 2006/24/EC of the European Parliament and of the Council of 15.03.2006 on the retention of data generated or processed in connection with the provision of publicly available electronic communications services or of public communications networks and amending Directive 2002/58/EC, OJ L 105 (13.04.2006), 54. To date 28 States have notified the Commission about the transposition of the Directive into their national law; of these States however, Germany and Belgium have only transposed the legislation partially.

395 CJEU, Joined cases C-293/12 and C-594/12 *Digital Rights Ireland v Minister for Communications, Marine and Natural Resources and Others, and Kärntner Landesregierung and Others,* Judgment of 08.04.2014.

396 A number of Member States, in accordance with their legislation, allow the access and use of retained data for purposes going beyond those covered by the Directive, including preventing and combating crime generally and the risk to life and limb. Access to the data is however in all Member States restricted to law enforcement authorities. Cf. European Commission, Report from the Commission to the Council and the European Parliament, *Evaluation Report on the Data Retention Directive (Directive 2006/24/EC)*, Com(2011) 225 final (18.04.2011), pp. 7 et seq. and pp. 10 et seq., http://eur-lex.europa.eu/LexUriServ/LexUriServ.do?uri=COM:2011:0225:FIN:en:PDF

397 Data preservation is distinct from data retention which requires the retention of all data. Cf. European Commission, *Report from the Commission to the Council and the European Parliament, Evaluation Report on the Data Retention Directive (Directive 2006/24/EC)*, Com(2011) 225 final (18.04.2011), p. 5.

Such "quick freeze" is valuable in many ways, but relies on the need or willingness of the Internet access providers to store these data for their own commercial purposes, and actually log IP addresses where they are dynamically allocated. If the data is logged, the question remains how long they are being retained for the purposes of the access providers. Considering that usually customers will enter into flatrate plans, there is often no need to preserve data for billing purposes for longer periods of time. Rights-holders thus have to be quick to file their requests for disclosure. In Germany, it has been shown that seven days of retention are long enough for rights-holders to exercise their right to information.[398] Due to the fundamental right impact of data disclosure, disclosure will only be granted under very strict conditions which will be evaluated in the second Chapter.

c) Anonymous Web Browsing

It is said that the Internet "interprets censorship as a form of damage and seeks to find ways around it".[399] Although intellectual property rights enforcement has nothing to do with censorship, this assumption also applies in this context.

Anonymous web browsing refers to browsing the Internet where the user´s IP address and other personally identifiable information is hidden from the websites that are visited. There are different ways of accomplishing anonymous web browsing such as for instance proxies or programs such as "The Onion Router" (TOR).

When a user requests a website, that request identifies the user's access provider and possibly sharing other computer information including the browser and operating system.[400] This information can be used to track the user. Anonymous web surfing services send the request as if it would stem from their own computers but pass on the received web page to the user.[401] The service provider will make some temporary records of the

---

398 See European Commission, *Synthesis of Comments on the Commission Report on the Application of Directive 2004/48/EC of the European Parliament and the Council of 29.04.2004 on the Enforcement of Intellectual Property Rights (July 2011)*, COM(2010) 779 final, p. 13.

399 Ian J. Lloyd, *Information Technology Law* (4th ed. 2004), p. 23.

400 Chris Reed, *Internet Law, Text and Materials* (2nd ed. 2004), p. 35.

401 *Ibid.*

user's originating IP address from which his identity might be discovered, but because there is no substantial delay between requesting a Web page and receiving it, these records need only to be maintained for a very short time.[402]

Proxy servers or virtual private network servers (VPN servers) work by redirecting the communication through themselves. The user's IP address is then only shared with the proxy server while the requested website only obtains the proxy server's information. Because proxies hide the origination of a request, they may also be used to bypass restrictions such as for instance geographical restrictions and visit websites that might be blocked in a specific country. The same may apply to circumvent local restrictions that for example often exist in relation to school networks. The disadvantages of proxy servers are that they often load websites slowly due to the rerouting of the requested information. Also browser add-ons like Flash player or Java plugin may nevertheless reveal the surfer's IP address.

Virtual private networks achieve anonymity also by allowing several users to access the Internet via a single gateway using the same IP address, so that the user cannot be identified as an individual but as belonging to a certain group of people who have access to that network.

With programs such as TOR, anonymity can be achieved by sending information through a net of routers to hide the original destination of the web page request.

All these variants may be used by users that want to ensure that their browsing session cannot be monitored. Although VPN services may be ordered to disclose information and logs if illegal activities take place, the fact that they regularly do not store such information any longer than necessary, makes them attractive for users.

With advances in mobile communication such as more sophisticated smartphones and high-speed data for mobile phones and data terminals[403], mobile communication may at some point also become attractive for file-sharers. Mobile phone telephony users may use prepaid SIM cards as a means of avoiding identification. In the case of prepaid SIM cards, the identification of the user of such a card depends on whether the number of the card was registered when purchased. Only few EU Member States

402 *Ibid.*

403 4G LTE as a standard for wireless communication is increasingly becoming available.

have adopted measures requiring the registration of prepaid SIM cards.[404] Accordingly, these users may surf the Internet anonymously.

3. The Difficulties to Delete or Block Access

The argument that is often brought forward against blocking[405] is that it is favourable to delete the infringing content whereby one would not only put an end to the infringement but also prevent its continuation. While this as such may be true, in practice deletion may just not be possible. Sometimes the operator of a website may just not be contactable. The domain registrant's data may be incomplete or just not correct. Commonly, operators of piracy websites are located in another jurisdiction – for obvious reasons. The operators of the "German" streaming websites kino.to, which inter alia communicated blockbuster movies prior to their release in Germany, run under a Tonga domain and had its servers located in Russia.[406] The operators paid attention that no Russian movies or movies with Russian subtitles were available in order to keep a low profile in Russia and not stir any interest of Russian authorities in investigating the matter.[407] The deletion of content outside of the EU, may thus also have its limits, where judgments are not recognised and enforceable and national authorities have no reason to pursue the matter any further. As copyright is territorial, content that is illegal in one country may not be so in another. Also different terms of protection may apply.

Where content is located outside a jurisdiction, for instance outside the EU where the *Brussels I Regulation* provides for the mutual recognition

---

404 As of April 2011, these Member States are Denmark, Spain, Italy, Greece, Slovakia and Bulgaria. See Report from the Commission to the Council and the European Parliament, *Evaluation Report on the Data Retention Directive (Directive 2006/24/EC)*, COM(2011) 225 final, p. 25.

405 The difficulties that may be encountered when trying to block access will be discussed in more detail in the third Chapter.

406 Ole Reißmann, *Geschäft mit Raubkopien: Wie kiNo.to Millionen verdiente,* Der Spiegel online (14.06.2012).

407 *Ibid.*

and enforcement of judgments in civil matters,[408] the enforcement of a deletion request may turn out inoperable.

Accordingly, blocking is a feasible alternative as its scope of application is domestic. Also Interpol has set its priority on blocking access to the most severe child sexual abuse materials worldwide to reduce the availability of such material on the web.[409] Equally, the COSPOL Internet Related Child Abusive Material Project (CIRCAMP), a European police collaboration project, promotes access blocking to child abuse materials as a crime prevention tool.[410] While law enforcement authorities are interested in monitoring usage of the websites in question to identify offenders, they also try to have the content removed. While server providers are willing to cooperate when it comes to child abuse content, the situation may – for the above mentioned reasons – be different when it comes to copyright infringements. Deletion requests may only be successful, where the rights-holders has obtained an injunction and this injunction can be enforced against a content or host provider.

Given the difficulties with extra-territorial deletion, the rights-holders increasingly seek to have access blocked to the infringing materials via the domestic Internet access providers.

The main disadvantage with access blocking is, that it does not let the infringing content disappear. As will be outlined in Chapter 3, the content remains on the Internet and will continue to be accessible for anybody capable of circumventing filters. Depending on the blocking technique that is being employed, no specific IT literacy is necessary, meaning that an average user is capable of accessing blocked materials.

---

408 *Council Regulation No. 44/2001 on jurisdiction and the recognition and enforcement of judgments in civil and commercial matters (Brussels I Regulation),* OJ L012 (16.01.2001), pp. 1–23.

409 See the website of Interpol at Interpol.com. Interpol operates a "worst of"-list which includes domains that contain the most severe child sexual abuse material according to set criteria.

410 See circamp.eu.

4. The Role of Technology in the Assessment of Interferences with Fundamental Rights

The interests of intellectual property rights owners in enforcing their rights often collide with the interests of Internet users and online intermediaries. Insofar as non-absolute rights are concerned, it will be necessary to determine whether interferences with the rights of these third parties are justified. This will ultimately require that a fair balance is struck between the colliding interests.

Within the proportionality test, the efficiency of an enforcement mechanism may play an important role: if an enforcement mechanism is not efficient, it may not justify an interference with the fundamental rights of third parties. In other words: if an enforcement mechanism is suitable for securing the attainment of copyright protection, but in fact is inefficient or ineffective, than it will not be proportionate – meaning that efficiency and effectiveness more or less becomes the premise for all enforcement mechanisms.

This applies in particular, where enforcement is directed against third parties, that have not committed, aided or abetted the infringement themselves, and are thus no copyright infringers. In online copyright enforcement it is not uncommon that third parties are addressed. The reasons for this are based on the technological challenges outlined above. In some cases, technology makes it difficult to identify the end-user that has committed an infringer. In a technological sense, the IP address does not allow to draw conclusions on the identity of an Internet user. The rights-holders will then usually search for actors that in some way contributed to the infringement and that are in a position to stop the infringement, such as the subscriber of an Internet access service, or an online intermediary. Where rights-holders are able to identify actors that are locatable, and situated within the same jurisdiction, they will seek to take action against them to put an end to infringements. Often the law provides for a cause of action in these scenarios – even though this scenario was not considered when the law was drafted. Thus, it will become necessary to evaluate whether enforcement, just because it is possible, is also justified. When input and control over material, or the subscription of an Internet access become the starting point for liability and subsequent enforcement, it becomes particularly important to assess the contribution of the addressee also from a technological point of view. This can for example mean that the feasibility of monitoring duties needs to be assessed within the proportionality test. The same applies for the aforementioned efficiency of an enforcement tool. Even where the mechanism may be suitable to attain the given objective, it must not put an excessive burden on the individual, in particular when the contribution of that individual to the actual infringement is minimal.

Finally, as technology hardly allows for action that solely affects the infringer (for instance over-blocking affects other users, Internet suspension may not only affect infringer), all consequences of a restriction, and not just the consequences for the parties to the case, need to be taken into consideration when applying the proportionality principle.

II. The Legal Challenges: The Fundamental Rights at Stake

Enforcing rights against third parties means that third parties are identified, deterred or sanctioned for violation of the rights in question. Without specifying any enforcement measures, it is already clear at this stage that copyright enforcement interferes with fundamental rights: the fundamental rights of Internet users and third parties whose cooperation is sought to terminate and prevent copyright infringements. At the same time the fundamental rights of intellectual property rights-holders may be infringed when states do not provide them with effective remedies. It must be born in mind that fundamental rights are positive and negative rights. They require states to avoid engaging in certain conduct, while also requiring states to take positive steps to enable protection of these rights.

As in any other situation where fundamental rights of different actors clash, copyright enforcement requires a fair balancing of contravening interests. In this respect, the Preamble to the *WIPO Copyright Treaty* states that a key element of global copyright policy is to ensure that the balance between the rights of authors and the general public interest is maintained, especially the public interest with respect to education, research and access to information.

In the light of the technology outlined above, it becomes clear that rights-holders are confronted with numerous difficulties when enforcing their intellectual property rights.

In constellations such as peer-to-peer file-sharing the IP address is the starting point to identify an infringer. But also websites that users visit may track the IP addresses of their visitors. Although the website owner will not know a user's name through their IP address, the data he may have logged, may prove helpful for a rights-holder to track down an infringer.

However, no matter whether a rights-holder has logged an IP address from where an infringement took place or a website owner tracks IP addresses of visitors, the rights-holder needs to find out to whom the IP address in question was allocated at the time of infringement. Here, it becomes crucial to balance the right of privacy against the right to identify an (anonymous) individual potentially involved in an illegal action in order to defend and enforce intellectual property rights.

Once the identity of the subscriber of a certain IP address has been identified, usually sanctions will be imposed. If warnings are send out to the subscriber concerning an infringement, someone must store this data. Depending on who will be involved in the administration of data, different fundamental rights may be concerned, for example, if the aid of an Internet service provider is needed, this may have an impact on his business or more precisely his right to conduct business.

Not just where measures are targeted at private individuals, but also where measures aim at the infringing content itself, the rights of Internet service providers and users will be affected.

No matter which enforcement measure is considered, they all intervene in some way with fundamental rights. As a number of fundamental rights of different actors including the IP address subscriber, the rights-holder and other third parties, in particular Internet service providers, need to be taken into account, the following section focusses on these aspect of the fundamental rights in question, that are likely to be affected. In this respect, the sources of the rights in question as well as their scope of application will be outlined.

1. Sources of Fundamental Rights

Originally, human rights where a matter of national law. A transformation of the substantive norms of fundamental rights law from national to international law was manifested in the promulgation of the *Universal Declaration of Human Rights* in 1948 (*UDHR*).[411] The *UDHR* inter alia enumer-

---

411 *Universal Declaration of Human Rights of 10.12.1948*, U.N.G.A. Res. 217 (III 1948). For a history of human rights in general and in Europe, see Mark W. Janis/ Richard S. Kay/Anthony Wilfred Bradley, *European Human Rights Law: Text*

ates traditional human rights norms at the level of international law. The *UDHR* together with the *International Covenant of on Civil and Political Rights* of 1966 with its two Optional Protocols and the *International Covenant on Economic, Social and Cultural Rights* of 1966 forms the so-called *International Bill of Human Rights*. Because neither *Universal Declaration* nor the accompanying Covenants provide a legal machinery to enforce human rights against recalcitrant states, it made sense for there to be regional international human rights machineries which – influenced by the *UDHR* provide enforcement mechanisms for individuals. In Europe, the first instrument of such kind was the Council of Europe's *European Convention on Human Rights (ECHR)*. As regards the European Union, the *Treaty on European Union* (*TEU*) and in specific the C*harter of Fundamental Rights of the EU* (*CFR*) provide enforcement mechanisms insofar as the respect of fundamental rights in the European Union law is concerned. When in the course of this work, the compatibility of enforcement mechanisms with fundamental rights will be examined, though reference will be made to the *International Bill of Human Rights*, the focus will be on the more specific *ECHR* and the Charter and the interpretation of the respective provisions by the ECtHR and the CJEU.

Accordingly, when assessing the legality of an enforcement measure by the EU or a Member State in terms of fundamental rights, two major sources will to be consulted: the *ECHR* and the *Charter of Fundamental Rights of the European Union* (*CFR*).

a) International Level: The International Bill of Human Rights

From 1948, when the *UDHR* was adopted and proclaimed, until 1976, when the International Covenants on Human Rights entered into force, the Declaration was the only completed portion of the *International Bill of Human Rights*. The UN Declaration, and at a later stage the Covenants, exercised a profound influence on the thoughts and actions of individuals and the governments of signatory states. The influence of the *UDHR* and the Covenants will be seen throughout the discussion of fundamental

---

and Materials (3rd ed. 2008), pp. 4 et seq; Antonio Cassese, *International Law* (2001), pp. 349 et seq.

rights in the following chapters as in particular the Declaration is fundamental to the European human rights instruments and their very existence.

aa) The Universal Declaration of Human Rights

The *Universal Declaration of Human Rights of 1948 (UDHR)*, which was signed in Rome on 4 November 1950, and entered into force on 3 September 1953, is recognized as a historic document providing a common definition of human dignity and values. Against the background of diverse political ideological regimes, nations with different economic and political structures as well as religious beliefs, the *UDHR* provides the lowest common denominator as regards the conception both of the relationship between State and individual, and of basic human rights.[412] In formal terms, the *UDHR* is not legally binding, and thus only provides for a moral and political force.[413] The Declaration focusses on civil and political rights rather than economic, social, and cultural rights. Due to its limitation, it can only provide a yardstick by which to measure the degree of respect for, and compliance with, international human rights standards.

bb) The International Covenant on Civil and Political Rights and the International Covenant on Economic, Social and Cultural Rights

The *International Covenant on Civil and Political Rights* (*ICCPR*) as well as the *International Covenant on Economic, Social and Cultural Rights* (*ICESCR*) were adopted in 1966 and entered into force in 1976. By the coming into force of the Covenants, States parties accepted a legal as well as a moral obligation to promote and protect fundamental rights and freedoms. The Covenants contain the measures of implementation required to ensure the realisation of the rights and freedoms set out in the Declaration. With regard to this book, it is necessary to mention that while the Covenants intend to cover the whole range of fundamental rights, the right of property is not included – arguably, this was due to the inability of East-

412 See Antonio Cassese, *International Law* (2001), pp. 357 et seq.
413 *Ibid*, p. 358.

ern and Western states to agree on the issue of compensation in case of expropriation.[414]

b) European Union Level: The European Convention for the Protection of Human Rights and Fundamental Freedoms, and the Charter of Fundamental Rights of the European Union

While the constituent *EC Treaty* did not initially contain express provisions for the protection of fundamental rights, the CJEU had recognised in its case law that such rights were enshrined in the general principles of Community law protected by it, and granted special significance to the *European Convention for the Protection of Human Rights and Fundamental Freedoms* (*ECHR*) as a source of such rights.[415]

Article 6(3) *TEU* now states that the European Union shall respect fundamental rights as general principles of Community law; the content of said fundamental rights recognised as general principles in EU law are to

---

414 *Ibid*, p. 359.

415 See ECtHR, *Bosphorus Hava Yollari Turzm ve Ticaret Anonim Sirketi v Ireland*, Judgement of 30.06.2005 – Application No. 45036/98, para. 159. At paras. 155 et seq. the Court found that the legal order of the Union offered satisfactory means to deal with alleged violations of the Convention, that "State action taken in compliance with such legal obligations [i.e. obligations flowing from its membership of an international organisation to which it has transferred part of its sovereignty] is justified as long as the relevant organisation is considered to protect fundamental rights, as regards both the substantive guarantees offered and the mechanisms controlling their observance, in a manner which can be considered at least equivalent to that for which the Convention provides [..]. By 'equivalent' the Court means 'comparable'; any requirement that the organisation's protection be 'identical' could run counter to the interest of international cooperation pursued (...). However, any such finding of equivalence could not be final and would be susceptible to review in the light of any relevant change in fundamental rights protection. If such equivalent protection is considered to be provided by the organisation, the presumption will be that a State has not departed from the requirements of the Convention when it does no more than implement legal obligations flowing from its membership of the organisation. However, any such presumption can be rebutted if, in the circumstances of a particular case, it is considered that the protection of Convention rights was manifestly deficient. In such cases, the interest of international cooperation would be outweighed by the Convention's role as a 'constitutional instrument of European public order' in the field of human rights."

be derived from *ECHR* and from the constitutional traditions common to the Member States. [416] Under the *CFR*, these implicit rights have been codified.

aa) The European Convention for the Protection of Human Rights and Fundamental Freedoms

The *European Convention for the Protection of Human Rights and Fundamental Freedoms* (*ECHR*) was enacted by the Council of Europe in 1950, not long after the *UDHR*.[417] The Council of Europe was created by the Treaty of London[418] with the express purpose of addressing issues of political and human rights concerns and provide for an enforcement mechanism for fundamental rights on a regional level.[419] Membership in the Council of Europe depends on signing the *ECHR* and its protocols. Vice-versa, the *ECHR* is a closed convention that can only be ratified by Council of Europe Member States. Only upon ratification, the *ECHR* will become binding for the Member States.[420]

---

416 The CJEU has repeatedly also noted the significance of relevant international Treaties, see for example "[I]n safeguarding [fundamental] rights, the Court is bound to draw inspiration from constitutional traditions common to the Member States, so that measures which are incompatible with the fundamental rights recognized by the constitutions of those States are unacceptable in the Community; and that, similarly, international treaties for the protection of human rights on which the Member states have collaborated or of which they are signatories, can supply guidelines which should be followed within the framework of Community law" (CJEU, Case C-44/79 *Hauer v Land Rheinland-Pfalz*, [1979] E.C.R. 3727, para. 15).

417 As regards the negotiations and competing ideologies when drafting the *ECHR*, see Danny Nicol, *Original Intent and the European Convention on Human Rights,* Public Law 2005, 152, 170 et seq.

418 *Statute of the Council of Europe* ("*Treaty of London*") of 05.05.1949, signed by the following states: Belgium Denmark, France Ireland, Italy, Luxembourg, the Netherlands, Norway, Sweden and the United Kingdom.

419 See only Jens Meyer-Ladewig, *EMRK, Handkommentar* (3rd ed. 2011), Introduction, para. 1.

420 *Ibid*, para. 32. It is up to the Member States to decide upon the means of implementation. In Germany, for instance, the *ECHR* became law in the rank of a domestic law, meaning that the *ECHR* is directly applicable and can be enforced in German courts.

The *ECHR*'s preamble provides for "the maintenance and further realization of human rights and fundamental freedoms," which "are the foundation of justice and peace in the world and are best maintained on the one hand by an effective political democracy and on the other by a common understanding and observance of the human rights upon which they depend."

The *ECHR* deals mainly with civil and political rights (Articles 1–18), but also lists the working mechanisms of the European Court and Commission (Articles 19–51), while Protocol 1, 4, 6, 7, and 12 include additional rights. Each Member State of the Council of Europe may refer to the European Court of Human Rights (ECtHR) in Strasbourg any alleged violation of the Convention and its Protocols by another contracting State (Article 33 *ECHR*).[421] In addition, any individual subject to the jurisdiction of any of the contracting States may address himself to the Court claiming to be the victim of a violation of the Convention or the Protocols (Article 34 *ECHR*).[422]

Article 53 *ECHR* sets forth the relationship between the protection offered by the Convention and that guaranteed by national constitutions or the legal order of the signatory states in general. The so-called subsidiarity clause permits the Convention to be invoked only insofar as it guarantees greater protection than that afforded by national orders.[423] The Convention

---

421 Inter-State cases are very rare, and so far only two have resulted in Judgments of the Court (*Ireland v the United Kingdom,* Judgment of 18.01.1978 – Application No. 5310/71 and *Cyprus v Turkey*, Judgment of 10.05.2001 – Application No. 25781/94).

422 According to Article 35(1) *ECHR* the Court can only examine the merits of applications where the applicant (State or individual applicant) has exhausted all domestic remedies in regards to the complaint. The admissibility criterion emphasises the subsidiary nature of the Court's system for enforcing the rights and freedoms enshrined in the *ECHR*. The Court's Judgments do not produce direct legal effect within the national legal system; they are only binding at the international level (Cf. for example Antonio Cassese, International Law (2001), pp. 366 et seq.). If a State is found responsible for a breach of the Convention or the Protocols and fails to comply with the Court's Judgment, Article 8 of the Statute of the Council of Europe provides that the State may be suspended from its rights of representation and requested by the Committee of Ministers to withdraw under Article 7.

423 As regards the notion of "subsidiarity clause" see Leonard Besselink, *Entrapped by the Maximum Standard: On Fundamental Rights and Subsidiarity in the European Union*, Common Market Law Review 1998, Vol. 35, 629–680.

cannot justify a reduction in fundamental rights as that guaranteed by the signatory Member States. It serves as a minimum standard, freely open to derogation in favour of greater protection within national orders.[424]

Whereas all EU Member States are also parties to the *ECHR*, the EU itself is currently not a member. This is however going to change in the near future.

bb) Charter of Fundamental Rights of the European Union

The Charter of Fundamental Rights of the European Union (*CFR*)[425], which became legally binding on the EU institutions and on national governments with the entry into force of the Treaty of Lisbon on 1 December 2009, further strengthens the protection of fundamental rights in the EU.[426]

Naturally, the *ECHR* can be seen as one of the primary influences on the Charter.[427] The *CFR* as such encompasses rights protected under the *ECHR* and further principles that have previously been recognised as fundamental rights in EU law. Article 6(1) *TEU* now also explicitly states that the rights granted under the Charter have the same legal status as those included in the foundational treaties.

The provisions of the *CFR* are addressed to the institutions and bodies of the EU with due regard for the principle of subsidiarity.[428] They are

---

424 Jens Meyer-Ladewig, *EMRK*, Handkommentar (3rd ed. 2011), Article 53, para. 2; Marta Cartabia in: William B. T. Mock/Gianmario Demuro, *Human Rights in Europe, Commentary on the Charter of Fundamental Rights of the European Union* (2010), Article 53, p. 338.

425 *Charter of Fundamental Rights of the European Union*, OJ C 83/389 (30.03.2010). For the history of the Charter see William B. T. Mock/Gianmario Demuro, Human Rights in Europe, *Commentary on the Charter of Fundamental Rights of the European Union* (2010), Foreword, p. ix et seq.

426 The *Charter of Fundamental Rights of the European Union* (*CFR*) was originally proclaimed by the European Parliament, Council and Commission at Nice in December 2000. As amended in December 2007, it became legally binding with the coming into force of the Treaty of Lisbon in December 2009.

427 William B. T. Mock/Gianmario Demuro, *Human Rights in Europe, Commentary on the Charter of Fundamental Rights of the European Union* (2010), Foreword, p. xvi.

428 With regard to the principle of subsidiarity see for instance Christian Calliess, *Die Charta der Grundrechte der Europäischen Union – Fragen der Konzeption,*

only addressed to the national authorities when they are implementing EU law, meaning that they will also have to apply the Charter when their authorities apply a national law implementing an EU Directive.

cc) The Relationship between the Convention and the Charter

Even though the EU is founded on the respect for fundamental rights, the observance of which is ensured by the CJEU, the *ECHR* and its judicial mechanism do not formally apply to EU acts. However, as all EU Member States are parties to the Convention, they have an obligation to respect the *ECHR* even when they are applying or implementing EU law.

In order to rectify this divergence, Article 6(2) of the *Lisbon Treaty*[429] requires the EU to become a party to the *ECHR*.[430] Further Article 59 *ECHR* as amended by Protocol 14 ("The European Union may accede to this Convention"), which entered into force on 1 June 2010, allows the EU to accede to the *ECHR*.[431] The EU's accession will submit the EU's legal system to an independent external control by ECtHR, and will provide European citizens with the same protection vis-à-vis acts of the EU as they presently enjoy from Member States.[432]

As of now, the relationship between different sources of fundamental rights in the EU has only partially been addressed in primary law; Article 6(3) TEU refers to the fundamental rights guaranteed by the *ECHR* as general principles of EU law.

As regards the *ECHR* and the *CFR*, Article 52(3) *CFR* stipulates: "In so far as this Charter contains rights which correspond to rights guaranteed

---

Kompetenz und Verbindlichkeit, Europäische Zeitschrift für Wirtschaftsrecht 2001, 261, 266 et seq.

429 *Treaty of Lisbon Amending the Treaty on European Union and the Treaty Establishing the European Community,* OJ C306 (13.12.2007), 1.

430 In this regard the current Draft Agreement on the Accession of the European Union to the Convention has been declared incompatible with Article 6(2) *TEU* or with Protocol (No 8) relating to Article 6(2) *TEU* by the CJEU on 18.12.2014. See CJEU, Opinion 2/13 of the Court of 18.12.2014.

431 As regards the necessity for EU accession to the *ECHR* and the proceedings, see Francoise Tulkens, *EU Accession to the European Convention on Human Rights* (2013).

432 It is further proposed that the EU join as a member of the Council of Europe now it has attained a single legal personality in the *Lisbon Treaty*.

by the Convention for the Protection of Human Rights and Fundamental Freedoms, the meaning and scope of those rights shall be the same as those laid down by the said Convention. This provision shall not prevent Union law providing more extensive protection."

According to the Explanations Relating to the Charter, Article 52(3) intends "to ensure the necessary consistency between the Charter and the *ECHR* by establishing the rule that, in so far as the rights in the [...] Charter correspond to rights guaranteed by the *ECHR*, the meaning and scope of those rights, including authorised limitations, are the same as those laid down by the *ECHR*. This means in particular that the legislator, in laying down limitations to those rights, must comply with the same standards as are fixed by the detailed limitation arrangements laid down in the *ECHR*, which are thus made applicable for the rights covered by this paragraph, without thereby adversely affecting the autonomy of Union law and of that of the Court of Justice of the European Union".[433]

In addition, Article 53 *CFR* sets forth: "Nothing in this Charter shall be interpreted as restricting or adversely affecting human rights and fundamental freedoms as recognised, in their respective fields of application, by Union law and international law and by international agreements to which the Union, the Community or all the Member States are party, including the European Convention for the Protection of Human Rights and Fundamental Freedoms, and by the Member States' constitutions."

The obvious purpose of Article 53 is to make it absolutely clear that the *CFR* does not intend to replace the various established forms of protection of fundamental rights, which exist in national, EU, and international legal orders.[434] In addition to safeguarding the standard of rights protection offered by the European Union, by national constitutions and international law, it is the *ECHR* "which constitutes a minimum standard in all cases".[435]

---

433 Praesidium of the European Convention, *Explanations relating to the Charter*, OJ C 303 (14.12.2007), 17, 33.

434 Marta Cartabia in: William B. T. Mock/Gianmario Demuro, *Human Rights in Europe, Commentary on the Charter of Fundamental Rights of the European Union* (2010), Article 53 *CFR*, p. 336.

435 Bureau of the Convention, Presidency Note, Draft Charter of Fundamental Rights of the European Union, Text of the explanations relating to the complete text of the Charter as set out in CHARTE 4422/00 CONVENT 45 (31.07.2000), CHARTE 4423/00, Convent 46, p. 37. The Council went on to explain that "The level of protection afforded by the Charter may not, in any instance, be lower

Article 53 *CFR*, although similar in wording to the above mentioned Article 53 *ECHR* (the "subsidiarity clause"), does not consider the Charter rights as a minimum standard. The Charter safeguards the pluralism of fundamental rights protection in Europe, whereas the *ECHR* acts as a unifying factor around a minimum standard for the signatory states.[436] These different roles depend to a great extent on the different fields in which the *ECHR* and the Charter operate: the *ECHR*'s field of application coincides with that of the Member States and the *ECHR* is the criterion for final review for the protection of fundamental rights, once all national judicial remedies have been tried; the *CFR* has its own field of application, which are the activities of the EU institutions, as well as the acts of Member States when they implement EU law.[437]

Thus, insofar as copyright enforcement mechanisms are the result of EU law, the conformity with fundamental rights has to be tested against the *CFR*. The question then arises, whether the *CFR* will be the exclusive source for fundamental rights. The cases that have been decided so far do not clearly indicate that the EU courts see the *CFR* merely as their point of departure for a fundamental rights analysis, or whether the *CFR* has become a (more or less) exclusive source for fundamental rights that eliminates the reference to the general principles of Community law.[438] However, there seems to be a general trend to use the *CFR* less as an exclusive source, but more as either a point of departure for a fundamental rights analysis or as one of several possible sources of law.[439]

There are cases, in which the CJEU started its analysis of fundamental rights with the rights arising from general principles of law,[440] while in

---

than that guaranteed by the Convention, with the result that the arrangements for limitations may not fall below the level provided for in the Convention".

436 *Ibid.*

437 *Ibid.*

438 Herwig Hofmann/Bucura Mihaescu, *The relation between the Charter's fundamental rights and the unwritten general principles of EU law: good administration as the test case,* European Constitutional Law Review 2013, Vol. 9 Issue 1, 73, 74 et seq.

439 *Ibid.*

440 For example in the *AJD Tuna* case, the CJEU stated that Article 47 CFR was merely "the reaffirmation of the principle of effective judicial protection, which is a general principle of Community law stemming from the constitutional traditions common to the Member States" instead of using Article 47 as a starting point for its analysis. See C-221/09 *AJD Tuna,* [2011] ECR I-1655 of 17.03.2011, para. 54 with reference to Case C-432/05 *Unibet* [2007] ECR I-2271, para. 37,

other cases, the different sources were applied in parallel.[441] In the latter, the Court linked the *CFR* rights to pre-existing case-law and stated that these rights had the character of general principles of law.[442]

Some scholars share what might be called a "hierarchic" understanding and place the *CFR* as the primary source of rights in the EU.[443] This approach has however been widely criticised for different reasons: it would result in an exclusive application of one or another source of rights which in turn runs counter to an understanding of several overlapping complementary sources applicable in parallel; it has difficulties explaining the presence of rights defined in the *CFR* only by way of example ("this right includes"). [444]

In practice, although some discussion exists as to the relationship of the Charter and the CJEU, the rights encompassed in the *CFR* are consistent with those under *ECHR* adopted in the framework of the Council of Europe: when the *CFR* contains rights that stem from the *ECHR*, their meaning and scope are the same.

In cases where the *CFR* does not apply, the protection of fundamental rights is guaranteed under the constitutions or constitutional traditions of EU countries and international conventions that the Member States have ratified such as the *ECHR*.

---

and Joined Cases C-402/05 P and C-415/05 P *Kadi and Al Barakaat* [2008] ECR I-6351, para. 335.

441 Case C-1/11 *Interseroh*, Judgment of 29.03.2012, para. 43.

442 See as example: *ibid.*

443 See for example European Convention, Working Group II "Intégration de la Charte/adhésion à la CEDH", *Speaking note of M. le juge Vassilios Skouris* (17.09.2002); Christian Calliess, *Die neue Europäische Union nach dem Vertrag von Lissabon (*2010), p. 322; Sacha Prechal, *Competence Creep and General Principles of Law*, Review of European Administrative Law 2010, Vol. 3 Issue 1, 5, 21.

444 For an overview of the arguments supporting a non-hierarchical, pluralistic understanding of sources, see Herwig Hofmann/Bucura Mihaescu, *The relation between the Charter's fundamental rights and the unwritten general principles of EU law: good administration as the test case,* European Constitutional Law Review 2013, Col. 9 Issue 1, 73, 77 et seq.

2. The Fundamental Rights of User at Stake

When copyrights are enforced, not only the copyright infringer may feel the consequences, but also third parties such as the user may be affected; in particular the user's freedom of expression in the form of freedom to seek, receive and impart information, his privacy, and in so far as criminal sanctions are concerned, his procedural rights are at stake. In the following section, the scope and application of these rights will be outlined.

a) Freedom of Expression in the Form of Freedom to Seek, Impart and Receive Information

Freedom of expression is essential for the creation and effective operation of pluralistic democracies, which are necessary to ensure respect for fundamental human rights.[445] Generally speaking, freedom of expression refers to the right to communicate one's opinions and ideas, and includes any act of seeking, receiving and imparting information or ideas, regardless of the medium used.

aa) Freedom of Expression in General

The right to freedom of expression is recognised as a human right under Article 19 *UDHR* and recognised in international human rights law in the *International Covenant on Civil and Political Rights (ICCPR)*. Article 19 *ICCPR* states that "[e]veryone shall have the right to hold opinions without interference" and "everyone shall have the right to freedom of expression; this right shall include freedom to seek, receive and impart information and ideas of all kinds, regardless of frontiers, either orally, in writing or in print, in the form of art, or through any other media of his choice". Article 19 goes on to say that the exercise of these rights carries "special duties and responsibilities" and may "therefore be subject to certain restrictions" when necessary "[f]or respect of the rights or reputation of

---

445 Monica Macovei, *Freedom of Expression, Council of Europe Human Rights Handbooks, No. 2* (2nd ed. 2004), pp. 6 et seq. With regard to the most protected class of freedom of expression, namely political expression see ECtHR, *Lingens v Austria*, Judgment of 08.07.1986 – Application No. 9815/82.

others" or "[f]or the protection of national security or of public order (order public), or of public health or morals".

On European Union level, the right to freedom of expression is enshrined within Article 10 *ECHR* and Article 11 *CFR*.[446] According to the Explanations Relating to the Charter the meaning and the scope of Article 11 *CFR* and Article 10 *ECHR* are the same.[447]

The first two sentences of Article 10(1) of the *ECHR* and Article 11(1) *CFR* stipulate that everyone has the right to freedom of expression, and that "this right shall include freedom to hold opinions and to receive and impart information and ideas without interference by public authority and regardless of frontiers". The third sentence of Article 10(1) *ECHR* expressly states, that this does "not prevent States from requiring the licensing of boradcasting, television or cinema enterprises". Article 11(2) *CFR* goes on to emphasise that "the freedom and pluralism of the media shall respected". In contrast, Article 10(2) *ECHR* provides an exhaustive list of legitimate aims that may justify an interference with the right to freedom of expression, i.e. "the interests of national security, territorial integrity or public safety", "the prevention of disorder or crime", "the protection of health or morals", "he protection of the reputation or rights of others", "preventing the disclosure of information received in confidence", and "maintaining the authority and impartiality of the judiciary". According to said Article any interference, in order to be justified, must (1) be prescribed by law, (2) safeguard one or more of the specified legitimate purposes, and (3) be necessary in a democratic society. Both, state acts and omission can restrict freedom of expression.[448]

---

446 Regarding freedom of expression and the Internet in general, see e.g. Eric Barendt, *Freedom of Speech* (2nd ed. 2007); Ronald Deibert/John Palfrey/Rafal Rohozinski/Jonathan Zittrain (eds.), *'Access Denied' – The Practice and Policy of Global Internet Filtering* (2008); and Rikke Frank Jørgensen (ed.), *Human Rights in the Global Information Society* (2006). Regarding freedom of expression and intellectual property rights see Dirk Voorhoof, *Freedom of expression and the right to information: Implications for copyright,* in Christophe Geiger (ed.), *Research handbook on human rights and intellectual property* (2015), pp. 331 – 353.

447 Praesidium of the European Convention, *Explanations relating to the Charter*, OJ C 303 (14.12.2007), 17, 33.

448 For an example of state acts cf. ECtHR, *Groppera Radio AG Others v Switzerland*, Judgment of 28.03.1990 – Application No 10890/84, Ser A No 173 (1990); for an example of a state omission cf. ECtHR, *Kenedi v Hungary*, Judgment of 26.05.2009 – Application No 31475/05, [2009] ECHR 786.

The Charter's drafters considered it appropriate to guarantee freedom of expression and information without expressly defining the limitations of these freedoms as the limitation of the Article 10(2) *ECHR* will be "applicable under Union law by virtue of the horizontal clause relating to the Convention".[449] It seems that even in absence of an express reference to Article 10(2) *ECHR*, the case law of the ECtHR provides a framework that can be consulted for the purposes of interpreting Article 11 *CFR*.[450]

The most protected class of expression has been political expression. [451] Political expression has been considered essential for the creation and effective operation of pluralistic democracies, which are necessary to ensure respect for fundamental human rights.[452] Since its first recognition, political expression has been expanded to encompass, inter alia, media comment on political figures[453], criticism of the government and its institutions,[454] political advertising,[455] and wider matters of political interest such as the freedom of academic opinion[456]. The scope of protection also expands to artistic expression,[457] as well as commercial expression.[458]

---

449 Bureau of the Convention, Draft Charter of Fundamental Rights of the European Union, New proposal for Articles 1 to 30 (Civil and political rights and citizens' rights) (05.05.2000), CHARTE 4284, Convent 28, p. 17: "Paragraph 2 has not been included but it is applicable under Union law by virtue of the horizontal clause relating to the Convention. The Court of Justice has endorsed the principle of freedom of expression on several occasions, first and foremost in the ERT Judgment (Judgment of 18.06.1991, Case C-260/89, ECR I-5485)".

450 Instead of many cf. Filippo Donati in: William B. T. Mock/Gianmario Demuro, *Human Rights in Europe, Commentary on the Charter of Fundamental Rights of the European Union* (2010), Article 11 *CFR*, p. 75.

451 Instead of many see ECtHR, *Lingens v Austria,* Judgment of 08.07.1986 – Application No. 9815/82.

452 *Ibid.*

453 ECtHR, *Oberschlick v Austria No. 2*, Judgment of 01.07.1997, Application No. 20834/92.

454 ECtHR, *Castells v Spain*, Judgment of 23.04.1992, Application No. 11798/85.

455 ECtHR, *TV Vest AS & Rogaland Pensjonistparti v Norway*, Judgment of 11.12.2008, Application No. 21132/05.

456 ECtHR, *Boldea v Romania*, Judgment of 15.02.2007, Application No. 19997/02.

457 Instead of many see ECtHR, *Müller and Others v Switzerland*, Judgement of 24.05.1985 – Application No. 10737/84. Artistic expression ranges from paintings *(ibid)* to poetry (ECtHR, *Karatas v Turkey*, Judgment of 08.07.1999 – Application No. 23168/94).

458 Instead of many see ECtHR, *Markt Intern Verlag GmbH and Klaus Beermann v Germany*, Judgment of 20.09.1989 – Application No. 10572/83.

Artistic expression has been an area, where the Court has granted States a wide margin of appreciation to restrict forms of artistic expression that national authorities consider offensive.[459]

Freedom of expression is guaranteed irrespective of the means of transmission; hence, it also applies to expression on the Internet. If in the Second Chapter, the termination of an Internet connection is discussed as a potential sanction, this needs to be taken into account. The same applies to the blocking of access to certain websites. Both enforcement mechanisms may entail a "violation" of Article 10 *ECHR* if they do not satisfy the conditions in Article 10(2), i.e. (1) are prescribed by law, (2) safeguard one or more specified legitimate purposes, and (3) are necessary in a democratic society.

As regards the "expression" protected, there is no limitation to words, written or spoken. The protection extends to inter alia pictures[460] and images[461]. Equally protected is the form of expression, which includes for instance printed documents,[462] radio broadcasts,[463] paintings[464] or films[465]. As regards this research, the focus is on the right to free expression on the Internet, and thus deals with the question of freedom to seek, receive and impart information and ideas as such, no matter whether written words or spoken words, videos or texts are concerned.

Since freedom of expression protects both information and ideas, also viewpoints and personal assessments, which are not susceptible of proof,

---

459 As regards obscene expression see ECtHR, *Müller and Others. Switzerland*, Judgement of 24.05.1985 – Application No. 10737/84. With regard to blasphemous expressions see ECtHR, *Otto-Preminger Institut v Austria*, Judgment of 20.09.1994 – Application No. 13470/87.

460 ECtHR, *Müller and Others v Switzerland*, Judgement of 24.05.1985 – Application No. 10737/84.

461 ECtHR, *Chorherr v Austria*, Judgment of 25.08.1993 – Application No. 13308/87.

462 ECtHR, *Handyside v The United Kingdom*, Judgment of 07.12.1976 – Application No. 5493/72.

463 ECtHR, *Groppera Radio AG and Others v Switzerland*, Judgment of 28.03.1990 – Application No. 10890/84.

464 ECtHR, *Müller and Others v Switzerland*, Judgement of 24.05.1985 – Application No. 10737/84.

465 ECtHR, *Otto-Preminger Institut v Austria*, Judgment of 20.09.1994 – Application No. 13470/87.

are protected.[466] The distinction between facts/information and ideas plays no role for this work, and further explanations are thus omitted.

The freedom of expression as such is most likely to be affected when the communication of individuals is monitored. Monitoring can have a chilling effect on the expression of information and opinions because the individual concerned may choose to not communicate his opinion if he knows that his expression will be monitored.[467] The CJEU only recently stated held in relation to the *Data Retention Directive* that even where only traffic data and no content of the communication is retained, it is not inconceivable that the retention of data might have an effect on the use of the Internet by Internet users, and consequently on their exercise of the freedom of expression.[468]

bb) The Right to Receive and Seek Information

The right to freedom of expression includes an active aspect (freedom to inform) and a passive aspect (freedom to receive information). The right to receive, seek and impart information is the preliminary right that renders effective the exercise of all the other fundamental rights and freedoms, including the freedom to hold opinions.[469] The right to receive information further implies the protection of a plurality of opinions and thereby fosters an active and informed population participating in the society.[470] Both aspects are of fundamental importance in a democratic society.[471]

---

466 Monica Macovei, *Freedom of Expression,* Council of Europe Human Rights Handbooks, No. 2 (2nd ed. 2004), pp. 9 et seq.

467 See ECtHR, *Telegraaf Media Nederland Landelijke Media B. V. and Others v the Netherlands*, Judgment of 22.11.2012 – Application No. 39315/06, para. 88; *Yefimenko v Russia*, Judgment of 12.02.2013 – Application No. 15204 152/04, paras. 154 et seq.

468 CJEU, Joined cases C-293/12 and C-594/12 *Digital Rights Ireland and Seitlinger and Others*, Judgment of 08.04.2014, para. 28.

469 See Filippo Donati in: William B. T. Mock/Gianmario Demuro, *Human Rights in Europe, Commentary on the Charter of Fundamental Rights of the European Union* (2010), Article 11 *CFR*, p. 72.

470 *Ibid.*

471 *Ibid.* Many national constitutions of EU Member States expressly guarantee these two aspects of the right to receive information, for instance Germany (Article 5

In contrast to Article 19 of the *ICCPR*, Article 10 *ECHR* does not explicitly mention "the right to freely search for information"; however, the ECtHR accepts that the right to freedom to seek and receive information is implicitly included in Article 10 *ECHR*.[472] With respect to the Charter, it has been assumed, that the drafters most likely agreed with this general opinion and considered it unnecessary to expressly mention the right to search for information in Article 11 *CFR*.[473]

As regards the content of information protected by the right to receive (or seek) information, protection "does not extend only to reports of events of public concern, but covers in principle also cultural expressions as well as pure entertainment".[474] As regards the access to a specific means of transmission, the ECtHR held in *Mustafa and Tarzibachi v Sweden* that although citizens may "obtain some news through … newspapers and radio programmes", "these sources of information only cover parts of what is available via television broadcasts and cannot in any way be equated with the later".[475] This case was seen as a precedent in order to ensure that citizens of the Member States have access to modern technology.[476] Hence, the right to receive information applies not only to the content of information but also to the technical means of transmission or reception.[477] In the case *Autronic v Switzerland*, the court held that an

---

Grundgesetz), Sweden (Chapter II, Article 1 *Regeringsformen*), Spain (Article 20 *Constitución española de 1978*).

472 Gerard Cohen-Jonathan in: Louis-Edmond Pettiti/Emmanuel Decaux/Pierre-Henri Imbert (eds.), *La Convention Européenne des Droits de l'Homme, Commentaire* (1999), Article 10, para.3.

473 Filippo Donati in: William B. T. Mock/Gianmario Demuro, *Human Rights in Europe, Commentary on the Charter of Fundamental Rights of the European Union* (2010), Article 11 *CFR*, p. 74.

474 ECtHR, *Khurshid Mustafa and Tarzibachi v Sweden*, Judgment of 16.12.2008 – Application No. 23883/06, para. 44.

475 *Ibid*, para. 45.

476 Robin Elizabeth Herr, *Can Human Rights Law support access to communication technology? A case study under Article 10 of the right to receive information*, Information & Communications Technology Law 2013, Vol. 22 Issue 1, 1, 8.

477 In contrast to Article 10 *ECHR* and Article 11 *CFR* which are silent with respect to forms of expression, Article 19 UDHR and Article 19 *ICCPR* explicitly provide for protection of the means by which the expression is communicated ("through any media"/"either orally, in writing or in print, in the form of art, or through any other media of his choice"). See also UN Human Rights Committee, *General comment No. 34. Article 19: Freedoms of opinion and expression*, CCPR/C/GC/34 (21.07.2011), p 4.

extensive interpretation is necessary "since any restriction imposed on the means necessarily interferes with the right to receive and impart information".[478] Accordingly, means of transmission or reception encompass any technical means.[479] Since the case law grants a broad scope of protection under Article 10 *ECHR*, there is a strong argument that the Internet falls within the ambit of protected technical means of transmission or reception.[480] In fact, the above cited case law has shown that new technologies shall not be excluded from the scope of application.[481] The ECtHR stated in several cases that Article 10 protects not only the substance of ideas and information expressed but also the form in which they are conveyed.[482]

Any interference with the transmission means may result in a violation of the freedom to receive information.

Protection will be granted to both direct state interferences and to interferences by private entities that are upheld by the State.[483] If these principles are applied to potential limitations on Internet access, it is possible that such legislative approaches could entail a violation of the freedom to receive and impart information.

It has long been unclear whether a state has a positive obligation to ensure that the right to receive information was protected in relations between individuals.[484] With its ruling in the case of *Mustafa and Tarz-*

---

478 ECtHR, *Autronic AG v Switzerland*, Judgment of 22.05.1990 – Application No. 12726/87, Ser A No. 178 (1990), para. 47.

479 Cf. *ibid.* For an analysis of the applicability to all communication technologies, see Robin Elizabeth Herr, *Can Human Rights Law support access to communication technology? A case study under Article 10 of the right to receive information,* Information & Communications Technology Law 2013, Vol. 22 Issue 1, 1–13.

480 Cf. Peter van Dijk/Godefridus J. H. Hoof, *Theory and Practice of the European Convention on Human Rights* (4th ed. 2006), p. 783.

481 See further also ECtHR, *Jersild v Denmark*, Judgement of 23.09.1994 – Application No 15890/89. In this case, the ECtHR analysed the role of the press in a democratic society and stated at para. 31 that "although primarily with regard to the print media, these principles doubtless apply also to the audiovisual media".

482 ECtHR, *Oberschlick v Austria*, Judgment of 23.05.1991 – Application No 11662/85, para. 57; ECtHR, *De Haes and Gijsels v Belgium*, Judgment of 24.02.1997 – Application No 19983/92, para. 48.

483 ECtHR, *Khurshid Mustafa and Tarzibachi v Sweden*, Judgment of 16.12.2008 – Application No. 23883/06, para. 34.

484 Robin Elizabeth Herr, *Can Human Rights Law support access to communication technology? A case study under Article 10 of the right to receive information,* Information & Communications Technology Law 2013, Vol. 22 Issue 1, 1, 6.

ibachi v Sweden[485], the ECtHR reiterated the rule that "the right of freedom to receive information basically prohibits a Government from restricting a person from receiving information that others wish or may be willing to impart to him or her".[486] Thereby, the Court confirmed that there is a positive obligation on the part of a state to protect communication between individuals. While traditionally, the identity and purpose of the speaker is critical in determining the level of scrutiny, this case showed that the right of the individual to have access to any type of information for private purposes, including leisure activities, is recognised by the *ECHR*.

Thus, when access is restricted in some way to a means of communication, this may interfere with his freedom of expression not only in the sense that his possibility to impart information may be affected, but more severely the right to receive information about issues of public interest.

cc) The Right to Impart Information

The right to impart information and ideas freely is complementary to the right to receive information and ideas. It is the active aspect of freedom of expression. The Court has consistently emphasised that Article 10 guarantees the right to impart information and the right of the public to receive it.[487] As stated above, the ECtHR clarified in several cases that Article 10 *ECHR* protects not only the substance of ideas and information expressed but also the form in which they are conveyed.[488] Moreover, with regard to imparting information and ideas via the Internet, the United Nations Human Rights Committee in its General Comment No. 34 on Article 19 *ICCPR* stated that: "Any restrictions on the operation of websites, blogs or any other Internet-based, electronic or other such information dissemination system, including systems to support such communication, such as Internet service providers or search engines, are only permissible to the

485 ECtHR, *Khurshid Mustafa and Tarzibachi v Sweden*, Judgment of 16.12.2008 – Application No. 23883/06, para. 44.

486 *Ibid*, para. 41.

487 See instead of many ECtHR, *Observer and Guardian v the United Kingdom*, Judgement of 26.11.1991 – Application No. 13585/88.

488 ECtHR, *Oberschlick v Austria*, Judgment of 23.05.1991 – Application No 11662/85, para. 57; ECtHR, *De Haes and Gijsels v Belgium*, Judgment of 24.02.1997 – Application No 19983/92, para. 48.

extent that they are compatible with paragraph 3. Permissible restrictions generally should be content-specific; generic bans on the operation of certain sites and systems are not compatible with paragraph 3. It is also inconsistent with paragraph 3 to prohibit a site or an information dissemination system from publishing material solely on the basis that it may be critical of the government or the political social system espoused by the government."[489] Thus, even on supra-European level, the Internet as a technical means for expression enjoys protection.

dd) The Right to Internet Access

Due to the ever-changing nature of society, also fundamental rights face with new challenges. While some challenges can be addressed by a more extensive interpretation of existing rights, some situations may require the evolution of new rights.[490] Historically, fundamental rights are situated rights and take shape in certain societies at certain moments of time.[491] In consideration of the omnipresent Internet and its increasing relevance in our everyday life, there has recently been some debate on a possible recognition of the use of the Internet as a fundamental right.[492] This idea stems from the growing necessity to have access to the Internet, be it for work purposes or private information exchange. The Internet is crucial for today´s knowledge-based economy: it fosters competitiveness as well as innovation. At the same the Internet promotes development and social

---

489 UN Human Rights Committee, *General comment No. 34. Article 19: Freedoms of opinion and expression,* CCPR/C/GC/34 (21.07.2011), p. 11.

490 For the future such rights may include for instance the right to genetic privacy. See Roger Brownsword/Morag Goodwin, *Law and the technologies of the Twenty-First Century* (2012), pp. 225–245.

491 Paul de Hert/Dariusz Kloza, *Internet (Access) as a New Fundamental Right. Inflating the Current Rights Framework?*, European Journal of Law and Technology 2012, Vol. 3 No. 3.

492 Wolfgang Benedek/Matthias C. Kettemann, *Freedom of expression and the Internet* (2014), pp. 41 et seq. For a summary of the debate as of 2012 see Paul de Hert/Dariusz Kloza, *Internet (Access) as a New Fundamental Right. Inflating the Current Rights Framework?*, European Journal of Law and Technology 2012, Vol. 3 No. 3; Stephen Tully, *A human right to access the Internet? Problems and Prospects*, Human Rights Law Review 2014, Vol. 14, 175–195; BBC World Service, *Four in five regard Internet access as a fundamental right: global poll*, BBC News (08.03.2010).

inclusion.[493] According to the European Parliament “the Internet has become a means of expression of choice for political dissidents, democracy activists, human rights defenders and independent journalists worldwide”.[494] Thus, one can also argue that the Internet advances democracy and a plurality of opinions.

Especially, if one considers that in contrast to traditional media, users are not only passive recipients of information but become publishers themselves, the World Wide Web boosts freedom of expression. The generation of so-called "digital natives" have increasingly depend on the Internet as a replacement for dictionaries, newspapers, written letters, music collections etc. Therefore the UN Special Rapporteur on the promotion of the right to freedom of opinion and expression, Frank La Rue, asks for as little content restriction as possible and to make the Internet available to all segments of population.[495]

The importance of Internet access for the freedom of expression becomes obvious when one looks at regimes that suppress certain opinions. Censorship and state control of the Internet is not just a matter of the East with the prominent great firewall of China or Iran's censorship, only recently Turkey blocked certain social media services before national elections.[496]

However, developments towards control and censorship may not convince everyone to grant human right status to Internet access. From an objective perspective, the Internet is nothing more than a content-neutral technology.[497]

In the classical human rights perspective, human rights (not to be confused with civic rights conferred upon humans by law) are understood as

---

493 Paul de Hert/Dariusz Kloza, *Internet (Access) as a New Fundamental Right. Inflating the Current Rights Framework?,* European Journal of Law and Technology 2012, Vol. 3 No. 3.

494 European Parliament, *Freedom of expression on the Internet*, resolution, P6_TA(2006)0324 (6.07.2006).

495 UN Human Rights Council, *Report of the Special Rapporteur on the promotion and protection of the right to freedom of opinion and expression, Frank La Rue,* A/HRC/17/27 (06.05.2011), p. 22.

496 See only Kevin Rawlinson, *Turkey Steps up Bid to Block Twitter after Users Flout Ban,* the Guardian (23.03.2014).

497 See only Paul de Hert/Dariusz Kloza, *Internet (Access) as a New Fundamental Right. Inflating the Current Rights Framework?,* European Journal of Law and Technology 2012, Vol. 3 No. 3.

basic moral guarantees that people have simply because they are people. The Internet as such is not necessary to lead a healthy, meaningful live. Some argue that we currently witness human rights inflation in general, which may lead to a practice of fragmentation. [498]

By recognising more and more rights as fundamental rights, the value of existing and core fundamental rights may diminish. Thus, one must ask, what the substantial added value of the protection of a right to Internet access would be and more importantly whether there would be an added value at all. This is difficult to assess, but the discussion of the right to freedom of expression in general and with regard to the freedom to receive, seek and impart information has already shown that these subcategories of freedom to expression can be invoked to protect both content and connectivity of the Internet against unlawful interferences. Against this background, the right to Internet access will not be treated as a separate subcategory of the freedom of expression. Interferences with Internet access and Internet content will be examined within the existing human rights framework, in particular the right to seek, receive and impart information and ideas, which as noted above also safegurads the means by which information is communicated.

On a national level, a few jurisdictions already explicitly provide in their constitutional system a positive obligation to ensure connectivity.[499] For instance in 2009, the French Constitutional Court declared that the freedom of expression under Article 11 of the Declaration on Human Rights implies freedom to access such services: "in the current state of online means of communication and in the light of the importance that these services have acquired for participation in democratic life and the expression of ideas and opinions, the right to freedom of expression implies the freedom of access to these services".[500] Having established

---

498 See *ibid.*

499 According to Paul de Hert/Dariusz Kloza in *ibid*, Article 5a (2) of the Greek Constitution states since 2001 that "all persons have the right to participate in the Information Society. Facilitation of access to electronically transmitted information, as well as the production, exchange and diffusion thereof, constitutes an obligation of the State, always in observance of the guarantees of articles 9 [privacy], 9A [personal data] and 19 [secrecy of correspondence]".

500 Conseil constitutionnel, Decision of 10.06.2009 – No. 2009-580 DC, Journal officiel de 13.06.2009, p. 9675, para. 12. An English version of the decision is available at http://www.conseil-constitutionnel.fr/conseil-constitutionnel/root/bank/ download/2009580DC2009_580dc.pdf (last accessed 17.05.2014).

this "right to access the Internet", the Court held that any infringement of this right must be strictly limited and is excessive if it comes from an administrative authority and not a judicial power.[501] The Court however laid down, that this right is not absolute and must be reconciled with other rights and freedom of the same rank such as author's rights protected by intellectual property, as laid down in Articles 2 and 17 of the French Declaration on Human Rights.[502] However, instead of developing a "new" fundamental right of Internet access, the French Court considers the right to Internet access as a subcategory of the freedom of expression. Thus the scope of application of freedom of expression is rather adjusted to encompass a new form of communication, a process which not necessarily can be equated with the emergence of a new fundamental right.

ee) Justification of Interference

In the European legal order, freedom of expression is not an absolute right.[503] Thus, limitations may be imposed on the freedom of expression as long as the interference is justified. In this respect, Article 11(2) *CFR* sets forth that "the freedom and pluralism of the media shall respected", while Article 10(2) *ECHR* provides an exhaustive list of legitimate aims that may justify an interference with the right to freedom of expression, i.e. "the interests of national security, territorial integrity or public safety", "the prevention of disorder or crime", "the protection of health or morals", "he protection of the reputation or rights of others", "preventing the disclosure of information received in confidence", and "maintaining the authority and impartiality of the judiciary". According to Article 10(2) *ECHR* any interference, in order to be justified, must (1) be prescribed by law, (2) safeguard one or more of the specified legitimate purposes, and (3) be necessary in a democratic society.[504] Given the extensive Article 10

501 See also Laure Marino, *Le droit d'accès à Internet, nouveau droit fondamental*, Recueil Dalloz 2009, Issue 30, 2045–2046.

502 Conseil constitutionnel, Decision of 10.06.2009 – No. 2009-580 DC, Journal officiel de 13.06.2009, p. 9675, para. 13.

503 Olivier de Schutter, *International Human Rights Law* (2010), pp. 257 et seq.

504 As regards an analysis of the similar test under Article 19 *ICCPR*, see UN Human Rights Council, *Report of the Special Rapporteur on the promotion and protection of the right to freedom of opinion and expression, Frank La Rue*, A/HRC/17/27 (06.05.2011).

ECHR case-law, the following will outline the justification test under said Article in consideration that this case law can be consulted for the purposes of interpreting Article 11 *CFR*.[505]

First of all, the notion of "prescribed by law" covers not only statute but also unwritten law such as common law.[506] In order to fulfil the requirement of "prescribed by law", firstly, the law must be adequately accessible, the citizen must be able to have an indication that is adequate in the circumstances of the legal rules applicable to a given case; secondly, the norm must be formulated with sufficient precision to enable the citizen to regulate his conduct – citizen must be able to foresee the consequences which a given action may entail.[507]

As regards the requirement of necessary in a democratic society, a balancing test is employed which generally follows the subsequent criteria: (1) the interference must correspond to a pressing social need, (2) it must be proportionate to the legitimate aim pursued, and (3) the reasons for the interference must be relevant and sufficient. According to the type of case at issue, the strictness of the criteria may vary. In addition, the States are given a margin of appreciation.

Interferences that are prescribed by law, must further have aims that are legitimate under Article 10(2) *ECHR*: they must be in the interests of national security, territorial integrity or public safety, for the prevention of disorder or crime, for the protection of health or morals, for the protection of the reputation or rights of others, for preventing the disclosure of information received in confidence, or for maintaining the authority and impartiality of the judiciary.

Interference must be "necessary in a democratic society": as regards an interference with the exercise of the rights and freedoms guaranteed in Article 10(1) *ECHR*, the ECtHR held that the "necessity for restricting them must be convincingly established".[508]

---

505 Instead of many cf. Filippo Donati in: William B. T. Mock/Gianmario Demuro, Human Rights in Europe, *Commentary on the Charter of Fundamental Rights of the European Union* (2010), Article 11 *CFR*, p. 75.

506 See ECtHR, *Sunday Times v the United Kingdom*, Judgment of 26.04.1979 – Application No. 6538/74, para. 47.

507 *Ibid*, para. 49.

508 ECtHR, *Autronic AG v Switzerland*, Judgment of 22.05.1990 – Application No. 12726/87, Ser A No. 178 (1990), para. 61.

While a restriction on the freedom of expression may comply with the first two of these conditions, the determining issue will always be whether the restriction on the freedom of expression complies with the third condition, i.e. is "necessary in a democratic society". In that respect, it is important to note that Article 10(2) *ECHR* leaves to the contracting States a margin of appreciation. Case law indicates that the extent of this margin of appreciation varies with, inter alia, the legitimate purposes of the restriction. The fact that copyright protection is a legitimate interest which is protected by the *ECHR* itself may increase the States' margin of appreciation. The margin of appreciation of a national court is in any case subject to the ECtHR's supervision with regard to the aim of the measure challenged and its "necessity", and it covers not only domestic legislation but also any decision to apply it.[509]

It follows from the case law of the ECtHR that a restriction will generally be considered "necessary in a democratic society" for a legitimate aim only if it answers a pressing social need and, in particular, is proportionate to the legitimate aim pursued.[510] Generally, the strongest protection is given to the media as providers of issues of public interest, but others who participate in the public debate or otherwise express opinions of public interest also enjoy a wide protection.

To answer "a pressing social need", the restriction must be justified by "relevant and sufficient" reasons.[511] Taking into consideration the large-scale copyright infringements taking place via the Internet, most of which rights-holders have so far been unable to stop using traditional enforcement measures, one may well argue that for example injunctions against Internet access providers performing mere conduit can generally be justified as answers to "a pressing social need" provided that they are proportionate to the legitimate aim pursued (the protection of copyright).

The test of whether interference was necessary in a democratic society cannot be applied in absolute terms.[512] Decisive in all case is going to be

509 See for example the ECtHR, Handyside v the United Kingdom, Judgment of 07.12.1976 – Application No. 5493/72, (1976) 1 EHRR 737, para. 49.

510 Instead of many see ECtHR, *Observer and Guardian v the United Kingdom*, Judgement of 26.11.1991 – Application No. 13585/88, para. 59.

511 *Ibid.* For the margin of appreciation of States to establish a pressing social need, see Wolfgang Benedek/Matthias C. Kettemann, *Freedom of expression and the Internet* (2014), pp. 48 et seq.

512 See recently ECtHR, *Fredrik Neij and Peter Sunde Kolmisoppi v Sweden*, Decision of 19.02.2013 -Application No. 40397/12.

the proportionality test. According to the principle of proportionality, any restriction on the freedom of expression must be proportionate to the legitimate aim pursued. The restrictions on the freedom of expression which may follow from an injunction against an Internet access provider or a user will depend largely on the specific circumstances of each case. Hence, the outcome of the proportionality test will also depend largely on the specific circumstances of each individual case.

When examining the proportionality of a measure, one needs to take into account the nature of the competing interests involved and the degree to which those interests require protection in the circumstances of the case.[513] Respect must also be paid to the nature and severity of the penalties imposed.[514]

Although there is an extensive amount of case law from the ECtHR with regard to the determination of "necessary in a democratic society", so far there is only one judgement referring to copyright law and restrictions on the Internet.[515]

For the first time in a judgment on the merits, the ECtHR clarified in the case of *Ashby Donald and others v France* that a conviction based on copyright law for illegally reproducing or publicly communicating copyright protected material can be regarded as an interference with the right of freedom of expression and information under Article 10 *ECHR*.

According to the ECtHR in *Ashby Donald*, it is no longer sufficient to justify a sanction or any other judicial order restricting one's (in this case: artistic or journalistic) freedom of expression on the basis that a copyright law provision has been infringed. Neither is it sufficient to consider that the unauthorised use, reproduction or public communication of a work cannot rely on one of the narrowly interpreted exceptions in the copyright law itself, including the application of the so-called three-step test[516].

---

513 *Ibid.*

514 See ECtHR, *Cumpănă and Mazăre v Romania* [GC], Judgment of 17.12.2004 – Application No. 33348/96, para. 111; *Skalka v Poland*, Judgment of 27.05.2003 – Application No. 43425/98, para. 41.

515 ECtHR, *Ashby Donald and others v France*, Judgment of 10.01.2013 – Application No. 36769/08. In the prior case of the founders of the Pirate Bay against Sweden challenging their criminal convictions, the Court declared the application inadmissible, see ECtHR, *Fredrik Neij and Peter Sunde Kolmisoppi v Sweden*, Decision of 19.02.2013 – Application No. 40397/12.

516 The three-step test is central to the regulation of limitations on copyright at an international level and has been encouraged to be applied by the IPR Enforce-

Recent case law also shows that where the speech is "commercial speech", meaning that it is merely money driven, it does not enjoy the added value of the protection guaranteed by Article 10 *ECHR*. Accordingly, there is a wider margin of appreciation available when freedom of expression is regulated in relation to speech in commercial matters or advertising.[517] This will be important when Internet service provider rely on the right to freely impart expression. However, it is not because a website is part of a commercial company, that the invoked freedom of expression will receive a lower degree of protection from the scope of Article 10 *ECHR*. What matter is whether the expression contributes to the very broadly defined debate of general interest.[518]

b) Privacy Rights

The notion of privacy is wide. It includes inter alia the right to private and family life. Due to the wide scope of application, the following outline will – following a general introduction – not address every aspect of privacy, but only focus on those aspects that may be affected in copyright enforcement scenarios.

---

ment Directive. For an outline of the potential implementation of the Three-Step Test in EU law, see Martin Senftleben, *The International Three-Step Test, A model provision for EC fair use legislation*, JIPITEC 2010, 67–82.

517 ECtHR, *Mouvement Raëlien Suisse v Switzerland*, Judgment of 13.07.2012 – Application No. 16354/06, para. 61, citing ECtHR, *Markt Intern Verlag GmbH and Klaus Beermann v Germany*, Judgment of 20.09.1989 – Application No. 10572/83. See also *Ashby Donald and others v France*, Judgment of 10.01.2013 – Application No. 36769/08.

518 Dirk Vorhoof, *Copyright vs Freedom of Expression Judment*, ECHR Blog (22.01.2013), with further references.

aa) Privacy Rights in General

Throughout history, the willingness of individuals to engage in debate on controversial subjects in the public sphere has been linked to being able to do so anonymously.[519]

The Internet allows individuals to access information and to engage in public debate without having to reveal their real identities; many services can be used without any identification, or verification of identity. As aforementioned, this anonymity may be real anonymity, but in most cases is only perceived as anonymity: the Internet presents tools and mechanisms through which both state as well as private actors have the ability to monitor and collect information about online communication and activities.[520] Technological progress means that large volumes of personal data are collected (often automatically) and stored by intermediaries.

A right to privacy is guaranteed by Article 12 *UDHR* and Article 17 *ICCPR*. The latter provides that "1. No one shall be subjected to arbitrary or unlawful interference with his privacy, family, home or correspondence, nor to unlawful attacks on his honour and reputation; 2. Everyone has the right to the protection of the law against such interference or attacks." Although "correspondence" primarily has been interpreted as written letters, this term today covers all forms of communication, including communication via the Internet.[521] The right to private correspondence obliges states to ensure that emails and other forms of online communication are actually delivered to the desired recipient without interference or monitoring by state organs or by third parties.[522]

The right to privacy in international law also encompasses the protection of personal data.[523] Article 17(2) *ICCPR* requires that the gathering and holding of automated personal data, whether by public authorities or

---

519 See UNHRC, *Report of the Special Rapporteur on the Promotion and Protection of the Right to Freedom of Opinion an Expression, Frank La Rue*, UN Doc A/HRC/17/27 (16.05.2011), p. 15.

520 *Ibid.*

521 *Ibid.*

522 Manfred Nowak, *U.N. Covenant on Civil and Political Rights, CCPR Commentary* (2005), Article 17, p. 401.

523 *Ibid.*

private parties must be regulated by law.[524] In order to guarantee effective protection of a person's private life, every individual should have rights to information as to what personal data is stored and for what purposes, and must have rights to correction and deletion of data.[525] However, the right to privacy is not granted without limits and can be subject to proportionate restrictions or limitations under clearly defined, exceptional circumstances for instance state surveillance measures for the purposes of administration of criminal justice or prevention of crime.[526]

As regards the definition of the right to privacy and the right to the confidentiality of communication under *ECHR* and EU law, the wording of Article 7 *CFR* corresponds almost exactly to Article 8 *ECHR*: Article 7 *CFR* sets forth that "everyone has the right to respect for his or her private and family life, home and communications", while Article 8(1) *ECHR* stipulates that "everyone has the right to respect for his private and family life, his home and his correspondence". Other than the Charter provision, Article 8 *ECHR* has a second paragraph which states that "there shall be no interference by a public authority with the exercise of this right except such as is in accordance with the law and is necessary in a democratic society in the interests of national security, public safety or the economic well-being of the country, for the prevention of disorder or crime, for the protection of health or morals, or for the protection of the rights and freedoms of others."

According to the Explanations Relating to the Charter the meaning and the scope of Article 7 of the Charter and Article 8 of the *ECHR* are the same.[527] In addition to these articles, Article 8 *CFR* expressly provides for a right to the protection of personal data.

---

524 UNHRC, *Report of the Special Rapporteur on the Promotion and Protection of the Right to Freedom of Opinion an Expression, Frank La Rue*, UN Doc A/HRC/17/27 (16.05.2011), p. 15.

525 Office of the High Commissioner for Human Rights, *General Comment No. 16: The Right to Respect of Privacy, Family, Home and Correspondence, and Protection of Honour and Reputation (Article 17),* CCPR General Comment No. 16 (08.04.1988), para. 10.

526 UNHRC, *Report of the Special Rapporteur on the Promotion and Protection of the Right to Freedom of Opinion an Expression, Frank La Rue*, UN Doc A/HRC/17/27 (16.05.2011), p. 15.

527 *Praesidium of the European Convention, Explanations relating to the Charter,* OJ C 303 (14.12.2007), 17, 33.

Although it is generally accepted that the right to privacy of the *ECHR*, the *UDHR* and the *ICCPR* encompasses the right to the protection of personal data, the drafters of the Treaty considered it necessary to specifically protect this fundamental right which is more and more threatened in light of the ever-expanding technological progress.[528] For the very same reason, this right will subsequently be dealt with separately from the general right to privacy.

Guidance as to the interpretation of the right to privacy and protection of personal data can be drawn from the *Strasbourg Data Protection Convention of 1981*[529], which assured to each person in the contracting parties' territories"the respect of his or her rights and his or her fundamental liberties, and in particular, the right to privacy, in relation to the automatic processing of personal data that concerns him or her".[530] As all Member States have ratified the Convention, these principles can be consulted when taking into account the common traditions of Member States in relation to data protection.

bb) Right to Respect for Family and Private Life

The right to respect for family and private life as it is provided by Article 8 *ECHR* and Article 7 *CFR* is to be understood in a very broad sense.[531] When the Charter refers to the right to respect for "communications"

528 Filippo Donati in: William B. T. Mock/Gianmario Demuro, *Human Rights in Europe, Commentary on the Charter of Fundamental Rights of the European Union* (2010), Article 8 *CFR*, p. 53.

529 Council of Europe, *Convention for Protection of Individuals with regard to Automatic Processing of Personal Data*, Council of Europe Treaties No. 108 of 28.01.1981. The Strasbourg Convention is an open convention and is accessible to any other non-member state of the Council of Europe that is invited to join the Convention by the Committee of Ministers. The Convention is currently being amended to allow accession by the EU itself. For a list of the parties to the Convention that have accepted the amendments allowing the EU to accede to the Convention, see http://conventions.coe.int/Treaty/Commun/ChercheSig.asp?NT=108&CL=ENG (last accessed on 17.05.2014).

530 Article 1 *Convention for Protection of Individuals with regard to Automatic Processing of Personal Data.*

531 Cf. EU Network of Independent Experts on Fundamental Rights, *Commentary of the Charter of Fundamental Rights of the European Union* (June 2006), Article 7 *CFR*, p. 78.

instead of "correspondence", this intends to take account of developments in technology.[532]

Various types of situations may involve the right to respect for family and private life, and the case-law of the ECtHR relating to this right and its general expressions of "private and family life" may serve as examples to illustrate the scope of the provision.[533]

The provision embraces a wide variety of matters including various spheres of life, and covers the physical and psychological integrity of a person.[534] It can therefore embrace multiple aspects of an individual's physical and social identity including the sphere of intimate relationships. Elements of privacy include gender identification, name und sexual orientation and sexual life.[535] The protected spheres further range from the social[536] and professional sphere to the protection of the environment.[537] Beyond a person's name, his private and family life may include other means of personal identification and of linking to a family.[538] In that respect the term "privacy" which is often used interchangeably must be understood as an umbrella term. [539]

---

532 Bureau of the Convention, Note from the Praesidium, *Draft Charter of Fundamental Rights of the European Union, Text of the Explanations Relating to the Complete Text of the Charter as set out in CHARTE 4487/00 CONVENT 50* (11.10.2000), CHARTE 4473/00, Convent 49, p. 10.

533 See EU Network of Independent Experts on Fundamental Rights, *Commentary of the Charter of Fundamental Rights of the European Union* (June 2006), Article 7 *CFR*, p. 78.

534 See ECtHR, *Pretty v the United Kingdom*, Judgment of 29.04.2002 – Application No. 2346/02, para. 61; Y. *F. v Turkey*, Judgment of 22.07.2003 – Application No. 24209/94, para. 33.

535 See for instance ECtHR, *Bensaid v the United Kingdom*, Judgment of 06.02.2001 – Application No. 44599/98, para. 47 with further references.

536 ECtHR, *Botta v Italy*, Judgment of 24.02.1998 – Application No. 21439/93, para. 32: the guarantees afforded by Article 8 *ECHR* intend inter alia "to ensure the development of each individual in his relations with other human beings".

537 See ECtHR, *Guerra and Others v Italy*, Judgment of 19.02.1998 – Application No. 14967/89. In this case (at para. 57), the Court considered the direct effect of toxic substances and inflammable gas emissions within the realm of the applicants' right to respect for their private and family life.

538 ECtHR, S. *and Marper v the United Kingdom*, Judgment of 04.12.2008 – Application Nos. 30562/04 and 30566/04, para. 66 with further references.

539 EU Network of Independent Experts on Fundamental Rights, *Commentary of the Charter of Fundamental Rights of the European Union* (June 2006), Article 7 *CFR*, p. 78.

The notion encompasses first of all "the right to be left alone",[540] and can be defined as freedom from unwarranted and arbitrary interference, i.e. contrary to established legal principles – from public authorities or private actors or bodies independent of the state, such as private electronic databases, into activities that society recognizes as belonging to the realm of individual autonomy (the private sphere).[541] The right to privacy is however not granted without limitations. Pursuant to the public order provision in Article 8(2) *ECHR*, interference with the right to privacy can be legitimate and may become necessary in a democratic society (see above). In addition to the general obligation to abstain from interferences, Article 8 *ECHR* also confers positive obligations on the State Parties to act in compliance with the Convention in protecting the rights of individuals.[542]

What is protected is not only the physical framework of personal life, but also a person's inner life as well, for instance his philosophical, religious or moral beliefs.[543]

The respect for private life thus requires, among other things, the right of individuals to non-interference with their decisions on ways to live their life.[544] The right shall also protect individuals from the disclosure or improper discovery by third persons of facts relating to their physical condition, health or personality.[545] This aspect may in the following become in so far relevant when warnings are sent to subscriber for alleged infringement of copyright, and the subscriber himself did not commit the infringement, however, the warning contains details about the files allegedly being shared. An extreme, yet likely scenario is that of a wife being informed that her husband allegedly shares hardcore gay pornography, or a politician whose employer is informed that he listens and shares

540 ECtHR, *Malone v the United Kingdom*, Judgment of 02.08.1984 – Application No. 8691/79, para. 51. See also EU Network of Independent Experts on Fundamental Rights, *Commentary of the Charter of Fundamental Rights of the European Union* (June 2006), Article 7 *CFR*, pp. 78 et seq.

541 *Ibid*, Article 7 *CFR*, p. 79.

542 ECtHR. *Marckx v Belgium*, Judgment of 13.06.1979 – Application No. 6833/74, para. 31.

543 EU Network of Independent Experts on Fundamental Rights, *Commentary of the Charter of Fundamental Rights of the European Union* (June 2006), Article 7 *CFR*, p. 79.

544 *Ibid.*

545 See ECtHR, *Eur. Comm. H.R., DVO v Belgium*, Judgment of 01.03.1979 – Application No. 7654/76.

songs which are deemed homophobe and racist. As regards the sexual private life, the ECtHR acknowledged that sexual life is part and parcel of private life.[546]

Intrinsically linked with the storing of personal data, which will be dealt with below is the subsequent use of information obtained. In Malone v United Kingdom, the British Post Office and the British Telephone Company collected data about phone numbers that had been dialled from particular telephones, as well as time and duration of these phone calls. In the following, the gathered data was released to the police without the consent of the subscriber. The ECtHR did not accept "that the use of data obtained [...] cannot give rise to an issue under Article 8. The records [...] contain information, in particular the numbers dialled, which is an integral element in the communications made by telephone".[547] Accordingly, the release of the information obtained to the police (without the consent of the subscriber) was held to constitute an interference with the right to private life.[548]

The right to respect for private life also includes the individual's right to have access to information stored about himself. Personal information held by third parties might be of vital interest for the individuals concerned.

Without going into too much detail at this point, different scenarios concerning copyright enforcement mechanisms are likely to affect the individual´s right to respect for his private life and family. These include scenarios where a subscriber is obliged to monitor the usage of his Internet access by family members; or where Internet traffic is monitored in general.

Likely scenarios include such where interferences exist with regard to an obligation of abstaining from interferences with the right to private life (for instance the imposition of an obligation upon individuals to monitor the Internet activities of their family members), as well as interferences with regard to positive obligations (for instance the denial of right to access personal data held by a state authority or third parties).

546 ECtHR, *Dudgeon v the United Kingdom*, Judgment of 22.10.1981 – Application No. 7525/76, para. 52.

547 ECtHR, *Malone v the United Kingdom*, Judgment of 02.08.1984 – Application No. 8691/79, para. 84.

548 *Ibid.*

cc) Right to the Confidentiality of Communications

Article 7 *CFR* and Article 8 *ECHR* also encompass the right to the confidentiality of communications. As mentioned above, the drafters of the Charter decided to depart from the notion of respect to privacy of correspondence and substituted the notion of "correspondence" by "communication" to take account of technological progress. However, even the notion "correspondence" is a broad one, and has historically been understood to include communications in writing and by telephone.[549]

In respect to communication via the telephone, not just the contents of telephone communications but also the telephone numbers dialled, i.e. traffic data, are protected under Article 8 *ECHR*.[550] The same principle applies to E-mail communication.[551]

Advances in modern technology have rendered certain forms of communication, such as mobile phones and email, particularly susceptible to improper surveillance by state authorities.[552] With a lot of communication taking place online, electronic surveillance is becoming more and more sophisticated, and may even allow for surveillance of communication channels where the individual has taken steps to encrypt his communication.[553] Comprehensive computerised file systems and electronic data banks as well as communication via the Internet entail many risks for the effective protection of private matters.[554] Further, telephone interception and other means of communication surveillance, in particular Internet surveillance, are considered by many states as a legitimate way of control-

---

549 The ECtHR established in *Klass* that telephone communications constitutes both "correspondence" and "private life". ECtHR, *Klass and Others v Germany*, Judgment of 06.09.1978 – Application No. 5029/71, para. 41.

550 See ECtHR, *Malone v the United Kingdom*, Judgment of 02.08.1984 – Application No. 8691/79, para. 84.

551 ECtHR, *Copland v the United Kingdom*, Judgment of 03.04.2007 – Application No. 62617/00, para. 43.

552 EU Network of Independent Experts on Fundamental Rights, *Commentary of the Charter of Fundamental Rights of the European Union* (June 2006), Article 7 *CFR*, p. 84.

553 With regard to encryption being cracked by state authorities see James Ball/Julian Borger/Glenn Greenwald, *Revealed: How US and UK spy agencies defeat Internet piracy and security*, The Guardian (06.09.2013).

554 EU Network of Independent Experts on Fundamental Rights, *Commentary of the Charter of Fundamental Rights of the European Union* (June 2006), Article 7 *CFR*, p. 85.

ling modern forms of crime including espionage and terrorism.[555] In the light of these developments, Article 7 *CFR* is also closely connected with the protection of telephone, email and other electronic means of communication from interception.[556]

Under the right to the confidentiality of communications, states are obliged to take all necessary measures to restrict unlawful obtaining of information by public authorities as well as by other private parties. Obviously, files or data gathered by authorities or third parties, which may well be the case with copyright enforcement schemes that encompass a warning mechanism, affect this right. In this respect, not only the fact that information is collected but also the methods used to gather and collect personal information may interfere with the right to confidentiality of communications.[557] In that respect, the fact that often information is gathered by third parties and then collected by state authorities needs to be examined.

555 This has only recently attracted a lot of public attention when it was revealed by Edward Snowden that the UK Government Communications Headquarters (GCHQ) as well as the US National Security Agency (NSA) not only monitor online communication but also have successfully cracked much of the online encryption relied upon by hundreds of millions of people to protect the privacy of their personal data, online transactions and emails. As regards the NSA's PRISM data-collection program see Washington Post, *NSA slides explain the PRISM data-collection program*, Washington Post (06.06.2013, updated 10.07.2013); as regards the GCHQs activities see James Ball/Julian Borger/Glenn Greenwald, *Revealed: How US and UK spy agencies defeat Internet piracy and security*, The Guardian (06.09.2013).

556 EU Network of Independent Experts on Fundamental Rights, *Commentary of the Charter of Fundamental Rights of the European Union* (June 2006), Article 7 *CFR*, p. 85. Nevertheless, secret surveillance, in particular telecommunications surveillance,can be legitimate according to the criteria in Article 8(2) *ECHR*, see for example ECtHR, *Klass and Others v Germany*, Judgment of 06.09.1978 – Application No. 5029/71, and *Malone v the United Kingdom*, Judgment of 02.08.1984 – Application No. 8691/79.

557 ECtHR, *Leander v Sweden*, Judgment of 26.03.1987 – Application No. 9248/81, para. 48; S. and Marper v the United Kingdom, Judgment of 04.12.2008 – Application Nos. 30562/04 and 30566/04, para. 67.

dd) Right to Protection of Personal Data

The right to protection of personal data forms a subset of the right to privacy, and is as such protected by Article 8 *ECHR*, Article 12 *UDHR* and Article 17 *ICCPR*. The EU legislator however considered it necessary to protect the protection of personal data expressly in Article 8 *CFR*.[558] Such necessity was based on the realisation that technological developments in the use of electronic and automated means of information management facilitate the creation of databases and the circulation of such data.[559] The use and exchange of personal data have become essential factors in the online economy. Article 8 *CFR*s sets forth that "1. Everyone has the right to the protection of personal data concerning him or her". According to paragraph 2 of said article, personal data "must be processed fairly for specified purposes and on the basis of the consent of the person concerned or some other legitimate basis laid down by law. Everyone has the right of access to data which has been collected concerning him or her, and the right to have it rectified". Further, compliance with these rules shall be subject to control by an independent authority (Article 8(3)). The right to protection of personal data is also expressly recognised in some European constitutions.[560] The progressive adoption of data protection legislation in EU Member States began with the Council of Europe Resolution on the Protection of the Privacy of Individuals vis-à-vis Electronic Data Banks in the Private Sector[561].

---

558 Filippo Donati in: William B. T. Mock/Gianmario Demuro, *Human Rights in Europe, Commentary on the Charter of Fundamental Rights of the European Union* (2010), Article 8 *CFR*, p. 53. Article 8 did not appear in the first drafts of the Charter, and was introduced during a more advanced stage of drafting.

559 *Ibid.*

560 The Constitution of Portugal for example contains a very detailed provision on the protection of personal data, see Article 35 (Utilização da informática) *Constituição da República Portuguesa.*

561 Council of Europe, *Parl. Ass. Resolution (73) 22 on the Protection of the Privacy of Individuals vis-à-vis Electronic Data Banks in the Private Sector of 26.09.1973.* This Resolution and the Resolution (74) 29 in reference to data banks in the public sector were non-binding instruments and as a result, legislation on the protection of privacy and the regulation of databases was not uniform in Europe.

At EU level, the right to protection of personal data is recognised in the *Data Protection Directive* [562], and Article 16 TFEU, which stipulates that everyone has the right to the protection of personal data.[563] In contrast to this non-binding instrument, the Strasbourg Data Protection Convention of 1981[564] assured to each person in the contracting parties' territories "the respect of his or her rights and his or her fundamental liberties, and in particular, the right to privacy, in relation to the automatic processing of personal data that concerns him or her".[565] The Convention sets forth basic principles for data processing such as that personal data must be obtained correctly and processed fairly and for lawful purposes, and that there exist duties to provide security measures and to allow interested persons access to the data that concern them.[566]

Moreover than the Convention, the EU *Data Protection Directive* of 24 October 1995 provides for a rather detailed common framework. The principles that are encompassed in Article 8 *CFR* have all previously been contained in said Directive. The purpose of the *Data Protection Directive*

---

562 *Directive 95/46/EC of the European Parliament and the European Council of 24.10.1995 on the Protection of Individuals with regard to the Processing of Personal Data and on the Free Movement of Such Date,* OJ L-281 (23.11.1995), 31.

563 Article 16 *TFEU* further states in its second paragraph that "The European Parliament and the Council, acting in accordance with the ordinary legislative procedure, shall lay down the rules relating to the protection of individuals with regard to the processing of personal data by Union institutions, bodies, offices and agencies, and by the Member States when carrying out activities which fall within the scope of Union law, and the rules relating to the free movement of such data. Compliance with these rules shall be subject to the control of independent authorities". The rules adopted on the basis of this Article shall be without prejudice to the specific rules laid down in Article 39 *TEU.*

564 Council of Europe, *Convention for Protection of Individuals with regard to Automatic Processing of Personal Data*, Council of Europe Treaties No. 108 of 28.01.1981. The Strasbourg Convention is an open convention and is accessible to any other non-member state of the Council of Europe that is invited to join the Convention by the Committee of Ministers. The Convention is currently being amended to allow accession by the EU itself. For a list of the parties to the Convention that have accepted the amendments allowing the EU to accede to the Convention, see http://conventions.coe.int/Treaty/ Commun/ChercheSig.asp?NT =108&CL=ENG (last accessed 17.05.2014).

565 Article 1 *Convention for Protection of Individuals with regard to Automatic Processing of Personal Data.*

566 Cf. Articles 4–11 *Convention for Protection of Individuals with regard to Automatic Processing of Personal Data.*

was to require Member States to adopt a uniform protection of individual rights and liberties with regard to data processing in order to eliminate obstacles to the movement of personal data and to permit the full development of the internal market. Accordingly, Articles 6 and 12 of the *Data Protection Directive* provide that very individual has the right to adequate protection of his personal data. Processing of personal data must be necessary, fair, lawful and proportionate. The data that individuals provide directly or indirectly must not be used for purposes other than those originally intended, nor can such data be passed on indiscriminately to entities that the individual has not chosen to be involved with. These rights apply to everyone, irrespective of nationality or place of residence.[567]

The importance of the right to protection of personal data was in the following acknowledged by the Treaty of Amsterdam, which introduced a new provision in the area of protection of personal data within the Treaty Establishing the European Community: Article 268(1) *EC Treaty* provided that Community law on the protection of individuals with regard to the treatment of personal data and the free movement of such data was to be applied to the institutions and all organisations instituted by the Treaty on European Union.[568] Further rules have been set up by the *E-Privacy Directive* of 12 July 2002[569].

One of the major discrepancies of Article 8 *CFR* and the *Data Protection Directive* is that the Charter limits the protection of personal data to physical persons. While the Directive defines the notion of processing of personal data as "any operation or set of operations which is performed

---

567 For certain categories of personal data, namely data revealing racial or ethnic origin, political opinions, religious or philosophical beliefs, trade-union membership, and the processing of data concerning health or sex life, processing is only permitted with explicit consent of the individual, where allowed by national legislation. See Article 8 *Data Protection Directive*.

568 Article 268 *EC Treaty* was replaced by Article 16 *TFEU* in the *Treaty of Lisbon.*

569 *Directive 2002/58/EC of the European Parliament and of the Council of 12.07.2002 Concerning the Processing of Personal Data and the Protection of Privacy in the Electronic Communications Sector (E-Privacy Directive),* OJ L-201 (31.07.2002), p. 37. Important regulations concerning data security in connection with the treatment of personal data are to be found in this Directive. The Directive emphasises the right to privacy for instance in its Article 4, which obliges the provider of a public available electronic communication service to take appropriate measures to protect the security of its services. If there is a particular risk of a breach of the security of the network, the provider must inform the subscribers of such a risk.

upon personal data, whether or not by automatic means, such as collection, recording, organization, storage, adaptation or alteration, retrieval, consultation, use, disclosure by transmission, dissemination or otherwise making available, alignment or combination, blocking, erasure or destruction"[570], the Charter goes not that far as providing definitions. The Travaux Préparatoires to the Charter suggest that a rather wide interpretation of "processing" was intended, so as to include any type of operation conducted with or without the aid of telematic means.[571] Being much shorter than the very detailed *Data Protection Directive*, Article 8 *CFR* only provides for a general yet fundamental framework and leaves room for interpretation. Nevertheless, it is much more detailed than previous fundamental rights instruments. Concerning the many indefinite legal notions encompassed in Article 8 *CFR*, it is assumed that the Charter's drafters intended to confer a protection at least equivalent to that protection already afforded by EU law.[572] Pursuant to Article 53 *CFR*, the guarantees recognised by Article 8 are additional to those guarantees already provided by EU law, and in particular by Article 16 *TFEU* and the *Data Protection Directive.*

ee) Justification of Interference

The right to privacy is not granted without limits. While Article 7 *CFR* remains silent as to the limits of this right, Article 8(2) *ECHR* set forth that "there shall be no interference by a public authority with the exercise of this right except such as is in accordance with the law and is necessary in a democratic society in the interests of national security, public safety or the economic well-being of the country, for the prevention of disorder or crime, for the protection of health or morals, or for the protection of the rights and freedoms of others." With regard to these limits, a note from the drafting Presidium indicates that the possible limits that can be placed on

570 Article 1(2) (b) *Data Protection Directive*.

571 See Filippo Donati in: William B. T. Mock/Gianmario Demuro, *Human Rights in Europe, Commentary on the Charter of Fundamental Rights of the European Union* (2010), Article 8 *CFR*, p. 57.

572 *Ibid.*

the rights protected in Article 7 are the same limits provided for in Article 8 *ECHR* by virtue of Article 52(3) *CFR*.[573]

A literal reading of Article 8(2) *ECHR* reflects that the objective is to constrain interferences by the public authorities. The limits of any possible interference are based on the law and are measures that fulfil one of the legitimate aims enlisted.

In order to be "in accordance with the law" under Article 8(2) *ECHR*, the impugned measure must have some basis in domestic law. Second, the domestic law must be compatible with the rule of law and accessible to the person concerned. Third, the person affected must be able to foresee the consequences of the domestic law for him.[574]

The ECtHR applies a wide margin of interpretation to the term "law". The notion not only enshrines statutory but also unwritten law,[575] and enactments of lower rank than statues.[576]

Foreseeability becomes more important in context with collection and storing of personal data. With regard to data protection, data harvesting often takes place in secrecy. Nevertheless, the criterion of foreseeability is an important factor, as precise formulations may enable the individual to regulate his behaviour and to foresee the consequences which his actions may entail.[577] However, especially in the context of secret surveillance, this does not mean "that an individual should be able to foresee when the authorities are likely to intercept his communications so that he can adapt his conduct accordingly".[578]

---

573 Bureau of the Convention, *Note from the Presidium, Draft Charter of Fundamental Rights of the European Union, New Proposal for Articles 1 to 12 (now 1 to 16)* (08.03.2000), CHARTE 4149/00, Convent 13, Article 12, p. 13: "Paragraph 2 on limitations has not been included but it is applicable under Union law pursuant to Article 6 of the TEU and the clause on limitations in the Charter".

574 See instead of many other authorities only ECtHR, *Rotaru v Romania*, Judgment of 04.05.2000 – Application No. 28341/95, para. 59.

575 ECtHR, *Sunday Times v the United Kingdom*, Judgment of 26.04.1979 – Application No. 6538/74, para. 47.

576 ECtHR, *De Wilde, Ooms and Versyp v Belgium*, Judgment of 18.06.1971 – Application No. 2832/66, para. 93: *Huvig v France*, Judgment of 24.04.1990 – Application No. 11105/84, para. 28.

577 See ECtHR, *Sunday Times v the United Kingdom*, Judgment of 26.04.1979 – Application No. 6538/74, para. 49.

578 ECtHR *Weber and Saravia v Germany*, Admissibility Decision of 29.06.2006 – Application No. 54934/00, para. 93.

The ECtHR reiterated the minimum safeguards in order to avoid abuses of power related to strategic secret measures of surveillance in *Rotaru v Romania* stating that "the law must indicate the scope of any such discretion conferred on the competent authorities and the manner of its exercise with sufficient clarity, having regard to the legitimate aim of the measure in question, to give the individual adequate protection against arbitrary interference."[579] The ECtHR has developed minimum safeguards that should be set out in statute law in order to avoid abuses of power, which are however of less relevance for this research as they refer to measures of secret surveillance of States, something that is not specifically foreseen in the field of copyright enforcement.[580]

There is no final definition of the aims enlisted in Article 8(2) *ECHR*. The ECtHR acknowledges a wide margin of appreciation to the Member States.[581] In the majority of cases, the emphasis within the justification test is put on the question of necessity because the examination of this question permits an exhausted analysis with regard to the conflicting interests. As regards copyright infringements, a legitimate aim could be the economic well-being of the country as adequate protection of intellectual property rights is relevant to the economic well-being of a country since successful participation in the global market is increasingly linked to strong protection of intellectual property rights including copyright and neighbouring rights.[582] As infringement of copyright under certain conditions, for instance relating to the scope, often also constitutes a criminal

---

579 ECtHR, *Rotaru v Romania*, Judgment of 04.05.2000 – Application No. 28341/95, para. 55 citing *Malone v the United Kingdom*, Judgment of 02.08.1984 – Application No. 8691/79, para. 67. The same also applies where non-general, but individual monitoring is concerned. See ECtHR, *Liberty and Others v the United Kingdom*, Judgment of 01.07.2008 – Application No. 58243/00, para. 63.

580 These safeguards that should be set out in statute law are: the nature of the offences which may give rise to an interception order; a definition of the categories of people liable to have their telephones tapped; a limit on the duration of telephone tapping; the procedure to be followed for examining, using and storing the data obtained; the precautions to be taken when communicating the data to other parties; and the circumstances in which recordings may or must be erased or the tapes destroyed. See inter alia ECtHR, *Huvig v France*, Judgment of 24.04.1990 – Application No. 11105/84, para. 34.

581 Birte Siemen, *Datenschutz als Europäisches Grundrecht* (2006), p. 151.

582 See Okechukwu Benjamin Vincents, *When rights clash online: The tracking of P2P copyright infringements vs. the EC Personal Data Directive*, International Journal of Law and Information Technology 2011, Vol.16 No. 3, 270, 288.

offence, the prevention of crime may also constitute a legitimate aim. Finally, more than any other, are the rights of others concerned, namely the intellectual property rights of the owners of copyright and related rights.

The achievement of the legitimate aim must remain within the scope of what is necessary in a democratic society. Member States enjoy a large margin of appreciation which is given both to the domestic legislator and the judicial bodies that are called upon to interpret and apply the law in force.[583]

When applying their margin of appreciation to interferences with the right to respect to private life, States have to pay regard to the relationship between the seriousness of the interference, the nature of the rights at stake and the scope accorded to the margin of appreciation, meaning that the more intimate or private the areas of private life affected are, the narrower the scope of the margin of appreciation will be.[584]

c) Procedural Rights

The *CFR* and the *ECHR* both provide for procedural rights. Beside a general fair trial guarantee in both civil and criminal litigation, specific guarantees are established for defendants in criminal proceedings. These guarantees may be affected when a user or subscriber is for instance sanctioned without a hearing.

aa) Right to a Fair Trial

First of all, Article 47 *CFR* guarantees the right to an effective remedy and to a fair trial.[585]

---

583 ECtHR, *Handyside v United Kingdom*, Judgment of 07.12.1976 – Application No. 5493/72, para. 48.

584 Birte Siemen, *Datenschutz als Europäisches Grundrecht* (2006), p. 156.

585 In order to strengthen trust in the criminal justice systems of the Member States, the European Parliament and the Council adopted *Directive 2012/13/EU on the right to information in criminal proceedings,* which codifies a right to information about procedural rights that is inferred from the case-law of the ECtHR. See *Directive 2012/13/EU of the European Parliament and of the Council of*

The second paragraph of Article 47 *CFR* sets forth that "everyone is entitled to a fair and public hearing within a reasonable time by an independent and impartial tribunal previously established by law. Everyone shall have the possibility of being advised, defended and represented".[586] The right to a fair hearing is guaranteed in all proceedings of criminal, civil and administrative nature. It provides that all its guarantees are to be respected upon the violation of rights and freedoms conferred by Community law.[587] The CJEU has consistently held that respect for the right to a fair hearing in any procedure brought against a person which may lead to an act adversely affecting him, in particular a procedure which may lead to sanctions being imposed, constitutes a fundamental principle of Community law. The right to fair hearing requires public authorities to hear interested parties before adopting a decision which concerns them.[588] Accordingly, any person on whom a sanction may be imposed must be given the opportunity to effectively express his view on the matters on the basis of which the sanction is imposed as well as be given the opportunity to produce evidence relevant to his defence.[589]

Article 47(2) *CFR* corresponds to Article 6(1) *ECHR* which provides a fair trial guarantee that applies respectively to both civil and criminal proceedings by stating that "In the determination of his civil rights and obligations or of any criminal charge against him, everyone is entitled to a fair and public hearing within a reasonable time by an independent and impartial tribunal established by law. Judgment shall be pronounced publicly but the press and public may be excluded from all or part of the trial in the

---

22.05.2012 on the right to information in criminal proceedings, OJ L 142 (01.06.2012), 1.

586 In EU law, the right to a fair hearing is not confined to disputes relating to civil law rights and obligations, which is one of the consequences of the fact that the European Union is a community based on the rule of law as stated by the CJEU in C-294/83 *Les Verts v European Parliament*, Judgment of 23.04.1986, [1986] ECR 1339.

587 For the right to a fair hearing to be observed in all proceedings, see CJEU C-85/76 *Hoffmann-La Roche v Commission*, Judgment of 13.02.1979, [1979] ECR 461.

588 CJEU, C-315/99 P *Ismeri Europea v Court of Auditors*, Judgment of 10.07.2001, [2001] ECR I-5281, para. 28.

589 CJEU, C-135/92 *Fiskano v Commission*, Judgment of 26.06.1994, [1994] ECR I-2885; C-142/87 *Belgium v Commission*, Order of 15.06.1987, [1990] ECR I-959; C-78/01 *BGL and Bundesrepublik Deutschland*, Judgment of 23.09.2003, [2003] ECR I-9543.

interests of morals, public order or national security in a democratic society, where the interests of juveniles or the protection of the private life of the parties so require, or to the extent strictly necessary in the opinion of the court in special circumstances where publicity would prejudice the interests of justice".

According to the Explanations Relating to the Charter, in all respects other than their scope, the guarantees afforded by the *ECHR* apply in a similar way to the Union.[590]

The fair hearing requirement in Article 6(1) *ECHR* has been interpreted by the ECtHR on numerous occasions[591] and includes a series of implicit protective principles, such as the right to a court as well as the principle of effective access to a court,[592] the right to participate effectively in proceedings,[593] the right to remain silent/privilege against self-incrimination[594] and the right to equality of arms[595]. The latter for instance relates to criminal proceedings being adversarial with due regard to an equality of arms between the prosecution and defence.[596]

In civil proceedings, the requirements inherent in the concept of "fair hearing" are not necessarily the same in cases concerning the determination of civil rights and obligations as they are in cases concerning the

---

590 Praesidium of the European Convention, *Explanations relating to the Charter*, OJ C 303 (14.12.2007), 17, 30.

591 In fact, the Court has delivered more judgments concerning this Article than any other right or freedom guaranteed by the Charter. See Alastair Mowbray, *Cases, materials and comments on the European Convention on Human Rights* (3rd ed. 2012), p. 344.

592 ECtHR, *Golder v the United Kingdom*, Judgment of 21.02.1975 – Application No. 4451/70.

593 ECtHR, *V. v the United Kingdom*, Judgment of 16.12.1999 – Application No. 24888/94.

594 ECtHR, *John Murray v the United Kingdom*, Judgment of 08.02.1996 – Application No. 18731/91.

595 ECtHR, *Borgers v Belgium*, Judgment of 30.10.1991 – Application No. 12005/86; *Rowe and Davis v the United Kingdom*, Judgment of 16.02.2000 – Application No. 28901/95.

596 ECtHR, *Rowe and Davis v the United Kingdom*, Judgment of 16.02.2000 – Application No. 28901/95, para. 60. However, there is no right to have access to all evidence in the hand of prosecution, when there is a general public interest to withhold certain evidence, for instance as regards the identity of anonymous witnesses, see in that regard the commentary to Article 6(1) *ECHR* in Jens Meyer-Ladewig, *EMRK*, Handkommentar, Article 6(1), para. 148.

determination of a criminal charge.[597] States are granted a greater latitude when dealing with civil cases concerning civil rights and obligations than they have when dealing with criminal cases.[598] As regards litigation involving opposing private interests, for instance the right to intellectual property and the freedom of expression, the right to equality of arms implies that each party must be afforded a reasonable opportunity to present his case – including his evidence – under conditions that do not place him at a substantial disadvantage vis-à-vis his opponent.[599] Civil proceedings must be adversarial, meaning that the parties must have the opportunity not only to make known any evidence needed for their claims to succeed, but also to have knowledge of, and comment on, all evidence filed by the opposing party.[600]

These principles are of relevance in intellectual property proceedings when it comes to the imposition of a sanction upon a user in criminal proceedings as well as in civil proceedings in relation to the alleged infringer being able to have an equal opportunity to submit its evidence.[601]

The right to fair trial, and in particular the right to remain silent, also plays a role where the subscriber of an Internet access service, that has been used to infringe copyright, is being charged for copyright infringement although it is technologically not possible to identify the user of an Internet access at the time of an infringement. The right to remain silent may in these cases be affected when silence leads to a conviction rather than the authorities having to identify the actual offender.

Though not specifically mentioned in Article 6 *ECHR*, the right to remain silent and the privilege against self-incrimination are encompassed as standards that lie at the heart of the notion of a fair trial. In general, the right not to incriminate oneself presupposes that the authorities seek to prove their case without resorting to evidence obtained through methods

---

597 ECtHR, *Dombo Beheer BV v the Netherlands*, Judgment of 27.10.1993 – Application No. 14448/88, para. 32.

598 *Ibid.*

599 Cf. *ibid*, para. 33 and ECtHR, *Komanicky v Slovakia*, Judgment of 04.06.2002 – Application No. 40437/07, para. 45.

600 ECtHR, *Komanicky v Slovakia*, Judgment of 04.06.2002 – Application No. 40437/07, para. 46.

601 As regards enforcement of intellectual property rights and the right to fair trial see Jonathan Griffiths, *Enforcement of intellectual property rights and the right to a fair trial,* in Christophe Geiger (ed.), *Research handbook on human rights and intellectual property* (2015), pp. 438-454.

of coercion or oppression in defiance of the will of the person charged.[602] As regards the right to remain silent, it is incompatible with the immunities under consideration to base a conviction solely or mainly on the accused's silence or on a refusal to answer questions or to give evidence himself.[603] However, the right to remain silent is not an absolute right; the right does not go that far as to preventing that the accused's silence, in situations "which clearly call for an explanation from him", are "taken into account in assessing the persuasiveness of the evidence adduced by the prosecution".[604] Hence, a national court cannot conclude that an accused is guilty merely because he decides to remain silent.[605] This may only be the case, where the evidence against the accused "calls" for an explanation and a failure to give that explanation "may as a matter of common sense allow the drawing of an inference that there is no explanation and that the accused is guilty".[606] Whether the drawing of adverse inferences from an accused's silence infringes Article 6 *ECHR* is a matter to be determined by taking into account all the circumstance of a case, with a particular regard to the situations where inferences may be drawn, and the weight attached to them by the national courts in their assessment of the evidence.[607]

bb) Presumption of Innocence and Right of Defence

The presumption of innocence as well as the right to defence may be of relevance in respect to criminal prosecutions for intellectual property rights infringements. Defendants must have the opportunity to challenge the validity of underlying rights, as well as to appeal the decision issued.

---

602 See for instance ECtHR, *J.B. v Switzerland*, Judgment of 03.05.2001 – Application No. 31827/96, para. 64. Protection against improper compulsion by the authorities serves the purpose of avoidance of miscarriages of justice and secures the aims of Article 6. See inter alia ECtHR, *John Murray v the United Kingdom*, Judgment of 08.02.1996 – Application No. 18731/91, para. 45; *Saunders v the United Kingdom*, Judgment of 17.12.1996 – Application No. 19187/91, paras. 68–69; ECtHR, *J.B. v Switzerland*, Judgment of 03.05.2001 – Application No. 31827/96, paras. 64 et seq.

603 ECtHR, *John Murray v the United Kingdom*, Judgment of 08.02.1996 – Application No. 18731/91, para. 47.

604 *Ibid.*

605 Cf. *Ibid*, para. 51.

606 *Ibid.*

607 *Ibid*, para. 47.

Whilst Article 6(1) *ECHR* provides for a general fair trial guarantee in both civil and criminal litigation, Article 6(2) and (3) establish specific guarantees for defendants in criminal trials.[608]

Article 48 *CFR*, which sets forth the presumption of innocence and the right of defence, is the same as Article 6(2) and (3) *ECHR*.[609] In accordance with Article 52(3) *CFR*, these rights have the same meaning and scope as the rights guaranteed by the *ECHR*.[610] Thus, when determining the scope of the law, the case law of the ECtHR can be consulted. With regard to a criminal offence, Article 6(2) *ECHR* provides for the presumption of innocence until proved guilty according to law. Accordingly, the burden of proving an offence must rest with the prosecution and any doubt should benefit the defendant.[611] In addition, said article has been held to restrict the application of presumptions of fact or law against a defendant in national law; they must be kept "within reasonable limits which take into account the importance of what is at stake and maintain the rights of the defence".[612] Thus, as elsewhere in the *ECHR*, a reasonable balance has to be held between the public interest and the interests of the individual. A derogation from the presumption of innocence requires justification.

In a case concerning trademarks infringements, the House of Lords summarised the approach to take when examining whether a burden of proof imposed upon a defendant exceeds reasonable limits. According to the House of Lords held in *R v Johnstone*[613] a "sound starting point is to remember that if an accused is required to prove a fact on the balance of probability to avoid conviction, this permits a conviction in spite of the fact-finding tribunal having a reasonable doubt as to the guilt of the accused. …This consequence of a reverse burden of proof should colour one's approach when evaluating the reasons why it is said that, in the absence of a persuasive burden on the accused, the public interest will be

608 Similarly, Article 14(3) of the *International Covenant on Civil and Political Rights* provides for minimum guarantees, including for instance the right against self-incrimination.

609 See also Praesidium of the European Convention, *Explanations relating to the Charter*, OJ C 303 (14.12.2007), 17, 30.

610 *Ibid.*

611 ECtHR, *Barberà, Messegué and Jabardo v Spain*, Judgment of 06.12.1988 – Application No. 10590/83, para. 77.

612 ECtHR, *Salabiaku v France*, Judgment of 07.10.1988 – Application No. 10519/83, para. 28.

613 House of Lords, *R v Johnstone* [2003] UKHL 28.

prejudiced to an extent which justifies placing a persuasive burden on the accused. The more serious the punishment which may flow from conviction, the more compelling must be the reasons. The extent and nature of the factual matters required to be proved by the accused, and their importance relative to the matters required to be proved by the prosecution, have to be taken into account. So also does the extent to which the burden on the accused relates to facts which, if they exist, are readily provable by him as matters within his own knowledge or to which he has ready access".[614]

In addition to the presumption of innocence in Article 6(2) *ECHR*, Article 6(3) *ECHR* grants a series of specific minimum entitlements to defendants, including the defendant's right to be informed of the accusation (Article 6(3)(a)),[615] the defendant's right to adequate time and facilities to prepare his defence (Article 6(3)(b)),[616] and the defendant's right to legal assistance (Article 6(3)(c))[617]. These minimum entitlements have been interpreted and applied by the ECtHR in ways that seek to ensure practical benefits for individuals.[618] As they are of no relevance in this research, further explanations as to their scope are omitted.

cc) Principles of Legality and Proportionality of Criminal Offences and Penalties

The principles of legality and proportionality of criminal offences and penalties follow the traditional rules of *nullum crimen sine lege* and *nul-*

614 *Ibid*, para. 50.

615 As to the scope of this right see ECtHR, *Brozicek v Italy*, Judgment of 19.12.1989 – Application No. 10964/84.

616 An example of a breach of this provision was found in ECtHR, *Öcalan v Turkey*, Judgment of 12.05.2005 – Application No. 46221/99.

617 See for instance ECtHR, *Artico v Italy,* Judgment of 13.05.1980 – Application No. 6694/74.

618 See Alastair Mowbray, *Cases, materials and comments on the European Convention on Human Rights* (3rd ed. 2012), p. 344.

lum poena sine lege.[619] They forbid the retroactive creation of crimes and retroactive creation or increase of criminal punishments.

These principles have been codified in Article 7 *ECHR*, which states that "1. No one shall be held guilty of any criminal offence on account of any act or omission which did not constitute a criminal offence under national or international law at the time when it was committed. Nor shall a heavier penalty be imposed than the one that was applicable at the time the criminal offence was committed. 2. This Article shall not prejudice the trial and punishment of any person for any act or omission which, at the time when it was committed, was criminal according to the general principles of law recognised by civilised nations". The first paragraph of Article 49 *CFR* is almost identical, but adds to the principle of *nullum crimen sine lege* and *nullum poena sine lege*, the rule of retroactivity of a more lenient penal law,[620] which exists in a number of Member States and which features in Article 15 *ICCPR*.[621]

Similar to Article 7(2) *ECHR*, Article 49(2) *CFR* provides said Article "shall not prejudice the trial and punishment of any person for any act or omission which, at the time when it was committed, was criminal according to the general principles recognised by the community of nations". The abstention from referring to "civilised nations" does not change the meaning of this paragraph. In accordance with Article 52(3) *CFR*, the right guaranteed under Article 49 *CFR* has the same meaning and scope as the right guaranteed by Article 7 *ECHR*.[622]

Paragraph 3 of Article 49 *CFR* further sets forth that "the severity of penalties must not be disproportionate to the criminal offence". The *ECHR*

---

619 For the concept of legality as a rule of customary international law see Kenneth S. Gallant, *Legality as a Rule of Customary International Law: Non-Retroactivity of Crimes and Punishments – research through 2010* (14.06.2011), UALR Bowen School Research Paper No. 11–12.

620 Article 49(1) *CFR* states : "No one shall be held guilty of any criminal offence on account of any act or omission which did not constitute a criminal offence under national law or international law at the time when it was committed. Nor shall a heavier penalty be imposed than that which was applicable at the time the criminal offence was committed. If, subsequent to the commission of a criminal offence, the law provides for a lighter penalty, that penalty shall be applicable".

621 Praesidium of the European Convention, *Explanations relating to the Charter*, OJ C 303 (14.12.2007), 17, 30.

622 *Ibid*, 31.

does not contain such a provision.[623] The general principle of proportionality between penalties and criminal offences derives from the common constitutional traditions of the EU Member States and the case-law of the CJEU.[624]

In the context of this research, only the principle of proportionality of penalties will be focussed on. When considering whether a provision of Community law complies with the principle of proportionality, the CJEU will ascertain whether the penalty exceeds what is appropriate and necessary to attain the objective pursued by the rules which have been breached.[625] More precisely, it is "necessary to ascertain whether the penalty laid down by the provision in question to achieve the aim in view corresponds with the importance of that aim and whether the disadvantages caused are not disproportionate to the aims pursued".[626] In accordance with the provisions of the Treaties, the CJEU applies the principle of proportionality not only to the exercise of the institutions' penal powers, but also to the legislative power and its control over the application of Community law by the national authorities.

---

623 In extreme cases, a severe sentence may violate Article 3 of the *ECHR*, which prohibits torture and inhuman or degrading treatment of punishment, but this is of no relevance for this research. Sentences passed in respect of conduct falling within the scope of a qualified right such as Articles 8 to 11, may rather only be considered as a disproportionate interference with such right in the context of this research. Cf. Jonathan Griffiths, *Criminal liability for intellectual property infringement in Europe: the role of fundamental rights*, in: Christophe Geiger (ed.), *Criminal enforcement of intellectual property* (2012), p. 204.

624 As regards the case law of the CJEU in respect to the principle of proportionality between penalites and criminal offences see CJEU, C-356/97 *Molkereigenossenschaft Widergeltingen eG v Hauptzollamt Lindau*, Judgment of 06.07.2000; C-213/99, *José Teodoro de Andrade v Director da Alfandega de Leixoes*, intervener: Ministério Público, Judgment of 07.12.2000.

625 CJEU, C-356/97 *Molkereigenossenschaft Widergeltingen eG v Hauptzollamt Lindau*, Judgment of 06.07.2000, para. 35 with reference to C-118/89 *Lingenfelser* [1990] ECR I-2637, para. 12; C-319/90 *Pressler* [1992] ECR I-203, para. 12; and C-354/95 *National Farmers' Union and Others* [1997] ECR I-4559, para. 49.

626 CJEU, C-356/97 *Molkereigenossenschaft Widergeltingen eG v Hauptzollamt Lindau*, Judgment of 06.07.2000, para. 35 with reference to C-8/89 *Zardi* [1990] ECR I-2515, para. 10; *Pressler*, cited above, para. 12; and Joined Cases C-133/93, C-300/93 and C-362/93 *Crispoltoni and Others* [1994] ECR I-4863, para. 41.

dd) Ne Bis in Idem Rule

The *ne bis in idem* rule refers to the right not to be tried or punished twice in criminal proceedings for the same criminal offence.

This right has been enshrined in Article 4 of Protocol No. 7 to the *ECHR*, which states that "1. No one shall be liable to be tried or punished again in criminal proceedings under the jurisdiction of the same State for an offence for which he has already been finally acquitted or convicted in accordance with the law and penal procedure of that State". The second paragraph goes on to clarify that this rule "shall not prevent the reopening of the case in accordance with the law and the penal procedure of the State concerned, if there is evidence of new or newly discovered facts, or if there has been a fundamental defect in the previous proceedings, which could affect the outcome of the case". The importance of this rule can be seen in paragraph 3 of said Article, which does not even allow for a derogation from said Article in times of emergency.

The ne bis in idem rule is also codified in Article 50 *CFR*, which reads as follows: "No one shall be liable to be tried or punished again in criminal proceedings for an offence for which he or she has already been finally acquitted or convicted within the Union in accordance with the law".[627]

The rule does not preclude the imposition of a combination of administrative and criminal penalties.[628] However, if the administrative penalty is criminal in nature, the ne bis in idem principle precludes criminal proceedings in respect of the same acts from being brought against the same person.[629] The CJEU employs a three criteria test to assess whether administrative penalties are criminal in nature.[630] The court will examine the legal classification of the offence under national law, the very nature of the offence as well as the nature and degree of severity of the penalty that the person concerned is liable to incur.[631] Thus, as long as an administrative

627 As regards the *ne bis in idem* rule in EU law in detail, see Bas van Bockel, *The Ne Bis In Idem Principle in EU Law* (2010).

628 For a combination of tax penalties and criminal penalties for the same acts of non-compliance with declaration obligations in the field of VAT see CJEU, C-617/10 *Åklagaren v Hans Åkerberg Fransson*, Judgment of 26.02.2013, para. 34.

629 *Ibid.*

630 *Ibid*, para. 35.

631 *Ibid* citing CJEU, C-489/10 *Bonda*, Judgment of 05.06.2012, para. 37.

penalty is not criminal in nature, a national court may impose a criminal sanction successively.

3. The Fundamental Rights of Internet Service Providers at Stake

The enforcement mechanisms described and analysed throughout this book often rely on the cooperation of online intermediaries such as access providers: they may be ordered to retain data on repeat infringers, send out warnings to their customers, filter the content hosted or transmitted and block access to infringing materials. Therefore their freedom to conduct business as well as their freedom of expression may be interfered with.

a) Freedom to Conduct Business

The freedom to conduct business of Access Providers may be concerned when they are obliged to retain data on repeat infringers and send out warnings to their customers. They may also be ordered to block access to infringing content. Host providers or search engine providers may be under an obligation to not only take-down infringing material but also prevent the continuation of the infringements by ensuring that they do not reappear.

Under the Charter, the freedom to conduct business is enshrined in Article 16, which provides that "[t]he freedom to conduct a business in accordance with European Union law and national laws and practices is recognised". It is the first time that the freedom to conduct business is being recognised in a formal sense in European sources.[632] It should however be

632 According to Alberto Lucarelli in: William B. T. Mock/Gianmario Demuro, *Human Rights in Europe, Commentary on the Charter of Fundamental Rights of the European Union* (2010), Article 16, p. 99, in the sphere of constitutions in Europem only the Spanish Constitution in its Article 38 expressly recognises the freedom of enterprise in the realm of the market economy, while the Luxembourgish constitution (Article 11(6)) guarantees the freedom of trade and industry, the Irish constitution (Article 45(3)) determines that the state must ensure private enterprise, the Portuguese constitution (Article 86) provides that the state encourages entrepreneurial activity, and the Finnish and Norwegian constitutions (Article 18 and Article 101 respectively) provide for a generic freedom commercial activity.

pointed out, that the freedom to pursue a trade or business belongs to the general principles of European Union law and has been recognised for several years.[633] Prior to the Charter, the CJEU and the ECtHR have been inferring from Article 1 of the Protocol No. 1 to the *ECHR* principles which concern the free exercise of economic activities.[634] The protection afforded by Article 16 *CFR* recognises individual economic freedom and covers the freedom to exercise an economic or commercial activity, [635] the freedom of contract[636] and free competition as recognised by Article 119(1) and (3) *TFEU*[637]. The freedom of contract includes for instance, the freedom to choose with whom to do business,[638] and the freedom to determine the price of a service[639]. As regards limitations on the freedom, the financial burdens on farmers resulting from an obligation to mark sheep and goats electronically and keep a holding register, was considered to be a limitation of the exercise of the freedom to conduct a business in general.[640]

---

633 CJEU, C-280/93 *Germany* v *Council* [1994] *ECR* I-4973, para. 78; Joined Cases C-20/00 and C-64/00 *Booker Aquaculture and Hydro Seafood* [2003] *ECR* I-7411, para. 68; Joined Cases C-154/04 and C-155/04 *Alliance for Natural Health and Others* [2005] *ECR* I-6451, para. 126; and Joined Cases C-453/03, C-11/04, C-12/04 and C-194/04 *ABNA and Others* [2005] *ECR* I-10423, para. 87. See also Andrea Usai, *The freedom to conduct a business in the EU, its limitations and its role in the European legal order: A new engine for deeper and stronger economic, social and political integration*, German Law Journal 2010, Vol. 14 No. 9, 1867–1888.

634 See Alberto Lucarelli in: William B. T. Mock/Gianmario Demuro, *Human Rights in Europe, Commentary on the Charter of Fundamental Rights of the European Union* (2010), Article 16, p. 99.

635 See CJEU, C-4/73 *Nold* [1974] ECR 491, para. 14; C-230/78 *SpA Eridiana and Others*, Judgment of 27.09.1979, [1979] ECR 2749, paras. 20 and 31.

636 Case C-151/78 *Sukkerfabriken Nykøbing* [1979] ECR 1, para. 19; Case C-240/97 *Spain v Commission* [1999] ECR I-6571, para. 99.

637 Praesidium of the European Convention, *Explanations relating to the Charter*, OJ C 303 (14.12.2007), 17, 23.

638 CJEU, Joined Cases C-90/90 and C-91/90 *Neu*, Judgment of 10.07.1991, [1991] ECR I-3617, para. 13.

639 CJEU, C-437/04 *Commission v Belgium*, Judgment of 22.03.2997, [2007] ECR I-2513, para. 51; C-213/10 *F-Tex SIA v Lietuvos-Anglijos UAB "Jadecloud-Vilma"*, Judgment of 09.04.2012, para. 45.

640 C-101/12 para. 24ff CJEU, C-101/12 *Herbert Schaible v Land Baden-Württemberg*, Judgment of 17.10.2013, para. 26.

Freedom to conduct a business is not absolute; moreover, it must be viewed in relation to its social function.[641] The CJEU has identified a series of social objectives, which it defines as "objectives of general interest" and that may limit the exercise of the freedom to conduct business.[642] Accordingly, the freedom to conduct a business may be subject to a broad range of interventions on the part of public authorities which may limit the exercise of economic activity in the public interest.[643]

Being subject to the limitations provided for in Article 52(1) *CFR*, interferences with the freedom must be provided for by law and respect the essence of those rights and freedoms and, in compliance with the principle of proportionality, must be necessary and actually meet objectives of general interest recognised by the European Union or the need to protect the rights and freedom of others.[644]

The *ECHR* does not mention the freedom to conduct a business as a fundamental right. The ECtHR has however used Article 1 of the Protocol No. 1 to the *ECHR* on the protection of private property as a basis for inferring the principles protecting the right to economic initiative. Interestingly, in the case of *Delfi v Estonia*, which concerned the liability of an Internet service provider for third part content and general monitoring obligations, the ECtHR did not discuss an interference with the freedom to conduct business although the service provider argued that due to the judgment of a national court, it was forced to alter its business model.[645] However, as the judgment did not become final, it remains to be seen

---

641 CJEU, Joined Cases C-184/02 and C-223/02 *Spain and Finland v Parliament and Council*, Judgment of 09.09.2004, [2004] ECR I-7789, paras. 51 and 52; C-544/10 *Deutsches Weintor*, Judgment of 06.09.2012, para. 54 with further references. See also Alberto Lucarelli in: William B. T. Mock/Gianmario Demuro, *Human Rights in Europe, Commentary on the Charter of Fundamental Rights of the European Union* (2010), Article 16, pp. 101 et seq.

642 See for example CJEU, C-44/09 *Hauer v Rheinland-Pfalz*, [1979] ECR 3727, para. 17.

643 CJEU, C-283/11 *Sky Österreich GmbH v Österreichischer Rundfunk*, Judgment of 22.01.2013, para. 46; C-101/12 *Herbert Schaible v Land Baden-Württemberg*, Judgment of 17.10.2013, para. 28.

644 See CJEU, C-283/11 *Sky Österreich GmbH v Österreichischer Rundfunk*, Judgment of 22.01.2013, paras. 47–48; C-101/12 *Herbert Schaible v Land Baden-Württemberg*, Judgment of 17.10.2013, para. 27.

645 Cf. ECtHR, *Delfi AS v Estonia*, Judgment of 10.10.2013 – Application No. 64569/09. However, this case has not become final because the Court decided to refer the matter to the Grand Chamber which has not yet rendered a decision.

whether the Grand Chamber of the ECtHR will discuss the freedom to conduct a business when measures are imposed upon an Internet service provider that would require him to change his business model completely.

b) Freedom of Expression

Host providers as well as search engine providers may not only be concerned in their freedom to conduct business but also in their freedom of expression.

Their freedom of expression may be concerned in so far as access providers may be ordered to block access to websites that host infringing materials. Article 10 *ECHR* guarantees freedom of expression to "everyone", both legal and natural persons.[646] No distinction is made according to whether the type of aim pursuit is a commercial activity or not.[647] Article 10 does not apply to certain types of information or expression; it also encompasses information of a commercial nature.[648] As the protection guaranteed by Article 11 *CFR* and Article 10 of the *ECHR* are intended to be the same,[649] freedom of expression of Internet service providers can also be invoked under Article 11 *CFR*.

4. Fundamental Rights of the Intellectual Property Rights Owners

Much has been said about fundamental rights of individuals affected by possible sanctions or other enforcement mechanisms. In that respect, it must not be ignored that the intellectual property rights-holders may themselves raise fundamental rights-based arguments when seeking protection of their rights.

---

646 ECtHR, *Autronic AG v Switzerland*, Judgment of 22.05.1990 – Application No. 12726/87, para. 47.

647 ECtHR, *Sunday Times v the United Kingdom,* Judgment of 26.04.1979 – Application No. 6538/74, paras. 42 et seq.; *Markt intern Verlag GmbH and Klaus Beermann v Germany,* Application No. 10572/83, para.25; *Groppera Radio AG and Others v Switzerland,* Application No. 10890/84, paras. 53 et seq.

648 See ECtHR, *Markt intern Verlag GmbH and Klaus Beermann v Germany*, Application No. 10572/83, Ser A No 165 (1989), para.25.

649 Praesidium of the European Convention, *Explanations relating to the Charter*, OJ C 303, 17 (14.12.2007), 33.

a) Right to Intellectual Property

First of all, the enjoyment of property and intellectual property rights is itself protected as a fundamental right. It falls within the right to property, which is a fundamental right common to all national constitutions in the EU[650] and enshrined in Article 17 *UDHR*.[651]

Because some European countries, or more precise their socialist-leaning post-WWII governments, were reluctant to include a right to property in the *ECHR*, the right to property was placed in an "Optional Protocol" to the Convention and phrased in rather general terms. Today, the right to property is effectively regarded as an integral part of the Convention, and all Member States of the Council of Europe have signed up to the respective Protocol.

Article 1 of the Protocol 1 to the *ECHR* provides that "every natural or legal person is entitled to the peaceful enjoyment of his possessions. No one shall be deprived of his possessions except in the public interest and subject to the conditions provided for by law and by the general principles of international law. The preceding provisions shall not, however, in any way impair the right of a State to enforce such laws as it deems necessary to control the use of property in accordance with the general interest or to secure the payment of taxes or other contributions or penalties".[652] Although there is no explicit mentioning of the right to intellectual property, the ECtHR held the enjoyment of intellectual property rights is a form

650 *Ibid*, 23.

651 As regards copyright as a human right under UDHR and the ICESCR, see Paul L. C. Torremans, *Is copyright a human right?,* Michigan State Law Review 2007, 271–291.

652 The jurisprudence on this Article is extensive. In *Sporrong and Lönnroth v Sweden* (ECtHR, Application No. No. 7151/75; 7152/75 – Judgment of 23.09.1982, para.61), it has been established for the first time that Article 1 of the Protocol 1 to the *ECHR* encompasses three separate rights: a right against deprivation of possessions, a right against the control of use of possessions and a general residual right against interferences with the peaceful enjoyment of possessions which constitute neither deprivation nor control of use.

of property interests. [653] Intellectual property has thus been recognised under the *ECHR* to be one aspect of property.

Article 17 (1) *CFR* was based on the aforementioned Article of the *ECHR* and states that "Everyone has the right to own, use, dispose of and bequeath his or her lawfully acquire possessions. No one may be deprived of his or her possessions, except in the public interest and in the cases and under the conditions provided for by law, subject to fair compensation being paid in good time for their loss. The use of property may be regulated by law in so far as is necessary for the general interest". Art 17(2) specifically confirms that intellectual property falls within this general guarantee, stating that: "Intellectual property shall be protected".

Although the wording of the two provisions is different, the meaning and scope of Article 17 *CFR* shall be the same as Article 1 of the Protocol 1 to the *ECHR*.[654] The change in wording results from the consideration that the *ECHR* provision is no more up-to-date.[655] Thus, concern, that has been expressed with regard to the protection of intellectual property seem-

---

653 See, for example, ECtHR, *Anheuser-Busch Inc. v Portugal* [GC], Application No. 73049/01, para. 72 (holding that Article 1 of Protocol No. 1 is applicable to intellectual property as well as the application for intellectual property rights if such an application gives rise to proprietary interests); *Dima v Romania*, Judgment of 16.11.2006 – Application No. 58472/00. For an analysis of the judgments see Laurence R. Helfer, *The new innovation frontier? Intellectual property and the European Court of Human Rights*, in: Paul L. C. Torremans (ed.), *Intellectual Property and Human Rights, Enhanced Edition of Copyright and Human Rights* (2008), pp. 25 et seq.; Council of Europe, *Internet: case-law of the European Court of Human Rights* (2011), pp. 18 et seq.

654 Praesidium of the European Convention*, Explanations relating to the Charter*, OJ C 303 (14.12.2007), 17, 23. See also Jonathan Griffiths, Constitutionalising or harmonising? – the Court of Justice, the right to property and European copyright law, European Law Review 2013, Vol. 38, 65–78, 68. When balancing the right to intellectual property against other rights, the scrutiny exercised by the CJEU and the ECtHR will differ in one significant aspect, namely, as regards the boundaries of intellectual property rights: the ECtHR has to distinguish between national decisions that interfere with an existing property right and those that serve only to define its boundaries; the CJEU however does not have to make this distinction because it usually has competence to determine the right as such and its boundaries (see *ibid*, 71).

655 Cf. *Praesidium of the European Convention, Explanations relating to the Charter*, OJ C 303 (14.12.2007), 17, 23, which state that "The wording has been updated".

ingly to be granted absolute under Art 17(2),[656] is unfounded. It has been intended by the *CFR* drafters that the limitations in Article 17 *CFR* may not exceed those provided for in the *ECHR*.[657] Its explicit mentioning only shows that the drafters of the Charter found it necessary to expressly guarantee its protection because of its growing importance and Community secondary legislation.[658]

In its recent judgment in *Scarlet Extended v SABAM*,[659] which will be discussed in the third Chapter, the Court of Justice accordingly stated that:

> "The protection of the right to intellectual property is indeed enshrined in Article 17(2) of the Charter...There is, however, nothing whatsoever in the wording of that provision or in the Court's case-law to suggest that that right is inviolable and must for that reason be absolutely protected."[660]

By this statement the CJEU reiterated that the right to intellectual property is not absolute and interferences may be justified. As regards interferences with the right to property as such, the CJEU has consistently held that

> "[W]hile the right to property forms part of the general principles of EU law, it is not an absolute right and must be viewed in relation to its social function. Consequently, its exercise may be restricted, provided that those restrictions in fact correspond to objectives of general interest pursued by the European Union and do not constitute disproportionate and intolerable interference, impairing the very substance of the rights guaranteed."[661]

The use of one's own intellectual property may thus be regulated by law insofar as it is necessary for the general interest. Accordingly, the CJEU reflects the principles under which interferences with intellectual property under the *ECHR* may be lawful.

The *ECHR* approach focuses upon the need to establish whether or not a contracting state has struck a "fair balance" between the protected right

---

656 See Christophe Geiger, *Intellectual Property Shall be Protected!? – Article 17(2) of the Charter of Fundamental Rights of the European Union: a Mysterious Provision with an Unclear Scope,* [2009] E.I.P.R. 115.

657 Cf. *Praesidium of the European Convention, Explanations relating to the Charter*, OJ C 303 (14.12.2007), 17, 23.

658 Cf. *Praesidium of the European Convention, Explanations relating to the Charter*, OJ C 303 (14.12.2007), 17, 23.

659 CJEU, C-70/10 *Scarlet Extended SA v SABAM*, Judgment of 16.02.2012, [2011] ECR I-11959.

660 *Ibid*, para. 43.

661 See CJEU, C-379/08 *Raffinerie Mediterranee (ERG) SpA v Ministero dello Sviluppo economico*, [2010] ECR I-2007, para. 80 and the case law cited therein.

and the general, public interest. [662] The "fair balance" test is quite similar to the necessity and proportionality tests applied under for example Articles 8 and 10 *ECHR* set out above. Although the wording of Article 17 *CFR* is similar to these articles and their corresponding provisions in the Charter ("....use of property may be regulated by law in so far as is necessary for the general interest"), the *ECHR* and EU approaches in respect of balancing property as a fundamental right with other fundamental rights are as good as the same.[663] Hence, "an instrument or measure that in some significant respect tilts the balance of protection manifestly unfairly in favour of one beneficiary of the right, and unfairly against others, or a procedure that fails to allow for the taking into account of the different, competing interests, but rather, stacks all the weight at one end, is incompatible with these fundamental European human rights instruments".[664]

With respect to the assessment of proportionality, the ECtHR accords national decision-makers a broader margin of appreciation under Article 1 of the Protocol 1 than it generally permits in the case of other qualified rights under the *ECHR*.[665]

This principle has also been reflected by the CJEU, when the Court noted in the case of Kadi, that for inferences with the right to property to be acceptable, there must "exist a reasonable relationship of proportionality between the means employed and the aim sought to be realised. The Court must determine whether a fair balance has been struck between the demands of the public interest and the interest of the individuals concerned. In so doing, the Court recognises that the legislature enjoys a wide margin of appreciation, with regard both to choosing the means of enforcement and to ascertaining whether the consequences of enforcement are justified in the public interest for the purpose of achieving the object of the law in question".[666]

---

662 Any procedure, instrument or measure taken must respect the fair balance required by Article 1 *First Protocol* and Article 17 *CFR*.

663 See Douwe Korff/Ian Brown, *Opinion on the Compatibility of ACTA with the ECHR and the EU Charter of Fundamental Rights* (2011), pp. 22 et seq.

664 *Ibid*, p. 23.

665 See Jonathan Griffiths, *Constitutionalising or harmonising? – the Court of Justice, the right to property and European copyright law,* European Law Review 2013, Vol. 38, 65, 68.

666 CJEU, Joined cases C-402/05P and C-415/05P *Kadi and Al Barakaat v Council of the European Union and Commission of the European Communities*, Judgment of 03.09.2008, [2008] ECR I-6351, para. 360.

The case law of the ECtHR on the fair balance test is more extensive than that of the CJEU and will thus be focussed on in the following.

The European Court of Human Rights has, for example, held that the concept of "possessions"[667] includes rights that arise as a result of legitimate expectations.[668] However, this does not include entitlements to property in future.[669]

The distinction between the aforementioned three forms of right to property plays a role in the context of compensation.[670] The ECtHR has established a strong presumption that compensation must be paid in cases of deprivation of property.[671] This presumption has been established as a rule in the Charter, when it states that "no one may deprived of his or her possessions, except ..., subject to fair compensation being paid in good time for their loss". No such presumption exists in relation to other forms of interferences that do not amount to total deprivation.[672] These principles may also be of relevance in relation to interferences with copyright.

It needs to be noted that in many copyright infringement cases not the authors themselves will invoke intellectual property rights, but collecting societies, record labels or other multinational corporations invoke rights. While some criticize that human rights protection also applies to non-individuals, such as these corporate owners of IPR,[673] the ECtHR does consid-

667 The concept of possessions which has autonomous Convention meaning and is therefore not restricted by concepts of national property law. See Jonathan Griffiths, *Constitutionalising or harmonising? – the Court of Justice, the right to property and European copyright law*, European Law Review 2013, Vol. 38, 65, 69.

668 ECtHR *Anheuser-Busch Inc. v Portugal* [GC], Judgment of 11.01.2007 – Application No. 73049/01, para. 49.

669 The *ECHR* only protects existing possessions and assets against interference. See, for example, ECtHR *Marckx v Belgium*, Judgment of 13.06.1979 – Application No. 6833/74, paras. 50 et seq.

670 See Jonathan Griffiths, *Constitutionalising or harmonising? – the Court of Justice, the right to property and European copyright law,* European Law Review 2013, Vol. 38, 65, 70.

671 *Ibid.*

672 *Ibid.*

673 Laurence R. Helfer/Graeme W. Austin, *Human rights and intellectual property: Mapping the global interface (2011), pp. 504 et seq. For further references see Peter K. Yu, Intellectual Property and Human Rights in the Nonmultilateral Era,* Florida Law Review 2012, Vol. 64, pp. 1045, 1066.

er the term "possessions" in Article 1 of Protocol No.1 to the *ECHR* to include intellectual property of corporations.[674]

Finally, beyond the protection of intellectual property rights against infringements, it has been discussed whether the right imposes positive duties upon states to take particular actions to secure intellectual property interests against third party violations.[675] In that respect, it needs to be remembered that the property guarantee under the *ECHR* and the *CFR* grants a considerable margin of appreciation to states to interfere with the enjoyment of property rights in order to secure conflicting public interests so long as a fair balance is maintained; there is nothing in the law that foresees positive duties to prevent intellectual property rights infringements.[676]

b) Right to an Effective Remedy

Article 47 *CFR* guarantees the right to an effective remedy and to a fair trial.

The first paragraph of Article 47 *CFR* sets forth that "everyone whose rights and freedoms guaranteed by the law of the Union are violated has the right to an effective remedy before a tribunal in compliance with the conditions laid down in this Article".

This paragraph is based on Article 13 *ECHR*, which states that "Everyone whose rights and freedoms as set forth in this Convention are violated shall have an effective remedy before a national authority notwithstanding that the violation has been committed by persons acting in an official capacity".

Already from the wording, it becomes clear that in EU law the protection is more extensive since it guarantees the right to an effective remedy before a court.[677]

---

674 See in relation to trademarks and trademark applications : ECtHR, *Anheuser-Busch Inc. v Portugal* [GC], Judgment of 11.01.2007 – Application No. 73049/01.

675 Jonathan Griffiths, *Criminal liability for intellectual property infringement in Europe: the role of fundamental rights,* in: Christophe Geiger (ed.), *Criminal enforcement of intellectual property* (2012), pp. 197 et seq.

676 *Ibid*, p. 198.

677 See also Praesidium of the European Convention, *Explanations relating to the Charter*, OJ C 303 (14.12.2007), 17, 29.

Prior to the Charter, the CJEU had recognised this right in its judgments in Johnston[678], Heylens[679] and Borelli[680] as a general principle of EU law, which also applies to the Member States when they are implementing EU law. The scope of application under EU law is thus limited to the institutions of the EU and of Member States when they are implementing EU law and applies for all rights guaranteed by EU law.[681]

In instances where the effective protection of a fundamental right is involved, the individuals concerned must be able to defend that right under the best possible conditions.[682] This may also include the possibility to acquire information that is necessary to pursue a claim. As such, the non-existence of an obligation to communicate personal data in the context of civil proceedings to prepare a claim may interfere with the victim's right to effective judicial protection.[683]

5. In Brief: The Balancing of Fundamental Rights

The outline of the scope of the conflicting rights has already shown that a fair balancing of these rights has a key function in the jurisprudence of the courts.

As regards the fundamental rights of the *CFR* outlined above, all interferences are subject to Article 52(1) *CFR*, which provides that:

> "[A]ny limitation on the exercise of the rights and freedoms recognised by this Charter must be provided for by law and respect the essence of those rights and freedoms. Subject to the principle of proportionality, limitations may be made only if they are necessary and genuinely meet objectives of general interest recognised by the Union or the need to protect the rights and freedoms of others." Where several rights and fundamental freedoms protected by

---

678 CJEU, C-222/84 *Johnston*, Judgment of 15.05.1986, [1986] ECR 1651.

679 CJEU, C-222/86 *Union nationale des entraineurs et cadres techniques professionnels du football (UNECTEF) v Georges Heylens,* Judgment of 15.10.1987, [1987] ECR 4097.

680 CJEU, C-97/91 *Borelli*, Judgment of 03.12.1992, [1992] ECR I-6313.

681 Praesidium of the European Convention, *Explanations relating to the Charter*, OJ C 303 (14.12.2007), 17, 29.

682 CJEU C-222/86 *Union nationale des entraineurs et cadres techniques professionnels du football (UNECTEF) v Georges Heylens,* Judgement of 15.10.1987, [1987] ECR 4097.

683 Cf. CJEU, C-275/06, *Productores de Música de España (Promusicae) v Telefónica de España SAU* [2008] ECR I-271.

> the European Union legal order are at issue, the assessment of the possible disproportionate nature of a provision of European Union law must be carried out with a view to reconciling the requirements of the protection of those different rights and freedoms and a fair balance between them.[684]
> Limitations on the freedom must be provided for by law and respect the essence of those rights and freedoms and, in compliance with the principle of proportionality, must be necessary and actually meet objectives of general interest recognised by the European Union or the need to protect the rights and freedom of others.[685] Thus, when there is a choice between several appropriate measures recourse must be had to the least onerous, and the disadvantages caused must not be disproportionate to the aims pursued.[686]
> Within 60 years of fundamental rights adjudication, the ECtHR has developed the principle of proportionality into an indispensable tool to balance conflicting rights.[687] The fundamental rigths granted by the *ECHR* are often principles that "guide decision-makers, but they rarely provide the sole basis for decision-making that involves, and requires, a significant measure of balancing of interests".[688]

When balancing for instance copyright against the right to privacy under Article 7 *CFR* and the right to the protection of personal data under Article 8 *CFR*, the CJEU will not only have to analyse whether a justification as prescribed by Article 8 *ECHR* exists, but also has to take into account that copyrights are "rights of others" within Article 8(2) *ECHR*/Article 52(1) Charter. Accordingly, these rights must be balanced against each other. Lord Steyn summarised the balancing test with regard to this rights as follows: First of all, neither Article as such has precedence over the other; secondly, where the values under two Articles are in conflict, an intense focus on the comparative importance of the specific rights being claimed in the individual case is necessary; thirdly, the justifications for interfering

---

684 See, to that effect, CJEU, C-275/06 *Productores de Música de España (Promusicae) v Telefónica de España SAU* [2008] ECR I-271, paras. 65 and 66.

685 In accordance with Article 52(1) *CFR*. See CJEU, C-283/11 *Sky Österreich GmbH v Österreichischer Rundfunk*, Judgment of 22.01.2013, paras. 47–48; CJEU, C-101/12 *Herbert Schaible v Land Baden-Württemberg*, Judgment of 17.10.2013, para. 27.

686 C-343/09 *Afton Chemical*, [2010] ECR I-7027, para. 45; Joined Cases C-581/10 and C-629/10 *Nelson and Others*, Judgment of 23.10.2012, para. 71; C-283/11 *Sky Österreich GmbH v Österreichischer Rundfunk*, Judgment of 22.01.2013, para. 50.

687 Jonas Christoffersen, *Human Rights and balancing: The principle of proportionality*, in: Christophe Geiger (ed.), *Research Handbook on Human rights and Intellectual Property* (2015), p. 19.

688 *Ibid*, p. 37.

with or restricting each right must be taken into account; and finally, the proportionality test in a strict sense, must be applied to each.[689]

689 House of Lords, *Re S,* [2004] UKHL 47, [2005] 1 AC 593, para 17.

Second Chapter: User-Targeted Responses

A. The Peer-to-Peer File-Sharer as the Addressee of Enforcement Measures

I. The Idea of Enforcement in Peer-to-Peer File-Sharing Networks

The Internet is about sharing information. The technical structure of the Internet does not limit the distribution of content to specific actors but invites everyone to connect and make information available. As outlined in the First Chapter, from the advent of the Internet being widely available, this always included copyrighted content. If information is transferred onto the Internet and hence made available worldwide, users often wrongly believe that its use must be free and unrestricted. They may also just ignore that online contents are subject to the same restriction as its tangible counterparts. The turn of the millennium meant that Napster made peer-to-peer file-sharing popular and almost omnipresent. In Napster's aftermath, new and more sophisticated peer-to-peer technologies entered the market and remained significant due to increased broadband access and developments in software. They had in common that the participating users not only downloaded content but at the same time made that content available. There is no dispute that the unauthorised making available of substantive parts of copyrighted content constitutes copyright infringement – even if it is done in a non-commercial context. As suing the innovators of improved file-sharing software for copyright infringement is deemed to fail, because the provision of the file-sharing infrastructure and software does not as such imply aiding and abetting an infringement, the next step for the rights-holders wassuing the users. The user is the one that commits the infringement, so it is obvious why a rights-holder would want to turn to the user to enforce his rights. The actual infringer may not only stop his activities but also compensate the rights holders for the infringement. Addressing users may also serve as a deterrent for other users to refrain from illegal file-sharing. This course of action thus has not only a punitive but also a specific and general deterrent role, and this even outside the context of criminal law as the examples of private litigation in this chapter will show. Intellectual property rights are private rights and the majority of enforcement procedures are civil: it is for the rights-holder to take action where an infringement has occurred. The aim of such action also goes beyond the deterrent role, educating users that their behaviour is not acceptable.[690] In an ideal world, users who no longer infringe copyright will become consumers of media content for which they pay.

Addressing users in this context may either refer to suing users, warning, or threatening users with lawsuits. In response to the high percentage of unauthorised downloads, a number of countries such as France,[691] the UK,[692] Ireland,[693] Spain,[694] New Zealand,[695] South Korea[696] or Taiwan[697] have implemented, or are drafting, laws to enforce 'graduated response' measures where content owners and Internet service providers join forces to fight online copyright infringement.

In most cases, users are sent a warning, which informs them about an infringement that has been committed via their Internet connection and asks them to refrain from infringing copyright. Following a certain number of warnings, they may face court action. In some jurisdictions, in particular in Germany[698], the warning letter may require the addressee to sign a declaration with a penalty clause that they will refrain from copyright infringements in the future. Repeat-infringers under a graduated response scheme may risk technical sanctions ranging from a proposed bandwidth reduction to temporary account suspension.

---

690 Lilian Edwards, *Role and responsibility of Internet intermediaries in the field of copyright and related rights* (2011), p. 26.

691 *Loi no 2009-669 du 12 juin 2009 favorisant la diffusion et la protection de la création sur Internet* – generally known as *Loi Hadopi.*

692 *Digital Economy Act 2010.*

693 Rónán Kennedy, *No three strikes for Ireland (yet): EU Copyright Law and individual liability in recent Internet file-sharing litigation,* Journal of Internet Law 2011, Vol. 14, 15–28.

694 *Ley 2/2011, de 4 de marzo, de Economía Sostenible (Ley Sinde).*

695 Jason Rudkin-Binks/Stephanie Melbourne, *The new 'three strikes' regime for copyright enforcement in New Zealand – requiring ISPs to step up to fight,* Entertainment Law Review 2009, Vol. 20, 146–149.

696 Doug Jay Lee/Kim Misung/Jong Won Hong, *Annual Report 2009*, Korea APAA Copyright Committee.

697 Erik Chen/Mark Brown, *Taiwan: Taiwan enacts ISP 'safe harbour' amendments to Copyright Act*, Computer Law & Security Review 2009, Vol. 25 Issue 4, 389–390.

698 Germany has not (yet) implemented a graduated response scheme although the introduction of such a system has been discussed recently.

The graduated response schemes were initially known as "three strikes" laws, based on the baseball rule of "three strikes and you're out". The batter is permitted two strikes before striked out by the third one. Because "three strikes" was understood to refer to physical assault, the approach is now primarily referred to as "graduated response".

The following chapter will analyse different enforcement schemes that are directed against the user. The analysis is divided into two major parts presenting enforcement schemes that work under criminal law and private litigation schemes.

A prerequisite for pursuing action against users under criminal and civil law, is that the user who committed the infringement can be identified. The only possible way of identifying the user is the IP address from which an infringement was committed. Obtaining the IP address already constitutes the first hurdle for the rights-holder. The easiest option is to become a member of a file-sharing network. In traditional file-sharing networks, including those operating BitTorrent technology, the IP address of sharers is visible. However this is not the case with file hosting services, and thus this Chapter solely focusses on enforcement schemes against users that engage in peer-to-peer file-sharing. The second hurdle is, that the rights-holder needs to obtain further information on the subscriber of an IP address, who either may be the infringer himself, hold further information on the infringer, or may be unaware of the situation. Nevertheless, the subscriber operates an Internet connection, for which he may have to be held responsible as it allows the commitment of infringements as shown later in Part B of this chapter.

However, compared to the introductory part, this section explores more in detail how peer-to-peer file-sharing works. It shows how file-sharers are typically identified by rights-holders, what evidence can be gathered and how, before in the following part of this chapter, national enforcement mechanisms including legal tools for identification will be presented and analysed. The analysis itself will focus on the compliance of the individual enforcement mechanism with secondary EU law and fundamental rights.

II. Peer-to-Peer File-Sharing: Scope, Specific Functioning and Consequences

There is a reason why users of peer-to-peer file-sharing networks are interesting targets for rights-holders: infiltration of the networks can be easy (depending on the design) and allows the identification of IP addresses of the users involved. The following paragraphs provide – in addition to the outline of peer-to-peer file-sharing in the First Chapter – a brief overview on the functioning of peer-to-peer file-sharing and its technological progress since the early days of Napster.

1. Peer-to-Peer File-Sharing Networks in General

Before the advent of peer-to-peer technology, different computers on one network could only communicate through a central server. In simple terms, peer-to-peer software eliminated the need for information being routed through a central server.

Peer-to-peer file-sharing provides for data-sharing between computers using a specific peer-to-peer software client.[699] Traditionally, a home computer needed to connect to a web server to download files that the users wanted to access. With increasing consumer demand, very large amounts of bandwidth have to be provided. Bandwidth is key to improving performance, but not the only solution when distributing content. Storing large files of data on a server is costly and ensuring that the files required are available on servers depends on a provider running servers that makes the files available. Due to deficits of a centralised system, the peer-to-peer technology which does not require a "major" server has been developed. Unlike a traditional content delivery network, peer-to-peer systems have no dedicated infrastructure. Basically, instead of accessing a central server, home computers connect to each other to download files from each other. By this, the resources of the computers are pooled to enhance performance.[700] A distinctive feature of peer-to-peer networks is, that each computer on the network can be a file server as well as a client. The term peers in this context refers to all the computers being used which can alternately act as a client to another peer, fetching its content, and as a server, providing content to other peers.[701] Everyone that joins the network for downloading participates in the distribution of content.

---

699 "Peers" are computer systems connected to each other through the Internet. The functioning has been outlined in the First Chapter, A. The Status Quo – or How Did We Get to Where We Are Today?.

700 Andrew Tanenbaum/David Wetherall, *Computer networks* (5th ed. 2011), p. 749.

701 *Ibid*, p. 748.

As has been outlined in the First Chapter, Peer-to-peer file-sharing emerged in 1999 with the launch of Napster, which managed to link users who had specific files with those who requested these files via a central server.[702] With Napster, users could share music via the Internet on a large scale, so that comprehensive digital music collections became available for them. Napster offered software and a service whereby a central server, operated by Napster itself, indexed all files currently available on the computers of its users then connected to the Internet. Users could search this catalogue for specific files and then download them from the computer they were located at. This provided a simple, fast and efficient search facility for users. This centralisation, however, turned out to be the final nail in Napster´s coffin: when A&M Records, a copyright owner in some of the music being downloaded by Napster users sued Napster for contributory and vicarious infringement, this ultimately resulted in the shut-down of the central server and eliminated an entire dissemination mechanism. Due to the centralised structure, US courts had no problems finding Napster liable for contributory and vicarious copyright infringement (see above First Chapter, B.).[703] Napster was ordered to take reasonable steps to prevent distribution of works in respect of which it had been notified of copyright ownership, but they did not succeed in complying with this obligation.[704]

As a consequence of the US Napster ruling, subsequent peer-to-peer network operators sought to decentralise file-sharing networks. Instead of conducting queries via a central server,[705] the second generation of net-

702 Cf. Chapter 1, p. 87. For an outline of the functioning of Napster, see also US Court of Appeals for the 9th Circuit, *A&M Records Inc. v Napster Inc.*, 239 F.3d 1004 (9th Cir. 2001).

703 17 US District Court for the Northern District of California, *A&M Records. Inc. v Napster Inc.,* 114 F. Supp. 2d 896 (N. D. Cal. 2000), confirmed by US Court of Appeals for the 9th Circuit, *A&M Records Inc. v Napster Inc.*, 239 F.3d 1004 (9th Cir. 2001).

704 Due to the fact that the centrally hosted catalogue was constantly being modified as users connected and disconnected from the Internet, it was in practice impossible to prevent infringing works from being exchanged.

705 See for example the original version of Napster. As regards Napster, central servers would index all of the current users and search their computers for shareable files. When a user searched for a file, the server would find all of the available copies of the requested file and present them to the user. The file would then be transferred between the two private computers. Napster allowed only for music files to be shared. As the downloading occurred via a central server, Nap-

works[706] connects users remotely to each other with the help of a software application that they need to install on their computers.[707] Catalogues of files are no longer kept centrally on the peer-to-peer intermediary's own website. Instead, each user maintains an index of files stored on his own computer, and each time he connects to the Internet, the software he has installed will search for other users running the same software[708]; if a user searches for a particular file he will need to send out a request which the peer-to-peer software in question will pass from user to user until it is met with a positive response. Following a positive response, the file download would be negotiated by the software directly between the user who has the file stored on his computer and the user who sent out the request. Some second generation protocols such as the FastTrack protocol used by Grokster, randomly (and unbeknownst to the user) assign computers in the system to operate as centralised connection points that index files and handle search requests, so called supernodes.[709] Other second generation protocols such as Gnutella, are fully decentralised and route searches serially through any available user on the network.[710] Typically, searches on individual computers are only possible within a particular folder that has been

---

ster was held liable of contributory and vicarious copyright infringement and ordered to monitor the activities of its network and to block access to infringing material when notified of that material's location (17 US District Court for the Northern District of California, *A&M Records. Inc. v Napster Inc.*, 114 F. Supp. 2d 896 (N. D. Cal. 2000), confirmed by *A&M Records, Inc. v Napster Inc.*, 239 F. 3d 1004 (9th Cir. 2001)). As Napster was unable to comply with the judgement it eventually shut down its service in July 2001. It later re-emerged as an online music store. For the history of Napster see also Nick Scharf, *Napster's long shadow: copyright and peer-to-peer technology*, *Journal of Intellectual Property Law & Practice* 2011, Vol. 6 Issue 11, 806–812.

706 Such as for example Gnutella or KaZaa.

707 For an outline of the functioning of KaZaa see Chris Reed, *Internet Law, Text and Materials* (2nd ed. 2004), pp. 98 et seq.

708 The default mode of most peer-to-peer software means that it starts running in the background whenever the computer on which it is installed is started. See expert report cited by Justice Arnold in *Dramatico Entertainment Ltd & others v British Sky Broadcasting Ltd & others* BitTorrent has emerged as the dominant P2P protocol, see [2012] EWHC 268, para. 19.

709 See US Supreme Court, *Metro-Goldwyn-Mayers Studios, Inc. v Grokster Ltd.*, 545 U.S. 913 (2005), 921.

710 The original Gnutella software application is no longer in circulation.

designated by the user to share with others.[711] Following a positive response to a search request, the file download is negotiated by the software directly between the user who has the file stored on his computer and the user who sent out the request. The difference between the first and second generation is that with the second generation the file-sharing software creates a new local database for each user every time he connects, which does not require any further involvement of the software provider. Acccordingly, the decentralised models have no central access point and cannot store a search index, identify users, or directly facilitate connections.[712] Some software applications, for example Gnutella, further distance themselves from liability, because they are open source protocols, meaning that rights-holders have difficulties to find someone to whom they may address their claims. Shutting down part of the system may also be ineffective because users can adapt copies of the program's code to keep a sharing network in place. This however means, that rights-holders need to change their approach from suing the provider of the network or software to the individual user.

The problem for users with peer-to-peer file-sharing is that each user (= client) that downloads a file onto his computer at the same time supplies the given file to the file-sharing network.[713] Most users seem to be unaware of this fact.[714] In some cases, the application used to allow the deactivation or blocking of the uploading function.[715] Sometimes the amount of the downloaded material and the downloading speed may depend on the extent to which the user makes files available himself.[716] Thus, it becomes attractive for users to keep a large number of files in their public folder.

Further technological advances mean, that the newest (third) generation of networks provides for files being searched and retrieved almost without

---

711 Mark Taylor/John Haggerty/David Gresty/Tom Berry, *Digital evidence from peer-to-peer networks*, Computer Law & Security Review 2011, Vol. 27, 647.

712 Cf. US Supreme Court, *Metro-Goldwyn-Mayers Studios, Inc. v Grokster Ltd.,* 545 U.S. 913 (2005), 920.

713 Rolf Schwartmann, *Filesharing, Sharehosting & Co, Funktionsweise und rechtliche Bewertung aktueller Erscheinungsformen von Urheberrechtsverletzungen im Internet,* Kommunikation und Recht 2011, Beihefter 2, 9.

714 European Parliament, DG for Internal Policies, Policy Department C: Citizens' Rights and Constitutional Affairs, *File Sharing* (2011), p. 6.

715 *Ibid.*

716 *Ibid.*

any form of database being involved. Current file-sharing protocols create a new network for every set of files instead of employing one big network of files.

2. The Third Generation of Peer-to-Peer File Sharing Networks

File sharing protocols of the newest (third) generation, BitTorrent protocols, also work decentralised but, in contrast to earlier protocols, files are not downloaded as one piece from one single user. As aforementioned, BitTorrent has proven to be very efficient,[717] and has thus become the leading file-sharing technology, in which peers cooperate in distributing files or content. [718] Its way of functioning is distinct from previous file-sharing applications and thus, needs to be looked at separately. Also, it is a complicated protocol to analyse in legal context due to many actors being involved in the act of sharing.[719] First of all, there is the web site which provides the client software; then there is the web site which provides "torrent" files which then aid the user in locating other users who hold all or parts of the file which this user seeks to download. With early versions of the BitTorrent protocol, tracker sites became necessary; they monitored the users contributing to the file transfer in order to pass their data to the client software. Finally there are the users using the BitTorrent protocol, who join in uploading bits of the file sought.

A rather allegorical and simplified description of the functioning of BitTorrent, which gives a first idea of the different actors, can be found in the 2010 first instance decision of the Australian case *Roadshow Films Pty Ltd v iiNet Ltd*:

"To use the rather colourful imagery that Internet piracy conjures up in a highly imperfect analogy, the file being shared in the swarm is the treasure, the BitTorrent client is the ship, the .torrent file is the treasure map, The Pirate Bay provides treasure maps free of charge and the tracker is the

717 Diane Rowland/Uta Kohl/Andrew Charlesworth, *Information Technology Law* (4th ed. 2012), p. 339; Lilian Edwards, *Role and responsibility of Internet intermediaries in the field of copyright and related rights* (2011), p. 17.

718 Gaetano Dimita, *Six characters in search of infringement: potential liability for creating, downloading, and disseminating.torrent files,* Journal of Intellectual Property Law & Practice 2012, Vol. 7 Issue 6, 466, 466.

719 See Lilian Edwards, *Role and responsibility of Internet intermediaries in the field of copyright and related rights* (2011), p. 17.

wise old man that needs to be consulted to understand the treasure map."[720]

Like with other peer-to-peer file-sharing programmes, the user, who is called a seeder (when he provides upload access) or a leecher (when he seeks to download),[721] needs to install a BitTorrent client on his computer. In BitTorrent terminology sharing a file is referred to as 'swarming a file'.[722] Users join a so called 'swarm' to download and upload from each other simultaneously a single set of files (also called a torrent file), which taken as a whole forms the desired content.

This works as follows: Before a file can be shared, the BitTorrent client needs to create the torrent file of the material to be swarmed. The client then has to disseminate the torrent file that describes metadata of the files being distributed to support the BitTorrent protocol, such as information on the blocks of data that are distributed, and how these blocks of data should be put together to form the desired content.[723] The torrent file does not itself contain any of the content to which it relates and can, in simple terms, be compared to a hyperlink leading to the desired content. The dissemination of the torrent file usually takes place via a website, where the user uploads the torrent file. BitTorrent does not offer facilities to search files: users need to find the torrent files by other means, and this has increased the popularity of the numerous websites which host, index, or link to them. Websites such as the PirateBay or FastTrack networks, such

720 Federal Court of Australia, *Roadshow Films Pty Ltd v iiNet Ltd*, [2010] FCA 24, para. 70. The decision was appealed, but the first instance judgement upheld, see [2011] FCAFC 23 (Full Court of the Federal Court of Australia) and [2012] HCA 16 (High Court of Australia).

721 BitTorrent software is designed so that users act as both downloaders and uploaders. The default setting in most cases, enables to do both simultaneously. This becomes important when users argue that they have only downloaded files (the donloading for private non-commercial purposes of a certain number of copies is for example in France a legal exception to copyright).

722 Gaetano Dimita, *Six characters in search of infringement: potential liability for creating, downloading, and disseminating torrent files,* Journal of Intellectual Property Law & Practice 2012, Vol. 7 Issue 6, 466, 466.

723 Joost Poort/Jorna Leenheer/Jeroen von der Ham/Cosmin Dumitru, *Baywatch: Two Approaches to Measure the Effects of Blocking Access to The Pirate Bay* (Working Paper, 22.08.2013), p. 2.

as LimeWire, provide a built-in torrent file search facility.[724] In most cases, these websites offer both a file index and a tracker. The latter are used to bootstrap and accelerate BitTorrent swarms so that they can provide a new peer with information on other peers participating in the swarm.[725] Hence, the tracker helps users to identify computers that are already downloading or uploading a requested file.[726] Accordingly, much of the communication still takes place with the aid of a central server, i.e. the tracker. The first versions of BitTorrent required such a central point to perform searches and aggregate torrent files, because during the sharing process, the identity of peers which can provide blocks of data that make up the file contents change regularly as other users acquire the content and make it available to others, so it became necessary for to keep track of the peers.[727] In simple terms, the tracker coordinates communication between peers attempting to download the payload of the torrents. Tracker also record data on each file they track including the "hash" of that file (a unique code that identifies that file alone and no other)[728] as well as the number of seeds (users holding an entire copy of the file), leechers (users in the act of downloading, that do not yet possess a full copy), and (in most cases) total completed downloads.

While the initial version of the BitTorrent protocol used trackers to locate and torrent files to describe content, newer versions have recently added another layer of distribution by storing the torrent files in a so called

---

724 Gaetano Dimita, *Six characters in search of infringement: potential liability for creating, downloading, and disseminating .torrent files,* Journal of Intellectual Property Law & Practice 2012, Vol. 7 Issue 6, 466, 466.

725 Joost Poort/Jorna Leenheer/Jeroen von der Ham/Cosmin Dumitru, *Baywatch: Two Approaches to Measure the Effects of Blocking Access to The Pirate Bay* (Working Paper, 22.08.2013), p. 2.

726 See expert report cited in High Court, *Dramatico Entertainment Ltd & others v British Sky Broadcasting Ltd & others,* [2012] EWHC 268, para. 19.

727 *Ibid.*

728 A "hash" is a unique alpha-numeric sequence used to identify files (movies, music, documents, etc) on bittorrent. On the bittorrent network, the hash is generated by an algorithm (e.g. the SHA1 algorithm) which creates a small identifier from a large file (such as for example a movie). Even trivial modifications to the original file result in a completely different hash. See Envisional, *Technical Report: An estimate of infringing use of the Internet* (2011), p. 8. See also Second Chapter, III. 3. a) The Copyright Infringement.

Distributed Hash Table (DHT) storage network created by all global peers.[729] A so-called magnet link[730] can then be used to address content in this DHT network, which provides the contents of a torrent file, and its participating peers.[731]

If a user wants to obtain a file, he connects to the user with the BitTorrent file and opens it with his BitTorrent client. The torrent file then tells the user how to connect to the peer users swarming that file. As already mentioned above, the desired content is divided into blocks of data (bits), which are downloaded from different peers. As each peer receives a new piece of the file he becomes a source for that segment for other peers. In this way, the original source will be relieved from sending out the requested piece as a whole to every user wishing a copy.[732] The segments will finally be reassembled into the correct order by the BitTorrent client.[733]

In contrast to the second generation peer-to-peer file-sharing technologies, there is no single file-sharing network where all the files are being shared. As mentioned above, a different network is created as soon as the first user obtains and launches a torrent file. [734] When everyone involved in a swarm has acquired a full copy, the network collapses. Like with earlier file-sharing protocols, much of the BitTorrent protocol operates invisibly to the user – after downloading a file, subsequent uploading takes place automatically if the user fails to close the programme.

It is important to understand that torrent files do not include any part, not even insubstantial parts, of the protected materials they have been cre-

---

729 Joost Poort/Jorna Leenheer/Jeroen von der Ham/Cosmin Dumitru, *Baywatch: Two Approaches to Measure the Effects of Blocking Access to The Pirate Bay* (Working Paper, 22.08.2013), p.2.

730 A provider of lists of magnet links is for example The Pirate Bay.

731 Joost Poort/Jorna Leenheer/Jeroen von der Ham/Cosmin Dumitru, *Baywatch: Two Approaches to Measure the Effects of Blocking Access to The Pirate Bay* (Working Paper, 22.08.2013), p2.

732 Decentralised file-sharing permits a reduction in the original distributor's hardware and bandwidth resources.

733 See Rolf Schwartmann, *Filesharing, Sharehosting & Co, Funktionsweise und rechtliche Bewertung aktueller Erscheinungsformen von Urheberrechtsverletzungen im Internet,* Kommunikation und Recht 2011, Beihefter 2, 9 with further references.

734 Gaetano Dimita, *Six characters in search of infringement: potential liability for creating, downloading, and disseminating torrent files,* Journal of Intellectual Property Law & Practice 2012, Vol. 7 Issue 6, 466, 466.

ated to disseminate.[735] No actual transmission of materials takes place before the actual swarm starts. The only way to determine whether a copyright infringement takes place is to join the swarm of the file.[736]

3. Peer-to-Peer File-Sharing in Numbers

The difficulties in measuring the scope and economic impact of file-sharing has already been outlined in the previous Chapter. However, at this point the numbers shall briefly be recalled, because all specifically implemented enforcement schemes were based on the assumption that the scope of copyright infringements in peer-to-peer networks requires specific legislation.

Peer-to-peer applications have long been considered to take up large amounts of the overall Internet traffic.[737] Traffic analysis in this regard suggest that BitTorrent is the most used file-sharing protocol worldwide, making up 14.6% of all Internet bandwidth worldwide in 2010.[738] Estimates for the future predict less traffic taken up by peer-to-peer file-sharing, but considering that the overall traffic is also increasing, even 2% of all worldwide traffic would mean that millions of users are using peer-to-peer networks.[739]

In 2011, the distributor of two of the most-used bittorent clients µTorrent and BitTorrent Mainline, claims that the clients have over 100 million unique users worldwide and 20 million daily users.[740]

---

735 *Ibid.*

736 *Ibid.*

737 Envisional, *Technical Report: An estimate of infringing use of the Internet* (2011), p. 47. See also Nick Scharf, *Napster's long shadow: copyright and peer-to-peer technology*, Journal of Intellectual Property Law & Practice 2011, Vol. 6 Issue 11, 806–812.

738 Envisional, *Technical Report: An estimate of infringing use of the Internet* (2011), p. 7. Envisional measured over eight million users simultaneously connected to the bitTorent network.

739 Cisco Systems Inc. predicts that in 2017 peer-to-peer file-sharing will take up 2% of the worldwide Internet traffic while other file transfer such as streaming will take up 27%. See Cisco Systems Inc., Cisco Visual Networking Index: *Forecast and Methodology, 2012-2017* (2013), p.11.

740 BitTorrent Inc., BitTorrent, inc. grows to over 100 million active monthly users (03.01.2011), Business Wire.

In 2010, it has been found that more than 99% of all material (with the exception of pornographic materials) in the top 10,000 file-sharing swarms was actually infringing copyrights.[741]

Also in 2012 and according to the British Record Music Industry, BitTorrent and other peer-to-peer applications remained the most popular methods of obtaining copyrighted material on the Internet.[742] Around four million users in the UK connected to peer-to-peer networks each month, accounting to 345 million unauthorised downloads via BitTorrent in the first half of 2012.[743] In contrast to the 345 million illegal copies, iTunes, Amazon and other authorised music distributors sold 91.7 million tracks and 14.7 million albums in the UK.[744] As this numbers have been released by the music industry, they have to be critically assessed, but clearly indicate that peer-to-peer file-sharing is a mass-scale phenomenon and nothing that is conducted by only small groups of the population.

4. The Copyright-Infringing Act

As outlined above, peer-to-peer file-sharing allows large amounts of data to be shared because users both download and upload the data. Users download files but necessarily also supply the files to the network as a start. It is the user that provides the opportunity to download. Irrespective of the intentional supply of files, users are often not aware of the fact, that by downloading, they also automatically supply the requested file.[745] The strength of peer-to-peer file-sharing is at the same time its biggest weakness: although users may only want to download a file, they regularly also become a contributor and thereby make the requested file available for third parties. By making it available, rights-holders or their agents, who

---

741 Envisional, Technical Report: An estimate of infringing use of the Internet (2011), p. 10.

742 British Record Music Industry (BPI), *Digital Music Nation 2013, the UK's legal and illegal digital music landscape* (2013), p. 26.

743 *Ibid.*

744 *Ibid.*

745 This explains the fact that a 2009 study analysing the web traffic of 21,766 hosts of a German Internet service provider showed that BitTorrent had nearly a balanced incoming and outgoing traffic (the upload was in fact 76% of the download traffic), see Amir Alsbih/Thomas Janson/Christian Schindelhauer, *Analysis of peer-to-peer traffic and user behaviour* (2009), p. 4.

have infiltrated the network by way of joining a swarm can log the IP address of the users.

a) Uploading Regularly Goes Along with Downloading

In simple terms, typical peer-to-peer applications require the user to designate directories in his hard drive as part of the peer-to-peer network and thereby making this content available for downloading throughout the network. Once a users starts downloading files, the bits and pieces that he has already obtained are automatically made available to his peers.

This however, infringes the right of copyright owners to prevent others from making copies of their work without authorisation, which is the most basic right under copyright law. Copyright owners have the exclusice rights to authorise reproduction and communication of works.[746] The right of reproduction may already be infringed when the user that initially plants a file by copying it in the designated directories for distribution via peer-to-peer technology.[747] When the files are then dissemintated through peer-to-peer networks, this infringes the right of communication to the public.[748]

Only a few peer-to-peer clients have the option of deactivating or blocking the uploading function.[749] The availability of this function is rare and usually discouraged amongst BitTorrent users because it goes against the basic principles of BitTorrent: the protocol depends on sharing and if no one uploaded content, then it would be useless. Therefore some peer-to-peer software keeps track of how much a user downloads compared to

---

746 See Article 2 of the *InfoSoc Directive*, whereby "Member states shall provide for the exclusive right to authorise or prohibit direct or indirect, temporary or permanent reproduction by any means and in any form, in whole or in part: (a) for authors of their work; for performers, of fixations of their performances; for phonogram producers, of their phonograms; for the producers of the first fixations of films, in respect of the original and copies of their films; for broadcasting organisations, of fixations of their broadcasts, whether those broadcasts are transmitted by wire or over the air, including by cable or satellite".

747 Cf. the wording of Article 2 of the *InfoSoc Directive*, which refers to the direct or indirect reproduction by any means and in any form.

748 Cf. Article 3(1) of the *InfoSoc Directive*.

749 Cf. European Parliament, DG for Internal Policies, Policy Department C: Citizens' Rights and Constitutional Affairs, *File Sharing* (2011), p. 6.

the quantity of his shared materials with the consequence that those who download more than they upload will have their download rate decreased or choked.[750]

BitTorrent for instance encourages users to upload data using incentives: users, who only download data (so called leeches) are punished by a reduced download rate.[751] The incentive principle means that a user will be able to download a requested file faster if he also contributes upload bandwidth.

As most users have asynchronous connections to the Internet, meaning that their download speed is significantly faster than their upload speed, uploading data to a peer-to-peer network can take some time. Thus, users often stay connected in order to even their upload – download ratio, which in turn means that the rights-holders have sufficient time to detect and log the data.

b) Parts of a Protected Work Enjoy Protection

Often users do not succeed in downloading a whole file; and obtain only parts or fragments of a copyrighted work.[752] There are different kinds of fragmented files, not all of them may be of use for the downloader. Most peer-to-peer file-sharing software mark fragmented data for instance by adding "part" to the file.[753] As a consequence media players cannot open the file.[754] Without going into detail, at this point, it shall only be noted,

---

750 *Ibid.* So called tit-for-tat incentive strategy.

751 This applies to the original BitTorrent protocol. Several newer clients deviate from the original protocol and may allow more downloads than uploads (e.g. BitTyrant) or even "free-riding" (e.g. BitThief). See Amir Alsbih/Thomas Janson/Christian Schindelhauer, *Analysis of peer-to-peer traffic and user behaviour* (2009), p. 2. See also Zhengye Liu/Prithula Dhungel/Di Wu/Chao Zhang/Keith W. Ross, *Understanding and improving incentives in private P2P communities* (year n.a.).

752 Considering that especially with large files or rare files it may take hours or even days until the download is completed it may happen that the source is suddenly no longer available. See Christian Solmecke/Jan Bärenfänger, *Urheberrechtliche Schutzfähigkeit von Dateifragmenten – Nutzlos = Schutzlos*, MultiMedia und Recht 2011, 567, 568.

753 *Ibid.*

754 *Ibid.*

that most music formats allow listening to fragments.[755] The same applies to most currently utilised video formats. As far as pictures are concerned, the files can regularly be opened once a certain file size has been reached, lacking file fragments will be left black.[756] Software and archive file, for instance .zip and .rar files are useless in fragments.[757] Relevant in practice are so-called "charts-container", i.e. files containing for instance the TOP 100 charts.[758] These charts-container are either distributed as open containers, or via an archive file. Open containers allow the download of individual files of the container whereas individual songs contained in a .zip or .rar archive cannot be downloaded separately and can only be played once the whole archive file is complete and the content has been unzipped.[759]

The question that arises in relation to fragmented files is whether the down- or upload of parts of a protected work constitutes a copyright infringement itself. First of all, this discussion can be limited to such files where the file fragments can be opened and used although the file is not complete.[760] The download of such file fragments constitutes an unauthorised reproduction and thus a copyright infringement.[761] Article 2(a) of the *InfoSoc Directive* provides that authors have the exclusive right to authorise or prohibit reproduction, in whole or in part, of their works. As regards parts of a work, these parts are not treated any differently from the work as a whole.[762] It follows that they are protected by copyright, if they share the originality of the whole work. Thus protection under Article 2(a) of the Directive is granted, provided that the parts contain elements which

755 For this, the fragmented file has to be renamed into .mp3 and must be open directly in the context menue, see *ibid.*

756 *Ibid.*

757 *Ibid.*

758 *Ibid.*

759 *Ibid.*

760 *Ibid*, 569.

761 See only *ibid*, 569.

762 See for instance CJEU, C-5/08 *Infopaq International v Danske Dagblades Forening*, para. 38. In this case the Court concluded that it may not be ruled out that certain isolated sentences, or even parts of sentences in the text in question, may be suitable for conveying to the reader the originality of a publication such as a newspaper or article, by communicating to that reader an element which is, in itself, the expression of the intellectual creation of the author of that article.

are the expression of the intellectual creation of the author of the work.[763] Insofar as the file fragment is of no use, i.e. cannot be consumed, it does not enjoy protection under this provision and copyright law in general, because it carries no expression of the intellectual creation of the author.[764]

However, the situation becomes more complicated, when national law as for instance section 16(3)(a) of the Copyright, Designs and Patents Act 1988 in the UK requires that the infringing act relates to the work as a whole or any substantial part of it.[765] It has also been argued, that even if the bits that are shared are too small to enjoy protection under copyright law,[766] there nevertheless is an infringing act. This shall be due to the fact, that already the making available to the public of the aggregate parts requires the copyright holder's permission.[767] Hence the relevance of this discussion remains limited.[768]

By uploading a file, or more precisely and insofar as Bittorrent networks are concerned fragments thereof, during the download process, the

763 *Ibid*, para. 39. In Germany for instance parts of a work enjoy protection when they themselve constitute an original personal creation. Instead of many see Winfried Bullinger in: Artur-Axel Wandtke/Winfried Bullinger, *Praxiskommentar zum Urheberrecht: UrhR* (3rd ed. 2009), § 2 *UrhG* para. 42; Gernot Schulze in: Thomas Dreier/Gernot Schulze, *Urheberrechtsgesetz* (4th ed. 2013), § 2 *UrhG* paras. 76 et seq.

764 Christian Solmecke/Jan Bärenfänger, *Urheberrechtliche Schutzfähigkeit von Dateifragmenten – Nutzlos = Schutzlos*, MultiMedia und Recht 2011, 567, 569.

765 See as regards the difficulties in the UK of determining the "taking of a substantial part" in file-sharing cases: James G.H. Griffin, *The effect of the Digital Economy Act 2010 upon 'Semiotic Democracy'*, International Review of Law, Computers & Technology 2010, Vol. 24 No. 3, 251, 258.

766 Nico van Eijk outlined in his report on file-sharing for the European Parliament the position that since no substantial part of a protected work can be recognised in the small bits that are exchanged via a BitTorrent network, there shall be no restricted act as an infringement shall usually require that the whole or substantial part of the protected work has been made available (Cf. European Parliament, DG for Internal Policies, Policy Department C: Citizens' Rights and Constitutional Affairs, *File Sharing* (2011), p.9. This conclusion was based on the assumption that national legislation as for example section 16 (3)(a) of *the Copyright, Designs and Patents Act 1988* in the UK requires that the work as a whole or a substantial part of it has been made available.

767 *Ibid.*

768 *Ibid.*

user makes the fragments publicly available.[769] The making available right is enshrined in Article 3 of the *InfoSoc Directive*. Again, where fragments are concerned that as such can be consumed, they enjoy protection and their upload infringes copyright.[770] For fragments that cannot be consumed independently, this does not apply. An infringement can only then be considered, when the user possesses the complete file.[771] In this case, the mere possibility that the file could be uploaded may amount to an infringement as "making publicly available" shall not require an actual upload.[772] In this context, it has been discussed whether the specific structure of peer-to-peer file-sharing networks requires a different assessment.[773] Although the individual fragments are as such of no use, for those users within a swarm, they are useful because they can obtain the missing fragments from multiple sources and complete the file.[774]

However, as all members of the file-sharing network act independently, the making available of non-protected fragments by others cannot be mutually attributed in terms of law.[775] The attribution of acts of third parties regularly requires intent to commit the infringing act together and intent to commit the infringement at all. File-sharing networks are commonly anonymous, participating users commonly do not know each other. Many users are also not aware that downloading a file implies that they make it available to others. Thus, it will in all cases be necessary to actual look at the file fragments in order to identify whether they enjoy protec-

---

769 As regards the notion of "making publicly available" cf. De Wolf & Partners, Study on the Application of Directive 2001/29/EC on Copyright and Related Rights in the Information Society (The "InfoSoc Directive") (2013), pp. 25 et seq. Recently, a first instance court in Germany discussed this particular subject matter with regard to fragments and concluded that the making available of "bits" of a protected work constitutes a copyright infringement, see see also AG München, Decision of 03.04.2012 – 161 C 19021/11, MultiMedia und Recht 2014, 197.

770 See Christian Solmecke/Jan Bärenfänger, *Urheberrechtliche Schutzfähigkeit von Dateifragmenten – Nutzlos = Schutzlos*, MultiMedia und Recht 2011, 567, 570.

771 *Ibid.*

772 This is at least the case in Germany, see Thomas Dreier in: Thomas Dreier/ Gernot Schulze, *Urheberrechtsgesetz* (3rd ed. 2008), § 19a, para. 6.

773 See Christian Solmecke/Jan Bärenfänger, *Urheberrechtliche Schutzfähigkeit von Dateifragmenten – Nutzlos = Schutzlos*, MultiMedia und Recht 2011, 567, 570 et seq.

774 *Ibid*, 571.

775 *Ibid*, 572.

tion before legal steps can be taken. As regards unprotected fragments, the claimant will have to prove that either a file has been downloaded completely or offered for download as a whole.[776] Evidence that only proves that a down- and upload has taken place at some point for a limited time, will regularly not suffice.

A further copyright-infringing act could be seen in the creation of a .torrent file.[777] The .torrent file as such does not contain any part of the related file that the user wants to share,[778] and therefore its creation arguably does not infringe reproduction rights.[779]

One might however argue that using the title of a protected work to name the .torrent file infringes copyright,[780] because even isolated sentences, or parts of sentences may be suitable for conveying to users the originality of a publication.[781] As regards the dissemination of a .torrent file by for instance posting the .torrent file on a website, this does not automatically imply that the related file is publicly available, as the .torrent file may be inactive or "dead".[782] Hence, the dissemination of a .torrent file does not necessarily involve the making available of protected material.[783] The .torrent file always has to be assessed in connection with the related file. Similarly, someone who downloads a .torrent file only

776 *Ibid.*

777 See Gaetano Dimita, *Six characters in search of infringement: potential liability for creating, downloading, and disseminating .torrent files,* Journal of Intellectual Property Law & Practice 2012, Vol. 7 Issue 6, 466–472.

778 Crossreference to functioning of peer-to-peer A. II. 3.

779 Gaetano Dimita, *Six characters in search of infringement: potential liability for creating, downloading, and disseminating .torrent files,* Journal of Intellectual Property Law & Practice 2012, Vol. 7 Issue 6, 466, 468.

780 *Ibid*, stating that even the protectability of a single word is not totally excluded by copyright law. This argument is supported by Court of Appeal, *Exxon Corp. v Exxon Insurance Consultants* [1981] 3 All E.R. 241; CJEU, C-5/08, *Infopaq International A/S v Danske Dagblades Forening*, [2009] ECDR 16; Court of Appeal, *Newspaper Licensing Agency Ltd v Meltwater Holding BV* [2011] EWCA Civ 890 (High Court, [2010] EWHC 3099 (Ch)).

781 See only CJEU, C-5/08, *Infopaq International A/S v Danske Dagblades Forening,* [2009] ECDR 16.

782 Gaetano Dimita, *Six characters in search of infringement: potential liability for creating, downloading, and disseminating .torrent files,* Journal of Intellectual Property Law & Practice 2012, Vol. 7 Issue 6, 466, 469. A .torrent file becomes "dead" or inactive when all members of a swarm have completed the download of the requested file and disconnect, see *ibid*, 466.

783 *Ibid*, 469.

infringes copyright when he subsequently also starts the download process of the related file. The mere download of the .torrent file does not suffice for infringing reproduction rights.[784]

c) Non-Applicability of the Private Copying Exception

Although a copyright infringement has been established, a user might escape liability if he could rely on the private copying defence. The concept of the "private copying exception" has already been outlined in the first Chapter in the context of lack of understanding by users of copyright law.[785] This concept, or defence, exists in most Member States, though in different variations.[786] Exception or limitation for private copying is enshrined in Article 5(2)(b) of the *InfoSoc Directive*, which foresees that "Member States may provide for exceptions or limitations to the reproduction right provided for in Article 2 in the following cases: ...(b) in respect of reproductions on any medium made by a natural person for private use and for ends that are neither directly nor indirectly commercial, on condition that the rightholders receive fair compensation which takes account of the application or non-application of technological measures referred to in Article 6 to the work or subject-matter concerned". First of all, a private copying exception requires that the copy is made for private use. While

---

784 *Ibid.*

785 See above First Chapter, I. 2. c) Lack of Understanding Intellectual Property Rights.

786 Notably, copyright law in the UK does currently not foresee a private copying exception. However, the UK government intends to introduce a narrow private copying exception which will allow individuals to copy content under the condition that they own the content, and have acquired the content lawfully. Under these circumstances, they will be allowed to copy the content to another medium or device for their own personal use. See HM Government, *Modernising Copyright: A modern, robust and flexible framework, Government Response to Consultation on Copyright Exceptions and Clarifying Copyright Law* (December 2012), p. 25. The House of Lords proposed to insert the following new clause into section 28 of the *Copyright Designs and Patents Act 1988*: "(5) Any provisions of this Chapter relating to an exception for private copying shall not apply where further copies of copyright works are commercially available, under the terms of the acquisition of the copy of the copyright work concerned, by or with the authority of the copyright owner." See *Intellectual Property Bill* [HL], Session 2012–14, 17.07.2013.

downloading materials from the Internet may be conducted for private use, the downloading from peer-to-peer networks, in particular BitTorrent networks, cannot be considered as copying for private use exclusively since the content is also distributed.

In the context of private copying, it is also being discussed whether it is of relevance that the copy has been made from an illegal source.[787] The question whether a law which allows copying from illegal sources for private use is compliant with EU copyright law has only recently been subject before the CJEU in Case C-435/12 *ACI Adam*. In its judgment the CJEU essentially followed the Opinion of the Advocate General[788] and held that the private copying exception may only apply to copies from legitimate sources.[789] Some national laws, for instance German law, required in this regard that the source has not been evidently illegal, which meant in practice that the exception could also apply to downloads from peer-to-peer networks, because the source could be a private copy from a lawfully obtained copy and thus not be *evidently* illegal.[790] In order to eliminate this loophole, the German Copyright Act now requires that the copying for private use is not permitted when the copy constitutes an evidently illegal reproduction or has been made available evidently illegally.[791]

While there is less discussion about what constitutes an illegal source (either the content copied is distributed without the rights-holder's permission or the file from which the content is downloaded has been created without the rights-holder's consent), the question is to determine when the illegality is evident.[792] The evidential illegality of a source has to be determined from the perspective of an objective bystander.[793] As an example for an unlawful copy that stems from an evidently illegal source, the Ger-

---

787 See above First Chapter, I. 2. c) Lack of Understanding Intellectual Property Rights.

788 See Opinion of the Advocate General in C-435/12 *ACI Adam v Stichting de Thuiskopie* of 09.01.2014.

789 CJEU, C-435/12 *ACI Adam v Stichting de Thuiskopie,* Judgment of 10.04.2014.

790 See version of § 53 I *UrhG* that was in force from 13.09.2003 to 31.12.2007.

791 As regards the intention of the legislator to amend the relevant provision see Deutscher Bundestag, *Bundestagsdrucksache 16/1828*, p. 18.

792 See for example Thomas Dreier in Thomas Dreier/Gernot Schulze, *Urheberrechtsgesetz* (4th ed. 2013), paras. 12 et seq. with further references.

793 At least this is the case in Germany, see Tobias Reinbacher, *Strafbarkeit der Privatkopie von offensichtlich rechtswidrig hergestellten oder öffentlich zugänglich*

man Federal Ministry of Justice stated that a download of a film or music file from an "illegal file-sharing network" would fall within that category.[794] Though the wording used by the Ministry of Justice is strictly speaking not correct in a legal sense as file-sharing networks are not per se illegal, the idea is well-founded. With regard to peer-to-peer file-sharing networks, the illegality of the source is commonly evident, because rightsholders will regularly not distribute their songs via file-sharing networks but use commercial on-demand services where users will have to pay.[795] Even if for instance a band wants to release a title for free, then they will regularly use their own website or that of a cooperating partner/sponsor/advertiser to do so. As a more in depth analysis of this subject matter would go beyond the scope of this work, at this point, it shall be born in mind that only in a limited number of cases, the private copy exception may apply.

5. Explaining the Demand for Enforcement Schemes Focussing on Peer-to-Peer Networks

As mentioned above, peer-to-peer file-sharing is a mass scale phenomenon. While the estimates about how much of the traffic is taken up by infringing materials vary, the sheer scope of it leads to the assumption that a lot of copyright infringements take place.

The aforementioned functioning of peer-to-peer networks where each member of a swarm of file-sharers commonly also aids in distributing the copyrighted materials explains why they have an interesting playing field for enforcement. First generation networks relied on a central authority to be addressed.[796] The newer protocols managed to make copyright enforcement more difficult on the one hand, but also made it more interesting for the rights-holders to go after the individual users that engage in peer-to-peer file-sharing.

---

gemachten Vorlagen, Gewerblicher Rechtsschutz und Urheberrecht 2008, 394, 397 with further references.

794 As the press release of 05.07.2007 is no longer available on the website of the Federal Ministry of Justice, see *ibid.*

795 See also *ibid*, 400 et seq.

796 As regards the liability of the operator of the central server see the Napster case outlined in the First Chapter, A. III. 1. Early Responses to File-Sharing: Legal Action against the Innovators.

Rights-holders are generally more interested in enforcing their rights against uploaders than mere downloaders. This has to do with a simple cost-benefit calculation: much time, cost and effort is required to identify infringers, thus, claims are rather brought against uploaders due to the scope of damage they have committed in comparison to a mere downloader. The maximum damage a mere downloader has produced is significantly less than the damage produced by an uploader. By joining a swarm of peer-to-peer file-sharing, the rights-holders can obtain information about who makes a file available. However, as this each swarm is only occupied with sharing one specific file, the acquisition of evidence of an infringement and the subsequent information requests on the identity of a user still involves a lot of time, costs and work. Thus, rights-holders have been lobbying for means to ease enforcement that is less costly for them but also fights copyright infringements effectively.[797]

III. Technological Challenges in Detecting and Identifying File-Sharers

In order to identify infringers, evidence needs to be gathered from a peer-to-peer network. As already mentioned, this is usually done by specialist companies and their forensic computer analysts. Due to the anonymity involved in the exchange of data, the data they may accumulate is not sufficient to identify an infringer. They will need to apply for a disclosure order[798] or (in the case of graduated response schemes) address themselves to a third party, i.e. the Internet access provider either directly or through an intermediary, that may then provide details of the identity of a

797 For an excellent, but also very critical analysis of the lobbying conducted by the creative industries to strengthen their position when it comes to enforcement issues, see Monica Horten, *The Copyright Enforcement Enigma, Internet Politics and the 'Telecoms Package'* (2012), and Monica Horten, *A Copyright Masquerade: How Corporate Lobbying Threatens Online Freedoms* (2013).

798 Regularly, obtaining information on the identity of the subscriber of an IP address requires a court order. Surprisingly, 15,5 % of the respondent to a question on the involvement of intermediaries to identify (alleged) infringers in a EU consultation stated that it had been possible for them to obtain such information directly from an intermediary without a court order, European Commission, DG Internal Market and Services, *Civil enforcement of intellectual property rights: Public Consultation of the efficiency of proceedings and accessibility of measures, synthesis of the responses* (July 2013), p.12.

potential infringer, or issue a warning to a potential infringer. In case of a disclosure order, the order forces the Internet access subscriber to match the IP address gathered by the rights-holder with the personal details of the Internet subscription holder.

1. In General: Collecting Digital Evidence

Commonly, online perpetrators are not easy to identify. Their identification and the identification of their unlawful activities usually requires real-time collection of traffic data and interception of content data. Many cases also require the search and confiscation of stored computer data similar to the search and seizure of tangible objects.[799] Such measures for evidence-gathering have an intrusive character, and interfere with the right to privacy and the freedom of communication. However, they are necessary because otherwise the prosecution of Internet crimes and other unlawful acts on the Internet could not be sanctioned. With regard to criminal procedure law, three principles have been identified by national legislators that need to be observed when law enforcement clashes with fundamental rights. These principles are: (1) to distinguish between serious and less serious crimes in order to respect the intrusive character of the above mentioned measures; intrusive measures are restricted to the serious crimes; (2) if the intrusive measures are lawful, their application must abide by the principle of proportionality, meaning that they shall be applied only to the minimum necessary extent; (3) the intrusive measures must follow strict procedural rules, that function as safeguards of fundamental rights, such as intrusive measures being subject to permission by judicial authorities or public prosecutors, and the measures being restricted in terms of time.[800]

However, in most copyright enforcement cases and in particular within the copyright enforcement schemes that will be discussed in the following, the evidence of an infringement is collected by the rights-holder himself or professionalised agents acting on his behalf. Within peer-to-peer file-sharing networks, they can track the IP address of a perpetrator like everyone else that is a member of that network and thus, do not need to employ

799 See as regards criminal proceedings, Articles 19–21 of the *Council of Europe Convention on Cybercrime*.

800 Cf. Dimitris Kioupis, *Criminal liability on the Internet*, in: Irini Stamatoudi (ed.), *Copyright enforcement on the Internet* (2010), p. 249.

secret surveillance techniques. In some cases, where the rights-holder also wants to press criminal charges, it is up for the respective law enforcement body to decide whether they need further evidence and apply for a search warrant. The initiation of criminal investigations used to be the only means for rights-holders to obtain information about the identity of the subscriber behind an IP address that they had identified. Establishing a connection between IP addresses and identities of real persons is only possible with the help of access providers. Although in the following it will be outlined that EU law does not "require Member States to lay down,..., an obligation to communicate personal data in order to ensure effective protection of copyright in the context of civil proceedings"[801], Member States may allow the release of data in their national law; if they do so, this must be in compliance with fundamental rights.

When national law allows the identification of the subscriber of a dynamic IP address, the effective application of any such information right presupposes that the Internet service provider is still in the possession of the data that connects the respective IP address to an individual subscriber. As has been mentioned previously, it is unlikely that private single connection subscribers have static IP addresses. They will commonly be allocated dynamic IP addresses. The identification of a subscriber consequently depends on two conditions, namely that the national law allows for the aforementioned disclosure of data by the Internet service provider, and that the Internet service provider retains the traffic data, so that when a request for disclosure is made, the matching of an IP address to a specific subscriber is made possible. Due to data protection laws, the retention of the relevant data is only allowed for billing purposes and must be deleted when payment can no longer be legally pursued. [802] With flatrate plans being the common subscription rate, access providers are not much interested in keeping the relevant records and are in general also not allowed to retain them. Although the *Data Retention Directive* in the EU requires the relevant records to be retained for a certain period of time ("no less than six months and no more than two years from the date of the communica-

801 CJEU, C-275/06, *Productores de Música de España (Promusicae) v Telefónica de España SAU* [2008] ECR 271.

802 Pursuant to Article 6(2) of the *E-Privacy Directive*, the retention is allowed for billing purposes but only as long as the statute of limitations allows the payment to be lawfully pursued.

tion"[803]), this does not mean that private parties can request the disclosure of this data. The purpose of data retention under said Directive is "to ensure that the data are available for the purpose of the investigation, detection and prosecution of serious crime".[804] Copyright infringements are not necessarily serious crimes, even if they are committed on a commercial scale. The use of the concept of commercial scale as a demarcation line between criminal and non-criminal copyright infringements is not without problems.[805] In general understanding, acts carried out on a commercial scale are intrinsically linked to some economic or commercial advantage, which would normally exclude acts carried out by end-consumers that may even act in good faith.[806] However, as the discussion in relation to commercial scale of file-sharing in Germany shows, end-consumers are often unsuccessful with their claim that they their sharing of files in peer-to-peer networks was not on a commercial scale. Although users make not a profit, they enjoy some commercial benefit because they download a file for free.[807] They certainly also cause financial damage to copyright owners because within peer-to-peer networks the downloader becomes at the same time a distributor of the requested file.[808] Accordingly, the concept of commercial scale alone does not suffice to distinguish a serious crime from other crimes.

As there is no legal obligation under EU law for Member State to provide for the retention of communications data for the purpose of pursuing private claims,[809] the disclosure of the identity of a subscriber depends on

---

803 See Article 6 of the *Data Retention Directive*.

804 Article 1(1) of the *Data Retention Directive.*

805 Cf. Dimitris Kioupis, *Criminal liability on the Internet,* in: Irini Stamatoudi (ed.), *Copyright enforcement on the Internet* (2010), p. 252.

806 Cf. Recital 14 to the *IPR Enforcement Directive*.

807 Dimitris Kioupis, *Criminal liability on the Internet,* in: Irini Stamatoudi (ed.), *Copyright enforcement on the Internet* (2010), p. 252.

808 See above, A. II. 4. a) Uploading Regularly Comes Along with Downloading.

809 See in this regard: European Observatory on Counterfeiting and Piracy, *Evidence and right of information in Intellectual Property Rights*, pp. 4 et seq., which outlines the example of Spain, in which, following the judgement of the CJEU in the Promusicae case (C-275/06 *Productores de Música de España (Promusicae) v Telefónica de España SAU* [2008] ECR 271), the domestic court "confirmed that Spanish data protection rules prevent Internet service providers from disclosing the identity of individual account holders to right holders for the purpose of civil proceedings, depriving right holders of a remedy altogether". Similarly the report states that in Austria, "in the case of on-line peer-to-peer infringements ('file

how long access providers store the data for their own business purposes. Because access providers have to respect the general data protection principles of data avoidance and data economy, which requires them to store data no longer than necessary, rights-holders have to be quick in filing their disclosure requests.

In practice, many rights-holders will ask for a so-called "quick freeze", i.e. either the rights-holder or a court will inform the provider about a detected infringement and ask him to refrain from deleting the data. Whether this is possible is a matter of national law, the "freezing" of data would need to be prescribed by law.[810] Usually, there is no obligation of access providers to comply with a quick freeze request, at least not with a request by a rights-holder.[811] However, most providers comply with such requests and freeze the relevant data until the rights-holder has obtained a court order requiring the disclosure of the information. In practice, most access providers store the relevant data for seven days for internal purposes.[812] This period of time will be prolonged if a disclosure request is filed with a court and the court has asked the provider to preserve the relevant data until the disclosure request has been dealt with. Once the disclosure is ordered, the data will be forwarded to the applicant, and subsequently deleted by the access provider. The latter poses a problem for the subscriber when he wants to prepare his defence: He will not be able to obtain log files from the provider. In that respect, subscribers are advised to activate the logging of IP addresses function of their router to keep a protocol of IP addresses that have been allocated to them as this will allow them to

---

sharing'), the provisions relating to the right of information are in practice not enforceable where information is requested from access providers, due to a decision of the Austrian Supreme Court restricting the retention and processing of dynamic IP addresses". It also has to be noted that the CJEU, in its judgment in the joined cases C-293/12 and C-594/12 *Digital Rights Ireland and Seitlinger and Others*, Judgment of 08.04.2014, has declared the *Data Retention Directive*, which provided for the retention of data for the purpose of the prevention, investigation, detection and preosecution of serious crime, to be invalid.

810 Data protection law prescribes that data pocessing and storing needs to be prescribed by law.

811 As regards Germany see LG München I, Decision of 20.08.2011 – 21 O 7841/11.

812 This has been confirmed by the Deutsche Telekom in Germany, see Holger Bleich/Joerg Heidrich/Thomas Stadler, *Schwierige Gegenwehr – Was tun bei unberechtigten Filesharing-Abmahnungen*?, c´t 19/2010.

identify mistimed logs by the rights-holder or simple transposed digits in IP addresses, i.e. wrongly forwarded IP addresses.[813]

2. The Necessary Evidence

All enforcement measures, irrespective whether criminal or private enforcement, require the identification of a copyright infringement. Relevant data in that context are not only the identification of the infringement as such but also the identification of the infringer or at least the IP address from which the infringement was committed. Whether the identification of the subscriber of that IP address suffices or the actual infringer needs to be identified varies from state to state. Who needs to be identified depends on the substance of the applicable law, i.e. whether it is the actual offender that is to be sanctioned for the copyright infringement or whether a norm exists that sanctions the subscriber for letting the infringement happen from his Internet access. Thus it will be necessary to clearly specify the alleged criminal activity. In addition to the IP address, it will also be necessary to log the access time at which the infringement was committed. Also, information as regards the way the file-sharing has been conducted may be required, such as for example the client used.

3. The Identifiable

In order to have a claim, a copyright infringement needs to be identified as well as the infringer or the information leading to the identification of the infringer. As concerns the latter, a file sharer in a peer-to-peer network can only be identified by his IP address. The problems connected with this will be outlined in the following. As regards the identification of an infringer, a public consultation by the European Commission on the civil enforcement of intellectual property rights showed, that many rights-holders have faced problems.[814]

813 *Ibid.*

814 Among the 146 respondents who answered questions relating to potential problems in the identification of infringers/alleged infringers of their IPR, 68 % declared having faced problems, European Commission, DG Internal Market and Services, *Civil Enforcement of Intellectual Property Rights: Public Consultation*

a) The Copyright Infringement

First of all, the copyright holder or someone acting on his behalf must identify an alleged copyright infringement. File-sharing normally can be qualified as an act of communication to the public, because copyright protected works are made available to the public. Some unauthorised files are easy to detect, because the file name carries the title of a song, album, film, or TV series. However, simply from the name of a file it cannot be instantly concluded that the file contains the content it is named after.[815] Therefore, someone will actually have to listen to the file in order to identify it as copyright infringing.[816] Alternatively, identical files can be identified by their hash value.[817] The term hash value refers to a piece of data that is given as the answer to a hash function. By a hash function, a computer creates a short reference code comprising a string of letters and numbers which represents a large piece of data. Every downloaded file has a unique hash value and can be identified on this basis. This hash value is being compared to a digital fingerprint for it is as unique as a human fingerprint.[818] In peer-to-peer file-sharing networks, the hash value is for example used to identify each piece of the content to be shared. This enables the tracker to recognise pieces of the content file as they are shared and is intended to ensure that the content files are correctly downloaded and unmodified.[819] Similar to the tracker within the file-sharing network, the rights-holder is able to identify a distributed file as infringing by the hash value. With almost certainty a matching hash value represents

---

of the Efficiency of Proceedings and Accessibility of Measures, Synthesis of the Responses (July 2013), p.12.

815 See for example Dennis Heinemeyer/Matthias Kreitlow/Arne Nordmeyer/André Sabellek: *Kampf gegen Filesharing als Modell verfehlter Mehrfachkompensation? – Fragen zur Schadenshöhe, zu Gesamtschuldnern und Beweisen bei Tauschbörsen,* MultiMedia und Recht 2012, 279.

816 Sara Weber, *Der Piraten-Jäger*, UniSpiegel 2012, Issue 3, 14–16.

817 Cf. in this regard Christian Solmecke/Jan Bärenfänger, *Urheberrechtliche Schutzfähigkeit von Dateifragmenten – Nutzlos = Schutzlos*, MultiMedia und Recht 2011, 567, 568; Holger Morgenstern, *Zuverlässigkeit von IP-Adressen-Ermittlungssoftware, Zur Sicherheit der eingesetzten Programme und Verfahren zur Verletzungsdokumentation,* Computer und Recht 2011, 203, 207.

818 *Ibid.*

819 See expert report cited by the High Court in *Dramatico Entertainment Ltd & others v British Sky Broadcasting Ltd & others*, [2012] EWHC 268, para. 19.

identical files.[820] However, even small alterations, for example cutting a music recording by one second, leads to a change in the hash value so that the hash value of the original file and the copy do not match anymore. As aforementioned, in these cases, it will be necessary for the rights-holder to actually verify the work by downloading it and watching/listening to it. This is also necessary with respect to one enforcement measure by the rights-holders themselves: namely, the so-called "poisoning" of peer-to-peer networks. The fact that protected works are commonly shared in different versions, e.g. radio edit, remix version, high quality, low quality, and thus, have different hash values was taken as their advantage by rights-holders: they started planting corrupt or invalid versions of their works in the networks.[821] These versions may for example contain white noise, advertisements, or warnings about the illegality of file-sharing.[822]

---

820 Christian Solmecke/Jan Bärenfänger, *Urheberrechtliche Schutzfähigkeit von Dateifragmenten – Nutzlos = Schutzlos*, MultiMedia und Recht 2011, 567, 568. Only few instances – under specific conditions – are known where the same hash value represented two different files. Technological progress also means that his is becoming less likely, See Dennis Heinemeyer/Matthias Kreitlow/Arne Nordmeyer/André Sabellek: *Kampf gegen Filesharing als Modell verfehlter Mehrfachkompensation? – Fragen zur Schadenshöhe, zu Gesamtschuldnern und Beweisen bei Tauschbörsen*, MultiMedia und Recht 2012, 279. File-sharing networks like BitTorrent no longer use the so-called MD5 functions, in which collisions could not be outruled and now uses SHA-1 instead, see http://www.bittorrent.org/beps/bep_0003.html (last accessed 17.05.2014) For the risks of collisions in MD5 see Xiaoyun Wang/Hongbo Yu, *How to Break MD5 and Other Hash Functions*, in: Ronald Cramer (ed.), *Advances in Cryptology – EUROCRYPT 2005: 24th Annual International Conference on the Theory and Applications of Cryptographic Techniques* (2005), Proceedings, Vol. 3494 of LNCS, pp. 19–35. This also makes BitTorrent very resistant against content poisoning. Content poisoning refers to the act by which copyright owners set up decoy peers that respond to download requests with corrupted or falsified files. The rationale behind such a deterring technique is that if users keep downloading falsified files, they will become frustrated and stop downloading from peer-to-peer networks, see Xiaosong Lou/Kai Hwang, *Adaptive content poisoning to prevent illegal file distribution in P2P networks* (2006).

821 See M. Eric Johnson/Dan McGuire/Nicholas D. Willey, *The evolution of the peer-to-peer file sharing industry and the security risks for users*, Proceedings of the 41st Hawaii International Conference on System Sciences 2008, p. 4.

822 See *ibid*, which also refers to Madonna having employed such tactics in the wake of releasing her album "An American Life". Users that downloaded songs from the album, or at least they thought so, ended up with a file in which Madonna herself questions the user about what he is doing. See also Gil Kaufman, *Madon-*

The idea behind this is clear: to frustrate users, who will spend as much time on downloading a corrupted file as they will spend on downloading a good file, and encourage them to switch to legitimate download offers.[823] Although advanced and sophisticated networks have developed strategies against polluted content and block results and requests from IP addresses that have been polluting,[824] this fact must not be ignored.

As regards the upload and download of parts of a protected work, it has already been outlined above, that these parts enjoy protection as long as they are "useful" and contain elements which are the expression of the intellectual creation of the author of the work.[825]

Insofar as unprotected fragments are concerned, the claimant will have to prove that either a file has been downloaded completely or offered for download as a whole. Evidence that only proves that a down- and upload has taken place at some point for a limited time, will regularly constitute no sufficient evidence.

b) The IP Address

Due to the technological functioning of peer-to-peer file-sharing, it is not possible to identify a potential infringer straight away. What can be identified is the IP address from which an alleged infringement has taken place. This IP address then needs to be matched against the subscriber to whom it was allocated at the time of the infringement. The problem is that the IP address is connected to a piece of hardware, i.e. router, not to an individual human being. So what can be identified from an IP address is the Internet connection subscriber behind an IP address at a given time. Time logging in that respect is particular important, as many Internet service providers (in IPv 4) allocate a pool of IP addresses as needed, rather than

---

na to pirates: 'What the F--- do you think you're doing?', Singer lashes out at file traders on P2P networks, MTV news (16.04.2003).

823 Apparently 50 % of popular songs on the FastTrack network were polluted in this way. Cf. *Ibid.*

824 See Michael Piatek/Tadayoshi Kohno/Arvind Krishnamurthy, *Challenges and directions for monitoring P2P file sharing networks – or – Why my printer received a DMCA takedown notice*, University of Washington Technical Report 2008, UW-CS, p. 4.

825 See above A. II. 4. b) Parts of a Protected Work Enjoy Protection.

assigning each computer a never-changing static IP address.[826] Whether the issue of correct time logging will still persist in IPv 6, where it will be possible to attribute a static IP address to each subscription remains to be seen.

With the IP address, the rights-holder will only be able to determine the Internet access provider that has allocated the IP address to a user.[827] In this regard, it is important to recall that dynamic IP addresses are not user-bound but provider-bound. Because public records are held in relation to which blocks of IP address have been assigned to particular access providers, a consultation of these public databases will tell the rights-holder the access provider to whom he needs to address his request.[828]

Having identified the Internet access provider, the rights-holder is only one step away from identifying the subscriber with whom the access provider contracted. However, it is evident that the person who pays for Internet access at a given location is not necessarily the same individual who allegedly downloaded a protected work from that access. An IP address provides only the location at which one of any number of computer devices may be deployed, much like a telephone number can be used for several telephones.

A US District Court Judge summarised the problem, that the rights-holders are confronted with, in a 2012 case as follows: "An IP address provides only the location at which one of any number of computer devices may be deployed, much like a telephone number can be used for any number of telephones….Thus, it is no more likely that the subscriber to an IP address carried out a particular computer function – here the purported illegal downloading of a single pornographic film – than to say an individual who pays the telephone bill made a specific telephone call".[829]

Like the US District Judge correctly summarised, the identification of an IP address in connection with an infringement is no proof that the subscriber of that particular IP address committed the infringement himself.

---

826 See above First Chapter, B. I. 1. b) IP Address Allocation.

827 For the functioning of IP address allocation, see Richard Clayton, *Online traceability: Who did that?, Technical expert report on collecting robust evidence of copyright infringement through peer-to-peer filesharing* (2012), pp. 14 et seq.

828 A simple whois search on the Internet allows everyone to find out which access provider allocates a specific IP address.

829 US District Court, Eastern District of New York, *K-Beech, Inc. v John Does 1-37*, CV 11-3995 (DRH)(GRB).

The IP address does not allow the identification of the individual user of a connection at the time of an infringement. If a router is used to share an Internet connection, the routers gets the IP address issued straight from the Internet service provider. It then creates and manages a subnet for all the computers connected to that router. It is common that connections are shared between several users, for example between members of a household. Also, subscribers may grant guests or neighbours access to their flatrate plan. For someone from outside of a household or a community sharing a connection, it is impossible to know who committed the infringement. This becomes even more difficult when business entities offer complementary and free Wi-Fi within their premises. It has for example become common standard for hotels to offer free Wi-Fi to their guests. Also coffee bars try to attract customers by complementary Wi-Fi.

Neither the criminal standard of proof, i.e. "beyond reasonable doubt", nor the civil standard of proof, i.e. "on the balance of probabilities", are likely to be met in terms of identifying an infringer when several users have access to a secured connection. That the criminal or civil standard of proof is met, becomes even more unlikely where the subscriber has not secured his Internet connection. In determining liability, it will be necessary to consider the level of security mechanisms that have been implemented to protect a Wi-Fi network.[830] Irrespective of the required security standard, many subscriber still do not realise or know how to secure their network. Even if they do, a likely, though rare scenario, is that Wi-Fi-networks are hacked by third parties.[831] With improved security standards,

---

830 Wireless routers have gained popularity in recent years (Wi-Fi penetration of households in 2011: UK 73.3 %, Germany 71.7 %, France 71.6 %. See Business Wire, *Strategy analytics: A quarter of households worldwide now have wireless home networks,* Business Wire (04.04.2012). Many Internet service providers provide a complimentary wireless router as part of their Internet access service. While wireless networks may be more convenient in terms that one does not have to run cables through the house to interconnect different computers to the router, it also means that the connection may be more vulnerable.

831 This issue was also raised by the Joint Committee on Human Rights in the UK when discussing the Digital Economy Bill, see House of Lords, House of Commons, Joint Committee on Human Rights, *Legislative Scrutiny: Digital Economy Bill, Fifth Report of Session 2009-10*, HL Paper 44 = HC 327 (05.02.2010), p. 87.

these incidents are declining in number, but cannot be ruled out as hackers may decrypt network keys.[832]

4. The Identifier

If a copyright infringement is suspected, the rights-holder needs to gather evidence of that alleged infringement. The process of identifying an infringement and the IP address from which an infringement took place is usually outsourced to private investigation companies that have specialised in this form of information gathering. They use various proprietary technologies, of which some will be discussed in the following. The details of the process are vital to prove an infringement in court. Advances in technologies mean that techniques for identification also progress, hence, the following will only briefly relate to a few recent detection and evidence gathering processes in order to give a basic idea of their functioning.

a) How Data Is Harvested

The collecting, or "harvesting" of IP addresses is usually conducted by a company specialised in the detection of online copyright infringements.[833] The right holders usually employ a third party company, for instance Logistep and Pro Media[834] in Germany, DtecNet in Ireland or Trident Media Guard[835] in France. These companies have specialised in the detection of file-sharing of copyrighted works and monitor peer-to-peer networks for incidents of illegal file-sharing by using special software. Usually a forensic computer analyst will install a peer-to-per client on his com-

---

832 In September 2013, German police arrested a man that hacked the Wi-Fi-networks of his neighbours to download child pornography. See Spiegel Online, *22-Jähriger festgenommen: Ermittler entdecken riesige Kinderporno-Sammlung in Köln*, Der Spiegel online (19.09.2013).

833 A detailed account on how data is harvested is given by Morgenstern in Holger Morgenstern, *Zuverlässigkeit von IP-Adressen-Ermittlungssoftware, Zur Sicherheit der eingesetzten Programme und Verfahren zur Verletzungsdokumentation*, Computer und Recht 2011, 203, 205.

834 Sara Weber, *Der Piraten-Jäger*, UniSpiegel 2012, Issue 3, 14–16.

835 http://www.tmg.eu/.

puter and will join a "swarm" of file-sharers.[836] He monitors the swarm and records the IP addresses of those connections that share the file. As most people under IPv 4 do not have static (i.e. unchanging) but dynamic IP addresses[837], the IP addresses only create a temporary reference point. Thus, it is important for the right holder that further data is collected to be able to identify a potential infringer and preserve evidence of an infringement. What information and how this information is being collected will be outlined by two examples, one from Germany and one from Ireland.[838] The restriction to two examples is based on the assumption that basically all harvesting takes place in a similar way and no detailed understanding of the software in use is necessary. The examples try to provide a general overview in a non-technical language.

Logistep in Germany for instance uses a self-developed monitoring software that collects information from various peer-to-peer networks. In particular, Logistep searches for copyright-protected works of their clients and logs – following a successful "test download" – the IP addresses of the participating users, as well as further information such as the actual time, the hash value of the file, the user's pseudonym within the sharing software, the name and version of the software.[839] Similarly, DtecNet, which is employed by EMI in Ireland, searches peer-to-peer networks for files being uploaded which are subject to copyright.[840] DtecNet does what any user of a peer-to-peer network does in order to obtain a file that is

---

836 For a general description of how a monitoring software will proceed to use a peer-to-peer system to download a copy of a file after it has obtained a torrent file, see Richard Clayton, *Online traceability: Who did that?, Technical expert report on collecting robust evidence of copyright infringement through peer-to-peer filesharing* (2012), pp. 8 et seq.

837 Dynamic means that the user's router will usually be given an IP address only for a certain period of time by the Internet service provider. Thus, the address will change from time to time, see above in the First Chapter, B. I. 2. b) Dynamic IP Addresses.

838 Although no Irish enforcement scheme will be analysed, the way data is harvested will be presented as the Irish High Court in *EMI v UPC* (Irish High Court, decision of 11.10.2010, [2009] no 5472 P) outlined in detail how the system deployed by "DtecNet" operated.

839 Cf. Felix Buchmann/Sebastian Brüggemann, *Der Preis des "Filesharing" – Streitwert, Schadensersatz und Kostendeckelung nach § 97 a Abs. 2 UrhG,* Kommunikation und Recht 2011, 368–373.

840 Irish High Court, *EMI v UPC*, Decision of 11.10.2010, [2009] no 5472 P, para. 34.

being shared: DtecNet searches peer-to-peer networks for copyrighted files being uploaded. If it finds such a file, it will request the file, which is subsequently transmitted to, and copied, by DtecNet's computer. Integral for this process is to obtain basic information about the uploader from whom the work is being transmitted: the user's pseudonym and the IP address of the user, the relevant time, data and identification of the copyright material.[841] If the IP address is registered to an Irish service provider, Dtecnet will identify how many copyrighted files were being made available "by that user on peer-to-peer software".[842] A list of these files will then be captured in the form of a log containing the name, size and hash value of user's shared files.[843] As regards the fact that with BitTorrent files are split into small blocks of data, the Irish High Court held in EMI v UPC that

> "Although a music file may be split up in several hundred pieces, each of them carries a sufficient identification through the file # for it to be fitted into an appropriate order of sense and sufficient to clearly identify that it is a portion of a work which is subject to copyright. In all of the examples of which the Court was provided evidence, there is nothing to suggest that if only a tiny portion of the work was being uploaded that that would be insufficient to identify it. Rather, what peer-to-peer involves is obtaining the entire music recording that is desired. The file # identifier ensures that it is put into a correct format and order. The process of DtecNet is automatic, in the sense that the handshake between the computers, in peer-to-peer terminology, is fully automated."[844]

As these "harvesting" techniques all require that the agent of the rightsholder infiltrates the network, friends-to-friends network, where the users know and/or trust each other, carry a natural barrier against detection. The software always needs to somehow obtain access to a swarm of file-sharers.

Regularly rumours occur, that rights-holders or third parties on their behalf plant so-called "honeypots" into file-sharing networks.[845] In file-

---

841 *Ibid.*

842 *Ibid.*

843 *Ibid.*

844 *Ibid.*

845 Cf. reports on notorious torrent sites such as extratorrent.cc which reported in March 2011 that *"Portugal created honeypot to fight piracy"* (see http://extratorrent.cc/article/1167/portugal+created+honeypot+to+fight+piracy.html [last accessed on 17.05.2014]). Apparently, the music industry in Portugal agreed to

sharing circles the term honeypot is used for websites and swarms specifically created in order to lure users into downloading copyrighted content. The honeypots serve as traps designed to gather the IP addresses of those who try downloading the content. As the user who joins the swarm is not in the position to acquire information whether the file was planted on purpose (and thus, authorised), or not, he may end up being charged for downloading from a lawful source without having a realistic chance to prove this.

Similar to the response to corrupted files, sophisticated networks may avoid systematic monitoring of peers by operating IP blacklists. [846] They will block the IP addresses of suspected monitoring agents, and thereby protect against direct monitoring techniques that involve actual data exchange between monitoring agents and peer-to-peer clients. It is however expected that rights-holders, or more precisely their enforcement agents will shift to more conclusive methods of identifying users.[847]

b) Reliability of Data Harvesting/Evidence

The question that follows from the employment of software to harvest data is the reliability of IP address evidence.[848] While cases that attract media attention are regularly those where a grandmother without a computer is accused of downloading indecent content,[849] from Germany instances are known where a court denied disclosure orders because it believed that an

---

grant Portuguese authorities the right to upload copyrighted files to file-sharing networks.

846 Michael Piatek/Tadayoshi Kohno/Arvind Krishnamurthy, *Challenges and directions for monitoring P2P file sharing networks – or – Why my printer received a DMCA takedown notice,* University of Washington Technical Report 2008, UW-CS, p. 4.

847 *Ibid.*

848 Holger Morgenstern, *Zuverlässigkeit von IP-Adressen-Ermittlungssoftware, Zur Sicherheit der eingesetzten Programme und Verfahren zur Verletzungsdokumentation,* Computer und Recht 2011, 203 – 208. For recommendations as to the standards that should be set in relation to monitoring systems to ensure that the collection of IP address of uploaders of copyright infringing materials on peer-to-peer networks is robust and error-free, see Richard Clayton, *Online traceability: Who did that?, Technical expert report on collecting robust evidence of copyright infringement through peer-to-peer filesharing* (2012).

849 Andrew Murray, *Information Technology Law* (2nd ed. 2013), p. 288.

error has occurred in the logging or transmission of IP addresses.[850] For instance, a court in Cologne refused a disclosure order where the request for disclosure contained numerous identical IP addresses. As the Internet service provider concerned allocates a new dynamic IP address every 24 hours to its users, and considering the amount of available IP addresses, the Court could not be convinced that a number of IP addresses were regularly involved in copyright infringements.[851] In 2008, the same court had previously denied access to criminal files to rights-holders arguing that the reliability of the harvested data had not been proven. Criminal investigations into alleged online copyright infringements had shown that more than 50% of the data harvested could not be allocated. In other cases, the error rate was more than 90%, assumingly due to mistimed logs.[852] Questions of validity of gathered evidence have also been raised in connection with recent copyright enforcement legislation.[853] Potential sources of error will be briefly outlined in the following. No claim is made that this list is complete.

aa) Manipulation of File-Sharing Clients

A 2008 study by researchers at the University of Washington revealed that DMCA takedown notices in the US are also sent based on inconclusive evidence—and sometimes even to printers and other devices that do not download music or movies at all.[854] Although the study did not examine a

---

850 OLG Köln, Decision of 10.02.2011 – 6 W 5/11, MultiMedia und Recht 2011, 322.

851 *Ibid*, 323.

852 See LG Köln, Order of 25.09.2008 – 109-1/08. For a comment on the case see Holger Bleich/Joerg Heidrich/Thomas Stadler, *Schwierige Gegenwehr – Was tun bei unberechtigten Filesharing-Abmahnungen?*, c´t 19/2010.

853 Cf. for instance House of Lords, House of Commons, Joint Committee on Human Rights, *Legislative Scrutiny: Digital Economy Bill, Fifth Report of Session 2009-10*, HL Paper 44 = HC 327 (05.02.2010), p. 87.

854 Michael Piatek/Tadayoshi Kohno/Arvind Krishnamurthy, *Challenges and directions for monitoring P2P file sharing networks – or – Why my printer received a DMCA takedown notice*, University of Washington Technical Report 2008, UW-CS. See also Richard Clayton, Expert Opinion in case *R (on the application of British Telecommunications Plc) v Secretary of State for Business, Innovation and Skills*, paras. 49 et seq.

software that is specifically being used in Europe to detect infringements, the findings give insight into the weaknesses of the process of detection.

They identified a main weakness in current methods of detecting copyright infringement in BitTorrent, namely the treatment of indirect reports as conclusive evidence of participation.[855] The research revealed that some rights-holders or companies acting on their behalf relied on information from the search phase of the protocol, and did not try to download a file and identify where it came from. The researchers run specialist BitTorrent programmes that looked as if they were doing file-sharing, but instead they were just recording statistics about the speed and effectiveness of the system. In the following, the researchers received cease and desist letters in which they were accused of copyright infringement. The tracker of the copyright holders had registered their interest in a particular file, which let to the rights-holder conclusion that the researchers were actually transferring the file. While other users whose IP addresses were present in the tracker file were actively file-sharing, the researchers were not. By default, BitTorrent trackers record the source IP address from the request as the actual address of the peer to be delivered to other peers, and from this the rights-holders had drawn their conclusion.

In the following, it could be proved that entries in the torrent files could be forged by providing IP addresses that were not involved in file-sharing at all. This has to do with some BitTorrent tracker implementations supporting "an optional extension to the peer request message that allows requesting clients to specify a different IP address that the tracker should record in its list of peers instead".[856] Accordingly, the researchers could frame arbitrary IP addresses for infringements ("IP spoofing").[857] Of 281 DMCA complaints, that they received, only 18 were for IP addresses that they attempted to implicate.[858] The majority of complaints targeted the IP addresses from which they launched their spoofed requests. Without going into too much detail, the experiment succeeded in proving that there are

855 Michael Piatek/Tadayoshi Kohno/Arvind Krishnamurthy, *Challenges and directions for monitoring P2P file sharing networks – or – Why my printer received a DMCA takedown notice,* University of Washington Technical Report 2008, UW-CS.

856 *Ibid*, p.3.

857 *Ibid.*

858 Ibid

BitTorrent trackers that do not record the IP source address and are open to IP spoofing.

Malicious users may further trigger misreporting, since the torrent meta data files that specify trackers are user-generated. A coordinating BitTorrent tracker can be manipulated so that he may falsely implicate an IP address in a swarm of file-sharers by simply returning that IP address as a peer regardless of participation.[859]

bb) Mistimed and Mismatched Logs

However, it is not necessary for false implications that malicious users are involved. Incorrect evidence may also be gathered in rather simpler ways.[860] Reports of logs can be mistimed.[861] Because IP addresses are allocated dynamically, the logging of the correct time is essential to identify an alleged infringer. Even an error in seconds may lead to the wrong subscriber being accused – depending on how fast the IP addresses are newly allocated.

Similar to mistimed logs, timestamps may be incorrectly translated: attention needs to be paid to the correct translation of time-zones.[862] In this regard, human error is the most likely pitfall.[863]

---

859 *Ibid.*

860 As regards the frequency of mistimed and inaccurate logs,see Holger Bleich/ Joerg Heidrich/Thomas Stadler, *Schwierige Gegenwehr – Was tun bei unberechtigten Filesharing-Abmahnungen?*, c´t 19/2010.

861 For different scenarios how this can happen see Michael Piatek/Tadayoshi Kohno/Arvind Krishnamurthy, *Challenges and directions for monitoring P2P file sharing networks – or – Why my printer received a DMCA takedown notice*, University of Washington Technical Report 2008, UW-CS.

862 Richard Clayton reports from a case where he was employed by the Crown Prosecution Service after flaws in the Internet traceability evidence were encountered during cross-examination of a witness in a 2009 UK murder trial. The Internet service provider in that case was asked to identify eight IP addresses, of which it initially could only match four due to incorrectly translated times in Pacific Daylight Saving Time (PDT) into Greenwich Mean Time (GMT). In addition, one event was incorrectly reported by the police to have occurred at 18:50 GMT, when it had in reality occurred one hour previous at 18:50 British Summer Time (BST). Richard Clayton, *Online traceability: Who did that?, Technical expert report on collecting robust evidence of copyright infringement through peer-to-peer filesharing* (2012), p. 28.

863 Cf. *ibid.*

cc) Misreporting by Trackers

Misreporting by trackers is the most straightforward way to falsely implicate an IP address in an infringement.[864] Misreporting takes place when the coordinating tracker in a BitTorrent network returns an IP address as a peer although that IP address is not participating in the swarm. This can happen through manipulation of the user-generated tracker by malicious users.[865]

dd) Problems Belonging to the Sphere of the Subscriber: Unsecured Computers and Wi-Fi Connections

Wi-Fi insecurity is fertile ground for cybercriminals.[866] A substantial percentage of users does not understand how to change the security settings on their Wi-Fi networks.[867] Many users are unsure whether their network is secure.[868] Innocent users may also be implicated for copyright infringement, if malware (malicious software) is running on their computer that downloads or hosts copyrighted content.[869] Malware can install itself if a computer does not run an anti-malware software. Also, their home network may have an open, or at least not appropriately secured Wi-Fi access point, which a non-authorised third party may use to share copyrighted content. In this regard, it will be for the courts to decide – if at all – which security standards are required when running a Wi-Fi access point.

---

864 *Ibid.*

865 *Ibid.*

866 Neil MacEwan, *A tricky situation: deception in cyberspace,* Journal of Criminal Law 2013, Vol. 77 Issue 5, 417, 422.

867 *Ibid* with further references.

868 *Ibid.*

869 Richard Clayton, *Online traceability: Who did that?, Technical expert report on collecting robust evidence of copyright infringement through peer-to-peer file-sharing* (2012), p. 28.

c) Evasion of Detection: Migration to (More) Secure Peer-to-Peer Networks

Almost as easy as IP addresses can be identified in peer-to-peer networks, users, that have some IT-literacy can evade detection. The logging of an IP address in Peer-to-Peer networks only works as long as the communication takes place "in public". Many variations of BitTorrent technology have evolved, which may avoid legal detection of copyright infringement by wither encrypting the content shared, or hide the IP addresses of the users sharing files. In addition, files may be changed in friend-to-friend networks, where users know and trust each other.

aa) Anonymous Peer-to-Peer Networks

Users that desire anonymity because they do not wish to be identified as copyright infringer may use anonymous or pseudonymous peer-to-peer technology. [870] The level of anonymity is different to that of conventional peer-to-peer networks, which is rather a perceived anonymity as long as the subscriber details of a certain IP address are not revealed.

Faced with increased enforcement actions against peer-to-peer file-shares, anonymous peer-to-peer communication systems provide an environment that is much more difficult for rights-holders to infiltrate and can also be more efficient for users. It is beyond the scope of this work to enter into detailed explanation of the technology that enables anonymous file-sharing over the Internet, hence it is only briefly outlined to acknowledge its existence.

Interest in such peer-to-peer system has increased for many reasons, ranging from the desire to legally share files without revealing one's network identity (IP address) due to concerns over mass surveillance and data retentions, to a desire to stay anonymous because one share copyright protected works and fears a lawsuit. Anonymity/pseudonymity is achieved by special routing overlay networks that hide the physical location of each node/participant from other participants. In this context pseudonymous communication refers to the fact that instead of being identified by their IP

870 For the development of anonymous peer-to-peer file-sharing see Jessica A. Wood, *The Darknet: A digital copyright revolution*, Richmond Journal of Law & Technology 2010, Vol. 16 Issue 4, pp. 1 et seq.

address, users are identified by pseudonyms such as cryptographic keys. Cryptographic keys can either be used to identify specific nodes (meaning that the participant will stay anonymous e.g. in the MUTE network), or to identify specific pieces of data (e.g. in Freenet).[871] Both types of networks are referred to as anonymous, because it is impossible – or at least difficult – to determine whether a node that sends a message originated the message or is simply forwarding it on behalf of another node. For Freenet[872] this means that clients retrieve files from other Freenet user's computers (= nodes), while a server relays requests and files for other Freenet clients on the network.[873] Files are retrieved and transmitted from node to node. The unique feature is that each node is only aware of nodes with which it can directly communicate. Hence, each user's computer may thus only know the IP address of the last node in the network of nodes that it had contact with. For a receiving node it is not possible to know whether that last node originated the file, or just passed on a copy from an earlier node.[874] In addition, unlike most peer-to-peer systems, Freenet users who wish to share a file do not simply make that file available, but create a "key" for the Freenet file, and insert the file into their node. As finally all communication between nodes is encrypted, it is impossible (or at least really difficult) for third parties to monitor the content of file requests.[875]

Anonymous peer-to-peer networks may also be truly anonymous, i.e. that the network nodes do not carry any identifiers, or pseudonymous, meaning that the nodes are identified by pseudonyms such as cryptographic keys. Like with Freenet, every node then acts as a universal sender and receiver, and forwards information for others on the network to prevent the determination of origin of a message. Anonymous peer-to-peer networks can either exist in the opennet or in the darknet/friend-to-friend network type. In opennet network, peer nodes are discovered automatically and there is little control available to the user which nodes become his peers. The majority of anonymous peer-to-peer systems are darknet/

---

871 As regards Freenet see *ibid*, pp. 19 et seq.

872 Freenet was founded in 2000 as a decentralised peer-to-peer system.

873 For the detailed functioning of Freenet, see Ryan Roemer, *The digital evolution: Freenet and the future of copyright in the Internet*, UCLA Journal of Law & Technology 2002, Vol. 6 Issue 2, 1, 5.

874 *Ibid.*

875 Ian Clarke/ Scott G. Miller/Theodore W. Hong/Oskar Sandberg/Brandon Wiley, *Protecting free expression online with Freenet* , Ieee Internet Computing 2011, Vol. 6 Issue 1, 40, 45.

friend-to-friend networks, where users manually establish connections with nodes that belong to users they actually know and trust.[876] These networks typically need more effort to set up because a node only has trusted nodes as peers.[877]

Darknet networks often also support indirect anonymous communication between users who do not know or trust each other: Users in these networks cannot find out who else is participating beyond their own circle of friends, but communication with remote nodes is possibly by sending messages across the overlay network without compromising anonymity. [878]

While it was already predicted in 2004 that Darknet is "[t]he collection of networks and other technologies that enable people to illegally share copyrighted digital files with little or no fear of detection",[879] in the wake of the latest US copyright enforcement initiatives,[880] increases in the usage of darknet/friend-to-friend networks have been reported.[881]

Where a user engages in anonymous peer-to-peer networks, it will be almost impossible to identify the origin of a file or part thereof and/or the identity of a participant in the network.

bb) Friends-to-Friends Networks

In addition, users may also opt to migrate to such file-sharing technologies that only allow the exchange of files between friends (friend-to-friend networks), or at least trusted members. The infiltration of such, rather "pri-

---

876 *See* Michael Rogers/Saleem Bhatti, *How to disappear completely: A survey of private peer-to-peer networks* (2007), available at http://www.cs.st-andrews.ac.uk/~saleem/papers/2007/space2007/space2007-rb2007.pdf. (last accessed 17.05.2014)

877 Lilian Edwards, *Role and responsibility of Internet intermediaries in the field of copyright and related rights* (2011), p. 19.

878 Tom Chothia/Konstantinos Chatzikokolakis, *A survey of anonymous peer-to-peer file-sharing*, pp.1 et seq.

879 Fred von Lohmann, *Measuring the Digital Millennium Copyright Act against the Darknet: Implications for the regulation of Technological Protection Measures,* Loyola of Los Angeles Entertainment Law Review 2004, Vol. 24, 635, 637.

880 Like *SOPA*, *PIPA* and *ACTA*.

881 Ernesto, *Anonymous, decentralized and uncensored file-sharing is booming*, TorrentFreak (03.03.2012) See also Nate Anderson, *Darknets and the future of P2P investigators,* Ars Technica (05.03.2009).

vate" peer-to-peer groups is much more difficult than public peer-to-peer networks.[882]

cc) VPN Clients, Proxies and TOR

Instead of Freenet or darknet/friend-to-friend networks, users may also use virtual private networks (VPN) to hide their identity. Simply speaking, VPNs create an encrypted tunnel between the user's computer and the host server, meaning that the user's Internet service provider will only see that he has connected to a VPN server, but will not be able to obtain information on the user's activites. Prominent examples of VPN networks are university networks. The VPN servers of a university network will however regularly log data when users connect. However, there are also providers of VPN, which are truly anonymous and do not keep logs.[883]

In contrast to VPN clients, proxy servers are computers that act as intermediaries between the user's computer and the Internet. All traffic is diverted through a proxy server and will appear to come from the proxy server's IP address. Thus, identification of the IP address will only help to identify the proxy.[884] Commercial anonymisation services are usually proxy-based.

As a further anonymisation mechanism, a user may also simply use TOR[885] to hide his original IP address. The advantage of TOR in comparison to an anonymising proxy or VPN client is that the user does not need to trust a single third party. Instead, in the TOR network, each client selects three proxies from a large number of available proxies. These encrypt the content transmitted and each proxy can only remove one layer

---

882 Cf. Electronic Frontier Foundation, *RIAA v The People; Five Years Later,* Electronic Frontier Foundation (30.09.2008).

883 See for example Enigmax, *Which are the best anonymous VPN providers*, TorrentFreak (07.10.2011).

884 In the UK, one of the difficulties with proxies alone is the costs involved to identify the "end-user". It has been argued that it can be "prohibitively expensive" to obtain orders against file-sharers who have used "proxy servers" to conceal their identities, because orders will be required from a number of Internet service providers and because the copyright owner is liable to meet the defendant's costs as well as his own. See Andrew Tibber, *Know your enemy*, Magazine of the Society for Computers and Law 2008, Vol. 19 Issue 4, 1, 3.

885 TOR = The Onion Router, see tor.org.

of encryption.[886] The first proxy (the "entry node") can only remove the first layer of encryption which will give information about the second proxy (the "middle node"). The middle node will be able to remove the second encryption layer, which will give information about the final proxy (the "exit node"). Providers of TOR services do not retain traffic data, so that the originating IP address cannot be identified. Even if the providers would be obliged to retain this data, TOR could always evade the retention of identifying data by using TOR servers in third countries.[887]

d) The Burden of Proof

Though usually the rights-holder will have to provide all evidence to support his claim, national law may foresee a shift of the burden of proof for some elements. As an analysis of this field would go beyond the scope of this research, the following will outline a few issues that have arisen in Germany with regard to the burden of proof.

The rights-holder is in a position to prove that an infringement has been committed from a particular IP address at a given time. He will however have difficulties to prove that the subscriber of that IP address has committed the infringement. In civil procedure law, the claimant usually carries the burden of proof for all circumstances that are necessary to establish a claim. Hence, he will not only have to prove that an infringement has been committed but he will commonly also have to identify the infringer. Sometimes the subscriber will admit that he committed the infringement, or it may be established that he was the only person using a secured connection (i.e. a connection that was protected against intruders from outside); but usually, without further information regarding the identity of the infringer, it is almost impossible to prove that the subscriber is the actual infringer.

Thus, national legislation will be necessary that provides for establishing liability without the need to identify the infringer. In the second part of this Chapter, we will see that for instance the national legislator in France recognised this issue and introduced a provision under which the subscriber will be liable for infringements that have been committed via his

886 Cf. Lukas Feiler, *Tor als Prüfstein der Data Retention Richtlinie* (2005).
887 *Ibid.*

connection. Although he will not be liable for infringing copyright as such, liability will arise for failure to prevent an infringement by securing his Internet connection and/or instructing third parties that are authorised to use his Internet access to refrain from copyright infringements.

Another approach to establish liability would be to shift the burden of proof in the sense that the subscriber would have to prove that he is innocent. However, rather than introducing a shift of the burden of proof the German Federal Court of Justice introduced an alleviation of the standard of proof: when a protected work has been made publicly available from a certain IP address, which has been allocated to a specific subscriber at the time of the infringement, there shall be an actual presumption that the subscriber is responsible for the infringement. In order to rebut this presumption, the subscriber will have to provide plausible arguments that another cause of action is possible.[888] This requirement will regularly be fulfilled, when the defendant can show that someone else - commonly family or other household members - used the connection.[889] This approach also seems to be taken by the UK when the *DEA 2010* requires a subscriber who wants to appeal a warning to prove that "the act constituting the apparent infringement to which the report relates was not done by the subscriber, and the subscriber took reasonable steps to prevent other persons infringing copyright by means of the Internet access service"[890]. Also the French approach is rather similar when it comes to rebutting the presumption of failure to comply with the obligation to secure one's Internet access: in that respect the subscriber will have to prove that he has taken reasonable steps to secure his Internet access, and instructed third parties,

888 The subscriber will not have to provide evidence but convince the court that someone else has committed the infringement. See Christian Solmecke/Felix Rüther/Thomas Herkens, *Uneinheitliche Darlegungs- und Beweislast in Filesharing-Verfahren – Abweichen von zivilprozessualen Grundsätzen zu Gunsten der Rechteinhaber?*, MultiMedia und Recht 2013, 217, 218; Christian Solmecke, *Darlegungs- und Beweislast in Filesharing-Verfahren – Eine Auswertung der Aktuellen Rechtsprechung*, in: Jürgen Taeger (ed.), *Law as a Service (LaaS) – Recht im Internet- und Cloud-Zeitalter* (2013), Band 1, pp. 447–459. See also BGH, Decisions of 11.06.2015 – I ZR 75/14; I ZR 7/14 and I ZR 19/14 (*Tauschbörse I – III*).

889 See *ibid* and OLG Köln, Decision of 16.05.2012 – 6 U 239/1, MultiMedia und Recht 2012, 549; LG Köln, Decision of 11.09.2012 – 33 O 353/11, Zeitschrift für Urheber- und Medienrecht 2013, 66.

890 See section 13(6) *DEA 2010.*

whom he allowed to use the connection, to refrain from copyright infringements.

IV. Resume

Peer-to-peer file-sharing is not just one of the most popular file-sharing mechanisms, but also a mechanisms were infringements can be detected without too much effort. However, detecting an infringement does not mean, that the rights-holder can enforce his rights by either pursuing a claim or sending out a warning. He will regularly only be able to obtain the IP address from where an infringement has been committed. Internet access providers possess the information necessary to become active against an infringer. How this information can be obtained from the access provider will be discussed in the context of national enforcement schemes as under certain schemes, the rights-holder will not be provided with information about the identity of a subscriber unless a certain number of infringements has been committed via his connection. The identification of a subscriber however does also not necessarily imply the identification of the actual infringer. Similar to phone numbers an IP address only allows the identification of the subscriber but not the identification of someone who did a specific call/committed an infringement. As regards the logging of the IP address in connection with an infringement and further data, that may serve as evidence for the existence of a copyright infringement, much depends on accuracy of logged traffic and reliability of the logging software. Minor defaults as for example incorrect logging of times may lead to the wrong subscriber in case of dynamic IP addresses. Particular attention also needs to be paid with regard to evidence of the copyright infringement as such. In the most popular form of peer-to-peer file-sharing, BitTorrent, the requested file is divided into small parts, which are then distributed. Although parts of a protected work also enjoy protection, the parts have to be useful, in the sense that they must be consumable. This can mean that a certain percentage of a works needs to be downloaded to establish an infringement. Also, the fact that the title of a file does not necessarily corresponds to its content, requires that the infringement is actually manually verified. Advances in technology also mean that sophisticated networks block suspected agents of rights-holders or render communication truly anonymous. As the latter still requires a certain degree of IT-literacy or at least some understanding of the functioning of peer-to-peer file-sharing, there are still huge numbers of users engaged in "normal" peer-to-peer networks, so that this field of action remains an interesting target for rights-holders.

B. National Enforcement Measures Against Users

Copyright enforcement against users can take different formats. Users may be addressed under criminal law, or may be sued under civil law. The following parts of this Chapter will first ouline the legal framework for seeking enforcement against individual users under European Union Law before enforcement on a national level is addressed. As regards the latter, a particular focus will be on statutory graduated response schemes that foresee as a final step a penal sanction. Because these schemes are met with controversy, the final section of this Chapter will also look at alternative enforcement means that exist under civil law such as cease and desist letters.

I. Legal Framework under European Union Law

Measures that target end-users by either sanctioning them under criminal law, or requesting compensation for damages from them, need to be in conformity with European law. European law sets up a common framework for all Member States, and needs to be obeyed by the Member States not only when setting up copyright enforcement provisions, but also when applying the law.

In response to the increased number of copyright infringements and in order to achieve equal protection and enforcement mechanisms in a harmonised market, a number of measures updated over recent years now exist at EU level that deal with infringements of intellectual property rights. In the following the regulations and directives which set up the legal framework for any user-targeted enforcements mechanisms in relation to peer-to-peer file-sharing will be briefly outlined.

In addition, to the following directives and regulations, the fundamental rights of the actors involved are of course of fundamental importance. When applying the framework, every measure needs to be weighed against the fundamental rights outlined in the first Chapter.

As Directives set forth objectives that need to be achieved by the Member States when transposing the Directive into national law, while leaving them the choice as to the forms and methods of implementation, some of the wording used in the Directives is relatively broad, and they contain a number of indefinite legal terms. They require interpretation by the CJEU, which will in this regard necessarily consider "not only its wording, but also the context in which it occurs and the objectives pursued by the rules of which it is part".[891] Hence, the outline of the legal framework will be complemented by some case law dealing with the interpretation of the legal objectives of the Directives. The case-law will be limited to landmark cases in respect to copyright enforcement.

1. Copyright Law Providing for Remedies against and Sanctions of Individual End-Users

At a European level, two fields of laws are important in the context of remedies against and sanctions of end-users, namely copyright law and data protection law. As regards copyright law, in particular the *IPR Enforcement Directive* provides for enforcement mechanisms against end-users, while the *InfoSoc Directive* specifies the notion of infringement in an online context. None of the Directives requires Member States to implement a specific mechanism for online copyright enforcement as long as enforcement of IP rights is ensured. The idea of graduated response schemes was however brought up during the legislative process of the Telecoms Package and resulted in the so-called Internet freedom provision which will also be outlined in the following.

---

891 CJEU, C-306/05 *Sociedad General de Autores y Editores de España v Rafael Hoteles SA* [2006] ECR I-11519, para. 34. See also C-156/98 *Germany v Commission* [2000] ECR I-6857, para. 50, and C-53/05 *Commission v Portugal* [2006] ECR I-6215, para. 20. In applying this basic rule of interpretation the CJEU routinely refers to the recitals of a measure as well as its operative provisions. In addition, the CJEU may – and frequently does so – refer to pre-legislative materials such as the Explanatory Memoranda which accompany the Commission's legislative proposals.

a) IPR Enforcement Directive 2004/48/EC

The *IPR Enforcement Directive*[892] contains minimum rules for the enforcement of intellectual property rights by providing for measures, procedures and remedies necessary to ensure the enforcement of such rights.[893] In that regard, the *IPR Enforcement Directive* requires Member States to make certain measures available to rights-holders, including information rights, the ability to apply for an (interlocutory or permanent) injunction intended to prevent an imminent infringement, or to forbid the continuation of the alleged infringement. These measures, like other procedures and remedies necessary to ensure the enforcement of the intellectual property rights covered by the *IPR Enforcement Directive*, "shall be fair and equitable and shall not be unnecessarily complicated or costly, or entail unreasonable time-limits or unwarranted delays" (Article 3(1) of the Directive). Pursuant to Article 3(2), they "shall also be effective, proportionate and dissuasive and shall be applied in such a manner as to avoid the creation of barriers to legitimate trade and to provide for safeguards against their abuse".[894]

The application of the Directive is not limited to infringements committed for commercial purposes or causing significant harm to rights-holders.[895] This is also clarified by Recital 14 of the Directive which states that although the measures provided for in Articles 6(2), 8(1) and 9(2) need to be applied only in respect of acts carried out on a commercial scale, this is without prejudice to the possibility for Member States to apply those measures also in respect of other acts. In that context, "acts carried out on a commercial scale" are defined as "those carried out for direct or indirect

892 *Directive 2004/48/EC of the European Parliament and of the Council of 29 April 2004 on the enforcement of Intellectual Property Rights,* OJ L 157 (30.04.2004), 16–25. The directive is also known as "(IPR) Enforcement Directive" or "IPRED".

893 See Article 1 *Enforcement Directive.*

894 Article 3 (1) and (2) of the Directive are very similar to Article 41 of *TRIPS*, and Article 8(1) and (2) of the *InfoSoc Directive*.

895 The original proposal for the Directive by the European Commission limited the scope of application to such infringements. See European Commission, *Proposal for a Directive of the European Parliament and of the Council on measures and procedures to ensure the enforcement of intellectual property rights*, COM (2003) 46 final (20.01.2003).

economic or commercial advantage; this would normally exclude acts carried out by end consumers acting in good faith".

The most important provision in terms of enforcing rights against end-users is the right to information enshrined in Article 8(1) of the Directive,[896] from which follows that Member States have to "ensure that in the context of proceedings concerning an infringement of an intellectual property right and in response to a justified and proportionate request of the claimant, the competent judicial authorities may order that information on the origin and distribution networks of the goods or services which infringe an intellectual property right be provided by the infringer and/or any other person". The right of information directed against other persons is a self-standing substantive right.[897] The other persons that are subject to the right of information, are those who: (a) were "found in possession of the infringing goods on a commercial scale"; (b) were "found to be using the infringing services on a commercial scale"; (c) were "found to be providing on a commercial scale services used in infringing activities"; and (d) were "indicated by the person referred to in point (a), (b) or (c) as being involved in the production, manufacture or distribution of the goods or the provision of the services".[898] Alternative (c) was the most controversial provision during the negotiations on the Directive, as it relates to information to be provided by Internet service providers.[899] Article 8 of the Directive goes much further than Article 47 TRIPS which only provides for a right of information but does not oblige contracting parties to introduce such a right, which is in addition also limited vis-à-vis the infringer.

The information to be provided for is described in Article 8(2) and includes "the names and addresses of the producers, manufacturers, distributors, suppliers and other previous holders of the goods or services, as well as the intended wholesalers and retailers", as well as information on

---

896 This provision is not only the most important provision in that regard – it has also been one of the most controversial provisions of the Directive during negotiations. See Jörg Reinbothe, *The EU Enforcement Directive 2004/48/EC as a tool for copyright enforcement*, in: Irini Stamatoudi (ed.), *Copyright enforcement and the Internet* (2010), p. 15.

897 *Ibid*, p. 16

898 Article 8(1) of the Directive.

899 See Jörg Reinbothe, *The EU Enforcement Directive 2004/48/EC as a tool for copyright enforcement,* in: Irini Stamatoudi (ed.), *Copyright enforcement and the Internet* (2010), p. 16.

the quantities produced, manufactured, delivered, received or ordered, as well as the price obtained for the goods or services in question".

Article 8(3)(a) confirms that the Directive provides for minimum standards with respect to the right of information and that national law may grant the rights-holders rights to receive additional information. The right of information shall further "apply without prejudice to other statutory provisions" which "(b) govern the use in civil or criminal proceedings of the information communicated pursuant to this Article; (c) govern responsibility for misuse of the right of information; or (d) afford an opportunity for refusing to provide information which would force the person referred to in paragraph 1 to admit to his/her own participation or that of his/her close relatives in an infringement of an intellectual property right; or (e) govern the protection of confidentiality of information sources or the processing of personal data". The right of information is thus subject to a number of conditions, and Member States are granted a certain degree of flexibility in implementing information rights into national law.

Such rights of information are crucial for rights-holders because information about the identity enables them to determine who is responsible for infringing conduct (or at least who "facilitated" the infringement)[900] and to determine the scope of an infringement. With this information they may then take legal steps against individuals. Relevant in the context of copyright infringements online is in particular the identification of the subscriber of an IP address at the time of an infringement. The only possible source for information on the identity of a potential infringer is the Internet service provider. It is decisive that there is a legal basis on which this information can be obtained from intermediaries who are not necessarily responsible for the infringement, but are likely to hold information about the identity of an infringer.

The right of information is restricted by data retention and data protection laws, meaning the ability of rights-holders to apply for an order against Internet service providers to disclose the identity of an account holder through which infringing material has been made available is restricted.

A further problem in relation to the information right which is however no problem arising from the right of such but relates to its scope in prac-

900 Facilitation in this context refers to the subscription of an Internet access service that was used to commit the infringement.

tice, is the fact that Internet access providers are not retaining data for longer than a few days due to domestic laws on data retention.[901]

As regards, the ability to apply for an (interlocutory or permanent) injunction intended to prevent an imminent infringement, the overriding purpose of injunctive relief is to ensure that IPR infringements cease as soon as possible. Article 9 requires Member States to ensure that rights-holders are able to apply for interlocutory injunctions intended to prevent imminent infringements of their intellectual property rights, or to order the cessation of effective infringements, on a provisional basis, subject, where appropriate, to recurring fines under national law for their continuation, or to make any such continuation subject to the depositing of a guarantee intended to ensure the compensation of the rights-holder. Similarly Article 11 provides for a permanent injunction.

According to Article 2(1) of the Directive, Member States may provide for sanctions and remedies that are more favourable to rights-holders.

b) Information Society Directive 2001/29/EC

The *Information Society Directive*[902], also known as *InfoSoc* or *Copyright Directive*, is an essential building block for the digital age.[903] Its objective

---

901 See in this regard: European Observatory on Counterfeiting and Piracy, *Evidence and right of information in intellectual property rights*, pp. 4 et seq., which outlines the example of Spain, in which, following the judgement of the CJEU in the Promusicae case (C-275/06 *Productores de Música de España (Promusicae) v Telefónica de España SAU* [2008] ECR 271), the domestic court "confirmed that Spanish data protection rules prevent Internet service providers from disclosing the identity of individual account holders to right holders for the purpose of civil proceedings, depriving right holders of a remedy altogether". Similarly the report states that in Austria, "in the case of on-line peer-to-peer infringements ('file sharing'), the provisions relating to the right of information are in practice not enforceable where information is requested from access providers, due to a decision of the Austrian Supreme Court restricting the retention and processing of dynamic IP addresses".

902 *Directive 2001/29/EC of the European Parliament and of the Council of 22 May 2001 on the harmonisation of certain aspects of copyright and related rights in the information society,* OJ L 167 (22.06.2001), pp. 10–19.

903 The EU committed itself to the establishment of an "Information Society" based on three interrelated prospects: (1) Continued improvements of ICT technology, that lead to (2) the establishment of a global knowledge and information based economy, which would (3) amount to widespread structural changes of the econ-

is to adapt legislation on copyright and related rights to reflect technological progress. In particular the Directive aims at resolving the legal uncertainty that existed with regard to on-demand transmission of copyright-protected works. With the *InfoSoc Directive* the EC transposed into Community law the main international obligations arising from the ratification of the 1996 WIPO Treaties (the WIPO Copyright Treaty and the WIPO Performances and Phonograms Treaty)[904].

The *InfoSoc Directive* as such does not provide any enforcement mechanisms.However, the Directive contains definitions of the exclusive rights granted to under copyright and related rights, distinguishing between the "reproduction right" (Article 2), the right of "communication to the public" and "making available to the public" (Article 3). The latter is specifically intended to cover publication and transmission on the Internet, and becomes relevant when determining under which circumstances a work is made available to the public in a peer-to-peer network.

Article 3(1) sets forth that "Member States shall provide authors with the exclusive right to authorise or prohibit any communication to the public of their works, by wire or wireless means, including the making available to the public of their works in such a way that members of the public may access them from a place and at a time individually chosen by them". In addition, under Article 3(2) "Member States shall provide for the exclusive right to authorise or prohibit the making available to the public, by wire or wireless means, in such a way that members of the public may access them from a place and at a time individually chosen by them: (a) for performers, of fixations of their performances; (b) for phonogram producers, of their phonograms; (c) for the producers of the first fixations of films, of the original and copies of their films; (d) for broadcasting organisations, of fixations of their broadcasts, whether these broadcasts are transmitted by wire or over the air, including by cable or satellite". Pursuant to Article 3(3), these rights shall not be exhausted by any act of

---

omy affecting society at large. In this context, it is considered necessary to establish and maintain an adequate regulatory framework to generate competition.

904 The Treaties supplement the *Berne Convention*. The *WIPO Copyright Treaty* followed *TRIPS* in many respects, but while *TRIPS* was driven by concern about international trade, the *WIPO Copyright Treaty* aims at responding to the problems created by the rise of the Internet. Accordingly, the *WIPO Copyright Treaty* adds rights to deal with distribution and public commuinication of works and to support the use of technological measures in the protection from unauthorised use of digitally recorded works, see Articles 6, 8, 11, 12 *WIPO Copyright Treaty*.

communication to the public or making available to the public as set out in Article 3.

Central to online copyright infringements is the notion of "making available to the public".[905] The making available right is protected as a species of the right of communication to the public.[906] It has to be distinguished from the broadcasting right (see Recital 25), where the sender controls the transmission of the work. Making available means in contrast that the user can choose when and where to access the works at his individual demand.[907]

The right also has to be distinguished from the distribution right in Article 4 of the *InfoSoc Directive*, which is restricted to tangible originals or copies of works or other subject matter.[908]

The making available right offers protection against the exploitation of works via computer networks. The "public" to which the work must be made available is not defined in the Directive but is to be understood as not being present at the place where the act of making available originates.[909] By including the notion of public, merely private communications are excluded from the scope of application.[910]

With regard to infringement of this right committed by users, Article 8 of the Directive provides for sanctions and remedies. This article provides as follows:

> "1. Member States shall provide appropriate sanctions and remedies in respect of infringements of the rights and obligations set out in this Directive and shall take all the measures necessary to ensure that those sanc-

---

905 For an excellent overview on the scope and limits of "making available to the public" see De Wolf & Partners, *Study on the Application of Directive 2001/29/EC on Copyright and Related Rights in the Information Society (The "InfoSoc Directive")* (2013), pp. 25 et seq.

906 In contrast, this is not necessarily the case for the making available right in the WIPO Treaties, see Brigitte Lindner, *The WIPO Treaties*, in: Brigitte Lindner/Ted Shapiro, *Copyright in the Information Society* (2011), p. 18.

907 De Wolf & Partners, *Study on the Application of Directive 2001/29/EC on Copyright and Related Rights in the Information Society (The "InfoSoc Directive")* (2013), p. 27.

908 See Recital 27 of the *InfoSoc Directive*.

909 See Recital 24 of the *InfoSoc Directive*.

910 De Wolf & Partners, *Study on the Application of Directive 2001/29/EC on Copyright and Related Rights in the Information Society (The "InfoSoc Directive")* (2013), p. 39.

> tions and remedies are applied. The sanctions thus provided for shall be effective, proportionate and dissuasive.
> 2. Each Member State shall take the measures necessary to ensure that rightholders whose interests are affected by an infringing activity carried out on its territory can bring an action for damages and/or apply for an injunction and, where appropriate, for the seizure of infringing material as well as of devices, products or components referred to in Article 6(2).
> 3. Member States shall ensure that rightholders are in a position to apply for an injunction against intermediaries whose services are used by a third party to infringe a copyright or related right."

Relevant in the context of enforcement of intellectual property rights are in particular recitals (2)–(4), (7)–(16) and (58)–(60). The recitals outline inter alia why a high level of protection of intellectual property rights is necessary from an economic as well as a cultural standpoint.[911] For present purposes, it is sufficient to refer to recital (58), which basically summarises Article 8 of the Directive by stipulating that "Member States should provide for effective sanctions and remedies for infringements of rights and obligations as set out in this Directive. They should take all the measures necessary to ensure that those sanctions and remedies are applied. The sanctions thus provided for should be effective, proportionate and dissuasive and should include the possibility of seeking damages and/or injunctive relief and, where appropriate, of applying for seizure of infringing material".

c) EU Telecoms Reform Package

In December 2009, the European Parliament approved the so called *Telecoms Reform Package*. The *Telecoms Reform Package* sets out a substantial reform of the regulatory framework for electronic communications.

---

911 Recitals (2)–(4) emphasise the importance of protection of intellectual property rights as an incentive for innovation and economic growth, while (7)–(9) stresses that a high level of protection is crucial to intellectual creation. Adequate legal protection of intellectual property rights is moreover necessary in order to guarantee the availability of appropriate reward for authors, performers and producers (see Recital (10)). The recitals further refer to copyright as one way of ensuring that European cultural creativity and production receive the necessary resources (Recital (11)).

The package consists of a regulation (*Regulation 1211/2009/EC*)[912] and two directives (*Directive 2009/136/EC*[913] and *Directive 2009/140/EC*[914]). As regards online copyright enforcement, the European Commission favoured in its 2007 draft version a graduated response scheme and asked EU Member States to make their broadband providers liable for applying sanctions to alleged copyright infringers.

This initial attempt has been widely criticised as an attempt to enable copyright enforcement on the Internet by amending telecoms law.[915]

A draft version by the European Commission of 13 November 2007 foresaw two amendments that favoured a graduated response scheme and asked Member States to mandate their broadband providers to co-operate with rights-holders.[916] These two provisions sparked a lot of controversy after they became public during the first reading at the European Parliament.

In the following, amendment 138 was drafted to hinder the legitimisation of graduated response schemes aiming at restricting end-users' access to the Internet under EU legislation. The amendment deliberately sought

---

912 *Regulation (EC) No 1211/2009 of the European Parliament and of the Council of 25 November 2009 establishing the Body of European Regulators for Electronic Communications (BEREC) and the Office,* OJ L 337/1 (18.12.2009).

913 *Directive 2009/136/EC of the European Parliament and of the Council of 25 November 2009 amending Directive 2002/22/EC on universal service and users' rights relating to electronic communications networks and services, Directive 2002/58/EC concerning the processing of personal data and the protection of privacy in the electronic communications sector and Regulation (EC) No 2006/2004 on cooperation between national authorities responsible for the enforcement of consumer protection laws (Universal Services and Users Rights Directive),* OJ L 337/11 (18.12.2009).

914 *Directive 2009/140/EC of the European Parliament and of the Council of 25 November 2009 amending Directives 2002/21/EC on a common regulatory framework for electronic communications networks and services, 2002/19/EC on access to, and interconnection of, electronic communications networks and associated facilities, and 2002/20/EC on the authorisation of electronic communications networks and services,* OJ L 337/37 (18.12.2009).

915 Instead of many see Monica Horten, *The Copyright Enforcement Enigma, Internet Politics and the 'Telecoms Package'* (2012), p. 1.

916 Annex 1, point 19 of the *Directive 2009/140/EC* and Amendment 20.6 to the Universal Services and Users Rights Directive. See Monica Horten, *The Copyright Enforcement Enigma, Internet Politics and the 'Telecoms Package'* (2012), p. 124.

to prevent the implementation of such measures by EU Member State governments by tightening the safeguards for Internet users.[917]

The text of amendment 138 required that "no restriction may be imposed on the fundamental rights and freedoms of end-users, without a prior ruling by the judicial authorities, notably in accordance with Article 11 of the Charter of Fundamental Rights of the European Union on freedom of expression and information, save when public security is threatened in which case the ruling may be subsequent." Thus, prior to any restriction on Internet access, a prior ruling by a court is necessary. Accordingly, private or voluntary agreements between Internet service providers and rights-holders are banned.

On 24 September 2008, amendment 138 was adopted by the European Parliament in the first reading plenary vote. It was also voted for again in the second reading. This caused some stir between the Parliament on the one hand, and the Commission and the Council of Ministers on the other.[918] The third reading let to a compromise provision that was finally agreed by all three EU institutions on 4 November 2009; Article 1(3)(a) of the Framework Directive now sets forth:

> "Measures taken by Member States regarding end-users access' to, or use of, services and applications through electronic communications networks shall respect the fundamental rights and freedoms of natural persons, as guaranteed by the European Convention for the Protection of Human Rights and Fundamental Freedoms and general principles of Community law. Any of these measures regarding end-users' access to, or use of services and applications through electronic communications networks liable to restrict those fundamental rights or freedoms, may only be imposed if they are appropriate, proportionate and necessary within a democratic society, and their implementation shall be subject to adequate procedural safeguards in conformity with the European Convention for the Protection of Human Rights and Fundamental Freedoms and with general principles of Community law, including effective judicial protection and due process. Accordingly, these measures may only be taken with due respect for the principle of the presumption of innocence and the right to privacy. A prior, fair and impartial procedure shall be guaranteed, including the right to be heard of the person or persons concerned, subject to the need for appropriate conditions and procedural arrangements in duly substantiated cases of urgency in conformity with the European Convention for

917 See Monica Horten, *The Copyright Enforcement Enigma, Internet Politics and the 'Telecoms Package'* (2012), p. 203.

918 *Ibid*, p. 202.

the Protection of Human Rights and Fundamental Freedoms. The right to effective and timely judicial review shall be guaranteed."[919]

Article 1(3)a of the Framework Directive is often also referred to as "Internet freedom provision" as it reinforces the presumption of innocence, the right to privacy, and the right to judicial review under any Internet sanctions.[920] However, it still allows "graduated response" laws and even Internet disconnections.[921] Pursuant to the provision disconnection orders may "only by imposed if they are appropriate, proportionate, and necessary within a democratic society" and shall be subject to judicial review. In that respect, the Parliament was primarily concerned to defend the right to due process, so that the right to a court hearing basically became the essence of Article 1(3)(a) of the Framework Directive.[922]

d) Rome II Regulation

Article 8 I of the Rome II Regulation sets forth that "the law applicable to a non-contractual obligation arising from an infringement of an intellectual property right shall be the law of the country for which protection is claimed". By Article 8 the EU opted for the so called *Schutzlandprinzip*.[923]

---

919 Article 1 (b) of *Directive 2009/140/EC of the European Parliament and of the Council of 25 November 2009 amending Directives 2002/21/EC on a common regulatory framework for electronic communications networks and services, 2002/19/EC on access to, and interconnection of, electronic communications networks and associated facilities, and 2002/20/EC on the authorisation of electronic communications networks and services, which inserts Article 3a into the Framework Directive (Directive 2002/21/EC).*

920 When the *Telecoms Reform Package* was passed, the *CFR* was not yet legally binding.

921 The Directives forming the *Telecoms Reform Package* had to become national law in each member state by May 2011.

922 See Monica Horten, *The Copyright Enforcement Enigma, Internet Politics and the 'Telecoms Package'* (2012), p. 203.

923 Marcus von Welser, in: Artur-Axel Wandtke/Winfried Bullinger, *Praxiskommentar zum Urheberrecht: UrhR* (3rd ed. 2009), before §§ 120 *UrhG* et seq., para. 3.

2. Data Protection Law and Information Rights

Data protection law plays an important role when it comes to information about the rights of rights-holders and the processing of data, in particular data relating to a specific IP address. The rights guaranteed in Articles 7 and 8 of *CFR* and Article 8 *ECHR* are concretised, at the Union level, in the *Data Protection Directive.* With the increasing use and advance of electronic data processing, the *Data Protection Directive* has been complemented by the *E-Privacy Directive* which has recently been amended by the *Data Retention Directive.* These data protection rules organise and control the way personal data are processed and thus are of relevance when information is processed about suspected infringers. They become inter alia relevant insofar as rights-holders may file requests to have the identity of a subscriber of a specific IP address disclosed, or where lists of repeat infringers are kept.

a) Data Protection Directive 95/46/EC

The *Data Protection Directive*[924] constitutes the fundamental legal framework for the processing of personal data in the EU. It was adopted to harmonise the legislation of the Member States with the twofold objective of protecting fundamental rights, namely the right to personal data protection, and ensuring the free flow of personal data between Member States within the context of the Internal Market. According to the *Data Protection Directive*, personal data must be processed fairly and lawfully, collected for specified, explicit and legitimate purposes (data minimisation principle) and not further processed in a way incompatible with those purposes (principle of finality). It sets up minimum standards of data protection that have to be implemented into the national laws of the Member States.

The Directive sets forth, that "in accordance with this Directive, Member States shall protect the fundamental rights and freedoms of natural persons, and in particular their right to privacy with respect to the processing of personal data" (Article 1 *Data Protection Directive*).

---

924 *Directive 95/46/EC on the protection of individuals with regard to the processing of personal data and on the free movement of such data (InfoSoc Directive),* OJ L 281 (23.11.1995), 31.

Personal data are defined in Article 2(a) as "any information relating to an identified or identifiable natural person ("data subject"); an person is one who can be identified, directly or indirectly, in particular by reference to an identification number or to one or more factors specific to his physical, physiological, mental, economic, cultural or social identity". Data are thus personal data when someone is able to link the information to a person, even if the person holding the data cannot make this link. This becomes of particular importance with regard to IP addresses, namely whether the IP address as such constitutes personal data.[925] If rights-holders seek the release of names and addresses of users or subscribers from Internet service providers, they clearly seek information relating to identified or identifiable natural persons, in accordance with the definition in Article 2(a) of the Directive.[926]

Pursuant to Article 2(b) of the Directive, the notion of processing refers to "any operation or set of operations which is performed upon personal data, whether or not by automatic means, such as collection, recording, organization, storage, adaptation or alteration, retrieval, consultation, use, disclosure by transmission, dissemination or otherwise making available, alignment or combination, blocking, erasure or destruction". In context of data processing, Article 2(d) of the Directive defines "controller" as a"natural or legal person, public authority, agency or any other body which alone or jointly with others determines the purposes and means of the processing of personal data; where the purposes and means of processing are determined by national or Community laws or regulations, the controller or the specific criteria for his nomination may be designated by national or Community law".

Thus, the Directive has a wide scope of applicability, but does expressly not apply to the processing of personal data by a natural person in the course of a purely personal or household activity.[927]

The Directive provides for the right of individuals to be given information on the purposes of the processing, how and by whom their data are processed and the rights to access, rectify and delete personal data (principle of transparency).[928] Service providers that qualify as data controllers

925 This will be discussed below within the section on Questions of Applicability of Data Protection Law: IP Address as Personal Data.

926 Cf. CJEU, C-101/01 *Lindqvist* [2003] ECR I-12971, para. 24.

927 Article 3(2) of the *Data Protection Directive.*

928 Articles 10 and 11 of the *Data Protection Directive.*

have to provide users with clear, easily understandable and affordable privacy notices in line with the requirements of the Directive.[929]

Data may be processed only under clearly defined circumstances, namely when the data subject has given his consent, when the processing is necessary for the performance of or the entering into a contract, when processing is necessary for compliance with a legal obligation, when processing is necessary in order to protect the vital interests of the data subject, when processing is necessary for the performance of a task carried out in the public interest or in the exercise of official authority vested in the controller or in a third party to whom the data are disclosed, and when processing is necessary for the purposes of the legitimate interests pursued by the controller or by the third party or parties to whom the data are disclosed, except where such interests are overridden by the interests for fundamental rights and freedoms of the data subject.[930]

Personal data can only be collected for specified, explicit and legitimate purposes and not further processed in a way incompatible with those purposes (Article 6(b)).

Member States are directed to provide that personal data should not be processed at all, except when certain conditions are met, which fall into three categories: transparency, legitimate purpose, and proportionality. Personal data may only be processed insofar as the processing is adequate, relevant and not excessive in relation to the purposes for which they are collected and processed (purpose limitation principle). In that regard Article 7 of the Directive requires Member States to ensure that personal data may be processed only in certain specified circumstances, for instance such circumstances where "processing is necessary for compliance with a legal obligation to which the controller is subject" (Article 7(c)), where "processing is necessary for the performance of a task carried out in the public interest or in the exercise of official authority vested in the controller or in a third party to whom the data are disclosed" (Article 7(e)), or

929 There is no express referral to the privacy notice or privacy policy in the Directive, but informing users has its grounds in Article 6(1)(a), which requires that the personal data be processed "fairly and lawfully", Article 10, which contains minimum information that must be provided to the data subject in cases where data is collected directly from him, Article 11, which contains minimum information that must be provided to the data subject in cases where data is collected from third parties and Article 14, which contains a requirement to inform the data subject before personal data is disclosed to third parties.

930 Article 7 of the *Data Protection Directive.*

in relation to "processing that is necessary for the purposes of the legitimate interests pursued by the controller or by the third party or parties to whom the data are disclosed, except where such interests are overridden by the interests for fundamental rights and freedoms of the data subject which require protection under Article 1(1)" (Article 7(f)).

Considering that copyright infringement claims may also be brought in relation to pornographic materials, and such materials may reveal sexual preferences of an Internet user, also Article 8(1) of the Directive may be of relevance. Article 8 erects a further hurdle in the case of special categories of data, in that it directs Member States to "prohibit the processing of personal data revealing racial or ethnic origin, political opinions, religious or philosophical beliefs, trade-union membership, and the processing of data concerning health or sex life." Article 8(2) provides a number of exceptions to that prohibition, which include at Article 8(2)(e) where "the processing relates to data which are manifestly made public by the data subject or is necessary for the establishment, exercise or defence of legal claims". Article 8(4) allows Member States, "subject to the provision of suitable safeguards", and "for reasons of substantial public interest", to lay down exemptions in addition to those laid down in Article 8(2), and provided that such derogations are notified to the Commission in accordance with Article 8(6).

Further Article 13 is of particular importance for this research. Article 13 specifies the situations where Member States may adopt legislative measures to restrict the scope of the obligations laid down in the Directive: pursuant to Article 13(1)(g), restrictions are allowed which constitute necessary measures to safeguard "the protection of the data subject or of the rights and freedoms of others".

b) E-Privacy Directive 2002/58/EC

The most significant instrument for E-Commerce and other online services is *Directive 2002/58 on Privacy and Electronic Communications*[931] as

931 *Directive 2002/58/EC of the European Parliament and of the Council of 12 July 2002 concerning the processing of personal data and the protection of privacy in the electronic communications sector (E-Privacy Directive),* OJ L 201/37 (31.07.2002).

amended by *Directive 2009/136/EC*[932], otherwise known as *E-Privacy Directive*, which complements the *Data Protection Directive*.

The *E-Privacy Directive* addresses the requirements of new digital technologies and aims at easing the advance of electronic communication services. Subject of the Directive is the "right to privacy in the electronic communication sector" as well as free movement of data, communication equipment and services.

The *E-Privacy Directive* applies to all matters which are not specifically covered by the *Data Protection Directive* and intends inter alia to give citizens control over which information is stored on or retrieved from their terminal equipment, including computers, smartphones or other devices connected to the Internet. The idea behind this is that users should be able to know and control who uses their information, and especially how this information is being used.

The Directive does not apply to issues concerning public security and defence, state security and criminal law. The interception of data is covered by the EU *Data Retention Directive*, the purpose of which is to amend the *E-Privacy Directive*. The Directive has been amended by Directive 2009/136, which introduced several changes, especially in what concerns cookies, but this is of no relevance for this work.

Pursuant to Article 5(1) of *E-Privacy Directive*, Member States must ensure the confidentiality of communications by means of a public communications network and publicly available electronic communications services, of its related traffic data, and they also must inter alia prohibit, in principle, the storage of that data by persons other than users, without the consent of the users concerned.

With regard to data retention in relation to traffic data by providers, the Directive sets forth that providers of services are obliged to erase or anonymise the traffic data processed when no longer needed (Article 6(1)). Retention is allowed for billing purposes but only as long as the statute of limitations allows the payment to be lawfully pursued (Article

---

932 *Directive 2009/136/EC of the European Parliament and of the Council of 25 November 2009 amending Directive 2002/22/EC on universal service and users' rights relating to electronic communications networks and services, Directive 2002/58/EC concerning the processing of personal data and the protection of privacy in the electronic communications sector and Regulation (EC) No 2006/2004 on cooperation between national authorities responsible for the enforcement of consumer protection laws,* OJ L 337/11 (18.12.2009).

6(2)). Data may be retained upon a user's consent for marketing and value-added services under the condition the data subject is informed why and for how long the data is being processed (Article 6(3)).

Important for this research is Article 15 of the *E-Privacy Directive*, which sets forth the situations in which Members States may adopt legislative measures to restrict the scope of the rights and obligations provided in the Directive. Article 15 must be read in conjunction with Article 13 of the *Data Protection Directive*, and allows Member States to restrict the scope of obligations provided in certain articles of the *E-Privacy Directive*, when this is necessary to safeguard the rights and freedoms of others, including the right to intellectual property in civil proceedings.[933]

c) Data Retention Directive 2006/24/EC

The *Data Retention Directive 2006/24/EC*[934] amends the *E-Privacy Directive*. The Directive introduces an obligation for providers of publicly available electronic communications services[935] (i.e. access provider[936]), or of public communications networks (i.e. persons who provide the network

---

933 See also CJEU, C-275/06 *Productores de Música de España (Promusicae) v Telefónica de España SAU* [2008] ECR 271.

934 *Directive 2006/24/EC of the European Parliament and of the Council of 15 March 2006 on the retention of data generated or processed in connection with the provision of publicly available electronic communications services or of public communications networks and amending Directive 2002/58/EC (Data Retention Directive),* OJ L105/54.

935 As regards the definition of "providers of publicly available electronic communications services" and providers of "public communications networks", Article 2(1) of the Directive refers to the definitions provided by the *Framework Directive 2002/21/EC* (*Directive 2002/21/EC of the European Parliament and of the Council of 7 March 2002 on a common regulatory framework for electronic communications networks and services*).

936 Art 2(c) *Framework Directive 2002/21/EC* defines the term "electronic communications service" as "a service normally provided for remuneration which consists wholly or mainly in the conveyance of signals on electronic communications networks". "[S]ervices providing, or exercising editorial control over, content transmitted using electronic communications networks and services" are explicitly excluded. In the context of the Directive, the most important question is whether only Internet access providers or also other providers (like mail service providers) provide an "electronic communications service". Art 2(c) *Framework Directive 2002/21/EC* requires that the service wholly or mainly consists "in the

infrastructure that permits the conveyance of signals) to retain traffic and location data for a period of six months up to two years for the purpose of the investigation, detection and prosecution of serious crime. The main objective of the Directive is to harmonise Member States' provisions concerning the retention of certain data which are generated or processed by providers of publicly available electronic communications services or of public communications networks.

aa) The Scope of Application of the Data Retention Directive

Article 3(1) determines the type of data that must be retained as data that the providers "generated or processed". "Processing" in that respect has to be construed according to Article 2(b) *Data Protection Directive*, which defines processing of data as "any operation or set of operations which is performed upon personal data, whether or not by automatic means". All data transmitted by a provider therefore is processed.

Article 5(2) provides that "no data revealing the content of the communication may be retained pursuant to this Directive".

Article 5(1) enumerates six categories of data to be retained: (a) data necessary to trace and identify the source of a communication; (b) data necessary to identify the destination of a communication; (c) data necessary to identify the date, time and duration of a communication; (d) data necessary to identify the type of communication; (e) data necessary to identify users' communication equipment or what purports to be their equipment and (f) data necessary to identify the location of mobile communication equipment. This traffic data is only to be retained in relation to fixed network telephony, mobile telephony, Internet access, Internet E-mail and Internet telephony.

In relation to online file-sharing, this means that in accordance with Article 5(1)(c) the Internet access provider has to retain the following data: the allocated IP address, user ID(s)[937], the calling telephone number

conveyance of signals on electronic communications networks". With respect to the Internet this definition only matches Internet access providers.

937 Article 2(2)(d) defines a user ID as a unique identifier allocated to persons when they subscribe to or register with the service in question. This could be a username when using a dial-up Internet connection.

in case of dial-up access[938], the name and address of the person to whom the IP address was allocated[939], the date and time of the log-in and log-off[940], and the DSL or other end point of the originator of the communication, i.e. the user[941]. In order to identify the type of communication, information about the Internet service uses must be retained.

With regard to dynamic IP addresses, it is important that the access provider identifies the date, time and duration of the communication correctly.

Article 6 of the Directive gives the Member States considerable flexibility in determining the retention period ("for periods of not less than six months and not more than two years of the date of the communication").

Although, it might come handy for rights-holders who seek disclosure of information, that data must be retained for at least six months, they are unlikely to gain access to this data. Article 4 of the Directive states that traffic data retained in accordance with the Directive shall be "provided only to the competent national authorities in specific cases and in accordance with national law". By means of an argumentum e contrario, Article 4 accordingly provides that the retained data must not be provided to private entities.

As the Directive itself does not state the conditions under which access may be granted to the retained data, the issue arose whether the data retention in itself constitutes an interference with the right to privacy.[942]

The necessity to release data only in limited cases is also provided for in the Preamble to the Directive; Recital 25 states that "under Article 8 of the *ECHR*, as interpreted by the European Court of Human Rights, interference by public authorities with privacy rights must meet the requirements of necessity and proportionality and must therefore serve specified,

---

938 See Article 5(1)(e)(3)(i) which explicitly mentions "dial-up access".

939 Article 5(1)(a)(2)(iii).

940 Article 5(1)(c)(2)(i).

941 Article 5(1)(e)(3)(ii) uses the phrase "end point of the originator of the communication" and hence applies to Internet access, Internet E-mail and Internet telephony.

942 With regard to the extensive protection granted by Article 8 *ECHR* and Articles 7 and 8 of the *CFR*, the retention of traffic data itself constitutes an interference with the right to privacy. According to Article 8 (2) *ECHR* any interference with the exercise of the right conferred by Article 8 (1) *ECHR* is only permissible if it is in accordance with the law and necessary in a democratic society for a legitimate purpose.

explicit and legitimate purposes and be exercised in a manner that is adequate, relevant and not excessive in relation to the purpose of the interference". The exceptional character of disclosure of retained data, taking into account conflicting fundamental rights, leads to the conclusion that disclosure of data that has been retained by access providers to fulfil their obligations under the *Data Retention Directive* is only legitimate in relation to serious crimes. This classification as serious crime, is principally a matter of national law and must not be confused with concept of "commercial scale" in other legal instruments of the EU. [943] Not all copyright infringements are crimes under national law, notwithstanding serious crimes. The issue of commercial scale is not directly relevant to determine what a serious crime is or should be.[944]

bb) The Declaration of the Invalidity of the Data Retention Directive: Joined cases C-293/12 and C-594/12 Digital Rights Ireland and Seitlinger and Others

Due to the concerns about the legitimacy of the Directive, Ireland brought an action for annulment under Article 230 EC requesting the CJEU to annul the Directive on the ground that it was not adopted on an appropriate legal basis.[945] Ireland's action did not relate to any possible infringement of fundamental rights arising from interference with the exercise of the right to privacy contained in the Directive. Ireland submitted that Article 95 EC, on which the Directive was based, nor any other provision of the EC Treaty is capable of providing an appropriate legal basis for the Directive. The CJEU did not follow Ireland's submission. The Court dismissed the action for annulment, based on the fact that the Directive regulates operations which are independent of the implementation of any police and judicial cooperation in criminal matter. Moreover, the substantive content of the Directive was held to be directed essentially at the

943 See in this regard Dimitris Kioupis, *Criminal liability on the Internet*, in: Irini Stamatoudi, *Copyright enforcement on the Internet*, pp. 251 et seq. The use of the concept of commercial scale as a demarcation line between criminal and non-criminal copyright infringements is not without problems.

944 See *ibid.*

945 See CJEU, C-301/06, *Ireland v European Parliament and Council of the European Union*, Judgement of 10.02.2009, ECR 2009 I-00593.

activities of service providers in the relevant sector of the internal market, and thus was held as to predominantly relate to the functioning of the internal market.

With for instance the German Constitutional criticising the German transposition of the *Data Retention Directive*, stating that the retention of data has the potential to generate a perception of surveillance which could impair the free exercise of fundamental rights,[946] it did not take long until the validity of the Directive was challenged again.

In course of a preliminary ruling procedure, the Irish High Court and the Austrian Constitutional Court asked the CJEU to examine the validity of the Directive, in particular in the light of two fundamental rights under the *CFR*, namely the fundamental right to respect for private life and the fundamental right to the protection of personal data.[947]

On 8 April 2014, the CJEU declared the *Data Retention Directive* to be invalid as it entails a wide-ranging and particularly serious interference with the rights to respect for private life and to the protection of personal data, without that interference being limited to what is strictly necessary.[948]

The Court observed first of all that the data to be retained make it possible, in particular, to know the identity of the person with whom a subscriber or registered user has communicated and by what means, to identify the time of the communication as well as the place from which that communication took place, and to know the frequency of the communications of a person with certain persons during a given period. Those data, may allow the determination of personal profiles as they may provide very

---

946 See for example the decision of the German Constitutional Court on the constitutionality of the German transposition of the *Data Retention Directive*, BVerfG 1 BvR 256/08.

947 The Irish High Court had to reseolve a dispute between the Irish company Digital Rights Ireland and the Irish authorities regarding the legality of national measures concerning the retention of data relating to electronic communications. The Austrian Vergfassungsgerichtshof had to decide on several constitutional action brought by the government of Kärnten and by Mr. Seitlinger and 11129 other applicants.The applicants sought the annulment of the national provision which transposes the Directive into Austrian law.

948 CJEU, Joined cases C-293/12 and C-594/12 *Digital Rights Ireland and Seitlinger and Others*, Judgment of 08.04.2014. Given that the Court has not limited the temporal effect of its judgment, the declaration of invalidity takes effect from the date on which the Directive entered into force.

precise information on the private lives of the persons whose data are retained, such as the habits of everyday life, permanent or temporary places of residence, daily or other movements, activities carried out, social relationships and the social environments frequented. The Court held that the retention of the data and access of competent national authorities to that data, constitutes a particularly serious interference with the fundamental rights to respect for private life and to the protection of personal data.

Given the risk that the retention and subsequent use of the data without informing the person concerned is likely to generate in the persons concerned a feeling that their private lives are the subject of constant surveillance.

Although Directive does not permit the acquisition of knowledge of the content of the communications as such and provides that service or network providers must respect certain principles of data protection and data security, and that the retention satisfies a general interest (fight against serious crime and public security), the Court concluded that the principle of proportionality was not respected.

In that context, the Court observes that, in view of the important role played by the protection of personal data in the light of the fundamental right to respect for private life and the extent and seriousness of the interference with that right caused by the directive, the EU legislature's discretion is reduced, with the result that review of that discretion should be strict.[949]

Although the objective pursued was legitimate, the wide-ranging and serious interference with the aforementioned fundamental rights was held to be not sufficiently circumscribed as to ensure that interferences with the rights are limited to what is strictly necessary.

This finding was based on the fact that the Directive covered, in a generalised manner, all individuals, all means of communication and all traffic data without any differentiation, limitation or exception being made in the light of the objective of fighting against serious crime.[950] Further, the Directive did not contain objective criteria which would ensure that the competent national authorities have access to the data only for the purposes of prevention, detection or criminal prosecutions concerning offences

949 *Ibid*, para. 48.
950 *Ibid*, paras. 56 et seq.

that may be considered to be sufficiently serious to justify such an interference woth the aforementioned rights.

In addition, the Directive fails to lay down substantive and procedural conditions under which national authorities may have access to the data and subsequently use them. In particular, the access to the data does not require prior review by a court or by an independent administrative body.[951]

Further, the Directive was held to fail to make any distinction between the categories of data or usefulness of data in relation to the objective pursued.

The Court also found that the Directive does not provide for sufficient safeguards to ensure effective protection of the data against the risk of abuse and against any unlawful access and use of the data.[952]

Accordingly, the legislature had exceeded the limits imposed by compliance with the principle of proportionality in the light of Articles 7, 8 and 52(1) *CFR*.

3. Liability Exemption for Access Providers under the E-Commerce Directive 2000/31

"Information society services" such as Internet service providers are exempted from liability under the *E-Commerce Directive* when they are involved in the business of mere conduit of data.[953] Mere conduits such as

---

951 *Ibid*, para. 62.

952 The Court noted, inter alia, that the directive permits service providers to have regard to economic considerations when determining the level of security which they apply (particularly as regards the costs of implementing security measures) and that it does not ensure the irreversible destruction of the data at the end of their retention period, see *ibid*, paras. 66 et seq. Further, there was no requirement for the data to be retained within the EU which does not ensure the compliance with the requirements of protection of individuals as regards the processing of personal data, see *ibid*, para. 68.

953 This immunity is parallel to the immunity commonly granted to traditional carriers such as telephone companies or the postal service. As regards the history of liability exemptions for Internet access providers and Article 12 of the *E-Commerce Directive* in specific cf. Uta Kohl, *The rise and rise of online intermediaries in the governance of the Internet and beyond – Connectivity intermediaries*, International Review of Law, Computers & Technology 2012, Vol. 26 Nos. 2–3 , 185–210.

access providers are naturally seen as attractive regulatory targets as they are an indispensable gateway to the Internet and relatively few in number.[954] One of the reasons why Article 12 of the *E-Commerce Directive* shields them from criminal[955] and civil liability is the fact that they have no control over the data flowing through their network. They have no influence on the information transmitted as their service is completely content-neutral. If they however got involved in the information transmitted, they would no longer account as mere conduits.

Article 12 of the *E-Commerce Directive* provides for two types of "mere conduit" activities. The first type consists of "the transmission in a communication network of information provided by a recipient of their service". The second type of mere conduit activity is the "provision of access to a communication network". Immunity from liability in civil or criminal law is granted for the information transmitted as long as the Internet service provider neither initiates the transmission nor selects the receiver of the transmission, or selects or modifies the information contained in the transmission.[956] Hence, as long as the provider acts as mere carrier and does not get involved in the information transmitted, he incurs no liability. This also applies if the transmission or the provision of access requires the "automatic, intermediate and transient storage of the information transmitted", in so far as it takes place for the sole purpose of carrying out the transmission in the communication network, and provided that the information is not stored for any period longer than is reasonably necessary for the transmission.[957] The activities of mere conduits are further described in recitals 43 to 45 of the Directive: recital 43 provides that an Internet service provider can benefit from the exemptions for a mere conduit "when he is in no way involved with the information transmitted". In contrast, the liability exemptions has its limits where an Internet service

954 *Ibid*, 191.

955 As reagrds, criminal liability, such liability will hardly arise where the immunities apply because of its dependance on a mens rea.

956 See Article 12(1) *E-Commerce Directive*.

957 See Article 12(2) *E-Commerce Directive*. This provision hence refers to the process of packet switching transmission, which allows Internet service providers to store information for a brief period of time in small pieces. The packet switching transmission process allows Internet service providers to provide mere conduit activities by making copies of the information to be transmitted for the sole purpose of carrying out the transmission of the information, without making the information available to subsequent users.

provider deliberately collaborates with one of the recipients of his service in order to undertake illegal acts (recital 44). Recital 45 further specifies that the limitations of the liability established in the directive "do not affect the possibility of injunctions of different kinds; such injunctions can in particular consist of orders by courts or administrative authorities requiring the termination or prevention of any infringement".

4. Relevant Jurisprudence of the CJEU

a) Disclosure of Traffic Data: C-275/06 Promusicae

In *Productores de Música de España (Promusicae) v Telefónica de España SAU*,[958] the CJEU had to deal with the question of whether Articles 15(2) and 18 of the *E-Commerce Directive*, Articles 8(1) and (2) of the *Data Protection Directive*, and Article 8 of the *IPR Enforcement Directive* permit Member States to limit the duty of operators of electronic communications networks and services to retain and make available connection and traffic information generated during the supply of their service for criminal investigations or the need to protect public safety and national defence, thus excluding civil proceedings. Basically, the referring Spanish court

958 CJEU, C-275/06, *Productores de Música de España (Promusicae) v Telefónica de España SAU* [2008] ECR I-271; [2008] 2 C.M.L.R. 17. For comments on the judgement see inter alia Henning Kahlert, *Urheberrecht kontra Datenschutz: EuGH bremst Forderungen nach einem zivilrechtlichen Auskunftsanspruch gegen Internet-Provider über die Identität von Tauschbörsen-Benutzern,* European Law Reporter 2008, 78–82; Laurent Szuskin/Maxime De Guillenschmidt, *L'arrêt « Promusicae » beaucoup de bruit pour rien?,* Droit de l'immatériel : informatique, médias, communication 2008, n° 37, 6–8; Emmanuel Derieux, *Le droit communautaire n'impose pas que les législations nationales prévoient l'obligation de communiquer des données à caractère personnel dans le cadre d'une procédure civile,* La Semaine Juridique – édition générale 2008, II 10099, 40–42; Gerald Spindler, *„Die Tür ist auf" – Europarechtliche Zulässigkeit von Auskunftsansprüchen gegenüber Providern,* Gewerblicher Rechtsschutz und Urheberrecht 2008, 574–577; Christopher Kuner, *Data Protection and Rights Protection on the Internet: The Promusicae Judgment of the European Court of Justice,* European Intellectual Property Review 2008, 199–202; Christian Czychowski/Jan Bernd Nordemann, *Vorratsdaten und Urheberrecht – Zulässige Nutzung gespeicherter Daten,* Neue Juristische Wochenschrift 2008, 3095–3099; Irini Stamatoudi, *Ethics, reality and the Law – The example of Promusicae v Telefonica & LSG v Tele 2,* Revue Hellénique de droit international 2010, 921–948.

wanted to know whether Member States were allowed under Community law to exclude the possibility of disclosing traffic data relating to copyright infringers in civil cases, while requiring such disclosure in criminal cases.

The underlying facts of the case giving rise for the reference for a preliminary ruling under Article 267 *TFEU* were as follows: Promusicae, a Spanish non-profit-making music rights-holder association made a request to Telefónica, Spain's leading Internet service provider, for personal data about its subscribers using particular dynamic IP addresses which Promusicae alleged were engaged in file-sharing. Telefónica argued that under the domestic law, the communication of the data sought by Promusicae was only authorised in a criminal investigation. Promusicae however argued that the national provisions must be interpreted in accordance with the *E-Commerce Directive*, the *IPR Enforcement Directive*, the *InfoSoc Directive* and with Articles 17(2) and 47 of the *CFR*EU. As mentioned above, Article 8(1) of the *IPR Enforcement Directive* in particular requires Member states to ensure that, in the context of proceedings concerning an IPR infringement and in response to a justified and proportionate request of the claimant, the competent judicial authorities may order the disclosure of information in relation to the infringement. As previously outlined, neither the IPR Enforcment Directive, nor Articles 15(2) and 18 of the *E-Commerce Directive* or Article 8(1) and (2) of the *InfoSoc Directive* require Member States to lay down an obligation to communicate personal data in the context of civil proceedings.[959]

The CJEU stated that European Union law does not require Member States to impose an obligation on Internet service providers to disclose their subscribers' personal data in a civil copyright case.[960] When implementing the aforementioned Directives, Member States must strike a fair balance between the various fundamental rights protected by community law.[961] Hence, each Member State had to reconcile the requirements of the

959 CJEU, C-275/06, *Productores de Música de España (Promusicae) v Telefónica de España SAU* [2008] ECR I-271, paras. 58 et seq. In addition, Articles 41, 42 and 47 of the *TRIPs Agreement*, relied on by Promusicae, do not provide for such an obligation, see *ibid*, para. 60.

960 *Ibid*, para. 70. The Court concluded that the Directives in question "do not require the Member States to lay down, in a situation such as that in the main proceedings, an obligation to communicate personal data in order to ensure effective protection of copyright in the context of civil proceedings".

961 *Ibid.*

protection of different fundamental rights, namely the right to respect for private life on the one hand and the right to protection of property (which includes intellectual property rights)[962] and to an effective remedy on the other[963]. In this regard, the *E-Privacy Directive* inter alia provides for rules which determine in what circumstances and to what extent the processing of personal data is lawful and sets forth the safeguards that must be provided for.[964] The Court stressed not only when implementing the measures transposing the Directives in question, but also the application of the measures must be consistent with the Directives: The authorities and courts of the Member States must not only interpret their national law in a manner consistent with the directives but must also make sure that they do not rely on an interpretation which would be in conflict with those fundamental rights or with the other general principles of Community law, such as the principle of proportionality.[965] From the CJEU's reasoning in the Promusicae case, it has in the following been concluded that the CJEU left the door open for the development of graduated response schemes in the form of mechanisms that respect data protection rights, while providing for effective enforcement of property rights.[966]

b) Disclosure of Traffic Data to Third Parties: C-557/07 LSG-Gesellschaft zur Wahrnehmung von Leistungsschutzrechten

In *LSG-Gesellschaft zur Wahrnehmung von Leistungsschutzrechten GmbH v Tele 2 Telecommunication GmbH (Tele2)*,[967] the CJEU considered the

---

962 See Case C-479/04 *Laserdisken* [2006] ECR I-8089, para. 65.

963 See Joined Cases C-154/04 and C-155/04 *Alliance for Natural Health and Others* [2005] ECR I-6451, para. 126 with further references, and Case C-432/05 *Unibet* [2007] ECR I-2271, para. 37 with further references.

964 CJEU, C-275/06, *Productores de Música de España (Promusicae) v Telefónica de España SAU* [2008] ECR I-271, para. 66.

965 *Ibid*, para. 68.

966 Cf. Christoph Kuner, *Data protection and rights protection on the Internet: The Promusicae Judgment of the European Court of Justice,* European Intellectual Property Review 2008, Issue 5, 199, 200

967 CJEU, C-557/07 *LSG-Gesellschaft zur Wahrnehmung von Leistungsschutzrechten GmbH v Tele 2 Telecommunication GmbH (Tele2)*, Judgment of 19.02.2009, [2009] ECR I-01227. For comments on the case see Jan Bernd Nordemann/ Martin Schaefer, V*ermittlereigenschaft eines Access-Providers*, Gewerblicher Rechtsschutz und Urheberrecht 2009, 583–584; Lionel Costes, *Peer to Peer et*

issue of whether Article 8(3) of the *IPR Enforcement Directive* and Articles 6 and 15 of the *E-Privacy Directive* should be interpreted as not permitting the disclosure of personal traffic data to private third parties for the purposes of civil proceedings for alleged copyright infringements.

LSG (a collecting society) applied for an order requiring Tele2 to disclose the names and addresses of the persons to whom it had provided an Internet access service and whose IP addresses, together with the day and time of the connection, were known. Tele2 believed that it was entitled to refuse the request. The CJEU considered the issue of whether Article8(3) of the *IPR Enforcement Directive* and arts 6 and 15 of the *E-Privacy Directive* should be interpreted as not permitting the disclosure of the data to private third parties for the purposes of civil proceedings. The court held that Community law – in particular, Article 8(3) of the *IPR Enforcement Directive*, read in conjunction with Article 15(1) of the *E-Privacy Directive* – does not preclude Member States from imposing an obligation to disclose to private third parties personal data relating to Internet traffic in order to enable them to bring civil proceedings for copyright infringement, but nor does it require those Member States to lay down such an obligation. [968] In Promusicae, the Court did not rule out the possibility that Member States may place Internet access providers under a duty of disclosure. Considering that under Article 8(3) of the *InfoSoc Directive*, Member States are to ensure that rights-holders are in a position to apply for an injunction against intermediaries whose services are used by a third party to infringe a copyright or related right, and that access providers provide such services that enable users to infringe copyright, the protection sought by the *InfoSoc Directive* would "substantially diminished" if access providers would not be considered as intermediaries in the sence of the *InfoSoc Directive*.[969] Repeating its response in Promusicae, the Court held that Community law requires Member States to ensure that, when transposing into national law the *E-Commerce Directive*, the *InfoSoc Directive*, the *E-Privacy Directive* and the *IPR Enforcement Directive*, they strike a fair balance between the various fundamental rights involved. Moreover,

---

recherche des contrefacteurs: les précisions de la CJCE, Droit de l'immatériel : informatique, médias, communication 2009, n° 48, 22–23.

968 CJEU, C-557/07 *LSG-Gesellschaft zur Wahrnehmung von Leistungsschutzrechten GmbH v Tele 2 Telecommunication GmbH (Tele2),* Judgment of 19.02.2009, [2009] ECR I-01227, para. 41.

969 *Ibid*, paras. 42 et seq.

the authorities and courts of Member States must not only interpret their national laws in a manner consistent with those directives but must also make sure that they do not rely on an interpretation of them which would conflict with those fundamental rights or with the other general principles of Community law such as the principle of proportionality.[970]

c) Legitimacy of National Disclosure Legislation : C-461/10 Bonnier Audio v Perfect Communication Sweden

In *Bonnier Audio AB v Perfect Communication Sweden AB*[971], the CJEU held that the *Data Retention Directive* does not preclude Member States from enacting laws that allow an Internet service provider to be ordered to supply information about subscribers whose IP addresses have allegedly been used for intellectual property infringing purposes.

Bonnier and the other claimants were all publishing companies, which held, inter alia, exclusive rights to the reproduction, publication and distribution to the public of 27 works in the form of audio books. They claimed that their exclusive rights were infringed by the unauthorised public distribution of these works by means of a FTP[972] server. The server facilitated online file-sharing and data transfer between users via ePhone, an Internet service provider. In order to prepare their claims for compensation, Bonnier and others applied for disclosure of data for the purpose of communicating the name and address of the person using the IP address from which it was assumed that the files in question had been sent. EPhone refused to forward the requested data, since it considered such an order contrary to the *Data Retention Directive*. The court of first instance granted disclosure

---

970 Cf. *ibid*, operative part of the judgement.

971 CJEU, C-461/10, *Bonnier Audio AB and Others v Perfect Communication Sweden AB,* Judgment of 19.04.2012. For comments on the case see inter alia Doris Möller, *Urheber-/Datenschutzrecht: Herausgabe gespeicherter Verkehrsdaten zur zivilrechtlichen Verfolgung von Urheberrechtsverletzungen,* Europäische Zeitschrift für Wirtschaftsrecht 2012, 519–520; Zuzana Hečko, *Data retention by Internet service providers for IP rights protection: Bonnier Audio (C-461/10),* Journal of Intellectual Property Law and Practice 2012, 449–456; Sandra Schmitz, *Die Verfolgung von Urheberrechtsverletzungen im Internet – Neues vom EUGH,* in: Jürgen Taeger (ed.), IT und Internet – Mit Recht gestalten (2012), pp. 227–243.

972 FTP = File transfer protocol.

of the data. EPhone appealed to the Stockholm Court of Appeal which held that the *Data Retention Directive* does not prevent a party to a civil dispute being ordered to disclose subscriber data to someone other than a public authority. As Bonnier and others however had not produced clear evidence that there had been an IP infringement, the order was set aside.

Bonnier and others then appealed to the Högsta domstolen, which referred two question for a preliminary ruling to the CJEU,[973] asking inter alia whether the *Data Retention Directive* precludes the application of a national provision based on Article 8 of the *IPR Enforcement Directive* which, "in order to identify a particular subscriber, permits an Internet service provider in civil proceedings to be ordered to give a copyright holder or its representative information on the subscriber to whom the Internet service provider provided an IP address which was allegedly used in the infringement".[974]

The CJEU held that the *Data Retention Directive* "…must be interpreted as not precluding the application of national legislation based on Article 8 of Directive 2004/48 ... which, in order to identify an Internet subscriber or user, permits an Internet service provider in civil proceedings to be ordered to give a copyright holder or its representative information on the subscriber to whom the Internet service provider provided an IP address which was allegedly used in an infringement, since that legislation does not fall within the material scope of Directive 2006/24".[975] It does not fall within the material scope, because the *Data Retention Directive* deals exclusively with the retention and handling of data generated or processed by Internet service providers for the purpose of the investigation,

973 The wording of the first question which is relevant for this research was as follows: "Does [Directive 2006/24], and in particular Articles 3 [to] 5 and 11 thereof, preclude the application of a national provision which is based on Article 8 [of Directive 2004/48, the *IPR Enforcement Directive*, which requires appropriate and proportionate disclosure orders to enable rights to be enforced] and which permits an Internet service provider in civil proceedings, in order to identify a particular subscriber, to be ordered to give a copyright holder or its representative information on the subscriber to whom the Internet service provider provided a specific IP address, which address, it is claimed, was used in the infringement? The question is based on the assumption that the applicant has adduced clear evidence of the infringement of a particular copyright and that the measure is proportionate".

974 CJEU, C-461/10, *Bonnier Audio AB and Others v Perfect Communication Sweden AB,* Judgment of 19.04.2012, para. 36.

975 *Ibid*, Operative part of the judgement.

detection and prosecution of serious crime, and does not cover the retention of data for civil proceedings.[976] Accordingly, it was irrelevant for the main proceedings that Sweden had not yet transposed the *Data Retention Directive* beside the period for transposition having expired.[977] The CJEU held that instead of the *Data Retention Directive*, the disclosure request constitutes personal data processing within the meaning of Article 2 of the *E-Privacy Directive*, and thus falls within the scope of the latter.[978]

Citing its decisions in Promusicae and in LSG – Gesellschaft zur Wahrnehmung von Leistungsschutzrechten, the Court recalled that the *E-Privacy Directive* and the *IPR Enforcement Directive* must be interpreted as not precluding national legislation that imposes an obligation to disclose to private persons personal data in order to enable them to bring civil proceedings for copyright infringements.[979]

The CJEU emphasised that the "national legislation in question requires, inter alia, that, for an order for disclosure of the data in question to be made, there be clear evidence of an infringement of an intellectual property right, that the information can be regarded as facilitating the investigation into an infringement of copyright or impairment of such a right and that the reasons for the measure outweigh the nuisance or other harm which the measure may entail for the person affected by it or for some other conflicting interest".[980]

Accordingly, the national legislation must enable "the national court seised of an application for an order for disclosure of personal data, made by a person who is entitled to act, to weigh the conflicting interests involved, on the basis of the facts of each case and taking due account of the requirements of the principle of proportionality".[981] The national court must strike a fair balance between the contravening interests, i.e. the pro-

---

976 *Ibid*, paras. 41 et seq. The Court explained that the *Data Retention Directive* constitutes a special and restricted set of rules, derogating from and replacing the *E-Privacy Directive* general in scope and, in particular Article 15(1) thereof.

977 *Ibid*, para. 46.

978 *Ibid*, para. 52.

979 *Ibid*, para. 55.

980 *Ibid*, para. 58.

981 *Ibid*, para. 59.

tection of intellectual property rights of the copyright-holders and the protection of personal data enjoyed by the Internet subscriber or users.[982]

In the light of Case C-275/06 Promusicae this was a predictable decision.

d) Prohibition of General Monitoring Duty: C-70/10 Scarlet Extended v SABAM

Relevant at this point is only one aspect of the preliminary ruling decision in *Scarlet Extended v SABAM* (which will be dealt with in detail in the Third Chapter): namely, the need for effective protection of intellectual property rights in the Member States. [983] In the context of a requested deletion and blocking of infringing content, the Court declared a general filtering obligation impermissible while at the same time stressing the need for effective protection of intellectual property as part of the right to property.[984] This will become relevant when balancing the rights concerned, where an emphasis needs to be put on the effectiveness of the measure. It also seems obvious from the findings in the Sabam case that providers are obliged to cooperate to enforce the rights of the rights-holders.[985]

The Court ultimately concluded that the installation of a "complicated, costly, permanent computer system" to monitor data at the expense of the service provider contravened Article 3(1) of the *IPR Enforcement Directive* (no measures that are unnecessarily complicated or costly), anddid not strike a fair balance between the interests of the service provider and copyright holders involved.[986]

---

982 *Ibid*, para. 60.

983 *Ibid*, para. 30.

984 Case C-70/10 *Scarlet Extended v SABAM*, Judgment of 14.11.2011, para. 43; Article 17 (2) *CFR*.

985 Rolf Schwartmann, *Vergleichende Studie über Modelle zur Versendung von Warnhinweisen durch Internet-Zugangsanbieter an Nutzer bei Urheberrechtsverletzungen, Studie im Auftrag des Bundesministerium für Wirtschaft und Technologie* (Januar 2012), p. 280.

986 CJEU, C-70/10 *Scarlet Extended v SABAM*, Judgment of 14.11.2011, paras. 48 et seq.

e) Practical Impact of the Decisions

The decisions of the CJEU confirm that there is no direct conflict as such between data protection and online copyright enforcement in the European legal framework. While the European legal framework does not preclude Member States from imposing an obligation to disclose to private third parties personal data relating to Internet traffic in order to provide them with the necessary information to pursue civil actions for copyright infringement, the Community law also does not require Member States to lay down an obligation to disclose personal data in order to ensure effective protection of copyright in the context of civil proceedings. The CJEU considers the law to be neutral in this respect. The most important point for the Court is that a fair balance is achieved between the fundamental rights of the parties involved. It is important that not only the national implementation, but also the interpretation of the national implementation is consistent with the directives and not in conflict with fundamental rights or other principles of Community law. The Court only provided little guidance in the Bonnier Audio case on how to strike a fair balance between the fundamental rights in question, namely that national legislation that foresees the disclosure of data must require that "there be clear evidence of an infringement of an intellectual property right, that the information can be regarded as facilitating the investigation into an infringement of copyright or impairment of such a right and that the reasons for the measure outweigh the nuisance or other harm which the measure may entail for the person affected by it or for some other conflicting interest".[987] The court seised must weigh the conflicting interests involved on the basis of the facts of each case presented and must strike a fair and proportionate balance between the interests involved. The judgement in Bonnier Audio does not constitute a carte blanche as regards the usage of retained data. It only clarified that national legislation that foresees the disclosure of data to pursue civil claims does not contravene the *Data Retention Directive* or other Community law. Such information rights are subject to national law which as aforementioned may or may not provide for these rights.

987 CJEU, C-461/10, *Bonnier Audio AB and Others v Perfect Communication Sweden AB,* Judgment of 19.04.2012, para. 58.

II. Copyright Enforcement in Member States through Criminal Sanctions: Graduated Response Schemes

One means of enforcing copyright is through criminal law. IP infringements are crimes in most jurisdictions, but also torts and thereby subjecting criminals to civil liability. A reason for supplementing civil liability with criminal sanctions is the necessity of deterrence as civil liability punishment can render certain crimes profitable.[988]

As a rule, making available protected works through file-sharing is covered by specific criminal provisions in the national copyright code or in the general criminal code.

Graduated response schemes, also referred to as "Three Strikes law", are one form of copyright enforcement against end-users that have recently attracted a lot of attention. This form of enforcement requires Internet service providers to play an active role in regulating the behaviour of their users by sending out warnings about infringements that have been committed, and ultimately applying sanctions to users that are alleged to have infringed copyright.[989] These sanctions are regularly criminal sanctions, at least under the schemes that will be analysed in the following. Although, it has been argued that those warning schemes, where an administrative authority is concerned with issuing warnings against users, this is rather a

---

988 Andrea Wechsler, *Criminal enforcement of intellectual property law: an economic approach,* in: Christophe Geiger (ed.), *Criminal enforcement of intellectual property* (2012), p. 129, at p.136.

989 The European Data Protection Supervisor summarised the functioning of graduated response schemes as follows: "In a nutshell, under three strikes Internet disconnection policies copyright holders using automated technical means, possibly provided by third parties, would identify alleged copyright infringement by engaging in monitoring of Internet users' activities, for example, via the surveillance of forums, blogs or by posing as file sharers in peer-to-peer networks to identify file sharers who allegedly exchange copyright material. After identifying Internet users alleged to be engaged in copyright violation by collecting their Internet Protocol addresses (IP addresses), copyright holders would send the IP addresses of those users to the relevant Internet service provider(s) who would warn the subscriber to whom the IP address belongs about his potential engagement in copyright infringement. Being warned by the Internet service provider a certain number of times would automatically result in the Internet service provider's termination or suspension of the subscriber's Internet connection." See *Opinion of the European Data Protection Supervisor on the current negotiations by the European Union of an Anti-Counterfeiting Trade Agreement (ACTA)*, OJ 2010 C-147/01, 3 et seq.

matter of administrative law,[990] this section is under the heading of enforcement through criminal sanctions as ultimately the subscriber of an Internet access service, or an identified infringer, will face a sanction under criminal law. In this regard, the determination of the prerequisites for warnings to be sent out, or the circumstances under which a user can be sanctioned under criminal law, requires a legal basis.

The necessary legal framework for employing such schemes have recently been implemented for instance in France and the UK. The core of the (initial) proposals includes the introduction of measures against individual users who do not take sufficient precautions to prevent infringements via their Internet connection, or who are themselves involved in copyright infringements.

The graduated response schemes that are discussed in this chapter, are no voluntary schemes where Internet service providers have entered into arrangements with rights-holder to enforce copyright against their customers,[991] because – as already mentioned – these schemes carry as an ultimate sanction a sanction under criminal law. Criminal enforcement requires statutory regulation, and more importantly the criminalisation of the behaviour that is subject to the sanction.[992]

Irrespective of the scheme employed, the analysis will show that they face the same challenges, in particular in relation to the identification of the actual infringer and the legal problems arising from this.

Subsequent to the outline of the schemes in France and the UK, the compliance of the enforcement schemes and secondary EU law will be focussed on, before the compatibility of the schemes with the fundamental rights of Internet users and Internet access providers will be analysed.

---

990 European Parliament, DG for Internal Policies, Policy Department C: Citizens' Rights and Constitutional Affairs, *File Sharing* (2011), p. 12.

991 Such as the Irish Eircom graduated response protocol: Under the system adopted by the Irish Internet service provider Eircom in 2010, customers suspected of sharing copyrighted material online are sent warning letters threatening disconnection from their broadband service. After a third warning letter, customers are disconnected for 12 months. See Eircom, *Eircom statement on illegal file sharing*, press release (2010).

992 For an overview on criminal sanctioning of intellectual property rigths infringements, see David Lefranc, *Historical perspective on criminal enforcement*, in: Christophe Geiger (ed), *Criminal enforcement of intellectual property* (2012), pp. 101–127.

1. France: the Graduated Response Scheme of the HADOPI Laws

France has been the first European country to pass anti-piracy legislation specifically combatting illegal downloads through peer-to-peer networks. Its warning scheme thus plays a leading role in the EU and has attracted a lot of attention even from outside France. The scheme goes beyond a mere warning mechanism insofar as the warning shall also educate users about intellectual property and its value for and benefits to society. At the end of a three-step warning system, more stringent measures can be imposed including the suspension of Internet access. The French graduated response scheme relies on new legislative measures, and on an administrative body, that has specifically been founded for the enforcement of copyright and will be in charge of the warning system including the cooperation with Internet service providers. In the following, the legal changes that paved the way of the graduated response scheme will be outlined before the different actors and the different warning steps will be focussed on. Finally, the conformity of the warning scheme with fundamental rights, and the way how it responds to technological challenges will be analysed.

a) Copyright Enforcement in France in General

aa) The Origin of Copyright in France

Intellectual property is protected by the right to property in the French constitution. The individual´s right to property appears in the list of the Rights of Man enshrined in Article 2 of the *Déclaration des Droits de l'Homme et du Citoyen of 26 August 1789*[993]. Article 17 of the *Declaration of 1789* foresees the individual´s right to property: "Since the right to property is inviolable and sacred, no one shall be deprived thereof, unless public necessity, legally ascertained, obviously requires it, and on condition that fair and prior compensation is given". The *Declaration of 1789* has been amended by the preamble of the French Constitution and as such benefits from the same standard of protection as the Constitution.[994]

993 In the following referred to as *Declaration of 1789*.

994 See: Preamble to the French Constitution of 4 October 1958: "The French people solemnly proclaim their attachment to the Rights of Man and the principles of

Although neither Article 2 nor Article 17 of the *Declaration of 1789* specifically mentions intellectual property rights, according to the French Constitutional Court, the Conseil Constitutionnel, intellectual property, especially copyright and related rights, are encompassed in the right to property of the *Declaration of 1789*. In a 2006 decision the Court recognised that "the purposes and conditions for exercising the right to property have since 1789 undergone changes in the form of an extension of the scope thereof to new fields; among the latter are to be found intellectual property rights and related rights in the information society".[995]

Also in its decision on the constitutionality of the Act furthering the diffusion and protection of creation on the Internet (*Loi HADOPI I*[996]), the Court stressed once more that "property is one of the rights of man enshrined in Articles 2 and 17 of the *Declaration of 1789*. The purposes and conditions of exercising the right to property have since 1789 undergone substantial changes characterized by the extension of the scope of this right to new fields. Among the latter exits the right, for copyright holders and holders of related rights to enjoy their intellectual property rights and protect the same within a framework set out by statute and in compliance with the international undertakings entered into by France".[997]

On a non-constitutional level, intellectual property has first gained protection by the *Loi n°57-298 du 11 mars 1957 sur la propriété littéraire et artistique,* which stated in its Article 1 that the author of an intellectual

---

national sovereignty as defined by the *Declaration of 1789*, confirmed and complemented by the Preamble to the Constitution of 1946, and to the rights and duties as defined in the Charter for the Environment of 2004." The English version of the French constitution is available at http://www.conseil-constitutionnel.fr/conseil-constitutionnel/english/constitution/constitution-of-4-october-1958.25742.html (last accessed 17.05.2014).

995 Conseil Constitutionnel, Decision of 27.07.2006 – No. 2006-540 DC, Journal officiel de la République Française of 03.08.2006, 11541, para. 15. An English version of the decision is available at http://www.conseil-constitutionnel.fr/conseil-constitutionnel/root/bank/download/2006540DCen2006_540dc.pdf (last accessed 17.05.2014).

996 *Loi no. 2009-669 du 12 juin 2009*, Journal officiel de la République Française of 13.06.2009, 9666.

997 Conseil Constitutionnel, Decision of 10.06.2009 – No. 2009-580 DC, Journal officiel de la République Française of 13.06.2009, 9675, para. 13. An English version of the decision is available at http://www.conseil-constitutionnel.fr/conseil-constitutionnel/root/bank/download/2009580DC2009_580dc.pdf (last accessed 17.05.2014).

work enjoys, as regards his work, an exclusive immaterial property right; This right encompasses the intellectual and moral as well as the financial exploitation of the work.

In recognition of the importance of intellectual property, in 1992, the French legislator united all laws and regulations regarding the protection of intellectual property in one single code of law, the Code de la propriété intellectuelle *(CPI)*.[998] According to Article L. 112-1 of the *CPI* all intellectual creations are protected irrespective of their genre, their form of expression, their value or their purpose.[999] A non-exhaustive list of subjects of protection can be found in Article L. 112-2 *CPI*.

bb) The Private Copying Exception

Article L. 122-5 *CPI* provides for an exception to the intellectual property rights by granting individuals a right to private copies. According to para. 2 of Article L. 122-5 *CPI* an individual may make copies of a protected work even without the consent of the rights-holder. A private copy is for personal use only. The applicability of the exception for private copying has been questioned when protected works were downloaded from the Internet: Does unauthorised downloading in itself constitute an unlawful act or not?[1000] There was some controversy as to whether the French private copy exception requires that a copy is made from a lawful source.[1001] Technically, answering this question with regard to peer-to-peer file-sharing is irrelevant, as with peer-to-peer technology the person who down-

---

998 *Loi no. 92-597 du 1er juillet 1992.*

999 « Toutes les oeuvres de l'esprit, quels qu'en soient le genre, la forme d'expression, le mérite ou la destination »-

1000 Christophe Geiger, C*ounterfeiting and the music industry: towards a criminalization of end users? The French 'HADOPI' example,* in: Christophe Geiger (ed), *Criminal enforcement of intellectual property* (2012), p. 391.

1001 The lawfulness of the source shall be irrelevant: Séverine Dussollier, *L'utilisation légitime de l'œuvre: un noveau sesame pour le benefice des exceptions en droit d'auteur?,* Communication commerce électronique November 2005, 19 ; Carine Bernault/Audrey Lebois, *Peer-to-peer filesharing and literary and artistic property, a feasibility study regarding a syste of compensation for the exchange of works via the Internet* (2006), p. 20; Christophe Geiger, *Les exceptions au droit d'auteur en France*, in: Christophe Geiger/Michele Bouyssi-Ruch/Reto M. Hilty (eds.), *Perspectives d'harmonisation du droit d'auteur en Europe*, p. 356.

loads a file at the same time makes the work available. The Cour d'Appel Montpellier held that the exception for private copying is applicable; On the basis of Arts. L. 122-3, L. 122-4 and L. 122-5 *CPI* the Court recalled that once a work has been made public, its author may not prohibit copying or reproduction that is strictly for the personal use of the person making the copy.[1002] As the public prosecutor as well as the rights owners and video publishing organisations appealed the decision, the Cour de Cassation had to decide on the matter. The Court found that the Cour d'Appel had not replied to their argument that the unlawful nature of the source of the copies, namely the download from the Internet, excluded the applicability of the private copy exception.[1003] Thus, the decision was overturned and referred to another appeal court.[1004] The Cour d'Appel Aix-en-Provence held that the private copy exception is not applicable where a protected work is downloaded from the Internet or where the protected work was borrowed from friends.[1005] Finally, the French legislator clarified in 2011 that reproductions made from an unlawful source are excluded from the scope of the private copy exception.[1006]

1002 The Court rejected the prosecution for counterfeiting of a defendant who had made copies of 488 films on CD-ROMs (one third of them had been downloaded from peer-to-peer networks while two thirds were copied from other CD-ROMs given to him by friends). Cour d'Appel de Montpellier, Decision of 10.03.2005, *Buena Vista Home Entertainment et al. v D.A.C.*, Legipresse of 22.06.2005, 120 with annotation by Isabelle Wekstein.

1003 Cour de Cassation, Decision of 30.05.2006 – RG No. 05-83335 (chambre criminelle).

1004 Article 593 of the Code of Criminal Procedure sets forth that "any judgment or order must include the reasons justifying the decision and answer the peremptory points contained in the parties' submissions. Insufficient or contradictory reasons are equivalent to their absence".

1005 Cour d'Appel d'Aix-en-Provence, Decision of 05.09.2007 – No. 2007/501, Gazette du Palais (10.05.2008), No. 131, 54 with annotation by Julien Guinot-Delery/Charles-Edouard Renault.

1006 Loi no. 2011-1898 du 20 décembre 2011 relative à la rémunération pour copie privée.

cc) Enforcement of Intellectual Property Rights upon Initiative of the Rights-Holder

In the context of private enforcement of IP rights it is important to know that French law does not provide for a right to information for rights-holders that seek to obtain information upon the identity of an infringer. There is also no obligation for access providers to store IP addresses for civil enforcement by rights-holders.[1007] The only possibility for French rights-holders to obtain such data was to press criminal charges against the not-yet identified infringer. Access providers are obliged to reveal the identity of subscriber to the judicial authorities in the course of the criminal proceedings, insofar as he still holds that information.[1008]

In the course of criminal proceedings, the rights-holder then is entitled to have a copy of the files of the inquiry. Damages may also be awarded in criminal proceedings; hence, it will not be necessary for the rights-holder to sue the infringer in a civil court as long as charges are pressed against him.

Due to new legislation being passed on an EU level which needed to be implemented on domestic level, French copyright law has lately seen a number of updates specifically in relation to the digital age. Law reforms in particular tried to strengthen the enforcement of copyright on the Internet, going further than required by the Enforcement Directive. Key to the law reforms is the graduated response scheme introduced by the *Loi HADOPI.*

1007 See Christoper Kuner/Cédric Burton/Jörg Hladjk/Oliver Proust, *Study on online copyright enforcement and data protection in selected Member States* (November 2009), p. 27.

1008 Until 14 June 2009, Article L.34-1 of the *Code des postes et des communications électroniques*, foresaw that traffic data must be deleted or anonymized by operators of electronic communications and may only be stored exceptionally for a period of up to one year for the purpose of investigating, detecting and prosecuting criminal offences , and with the sole purpose of making information available, as appropriate, to the judicial Authorities, or invoicing and payment of electronic communications services.

b) Setting the Framework for a Graduated Response Scheme

In response to an online copyright enforcement regime, that was perceived as weak, the French legislator aimed at finding a legislative solution to the problem of online file-sharing. Central to the law reforms was the determination of conditions in which certain offences provided for in the code de la propriéte intellectuelle could be ascertained, prosecuted and tried in the event of set offences being committed via a public online communication service. They opted for a so-called graduated response scheme, which introduces a supplementary penalty of suspension of Internet access.

The French legislation concerning illegal file-sharing was constructed in two subsequent stages: *DADVSI* and *HADOPI*.[1009] The initiatives leading to the current graduated response scheme governed by the *Loi HADOPI* are based on the assumption (1) that the Internet user himself may not be familiar with copyright law and needs to be educated about the consequences of his behaviour before he is faced with sanction and (2) that there are not sufficient established legal alternatives to access content online.

Prior to the Loi Hadopi, French Internet users were faced with almost no sanctions for online copyright infringements. The reason for this was the fact that only the police and the Gendarmerie[1010] were entitled to investigate to whom an IP address was assigned to. The French law did not grant holders of copyright or related rights a separate information right. The enforcement of copyright infringements was therefore dependent on criminal investigations by the investigative authorities.

In practice, investigations in relation to online copyright infringements were not within the priorities of the investigative authorities which rather

---

1009 Although it involved three laws and a multitude of implementation decrees, the two HADOPI laws will be considered as one stage as they are so closely linked. See also Christophe Geiger, *Honourable attempt but (ultimately) disproportionately offensive against peer-to-peer on the internet (HADOPI) – a critical analysis of the recent anti-file-sharing legislation in France*, International Review of Intellectual Property and Competition Law 2011, Vol. 42, 457, 459.

1010 See Rolf Schwartmann, *Vergleichende Studie über Modelle zur Versendung von Warnhinweisen durch Internet-Zugangsanbieter an Nutzer bei Urheberrechtsverletzungen, Studie im Auftrag des Bundesministerium für Wirtschaft und Technologie* (January 2012), p. 85.

focussed on child pornography.[1011] Thus, owners of copyright or related rights were left with a blunt instrument.

aa) Loi Relative au Droit d'Auteur et aux Droits Voisins dans la Société de l'Information – Loi DADVSI

Parliamentary discussions on the regulation of file-sharing only started in the implementation proceedings of the *InfoSoc Directive*.[1012] The French legislature decided to integrate in the bill the question of file-sharing through peer-to-peer networks although this question was not directly addressed in the Directive.[1013]

By the *Loi relative au droit dáuteur et aux droits voisins dans la société de l'information*[1014] of 1 August 2006 France transposed the *InfoSoc Directive* into national law. During the legislative process there was some discussion as to the role of misuse of peer-to-peer networks on the Internet.[1015] Due to the scope of illegal use of peer-to-peer technology, it was suggested to legalise file-sharing via peer-to-peer networks by a natural person for private use and introduce a flat-rate remuneration.[1016] Downloading would have been the subject of a kind of compulsory license by

---

1011 *Ibid.*

1012 Christophe Geiger, *Honourable attempt but (ultimately) disproportionately offensive against peer-to-peer on the internet (HADOPI) – a critical analysis of the recent anti-file-sharing legislation in France,* International Review of Intellectual Property and Competition Law 2011, Vol. 42, 457, 459.

1013 *Ibid.*

1014 *Loi no. 2006-961 du 1 août 2006 relative au droit dáuteur et aux droits voisins dans la société de l'information (DADVSI).*

1015 Rolf Schwartmann, *Vergleichende Studie über Modelle zur Versendung von Warnhinweisen durch Internet-Zugangsanbieter an Nutzer bei Urheberrechtsverletzungen, Studie im Auftrag des Bundesministerium für Wirtschaft und Technologie* (Januar 2012), p. 80.

1016 Lionel Thoumyre, *La licence globale optionelle: un pare-feu contre le bugs de la repression*, Revue Lamy Droit de l'Immateriél 2006, 80–84. The text of the amendment adopted on 21.12.2005 which was later reversed: "Similarly, the author cannot forbid reproductions made on all media on the basis of an online communication service by a physical person for his private use for purposes that are not directly or indirectly commercial, with the exception of copies of software other than a backup copy, provided that such reproductions are the subject of a remuneration as laid down in Article L. 311-4" (translation by Christophe Geiger, *Counterfeiting and the music industry: towards a criminalization of end*

analogy with the private copy exception, while the upload of a file to the system would probably have been subjected to a system of mandatory collective management.[1017] This system, which in the end was not adopted, was also referred to as a system of 'global licence'[1018]. Instead, Article 24 of the *Loi DADVSI* made the unauthorised reproduction for personal use as well as the online communication to the public for non-commercial purposes of protected works via peer-to-peer networks a summary offence ("contravention") rather than a felony ("délit").[1019] Hence, an illegal downloader using peer-to-peer networks faced a 'reduced' penalty for copyright infringements.[1020] The law also imposed on Internet access holders an obligation to monitor their access. Article 25 of the *Loi DADVSI* required Internet access holders to make sure, if requested to do so, that their Internet access is not used for the exchange of copyrighted material without the rights-holders' consent or authorisation.[1021] However, since a breach of that obligation did not trigger any sanctions, this obligation did not affect the Internet access holders in practice.[1022]

---

users? The French 'HADOPI' example, in: Christophe Geiger (ed), *Criminal enforcement of intellectual property* (2012), p. 388.

1017 The members of parliament did not decide on the latter. See Christophe Geiger, *Counterfeiting and the music industry: towards a criminalization of end users? The French 'HADOPI' example*, in: Christophe Geiger (ed), *Criminal enforcement of intellectual property* (2012), p. 389.

1018 Lionel Thoumyre, *La licence globale optionelle: un pare-feu contre le bugs de la repression,* Revue Lamy Droit de l'Immateriél 2006, 80–84.

1019 Amélie Blocman, *Adoption of the Act on Copyright and Neighbouring Rights in the Information Society* (2006). Under Article 111-1 of the *Code Pénal*, offences are classified according to their seriousness as crimes, délits and contraventions. A contravention is punishable solely by a fine. The Penal Code differentiates between five types of contraventions, with varying fines up to a maximum of EUR 1,500. A délit is punishable by a prison sentence of up to ten years, or by a fine of at least EUR 3,750. A crime carries a longer prison sentence (from 15 years to life).

1020 Christophe Geiger, *Honourable attempt but (ultimately) disproportionately offensive against peer-to-peer on the internet (HADOPI) – a critical analysis of the recent anti-file-sharing legislation in France,* International Review of Intellectual Property and Competition Law 2011, Vol. 42, 457, 462.

1021 Article 25 inserted Article L. 335-12 into the *CPI.* This Article has however been abolished by the *Loi HADOPI I* and the obligation is now incorporated in Article L. 336-3 *CPI.*

1022 Christophe Geiger, *Honourable attempt but (ultimately) disproportionately offensive against peer-to-peer on the internet (HADOPI) – a critical analysis of*

Following a referral to the Conseil Constitutionnel for review of the constitutionality of the proposed *Loi DADVSI*, some adaptions were necessary. The Conseil Constitutionnel inter alia set aside the provision, which set forth less severe sanctions for users that made unauthorised copies of protected works via peer-to-peer networks for their personal use.[1023] The Court held that it was not possible to differentiate between piracy using eMail, blogs, or any other means of online communication and piracy carried out via peer-to-peer networks.[1024] The particularities of peer-to-peer networks cannot justify the difference in treatment that had been introduced by Article 24 of the *Loi DADVSI*. The contested provision was consideredcontrary to the principle of equality prescribed by Article 6 of the *Declaration of 1789* and thus held to be unconstitutional.[1025] Accordingly, unauthorised file-sharing via peer-to-peer networks remains a criminal offence, punishable with a fine of up to EUR 300,000 and three years imprisonment.[1026] With the monitoring obligation not being linked to any sanctions, the legislation combatting illegal file-sharing remained somehow incomplete. For this reason, the public authorities commissioned a report, which subsequently formed the basis for the HADOPI laws.

bb) Loi Favorisant la Diffusion et la Protection de la Création sur Internet – Loi HADOPI I

In September 2007, the French Minister of Culture and Communication, Christine Albanel, asked the former CEO of the major French entertainment retailer FNAC, Denis Olivennes, to lead a task force of four experts to investigate the economical, legal and technological requirements of a

---

the recent anti-file-sharing legislation in France, International Review of Intellectual Property and Competition Law 2011, Vol. 42, 457, 464.

1023 Conseil Constitutionnel, Decision of 27.07.2006 – No. 2006-540 DC, Journal officiel de la République Française of 03.08.2006, 11541. An English translation of the decision is available at http://www.conseil-constitutionnel.fr/conseil-constitutionnel/root/bank/download/2006540DCen2006_540dc.pdf (last accessed 17.05.2014).

1024 *Ibid*, para. 64 et seq.

1025 *Ibid*, para. 65.

1026 See Article L.335-4 *CPI*.

graduated response scheme in France.[1027] Following a consultation of representatives of the entertainment industry, Internet service providers and consumer associations, the Olivennes committee submitted its report, entitled "Le developpement et la protection des oeuvres culturelles sur les nouveaux reseaux", in November 2007.[1028] The Olivennes Report found that copyright protection measures in music files (DRM) hinder interoperability and should be abandoned.[1029] Legally purchased music must be readable more easily on all types of devices. The report also found that users want faster access to audiovisual works on digital networks and respective solutions should be provided.[1030] The report further suggested the establishment of a single agency in the form of an independent admininstrative authority that takes action against online piracy in its entirety and promotes legal offers of online distribution of content.[1031] Also, Internet service providers shall commit themselves to developing and operating – in cooperation with rights-holders – identification systems to detect legal offers (e.g. digital fingerprints). Most notably, the report proposes the introduction of a graduated response scheme with an Internet suspension as final sanction..[1032]

The report was signed by more than 40 entities from the film, music, TV and Internet service provider sector at the Elysée palace and presented as the "Olivennes Agreement".[1033] The Agreement has been historic: it was the first of its kind where the creative industries agreed on solutions to fight online piracy and where a consensus in that respect was reached with Internet access providers.[1034] The signatories of the Agreement committed themselves to contribute to finding a solution against online piracy and to

---

1027 Further members of the task force were Olivier Bomsel (Professor in Economics, Centre d'économie industrielle de l'Ecole des Mines), Pascal Faure (Privy councillor, general delegate and president of the Conseil d'orientation du Forum des droits sur l'Internet) and Isabelle Falque-Pierrotin (Vice president of the Conseil Général des Technologies de l'Information).

1028 The full report is available online at http://www.culture.gouv.fr/culture/actualites/conferen/albanel/rapportolivennes 231107.pdf (last accessed 17.05.2014).

1029 *Ibid*, p. 25.

1030 *Ibid.*

1031 *Ibid.*

1032 *Ibid.*

1033 It has later been renamed to "Elysée agreement".

1034 See Sénat, *Explanatory Memorandum, Projet de loi favorisant la diffusion et la protection de la création sur Internet, Annexe au procès-verbal de la séance du 18.06.2008.*

promote ways to use the Internet as a legal distribution channel for content.

The conclusions drawn in the Olivennes Report led to a new law project in 2008. The French senate recognised that although sanctions exist for illegal file-sharing on the basis of copyright infringements, the existing regime was unsuitable to respond to the mass phenomenon of online piracy.[1035] The Senate also accepted as fact that Internet users are often unaware of the wrongfulness of their actions.[1036] At that time Article L. 335-12 of the *CPI*, which was introduced by *Loi DADVSI* and obliged Internet access holders to ensure that their access is not used for intellectual property rights infringements, did not provide any sanction for a breach of that obligation.[1037]

In order to meet the goals set forth in the Elysée Agreement, the law project aimed to introduce a system of graduated response. Therefore, it proposed to widen the competences of the Autorité de regulation des mesure techniques, which had been established by the Senate in 2006 and which was responsible for the interoperability and implementation of technical protections measures. The Autorité de regulation des mesure techniques was renamed Haute Autorité pour la diffusion des œuvres et la protection des droits sur Internet (HADOPI)[1038] to reflect the new scope of its powers.[1039] Under its new mission the independent HADOPI's function is to discourage Internet users from unauthorised copying via the Internet by a gradual intervention: HADOPI will send out warning notices on behalf of rights-holders to users. These warnings are known as "recommendation" and precede possible sanctions.

Following two warnings HADOPI was foreseen to adopt, subject to judicial review, a sanction in the form of temporary suspension of an Internet acccess from three months to one year combined with a prohibition to re-subscribe for another Internet access service for that period. The Senate

1035 See *Ibid.*

1036 *Ibid.*

1037 *Ibid.*

1038 "High Authority for the diffusion of works and protection of copyright on the Internet", in the following referred to as HADOPI.

1039 See Section 2 of the *Projet de loi favorisant la diffusion et la protection de la création sur Internet, Annexe au procès-verbal de la séance du 18.06.2008.*

assessed the future of a scheme of graduated response as a success story based on several industry-led studies.[1040]

As a first step, Article L.335-12 *CPI*was to be amended to provide for a sanction for breaching the obligation to monitor one´s Internet connection. [1041] According to the new Article L.336-3 *CPI*, no penalty should be imposed on an Internet access subscriber if he had installed effective means to secure his connection. For this purpose HADOPI set up a list of security means which it would consider effective to prevent a breach of the monitoring duty.

The law project saw numerous amendments, in particular concerning the system of graduated response[1042] before it was finally adopted by the Assemblée nationale on 12 May 2009 and by the Sénat on 13 May 2009. Being controversial from the start,[1043] it took less than a week after the final vote of the assembly until the law was legally challenged.[1044] At least 60 members of the national assembly referred the *Loi HADOPI I* to the Conseil constitutionnel for review, claiming that several parts of the

1040 Sénat, *Explanatory Memorandum, Projet de loi favorisant la diffusion et la protection de la création sur Internet, Annexe au procès-verbal de la séance du 18.06.2008*. The Senate quoted several studies that allegedly confirm the future success of graduate response schemes: a US study allegedly found that in US digital networks where a similar solution had been implemented 70% of Internet users refrained from further downloads upon a first warning , 85 to 90% upon a second warning and 97% upon receiving a third warning. According to the Senat an IPSOS (www.ipsos.fr) poll conducted in France in May 2008 showed that a warning system could have a comparable effect in France with 90% of the interviewees responding that they would refrain from illegal downloads following a second warning. Further the Senate relied on a study conducted by Entertainment Media Research which alleged that 70% of users that received a first warning and 90% of users that received a second warning would refrain from futher infringements.

1041 *Ibid*, Article 4 of *Projet de loi favorisant la diffusion et la protection de la création sur Internet.*

1042 See http://www.assemblee-nationale.fr/13/dossiers/Internet.asp (last accessed 17.05.2014).

1043 In the Assemblée nationale 296 members voted in favour of the law and 233 against it.

1044 According to Article 61 para. 2 of the French Constitution, the Conseil constitutionnel can exercise a priori and abstract control over the constitutionality of laws before they enter into force.

statute were unconstitutional.[1045] In particular, they contended unconstitutionality of Articles 5, 10 and 11 of the law. One of the key claims was that the sanctions on copyright infringers were disproportionate, and that the imposition of a suspension order should be left to judicial authorities rather than to HADOPI.[1046]

On 10 June 2009, the Conseil constitutionnel declared several provisions encompassed in Article 5 and 11 of the *Loi HADOPI I* unconstitutional: They were not in compliance with procedural safeguards in case of

---

1045 *Saisine du Conseil constitutionnel en date du 19 mai 2009 présentée par au moins soixante députés, en application de l'article 61, alinéa 2, de la Constitution, et visée dans la décision no 2009-580 DC,* Journal officiel de la République Française of 13.06.2009, texte 4 sur 148.

1046 Conseil constitutionnel, Decision of 10.06.2009 – No. 2009-580 DC, Journal officiel de la République Française of 13.06.2009, 9675, paras. 2 et seq. An English version of the decision is available at http://www.conseil-constitutionnel.fr/conseil-constitutionnel/root/bank/download/2009580DC2009_580dc.pdf (last accessed 17.05.2014). For an analysis of the decision see also William Benassiano, *L'inconstitutionnalité, sanction de l'identification d'un pouvoir de répression pénale dévalué. Décision no 2009-580 DC du 10 juin 2009*, Revue française de droit constitutionnel 2010, no 81, 168–174; Aurélie Binet-Grosclaude, *La décision du Conseil constitutionnel du 10 juin 2009 relative à la loi favorisant la diffusion et la protection de la création sur internet : un coup d'arrêt au pouvoir de sanction des AAI ?*, Droit Pénal 2009, no 11, 11–17; Iliana Boubekeur, *De la « loi HADOPI » à la « loi HADOPI 2 ». Analyse de la décision du Conseil constitutionnel 2009-580 DC et de ses conséquences*, Revue Lamy Droit de l'Immatériel 2009, no 51, 107–113; Jacques Francillon, *Téléchargement illégal. Heur et malheur de la loi Création et Internet : la loi HADOPI censurée par le Conseil constitutionnel*, Revue de science criminelle et de droit pénal comparé 2009, no 3, 609–622; Gautron, Allan, *La « réponse graduée » (à nouveau) épinglée par le Conseil constitutionnel. Ou la délicate adéquation des moyens aux fins*, Revue Lamy Droit de l'Immatériel 2009,no 51, 63–73; Laure Marino, *Le droit d'accès à internet, nouveau droit fondamental*, Recueil Dalloz 2009, 2045–2046; Thierry Revet, *Droit de propriété sur droit de propriété ne vaut*, Revue trimestrielle de droit civil 2009, no 4, 754–756; Thierry Revet, *La consécration de la liberté d'accéder aux services de communication au public en ligne, protection comme res de la position contractuelle permettant l'accès au réseau internet ?*, Revue trimestrielle de droit civil 2009, no 4, 756–757; Dominique Rousseau, *Hado-pirate la Constitution : le Conseil sanctionne !*, Revue Lamy Droit de l'Immatériel 2009, no 51, 103–105; Charles Simon, *Les adresses IP sont des données personnelles selon le Conseil constitutionnel*, Revue Lamy Droit de l'Immatériel 2009, no 51, 114–115.

sanctions, and most notably, were held to infringe freedom of expression. [1047]

Article 5 of the HADOPI I Law which was referred for review inserted into the *CPI* the section regulating the HADOPI. HADOPI was supposed to be composed of a board and a committee for the protection of copyright. While the board should be responsible for promoting and furthering the lawful offer of intellectual property, the task of the Committee for the protection of copyright is to trigger the new warning mechanisms and administrative penalties incurred by Internet access holders who failed to monitor their connection.[1048]

The provisions on the warning scheme were to be incorporated in Article L.331-27 of the *CPI*, which was supposed to set forth the following:

"When it has been ascertained that the subscriber has failed to comply with the duty defined in Article L 336-3 in the year following receipt of a recommendation addressed by the Committee for the protection of copyright accompanied by a signed acknowledgment of receipt or any other means likely to prove the date of the sending of said recommendation and its receipt by the subscriber, the Committee may, after a full hearing of all parties, impose one of the following penalties depending on the seriousness of the failure to comply and the use of Internet access:

1° Suspension of access to the Internet for a period of between two months and one year accompanied by the impossibility for the subscriber to enter into any other contract with any other operator for access to online public communication services

2° An injunction to take, within a period determined by the Committee, measures designed to prevent any repetition of the breach of duty ascertained, in particular by installing a security device from among those listed in paragraph 2 of Article L 331-32, and to account for the same to the High Authority on pain, if need be, of payment of a financial penalty."[1049]

It was foreseen that under Article L.331-28, HADOPI's Committee for the protection of copyright may, before initiating penalty proceedings, propose an amicable arrangement whereby the subscriber concerned has his connection suspended for a period of one to three months, or is put under a duty to prevent the re-occurrence of said breach of duty. In addition Arti-

1047 Conseil constitutionnel, Decision of 10.06.2009 – No. 2009-580 DC, Journal officiel de la République Française of 13.06.2009, 9675.

1048 *Ibid*, para. 4.

1049 *Ibid*, para. 9.

cle L.331-29 was supposed to authorise the Committee to impose the penalties provided for in Article L.331-27 in the event of non-compliance with the amicable agreement.[1050] In addition, Article L.331-30 specified the contractual consequences of a suspension order, while Article L. 331-32 determined the manner for drawing up the list of devices to be installed in order to exonerate the access holder from all penalties; Arts. L. 331-33 and L.331-34 set up a national register of names of persons whose access has been suspended. The Committee for the protection of copyright was supposed to retain the technical data supplied to it until an Internet access has been completely suspended (Article L.331-36).

These provisions have all been declared unconstitutional by the Conseil constitutionnel. In analysing the provisions, the Court paid regard to the importance of access to the Internet in a networked world for the participation in democracy and the expression of ideas and opinions and concluded that Article 11 of the *Declaration of 1789* implies the freedom to access online communication services.[1051] Article 11 of the *Declaration of 1789* proclaims: "The free communication of ideas and opinions is one of the most precious rights of man. Every citizen may thus speak, write and publish freely, except when such freedom is misused in cases determined by Law".

Having regard to the nature of the freedom guaranteed by Article 11 of the *Declaration of 1789*, the Court held that the legislature could not entrust the Committee for the protection of copyright, an administrative authority, with such powers to impose penalties created by the challenged provisions of Articles 5 and 11 of the *Loi HADOPI I.*[1052] Considering that the powers to suspense access were not limited to a specific category of persons but extended to the entire French population, the powers of the Committee have the potential to restrict the right of any person to exercise his right to free expression and communication, in particular from his own home.[1053] As freedom of expression and communication are considered as the cornerstones of a democratic society and a prerequisite for other rights and freedoms, any restriction placed on these freedoms has to be proportionate in achieving its goal.[1054] The Court concluded that the principle of

---

1050 *Ibid*, para. 10.
1051 *Ibid*, para. 12.
1052 *Ibid*, para. 16.
1053 *Ibid*, para. 16.
1054 *Ibid*, para. 15.

proportionality had not been respected, although the goal of the challenged provisions was legitimate, namely the protection of copyrights and related rights enshrined in Arts. 2 and 17 of the *Declaration of 1789*.[1055]

Considering that, pursuant to Article 9 of the *Declaration of 1789* every man is presumed innocent until proven guilty, the introduction of a reversal of the burden of proof by presuming guilt on the part of an Internet access holder was also held unconstitutional.[1056]

As regards the right to privacy enshrined in Article 2 of the *Declaration of 1789*, the Court stressed that the Constitution requires the right to privacy and other constitutional rights such as the right to property to be balanced.[1057] In that regard, allowing private entities to collect data that allows the identification of Internet access subscribers was held to be a disproportionate infringement of the right to privacy.[1058] However, the Court did not agree with the referring parties that "the possibility of blocking, by measures and injunctions, the functioning of telecommunications infrastructures … might deprive many Internet users of the right to receive information".[1059]

In summary, the Court did not criticise the sanction of Internet access suspension as such. However, the Court concluded that authorising an administrative authority to order said suspension infringes Article 11 of the *Declaration of 1789*. A sanction which may have such a severe impact on the fundamental rights and freedoms of an individual requires a decision by a judge.

cc) Loi Relative à la Protection Pénale de la Propriété Littéraire et Artistique sur Internet – Loi HADOPI II

Following the decision of the Conseil constitutionnel and the removal of the penal aspects from the law, the *Loi HADOPI II* was drafted. The *Loi no. 2009-1311 du 28 octobre 2009 relative à la protection pénale de la*

1055 *Ibid*, para. 13.

1056 *Ibid*, para. 18.

1057 *Ibid*, paras. 22 et seq.

1058 *Ibid*, para. 27. It must be noted, that the Court did not declare the provisions on the gathering of data by private entities (acting on behalf of the rightholders) to identify Internet access subscribers unconstitutional.

1059 *Ibid*, para. 37.

propriété littéraire et artistique sur Internet – Loi HADOPI II[1060] was designed to complete the then incomplete *Loi HADOPI I.* In essence, it lays down the competences of the different actors involved in the execution of the warning procedures as well as the role of courts in this system. Most importantly, Article 2 introduces Article L. 335-7 into the *CPI,* which foresees a sanction for gross negligent non-compliance with the aforementioned obligation to secure an Internet access.[1061] The mere abstention from securing a connection does not in itself constitute the offence: Gross negligence will only be established where an Internet connection is actually used for the purposes of copyright infringement within one year following a second warning by HADOPI[1062] and when it appears that without justification the Internet subscriber has failed to implement security mechanisms. At procedural level, it was foreseen that the public prosecutor would be in charge to bring an action before a criminal court for alleged infringements.[1063]

HADOPI II also introduced two further offences: an infringement of the prohibition on the Internet user to sign up with another access provider during the suspension period,[1064] and the failure of the access provider to suspend access after notification by HADOPI.[1065]

Essemtially, the *Loi HADOPI II* reinforces the repressive nature of the law: this is not so much because a judge may impose a EUR 1,500 fine combined with a maximum one month Internet access suspension, when an Internet access subscriber fails to comply with his obligation to monitor his connection. It is rather the cumulation of penalties, namely that an infringer faces a fine, suspension of Internet access combined with the

---

1060 Available online at http://www.legifrance.gouv.fr/affichTexte.do?cidTexte=JORFTEXT000021208046&dateTexte=& categorieLien=id (last accessed 17.05.2014).

1061 The term used in Article L. 335-7-1 is "négligence caractérisée". Christophe Geiger uses the translation "blatant negligence", see Christophe Geiger, *Honourable attempt but (ultimately) disproportionately offensive against peer-to-peer on the internet (HADOPI) – a critical analysis of the recent anti-file-sharing legislation in France*, International Review of Intellectual Property and Competition Law 2011, Vol. 42, 457, 468, Fn. 49.

1062 It was foreseen that the first warning was sent by email, while the second warning would have to be sent by registered letter against signature.

1063 Article 398 of the *Code de Procédure Pénale (CPP).*

1064 Article L. 335-7-1 of the *CPI.*

1065 Article L. 335-7 of the *CPI.*

prohibition to sign up for another contract and the obligation to pay the subscription fee, that gave rise to concern.[1066] However, such a cumulation is nothing special in law, considering that speeding in a car may also be sanctioned with a fine and a driving ban.

At all, it came to no surprise when members of the National Assembly addressed the Conseil Constitutionnel contending that Articles 1, 6 to 8 and 11 *Loi HADOPI II* were unconstitutional.[1067]

The Conseil constitutionnel held the challenged provisions essentially to be constitutional with the exception of Article 6 II *Loi HADOPI II.*[1068] Article 6 of the *Loi HADOPI II* introduced a specific procedure applicable to copyright infringements committed via Internet. The second paragraph of Article 6 set forth that requests for damages will be decided upon by a single judge in the course of a summary order. Details of the proceedings such as for instance the effects of possible objections by the defendant would have been subject to future regulations, which in particular was held to be unconstitutional.[1069] Although this did not have any impact on the revised graduated response scheme, it was nevertheless quickly addressed by the legislator.

1066 Cf. Christophe Geiger, *Counterfeiting and the music industry: towards a criminalization of end users? The French 'HADOPI' example,* in: Christophe Geiger (ed), *Criminal enforcement of intellectual property* (2012), pp. 397 et seq.

1067 Conseil constitutionnel, Decision of 22.10.2009 – no. 2009-590 DC, Journal officiel de la République Française of 29.10.2009, 18292. An English version of the decision is available at http://www.conseil-constitutionnel.fr/conseil-constitutionnel/root/bank/ download/2009590DCen2009_590dc.pdf (last accessed 17.05.2014). For an analysis of this decision, see William Benassiano, *Décision no 2009-590 Dc du 22 octobre 2009, La sanction de l'incompétence négative*, Revue française de droit constitutionnel 2010, 390–396; Florence Chaltiel, *La loi HADOPI II de nouveau censurée*, Petites affiches 2009, no 235 (25.11.2009), 7–13; Emmanuel Derieux, *Validation par le Conseil constitutionnel de l'essentiel des dispositions de la loi 'HADOPI 2'*, Revue Lamy Droit de l'Immatériel 2009, no 54, 6–8; Dominique Rousseau, *Après HADOPI 1et HADOPI 2, HADOPI 3? La décision du Conseil constitutionnel du 22 octobre 2009*, Légipresse 2009, no 267, 173–174; Michel Verpeaux, *Loi Hadopi 2, contrôle à double détente : 1. A propos de la décision du Conseil constitutionnel du 22 octobre 2009*, La Semaine Juridique, Édition générale 2009, no 46, 15–17.

1068 Art. 6 II *Loi HADOPI II* would have amended Article 495-6-1 *Code de procédure pénale*.

1069 The offence may be tried before a criminal court (*tribunal correctionnel*) sitting with a single judge or under the summary procedure of a criminal order.

dd) Summary

The graduated response scheme, that results from the *Loi HADOPI II* and that will be analysed in the following, has not been the first French legislative effort to find a legal solution to the problem of unauthorised file-sharing via peer-to-peer networks. It rather constitutes the preliminary end to a struggle to find a solution that aims at respecting not only the interests of the rights owners but also the fundamental rights of the users. The foundation for *Loi HADOPI I* and *II* was laid by the *Loi DADVSI* which imposed upon Internet access subscribers an obligation to monitor their access, when it laid down that Internet access subscribers must ensure that their access is not used for the purpose of reproducing or presenting intellectual works without the rights-holders' authorisation. The need for the HADOPI laws arose from the fact that the monitoring obligation somehow was a blunt instrument, because it was not associated with any sanctions and enforcement mechanisms. A system intended to combat unauthorised file-sharing was left incomplete, until the *HADOPI I* and *II* laws were passed aiming to close that gap. While the *HADOPI I* and *II* laws were passed under the pretence to prefer an "educational and preventive approach" to a repressive solution, they centre around a system that beside education clearly focusses on sanctioning potential infringers. This regime that provides for a system based on the failure to comply with an obligation to monitor, is no substitution for criminal prosecution but amends them.[1070]

c) Outline and Functioning of the Current Graduated Response Scheme

The warning model foreseen by the *Loi HADOPI II* has both a preventive and educational character, as well as a repressive character. The model where warnings precede a sanction intends to hinder further infringements by teaching the Internet access holders about the legal situation. The Inter-

---

1070 The absence of a rule to prevent the cumulation of penalties has been criticised by scholars. See Alain Strowel, *La loi création et Internet : de la confirmation d'un 'droit d'accès' en droit d'auteur à l'analyse de la proportionalité de la réponse graduée*, in : Institut de Recherche en Propriété Intellectuelle (ed.), *Contrefaçon sur Internet : Les enjeux du droit d'auteur sur le Web 2.0* (2009), p. 119.

net user or more precisely the Internet access subscriber that potentially does not know that unauthorised file-sharing contravenes the law, will be exempted from legal consequences for a first and even a second infringement.

Due to the central role of HADOPI (= the High Authority) the following analysis will first outline the role and composition of the Authority before focussing on the details of the graduated response scheme.

aa) The Missions and Powers of HADOPI

Article L. 331-13 *CPI* vests three missions to Haute Autorité pour la diffusion des oeuvres et la protection des droits sur Internet (HADOPI): (i) to promote the development of legal content services, and monitor the legal and illegal use of works that are subject to a copyright or neighbouring right on digital communications networks used to provide public online communications services, (2) to protect these works against infringements of these rights committed on electronic communications networks, and (iii) to regulate and monitor in the field of technical measures to protect and identify copyright-protected works and objects. HADOPI has been given extensive competences to prevent online copyright infringements, to prosecute and sanction them. Essential in this system is the education and warning of Internet users.

HADOPI has the status of a so-called "Autorité publique indépendante". As such, HADOPI carries out public tasks without being under the auspices of a French ministry. The Authority is composed by a board and the so called Rights Protection Commission,[1071] with the latter being in charge of executing the measures laid down by the HADOPI law.[1072] The execution of these measures means that the Rights Protection Commission oversees the graduated response procedure set forth in Article L. 331-25 *CPI* that will be initiated if the Commission has evidence proving a failure of an Internet subscriber to meet his obligation to ensure that his Internet access is not used to commit copyright infringements. In that respect, the Commission has powers to receive claims, and as regards the gathering of evidence, the Rights Protection Commission is also vested with police

---

1071 L. 331-15 *CPI.*

1072 For the organisational structure of HADOPI see HADOPI, *2010 Activity Report* (2011), p. 20.

powers.[1073] Accordingly, the Commission may conduct investigations, question the accused and gather further information in relation to the offence. Pursuant to Articles 431 and 537 *Code de procédure pénale (CPP)*, the reports of the Rights Protection Commission serve as evidence until the contrary is proven. In executing its mandate under the HADOPI laws, the Rights Protection Commission is not bound by the terms and conditions of Article 40 *CPP*, meaning that when in possession of material evidence of an infringement and information about the subscriber, the Rights Protection Commission is not obliged to forward the information to the public prosecutor. An obligation as under Article 40 *CPP*, namely the obligation to inform public prosecution upon acquiring knowledge of an offence while carrying out public tasks, would render the graduated response procedure ineffective.[1074]

As regards the sending out of warnings under the graduated response scheme, the Rights Protection Commission is free to decide whether it sends a warning or not. HADOPI is also free to forward a case to the public prosecutor, even where it has previously sent out two warnings.[1075]

bb) How the Graduated Response Scheme Works

In the following, the different steps of the graduated response procedure and the consequences at the end of the procedure are outlined.

(1) Gathering of Information of Infringements

Prior to the HADOPI laws, the collection and processing of IP addresses of users suspected of committing online infringements were solely cov-

---

1073 This constitutes a major change to the previous legal regime: It is no longer the police and the gendarmerie that are vested with these powers and are solely in charge of the preliminary investigations, see Articles 15 and 28 *CPP*.

1074 HADOPI, *2010 Activity Report* (2011), p. 31.

1075 Cf. Article 331-25 *CPI*, which does not state at any point that HADOPI is obliged to send a warning or forward a report to the public prosecuor's office. This power departs from the provisions in Article 40 *CPP*, but only for offences regulated by the HADOPI laws, i.e. Articles L. 335-2, L. 335-3, L. 335-4 and R. 335-5 *CPI*.

ered by the Loi informatique et libertés de 1978.[1076] Article 9 of said law expressly allows some legal entities representing the right owner (in particular collecting societies) to collect and process the data that is necessary to enforce copyright infringement. The *LOI HADOPI I* now provides that online copyright infringements may be reported to HADOPI by the public prosecution or sworn agents of rights-holders (including collecting societies) that have been accredited by the Ministry of Culture.[1077] Pursuant to Article 9(4) of the Loi informatique et libertés, these sworn agents acting by virtue of the rights they administer, or on behalf of victims of copyright infringements, and for the purposes of ensuring the enforcement of these rights, may process personal data relating to offences under the condition that this data processing activity is authorised by the CNIL[1078] as requires by Article 35 the Loi informatique et libertés.

In practice, the rights-holders have instructed the private company Trident Media Guard[1079] to search peer-to-peer networks for copyrighted material and retrieve IP addresses of potential copyright infringers. Although the HADOPI laws do not limit the scope of the graduated response scheme to a specific uploading or downloading technique, the decree on the automated processing of personal data[1080], that has to be obeyed by the Rights Protection Commission when administering the warning letters, only refers to illegal acts of uploading and downloading committed on peer-to-peer networks, and thereby narrows the scope of application.[1081]

Trident Media Guard has a catalogue of works for which it monitors peer-to-peer networks.[1082] Once Trident Media Guard has detected that an Internet access has been used to disseminate copyrighted works, they will save a file containing an extract of the infringing work (so-called 'chunk')

1076 *Loi n° 78-17 du 6 janvier 1978 relative à l'informatique, aux fichiers et aux libertés.*

1077 L. 331-24 and L.331-2 of the *CPI.*

1078 The Commission Nationale de l'Informatique et des Libertés (CNIL) is the French data protection authority.

1079 www.tmg.eu.

1080 *Décret no 2010-236 du 5 mars 2010 relatif au traitement automatisé de données à caractère personnel autorisé par l'article L. 331-29 du CPI dénommé « Système de gestion des mesures pour la protection des œuvres sur Internet ».*

1081 HADOPI, *2010 Activity Report* (2011), p. 34.

1082 *Ibid.*

that they may then refer to the Rights Protection Commission.[1083] It is important for them to provide HADOPI with as much evidence as possible, because HADOPI decides – based on the notification – whether it will initiate the graduated response procedure. The rights-holder may also choose to address the criminal justice system directly on grounds of infringement – a way that the rights-holders could also pursue prior to the passing of the HADOPI laws.[1084] In that respect, they would have to prove that they have identified the actual infringer, which is far more difficult than entering the warning procedure, due to the limited information that can be retrieved from a peer-to-peer network. The warning procedure only requires evidence with respect to an infringement that has happened online and has been committed from a specific IP address, which can be provided to HADOPI.[1085] In particular, in addition to the extract from the infringing work, the Rights Protection Commission needs to be presented with the following evidence: (i) proof of the information relating to the sworn agent who signed the claim; (ii) proof of the information relating to the acts observed: the acts must have occurred within the previous six months,[1086] the date and time of the observation, the peer-to-peer protocol used, information on the copyright-protected works and the file name; (iii) proof of the information regarding the identity of the infringer: the IP address retrieved on the date and at the time of the infringement, the Internet service provider used, and the pseudonyms used on the peer-to-peer network by the infringer; (iv) proof of the presence of a sworn statement certifying that the person filing the claim is authorised to act on behalf of the copyright holder.[1087]

1083 Mireille Imbert-Quaretta/Jean-Yves Monfort/Jean-Baptiste Carpentier, *La contravention de négligence caractérisée à la lumière de la mise en œuvre de la procédure de réponse graduée*, La Semaine Juridique–Édition Générale 2012, no 19, 966, 969.

1084 HADOPI, *2010 Activity Report* (2011), p. 30.

1085 A prerequisite to be charged with the failure to secure an Internet access is that the subscriber has been notified about infringements taking place via his connection.

1086 Article 331-24 *CPI*.

1087 HADOPI, *2010 Activity Report* (2011), p. 35. As regards the data processed see also the annex to *Décret no 2010-236 du 5 mars 2010 relatif au traitement automatisé de données à caractère personnel autorisé par l'article L. 331-29 du CPI dénommé « Système de gestion des mesures pour la protection des œuvres sur Internet »*.

Only following the submission of the required evidence of the alleged infringement by the rights-holder, or a prosecutor, HADOPI will initiate its warning procedure.[1088]

If HADOPI opens a *dossier*, they are entitled to obtain all documents relevant for the case from electronic communication operators and service providers mentioned in Article 6-1 and 2 of the *Loi de 21 juin 2004 pour la confiance dans l'économie numérique (LCEN).* In particular, HADOPI has an information right as regards the identity of a subscriber behind a certain IP address at a given time. The Rights Protection Commission will send disclosure requests to the respective Internet service providers who are obliged to provide the following information on the subscriber within eight days: full name, telephone number, address where the subscriber's telephone line is installed, postal and email addresses.[1089] The email address is the one that the Internet service provider himself uses to contact the subscriber. It can either be an address created for the subscriber when he signed up for the subscription plan, or an address that was given to the service provider by the subscriber when the subscription started.[1090] Only HADOPI will have access to the transmitted data.[1091] In order to ensure that the required data is available from access providers, Article L.34-1 *Code des postes et des communications électroniques* provides that access providers are obliged to store traffic data for a period of up to one year for the purpose of investigating, detecting and prosecuting criminal offences as well as copyright infringements, and with the sole purpose of making information available, as appropriate, to the judicial authorities and to the Hadopi (in compliance with Article L.331-12 *CPI*). Rights-holders and their representatives cannot cooperate directly with access providers to

---

1088 Article L. 331-24, 331-25 *CPI.*

1089 The obligation arises from R. 331-37 and R. 331-38 of the *CPI.* Internet service providers who do not disclose the identity of an Internet access subscriber face a fine under Article L. 331-38. In order to ease communication with the five largest Internet access providers in France, an electronic information network has been established by HADOPI with the respective providers, see HADOPI, *2010 Activity Report* (2011), p. 42.

1090 *Ibid*, p. 35.

1091 Article 4 of *Décret no 2010-236 du 5 mars 2010 relatif au traitement automatisé de données à caractère personnel autorisé par l'article L. 331-29 du CPI dénommé «Système de gestion des mesures pour la protection des œuvres sur Internet».*

obtain from them data identifying a subscriber for the purpose of copyright enforcement.

If HADOPI has doubts that an alleged infringement has taken place, the Authority may conduct a hearing of the applying rights-holder and the Internet subscriber concerned at any stage.[1092] If the Authority concludes that an infringement has taken place, its Rights Protection Commission may forward the case to the competent prosecutor. There is no obligation to forward the case, but HADOPI has discretion to do so.[1093] Usually, if there is sufficient evidence that an infringement has taken place, HADOPI will issue a warning.

(2) The Warning Procedure

As aforementioned, the French warning scheme is a three strikes model, in which an alleged infringer of copyright may be sanctioned following three alleged infringements. Basis for all warnings is the amendment in the *CPI* that an Internet access subscriber must ensure that his connection is not used for copyright infringements.[1094] If an infringement is detected in the manner mentioned above, it will be assumed that the Internet connection subscriber has not sufficiently secured his connection. He will receive a warning by HADOPI. The warning has to be sent within two months fol-

---

1092 Christophe Geiger, *Honourable attempt but (ultimately) disproportionately offensive against peer-to-peer on the internet (HADOPI) – a critical analysis of the recent anti-file-sharing legislation in France,* International Review of Intellectual Property and Competition Law 2011, Vol. 42, 457, 466.

1093 Mireille Imbert-Quaretta/Jean-Yves Monfort/Jean-Baptiste Carpentier, *La contravention de négligence caractérisée à la lumière de la mise en œuvre de la procédure de réponse graduée*, La Semaine Juridique – Édition Générale (2012), no 19, 966, 971.

1094 Cf. The wording of the first paragraph of Article L.336-3 *CPI*: "A person who has subscribed to Internet access to online public communication services is under a duty to ensure that said access is not used for reproducing, showing, making available or communicating to the public works or property protected by copyright or a related right without the authorization of the copyright holders provided for in Books I and II when such authorization is required". The English translation is taken from the official English translation of the Decision of the Conseil Constitutionnel (Decision of 10.06.2009 – No. 2009-580), available at http://www.conseil-constitutionnel.fr/conseil-constitutionnel/root/bank_mm/anglais/2009_580dc.pdf (last accessed 17.05.2014).

lowing the notification of an infringement to HADOPI.[1095] The warning does not contain any information about the file that has been shared,[1096] or any pseudonyms used by the file-sharer,[1097] but indicates the date and time of the allegedly infringing acts, as well as the contact details of HADOPI, so that the subscriber can request further information.[1098] Originally, it did also not mention the peer-to-peer protocol,[1099] but this has subsequently been changed to allow the subscriber to understand the origin of the facts with which he is confronted.[1100] The warning further contains information about the subscriber's obligation to secure and monitor his Internet access and information about how an Internet connection can be secured.[1101] He will also be informed about the legal consequences for non-compliance. In addition, the warning also informs about existing legal download alternatives on the Internet and the negative effects for the cultural sector and creative industries, when intellectual property rights are not respected.[1102] By the latter, the French warning system intends to give priority to an educational and preventive approach.[1103] It is not required that the person that

1095 Article 2 of the *Decrét no 2010-236 du 5 mars 2010* sets forth that the data contained in any claim submitted to the Rights Protection Commission must be deleted from the Commission's information system two months after receipt if the Commission has not sent a warning to the subscriber within that time.

1096 Article L. 331-25 *CPI* expressly stipulates that the warnings "do not disclose the content of the copyright-protected works" in question. Thereby, the legislator wanted to pay regard to the fact that the actual infringer does not necessarily have to be the subscriber. The privacy of the infringer was intended to be kept confidential, cf. HADOPI, *2010 Activity Report* (2011), p. 37.

1097 *Ibid*, p. 38.

1098 Alain Stowel, *The "Graduated Response" in France,* in: Irini Stamatoudi, *Copyright enforcement and the Internet,* p. 147, 149.

1099 HADOPI, *2010 Activity Report* (2011), p. 38.

1100 HADOPI, *Rapport Annuel 2012/2013* (2013), p.9.

1101 Article L. 331-25 para. 1 *CPI.* As regards the protection of an Internet connection, the HADOPI has the competence to establish a list of adequate security measures, see Article L.331-26 para. 2 *CPI.*

1102 *Ibid.* By 2013, the first warning provides the subscriber with a link to a video by HADOPI, by which the Authority tries to raise awareness of intellectual property rights and educate the recipients about such rights. See HADOPI, *Rapport Annuel 2012/2013* (2013), p.9.

1103 Christophe Geiger, *Honourable attempt but (ultimately) disproportionately offensive against peer-to-peer on the internet (HADOPI) – a critical analysis of the recent anti-file-sharing legislation in France,* International Review of Intellectual Property and Competition Law 2011, Vol. 42, 457.

carried out the infringement is identified. The first warning is sent by email via the access provider to the Internet access subscriber.[1104] As mentioned above, the email address is the one used by the Internet access provider in its communication with the subscriber.[1105]

Once the first warning is sent, the graduated response scheme becomes adversarial because now the subscriber can obtain information on the infringement and request a hearing by the Rights Protection Commission.[1106]

If a particular Internet access subscriber's IP address is detected again for alleged copyright infringement within a period of six months following the first warning, a second warning will be sent.[1107] In contrast to the first warning, the second warning will be sent by registered mail with confirmation of receipt.[1108] However, the content will be the same as in the first warning. The second warning is one of the constitutive elements of the offence of gross negligent failure to implement security measures with regard to an Internet access.

If within one year of the receipt of the second warning, a further infringement is established from that very Internet access, the subscriber will be informed about possible criminal sanctions by a registered letter delivered against signature (so-called *délibération*).[1109] In detail, the letter informs him about the evidence collected that may lead to a sanction under the gross negligence offence, and that the file can be forwarded to the public prosecutor so that he may take legal action. The subscriber is granted a 15 day period to deliver his comments or request a hearing.[1110] At the same time he is requested to specify his financial resources.[1111] Because HADOPI will assess and review the facts, and has discretion

---

1104 According to *Décret no 2010–1202 du 12 octobre 2010 modifiant l'article R. 331-37 du CPI*, the Internet access subscribers are obliged to forward the warning to their subscribers within 24 hours.

1105 This may either be an email adress specifically created by the Internet service provider for the subscriber when he signed up for the subscription plan, or an address that the service provider was informed of by the subscriber when the subscription plan started. HADOPI, *2010 Activity Report* (2011).

1106 *Ibid*, p. 36.

1107 Article L.331-25 para. 2 *CPI.*

1108 *Ibid.*

1109 Article L.335-7 para. 1 and R.335-5 II para. 2 *CPI.*

1110 Article R.335-40 *CPI.*

1111 *Ibid.*

whether it forwards a case to the prosecutor's office; accordingly, a third time detection does not necessarily mean that the case is forwarded to the public prosecutor.[1112]

The processing of personal data by HADOPI is regulated by a decree, which inter alia sets forth that only HADOPI has access to its database of potential infringers, and also stipulates the time frame after which personal data has to be deleted.[1113] In general, all personal data must be deleted, when no further measures can be taken by HADOPI against the person to whom the data refers.[1114]

(3) Consequences: Referral to the Prosecutor's Office and Criminal Proceedings

Originally, the HADOPI law foresaw that HADOPI itself had punitive powers and could order the suspension of an Internet access, but this provision has been declared unconstitutional by the Conseil Constitutionnel.[1115] The *Loi HADOPI II* now provides that HADOPI can hand a sum-

1112 If HADOPI decides to hear the subscriber concerned (who is also entitled to request a hearing), an official report of the hearing will be sent to the subscriber. See Alain Stowel, *The "Graduated Response" in France*, in: Irini Stamatoudi, *Copyright enforcement and the Internet*, pp. 147, 150.

1113 *Décret no 2010-236 du 5 mars 2010 relatif au traitement automatisé de données à caractère personnel autorisé par l'article L. 331-29 du CPI dénommé« Système de gestion des mesures pour la protection des œuvres sur Internet ».*

1114 See *ibid*, Article 3. The Décret also stipulates that only HADOPI has access to the stored data. For instance, personal data must be deleted: in cases where no warning was issued following a first time notification, the personal data (= evidence provided to HADOPI, as well as full name, telephone number, address where the subscriber's telephone line is installed, postal and email addresses) has to be deleted within two months; in cases where a first warning was issued, but there has been no second detection of that particular subscriber, the data has to be deleted within 14 months; in cases where two warnings have been issued, but no report was forwarded to the public prosecutor's office, the data has to be deleted within 21 months; in case a report has been issued to the public prosecutor's office and the prosecutor did not bring charges, the data has to be deleted one year following the issue of the report.

1115 Conseil Constitutionnel, Decision of 10.06.2009 – No. 2009-580 DC, Journal officiel de la République Française of 13.6.2009, 9675. The unconstitutional parts of the Loi HADOPI I have been replaced by *Loi n°2009-1311 du*

mary report to the public prosecutor's office of the competent district court,[1116] which will then have to decide whether criminal proceedings will be initiated.[1117]

The public prosecutor may also pursue further investigations in order to establish whether the concerned subscriber has himself infringed copyright (for example by searching for infringing copies on his computer). The public prosecutor also decides whether he brings charges for wilful copyright infringement against the subscriber, or whether he charges the subscriber over the gross negligent failure to implement security measures with regard to his Internet access. The latter is punishable by a fine of up to EUR 1,500,[1118] while wilful copyright infringement via the Internet is punishable by up to three years' imprisonment, a fine of up to EUR 300,000 and the suspension of the infringer Internet access of up to one year.[1119] Until 10 July 2013, the gross negligent failure to implement

---

28.10.2009 relative à la protection pénale de la propriété littéraire et artistique sur Internet (Loi HADOPI II).

1116 Article R.331-43 *CPI.*

1117 Article 398 *CPP.*

1118 Article L.335-7-1 *CPI* states that "For offences in class 5 provided for by this code,…, the supplementary penalty defined in Article L. 355-7 may be imposed in the same manner, in the event of gross negligence, on the holder of a right of access to a public online communication service to whom the Committee for the Protection of Copyright, pursuant to Article L.331-25, has previously sent by registered letter delivered in person and duly signed for or by any other method ensuring proof of the date of receipt thereof, a recommendation asking said holder of access to implement security tools for its Internet access. Gross negligence shall be assessed on the basis of acts committed no later than one year from receipt by the holder of the recommendation referred to in the foregoing paragraph. In such cases, the maximum period of suspension shall be of one month. Failure by any person who has been the object of the supplementary penalty provided for herein to comply with the prohibition on entering into another contract for access to a public online communication service during the period of suspension shall render said person liable to a maximum fine of EUR 3,750." English translation of Article L.335-7-1 *CPI* taken from Conseil constitutionnel, Decision of 22.10.2009 – no. 2009-590 DC, http://www.conseil-constitutionnel.fr/conseil-constitutionnel/root/bank/download/2009590DCen2009_590dc.pdf.

1119 Article 335-7 *CPI.* Article L. 335-7 of the *CPI* introduces a supplementary penalty for copyright infringements committed via the Internet and consists of suspending access to the Internet for a maximum period of one year, together with a prohibition on entering into another access contract with any other Internet access provider. In detail said article states:

security measures was also punishable by the suspension of Internet access of up to one month.[1120]

The offence of gross negligence was created by *Loi HADOPI I* which introduced Article R. 335-5 into the *CPI*. Article R. 335-5 states that gross negligence is provided where an Internet access holder has not implemented means to secure his access or has lacked diligence in implementing the security means. According to para. 2 of Article R. 335-5, this article is only applicable if the following conditions are met: (1) the subscriber concerned has received a second warning by HADOPI via registered mail against signature to implement security means to prevent further infringements of copyright or related rights, and (2) in the year following the receipt of this warning, his access has been used again for an infringe-

---

"When the offence has been committed by the use of a public online communication service, persons guilty of the offences provided for in Articles L. 335-2, L. 335-3 and L. 335-4 may also be liable to imposition of a supplementary penalty of suspension of access to a public online communication service for a maximum period of one year, together with a prohibition on taking out any other contract of a similar nature with another online access provider for the same period. When such a service is purchased as part of a commercial package including other types of service such as telephone or television connections, the decision to suspend online access shall not affect subscriptions to these other services. Suspension of access shall not, per se, affect the payment of the subscription fee to the service provider. Article L. 121-84 of the Consumer Code shall not apply during the suspension period.The costs of any termination of subscription during the suspension period shall be borne by the subscriber. When the decision is executory, the High Authority for the Diffusion of Works and Protection of Copyright on the Internet shall be informed of the supplementary penalty provided for herein and shall in turn notify the provider of access to public online communication services of the same in order for the latter to proceed to suspend access of the subscriber involved no later than 15 days of said notice. Failure by any provider of access to public online communication services to implement the notified order to suspend access shall carry a maximum fine of EUR 5,000. 3° of Article 777 of the Code of Criminal Procedure shall not apply to the supplementary penalty provided herein". English translation of Article L. 335-7 of the *CPI* taken from Conseil constitutionnel, Decision of 22.10.2009 – no. 2009-590 DC, http://www.conseil-constitutionnel.fr/conseil-constitutionnel/ root/bank/download/2009590DCen2009_590dc.pdf.

1120 See Article R. 335-5 *CPI* in the version that was in force from 27.06.2010 to 10.07.2013.

ment.[1121] Thus, charges under this offence can only be brought, where the rights-holder decided to initiate the graduated response scheme instead of addressing his claims directly to the public prosecutor. The new offence has its legal basis in Article L. 336-3, which imposes an obligation upon Internet access subscribers to ensure that their access is not being used for infringements of copyright or related rights. Committing the offence does not require mens rea: A "contravention" requires neither an intention to violate the law, nor an act of imprudence or negligence on behalf of the infringer.[1122] However, the subjective element of the offence is narrower than mere negligence and is comparable to a breach of due diligence in tort law.[1123] Only when the subscriber has been informed about his obligation to secure his Internet access by HADOPI, he may breach a known duty of law and be held liable.[1124] It will then be his persistence to omit the implementation of security measures that is eventually punished under the condition that a further infringement is committed.

The required security means are not defined from a technical point of view.[1125] According to the wording of Article R. 335-5 of the *CPI,* the failure can take two forms: the total failure to secure an Internet connection, and the lack of diligence in installing a security mechanism. According to HADOPI, the latter covers those cases, where the security solution is ineffective, because, for instance, it had not been activated.[1126] The law

1121 The offence can only be committed by accumulating three different infringements while the Internet access holder has not sufficiently secured his connection.

1122 HADOPI, *2010 Activity Report* (2011), p. 33. Mireille Imbert-Quaretta/Jean-Yves Monfort/Jean-Baptiste Carpentier, *La contravention de négligence caractérisée à la lumière de la mise en œuvre de la procédure de réponse graduée,* La Semaine Juridique –Édition Générale (2012), no 19, 966, 969. The committing of the actus reus is sufficient to fulfil the requirements of an "contravention".

1123 *Ibid.*

1124 Mireille Imbert-Quaretta/Jean-Yves Monfort/Jean-Baptiste Carpentier, *La contravention de négligence caractérisée à la lumière de la mise en œuvre de la procédure de réponse graduée*, La Semaine Juridique – Édition Générale (2012), no 19, 966, 969.

1125 HADOPI, *2010 Activity Report* (2011), p. 33. Mireille Imbert-Quaretta/Jean-Yves Monfort/Jean-Baptiste Carpentier, *La contravention de négligence caractérisée à la lumière de la mise en œuvre de la procédure de réponse graduée,* La Semaine Juridique – Édition Générale (2012), no 19, 966, 969.

1126 HADOPI, *2010 Activity Report* (2011), p. 33.

itself does not impose the installation of a specific security means upon Internet access subscribers. Although HADOPI specifies security means in its warning letters, the law does not require the implementation of a security means approved by HADOPI. It is up to the Internet access holder to decide which method is appropriate to secure his connection.[1127]

In this regard, HADOPI concludes that a subscriber that decides to lock down his computer to stop people in his household from committing copyright infringements, implements an appropriate security means.[1128] However, this can only be an appropriate means if the subscriber does not run an unsecured Wi-Fi router to which third parties may connect. It has been suggested that where a subscriber allows a third party to use his access, he will have to change the password following misuse by the third party in order to comply with the obligation to have his access secured.[1129]

If the public prosecutor decides to bring charges against a subscriber, he can decide whether the case will be dealt with in simplified proceedings before a single judge or in standard criminal proceedings.[1130] Article 335-7-2 *CPI* sets forth that when considering the suspension of an Internet access, the court must take into account the circumstances and seriousness of the violation, the personality of the infringer including his professional and social activites and his economic situation.[1131] The duration of the imposed suspension has to reflect a balancing of the fundamental rights

---

1127 Mireille Imbert-Quaretta/Jean-Yves Monfort/Jean-Baptiste Carpentier, *La contravention de négligence caractérisée à la lumière de la mise en œuvre de la procédure de réponse graduée*, La Semaine Juridique – Édition Générale (2012), no 19, 966, 969.

1128 HADOPI, *2010 Activity Report* (2011), p. 33. A further not very helpful suggestion by the Rights Protection Commission was the statement that the only effective security means for someone that has committed a first infringement is to stop downloading. See Mireille Imbert-Quaretta/Jean-Yves Monfort/Jean-Baptiste Carpentier, *La contravention de négligence caractérisée à la lumière de la mise en œuvre de la procédure de réponse graduée*, La Semaine Juridique – Édition Générale (2012), no 19, 966, 969.

1129 Mireille Imbert-Quaretta/Jean-Yves Monfort/Jean-Baptiste Carpentier, *La contravention de négligence caractérisée à la lumière de la mise en œuvre de la procédure de réponse graduée*, La Semaine Juridique – Édition Générale (2012), no 19, 966, 969.

1130 Article 495 para. II No. 12 *CPP*. Alain Stowel, *The "Graduated Response" in France*, in: Irini Stamatoudi, *Copyright enforcement and the Internet*, p. 147, 150.

1131 Article L.335-7-2 *CPI*.

concerned, notably the protection of the respective intellectual property rights and the right of the subscriber to freedom of expression and communication, in particular in his home.[1132]

The HADOPI laws do not distinguish between natural and legal persons.[1133] Accordingly, not only natural persons face a disconnection of their Internet connection but also legal persons. However, as regards the latter a suspension would, in most cases, disproportionately affect their business, and is thus, unlikely to be imposed.

If the court imposes the suspension of an Internet access, the convicted subscriber will be prohibited from entering into a contract with another Internet access provider for the stipulated period.[1134] The Internet access suspension does not affect the subscriber's obligation to pay his subscription fees.[1135] If he has a "multiple play" subscription, meaning bundled TV, Internet and phone access, the suspension sanction only applies to the Internet access.[1136] If the public prosecutor has seized the standard criminal court, this court will also be competent to rule on damages that the copyright holder may claim.[1137]

Within the criminal proceedings and irrespective whether the subscriber is charged with direct infringement or failure to secure his Internet access, it needs to be established whether an infringement has been committed from the subscriber's Internet access. The existence of material facts of illegal downloading does not necessarily imply an infringement. The Internet access holder may invoke force majeure or authorisation by law as justification.[1138] Thus, the subscriber may claim that he had a legitimate reason to breach his monitoring duty and shall be exempted from criminal

---

1132 *Ibid.*

1133 However, Article 131-38 *Code Penal* foresees that fines are five times higher for legal persons. Accordingly, the maximum fine for legal persons in case of the negligence offence will be EUR 7,500.

1134 Article L. 335-7-1 *CPI* sets forth that entering into a contract with another Internet access provider constitutes an offense.The subscriber faces a fine of up to EUR 3,750.

1135 Article 335-7 *CPI.*

1136 Alain Stowel, *The "Graduated Response" in France,* in: Irini Stamatoudi, *Copyright enforcement and the Internet,* p. 147, 151.

1137 *Ibid.*

1138 Mireille Imbert-Quaretta/Jean-Yves Monfort/Jean-Baptiste Carpentier, *La contravention de négligence caractérisée à la lumière de la mise en œuvre de la procédure de réponse graduée*, La Semaine Juridique – Édition Générale (2012), no 19, 966, 970.

liability.[1139] If the subscriber is only accused for non-compliance with his obligation to monitor and secure his Internet access, it does not make a difference whether he can prove that he himself did not commit the offence, because liability results solely from the failure to secure his Internet access. An accusation for the gross negligence offence does at no point suggest that the subscriber has committed a copyright infringement himself. Hence, he will have to prove that he had legitimate reason for not implementing security mechanisms.

The procedure, as it stands, means that before any decision will be rendered by a court, the case will be assessed two times outside of the court: once, when the Rights Protection Commission makes its decision whether to forward a *dossier* to the public prosecutor; once more, when the public prosecutor decides whether to bring charges against a subscriber.

If a subscriber is convicted, he will also have a right to appeal the decision.[1140]

d) The Status quo

The graduated response scheme was expected to lead to a significant reduction in unauthorised file-sharing by its two-fold approach of education and sanctions following two warnings. In the following section, an analysis of HADOPI's statistics on the graduated response scheme will show that at least the mere existence of the graduated response scheme does not lead to a reduction in the numbers of first time infringers. Also, what can be seen is that the actual risk of being taken to court is rather low. In the subsequent section the cost-benefit relation of HADOPI as well as the public perception of the graduated response scheme will be briefly discussed before we look at the future of the HADOPI laws.

aa) The Graduated Response Scheme in Numbers

The graduated response scheme entered into force in 2010, and in August 2010, HADOPI received the first actionable claims from rights-hold-

---

1139 *Ibid.*

1140 See Alain Stowel, *The "Graduated Response" in France, in: Irini Stamatoudi, Copyright enforcement and the Internet,* pp. 147, 151.

ers.[1141] In September 2010, the first requests for identification were sent to an Internet access provider.[1142] In October 2010, for the first time, warnings were sent to Internet subscribers by email.[1143] It took a further four months until in February 2011 the second stage of warnings was initiated for the first time.[1144] While the first court decisions were expected to be rendered in 2011, it took much longer than anticipated for the first case to be brought before court: in September 2012, the first subscriber was convicted on the basis of the HADOPI laws.[1145] The first suspension of an Internet access was ordered by a court in Seine-Saint-Denis in May 2013 for the failure to secure an Internet access.[1146] In addition to an Internet suspension of 15 days, the subscriber was fined EUR 600. The Court refrained however from imposing a total Internet ban on the subscriber and ordered instead that – irrespective of the sanction – the subscriber shall be granted access to email, messenger and VoIP services.[1147]

That the first judgements were rendered relatively late came as a surprise, considering that until the end of 2011 alone more than 824,000 first warnings and more than 68,000 second warnings had been sent out.[1148] In 114 cases, a *délibération* had been issued.[1149] If one looks at the recent statistics by HADOPI, there is even an upward trend as regards the warnings: In 2013, in average 84,000 first warnings and more than 11,000 sec-

1141 HADOPI, *2010 Activity Report* (2011), p. 11.

1142 *Ibid.*

1143 *Ibid.*

1144 *Ibid.*

1145 AFP, *HADOPI : Première condamnation d'un internaute*, Libération (13.09.2012). The subscriber argued that he did not possess the required technological knowledge to download files from the Internet. Although his living-in partner confessed the unauthorised download of two Rihanna songs, the subscriber was fined EUR 150. The basis for his conviction, was the failure to secure his Internet connection. Pascal Lainé, *Belfortain poursuivi pour téléchargement illégal : EUR 150 d'amende*, Le Pays (13/09/2012).

1146 Marc Rees, *Hadopi : EUR 600 d'amende et quinze jours de suspension pour un abonné*, PC Inpact (12.06.2013). This suspension was also the one and only suspension imposed upon a subscriber for the offence of gross negligence, see below.

1147 As reported by the PC magazine PC Inpact, see *ibid.*

1148 The statistics are updated by HADOPI on a monthly basis and can be accessed via http://www.hadopi.fr/actualites/reponse-graduee/chiffres-cles.

1149 *Ibid.*

ond warnings were issued per month.[1150] October 2013 topped all previous months with 138,000 first warnings, and two years on, in June 2015 an all-time high was reached with 231,000 first warnings been sent out.[1151] In total, until July 2015, almost 4.9 million first warnings have been sent out.[1152] In the light of these numbers, one might expect an increase in cases being filed to court, but the increase in warnings is not reflected in the reports forwarded to the public prosecutor's office. According to HADOPI's annual report 2013, only 51 *dossiers* have been transferred to public prosecution, although 663 *délibérations* had been issued.[1153] Thus, in almost 9 out of 10 cases, the Rights Protection Commission decided against forwarding the case.[1154] These decisions were not just influenced by the submissions by the subscribers, and the efforts they took to prevent that further infringements are committed via their connection during the whole warning procedure.[1155] Often, the motivation for referring only such a small number of cases to the public prosecution was the absence of further infringements following the *délibération*.[1156] In practice, the Commission only forwards a report to the public prosecutor when a new infringement took place within one year following the *délibération*. Hence, one may speak of a "fourth phase" within the three strikes procedure that has recently developed in practice.[1157] One can assume that the Rights Protection Commission only forwarded such cases where they were convinced that the subscriber would be convicted. All eleven court decisions that have been rendered until June 2013, resulted in a guilty verdict.[1158] The decisions were of a diverse nature, but all concerned the gross negligence

1150 HADOPI, *Réponse graduée – Les chiffres clés* (06.11.2013). Monthly updated statistics are available at http://www.hadopi.fr/actualites/reponse-graduee/chiffres-cles.

1151 HADOPI, *Réponse graduée – Les chiffres clés* (30.05.2015). Monthly updated statistics are available at http://www.hadopi.fr/actualites/reponse-graduee/chiffres-cles.

1152 *Ibid.*

1153 HADOPI, *Rapport Annuel 2012/2013* (2013), p.9. The Report was published in October 2013.

1154 *Ibid.*

1155 *Ibid.*

1156 *Ibid.*

1157 *Ibid.* One reason for this are the findings of the Lescure Rapport which will discussed below.

1158 HADOPI, *Rapport Annuel 2012/2013* (2013), p. 9.

offence, i.e. a breach of the obligation to secure one´s Internet access.[1159] The sanctions imposed varied from a warning to a fine of between EUR 50 and EUR 600, and in one case an Internet access suspension of 15 days was imposed. [1160] Until now, no case has become public in which – following the initiation of the graduated response procedure – a subscriber was accused of wilful copyright infringement by the public prosecutor upon receipt of a *dossier* from HADOPI. Both, the Rights Protection Commission and the public prosecutors took advantage of the wide margin of appreciation granted to them, and only pursued few carefully selected cases.

bb) The Unsatisfying Results of HADOPI

The first court decision in application of the HADOPI laws was eagerly anticipated by the public, even outside France.[1161]

As mentioned above, it took much longer than expected until the first decisions were rendered. In fact, in 2012, only three decisions were rendered by criminal courts.[1162] In the first case, a fine was imposed upon a subscriber, in the second case a warning was issued by the criminal court, and in the third 2012 case the alleged infringer was pronounced not guilty.[1163]

No subscriber has yet been faced with the threat of having his Internet connection suspended for up to one year as prescribed by Article 335-7 *CPI*. It is rather likely that the public prosecutor will bring charges for gross negligence, i.e. failure to implement adequate security measures.

1159 *Ibid.*

1160 *Ibid*, p. 10.

1161 Sébastien Thévenet, *Hadopi: Un Premier Internaute Condamné*, Le Figaro (13.09.2012); AFP, *Hadopi: Première Condamnation d'un Internaute*, Libération (13.09.2012); Thomas Pany, *Beginnt jetzt die Sanktionsphase von Hadopi?*, heise.de blogs (05.07.2011); Henning Steier, *Ersten Piraten Drohen Netzsperren*, Neue Züricher Zeitung (07.10.2011); Valéry Marchive, *Three years and millions of euros later, Hadopi has its first conviction. Now what?*, ZDnet (30.10.2012); Kimber Streams, *France's Controversial Hadopi Piracy Law Nets its First Conviction, a Man Who Says He Didn't Do It*, The Verge (14.09.2012).

1162 Assemblée Nationale, Réponse à la Question écrite No. 3096, Journal Officiel de la Republique Francaise of 25.12.2012, 7918.

1163 *Ibid.*

The reason for this is obvious: the evidence collected by HADOPI only suffices to prove that an infringement has been committed via a particular Internet access. The reason for this has been outlined in the introduction, namely, that with per-to-peer file-sharing, the identifiable is regularly only the IP address.

As has been outlined in the first Chapter, an IP address does not provide evidence about the identity of the actual infringer. Although further investigations may be conducted as to the identity of an infringer, these do not necessarily provide further information, when for instance computers are shared within a household, or no device with the files in question can be obtained. The offence of gross negligent failure to implement security measures is far easier to be fullfilled. This legal concept, which has been introduced by the HADOPI laws, establishes liability irrespective of the identity of the actual copyright infringer. In any case will the subscriber at least have received a registered letter informing him about infringements taking place from his access; the offence is committed if nevertheless another infringement takes place in the consecutive year. In that context the failure to secure a connection does not only apply to technical measures but also the mere prevention of copyright infringement committed by third parties, which are authorised by the subscriber to use the connection.

Whereas the HADOPI has sent more than two million messages to Internet users carrying out illegal downloading since October 2010, the sanction of Internet access suspension has only been applied once: on 3 June 2013, the magistrates court in Montreuil convicted a subscriber for failing to secure access to an on-line communication service without legitimate reason (covered and punished by Articles R. 335-5, L. 335-7-1(2), L. 331-25, and L. 335-7-1(1) and (3) of the *CPI*).[1164] In absence, the subscriber was fined EUR 600 as the principal penalty, while his Internet access was suspended for 15 days as an additional penalty.

With few convictions and few cases pending, one might assume that the French graduate response scheme is a success story. This assumption is supported by the director of HADOPI, who argues that the small number

1164 TP Montreuil, Decision of 03.06.2013, parquet no12053081381, accessible via http://www.alain-bensoussan.com/ hadopi-condamnation-pour-absence-securisation-acces/2013/06/26/.

of convictions proves the success of the scheme.[1165] Figures presented by HADOPI in its first full report in 2012 suggest that illegal downloading is significantly on the decline in France.[1166] The sources cited by HADOPI found a decline in audiences of websites offering links to peer-to-peer files and applications by 17%, as well as a 29% drop in audience to the ecosystems developed around certain peer-to-peer clients in 2011.[1167] Furthermore, figures suggest an overall drop of at least 43% in illegal file-sharing via peer-to-peer technology in 2011.[1168] A study cited by HADOPI reported a decrease of approximately 66% in the illegal sharing of films on peer-to-peer networks.[1169] In addition, HADOPI found that there was no evidence that users transferred to streaming and direct download services.[1170]

However, at the same time, sales figures in the music industry are still on decline. The first quarter results for 2013 by the Syndicat National de l'édition Phonographique (SNEP), an industry anti-piracy group, show no halt to the slide in music sales. In the first quarter of 2013, the wholesale market for recorded music in France was worth 107.9 million euros in France, down 6.7% on the same period last year. [1171] Overall in 2012, sales fell by 4.4%.[1172] This trend has been continuing in 2013 with physical sales (CDs etc.) going down by 7.3% and for the first time also digital sales (iTunes etc.) were affected (-5.2%).[1173]

1165 Guénaël Pépin, La Hadopi défend le bilan de la réponse graduée, Le Monde (05.09.2012).

1166 HADOPI, *HADOPI – 1 ½ year after the launch* (March 2012), p.4.

1167 *Ibid.*

1168 *Ibid*, p. 5.

1169 *Ibid*, p. 6.

1170 *Ibid*, p. 7.

1171 Syndicat National de l'édition Phonographique (SNEP), *Presentation des Resultats du 1er semestre 2013* (18.09.2013).

1172 Syndicat National de l'Edition Phonographique, *Bilan Economique 2012* (2013), p. 2.

1173 Syndicat National de l'édition Phonographique (SNEP), *Presentation des Resultats du 1er semestre 2013* (18.09.2013). Previously, an Event Study suggested that the HADOPI laws have positively influenced the sales figures of iTunes in France. See Brett Danaher/Michael D. Smith/Rahul Telang/Siwen Chen, *The effect of graduated response anti-piracy laws on music sales: Evidence from an Event Study in France* (2012).

Considering that the annual costs for administering HADOPI are 12 million Euros,[1174] the new French Minister of Culture and Communication, Aurélie Filippetti stated that "12 million Euros are too much for sending out 1 million emails".[1175] According to the newly elected French government, HADOPI has also failed its primary and key mission, namely the promotion of services that respect intellectual property rights as well as the responsible use of intellectual property. Hence, in August 2012, Fillippetti announced as a preliminary measure a budget cut for HADOPI.[1176] Fillippetti also repeatedly declared that she does not support the graduated response scheme because she considers the sanction of Internet suspension to be disproportionate and a threat to the freedom of communication. Also based on her initiative, a review of the *Loi HADOPI II* was launched under the auspices of Pierre Lescure[1177]. The aim of this initiative has been obvious: an abolishment of HADOPI and potentially the abrogation of the graduated response scheme. An abrogation of the latter had already been promised by President François Hollande during his election campaign.[1178] It came thus as no surprise when Hollande declared in July 2012, that the outcome of the consultation on the *Loi HADOPI II* should be a new legal framework in the first half of 2013.[1179] In May 2013, the final report of the consultation, the so-called Lescure Rapport was published.[1180] The report affirms previous expectations[1181]: HADOPI will be abolished. However, this does not imply the end of the graduated response scheme, only the end of the High Authority has been sealed.

1174 Lemonde.fr, Le budget de la Hadopi passe à 8 millions d'euros, Le Monde (03.10.2012).

1175 Boris Manenti, *Aurélie Filippetti : « Je vais réduire les crédits de l'Hadopi »,* Le nouvel Observateur (01.08.2012).

1176 *Ibid.*

1177 Pierre Lescure is the former president of the French TV channel Canal+.

1178 Boris Manenti, *L'abrogation de l'Hadopi est en marche*, Le nouvel Observateur (03.07.2012).

1179 *Ibid.*

1180 Pierre Lescure, *Culture-acte 2, Mission « Acte II de l'exception culturelle », Contribution aux politiques culturelles à l'ére numérique* (May 2013).

1181 See for instance Leparisien.fr, *Téléchargement illégal: Fleur Pellerin confirme qu'HADOPI va disparaître, Le Parisien* (24.05.2013).

e) A Sustainable Model Regime? The Order of 8 July 2013 and the Lescure Rapport

As mentioned above, the Lescure Rapport recommended the liquidation of HADOPI. The tasks of HADOPI will in the future be executed by the regulatory body for audiovisual services, the Conseil supérieur de l'audiovisuel (CSA).[1182] As Lescure considers the deterrent and educational effect of the warning scheme as proven, he explicitly recommends the adherence of the graduated response scheme.[1183] However, Lescure recommended several changes not only in the administration of the warning scheme but also the scheme as such.

First of all, he demands the abolition of the Internet suspension sanction for the gross negligence offence. This means, that while the Internet suspension order of June 2013 imposed by the Montreuil court has been the first suspension order for the gross negligence offence, it has also been the last. Less than two months following the publication of the Lescure Rapport, a Decree implements Lescure's recommendation: Article 2 of the Decree of 8 July 2013[1184] repeals the provision of the Code de la propriété intellectuelle that allows a court to temporary suspend a person's Internet access for up to one month where such person had failed to secure his Internet access adequately. Accordingly, it is now only possible to issue a fine in the fifth category (EUR 1,500) in the event of an Internet user showing gross negligence by failing to secure his Internet access.[1185] The Decree of 8 July 2013 does however not affect a court's power to order an Internet suspension for up to one year as a complementary penalty for the actual infringer. Thus, the sanction remains available if a person is con-

---

1182 Pierre Lescure, *Culture-acte 2, Mission « Acte II de l'exception culturelle », Contribution aux politiques culturelles à l'ére numérique* (May 2013), p. 381.

1183 *Ibid*, pp. 32 et seq. and pp. 379 et seq.

1184 *Décret no 2013-596 du 08.07.2013 supprimant la peine contraventionnelle complémentaire de suspension de l'accès à un service de communication au public en ligne et relatif aux modalités de transmission des informations prévue à l'article L. 331-21 du code de la propriété intellectuelle.*

1185 A sanction of one year's suspension may nevertheless still be imposed, as an additional penalty, on anyone prosecuted for infringing copyright, punishable by three years' imprisonment and a fine of up to EUR 300,000 under Article L. 335-7 of the *CPI*. The continuing existence of the sanction will have practically no effect, as it is not forseeable that courts will – due to lacking evidence – convict subscribers for having committed the copyright infringement themselves.

victed under the traditional copyright infringement provision (Article L 335-7 *CPI*).

The Decree of 9 July 2013 as such is already part of much wider reforms that may possibly include a future incorporation of HADOPI into the CSA.[1186] The CSA then may also be assigned further tasks such as combatting "commercial sites carrying out illegal downloading and providing the public with access to files which may or may not be protected by copyright".[1187]

The first legislative measure taken in relation to the graduated response scheme as such, does not go as far as requested by Lescure. Lescure does not only recommend the abrogation of the sanction of Internet suspension but also demands a decriminalisation of the gross negligence offence. Instead of criminally sanctioning the failure to secure an Internet connection, and the lack of diligence in installing a security mechanism, the repeated use of a certain Internet access for copyright infringements shall constitute an administrative offence.[1188] Accordingly, a third warning shall not result in charges being brought against the offender, but allow the imposition of an administrative fine of EUR 60.[1189] The amount of EUR 60 was assumed to correspond to an annual subscription fee for an online music streaming service or 12 movies on a video-on-demand service.[1190] It remains to be seen whether a fine of EUR 60 will have a dissuasive effect at all. One may argue that potential file-shares may be tempted to do a simple cost-benefit calculation in ignorance that a conviction for copyright infringement still carries higher sanctions and a possible Internet suspension. Lescure obviously departs from penalising subscriber

---

1186 Cf. Amélie Blocman, *Illegal Downloading: Penalty of Refusing Internet Access Abolished,* IRIS 2013-8:1/16. However, in February 2015 the French culture minister announced that an incorporation of HADOPI into the CSA has no priority in French anti-piracy politics, see Guillaume Champeau, *Le transfert HADOPI > CSA n'est "plus l'axe prioritaire",* Numerama.com (19.02.2015).

1187 Amélie Blocman, *Illegal Downloading: Penalty of Refusing Internet Access Abolished,* IRIS 2013-8:1/16 quoting Aurélie Filippetti.

1188 Pierre Lescure, *Culture-acte 2, Mission « Acte II de l'exception culturelle », Contribution aux politiques culturelles à l'ére numérique* (May 2013), pp. 380 et seq. The report emphasises that under the condition that the behaviour only constitutes an administrative offence, the subscriber will not face being entered into criminal records.

1189 *Ibid*, p. 381.

1190 *Ibid.*

that cannot be convicted for copyright infringements and relies on the persuasive effect of warnings. Only in case of repeat infringements following the third warning, the fine of EUR 60 may be increased.[1191] This also constitutes a fundamental change in comparison to the existing system: under the latter, the warning mechanisms would start from a new following a conviction. Further the CSA shall be competent to adapt the number of warnings to the number of downloads and the good faith *("bonne foi")* of the subscriber, meaning that a third warning will not necessarily imply a sanction.[1192] During the administrative-fine proceedings the subscriber shall be heard and he will be able to recourse to the administrative courts.[1193] Within the CSA there shall be a strict segregation between the department in charge of the warnings and the department in charge of the fines. For transparency reasons all imposed sanction will be published in an anonymised manner.[1194]

A press release by the French Ministry of Culture and Communication complementing the Decree of 8 July 2013 confirms, that the future fight against online copyright infringement will focus on the fight against commercial online piracy.[1195] This will also encompass further measures educating the public and enhancing people's awareness towards copyright law and the consequences of infringements as foreseen in the Lescure Rapport. In the light of research conducted by or on behalf of HADOPI, Lescure concluded that still a large number of Internet users is not able to determine whether an online content is legal or illegal.[1196] For instance, in a HADOPI study, 52% of Internet users stated that they assume, that creative content for which they need to pay is in any case legal.[1197] Ignorance of the existence and scope of intellectual property rights still is a

---

1191 *Ibid.*

1192 *Ibid.*

1193 *Ibid.*

1194 *Ibid.*

1195 Ministère de la Culture et de la Communication, *Publication du décret supprimant la peine complémentaire de la suspension d'accès á Internet,* Press release (09.07.2013).

1196 Pierre Lescure, *Culture-acte 2, Mission « Acte II de l'exception culturelle », Contribution aux politiques culturelles à l'ére numérique* (May 2013), p. 383.

1197 HADOPI, *Biens culturels et usages d'Internet : pratiques et perceptions des internautes français* (January 2013), p. 17.

widespread phenomenon, and requires equally widespread educational measures.[1198]

In order to curtail commercial online piracy, the Lescure Rapport asks for cooperation by the intermediaries. As a first step, providers of search engines and social networks shall adapt code of conducts, and obligate themselves therein to delist copyright infringing content from their search results.[1199] Furthermore, payment service providers shall adapt a code of conduct, by which they obligate themselves to include the fight against intellectual property rights infringements into their terms and conditions, and implement measures that are suitable to take action against violations of their terms and conditions.[1200] Although the adaption of these codes of conducts shall be entirely voluntarily, the suggestion of these shows a change in attitude from sanctioning consumers to seeking cooperation of intermediaries to fight those benefiting financially from copyright infringements. However, the Lescure's suggestions do not stop here. Lescure clearly states in his report that he also considers the blocking of content as an effective remedy to put an end to copyright infringements.[1201] In how far such blocking requires law reforms and how much it already takes place in France will be dealt with in the third Chapter.

Following the Lescure Rapport it seemed that the days of the previously outlined graduated response scheme are numbered. However, latest statistics of June 2015 show that there has even been an increase in warning letters being sent out, with a record breaking number of first warnings in June 2015 (i.e. 231,000 first warnings per June).[1202] In the same month, 21,400 second warnings and 104 *delibérations* were issued.[1203] Surprisingly, the number of court cases remains low, only sporadically cases become public. It seems that recently right-holders are making increased use of HADOPI and the graduated response system to strengthen their position as to the necessity of a strong enforcement tool in view of upcom-

---

1198 *Ibid*, p. 383.

1199 *Ibid*, p. 411.

1200 *Ibid*, p. 417.

1201 *Ibid*, pp. 419 et seq. He also suggests a tax on smartphones, tablets and other Internet-linked devices to help fund the production of French art, films and music.

1202 HADOPI, *Réponse graduée – Les chiffres clés* (30.05.2015). Monthly updated statistics are available at http://www.hadopi.fr/actualites/reponse-graduee/chiffres-cles.

1203 *Ibid*.

ing law reforms in summer 2015. In the light of the number of warnings and their limited impact on file-sharing activities of the public, action in terms of legislative reforms are certain while the future of the graduate response system is questionable.

2. UK: The Graduated Response Scheme of the DEA 2010

The *Digital Economy Act 2010* imposes new obligations on Internet service providers to cooperate in an attempt to reduce copyright infringements and send out notifications to their subscribers following receipt of reports of copyright infringements from copyright holders. They must also record the number of reports made against their subscribers and provide copyright holders on request with an anonymised list which enables the rights-holders to see which of the reports it has made are linked to the same subscriber. The *DEA 2010* is the result of the Digital Britain report of 2009[1204] and entered into force in June 2010. However, disputes regarding the implementation of the obligations under the Act mean that the actual employment of the warning procedure has not taken place yet. Already during the legislative proceedings, the Act was highly disputed.[1205]

Although, practically, the warning scheme of the *DEA 2010* is not being employed yet, it is of particular interest to see how one could administer a warning scheme without relying on a central authority like in France. Hence, the following will go into detail where the schemes depart from each other and only briefly address common features.

1204 Department for Culture, Media and Sport and Department for Business, Innovation and Skills, *Digital Britain Report* (2009), p. 111.

1205 Siehe Dinusha Mendis, *Digital Economy Act 2010: fighting a losing battle? Why the 'three strikes' law is not the answer to copyright law's latest challenge,* International Review of Law, Computers & Technology 2013, 60 with further references; Struan Robertson, *The Legislative Farce of the Digital Economy Bill,* out-law.com (07.04.2010).

a) Copyright Enforcement in the UK in General

aa) The Origins of Copyright in the UK

Copyright is primarily a statutory right, there is no copyright at common law in published works.[1206] The first formal legal recognition of copyright of authors can be found in the *Copyright Act of 1709*, also referred to as *Statute* or *Act of Anne.*[1207] The Act created a single regime for application in both Scotland and England and gave the "sole right and liberty of printing books" to the authors of the books and not the printers. The Act also enabled authors to transfer his rights to third parties ("assigns"), typically printers. Since the 18th century, copyright primarily developed by statute with further acts being passed that extended protection in terms of inter alia time and scope of artistic works.

The UK implemented the *Berne Convention* in the *Copyright Act 1911* which also replaced previous copyright statutes as well as the common law copyright in unpublished works. Following the *Copyright Act 1956*, intellectual property is now protected by the *Copyright, Designs and Patents Act 1988* (*CDPA 1988*). The *CDPA 1988* removed the previous distinction between "works" (literary, dramatic, musical or artistic works) and "subject matter" (sound recordings films, broadcasts, cable programmes and typographical arrangements). It now forms the basis of contemporary copyright law and has been amended several times, mostly by European Directives. The Directives were generally implemented by way of regulations.

1206 The court of Session (*Hinton v Donaldson*, 1772 Mor 8307) and the House of Lords (*Donaldson v Beckett* [1774] 2 Bro PC 129) held that no copyright exists under common law in works which had been published and enjoyed copyright under the *Copyright Act of 1709*. Copyright at common law however existed with regard to unpublished works and remained significant until the beginning of the 20th century.

1207 After Queen Anne, who reigned from 1702 to 1714, the Act entered into force in 1710.

bb) The Fair Dealing Exception

Chapter III of the *CDPA 1988* detail several exceptions to copyright infringement.[1208] These exceptions are typically non-commercial and not-for-profit in nature, although they are possibly carried out by commercial entities. [1209] There is no private copying exemption as foreseen in the French Code de la propriété intellectuelle.[1210] Of the various permitted acts of Chapter III of the *CDPA 1988*, the most well-known is the fair dealing defence.[1211] In that respect, the fair dealing defence most likely to be invoked by users, is the copying for the purposes of research or private study of section 29(1). Private research or study does not require an academic context.[1212] However, the defence applies only where the dealing takes place with literary, dramatic, musical, and artistic works, as well as to the typographical formats of published works.[1213] It does not apply to broadcasts, cable programme, sound recordings, or film.[1214] Hence, even for private research or study the reproduction of films or sound recordings would not be permissible.

cc) Enforcement of IP Rights upon Initiative of the Rights-Holder

The legislative regime that existed prior to the *DEA 2010* provided (and still provides) civil and criminal penalties for copyright infringements.

1208 These exceptions have recently been described as striking a balance between the rights of copyright owners and the benefits of wider use of intellectual property. See Proudman J in High Court, *Newspaper Licensing Agency and Others v Meltwater BV and Others* (2010) EWHC 3099 (Ch), para. 115.

1209 Cf. Antony W. Dnes, *Should the UK Move to a Fair-Use Copyright Exception*, International Review of Intellectual Property and Competition Law 2013, 418, 424.

1210 As regards the controversy on private copying in the UK, see Ian J. Lloyd, *Information Technology Law* (6th ed. 2011), pp. 380 et seq.

1211 The fair dealing defences can be found in sections 29 and 30 of the *CDPA*: research and private study excluding broadcasts and sound recordings (Section 29(1)), criticism and review and news reporting (Section 30(1)) and news reporting of current affairs (Section 30(2)).

1212 Lionel Bentley/Brad Sherman, *Intellectual Property Law* (2001), p. 199.

1213 See *ibid.* As regards the requirement that the dealing must be fair, see pp. 195 and 200.

1214 See High Court, Pro Sieben Media v Carlton UK Television [1997] EMLR 509.

However, there were no particular provisions targeting file-sharing as such, or addressing the prevention of copyright infringements on the Internet.

Under existing law, a user who downloads a file from a peer-to-peer platform performs the infringing act of copying by electronic means under section 16(1)(a) of the *CDPA 1988*.[1215] A user who uploads a file performs the restricting act of "communicating the work to the public" under section 16(1)(d) *CDPA 1988*, because communication to the public includes making the work available by electronic transmission under section 20(2)(b) of the Act. In that respect, Collins J held in Polydor v Brown that "connecting a computer to the Internet, where the computer is running P2P software, and in which music files containing copies of the claimant's copyright works are placed in a shared directory falls within the infringing act [under s.16(1)(d)]".[1216]

If rights-holders want to pursue civil claims, they can either press criminal charges[1217] in order to obtain information about the identity of the subscriber of an Internet access that could be connected to copyright infringements, or they can seek information as to the identity of an alleged infringer by way of a Norwich Pharmacal Order.[1218] Identification of an alleged infringer is necessary prior to civil proceedings because UK common law requires there to be an identifiable defendant to a claim. Under UK common law, possessors of information are under a duty to assist a wronged party by disclosing the identity of anonymous actors in certain circumstances.[1219] In relation to costs, the court will usually order the

---

1215 Section 17(2) of the *CDPA* states that copying includes storing the work in any medium and that includes by "electronic means".

1216 High Court, *Polydor Ltd v Brown*, [2005] EWHC 3191 (Ch), (2006) 29(3) IPD 29021, para. 7.

1217 As regards the criminal liability for copyright infringements, see Hector MacQueen/Charlotte Waelde/Graeme Laurie/Abbe Brown, *Contemporary intellectual property, Law and policy* (2nd ed. 2011), p. 253.

1218 The power to make a Norwich Pharmacal order is preserved by Civil Procedures Rules 31.18. This instrument will be discussed in detail below within the analysis of enforcement through private litigation.

1219 Website operators and Internet service providers do not usually voluntarily disclose user details due to contractual confidentiality obligations or due to the fact that such disclosure may be in breach of statutory obligations under UK data protection legislation not to disclose personal data without the consent of the data subject or an order of the court. In *Norwich Pharmacal v Excise Commissioners* (House of Lords, [1974] AC 133, at 175), it was held that even where an

applicant to pay the costs of the party making the disclosure- including the costs of complying with the order, where the respondent was not involved in the unlawful act. The applicant then has to recover those costs in the main proceedings against the wrong-doer.[1220]

Hence, even prior legislative action to strengthen copyright enforcement on the Internet, the law provided mechanisms for rights-holders to seek redress even if they had no more information than the data logged in connection with an infringement.

However, these tools, in particular the Norwich Pharmacal Order to obtain data, was apparently considered as not efficient enough, so that further enforcement mechanisms were sought after. The Secretary of State for Business, Innovation and Skills stated in that regard, that the fact that rights-holders have to rely on obtaining a Norwich Pharmacal order will require an Internet service provider to reveal the physical address behind an IP address, provided them with no means of identifying the most serious and persistent infringers.[1221] As it cannot be ignored that online copyright infringements are a mass phenomenon, the basic idea of *Digital Economy Act* becomes obvious: sanctioning notorious and mass infringers instead of spending time and money obtaining orders to identify the subscriber of each and every IP address logged in connection with an infringement.

b) Paving the Way for a Future Graduated Response Scheme

UK copyright law has lately seen a number of updates specifically in relation to the digitalisation of copyright materials. Key to the law reforms is obviously the *DEA 2010,* and in specific the graduated response scheme that is still awaiting application and which will be outlined in the follow-

---

"involved" third party incurred no personal liability for the tortious acts of others, it nonetheless had a duty to assist a wronged party by disclosing information that it possesses in order to enable the claimant to identify a wrongdoer, where otherwise he would not have been able to do so.

1220 See Patents Court, *Smith Kline and French Laboratories Ltd v R.D. Harbottle (Mercantile) Ltd* [1980] RPC 363.

1221 See House of Lords and House of Commons, Joint Committee on Human Rights, *Legislative Scrutiny: Digital Economy Bill, 5th Report of session 2009-10*, HL Paper 44 = HC 327, p. 32.

ing. In contrast to France, the foreseen UK graduated response scheme does not require a change in copyright law as such.[1222]

aa) Digital Britain Report

In June 2009, the Government published the *Digital Britain Report* on the future of the digital and communications industries.[1223] The Report followed a number of policy developments related to online copyright enforcement including the *Gowers Review of the UK Intellectual Property Framework* of 2006[1224] and the industry-led *Memorandum of Understanding process to trial subscriber notifications* of 2008[1225].

The *Digital Britain Report* recommended several reforms relating to copyright, such as for example licensing the use of orphan works or extending public lending rights to non-traditional book formats, such as e-books. The Report also addressed the issue of online copyright infringements and made proposals for reducing these.[1226] It estimated that an Act

1222 In France, the graduated response scheme required that the non- or not sufficient securisation of an Internet access is punishable in order to establish responsibility of the subscriber.

1223 Department for Culture, Media and Sport and Department of Business, Innovation and Skills, *Digital Britain, Final Report* (June 2009).

1224 In 2006, the current state of intellectual property law framework was reviewed. In commissioning the Review in 2005, the government wanted to know whether the current system was fit for purpose in an era of globalisation, digitisation and increasing economic specialisation. Against the background of growing importance of IP and of the challenges brought by the changing economic environment, the Gowers Review supported the development of a Best Common Practice document that encouraged cooperation between Internet service providers and rights-holders to change public attitudes and behaviours. However, the Review also noted that if this approach had not proved successful by the end of 2007, the government should consider whether to pass new legislation that provides for an effective and dissuasive system of damages for civil IP cases. Such an effective and dissuasive system would for instance require the matching of penalties in the physical and digital world for IP infringement, which was – as of then – not the case. See Andrew Gowers, *Gowers Review of Intellectual Property* (December 2006), in particular pp. 102 et seq.

1225 Cf. Ofcom, Online infringement of copyright and the Digital Economy Act 2010, Notice of Ofcom's proposal to make by order a code for regulating the initial obligations (26.06.2012).

1226 Department for Culture, Media and Sport and Department of Business, Innovation and Skills, *Digital Britain, Final Report* (June 2009), pp. 111 et seq.

implementing the proposals might lead to a reduction of unlawful file-sharing in the UK by 70 to 80%.[1227] One of the proposals was the passing of legislation to reduce online piracy. The Government was thus consulting on a proposal to legislate to give Ofcom a duty to take steps aimed at reducing copyright infringement. In order to fulfil that duty, it suggests that Ofcom places obligations on Internet service providers to require them to notify alleged infringers of copyright (subject to reasonable levels of proof from rights-holders) that their conduct is unlawful. In addition, Internet service providers shall be obliged to collect anonymised information on serious repeat infringers (derived from their notification activities), to be made available to rights-holders together with personal details on receipt of a court order.[1228] This shall then allow the identification of the minority of serious repeat infringers to allow targeted court action against those responsible for the most damaging breaches of copyright.[1229]

The Report called upon rights-holders and Internet service providers in particular to provide input to a code of practice that would underpin these obligations. The Government held the view that such a notification procedure should significantly reduce file-sharing. However, it also recognises, that if the notification procedure proves to go not far enough, then further action will need to be taken. In that respect, the Report suggests to give Ofcom "the power to specify, by Statutory Instrument, other conditions to be imposed on Internet service providers aimed at preventing, deterring or reducing online copyright infringement, such as ... port blocking, bandwidth capping (capping the speed of a subscriber's Internet connection and/or capping the volume of data traffic which a subscriber can access); bandwidth shaping (limiting the speed of a subscriber's access to selected protocols/services and/or capping the volume of data to selected protocols/services)".[1230]

bb) Digital Economy Act

The government's answer to the *Digital Britain Report* was the controversial Digital Economy Bill, which sought to implement many aspects of the

1227 *Ibid*, p.110.
1228 *Ibid*, pp. 111 et seq.
1229 *Ibid*, p. 111.
1230 *Ibid*, p. 113.

Digital Britain Report.[1231] The subsequent Digital Economy Act was passed by the House of Commons on 7 April 2010 as part of the parliamentary "wash-up" procedure with only 6% of MPs attending the debate that let to its passing. [1232] It then received Royal Assent on the following day.

The provisions of the *DEA 2010* cover a wide range of areas including public service broadcasting, network infrastructure and digital safety. The *DEA 2010* in particular inserts amendments to the *Communications Act 2003 (CA 2003).* Controversial were primarily the provisions relating to online copyright infringement and more specifically measures targeting illegal peer-to-peer file-sharing.

These measures form part of a multi-pronged approach by the Government aimed at reducing online copyright infringement through a complementary mix of enforcement, consumer education and encouragement to industry, to develop and promote online services offering lawful access to copyright works.[1233]

Key to the *DEA 2010* in the context of responses to online copyright infringements are sections 3 to 18 relating to the "online infringement of copyright" and in particular the mass notification system of sections 3 to 8[1234]. Unauthorised file-sharing will be dealt with in a two-stage process:

1231 On the controversy surrounding the Digital Economy Act see the Memorandums submitted to the Joint Committee on Human Rights in House of Lords, House of Commons, Joint Committee on Human Rights, *Legislative Scrutiny: Digital Economy Bill, Fifth Report of Session 2009-10*, HL Paper 44 = HC 327 (05.02.2010), pp. 30 et seq.

1232 The wash-up period refers to the last few days while a Parliament continues to sit after the Prime Minister has announced the date when Parliament will be dissolved so a general election can be held but before Parliament has been formally adjourned, prorogued or dissolved. During this period, the Government attempts to pass unfinished business. Traditionally, Parliamentary bills cannot be carried forward from one session of Parliament to another after a general election. Hence, if a Bill does not receive Royal Assent before Parliament rises, it will be lost, although a new Bill could be reintroduced after the general election. Out of 643 MPs only 40 MPs were present during the Second Reading of the *DEA Bill.* When the Bill was passed 227 MPs were present, of which 189 voted in favour of the Bill. See Parliament, Hansard (House of Commons), Column 1142 (07.04.2010).

1233 See Ofcom, Online infringement of copyright and the Digital Economy Act 2010, Notice of Ofcom's proposal to make by order a code for regulating the initial obligations (26.06.2012).

1234 Sections 3 to 8 *DEA 2010* insert ss. 124A to 124F into the *CA 2003.*

first, access providers will issue notifications to their customers which are suspected to have infringed copyrights; and second, copyright holders will be able to obtain lists of users that have been issued several notifications against whom they can then pursue ordinary civil proceedings. Section 9 *DEA 2010* also foresees that in the future technical sanctions may be imposed on repeat infringers.

Unlike the French HADOPI laws, the *DEA 2010* only provides a framework for the copyright infringement provisions, while the operational details are subject to and specified by a series of regulatory codes produced or to be produced by Ofcom. This means in practice, that while the majority of the *DEA 2010* is in force, the copyright enforcement provisions will not have any impact until the regulatory codes are finalised. Section 3 of the *DEA 2010* (new section 124A *CA 2003*) for example provides that a copyright owner "may make a copyright infringement report to the Internet service provider who provided the Internet access service if a code in force under section 124C or 124D (an "initial obligations code") allows the owner to do so". Equally, the number of reports that a subscriber will have to have reached until he will face any consequences, is left to the Code.

Crucial for the start of sending out notifications are the *Initial Obligations Code* and the *Sharing of Costs Order*, whereas the *Technical Obligations Code* does not have a direct effect on the applicability of the copyright enforcement provisions at this stage. One of the main reasons for the delay in passing the codes is that access providers have fought vigorously against the new enforcement system. The Internet service providers BT and Talk Talk instigated a judicial review of the Act relating to the compatibility of the online copyright infringement provisions of the *DEA 2010* and the *draft Copyright (Initial Obligations) (Sharing of Costs) Order* with EU law.[1235] The applicants argued that the *DEA 2010* infringes users'

1235 The service providers inter alia asked the Court whether the contested provisions were incompatible with the eCommerce Directive 2000/31, the *Data Protection Directive* 95/46, the *E-Privacy Directive 2002/58* and/or the *Authorisation Directive 2002/20*. See High Court, *R. (on the application of British Telecommunications Plc) v Secretary of State for Business, Innovation and Skills*, 2011] EWHC 1021 (Admin), [2011] 3 C.M.L.R. 5, and the appeal Court of Appeal, *R. (on the application of British Telecommunications Plc) v Secretary of State for Business, Innovation and Skills*, [2012] EWCA Civ 232. For an analysis of the High Court decision see also Monica Horten, *The Digital Economy Act in the Dock: A Proportionate Ruling?* Journal of Intellectual Property, Infor-

rights and freedoms and that the statute was rushed through parliament without sufficient scrutiny.[1236] The challenged parts of the Act inserted new sections into the *Communications Act 2003* that imposed "initial obligations" on Internet service providers based on the premise that an "initial obligations code" was in force. These "initial obligations" encompass the obligation of Internet service providers to notify their subscribers of copyright infringement reports received from copyright owners and to provide anonymous records of copyright infringement to copyright owners. Rights-holders, upon obtaining a court order, would then be able to sue those subscribers for copyright infringements. The contested parts of the Act made provision for the approval or making of an initial obligations code and as to the content of such a code, and empowered the secretary of state to specify provisions that had to be included in the code about the costs incurred.

The notification procedure survived the challenge of judicial review with Mr. Justice Kenneth Parker holding that "from the point of view of both copyright owner and subscriber, the DEA represents a more efficient,

---

mation Technology and Electronic Commerce Law 2012, 81–87; Julia Hörnle, *Premature or Stillborn? – The Recent Challenge to the Digital Economy Act*, Computer Law & Security Review 2012, Vol. 28, 83 – 89; Robin Mansell/W. Edward Steinmueller, *Copyright Infringement Online: The Case of the Digital Economy Act Judicial Review in the United Kingdom*, New Media & Society 2013, Vol. 15, 1312 – 1328.

1236 Specifically, the challenged the Act on five grounds: (1) that the provisions of the *DEA 2010* constituted a technical regulation, which according to the *Technical Standards Directive 98/34/EC*, as amended by *Directive 98/48/EC* should have been notified to the European Commission and were therefore unenforceable; (2) that the *DEA 2010* was infringing Articles 3 (country-of-origin principle), 12 (liability exemption for mere conduits) and 15 (no general obligation to monitor) of the *E-Commerce Directive*; (3) that the processing of personal data under the *DEA 2010* was in breach of the *Data Protection Directive* and that the processing did not comply with Articles 6 and 15 of the *E-Privacy Directive*; (4) that the provisions of the *DEA 2010* were contrary to the *Authorisations Directive 2009/140* and in particular Article 12 thereof (which relates to administrative costs); and (5) that the *DEA 2010* infringes free movement of services under Articles 56, 61 and 52 *TEU*, freedom of expression (in particular the right to receive and impart information) and the right to privacy under Articles 7 and 8 *CFR* and Articles 8 and 10 *ECHR*.

focused and fair system than the current arrangements".[1237] The applicants however appealed the decision on the basis that the *DEA 2010* was not consistent with the Technical Standards Directive[1238], the Authorisations Directive[1239], the *E-Commerce Directive* and the *E-Privacy Directive.* They dropped the challenge on proportionality of the graduated response scheme, as the High Court held that the *DEA 2010* could not be considered a disproportionate response to file-sharing prior to the publication of Ofcom's code of practice. The Court of Appeal finally confirmed in March 2012 that the contested provisions were compatible with European law; only the provisions of the *Draft Costs Order* were held to breach Article 12 of the *Authorisations Directive* in respect of "qualifying costs", namely the costs incurred by Ofcom or the appeals body in carrying out assigned tasks under the copyright infringement provisions. These costs could not be imposed on Internet service providers, as they were administrative charges. That being clarified, the legislator could finalise amended drafts for the regulatory codes.

cc) The Regulatory Codes that Accompany the Digital Economy Act

The Digital Economy Act only provides a general framework and depends on more detailed regulatory codes, which have not been passed yet.

(1) Online Infringement of Copyright Initial Obligations Code

The *DEA 2010* inserted amendments to the Communications Act to create two new obligations for Internet service providers, which are referred to as the "initial obligations" and must be set out in a regulatory code. These initial obligations include the notification of subscribers whose IP address has been reported by copyright-holders as being used to infringe copy-

---

1237 High Court, *R. (on the application of British Telecommunications Plc) v Secretary of State for Business, Innovation and Skills,* [2011] EWHC 1021 (Admin), [2011] 3 C.M.L.R. 5, para. 228.

1238 *Technical Standards Directive 98/34/EC as amended by Directive 98/48/EC, OJ 1998 L204 and OJ 1998 L217.*

1239 *Authorisations Directive 2002/20/EC as amended by Directive 2009/140, OJ 2002 L108 and OJ 2009 L337.*

right, and the obligation to keep track of the number of reports about each subscriber, by compiling a list of those subscribers who have been reported on above a threshold to be set out in the *Initial Obligations Code*.

The Online Infringement of Copyright *Initial Obligations Code (Initial Obligations Code)* thus plays a vital role for enforcing the provisions of the *DEA*. The Explanatory Notes to the *DEA 2010* explain that the *Initial Obligations Code* will either be an industry code or will be made by Ofcom. In the absence of an approved code set up and agreed by industry, it fell to Ofcom to draw up a code in accordance with the requirements of the *DEA 2010* provisions.[1240]

While the *DEA 2010* is very precise on how Ofcom should implement many elements of the measures, there is also discretion left in some parts. In order to pay utmost respect to the interests of citizens and consumers, Ofcom opened up a consultation on a first draft published in May 2010.[1241]

The draft Code has been subject to extensive criticism.[1242] The publication of a statement summarising the results of the consultation and a slightly revised draft code has subsequently been delayed due to a number of factors, including the judicial review of the DEA, and the revision by the Government of secondary legislation in relation to the cost sharing arrangements as a result of the judicial review.

Finally, the new draft *Initial Obligations Code* has been published on 26 June 2012.[1243] The key proposals of the original draft remain unchanged. However, the changes that have been made reflect stakeholder responses to the 2010 consultation and instructions given by Government in accordance with the approvals process set out in the DEA.[1244]

1240 Ofcom, *Online infringement of copyright and the Digital Economy Act 2010, Notice of Ofcom's proposal to make by order a code for regulating the initial obligations* (26.06.2012), p. 2.

1241 Ofcom *Consultation Report, Online Infringement of Copyright and the Digital Economy Act 2010: Draft Initial Obligations Code* (28.05.2010).

1242 See Sam de Silva/Faye Weedon, *The Digital Economy Act 2010: Past, present and a future "in limbo"*, Computer and Telecommuncations Law Review 2011, 17(3), 55, 57.

1243 Ofcom, Online infringement of copyright and the Digital Economy Act 2010, Notice of Ofcom's proposal to make by order a code for regulating the initial obligations (26.06.2012), Annex 3.

1244 *Ibid*, p. 3.

The draft Code now sets forth that mass notification obligations only apply to fixed-line Internet service providers with over 400,000 broad-band-enabled lines.[1245] Internet access providers, who do not meet this criterion, for example mobile network operators and providers of Wi-Fi services, are outside the scope of the Code.[1246] Accordingly, only the seven largest Internet service providers (BT, Orange, O2, the Post Office, Sky, Talk Talk and Virgin Media) would be concerned. Internet service providers cannot avoid being considered a qualifying Internet service provider by making changes to their corporate structure; groups of Internet service providers as defined in section 1261 of the *Companies Act 2006* that provide Internet access services to more than 400,000 subscribers will each be a qualifying Internet service provider.[1247] The sole reason for excluding smaller Internet service providers is "that costs of participation would be disproportionately high compared to the expected low reduction in overall levels of online copyright infringement that participation would bring".[1248] If an Internet service provider falls below the qualification threshold, it will remain subject to the initial obligations for the duration of the notification period[1249] to ensure that copyright holders, who have invested in copyright infringement reports can benefit from their investment.[1250]

Further details of the draft *Initial Obligations Code* will be referred to when appropriate in the following.[1251] The subsequent outset of the func-

1245 The 400,000+ line threshold covers 93.5% of the retail broadband market and covers every Internet service provider with significant scale. See *ibid*, p. 36.

1246 *Ibid*, p. 3.

1247 See section 2(1)(b) *Initial Obligations Code* (June 2012).

1248 Ofcom, Online infringement of copyright and the Digital Economy Act 2010, Notice of Ofcom's proposal to make by order a code for regulating the initial obligations (26.06.2012), p. 3.

1249 See section 2(6) *Initial Obligations Code* (June 2012).

1250 Ofcom, Online infringement of copyright and the Digital Economy Act 2010, Notice of Ofcom's proposal to make by order a code for regulating the initial obligations (26.06.2012), p. 4.

1251 The Draft Code sets forth the precise circumstances when and how a notification must be issued and the information which it may contain. In addition, it also outlines the appeal procedures.

tioning of the graduated response scheme under the *DEA 2010* relies on the *Initial Obligations Code* as published on 26 June 2012.[1252]

(2) Online Infringement of Copyright (Initial Obligations) (Sharing of Costs) Order

The *Online Infringement of Copyright (Initial Obligations) (Sharing of Costs) Order 2011* has been published in February 2011 and was subject to the legal review. In order to come into force, the draft order needs approval by resolution of each House of Parliament, and must be notified to the European Commission. The *Sharing of Costs Order* specifies provisions that must be included in the *Initial Obligations Code* about payment by copyright owners and Internet service providers of contributions towards costs incurred under the copyright infringement provisions that will be inserted into the *CA 2003* by the *DEA 2010*. The latest development with regard to secondary legislation to the *DEA 2010* has been the withdrawal of the *Sharing of Costs Order* in February 2013, by the Government, in response to the need to make "technical changes".[1253] Since then, no new draft code has been published, leading to a further delay in implementing the graduated response scheme.

(3) Technical Obligations Code

If the Initial Obligations are not as effective as expected, the next stage foreseen in section 10 *DEA 2010* allows the Secretary of State, to impose technical obligations on Internet service providers, by order, to take certain actions against subscribers who have received a prescribed number of notifications. Technical obligations have the purpose of preventing or reducing online copyright infringements. The measures to be taken are enlisted in section 9 *DEA 2010* and encompass the limitation of speed or other capacity of the service provided, the prevention, or limitation of use,

---

1252 See Ofcom, Online infringement of copyright and the Digital Economy Act 2010, Notice of Ofcom's proposal to make by order a code for regulating the initial obligations (26.06.2012), Annex 3.

1253 See BBC News, UK Piracy Warning Letters Delayed until 2015, BBC News (06.06.2013).

of the service to gain access to particular material such as for instance particular sites, the suspension of Internet service, or other limitations on the service provided.[1254] They will be introduced, when regulators and Parliament feel that the notification system does not have the desired impact. No *Technical Obligations Code* can be made until the *Initial Obligations Code* has been in force for at least 12 months. Hence, as of now, it is too early to predict how exactly a future *Technical Obligations Code* will implement these obligations.

dd) Summary

While the *DEA 2010* has been passed in 2010, the actual application of the graduated response scheme is still in the waiting. The first delay was due to the fierce resistance by Internet access providers who feared that a disproportionate burden was placed upon them. Their challenge of the Act has however only been the starting point for further delays.

With none of the accompanying codes yet in force, the future of the *DEA 2010* at this stage is more than vague.

c) Outline and Functioning of the Graduated Response Scheme

Similar to the French model, the *DEA 2010* foresees a sanction against a subscriber whose Internet access was used three times to commit copyright infringements. Though the basic idea is the same, the two models work fundamentally different. In contrast to the French scheme, there is no central authority administering the notifications of infringements and issues warnings to the users. Instead the Internet access providers play an important role. Consequently, sensitive data, i.e. data in relation to infringements committed by their customers, is stored and processed by private entities. As this will be in the focus on the subsequent legal analysis, the description of the functioning of the UK scheme will only go into detail where the scheme departs from the French scheme.

1254 See Section 9 *DEA 2010*, that inserts section 124G into the *CA 2003*.

aa) The Role of the Ofcom

Although new responsibilities have been imposed upon the Office of Communications (Ofcom) by the *DEA 2010*, Ofcom does not play a central role in the execution and administration of the warning scheme.[1255] Ofcom's role is primarily of a supervisory character and also involves the approving and adopting of codes of practice for the procedure and enforcement of new Internet service provider obligations. In that regard, Ofcom is for instance responsible for passing of an *Initial Obligations Code* that details the graduated response scheme. Ofcom also may take steps to prepare a proposed *Technical Obligations Code.*[1256] Under the *DEA 2010* Ofcom is further tasked with reporting on various communications matters;[1257] for instance new section 124F *CA 2003*[1258] imposes a duty on Ofcom to prepare reports on the extent of infringement of copyright by Internet users.

bb) How the Graduated Response Scheme (should) Work

The *DEA 2010* requires Internet Service Providers to notify subscribers of their alleged illegal file-sharing based on evidence collected by investigatory agents' monitoring software, and to retain Copyright Infringement Lists (CIL) of alleged repeat infringers. While copyright owners can already seek court orders against online infringers, the DEA2010 is designed to enable them to target legal action against the most persistent alleged infringers.

As no *Initial Obligations Code* has entered into force yet, reference will be made to the draft *Initial Obligations Code* of June 2012.

1255 Although Ofcom's role has been described as key (see for instance Rachel Burnett, *The Role of Ofcom*, ITNOW 2010, Vol. 52 Issue 6, 24), this view is slightly exagerated if one compares the role to that of HADOPI.

1256 See section 9 *DEA 2010.*

1257 Sections 1 and 2 *DEA 2010.*

1258 As inserted by section 8 *DEA 2010.*

(1) Gathering of Information of Infringements

Copyright holders gather data relating to IP addresses that they believe have infringed their rights by connecting to peer-to-peer file-sharing networks and downloading their work.

Copyright holders are required to submit their evidence gathering procedures for approval to Ofcom before they can send any reports of apparent copyright infringements to Internet service providers.[1259] Ofcom expects that copyright-holders will be well placed to secure approval from Ofcom if they adopt evidence-gathering procedures that comply with a publicly available specification, which Ofcom is prepared to sponsor.[1260] Provided that the rights-holder wants to pursue the matter, he will have to provide the relevant access provider with a so called copyright infringement report (CIR) within a month of becoming aware of the alleged infringement.[1261] The draft *Initial Obligations Code* clarifies the standard for obtaining evidence of copyright infringements: a copyright-holder may only file a CIR to an access provider if he has gathered evidence in accordance with his approved evidence-gathering procedures "which gives reasonable grounds to believe that (a) a subscriber to an Internet access service has infringed the owner's copyright by means of the service; or (b) has allowed another person to use that service and that person has infringed the owner's copyright by means of that service".[1262] As regards the latter, it has been speculated that this section could apply, for example, to businesses that provide Wi-Fi as a service, as well as to domestic unsecured Wi-Fi networks, and organisations such as for instance universities, hotels or pubs, that provide access to the Internet to their customers.[1263]

The CIR must contain evidence about the infringement that has occurred, and must state the name and address of the copyright owner (or

---

1259 Section 6 *Initial Obligations Code* (June 2012).

1260 Ofcom, Online infringement of copyright and the Digital Economy Act 2010, Notice of Ofcom's proposal to make by order a code for regulating the initial obligations (26.06.2012), p. 4.

1261 Section 3(1)(a)-(b) *DEA 2010* and section 4(4)(a)-(b) *Initial Obligations Code*. The requirement that the CIR must be filed within a month is regulated in section 4(5) *Initial Obligations Code*.

1262 Section 4(4) *Initial Obligations Code* (June 2012). See also new section 124A(2) *CA 2003* inserted by section 3 *DEA 2010*.

1263 Diane Rowland/Uta Kohl/Andrew Charlesworth, *Information Technology Law* (4th ed. 2012), p. 347.

respectively the name and address of the person on whose behalf the copyright owner is authorised to act and evidence of authorisation), an identification of the copyright work,[1264] a statement that there appears to have been a copyright infringement in the respective work, a description of the apparent infringement and the evidence gathered of that apparent infringement,[1265] a statement that the copyright owner has not given consent to the act giving rise to the apparent infringement, the start time, end time and date of the online session during which the evidence was gathered,[1266] the day on which the infringement is believed to have taken place, the IP address associated with the infringement, the relevant port numbers used to commit the infringement as well as the website protocol, application, online location, Internet-based service or system through which the apparent infringement occurred. [1267] Further, the CIR must contain a unique numerical identifier allocated to the CIR by the copyright owner as well as the date and time of issue of the CIR. [1268]

Upon receipt of a CIR, the access provider must identify the subscriber to which the IP address related at the time of the alleged infringement.[1269] Access providers are not required to have their internal subscriber identification processes approved by Ofcom, though failure to comply with the requirement for accurate address matching may constitute a material breach of the *Initial Obligations Code* that triggers a sanction.[1270] Match-

---

1264 This must include the title of the work and a description of the nature of the work (see section 5(c) *Initial Obligations Code* (June 2012)).

1265 The information about the infringement must provide sufficient information to enable the subscriber to identify the means used to obtain evidence of the copyright infringement, cf. section 5(e) *Initial Obligations Code* (June 2012).

1266 As regards the time, the Code requires the use of Coordinated Universal Time, see section 5(g) *Initial Obligations Code* (June 2012).

1267 Section 5 *Initial Obligations Code* (June 2012).

1268 *Ibid.*

1269 Section 8(1) *Initial Obligations Code* (June 2012). Exceptions to this rule exist where for instance the CIR is not complete, the IP address was not allocated to the Internet service provider in question, the Internet service provider does not hold a postal address for a subscriber, or the rights-holder has not paid the Internet service provider notification fees in full for the relevant notification period (cf. section 18 of the draft Code).

1270 Ofcom also argues that it is in their own interest for Internet service providers to ensure that their processes are robust in order to avoid reputational damage. See Ofcom, *Online infringement of copyright and the Digital Economy Act 2010, Notice of Ofcom's proposal to make by order a code for regulating the initial obligations* (26.06.2012), p. 4.

ing an IP address to a subscriber is possible for a period of 12 months, since section 5 of the Data Retention (EC Directive) Regulations 2009 sets forth that communications data has to be retained for 12 months. Pursuant to section 7 of the Regulations, access to retained data may be obtained only "(a) in specific cases, and (b) in circumstances in which disclosure of the data is permitted or required by law". Since the *DEA 2010* foresees the identification of subscribers, it indirectly contains such permission for disclosure of retained data.

(2) The Warnings: Applicant, Content and Proceedings

Once the subscriber has been identified, the access provider must send a written notification to the subscriber provided that it does not hold another current CIR.[1271]

Pursuant to section 11(2) and (16) of the draft *Initial Obligations Code* (June 2012) and new section 124A(6) CA 2013[1272], the notification must contain inter alia a statement that the IP address allocated to the subscriber has been identified in relation to an apparent copyright infringement which needs to be described, that the statement is sent in response to a CIR, information about the CIR as well as the number of CIRs relating to the subscriber which the Internet service provider holds prior to sending the notification.[1273] In addition, the subscriber must be informed about the possibility and conditions of an appeal procedure.[1274] Similar to a notification under the HADOPI laws, the notification shall educate the subscriber about copyright and its purpose including the ability of a rights-holder to bring legal action for damages.[1275] Also, advice shall be given on how to

---

1271 Section 11(1)(b) *Initial Obligations Code* (June 2012).

1272 This section is to be inserted by section 3 *DEA 2010.*

1273 Information about the number of CIRs held is intended to provide more complete information to the subscriber about allegations of infringement that have been made to their Internet service provider and help them assess whether to seek copies of these additional CIRs. See Ofcom, *Online infringement of copyright and the Digital Economy Act 2010, Notice of Ofcom's proposal to make by order a code for regulating the initial obligations* (26.06.2012), p. 5. Section 11(1)(b) *Initial Obligations Code* (June 2012).

1274 Section 16(1)(d) *Initial Obligations Code* (June 2012).The subscriber appeals procedure is set out in Part 8 of the Code.

1275 Section 16(1)(f) *Initial Obligations Code* (June 2012).

lawfully obtain access to copyright works, and inform the subscriber about steps that he can take to protect his Internet access service from unauthorised use.[1276] Furthermore, the subscriber will be informed that the access provider will store information in relation to the CIR no longer than necessary, i.e. twelve months.[1277] Finally, the subscriber will be made aware that further CIRs may lead to the sending of further notifications, and may give rise to a claim before a court by the rights owners.[1278]

It should be noted, that until the rights-holder has paid the fees due to the Internet access provider in full, the access provider is not required to send notifications to its subscribers in relation to a CIR. In contrast, a failure to pay the fees owed to Ofcom does not hinder the processing of CIRs, but as a consequence Ofcom may initiate enforcement action against the rights-holder for recovery of the amount owed.[1279]

All notifications must be submitted in writing and be posted using first class mail.[1280] If a subscriber has been identified again in connection with an infringement within a twelve-month period following the first notification, he will be sent a second notification (so-called "intermediate notification").[1281] If a third apparent infringement is been committed within the 12-month period triggered by the first infringement, a third notification (so-called infringement list notification) will be sent.[1282] A second and third notification will only be send if the previous notification was sent

1276 Section 16(1)(g)-(h) *Initial Obligations Code* (June 2012).

1277 Section 16(1)(j) *Initial Obligations Code* (June 2012).

1278 Section 11(2)(b)-(c) *Initial Obligations Code* (June 2012).

1279 In an earlier consultation of May 2010, Ofcom had suggested that a copyright owner could only participate in the notification scheme if it had paid the fees due to Internet service providers and Ofcom. The draft *Initial Obligations Code* of June 2012 no longer requires an advance payment for the ability to send CIRs to an Internet service provider.

1280 Section 15 *Initial Obligations Code* (June 2012). In an early draft version of the *Initial Obligations Code*, it was foreseen that the first and second notifications could be emailed by the access provider to the subscribers, and that only the third notification should be posted by recorded delivery. The new framework now addresses concerns, that access providers may not always have the relevant email address of their customers. Cf. Ofcom, *Online infringement of copyright and the Digital Economy Act 2010, Notice of Ofcom's proposal to make by order a code for regulating the initial obligations* (26.06.2012), p. 5.

1281 As regards the details see section 12 *Initial Obligations Code* (June 2012).

1282 For details see section 13(1) *Initial Obligations Code* (June 2012). The *Initial Obligations Code* does not outrule the sending of further notifications, see section 14.

more than a month ago.[1283] It seems that this shall allow users to change their behaviour. In addition to the information contained in any first notification, the second warning will also inform the subscriber that if further notifications have to be sent, a CIL, which sets out the CIRs made, by a copyright owner in relation to the subscriber may be provided to that copyright owner by the Internet service provider on request.[1284] The third notification will then state that the subscriber is put on the CIL of repeat infringers. He will remain on the list until 12 months after the date on which the last notification is received.[1285]

CILs are records of the CIR linked to each subscriber along with a record of which copyright owner sent the report.[1286] These lists intend to help the rights-holders to identify notorious and persistent infringers and target litigation against them.[1287] CILs are administered by the relevant Internet access providers. A CIL will never reveal the identity of the relevant subscribers to the copyright owner, instead an anonymised list will be provided upon request to comply with data protection legislation.[1288] CILs can be requested on a monthly basis[1289], but must be limited to a maximum period of twelve months.[1290]

The access provider will only submit those parts of the CIL to a copyright owner, that relate to that specific rights-holder. Hence, the material provided upon request does not include CIRs relating to other copyright

---

1283 Sections 12(1)(b) and 13(1)(b) *Initial Obligations Code* (June 2012).

1284 Section 4(1)(a) and (3)*DEA 2010* , Section 12(2)(c) *Initial Obligations Code* (June 2012).

1285 See also Ofcom, *Online infringement of copyright and the Digital Economy Act 2010, Notice of Ofcom's proposal to make by order a code for regulating the initial obligations* (26.06.2012), p. 65.

1286 Section 4(2)(a) *DEA 2010* .

1287 Ofcom, *Online infringement of copyright and the Digital Economy Act 2010, Notice of Ofcom's proposal to make by order a code for regulating the initial obligations* (26.06.2012), p. 62.

1288 Section 4(2)(b) *DEA 2010* which inserts new section 124B *CA 2003.* See also Ofcom, *Online infringement of copyright and the Digital Economy Act 2010, Notice of Ofcom's proposal to make by order a code for regulating the initial obligations* (26.06.2012), p. 62.

1289 Section 19(5) *Initial Obligations Code* (June 2012).

1290 Section 19(4) *Initial Obligations Code* (June 2012).

owners.[1291] Accordingly, although a subscriber has received multiple notifications, the copyright owner will only be informed about such infringements that relate to his rights. The threshold however to be put on the list is three notifications in total irrespective of the injured party. It remains to be seen whether a third party acting on behalf of a number of copyright owners will be treated as a single copyright owner or several.[1292] From the Notice of Ofcom's proposal for an initial obligations code, it seems that a third party must file a request for each copyright owner on which behalf he becomes active.

As mentioned previously, an appeals process will be available to subscribers. Appeals are available at a relatively early stage compared to the French graduated response scheme: namely, appeals can already be brought regarding CIRs.[1293] In that respect, an independent body will be set up to hear these appeals.[1294] An appeal may be made where the alleged apparent infringement is not an infringement, the infringement does not relate to the subscriber's IP address at the specified time, and/or the copyright holder and/or the Internet service provider failed to comply with the regulatory codes.[1295] The most relevant ground for appeal is likely to be

---

1291 Cf. Ofcom, *Online infringement of copyright and the Digital Economy Act 2010, Notice of Ofcom's proposal to make by order a code for regulating the initial obligations* (26.06.2012), pp. 66 et sq.

1292 Several stakeholders, including BT and Internet service providerA, raised concerns regarding who precisely could request a copyright infringement list in such a case. See *ibid.*

1293 Section 124K(3) *CA 2003* as inserted by section 13(3) *DEA 2010*. In section 6(1) *Online Infringement of Copyright (Initial Obligations) (Sharing of Costs) Order 2011* (*Draft Costs Order*), it was foreseen as a formal requirement that the subscriber pays a GBP 20 fee to have his appeal admitted. However, following the withdrawal of the *Draft Costs Order* in February 2013 and no new draft being published, it is doubtful whether this provision will survive. The consumer rights organisation Consumer Focus has already filed a submission to the Lords Committee in which it expressed its concern that "a GBP 20 appeals fee will prevent low income consumers, be they benefit recipients or minimum-wage workers, from bringing legitimate appeals against notifications that copyright owners suspect that their Internet connection has been used for copyright infringement." See Consumer Focus, *Consumer Focus Submission to the Secondary Legislation Scrutiny Committee on the Digital Economy Cost Sharing Order* (July 2012).

1294 Section 13(2)(c) *DEA 2010* .

1295 Section 124K(3) and (4) *CA 2003* as inserted by section 13 *DEA 2010* .

that the subscriber has not committed the infringement himself.[1296] The subscriber must then prove during the procedure that the act constituting the "apparent infringement" was not committed by him, and that he took "reasonable steps" to prevent other persons infringing copyright by means of the Internet access service.[1297] The draft *Initial Obligations Code* simply states with regard to the requirement of "reasonable steps" that the appeals body may require "any information it considers necessary" from copyright owners.

According to Ofcom, it is for the appeals body to assess the evidence presented by subscribers and to determine the basis on which it will assess the reasonableness of any steps that the subscriber may have taken to secure its Internet access service.[1298] Because the appeals body should be able to impose an objective standard of reasonableness, Ofcom removed from its earlier draft of the *Initial Obligations Code* the requirement that it should take into account the technical ability and knowledge of the subscriber in making its determination.[1299]

Once a *Technical Obligations Code* has been passed, and technical measures are being applied, the subscriber will be able to appeal any such measure. In contrast to appeals made against CIR, an appeal against a technical measure will be made to a first-tier tribunal.[1300]

(3) Consequences

It is intended that the notification process will itself deter copyright infringements.[1301] However, as new sections 124F-J *CA 2003* suggest, the

---

1296 The burden of proof for a copyright infringement claim and for the accuracy of the IP address falls on the copyright holder and the Internet service provider. See Sam de Silva/Faye Weedon, *The Digital Economy Act 2010: Past, Present and a Future "in Limbo"*, Computer and Telecommuncations Law Review 2011, Vol. 17 Issue 3, 55, 57.

1297 Section 13(6) *DEA 2010.*

1298 Ofcom, Online infringement of copyright and the Digital Economy Act 2010, Notice of Ofcom's proposal to make by order a code for regulating the initial obligations (26.06.2012), p. 75.

1299 *Ibid.*

1300 Section 124K(10) *CA 2003* as inserted by section 13 *DEA 2010* .

1301 Diane Rowland/Uta Kohl/Andrew Charlesworth, *Information Technology Law* (4th ed. 2012), p. 347. See also High Court, *R. (on the application of British Telecommunications Plc.) v Secretary of State for Business, Innovation and*

legislator has well recognised the possibility that notifications alone may be not efficient enough to prevent future infringements. Thus, said sections make provision for subsequent action in the event that the notifications are not enough deterrents.[1302]

If infringements persist, the Secretary of State may direct Ofcom to assess whether technical obligations should be imposed on Internet service providers and prepare for the obligations.[1303] The *DEA 2010* does not set out which technical obligations should be introduced. A "technical obligation" in relation to an Internet service provider is merely defined as "an obligation for the provider to take a technical measure against some or all relevant subscribers to its service for the purpose of preventing or reducing infringement of copyright by means of the Internet".[1304] Pursuant to Article 9 *DEA 2010*, a technical measure is a measure that limits the speed or other capacity of the service provided to a subscriber, prevents a subscriber from using the service to gain access to particular material, or limits such use, suspends the service provided to a subscriber, or limits the service in another way. The list is thus merely indicative. [1305]

The Secretary of State may by order impose a technical obligation on Internet service providers depending on the results of the assessment by Ofcom, on whether such technical obligations should be imposed.[1306] As of now, it is difficult to predict the conditions for taking a technical measure against an infringer beside the fact that he must have received at least three notifications within a 12-month period. The *DEA 2010* only provides a very general framework containing a number of uncertain legal terms. The Act requires the provisions of a Technical Obligations Code in relation to technical measure to be "objectively justifiable in relation to the

---

Skills [2011] EWHC 1021 (Admin), [2011] CMLR 5, para. 254.Cf. in addtion the Explanatory Note to the *DEA 2010* at para. 62, which states that the Initial Obligations are expected to "significantly reduce online copyright infringement".

1302 Diane Rowland/Uta Kohl/Andrew Charlesworth, *Information Technology Law* (4th ed. 2012), p. 347.

1303 New Section 124G(1) *CA 2003* as inserted by section 9 *DEA 2010* .

1304 New Section 124G(2) *CA 2003* as inserted by section 9 *DEA 2010* .

1305 See Julia Hörnle, *Premature or Stillborn? – The Recent Challenge to the Digital Economy Act*, Computer Law & Security Review 2012, Vol 28, 83, 84.

1306 New Sections 124G and 124H *CA 2003* as inserted by sections 9 and 10 *DEA 2010.* The Secretary of State must lay a draft of the order before Parliament. It must be approved by a resolution of each House.

matters to which it relates", "not…to discriminate unduly against particular persons or against a particular description of persons", to be "proportionate to what they are intended to achieve", and to be transparent "in relation to what those provisions are intended to achieve".[1307] In simple words, this means nothing more as that they have to be legitimate. While it is a long way to go until technical measures may be taken against repeat infringers, copyright owners are free to take the traditional path of private litigation.

Copyright owners may use the information contained in a CIL to apply to a court for a Norwich Pharmacal order[1308] requiring the Internet service provider to reveal the subscriber's personal detail. This option however does not even require that the user has been put on the CIL for receiving three or more notifications. A disclosure request may already be filed once evidence is collected with regard to an infringement and an IP address has been identified in connection with that infringement.

d) The Status Quo

As of 2014, the graduated response scheme is far from being employed. Little progress has been made since 2010. When the *DEA 2010* was rushed through Parliament in 2010, it was expected that it would not take long until the first warning letters were sent out. Already in August 2011, the first warnings were expected to be delayed until the second half of 2012 – more than a year later than originally planned.[1309] As of June 2012, Ofcom announced that the first warning letters would probably be sent out in March 2014.[1310] This delay was partly due to the judicial review of the

1307 New Section 124J *CA 2003* as inserted by section 12 *DEA 2010.*

1308 A Norwich Pharmacal order requires a respondent to disclose information to the applicant so that the applicant can pursue proceedings against an infringer. The respondent must be a party who is involved or mixed up in alleged wrongdoing, whether innocently or not, but who is not likely to be party to the proceedings. The prerequisites for obtaining a Norwich Pharmacal Order are outlined in this Chapter under III. 2.a).

1309 See Jeremy Philips, *Digital Opportunity Knocks...,* IPkat (03.08.2011.

1310 See Ofcom, *New Measures to Protect Online Copyright and Inform Consumers* (26.06.2012).

DEA 2010, which took until March 2012.[1311] The copyright enforcement legislation had been the focal point of a two-year battle between rightsholders and Internet service providers, who argued that they should not pay the costs for enforcing the private and exclusive rights of the copyright owners.[1312] In that context, Ofcom's first draft of the *Initial Obligations Code* published in May 2010[1313] was revised with a final draft published in June 2012[1314]. Contrary to expectations, this draft was not passed through Parliament by the end of 2012.[1315] Even if that timeframe had been respected, given the logistics involved in establishing an appeals body and other elements necessary to police the *Initial Obligations Code*, Internet users would not have received letters before 1 March 2014.[1316] While the *Initial Obligations Code* was awaiting full approval, the Government withdrew the *Initial Obligations Sharing of Costs Order* in February 2013, citing the need to make "technical changes".[1317] On current plans and subject to parliamentary approval, the first customer notification letters are expected in late 2015 or even later.[1318] Thus, from passing the *DEA 2010* to sending out warnings to subscribers more than five years will have gone by. By that time, the *DEA 2010* will have produced significant costs without having any effects. Up until March 2011, the *DEA 2010* has already produced several millions of costs, for instance over GBP 2

1311 High Court, *R. (on the application of British Telecommunications Plc) v Secretary of State for Business, Innovation and Skills,* [2011] EWHC 1021 (Admin), [2011] 3 C.M.L.R. 5; Court of Appeal, *R (on the application of British Telecommunications plc. and another) v Secretary of State for Culture, Olympics, Media and Sport* [2012] EWCA Civ 232.

1312 See Mark Sweney, *Ofcom outlines new anti-piracy rules,* The Guardian (26.06.2012).

1313 Ofcom Consultation Report, *Online Infringement of Copyright and the Digital Economy Act 2010: Draft Initial Obligations Code* (28.05.2010).

1314 Ofcom, *Online infringement of copyright and the Digital Economy Act 2010, Notice of Ofcom's proposal to make by order a code for regulating the initial obligations* (26.06.2012), Annex 3.

1315 According to news reports, the draft code was expected to pass through Parliament following a consultation period by the end of that year, i.e. 2012. See Mark Sweney, *Ofcom outlines new anti-piracy rules*, The Guardian (26.06.2012).

1316 *Ibid.*

1317 See BBC News, *UK Piracy Warning Letters Delayed until 2015,* BBC News (06.06.2013).

1318 House of Commons, *Digital Economy Act: Copyright*, Standard Note: SN/HA/5515 (28 June 2013)

million in consultation fees.[1319] Ofcom estimated in 2012 that the costs for setting up and running the *DEA 2010's* copyright enforcement regime would be up to GBP 10.5m between 2010 and 2015.[1320]

As mentioned before, the delay in implementing the graduated response scheme can primarily be based on the concerns as regards the costs to be covered by Internet service providers. The initial draft *Sharing of Costs Order* required rights-holders to carry 75% of the costs involved to set up and run the new system.[1321] The costs that Internet service providers were to carry were set at 25% of the costs involved.[1322] According to Ofcom, if 70,000 CIRs are sent by rights-holders to the biggest Internet service providers[1323] each month, the total costs to rights-holders would be GBP 14.4m, with each letter costing GBP 17.[1324] It has been estimated that the costs for individual letters will drop, if more CIRs are filed.[1325] However, this would still leave a significant amount of costs on the access providers. In that context, it has been suggested that the reason for the withdrawal of the *Sharing of Costs Order* have been concerns by the Treasury that requiring Internet service providers to bear their share of costs in complying with the regime would amount to levying a tax on the providers. This is however something the Treasury said it would need to sanction.[1326]

1319 See HC Debate of 21 March 2011, vol. 525, col 765W.

1320 Mark Sweney, *Ofcom outlines new anti-piracy rules*, The Guardian (26.06.2012).

1321 Article 3 sections 1 (6)(b), 3(3) and 4(2) of the draft Online Infringement of Copyright (Initial Obligations)(Sharing of Costs) Order 2011.

1322 *Ibid.* Non-compliance of Internet service providers with their obligations under the Act, would lead to penalty fees.

1323 This would be BT, Virgin, TalkTalk and BskyB.

1324 See Mark Sweney, *Ofcom outlines new anti-piracy rules*, The Guardian (26.06.2012).

1325 "The forecast is for it to become more cost effective for the rights holders to foot the bill for significantly more copyright infringement reports to go out to Internet service providers each month – 175,000 will cost them GBP 15.2m, however the cost-per-letter drops to GBP 7.20." See Mark Sweney, *Ofcom outlines new anti-piracy rules*, The Guardian (26.06.2012).

1326 Cf. Pinsent Masons, *Ofcom anti-piracy code delayed until 2015*, out-law.com (10.06.2013).

On the other hand, the graduated response scheme may be beneficial for Internet service providers considering that file-sharers take up large volumes of bandwidth and "congest[ing] the network".[1327]

Irrespective of whether the *Sharing of Costs Order* would impose a tax levy upon providers, it is obvious that any additional costs, that access providers would have to carry (in administering the CIRs and CILs, and sending out the notifications), will be transferred upon subscribers. Thus, in the end, for the subscribers the situation will not be too much different from France, where the taxpayer carries the costs of the administrative authority occupied with administering and sending out the notifications – with the exception that only Internet access subscriber will be paying. However, considering the household penetration of broadband Internet access, almost every household will contribute its share for rights-holders being able to protect and enforce their own exclusive rights. Not surprisingly, it has been argued that systems such as the one that will be imposed by the *DEA 2010* "mutualize[s] the costs of the fight against piracy within the whole society".[1328] As for now, it remains to be seen, what kind of "technical changes" will be made to the *Initial Obligations Sharing of Costs Order* and what effect this will have on access providers.

Considering the delay of the copyright enforcement scheme, the delay clearly shows that the Act was passed without sufficient scrutiny and that too much was left for secondary legislation. This secondary legislation seems to be a never-ending story: bearing in mind, that any Technical Obligations Code requires the *Initial Obligations Code* to be in force for 12 months, and requires an assessment of the impact of the warning scheme prior to drafting a Technical Obligations Code, it seems rather unlikely that such a Code will ever come into force. It will be no earlier than 2016, until such a Code may be drafted. The benefit of course, will be that the Code adapts to technological progress. On the other hand, by 2016 or 2017, considering previous delays, may have brought changes in user behaviour with new models of unauthorised downloads. The *DEA 2010,* as well as the HADOPI, relies however on peer-to-peer file-sharing models of 2010.

1327 See Peter Yu, *The Graduated Response*, Florida Law Review 2010, Vol 62, 1373, 1385.

1328 See Valérie-Laure Benabou, The French Insight into the 'Three Strikes' System', in: Irini A. Stamatoudi (ed.), Copyright enforcement and the Internet (2010), 180.

Finally, sanctions such as the suspension of an Internet access, or any limitations on such access, are highly controversial and may interfere with fundamental rights (as will be discussed in the following). While in the UK, these sanctions are formally still on the agenda, France has already abolished such sanctions for peer-to-peer file-sharing scenarios if no actual infringer can be identified.

Without technical sanctions, the copyright enforcement scheme against subscribers leaves the copyright-holders with a rather blunt instrument: the identity of infringers will only be revealed upon them, once they have obtained a disclosure order before a court. This is however nothing new, but an existing instrument under common law. The graduated response scheme will only allow them to filter out the most persistent infringers, while having to pay a significant amount of money to do this. The benefit for rights-holders may only be that these notorious infringers are also those, were legal action promises to be successful. In that regard, what is lacking is the court-proof identification of the actual infringer. Hence, unless the notifications are deterrent enough, the graduated response scheme without a real graduated response is theoretically only beneficial for infringers as they will know that they are only likely to be sued once they have been detected at least three times within a 12 month period. Of course, without a system of notifications, claims are likely to be made against a subscriber who has not himself committed an infringement and has not secured his Wi-Fi adequately or allowed third parties to use his connection. Thus, "innocent" subscribers will not have the chance to review their security settings or educate others using their connection to not infringe copyright. The question then however is, if rights-holders should have to pay to make subscribers aware of their very own negligence. Without a system of notifications, fewer subscribers will be made aware of infringements committed from their access, because disclosure orders are more costly than notifications under the *DEA*. So in fact, as the *DEA 2010* stands today, the copyright enforcement provisions against users are rather an educational tool than a real enforcement mechanism.

e) The DEA's Future in Limbo

The DEA's future is uncertain. The costs involved as well as potentially disproportionate sanctions are not the only controversy about the copyright enforcement scheme of the *DEA 2010*. As such, the *DEA 2010* was perceived as being not as forward-looking as the *Digital Britain Report*, for example in terms of creating an infrastructure for super-fast broadband access.[1329] In terms of fast developing technology, it is questionable whether the *DEA 2010* is able to keep up with the challenges of the digital age. It has been criticised for not providing future-proofing against current and future technological developments, allowing infringers to simply use other methods for illegally obtaining copyrighted material, for example use of sharehosters, proxy servers and data encryption to avoid detection of an IP address.[1330]

It remains to be seen whether the system will not just only benefit large copyright holders who have the financial means to support the costs involved.[1331]

It also remains to be seen how open Wi-Fi services will be addressed, such as coffee shops, libraries or universities. It is uncertain whether in the end they may not become liable as subscribers.[1332] In its proposal for an *Initial Obligations Code*, Ofcom only addressed the issue whether the providers of Wi-Fi hotspots would fall into the category of Internet service providers (although they would not fall within the required category of broadband providers).[1333] In this regard, Ofcom distinguished providers of commercial hotspots such as BT and his Openzone service, from commercial entities that offer Internet access in addition to their primary business, such as hotels or cafés that allow their customers to use their Wi-Fi network. With regard to his Openzone service, British provider BT had stated that the "vast majority" of Openzone users purchase on a pay-as-you-go

1329 Sam de Silva/Faye Weedon, *The Digital Economy Act 2010: Past, present and a future "in limbo"*, Computer and Telecommuncations Law Review 2011, Vol. 17 Issue 3, 55.

1330 *Ibid*, 60.

1331 Cf. *ibid*.

1332 In this regard, the preliminary ruling decision of the CJEU in C-484/14 (*Tobias McFadden v Sony Music Entertainment Germany GmbH*) is eagerly awaited. The request for a preliminary ruling by a German court seeks clarification as to whether the provider of an open Wi-Fi network, i.e. a free non-password-protected Wi-Fi, may be liable for third-party copyright infringements or whether said provider may be shielded from liability on the basis that he falls within the category of "mere conduit" provider under Art. 12 of the *E-Commerce Directive*.

1333 Ofcom, *Online infringement of copyright and the Digital Economy Act 2010, Notice of Ofcom's proposal to make by order a code for regulating the initial obligations* (26.06.2012), pp. 29 et seq.

basis, rather than via subscription, and[1334] Ofcom recognised that where providers offer Wi-Fi in this way, in many instances the subscriber address data collected for pay-as-you-go consumers will be neither reliable nor easily verifiable.[1335] Therefore Wi-Fi providers are excluded from the Scope of the Code on the basis that inclusion "is likely to lead to them incurring substantial costs to achieve a minimal reduction in overall levels of online copyright infringements".[1336]

According to Ofcom, also commercial enterprises that offer Wi-Fi services to their customers like hotels or cafés, as well as public bodies like libraries or universities, fall within the definition of an Internet service provider, but are exempted from any obligations under the *DEA*. This is due to the fact that they do not fall within the category of qualifying Internet service provider, meaning broadband providers with more than 40,000 customers.[1337]

One of the most controversial issues of the graduated response scheme has been the fact that notifications may also be send to subscribers for allowing "another person to use that service and that person has infringed the owner's copyright by means of that service"[1338]. As regards the notion of "allowing", it has been argued, that "it is unjustifiable for an Internet subscriber to be held vicariously liable for the actions of others".[1339] It was feared that entities that offer free Internet access without further regis-

---

1334 *Ibid.*

1335 *Ibid.*

1336 *Ibid*, p. 30.

1337 *Ibid*, p. 99. If a pay-as-you go broadband provider suddenly has more customers than the initial threshold set by the *Initial Obligations Code*, he will nevertheless not be required to collect contact details of existing customers once it becomes a qualifying Internet service provider. Ofcom departs in this regard from its previous opinion (from its 2010 consultation), that operators that do not hold information necessary for notifying subscribers, must, at such a time as they become a qualifying Internet service provider, ensure that they do collect this data so as to be able to comply with the obligations in the *DEA 2010* and the *Initial Obligations Code* (see p. 95).

1338 Section 4(4) *Initial Obligations Code* (June 2012). See also new section 124A(2) *CA 2003* inserted by section 3 DEA.

1339 Cf. for instance Sam de Silva/Faye Weedon, *The Digital Economy Act 2010: Past, present and a future "in limbo"*, Computer and Telecommuncations Law Review 2011, Vol. 17 Issue 3, 55, 60.

tration to their customers, would be held liable for infringements committed by their customers.[1340]

However, the fact, that warnings may be send to subscribers for allowing third parties to use their service does not in itself carry a sanction. The warning has primarily a deterring function, and only secondly a preparatory function for future legal action. If the subscriber is taken to court, the court will have to examine whether he has either committed the infringement himself or authorised a third party to do so. The *CDPA 1988* does not speak of "allowing a third party" but instead uses the notion of "authorisation". There is a distinctive difference between the two concepts. "Allowing" cannot be equalled with the legal concept of "authorising".[1341]

Another issue that may give rise to concern is whether it still makes sense to apply provisions of the *DEA 2010* only to the big broadband providers. While it is understandable, that the business models of small providers may be put on risk if they face huge costs for implementing and enforcing the graduated response scheme, it is questionable whether it makes sense to limit the application of the copyright enforcement scheme on big broadband providers. In 2014, the LTE[1342] wireless communication standard of high-speed data for mobile phones and data terminals will mean that peer-to-peer file-sharing becomes also possible via mobile communication.[1343] Although, data transfer rates of up to 300 Mbit/s will not be available everywhere, the improvements indicate the future developments in mobile communication. With more and more users using mobile surfsticks to go online wherever they are, a huge number of end-users are

1340 Lilian Edwards, *Mandy and Me: Some Thoughts on the Digital Economy Bill*, ScriptED 2009, Vol. 6 Issue 3, 535, 536.

1341 In that respect, HJ Birss QC already pointed out in *Media CAT v Adams* that allowing a third party to use an Internet connection does not alone equate authorising an infringement by that person (Patents County Court, *Media C.A.T. v Adams* [2011] EWPCC 6, [2011] FSR 8, para. 30). UK courts have not yet decided whether the act of authorising use of an Internet connection turn the person doing the authorising into a person authorising the infringement within section 16(2) *CDPA 1988*.

1342 LTE is an initialism of Long Term Evolution and is marketed as 4G LTE. In Germany, LTE was first introduced in 2010 in selected areas and since then has been expanding. See Alexander Spier, *Darf's ein bisschen schneller sein? Wie sich LTE im mobilen Alltag schlägt*, c't 22/2012, 84.

1343 The transfer volume will be increased up to 300MBit per second. See heise.de, *LTE-A-Modems liefern bald bis zu 300 MBit/s*, Heise (11.09.2013).

not covered by the *DEA*, i.e. subscribers of small Internet service providers or wireless data communication technology.

A solution must be found that provides for adequate legislative intervention, but also recognises legitimate interests of parties other than the copyright-holders.

Considering the delay, it is rather unlikely that subscribers in the UK must fear technical measures based on the *DEA 2010* in the future. The new Government has indicated that it does not propose to bring into effect provisions relating to limiting or excluding a particular subscriber's access to the Internet.[1344] Further, it seems that by further delays stakeholders will rather lose interest in the graduated response enforcement procedure before the first notification is sent out. Realistically, they have to ask themselves, what the *DEA 2010* has given them so far: Internet access providers challenged the act unsuccessfully and were left with the costs for this; the same access providers have to work out internal systems for handling CIRs and CILs that respect the relevant data protection law; in addition, public consultations have already cost more than 2 million pounds. As of now, only costs have been involved. In contrast to France, these costs are not exclusively born by the state. As outlined above, rights-holders have to bear 75% of the costs involved in the warning scheme. Thus, it comes to no surprise that rights-holders are not really pushing the implementation of the warning scheme forward. Moreover, rights-holders are seeking alternative ways to enforce their rights and reduce unauthorised copying: they send out their own warnings in the form of letters before claim threatening subscribers to sue them;[1345] but primarily, they are starting to target enforcement against websites that facilitate piracy and have successfully obtained blocking orders against notorious websites.[1346]

1344 See Ian J. Lloyd, *Information Technology Law* (6th ed. 2011), p. 385.

1345 See below B. III. 2. UK: Out of Court Settlement by Pre-Litigation Letters: A fundamently Different Approach?.

1346 For content- and intermediary-targeted responses see below in the Third Chapter.

3. Graduated Response Schemes: Concerns Relating to Technology and Fundamental Rights

The graduated response scheme foreseen by the *DEA 2010* in the UK has been criticised for similar reasons as the graduated response scheme under the HADOPI laws. Both schemes have been challenged before national courts, but those decisions left many questions unanswered. There has been no thorough analysis of the law: in France, the law was tested against the French Constitution and important issues such as for instance the fundamental rights of the subscribers and his household members have been touched in no more than a few sentences. The UK review of the *DEA 2010* also only discussed some issues on a very general level due to the details of the schemes being left for secondary legislation. The following analysis aims at closing the gaps, and will discuss whether and how a graduated response scheme that duly respects the fundamental rights of all parties involved, may be structured by pointing at the most controversial points of the French and UK example. In the following, it will be examined whether and how the graduated response scheme interfere with fundamental rights of the subscribers, their families and household members, and the rights of access providers under the *CFR* and *ECHR*. Considering the scope of this research, some points may only be touched briefly, while others will be completely ignored, to leave room for the most important issues such as for instance interferences with the right to receive and impart information, privacy and data protection in general. In doing so, also questions that are not obvious at first need to be addressed, such as for example the question whether IP addresses constitute personal data, so that the data protection provisions of the *CFR* and *ECHR* are applicable. The analysis will also look at how technology as such and in particular technological concerns are addressed, for instance in how far subscribers have to secure their Wi-Fi connection.

a) Dealing with Technological Matters

In the following, it will be addressed how the graduated response schemes respond to the technological issues that have been outlined in the First Chapter.

aa) The Identifiable

As regards the question of what can be identified, the question of determination of a copyright infringement as well as the problem that the subscriber is not necessarily the infringer will be addressed.

(1) Determination of a Copyright Infringement

In the introductory section[1347], it has been outlined that the detection of a file being exchanged that carries the name of a protected work cannot be sufficient evidence for an infringement. In France, Rights Protection Commission within HADOPI is occupied with determining whether an infringement has taken place. The rights-holders are therefore advised to provide a file containing an extract of the infringing work to the Commission in order to prove that their intellectual property has been infringed.[1348] Although law does not prescribe this, rights-holders are well-advised to present only evident infringements to HADOPI. Only when HADOPI is satisfied that an infringement has taken place, it will initiate a warning. Though a presentation of chunks of the file in question suffices, it seems to be accepted that they need to be useful chunks, i.e. they must actually contain a useful part of the work in question.[1349] If HADOPI has doubts that an alleged infringement has taken place, the Authority may conduct a hearing of the applying rights-holder and the Internet subscriber concerned at any stage.[1350] In addition to evidence of the infringement, the authority needs to be presented inter alia with proof of the information relating to the acts observed, such as the date and time of the observation, the peer-to-peer protocol used, information on the copyright-protected works and the file name, and proof of the information

---

1347 See above, A. III. 3. a) The Copyright Infringement.

1348 Mireille Imbert-Quaretta/Jean-Yves Monfort/Jean-Baptiste Carpentier, *La contravention de négligence caractérisée à la lumière de la mise en œuvre de la procédure de réponse graduée*, La Semaine Juridique – Édition Générale 2012, no 19, 966, 969.

1349 See above A. II. 4.

1350 Christophe Geiger, *Honourable attempt but (ultimately) disproportionately offensive against peer-to-peer on the internet (HADOPI) – a critical analysis of the recent anti-file-sharing legislation in France,* International Review of Intellectual Property and Competition Law 2011, Vol. 42, 457, 466.

regarding the identity of the infringer such as the IP address retrieved on the date and at the time of the infringement, the Internet service provider used, and the pseudonyms used on the peer-to-peer network by the infringer.[1351] It is also necessary for any agent acting on behalf of the rights-holder to prove that he has been officially authorised by the rights-holder to pursue his intellectual property rights. Thus, professional copyright enforcement companies must also provide documents in relation to their mandate to HADOPI.

While the French graduated response scheme requires a review of the evidence at an early stage, namely prior to the submission of a warning, the UK regime does not foresee the establishment of an infringement before a public authority. Instead, rights-holders have to provide evidence to the relevant access provider, who will then issue a warning without a third party overlooking the matter. In that respect, the draft *Initial Obligations Code* prescribes the standard for obtaining evidence of copyright infringements, but it does not foresee that the access provider examines the facts and in particular, whether the facts provided suffice to establish a copyright infringement. Moreover the law only requires a CIR to contain a statement that there "appears" to have been a copyright infringement in the respective work, as well as a description of the apparent infringement and the evidence gathered of that apparent infringement.[1352] A test, whether the accused act constitutes a copyright infringement will only be conducted upon appeal by the subscriber, or when the rights-holder decides to file a claim before a civil court.

(2) Fact that IP Address Identification Does Not Necessarily Identify the Actual Infringer

Matching an IP address to a subscriber only provides the name of the subscriber of the Internet access service, and not the name of the person who

1351 HADOPI, 2010 Activity Report (2011), p. 35. As regards the data processed see also the annex to *Décret n° 2010-236 du 5 mars 2010 relatif au traitement automatisé de données à caractère personnel autorisé par l'article L. 331-29 du CPI dénommé «Système de gestion des mesures pour la protection des œuvres sur Internet»*.

1352 The information about the infringement must provide sufficient information to enable the subscriber to identify the means used to obtain evidence of the copyright infringement, cf. section 5(e) *Initial Obligations Code* (June 2012).

was engaged in the wrongful conduct at issue. A criminal charge as well as a plausible claim in civil law, requires the presentation of factual allegations establishing that the particular person identified was, in fact, the individual who engaged in wrongful conduct.

The French graduated response scheme addressed this issue by introducing a new criminal offence in the national copyright code: Article L. 336-3 *CPI* now requires subscribers to an Internet access to ensure, that their Internet access is not used for infringements of copyrighted materials.[1353] A subscriber is thus obliged to secure and monitor his Internet access. A violation of this obligation constitutes a "contravention", which neither requires an intention to violate the law, nor an act of imprudence or negligence on behalf of the infringer. As outlined previously, the subjective element of the offence is narrower than mere negligence and is comparable to a breach of due diligence in tort law.[1354] Only when the subscriber has been informed about his obligation to secure his Internet access by HADOPI, he may breach a known duty of law and be held liable. It will then be his persistence to omit the implementation of security measures that is eventually punished under the condition that a further infringement can be established. Thus, subscribers who have not secured and/or monitored their access adequately will not be directly liable for the copyright infringement. There is no known peer-to-peer file-sharing case where a subscriber was actually prosecuted for committing the copyright infringement himself. The prosecutor's office will regularly only pursue proceedings for this negligence offence as it seems that they are very well aware of the fact that it is impossible without further information than the IP address to prosecute a subscriber. Accordingly, the French regime makes it obsolete to identify the actual infringer by sanctioning subscribers for their reluctance to control their Internet access following three notifications.

In contrast, the UK system as it stands today does not address the problem of identifying the actual infringer. Although the *DEA 2010* provides the legal basis for sending out notifications to subscribers in relation to infringements that have been committed via their access, the regime does not provide for a final sanction of the subscriber. As long as no Technical Obligations Code has been passed, the subscriber may be faced with pri-

---

1353 See B. II. 1. B).

1354 See above, B. II. 1. c) bb) (3) Consequences: Referral to the Prosecutor's Office and Criminal Proceedings.

vate legal action by the copright-holders. In civil proceedings, they will however be required to provide evidence that the subscriber is liable for the copyright infringement. Liability will be established, if the subscriber has himself committed the copyright infringement or has authorised an infringement by another person. In that respect, HJ Birss QC already pointed out in Media CAT v Adams, that allowing a third party to use an Internet connection does not alone equate authorising an infringement by that person.[1355] UK courts have not yet decided whether the act of authorising use of an Internet connection turn the person doing the authorising into a person authorising the infringement within section 16(2) *CDPA 1988*. As mentioned previously, the notification procedure under the *DEA 2010* is a rather blunt instrument, unless a Technical Obligations Code is being passed. How such a Code will address the issue that the subscriber is not necessarily identical with the actual infringer remains to be seen. The *DEA 2010* alone does not provide a solution to this problem, when it foresees that technical measures may be imposed upon subscribers that have received at least three warnings. Considering that a subscriber may appeal a CIR with inter alia the argument that the alleged apparent infringement is not an infringement or the infringement does not relate to the subscriber's IP address at the specified time and that the will succeed with his appeal when he shows that "the act constituting the apparent infringement to which the report relates was not done by the subscriber, and the subscriber took reasonable steps to prevent other persons infringing copyright by means of the Internet access service"[1356], the basic principle is the same as in France: a sanction may only be imposed where the subscriber has not adequately secured his access. While the French legislator introduced a statutory criminal offence in the *CPI* for failure to comply with the obligation to secure and monitor an Internet access, the UK legislator refrained from introducing such an obligation from the start. However, the UK legislator may introduce this obligation indirectly through the backdoor left by the power to pass a Technical Obligations Code.

Both regimes leave it to the courts and appeal bodies to determine the conditions for reasonable steps to prevent other persons from infringing copyright by means of an Internet access service, and the reasonable steps to take to technologically secure an access as such.

1355 Patents County Court, *Media C.A.T. v Adams* [2011] EWPCC 6, [2011] FSR 8, para. 30.

1356 Section 124K(3), (4) and (6) CA 2003 as inserted by section 13 *DEA 2010*.

bb) The Identifier

As regards the identifier, the concerns in relation to the reliability of data harvesting and data as such as well as potential responses to evasion of detection will be looked at.

(1) Concerns in Relation to Reliability of Data

Both regimes provide for judicial oversight of sanctions. While in France, the warnings as such cannot be appealed, the UK system foresees appeals at an early stage. At these levels, the subscribers can challenge the reliability of the data that has been collected in relation to the respective alleged infringement. How a subscriber may succeed to prove a misconfiguration of logs remains to be seen, but it is likely that he will only succeed if he can rebut the allegation that he himself has committed the infringement, or any party whom he allowed to use his Internet access service, and his connection has been adequately secured.

In order to limit risks posed by harvesting software, copyright-holders in the UK are required to submit their evidence gathering procedures for approval to Ofcom before they can send any reports of apparent copyright infringements to access providers.[1357] Ofcom also advises copyright-holders to secure approval from Ofcom if they adopt evidence-gathering procedures; further, Ofcom is prepared to sponsor specifications for such procedures.[1358] However, as the outline of the concerns in relation to reliability of data show, there are more sources of error than unreliable software. Whether data is unreliable, is solely left for the subscriber to prove. In this regard, probably witness statements by technical experts are necessary. Also, courts need to be made aware that the matching of an IP address to a subscriber in connection with an infringement may not be accurate.

1357 Section 6 *Initial Obligations Code* (June 2012).

1358 Ofcom, *Online infringement of copyright and the Digital Economy Act 2010, Notice of Ofcom's proposal to make by order a code for regulating the initial obligations* (26.06.2012), p. 4.

(2) Responses to Evasion of Detection

With respect to users that try to evade detection, no measures are taken. It seems to be generally accepted that it is impossible to hinder copyright infringements as such. One may also argue that there is a battle of arms between persistent infringers and rights-holders: migration to more secure networks also means that specialised copyright enforcement companies are searching for ways to infiltrate these networks. However, as long as many users stick to conventional peer-to-peer file-sharing, there is still much work to handle. Recent numbers published by HADOPI have shown that there is no decline in copyright infringement notifications to HADOPI. While in 2013, in average 84,000 first warnings were issued per month,[1359] in October 2013 138,000 first warnings were issued.[1360] Thus, it is doubtful, whether rights-holder will invest many resources to go after sophisticated infringers as long as there is such a vast number of easily detectable infringers.

cc) Enforcement of Internet Suspension or Restriction

The legislators have said little regarding the practical enforcement of a sanction that suspends or limits access to the Internet. While the French system foresaw that Internet access providers, that offered Internet access service to someone who has been convicted to an Internet suspension, could be fined, no reference could be found as regards the other individuals allowing the offender to use their connection. This may be due to the fact, that the usage of another private connection by the offender will hardly be detected. The question becomes however interesting, when someone else who lives in the household of the offender will order a new Internet access service for the household. Then the Internet suspension or restriction will have no effect. The new subscriber does not fall within the category of an Internet access service provider and will thus not be obliged to refrain from granting access to the offender. In turn, the Internet access service provider who provides the new service will not know who

---

1359 HADOPI, *Réponse graduée – Les chiffres clés* (06.11.2013), Monthly updated statistics are available at http://www.hadopi.fr/actualites/reponse-graduee/chiffres-cles.

1360 *Ibid.*

else than the subscriber will use the connection. In order to have at least some effect, the suspension or restriction order would have to extent to everyone living under the offender's address. This however would have an even more severe impact on potentially innocent third parties than the sanction extending to the subscriber alone. It can only be speculated, that the legislators considered that no one upon whom that sanction has been imposed would ask a third party to order a new Internet access service as those are usually connected to a minimum subscription time. However, it seems more likely that they rather ignore the alternatives for an offender to obtain access to the Internet. Also, the court that imposed the first Internet suspension order did not discuss this matter any further. Similarly – though in a case concerning blackmailing -, a German court ordered a 21-year-old to refrain from using social media including Facebook, WhatsApp and Instagram for six months.[1361] He will have to delete his respective social media accounts. It is highly questionable how such an order can be legitimately enforced without monitoring the online behaviour of the person in question. Whether such interference with the privacy rights of the person concerned can be justified is rather unlikely.

dd) No Prescribed Standard for Securing Internet Access

One aspect that gives rise to concern and that has already been referred to when discussing that an IP address only relates to a subscriber and not necessarily an individual user, is the required security means to protect a Wi-Fi network. These means are not defined from a technical point of view. According to the wording of Article R. 335-5 *CPI*, the failure can take two forms: the total failure to secure an Internet connection, and the lack of due diligence in installing a security mechanism. According to HADOPI, the latter covers those cases, where the security solution is ineffective, because, for instance, it had not been activated. The law itself does not impose the installation of a specific security means upon Internet access subscribers. Although HADOPI specifies security means in its warning letters, the law does not require the implementation of a security means approved by HADOPI.

1361 See Der Spiegel, *Erpressung im Internet: 21-jähriger Münchner zu Facebook-Verbot verurteilt,* Der Spiegel online (25.03.2014).

As of now, also in the UK no specific standard for securing an Internet access against intruders from outside is prescribed by law or has been established by case law.

b) Compliance of the Graduated Response Schemes With Secondary EU Law

The focus of this research is primarily on the impact on fundamental rights of users and access providers while observing the fundamental rights of copyright-holders. However, as a starting point, the graduated responses are briefly analysed in terms of their compliance with EU secondary legislation as described above. Within this analysis the most controversial issues are focussed on while trying to outline under which conditions graduated response schemes are in compliance with secondary EU law.

aa) Compliance of Graduated Response Schemes with Secondary EU Law in General

First of all, it has to be recalled that the graduated response schemes that have been discussed above do not alter existing enforcement mechanisms, but provide for an alternative measure to enable the minority of serious repeat infringers to be identified. The graduated response schemes intend to warn and educate subscribers and users prior to sanctioning persistent infringers. Instead of requiring rights-holders to initiate criminal proceedings or address themselves to a civil court for obtaining a disclosure order, an public administrative authority or a third party (i.e. in the UK the access providers) sends warning to first, second or third-time infringers without revealing the identity of the potential infringer to the rights-holder.

There is no obligation in secondary EU law to introduce alternative enforcement mechanisms such as graduated response schemes in addition to existing copyright enforcement law that respects the minimum standards set forth in the *IPR Enforcement Directive*.[1362] If alternative enforcement measures are introduced, they nevertheless have to be in accordance with framework provided for in said Directive. Article 3 of the *IPR*

1362 With regard to copyright enforcement, the *IPR Enforcement Directive* has been implemented by all Member States.

Enforcement Directive contains rather general provisions on sanctions and remedies for intellectual property rights infringements. According to Article 2(1) of the Directive, Member States may provide for sanctions and remedies that are more favourable to rights-holders. However for all enforcement measures it is necessary that Member States ensure that the enforcement of the intellectual property rights covered by the Directive, are "fair and equitable" and not "unnecessarily complicated or costly, or entail unreasonable time-limits or unwarranted delays", are "effective, proportionate and dissuasive" as well as "applied in such a manner as to avoid the creation of barriers to legitimate trade and to provide for safeguards against their abuse".[1363]

Already when it comes to the notion of "fair and equitable", it is questionable whether the warning and subsequent sanctioning of subscribers is fair. The fact that in most cases, it will only be possible to identify the subscriber of an Internet access service and not the actual infringer is however no specific problem of graduated response schemes. The graduated response scheme in fact targets in particular the issue that innocent parties shall not be prosecuted or at least not be confronted with prosecutions.[1364] To achieve this aim, the schemes requires a subscriber to be warned prior to sanctions in order to allow him to stop infringing copyright or prevent others from using his Internet access to infringe copyright. Without prior warnings, a subscriber may be faced with criminal charges or civil proceedings following a first incident. As this would be the common practice under existing law, the graduated enforcement scheme is rather beneficial for subscribers.

As regards the requirement of "unnecessarily complicated or costly", the initial obligation in the UK to hold access providers partly accountable for the costs of sending out warnings and administering the CILs gives rise to concerns. However, as the initially foreseen sharing of costs, were access providers were held to carry 25% of the costs involved, was recently recalled, it remains to be seen whether future *Sharing of Costs Order*s comply with Article 2(1). In terms of cost, one may also argue that the

1363 Article 3 of the *IPR Enforcement Directive.*

1364 In France, civil legal proceedings against alleged infringers had "appalling effects" for rights-holders, so that they decided to refrain from this option of enforcing their rights. See Valérie-Laure Benabou, *The Chase: The French Insight into the 'Three Strikes' System*, in: Irini Stamatoudi (ed.), *Copyright enforcement and the Internet* (2010), p. 164.

storing of traffic data for the purpose of identifying infringers may come costly for the access providers. However, the graduated response schemes discussed above do not impose further data retention duties upon access providers. Instead for instance the *DEA 2010* foresees that for these purposes the data retained in accordance with the *Data Retention Directive* can be accessed. For rights-holders the advantage of graduated response schemes in relation to costs is the fact, that instead of addressing themselves to a court to obtain information about the identity of an infringer, or right away press criminal charges against a subscriber, they forward the collected evidence about an infringement to a third party which will then deal with the matter. Although the initiation of criminal investigations comes at no costs for the rights-holder, considering the scale of infringements, it is in practice rather unlikely that the police or public prosecutor will investigate the matters any further than identifying the subscriber. Regularly, they will then have to drop charges because they do not succeed in identifying the actual infringer. Although the graduated response schemes are costly as such, they are not "unnecessarily costly". There are also no unreasonable time-limits or unwarranted delays. In terms of effectiveness one may argue that the effectiveness of the schemes is limited. This may be based on the continuing high number of first warnings being sent out in France.[1365] On the other hand, HADOPI argues that the scheme is being effective in that peer-to-peer file-sharing is on the decline.[1366] However, as already the scope and impact of online file-sharing as such is difficult to measure and there are hardly any robust statistics on this subject-matter, the effect is equally difficult to measure. From an ex-ante perspective, graduated response schemes seem however be promising given the lack of understanding about copyright and the lack of understanding towards security settings of Wi-Fi routers, it cannot be ignored that many infringements happen out of ignorance.[1367] Given the educational part of

1365 Cf. current statistics with monthly updates see http://www.hadopi.fr/actualites/reponse-graduee/chiffres-cles. For the highest number of warnings in October 2013 see HADOPI, *Réponse graduée – Les chiffres clés* (06.11.2013), http://www.hadopi.fr/sites/default/files/Chiffres_reponsegraduee_Octobre2013.pdf.

1366 A study cited by HADOPI reported a decrease of approximately 66 % in the illegal sharing of films on peer-to-peer networks, see HADOPI, *HADOPI – 1 ½ year after the launch* (March 2012), p. 6

1367 Cf. as regards the lack of understanding what is legal: Pierre Lescure, Culture-acte 2, Mission « Acte II de l'exception culturelle», Contribution aux politiques culturelles à l'ére numérique (May 2013), p. 383.

the warnings they may well have a persuasive effect. Also, warnings may have a dissuasive effect as subscribers are made aware of the legal consequences of their behaviour or reluctance. Considering that in relation to the principle of effectiveness[1368], rules of national law must be designed in such a way that the objective pursued by the directive *may* be achieved,[1369] and the objective pursued by the *IPR Enforcement Directive* is that the Member States should ensure effective protection of intellectual property in an online environment,[1370] it is not necessary that the measures in question put an end to all infringements. Rather national measures amount to effective measures, when they contribute to the protection of intellectual property on the Internet. The system to be implemented in the UK raises doubts in terms of its potential capacity to reduce online piracy. During the first stage of implementation (i.e. without a Technical Obligations Code), the instrument is a rather blunt instrument, because subscriber face warnings but no sanctions connected with these.[1371] However, although they face no sanctions resulting from the *DEA 2010*, the scheme serves as a preparatory element for civil proceedings by identifying persistent infringers. It thus servers as some kind of filtering mechanism to make it possible for rights-holders to initiate legal proceedings against the most promising potential infringers: it may be easier to establish claims against subscriber listed on the CILs. This presumption however ignores the fact that subscribers are not necessarily infringers, and that it is doubtful that a court will find that allowing a third party to use an Internet access service can be equalled with authorising a third party to commit a copyright infringement.[1372] In that respect, one also needs to consider that

1368 As regards the principle of effectiveness which sets forth that the measures must not render virtually impossible or excessively difficult the exercise of rights conferred by Community law, see CJEU, Joined Cases C-430/93 and C-431/93 *Van Schijndel and van Veen* [1995] ECR I-4705, para. 17; Joined Cases C-222/05 to C-225/05 *van der Weerd and Others* [2007] ECR I-4233, para. 28, and Joined Cases C-145/08 and C-149/08 *Club Hotel Loutraki and Others* [2010] ECR I-0000, para. 74.

1369 Cf. CJEU, C-324/09 *L'Oréal v eBay* [2011] ECR I-06011, para. 136.

1370 Cf. also *ibid*, para. 131.

1371 See above, B. II. 2. e) The DEA's Future in Limbo.

1372 *Ibid.*

even the threat with civil proceedings or the initiation of criminal proceedings has some effect on those exposed to such threats.[1373]

As regards the proportionality of measures, this will be discussed in detail within balancing of fundamental rights below. At this point, it shall only be noted, that the warning system prior to sanctioning follows a legitimate aim, which is the effective protection of intellectual property, is suitable to achieve the aim, and provides a less onerous way than conventional enforcement measures. Whether the sanctioning of subscribers is reasonable in consideration of the contravening interests, is a matter of how far such sanctioning pays regard to a fair balancing of fundamental rights. When analysing whether a Member State's measure related to a consumer's access to or use of services constitutes an interference with fundamental rights of users, Artice 1(3a) of the Framework Directive further requires that restrictions on the fundamental rights or freedoms of users can only be imposed if appropriate, proportionate and necessary within a democratic society.[1374]

In addition, the general obligations on national measures in Article 3 of the *IPR Enforcement Directive* require the measures to be "applied in such a manner as to avoid the creation of barriers to legitimate trade and to provide for safeguards against their abuse". There are no claims that graduated response schemes may create barriers to legitimate trade as long as access providers are not unnecessarily and disproportionately burdened. Both schemes that have been presented also provide for safeguards against their abuse: the UK system by introducing appeals already at the stage of warnings, and the French system by requiring HADOPI to assess whether there is sufficient evidence for an infringement before sending out a warning. At the sanctioning stage, it is further required that sanctions can only be imposed by a court. Thus, subscribers are protected against unjustified claims.

1373 In Germany, where instead of warnings cease and desist letters in connection with a claim for compensatory damages are send out by rights-holders, a substantive number of subscribers pay the amount asked for because they fear court proceedings.

1374 Cf. also EU Commission, *Code of EU online rights* (2012), p. 5.

bb) Compliance of the Data Processing with Secondary EU Law

Irrespective of whether a central authority administers the claims or the access providers are administering these, both alternatives require the processing of personal data. At a first stage, data is collected by rights-holders to prove that an infringement has been committed from a certain IP address at a given time. At a second stage, this data is forwarded to either an administrative authority (France) or the relevant Internet access provider (UK) in order to issue a warning. The administrative authority, as well as the access providers, further process the data in order to identify repeat infringers.

It is now to determine to what extent the processing of personal data is lawful and what safeguards must be provided for. As to the applicable Directives as such, their provisions are relatively general, since they have to be applied to a large number of different situations which may arise in any of the Member States. Consequently, they include rules, which leave the Member States with discretion to define transposition measures, which then may be adapted to the various situations that may arise.[1375]

(1) Questions of Applicability of Data Protection Law: IP Address as Personal Data

At the heart of the data protection-related discussion towards criminal enforcement of copyright infringements lays the question whether an IP addresses are data relating to an identifiable person. As an IP address does not directly allow the identification of a subscriber because it refers to an account only, there has – and to some degree still is – vivid discussion whether it nevertheless qualifies as personal data.[1376] The answer to this

1375 See to that effect CJEU, C-101/01 *Lindqvist*, Judgment of 06.11.2008, para. 84.

1376 A detailed discussion would go beyond the scope of this work. For an excellent overview on this subject matter, see Eneken Tikk, *IP Addresses Subject to Personal Data Regulation*, in: Eneken Tikk/Anna-Maria Talihärm (eds.), *International Cyber Security Legal & Policy Proceedings* (2010), pp. 24–39. See also Okechukwu Benjamin Vincents, *When rights clash online: The tracking of P2P copyright infringements vs. the EC Personal Data Directive*, International Journal of Law and Information Technology 2011, Vol.16, No.3, 270, 285 et seq. and Rolf Schwartmann, *Vergleichende Studie über Modelle zur Versendung von Warnhinweisen durch Internet-Zugangsanbieter an Nutzer bei Urheber-*

question is essential because the classification determines the applicable law.

Fact is, that Internet access providers and managers of local area networks have the means and capacity to identify subscribers to whom they have attributed IP addresses as they normally systematically "log" in a file the date, time, duration and dynamic IP address given to the Internet user.[1377] The same applies to Internet service providers that keep logbooks on their HTTP servers.[1378] Hence, since the subscriber can be identified through a dynamic IP address, he can also be identified as the person who has at least "facilitated" the infringement if he has not committed the infringement himself.[1379]

Information relevant from a data protection point of view is only that information that refers to an identified or identifiable person. This requires that the information refers to a natural person and has the capacity to identify this person. Article 2(a) of *Data Protection Directive* 95/46/EC defines "personal data" to mean:

> "any information relating to an identified or identifiable natural person ("data subject"); an identifiable person is one who can be identified, directly or indirectly, in particular by reference to an identification number or to one or more factors specific to his physical, physiological, mental, economic, cultural or social identity."

The definition of personal data in Article 2 of the Directive is complemented by Recital 26 which states that "whereas the principles of protec-

---

rechtsverletzungen, Studie im Auftrag des Bundesministerium für Wirtschaft und Technologie (Januar 2012), pp. 295 et seq. For a more detailed discussion on this issue from a German perspective see for example Per Meyerdierks, *Sind IP-Adressen personenbezogene Daten*, MultiMedia und Recht 2009, 8; Sven Venzke, *Die Personenbezogenheit der IP-Adresse*, Zeitschrift für Datenschutz 2011, 114; Stefan Krüger/Svenja-Ariane Maucher, *IP-Adresse wirklich ein personenbezogenes Datum? – Ein falscher Trend mit großen Auswirkungen auf die Praxis*, MultiMedia und Recht 2011, 433. For a comparative overview on the treatment of IP addresses as personal data, see Christoper Kuner/Cédric Burton/Jörg Hladjk/Oliver Proust, *Study on Online Copyright Enforcement and Data Protection in Selected Member States* (November 2009).

1377 For more details see Article 29 Data Protection Working Party, *WP 37: Privacy on the Internet – An integrated EU Approach to Online Data Protection,* adopted on 21.11.2000.

1378 *Ibid.*

1379 "Facilitation" in this context shall refer to either allowing third parties to use the Internet access service in question or running an unsecure wifi network.

tion must apply to any information concerning an identified or identifiable person; whereas, to determine whether a person is identifiable, account should be taken of all the means likely reasonably to be used either by the controller or by any other person to identify the said person; whereas the principles of protection shall not apply to data rendered anonymous in such a way that the data subject is no longer identifiable; ..."

During the discussion on ACTA, the European Data Protection Supervisor has taken the view that in the context of graduated response schemes IP addresses should be considered as personal data.[1380] His explanation for this conclusion was as follows:

"IP addresses are identifiers which look like a string of numbers separated by dots, such as 122.41.123.45. A subscription to an Internet access provider will give the subscriber access to the Internet. Every time the subscriber wishes to go onto the Internet, he will be attributed an IP address through the device he is using to access the Internet (a computer, for example). If a user engages in a given activity, for example, uploads material onto the Internet, the user may be identified by third parties through the IP address he/she used. For example, the user holding IP address 122.41.123.45 uploaded allegedly copyright infringing material onto a P2P service at 3 p.m. on 1 January 2010. The Internet service provider will then be able to connect such IP address to the name of the subscriber to whom it assigned this address and thus ascertain his/her identity. If one considers the definition of personal data provided in Article 2 of Directive 95/46/EC, 'any information relating to an identified or identifiable natural person (data subject); an identifiable person is one who can be identified, directly or indirectly, in particular by reference to an identification number', it is only possible to conclude that IP addresses and the information about the activities linked to such addresses constitutes personal data in all cases relevant here. Indeed, an IP address serves as an identification number, which allows finding out the name of the subscriber to whom such IP address has been assigned. Furthermore, the information collected about the subscriber who holds such IP address ('he/she uploaded certain material onto the Web site ZS at 3 p.m. on 1 January 2010') relates to, i.e. is clearly about the activities of an identifiable

---

1380 European Data Protection Supervisor, *Opinion of the European Data Protection Supervisor on the current negotiations by the European Union of an Anti-Counterfeiting Trade Agreement (ACTA)*, OJ C 147 (05.06.2010), 1 para. 25.

individual (the holder of the IP address), and thus must also be considered personal data."[1381]

The European Data Protection Supervisor further continues that for the purposes of ACTA:

> "Traffic data such as IP addresses may only be collected and stored for reasons directly related to the communication itself, including billing, traffic management and fraud prevention purposes. Afterwards, the data must be erased. This is without prejudice to the obligations under the *Data Retention Directive* which, as discussed, requires the conservation of traffic data and its release to police and prosecutors to aid in the investigation of a serious crime only. This means that, when contacted by copyright holders, unless such contact occurred within the limited period outlined above, Internet service providers should not have the log files linking the IP addresses to the relevant subscribers. Retaining the log files beyond such period should only be done for justified reasons within the scope of the purposes provided by law."[1382]

Also, the Article 29 Data Protection Working Party[1383] has repeatedly advised that IP addresses should be considered personal data and in this regard shares the opinion of the European Data Protection Supervisor. According to the Working Party a natural person can be considered identifiable "when, within a group of persons, (s)he can be distinguished from others and consequently be treated differently".[1384] In explicit reference to cases where the processing of IP addresses is carried out with the purpose of identifying the users of an Internet access by copyright holders in order to prosecute them for violation of intellectual property rights, the Working Party stated "that the 'means likely reasonably to be used' to identify the persons will be available e.g. through the courts appealed to (otherwise the collection of the information makes no sense), and therefore the information should be considered as personal data".[1385] The Working Party also recognises that in some circumstances IP addresses may not relate to an

1381 *Ibid*, paras. 25–27.

1382 *Ibid*, paras. 57–59.

1383 The Article 29 Data Protection Working Party, which is set up under Article 29 *Data Protection Directive*, is an independent European advisory body on data protection and privacy; Its tasks are set out in Article 30 *Data Protection Directive* and Article 15 *E-Privacy Directive*.

1384 Cf. only Article 29 Data Protection Working Party, *Statement of the Working Party on Current Discussions Regarding the Data Protection Reform Package* (27.02.2013).

1385 Article 29 Data Protection Working Party, *Opinion 4/2007 on the Concept of Personal Data*, 01248/07/EN WP 136 of 20.06.2007, p. 17.

identifiable person: for instance in the case of Internet cafés, where no identification of the customers is requested, an IP address does not relate to an identifiable person. However, as the Internet access provider is not in a position to know that the person can hardly be identified, he needs to treat the IP address as personal data. In specific, the Working Party stated that "unless the Internet service provider is in a position to distinguish with absolute certainty that the data corresponds to users that cannot be identified, it will have to treat all IP information as personal data, to be on the safe side".[1386] Thus, an IP address is not per se considered as personal data, but rather in general with exceptional circumstances where it is seen necessary to depart from this general rule.

In its subsequent opinion on search engines, the Working Party observed that though IP addresses are in most cases not directly identifiable by search engines, identification can be achieved by a third party, meaning that law enforcement and national security authorities can gain access to such data as well (under some national laws) private parties through civil litigation.[1387] The Party then concluded that in most cases – including cases with dynamic IP address allocation – the necessary data would be available to identify the user(s) of the IP address.[1388] Accordingly, the presumption that an IP address is to be considered as personal data has been reinforced.

This view, in particular the view that IP addresses are personal data where the processing of an IP address is carried out with the purpose of identifying the data subject, has not been shared by all Member States. [1389]

1386 *Ibid.* The Working Party also noted that in the Internet café example "It could be argued that the data collected on the use of computer X during a certain timeframe does not allow identification of the user with reasonable means, and therefore it is not personal data. However, it should be noted that the Internet Service Providers will most probably not know either whether the IP address in question is one allowing identification or not, and that they will process the data associated with that IP in the same way as they treat information associated with IP addresses of users that are duly registered and are identifiable".

1387 See Article 29 Data Protection Working Party, *Opinion 01/2008 on Data Protection Issues related to Search Engines*, 00737/EN, WP 148 of 04.04.2008, p. 8.

1388 *Ibid.*

1389 For example in Ireland the High Court ruled with regard to disclosure orders in relation to online copyright infringements that IP addresses are not personal data, see *EMI Records (Ireland) Ltd., Sony B. G. Music Entertainment (Ireland) Ltd., Universal Music Ireland Ltd. and Warner Music Ireland Ltd. v Eircom Ltd.* , Charleton J., 16.04.2010, [2010] IEHC 108, paras. 18 et seq. For an

A harmonised interpretation of the concept of personal data in relation to IP addresses may however be achieved by the CJEU's judgment in *Scarlet Extended v SABAM.*[1390] In this case, the CJEU took the view that IP addresses are personal data as defined by the *Data Protection Directive* 95/46/EC when the Court considered that the filtering system in question, whereby an access provider would have to monitor its customers, may infringe the fundamental rights of said customers. According to the CJEU, IP addresses are protected personal data "because they allow the users to be precisely identified".[1391]

The CJEU did not discuss if it makes a difference whether the IP address that the access provider has attributed to the individual is static (i.e. always the same for every time the customer surfs the web), or dynamic (i.e. a different IP address is allocated each time the customers connects to the Internet).[1392] It seems that the fact, that the access provider can connect the IP address to the subscriber's account to whom it has assigned the IP address is sufficient to satisfy the criteria for personal data.

However, while the discussion above focussed on Internet access providers, the situation is somewhat different when it comes to other

---

overview on how and whether IP addresses are considered personal data in Austria, Belgium, France, Germany, Spain and Sweden, see European Commission, DG Internal Market, *Study on Online Copyright Enforcement and Data Protection in Selected Member States* (November 2009).

1390 CJEU, C-70/10 *Scarlet Extended v SABAM*, Judgment of 24.11.2011.

1391 *Ibid.* Para. 51 of the judgement reads as follows: "It is common ground, first, that the injunction requiring installation of the contested filtering system would involve a systematic analysis of all content and the collection and identification of users' IP addresses from which unlawful content on the network is sent. Those addresses are protected personal data because they allow those users to be precisely identified." In Belgium, from where the case was referred to the CJEU for a preliminary ruling, the judgment will not change the existing practice because Belgian courts treat IP addresses already as personal data and thereby have confirmed the view taken by the domestic Data Protection Authority (Commissie voor de bescherming van de persoonlijke levenssfeer / Commission de la protection de la vie privée).

1392 As regards the necessity to distinguish between dynamic and static IP addresses in relation to the logging of IP addresses by website providers, see Per Meyerdierks, *Personenbeziehbarkeit Statischer IP-Adressen – Datenschutzrechtliche Einordnung der Verarbeitung durch Betreiber von Webseiten*, MultiMedia und Recht 2013, 705–708.

online intermediaries.[1393] If other online intermediaries do not use IP addresses to distinguish an individual, they could successfully argue that they do not process personal data.[1394] Like the Article 29 Data Protection Working Party has mentioned above, the classification of an IP address as personal data depends on the service provider's ability to connect the IP address with a certain account. Similarly the Advocate General noted in Scarlet Extended v SABAM that "The question is,..., to determine not so much the legal status of IP addresses as the circumstances in which and the purposes for which they may be collected, the circumstances in which the resulting personal data may be resolved and processed, or even the conditions under which their collection and resolution may be requested".[1395] Accordingly, while it is possible for an access provider to tie an IP address to a specific subscriber, the operator of a website may not so easily identify the subscriber of an IP address.[1396] The latter depends on third parties to resolve an IP address to an account, and may only be successful with a request where laws exist that would give them information rights as to the identity of a subscriber. Thus, it is doubtful whether for them the IP address constitutes personal data. Referring back to the Working Party´s wording in its Opinion on the Concept of Personal Data, such connection can only be made where "the 'means likely reasonably to be used' to identify the persons will be available e.g. through the courts appealed

---

1393 See also Stefan Kulk/Frederik Zuiderveen Borgesius, *Filtering for Copyright Enforcement in Europe after the SABAM cases,* European Intellectual Property Review 2012, 54, 56.

1394 Article 29 Data Protection Working Party, *Opinion 4/2007 on the Concept of Personal Data*, 01248/07/EN WP 136 of 20.06.2007, p. 17.

1395 Opinion of Advocate General Cruz Villalón delivered on 14.04.2011 in Case C-70/10 *Scarlet Extended v SABAM*, para. 79.

1396 For a more detailed discussion on this subject matter see Rolf Schwartmann, *Vergleichende Studie über Modelle zur Versendung von Warnhinweisen durch Internet-Zugangsanbieter an Nutzer bei Urheberrechtsverletzungen, Studie im Auftrag des Bundesministerium für Wirtschaft und Technologie* (Januar 2012), p. 299, with further references as to the situation in Germany. That an IP address is no personal data for website operators, cf. Stefan Krüger/Svenja-Ariane Maucher, *IP-Adresse wirklich ein personenbezogenes Datum? – Ein falscher Trend mit großen Auswirkungen auf die Praxis*, MultiMedia und Recht 2011, 433, 433 et seq.; Per Meyerdierks, *Sind IP-Adressen personenbezogene Daten,* MultiMedia und Recht 2009, 8, 9 et seq.; Flemming Moos, *Die Entwicklung des Datenschutzrechts im Jahr 2007,* Kommunikation und Recht 2008, 137, 139.

to…".[1397] A strict application of this conclusion would mean that even for the rights-holders the IP addresses they collect in peer-to-peer networks would constitute personal data. Accordingly, the French legislator, in the course of the HADOPI laws, and albeit the lack of an explicit classification in France[1398], chose to pass a statutory clause that expressly enables the agents of the rights-holders to collect personal data in relation to an infringement including the IP address of the user.[1399] Previously, the French Data Protection Authority had repeatedly declared that IP addresses are personal data, and some courts followed that proposition.[1400] In contrast, in Germany, the majority view seems to be that "harvesting" of data in relation to copyright infringements, i.e. the logging of dynamic IP addresses in peer-to-peer networks by rights-holders does not constitute the collecting of personal data.[1401] This view pays regard to the fact that the (dynamic) IP address as such without any further elements or steps taken for identification, does not allow parties other than access providers

---

1397 Article 29 Data Protection Working Party, *Opinion 4/2007 on the Concept of Personal Data*, 01248/07/EN WP 136 of 20.06.2007, p. 17.

1398 Cf. Yves Détraigne/Anne-Marie Escoffier, *Rapport d'information fait au nom de la Commission des lois constitutionnelles, de législation, du suffrage universel, du Règlement et d'administration générale, par le groupe de travail relatif au respect de la vie privée à l'heure des mémoires numériques* (27.05.2009).

1399 In that regard, the *Décret no 2010-236 du 5 mars 2010 relatif au traitement automatisé de données à caractère personnel autorisé par l'article L. 331-29 du code de la propriété intellectuelle dénommé «Système de gestion des mesures pour la protection des œuvres sur Internet»* expressly refers to the IP address as a personal data. The Annex to said Decret enumerates what is considered as personal data and this includes the IP address.

1400 See Christoper Kuner/Cédric Burton/Jörg Hladjk/Oliver Proust, *Study on online copyright enforcement and data protection in selected Member States* (November 2009), pp. 23 et seq. The authors cite a decision by the TGI Paris from 24 June 2009, in which the TGI stated that an IP address is personal data since "it corresponds to a number provided by an Internet service provider which identifies a computer connected to the network (...). With regard to the existing technology, this address appears to be the only means enabling to track a natural person who has posted content online".

1401 Instead of many, see Rolf Schwartmann, *Vergleichende Studie über Modelle zur Versendung von Warnhinweisen durch Internet-Zugangsanbieter an Nutzer bei Urheberrechtsverletzungen, Studie im Auftrag des Bundesministerium für Wirtschaft und Technologie* (Januar 2012), p. 300.

to identify an access subscriber.[1402] Thus, the determination of IP addresses as personal data depends on the perspective: while for access providers IP addresses are personal data, for rights-holder they are no personal data but may become so once a court order for disclosure against the access provider is obtained. However, also in Germany, this view is contested with some scholars and data protection commissioners arguing that IP addresses are in general personal data.[1403] The UK approach shows that it is difficult to view the IP address separate from the information about the infringing content that has been identified. During the judicial review of the Digital Economy Act in the UK, the High Court proceeded on the assumption that dynamic IP addresses are personal data citing inter alia the Opinion of the Article 29 Working Party.[1404] This conclusion was further based on the fact that the data collected to prepare a notification of an infringement also identifies the nature of the digital material that has been unlawfully copied; the nature of this material however may reveal special categories of personal data that may inter alia relate to racial, or ethnic origin, political opinions, or sex life of an individual. An identified or identifiable person (the subscriber) will thus be "inevitably linked, through the dynamic IP address, to material that might, for example, tend to show unusual sexual proclivities".[1405] While an isolated IP address may not carry any such information, in the context of copyright enforcement, they always need to be processed together with the materials that have been up- or downloaded through that address. Hence, in connection with the fact that there are means available to identify the subscriber of that address, who will at least have "facilitated" the infringement, there is a strong argument to treat IP addresses as personal data.

1402 Peter Schmitz, *Datenschutz im Internet*, Part. 16.2, paras. 80 and 83, in: Thomas Hoeren/Ulrich Sieber/Bernd Holznagel, *Handbuch Multimedia-Recht* (36th ed. 2013).

1403 Instead of many cf. Peter Schaar, *Datenschutz im Internet* (2002), para. 174 and Alexander Dix, *Vorratsdatenspeicherung von IP-Adressen?*, Datenschutz und Datensicherheit 2003, 234–235.

1404 High Court, *R. (on the application of British Telecommunications Plc) v Secretary of State for Business, Innovation and Skills,* [2011] EWHC 1021 (Admin), [2011] 3 C.M.L.R. 5, paras. 152–157.

1405 *Ibid*, para. 156.

This conclusion can be supported on an EU law level by reference to the *Data Retention Directive*[1406]. For the purposes of the *Data Retention Directive*, data means traffic data, location data and the related data necessary to identify the subscriber or the users.[1407] A starting point to trace and identify a particular user or at least the subscriber will be the IP address used.[1408] IP addresses and further data to trace the origin of a communication shall be retained "to the extent that those data are generated or processed by providers of publicly available electronic communications services or of a public communications network within their jurisdiction in the process of supplying the communications services concerned".[1409] If one again takes into account the Opinion of the Article 29 Working Party as regards the determination of IP addresses as personal data, namely, that IP address are personal data when information about the subscriber is available to national authorities upon request, IP addresses are personal data at least for the stipulated retention time foreseen in the national transposition of the *Data Retention Directive*.[1410] However, considering that the *Data Retention Directive* only requires the disclosure of data to national authorities in relation to serious crime, the awkward result would be that for national authorities, IP addresses would only fall within the scope of personal data when they relate to serious crime, because only then, it would be possible for the national authorities to identify a subscriber. For access providers, the data however constitutes personal data from the allocation of an IP address and the retention of this data onwards. This shows that for different stakeholders IP addresses have a different quality.[1411]

1406 *Directive 2006/24/EC of the European Parliament and of the Council of 15 March 2006 on the retention of data generated or processed in connection with the provision of publicly available electronic communications services or of public communications networks and amending Directive 2002/58/EC,* OJ 2006 L 105, p. 54.

1407 See Article 2(a) of the *Data Retention Directive*.

1408 See Article 5(1)(a)(2)(iii) of the *Data Retention Directive;* Eneken Tikk, *IP Addresses Subject to Personal Data Regulation,* in: Eneken Tikk/Anna-Maria Talihärm (eds.), *International Cyber Security Legal & Policy Proceedings* (2010), 35.

1409 Article 3(1) of the Data Retention Directive.

1410 See in this regard also Eneken Tikk, *IP Addresses Subject to Personal Data Regulation,* in: Eneken Tikk/Anna-Maria Talihärm (eds.), *International Cyber Security Legal & Policy Proceedings* (2010), 35.

1411 Cf. Rolf Schwartmann, *Vergleichende Studie über Modelle zur Versendung von Warnhinweisen durch Internet-Zugangsanbieter an Nutzer bei Urheber-*

In the following, it is thus proceeded on the basis that IP addresses, including dynamic IP addresses, are personal data as long as there are means likely reasonably to be used to identify the persons including through court orders or the initiation of criminal investigations – meaning that as long as a rights-holder or website operator has the possibility to obtain a disclosure order, an IP address constitutes personal data. Once a court denies a disclosure order or a disclosure is not possible because the service provider has already deleted the data required to match the address to a subscriber, an IP address will no longer constitute personal data.

(2) Processing of Data

The graduated response schemes that have been presented both require access providers to process "personal data" within the meaning of Articles 2(a) and (b) of the *Data Protection Directive*: the access providers must link the IP address provided by the copyright owner (or in the case of France: HADOPI), and either notify them about the infringement or provide an authority with the identity of a subscriber. In the UK, the access provider will further be under a legal obligation to complete copyright infringement lists. Considering that the information processed constitutes "personal data" as the processing of IP addresses is carried out with the purpose of identifying the subscriber,[1412] the procedures have to be in conformity with the *Data Protection Directive*. This applies in particular as the reports on copyright infringements, be it the French *dossiers* that are forwarded to HADOPI or the UK CIRs that are forwarded to the access providers, identify the nature of the material that has been unlawfully copied by a subscriber or someone else using his connection. Even if the IP address may only help to identify the subscriber, the data nonetheless relates to an identified or identifiable person because the subscriber who can be identified is "inevitably linked to the data"[1413] as the person, who

---

rechtsverletzungen, Studie im Auftrag des Bundesministerium für Wirtschaft und Technologie (Januar 2012), pp. 299 et seq.

1412 See the above discussion of IP address as personal data.

1413 Cf. High Court, *R. (on the application of British Telecommunications Plc) v Secretary of State for Business, Innovation and Skills,* [2011] EWHC 1021 (Admin), [2011] 3 C.M.L.R. 5, para. 156.

has "facilitated" the infringement, even if he is not the infringer and could incur no legal liability for the infringement.

The question is whether already the collection of evidence by rights-holders or their agents as well as the assessment of notifications by HADOPI prior to matching the information to subscribers with the help of access providers amounts to the processing of *personal* data. In contrast to the access providers, neither the rights-holders nor HADOPI at an early stage have the capacity to link an identifiable person to the dynamic IP addresses. However, as stated in the introduction, dynamic IP addresses are personal data as long as there are means likely reasonably to be used to identify the persons including through court orders or the initiation of criminal investigations – meaning that as long as a rights-holder or website operator has the possibility to legally obtain information on the identity of a source of communication, an IP address constitutes personal data. Once a court denies a disclosure order or a disclosure is not possible because the service provider has already deleted the data required to match the address to a subscriber, the address will no longer constitute personal data.

Even if IP addresses are considered to be solely traffic data, they may only be processed in a limited number of circumstances and for specific purposes (such as billing, invoicing, compliance with a legal obligation, or the legitimate interests pursued by the controller or a third party to whom the data are disclosed).[1414] The processing for other purposes (such as online copyright enforcement) generally requires consent.[1415]

The traffic data in question is originally being processed by access providers for the purposes of Article 2 *E-Privacy Directive*, namely, "for the purpose of the conveyance of a communication on an electronic communications network or for the billing thereof".

The processing of traffic data by both rights-holders, the administrative authority and access providers under the graduated response schemes at a first sight contravenes the obligation on Member States under Article 5 of the E-.Privacy Directive to "ensure the confidentiality of communications and the related traffic data". Pursuant to Article 5(1) of *E-Privacy Directive*, Member States must ensure the confidentiality of communications by means of a public communications network and publicly available elec-

1414 See Article 7 of the *Data Protection Directive.*

1415 Cf. European Commission, DG Internal Market, *Study on Online Copyright Enforcement and Data Protection in Selected Member States* (November 2009).

tronic communications services, and of the related traffic data, and must inter alia prohibit, in principle, the storage of that data by persons other than users, without the consent of the users concerned. There are only two exceptions to that rule, namely the exceptions related to persons lawfully authorised in accordance with Article 15(1) of the Directive and the technical storage necessary for conveyance of a communication.

In addition, as regards traffic data, Article 6(1) of *E-Privacy Directive* provides that stored traffic data must be deleted or rendered anonymous when it is no longer needed for the purpose of the transmission of a communication. As regards Article 6(2), (3) and (5), which concern the processing of traffic data for billing and marketing purposes as well as the provision of value-added services, these provisions do not concern the communication of the respective data to third parties. They thus can only relate to disputes between service providers and users concerning the grounds for data storage.[1416]

However, Article 15(1) *E-Privacy Directive* contains exceptions to Articles 5 and 6 of the *E-Privacy Directive* and allows Member States to adopt legislative measures restricting the confidentiality obligations with regard to users' communications and related traffic data. Thus, the compatibility of the collecting and processing activities with the *E-Privacy Directive* depend on whether these activities come within the scope of one of the derogations set forth in Article 15(1). Article 15(1) stipulates that "Member States may adopt legislative measures to restrict the scope of the rights and obligations provided for in Article 5, Article 6, Article 8(1), (2), (3) and (4), and Article 9 of this Directive when such restriction constitutes a necessary, appropriate and proportionate measure within a democratic society to safeguard national security (i.e. State security), defence, public security, and the prevention, investigation, detection and prosecution of criminal offences or of unauthorised use of the electronic communication system, as referred to in Article 13(1) of the *Data Protection Directive*. To this end, Member States may, inter alia, adopt legislative measures providing for the retention of data for a limited period justified on the grounds laid down in this paragraph. All the measures referred to in this paragraph shall be in accordance with the general principles of Community law, including those referred to in Article 6(1) and (2) of the Treaty on Euro-

1416 See CJEU, C-275/06, *Productores de Música de España (Promusicae) v Telefónica de España SAU* [2008] ECR I-271, para. 48.

pean Union".[1417] Although the protection of (intellectual) property is not explicitly referred to in Article 15, it may be included by Article 15(1) ending the list of exceptions with an express reference to Article 13(1) of the *Data Protection Directive.* Said paragraph sets forth further purposes for which Member States may restrict the right to privacy in respect for the processing of personal data, including where the restriction is necessary for "(g) the protection of the data subject or of the rights and freedoms of others". In the *Promusicae* case, the CJEU held that Article 13(1) of the *Data Protection Directive* is incorporated by said reference into the *E-Privacy Directive.*[1418] Accordingly, Article 15(1) *E-Privacy Directive* has to be interpreted as expressing the Community legislature's intention not to exclude from its scope of protection the right to (intellectual) property or situations in which authors seek to obtain that protection in civil proceedings.[1419] As a consequence, Article 15(1) of the *E-Privacy Directive* allows the restriction of the obligations under the Directive not only in the circumstances explicitly mentioned in Article 15(1), but also in situations "that may give rise to civil proceedings".[1420] Therefore the question referred to the Court in Promusicae was answered as follows: although EU law does not require Member States to implement in their national laws an obligation to disclose personal data in the context of civil proceedings in order to ensure the effective protection of copyright, it does not preclude this either.[1421] EU law requires however, that Member States transposing the relevant Directives interpret them in a way that "allows a fair balance to be struck between the various fundamental rights protected by the Community legal order"; also when applying their national law, this has to interpreted in such a way as to not be in conflict with EU law.[1422]

1417 Article 15(1a) further provides that "Paragraph 1 shall not apply to data specifically required by Directive 2006/24/EC of the European Parliament and of the Council of 15 March 2006 on the retention of data generated or processed in connection with the provision of publicly available electronic communications services or of public communications networks to be retained for the purposes referred to in Article 1(1) of that Directive".

1418 CJEU, C-275/06, *Productores de Música de España (Promusicae) v Telefónica de España SAU* [2008] ECR I-271, para. 52.

1419 *Ibid*, para. 53.

1420 *Ibid.*

1421 *Ibid.*

1422 *Ibid*, paras. 68 et seq.

Applying this guidance the CJEU, the collecting and processing of personal data in the context of graduated response schemes must protect the right to intellectual property or be in situations in which authors seek to obtain that protection in civil proceedings. None of the graduated response schemes solely focusses on situations in which authors seek to obtain protection of intellectual property rights in civil proceedings. Although, the UK systems intends to identify repeat infringers to allow rights-holders targeted actions against persistent infringers, it does not require rights-holders to seek protection in civil proceedings. The main intention is rather to warn and inform users. Therefore the scheme does not foresee any further information rights of rights-holder than the anonymised CIL, instead further information rights are subject to common law. In France, the whole scheme is outside the context of civil proceedings, as its purpose is to sanction repeat infringers under criminal law. Thus, neither rights-holders collect nor HADOPI or access providers (in the case of UK) process data to obtain protection of copyright in civil proceedings. Because the collecting and processing of personal data takes place outside of civil proceedings, the present situation is different from the issues raised in the Promusicae case. In particular, the disclosure of information in relation to IP addresses by the access providers to HADOPI requires no judicial oversight. In that respect, one has to consider that enforcement by public authorities means that there is potentially more respect to privacy than enforcement by private parties. Moreover, in her opinion in the Promusicae case, the Advocate General concluded that enforcement by public authorities necessarily results in greater respect for fundamental rights than does enforcement by private parties.[1423] Thus, there are less concerns involved when public authorities process personal data. The CJEU however, did not discuss this contention, and thus seems to place enforcement by private entities on the same level as enforcement by public authorities.[1424] One may argue that the court thereby indirectly recognised that law enforcement authorities in practice do not have the capacities to deal with online copyright infringements by end-users.[1425] While this may be

1423 Opinion of Advocate General Kokott in Case C-275/06, *Productores de Musica de España (Promusicae) v Telefonica de España SAU,* para. 114.

1424 Cf. Christoph Kuner, *Data Protection and Rights Protection on the Internet: The Promusicae Judgment of the European Court of Justice,* European Intellectual Property Review 2008, Issue 5, 199, 201.

1425 See *ibid.*

the case considering the large number of warnings being send out each month by HADOPI, one should at this point not confuse the administration of warnings by a public authority and law enforcement by the police and public prosecutor. The fact, that the CJEU did not discuss the Advocate General´s contention should rather be considered as there being no need to discuss this subject-matter.

With respect to the collecting and processing of personal data outside of civil proceedings, one must pay consideration to the fact, that the CJEU in Promusicae also set forth that such processing is permitted for the protection of the right to property within the scope of the "protection of the rights and freedoms of others" under Article 15(1).[1426] The CJEU's ruling went beyond protection in the context of civil proceedings. The graduated response schemes and the data processing connected with them are intended to promote the protection of copyright and thus are covered by the exceptions provided for in Article 15(1) *E-Privacy Directive* read in conjunction with Article 13(1) *Data Protection Directive*.[1427] This does not mean that the graduated response schemes are in compliance with EU law.

According to the principle of proportionality in EU law, a balance needs to be struck between the means used and the intended aim of their actions.

Neither data protection nor protection of IP rights is given precedence over the other.[1428] The CJEU considers the law to be neutral in this respect. The most important point for the Court is that a fair balance is achieved between the fundamental rights of the parties involved. It is important that not only the national implementation, but also the interpretation of the national implementation is consistent with the directives and not in conflict with fundamental rights or other principles of Community law.

1426 CJEU, C-275/06, *Productores de Música de España (Promusicae) v Telefónica de España SAU* [2008] ECR I-271, para. 53.

1427 The same conclusion was reached by the High Court in *R (on the Application of British Telecommunications Plc and Others) v The Secretary of State for Business, Innovation and Skills* [2011] EWHC 1021 (Admin), Judgment of 20.04.2011. See also Anne Barron, *'Graduated Response' à l'Anglaise: Online Copyright Infringement and the Digital Economy Act 2010,* Journal of Media Law 2011, Vol. 3 Issue 2, 305, 332.

1428 See instead of many Case C-275/06 *Productores de Musica de España (Promusicae) v Telefonica de España SAU*, [2008] ECR I-271, paras. 61 et seq.

(3) Disclosure of Personal Data

As regards the disclosure of personal data to rights-holders, the CJEU only provided little guidance in the Bonnier Audio case on how to strike a fair balance between the fundamental rights in question, namely that national legislation that foresees the disclosure of data must require that "there be clear evidence of an infringement of an intellectual property right, that the information can be regarded as facilitating the investigation into an infringement of copyright or impairment of such a right and that the reasons for the measure outweigh the nuisance or other harm which the measure may entail for the person affected by it or for some other conflicting interest".[1429] The court seised must weigh the conflicting interests involved on the basis of the facts of each case presented and must strike a fair and proportionate balance between the interests involved. The same applies to the disclosure of personal data by access providers to HADOPI. The judgement in Bonnier Audio does not constitute a carte blanche as regards the usage of retained data. It only clarifies that national legislation, that foresees the disclosure of data to pursue civil claims, does not contravene the *Data Retention Directive* or other Community law. Such information rights are subject to national law, which as aforementioned may or may not provide for these rights. The French data protection law provides that HADOPI may request the disclosure of personal data, that access provider have to retain for the prosecution of serious crimes. Similarly, access providers in the UK have to use the data retained for these purposes to send out warnings. These statutory changes were necessary to guarantee that warnings could be send out in first place because Internet access providers were not retaining data for longer than a few days due to existing domestic laws on data retention.[1430]

1429 *Ibid*, para. 58.

1430 See in this regard: European Observatory on Counterfeiting and Piracy, *Evidence and Right of Information in Intellectual Property Rights* (2010), pp. 4 et seq., which outlines the example of Spain, in which, following the judgement of the CJEU in the Promusicae case, the domestic court "confirmed that Spanish data protection rules prevent Internet service providers from disclosing the identity of individual account holders to right holders for the purpose of civil proceedings, depriving right holders of a remedy altogether". Similarly the report states that in Austria, "in the case of on-line peer-to-peer infringements ('file sharing'), the provisions relating to the right of information are in practice not enforceable where information is requested from access providers, due to a deci-

Following the CJEU's ruling in Bonnier Audio, it has been clarified that Member States are free to introduce obligations upon Internet service providers to forward information under the condition that this is in compliance with data protection law. From what has been said above, EU data protection law does not preclude such processing that is intended to protect copyright.

(4) Processing of Sensitive Data

The data that is processed in connection with a copyright infringement also contains information about the materials that have been shared. Depending on the materials this data may constitute sensitive data. Sensitive data is defined as personal data that reveals racial or ethnic origin, political opinions, religious or philosophical beliefs, trade-union membership, or relates to health or sex life.[1431] The material collected in relation to the subscriber may also reveal such special categories of personal data, relating in particular to the sex life of an individual insofar as pornographic materials are concerned.[1432] For instance, a subscriber may be linked to unusual sexual proclivities. The processing of such sensitive personal data must be justified.

As regards the processing of special categories of personal data within Article 8 of the *Data Protection Directive*, Article 8(2)(e) provides a justification for the processing if the processing is necessary for "the establishment, exercise or defence of legal claims". The graduated response schemes presented have precisely this purpose, namely putting the copyright owner in a position to establish that there has been an infringement of copyright, and identify the person responsible for the infringement. The initiation of a warning procedure does not exclude future civil legal proceedings. The information gathered however allows the preparation of such proceedings. Article 8(2)(e) also does not require that the copyright

sion of the Austrian Supreme Court restricting the retention and processing of dynamic IP addresses".

1431 See Article 8(1) of the *Data Protection Directive*.

1432 See the above discussion on IP addresses as personal data.

owner will in the end commence legal proceedings.[1433] At the time, the rights-holder gathers the data, he can never be a hundred percent sure that he will at a later stage take legal action. Whether a claim is pursued can regularly only be decided once the identity of a subscriber is revealed; following pre-litigation correspondence, the rights-holder will be able to estimate his chances of a successful claim.[1434] Successful in that respect not only relates to a successful claim, but also to enforceability (the defendant for example may be bankrupt).

The circumstances described in Article 8(2)(e) *Data Protection Directive* also fall within Article 7(f) of the Directive as "processing…necessary for the purposes of the legitimate interests pursued by the controller or by the third party or parties to whom the data are controlled".[1435] The justification applies to all categories of personal data, i.e. sensitive and non-sensitive data because otherwise the scope of protection for sensitive data would be narrower than the one for non-sensitive personal data.[1436]

cc) Compliance of Internet Suspension or Restriction Orders with Secondary EU Law

As of now, none of the graduated response schemes foresees the imposition of sanctions that may interfere with the user's possibility to access the Internet. The initial version of the French system however foresaw the

1433 Cf. also High Court, *R. (on the application of British Telecommunications Plc) v Secretary of State for Business, Innovation and Skills,* [2011] EWHC 1021 (Admin), [2011] 3 C.M.L.R. 5, para. 160.

1434 In *ibid*, para. 161, it has similarly been argued that "The data controller might not know at an early stage in processing the relevant data whether he intended at the end of the process to commence legal proceedings, and the processing could be rendered impermissible if in the event he did not commence such proceedings; and it might be only after the relevant data processing that he could sensibly decide whether it was appropriate to commence proceedings. The data controller might change his mind during the course of processing, and the legal position would be obscure".

1435 See *ibid*. The Court also stated that if there were any doubts about the application of Article 8(2)(e) to the relevant processing, the UK legislator could, before the Code came into legal effect, lay down an exemption under Article 8(4), based upon a "substantial public interest", namely, the better protection of the rights of copyright owners.

1436 Cf. *ibid*.

suspension of an Internet access as the ultimate sanction, and also the UK legislator foresees the passing of a Code providing for such sanctions. It is obvious, that these kind of sanctions interfere with fundamental rights. This has also been recognised by the EU legislators during the negotiations of the Telecoms Reform Package. Article 1(3) of the Universal Service Directive now provides that measures taken by Member States regarding end-users' access to, or use of, the Internet "shall respect the fundamental rights and freedoms of natural persons, including in relation to privacy and due process."

In addition, Article 1(3)(a) of the Framework Directive further stipulates that where fundamental rights are engaged by such measures, the latter can only be imposed if appropriate, proportionate, necessary within a democratic society, and subject to adequate procedural safeguards including effective judicial protection and due process. Thus, in general, the new provisions inserted by the *Telecoms Reforms Package* do not preclude the introduction of sanctions that ultimately limit end-users' access to the Internet. Any such sanction is however, subject to the conditions set forth in Article 1(3)(a) of the Framework Directive. Accordingly, such intrusive measures may only be taken with due respect for the fundamental rights of users including the principle of the presumption of innocence and the right to privacy. A prior, fair and impartial procedure must be guaranteed, including the right of the person concerned to be heard.[1437] Also the right to effective and timely judicial review must be guaranteed. EU law thus recognises that interferences with an end-user's Internet access may be legitimated. The European Parliament took the position that it is not impossible to justify restrictions on Internet access as long as due respect is paid to the fundamental rights of the end-users concerned by such a measure.[1438] Whether and under which circumstances the fundamental rights and freedoms of end-users are respected will be discussed in the following section on the impact of such measures on fundamental rights.

As regards other restrictions of Internet access, ony may also refer to Article 12(3) of the *E-Commerce Directive*, which provides that mere con-

---

1437 See also Anne Barron, *'Graduated Response' à l'Anglaise: Online Copyright Infringement and the Digital Economy Act 2010,* Journal of Media Law 2011, Vol. 3 issue 2, 305, 321.

1438 This view is also shared by the French Constitutional Court in its decision on the HADOPI I law, see Conseil constitutionnel, Decision of 10 June 2009 – No. 2009-580 DC, Journal officiel 13.06.2009, 9675.

duits, that is Internet access providers, may come under an obligation to terminate or prevent an infringement by using its technical facilities to end or prevent an infringement committed by a third party or to facilitate a copyright owner in pursuing his rights against an infringing party. Thus, the E-Commerce itself foresees the cooperation of access providers to not only terminate infringements but also to hinder users to commit further infringements as long as such restriction is imposed by a court or administrative authority.

dd) Compliance of Cost-Sharing with Secondary EU Law

One of the reasons why the implementation of a graduated response scheme in the UK has been delayed was the strong opposition by access providers. They in particular fought the obligation to bear 25% of the implementation costs and the costs of appeals as well as their own costs in implementing the system.[1439] They further challenged the provision under which they could be exposed to financial penalties in the event of failure to comply the Codes.[1440] An obligation to bear costs in order to allow third parties to enforce their private rights as well as the threat of penalties could potentially be equalled with rendering the access providers "liable for the information transmitted". In that regard, Article 12 of the *E-Commerce Directive* provides that mere conduits are not liable for any of the information transmitted. As long as access providers only act as mere carriers and neither initiate the transmission, nor select the receiver of the transmission or select or modify the information contained in the transmission,[1441] and within the service concerned do not store information longer than is necessary for transmission,[1442] the providers fall (as concerns the

1439 *R. (on the application of British Telecommunications Plc) v Secretary of State for Business, Innovation and Skills,* [2011] EWHC 1021 (Admin), [2011] 3 C.M.L.R. 5, para. 107.

1440 Cf. new Section 124L of the *CA 2003*.

1441 As regards these requirements see Article 12(1) *E-Commerce Directive*

1442 As regards these requirements see Article 12(2) *E-Commerce Directive*. Article 12(2) *E-Commerce Directive*refers to the process of packet switching transmission, which allows Internet service providers to store information for a brief period of time in small pieces. The packet switching transmission process allows Internet service providers to provide mere conduit activities by making copies of the information to be transmitted for the sole purpose of carrying out

provision of Internet access service) within the category of mere conduits.[1443] The liability exemption of Article 12 *E-Commerce Directive* shields mere conduits from liability such as criminal liability but also from regulatory fines or damages and other compensation payable to the copyright owner when their rights have been infringed via the connectivity service.[1444]

It is thus necessary to determine whether the obligations on access providers impose liability for the information transmitted by the providers. The penalties foreseen for non-compliance with the specific scheme established by the *DEA 2010* do not constitute any liability "for the information transmitted", i.e. for the underlying copyright infringement.[1445] The penalties derive from an infringement of obligations under the *DEA 2010*. As long as the penalties do not arise because there has been an infringement of copyright for which the access providers will be held liable, provisions that foresee the imposition of penalities are in compliance with the *E-Commerce Directive*. The same applies to the costs involved in implementing and administering the *DEA 2010* scheme. They do not constitute liability for information transmitted but are part of the *DEA 2010* scheme. The natural meaning of the wording "liable for the information transmitted" cannot be extended to also cover an economic burden imposed on an access provider for transmitting copyright-infringing information.[1446]

As already stated in the introduction to this section, the (partial) imposition of the costs for the scheme upon access providers could infringe Aricle 3(1) of the *IPR Enforcement Directive*. Said provision foresees that procedures and remedies necessary to ensure the enforcement of the intel-

---

the transmission of the information, without making the information available to subsequent users.

1443 See also recitals 43 to 45 of the *E-Commerce Directive*.

1444 See Julia Hörnle, *Premature or stillborn? – The recent challenge to the Digital Economy Act,* Computer Law & Security Review 2012, Vol. 28, 83, 85 with reference to *R. (on the application of British Telecommunications Plc) v Secretary of State for Business, Innovation and Skills,* [2011] EWHC 1021 (Admin), [2011] 3 C.M.L.R. 5, para. 102.

1445 See *R. (on the application of British Telecommunications Plc) v Secretary of State for Business, Innovation and Skills,* [2011] EWHC 1021 (Admin), [2011] 3 C.M.L.R. 5, para. 107 confirmed by [2012] EWCA Civ 232. The Court noted that "the legal test is not whether a liability has arisen because there was an initial infringement of copyright; the liability must arise in respect of that underlying infringement, so that the liability is for the information transmitted".

1446 Cf. *ibid*, at 108.

lectual property rights covered by the *IPR Enforcement Directive*, "shall be fair and equitable and shall not be unnecessarily complicated or costly, or entail unreasonable time-limits or unwarranted delays". Pursuant to Article 3(2), they "shall also be effective, proportionate and dissuasive and shall be applied in such a manner as to avoid the creation of barriers to legitimate trade and to provide for safeguards against their abuse". If one takes the robust data from France in relation to the number of infringements being send out, the access providers will look at costs of hundreds of thousands GBP, which makes the scheme costly for them. Considering that access providers are completely neutral providers and do not interfere with the content transmitted, the bearance of such a high sum seems unnecessarily costly – at least if its proportionality cannot be established.[1447]

c) Conformity with the Fundamental Rights of Internet Users

The above analysis shows that as such graduated response schemes do not contravene secondary EU law, even if they foresee as an ultimate sanction the suspension of a subscriber's Internet access service. This however applies under the condition that there is a fair balancing of fundamental rights. In this regard not only the legislation as such but also their application must not be in conflict with fundamental rights or other principles of Community law. First of all, the impact on the fundamental rights of Internet users will be in the focus as they are those against whom copyright will be enforced.

aa) Sanctions Interfering with a User's Right to Freedom to Expression in the Form of Freedom to Seek, Impart and Receive Information

The most controversial aspect of graduated response schemes has been the suspension or restriction of Internet access as an ultimate sanction.

Although the suspension of an Internet access service has been abolished in France for the offence of gross negligence and in the UK such a technical measure is far from becoming a statutory sanction, the impact on

---

1447 Cf. the CJEU's findings in C-70/10 *Scarlet Extended v SABAM*, Judgment of 14.11.2011, paras. 48 et seq.

the freedom to receive and impart information needs to discussed briefly, in particular with regard to the fact that the UK foresees as a possible alternative reductions in bandwidth, or limited access to the Internet.

It must also be noted that all these sanctions assume that the subscriber is the only person involved. This is however not true in most scenarios. Commonly, private single connections are shared, either between family members, third parties within a communal household or flatshare. The situation becomes more complicated where parties open up their Wi-Fi to the general public, for instance in the course of their business, such as hotels, coffee bars or pubs. Also, libraries and universities usually provide Internet facilities, however often under the condition that users register, which would allow identification of an infringer if logging data is retained for a certain time. At this point, the discussion will focus on private single connections. Practice has shown that it is possible for third parties to take control of a network from the outside without the owner's knowledge.[1448] This may be achieved by installing malware or hacking into the Wi-Fi network. Often access to Wi-Fi networks is not difficult for people with some IT-literacy. Where insecure wireless connections are operated, access is even simpler. Since the advent of private Wi-Fi networks, it was popular with certain IT-literate people to drive through neighbourhoods and search for unsecured Wi-Fi networks using a portable computer (so-called "wardriving"[1449]). With smartphone or other Internet usable devices such as tablets on the rise, this activity may raise to popularity again, especially since software for searching for networks is freely available on the Internet.[1450]

Accordingly, sanctions against a subscriber will not only hinder illegitimate users, but also legitimate users.[1451] Legitimate users in this context

1448 Cf. for example House of Lords, House of Commons, Joint Committee on Human Rights, *Legislative Scrutiny: Digital Economy Bill, Fifth Report of Session 2009–10*, HL Paper 44 = HC 327 (05.02.2010), p. 87.

1449 See Benjamin D. Kern, *Whacking, joyriding and war-driving: Roaming use of Wi-Fi and the Law*, CIPerati – a Cyberspace and I.P. law newsletter 2005, Vol. 2 Issue 4.

1450 Such as for example NetStumbler for Windows, SWScanner for Linux or Wi-Fi-Where for iPhones.

1451 House of Lords, House of Commons, Joint Committee on Human Rights, *Legislative Scrutiny: Digital Economy Bill, Fifth Report of Session 2009-10*, HL Paper 44 = HC 327 (05.02.2010), p. 87.

encompass all those parties that the subscriber has allowed to use his Internet access service.

The following paragraphs will outline the interference of the poposed severe penal sanctions with freedom of expression and discuss a potential justification.

In this regard, the preamble to the Declaration of the Committee of Ministers on human rights and the rule of law in the Information Society recognises that "limited or no access to information and communication technologies can deprive individuals of the ability to exercise fully their human rights".[1452]

The first chapter of the Declaration, entitled "Human rights in the Information Society" further provides that "1. [...] Freedom of expression, information and communication should be respected in a digital as well as in a non-digital environment, and should not be subject to restrictions other than those provided for in Article 10 of the ECHR, simply because communication is carried in digital form". This statement seems to indicate that a comparison must be drawn between sanctions for infringments committed in the "offline" and "online" world. Thus, one may conclude that no additional sanction should be imposed on offenders simply because they use new technologies to commit the offence. Sanctions that interfere with a user's right to freedom to expression, that only exist because the offence has been committed online, thus seem to be unjustifiable if no such sanction would exist for the same offence being committed offline, for instance by making unauthorised copies of a CD and distributing those.

Irrespective of similar sanctions existing for online and offline behaviour, the main concern is the seriousness of the interference and a justification being available. These questions will be addressed in the following.

(1) Interference

The right to freedom of expression enshrined in Article 10 *ECHR* and Article 11 *CFR* includes an active aspect (the freedom to inform) and a

---

1452 Council of Europe, *Declaration of the Committee of Ministers on human rights and the rule of law in the information society* (13.05.2005), CM(2005)56 final.

passive aspect (freedom to receive information). The right imposes on the State a negative duty not to interfere with the freedom to seek, receive and impart information.

When sanctions are imposed upon Internet access subscribers that suspend or in some other way restrict the subscriber's access to the Internet, this interferes with his right to freedom of expression in the form of freedom to seek, impart and receive information. Access to the Internet ios important in the sense to have access to mass media and to be able to consume and exchange ideas and information.

The suspension of an Internet access service may cause substantial harm to the legitimate interests of all users of the Internet connection in question. One only needs to imagine that the Internet connection is used for professional purposes.

As outlined in the first Chapter, freedom to expression is not limited to certain kinds of expressions but encompasses cultural expressions as well as pure entertainment.[1453] Thus, even when access is limited to certain services or bandwidth is restricted so that the user may no longer be able to engage in peer-to-peer networks, watch movie streams or use other services that take up large bandwidth, this interferes with his freedom of expression. One may argue, that the user may use alternative means of communication instead. However, as outlined in the first Chapter, the right to freedom of expression also covers access to specific technical means of transmission since any restriction imposed on the latter necessarily interferes with the right to receive and impart information.[1454] Freedom of expression does not only guarantee the right to impart information but also the right of the public to receive it.[1455] As regards the access to a specific means of transmission, the ECtHR held in that although citizens may "obtain some news through … newspapers and radio programmes", "these sources of information only cover parts of what is available via television broadcasts and cannot in any way be equated with the later".[1456] Consider-

1453 See ECtHR, *Khurshid Mustafa and Tarzibachi v Sweden*, Application No. 23883/06, para. 45.

1454 ECtHR, *Autronic AG v Switzerland*, Judgment of 22.05.1990 – Application No. 12726/87, Ser A No. 178 (1990), para. 47.

1455 See instead of many ECtHR, *Observer and Guardian v the United Kingdom*, Judgement of 26.11.1991 – Application no. 13585/88, para. 59.

1456 ECtHR, *Khurshid Mustafa and Tarzibachi v Sweden*, Application No. 23883/06, para. 45.

ing the nature and scope of information that is available on the Internet, the Internet as a source of information as well as an audience for own expressions, the same must apply to the Internet. The findings in *Mustafa and Tarzibachi v Sweden* must be interpreted in the light of the present-day conditions.[1457] The dissemination factor of the Internet is unreachable for traditional media and traditional sources only cover parts of what is available via the Internet. Even mere bandwidth restrictions would thus interfere with Article 10 *ECHR* – and with Article 11 *CFR*, if the sanction was based on EU legislation.[1458]

(2) Justification of Interference

Interferences with the right to freedom of expression can be justified if they are in accordance with the law, have aims that are legitimate under Article 10(2) *ECHR* and are necessary in a democratic society.

Thus, first of all, domestic law must prescribe the interference. The restrictions on Internet access that existed in France and are discussed in the UK constitute penal sanctions, and were/will be prescribed by statute.

Secondly, the interference must have aims that are legitimate under Article 10(2) *ECHR*. The criminal sanctions concerned pursue the legitimate aim of protection of the rights of others. The rights of others include legal rights, such as proprietary rights.[1459] Further, as the sanctions may have a dissuasive effect on the individual concerned and on the general

---

1457 Cf. See Council of Europe, *Internet: Case-Law of the European Court of Human Rights* (June 2011).

1458 The latter is not the case in the described scenarios, which relate to enforcement schemes that have been implemented under national legislation. One may also argue that the duty to pay the subscription fees for the duration of a suspension is a disproportionate penalty. However, the obligation to pay the subscription fees is no penalty as such as the obligation to pay the subscription fee in the absence of a termination of a contract is an obligation under civil law. It is not a measure of a punitive nature. The obligation rather stems from a breach of contract attributable to the subscriber. See in that regard also Conseil constitutionnel, Decision of 22 October 2009 – no. 2009-590 DC, Journal officiel 29.10.2009, 18292, para. 17.

1459 Alastair Mowbray, *Cases, Materials, and Commentary on the European Convention on Human Rigths* (2nd ed. 2007), p. 726. See also the recent case of ECtHR, *Ashby Donald and others v France*, Judgement of 10.01.2013 – Application No. 36769/08 with further references, and ECtHR, *Fredrik Neij and*

public to infringe copyright, the sanctions also pursue the legitimate aim of prevention of crime.[1460] Restrictions on or suspension of Internet access are theoretically capable to put an end to infringements.

Most importantly, the interference must be necessary in a democratic society. The Court's judgments relating to Article 10 – starting with Handyside[1461] – enounce the following major principles. Freedom of expression constitutes one of the essential foundations of a democratic society, exceptions to free expression must thus be narrowly interpreted and the necessity for any restrictions must be convincingly established. The notion "necessary" is not synonymous with "indispensable".[1462] "Necessary", within the meaning of Article 10(2) implies the existence of a "pressing social need".[1463] The Contracting States have a certain margin of appreciation in assessing whether a pressing social need exists. Such a need could well be the combat against copyright infringements on the Internet as such. Nevertheless, it is necessary to weigh the interests of Internet users to have unrestricted access to the Internet and the interests of intellectual property rights-holder to have their rights protected. It has to be noted at this point that intellectual property is protected by Article 1 of Protocol No. 1 to the *ECHR*[1464] and Article 17 *CFR*. The genuine, effective exercise of property rights does not depend merely on the State's duty not to interfere, but may require positive measures of protection.[1465] Thus, it is necessary to balance the two competing interests of which both enjoy fundamental rights protection. Within the balancing test, it is necessary to consider the type of expression and information that is interfered with. In the present case, a suspension would prevent access to all differ-

---

Peter Sunde Kolmisoppi v Sweden, Decision of 19.02.2013 – Application No. 40397/12.

1460 Cf. also ECtHR, *Fredrik Neij and Peter Sunde Kolmisoppi v Sweden*, Decision of 19.02.2013 – Application No. 40397/12.

1461 ECtHR, *Handyside v the United Kingdom*, Judgment of 07.12.1976 – Application no. 5493/72.

1462 ECtHR, *Handyside v the United Kingdom*, Judgment of 07.12.1976 – Application no. 5493/72, para. 48.

1463 Instead of many see ECtHR, *Observer and Guardian v the United Kingdom*, Judgment of 26.11.1991 – Application no. 13585/88, para. 59.

1464 See for example, ECtHR, *Anheuser-Busch Inc. v Portugal [GC],* Application no. 73049/01, § 72, *ECHR* 2007-I.

1465 See for example ECtHR, *Öneryıldız v Turkey [GC],* Application no. 48939/99, para. 134.

ent kinds of speech including the access to various mass media which in turn is fundamental to develop own opinions. In light of its accessibility and its capacity to store and communicate vast amounts of information, the Internet plays an important role in enhancing the public's access to news and facilitating the dissemination of information generally.[1466]

The impact on freedom of expression may not be as severe where only restrictions on access exist. As regards restrictions to Internet access, the ECtHR held in *Yildirim v Turkey* that even though effects of a restriction may be limited, this "does not diminish its significance, especially since the Internet has now become one of the principal means by which individuals exercise their right to freedom of expression and information, providing as it does essential tools for participation in activities and discussions concerning political issues and issues of general interest".[1467] Thus, restrictions on access are still interferences with freedom of expression and information.

Further, it needs to assess who will be affected by the sanction. Neither the French nor the UK graduated response scheme determines what needs to be done when the subscriber shares an Internet access with third parties. The fact that third parties may be affected by a suspension or restriction order is just being ignored. Moreover, the legitimate interests of third parties need also to be taken into consideration when assessing whether an interference with the freedom of expression is proportionate.

Considering that also the subscriber must not necessarily be the infringer, and may just have recklessly not secured his Internet access sufficiently or may be wrongly accused of copyright infringement.[1468] Also, the criminal offence for which the sanction is imposed is of a minor nature considering that the download (and necessary upload) of three songs from a peer-to-peer network will be enough to reach the sanctioning stage of the graduated response schemes in question. Although the court imposing the sanction will regularly take into account whether the subscriber has taken any action to prevent further infringements from being committed via his Internet access, a strict application of the law does not make such an assessement a necessity. Even if one assumes that against persistent

---

1466 ECtHR, *Times Newspapers Ltd v the United Kingdom* (nos. 1 and 2), Application nos. 3002/03 and 23676/03, para. 27.

1467 ECtHR, *Yildirim v Turkey*, Judgment of 18.12.2012 – Application no. 3111/10, para. 54.

1468 See above A. III. 4. The Identifier.

infringers that wilfully infringe copyright, an Internet restriction order may outweigh his right to freedom of seek, receive and impart information and ideas, this may only be the case as long as innocent third parties are not affected. To guarantee that only in these cases restrictions may apply, it will be necessary to draft provisions that foresee the application of the Internet restriction sanction under certain further conditions including the wilfull infringement of copyright for which the subscriber himself is liable. In France such a provision existed with Article 335-7-2 of the Code de la proriété intellectuelle, which set forth that when considering the suspension of an Internet access, the court must take into account the circumstances and seriousness of the violation, the personality of the infringer including his professional and social activites and his economic situation. Nevertheless, the law foresaw the suspension of an Internet access even where the subscriber was not the infringer and still encompassed a multiplicity of cases where a sanction could be imposed. In that regard and considering the severity of the interference, it cannot be enough to merely allow third parties to use an Internet access, especially if the third party may be instructed not to interfere with intellectual property rights.

In light of the importance of Internet in a networked world, the only conclusion that can be drawn that the sanctions as they stood/stand interfere with the rights of the subscriber and moreover third parties in a non-justifiable way. They may restrict a broad circle of users' access to impart or receive information. The rights of the intellectual property rights-holders can further be protected by less intrusive means including fines.

This result corresponds with the findings of the Special Rapporteur for the UN's Human Rights Council Frank La Rue's findings in his Report on Freedom of Expression. La Rue considered cutting off users from Internet access, regardless of the justification provided, including the intellectual property rights of the copyright owners, to be disproportionate and thus a violation Article 19(3) of the ICCPR.[1469]

1469 See UNHRC, *Report of the Special Rapporteur on the Promotion and Protection of the Right to Freedom of Opinion an Expression, Frank La Rue* (16.05.2011), UN Doc A/HRC/17/27, paras. 78–79. The Special Rapporteur also called upon States to ensure that Internet access is maintained at all times, including during times of political unrest. States should repeal or amend existing intellectual property laws and refrain from adopting laws which forsee the disconnection of users from Internet access.

bb) Collecting and Processing of Communications and Personal Data Interfering with Privacy Rights

The privacy rights enshrined in Article 8 *ECHR* and Articles 7 and 8 *CFR* are obviously implicated in the enforcement schemes.

First of all, privacy rights may be concerned when rights-holders monitor peer-to-peer networks for online infringements and harvest IP addresses. Secondly, they may be concerned when rights- holders seek to unmask the person behind the harvested IP address.

While these are obvious scenarios where privacy rights may be concerned, there are further aspects that are not so obvious that may give rise to concern. One of these will be discussed in the following, which is the information concerning the infringement that is forwarded to the subscriber who must not necessarily have committed the infringement himself.

(1) Interference with the Right to Respect for Family and Private Life

The most likely aspect to be concerned with regard to the right to respect for family and private life under Article 8 *ECHR* and Article 7 *CFR*, is the private life of the alleged infringer.[1470] As mentioned above, where information is disclosed to the subscriber as regards the infringing work in question, from which he may draw conclusions in relation to the sexual preferences (see above) or radical views of another person that uses his Internet access, this clearly interferes with the right to respect for private life of that person. Although within none of the graduated response scheme such information will be contained in the warning, at least under the *DEA 2010* scheme, the subscriber may ask for further information.

But not only where information is disclosed to the subscriber as regards the content that has been shared, the private life of an Internet user will be affected. When access providers in the UK are obliged to keep records, the so-called copyright infringement lists, or HADOPI collects data relating to infringements, the private life of subscribers is interfered with. It is his private life and potentially his intimate sphere that will be affected when

1470 With regard to the scope of protection see above, First Chapter, B. II. 2. b) bb) Right to Respect for Family and Private Life.

public authorities or private actors hold electronic databases with the respective (sensitive) data.[1471]

The UK legislator has recognised this risk and therefore the *DEA 2010* foresees that data held by the access provider is being anonymised. In France all data is processed and retained by HADOPI, with only HADOPI having access to the data that is retained. As regards public authorities, domestic laws usually foresee transparency and supervision as to data processing, whereas with private actors there is less supervision, which may be one of the reasons why HADOPI is not required to keep anonymised lists.[1472] Both schemes foresee the deletion of data within a certain time frame and thereby aim to respect the principle of proportionality. Whether the interference can be justified will be examined following an outline of further aspects of privacy that may be affected.

Not to be neglected in the context of respect for family and private life is the provision in the *DEA 2010*, whereby a subscriber may be sanctioned for "allowing" another person to use the service and infringe copyright. [1473] The notion of "allowing" cannot be equalled with "authorising". In that respect, HJ Birss QC pointed out in Media CAT v Adams that allowing a third party to use an Internet connection does not alone equate authorising an infringement by that person.[1474] UK courts have not yet decided whether the act of authorising use of an Internet connection turn the person doing the authorising into a person authorising the infringement within section 16(2) *CDPA 1988*. So, if the *DEA 2010* introduces a new liability provision, the question is: what is meant by "allowing"? Should the subscriber be obliged to monitor the activities of his family members

---

1471 Cf. EU Network of Independent Experts on Fundamental Rights, *Commentary of the Charter of Fundamental Rights of the European Union* (June 2006), Article 7 *CFR*, p. 79.

1472 In her opinion in the Promusicae case, the Advocate General concluded that enforcement by public authorities necessarily results in greater respect for fundamental rights than does enforcement by private parties, see Opinion of the Advocate General Kokott in Case C-275/06 *Productores de Musica de España (Promusicae) v Telefonica de España SAU.*

1473 See Section 4(4) *Initial Obligations Code* (June 2012). See also new section 124A(2) *CA 2003* inserted by section 3 *DEA 2010*.

1474 Patents County Court, *Media C.A.T. v Adams* [2011] EWPCC 6, [2011] FSR 8, para. 30.

or flatmates? This would clearly interfere with the guarantee to private life of the persons concerned.[1475]

(2) Interference with the Right to the Confidentiality of Communications

If Internet service providers are under an obligation to link IP addresses listed in CIRs or notifications by HADOPI to the subscriber's personal details and in the case of CILs pass this information on, these acts of data processing could interfere with data protection principles such as the confidentiality of communications guaranteed under Article 7 *CFR* and Article 8 *ECHR*. Article 7 *CFR* and Article 8 *ECHR* do not only protect the contents of communication but also traffic data.[1476] Under the right to confidentiality of communications, states are obliged to take all necessary measures to restrict unlawful obtaining of information by public authorities and private parties.[1477] In that respect not just the contents of communications is protected, but also traffic data.[1478] Already the collecting of data that by rights-holders or their agents thus affects the confidentiality of communications by subscribers and other Internet users. However, the question is, whether the gathering of information is unlawful. In that regard, it is also necessary to look at the methods used to gather and collect personal information.[1479] No specific method is addressed in the laws, in particular does none of the graduated response schemes foresee the monitoring of detected infringers. The information is not obtained through secret surveillance, but by crawling peer-to-peer networks. The right-holders do nothing else than taking the role of a user and join a swarm of peer-to-peer file-sharers. One may argue, that at this stage, they do not interfere with the confidentiality of communications when they colllect data necessary to trace and identify the source of a communication and its destina-

---

1475 See Lilian Edwards, *Mandy and me: Some thoughts on the Digital Economy Bill*, Scripted 2009, Vol. 6 Issue 3, 535, 536.

1476 See ECtHR, *Malone v The United Kingdom*, Judgement of 02.08.1984 – Application No. 8692/79, para. 84.

1477 See above First Chapter, B. II. 2. b) aa) Privacy Rights in General.

1478 See above First Chapter, B. II. 2. b) cc) Right to the Confidentiality of Communications.

1479 Cf. ECtHR, *Leander v Sweden*, Judgment of 26.03.1987 – Application no. 9248/81, para. 48; S. and Marper v United Kingdom, Judgment of 04.12.2008 – Application nos. 30562/04 and 30566/04, para. 67.

tion, i.e. the date, time, duration and type of communication. However, considering that they may – in addition to the graduated response scheme – have information rights under civil law (as for instance in the UK[1480]), the IP addresses lead to an identifiable person (=the subscriber) and thus, fall within the category of personal data. The collecting of IP address thus already constitutes collecting of personal data.

Once rights-holders have logged IP addresses and further information relating to an infringement and forward this information to the access provider (UK) or HADOPI, this data is processed. Both, access providers and HADOPI are empowered to match the IP address to a subscriber. When access providers are obliged to disclose information about their customers in relation to a user's communication to a public authority, the confidentiality of communication will be affected.

In consideration of the recent decision of the CJEU in relation to the *Data Retention Directive*,[1481] it also becomes necessary to analyse which kind of data access providers may be obliged to disclose. This question also relates to the context and purpose for which the requested data has been retained. In the UK, access providers will for instance be required to disclose data that they have retained in order to comply with the national transposition of the *Data Retention Directive*. This provision has not become invalid simply because the *Data Retention Directive* has been declared invalid by the CJEU. The national transposition will in itself have to be analysed as regards its compliance with EU law. As this would go beyond the scope of this research, it shall only be noted that the collecting and retention of data derogates from the system of protection of the right to privacy established by *Data Protection* and *E-Privacy Directive*, which provide for the confidentiality of communications. To establish the existence of an interference with the fundamental right to privacy, it does not matter whether the information on the private lives concerned is sensitive

---

1480 See below B. III. 2. A) aa) The Service of Disclosure Orders in the UK – Right to Information and Norwich Pharmacal Orders.

1481 CJEU, Joined cases C-293/12 and C-594/12 *Digital Rights Ireland and Seitlinger and Others*, Judgment of 08.04.2014. Given that the Court has not limited the temporal effect of its judgment, the declaration of invalidity takes effect from the date on which the Directive entered into force.

or whether the persons concerned have been inconvenienced in any way.[1482] If one compares the general framework with the findings of the CJEU in the case challenging the validity of the *Data Retention Directive*, one may draw the conclusion that, the obligation imposed by the domestic law on access providers to retain, for a certain period, data relating to a person's private life and his communications, constitutes an interference with the right to privacy under Article 7 *CFR* (and Article 8 *ECHR*).[1483] The CJEU also noted in that case that the fact that data are retained and subsequently used without the subscriber being informed is likely to generate in the minds of the persons concerned the feeling that their private lives are the subject of constant surveillance.[1484] With regard to this point the graduated response schemes can be distinguished as the data is used with the intention to inform the subscriber concerned.

As regards the retention of data, attention needs to be paid within the balancing of contravening interests whether there was a reason for the collecting and retention of data. Where the individual concerned gave reason to have his data collected, for instance because he has committed an offence, an interference will be considered less severe than where he has not given reason for the data collecting.[1485]

(3) Interference with the Right to the Protection of Personal Data

As mentioned above, the collecting of traffic data by the rights-holders also amounts to the processing of personal data, because it is conducted with the purpose of identifying a copyright infringer – at least for the public authorities or the access providers. Further, the processing of data by the access providers (UK) and the disclosure of data towards HADOPI

1482 CJEU, Joined cases C-293/12 and C-594/12 *Digital Rights Ireland and Seitlinger and Others*, Judgment of 08.04.2014, para. 33 refering to CJEU C-465/00, C-138/01 *Österreichischer Rundfunk and Others*, ECR I-4989, para. 75.

1483 Cf. CJEU, Joined cases C-293/12 and C-594/12 *Digital Rights Ireland and Seitlinger and Others*, Judgment of 08.04.2014, para. 34.

1484 *Ibid*, para. 35.

1485 Cf. for example the judgment of the German constitutional court in relation to the scanning of number plates of all drivers. BVerfG, Judgment of 11.03.2008 – 1 BvR 2074/05, 1 BvR 1254/07 (*Automatisierte Erfassung von Autokennzeichen*), Neue Juristische Wochenschrift 2008, 1505.

interferes with the right to protection of personal data under Article 8 *ECHR* and Article 8 *CFR*, because the identity of an individual and his contact details are revealed by the data controller to a third party. Although this is prescribed by national law and conducted in accordance with the *Data Protection Directive* and *E-Privacy Directive* (see above) for the protection of the rights of others, it needs to be examined whether such disclosure is proportionate. According to the principle of proportionality in EU law, a balance needs to be struck between the means used and the intended aim of their actions.

(4) Justification

Under Article 8(2) *ECHR* framework, an interference may be justified, when it had a legal basis in domestic law, and the interference "is necessary in a democratic society in the interests of national security, public safety or the economic well-being of the country, for the prevention of disorder or crime, for the protection of health or morals, or for the protection of the rights and freedoms of others".[1486] This test is quite similar to the test under EU law, which requires compliance with EU law and a balancing of the interests concerned. With regard to any limitations on Articles 7 and 8 *CFR*, a note from the drafting Presidium indicates that the possible limitation that can be placed on the rights protected in Article 7 *CFR* are the same limits provided for in Article 8 *ECHR* by virtue of Article 52(3) *CFR*.[1487] The graduated response schemes must however only comply with *CFR* standards insofar as EU law is concerned, meaning inter alia that states will have to respect the rights guaranteed by the Charter when their authorities apply a national law that implements an EU Directive. As the data protection aspects with which national copyright enforcement

---

1486 Article 8(2) *ECHR*. These limits can also be placed on the rights protected in Article 7 *CFR*, see above First Chapter, B. II. 2. b) ee) Justification of Interference.

1487 With regard to Article 7 CFR see Bureau of the Convention, Note from the Presidium, Draft Charter of Fundamental Rights of the European Union, New Proposal for Articles 1 to 12 (now 1 to 16) (08.03.2000), CHARTE 4149/00, Convent 13, Article 12, p. 13: "Paragraph 2 on limitations has not been included but it is applicable under Union law pursuant to Article 6 of the TEU and the clause on limitations in the Charter".

schemes interefer have been regulated by EU Directives, the guarantees provided for in the Charter need to be observed.

Irrespective of whether the copyright enforcement procedures serve the economic well-being of a state, and the fact that the schemes aim at the prevention of crime, the only focus in the following analysis will be the balancing of the intellectual property rights of the copright owners and the privacy rights of the subscriber of an Internet access service and further users of that access. Within the balancing of rights, specific regard will be paid to the necessity of a limitation on the right to privacy.

First of all the required retention of data with regard to the content and name of the copyrighted work in question interferes with the right to respect for family life in two aspects: a public authority (France) or the Internet access provider (UK) will keep a record of the infringements and thus may be able to draw conclusions as to the private and even intimate life of a subscriber from that records; and a subscriber may obtain information as to the personal preferences of other persons that use his connection. However, without information regarding the copyrighted work, it would be impossible in future criminal proceedings to obtain a judgment, or for the copyright owner to bring a successful claim before a civil court due to missing evidence. The success of criminal or civil proceedings depends on sufficient information being available as to the copyright infringement as such and the coprighted work in question. Without retention of data regarding the work in question, the aim of copyright enforcement would be rendered ad absurdum. At a first glance, it thus seems as if the copyright owner's interest in protecting their intellectual property rights would definitely prevail. This conclusion is deceiving. One needs to take into consideration that in particular the access providers under the *DEA 2010* will have to keep records which may relate to numerous works which in turn may allow to draw information on the personality of the subscriber. Other than the data that is automatically processed when providing Internet access, the provider will have to administer detailed lists relating to content that the subscriber is interested in. In contrast to the French system, an access provider may be under an obligation to keep more extensive lists than HADOPI, as a third warning does not trigger a sanction. Moreover a third warning will only mean that the subscriber will be entered on a Copyright Infringement List (CIL), of which an anonymised version can be obtained by rights-holders on a monthly basis.[1488] A CIL may thus contain more than three infringement reports and allow to draw a more precise personal profile than would be possible from only three warnings. Considering that the processing of sensitive data can be justified under the *Data Protection Directive* as necessary for the establishment, exercise or defence of legal claims (Article 8(2)(e)) and for the purpose of legitimate interests by a third party (Article 7(f)), the data protection framework of the EU hints that even the processing of sensitive data can be legitimate for the enforcement of intellectual property rights. Considering that the *DEA 2010* foresees relatively short timeframes for the retention of that data and thereby hinders the development of large profiles and foresees the notification of subscribers with every new "entry" on its records as well as the possibility of subscribers to appeal a CIR, the *DEA 2010* provides for a fair balance between the right to respect for private life and the interests of the copyright owners insofar as the records kept by the access providers are concerned. Further the retention is necessary to provide the copyright-holders with an effective remedy. The same applies to the records kept by HADOPI, which instead of an appeal procedure foresees hearings following a first warning.

As regards the scenario where not the subscriber himself has committed an infringement and he may obtain information about the work that has been shared, it needs to be stressed that in France a warning will not contain any information as to the work that has been shared,[1489] or any pseudonyms used by the file-sharer.[1490] As is understood from the HADOPI laws, such information will only be disclosed when the prosecutor decides to pursue criminal charges. Hence, a subscriber will not know which files third parties that use his connections have been sharing. In order to understand the origin of the copyright infringement, he will only be informed of the file-sharing client that has been used. In contrast a

1488 Section 4(2)(b) *DEA 2010* which inserts new section 124B *CA 2003*. See also Ofcom, *Online infringement of copyright and the Digital Economy Act 2010, Notice of Ofcom's proposal to make by order a code for regulating the initial obligations* (26.06.2012), p. 62.

1489 Article L. 331-25 *CPI* expressly stipulates that the warnings "do not disclose the content of the copyright-protected works" in question. Thereby, the legislator wanted to pay regard to the fact that the actual infringer does not necessarily have to be the subscriber. The privacy of the infringer was intended to be kept confidential, cf. HADOPI, *2010 Activity Report* (2011), p. 37.

1490 HADOPI, *2010 Activity Report* (2011), p. 38.

warning under the *DEA 2010* will also contain information on the copyright-protected work in question. This information is necessary in order to allow the subscriber to appeal a warning at an early stage. Hence, while the French provision protects third parties directly, the UK provision protects third parties indirectly by allowing them at an early stage to contest false allegations. Given that the third parties might have downloaded for instance hardcore pornography that reveals certain proclivities and the subscriber is informed about this, they seem to deserve less protection if they have actually (mis-)used a third party's connection. Moreover, less weight must be attributed to their rights, because if they have used a third party's Internet access, they must have been aware that a warning will be addressed to the subscriber. They are in a position where they may foresee the consequences of their behaviour, which then also satisfies the criterion of foreseeability under Article 8(2) *ECHR*. Hence, although there may be an interference with the interests of third parties to have sensitive information about them protected, their interest does not prevail over the interests of the intellectual property rights owners. Both approaches are careful in providing for safeguards against intrusive measures.

Secondly, the sanctioning of "allowing" third parties to use an Internet access and commit an infringement, would as a consequence lead to an obligation to monitor third parties. Although the scope of the provision is not clear and an instruction of fellow users as to the legal use of information technology may suffice, it shall be noted at this point, that the provision does not respect the principle of foreseeability. Less intrusive measures such as instructing fellow users when there is reason to believe that they may infringe copyright would rather be justifiable and allow a fair balance between privacy rights and copyright.

Thirdly, the matching of IP addresses listed to the subscriber's personal details by the access provider, and the disclosure of that data to HADOPI or to the rights-holders in the UK, interferes with the confidentiality of communications guaranteed under Article 7 *CFR* and Article 8 *ECHR*. Again, this interference is a direct result of copyright enforcement. Due to the prevalence of dynamic IP addresses, the identification of an alleged infringer is not possible other than by the matching of an IP address by an access provider. Some guidance was given as to the disclosure of personal data in these scenarios in the Bonnier Audio case[1491] before the CJEU. The CJEU held that national legislation that foresees the disclosure of data must require that "there be clear evidence of an infringement of an intellectual property right, that the information can be regarded as facilitating the investigation into an infringement of copyright or impairment of such a right and that the reasons for the measure outweigh the nuisance or other harm which the measure may entail for the person affected by it or for some other conflicting interest".[1492] French law foresees that HADOPI examines the evidence provided by the rights-holder, and only if it is satisfied that an infringement has taken place, HADOPI will ask for the disclosure of subscriber data and forward the case without informing the rights-holder of the identity of a subscriber. In the UK, the situation is fundamentally different: there is no independent public authority that assesses the allegations and the evidence presented. While the law foresees that the infringement must be apparent, there is no oversight whether the evidence presented suffices. The access provider only forwards the claims, but does not assess the matter. In order to provide a remedy to subscribers for unfounded allegations, the *DEA 2010* foresees a subscriber appeals procedure.[1493] At this point no data will have been disclosed to the rights-holder. In fact, the *DEA 2010* foresees at no stage the disclosure of personal data to the rights-holder. Rather the rights-holder will have to apply for a Norwich Pharmacal Order to have the identity of a subscriber revealed and be able to initiate criminal or civil proceedings. A civil court will hence assess whether the criteria set forth by the CJEU are fulfilled.

Both schemes try to withhold personal data from the copyright owner as long as possible without rendering the enforcement of copyright inoperable. They rather protect alleged infringers from long and costly court proceedings while at the same time trying to ensure that repeat infringers are prosecuted (France), or ensure that repeat infringers can be sued or prosecuted (UK). The UK system may even achieve to filter out falsely accused subscribers by an appeal procedure at an early stage and disclosure of personal data will only be granted under Norwich Pharmacal orders, meaning

---

1491 CJEU, C-461/10, *Bonnier Audio AB and Others v Perfect Communication Sweden AB,* Judgment of 19.04.2012.

1492 *Ibid*, para. 58.

1493 As previously outlined after paying a GBP 20 fee, the subscriber can rely on four grounds to appeal each warning letter and each CIR included in the warning letter; and the appeals body resolves the appeal.

that a court will have to order a disclosure. In France, disclosure of personal data of alleged infringer does not take place at all, although in due course of criminal proceedings, the copyright owner may ultimately acquire information on the identity of an alleged infringer. Against this background both schemes have achieved a fair balance of the contravening interests.

(5) In Specific: Data Retention Requirements for Access Providers

The French data protection law provides that HADOPI may request the disclosure of personal data, that access provider must retain for the prosecution of serious crimes. Similarly, access provider in the UK have to use the data retained for these purposes to send out warnings. Since the *Data Retention Directive* has been declared invalid by the CJEU, it is clear, that the retention of all communications data derogates from the system of protection of the right to privacy established by the *Data Protection Directive* and *E-Privacy Directive*.[1494] In particular the UK provision on data retention and access to that data seems to be too wide. Pursuant to section 7 of the *Data Retention (EC Directive) Regulations 2009*, access to retained data may be obtained "(a) in specific cases, and (b) in circumstances in which disclosure of the data is permitted or required by law". The Regulations do not make any reference as to the objective of the data retention or disclosure being limited to cases of serious crime. Since, this data can be used to sent out warnings, it can actually be used for minor offences, for instance single instances of copyright infringement. Considering that the CJEU declared the retention of data for the fight against serious crime as disproportionate, there can be no fair balance between the nature and seriousness of the interference of privacy rights in relation to the data retention and the object pursued by the interference in cases of copyright infringement. Although the data retention may be appropriate for attaining the objective of fighting criminal offences including copyright infringements, an objective of general interest does not in itself justify a retention measure to be necessary for the purpose of that fight.[1495] It is doubtful that

---

1494 Cf. CJEU, Joined cases C-293/12 and C-594/12 *Digital Rights Ireland and Seitlinger and Others*, Judgment of 08.04.2014, para. 32.

1495 Cf. *Ibid*, para. 49. Cf. also ECtHR, *S. and Marper v the United Kindgom*, Judgment of 04.12.2008 – Application nos. 30562/04 and 30566/04.

the Data Retention Regulations in question lay down sufficiently clear and precise rules governing the retention. [1496] Considering that the required retention encompasses all traffic data concerning all means of electronic communication and all users, it entails an interference with the fundamental rights of all people in the UK. Retention is not to be ordered following an assessment on a case by case basis, but the obligation applies in general.[1497] There is no differentiation, limitation or exception being made in the light of the objective of fighting against crime. Every user becomes a suspect without giving a reason for his monitoring. Data is to be retained even where there is no evidence capable of suggesting that the individual concerned can be linked with crime. Similar to the Data Retention Directive, the Data Retention Regulations do not provide for exceptions with the result that it seems to apply even to persons whose communications are subject to the obligation of professional secrecy. [1498] Also similar to the Data Retention Directive, the Data Retention Regulations does not distinguish between different kinds of data and possible distinct retention periods.

Considering that the Regulations are not more precise than the Directive and provide for interferences with the rights of users in a too generalised manner, the intereferences cannot be justified.

cc) Interferences with Procedural Rights

The graduated response schemes as outlined above could infringe several procedural rights that are guaranteed under the *ECHR* and the *CFR*, including the fair trial right (Article 47 *CFR* and Article 6(1) *ECHR*), presumption of innocence (Article 48 *CFR* and Article 6(2) *ECHR*) and the

---

1496 As regards the *Data Retention Directive*, cf., CJEU, Joined cases C-293/12 and C-594/12 *Digital Rights Ireland and Seitlinger and Others*, Judgment of 08.04.2014, para. 54 wit further references to the jurisprudence of the ECtHR such as inter alia *Liberty and Others v the United Kingdom*, Judgment of 01.07.2008 – Application no. 58243/00, paras. 62 and 63.

1497 As regards the incompatibility of such a general obligation with the rights of the subscribers and registered users, see also Stafan Maaßen, *Urheberrechtlicher Auskunftsanspruch und Vorratsdatenspeicherung*, MultiMedia und Recht 2009, 511, 514.

1498 As regards the *Data Retention Directive*, cf. *ibid*, para. 58.

principle of proportionality of sanctions (Article 49(3) *CFR*).[1499] Given that the criminal enforcement of copyright infringements is not (yet) provided for on an EU basis, the following procedural rights will only be examined under the *ECHR* framework. The potential interferences discussed are only such that derive from the graduated response schemes as such. Thus, the discussion will not go as far as exposing in general the conditions for a fair trial.

(1) Right to a Fair Trial

The fair trial principle could in particular be infringed with regard to the the admissibility of evidence and the right to remain silent.

As regards the right to fair trial in general, the French legislator leaves it to a non-judicial authority to initiate proceedings against a potential infringer. While this is not an issue per se, the fact that judicial authorities are able to intervene only at a late stage in the procedure, may affect the the right to a fair trial of the subscriber concerned. Other than the *DEA 2010*, it is not possible under the French scheme to formally appeal a single warning; law only forsees a hearing. Irrepsective of the fact that the identification of a subscriber does not necessarily mean that the actual infringer has been identified, it will be the subscriber that receives the warnings and against whom criminal charges may be brought. It is understandable that the warning needs to be send to "someone", considering that there are no means to identify the actual user that connected to the peer-to-peer file-sharing network at the given time. However, three warnings may lead to the subscriber being charged before a court (France), or to have CILs forwarded to copyright owners, so that they are in a position to target "any litigation" against repeat infringers.[1500] The subscriber may however find it difficult to defend his case, if he has not himself commit-

1499 For an in-depth analysis of the subscriber's appeal process in the UK and its conformity with Article 6 *ECHR* see Felipe Romero Moreno, *Incompatibility of the Digital Economy Act 2010 subscriber appeal process provisions with Article 6 of the ECHR*, International Review of Law, Computers & Technology 2014, 1–17. Romero Moreno considers that also the principle of equality of arms is infringed with regard to the *DEA 2010* procedures.

1500 See Ofcom, *Online Infringement of Copyright and the Digital Economy Act 2010 – Notice of Ofcom's Proposal to Make by Order a Code for Regulating the Initial Obligations*, p. 62.

ted the infringement. The French warnings, for instance, will not give him any further information as to the work that has been shared, so that he could investigate the matter at his home.

Article 6(1) *ECHR* provides a fair trial guarantee that applies respectively to both civil and criminal proceedings by stating that "In the determination of his civil rights and obligations or of any criminal charge against him, everyone is entitled to a fair and public hearing within a reasonable time by an independent and impartial tribunal established by law". While the UK system foresees appeals against each warning before an independent appeals body, the French system does not.[1501] However, as none of the warnings brings with it criminal charges, but is a "warning", it only needs to be examined whether the case will be heard before a court at the sanctioning stage. This is the case.

The right to fair trial, and in particular the aspect of the right to remain silent, also plays a role where the subscriber of an Internet access service, that has been used to infringe copyright, is being charged for copyright infringement, although it is technologically not possible to identify the user of an Internet access at the time of an infringement. The right to remain silent may in these cases be affected when silence leads to conviction rather than requiring the authorities to identify the actual offender.

Though not specifically mentioned in Article 6 *ECHR*, the right to remain silent and the privilege against self-incrimination are encompassed as standards that lie at the heart of the notion of a fair trial. In general, the right not to incriminate oneself presupposes that the authorities seek to prove their case without resorting to evidence obtained through methods of coercion or oppression in defiance of the will of the person charged.[1502] It is incompatible with the right to remain silent to base a conviction solely or mainly on the accused's silence or on a refusal to answer questions or to

---

1501 If HADOPI foresees that the subscriber may be heard following a warning, this is not an appeals procedure in a formal sense.

1502 See for instance ECtHR, *J.B. v Switzerland*, Judgment of 03.05.2001 – Application no. 31827/96, para. 64. Protection against improper compulsion by the authorities serves the purpose of avoidance of miscarriages of justice and secures the aims of Article 6. See inter alia ECtHR, *John Murray v the United Kingdom*, Judgment of 08.02.1996 – Application no. 18731/91, para. 45; *Saunders v the United Kingdom*, Judgment of 17.12.1996 – Application no. 19187/91, paras. 68–69; ECtHR, *J.B. v Switzerland*, Judgment of 03.05.2001 – Application no. 31827/96, paras. 64 et seq.

give evidence himself.[1503] However, the right to remain silent is not an absolute right; the right does not go that far as to preventing that the accused's silence, in situations "which clearly call for an explanation from him", are "taken into account in assessing the persuasiveness of the evidence adduced by the prosecution".[1504] Hence, a national court cannot conclude that an accused is guilty merely because he decides to remain silent.[1505] This may only be the case, where the evidence against the accused "calls" for an explanation and a failure to give that explanation "may as a matter of common sense allow the drawing of an inference that there is no explanation and that the accused is guilty".[1506] Whether the drawing of adverse inferences from an accused's silence infringes Article 6 *ECHR* is a matter to be determined by taking into account all the circumstance of a case, with a particular regard to the situations where inferences may be drawn, and the weight attached to them by the national courts in their assessment of the evidence. The right exists where criminal charges are brought against the subscriber, and does not already apply at the stage of the warnings, which individually have no direct legal consequences. Taking the example of France, silence will obviously lead to a conviction of the subscriber. A conviction will however never be based on the mere fact that the defendant remains silent as to the accusations. Due to the lacking possibility to identify the actual infringer, subscribers will usually be charged with the gross negligence offence, meaning the failure to secure their Internet access. The evidence collected in online copyright infringement cases calls for an explanation of the defendant. Only he will be in the position to tell whether he has instructed third parties not to misuse his access, whether his Wi-Fi was protected at the time of the infringement, or whether his computer was for instance password protected. Of course, the prosecution may also try to obtain further evidence establishing the defendant's guilt by seizing the accused's computer, but considering the time that has passed since the first infringement took place, the data may not exist anymore. Even if the data that has initially not been collected by law enforcement agencies but by the rigths-holder is error-prone, the fact that only following at least three warnings charges are

---

1503 ECtHR, *John Murray v the United Kingdom*, Judgment of 08.02.1996 – Application no. 18731/91, para. 47.

1504 *Ibid.*

1505 Cf. *Ibid*, para. 51.

1506 *Ibid.*

brought should ensure that at least an infringement has taken place. Hence, there is no infringement with the right to remain silent.

(2) Presumption of Innocence

Also the privilege against self-incrimination as an aspect of the presumption of innocence under Article 6(2) *ECHR* might be infringed, if a subscriber was not presumed innocent until proven guilty according to law. As remains to be seen how exactly the UK courts will deal with the sanctioning stage, at this point the focus will again be on the French system.[1507]

For a start, the burden of proof in relation to an offence must rest with the prosecution and any doubt should benefit the defendant.[1508] This is respected by the French system, because subscriber will be charged with the gross negligence offence that has been introduced in order to provide for conviction where there is doubt as to the wilful commitment of an infringing act. The accused may escape a conviction for gross negligence, if he succeeds in proving that no one else used his access to commit copyright infringements and his access was adequately secured. Similarly in the UK, subscribers could see themselves exposed to warnings or CILs, unless they can demonstrate that they have taken "reasonable measures" to prevent copyright infringements.[1509] Principally, the burden of proof could legitimately shift to the accused.[1510] For reverse onus of proof provisions to be compatible with Article 6(2) *ECHR*, Member States must remain within reasonable limits. There is nothing in France that would suggest that the French legislator overstepped this mark. Taking into acoount the importance of what is at stake, the more serious the punishment which

---

1507 For a discussion of the principle of presumption of innocence in relation to the *DEA 2010* see Felipe Romero Moreno, *Incompatibility of the Digital Economy Act 2010 subscriber appeal process provisions with Article 6 of the ECHR*, International Review of Law, Computers & Technology 2014, 1, 8 et sq.

1508 ECtHR, *Barberà, Messegué and Jabardo v Spain*, Judgment of 06.12.1988 – Application no. 10590/83, para. 77.

1509 Cf. High Court, *R (on the application of BT PLC and Talk Talk PLC) v Secretary of State for Business Innovation and Skills and others* [2011] EWHC 1021 (Admin), para. 238. It has to born in mind, that this is pre-trial stage.

1510 See ECtHR, *Salabiaku v France*, Judgment of 07.10.1988 – Application no. 1951/83, para. 28.

may flow from conviction, the more compelling the reasons must be. With the abolition of the Internet suspension sanction, the subscriber faces a fine.[1511] The fines imposed by courts so far, have been considerably low. There is thus no severe punishment. If one further takes into account the extent to which the burden on the accused relates to facts, which, if they exist, are readily provable by him as matters within his own knowledge or to which he has ready access,[1512] no violation of the presumption of innocence can be established.[1513]

(3) Principles of Legality and Proportionality of Criminal Offences and Penalties

The suspension or other interferences with an Internet access service may amount to disproportionate penalties, which would contravene the principle of proportionality of criminal offences and penalties. Article 49(3) *CFR* sets forth that "the severity of penalties must not be disproportionate to the criminal offence". However, there is no provision in EU law that foresees the imposition of disconnection orders, nor where the sanctions based on any Community legislation. Therefore the severity of the sanctions can only have an impact when assessing the proportionality of interferences with other rights.

1511 With respect to the suspension of an Internet access, also the Article 1(b) *European Framework Directive* emphasises that "measures regarding end-users' access to...electronic communications networks...may only be imposed if...taken with due respect for the principle of the presumption of innocence".

1512 Cf. House of Lords, *R v Johnstone* [2003] UKHL 28, para. 50.

1513 Another conclusion with regard to the UK graduated response scheme has been reached by Felipe Romero Moreno, *Incompatibility of the Digital Economy Act 2010 subscriber appeal process provisions with Article 6 of the ECHR*, International Review of Law, Computers & Technology 2014, 1, 8 et seq. This result is questionable, as the author reaches this conclusion by examining the fact that subscribers may be exposed to CIRs or CILs. At this stage one may however not yet speak of "criminal proceedings".Although Article 6(2) *ECHR* also applies prior to charges being brought against an alleged offender, the warning scheme in the UK as it stands now, is merely preparatory for "any litigation" targeted by copyright owners against alleged infringers. Neither the sending out of CIRs nor CILS involves state or moreover law enforcement authorities.

d) Conformity with the Fundamental Rights of Internet Service Providers

With regard to the fundamental rights of Internet service providers, two rights may be affected: their freedom to conduct business and their right to impart information. The following analysis will however limit itself to the freedom to conduct business as the interference with the right to impart information is only of a minor nature as not the nucleus of the service to impart of information, but the circumstances under which this service can be provided is affected. The more controversial aspect is the interference with the provision of the service as such in terms of the freedom to conduct business. The analysis will not be restricted to access providers alone, but will also look at the impact of graduated response schemes on commercial Wi-Fi providers and entities that provide in addition to their primary business Internet access to their customers. Because only the UK scheme requires active cooperation of access providers, requiring them to administer and send out the warning letters, the following analysis will solely look at the conformity of the foreseen UK scheme with the fundamental rights of the service providers.

aa) Freedom to Conduct Business of Traditional Access Providers

It is obvious, that by the proposed *Initial Obligations (Sharing of Costs) Order* the State interferes with the acess providers's freedom to conduct business because the access providers will need to bear substantial financial burdens. This has already briefly been addressed above when the compliance of the scheme with Article 3(1) of the *IPR Enforcement Directive* was outlined. The question to be answered is now, whether the financial burden is not a disproportionate burden and can thus be justified under Arrticle 1 of the Protocol No. 1 to the *ECHR* and – since the *IPR Enforcement Directive* is applicable – Article 16 *CFR*. In that respect, it needs to be recalled that access providers are completely neutral providers and do not interfere with the content transmitted.

Similar to the financial burdens on farmers resulting from an obligation to mark sheep and goats electronically and keep a holding register, the obligation to administer the warning scheme and bear substantial costs of the scheme is a limitation of the exercise of the freedom to conduct a business in general.[1514]

Neither under the *ECHR* nor under the Charter, freedom to conduct a business enjoys absolute protection; moreover, it must be viewed in relation to its social function.[1515] The CJEU has identified a series of social objectives, which it defines as "objectives of general interest" and that may limit the exercise of the freedom to conduct business.[1516] Accordingly, the freedom to conduct a business may be subject to a broad range of interventions on the part of public authorities, which may limit the exercise of economic activity in the public interest.[1517] Being subject to the limitations provided for in Article 52(1) *CFR*, interferences with the freedom must be provided for by law and respect the essence of those rights and freedoms and, in compliance with the principle of proportionality, must be necessary and actually meet objectives of general interest (recognised by the European Union) or the need to protect the rights and freedom of others.[1518] Other than the aforementioned sheep holding register which had the aim to allow for appropriate responses in case of the outbreak of a disease and was thus necessary and in the general interest, the administration of the warnings and the records of repeat infringers does not serve such a general interest of public concern. Although one may argue that the economic well-being of a country is affected when intellectual property rights are not guaranteed adequate protection, it needs to be recalled that the graduated response scheme is only an additional measure to conventional enforcement mechanisms provided for by UK law. The

1514 Cf. CJEU, C-101/12 *Herbert Schaible v Land Baden-Württemberg*, Judgment of 17.10.2013, paras. 24ff.

1515 CJEU, Joined Cases C-184/02 and C-223/02 *Spain and Finland v Parliament and Council*, Judgment of 09.09.2004, [2004] ECR I-7789, paras. 51 and 52; C-544/10 *Deutsches Weintor*, Judgment of 06.09.2012, para. 54 with further references. See also Alberto Lucarelli in: William B. T. Mock/Gianmario Demuro, *Human Rights in Europe, Commentary on the Charter of Fundamental Rights of the European Union* (2010), Article 16, pp. 101 et seq.

1516 See for example CJEU, C-44/09 *Hauer v Rheinland-Pfalz*, [1979] ECR 3727, para. 17.

1517 CJEU, C-283/11 *Sky Österreich GmbH v Österreichischer Rundfunk*, Judgment of 22.01.2013, para. 46; C-101/12 para. 24ff CJEU, C-101/12 *Herbert Schaible v Land Baden-Württemberg*, Judgment of 17.10.2013, para. 28.

1518 See CJEU, C-283/11 *Sky Österreich GmbH v Österreichischer Rundfunk*, Judgment of 22.01.2013, paras. 47–48; CJEU, C-101/12 *Herbert Schaible v Land Baden-Württemberg*, Judgment of 17.10.2013, para. 27.

purpose of the scheme can hence be achieved otherwise. Also at this stage, the graduated response scheme does not result in any sanctioning of alleged infringers, but rather allows copyright owners to filter out the potentially most notorious infringers. The scheme is thus only beneficial to rights-holders, which under UK law, would otherwise also face costly procedures against first time infringers, or infringers where the chances of winning in civil litigation are not promising. Even evidence is pre-filtered in some way by providing for an appeals procedure in which subscriber may present evidence as to their innocence. This all is conducted at the cost of the access provider, which by law has to bear a substantial share of the costs. Further the imposition of costs upon the providers is not necessary to achieve adequate copyright protection or to employ a graduate response scheme. As private parties aim at protecting their private rights, they could also be asked to cover the costs for this. Under the purpose of economic well-being of a state, one may also think of the state covering a share of the costs rather than access providers.

The obligations imposed upon access providers do not allow a fair balance to be struck between the interests of the access providers and the interests of copyright owners, and thus constitute a violation of the access providers' freedom to conduct business.

In addition, it is also questionable whether the system can be fair, when only providers with more than 40.000 customers have to issue warnings. By restricting the application of said obligations to only large providers, the legislator himself recognises the severity of the financial burdens that the administration of the scheme brings with it.

bb) Freedom to Conduct Business of Providers of Free Wi-Fi Services

The graduated response schemes may also have a chilling effect on providers of free Wi-Fi such as libraries, cafés, hotels, etc, which offer free Internet access to their customers. As the subscriber of the Internet access will be the recipient of any warning, these providers may opt not to allow free access or restrict access in some way (e.g. bandwidth restriction). In this case the freedom of expression of their customers would be concerned as well as their freedom to conduct business. It has to be noted that not the core of their business would be affected; they could still pursue their main business, such as running a hotel or café. What would rather cause concerns their position on the market. Customers nowadays expect to have free Wi-Fi in hotels or even pubs and cafés and they may make this a requirement when searching for a respective establishment. Though all businesses are under the same risk, some may cancel free Wi-Fi for their guests in order not to be faced with warnings or sanctions.[1519] How France will deal with these situations remains rather unclear. Ofcom however took these scenarios into consideration when making its proposal for a code for regulationg the intitial obligations under the *DEA 2010.* [1520] Commercial entities that provide Internet access as a supplement for their primary business, as well as public bodies like libraries or universities would not fall within the definition of a qualifying Internet service provider. This means that they would be exempted from any obligations under the *DEA 2010*, because they are no broadband providers with more than 40,000 customers.[1521] Only to the latter the *DEA 2010* provisions apply. A chilling effect on the providers of free Wi-Fi is thus avoided.

With regard to such complementary Wi-Fi services and private initiatives to provide free Wi-Fi to the public, the decision of the CJEU in Tobias McFadden v Sony Music Entertainment Germany GmbH is eagerly awaited.[1522]

1519 The High Court also elaborated that subscribers, and this may include the provider of open or free Wi-Fi access, to take preventive measures that exceed what was necessary to exonerate them from liability, see *R (on the application of BT PLC and Talk Talk PLC) v Secretary of State for Business Innovation and Skills and others* [2011] EWHC 1021 (Admin), para. 235.

1520 Ofcom, *Online infringement of copyright and the Digital Economy Act 2010, Notice of Ofcom's proposal to make by order a code for regulating the initial obligations* (26.06.2012), pp. 29 et seq.

1521 *Ibid*, p. 99. If a pay-as-you go broadband provider suddenly has more customers than the initial threshold set by the *Initial Obligations Code*, he will nevertheless not be required to collect contact details of existing customers once it becomes a qualifying Internet service provider. Ofcom departs in this regard from its previous opinion (from its 2010 consultation), that operators that do not hold information necessary for notifying subscribers, must, at such a time as they become a qualifying Internet service provider, ensure that they do collect this data so as to be able to comply with the obligations in the *DEA 2010* and the *Initial Obligations Code* (see p. 95).

1522 CJEU, C-484/14, request for a preliminar ruling from the Landgericht München I (Germany) of 03.11.2014 (*Tobias McFadden v Sony Music Entertainment Germany GmbH*). The request for a preliminary ruling to the CJEU seeks clarification as to whether the provider of an open Wi-Fi network, i.e. a free non-password-protected Wi-Fi, may be liable for third-party copyright infringements or whether said provider may be shielded from liability on the basis that he falls

cc) Freedom to Conduct Business of Commercial Wi-Fi Operators

Also operators of commercial hotspots such as BT and its Openzone service would not be affected in their freedom to conduct business if Ofcom's proposal becomes law. Wi-Fi providers would be excluded from the Scope of the Code on the basis that inclusion "is likely to lead to them incurring substantial costs to achieve a minimal reduction in overall levels of online copyright infringements".[1523] The reason for this is that, as BT stated, the "vast majority" of Openzone users purchase on a pay-as-you-go basis, rather than via subscription. Ofcom recognised that where providers offer Wi-Fi in this way, in many instances the subscriber address data collected for pay-as-you-go consumers will be neither reliable nor easily verifiable.[1524] Again, the legislator recognised that the implementation of the graduated response scheme may affect certain providers disproportionally, in this case by requiring an overly complicated and costly system.

dd) The UK Graduated Response Scheme Violates the Rights of Access Providers

Thc consequence being drawn from the exception for commercial Wi-Fi operators is that yet another exception is added for certain type of providers. With each exception, the system is however somehow turned ab adsurdum because it presents more and more loopholes for wilful infrignes to escape detection, while at the other hand affecting the market position of large providers. Although, it is rather unlikely that substantial amounts of users will change to small providers (considering the number of these, some of them will reach the threshold of 40,000 customers), notorious infringers are considerably likely to take advantage of the "loopholes" to avoid being exposed to warnings.

Considering the obligations imposed on qualifying access providers (i.e. more than 40,000 customers), these violate the freedom of access

---

within the category of "mere conduit" provider under Art. 12 of the *E-Commerce Directive*.

1523 Ofcom, *Online infringement of copyright and the Digital Economy Act 2010, Notice of Ofcom's proposal to make by order a code for regulating the initial obligations* (26.06.2012), p. 30.

1524 *Ibid.*

providers to pursue business. Even though they do not affect the core of the provision of Internet access service, the financial burdens that they impose upon providers are not justifiable, in particular in light of the aim that is pursued. It is not proportionate to confer the costs for enforcing private rights upon "innocent" third parties. Other than host providers, access providers cannot legitimately interfere with the information that is transmitted via their service.

e) Achieving a Fair Balance of the Contravening Interests

Following the above analysis, the main conclusion to be drawn is, that neither secondary EU law nor fundamental rights rule out the construction of a regulatory scheme, where warning letters are sent out to alleged infringers and repeat infringers are sanctioned.

The Joint Committee on Human Rights in the UK parliament held in that regard, that:

> "Articles 8 and 10 are qualified rights and it is acceptable under the Convention to interfere with these rights if it is in accordance with the law and it is necessary in a democratic society…the receipt of a notification does not impede the subscriber's access to the Internet in any way. Article 1 Protocol 1 is also a qualified right and it is acceptable under the Convention to interfere with this right in the public interest and subject to the conditions provided for by law. Article 1 provides that the right of the State to enforce such laws as it deems necessary to control the use of property is not impaired in any way. The sending of notifications is in the public interest. Copyright holders should be able to protect their copyright and enforce their rights. In the case of online copyright infringement, the involvement of Internet service providers is needed for them to do so".[1525]

While it is true that the interferences with privacy rights and the freedom of expression can be justified, the initial graduated response schemes that forsaw/foresee the suspension of an Internet access service or other technical measures with regard to that service, violate the freedom of expression. The importance of Internet access in today's society had been ignored or at least incorrectly weighted by the legislator. The Internet is no more pure entertainment. In today's society, Internet access is essential for work,

---

1525 House of Lords, House of Commons, Joint Committee on Human Rights, *Legislative Scrutiny: Digital Economy Bill, Fifth Report of Session 2009-10*, HL Paper 44 = HC 327 (05.02.2010), p. 10.

education, keeping informed of the news, keeping in touch with friends and family. In E-Commerce not only large business but also small businesses that are run from a family's home, depend on the Internet access. A number of banks, so called direct banks, do no longer maintain branches but rely solely on online banking. Consequently, the Internet has become a relied upon service, that cannot be compared to the telephone, fax or other media. Accordingly, disconnection can only be justified in very narrow circumstances, for example for prison inmates. The disconnection as a sanction for misusing the service would even where a due trial has taken place violate freedom of expression of the subscriber of the Internet access.[1526] It has to be recalled, that the identification of a subscriber does not necessarily lead to the identification of the actual copyright infringer. But even where the infringer would be identified, copyright infringements cannot justify such a severe interference with his freedom to seek, receive and impart information. When assessing the proportionality of a measure, the damage that has been caused needs also to be taken into consideration. In this respect, the damages awarded in civil proceedings for copyright infringement are not set as high as they are in the US and are usually calculated based on licence analogy. When the law foresees disconnection orders or technical measures already following the infringement of three separate works, this can hardly be proportionate in terms of the damage caused. Ultimately, there is no justification for interfering with the alleged infringer's freedom of expression.

When the Joint Committee on Human Rights argues that he sending of warnings is in the public interest, and copyright holders should be able to protect their copyright and enforce their rights with the help of Internet service providers, this conclusion is not followed.

As has been outlined above, the cooperation of Internet access providers, in particular their financial contribution violates their freedom to conduct business. Neither the right to property of the copyright owners nor the general interest in protecting the economic well-being of the state or the prevention of crime may justify that access providers have to share 25 % of the costs of copyright enforcement under the graduate response scheme in the UK. The above analysis has shown that the UK graduate response scheme is beneficial to copyright owners as it allows for the fil-

---

1526 According to the UK Joint Committee on Human Rights, a disconnection may be justified under the condition that there must be a fair trial for those involved before any action can be taken against them. See *ibid*, p. 86.

tering of infringers in order to identify the most notorious ones against which civil and criminal litigation will be successful. It is not proportionate to impose the costs for this benefit on the neutral transmitter of information.

With regard to privacy, one may conclude that although limitations of privacy rights exist, there are sufficient safeguards foreseen in the laws to justify interferences. Both schemes foresee that already at the stage of warnings, the recipients of a warning may be heard although a warning as such has no direct legal consequences. At no point will personal data be disclosed to the rights-holders in addition to possible information rights that already exist under domestic law.

Finally, the effictiveness of the schemes presented is questionable.

During the first phase of the *DEA 2010* scheme in the UK, warnings will not be followed by a sanction. Instead copyright owners may ask for the anonymised CILs to be handed over. This is intended to allow them to identify the most notorious infringers. They may then apply for a Norwich Pharmacal Order for disclosure of the identity of a subscriber on the list. Although it may be beneficial for the rights-holder to have potential targets of litigation pre-selected, the question is whether in practice this will lead to fewer costs for them to enforce copyright. They will have to pay the majority of costs for the administration of warnings. Only if a subscriber's access has been identified several times within a certain time, he will be put on the CIL. Although rights-holder may be tempted to send a warning where they otherwise would not apply for a Norwich Pharmacal order or press criminal charges under the existing law (simply because it is does not carry "much" costs), the costs for warnings may quickly sum up. We are then in a situation where the rights-holders in addition to the costs connected with the detection of an infringement, have to invest money to notify potential infringers of their alleged wrongdoing for which they will not be able to claim compensation (because only few disclosure orders will ultimately be applied for). The question then is, whether the costs for such a complicated system of educationary measures, shall be solely left to the rights-holder and not be covered by the State as in France.

Where in the second phase of implementation of the UK system, sanctions may be imposed upon subscribers also in cases in which they have allowed other persons to use their access and those have infringed copyright, this is in stark contrast to existing UK copyright law, where liability would only exist when the subscriber has "authorised" the infringement.[1527] There is no case law that suggests under which circumstances an allowance of Internet access usage would amount to "authorisation" of an infringement. Will it be sufficient for a subscriber to escape liability if he can prove that he instructed fellow users not to commit copyright infringements? Will the inadequate securisation of a Wi-Fi network amount to allowing infringements? The practical effect of the sanctioning provision remains unclear.In France, the gross negligence offence, which provides for sanctions against subscribers for inadequate securisation of their Internet access, constitutes a fundamental different approach. Here, the subscriber will not be held liable for the infringement as such but for not preventing that infringements are committed via his access. Although questions also arise as to what security measures have to be implemented to escape liability, the provision is far more precise as the UK provision for sanctions.

Looking at the experiences of France with the graduate response scheme, one may argue that a system of warnings prior to the imposition of sanctions is not effective. An ineffective system however would not allow interferences with fundamental rights to be justified.

An academic study indicated that the HADOPI laws have had a positive effect on iTunes sales in France, suggesting they are significantly higher than they would have been without the legislation.[1528] This however does not pay the necessary regard to the fact that Apple devices saw a massive increase in sale in the same timeframe and consequently the number of iTunes users rose. At the beginning of 2012, Apple announced that its net profit increases 94% year over year.[1529] Thus, there is also an alternative explanation for higher iTunes sales in France. Also, the number of warnings that is still being send out per month, does not suggest that the warning scheme is effective in reaching its aim of less copyright infringements. Statitistics presented by HADOPI in turn assume that most users will refrain from sharing files via peer-to-peer networks following at least the second warning. This explains why only few cases have reached trial

1527 See section 16 of the *CDPA 1988*.

1528 Brett Danaher/Michael D. Smith/Rahul Telang/Siwen Chen, *The effect of graduated response anti-piracy Laws on music sales: Evidence from an Event Study in France* (2012), p. 18.

1529 Apple, *Apple reports second quarter results, net profit increases 94 % year-over-year*, Press release (24.04.2012).

stage. Considering that the goal of any graduated response system can never be to eliminate online copyright infringement once and for all,[1530] the French warning scheme seems in general to be successful. With the abolition of the Internet suspension sanction, it now also pays regard to the fundamental rights of users.

In contrast, the UK *DEA 2010* scheme has far too many pitfalls that lacks respect for the fundamental rights of subscribers/Internet users and access providers.

Generally speaking, it must be concluded that a warning scheme that either foresees the suspension of an alleged infringer's Internet access, or in another way interferes with Internet access service cannot be justified under the *CFR* and the *ECHR*. In contrast, a graduated response scheme may comply with the *CFR* and *ECHR*, if third parties, such as access providers, do not have to invest substantial amounts of money to implement and administer the scheme. A fair balance can only be achieved when access providers do not have to bear substantial costs in in connection with the enforcement of private rights of others.

III. Copyright Enforcement in Member States Through Private Litigation

Intellectual property rights are private rights and the majority of enforcement procedures are civil: it is for the rights-holder to take action where an infringement has occurred. While criminal cases require knowledge on behalf of the infringer, this is not the case in civil cases and considering that criminal cases may not carry the same remedies as those available in civil proceedings, a lot more cases are dealt with in civil litigation.

In civil law, specific regulations for instance under copyright law itself and general regulations of a civil or procedural nature are used for enforcement purposes and as such also mentioned in the *IPR Enforcement Directive*. These instruments include injunctive relief and damages, as well as information rights regarding the identity of potential infringers.

Different approach taken which does not foresee a warning before an infringer is taken to court, but relies on pre-litigation settlement.

1530 Cf. Peter Yu, *The Graduated Response*, Florida Law Review 2010, Vol. 62, 1373, 1382.

While the graduated response schemes involve a third actor responsible for sending out the warnings and thus, the rights-holder does not directly contact the alleged infringer, private litigation models foresee direct litigation between the rights-holder and the alleged infringer.

When most people think of copyright enforcement through private litigation, what comes to their mind is the massive amount of lawsuits that have been launched against individual file sharers in the US.[1531] While RIAA mass John Doe lawsuits[1532] and volume pre-litigation letters[1533] gained worldwide attention, it is often ignored that in Germany, peer-to-peer file-sharing is almost exclusively dealt with in private litigation.[1534]

1531 From 2003 until 2008, about 35,000 people have been sued for illegal file-sharing in the US. In 2008, RIAA announced that it would end volume litigation. See Sarah McBride/Ethan Smith, *Music Industry to Abandon Mass Suits* (19.12.2008), Wall Street Journal. For an in-depth legal account of the RIAA lawsuits in the US, see Art Neill, *Does a new wave of filesharing lawsuits represent a new business model for copyright owners?,* Journal of Internet Law 2011, Vol. 14, No.12, 1–17.

1532 In these lawsuits, the lawyers of members of the RIAA (Recording Industry Association of America) sued unidentified "John Doe" uploaders that their specialised investigators had traced to an IP address. After filing the lawsuit, the record labels would ask the court to authorise subpoenas against the Internet access providers. After delivering these subpoenas and obtaining the real name of the subscriber behind the logged IP address, the lawyers of the record labels would then either send a letter demanding a settlement or amend their lawsuit to name the identified individual. From 2003 to October 2007, record labels have brought legal action against about 30,000 people (see Jeff Leeds, *Labels win suit against song sharer, New York Times* (05.10.2007). Most lawsuit targets settle their cases for amounts ranging between USD 3,000 and USD 11,000 (see Electronic Frontier Foundation, *RIAA v the People: Five years later* (2008), p. 5.

1533 Instead of initiating lawsuits, the RIAA sent out hundreds of pre-litigation letters each month to various universities in the US with the request to forward these letters to unidentified students (see Thomas Mennecke, *RIAA announces new campus lawsuit strategy,* Slyck News (28.02.2007). The letters identify the IP address of the alleged infringer and threaten future legal action with damages upwards of USD 750 per song. They also offer a reduced settlement if the student agrees to pay a non-negotiable amount (around USD 3000) within a certain time after receiving the letter (Ken Fisher, *Students largely ignore RIAA instant settlement offers,* Ars technica [26.03.2007]). According to news reports, the RIAA had sent over 5,400 letters to 160 different schools within one year (Eric Bangemann, *Pass or fail? RIAA's college litigation campaign turns one,* Ars Technica (28.02.2008)).

1534 For example in European Parliament, DG for Internal Policies, Policy Department C: Citizens' Rights and Constitutional Affairs, *File Sharing* (2011), p. 11,

Usually, a rights-holder will send a letter before claim to an Internet subscriber stating that the connection of the recipient was used in an infringement of copyright. In the letter the rights-holder will not only ask the recipient to sign an undertaking that he will abstain from infringing copyright in the future, but also claim compensation for the costs occurred in pursuing the claim and damages for the infringement. The contact details of the Internet subscribers will have been obtained by means of a disclosure order against their access provider.

The following paragraphs will focus on the German enforcement instrument of *Abmahnungen*, a private pre-settlement litigation tool, and how it has been employed in relation to copyright infringements in peer-to-peer networks. In this regard, a critical approach is taken, which will also analyse the deficits of the system. It is then worth to study the UK model of letters before claim, which is very similar to the German enforcement instrument of *Abmahnung* to see how courts in the UK address the deficits identified beforehand.

1. Germany: Abmahnungen

Although the introduction of graduated response schemes has been widely discussed in Germany,[1535] including a research study on the feasibility of such a system conducted on behalf of the German Federal Ministry for Economic Affairs [1536], Germany has until now refrained from introducing a graduated response scheme. One reason for this reluctance is the fact, that online copyright infringements are on a large scale dealt with in private litigation: German private law provides sufficient means to compensate rights-holders but also serves as a deterrent that prevents users from committing a certain infringement again.

The system at hand for rights-holders consists of cease-and-desist letters, so called *Abmahnungen*. These letters are sent out by lawyers on

---

it has been stated that the deployment of civil law enforcement instruments against individual users is not common practice in Europe.

1535 Cf. for example Thomas Hoeren, *Kurzgutachten zur BMWi-Studie über Modelle zur Versendung von Warnhinweisen durch Internet-Zugangsanbieter an Nutzer bei Urheberrechtsverletzungen* (2012).

1536 Rolf Schwartmann, *Vergleichende Studie über Modelle zur Versendung von Warnhinweisen durch Internet-Zugangsanbieter an Nutzer bei Urheberrechtsverletzungen, Bundesministerium für Wirtschaft und Technologie* (2012).

behalf of the rights-holders and inform the recipient that an infringement has been committed from his Internet access. The letter also contains a request to compensate the sender for the work involved to issue the warning (which according to the German law is beneficial to him) and regularly asserts a claim for damages. Furthermore, it is usually linked with a desist request which sets up penalty for further similar infringements. If the recipient signs the request he will have to pay the penalty for breaching his cease and desist promise.

At a first glance, this system seems to be fair and just. However, since a whole business has evolved with specialised law firms sending out dozens of cease and desist letters each day[1537] and advertising this business with the promise to "turn piracy into profit".[1538]

In the following the legal framework for the pre-litigation letters will be outlined before the system will be analysed in detail. In this context, the legal framework for information requests will be outlined and it will be evaluated how information requests are dealt with.

1537 In 2010, activists against *Abmahnungen* as a business modell suggested that 575,000 letters had been sent out to users. See Annual statistic 2010 of *Verein zur Hilfe und Unterstützung gegen den Abmahnwahn e.V.*, available at http://www.verein-gegen-den-abmahnwahn.de/zentrale/download/statistiken/2010/jahresbilanz_2010.html (last accessed 16.06.2011). This estimate stems from an association that lobbies against the instrument *Abmahnung*; therefore the number should be viewed critically. However, considering that according to the German association of the Internet industry *eco* information on subscribers of 300,.000 IP addresses are disclosed via court order per month, the estimated number of warning letters even seems to be too low. See eco press release *„300.000 Adressen pro Monat: erfolgreicher Kampf gegen illegale Downloads"* of 31.05.2011 http://www.eco.de/verband/202_9137.htm (last accessed 16.06.2011).

1538 See Sandra Schmitz/Thorsten Ries, *Three songs and you are disconnected from Cyberspace? Not in Germany where the industry may "turn Piracy into Profit"*, European Journal of Law and Technology 2012, Vol. 3 No. 1. For a discourse on a similar business modell in the US see Art Neill, *Does a new wave of filesharing lawsuits represent a new business model for copyright owners?,* Journal of Internet Law 2011, Vol. 14, No. 12, 1–17.

a) Legal Framework for Private Copyright Enforcement in Germany

German copyright law protects rights-holders under both civil and criminal law. In copyright infringement matters, especially with regard to illegal file-sharing, a civil action is the far more common way to proceed as criminal charges may not be pursued by the prosecutor if there has been no mass-scale infringement.

aa) Liability for Copyright Infringements

Under German civil law, any infringement of an exclusive right of an author, an author's moral right, or a neighbouring right protected under the *Gesetz über Urheberrecht und verwandte Schutzrechte – UrhG* ("Act on Copyright and Neighbouring Rights") could lead to a claim for removal of derogation or for injunctive relief[1539], damages[1540], unjust enrichment[1541] as well as destruction, recall or restitution of infringing goods[1542]. Copy-

---

1539 § 97 I *UrhG*: "The infringed party may assert a claim against any person who unlawfully infringes a copyright or another right protected by this Act for removal of the derogation or, in case of risk of recurrence, for injunctive relief. A claim for injunctive relief shall also exist where an infringement impends for the first time." (Translation by Alexander Klett/Matthias Sonntag/Stephan Wilske, *Intellectual Property Law in Germany* (2008), p. 340).

1540 § 97 II *UrhG:* "Any party who undertakes such action intentionally or negligently shall be liable for compensation to the infringed party for the damage suffered. When assessing damages, the profit made by the infringing party as a result of the infringement may also be taken into account. The claim for damages may also be calculated on the basis of the amount payable by the infringing party as appropriate remuneration had it obtained permission to use the infringed right. Authors, authors of scientific editions (§ 70), photographers (§ 72) and performing artists (§ 73) may also demand compensation in money for non-pecuniary losses if and to the extent that this is equitable." (Translation by Alexander Klett/Matthias Sonntag/Stephan Wilske, *Intellectual Property Law in Germany* (2008), p. 340).

1541 It is generally accepted in German law that the provisions in the German Civil Code on unjust enrichment also apply in the intellectual property area. Consequently, the infringer will have to surrender the value of what he gained due to the infringement according to the provisions on unjust enrichment. See also Alexander Klett/Matthias Sonntag/Stephan Wilske, *Intellectual Property Law in Germany* (2008), p.71.

1542 § 98 *UrhG*: "(1) Any person who unlawfully infringes a copyright or another right protected by this Act may be required by the infringed party to destroy all

right infringement also constitutes a criminal offence punishable with up to three years of imprisonment or a fine.[1543]

While infringers and those that contribute culpably to an infringement are fully liable, German law also recognises limited liability where a third party otherwise contributes or facilitates an infringement. The latter, which is also known as *Störerhaftung*, is of particular relevance in the context of file-sharing. Therefore direct and vicarious liability will only be dealt with in brief, whereas the concept of *"Störerhaftung"* will be outlined in detail.

(1) Direct, Contributory and Vicarious Liability

German law distinguishes between direct infringements, and contributory and vicarious liability. Direct infringers are those, who commit the infringement themselves, and will be directly liable. Besides those that are aiding and abetting the infringement, this also includes those that contribute to an infringement in a legally relevant way. In that regard, legally relevant are material contributions to the act or enabling the infringing act with knowledge of the act being a key element. Individuals involved in an

---

unlawfully produced and distributed copies or copies intended for unlawful distribution held or owned by the infringing party. Sentence 1 shall apply *mutatis mutandis* to the devices owned by the infringing party that mainly served to produce such copies. (2) Any person who unlawfully infringes a copyright or another right protected by this Act, may be required by the infringed party to recall unlawfully produced and distributed copies or copies intended for unlawful distribution or to remove these permanently from the distribution channels. (3) Instead of the measures provided for in subsection 1, the infringed party may demand that the copies owned by the infringing party be handed over to it in return for payment of appropriate remuneration which may not exceed the costs of production. (4) The claims arising from sections 1 to 3 shall be excluded if the measure is disproportionate in the individual case. The legitimate interests of third parties shall also be taken into consideration when assessing proportionality. (5) Buildings and separable parts of copies and devices of which production and distribution is not unlawful shall not be subject to the measures provided for in sections 1 to 3." (Translation by Alexander Klett/Matthias Sonntag/ Stephan Wilske, *Intellectual Property Law in Germany* (2008), p.341).

1543 See § 106 *UrhG*. For infringements committed on a commercial scale the maximum sentence is five years imprisonment (§ 108a *UrhG*). Criminal investigations in copyright matters are only successful where the infringement is of some severity.

infringement may hence be liable if they induced the infringement and act culpably.[1544] This can apply, for example, to somebody who knowingly rents out a venue for an infringing show,[1545] organises an infringing show[1546] or to the publisher or the printer of an infringing book. The decisive criterion for liability in this context is that the individual in question has contributed significantly to the infringement in an organisational or financial way.[1547] In contrast, liability will be excluded when the infringing acts take place outside his sphere of influence.[1548]

Contributory liability has its limits where the contribution to the infringement is nothing more than the provision of mere help[1549] or technical infrastructure.[1550]

In addition to direct and contributory liability, German copyright law also recognises vicarious liability. Vicarious liability is related to contributory liability and applies where someone provides a non-infringing device to a third party while knowing that the third party will use the device to commit an infringement.[1551] The notion of infringer in that context is interpreted relatively wide and includes for instance copy shop owners

---

1544 Cf. Gerald Spindler, in: Gerald Spindler/Fabian Schuster, *Recht der elektronischen Medien* (2nd ed. 2011), § 97 *UrhG* paras. 16 et seq.; Jörg-Alexander Paul, in: Thomas Hoeren/Ulrich Sieber/Bernd Holznagel, *Multimedia-Recht* (36th supplementary sheets 2013), Part 7.4, paras. 167 et seq.

1545 OLG München, Decision of 21.09.1978 – 6 U 4941/77 *(Transvestiten-Show),* Gewerblicher Rechtsschutz und Urheberrecht 1979, 152.

1546 BGH, Decision of 16.06.1971 – I ZR 120/69 *(Konzertveranstalter),* Gewerblicher Rechtsschutz und Urheberrecht 1972, 141, 142; BGH, Decision of 18.03.1960 – I ZR 75/58 *(Eisrevue II),* Gewerblicher Rechtsschutz und Urheberrecht 1960, 606, 607.

1547 Gerald Spindler, in: Gerald Spindler/Fabian Schuster, *Recht der elektronischen Medien* (2nd ed. 2011), § 97 *UrhG* para. 16.

1548 BGH, Decision of 16.06.1971 – I ZR 120/69 *(Konzertveranstalter),* Gewerblicher Rechtsschutz und Urheberrecht 1972, 141, 142.

1549 For instance the person that merely sells tickets to an unauthorised movie screening, or the paper boy that delivers a newspaper with infringing content will not be liable for the infringements. See also *KG,* Gewerblicher Rechtsschutz und Urheberrecht 1959, 150 *(Musikboxaufsteller).*

1550 See Jörg-Alexander Paul in: Thomas Hoeren/Ulrich Sieber/Bernd Holznagel, *Multimedia-Recht* (36th supplementary sheets 2013), Part 7.4, paras. 168 with further references.

1551 Gerald Spindler, in: Gerald Spindler/Fabian Schuster, *Recht der elektronischen Medien* (2nd ed. 2011), § 97 *UrhG* para. 17.

who do not take reasonable measures in order to prevent illegal copying by their customers.[1552]

Vicarious liability also applies where an employee or authorised person within a company has unlawfully infringed a right protected under copyright law. In this case, the owner of the company will be liable for claims arising from §§ 97 I and 98 *UrhG.*[1553]

(2) Störerhaftung: Liability as a Disturber

In addition to contributory and vicarious liability, German law also foresees liability, where there has been a lesser degree of involvement of a third party. This concept of liability is called *Störerhaftung* and may be literally translated as "liability as a disturber". [1554] It is in some way also a form of contributory liability, but instead of being fully liable as it is the case under vicarious liability, the disturber *(Störer)* will only be liable to cease and desist. *Störerhaftung* is rooted in the tort theory of liability for dangerous property and holds the third party liable based on the third party's relationship with the infringement. The concept must not be confused with the US concept of contributory liability as outlined by the court in Gershwin Publishing Corp. v Columbia Artists as "one who, with knowledge of the infringing activity, induces, causes, or materially contributes"[1555]. This definition would be too wide for the German *Störer* concept. *Störerhaftung* is of particular relevance in the context of copyright infringements on the Internet because in most constellations a third party either provides the infrastructure or other technical means to commit

1552 A clearly visible sign indicating that copyrights have to be observed may constitute such a measure. BGH, Decision of 09.06.1983 – I ZR 70/81 *(Kopierläden),* Gewerblicher Rechtsschutz und Urheberrecht 1984, 54.

1553 See § 99 *UrhG* : "If an employee or authorized person within a company has unlawfully infringed a right protected under this Act, the infringed party shall also be entitled to the claims arising from § 97(1) and § 98 against the owner of the company". (Translation by Alexander Klett/Matthias Sonntag/Stephan Wilske, *Intellectual Property Law in Germany* (2008), p.341).

1554 For an outline of the concept and a comparison with other secondary liability schemes in Europe see Matthias Leistner, *Structural aspects of secondary (provider) liability in Europe*, Journal of Intellectual Property and Practice 2014, Vol. 9 No. 1, 75, 78 et seq.

1555 *Gershwin Publishing Corp. v Columbia Artists,* 443 F. 2d 1159 (2d Cir. 1971).

an infringement. For instance host providers facilitate infringements by hosting third party content, while access providers provide the infrastructure to infringe protected rights. Especially, where the actual infringer cannot be identified and vicarious liability does not apply, *Störerhaftung* provides a means by which the rights-holder can at least achieve that the infringing content is removed or blocked. As the *Störer* will be obliged to cease and desist, the relevance in peer-to-peer file-sharing cases becomes obvious: if one cannot establish direct liability of a subscriber but liability as a *Störer*, the subscriber might be obliged to prevent similar infringements in the future. In how far, this applies and under which circumstances liability as a *Störer* can be established will be discussed in the following.

As previously mentioned, the liability concept derives from the tortious liability for dangerous property. Under *Störerhaftung*, liability will be established if the third party knowingly contributes to the infringement of a protected right.[1556] This liability concept originally applied to cases where a person had constructive control over dangerous property and was therefore held liable under public law – irrespective of intentional or negligent behaviour – for any foreseeable harm arising from such source of danger. Under private law, the notion of *Störer* characterizes a person who is liable under § 1004 *Bürgerliches Gesetzbuch (BGB)* to cease any interference with the property of another that is not caused by removal or retention of the possession.[1557] The *Störer* does not himself interfere with the rights of a third party, but in another way contributes deliberately and adequately causal to the infringement of a protected right without being

---

1556 BGH, Decision of 11.03.2004 – I ZR 304/01 *(Internetversteigerung I),* MultiMedia und Recht 2004, 668 et seq. with a case comment by Thomas Hoeren; concerning the specific requirements in detail: Markus Köhler/Hans-Wolfgang Arndt/Thomas Fetzer *Recht des Internet* (6th ed. 2008), para.774 et seq.; Gerald Spindler/Katharina Anton in: Gerald Spindler/Fabian Schuster, *Recht der elektronischen Medien* (2nd ed. 2011), § 1004 *BGB* para. 8 et seq. with further references, as well as Gerald Spindler in *ibid,* § 97 *UrhG* paras. 16–33.

1557 § 1004 *BGB*: "(1) If the ownership is interfered with by means other than removal or retention of possession, the owner may require the disturber to remove the interference. If further interferences are to be feared, the owner may seek a prohibitory injunction. (2) The claim is excluded if the owner is obliged to tolerate the interference". Translation provided by the Langenscheidt Translation Service on the homepage of the Ministry of Justice, www.gesetzeiminternet.de (last accessed on 21.03.2011).

the perpetrator or an accessory.[1558] In addition, the Strörer must be someone who has the legal and effective means to cease the infringement and prevent future infringements of the same kind.[1559]

The concept has been applied by analogy also to interferences with intellectual property rights. This analogy also encompassed interferences on the Internet. In an Internet context, the *Störerhaftung* has been discussed by the Federal Court of Justice at first in relation to Internet auction platforms.[1560]

Providers of Internet auction platforms were held liable as *Störer* for trademark infringements committed by third party sellers on their platforms based on the conclusion that their service constitutes a source of danger, which facilitates the commitment of infringements of intellectual property rights.[1561] Although the platform providers neither committed the infringements themselves nor aided or abetted the infringement or were vicarious liable, they were held to otherwise contribute deliberately and adequately causal to the infringements by the provision of their ser-

---

1558 Cf. in the context of *Störer* liability on the Internet BGH, Decision of 11.03.2004 – I ZR 304/01 *(Internetversteigerung I),* MultiMedia und Recht 2004, 668 et seq. with a case comment by Thomas Hoeren.

1559 In an Internet context, see BGH, Decision of 17.05.2001 – I ZR 251/99 *(ambiente.de),* MultiMedia und Recht 2001, 671; BGH, Decision of 01.04.2004 – I ZR 317/01 *(Schöner Wetten),* Gewerblicher Rechtsschutz und Urheberrecht 2004, 693; BGH, Decision of 11.03.2004 – I ZR 304/01 *(Internetversteigerung I),* MultiMedia und Recht 2004, 668.

1560 BGH, Decision of 11.03.2004 – I ZR 304/01 *(Internetversteigerung I),* MultiMedia und Recht 2004, 668 et seq. with a case comment by Thomas Hoeren; concerning the specific requirements in detail: Markus Köhler/Hans-Wolfgang Arndt/Thomas Fetzer, *Recht des Internet* (6th ed. 2008), paras.774 et seq.; Gerald Spindler/Katharina Anton in: Gerald Spindler/Fabian Schuster, *Recht der elektronischen Medien* (2nd ed. 2011), § 1004 *BGB* paras. 8 et seq. with further references; Thomas Dreier in: Thomas Dreier/Gernot Schulze, *Urheberrechtsgesetz* (4th ed. 2013), § 97 para .33 with further references. For a detailed discussion of *Störerhaftung* in relation to Internet auction platforms see Gerald Spindler in: Gerald Spindler/Andreas Wiebe, *Internet-Auktionen und elektronische Marktplätze* (2nd ed. 2005), pp. 231 et seq. The liability of host providers will further be discussed in the Third Chapter.

1561 See only BGH, Decision of 11.03.2004 – I ZR 304/01 *(Internetversteigerung I),* MultiMedia und Recht 2004, 668. For an evaluation of the concept in English and its applicability on Auctioning websites see Andreas Rühmkorf, *The Liability of online auction portals: Towards a Uniform Approach?,* Journal of Internet Law 2010, Vol. 14 Issue 4, 3–10.

vice. [1562] The same conclusion was drawn as regards subscribers of Internet connections. The operation of an Internet access was equalled to operating a source of danger.

Liability is not extended without limits upon third parties: Considering that a *Störer* will be liable to cease and desist,[1563] *Störer* liability requires that the *Störer* has breached a reasonable duty to examine when he had reason to believe that he is actually supporting an infringing act. Generally speaking, liability requires a breach of due diligence or monitoring duties and is also restricted by the principle of proportionality.

(3) Application of the Liability Concepts to the Subscriber of an IP Address

Regularly, the rights-holder will address the subscriber of an Internet access as the direct infringer. The rights-holder bears the burden of proof that the subscriber has actually committed the infringement. There is a presumption of proof concerning the perpetration of a copyright infringement committed online, namely that the subscriber of the IP address from which the work has been made available has committed the infringement.[1564] This assumption is based on the concept of prima facie evidence: it is assumed that it is in the first place the subscriber who uses his Internet access and in relation to others using the connection, he is in the position to control to whom he grants access. The assumption of the subscriber being the infringer can however be rebutted when there are reasons to believe that someone else may have committed an infringement.[1565] It will be sufficient for the subscriber to proof that he shares his Internet connec-

---

1562 See only BGH, Decision of 11 March 2004 – I ZR 304/01 *(Internetversteigerung I),* MultiMedia und Recht 2004, 668 with a case comment by Thomas Hoeren; concerning the specific requirements in detail: Markus Köhler/ Hans-Wolfgang Arndt/Thomas Fetzer, *Recht des Internet* (6th ed. 2008), para. 774 et seq.; Gerald Spindler/Katharina Anton in: Gerald Spindler/Fabian Schuster, *Recht der elektronischen Medien* (2nd ed. 2011), § 1004 *BGB* paras. 8 et seq. with further references.

1563 As previously mentioned, the *Störer* will not be liable for damages, he will only be liable to cease and desist.

1564 BGH, Decision of 12.05.2010 – I ZR 121/08 *(Sommer unseres Lebens),* Neue Juristische Wochenschrift 2010, 2061.

1565 *Ibid.*

tion. He is not required to investigate who else has actually committed the infringement.[1566] The subscriber only bears the burden of proof that someone else has committed the infringement.[1567] In order to satisfy this burden of proof, he will have to provide evidence that he was not the only one that used the connection. As most connections are being shared, the subscriber will regularly succeed to absolve himself from liability. However, this only applies to his liability as the actual perpetrator and does not extend to his liability as a *Störer*. Moreover, there are only view constellations, where a subscriber will also be exempted from liability as *Störer*.

Considering that liability as a *Störer* requires that the *Störer* has breached a reasonable duty of care, the subscriber of an Internet access has to take duly diligent efforts to prevent misuse of that access. [1568] His efforts has to be reasonable, and amount to what can be reasonably expected from an average person.[1569] A subscriber may thus be a *Störer* when he has breached a monitoring duty. Monitoring duties exist not per se, but may arise, if a *Störer* allows third parties to use his Internet connection. The existence and scope of potential monitoring duties have been subject to a number of lawsuits where the subscriber allowed family or household members to use his connection.[1570]

The jurisprudence on this subject-matter has long been inconsistent and only recently the Federal Court of Justice clarified some issues. In early

---

1566 See OLG Hamm, Zeitschrift für Urheber- und Medienrecht 2012, 254.

1567 BGH, Decision of 12.05.2010 – I ZR 121/08 *(Sommer unseres Lebens),* Neue Juristische Wochenschrift 2010, 2061.

1568 *Ibid.* In this case the Federal Court of Justice had to decide whether someone who was evidently not at home at the time when the alleged infringement took place, is liable for the copyright infringement committed via his WiFi Internet access.

1569 In relation to online marketplaces, it was held that the provider of such a marketplace has to make sure that sellers of adult material employ a functioning age verification system, BGH, Decision of 12.07.2007 – I ZR 18/04 *(Jugendgefährdende Medien bei eBay),* Zeitschrift für Urheber- und Medienrecht 2007, 846, 852. A marketplace provider will however not be required to determine which goods are not to be sold to minors, *ibid.* This would be beyond reasonableness and cannot be expected from the online marketplace provider.

1570 For instance LG Hamburg, Decision of 19.04. 2006– 308 O 92/06, Zeitschrift für Urheber- und Medienrecht 2006, 661; OLG Düsseldorf, Decision of 27.12.2007 – I-20 W 157/07, Zeitschrift für Urheber- und Medienrecht-RD 2008, 170; LG Köln, Decision of 27.01.2010 – 28 O 241/09, Zeitschrift für Urheber- und Medienrecht-RD 2010, 277.

cases, some courts have established liability of the subscriber based on the fact that he did not use available technical measures as for example a firewall or tools restricting the installation or use of peer-to-peer software in order to prevent copyright infringements by other authorised users of his computer.[1571]

As regards the notion of "authorised" users, these are users to whom the subscriber grants access to his Internet connection. In this regard, the jurisprudence distinguishes between family members and other third parties using a connection. As regards the latter, initial instruction and monitoring duties are easier established because their behaviour is not as foreseeable as that of family members that live in the same household.[1572] However, the manner and scope of such instruction and monitoring in relation to non-family members has not yet been established by the courts. The German Constitutional Court stressed in its file-sharing decision in 2012 that the question of instruction and monitoring duties towards non-family members is of fundamental importance.[1573] Irrespective of the Constitutional Court's appeal, guidance only exists in relation to family members. While the jurisprudence on this subject matter has been quite diverse on the lower court level, the Federal Court of Justice has recently clarified some issues.

With regard to children, there is consensus, that children should be instructed by their parents before they were allowed to access the Internet. In November 2012, the Federal Court of Justice held in the *Morpheus* case, that parents have to instruct their underage children, that they are not allowed to use file-sharing networks. [1574] This shall be sufficient to comply with due diligence.[1575] However, the Court also curtailed this liability

---

1571 OLG Hamburg, Decision of 11.10.2006 – 5 W 152/06, BeckRS 2008, 14864; LG Köln, Decision of 28.02.2007 – 28 O 10/07, Zeitschrift für Urheber- und Medienrecht-RD 2008, 93, 95; LG Frankfurt/M., Decision of 12.04.2007 – 2/03 O 824/06, MultiMedia und Recht 2007, 804, 805.

1572 OLG Frankfurt/M., MultiMedia und Recht 2008, 169, 179.

1573 BVerfG, Zeitschrift für Urheber- und Medienrecht 2012, 471 *(Unerlaubtes Filesharing im Internet)*.

1574 BGH, Decision of 15.11.2012 – I ZR 74/12 *(Morpheus)*, Gewerblicher Rechtsschutz und Urheberrecht 2013, 511. The decision has recently been confirmed by BGH, Decision of 11.06.2015 – I ZR 7/14 (*Tauschbörse III*).

1575 As parents will be required in court to provide evidence for the initial instruction on the prohibition of file-sharing, lawyers advise their clients to let the children sign a written declaration that stipulates the modalities of their Internet use.

exemption in so far as this should only apply to a normally developed child that generally obeys his parents' orders. Only in this case, it is not required that the parents further monitor the online activities of minors by for example installing software on their computer. If the parents have concrete reasons to believe that their child will not obey their order, the parents are under an obligation to implement measure that hinder file-sharing.[1576] The requirements for instruction and monitoring have to be determined on a case-by-case basis and depend on the age of the child and the child's capacity to understand the wrongfulness of file-sharing.[1577]

Previous to the decision of the Federal Court of Justice in *Morpheus*, lower courts held that parents have to monitor the surfing habits of even an adult child on a random basis when the child uses his parents' Internet connection.[1578] Some courts even considered that instruction or monitoring duties exist in relation to the subscriber's spouse.[1579] In relation to

---

See for instance WBS Law, *Nach dem BGH Filesharing Urteil (Morpheus) – Wie geht es nun weiter?* (16.11.2012).

1576 This had also previously been held by OLG Frankfurt/M., Gewerblicher Rechtsschutz und Urheberrecht, Rechtsprechungs-Report 2008, 73, 74; LG Mannheim, MultiMedia und Recht 2007, 267, 268; Zeitschrift für Urheber- und Medienrecht-RD 2007, 252, 254 et seq.; MultiMedia und Recht 2007, 459, 460; see also Lambert Grosskopf, *Anmerkung zum Urteil des LG Hamburg: Störerhaftung des Internanschlussinhabers für Urheberrechtsverletzungen,* Computer und Recht 2007, 122–124; Markus Peter, *Störer im Internet – Haften Eltern für ihre Kinder?,* Kommunikation und Recht 2007, 371, 373; Matthias Leistner/Felix Stang, *Die Neuerung der wettbewerbsrechtlichen Verkehrspflichten – Ein Siegeszug der Prüfungspflichten?,* Wettbewerb in Recht und Praxis 2008, 533, 549; Sven Mühlberger, *Die Haftung des Internetanschlussinhabers bei Filesharing-Konstellationen nach den Grundsätzen der Störerhaftung,* Gewerblicher Rechtsschutz und Urheberrecht 2009, 1022, 1025 et seq.; Gerald Spindler, in: Georg Bamberger/Herbert Roth, *BeckOK-BGB* (updated: 01.08.2012), § 832 para. 31 a.

1577 BGH, Decision of 15.11.2012 – I ZR 74/12 *(Morpheus),* Gewerblicher Rechtsschutz und Urheberrecht 2013, 511, 513.

1578 OLG Hamburg, Decision of 11.10.2006 – 5 W 152/06, BeckRS 2008, 14864; LG Düsseldorf, Decision of 27.05.2009 – 12 O 134/09, MultiMedia und Recht 2009, 780.

1579 The Higher Regional Court of Cologne for instance expressed doubts whether a subscriber has instruction or monitoring duties with regard to his/her spouse, and thus, set aside a prior decision that denied legal aid to the defendants based on the assumption that a subscriber must monitor the online activities of her spouse, see OLG Köln, Decision of 24.03.2011 – 6 W 427/11, Neue Juristische Online Zeitschrift 2011, 1239, 1240.

adult children, monitoring and instruction duties were also controversially discussed.[1580] The majority of courts held that protective measures only have to be employed when there are indications that an infringement has already happened: an on-going supervision without cause for action is unreasonable.[1581]

In January 2014, the Federal Court of Justice finally provided some guidance as regards the emergence of monitoring duties in relation to adult family members.[1582] According to the Court, a subscriber's decision to allow family members to use his Internet access is based on family ties. Considering that adults are fully responsible for their own acts and considering that within families there is usually a climate of trust, the Court held that subscribers have no duty to instruct or monitor adult family members when they use a shared Internet connection. Only when there is concrete reason to believe that an adult family member will use the Internet access to commit copyright infringements, the subscriber will be obliged to implement the necessary measures to hinder the commitment of infringements. The Court stressed that such "concrete reason to believe" can be acquired by notification of the rights-holder.[1583]

Further scenarios of shared connections where a subscriber may be held liable as a *Störer* are those of employers in relation to their employees, or providers of open Wi-Fis, for instance in hotel or restaurants, in relation to their users.

There is almost no case law dealing with the liability of employers for illegal file-sharing by their employees. So far the Regional Court of Munich held, that employers are not liable as *Störer* for illegal file-sharing

1580 Some courts assumed that children may well be more advanced in the use of information technologies and therefore specifically adult children do not have to be instructed or monitored by their parents when surfing the Internet, see LG Mannheim, Decision of 29.09.2006 – 7 O 76/06, MultiMedia und Recht 2007, 267. No need to instruct adult family member: see also AG Frankfurt am Main, Decision of 12.02.2010 – 32 C 1634/09-72, Zeitschrift für Urheber- und Medienrecht-RD 2011, 116.

1581 OLG Frankfurt/M., Decision of 20.12.2007 – 11 W 58/07, MultiMedia und Recht 2008, 169.

1582 BGH, Decision of 08.01.2014 – I ZR 169/12 *(BearShare),* Zeitschrift für Urheber- und Medienrecht 2014, 707.

1583 Such notification usually takes the form of a cease and desist letter before claim, which will be outlined in this chapter in the following.

committed by their employees, when they had no reason to foresee the illegal activities.[1584]

As regards the *Störer* liability of providers of Wi-Fi access points in course of the commercial activity, for instance the aforementioned hotel or restaurant owner, there is only limited guidance to the necessary duty of care. This may also be due to the fact, that there have been only two cases that have been published so far. In one case the owner of an Internet café was held liable as a *Störer* because he did not implement protective measures to prevent copyright infringements in his café.[1585] In another case, the owner of a hotel was exempted from liability as a disturber because he instructed his guests to respect the laws before granting access to the hotel's secured Wi-Fi network.[1586] In these scenarios there is other than in a family no relationship of trust between the subscriber and the third parties that are allowed to use the Internet connection. The conclusion one may draw from these two cases is, that it is necessary to instruct the users before granting access to the Internet.

To be distinguished from these scenarios, where the subscriber expressly or implicitly allows third parties to use his Internet access, is the unauthorised use by third parties. As most subscribers have wireless routers, there is always a risk that non-authorised third parties acquire access to the network. The subscriber has to take efforts to control who has access to his connection and uses it.[1587] First of all, the prevention of misuse requires the implementation of standard security measures for Wi-Fi networks. His duty exists per se and does not only arise where the subscriber has reason to believe that infringements are taking place via his connection.[1588] If the subscriber runs a Wi-Fi router, he will be expected to have

---

1584 LG München I, MultiMedia und Recht 2008, 422, 423.

1585 LG Hamburg, Decision of 25.11.2010 – 310 O 433/10, BeckRS 2011, 03015.

1586 LG Frankfurt am Main, Zeitschrift für Urheber- und Medienrecht-RD 2011, 371.

1587 See Georg Borges, *Pflichten und Haftung beim Betrieb privater WLAN,* Neue Juristische Wochenschrift 2010, 2624.

1588 BGH, Decision of 12.05.2010 – I ZR 121/08 *(Sommer unseres Lebens),* Neue Juristische Wochenschrift 2010, 2061. See also Patrick Breyer, *Die Haftung für Mitbenutzer von Telekommunikationsanschlüssen,* Neue Juristische Online Zeitschrift 2010, 1085 et seq.; Georg Borges, *Pflichten und Haftung beim Betrieb privater WLAN*, Neue Juristische Wochenschrift 2010, 2624 et seq.; Gerald Spindler in: Gerald Spindler/Fabian Schuster, *Recht der elektronischen Medien* (2nd ed. 2011), § 97 *UrhG,* para. 20.

it adequately secured so that no unauthorised third party can access his connection.[1589] This means in the first place that he has a sufficiently secure password. According to the Federal Court of Justice a sufficiently secure password is such a password that is distinct and sufficiently long, and fulfils the general security standards at the time of purchase of the router.[1590] There is no need to update the security settings to keep track with technological developments. By its findings, the Court took into account that private users who have a Wi-Fi router at home are not necessarily IT-literate and can therefore not be reasonably expected to inform themselves about current security standards. In practice, this may lead to unfair results, when those who run an old router with out-dated security mechanisms are less likely to be held liable for infringements committed via their connection – assuming that it is relatively easy for a third party to connect to the network.

Other than with the graduated response schemes discussed previously, there is no centrally administered list of infringers/*Störer*. As a consequence, unless the respective rights-holders' rights have been previously infringed, *Störer* liability will hardly be established in those scenarios where a duty of care in the shape of a monitoring duty only emerges following a first time infringement (or concrete reason to believe that an infringement has taken place) although an infringement might already have been committed via the subscriber's Internet access.

bb) Remedies for Copyright Infringement

As mentioned above, the rights-holder is entitled to a claim for removal of derogation or for injunctive relief in case of risk of recurrence ("cease and desist"), damages, unjust enrichment as well as destruction, recall or resti-

---

1589 BGH, Decision of 12.05.2010 – I ZR 121/08 *(Sommer unseres Lebens),* Neue Juristische Wochenschrift 2010, 2061.

1590 *Ibid.* Accordingly, WPA2 is likely to be considered as the current standard for private users. WPA2 (Wi-Fi Protected Access 2) is an implementation of an IEEE ("The Institute of Electrical and Electronics Engineers, Incorporated", a New York not-for-profit corporation) security standard for Wi-Fi networks and the most used Wi-Fi protection nowadays in both, home and professional networks. Based on the Advanced Encryption Standard (AES), the current standard specification for the encryption of data, WPA2 provides strong security and vulnerabilities are currently only known in regard to weak passphrases.

tution of infringing goods. In case of online copyright infringements, the remedies sought after are the removal of the infringing content from the Internet and a desist declaration by the potential infringer to refrain from infringements in the future. In addition, rights-holders seek compensation for the damage suffered.

(1) Damages

In relation to the actual infringer, i.e. in a case of direct, contributory or vicarious liability, the rights-holder regularly seeks to have his actual damages compensated. If the infringer acts intentionally or negligently he will be liable for the actual damages suffered by the rights-holder (§ 97 II *UrhG*). In German law, there are three different ways of calculating damages in copyright infringement matters. The rights-holder may claim compensation for his profits lost due to the infringement, reasonable royalties in relation to the infringement (by the way of license analogy), or to have the actual profits generated by the infringer conveyed to him.[1591] Although under German law only actual damages can be compensated, meaning that there are no punitive damages, in certain limited circumstances "immaterial damages" may also be compensated.[1592] The *UrhG* provides for a compensation of non-pecuniary losses by authors, editors of scientific editions, photographers and performing artists if and to the extent that this is equitable (§ 97 II *UrhG*). The intention behind this provision is to compensate

1591 For the calculation of damages see: Bodo von Wolff, in: Artur-Axel Wandtke/Winfried Bullinger, *Praxiskommentar zum Urheberrecht: UrhR* (3rd ed. 2009), § 97 *UrhG* paras. 58–83; Thomas Dreier in: Thomas Dreier/Gernot Schulze, *Urheberrechtsgesetz* (3rd ed. 2008), § 97 paras. 58–70; P. Meier-Beck, *Herausgabe des Verletzergewinns – Strafschadensersatz nach deutschem Recht,* Gewerblicher Rechtsschutz und Urheberrecht 2005, 617–623; R. Kraßer, *Schadensersatz für Verletzungen von gewerblichen Schutzrechten und Urheberrechten nach deutschem Recht,* Gewerblicher Rechtsschutz und Urheberrecht, Internationaler Teil 1980, 259–272, all with further references. In copyright infringement matters via peer-to-peer networks, the license analogy is the most commonly used way to calculate damages.

1592 Cf. Bodo von Wolff, in: Artur-Axel Wandtke/Winfried Bullinger, *Praxiskommentar zum Urheberrecht: UrhR* (3rd ed. 2009), § 97 *UrhG* paras. 58–83; Thomas Dreier in: Thomas Dreier/Gernot Schulze, *Urheberrechtsgesetz* (3rd ed. 2008), § 97 paras. 84–90.

particularly for the infringement of moral rights.[1593] If damages claims cannot be brought,[1594] the rights-holder may base his claims on the unjust enrichment provisions in §§ 812 et seqq. *BGB*. Under unjust enrichment, the infringer will be liable for restitution of the value of what he gained due to the infringement.

In order to be able to calculate damages, rights-holders are also attributed claims for information regarding the origin and distribution channels of the infringing products and rendering of accounts.[1595]

Pursuant to § 98 *UrhG*, the rights-holder may also demand destruction, recall or restitution of infringing copies and equipment.

(2) Cease and Desist

As outlined above, in most peer-to-peer file-sharing cases direct, contributory or vicarious liability will be hardly established. While the actual infringer will be liable for damages and cease the interference, the *Störer* will only be liable to cease and desist.

1593 Cf. *ibid.*

1594 One reason may be for example that the infringer has not acted at least negligently. However, as in copyright matters regularly at least negligence on part of the infringer is established, claims for unjust enrichment are primarily relevant with respect to compensation claims against owners of businesses in which an infringement occurred. See Alexander Klett/Matthias Sonntag/Stephan Wilske, *Intellectual Property Law in Germany* (2008), p. 71.

1595 Thomas Dreier in: Thomas Dreier/Gernot Schulze, *Urheberrechtsgesetz* (3rd ed. 2008), § 97 para. 78. The implementation of the Enforcement Directive into national law introduced further information rights into the UrhG: Information on the origin and distribution of the infringing copies can now also be claimed from a third party which – on a commercial scale – was found (1) in possession of infringing goods, (2) to be using infringing services, (3) to be providing services used in infringing activities, or (4) was indicated by the person referred to in point 1, 2 or 3 as being involved in the production, manufacture, or distribution of the copies, other goods or services (§ 101 II UrhG, which transposes Article 8 of the Enforcement Directive into national law). There is no statutory definition of the notion of "commercial scale" beside Recital 14 of the Enforcement Directive referring to acts on a commercial scale as those that are carried out for direct or indirect economic or commercial advantage, which would normally exclude acts carried out by end-consumers acting in good faith.

Both, *Störer* and actual infringers are obliged to cease the interference once liability is established. They also will be requested to prevent identical infringements in the future.

Usually, the rights-holder will ask the infringer or *Störer* to sign a predrafted cease and desist letter, in which the recipient declares that he will cease and desist from the declared infringement, meaning that he will not only cease the infringement but also refrain from committing the infringement in question in the future. The declaration will usually contain a penalty clause as an additional enforcement mechanism.

The scope of the obligation to refrain from committing the infringement in question in the future has been subject to numerous lawsuits.[1596] Although this is of more relevance when host providers are asked to prevent the re-appearance of infringing content, this issue shall already be briefly addressed at this point. The discussion usually focusses on the question what kind of infringement is to be omitted in the future: is it the infringement of rights in relation to all works of the rights-holder in question? Is it the infringement of rights in relation to one particular work? Is it the infringement of rights of the rights-holder committed by the subscriber/one particular user? Is it the infringement of rights of the rights-holder committed by specific means e.g. in peer-to-peer networks?[1597]

In file-sharing cases, the rights-holder will only be entitled to ask for a discontinuation of infringements of works of which he is the rights-holder

---

1596 For a summary of the latest copyright infringement cases, that reached the Federal Court of Justice, see Markus Bölling, *Unterlassungsantrag und Streitgegenstand im Falle der Störerhaftung*, Gewerblicher Rechtsschutz und Urheberrecht 2013, 1092–1099.

1597 These questions have been first addressed by the Federal Court of Justice in its various Internet auction decisions (BGH, Decision of 11.03.2004 – I ZR 304/01 *[Internet auction I]*, MultiMedia und Recht 2004, 668; BGH, Decision of 19.04.2007 – I ZR 35/04 *[Internet Auction II]*, MultiMedia und Recht 2007, 507; BGH, Decision of 30.04.2008 – I ZR 73/05 *[Internet auction III]*; BGH, Decision of 22.07.2010 – I ZR 139/08 *[Kinderhochstühle im Internet]*, Gewerblicher Rechtsschutz und Urheberrecht 2011, 152): Insofar as auctions of counterfeited goods are concerned, the provider of an Internet auction platform must not only disable access to an infringing offer without undue delay, but must also take reasonable precautions to prevent "identical" infringements in the future, see only BGH, Decision of 11.03.2004 – I ZR 304/01 *(Internet auction I)*, MultiMedia und Recht 2004, 668, 671.

of, and of which he can prove that they have already been shared via the subscriber's Internet access.[1598]

If the subscriber refrains to sign a cease and desist declaration, rights-holders regularly seek to obtain an injunction against the subscriber.[1599]

cc) Information Rights

It has previously been addressed numerous times, that in most cases where the infringement has been committed online, the evidence collected about an infringement will only identify the IP address from which an alleged infringement has taken place. This IP address then needs to be matched against the subscriber to whom it was allocated at the time of the infringement. Similar to the Norwich Pharmacal orders, the *UrhG* forsees that rights-holders can seek disclosure of information on communications traffic data to identify a subscriber from Internet access providers by way of a judicial disclosure order.[1600] Pursuant to § 101 II, IX *UrhG*, a disclosure order against a third party will be granted, if an obvious infringement has been committed, and the third party from whom disclosure is sought provided the services used to commit an infringement on a commercial

---

1598 Urs Verweyen, *Grenzen der Störerhaftung in Peer to Peer-Netzwerken,* Multi-Media und Recht 2009, 590–594 with further references to case-law.

1599 An interim injunction may be granted if interim legal protection is sought before an actual decision in the main proceedings, whereas injunctive relief may also be granted permanently in normal proceedings.

1600 The information in question relates to communications traffic data (§ 3 No. 3 *Telekommunikationsgesetz – TKG*), which requires a judicial order on the permissibility of its use. The data that can legitimately retained by communication service providers is enumerated in § 96 I *TKG*: "(1) the number or other identification of the lines in question or of the terminal, personal authorisation codes, additionally the card number when customer cards are used, additionally the location data when mobile handsets are used; (2) the beginning and end of the connection, indicated by date and time and, where relevant to the charges, the volume of data transmitted; (3) the telecommunications service used by the user; (4) the termination points of fixed connections, the beginning and end of their use, indicated by date and time and, where relevant to the charges, the volume of data transmitted; (5) any other traffic data required for setup and maintenance of the telecommunications connection and for billing purposes" (Translation by Bundesbeauftragter für den Datenschutz und die Informationsfreiheit, available at http://www.bfdi.bund.de/cae/servlet/contentblob/411286/publicationFile/25386/TelecommunicationsAct-TKG.pdf (last accessed on 16.06.2011)).

scale.[1601] § 101 IV *UrhG* requires the court to respect the principle of proportionality, when assessing whether to grant a disclosure order.

Accordingly, information can be acquired from an Internet access provider with regard to the identity of an Internet access service subscriber.

dd) The Abmahnung

As already mentioned, the author of a work, the right-holder of neighbouring rights, and the owner of exclusive rights of use with respect to an infringed work may sue for copyright infringement.[1602] Before bringing a case to court, rights-holders are advised to send an *Abmahnung* to the infringer asking him to cease and desist from the infringement and sign an undertaking that he will subject himself to a cease and desist obligation with an appropriate penalty clause.[1603] Although the issue of a *Abmahnung* is not a prerequisite for subsequent court proceedings, § 97a I *UrhG*

1601 The "commercial scale" requirement stems from Article 8 of the *IPR Enforcement Directive*. With its introduction, the European legislator intended to regulate the proceedings for disclosure of information in the sense that information rights are restricted to acts carried out for direct or indirect economic or commercial advantage (Recital 14 of the *IPR Enforcement Directive*). Prior to the decision of the Federal Court of Justice regarding a song by German singer and songwriter Xavier Naidoo in 2012 (BGH, Decision of 19.04.2012 – 1 ZB 80/11, Neue Juristische Wochenschrift 2012, 2958), it has long been assumed that the infringement itself must have been committed on a commercial scale. This condition had been interpreted by German courts very broadly, with the upload of one music album or one film satisfying this condition (Cf. Sandra Schmitz/Thorsten Ries, *Three songs and you are disconnected from cyberspace? Not in Germany where the industry may "turn piracy into profit"*, European Journal of Law and Technology 2012, Vol. 3 No. 1). However, in the Xavier Naidoo case, the Federal Court of Justice once and for all clarified that not the infringement must have been committed on a commercial scale. Instead the notion of commercial scale refers to the service provided by the third party from whom disclosure is sought.

1602 The owners of non-exclusive rights of use, however, do not have standing to sue for copyright infringement unless the right holder agreed (either separately for purposes of the infringement action or in the license agreement) that the licensee should be entitled to sue on behalf of the right holder.

1603 The penalty clause serves as a means to express the seriousness of the cease and desist promise.

provides that the infringed party should send a cease and desist letter to the infringing party prior to the instigation of court proceedings to give him an opportunity to settle the dispute without court action. In addition, § 93 *ZPO*[1604] provides that the claimant has to bear the defendant's costs if the defendant acknowledges the claim straight away in litigation and the claimant had not sent a cease and desist letter prior to filing his claim. Thus, it is advisable to send an *Abmahnung*; the initiation of court action right away should only be pursued where the matter is extremely urgent and a preliminary injunction is needed immediately or where the claimant is certain that the defendant will defend himself against the claims and would not sign a cease and desist declaration out of court.

The *Abmahnung* as a letter before claim, is usually sent by a lawyer *(Rechtsanwalt)* on behalf of the infringed party.[1605]

The recipient of an *Abmahnung* has to compensate the rights-holders for the costs involved, if the claim is justified.[1606] Pursuant to § 97a III *UrhG*, the recoverable costs are limited to the necessary expenses.[1607] The necessary expenses regularly include the lawyer's fees and the costs for identifying the infringement and the infringer.[1608] The lawyer's fees depend on the value of the claim.[1609] In addition to the costs for the *Abmahnung*, the rights-holders usually also claim damages in the same letter.

1604 *Zivilprozessordnung – ZPO* ("Civil Procedure Code").

1605 The lawyer's fees can be claimed from the infringer if the claim is justified.

1606 Nikolaus Reber, in: Hartwig Ahlberg/Horst-Peter Götting, *Beck'scher Online-Kommentar* (4th ed. 09.10.2013), § 97a para. 18.

1607 If an *Abmahnung* is justified, it avoids a costly court litigation and thus, it is assumed that it is a necessary means for settlement and in the interest of the infringing party.

1608 The latter may include costs for private investigators, travelling expensis, costs for technical assistance etc. See Nikolaus Reber, in: Hartwig Ahlberg/Horst-Peter Götting, *Beck'scher Online-Kommentar* (4th ed. 09.10.2013), § 97a para. 23.

1609 Lawyers' fees for litigation work in civil law are regulated in the *Attorneys Remuneration Act (Gesetz über die Vergütung von Rechtsanwältinnen und Rechtsanwälten – RVG)* which details schedules of the statutory fees payable on a claim-value basis and payable in stages for the proceedings and court hearings. See § 11 of the *Attorneys Remuneration Act* and its Appendix. Court costs in civil matters rise on a scale depending on the value of the claim which is not uniformly proportional. They are determined by reference to the statutory scales, primarily the Court Fees Act.

Since 2008, the § 97a II *UrhG* forsaw that no more than EUR 100 may be claimed as the "necessary expenses" for "non-complex cases with only an immaterial infringement of rights outside of commercial transactions". This provision has been replaced on 01 October 2013 by a more detailed provision aiming to ban unfounded claims and claims that are solely made to generate profit.[1610]

b) Outline and Functioning of Pre-Litigation Settlement

The pre-litigation settlement requires several steps to be taken: first of all, the rights-holder must obtain evidence on an infringement, which he will then present to a court in order to obtain a disclosure order against an Internet access provider; once the identity of a subscriber is revealed, he will send a cease and desist letter, the *Abmahnung*, to the alleged infringer. If the alleged infringer does not sign the cease and desist declaration, the rights-holder may seek injunctive relief before a court.

aa) Gathering of Information on Infringements

Similar to the previously discussed graduated response schemes, most rights-holder will entrust specialised companies with the identification of infringements and the collecting of evidence.[1611] These companies monitor peer-to-peer networks for incidents of illegal file-sharing by using software such as, for example, *Filewatch* which is/was used by Media Protector.[1612] *Filewatch* connects to a peer-to-peer server and requests a copyrighted file. As every downloaded file has a unique hash value and can be identified on this basis, a search will be conducted for identical files with the same hash value. The software records all the IP addresses that offer the file and starts a download. For every hit, the actual time, the hash value of the file, the user's pseudonym within the sharing software, a hash value that identifies the software client within the network, the name and

1610 The new wording will discussed at the end of this section.

1611 There are several companies that are active in Germany.

1612 See http://stop-p2p-piracy.com/site/filewatch-merkmale for more information (last accessed on 16.03.2013). The following procedure that is being described is that of Media Protector, which uses or at least used Filewatch.

version of the software, the number of packets which the client has already downloaded and most importantly the IP address of the client's Internet connection as well as the name of the corresponding Internet service provider at the time of the incident, are logged. Procedures may vary depending on the software being used and the networks that are crawled.

bb) Disclosure Orders

Pursuant to § 101 II, IX *UrhG*, a disclosure order against a third party will be granted, if an obvious infringement has been committed, and the third party from whom disclosure is sought provided the services used to commit an infringement on a commercial scale.[1613] The condition of an "obvious" infringement is fulfilled when the infringement is so clear, that an unjustified burden upon the access provider is almost impossible.[1614]

Although § 101 IV *UrhG* requires the court to respect the principle of proportionality, the courts will in fact hardly conduct a balancing test considering the workload they are faced with. In addition, the Federal Court of Justice held that the requirement for disclosure, namely an obvious

---

1613 The "commercial scale" requirement stems from Article 8 of the *IPR Enforcement Directive*. With its introduction, the European legislator intended to regulate the proceedings for disclosure of information in the sense that information rights are restricted to acts carried out for direct or indirect economic or commercial advantage (Recital 14 of the *IPR Enforcement Directive*). Prior to the decision of the Federal Court of Justice regarding a song by German singer and songwriter Xavier Naidoo in 2012 (BGH, Decision of 19.04.2012 – 1 ZB 80/11, Neue Juristische Wochenschrift 2012, 2958), it has long been assumed that the infringement itself must have been committed on a commercial scale. This condition had been interpreted by German courts very broadly, with the upload of one music album or one film satisfying this condition (Cf. Sandra Schmitz/ Thorsten Ries, *Three songs and you are disconnected from cyberspace? Not in Germany where the industry may "turn piracy into profit"*, European Journal of Law and Technology 2012, Vol. 3 No. 1). However, in the Xavier Naidoo case, the Federal Court of Justice once and for all clarified that not the infringement must have been committed on a commercial scale. Instead the notion of commercial scale refers to the service provided by the third party from whom disclosure is sought.

1614 Cf. Deutscher Bundestag, Bundestagsdrucksache 11/4792, p. 32; Thomas Dreier in: Thomas Dreier/Gernot Schulze, *Urheberrechtsgesetz* (4th ed. 2013), § 101, para. 28 with further references.

infringement suffices to guarantee a fair balance of the fundamental rights involved and to prevent unfounded claims.[1615]

In addition, it is not required that the infringement is proven. Moreover, in proceedings for interim measures, it is only necessary for the applicant to credibly show that an obvious infringement has taken place via a certain IP address.[1616] As regards the reliability of the logging software, it is sufficient that the applicant issues a statutory declaration that the software is reliable.[1617]

Once disclosure is ordered, the Internet access provider will have to match the IP address in question against the subscriber data that he holds and reveal the identity of the subscriber of the IP address in question at the given time. As data in relation to the allocation of IP address to customers is only held for a limited time for billing purposes, the rights-holders will usually inform the provider about their foreseen disclosure request so that the traffic data in question can be frozen.[1618] However, a legal obligation for data preservation in the sense of "expedited preservation of stored data or 'quick freeze'" does not exist in Germany.[1619]

German law provides no legal basis for rights-holders to obligate the preservation of data by access providers.[1620] § 101 II No. 3 and IX only attribute information rights to the rights-holders but do not oblige access providers to preserve data upon receipt of a copyright infringement report

---

1615 BGH, Decision of 19.04.2012 – 1 ZB 80/11, Neue Juristische Wochenschrift 2012, 2958 with annotation by Karl-Heinz Ladeur.

1616 So-called *Glaubhaftmachung*, which suffices in proceedings for interim measures under § 101 VII *UrhG*.

1617 See Thomas Dreier in: Thomas Dreier/Gernot Schulze, *Urheberrechtsgesetz* (4th ed. 2013), § 101 *UrhG*, para. 28.

1618 Access provider usually store IP address data for a short period time based on §§ 96 *TKG* for their own purposes. This period of time in general varies from three to seven days (See Stefan Maaßen, Annotation to OLG Frankfurt/Main, Decision of 12.11.2009 – 11 W 41/09, MultiMedia und Recht 2010, 62, 63.).

1619 OLG Hamm, Decision of 02.11.2010 – 4 W 119/10, Gewerblicher Rechtsschutz und Urheberrecht, Rechtsprechungs-Report 2011, 90; OLG Frankfurt/Main, Decision of 12.11.2009 – 11 W 41/09, MultiMedia und Recht 2010, 62; OLG Düsseldorf, Decision of 15.03.2011 – I-20 U 136/10, MultiMedia und Recht 2011, 546. An expedited preservation of data has been favoured by the German Data Protection Commissioner as an alternative to data retention under the *Data Retention Directive*, but is not enshrined in German law.

1620 *Ibid.*

by a rights-holder.[1621] Only once a court has ordered the disclosure of the requested data, the access provider is obliged to preserve this data.[1622] If he nevertheless deletes the data, the rights-holder will be entitled to damages under §§ 280 I, 281 *BGB* in connection with § 101 II *UrhG*.[1623]

The rights-holders may apply for interim measures which forbid the deletion of the IP address data concerned until a decision is taken in relation to their – usually in parallel – filed request for disclosure of this data pursuant to § 101 IX *UrhG*.[1624] Once the proceedings under § 101 *UrhG* are completed and the court has granted information rights to the rights-holders, the access provider will have to disclose the identity of those subscribers behind the IP addresses concerned.

No disclosure can be ordered with regard to information that is retained by an access provider to comply with his obligations of the national transposition of the *Data Retention Directive*.[1625] Data that has been retained to comply with an obligation stemming from the *Data Retention Directive*, cannot be obtained by private parties.[1626]

cc) Pre-Litigation Correspondence: Request to Cease and Desist and Claim for Damages

Once the rights-holder has obtained information about the identity of the subscriber of an Internet access service from which an infringement has been committed, he will send a cease and desist letter to the subscriber.

1621 See also Bundesrat, Bundesratsdrucksache 798/1/07 and Bundestag, Bundestagsdrucksache 16/5048.

1622 Cf. for example OLG Frankfurt/Main, Decision of 12.11.2009 – 11 W 41/09, MultiMedia und Recht 2010, 62, 63.

1623 Cf. OLG Frankfurt/Main, Decision of 12.05.2009 – 11 W 21/09, MultiMedia und Recht 2009, 542.

1624 *Ibid.*

1625 If an access provider stores IP address data not for his own purposes but to fulfil his obligations under § 113a *TKG* which transposes the storing obligations of the *Data Retention Directive* into national law, the rights-holders' request for disclosure will consequently have no success.

1626 Under these circumstances, rights-holders may only obtain access to the data by pressing criminal charges and then requesting access to the investigation files via their lawyer, see Stefan Maaßen, Annotation to OLG Frankfurt/Main, Decision of 12.11.2009 – 11 W 41/09, MultiMedia und Recht 2010, 62, 63.

The reasons, why it is advisable for the rights-holder to send this letter before claim instead of filing a claim have already been addressed:

First of all the rights-holder shall give the alleged infringer or *Störer* an opportunity to settle the dispute without court action;[1627] secondly, it prevents that the rights-holder has to pay the court fees if the alleged infringer admits the infringement after a claim has been filed.[1628]

It is common practice that *Abmahnungen* are sent by an attorney on behalf of the infringed rights-holder. Similar to companies that have specialised in the detection of online copyright infringements, law firms exist that have specialised in pursuing these claims of copyright infringements. They work closely together with the aforementioned companies. Together, they have optimised the procedures: the companies collect thousands of IP addresses, for which bundled disclosure requests are applied for.

As aforementioned, the cease and desist letter will inform the recipient of the alleged infringement and provide details on the infringement such as date and time, the software client used, the work that has been infringed, and the access provider. The letter will also provide details on how information of identity of the subscriber was obtained by stating the file number and the court that has ordered the disclosure. The lawyer will also detail the position of the rights-holder with regard to the infringement and the assumed legal obligations deriving from this. Accordingly, the letter will ask the recipient to sign a pre-drafted cease and desist declaration, which regularly contains a penalty clause. The cease and desist promise will relate to the work, that has been infringed, but subscribers are advised to check whether the cease and desist promise is not drafted too wide. They will only be obliged to refrain from infringing again the work that he has previously infringed, and not for instance all songs performed by the artist in question.[1629] The penalty clause shall express the seriousness of the declaration. Regularly, the subscriber is addressed as the actual infringer, which means that the rights-holder will also claim damages for the infringement of his exclusive rights.

1627 See § 97 *UrhG*.

1628 According to § 93 *ZPO*, the claimant has to pay the defendant's costs if the defendant acknowledges the claim straight away in litigation and the claimant had not sent a cease and desist letter prior to filing the action.

1629 Markus Bölling, *Unterlassungsantrag und Streitgegenstand im Falle der Störerhaftung*, Gewerblicher Rechtsschutz und Urheberrecht 2013, 1092 et seq.

The rights-holder will also fix a time-limit within which the recipient of the letter will have to comply with the requested acts.

If an *Abmahnung* has been sent via a lawyer, the lawyer's invoice will be attached.

The recipient of an *Abmahnung* has to compensate the rights-holders for the costs involved, if the claim is justified.[1630] Pursuant to § 97a III *UrhG*, the recoverable costs are limited to the necessary expenses.[1631] The necessary expenses regularly include the lawyer's fees and the costs for identifying the infringement and the infringer.[1632] The lawyer's fees depend on the value of the claim.[1633] In cases involving peer-to-peer sharing of music files, the value of the claim was regularly set at EUR 10,000 per file by the rights-holders.[1634] Case law however shows that although courts may confirm this value for a single claim,[1635] in cases where more than one music title is involved, they regularly reduce the total value of the claim. For instance, in a case where several music files had been exchanged without authorisation of the rights-holder, the value for the first title was set at EUR 10,000 and at EUR 5,000 for any subsequent

---

1630 Nikolaus Reber, in: Hartwig Ahlberg/Horst-Peter Götting, *Beck'scher Online-Kommentar* (4th ed. 09.10.2013), § 97a para. 18.

1631 If an *Abmahnung* is justified, it avoids a costly court litigation and thus, it is assumed that it is a necessary means for settlement and in the interest of the infringing party.

1632 The latter may include costs for private investigators, travelling expensis, costs for technical assistance etc. See Nikolaus Reber, in: Hartwig Ahlberg/Horst-Peter Götting, *Beck'scher Online-Kommentar* (4th ed. 09.10.2013), § 97a para. 23.

1633 Lawyers' fees for litigation work in civil law are regulated in the *Attorneys Remuneration Act (Gesetz über die Vergütung von Rechtsanwältinnen und Rechtsanwälten – RVG)* which details schedules of the statutory fees payable on a claim-value basis and payable in stages for the proceedings and court hearings. See § 11 of the Attorneys Remuneration Act and its Appendix. Court costs in civil matters rise on a scale depending on the value of the claim which is not uniformly proportional. They are determined by reference to the statutory scales, primarily the Court Fees Act.

1634 See Frank Tyra, Ausgewählte Probleme aus der Abmahnpraxis bei Privatnutzungen in Musiktauschsystemen, Zeitschrift für Urheber- und Medienrecht 2009, 934, 940; Christian Solmecke, *LG Köln: Erstattung von Anwaltskosten einer (Massen-) Abmahnung wegen P2P-Urheberrechtsverletzung,* MultiMedia und Recht 2008, 129–130.

1635 The courts are free to set a lower value. The OLG Frankfurt tends to set the value at EUR 2,500 see only OLG Frankfurt, decision of 21.12.2010 – 11 O 52/07.

titles.[1636] The Regional Court of Cologne set the claim value for 964 shared music files at EUR 50,000.[1637] Further, courts tend to distinguish whether the actual infringer could be identified or whether the Internet access service subscriber is sued for an infringement that he has not himself committed.[1638]

As regards damages that are claimed by the rights-holder, these damages are usually calculated by way of licence analogy.[1639] Insofar a damages are concernced, it must be recalled that the subscriber will regularly only have to pay the costs of the cease and desist letter if no more than *Störer* liability can be established. Although there is an actual presumption, that when a work has been made publicly available from a certain IP address, the subscriber of that IP address is liable for the infringement,[1640] recent case-law of the Federal Court of Justice has determined conditions under which this presumption can be rebutted. Accordingly, *Störer* liability will no longer easily be established with regard to underaged children, when no monitoring duty exists towards their online behaviour, and the subscriber succeeds in proving that the child has committed the infringe-

---

1636 See LG Hamburg, Decision of 21.04.2006 – 308 O 139/06, published in parts in Zeitschrift für Urheber- und Medienrecht 2006, 661.

1637 OLG Köln, Decision of 23.12. 2009 – 6 U 101/09, MultiMedia und Recht 2010, 281. In this case the four claimants argued that the value of the claim was EUR 400,000 (four claimants, each EUR 100,000) and demanded to be reimbursed for attorney's fees of EUR 5,832.40 altogether. The court however held – inter alia taking into account that the shared music files were not current releases and therefore it was unlikely that they were downloaded by many people – a claim-value of EUR 50,000 each adequate.

1638 Frank Tyra, *Ausgewählte Probleme aus der Abmahnpraxis bei Privatnutzungen in Musiktauschsystemen,* Zeitschrift für Urheber- und Medienrecht 2009, 934, 940 with further references.

1639 To name a few examples: The licence costs for a song were set at EUR 150 (AG Frankfurt/M, Decision of 29.01.2010 – 31 C 1078/09 – 78, MultiMedia und Recht 2010, 262; Decision of 16.04.2010 – 30 C 562/07 – 47; Decision of 04.02.2009 – 29 C 549/08 – 81, MultiMedia und Recht 2009, 724) or EUR 200 (BGH, Decisions of 11.06.2015 – I ZR 75/14; I ZR 7/14 and I ZR 19/14 (*Tauschbörse I – III*); for a porn movie at EUR 100 (plus EUR 75 for investigation, AG Halle, Decision of 14.11.2009 – 95 C 3258/09); for the Brockhaus encyclopedia at EUR 3,000 (AG Magdeburg, Decision of 12.05.2010 – 140 C 2323/09).

1640 BGH, Decision of 12.05.2010 – case.no. I ZR 121/08 *(Sommer unsers Lebens),* Neue Juristische Wochenschrift 2010, 2061.

ment.[1641] Though there still is an alleviation of the burden of proof, the subscriber may succeed in escaping *Störer* liability if he can prove that he has obeyed a required duty of care such as the instruction of minor family members, and the securisation of his Wi-Fi network, and can thus prove that an alternative cause of action is plausible.[1642]

c) The Status Quo: How Abmahungen (almost) Became a Profitable Tool for Rights-holders

No legal instrument in Germany has in the rise of the World Wide Web encountered as many criticisms as the *Abmahnung*. The reasons for this are magnifold, but are primarily based on the fact that some rights-holder "abuse" the system. The public perception of the system is impaired by the volume of cease and desist letters being sent out by only a few lawyers, and the amount of compensation that is claimed. Subscribers often feel intimidated by the language used and faced with a very short time-limit to comply with the cease and desist and compensation demand, they are rather tempted to comply. Considering that they may actually have committed a wrong, this does not explain why the use of *Abmahnungen* is perceived as abusive. Thus, the following paragraphs will examine the deficits of the system that laid the basis for the negative perception of the instrument by the general public.

The *Abmahnung* is nothing new, but a legal instrument that has existed in German law long before. However, only recently has the usage of this instrument increased significantly and while up to the mid-90s such letters were primarily targeted at business entities, it is now the private computer user, or more specifically the subscriber of an Internet access service, who is the focus of cease and desist requests. The reason for this shift of focus is that modern technologies – as has been explained in the first Chapter –

1641 BGH, Decision of 15.11.2012 – I ZR 74/12 *(Morpheus),* Gewerblicher Rechtsschutz und Urheberrecht 2013, 511. See also BGH, Decisions of 11.06.2015 – I ZR 75/14; I ZR 7/14 and I ZR 19/14 (*Tauschbörse I – III*), which confirm the findings in *Morpheus*.

1642 See in that regard also Christian Solmecke, *Darlegungs- und Beweislast in Filesharing-Verfahren – Eine Auswertung der aktuellen Rechtsprechung,* in: Jürgen Taeger (ed.), *Law as a Service (LaaS) – Recht im Internet- und Cloud-Zeitalter* (2013), Band 1, p. 447–459.

allow users to engage in potential illicit behaviour on a scale never encountered before.

aa) Information Requests Are not Thoroughly Assessed

First of all, the key idea of the *Abmahnung* has to be recalled: the sender makes the recipient aware of an illegal behaviour. The aim is to settle a potential lawsuit out of court and not to burden courts with unnecessary work. Likewise, the potential infringer shall be able to avoid the legal costs of court proceedings. The time and effort for the rights-holder to issue a warning letter is minimal. Thus, at a first glance, the system provides advantages for both sides.

However, the more the procedure is optimised and if many warning letters are sent out, they might become a separate profitable business model. Although it was not the intention of the legislator to turn the *Abmahnung* into a source of income, he has cleared the way for it. Each warning letter requires that the infringement and the infringer are identified. With the introduction of information rights in 2008,[1643] the first step was taken to ease proceedings. Prior to the possibility of a disclosure order, rights-holders had to press criminal charges against the unknown subscriber of an IP address. In the course of criminal investigations, the rights-holder could then be granted access to the records and thereby obtain information about the identity of the subscriber of the IP address in question. Obviously, police and public prosecution were not happy with this situation as they would have to spend time on seeking information on the IP address subscriber, but would regularly not pursue the matter any further due to the minor wrong that had been committed and the fact that a subscriber is not necessarily the infringer.

The new civil information right, enshrined in § 101 *UrhG*, requires that an obvious infringement has been committed.

1643 The *Gesetz zur Verbesserung der Durchsetzung von Rechten des geistigen Eigentums* (Act to Improve Enforcement of Intellectual Property Rights) came into force on 1 September 2008 and introduced information rights by which rightholders and their lawyers may now request a judicial order against an access provider to disclose information on communications traffic data to identify the infringer.

Although § 101 IV *UrhG* requires the court to respect the principle of proportionality, in practice, the courts do not thoroughly balance the contravening interests. On the one hand, the Federal Court of Justice held that the establishment of an obvious infringement suffices to guarantee a fair balance of the fundamental rights,[1644] on the other hand, the courts are faced with so many requests that they can hardly examine each case any further. Whether this conclusion satisfies the CJEU's criterion that national legislation must enable "the national court seised of an application for an order for disclosure of personal data, made by a person who is entitled to act, to weigh the conflicting interests involved, on the basis of the facts of each case and taking due account of the requirements of the principle of proportionality", remains to be seen.[1645]

As regards the number of disclosure requests, incidents have been reported where one request relates to up to 3,500 IP addresses.[1646] Within 9 months in 2009, 2824 disclosure orders were sought after in Cologne alone, each relating to several hundreds of IP addresses.[1647] The German access provider Deutsche Telekom reported that it had to disclose the identity of subscribers behind 2.4 million IP addresses in 2010 alone.[1648]

The number of applications for disclosure of information leads to thousands of subscriber identities being disclosed; according to estimates, in

---

1644 BGH, Decision of 19.04.2012 – 1 ZB 80/11, Neue Juristische Wochenschrift 2012, 2958 with annotation by Karl-Heinz Ladeur.

1645 Case C-461/10, *Bonnier Audio AB and Others v Perfect Communication Sweden AB*, ECR 2012 p.000. For comments on the case see inter alia Doris Möller, Urheber-/Datenschutzrecht: *Herausgabe gespeicherter Verkehrsdaten zur zivilrechtlichen Verfolgung von Urheberrechtsverletzungen,* Europäische Zeitschrift für Wirtschaftsrecht 2012, 519-520; Zuzana Hečko, *Data retention by Internet service providers for IP rights protection: Bonnier Audio (C-461/10),* Journal of Intellectual Property Law and Practice 2012, 449–456; Sandra Schmitz, *Die Verfolgung von Urheberrechtsverletzungen im Internet – Neues vom EUGH,* in: Jürgen Taeger (ed.), *IT und Internet – Mit Recht gestalten* (2012), pp. 227–243.

1646 Holger Bleich, *Die Abmahn-Industrie – Wie mit dem Missbrauch des Urheberrechts Kasse gemacht wird,* c't 2010, No. 1, 154, 155. In October 2009, the Regional Court of Cologne ordered the disclosure of the identity behind 11,000 IP-adresses from major provider Telekom. Thus, one single application regarding the sharing of one music title led to potentially 11,000 *Abmahnungen* being sent out.

1647 *Ibid.*

1648 These numbers relate to copyright infringement cases alone. See Thomas Darnstädt, *Urheberrecht: Wem gehören die Gedanken?, 2. Teil: Die Jagd auf IP-Daten Verdächtiger geht weiter,* Der Spiegel online (21.05.2012).

2010 more than half a million *Abmahnungen* had been issued.[1649] Obviously not much time can be spent on examining the facts of these cases.[1650]

This assumption has lately been proven right by the Redtube.com incident.[1651] Redtube.com is a streaming website for pornographic movies and clips. In December 2013, ten-thousands of Redtube users received cease and desist letters in which they were accused of copyright infringements by "using" specified movie streams.[1652] The recipients were asked to sign a cease and desist declaration and pay EUR 250 in compensation.[1653] It is unknown, how the law firm managed to log the IP addresses of the subscribers concerned.[1654] Other than the actual logging of the IP addresses, it is known, where the rights-holders got the subscriber details from: the Landgericht Köln ordered the Internet service provider Deutsche Telekom to disclose the identity of the subscribers of hundreds of logged IP address at a given time.[1655] Considering that each of the 62 successful applications

---

1649 *Ibid.*

1650 Solmecke states in that context, that the courts "wave" the requests "through". See Christian Solmecke, *Wenn sich die Abmahnindustrie verzockt – Rechtsprobleme bei Massenabmahnungen im Internet,* in: Jürgen Taeger (ed.), *Digitale Evolution – Herausforderungen für das Informations- und Medienrecht* (2010), p. 627.

1651 For a detailed outline of the facts of the case and its legal implications, see Sandra Schmitz, *The RedTube copyright infringement affair in Germany: Shame on who?,* International Review of Law, Computers & Technology 2015, Vol. 29 Issue 1, 33 et seq.

1652 The following films are subject to the claims: Miriam's Adventures, Hot Stories, Amanda's Secrets,
Dream Trip and Glamour Show Girls. See Christian Solmecke, *Redtube: Wave of Streaming Letters hits Germany* (12.12.2013).

1653 This amount is comprised of EUR 149.50 lawyers' fees, EUR 20 standard fee for postage and telecommunication, EUR 15.50 damages and EUR 65 expenses for investigating the alleged copyright infringements. The claim value, from which the lawyrs' fees are calculated, is set at EUR 1,000

1654 See Sandra Schmitz, *The RedTube copyright infringement affair in Germany: Shame on who*?, International Review of Law, Computers & Technology 2015, Vol. 29 Issue 1, 33, 38.

1655 The law firm filed 89 applications, of which each contained disclosure requests in relation to 400 to 1,000 IP addresses. Sixteen different chambers of the Landgericht Köln had to deal with the applications. Out of the filed 89 applications, 62 were sucessful. See Carl Christian Müller, *Abmahnwelle gegen Redtube-Nutzer, Vom Leerlaufen des Richtervorbehalts,* Legal Tribune Online (12.12.2013).

referred to up to 1,000 IP addresses, a maximum of 62,000 subscribers could be faced with cease and desist letters; even if one assumes an average of 700 IP addresses, this still leads to a five digit number of potential recipients.[1656] What the court ignored was the fact that already the commitment of an obvious infringement was less than clear. Whether the consumption of a stream constitutes a copyright infringement has not yet been decided by a court. § 53 *UrhG* provides for a right to make private copies of copyright-protected material under the condition that the source has not been disseminated in an evidently illegal manner, meaning that the source is neither an evidently illegal reproduction or has been made available evidently illegally.[1657] In the case of Redtube evident illegality of the source cannot be established, because onstreaming sites for pornography, the rightsholders themselves commonly make available clips or low resolution versions of their repertoire to incite user to buy the full copy or full stream.[1658] This makes it particularly difficult for users to distinguish whether a clip has been uploaded by the rights-holder or with his authorisation, or is infringing copyright. Thus, also an objective bystander may not succeed in establishing that a clip has been disseminated in evidently illegal manner, and therefore the illegality is not obvious. Moreover, even if one assumes that the consumption of a stream constitutes "copying", the consumer would be able to rely on the private copying defence. Further, any copy generated during streaming on the user's hardware is no illegal reproduction. These kind of copies may fall within the permitted temporary acts of reproduction under § 44a *UrhG*.[1659] Against this background,

---

1656 *Ibid.*

1657 The question whether a law which allows copying from illegal sources for private use is compliant with EU copyright law has only recently been decided by the CJEU in Case *ACI Adam v Stichting de Thuiskopie,* Judgment of 10.04.2014. The Advocate General stated in his opinion that the private copying exception only applies to copies from legitimate sources (See Opinion of the Advocate General in Case C-435/12 *ACI Adam v Stichting de Thuiskopie* of 09.01.2014). The CJEU essentially followed the Opinion of the AG.

1658 See Sandra Schmitz, *The RedTube copyright infringement affair in Germany: Shame on who?, International Review of Law, Computers & Technology 2015, Vol. 29 Issue 1, 33.*

1659 Ronny Hauck/Sebastian Heim, *Schwerpunktbereich Urheberrecht: Die rechtliche Bewertung von "Filesharing"- und "Streaming"- Sachverhalten,* JUS 2014, 303, 306.

it becomes evident, that the court did not assess whether there was an obvious infringement and just waved the disclosure requests through.

bb) A Narrow Interpretation of "Non-Complex" Cases

Since 2008, § 97a II *UrhG* foresaw that no more than EUR 100 could be claimed as "necessary expenses" for "non-complex cases with only an immaterial infringement of rights outside of commercial transactions". The impact of this provision has however been limited, an analysis of the case-law so far shows that courts interpret the limitation clause restrictively and consider file-sharing cases as complex cases.[1660] According to the German legislator, the making publicly available of excerpts from a city map on a website, or the making publicy available of a songtext, or the infringing use of an image on an Internet auction platform will constitute non-complex cases.[1661] In recognition of the limited effect of the provision, it has been replaced in October 2013.[1662]

cc) Optimisation of Pre-Litigation Correspondence

With many disclosed identities at hand, pre-litigation correspondence has been optimised by a few law firms that have specialised in *Abmahnungen* in the context of copyright infringements.

Recently, the German Pirate Party leaked a secret agreement between one of the law firms involved in the aforementioned Redtube incident and another rights-holder that suggests that they were operating a business model to turn piracy into profit.[1663] The parties basically agreed on a no

---

1660 See Nikolaus Reber, in: Hartwig Ahlberg/Horst-Peter Götting, *Beck'scher Online-Kommentar* (4th ed. 09.10.2013), § 97a para. 27–28; Sandra Schmitz/ Thorsten Ries, *Three songs and you are disconnected from cyberspace? Not in Germany where the industry may "turn piracy into profit"*, European Journal of Law and Technology 2012, Vol. 3 No. 1.

1661 Deutscher Bundestag, *Bundestag-Drs. 16/5048,* p. 50.

1662 The new wording and scope of § 97a *UrhG* will be discussed at the end of this section.

1663 Legal Tribune online, *Entwicklungen in Sachen Redtube – Gegenwind für Abmahnanwälte, Neues zu IP-Ermittlung* (13.12.2013). The slogan "turn piracy into profit" was formerly used by the company DigiProtect, Gesellschaft zum

win no fee arrangement for pursuing the copyright infringement claims.[1664] Law firms and rights-holders may secretly create "joint ventures" with no risks of costs for the rights-holder.[1665] This however infringes § 49b II *BRAO*[1666]. If in such cases the rights-holder asks for compensation of the costs incurred in issuing the *Abmahnung*, this may even constitute fraud because compensation can only be claimed for costs that have actually occured.[1667]

Irrespective of the existence of such an agreement, it becomes clear, that some rights-holders do not just consider the *Abmahnung* as an instrument to stop copyright infringements and to prevent the continuation of infringements, but primarily as a source of income.[1668]

The following shows an example for recoverable costs of a cease and desist request only: cost of third party investigating the infringement EUR 50 plus costs of Internet service provider EUR 2.33 and if value of claim set at EUR 2,500 and lawyer claims average fees, then these are EUR 232.45 (including EUR 20 communication flat fee and EUR 3.15 costs for disclosure order) – in total EUR 284.78.[1669]

Schutze digitaler Medien mbH. The advertising brochure containing this slogan is not accessible on their website www.digiprotect.org anymore, but is available via the following link: http://pdfcast.org/pdf/digiprotect-turn-piracy-into-profit-praesentation (last accessed 16.06.2011).

1664 Such information had also already been leaked in 2010 in relation to another joint venture, where the law firm kept 37.5 % of the amount paid by the alleged infringers and the remaining 62.5 % went to the rights-holder. See Christian Solmecke, *Wenn sich die Abmahnindustrie verzockt – Rechtsprobleme bei Massenabmahnungen im Internet,* in: Jürgen Taeger (ed.), *Digitale Evolution – Herausforderungen für das Informations- und Medienrecht* (2010), p. 629.

1665 *Ibid.*

1666 *Bundesrechtsanwaltsordnung* (*BRAO* – Federal Regulation of Attorneys).

1667 Legal Tribune online, Entwicklungen in Sachen Redtube – Gegenwind für Abmahnanwälte, Neues zu IP-Ermittlung (13.12.2013).

1668 Cf. Christian Solmecke, *Wenn sich die Abmahnindustrie verzockt – Rechtsprobleme bei Massenabmahnungen im Internet,* in: Jürgen Taeger (ed.), Digitale Evolution – Herausforderungen für das Informations- und Medienrecht (2010), pp. 626 et seq.; Sandra Schmitz/Thorsten Ries, *Three songs and you are disconnected from cyberspace? Not in Germany where the industry may "turn piracy into profit",* European Journal of Law and Technology 2012, Vol. 3 No. 1.

1669 See AG Düsseldorf, Decision of 05.04.2011 – 57 C 15740/09, BeckRS 2011, 14473.

Although in most cases sums between EUR 800 and EUR 2,500 (incl. damages) are claimed,[1670] a rather low sum can turn out more profitable. It may prevent recipients of an *Abmahnung* to consult a lawyer. A consultation of a lawyer to have the claim assessed will usually cost approx. EUR 170.[1671] The difference to the amount claimed is small. Recipients of *Abmahnungen* often pay the costs without consulting a lawyer or negotiate a settlement themselves where they will then pay an agreed amount of money. The incentives for paying even if they claim to be unaware of having committed an infringement are high: the letter usually informs them that in case of non-compliance they will be taken to court and that this will involve further costs. Even if the recipient has not committed the infringement himself, he may be tempted to pay because he fears that he cannot prove his innocence and may have to pay his lawyer's costs in addition.

Hence, even if smaller sums are claimed, the sheer volume of letters being sent out, and the optimisation in handling the cases by specialised law forms, means that *Abmahnungen* provide an income for lawyers and companies that detect infringements, while at the same time compensating the infringed rights-holders.

Activists against the system of *Abmahnungen* claim that a large amount of cease and desist letters is being sent out in relation to copyright infringements of hardcore porn movies.[1672]

The reason for this obvious, the subject of hardcore porn movies may promise a higher "success rate", meaning that many recipients of an *Abmahnung* may rather pay the requested compensation than challenge the claim. The recipients of the cease and desist letter may rather pay to avoid embarrassing discussions with their family members. They may also feel too embarrassed to consult a lawyer.

1670 Alexander Klett/Matthias Sonntag/Stephan Wilske, *Intellectual Property Law in Germany* (2008), pp. 74 et seq.

1671 Based on the value of the claim and a EUR 20 flat fee for postage and communication.

1672 See for instance Verein zur Hilfe und Unterstützung gegen den Abmahnwahn e.V., Die Große Jahresstatistik 2010, available at http://www.verein-gegen-den-abmahnwahn.de/zentrale/download/statistiken/2010/jahresbilanz_2010.html (last accessed 16.06.2011).

dd) False Allegations – The Redtube.com Case

As already outlined above, the Redtube.com case concerned the streaming of porn clips on Redtube. To date, it has not become clear, how the rights-holder, the Swiss company the Archive AG, managed to log the IP addresses of the stream consumer. Redtube itself denies the allegations that it has forwarded any data.[1673]

According to the disclosure orders, the IP addressed had been harvested by a software name GLADII 1.1.3 by the company IPGuards, which claims that it allows the monitoring of download platforms. A technical expert statement as regards the reliability of GLADII 1.1.3 had been leaked but did not provide any details as regards the functioning of the software, in particular references regarding the monitoring of Redtube were omitted.[1674] Redtube's Vice-President considers it unlikely that the monitoring software managed to log IP addresses. This would only be possible in peer-to-peer file-sharing networks and not with streaming sites.[1675] To obtain the information in question, it would thus have been necessary to have monitoring software installed by the streaming provider on its servers or on the computers of its users – something the streaming provider denies.[1676] Research by the online news portal heise.de, which specialises in IT-related news suggests that users were redirected to the copyrighted clips without noticing that they were redirected.[1677] Users reported that prior to accessing Redtube.com, they were connected to trafficholder.com, which redirected them via retdube.net to Redtube.com.[1678] According to heise.de, trafficholder sells redirection of traffic.[1679] Further investigations conducted by heise.de suggests that in fact the rights-hold-

1673 Mathhias Kremp, *Streaming-Portal: Redtube will für Recht auf Porno kämpfen,* Spiegel online (20.12.2013).

1674 The expert statement can be accessed via http://abmahnung-medienrecht.de/wp-content/uploads/2014/01/ Gutachten_ zur_ Software_ GLADII_1_1_3.pdf

1675 Mathhias Kremp, *Streaming-Portal: Redtube will für Recht auf Porno kämpfen,* Spiegel online (20.12.2013).-

1676 *Ibid.*

1677 heise.de, *Porno-Abmahnungen: Indizienkette zur IP-Adressen-Ermittlung verdichtet sich* (13.12.2013).

1678 *Ibid.*

1679 *Ibid.*

ers used fake domains as honeypots, which logged the IP addresses while at the same time presenting the video stream on Redtube to the user.[1680]

If this allegations turn out to be true, then the *Abmahnungen*, that have been sent out will amount to fraud. In January 2014, the prosecutor's office in Cologne initiated criminal investigations.

d) Steps Taken to Prevent that "Piracy Turns into Profit"

In 2012, the German Constitutional Court announced as an obiter dictum, that it is questionable whether an *Abmahnung* constitutes a useful service of a lawyer and should be compensated.[1681] Thereby the Court indirectly expressed criticism on the mass scale sending out of cease and desist letters. Against the deficits described above, the criticism is in many instances justified. Especially since reports had previously emerged that a company that specialised in the detection of copyright infringement in file-sharing networks, advertised its business model as generating more income for rights-holders than online music sales: whereas a legal download generates an income of EUR 0.60, illegal downloads may generate EUR 90.[1682] Accordingly, the enforcement of copyrights via warning letters has a distinctive economic value in itself, which is even higher than the legal download market.

In 2010, approximately half a million *Abmahnungen* have been issued, leading to approximately claims of 400 million Euros in total.[1683]

In particular the Redtube case highlights that the *Abmahnung,* which has been designed as an easy, fast and claimant- and defendant-friendly tool for out-of-court settlement, is prone to misuse. Although theoretically

---

1680 Holger Bleich, *Briefkasten-Ermittlungen,* c't 2014, Issue 5, 28.

1681 The Court questioned whether the Abmahnung constitutes "überhaupt eine grundsätzlich brauchbare anwaltliche Dienstleistung darstellt und insoweit ersatzfähige Rechtsverfolgungskosten auslöst", BVerfG, Order of 21.03.2012 – 1 BvR 2365/11 *(Unerlaubtes Filesharing im Internet),* Zeitschrift für Urheber- und Medienrecht 2012, 471, 474.

1682 Holger Bleich, *Die Abmahn-Industrie – Wie mit dem Missbrauch des Urheberrechts Kasse gemacht wird,* c´t 2010, No. 1, 154, 155; Christian Solmecke, *Wenn sich die Abmahnindustrie verzockt – Rechtsprobleme bei Massenabmahnungen im Internet,* in: Jürgen Taeger (ed.), *Digitale Evolution – Herausforderungen für das Informations- und Medienrecht* (2010), p. 629.

1683 *Ibid.*

the system is fair and just, its application does not fulfil these expectations. The basic idea is to avoid court litigation and settle disputes out of court. This shall not only safe time but also costs. It is the right of the infringed party to inform the infringer of his misconduct and to be compensated for the costs involved for this informing which is also in the interest of the infringed party. The latter may not be aware of his infringing behaviour, and following the *Abmahnung* may be able to cease and desist from the infringing conduct.

However, as long as allegedly infringed parties are successful with dubious claims the public perception of the instrument is negative. But it is not just the wilful abusers of the systems that must to be blamed for this negative perception; it is also the jurisprudence of the courts issuing the disclosure orders. In addition, the restrictive interpretation of § 97a II *UrhG,* which until October 2013 limited the recoverable necessary expenses to EUR 100 for "non-complex cases with only an immaterial infringement of rights outside of commercial transactions" added to the misapprehension regards the *Abmahnung*.

Undeniably, there are (mis-) and (ab-)users of the system that try to turn piracy into profit. Undeniably, there are also rights-holders that need quick, effective and inexpensive instruments to enforce their rights. That is why the legislator and the courts need to close the loopholes that facilitate the abuse of the system. A first step into the right direction has been taken in 2013, when the *Gesetz gegen unseriöse Geschäftspraktiken*[1684] was passed, and subsequently took effect in October 2013. The Law requires transparency, meaning that every *Abmahnung* that is issued in relation to copyright infringements, must be transparent: it must list all costs and damages claimed separately and not as one lump sum.[1685] Further the law sets the value of a claim for a first *Abmahnung* against a consumer at EUR 1,000 maximum, which would limit the lawyer's fees that must be compensated in addition to damages, to EUR 130.[1686] However,

1684 This can be translated as "Law against dubious business practices".

1685 See Article 8 of the *Gesetz gegen unseriöse Geschäftspraktiken,* which inserts § 97a *UrhG* into the German copyright code.

1686 *Ibid.* There is no limitation on damages in the law, so the rights-holders may still claim hypothetic licence costs. Prior to the enactment of the law, it had been assumed that if the bill becomes law, rights-holders would concentrate on damages and their calculation, see Konrad Lischka, *Anti-Abzock-Gesetz: Das Märchen von der Abmahn-Deckelung* (30.01.2013).

this limitation shall not apply when the limitation would be unreasonable in light of the specific circumstances of the case in question. The previous limitation in § 97a *UrhG*, that existed from 2008 to October 2013, did not succeed in curtailing the perceived abuse of the system due to a considerably strict interpretation of "non-complex" cases. No file-sharing case has been reported, where a court held a file-sharing case to be "non-complex". A "non-complex" case is no longer a condidtion for the limitation, and now, a lot depends on the determination of what could be considered unreasonable in light of the specific circumstance of the case. Scholars doubt that the new law will lead to any changes and predict that the notion of "specific circumstances of the individual case" will be read by judges as "do whatever you want".[1687] However, with the first cases emerging recently, it seems that courts are willing to interpret the provision wide, and are likely to accept the limitation in peer-to-peer file-sharing scenarios.

The law also foresees that in case of unfounded claims, the recipient of an *Abmahnung* may claim compensation for his lawyer's costs.[1688] Also, the law introduces a new jurisdiction rule, establishing exclusive competence of the court at the place of residence of the alleged infringer.[1689] As a consequence, all courts will be confronted with claims, which will no longer be concentrated in Munich and Hamburg as it is the case today.[1690] This will probably lead to a less uniform jurisprudence.

Although the law contains some welcomed changes, it still leaves enough room for abuse. Especially, since the courts obviously lack expertise when it comes to Internet disputes. If the Landgericht Köln judges had paid attention to the fact that there are many different ways to download, upload, share or streams protected works on the Internet, they might have questioned the obviousness of infringements in the disclosure requests. Their attitude towards handling the disclosure requests is in clear disrespect of the law, even if they only need to examine the obviousness in summary proceedings. What is needed in that respect are specialised

1687 See *ibid.*

1688 *Ibid.*

1689 See Article 8 of the *Gesetz gegen unseriöse Geschäftspraktiken,* which inserts § 104a *UrhG* into the German copyright code.

1690 The courts in Munich and Hamburg are alleged to be particularly claimant (=rights-holder)-friendly.

"cyber"chambers that deal with nothing else than these requests.[1691] It needs to be guaranteed that the law which foresees a balancing of interests, is also applied in that way, especially since the disclosure of personal data interferes with the privacy and data protection rights of the subscriber.

It may also be helpful for consumer to regulate the content of an *Abmahnung*, for instance making it obligatory to inform the recipient that only the actual infringer is obliged to pay damages. Although many forums and websites discuss the issue of who is obliged to pay damages, the majority of recipients is unaware of this fact.

That the *Gesetz gegen unseriöse Geschäftspraktiken* is no more than a good start for shaping a framework for online infringements of copyright has been proven by the Redtube case: at the time the *Abmahnungen* were sent out, the Law was already in force and could not prevent the shameful consequences. Although the mass-scale sending of cease and desist letters is unlikely to end, the rights-holders and their aides will be required to spend more time on assessing their claim and draft the letters more precisely. At least the time where hundreds of Euros could be claimed just for sending the letter (excluding damages) has reached its end. Recent case-law suggests that courts no longer accept claim values of more than EUR 1,000 in file-sharing cases. As a consequence, it has become more difficult to pursue *Abmahnungen* as a tool that turns piracy into money. A lower claim value, however, also means that the recipient of an *Abmahnung* may be less likely to consult a lawyer, because the costs for consultation, and the compensation that is claimed are almost equal. But then one must ask, whether someone that has not committed a wrongful act is likely to comply with the request or challenge it. If users understood the concept of *Störerhaftung*, this would help to change the public perception of *Abmahnungen* as a money-making instrument. As most of the subscribers that share a connection, will escape liability for damages, what will be left of the *Abmahnung* is a warning and the cease and desist request. For this act, which is in the interest of the subscriber as it will inform him, that either his Internet access is not adequately secured or someone else is

1691 It must be noted that almost all German states have passed regulations (based on § 105 *UrhG*) that grant jurisdiction in copyright infringement cases to specific courts. However this does not mean that the judges at these courts have received specific training with regard to digital evidence or the functioning of the Internet as such.

using his connection to commit infringement, it is reasonable to claim compensation from the subscriber instead of having the taxpayer (French gradutated response), or the rights-holder and access provider (UK graduated response) pay. One may only ask if the EUR 1,000 limitation on the claim value is not still too high.

What remains to be solved, are claims against non-consumers like hotels or pubs that offer free Wi-Fi to their customers. These cases do not fall under the new limitation within § 97a *UrhG.*

2. UK: Out of Court Settlement by Pre-Litigation Letters: A fundamentally Different Approach?

While *Abmahnungen* have been sent out to alleged file-sharers in Germany for several years, reports of such letters being sent to UK customers only evolved after German antipiracy company became active in the UK in 2007.[1692] They tried to import their time-tested businell model to the UK. First cases of cease and desist letters similar to the German *Abmahnung* have been reported as early as 2007, but have in 2012 raised attention when the scheme was subject to a case before the High Court. However, the letters never became such a successful – in terms of generating revenues for the rights-holders – tool as in Germany. The following paragraphs will outline the practice of letters before claim in the UK, analyse their legal basis and look into similarities to the *Abmahnungen* in Germany.

Although jurisprudence recognises the legitimate right of companies to seek redress for copyright infringement, the courts require that the legitimate interests of consumers must be properly safeguarded.

This has been highlighted in the case of *Golden Eye (International) Ltd and others v Telefonica UK Ltd, Consumer Focus intervening,*[1693] where the High Court expressed its concern about a business model that often has been referred to as "speculative invoicing".

Like in Germany, it seems that abuses exceed the schemes' potential as a viable solution to enforcing copyright out of court.

1692 Andrew Murray, *Information Technology Law,* The law and society (2nd ed. 2013), p. 287.

1693 *Golden Eye (International) Ltd and others v Telefonica UK Ltd, Consumer Focus intervening* [2012] EWHC 723 (Ch).

Due to the minor relevance of the pre-litigation letters in the UK, the following paragraphs will not go into depth when it comes to the basic framework for copyright infringements and remedies, and only address these briefly. The focus will be clearly on how the High Court dealt with the deficits of the system that have been outlined in the analysis of the German system of *Abmahnungen.*

a) In Brief: Legal Framework for Private Copyright Enforcement in the UK

Other than in Germany, the UK does not have a statutory information right against third parties in relation to copyright infringements. This does however not mean, that there are no information rights. Rights-holders in the UK will have to apply for a so called Norwich Pharmacal order, that has already been addressed in the context of the *DEA 2010* graduated response scheme and will at this point be outlined in detail.

aa) The Service of Disclosure Orders in the UK – Right to Information and Norwich Pharmacal orders

A copyright owner contemplating legal action against a copyright infringer in the UK also faces the aforementioned hurdles in relation to bringing his claim. In order to be able to call an identifiable party to account, the UK common law system places possessors of information under a duty to assist a wronged party by disclosing the identity of anonymous actors in certain circumstances. Website operators and Internet service providers do not usually voluntarily disclose user details due to contractual confidentiality obligations or due to the fact that such disclosure may be in breach of statutory obligations under UK data protection legislation not to disclose personal data without the consent of the data subject or an order of the court.

While in Germany, the copyright code contains an explicit provision on third party disclosure orders,[1694] the *Copyright, Designs and Patents Act 1988* remains silent as to such a statutory right. When Article 8(1)(c) *IPR*

1694 § 101 II, IX *UrhG.*

Enforcement Directive[1695] however requires Member States to ensure that, in the context of proceedings concerning IPR infringements and in response to a justified and proportionate request of a claimant, judicial authorities may order the disclosure of information leading to the origin of the infringement, this does not mean that the Member State has to introduce a separate provision on third party disclosure in proceedings concerning IPR infringements. The *Enforcement Directive* only requires Member States to "ensure" that the possibility for third party disclosure exists. In the UK such a remedy exists in the form of an application for a Norwich Pharmacal order. In *Norwich Pharmacal v Excise Commissioners*[1696], it had been judicially determined that even where an "involved" third party incurred no personal liability for the tortious acts of others, it nonetheless had a duty to assist a wronged party by disclosing information that it possesses enabling the claimant to identify a wrongdoer where otherwise he would not be able to do so.[1697] Jurisdiction of a court to order disclosure under the Norwich Pharmacal principles against third parties is only to be exercised if the third party is the only practicable source of the information sought and thus is a remedy of last resort.[1698] In subsequent

---

1695 Article 8 of the *IPR Enforcement Directive* reads as follows: "1. Member States shall ensure that, in the context of proceedings concerning an infringement of an intellectual property right and in response to a justified and proportionate request of the claimant, the competent judicial authorities may order that information on the origin and distribution networks of the goods or services which infringe an intellectual property right be provided by the infringer and/or any other person who: [...] (c) was found to be providing on a commercial scale services used in infringing activities".

1696 Norwich Pharmacal Co. and others v Customs and Excise Commissioners [1974] AC 133.

1697 *Norwich Pharmacal Co. and others v Customs and Excise Commissioners* [1974] AC 133, at 175. Lord Reid described the principle as follows: "...if through no fault of his own a person gets mixed up in the tortious acts of others so as to facilitate their wrong-doing he may incur no personal liability but he comes under a duty to assist the person who has been wronged by giving him full information and disclosing the identity of the wrongdoers. I do not think that it matters whether he became so mixed up by voluntary action on his part or because it was his duty to do what he did. It may be that if this causes him expense the person seeking the information ought to reimburse him. But justice requires that he should co-operate in righting the wrong if he unwittingly facilitated its perpetration."

1698 *Mitsui & Co Ltd v Nexen Petroleum UK Ltd* [2005] EWHC 625 (Ch), [2005] 3 All E.R. 511, at 24.

cases, the courts have extended the application of the principle,[1699] which as a common law instrument is a flexible remedy, capable of adaption to new circumstances.[1700] In *Mitsui & Co Ltd v Nexen Petroleum UK Ltd* the High Court summarised the conditions that have to be satisfied for the court to exercise the power to order Norwich Pharmacal Relief:

> "i) a wrong must have been carried out, or arguably carried out, by an ultimate wrongdoer;
> ii) there must be the need for an order to enable action to be brought against the ultimate wrongdoer; and
> iii) the person against whom the order is sought must: (a) be mixed up in so as to have facilitated the wrongdoing; and (b) be able or likely to be able to provide the information necessary to enable the ultimate wrongdoer to be sued."[1701]

As regards the first requirement, a Norwich Pharmacal applicant will have to provide evidence that an infringement has taken place. In peer-to-peer file-sharing cases, applicants may submit statements by IT scientist outlining the operation of software used to monitor peer-to-peer file-sharing[1702]

1699 E.g. the jurisdiction is not confined anymore to circumstances where there has been tortious wrongdoing and is now also available where there has been contractual wrongdoing, see *P v T Limited* [1997] 1 WLR 1309; *Carlton Film Distributors Ltd v VCI Plc* [2003] FSR 47. In addition, jurisdiction is no more limited to cases where the identity of the wrongdoer is unknown but extends to cases where the identity of the wrongdoer is known, but where the claimant requires disclosure of crucial information in order to able to bring his claim, see *Axa Equity & Law Life Assurance Society Plc v National Westminster Bank (CA)* [1998] CLC, 1177, *Aoot Kalmneft v Denton Wilde Sapte* [2002] 1 *Lloyds Rep 417, Carlton Film Distributors Ltd v VCI Plc* [2003] FSR 47. Also, the third party from whom information is sought does not need to be an innocent party anymore, he may as well be a wrongdoer himself, see *CHC Software Care v Hopkins and Wood* [1993] FSR 241.

1700 *Ashworth Hospital Authority v MGN Ltd* [2002] 1 WLR 2033, per Lord Woolf CJ at 2049F.

1701 *Mitsui & Co Ltd v Nexen Petroleum UK Ltd* [2005] EWHC 625 (Ch), [2005] 3 All E.R. 511, at 21.

1702 They described the test carried out to verify that the computer application that had been in use, was "able to identify the source of a file transmitted over the Internet through certain P2P networks, namely transmissions involving the eDonkey network and the BitTorrent protocol, correctly identified the IP addresses and dates and times of uploading of a number of test files which he had uploaded. Mr Vogler [the expert] explains he did not have Xtrack installed on his computer, and did not concern himself with how it worked, but treated it as a "black box". He simply presented it with inputs, namely his test files, and

as evidence provided by experts in the sense of *CPR* r.35.2(1)[1703], which is admissible under section 3 of the *Civil Evidence Act 1972*.

The necessity of a disclosure order is often immanent in the medium Internet where anonymous or pseudonymous communication is usually the case.

Thus Norwich Pharmacal orders were granted in cases of anonymous online communication in relation to defamation cases[1704] and online privacy violations[1705]. Accordingly, host providers were ordered to disclose information leading to the identification of their users to enable the applicants to sue them.

---

examined the outputs to see if they corresponded to his inputs. He was satisfied that they did correspond… In section 6 of his report, Mr Vogler explains that an IP address identifies a device, which may be a computer or a router. Although Internet service providers often assign IP addresses dynamically, they retain records which enable the customer to whom the IP address had been assigned to be identified. He goes on to say that the actual user of the computer at the relevant time may or may not be the customer registered with the Internet service provider. He also acknowledges two possible circumstances in which Xtrack might wrongly identify someone as the source of an upload, the more straightforward of which is where the victim's computer has been taken over by a trojan which enables a third party to control the computer." (*Golden Eye (International) Ltd and others v Telefonica UK Ltd, Consumer Focus intervening* [2012] EWHC 723 (Ch), para. 26–27).

1703 CPR r. 35.2(1), that is to say, "a person who has been instructed to give or prepare expert evidence for the purpose of proceedings". Although CPR Part 35 does not define "expert evidence" as such. it is generally accepted that expert evidence is evidence the giving of which requires particular expertise in the field in question by virtue of study and/or experience (see Evans-Lombe J held in *Barings plc v Coopers & Lybrand* [2001] PNLR 22 at [45]).

1704 See e.g. Court of Appeal, *Totalise plc v Motley Fool Ltd* [2001] EWCA Civ 1897, [2002] 1 WLR 1233; High Court, *Sheffield Wednesday Football Club Ltd v Hargreaves* [2007] EWHC 2375 (QB); *Jane Clift v Martin Clark* [2011] EWHC 1164 (QB).

1705 High Court, *G and G v Wikimedia Foundation Inc* [2009] EWHC 3148 (QB). In this case the applicants, a mother and her child, sought an anonymous user's details from the Wikimedia Foundation so as to identify an individual who had anonymously posted private and confidential information about them on the Wikipedia website. See also High Court, *Applause Store Productions Ltd v Grant Raphael* [2008] EWHC 1781, which concerned a fake profile on Facebook and an order seeking to have the identity of the person who set up the profile revealed.

From a data protection point of view, the court will have to consider whether the disclosure is warranted having regard to the rights and freedoms or the legitimate interests of the data subject.[1706] Thus, in addition to being necessary, the order must be proportionate.[1707]

A disclosure order regularly invades the right to privacy of an individual (as enshrined in section 6 of the *Human Rights Act 1998*, Article 8(1) of the *ECHR* and Arts. 7 of the *CFR*) as well as the right to the protection of personal data under Article 8 of the *CFR* and in the light of those provisions, the *Data Protection Directive* and section 35 of the *Data Protection Act 1998* – especially when that individual is in the nature of things not before the court.[1708] Therefore, the court must ensure that the invasion is justified.[1709] Anonymity is not merely a mask for wrongdoers but has social values in its own right. In this regard, Article 10 *ECHR* and the Charter also protect the anonymous individual.[1710]

Thus, there must be an infringement of some severity so that a disclosure would not disproportionate. In copyright law, section 16(3)(a) of the *CDPA 1988* requires that the sharing related to the work as a whole or any substantial part of it. The rights-holder will have to demonstrate that if a work had been shared, a substantial part of it was been made available.[1711] It remains to be seen whether the sharing of only parts of a work as it is common in bittorrent networks will qualify as substantial parts of a work, and subsequently be able to outweigh the rights of the not-yet identified defendant. Defamation case law suggests that minor infringements are not capable of outweighing the interests of the anonymous defendant.

In a defamation case, a judge concluded that it would be "disproportionate and unjustifiable intrusive" to make an order for the disclosure of the identities of users who had posted messages which were barely defam-

---

1706 Court of Appeal, *Totalise plc v Motley Fool Ltd* [2001] EWCA Civ 1897, [2002] 1 WLR 1233, para. 24.

1707 Court of Appeal, *Rugby Union v Viagogo Ltd* [2011] EWCA Civ 1585, para. 27 et seq.

1708 See Court of Appeal, *Totalise plc v Motley Fool Ltd* [2001] EWCA Civ 1897, [2002] 1 WLR 1233, para. 24 and *Rugby Union v Viagogo Ltd* [2011] EWCA Civ 1585, para. 27.

1709 Court of Appeal, *Totalise plc v Motley Fool Ltd* [2001] EWCA Civ 1897, [2002] 1 WLR 1233, para. 25.

1710 Cf. *ibid.*

1711 This will be difficult to prove if a bittorrent file-sharing programme was used, where usually a number of peers will each share a small portion of the file.

atory or little more than abusive or likely to be understood as jokes.[1712] Only in the case of those comments that could reasonably be understood "to allege greed, selfishness, untrustworthiness and dishonest behaviour on the part of the claimants"[1713], the rights of the defamed could outweigh the right of the authors to protect their anonymity.

However, in some cases, necessity and proportionality may go hand in hand, meaning that once an arguable wrongdoing by an unidentified individual is established and there is no realistic way of discovering the identity of the individual other than a Norwich Pharmacal order, it will usually be proportionate to make such an order.[1714] Hence, where a whole work has been made available to the public, it is unlikely that the rights of the not yet identified defendant will outweigh the interests of the rightholders.

As outlined above in the section on Germany, it is evident that disclosure orders may not be as effective in revealing usable information as they initially appear, for example when they lead to an Internet café or unsecured Wi-Fi networks. Also, any application for a Norwich Pharmacal order has to be made swiftly because access providers do not preserve relevant data for a long period.

The claimant will have to argue that the subscriber of an Internet connection identified was making a copyright protected work available contrary to section 20 *CDPA 1988* and authorising within the meaning of section 16 *CDPA 1988* the downloading of films which involved the making of infringing copies or substantial parts thereof, and/or acting as joint tortfeasor with the downloaders.

bb) Remedies for Copyright Infringement in the UK

Similar to the remedies available in Germany, the remedies available to a successful claimant in a private civil infringement action include inter alia relief by way of damages, injunctions, or accounts.[1715]

1712 High Court, *Sheffield Wednesday Football Club Ltd v Hargreaves* [2007] EWHC 2375 (QB), para. 17.

1713 *Ibid,* para. 18.

1714 Court of Appeal, *Rugby Union v Viagogo Ltd* [2011] EWCA Civ 1585, para. 28 et seq.

1715 See Section 96(2) *CDPA 1988.*

The rights-owner is entitled to deprive the infringer of the unjust enrichment that has accrued to him as a result of his unlawful activites. In the context of intellectual property rights infringements, the claimant may claim damages, or alternatively an account of profits. As regards the account of profits, the claimant will be entitled to the profits made by the defendant as a result of his infringement.[1716]

As regards a claim for damages, the claimant will be entitled to be compensated for the invasion of his rights. This compensatory remedy will put the claimant in the position he would have been in if there had been no infringement.

Additional statutory damagaes can be awarded under section 97(2) *CDPA 1988*, where ordinary damages would not be sufficient to compensate.[1717]

In file-sharing case, the rights-holder will usually claim damages because the infringer commonly does not make any profits from infringing copyright.

In relation to the calculation of damages a distinction is made between a rights-holder who himself exploits the intellectual property rights and a rights-holder who does not. The latter will only be able to claim a licence fee as damages. The licence fee is the fee that would have been paid by the infringer if he had acquired a licence from the rights-holder for the act that gave rise to the claim.

An interesting case in relation to damages for online copyright infringements has been rendered by the Court of Appeal in 2012.[1718] In *Sullivan v Bristol Studios*, the claimant, a hiphop artist, demanded damages from the defendant for uploading a music video of him without his consent on YouTube. Precisely, the claimant sought damages of GBP 800,000 for "breach of statutory duty, infringement of copyright and...loss of a chance". It was calculated that the video would have been seen by the defendant film company's staff plus a maximum of 50 people. The claim was transferred to the Chancery Division, where its value was assessed at just GBP 50. The defendant applied successfully to have the claim struck

---

1716 As regards the account of profits see Hector MacQueen/Charlotte Waelde/ Graeme Laurie/Abbe Brown, *Contemporary intellectual property*, Law and policy (2nd ed. 2011), p. 972.

1717 As regards the award of additional damages see *ibid,* p. 970.

1718 Court of Appeal, *Tony D Sullivan (aka Rudey Soloman) v Bristol Film Studios Ltd,* [2012] EWCA civ 570.

out on the basis that a claim for such a small sum was a disproportionate use of the court's time and resources.

In addition to damages, the rights-holder is also entitled to obtain an injunction to stop any further infringement. In this context the distinction between the different types of actors is not as relevant as in Germany.

b) Lessons Learned from Germany: The Phenomenon of Cease and Desist Letters in the UK and Speculative Invoicing

It did not take long after the first letters before claim asking for damages had been sent out in the UK that they were deemed as "speculative invoicing". Soon they attracted considerable media attention as they usually request the Internet subscriber to pay a specified sum of several hundred pounds[1719] to compensate the copyright holder for any damage caused by the alleged copyright infringement and the costs incurred in enforcing the claim outside of court.

The attention, this practice gained, was not in regard to the practice as such, but to the fact that the sums demanded were out of proportion and that the rights-holders or those acting on their behalf did not seek to confirm whether the Internet subscriber was actually responsible for the copyright infringement that had been detected.[1720]

Soon it emerged that antipiracy companies are running a quite profitable business model. In the following this business model and its public perception will be outlined before it will be analysed how the High Court tries to set boundaries on a scheme that turns piracy into profit.

aa) Introducing the Antipiracy Industry in the UK

Copyright infringements in peer-to-peer networks are usually detected by "antipiracy" companies that are specialised in searching the networks for infringements. After their business model has proven successful in Ger-

---

1719 According to Consumer Focus typical sums demanded are in the range of GBP 500 to GBP 1,000, see High Court, *Golden Eye (International) Ltd and others v Telefonica UK Ltd, Consumer Focus intervening* [2012] EWHC 723 (Ch), para. 36.

1720 *Ibid.*

many with a number of court cases won in German courts, the companies were confident that they can do the same in the UK and started entering the UK market from 2008 onwards.[1721]

Their business model is the same as in Germany:

The antipiracy company acquires the right to distribute movies, music or computer games from the rights-holders or as stated by HHJ Birss QC in Media CAT v Adams citing an agreement between an antipiracy company and a rights-holder: "At best it is a company with a contract which gives it 'all rights necessary to allow [*Med T*] to inquire claim demand and prosecute through the civil courts where necessary any person or persons identified as having made available for download a film for which [*an agreement*] has expressly licensed'".[1722]

The antipiracy companies then access peer-to-peer networks and, acting as fictitious users (or peers), pretend, that they wish to access copyrighted material. The companies use their software to make connections with individuals who indicate that they had works of the rights-holders they represent or works for which they have acquired the distribution rights. They then download the work or parts of it onto the companies' computers and compare the download with the original material in order to see whether it corresponds. Besides searching peer-to-peer networks for copyright infringements, critics accuse the companies to also set up "honey traps" for file-sharers by themselves making copyrighted material available for download in peer-to-peer networks.[1723] This practice allows them to easily record the IP address of incoming connections that download and at the same time upload the file. While this is only an allegation, these allegations have in particular been raised in relation to hardcore pornography. When sending out the letter before claim informing the identified subscriber about the alleged infringement, they obviously expect that a sub-

1721 Miles Brignall, *File sharers targeted with legal action over music downloads*, The Guardian (17.07.2010), see also Tony Levene, *Porn bill for couple who can't download*, The Guardian (29.11.2008). The most famous German companies specifically active in the field of copyright enforcement in peer-to-peer networks are DigiProtect, DigiRights Solutions or Logistep.

1722 *Media C.A.T. Ltd v Adams and others* [2011] EWPCC 6, para. 5. HHJ Bliss QC refers to an agreement between Media CAT and Sheptonhurst Ltd, which are the owners of copyright in pornographic films. The agreement purport to give Media CAT the right described as well as the sole and exclusive right to demand, collect and receive all revenues in respect of illegal file-sharing.

1723 Ernesto, *When pirates become copyright cash cows*, TorrentFreak (30.08.2009).

stantive number of recipients will rather pay the requested fee than start negotiating or denying the claim – especially when pornography is concerned.[1724] Letters before claim are not required by law in the UK. There is no formal pre-action conduct, which applies to intellectual property disputes.

The antipiracy companies have optimised the detection of copyright infringements by acting and enforcing the rights of numerous artists. Like in Germany, they would cooperate with law firms that are themselves specialised in assisting intellectual property rights-holders exploiting and enforcing their rights globally.

With these law firms, the companies would have "revenue sharing agreements" whereby they would share the sums recovered by sending the letters before claim to alleged infringers. The rights-holders would be invoiced for the law firm's professional fees.

It is recognised that copyright owners have a legitimate interest in obtaining legal remedies against copyright infringements. But it is not clear whether this legitimate interest can be satisfied by sending out speculative invoices. Given the profit-sharing agreements and the fact that the party conducting the litigation gets a higher share than the author of the copyright protected work, antipiracy companies are considered as acting with the sole intention of soliciting money rather than enforcing copyright.

bb) The History of Speculative Invoicing in the UK

The practice of speculative invoicing emerged in March 2007, when 500 individuals were accused of having shared a computer game.[1725] The National Association of Citizens Advice Bureaux reported in 2010 about several incidents where individuals seeked for advice after receiving let-

1724 Miles Brignall, *File sharers targeted with legal action over music downloads*, The Guardian (17.07.2010). In Germany, it has been reported that the exploitation rights of cheap-produced amateur pornography have been sold by the copyright holder to third parties way above its original value so that the monetary compensation the third party could claim and which depends in Germany on the market value of the movie increases. Considering that Internet subscriber that receive a letter accusing them of sharing porn movies might be too embarrassed to risk being sued, this can became a quite lucrative business scheme.

1725 Andrew Murray, *Information Technology Law, The law and society* (2nd ed. 2013), p.287.

ters asking for damages.[1726] These individuals seeked advice because they believed they were innocent of the alleged infringement and had been wrongly identified or because someone else might have used their Internet connection and downloaded the work in question. Many of the recipients of letters claim that they have been shocked and worried at having received a demand for payment and want to know how to refute the claim. Typical examples for those seeking advice would be the following:

> "A Derbyshire CAB client was one of many reported by this bureau who thought a demand received for GBP 295 for a claimed music download was a scam. The client explained that he never downloaded music and did not even listen to the type of music detailed in the letter. He was the only person able to access his computer. He was worried about the threat of court action and the stress this was causing his partner who had recently suffered a stroke."[1727]
> "A CAB client in Buckinghamshire received a letter claiming GBP 495 for downloading material protected by copyright. He was certain this had not happened in his home. At the time the download had allegedly occurred, he was getting married."[1728]
> "A CAB client in Buckinghamshire was worried about the consequences of not paying a GBP 295 demand for copyright breach despite being certain that no breach had occurred in her household. At the time of the claimed download the client was at work, her eldest child was away at university and the two younger children were at school. She checked the download history of all the computers and found no evidence to substantiate the claim."[1729]

Interestingly, only a few actors could be identified in the UK since 2007 that have been involved in speculative invoicing.[1730] The most prominent law firms involved were Davenport Lyons and ACS:Law, with the latter taking over Davenport Lyons' work from April 2009 onwards. It was Devenport Lyons that had originally developed and pursued a scheme for recovering compensation for copyright owners whose copyright had been infringed. In April 2009, ACS:Law took over this scheme from Davenport

1726 National Association of Citizens Advice Bureaux, *Online infringement of copyright and the Digital Economy Act 2010 – Draft Initial Obligations Code, Response from Citizens Advice to Ofcom* (July 2010), p.4 et seq.

1727 *Ibid*, p.4.

1728 *Ibid.*

1729 *Ibid*, p.5.

1730 Max Rowlands, *UK: "Speculative invoicing" schemes target internet file-sharers and individuals accused of minor retail crime* (2011), p. 4; Andrew Murray, Information Technology Law, The law and society (2nd ed. 2013), p.287.

Lyons, including the client list and staff involved being transferred from one law firm to another.[1731]

ACS:Law had obtained the right to identify, pursue and prosecute instances of copyright infringement from some copyright owners. Several antipiracy companies were instructed to conduct monitoring of IP addresses in peer-to-peer networks for infringements of its clients' copyrights. Once an antipiracy company detected an IP addresses involved in file-sharing, ACS:Law would apply for a Norwich Pharmacal order on behalf of its clients against the Internet service provider. Once ACS:Law had obtained the names and contact details, it sent letters of claim demanding payment of a specified sum as compensation to the Internet subscribers.[1732] The compensation was said to include damages, Internet service provider administration costs (and its legal costs where applicable), as well as a contribution to the rights-holders' legal costs incurred to date and "additional costs".[1733] No breakdown is made of the figure given, so it was not possible to identify what exactly was claimed.

In the case of *Media CAT v Adams*,[1734] the owner of copyright in relation to a number of pornographic films, the sum demanded was initially GBP 540 and later GBP 495.[1735] According to Mr Crossley's own evidence was that the reason for the reduction that "the client wants to bring the figure below GBP 500 because he believes there is a psychological barrier at GBP 500 that prevents people from paying so he is trying to optimise revenue on settlement".[1736]

The letter also informs the subscriber that if the sum is agreed no further payment will be sought in relation to the infringements referred to.

1731 Max Rowlands, *UK: "Speculative invoicing" schemes target internet file-sharers and individuals accused of minor retail crime* (2011), pp. 4 et seq.

1732 For a description of the procedure see High Court, *Golden Eye (International) Ltd and others v Telefonica UK Ltd, Consumer Focus intervening* [2012] EWHC 723 (Ch), para. 41 et seq.

1733 Cf. e.g. Patents County Court, *Media C.A.T. Ltd v Adams and others* [2011] EWPCC 6, para. 19.

1734 *Ibid.* For a comment on the case see Gary Moss, *Media CAT v Adams: the CAT that did not get the cream,* Journal of Intellectual Property Law & Practice 2011, Vol. 6 No. 11, 813 – 820.

1735 For a description of the procedure see High Court, *Golden Eye (International) Ltd and others v Telefonica UK Ltd, Consumer Focus intervening* [2012] EWHC 723 (Ch), para. 42.

1736 *Ibid.*

Leaked documents of correspondence between Davenport Lyons and DigiProtect suggested that the antipiracy companies also carefully selected against whom they will pursue their claim, leading to the conclusion that they do not necessarily have the intention to sue alleged infringers.[1737] The recipients of the letters were ranked out of ten on the basis of how likely they were to comply and then targeted accordingly.[1738] In ranking the recipients, they carefully considered the recipient's financial means, legal knowledge, and the potential for negative publicity. Whether a claim was pursued was made dependent on the ranking.

It has also been reported that ACS:Law sent questionnaires to those who refuted the allegations.[1739] The questionnaire had the potential to be used against the recipient in further proceedings by asking inter alia whether the recipient used file-sharing software and why, whether some-one else had access to the Internet connection and whether they would be willing to submit their computer(s) for forensic analysis.[1740] They usually do not have sufficient evidence to enforce their claim unless a user con-fesses to illegally downloading/uploading a file. The Internet is awash with complaints from users who insist that they have not downloaded the files of which they have been accused of infringing copyright.[1741] At this point, it needs to be clarified that the letters – in – in a strict sense – do not accuse the recipients of illegal downloading but inform them that the antipiracy company has evidence that one of their clients'copyrighted works was made available through a file-sharing network to others from the recipient's Internet connection. They thus, allege the unauthorised making available of a copyrighted work from a specific Internet connec-tion and not a download by the recipient.

The scheme needed to be profitable for the actors involved otherwise the engagement of antipiracy firms would be obsolete. It is known that ACS:Law entered into retainers for "non-contentious" work with its

1737 The documents can be accessed at http://www.wikileaks.com/wiki/Davenport_Lyons_and_DigiProtect_Actionpoints_for_filesharers%2C_14_Jan_2009 (last accessed on 17.03.2013).

1738 *Ibid.*

1739 Max Rowlands, *UK: "Speculative invoicing" schemes target internet file-shar-ers and individuals accused of minor retail crime* (2011), p. 5.

1740 *Ibid.*

1741 Miles Brignall, *File sharers targeted with legal action over music downloads,* The Guardian (17.07.2010), see also Tony Levene, *Porn bill for couple who can't download,* The Guardian (29.11.2008).

clients which provided for the damages and costs paid by the alleged infringers (minus applicable disbursements and the Internet service providers' costs) to be split between ACS:Law, the antipiracy company and the rights-holder. An agreement referred to in the disciplinary proceedings against the head of ACS:Law, Anthony Crossley, set out the share of the net recoveries between each of the parties involved: in relation to the works of one specific copyright owner copyright owner was to receive 25% of the net recoveries, the law firm was to receive 42% and the antipiracy company was to receive 33%, in another case, the rights-holder was to receive 35% of the net recoveries, the law firm was to receive 52.5% and the monitoring firm was to receive 12.5%.[1742] DigiRights Solutions, which is one of the antipiracy companies, that had an agreement with ACS:Law, claims that in Germany roughly 25% of people to whom they send a letter pay an average fee of around EUR 450, making the letters before claim a lucrative revenue stream considering that DigiRights Solution receives 80% of the money and forward 20% to the copyright holder.[1743] As of 30 June 2010, ACS:Law had sent 20,323 letters of claim and thereby recovered the total sum of GBP 936,570.92, of which ACS:Law received GBP 341,078.92.[1744] In September 2010, ACS:Law accidentally published its email archive online, so that it could be revealed that the company had even made over GBP 636,000 from alleged file-sharers in less than two years activity.[1745]

But it is not just the generated revenues as such that are not well perceived, it is the individual fee that is claimed.[1746] The antipiracy companies would often ask for the same amount of money from every alleged infringer without distinguishing between the work that has been shared or the number of files shared, which indicates that the actual damages incurred by the rights-holder seem not to be taken into consideration. Like

1742 *Solicitors Regulation Authority v Andrew Jonathan Crossley,* Case no. 10726 (06.02.2012), paras. 33 and 45.

1743 See Max Rowlands, *UK: "Speculative invoicing" schemes target internet file-sharers and individuals accused of minor retail crime* (2011), p. 4.

1744 High Court, *Golden Eye (International) Ltd and others v Telefonica UK Ltd, Consumer Focus intervening* [2012] EWHC 723 (Ch), para. 44.

1745 Ernesto, *Leaked emails reveal profits of anti-piracy cash scheme,* TorrentFreak (26.09.2010).

1746 For early cases see Tony Levene, *Porn bill for couple who can't download,* The Guardian (29.11.2008).

in Germany, the sum demanded would not be broken down into costs and damages.

Finally, until November 2010, ACS:Law commenced only 27 cases on behalf of the rights-holder Media CAT, for which it had previously sent out tens of thousands of letters threatening legal action.[1747] Considering that it is very unlikely that out of 10,000 letters only 27 recipients refused to pay, one may ask where all the announced legal actions are. When HHJ Birss QC convened a hearing for directions in all 27 Media CAT cases commenced before the Patents County Court in January 2011[1748], ACS:Law attended the court office with 27 notices of discontinuance. The notices of discontinuance were however set aside by HHJ Birss QC as an abuse of process for two reasons: "First, they would give the copyright owners, who had not been joined to the proceedings, an unwarranted collateral advantage stemming from a breach of section 102 of the *CDPA 1988* and the avoidance of CPR r. 19.3, namely that the copyright owners would avoid being subject to CPR r. 38.7. Secondly, they would give Media CAT, ACS:Law and the copyright owners an unwarranted collateral advantage of avoiding judicial scrutiny of the underlying claims on which the *Norwich Pharmacal* orders were based".[1749] He found that "a wholesale letter writing campaign" was being conducted to generate revenues based on the threat of legal proceedings.[1750] In this regard, the court assumed that simple arithmetic shows that the actors involved would make more than one million pounds even if 80% of the recipients refused to pay. Taking a very pragmatic view, the court concluded that it is unlikely that cases are being taken to court if one could make such an amount of many just with the threat of legal proceedings.[1751] To date there is no known case of proceedings being issued by ACS:Law.

Overall, HHJ Birss QC had been very critical about the letters before claim scheme. He concluded that ordinary members of the public could have a wrong understanding of the content of such a letter, in particular do

1747 Patents County Court, *Media C.A.T. v Adams* [2011] EWPCC 6, [2011] FSR 8, para. 22 et seq.

1748 See Patents County Court, *Media C.A.T. v Billington* [2010] EWPCC 18.

1749 HHJ Birss QC in *Golden Eye (International) Ltd and others v Telefonica UK Ltd, Consumer Focus intervening* [2012] EWHC 723 (Ch), para. 52, referring to *Media C.A.T. v Adams* [2011] EWPCC 6, [2011] FSR 8, para. 98 et seq.

1750 Patents County Court, *Media C.A.T. v Adams* [2011] EWPCC 6, [2011] FSR 8, para. 98.

1751 *Ibid*, para. 100.

lay members if the public do not know that a Norwich Pharmacal order is not based on a finding of infringement by the court.[1752]

Considering the above described activities of ACS:Law, it is not surprising that the Solicitors' Regulation authority received more than 500 complaints about ACS:Law within less than one and a half year of their activities in this regard.[1753]

These concerns also attracted the attention of politicians. During a debate on the Digital Economy Bill in the House of Lords, the issue of letters before claim and the way they are used in other jurisdictions, has been raised in the context of the notification procedure foreseen in the Digital Economy Act. Several members of the House of Lords referred to the way letters before claims are used as "bullying tactics…to get people to pay up".[1754] Lord Clement-Jones recognised that the letter before claim tactic is becoming a "big business" and does not protect the proper and legitimate rights of copyright owners while causing distress to the recipients of the letters.[1755] Already in 2010, voices have been raised in the House of Lords to put an end to the scheme.[1756]

The concerns of the House of Lords have been shared by the Ministry of Justice in a letter sent by the Parliamentary Under Secretary of State, Bridget Prentice, to Lord Young of Norwood Green.[1757]

On a wide basis, the scheme is rather seen as an economic model than a model of copyright enforcement.

Even BPI, the body that represents the UK recorded music industry, does not condone the mass-mailing of alleged infringers but stresses that it

---

1752 *Ibid*, para. 21.

1753 High Court, *Golden Eye (International) Ltd and others v Telefonica UK Ltd, Consumer Focus intervening* [2012] EWHC 723 (Ch), para. 45.

1754 House of Lords, *Hansard*, Debate 18 January 2010, Columns 792 et seq., 4.15 pm, http://www.publications.parliament.uk/pa/ ld200910/ldhansrd/text/100118-0004.htm#1001185000078.

1755 House of Lords debate (18.01.2010), http://www.youtube.com/watch?v=ORBfs 3QCvTY.

1756 Lord Lucas in House of Lords debate, (01.03.2010), http://www.youtube.com/w atch?v=dwKbQVzRHEg.

1757 Letter dated 08 February 2010 from Bridget Prentice, Ministry of Justice, to Lord Young of Norwood Green, Minister for Postal Affairs and Employment Relations, http://webarchive.nationalarchives.gov.uk/+/interactive.bis.gov.uk/di gitalbritain/ wp-content/uploads/ 2010/02/Bridget%20Prentice%20MP%20letter -%208%20Feb%202010.pdf.

considers that legal action is best reserved for the most persistent or serious offenders, rather than being widely used as a first response.[1758]

Thus, it came to no surprise when the British national consumer association, Consumer Focus[1759], concluded that the letter before claim scheme as it is operated to date is indiscriminate and potentially causes distress on part of consumers.[1760]

Notably, the owner of law firm ACS:Law, Anthony Crossley, has been referred to the Solicitors Disciplinary Tribunal by the Solicitors Regulation Authority, and in February 2012, has been suspended from practising for two years for breaching several rules of the Solicitors Code of Conduct 2007.[1761]

Although it seemed that the awareness and the proceedings against ACS:Law before the Solicitors' Disciplinary Tribunal let to a decrease in

---

1758 Miles Brignall, *File sharers targeted with legal action over music downloads,* The Guardian (17.07.2010).

1759 The National Consumer Council, which operated until May 2013 as Consumer Focus and is now operating as Consumer Futures, is a non-departmental public body and statutory consumer organisation in England, Wales, Scotland, and, for postal services, Northern Ireland. It was established by the Consumers, Estate Agents and Redress Act 2007, and began operations in 2008 by the merging Postwatch, Energywatch and the Welsh, Scottish and National Consumer Councils under the Consumer Focus brand.

1760 High Court, *Golden Eye (International) Ltd and others v Telefonica UK Ltd, Consumer Focus intervening* [2012] EWHC 723 (Ch), para. 37.

1761 In specific, he breached Rule 1.03 by allowing his independence to be compromised ; he breached Rule 1.04 by acting contrary to the best interests of his clients ; he breached Rule 1.06 by acting in a way that was likely to diminish the trust of the public places in him or in the legal profession ; he breached Rule 2.04(1) by entering into arrangements to receive contingency fees for work done in prosecuting or defending contentious proceedings before the courts except as permitted by statute or the common law; he breached Rule 3.01 by acting where there was a conflict of interest in circumstances not permitted under the Rules, in particular because there was a conflict or significant risk that the Respondent's interest were in conflict with those of his clients; he breached Rule 10.01 by using his position as a solicitor to take or attempt to take unfair advantage of other persons, being recipients of letters of claim wither for his own benefit or the benefit of his clients; he breached Rule 1.06 and 5.01(g) by failing to take adequate steps to ensure that appropriate technical and organisational safeguards were in place at his firm to protect against the accidental loss of personal data and documents. See *Solicitors Regulation Authority v Andrew Jonathan Crossley*, Case no. 10726 (06.02.2012).

letters being sent out, in 2012 more and more disclosure orders were applied for.

cc) Putting the Rule to the Test: Piracy Cannot Be Turned into Profit

As outlined above, the only way in which it is possible to obtain information about the names and addresses of subscribers to whom logged IP addresses had been assigned at the relevant time is to obtain disclosure from the Internet service provider.

In the case of *Golden Eye (International) Ltd and others v Telefonica UK Ltd, Consumer Focus intervening* [2012] EWHC 723 (Ch), the court took the opportunity to discuss fundamental questions as to the operation of the Norwich Pharmacal Regime and the legitimacy of so called "speculative invoicing". With regard to the latter, the court in particular dealt with the question how to balance the rights of copyright owners and consumers.

(1) Golden Eye v Telefonica UK: Facts of the Case

In short, Golden Eye and its fellow claimants[1762] were the owners of the copyright in a number of pornographic films which they suspected had been the subject of unauthorized peer-to-peer file-sharing. The claimant Ben Dover Productions had granted Golden Eye a royalty-free worldwide

---

1762 Golden Eye also acted for the other 13 applicants in the application. One claimant (Ben Dover Productions) had granted Golden Eye a royalty free worldwide exclusive licence of all copyrights and rights in the nature of copyright in a number of pornographic films for a period of five years. The third to fourteenth claimants were also owners of copyrights in pornographic films and each of them had entered into an agreement with Golden Eye granting Golden Eye the exclusive right to act for them in relation to any alleged breaches of copyright arising out of peer-to-peer copying of material across the Internet. This included allowing Golden Eye to bring a claim for breach of copyright on their behalf. Under the agreements, Golden Eye agreed to pay the licensor 25% (in some agreements the figure specified was up to 37.5%) of any revenue. See High Court, *Golden Eye (International) Ltd and others v Telefonica UK Ltd, Consumer Focus intervening* [2012] EWHC 723 (Ch), paras. 10-14. For a comment on the case see Gary Moss, *Golden Eye v Telefonica: Media CAT revisited*, Journal of Intellectual Property Law & Practice 2012, Vol. 7 No. 12, 872 – 878.

exclusive licence of all copyrights and rights in the nature of copyright in a number of pornographic films for a period of five years. The other claimants had entered into an agreement with Golden Eye, which granted Golden Eye the exclusive right to act for them in relation to any alleged breaches of copyright arising out of peer-to-peer file-sharing, including allowing Golden Eye to bring a claim for breach of copyright on their behalf. They had logged data of 9,124 users of the access provider O2 in connection with infringements of their copyrights. In the following, Golden Eye, acting as well for the other 13 applicants, applied for a Norwich Pharmacal order seeking disclosure from the access provider of details of their subscribers so that they could then sent cease and desist letters to the subscriber whom they suspected of copyright infringement. The business model operated by Golden Eye is identical to the ones described above: Golden Eye would receive between 25% and 37.5% of the damages collected for its clients. Although the letters that had been sent out to the Internet subscribers threatened them with legal proceedings, Golden Eye seemed to be reluctant to pursue its claims. Arising out of information obtained by virtue of Norwich Pharmacal orders in previous cases, Golden Eye had only brought three claims for infringement.[1763] In two of these cases, Golden Eye served a notice of discontinuance after the claims had been transferred to the Patents County Court, while in the third case, Golden Eye obtain a default judgement.[1764]

In Golden Eye v Telefonica UK the draft letter, which was intended to be sent out and which was presented in the proceedings for the disclosure order against Telefonica, asked the recipients to sign an undertaking that they will abstain from infringing intellectual property rights and threatened to sue them if they did not pay the sum of GBP 700 by way of compensation for the infringement that had already occurred. Similar to the letters sent out by ACS:Law, the draft letter suggested that the subscribers were responsible for any copyright infringement that took place via their Internet connection even if it was committed by a third party whom they permitted the use of that connection.The following are extracts from the original draft letter:

1763 See *ibid*, para. 56.

1764 See Patents County Court, *Golden Eye (International) Ltd v Mohamed Maricar* [2011] EWPCC 27, and High Court, *Golden Eye (International) Ltd and others v Telefonica UK Ltd, Consumer Focus intervening* [2012] EWHC 723 (Ch), para. 58.

- "Forensic Analyst
  We have obtained the services of a forensic computer analyst to search for and identify Internet addresses from which out copyright works (including the Work) are being made available on so called 'peer to peer' (P2P) Internet sites for the purposes of making them available for download by third parties without our client's consent or licence.
- Evidence
  GEIL's forensic computer analyst has provided us with evidence that the following UK date and time, [**B**] [**C**], all or part of the Work was made available from the Internet protocol (or IP) address [**Applicant**], specifically for the purpose of downloading by third parties…On 2011 Mr Justice,…, ordered O2 to give us disclosure of your name and address for the purpose of this letter. For your information we enclose a copy of that Order….
- Infringing Acts
  The act of file sharing the Work without the consent of GEIL is unlawful and, in particular, has caused damage to our business. In effect, every copy of the Work that is downloaded represents a potential lost sale. … File sharing also results in lost royalty revenue and weakening of the brands saleability. We have set out below the infringing acts you are liable for to GEIL: 1. either for copying the Work on to the hard drive of your personal (or office) computer…and/or for 2. making the Work available to third parties for downloading (pursuant to sections 16(1)(d) and 20 of the Act). Please note that such making available can be caused simply by a person connected to your Internet connection downloading the Work, during the course of which the part downloaded is then made available to other third parties connected to the network in question. In the event that you were not responsible for the infringing acts outlined above, you should make full disclosure to us of the other parties at your residence using your Internet connection to make the Work available for download.
- Legal Consequences
  … In the event that this matter cannot be resolved, it may become necessary for GEIL to being a claim against you for copyright infringement. This claim would be brought in the civil court, where liability is determined on the balance of probabilities. In that event, we must make you aware that if successful, we will be entitled to recover from you damages and possibly a contribution towards the legal costs if you choose to instruct lawyers. …

- Proposed Settlement
  ... Our offer is that you: 1. promise in a written undertaking not to upload, download, make available or otherwise share the Work or any of GEIL works (or other intellectual property) and/or permit others to do the same using your Internet connection, at any time in the future, either from the above IP address or any other; 2. agree to delete any copies of the Work (and any other intellectual property of GEIL from your hard drive and/or operating system and/or any copies saved to disk (or other media), other than those that were purchased by you from a legitimate source; and 3. pay GBP 700.00 as compensation to GEIL for its losses.
- Next Steps – payment and undertakings
  ... For the avoidance of doubt, these undertakings will represent an agreement between you and GEIL and if you act in breach of that agreement, we will have no option but to take further action against you. ... In the event that either the payment or undertakings are not received within fourteen days of the date of this letter, GEIL reserves the right to take further action which could include commencement of proceedings and possibly an application to your ISP to slow down or terminate your Internet connection."[1765]

The content of the letter and the way it was drafted clearly suggested to a recipient without any legal knowledge that he needs to pay the requested sum.

(2) The Conditions for Granting Norwich Pharmacal Relief in Relation to Peer-to-Peer File-Sharing Cases and Speculative Invoicing

Although Arnold J found that there was a *prima facie* case that each of the respective subscribers associated with the IP addresses provided by the claimants had illicitly copied one or more of each of the applicants' works for the purpose of making them available via file-sharing websites for third parties to download, it took the court 152 paragraphs to grant disclo-

1765 High Court, *Golden Eye (International) Ltd and others v Telefonica UK Ltd, Consumer Focus intervening* [2012] EWHC 723 (Ch), para. 33. Golden Eye argued that the letter would be suitably adapted in the case of claims concerning infringements of copyrights owned by the fellow claimants.

sure of "the name and postal address of the registered owner or owners of each of the Internet account or accounts that were assigned to the Internet protocol address"

The High Court took the opportunity to set a precedent after four years of speculative invoicing. Although the court granted Norwich Pharmacal orders in relation to Golden Eye and one other claimant out of 14[1766], it stated that any claim letter sent by copyright owners or their representatives must properly safeguard the legitimate interests of the recipients. Thus, when considering the proportionality of the order, the court balanced not just the rights of the copyright holders against those of the access provider from whom they demand disclosure of information but also took into account the rights of the not-yet-identified subscribers by examining the wording of the draft cease and desist letter. While the general prerequisites for a Norwich Pharmacal order could be established without doubt, the Court put an emphasis on the question of whether the request of the claimant was "justified and proportionate".[1767]

(3) Establishment of Genuine Intent to Seek Redress for Arguable Wrongs

Before the Court could deal with question of whether the claimants' requests were justified and proportionate, it examined whether the claimants were genuinely seeking redress.

In this regard, it was irrelevant that the applicants might not bring proceedings against the wrongdoer in the future. It is not a requirement for the grant of Norwich Pharmacal relief that the applicant intends to bring proceedings against the wrongdoer.[1768]

1766 Golden Eye had only entered into an agreement with one of the other claimants that would give Golden Exe an exclusive licence in accordance with section section 92(1) *CDPA 1988*, and thus a title to sue. With regard to the other claimants, Golden Exe was not licensed by the copyright owner to do any of the acts restricted by the copyrights in the works, but only to act for them in relation to any alleged breaches of copyright arising out of P2P file-sharing.

1767 Akash Sachdeva/Jonathan McDonald, *The use of Norwich Pharmacal orders to identify online infringers – an old remedy updated for modern times,* Entertainment Law Review 2013, Vol. 24 Issue 3, 103, 106.

1768 High Court, *Golden Eye (International) Ltd and others v Telefonica UK Ltd, Consumer Focus intervening* [2012] EWHC 723 (Ch), para. 109.

Sending a letter before action with to the intention of persuading the wrongdoer to agree to pay compensation and to give an undertaking not to infringe in the future was considered as one legitimate way of seeking redress.[1769] There is no requirement for the intending claimant to commit himself at such an early stage to bring proceedings if redress cannot be obtained consensually.[1770] The intending claimant is entitled to be selective as to whom he pursues proceedings against.[1771] Bearing the costs of litigation in mind, litigating for damages of GBP 700 is likely to be uneconomic and thus, a claimant may not want to sue, except perhaps as a test case.[1772] This may even be the case under the new small claims track for copyright claims in the Patents County Court which has been introduced in October 2012 as a lower cost solution for litigants with a maximum damages award of GBP 10,000 and minimal costs recovery and exposure.[1773] Against this background, an applicant seeking redress for a large number of low-value infringements cannot be criticised for being selective or not pursuing claims at all.[1774] It was also legitimate for Golden Eye and the other claimants to enter into commercial arrangements under which Golden Eye undertakes the effort, cost and risk of applying for *Norwich Pharmacal* orders and making claims against alleged infringers, including the costs of instructing solicitors and counsel, in return for a handsome share of the proceeds. Such an agreement does not as such imperil the ability of the court properly to control the circumstances in which an order will be granted and the use which may be made of the information obtained if an order is granted or to control the conduct of subsequent claims against the intended Defendants.[1775]

1769 *Ibid*, para. 109.

1770 *Ibid*, para. 109.

1771 *Ibid*, para. 110.

1772 *Ibid*, para. 110.

1773 If the amount that is claimed is excessive, then even bringing a small claim may be unattractive.

1774 High Court, *Golden Eye (International) Ltd and others. v Telefonica UK Ltd, Consumer Focus intervening* [2012] EWHC 723 (Ch), para. 111.

1775 *Ibid*, para. 99. Consumer Focus which intervened on behalf of the not-yet-identified subscriber had argued that "profit-sharing-agreements" between Golden Eye and the other claimants are champertous and thus jeopardise the proper administration of justice. The Court did not find that the agreements in question were "agreements to conduct litigation in the sense of the champertous agreements" in *Sibthorpe v Southwark London Borough Council* [2011] EWCA Civ 25, [2011] 1 WLR 2111.

The court rejected the allegation that the division of revenue between Golden Eye and the other Claimants had all the hallmarks of a money-making exercise for Golden Eye, (ii) the sum of GBP 700 requested in the draft letter was unsupported and unsupportable, (iii) the Claimants were equivocal about their willingness to pursue infringement actions and (iv) the conduct of the three claims brought by Golden Eye against alleged infringers suggested a desire to avoid judicial scrutiny.[1776]

(4) Disclosure Order Must be Necessary to Pursue Redress

The applicants are owners of copyrights, which have been infringed by individuals who have been engaged in peer-to-peer file-sharing. The only way in which the applicants could ascertain the identity of the Internet subscribers and seek compensation for past infringements would be the disclosure of names and addresses of the subscribers of the logged IP addresses. Without the information sought by the application for Norwich Pharmacal relief, the claimants cannot issue proceedings to engage in pre-action correspondence with the intended defendants. When the claimants's copyrights have been infringed, it is necessary for the alleged wrongdoers to be identified so that the claimants are able to protect their rights by seeking redress.[1777]

(5) Proportionality of a Disclosure Order

When considering the proportionality of the order sought, a court will have to take into account the precise terms of the order sought and in this regard also the terms of the draft letter of claim. Although the order sought may be proportionate between the applicants and the Internet service provider, it does not follow that it is proportionate as between the applicants and the intended defendants.[1778] With regard to the latter, it is necessary to examine the terms of the draft letter of claim.

1776 High Court, *Golden Eye (International) Ltd and others v Telefonica UK Ltd, Consumer Focus intervening* [2012] EWHC 723 (Ch), para. 108 et seq.

1777 See *ibid*, para. 114 et seq.

1778 *Ibid*, para. 120.

The draft letter must be worded so as properly safeguard the legitimate interests of the intended defendants, and in particular the interests of intended defendants who have not committed the alleged infringements. A disclosure order can only be proportionate, if the legitimate interests of the intended defendants in protecting their privacy and data protection rights are safeguarded. This was not the case in the Golden Eye case for several reasons: As regards the letter of claim in the Golden Eye case, Arnold J criticised that the letter failed to state clearly that the merits of the infringement allegations against the intended defendant had not yet been considered by the court.[1779] The letter further suggested that the recipient was liable for copyright infringement without clearly stating that that person might not be responsible at all for the infringing acts.[1780] Liability for a third party that used an Internet connection to infringe copyright may only arise where the subscriber has authorised within the meaning of section 16 of the *CDPA 1988* the downloading of films which involved the making of infringing copies. [1781] Allowing a third party to use an Internet connection in general cannot be equated with authorising a third party to commit infringements. The Court also recognised that an Internet connection may be unsecured and utilised unbeknownst to the owner.[1782] Further the letter was considered one-sided in that it listed the legal consequences to the intended defendant of a successful claim without mentioning the consequences to the relevant claimant of an unsuccessful claim.[1783] In addition, it was also unjustified to refer to "other intellectual property" under the heading "Proposed Settlement" when there was no evidence that any IP rights of the claimants have been infringed.[1784] Also, it was unrea-

1779 *Ibid*, para. 125.

1780 *Ibid*, para. 126.

1781 To authorise an infringement is to "sanction, approve, or countenance" it, see High Court, *Monckton v Pathe Freres Pathephone Ltd* [1914] 1 KB 395 and High Court, *Evans v Hulton & Co Ltd* [1924] WN 130 (KB). An apparent willingness of the courts to treat indifference as capable of being authorisation, has been identified, cf. Hector MacQueen/Charlotte Waelde/Graeme Laurie/Abbe Brown, *Contemporary intellectual property, Law and policy* (2nd ed. 2011), p. 159 with further references.

1782 In this regard cf. also HHJ Birss QC's arguments against equating allowing and authorising in *Media C.A.T. v Adams* [2011] EWPCC 6, [2011] FSR 8, para. 30.

1783 High Court, *Golden Eye (International) Ltd and others v Telefonica UK Ltd, Consumer Focus intervening* [2012] EWHC 723 (Ch), para. 127.

1784 *Ibid*, para. 128.

sonable to require a response from the intended defendants within 14 days, in particular, as they were consumers.[1785] Finally, it was unjustified to threaten further legal action in the form of an "application" to the Internet service provider to slow down or terminate the subscriber's Internet connection.[1786]

As regards the claim for GBP 700, the claimants are not justified to demand from every intended defendant the payment of GBP 700. The figure was unsupportable for several reasons: (i) an unknown percentage of the intended defendants would not be infringers, and would thus not liable to pay any sum; (ii) the scale of the infringement committed by each infringer is unknown; (iii) the royalties must not necessarily be assessed on the basis of a time limited license to exploit a work worldwide; (iv) additional damages will not necessarily be awarded; (v) the sum seems to be selected so as to maximise the revenue obtained from the letters of claim and was not a realistic estimate of recoverable damages.[1787]

The Court took the position that instead of specifying a figure in the initial letter it would rather be acceptable for the claimants to explain that they are prepared to accept a lump sum in settlement of their claims.[1788] Accordingly, the claimants should individually negotiate the settlement sum with each intended defendant.[1789]

In summary, a legitimate course was to inform the intended defendants about the meaning of a Norwich Pharmacal, and require those who admit infringing to disclose information about the extent to which they did so and then negotiate a settlement on a case-by-case basis.

If the claim for a Norwich Pharmacal order takes into account the concerns above, the claimants' interests in enforcing their copyrights outweigh the intended defendants' interests in protecting their privacy and data protection rights. This meant for Golden Eye, that the order was granted under the condition that Golden Eye amends the draft order and the draft letter so as to eliminate the concerns expressed.

1785 *Ibid*, para. 129.
1786 *Ibid*, para. 130.
1787 *Ibid*, paras. 133–137.
1788 *Ibid*, para. 138.
1789 *Ibid.*

(6) Control of the litigation

The claimants in the Golden Eye case were divided into two groups. The Court distinguished between Golden Eye and Ben Dover Productions, and the other claimants. While with regard to Golden Eye and Ben Dover Norwich Pharmacal relief was granted, it was denied in relation to the other claimants.

The reason for this were the terms of agreements that Golden Eye had entered in with the other claimants. Ben Dover Productions was the only claimant that had entered into a worldwide licensing agreement with Golden Eye under which Golden Eye had the exclusive licence of all copyrights and rights in the nature of copyrights in specified Ben Dover films for a period of five years. Thus, Golden Eye could bring a claim in its own right. However, as regards the other twelve claimants, the situation was different as they had only granted Golden Eye the exclusive right to act for them in relation to alleged breaches of copyright arising out of peer-to-peer file-sharing. Norwich Pharmacal relief was denied in regard to these twelve claimants as this kind of relief was considered as "tantamount to the court sanctioning the scale of the intended defendants' privacy and data protection rights to the highest bidder".[1790] Hence, a disclosure order would not be proportionate and fair. If these claimants had applied themselves, orders would have been granted in their favour.[1791] This decision was however reversed by the Court of Appeal.[1792]

dd) Summary

The Golden Eye case clarifies that revenue-sharing agreements in this context are not per se champertous and that the business model operated by Golden Eye is legitimate. As long as the applicant for a Norwich Pharmacal order can demonstrate that he has a genuine commercial desire to

1790 High Court, *Golden Eye (International) Ltd and others v Telefonica UK Ltd, Consumer Focus intervening* [2012] EWHC 723 (Ch), para. 146.

1791 *Ibid.*

1792 Court of Appeal, Golden Eye (International) Ltd and others v Telefonica UK Ltd [2012] EWCA Civ 1740. For a comment on the appeal see Mark Hyland, *The seductive interface between adult entertainment and Norwich Pharmacal Relief*, Communications Law 2013, Vol. 18 Issue 2, 56 – 60.

obtain compensation for infringement of his copyrights, he is entitled to the order sought. Although speculative invoicing as a method of seeking redress for infringement was not condemned by the court, Arnold J.'s comments on the content and wording of letters before claim provides useful guidelines for future enforcement campaigns. [1793] Intended threatening behaviour in the letters before claim, in particular with regard to cut down or slow down a potential infringer's Internet connection will not be considered favourably by a court.

In Golden Eye, the High Court confirmed what has been previously set out by HJ Birss QC in *Media CAT v Adams*,[1794] namely, that a court, when asked to grant Norwich Pharmacal relief, has to carefully consider the terms of the draft letter of claim and its impact upon ordinary consumers who may be innocent, who may not have access to specialised legal advice and who may be embarrassed or distressed at the allegations. The draft letter in Golden Eye failed this test as it failed to state clearly that the merits of the infringement allegations had not yet been proven, and was one-sided as well as of a threatening nature. A letter that is drafted in such a way and demands a lump sum for compensation without acknowledging that an unknown percentage of recipients would be non-infringers and the scale of infringements is unknown and differs from recipient to recipient.

The pre-action correspondence needs to be adapted on a case-by-case basis. As at the time of application for disclosure the scale of infringement is unknown and it is not clear that the intended defendant is the actual infringer, the rights-holder may only express that he is willing to accept a lump sum as compensation but may not demand a sum that is not a realistic estimate of losses and costs incurred. Hence, a court is not going to approve standardised mass letters, which are not adapted on a case-by-case basis.

In addition to what has been said, the comparable low number of warnings being send out, may also be based on the fact that in the UK, suing users "has been seen as something of a last resort because of the damage it causes to public relations".[1795] If this is true for the UK, than it becomes

1793 Paul Joseph/Charlotte Ward, *Golden Eye (International) Ltd v Telefonica UK Ltd*, Entertainment Law Review 2012, Vol 23 Issue 6, 183, 185.

1794 Patents County Court, *Media C.A.T. v Adams* [2011] EWPCC 6, [2011] FSR 8, para. 30.

1795 Lilian Edwards, *Role and responsibility of Internet intermediaries in the field of copyright and related rights* (2011), p. 25.

clear why primarily adult film copyright owner rather than the mainstream industries have been involved in volume litigation.

ee) The UK Application Departs from the German Approach

In comparison to the German pre-litigation settlement scheme, there is, first of all, a significant conceptual difference. In Germany a subscriber is likely to be liable as a *Störer*, in the UK such concept does not exists. Thus, a subscriber who has not committed an infringement himself or authorised another person to do infringe copyright pursuant to s. 16(2) *CDPA 1988*, is not liable at all. Authorisation of infringement is sanctioning, countenancing or approving another person's primary infringement where one has authority or control over a primary infringer. In copyright infringement cases where authorisation pursuant to s. 16(2) *CDPA 1988* took place, there has always been a direct and immediate link between the act of the defendant and the infringement which followed.[1796] This however, differs from the German concept of *Störerhaftung* as it requires more than creating an opportunity for others to infringe. Although it has been argued that where the complaint is about the provision to others of opportunity to infringe and it can be coupled with the necessary degree of control over those others and specific instances of infringement, then there may be liability for infringement,[1797] this does not equate the *Störerhaftung*. HJ Birss QC already pointed out in Media CAT v Adams that allowing a third party to use an Internet connection does not alone equate authorising an infringement by this person.[1798] UK courts have not yet decided whether the act of authorising use of an Internet connection turn the person doing the authorising into a person authorising the infringement within section 16(2), but in the light of the decision in Golden Eye it is unlikely that they will equate authorised use of an Internet connection with authorised use to infringe copyright.

1796 Cf. Hector MacQueen/Charlotte Waelde/Graeme Laurie/Abbe Brown, *Contemporary intellectual property, Law and policy* (2nd ed. 2011), p. 161 with further references.

1797 *Ibid*, p. 161.

1798 Patents County Court, *Media C.A.T. v Adams* [2011] EWPCC 6, [2011] FSR 8, para. 30.

Another difference is the applicable law, concerns the granting of a disclosure order. While in Germany a court will only assess in summary proceedings whether an obvious infringement has been committed, the UK court has to assess the contravening interests even of the non-identified subscribers. In this regard, he will also have to take into account the concrete allegations and the terms of pre-action letter of claims. This of course leads to much more workload of a court confronted with an application for Norwich Pharmacal relief. However, it is not foreseeable that UK courts will be overrun with disclosure request like German courts are. The reasons for this are:

UK courts do not approve the mass scale sending out of standardised letters before claim. Instead of specifying a figure in the letter before claim, they rather consider it acceptable for the claimants to explain that they are prepared to accept a lump sum in settlement of their claims.[1799] Only if the recipient of the letter admits an infringement (either committed by himself or authorised) and in particular also the scale of the infringement, the claimants should individually negotiate the settlement sum with the intended defendant.

3. Pre-Litigation Letters: Concerns Relating toTechnology and Fundamental Rights

While in Germany the pre-litigation settlement plays a major role and is primarily relied on in copyright infringement cases, in the UK courts are rather careful to grant the disclosure orders necessary to prepare for cease and desist letters. The difference in numbers is based on mainly two grounds: there are only few actors in the UK, that send out the cease and desist letters in online copyright infringement cases,[1800] and the courts dealing with the disclosure request will more thoroughly examine the application for disclosure.

Other than the graduated response schemes, questions as to the standards for establishing an infringement or the evasion of detection will not

---

1799 High Court, *Golden Eye (International) Ltd and others v Telefonica UK Ltd, Consumer Focus intervening* [2012] EWHC 723 (Ch), para. 138.

1800 As of 2013, apparently only one practioner firm is sending out speculative invoicing letters, see Andrew Murray, *Information Technology Law, The law and society* (2nd ed. 2013), p.287.

be addressed. Especially the latter does not play a role, when it comes to the efficiency of the system in the fundamental rights assessment. The pre-litigation letters are no instruments that prepare criminal proceedings; they are instruments for out-of-court settlement in civil matters. The rights-holders are free to decide whether and against whom they want to pursue their claims.

In the following, it will be briefly outlined how the technological problems that have previously identified are dealt with under civil law, in particular the fact that the IP address subscriber must not necessarily be the infringer as well as the securisation of Wi-Fi networks will be addressed.

In terms of compliance with secondary EU law, only the disclosure of personal data is of relevance as this is based on Article 8 of the IPR Enforcment Directive. Also, the assessment of fundamental rights can be kept brief, as in the context of civil proceedings; we have private parties on the claimant and defendant side instead of a subordination relationship.

a) Dealing with Technological Matters

The question of how the fact is dealt with that the IP address does not necessarily lead to the actual infringer, is a matter of general copyright law: namely, whether subscribers can be liable for copyright infringements that have been committed via their Internet connection. The question of determination of an infringement is of no relevance in this discussion, because there is no third party or authority that needs to determine whether an infringement has actually been committed. If a recipient of a cease and desist letter challenges the allegations, the rights-holder may sue him before a civil court, which will then assess the case based on the evidence provided by the parties. As this research is not so much concerned with the determination of copyright infringements in court, the determination of an infringement in civil proceedings will not be analysed any further than it has already been done when outlining the pre-litigation settlement in Germany and the UK. The emphasis of this section is put on the disclosure procedure and the liability of a subscriber for wrongful act committed via his Internet access.

aa) IP Address Subscribers Must Not be Equalled with Actual Infringers

In Germany, the rightholder carries the burden of proof that the Internet access subscriber was the actual infringer. This proof is regularly difficult to produce unless the subscriber does not admit to be the actual infringer and only the actual infringer is liable for damages. The subscriber may always rely on his right to refuse to give evidence (§ 383 *ZPO*) as far as family members are concerned.[1801] He may argue that he was not the infringer, but does not have to name the family member who committed the infringement. Accordingly, where the subscriber can prove that not only he but also third parties used a connection, he may only be liable as a *Störer*. The burden of proof is alleviated for the *Störerhaftung* relating solely to an obligation to cease and desist. Liability as a *Störer* is – as mentioned before[1802] – only established where the Internet access subscriber breached a duty to of care in relation to his Internet access. Such a duty is regularly established where the subscriber shares his Internet access service with other persons. It is up to the subscriber to prove that he has not breached a duty.

This concept allows to issue cease and desist letters to IP address subscribers without having to identify the actual infringer. The disadvantage for rights-holders is that they will not be entitled to damages against the mere *Störer*. However, they will nevertheless usually also demand damages from the addresses of their cease and desist request as there is a presumption that the subscriber has also committed the infringement. It is then up to the subscriber to rebut the presumption.

What makes the *Abmahnungen* an attractive instrument for rights-holders is the fact, that the subscriber will have to pay the costs of the *Abmahung* even if only *Störerhaftung* can be established. As in most cases, liability as a *Störer* will be established, the rights-holder will not have to bear any costs for informing the subscriber about the infringement that has been committed.

1801 Similarly in the UK, a party has the right in civil proceedings to refuse to answer any question or produce any document or thing if to do so would tend to expose him (or spouse) to criminal proceedings, section 14 of the *Civil Evidence Act 1968*.

1802 See above B. III. 1. A) aa) (3) Application of the Liability Concepts to the Subscriber of an IP Address.

In the UK, liability for a third party that used an Internet connection to infringe copyright may only arise where the subscriber has "authorised" within the meaning of section 16 of the *CDPA 1988* the downloading of copyrighted materials which involved the making of infringing copies. [1803] "Authorisation" cannot be equated with the conditions for *Störerhaftung*. Allowing a third party to use an Internet connection in general can also not be equated with authorising a third party to commit infringements. [1804] UK courts have not yet decided whether the act of authorising use of an Internet connection may turn the person doing the authorising into a person authorising the infringement within section 16(2). However, in the light of the decision in Golden Eye it is unlikely that they will equate authorised use of an Internet connection with authorised infringement of copyright.

The High Court also recognised that an Internet connection may be unsecured and utilised unbeknownst to the owner.[1805] Accordingly, in cases were the actual infringer cannot be identified, the pre-litigation letter will have no more effect than informing the subscriber of a wrong that has been committed via his connection. For this information, the rights-holder will have to bear the costs.

bb) Obligations to Secure a Wi-Fi Connection under Private Law

There is not statutory provision that sets forth, whether a Wi-Fi network that is operated by a private person has to be secured. The non-adequate securisation may however lead to liability as a *Störer* if the subscriber succeeds in proving that he has not himself committed the infringement. The German Federal Court of Justice held in the *Sommer unseres Lebens*

1803 To authorise an infringement is to "sanction, approve, or countenance" it, see *Monckton v Pathe Freres Pathephone Ltd* [1914] 1 KB 395 and *Evans v Hulton & Co Ltd* [1924] WN 130. An apparent willingness of the courts to treat indifference as capable of being authorisation, has been identified, cf. Hector MacQueen/Charlotte Waelde/Graeme Laurie/Abbe Brown, *Contemporary intellectual property, Law and policy* (2nd ed. 2011), p. 159 with further references.

1804 Patents County Court, *Media C.A.T. v Adams* [2011] EWPCC 6, [2011] FSR 8, para. 30.

1805 In this regard cf. also HHJ Birss QC's arguments against equating allowing and authorising in *ibid*, para. 30.

case[1806], that private persons that operate a Wi-Fi have to have a sufficiently secure password defined as one that is individual and sufficiently long, and have to obey the security standards at the time of purchase. Accordingly, WPA2[1807] is likely to be considered as the current standard for private users. This finding recognises that Wi-Fi has become a common standard, even for non-IT-literate persons. They are not required to update the security settings on a regular basis. However, this conclusion leads to unfair results, namely that those who have an old router with outdated security mechanisms are less likely to be liable for infringements committed via their Internet connection. Whether the Court intended such a result is questionable.

In the UK the question of security standard, or more general, of securisation of Wi-Fi routers has not been addressed by courts yet.

cc) Concerns in Relation to Reliability of Data

Although concern in relation to reliability of data is a question of a more general nature, it shall be addressed briefly at this point and by looking at the German case law. Usually the disclosure requests will contain an expert's statement on the reliability of the data harvesting procedure. Unfortunately, to date, courts have not questioned these reports and relied on the accuracy of logged traffic data. The Redtube case has recently shown, that more attention needs to be paid on assessing how IP address data was collected. In order to be able to assess the expert's statement and the functioning of the software in the specific case, the courts will need additional training or experts themselves that instruct them on IT-related issues. In civil proceedings the parties to the case have to present the evidence that supports their claim/defence, and only in conflicts that cannot be resolved other than by the appointment of an independent expert such

1806 BGH, Decision of 12.05.2010 – I ZR 121/08, Neue Juristische Wochenschrift 2010, 2061.

1807 WPA2 (Wi-Fi Protected Access 2) is an implementation of an IEEE ('The Institute of Electrical and Electronics Engineers, Incorporated', a New York not-for-profit corporation) security standard for Wi-Fi networks and the most used Wi-Fi protection nowadays in both, home and professional networks. Based on the Advanced Encryption Standard (AES), the current standard specification for the encryption of data, WPA2 provides strong security and vulnerabilities are currently only known in regard to weak passphrases.

an expert will be appointed. In this respect, the Redtube case and also the reasoning of the High Court in *Golden Eye* have shown that in procedures were the future defendant is not yet named, more scrutiny in examining the infringement is required by the court.

In February 2011, the Higher Regional Court of Cologne for instance raised doubts on the reliability of the traffic data stored by a major Internet access provider.[1808] This provider forces a re-connect of the Internet connection every 24 hours. Additionally, when users disconnect and re-connect, they are most likely allocated a new IP address. In the application for disclosure of information, the Internet service provider confirmed that the complainant was given a new IP several times during the period in question (three consecutive days).[1809] Concluding from the way IP addresses were assigned, it was considered to be very unlikely that one person will be allocated the same IP address several times in a row. The Court had doubts whether the complainant could be identified behind one single IP address for a period of three days or whether this fact was based on a faulty transmission, collection or transfer of IP addresses. Thus, the court revoked the previous order of the Regional Court of Cologne for disclosure of information.

This case has unfortunately been a single incident, but shows in connection with the Redtube incident, that IP address logging and transmission of data is prone to error and that attention needs to be paid to that fact.

b) Compliance of Information Disclosure with Secondary EU Law

The compliance of disclosure of personal data with secondary EU law has also already been discussed in the context of graduate response schemes. As in the context of France the disclosure was made in preparation of criminal proceedings and, at this point, it needs to be examined, whether the disclosure of personal data in civil proceedings for the benefit of a copyright holder (to prepare a civil claim against a potential infringer) is in compliance with EU law.

1808 OLG Köln, Decision of 10.02.2011 – 6 W 5/11, BeckRS 2011, 04582.

1809 In this case the same dynamic IP address was allegedly allocated to the complainant on 12.06.2010 at 9:30 pm, on 13.06.2010 at 11:01 pm and on 14.06.2010 at 8:37 pm.

First of all, he communication sought constitutes the processing of personal data within the meaning of Article 2 of the *E-Privacy Directive*, read in conjunction with Article 2(b) of the *Data Protection Directive*. That communication thus falls within the scope of the latter.[1810]

In *Promusicae*[1811] and in *LSG – Gesellschaft zur Wahrnehmung von Leistungsschutzrechten*[1812], the CJEU clarified that the *E-Privacy Directive* and the *IPR Enforcement Directive* must be interpreted as not precluding national legislation that imposes an obligation to disclose to private persons personal data in order to enable them to bring civil proceedings for copyright infringements. Article 8(3) of the *IPR Enforcement Directive* and Articles 6 and 15 of the *E-Privacy Directive* are to be interpreted as permitting the disclosure of personal traffic data to private third parties for the purposes of civil proceedings for alleged copyright infringements. The Court held that Community law – in particular said articles – does not preclude Member States from imposing an obligation to disclose to private third parties personal data relating to Internet traffic in order to enable them to bring civil proceedings for copyright infringement, but nor does it require those Member States to lay down such an obligation.[1813]

In the *Bonnier Audio* case, the CJEU further held that the *Data Retention Directive* "...must be interpreted as not precluding the application of national legislation based on Article 8 of Directive 2004/48 ... which, in order to identify an Internet subscriber or user, permits an Internet service provider in civil proceedings to be ordered to give a copyright holder or its representative information on the subscriber to whom the Internet service provider provided an IP address which was allegedly used in an infringement, since that legislation does not fall within the material scope of Directive 2006/24".[1814] Information rights enabling rights-holder to bring civil proceedings do not fall within the material scope of the *Data Retention Directive*, because the *Data Retention Directive* deals exclusively

---

1810 See CJEU, C-461/10 *Bonnier Audio AB and Others v Perfect Communication Sweden AB,* Judgment of 19.04.2012, para. 52.

1811 CJEU, C-275/06 *Productores de Musica de España (Promusicae) v Telefonica de España SAU* [2008] ECR I-271.

1812 CJEU, C-557/07 *LSG-Gesellschaft zur Wahrnehmung von Leistungsschutzrechten GmbH v Tele 2 Telecommunication GmbH* (Tele2), Judgment of 19.02.2009, [2009] ECR I-01227.

1813 *Ibid*, para. 41.

1814 CJEU, C-461/10, *Bonnier Audio AB and Others v Perfect Communication Sweden AB*, Judgment of 19.04.2012, operative part of the judgement.

with the retention and handling of data generated or processed by Internet service providers for the purpose of the investigation, detection and prosecution of serious crime, and does not cover the retention of data for civil proceedings.[1815]

According to the ruling of the CJEU in the case of *Bonnier Audio,* national legislation must enable "the national court seised of an application for an order for disclosure of personal data, made by a person who is entitled to act, to weigh the conflicting interests involved, on the basis of the facts of each case and taking due account of the requirements of the principle of proportionality".[1816] The national court must strike a fair balance between the contravening interests, i.e. the protection of intellectual property rights of the copyright-holders guaranteed by Article 17(2) *CFR* and the protection of the fundamental rights of individuals who are affected by such measures, in particular the rights safeguarded by Articles 8(1) *ECHR*/Article 7 *CFR* and Article 8 *CFR*.[1817]

The general obligation to consider the proportionality of remedies for the infringement of intellectual property rights, including orders for the disclosure of the identities of infringers derives from Article 3(2) of the *IPR Enforcement Directive.*

Both, the common law in the UK as well as the statutory information right in Germany require the court to conduct a proportionality assessment. Thus, the law as such is conform with EU secondary law. However, not only the law but also the application of the law must be in compliance with EU law. In this respect, the practice in Germany, where courts "wave" through information requests, is questionable. In the context of fundamental rights conformity, the proportionality of the application in Germany will be assessed.

1815 *Ibid*, paras. 41 et seq. The Court explained that the *Data Retention Directive* constitutes a special and restricted set of rules, derogating from and replacing the *E-Privacy Directive* general in scope and, in particular Article 15(1) thereof.

1816 *Ibid*, para. 59.

1817 Ibid, para. 60. See also C-275/06 *Productores de Musica de España (Promusicae) v Telefonica de España SAU* [2008] ECR I-271, paras. 61- 68.

c) Conformity with the Fundamental Rights of Internet Users

While with regard to the graduated response schemes a thorough analysis of the fundamental rights has been conducted, the following analysis will concentrate on only two aspects: the compliance of the disclosure of personal data with fundamental rights and the fact that German courts do not pay sufficient regard to how data is harvested. As rights-holders often do not make transparent how they have obtained the data, and the courts are often unwilling to require more information, this could interfere with the right to fair trial of the subscriber.

aa) Collecting of Personal Data Interfering with Privacy Rights

The collecting of personal data and its impact on the privacy rights of the subscribers has only briefly been addressed within the assessment of the graduated response schemes. When dynamic IP addresses are collected with the intention to have the identity of the subscriber behind an IP address disclosed, the rights-holders collect personal data.[1818] It has been argued that automatised IP address "harvesting" is a disproportionate interference with the privacy rights, in particular the right to confidentiality of communication, because data is collected in a general manner without knowing whether the subscriber is liable.[1819] Such a conclusion would however render the IP collecting per se illegitimate, because without information on the identity of the subscriber of an Internet access service, it is impossible to tell whether the subscriber will be liable as Störer or infringer, or will not be liable at all. In fact IP collecting would then only be legitimate if the national law provided for liability for activities conducted via the addressee's Internet access similar to the gross negligence offence in France that has been discussed in the context of graduated response schemes. However, even such a far-reaching liability requires the breach of duties to secure an Internet access and shield the connection from abusive use. This would mean, that rights-holders would have no

1818 See above B. II. c) bb) (2) Interferrence with the Right to the Confidentiality of Communications. See also Stefan Maaßen, *Urheberrechtlicher Auskunftsanspruch und Vorratsdatenspeicherung*, MultiMedia und Recht 2009, 511, 513.

1819 Stefan Maaßen, *Urheberrechtlicher Auskunftsanspruch und Vorratsdatenspeicherung*, MultiMedia und Recht 2009, 511, 513.

possibility to obtain information about the identity of an infringer, and would not allow a fair balance to be struck between the rights and interests of copyright owners and Internet users.

When assessing the proportionality of the interference with the privacy rights of users, one must take into account that at this point (i.e. prior to a disclosure order), no identity is yet revealed. Moreover identity can only be revealed following an assessment by a court and by a court order. Thus, there is a (theoretic) safeguard that shall hinder an abuse of information requests.

Further, the logging of a dynamic IP address in connection with the infringement of a protected work, and the subsequent second logging of that IP address does not mean that two infringements by one and the same subscriber have been identified. IP addresses are attributed dynamically and the logging of the same address may refer to two different persons, so that the drawing up of personal profiles is rather unlikely. With the information collected at hand, they are not able to attribute several infringements to a specific Internet access service subscriber. Other than HADOPI or UK access providers, no repeat infringer lists can be set up.

Further, in contrast to the data retention by access providers under the Data Retention Directive, which was held to be illegitimate, because all data of all customers will be retained, the rights-holder or their agents will rather not log all data of all the participants of a peer-to-peer network, their software crawls for specific pre-defined infringements only. Accordingly, there is no general surveillance of peer-to-peer traffic, but monitoring for pre-defined content, of which the distribution would constitute a copyright infringement.

Due to the limited scope of the data collecting, the interference with privacy rights that is necessary to pursue civil claims for copyright infringements is proportionate, and thus can be justified.[1820]

bb) Disclosure of Personal Data Interfering with Privacy Rights

First of all, it has to be recalled, that other than under the graduated response scheme in France, disclosure of personal data can only be

1820 Stefan Maaßen in *ibid* concludes that the collecting of personal data by rights-holders is not legitimate under German law.

ordered by a court. In the context of pre-litigation correspondence, it is necessary to bear in mind that the applicants for a disclosure order seek the communication of the name and address of an Internet subscriber using the IP address from which it is presumed that an unlawful exchange of files containing protected works took place, in order to identify that person. As stated above, granting a disclosure order interferes with the privacy rights under Article 8 *ECHR* and Articles 7 and 8 *CFR*. An interference of right to confidentiality of communication and data protection rights needs to be in accordance with the law and pursue a legitimate aim. Such a legitimate aim is the protection of the rights and freedoms of others.[1821] The claimants's copyrights, which are protected under Article 1 of the Protocol 1 to the *ECHR* and Article 17(2) *CFR* are "rights of others" within Article 8(2) *ECHR* and Article 52(1) of the Charter. The same applies to the rights-holders' right to an effective remedy.

Where a balance falls to be struck between the right to intellectual property and the right to an effective remedy on the one hand and privacy rights on the other hand, neither right as such has precedence over the other. The interests need to be reconciled. The mechanisms allowing these rights and interests to be balanced are, first of all, contained in the *E-Privacy Directive* itself, in that it provides for rules which determine in what circumstances and to what extent the processing of personal data is lawful and what safeguards must be provided for.[1822] The national implementations comply with the Directive. However, as mentioned above, the authorities and courts of the Member States must not only interpret their national law in a manner consistent with the Directives but also make sure that they do not rely on an interpretation of them which would be in conflict with the aforementioned fundamental rights or with the other general principles of Community law, such as the principle of proportionality.[1823]

It must be noted that the national legislation in question requires, first of all, that disclosure can only be granted by a court. The court will have to assess, inter alia, that, for an order for disclosure of personal data, there be clear evidenceof an infringement of an intellectual property right (in Germany: "obvious infringement"). Further the information requested must be necessary for the infringed party to pursue his claim in the main

---

1821 See Article 8(2) *ECHR* and Article 52(1) *CFR*.

1822 See CJEU, C-275/06, *Productores de Musica de España (Promusicae) v Telefonica de España SAU* [2008] ECR I-271, para. 66.

1823 *Ibid*, para. 68 with further references.

proceedings. Both, the German statutory provision in § 101 UrhG and the Norwich Pharmacal relief in the UK require the court concerned to respect the principle of proportionality. However, although § 101 IV *UrhG* requires German courts to respect the principle of proportionality, the courts will in fact hardly conduct a balancing test. In practice, they will "wave" the requests "through" considering the workload they are faced with and due to the fact that the Federal Court of Justice held that the establishment of an obvious infringement suffices to guarantee a fair balance of the fundamental rights involved and to prevent unfounded claims.[1824] As regards the latter, this would mean that the court would have to thoroughly assess the obviousness of an infringement in summary proceedings, which is regularly not the case. Hence, there is a strong presumption that the German courts do not satisfy the condition for a fair balancing of rights – especially since this would not be practicable for them when they are faced with mass volume requests that contain hundreds of IP addresses each.

A further reason for the reluctance to conduct a proportionality test is, that disclosure is commonly applied for in proceedings for interim measures. Under these proceedings, it is sufficient that the applicant makes a credible claim.[1825] This means that there will be no assessment of the evidence, for example on the reliability of logging software that has been used. Whether the methods of data collecting are comprehensible and the software that is used is reliable, is not questioned. Instead it is sufficient that the applicant gives a statutory declaration that his methods of data collecting are validated.[1826] Validated in that respect does not mean approved by an independent body, it rather means that the applicant declares that the software is reliable. Under these circumstances it is questionable how a fair balance can be struck between the contravening interests since the rights-holder basically approves his own methods of data collecting, which he does not disclose and which are not questioned by the court. Considering that a disclosure order will interfere with privacy rights of individuals, a proportionate interference can only exist, where it is established that an infringement has taken place.

1824 BGH, Decision of 19.04.2012 – 1 ZB 80/11, Neue Juristische Wochenschrift 2012, 2958 with annotation by Karl-Heinz Ladeur.

1825 See Thomas Dreier in: Thomas Dreier/Gernot Schulze, *Urheberrechtsgesetz* (4th ed. 2013), § 101 *UrhG*, para. 28.

1826 *Ibid.*

In the UK, the courts will regularly conduct a more thorough assessment and balance the rights of the concerned parties in detail. In the *Golden Eye* case, the High court set forth, that when considering the proportionality of the order sought, a court needs to take into account the terms of the draft cease and desist letter. The intended defendants must not be given a wrong impression about what the Court decided when it made the order or why. In particular, should the order not be worded in such a way as to cause the intended defendants unnecessary anxiety or distress.[1827] Although a court would not usually supervise pre-action correspondence, the draft order requires the letter of claim to be in the form as handed in with the application.[1828] The practice of ACS:Law indicates that it is appropriate for the court that is concerned with the Norwich Pharmacal request to consider the terms of the draft letter of claim.[1829] In this respect, it was held appropriate for the court to consider the impact of the letter of claim upon ordinary consumers. Accordingly, UK courts will put a lot of weight on the interests of the to-be-identified recipients of the cease and desist letters and will also ensure that information is only disclosed when the letter before claim does not amount to unnecessary distress. At the same time, it is guaranteed that the rights-holder has a chance to be compensated for the wrongful act.

The principle of proportionality is thus observed in the UK. In Germany, the situation is slightly different: whereas the statutory provision pays due regard to the contravening interests, there seems to be a deficit in the application of that provision, which needs to be addressed by the judiciary. It seems obvious that a proportionality test is not conducted in proceedings for interim measures within which disclosure is commonly ordered.

In determining under which circumstances a disclosure order would be proportionate in Germany, it needs to be taken into account, that other than in the UK, a German Internet access subscriber may be liable as a Störer – a concept that does not exist in the UK.

As it is not possible to determine the scope of liability prior to identification of the subscriber and an analysis of his defence, German courts could either require rights-holders to submit a draft of their cease and

---

1827 *Golden Eye (International) Ltd and others v Telefonica UK Ltd, Consumer Focus intervening* [2012] EWHC 723 (Ch), para. 121.

1828 *Ibid*, para. 123.

1829 *Ibid.*

desist letters or examine the alleged infringement in more detail. Requiring an analysis of the draft cease and desist letter would amount to a supervision of pre-action correspondence, which would be quite far-reaching. To be able to assess the proportionality of an order, it could rather be sufficient to provide the court with an estimate of the damage that has been caused. This would however only rule out bagatelle claims being made and would encourage rights-holders to provide high estimates. The Redtube case has shown, that the crux is rather the establishment of the infringement as such. Instead of only claiming that from a specific IP address at a given time via client xy an infringement has been committed, the rights-holders should be required to provide more details about the evidence that they have collected. In some cases of BitTorrent peer-to-peer file-sharing, they may only have evidence about a small part of a work being uploaded by a user. The courts addressed need to look at the evidence in more detail, even if information requests are dealt with in summary proceedings. Only when they are convinced that an infringement has taken place that goes beyond a mere bagatelle infringement, they could be satisfied that a fair balance is struck between the contravening interests. It is understood, that it will be necessary to define "bagatelle" infringement, but in this regard, the courts will also need to take into account the overall circumstances of the case. For instance, insofar as copyright infringements outside of peer-to-peer networks are committed, such as replication of images on websites or a video where someone mimes to a song that has been uploaded onto YouTube, the court could assess whether the rights-holder has also sought to have the infringing file removed simultaneously or prior to filing for disclosure. Such a behaviour could support the seriousness of the rights-holder to pursue his claim. As was seen in Redtube, no such initiative was taken by the rights-holders, and their interest in the cessation of an infringement was thus questionable.

This being said, disclosure orders are not per see disproportionate. In order for the interference with the privacy rights of the intended defendants to be justified, the court that assess the disclosure requests will need to strike a fair balance between the interests concerned by assessing the evidence provided and the seriousness of the rights-holders to pursue their claims. A fair balance does not require a supervision of the pre-action correspondence.

cc) Right to Fair Trial of Alleged Infringers

The right to fair trial plays a role where the subscriber of an Internet access service, that has been used to infringe copyright, is being sued and carries the burden of proof, that he himself has not committed the infringement. It is difficult for a subscriber to prove that he has not infringed copyright. In the light of the aforementioned case law from Germany, an alibi, i.e. proof that he himself did not have access to the Internet access service in question would not suffice as long as he cannot prove that no third party whom he allowed to use the connection committed the infringement. Even if the subscriber was absent at the time of the infringement, and no one else had access to the service in question, he would still need to prove that his router was secured adequately. Often, the subscriber will not succeed in providing the required evidence for various reasons, for instance that he may have no memory of where he had been at the time of the infringement. Further, he may not escape disturber liability even if he has instructed his children that they should not infringe copyright. Thus, although he may be innocent, he may not be able to succeed in providing satisfying evidence. This is particularly likely in cases, where IP addresses have been logged incorrectly.

The alleged infringer must have access to information about the logging of IP addresses by the rights-holder. As usually the subscriber will have to prove that he has not himself committed an infringement, he has to rely on the evidence of the claimant in order to prepare his defence – he may for instance argue, that the software used was not reliable, or that human error occurred when analysing the data harvested. Currently, rights-holders, or more precisely the specialised agencies collecting evidence on their behalf, keep relatively quiet when it comes to the functioning of their harvesting software. In the German RedTube case, the rights-holders presented an expert statement to the court, which did not refer to the functioning as such, but to tests proving the reliability of the logging software. It was not revealed how they could succeed in logging the data in the first place. The court however was satisfied with the evidence and granted a disclosure order. If they were also satisfied with such evidence in the main proceedings, this could interfere with subscriber's right to defend himself as for this he has to know exactly how the harvesting system in place worked. For him or an expert appointed by him, it is necessary to understand how evidence was gathered if he believes that an error has occurred. If rights-holder were not asked to present more details on their evidence gathering methods, this would interfere with the defendant's right to fair trial, because, under Article 6(1) of the *ECHR*, civil proceedings must be adversarial, meaning that the parties must have the opportunity not only to make known any evidence needed for their claims to succeed, but also to have knowledge of, and comment on, all evidence filed by the opposing party.[1830] A fair balance can otherwise not be achieved, considering that there is regularly a reversal of the burden of proof upon the subscriber, meaning that he will have to rebut the presumption that he has committed the infringement.

One may also need to consider whether or not access providers should be obliged to retain data that they have disclosed for a certain period in order to allow subscribers to access this data when preparing their defence in copyright infringement proceedings. As access providers will regularly delete the data once they have disclosed it, the subscriber will not be able to check whether for example human error has occurred when the data was transmitted.

As of today, it cannot be concluded that courts are reluctant to pay due regard to the fair trial principle in copyright infringement proceedings. However, a lack of understanding of technology, and a lack of questioning digital evidence as could be witnessed in the disclosure proceedings in the *Redtube* case pose a threat to these rights.

Finally, access to judicial review must not be overly complicated or expensive in order to sufficiently protect the defendants.

d) Achieving a Fair Balance of the Contravening Interests

First of all, the civil pre-litigation settlement does not raise as much concerns as the graduated response schemes. There are basically two reasons for this: the subscriber of an Internet access may not be subject to sanctions such as disconnection orders, and not private party or state authority will keep records of infringers. Thus, when it comes to intereferences with fundamental rigths, questions primarily arise with regard to the disclosure of personal data to rights-holders by the access providers.

1830 ECtHR, *Komanicky v Slovakia*, Judgment of 04.06.2002 – Application no. 40437/07, para. 46.

As outlined before, the *IPR Enforcement Directive* provides for minimum standards and Member States are free to provide for enforcement measures as well as information rights that go beyond those standards. While the European legal framework does not preclude Member States from imposing an obligation to disclose to private third parties personal data relating to Internet traffic in order to provide them with the necessary information to pursue civil actions for copyright infringement, Community law also does not require Member States to lay down an obligation to disclose personal data in order to ensure effective protection of copyright in the context of civil proceedings.[1831] Until the judgement in *Promusicae*, there had been a lack of legal certainty regarding the extent to which personal data may be disclosed for the enforcement of private rights. National data protection authorities had reached different conclusions on the conditions under which parties may process IP addresses for enforcement purposes.[1832]

The *IPR Enforcement Directive* does even not preclude Member States from introducing information rights against third parties where the infringement in question does not amount to commercial scale.[1833] With regard to the right to information, this is explicitly clarified in Recital 14.[1834]

1831 In Promusicae, the CJEU has answered the question whether the *E-Privacy Directive* precludes Member States from laying down, with a view to ensuring effective protection of copyright, an obligation to communicate personal data which enables a copyright-holder to bring civil proceedings. The CJEU concluded that Article 15(1) of the *E-Privacy Directive* in conjunction with Article 13 of the *Data Protection Directive* does not preclude Member States from laying down an obligation to disclose personal data in the context of civil proceedings. When introducing such an obligation Member States are bound to allow a fair balance to be struck between the various fundamental rights involved (para. 54).

1832 Cf. Christoph Kuner, *Data Protection and Rights Protection on the Internet: The Promusicae Judgment of the European Court of Justice,* European Intellectual Property Review 2008, Issue 5, 199, 200.

1833 Michel Walter/Dominik Göbel, in: Michel Walter/Silke von Lewinski, *European Copyright Law* (2010), para. 13.8.16. This view is not shared by the German Governement see Deutscher Bundestag, *Bundestagsdrucksache 16/5048*, p. 65.

1834 Recital 14 states that the measures provided for in inter alia Article 8(1) need to be applied only in respect of acts carried out on a commercial scale, but Member States are free to apply those measures also in respect of other acts. Acts carried out on a commercial scale are those carried out for direct or indirect eco-

Due to the intrusive nature of information requests, Article 8(1) of the *IPR Enforcement Directive* sets forth that any such obligation has to respect certain conditions.

In that respect the proportionality of the interference of the rights of the subjects to an information request are essential. The subscribers of an Internet access service must not be disproportionately affected. As has been outlined above, the main safeguard is the judicial oversight over any disclosure. For data protection reasons, disclosure would either require the consent of the data subject, or a court order. The court order in itself must be proportionate, and thus, not only the law providing for the information disclosure but also the application of that law must pay due regard to the rights and interests of the parties concerned. This assessment is key to proceedings for disclosure in the UK. The court will not only examine the claim that has been made by the rights-holder, but also look at how they wish to enforce their rights. This procedure departs fundamentally from the German approach, where it will be sufficient for the rights-holder to prove that an infringement has taken place. By taking the legitimate interests of the intended defendants into consideration, a UK court is likely to come to a different conclusion in a number of cases. First of all, the court will exmine the wording of the cease and desist letter in order to rule out that the intended defendant will be faced with unfounded allegations, and put under pressure. This approach clearly intends to prevent an establishing of a system of cease and desist letters similar to the one in Germany. The supervision of pre-action correspondence seems however to be too far-reaching. While it is understandable that the intended defendants shall not be exposed to unfounded claims, the supervision of this correspondence is not feasible when large numbers of letters are being sent out. The sending out of large numbers of unfounded claims should rather be subject to proceedings before the respective lawyers' tribunal. As regards the content of the cease and desist letters, the German legislator recognised that this may potentially be threatening and causing distress, and thus passed the *Gesetz gegen unseriöse Geschäftspraktiken,* which requires first of all, that any claims for compensation must be detailed. Further, it limits the maximum amount that can be claimed for lawyer's fees, and provides for a right to compensation of the costs that occurred for consulting a lawyer

nomic or commercial advantage; this would normally exclude acts carried out by end consumers acting in good faith.

in case of unfounded claims. By ensuring that no exaggerated costs can be claimed, and by providing a deterrent for unfounded claims, safeguards are provided that subscribers shall not be faced with unfounded allegations. Thus, the *UrhG* in itself makes a supervision of pre-action correspondence unnecessary. Accordingly, where the law provides safeguards against unfounded and exaggerated claims, the rights of the not yet identified defendants are not disproportionately affected by a disclosure order.

Third Chapter: Content- or Intermediary-Targeted Responses

A. Online Intermediaries as the Addressees of Enforcement Measures

I. The Idea of Enforcement via Online Intermediaries

It has been established that consumers are increasingly consuming media and entertainment online. While two decades ago, consumers would go to a record store to purchase music CDs or video tapes, they now either buy such content online, or consume it directly online via streams on platforms such as Amazon or Netflix. Whilst consumer demand for easy access to attractive content that can be played on the various digital devices that they possess grows, the availability of offers responding to that demand also increases. The creative industries clearly seek to capitalise on this demand.[1835] As already outlined in the First Chapter, Napster was the first successful online music database – albeit the fact that it infringed copyright. So from the start, lawful services had to compete with services that enable users to share or access content unlawfully. With increased broadband capacity, high quality like HD in movies is increasingly available. Other than with peer-to-peer networks, services that are used to disseminate unauthorised copies are not per se free of charge. Many such services employ freemium models, where users may access a limited amount of data for free, and upon paying a subscription can bypass waiting lines and receives an increased download rata. Often, it becomes difficult for users to distinguish unlawful services or services that are unlawfully used from their lawful competitors.

In addition, third party operators may collect information about torrent files and provide users with link directories that allows them to find copies of the desired content on the worldwide web.

1835 Ofcom, *'Site blocking' to reduce online copyright infringement: A review of sections 17 and 18 of the Digital Economy Act* (27.05.2011), p. 12.

Recently, there has been an increase in lawsuits against intermediaries for aiding and abetting or in some other way facilitating copyright infringements.[1836]

Awareness has been raised that going against end-users may not present the ideal solution to combat mass-scale copyright infringements on the Internet. From a public relations point of view, volume litigation against end-users has become publicly regarded as disproportionate, fraudulent, and, due to the threatening nature of some warnings, as a modern form of blackmailing. For some artists, it took its toll on their popularity and reputation.[1837] In addition, modern third generation peer-to-peer technology with advanced security, as noted above, makes it more difficult for rights-holders to identify infringers and infringements. With the exception of Germany, rights-holders may refrain from litigation against individual users because litigation may be too lengthy and too expensive with a low likelihood of being compensated at the end and difficulties in successfully

---

1836 For example in Germany: OLG Hamburg, Decision of 30.09.2009 – 5 U 111/08 (*Sharehoster II – Rapidshare*), MultiMedia und Recht 2010, 51; OLG Hamburg, Decision of 02.07.2008 – 5 U 73/07 (*Sharehoster I – Rapidshare*), MultiMedia und Recht 2008, 823; OLG Hamburg, Decision of 14.01.2009 – 5 U 113/07 (*Usenet I – Spring nicht*), MultiMedia und Recht 2009, 631; OLG Hamburg, Decision of 28.01.2009 – 5 U 255/07 (*Alphaload*), MultiMedia und Recht 2009, 405; OLG Düsseldorf, Decision of 27.04.2010 – I-20 U 166/09 (*Rapidshare – An American Crime et al*), MultiMedia und Recht 2010, 483; OLG Düsseldorf, Decision of 21.12.2010 – I-20 U 59/10 (*Rapidshare III – Alone in the Dark*), MultiMedia und Recht 2011, 250; OLG Köln, Decision of 21.09.2007 – 6 U 86/07 (*Haftung eines Sharehoster-Dienstes*), MultiMedia und Recht 2007, 786; OLG Hamburg, Decision of 14.03.2012 – 5 U 87/09 (*GEMA v Rapidshare*), MultiMedia und Recht 2012, 393; in the Netherlands: RB Den Haag, Decision of 24 October 2012 (*BREIN v XS Networks*); RB 's Gravenhage, Decision of 11.01. 2012 (*BREIN v Ziggo and XS4ALL*); RB s'Gravenhage, Decision of 10.05.2012 (*Blocking of The Pirate Bay: BREIN v providers*); in Sweden: Svea Hovrätt, Decision of 26.11.2010 – file no. B 4041-09 (*The Pirate Bay*); in Belgium: Enigmax, *Belgian ISPs ordered to block The Pirate Bay*, TorrentFreak (04.10.2011).

1837 The German rap artist Bushido has also been nicknamed the "Abmahnrapper" for being particularly active in the field of sending out *Abmahnungen*, see Peter Mühlbauer, *Die Geister, die er rief...*, Heise online (25.03.2010). As regards the scale of Abmahnungen see Katrin Löhr, *Skandal-Rapper fordert Ablasszahlung – Vorwurf Musik-Klau! So jagt Bushido seine Fans*, Bild (17.04.2010).

proving an infringement to the required standard.[1838] Even the French graduated response scheme which does not require the identification of the actual infringer does not satisfy a cost-benefit-calculation: infringements are still taking place, while the rights-holders have to bear the costs for identifying infringements.

Focussing on end-users also distracts attention from pursuing large scale commercial infringers. The majority of right-holders perceive restraining infringements committed for profit as more important than doing so for non-profit infringements by end-users.[1839] Speaking of commercial infringers, this does not only refer to notorious pirate sites that generate profits from advertisements, but also includes the providers of websites with user-generated content. File-hosting services or streaming sites such as YouTube are also being used to distribute copyrighted works without authorisation. The more users are attracted by these websites, the more revenues may be generated from advertisements, meaning that attractive content can be essential for the business model. When self-regulation fails and widespread unauthorised postings of copyrighted content is not (successfully) policed, the responsibility of these service providers needs to be looked at.

In addition, the main intentions of most copyright holders for instituting civil law proceedings concerning intellectual property rights infringements can be identified as: stopping the infringing activity and preventing future infringements of the same kind.[1840]

The best addressee to achieve these intentions has been identified as those hosting the infringing content or facilitating access to it. The lawsuits against the Pirate Bay are a good example of all this. Simply speaking, the Pirate Bay can be compared to a bulletin board,[1841] where magnet links are posted that serve as reference resources for content that is available via peer-to-peer networks.[1842] Although the operators of the Pirate Bay argued before the Swedish courts that the Pirate Bay is merely a

---

1838 European Commission, *Synthesis of the responses „Civil enforcement of intellectual property rights: public consultation on the efficiency of proceedings and accessibility of measures"* (July 2013), p. 7.

1839 *Ibid.*

1840 *Ibid.*

1841 Stefan Larsson, *Metaphors, law and digital phenomena: the Swedish pirate bay court case*, International Journal of Law and Information Technology 2013, Vol. 21 No. 4, 354, 370 with further references.

1842 Before switching to magnet links in 2012, the Pirate Bay provided .torrent files.

transmission service and that they were doing nothing different than search engines like Google, they were convicted.[1843] Irrespective to the convictions, the Pirate Bay site is still up regardless of the convictions of its founders,[1844] having moved its servers to other countries including Iceland and the Caribbean island of St. Martin to avoid police action.[1845] Physically closing down the Pirate Bay is been proving difficult, and albeit the conviction of its founders and original operators, the website is still up and running.[1846]

1843 Svea Hovrätt, Decision of 26.11.2010 – file no. B 4041-09 (*The Pirate Bay*). According to the Court and contrary to the common public perception, the Pirate Bay operators were not altruistic anarchists, but generating a decent amount of revenues from advertisements on the website. The Court had no problem to establish actual knowledge of copyright infringements on behalf of the operators since they posted take down letters sent in by copyright owners on the Pirate Bay website to ridicule. For an analysis of the decision see, Stefan Larsson, *Metaphors, law and digital phenomena: the Swedish pirate bay court case*, International Journal of Law and Information Technology 2013, Vol. 21 No. 4, 354–379.

1844 Stefan Larsson, *Metaphors, law and digital phenomena: the Swedish pirate bay court case*, International Journal of Law and Information Technology 2013, Vol. 21 No. 4, 354, 358.

1845 Ryan W. Neal, *Pirates of the Caribbean: The Pirate Bay moves to island of St. Martin,* International Business Times (30.04.2013). At one point, The Pirate Bay operators discussed buying an island just offshore the British coast ("Sealand"), and even considered munting their servers in space on a satellite. See Ernesto, *Pirate parties plan to shoot torrent site into orbit* , TorrentFreak (20.10.2010). Following, an odyssey of domain changes, Pirate Bay recently returned to Sweden, see Cyrus Farivar, *After sailing the domain name seas, Pirate Bay returns to Sweden*, ars technica (19.12.2013).

1846 Although the operators of the Pirate Bay were convicted in their home country Sweden for copyright infringements in 2010, the website is still being in operation. According to the Rechtbank s'Gravenhage in its the Pirate Bay decision, as of 2012, the Pirate Bay still was the world largest indexing and one of the most visited websites. At the time of the decision the website contained 4.3 million links of which at least 90 % referred to content that had been made available without authorisation of the right holders (see RB s'Gravenhage, Decision of 10.05.2012 (*Blocking of The Pirate Bay: BREIN v providers*), paras. 2.12 et seq,. As regards the struggle of rights-holders to block access to the Pirate Bay in the Netherlands, see Arno R. Lodder/Nicole S. van der Meulen, *Evaluation of the role of access providers, Discussion of Dutch Pirate Bay case law and introducing principles on directness, effectiveness, costs, relevance, and time*, Journal of Intellectual Property, Information Technology and Electronic Commerce Law 2013, Vol. 4 Issue 2, 130–141.

Like the Pirate Bay, pirate websites in general set themselves up out of jurisdiction, some cloak themselves in anonymity, others refuse to engage with legal processes. Ultimately, most of the true pirate sites, meaning that they are obviously dedicated to piracy, make very unattractive targets for litigation.[1847] Hence, rights-holders are increasingly seeking Internet service provider cooperation. This cooperation can either achieved by voluntary agreement, or through court orders.

While the measures presented in the first part of this research study focus on the individual user that disseminates an unauthorised copy of a copyrighted work, this part will look at measures that target the copyright infringing content as such. There have been numerous approaches to remove illegal materials from the web instead of investing a lot of time and effort to go for small scale infringers. While peer-to-peer networks have long been deemed to be the centre of large scale copyright infringement, a new area of online copyright infringement had long begun. File-hosting services like Megaupload.com or Rapidshare no longer turn downloaders at the same time into uploaders and thus, make it difficult to identify infringers. Also, the original uploader may be difficult to identify. Hence, rights-holders seek ways to go for the hosting services as such, or seek the blocking of access to the service. The latter is also sought for websites that are vital to gain access to the infringing materials such as link directories or torrent sites.

This being said, numerous lawsuits in the recent past were targeted against major file-hosting services, the entities that, from the position of the rights-holders, provide the means for the unauthorised dissemination of works. While peer-to-peer file-sharing becomes for some users less attractive because they get to understand that they can easily be detected and may be sanctioned, file-hosting services are gaining popularity.[1848] This shall not mean, that peer-to-peer file-sharing has disappeared – BitTorrent is still popular, but even non-IT literate users are becoming more and more sensitive about the risks involved. For both, file-hosting services as well as BitTorrent networks, access to files depends on links about the location being disseminated.

1847 See Darren Meale, *Premier League 1, Internet pirates 0: sports streaming website the latest to be blocked*, Journal of Intellectual Property Law & Practice 2013, Vol. 8 No. 11, 821.

1848 Jan Mölleken, *Filehoster: Hehler oder Helfer*, Der Spiegel online (14.09.2010).

Rights-holders are thus not only seeking to have access blocked to link directories but also to torrent trackers. In addition, with for instance 14 million Internet connectable TVs being sold in Germany alone until December 2013,[1849] and smart devices increasingly becoming standard, online streaming is posing a new threat to rights-holders. Although smart TVs are unlikely to have pirate streaming apps pre-installed, installation of new apps is easy. While it was previously necessary to connect a PC to a TV in order to watch downloaded copies or streams on TV, smart TVs allow even non-tech savvy consumers to watch streams.

What can be witnessed with regard to file-hosting services, torrent sites and streaming is, that rights-holders return to Internet service providers as the natural gatekeepers to the Internet.[1850] Accessing the Internet and communicating online is impossible without them. They are the chokepoints for communication and as such have access to third party information. This makes them an attractive target for Internet regulation, – and with regard to this research – an attractive target for the enforcement of copyright.[1851]

In their comments on the 2010 European Commission report on the application of the *Enforcement Directive*, rights-holders and collecting societies thus demanded a greater involvement of access providers and other intermediaries, identifying them as key actors in combating intellectual property infringements in the digital world.[1852] One of the reasons identified in the comments was the issue of anonymity of users and the perceived lack of verification, by Internet service providers, of information provided by subscribers/customers, both of which were claimed to facilitate infringements these customers and thus and hinder enforcement.[1853]

1849 Markus Brauck/Isabell Hülsen/Alexander Kühn/Ann-Kathrin Nezik, *Was glotzen Sie so?*, Der Spiegel online (13.01.2014).

1850 Uta Kohl, *The rise and rise of online intermediaries in the governance of the Internet and beyond – connectivity intermediaries,* International Review of Law, Computers & Technology 2012, Vol. 26 Issue 2–3, 185, 188.

1851 *Ibid.*

1852 European Commission, Synthesis of comments on the Commission Report on the application of Directive 2004/48/EC of the European Parliament and the Council of 29.04.2004 on the enforcement of intellectual property rights (July 2011), COM(2010) 779 final, p. 4.

1853 *Ibid*, p. 5.

Intermediaries are seen in the position to not only put an end to persisting infringements but also to prevent further infringements taking place.[1854] Taking intermediaries into responsibility has also been referred to as "taming the Internet through the use of online intermediaries as a regulatory tool".[1855] *Kohl* describes the multiple intermediary layers as bringing "the utopia of a perfect panopticon applied to society generally much closer to reality".[1856] Hypothetically, in this panopticon "the government is the omniscient and omipotent actor".[1857] Figuratively speaking, in this environment, private actors ask governments to protect their property rights by using online intermediaries as guardsmen.[1858] Considering that the Chinese government actually obliges intermediaries to block certain content, often referred to as the Great Firewall of China, this scenario is not everywhere hypothetical. Surveillance of online communication for other reasons, for instance the fight against serious crime or terrorism, is at least tolerated by governments even in the Western hemisphere. However, having the infrastructure for total surveillance does not mean that it will be allowed to use it for that purposes, especially with regard to property rights of third parties. In the EU, strict rules already apply when it comes to monitoring systems for governmental purposes, leaving not much room for monitoring put in place for private interests. Enforcement of private rights remains private and governments so far refrain from requiring online intermediaries to monitor third party content for copyright infringing materials. This been said, when it comes to public interests such as the fight against child pornography, online intermediaries are being asked to scan content they transmit. Having such infrastructure in place, raises the interests of private actors to "piggy-back" on these monitoring schemes.[1859] One example of such "piggy-backing", that will be outlined

---

1854 In their comments on the Commission Report on the application of the *Enforcement Directive*, right holders and collecting societies criticised the shortcomings of the *Enforcement Directive* as transposed into national law especially in terms of how it frames the role of intermediaries as well as its perceived failure to stem the increase in online copyright infringements. See *ibid*, p. 4.

1855 Uta Kohl, *The rise and rise of online intermediaries in the governance of the Internet and beyond – connectivity intermediaries,* International Review of Law, Computers & Technology 2012, Vol. 26 Issue 2–3, 185.

1856 *Ibid*, 188.

1857 *Ibid.*

1858 Cf. *ibid.*

1859 *Ibid.*

in this Chapter, is the CleanFeed software employed by the Internet Watch Foundation in the UK to filter out child pornography. This software is lately also being used to block access to obnoxious copyright infringing websites. Again, this was not imposed by the government but by the judiciary, confirming previous fears that child pornography will be a test case for further filtering.

With the online intermediaries as omnipotent guardsmen, the intention to address the intermediary rather than the primary wrongdoer is however clear: those with the power to not only block infringing materials but also prevent them from happing in the first place are addressed as being in the best position to enforce third party property rights.

As early as 1991, German universities for instance started blocking access to several Usenet groups which allegedly were misused for the consumption of pornography by University staff.[1860] Although this was a pure private and voluntary initiative, it shows that even in the early days of the Internet, where the Internet was not such a mass phenomenon as of today, individuals were seeking ways to ban unwanted content from the Internet via the gatekeepers. With regard to copyright infringing content on the Internet, we will see that nowadays the preferred course of action lays in suing host providers and access providers in order to obtain injunctions ordering them to block specific content, or as regards access providers, to block access to third party websites.

II. The Services and Activities of Online Intermediaries that Are Targeted: Scope, Specific Functioning and Consequences

When enforcement against intermediaries is discussed, this encompasses not only providers that host infringing contents; moreover, there are complementary services such as link directories and indexing websites that accommodate file-sharing and copyright infringements. The way how they interact or relate to each other will be outlined in the following. In that context, also the relevance of indexing sites in relation to peer-to-peer networks will be addressed. Parallel to the rise in popularity of file-hosting services, streaming is increasingly used for the consumption of copyright-

1860 The actual content blocking ended in special interest groups being blocked, that did not engage in the dissemination of pornography but served as discussion fora for sexual minorities.

ed works. In this regard, youTube obviously has long been used by consumers to upload protected works without authorisation – however, youTube as such has never been solely dedicated to on-demand streaming of protected works. Lately, various platforms have appeared that are committed to the latter. Due to their popularity, streaming technology and its role in copyright infringements will also be outlined in brief.

1. File-Hosting Services, Indexing Sites and Link Directories

With technological progress the cost of data storage declined. This factor combined with the increasing use of the web as the most important and central part of the Internet for most users have led to the appearance and increasing use of file-hosting services : centralised file storage services to which users can upload materials for access by themselves or others. [1861] There are numerous services of this kind, which also have become widely known as "one-click hosters", "sharehosters" or "cyberlockers",[1862] with the most prominent being Megaupload, 4Shared and Rapidshare.

Their use requires little technical expertise. In order to store or access content on a file-hosting service, users only need a web browser – whereas with Peer-to-peer file-sharing, users need to run peer-to-peer programmes like BitTorrent or eMule. On high bandwith connections, a download from a file-hosting service can be quicker than peer-to-peer file-sharing.[1863] Another advantage for users is, that it is more anonymous than peer-to-peer file-sharing. Users can freely upload any material to such sites. They are then provided with a link by which anyone in possession of that link can access the content.

Most file-hosting services offer a basic service for free and charge users for premium accounts. Often, when the service is offered free of charge, content remains on the service for a limited period only. It may also only be downloaded a certain number of times.[1864] Most service providers allow downloads only after a waiting period of a minute or so while the

---

1861 Envisional, Technical Report: An Estimate of Infringing Use of the Internet (2011), p. 15.

1862 Jan Mölleken, *Filehoster: Hehler oder Helfer*, Der Spiegel online (14.09.2010).

1863 *Ibid.*

1864 *Ibid.*

potential downloader is presented with various advertisements.[1865] Usually, download speeds are limited unless a premium account is purchased that often allows downloads at speeds which may be as fast as the user's broadband capacity. Premium subscribers[1866] may store content for longer and – more importantly for downloaders – may download instantly. While basic users are often granted limited traffic, premium subscribers have unlimited traffic.[1867]

Significantly, the majority of file-hosting services do not allow the content they store to be searched in the same manner as a .torrent file portal: they do not provide for queries for a specific file by typing a search term into a search engine. Searching for the latest Sherlock Holmes film by typing its title into a box is thus not possible. A potential downloader needs to be provided with the hyperlink that was given to the uploader in order to be able to access a particular file.

One may argue that the fact that the file-hosting services do not provide for a search of the files they store, limits the attraction of these sites for piracy purposes. However, this is not the case. Almost parallel to the raise of file hosting services, hundreds of third-party file-hosting indexing sites and link sites, such as NewzBin.com or serienjunkies.org, have appeared on the scene. They basically provide inventories of available files. As many files are uploaded under cryptic names, the indexing sites also unlock these and thus play an important role.[1868]

In practice, many users that uploaded a file to a file-hosting service, subsequently post the link to that file on one of the many indexing sites, bulletin boards or forums directed to potential downloaders. Once a link is published, any user may click to obtain the material. There are notorious indexing sites that arrange and sort the links and also allow for searches within their lists. Alternatively, links are posted on bulletin boards or notorious online forums.

While these indexes refer to content stored on file-hosting services, there are also sites dedicated to search for content in peer-to-peer networks. While previously these sites offered .torrent files for download,

---

1865 *Ibid.*

1866 Premium membership usually costs about EUR 10 per month. See for example https://rapidshare.com/#!buyrapids (last accessed on 12.01.2013).

1867 See for example *ibid.*

1868 See European Parliament, DG for Internal Policies, Policy Department C: Citizens' Rights and Constitutional Affairs, *File Sharing* (2011), p. 6.

many of them have now switched to providing magnet links to resources available for download via peer-to-peer networks. [1869] When magnet links are opened in a BitTorrent client, they begin downloading the desired content. In contrast to BitTorrent files, which contain metadata necessary to download the data files from other peers (and require a torrent client to calculate a torrent hash based on the file it relates to, and seek the addresses of peers from a tracker before connecting to those peers), magnet links point to a particular file based on the hash value of its contents.[1870] With the torrent hash, clients immediately seek the addresses of peers and connect to them to download first the torrent file, and then the desired content.[1871] The Pirate Bay is probably the most famous and world largest website that provides magnet links to facilitate peer-to-peer file-sharing using the BitTorrent protocol.[1872] The platform has undergone a change from its early days, where it also offered torrent files.[1873] Usually the indexing site features a browse function that enables users to see what is available in different categories, like movie files, games or music, with sub-categories like music genres.

1869 The Magnet Unified Resource Identifier (URI) scheme is a standard defining a URI scheme for Magnet links, which mainly refer to resources available for download via peer-to-peer networks. The most common use of Magnet URIs is to point to a particular file based on the hash value of its contents, producing a unique identifier for the file, similar to an ISBN or catalogue number. The Pirate Bay switched for instance in 2012 from –torrent files to magnet links.

1870 See Ernesto, *BitTorrent's Future? DHT, PEX and magnet Links explained,* Torrentfreak.com (20.11.2009).

1871 See *Ibid.*

1872 According to the Rechtbank s'Gravenhage in it's the Pirate Bay decision, The Pirate Bay is currently the world largest indexing and one of the most visited websites. At the time of the decision the website contained 4.3 million links of which at least 90 % referred to content that had been made available without authorisation of the right holders (see RB s'Gravenhage, Decision of 10.05.2012 *[Blocking of The Pirate Bay: BREIN v providers]*, paras. 2.12 et seq.).

1873 Since 29.02.2012, The Pirate Bay like most other indexing sites, no longer offers torrent files, and instead provides only magnet links. The site commented: "Not having torrents will be a bit cheaper for us but it will also make it harder for our common enemies to stop us". See Ernesto, *The Pirate Bay, Now without torrents,* TorrentFreak (28.02.2012).

As magnet link providers and file-hosting services neither store the IP addresses of uploaders nor those of downloaders,[1874] it is difficult for right holders to identify copyright infringers. For this particular reason, many right holders have now turned to suing the service providers, or try to obtain orders whereby access providers have to block access to notorious websites.

2. Streaming

During the past years, streaming has become a standard technology for the online distribution of digital works.[1875] Video streaming is being used by many broadcasting networks such as for example the BBC in the UK or ARD and ZDF in Germany, or social media sites like YouTube. Similarly, audio streaming is used for transmission of radio shows via the web and mere audio streaming sites like for instance Spotify are increasingly becoming available. According to a study by the German Bundesverband Informationswirtschaft, Telekommunikation und neue Medien (Bitkom), more than 4.5 million Germans used music streaming platforms regularly by July 2012.[1876]

The popularity with streaming services came along with increased bandwidth and flatrate plans being available to many customers. In addition, TV sets with smart TV functions allow immediate connection to the Internet via Wi-Fi. Pre-installed apps facilitate access to online content. There clearly is a trend to make media content available at anytime and anywhere in high quality. While music streaming services like Spotify or Simfy, and video streaming platforms like Amazon Lovefilm or Maxdome offer on-demand access to thousands of copyrighted works legally, there are also platforms that make available creative works without authorisation by the rights-holders. One of the most notorious platforms in that

---

1874 Rolf Schwartmann, Vergleichende Studie über Modelle zur Versendung von Warnhinweisen durch Internet-Zugangsanbieter an Nutzer bei Urheberrechtsverletzungen, p. 37.

1875 Maurizio Borghi, *Chasing copyright infringement in the streaming landscape*, International Review of Intellectual Property and Competition Law 2011, 316–343, 317.

1876 See Bitkom, *Trend zu Musik-Streaming per Internet*, Press release of 10.07.2012.

regard has probably been kino.to, which was shut down and their operators arrested in June 2011.

The notion of streaming refers to a particular method of delivering content to end-users, while the content delivered is a "stream".[1877] During streaming of media content, data is constantly received by and presented to an end-user. The user will need to install a client media player on his computer in order to be able to play the data. As regards the functioning, one first has to distinguish between on-demand streaming and live streaming. Live streams are only available at one time only and enable the user to view or listen to the content in real time.[1878] In this respect, streaming provides an alternative to traditional broadcasting. Therefore much of the discussion on the legality of the provision of live streams revolves around the question whether the providers of live streams of television programmes are retransmitting television for which as an act of communication to the public they would need authorisation from the rights-holder.[1879]

Live streams are generally provided by means called true streaming, where the information is sent straight to the end-user's computer or device without saving the file to a hard disk. This kind of transmission is regularly used to cover live events and is only available at one time only. Live streams are regularly multicast, meaning that the content is transmitted to

---

1877 For a more detailed description of the functioning of streaming see Malte Stieper, *Rezeptiver Werkgenuss als rechtmäßige Nutzung*, MultiMedia und Recht 2012, 12–17.

1878 See Maurizio Borghi, *Chasing copyright infringement in the streaming landscape*, International Review of Intellectual Property and Competition Law 2011, 316, 317.

1879 Cf. only the recent judgement of the UK High Court in the TVCatchup case, High Court, *ITV Broadcasting Ltd. et al v TVCatchup Ltd* [2013] EHWC 3638 (CH). In this case the High Court issued an order prohibiting TVCatchup from providing streams to mobile devices of all the claimants' television channels and online streams of selected digital channels. The order followed a preliminary ruling decision by the CJEU in that subject matter. The CJEU had ruled that the concept of 'communication to the public', within the meaning of Article 3(1) of the *InfoSoc Directive*, must be interpreted as meaning that it covers a retransmission of the works included in a terrestrial television broadcast where the retransmission is made by an organisation other than the original broadcaster, by means of an Internet stream made available to the subscribers of that other organisation who may receive that retransmission by logging on to its server, even though those subscribers are within the area of reception of that terrestrial television broadcast and may lawfully receive the broadcast on a television receiver.

multiple users simultaneously from a single source.[1880] Live-Streams can be compared to television or radio broadcasts. The data is transmitted on a constant rate to the user.

In contrast, with on-demand streaming, transmission of the file starts upon request by a user for that user only (unicast).[1881] This allows the user to pause the replay, forward or rewind.[1882] On-demand streaming is the principal method to make videos available on the Internet, and is also used by most music streaming sites that make content available upon request.[1883]

In relation to on-demand streaming, one must differentiate between progressive download and progressive streaming: progressive downloading means that the transmitted data is stored on the hard disk of the user's device. The requested file is sent to the hard disk of the computer or device and then played from that location, both upon request by a user (so-called push technology); the download ends once the entire file has been transferred or the transmission is interrupted by the user.[1884] Whether the copy made on the user's device is only temporary or permanent depends on the software used and its settings. Data that is temporary stored in the browser cache[1885] will be deleted once the browser is being closed or the device is shut down.[1886] Caching may thus be referred to as a temporary storage in the permanent memory, which is not part of the streaming pro-

---

1880 Maurizio Borghi, *Chasing copyright infringement in the streaming landscape*, International Review of Intellectual Property and Competition Law 2011, 316, 318.

1881 This is in contrast to live-streaming, which is multicast, meaning that the content is transmitted to multiple users at the same time.

1882 Malte Stieper, *Rezeptiver Werkgenuss als rechtmäßige Nutzung*, MultiMedia und Recht 2012, 12 et seq.

1883 Maurizio Borghi, *Chasing copyright infringement in the streaming landscape*, International Review of Intellectual Property and Competition Law 2011, 316, 319.

1884 See Ulrich Sieber in: Thomas Hoeren/Ulrich Sieber/Bernd Holznagel, *Handbuch Multimedia-Recht* (36th amended ed. 2013), Teil 1 para. 134.

1885 Usually, cache copies are saved into a hidden folder called "temporary Internet files" on the user's hardware.

1886 Depending on the settings of the operating system, older data may automatically be cancelled to be replaced by

cess but is associated with it for technical reasons.[1887] In contrast, progressive streaming does not require a complete, permanent storage on the user's computer.[1888] Temporary storage takes place within the client buffer[1889] in order to compensate a potential difference between the rate at which data is received and the rate at which it can be processed. The scope of temporary storage depends on the individually set size of the buffer, often storage of two to five seconds is recommended.[1890] Data segments are overwritten once the client programme has read and replayed the segments in order to make available storage space for new data segments. At no time will the entire file be stored on the user´s device.[1891] Consumption of the media content is already possible once a certain amount of data has been transferred, which makes it obsolete to have an entire file stored.

Irrespective of the technology used, streaming must not be confused with traditional download, where data is stored on a permanent memory.[1892] Although some streaming providers may also allow the users to download the content, on-demand streams are generally only saved for a limited amount of time. The buffering process is only necessary in order to overcome jitters and allow a non-interrupted playing of the data.

Similar to peer-to-peer platforms, streaming technology is neutral and not illegal. Moreover, streaming is increasingly being used by rights-holders and there are many legal offers available of which some even are for free.

As such, the distribution of content via streaming platforms is advantageous for rights-holders: user can regularly only consume the media, but do not download the file, so that the rights-holder has more control over further distribution, meaning that users are not able to further disseminate digital copies themselves.

1887 Cf. Maurizio Borghi, *Chasing copyright infringement in the streaming landscape*, International Review of Intellectual Property and Competition Law 2011, 316, 328.

1888 As regards the distinction between buffering and caching see *ibid*, 327.

1889 The buffer can be described as a „waiting room for data to be read by a media player or any other application", see *ibid.*

1890 see Malte Stieper, *Rezeptiver Werkgenuss als rechtmäßige Nutzung*, MultiMedia und Recht 2012, 12, 13.

1891 *Ibid.*

1892 Ulrich Sieber in: Thomas Hoeren/Ulrich Sieber/Bernd Holznagel, *Handbuch Multimedia-Recht* (36th amended ed. 2013), Teil 1 para. 136.

The advantages for users are, that they do not have to wait until a download is completed, but may start playing the content immediately. In addition, they no longer need huge storage capacities and thus only limited resources.[1893]

Websites that offer live and/or on-demand streaming may either themselves host the content. Often – as for example with YouTube – the content is user-generated, meaning that users can upload videos and other materials which are then made available on-demand to consumers. Websites may also only act as user-contributed video directories for television programs and films, and thus act as a portal that directs users to content that is available via streaming.

3. File Hosting and Streaming Websites in Numbers

One of the reasons why file-hosting services and streaming provider saw a massive increase in use recently, in addition to increased bandwidth and an increased number of smart devices being used, is the fact, that these content-sharing models operate different from Peer-to-Peer file-sharing. Users that download a file do not simultaneously offer the file for download, i.e. they do not become a disseminator themselves, and thus are unlikely to become the target of enforcement measures.[1894]

As of April 2012, the file-hosting service 4shared.com is ranked 82 at the global three-month Alexa traffic rank.[1895] As of April 2014, it is still ranked within the 200 most popular websites worldwide. Before the arrest of Megaupload.com's owner, the website was also ranked in the TOP100 Alexa traffic rankings.[1896] A report published in January 2011, claimed

---

1893 Maurizio Borghi, *Chasing copyright infringement in the streaming landscape*, International Review of Intellectual Property and Competition Law 2011, 316, 317.

1894 Jan Mölleken, *Filehoster: Hehler oder Helfer?*, Der Spiegel online (14.09.2010).

1895 4shared.com is thereby more popular than ThePirateBay.se which is – as of April 2012 – not listed within the TOP100 three-month Alexa traffic rankings. Alexa is a leading provider of free, global web metrics and publishes its statistics at Alexa.com.

1896 As regards the arrest of Kim Dotcom see U.S. Department of Justice, *Justice Department Charges Leaders of Megaupload with Widespread Online Copyright Infringement,* Press release of 29.01.2012-

that the 16 largest file-hosting services of that time were among the most popular websites in the world.[1897] In this report, it was also alleged that 4Shared and Megaupload had around 78 million unique users each month.[1898] Currently, Filehostwatch.com lists more than 1,400 file-hosters. Interestingly, (non-cloud-based) file-hosting websites are more popular in Europe than they are in North America.[1899] While most of the previously popular web server-based services have been losing traffic since 2012, cloud –based storage services are on the rise. Again, the fast development of technology means that users shift to more convenient services. Dropbox.com for instance, which offers cloud storage and file synchronisation services, also allows users to share folders with third parties, and is ranked as the 111th most popular website in April 2014.[1900]This may also have to do with the increased use of smartphones and other portable devices, which on the one hand do not have much storage capacity and on the other hand the multitude of devices being used requiring file synchronisation.

Already in 2011, it had been estimated that file-hosters are responsible for at least 5% of all Internet traffic.[1901] This number should have risen by now. More interesting with regard to the traffic, that these services take up, is data that provides information as to the copyrighted works being shared this way. It has been estimated that as of May 2012 80% of all copyright infringements take place via file-hosting services.[1902] The German music industry association for example claims that in Germany file-hosters are the main source for illegal downloads.[1903] However, estimating the amount of copyright infringing content stored on file-hosters is more difficult than with peer-to-peer file-sharing networks as such sites do not

---

1897 Envisional, *Technical Report: An Estimate of Infringing Use of the Internet* (2011), p. 16.

1898 With 78 million unique users, 4Shared and MegaUpload had twice as many users as ThePirateBay. In addition, Rapidshare had 60 million and Hotfile 53 million unique users. *Ibid.*

1899 Envisional, *Technical Report: An Estimate of Infringing Use of the Internet* (2011), p. 46.

1900 See Alexa.com.

1901 Envisional, *Technical Report: An Estimate of Infringing Use of the Internet* (2011), p. 46.

1902 Thomas Darnstädt, *Wem gehören die Gedanken?* Der Spiegel Online (21.05.2012).

1903 GfK Consumer Panel, *Studie zur digitalen Content-Nutzung (DCN-Studie) 2011* (2011).

usually allow stored content to be searched. To check the representative nature of content stored on file-hosters, *Envisional* collected a random sample of 2,000 file-hoster links and determined the type of content and whether it was copyrighted.[1904] Based on their findings they concluded that over 90% of the content was copyrighted material.[1905] However, considering that the sample of file-hoster links collected, i.e. links that provide third parties with the necessary information to access a file, must have been publicly available, the estimates of Envisional are highly questionable. It ignores that consumers may use file-hosters to back up their data, or to share content of which they own the copyright with friends, and thus do not publish the file-hoster link to the general public.

Parallel to file-hosters remaining popular, users are also increasingly using on-demand streaming. As has been outlined above, streaming is popular with smart TVs, allowing users to access the media databases of broadcasters to catch up with TV programmes that they have missed. Apps that can be installed on mobile Internet devices also allow the consumption of TV broadcasts independent from a traditional TV device. Instead of video lending stores, users may now subscribe to video on-demand providers to access the latest blockbusters or their favourite TV series from anywhere at any time and with less costs. Parallel to these developments, they may also access streaming websites that grant access to copyrighted works without the consent of the rights-holders. Famous examples for streaming websites that have been the target of enforcement action by rights-holders are kino.to and Movie4k.to, formerly known as Movie2k.to.[1906] While kino.to also hosted content or at least paid third

1904 Envisional, *Technical Report: An Estimate of Infringing Use of the Internet* (2011), p.17.

1905 *Ibid.*

1906 While kino.to was ultimately shut down in Germany following the arrest of its operators, Movie4k.to was the 202nd most popular website in the world in May 2013. It is a website aggregator acting as a search index for online videos. In May 2013, its predecessor, Movie2k.to, was shut down by the Motion Picture Association of America (MPAA) due to copyright infringement concerns, and morphed into Movie4k.to shortly after. It primarily addresses English and German-speaking users. Following, the blocking of the site by ISPs in the UK and parts of the USA, proxies were used on the original site "movie2k.to" to bypass blocking. How this can be done will be addressed in the following section of this chapter. The website provides a detailing listing of television programs and films, but does not host any content – instead the site acts as a search index for streaming sources. The directory supports user-submitted links by registered

parties to contribute content, movie4k.to rather falls into the category of indexing sites and link directories. As of April 2014, the latter was ranked the 60th most popular website in Germany,[1907] which gives an impression of the popularity of streaming sites in a wider context.

4. The Copyright-Infringing Act

It has already been briefly mentioned that streaming as such is not illegal. However, providing streams of copyrighted works without authorisation by the copyright owner generally infringes the tight to communication to the public as defined by Article 3(1) of the *InfoSoc Directive*.[1908] The provision of a stream is an act of making publicly available that fall under the exclusive rights of the authors . While this seems obvious, the issue had to be clarified in relation to Internet television broadcasting services that make live television programmes of third parties available on the Internet. In this regard, without going into detail, the recent judgements of the CJEU in the Karen Murphy case as well as in the TVCatchup case will be outlined. In the following, a brief analysis will be given on whether end-users that consume unauthorised streams commit a copyright infringement themselves by interfering with the reproduction right of the rights-holders.

a) The Legality of the Provision of File Hosting Services

Like peer-to-peer file-sharing, the provision of file-hosting services is content neutral, but the technology may be used to commit copyright infringements. The possibility that a service is abused by its users does not per se

---

editors, and is thus rather falls into the category of indexing sites and link directories.

1907 Cf. the data on the web-ranking service Alexa of April 2014, accessible via http://www.alexa.com/siteinfo/movie4k.to (last accessed on 17.05.2014).

1908 Article 3 of the *InfoSoc Directive*, headed "Right of communication to the public of works and right of making available to the public other subject-matter", provides in paragraph 2 that "Member States shall provide for the exclusive right to authorise or prohibit the making available to the public, by wire or wireless means, in such a way that members of the public may access them from a place and at a time individually chosen by them: ... (c) for the producers of the first fixations of films, of the original and copies of their films...".

render the service illegitimate, in particular if the operator does not interfere with the content. The border between mere neutrality and an active role in committing infringements are often difficult to determine, and may be blurred. In the second part of this Chapter, this will be addressed in the context of monitoring duties that may arise following notification of a copyright infringement. At this point, it shall be borne in mind, that file-hosting services fall within the category of host providers, that benefit from a liability exemption under the *E-Commerce Directive*.

b) The Illegality of Making Available Links to the General Public

By making available links to content hosted on a file-hosting service available, access to that file is granted to the general public. Thus, there are no difficulties in establishing an infringing act, namely the act of making publicly available protected works contra Article 3 of the *InfoSoc Directive*.

When link directories or indexing websites host these links, they host illegal content, and may thus be required – upon acquiring actual knowledge of the illegality of that content – to remove or block access to the content in question, which will be outline in the second part of this Chapter.

c) The (Il)Legality of Unauthorised Streaming

While peer-to-peer technology is challenging the music industry since more than a decade and direct downloaders have been entering the market, various platforms such as TVCatchup or kino.to now place additional new challenges on the broadcasting and film industry. The difference of these platforms to peer-to-peer technology or direct downloaders is that current battle-lines are drawn around retransmission or streaming of broadcasts where there is or may be no file or fixed copy and only the transient display of sound and images. Undisputed is the fact that by providing streams of copyrighted works without the consent of the copyright owners, the provider is making a copyrighted work publicly available and thereby infringes copyright.[1909] It follows from Article 3(1) of the *InfoSoc Directive* that for there to be a communication to the public, it is sufficient that the work is made available to the public in such a way that the persons forming that public may access it. Article 3(2) of the *InfoSoc Directive*, further provides for the right of making available to the public of enumerated subject matter. [1910] Recital 23 of said Directive defines the public communication right as covering "all communication to the public not present at the place where the communication originates". As such the public communication right encompasses two distinct rights: the right to broadcast a work to the public, and the right to make the work available from a place and at a time individually chosen by members of the public.[1911]

In particular, the scope of the right to broadcast a work to the public has been challenged by operators of live streaming of third party TV programmes via the Internet.[1912]

In the US, the US Supreme Court only recently agreed to hear the ongoing dispute between several US broadcast networks, including Fox and CBS, and Aereo, a small Internet company that uses transmitters to stream television programmes over the Internet.[1913] In streaming TV programmes

1909 Cf. in that respect and with regard to the platform kino.to CJEU, C-314/12 *UPC Telekabel Wien GmbH v Constantin Film Verleih GmbH and Wega Filmproduktionsgesellschaft GmbH*, Judgment of 27.03.2014, paras. 24 et seq.

1910 CJEU, C-306/05 *Sociedad General de Autores y Editores de España (SGAE) v Rafael Hoteles SA,* Judgment of 07.12.2006, para. 43

1911 Maurizio Borghi, *Chasing copyright infringement in the streaming landscape*, International Review of Intellectual Property and Competition Law 2011, 316, 320.

1912 It has to be noted that the distinction between a broadcasting and making available right is important, since these rights are subject to different legal regimes under European copyright law. In cases of making available, authors as well as holders of related rights enjoy an exclusive right to make the work available to the public. In contrast, in cases of broadcasting, holders of rights in performances and in phonogram records have only a right to an equitable remuneration under Article 8(2) of the Rental and Lending Right Directive. In addition, broadcasting is subject to the "cable retransmission right" (provided for in Articles 9–12 of the Satellite and Cable Directive). For more information on this distinction and its relevance with regard to streaming, see Maurizio Borghi, *Chasing copyright infringement in the streaming landscape*, International Review of Intellectual Property and Competition Law 2011, 316, 321 et seq.

1913 Aereo, Statement from Aereo CEO and founder Chet Kanoja, Press release of 10.01.2014. For the decision of the US Court of Appeals for the Second Circuit

over the Internet, Aero responds to consumers demanding flexibility as to the consumption of TV programmes, meaning that they want to watch programmes on their mobile devices at any chosen time. Not surprisingly, the broadcast networks fear a loss in revenues when they lose their ability to control the use of their content: Retransmission rights are highly lucrative and are nothing that the broadcasters want to give away for free.

This issue has been addressed by the CJEU in the Karen Murphy case[1914] in relation to the streaming of football matches via foreign decoding devices to avoid expensive programme reception charges. According to the CJEU's reasoning, one has to distinguish between a copyright holder's right to control the unauthorised use of his content and the right to control the medium or channels through which his content is accessed.

The central question in relation to the streaming of TV broadcasts is whether the making available of content through retransmission via another medium constitutes an infringement of the underlying work or broadcast.

In 2013, the CJEU had to consider this question in the TVCatchup case when various UK broadcasters took legal action against the Internet television broadcasting service TVCatchup.[1915] In this case the question arose, whether, in using streaming technology to make regular terrestrial television programmes (i.e. broadcasts that had been provided "free-to-air")

---

of 30.11.2012, see https://www.eff.org/files/filenode/aereo_opinion.pdf. Also see the previous case of US Supreme Court, *Cartoon Network LP v CSC Holdings*, 536 F3d 2008, where the Court held that retransmission over the Internet does not infringe the underlying broadcast and broadcasters' rights based on the finding that the notion of "public" performance requires the presence of multiple persons at once and does not include the transmission of a recording to a viewer.

1914 CJEU, Joint cases C-403/08 *Football Association Premier League Ltd and others v OC Leisure and others*, and C-429/08 *Karen Murphy v Media Protection Services Ltd.*, Judgement of 04.10.2011. For comments on the case see Thomas Hoeren/Julia Ariella Bilek, *Die territoriale Exklusivitätsvereinbarung bei Fußball-Übertragungen – Ein Modell der Vergangenheit!*, Computer und Recht 2011, 735; Bartosz Sujecki, *Wettbewerbsverstoß durch territoriale Exklusivitätsvereinbarungen bei Fußball-Übertragungen, Anmerkung,* Neue Juristische Wochenschrift 2012, 213–214.

1915 CJEU, C-607/11 *ITV Broadcasting Ltd et al. v TVCatchup Ltd., Judgement of 07.03.2013. For a comment on the case, see Wolfgang Frhr. Raitz von Frentz/ Christian L. Masch, Anmerkung zu EuGH, Urteil vom 7. März 2013 – EUGH 2013-03-07 Aktenzeichen C-607/11 – Livestreaming, ITV Broadcasting Ltd. u. a./TVCatchup Ltd., Zeitschrift für Urheber- und Medienrecht 2013, 393–395.*

available over the Internet, TVCatchup had infringed the broadcasters' rights.

The claimants had argued before the High Court of Justice that the streaming conducted by TVCatchup constitutes a communication of the works to the public which is prohibited by section 20 of the Copyright, Designs and Patents Act 1988, and by Article 3(1) of the *InfoSoc Directive* 2001/29.[1916]

The operators of TVCatchup argued that the streaming was only transmitting or retransmitting what was anyway publicly available to viewers, and that their service was only adding another medium to view the programmes which did neither constitute an interference with the respective works nor an unauthorised use of the works.

The CJEU held, that the right to communication to the public includes the retransmission of programmes even though they may have been provided "free-to-air" available to the public in the same area as the retransmission took place.[1917]

Hence, TVCatchup needs to obtain a licence from the broadcasters if it wants to continue its retransmission service.[1918] However, where public service broadcasters are concerned and TVCatchup receives and immediately re-transmits the content via cable, the cable re-transmission defence of section 73 *CDPA* applies.[1919]

1916 CJEU, C-607/11 *ITV Broadcasting Ltd et al. v TVCatchup Ltd., Judgement of 07.03.2013,* para.16.

1917 *Ibid*, paras. 26, 40 et seq.

1918 The broadcasters obtained a restraining order in the High Court requiring TVCatchup to refrain from retransmission without obtaining a licence. The Order does, however, allow TVCatchup to continue to stream public service broadcaster (**PSB**) channels (i.e. ITV1, Channel 4 and Channel 5) live via cable in the UK, by virtue of the cable re-transmission defence under section 73 of the *CDPA 1988*. See High Court, Order of 07.10.2013 – Claim no. HC10C01057, available at http://presscentre.itvstatic.com/presscentre/sites/presscentre/files/TVCatchup.pdf (last accessed on 17.05.2014).

1919 This defence was originally designed to encourage cable roll-out in the 1980s and 1990s, see Gillie Abbotts, *A catch for TVCatchup – Limits of the cable defence*, Entertainment Law Review 2014, Vol. 25 Issue 1, 17, 18.

d) The (Il)Legality of Consumption of Streams

The consumption of illegal copies by way of streaming has long been considered as being somehow in a grey area, being neither legal nor illegal. The reason for this uncertainty was the fact that while the stream is consumed, the computer produces a temporary copy of the stream to allow uninterrupted playing of the file.

While diverging views may exist throughout Europe when it comes to determining whether the end-user commits a copyright infringement by consuming streams, and this question is of no relevance for this research, the following discussion will focus on this determination under German law. By focussing on one jurisdiction only, the main issues surrounding the legality of the behaviour of end-users shall be best elaborated.

First of all, it is helpful to look at the position of the rights-holders to understand the underlying problem. The rights-holders argue that the end-user produces a copy from an illegal source,[1920] which under German law – in contrast to for instance Dutch law – constitutes a copyright infringement. Because streaming requires a temporary storage, rights-holders will conclude that this constitutes a reproduction in the sense of § 16 *UrhG*.[1921] For such a reproduction the users would need the authorisation of the copyright owners.[1922]

The majority view taken by scholars has been that the consumption of movie or music streams is in most cases not illegal even if the making available of the file by the streaming provider infringes copyright.

First of all, § 53 *UrhG* provides for a right to make private copies of copyright-protected material under the condition that the source has not been disseminated in an evidently illegal manner, meaning that the source is neither an evidently illegal reproduction or has been made available evi-

1920 Christian Solmecke, *Redtube: Wave of Streaming Letters hits Germany* (12.12.2013), http://www.wbs-law.de/eng/streaming/redtube-wave-streaming-warning-letters-hits-germany-49182/.

1921 *Ibid.*

1922 For an outline of the reproduction right in EU copyright law with a focus on digital reproductions and an analysis whether reproduction in part or temporary reproduction infringes the reproduction rights of the author, see Maurizio Borghi, *Chasing copyright infringement in the streaming landscape*, International Review of Intellectual Property and Competition Law 2011, 316, 329 et seq.

dently illegally.[1923] The evident illegality of a source has to be determined from the perspective of an objective bystander.[1924] The illegality must be obvious to the objective bystander, who carries no further burden to investigate the subject-matter.[1925] With regard to platforms such as kino.to the illegality of the source has been considered obvious, as Kino.to's repertoire included mainstream movies parallel or even prior to their release in cinemas, movies with warnings that they shall only be shown to the press as well as US serial dramas and comedy prior to their release in Europe. However, there are other platforms, where the illegality of the source is not so obvious. This may include YouTube, which has many legal offers but sometimes users may upload content for which they do not hold any communication rights. Equally, the content of streaming sites that contain porn movies and snippets from porn movies, may be considered as not being an evidently illegal source.[1926] With platforms that host porn movies, it is common that rights-holders make available clips or low resolution versions of their repertoire to incite user to buy the full copy or full stream. Youporn.com, the major adult movie platform where users may upload their own films, contains many clips that have been uploaded by the rights-holders themselves. This makes it particularly difficult for users to distinguish whether a clip has been uploaded by the rights-holder or with his authorisation, or is infringing copyright. Thus, also an objective

1923 The question whether a law which allows copying from illegal sources for private use is compliant with EU copyright law has recently been decided by the CJEU in Case C-435/12 *ACI Adam v Stichting de Thuiskopie*. The Advocate General stated in his opinion that the private copying exception only applies to copies from legitimate sources (See Opinion of the Advocate General in Case C-435/12 *ACI Adam v Stichting de Thuiskopie* of 09.01.2014). The CJEU essentially followed the Opinion of the AG, see CJEU, C-435/12 *ACI Adam v Stichting de Thuiskopie,* Judgment of 10.04.2014.

1924 See Ulrike Grübler in: Hartwig Ahlberg/Horst-Peter Götting, *Beck'scher Onlinekommentar Urheberrecht* (updated 01.02.2014), § 53 para. 13 with further references; Tobias Reinbacher, *Strafbarkeit der Privatkopie von offensichtlich rechtswidrig hergestellten oder öffentlich zugänglich gemachten Vorlagen,* Gewerblicher Rechtsschutz und Urheberrecht 2008, 394, 397 with further references.

1925 Ulrike Grübler in: Hartwig Ahlberg/Horst-Peter Götting, *Beck'scher Onlinekommentar Urheberrecht* (updated 01.02.2014), § 53 para. 13.

1926 This has for example been the case with the Germany directed pornography streaming site Redtube.com, see Christian Solmecke, *Redtube: Wave of Streaming Letters hits Germany* (12.12.2013), http://www.wbs-law.de/eng/streaming/redtube-wave-streaming-warning-letters-hits-germany-49182/.

bystander may not succeed in establishing that a clip has been disseminated in evidently illegal manner, and therefore the illegality is not obvious.

Accordingly, even if one assumes that the consumption of a stream constitutes "copying", the consumer would be able to rely on the private copying defence.

Further, any copy generated during streaming on the user's hardware is no illegal reproduction. These kind of copies may fall within the permitted temporary acts of reproduction under § 44a *UrhG.*[1927] § 44a No.2 *UrhG* sets forth that "admissible acts of reproduction are temporary acts of reproduction which are brief or of an accompanying nature and which represent an integral and essential part of a technical procedure and serve the sole purpose of making possible…2. a lawful use of a work or other subject matter of protection and which are not of any independent economic significance".[1928] As regards streaming, copies are only stored for a very short time period. They have no commercial value[1929] in the sense that

1927 Ronny Hauck/Sebastian Heim, Schwerpunktbereich Urheberrecht: Die rechtliche Bewertung von „Filesharing"- und „Streaming"- Sachverhalten, Juristische Schulung 2014, 303, 306; Kathleen Fangerow/Daniela Schulz, Die Nutzung von Angeboten auf www.kino.to, Eine urheberrechtliche Analyse des Film-Streamings im Internet, Gewerblicher Rechtsschutz und Urheberrecht 2010, 677, 680 et seq.; Artur-Axel Wandtke/Felix-Tessen von Gerlach, Die urheberrechtliche Rechtmäßigkeit der Nutzung von Audio-Video Streaminginhalten im Internet, Gewerblicher Rechtsschutz und Urheberrecht 2013, 676 et seq.See also as regards the exemption for temporary acts of reproduction under EU copyright law, Maurizio Borghi, Chasing copyright infringement in the streaming landscape, International Review of Intellectual Property and Competition Law 2011, 316, 332 et seq.

1928 This corresponds to the explanation of the CJEU in the *Infopaq* case (CJEU, C-5/08 *Infopaq International A/S v Danske Dagblades Forening*) with regard to the conditions for an act of reproduction to fall under the temporary act of reproduction exception, namely that the act must be (i) temporary, (ii) transient or incidental, (iii) an integral and essential part of a technological process, and (iv) that the sole purpose of that process must be that of enabling either a transmission in a network between third parties by an intermediary or a lawful use of the work, as well as (v) that the act must have no independent economic significance.

1929 Christian Solmecke, *Redtube: Wave of Streaming Letters hits Germany* (12.12.2013), http://www.wbs-law.de/eng/streaming/redtube-wave-streaming-warning-letters-hits-germany-49182/.

they allow further exploitation of the work.[1930] They further constitute necessary technical measures to make a lawful use possible. The lawful use requirement does not refer to the act of temporary copying but to the consumption of the stream.[1931]

Thus, even if one assumes that users have "stored"[1932] a copy of the protected work in the volatile memory (RAM) of their computer, this act would be protected by § 44a *UrhG*.

Considering, that when copyright works are available in digital format, any normal use of the works involves a technical act of reproduction (e.g. browsing the net produces at least temporary copies on the user's computer), it has been observed that the making of copies is no longer "a good predictor of whether there will be distribution to the public", and consequently of an "intent to infringe".[1933]

5. The Reasons for Targeting these Services

Notably, as with Peer-to-Peer file-sharing, the file-hosting as such is not illegal. However, it provides the infrastructure and means to allow large scale distribution of large files. Due to the latter, file-hosters have become specifically popular for the distribution of movies.[1934] With many services it is not even necessary to download a file as one may also watch a video stream.[1935] Streaming – from a user perspective – is in most jurisdictions no infringement of copyright or it is still not clear whether it may constitute an infringement. Thus, for example the US SOPA Bill contained a respective provision criminalising streaming in order to provide for legal

---

1930 Ronny Hauck/Sebastian Heim, Schwerpunktbereich Urheberrecht: Die rechtliche Bewertung von „Filesharing"- und „Streaming"- Sachverhalten, Juristische Schulung 2014, 303, 306.

1931 *Ibid.*

1932 Stored in that context has to distinguished from downloading.

1933 Maurizio Borghi, *Chasing copyright infringement in the streaming landscape*, International Review of Intellectual Property and Competition Law 2011, 316, 343 quoting Ernest *Miller*/ Joan *Feigenbaum*, T*aking the copy out of copyright*, in: Tomas Sander (ed.), *Security and Privacy in Digital Rights Management*, ACM CSS-8 Workshop DRM 2001 (2002), 233, 236.

1934 Jan Mölleken, *Filehoster: Hehler oder Helfer?*, Der Spiegel online (14.09.2010).

1935 *Ibid.*

certainty and make it clear to users that streaming will not be tolerated. Streaming is easy and ironically, often even easier as using one of the pay-per-view offers of the entertainment industry.[1936] They do not require specific IT literacy, registration, payment or the installation of specific software. Significantly, many users are unaware how file-hosters work. Firstly, file-hosters provide storage space on webservers allowing the storage of data. The services allow users to upload files to the host's server – regularly free of charge and without prior registration. Often an upload does not require more than two clicks.[1937] The file-hoster returns a URL to the uploader. By entering the URL into a browser or simply clicking on the hyperlink the file can then be downloaded, or – depending on the file type – watch a movie stream. Anyone that gets hold of the URL may download the file without registering or logging in. This functioning has made the service to compete with traditional Peer-to-Peer file-sharing services. URLs may disseminated at no time and thereby allow access for an undefined number of users. Usually, files cannot be accessed without the respective link. However some providers, for example 4shared.com allow anyone to search the files that users have set on public.[1938] There are also a number of search masks that scan the Internet for links to files on share hosting services. Further, indexing sites like serienjunkies.org list thousands of URLs by which users may access files.

Due to the bandwidth cost involved , many services slow down downloading speeds in order to encourage users to subscribe to the service with a paid premium account offering increased downloading capacity, pace and/or straight access to a file. Users without subscription often have to queue for several hours in a waiting line until they may download a file. These premium accounts may be the sole income of the provider; however, most services make money from selling advertisement space. File hosting can be profitable. In fact, for example British website NewzBin

1936 *Ibid.*

1937 *Ibid.*

1938 See 4shared's FAQ question 31: "4shared users can search among your files only if you allow them access. To make your files from a particular folder available for public search, check the box "Public search" when sharing the folder. If you want to make all files from your account accessible for public search choose the tab "Settings" in "My Account" and then click the box "Allow to show my files in public search results". It takes 24 – 48 hours to index the files for our search system." http://www.4shared.com/faq.jsp#q31 (last accessed on 17.05.2014).

had in 2009 a turnover in excess of GBP 1million, amounting to a profit in excess of GBP 360,000 and paid dividends on ordinary shares of GBP 415,000.[1939] Although NewzBin was not a file-hosting service itself, but a mere indexing website that linked to downloadable files and offered premium accounts to its users, these figures indicate the potential for such services. Access to content on the basis of a paid subscription means in fact, that users are not getting (infringing) content for free.

The money-generating aspect is of course a thorn in the flesh of rightsholders. While with peer-to-peer file-sharing, users were able to obtain files for "free", the use of file-hosting services means that a third party indirectly even may generate revenues from copyright infringements.

Even though, major file-hosting services such as Rapidshare or 4shared.com claim that they take copyright infringement serious and do not allow users to use their service for copyright infringement,[1940] rightsholders struggle to accept this and argue that they wilfully turn a blind eye on copyright infringements or even incite those. Of course, they are also a number of "black sheep" that act under the disguise of providing a legal service. Following the investigations into the activities of Megaupload.com, which was shut down by US authorities in January 2012, the US Ministry of Justice announced, that Megaupload was more than willing to turn a blind eye on copyright infringement.[1941]

Finally, even if the operators of file-hosting platforms cooperate in stopping copyright infringements, the storage of a file on their service is not illegal, and thus it is doubtful whether they can be forced to delete the file. The infringing act is the making available of the URL leading to a file. How courts deal with this issue will be central to the analyses in this Chapter.

1939 High Court, *Twentieth Century Fox Film Corporation and others v NewzBin Ltd* [2010] EWHC 608 (Ch) (NewzBin 1), para. 15.

1940 See for example 4shared's policy towards copyright infringement, stating that "4shared.com takes copyright violation very seriously and is committed to protecting the rights of copyright owners", http://www.4shared.com/dmca.jsp (last accessed on 17.05.2014).

1941 Felix Knoke, *Kim Dotcom: US-Justizministerium legt seine Erkenntnisse gegen Megaupload vor*, Der Spiegel online (23.12.2013). It has even be reported that employees of Megaupload themselves uploaded materials.

III. Technological Challenges

If the actual infringer of copyright i.e. the person that uploaded a file or made a file available to the public, cannot be identified or resides outside the jurisdiction concerned, it will usually be the content that will be targeted. Targeted in that sense means that either the content is deleted or access is blocked. This research focuses on the latter, namely cases where deletion of content is not possible, because for instance the host provider does not cooperate (if outside jurisdiction) or because deletion cannot be required. There are a number of mechanisms for blocking access to particular content. In the following blocking refers to refusing users access to certain web pages without the cooperation of the content provider, the host provider and the owner of the client machine.[1942] Thus, the sole focus will be at blocking measures implemented or to be implemented by access providers.

The following paragraphs will look into the technical details of different ways of blocking including their implementation, cost and side effects. When analysing the proportionality of filtering in terms of potential violations of fundamental rights, the focus will shift to the efficacy of any of these filtering schemes. In this context, tools enabling the circumvention of blocking will be looked at.

1. Filtering and Blocking Techniques

Several techniques are available to block access to websites with infringing content. Four currently-available techniques as well as hybrid options that could potentially be used to improve the accuracy and robustness of blocking are briefly outlined in the following.

1942 Cf. The similar definition in Maximilian Dornseif, *Government mandated blocking of foreign Web content*, in: Jan von Knop/Wilhelm Haverkamp/Eike Jessen (eds.), *Security, E-Learning, E-Services: Proceedings of the 17. DFN-Arbeitstagung über Kommunikationsnetze* (2013), Lecture Notes in Informatics, p. 618.

a) Internet Protocol Address Blocking

Internet Protocol (IP) address blocking or IP blocking refers to the blocking of particular IP addresses by discarding Internet traffic destined for the blocked website.

As outlined in the first Chapter, in Internet based communication, computers are addressed by their IP address, which identifies a host taking part in Internet communication. The IP address is a number in the range between 0 and 4 billion, usually written as four numbers separated by dots, e.g. 158.64.76.51.

IP address blocking is implemented in network devices (known as border gateway routers) which Internet access providers operate to send user communications to their destinations based on the destination IP address.

An Internet access provider can modify its routers to discard communications destined for the IP address of the website in question (packet dropping) or route them to an IP address defined by the Internet service provider that is different from the actual IP address of the requested website.[1943] Thus, the user's communication to a website is blocked although his computer uses the correct IP address for the website.

IP address blocking can be a low cost model depending on the scope of blocking i.e. the number of IPs to be blocked.[1944] The key problem with IP address blocking is that many addresses are shared between multiple content providers (shared webhosting).[1945] If a particular IP address is blocked, then all of the web content under that particular IP address will become inaccessible.[1946] Hence, there is an obvious risk of over-blocking when barring particular IP addresses. Websites that share the same IP address will be unavailable.[1947]

1943 See Ofcom, *'Site blocking' to reduce online copyright infringement: A review of sections 17 and 18 of the Digital Economy Act* (27.05.2011), p. 28.

1944 Richard Clayton, *Harmful Content on the Internet and in Video Games* (2008), p. 1.

1945 Richard Clayton, *Anonymity and traceability in cyberspace* (2005), Technical Report UCAM-CL-TR-653, p. 118; See also Benjamin Edelman, *Web sites sharing IP addresses: Prevalence and Significance* (September 2003) .

1946 See Holger Bleich/Axel Kossel, *Verschleierungstaktik: Die Argumente für Kinderporno-Sperren laufen ins Leere,* Der Spiegel Online (17.04.2009).

1947 Richard Clayton, *Anonymity and traceability in cyberspace* (2005), Technical Report UCAM-CL-TR-653, p. 115.

When the German Internet access provider Arcor in 2007 used IP blocking to block access to several pornographic websites, this led to massive collateral damage.[1948] One of the websites Arcor had been asked to block was Privatamateure.com, which was attributed the IP address 64.202.189.170.[1949] Under this address not only Privatamateure.com could be found but also more than 3.5 million single websites, for example a Bollywood fanpage, a Linux-Kernel-Debugger, a Wi-Fi network initiative and an ICT congress.[1950] Users that tried to access one of the websites were confronted with an error message "Netzwerk-Zeitüberschreitung".

Furthermore, IP address locking does not differentiate between a whole platform as such and individual subpages. Only the whole of a website could be blocked, rather than the individual part identified as illegal. Thus, if Facebook.com contained illegal content on one user's profile, the whole of Facebook would be affected by the blocking of its IP address.

b) Domain Name System Name Blocking

It is also possible to subvert the Domain Name System (DNS) so that websites cannot be located. This is also known as DNS poisoning[1951] and was considered by Ofcom to be the blocking technique that could be implemented with least delay.[1952]

As mentioned before, the DNS is the system that associates/"translates" a cryptic IP address (such as: 158.64.76.51) that Internet service providers use to route traffic to the web server which operates a website to domain name (such as: www.uni.lu) which are easier to remember than mere sequences of numbers. Internet service providers operate DNS servers that

---

1948 The blocking attempt was a pure voluntary measure by Arcor. See Urs Mansmann, *Arcor sperrte zahlreiche Websites*, Heise online (17.09.2007).

1949 Stefan Krempl, *Arcor muss YouPorn sperren*, Heise online (19.10.2007); Konrad Lischka, *Fehlerhafte Zensur-Methode: Arcor stoppt den Porno-Filter*, Der Spiegel online (17.09.2007).

1950 *Ibid.*

1951 Richard Clayton, *Anonymity and traceability in cyberspace* (2005), Technical Report UCAM-CL-TR-653, p.118.

1952 Ofcom, *'Site blocking' to reduce online copyright infringement: A review of sections 17 and 18 of the Digital Economy Act* (27.05.2011), p. 43. As regards a detailed outline of the functioning of DNS name blocking see *Ibid*, pp. 31 et seq.

their customers' computers automatically call upon to identify which IP address corresponds to a particular DNS name.[1953] This is necessary in order to resolve the website in question. In simple terms, DNS name blocking would block that translation. This can be done by manipulating the domain name resolution by way of removing or modifying the records of the IP address for a particular DNS name. Instead of resolving the domain name to an IP address, an invalid response along the lines of "host not found" will be given.[1954]

A user may also be directed to an IP address defined by the Internet service provider that in actuality does not correspond to the DNS name. This makes all content hosted within a particular domain inaccessible.[1955]

This scheme permits the blocking of individual websites without intervening with further sites that share the same IP address. The scheme is even low cost if thousands of domain names are blocked.[1956]

One of the drawbacks of DNS Blocking is that it – like IP Blocking – does not distinguish between a large website as such and only parts thereof.[1957] Thus, it is a hardly feasible solution for blocking of certain content on for example facebook.com.

An advantage is that – although over-blocking exists – over-blocking does not take place in the same scope as with IP blocking, because the blocking does not extend to other websites that are hosted under the same IP address. Nevertheless, the blocking extends to other websites under the same domain, which may have nothing to do with the illegal content that is targeted.

DNS name blocking is also easy to circumvent, because the websites are still accessible by typing the numeric IP address into the address

1953 Each Internet service provider operates its own DNS servers, which he may easily manipulate. See Holger Bleich/Axel Kossel, *Verschleierungstaktik: Die Argumente für Kinderporno-Sperren laufen ins Leere*, Der Spiegel online (17.04.2009).

1954 Maximilian Dornseif, *Government mandated blocking of foreign Web content,* in: Jan von Knop/Wilhelm Haverkamp/Eike Jessen (eds.), *Security, E-Learning, E-Services: Proceedings of the 17. DFN-Arbeitstagung über Kommunikationsnetze, Lecture Notes in Informatics* (2013), p. 624.

1955 Richard Clayton, *Anonymity and traceability in cyberspace* (2005), Technical Report UCAM-CL-TR-653, p.118.

1956 *Ibid.*

1957 *Ibid;* Ofcom, '*Site blocking' to reduce online copyright infringement: A review of sections 17 and 18 of the Digital Economy Act* (27.05.2011), p. 34.

field.[1958] Alternatively, users may enter a foreign DNS server into their operating system, which does not block the translation.[1959]

DNS name blocking may be of limited value in the longer term.[1960] First of all, it puts at risks the fundamental interconnection principle, which lies at the very heart of the Internet, by letting single jurisdictions decide unilaterally who can find what on the Internet. The principle of domain name universality requires that all domain name servers, irrespective of their location, will return the same answer when queried with respect to an Internet address.[1961] This core principle would be undermined if domain name servers ceased resolving specific domain names to the respective IP address. According to a technical study by experts in the field of network security, DNS blocking indeed poses a serious threat to cybersecurity.[1962] DNS is one of the protocols upon which almost every other protocol and most applications rely upon to operate correctly.

Furthermore, DNS blocking would break on-going attempts to make the Internet more secure against malicious use.[1963] It would for example render the planned security protocol Domain Name System Security Extensions (DNSSEC)[1964] inoperable.[1965] DNSSEC will authenticate and verify domain name queries to reduce the illegal use of computers, for example by Trojans via a DNS change. Under DNSSEC, users attempting to access a blocked site would no longer be re-directed to an alternative webpage and thus, would be unable to figure out whether they are faced with a law-

---

1958 It has been argued that this blocking mechanism is a blocking for "Fritzchen Doof", see Holger Bleich/Axel Kossel, *Verschleierungstaktik: Die Argumente für Kinderporno-Sperren laufen ins Leere*, Der Spiegel Online (17.04.2009).

1959 *Ibid.*

1960 See Ofcom, 'Site blocking' to reduce online copyright infringement: A review of sections 17 and 18 of the *Digital Economy Act* (27.05.2011), p. 5.

1961 Mark Lemley/David Levine/David Post, *Don't break the Internet*, Stanford Law Review Online 2011, Vol. 64, 34, 35.

1962 Steve Crocker/David Dagon/Dan Kaminsky/Danny McPherson/Paul Vixie, *Security and other technical concerns raised by the DNS filtering requirements in the PROTECT IP Bil*l (2011).

1963 Mark Lemley/David Levine/David Post, *Don't break the Internet*, Stanford Law Review Online 2011, Vol. 64, 34, 35.

1964 DNSSEC is a new technology designed to add confidence and trust to the Internet. DNSSEC ensures that DNS data are not modified by anyone between the data provider and the consumer.

1965 Cf. Ofcom, '*Site blocking' to reduce online copyright infringement: A review of sections 17 and 18 of the Digital Economy Act* (27.05.2011), p. 42.

ful blocking sanction imposed by a court or malicious activity on their DNS query.[1966]

As relates DNS blocking even the US White House, which otherwise has been fond of access blocking to piracy websites, declared during the discussions on anti-piracy bills that DNS blocking poses a risk to cybersecurity, and legislation that drives users to dangerous, unreliable DNS servers must be avoided.[1967]

c) Uniform Resource Locator Site Blocking

A rather precise technology for barring access to content is uniform resource locator (URL) site blocking, also known as URL filtering.[1968]

In comparison to IP or DNS blocking, URL filtering allows for quite precise blocking of specific parts, i.e. a specific file, directory or server. This scheme involves the use of proxy machines that interpose themselves between the requestor and the remote content.[1969]

This means, that the Internet service provider arranges that a request is transferred to a proxy which pretends to be the requested machine. The proxy can filter materials that pass through and search for the URLs of for instance images or videos that are on a blacklist.[1970] As mentioned above, this allows filtering to be rather precise. Overblocking as with IP or DNS blocking may hence be avoided.

The drawback of URL filtering is, that it is very costly. It can be extremely expensive for Internet service provider to implement URL filtering as all traffic must be processed over the proxy.[1971] In practice, service providers would have to run multiple proxies in order to avoid single

---

1966 See *ibid*, p. 5.

1967 Victoria Espinel/Aneesh Chopra/Howard Schmidt, *Combating online piracy while protecting an open and innovative Internet: Official White House response to stop the E-PARASITE Act* (2012).

1968 For a detailed account of the functioning of URL blocking see Ofcom, *'Site blocking' to reduce online copyright infringement: A review of sections 17 and 18 of the Digital Economy Act* (27.05.2011), pp. 35 et seq.

1969 *Ibid*, p. 36.

1970 *Ibid*, p. 2.

1971 See Holger Bleich/Axel Kossel, *Verschleierungstaktik: Die Argumente für Kinderporno-Sperren laufen ins Leere,* Der Spiegel Online (17.04.2009).

points of failure.[1972] A redundant performance would thus require huge hardware resources.

d) Deep Packet Inspection-Based Blocking

Deep packet inspection (DPI) schemes examine the content of communication.[1973] The service provider's network management system will be configured to monitor traffic, i.e. the packets of data to and from customers. This packet inspection can be applied at two levels, namely shallow and deep.

Shallow packet inspection is conducted by monitoring and blocking traffic to specific IP addresses, port and protocol combinations.[1974]

By deep packet inspection the content of a network packet will be examined for prior defined characteristics or values.[1975] Where packets are fragmented during transmission, the DPI device will reassemble those packets in order to analyse their content. If content is detected that matches certain pre-defined properties, for instance traffic destined for a blocked site, the DPI device can break the connection or drop traffic destined for the blocked website.[1976] It is also possible to block outbound encrypted traffic connection requests to a known, specific IP address by so called access control lists (ACL). [1977] The user's connection to the URLs on the ACL will be reset or blocked. However, unlike with URL filtering, there are no proxies involved in the filtering process. If the network management system detects a bad connection, further packets will be discarded.

1972 *Ibid.*

1973 For an overview of discussions about deep packet inspection for copyright enforcement in Europe and the US see Milton Mueller/Andreas Kuehn/Stephanie Michelle Santoso, *Policing the Network: Using DPI for Copyright Enforcement*, Surveillance & Society 2012, Vol. 9 Issue 4, 348–364. For a detailed account of the functioning and robustness of deep packet inspection see also Ofcom, *"Site blocking" to reduce online copyright infringement: A Review of sections 17 and 18 of the Digital Economy Act* (27.05.2011), pp. 39 et seq.

1974 See Ofcom, *"Site blocking" to reduce online copyright infringement: A Review of sections 17 and 18 of the Digital Economy Act* (27.05.2011), p. 39.

1975 *Ibid.*

1976 *Ibid.*

1977 *Ibid.*

Of all the techniques outlined, DPI-based filtering is the only one to be able to catch all forms of unencrypted traffic.

Deep packet inspection is an expensive but yet cheaper scheme than URL filtering,[1978] however, it may only be deployed by larger Internet service providers considering the investment that must be taken.[1979]

Deep packet inspection as a filtering mechanism is known for being employed by the Chinese Government to censor the Internet for its residents.[1980] It is a key part of the Chinese "Great Firewall of China".[1981]

e) Hybrid Systems – The Example of CleanFeed

Hybrid systems combine at least two of the above enlisted blocking schemes. The result may be a cheaper, but yet more effective and precise means for content blocking. One may couple DNS name blocking with shallow packet inspection, DNS name blocking with URL blocking and DNS blocking with DPI-based blocking. By for example combining DPI-based blocking with URL blocking, one may avoid the blocking of further websites that share the IP address with the target website. The combination also allows for the blocking of only a portion of a website while leaving the remainder of the site accessible.

The UK looks back at a relatively long experience with a hybrid content blocking system. CleanFeed was created in 2003 and implemented in June 2004 by Britain's then largest Internet Provider British Telecom (BT).[1982] All UK Internet service providers were instructed by the Home Office to implement a version of Cleanfeed by the end of 2007 on a voluntary basis or face legal compulsion.

CleanFeed as a government-mandated programme was initially designed to target solely child sexual abuse materials identified as such by the UK Internet Watch Foundation (IWF).[1983] The programme attempts to

1978 *Ibid.*

1979 *Ibid*, p. 40.

1980 *Ibid.*

1981 *Ibid.*

1982 Martin Bright, *BT puts block on child porn sites,* The Observer (06.06.2004).

1983 As regards the status and the role of the IWF: In 1996 the Metropolitan Police notified the Internet Service Providers Association (ISPA) that some newsgroup content being carried by UK Internet service providers (ISPs) were indecent images of children. The police believed this may have constituted a publication

block such content that is located outside of the UK.[1984] The filtering system is a hybrid system of IP address blocking and DPI-based URL filtering and treats particular IP addresses special. It thus incorporates both redirection of traffic and the use of web proxies.[1985] It is intended to be very precise in what it blocks, while at the same time being a low-cost model to build and operate. Accordingly, Internet traffic is filtered in a two-stage process. First of all, the IWF maintains a database of URLs that

offence under the Protection of Children Act 1978 (England and Wales) by the ISPs. Efforts were then undertaken to find a way to combat the hosting of such content in the UK whilst protecting the Internet industry from being held criminally liable for providing access to the content. Following discussions between the former Department of Trade and Industry (DTI), the Home Office, the Metropolitan Police, some ISPs and the Safety Net Foundation (formed by the Dawe Charitable Trust) an R3 Safety Net Agreement regarding rating, reporting and responsibility was created by ISPA, the London Internet Exchange (LINX) and the Safety Net Foundation. A key outcome of the Agreement was the formation of the Internet Watch Foundation (IWF). The IWF as a Hotline was formally launched in December 1996 to combat child sexual abuse images and criminally obscene adult content hosted in the UK. The IWF was established to fulfil an independent role in receiving, assessing and tracing public complaints about child sexual abuse content on the Internet and to support the development of website rating systems. The intention was to provide members of the public with one single point of contact to report on the presence of child abuse materials on the Internet. Since its formation the IWF has been actively engaged in operating this Hotline service for the public to report potentially criminal content and providing a "notice and takedown" service to advise ISPs in partnership with the Police Services in the UK to effect its removal. See Internet Watch Foundation, *IWF History*, https://www.iwf.org.uk/about-iwf/iwf-history (last accessed on 17.05.2014).

1984 It has to be noted that for content inside the UK, law enforcement authorities will address the provider of that content directly as he is under UK jurisdiction. The experts at the IWF are to establish whether a report referred to an illegal image of a child. If illegality is established then the URL on which the material is hosted will be put on the IWF blacklist. The ISPs then have to remove the content from all of their news servers (in case of Usenet) or block access to this content on websites they do not control. The blacklist is updated twice daily. The IWF accepts reports of content irrespective of where in the world it is hosted. The UK police also reports UK material directly. Materials hosted outside the UK are reported to the National Criminal Intelligence Service (NCIS) which will pass the report via Interpol to the relevant national authority where the website is hosted (see Richard Clayton, *Anonymity and traceability in cyberspace* (2005), Technical Report UCAM-CL-TR-653, p. 116).

1985 Richard Clayton, *Anonymity and traceability in cyberspace* (2005), Technical Report UCAM-CL-TR-653, p. 116

have been inspected and keep a record/blacklist of when they led to illegal material. While some websites remained accessible for a considerable time, some countries take down illegal content upon notification expeditiously. If illegal content is not removed or blocked at its origin, Cleanfeed comes into play. The routers at the Internet service providers redirect traffic to IP addresses that match domains appearing in URLs on the IWF blacklist. Instead of simply blocking the addresses in question, they are passed through HTTP proxy servers which then conduct the actual filtering by matching HTTP requests to destinations on a more specific blacklist. By combining the easy and cheap IP blocking with the more cost-intensive and elaborated URL filtering, it is a more exact scheme for less cost. It has the exactness of the proxy scheme, and in comparison to the single URL filtering has to deal with less traffic.[1986] Proxies can be smaller and thus cheaper. When the German Internet access provider Arcor used IP blocking to block access to several pornographic websites, for example Privatamateure.com, this led to the traffic to Privateamateure.com and inter alia a Bollywood fan page under the same IP address being blocked in 2007.[1987] By employing a hybrid system like Cleanfeed, the traffic would have been redirected to a proxy, that would permit access to the fan page whilst blocking the adult content.

However, Cleanfeed is not immune against producing collateral damage as could be learned from the Virgin Killer cover incident.[1988] The depiction of the album cover the German rock band Scorpions was reported as potentially illegal content (indecent image of a child) to the IWF, which subsequently put the URL of the Wikipedia article on the album on their blacklist.[1989] As a direct consequence the article and image was not accessible for UK based readers of the English Wikipedia. However, indirectly, all editors using the UK Internet access providers were prevented from contributing to or editing any page of Wikipedia.[1990] This was due to the

---

1986 Richard Clayton, *Harmful Content on the Internet and in Video Games*, p. 2.

1987 See Urs Mansmann, *Arcor sperrte zahlreiche Websites*, Heise online (17.09.2007).

1988 The incident concerned a depiction of the cover of German rock band Scorpions' 1976 studio album Virgin Killer on Wikipedia. The controversial cover artwork depicted a young girl posing nude, with a faux glass shatter obscuring her genitalia. See Raphael Satter, *Wikipedia article blocked in UK over child photo*, The Independent (08.12.2008).

1989 *Ibid.*

1990 *Ibid.*

proxies used to access Wikipedia, as Wikipedia implements a blocking policy whereby contributors can be blocked if they vandalise the encyclopaedia. As all traffic towards Wikipedia was redirected through proxies, the affected Internet service providers shared a relatively small number of IP addresses.[1991] Consequently, vandalism directed through a proxy, would lead to the IP address of that proxy being blocked by Wikipedia. In the end, Wikipedia could no more distinguish users committing vandalism from others complying with Wikipedia's terms of use.[1992]

The editing ban for most UK users was the result of two mutually incompatible content regulation systems. Although Cleanfeed did not directly cause the Wikipedia editing ban, the incident shows that filtering can have severe effects on network accessibility and infrastructure.

2. Circumvention Tools

It has been argued that all the existing content blocking schemes are relatively easy to circumvent or as an expert puts it "trivial to evade". [1993] An in-depth analysis of circumvention tools would go beyond the scope of this research, thus, in the following the different tools will only be addressed briefly. Two of the major tools to circumvent blocking are encryption and proxy services. Taking into account further available tools, one may distinguish between circumvention tools available to website operators and users. In light of the available circumvention techniques, it should be possible to get an estimate of the efficacy of the various blocking schemes.

1991 Becky Hogge, *IWF censors Wikipedia, chaos ensues*, Open Rights Group (08.12.2008).

1992 *Ibid.*

1993 See Thorsten Schreier, *Düsseldorfer Sperrungsverfügung: Warum ein Provider erfolgreich war*, MultiMedia und Recht 3004, 297 – 298; Ofcom, "*Site blocking" to reduce online copyright infringement: A Review of sections 17 and 18 of the Digital Economy Act* (27.05.2011), p. 5.

a) Circumvention Tools available to Website Operators

The following only lists a few examples that particularly illustrate different approaches to circumvent blocking by the website providers themselves.

aa) Change of IP Address and/or Additional Domain Names

This sounds rather trivial but is highly effective to bypass court orders that order the blocking of access to the website. It is an effective tool where the blocking is conducted by IP filtering.

The content provider simply changes the IP address of the host running the web server software. The DNS will automatically allow the user's web browser to start communication with the new IP address.[1994] However as simple as this may sound, it can get rather complicated if the IP address needs to be changed several times a day.[1995]

Similarly website operators could operate a so-called Fast Flux network, whereby – in simple terms – users of a blocked site could choose to use specific software which would associate hundreds or thousands of IP addresses with a blocked website which could change as often as every few minutes.[1996]

If blocking is conducted via DNS poising or filtering http proxies, a simple yet effective measure is the change of the domain name. Alternative domain names will regularly not be subject to the blocking order.[1997]

1994 Maximilian Dornseif, *Government mandated blocking of foreign Web content*, in: Jan von Knop/Wilhelm Haverkamp/Eike Jessen (eds.), *Security, E-Learning, E-Services: Proceedings of the 17. DFN-Arbeitstagung über Kommunikationsnetze*, Lecture Notes in Informatics (2013), pp. 617 et seq.

1995 *Ibid.* Dornseif refers to an example that was often referred to in Literature at that time, namely the Dutch provider xs4all which in 1997 was changing IP addresses on an hourly basis to circumvent being blocked.

1996 For a thorough technical account of the functioning of a Fast Flux Network, see Jamie Riden, *How Fast-Flux service networks work*, The Honeynet Project (16.08.2008).

1997 Dornseif states that for instance http://nazi-lauck-nsdapao.com/, a website that was ordered to be blocked in Germany, was subsequently accessible via the domain names auschwitz.biz, bundesinnenministerium.biz, bundesinnenministerium.us, bundesjustizministerium.com, bundesjustizministerium.net, bundesjustizministerium.org, bundesjustizministerium.us, bundesrepublikdeutsch-

The content provider can thus evade blocking by using additional domain names pointing to the same content on the same host server.[1998] Although, the user needs to be informed somehow of the new domain name so that he will be able to access it at all, it seems that such information spreads relatively quickly. For example, following an order by a Belgian court requiring Belgian Internet service providers to initiate DNS blockades of domains connected to the Pirate Bay, the Pirate Bay registered a new domain: depiraatbaai.be, which is the literal translation of The Pirate Bay in Dutch.[1999] Users that accessed the standard domain from a Belgian IP-address were instantly redirected to the new home.

bb) Proxy Services, Anonymising Services and Virtual Private Networking

Operators of blocked websites may make use of anonymous web proxy providers. A server will then act as an intermediary between the end-user and the website operator; equally, anonymising services may prevent that the Internet access provider becomes aware that the end-user is seeking access to the blocked website.[2000]

In order to bypass IP address, DNS name or URL blocking, the operator of a blocked website may offer encrypted network services which obscure the true network address. [2001] Virtual private networks (VPN) and anonymous proxies may be used to bypass inter alia DPI-based blocking or URL blocking. VPNs enable the extension of private networks across the Internet. This means that data is sent and received across the Internet as if

---

land.us, hitlerwasright.info, kanzleramt.us, nordrhein-westfalen.biz, nsdap.info, verfassungsschutz.biz, verfassungsschutz.us, zensurfrei.com and zuwanderungskommission.com. See Maximilian Dornseif, *Government mandated blocking of foreign Web content*, in: Jan von Knop/Wilhelm Haverkamp/Eike Jessen (eds.), *Security, E-Learning, E-Services: Proceedings of the 17. DFN-Arbeitstagung über Kommunikationsnetze*, Lecture Notes in Informatics (2013), p. 617.

1998 *Ibid.*

1999 Ernesto, *The Pirate Bay adds domain to bypass court order,* TorrentFreak (05.10.2011).

2000 Ofcom, *"Site blocking" to reduce online copyright infringement: A Review of sections 17 and 18 of the Digital Economy Act* (27.05.2011), p. 29.

2001 *Ibid.*

it is directly connected to the private network. Encryption and other security measures are deployed to guarantee that the data cannot be viewed by third parties.[2002]

cc) Mirroring

Mirroring is strictly speaking not a circumvention tool as it does not circumvent a blocking mechanism. It rather refers to copies of the content being made available from different host location. The technique is commonly used to reduce resource usage on a host and to increase availability of content.

A mirror is a host that retrieves the content from the original source and publishes it as a website.[2003]

Retrieval and publication takes place regularly and often automated.

The effect of mirroring is that the content is made available from more than one source. Thus, although content from one source may be blocked, it will still be accessible on the mirrored site as long as this site is not blocked as well.

With web 1.0 websites, i.e. websites that were rather static with little interactive features, mirroring could easily be done. However, modern, dynamic systems where user contribute content or database driven websites require great effort for mirroring.[2004] Thus, although practicable when it comes to the circumvention of blocking, this technique has become of very limited relevance.

b) Circumvention Tools available to Users

As with the circumvention tools available to website operatory, the following only lists a few examples that particularly illustrate different approaches to circumvent blocking by end-users. While some of them are only

---

2002 *Ibid,* p. 33.

2003 Maximilian Dornseif, *Government mandated blocking of foreign Web content,* in: Jan von Knop/Wilhelm Haverkamp/Eike Jessen (eds.), *Security, E-Learning, E-Services: Proceedings of the 17. DFN-Arbeitstagung über Kommunikationsnetze, Lecture Notes in Informatics* (2013), p. 632.

2004 *Ibid*, pp. 632 et seq.

addressed very briefly, a closer look will be taken on the functioning of TOR as a tool to hide the origin of a request.

aa) Encryption

Encryption became popular in peer-to-peer file-sharing as it allowed file-sharing to continue at full speed where it was otherwise slowed down by blocking systems and traffic shaping.

If traffic is encrypted, schemes that examine packets to determine what they contain, are no longer of use. It is not feasible to block any encrypted traffic on the assumption that it contains illegal materials – a lot of traffic is encrypted anyway for example such that contains personal data when shopping online. However, encrypted traffic defeats any system that relies on examining packets in order to determine what they contain.[2005]

bb) Proxy Services, Anonymising Services and Virtual Private Networking

In order to bypass inter alia DNS name blocking, end-users may use anonymous web proxy services or other anonymising services.[2006]

Proxy services hide the IP addresses of their users from the public. With servers outside of the jurisdiction concerned, this means that domestic blocking can be bypassed.

Accordingly, a German user may want to use a Swiss proxy which is not bound on German rules on what to block. The Swiss proxy will not filter and thereby allow access to otherwise blocked content. Connections to proxies are encrypted.[2007] Encryption allows for anonymity and some individuals rely on anonymity for legitimate use of the Internet (for exam-

2005 See UK Parliament, Select Committee on Culture, Media and Sport, *Memorandum submitted by Dr Richard Clayton* (2008), para. 11.

2006 For an account of which proxies are available, see Enigmax/Ernesto, *Review: Is your VPN service really anonymous?*, TorrentFreak (02.01.2014). For the functioning of the anonymising service BTGuard see Ernesto, *BTGuard review: How does it work?*, TorrentFreak (19.01.2013).

2007 *Ibid.*

ple those posting from the Arab Spring), thus blocking proxies will have a severe impact on human rights.

The use of proxies is easy, even for non-It-literate end-users.

There are also more complex anonymity systems available such as TOR[2008], where the concealing of origin allows the circumvention of access blocking. Initially, TOR was developed by the US Navy to permit them surfing the Internet without revealing their identity. The abbreviation TOR stands for "the onion router". "Onion routing" refers to the layers of encryption used when using TOR. The TOR software directs Internet traffic through a volunteer-run network consisting of numerous relays to conceal a user's location or usage from anyone conducting network surveillance or traffic analysis.[2009] Instead of a taking a direct route from source to destination, data packets are encrypted and re-encrypted multiple times, and take a random pathway through several TOR relays that cover the user's tracks so no observer at any single point can tell where the data packet came from or where it is going.[2010] By this, TOR prevents that third parties monitor which websites are accessed from a certain IP address, but it also lets the TOR user access websites which are blocked by evading geographic content-blocking. This means that a TOR user located in Germany may be assigned a Russian IP address; as for Russian users for example www.kino.to is not blocked, he may then access the website. A user that wants to use TOR has to install the TOR software on his computer. But there is also a version of TOR, the TOR-Browser-Bundle[2011], which does not require the installation of any TOR software: it runs off a USB flash drive, comes with a pre-configured web browser and is self-contained. Hence, the usage of this circumvention tool does not require IT literacy anymore.

2008 See www.torproject.org.

2009 The distributed network of relays used by the TOR software is run by volunteers around the world, such as for example the Chaos Computer Club in Germany.

2010 See Tor project: Overview, https://www.torproject.org/about/overview.html.en (last accessed on 13.08.2013).

2011 https://www.torproject.org/projects/torbrowser.html.en (last accessed on 13.08.2013).

Also the modified Firefox browser that is offered by The Pirate Bay in order to guarantee access to their website which is blocked in at least seven European countries[2012], uses the TOR-Browser-Bundle.[2013]

Users may also turn to VPN clients to bypass blocking. VPNs enable the extension of private networks across the Internet, meaning that data is sent and received across the Internet as if it is directly connected to the private network.

c) The Efficiency of Blocking

The analysis shows that even if Internet service providers are forced to implement blocking schemes, their subscribers may succeed in accessing the blocked materials, either because they circumvent the blocking themselves or the operator of a blocked website changes the location of the websites in question. However, just because it is possible for the end-users and website operators to circumvent blocking, this does not mean that in practice they will all do so.[2014] Several factors may play a role, when it comes to the usage of circumvention techniques including the convenience and prevalence of such techniques.[2015]

It can however be established, that none of the techniques available to users necessarily requires a high level of technical expertise. It may rather require the acquisition of additional expertise beyond the knowledge an ordinary Internet user already possesses. In that respect, the Ofcom report on website blocking found that "knowledge of how site operators and end users can work around blocks is widely distributed and easily accessible on the Internet".[2016] The question then is whether users are willing to expend time and effort to expand their knowledge on blocking and circumvention. As Ofcom noted, bypassing of blocking is "not technically

2012 For example in the UK: High Court, *Dramatico Entertainment Ltd and others v BT PLC and orthers* [2012] EWHC 268 (Ch).

2013 Spiegel Online, "*The Pirate Bay": IT-Experten warnen vor Piraten-Browser*, Der Spiegel Online (13.08.2013). The Pirate Bay announced the launch of the browser under the heading "no more Censorship" right in time for the 10th year anniversary of the platform.

2014 See Ofcom, *'Site blocking' to reduce online copyright infringement: A review of sections 17 and 18 of the Digital Economy Act* (27.05.2011), p. 6.

2015 *Ibid.*

2016 *Ibid*, p. 51.

challenging and does not require a particularly high level of skill or expertise",[2017] which would also mean that the necessary time and effort is limited.

Even elaborated hybrid blocking mechanisms like Cleanfeed can as easy be circumvented as single blocking schemes, for instance via VPNs or anonymising services.[2018]

Ultimately, blocking is never perfect, and may only undermine the viability of infringing content for some users – though these users may amount to the majority of Internet users. Blocking rather makes accidental access of blocked websites unlikely, access requires a certain degree of active circumvention, so that casual and unintentional infringers are deterred (in case that they do not use the circumvention tools described above by default).

IV. Resume

The circumstances have been outlined that make it attractive for rights-holders to address online intermediaries, access providers and host providers, as the natural gatekeepers to online communication. With online intermediaries having the capacities to act as guardsmen, they have been targeted by rights-holders since the advent of the Internet. While targeting enforcement against individual users can be costly and lengthy, and seems to have limited effect as concerns the scope of infringements, targeting intermediaries is considered more promising.

New services that have become subject to legal action in the recent past include file-hosting services, streaming services, link directories and torrent indexing sites. The popularity of file-hosting and streaming is not only owed to users migrating from peer-to-peer file-sharing because they fear detection, but is also owed to technological progress. Smart devices, such as smart TVs, smartphones and tablet pcs, are changing the way media is consumed. It is no longer necessary to download files as they can be consumed via streaming technology everywhere and at any time. File-hosting services, especially cloud storage services, are also becoming essential for back-ups of mobile devices, and to allow access to materials

---

2017 *Ibid.*

2018 Holger Bleich/Axel Kossel, *Verschleierungstaktik: Die Argumente für Kinderporno-Sperren laufen ins Leere,* Spiegel Online (17.04.2009).

from different locations and different devices. While streaming and file-hosting services are content neutral, they, similar to peer-to-peer technology, provide the infrastructure to commit copyright infringements. There is consensus that the providers of these services are under no general monitoring duty. However, we will see in the following that specific monitoring duties may arise in relation to defined content. Irrespective of the technology being neutral, the business model of a few file-hosting services is based on the service being (ab)used for copyright infringements. The same applies for streaming website, where the technology is used to make publicly available unauthorised copies of protected works. Similarly link directories exist, that provide hyperlinks to content stored on file-hosting services, and thereby makes this content publicly available. Indexing websites list content that is available on peer-to-peer networks that would otherwise be impossible or hard to find. In each of these scenarios, suing the individual infringer may be ineffective, or the identity of the infringer not traceable. Thus, copyright owners resort to suing the platform as such instead of going for the individual infringer.

When online intermediaries are addressed to enforce copyright, one needs to distinguish between action that is taken against access providers and action that is taken against host providers. Host providers will usually be addressed, when they are located in the same jurisdiction, or are likely to comply with a court order. In these cases, the aim will regularly be that the provider deletes or blocks access to the infringing materials and hinders the reappearance of the infringement. In contrast, access providers will be addressed when legal action against the host is not possible, or has failed. In this context, it may also be important that intellectual property rights are regulated domestically, and thus are not universally the same. Accordingly, enforcement of IP rights may have its limits where the content in question is hosted abroad. Based on the limited effectiveness of domestic law, rights-holders are increasingly seeking to have access to the infringing content, or moreover the infringing website, blocked. Blocking access to content that is outside of a state's jurisdiction is a recent phenomenon predominantly encountered in relation to child abuse materials. Already in this context, meaning with regard to content that is almost universally deemed illegal, there has been some controversy as to the legitimacy of blocking.[2019] Accordingly, an assessment of the legitimacy of blocking with a particular focus on the proportionality of any such measure will be central to the subsequent discussion of selected access blocking schemes.

As regards access blocking in general, it is essential to understand that blocking can only practically be done at individual online intermediaries. As Richard Clayton puts it "there is no Internet backbone where it can be done for everyone at once".[2020] Thus, even blocking schemes at national levels require the cooperation of every single domestic Internet service provider. In addition, service providers have different network designs and hence, need to deploy different content blocking schemes.[2021] None of the existing blocking schemes is a 100% effective. Circumvention tools exist for both, content providers and users that still allow access, even if it is blocked by the access provider. Depending on the blocking scheme that is being deployed, circumvention of blocking is feasible for every user without an IT background. Thus, access blocking may only undermine the viability of infringing content for some users – though these users may amount to the majority of Internet users. Blocking rather makes accidental access of blocked websites unlikely, which is often already considered an achievement.

However, almost all blocking carries the risk of over-blocking, i.e. blocking of legitimate content. When assessing the legitimacy of any blocking measure, it thus does not only need to be considered that blocking does not mean that content is no longer accessible, it must also be considered, that legitimate content may be affected. This being said, it becomes already obvious at this stage, that blocking interferes with the fundamental right of freedom to seek, receive and impart information.

B. *Enforcement Measures Directed at Intermediaries*

Intermediaries may be taken into responsibility in various ways: by way of criminal law, civil law or even public law with administrative authorities

---

2019 See Yaman Akdeniz, *To block or not to block: European approaches to content regulation, and implications for freedom of expression,* Computer Law & Security Review 2010, 260, 269 et seq.

2020 Richard Clayton, *Harmful Content on the Internet and in Video Games,* p. 1.

2021 *Ibid.*

ordering the deletion or blocking of access to illegal content. As it would go beyond the scope of this research to address all constellations in detail, the focus will be on the enforcement via civil law. However, as the *DEA 2010* initially foresaw provisions that would allow website blocking by administrative authorities, this issue will be briefly addressed. In that context, it will be outlined by looking at the practice in France and Germany why access blocking orders by administrative authorities are a highly controversial issue. We will see that even with regard to child abuse content, blocking is rarely ordered by administrative authorities. Thus, administrative blocking orders are not an issue when it comes to the enforcement of merely private intellectual property rights. As the focus of this Chapter is primarily on civil rights enforcement, respectively content blocking to enforce intellectual property, criminal law will not be a core subject of this chapter. Although "websites" have been seised and operators of piracy websites been convicted for large-scale intellectual property rights infringements, this research considers it more interesting to analyse the framework for civil rights enforcement and examine the efficiency of orders requiring online intermediaries to monitor content and block access or even delete third party content.

Depending on their status, meaning whether they are a mere technical facilitator of online communication and provide access to the Internet (access provider), or host third party information, the liability regimes vary. In the context of this work, caching will not be addressed.

I. EU Legal Framework

While in the Second Chapter, the outline of the EU legal framework focussed on user-targeted enforcements mechanisms in relation to peer-to-peer file-sharing, the following section focusses on enforcement mechanisms that rely on the involvement of third parties that are innocent from a tort law perspective. In that respect, the discussion is limited to obligations of access and host providers. Some legal provisions that have been outlined in Chapter 2, are also relevant when it comes to enforcement actions against intermediaries; these provisions will not be presented again but only referred to in the analysis.

1. Liability of Intermediaries in General: The E-Commerce Directive 2000/31

Intermediary liability is addressed in the *E-Commerce Directive*. The Directive itself does not establish liability, but determines the circumstances in which the liability of certain online intermediaries should be limited.[2022]

The exemptions for online intermediaries that are provided for in the *E-Commerce Directive* have already been outlined in the first Chapter. At this point, the most important aspects with regard to access and host provider liability will be recalled.

First of all, Recital 45 in the preamble to the Directive clarifies that the limitations of the liability of intermediary service providers established in this Directive do not affect the possibility of injunctions of different kinds: "such injunctions can in particular consist of orders by courts or administrative authorities requiring the termination or prevention of any infringement, including the removal of illegal information or the disabling of access to it". In the following, Recital 47 states that "Member States are prevented from imposing a monitoring obligation on service providers only with respect to obligations of a general nature; this does not concern monitoring obligations in a specific case and, in particular, does not affect orders by national authorities in accordance with national legislation".

Provisions on the liability of intermediaries can be found in Articles 12 to 15 of the *E-Commerce Directive.*

In the context of this research Articles 12, 14 and 15 are of relevance. Article 12(1) provides that a service providers whose service "consists of the transmission in a communication network of information provided by a recipient of the service, or the provision of access to a communication network" is not liable for the information transmitted, on condition that the provider "(a) does not initiate the transmission; (b) does not select the receiver of the transmission; and (c) does not select or modify the information contained in the transmission". Pursuant to section 3 of said Arti-

---

2022 Accordingly, the Directive lacks EU-wide criminal intermediary liability, because there is no EU-wide criminalisation of copyright infringement. In that regard, the European Commission withdrew a proposal for a European Parliament and Council Directive on criminal measures aimed at ensuring the enforcement of intellectual property rights (Com(2005) 276/1), See OJ C 252 (18.09.2010), 9.

cle, this "does not affect the possibility for a court or administrative authority, in accordance with Member States' legal systems, of requiring the service provider to terminate or prevent an infringement".

The relevant Article in relation to enforcement against host providers is Arrticle 14 of the *E-Commerce Directive.* A host provider is defined as providing a service that "consist of the storage of information provided by a recipient of the service". Furthmore hosting services are "of a mere technical, automatic and passive nature, which implies that the information society service provider has neither knowledge of nor control over the information which is transmitted or stored".[2023]

Under Article 14 of the *E-Commerce Directive* a host provider shall not be liable for the information stored at the request of a recipient on the condition that :

> "(a) the provider does not have actual knowledge of illegal activity or information and, as regards claims for damages, is not aware of facts or circumstances from which the illegal activity or information is apparent; or
> (b) the provider, upon obtaining such knowledge or awareness, acts expeditiously to remove or to disable access to the information."

The last condition imposes a duty of care on the provider. He has to take expeditious action if he obtains knowledge or awareness of the illegality of information. Recital 48 provides that the Directive does not affect the possibility for Member States to require host providers to apply duties of care, which can reasonably be expected from them and which are specified by national law, in order to detect and prevent certain types of illegal activities.[2024]

Even if a host provider receives notice of unlawful content, it can avoid liability under the condition that it takes down or blocks access to that content expeditiously. Member States are merely encouraged to implement "rapid and reliable procedures for removing and disabling access to illegal information".[2025]

2023 Recital 42 of the *E-Commerce Directive*.

2024 It has been understood that such duties of care mean those imposed by criminal or public law e.g. aid in investigation of crime or security matters, not as extending to duties under private law, such as to help prevent copyright infringement – since that would negate the point of Article 15 as well as that of Article 14 generally. See Cf. Lilian Edwards, *Role and responsibility of Internet intermediaries in the field of copyright and related rights*, p. 10.

2025 Recital 40 of the *E-Commerce Directive*.

Article 15(1) prohibits Member States from imposing a general obligation on providers, when providing the above mentioned services," to monitor the information which they transmit or store, nor a general obligation actively to seek facts or circumstances indicating unlawful activity". In that context, Member States may however establish obligations for the service providers promptly to inform the competent public authorities of alleged unlawful activities undertaken or information provided by recipients of their service or obligations to communicate to the competent authorities, at their request, information enabling the identification of recipients of their service with whom they have storage agreements".[2026] This does not mean that monitoring is in general prohibited. Moreover, Article 14(3) clarifies that the prohibition of general monitoring does not affect the possibility for a court or national authority of requiring the service provider to terminate or prevent an infringement, or of establishing procedures governing the removal or disabling of access to information.

Article 15 leads to the question whether a measure that would require an online intermediary to actively search its systems infringes the prohibition to impose general monitoring. In that respect, Article 18 of the *E-Commerce Directive* requires Member States to adopt "measures designed to terminate any alleged infringement *and to prevent any further impairment of the interests involved*" (emphasis added).

2. Copyright Law Providing for Injunctions

As most intermediaries do not themselves infringe copyright, but provide the technical means for such to third parties, the EU legal framework provides for sanctions to be issued against intermediaries.

2026 Article 15(2) *E-Commerce Directive*.

a) Information Society Directive 2001/29/EC

The *InfoSoc Directive*[2027] does not only play a role when it comes to measures targeting end-users that infringe copyright, but also is relevant in the context of measures against intermediaries whose services have been used to infringe copyright.

As regards the Recitals of the *InfoSoc Directive*, Recital 9 defines the objective pursued by the Directive as to guarantee rights-holders a high level of protection. Recital 13 then calls for common search for, and consistent application at European level of, technical measures to protect intellectual property.

Recital 59 in the preamble to the *InfoSoc Directive* further states that "In the digital environment, in particular, the services of intermediaries may increasingly be used by third parties for infringing activities. In many cases such intermediaries are best placed to bring such infringing activities to an end. Therefore, without prejudice to any other sanctions and remedies available, rights-holders should have the possibility of applying for an injunction against an intermediary who carries a third party's infringement of a protected work or other subject-matter in a network. … The conditions and modalities relating to such injunctions should be left to the national law of the Member States".[2028]

In this regard, Articles 8 requires Member States to provide appropriate sanctions and remedies in respect of intellectual property rights infringements. The sanctions provided for shall be effective, proportionate and dissuasive. Accordingly, Article 8(3) *InfoSoc Directive* obliges Member States to ensure that rights-holders are in a position to apply for an injunction against intermediaries whose services are used by a third party to infringe copyright or related rights.[2029] This provision applies irrespective

---

2027 *Directive 2001/29/EC of the European Parliament and of the Council of 22.05.2001 on the harmonisation of certain aspects of copyright and related rights in the information society (InfoSoc Directive),* OJ L 167 (22.6.2001), 10-19.

2028 Recital 59 has been interpreted as providing a "cheapest cost avoider" argument for intermediary liability. See High Court, *L'Oréal v eBay*, [2009] EWHC 1094 (Ch), para. 277 and Matthias Leistner, *Grundlagen und Perspektiven der Haftung für Urheberrechtsverletzungen im Internet*, Zeitschrift für Urheber- und Medienrecht 2012, 722, 723.

2029 In a limited number of Member States (Austria, Greece, Latvia, Belgium), Article 8(3) has been implemented in national legislation. In other Member States,

of whether the relevant acts come under the exception for acts of temporary copying under Article 5(1) and irrespective of whether they are covered by exceptions from liability under the relevant provisions of the *E-Commerce Directive*. For Article 8(3) to apply, it suffices that the existence of copyright infringement by a third party is established.[2030] As regards the definition of "intermediary" in the sense of Articles 5(1)(a) and 8(3) *InfoSoc Directive*, this does not just refer to host providers but also includes access providers which merely provide users with Internet.[2031]

With respect to the relation of the *InfoSoc Directive* to the *E-Commerce Directive*, Recital (16) clarifies that the *InfoSoc Directive* is without prejudice to provisions relating to liability in that Directive.

b) IPR Enforcement Directive 2004/48/EC

Article 8 of the *IPR Enforcement Directive*[2032], which provides for information rights being available for righta-holders has already been discussed in the previous Chapter.

The *IPR Enforcement Directive* does however not only provide for information rights, but also provides for injunctions being available for right holders against infringers and intermediaries.

Of specific interest in relation to stop an on-going infringement and copyright enforcement via intermediaries, is Article11 of the *Enforcement Directive*, which explicitly requires Member States to provide for an injunction to prohibit the continuation of an infringement:

Article 8(3) comes under the scope of existing legislation. See Commission of the European Communities, *Commission Staff Working Document, Report to the Council, the European Parliament and the Economic and Social Committee on the application of Directive 2001/29/EC on the harmonisation of certain aspects of copyright and related rights in the information society* (30.11.2007), SEC(2007) 1556, p. 9.

2030 *Ibid.*

2031 CJEU, C-557/07 *LSG-Gesellschaft zur Wahrnehmung von Leistungsschutzrechten GmbH v Tele2 Telecommunication GmbH* [2009] ECR I-1227.

2032 *Directive 2004/48/EC of the European Parliament and of the Council of 29 April 2004 on the enforcement of Intellectual Property Rights,* OJ L 157 (30.04.2004), pp. 16–25. The directive is also known as "(IPR) Enforcement Directive" or "IPRED".

> "Member States shall ensure that, where a judicial decision is taken finding an infringement of an intellectual property right, the judicial authorities may issue against the infringer an injunction aimed at prohibiting the continuation of the infringement. Where provided for by national law, non-compliance with an injunction shall, where appropriate, be subject to a recurring penalty payment, with a view to ensuring compliance. Member States shall also ensure that rights-holders are in a position to apply for an injunction against intermediaries whose services are used by a third party to infringe an intellectual property right, without prejudice to Article 8(3) of Directive 2001/29/EC."

Article 11 thereby forms a common basis for the availability of injunctions in the Member States. In this respect, Article 2(3) makes it clear that the *Enforcement Directive* "shall not affect" the provisions of the *E-Commerce Directive* as well as the substantive law on intellectual property and the Data Protection Directive. Thus, any injunction granted must not affect the provision in Article 15 *E-Commerce Directive* which prohibits the imposition of a general monitoring obligation onto intermediaries.

In addition to Article 11 injunctions, Article 9 of the Directive provides an equivalent provision for interlocutory injunctions. For both types of injunctions, Article 3 requires that they "[S]hall be fair and equitable and shall not be unnecessarily complicated or costly, or entail unreasonable time-limits or unwarranted delays [and] shall also be effective, proportionate and dissuasive and shall be applied in such a manner as to avoid the creation of barriers to legitimate trade and to provide for safeguards against their abuse."[2033]

This implies that, in a case which concerns possible infringements of trade marks on an online marketplace, the injunction obtained against the service provider cannot have as its object or effect a general and permanent prohibition on the selling, on that marketplace, of goods bearing those trade marks.[2034]

Some guidance as to the interpretation of Articles 3 and 11 of the Directive can also be drawn from the Recitals. Of a mere 32 Recitals, the relevant Recitals are Recitals (22)–(24), which read as follows:

"(22) It is also essential to provide for provisional measures for the immediate termination of infringements, without awaiting a decision on the substance of the case, while observing the rights of the defence, ensur-

2033 In fact, Article 3 applies to all remedies which includes injunctions.

2034 CJEU, C-324/09 *L'Oréal v eBay* [2011] ECR I-06011, para. 140. This case will be discussed in detail below.

ing the proportionality of the provisional measures as appropriate to the characteristics of the case in question and providing the guarantees needed to cover the costs and the injury caused to the defendant by an unjustified request. Such measures are particularly justified where any delay would cause irreparable harm to the holder of an intellectual property right.

> (23) Without prejudice to any other measures, procedures and remedies available, rights-holders should have the possibility of applying for an injunction against an intermediary whose services are being used by a third party to infringe the rights-holder's industrial property right. The conditions and procedures relating to such injunctions should be left to the national law of the Member States. As far as infringements of copyright and related rights are concerned, a comprehensive level of harmonisation is already provided for in Directive 2001/29/EC. Article 8(3) of Directive 2001/29/EC should therefore not be affected by this Directive.
> (24) Depending on the particular case, and if justified by the circumstances, the measures, procedures and remedies to be provided for should include prohibitory measures aimed at preventing further infringements of intellectual property rights. Moreover there should be corrective measures, where appropriate at the expense of the infringer, such as the recall and definitive removal from the channels of commerce, or destruction, of the infringing goods and, in appropriate cases, of the materials and implements principally used in the creation or manufacture of these goods. These corrective measures should take account of the interests of third parties including, in particular, consumers and private parties acting in good faith."

As is clear from Recital 23 to the *Enforcement Directive*, the rules for the operation of the injunctions for which the Member States must provide under Articles 9 and 11 of the Directive, such as those relating to the conditions to be met and to the procedure to be followed, are solely a matter for national law.[2035]

In July 2011, the European Commission published comments that it had received on its 2010 report on the impact of the *Enforcement Directive* which specifically addressed intermediaries and the workability of injunctions. Most rights-holders and all collecting societies that took a position on the issue called for a stronger involvement of intermediaries and for clearer rules regarding the conditions under which injunctions may be granted.[2036] Many stakeholders expressed their concerns regarding the

2035 This is also the case with the *InfoSoc Directive*.

2036 European Commission, *Synthesis of comments on the Commission Report on the application of Directive 2004/48/EC of the European Parliament and the Coun-*

scope of injunctions available to prevent repeat infringements as there is no exact guidance in the Directive.[2037]

c) Data Protection Framework: E-Privacy Directive 2002/58

When monitoring of online communication is concerned, the actors have to respect the data protection rules set out in the *E-Privacy Directive*. Article 5(1) of the *E-Privacy Directive* provides for the secrecy of communication by requiring Member States to "ensure the confidentiality of communications and the related traffic data by means of a public communications network and publicly available electronic communications services, through national legislation. In particular, they shall prohibit listening, tapping, storage or other kinds of interception or surveillance of communications and the related traffic data by persons other than users, without the consent of the users concerned, except when legally authorised to do so in accordance with Article 15(1) …".

Surfing the Internet falls under the definition of "communication" as defined in Article 2(d) *E-Privacy Directive*.

3. Relevant Jurisprudence of the CJEU

In recent cases, the CJEU had been asked on the interpretation of the aforementioned legal framework in the context of injunctions ordering the cessation of copyright infringements. The injunctions sought after by rights-holders were addressed at host providers as well as access providers. Considering the liability exemptions for intermediaries, it does not come as a surprise that intermediaries oppose any monitoring and filtering obligations. [2038] Online intermediaries argued and are still arguing that they are not in a position to make qualitative judgements as to the legality of content, and thus consider that injunctions should remain limited to the elimination of a concrete and actual infringement, and not apply

---

cil of 29.04.2004 on the enforcement of intellectual property rights (July 2011), COM/2010/779 final, p. 8.

2037 *Ibid*, p.10.

2038 *Ibid.*

in view of possible future infringements.[2039] Further, where access providers have been addressed, these intermediaries do not consider themselves as the correct addressee for costly filtering schemes. The following case law shows, that the compatibility of such injunctions with EU law, in particular with the prohibition of general monitoring obligations as set forth in the *E-Commerce Directive*, has been central to the disputes. A key question has been the scope of any monitoring obligation, which may not only aim at stopping an on-going infringement, but also constitute a preventive measure with a view to possible future infringements.[2040]

Although *Louis Vuitton v Google France*[2041] was the first case in which the CJEU elaborated on the liability exemptions in the *E-Commerce Directive*, this case will not be discussed any further as it primarily dealt with the question of whether Google could be considered a host provider. An evaluation of host provider liability in general would go beyond the scope of this research. At this point it is sufficient to know, that the host provider's service has to be neutral with the provider taking a mere technical, automatic and passive role.[2042]

a) Injunctions in General: Case C-324/09 L'Oréal v eBay

Important guidance as regards injunctions to prevent further infringements of copyright was given by the CJEU in its preliminary ruling decision in

2039 *Ibid.*

2040 This has previously been discussed as a development from notice and takedown to a notice and stay down.

2041 CJEU, C-236/08 to C-238/08 *Google France v Louis Vuitton* [2010] E.T.M.R. 30.

2042 *Ibid*, para. 113.

the case of *L'Oréal v eBay*[2043]. This case provided precedent for further cases concerning copyright infringements.

L'Oréal took action against the online auction platform eBay because users of eBay were selling counterfeit L'Oréal products and products sourced from outside the EU/EEA, all of which L'Oréal claimed infringed its trade mark rights. The High Court of England and Wales was satisfied that it had the power under the *Senior Courts Act 1981* and its equitable

2043 CJEU, C-324/09 *L'Oréal v eBay* [2011] ECR I-06011. This case has triggered numerous comments and annotations. For an analysis of the decision see for instance Patrick Van Eecke/Maarten Truyens, *L'Oréal v eBay: Is the tide finally turning for hosting providers?*, Computer und Recht 2011, 1–8; Patrick Van Eecke/Maarten Truyens, L'Oréal v eBay: *The Court of Justice clarifies the position of online auction providers*, Computer Law Review International 2011, Issue 5, 129–136; Birgit Brömmekamp, *Der Fall L'Oréal gegen eBay: Prüfstein für die Informationsgesellschaft*, Wettbewerb in Recht und Praxis 2011, 306–316; François Terré, *Être ou ne pas être... responsable – À propos des prestataires de service par Internet*, La Semaine Juridique – édition générale 2011, n° 43–44, 1943–1948; Markus Rössel, *Filterpflichten des Providers im Lichte des EuGH – Eine Entlastung des I. Zivilsenates*, Computer und Recht 2011, 589–597; Hans-Peter Roth, *Verantwortlichkeit von Betreibern von Internet-Marktplätzen für Markenrechtsverletzungen durch Nutzer: L'Oréal gegen eBay*, Wettbewerb in Recht und Praxis 2011, 1258–1268; Stéphane Lemarchand/Anne-Sophie Lampe, *L'arrêt eBay c/ L'Oréal de la CJUE du 12 juillet 2011 revisite les conditions de la qualification de fournisseur d'hébergement au sens de l'article 14 de la directive « e-commerce »*, Droit de l'immatériel : informatique, médias, communication 2011, n° 75, 53–58; Marlous Schrijvers, *European Court rules on the position of eBay regarding the sale of infringing products: L'Oréal v eBay*, European Intellectual Property Review 2011, Vol. 33 Issue 11, 723-724; Jan Bernd Nordemann, *Haftung von Providern im Urheberrecht*, Gewerblicher Rechtsschutz und Urheberrecht 2011, 977–981; Gerald Spindler, *Europarechtliche Rahmenbedingungen der Störerhaftung im Internet*, Multimedia und Recht 2011, 703–707; Georg Borges, *Zur Haftung des Betreibers einer Handelsplattform für Markenverletzungen der Nutzer ("L'Oréal/eBay")*, Entscheidungen zum Wirtschaftsrecht 2011, 823–824; Catherine Smits/Johanne Ligot, *Arrêt "L'Oréal": clarifications sur le cadre légal des activités et des responsabilités des hébergeurs de sites Internet*, Journal de droit européen 2011, n° 184, 294–296; Eduard Salsas/Niko Härting, *L'Oréal v eBay – Consequences for EU Member States*, Computer Law Review International 2011, Issue 5, 137–142; Dennis Lievens, *L'Oréal v eBay – Welcomed in France, resented in England*, International Review of Intellectual Property and Competition Law 2012, 68–76; Toby Headdon, *Beyond liability: on the availability and scope of injunctions against online intermediaries after L'Oréal v eBay*, European Intellectual Property Review 2012, Vol 34 Issue 3, 137–144.

jurisdiction to grant an injunction against an intermediary that was not itself liable, but decided to stay the proceedings and refer inter alia the following questions to the CJEU for a preliminary ruling[2044]: (1) Whether eBay itself had infringed L'Oréal's trademarks by sponsoring Internet links which led to listings on eBay's site, including listings for infringing goods; (2) Whether the service provided by eBay is covered by Article 14(1) of the *E-Commerce Directive*, and if so, in what circumstances it may be concluded that the operator of an online marketplace has "awareness" within the meaning of Article 14(1); (3) whether Article 11 of the *IPR Enforcement Directive* requires Member States to ensure that the trade mark proprietor can obtain an injunction against the intermediary to prevent further infringements of the said trade mark, as opposed to continuation that specific act of infringement, where the services of an intermediary have been used by a third party to infringe a registered trade mark; if so, what the scope of that injunction is.

For host providers, it is of fundamental importance to know exactly under which circumstances they may be liable for third party content they host. While it is apparent from the definition of "information society service"[2045], that the liability exemptions of Article 12 to 15 of the *E-Commerce Directive* apply to services provided at a distance by means of electronic equipment for the processing and storage of data, at the individual request of a recipient of services (normally) for remuneration, the fact that the service provider stores information transmitted by its customers is not in itself sufficient ground for concluding that that service falls within the scope of Article 14(1) *E-Commerce Directive* (hosting). Where a service provider provides "assistance which entails, in particular, optimising the

---

2044 By questions 1 to 4 the High Court asked the CJEU to decide if the sale of tester and dramming products and unboxed products amounts to an infringement of the trademarks according to Article 7 of the Trade Marks Directive 89/104. However, as these questions only relate to the liability of the individual sellers and not to eBay it will not be discussed here.

2045 Article 2(a) of the *E-Commerce Directive* defines "information society services" by reference to Article 1(2) of Directive 98/34/EC of the European Parliament and of the Council of 22.06.1998 laying down a procedure for the provision of information in the field of technical standards and regulations and of rules on Information Society services (OJ 1998 L 204, p. 37), as amended by Directive 98/48/EC of 20.07.1998 (OJ 1998 L 217, p. 18), which refers to "any service normally provided for remuneration, at a distance, by electronic means and at the individual request of a recipient of services".

presentation of the offers for sale in question or promoting those offers, it must be considered not to have taken a neutral position between the customer-seller concerned and potential buyers but to have played an active role of such a kind as to give it knowledge of, or control over, the data relating to those offers for sale".[2046] In this case, the service provider cannot rely on the exemption from liability referred to in Article 14(1) *E-Commerce Directive*. The liability exemption for host providers does not lead to a broad overall liability exemption. It applies to specific activities at a micro-level. Acting non-neutrally in relation to some types of third party content does not affect the status for other third party content for which neutrality has been maintained.

Only "in situations in what the provider has confined itself to a merely technical and automatic processing of data", Article 14(1) will apply, meaning that the provider may be exempt, from any liability for unlawful data that it has stored on condition that it has not had "actual knowledge of illegal activity or information" and, as regards claims for damages, has not been aware of facts or circumstances on which a diligent economic operator should have realised that the offers for sale in question were unlawful and, in the event of it being so aware, failed to act expeditiously to remove, or disable access to, the information.[2047]

With respect to notice and take down requests, which service providers regularly face under the *E-Commerce Directive's* limited liability scheme, the question regarding the scope of a possible injunction regardless of any liability of the service provider himself is of great importance. Whilst an injunction against an infringer logically entails preventing that person from continuing the infringement, the situation is somewhat different when an injunction is sought for against the service provider that provides the means by which the infringement is committed. Service providers would obviously argue that an injunction within the meaning of the third sentence of Article 11 of the *IPR Enforcement Directive* may relate only to specific and clearly identified infringements of an intellectual property right, while right holders would argue that injunctions under the *Enforcement Directive* also cover the prevention of future infringements.[2048] It was in *L'Oréal v eBay*, that the CJEU for the first time discussed whether the third sentence of Article 11 of the *Enforcement Directive* requires

2046 CJEU, C-324/09 *L'Oréal v eBay* [2011] ECR I-06011, para. 116.
2047 *Ibid*, paras. 119 and 124.
2048 *Ibid*, paras. 125 et seq.

injunctions to prevent future infringements of intellectual property rights, rather than just bringing to an end specific existing infringements. According to the CJEU, an injunction as referred to in this particular third sentence cannot be equated with an "injunction aimed at prohibiting the continuation of the infringement" as referred to in the first sentence of Article 11.[2049] National courts must be able to order service providers to take measures that go beyond a mere take down, and contribute to the prevention of future infringements.[2050] The reason for this was that if Article 11 *Enforcement Directive* was interpreted in a manner that meant injunctions were not available to prevent "further impairment", the scope of the obligation in Article 18 of the *E-Commerce Directive* would be narrowed[2051] – which would be contrary to Article 2(3) of the *Enforcement Directive*. The Court also cited Recital 24 of the *E-Commerce Directive*, which explicitly states that measures aimed at preventing further infringements of intellectual property rights must be provided for.[2052] Unfortunately, the CJEU did not elaborate what is meant by "future" infringements or "further impairments". The conditions and procedures for injunctions are the responsibility of the national courts of the Member States, and thus the definition of prevention of future infringements is also a matter for national law.[2053] The Court also side-stepped the elaboration of the "double requirement of

2049 *Ibid*, para. 130.

2050 *Ibid*, para. 131.

2051 *Ibid*, paras. 132 et seq. Under said Article of the *E-Commerce Directive*, Member States are required to adopt "measures designed to terminate any alleged infringement and to prevent any further impairment of the interests involved".

2052 *Ibid*, para. 134.

2053 *Ibid*, para. 135. In comparison, the Advocate General Jääskinen's opinion was rather detailed on this point: first, he stated that third sentence of Article 11 of the *Enforcement Directive* does not provide for an injunction against an intermediary to prevent any further infringement of that type (L'Oréal's trade marks) as this would be inconsistent with the principle of proportionality. Secondly, he concluded that an injunction may be available against an intermediary to prevent not only the continuation of a specific act of infringement, but also the repetition of the same or a similar infringement in the future, where such injunctions are available under national law. However, he did not specify what may be considered a "similar" infringement. Finally, the Advocate General suggested that an appropriate limit may be to impose a "double requirement of identity", which basically means that the future infringements would have to be committed by the same third party and in respect of the same trade mark. Hence, an injunction could be given against an intermediary to prevent the continuation or repetition of an infringement of a certain trade mark by a certain user. See Opin-

identity" suggested by the Advocate General in his opinion. Under the double requirement of identity, a service provider would be obliged to prevent future infringements committed by the same user and in respect to the same intellectual property right that had previously been infringed.[2054] Instead the Court considered it more important to stress that it follows from Article 15(1) *E-Commerce Directive* in conjunction with Article 2(3) *IPR Enforcement Directive*s that the measures required of the service provider concerned "cannot consist in an active monitoring of all the data of each of its customers in order to prevent any future infringement of intellectual property rights via the provider's website".[2055] Furthermore, a general monitoring obligation would be incompatible with Article 3 *IPR Enforcement Directive*, which states that the measures referred to by the Directive must be fair and proportionate and must not be excessively costly.[2056] Finally, measures which may be imposed in the form of an injunction under the third sentence of Article 11 *IPR Enforcement Directive* must strike a fair balance between the various rights and interests concerned, and must not create barriers to legitimate trade.[2057]

In summary, the Court set up basic rules for injunctions under the third sentence of Article 11 *Enforcement Directive*, which must be interpreted as requiring the Member States to ensure that the national courts are able to order a host service provider to take measures which contribute, not only to bringing to an end infringements of intellectual property rights by users of that service, but also to preventing further infringements of that kind. The measures that need to be imposed will be determined by the scope of the injunction required, which further will be determined by the effectiveness, cost, proportionality and dissuasiveness of the measures that might be taken. The Court however refrained from providing further guidance on the determination of "future infringement" to which an injunction may apply.

---

ion of Advocate General Jääskinen in case C-324/09 *L'Oréal v eBay*, delivered on 09.12.2010, paras. 169 to 182.

2054 See Opinion of Advocate General Jääskinen in case C-324/09 L'Oréal v Ebay, delivered on 09.12.2010, para. 182.

2055 CJEU, C-324/09 *L'Oréal v eBay* [2011] ECR I-06011, para. 139.

2056 *Ibid.*

2057 In this regard, the Court referred to Case C-275/06 *Promusicae v Telefónica de Espana* [2008] ECRI-271, paras. 65–68.

b) Injunctions against Access Providers: Case C-70/10 Scarlet Extended v SABAM

It did not take long until the CJEU was asked whether a particular filtering obligation imposed by a national court fulfills the general criteria set forth in the *L'Oréal v eBay* ruling. In *Scarlet Extended v SABAM*[2058], the CJEU concluded that the terms of an injunction granted by a Belgian court requiring the Internet access provider Scarlet to install and maintain at its own expense a filtering system to prevent illegal file-sharing was contrary to EU law.

This case was referred to the CJEU by the Belgian Court of Appeal and concerned an appeal by Scarlet against an injunction obtained by SABAM, a Belgian collective rights management organisation (which acted on behalf of various copyright owners). SABAM had determined that Internet users were using Scarlet's services to illegally download their clients' content, and therefore sought an injunction requiring Scarlet to bring this activity to an end by making it impossible for its users to send and receive SABAM's content using peer-to-peer software. The injunction required Scarlet to monitor all electronic communications of all customers at its own expense for an unlimited period of time.

The proposed injunction effectively required Scarlet to (1) identify within all of the electronic communications of all of its customers those files relating to peer-to-peer traffic; (2) identify within that traffic the files containing works in which the right owners claimed rights; (3) determine

2058 CJEU, C-70/10 *Scarlet Extended v SABAM*, Judgment of 14.11.2011, ECR I-11959. For comments on the judgement, see inter alia Sandra Schmitz, *Die Verfolgung von Urheberrechtsverletzungen im Internet – Neues vom EUGH*, in: Jürgen Taeger (ed.), *IT und Internet – Mit Recht gestalten*, Tagungsband Herbstakademie 2012 (2012), pp. 227–243; Stefan Kulk/Frederik Zuiderveen Borgesius, *Filtering for Copyright Enforcement in Europe after the SABAM cases*, European Intellectual Property Review 2012, 54–58; Evangelia Psychogiopoulou, *Copyright enforcement, human rights protection and the responsibilities of Internet service providers after Scarlet*, European Intellectual Property Review 2012, 552–555; Hans-Peter Roth, *Überwachungs- und Prüfungspflicht von Providern im Lichte der aktuellen EuGH-Rechtsprechung, zugleich Anm. zu EuGH, Urteil vom 24-11.2011 – C-70/10*, Zeitschrift für Urheber- und Medienrecht 2012, 125–128; Darren Meale, *SABAM v Scarlet: of course blanket filtering of the Internet is unlawful, but this isn't the end of the story*, European Intellectual Property Review 2012, Vol. 34 Issue 7, 429–432.

which of those files are being shared unlawfully; and (4) block the file-sharing which it considers to be unlawful.

The central question in the case was whether the *InfoSoc Directive* and the *IPR Enforcement Directive*, interpreted in the light of the *E-Commerce Directive*, the *Data Protection Directive,* the *E-Privacy Directive* and fundamental rights, preclude such a filter obligation.

The installation of the contested filtering system namely obliged the Internet service provider to actively monitor all the data relating to each of its customers in order to prevent future infringements. The CJEU concluded that the extent of the obligations placed upon Scarlet corresponded to a general monitoring obligation, which is prohibited by Article 15(1) of the *E-Commerce Directive*.[2059] When assessing whether that injunction was consistent with EU law, account was also taken of the requirements that stem from the protection of the applicable fundamental rights. In that regard, as paragraphs 62 to 68 of the judgment in case C-275/06 *Promusicae*[2060] make clear, the protection of the fundamental right to property, which includes the rights linked to intellectual property, must be balanced against the protection of other fundamental rights. Hence, a fair balance must be struck between the intellectual property right enjoyed by the copyright holders and the right to freedom to conduct a business enjoyed by the Internet service provider under Article 16 *CFR*. The installation of a "complicated, costly, permanent computer system" at the expense of the service provider, thus did not only contravene Article 3(1) of the *IPR Enforcement Directive* (no measures that are unnecessarily complicated or costly), but also did not strike a fair balance between the interests of the service provider and copyright holders involved.[2061] Moreover, as the filtering "would involve a systematic analysis of all content" and "the collection and identification of users' IP addresses from which unlawful content on the network is sent",[2062] this also infringed the fundamental rights of the Internet service provider's customers, namely their right to protection of their personal data (Article 8 *CFR*) and their freedom to receive or

2059 CJEU, C-70/10 *Scarlet Extended v SABAM*, Judgment of 14.11.2011, ECR I-11959, paras. 35 et seq.In this respect, the CJEU also referred to its ruling in *L'Oréal v eBay*, para. 139.

2060 CJEU, C-275/06 *Promusicae* [2008] ECR I-271.

2061 CJEU, C-70/10 *Scarlet Extended v SABAM*, Judgment of 14.11.2011, paras. 48 et seq.

2062 *Ibid*, para. 51.

impart information (Article 11 *CFR*).[2063] The Court considered the collection and identification of users' IP addresses as protected personal data because "they allow those users to be precisely identified".[2064] The proposed injunction was further held to potentially undermine freedom of information since that system might not distinguish adequately between unlawful content and lawful content, "with the result that its introduction could lead to the blocking of lawful communications".[2065]

c) Injunctions against Host Providers: Case C-360/10 SABAM v Netlog

While the case of *Scarlet Extended v SABAM* concerned a filtering obligation imposed on an Internet access provider, the case *of SABAM v Netlog*[2066] concerned a similar obligation imposed on a social network provider.[2067] SABAM had applied before a Belgian court to order Netlog to cease unlawfully making available musical or audio-visual works from SABAM's repertoire and to pay a penalty for each day of delay in complying with the order. The Belgian Court in that respect referred the following question to the CJEU for a preliminary ruling:

"Do Directives 2001/29 and 2004/48, in conjunction with Directives 95/46, 2000/31 and 2002/58, construed in particular in the light of Articles

---

2063 *Ibid*, para. 50.

2064 *Ibid*, para. 51.

2065 *Ibid*, oara. 52.

2066 CJEU, C-360/10, *SABAM v Netlog NV*, Judgment of 16.02.2012. For comments on the judgment see inter alia Axel Metzger, *Anm. zu EuGH: Keine Pflicht für Betreiber sozialer Netzwerke zu umfa-senden Überwachungs- und Filtersystemen,* Gewerblicher Rechtsschutz und Urheberrecht 2012, 382–385; Sandra Schmitz, *Die Verfolgung von Urheberrechtsverletzungen im Internet – Neues vom EUGH,* in: Jürgen Taeger (ed.), *IT und Internet – Mit Recht gestalten* (2012), pp. 227–243; Stefan Kulk/Frederik Zuiderveen Borgesius, *Filtering for Copyright Enforcement in Europe after the SABAM cases,* European Intellectual Property Review 2012, 54–58; Evangelia Psychogiopoulou, *Copyright enforcement, human rights protection and the responsibilities of Internet service providers after Scarlet,* European Intellectual Property Review 2012, 552–555.

2067 Netlog runs an online social networking platform where users who register acquire a personal space known as a "profile" which the user can complete himself and which allows him to participate in virtual communities through which the users can communicate with each other and develop friendships. On their profile, users can enter information about themselves, keep a diary, and inter alia, display images or publish video clips.

8 and 10 of the European Convention on the Protection of Human Rights and Fundamental Freedoms [signed in Rome on 4 November 1950], permit Member States to authorise a national court, before which substantive proceedings have been brought and on the basis merely of a statutory provision stating that "[the national courts] may also issue an injunction against intermediaries whose services are used by a third party to infringe a copyright or related right", to order a hosting service provider to introduce, for all its customers, in abstracto and as a preventive measure, at its own cost and for an unlimited period, a system for filtering most of the information which is stored on its servers in order to identify on its servers electronic files containing musical, cinematographic or audio-visual work in respect of which SABAM claims to hold rights, and subsequently to block the exchange of such files?".

Because the CJEU's judgment resembles the prior judgment in Scarlet Extended, the following outline only refers to aspects where the judgment departs from Scarlet Extended.

First of all the CJEU established that the social network provider in question can be considered as hosting providers, as it "stores information provided by the users of that platform, relating to their profile, on its servers".[2068] As the court had already ruled in *Scarlet Extended v SABAM* that the prohibition of general monitoring applies in particular to national measures which would require an intermediary provider to actively monitor all the data of each of its customers in order to prevent any future infringement of intellectual property rights, the CJEU only had to examine whether the contested filtering system would oblige Netlog to actively monitor all its customers' data.[2069] As this was the case, the CJEU almost literally reiterated its findings in the *Scarlet Extended* case and concluded that the *E-Commerce Directive*, the *InfoSoc Directive* and the *IPR Enforcement Directive* "read together and construed in the light of the requirements stemming from the protection of the applicable fundamental rights, must be interpreted as precluding a national court from issuing an injunction against a hosting service provider which requires it to install a system for filtering: information which is stored on its servers by its service users, which applies indiscriminately to all of those users, as a preventative measure, exclusively at its expense, and for an unlimited period,

2068 CJEU, C-360/10, *SABAM v Netlog NV*, Judgment of 16.02.2012, para. 27.
2069 See *ibid*, paras. 34 et seq.

which is capable of identifying electronic files containing musical, cinematographic or audio-visual work in respect of which the applicant for the injunction claims to hold intellectual property rights, with a view to preventing those works from being made available to the public in breach of copyright".[2070]

d) Injunctions Specifying the Means of Access Blocking: Case C-314/12 UPC Telekabel Wien v Constantin Film Verleih

In the case of *UPC Telekabel Wien v Constantin Film Verleih*[2071], the CJEU had to inter alia deal with the question whether it is compatible with EU law, to require an Internet access provider to take specific measures to make it more difficult for its customers to access a piracy website without any further determination of the measures to be adopted.

Constantin Film and Wega, two film production companies applied for interim measures with an Austrian in order to enjoin UPC Telekabel, an Internet service provider, to block the access of its customers to the website kino.to. The website in question made available to the public without their consent, cinematographic works over which Constantin Film and Wega hold a right related to copyright.[2072] By order of 13 May 2011, the Handelsgericht Wien prohibited UPC Telekabel from providing its customers with access to said website. In particular, this prohibition was to be carried out by blocking that kino.to's domain name and current IP address and any other IP address of that site of which UPC Telekabel might be aware. In June 2011, kino.to ceased its operation. By order of 27 October 2011, the Oberlandesgericht Wien, as an appeal court, partially reversed the order of the court of first instance, in so far as the Handelsgericht had specified the means that UPC Telekabel had to introduce in order to block access to kino.to. The Oberlandesgericht Wien held that UPC Telekabel as an intermediary whose services were used to infringe a right related to copyright could be required to forbid its customers access to kino.to, but

2070 *Ibid*, grounds.

2071 CJEU, C-314/12 *UPC Telekabel Wien GmbH v Constantin Film Verleih GmbH and Wega Filmproduktionsgesellschaft GmbH,* Judgment of 27.03.2014.

2072 It was undisputed that the protected works were made available to users of the website without the consent of the rights-holders mentioned in Article 3(2) of the *InfoSoc Directive*.

was free to decide the means to be used. Upon appeal by UPC Telekabel, the Oberster Gerichtshof referred the case to the CJEU for a preliminary ruling on inter alia the interpretation of Article 8(3) of the *InfoSoc Directive*.[2073]

The CJEU held that when protected subject-matter is made available to users of a website without the consent of the rights-holder, this infringes Article 3 of the *InfoSoc Directive*.[2074] In order to remedy this infringement, Article 8(3) *InfoSoc Directive* provides rights-holders with the possibility to apply for an injunction against the intermediary whose services are used to infringe copyright or related rights. It follows from Recital 59 of said Directive that the term "intermediary" in Article 8 encompasses any person who carries a third party's infringement in a network.[2075] UPC Telekabel as an access provider was held to be an inevitable actor in any transmission of an infringement over the Internet between one of its customers and a third party, since, in granting access to the network, it makes tat transmission possible. [2076] The CJEU confirmed its findings in the SABAM cases that the *InfoSoc Directive* requires that the requested injunction must not only aim at bringing to an end infringements of copyright and of related rights, but also at preventing them.[2077]

In the following the CJEU reiterates that in order to assess whether an injunction such as that at issue in the main proceedings, taken on the basis of Article 8(3) *InfoSoc Directive*, is consistent with EU law, it is necessary to take account in particular of the requirements that stem from the protection of the applicable fundamental rights.[2078] The Court arrived at outlin-

---

2073 ÖOGH, Decision of 11.05.2012 – 4 Ob 6/12d.

2074 CJEU, C-314/12 *UPC Telekabel Wien GmbH v Constantin Film Verleih GmbH and Wega Filmproduktionsgesellschaft GmbH,* Judgment of 27.03.2014, paras. 24 et seq.

2075 *Ibid*, para. 30.

2076 *Ibid*, para. 32 with reference to CJEU, C-557/07 *LSG-Gesellschaft zur Wahrnehmung von Leistungsschutzrechten* [2009] ECR I-1227, para. 44. In LSG the CJEU held that "Access providers which merely provide users with Internet access, without offering other services such as email, FTP or file-sharing services or exercising any control, whether de iure or de facto, over the services which users make use of, must be regarded as 'intermediaries' within the meaning of Article 8(3) of the [Information Society] Directive".

2077 *Ibid*, para. 37.

2078 *Ibid*, para. 45.

ing and balancing the fundamental rights concerned in a more detailed account than in the SABAM cases.

As regards the freedom to conduct a business, the Court held that this includes inter alia "the right for any business to be able to freely use, within the limits of its liability for its own acts, the economic, technical and financial resources available to it".[2079] The injunction at issue, which obliges the access provider to take measures which may represent a significant cost for him, constrains the access provider in a manner which restricts the free use of the resources at his disposal.[2080] The measure would have a considerable impact on the organisation of his activities or require difficult and complex technical solutions.[2081] However, the measure in question would not infringe the core of the freedom to conduct business as it leaves the access provider to determine the specific measures to be taken in order to achieve the requested result. Hence, he can choose to put in place measures which are "best adapted to the resources and abilities available to him".[2082] Having implemented measures that are reasonable for him, the access provider will be exempted from liability.[2083] The law does not require the addressee of an injunction to make unbearable sacrifices, which the Court considers as justified in the light of the fact the service provider is not the author of the infringement in question.[2084] In that regard, the CJEU also stated that, "in accordance with the principle of legal certainty, it must be possible for the addressee of an injunction such as that at issue in the main proceedings to maintain before the court, once the implementing measures which he has taken are known and before any decision imposing a penalty on him is adopted, that the measures taken were indeed those which could be expected of him in order to prevent the proscribed result".[2085]

However, not only the interests of the addressee of the injunction and the copyright owners must be balanced, when adopting a measure, the ser-

2079 *Ibid*, para. 49.
2080 *Ibid*, para. 50.
2081 *Ibid.*
2082 *Ibid*, para. 52.
2083 *Ibid*, para. 53.
2084 *Ibid.*
2085 *Ibid*, para. 54.

vice provider must also ensure compliance with the fundamental right of Internet users to freedom of information.[2086]

The adopted measures "must be strictly targeted, in the sense that they must serve to bring an end to a third party's infringement of copyright or of a related right but without thereby affecting Internet users who are using the provider's services in order to lawfully access information".[2087] Otherwise, there would be an unjustified interference in the freedom of information of those users. A review of the compliance with this requirement can practically not be carried out at the stage of the enforcement proceedings if the adopted measures are not challenged.[2088] Accordingly, the CJEU held that – in order to prevent that fundamental rights preclude the adoption of an injunction – national procedural rules must provide a possibility for Internet users to assert their rights before the court once the concrete measures that have been taken by the service provider are known.[2089]

In the following, the CJEU recognised that it is possible that an injunction may not lead to a complete cessation of the intellectual property rights infringements.[2090] First, as mentioned above, the addressee of an injunction may escape liability, when measures that may be achievable, constitute unreasonable measures for him.[2091] Secondly, means, that put an end to the infringements in question, may not exist, or the complete cessation of the infringements may in practice not be achievable as users may circumvent the blocking.[2092] Nevertheless, the measures adopted "must be sufficiently effective to ensure genuine protection of the fundamental rights at issue", meaning that "they must have the effect of preventing unauthorised access to the protected subject-matter or, at least, of making it difficult to achieve and of seriously discouraging Internet users who are using the services of the addressee of that injunction from accessing the subject-matter made available to them in breach of that fundamental right".[2093]

2086 *Ibid*, para. 55.
2087 *Ibid*, para. 56.
2088 *Ibid*, para. 57.
2089 *Ibid*, para. 57.
2090 *Ibid*, para. 58.
2091 *Ibid*, para. 59.
2092 *Ibid*, para. 60.
2093 *Ibid*, para. 62.

As a consequence, even where measures do not achieve the cessation of an infringement at 100%, they cannot per se be considered to be incompatible with the requirement of striking a fair balance between the applicable fundamental rights.[2094]

e) Summary of the Case Law of the CJEU

From the *E-Commerce Directive*, the *InfoSoc Directive* and the *IPR Enforcement Directive* follows, that – regardless of the liability exemptions in the *E-Commerce Directive* – national courts can impose injunctions on online intermediaries.

The *InfoSoc Directive* and the *Enforcement Directive* foresee the possibility for rights-holders to apply for an injunction against an infringer, aiming at the prohibition of the continuation of an infringement. The case law outlined above clarifies that rights-holders may also apply for an injunction against online intermediaries who are not themselves liable for the infringement but whose services have been used by a third party to infringe intellectual property rights.

While the possibility for injunctions is settled case law, the scope of any such injunction remains rather unclear. So far, the CJEU has established that a general monitoring obligation would be incompatible with Article 3 of the *IPR Enforcement Directive*, which states that the measures referred to by the Directive must be fair and proportionate and must not be excessively costly. [2095] As regards the scope of any injunction, Article 11 of the *IPR Enforcement Directive* must be interpreted as requiring the Member States to ensure that the national courts are able to order a host service provider to take measures which contribute, not only to bringing to an end infringements of intellectual property rights by users of that service, but also to preventing further infringements of that kind. The measures that need to be imposed will be determined by the scope of the injunction required, which further will be determined by the effectiveness, cost, proportionality and dissuasiveness of the measures that might be taken. So far, it remains unclear which kind of infringements would amount to "future infringements", for instance whether that means the repertoire of

2094 *Ibid*, para. 63.
2095 CJEU, C-324/09 *L'Oréal and Others v eBay* [2011], para. 141.

the rights-holder, the protected work that has previously been infringed, and whether that would apply to infringements committed by the previous infringer or any potential user.

Some guidance has however been given in the SABAM cases as to what kind of monitoring obligations are not fair and equitable, unnecessarily complicated or costly and entail unreasonable time-limits. In the words of the CJEU, injunctions shall be precluded that require an Internet access to install a system for filtering all electronic communications passing via its services, which applies indiscriminately to all its customers, as a preventive measure, exclusively at its own expense, and for an unlimited period, which is capable of identifying on that provider's network the movement of electronic files containing a musical, cinematographic or audiovisual work in respect of which the applicant claims to hold intellectual-property rights, with a view to blocking the transfer of files the sharing of which infringes copyright. Similarly, host providers cannot be obliged to install a system for filtering information which is stored on its servers by its service users, which applies indiscriminately to all of those users, as a preventative measure, exclusively at its expense, and for an unlimited period, which is capable of identifying electronic files containing musical, cinematographic or audio-visual work in respect of which the applicant for the injunction claims to hold intellectual property rights, with a view to preventing those works from being made available to the public in breach of copyright. In simple terms, an injunction requiring access or host providers to filter traffic/content must not be a complicated, costly and permanent computer system at the expense of the service provider, and must not amount to a general obligation to monitor all data of each of its customers.

Hence, rather than providing guidance on the design of such a monitoring system, and the scope of an injunction in terms of the prevention of future infringements of intellectual property rights, the CJEU only did not go any further than making clear that the suggested filtering and monitoring systems infringed EU law.

In reaching its conclusion, the CJEU also briefly discussed the fundamental rights of the service providers (freedom to conduct a business), the copyright owners (right to intellectual property) and the Internet service users (right to protection of their personal data and freedom to receive or impart information). A filtering obligation that is complicated, costly and permanent and at the expense of the service provider would disproportionately affect the service provider's freedom to conduct a business. A systematic analysis of all content and the collection and identification of users' IP addresses from which unlawful content on the network is sent would also interfere with protected personal data. At the same time, such filtering could potentially limit the Internet user's freedom of information, because the filter may not adequately distinguish legal from illegal content. Unfortunately, the CJEU did not develop the argument of IP addresses as personal data any further, nor did the Court discuss the secrecy of communications[2096] or the right to respect for private life in the context of monitoring.[2097] As regards the guarantee secrecy of communications, the CJEU had already clarified in the *Promusicae* case that Member States may establish exceptions on that obligation to enable copyright enforcement.[2098]

In the *UPC Telekabel Wien* case, the CJEU finally conducted a more detailed analysis of at least the fundamental rights of the addressee of an injunction, and the balancing of the fundamental rights that are applicable. In this very recent case, the CJEU set forth that the fundamental rights recognised by EU law must be interpreted as not precluding a court injunction prohibiting an Internet service provider from allowing its customers to access an intellectual property rights-infringing website when that injunction does not specify the measures which the access provider must take. There is no requirement in EU law that would require a court to determine the appropriate filtering and blocking measures. Further, EU law does not preclude such an injunction, when the access provider can avoid incurring coercive penalties for breach of that injunction by showing that it has taken all reasonable measures, provided that (i) the measures

---

2096 The filtering system as requested by SABAM would require DPI-based filtering, meaning that all communication would have to be inspected. Article 5(1) of the E-*Privacy Directive* however requires that "Member States shall ensure the confidentiality of communications and the related traffic data by means of a public communications network and publicly available electronic communications services, through national legislation. In particular, they shall prohibit listening, tapping, storage or other kinds of interception or surveillance of communications and the related traffic data by persons other than users, without the consent of the users concerned, except when legally authorised to do so in accordance with Article 15(1) …".

2097 Stefan Kulk/Frederik Zuiderveen Borgesius, *Filtering for Copyright Enforcement in Europe after the SABAM cases,* European Intellectual Property Review 2012, 54, 56.

2098 CJEU, *Promusicae v Telefonica de Espana*, [2008] ECR I-271, para. 53. This case has been discussed in the Second Chapter.

taken do not unnecessarily deprive Internet users of the possibility of lawfully accessing the information available, and (ii) that those measures have the effect of preventing unauthorised access to the protected subject-matter or, at least, of making it difficult to access, and may seriously discourage Internet users from accessing the infringing subject-matter. Whether these conditions are fulfilled is a matter for the national authorities and courts to establish.

Finally, as the Court has not outruled the employment of filtering systems to enforce copyright and has provided little guidance as to where the balance should lie between the fundamental rights concerned, it does not only need to be examined in the following whether national measures obliging online intermediaries to monitor and filter content respect secondary EU law, but also whether they adequately respect the fundamental rights of the actors involved.

4. Jurisprudence of the ECtHR

Other than with regard to measures directed at users, there is case law of the ECtHR in respect to access blocking and online intermediary liability. In order to understand the weighting of the different interests involved under the *ECHR*, the cases will be outlined briefly in addition to the case law of the CJEU.

a) Access Blocking: Yildirim v Turkey

In the case of *Yildirim v Turkey* in 2012, the ECtHR reviewed whether the blocking of access to the domain sites.google.com was legitimate.[2099] The crux with the Turkish blocking order requiring Turkish access providers to block access to sites.google.com was the fact in order to block access to one website hosted under that domain which was disseminating content in violation of Turkish law, all websites hosted under the domain were blocked. The applicant in that case also had his personal website hosted under the domain in question, and was thus, also affected by the blocking order. Therefore, the applicant asked the ECtHR to review whether an

2099 ECtHR, *Yildirim v Turkey*, Judgment of 18.12.2012 – Application no. 3111/10.

interference with his right to freedom of expression was prescribed by law, pursued legitimate aims and was necessary in a democratic society as required by Article 10(2) *ECHR*.

The Court reiterated that Article 10 does not prohibit prior restraints on publication as such.[2100] In its assessment of whether there was an interference with Article 10, the Court considered that the Internet had now become one of the principal means of exercising the right to freedom of expression and information. This role of the Internet in modern society was seen as an aggravating factor in determining the illegality of the measures in question taken by Turkish authorities. Because Article 10 protects not only the content of information but also the means of dissemination,[2101] the preventive order to block access to a Google Sites amounted to an interference by public authority with the applicant's right to freedom of expression.[2102]

In terms of justification of the interference, the Court examined whether, at the time the blocking order was issued, a clear and precise rule existed, which enabled the applicant to regulate his conduct in the matter.[2103] The problem in this regard was, that the Turkish law provided for the blocking of access to Internet publications if the content amounted to "offences". Neither the content of the applicant's website nor that of Google Sites per se was illegal. Neither the applicant's website nor Google Sites was the subject of judicial proceedings. Further, it had not been maintained that the law authorised the blocking of an entire Internet domain like Google Sites, and Google was not notified that it was hosting illegal content. Considering that prior restraints are not necessarily incompatible with the ECHR as a matter of principle, the Court also reiterated that such restraints would need a legal framework that ensures both tight control over the scope of bans and effective judicial review to prevent any abuse of power.[2104] Precise and specific rules are required regarding the application of preventive restriction on freedom of expression. These rules

---

2100 *Ibid*, para. 46 with reference to ECtHR, *Sunday Times v United Kingdom*, Judgment of 26.04.1979 – Application no. 6538/74, and *Markt intern Verlag GmbH and Klaus Beermann v Germany*, Application No. 10572/83, Ser A No 165 (1989).

2101 *Ibid*, para 50 with reference to ECtHR, *Autronic AG v Switzerland*, Judgment of 22.05.1990 – Application No. 12726/87, Ser A No. 178 (1990), para. 47.

2102 *Ibid*, para. 55.

2103 *Ibid*, paras. 60 et seq.

2104 *Ibid*, para. 64.

must also be designed to strike a balance between the competing interests.[2105] When the Turkish court of first instance decided to block access to Google Sites in general, it did not weigh up the various interests at stake, in particular did the court no assess the need to block access to Google Sites as such.[2106] According to the ECtHR, this shortcoming was a consequence of the Turkish law, which did not lay down any obligation for the domestic courts to examine the necessity to block access to the whole domain.[2107] The obligation to consider the fact that such a measure substantially restricted the rights of Internet users and had a significant collateral effect was held to flow directly from the Convention and the case-law of the Convention institutions.[2108] In the light of these considerations, the ECtHR concluded that the interference, which resulted from the application of Turkish law, did not satisfy the foreseeability requirement under the ECHR and did not afford the applicant the degree of protection to which he was entitled by the rule of law in a democratic society.[2109] The measure in question could not be said to have been aimed solely at blocking access to the offending website, since it consisted in the blocking of a whole domain.

b) Criminal Liability of Intermediaries: Neij and Sunde Kolmisoppi v Sweden

Some guidance as regards the (criminal) liability of operators of a link directory for .torrent files[2110] can be drawn from the ECtHR's decision in the case of *Neij and Sunde Kolmisoppi v Sweden*[2111], which concerned the

2105 *Ibid.*
2106 *Ibid*, para. 66.
2107 *Ibid.*
2108 *Ibid.*
2109 *Ibid*, paras. 67
2110 At the time of the Swedish court proceedings, the Pirate Bay was hosting .torrent files.
2111 ECtHR, *Neij and Sunde Kolmisoppi v Sweden,* Inadmissibility order of 19.02.2013 – Application no. 40397/12. For a comment on the case see Joseph Jones, *Internet pirates walk the plank with Article 10 kept at bay: Neij and Sunde Kolmisoppi v Sweden,* European Intellectual Property Review 2013, Vol. 35 Issue 11, 695–700. See also Dirk Voorhoof, *Freedom of expression and the right to information: Implications for copyright,* in Christophe Geiger (ed.),

operators of the (in)famous link directory for .torrent files, and lately magnet links, the Pirate Bay.

The applicants complained that their convictions interfered with their right to freedom of expression under Article 10 *ECHR*. In consideration that Article 10 guarantees the right to impart information and the right of the public to receive it, the ECtHR emphasised the important role of in enhancing the public's access to news and facilitating the sharing and dissemination of information generally.[2112] Further, Article 10 applies not only to the content of the information but also to the means of transmission or reception since any restriction imposed on the means necessarily interferes with the right to receive and impart information.[2113]

Article 10 also guarantees freedom of expression to "everyone", and does not distinguish whether the aim pursued is profit-making or not.[2114]

By providing third parties with the means to impart and receive information within the meaning of Article 10 *ECHR*, the applicants were also afforded protection under Article 10(1) *ECHR*. Consequently, their convictions by a Swedish court interfered with their right to freedom of expression. Such interference was held to breach Article 10 unless it was "prescribed by law", pursued one or more of the legitimate aims referred to in Article 10(2) and was "necessary in a democratic society" to attain such aim or aims. The conviction were based on the Swedish Copyright Act and the Criminal Code, and therefore prescribed by law. Because the conviction aimed at protecting the copyright of others and preventing crime, the aim pursued by the interference was legitimate within the meaning of Article 10(2).

In order to determine whether the interference was necessary in a democratic society, the ECtHR examined the interference corresponded to a "pressing social need". With respect to the test, the Court took into account the nature of the competing interest involved and the degree to

---

Research handbook on human rights and intellectual property (2015), pp. 331 – 353.

2112 In that respect the ECtHR referred to its previous Judgments in *Times Newspapers Ltd v the United Kingdom (nos. 1 and 2)*, Application No. 3002/03 and 23676/03 and *Ashby Donald and Others v France*, Judgment of 10.01.2013 – Application no. 36769/08.

2113 The ECtHR cited its judgment in *Öztürk v Turkey*, Application no. 22479/93, para. 49.

2114 See ECtHR, *Autronic AG v Switzerland*, Judgment of 22.05.1990 – Application No. 12726/87, Ser A No. 178 (1990), para. 47.

which those interests require protection in the circumstances of the case. Accordingly, the Court weighed the interest of the applicants to facilitate the sharing of the information in question and, against the interest in protecting the rights of the copyright-holders. As to the weight afforded to the interest of protecting the copyright-holders rights enshrined in Article 1 of the Protocol 1 to the *ECHR*, the Court reiterated the principle that genuine, effective exercise of the rights protected by that provision does not depend merely on the State's duty not to interfere, but may require positive measures of protection.[2115]

As regards the width of the margin of appreciation afforded to States, this varies depending on a number of factors, among which the type of information at issue is of particular importance. The protection afforded to the distributed material did not reach the same level as that afforded to political expression and debate. Because the Swedish authorities were under an obligation to protect the property rights of the copyright-holders in accordance with the Swedish Copyright Act and the *ECHR*, the ECtHR held that there were weighty reasons for the restriction of the applicants' freedom of expression. This included the fact that the activities of the applicants within the commercially run platform the Pirate Bay amounted to criminal conduct requiring appropriate punishment.

Finally, the Court reiterated that the nature and severity of the penalties imposed are factors to be taken into account when assessing the proportionality of interference with the freedom of expression guaranteed by Article 10 *ECHR*. As the applicants had not taken any action to remove the files in question when asked to do so, the Court concluded the prison sentence and award of damages cannot be regarded as disproportionate, and was thus "necessary in a democratic society" within the meaning of Article 10(2) *ECHR*.

Hence, the ECtHR rejected the application as manifestly ill-founded.

2115 See also ECtHR, *Öneryildiz v Turkey*, Judgment of 30.11.2004 – Application no. 48939/99, para. 134.

c) Civil Liability of Intermediaries: Delfi v Estonia

In the case of *Delfi AS v Estonia* the ECtHR handed down its first judgment with regard to Internet service provider liability. [2116] The case concerns the question of liability of Delfi, an Internet news portal, for third party comments made on its website under one of the news items. This news item, which concerned a ferry company and its decision to change some of its routes which caused ice to break where ice roads could have been made in the near future, triggered many user comments, [2117] which were found by an Estonian court to be defamatory. Further the domestic court held Delfi responsible for the defamatory comments and Delfi was ordered to pay damages to the ferry company. In reaching this decision, the domestic courts rejected Delfi's argument that it falls under the host provider liability exemption encompassed in the *E-Commerce Directive*. Relying on Article 10 *ECHR*, Delfi complained that the Estonian civil courts had found Delfi liable for comments written by its readers. The Strasbourg Court was thus faced with making an Article 10 evaluation of the consequences of a very narrow interpretation of the *E-Commerce Directive*'s liability exemption for hosting content. The ECtHR held unanimously, that there had been no violation of Article 10 *ECHR*.[2118] It found

2116 ECtHR, *Delfi AS v Estonia,* Judgment of 10.10.2013 – Application no. 64569/09. For comments on the case see Leo Schapiro, *Anhaltende Rechtsunsicherheit für die Betreiber von Internetmeinungsportalen?, Das Urteil des EGMR »Delfi AS v Estonia« und seine Auswirkungen auf die deutsche Rechtslage,* Zeitschrift für Urheber- und Medienrecht 2014, 201 – 210; Alexander Milstein, Anmerkung zu EGMR: Haftung eines Forenbetreibers für anonyme Nutzerkommentare mit Meinungsfreiheit vereinbar, MultiMedia und Recht 2014, 41–42.

2117 The comments were not moderated on a routine bases, although there was evidence that on some occasions the website had proactively removed comments. Comments containing certain obscene words were automatically deleted. There was a notice and take down procedure in place for victims of defamatory comments. Any user could flag comments as abusive, which were subsequently taken down expeditiously. About 10,000 comments were posted per day, the majority under pseudonyms. Once a user posted a comment he could not edit or delete the comment.

2118 The Court accepted the Estonian courts' view that Delfi was not an intermediary but a publisher as it had an economic interest in the comments and had the sole control over the comments once they were posted; in particular, users could not change or delete their comments, they could merely report obscene comments. Unfortunately, the Court did not examine itself whether Delfi, a Internet news

that the finding of liability by the Estonian courts was a justified and proportionate restriction on the portal's right to freedom of expression, in particular, because: the comments were highly offensive; the portal failed to prevent them from becoming public, profited from their existence, but allowed their authors to remain anonymous; and, the fine imposed by the Estonian courts was not excessive. This conclusion has been widely criticised by free speech activists[2119] as well as scholars[2120] and news providers[2121] for not adequately respecting the freedom of expression online but also for misunderstanding the EU legal framework regulating intermediary liability. Delfi subsequently argued that the decision may have a chilling effect on free speech, when anonymous expression of opinions is not protected as the Court indirectly requires the registration of users and monitoring of third party content.[2122]

It can be established, that the ECtHR avoided to determine whether the service provider qualified as host as it was not its role to take the place of the domestic courts.

The ECtHR also subsequently recognised the importance of the case and decided on 17 February 2014 to refer the case to the Grand Chamber

---

site, that published 330 articles a day and employed – as common on newspaper sites – an "add your comment" section at the end of each article, is a publisher or intermediary. It would have been interesting to see the Court determining on the facts before it whether a service provider like Delfi is an intermediary or a publisher before analysing the Article 10 in the light of this finding. See in specific, ECtHR, *Delfi AS v Estonia*, Judgment of 10.10.2013 – Application no. 64569/09, para. 86.

2119 See for instance Gabrielle Guillemin, *Case Law, Strasbourg: Delfi AS v Estonia: Court Strikes Serious Blow to Free Speech Online,* Inform's blog (15.10.2013); Graham Smith, *Who will sort out the Delfi mess?,* Cyberleagle blog (16.10.2013).

2120 See for instance Dirk Voorhoof, *Treating a news portal as publisher of users' comment may have far-reaching consequences for online freedom of expression,* Inform's blog (29.10.2013).

2121 See the open letter to the ECtHR's president signed by 69 news organisations, Algemene Vereniging van Beroepsjournalisten in Belgie et al., *Open letter to President Dean Spielmann of 13.01.2014.*

2122 Delfi's request for referral to the Grand Chamber can be accessed online at http://www.psw.ugent.be/cms_global/uploads/ publicaties/dv/REQUEST%20FOR%20REFERRAL%20TO%20THE%20GRAND%20CHAMBER_DELFI_2014%2001%2008%20FINALDV.pdf (last accessed 30.04.2014).

at the request of Delfi.[2123] As a consequence the Delfi judgment did not become final. By accepting to review the case, the Grand Chamber Panel recognised the case as exceptional and raising a serious question that affects the interpretation or application of the *ECHR* or its protocols, or raising a serious issue of general importance.[2124]

In its much-awaited judgment the Grand Chamber Panel confirmed the previous Chamber judgement in June 2015.[2125] The judgment contains two concurring and one dissenting opinions and in particular the harsh joint dissenting opinion of judges Sajó and Tsotsoria and the great length of the judgment may explain why the release of the judgment took some time. The judgment has to be criticised for in effect requiring a pre-monitoring of user comments by Delfi and Internet news portals in general. Interestingly, the Court distinguishes between different types of platforms that exist for and curating information, when stating that "the case ase does not concern other fora on the Internet where third-party comments can be disseminated, for example an Internet discussion forum or a bulletin board where users can freely set out their ideas on any topics without the discussion being channelled by any input from the forum's manager; or a social media platform where the platform provider does not offer any content and where the content provider may be a private person running the website or a blog as a hobby"[2126]. Delfi, however, was held to be "a large professionally managed Internet news portal run on a commercial basis"[2127] and thus, the Grand Chamber concluded that the portal had control over user-generated content. The concurring opinion of judges Raimondi, Karakas, de Gaetano and Kjølbro goes to great length to draw a

---

2123 ECtHR, Grand Chamber Panel's decisions of 18.02.2014, available at http://hudoc.echr.coe.int/webservices/content/pdf/003-4674833-5667824 (last accessed 30.04.2014).

2124 Under article 43 of the *ECHR*, within three months from the date of a Chamber judgment, any party to the case may, in exceptional cases, request that the case be referred to the 17 member Grand Chamber of the ECtHR. In that event, a panel of five judges considers whether the case raises a serious question affecting the interpretation or application of the Convention or its protocols, or a serious issue of general importance, in which case the Grand Chamber will deliver a final judgment. If no such question or issue arises, the panel will reject the request, at which point the judgment becomes final.

2125 ECtHR, *Delfi AS v Estonia,* Judgment of 16.06.2015 – Application no. 64569/09 (Grand Chamber).

2126 *Ibid*, para. 116.

2127 *Ibid*, para. 144.

line between liability for failure to prevent unlawful comments and liability for not subsequently removing such comments. This distinction is not made by the majority judges and indicates a lack of understanding of practical control of user-generated content; as well as of the consequences that their findings have, namely an obligation to pre-monitor user-generated content. The latter would have to be considered when balancing the contravening rights, as pre-monitoring is a clear burden for any portal provider.[2128] However, the concurring opinion also makes clear that the majority judges have adopted case-specific reasoning and have left the relevant principles to be developed more clearly in subsequent case-law.[2129] Thus, the case does not set a clear precedent: it only concerns the assessement of the Estonian ruling in the context of the *ECHR* and does not create a strict liability for host providers.

The conclusion that can be drawn from the Delfi case is that the *ECHR* permits pre-monitoring of user-generated content. Considering that EU law prohibits general monitoring duties, there is some potential for conflict. The Estonian courts would have been well-advised to submit a question for a preliminary ruling to the CJEU on the application of EU law, instead of seemingly misapplying the EU liability regime for host providers that resulted in the ECtHR judgment. This being said, the Delfi judgment must not be generalised and is for the above stated reasons very limited in its precedence for future cases of liability for user-generated content.

d) Summary of the Case-Law of the ECtHR

The case law of the ECtHR shows, that any restriction on the access to content on the Internet will interfere with end-users' right to receive, seek and impart information. The ECtHR in this context recognises that the Internet has become one of the principle means of transmission of free speech and information. In order to determine whether an interference with Article 10 *ECHR* is necessary in a democratic society, the ECtHR will examine whether the interference corresponds to a "pressing social need". With respect to the test, one needs to take into account the nature of

2128 Cf. concurring opinion of judges Raimondi, Karakas, de Gaetano and Kjølbro at para. 7.

2129 *Ibid*, paras. 8 et seq.

the competing interest involved and the degree to which those interests require protection in the circumstances of the case. In the context of copyright infringements, this means that the interests of the Internet users to access or share the information in question, and the interests of website operators to impart information, have to be weighed against the interest in protecting the intellectual property rights of the copyright-holders. As regards the width of the margin of appreciation afforded to States, this varies depending on a number of factors, among which the type of information at issue is of particular importance. If as for instance in the Pirate Bay case, the information at issue amounted to criminal conduct, this could well require criminal prosecution.

With regard to access blocking to infringing content via access provider, the quantitative assessment of the foreseeable success of the blocking measure is one factor to be weighed. Thus, collateral effects that may be caused by the blocking need to be taken into consideration when assessing the proportionality of a measure. Prior to the proportionality test however, it needs to be examined whether the national law, that prescribes the interference with users' Article 10 rights, satisfies the requirement under Article 10(2) *ECHR* that any law restricting freedom of expression must be formulated with sufficient precision to enable individuals to regulate their conduct. Thus, third parties, which may eventually affected by access blocking, must be able to foresee that this may be the case.

Proportionality is also unlikely to be achieved, where the host provider that hosts the infringing content is not informed of the illegal content prior to the blocking.

In addition, laws that provide for the blocking of access to illegal materials must provide sufficient safeguards against potential abuses such as a guarantee of judicial review.

While the ECtHR has recognised the significance of the Internet in contemporary communication, the judgment in *Yildirim v Turkey* does not mean that no access blocking orders directed at access providers can comply with Article 10 *ECHR*. Moreover, the case makes clear that laws, that set forth access blocking, must be carefully drafted, so that orders are targeted at the infringing content only, and that there must be a thorough assessment of the contravening interests before any measure may be imposed.

II. Enforcement upon Initiative of Administrative Authorities

Insofar as access blocking to content is concerned, the most likely scenario is that rights-holders will apply for a court order before a civil court. Regularly, there have been attempts to extend the competence for blocking orders to administrative authorities as a quick, less costly and efficient alternative. In particular with regard to gambling and pornography, state authorities are addressed for regulation. The following paragraphs give a brief outline explaining how and why administrative authorities rarely order the blocking of access to certain content and why government are reluctant to pass laws that would allow for access blocking upon initiative of administrative authorities. While France does not grant any competence to administrative authorities to order the blocking of access to illegal materials, Germany has been rather progressive in this field – though of limited success and excluding the enforcement of private rights such as intellectual property rights by administrative authorities. In light of the controversy of access blocking by administrative authorities, the UK part will solely focus on the initially foreseen access blocking under the *DEA 2010*.

1. France: No Competence of Administrative Authorities to Order Access Blocking to Illegal Materials

When it comes to blocking obligations under French law, French law foresees that administrative authorities as well as courts may order an Internet service provider to block access to specified content. However, as to date no blocking has been ordered by an administrative authority.

In France, the issue of blocking is dealt with on a vertical level, meaning that for different areas of law, specified rules may exist. The first provision that was passed granting administrative authorities the power to order access blocking was in the course of the transposition of the *E-Commerce Directive* into national law by the *Loi de 21 juin 2004 pour la confiance dans l'économie numérique (LCEN)* in 2004, and was restricted to violations or risks of violations of fundamental state interests. It requires the Conseil d'Etat to pass an order determining the conditions under which administrative authorities may order access blocking. Until September 2013, no such executive order has been passed, meaning that no blocking may be ordered by administrative authorities to date in the course of Article 18 *LCEN*. A similar fate has been encountered by a provision that foresees the blocking of access to child pornography that has been inserted into the Article 6 *LCEN* by the Law on guidelines and programming for the performance of internal security (*LOPPSI 2*) in 2011. Hence, as of September 2013, there is no provision based on which an administrative authority may actually order intermediaries to block access to illegal content.

Pursuant to Article 18 of the *LCEN*, the Conseil d'Etat may pass an order that may lay down the conditions under which administrative authorities may impose restrictions on eCommerce in case of violation, or where there is a serious risk of violation, of the maintenance of public order and security, the protection of minors, the protection of public health, the preservation of interests of the national defense, or the protection of physical persons". Ecommerce in that context encompasses providers of online information, commercial communications and search tools, access and recovery tools, access to a communications networks or data hosting, even if they are not paid by those who benefit from them.[2130] A first draft of an executive order was discussed in 2011, but did not come into force. The draft order of June 2011 implementing Article 18 of the *LCEN* foresaw that the Ministries of Defense, of Justice, of the Interior, of the Economy, of Communication, of Health, of the Digital Economy, and the National Authority for the Defense of Information System would have the power to take down or block Internet content they deem harmful.[2131] These ministries would be able to start a three-step process: (i) first, the operator of the website will be requested to cease publication of the content in concern or block access to it, or to remove it from the net entirely; (ii) If there is no reaction within 72 hours, the hosting provider will be notified to delete the content or block its publication; and (iii) finally, if there is no reaction from the hosting provider, Internet service providers will be prompted to block the website.[2132] In case of emergency, the Inter-

2130 Cf. Article 14 *LCEN*.

2131 The draft executive order became public after the new French Conseil National du Numérique (CNN; National Digital Council) published an opinion on the proposal. Conseil National du Numérique, *Avis n° 2 du Conseil National du Numérique relatif au projet de décret pris pour l'application de l'article 18 de la loi pour la confiance dans l'économie numérique* (20.06.2011).

2132 See Simon Columbus, *French Government plans to extend Internet censorship*, OpenNet Initiative (21.06.2011).

net service providers could also be ordered to block the respective content straight away. The order foresaw that Internet service providers would be compensated for their efforts. In case of non-compliance with a blocking request, the non-compliant party would face a fine of up to 1500 Euros as well as confiscation measures.[2133] Presumably due to severe criticism relating to the power given by the Ministries to impose blocking order without judicial oversight,[2134] the draft order did not become law.

The situation has been similar with regard to Article 4 of *LOPPSI 2*, which inserted into Article 6 I 7 *LCEN* that "Where justified by the requirements of combating the distribution of pictures or representations of minors falling under Article 227-23 *Code Pénal*, the administrative authority shall notify the electronic addresses of public online communications services which breach the provisions of this Article to the persons mentioned under paragraph I(1) hereof, which must promptly block access to these sites". While Article 4 *LOPPSI 2* laid down the competence of administrative authorities to order access blocking, it also made the blocking dependent on an executive order that should set forth the procedures for any website blocking under this provision including the compensation of intermediaries concerned. The provision itself was widely criticised by Internet activists as constituting censorship[2135] and was referred to the Conseil Constitutionnel for review by members of the French parliament[2136]. Although the Conseil Constitutionnel did not consider the provision unconstitutional, in specific not constituting a violation of the right to freedom of communication guaranteed under Article 11 of the *Declaration of the Rights of man and the Citizen of 1789*,[2137] the French government

2133 *Ibid.*

2134 See for example the statements by the digital rights advocacy group La Quadrature du Net: Félix Tréguer, *France on its way to total Internet censorship*?, Index on Censorship (27.06.2011).

2135 La Quadrature du Net, *French LOPPSI Bill adopted: the Internet under control?,* La Quadrature du Net (09.02.2011); Philippe Berry, *LOPPSI 2 donne les pleins pouvoirs au ministère de l'Intérieur pour censurer le Net,* 20 minutes (21.12.2010); Le Monde, RSF critique le filtrage du Net prévu par la Loppsi 2, Le Monde (16.09.2010).

2136 Notably by members of the opposition.

2137 Conseil Constitutionnel, Decision of 10.03.2011 – decision no 2011-625 DC, paras. 7 et seq. English version available at http://www.conseil-constitutionnel.fr/conseil-constitutionnel/francais/les-decisions/acces-par-date/decisions-depuis-1959/2011/2011-6 25-dc/decision-n-2011-625-dc-du-10-mars-2011.94924.html (last accessed on 17.05.2014). The Constitutional Court stressed in its decision

decided to refrain from passing an executive order on the application of Article 4 *LOPPSI 2*.[2138] Hence, until today, there is no order in force that stipulates the conditions under which administrative authorities may impose blocking orders on online service providers.

Considering that even for child abuse images, French law does not foresee the possibility for administrative authorities to order the blocking of access to that clearly illegal material, it is highly unlikely that such a competence will ever be granted to protect private rights.

---

on the constitutionality of the website blocking provision that it is restricted in its analysis to examine whether the procedures adopted by the law were manifestly inappropriate for the objective pursued. The Court does not have the competence to assess whether the objectives of the law (combatting child pornography) can be achieved by other means as its general power of assessment and decision is limited and not as far reaching as that of the legislator. Thus, the Court did not have to examine alternative means to prevent access to illegal materials, unless it could establish that the procedures adopted by the law were manifestly inappropriate for the objective pursued. Such a manifest error of assessment by the legislator could not be established (It was in particular not manifestly appropriate to use public funds to compensate Internet service provider for the costs incurred resulting from the obligation to block access.). When assessing the proportionality of granting the administrative authority the power to limit access to online content, the Court took into account that (i) the aim was to protect Internet users from accessing child pornography and that the power to limit access was restricted to child pornography, and (ii) that a decision of the administrative authority to impose blocking obligations may be challenged at any time by any party concerned before a court (also in proceedings for interim injunctive relief). Due to the very restricted scope of application of the provision and the possibility of judicial review, the interference with freedom of communication guaranteed under Article 11 of the *Declaration of the Rights of man and the Citizen of 1789* was not considered disproportionate.

2138 Mark Rees, *LOPPSI: le gouvernement abandonne le blocage de sites sans juge,* PC Inpact (25.07.2012); Le Monde, *Loppsi 2: le gouvernement pourrait abandonner le blocage des sites sans juge,* Le Monde (25.07.2012).

2. Germany: Regional Initiatives and Legislative Attempts to Provide for Access Blocking Have Limited Success

In Germany, website blocking by administrative authorities is highly controversial[2139] and most authorities refrain from ordering access blocking to specific content. Due to this controversy, there is basically just one administrative authority, namely the Bezirksregierung Düsseldorf that has ordered access blocking on various occasions. As a consequence, this regional public authority has become (in)famous for this practice.[2140] However, none of its orders aimed at blocking access to content that infringed intellectual property rights. The reasons for this will be addressed when discussing the access blocking orders of the Düsseldorf authority. The best example for the tough climate for administrative blocking orders has recently been the *Zugangserschwerungsgesetz* – a statute providing for the blocking of child abuse content that has already been recalled. Finally, the following paragraphs will also examine whether in the highly regulated field of online gambling, access blocking can be ordered by regulatory authorities.

a) "Düsseldorfer Sperrverfügungen"

In 2002 the Bezirksregierung Düsseldorf (Regional Administrative Authority) orderd 80 commercial and University Internet service providers

---

2139 Cf. for instance Stefan Krempl, *SPD-Sprecher verreißt die rheinischen Sperrungsverfügungen*, Heise online (20.02.2002); Thomas Stadler, *Sperrungsverfügung gegen Access-Provider*, MultiMedia und Recht 2002, 343–347.

2140 Cf. Peter *Mankowski, Die Düsseldorfer Sperrungsverfügung – alles andere als rheinischer Karneval,* MultiMedia und Recht 2002, 277–278; Christoph Engel, *Die Internet-Service-Provider als Geiseln deutscher Ordnungsbehörden – Eine Kritik an den Verfügungen der Bezirksregierung Düsseldorf,* MultiMedia und Recht 2003, Beilage 4; Thomas Stadler, *Sperrungsverfügungen gegen Access-Provider*, MultiMedia und Recht 2002, 343–347; Ulrich Sieber/Christian Volkmann, *Die öffentlich-rechtliche Störerhaftung der Access-Provider*, Kommunikation und Recht 2002, 398–409. There are even Ph.D. theses being written solely about the blocking orders of the Bezirksregierung Düsseldorf, which indicates the controversial nature of these orders, for instance Eva Billmeier, Die Düsseldorfer Sperrungsverfügung: ein Beispiel für verfassungs- und gefahrenabwehrrechtliche Probleme der Inhaltsregulierung in der Informationsgesellschaft (2007).

to block access to two web pages with right-wing extremist content.[2141] The blocking orders were based on the then existing §§ 8 and 18 *Mediendienste-Staatsvertrag* (*MDStV*) [2142]. According to the Bezirksregierung Düsseldorf, the content on the respective websites was in violation of § 8 *MDStV*[2143] which determined content that is considered illegal, namely

---

2141 See Stefan Krempl, *Provider in Nordrhein-Westfalen erhalten Sperrungsverfügungen*, Heise online (08.02.2002). Initially, it was also planned to block access to the website rotten.com which depicts inter alia terrorism, murders, suicides and rape. The blocking order issued in February 2002 ordered the blocking of http://www.stormfront.org and http://www.nazi-lauck-nsdapao.com (for a professional translation of the administrative blocking order see Maximilian Dornseif, *Government mandated blocking of foreign Web content*, in: Jan von Knop/Wilhelm Haverkamp/Eike Jessen (eds.), *Security, E-Learning, E-Services: Proceedings of the 17. DFN-Arbeitstagung über Kommunikationsnetze*, Lecture Notes in Informatics (2013), pp. 617–648). It has to be noted that Universities were exempted from the blocking obligation to the extent that they need to make these websites available for the purpose of research or teaching. For a critical assessment of the blocking orders see Christoph Engel, *Die Interrnet-Service-Provider als Geiseln deutscher Ordnungsbehörden*, MultiMedia und Recht 2003, Beilage 4; Timo Rosenkranz, *Sperrungsverfügungen gegen Access-Provider*, JurPC 2003, Web–Dok. 16/2003; Thomas Stadler, *Sperrungsverfügungen gegen Access Provider*, MultiMedia und Recht 2002, 343–347; Peter Mankowski. *Die Düsseldorfer Sperrungsverfügung – alles andere als rheinischer Karneval*, MultiMedia und Recht 2002, 277–278.

2142 *Mediendienste-Staatsvertrag – MDStV* (State Treaty on Media Services). From April 2003 to 2007, the provisions could be found in §§ 12 and 22 *MDStV*, which have now been integrated in § 59 *Rundfunk-Staatsvertrag – RStV* (State Treaty on Broadcasting). As regards the competences of administrative authorities to issue blocking orders based on the *MDStV* see Ulrich Sieber/Malaika Nolde, *Sperrverfügungen im Internet, Territoriale Rechtsgeltung im globalen Cyberspace?* (2008), pp. 4 et seq.

2143 The successor to § 8 *MDStV*, § 12 *MDStV* refers to the *Jugendmedienschutz-Staatsvertrag – JMStV* (State Treaty on Media Protection of Minors) which in its § 4 defines illegal content. Illegal content includes – without prejudice to any liability under the German Criminal Code, content that represents propaganda instruments as defined in § 86 *StGB*, content which is directed against the free and democratic order or the spirit of understanding among the nations,…, incites to hatred against parts of the population or against a national, racial, religious or ethnic group, encourages violent or arbitrary action against such a group or violates the human dignity of a person or group by insulting, maliciously degrading or defaming parts of the population or any of the aforementioned groups, content that denies or plays down acts committed under the Nazi regime, content which disturbs public peace, presents cruel or otherwise inhuman acts of violence against a person in a manner devised to glorify or trivialise such content that violates provisions of the *Strafgesetzbuch* (*StGB*)[2144], glorifies war, is evidently obscene, depicts human beings that are dying or suffering grievous bodily harm or mental cruelty without respecting their human dignity, or in other ways infringes human dignity. Under § 18 II *MDStV*[2145], the authority competent to regulate media could take measures against the provider of illegal content to remove the content in question. In particular, the authority could forbid Internet service providers to offer certain content and may order this content to be blocked. In the 2002 blocking order by the Bezirksregierung Düsseldorf, the websites concerned hosted right-wing extremist content that was in violation of § 130 *StGB* and § 8 *MDStV*. As regards the blocking of access to said content, the Bezirksregierung Düsseldorf stated that the present state of the art foresees three possibilities of blocking: excluding domains on the domain server, use of a proxy server, or excluding IP addresses by blocking them at a router level.[2146] The Bezirksregierung argued that the blocking was

---

such acts of violence or devised to present the cruel or inhuman nature of the act in a manner which violates human dignity,…, content which violates human dignity, especially by presenting persons who are or were dying or exposed to serious physical or mental suffering while reporting actual facts without any justified public interest in such form of presentation or reporting being given…., content which presents children or adolescents in unnatural poses (this explicitly also applies to virtual presentations), content which is pornographic and has as its subject acts of violence, the sexual abuse of children or adolescents or sexual acts of persons involving animals (again this explicitly also applies to virtual presentations). According to subsection 2 of said paragraph content is furthermore illegal if it is inter alia pornographic in any other manner, or evidently suited to seriously impair the development of children and adolescents or their education into self-responsible and socially competent personalities, taking into account the specific effect of the media via which the content is provided. In contrast to the content listed in § 4 I *JMStV*, this content is legal if the telemedia service provider has ensured that such content is accessible for adult persons only (closed user group).

2144 *Strafgesetzbuch StGB* (Criminal Code).

2145 § 18 (later § 22) *MDStV* specified the competent administrative authorities to enforce the provisions of the *Mediendienste-Staatsvertrag*. Subsection 3 of set paragraph also grants the competent authorities the power to order third parties to block access to unlawful content in the interest of public weal.

2146 As to the specific functioning of these blocking methods foreseen in the order see Maximilian Dornseif, *Government mandated blocking of foreign Web content*, in: Jan von Knop/Wilhelm Haverkamp/Eike Jessen (eds.), *Security, E-Learning, E-Services: Proceedings of the 17. DFN-Arbeitstagung über Kommunikationsnetze*, Lecture Notes in Informatics (2013), pp. 617 et seq.

reasonable and does not impose a heavy burden upon providers. In the following court proceedings, it was argued that although the blocking may not succeed in preventing access for everyone to all the materials, it was nevertheless proportionate.[2147] The legitimate aim, barring access to illegal materials, must only be achieved in the sense that the legitimate aim is promoted and access is limited.[2148] The providers faced fines of up to DM 1 million (approx. EUR 0.5 million) or court proceedings in case of non-compliance. Some of the Internet service providers complied with the order, while others took action. In June 2005, the Verwaltungsgericht Düsseldorf declared the blocking order lawful.[2149] The court held that § 22 *MDStV*, which at that time granted competence to the administrative authority similar to its predecessor § 18 *MDStV* (before 2003), contained a legitimate basis for ordering access blocking and that this does not violate Article 12(3) of the *E-Commerce Directive*.[2150] According to said Article of the *E-Commerce Directive* the liability exemption for access providers shall explicitly not affect the possibility for a court or administrative

2147 Cf. for instance VG Köln, Decision of 03.03.2005 – 6 K 7151/02, MultiMedia und Recht 2005, 399, 402.

2148 Cf. Bodo Pieroth/Bernhard Schlink/Michael Kniesel, *Polizei- und Ordnungsrecht* (2002), § 10 para. 22; Wolf-Rüdiger Schenke, *Polizei- und Ordnungsrecht* (3rd ed. 2004), para. 333. In the main proceedings against the blocking order, the VG Köln for instance explicitly recognised that IT-literate users will have many ways to circumvent access blocking to certain websites. However, against "normal" users, the blocking was predicted to have some effect. See VG Köln, Decision of 03.03.2005 – 6 K 7151/02, MultiMedia und Recht 2005, 399, 402.

2149 As regards the proceedings for interim relief: VG Düsseldorf, Decision of 19.12.2002 – 15 L 4148/02, MultiMedia und Recht 2003, 205. The decision was affirmed by OVG Münster, Decision of 19.03.2003 – 8 B 2567/02, MultiMedia und Recht 2003, 348 with comment by Gerald Spindler/Christian Volkmann. These decisions concerned only the claims for injunctive relief by the service providers and thus, only required a summary examination by the courts addressed. The final decision in this subject matter was rendered by the VG Düsseldorf in May 2005 (27 K 5968/02, Zeitschrift für Urheber- und Medienrecht-RD 2006, 150), which ultimately affirmed the blocking orders by the Bezirksregierung Düsseldorf.

2150 *VG Düsseldorf*, Decision of 10.05.2005 – 27 K 5968/02, Zeitschrift für Urheber- und Medienrecht-RD 2006, 150. Cf. also the similar judgements of *VG Arnsberg*, Decision of 26.11.2004 – 13 K 3173/02; *VG Gelsenkirchen*, Decision of 28.7.2006 – 15 K 2170/03; VG Köln, Decision of 03.03.2005 – 6 K 7151/02, MultiMedia und Recht 2005, 399.

authority, in accordance with Member States' legal systems, of requiring the service provider to terminate or prevent an infringement.

Since 2007, the legal grounds on which the Bezirksregierung based its blocking orders are enshrined in § 59 III and IV Rundfunk-Staatsvertrag – *RStV*.[2151] Said paragraph foresees that the competent regulatory authorities may forbid or order providers to remove content that infringes the provisions of said treaty or data protection provisions of the Telemediengesetz – *TMG* if this measure would not be disproportionate.[2152] Subparagraph 4 provides that a blocking order may also be directed against access or hosts providers.

In practice, the new legal basis for blocking orders by administrative authorities did not trigger any decisive changes. First of all, the provision is still similar to its predecessors. Its main field of application is set to be the contents already addressed by the Bezirksregierung Düsseldorf, namely pornography (in particular hardcore pornography and child abuse content)[2153] and right-wing extremist speech[2154], which is – due to German history – a very sensitive subject in Germany, as well as content that is in violation of human dignity[2155].

While the Bezirksregierung Düsseldorf succeeded before the courts, subsequent attempts by providers of pornographic content and intellectual property rights-holders to obtain injunctions against access providers to order them to block access to websites that infringed their rights based on competition law, or intellectual property law respectively, failed.[2156]

Although this did not concern blocking by administrative authorities, it shows that following the Düsseldorf blocking orders and the controversy about blocking in general that arose in the aftermath, produced a tough cli-

---

2151 As regards the legislative developments from *MDStV* to *RStV*, see Ulrich Sieber/Malaika Nolde, *Sperrverfügungen im Internet, Territoriale Rechtsgeltung im globalen Cyberspace?* (2008), pp. 4 et seq.

2152 Accordingly, also content that is in violation of § 20 Abs. 4 *JMStV* is encompassed.

2153 Ulrich Sieber/Malaika Nolde, Sperrverfügungen im Internet, Territoriale Rechtsgeltung im globalen Cyberspace? (2008), pp. 9 et seq. with further references.

2154 *Ibid*, pp. 13 et seq. with further references.

2155 *Ibid*, pp. 18 et seq. with further references.

2156 Dieter Frey /Matthias Rudolph/Jan Oster, *Internetsperren und der Schutz der Kommunikation im Internet, Am Beispiel behördlicher und gerichtlicher Sperrungsverfügungen im Bereich des Glücksspiel- und Urheberrechts,* MultiMedia und Recht-Beilage 2012 to Issue 3, 3 et seq.

mate for blocking orders and legislation that foresees such blocking.[2157] Hence, no attempts were made by administrative authorities to block access to content that may infringe the feelings of certain religious groups[2158], supports terrorism[2159] or violates the private rights of others[2160]. As regards the latter, § 59 V *RStV* explicitly sets forth that insofar as administrative measures aim at the enforcement of private rights, such measures shall be subsidiary to the individual pursuing his claims in ordinary proceedings.[2161] The basic principle of the law governing public security that gives priority to the protection of individual rights via the due process of law is also applied to administrative blocking orders.[2162] The administrative authorities shall only become active in matters of general public interest.[2163] The intention of this approach is obvious, namely to prevent the escalation of requests to administrative authorities aiming at the enforcement of mere private rights,[2164] and thus protecting public resources. Against this background and considering that already in regard to content that is harmful for children and/or violates human dignity, administrative blocking orders are disputed, blocking orders in the context of intellectual property rights infringements are not on the agenda of administrative regulatory authorities.

b) The Fate of the "Zugangserschwerungsgesetz"

The controversy about access blocking reached its peak during the legislative procedure leading to the passing of the *Zugangserschwerungsgesetz*

2157 *Ibid*, 5.

2158 Ulrich Sieber/Malaika Nolde, *Sperrverfügungen im Internet, Territoriale Rechtsgeltung im globalen Cyberspace?* (2008), p. 24.

2159 *Ibid*, p. 25.

2160 *Ibid*, p. 26.

2161 *Ibid*, pp. 26 et seq.; Christian Volkmann in: Gerald Spindler/Fabian Schuster, *Recht der elektronischen Medien* (2nd ed. 2011), § 59 *RStV*, para. 75.

2162 Cf. Arved Greiner, Die Verhinderung verbotener Internetinhalte im Wege polizeilicher Gefahrenabwehr (2001), p. 139.

2163 See § 59 V *RStV*.

2164 Christian Volkmann in: Gerald Spindler/Fabian Schuster, *Recht der elektronischen Medien* (2nd ed. 2011), § 59 *RStV*, para. 75.

– *ZugErschwG*[2165].[2166] In order to block access to child abuse materials, the German legislator decided in 2009 to introduce a federal statute on access blocking to such content.[2167]

Pursuant to § 2 of the *ZugErschwG* access provider were supposed to block access to websites listed on a "black list" at least at the DNS level and redirect users to a website of the Federal Criminal Police Office displaying a stop sign.[2168] The "black list" should have been administered by said authority, meaning that the Federal Criminal Police Office would also have been in charge of deciding which websites were to be included in the list.

The *ZugErschwG* raised a lot of controversy between the political parties and society, particular the Internet community.[2169] Due to a new political situation in Germany in 2011 with a coalition of the Christian Democrats, CDU, and the liberal Party, FDP, where especially the FDP opposes restrictions on the use and access to the Internet, the controversial *ZugErschwG* is now history.[2170]

2165 The full title was Gesetz zur Erschwerung des Zugangs zu kinderpornographischen Inhalten in Kommunikationsnetzen.

2166 See for instance Dieter Frey/Matthias Rudolph, *Zugangserschwerungsgesetz: Schnellschuss mit Risiken und Nebenwirkungen,* Computer und Recht 2009, 644; Christoph Schnabel, *Das Zugangserschwerungsgesetz – Zum Access-Blocking als ultima ratio des Jugendschutzes,* Juristenzeitung 2009, 996; Ulrich Sieber, Sperrverpflichtungen gegen Kinderpornografie im Internet, Juristenzeitung 2009, 653.

2167 For an overview of the rise and fall of the statute, see Jenny Kortlander, *Is filtering the new silver bullet in the fight against child pornography on the Internet? A legal study into the experiences of Australia and Germany,* Computer and Telecommunications Law Review 2011, Vol. 17 Issue 7, 199, 204 et seq.

2168 For a comment on § 2 *ZugErschwG* see Christian Volkmann in: Gerald Spindler/Fabian Schuster, *Recht der elektronischen Medien* (2nd ed. 2011), § 2 *ZugErschwG*.

2169 See Jenny Kortlander, *Is filtering the new silver bullet in the fight against child pornography on the Internet? A legal study into the experiences of Australia and Germany,* Computer and Telecommunications Law Review 2011, Vol. 17 Issue 7, 199, 200 with further references.

2170 The Bill was originally proposed by the previous coalition government of the Christian Democrats and the Social-Democrats in April 2009. After the national federal election in September 2009 the German CDU/CSU/SPD coalition government ended in a somewhat awkward situation: The then elected CDU/CSU/FDP coalition government did not want the Act anymore. In the following the new coalition government agreed upon a "non application directive" for the law. Germany's new justice secretary Sabine Leutheusser-Schnarren-

Besides a questionable federal competence for a preventive measure in the field of public security,[2171] concerns were also raised in regard to the compliance of the Act with secondary EU legislation. As regards the latter, the *ZugErschwG*, and in specific its blocking provision, constituted a technical regulation, which – according to the *Technical Standards Directive 98/34/EC* as amended by the *Transparency Directive 98/48/EC* – should have been notified to the European Commission without undue delay. This however had been neglected prior to the passage of the Act.[2172]

Further, the Act had been criticised for being disproportionate: while § 59 *RStV* requires the competent regulatory authorities of the Länder to examine each single measure in terms of proportionality and their decision being subject to judicial review if challenged, the *ZugErschwG* does not foresee any such examination.[2173]

The main point of criticism has been the risk of over-blocking,[2174] meaning that not only child abuse content would be blocked but also legitimate content. This "collateral damage" is inevitable with most blocking

berger stated that the German government has agreed that access blocking will not be conducted. For one year, the access blocking should be replaced by stronger efforts to tighten international cooperation regarding deletion of incriminated sites. In November 2009, the German President of that time, Horst Köhler, refused to sign the Act into law. This led to the situation that – without the president's signature, a mere formal act, the law was not in force, but in case he would sign it, it still would not be applied. Surprisingly for the new government, the president signed the Bill after all on 17.02.2010, expressing that he does not have any significant concerns regarding the law's compatibility with the German constitution. Five days later the law was officially published and came into force on 23.02.2010. Germany then had a law that no one wanted to apply. Even the SPD party, which in 2009 voted for the law, had changed its opinion on the subject.

2171 Thomas Stadler, *Kein erschwerter Zugang*, MultiMedia und Recht 2009, 581, 582.

2172 See Christoph Schnabel, Das Zugangserschwerungsgesetz – Zum Access-Blocking als ultima ratio des Jugendschutzes, JZ 2009, 996, 997; Dieter Frey/ Matthias Rudolph, *Zugangserschwerungsgesetz: Schnellschuss mit Risiken und Nebenwirkungen,* Computer und Recht 2009, 644, 645.

2173 While judicial review is possible concerning the inclusion of a service on the black list, no appeal is possible against the concrete measure that is taken to block access to the content in question. See Christian Volkmann in: Gerald Spindler/Fabian Schuster, *Recht der elektronischen Medien* (2nd ed. 2011), Vorbem. *ZugErschwG*, para. 6.

2174 Ulrich Sieber, *Sperrverpflichtungen gegen Kinderpornografie im Internet,* Juristenzeitung 2009, 653, 657.

means.[2175] Where legitimate content is blocked, this obviously violates the disseminator's right to free speech. In addition, the users' right to information freedom (Article 5 I *GG*) is interfered with. Access blocking has also been and still is criticised for interfering with the access providers' rights out to pursue their business and their right to property (Article 12 *GG* and Article 10 *GG*).[2176] These issues will be further discussed in the context of the legitimacy of access blocking.[2177]

Finally, the usefulness of the *ZugErschwG* remained questionable. Considering the ease by which blocking can be circumvented, blocking does not seem an appropriate tool to limit the dissemination of child abuse content.[2178] In that context the particular subject of child pornography may also play a significant role. Such content is rarely freely distributed on the web. Instead secretive channels are used, such as hidden fora, friends-to-friends networks or other means of trusted communication. Thus, the aim of the *ZugErschwG*, limiting access to child pornography, is already hardly to achieve where those disseminating, exchanging and trading the content act secretively, and may well be aware of how to hide their traces. At the same time, anyone with some IT literacy is able to circumvent access blocking means.

c) No Positive Future for Access Blocking by Administrative Authorities in Germany

Interestingly, parallel the legislative process of the Act, courts in Hamburg were asked to block access to inter alia copyright-infringing content. In one case, rights-holders requested the blocking of the Indian website g-stream.in, which made publicly available copyrighted works without authorisation. Against the background of the at this time on-going legislative process of the *ZugErschwG*, the Higher Regional Court Hamburg analysed the impact of DNS blocking on legitimate content and referred to

2175 The Act as such did not prescribe a specific way of blocking, so that access providers were free to decide upon the means.

2176 Christian Volkmann in: Gerald Spindler/Fabian Schuster, *Recht der elektronischen Medien* (2nd ed. 2011), Vorbem. *ZugErschwG*, para. 6.

2177 See III. 3. e) Striking a fair balance between the contravening interests, p. 657.

2178 See Thomas Stadler, *Kein erschwerter Zugang*, MultiMedia und Recht 2009, 581, 582; Holger Bleich/Axel Kossel, *Verschleierungstaktik: Die Argumente für Kinderporno-Sperren laufen ins Leere*, Der Spiegel Online (17.04.2009).

the controversy on blocking as censorship. Referring also to the controversy surrounding the *ZugErschwG*, the Court stated that if already the efficacy of blocking of child abuse content is not clear then the Court can hardly order access providers to block access to copyright infringements.[2179]

Although one may make out a tendency to refrain from blocking against access providers, the Bezirksregierung Düsseldorf lately has again turned to ordering the blocking of access to certain online content.[2180] This time, subject of the orders were gambling websites outside the territory of Germany. The Bezirksregierung sought to base the orders on the new *Glücksspielstaatsvertrag* (*GlüStV*)[2181], which foresees in § 9 I No. 5 that the regulatory authority may order service providers, insofar as they are liable under law, to desist from assisting to give access to non-permitted gambling services. Administrative courts rejected the enforcement of the orders against several access providers based on the findings that the orders lacked a legitimate basis.[2182] Other than § 22 *MDStV* and § 59 *RStV*, the *GlüStV* does not foresee that third parties that are not liable for the infringing content can be ordered to block access.

Finally, an analysis of the blocking under the Düsseldorf order namely showed that all providers on the one hand blocked more content than ordered and on the other hand blocked not all content that they were required to block.[2183]

2179 OLG Hamburg, Decision of 22.12.2010 – 5 U 36/09, Computer und Recht 2011, 735L

2180 Torsten Kleinz, *Sperrverfügungen gegen Wettanbieter in NRW*, Heise online (04.05.2011).

2181 *Glücksspielstaatsvertrag* (*GlüStV*) – State Treaty on Gambling. The Treaty entered into force on 01.01.2008.

2182 See inter alia VG Düsseldorf, Decision of 29.11.2011 – 27 K 5887/10, Computer und Recht 2012, 155; VG Düsseldorf, Decision of 08.11.2011 – 27 K 5887/10, Zeitschrift für Urheber- und Medienrecht-RD 2012, 362. This outcome has already been predicted by Sieber and Nolde in their 2008 study on access blocking, see Ulrich Sieber/Malaika Nolde, *Sperrverfügungen im Internet, Territoriale Rechtsgeltung im globalen Cyberspace?* (2008), p. 23.

2183 Holger Bleich/Axel Kossel, *Verschleierungstaktik.Die Argumente für Kinderporno-Sperren laufen ins Leere,* Der Spiegel Online (17.04.2009).

3. UK: The Fate of the Website Blocking Provisions of the DEA 2010

The *Digital Economy Bill 2009-10*, which led to the passage of the *Digital Economy Act 2010*, did not only foresee the graduated response scheme discussed in the previous Chapter. During the wash-up period, Conservative and Liberal Democrats introduced Clause 17 on website blocking for copyright infringement into the Bill which was subsequently removed in the House of Commons committee stage.[2184] The originally intended website blocking clause[2185] was replaced by two new clauses, now sections 17 and 18 of the Act, empowering the Secretary of State to bring in regulations for website blocking – subject to a superaffirmative procedure.

a) Legal Framework foreseen in the DEA 2010

Sections 17 and 18 set forth that the Secretary of State could make website blocking regulations, but only a court could order the blocking of a website once such regulations provide for this. Section 17 of the *DEA 2010* provides that "the Secretary of State may by regulations make provision about the granting by a court of a blocking injunction in respect of a location on the Internet which the court is satisfied has been, is being or is likely to be used for or in connection with an activity that infringes copyright". In that context "blocking injunction" refers to "an injunction that requires a service provider to prevent its service being used to gain access to the location".[2186] No regulations shall be made unless satisfied that "(a) the use of the Internet for activities that infringe copyright is having a serious adverse effect on businesses or consumers, (b) making the regulations is a proportionate way to address that effect, and (c) making the regulations would not prejudice national security or the prevention or detection of crime" (section 17(3)). As regards a regulation as such, it must provide that a court may not grant a blocking injunction unless from or at the location in question a substantial amount of infringing material has been, is

---

2184 See Dinusha Mendis, *Digital Economy Act 2010: fighting a losing battle? Why the 'three strikes' law is not the answer to copyright law's latest challenge,* International Review of Law, Computers & Technology 2013, Vol.27 Nos. 1-2, 60, 69.

2185 Clause 18 Bill 89 2009-10.

2186 Section 17 (2) of the *DEA 2010.*

being or is likely to be obtained or made available, or the location in question facilitates access to infringing materials (section 17(4)). Hence the court would need to be satisfied that such websites are used, or are likely to be used, to infringe copyright. When determining whether to grant an order, the regulations must ensure that the court also takes into account the steps already taken by the service provider, or by an operator of the location in question, to prevent infringement of copyright. As regards the speed of granting an injunction, copyright owners will first have to give notice of the application to the site owner (section 17(6)), Section 17 enumerates further general principles that must be considered by a court when granting an injunction such as the importance of freedom of expression and the principle of proportionality.[2187] Section 18, which is entitled "Consultation and Parliamentary Scrutiny", sets forth the steps that the Secretary of State should follow before making regulations under section 17. Not surprisingly, "the music industry was mad keen – as indeed were many broadcasters and sports organisations" about such extensive legal basis for blocking of copyright infringing content.[2188] However, their delight did not last long as said sections will soon be abolished.

b) Sections 17 and 18 of the DEA 2010: Unnecessary?

Already in August 2011, the government announced in its paper "Next steps for the implementation of the Digital Economy Act" that it would not make regulations on the basis of sections 17 and 18. This opinion is still upheld and accordingly, no regulations have been passed.[2189] Moreover, the *Draft Deregulation Bill* of July 2013 foresees the repeal of sections 17 and 18 of the *DEA 2010*.[2190]

2187 Section 17 (5) of the *DEA 2010*.

2188 Hansard (House of Lords) Lord Clement-Jones, Column 472 (15.03.2010).

2189 House of Commons, Digital Economy Act: Copyright, Standard Note: SN/HA/5515 (28.06.2013), p.1.

2190 Clause 26 of *Draft Deregulation Bill* presented to Parliament by the Minister for Government Policy and the Minister without Portfolio by Command of Her Majesty (July 2013), https://www.gov.uk/government/uploads/system/uploads/attachment_data/file/210035/130701_CM_8642_Draft_Deregulation_Bill.pdf (last accessed on 17.05.2014).

This came to no surprise as previously an Ofcom report on the practicability of website blocking questioned the practicability of sections 17 and 18, and concluded that the specific blocking injunctions were unlikely to be effective in practice.[2191] The report stated that whilst it is possible to block access to websites by using techniques such as IP addresses, DNS, URL and packet inspection, there were some serious concerns that need to be taken into account.[2192] The expectations of copyright owners, to achieve blocking of infringing materials potentially within hours of an application being made, and thus, having a much speedier procedure than before a court, do not appear realistic given the constraints imposed on the courts by the *DEA 2010*.[2193] These constraints include inter alia a notice to the website operator in order to guarantee a process which is fair to the legitimate interest of website operators and end-users.[2194] Hence, any injunction scheme operated under sections 17 and 18 was considered unlikely to give rise to a sufficient level of actions to have a material impact on levels of copyright infringement.

Ofcom concluded that it is not possible to deliver a framework under the *DEA* for website blocking that would be effective.[2195]

The decision to repeal the power to make regulations on website blocking can also be seen as a consequence of copyright owners having brought successful court actions against infringing websites under existing laws. It was right after the precedent under section 97A of the *CDPA 1988* by the decision in *NewzBin II*[2196] and obviously as a consequence of the review by Ofcom, that the Government first recommended the abolition of section 17 in their response to the Hargreaves Report.[2197] The government's response to the Hargreaves Report referring to website blocking established that "the approach set out in the *DEA* is unlikely to be effective

2191 Ofcom, *'Site blocking' to reduce online copyright infringement: A review of sections 17 and 18 of the Digital Economy Act* (27.05.2011), pp. 46 et seq.

2192 *Ibid.*

2193 See *Ibid*, p. 48.

2194 *Ibid.*

2195 *Ibid.*

2196 High Court, *Twentieth Century Fox Film Corp v British Telecommunications Plc* [2011] EWHC 1981 (Ch).

2197 See Dinusha Mendis, *Digital Economy Act 2010: fighting a losing battle? Why the 'three strikes' law is not the answer to copyright law's latest challenge,* International Review of Law, Computers & Technology 2013, Vol.27 Nos. 1–2, 60, 69.

because of the slow sped that would be expected from a full court process. This would provide site operators with the opportunity to change the location of the site long before any injunction could come into force".[2198]

The *NewzBin II* decision, which will be discussed in detail in the second part of this Chapter, put the final nail in the coffin of sections 17 and 18. At the time the *NewzBin II* case entered the court, sections 17 and 18 where already met with controversy.[2199] The counsel for BT as well as Arnold J expressed their concerns during the hearings. The counsel for BT questioned in particular the necessity of a new blocking provision, "if section 97A of the *CDPA 1988* already allowed a 'blocking injunction' to be granted where a website has been, is being or is likely to be used to infringe copyright".[2200] This argument summarises the major point of criticism: the significance of section 17 is unclear, considering that section 97A of *CDPA 1988* can carry out the same function as section 17.[2201]

In fact, the requirements that a provision based on section 17 will have to take into account, do not go any further than the existing law already does.[2202] In specific, when section 17(5) requires that the importance of freedom of expression needs to be taken into account as well as the principle of proportionality, then this does nothing more than summarising existing legal principles.

Hence, it must be seen as coming to no surprise that the government will repeal sections 17 and 18 of the *DEA 2010*.

2198 *Government's Response to Hargreaves Review: 'Next steps for implementation of the Digital Economy Act'* (August 2011), p. 7, http://www.culture.gov.uk/images/publications/Next-steps-for-implementation-of-the-Digital-Economy-Act.pdf (last accessed on 17.05.2014).

2199 Cf. for example Benjamin Farrand, *The Digital Economy Act 2010: A cause for celebration, or a cause for concern*, European Intellectual Property Review 2010, Vol. 32 Issue 10, 536–541.

2200 High Court, *Twentieth Century Fox Film Corp v British Telecommunications Plc* [2011] EWHC 1981 (Ch), para. 149.

2201 The scope of blocking injunctions under section 97A *CDPA 1988* will be discussed below 1. UK: Injunctions to Block Access against Access Providers, pp. 622 et seq.

2202 For a comparison of the requirements for injunctions under section 97A CDPA 1988 and injunctions under the *DEA 2010* provisions see Ofcom, *"Site blocking" to reduce online copyright infringement: A Review of sections 17 and 18 of the Digital Economy Act* (27.05.2011), p. 47.

4. Resume: No Blocking of Copyright Infringing Content to Be Ordered by Administrative Authorities

None of the states that are subject of this research foresees that the blocking of access to copyright infringing materials can be ordered by administrative authorities.[2203]

First of all, secondary EU law would not forbid blocking orders by administrative authorities. Article 15 of the *E-Commerce Directive* does only forbid the imposition of general filtering obligations on access providers. Although, Article 12(1) of the *E-Commerce Directive* provides that mere conduits are not liable for information they transmit, this does not prevent an injunction being imposed. In fact, Article 12(3) of the *E-Commerce Directive* makes it clear that the liability exemption "does not affect the possibility for a court or administrative authority, in accordance with Member States' legal systems, of requiring the service provider to terminate or prevent an infringement". The same applies for host providers under Article 14 of the *E-Commerce Directive*.

Blocking as such is a controversial subject due to its technological implications: depending on the blocking system used, there is a risk of over-blocking; depending on the blocking system used, blocking can be expensive. The above discussion shows that even where evidently illegal content such as child pornography is concerned, access blocking by administrative authorities is not met with acceptance, although there is consensus that such materials should not be accessible.

2203 Within the EU, Spanish and Italian administative authorities have so far issued administrative blocking orders. In 2014, the Italian Communication Authority (AGCOM) passsed a regulation on online copyright enforcement (*Allegato A alla Delibera n. 680/13/CONS del 12.12.2013*), which – in cases of copyright infringement - provides fort he selective takedown of content hosted in Italy, or the blocking of a whole website issued against Italian access providers if there is massive infringement or the website is hosted outside Italy. Less than a month after the regulation entered into force in March 2014, the first Italian administrative blocking injunction against the website www.cineblog-01net was issued and access providers operating in Italy were required to disable access to said website (the order can be accessed via AGCOM's website, see http://www.agcom.it/documents/10179/1260293/Delibera+41-14-CSP/70e102fa-b552-4064-9513-a3b41b1117e8?version=1.2 (last accessed 07.07.2015). In Spain, the first blocking order by an administrative court was released following a complaint filed tby the Spanish Association of Intellectual Rights Management (AGEDI) in March 2015.

The main reason for refraining from introducing access blocking by administrative authorities is the risk of over-blocking and the impact of over-blocking on fundamental rights. If legitimate content is blocked by way of "collateral damage", the blocking interferes with the disseminator's right to free speech that is guaranteed by Article 10 *ECHR* (and Article 11 *CFR*). If end-users can no longer access legitimate content that has been blocked unintentionally, this also interferes with the users' rights to receive information, which is equally guaranteed by said Articles. Furthermore access blocking interferes with the access providers' rights out to pursue business and their right to property as guaranteed by Article 1 of the Protocol No. 1 to the *ECHR* (and Articles 16 and 17 *CFR*). When assessing the proportionality of a measure, the effectiveness of a blocking measure needs to be taken into account. As aforementioned, there are many ways to circumvent blocking, which may even be used by non-IT-literate users. This would mean effectively, that the blocking would not fundamentally affect notorious, wilful infringers as they would be able to make their way around the blocking mechanism. Finally, considering that there would be no judicial oversight before blocking would be ordered, it cannot be imagined how the interferences could be justified even if they pursue the legitimate aim of protecting the right to intellectual property of others.

III. Enforcement upon Initiative of the Rights-holders via Access Providers

Enforcement via access providers is one route that has become specifically popular in the UK. Enforcement via access providers in this context refers to rights-holders applying for injunctions against access providers that require the providers to block access to infringing materials. This route is usually taken when addressing the website hosting the infringing materials is not practical: the website is located outside of the domestic jurisdiction, it moves its location on a regular basis, and/or does not pay regard to take down requests.

1. UK: Injunctions to Block Access against Access Providers

Content access restrictions to infringements of intellectual property rights are a relatively new scenario in the UK. Cleanfeed, a software that is being used to block access to child abuse materials, has been tried and run for several years until the first court suggested that it might also be used for online copyright enforcement.

a) The Legal Framework: Section 97A CDPA 1988

Section 97A was inserted into the *CDPA 1988* in 2003 by the implementing regulations for the *InfoSoc Directive*. Precisely, it implements Article 8(3) of said Directive, which provides that rights-holders must be "in a position to apply for an injunction against intermediaries whose services are used by a third party to infringe a copyright". Section 97A(1) *CDPA 1988* in that regard provides that "the High Court [...] shall have power to grant an injunction against a service provider, where that service provider has actual knowledge of another person using their service to infringe copyright". Section 97A(2) defines the condition for determining "actual knowledge", namely that "a court shall take into account all matters which appear to it in the particular circumstances to be relevant and, amongst other things, shall have regard to— (a)whether a service provider has received a notice through a means of contact made available in accordance with regulation 6(1)(c) of the *Electronic Commerce (EC Directive) Regulations 2002* (SI 2002/2013); and (b)the extent to which any notice includes— (i) the full name and address of the sender of the notice; (ii)details of the infringement in question".

b) Setting the Precedent: Twentieth Century Fox v BT

In 2011, the High Court ruled that BT must block access to NewzBin.[2204] NewzBin provided a search service for UseNet content, which included unauthorised copies of protected works. Already in 2010, Twentieth Century Fox Film Corporation and others had taken joint legal action against

2204 High Court, *Twentieth Century Fox Film Corp v British Telecommunications Plc* [2011] EWHC 1981.

NewzBin for copyright infringement. [2205] Although the rights-holders won their case against NewzBin, their success showed little effect when NewzBin reappeared as NewzBin2, this time located abroad with little chances to enforce a British judgment.

aa) Excursus: From NewzBin1 (Twentieth Century Fox v NewzBin) to NewzBin2 (Twentieth Century Fox v BT)

NewzBin was a British Usenet indexing website intended to facilitate access to content on Usenet, one of the oldest communications arenas on the Internet.[2206]

Usenet is strictly speaking also a form of peer-to-peer network, files are placed into news groups on decentralized servers, from where they can be retrieved by the news group participants.[2207] An important difference with the forms of peer-to-peer described earlier is the fact that the user does not need to be active in supplying files. Users may also just download files. Usenet allows its users to upload and view messages on an electronic equivalent of public bulletin boards. Usenet had been developed in the early 1980s and predated the World Wide Web by some years. It was originally designed as a text-based medium and supported text content only, but evolved in the following so as to support binary i.e. non-text content. The infrastructure for the system is provided by interconnected servers that store the content uploaded to them in a hierarchy of newsgroups that are usually named in such a way as to reflect their content.

Text content on Usenet is designed to be read by other users without further processing. As Usenet however was initially designed to deal with text only, binary materials require further processing. They are encoded in

---

2205 High Court, *Twentieth Century Fox Film Corporation and others v NewzBin Ltd* [2010] EWHC 608 (Ch) (NewzBin 1). For a comment on the case see Ryan Hocking, *Secondary liability in copyright infringement: still no Newz?*, Entertainment Law Review 2012, Vol. 23 Issue 4, 83 – 90.

2206 Usenet is a worldwide distributed Internet discussion forum. It resembles an online bulletin board, but is distributed among a large, constantly changing conglomeration of servers that store and forward messages to one another in so-called news feeds. See First Chapter, A. II. 3. USENET.

2207 European Parliament, DG for Internal Policies, Policy Department C: Citizens' Rights and Constitutional Affairs, *File Sharing* (2011), p. 6.

text form and in the following split into multiple parts so that they can be posted as a set of individual but related messages.

The consequences for users are that they need a news client to post messages to or download messages from newsgroups. The user has to enter details of his chosen server to the news client. He then selects the newsgroups to which he would like access and to which he will post or from which he will download messages.

Binary materials are often split up by RAR encoding - meaning that a large file will be split into a series of smaller parts called RAR archive files, each of which is again split into 50 or more messages. Each of these messages is posted to the newsgroup separately. This results in for example a movie file being distributed across potentially hundreds or thousands of messages. Hence, if a user wants to download a copy of the movie, he must identify every one of those messages from a list of messages available on the Usenet server to which he has access. Usually, the server will list these messages in the order in which it has received them. As a result, messages comprising one movie get mixed up with other messages added to the newsgroup during the time the upload of the movie was completed. Consequently, each message file must be downloaded into appropriate RAR archive files and must then be assembled together to form the whole copy.

Some years ago, the operators of NewzBin created the "NZB" system for quickly retrieving large files from Usenet. The NZB system facilitated access to files on Usenet.

Access to NewzBin itself was restricted to members and membership was only granted to users who had had an invitation from someone who already was a member to NewzBin. The service was free for basic members, which were not given the ability to download files sourced using NewzBin1. Premium members, who had to pay a membership fee, however could download files.

Contents of NewzBin1 were indexed either as "reports" or "files" and tools were provided to search them. The focus of the site was binary content; information about films, television programmes and other works were processed and stored in three main indices: RAW index, Condensed index and NewzBin index. The NewzBin index was the highest level index and showed entries with reports, which had been created by a team of about 250 'editors'. These editors checked that the subject matter of a report related to a complete set of Usenet messages. Within the NewzBin index reports were listed by the title of the film or work in question. Also, further descriptive information was added by the editors, such as the file size in total and details of other attributes such as genre, source and language of the work. Typically information in relation to films linked to an Internet address with further information, for example Amazon or a movie database. Remarkably, reports often also included information or a file in which the uploader of the infringing copy identified himself.

Premium members of NewzBin1 could download file sets suitable for burning to a DVD by a facility that created so called "NZB" files. A NZB file contained all the information necessary for a news client to fetch all the Usenet messages to assemble the original binary work. Thus, the features "Create NZB" or "Download Report NZB" make the download process much easier for the user. He does not have to identify and individually download all the messages required to assemble the original file. He also does not need a separate software application to assemble the messages.

NewzBin1 premium members could also search the NewzBin indices by reference to a specific category. NewzBin1 grouped Usenet messages into various categories such us for example "books", "Games" or "Movies". These categories were often divided into subcategories by source (e.g. DVD, BluRay, CAM, Screener), video format (e.g. DivX, XviD, BluRay). From some of the subcategories names it was obvious that they contained pirated content. CAM for example, referred to the use of a handheld cam in a cinema to record a film shown there.[2208]

An analysis of 50,000 reports in the movies category showed that 97.5% were linked to the IMDb site[2209], whereas only 0.3% of them were not shown to be commercially available.

Twentieth Century Fox and other film rights holders accused NewzBin of locating and categorising unlawful copies of films and (1) displaying the titles of these copies in its indices, (ii) providing a facility for its users to search for particular unlawful copies, (iii) displaying their search results and (iv) providing a simple one-click mechanism for users to acquire the

2208 The same applies to the sources Telesync, referring to a copy of a film made in a cinema using professional camera equipment, and Screener, referring to a copy of a film supplied on a restricted basis to persons within the industry before the film has been released commercially.

2209 IMDb is an Amazon company, and, according to Amazon, "is the world's most popular and authoritative source for movie, TV and celebrity content".

unlawful copies of their choice.[2210] NewzBin argued that its website was simply a search engine like Google – though not directed to the whole Internet but merely to Usenet -, and played no part in copyright infringements.

The High Court held that NewzBin Ltd knew that its service was used mainly by its members for the unauthorised downloading of infringing copies of the claimant's films. The argument of NewzBin Ltd that it had no knowledge of infringement occurring on its service and did not encourage copyright infringement was rejected as "simply not credible".[2211] Kitchin J found that NewzBin knew that the vast majority of films in the movies category were commercial and very likely to be protected by copyright and that users that used the NZB facility to download those materials were infringing copyright.[2212] Thus, "a reasonable member would deduce from the defendant's activities that it purports to possess the authority to grant any required permission to copy any film that a member may choose from the Movies category on NewzBin and that the defendant has sanctioned, approved and countenanced the copying of the claimants' films ...".[2213] While "mere (or even knowing) assistance or facilitation of the primary infringement is not enough", the Court found that NewzBin had involved itself so the infringement was made its own.[2214] Based on the ECJ's ruling in *Sociedad General de Autores e Editores de Espana v Rafael Hoteles SA*[2215], the Court further held that NewzBin communicated unauthorised copies of protected works available to the public.[2216]

Kitchin J held that NewzBin had infringed the claimants' copyrights in three ways: (i) It had authorised its premium members to make infringing copies of the Studios' films because a reasonable member would deduce from its activities that it purported to possess the authority to grant any required permission to copy any film that a member may choose from the

2210 High Court, Twentieth Century Fox Film Corporation and others v NewzBin Ltd [2010] EWHC 608 (Ch) (NewzBin 1)

2211 *Ibid,* para.63.

2212 *Ibid,* para. 78.

2213 *Ibid,* para. 102.

2214 *Ibid,* para. 108.

2215 CJEU, C-306/05 *Sociedad General de Autores y Editores de España (SGAE) v Rafael Hoteles SA,* Judgment of 07.12.2006.

2216 NewzBin's premium subscribers downloaded the protected works from a place and at a time individually chosen by them, and considered NewzBin to be making the films available to them.

Movies category on NewzBin1, and it had sanctioned, approved and countenanced the copying of the Studios' films, including each of the films specifically relied on.[2217] (ii) For similar reasons, it had procured the premium members to infringe, had participated in a common design with the premium members to infringe, the Studios' copyrights. It was immaterial that the Studios were not able to point to specific acts of infringement by particular infringers which NewzBin Ltd might be said to have procured.[2218] (iii) NewzBin Ltd had itself infringed the Studios' copyrights by communicating the copyright works to the public, specifically by making each work available to the public by electronic transmission in such a way that members of the public may access it from a place and at a time chosen by them within section 20(2)(b) *CDPA 1988* which implements Article 3(2) of the *InfoSoc Directive*.[2219]

The Court concluded that, so far relief was concerned, it was appropriate and necessary to grant an injunction restraining infringement of the copyrights in the claimants'repertoire.[2220] Kitchin J declined however, to grant an injunction pursuant section 97A *CDPA1988* restraining NewzBin Ltd from including in its indices or databases entries identifying any material posted to or distributed through any Usenet group in infringement of copyright.[2221]

2217 *Twentieth Century Fox Film Corporation and others v NewzBin Ltd* [2010] EWHC 608 (Ch) (NewzBin 1), paras. 85–102.

2218 See *ibid*, paras. 103–112

2219 See *ibid*, paras. 113–125.

2220 *Ibid,* para. 129.

2221 High Court, *Twentieth Century Fox Film Corporation and others v NewzBin Ltd* [2010] EWHC 608 (Ch) (NewzBin 1), paras. 130–135. Section 97A of the *CDPA 1988* states: "97A Injunctions against service providers
(1) The High Court (in Scotland, the Court of Session) shall have power to grant an injunction against a service provider, where that service provider has actual knowledge of another person using their service to infringe copyright. (2) In determining whether a service provider has actual knowledge for the purpose of this section, a court shall take into account all matters which appear to it in the particular circumstances to be relevant and, amongst other things, shall have regard to – (a) whether a service provider has received a notice through a means of contact made available in accordance with regulation 6(1)(c) of the Electronic Commerce (EC Directive) Regulations 2002 (SI 2001/2013); and (b) the extent to which any notice includes – (i) the full name and address of the sender of the notice; (ii) details of the infringement in question. (3) In this section "service provider" has the meaning given to it by regulation 2 of the Electronic Commerce (EC Directive) Regulations 2002".

Following a further hearing in April 2010, Kitchin J granted the injunctions restraining NewzBin from infringing copyright in or relating to the motion pictures and television programmes enlisted by the applicants. The order also applied to content notified after the decision. The Newzbin operators were ordered to ensure that users of the NewzBin Website or any other service, by use of the said website or service, do not infringe copyright in or relating to the content in question.[2222] Accordingly, the injunction did not only cover the Studios' existing repertoire, but also future additions to the repertoire as long as they would be notified to the operators of NewzBin.

bb) The Injunctions against BT in NewzBin2

In April 2010 NewzBin Ltd entered into voluntary liquidation and NewzBin1 ceased to operate shortly thereafter.[2223] However, already in May 2010 the very similar NewzBin2 website went online. The design and manner of NewzBin2 became substantially the same as that of NewzBin1. The only significant difference was that the website's starting page revealed listings of content available and that the name NewzBin was followed by the numeral 2. NewzBin2 was hosted in Sweden and the domain name www.newzbin.com registered to a company in the Seychelles.[2224] The website used the same code and database including the same categorisation mode for content as its predecessor.[2225] Again, membership to NewzBin was subject to a fee, payable in Pounds Sterling, accordingly NewzBin2 was obviously directed at UK users.[2226] As with NewzBin1, the main focus of NewzBin2 was film and television programmes.[2227] The Court found that "it appears to be quite hard to find any content on NewzBin2 that is not protected by copyright".[2228]

2222 High Court, *Twentieth Century Fox Film Corp v British Telecommunications Plc* [2011] EWHC 1981, para. 43.

2223 *Ibid*, paras. 45–47.

2224 *Ibid*, para. 58. As of 27.04.2012, a whois search showed that the server is still located in Linkoping, Sweden. However, since NewzBin.com has been closed down in February 2012, NewzBin migrated to www.newzbin2.es.

2225 *Ibid*, para. 48.

2226 *Ibid*, para. 49.

2227 *Ibid*, para. 53.

2228 *Ibid*, para. 55.

On 28 July 2011, the High Court ruled that BT must block access to NewzBin2 using Cleanfeed as NewzBin2 and its users were infringing copyright of the movie studies that applied for injunctive relief.[2229] The same service was thus required to be used to block access to copyright infringing materials as is deployed to block access to child pornography: IP address blocking, using the unique IP address of a website and DPI-based URL blocking.

Justice Arnold concluded that users of BT's service infringe the studios' copyrights.[2230] He ruled that BT had actual knowledge regarding other persons using its service to infringe copyright: 'it knows that users and operators of NewzBin2 infringe copyright on a large scale, and in particular infringe the copyrights of the Studios in large numbers of their films and television programmes'.[2231] This knowledge satisfied the requirements of section 97A(1) of the *CDPA 1988*.[2232] Thus, the Court had jurisdiction to grant an injunction against BT pursuant to section 97A.

The Court clarified that the obligation to monitor traffic and disrupt traffic between BT's users and the NewzBin2 website does not involve a general obligation to monitor, but constitutes rather a specific and limited one.[2233] It distinguished the case from *Scarlet Extended v SABAM*.[2234] In contrast to SABAM, the studios are not seeking an order that BT has to "introduce, for all its customers, in abstracto and as a preventive measure, exclusively at [its] cost … and for an unlimited period, a system for filtering all electronic communications, both incoming and outgoing, passing via its services, in particular those involving the use of peer-to-peer software, in order to identify on its network the sharing of electronic files containing a musical, cinematographic or audio-visual work in respect of which the applicant claims to hold rights, and subsequently to block the

---

2229 Twentieth Century Fox Film Corporation, Universal City Studios Productions LLLP, Warner Bros. Entertainment Inc, Paramount Pictures Corporation, Disney Enterprises, Inc and Columbia Pictures Industries Inc. The Studios are members of the Motion Picture Association of America Inc, and they bring this application in a representative capacity on behalf of all group companies of the Studios that are owners or exclusive licensees of copyrights in films and television programmes, see *ibid*, para. 1.

2230 *Ibid*, para. 108.

2231 *Ibid*, para. 157.

2232 *Ibid*, para. 157.

2233 *Ibid*, para. 161.

2234 *Ibid*, para. 177.

transfer of such files, either at the point at which they are requested or at which they are sent".[2235] As regards NewzBin2 the Studios sought a clear and precise order that merely required BT to implement an existing technical solution. This technical solution is already employed by BT for a different purpose, namely child abuse images identified as such by the Internet Watch Foundation. BT itself accepted that the solution is technically feasible and that the cost is not excessive.[2236] In addition, a provision was made to enable the order to be varied or discharged in the event of a future change in circumstances. Therefore, Justice Arnold held requested order to be foreseeable by Internet service providers on the basis of Section 97A as well as Article 8(3) of the *InfoSoc Directive*.[2237] He also concluded that the order is "prescribed by law" within the meaning of Article 10(2) *ECHR*.[2238]

The Studios will not have to identify individual URLs corresponding to individual NZB files as indexed by NewzBin2 that relate to infringing copies of individual works.[2239] The Court considered such a precise identification of infringing files as not practicable since it would require the Studios to invest a lot of effort and cost in notifying long lists of URLs to BT on a daily basis.[2240] Such a requirement would also have been disproportionate for the same reasons.

Interestingly, while Justice Arnold recognised that the order would potentially prevent BT subscribers from making legitimate i.e. non-infringing use of NewzBin2, he concluded that – on the evidence – such uses are de minimis.[2241] Of course, every case has to be decided on its individual circumstances and any order has to be proportionate, this very finding of Justice Arnold indicates that if there is proof that the network is used for legitimate purposes on a large scale, an order might not be granted.

BT feared that in the wake of the order countless other applicants may demand that BT blocks access to further websites including such that con-

2235 *Ibid*, para. 177.
2236 *Ibid*, para. 177.
2237 *Ibid*, para. 177.
2238 *Ibid*, para. 177.
2239 *Ibid*, para. 201.
2240 *Ibid*, para. 201.
2241 Cf. *Ibid*, para. 186.

tain defamatory statements or private information.[2242] It was concerned that numerous replications of the order would undermine the Cleanfeed blocking system and/or put strain on BT's network itself.[2243] This could involve substantial compliance costs for BT.[2244]

However, considering the effort and expenditure necessary for an application to be successful, rights-holders are unlikely to undertake an application lightly.[2245]

c) Applying the Precedent

The NewzBin2 case seems to have encouraged further cases. In February 2012, the High Court was asked by several UK record companies[2246] to

2242 *Ibid*, paras. 187 and 191.

2243 *Ibid*, para. 190.

2244 *Ibid*, para. 190.

2245 See also *ibid*, para. 189.

2246 Dramatico Entertainment Ltd, Emi Records Ltd, Mercury Records Ltd, Polydor Ltd, Rough Trade Records Ltd, Sony Music Entertainment UK Ltd, Virgin Records Ltd, Warner Music UK Ltd and 679 Recordings Ltd. They claimed on their own behalf and in a representative capacity on behalf of the other members of BPI (British Recorded Music Industry) Ltd ("BPI") and Phonographic Performance Ltd ("PPL"), see High Court, *Dramatico Entertainment Ltd & others v British Sky Broadcasting Ltd & others* [2012] EWHC 268. For a comment on the case see Darren Meale, *Avast, ye file sharers! The Pirate Bay is sunk*, Journal of Intellectual Property Law & Practice 2012, Vol. 7 No. 9, 646; Alexander Ross/Claire Livingstone, *Communication to the public: Part 2*, Entertainment Law Review 2012, Vol. 23 Issue 7, 209–213; Ruth Hoy/John Wilks/Nick Edbrooke, *Dramatico Entertainment v BskyB: Pirate Bay runs aground in English waters*, Entertainment Law Review 2012, Vol. 23 Issue 5, 151–153; Joel Smith/Sarah Burke, *Record companies win first round v The Pirate Bay in the United Kingdom but pirates remain at large: Dramatico Entertainment Ltd v British Sky Broadcasting Ltd*, European Intellectual Property Review 2012, Vol. 34 Issue 6, 416–419.

order six ISPs[2247] to block access to the Pirate Bay.[2248] Largely based on his findings in NewzBin2 Justice Arnold ruled that both users and the operators of the Pirate Bay infringe copyrights of the claimants and those they represent in the UK.[2249]

Like the operator of NewzBin1 and NewzBin2, the operators of the Pirate Bay were held to "authorise its users' infringing acts of copying and communication to the public".[2250] Justice Arnold even came to the conclusion that "if anything, it is a stronger case' of infringement than NewzBin".[2251] Accordingly, major Internet service providers were ordered to block access to the Pirate Bay.

In 2013, EMI Records Ltd and others sought the blocking of three popular BitTorrent trackers, namely KAT (KickassTorrents), H22T and Fenopy.[2252] Like the early Pirate Bay, these trackers provided users with user-uploaded descriptions of copyrighted material, i.e. metadata including .torrent files) in indexed and searchable form. Users could use that metadata to download infringing copies of protected works using the BitTorrent file-sharing protocol. The rights-holders argued that the operators of the trackers in question communicated sound recordings to the public, committed the tort of authorising infringements, and were jointly liable as accessories for infringements.[2253] The reasoning of the Court basically fol-

2247 British Sky Broadcasting Ltd, BT Plc, Everything Everywhere Ltd, TalkTalk Telecom Group PLC, Telefónica UK Ltd and Virgin Media Ltd. They are the six main retail Internet service providers in the UK with a fixed line market share of some 94 % of UK Internet users between them, see *Dramatico Entertainment Ltd & others v British Sky Broadcasting Ltd & others* [2012] EWHC 268, para. 1.

2248 Dramatico Entertainment Ltd & others v British Sky Broadcasting Ltd & others [2012] EWHC 268.

2249 *Ibid*, para. 84.

2250 *Ibid*, para. 81.

2251 *Ibid.*

2252 High Court, *EMI Records Ltd and others v British Sky Broadcasting Ltd and others* [2013] EWHC 379 (Ch). For a comment on the case see Darren Meale, *A triple strike against piracy as the music industry secures three more blocking injunctions,* Journal of Intellectual Property Law & Practice 2013, Vol. 8, No. 8, 591–594; Paddy Gardiner/Gillie Abbotts, Sky's the limit for ISP blocking orders, Entertainment Law Review 2013, Vol. 24 Issue 6, 217–219.

2253 High Court, *EMI Records Ltd and others v British Sky Broadcasting Ltd and others* [2013] EWHC 379 (Ch), para. 43. In contrast, in the earlier case of the Pirate Bay (*Dramatico Entertainment Ltd & others v British Sky Broadcasting Ltd & others* [2012] EWHC 268), only the last two causes were pursued.

lowed previous cases. It was held that the service provided by the trackers in question was not purely passive and that the operators had intervened in an active manner by having a mechanism specifically designed to allow users to provide actual content. Arnold J further concluded that even if this conclusion was wrong, the operators might still be liable on the grounds of authorisation and joint tortfeasance.[2254] In reaching this conclusion, Arnold J spent some time on discussing the take down policy that was employed by the operators of the tracker websites. The deletion of individual links was held to be impractical and ineffective because users might have uploaded multiple versions of each infringing recording and were constantly uploading additional ones. According to the Court, a cessation of an infringement could thus not be achieved by deleting one URL. Moreover, a cessation would require a constant monitoring of the website by the rights-holder in order to notify each and every link. Other than in the previous cases, the access providers concerned did not actively oppose the blocking application.[2255]

The same conclusions were applied in the context of video streams. In *Football Association Premier League Ltd v Sky*,[2256] a website, FirstRow, that provided links to various user-generated sports video streams, was considered analogous to .torrent trackers, because it aggregated, indexed and provided users a link to access the streams.[2257] A visitor to the FirstRow website would be presented with lists of links, organised by sport and time of the day, to streams containing live coverage of a wide range of sporting events, including in particular Premier League matches and events organised by the other supporting rights-holders in this case. Upon clicking on one of those links, the user was taken to a new page,

2254 *Ibid*, paras. 44–46.

2255 Without an oral hearing and the rather fast CPR Par 8 alternative claims procedure being employed, the costs for the blocking applications have been lower for the rights-holders than in previous cases. See Darren Meale, *A triple strike against piracy as the music industry secures three more blocking injunctions*, Journal of Intellectual Property Law & Practice 2013, Vol. 8, No. 8, 591, 594.

2256 High Court, *Football Association Premier League Ltd v British Sky Broadcasting Ltd.* [2013] EWHC 2058. For a comment on the case see Rachel Alexander, *FirstRow – access denied*, Entertainment Law Review 2013, Vol. 24 Issue 8, 280–283; Darren Meale, *Premier League 1, Internet pirates 0: sports streaming website the latest to be blocked*, Jounral of Intellectual Proporty Law & Practice 2013, Vol. 8 No. 11, 821–823.

2257 *Ibid*, paras. 40 et seq.

which featured a "frame" or window in which that live coverage then appeared, accompanied by advertising. The streams were provided by third party streamers using one of a number of user-generated content websites.[2258] By presenting the content within a frame, it seemed as if the stream originated from FirstRow. In these scenarios, it is commonly discussed whether the provider is directly liable for raising the impression that he presents "own" content.[2259] Due to the framing and the aggregation and indexing, the operator of *Football Association Premier League Ltd* was held directly liable for communication to the public. In a subsequent blocking injunction relating to the similar functioning SolarMovie and TubePlus websites, Arnold J. discussed his previous conclusion in the light of recent CJEU referrals and acknowledged that it is arguable whether the provision of hyperlinks amounts to communication to the

2258 The Court explained that the presentation of a stream to the end-users was the result of a process involving several stages. First of all, a third party needed to digitally capture a broadcast of a live sports event on his computer. The captured broadcast may be one that the streamer is receiving legally, for instance via a legitimate subscription, or may be an illegal stream. Secondly, the streamer would have to send the captured images in real time to the server of a user-generated content website. Thirdly, the streamer would use the user-generated content site to create an "embed code" which enables the stream player to be embedded into a website like FirstRow. Finally, the streamer would have to submit the embed code to FirstRow, which would then list the code as a link on its website. By clicking on the link, the users would be able to watch the stream. See *ibid*, para. 15.

2259 In particular in German case law, one can find lengthy discussion whether embedding and framing amounts to "Zueigenmachen" ("making the content own content"). For content that is user-generated but perceived as "own content", the host provider will be directly liable as he would be for own content. Unfortunately, the Court did not evaluate this question in *Football Association Premier League Ltd v British Sky Broadcasting Ltd.* The question of whether hyperlinking constitutes communication to the public as "making available" has recently been discussed by the CJEU in C-466/12 *Svensson*, Judgment of 13.02.2014 (for a comment on this decision see Frank Michael Höfinger, *Anmerkung zu EuGH, Urteil vom 13. Februar 2014 – C-466/12 – Nils Svensson u.a./Retriever Sverige AB,* Zeitschrift für Urheber- und Medienrect 2014, 293–295). Questions to embedding and framing have recently been decided by the CJEU in C-279/13, *C More Entertainment,* Judgment of 26.03.2015 and C-348/13, *BestWater International*, Order of 21.10.2014.

public.[2260] This did however not affect the outcome, and the blocking of access to the websites was ordered.

As regards the scope of blocking injunctions, the High Court does not necessarily require Cleanfeed to be used for access blocking. For instance, in the case of *Football Association Premier League Ltd v Sky*, the Court ordered IP address blocking of the IP address of FirstRow's domain name firstrow1.eu because the Court was convinced that this would not result in over-blocking since that IP address is not shared. Further, the orders also required IP address re-routing and URL blocking for URLs at any shared IP addresses.[2261]

With the case of *Football Association Premier League Ltd v Sky,* the High Court's approach to evaluating the proportionality has also changed slightly. Whereas previously, the Court concluded that circumvention of blocking requires some technical expertise, the Court has now accepted that the "narrow and targeted" blocking is "unlikely to be completely efficacious, since some users will be able to circumvent the technical measures which the orders require the Defendants to adopt".[2262] Nevertheless, the Court is convinced that blocking is likely to be reasonably effective.

d) Injunctions under Section 97A CDPA 1988: A Pyrrhic Victory for Copyright Owners

In a series of cases that began with the NewzBin case, the High Court has awarded injunctions under section 97A *CDPA 1988* requiring access providers to take measures to block or at least impede access by their customers to peer-to-peer file-sharing websites using Cleanfeed or similar technologies.

All blocking orders were based on the fact that the websites in question were held themselves to infringe copyright. In *NewzBin*, liability of the NewzBin operators was established because the operators went beyond

---

2260 See High Court, *Paramount Home Entertainment International Ltd v British Sky Broadcasting Ltd* [2013] EWHC 3479 (Ch), paras. 13–22. For a comment on the case see Paddy Gardiner/Juliane Althoff, *High Court grants further blocking injunction against film and TV streaming websites,* Entertainment Law Review 2014, Vol. 25 Issue 3, 108–110.

2261 High Court, *Football Association Premier League Ltd v British Sky Broadcasting Ltd.* [2013] EWHC 2058, para. 56.

2262 *Ibid*, para. 55.

merely enabling and assisting the users to infringe copyright; the operators were held to have inter alia authorised its premium members to make infringing copies of the Studios' films, and to have itself infringed the Studios' copyrights by communicating the copyright works to the public. In *Dramatico v Sky*, the Pirate Bay operators were held to have authorised infringement and be jointly liable as accessories. In *EMI v Sky*, the operators of KAT, H33T and Fenopy were held liable for communicating sound recordings to the public by indexing .torrent files and providing a search function to these files. In *Football Association Premier League Ltd v Sky*, the operator of FirstRow was held directly liable for communication to the public. While the liability can be questioned, an analysis of liability for the different services provided would go beyond the scope of this research, which focuses on the response to an established infringement. It shall only be mentioned at this point that in particular the authorisation of an infringement is not such a clear case as the rights-holders want it to be. Beside its dictionary meaning of sanction, approve and countenance, authorisation can also be defined as to "grant or purport to grant to a third person the right to do the act complained of, whether the intention is that the grantee shall do the act on his own account, or only on account of the grantor".[2263] Authorisation does not extend to mere enablement, assistance or even encouragement.[2264] It seems that we can witness a shift in the interpretation of authorisation towards "allowing facilitation".[2265]

As regards the establishment of liability, it may be more appropriate to take the route of joint tortfeasance. The principles of joint tortfeasance have already been applied in NewzBin 1 and Dramatico. Joint tortfeasance exists where someone is "so involved in the commission of the tort as to make the infringing act their own".[2266] The concept thus introduces a component of blameworthiness to the liability standard, and this is exactly what the courts were trying to establish in all cases.[2267]

2263 High Court, *Falcon v Famous Players Film Co.* [1926] 2 KB 474, 499.

2264 See Pekka Savola, *Blocking injunctions and website operators' liability for copyright infringement for user-generated links,* European Intellectual Property Review 2014, Vol. 36 Issue 5, 279, 285.

2265 See *ibid*, 286.

2266 Court of Appeal, *SABAF SpA v MFI Furniture* [2003] RPC 14, para. 59.

2267 Christina Angelopoulos, *Beyond the Safe Harbours: Harmonising substantive intermediary liability for copyright infringement in Europe,* p. 6.

Irrespective of how the court arrived at establishing liability, once liability is established, blocking will be considered as an appropriate remedy.

In NewzBin2, the Court discussed in detail the proportionality of the order sought and concluded that the blocking of access to NewzBin "is necessary and appropriate to protect the Article 1 *First Protocol* rights of the Studios and other copyright owners".[2268] In all subsequent cases that have been addressed above the interests of the rights-holders in enforcing their copyrights were held to outweigh the Article 10 *ECHR*/Article 11 *CFR* rights of the users of the service in question. Besides the arguments brought forward in NewzBin, it must also be noted that in *Football Association Premier League Ltd v Sky*, the Court also noted that the users could obtain the blocked content from available lawful source.[2269] The outweighing was considered to be even more clearly in relation to the rights of operators of the websites in question, in particular when they were profiting from large scale infringement.[2270] The rights-holders interests were also always held to outweigh the access providers' freedom of expression rights to the extent that they were engaged.

Decisive was inter alia that the order is a narrow and targeted one, and that it contains "safeguards in the event of any change of circumstances".[2271] Also the cost of implementation for the access provider was considered modest and proportionate considering that access providers already use Cleanfeed to filter out child abuse materials.

The High Court however underestimated the circumvention measures available to users.[2272] Although the High Court acknowledged that the operators of NewzBin2 were already making plans to assist users to circumvent blocking, at the same time, the Court concluded that blocking would require the acquisition of additional technical expertise that goes beyond the expertise of ordinary users.[2273] This would require that users

---

2268 High Court, *Twentieth Century Fox Film Corp v British Telecommunications Plc* [2011] EWHC 1981, para. 200.

2269 High Court, *Football Association Premier League Ltd v British Sky Broadcasting Ltd.* [2013] EWHC 2058, para. 59.

2270 See only *ibid*, para. 59 and High Court, *Twentieth Century Fox Film Corp v British Telecommunications Plc* [2011] EWHC 1981. 200.

2271 High Court, *Twentieth Century Fox Film Corp v British Telecommunications Plc* [2011] EWHC 1981, para. 200.

2272 Cf. *Ibid*, paras. 192 et seq.

2273 Cf. *Ibid*, paras. 194 et seq.

spent time and effort, which not all users would be willing to invest.[2274] The Court was also convinced that circumvention measures would result in slower performance and lower quality downloads unless users were prepared to pay for circumvention services (such as for instance a good proxy) – which again not all users would be willing to do.[2275] Considering the added costs, the Court concluded that the gap between lawful services and the use of NewzBin2 would diminish, in particular, for less active users.[2276] Finally, the order as such may reduce usage of NewzBin2,[2277] and thus, efficacy was attributed to the blocking.

This reasoning ignores that already four months before the judgment was rendered, NEwzBin2 had announced a new web address to which users could navigate using the free-of-charge TOR network.[2278] The latter is impossible for access providers to block.

As outlined under the technological challenges in this Chapter, current blocking measures are imperfect and circumvention is available for all of them. Other than the High Court concluded, employing a circumvention tool is also not complicated and not necessarily connected to costs. A lot of circumvention services are free. While it is true for most of the tools available to users, that download speed will decrease, the Court simply ignored that the easiest way is that the site operators themselves circumvent blocking by relocating their service.[2279] Considering that already four months prior to the judgment, the NewzBin2 operators already provided for the circumvention, the efficacy of the blocking is more than questionable. Moreover, the victory for the rights-holders only existed on paper, but not in reality.

On the other hand, the Court also acknowledged that legitimate content may become victim of the blocking. This was however not considered to have enough impact on the legitimacy of the blocking order as the percentage of legal content to be blocked was held to be de minimis. Legal in that context can however not refer to the sharing of non-copyrighted works, legal must also include copyrighted content where the rights-hold-

2274 *Ibid*, para. 194.

2275 Cf. *Ibid*, para. 195.

2276 *Ibid*, para. 196.

2277 *Ibid*, para. 197.

2278 See Darren Meale, *NewzBin2: the first section 97A injunction against an ISP*, Journal of Intellectual Property Law & Practice 2011, Vol. 6 No. 12, 854, 856.

2279 *Ibid.*

ers do not take action to have access blocked. Rights-holder may also have reasons not to intervene. Bands may use peer-to-peer networks for promotion; the band Georgia Wonder for instance seeded its songs in peer-to-peer network to become the 14th most downloaded band in the world.[2280] By blocking access to torrent indexing sites, one automatically cuts off access to platforms that can be used for free promotion by artists. The High Court failed to take into consideration the rights and interests of third parties. Although one might argue, that Georgia Wonder could have also set up its own website, the disseminating factor of peer-to-peer networks cannot be neglected.

However, the strongest argument against access blocking by access providers is, that it is a costly system that is easy to circumvent and thus, has little effect.

As regards the access providers the latest case shows their resignation in fighting the applications. Moreover, they agree their terms with the rights-holders, and include a clause whereby operators of third party websites, who claim to be affected by the order, are enabled to apply to vary or discharge an order.[2281]

With less opposition on behalf of the providers, less court costs and a swift procedure, it can thus be predicted that rights-holders will increasingly seek blocking injunctions and be successful with their applications.[2282] Considering that already the NewzBin case was more of a "catch me if you can" matter, there is a strong presumption that successful applications are rather pyrrhic victories.

2. Germany: No Injunctions against Access Providers

While in the UK copyright may be enforced through access providers, German laws as it stands today does not provide a legal basis for measures

---

2280 Techradar, *Cheap promotion, Twitter and peer-to-peer, How one band used YouTube, Twitter and file-sharing to create a community of fans,* Techradar (16.01.2010).

2281 Rachel Alexander, *FirstRow – access denied*, Entertainment Law Review 2013, Vol. 24 Issue 8, 280, 282.

2282 Paddy Gardiner/Gillie Abbotts, *Sky's the limit for ISP blocking orders*, Entertainment Law Review 2013, Vol. 24 Issue 6, 217, 219; Darren Meale, *Premier League 1, Internet pirates 0: sports streaming website the latest to be blocked*, Journal of Intellectual Property Law & Practice 2013, Vol. 8 No. 11, 821, 822.

that would require access providers to enforce copyright. In order to provide a contrasting approach to the one conducted in the UK, this section will briefly look at the very short history of access blocking by access providers in Germany.

Between 11 and 17 September 2007, the German Internet access provider Arcor blocked access for all its 2.4 million customers to YouPorn and further websites that allowed free access to pornographic materials. According to Arcor the blocking was voluntarily following the request of a Kirchberg Logistik GmbH that charged its customers for downloads of erotica and argued that pursuant to German youth media protection laws, access to pornography without proof of age is not permissible.[2283] These cases thus did not concern liability for copyright infringements, but claims under unfair competition law.

Blocking was lifted when it became clear that by the blocking of the IP addresses of the websites in question led to over-blocking; further sites that did not contain pornographic content were also blocked.[2284] Ironically, the website of an IT Conference belonged to the sites affected.[2285]

On 19 October 2007, Kirchberg Logistik GmbH obtained an injunction before the Regional Court of Frankfurt am Main against Arcor, requiring Arcor to block content to the websites in question. [2286] Arcor then opted for DNS manipulation in order to block access.[2287] In the following, Kirchberg sent out several cease and desist letters demanding further German Internet service providers to block access as well. As they did not comply with the cease and desist requests, Kirchberg applied for preliminary injunctions against several providers. On 23 November 2007, the Regional Court of Kiel rejected Kirchberg's claim arguing that the provision of Internet access is content neutral and access providers are not liable for the content of websites.[2288] In addition, the Regional Court of

2283 Urs Mansmann, *Arcor sperrt Zugriff auf Porno-Seiten*, Heise online (10.09.2007).

2284 Konrad Lischka, *Fehlerhafte Zensur-Methode: Arcor stoppt den Porno-Filter*, Spiegel Online (17.09.2007).

2285 *Ibid.*

2286 Stefan Krempl, *Arcor muss YouPorn sperren*, Heise online (19.10.2007).

2287 Stefan Krempl, *Arcor installiert leicht umgehbare Netzsperre für YouPorn*, Heise online (24.10.2007).

2288 LG Kiel, Decision of 23.11.2007 – 14 O 125/07, MultiMedia und Recht 2008, 123 with comment by Christoph Schnabel.

Düsseldorf refused to issue an injunction against an access provider.[2289] The obligation imposed upon Arcor to block access to YouPorn has later been annulled by the Regional Court Frankfurt.[2290]

Further attempts by providers of pornographic content to have access blocked to for instance google.com and google.de, based on the fact that the search engines list links to pornographic content without limiting access to adults, were unsuccessful.[2291]

Recently, there seems to be a consensus that the imposition of filtering and blocking duties upon access providers infringes the fundamental rights of users, in particular Article 10 II *GG* which protects the confidentiality of communications.[2292] Considering that blocking as such is not prescribed by law in Germany, a blocking order could solely be based on the *Störerhaftung*,[2293] which in turn is not considered sufficient to justify an infringement of Article 10 II *GG*.[2294] As regards copyright infringements, the majority of courts and scholars even rule out the possibility of *Störerhaftung* of access providers.[2295]

When examining whether the DNS and IP blocking which was requested by rights-holders could be justified, courts have first acknowledged that this would require the access provider to monitor the data communications

---

2289 LG Düsseldorf, Decision of 13.12.2007 – 12 O 550/07, MultiMedia und Recht 2008, 349.

2290 LG Frankfurt/M., Urteil vom 8.2.2008 – 3-12 O 171/07, MultiMedia und Recht 2008, 344.

2291 See OLG Frankfurt, Decision of 22.01.2008 – 6 W 10/08, MultiMedia und Recht 2008, 166 with comment by Gerald Spindler.

2292 Dieter Frey /Matthias Rudolph/Jan Oster, *Internetsperren und der Schutz der Kommunikation im Internet, Am Beispiel behördlicher und gerichtlicher Sperrungsverfügungen im Bereich des Glücksspiel- und Urheberrechts,* MultiMedia und Recht-Beilage 2012 to Issue 3, 5.

2293 The concept of *Störerhaftung* has already been discussed in the context of pre-litigation settlement in Chapter 2. In relation to host providers, the concept will be evaluated in the context of monitoring and filtering obligations.

2294 LG Köln, Decision of 31.08.2011 – 28 O 362/10, MultiMedia und Recht 2011, 833 with comment by Christoph Schnabel.

2295 See Thomas Hoeren/Silviya Yankova, *The Liability of Internet Intermediaries – The German Perspective*, International Review of Intellectual Property and Competition Law 2012, 501, 518 with further references. Thomas Hoeren in: Thomas Hoeren/Ulrich Sieber/Bernd Holznagel, *Multimedia-Recht* (37th amended ed. 2014), para. 79. As regards jurisprudence cf. only OLG Hamburg, Decision of 21.11.2013 – 5 U 68/10 (*3dl.am*), Gewerblicher Rechtsschutz und Urheberrecht-RR 2014, 140.

of all his customers, which would also mean that the providers acquires knowledge of the circumstances of communication including the content.[2296] The acquisition of such knowledge was held to constitute a serious interference with the right to confidentiality of communications.[2297] In this context, German courts have also recognised that DNS or IP blocking does not constitute a feasible means to prevent further infringements.[2298] Blocking by access providers would not be allowed to go so far as to block access to an indexing service, as this would also mean that legitimate content and the rights and interests of third parties were concerned.[2299] The courts paid regard to the fact, that if the service provider of the targeted service added one digit to the URL concerned, this would mean that the illegal content would still be available under the same domain but under another URL. This would then require that the claimant applies for new injunctions or amends his request with each and every change.[2300] Consequently, effective blocking by access providers would require the provider to implement the technical infrastructure for access blocking and invest human resources to comply with the requests. Considering that a *Störer* does not himself interfere with the rights of another party, but in another way contributes deliberately and adequately causal to the infringement of a protected right, such contributions by the access providers are not considered proportionate.[2301]

As rights-holders are still trying to obtain injunctions against access providers, the question of whether access providers could be obliged as Störer to bar access to copyright infringing materials irrespective of a statutory basis has recently been referred to the Federal Court of Justice

2296 *Ibid*, 834. See also LG Hamburg, Decision of 12.3.2010 – 308 O 640/08, MultiMedia und Recht 2010, 488, 490 and OLG Hamburg, Decision of 22.12.2010 – 5 U 36/09, Computer und Recht 2011, 735.

2297 *Ibid.*

2298 LG Köln, Decision of 31.08.2011 – 28 O 362/10, MultiMedia und Recht 2011, 833; see also Christoph Schnabel, *Anmerkung zu Urteil des LG Kiel*, MultiMedia und Recht 2008, 123, 125.

2299 LG Köln, Decision of 31.08.2011 – 28 O 362/10, MultiMedia und Recht 2011, 833, 834. See also LG Hamburg, Decision of 12.3.2010 – 308 O 640/08, MultiMedia und Recht 2010, 488, 490 and OLG Hamburg, Decision of 22.12.2010 – 5 U 36/09, Computer und Recht 2011, 735.

2300 *Ibid.*

2301 *Ibid.* See also see also Christian Czychowski/Jan Bernd Nordemann, *Grenzenloses Internet – entgrenzte Haftung?*, Gewerblicher Rechtsschutz und Urheberrecht-Beilage 2014, 3, 9.

for clarification.[2302] As of now, no injunctions will be issued until the Federal Court has answered this question.

3. Access Blocking by Access Providers: Concerns relating to Technology and Fundamental Rights

Many of the issues that arise from technology in relation to blocking have already been addressed in the above analyses. The focus of this section shall thus be on the conformity with fundamental rights.

a) Technological Concerns in Relation to Access Blocking

The reason for access blocking lies in the difficulty to provide an effective remedy to rights-holders. Operators of piracy sites, that index .torrent files or provide link directories often change their domain names, so that seizures of domains like for example conducted in the case of FirstRow[2303] by the US Department of Homeland Security, are ineffective. The operators are difficult to catch, they cloak themselves in anonymity, and do not respond to take down requests. For instance in respect to FirstRow, the rights-holders concerned were not even able to establish who the operators of FirstRow were, and where they could be contacted.[2304] Cease and desist letters on behalf of the rights-holders were not responded to.[2305]

In particular in the UK, rights-holders are thus applying for injunctions against domestic access providers requiring the blocking of access of such

---

2302 OLG Hamburg, Decision of 21.11.2013 – 5 U 68/10 (*3dl.am*), Gewerblicher Rechtsschutz und Urheberrecht-RR 2014, 140. The case is pending with the Federal Court of Justice (BGH, file no. I ZR 3/14), a decision is expected in autumn 2015.

2303 FirstRow was subject of the order sought in *Football Association Premier League Ltd v Sky,* see High Court, *Football Association Premier League Ltd v British Sky Broadcasting Ltd.* [2013] EWHC 2058, para. 14.

2304 FirstRow had been registred under many different domain names, using a mixture of what appeared to be fals name and address details and registrations via proxy registration firms. At the time the case was before the High Court, the website was hosted in Sweden. *Ibid*, paras. 21–22.

2305 *Ibid*, para. 22.

websites. The main difference between the German and UK approach in relation to access blocking by access providers is, that German law does not provide legal grounds for such a far-reaching measure. In addition, German courts also considered that DNS or IP blocking do not constitute feasible means to prevent further infringements, and that it is easy for website operators to escape blocking. Consequently, blocking does not only lack a legal basis but is also considered ineffective.

In contrast to German law, in the UK, section 97A *CDPA 1988* provides a legal basis for court orders in relation to access blocking. The first problem of a technological nature in relation to section 97A injunctions is that of actual knowledge of the access provider. Access providers do not monitor the content they transmit, so how can they acquire actual knowledge that their service is being used by a third party to infringe a copyright. In NewzBin2 knowledge was established, because BT knew of the judgment against NewzBin1, was aware of the service provided by NewzBin2 and aware that its customers accessed NewzBin2. Knowledge does not require that the access provider is aware of a particular user accessing NewBin, or a particular infringing act was committed. The actual knowledge condition can thus be justified by a general knowledge of infringing acts. Rightsholders will send pre-litigation letters to the access providers informing them about the infringements and the action that they are intending to take.

The UK case law has shown that section 97A injunctions are increasingly applied for to bar access to "infringing websites". While the Turkish order in the *Yildirim* case before the ECtHR concerned the blocking of a whole domain, UK orders are more precise and require the blocking of a specified website. Blocking will be conducted by using Cleanfeed, a hybrid blocking system of IP address blocking and DPI-based URL filtering Cleanfeed incorporates both redirection of traffic and the use of web proxies.[2306] While it is particularly precise in what it blocks, it is also a low-cost model to build and operate. Referring to Cleanfeed as "particularly precise" already indicates that it is not a 100% precise system that does not have the potential to produce collateral damage. The Virgin

2306 Richard Clayton, *Anonymity and traceability in cyberspace* (2005), Technical Report UCAM-CL-TR-653, p.116. The functioning has already been outlined above; see above A. III. 1. e) Hybrid Systems – The Example of CleanFeed.

Killer incident,[2307] which has previously been described, has proven that it may clash with other content regulation systems and have a severe effect on network accessibility and infrastructure.

In addition, and this relates to one of the concerns, that the German courts addressed, even elaborated hybrid blocking mechanisms like Cleanfeed can as easy be circumvented as single blocking schemes. Users may circumvent the blocking system for instance via VPNs or anonymising services.[2308] The blocking does rather prevent the accidental access of the blocked website, whereas users that want to access the website may still do so. In particular notorious infringes, may not be affected as they will now how to access the materials.

Taking the example of *Football Association Premier League Ltd v Sky,* this case also shows like many others, that the operators of piracy sites change their domain names quite often and migrate from one country to another, so that blocking will need to be adapted with every move they take. It is unclear in how far a section *97A CDPA 1988* injunction would cover the reappearance of a blocked service under a new name. While in NewzBin2, the Court had no difficulties in establishing that NewzBin2 was an identical service to NewzBin1, the case may not always be so clear cut.

Further, access blocking does not mean that the content disappears. The access blocking orders that have so far been issued by the UK courts did not relate to host providers that hosted the materials as such. Instead the blocking of .torrent trackers, indexing sites and streaming portals, that framed third party content were targeted. Metaphorically speaking, the phonebook was deleted, but the phone numbers persisted. The content remained, and only one way to get information about its location was cut off, or more precisely, "hidden" from the public.

Finally, the access blocking orders were always directed at a whole website, once the court was convinced that it had substantial infringing use. Considering that for instance in the case of *Football Association Pre-*

2307 The incident concerned a depiction of the cover of German rock band Scorpions' 1976 studio album Virgin Killer on Wikipedia. The controversial cover artwork depicted a young girl posing nude, with a faux glass shatter obscuring her genitalia. See Raphael Satter, *Wikipedia article blocked in UK over child photo*, The Independent (08.12.2008).

2308 Holger Bleich/Axel Kossel, *Verschleierungstaktik: Die Argumente für Kinderporno-Sperren laufen ins Leere,* Der Spiegel Online (17.04.2009).

mier League Ltd v Sky, access to FirstRow as such was blocked, also access to content that did not belong to the Premier League Ltd was blocked as well. FirstRow was not solely dedicated to Premier League matches, but to all kinds of sports events. Although the High Court acknowledges that legitimate content may become victim of blocking, this is not considered to have enough impact on the legitimacy of the blocking order as the percentage of legal content to be blocked is regularly held to be de minimis. Notably, in the UK cases, it is true, that the websites in question, were dedicated to piracy. However, no assessment was made as to whether there was a substantial non-infringing use of the platforms that could be affected. It will be interesting to see, how the courts will deal with cases where website operators do not respond to take down requests of certain infringing content, but also provide for substantial non-infringing use. This may in particular be the case with file-hosting services, which are used for both, legal and illegal acts.[2309]

With generations of digital natives growing up, it may be likely that blocking becomes less and less effective, because they will find it easy to circumvent blocking. Thus, one may witness a "technological arms race"[2310], where to new forms of blocking, new ways of circumvention will be developed.

b) Compliance with Secondary EU Law

In contrast to the assessment of whether graduated response schemes comply with secondary EU law, the analysis can be cut short in relation to access blocking orders against access providers. As already stated in the context of access blocking upon orders by an administrative authority, although, Article 12(1) of the *E-Commerce Directive* provides that mere conduits are not liable for information they transmit, this does not prevent an injunction being imposed. In fact, Article 12(3) *E-Commerce Directive* makes it clear that the liability exemption "does not affect the possibility

2309 Lilian Edwards refers to websites that host both infringing and non-infrining content as "dual purpose" sites, see Lilian Edwards, *Role and responsibility of Internet intermediaries in the field of copyright and related rights*, p. 52.

2310 Toby Headdon, *Beyond liability: on the availability and scope of injunctions against online intermediaries after L'Oréal v eBay,* European Intellectual Property Review 2012, Vol. 34 Issue 3, 137, 144.

for a court or administrative authority, in accordance with Member States' legal systems, of requiring the service provider to terminate or prevent an infringement". Under Article 8(3) of the *InfoSoc Directive* injunctive relief is available against intermediaries specifically in relation to preventing infringements of intellectual property rights.

When Article 15(1) *E-Commerce Directive* forbids Member States to impose general obligations on online intermediaries to monitor the information they transmit, this does for instance exclude an "active monitoring of all the data of each of a website's customers in order to prevent any future infringement via the provider's website".[2311]

c) Conformity with Fundamental Rights of Internet Users

The fundamental rights of Internet users in the context of blocking have already been briefly addressed in relation to access blocking orders by administrative authorities and will be analysed in more detail at this point.

aa) Interference with Users' Rights to Seek, Receive and Impart Information

If legitimate content is blocked by way of "collateral damage", the blocking interferes with the disseminator's right to freedom of expression that is guaranteed by Article 10 *ECHR* (and Article 11 *CFR*). If end-users can no longer access legitimate content that has been blocked unintentionally, this also interferes with the users' rights to receive information, which is equally guaranteed by said Articles.

As regards filtering and blocking of content on the Internet, the first Chapter of the Declaration of the Committee of Ministers on human rights and the rule of law in the Information Society recognises that "1. [...] ICTs provide unprecedented opportunities for all to enjoy freedom of expression. However, ICTs also pose many serious challenges to that freedom, such as state and private censorship".[2312] In the preamble to their Declaration of 28 May 2003 on freedom of communication on the Inter-

2311 CJEU, C-324/09 *L'Oréal v eBay* [2011] ECR I-06011, para. 139.

2312 Council of Europe, *Declaration of the Committee of Ministers on human rights and the rule of law in the information society* (13.05.2005), CM(2005)56 final.

net, the Committee of Ministers went on to state that prior control of communications on the Internet, regardless of frontiers, should remain an exception.[2313] While this relates to censorship as such, the Declaration clarified that "Principle 3: […] Public authorities should not, through general blocking or filtering measures, deny access by the public to information and other communication on the Internet, regardless of frontiers. This does not prevent the installation of filters for the protection of minors, in particular in places accessible to them, such as schools or libraries. Provided that the safeguards of Article 10, paragraph 2, of the Convention for the Protection of Human Rights and Fundamental Freedoms are respected, measures may be taken to enforce the removal of clearly identifiable Internet content or, alternatively, the blockage of access to it, if the competent national authorities have taken a provisional or final decision on its illegality". The Council of Europe thus recognises that courts may order the deletion or blocking of clearly identifiable content, given that the competent national authorities have taken a decision on the illegality of the content. Hence, filtering or monitoring obligations are not as such forbidden by the *ECHR*. The same applies for monitoring and filtering obligations under EU law. Decisive is under both frameworks, whether the monitoring and filtering regime respects freedom of expression.

As with all interferences to be justified, they must be prescribed by law. Already the requirement that any interference must be "prescribed by law" is doubtful. For the interference to be prescribed by law, the measure in question must have a legal basis. This legal basis must, firstly, be adequately accessible (the individual must be able to have an indication that is adequate in the circumstances of the legal rules applicable to a given case); secondly, be formulated with sufficient precision to enable individuals to regulate their conduct (they must be able to foresee the consequences which a given action may entail).[2314]

In Germany, there is consensus that the *Störerhaftung* does not provide a sufficiently precise legal basis for access blocking orders against access providers. In the UK, section 97A of the *CDPA 1988* has been considered to be foreseeable enough, although it only provides a basis for injunctions

2313 Council of Europe, *Freedom of communication on the Internet*, Declaration adopted by the Committee of Ministers on 28.05.2003 at the 840th meeting of the Ministers' Deputies and explanatory note (2003), preamble.

2314 ECtHR, *Sunday Times v the United Kingdom*, Application No, Ser A No 30 (1979), para. 49.

in a rather general manner. While the general concept of *Störerhaftung* does not precisely determine that access providers fall within its scope, section 97A *CDPA 1988* specifically targets service providers including access providers. In that regard, the provision is much more precise than its German counterpart. Considering that in Germany, the crux was that it was not sufficiently foreseeable that access providers may be liable as *Störer*, in the UK access providers could foresee that they may be subject to an injunctions for actions of their users as section 97A *CDPA 1988* set forth that injunctions may be granted against a service provider, where that service provider has actual knowledge of another person using their service to infringe copyright. Considering that access providers in the UK already employ a blocking system in relation to child pornography, one may conclude that an order to block copyright infringing materials pursuant to section 97A *CDPA 1988* is foreseeable.

The same applies with regard to the foreseeability of users that have uploaded content, which is no longer accessible following a blocking order. In this context, it must be noted that they can hardly rely that content remains accessible, if the content is illegal. As regards legitimate content, it must be noted, that the blocking orders that have been issued in the UK, only related to sites that facilitated access to infringing materials, they did not themselves host the data as such. By only blocking links and trackers that have been published on one website, the orders did not interfere with the materials as such. Further, the websites concerned where evidently piracy sites. In cases where it is not obvious, that a website is dedicated to infringing use, and a user uploads a legitimate link or .torrent file, it is more difficult to establish foreseeability in that particular case. However, as blocking exist, users must foresee that they may be affected.

Considering that the access blocking measure would be foreseeable, the question remains whether the interference can be justified.

Although the access blocking in general protects the rights of the copyright owners, it is questionable whether it is proportionate.

As regards the proportionality of any blocking measure, it must be ensured that the blocking is a matter of last resort, meaning that no less intrusive measure is available. In all UK cases, that have been discussed above, the website operator did not respond to take down requests and thus, did not comply with a legal obligation. This has been considered by the court, which also discussed the fact that some of the operators shielded their identity, and contact was not possible.

In *Scarlet Extended v SABAM*, the CJEU held that the installation of a "complicated, costly, permanent computer system" at the expense of the service provider did not strike a fair balance between the interests of the access provider and copyright holders involved.[2315] The proposed filtering "would involve a systematic analysis of all content" and "the collection and identification of users' IP addresses from which unlawful content on the network is sent",[2316] and thus infringed the fundamental rights of the access provider's customers, namely their right to protection of their personal data (Article 8 *CFR*) and their freedom to receive or impart information (Article 11 *CFR*).[2317] The proposed injunction was further held to potentially undermine freedom of information since that system might not distinguish adequately between unlawful content and lawful content, "with the result that its introduction could lead to the blocking of lawful communications".[2318]

Accordingly, injunctions that would require a systematic analysis of all content and which do not distinguish adequately between unlawful content and lawful content so that they also result in the blocking of lawful content cannot be justified. When in NewzBin2 films and television programmes comprised about 70% of the material accessible via Newzbin2 and about 30% of that material consisted of other types of content, this means that not all content necessarily constituted unlawful content.[2319] More precisely only 70% of NewzBin2's content related to materials of the claimants. The other 30% of the content was owned by an uncertain number of third parties that were not parties to the case. The High Court concluded that the non-infringing uses of NewzBin2 that were affected by the injunction were de minimis, and thus blocking proportionate. This conclusion however goes too far. Having not established whether the rights-holders in the 30% of content did just not care about the dissemination of their materials via NewzBin, it cannot be certain that NewzBin had no substantial non-infringing use. The latest injunctions thus provide for the possibility of third parties that are affected by the blocking orders to apply to vary or

---

2315 CJEU, C-70/10 *Scarlet Extended v SABAM*, Judgment of 14.11.2011, ECR I-11959, paras. 48 et seq.

2316 Ibid, para. 51.

2317 *Ibid*, para. 50.

2318 *Ibid*, oara. 52.

2319 High Court, *Twentieth Century Fox Film Corp v British Telecommunications Plc* [2011] EWHC 1981, para. 179.

discharge the order insofar as it affects that applicant.[2320] Naturally, this safeguard only becomes effective following the order being applied, because only then will the party concerned obtain knowledge of the order. Considering that access is only blocked, or more precisely the "sign" to the location of content is turned "invisible", the blocking can be reversed easily and the content still be accessed. Without such safeguard, it is difficult to see, how an order can be proportionate if national law does not provide for a third party appeal to an order by which the third party is affected in its fundamental rights.

As regards users that want to access content, an argument in favour of blocking may be the fact that content can be obtained from legal sources as an alternative. It is not that they no longer can access the content as such, but they can no longer access it for free or from that specific source. This argument is valid, insofar as commercialised content is concerned, that is otherwise available. It is relevant with regard to the claimants in the aforementioned cases as they pursued legal action to ensure that they alone can commercially exploit the protected works. However, as the blocking extends to whole platforms, and to content, where it is not certain that it is otherwise available, or which is legally disseminated, this argument loses strength.

When assessing the proportionality of a measure, the efficacy of a blocking measure needs to be taken into account. As aforementioned, there are many ways to circumvent blocking, which may even be used by non-IT-literate users. This would mean effectively, that the blocking would not fundamentally affect notorious, wilful infringers, as they would be able to make their way around the blocking mechanism. In addition, as mentioned above, access blocking to indexing sites and .torrent trackers does not hinder the distribution of the content as such: Links may exist on other platforms, or can be distributed anew. The content as such is not banned, but merely the "sign" to where it can be found. While the latter may not apply where file-hosting services are targeted, an application of blocking orders to these services seems unlikely, because they provide for substantial non-infringing use.

2320 See for instance High Court, *Football Association Premier League Ltd v British Sky Broadcasting Ltd.* [2013] EWHC 2058, para. 57.

The lack in efficacy has been addressed by the High Court as being not so severe as to render blocking disproportionate.[2321] The Court cited research that blocking to the Pirate Bay in Italy let to a 73% reduction in audience accessing the Pirate Bay in Italy.[2322] Similarly, following the blocking of the Pirate Bay in UK, the website dropped from rank 43 in the Alexa rating to rank 293.[2323] The latter indicates that the Pirate Bay is still popular and that many users find their way round the blocking. As regards the efficacy of blocking, also the CJEU acknowledged in the *UPC Telekabel Wien* case, that access blocking may not lead to a complete cessation of the intellectual property rights infringements.[2324] Accordingly, it is accepted, that a complete cessation of copyright infringements may in practice not be achievable as users may circumvent the blocking.[2325] The standard thus has to be to provide for "sufficiently effective" measures "to ensure genuine protection of the fundamental rights at issue", meaning that "they must have the effect of preventing unauthorised access to the protected subject-matter or, at least, of making it difficult to achieve and of seriously discouraging Internet users who are using the services of the addressee of that injunction from accessing the subject-matter made available to them in breach of that fundamental right".[2326] Simply speaking, this means that it is sufficient that access is rendered more difficult, and accessing the content is discouraged. At least for casual users, circumventing the blocking may be too much hassle. Further, unintentional access is avoided. Users that search for a specific file may not be pointed to an illegal offer.

This being said, what is left, is a very narrow scope of application of blocking injunctions under section 97A *CDPA 1988*. A blocking order can only be proportionate under very narrow circumstances. In its blocking orders, the High Court has repeatedly acknowledged that it only grants targeted and narrow orders. However, the "narrow" in the above assessment

---

2321 Cf. High Court, *Twentieth Century Fox Film Corp v British Telecommunications Plc* [2011] EWHC 1981, paras. 192 – 198.

2322 *Ibid*, para. 197.

2323 High Court, *EMI Records Ltd and others v British Sky Broadcasting Ltd and others* [2013] EWHC 379 (Ch), para. 106.

2324 CJEU, C-314/12 *UPC Telekabel Wien GmbH v Constantin Film Verleih GmbH and Wega Filmproduktionsgesellschaft GmbH,* Judgment of 27.03.2014, paras. 58 et seq.

2325 *Ibid*, para. 60.

2326 *Ibid*, para. 62.

does not refer to the injunction being "narrowly" addressed at a certain website; it rather means, that only very few websites can be considered for blocking. As soon as a website is also used for legitimate purposes, access blocking cannot be ordered.

The Court needs to be convinced that the website in question is substantially infringing. In most of the aforementioned cases, this could be established. In order to prevent disproportionate interferences with third party rights, a further safeguard has been established, allowing third parties that are affected by a blocking injunction, to rebut the presumption of illegality by applying for a variation of the order or a discharge. This safeguard satisfies the criteria set up by the CJEU in the *UPC Telekabel Wien* case. The CJEU held that – in order to prevent that fundamental rights preclude the adoption of an injunction – national procedural rules must provide a possibility for Internet users to assert their rights before the court once the concrete measures that have been taken by the service provider are known and by which they are affected.[2327]

Finally, access blocking can be proportionate, but only in very limited cases. As soon as an indexing feature or a .torrent tracker does not almost exclusively refer to infringing content, blocking is likely to be disproportionate in terms of an interference with the rights of users. It will be interesting to see, whether a court will discharge or vary an injunction when a third party is affected by the blocking.

bb) Interference with the Users' Privacy Rights

In addition to what has been said above, blocking may also interfere with privacy rights, in particular where DPI-based blocking is deployed.[2328] Deep packet inspection schemes examine the content of communication,[2329] which is something an access provider would normally not do.

2327 *Ibid*, para. 57.

2328 See in this regard, Lilian Edwards refers to websites that host both infringing and non-infrining content as "dual purpose" sites, see Lilian Edwards, *Role and responsibility of Internet intermediaries in the field of copyright and related rights*, p. 54.

2329 For a detailed account of the functioning and robustness of deep packet inspection see also Ofcom, *"Site blocking" to reduce online copyright infringement: A Review of sections 17 and 18 of the Digital Economy Act* (27.05.2011), pp. 39 et seq.

Such filtering would amount to blanket monitoring of users, something that has been rejected by the CJEU in the *Scarlet Extended v SABAM* case.[2330] Due to its functioning, DPI-based blocking "would involve a systematic analysis of all content" and "the collection and identification of users' IP addresses from which unlawful content on the network is sent";[2331] this would infringe the fundamental rights of the access provider's customers, including their right to protection of their personal data (Article 8 *CFR*).[2332]

In the aforementioned access blocking cases, DPI-based blocking has not been ordered.

Instead, the Cleanfeed blocking scheme was ordered to be employed, for instance in the *NewzBin2* case. The filtering system is a hybrid system of IP address blocking and DPI-based URL filtering and treats particular IP addresses special. It thus incorporates both redirection of traffic and the use of web proxies.[2333] Only suspicious requests are thus examined, which does not amount to a systematic analysis of all content, even though all requests would be filtered. Further Cleanfeed does not log any user data.

Thus, depending on the blocking scheme that is used, there is a risk of disproportionate interference with users' privacy rights.

d) Conformity with Fundamental Rights of Access Providers

Access blocking interferes with the access providers' rights to pursue business and their right to property as guaranteed by Article 1 of the Protocol No. 1 to the *ECHR* (and Articles 16 and 17 *CFR*). Injunctions against provider to block access to certain materials or website further constitute a restriction of freedom of expression and information. Although it is true that, in substance, the expressions of opinion and information in question are those of the access provider's customers, the provider can nevertheless rely on that fundamental right by virtue of its function of publishing its customers' expressions of opinion and providing

---

2330 CJEU, C-70/10 *Scarlet Extended v SABAM*, Judgment of 14.11.2011, ECR I-11959.

2331 *Ibid*, para. 51.

2332 *Ibid*, para. 50.

2333 Richard Clayton, *Anonymity and traceability in cyberspace* (2005), Technical Report UCAM-CL-TR-653, p.116

them with information. It must be ensured in that regard that the blocking measure does actually affect infringing material and that there is no danger of blocking access to lawful material.[2334]

As regards the freedom to conduct a business, that is guaranteed under the CFR, the CJEU held in *UPC Telekabel Wien* that this includes inter alia "the right for any business to be able to freely use, within the limits of its liability for its own acts, the economic, technical and financial resources available to it".[2335]

This being said, an injunction, which obliges an access provider to take measures which may represent a significant cost for him, is considered to constrain the access provider in a manner which restricts the free use of the resources at his disposal.[2336] This shall in particular apply, where the measure would have a considerable impact on the organisation of his activities or require difficult and complex technical solutions.[2337] It needs to be stressed that the domestic law must not require the addressee of an injunction to make unbearable sacrifices. A blocking injunction is, in that respect, not proportionate if it jeopardises an access provider's business activity as such, that is, the commercial activity of making Internet access.[2338]

Similar to the administration of copyright infringement reports and lists in the context of a graduated response scheme, the imposition of a blocking obligation requires expenditures by the access provider, but does not jeopardise the business activity of providing Internet access as such. As has been explained in the introductory section, the more precise a blocking mechanism is, the more costly is its implementation. Irrespective of the expenditures, a blocking obligation may not infringe the core of the freedom to conduct business when it leaves the access provider to determine the specific measures to be taken in order to achieve the requested

---

2334 See Opinion of the AG Cruz Villalón of 26.11.2013 in -314/12 *UPC Telekabel Wien GmbH v Constantin Film Verleih GmbH and Wega Filmproduktionsgesellschaft GmbH,* para. 82.

2335 CJEU, C-314/12 *UPC Telekabel Wien GmbH v Constantin Film Verleih GmbH and Wega Filmproduktionsgesellschaft GmbH,* Judgment of 27.03.2014, para. 49.

2336 *Ibid*, para. 50.

2337 *Ibid.*

2338 Opinion of the AG Cruz Villalón of 26.11.2013 in -314/12 *UPC Telekabel Wien GmbH v Constantin Film Verleih GmbH and Wega Filmproduktionsgesellschaft GmbH,* para. 108

result.[2339] In the *UPC Telekabel Wien* case, this meant that the provider could choose to put in place measures which are "best adapted to the resources and abilities available to him".[2340] The blocking ordered in the UK can be distinguished from the Austrian case insofar as the measures to be taken were already specified in the injunction. Thus, the Court also assessed the costs involved, which were considered to be not very high as no blocking scheme had to be implemented anew, but a scheme that was already being deployed to block access to child abuse materials was to be used. Hence, although the measures could not be chosen by the access provider, it was guaranteed that they were adapted to the resources and abilities available to the provider, i.e. requiring the usage of a system that was already in use. Accordingly, in the UK cases, the blocking can be considered reasonable to achieve the aim of protection of third party copyright. Obligations that would go further than those outlined above would be unjustifiable in the light of the fact that the service provider is not the author of the infringement in question.[2341] This being said, it is questionable whether the Austrian approach in the *UPC Telekabel Wien* case can amount to a fair balancing of rights.[2342] As has already been outlined in the first section of this Chapter, there are a number of measures available to block a website. They include simple and cheap methods as well as highly complex methods, which are difficult to implement. Some are prone to over-blocking, others are very precise. The degree of interference with the fundamental rights of the access provider thus differs. It would then be left for the access provider to assess the reasonability of a blocking measure, which is however something that the court ordering the blocking should assess. As has been noted by the Advocate General Cruz Villalón in his opinion in the *UPC Telekabel Wien* case, "according to the case-law, the balance between the fundamental rights must be observed when the injunction is issued".[2343] Consideration relevant to fundamental rights

2339 CJEU, C-314/12 *UPC Telekabel Wien GmbH v Constantin Film Verleih GmbH and Wega Filmproduktionsgesellschaft GmbH,* Judgment of 27.03.2014, para. 52.

2340 *Ibid*, para. 52.

2341 Cf. *Ibid*, para. 53.

2342 See also Opinion of the AG Cruz Villalón of 26.11.2013 in -314/12 *UPC Telekabel Wien GmbH v Constantin Film Verleih GmbH and Wega Filmproduktionsgesellschaft GmbH,* paras. 86 et seq.

2343 *Ibid*, para. 88.

must not be examined at a later stage.[2344] The possibility of a judicial review of the standard adopted by the access provider as suggested by the CJEU does not heal the lacking assessment of a fair balance. The procedural guarantee does not heal the severe impact of the access blocking order on the fundamental rights of an access provider. If an access provider would opt for a mild blocking in order not to interfere too much with user rights, he must fear a dispute for non-compliance with the blocking order.[2345] If he opts for an extensive yet not overly complex blocking measure, he must fear disputes with his customers for over-blocking.[2346] Considering the extent some blocking measures may have on users' rights to freedom of expression and information, it should be for a court to assess what kind of blocking is reasonable and justified in order not to leave the service provider in legal uncertainty.

e) Striking a Fair Balance between the Contravening Interests

Following the analysis above, it is established that access blocking interferes with the rights of users to freedom of expression and information as well as privacy rights. Further access blocking orders against access providers interfere with the providers' right to freedom of expression and information and their freedom to pursue business. In order for a measure that seeks to stop and prevent copyright infringements to be justified a fair balance needs to be struck between the contravening interests. The proportionality of blocking obligations particularly depends on three factors: their effectiveness, the severity of the interference, and the presence of adequate and effective measures against abuse. The European Court of Human Rights has repeatedly held that "adequate and effective measures against abuse" need to be present in order for an interference to be proportional.[2347]

2344 *Ibid.*

2345 Cf. *ibid*, para. 89.

2346 Cf. *ibid.*

2347 ECtHR, *Klass and Others v Germany*, Judgment of 06.09.1978 – Application No. 5029/71, para. 50; see also *Rotaru v Romania*, Judgment of 04.05.2000 – Application No. 28341/95, para. 59, which uses the term "safeguards" instead of guarantees.

Access blocking orders seek to protect copyright and undoubtedly pursue a legitimate aim. What is questionable is the appropriateness of access blocking for the furtherance of the aim, meaning whether they make a contribution to the attainment of the aim. Doubts exist in this regard, because the blocking measures that are available can be circumvented. As with traditional crimes, offenders will always try to find a way to evade detection and prosecution. Only because some users will succeed in circumventing the blocking, the enforcement mechanism is not being rendered inappropriate per se. With online copyright infringement, the aim has to be the reduction of the scale of infringements in order to ensure revenues for creative works. Even if there is not just the possibility of evasion but facts that some circumvention of the technical measures is going to happen, this does not mean that these measures are not appropriate and cannot be justified. The Advocate General rightly noted in this respect that the presumption of "an intention of the part of every user to gain access to a website despite a block would […] mean that one assumes inadmissibly that every user intends to further a breach of the law".[2348] Furthermore, it must be observed that, while quite a few users will know how to circumvent a blocking, this does not mean that all users will do so. Similarly, the possibility that the operator of the website to be blocked migrates to another domain/different IP address does not, in principle, preclude the appropriateness of blocking measures. In this regard the Advocate General in the *UPC Telekabel Wien* case concluded that an initial blocking will raise awareness of the illegality of the website and its service in question, and thereby possibly also prevent users from accessing the website.[2349] However, this prominence may also make the website even more known to users that have previously never heard of that platform.[2350] This being said, the quantitative assessment of the foreseeable success of the blocking measure sought after is one factor to be weighed in the proportionality test.

2348 Opinion of the AG Cruz Villalón of 26.11.2013 in -314/12 *UPC Telekabel Wien GmbH v Constantin Film Verleih GmbH and Wega Filmproduktionsgesellschaft GmbH,* paras. 86 et seq., para. 101.

2349 *Ibid.*

2350 This phenomenon falls into the catgory of Streisand effect, meaning that the attempt to hide, remove or block access to a piece of information has the unintended consequence of attracting attention to that information, which results in more people trying to access the information.

A blocking measure must also not go beyond what is necessary to achieve the objective pursued, and of several appropriate measures, recourse must be had to the least onerous.[2351] As mentioned previously, a less intrusive measure would be the deletion of the infringing content by the host provider. However, in those cases cited above, the host providers, or respectively the joint tortfeasors, did not respond to take down requests or were not contactable at all. Educating users about the illegal nature of the acts in question does not promise to be equally effective. Although education of users is a track that should be pursued, an amelioration of media competence does not lead to instant results and is an on-going process.

Finally, the legitimacy of a blocking measure depends on whether the disadvantages caused by the measure are proportionate to the aim pursued. According to the CJEU's case law, in particular the case of *Scarlet Extended v SABAM*, the complexity, costs and duration of the measure sought for must be weighed with the other factors. The effect of the ruling in SABAM was, that general filtering is incompatible with fundamental rights, but specific (in the sense of "targeted at a clearly indicated website") blocking injunctions are permissible, as long as they do not unreasonably infringe the fundamental rights of users and access providers.

This was the case in the UK cases where a narrow and targeted blocking obligation was imposed upon access providers that also specified the measure to be taken. Further, a remedy was provided for third parties affected by the order to have an order discharged or varied upon application to a Court. The most important aspect was however, that the Court assessed the contravening interests in light of the specified measure. Having specified the measure, the Court was in a position to analyse the costs that the access provider was faced with, potential risks of over-blocking, the rights of users affected etc.. The High Court also put weight on the fact that the website operators of the sites to be blocked were profiting from infringement on an industrial scale.[2352] Considering that the measures imposed were all directed against indexing sites and .torrent trackers, the effect on potential legal user content was also minimal.[2353]

2351 CJEU, C-375/96 *Zaninotto* [1998] ECR I-6629, para. 63.

2352 Cf. for instance High Court, *Football Association Premier League Ltd v British Sky Broadcasting Ltd.* [2013] EWHC 2058, para. 59.

2353 See above B. III. 3. c) aa) Interference with Users' Rights to Seek, Receive and Impart Information.

Other than concluded by the CJEU in the *UPC Telekabel Wien* case, it must be for the national court that is addressed by the rights-holder to examine the proportionality of the measure envisaged in the specific case. The Court must not pass on the assessment of the proportionality of a measure to the access providers.[2354]

In this context, the measures employed, "must be sufficiently effective to ensure genuine protection, that is to say that they must have the effect of preventing unauthorised access to the protected subject-matter or, at least, of making it difficult to achieve and of seriously discouraging Internet users who are using the services of the addressee of that injunction from accessing the subject-matter made available to them in breach of that fundamental right."[2355] It is evident, that the effectiveness of site blocking may be limited in a wider context, due to an inherent flaw in the very concept of blocking websites. Shortly after the *Pirate Bay* trial in Sweden, the website returned to cyberspace with more users than ever. Following the judgement declaring that NewzBin was infringing copyright, the service was back online within weeks after the trial as "NewzBin v. 2.0", laughing off the loss in court on the main page. New services continue to enter the market. Every time a website is blocked, new ones appear to take over their place; more than that, the same website might return under a slightly different address. It is evident that site blocking can never achieve a total cessation of copyright infringements. However, once a website is blocked, it disappears for most users in the wide world of the Web. New services that appear must first be brought to the awareness of users, thus there will always be a delay until they reach high traffic volume. With blocking injunctions in the UK being granted more quickly than ever, many UK Internet users may find it more and more difficult to find the content they search for. In parallel, the blocking orders also raise attention about the illegality of the activities and may have a dissuasive effect. As of now, there is no reliable and robust evidene on this. Similarly, it would be interesting to know whether – in consideration of more and more smart devices (smartphones, smart TV and tablets) being used and cheap flatrates available to content databases, convenient access to audio and audio-visual

---

2354 See above B. III. 3. d) Conformity with Fundamental Rights of Access Providers.

2355 CJEU, C-314/12 *UPC Telekabel Wien GmbH v Constantin Film Verleih GmbH and Wega Filmproduktionsgesellschaft GmbH,* Judgment of 27.03.2014, para. 62.

media gains in importance over free access. Thus, it is not only made difficult to obtain files from the service that is being blocked, but users are also seriously discouraged to access the service in question and potentially also its successors.

Whether access blocking discourages users to access particular and even similar services has been subject to a Dutch research study. With regard to access blocking to in particular the Pirate Bay, evidence from that study suggests that blocking of the Pirate Bay significantly reduced the number of unique visitors of this site.[2356] Although this seems to support the thesis that blocking is an appropriate means to reduce piracy, the researchers could not establish a long-term effect of the blocking. In fact, the researchers reached the conclusion that the blocking of the Pirate Bay by Dutch access providers has no lasting net impact on the percentage of the Dutch population downloading from illegal sources, as users turn to alternatives to the Pirate Bay.[2357] While this may still support blocking of indexing sites as a means to reduce peer-to-peer file-sharing as an additional means to further measures, the study also suggests that users may learn how to circumvent blocking and education effects may wear off after a few months.[2358] This in turn means that the effect of blocking in the long run is close to zero. Consequently, one must ask whether an enforcement action that results in the blocking of content, but has practically no or little effect on piracy in general can be considered as an appropriate means to fight copyright infringements. In order to answer that question, one must first determine whether effectiveness relates to piracy in general.[2359] If effectiveness is interpreted as reducing piracy in general,[2360] one may argue that the described access blocking is not effective. However, as stated above, the CJEU interprets effective as having the effect of preventing "unauthorised access to the protected subject-matter or, at least, of making

---

2356 Joost Poort/Jorna Leenheer/Jeroen von der Ham/Cosmin Dumitru, *Baywatch: Two Approaches to Measure the Effects of Blocking Access to The Pirate Bay,* Telecommunications Policy 2014, Vol. 38 Issue 4, 383–392.

2357 *Ibid.*

2358 *Ibid,* p. 390.

2359 T.J. McIntyre, *Child abuse images and Cleanfeeds: Assessing Internet Blocking Systems,* in: Ian Brown (ed.), *Research handbook on governance of the Internet* (2012), 299, section 5.7.

2360 See in the context of graduated response schemes Rebecca Giblin, *Evaluating graduated response,* Columbia Journal of Law & the Arts 2014, Vol. 37 No.2, 147, 208.

it difficult to achieve and of seriously discouraging Internet users ... from accessing the subject-matter made available to them in breach of that fundamental right".[2361] Thus, effectiveness must not be understand as requiring evidence demonstrating a causal link between the blocking and an overall reduction of infringements.[2362] Accordingly, even the introduction of obstacles towards the respective content is sufficient to satisfy the criterion of effectiveness.

The discussion of effectiveness of blocking measures also exists in the context of the fight against child pornography, namely whether access blocking can be an effective means to combat the dissemination of child abuse images on the Internet.[2363] The dominant argument in favour of blocking is that accidental exposure shall be prevented.[2364] In the context of child abuse materials, this argument seems to be strong at a first glance, but in fact ignores that such content is rarely freely distributed on the web. Instead secretive channels are used, such as hidden fora, friends-to-friends networks or other means of trusted communication. In the context of copyright infringement the argument of accidental access however becomes stronger: if an Internet user searches for a particular file on the Internet – be it either via a search engine or the search function of an indexing website, he will be confronted with many search results that lead to unauthorised copies. Thus, it is not necessary to determine whether evidence exists that accidental or casual access is a significant problem.

Further, while in relation to child abuse images, blocking has also been considered as counterproductive – as it may distract attention from international attempts to achieve the removal of the materials at source,[2365] there are no international attempts to remove IP infringing contents from the Internet. There is an obvious reason for the latter: IP rights are territorial and may differ, in particular as terms of protection and exceptions such

---

2361 CJEU, C-314/12 *UPC Telekabel Wien GmbH v Constantin Film Verleih GmbH and Wega Filmproduktionsgesellschaft GmbH,* Judgment of 27.03.2014, para. 62.

2362 This has been criticised by Giblin in relation to graduated response schemes, see Rebecca Giblin, *Evaluating graduated response,* Columbia Journal of Law & the Arts 2014, Vol. 37 No.2, 147, 208.

2363 See for instance T.J. McIntyre, *Child abuse images and Cleanfeeds: Assessing Internet Blocking Systems,* in: Ian Brown (ed.), *Research handbook on governance of the Internet* (2012), pp. 299 et seq.

2364 See *ibid*, section 5.7 with further references.

2365 See *ibid*, with further references.

as fair use are concerned. Thus, while some consider child abuse images the best case scenario for blocking, in fact copyright may present an equally good scenario: the lack of a common determination of illegality of the acts concerned makes the removal of infringing materials from the Internet almost impossible if hosted abroad.

Ultimately, the proportionality test also needs to take into consideration that in case of an interference with Article 10 *ECHR*, the ECtHR requires a "pressing social need" for the interference. With respect to the test, one needs to take into account the nature of the competing interest involved and the degree to which those interests require protection in the circumstances of the case. In the context of copyright infringements, this means that the interests of the Internet users to access the materials in question, and the interests of website operators to impart information, have to be weighed against the interest in protecting the intellectual property rights of the copyright-holders.

As to the weight to be afforded to the interest of protecting the copyright-holders rights enshrined in Article 1 of the Protocol 1 to the *ECHR*, the Court reiterated in *Neji and Sunde Kolmisoppi v Sweden*[2366] the principle that genuine, effective exercise of the rights protected by that provision also encompasses positive measures of protection by States.[2367] The protection of a genuine, effective exercise of copyright can accordingly be necessary in a democratic society and amount to a pressing social need.

As regards the width of the margin of appreciation afforded to States, this varies depending on a number of factors, among which the type of information at issue is of particular importance. If it can be established that the materials are copyright infringing music or film files, the protection granted does not reach the same level of protection as that afforded to political expression and debate. In the summary proportionality test in *Neji and Sunde Kolmisoppi v Sweden* the ECtHR paid regard to the fact, that the applicants did not respond to take-down requests and thus upheld their activities that were criminal under Swedish law. Accordingly, it becomes

---

2366 ECtHR, *Neij and Sunde Kolmisoppi v Sweden,* Inadmissibility order of 19.02.2013 – Application no. 40397/12. For a comment on the case see Joseph Jones, *Internet pirates walk the plank with Article 10 kept at bay: Neij and Sunde Kolmisoppi v Sweden,* European Intellectual Property Review 2013, Vol. 35 Issue 11, 695–700.

2367 See also ECtHR, *Öneryildiz v Turkey*, Judgment of 30.11.2004 – Application no. 48939/99, para. 134.

clear that access blocking can only be proportionate in very limited scenarios: where there is no contactable, identifiable defendant or that defendant does not comply with legitimate take-down requests. Further, no other domestic means of enforcement against the defendant must be available. Blocking is ultima ratio. Taking into account also the interests of the uploader of links and interested Internet users, it must further be established that effects on legitimate content are excluded or marginal. Only then can a blocking measure be proportionate. Obviously, the scenarios of legitimate blocking are very limited and may in fact only concern such websites that are dedicated to piracy. If their service is evidently supporting piracy and profits are generated, there is a strong presumption that copyright will outweigh the interest of the website provider and its users. However, this has to be decided on a case by case basis.

In accordance with these conclusions, fundamental rights do not preclude the blocking of access to infringing website even if a complete cessation of infringements might not be possible or achievable in practice. However, in contrast to the findings of the CJEU in the *UPC Telekabel Wien* case, in order to achieve a fair balance of the contravening interests, the court addressed must specify the concrete measure to be taken by the access provider. Open-textured injunctions leave too much legal uncertainty to access provider, and carry the risk that either not enough or too much content is blocked, which in turn will affect Internet users as well. Thus, irrespective of the overall effect of a single blocking order on piracy in general, access blocking can be legitimate under very restrictive conditions.

IV. Enforcement upon Initiative of the Rights-Holders via Host Providers

Having established that European law and fundamental rights do not preclude the targeted and narrow access blocking to illegal content by access blockers, the closing section of this Chapter will look at enforcement procedures against host providers. As has already been addressed previously, such proceedings only promise to be effective where the sites targeted are within the same jurisdiction, or voluntarily comply with the legal obligations imposed upon them. The following analysis will focus on France and Germany, because they provide two similar, but yet diverging approaches. The primary focus will be on the German approach as the numerous cases within the last years perfectly highlights the problems courts have encountered when trying to determine possible take down and monitoring obligations of host providers under the regime introduced by the *E-Commerce Directive*. This section will show that courts struggle to apply the *E-Commerce Directive* regime, that was developed at the turn of the millennium to the participatory Internet that exists today.

1. Germany: Obligations of Host Providers to Prevent Similar Infringements

In the absence of the possibility to obtain blocking injunctions against access providers, rights-holders resort to seeking injunctions against host providers requiring them not only to stop an infringement but also achieve its cessation.

The legal basis for such injunctions lies in the *E-Commerce Directive* and the respective provision in the national implementation of the Directive. In particular when infringers or Internet access subscribers cannot be or prove difficult to be identified, the rights-holders are increasingly relying on the liability provisions from the start of this millennium. This being said, it must be recalled that the legal action against host providers only promises success where the host provider is located within the jurisdiction, or will voluntarily comply with an injunction.

The following section will show that often it will not even be necessary to take a matter before the court, as the German courts interpret the obligation to delete or block access to an infringement quite wide so that the obligation that stems from the E-Commerce Directive will also extend to the prevention of future identical infringements.

a) The Legal Framework

In order to determine whether host providers may incur liability for third party content that they host, the following paragraphs outline the liability exemptions for host providers in the *Telemediengesetz* (*TMG*)[2368] and the concept of liability as a disturber (*Störerhaftung*). The latter has already

2368 *Telemedia Act.*

been discussed on several occasions throughout this work, and at this point shall only be addressed briefly with a focus on host providers.

aa) Telemediengesetz

In the first Chapter, the concept of limited liabiltiy for host providers under the *E-Commerce Directive* has already been touched upon, and the necessity to go beyond notice and take down has been identified.

In Germany the relevant provisions of the *E-Commerce Directive* on limited liability for online intermediaries can be found in the *Telemediengesetz* (*TMG*). The German legislator implemented the provision first in §§ 6–9 *Mediendienstestaatsvertrag* (*MDStV*)[2369] and §§ 8–11 *Teledienstegesetz* (*TDG*).[2370] These statutes have been merged without any material changes into the *TMG*.[2371] Structure and wording of the German statutory provisions are very similar to the wording of Articles 12–15 of the *E-Commerce Directive*.

§ 10 *TMG* provides that service providers are not liable for third-party content that they store for a user "if they do not have knowledge of the illegal act or information and as regards claims for damages, are not aware of facts or circumstances from which the illegal act or information is apparent or, upon obtaining such knowledge, act expeditiously to remove or to disable access to the information". The wording of § 10 *TMG* is almost exactly the same as in the German language version of Article 14(1) and (2) of the *E-Commerce Directive* but with the slight difference that where the Directive requires that the host provider does not have "actual" knowledge the German national provision just refers to knowledge as such. As becomes clear from § 7 *TMG* – which is entitled "General Principles" – exemption from liability depends on whether the content provided derives from a third party and is not adopted as own content. For own content providers are liable according to the general laws. Pursuant to § 7 II *TMG* service providers are not obliged to monitor information that they host or transmit, or to search for circumstances which indicate illegal

2369 *Media services State Treaty.*

2370 *Teleservices Act.*

2371 The *TDG* formerly applied to teleservices, whereas the *MDStV* applied to media services. To distinguish between these two types of services has proven difficult. With the implementation of the *TMG* any distinction is now obsolete.

activities. This privilege must not be rendered invalid by imposing general and proactive monitoring duties upon service providers.

The liability privileges for hosting, caching and the provision of access to the Internet (§§ 8 to 10 *TMG*) do only apply for claims of damages and criminal liability. They do not affect the possibility to impose injunctions upon these intermediaries. Injunctive relief is often the only remedy available for rights-holders when the actual infringers cannot be identified. As intermediaries are considered in a position to cease infringement, it is obvious that rights-holders will seek their cooperation.

bb) Störerhaftung

Irrespective of the liability exemption for online intermediaries that originate from the *E-Commerce Directive*, online intermediaries may be obliged to terminate and prevent infringements once they have acquired knowledge of a particular infringement. In these cases, responsibility will be construed under the concept of *Störerhaftung* (liability as a disturber).[2372]

As stated above, someone who is not a direct infringer or accessory will not be liable for damages. Nevertheless, non-infringers (as well as infringers) may be obliged upon obtaining knowledge of an illegal act or information to act expeditiously to remove or to disable access to the information. This obligation derives from the doctrine of *Störerhaftung*. Under this doctrine, he will also be required to prevent similar infringements in the future.[2373]

According to the doctrine of *Störerhaftung*, liability will be established if the provider knowingly contributes to the infringement of a protected right.[2374] It needs to be recalled that the *Störer* does not himself interfere

2372 See above Second Chapter, B. III. 1. a) aa) (2) Störerhaftung: Liability as a Disturber.

2373 For an evaluation of the concept in English and its applicability on Auctioning websites see Andreas Rühmkorf, *The Liability of online auction portals: Towards a Uniform Approach?*, Journal of Internet Law 2010, Vol. 14 Issue 4, 3–10.

2374 BGH, Decision of 15.10.1998 – 1 ZR 120/96 (*Möbelklassiker*), Gewerblicher Rechtsschutz und Urheberrecht 1999, 419; BGH, Decision of 11.03.2004 – I ZR 304/01 (*Internetversteigerung I*), MultiMedia und Recht 2004, 668 with a case comment by Thomas Hoeren; concerning the specific requirements in detail see

with the rights of another party, but in another way contributes deliberately and adequately causal to the infringement of a protected right without being the perpetrator or an accessory. Hence, where the service provider cannot be held liable for damages, the claimant will regularly try to institute proceedings for an injunction against the *Störer*. Injunctions can be issued regardless of negligence or fault.[2375] Accordingly, it is not only the perpetrator himself, i.e. the direct infringer, and accessories, i.e. abettors to the infringement, that can be subject to an injunction claim, but also the so-called *Störer*. As stated before, this doctrine originally applied to cases where a person had constructive control over dangerous property and was therefore held liable under public law – irrespective of intentional or negligent behaviour – for any foreseeable harm arising from such source of danger. Under private law, the notion of *Störer* characterises a person who is liable under § 1004 *BGB* to cease any interference with the property of another that is not caused by removal or retention of the possession.[2376] The concept of *Störerhaftung* has been applied by analogy to other kind of interferences, in particular to determine responsibility for unlawful content on a website.[2377] Service providers that provide online communication services are considered to run a "source of danger" as their service provides

---

Markus Köhler/Hans-Wolfgang Arndt/Thomas Fetzer, *Recht des Internet* (7th ed. 2011), para. 774 et seq.; Gerald Spindler/Katharina Anton in: Gerald Spindler/Fabian Schuster, *Recht der elektronischen Medien* (2nd ed. 2011), § 1004 BGB para. 8 et seq. with further references.

2375 BGH, Decision of 11.03.2004 – I ZR 304/01 (*Internetversteigerung I*), MultiMedia und Recht 2004, 668. For an analysis of the first Internet auction case in English see Joachim Bornkamm, *E-Commerce Directive vs. IP rights enforcement – Legal balance achieved?*, Gewerblicher Rechtsschutz und Urheberrecht – Internationaler Teil 2007, 642–644.

2376 § 1004 *BGB*: "(1) If the ownership is interfered with by means other than removal or retention of possession, the owner may require the disturber to remove the interference. If further interferences are to be feared, the owner may seek a prohibitory injunction. (2) The claim is excluded if the owner is obliged to tolerate the interference". Translation provided by the Langenscheidt Translation Service at the homepage of the Ministry of Justice, www.gesetzeimInternet.de (last accessed: 21.03.2014).

2377 BGH, Decision of 11.03.2004 – I ZR 304/01 (*Internetversteigerung I*), MultiMedia und Recht 2004, 668 et seq. with a case comment by Thomas Hoeren; concerning the specific requirements in detail see Markus Köhler/Hans-Wolfgang Arndt/Thomas Fetzer, *Recht des Internet* (7th ed. 2011), para.774 et seq.; Gerald Spindler/Katharina Anton in: Gerald Spindler/Fabian Schuster, *Recht der elektronischen Medien* (2nd ed. 2011), § 1004 BGB para. 8 et seq. with further

the infrastructure for infringements of intellectual property rights.[2378] Accordingly, a host provider, that is neither infringer nor abettor to an infringement, will be obliged to terminate and prevent any infringement of a third party's right if he deliberately and causally contributes to the infringement, and has the legal and effective means to prevent the infringement.[2379]

Liability is not extended without limits upon third parties: Considering that a *Störer* will be liable to cease AND desist, liability requires a breach of due diligence or monitoring duties and is also restricted by the principle of proportionality. In relation to online marketplaces it was held that the provider of such a platform has to ensure that sellers of adult material employ a functioning age verification system.[2380] He will however not be required to determine which goods are not to be sold to minors.[2381] This would be beyond reasonableness and cannot be expected from the online marketplace provider.

In general, a monitoring duty may only then arise, if a *Störer* has acquired knowledge of an infringement. The duty only arises if and in so far as it can be reasonably expected from the *Störer*. This particularly applies where third parties use the structural and technical means provided by the *Störer* to infringe intellectual property rights. As mentioned above, a monitoring duty does not exist per se; this would contravene § 7 II *TMG* (which transposes Article 15(1) *E-Commerce Directive* into German law).

Hence, where the service provider cannot be held liable for damages, the claimant will regularly try to institute proceedings for an injunction

---

references; Thomas Dreier in: Thomas Dreier/Gernot Schulze, *Urheberrechtsgesetz* (4th ed. 2013), § 97 para. 33 with further references.

2378 Rolf Schwartmann, *Vergleichende Studie über Modelle zur Versendung von Warnhinweisen durch Internet-Zugangsanbieter an Nutzer bei Urheberrechtsverletzungen* (2012), p. 232.

2379 BGH, Decision of 17.05.2001 – I ZR 251/99 (*ambiente.de*), MultiMedia und Recht 2001, 671; BGH, Decision of 01.04.2004 – I ZR 317/01 (*Schöner Wetten*), Gewerblicher Rechtsschutz und Urheberrecht 2004, 693; BGH, Decision of 11.03.2004 – I ZR 304/01 (*Internetversteigerung I*), MultiMedia und Recht 2004, 668.

2380 BGH, Decision of 12.07.2007 – I ZR 18/04 *(Jugendgefährdende Medien bei eBay),* Zeitschrift für Urheber- und Medienrecht 2007, 846, 852.

2381 *Ibid.* Whether the sale to minors is prohibited, is subject to the determination by the respective authorities or self-regulatory bodies.

against the *Störer*. Injunctions can be issued regardless of negligence or fault.[2382]

Usually, the rights-holder will ask the infringer or *Störer* to sign a pre-drafted cease and desist letter (so-called *Abmahnung*),[2383] in which the recipient declares that he will cease and desist from the declared infringement, meaning that he will not only cease the infringement but also refrain from committing that the infringement in question in the future. The declaration will usually contain a penalty clause as an additional enforcement mechanism.

cc) The Scope of Monitoring Duties of Host Providers

In the case of host providers a monitoring duty arises following a first time infringement of which the provider has gained knowledge. Knowledge requires knowledge of the act/activity or information and its illegality and does not mean mere knowledge of the existence of the act/activity or information alone.[2384] Usually, knowledge is acquired by notification by the injured rights-holder.[2385]

Whether and if a monitoring duty is reasonable is to be determined in due consideration of the individual rights of the infringer, the host

2382 BGH, Decision of 11.03.2004 – I ZR 304/01 (*Internetversteigerung I*), MultiMedia und Recht 2004, 668.

2383 The practice of cease and desist letters as enforcement mechansisms has already been addressed in the Second Chapter, see Second Chapter, B. III. 1. Germany: Abmahnungen.

2384 Helmut Hoffmann in: Gerald Spindler/Fabian Schuster, Gerald Spindler/Fabian Schuster, *Recht der elektronischen Medien* (2nd ed. 2011), § 10 *TMG* para. 23; Dirk Heckmann, *Juris PraxisKommentar Internetrecht*, Chapter 1.10 para. 17; Gerald Spindler, *Das Gesetz zum elektronischen Geschäftsverkehr – Verantwortlichkeit der Diensteanbieter und Herkunftslandprinzip*, Neue Juristische Wochenschrift 2002, 921, 924.

2385 Knowledge as such can only be obtained by physical persons and not by automatic transmission or storage. See Gerald Spindler, *Die zivilrechtliche Verantwortlichkeit von Internetauktionshäusern – Haftung für automatisch registrierte und publizierte Inhalte?*, MultiMedia und Recht 2001, 737, 740; OLG Brandenburg, Decision of 16.12.2003 – 6 U 161/U (*Haftung eines Onlineauktionshauses*), MultiMedia und Recht 2004, 330, 332.

provider and the rights-holder.[2386] Criteria that may have an impact on the reasonableness are for example economic advantages of the host provider due to the infringing content,[2387] quantity and quality of the infringements,[2388] or the possibility of filtering.[2389]

If liability as a *Störer* has been established, the *Störer* may also be liable for damages for repeated similar infringements, specifically in the field of copyright law.[2390] At first sight this may sound contrary to what has been said before about this concept. However, the obligation following a first infringement implies the duty to prevent identical and even similar infringements in the future. If a service provider does not implement measures to prevent similar infringements in the future, he will basically be in the same position as someone who is aware of an infringement.[2391]

Host providers are often sued for non-compliance with monitoring duties following a first infringement. In fact, non-implementation of precautionary measures to prevent similar infringements is the most common scenario where host providers face legal action. German courts have developed an elaborated system of what constitutes a "similar" infringement and what can be expected in relation to the prevention of such an infringement.

2386 OLG Hamburg, Decision of 02.07.2008 – 5 U 73/07 *(Rapidshare I),* MultiMedia und Recht 2008, 823; OLG Hamburg, Decision of 30.09.2009 – 5 U 111/08 *(Rapidshare II),* MultiMedia und Recht 2010, 51, 53.

2387 *Ibid.*

2388 Thomas Wilmer, *Überspannte Prüfpflichten für Host-Provider? – Vorschlag für eine Haftungsmatrix*, Neue Juristische Wochenschrift 2008, 1845, 1849 with further references.

2389 BGH, Decision of 19.04.2007 – I ZR 35/04 *(Internetversteigerung II),* MultiMedia und Recht 2007, 507; *Ibid.*

2390 Stefan Krüger/Simon Apel, *Haftung von Plattformbetreibern für urheberrechtlich geschützte Inhalte – Wie weit geht die Haftung und wann droht Schadensersatz?,* MultiMedia und Recht 2012, 144, 149.

2391 See: Stefan Krüger/Simon Apel, Haftung von Plattformbetreibern für urheberrechtlich geschützte Inhalte – Wie weit geht die Haftung und wann droht Schadensersatz?, MultiMedia und Recht 2012, 144, 149 with further references.

The case law on Internet auction platforms[2392] has shown that the extent of a monitoring duty is subject to a test of reasonableness. What is reasonable depends on the specific facts of the individual case, and thus, needs to be determined on a case by case basis.

Some guidance can however be drawn from these cases, namely that a monitoring duty following a first infringement does not mean that a host provider has to actively monitor every single posting/offer for sale prior to its publication. The monitoring duties are specific monitoring duties in accordance with Article 15(1) of the *E-Commerce Directive* and can only apply under certain circumstances.[2393] This means for Internet auction providers that they must disable access to an infringing offer without undue delay upon becoming aware of the infringement, AND take reasonable steps to prevent similar infringements in the future.[2394] As regards eBay and the sale of counterfeited goods, the Federal Court of Justice held that a host provider could be required to use filter software to detect suspicious offers for sale which could subsequently be checked manually for identical infringements of intellectual property rights.[2395] Such a filtering duty was assumed to bring the colliding interests of eBay in pursuing its business and the interests of intellectual property rights owners in protecting their brand into a fair balance.

The host provider's role in relation to an infringement as well as the means in terms of human or financial resources available to him, are important criteria that need to be taken into account.[2396] As concerns the role of the host provider, courts will examine whether the provider got a

2392 BGH, Decision of 11.03.2004 – I ZR 304/01 *(Internetversteigerung I),* MultiMedia und Recht 2004, 668; Decision of 19.04.2007 – I ZR 35/04 *(Internetversteigerung II),* MultiMedia und Recht 2007, 507; Decision of 30.04.2008 – I ZR 73/05 *(Internet-Versteigerung III);* Decision of 22. 07. 2010 – I ZR 139/08 *(Kinderhochstühle im Internet),* Gewerblicher Rechtsschutz und Urheberrecht 2011, 152.

2393 BGH, Decision of 11.03.2004 – I ZR 304/01 *(Internetversteigerung I),* MultiMedia und Recht 2004, 668. See also BGH, Decision of 22. 07. 2010 – I ZR 139/08 *(Kinderhochstühle im Internet),* Gewerblicher Rechtsschutz und Urheberrecht, 2011, 152.

2394 BGH, Decision of 11.03.2004 – I ZR 304/01 *(Internetversteigerung I),* MultiMedia und Recht 2004, 668, 671.

2395 *Ibid*, 672; BGH, Decision of 22. 07. 2010 – I ZR 139/08 (*Kinderhochstühle im Internet*), Gewerblicher Rechtsschutz und Urheberrecht 2011, 152.

2396 See only BGH, Decision of 11.03.2004 – I ZR 304/01 *(Internetversteigerung I),* MultiMedia und Recht 2004, 668 et seq.; BGH, Decision of 12.07.2007 – I ZR

financial gain from infringements of intellectual property rights,[2397] or whether the provider facilitated infringements by providing users with the necessary means for example specific software.[2398] Monitoring duties shall not reach so far as compliance would challenge the business model.[2399] Concerning the feasibility of monitoring duties, the courts will have to examine the necessary financial effort with regard to the implementation of a monitoring system, [2400] as well as the efficacy of monitoring and filtering measures.[2401] Measures are not necessarily unreasonable if the host provider has to employ further staff to comply with the monitoring duty.[2402] Unreasonable are only those duties that challenge the business model as a whole.[2403] A provider will not be required to implement software that does not distinguish between potential infringements and legitimate offers in its result list.[2404] For example if eBay runs a software that instead of potential infringements of a certain trademark lists all offers referring to that trademark, the host provider will not be expected to check all results manually for potential infringements.[2405]

18/04 *(Jugendgefährdende Medien bei eBay),* Zeitschrift für Urheber- und Medienrecht 2007, 846, 849 et seq.

2397 See only BGH, Decision of 11.03.2004 – I ZR 304/01 *(Internetversteigerung I),* MultiMedia und Recht 2004, 668, 671 et seq.

2398 OLG Hamburg, Decision of 28.01. 2009 – 5 U 255/07 *(Alphaload/Usenet II),* MultiMedia und Recht 2009, 405, 407.

2399 See only BGH, Decision of 11.03.2004 – I ZR 304/01 *(Internetversteigerung I),* MultiMedia und Recht 2004, 668, 671 et seq.

2400 LG Hamburg, Decision of 12.11.2008 – 308 O 548/08, Kommunikation und Recht 2009, 272, 275 with comment by Flemming Moos/Anna Gosche.

2401 *Ibid.* Cf. also in relation to Usenet LG München I, Decision of 19.04.2007 – 7 O 3950/07, MultiMedia und Recht 2007, 453, 456; OLG Hamburg, Decision of 14.01. 2009 – 5 U 113/07 *(Spring nicht – Usenet I),* MultiMedia und Recht 2009, 631, 634.

2402 OLG Köln, Decision of 21.09.2007 – 6 U 86/07, Zeitschrift für Urheber- und Medienrecht 2007, 927, 930.

2403 BGH, Decision of 12.07.2007 – I ZR 18/04 *(Jugendgefährdende Medien bei eBay),* Zeitschrift für Urheber- und Medienrecht 2007, 846, 849; BGH, Decision of 12.05.2010 – I ZR 121/08 *(Sommer unseres Lebens).*

2404 BGH, Decision of 22. 07. 2010 – I ZR 139/08 *(Kinderhochstühle im Internet),* Gewerblicher Rechtsschutz und Urheberrecht 2011, 152, 155; Helmut Redeker, IT-Recht (5th ed. 2012), para. 1286.

2405 Cf. BGH, Decision of 22. 07. 2010 – I ZR 139/08 *(Kinderhochstühle im Internet),* Gewerblicher Rechtsschutz und Urheberrecht 2011, 152, 155.

Accordingly, the manual control of all data, where large volumes of data are concerned, is not reasonable,[2406] whereas the manual control of filtered data is not necessarily disproportionate.[2407] However, recently the Court held that eBay does not have to check the results of a word filter search manually in order to detect intellectual property right infringements due to the sheer volume of data.[2408] In this case, such an obligation was considered disproportionate and challenging eBay's business model. The lesser time and effort is needed to control hosted content, the more likely a certain type of control will be considered reasonable.[2409]

As regards the limitation to "similar" infringements, the Court also determined what kind of infringements fall within the category of similar. This was necessary as the notion of "similar" is not particularly precise, and could refer to infringements by a specific infringer, within a certain category, or with regard to all products by the injured party. As far as auctions of counterfeited goods are concerned, not only repeated auctions of such goods by the same infringer, but also auctions of counterfeited goods by other users will amount to "similar" infringements.[2410] This conclusion was based on the fact, that users may re-register to the auctioning website using another pseudonym, and the real identity of an infringer is difficult to establish.[2411] Further, the Federal Court of Justice held in the context of unfair competition law, that "similar" infringing sales on eBay include infringements committed by the same user in relation to the same carrier

---

2406 Ibid; BGH, Decision of 11.03.2004 – I ZR 304/01 (Internetversteigerung I), MultiMedia und Recht 2004, 668, 671 et seq.; Gerald Spindler, *Präzisierungen der Störerhaftung im Internet – Besprechung des BGH-Urteils „Kinderhochstühle im Internet"*, Gewerblicher Rechtsschutz und Urheberrecht 2011, 101, 104 with further references.

2407 BGH, Decision of 12.07.2007 – I ZR 18/04 *(Jugendgefährdende Medien bei eBay),* Zeitschrift für Urheber- und Medienrecht 2007, 846, 852; BGH, Decision of 30.04.2008 – I ZR 73/05 *(Internetversteigerung III),* MultiMedia und Recht 2008, 531, 533.

2408 BGH, Decision of 22.07.2010 – I ZR 139/08 *(Kinderhochstühle im Internet),* MultiMedia und Recht 2011, 172.

2409 Jürgen Ensthaler/Jürgen Heinemann, *Die Fortentwicklung der Providerhaftung durch die Rechtsprechung*, Gewerblicher Rechtsschutz und Urheberrecht 2012, 433, 438.

2410 BGH, Decision of 11.03.2004 – I ZR 304/01(*Internetversteigerung I*), MultiMedia und Recht 2004, 668, 672

2411 *Ibid.*

medium in the same category of goods (e.g. Nazi propaganda, pornography).[2412]

In conclusion it has been suggested that the monitoring duty stipulated in the Internet auction cases shall be understood as "not turning a blind eye to illegality".[2413]

In practice, rights-holders as well as host providers use Hash value filters,[2414] and for instance software, that can detect certain images in copyrighted video files[2415] in order to identify copyright infringements. Hash value filters will however only allow the identification of files that are a 100% identical with the original file – cutting less than a second of an audio file or altering it otherwise will mean that the file cannot be detected.[2416] Obviously, the host provider can only successfully deploy such a filter if he has been notified of a first infringement.

In summary, the duty to monitor emerges when a host provider has been notified of a first infringement. In simple terms, liability as a *Störer* is interlinked with the violation of the duty to monitor – those who, after being notified do not monitor are liable. Once an infringement has been notified, the provider is under an obligation to take all technically and economically possible and reasonable measures to prevent similar infringements in the future. The following paragraphs will explore what this means in particular for providers of file-hosting services.

2412 BGH, Decision of 12. Juli 2007 – I ZR 18/04 (*Jugendgefährdende Medien bei eBay*), Zeitschrift für Urheber- und Medienrecht 2007, 846, 851.

2413 Thomas Hoeren, *The European Liability and Responsibility of Providers of Online-Platforms such as "Second Life"*, Journal of Information, Law & Technology 2009, Issue 1, 1, 10, http://go.warwick.ac.uk/jilt/2009_1/hoeren.

2414 Jan Bernd Nordemann, *Störerhaftung für Urheberrechtsverletzungen – Welche konkreten Prüfpflichten haben Hostprovider (Contentprovider)?*, Computer und Recht 2010, 653, 656 and 659; Stefan Krüger/Simon Apel, *Haftung von Plattformbetreibern für urheberrechtlich geschützte Inhalte – Wie weit geht die Haftung und wann droht Schadensersatz?,* MultiMedia und Recht 2012, 144, 150.

2415 As regards the content-ID filter employed by YouTube see http://www.youtube.com/t/contentid. In April 2012, the LG Hamburg declared such a contentID filter as not sufficient to escape liability, see LG Hamburg, Decision of 20.04.2012 – 310 O 461/10 (GEMA v YouTube), Zeitschrift für Urheber- und Medienrecht 2012, 596.

2416 If only one second of a song is missing, the hash value will differ from the hash value of the original file.

b) Liability of File-Hosting Services in General

The liability of file-hosting services for hosted content has been subject to a number of court decisions in Germany with the result of extensive yet inconsistent jurisprudence.

First of all, German courts categorise the providers of file-hosting services as host providers, to whom the limited liability under § 10 *TMG* (Article 14 *E-Commerce Directive*) applies. The fact that the file-hoster charges fees for a premium service does not change its status. Hence, a file-hoster will only be liable if he has knowledge of the illegal act or information and as regards claims for damages, is aware of facts or circumstances from which the illegal act or information is apparent, or, upon obtaining such knowledge, does not act expeditiously to remove or disable access to the content.

Early judgements held that users committed a copyright infringement by uploading a file onto the servers of a file-hosting service or social media platform.[2417] There is now consensus, that file-hosting services as such and cloud-computing services in particular are online data storage services and both offer to a large extent neutral services.[2418] Accordingly, the mere upload upon a file-hoster´s servers is no longer considered as an act of making a work publicly available.[2419] Instead a work is made publicly available when the URL via which it can be accessed is published. The act of link publication thus constitutes the infringing act. This change in reasoning was necessary, because otherwise the emerging business model of Cloud-Computing services, on which many smart devices rely,

2417 See for instance OLG Hamburg, Decision of 02.07.2008 – 5 U 73/07 *(Sharehoster I – Rapidshare)*, MultiMedia und Recht 2008, 823.

2418 Cf. OLG Hamburg, Decision of 14.03.2012 – 5 U 87/09 *(GEMA v Rapidshare)*, MultiMedia und Recht 2012, 393 with comment by Markus Schröder. Previously, i.e. before 1 July 2010, Rapidshare employed a rewards program that allowed the user to trade "RapidPoints" for a selection of products depending on the number of points the user had collected. In June 2010, RapidShare announced that it would stop this program along with RapidDonations on 1 July 2010 in order to avoid the impression it rewarded its users for uploading copyrighted material.

2419 OLG Hamburg, Decision of 14.03.2012 – 5 U 87/09 *(GEMA v Rapidshare)*, MultiMedia und Recht 2012, 393

would have been under serious threat.[2420] Moreover, external storage of date would have been legally impossible.

In July 2012, in the *Alone in the dark* case[2421], the German Federal Court of Justice gave its first ruling on the liability of file-hosting services that confirmed this approach.[2422] It held that file-hosting services are only liable for copyright infringements committed via their service if they have previously been made aware of an obvious similar infringement. The facts of the case were as follows: Atari Europe requested that the provider of Rapidshare, a popular file-hosting service, should cease and desist from making publicly available copies of the popular computer game Alone in the dark on the website www.rapidshare.com. Rapidshare provides storage space; the service provided is comprable to the provision of an online backup service. Rapidshare is a classic file-hoster/sharehoster/one-click hoster. Users of Rapidshare upload files via the Rapidshare website, which are then stored on Rapidshare's servers. Upon uploading, the user is supplied with a unique download URL which enables anyone with whom the uploader shares the URL to access and download the file. Users can register for a premium service for which they will have to pay but in return receive inter alia unlimited download speed, the possibility of immediate download (instead of a waiting period), simultaneous download of several files, and significantly more storage space. Rapidshare does not provide a file index or allows to search its server for content. However, certain search engines, so-called "indexing sites"[2423] allow searches of enlisted files with Rapidshare URLs.[2424]

When the computer game "Alone in the dark" had been made available for download on Rapidshare's servers, the rights-holder filed for injunctive relief arguing that the possibility to download the file constituted a copyright infringement. The Regional Court Düsseldorf granted injunctive relief. An appeal by Rapidshare was subsequently dismissed by the Higher Regional Court Düsseldorf.[2425] The Federal Court of Justice annulled the

---

2420 *Ibid.*

2421 *Ibid.*

2422 BGH, Decision of 12.07.2012 – I ZR 18/11 *(Alone in the Dark),* MultiMedia und Recht 2013, 185.

2423 The German court uses the term "Link-Sammlungen" (link collections).

2424 These indexing sites contain data collected and entered by users, see above A. II. 1. File-Hosting Services, Indexing Sites and Link Directories.

2425 OLG Düsseldorf, Decision of 21.12.2010 – I-20 U 59/10 *(Rapidshare III – Alone in the Dark),* MultiMedia und Recht 2011, 250.

judgement and referred the case back to the Higher Regional Court.[2426] The Court held that Rapidshare is neither infringer nor abettor as user had uploaded the files without prior knowledge by Rapidshare. Rapidshare is a host provider and is as such not obliged to monitor information hosted on its server. This applies even where the service provided is prone to copyright infringements. However, Rapidshare was held to be liable as a *Störer* to cease the infringement and prevent further similar infringements.

c) Notice and Stay-Down: Scope of Specific Monitoring Duties of File-Hosting Services

A specific monitoring duty in relation to the prevention of identical infringements emerges once a host provider has been notified of infringing material. Similar to the controversy on the liability of file-hosting service for third party content in general, controversy existed with regard to the scope of specific monitoring duties that arise following an infringement with in particular the courts in Hamburg arguing that the business model of file-hosting as such triggers monitoring duties.

Two major contradicting views existed prior to the decision of the Federal Court of Justice in the *Alone in the Dark* case:

The courts in Hamburg held that the provider of a file-hosting service is under an increased monitoring duty following notification of an infringement. [2427] The provider has to disable access to the file and prevent similar infringements.[2428] The Higher Regional Court of Hamburg specified this obligation and held that the provider is obliged to monitor all content of such users that in the past have committed copyright infringements via the platform. Even a specific control of content during its upload was consid-

2426 BGH, Decision of 12.07.2012 – I ZR 18/11 *(Alone in the Dark),* MultiMedia und Recht 2013, 185.

2427 LG Hamburg, Decision of 12.06. 2009 – 310 O 93/08, Zeitschrift für Urheber- und Medienrecht 2009, 863, 864; OLG Hamburg, Decision of 30.09.2009 – 5 U 111/08 *(Sharehoster II – Rapidshare),* MultiMedia und Recht 2010, 51, 54; OLG Hamburg, Decision of 02.07.2008 – 5 U 73/07 *(Sharehoster I – Rapidshare),* MultiMedia und Recht 2008, 823; see also OLG Hamburg, Decision of 14.01.2009 – 5 U 113/07 *(Usenet I – Spring nicht),* MultiMedia und Recht 2009, 631; OLG Hamburg, Decision of 28.01.2009 – 5 U 255/07 *(Alphaload),* MultiMedia und Recht 2009, 405.

2428 *Ibid.*

erate reasonable.[2429] In its first file-hoster case, the Hamburg Court made clear that it considers the upload of a work on a file-hosting service as the act of making a work available to the public.[2430] This conclusion ignored that under German law, user have a right to private copy (§ 53 I *UrhG*)[2431] and that the materials are not available to the public by the upload alone; publication requires the distribution of the hyperlink leading to the materials in question. According to the Hamburg court, the implementation of an "abuse" department, password encryption, word filters and the checking of notorious piracy websites for hyperlinks leading to content on the file-hoster´s servers does not satisfy the required monitoring obligations if the service is prone to copyright infringements.[2432] Moreover, the Court did not consider file-hosting as conducted by Rapidshare as a legitimate business model at all.[2433] Later on the Hamburg courts departed from these findings, but nevertheless requested extensive monitoring. The Hamburg Regional Court for instance requested that the social media platform YouTube, in addition to an effective notice and take down regime and its complex and costly content-ID filtering system, has to block user accounts that have been used for copyright infringements, use word filtering to detect further similar infringements and implement a dispute settlement procedure.[2434] The latter was considered necessary as a response to potential over-blocking.[2435]

In comparison, the Higher Regional Court of Düsseldorf considers the extensive monitoring duties discussed by the Hamburg courts unreasonable.[2436] The Düsseldorf Court argued that the file-hoster Rapidshare offers a completely neutral service and is not only exempted from direct

---

2429 See for example: OLG Hamburg, Decision of 02.07.2008 – 5 U 73/07 *(Sharehoster I – Rapidshare),* MultiMedia und Recht 2008, 823, 827.

2430 OLG Hamburg, Decision of 02.07.2008 – 5 U 73/07 *(Sharehoster I – Rapidshare),* MultiMedia und Recht 2008, 823.

2431 See above Second Chapter, A. II. 4. c) Non-Applicability of the Private Copying Exception.See also Alexander Klett, *Cloud und Privatkopie*, Zeitschrift für Urheber- und Medienrecht 2014, 18–22.

2432 OLG Hamburg, Decision of 30.09.2009 – 5 U 111/08 *(Sharehoster II – Rapidshare),* MultiMedia und Recht 2010, 51.

2433 *Ibid.*

2434 LG Hamburg, Decision of 20.04.2012 – 310 O 461/10 *(GEMA v YouTube),* Zeitschrift für Urheber- und Medienrecht 2012, 596.

2435 *Ibid*, 605.

2436 OLG Düsseldorf, Decision of 27.04.2010 – I-20 U 166/09 *(Rapidshare – An American Crime et al),* MultiMedia und Recht 2010, 483, 484.

liability, but also from liability as a *Störer*. Liability as a *Störer* would require that there are feasible monitoring options. However, according to the Court this is not the case: by blocking certain files via word or text filters, it is impossible to achieve the aim pursued, while manual checks are considered disproportionate due to the quantity of content and the disambiguity of search terms.[2437] Furthermore, manual searches on Google would require unreasonable human resources.[2438] The Court also held that the blocking of certain IP addresses that have been used for infringements in the past is also not feasible as IP addresses are regularly not used by one single person.[2439] In addition to the possibility of shared connections, the Court recognised that IP addresses are often allocated dynamically. As regards link directories, the Düsseldorf Court analysed the feasibility of monitoring notorious link directories in detail, but did not considered their monitoring as a reasonable way to go.[2440] A similar conclusion was drawn by the Higher Regional Court of Köln, which held that automatic monitoring of uploads is not possible to detect infringements as the upload as such can be legal, i.e. a private copy without making available to the public.[2441] However, the regular manual checking of notorious link directories that are known for disseminating links to infringing content was considered reasonable.

Due to different standards of monitoring being requested by different courts throughout Germany, guidance by the Federal Court of Justice that would put an end to the discrepancies was eagerly awaited.

The Higher Regional Court recognised in the matter of Alone in the Dark, that "most people utilize RapidShare for legal use" and that, if the contrary were assumed, it would mean "a general suspicion against shared hosting services and their users which is not justified".[2442] One may argue

---

2437 OLG Düsseldorf, Decision of 27.04.2010 – I-20 U 166/09 *(Rapidshare – An American Crime et al),* MultiMedia und Recht 2010, 483, 485. See also OLG Düsseldorf, Decision of 06.07.2010 – I-20 U 8/10 *(Rapidshare II – Inside a Skinhead),* MMR 2010, 702.

2438 *Ibid.*

2439 *Ibid.*

2440 OLG Düsseldorf, Decision of 21.12.2010 – I-20 U 59/10 *(Rapidshare III – Alone in the Dark),* MultiMedia und Recht 2011, 250.

2441 OLG Köln, Decision of 21.09.2007 – 6 U 86/07 *(Haftung eines Sharehoster-Dienstes),* MultiMedia und Recht 2007, 786, 788.

2442 *OLG Düsseldorf, Decision of 21.12.2010 – I-20 U 59/10 (Rapidshare III – Alone in the Dark)*, MultiMedia und Recht 2011, 250.

that this was a surprising conclusion, namely, just because it is not appropriate to have such a suspicion, it should be presumed that most people utilise the services legitimately. The Court did not find it justified to obligate RapidShare, in addition to take down illegal copies when duly notified, to prevent, through a filtering system, repeated uploading of illegal copies of the same works.

The Federal Court of Justice saw the factual situation more realistically[2443] and reversed the ruling of the Düsseldorf court.[2444] Although it stated that, in principle, file-hosting services are to be recognized as an appropriate business model, it also ruled that they should duly cooperate with copyright owners not only by removing illegal copies from their system but also by preventing repeated uploading thereof, i.e. if illegal copies of a work are taken down, they should stay down. If Rapidshare does not apply a reasonable filtering system for this purpose, it will be liable for the infringements. Accordingly, it was not sufficient that Rapidshare upon notification in August 2008, removed the respective file immediately, but did not check whether other users had also uploaded a copy of the computer game to its servers, and if so, whether these files were still accessible.

It did not come as a surprise that the Court held that it was not sufficient to bar access to only the concrete infringing file that Rapidshare had been made aware of. From the Internet auction cases, it was known, that host providers are obliged to do everything that is technically and economically reasonable – without challenging their business model – to prevent, that the infringements reappears. As regards the computer game Alone in the Dark, this meant that Rapidshare had to prevent that the game could be made available to third parties via its servers. The Court held that this duty had potentially been infringed by the non-implementation of a word filter which scans all uploaded data for the word sequence “Alone in the Dark”. In order to prevent over-blocking, the results of the word would have to be checked manually for infringements. Additionally, the judges considered that the examination of third party indexing sites with “link collections” is generally reasonable to put an end to similar infringements. This being said, Rapidshare can be required to check pertinent indexing sites for results to the search term “Alone in the Dark” in order to identify files that

2443 This is reflected, for example, by the remark that after all “[t]he company is called RapidShare and not RapidStore.”

2444 BGH, Decision of 12.07.2012 – I ZR 18/11 (*Alone in the Dark*), MultiMedia und Recht 2013, 185.

it cannot itself detect on its own servers by the word filter running on its site. Although the defendant is not the provider of the link indexing site, the defendant can subsequently delete the files containing the computer game on its own servers and thereby prevent access to them. Unfortunately, the Federal Court did not render a final judgment in this matter, but referred the case back to the Higher Regional Court of Düsseldorf[2445] holding that the Court had not sufficiently established that the outlined monitoring duties were unreasonable in the specific case.

Finally, in September 2013, the Federal Court of Justice clarified in the case of *GEMA v Rapidshare* that a file-hosting service is under an obligation to monitor indexing websites, if his business model "supports" copyright infringements.[2446] Although Rapidshare's service was not dedicated to copyright infringements, it was noted that the risk of copyright-infringing use was supported by Rapidshare.[2447] Already the Higher Regional Court of Hamburg held in this case that Rapidshare is more than a neutral provider, and rather takes over an "active role". Decisive for establishing an "active role" of Rapidshare in relation to the copyright infringements was the fact that Rapidshare tried to gain financial advantages from potentially infringing services. At the time the claim was made, Rapidshare had employed an awards program for content upload, which has however been ceased in July 2010 in order to avoid the impression that Rapidshare rewards its users for uploading copyrighted material. Accordingly, it can be said, that once a "tendency" can be established that a host provider influences its users to infringe copyright and the host provider benefits indirectly from the infringements, an active role will be attributed to the

---

2445 OLG Düsseldorf, Decision of 21.12.2010 – I-20 U 59/10 *(Rapidshare III – Alone in the Dark)*, MultiMedia und Recht 2011, 250.

2446 BGH, Decision of 15.08.2013 – I ZR 80/12 *(GEMA v Rapidshare).* In this case GEMA, a German collecting society, claimed that 4815 music files that belonged to its repertoire were downloadable on Rapidshare without its authorisation. For a comment on the case see Barbara Völzmann-Stickelbrock, *BGH: Prüfpflichten für Sharehoster im Rahmen der Störerhaftung – File-Hosting-Dienst*, Kommentierte BGH-Rechtsprechung Lindenmaier-Möhring 2013, 352737, and Manuel Finger/Simon Apel, *Anmerkung zu BGH, Urteil vom 15. August 2013 – I ZR 80/12 – File-Hosting Dienst*, Zeitschrift für Urheber- und Medienrecht 2013, 879–882.

2447 Cf. the findings of the previous instance court OLG Hamburg, Decision of 14.03.2012 – 5 U 87/09 *(GEMA v Rapidshare),* MultiMedia und Recht 2012, 393.

provider.[2448] An active role means that increased duties exist to prevent further similar infringements. Although most file-hosters have recognised by now, that they must not in any way influence the content upload, the "active role" condition has not become obsolete. An increased duty of care was also based on the fact that Rapidshare allows its users to use the service anonymous. Anonymity was held to be an incentive for illegal behaviour, because users can be practically certain that they will not be sued.[2449] File-hosting services that provide for the anonymous use of their service are thus not considered a mere neutral provider.[2450] In addition, Rapidshare sells premium accounts for massive downloaders, which are rather attractive for downloading copyrighted materials. Having established an active role of the host provider, extensive monitoring duties arise. With regard to Rapidshare, they currently consist of the following: (i) once an "illegal" link has been notified, similar links have to searched for and checked whether they relate to the protected work in question; (ii) when monitoring link directories/indexing sites, the file-hoster will not only have to check for links containing the file name, but must also search the description of files to identify similar files, i.e. scanning will not be sufficient, the descriptions have to be actually read; (iii) in addition to notorious link directories/indexing sites, the file-hoster will also have to resort to common search engines like "Google, Facebook or Twitter" to search for information about infringing links; potentially also web crawlers may be deployed.[2451]

2448 See Adrian Schneider, OLG Hamburg: Die Rapidshare-Entscheidung, ein Meilenstein?, Telemedicus (29.03.2012).

2449 *Ibid.* See with regard to anonymity and illegal behaviour in general Sandra Schmitz, *Facebook's real name policy, Bye-bye, Max Mustermann?*, Journal of Intellectual Property, Information Technology and E-Commerce Law 2013, Vol. 4 Issue 3, 190–204.

2450 OLG Hamburg, Decision of 14.03.2012 – 5 U 87/09 (*GEMA v Rapidshare*), MultiMedia und Recht 2012, 393 et seq.

2451 BGH, Decision of 15.08.2013 – I ZR 80/12 *(GEMA v Rapidshare),* Kommunikation und Recht 2013, 655.

d) Extensive Monitoring in Practice

The German monitoring duty is rather high,[2452] considering that it is not sufficient for host providers to remove notified infringing content, but also prevent similar infringements in the future. After being notified of an infringement, the prevention of similar infringements in the future means that the provider has to check constantly – insofar as technically and economically reasonable – all content. The recent case-law has shown, that courts struggled to find a common approach to determine the scope of these monitoring duties. This can be based on the fact, that the reasonable duties of care requested by the providers are not specified in statutory law.

It is questionable whether the monitoring duties as finally confirmed by the Federal Court of Justice in compliance with the *E-Commerce Directive*.[2453] The standard required is considerably high in comparison to that required by the jurisprudence of the CJEU. The CJEU requires a fair balance to be struck between the contravening interests of rights-holders, third parties and users, and takes into consideration the economic and legal implications of complex and costly filtering technologies.[2454] In contrast, the German courts concentrate solely on assessing what could be reasonably requested from the service provider without a real balancing of interests. It seems that as long as the monitoring duties do not challenge the business model of the service provider as such, they will be considered reasonable. However, following in particular the case-law of the courts in Hamburg, host providers must have gained the impression that their attempts to filter content are not valued enough. Sophisticated filtering as the Content-ID filter deployed by social media platform YouTube had been declared insufficient without the court having assessed the functioning in detail.[2455] As a consequence, it has been argued by scholars that no incentive existed for host-providers to employ filtering mechanisms voluntarily, and to invest resources into research and the implementation of

---

2452 See Georg Nolte/Jörg Wimmers, *Wer stört? Gedanken zur Haftung von Intermediären im Internet*, GRUR-Beilage 2014, 58, 64.

2453 This will be discussed below.

2454 See only with regard to host providers CJEU, C-360/10, *SABAM v Netlog NV*, Judgment of 16.02.2012, [2012] 2 C.M.L.R. 18.

2455 The same applied to the VeRI filter deployed by eBay, see Georg Nolte/Jörg Wimmers, *Wer stört? Gedanken zur Haftung von Intermediären im Internet,* GRUR-Beilage 2014, 58, 64.

complex filtering tools.[2456] In particular the courts in Hamburg were difficult to satisfy, and thus became attractive for rights-holders seeking to put extensive filtering obligations upon host providers. The Hamburg courts were happy to respond to these demands by introducing extensive monitoring obligations that did pay little regard to the feasibility and appropriateness of certain filtering mechanisms.[2457] The argument of potential over-blocking resulting from extensive blocking was considered invalid as long as a dispute settlement procedure was in place.[2458]

A repeated target for enforcement action has been the Swiss file-hosting service Rapidshare, which – following the judgments of the Federal Court of Justice in the *Alone in the Dark* case and *GEMA v Rapidshare* – will have to implement a word filter to filter for similar infringements following notification of a first infringement. The monitoring duties however go beyond the a monitoring of the service provided by the file-hoster and encompass the monitoring of notorious link directories/indexing sites and searches to be conducted via search engines. The file-hoster is obliged to identify not only links that contain the title of the work in question, but also look out for descriptions of the content to which a link leads. This is such a far-reaching duty that it is questionable, whether in practice a file-hoster will be able to fulfil this obligation.[2459] In this respect one also needs to take into account, that for example GEMA requested Rapidshare to cease and prevent copyright infringements in relation to more than 4800 works. GEMA holds the rights in several millions of works. If a file-hoster was only obliged to manually check a small percentage of this repertoire, the provider would most certainly reach his capacities in terms of human,

---

2456 Per Christiansen, *Störerhaftung des Betreibers einer Video-Plattform wegen Urheberrechtsverletzung, Anmerkung zu LG Hamburg, 310 O 461/10 vom 20.04.2012,* Kommunikation & Recht 2012, 533, 534.

2457 Cf. *ibid*; Georg Nolte/Jörg Wimmers, *Wer stört? Gedanken zur Haftung von Intermediären im Internet*, GRUR-Beilage 2014, 58, 64. See also LG Hamburg, Decision of 20.04.2012 – 310 O 461/10 *(GEMA v YouTube),* Zeitschrift für Urheber- und Medienrecht 2012, 596

2458 LG Hamburg, Decision of 20.04.2012 – 310 O 461/10 *(GEMA v YouTube),* Zeitschrift für Urheber- und Medienrecht 2012, 596, 605.

2459 The practicability has been questioned by Thomas Hoeren, *Anmerkung zu BGH: Störerhaftung von RapidShare – Alone in the Dark*, MultiMedia und Recht 2013, 185, 188.

organisational and economical resources.[2460] Reaching its capacities may in turn mean that the business model as such is under threat. The question remains what the file-hosting service provider can do in order to escape the attribution of having an "active role" in copyright infringements. From the reasoning of the Federal Court of Justice it seems that one option would be to disable the anonymous use of the service. Anonymous use of the Internet has traditionally been thought to be more likely to create negative outcomes.[2461] This assumption is for instance one of the reasons the providers of Facebook put forward to enforce their real name policy.[2462] Obviously, anonymous speech poses challenges to unwanted behaviour,[2463] but it is also one of the safeguards for free speech on the Internet.[2464] It would not be appropriate to require all services that could potentially be abused for copyright infringements to introduce real name registration procedures – considering that this would basically include all websites with user-generated content. This would mean that free speech was only free as long as the host provider holds information about the identity of the speaker. The implications of this conclusion are severe.[2465] This being said, the sixth senate of the Federal Court of Justice[2466] introduced as reasonable monitoring obligation in relation to host providers of blogs a "ping-pong" notice and take down procedure similar to the proce-

2460 See Georg Nolte/Jörg Wimmers, *Wer stört? Gedanken zur Haftung von Intermediären im Internet,* GRUR-Beilage 2014, 58, 65.

2461 Kimberly M. Christopherson, *The positive and negative implications of anonymity in Internet social interaction: "On the Internet, nobody knows you're a dog",* Computers in Human Behaviour 2007, Vol. 23 Issue 6, 3038, 3042 with further references.

2462 See Sandra Schmitz, *Facebook's real name policy, Bye-bye, Max Mustermann?*, Journal of Intellectual Property, Information Technology and E-Commerce Law 2013, Vol. 4 Issue 3, 190, 198.

2463 Anna Vamialis, *Online defamation: confronting anonymity*, International Journal of Law and Information Technology 2013, Vol. 21, 31, 61.

2464 See Sandra Schmitz, *Facebook's real name policy, Bye-bye, Max Mustermann?*, Journal of Intellectual Property, Information Technology and E-Commerce Law 2013, Vol. 4 Issue 3, 190, 198.

2465 The evaluation of this subject matter would go beyond the scope of this research.

2466 In contrast to the file-hoster cases, which were decided by the first senate, the *Blog* case was decided by the sixth senate. See BGH, Decision of 25.10.2011 – VI ZR 93/10 *(Blog),* MultiMedia und Recht 2012, 124 with a case comment by Thomas Hoeren.

dure enshrined in the US DMCA.[2467] If someone claims that a certain blog posting infringes his rights, the provider must forward the complaint to the blogger in question. If the blogger does not respond within a defined time frame, the host provider will have to delete the posting. If the author of the posting substantiates that the posting does not infringe the rights of the claimant, the host provider will have to forward this information to the claimant and ask him to provide evidence for his allegations. In case, the claimant does not respond to this request, the host provider is under no further obligations to monitor. Although in the concrete case before the Court, personality rights infringements were concerned, it has been suggested that this approach could also be applied to infringements of copyright.[2468]

In conclusion, it remains to be seen whether the efforts undertaken by file-hosters to prevent similar infringements will satisfy the required extensive duty of care. As of now, no real assessment of the reasonableness has been conducted that also pays regard to the technical feasibility and appropriateness of monitoring and active searching for infringements.[2469] It is about time, that the Federal Court of Justice turns to the CJEU for a preliminary ruling decision on whether such extensive monitoring is in compliance with the prohibition of general monitoring under the E-Commerce Directive.[2470]

2467 As regards the DMCA procedure, see First Chapter, A. III. 2. a) aa) The US Digital Millenium Copyright Act.

2468 Cf. Andreas Leupold in: Andreas Leupold/Silke Glossner, *Münchener Anwaltshandbuch IT-Recht* (3rd ed. 2013), Part 2 para. 667.

2469 This has been criticised by inter alia Christian Volkmann, *Aktuelle Entwicklungen in der Providerhaftung im Jahr 2013*, Kommunikation & Recht 2014, 375; Andreas Sesing, *Anmerkung zur Entscheidung des BGH-Urteil vom 15.08.2013 (I ZR 80/12, MMR 2013, 733) – Zur Frage der Prüfungs- und Handlungspflichten für Sharehoster*, MultiMedia und Recht 2013, 737, 739 and Thomas Hoeren, *Anmerkung zu BGH: Störerhaftung von RapidShare – Alone in the Dark,* MultiMedia und Recht 2013, 185, 188.

2470 Cf. Andreas Leupold in: Andreas Leupold/Silke Glossner, *Münchener Anwaltshandbuch IT-Recht* (3rd ed. 2013), Part 2 para. 660 et seq.

2. France

In accordance with the *E-Commerce Directive*, French law requires host providers to remove or block access to materials that are illegal upon receiving notice of such materials. Like in Germany, the question in that context is whether notice and take down has to be interpreted as notice and stay-down. Similar to Germany, this question has also been subject to a number of court decisions where rights-holders tried to obtain injunctions against host providers in order to prevent the continuation of infringements. However, in contrast to Germany, host providers will not have to monitor third party websites, but search engines themselves may be under an obligation – following notification – to prevent listings of links directing users to copyright infringing materials.

Finally, the case law shows that the assumption made in the introduction, namely, that courts struggle to apply the concepts developed in the advent of user-generated content to new forms of services provided by online service providers, also applies to France. This in particular applies to host providers. Thus, the analysis of potential monitoring obligations needs to be preceded by a short analysis of the concept of host provider and how the original concept has been reshaped and extended to encompass new phenomena.

a) Legal Framework: Loi pour la confiance dans l'économie numerique

The *E-Commerce Directive* was transposed into French national law by means *of Loi n° 2004-575 de 21 juin 2004* pour la confiance dans l'économie numérique (LCEN)[2471]. The liability exemptions of the *E-Commerce Directive* for different kinds of provider are incorporated into one single article, Article 6 of the *LCEN.*

Under Article 6-I-2 *LCEN* a host provider may not be held civilly liable for the activities or information stored at the request of a recipient of these services if they did not have actual knowledge of their unlawful nature or of facts or circumstances making this nature apparent, or if, as soon as they obtained such knowledge, they acted expeditiously to remove or to disable access to these data. Further a host provider may not be held crimi-

2471 Law on Trust in the Digital Economy.

nal liable for the information stored at the request of a recipient of these services if they did not have actual knowledge of the unlawful activity or information, or if, as soon as they obtained such knowledge, they acted expeditiously to remove or to disable access to these information.[2472]

Departing from the wording of the *E-Commerce Directive Directive*, the *LCEN* sets forth how knowledge of infringing content can be acquired by way of notification. Article 6-I-5° of the *LCEN* also serves as a rule of evidence to establish "knowledge" in court proceedings.[2473] Accordingly, where a notification does not fulfil the requirements of Article 6-I-5 *LCEN*, the notification will be void and will not trigger liability of the host provider.[2474] One of the requirements for a valid notification under Article 6-I-5 *LCEN* relates to the precise location of the notified content, because otherwise the hosting provider would in most cases not be able to identify and remove the litigious content. The French legislator added further aspects to the *LCEN*: pursuant to Article 6-II the host provider is legally obliged to obtain and to keep data of its users that allows their identification in case of dispute. It has been argued that this provision has the potential to ease the handling of liability cases involving host providers.[2475]

In order not to put host providers into the position of a judge deciding over the legality of the content, the Constitutional Council clarified that liability of host providers only arises where content is clearly unlawful or where the removal of the content was ordered by a judge.[2476] In general,

---

2472 See Article 6-I-3° *LCEN*.

2473 According to said Article knowledge of illegal content will be assumed, if someone asks for the withdrawal of information giving his name, describing the facts clearly and the reasons for its withdrawal request. The notification has to contain the following: (i) notification date; (ii) details about the notifier (iii) the name and address of the addressee; (iv) a description of the illegal activity and its precise localisation; (v) the reasons why the content should be removed including reference to the legal and factual grounds; (vi) a copy of the correspondence with the author or editor of the illegal information or activities asking for their interruption, removal or modification. In order to deter third parties from filing false notifications, the filing of abusive notifications is an offence and punishable with imprisonment of up to one year and a fine of EUR 15,000.

2474 Cour de cassation, Decision of 17.02.2011 *(affaires Dailymotion, Fuzz et Amen)*.

2475 Thomas Hoeren, *The European liability and responsibility of providers of online-platforms such as "Second Life"*, Journal of Information, Law & Technology 2009, Issue 1, 10.

2476 Initially, only content of such nature as enlisted in Article 6-I-7 *LCEN* (child pornography, denial of crimes against humanity and incitement of racial hatred)

the notion of host provider is interpreted broadly by French courts. This has been widely criticised, and it is being suggested to revise the concept of host to reflect the diversity of service providers that exist today in contrast to the time the *E-Commerce Directive* was drafted.[2477] A recent parliamentary report[2478] proposed to create – alongside host providers and publishers – the category of "éditeur de services"[2479] which gain a direct economic benefit from users accessing hosted content, and to impose upon these éditeurs de services the obligation to monitor the hosted content.[2480]

As regards the monitoring of content, Article 6-I-7 *LCEN* restates the principle of Article 15(1) *E-Commerce Directive* that the host or access provider is under no general obligation to actively monitor content transmitted or stored on his website. In accordance with Article 14(3) *E-Commerce Directive*, the second paragraph of Article 6-I-7 *LCEN* allows the judiciary to order host providers to implement targeted and temporary

---

was held to be manifestly illegal. However, courts held that also defamation (TGI Paris, Decision of 15.11.2004) and infringements of intellectual property rights (CA Paris, Decision of 07.06.2006 *(Tiscali Media v Dargaud)*) fulfil the requirements of manifestly illegal.

2477 See Pierre Lescure, *Culture-acte 2, Mission «Acte II de l'exception culturelle», Contribution aux politiques culturelles à l'ére numérique* (May 2013), p. 400.

2478 Rapport d'information des sénateurs Laurent Béteille et Richard Yung, *La lutte contre la contrefaçon : premier bilan de la loi du 29 octobre 2007* (February 2011), http://www.senat.fr/rap/r10-296/r10-2960.html (last accessed on 17.05.2014).

2479 "Éditeurs de services" may best be translated as "publishing services".

2480 This suggestion has to be seen in the context of the ongoing struggle of courts to hold user-generated content platforms liable for third party content from which they generate remarkable revenues by selling advertising space. One exemplary case in this regard is the judgment of the Paris High Court in *TF1 v YouTube* (TGI Paris, Decision of 29.05.2012 – RG no. 10/11205). Applying the principles of *SABAM v Netlog*, the Court concluded that YouTube was a hosting provider and thus, it only had the duty to remove infringing copies of the work in question when it was notified. However, although a five-day delay in removing content was considered unreasonably long, YouTube did not incur any liability for that delay. This conclusion was based on the finding that the conditions of Article L.216-1 *Code de la propriété intellectuelle* were not met: Article L.216-1 contemplates an infringement where programmes are telecasts or communicated to the public in a place open to the public in exchange for an entrance fee; although the notion of telecasts does not require that access to the site is only granted in exchange for payment, the court concluded that telecasts with free access do not infringe Article L.216-1.

surveillance with regard to specific contents. Article 6-I-8 *LCEN* stipulates a principle of subsidiarity for injunctions.[2481]

The French law thus also foresees for injunctions requiring the service provider to cease and desist from an infringement as required by Article 8(3) *InfoSoc Directive*. French courts imposed an obligation to monitor third-party content with regard to subsequent infringements of a specific subject matter for example on the video platform Dailymotion.[2482] This decision has however been overturned on appeal and Dailymotion excluded from liability for further copyright infringing uploads by its users of the disputed content.[2483] Although the *LCEN* does not explicitly state that monitoring of subsequent publications is required by law, French courts recently tend to impose such an obligation on host providers. [2484] What can be witnessed is a shift from a notice and take down rule to a notice and stay-down rule, which will be examined in the following.

2481 As regards the subsidiarity principle in practice see TGI Paris, Decision of 13.06.2005 – RG no. 05/53871 *(UEJF, J'Accuse, SOS Racisme et autres v SA Tiscali [Telecom Italia], AFA, France Telecom et autres);* Decision of 20.04.2005 – RG no. 05/52674 – 05/53871 *(UEJF, J'Accuse, SOS Racisme et autres v Olm LLC et autres),* affirmed by CA Paris, Decision of 24.11.2006 – RG no. 05/15722 *(SA Tiscali (Telecom Italia), AFA, France Telecom et a. v UEJF, J'Accuse, SOS Racisme et autres),* affirmed by Cour de Cassation, Decision of 19.06.2008 – RG no. 07/12244; see also Étienne Montéro/Quentin van Enis, *Ménager la liberté d'expression au regard des mesures de filtrage imposées aux intermédiaires de l'Internet : la quadrature du cercle ?*, Revue Lamy Droit de l'Immatériel 2008, No. 40, 86, 97.

2482 TGI Paris, Decision of 13.07.2007 *(Christian C., Nord-Ouest Production et UGC Images v Dailymotion).* The findings were partly revised by the Court of Appeal of Paris in CA Paris, Decision of 06.05.2009 *(Christian C., Nord-Ouest Production et UGC Images v Dailymotion),* which was also affirmed by Court de Cassation, Decision of 17.02.2011 *(Christian C., Nord-Ouest Production et UGC Images v Dailymotion).*

2483 CA Paris, Decision of 6.05.2009 *(Christian C., Nord-Ouest Production et UGC Images v Dailymotion),* affirmed by Court de Cassation, Decision of 17.02.2011 *(Christian C., Nord-Ouest Production et UGC Images v Dailymotion).*

2484 Cf. Catherine Jasserand, *YouTube guilty but not liable for late removal of infringing material*, Journal of Intellectual Property Law & Practice 2012, Vol. 7 Issue 11, 790–791.

b) Scope of Any Blocking Obligation: Take down and Stay Down?

As aforementioned, the effect of a notice complying with the legal requirements of a valid notification has long been uncertain. The reason for this uncertainty was the underlying question whether the obligation to remove content expeditiously is met as soon as the provider removes the notified content, or whether he must also ensure that the same content is not re-posted in the future.

The re-appearance of content that has been removed upon request significantly limits the effectiveness of the procedures laid down in the *LCEN*: notification relates to specific content at a specific location, however, the litigious content can be available at several locations on a website or reappear quickly after removal. Thus, rights owners usually demand that the obligation of take down following notification of the illegality of content shall encompass an obligation to prevent further infringements of the same kind: notice and take down shall be interpreted as notice and stay down and in case of reappearance of the content in question, the host shall incur liability.[2485] If host providers do not comply with this request the rights-holders usually try to obtain an injunction pursuant to Article L 336-2 *CPI.* Article L 336-2 *CPI*, which was inserted into the *CPI* by the *Loi HADOPI I*, sets forth that where an infringement of copyright or a related right is caused by the content of an online public communication service, the regional court may order (at request of the rights-holder) any measure necessary to prevent or put an end to an infringement of copyright or a related right in respect of any person likely to contribute to resolving the problem without taking into account any liability and without demanding that the measure should be totally effective.[2486] The rights owners will usually request the broadest injunction pos-

---

2485 Cf. Pierre Lescure, *Culture-acte 2, Mission «Acte II de l'exception culturelle», Contribution aux politiques culturelles à l'ére numérique* (May 2013), p. 401.

2486 This provision was also challenged before the Conseil Constitutionnel, which held that the provision is not unconstitutionnel. The applicants argued that the possibility of blocking might deprive many Internet users of the right to receive information and ideas, and that the wording of the provision is too wide and uncertain, so that providers concerned may preventively restrict access to the Internet. The Court rejected these arguments, stressing that it is incumbent upon a court that has to deal with such a request to order solely such measures that are strictly necessary to preserve the rights involved. See Conseil Constitutionnel, Decision of 27.07.2006, no. 2006-540 DC, paras. 37 et seq.

sible by relying on the possibility that a court may "*order a measure of such a kind as to prevent or end the damage related to the current content of the website in question*".[2487]

Like in Germany, the re-posting of content that is identical or similar to content, which had been notified and deleted, became subject to numerous disputes. There was legal uncertainty, whether – in order to keep notifications to a minimum – the obligation to end and prevent damage amounts to a prevention of future infringements of the litigious content. In this respect, host providers obviously wanted to keep their efforts to a minimum and only delete upon notification.

Various courts concluded that notice and take down amounts to notice and stay down, and imposed upon host providers a proactive specific monitoring duty requiring them to prevent any future infringements of notified works.[2488] Accordingly, liability of a host provider was established for re-posted content identical to the content that had previously been notified and that infringed the same intellectual property rights.[2489] The obligation to prevent infringements was held to not only include the prevention of re-posts of the litigious content by the same user responsible for the first infringement, but also to extend to other users.[2490] Accordingly, the rights-holder would not have to notify the host provider every time the content is uploaded again, irrespective of the identity of the uploader.

At the same time when the German Federal Court of Justice was asked to rule on the scope of monitoring duties, the French Supreme Court was addressed with this question as well. In three separate but similar judgments rendered on 12 July 2012 the French Supreme Court held that the

2487 Cf. Christelle Coslin/Christine Gateau, *No 'stay down' obligation for hosting providers in France*, Society for Computers and Law (02.07.2013).

2488 See for example CA Paris, Decision of 09.04.2010 *(Google v Flach Films and others);* CA Paris, Decision of 03.12.2010 *(Dailymotion v Zadig Production);* CA Paris, Decision of 14.01. 2011 *(Google Inc. v Bac Films and others);* CA Paris, Decision of 04.02.2011 – RG no. 09/21941 *(André Rau v Google & AuFeminin.com);* TGI Paris, Decision of 11.06.2010 *(La Chauve Souris and 120 Films v Dailymotion);* TGI Paris, Decision of 13.01.2011 *(Calt Production v Dailymotion);* TGI Créteil, Decision of 14.12.2010 *(INA v YouTube).* These cases concerned either films that could be streamed or downloaded from host providers and/or through links on Google's video service, or reproductions of photographs on the website aufeminin.com, that were used by Google Images.

2489 CA Paris, Decision of 04.02.2011 – RG no. 09/21941 *(André Rau v Google & AuFeminin.com).*

2490 *Ibid.*

subsequent unauthorised upload of litigious content by a different user must be considered as a new infringement that requires a new notification.[2491] The Court recalled that such a notification is required for the host provider to have actual knowledge of the illicit nature and the location of the litigious content. Intermediaries do not have any obligation to actively search for illicit content. However, a duty to prevent any future infringements of the litigious content by any users of the service (= stay down) would require an intermediary to search for these infringement, which vice versa would impose upon intermediaries a general obligation to monitor all content.[2492] In particular, the Supreme Court criticised the imposition of a monitoring duty that is not restricted in time; only temporary measures shall be allowed.[2493] Non-temporary injunctions were held to be prohibited by Article 6-I-7 LCEN, which implements Article 15 of the *E-Commerce Directive*. The Court emphasised that every restriction of the freedom to receive and impart information must be necessary in a democratic society and strictly proportionate with regard to the aim pursued; the wide stay down obligation in question failed that test.

However, the decisions of the Supreme Court do not exclude that the judge can require a host provider to implement measures that aim at preventing the reappearance of the content in question when restricted to a limited number of content and limited in time.[2494] This has to be decided on a case by case basis.

The French Supreme Court followed the guidelines set up by the CJEU in the SABAM cases (*Scarlet Extended v SABAM*, *SABAM v Netlog*) without explicitly referring to them: namely, that injunctions that aim at the prevention of infringements of intellectual property rights must be effect-

---

2491 Cour de cassation, Decision of 12.07.2012 – Arrêt n° 830 *(André Rau v Google & AuFeminin.com);* Decision of 12.07.2012 – Arrêt n° 831 *(Bac Films v Google France and Inc [1 & 2]);* Decision of 12.07.2012 – Arrêt n° 832 *(SNEP v Google France).*

2492 Instead of many see Cour de casssation, Decision of 12.07.2012 – Arrêt n° 831 (*Bach Films v Google France and Inc [1 & 2]*), para. "sur le quatrième moyen".

2493 *Ibid.*

2494 See also Pierre Lescure, Culture-acte 2, Mission «Acte II de l'exception culturelle», Contribution aux politiques culturelles à l'ére numérique (May 2013), p. 401.

ive, proportionate and dissuasive.[2495] National courts must not enjoin intermediaries to implement preventive filtering systems of all the electronic communications passing through their services that would indistinctly apply to all their customers at their exclusive expense and without any limitation in time.

It is interesting to see, that while the CJEU in *SABAM v Netlog* set up cumulative criteria that would render a blocking measure disproportionate, the French Supreme Court considered that the "no limitation in time" criterion suffices to qualify proactive filtering as disproportionate. Following the decisions of the French Supreme Court, rights owners will have to send a notice each time content infringing their rights is posted online.[2496] This puts them in an unsatisfactory position: they will have to monitor numerous websites for intellectual property rights infringements, while some of the most popular sites (directly or indirectly) benefit financially from the content that is posted on their platforms. The French Supreme Court had no issues basing its conclusion on only one criterion from the *SABAM v Netlog* reasoning. It is doubtful whether that was the interpretation intended to be given to Article 15 *E-Commerce Directive* by the CJEU in *SABAM v Netlog*. As mentioned above, the CJEU test is a cumulative test. The CJEU did not state that where one of the criteria ((i) filtering of all communication, (ii) all customers, (iii) at its exclusive expense and (iv) without any limitation in time) is not fulfilled the filtering will be disproportionate. In this regard the French Supreme Court may have overshot the mark. The Court also did not give reasons why the lack of a time limit rendered the monitoring obligation disproportionate. It is one thing to state that a measure is disproportionate, but another thing to give an explanation. Further, like in Germany, but this time in favour of the host provider, there was no real balancing of interests conducted. In addition, the Court did not give any guidance as to how the disproportionality could be eliminated. One may draw the conclusion that as long as proactive filtering is imposed temporary, the interests of the rights owners are likely to prevail.

2495 CJEU, C-70/10 *Scarlet Extended v SABAM*, Judgment of 14.11.2011, ECR I-11959; CJEU, C-360/10, *SABAM v Netlog NV*, Judgment of 16.02.2012, [2012] 2 C.M.L.R. 18.

2496 See also Pierre Lescure, *Culture-acte 2, Mission «Acte II de l'exception culturelle», Contribution aux politiques culturelles à l'ére numérique* (May 2013), p. 401.

Although the reactions to the judgments of the Supreme Court were mixed,[2497] most commentaries concentrated on the prohibition of proactive filtering as such, and ignored that the Court also mentioned – but unfortunately did not discuss – the feasibility of proactive filtering.[2498] As relates to Google, it needs to be stressed that the Supreme Court recognised Google's argument that proactive filtering is not possible with regard to the automatic indexing on its Google video site. Google in relation to its Google Video service however is not a classical provider of hosting services, but rather a search engine. There was no analysis as to whether, and ultimately how, the provision of a search engine differs from that of a provider of a social network like Netlog, and thus, it was not addressed whether the *Netlog* criteria could be applied at all. Considering the advancements in filtering and blocking technology, stay down obligations may easier be imposed where users upload content on the service provider's own servers. Of course, the courts will then have to examine the temporary scope of any request for an injunction sought by rights owners.

The cases before the Cour de cassation indicate, that courts struggle to apply a system, that has been developed in the last century and was created to achieve an appropriate balance in a time where only few types of services existed, to new forms of services.

c) Limits of Notice and Take down and the Shift to Content Blocking by Search Engines

As mentioned above, French courts will need to examine whether an injunction requested by rights-holders is temporary and may thus be proportionate. As convenient the injunction may be, their effect is also limi-

---

2497 Christophe Caron, *Responsabilité des hébergeurs : requiem pour le «take down, stay down»*, Communication Commerce éléctronique 2012, Vol. 14 Issue 9, 28–30; Milhály J. Fiscor, *The WIPO "Internet Treaties" and copyright in the "cloud"*, ALAI 2012 Congress, pp.40 et seq.; Christelle Coslin/Christine Gateau, *No "stay down" obligation for hosting providers in France*, Society for Computers and Law (02.07.2013).

2498 See for example Milhály J. Fiscor, *The WIPO "Internet Treaties" and copyright in the "cloud"*, ALAI 2012 Congress, pp.40 et seq.; Christelle Coslin/Christine Gateau, *No "stay down" obligation for hosting providers in France*, Society for Computers and Law (02.07.2013).

ted. They are only ever an effective mechanism when the host providers are within French jurisdiction or otherwise comply with the order. Further, rights-holders may also find it particularly time and cost consuming to send out notifications if content expeditiously reappears after its been taken down and/or where the sheer mass of files requires constant monitoring in order to reduce unauthorised copying. Hence, the French national syndicate of music producers (Le Syndicat national de l'édition phonographique – SNEP) decided to turn to Google as the provider of one of the most popular search engines to bar access to unauthorised copies. The reason for this was the fact that Google's suggest service provided the suggestions "Torrent", "Megaupload" and "Rapidshare" when users typed the names of artists or music bands in the Google search bar. Google Suggest autocompletes search queries based on the most popular search terms by other users associated with the term that is being typed in the search bar. As Google would not comply with SNEP's request, SNEP sued Google to refrain from providing these suggestions, arguing that the search tool made it possible to infringe copyright and related rights by directing users to services that offer illegal downloading. Both, the Court of First Instance[2499] and the Appellate Court[2500], rejected SNEP's demands based on the findings that the suggested search results were not illegal in themselves. In addition, the blocking of the requested terms would simply make it less easy to find these sites for users that do not already know them, but would in fact not hinder the illegal download of protected works as such.

The Supreme Court overturned these rulings, and held (i) that Google's suggest feature actually "provided the means to infringe copyright and related rights" by systematically directing users towards downloading portals, and (ii) that the measures requested by SNEP, while not being totally effective, could in fact "prevent or terminate such infringements" by making it more difficult to find the websites in question.[2501] The Court did not

---

2499 TGI Paris, Decision of 10.09.2010 – RG no. 10/53985 *(SNEP v Google France).*

2500 CA Paris, Decision of 03.05.2011 – RG no. 10/19845 *(SNEP v Google France).*

2501 Cour de Cassation, Decision of 12.07.2012 – Arrêt n° 832 *(SNEP v Google France).* The case has been referred back to a lower court to be reassessed. Interestingly, six months before the ruling by the Supreme Court, Google voluntarily removed "Rapidshare", "uTorrent" and "MegaUpload" from its Google Suggest service.

discuss whether ordering Google to abolish the suggestions in question when users typed the names of SNEP's artists into the search bar was proportionate.[2502] This would have been particularly interesting as the omission of particular suggestions based on popular queries does not effectively block access to the downloading sites. The only effective result of such omission would be that users would not be automatically be confronted with these suggestions, but would need to specifically search for these sites in connection with the artists in question. Although the decision remained silent on many interesting aspects, it indicates a tendency which at the same time could also be seen in German courts in a different context: namely, a differentiation based on whether information is pushed to the attention of a user or whether the information needs to be actively searched for by the user.[2503] One may thus say that there is a differentia-

2502 This was not necessary because the court annulled the previous judgment of the Court of Appeal in Paris and referred the case to the Court of Appeal in Versailles. The proportionality test needs to be conducted by the Court of Appeal Versailles to whom the case was referred to for reassessment taking into account the finding that Google Suggest provides the means to infringe intellectual property rights.

2503 See Lawrence Siry/Sandra Schmitz, *A right to be forgotten? – How recent developments in Germany may affect the Internet publishers in the US*, European Journal of Law and Technology, Vol.3 No. 1, 2012, pp. 3 et seq. The German cases concerned two brothers that were convicted of the murder of the famous German actor Walter Sedlmayr. They both denied and still deny the accusations. The murder, and the subsequent trial and conviction of the brothers, received extensive media coverage in Germany, especially due to controversies surrounding the investigations. When one of them was released from prison, they began to sue publishers in an effort to have their names deleted from archived stories. While archived stories identifying the brothers are legitimate, any new publication must respect their right to rehabilitation meaning that in balancing the interests of those concerned, the personality rights of the brothers would outweigh the interest of the publishers to inform and the public to be informed, In the proceedings, the question arose whether the easy accessibility of these stories, amounts to another quality of the stories that equals that of new reports on the subject matter. While new reports would certainly fail the test of proportionality (time has passed, offenders due to be released, interest of public to be informed about trial and proceedings satisfied), the archived stories are not new publications. Some lower courts have found that the storage of old news stories in online archives equals a current dissemination of the story, thus having the quality of completely new reports (LG Hamburg, Decision of 01.06.2007 – 324 O 717/06, MultiMedia und Recht 2007, 666; LG Hamburg: Decision of 29.02.2008 – 324 O 469/07, BeckRS 2009, 22552; LG Hamburg, Decision of

tion between push and pull effect or active and passive access. In Germany, the cases where the Federal Court of Justice conducted this differentiation concerned information in online archives that interfered with the personality rights of the claimants. Although the context of online archives cases is different, in that it concerned personality rights, the similarities in the conclusion are striking similar. The German Federal Court of Justice held, that the provision of out-dated news stories in online archives is legal as long as the archived story does not give the impression that it is up to date or presents or has the characteristics of an afresh publication.[2504] In this context it is relevant to know that while news reports on criminal cases may allow the identification of the accused, the personality rights of a criminal will outweigh the public interest in reports about him if time has passed. The easy accessibility of old and often out-dated news stories by search engines as such does not constitute sufficient reason to eliminate "historical memory".[2505] Hence, where articles are clearly identifiable as archived reports, the provision of the article in an online archive is legitimate. In this case, the user will need to actively search for the story. The story will not be dragged to his attention by the publisher, meaning that it

---

28.02.2008 – 324 O 459/07, BeckRS 2010, 03447; LG Hamburg, Decision of 18.01. 2008 – 324 O 507/07, Neue Juristische Wochenschrift-RR 2009, 120, 121). Other lower courts have found that online archives are comparable to traditional archives for printed works and accordingly, came to the conclusion that there is "no renewal of former statements" (OLG Frankfurt, Decisions of 20.09.2006 – 16 W 55/06 and 16 W 57/06, see also KG Berlin, Decision of 19.10.2001 – 9 W 132/01, BeckRS 2007 02224; LG München I, Decision of 13 June2007 – 9 O 2295/07, BeckRS 2008 03243). The Federal Court of Justice finally held that as long as the story is not pushed to the attention of the reader but is clearly marked as an archived report and requires an active search by the users in order to be accessed, the provision of the news story in an online archive is legal (BGH, Decision of 10.11.2009 – VI ZR 217/08 *(rainbow.at);* Decisions of 15.12.2009 – VI ZR 227/08 and 228/08 (*Deutschlandradio*); Decisions of 09.02.2010 – VI ZR 243/08 and 244/08 *(Spiegel online);* Decisions of 20.04.2010 – VI ZR 245/08 and 246/08 (*morgenweb.de*)).

2504 BGH, Decision of 10.11.2009 – VI ZR 217/08 *(rainbow.at);* Decisions of 15.12.2009 – VI ZR 227/08 and 228/08 *(Deutschlandradio);* Decisions of 09.02.2010 – VI ZR 243/08 and 244/08 *(Spiegel online);* Decisions of 20.04.2010 – VI ZR 245/08 and 246/08 *(morgenweb.de).*

2505 See also Walter Seitz in: Thomas Hoeren/Ulrich Sieber, *Handbuch Multimedia-Recht* (2010), Part 8 C, para. 62a.

is not "pushed" to the reader by for example linking it in a current news story.[2506]

Similarly the French Supreme Court did not argue that the provision of links to file-hosters or torrent indexing sites is illegal, whereas dragging the attention of users to these sites by suggesting them as search terms in connection with the repertoire of the claimants, was providing the means to infringe copyright. Although the decision may be criticised for concluding that the suggestion as such constitutes a means to infringe copyright, hence interpreting the notion of means very wide, the decision shows the same tendency as those by the German court in the online archive cases.

The push and pull differentiation requires the court to examine the degree of involvement of the provider in making content available to the public. In this regard, it is important whether the user plays a rather passive role, and the provider actively supports him in accessing files by suggesting search results or links, or whether the provider remains passive and only responds to queries by the active user.

3. Host Provider Obligations: Concerns Relating to Technology and Fundamental Rights

a) Dealing with Technological Matters: The Difficulties to Identify Similar or Identical Infringements

At this point, the discussion shall be restricted to the difficulties to identify similar or identical infringements, because this lies at the heart of the ability to prevent the continuation of an infringement. Other than the access blocking conducted by access providers, host providers may block access and delete content to infringing materials. As they store the materials in question, they can target only the infringing file and one may assume that do not carry risks of over-blocking. The latter is however not true, insofar as the monitoring duties imposed by German courts are rather extensive and also require the blocking of access or deletion of identical infringements.

It has already been outlined that hash value filters may only detect identical infringements that have exactly the same hash value as the original

2506 See Sandra Schmitz/Lawrence Siry, *Online-Archive – "Der ewige Pranger im Internet"?* in: Jürgen Taeger (ed.), *Digitale Evolution* (2010), pp. 217 et seq.

work. If only less than a second is cut off from a song, this would mean that the hash value filter is unable to identify a file as identical. Word filters are also only successful, where the title of the work in question is included in the file name. Users may however change the name of a file in order to prevent the blocking of a file. Sophisticated filtering like for instance YouTube's content-ID filter requires the provision of reference data by the rights-holder and thus requires mutual cooperation.[2507] However, no matter how sophisticated filtering systems are, there success is mostly limited to identify content that is hosted on the host provider's servers. With social media platforms or other user-generated content platforms, this will suffice to identify most infringements. The situation with file-hosters is however different. The essence of the service provided is the storage of the protected work, which is legal as long as the link by which the file can be accessed is not made publicly available. Thus, even a (hypothetical) manual check of all uploaded files containing a protected work would not in itself be sufficient to identify an infringement. German courts responded to this problem quite rigorous and require file-hosters upon notification of an infringement to monitor pertinent link directories for links in relation to the litigious content hosted on its servers. In this context, the deployment of web crawlers searching for the content would however not be enough to comply with the monitoring obligations. Moreover, it is required to check not only the file names, but also look for materials that are hidden behind other file names to disguise infringements. In addition, searches must be conducted via search engines to identify further links. Obviously, the German Federal Court recognised that word filters are unlikely to identify all infringements and carry the risk of false positives.[2508] The same applies to searches on notorious link directories. However, while the Court certainly recognised that links can be distributed in various ways and references to the content be disguised, the Court ignored the complexity of identifying the links. It is obvious that such extensive

2507 As regards the content-ID filter employed by YouTube see http://www.youtube.com/t/contentid. In April 2012, the LG Hamburg declared such a content-ID filter as not sufficient to escape liability, see LG Hamburg, Decision of 20.04.2012 – 310 O 461/10 (*GEMA v YouTube*), Zeitschrift für Urheber- und Medienrecht 2012, 596.

2508 Matthias Leistner, *Grundlagen und Perspektiven der Haftung für Urheberrechtsverletzungen im Internet,* Zeitschrift für Urheber- und Medienrecht 2012, 722, 733.

filtering would not only require complex filtering technology but also manual searches. Considering the sheer volume of data and the number of link directories, fora and indexing sites, the file-hosters are faced with a near impossible task.

It is obvious, that the Courts felt the need to respond to the increased use of file-hosters for copyright infringements while recognising that a deletion of the actual infringing act, the publication of the hyperlink, is not feasible because the providers of link directories regularly do not respond to take down requests, and are regularly located outside jurisdiction. The deletion of the content, or at least the blocking of access to the litigious content, thus is considered the easier way to go as the links will no longer be of any use.

It is highly questionable whether the monitoring that goes beyond the monitoring of the own service provided and extends to third party platforms is in compliance with secondary EU law and fundamental rights.

b) Compliance with Secondary EU Law

The basic question that needs to be addressed in respect to all filtering obligations is whether the *InfoSoc Directive* and the *Enforcement Directive*, in the light of the *E-Commerce Directive*, the *Data Protection Directive*, the *E-Privacy Directive* and fundamental rights as guaranteed by the ECHR and CFR preclude such a filter obligation. Since the CJEU's decision in *L'Oréal v eBay,* and most recently *SABAM v Netlog*, it is clear that the Directives do not exclude the imposition of specific filtering obligations upon host providers. Thus, the following analysis can be restricted to compliance with the findings in these cases.

First of all, the providers in question must fall within the definition of host providers in relation to the content in question. This has not disputed as file-hoster as well as social media platforms "store information provided by the users of that platform, [….], on its servers".[2509] For host providers, the prohibition of general monitoring applies in particular to national measures which would require the host provider to actively moni-

2509 Cf. CJEU, C-360/10, *SABAM v Netlog NV*, Judgment of 16.02.2012, [2012] 2 C.M.L.R. 18, para. 27.

tor all the data of each of its customers in order to prevent any future infringement of intellectual property rights.

According to the CJEU in *SABAM v Netlog* the *E-Commerce Directive*, the *InfoSoc Directive* and the *IPR Enforcement Directive* and thereby the prohibition of a general filtering obligation "must be interpreted as precluding a national court from issuing an injunction against a hosting service provider which requires it to install a system for filtering:

- information which is stored on its servers by its service users;
- which applies indiscriminately to all of those users;
- as a preventative measure;
- exclusively at its expense;
- and for an unlimited period,

which is capable of identifying electronic files containing musical, cinematographic or audio-visual work in respect of which the applicant for the injunction claims to hold intellectual property rights, with a view to preventing those works from being made available to the public in breach of copyright".[2510] This prohibition outlines the archetype of general monitoring which infringes Article 15 of the E-Commerce Directive,[2511] and does not give any further guidance as to what would be appropriate specific monitoring. This had to do with the question referred to the CJEU for preliminary reference being drafted rather general. The test as such is a cumulative test, meaning that a filtering obligation that fulfils all the criteria is prohibited.

Taking the example of Germany, one may argue that host providers are obliged to install exactly such as system as the one precluded by the CJEU, namely a system for filtering of information which is stored on its servers by its users which applies indiscriminately to all service users as a preventative measure exclusively at its expense and for an unlimited period. Although the Federal Court of Justice restricted the monitoring duty to the litigious work and not any further, it requires the active search for infringements in relation to all content stored by all of its users without a limitation in time. Similar monitoring duties were rejected by the French Supreme Court in due consideration that the monitoring of all users in

2510 *Ibid*, grounds.

2511 Matthias Leistner, Grundlagen und Perspektiven der Haftung für Urheberrechtsverletzungen im Internet, Zeitschrift für Urheber- und Medienrecht 2012, 722, 728.

relation to the litigious content that is not limited in time is disproportionate and not in compliance with EU law. The monitoring obligation in France thus has its limits where content of other users than the original infringer is concerned and where not limitation in time is prescribed. There is no doubt that such a limited monitoring duty is in compliance with the *SABAM v Netlog* criteria. In contrast, the German approach goes too far and amounts to a general monitoring obligation.[2512] From the wording of the CJEU in *SABAM v Netlog*, it becomes clear that the monitoring of all data in relation to a specific infringement (the "work in respect of which the applicant for the injunction claims to hold intellectual property rights, with a view to preventing those works from being made available") in the aforementioned scope is prohibited, and not as one may argue, the active search for infringements in general. Thus, the obligation has either to be restricted to specific user(s) or data, and/or be limited in time. Although it is understandable that it is necessary for the identification of infringements to check whether the links granting access to the litigious content have been made publicly available, a monitoring that even goes beyond pertinent link directories goes even further than the monitoring of content stored on own servers. In addition, the technical feasibility of such monitoring and its effectiveness and the necessary efforts to be taken when thousands of works are concerned, has not been addressed by the courts. The necessary measures to prevent identical infringements have also not been construed in the light of the requirements stemming from the protection of the applicable fundamental rights. The German Federal Court of Justice did not even take into consideration the judgment of the CJEU in *SABAM v Netlog*, and only briefly noted that the extensive monitoring would be in compliance with the findings of the CJEU in *L'Oréal v eBay*.

Obviously the Court sought to respond with its extensive monitoring obligation to the problem that the anonymised usage of file-hosters makes it difficult to pursue action against direct infringers. This intention does however not justify setting aside almost completely a fair balancing of the contravening interests.

If courts want to impose extensive monitoring duties upon service providers, they can do so as long as the service providers are not classified

---

2512 Cf. Andreas Leupold in: Andreas Leupold/Silke Glossner, *Münchener Anwaltshandbuch IT-Recht* (3rd ed. 2013), Part 2 para. 660 et seq.

as host providers to which Article 15 of the *E-Commerce Directive* applies. The approach taken, i.e. to accredit an active role to a service provider in order to base on this active role increased monitoring duties, and nevertheless classify the provider as a host provider is not possible under the current regime.

This being said, the Federal Court of Justice ignored the jurisprudence of the CJEU on the interpretation of the aforementioned Directives. The obligations imposed upon file-hosters are not in compliance with secondary EU law, in particular Article 15 of the E-*Commerce Directive.*

c) Conformity with Fundamental Rights of Host Providers

Monitoring obligations that are imposed upon host providers interfere with their freedom to pursue business and their right to impart information by third parties.

aa) Freedom to Pursue Business and Property Rights

Filtering and monitoring obligations interfere with the host providers' rights to pursue business and their right to property as guaranteed by Article 1 of the Protocol No. 1 to the *ECHR* (and Articles 16 and 17 *CFR*).

The freedom to conduct a business includes, inter alia, the right for any business to be able to freely use, within the limits of its liability for own acts, the economic, technical and financial resources available to it.[2513] The adoption of monitoring duties such as those discussed above constrains its addressee, the host provider, in a manner which restricts the free use of the resources at his disposal because it obliges him to take measures which may represent significant cost for him.[2514] Similar to the administration of copyright infringement reports and lists in the context of a graduated response scheme, the imposition of monitoring obligations, that even go beyond the monitoring of the own platform have also a considerable impact on his human resources and require in addition complex tech-

---

2513 Cf. CJEU, C-314/12 *UPC Telekabel Wien GmbH v Constantin Film Verleih GmbH and Wega Filmproduktionsgesellschaft GmbH,* Judgment of 27.03.2014, para. 49.

2514 Cf. *ibid*, para. 50.

nical solutions. However, at least in France, the obligation does not seem to infringe the very substance of the freedom of host providers to conduct their legitimate business models. The situation may be different in Germany where monitoring extends to pertinent link directories and searches via popular search engines. In that context, it needs to be recalled, how and to what extent host providers in Germany are required to monitor external content. First of all, it needs to be noted that monitoring duties increase in parallel to the active involvement of the provider in the infringements. Although this is rather of relevance in the ultimate balancing test, at this point it is necessary to look at the extent in order to determine what kind of monitoring is still considered to be legitimate by German courts (irrespective of whether it is non-compliant with the *E-Commerce Directive*). The increased monitoring as described above relates so far to file-hosters only because they are considered to be more than neutral intermediaries by allowing anonymous usage of service and benefitting financially from high traffic volume as well as an established high number of infringements. An obligation such as that at issue leaves it to the file-hosters to determine the specific means to be taken in order to achieve the result sought, thereby allowing the file-hosters to put in place measures which are best adapted to the resources and abilities available to him. However, the courts also declared what measures they will not consider sufficient, leaving in practice not much discretion to the file-hosters. By proving that he has taken all reasonable measures, the file-hoster would avoid liability. The possibility of exoneration has the effect that the file-hoster will not be required to make unbearable sacrifices considering that he is not the author of copyright infringements. However, the question of reasonableness is a question that has not been properly assessed by German courts.

If a host provider is obliged to actively search for further infringements of the same kind, he essentially has two choices: to implement a monitoring system that would search the hosted content for infringements. However, as noted above hash value filters only identify exact copies of the original work and not slightly modified versions, while word filters may return false positives and only identify files that carry the name of a protected work, which can in turns be inconclusive. Word filtering brings with it false positives and a risk of over-blocking. However the latter can be reduced by blocking the content first and implement a dispute settlement scheme which allows users to file a complaint if their legitimate content is blocked.[2515] Alternatively, in order to avoid over-blocking, the host provider would have to check results manually as well. When in Germany the monitoring duty would go as far as requiring the screening of notorious indexing websites and link directories, it seems obvious that additional manpower would be needed. Though this may be just and fair considering that many file-hosting services generate profits from the provision of their services, no excessive financial burden must be placed on them that would render their business model inoperable. Although it is not yet known how much a monitoring system that would be able to satisfy the monitoring duty imposed on for instance Rapidshare would cost, it seems obvious that the core of the business is interfered with. The extent of monitoring required is hardly feasible from a technical perspective, and as mentioned above, clearly requires manual checks. Considering that 500,000 files are uploaded per day, the court concluded that this results in 30,000 infringements.[2516] The German rights-holders association GEMA applied for an injunction with regard to more than 4,800 by one single application. Considering that the deployment of software would not be sufficient according to the court, and disguised or hidden files must be manually searched for, the personal and financial resources necessary pose a severe threat to small businesses and also severely affect the service of file-hosting as such. It is questionable whether file-hosting can comply with the obligations and be economically feasible.[2517]

The German Federal Court of Justice was not satisfied that less intrusive measures may be available to file-hosters such as for instance the content-ID filtering system as deployed by YouTube. The software is able to detect infringements by using reference data; the software is able to identify whether content corresponds – even in part – to that reference data.[2518] Content-ID also allows rights-holders to decide, what the users

2515 Matthias Leistner, *Grundlagen und Perspektiven der Haftung für Urheberrechtsverletzungen im Internet,* Zeitschrift für Urheber- und Medienrecht 2012, 722, 733.

2516 BGH, Decision of 15.08.2013 – I ZR 80/12, Kommunikation & Recht 2013, 655, 658.

2517 See Joerg Heidrich, *Weitergehende Prüfpflichten bei besonderer Gefahrengeneigtheit eines File-Hosting-Diensts,* K&R-Kommentar, Kommunikation & Recht 2013, 655, 659.

2518 As regards the functioning of the Content-ID filter see Georg Nolte/Jörg Wimmers, *Wer stört? Gedanken zur Haftung von Intermediären im Internet,* GRUR-Beilage 2014, 58, 65.

may do with their repertoire. Parallel to the system of Content-ID filter, YouTube deploys a dispute settlement procedure by which disputes can be settled between the uploader and the rights-holder.

However, this system is a purely voluntary system and depends on cooperation between the rights-holders and the host provider.

Another less intrusive measure that would also be in conformity with Article 15 of the *E-Commerce Directive* would be the monitoring of accounts of those that have already infringed copyright instead of monitoring the data of all users. As previously mentioned the mere upload of a file onto the file-hoster's servers does not infringe copyright. Only when the link is made publicly available an infringement is established. Thus monitoring the data of all users on the platform to identify copies of the litigious content is useless without checking whether the access link has been distributed. If only the accounts of those that have infringed copyright before, or even those accounts that have infringed copyright in the litigious work, were monitored, this would already reduce the amount of data to be checked tremendously.

Further, a specific monitoring obligation must be clearly defined in order to make it practicable. When in Germany courts order the prevention of similar infringements by all users and in relation to all data hosted in the future, in practice, this may amount to a general obligation to monitor content. Although, the monitoring obligations as such pursue a legitimate aim, namely the protection of the intellectual property rights of the copyright owners, the interference with the host providers' rights cannot be justified when they have to monitor all content of all users at their own expense without a limitation in time.

bb) Right to Impart Information Created by Third Parties

Monitoring obligations also interfere with the service provider's right to impart information created by third parties. This interference is however only minor in comparison to the interference with their right to pursue business. Further, when file-hosting services are concerned, one needs to be aware that their primary aim is not the dissemination of information but the provision of external storage capacities. It may however play a role where indexing sites and link directories are concerned. In this regard, it also needs to be taken into consideration that especially the ECtHR differentiates between, on the one hand, expression and content that is message driven, and on the other hand, "commercial speech". [2519]The latter, which is merely money driven does not enjoy the added value of the protection guaranteed by Article 10 *ECHR*, and thus, the margin of appreciation of domestic courts is rather wide.[2520]

As the monitoring would not just apply to the accounts of users that have infringed copyright before, but to all users and all data hosted, Internet users who are using the file-hoster's service in a lawful manner for example for lawful data back-ups or the storage of own works, would also be affected by the monitoring in their right to freedom of information.

In this respect, the CJEU held in *UPC Telekabel Wien*, that measures adopted by the service provider must be strictly targeted, in the sense that they must serve to bring an end to a third party's infringement of copyright but without thereby affecting Internet users who are using the provider's service in order to lawfully access information.[2521] This can be applied by analogy also to host providers, meaning that the obligation must not be targeted against all users of the service when there are also users that use the service in a lawful manner. Failure to strictly target the monitoring, results in an unjustifiable interference in the freedom of information of the legitimate users in the light of the objective pursued.[2522]

d) Extensive Monitoring and a Fair Balance of Rights

From the above analysis it becomes obvious that extensive monitoring does not put sufficient weight on the rights of host providers. A fair balance can hardly be achieved when already the legitimate business as such is substantially affected. This does not mean that there is no appropriate filtering that goes beyond the mere deletion of notified content as required in France and at the same time is less intrusive than the general monitoring obligation imposed upon file-hosters in Germany.

2519 ECtHR, *Mouvement Raëlien Suisse v Switzerland*, Judgment of 13.07.2012 – Application No. 16354/06, para. 61 with reference to *Markt Intern Verlag GmbH and Klaus Beermann v Germany*, Judgment 20.09.1989 – Application No. 10572/83.

2520 *Ibid.*

2521 CJEU, C-314/12 *UPC Telekabel Wien GmbH v Constantin Film Verleih GmbH and Wega Filmproduktionsgesellschaft GmbH,* Judgment of 27.03.2014, para. 56.

2522 Cf. *ibid.*

First of all, in addition to the severe interference with the rights of host providers, it shall only briefly be mentioned that the (German) national courts have ignored, that the systematic monitoring of data, may interfere with the privacy rights of users, in particular when users have registered for the premium service and provided payment details. As regards the rights and interests of users, the German courts limited the discussion to safeguards against over-blocking, by suggesting the implementation of an internal dispute settlement procedure, where user could appeal unjustified content blocking. This indicates that host providers are advised to block access rather than delete in order to avoid the deletion of legitimate content. Considering that the content may constitute own data of the users, the deletion of such content would also interfere with the property rights of users. It is difficult to assess the rights of users in abstracto as the severity of interferences with their rights and interests depends on the particular filtering regime employed. As stated above, the extensive monitoring obligations imposed by the German courts are likely to be disproportionate when the service that is targeted is used by many users legitimately. In this case the monitoring of the content of all users appears to assume that all users are infringing and thus give a reason to be monitored. It is difficult to determine when exactly users are triggering monitoring.

As regards file-hosting providers, monitoring duties increase in parallel to the active involvement of the provider in the infringements. Although still considered to be host providers, from allowing anonymous usage of their service and benefitting financially from high traffic volume, in connection with the establishment of a high number of infringements,[2523] it seems that the courts draw the conclusion that the provider "turned a blind eye" to copyright infringements. At least these factors are considered as risk factors that – according to a German court – may justify increased obligations to prevent identical infringements in the sense of the prevention of all infringements of the litigious content without any limitations.

The main issue with monitoring obligations is, that as long as they are not clearly defined, they create legal uncertainty. The determination of what is technologically and economically reasonable monitoring is however important for the Internet economy. Service providers must be in a

---

2523 Rapidshare itself admitted that approximately 5 to 6% of uploads will be infringing. Considering that 500,000 files are uploaded per day, the court calculated that this makes 30,000 infringements. BGH, Decision of 15.08.2013 – I ZR 80/12, Kommunikation & Recht 2013, 655, 658.

position so as to calculate the risks they may be confronted with – as well as to foresee the costs associated with risk-avoidance.

The Federal Court of Justice is correct in concluding that file-hosters are not ordinary host providers. In particular in the early years of file-hosting, the operators of these services provided incentives for users to use the service unlawfully. Thus, it is understandable that they could not be considered to benefit from the liability exemptions under the *E-Commerce Directive* in the same way as completely neutral providers. However, in particular Rapidshare had abolished its early reward model and had taken a number of measures to prevent copyright infringements. The company had founded an abuse department, which responded to take down requests considerably quick.[2524] Further Rapidshare deployed a MD5 filter[2525], a hash value filter that is able to detect identical infringements. In addition, Rapidshare also created an interface for rights-holders that allowed them to delete infringing data themselves.[2526] Even the combination of these preventive measures did not satisfy the extensive monitoring duties that arise in relation to a protected work following a first infringement. The German Federal Court of Justice held that the omission to also check pertinent "link collections" for the litigious content infringed the monitoring duties. Following the decision in *GEMA v Rapidshare*, the monitoring extended even to unspecified pertinent links collections. A file-hoster will not only have to check the link collections for litigious content but also examine the description of the files as it may not be evident from the link as such or the heading that it relates to the work in question. Further, popular search engines like Google or social media like Twitter should be checked for infringements. The Court ignored that this basically means that file-hosters will have to search the whole World Wide Web. First of all, they can never be sure, what "link collections" will be considered pertinent. The case law from the UK that has been addressed above in the context of access blocking by access provider has shown, how fast content is moved, platforms may reappear under a new domain, and new link

2524 Joerg Heidrich, *Weitergehende Prüfpflichten bei besonderer Gefahrengeneigtheit eines File-Hosting-Diensts,* K&R-Kommentar, Kommunikation & Recht 2013, 655, 660.

2525 MD5 stands for Message-Digest algorithm 5.

2526 See Joerg Heidrich, *Weitergehende Prüfpflichten bei besonderer Gefahrengeneigtheit eines File-Hosting-Diensts,* K&R-Kommentar, Kommunikation & Recht 2013, 655, 660.

directories enter the market. Links may also be distributed in chats, via Usenet, etc.. Considering the aforementioned amount of data, it is evident that additional staff would be required to comply with the monitoring duties. In addition, it remains unclear what searches shall be conducted via search engines. In this context, it must be noted that the Court addressed Facebook and Twitter as "common search engines" which indicates the lack of understanding of social media platforms, and moreover of technology as such, by the Court.[2527] It must be noted that the search query "Alone in the Dark" on google.de listed 24,300,000 results as of June 2014, while the query "Alone in the Dark" and Rapidshare still returned 209,000 results. Considering that the *GEMA v Rapidshare* case alone related to 4,800 works, it seems that the Court underestimated the personal and economical capacities of Rapidshare which at the time in question had 60 staff members.[2528] In addition, following blocking injunctions against search engine providers like in France, search engine may not only block results for French users, but do so elsewhere as well, which adds to the difficulties for file-hoster to find infringing content.

The Court also overshot the mark of what is required by the Störerhaftung, which does not require a 100% prevention of infringements, but merely a reduction of the risk of infringements.[2529] In this respect, Article 11 of the *IPR Enforcement Directive* sets forth that an injunction must be "aimed at prohibiting the continuation" of an infringement. In connection with the requirement that all measures must be proportionate, it is clear that non-infringers that in some way contribute to an infringement are not required to guarantee the cessation of infringements.

Another point for criticism is the rather negative perception of the Federal Court of Justice of anonymous use of Rapidshare that is not only considered to prevent legal action against the direct infringer, but also as lowering the threshold for illegal behaviour. Considering that in Germany, telemedia services are obliged to provide for the anonymous or pseudonymous use of their service,[2530] this can be seen as an open criticism on the weight attributed to data protection.

2527 *Ibid.*

2528 See *ibid.*

2529 Matthias Leistner, *Grundlagen und Perspektiven der Haftung für Urheberrechtsverletzungen im Internet,* Zeitschrift für Urheber- und Medienrecht 2012, 722, 732.

2530 See § 13 VI *TMG.*

The conclusion reached by the Federal Court of Justice is ultimately the result of a misjudgement of what is technologically and economically feasible monitoring, and did not assess the proportionality of the obligations imposed in an appropriate manner. In particular little regard was paid to less intrusive measures such as requiring a registration of users under their real name (which would have to be balanced against the interest of the users in protecting their personal data), or limitations of downloads or traffic as such. While the deletion of accounts is regularly considered as insufficient,[2531] the situation may have been different with regard to Rapidshare. The service of Rapidshare was only convenient when users subscribed to a premium account. Thus, it is questionable whether blocking of users could not be conducted based on the fact that they are unlikely to subscribe to several new accounts once they have already paid. While this may more likely be a less intrusive measure for users that up- and download, pure uploaders would at least face new registrations with every account blocked. Another feasible monitoring would also be an internal filtering for litigious content and a subsequent check of downloads of that content from one particular account. This could also be automatized. By identifying irregular numbers of downloads of a protected work, this content could at least be blocked.

A solution on how to determine reasonable and appropriate filtering in general could be to require the rights-holder to define in his application for an injunction the means that he considers appropriate. The host provider that is targeted should then be able to rebut the appropriateness of specific measures by explaining why these measures are not feasible or reasonable in his particular case. However, this would not avoid the fragmentation of intermediary liability that has been encountered not only throughout Europe, but even within individual jurisdictions.[2532] What is needed is clear guidance by the CJEU on whether the prevention of identical infringements must be interpreted as to extend to all infringements of the litigious content on the platform in question, or needs to be restricted any further.[2533] With regard to the latter, the double identity requirement suggest-

---

2531 Cf. the Internet auction cases of the Federal Court of Justice cited above.

2532 Cf. With regard to the UK Daithí Mac Síthigh, *The fragmentation of intermediary liability in the UK*, Journal of Intellectual Property Law & Practice 2013, Vol. 8 No. 7, 521-531.

2533 Cf. Andreas Leupold in: Andreas Leupold/Silke Glossner, *Münchener Anwaltshandbuch IT-Recht* (3rd ed. 2013), Part 2 para. 661.

ed by the Advocate General Jääskinen in *L'Oréal v eBay* could also be reconsidered in defining the notion of "identical infringement".[2534] Under such a double requirement of identity, a host provider could comply with specific monitoring duties if he shuts down the account of the infringing user to prevent future infringements committed by the same user and in respect to the same work that had previously been infringed.[2535] Limiting "identical infringement" to infringements by the same user in respect to the litigious content would not only put host providers in a position to determine whether an"identical infringement"occurred. It would also mean that host providers must not actively search all content hosted for infringements.

Rapidshare had drawn consequences from being faced with extensive monitoring obligations: Already following the *Alone in the Dark* case, Rapidshare reduced the maximum traffic per upload and has thereby rendered its service unattractive for mass-scale downloads.[2536] However, it must be noted, that this had little effect on the problem of file-hosting and copyright infringements. New file-hosters entered the market, which is currently more diverse than ever. While in the aftermath of the copyright disputes Rapidshare's popularity declined and as a consequence the service was ultimately shut down in March 2015, new services emerged with locations in considerably safe harbours like the Carribean or Eastern Europe; these services do not even respond to take down requests.[2537] Thus, making a service, that was willing to cooperate in putting an end to infringements, unattractive for users, turned out to be Pyrrhus victory like the access blocking to link directories and indexing sites in the UK. With every service that is shut-down or blocked, new services emerge – and are welcomed by consumers.This assumption is supported by evidence from a Dutch research study, that has been discussed in context of blocking under section 97A *CDPA 1988* in the UK: blocking has no lasting net impact on

2534 See Opinion of Advocate General Jääskinen in case C-324/09 *L'Oréal v eBay*, delivered on 09.12.2010, paras. 169 to 182.

2535 Cf. *ibid*, para. 182.

2536 See Joerg Heidrich, *Weitergehende Prüfpflichten bei besonderer Gefahrengeneigtheit eines File-Hosting-Diensts,* K&R-Kommentar, Kommunikation & Recht 2013, 655, 661.

2537 *Ibid*, 662.

the percentage of users downloading from illegal sources, as users turn to alternatives to the blocked website.[2538]

Further, the French Supreme Court's decision against "notice- and stay down" does also fail to provide an answer to the ongoing debate on the future of specific monitoring. It rather leaves rights-holders with a blunt instrument to enforce their rights. File-sharing networks or other websites where files are shared are essentially about sharing, meaning that once a file has been uploaded, it will be copied, and leaving numerous copies in circulation. The rights-holder will need to send a copyright infringement notification relating to each single copy that is being disseminated. There is no chance of obtaining an injunction requiring the service provider to prevent the re-distribution of a particular work; an injunction is limited in scope to the work being made available by one particular user. So it becomes understandable that rights-holders are now also turning to an indirect mechanism of information control by addressing search engines in order to make it more difficult to find information about the location of unauthorised copies or infringing files. As mentioned before, file-hosters for instance do no provide a search function for the materials stored on their servers. Thus, users will either directly access pertinent link directories or, and this is probably the most easy way or a good starting point, conduct a search via a search engine to find out on which link directory or indexing site information about the location of a requested file is stored. Considering the amount of data on the World Wide Web, search engines are essential to find information.[2539] The effective use of the Internet is only guaranteed when search engines facilitate access to content. It has been said that for information to exist on the Internet, it has to be indexed by a search engine.[2540] Online content that cannot be found via a search engine is factual non-existent for the general public. Users depend in general on search engine technology to be able to find and access information.[2541] By blocking certain search results, the blocked information

---

2538 *Ibid.*

2539 Cf. Wolfgang Schulz/Thorsten Held/Arne Laudien, *Search engines as gatekeepers of public communication: Analysis of the German framework applicable to Internet search engines including Media Law and Anti-trust Law,* German Law Journal 2005, 1419–1432.

2540 See Lucas D. Introna/Helen Nissenbaum, *Shaping the Web: Why the politics of search engine matters*, The Information Society 2000, Vol. 16, 169, 171.

2541 See Inka Frederike Brunn, *Cache Me if You Can* (2012), pp. 189 et seq. with further references. Therefore one may argue that there is a common interest to

becomes "less visible" and basically vanishes in the Deep Web, the "unindexed … terrain of the Internet".[2542] Search engines are critical chokepoints acting as the link between readers and information by making information accessible.[2543] In addition to facilitating access to online content, search engines also have an influence on which content is received.[2544]

In 2004, a German research study has found that 74% of German Internet users rely on search engines as their primary tool to find information on the web.[2545] The approach to require Google and co. to refrain from displaying certain search results also seems to be in compliance with the reasonableness requirement.[2546] It does neither require host providers to search the notorious websites themselves, nor conduct searches via search

---

guarantee the overall functioning of search engines, cf. LG Frankfurt, NJW-RR 2002, 545, 546.

2542 See Emily Laidlaw, *Internet gatekeepers, human rights and corporate social responsibilities* (2012), p. 165.

2543 Emily Laidlaw, *Internet gatekeepers, human rights and corporate social responsibilities* (2012), p. 166; for search engines as gatekeepers see also Wolfgang Schulz/Thorsten Held/Arne Laudien, *Suchmaschine als Gatekeeper*, pp. 13 et seq. with further references.

2544 Inka Frederike Brunn, *Cache Me if You Can* (2012), pp. 190 et seq. The selective and prioritised presentation of content has some influence on media consumption by the users (see Burkhard Danckert/Frank Joachim Mayer, *Die vorherrschende Meinungsmacht von Google – Bedrohung durch einen Informationsmonopolisten?,* MultiMedia und Recht 2010, 219). Hence, search engines do not only provide access to information; in providing access, they also have an editorial and selective role (Inka Frederike Brunn, *Cache Me if You Can* (2012), p. 191). One may thus pose the question whether search results are expressions by the search engine provider. As a consequence, there would also be an interference with the search engine provider's freedom of expression. This question may in particular arise with regard to autocomplete functions, where the search engine suggests further search terms in connection to the search the user has started, for instance if a user searches for a song and the search engine autocompletes this search with "bitTorrent". It is difficult to see, how programming of algorithms that autocomplete searches with popular search terms or influence page ranking could be considered as expression of opinion by the search engine provider.

2545 Birgit van Eimeren/Heinz Gerhard/Beate Frees, *ARD/ZDF-Online-Studie 2004, Internetverbreitung in Deutschland: Potenzial vorerst ausgeschöpft?,* Media Perspektiven 2004, No. 8, 350, 355.

2546 As regards the measures being reasonable for search engines see above B. IV. 2. c) Limits of Notice and Take down and the Shift to Content Blocking by Search Engines.

engines for infringing content. Further, search engines are likely to comply with the requests/injunctions as their service usually falls within national jurisdiction.[2547] In contrast, notorious services are commonly located abroad, operators hide identities, and no point of contact is provided in order to not be bothered with legal obligations.

Finally, the German case-law shows that courts can also be rather creative in constructing monitoring duties of services that are already trying to comply with domestic laws as they have an economic interest to conduct business within national jurisdiction. Nevertheless the courts have construed far-reaching duties that they consider to be still permissible under the *E-Commerce Directive* as specific monitoring duties although they extent to a systematic filtering of all data passing through their service. In doing so, the German judges unfortunately revealed a lack of understanding of technology by demanding the (rather) impossible. Extensive filtering is being justified by way of a neutrality test that allows for far-reaching duties if the provider has an active role in relation to the copyright infringements. The filtering in question however blurs the lines between specific and general monitoring; this is something that must be avoided. In France, this led to the discussion of whether another category of provider needs to be introduced that is something in-between content and a host provider – a category that also seems to be favoured by the Federal Court of Justice in Germany, when it requires more extensive filtering from file-hosters than ordinary host providers. It is urgently required that the CJEU specifies the guidance given in the *SABAM* cases, in order to provide for a uniform interpretation of the relevant EU Directives and an approach that considers the fundamental rights of all actors involved.

2547 With regard to Google and Spanish jurisdiction see CJEU, C-131/12, *Google Spain and Google Inc v Agencia Española de Protección de Datos (AEPD)*, Judgment of 13.05.2014.

General Conclusions

The above analysis of different copyright enforcement schemes has shown that the adaption of existing copyright enforcement systems to the 21st century proves difficult. However, equally difficult is the drafting of new enforcement legislation. Some of the very recent legislation that has been subject to this research shows blindness to the limits on these laws' ability to exercise control over Internet users. Similarly, the application of traditional copyright regimes is characterised by a result-oriented approach that too often expresses a lack of understanding of technology.

Graduated response schemes that were deemed to be the silver bullet against copyright infringements, do not seem to be as successful as predicted. While the French model is currently under revision for being too expensive in light of the results achieved, the UK scheme makes little progress in its implementation. The legal analysis has proven that the UK is well advised to refrain from implementing the current draft as it fails to strike a fair balance between the interests of copyright owners on the one hand and Internet access providers and Internet users on the other hand – irrespective of whether the final sanction would mean a suspension or limitation of Internet access. As regards the latter, this research has proven that interferences with Internet access constitute an unjustifiable violation of Internet users' right to seek, receive and impart information and opinions.

In contrast to the graduated response schemes, civil enforcement against users does not put any burdens on access providers, but is prone to abuse when scare tactics are used to achieve compliance.

The analysis has shown that the weakness of user-targeted sanctions is the difficulty to identify the actual infringer. With action being targeted against potential non-infringers, it is difficult to respect the principle of proportionality, and to achieve that enforcement is perceived as fair and just.

Hence, it is not surprising that rights-holders are returning to third parties to enforce their intellectual property rights. While in the early days of the Internet, legal action was directed against the innovators, there has now been a shift to online intermediaries. Online intermediaries, no matter whether access providers, host providers or search engines are considered as gatekeepers and as such to be in a position to not only regulate user behaviour but also to limit access to infringing materials. In this regard, issues arise in relation to the scope of monitoring and blocking that can be legitimately required. In this respect, the focus must not be solely on what is technologically feasible; attention must be paid to the capacities of the service provider concerned because otherwise the operation of legitimate and innovative services is at risk.

This being said, the following final conclusions recapitulate some of the main problems identified by this research before the prospects of copyright enforcement are addressed.

A. Problems Encountered in Copyright Enforcement

I. Copyright Enforcement on the Internet is a Struggle to Find the Right Target

As has been shown in this research, there is no uniform approach to enforce copyright online. Although national enforcement is based on European law, the fact that the area of enforcement is regulated by Directives leaves room for different interpretations and determinations of enforcement. Thus, though similar, national approaches to copyright enforcement on the Internet vary. A common tendency throughout the EU Member States presented in this work is the targeting of online intermediaries. The reason for this has been addressed in various contexts and in simple terms is the response to the struggle to find an identifiable, locatable defendant that is also located within jurisdiction of the place of damage. In the early days of the Internet, innovators of technology were considered ideal targets that also fulfil the above criteria. For this very reason, for instance Napster was shut-down. However, suing the innovators had its limits where the involvement of the innovators in the actual infringing act diminished and their contribution did not go beyond the mere provision of technology. The example addressed in the first Chapter in this context is peer-to-peer file-sharing. With technological progress, the central server that was Napster's fate disappeared and was replaced by a centralised system with no central server. Without any involvement of the innovators of the technology in the actual act of sharing and infringing copyright, and no incitement of the innovators of peer-to-peer clients, the easy identifiable and locatable actor was gone.

Thus, new targets were searched for and quickly identified. With users being uploaders and downloaders in peer-to-peer file-sharing networks, and technology providing information about the user from which a file was being obtained, rights-holders could identify infringers by joining the network. However, what they were left with was the IP address of the infringer and nothing more. While the IP address allows for identification of the Internet access service provider and thus, the general location, and hence jurisdiction, of an infringer, it does not give any information about the identity of an actual infringer. Further information rights were necessary to sue users. This did however not solve the issue of whether the subscriber of an Internet access service is the right target. A subscriber must not necessarily be the actual infringer. While German courts succeeded in constructing a liability regime by analogy to a public law institute of liability for a source of danger, other jurisdictions struggled to establish such liability. Thus, new legislation was drafted to allow action against Internet access subscribers.[2548] In parallel, alternative targets for action were identified in the services that facilitate the infringements by providing the technology for sharing files. While courts in Germany are considering the contribution of access providers too minimal to allow action against them, rights-holders in the UK have successfully obtained injunctions against access providers to block access to indexing sites. The effect is, however, minimal: Like a hydra, with every website cut off, new sites appear, making it difficult to take legal action with efficient results. With news forms of file-sharing such as via file-hosting services or new forms of media consumption such as streaming, host providers have also been identified as attractive targets. As legal action against host providers only produces effective results when the host providers fulfil the aforementioned criteria of identifiable, locatable and complying with obligations and injunctions , new targets for legal action were identified in search engine providers. With search engines being the navigators through the vastness of Cyberspace, they are essentially *the* gatekeepers to information. With the quasi-monopoly of Google, it also becomes easy to identify a promising target. Although this means that the visibility instead of the existence of infringing copies disappears, it may have some temporary impact on users – until the next search engine appears or information is passed on within the community of Internet users about the location of the desired content.

2548 For instance the French *Loi HADOPI* and the *UK Digital Economy Act 2010*.

II. Copyright Enforcement on the Internet Puts Disproportionate Weight on Intellectual Property Rights

The research has shown that some copyright enforcement mechanisms in an Internet context put a disproportionate weight on intellectual property rights. They thereby not only trigger the feeling of consumers that they are under constant surveillance, but also put businesses at risk and interfere disproportionately with fundamental rights. They further target non-infringers by construing responsibility by the provision of an Internet service, i.e. hosting and providing access to the Internet.

When in the analogue world, people made copies of records that they had purchased for their friends, there was hardly a way that this came to the attention of the record companies. The same applied to movies recorded from TV. At that time, rights-holders concentrated their legal action against the inventors of technology.

Whether they would have gone after users for making a copy of a TV screening is hard to imagine. One may argue that consumers today do nothing else than they did before, they make copies of their mp3s or CDs for their friends, and they "record" TV programme on their hard drives. However, what has changed is that instead of handing over the copies from one-to-one, they distribute it one-to-many and also obtain data that way. They do it because technology allows them to do it. As regards the distribution and acquisition of media via peer-to-peer file-sharing, the only way to try to effectively put an end to file-sharing – besides educating consumers – would be the surveillance of all file-sharing networks. This is something that is just not possible. Although the activities of specialised companies that join networks to harvest IP addresses of infringers, is often perceived by users as general surveillance, this is actually not true. This research has shown that the "IP harvesting" is legitimate if it is limited to identify infringers of certain works and in order to prepare civil proceedings. However, already at this point, one may question this behaviour, because every download comes along with an upload, meaning that the rights-holders themselves become distributors if they have not deactivated this function. If one looks at other ways to distribute copyrighted materials without authorisation, such as file-hosting services or streaming sites, it becomes even more obvious that user-targeted action would require surveillance of everybody's communication as there is no way to separate private communication from copyright infringements without checking the content of the data transmitted. This would mean that privacy of communication would no longer exist. The access blocking by access providers in the UK already goes into that direction by requiring all communication to be filtered – although the technology used is highly sophisticated in order not to violate fundamental rights (see Third Chapter B. III.).

A disproportionate shifting of weight on copyright protection can clearly be witnessed when host providers are required to not only block certain materials but also monitor third party websites for infringements (cf. Third Chapter B. IV 1). This basically means that they would either have to monitor the "whole" World Wide Web or implement a blocking policy that would block access to all materials that can be linked to the content in question on their servers. The incentive to over-block, i.e. also block access to legitimate private back-up copies or materials with the same file name, and thereby comply with monitoring duties is rather high. It thus, does not come as a surprise that the formerly globally largest file-hosting service Rapidshare saw a massive decline in user numbers.[2549] Although the legitimacy of the service provided was confirmed by German courts, the burden put upon the provider to prevent future identical infringements is putting the business model at risk. Even though Rapidshare changed its focus on cloud storage services for businesses, the formerly pioneering and flourishing service provider ultimately shut down ist service in March 2015 .[2550]

Over-blocking is also a serious matter when access providers are obliged to block access to piracy websites, with UK courts granting orders once they are satisfied that the website to be blocked is "so involved in the commission of the tort as to make the infringing act their own"[2551] and "it appears to be quite hard to find any content… that is not protected by

2549 As of June 2014, only 2.7% of Rapidshare users were located in Germany, its overall global rank is dropping since 2010 with a remarkable decline by the end of 2012 following the implementation of anti-piracy measures such as reduction of download speed for non-premium users and a limitation on the amount of outbound public traffic that could be generated by a single user, see Enigmax, *Rapidshare: Traffic and piracy dipped after new business model kicked in,* TorrentFreak (09.01.2013).

2550 The shut-down followed an announcement on RapidShare's website in February 2015 that it would shut down ist service permanently. See also Simon Gröflin, *RapidShare ohne Führung und Angestellte*, PC Tipp (25.02.2014).

2551 Court of Appeal, *SABAF SpA v MFI Furniture* [2003] RPC 14, para. 59.

copyright".[2552] Finding it hard to find legitimate content, does not mean that legitimate content does not exist. The case law that derives from the UK so far can however not be generalised as the cases were exceptional in the sense that the website operators were ignorant to any take-down requests or were not identifiable at all. They also did not challenge the blocking orders, presumably because they were well aware that they were facilitating access to unauthorised copies.

Beside enforcement models that provide for action against online intermediaries, enforcement schemes are discussed or implemented that allow action against subscribers of Internet access services. Subscribers are held responsible for infringements committed via their Internet connection. Sanctions may be imposed upon subscribers that would result in restricting their access to the Internet. This violates not only their right to freely seek, receive and impart information and opinions in an unjustifiable way, but also that of third parties using the same connection. Theoretically the download of only parts of three songs within a period of several months may trigger this sanction. Even when courts are required to assess the proportionality of such a sanction, it is difficult to foresee, in what circumstances a measure will be seen as disproportionate. At the same time, it is often unclear, what kind of security measures can be expected from a subscriber in relation to his Internet access. Although the warnings send out in France or the UK propose certain measures, it remains to be seen whether they will be considered sufficient by a court.[2553]In particular, it remains unclear, how a subscriber could comply with his obligation to ensure that no third parties commit infringements via his connection. Obviously, he will have to instruct third parties, but will he also have to monitor them? And to what extent? In this respect, privacy rights need to be observed as well as free speech which may be under serious threat if online behaviour is supervised. The situation becomes even more unclear, when a subscriber allows not only family members and flatmates to use his Internet access but also other third parties for instance in the course of his business. Consumers expect today that hotel owners, pub landlords, or café owners provide free Wi-Fi access to them. While in the UK most pubs

2552 High Court, *Twentieth Century Fox Film Corp v British Telecommunications Plc* [2011] EWHC 1981, para. 55.

2553 In contrast, German courts clarified that the security standard for Wi-Fi routers only has to comply with the technical standard at the time of purchase of the router.

offer Wi-Fi access, the situation is different in Germany, where landlords are under fear to be held liable for abusive use of their connection, in particular with regard to copyright infringements. With liability being unforeseeable, copyright indirectly prevails of the provision of communication services.[2554]

III. Copyright Enforcement Discourages Innovation and Creativity

Referring to what has just been stated above, Wi-Fi access points are a risky matter as long as it is uncertain whether the service providers will be held liable. Innovative projects of providing Wi-Fi access (such as HOTCITY in Luxembourg)[2555] to an ever increasing number of smartphone users that are frustrated by weak 3G/LTE coverage, slow speeds and service restrictions, are rarely implemented due to unclear responsibilities when the system is abused. Obviously, innovation is discouraged for the sake of copyright protection.

If one takes the example of the Lawrence Lessig lecture being blocked in YouTube[2556], one gets the impression that copyright protection sometimes goes further than it was originally intended. The need to protect creators is undeniable, but it may be necessary to focus rather on the core idea of copyright as an incentive to create and secure income, which is not harmed by such activities.[2557]

2554 It remains to be seen, whether the eagerly awaited decision of the CJEU in C-484/14 (*Tobias McFadden v Sony Music Entertainment Germany GmbH*) will provide legal certainty. The request for a preliminary ruling to the CJEU by the Landgericht München I seeks clarification as to whether the provider of an open Wi-Fi network, i.e. a free non-password-protected Wi-Fi, may be liable for third-party copyright infringements or whether said provider may be shielded from liability on the basis that he falls within the category of "mere conduit" provider under Art. 12 of the *E-Commerce Directive*.

2555 See www.hotcity.lu.

2556 See Introduction, D. The Research Topic: Copyright Infringement on the Internet.

2557 Chris Reed suggests in that context to reframe copyright infringement in terms of the "use" of works. Use of a protected work that amounts to commercial exploitation should amount to infringements, because it is commercial exploitation that secures a return for creators. See Chris Reed, *Making laws for Cyberspace (2012),* pp. 154 et seq. and 237 et seq.

It is also necessary to take into consideration that the availability of content on the Internet also triggers demand to use that content. For instance, in order to give directions to a locality, many users and businesses alike rely on Google Maps. However, those that have ever tried to obtain a licence from Google for a screenshot of a map, are faced with complicated terms of use and even the "Frequently Asked Questions" are of little help. Instead Google states that it cannot make judgements of fair use or dealing and advises users to consult a lawyer.[2558] At the same time, Google states that due to limited resources, they are not able to sign individual letters asking for licences.[2559] This triggers the question why rightsholders make it so difficult to obtain licences, while at the same time it is so easy to infringe copyright.

Beyond the issues discussed in this research, copyright enforcement also prevents or restricts user from being "prosumers" that publish their samples or voice-overs for instance on YouTube or post adapted images on their Facebook profile. Assuming that they do not commercially exploit copyrighted works, users are often left in a grey zone were they do not know whether their activities are still legitimate or not. While ignorance of the law is no defence, it is necessary to educate users about legitimate use.

IV. Copyright Enforcement on the Internet Targets End-Users Rather than Commercial Infringers

From the John Doe letters by RIAA in the US to graduated response schemes in the UK and France and cease and desist letters in Germany, these measures have in common that they target end-users. Although legal action is also pursued against commercial infringers, it is striking that the principal legislative projects target users. At times, there seems to be capitulation when it comes to enforcement against commercial infringers. Only lately, for instance the blocking injunctions in the UK, enforcement is addressing those that benefit commercially from the infringements. Although previously, some services have also been prominently shut-

2558 See http://www.google.de/intl/de/permissions/geoguidelines.html (last accessed on 06.06.2014).

2559 *Ibid.*

down, for example the streaming portal kino.to,[2560] quantitatively the end-user was the focus of legal action. For a substantial number of users, it is difficult to tell what constitutes legitimate use and what not. Streaming websites may provide content that is not evidently illegal. Infringing services may not always be as easy to distinguish from piracy services as it was the case with kino.to. Most prominently users have been threatened with lawsuits were it was not even established that the streams were infringing copyright. While the user is the direct infringer, the saying that "opportunity makes a thief" is truer than ever in Cyberspace. With availability creating demand, users are tempted to download or consume works that are not yet, or not at all, available in their region. This shall not trivialise that copyright is infringed on a large scale, but highlight that not all infringements are committed in bad faith or are actually replacing sale. At the same time, as has been outlined on a few occasions, piracy services are not particularly reliable to use. Content may be defected, be infected with viruses, be slowly transmitted and numerous advertisement windows pop-up in the process of getting information about the content and downloading it. In order to obtain information about the availability and location of desired content, indexing sites and link directories need to be consulted. These are rarely run by volunteers, but by service providers that generate revenues by having advertisements placed on these sites. Thus, someone is "cashing in" on what is supposed to support creators. Further, with services like Rapidshare having to almost shut-down due to legal obligations although trying their best to comply with the law, new services emerge where the operators are hardly identifiable, locatable or willing to comply with legal obligations. These providers do not run their service out of altruistic reasons but to generate profit. In most cases profit is generated through advertisements or premium services.[2561] The question arises, whether it should not rather be the commercial providers that generate profits that should be the focus of legal action.[2562] Similar thoughts are also brought forward when it comes to the fight against illegal substances, where the focus is today on those dealing with drugs instead of the con-

2560 See Ole Reißmann, *Geschäft mit Raubkopien: Wie kino.to Millionen verdiente,* Der Spiegel Online (14.06.2012).

2561 See below B. III. A Promising Alternative: Follow the Money.

2562 Cf. Bart Cammaerts/Robin Mansell/Bingchun Meng, *Copyright & Creation, A case for promoting inclusive online sharing* (September 2013), London School of Economics and Political Science, Media Policy Brief 9, p. 14.

sumers (who typically equally commit a criminal offence by possessing the substance). On an international level, legislation for instance against money laundering aims at combatting the drug trade. Whether addressing the revenue streams of piracy sites is more promising than investing vast resources in the warning or sanctioning of users will be briefly addressed below.

V. No Evidence of Effectiveness of Current Initiatives

There is hardly any obust and reliable evidence on the effects of graduated response schemes or other anti-piracy measures. In fact, it appears that there is no evidence that a causal link exists between current enforcement and reduced infringement.[2563] The creative industries tend to oversell achievements. Moreover, we are left with the question whether current copyright enforcement measures help to achieve any of the underlying aims of copyright law.

Do current regimes establish an incentive to create? Do current regimes have an effect on sales? Would sales be declining without a graduated response scheme being in force? More specifically, what effect do warnings have on infringers? In that context, it would be interesting to know whether they migrate to other services where they are more difficult to track. In France, for instance, there is a persistent high number of first warnings, while the number of second warnings is low. This does however not mean that the graduated response is effective. The second warning only follows if a subscriber's IP address is detected for a second time within a period of six months following the first warning.[2564] Thus, some Internet access subscribers may have received several first warnings. Thus, it is difficult to determine whether the warning has an effect on user behaviour; taking the high number of first warnings and the considerably low number of second warnings in consideration, one may also conclude that warnings have an effect on those that have received a warning but not on users in general.

2563 As regards graduated response schemes and a lack of evidence on its impact on a reduction of infringements see Rebecca Giblin, *Evaluating graduated response,* Columbia Journal of Law & the Arts 2014, Vol. 37 No. 2, pp. 147 et seq.

2564 Article L.331-25 para. 2 *CPI.*

In addition, it has not been established whether reduced infringement increases legitimate sales. Little regard is paid as to whether we have a change in consumption of music, and whether declining sales are the result of that change in consumption. With new legitimate streaming services entering the market, we are likely to see a shift towards consuming rather than possessing. This may apply in particular against the background that web-enabled devices are omnipresent. Considering that streaming does not count as sale even if money is being paid for the service, a substantial number of uses of copyrighted works does not appear in the sales statistics.

Ultimately, it will also be necessary to reconsider how effectiveness is to be measured: considering the underlying aims of copyright, this should be a decrease in sharing unauthorised copies and an increase in assessing legal content.

VI. Access Blocking is Playing Cat and Mouse

It has repeatedly been addressed that copyright enforcement has its limits at national borders – even within the European Union. In the third Chapter, it has been shown that this also applies to access blocking. Nevertheless, in particular the UK employs access blocking to respond to copyright infringements where they lack an identifiable, locatable defendant, or that defendant does not respond to take down requests or orders to cease an infringement. Access blocking is however playing cat and mouse in light of the many circumvention methods available. Already in the early 1990s, the computer scientist and civil libertarian John Gilmore concluded in the context of blocking access to unwanted materials on Usenet that "the Net interprets censorship as damage and routes around it".[2565] There will always be a way to circumvent blocking and it needs to be accepted as a fact that eventually blocking may only delay access.

In particular the blocking of access to indexing sites and link directories are phyrric victories as the operator will just migrate his service to another web address. Nevertheless the increased use of section 97A *CDPA 1998*

2565 According to John Gilmore this conclusion was quoted by Philip Elmer-DeWitt in his article *First Nation in Cyberspace* in the Time Magazine of 06.12.1993. See John Gilmore's homepage at http://www.toad.com/gnu/ (last accessed on 30.09.2014).

injunctions in the UK indicates that rights-holders consider this mechanism as a feasible means. To some regard this consideration is true, for instance when the service provider does not change its IP address or domain name. It is generally assumed that although circumvention does not require distinguished IT literacy, not all users will try to circumvent the blocking. Accordingly, access blocking is commonly justified on the basis that the enforcement measure must only achieve a reduction of the scale of infringements and may as such also raise awareness of the illegality of the blocked content or service [see Third Chapter B. III. 3. E]). In this context, it must be noted that access blocking that avoids over-blocking is a costly matter. Where access providers do not employ an access blocking system in a different context, most likely in relation to child pornography, a blocking obligation may constitute a "complicated, costly, permanent computer system" at the expense of the service provider". It may also fail to strike a fair balance between the interests of the access provider and copyright holders involved.[2566]

B. Prospects

Beyond the findings above and the concluding summaries in the second Chapter (B. II. 3. and B. III. 3.) and the third Chapter (B. III. 3. and B. IV. 3.), there is also a need to refer to some general observations that may also provide some perspective for the future of online copyright infringement.

I. The German Cease and Desist Letter Regime: Not so Bad as it May Seem

The German system of cease and desist letters, the so-called *Abmahnungen*, has been analysed in great detail in the second Chapter (B. II. 1.). In this context, also the deficits of the system have been highlighted such as the perceived "abusive" use of warning letters (B. II. 1. c) to d)). However, the core of the system, namely the warning of potential infringers at their very own cost, is not unfair. In contrast to the graduated response scheme, no cost and effort of third parties is required in the administration and

2566 Cf. CJEU, C-70/10 *Scarlet Extended v SABAM*, Judgment of 14.11.2011, ECR I-11959, paras. 48 et seq.

issuing of the letters before claim. The letters intend to notify a subscriber that an infringement has been committed via his Internet access. If the subscriber has not himself committed the infringement, he will not be liable for damages. If he has not secured his Internet access adequately, or shares his connection with others that may have committed the infringement, he will only be liable to cease and desist. In both cases, he will also have to carry the costs of the cease and desist letter. The main drawback of this system has been that the letters are drafted in a way as to suggest liability for damages, and demanded relatively high damages and consequently high lawyer's fees. In a response to the perceived abusive use, the legislator reformed the law with the intent to put an end to disproportionately high claims and the fact that the letters were turned in a profitable tool (See Second Chapter B. III. 1. d)). The core of the letters has to be the cessation of an infringement and not being a separate instrument to generate revenues. If it can be guaranteed that rights-holders do not carry any further costs and the recipients of the letters, which can hardly be proven guilty as direct infringers, do not face excessive costs, the cease and desist letter may well be a reasonable means to limit copyright infringements. It does not only have a deterrent effect on the recipient himself, but also a dissuasive effect on other users. By abolishing the side-effect that *Abmahnungen* can be profitable in themselves, a decline in the number of *Abmahnungen* could recently be witnessed. Although there are no statistics on *Abmahnungen* in general, and on a decline since the latest legal reform in particular, German lawyers reported at an annual conference on law and informatics that they have experienced a decline in clients seeking advice on *Abmahnung*en.[2567] Thus, rights-holders seem to limit the initiation of the enforcement mechanism to cases where they have a real interest in protecting their rights. The time where rights-holders in porn movies could generate substantial income by sending out thousands of *Abmahnungen* seem to be gone. It remains to be seen, whether rights-holders will now use their capacities to concentrate on commercial infringers, which are more difficult to get hold of than end-users.

2567 There are no official statistics, understandably no law firm publishes such figures. However, within personal conversation, the author was told that the decline in clients that are alleged of online copyright infringements is remarkable. A small law firm that is specialised in advising clients on *Abmahnungen* reported of a decline of 100 mandates per month on average solely relating to *Abmahnungen* for copyright infringements on the Internet.

II. Search Engines as Law Enforcement Officers: Limiting Visibility of Illegal Materials

In the third Chapter, it has been shown that online intermediaries such as Internet access providers and host providers are crucial in the production and distribution of cultural goods, as well as in the enforcement of copyright. In addition, search engine providers have been identified as important chokepoints that have the potential to play a role in copyright enforcement. Considering the amount of data on the World Wide Web, search engines are vital to find and access information.[2568] Content that is not indexed by a search engine, is factual non-inexistent.[2569] Users depend in general on search engine technology to be able to find and access information and this makes the basically vanishes in the Deep Web, the "unindexed ... terrain of the Internet".[2570] Considering that there are also only few actors on the scene, turning to search engines to combat copyright infringements gains even more attractiveness. In addition, search engines are likely to comply with blocking requests or injunctions, because their service usually falls within national jurisdiction.[2571]

However, one also has to consider in this regard, that in particular Google has a quasi-monopoly role in many States.[2572] Against this background, Google is almost taking over a governmental role if it becomes THE gatekeeper to information. When gatekeepers like Google are turned into auxiliary policemen acting on behalf and upon notification of the rights-holders, this needs to be carefully watched. It will be necessary to provide clear rules when and under which circumstances results may be

---

2568 Cf. Wolfgang Schulz/Thorsten Held/Arne Laudien, *Search engines as gatekeepers of public communication: Analysis of the German framework applicable to Internet search engines including Media Law and Anti-trust Law,* German Law Journal 2005, 1419–1432.

2569 See Lucas D. Introna/Helen Nissenbaum, *Shaping the Web: Why the politics of search engine matters,* The Information Society 2000, Vol. 16, 169, 171.

2570 See Emily Laidlaw, *Internet gatekeepers, human rights and corporate social responsibilities* (2012), p. 165.

2571 With regard to Google and Spanish jurisdiction see CJEU, C-131/12, *Google Spain and Google Inc v Agencia Española de Protección de Datos (AEPD),* Judgment of 13.05.2014.

2572 The European Commission is for instance conduction antitrust investigations on online search against Google. See European Commission, *Antitrust: Commission obtains from Google comparable display of specialised search rivals,* Press release of 05.02.2014.

blogged and what evidence needs to be provided by the requesting party. In this regard, one may introduce a system of notification and counter-notification as required by § 512 (g) of the *US DMCA* (see First Chapter, A. I. 2. a) aa)). Also, there must be a right to appeal de-listing, considering that the removal from search results could ruin legitimate businesses if they can no longer be found in the World Wide Web.

III. A Promising Alternative: Follow the Money

Both, the UK Hargreaves Report[2573] as well as the Lescure Report in France[2574], suggest as an alternative means the aforementioned "follow the money" approach.[2575] This approach has also been part of the US SOPA and PIPA Bills that have been outlined in the Introduction. The advantage of addressing payment and advertisement services is that they may be, and often are, physically located in the US or Europe.

Undeniably, major sectors like the online advertising industry could make it considerably harder for the operators of piracy sites to unfairly take revenues away from the creative industries. In fact, research has shown that pirate websites, i.e. websites that either provide access to copyright-infringing content or information about the location of such content, are most commonly funded in part or in combination by either advertising or payments (including subscriptions, donations, and transactions).[2576] Where operators of pirate websites rely on payment collection, in most

---

2573 Ian Hargreaves, *Digital Opportunity, A Review of Intellectual Property and Growth* (2011), 10 key recommendations.

2574 Pierre Lescure, *Culture-acte 2, Mission « Acte II de l'exception culturelle », Contribution aux politiques culturelles à l'ére numérique* (May 2013), pp. 413 et seq.

2575 In Germany, this approach has also been suggested by scholars in the context of illegal online gambling websites, see Matthias Steegmann, *Die Haftung der Basisinfrastruktur bei rechtswidrigen Internetangeboten* (2010), pp. 207 – 218.

2576 See Google/PRS for Music/BAE Systems Detica, *The six business models for copyright infringement* (27.06.2012). Relying on data provided by the Google Transparency Report (see http://www.google.com/transparencyreport/removals/copyright/domains/?r=last-year (last accessed on 05.05.2014)), research by the University of Southern California evidenced that "in the last five years, a large number of new advertising networks now service the seemingly infinite advertising inventory of the broadband era [and that] much of that inventory sits on more than 150,000 pirate entertainment sites". See Jonathan Taplin and Others,

cases card processors or other electronic payment processors such as PayPal are used for payment collection.[2577]

Advertising plays a key role in commercial online piracy. Fact is that many pirate websites make large amounts of money from advertiser because millions of users visit their website every month. Considering that those users often have the age profile that web advertisers are keen to reach and that they are often forced to look at advertisements first before they can access the desired materials, these websites constitute an interesting market for online advertising networks. Also, advertisements are regularly the only possibility for the operators of these websites to generate revenues.

It has been reported that one British website[2578] that linked to pirate content generated GBP 35,000 per month from on-site advertisements before its owner was imprisoned.[2579] The Pirate Bay pre-trial investigation revealed email correspondence between the founders of the Pirate Bay and their "ad man" confirming that the website was profitable from 2005 onwards with a monthly turnover of SEK 30,000 to 40,000[2580].[2581] While this was prior The Pirate Bay engaging seriously in the field of advertisements, mails from The Pirate Bay revealed ahead to its founders' trial showed it was offered GBP 65,000 per month to run online gambling advertisements alone.[2582] In so far as advertisements are concerned, for instance the German website heftig.co,[2583] which is only directed at a Ger-

---

Advertising transparency report, monthly updates are available at http://www.annenberglab.com/projects/ad-piracy-report-0 (last accessed on 06.06.2014).

2577 *Ibid.*

2578 I.e. Surfthechannel.

2579 Charles Arthur/Stuart Dredge, *Google ads to be blocked from sites offering pirated content*, The Guardian (16.07.2013).

2580 This corresponds to approximately EUR 3,400 – 4,500. The cost of internet lines, server-hosting etc. was less, making The Pirate Bay profitable. See Helienne Lindvall, *Piracy sites are raking in ad money from some of the World's biggest brands*, Business Insider (05.02.2013).

2581 *Ibid.*

2582 *Ibid.*

2583 As of June 2014, heftig.co was ranked as the 84th most popular website in Germany. See the page ranking by Alexa at http://www.alexa.com/siteinfo/heftig.co (last accessed on 06.06.2014). As of June 2006, the website also had more than 800.000 Facebook fans and as of July 2015, it had acquired more than 1.5 million fans.

man-speaking audience, generated estimated 6 digit figures profits from advertisements.[2584]

The bigger the websites are and the more infrastructures are needed to operate them, the operators more or less depend on advertisement as a revenue source because it means that they will not have to charge their customers. Although popular portals like for instance Megaupload also set up merchant accounts with payment providers to process payments from customers, numerous sites refrain because they attract users that would anyway be unwilling to pay. Also, many operators may want to receive as little information as possible about their users to avoid being confronted with information requests.

Many top advertising networks place advertisements on websites that feature pirated content. The University of Southern California's Annenberg Innovation Lab for instance ranked Google and Yahoo among the top 10 advertising networks that actually support major piracy sites around the world, based on the lab's analysis of online advertisements that receive the most copyright infringement notices.[2585] Google itself lists in its Transpareny Report internet sites that receive the most take-down notices from the creative industries to remove copyrighted works.[2586] Software by the Annenberg Innovation Lab obtained the name of the ad network once an ad appeared on of pirate sites that had been identified as leading by Google. Although Google believes that the extent by which Google ads are a major source of funds for major pirate sites is mistaken by the USC lab, further studies, such as for instance a UK study by Google and the Performing Rights Society for Music in Britain with research conducted

---

2584 Lars Wienand, *Das ist heftig: Die Viralseiten-Macher und ihr Verhältnis zu Urheberrechten*, Rhein-Zeitung (27.05.2014).

2585 From January 2013 to May 2013 the Innovation lab published on its website a monthly report on online advertisements which aims to raise awareness of major brands which ad networks put ads on pirate sites so that they could avoid these networks, *see* Jonathan Taplin and Others, *Advertising transparency report*, http://www.annenberglab.com/projects/ad-piracy-report-0 (last accessed on 06.06.2014). See also Dawn C. Chmielewski, *Report links Google, Yahoo to Internet piracy sites*, LA Times (02.01.2013).

2586 For the weekly updated Google Transparency Report, see http://www.google.com/transparencyreport/removals/ copyright/domains/?r =last-year (last accessed on 05.05.2014).

by BAE Systems Detica,[2587] suggest that most of the financing for piracy sites is related to advertising.[2588] In fact, the UK study found that 86% of the financing of peer-to-peer communities and 67% of the financing of live TV Gateways (streaming)[2589] is provided by advertising.[2590]

While the Annenberg Innovation Lab intends to make major brands aware which advertising networks put ads on websites that they have identified as piracy websites, the British music industry body BPI is working with the UK Internet Advertising Bureau on a scheme that will involve a central database of piracy sites for ad networks, agencies and brands to consult in order to avoid advertisements on these sites.[2591] The latter is a welcomed policy with regard to limiting revenues from advertisements. However, it is unlikely to be sufficient to "dry out" piracy providers.

Requiring third parties to cease providing services to an "infringing" site had already been tested in practice and proved partly successful in the case of WikiLeaks. WikiLeaks as such could not be stopped from providing access to leaked secret dossiers when it moved its content to a Swedish storage provider, but WikiLeaks suffered a severe loss in revenue when payment system providers stopped servicing WikiLeaks.[2592]

Against this background, it must be evaluated how revenue streams could be cut off legitimately, in particular with regard to the extra-territorial effect of such measures. In this regard one could think about creating a legal basis for court orders requiring advertisement providers to refrain from placing advertisement on certain platforms. In relation to payment

---

2587 Google/PRS for Music/BAE Systems Detica, *The six business models for copyright infringement* (27.06.2012).

2588 See also Dawn C. Chmielewski, *Report links Google, Yahoo to Internet piracy sites*, LA Times (02.01.2013).

2589 The study describes Live TV Gateways as websites that predominantly offer links to streams of livefree-to-air and pay TV. They typically also provide links to downloads with content being centrally hosted (as opposed to peer-to-peer networks) in a different location from the site. Google/PRS for Music/BAE Systems Detica, *The six business models for copyright infringement* (27.06.2012), p. 5.

2590 *Ibid*, pp. 3 and 11.

2591 Cf. Charles Arthur/Stuart Dredge, *Google Ads to be blocked from sites offering pirated content*, The Guardian (16.07.2013).

2592 For a summary of the events leading to WikiLeaks moving its content to Sweden and the denial of service by payment services see Yochai Benkler, *WikiLeaks and the PROTECT-IP Act: A new public-private threat to the Internet Commons*, Daedalus 2011, Vol. 140 Issue 4, 154, 156 et seq.

providers, a criminal law provision could be considered that would allow for the blocking of money processing or freeze payments in order to render the operation of a piracy website unattractive.

IV. In Parallel: Protecting Copyright and Users

Within this work, it has become obvious that copyright enforcement must not only protect copyright but also pay regard to the rights and interests of users that are affected by enforcement. What must be avoided is over-regulation of activities which do not prejudice the central objective of copyright – the provision of incentives to creators. Thus, it will be necessary to clear up outdated rules, such as existing laws on format shifting which mean that it is illegal to download a CD on to an mp3 player;[2593] ensure that there is a private copying exception[2594] and clarify the (il)legality of streaming. The legislators must be called upon to adapt legislation to the altered distribution environment.[2595]

In the following two specific aspects will be addressed that are essential for the promotion of copyright, namely that it should be made easier for people who want to try new business models to do so legally by making it easier for them to acquire the rights to the content that they don't have.[2596] At the same time, the education of users and the promotion of legitimate offers should have a priority on the policy agenda.

2593 Ian Hargreaves, *Digital Opportunity, A Review of Intellectual Property and Growth* (2011), Recommendation 5, p. 99.

2594 This has not only been demanded by Ian Hargreaves in *ibid*, but also by Pierre Lescure in his report, see Pierre Lescure, *Culture-acte 2, Mission « Acte II de l'exception culturelle », Contribution aux politiques culturelles à l'ère numérique* (May 2013), pp. 352 et seq.

2595 Cf. James Griffin, *Copyright evolution – creation, regulation and the decline of substantively rational copyright law,* Intellectual Property Quarterly 2013, 234, 252.

2596 Ian Hargreaves, *Digital Opportunity, A Review of Intellectual Property and Growth* (2011), pp. 3 et seq.

1. In Specific: Remove Obstacles to the Provision of Cross-Border Digital Content Services

As regards the consumption of music, a transition is taking place in younger generations from an ownership to an access model of consuming music and radio, with younger generations buying and owning less CDs and instead accessing music on services like Youtube, Spotify and Mixcloud.[2597] These legitimate services are also interested in solutions that make it easier for them to acquire licenses, preferably via a one-stop shop for Europe, as they have to compete with piracy.[2598] The principle of territoriality that applies to copyright as well as licensing practices means that often it is necessary to obtain separate licences for each territory. Evidently, this constitutes an obstacle to the provision of cross-border digital content services.[2599] It also leads to frustration by users, where popular and legitimate service provider block contents for certain territories.

Obstacles are clearly put in the way of legal platforms in so far as the licensing of content is concerned. Copyright-holders can choose between individual rights management, or collective management of their rights. The latter is mostly carried out by collective management organisation, i.e. collecting societies.[2600] The advantage for commercial users is that they can clear rights for a large number of works instead of negotiating with each individual rights-holder. Collecting societies however usually tend to be concerned with activities only within a particular territory.[2601] Opera-

2597 See Nico Perez, *New creative- and content-delivery services,* in: Ian Hargreaves/ Paul Hofheinz (eds.), *Intellectual property and innovation. A framework for 21st century growth and jobs,* p. 25.

2598 *Ibid.*

2599 Territorial licensing practices were also the subject of a case before the CJEU in 2012 that was widely discussed not only by legal scholars but also the general public. The Murphy case concerned the restriction of access by means of conditional access technology, in specific decoder cards, to Premier league broadcasts which were transmitted via satellite in various Member States. Premier league brought actions against a number of UK pubs using Greek pay-tv subscriptions to show live football matches, see CJEU, C-430/08, Football Association Premier League Ltd v QC Leisure and C-429/08, *Karen Murphy v Media Protection Services Limited*, Judgment of 04.10.2011.

2600 For a brief overview on collective licensing see Hector MacQueen/Charlotte Waelde/Graeme Laurie/Abbe Brown, *Contemporary Intellectual Property – Law and Policy* (2nd ed. 2011), pp. 935 et seq.

2601 *Ibid*, p. 938.

tion between territories only took place by means of reciprocal agreements. Due to negotiations pending or difficulties in acquiring licenses, legal offers often operate only within a certain jurisdiction and/or offer a limited catalogue of works. For licensing reasons, streams of TV broadcasts may be blocked for users outside the original broadcast area as it is the case with for example the BBC iPlayer for users outside the UK. The same applies for music streaming services, where the operators have not succeeded in obtaining multi-territorial licences. Spotify[2602] for instance had only been made available in Luxembourg in November 2012, a time at which it had already acquired the status of the second most used digital music platform after iTunes and an estimated 10% of the UK population using the service.[2603] Many collective management organisations today are not ready to cater the needs of services such as Spotify: they do not even have the capacity to process data from online service providers on music downloads and streaming, or to match this data with their repertoire.[2604]

The slow pace in expanding innovative business models was frustrating for users as well as rights-holders that want to obtain their fair share of revenues.

While on the one hand, legal services find it difficult to enter multiple markets, illegal offers that do not respect any rights at all, often provided a more attractive service. As long as collective management organisations are not ready to satisfy the needs of online service providers, namely the

2602 Spotify is a commercial music streaming service providing digital rights management-restricted content from many record labels. Spotify principally operates under the so-called "Freemium" model: basic services are free with advertisements, while more advanced, ad-free services need to be paid for.

2603 Adam Walder, *Popular music platform "Spotify" launches in Luxembourg*, Luxemburger Wort (13.11.2012). The press release in relation to the adoption by the European Parliament of a new directive directive on collective management of copyright and related rights and multi-territorial licensing explicitly mentions Luxembourg alongside Malta, Cyprus, Slovenia, Hungary, Estonia, Latvia, Lithuania, Bulgaria, Greece and Romania, as being a Member State where fewer music services are available to consumers. See European Commission, *Directive on collective management of copyright and related rights and multi-territorial licensing – frequently asked questions*, MEMO/14/79 of 04.02.2014, p. 4. As a consequence, there is also a risk of incorrect invoicing.

2604 European Commission, *Directive on collective management of copyright and related rights and multi-territorial licensing – frequently asked questions*, MEMO/14/79 of 04.02.2014, p. 4.

provision of their services within a multitude of territories covering a large catalogue of music, this situation was not going to change.[2605]

As early as 2004, it was therefore suggested that the existing regulation of collecting societies under competition law should be complemented by a legislative framework to tackle inter alia the above mentioned issues in order to achieve a genuine internal market for both the offline and online exploitation of intellectual property.[2606] The abstention from legislative action was not considered an option anymore, as soft law appeared to be not appropriate.[2607] Almost ten years on, on 4 February 2014, the EU Parliament finally adopted a directive on collective management of copyright and related rights and multi-territorial licensing.[2608] Legislation in this field had been proposed by the Commission after concerns had been raised in relation to the transparency, governance and the handling of revenues collected on behalf of rights-holders by some collective management organisations. The Commission also recognised that collective management of rights is important for the licensing of online service providers such as music download services and streaming services.[2609] Without a solution to these issues, it was feared that fewer music services would be available to

2605 See *ibid.*

2606 European Commission, *Communication from the Commission to the Council, the European Parliament and the European Economic and Social Committee, The Management of Copyright and Related Rights in the Internal Market,* COM(2004) 0261 final.

2607 *Ibid.*

2608 European Parliament, *Legislative resolution of 4 February 2014 on the proposal for a Directive of the European Parliament and of the Council on collective management of copyright and related rights and multi-territorial licensing of rights in musical works for online uses in the internal market* (COM[2012] 0372 – C7-0183/2012 – 2012/0180[COD]). For a critical analysis of the "proposal for a Directive of the European Parliament and of the Council on collective management of copyright and related rights and multi-territorial licensing of rights in musical works for online uses in the internal market" of 2012 see Josef Drexl/ Sylvie Nérisson/Felix Trumpke/Reto M. Hilty, *Comments of the Max Planck Institute for Intellectual Property and Competition Law on the Proposal for a Directive of the European Parliament and of the Council on collective management of copyright and related rights and multi-territorial licensing of rights in musical works for online uses in the internal market* COM (2012)372.

2609 See European Commission, *Directive on collective management of copyright and related rights and multi-territorial licensing – frequently asked questions,* MEMO/14/79 of 04.02.2014, p. 4, http://europa.eu/rapid/press-release_MEMO-14-79_en.pdf.

consumers across the EU, along with a slower uptake of innovative services and poor allocation of revenue to rights-holders.[2610] The new Directive thus intends to create conditions that can expand the legal offer of online music and also allows online content services to test new business models.[2611] As a first step to facilitate invoicing and administration of repertoires, Articles 23 et seq. of the Directive require collecting societies to set up proper databases to be able to keep better track of their own repertoire. In future, collect management societies shall function better and it will be easier for service providers to clear rights.[2612]

For users this will mean that they will have access to wider variety of content.[2613]At the same time, rights-holders shall exercise more control over collecting societies. Increased business opportunities and the aforementioned improvements in administering the rights shall ultimately result in increased revenue distributed to the creative industries and thereby also be an incentive to create.[2614] Because as of now, the Directive has only been adopted by the Parliament, it remains to be seen how the final provisions will be worded. However, the Directive constitutes a long-awaited and necessary step for the improvement of legal offers on the Internet – in particular, as there are many examples that users are also willing to pay for content. As could be witnessed with iTunes, users also accept payment models as long as they are easy to use and convenient. Though it is not the one and only solution, it clearly is one step on the way for a just and fair system for creators and users.

2. In Specific: Education of Users and Promotion of Legal Offers

The scale of copyright infringement[2615] proves that users are often ignorant of the law. Ignorant however does not only mean that they necessarily

2610 *Ibid.*

2611 *Ibid.*

2612 *Ibid*, p. 5.

2613 *Ibid.*

2614 *Ibid.*

2615 As outlined in the First Chapter, the scale of copyright infringement is difficult to establish. As many studies on the scale of infringements are commissioned by the rights-holders, the results have to be carefully assessed. However, it cannot be denied that many copyright infringements take place, especially if one looks at the number of warnings sent out in France, on which one has reliable data.

wilfully ignore the law, but also means that they lack understanding of the law as it stands. At the same time, copyright enforcement can lead to frustration, when for instance it is difficult for users to understand why content is blocked in their place of residence but freely available elsewhere.[2616] It may also be difficult to understand why it is allowed to copy music from the radio or a non-DRM-protected CD and give it to close friends, but often not allowed to download content from the Internet. For the user the difference in these acts is hard to understand in particular in the light of increased dematerialisation of content. What is thus needed is to accept the reality and invest into the education of Internet users.[2617] The latter was also important to the legislators when they drafted the graduated response schemes. Both schemes that have previously been discussed put an emphasis on educating users. Warnings should not only have a dissuasive but also persuasive effect, and thus shall inform users about copyright as such and legal alternatives. It is not necessary that users will fully understand all the details of intellectual property law, but they must be sensitised to understand which behaviour and activities can be problematic in terms of copyright. Copyright as one aspect of media competence must be taught at school level. With more and more children and teens owning smartphones, they must not only learn how to use technology but also how to use it responsibly. In addition, educational campaigns are necessary that do not depict users as criminals as it has been done in the German cam-

2616 A further prominent example for this – beside the aforementioned BBC iPlayer – is YouTube, where many content is blocked for German users due to a unfruitful negotiations regarding a licence between the German collecting society GEMA and YouTube. Without a licence agreement, GEMA has repeatedly obtained injunctions against YouTube to block materials of which GEMA holds the licence. GEMA even succeeded in having the wording of the blocking message that appears when users try to access content changed (LG München I, Decision of 25.02.2014 – 1 HK O 1401/13, Gewerblicher Rechtsschutz und Urheberrecht, Praxis im Immaterialgüter und Wettbewerbsrecht 2014, 140 with comment by Manuel Kleinemenke). GEMA no longer wanted to be the sole scapegoat for the lacking licensing agreement. In fact, what GEMA wants is a fair renumeration. What it achieves is that users consider GEMA as non-consumer-friendly and thus, may rarely develop guilt when they follow the instructions of PC magazines to circumvent blocking (See PC Magazin, *Youtube-GEMA-Sperre umgehen – so geht's*, PC Magazin (16.05.2014)).

2617 See in this regard also Ian Hargreaves, *Digital Opportunity, A Review of Intellectual Property and Growth* (2011), pp. 78 et seq.

paign of “Raubkopierer sind Verbrecher”,[2618] because copyright is too complex as to justify the equation “copyright infringers are criminals”. Users need to understand what copyright is and why it matters. In this regard, it is also necessary to look beyond copyright infringements from an economical perspective. It may also be that with increased use of smart phones and tablets and a new culture of sharing information, more users themselves become victims of copyright infringements, when other users make use of the images they have uploaded on social media platforms. In that regard, equations such as the above are out of place, insofar as primarily moral rights will be infringed.

In parallel, legitimate offers and services need to be promoted. This may be done by enhancing the availability of legal online content in all markets (see above), or clear marking of legal content.[2619] Most importantly, it must be prevented that legitimate services have to compete with piracy. In his “Digital Opportunity Report”, Ian Hargreaves refers to a US study that found that pragmatic issues of price and availability usually override moral considerations.[2620] Thus, not only promotion of legitimate service is necessary, but service providers and rights-holder must reassess what users get when they buy digital content. As has been outlined in the introduction, online purchase of music in a digital format means that the buyer only acquires a licence to use the digital content. If these copies are sold at the same price as a CD, users will obtain a good that actually has less value. Amazon for instance has recognised this discrepancy and is providing an audio-rip version to most CDs that can be purchased on Amazon’s platform. With such additional services that are easy to use and most importantly reliable, the incentive to pay for content may rise.

The education of users and promotion of legitimate content can however never be the only means to fight online piracy; what is necessary is an integrated approach based upon enforcement, promotion of legal services and education.

2618 See Nathalie Waehlisch, *Kampagne der Filmindustrie: “Raubkopierer sind Verbrecher“,* Der Spiegel online (27.11.2003).

2619 See Lilian Edwards, *Next steps in the UK*, in: Ian Hargreaves/Paul Hofheinz (eds.), *Intellectual property and innovation. A framework for 21st century growth and jobs*, p. 38.

2620 Ian Hargreaves, *Digital Opportunity, A Review of Intellectual Property and Growth* (2011), p. 79.

V. Exciting Time with Pitfalls

The digital age brings with it many challenges, in particular when it comes to the protection of copyright. These challenges are responded to in different ways of which graduated response schemes and *ACTA* are the most controversial. As such, policymaking in the digital intellectual property arena is controversial matter, and has been described as being "bedevilled by a well-funded lobbying community and a lack of technological expertise among legislators".[2621]

With no consensus achievable on macro-level, also regional initiatives like the revision of the *IPR Enforcement Directive* are taking their time. So what we are faced with is micro-level regulation that has led to some fragmentation, although there still is a common basis and most aspects are basically regulated by EU Directives. Nevertheless the Directives leave room for interpretation which needs to be addressed. As of now, the interpretation in Member States does not diverge fundamentally and the analysis above has shown that the differences are not as severe as they may seem at first glance. Even though there is for instance a discrepancy when it comes to monitoring duties of host providers in order to prevent identical infringements, the interpretation of this notion does not depart essentially. The lacking guidance by the CJEU on the interpretation of this notion is obviously a shortcoming, but the real problem – at least in some occasions – is the lack of understanding of technology by courts. For instance, German courts require file-hosting services to monitor not only their own platform but also basically the whole Internet in order to identify links that have been published and direct to copyrighted works stored on their servers. The courts misinterpreted the feasibility of such extensive monitoring, and only therefore have been able to reach the conclusion that such monitoring is reasonable and proportionate. This shows that it is not only necessary to educate users about copyright but also the judiciary about technology. Unjust balancing of interests of the parties to a case is the result of a lack of understanding of technology by judges. They arrive at constructing result-oriented monitoring duties without paying regard to the technological and economical means of the service providers concerned. It may thus be necessary to introduce "Cyber"-chambers that

---

2621 Lilian Edwards, *Next steps in the UK,* in: Ian Hargreaves/Paul Hofheinz (eds.), *Intellectual property and innovation. A framework for 21st century growth and jobs,* p. 38.

would solely deal with cases that require an assessment on the interface of law and technology.

This example also shows that in this exciting time, many pitfalls exist. With new targets for enforcement action being identified, it is necessary to rethink where we are and where we go; and whether that is really where we want to go.

Finally, with new technologies attracting the attention of users and smart devices becoming everyday commodities, user behaviour may also be changing. In particular smart devices such as smartphones, smart TVs or tablet PCs are increasingly being used. As of now, these devices have in common that they only have limited storage capacities and thus, it is the technology itself that is turning downloads unattractive.[2622] Instead users may be more interested in streaming content. Accordingly, while legislators and rights-holders are concentrating on the combat against peer-to-peer file-sharing, this way of sharing may not attract as many users in the near future as it used to. Considering that the graduated response scheme in the UK is still not being applied, one must wonder whether it will ever be employed and what effect it will have. As of now, it is more than likely that it will never come into force. The *DEA 2010* is the perfect example how legislative projects struggle to keep up with technology.

In these exciting times, there is also light at the end of the tunnel: the music industry has experienced an overall revenue growth recently, also in regard to digital sales.[2623] Furthermore, despite the Motion Picture Association of America's (MPAA) claiming that online piracy is ruining the movie industry, Hollywood achieved record-breaking global box office revenues of USD 35 billion in 2012.[2624] At the same time, the publishing industry has encountered a record of revenue stabilisation thanks to an increase in sales of E-books.[2625] Thus, the overall situation of the creative industries is not as bad as they may want us to believe. Although copy-

---

2622 It must nevertheless be noted that peer-to-peer file-sharing apps for smartphones exist, such as for instances BitTorrent, Kazaa Lite and BitComet.

2623 Bart Cammaerts/Robin Mansell/Bingchun Meng, *Copyright & Creation, A case for promoting inclusive online sharing* (September 2013), London School of Economics and Political Science, Media Policy Brief 9, p. 7. In 2013, for the first time, UK revenues from online music were higher than revenues from CDs and vinyl combined, see *ibid.*

2624 See *ibid*, p. 8.

2625 "In 2013, the global book publishing industry was worth some USD 102 billion, larger than the film, music or video games industries. Although revenues from

right is evidently infringed in new dimensions, a lot of factors influence the sale of creative works; neither strict enforcement alone nor education on its own may prevent that pirates become competitors to legitimate offers. An integrated approach is needed that guarantees a fair balance to be struck between the interests of rights-holders, Internet users and online intermediaries.

Finally, it remains to be seen if the problems in online copyright enforcement that we encounter today will persist in the future or may be resolved by media convergence and new revenue schemes.

---

print book sales have declined, this has been offset by increases in sales of eBooks and the rate of growth is not declining", see *ibid*, pp. 8 et seq.

List of References

Books and Commentaries

Ahlberg, Hartwig/Götting, Horst-Peter, Beck'scher Online-Kommentar Urheberrecht (updated 01.02.2014)

Barendt, Eric, Freedom of Speech (2nd ed. 2007)

Benedek, Wolfgang/Kettemann, Matthias C., Freedom of expression and the Internet (2014)

Bentley, Lionel/Sherman, Brad, Intellectual Property Law (2001)

Berners-Lee, Tim, Weaving the Web: The original design and ultimate destiny of the World Wide Web by its inventor (2000)

Billmeier, Eva, Die Düsseldorfer Sperrungsverfügung: ein Beispiel für verfassungs- und gefahrenabwehrrechtliche Probleme der Inhaltsregulierung in der Informationsgesellschaft (2007)

Brownsword, Roger/Goodwin, Morag, Law and the technologies of the twenty-first century (2012)

Brunn, Inka Frederike, Cache me if you can (2012)

Calliess, Christian, Die neue Europäische Union nach dem Vertrag von Lissabon (2010)

Cassese, Antonio, International Law (2001)

de Schutter, Olivier, International Human Rights Law (2010)

Deibert, Ronald/Palfrey, John/Rohozinski, Rafal/Zittrain, Jonathan (eds.), 'Access denied' – The practice and policy of global Internet filtering (2008)

Dreier, Thomas/Schulze, Gernot, UrhG, Kommentar (3rd ed. 2008)

Dreier, Thomas/Schulze, Gernot, UrhG, Kommentar (4th ed. 2013)

Greiner, Arved, Die Verhinderung verbotener Internetinhalte im Wege polizeilicher Gefahrenabwehr (2001)

Heckmann, Dirk, Juris PraxisKommentar Internetrecht, (2nd ed. 2009)

Helfer, Laurence R./Austin, Graeme W., Human rights and intellectual property: Mapping the global interface (2011)

Hoeren, Thomas/Sieber, Ulrich/Holznagel, Bernd (eds.), Handbuch Multimedia-Recht (36th amended ed. 2013)

Horten, Monica, A copyright masquerade: How corporate lobbying threatens online freedoms (2013)

Horten, Monica, The copyright enforcement enigma, Internet politics and the 'Telecoms Package' (2011)

Ibing, Stefan, Die Einschränkung der europäischen Grundrechte durch Gemeinschaftsrecht (2006)

Janis, Mark W./Kay, Richard S./Bradley, Anthony Wilfred, European Human Rights Law: Text and Materials (3rd ed. 2008)

Jørgensen, Rikke Frank (ed.), Human Rights in the global information society (2006)

Klett, Alexander/Sonntag, Matthias/Wilske, Stephan, Intellectual Property Law in Germany (2008)

Köhler, Markus/Arndt, Hans-Wolfgang/Fetzer, Thomas, Recht des Internet, (7th ed. 2011)

Laidlaw, Emily, Internet gatekeepers, human rights and corporate social responsibilities (2012), http://etheses.lse.ac.uk/317/1/Laidlaw_Internet%20Gatekeepers,%20 Human%20 Rights%20and%20Corporate%20Social%20Responsibilities.pdf (last accessed 17.05.2014)

Lessig, Lawrence, Code: Version 2.0 (2006)

Leupold, Andreas/Glossner, Silke, Münchener Anwaltshandbuch IT-Recht (3rd ed. 2013)

Lloyd, Ian J., Information Technology Law (6th ed. 2011)

Löwenheim, Ulrich (ed.), Handbuch des Urheberrechts (2nd ed. 2010)

MacQueen, Hector/Waelde, Charlotte/Laurie, Graeme/Brown, Abbe, Contemporary intellectual property, Law and policy (2nd ed. 2011)

Marsden, Christopher, Net neutrality: Towards a co-regulatory solution (2010)

Meyer-Ladewig, Jens, EMRK, Handkommentar (3rd ed. 2011)

Mock, William B. T./Demuro, Gianmario (eds.), Human Rights in Europe, Commentary on the Charter of Fundamental Rights of the European Union (2010)

Mowbray, Alastair, Cases, materials and comments on the European Convention on Human Rights (3rd ed. 2012)

Murray, Andrew, Information Technology Law, The law and society (2nd ed. 2013)

Nowak, Manfred, U.N. Covenant on Civil and Political Rights, CCPR Commentary (2005)

Pettiti, Louis-Edmond/Decaux, Emmanuel/Imbert, Pierre-Henri (eds.), La Convention Euro–péenne des Droits de l'Homme, Commentaire (1999)

Pieroth, Bodo/Schlink, Bernhard/Kniesel, Michael, Polizei- und Ordnungsrecht (2002)

Reed, Chris, Making laws for cyberspace (2012)

Reed, Chris, Internet Law, Text and Materials (2nd ed. 2004)

Rowland, Diane/Kohl, Uta/Charlesworth, Andrew, Information Technology Law (4th ed. 2012)

Schaar, Peter, Datenschutz im Internet (2002)

Schulz, Wolfgang/Held, Thorsten/Laudien, Arne, Suchmaschinen als Gatekeeper in der öffentlichen Kommunikation: Rechtliche Anforderungen an Zugangsoffenheit und Transparenz bei Suchmaschinen im WWW (2005)

Siemen, Birte, Datenschutz als Europäisches Grundrecht (2006)

Spindler, Gerald/Schuster, Fabian, Recht der elektronischen Medien (2nd ed. 2011)

Spindler, Gerald/Wiebe, Andreas, Internet-Auktionen und elektronische Marktplätze (2nd ed. 2005)

Steegmann, Matthias, Die Haftung der Basisinfrastruktur bei rechtswidrigen Internetangeboten, Verantwortlichkeit von Internet- und Finanzdienstleistern im Rahmen des illegalen Online-Glücksspiels (2010)

Stokes, Simon, Digital Copyright (2nd ed. 2005)

Tanenbaum, Andrew/Wetherall, David, Computer Networks (5th ed. 2011)

van Bockel, Bas, The Ne Bis In Idem Principle in EU Law (2010)

van Dijk, Peter/Hoof, Godefridus J. H. (eds.), Theory and Practice of the European Convention on Human Rights (4th ed. 2006)

Walter, Michel/von Lewinski, Silke, European Copyright Law (2010)

Wandtke, Artur-Axel/Bullinger, Winfried, Praxiskommentar zum Urheberrecht (3rd ed. 2009)

Scientific Papers and Journal Articles

Abbotts, Gillie, A catch for TVCatchup – Limits of the cable defence, Entertainment Law Review 2014, Vol. 25 Issue 1, 17–18

Adermon, Adrian / Liang, Che-Yuan, Piracy, music, and movies: A natural experiment, Uppsala Universitet Working Paper 2010: 18, http://www.nek.uu.se/Pdf/wp201018.pdf (last accessed on 20.04.2014)

Aguiar, Luis/Martens, Bertin, Digital music consumption on the Internet: Evidence from clickstream data (2013), European Commission JRC Technical Reports, Institute for Prospective Technological Studies, http://ftp.jrc.es/EURdoc/JRC79605.pdf (last accessed 30.04.2014)

Ahlert, Christian/Marsden, Chris/Yung, Chester, How "liberty" disappeared from Cyberspace: The mystery shopper tests Internet content self-regulation, http://www.rootsecure.net/content/downloads/pdf/liberty_disappeared_from_cyberspace.pdf (last accessed on 30.04.2014)

Akdeniz, Yaman, To block or not to block: European approaches to content regulation, and implications for freedom of expression, Computer Law & Security Review 2010, 260–272

Alexander, Rachel, FirstRow – access denied, Entertainment Law Review 2013, Vol. 24 Issue 8, 280–283

Alsbih, Amir/Janson, Thomas/Schindelhauer, Christian, Analysis of peer-to-peer traffic and user behaviour (2009), http://archive.cone.informatik.uni-freiburg.de/pubs/ITA 11_bittorrent_alsbih_janson_schindelhauer.pdf (last accessed on 17.05.2014)

Angelopoulos, Christina, Beyond the Safe Harbours: Harmonising substantive intermediary liability for copyright infringement in Europe, http://www.ivir.nl/publicatio ns/angelopoulos/IPQ_2013_3.pdf

Barron, Anne, 'Graduated Response' à l'Anglaise: Online Copyright Infringement and the Digital Economy Act 2010, Journal of Media Law 2011, Vol. 3 Issue 2, 305–347

Bastard Irène/Bourreau, Marc/Moreau, François, L'impact du piratage sur l'achat et le telechargement legal: une comparaison de quatre filieres culturelles (2012), Working paper, http://manzanamecanica.org/files/Piratage4filieres_06avril2012.pdf (last accessed on 30.04.2014*)*

Benabou, Valérie-Laure, The Chase: The French insight into the 'Three Strikes' system, in: *Stamatoudi, Irini A. (ed.)*, Copyright enforcement and the Internet (2010), 163–182

Benassiano, William, Décision n° 2009-590 DC du 22 octobre 2009, La sanction de l'incompétence négative, Revue française de droit constitutionnel 2010, 390–396

Benassiano, William, L'inconstitutionnalité, sanction de l'identification d'un pouvoir de répression pénale dévalué. Décision no 2009-580 DC du 10 juin 2009, Revue française de droit consti-tutionnel 2010, no 81, 168–174

Benkler, Yochai, WikiLeaks and the PROTECT-IP Act: A new public-private threat to the Internet Commons, Daedalus 2011, Vol. 140 Issue 4, 154–164

Bernault, Carine/Lebois, Audrey, Peer-to-peer file sharing and literary and artistic property, A feasibility study regarding a system of compensation for the exchange of works via the Internet (2005), http://privatkopie.net/files/Feasibility-Study-peer-to-peer-acs_Nantes.pdf (last accessed on 17.05.2014)

Besselink, Leonard, Entrapped by the maximum standard: On fundamental rights and subsidiarity in the European Union, Common Market Law Review 1998, Vol. 35, 629–680

Binet-Grosclaude, Aurélie, La décision du Conseil constitutionnel du 10 juin 2009 relative à la loi favorisant la diffusion et la protection de la création sur internet : un coup d'arrêt au pouvoir de sanction des AAI ?, Droit Pénal 2009, No. 11, 11–17

Bölling, Markus, Unterlassungsantrag und Streitgegenstand im Falle der Störerhaftung, Gewerblicher Rechtsschutz und Urheberrecht 2013, 1092–1099

Borges, Georg, Pflichten und Haftung beim Betrieb privater WLAN, Neue Juristische Wochenschrift 2010, 2624–2627

Borges, Georg, Zur Haftung des Betreibers einer Handelsplattform für Markenverletzungen der Nutzer („L'Oréal/eBay"), Entscheidungen zum Wirtschaftsrecht 2011, 823–824

Borghi, Maurizio, Chasing copyright infringement in the streaming landscape, International Review of Intellectual Property and Competition Law 2011, 316–343

Bornkamm, Joachim, E-Commerce Directive vs. IP rights enforcement – Legal balance achieved?, Gewerblicher Rechtsschutz und Urheberrecht – Internationaler Teil 2007, 642–644

Boubekeur, Iliana, De la « loi HADOPI » à la « loi HADOPI 2 ». Analyse de la décision du Conseil constitutionnel 2009-580 DC et de ses conséquences, Revue Lamy Droit de l'Immatériel 2009, No. 51, 107–113

Brömmekamp, Birgit, Der Fall L'Oréal gegen eBay: Prüfstein für die Informationsgesellschaft, Wettbewerb in Recht und Praxis 2011, 306–316

Buchmann, Felix/Brüggemann, Sebastian, Der Preis des „Filesharing" – Streitwert, Schadensersatz und Kostendeckelung nach § 97 a Abs. 2 UrhG, Kommunikation und Recht 2011, 368–373

Burnett, Rachel, The role of Ofcom, ITNOW 2010, Vol. 52 Issue 6, 24

Calliess, Christian, Die Charta der Grundrechte der Europäischen Union – Fragen der Konzeption, Kompetenz und Verbindlichkeit, Europäische Zeitschrift für Wirtschaftsrecht 2001, 261–268

Cammaerts, Bart/Mansell, Robin/Meng, Bingchun, Copyright & Creation, A case for promoting inclusive online sharing (September 2013), London School of Economics and Political Science, Media Policy Brief 9, http://www.lse.ac.uk/media@lse/documents/MPP/LSE-MPP-Policy-Brief-9-Copyright-and-Creation.pdf (last accessed on 06.06.2014)

Caron, Christophe, Responsabilité des hébergeurs : requiem pour le «take down, stay down», Communication Commerce éléctronique 2012, Vol. 14 Issue 9, 28–30

Chaltiel, Florence, La loi HADOPI II de nouveau censurée, Petites affiches 2009, No. 235 (25.11.2009), 7–13

Chang, Liliana, The red flag test for apparent knowledge under the *DMCA* § 512 (c) Safe Harbor, Cardozo Arts & Entertainment Law Journal, Vol. 28, 195–222

Chen, Erik/Brown, Mark, Taiwan: Taiwan enacts ISP 'safe harbour' amendments to Copyright Act, Computer Law & Security Review 2009, Vol. 25 Issue 4, 389–390

Chothia, Tom/Chatzikokolakis, Konstantinos, A survey of anonymous peer-to-peer file-sharing, http://www.lix.polytechnique.fr/~tomc/P2P/Papers/AnonP2PSurvey.pdf (last accessed on 13.08.2013)

Christiansen, Per, Störerhaftung des Betreibers einer Video-Plattform wegen Urheberrechtsverletzung, Anmerkung zu LG Hamburg, 310 O 461/10 vom 20.04.2012, Kommunikation & Recht 2012, 533

Christoffersen, Jonas, Human Rights and balancing: The principle of proportionality, in: *Geiger, Christophe (ed.),* Research Handbook on Human rights and Intellectual Property (2015), pp. 19 – 38

Christopherson, Kimberly M., The positive and negative implications of anonymity in Internet social interaction: "On the Internet, nobody knows you're a dog", Computers in Human Behaviour 2007, Vol. 23 Issue 6, 3038–3056

Clarke, Ian/Miller, Scott G./Hong, Theodore W./Sandberg, Oskar/Wiley, Brandon, Protecting free expression online with Freenet, IEEE Internet Computing 2011, Vol. 6 Issue 1, 40–49

Clayton, Richard, Anonymity and traceability in cyberspace (August 2005), Technical Report UCAM-CL-TR-653, http://www.cl.cam.ac.uk/techreports/UCAM-CL-TR-653.pdf (last accessed on 17.05.2014)

Clayton, Richard, Expert Opinion in case R (on the application of British Telecommunications Plc) v Secretary of State for Business, Innovation and Skills, https://www.openrightsgroup.org/assets/JK1RC.pdf (last accessed 30.04.2014)

Clayton, Richard, Harmful Content on the Internet and in Video Games (2008), http://www.cl.cam.ac.uk/~rnc1/080129-cms.pdf (last accessed 13.04.2012)

Clayton, Richard, Online traceability: Who did that?, Technical expert report on collecting robust evidence of copyright infringement through peer-to-peer filesharing (2012), http://www.consumerfocus.org.uk/files/2012/07/Online-traceability.pdf (last accessed 30.04.2014)

Clayton, Richard/et al., A study of Whois privacy and proxy services abuse, National Physical Laboratory (20.09.2013), http://gnso.icann.org/en/issues/whois/pp-abuse-study-20sep13-en.pdf (last accessed on 17.05.2014)

Costes, Lionel, Peer to Peer et recherche des contrefacteurs: les précisions de la CJCE, Droit de l'immatériel : informatique, médias, communication 2009, No. 48, 22–23

Czychowski, Christian/Nordemann, Jan Bernd, Grenzenloses Internet – entgrenzte Haftung?, Gewerblicher Rechtsschutz und Urheberrecht-Beilage 2014, 3–13

Czychowski, Christian/Nordemann, Jan Bernd, Vorratsdaten und Urheberrecht – Zulässige Nutzung gespeicherter Daten, Neue Juristische Wochenschrift 2008, 3095–3099

D'Erme, Roberto/Geiger, Christophe/Große Ruse-Khan, Henning/ Heinze, Christian/ Jaeger, Thomas and Others, Opinion of European academics on anti-counterfeiting trade agreement, Journal of Intellectual Property, Information Technology and E-Commerce Law 2011, Vol. 2 Issue 1, 65–72

Danaher, Brett/Smith, Michael D/Telang, Rahul/Chen, Siwen, The Effect of Graduated Response Anti-Piracy Laws on Music Sales: Evidence from an Event Study in France (2012), http://papers.ssrn.com/sol3/papers.cfm?abstract_id=1989240 (last accessed on 15.05.2014)

Danckert, Burkhard/Mayer, Frank Joachim, Die vorherrschende Meinungsmacht von Google – Bedrohung durch einen Informationsmonopolisten?, MultiMedia und Recht 2010, 219–222

Danckwerts, Rolf, Neues vom Störer: Was ist ein „von der Rechtsordnung gebilligtes Geschäftsmodell"?, Gewerblicher Rechtsschutz und Urheberecht-Prax 2011, 260–262

Dara, Rishabh, Intermediary liability in India: Chilling effects on free expression on the Internet (2011), http://cis-india.org/internet-governance/intermediary-liability-in-india.pdf/view (last accessed on 17.05.2014)

de Hert, Paul/Kloza, Dariusz, Internet (Access) as a new fundamental right. Inflating the current rights framework?, European Journal of Law and Technology 2012, Vol. 3 No. 3, http://ejlt.org/article/view/123/268 (last acccessed on 17.05.2014)

de Silva, Sam/Weedon, Faye, The Digital Economy Act 2010: Past, present and a future "in limbo", Computer and Telecommuncations Law Review 2011, Vol. 17 No. 3, 55–62

Derieux, Emmanuel, Le droit communautaire n'impose pas que les législations nationales prévoient l'obligation de communiquer des données à caractère personnel dans le cadre d'une procédure civile, La Semaine Juridique – édition générale 2008, No. 21 (21.05.2008), 40–42

Derieux, Emmanuel, Validation par le Conseil constitutionnel de l'essentiel des dispositions de la loi 'HADOPI 2', Revue Lamy Droit de l'Immatériel 2009, No. 54, 6–8

Devigne, Luc Pierre/Velasco-Martins, Pedro/Iliopoulou, Alexandra, Where is ACTA taking us? Policies and politics, in: *Irini Stamatoudi (ed.),* Copyright enforcement and the Internet (2010), pp. 29–42

Dimita, Gaetano, Six characters in search of infringement: potential liability for creating, downloading, and disseminating .torrent files, *Journal of Intellectual Property Law & Practice* 2012, Vol. 7 Issue 6, 466–472

Dix, Alexander, Vorratsdatenspeicherung von IP-Adressen?, Datenschutz und Datensicherheit 2003, 234–235

Dnes, Antony W., Should the UK Move to a Fair-Use Copyright Exception, International Review of Intellectual Property and Competition Law 2013, 418–444

Dornseif, Maximilian, Government mandated blocking of foreign Web content, in: *von Knop, Jan/Haverkamp, Wilhelm/Jessen, Eike (eds.),* Security, E-Learning, E-Services: Proceedings of the 17. DFN-Arbeitstagung über Kommunikationsnetze (2013), Lecture Notes in Informatics, pp. 617–647

Drexl, Josef Nérisson, Sylvie/Trumpke, Felix/Hilty, Reto M., Comments of the Max Planck Institute for Intellectual Property and Competition Law on the Proposal for a Directive of the European Parliament and of the Council on collective management of copyright and related rights and multi-territorial licensing of rights in musical works for online uses in the internal market COM (2012)372

Dussollier, Séverine, L'utilisation légitime de l'œuvre: un noveau sesame pour le benefice des exceptions en droit d'auteur?, Communication commerce électronique November 2005, No. 11, 19

Edelman, Benjamin, Web sites sharing IP addresses: Prevalence and Significance (September 2003), http://cyber.law.harvard.edu/archived_content/people/edelman/ip-sharing/ ((last accessed on 17.05.2014)

Edstrom, Jerker/Nillson, Henrik, The Pirate Bay verdict – predictable, and yet…, European Intellectual Property Review 2009, Vol. 31 No. 9, 483–487

Edwards, Lilian, Next steps in the UK, in: *Hargreaves, Ian /Hofheinz, Paul (eds.),* Intellectual property and innovation. A framework for 21st century growth and jobs, pp. 37–41 http://www.lisboncouncil.net/index.php?option=com_downloads&id=693 (last accessed on 06.06.2014)

Edwards, Lilian, Mandy and Me: Some Thoughts on the Digital Economy Bill, Script-ED 2009, Vol. 6 Issue 3, 534–537

Edwards, Lilian/Waelde, Charlotte, Online intermediaries and liability for copyright infringement, WIPO Workshop Keynote Paper (2005), http://papers.ssrn.com/sol3/papers.cfm?abstract_id=1159640 (last accessed 16.06.2009)

Engel, Christoph, Die Internet-Service-Provider als Geiseln deutscher Ordnungsbehörden – Eine Kritik an den Verfügungen der Bezirksregierung Düsseldorf, MultiMedia und Recht 2003, Beilage 4

Engström, Christian/Falkvinge, Rick, The case for copyright reform (2012), http://www.copyrightreform.eu/sites/copyrightreform.eu/files/The_Case_for_Copyright_Reform.pdf (last accessed on 06.06.2014)

Ensthaler, Jürgen/Heinemann, Jürgen, Die Fortentwicklung der Providerhaftung durch die Rechtsprechung, Gewerblicher Rechtsschutz und Urheberrecht 2012, 433–440

Fangerow, Kathleen/Schulz, Daniela, Die Nutzung von Angeboten auf www.kino.to, Eine urheberrechtliche Analyse des Film-Streamings im Internet, Gewerblicher Rechtsschutz und Urheberrecht 2010, 677–682

Farrand, Benjamin, The Digital Economy Act 2010: A cause for celebration, or a cause for concern, European Intellectual Property Review 2010, Vol. 32 Issue 10, 536–541

Feeman, Vickie L./Coats, William S./Rafter, Heather D./Given, John G., Revenge of the Record Industry Association of America: The rise and fall of Napster, Villanova Sports & Entertainment Law Journal 2002, Vol. 9, 35–36

Feiler, Lukas, Tor als Prüfstein der Data Retention Richtlinie (2005), http://www.lukas feiler.com/Tor.pdf (last accessed on 17.05.2014)

Finger, Manuel/Apel, Simon, Anmerkung zu BGH, Urteil vom 15. August 2013 – I ZR 80/12 – File-Hosting Dienst, Zeitschrift für Urheber- und Medienrecht 2013, 879–882

Fiscor, Milhály J., The WIPO "Internet Treaties" and copyright in the "cloud", ALAI 2012 Congress, pp.40 et seq., http://www.alai.jp/ALAI2012/program/paper/The%20WIPO%20Internet%20Treaties%20and%20copyright%20in%20the%20Cloud%20%EF%BC%88Dr.%20Mih%C3%A1ly%20J.%20Ficsor%EF%BC%89.pdf

Francillon, Jacques, Téléchargement illégal. Heur et malheur de la loi Création et Internet : la loi HADOPI censurée par le Conseil constitutionnel, Revue de science criminelle et de droit pénal comparé 2009, No. 3, 609–622

Frey, Dieter/Rudolph, Matthias, Zugangserschwerungsgesetz: Schnellschuss mit Risiken und Nebenwirkungen, Computer und Recht 2009, 644–651

Frey, Dieter/Rudolph, Matthias/Oster, Jan, Internetsperren und der Schutz der Kommunikation im Internet, Am Beispiel behördlicher und gerichtlicher Sperrungsverfügungen im Bereich des Glücksspiel- und Urheberrechts, MultiMedia und Recht-Beilage 2012 to Issue 3, 1–26

Frhr. Raitz von Frentz, Wolfgang/Masch, Christian L., Anmerkung zu EuGH, Urteil vom 7. März 2013 – EUGH 2013-03-07 Aktenzeichen C-607/11 – Livestreaming, ITV Broadcasting Ltd. u. a./ TVCatchup Ltd., Zeitschrift für Urheber- und Medienrecht 2013, 393–395

Gallant, Kenneth S., Legality as a Rule of Customary International Law: Non-Retroactivity of Crimes and Punishments – research through 2010 (14.06.2011), UALR Bowen School Research Paper No. 11–12, http://ssrn.com/abstract=1864930 (last accessed on 17.05.2014)

Gardiner, Paddy/Abbotts, Gillie, Sky's the limit for ISP blocking orders, Entertainment Law Review 2013, Vol. 24 Issue 6, 217–219

Gardiner, Paddy/Althoff, Juliane, High Court grants further blocking injunction against film and TV streaming websites, Entertainment Law Review 2014, Vol. 25 Issue 3, 108–110

Gautron, Allan, La « réponse graduée » (à nouveau) épinglée par le Conseil constitutionnel. Ou la délicate adéquation des moyens aux fins, Revue Lamy Droit de l'Immatériel 2009, No. 51, 63–73

Geiger, Christophe, Counterfeiting and the music industry: towards a criminalization of end users? The French 'HADOPI' example, in: *Geiger, Christophe (ed.)*, Criminal enforcement of intellectual property (2012), pp. 386–402

Geiger, Christophe, Honourable attempt but (ultimately) dis-proportionately offensive against peer-to-peer on the internet (HADOPI) – a critical analysis of the recent anti-file-sharing legislation in France, International Review of Intellectual Property and Competition Law 2011, Vol. 42, 457–472

Geiger, Christophe, Intellectual Property Shall be Protected!? – Article 17(2) of the Charter of Fundamental Rights of the European Union: a Mysterious Provision with an Unclear Scope, European Intellectual Property Review 2009, 113–117

Geiger, Christophe, Les exceptions au droit d'auteur en France, in: *Geiger, Christophe/ Bouyssi-Ruch, Michele/Hilty, Reto M. (eds.),* Perspectives d'harmonisation du droit d'auteur en Europe, pp. 335–360

Giblin, Rebecca, Evaluating graduated response, Columbia Journal of Law & the Arts 2014, Vol. 37 No. 2, 147–209

Griffin, James, Copyright evolution – creation, regulation and the decline of substantively rational copyright law, Intellectual Property Quarterly 2013, 234–252

Griffin, James G. H., The effect of the Digital Economy Act 2010 upon 'Semiotic Democracy', International Review of Law, Computers & Technology 2010, Vol. 24 No. 3, 251–262

Griffiths, Jonathan, Constitutionalising or harmonising? – the Court of Justice, the right to property and European copyright law, European Law Review 2013, Vol. 38, 65–78

Griffiths, Jonathan, Criminal liability for intellectual property infringement in Europe: the role of fundamental rights, in: *Geiger, Christophe (ed.)*, Criminal enforcement of intellectual property (2012), pp. 191–212

Griffiths, Jonathan, Enforcement of intellectual property rights and the right to a fair trial, in: *Geiger, Christophe (ed.),* Research handbook on human rights and intellectual property (2015), pp. 438 - 454

Grosskopf, Lambert, Anmerkung zum Urteil des LG Hamburg: Störerhaftung des Internanschlussinhabers für Urheberrechtsverletzungen, Computer und Recht 2007, 122–124

Hammond, Robert G., Profit Leak? Pre-released file-sharing and the music industry (2013), Working paper, http://www4.ncsu.edu/~rghammon/Hammond_File_Sharing _Leak.pdf (last accessed on 17.05.2014)

Hauck, Ronny/Heim, Sebastian, Schwerpunktbereich Urheberrecht: Die rechtliche Bewertung von „Filesharing"- und „Streaming"- Sachverhalten, Juristische Schulung 2014, 303–307

Headdon, Toby, Beyond liability: on the availability and scope of injunctions against online intermediaries after L'Oréal v eBay, European Intellectual Property Review 2012, Vol 34 Issue 3, 137–144

Hečko, Zuzana, Data retention by Internet service providers for IP rights protection: Bonnier Audio (C-461/10), Journal of Intellectual Property Law and Practice 2012, 449–456

Heidrich, Joerg, Weitergehende Prüfpflichten bei besonderer Gefahrengeneigtheit eines File-Hosting-Diensts, K&R-Kommentar, Kommunikation & Recht 2013, 655–662

Heinemeyer, Dennis/Kreitlow, Matthias/Nordmeyer, Arne/Sabellek, André: Kampf gegen Filesharing als Modell verfehlter Mehrfachkompensation? – Fragen zur Schadenshöhe, zu Gesamtschuldnern und Beweisen bei Tauschbörsen, MultiMedia und Recht 2012, 279–284

Helfer, Laurence R., The new innovation frontier? Intellectual property and the European Court of Human Rights, in: *Torremans, Paul L. C. (ed.)*, Intellectual Property and Human Rights, Enhanced Edition of Copyright and Human Rights (2008), pp. 25–76

Herr, Robin Elizabeth, Can Human Rights Law Support Access to Communication Technology? A Case Study under Article 10 of the Right to Receive Information, Information & Communications Technology Law 2013, Vol. 22, No. 1, 1–13

Hocking, Ryan, Secondary liability in copyright infringement: still no 'Newz'?, Entertainment Law Review 2012, Vol. 23 Issue 4, 83–90

Hoeren, Thomas, Anmerkung zu BGH: Störerhaftung von RapidShare – Alone in the Dark, MultiMedia und Recht 2013, 185–189

Hoeren, Thomas, Kurzgutachten zur BMWi-Studie über Modelle zur Versendung von Warnhinweisen durch Internet-Zugangsanbieter an Nutzer bei Urheberrechtsverletzungen (2012), http://politik.eco.de/files/2012/03/20120227-Hoeren-eco-Gutachten_final-2702.pdf (last accessed on 10.03.2013)

Hoeren, Thomas, The European liability and responsibility of providers of online-platforms such as "Second Life", Journal of Information, Law & Technology 2009, Issue 1, http://go.warwick.ac.uk/jilt/2009_1/hoeren (last accessed on 10.03.2013)

Hoeren, Thomas/Bilek, Julia Ariella, Die territoriale Exklusivitätsvereinbarung bei Fußball-Übertragungen – Ein Modell der Vergangenheit!, Computer und Recht 2011, 735–741

Hoeren, Thomas/Yankova, Silviya, The liability of Internet intermediaries – The German perspective, International Review of Intellectual Property and Competition Law 2012, 501–531

Höfinger, Frank Michael, Anmerkung zu EuGH, Urteil vom 13. Februar 2014 – C-466/12 – Nils Svensson u.a./Retriever Sverige AB, Zeitschrift für Urheber- und Medienrect 2014, 293–295

Hofmann, Herwig/Mihaescu, Bucura, The relation between the Charter's fundamental rights and the unwritten general principles of EU law: good administration as the test case, European Constitutional Law Review 2013, Vol. 9. No. 1, 73–101

Hörnle, Julia, Premature or Stillborn? – The Recent Challenge to the Digital Economy Act, Computer Law & Security Review 2012, Vol. 28, 83–89

Horten, Monica, The Digital Economy Act in the dock: A proportionate ruling? Journal of Intellectual Property, Information Technology and Electronic Commerce Law 2012, 81–87

Hoy, Ruth/Wilks, John/Edbrooke, Nick, Dramatico Entertainment v BskyB: Pirate Bay runs aground in English waters, Entertainment Law Review 2012, Vol. 23 Issue 5, 151–153

Hyland, Mark, The seductive interface between adult entertainment and Norwich Pharmacal Relief, Communications Law 2013, Vol. 18 Issue 2, 56–60

Imbert-Quaretta, Mireille/Monfort, Jean-Yves/Carpentier, Jean-Baptiste, La contravention de négligence caractérisée à la lumière de la mise en œuvre de la procédure de réponse graduée, La Semaine Juridique – Édition Générale 2012, No. 19, 966–971

Introna, Lucas D./Nissenbaum, Helen, Shaping the Web: Why the politics of search engine matters, The Information Society 2000, Vol. 16, 169–185

Jasserand, Catherine, YouTube guilty but not liable for late removal of infringing material, Journal of Intellectual Property Law & Practice 2012, Vol. 7 Issue 11, 790–791

Lynn, Jeff, Copyright for growth, in: *Hargreaves, Ian/Hofheinz, Paul (eds.),* Intellectual property and innovation. A framework for 21st century growth and jobs, pp. 11-16, http://www.lisboncouncil.net/index.php?option=com_downloads&id=693 (last accessed on 06.06.2014)

Johnson, M. Eric/McGuire, Dan/Willey, Nicholas D., The evolution of the peer-to-peer file sharing industry and the security risks for users, Proceedings of the 41st Hawaii International Conference on System Sciences 2008, http://cds.tuck.dartmouth.edu/digital/assets/images/30750383.pdf (last accessed 13.03.2013)

Jones, Joseph, Internet pirates walk the plank with Article 10 kept at bay: Neij and Sunde Kolmisoppi v Sweden, European Intellectual Property Review 2013, Vol. 35 Issue 11, 695–700

Joseph, Paul/Ward, Charlotte, Golden Eye (International) Ltd v Telefonica UK Ltd, Entertainment Law Review 2012, Vol. 23 Issue 6, 183–185

Kahlert, Henning, Urheberrecht kontra Datenschutz: EuGH bremst Forderungen nach einem zivilrechtlichen Auskunftsanspruch gegen Internet-Provider über die Identität von Tauschbörsen-Benutzern, European Law Reporter 2008, 7882

Kennedy, Rónán, No Three Strikes for Ireland (yet): EU Copyright Law and individual liability in recent Internet file sharing litigation, Journal of Internet Law 2011, Vol. 14, 15–28

Keplinger, Michael, Enforcement of IP rights in the digital environment: The role of the World Intellectual Property Organisation, Gewerblicher Rechtsschutz und Urheberrecht – Internationaler Teil 2007, 648–649

Kern, Benjamin D., Whacking, joyriding and war-driving: Roaming use of Wi-Fi and the Law, CIPerati – a Cyberspace and I.P. Law newsletter 2005, Vol. 2 Issue 4, http://apps.americanbar.org/buslaw/committees/CL320010pub/newsletter/0009/ (last accessed on 17.05.2014)

Kioupis, Dimitris, Criminal liability on the Internet, *in: Stamatoudi, Irini (ed.)*, Copyright enforcement on the Internet (2010), pp. 233–254

Klett, Alexander, Cloud und Privatkopie, Zeitschrift für Urheber- und Medienrecht 2014, 18–22

Kohl, Uta, The rise and rise of online intermediaries in the governance of the Internet and beyond – connectivity intermediaries, International Review of Law, Computers & Technology 2012, Vol. 26 Issue 2–3, 185–210

Kortlander, Jenny, Is filtering the new silver bullet in the fight against child pornography on the Internet? A legal study into the experiences of Australia and Germany, Computer and Telecommunications Law Review, 2011, Vol. 17 Issue 7, 199–208

Kraßer, Rudolf, Schadensersatz für Verletzungen von gewerblichen Schutzrechten und Urheberrechten nach deutschem Recht, Gewerblicher Rechtsschutz und Urheberrecht, Internationaler Teil 1980, 259–272

Krüger, Stefan/Apel, Simon, Haftung von Plattformbetreibern für urheberrechtlich geschützte Inhalte – Wie weit geht die Haftung und wann droht Schadensersatz?, MultiMedia und Recht 2012, 144–151

Krüger, Stefan/Maucher, Svenja-Ariane, IP-Adresse wirklich ein personenbezogenes Datum? – Ein falscher Trend mit großen Auswirkungen auf die Praxis, MultiMedia und Recht 2011, 433–439

Kulk, Stefan/Zuiderveen Borgesius, Frederik, Filtering for Copyright Enforcement in Europe after the SABAM cases, European Intellectual Property Review 2012, 54–58

Kuner, Christopher, Data Protection and Rights Protection on the Internet: The Promusicae Judgment of the European Court of Justice, European Intellectual Property Review 2008, 199–202

Larsson, Stefan, Metaphors, Law and digital phenomena: the Swedish pirate bay court case, International Journal of Law and Information Technology 2013, Vol. 21 No. 4, 354–379

Larusson, Haflidi Kristjan, Uncertainty in the scope of copyright: the case of illegal file-sharing in the UK, European Intellectual Property Review 2009, Vol. 31 No. 3, 124–134

Lauinger, Tobias/Kirda, Engin/Michiardi, Pietro, Paying for piracy? An analysis of one-click hosters' controversial reward schemes, in: *Balzarotti, Davide/Stolfo, Salvatore J./Cova, Marco (eds.),* Research in attacks, intrusions, and defenses (2012), Lecture Notes in Computer Science Vol. 7462, pp. 169–189

Leistner, Matthias, Grundlagen und Perspektiven der Haftung für Urheberrechtsverletzungen im Internet, Zeitschrift für Urheber- und Medienrecht 2012, 722–740

Leistner, Matthias, Structural aspects of secondary (provider) liability in Europe, Journal of Intellectual Property and Practice 2014, Vol. 9 No. 1, 75–90.

Leistner, Matthias/Stang, Felix, Die Neuerung der wettbewerbsrechtlichen Verkehrspflichten – Ein Siegeszug der Prüfungspflichten? Wettbewerb in Recht und Praxis 2008, 533–555

Lemarchand, Stéphane/Lampe, Anne-Sophie, L'arrêt eBay c/ L'Oréal de la CJUE du 12 juillet 2011 revisite les conditions de la qualification de fournisseur d'hébergement au sens de l'article 14 de la directive « e-commerce », Droit de l'immatériel : informatique, médias, communication 2011, No. 75, 53–58

Lemley, Mark/Levine, David/Post, David, Don't break the Internet, Stanford Law Review Online 2011, Vol. 64, 34–38, http://www.stanfordlawreview.org/online/dont-break-internet (last accessed on 12.06.2012)

Lievens, Dennis, L'Oréal v. eBay – Welcomed in France, resented in England, International Review of Intellectual Property and Competition Law 2012, 68–76

Lindner, Brigitte, The WIPO Treaties, in: *Lindner, Brigitte/Shapiro, Ted*, Copyright in the Information Society (2011), pp. 3–26

Liu, Zhengye/Dhungel, Prithula/Wu, Di/Zhang, Chao/Ross, Keith W., Understanding and improving incentives in private P2P communities (2010), http://www.cis.poly.edu/~ross/papers/private_incentive.pdf (last accessed on 20.04.2013)

Lodder, Arno R./van der Meulen, Nicole S., Evaluation of the role of access providers, Discussion of Dutch Pirate Bay case law and introducing principles on directness, effectiveness, costs, relevance, and time, Journal of Intellectual Property, Information Technology and Electronic Commerce Law 2013, Vol. 4 Issue 2, 130–141

Lou, Xiaosong/Hwang, Kai, Adaptive content poisoning to prevent illegal file distribution in P2P networks (2006), http://gridsec.usc.edu/files/publications/IEEE-TC-Lou-Hwang-Aug24-2006.pdf (last accessed on 20.04.2013)

Maaßen, Stefan, Urheberrechtlicher Auskunftsanspruch und Vorratsdatenspeicherung, MultiMedia und Recht 2009, 511–515

MacEwan, Neil, A tricky situation: deception in cyberspace, Journal of Criminal Law 2013, Vol. 77 Issue 5, 417–432

Mac Síthigh, Daithí, The fragmentation of intermediary liability in the UK, Journal of Intellectual Property Law & Practice 2013, Vol. 8 No. 7, 521-531

Mankowski, Peter, Die Düsseldorfer Sperrungsverfügung – alles andere als rheinischer Karneval, MultiMedia und Recht 2002, 277–278

Mansell, Robin/Steinmueller, W. Edward, Copyright infringement online: The case of the Digital Economy Act Judicial Review in the United Kingdom, New Media & Society 2013, Vol. 15, 1312–1328

Marino, Laure, Le droit d'accès à internet, nouveau droit fondamental, Recueil Dalloz 2009, Issue 30, 2045–2046

Matthews, Duncan/Zikovska, Petra, The rise and fall of the Anti-counterfeiting Trade Agreement (ACTA): lessons for the European Union, International Review of Intellectual Property and Competition Law 2013, Vol. 44 Issue 6, 626–655

McIntyre, T.J., Child abuse images and Cleanfeeds: Assessing Internet blocking systems, in: Ian Brown (ed.), Research handbook on governance of the Internet (2012), 277–302

Meale, Darren, A triple strike against piracy as the music industry secures three more blocking injunctions, Journal of Intellectual Property Law & Practice 2013, Vol. 8, No. 8, 591–594

Meale, Darren, Avast, ye file sharers! The Pirate Bay is sunk, Journal of Intellectual Property Law & Practice 2012, Vol. 7 No. 9, 646–648

Meale, Darren, NewzBin2: the first section 97A injunction against an ISP, Journal of Intellectual Property Law & Practice 2011, Vol. 6 No. 12, 854–857

Meale, Darren, Premier League 1, Internet pirates 0: sports streaming website the latest to be blocked, Journal of Intellectual Property Law & Practice 2013, Vol. 8 No. 11, 821–823

Meale, Darren, SABAM v Scarlet: of course blanket filtering of the Internet is unlawful, but this isn't the end of the story, European Intellectual Property Review 2012, Vol. 34 Issue 7, 429–432

Meier-Beck, Peter, Herausgabe des Verletzergewinns – Strafschadensersatz nach deutschem Recht, Gewerblicher Rechtsschutz und Urheberrecht 2005, 617–623

Mendis, Dinusha, Digital Economy Act 2010: fighting a losing battle? Why the 'three strikes' law is not the answer to copyright law's latest challenge, International Review of Law, Computers & Technology 2013, Vol. 27 Issue 1–2, 60–84

Meyerdierks, Per, Personenbeziehbarkeit Statischer IP-Adressen – Datenschutzrechtliche Einordnung der Verarbeitung durch Betreiber von Webseiten, MultiMedia und Recht 2013, 705–708

Meyerdierks, Per, Sind IP-Adressen personenbezogene Daten, MultiMedia und Recht 2009, 8–14

Michel, Norbert, The impact of digital file sharing on the music industry: An empirical analysis, B.E. Journal of Economic Analysis & Policy 2006, Vol. 6 Issue 1, 1–24

Miller, Ernest/*Feigenbaum*, Joan, Taking the copy out of copyright, in: *Sander, Tomas (ed.),* Security and Privacy in Digital Rights Management, ACM CSS-8 Workshop DRM 2001 (2002), 233–244

Milstein, Alexander, Anmerkung zu EGMR: Haftung eines Forenbetreibers für anonyme Nutzerkommentare mit Meinungsfreiheit vereinbar, MultiMedia und Recht 2014, 41–42

Möller, Doris, Urheber-/Datenschutzrecht: Herausgabe gespeicherter Verkehrsdaten zur zivilrechtlichen Verfolgung von Urheberrechtsverletzungen, Europäische Zeitschrift für Wirtschaftsrecht 2012, 519–520

Montéro, Étienne/van Enis, Quentin, Ménager la liberté d'expression au regard des mesures de filtrage imposées aux intermédiaires de l'internet : la quadrature du cercle ?, Revue Lamy Droit de l'Immatériel 2008, No. 40

Moos, Flemming, Die Entwicklung des Datenschutzrechts im Jahr 2007, Kommunikation & Recht 2008, 137–145

Moreno, Felipe Romero, Incompatibility of the Digital Economy Act 2010 subscriber appeal process provisions with Article 6 of the ECHR, International Review of Law, Computers & Technology 2014, 1–17

Morgenstern, Holger, Zuverlässigkeit von IP-Adressen-Ermittlungssoftware, Zur Sicherheit der eingesetzten Programme und Verfahren zur Verletzungsdokumentation, Computer und Recht 2011, 203–208

Moss, Gary, Golden Eye v Telefonica: Media CAT revisited, Journal of Intellectual Property Law & Practice 2012, Vol. 7 No. 12, 872–878

Moss, Gary, Media CAT v Adams: the CAT that did not get the cream, Journal of Intellectual Property Law & Practice 2011, Vol. 6 No. 11, 813–820

Mueller, Milton/Kuehn, Andreas/Santoso, Stephanie Michelle, Policing the Network: Using DPI for Copyright Enforcement, Surveillance & Society 2012, Vol. 9 Issue 4, 348–364

Mühlberger, Sven, Die Haftung des Internetanschlussinhabers bei Filesharing-Konstellationen nach den Grundsätzen der Störer-haftung, Gewerblicher Rechtsschutz und Urheberrecht 2009, 1022–1027

Nas, Sjoera, The Multatuli Project ISP Notice & take down, revised article (27.10.2004), http://www.bof.nl/docs/researchpaperSANE.pdf (last accessed on 24.06.2009)

Nasir, Colin, Taming the beast of file-sharing—Legal and technological solutions to the problem of copyright infringement over the Internet: Part 2, Entertainment Law Review 2005, Vol. 16 No. 4, 82–88

Neill, Art, Does a new wave of filesharing lawsuits represent a new business model for copyright owners?, Journal of Internet Law 2011, Vol. 14 No.12, 1–17

Nguyen, Godefroy Dang/Dejean, Sylvain/Moreau, François, Are streaming and other music consumption modes substitutes or complements? (2012), http://ssrn.com/abstract=2025071 (last accessed on 30.04.2014)

Nicol, Danny, Original Intent and the European Convention on Human Rights, Public Law 2005, 152–172

Nolte, Georg/Wimmers, Jörg, Wer stört? Gedanken zur Haftung von Intermediären im Internet, GRUR-Beilage 2014, 58–69

Nordemann, Jan Bernd, Haftung von Providern im Urheberrecht, Gewerblicher Rechtsschutz und Urheberrecht 2011, 977–981

Nordemann, Jan Bernd, Störerhaftung für Urheberrechtsverletzungen – Welche konkreten Prüfpflichten haben Hostprovider (Contentprovider)?, Computer und Recht 2010, 653–661

Nordemann, Jan Bernd/Schaefer, Martin, Vermittlereigenschaft eines Access-Providers, Gewerblicher Rechtsschutz und Urheberrecht 2009, 583–584

Oberholzer-Gee, Felix/Strumpf, Koleman, The effect of file sharing on record sales: An empirical analysis, Journal of Political Economy 2007, Vol. 115 Issue 1, 1–42

Paal, Boris/Hennemann, Moritz, Schutz von Urheberrechten im Internet, ACTA, Warnhinweismodell und Europarecht, MultiMedia und Recht 2012, 288–293

Peguera, Miquel, The DMCA safe harbors and their European counterparts: A comparative analysis of some common problems, Columbia Journal of Law & the Arts 2009, Vol. 32, 481–482

Peitz, Martin/Waelbroeck, Patrick, The effect of internet piracy on music sales: Cross-section evidence, Review of Economic Research on Copyright Issues 2004, Vol. 1 Issue 2, 71–79

Perez, Nico, New creative- and content-delivery services, in: *Hargreaves, Ian/ Hofheinz, Paul (eds.),* Intellectual property and innovation. A framework for 21st century growth and jobs, pp. 22–26, http://www.lisboncouncil.net/index.php?option=com_downloads&id=693 (last accessed on 06.06.2014)

Peter, Markus, Störer im Internet – Haften Eltern für ihre Kinder? Kommunikation und Recht 2007, 371–375

Piasentin, Robert C., Unlawful? Innovative? Unstoppable? A comparative analysis of the potential legal liability facing P2P end-users in the United States, United Kingdom and Canada, International Journal of Law and Information Technology 2006, No. 14, 195–241

Piatek, Michael/Kohno, Tadayoshi/Krishnamurthy, Arvind, Challenges and directions for monitoring P2P file sharing networks – or – Why my printer received a DMCA takedown notice, University of Washington Technical Report 2008, UW-CS, http://dmca.cs.washington.edu/uwcse_dmca_tr.pdf (last accessed on 17.05.2014)

Poort, Joost/Leenheer, Jorna/von der Ham, Jeroen/Dumitru, Cosmin, Baywatch: Two approaches to measure the effects of blocking access to the Pirate Bay, Telecommunications Policy 2014, Vol. 38 Issue 4, 383–392

Prechal, Sacha, Competence creep and general principles of Law, Review of European Administrative Law 2010, Vol. 3 Issue 1, 5–22

Psychogiopoulou, Evangelia, Copyright enforcement, human rights protection and the responsibilities of Internet service providers after Scarlet, European Intellectual Property Review 2012, 552–555

Reinbacher, Tobias, Strafbarkeit der Privatkopie von offensichtlich rechtswidrig hergestellten oder öffentlich zugänglich gemachten Vorlagen, Gewerblicher Rechtsschutz und Urheberrecht 2008, 394–401

Reinbothe, Jörg, The EU Enforcement Directive 2004/48/EC as a tool for copyright enforcement, in: *Stamatoudi, Irini (ed.)*, Copyright enforcement and the Internet (2010), pp. 3–28

Revet, Thierry, Droit de propriété sur droit de propriété ne vaut, Revue trimestrielle de droit civil 2009, No. 4, 754–756

Revet, Thierry, La consécration de la liberté d'accéder aux services de communication au public en ligne, protection comme res de la position contractuelle permettant l'accès au réseau internet ?, Revue trimestrielle de droit civil 2009, No. 4, 756–757

Ricke, Thorsten/Wild, Fabian, Konten in Sachen „kino.to" beschlagnahmt, MultiMedia und Recht-Aktuell 2011, 319492

Roemer, Ryan, The digital evolution: Freenet and the future of copyright in the Internet, UCLA Journal of Law & Technology 2002, Vol. 6 Issue 2, 1–28

Rogers, Michael/Bhatti, Saleem, How to disappear completely: A survey of private peer-to-peer networks 2 (2007), http://www.cs.st-andrews.ac.uk/~saleem/papers/2007/space2007/space2007-rb2007.pdf (last accessed on 17.05.2014)

Rosenkranz, Timo, Sperrungsverfügungen gegen Access-Provider, JurPC 2003, Web–Dok. 16/2003, http://www.jurpc.de/jurpc/show?id=20030016 (last accessed on 17.05.2014)

Rösler, Hannes, Comment to OLG Hamburg, Decision of 08.02.2006 – 5 U 78/05 (Cybersky), International Review of Intellectual Property and Competition Law 2006, 994–996

Ross, Alexander/Livingstone, Claire, Communication to the public: Part 2, Entertainment Law Review 2012, Vol. 23 Issue 7, 209–213

Rössel, Markus, Filterpflichten des Providers im Lichte des EuGH – Eine Entlastung des I. Zivilsenates, Computer und Recht 2011, 589–597

Roth, Hans-Peter, Überwachungs- und Prüfungspflicht von Providern im Lichte der aktuellen EuGH-Rechtsprechung, zugleich Anm. zu EuGH, Urteil vom 24..11.2011 – C-70/10, Zeitschrift für Urheber- und Medienrecht 2012, 125–128

Roth, Hans-Peter, Verantwortlichkeit von Betreibern von Internet-Marktplätzen für Markenrechtsverletzungen durch Nutzer: L'Oréal gegen eBay, Wettbewerb in Recht und Praxis 2011, 1258–1268

Rousseau, Dominique, Après HADOPI 1et HADOPI 2, HADOPI 3 ? La décision du Conseil constitutionnel du 22 octobre 2009, Légipresse 2009, No. 267, 173–174

Rousseau, Dominique, Hado-pirate la Constitution : le Conseil sanctionne !, Revue Lamy Droit de l'Immatériel 2009, No. 51, 103–105

Rudkin-Binks, Jason/Melbourne Stephanie, The new 'three strikes' regime for copyright enforcement in New Zealand – requiring ISPs to step up to fight, Entertainment Law Review 2009, Vol. 20, 146–149

Rühmkorf, Andreas, The Liability of online auction portals: Towards a Uniform Approach?, Journal of Internet Law 2010, Vol. 14 Issue 4, 3–10

Sachdeva, Akash/McDonald, Jonathan, The use of Norwich Pharmacal orders to identify online infringers – an old remedy updated for modern times, Entertainment Law Review 2013, Vol. 24 Issue 3, 103–106

Salsas, Eduard/Härting, Niko, L'Oréal v. eBay – Consequences for EU Member States, Computer Law Review International 2011, Issue 5, 137–142

Savola, Pekka, Blocking injunctions and website operators' liability for copyright infringement for user-generated links, European Intellectual Property Review 2014, Vol. 36 Issue 5, 279–288

Schapiro, Leo, Anhaltende Rechtsunsicherheit für die Betreiber von Internetmeinungsportalen?, Das Urteil des EGMR „Delfi AS v. Estonia" und seine Auswirkungen auf die deutsche Rechtslage, Zeitschrift für Urheber- und Medienrecht 2014, 201–210.

Scharf Nick, Napster's long shadow: copyright and peer-to-peer technology, Journal of Intellectual Property Law & Practice 2011, Vol. 6 No. 11, 806–812

Schmitz, Sandra, The US SOPA and PIPA – A European Perspective, International Review of Law, Computers & Technology 2013, Vol. 27 Issue 1-2, 213–229

Schmitz, Sandra, Die Verfolgung von Urheberrechtsverletzungen im Internet – Neues vom EUGH, in: *Taeger, Jürgen (ed.)*, IT und Internet – Mit Recht gestalten, Tagungsband Herbstakademie 2012 (2012), pp. 227–243

Schmitz, Sandra, Facebook's real name policy, Bye-bye, Max Mustermann?, Journal of Intellectual Property, Information Technology and E-Commerce Law 2013, Vol. 4 Issue 3, 190–204

Schmitz, Sandra, The RedTube copyright infringement affair in Germany: Shame on who?, International Review of Law, Computers & Technology 2015, Vol. 29 Issue 1, pp. 33 - 49

Schmitz, Sandra/Ries, Thorsten, Three songs and you are disconnected from Cyberspace? Not in Germany where the industry may "turn Piracy into Profit", European Journal of Law and Technology 2012, Vol. 3 No. 1

Schmitz, Sandra/Siry, Lawrence, Online-Archive – „Der ewige Pranger im Internet"? in: *Taeger, Jürgen (ed.),* Digitale Evolution, Tagungsband Herbstakademie 2010 (2010), pp. 217–232

Schnabel, Christoph, Das Zugangserschwerungsgesetz – Zum Access-Blocking als ultima ratio des Jugendschutzes, Juristenzeitung 2009, 996–1001

Schreier, Thorsten, Düsseldorfer Sperrungsverfügung: Warum ein Provider erfolgreich war, MultiMedia und Recht 2004, 297–302

Schrijvers, Marlous, European Court rules on the position of eBay regarding the sale of infringing products: L'Oréal v eBay, European Intellectual Property Review 2011, Vol. 33 Issue 11, 723–724

Schwartmann, Rolf, Filesharing, Sharehosting & Co, Funktionsweise und rechtliche Bewertung aktueller Erscheinungsformen von Urheberrechtsverletzungen im Internet, Kommunikation und Recht 2011, Beihefter 2

Seltzer, Wendy, Free speech unmoored in copyright's safe harbor: Chilling effects of the DMCA on the First Amendment, Harvard Journal of Law & Technology 2010, Vol. 24 No. 1, 171–232

Senftleben, Martin, The International Three-Step Test, A model provision for EC fair use legislation, Journal of Intellectual Property, Information Technology and Electronic Commerce Law 2010, 67–82

Sesing, Andreas, Anmerkung zur Entscheidung des BGH-Urteil vom 15.08.2013 (I ZR 80/12, MMR 2013, 733) – Zur Frage der Prüfungs- und Handlungspflichten für Sharehoster, MultiMedia und Recht 2013, 737–739

Sieber, Ulrich, Sperrverpflichtungen gegen Kinderpornografie im Internet, Juristenzeitung 2009, 653–662

Sieber, Ulrich/Nolde, Malaika, Sperrverfügungen im Internet, Territoriale Rechtsgeltung im globalen Cyberspace? (2008), http://www.mpicc.de/de/data/pdf/mpi_sperrverfuegungen_pm-gutachten.pdf (last accessed on 17.05.2014)

Sieber, Ulrich/Volkmann, Christian, Die öffentlich-rechtliche Störerhaftung der Access-Provider, Kommunikation & Recht 2002, 398–409

Simon, Charles, Les adresses IP sont des données personnelles selon le Conseil constitutionnel, Revue Lamy Droit de l'Immatériel 2009, No. 51, 114–115

Siry, Lawrence/Schmitz, Sandra, A right to be forgotten? – How recent developments in Germany may affect the internet publishers in the US, European Journal of Law and Technology, Vol.3, No. 1, 2012, 1–12

Smith, Joel/Burke, Sarah, Record companies win first round v The Pirate Bay in the United Kingdom but pirates remain at large: Dramatico Entertainment Ltd v British Sky Broadcasting Ltd, European Intellectual Property Review 2012, Vol. 34 Issue 6, 416–419

Smits, Catherine/Ligot, Johanne, Arrêt « L'Oréal » : clarifications sur le cadre légal des activités et des responsabilités des hébergeurs de sites internet, Journal de droit européen 2011, No. 184, 294–296

Solmecke, Christian, Darlegungs- und Beweislast in Filesharing-Verfahren – Eine Auswertung der Aktuellen Rechtsprechung, in: *Taeger, Jürgen (ed.),* Law as a Service (LaaS) – Recht im Internet- und Cloud-Zeitalter (2013), Band 1, pp. 447–459

Solmecke, Christian, LG Köln: Erstattung von Anwaltskosten einer (Massen-) Abmahnung wegen P2P-Urheberrechtsverletzung, MultiMedia und Recht 2008, 129–130

Solmecke, Christian, Wenn sich die Abmahnindustrie verzockt – Rechtsprobleme bei Massenabmahnungen im Internet, in: *Taeger, Jürgen (ed.),* Digitale Evolution – Herausforderungen für das Informations- und Medienrecht (2010), pp. 627–633

Solmecke, Christian/Bärenfänger, Jan, Urheberrechtliche Schutzfähigkeit von Dateifragmenten – Nutzlos = Schutzlos, MultiMedia und Recht 2011, 567–573

Solmecke, Christian/Rüther, Felix/Herkens, Thomas, Uneinheitliche Darlegungs- und Beweislast in Filesharing-Verfahren – Abweichen von zivilprozessualen Grundsätzen zu Gunsten der Rechteinhaber?, MultiMedia und Recht 2013, 217–221

Spindler, Gerald, „Die Tür ist auf" – Europarechtliche Zulässigkeit von Auskunftsansprüchen gegenüber Providern, Gewerblicher Rechtsschutz und Urheberrecht 2008, 574–577

Spindler, Gerald, Das Gesetz zum elektronischen Geschäftsverkehr – Verantwortlichkeit der Diensteanbieter und Herkunftslandprinzip, Neue Juristische Wochenschrift 2002, 921–927

Spindler, Gerald, Die zivilrechtliche Verantwortlichkeit von Internetauktionshäusern – Haftung für automatisch registrierte und publizierte Inhalte?, MultiMedia und Recht 2001, 737–743

Spindler, Gerald, Europarechtliche Rahmenbedingungen der Störerhaftung im Internet, Multimedia und Recht 2011, 703–707

Spindler, Gerald, Präzisierungen der Störerhaftung im Internet – Besprechung des BGH-Urteils „Kinderhochstühle im Internet" Gewerblicher Rechtsschutz und Urheberrecht 2011, 101–108

Stadler, Thomas, Kein erschwerter Zugang, MultiMedia und Recht 2009, 581–582

Stadler, Thomas, Sperrungsverfügungen gegen Access-Provider, MultiMedia und Recht 2002, 343–347

Stamatoudi, Irini, Ethics, reality and the Law – The example of Promusicae v Telefonica & LSG v Tele 2, Revue Hellénique de droit international 2010, 921–948

Stieper, Malte, Rezeptiver Werkgenuss als rechtmäßige Nutzung, MultiMedia und Recht 2012, 12–17

Strowel, Alain, La loi création et Internet : de la confirmation d'un 'droit d'accès' en droit d'auteur à l'analyse de la proportionalité de la réponse graduée, in : *Institut de Recherche en Propriété Intellectuelle (ed.)*, Contrefaçon sur Internet : Les enjeux du droit d'auteur sur le Web 2.0 (2009), pp. 99–121

Strowel, Alain, The "Graduated Response" in France, in: *Stamatoudi, Irini*, Copyright enforcement and the Internet (2010), pp. 147–162

Sujecki, Bartosz, Wettbewerbsverstoß durch territoriale Exklusivitätsvereinbarungen bei Fußball-Übertragungen, Anmerkung, Neue Juristische Wochenschrift 2012, 214

Szuskin, Laurent/De Guillenschmidt, Maxime, L'arrêt « Promusicae » beaucoup de bruit pour rien?, Droit de l'immatériel : informatique, médias, communication 2008, No. 37, 6–8

Taylor, Mark/Haggerty, John/Gresty, David/Berry, Tom, Digital evidence from peer-to-peer networks, Computer Law & Security Review 2011, Vol. 27, 647–652

Terré, François, Être ou ne pas être… responsable – À propos des prestataires de service par Internet, La Semaine Juridique – édition générale 2011, Nos. 43–44, 1943–1948

Thoumyre, Lionel, La licence globale optionelle: un pare-feu contre le bugs de la repression, Revue Lamy Droit de l'Immateriél 2006, 80–84

Tibber, Andrew, Know your enemy, Magazine of the Society for Computers and Law 2008, Vol. 19 Issue 4, 1–3

Tikk, Eneken, IP Addresses Subject to Personal Data Regulation, in: *Tikk, Eneken/ Talihärm, Anna-Mari (eds.)*, International Cyber Security Legal & Policy Proceedings (2010), pp. 24–39

Tully, Stephen, A human right to access the Internet? Problems and Prospects, Human Rights Law Review 2014, Vol. 14, 175–195

Tyra, Frank, Ausgewählte Probleme aus der Abmahnpraxis bei Privatnutzungen in Musiktauschsystemen, Zeitschrift für Urheber- und Medienrecht 2009, 934–944

Usai, Andrea, The freedom to conduct a business in the EU, its limitations and its role in the European legal order: A new engine for deeper and stronger economic, social and political integration, German Law Journal 2010, Vol. 14 No. 9, 1867–1888

Vamialis, Anna, Online defamation: confronting anonymity, International Journal of Law and Information Technology 2013, Vol. 21 Issue 1, 31–65

van Eecke, Patrick/Truyens, Maarten, L'Oréal v eBay: Is the tide finally turning for hosting providers?, Computer und Recht 2011, 1–8

van Eecke, Patrick/Truyens, Maarten, L'Oréal v. eBay: The Court of Justice clarifies the position of online auction providers, Computer Law Review International 2011, Issue 5, 129–136

van Eimeren, Birgit/Gerhard, Heinz/Frees, Beate, ARD/ZDF-Online-Studie 2004, Internetverbreitung in Deutschland: Potenzial vorerst ausgeschöpft?, Media Perspektiven 2004, No. 8, 350–370

Venzke, Sven, Die Personenbezogenheit der IP-Adresse, Zeitschrift für Datenschutz 2011, 114–118

Verpeaux, Michel, Loi Hadopi 2, contrôle à double détente : 1. A propos de la décision du Conseil constitutionnel du 22 octobre 2009, La Semaine Juridique, Édition générale 2009, No. 46, 15–17

Verweyen, Urs, Grenzen der Störerhaftung in Peer to Peer-Netzwerken, MultiMedia und Recht 2009, 590–594

Vincents, Okechukwu Benjamin, When Rights Clash Online: The tracking of P2P copyright infringements vs. the EC Personal Data Directive, International Journal of Law and Information Technology 2011, Vol.16, No.3, 270–296

Volkmann, Christian, Aktuelle Entwicklungen in der Providerhaftung im Jahr 2013, Kommunikation & Recht 2014, 375–381

Völzmann-Stickelbrock, Barbara, BGH: Prüfpflichten für Sharehoster im Rahmen der Störerhaftung – File-Hosting-Dienst, Kommentierte BGH-Rechtsprechung Lindenmaier-Möhring 2013, 352737

von Lohmann, Fred, Measuring the Digital Millennium Copyright Act against the Darknet: Implications for the regulation of Technological Protection Measures, Loyola of Los Angeles Entertainment Law Review 2004, Vol. 24, 635–648

Voorhoof, Dirk, Freedom of expression and the right to information: Implications for copyright, in *Geiger, Christophe (ed.)*, Research Handbook on Human Rights and Intellectual Property (2015), pp. 331 – 353

Wandtke, Artur-Axel/von Gerlach, Felix-Tessen, Die urheberrechtliche Rechtmäßigkeit der Nutzung von Audio-Video Streaminginhalten im Internet, Gewerblicher Rechtsschutz und Urheberrecht 2013, 676–683

Wang, Xiaoyun/Yu, Hongbo, How to break MD5 and other hash functions, in: *Cramer, Ronald (ed.)*, Advances in Cryptology – EUROCRYPT 2005: 24th Annual International Conference on the Theory and Applications of Cryptographic Techniques, Proceedings, Lecture Notes in Computer Science Vol. 3494 (2005), pp. 19–35

Wechsler, Andrea, Criminal enforcement of intellectual property law: an economic approach, in: *Geiger, Christophe (ed.)*, Criminal enforcement of intellectual property (2012), pp. 128–150

Weinstein, Debra, Defining Expeditious: Uncharted territory of the DMCA safe harbor provision – A survey of what we know and do not know about the expeditiousness of service provider responses to takedown notifications, Cardozo Arts & Entertainment Law Journal 2009, Vol. 26, 589–621

Wilmer, Thomas, Überspannte Prüfpflichten für Host-Provider? – Vorschlag für eine Haftungsmatrix, 61 Neue Juristische Wochenschrift 2008, 1845–1851

Wolfgang Schulz/Thorsten Held/Arne Laudien, Search engines as gatekeepers of public communication: Analysis of the German framework applicable to Internet search engines including Media Law and Anti-trust Law, German Law Journal 2005, 1419–1432

Wood, Jessica A., The Darknet: A digital copyright revolution, Richmond Journal of Law & Technology 2010, Vol. 16 Issue 4, Article 14

Yu, Peter K., Six secret (and now open) fears of ACTA, Southern Methodist University Law Review 2011, Vol. 64 Issue 3975–1094

Yu, Peter K., Intellectual Property and Human Rights in the Nonmultilateral Era, Florida Law Review 2012, Vol. 64, 1045–1100

Yu, Peter K., The Graduated Response, Florida Law Review 2010, Vol 62, 1373–1430

Zentner, Alejandro, Measuring the effect of file sharing on music purchases, Journal of Law and Economics 2006, Vol. 49 Issue 1, 63–90

Government Materials and Official Documents

Article 29 Data Protection Working Party, Opinion 01/2008 on Data Protection Issues related to Search Engines, 00737/EN, WP 148 of 04.04.2008, http://ec.europa.eu/justice/policies/privacy/docs/wpdocs/2008/wp148_en.pdf (last accessed on 17.05.2014)

Article 29 Data Protection Working Party, Opinion 4/2007 on the Concept of Personal Data, 01248/07/EN, WP 136 of 20.06.2007, http://ec.europa.eu/justice/policies/privacy/docs/wpdocs/2007/wp136_en.pdf (last accessed on 17.05.2014)

Article 29 Data Protection Working Party, Statement of the Working Party on Current Discussions Regarding the Data Protection Reform Package (27.02.2013), http://ec.europa.eu/justice/data-protection/article-29/documentation/other-document/files/2013/20130227_statement_dp_reform_package_en.pdf (last accessed on 17.05.2014)

Article 29 Data Protection Working Party, WP 37: Privacy on the Internet – An integrated EU Approach to Online Data Protection, 5063/00/EN/FINAL, WP 37 of 21.11.2000 http://ec.europa.eu/justice/data-protection/article-29/documentation/opinion-recommendation/files/2000/wp37_en.pdf (last accessed on 17.05.2014)

Assemblée Nationale, Réponse à la Question écrite No. 3096, Journal Officiel de la Republique Francaise of 25.12.2012, 7918, http://questions.assemblee-nationale.fr/q14/14-3096QE.htm (last accessed on 17.05.2014)

Bundesministerium für Wirtschaft und Technologie, Gesamt-wirtschaftliche Perspektiven der Kultur- und Kreativwirtschaft in Deutschland, Forschungsbericht Nr. 577, http://www.kultur-kreativ-wirtschaft.de/Dateien/KuK/PDF/doku-577-gesamtwirtschaftliche-perspektiven-kultur-und-kreativwirtschaft-kurzfassung,property=pdf,bereich=kuk,sprache=de,rwb=true.pdf (last accessed on 15.05.2014)

Bundesministerium für Wirtschaft und Technologie, Monitoring zu ausgewählten wirtschaftlichen Eckdaten der Kultur- und Kreativwirtschaft 2009, Forschungsbericht Nr. 589 (2010), http://www.creative.nrw.de/fileadmin/files/downloads/Publikationen/589_BMWI_StudieKuK2009.pdf (last accessed on 15.05.2014)

Bundesverband Musikindustrie, Musikindustrie in Zahlen 2009, http://www.musikindustrie.de/uploads/media/MiZ_2009_gesamt_01.pdf (last accessed on 30.04.2014)

Bureau of the Convention, Draft Charter of Fundamental Rights of the European Union, New proposal for Articles 1 to 30 (Civil and political rights and citizens' rights) (05.05.2000), CHARTE 4284, Convent 28

Bureau of the Convention, Note from the Praesidium, Draft Charter of Fundamental Rights of the European Union, Text of the Explanations Relating to the Complete Text of the Charter as set out in CHARTE 4487/00 CONVENT 50 (11.10.2000), CHARTE 4473/00, Convent 49

Bureau of the Convention, Note from the Presidium, Draft Charter of Fundamental Rights of the European Union, New Proposal for Articles 1 to 12 (now 1 to 16) (08.03.2000), CHARTE 4149/00, Convent 13

Bureau of the Convention, Presidency Note, Draft Charter of Fundamental Rights of the European Union, Text of the explanations relating to the complete text of the Charter as set out in CHARTE 4422/00 CONVENT 45 (31.07.2000), CHARTE 4423/00, Convent 46

Commission of the European Communities, Commission Staff Working Document, Report to the Council, the European Parliament and the Economic and Social Committee on the application of Directive 2001/29/EC on the harmonisation of certain aspects of copyright and related rights in the information society (30.11.2007), SEC(2007) 1556, http://ec.europa.eu/internal_market/copyright/docs/copyright-infso/application-report_en.pdf (last accessed on 30.04.2014)

Commission of the European Communities, Green Paper, Copyright in the Knowledge Economy (16.07.2008), COM(2008) 466 final, http://eur-lex.europa.eu/LexUriServ/LexUriServ.do?uri=COM:2008:0466:FIN:EN:PDF (last accessed on 30.04.2014)

Commission of the European Parliament, First Report on the Application of Directive 2000/31/EC of the European Parliament and of the Council of 8 June 2000 on Certain Legal Aspects of Information Society Services, in particular Electronic Commerce, in the Internal Market (Directive on Electronic Commerce) COM(2003) 702 final, http://eur-lex.europa.eu/LexUriServ/LexUriServ.do?uri=COM:2003:0702:FIN:EN:PDF (last accessed on 30.04.2014)

Council of Europe, Internet: Case-Law of the European Court of Human Rights (June 2011), http://www.echr.coe.int/Documents/Research_report_Internet_ENG.pdf (last accessed on 05.05.2014)

De Wolf & Partners, Study on the Application of Directive 2001/29/EC on Copyright and Related Rights in the Information Society (The "InfoSoc Directive") (2013), http://ec.europa.eu/internal_market/copyright/docs/studies/131216_study_en.pdf (last accessed on 15.05.2014)

Department for Culture, Media and Sport and Department for Business, Innovation and Skills, Digital Britain Report (2009), http://www.official-documents.gov.uk/document/cm76/7650/7650.pdf (last accessed on 30.04.2014)

Department of Trade and Industry, Consultation Document on Electronic Commerce Directive: the liability of Hyperlinkers, Location Tool Services and Content Aggregators (June 2005), http://www.berr.gov.uk/files/file13986.pdf (last accessed on 30.04.2014)

Détraigne, Yves/Escoffier, Anne-Marie, Rapport d'information fait au nom de la Commission des lois constitutionnelles, de législation, du suffrage universel, du Règlement et d'administration générale, par le groupe de travail relatif au respect de la vie privée à l'heure des mémoires numériques (27.05.2009), http://www.senat.fr/rap/r08-441/r08-441.html (last accessed on 30.04.2014)

Deutscher Bundesrat, Empfehlungen der Ausschüsse zum Gesetz zur Neuregelung der Telekommunikationsüberwachung und anderer verdeckter Ermittlungsmaßnahmen sowie zur Umsetzung der Richtlinie 2006/24/EC, Bundesratsdrucksache 798/1/07 (19.11.2007)

Deutscher Bundestag, Bundestagsdrucksache 16/5048 (20.04.2007)

Deutscher Bundestag, Dritter Zwischenbericht der Enquete-Kommission 'Internet und digitale Gesellschaft', Bundestagsdrucksache 17/7899 (23.11.2011)

Deutscher Bundestag, Entwurf eines Gesetzes zur Produktpiraterie, Bundestagsdrucksache 11/4792 (15.06.1989)

Deutscher Bundestag, Entwurf eines Zweiten Gesetzes zur Regeleung des Urheberrechts in der Informationsgesellschaft, Bundestagsdrucksache 16/1828 (05.06.2006)

Edwards, Lilian, Role and responsibility of Internet intermediaries in the field of copyright and related rights (2011), http://www.wipo.int/export/sites/www/copyright/en/doc/role_and_responsibility_of_the_Internet_intermediaries_final.pdf (last accessed on 17.05.2014)

Espinel, Victoria / Chopra, Aneesh / Schmidt, Howard, Combating online piracy while protecting an open and innovative Internet: Official White House response to stop the E-PARASITE Act (2012), https://wwws.whitehouse.gov/petition-tool/response/combating-online-piracy-while-protecting-open-and-innovative-internet (last accessed: 12.07.2012)

Espinel, Victoria/Chopra, Aneesh/Schmidt, Howard, Combating online piracy while protecting an open and innovative Internet, Official White House response to the petitions "Stop the E-Parasite Act" and "VETO the SOPA bill and any other future bills that threaten to diminish the free flow of information" (14.01.2012), https://petitions.whitehouse.gov/response/combating-online-piracy-while-protecting-open-and-innovative-internet (last accessed on 06.06.2014)

EU Commission, Code of EU online rights (2012), https://ec.europa.eu/digital-agenda/sites/digital-agenda/files/Code%20EU%20online%20rights%20EN%20final%202.pdf (last accessed on 30.04.2014)

EU Network of Independent Experts on Fundamental Rights, Commentary of the Charter of Fundamental Rights of the European Union (June 2006), http://ec.europa.eu/justice/fundamental-rights/files/networkcommentaryfinal_en.pdf, Article 7 CFR (last accessed on 30.04.2014)

European Commission, Antitrust: Commission obtains from Google comparable display of specialised search rivals, Press release of 05.02.2014, http://europa.eu/rapid/press-release_IP-14-116_en.htm (last accessed on 06.06.2014)

European Commission, Civil enforcement of intellectual property rights: public consultation on the efficiency of proceedings and accessibility of measures, consultation period 30.11.2012 to 30.03.2013 (July 2013), http://ec.europa.eu/internal_market/consultations/docs/2012/intellectual-property-rights/questionnaire_en.pdf (last accessed on 06.06.2014)

European Commission, Communication from the Commission to the Council, the European Parliament and the European Economic and Social Committee, The Management of Copyright and Related Rights in the Internal Market, COM(2004) 0261 final, http://eur-lex.europa.eu/LexUriServ/LexUriServ.do?uri=CELEX:52004DC0261:EN:NOT (last accessed on 06.06.2014)

European Commission, Communication from the Commission to the European Parliament, the Council, the European Economic and Social Committee and the Committee of the Regions, A Single Market for intellectual property rights – Boosting creativity and innovation to provide economic growth, high quality jobs and first class products and services in Europe, Com(2011) 287 final, http://ec.europa.eu/internal_market/copyright/docs/ipr_strategy/COM_2011_287_en.pdf (last accessed on 30.04.2014)

European Commission, DG Internal Market and Services, Civil enforcement of intellectual property rights: Public Consultation of the efficiency of proceedings and accessibility of measures, synthesis of the responses (July 2013), http://ec.europa.eu/internal_market/consultations/docs/2012/intellectual-property-rights/summary-of-responses_en.pdf (last accessed on 30.04.2014)

European Commission, DG Internal Market and Services, Study on Online Copyright Enforcement and Data Protection in Selected Member States (November 2009), http://ec.europa.eu/internal_market/iprenforcement/docs/study-online-enforcement_en.pdf (last accessed on 30.04.2014)

European Commission, Directive on collective management of copyright and related rights and multi-territorial licensing - frequently asked questions, MEMO/14/79 of 04.02.2014, http://europa.eu/rapid/press-release_MEMO-14-79_en.pdf (last accessed on 06.06.2014)

European Commission, Evidence Dossier – Evidence for Necessity of Data Retention in the EU (2013) http://ec.europa.eu/dgs/home-affairs/pdf/policies/police_cooperation/evidence_en.pdf (last accessed on 30.04.2014)

European Commission, Proposal for a Directive of the European Parliament and of the Council on measures and procedures to ensure the enforcement of intellectual property rights, COM (2003) 46 final (20.01.2003), http://eur-lex.europa.eu/LexUriServ/LexUriServ.do?uri=COM:2003:0046:FIN:EN:PDF (last accessed on 30.04.2014)

European Commission, Proposal for a European Parliament and Council Directive on criminal measures aimed at ensuring the enforcement of intellectual property rights, COM(2005) 276 final (12.07.2005), http://www.europarl.europa.eu/registre/docs_autres_institutions/commission_europeenne/com/2005/0276/COM_COM%282005%290276_EN.pdf (last accessed on 06.06.2014)

European Commission, Proposal for a revision of the Directive on the enforcement of intellectual property rights (Directive 2004/48/EC), http://ec.europa.eu/smart-regulation/impact/planned_ia/docs/2011_markt_006_review_enforcement_directive_ipr_en.pdf (last accessed on 06.06.2014)

European Commission, Report from the Commission to the Council and the European Parliament, Evaluation Report on the Data Retention Directive (Directive 2006/24/EC), Com(2011) 225 final (18.04.2011), http://eur-lex.europa.eu/LexUriServ/LexUriServ.do?uri=COM:2011:0225:FIN:en:PDF (last accessed on 30.04.2014)

European Commission, Strategy for the enforcement of intellectual property rights in third countries, OJ C 129 (26.05.2005), pp. 3–16. http://trade.ec.europa.eu/doclib/docs/2010/december/tradoc_147070.pdf (last accessed on 06.06.2014)

European Commission, Synthesis of Comments on the Commission Report on the Application of Directive 2004/48/EC of the European Parliament and the Council of 29 April 2004 on the Enforcement of Intellectual Property Rights (July 2011), COM(2010) 779 final, http://ec.europa.eu/internal_market/consultations/docs/2011/intellectual_property_rights/summary_report_replies_consultation_en.pdf (last accessed on 30.04.2014)

European Commission, Synthesis of the responses "Civil enforcement of intellectual property rights: public consultation on the efficiency of proceedings and accessibility of measures" (July 2013), http://ec.europa.eu/internal_market/consultations/docs/2012/intellectual-property-rights/summary-of-responses_en.pdf (last accessed on 30.04.2014)

European Convention, Working Group II "Intégration de la Charte/adhésion à la CEDH", Speaking note of M. le juge Vassilios Skouris (17.09.2002), http://european-convention.eu.int/ docs/wd2/3063.pdf (last accessed on 30.04.2014)

European Data Protection Supervisor, Opinion of the European Data Protection Supervisor on the current negotiations by the European Union of an Anti-Counterfeiting Trade Agreement (ACTA), OJ C 147 (05.06.2010), 1, http://eur-lex.europa.eu/LexUriServ/LexUriServ.do?uri=OJ:C:2010:147:0001:0013:EN:PDF (last accessed on 30.04.2014)

European Observatory on Counterfeiting and Piracy, Evidence and right of information in Intellectual Property Rights (2010), http://ec.europa.eu/internal_market/iprenforcement/docs/evidence_en.pdf. (last accessed on 30.04.2014)

European Parliament, ACTA before the European Parliament, press release Ref. no. 20120217BKG38488 of 04.06.2012, http://www.europarl.europa.eu/news/en/pressroom/content/20120217BKG38488/ht (last accessed on 06.06.2014)

European Parliament, DG for Internal Policies, Policy Department C: Citizens' Rights and Constitutional Affairs, File Sharing (2011), http://www.ivir.nl/publications/vaneijk/pe432775_en-rev-fin.pdf (last accessed on 15.05.2014)

European Parliament, Freedom of expression on the Internet, resolution, P6_TA(2006)0324 (6.07.2006), http://www.europarl.europa.eu/sides/getDoc.do?type=TA&reference=P6-TA-2006-0324&language=EN

European Parliament, Legislative resolution of 4 February 2014 on the proposal for a directive of the European Parliament and of the Council on collective management of copyright and related rights and multi-territorial licensing of rights in musical works for online uses in the internal market (COM(2012) 0372 – C7-0183/2012 – 2012/0180(COD)), http://www.europarl.europa.eu/sides/getDoc.do?pubRef=-//EP//TEXT+TA+P7-TA-2014-0056+0+DOC+XML+V0//EN (last accessed on 06.06.2014)

European Telecommunications Standards Institute, ETSI TS 101 331 (August 2001), http://www.etsi.org/deliver/etsi_ts/101300_101399/101331/01.01.01_60/ts_101331v010101p.pdf (last accessed on 15.05.2014)

Executive Office of the President of the United States, US Intellectual Property Enforcement Coordinator, Joint Strategic Plan on Intellectual Property Enforcement (June 2010), http://www.whitehouse.gov/sites/default/files/omb/assets/intellectualproperty/intellectualproperty_strategic_plan.pdf (last accessed on 06.06.2014)

Gowers, Andrew, Gowers Review of Intellectual Property (December 2006), http://www.official-documents.gov.uk/document/other/0118404830/0118404830.pdf (last accessed on 30.04.2014)

HADOPI, 2010 Activity Report (2011), http://hadopi.fr/sites/default/files/page/pdf/Hadopi_Rapportannuel_ENG.pdf (last accessed on 30.04.2014)

HADOPI, Biens culturels et usages d'Internet : pratiques et perceptions des internautes français (January 2013), http://hadopi.fr/sites/default/files/page/pdf/HADOPI-160113-BU2-Complet.pdf (last accessed on 30.04.2014)

HADOPI, HADOPI – 1 ½ year after the launch (March 2012), http://www.hadopi.fr/sites/default/files/page/pdf/note17_en.pdf (last accessed on 30.04.2014)

HADOPI, Rapport Annuel 2012/2013 (2013), http://www.hadopi.fr/sites/default/files/page/pdf/HADOPI_RapportAnnuel_2013.pdf (last accessed on 30.04.2014)

HADOPI, Réponse graduée – Les chiffres clés (06.11.2013), http://www.hadopi.fr/sites/default/files/Chiffres_reponsegraduee_Octobre2013.pdf (last accessed on 30.04.2014)

Hargreaves, Ian, Digital Opportunity, A Review of Intellectual Property and Growth (2011), http://www.ipo.gov.uk/ipreview-finalreport.pdf (last accessed on 15.05.2014)

HM Government, Modernising Copyright: A modern, robust and flexible framework, Government Response to Consultation on Copyright Exceptions and Clarifying Copyright Law (December 2012), http://www.ipo.gov.uk/response-2011-copyright-final.pdf (last accessed on 30.04.2014)

House of Commons, Digital Economy Act: Copyright, Standard Note: SN/HA/5515 (28.06.2013), www.parliament.uk/briefing-papers/sn05515.pdf (last accessed on 30.04.2014)

House of Lords, Hansard, Debate 18.01.2010, http://www.publications.parliament.uk/pa/ld200910/ldhansrd/text/100118-0004.htm#1001185000078 (last accessed on 30.04.2014)

House of Lords, House of Commons, Joint Committee on Human Rights, Legislative Scrutiny: Digital Economy Bill, Fifth Report of Session 2009-10, HL Paper 44 = HC 327 (05.02.2010), http://www.publications.parliament.uk/pa/jt200910/jtselect/jtrights/44/44.pdf (last accessed on 30.04.2014)

House of Representatives, Digital Millennium Copyright Act of 1998, Report, H.R. Rep. No. 105–551, Part II, 49 (1998), http://frwebgate.access.gpo.gov/cgi-bin/getdoc.cgi?dbname =105_cong_reports&docid=f:hr551p2.105.pdf (last accessed on 30.04.2014)

International Telecommunication Union, Understanding Cybercrime: A guide for developing countries (April 2009), http://www.itu.int/dms_pub/itu-d/oth/01/0B/D010B0000073301PDFE.pdf (last accessed on 30.04.2014)

Joint Committee on Human Rights, Legislative Scrutiny: Digital Economy Bill, Fifth Report of Session 2009 – 10, http://www.publications.parliament.uk/pa/jt200910/jtselect/jtrights/44/44.pdf (last accessed on 15.05.2014)

Kuner, Christoper/Burton, Cédric/Hladjk, Jörg/Proust, Oliver, Study on online copyright enforcement and data protection in selected Member States (November 2009), http://ec.europa.eu/internal_market/iprenforcement/docs/study-online-enforcement_en.pdf (last accessed on 15.05.2014)

Lescure, Pierre, Culture-acte 2, Mission « Acte II de l'exception culturelle », Contribution aux politiques culturelles à l'ére numérique (May 2013), http://www.culturecommunication.gouv.fr/content/download/67159/514925/version/1/file/Rapport_Lescure.pdf (last accessed on 30.04.2014)

Macovei, Monica, Freedom of Expression, Council of Europe Human Rights Handbooks, No. 2 (2nd ed. 2004), http://www.coe.int/t/dgi/publications/hrhandbooks/HRHAND-02%282004%29_en.pdf (last accessed on 20.04.2013)

Ministère de la Culture et de la Communication, Publication du décret supprimant la peine complémentaire de la suspension d'accès á Internet, Press release (09.07.2013), http://culturecommunication.gouv.fr/Espace-Presse/Communiques/Publication-du-decret-supprimant-la-peine-complementaire-de-la-suspension-d-acces-a-Internet (last accessed on 30.04.2014)

OECD, Directorate for Science, Technology and Industry, Committee for Information, Computer and Communications Policy, Working Party on the Information Economy, Participative Web: User-Created Content (12.04.2007), DSTI/ICCP/IE(2006)7/FINAL, http://www.oecd.org/sti/38393115.pdf (last accessed on 30.04.2014)

OECD, Magnitude of counterfeiting and piracy of tangible products – November 2009 update, http://www.oecd.org/document/23/0,3343,en_2649_34173_44088983_1_1_1_1,00.html (last accessed on 30.04.2014)

Ofcom, "Site Blocking" to reduce online copyright infringement: A review of sections 17 and 18 of the Digital Economy Act (2011), http://stakeholders.ofcom.org.uk/binaries/internet/site-blocking.pdf (last accessed 30.04.2014)

Office of the High Commissioner for Human Rights, General Comment No. 16: The right to respect of privacy, family, home and correspondence, and protection of honour and reputation (Article 17), CCPR General Comment No. 16 (08.04.1988)

Parliament, Hansard (House of Commons), Column 1142 (07.04.2010), http://www.publications.parliament.uk/pa/cm200910/cmhansrd/cm100407/debtext/100407-0032.htm (last accessed 30.04.2014)

Parliament, Select Committee on Culture, Media and Sport, Memorandum submitted by Dr Richard Clayton (2008), http://www.publications.parliament.uk/pa/cm200708/cmselect/cmcumeds/353/353we05.htm (last accessed 17.05.2014)

Praesidium of the European Convention, Explanations relating to the Charter, OJ C 303 (14.12.2007), 17–35, http://eur-lex.europa.eu/LexUriServ/LexUriServ.do?uri=OJ:C:2007:303:0017:0035:EN:PDF (last accessed 17.05.2014)

Schwartmann, Rolf, Vergleichende Studie über Modelle zur Versendung von Warnhinweisen durch Internet-Zugangsanbieter an Nutzer bei Urheberrechtsverletzungen, Studie im Auftrag des Bundesministerium für Wirtschaft und Technologie (Januar 2012), http://bmwi.de/BMWi/Redaktion/PDF/Publikationen/Technologie-und-Innovation/warnhinweise-lang,property=pdf,bereich=bmwi,sprache=de,rwb=true.pdf (last accessed on 06.05.2014)

Sénat, Explanatory Memorandum, Projet de loi favorisant la diffusion et la protection de la création sur Internet, Annexe au procès-verbal de la séance du 18.06.2008, http://www.senat.fr/leg/pjl07-405.html (last accessed 30.04.2014)

Senate, Digital Millennium Copyright Act, S. Rep. No. 105-190, (1998), http://frwebgate.access.gpo.gov/cgi-bin/getdoc.cgi?dbname=105_cong_reports&docid=f:sr190.105.pdf (last accessed 30.04.2014)

Söndermann, Michael / Backes, Christoph / Arndt, Olaf, Gesamtwirtschaftliche Perspektiven der Kultur- und Kreativwirtschaft in Deutschland, Bundesministerium für Wirtschaft und Technologie, Forschungsbericht Nr. 577 (2009), http://www.kultur-kreativ-wirtschaft.de/Dateien/KuK/PDF/doku-577-gesamtwirtschaftliche-perspektiven-kultur-und-kreativwirtschaft-kurzfassung,property=pdf,bereich=kuk,sprache=de,rwb=true.pdf (last accessed on 17.05.2014)

United Nations Conference on Trade and Development, Information Economy Report 2005, UNCTAD/SDTE/ECB/2005/1, http://www.unctad.org/en/docs/sdteecb20051ch6_en.pdf (last accessed on 30.04.2014)

United Nations Human Rights Committee, General comment No. 34. Article 19: Freedoms of opinion and expression, CCPR/C/GC/34 (21.07.2011), http://www2.ohchr.org/english/bodies/hrc/docs/gc34.pdf (last accessed 30.04.2014)

United Nations Human Rights Council, Report of the Special Rapporteur on the promotion and protection of the right to freedom of opinion and expression, Frank La Rue (16.05.2011), A/HRC/17/27, http://www2.ohchr.org/english/bodies/hrcouncil/docs/17session/A.HRC.17.27_en.pdf (last accessed 30.04.2014)

United States Department of Justice, *Justice Department Charges Leaders of Megaupload with Widespread Online Copyright Infringement,* Press release of 29.01.2012, http://www.justice.gov/opa/pr/2012/January/12-crm-074.html (last accessed 17.05.2014)

United States Government Accountability Office, Observations on Efforts to Quantify the Economic Effects of Counterfeit and Pirated Goods, Report to Congressional Committees (12.04.2010) http://www.gao.gov/new.items/d10423.pdf (last accessed on 15.05.2014)

US Senate, Committee on the Judiciary, Statement from Chairman Smith on Senate Delay of Vote on PROTECT IP Act, Senate press release of 20.01.2012, http://judiciary.house.gov/index.cfm/2012/1/statementfromchairmansmithonsenatedelayofvoteonprotectipact (last accessed on 06.06.2014)

Other Sources

Aereo, Statement from Aereo CEO and founder Chet Kanoja, Press release of 10.01.2014, http://blog.aereo.com/2014/01/statement-aereo-ceo-founder-chet-kanoji a-2/ (last accessed on 17.05.2014)

AFP, HADOPI : Première condamnation d'un internaute, Libération (13.09.2012), http://www.liberation.fr/cultuere/2012/09/13/premiere-condamnation-d-un-internau te-dans-le-cadre-de-hadopi_846042 (last accessed on 17.05.2014)

Algemene Vereniging van Beroepsjournalisten in Belgie et al., Open letter to President Dean Spielmann of 13.01.2014, www.mediadefence.org/sites/default/files/DelfiSup portLetter.pdf (last accessed 05.05.2014).

Anderson, Nate, Darknets and the future of P2P investigators, Ars Technica (05.03.2009), http://arstechnica.com/tech-policy/2009/03/the-new-version-of-p2p/ (last accessed on 17.05.2014)

Apple, Apple reports second quarter results, net profit increases 94 % year-over-year, Press release (24.04.2012), http://www.apple.com/pr/library/2012/04/24Apple-Rep orts-Second-Quarter-Results.html (last accessed 30.04.2014)

Arthur, Charles, Are downloads really killing the music industry? Or is it something else?, The Guardian (09.06.2009), http://www.theguardian.com/news/datablog/200 9/jun/09/games-dvd-music-downloads-piracy (last accessed on 17.05.2014)

Arthur, Charles/Dredge, Stuart, Google ads to be blocked from sites offering pirated content, The Guardian (16.07.2013), http://www.theguardian.com/technology/2013/ jul/16/google-ads-block-pirated-content (last accessed on 06.06.2014)

Ball, James/Borger, Julian/Greenwald, Glenn, Revealed: How US and UK spy agencies defeat Internet piracy and security, The Guardian (06.09.2013), http://www.the guardian.com/world/2013/sep/05/nsa-gchq-encryption-codes-security/print (last accessed on 17.05.2014)

Bangemann, Eric, Pass or fail? RIAA's college litigation campaign turns one, Ars Technica (28.02.2008), http://arstechnica.com/tech-policy/2008/02/riaa-college-law suit-anniversary/ (last accessed on 17.05.2014)

Barnett, Emma, Wikipedia founder Jimmy Wales defends SOPA protest blackout, The Telegraph (17.01.2012), http://www.telegraph.co.uk/technology/wikipedia/9020053/Wikipedia-founder-Jimmy-Wales-defends-SOPA-protest-blackout.html (last accessed on 17.05.2014)

BBC News, Music fans back legal downloads, BBC News (12.10.2008), http://news.bbc.co.uk/2/hi/technology/7664088.stm (last accessed on 17.05.2014)

BBC News, UK piracy warning letters delayed until 2015, BBC News (06.06.2013), http://www.bbc.com/news/technology-22796723 (last accessed on 17.05.2014)

BBC World Service, Four in five regard Internet access as a fundamental right: global poll, BBC News (08.03.2010), www.bbc.co.uk/pressoffice/pressreleases/stories/2010/03_march/07/poll.shtml (last accessed on 17.05.2014)

Beckedahl, Markus/Lüke, Falk, Wie die Musikbranche zum Internet-gegner wurde, Der Spiegel Online (23.05.2012), http://www.spiegel.de/netzwelt/netzpolitik/die-digitale-gesellschaft-ein-buchauszug-a-834398.html (last accessed on 15.05.2014)

Berry, Philippe, LOPPSI 2 donne les pleins pouvoirs au ministère de l'Intérieur pour censurer le Net, 20 minutes (21.12.2010), http://www.20minutes.fr/web/642783-web-loppsi-2-donne-pleins-pouvoirs-ministere-interieur-censurer-net (last accessed on 17.05.2014)

Bitkom, Trend zu Musik-Streaming per Internet, Press release of 10.07.2012, http://www.bitkom.org/files/documents/BITKOM-Presseinfo_Musik-Streaming_10_07_2012%281%29.pdf (last accessed on 17.05.2014)

BitTorrent Inc., BitTorrent, inc. grows to over 100 million active monthly users (03.01.2011), Business Wire, http://www.businesswire.com/news/home/20110103005337/en/BitTorrentGrows-100-Million-Active-Monthly-Users (last accessed on 17.05.2014)

Bleich Holger, Die Abmahn-Industrie – Wie mit dem Missbrauch des Urheberrechts Kasse gemacht wird, c´t 2010, Issue 1, 154–156

Bleich, Holger, Briefkasten-Ermittlungen, c't 2014, Issue 5, 28, http://www.heise.de/ct/heft/2014-5-Pornostreaming-Richter-geben-Fehler-in-Auskunftsverfahren-zu-2107127.html (last accessed on 15.05.2014)

Bleich, Holger/Heidrich, Joerg/Stadler, Thomas, Schwierige Gegenwehr – Was tun bei unberechtigten Filesharing-Abmahnungen?, c´t 2010, Issue 19, http://www.heise.de/ct/artikel/Schwierige-Gegenwehr-1069835.html (last accessed on 15.05.2014)

Bleich, Holger/Kossel, Axel, Verschleierungstaktik: Die Argumente für Kinderporno-Sperren laufen ins Leere, Der Spiegel online (17.04.2009), http://www.spiegel.de/netzwelt/web/verschleierungstaktik-die-argumente-fuer-kinderporno-sperren-laufen-ins-leere-a-619505.html (last accessed on 17.05.2014)

Blocman, Amélie, Adoption of the Act on Copyright and Neighbouring Rights in the Information Society (2006), http://merlin.obs.coe.int/iris/2006/7/article20.en.html (last accessed on 17.05.2014)

Blocman, Amélie, Illegal downloading: Penalty of refusing Internet access abolished, IRIS 2013-8:1/16, http://merlin.obs.coe.int/iris/2013/8/article16.en.html (last accessed on 17.05.2014)

Brauck, Markus/Hülsen, Isabell/Kühn, Alexander/Nezik, Ann-Kathrin, Was glotzen Sie so?, Der Spiegel online (13.01.2014), http://www.spiegel.de/spiegel/print/d-124381 357.html (last accessed on 17.05.2014)

Bright, Martin, BT puts block on child porn sites, The Observer (06.06.2004), http://w ww.theguardian.com/technology/2004/jun/06/childrensservices.childprotection (last accessed on 17.05.2014)

Brignall, Miles, File sharers targeted with legal action over music downloads, The Guardian (17.07.2010), http://www.theguardian.com/money/2010/jul/17/file-sharer s-legal-action-music-downloads (last accessed on 17.05.2014)

British Record Music Industry (BPI), Digital Music Nation 2013, the UK's legal and illegal digital music landscape (2013), http://www.bpi.co.uk/assets/files/BPI_Digita l_Music_Nation_2013.PDF (last accessed on 17.05.2014)

Business Wire, BitTorrent, Inc. grows to over 100 million active monthly users, Business Wire (03.01.2011), http://www.businesswire.com/news/home/2011010300533 7/en/BitTorrent-Grows-100-Million-Active-Monthly-Users (last accessed on 17.05.2014)

Business Wire, Strategy Analytics: A Quarter of Households Worldwide Now Have Wireless Home Networks, Business Wire (04.04.2012), http://www.businesswire.co m/news/home/20120404006331/en/Strategy-Analytics-Quarter-Households-World wide-Wireless-Home (last accessed on 15.05.2014)

Champeau, Guillaume, Le transfert HADOPI > CSA n'est "plus l'axe prioritaire", Numerama.com (19.02.2015), http://www.numerama.com/magazine/32267-le-trans fert-hadopi-csa-n-est-plus-l-axe-prioritaire.html (last accessed on 07.07.2015)

Chmielewski, Dawn C., Report links Google, Yahoo to Internet piracy sites, LA Times (02.01.2013), http://articles.latimes.com/2013/jan/02/entertainment/la-et-ct-piracy-a ds-20130102 (last accessed on 06.06.2014)

Cisco Systems Inc., Cisco Visual Networking Index: Forecast and Methodology, 2012–2017 (2013), http://www.cisco.com/c/en/us/solutions/collateral/service-provider/ip-ngn-ip-next-generation-network/white_paper_c11-481360.pdf (last accessed on 17.05.2014)

Columbus, Simon, French Government plans to extend internet censorship, OpenNet Initiative (21.06.2011), https://opennet.net/blog/2011/06/french-government-plans-e xtend-internet-censorship (last accessed on 17.05.2014)

Conseil National du Numérique, Avis n° 2 du Conseil National du Numérique relatif au projet de décret pris pour l'application de l'article 18 de la loi pour la confiance dans l'économie numérique (20.06.2011), http://www.cnnumerique.fr/wp-content/u ploads/2012/02/2011-06-20_CP_LCENArticle8.pdf (last accessed on 17.05.2014).

Consumer Focus, Consumer Focus Submission to the Secondary Legislation Scrutiny Committee on the Digital Economy Cost Sharing Order (July 2012), http://www.co nsumerfocus.org.uk/files/2010/10/Consumer-Focus-submission-to-the-Secondary-le gislation-Scrutiny-Committee-on-the-Digital-Economy-cost-sharing-order.pdf (last accessed on 17.05.2014)

Consumer Focus, Outdated copyright law confuses consumers, press release (24.02.2010), http://www.consumerfocus.org.uk/news/outdated-copyright-law-conf uses-consumers (last accessed on 15.05.2014)

Coslin, Christelle/Gateau, Christine, No 'stay down' obligation for hosting providers in France, Society for Computers and Law (02.07.2013), http://www.scl.org/site.aspx?i=ed32661 (last accessed on 17.05.2014)

Cowell, Simon/Daltrey, Roger/Professor Green/John, Elton/Lloyd-Webber, Andrew/May, Brian/ Plant, Robert/Taylor, Roger/Tinie Tempah/Townshend, Pete, Musicians need strong copyright laws to excel globally, The Telegraph (24.07.2012), http://www.telegraph.co.uk/comment/letters/9421416/Musicians-need-strong-copyright-laws-to-excel-globally.html (last accessed on 06.06.2014)

Crocker, Steve/Dagon, David/Kaminsky, Dan/McPherson, Danny/Vixie, Paul, Security and other technical concerns raised by the DNS filtering requirements in the PROTECT IP Bill (May 2011), http://domainincite.com/docs/PROTECT-IP-Technical-Whitepaper-Final.pdf (last accessed: 12.06.2012)

Darnstädt, Thomas, Wem gehören die Gedanken? Der Spiegel online (21.05.2012), http://www.spiegel.de/spiegel/urheberrecht-a-833984.html (last accessed on 17.05.2014)

Der Spiegel, Erpressung im Internet: 21-jähriger Münchner zu Facebook-Verbot verurteilt, Der Spiegel online (25.03.2014), http://www.spiegel.de/panorama/justiz/muenchner-zu-facebook-verbot-verurteilt-a-960688.html (last accessed on 17.05.2014)

Eckersley, Peter/Higgins, Parker, An Open Letter From Internet Engineers to the U.S. Congress, EFF (15.12.2011), https://www.eff.org/deeplinks/2011/12/internet-inventors-warn-against-sopa-and-pipa (last accessed on 06.06.2014)

Eco, 300.000 Adressen pro Monat: erfolgreicher Kampf gegen illegale Downloads, Press release (31.05.2011), http://www.eco.de/verband/202_9137.htm (last accessed 16.06.2011)

Electronic Frontier Foundation, Lawrence Lessig settles fair use lawsuit over Phoenix music snippets, EFF press release of 27.02.2014, https://www.eff.org/press/releases/lawrence-lessig-settles-fair-use-lawsuit-over-phoenix-music-snippets (last accessed on 06.06.2014)

Electronic Frontier Foundation, Lawrence Lessig strikes back against bogus copyright takedown, EFF press release of 22.08.2013, https://www.eff.org/press/releases/lawrence-lessig-strikes-back-against-bogus-copyright-takedown (last accessed on 06.06.2014)

Electronic Frontier Foundation, Lenz v Universal, https://www.eff.org/cases/lenz-v-universal (last accessed on 06.06.2014)

Electronic Frontier Foundation, RIAA v. the People: Five years later (2008), https://www.eff.org/files/eff-riaa-whitepaper.pdf (last accessed on 15.05.2014)

Enigmax (= Maxwell, Andy), Which are the best anonymous VPN providers, TorrentFreak (07.10.2011), http://torrentfreak.com/which-vpn-providers-really-take-anonymity-seriously111007/ (last accessed on 15.05.2014)

Enigmax, Rapidshare: Traffic and piracy dipped after new business model kicked in, TorrentFreak (09.01.2013), http://torrentfreak.com/rapidshare-traffic-and-piracy-dipped-after-new-business-model-kicked-in-130109/ (last accessed on 06.06.2014)

Enigmax/Ernesto, Review: Is your VPN service really anonymous?, TorrentFreak (02.01.2014), http://torrentfreak.com/vpn-services-that-take-your-anonymity-seriously-2013-edition/ (last accessed on 17.05.2014)

Envisional, Technical Report: An Estimate of Infringing Use of the Internet (2011), http://documents.envisional.com/docs/Envisional-Internet_Usage-Jan2011.pdf (last accessed on 15.05.2014)

Ernesto (= Renkema, Lennart), Anonymous, decentralized and uncensored file-sharing is booming, TorrentFreak (03.03.2012), https://torrentfreak.com/anonymous-decentralized-and-uncensored-file-sharing-is-booming-120302/ (last accessed on 15.05.2014)

Ernesto, BitTorrent's Future? DHT, PEX and magnet Links explained, TorrentFreak (20.11.2009), http://torrentfreak.com/bittorrents-future-dht-pex-and-magnet-links-explained-091120/ (last accessed on 17.05.2014)

Ernesto, BTGuard review: How does it work?, TorrentFreak (19.01.2013), http://torrentfreak.com/make-bittorrent-transfers-anonymous-with-btguard-100419/ (last accessed on 17.05.2014)

Ernesto, Leaked emails reveal profits of anti-piracy cash scheme, TorrentFreak (26.09.2010), http://torrentfreak.com/leaked-emails-reveal-profits-of-anti-piracy-cash-scheme-100926/ (last accessed on 15.05.2014)

Ernesto, Pirate parties plan to shoot torrent site into orbit, TorrentFreak (20.10.2010), http://torrentfreak.com/pirate-parties-plan-to-shoot-torrent-site-into-orbit-101020/ (last accessed on 17.05.2014)

Ernesto, The Pirate Bay adds domain to bypass court order, TorrentFreak (05.10.2011), https://torrentfreak.com/the-pirate-bay-adds-domain-to-bypass-court-order-111005/ (last accessed on 17.05.2014)

Ernesto, The Pirate Bay, now without torrents, TorrentFreak (28.02.2012), https://torrentfreak.com/the-pirate-bay-dumps-torrents-120228/ (last accessed on 17.05.2014)

Ernesto, When pirates become copyright cash cows, Torrentfreak.com (30.08.2009), http://torrentfreak.com/when-pirates-become-copyright-cash-cows-090830/ (last accessed on 15.05.2014)

European Digital Rights, ACTA fact sheet, EDRi (02.02.2012), http://www.edri.org/ACTAfactsheet (last accessed on 06.06.2014)

Farivar, Cyrus, After sailing the domain name seas, Pirate Bay returns to Sweden, ars technica (19.12.2013), http://arstechnica.com/tech-policy/2013/12/after-sailing-the-domain-name-seas-pirate-bay-returns-to-sweden/ (last accessed on 17.05.2014)

Fisher, David, Dotcom trial may not occur, The New Zealand Herald (21.04.2012), http://www.nzherald.co.nz/nz/news/article.cfm?c_id=1&objectid=10800409 (last accessed on 17.05.2014)

Fisher, Ken, Students largely ignore RIAA instant settlement offers, Ars technica (26.03.2007), http://arstechnica.com/tech-policy/2007/03/students-largely-ignore-riaa-instant-settlement-offers/ (last accessed on 17.05.2014)

Fleishman, Glenn, Cartoon Captures Spirit of the Internet, The New York Times (14.12.2000), http://www.nytimes.com/2000/12/14/technology/14DOGG.html (last accessed on 17.05.2014)

GfK Consumer Panel, Studie zur digitalen Content-Nutzung (DCN-Studie) 2011 (2011), http://www.musikindustrie.de/uploads/media/DCN-Studie_2011_Pressevers ion_FINAL.pdf (last accessed on 15.05.2014)

Gillmor, Dan, The Bruce Willis dilemma? In the digital era, we own nothing, The Guardian (03.09.2012), http://www.theguardian.com/commentisfree/2012/sep/03/br uce-willis-dilemmadigital-era-own-nothing (last accessed on 06.06.2014)

Google, Google Transparency Report (updated weekly), http://www.google.com/transp arencyreport/removals/copyright/domains/?r=last-year (last accessed on 05.05.2014)

Google/PRS for Music/BAE Systems Detica, The six business models for copyright infringement (27.06.2012), http://www.prsformusic.com/aboutus/policyandresearch /researchandeconomics/Documents/TheSixBusinessModelsofCopyrightInfringemen t.pdf (last accessed on 06.06.2014)

Gröflin, Simon, RapidShare ohne Führung und Angestellte, PC Tipp (25.02.2014), http://www.pctipp.ch/news/firmen/artikel/rapidshare-ohne-fuehrung-und-angestellte -70690/ (last accessed on 06.06.2014)

Guillemin, Gabrielle, Case Law, Strasbourg: Delfi AS v Estonia: Court strikes serious blow to free speech online, Inform's blog (15.10.2013), http://inforrm.wordpress.co m/2013/10/15/case-law-strasbourg-delfi-as-v-estonia-court-strikes-serious-blow-to-free-speech-online-gabrielle-guillemin/ (last accessed: 05.05.2014)

heise.de, LTE-A-Modems liefern bald bis zu 300 MBit/s, Heise online (11.09.2013), http://www.heise.de/netze/meldung/LTE-A-Modems-liefern-bald-bis-zu-300-MBit-s-1953525.html (last accessed on 15.05.2014)

heise.de, Porno-Abmahnungen: Indizienkette zur IP-Adressen-Ermittlung verdichtet sich, Heise online (13.12.2013), http://www.heise.de/newsticker/meldung/Porno-Ab mahnungen-Indizienkette-zur-IP-Adressen-Ermittlung-verdichtet-sich-2065879.htm l (last accessed on 15.05.2014)

Hogge, Becky, IWF censors Wikipedia, chaos ensues, Open Rights Group (08.12.2008), http://www.openrightsgroup.org/blog/2008/iwf-censors-wikipedia-ch aos-ensues (last accessed on 17.05.2014)

Holzel, Mark, The connected TV landscape: Why smart TVs and streaming gadgets are conquering the living room, Business Insider (03.03.2014), http://www.business insider.com/the-connected-tv-landscape-why-smart-tvs-and-streaming-gadgets-are-conquering-the-living-room-2-2014-2 (last accessed on 30.04.2014)

Kaufman, Gil, Madonna to pirates: 'What the F--- do you think you're doing?', Singer lashes out at file traders on P2P networks, MTV news (16.04.2003), http://www.mt v.com/news/articles/1471321/madonna-rips-file-traders.jhtml (last accessed on 15.05.2014)

Kleinz, Torsten, Sperrverfügungen gegen Wettanbieter in NRW, Heise online (04.05.2011), http://www.heise.de/newsticker/meldung/Sperrverfuegungen-gegen-Wettanbieter-in-NRW-1237731.html (last accessed on 17.05.2014)

Knoke, Felix, Kim Dotcom: US-Justizministerium legt seine Erkenntnisse gegen Megaupload vor, Der Spiegel online (23.12.2013), http://www.spiegel.de/netzwelt/ web/us-justizministerium-legt-erkenntnisse-gegen-megaupload-vor-a-940627.html (last accessed on 17.05.2014)

Knoke, Felix, Streaming: Disney löscht Weihnachtsfilm für Amazon-Kunden, Der Spiegel Online (16.12.2013), http://www.spiegel.de/netzwelt/web/streaming-disney-loescht-weihnachtsfilm-fuer-amazon-kunden-a-939297.html (last accessed on 06.06.2014)

Korff, Douwe/Brown, Ian, Opinion on the compatibility of ACTA with the ECHR and the EU Charter of Fundamental Rights (2011), http://www.greens-efa.eu/fileadmin/dam/Documents/Studies/ACTA_fundamental_rights_assessment.pdf (last accessed on 15.05.2014)

Kremp, Matthias, Streaming-Portal: Redtube will für Recht auf Porno kämpfen, Der Spiegel online (20.12.2013), http://www.spiegel.de/netzwelt/web/redtube-betreiber-alex-taylor-bestreitet-weitergabe-von-ip-adressen-a-940113.html (last accessed on 17.05.2014)

Krempl, Stefan SPD-Sprecher verreißt die rheinischen Sperrungsverfügungen, Heise online (20.02.2002), http://www.heise.de/newsticker/meldung/SPD-Sprecher-verreisst-die-rheinischen-Sperrungsverfuegungen-56316.html (last accessed on 17.05.2014)

Krempl, Stefan, Arcor installiert leicht umgehbare Netzsperre für YouPorn, Heise online (24.10.2007), http://www.heise.de/newsticker/meldung/Arcor-installiert-leicht-umgehbare-Netzsperre-fuer-YouPorn-188617.html (last accessed: 04.12.2012)

Krempl, Stefan, Arcor muss YouPorn sperren, Heise online (19.10.2007), http://www.heise.de/newsticker/meldung/Arcor-muss-YouPorn-sperren-Update-187184.html (last accessed on 17.05.2014)

Krempl, Stefan, Provider in Nordrhein-Westfalen erhalten Sperrungsverfügungen, Heise online (08.02.2002), http://www.heise.de/newsticker/meldung/Provider-in-Nordrhein-Westfalen-erhalten-Sperrungsverfuegungen-53926.html (last accessed on 17.05.2014)

La Quadrature du Net, French LOPPSI Bill adopted: the Internet under control?, La Quadrature du Net (09.02.2011), http://www.laquadrature.net/en/french-loppsi-bill-adopted-the-Internet-under-control (last accessed on 17.05.2014)

Lainé, Pascal, Belfortain poursuivi pour téléchargement illégal : 150 € d'amende, LePays.fr (13/09/2012), http://www.lepays.fr/faits-divers/2012/09/13/belfort-un-quadragenaire-poursuivi-pour-Telechargement-illegal-hadopi-mp3-lepuix (last accessed on 15.05.2014)

Le Monde, Le budget de la Hadopi passe à 8 millions d'euros, Le Monde (03.10.2012), http://www.lemonde.fr/technologies/article/2012/10/03/le-budget-de-la-hadopi-reduit-a-8-millions-d-euros_1769154_651865.html (last accessed on 17.05.2014)

Le Monde, Loppsi 2: le gouvernement pourrait abandonner le blocage des sites sans juge, Le Monde (25.07.2012), http://www.lemonde.fr/technologies/article/2012/07/25/loppsi-2-le-gouvernement-pourrait-abandonner-le-blocage-des-sites-sans-juge_1738020_651865.html (last accessed on 17.05.2014)

Le Monde, RSF critique le filtrage du Net prévu par la Loppsi 2, Le Monde (16.09.2010), http://www.lemonde.fr/technologies/article/2010/09/16/rsf-critique-le-filtrage-du-net-prevu-par-la-loppsi-2_1411897_651865.html (last accessed on 17.05.2014)

Lee, Doug Jay/Kim, Misung/Hong, Jong Won, Annual Report 2009, Korea APAA Copyright Committee, http://www.apaaonline.org/pdf/APAA_56th_&_57th_council_meeting/copyright/2-Korea%20Copyright%20Cttee%20Country%20Report%202009.pdf (last accessed on 17.05.2014)

Leeds, Jeff, Labels win suit against song sharer, The New York Times (05.10.2007), http://www.nytimes.com/2007/10/05/business/media/05music.html?_r=0 (last accessed on 17.05.2014)

Leparisien.fr, Téléchargement illégal: Fleur Pellerin confirme qu'HADOPI va disparaître, Le Parisien (24.05.2013), http://www.leparisien.fr/high-tech/telechargement-illegal-fleur-pellerin-confirme-qu-hadopi-va-disparaitre-24-05-2013-2831541.php (last accessed on 17.05.2014)

Levene, Tony, Porn bill for couple who can't download, The Guardian (29.11.2008), http://www.theguardian.com/money/2008/nov/28/internet-porn-bill-mistake (last accessed on 17.05.2014)

Lewis, Rita, What is DRM and why should I care?, Firefox News (08.01.2008), http://firefox.org/news/articles/1045/1/What-is-DRM-and-why-should-I-care/Page1.html (last accessed on 30.04.2014)

Lindvall, Helienne, Piracy sites are raking in ad money from some of the World's biggest brands, Business Insider (05.02.2013), http://www.businessinsider.com/piracy-sites-raking-in-ad-money-2013-2 (last accessed on 06.06.2014)

Lischka, Konrad, Anti-Abzock-Gesetz: Das Märchen von der Abmahn-Deckelung, Der Spiegel Online (30.01.2013), http://www.spiegel.de/netzwelt/netzpolitik/anti-abzock-gesetz-das-maerchen-von-der-abmahn-deckelung-a-880503.html (last accessed on 17.05.2014)

Lischka, Konrad, Fehlerhafte Zensur-Methode: Arcor stoppt den Porno-Filter, Der Spiegel online (17.09.2007), http://www.spiegel.de/netzwelt/web/fehlerhafte-zensur-methode-arcor-stoppt-den-porno-filter-a-506143.html (last accessed on 17.05.2014)

Löhr, Katrin, Skandal-Rapper fordert Ablasszahlung – Vorwurf Musik-Klau! So jagt Bushido seine Fans, Bild (17.04.2010), http://www.bild.de/unterhaltung/musik/bushido/jagt-weiter-fans-wegen-musik-klau-12228662.bild.html (last accessed on 17.05.2014)

LTO-Redaktion, Entwicklungen in Sachen Redtube – Gegenwind für Abmahnanwälte, Neues zu IP-Ermittlung, Legal Tribune online (13.12.2013), http://www.lto.de/recht/nachrichten/n/abmahnwelle-redtube-strafanzeige-erfolgshonorar-mandantenvereinbarung/ (last accessed on 17.05.2014)

Manenti, Boris, Aurélie Filippetti : « Je vais réduire les crédits de l'Hadopi », Le nouvel Observateur (01.08.2012), http://obsession.nouvelobs.com/high-tech/20120801.OBS8587/aurelie-filippetti-je-vais-reduire-les-credits-de-l-hadopi.html (last accessed on 17.05.2014)

Manenti, Boris, L'abrogation de l'Hadopi est en marche, Le nouvel Observateur (03.07.2012), http://obsession.nouvelobs.com/high-tech/20120703.OBS5858/l-hadopi-court-toujours.html (last accessed on 17.05.2014)

Mansmann, Urs, Arcor sperrte zahlreiche Websites, Heise online (17.09.2007), http://www.heise.de/newsticker/meldung/Arcor-sperrte-zahlreiche-Websites-Update-1759 06.html (last accessed on 17.05.2014)

Marchive, Valéry, Three years and millions of euros later, Hadopi has its first conviction. Now what?, ZDnet (30.10.2012), http://www.zdnet.com/three-years-and-milli ons-of-euros-later-hadopi-has-its-first-conviction-now-what-7000006612/ (last accessed on 17.05.2014)

Masons, Pinsent, Ofcom anti-piracy code delayed until 2015, out-law.com (10.06.2013), http://www.out-law.com/en/articles/2013/june/ofcom-anti-piracy-cod e-delayed-until-2015/ (last accessed on 17.05.2014)

McBride, Sarah / Smith, Ethan, Music Industry to Abandon Mass Suits (19.12.2008), Wall Street Journal, http://online.wsj.com/news/articles/SB122966038836021137 (last accessed on 17.05.2014)

Meller, Paul, Leaked ACTA draft reveals plans for Internet clampdown, Computerworld (20.02.2010), http://www.computerworld.co.nz/article/490341/leaked_acta_d raft_reveals_plans_internet_clampdown/ (last accessed on 06.06.2014)

Mennecke, Thomas, RIAA announces new campus lawsuit strategy, Slyck News (28.02.2007), http://www.slyck.com/story1422.html (last accessed on 17.05.2014)

Mölleken, Jan, Filehoster: Hehler oder Helfer ?, Der Spiegel online (14.09.2010), http://www.spiegel.de/netzwelt/web/0,1518,717333,00.html (last accessed on 17.05.2014)

Mühlbauer, Peter, Die Geister, die er rief..., Heise online (25.03.2010), http://www.hei se.de/tp/artikel/32/32327/1.html (last accessed on 17.05.2014)

Müller, Carl Christian, Abmahnwelle gegen Redtube-Nutzer, Vom Leerlaufen des Richtervorbehalts, Legal Tribune Online (12.12.2013), http://www.lto.de/recht/hint ergruende/h/redtube-streaming-abmahnung-Internetporno-urmann/ (last accessed on 17.05.2014)

National Association of Citizens Advice Bureaux, Online infringement of copyright and the Digital Economy Act 2010 – Draft Initial Obligations Code, Response from Citizens Advice to Ofcom (July 2010)

Neal, Ryan W., Pirates of the Caribbean: The Pirate Bay moves to island of St. Martin (30.04.2013), International Business Times, http://www.ibtimes.com/pirates-caribb ean-pirate-bay-moves-island-st-martin-1226787 (last accessed on 17.05.2014)

Ofcom Consultation Report, Online infringement of copyright and the Digital Economy Act 2010: Draft Initial Obligations Code (28.05.2010), http://www.ofcom.org.u k/consult/condocs/copyright-infringement/condoc.pdf (last accessed on 17.05.2014)

Ofcom, New Measures to Protect Online Copyright and Inform Consumers (26.06.2012), http://media.ofcom.org.uk/2012/06/26/new-measures-to-protect-onlin e-copyright-and-inform-consumers/ (last accessed on 17.05.2014)

Ofcom, Online infringement of copyright and the Digital Economy Act 2010, Notice of Ofcom's proposal to make by order a code for regulating the initial obligations (26.06.2012), http://stakeholders.ofcom.org.uk/binaries/consultations/online-notice/summary/notice.pdf (last accessed on 17.05.2014)

Pany, Thomas, Beginnt jetzt die Sanktionsphase von Hadopi?, heise.de blogs (05.07.2011), http://www.heise.de/tp/blogs/6/150095 (last accessed on 17.05.2014)

PC Magazin, Youtube-GEMA-Sperre umgehen – so geht's, PC Magazin (16.05.2014), http://www.pc-magazin.de/ratgeber/youtube-sperre-gema-umgehen-1343989.html (last accessed on 06.06.2014)

Pépin, Guénaël, La Hadopi défend le bilan de la réponse graduée, Le Monde (05.09.2012), http://www.lemonde.fr/technologies/article/2012/09/05/la-hadopi-defend-le-bilan-de-la-reponse-graduee_1755909_651865.html (last accessed on 17.05.2014)

Pepitone, Julianne, SOPA explained: What is is and why it matters, CNN (20.01.2012), http://money.cnn.com/2012/01/17/technology/sopa_explained/ (last accessed on 06.06.2014)

Philips, Jeremy, Digital Opportunity Knocks..., IPkat (03.08.2011), http://ipkitten.blogspot.de/2011/08/digital-opportunity-knocks.html (last accessed on 17.05.2014)

Poort, Joost/ Leenheer, Jorna/ von der Ham, Jeroen/ Dumitru, Cosmin, Baywatch : Two Approaches to Measure the Effects of Blocking Access to The Pirate Bay (Working Paper, 22.08.2013), available via http://papers.ssrn.com/sol3/papers.cfm?abstract_id=2314297 (last accessed on 17.05.2014)

Ramalho, Ana, The EU mandate to negotiate the TTIP: should copyright be an outcast?, Kluwer Copyright Blog (21.05.2013), http://kluwercopyrightblog.com/2013/05/21/the-eu-mandate-to-negotiate-the-ttip-should-copyright-be-an-outcast/ (last accessed 07.07.2015)

Rawlinson, Kevin, Turkey Steps up Bid to Block Twitter after Users Flout Ban, The Guardian (23.03.2014), http://www.theguardian.com/world/2014/mar/23/turkey-twitter-ban (last accessed on 17.05.2014)

Rees, Marc, Hadopi : 600 € d'amende et quinze jours de suspension pour un abonné , PC Inpact (12.06.2013), http://www.pcinpact.com/news/80487-hadopi-600-d-amende-et-quinze-jours-suspension-pour-abonne.htm (last accessed on 17.05.2014)

Rees, Mark, LOPPSI: le gouvernement abandonne le blocage de sites sans juge, PC Inpact (25.07.2012), http://www.pcinpact.com/news/72658-loppsi-gouvernement-abandonne-blocage-sites-sans-juge.htm (last accessed on 17.05.2014)

Reißmann, Ole, Geschäft mit Raubkopien: Wie kino.to Millionen verdiente, Der Spiegel online (14.06.2012), http://www.spiegel.de/netzwelt/netzpolitik/die-geschichte-von-kino-to-wer-mit-den-raubkopien-verdiente-a-838816.html (last accessed on 30.04.2014)

Riden, Jamie, How Fast-Flux service networks work, The Honeynet Project (16.08.2008), http://www.honeynet.org/node/132 (last accessed on 17.05.2014)

Robertson, Struan, The legislative farce of the Digital Economy Bill, out-law.com (07.04.2010), http://www.out-law.com/page-10900 (last accessed on 17.05.2014)

Rowlands, Max, UK: "Speculative invoicing" schemes target internet file-sharers and individuals accused of minor retail crime (2011), http://www.statewatch.org/analyses/no-156-speculative-invoicing.pdf (last accessed on 17.05.2014)

Rundle, Micheal, Government Scraps Plans to Block Content-Sharing Websites, Huffington Post (03.08.2011), http://www.huffingtonpost.co.uk/2011/08/03/website-blocking-plans-sc_n_916826.html (last accessed on 17.05.2014)

Salzenberg, Chip/Spafford, Gene/Moraes, Mark, What is Usenet? (1998), http://cyber.law.harvard.edu/lawofcyberspace/news.html (last accessed on 17.05.2014)

Satter, Raphael, Wikipedia article blocked in UK over child photo, The Independent (08.12.2008), http://www.independent.co.uk/life-style/gadgets-and-tech/news/wikipedia-article-blocked-in-uk-over-child-photo-1057010.html (last accessed on 17.05.2014)

Schneider, Adrian, OLG Hamburg: Die Rapidshare-Entscheidung, ein Meilenstein?, Telemedicus (29.03.2012), http://www.telemedicus.info/article/2229-OLG-Hamburg-Die-Rapidshare-Entscheidung,-ein-Meilenstein.html (last accessed on 17.05.2014)

Schumpeter, Joseph, Net Neutraliy, More equal than others, The Economist (25.04.2014), http://www.economist.com/blogs/schumpeter/2014/04/net-neutrality (last accessed on 17.05.2014)

Sisario, Ben, 7 Charged as F.B.I. closes a top file-sharing site, The New York Times (20.01.2012), http://www.nytimes.com/2012/01/21/technology/megaupload-indictment-Internet-piracy.html?ref=technology (last accessed on 17.05.2014)

Smith, Graham, Who will sort out the Delfi mess?, Cyberleagle blog (16.10.2013), http://cyberleagle.blogspot.co.uk/2013/10/who-will-sort-out-delfi-mess.html (last accessed 05.05.2014)

Software & Information Industry Association (SIIA), SIIA Releases Sequel to Classic Anti-Piracy Music Video "Don't Copy That Floppy", Reuters (09.09.2009), http://www.reuters.com/article/2009/09/09/idUS141575+09-Sep-2009+PRN20090909 (last accessed on 17.05.2014)

Solmecke, Christian, Redtube: Wave of Streaming Letters hits Germany (12.12.2013), http://www.wbs-law.de/eng/streaming/redtube-wave-streaming-warning-letters-hits-germany-49182/ (last accessed on 17.05.2014)

Spiegel Online, "The Pirate Bay": IT-Experten warnen vor Piraten-Browser, Der Spiegel online (13.08.2013), http://www.spiegel.de/netzwelt/web/piratebrowser-it-experten-warnen-vor-piraten-browser-a-916279.html (last accessed 13.08.2013)

Spiegel Online, 22-Jähriger festgenommen: Ermittler entdecken riesige Kinderporno-Sammlung in Köln, Der Spiegel online (19.09.2013), http://www.spiegel.de/panorama/koeln-ermittler-entdecken-riesige-kinderporno-sammlung-a-923284.html (last accessed on 17.05.2014)

Spiegel Online, Gesetz gegen Abzocke: Bundestag setzt Massenabmahnungen Grenzen, Der Spiegel online (27.06.2013), http://www.spiegel.de/wirtschaft/service/gesetz-gegen-abzocke-bundestag-setzt-massenabmahnungen-grenzen-a-908267.html (last accessed on 06.06.2014)

Spiegel Online, Sven Regener zum Urheberrecht: "Man pinkelt uns ins Gesicht!", Der Spiegel Online (22.03.2012), http://www.spiegel.de/kultur/gesellschaft/sven-regener-im-bayerischen-rundfunk-zum-urheberrecht-a-823144.html (last accessed on 06.06.2014)

Spiegel Online, Urheberrechtskampagne: 1500 Künstler gegen Gier und Geiz, Der Spiegel Online (10.05.2012), http://www.spiegel.de/netzwelt/netzpolitik/kuenstler-schreiben-offenen-brief-fuer-das-urheberrecht-a-832538.html (last accessed on 06.06.2014)

Spier, Alexander, Darf's ein bisschen schneller sein? Wie sich LTE im mobilen Alltag schlägt, c't 2012, Issue 22, http://www.heise.de/ct/artikel/Darf-s-ein-bisschen-schneller-sein-1722006.html (last accessed on 17.05.2014)

Steier, Henning, Ersten Piraten Drohen Netzsperren, Neue Züricher Zeitung (07.10.2011), http://www.nzz.ch/aktuell/digital/frankreich-hadopi-bilanz-1.12873303 (last accessed on 17.05.2014)

Streams, Kimber, France's controversial Hadopi piracy law nets its first conviction, a man who says he didn't do It, The Verge (14.09.2012), http://www.theverge.com/2012/9/14/3332056/france-hadopi-piracy-law-conviction-alain-prevost (last accessed on 17.05.2014)

Sweney, Mark, Ofcom outlines new anti-piracy rules, The Guardian (26.06.2012), http://www.guardian.co.uk/technology/2012/jun/26/ofcom-outlines-anti-piracy-rules (last accessed on 17.05.2014)

Syndicat National de l'édition Phonographique (SNEP), Presentation des Resultats du 1er semestre 2013 (18.09.2013), http://www.actu.snepmusique.com/snep/actualites-du-snep/presentation-des-resultats-du-1er-semestre-2013/ (last accessed on 17.05.2014)

Syndicat National de l'Edition Phonographique, Bilan Economique 2012 (2013), http://proxy.siteo.com.s3.amazonaws.com/www.snepmusique.com/file/bilaneconomiquesnepmidem2013etpresentationmidem.pdf (last accessed on 17.05.2014)

Tait, Morgan, Dotcom extradition hearing delayed, The New Zealand Herald (01.05.2015), http://www.nzherald.co.nz/nz/news/article.cfm?c_id=1&objectid=11441894 (last accessed on 07.07.2015).

Taplin, Jonathan and Others, Advertising transparency report, monthly updates are available at http://www.annenberglab.com/projects/ad-piracy-report-0 (last accessed on 06.06.2014)

Techradar, Cheap promotion, Twitter and peer-to-peer, How one band used YouTube, Twitter and file-sharing to create a community of fans, Techradar (16.01.2010), http://www.techradar.com/news/internet/how-to-get-famous-online-663244/2 (last accessed on 17.05.2014)

The British Record Music Industry (BPI), Digital Music Nation 2010, the UK's legal and illegal digital music landscape (2010), http://www.bpi.co.uk/assets/files/Digital%20Music%20Nation%202010.pdf (last accessed on 17.05.2014)

The Economist, Criminalising the consumer – Where digital rights went wrong, The Economist (27.04.2007), http://www.economist.com/node/9096421 (last accessed on 30.04.2014)

Thévenet, Sébastien, Hadopi: Un premier internaute condamné, Le Figaro (13.09.2012), http://www.lefigaro.fr/secteur/high-tech/2012/09/13/01007-20120913ARTFIG00599-hadopi-un-premier-internaute-condamne.php (last accessed on 17.05.2014)

Tréguer, Félix, France on its way to total Internet censorship?, Index on Censorship (27.06.2011), http://www.indexoncensorship.org/2011/06/france-on-its-way-to-total-internet-censorship/ (last accessed on 17.05.2014)

Tulkens, Francoise, EU Accession to the European Convention on Human Rights (2013), http://www.ejtn.eu/Documents/About%20EJTN/Independent%20Seminars/Human%20Rights%20and%20Access%20to%20Justice%20Seminar/Krakow_Tulkens_final.pdf (last accessed on 17.05.2014)

Verein zur Hilfe und Unterstützung gegen den Abmahnwahn e.V., Annual statistic 2010, http://www.verein-gegen-den-abmahnwahn.de/zentrale/download/statistiken/2010/jahresbilanz_2010.html (last accessed 16.06.2011)

Voorhoof, Dirk, Copyright vs Freedom of Expression Judment, ECHR Blog (22.01.2013), http://echrblog.blogspot.de/2013/01/copyright-vs-freedom-of-expression.html (last accessed on 17.05.2014)

Voorhoof, Dirk, Treating a news portal as publisher of users' comment may have far-reaching consequences for online freedom of expression, Inform's blog (29.10.2013), http://inforrm.wordpress.com/2013/10/29/treating-a-news-portal-as-publisher-of-users-comment-may-have-far-reaching-consequences-for-online-freedom-of-expression-dirk-voorhoof/ (last accessed on 05.05.2014)

Waehlisch, Nathalie, Kampagne der Filmindustrie: "Raubkopierer sind Verbrecher", Der Spiegel online (27.11.2003), http://www.spiegel.de/netzwelt/web/kampagne-der-filmindustrie-raubkopierer-sind-verbrecher-a-275867.html (last accessed on 06.06.2014)

Walder, Adam, Popular music platform 'Spotify' launches in Luxembourg, Luxemburger Wort (13.11.2012), http://www.wort.lu/en/view/popular-music-platform-spotify-launches-in-luxembourg-50a26ee3e4b0f09219140f0a (last accessed on 06.06.2014)

Washington Post, NSA slides explain the PRISM data-collection program, The Washington Post (06.06.2013, updated 10.07.2013), http://www.washingtonpost.com/wp-srv/special/politics/prism-collection-documents/ (last accessed on 17.05.2014)

WBS Law, Nach dem BGH Filesharing Urteil (Morpheus) – Wie geht es nun weiter? (16.11.2012), http://www.wbs-law.de/abmahnung-filesharing/nach-dem-bgh-filesharing-urteil-morpheus-wie-geht-es-nun-weiter-32204/ (last accessed on 17.05.2014)

Weber, Sara, Der Piraten-Jäger, UniSpiegel 2012, Issue 3, 14–16, (last accessed on 15.05.2014)

Wienand, Lars, Das ist heftig: Die Viralseiten-Macher und ihr Verhältnis zu Urheberrechten, Rhein-Zeitung (27.05.2014), http://www.rhein-zeitung.de/nachrichten/netzwelt/news_artikel,-Das-ist-heftig-Die-Viralseiten-Macher-und-ihr-Verhaeltnis-zu-Urheberrechten-_arid,1158093.html#.U5HapSiuNEP (last accessed on 06.06.2014)

Williams, Christopher, E-books Drive Older Women to Piracy, The Telegraph (17.05.2011), http://www.telegraph.co.uk/technology/news/8518755/E-books-drive-older-women-to-digital-piracy.html (last accessed on 06.06.2014)

Wyatt, Edward, Rebuffing F.C.C. in 'Net Neutrality' Case, court allows streaming deals, The New York Times (14.01.2014), http://www.nytimes.com/2014/01/15/technology/appeals-court-rejects-fcc-rules-on-Internet-service-providers.html?_r=0 (last accessed on 17.05.2014)

Table of Cases

Court of Justice of the European Union

CJEU, Joined Cases C-453/03, C-11/04, C-12/04 and C-194/04 *ABNA and Others,* [2005] ECR I-10423

CJEU, Case C-435/12 *ACI Adam v Stichting de Thuiskopie*, Judgment of 10.04.2014

CJEU, Case C-343/09 *Afton Chemical*, [2010] ECR I-7027

CJEU, Case C-221/09 *AJD Tuna*, [2011] ECR I-1655

CJEU, Case C-617/10 *Åklagaren v Hans Åkerberg Fransson*, Judgment of 26 .02.2013

CJEU, Joined Cases C-154/04 and C-155/04 *Alliance for Natural Health and Others,* [2005] ECR I-6451

CJEU, Case C-142/87 *Belgium v Commission*, Order of 15.06.1987, [1990] ECR I-959

CJEU, C-348/13 *BestWater International*, Order of 21.10.2014

CJEU, Case C-78/01 *BGL and Bundesrepublik Deutschland*, Judgment of 23.09.2003, [2003] ECR I-9543

CJEU, Case C-489/10 *Bonda*, Judgment of 05.06.2012

CJEU, Case C-461/10 *Bonnier Audio AB and Others v Perfect Communication Sweden AB*, Judgment of 19.04.2012

CJEU, Joined Cases C-20/00 and C-64/00 *Booker Aquaculture and Hydro Seafood,* [2003] ECR I-7411

CJEU, Case C-97/91 *Borelli*, [1992] ECR I-6313

CJEU, Case C-279/13, *C More Entertainment*, Judgment of 26.03.2015

CJEU, Joined Cases C-145/08 and C-149/08 *Club Hotel Loutraki and Others*, [2010] ECR I- 4165

CJEU, Case C-437/04 *Commission v Belgium*, [2007] ECR I-2513

CJEU, Case C-53/05 *Commission v Portugal*, [2006] ECR I-6215

CJEU, Joined Cases C-133/93, C-300/93 and C-362/93 *Crispoltoni and Others,* [1994] ECR I-4863

CJEU, Case C-544/10 *Deutsches Weintor*, Judgment of 06.09.2012

CJEU, Joined cases C-293/12 and C-594/12 *Digital Rights Ireland v Minister for Communications, Marine and Natural Resources and Others, and Kärntner Landesregierung and Others*, Judgment of 08.04.2014

CJEU, Case C-260/89 *ERT v DEP*, [1991] ECR I-5485

CJEU, Joint Cases C-403/08 *Football Association Premier League Ltd and others v OC Leisure and others*, and C-429/08 *Karen Murphy v Media Protection Services Ltd.*, [2011] ECR I-9083

CJEU, Case C-213/10 F-*Tex SIA v Lietuvos-Anglijos UAB "Jadecloud-Vilma"*, Judgment of 09.04.2012

CJEU, Case C-135/92 *Fiskano v Commission*, [1994] ECR I-2885

CJEU, Case C-280/93 *Germany* v *Council*, [1994] ECR I-4973

CJEU, Case C-156/98 *Germany v Commission*, [2000] ECR I-6857

CJEU, Joined Cases C-236/08 to C-238/08, *Google France, Google Inc. v Louis Vuitton Malletier, Google France v Viaticum Luteciel, Google France v CNRRH Pierre-Alexis Thonet, Bruno Raboin, Tiger, a franchisee of Unicis,* [2010] ECR I-02417 *(Google Adwords)*

CJEU, Case C-131/12, *Google Spain and Google Inc v Agencia Española de Protección de Datos (AEPD)*, Judgment of 13.05.2014

CJEU, Case C-44/79 *Hauer v Land Rheinland-Pfalz*, [1979] ECR 3727

CJEU, Case C-101/12 *Herbert Schaible v Land Baden-Württemberg,* Judgment of 17.10.2013

CJEU, Case C-85/76 *Hoffmann-La Roche v Commission*, Judgment of 13.02.1979 [1979] ECR 461

CJEU, Case C-5/08 *Infopaq International v Danske Dagblades Forening*, [2009] ECR I-6569

CJEU, Case C-1/11 *Interseroh*, Judgment of 29.03.2012

CJEU, Case C-301/06 *Ireland v European Parliament and Council of the European Union*, [2009] ECR I-593

CJEU, Case C-315/99 P *Ismeri Europea v Court of Auditors*, [2001] ECR I-5281

CJEU, Case C-607/11 *ITV Broadcasting Ltd et al. v TVCatchup* Ltd., Judgment of 07.03.2013

CJEU, Case C-222/84 *Johnston*, [1986] ECR 1651

CJEU, Case C-213/99 *José Teodoro de Andrade v Director da Alfandega de Leixoes, intervener: Ministério Público*, [2000] ECR I-11083

CJEU, Joined Cases C-402/05P and C-415/05P *Kadi and Al Barakaat v Council of the European Union and Commission of the European Communities,* [2008] ECR I-6351

CJEU, Case C-479/04 *Laserdisken*, [2006] ECR I-8089

CJEU, Case C-294/83 *Les Verts v European Parliament*, [1986] ECR 1339

CJEU, Case C-118/89 *Lingenfelser,* [1990] ECR I-2637

CJEU, Case C-101/01 *Lindqvist*, [2003] ECR I-12971

CJEU, Case C-324/09 *L'Oréal v eBay*, [2011] ECR I-6011

CJEU, Case C-557/07 *LSG-Gesellschaft zur Wahrnehmung von Leistungsschutzrechten GmbH v Tele 2 Telecommunication GmbH (Tele2)*, [2009] ECR I-01227

CJEU, Joined Cases C-402/05 P and C-415/05 P *Kadi and Al Barakaat*, [2008] ECR I-6351

CJEU, Case C-356/97 *Molkereigenossenschaft Widergeltingen eG v Hauptzollamt Lindau*, [2000] ECR I-5461

CJEU, Case C-354/95 *National Farmers' Union and Others,* [1997] ECR I-4559

CJEU, Joined Cases C-581/10 and C-629/10 *Nelson and Others*, Judgment of 23.10.2012

CJEU, Joined Cases C-90/90 and C-91/90 *Neu,* [1991] ECR I-3617

CJEU, Case C-4/73 *Nold,* [1974] ECR 491

CJEU, Case C-465/00 C-138/01 *Österreichischer Rundfunk and Others,* [2003] ECR I-4989

CJEU, Case C-319/90 *Pressler,* [1992] ECR I-203

CJEU, Case C-275/06 *Productores de Música de España (Promusicae) v Telefónica de España SAU*, [2008] ECR I-271

CJEU, Case C-379/08 *Raffinerie Mediterranee (ERG) SpA v Ministero dello Sviluppo economic*, [2010] ECR I-2007

CJEU, Case C-360/10 *SABAM v Netlog NV*, Judgment of 16.02.2012

CJEU, Case C-70/10 *Scarlet Extended SA v SABAM*, [2012] ECR I-11959

CJEU, Case C-283/11 *Sky Österreich GmbH v Österreichischer Rundfunk*, Judgment of 22.01.2013

CJEU, Case C-306/05 Sociedad General de Autores y Editores de España v Rafael Hoteles SA, [2006] ECR I-11519

CJEU, Case C-230/78 *SpA Eridiana and Other*s, [1979] ECR 2749

CJEU, Case C-240/97 *Spain v Commission,* [1999] ECR I-6571

CJEU, Joined Cases C-184/02 and C-223/02 *Spain and Finland v Parliament and Council,* [2004] ECR I-7789

CJEU, Case C-151/78 *Sukkerfabriken Nykøbing,* [1979] ECR 1

CJEU, Case C-466/12 *Svensson*, Judgment of 13.02.2014

CJEU, Case C-432/05 *Unibet*, [2007] ECR I-2271

CJEU, Case C-314/12 *UPC Telekabel Wien GmbH v Constantin Film Verleih GmbH and Wega Filmproduktionsgesellschaft GmbH*, Judgment of 27.03.2014

CJEU, Case C-222/86 *Union nationale des entraineurs et cadres techniques professionnels du football (UNECTEF) v Georges Heylens,* Judgment of 15.10.1987, [1987] ECR 4097

CJEU, Joined Cases C-222/05 to C-225/05 *Van der Weerd and Others*, [2007] ECR I-4233

CJEU, Joined Cases C-430/93 and C-431/93 *Van Schijndel and van Veen*, [1995] ECR I-4705

CJEU, Case C-375/96 *Zaninotto* [1998] ECR I-6629

CJEU, Case C-8/89 *Zardi,* [1990] ECR I-2515

European Court of Human Rights

ECtHR, *Anheuser-Busch Inc. v Portugal,* Judgment of 11.01.2007, Application No. 73049/01

ECtHR, *Artico v Italy*, Judgment of 13.05.1980, Application No. 6694/74

ECtHR, *Ashby Donald and others v France*, Judgment of 10.01.2013, Application No. 36769/08

ECtHR, *Autronic AG v Switzerland*, Judgment of 22.05.1990, Application No. 12726/87

ECtHR, *Barberà, Messegué and Jabardo v Spain*, Judgment of 06.12.1988, Application No. 10590/83

ECtHR, *Bensaid v The United Kingdom*, Judgment of 06.02.2001, Application No. 44599/98

ECtHR, *Boldea v Romania*, Judgment of 15.02.2007, Application No. 19997/02

ECtHR, Borgers v Belgium, Judgment of 30.10.1991, Application No. 12005/86

ECtHR, Bosphorus Hava Yollari Turzm ve Ticaret Anonim Sirketi v Ireland, Judgment of 30.06.2005, Application No. 45036/98

ECtHR, *Botta v Italy*, Judgment of 24.02.1998, Application No. 21439/93

ECtHR, *Brozicek v Italy*, Judgment of 19.12.1989, Application No. 10964/84

ECtHR, *Castells v Spain*, Judgment of 23.04.1992, Application No. 11798/85

ECtHR, *Copland v The United Kingdom*, Judgment of 03.04.2007, Application No. 62617/00

ECtHR, *Cumpănă and Mazăre v Romania*, Judgment of 17.12.2004, Application No. 33348/96

ECtHR, *Cyprus v Turkey*, Judgment of 10.05.2001, Application No. 25781/94

ECtHR, *Chorherr v Austria*, Judgment of 25.08.1993, Application No. 13308/87

ECtHR, *De Haes and Gijsels v Belgium*, Judgment of 24.02.1997, Application No. 19983/92

ECtHR, *Delfi AS v Estonia*, Judgment of 10.10.2013, Application No. 64569/09, and Judgment of 16.06.2015, Application no. 64569/09 (Grand Chamber)

ECtHR, *De Wilde, Ooms and Versyp v Belgium*, Judgment of 18.06.1971, Application No. 2832/66

ECtHR, *Dima v Romania*, Judgment of 16.11.2006, Application No. 58472/00

ECtHR, *Dombo Beheer BV v the Netherlands*, Judgment of 27.10.1993, Application No. 14448/88

ECtHR, *Eur. Comm. H.R., DVO v Belgium*, Judgment of 01.03.1979, Application No. 7654/76

ECtHR, *Fredrik Neij and Peter Sunde Kolmisoppi v Sweden*, Decision of 19.02.2013, Application No. 40397/12

ECtHR, *Golder v The United Kingdom*, Judgment of 21.02.1975, Application No. 4451/70

ECtHR, *Groppera Radio AG Others v Switzerland*, Judgment of 28.03.1990, Application No. 10890/84

ECtHR, *Guerra and Others v Italy*, Judgment of 19.02.1998, Application No. 14967/89

ECtHR, *Handyside v The United Kingdom*, Judgment of 07.12.1976, Application No. 5493/72

ECtHR, *Rotaru v Romania*, Judgment of 04.05.2000, Application No. 28341/95

ECtHR, *Rowe and Davis v The United Kingdom*, Judgment of 16.02.2000, Application No. 28901/95

ECtHR, *S. and Marper v The United Kingdom*, Judgment of 04.12.2008, Application Nos. 30562/04 and 30566/04

ECtHR, *Salabiaku v France*, Judgment of 07.10.1988, Application No. 10519/83

ECtHR, *Saunders v The United Kingdom*, Judgment of 17.12.1996, Application No. 19187/91

ECtHR, *Sporrong and Lönnroth v Sweden*, Judgment of 23.09.1982, Application No. 7152/75

ECtHR, *Sunday Times v The United Kingdom*, Judgment of 26.04.1979, Application No. 6538/74

ECtHR, *Skalka v Poland*, Judgment of 27.05.2003, Application No. 43425/98

ECtHR, *Telegraaf Media Nederland Landelijke Media B. V and Others v the Netherlands*, Judgment of 22.11.2012, Application No. 39315/06

ECtHR, *Times Newspapers Ltd v The United Kingdom* (nos. 1 and 2), Judgment of 10.06.2009, Application Nos. 3002/03 and 23676/03

ECtHR, *TV Vest AS & Rogaland Pensjonistparti v Norway*, Judgment of 11.12.2008, Application No. 21132/05

ECtHR, *V. v The United Kingdom*, Judgment of 16.12.1999, Application No. 24888/94

ECtHR, *Weber and Saravia v Germany*, Admissibility Decision of 29.06.2006, Application No. 54934/00

ECtHR, *Yefimenko v Russia*, Judgment of 12.02.2013, Application No. 152/04

ECtHR, *Y. F. v Turkey*, Judgment of 22.07.2003, Application No. 24209/94

ECtHR, *Yildirim v Turkey*, Judgment of 18.12.2012, Application No. 3111/10

National courts

Australia

Federal Court of Australia, *Roadshow Films Pty Ltd v iiNet Ltd*, [2010] FCA 24

Federal Court of Australia, *Roadshow Films Pty Ltd v iiNet Ltd*, [2011] FCAFC 23

Federal Court of Australia, *Universal Music Australia Pty Ltd v Sharman License Holdings Ltd,* [2005] FCA 1242

High Court of Australia, *Roadshow Films Pty Ltd v iiNet Ltd*, [2012] HCA 16

Austria

ÖOGH, Decision of 11.05.2012 – 4 Ob 6/12d

OGH, Decision of 21.12.2006 – 6 Ob 178/04a

France

CA Paris, Decision of 04.02.2011 – RG no. 09/21941 *(André Rau v Google & AuFeminin.com)*

CA Paris, Decision of 09.04.2010 *(Google v Flach Films and others)*

CA Paris, Decision of 03.12.2010 *(Dailymotion v Zadig Production)*

CA Paris, Decision of 14.01.2011 *(Google Inc. v Bac Films and others)*

Cour de Cassation, Decision of 17.02.2011, RG no. 09/67896 *(Christian C., Nord-Ouest Production et UGC Images v Dailymotion)*

Cour de Cassation, Decision of 12.07.2012, Arrêt no. 830 *(André Rau v Google & AuFeminin.com)*

Cour de Cassation, Decision of 12.07.2012, Arrêt no. 831 *(Bach Films v Google France and Inc [1 & 2])*

Cour de Cassation, Decision of 12.07.2012, Arrêt no. 832 *(*SNEP v Google France*)*

Cour d'Appel d'Aix-en-Provence, Decision of 05.09.2007, Arrêt no. 501

Cour d'Appel de Montpellier, Decision of 10.03.2005 *(Buena Vista Home Entertainment et al. v D.A.C.)*

Cour d'Appel Paris, Decision of 03.05.2011, RG no. 10/19845 *(SNEP v Google France)*

Cour d'Appel Paris, Decision of 24.11.2006, RG no. 05/15722 *(SA Tiscali [Telecom Italia])*

Cour de Cassation, Decision of 30.05.2006, RG no. 05/83335

Cour de Cassation, Decisions of 17.02.2011 *(affaires Dailymotion, Fuzz et Amen)*

Conseil Constitutionnel, Decision of 27.07.2006, no. 2006-540 DC

Conseil Constitutionnel, Decision of 10.06.2009, no. 2009-580 DC

Conseil Constitutionnel, Decision of 22.10.2009, no. 2009-590 DC

Conseil Constitutionnel, Decision of 10.03.2011, no. 2011-625 DC

TP Montreuil, Decision of 03.06.2013, parquet no. 12053081381

TGI Créteil, Decision of 14.12.2010 *(INA v YouTube)*

TGI Paris, Decision of 20 November 2000 – RG no. 00/05308 *(La Ligue contre le racisme et l'antisémitisme et al. v Yahoo Inc)*

TGI Paris, Decision of 13.06.2005, RG no. 05/53871

TGI Paris, Decision of 11.06.2010 *(La Chauve Souris and 120 Films v Dailymotion)*

TGI Paris, Decision of 10.09.2010, RG no. 10/53985 *(SNEP v Google France)*

TGI Paris, Decision of 13.01.2011 *(Calt Production v Dailymotion)*

TGI Paris, Decision of 29.05.2012, RG No. 10/11205

Germany

AG Düsseldorf, Decision of 05.04.2011 – 57 C 15740/09

AG Frankfurt/M., Decision of 04.02.2009 – 29 C 549/08 – 81

AG Frankfurt/M., Decision of 29.01.2010 – 31 C 1078/09 – 78

AG Frankfurt/M., Decision of 12.02.2010 – 32 C 1634/09-72

AG Frankfurt/M., Decision of 16.04.2010 – 30 C 562/07 – 47

AG Halle, Decision of 14.11.2009 – 95 C 3258/09

AG Magdeburg, Decision of 12.05.2010 – 140 C 2323/09

BGH, Decision of 18.03.1960 – I ZR 75/58 *(Eisrevue II)*

BGH, Decision of 16.06.1971 – I ZR 120/69 *(Konzertveranstalter)*

BGH, Decision of 15.10.1998 I ZR 120 / 96 *(Möbelklassiker)*

BGH, Decision of 17.05.2001 – I ZR 251/99 *(ambiente.de)*

BGH, Decision of 11.03.2004 – I ZR 304/01 *(Internetversteigerung I)*

BGH, Decision of 01.04.2004 – I ZR 317/01 *(Schöner Wetten)*

BGH, Decision of 19.04.2007 – I ZR 35/04 *(Internetversteigerung II)*

BGH, Decision of 12.07.2007 – I ZR 18/04 *(Jugendgefährdende Medien bei eBay)*

BGH, Decision of 30.04.2008 – I ZR 73/05 *(Internetversteigerung III)*

BGH, Decision of 10.11.2009 – VI ZR 217/08 *(rainbow.at)*

BGH, Decisions of 15.12.2009 – VI ZR 227/08 and 228/08 *(Deutschlandradio)*

BGH, Decisions of 09.02.2010 – VI ZR 243/08 and 244/08 *(Spiegel online)*

BGH, Decisions of 20.04.2010 – VI ZR 245/08 and 246/08 *(morgenweb.de)*

BGH, Decision of 12.05.2010 – I ZR 121/08 *(Sommer unseres Lebens)*

BGH, Decision of 22.07.2010 – I ZR 139/08 *(Kinderhochstühle im Internet)*

BGH, Decision of 25.10.2011 – VI ZR 93/10 *(Blog)*

BGH, Decision of 19.04.2012 – 1 ZB 80/11 *(Alles kann besser werden)*

BGH, Decision of 12.07.2012 – I ZR 18/11 *(Alone in the Dark)*

BGH, Decision of 15.11.2012 – I ZR 74/12 *(Morpheus)*

BGH, Decision of 15.08.2013 – I ZR 80/12 *(GEMA v Rapidshare)*

BGH, Decision of 08.01.2014 – I ZR 169/12 *(BearShare)*

BGH, Decisions of 11.06.2015 – I ZR 75/14; I ZR 7/14 and I ZR 19/14 (*Tauschbörse I – III*)

BVerfG, 1 BvR 256/08 *(Vorratsdatenspeicherung)*

BVerfG, 1 BvR 2074/05, 1 BvR 1254/07 *(Automatisierte Erfassung von Autokennzeichen)*

BVerfG, Order of 21.03.2012 – 1 BvR 2365/11 *(Unerlaubtes Filesharing im Internet)*

KG Berlin, Decision of 19 October2001 – 9 W 132/01

LG Düsseldorf, Decision of 13.12.2007 – 12 O 550/07

LG Düsseldorf, Decision of 27.05.2009 – 12 O 134/09

LG Frankfurt/M., Decision of 12.04.2007 – 2/03 O 824/06

LG Frankfurt/M., Decision of 08.02.2008 – 3-12 O 171/07

LG Frankfurt/M., Decision of 18.08.2010 – 2-6 S 19/09

LG Hamburg, Decision of 19.04.2006 – 308 O 92/06

LG Hamburg, Decision of 21.04.2006 – 308 O 139/06

LG Hamburg, Decision of 01.06.2007 – 324 O 717/06
LG Hamburg, Decision of 18.01.2008 – 324 O 507/07
LG Hamburg: Decision of 28.02.2008 – 324 O 459/07
LG Hamburg: Decision of 29.02.2008 – 324 O 469/07
LG Hamburg, Decision of 15.07.2008 – 310 O 144/08
LG Hamburg, Decision of 12.11.2008 – 308 O 548/08
LG Hamburg, Decision of 12.06.2009 – 310 O 93/08
LG Hamburg, Decision of 25.11.2010 – 310 O 433/10
LG Hamburg, Decision of 12.3.2010 – 308 O 640/08
LG Hamburg, Decision of 20.04.2012 – 310 O 461/10 *(GEMA v YouTube)*
LG Kiel, Decision of 23.11.2007 – 14 O 125/07
LG Köln, Decision of 28.02.2007 – 28 O 10/07
LG Köln, Decision of 27.01.2010 – 28 O 241/09
LG Köln, Decision of 31.08.2011 – 28 O 362/10
LG Leipzig, Decision of 14.06.2012 – 11 KLs 390 Js 191/11 *(kino.to)*
LG Mannheim, Decision of 29.09.2006 – 7 O 76/06
LG München I, Decision of 19.04.2007 – 7 O 3950/07
LG München I, Decision of 13.06.2007 – 9 O 2295/07
LG München I, Decision of 19.06.2008 – 7 O 16402/07
LG München I, Decision of 25.02.2014 – 1 HK O 1401/13
OLG Brandenburg, Decision of 16.12.2003 – 6 U 161/U
OLG Düsseldorf, Decision of 27.12.2007 – I-20 W 157/07
OLG Düsseldorf, Decision of 27.04.2010 – I-20 U 166/09 *(Rapidshare – An American Crime et al)*
OLG Düsseldorf, Decision of 06.07.2010 – I-20 U 8/10 *(Rapidshare II – Inside a Skinhead)*
OLG Düsseldorf, Decision of 21.12.2010 – I-20 U 59/10 *(Rapidshare III – Alone in the Dark)*
OLG Düsseldorf, Decision of 15.03.2011 – I-20 U 136/10
OLG Frankfurt/M., Decision of 22.01.2008 – 6 W 10/08
OLG Frankfurt/M., Decision of 20. 12. 2007 – 11 W 58/07
OLG Frankfurt/M., Decisions of 20.09.2006 – 16 W 55/06 and 16 W 57/06
OLG Frankfurt/M., Decision of 20.12.2007 – 11 W 58/07
OLG Frankfurt/M., Decision of 12.05.2009 – 11 W 21/09
OLG Frankfurt/M., Decision of 12.11.2009 – 11 W 41/09
OLG Frankfurt/M., Decision of 21.12.2010 – 11 O 52/07
OLG Hamburg, decision of 08.02.2006 – 5 U 78/05 *(Cybersky)*
OLG Hamburg, Decision of 11.10.2006 – 5 W 152/06
OLG Hamburg, Decision of 02.07.2008 – 5 U 73/07 *(Sharehoster I – Rapidshare)*

OLG Hamburg, Decision of 14.01.2009 – 5 U 113/07 *(Spring nicht – Usenet I)*

OLG Hamburg, Decision of 28.01.2009 – 5 U 255/07 *(Alphaload – Usenet II)*

OLG Hamburg, Decision of 30.09.2009 – 5 U 111/08 *(Sharehoster II – Rapidshare)*

OLG Hamburg, Decision of 22.12.2010 – 5 U 36/09

OLG Hamburg, Decision of 14.03.2012 – 5 U 87/09 *(GEMA v Rapidshare)*

OLG Hamburg, Decision of 21.11.2013 – 5 U 68/10 *(3dl.am)*

OLG Hamm, Decision of 02.11.2010 – 4 W 119/10

OLG Hamm, Decision of 27.10.2011 – I-22 W 82/11

OLG Köln, Decision of 21.09.2007 – 6 U 86/07 *(Haftung eines Sharehoster-Dienstes)*

OLG Köln, Decision of 23.12.2009 – 6 U 101/09

OLG Köln, Decision of 10.02.2011 – 6 W 5/11

OLG Köln, Decision of 24.03.2011 – 6 W 427/11

OLG Köln, Decision of 16.05.2012 – 6 U 239/1

OLG München, Decision of 21.09.1978 – 6 U 4941/77 *(Transvestiten-Show)*

OVG Münster, Decision of 19.03.2003 – 8 B 2567/02

VG Arnsberg, Decision of 26.11.2004 – 13 K 3173/02

VG Düsseldorf, Decision of 19.12.2002 – 15 L 4148/02

VG Düsseldorf, Decision of 10.05.2005 – 27 K 5968/02

VG Düsseldorf, Decision of 08.11.2011 – 27 K 5887/10

VG Düsseldorf, Decision of 29.11.2011 – 27 K 5887/10

VG Gelsenkirchen, Decision of 28.7.2006 – 15 K 2170/03

VG Köln, Decision of 03.03.2005 – 6 K 7151/02

Ireland

Irish High Court, *EMI v UPC,* Decision of 11.10.2010, [2009] no 5472

Sweden

Svea Hovrätt, Decision of 26.11.2010 – B 4041-09 *(The Pirate Bay)*

The Netherlands

Gerechtshof Amsterdam, Decision of 28.03.2002, – 1370/01SKG *(KAZAA B.V v BUMA/STEMRA)*

RB Den Haag, Decision of 24.10.2012 *(BREIN v XS Networks)*

RB 's Gravenhage, Decision of 11.01.2012 *(BREIN v Ziggo and XS4ALL)*

RB 's Gravenhage, Decision of 10.05.2012 *(Blocking of The Pirate Bay: BREIN v providers)*

The United Kingdom

Court of Appeal, *Axa Equity & Law Life Assurance Society Plc v National Westminster Bank* [1998] CLC 1177

Court of Appeal, *Newspaper Licensing Agency Ltd v Meltwater Holding BV* [2011] EWCA Civ 890,

Court of Appeal, *Rugby Union v Viagogo Ltd* [2011] EWCA Civ 1585

Court of Appeal, *SABAF SpA v MFI Furniture* [2003] RPC 14

Court of Appeal, *Sibthorpe v Southwark London Borough Council* [2011] EWCA Civ 25

Court of Appeal, *Tony D Sullivan (aka Rudey Soloman) v Bristol Film Studios Ltd* [2012] EWCA civ 570

Court of Appeal, *Totalise plc v Motley Fool Ltd* [2001] EWCA Civ 1897

High Court, *Aoot Kalmneft v Denton Wilde Sapte* [2002] 1 Lloyds Rep 417

High Court, *Applause Store Productions Ltd v Grant Raphael* [2008] EWHC 1781

High Court, *Barings Plc v Coopers & Lybrand* [2001] PNLR 22

High Court, *Carlton Film Distributors Ltd v VCI Plc* [2003] EWHC 616

High Court, *CHC Software Care v Hopkins and Wood* [1993] FSR 241

High Court, *Dramatico Entertainment Ltd and others v British Sky Broadcasting Ltd and others* [2012] EWHC 268

High Court, *EMI Records Ltd and others v British Sky Broadcasting Ltd and others* [2013] EWHC 379 (Ch)

High Court, *Exxon Corp. v Exxon Insurance Consultants* [1982] Ch 119

High Court, *Falcon v Famous Players Film Co.* [1926] 2 KB 474

High Court, *Football Association Premier League Ltd v British Sky Broadcasting Ltd* [2013] EWHC 2058

High Court, *G and G v Wikimedia Foundation Inc* [2009] EWHC 3148 (QB)

High Court, *Golden Eye (International) Ltd and others v Telefonica UK Ltd, Consumer Focus intervening* [2012] EWHC 723 (Ch)

High Court, *ITV Broadcasting Ltd and others v TVCatchup Ltd* [2013] EHWC 3638 (CH)

High Court, *Jane Clift v Martin Clark* [2011] EWHC 1164 (QB)

High Court, *L'Oréal v eBay* [2009] EWHC 1094 (Ch)

High Court, *Mitsui & Co Ltd v Nexen Petroleum UK Ltd* [2005] EWHC 625 (Ch)

High Court, *Newspaper Licensing Agency Ltd v Meltwater Holding BV* [2010] EWHC 3099 (Ch)

High Court, *Paramount Home Entertainment International Ltd v British Sky Broadcasting Ltd* [2013] EWHC 3479 (Ch)

High Court, *Polydor Ltd v Brown* [2005] EWHC 3191 (Ch)

High Court, *Pro Sieben Media v Carlton UK Television* [1997] EMLR 509

High Court, *R. (on the application of British Telecommunications Plc) v Secretary of State for Business, Innovation and Skills,* [2011] EWHC 1021 (Admin)

High Court, *Sheffield Wednesday Football Club Ltd v Hargreaves* [2007] EWHC 2375 (QB)

High Court, *Twentieth Century Fox Film Corp and others v British Telecommunications Plc* [2011] EWHC 1981

High Court, *Twentieth Century Fox Film Corporation and others v NewzBin Ltd* [2010] EWHC 608 (Ch)

House of Lords, *Ashworth Hospital Authority v MGN Ltd* [2002] UKHL 29

House of Lords, *CBS Songs v Amstrad* [1988] AC 1013

House of Lords, *Norwich Pharmacal Co. and others v Customs and Excise Commissioners* [1974] AC 133

House of Lords, *R v Johnstone* [2003] UKHL 28

House of Lords, *Re S* [2004] UKHL 47

Patents County Court, *Media C.A.T. v Adams* [2011] EWPCC 6, [2011] FSR 8

Patents Court, *Smith Kline and French Laboratories Ltd v R.D. Harbottle (Mercantile) Ltd* [1980] RPC 363

Solicitors Disciplinary Tribunal, *Solicitors Regulation Authority v Andrew Jonathan Crossley*, Case no. 10726 (06.02.2012)

The United States of America

17 U.S.C. A&*M Records. Inc. v Napster Inc.* (N. D. Cal. 2000),

A&M Records Inc. v Napster Inc., 239 F.3d 1004 (9th Cir. 2001)

Corbis Corp. v Amazon.com Inc., 351 F. Supp. 2d 1090 (W.D. Wash. 2004)

CoStar Group Inc. v LoopNet Inc., 164 F.Supp. 2d 688 (D. Md. 2001)

CoStar Group Inc. v LoopNet Inc., 373 F.3d 544 (4th Cir. 2004)

Cubby v CompuServe, 766 F Supp 135 (SDNY 1991)

Gershwin Publishing Corp. v Columbia Artists, 443 F. 2d 1159 (2nd Cir. 1971)

Hendrickson v eBay Inc., 165 F. Supp. 2d 1082 (C.D. Cal. 2001)

In Re: Aimster Copyright Litigation, 252 F.Supp.2d 634 (N.D. Ill. 2002)

In Re: Aimster Copyright Litigation, 334 F 3d 643 (7th Cir. 2003)

IO Group Inc. v Veoh Networks Inc., 586 F. Supp. 2d 1132 (N.D. Cal. 2008)

K-Beech, Inc. v John Does 1-37, CV 11-3995 (DRH)(GRB) (United States District Court, Eastern District of New York)

Metro-Goldwyn-Mayer Studios Inc. v Grokster Ltd., 125 S. Ct. 2764 (U.S.S.C. 2005)

Metro-Goldwyn-Mayer Studios Inc. v Grokster Ltd., 259 F.Supp.2d 1029 (C.D. Calif. 2003)

Metro-Goldwyn-Mayer Studios Inc. v Grokster Ltd., 380 F.3d 1154 (9th Cir. 2004)

Perfect 10 Inc. V CCBill LLC, 488 F.3d 1102, 1117 (9th Cir. 200)

Sony Corp. of America v Universal City Studios, 464 U.S. 417 (1984)

Stratton Oakmont Inc. v Prodigy Services Co., 1995 WL 323710 (NY Sup. Ct. 1995)